36-N.M.-6

◀ *View of Acoma Pueblo (Sky City), Block Number 3 from the southeast, Casa Blanca vicinity, Valencia County, New Mexico. Photograph by M. James Slack, April 1934 (HABS NM,31-ACOMP,1-32).*

North elevation, Independence Hall, Philadelphia, Philadelphia County, Pennsylvania. Measured drawing plotted by Bruce A. Harms, 1986; delineated by Marie A. Neubauer, 1986-87 (HABS PA -1430, sheet 16 of 45). ▶

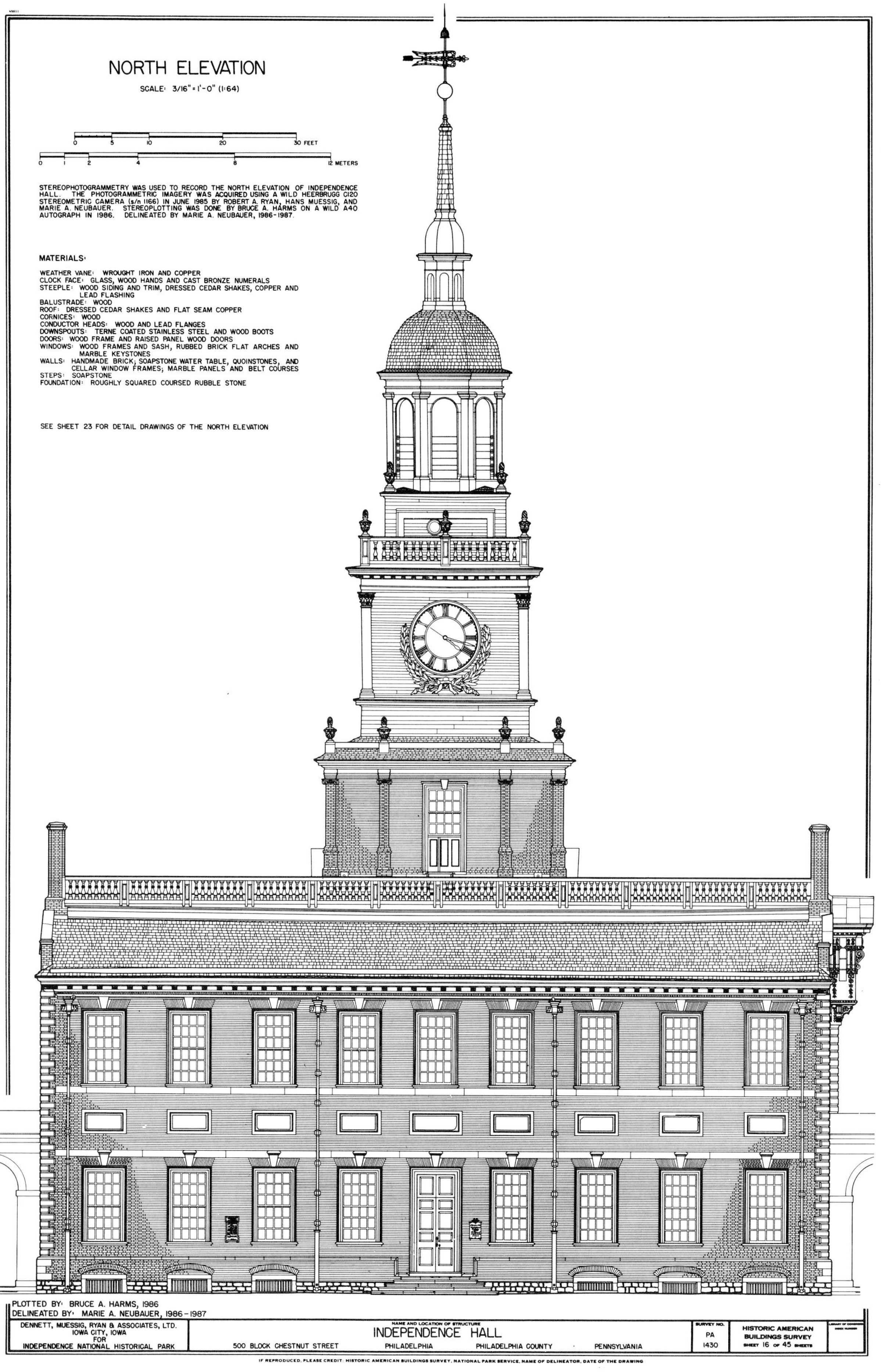

NORTH ELEVATION
SCALE: 3/16" = 1'-0" (1:64)
0 5 10 20 30 FEET
0 1 2 4 8 12 METERS
STEREOPHOTOGRAMMETRY WAS USED TO RECORD THE NORTH ELEVATION OF INDEPENDENCE HALL. THE PHOTOGRAMMETRIC IMAGERY WAS ACQUIRED USING A WILD HEERBRUGG C120 STEREOMETRIC CAMERA (s/n 1166) IN JUNE 1985 BY ROBERT A. RYAN, HANS MUESSIG, AND MARIE A. NEUBAUER. STEREOPLOTTING WAS DONE BY BRUCE A. HARMS ON A WILD A40 AUTOGRAPH IN 1986. DELINEATED BY MARIE A. NEUBAUER, 1986-1987.
MATERIALS:
WEATHER VANE: WROUGHT IRON AND COPPER
CLOCK FACE: GLASS, WOOD HANDS AND CAST BRONZE NUMERALS
STEEPLE: WOOD SIDING AND TRIM, DRESSED CEDAR SHAKES, COPPER AND LEAD FLASHING
BALUSTRADE: WOOD
ROOF: DRESSED CEDAR SHAKES AND FLAT SEAM COPPER
CORNICES: WOOD
CONDUCTOR HEADS: WOOD AND LEAD FLANGES
DOWNSPOUTS: TERNE COATED STAINLESS STEEL AND WOOD BOOTS
DOORS: WOOD FRAME AND RAISED PANEL WOOD DOORS
WINDOWS: WOOD FRAMES AND SASH, RUBBED BRICK FLAT ARCHES AND MARBLE KEYSTONES
WALLS: HANDMADE BRICK; SOAPSTONE WATER TABLE, QUOINSTONES, AND CELLAR WINDOW FRAMES; MARBLE PANELS AND BELT COURSES
STEPS: SOAPSTONE
FOUNDATION: ROUGHLY SQUARED COURSED RUBBLE STONE
SEE SHEET 23 FOR DETAIL DRAWINGS OF THE NORTH ELEVATION
PLOTTED BY: BRUCE A. HARMS, 1986
DELINEATED BY: MARIE A. NEUBAUER, 1986-1987
DENNETT, MUESSIG, RYAN & ASSOCIATES, LTD.
IOWA CITY, IOWA
FOR
INDEPENDENCE NATIONAL HISTORICAL PARK
NAME AND LOCATION OF STRUCTURE
INDEPENDENCE HALL
500 BLOCK CHESTNUT STREET
PHILADELPHIA
PHILADELPHIA COUNTY
PENNSYLVANIA
SURVEY NO.
PA
1430
HISTORIC AMERICAN BUILDINGS SURVEY
SHEET 16 OF 45 SHEETS
IF REPRODUCED, PLEASE CREDIT: HISTORIC AMERICAN BUILDINGS SURVEY, NATIONAL PARK SERVICE, NAME OF DELINEATOR, DATE OF THE DRAWING

AMERICA PRESERVED

A CHECKLIST OF HISTORIC BUILDINGS, STRUCTURES, AND SITES

Detail of porch, Carson House, Eureka, Humboldt County, California. One of the grand examples of Victorian American architecture in wood, this Stick-style mansion was built for lumber baron William Carson in 1885. Photograph by Jack E. Boucher, October 1960 (HABS CAL,12-EUR,6-13).

Published on the occasion of the 60th anniversary of the Historic American Buildings Survey and the 25th anniversary of the Historic American Engineering Record

AMERICA PRESERVED

A CHECKLIST OF HISTORIC BUILDINGS, STRUCTURES, AND SITES

Recorded by The Historic American Buildings Survey/ Historic American Engineering Record

Introduction by Marilyn Ibach and Georgette R. Wilson

LIBRARY OF CONGRESS, CATALOGING DISTRIBUTION SERVICE
Washington, D.C. 1995

NOTE ON ORDERING REPRODUCTIONS: The numbers in parentheses at the end of each illustration caption are for use in ordering reproductions. Contact the Photoduplication Service, Library of Congress, Washington, D.C. 20540, for information on prices and how to order reproductions.

Published for the Sixtieth Anniversary of the Historic American Buildings Survey and the Twenty-fifth Anniversary of the Historic American Engineering Record, *America Preserved* was prepared by the staffs of the Historic American Buildings Survey/Historic American Engineering Record Division of the National Park Service and the Prints and Photographs Division of the Library of Congress.

Library of Congress Cataloging-in-Publication

Main entry under title:
America Preserved: A Checklist of Buildings,
Structures, and Sites/ recorded by The Historic American Buildings Survey/Historic American Engineering Record ; introduction prepared by the Prints and Photographs Division of the Library of Congress, and the Historic American Buildings Survey/Historic American Engineering Record of the National Park Service. -- 60th anniversary ed.
p. cm.
Chiefly a checklist and index to the collections of the Historic American Buildings Survey/Historic American Engineering Record housed in the Library of Congress, Prints and Photographs Division.
Includes index.
1. Historic buildings--United States. 2. Historic sites--United States. 3. Architecture--United States. I. Historic American Buildings Survey/ Historic American Engineering Record. II. Library of Congress. Prints and Photographs Division.
E159.A37 1995 94-19453
973--dc20 CIP

ISBN 0-16-045255-4

For sale by the Cataloging Distribution Service,
Library of Congress
Washington, D.C. 20541

Also for sale by the U.S. Government Printing Office
Superintendent of Documents, Mail Stop: SSOP, Washington, DC 20402-9328

Table of Contents

x Dedication

xi Foreword

xiii Acknowledgements

xv Introduction
by MARILYN IBACH and GEORGETTE R. WILSON

1 Checklist of Historic Buildings, Structures, and Sites
(listing of States and Territories, page viii)

1117 Index to County by City

CHECKLIST OF HISTORIC BUILDINGS, STRUCTURES, AND SITES

LISTING OF STATES AND TERRITORIES

3 Alabama

49 Alaska

65 Arizona

77 Arkansas

85 California

145 Canal Zone

147 Colorado

159 Connecticut

179 Delaware

193 District of Columbia

225 Florida

239 Georgia

263 Guam

265 Hawaii

277 Idaho

287 Illinois

315 Indiana

329 Iowa

345 Kansas

353 Kentucky

365 Louisiana

379 Maine

389 Maryland

441 Massachusetts

491 Michigan

503 Minnesota

517 Mississippi

529 Missouri

569 Montana

581 Nebraska

585 Nevada

591 New Hampshire

601 New Jersey

649 New Mexico

657 New York

717 North Carolina

737 North Dakota

741 Ohio

765 Oklahoma

769 Oregon

781 Pennsylvania
877 Puerto Rico
885 Rhode Island
899 South Carolina
929 South Dakota
933 Tennessee
945 Texas
971 Utah
987 Vermont
993 Virgin Islands
1001 Virginia
1061 Washington
1079 West Virginia
1095 Wisconsin
1109 Wyoming

DEDICATION

KENNETH LANIER ANDERSON, AIA

Former Principal Architect of the Historic American Buildings Survey (HABS) and later Chief of the program, Kenneth Anderson served HABS for almost two decades with intense loyalty. Mr. Anderson was unique among the many talented architects associated with HABS throughout its sixty year history. None other has come close to developing the number of projects that Mr. Anderson did, nor has any other architect overseen the production of as many measured drawings deposited in the HABS collection in the Library of Congress. In remembrance of that loyalty and his wonderful sense of humor.

VIRGINIA DAIKER

For over forty years, from the inception of the Historic American Buildings Survey collections at the Library of Congress, Virginia Daiker provided guidance to thousands of researchers, scholars, students, and architects, first as a cataloger, later as a reference librarian and reading room head, and ultimately as a specialist in American architecture. Her knowledge of and devotion to the care and service of these collections, together with her calm and steady nature, are remembered warmly by all who were privileged to work with her. Her career spanned the renewal of interest in the nation's architectural heritage and the emergence and growth of the fields of architectural history and historic preservation. Miss Daiker and the collections which she made available at the Library of Congress were inseparable and indispensable resources for these developments. In remembrance of a lifetime of public service.

SALLY KRESS TOMPKINS

Former Deputy Chief of the Historic American Buildings Survey/Historic American Engineering Record (HABS/HAER) through the decade of the 1980s, Sally Kress Tompkins was primarily responsible for the preservation and revitalization of the HABS/HAER program during this period. Among her countless contributions, the reestablishment of the maritime recording program, dormant for almost forty years, stands out as one of her principal achievements. In remembrance of her many contributions to the program and the very engaging manner in which she pursued her work.

FOREWORD

In 1933, when the National Park Service, the American Institute of Architects, and the Library of Congress joined together to create the Historic American Buildings Survey, the nation was in the midst of its greatest economic crisis. Promising a "New Deal" Franklin Delano Roosevelt's administration launched many public works programs to offer immediate relief to thousands of unemployed Americans. These efforts produced much of enduring value, including creative efforts as various as the Federal Writers' Program, the Federal Theatre Project, and the Index of American Design. Of these programs begun in the 1930s, however, only the Historic American Buildings Survey continues today.

The Historic American Buildings Survey was the government's first attempt to systematically record America's built environment through graphic and written records. In the 1930's and early 1940's, the Survey put unemployed architects to work. Since the 1950's, it has employed and provided "on-the-job" training for students of architecture, historians, photographers, and others in historic principles of design, construction, and technology. From the beginning it has provided a resource for writers, researchers, and scholars in many fields. Countless publications continue to draw upon its images and records, copies of which are widely available internationally.

The idea for such a survey originated with Charles E. Peterson, Chief of the Eastern Division of the Branch of Plans and Design in the National Park Service, who recognized the opportunity to employ jobless architects to record a vanishing architectural heritage. He seized upon the moment to convince his superior, Arthur E. Demaray, of the feasibility of such a program. Peterson enlisted the cooperation of the American Institute of Architects (AIA), through Edward C. Kemper, and the Library of Congress, with the help of Leicester B. Holland, who was Chief of the Library's Fine Arts Division and Chairman of the AIA's Committee on the Preservation of Historic Buildings. Besides securing initial funding, Peterson recruited the staff to produce the Survey's original records. Meanwhile, Holland adapted an existing system at the Library of Congress to receive and organize these records for public use.

Work began in late 1933 under the direction of Thomas C. Vint, Chief of Design and Construction, National Park Service. In January 1934, a national advisory committee was convened by William Graves Perry, head of the firm noted for its architectural work at Colonial Williamsburg. The tripartite agreement among the National Park Service, the American Institute of Architects, and the Library of Congress became effective on July 23 of that same year. The Historic American Buildings Survey (HABS) has operated under that agreement ever since. The program received its legislative mandate through the Historic Sites, Buildings, and Antiquities Act of 1935.

In January 1969, the Historic American Engineering Record (HAER) was established by a tripartite agreement among the National Park Service, the American Society of Civil Engineers, and the Library of Congress. This agreement was later ratified by four other American engineering societies: the American Society of Mechanical Engineers, the American Institute of Chemical Engineers, the Institute of Electrical and Electronic Engineers, and the American Institute of Mining, Metallurgical, and Petroleum Engineers. All partners continue in a productive and unparalleled cooperative venture that includes both the public and the private sectors.

Reciting the history of HABS and HAER does not begin to introduce them adequately. They are, after all, the results of inspired visions brilliantly realized. Along with the Civil War and the Farm Security Administration photographs, they share the distinction of being among the most heavily used collections in the Prints and Photographs Division. They are in almost constant demand for a wide range of projects to include writing architectural and social histories, preserving historic buildings, and restoring private homes that are cherished by their occupants. Although HABS and HAER's documentation of structures has not been able to be systematic, it has encompassed an extraordinary range of building types and locations. Further, the collections have reached sufficient critical mass to make them a uniquely rich resource for studying America's built environment. They are all the more important because so many of the structures they document no longer exist, except as HABS/HAER measured drawings, photographs, and field notes.

In the preface to his book, *Back of the Big House*, John Michael Vlach rightfully praises the thoroughness and high standards of architectural documentation achieved by HABS and succinctly provides a stunning insight into the impact of this collection. These few sentences summarize what HABS and HAER have achieved and illustrate the high praise that they deserve:

"Look at the pictures. Pore over the drawings. Check their details. Do it carefully, and you can develop almost a tangible sense of the buildings..." (Preface xiii).

Robert J. Kapsch
Chief, Historic American Buildings Survey/
Historic American Engineering Record
National Park Service

Stephen E. Ostrow
Chief, Prints and Photographs Division
Library of Congress

ACKNOWLEDGEMENTS

Many people contributed to this publication. Robert J. Kapsch, Chief of the Historic American Buildings Survey/Historic American Engineering Record (HABS/HAER), and Stephen E. Ostrow, Chief, Prints and Photographs Division, Library of Congress, provided managerial support to this undertaking.

Georgette R. Wilson, Collections Management Administrator, HABS/HAER, wrote the section of the introduction entitled "Using the Checklist," provided consultation for the HABS/HAER computerized checklist data, assisted with the selection of photographs and drawings, and coordinated the overall publication effort for the Historic American Buildings Survey/Historic American Engineering Record.

Marilyn Ibach, Reference Specialist in the Prints and Photographs Division, Library of Congress, coordinated the contribution of the Prints and Photographs Division, wrote sections of the introduction, made the first selection of most of the illustrations, and provided illustration captions.

Other contributors to the checklist include the staff at the HABS/HAER offices at the National Park Service and the Prints and Photographs Division at the Library of Congress. HABS/HAER Deputy Chief John A. Burns directed the efforts of staff members Brian L. Cary, Paul D. Dolinsky, Alison K. Hoagland, Monica P. Murphy, and Georgette R. Wilson. From the National Park Service's Interagency Resources Division, computer specialist John Byrne provided technical expertise. Participants from the Library of Congress Prints and Photographs Division include Cristina Carbone, Sam Daniel, Marilyn Ibach, Mary M. Ison, Megan E. Keister, Greg Marcangelo, Elisabeth B. Parker, C. Ford Peatross, Bernard Reilly, and Helena Zinkham.

Participants from the Library's Cataloging Distribution Service include several staff members from the Product Development Unit and the Marketing Unit of the Customer Services Section and from the Computer Applications Section, all of whom assisted in the development, editing, and production of this publication. The cover design and all graphic preparation were done by Kimberly Lord, of the Library's Office Systems Services/Graphics Unit.

Without the contributions of these people, this book would not have been possible.

The technology of documenting structures has changed dramatically since 1933 when HABS was founded. At upper left: *a 1930's recording team in the act of measuring the columns of the Kentucky School for the Blind in Louisville (HABS KY,56-LOUVI,2-7).* Second photo on the left: *historians working on written documentation which serves as resource data. Documentation requires more than the skills of historians and architectural photographers; it requires architectural draftsmanship as well.* Bottom photo: *a team uses computer-aided drafting (CAD) on the AutoCAD program at HABS/HAER CAD/Photogrammetry Laboratory for the Lincoln Memorial project.* Photo at right: *Jack Boucher, an architectural photographer, taking large-format photographs of Jefferson's retreat Poplar Forest in Bedford County, Virginia. All contribute to the production of the documentation which appears in this checklist.*

INTRODUCTION

by MARILYN IBACH and GEORGETTE R. WILSON

From the inception of the Historic American Buildings Survey (HABS) in 1933 and of its sister program the Historic American Engineering Record (HAER) in 1969, the guiding purpose for these two programs has been to document the nation's architectural, industrial, and technological legacy and to make the documentation easily accessible to a vast audience. Therefore, the Library of Congress and the National Park Service share a continuing interest in making available national catalogs of the two collections. The 1983 publication *Historic America* was the first to act as a catalog for both collections. *America Preserved* expands upon the 1983 checklist by adding 14,000 more structures, providing quantities for all formal documentation (measured drawings, photographs, pages of written historical and descriptive data, and pages of photo captions), including references to informal documentation contained in field records, and citing full shelflist numbers to facilitate the ordering of copies. Further, it indicates the presence of large format color transparencies that, although not accessible now, are scheduled to be transferred to the Library and made available in the future.

The HABS and HAER collections continue to grow daily, making the current checklist a snapshot in time generated from a computerized database as of March 31, 1994. Statistics for the HABS and HAER collections at the time of publication are as follows:

Number of structures:	30,097
Number of photographs:	160,517
Number of drawings:	96,242
Number of pages of written data:	15,464

USING THE CHECKLIST

The arrangement of the checklist entries follows the geographical organization used by the Library of Congress. A sample entry found on the inside covers of this book and at the end of this introduction illustrates this arrangement. The elements of the entry are labeled numerically in order of appearance.

1-3. State, County, and City or Nearest Vicinity

Elements 1 through 3 locate a site first by state, then by county, and then by city, town, or nearest vicinity. States and territories are listed alphabetically. Within each state or territory, counties, parishes and divisions are listed alphabetically. Independent cities are given the same status as counties and are listed alphabetically among them, followed by the word "CITY" in parentheses, for example, "Richmond (CITY)" or, independent cities within counties of the same name, such as "Baltimore (CITY)." If a rural structure is not in the vicinity of a city or town, it appears alphabetically at the beginning of the appropriate county listing.

4. Structure or Site Name (Record Name)

Element 4 in the sample entry shows the structure or site name, also referred to as the record name. After structures or sites are grouped geographically within state, county, and city, they are listed alphabetically by the structure's name, for instance, "Chesterfield Blacksmith Shop." Personal names that have become part of building names are listed by last name, first name, and descriptive building type, as in "Eddy, Zachariah, Law Office." Several special situations may occur with the structure, site, or record name. These include secondary names, the use of an address as structure or site name, historic districts, and complexes.

Secondary Names. When a structure has more than one name, each of the secondary or alternate names appears in parentheses following the main entry, for example, "Sterne, Augustus, House" followed by the secondary name "(Hoya Library)." Each secondary name is also listed in alphabetical sequence as a cross-reference entry that refers the reader back to the primary entry.

Address Used as Structure or Site Name. When the street address is listed as the structure or site name, it is alphabetized by the name of the street and is followed by the building type, for example, "301 Elm Street (House)," is listed under "Elm." A numerical street name is spelled out, as in "1919 Twenty-first Street (House)" and alphabetized under "T." A street address preceded by North, South, East, or West is alphabetized by that designation. A building in a rural location with no specific address is listed by the building type, for example, "Farm House."

Historic Districts. Historic districts are comprised of structures with separate addresses but united by a historic district designation or some other historic, geographic, or administrative link. Structures located within a historic district are listed in one of two ways: 1) for older surveys (up to December 1989) the structures are listed under the name of the historic district, followed by the name of the individual structure, for example, "Strand Historic District" followed by "Ufford, E.L., Building"; and 2) for recent surveys (since January 1990) the structure name is listed first, followed by the historic district designation, for example, "Worthman General Store" followed by the historic district designation "Old Town."

Complex. A complex represents small groupings of related buildings. The complex receives an overall HABS or HAER survey number and each structure within the complex also receives the overall HABS or HAER survey number with a designation of A, B, C, etc. For these entries, the complex name is listed first, followed by the individual structure name, for example, HAER OH-79-A is listed as "Wright-Patterson Air Force Base [complex name], Hangar No. 1 [structure name]."

5. Address

Element 5 in the sample entry shows the address, which follows the structure or site name. If the address is listed as the name of the structure, it is not repeated. A moved structure is identified with a parenthetical note following the address, stating that the structure was either "moved to" or "moved from" another address, with the town or vicinity name and the two-letter state abbreviation, for instance "103 Elm Street (moved from 600 Blacksmith Street, Binghamton, NY)." A moved structure is listed under the location at the time of recording by HABS or HAER. Structures moved across cities or counties are not cross-referenced but are listed twice, once under each location. A structure moved within a city, however, appears once, with the alternate street address following either "moved to" or "moved from."

6. HABS or HAER Survey Number

Element 6 in the sample entry shows the HABS or HAER Survey number. This number identifies either the HABS or HAER program designation, the two-letter state abbreviation as used by the Postal Service, and the structure or site number representing the approximate numerical sequence in which the structure was recorded by HABS or HAER in that state, i.e., HAER [program] VA- [state] 103 [approximate sequence recorded]. For complexes, an identifier of A, B, C, etc., is given for structures associated with the overall record entry, for example, HABS TN-1033 (single structure) and HAER TN-1033-A ("A" indicating a complex). If a structure or site has been recorded by both HABS and HAER, the entry lists both survey numbers.

7. Library of Congress Shelflist Number

Element 7 in the sample entry shows the shelflist number printed in italics. This is the number used for ordering reproductions. The Library of Congress shelflist number groups HABS and HAER materials by geographic order and is important for locating documentation at the Library and on the microfiche. Following the imaginary example in this section, HABS RI,16-ASH,101- , the components of the shelflist number are:

1) the collection (HABS)
2) the state (RI, for Rhode Island)
3) the county (16- for Kramer, the sixteenth county alphabetized in Rhode Island)
4) the city (ASH, being the abbreviation for the town of Ashland)
5) 101- (the unique number assigned for the building within the town of Ashland).

If the number in this element is in a different form, it is an accession number, for example, *1993 (HAER): 119*, and indicates that, as of March 1994, the records had not yet been processed and made available for public use.

8-13. Documentation

HABS/HAER records cited in this checklist include both formal and informal documentation. Formal documentation includes information recorded in standardized formats: measured drawings, photographs from large-format negatives, and data pages. Once processed into the collections at the Library of Congress, they are readily available for use. Informal documentation consists of non-standardized field records and other materials that are difficult to serve to researchers and are not readily available. However, in circumstances where the building is undergoing restoration or is the subject of advanced scholarly research, the scholar or restorer may want to apply to the Prints and Photographs Division to view field records, which can normally be made available with advance notice and an appointment.

Formal Documentation. Measured drawings are produced from recorded, accurate measurements. The drawings are in ink or graphite and are on translucent and archivally stable materials, such as mylar. They are produced in three standard sizes: 19 x 24 inches, 24 x 36 inches, and 33 x 44 inches. Black-and-white photographic contact prints are made from 4 x 5 inch, 5 x 7 inch, or 8 x 10 inch large format negatives. Large format negatives permit maximum enlargement without reduction of the sharpness of the image; large format cameras permit photography of tall or wide structures without distortion, to increase depth of field, and to displace obstructions blocking the view of the structure being photographed. In some cases, photographs are reference copies of photogrammetric images, commonly one plate of a stereopair, the original of which can be plotted for measured drawings.

Written documentation includes pages of written historical and descriptive data (referred to as "pages of text" in the footers within the checklist) and pages of photo captions that identify the photographs. The historical and descriptive data are based on primary sources to the greatest extent possible and generally specify the name of the researcher, date of research, sources, and limitations of the project. Photo caption pages cite the name of the photographer, date(s) the photographs were taken, and captions for each photograph. In some cases, they also cite the quantities of other documentation for a particular structure. All data pages are on 8-1/2 x 11 inch or 8 x 10-1/2 inch archival bond paper.

Large format color transparencies are cataloged in this checklist for the first time. The color transparencies generally duplicate black-and-white large format photograph views of the same structure and are made when information can be added by the use of color. When incorporated into the collection, a color xerographic image will be placed with the other documentation for that structure to alert the reader to the presence of a color transparency; the original transparency will be placed in cold storage. While not yet available to researchers, their notation in the checklist reflects an accurate picture of HABS/HAER documentation to date and indicates future availability.

Informal Documentation. Field records are considered informal documentation because they do not meet one or more HABS/HAER standards (content, quality, materials, or presentation). Field records from the 1930's usually consist of measured sketches of plans, elevations, sections, or details on graph paper in bound notebooks. Later field records can be diverse; they might include 35mm black-and-white negatives, contact sheets of field photographs, preliminary sketches of measured drawings, oversize blueprints with written notations and measurements, photographs from outside sources, or written material. Photogrammetric glass plate negatives are also considered informal documentation. Reference prints and copy film negatives for the most informative plates are incorporated into the formal HABS/HAER documentation, but the glass photogrammetric plates themselves are too fragile to be routinely served.

In elements 8 through 13 in the sample entry, symbols are used to designate the different types of documentation as follows:

dr = measured drawings
ph = large format photographs (black and white)
pg = pages of written data or text
pc = photo caption pages for photographs
ct = large format color transparencies
fr = field records

The number in front of a symbol indicates the quantity of that type of documentation. The symbol "fr" indicates the presence of field records but not the quantity. The absence of a symbol indicates that documentation of that type currently does not exist.

14-15. Location

Elements 14 and 15 in the sample entry show the location of the documentation, which is either the Library of Congress (L) or the HABS/HAER Washington office (H). In some instances, documentation can be at both places. This occurs when additional information has been recorded by HABS/HAER at a later date but has not yet been transmitted to the Library of Congress. When the location code appears as "L," even with an "H," please contact the Library of Congress, Prints and Photographs Division to determine what material is available. When the location code appears as "H" alone, the documentation is at the HABS/HAER Washington office and is considered work-in-progress, not available to the public until transmitted to the Library of Congress.

USING THE COLLECTIONS AT THE LIBRARY OF CONGRESS

The HABS and HAER collections are housed in the Prints and Photographs Division Reading Room of the Library of Congress. Researchers are welcome to visit the collections at that site and examine the records and finding aids in person. Space is limited and advance appointments are encouraged. General information about the Reading Room's hours and rules is available by telephone or letter.

Readers will find the HABS and HAER collections in ring binders in open stacks in the Reading Room, retrievable by shelflist number and arranged in geographic hierarchical order: state, county, city or vicinity, and by the sequence in which the building was recorded within the given city or vicinity. The order for the material for each structure in the ring binder is: 1) captioned black-and-white photographs (some later photographs are preceded by a photo caption page); 2) written historical and descriptive data; 3) reduced-size copies of measured drawings (8-1/2 x 11 inches).

continued on page xxii

This page, top photo : *Georgette R. Wilson, HABS / HAER Collections Management Administrator, Brian L. Cary, Collections Management Architect, and Monica P. Murphy, Collections Management Historian, in the HABS/HAER Washington, D.C. office, preparing HABS documentation of the Burnside Bridge at Antietam National Battlefield for transmittal to the Library of Congress. Photograph by Jack Boucher, 1994.*

Bottom left photo : *HABS/HAER documents are filed in easy-to-use formats and sizes. All forms of documentation — measured drawings, photographs, and data pages — are filed in ring binders in the Prints and Photographs Reading Room. Their retrieval is simple; readers refer to the card catalog for the geographic location and name of the structure, then consult the notebooks in open stacks in the reading room. Photograph by Jim Higgins, 1994.*

Bottom right photo : *HABS and HAER notebooks are easily accessible in the Prints and Photographs Reading Room. Patrons can retrieve notebooks within a specific city or county and browse to find the images they want. Photograph by Jim Higgins, 1994.*

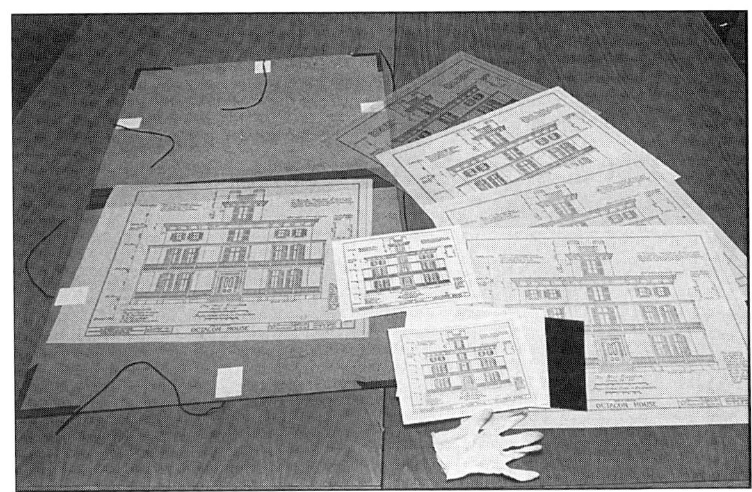

This page, top photo : *The various types of reproductions available from the Library of Congress Photoduplication Service are displayed using a 1936 measured drawing of the Octagon House, Watertown, Jefferson County, Wisconsin (HABS WI-135, sheet 3 of 5). Counterclockwise, from upper left: the original reproducible measured drawing, an 8-1/2 x 11-inch electrostatic positive print (xerox), an 8 x 10-inch glossy black-and-white photoprint, an 8 x 10-inch black-and-white negative, a full-size blue-line diazo print, a full-size black-line diazo print, a photodirect positive print, and a full-size mylar reproducible. The Photoduplication Service also provides transparencies and exhibition-quality prints. Photograph by Jim Higgins, 1994.*

Bottom left photo : *Readers able to visit the Prints and Photographs Reading Room can call on the experienced reference staff for specialized reference assistance. Copies of HABS/HAER materials at the Library of Congress can be obtained through the Library's central copying service, the Photoduplication Service, which can provide information on prices and products. Photograph by Jim Higgins, 1994.*

Bottom right photo : *The HABS/HAER card catalog lists all available documentation. The main access is by geographic area. Additional card indexes below give access by subject, style of building, date of the structure, and name of architect or engineer. Photograph by Jim Higgins, 1994.*

continued from page xix
Photographic negatives and original full-size measured drawings are filed separately.

The geographic arrangement of the HABS and HAER collections is reflected in the shelflist number assigned to each structure, as described above. This arrangement serves readers well, as it enables them to easily find records for areas of the country, for individual states, for portions of states, or for individual structures. In many cases the card catalog need not even be consulted. For example, if a reader wishes to examine records of domestic architecture in the "Eastern Shore" area of Virginia and Maryland, he or she can determine the counties which make up this area, look up the numbers for each county, retrieve the notebooks for all the materials in those numbers, and easily browse the records to find appropriate material.

A master card catalog, which also follows the hierarchical geographic arrangement, provides an entry for each structure or site and lists the amount of documentation and applicable call numbers. Several card indexes, all in progress, have been developed to supplement the geographic catalog. The largest index is by subject, which includes types of buildings (such as barns), specific materials (such as stone buildings), and details (such as murals). The subject index also includes building styles ranging from Federal to International. A smaller index lists structures chronologically. Another card index includes the names of architects, engineers, or firms, allowing a reader interested in the work of a particular architect or engineer to determine which works by that architect are included in HABS/HAER.

A vertical file provides additional subject access. This file contains duplicates of the reduced-size measured drawings, as well as miscellaneous lists, pamphlets, and photographs arranged in folders by subject.

New material is added to the ring binders regularly. All records received through 1988 are available in the binders. Records received from 1989 to 1993 are scheduled for processing in 1994-96.

HOW TO ORDER REPRODUCTIONS

Copies of HABS/HAER formal records that have been transferred to the Library and made available for use can be ordered from the Library's Photoduplication Service. Such materials are noted by an "L" in the location field of the checklist and have an LC shelflist number in the shelflist number field, as noted above. Patrons may telephone or write the Photoduplication Service (at 202 707-5640 or the Photoduplication Service, Library of Congress, Washington, D.C. 20540-5230) for information on the reproduction services available and corresponding prices and use this information to choose the type of reproduction wanted and to calculate pricing. Orders, which must be prepaid, can then be placed directly with the Photoduplication Service. Patrons should send a written request to the Photoduplication Service, providing a copy of the checklist entry, citing the documentation wanted, and supplying a MasterCard or Visa credit card number or a check. The Photoduplication Service will make the copies and send them to the patron.

When the location field contains either an "H" or "L H," it is an indication that some or all of the records have not yet been transferred to the Library. When the entry does not have an LC shelflist number or has an accession number, as described above, the materials are likely to be unavailable. Also, as noted above, color transparencies are not yet available for use. Patrons are welcome to contact the Prints and Photographs Division reference staff for the status of a particular project and an accurate count of available records.

HABS/HAER PUBLICATIONS

America Preserved is the most recent book in a long history of HABS/HAER publications. The first published catalog of the HABS collection was issued in 1938, only five years after the Survey was created. Another complete catalog followed in 1941, and a supplement to that publication was published in 1959. After 1959, the size of the HABS collection necessitated publishing by state, rather than publishing one large catalog, and a program of publishing building lists by state and region was instituted. State catalogs for Alabama, California, the District of Columbia, Georgia, Indiana, Iowa, Maine, Massachusetts, Michigan, New Hampshire, New Jersey, Texas, Utah, Virginia, and Wisconsin followed. The Historic American Engineering Record published its first catalog in 1976, only eight years after HAER was established, and a second in 1985. The 1983 publication *Historic America: Buildings, Structures, and Sites* was the first complete catalog of both the HABS and HAER collections. It included a checklist of both collections, accompanied by essays about the collections by authors from various fields. Intended to serve as a major guide for persons unable to visit the collections in Washington, D.C., and to place them in a larger historical context, the publication sold over 4,000 copies before going out-of-print in late 1991.

A complete list of HABS/HAER publications is found in *Historic American Buildings Survey / Historic American Engineering Record: An Annotated Bibliography,* compiled by James C. Massey, Nancy B. Schwartz, and Shirley Maxwell (Washington, D.C.: U.S. Department of the Interior, 1992). This bibliography cites all HABS and HAER national and state catalogs and manuscripts, microforms and films, documentary publications by HABS/HAER and HABS/HAER cooperators, publications about the history and operations of HABS/HAER, recording specifications and instructions, official documents, and miscellaneous publications.

Three microfiche publications of the collections have been or are being published by Chadwyck-Healey, Ltd., 1101 King Street, Suite 380, Alexandria, Virginia 22314 (703 683-4890 or 800 752-0515). The first of these, *The Historic American Buildings Survey, Part I*, is a microfiche edition of 45,000 photographs and 35,000 pages of written histories in the Library's cataloged collections as of January 1979, describing 20,000 sites and structures. It is arranged geographically.

The Historic American Buildings Survey, Part II (1980-1988) is currently being published state-by-state and will include **all** drawings received from 1933 to 1988 and photographs and written records received from 1980-1988. The microfiche for the states of Alabama, Arizona, Colorado, the District of Columbia, Florida, Georgia, Idaho, Illinois, Indiana, Kentucky, Massachusetts, Michigan, Missouri, Nebraska, Nevada, New Hampshire, New Mexico, New York, Ohio, Pennsylvania,

South Carolina, Texas, and Virginia were available as of December 31, 1993. Significantly, the checklist *America Preserved* can be used as a finding aid for the documentation in the microfiche sets. The microfiche documentation was filmed in shelflist number order, so the checklist may be used to find the documentation on the microfiche.

Chadwyck-Healey also is currently publishing the microfiche *Historic American Engineering Record* state by state; this microfiche will include all drawings, photographs, and written records from 1969 to 1988. The same states available as of December 31, 1993, for HABS in *Historic American Buildings Survey, Part II* are also available for HAER.

As a preservation measure, the Library microfilmed all of the original HABS measured drawings in its collection in 1974, by state, on 63 reels (P&P LOT 12023). The order of the drawings within each state is not consistent by county or city name, and the microfilm should be viewed primarily as an inexpensive browsing tool. However, the Library's Photoduplication Service can make good quality xerox copies ("copyflo") from the microfilm and the resulting drawings can be arranged in file folders or notebooks as patrons desire.

These microform publications are available in many libraries throughout the country.

THE AUTOMATED INVENTORY (HABS/HAER Database)

An automated inventory, or database, of the HABS and HAER collections was established in 1982 by the National Park Service for administrative purposes, including indexing and statistical reports. This database is the basis for the checklist for *America Preserved.* Computer printouts of the database are used in the Prints and Photographs Division Reading Room for quick reference to the collection, and the Library can do some on-line searching. This searching, while limited, does provide access not available through existing catalogs and indexes. For example, a reader searching for mills in a particular state could request an automated search; the search will find all mills in the state if the primary name of the building includes the word "mill," as in "Swain's Mill." These searches must be requested in advance; "on-the-spot" automated searches are not yet available.

FOR MORE INFORMATION

Specialized reference assistance for the HABS and HAER collections at the Library of Congress is available from the Prints and Photographs Division, Library of Congress, Washington, D.C. 20540-4840 (202 707-6394). Information about the HABS/HAER program and upcoming projects is available from HABS/HAER, Box 37127, Washington, D.C. 20013-7127 (202 343-9618). Information on reproduction services and prices is available from the Photoduplication Service, Library of Congress, Washington, D.C. 20540-5230 (202 707-5640).

Sample Entry

1 **Rhode Island**

2 KRAMER COUNTY

3 *ASHLAND*

4 **Summer's Point Mill**
5 825 Main St.
6 HABS RI-1230
HAER RI-45
7 *HABS/HAER RI,16-ASH,101-*
8-9 45dr/15ph/
10-13 16pg/25pc/2ct/fr L H 14-15

1. State
2. County
3. City
4. Name of building, structure, or site (record name)
5. Address
6. HABS or HAER Survey Number
   HABS=Historic American Buildings Survey
   HAER=Historic American Engineering Record

Each number is preceded by the Postal Service two-letter abbreviation for the state where the building, structure, or site is located, here RI for Rhode Island. In this imaginary example, both HABS and HAER have recorded this site.

7. Shelflist number (in *italics*)
   Each number is preceded by a 2-4 letter code representing the state where the building structure, or site is located, here RI for Rhode Island.

Documentation

8. dr = sheets of measured drawings
9. ph = photographs
10. pg = pages of written data
11. pc = pages of photo captions
12. ct = color transparencies
13. fr = field records

This imaginary example illustrates each category of documentation. In the actual checklist, if there is no documentation for a particular category, that category does not appear.

Location

14. L=Library of Congress
15. H=HABS/HAER Office, National Park Service

Checklist of Historic Buildings, Structures, and Sites

The arrangement of cities and towns within the checklist is alphabetical **by county** within each state. To determine in which county a city or town is located, consult the *Index to County by City*, which follows this checklist and which lists all cities and towns by state and indicates the county in which they are located.

Independent cities—those cities that are legally separate from any county—are identified by the word "(CITY)" following the city name. In the checklist, they are interfiled in the same alphabet as the counties. In the index independent cities are listed without reference to a county name.

This checklist was computer generated. Occasionally, inconsistencies in spelling, spacing, and punctuation may cause sorting irregularities. If you have difficulty in finding a site, please look to the beginning of the state or county in which the site is located, or look for irregular spellings of the site or city name. We regret any inconvenience these irregularities may cause.

Octavia Adkinson House, Peachburg vicinity, Bullock County, Alabama. Finish of railroad at top of hill [Mrs. Adkinson with bucket pulley for well]. Photograph by W.N. Manning, July 17, 1935 (HABS ALA,6-PECH.V,1A-2).

Alabama

AUTAUGA COUNTY

MULBERRY VIC.

Ivy Creek Methodist Church
State Hwy. 14
HABS AL-724
HABS ALA,1-MUL.V,1-
3ph/2pg/3pc/fr L

PRATTVILLE

Coe-Swift-Fay House; see Fay,Thomas Avery,House

Continental Gin Company; see Pratt,Daniel,Cotton Gin Factory Complex

Fay,Thomas Avery,House
(Coe-Swift-Fay House)
203 Washington St.
HABS AL-653
HABS ALA,1-PRAVI,4-
4ph L

Pratt,Daniel,Cotton Gin Factory Complex (Continental Gin Company)
Autauga Creek
HABS AL-685
HAER AL-5
HABS/HAER ALA,1-PRAVI,3-
9ph/1pg/1pc L

Pratt,Daniel,House
Autauga Creek
HABS AL-686
HABS ALA,1-PRAVI,2-
16ph L

Smith Racing Stables
County Rd. 75
HABS AL-669
HABS ALA,1-PRAVI,1-
3ph L

PRATTVILLE VIC.

Buena Vista; see Montgomery-Jones-Whitaker House

Golson,John B.,House; see Pope-Golson House

Montgomery-Jones-Whitaker House
(Buena Vista)
County Rd. 4 (Reynolds Mill Rd.)
HABS AL-695
HABS ALA,1-PRAVI.V,1-
19ph L

Pope-Alexander-Golson House; see Pope-Golson House

Pope-Golson House (Golson,John B.,House; Pope-Alexander-Golson House)
815 Shadow Ln. (moved from original location)
HABS AL-654
HABS ALA,1-PRAVI.V,1-
14ph L

BALDWIN COUNTY

BLAKELY

Double House,French-type; see Reingard Double House

8-10 N. Jackson Street (Double House); see Reingard Double House

Reingard Double House (8-10 N. Jackson Street (Double House); Double House,French-type)
(See MOBILE CO.,MOBILE for documentation)
HABS AL-25
HABS ALA,49-MOBI,27-
1dr/10ph/2pg/fr L

GULF SHORES VIC.

Fort Morgan
HABS AL-101
HABS ALA,2-GULSH.V,1-
2ph/1pg/1pc L

POINT CLEAR

Battle House (Gunnison House)
U.S. Hwy. 98 (State Hwy. 42)
HABS AL-120
HABS ALA,2-POCLI,1-
3ph/2pg L

Gunnison House; see Battle House

STOCKTON

House,Old; see McMillan House

Kitchen-McMillan House; see McMillan House

McMillan House (Kitchen-McMillan House; House,Old)
County Rd. 21
HABS AL-118
HABS ALA,2-STOCK,1-
2ph L

TENSAW

Atkinson-Till House
State Hwy. 59
HABS AL-116
HABS ALA,2-TENSA,2-
3ph L

Tunstall House (Woolf House)
State Hwy. 59
HABS AL-115
HABS ALA,2-TENSA,2-
1ph L

Woolf House; see Tunstall House

BARBOUR COUNTY

EUFAULA

Alabama National Bank; see Eastern Bank of Alabama

Alexander-McDonald-Smartt House; see McDonald-Smartt House

Baptist Church (St. Luke's African Methodist Episcopal Church)
234 S. Van Buren St.
HABS AL-590
HABS ALA,3-EUFA,4-
5ph L

Cato,Lewis Llewellyn,House
823 W. Barbour St.
HABS AL-554
HABS ALA,3-EUFA,7-
10ph L

Cowan-Ramser House
441 E. Barbour St.
HABS AL-519
HABS ALA,3-EUFA,2-
10ph L

East Alabama National Bank; see Eastern Bank of Alabama

Eastern Bank of Alabama (East Alabama National Bank; McNab Bank Building; Alabama National Bank)
201 Broad St.
HABS AL-592
HABS ALA,3-EUFA,8-
17ph L

Ferrell's Gardens; see Irwinton Inn

Hart-Milton House
211 Eufaula St.
HABS AL-591
HABS ALA,3-EUFA,5-
16ph L

Irwinton Inn (Tavern,The; Marshburn House; Pease Tavern; Ferrell's Gardens)
105 Riverside Dr.
HABS AL-516
HABS ALA,3-EUFA,1-
6ph/2pg L

Marshburn House; see Irwinton Inn

McDonald-Smartt House
(Alexander-McDonald-Smartt House)
315 N. Randolph St.
HABS AL-517
HABS ALA,3-EUFA,6-
9ph/2pg L

McNab Bank Building; see Eastern Bank of Alabama

Pease Tavern; see Irwinton Inn

St. Luke's African Methodist Episcopal Church; see Baptist Church

Tavern,The; see Irwinton Inn

Thomas-Wills House; see Wellborn,Dr. Levi Thomas,House

Wellborn,Dr. Levi Thomas,House
(Thomas-Wills House)
Broad St. (moved from 134 Livingston St.)
HABS AL-520
HABS ALA,3-EUFA,3-
9ph L

BIBB COUNTY

BRIERFIELD

Bibb Naval Furnaces; see Brierfield Furnace

Birmingham Industrial District; see Brierfield Furnace

Brierfield Furnace (Brierfield Ironworks; Brierfield Ironworks Park-Tannehill St. Hist. Park Bibb Naval Furnaces; Birmingham Industrial District)
St. Hwy. 25
HAER AL-30
H

Brierfield Ironworks; see Brierfield Furnace

Brierfield Ironworks Park-Tannehill St. Hist. Park; see Brierfield Furnace

WEST BLOCTON

Birmingham Industrial District; see West Blocton Commercial District (Streetscapes)

West Blocton Commercial District (Streetscapes) (Birmingham Industrial District)
County Rd. 24
HABS AL-922
H

BULLOCK COUNTY

HIGH RIDGE VIC.

Berry House (Berry-Braswell House; Braswell,E. B.,House)
County Rd. 14
HABS AL-595
HABS ALA,6-HIRI,1-
5ph L

Berry-Braswell House; see Berry House

Braswell,E. B.,House; see Berry House

Chancey,John,House
HABS AL-572
HABS ALA,6-HIRI.V,2-
2ph L

Howe-Roughton House
County Rd. 14
HABS AL-561
HABS ALA,6-HIRI.V,1-
4ph L

PEACHBURG

Seale-Mosley House
(Seale,Arnold,House)
County Rd. 40 (moved from original location)
HABS AL-546
HABS ALA,6-PECH,1-
9ph L

Seale,Arnold,House; see Seale-Mosley House

PEACHBURG VIC.

Atkinson,Octavia House
(Cunningham-Atkinson House)
Wilson Rd.
HABS AL-539
HABS ALA,6-PECH.V,1-
5ph L

Cunningham-Atkinson House; see Atkinson,Octavia House

Evergreen Bower; see Walker,Col. Luther,House

Frazier,Sen. Thomas Sidney,House
(Walker-Frazier-Adams House)
County Rd. 40
HABS AL-538
HABS ALA,6-PECH.V,2-
5ph L

Mulberry; see Walker,Col. Luther,House

Walker-Adams House; see Walker,Col. Luther,House

Walker-Frazier-Adams House; see Frazier,Sen. Thomas Sidney,House

Walker,Col. Luther,House (Evergreen Bower; Walker-Adams House; Mulberry)
County Rd. 40
HABS AL-598
HABS ALA,6-PECH.V,3-
11ph/fr L

UNION SPRINGS

Atkinson,Octavia,House
(Cunningham-Atkinson House)
(See BULLOCK CO.,PEACHBURG VIC. for documtatn.)
HABS AL-539
HABS ALA,6-PECH.V,1-
L

Cunningham-Atkinson House; see Atkinson,Octavia,House

Foster-Bryan-Brown House; see Foster,Mrs. Hugh,House

Foster,Mrs. Hugh,House
(Foster-Bryan-Brown House; Laurel Hill)
201 Kennon St.
HABS AL-599
HABS ALA,6-UNSP,1-
14ph L

Laurel Hill; see Foster,Mrs. Hugh,House

UNION SPRINGS VIC.

Evergreen Bower; see Walker,Col. Luther,House

Frazier,Sen. Thomas Sidney,House
(Walker-Frazier-Adams House)
(See BULLOCK CO,PEACHBURG for documentation)
HABS AL-538
HABS ALA,6-PECH.V,2-
5ph L

Mulberry; see Walker,Col. Luther,House

Walker-Adams House; see Walker,Col. Luther,House

Walker-Frazier-Adams House; see Frazier,Sen. Thomas Sidney,House

Walker,Col. Luther,House (Evergreen Bower; Walker-Adams House; Mulberry)
(See BULLOCK CO.,PEACHBURG VIC. for documentation)
HABS AL-598
HABS ALA,6-PECH.V,3-
11ph/fr L

BUTLER COUNTY

GREENVILLE

Beeland-Stanley House (Beeland,Judge Henry,House)
218 E. Commerce St.
HABS AL-692
HABS ALA,7-GRENV,3-
8ph L

Beeland,Judge Henry,House; see Beeland-Stanley House

Beeland,Leavy,House; see Beeland,Leroy,House

Beeland,Leroy,House
(Dunklin-Beeland-Kendrick House; Beeland,Leavy,House)
504 Ft. Dale Rd.
HABS AL-693
HABS ALA,7-GRENV,4-
2ph L

Beeland,R. A.,House; see Dunklin,Major James,House

Burnett-Dunklin-Smith House; see Smith,Earl,House

Dunkin-Smith House; see Smith,Earl,House

Dunklin-Beeland House; see Dunklin,Major James,House

Dunklin-Beeland-Kendrick House; see Beeland,Leroy,House

Documentation: **ct** color transparencies **dr** measured drawings **fr** field records **pc** photograph captions **pg** pages of text **ph** photographs

Dunklin,Major James,House (Dunklin-Beeland House; Beeland,R. A.,House)
111 Herbert St.
HABS AL-688
HABS ALA,7-GRENV,1-
2ph L

Magnolia Cemetery,Grave House; see Pine Crest Cemetery,Grave House

Pine Crest Cemetery,Grave House (Magnolia Cemetery,Grave House)
W. Commerce St.
HABS AL-689-A
HABS ALA,7-GRENV,5-
1ph L

Smith,Earl,House (Dunkin-Smith House; Waller House; Burnett-Dunklin-Smith House)
Commerce & Pine Sts.
HABS AL-691
HABS ALA,7-GRENVI,2-
9ph L

Waller House; see Smith,Earl,House

GREENVILLE VIC.

Crenshaw,Judge Anderson,House (Crenshaw,Nolan,House)
County Rd. 54
HABS AL-690-B
HABS ALA,7- ,5-
2ph L

Crenshaw,Nolan,House; see Crenshaw,Judge Anderson,House

Crenshaw,Walter H.,Plantation (House); see Crenshaw,Will,Plantation (House)

Crenshaw,Will,Plantation (House) (Crenshaw,Walter H.,Plantation (House))
County Rd. 54
HABS AL-690
HABS ALA,7- ,1- & 2-
13ph L

Fort Dale Cemetery,Grave Houses
State Hwy. 185
HABS AL-689-B
HABS ALA,7-GRENV.V,1-
1ph L

Grave House
County Rd. 54 (see AL,Manningham Vic.)
HABS AL-689-C
HABS ALA,7-MAN.V,1-
1ph L

Hartley,Joseph,House; see Tavern & Stage Inn

Palings,The; see Tavern & Stage Inn

Stagecoach Inn; see Tavern & Stage Inn

Tavern & Stage Inn (Hartley,Joseph,House; Stagecoach Inn; Palings,The)
County Rd. 58
HABS AL-694
HABS ALA,7-GRENV.V,2-
4ph L

Womack-Crenshaw House
County Rd. 54
HABS AL-690-A
HABS ALA,7- ,4-
20ph L

Womack,T. Augustus (Gus) House
County Rd. 54
HABS AL-690-C
HABS ALA,7- ,3-
1ph L

MANNINGHAM VIC.

Crenshaw,Judge Anderson,House (Crenshaw,Nolan,House)
(See BUTLER CO.,GREENVILLE VIC. for documentation)
HABS AL-690-B
HABS ALA,7- ,5-
2ph L

Crenshaw,Nolan,House; see Crenshaw,Judge Anderson,House

Crenshaw,Walter,Plantation (House); see Crenshaw,Will,Plantation (House)

Crenshaw,Will,Plantation (House) (Crenshaw,Walter,Plantation (House))
(See BUTLER CO.,GREENVILLE VIC. for documentation)
HABS AL-690
HABS ALA,7- ,1- & 2-
13ph L

Grave House
County Rd. 54 (see AL,Greenville Vic.)
HABS AL-689-C
HABS ALA,7-MAN.V,1-
1ph L

RIDGEVILLE

Womack-Crenshaw House
(See BUTLER CO.,GREENVILLE VIC. for documentation)
HABS AL-690-A
HABS ALA,7- ,4-
20ph L

Womack,T. Augustus (Gus),House
(See BUTLER CO.,GREENVILLE VIC. for documentation)
HABS AL-690-C
L

CALHOUN COUNTY

ALEXANDRIA

Green-Woodruff House
Alexandria-Jacksonville Rd.
HABS AL-468
HABS ALA,8-ALEX,1-
11ph L

ANNISTON VIC.

Aderholdt's Mill; see Mill with Water Wheel

Anniston Army Depot (Coosa River Storage Annex)
HAER AL-10
HAER ALA,8-ANNI.V,2-
45pg/fr L

Coosa River Storage Annex; see Anniston Army Depot

Mill with Water Wheel (Aderholdt's Mill; Water Mill)
Aderholdt's Mill Rd.
HABS AL-421
HABS ALA,8-ANNI.V,1-
7ph L

Water Mill; see Mill with Water Wheel

JACKSONVILLE

Arnold-Rowan House (Snow-Arnold-Rowan House)
201 Murphy St.
HABS AL-450
HABS ALA,8-JACVI,8-
8ph L

Crow Building; see Tavern,Old

Daugette,Dr. E. W.,House (Magnolias,The; Walker-Daugette House)
601 N. Pelham Rd.
HABS AL-415
HABS ALA,8-JACVI,5-
13ph/2pg L

Greenleaf,W. I.,House (Williams-Greenleaf House)
Pelham Rd.
HABS AL-417
HABS ALA,8-JACVI,6-
10ph L

Greenleaf's Store; see Tavern,Old

Hope House (Hotel,Old)
N. Pelham Rd. & Clinton Sts.
HABS AL-481
HABS ALA,8-JACVI,9-
1ph L

Hotel,Old; see Hope House

Magnolias,The; see Daugette,Dr. E. W.,House

Martin,Thomas House (McCampbell-Martin House)
N. Pelham Rd.
HABS AL-480
HABS ALA,8-JACVI,4-
3ph L

McCampbell-Martin House; see Martin,Thomas House

Nisbet-Weaver House; see Weaver House

Presbyterian Church
N. Chinabee & E. Clinton Sts.
HABS AL-419
HABS ALA,8-JACVI,3-
7dr/7ph/2pg/fr L

Snow-Arnold-Rowan House; see Arnold-Rowan House

Tavern,Old (Greenleaf's Store; Crow Building)
E. Clinton & E. Square Sts.
HABS AL-416
HABS ALA,8-JACVI,1-
4dr/10ph/2pg/fr L

Walker-Daugette House; see Daugette,Dr. E. W.,House

Weaver House (Nisbet-Weaver House)
420 E. Ladiga St.
HABS AL-420
HABS ALA,8-JACVI,7-
6ph L

Williams-Greenleaf House; see Greenleaf,W. I.,House

Wood-Crook-Treadway House; see Wood-Treadway House

Wood-Treadway House
(Wood-Crook-Treadway House)
517 N. Pelham Rd.
HABS AL-418
HABS ALA,8-JACVI,2-
4ph L

JACKSONVILLE VIC.

Aderholdt's Mill; see Mill with Water Wheel

Mill with Water Wheel (Aderholdt's Mill; Water Mill)
(See CALHOUN CO.,ANNISTON VIC. for documtatn.)
HABS AL-421
HABS ALA,8-ANNI.V,1-
7ph L

Water Mill; see Mill with Water Wheel

OXFORD

Boiling Spring; see Freeman-Caver-Christian House

Caver-Christian House; see Freeman-Caver-Christian House

Freeman-Caver-Christian House
(Boiling Spring; Caver-Christian House)
Upper Friendship Rd.
HABS AL-470
HABS ALA,8-OXFO.V,1-
16ph L

Snow,Dudley,House
704 Snow St.
HABS AL-465
HABS ALA,8-OXFO,1-
9ph L

OXFORD VIC.

Borders-Blackman House
DeArmanville-Choccolocco Rd.
HABS AL-471
HABS ALA,8-OXFO.V,2-
14ph L

WEAVER

Kelly House
Peachburg Rd.
HABS AL-467
HABS ALA,8-WEAV.V,1-
3ph L

Weaver-Rowe House; see Weaver,D. F.,House

Weaver,D. F.,House (Weaver-Rowe House)
Weaver Rd.
HABS AL-464
HABS ALA,8-WEAV,1-
8ph L

WEAVER VIC.

Glover-Pollack House; see Glover,Doctor,House

Glover,Doctor,House (Lenlock; Glover-Pollack House)
Weaver Rd.
HABS AL-466
HABS ALA,8-WEAV.V,2-
11ph L

Lenlock; see Glover,Doctor,House

WHITE PLAINS

Cobb,Tom,House; see Cook-Johnson House

Cook-Johnson House (Cobb,Tom,House)
HABS AL-469
HABS ALA,8-WHIPL,1-
2ph L

CHAMBERS COUNTY

LAFAYETTE

Andrews House (Andrews-Allen House)
S. Lafayette St. (U.S. Rt. 431)
HABS AL-553
HABS ALA,9-LAFA,3-
9ph L

Andrews-Allen House; see Andrews House

Goodman-Towers-Tatum House; see Tatum,A. A.,House

Hightower Building
15 S. Lafayette St.
HABS AL-890
HABS 1991(HABS):33
14dr/18pg/fr L

McLemore,Betty,House
(McNamee-Kinsey-McLemore House)
342 N. Lafayette St.
HABS AL-530
HABS ALA,9-LAFA,1-
12ph L

McNamee-Kinsey-McLemore House; see McLemore,Betty,House

Tatum,A. A.,House
(Goodman-Towers-Tatum House)
226 N. Lafayette St.
HABS AL-535
HABS ALA,9-LAFA,2-
11ph L

OAK BOWERY

Bullard,Gen. Robert Lee,House
(Dowdell-Mathews-Bullard House)
U.S. Rt. 431 (State Rt. 37)
HABS AL-506
HABS ALA,9-OKBO,1-
3dr/2ph/2pg/fr L

Dowdell-Mathews-Bullard House; see Bullard,Gen. Robert Lee,House

CLARKE COUNTY

GROVE HILL VIC.

Figures-York House; see Vickers-Chapman-Gordon House

Vickers-Chapman-Gordon House
(Figures-York House)
State Hwy. 69
HABS AL-110
HABS ALA,13-GROHI.V,1-
2ph L

SUGGSVILLE

Wilson,Albert,House
County Rd. 35
HABS AL-109
HABS ALA,13-SUGVI,1-
1ph L

CLEBURNE COUNTY

EDWARDSVILLE

Cleburne County Courthouse
U. S. Rt. 78
HABS AL-775
HABS ALA,15-EDWA,1-
13dr L

COLBERT COUNTY

ALLSBORO VIC.

Big Bear Creek Covered Bridge
Spanning Big Bear Creek on County Rd. 7
HABS AL-361-A
HABS ALA,17-ALBO.V,2-
4ph L

Cripple Deer Creek Covered Bridge
Spanning Cripple Deer Creek on County Rd. 1
HABS AL-361
HABS ALA,17-ALBO.V,1-
6ph L

BRICK VIC.

Mt. Pleasant Cumberland Presbyterian Meetinghouse; see Presbyterian Church

Presbyterian Church (Mt. Pleasant Cumberland Presbyterian Meetinghouse)
Mt. Pleasant Rd.
HABS AL-382
HABS ALA,17-BRIC.V,1-
1ph L

CHEROKEE VIC.

Barton Hall; see Cunningham Plantation

Buzzard Roost Covered Bridge
Old Memphis Rd. (Gaines Trace Rd.)
HABS AL-361-B
HABS ALA,17-CHER.V,2-
2ph L

Cunningham Plantation (Barton Hall)
Old Memphis Rd. (Gaines Trace Rd.)
HABS AL-337
HABS ALA,17-CHER.V,1-
13dr/31ph/2pg L

LEIGHTON

Leckey,Hugh C.,House
State Hwy. 20 & County Rd. 48
HABS AL-863
HABS ALA,17-LEIT,1-
2ph/1pg/1pc L

Oaks,The (Ricks,Abraham,House)
Ricks Ln.
HABS AL-362
HABS ALA,17-LEIT.V,1-
12ph/2pg L

Ricks,Abraham,House; see Oaks,The

LEIGHTON VIC.

Mt. Pleasant Cumberland Presbyterian Meetinghouse; see Presbyterian Church

Presbyterian Church (Mt. Pleasant Cumberland Presbyterian Meetinghouse)
(See COLCERT CO.,BRICK VIC. for documentation)
HABS AL-382
HABS ALA,17-BRIC.V,1-
1ph L

Vinson,Drury,House
County Rd. 63
HABS AL-381
HABS ALA,17-LEIT.V,2-
6ph L

SHEFFIELD

Barner House; see Bonner House

Bonner House (Barner House; Winter-Barner House)
2708 Tenth Ave.
HABS AL-323
HABS ALA,17-SHEF,1-
3ph L

Jackson,Andrew,House; see Winston,Anthony,House

Winston,Anthony,House (Jackson,Andrew,House)
(See COLBERT CO.,TUSCUMBIA VIC. for documtatn.)
HABS AL-316-A
HABS ALA,17-TUSM,9-
2ph L

Winter-Barner House; see Bonner House

SHEFFIELD VIC.

House (Kernachan House)
County Rd. 40 (River Rd.)
HABS AL-862
HABS ALA,17-SHEF.V,1-
1ph/1pg/1pc L

Kernachan House; see House

SPRING VALLEY VIC.

Belmont (Thornton,Henry P.,Plantation)
U.S. Hwy. 43
HABS AL-388
HABS ALA,17-SPRIVA.V,1-
13dr/44ph/fr L

Thornton,Henry P.,Plantation; see Belmont

TUSCUMBIA

Aycock,Tom,House
205 W. Jefferson St.
HABS AL-350
HABS ALA,17-TUSM,10-
10ph L

Barber's House (306 West Fifth Street (House))
HABS AL-351
HABS ALA,17-TUSM,18-
1ph L

Bell-Prout-Edwards House; see Edwards House

Carriage Factory (Young's Carriage Shop; Post Office; Keller,Helen,Library)
Main & E. Fourth Sts.
HABS AL-315
HABS ALA,17-TUSM,3-
3dr/3ph/2pg L

Carroll House; see Minor House

Carroll-Johnson House; see Carroll,G. W.,House

Carroll,G. W.,House (Carroll-Johnson House)
801 E. North Commons
HABS AL-322
HABS ALA,17-TUSM,8-
13ph/1pg L

Christian-Lindsay House; see Lindsay,Gov. Robert,House

City Clerk's Office; see First Methodist Church,Old

City Fire Station; see First Methodist Church,Old

Commercial Row
Fifth St.
HABS AL-360
HABS ALA,17-TUSM,15-
3ph L

Coons-Steele-Armistead House; see Goodlow,Judith,House

107 & 109 East Fifth Street (Commercial Buildings); see Morgan House

Edwards House (Bell-Prout-Edwards House)
Dickson & E. Second Sts.
HABS AL-354
HABS ALA,17-TUSM,19-
3ph L

First Methodist Church,Old (City Clerk's Office; City Fire Station)
Dickson & E. Seventh Sts.
HABS AL-313
HABS ALA,17-TUSM,17-
2ph L

First Presbyterian Church
E. Fourth & N. Broad Sts.
HABS AL-314
HABS ALA,17-TUSM,2-
8dr/8ph L

Garmon,Kate,House; see Johnson,John,House

Goodlow,Judith,House (Coons-Steele-Armistead House)
406 N. Main St.
HABS AL-356
HABS ALA,17-TUSM,13-
5ph/1pg L

Gresham House (Stonecroft)
608 E. Fifth St.
HABS AL-319
HABS ALA,17-TUSM,6-
6ph L

Houston-Abernathy-Minor House; see Newson-Minor House

Ivy Green; see Keller,Helen,House

Johnson,John,House (Garmon,Kate,House)
Broad St.
HABS AL-357
HABS ALA,17-TUSM,14-
3ph L

Jones-Winston-Rand House; see Rand,Carl,House

Keller,Helen,House (Ivy Green; Rose & Honeysuckle House)
300 W. North Commons
HABS AL-317
HABS ALA,17-TUSM,4-
8ph/3pg L

Keller,Helen,Library; see Carriage Factory

Lindsay,Gov. Robert,House (Christian-Lindsay House; Tennessee Valley Country Club)
U. S. Hwy. 72
HABS AL-312
HABS ALA,17-TUSM,1-
17ph L

Locust Hill; see Rather,John Daniel,House

Minor House (Carroll House)
HABS AL-384
HABS ALA,17-TUSM,21-
1pg L

Minor House; see Newson-Minor House

Morgan House (107 & 109 East Fifth Street (Commercial Buildings)
HABS AL-321
HABS ALA,17-TUSM,7-
5ph L

Newson-Minor House (Minor House; Houston-Abernathy-Minor House)
204 N. Main St.
HABS AL-355
HABS ALA,17-TUSM,20-
7ph L

Post Office; see Carriage Factory

Rand,Carl,House (Jones-Winston-Rand House)
501 E. Third St.
HABS AL-352
HABS ALA,17-TUSM,16-
11ph L

Rand,Dr. R. A.,House (Violet Hall)
402 N. Commons St.
HABS AL-353
HABS ALA,17-TUSM,12-
5ph/1pg L

Rather,John Daniel,House (Locust Hill)
209 S. Cave St.
HABS AL-318
HABS ALA,17-TUSM,5-
3ph L

Rose & Honeysuckle House; see Keller,Helen,House

Stein House; see Stine House

Stine House (Young-Stine House; Stein House)
407 W. Second St.
HABS AL-349
HABS ALA,17-TUSM,9-
7ph/3pg L

Stonecroft; see Gresham House

Tennessee Valley Country Club; see Lindsay,Gov. Robert,House

Violet Hall; see Rand,Dr. R. A.,House

306 West Fifth Street (House); see Barber's House

Winston,William,House
North Commons St,
HABS AL-316
HABS ALA,17-TUSM.V,1-
2ph L

Young-Stine House; see Stine House

Young's Carriage Shop; see Carriage Factory

TUSCUMBIA VIC.

Belmont (Thornton,Henry P.,Plantation) (See COLBERT CO.,SPRING VALLEY VIC. for documtn.)
HABS AL-388
HABS ALA,17-SPRIVA.V,1-
13dr/44ph/fr L

Goodloe,Colonel,House
HABS AL-380
HABS ALA,17-CHER.V,3-
23ph L

Jackson,Andrew,House; see Winston,Anthony,House

Thornton,Henry P.,Plantation; see Belmont

Vinson,Drury,House
(See COLBERT CO.,LEIGHTON VIC. for documentation)
HABS AL-381
HABS ALA,17-LEIT.V,2-
6ph L

Winston,Anthony,House
(Jackson,Andrew,House)
Eighth St. & Fourteenth Ave.
HABS AL-316-A
HABS ALA,17-TUSM,11-
2ph L

COVINGTON COUNTY

ANDALUSIA VIC.

Camp Chapel; see Methodist Church

Methodist Church (Camp Chapel) (See GREENE CO.,FORKLAND for documentation)
HABS AL-256
HABS ALA,32-FORK,2-
4ph L

CRENSHAW COUNTY

LUVERNE VIC.

Grave Houses
Local Cemetery
HABS AL-689-D
HABS ALA,21-LUV.V,1-
2ph L

MOUNT IDA VIC.

Carlton-Autrey House; see Jenkins-Carlton-Autrey House

Jenkins-Carlton-Autrey House
(Carlton-Autrey House)
County Rd. 52
HABS AL-449
HABS ALA,21-MOUTI.V,1-
9ph L

DALLAS COUNTY

CAHABA

Barker-Kirkpatrick House; see Kirkpatrick House

Bell House (Fambro-Troy House)
First North & Oak Sts.
HABS AL-731
HABS ALA,24-CAHA,4-
4ph L

Crocheron House (Remains)
(Crocheron-Matthews House (Remains))
Second North St.
HABS AL-728
HABS ALA,24-CAHA,3-
1ph L

Crocheron-Matthews House (Remains); see Crocheron House (Remains)

Duke,Captain,House; see Evans,Grace,House

Evans,Grace,House
(Duke,Captain,House)
Alabama River Vic.
HABS AL-729
HABS ALA,24-CAHA,7-
1ph L

Fambro-Troy House; see Bell House

First State Capitol Marker; see Monument

Gayle,Col. Rees D.,House
Oak & First South Sts.
HABS AL-732
HABS ALA,24-CAHA,5-
1ph L

Kirkpatrick House (Barker-Kirkpatrick House)
Oak St.
HABS AL-727
HABS ALA,24-CAHA,2-
6ph L

Methodist Church
Walnut St.
HABS AL-726
HABS ALA,24-CAHA,1-
6dr/3ph/2pg/fr L

Monument (First State Capitol Marker)
HABS AL-725
HABS ALA,24-CAHA,6-
1ph L

St. Luke's Episcopal Church
(See DALLAS CO.,MARTIN'S STATION for documtatn.)
HABS AL-734
HABS ALA,24-MART,1-
L

MARTIN'S STATION

St. Luke's Episcopal Church
(Moved from Cahaba,AL)
HABS AL-734
HABS ALA,24-MART,1-
6dr/4ph/5pg L

ORRVILLE

Craig-Wilson House
County Rd. 2
HABS AL-738
HABS ALA,24-ORVI,5-
1ph L

Dunaway,Ben Ellis,House (Orrville Male Academy)
State Hwy. 22
HABS AL-737
HABS ALA,24-ORVI,3-
3ph L

Kelley-Bland-Ward House
County Rd. 2 Vic.
HABS AL-755
HABS ALA,24-ORVI,4-
4ph L

Milhous-Albritton House; see Mill-Albritton House

Mill-Albritton House (Milhous-Albritton House)
State Hwy. 22
HABS AL-736
HABS ALA,24-ORVI,2-
1ph L

Molette Houses
County Rds. 33 & 31 Vic.
HABS AL-753
HABS ALA,24-ORVI,6-
2ph L

Orrville Male Academy; see Dunaway,Ben Ellis,House

Smith-Sutton House
State Hwy. 22
HABS AL-735
HABS ALA,24-ORVI,1-
1ph L

ORRVILLE VIC.

Bland House (Bland-Chestnut House)
County Rd. 11 Vic.
HABS AL-749
HABS ALA,24-ORVI.V,1-
5ph L

Bland-Chestnut House; see Bland House

Cochran House (Cochran-Crumpton House; McCreary House; Crumptonia)
County Rd. 21
HABS AL-750
HABS ALA,24, ,1-
4ph L

Cochran-Crumpton House; see Cochran House

Crumptonia; see Cochran House

McCreary House; see Cochran House

McMillan,Lewis,House
County Rd. 31
HABS AL-752
HABS ALA,24- ,3-
2ph L

Moseley-Seal House; see Seal House

Seal House (Moseley-Seal House)
County Rd. 33 Vic.
HABS AL-751
HABS ALA,24- ,2-
3ph L

St. Luke's Episcopal Church
(See DALLAS CO.,MARTIN'S STATION for documtatn.)
HABS AL-734
HABS ALA,24-MART,1-
fr L

SELMA

Beel-Bennett House (Burns-Bell House; Bell House)
412 Lauderdale Ave.
HABS AL-707
HABS ALA,24-SEL,12-
2ph L

Bell House; see Beel-Bennett House

Blake,Samuel R.,House; see McKee,Harvey L.,House

Brantley Hotel; see St. James Hotel

504 Broad Street (House); see Pitts,L. B.,House

Burns-Bell House; see Beel-Bennett House

Dawson-Vaughan House
704 Tremont St.
HABS AL-711
HABS ALA,24-SEL,14-
11ph L

First Christian Church Property (House) (207 Franklin Street (House))
HABS AL-710
HABS ALA,24-SEL,6-
1ph L

207 Franklin Street (House); see First Christian Church Property (House)

Franklin,H. F.,House; see White-Franklin House

819 Jefferson Davis Avenue (House); see White-Franklin House

Jones,C.,House (433 Lauderdale Avenue (House))
HABS AL-706
HABS ALA,24-SEL,11-
2ph L

King-Welch House
607 Union St.
HABS AL-703
HABS ALA,24-SEL,3-
1ph L

Kirkpatrick,Doctor,House (601 Washington Street (House))
HABS AL-709
HABS ALA,24-SEL,13-
3ph L

433 Lauderdale Avenue (House); see Jones,C.,House

Mabry-Jones House; see Mabry,A. T.,House

Mabry,A. T.,House (Mabry-Jones House)
629 Tremont St.
HABS AL-705
HABS ALA,24-SEL,4-
5ph/fr L

Marks House; see Plattenburg House

Marks-Plattenburg House; see Plattenburg House

McKee,Harvey L.,House (Blake,Samuel R.,House; Suttle House)
911 Mabry St.
HABS AL-701
HABS ALA,24-SEL,9-
5ph L

Morgan-Agee House
(Wetmore-Morgan-Agee House; Morgan,Sen. John T.,House)
719 Tremont St.
HABS AL-712
HABS ALA,24-SEL,7-
5ph L

Morgan,Sen. John T.,House; see Morgan-Agee House

Pitts,L. B.,House (504 Broad Street (House))
HABS AL-708
HABS ALA,24-SEL,5-
2ph L

Planters' Hotel; see St. James Hotel

Plattenburg House (Marks-Plattenburg House; Marks House)
1009 N. Lapsley St.
HABS AL-702
HABS ALA,24-SEL,2-
8ph L

St. James Hotel (Brantley Hotel; Planters' Hotel; Troupe House; Warehouse)
1200 Water Ave.
HABS AL-713
HABS ALA,24-SEL,8-
13ph L

Sturdivant Hall; see Watts-Parkman-Gillman House

Sturdivant House; see Watts-Parkman-Gillman House

Suttle House; see McKee,Harvey L.,House

Troupe House; see St. James Hotel

Warehouse; see St. James Hotel

601 Washington Street (House); see Kirkpatrick,Doctor,House

Watts-Parkman-Gillman House
(Sturdivant House; Sturdivant Hall)
713 Mabry St.
HABS AL-700
HABS ALA,24-SEL,1-
10ph/fr L

Wetmore-Morgan-Agee House; see Morgan-Agee House

White-Franklin House (Franklin,H. F.,House; 819 Jefferson Davis Avenue (House))
HABS AL-704
HABS ALA,24-SEL,10-
5ph L

SELMA VIC.

Harper,Doctor,House
(Harrison-Hunter-Harper House; Oaks,The)
State Hwy. 219 & County Rd. 344
HABS AL-754
HABS ALA,24-SEL.V,2-
6ph L

Harrison-Hunter-Harper House; see Harper,Doctor,House

Kenan,Dan,House
Summerfield Rd. (County Rd. 37)
HABS AL-739
HABS ALA,24-SEL.V,1-
12ph L

Oaks,The; see Harper,Doctor,House

SUMMERFIELD

Blacksmith Shop
Centenary & Main Sts.
HABS AL-763
HABS ALA,24-SUM,10-
1ph L

Boys' Methodist College (Summerfield College,Boys' Dormitory; Centenary Institute,Boys' Dormitory)
Centenary & Main Sts.
HABS AL-746
HABS ALA,24-SUM,5-
2ph L

Centenary Institute,Boys' Dormitory; see Boys' Methodist College

Centenary Institute,Dr. Hudson Building; see Summerfield College,Dr. Hudson Building

Centenary Institute,Dr. Jackson Building; see Summerfield College,Dr. Jackson Building

Centenary Institute,Main Building; see Summerfield College,Main Building

Centenary Institute,Music Building; see Summerfield College,Music Building

Childers-Tate House
Centenary St.
HABS AL-730
HABS ALA,24-SUM,1-
1ph L

Hudson Summer House (Moore-Hudson House)
County Rd. 37
HABS AL-744
HABS ALA,24-SUM,3-
1ph L

King House (Mitchell-King House; Mitchell House)
Centenary St.
HABS AL-758
HABS ALA,24-SUM,9-
1ph L

Main Street (Bank Building)
HABS AL-757
HABS ALA,24-SUM,8-
1ph L

Methodist Church; see Methodist Episcopal Church

Methodist Episcopal Church
(Methodist Church)
College St.
HABS AL-748
HABS ALA,24-SUM,7-
1ph L

Methodist Orphans' Home; see Summerfield College,Main Building

Mitchell House; see King House

Mitchell-King House; see King House

Moore House (Swift-Moore-Cottingham House)
Persimmon St.
HABS AL-747
HABS ALA,24-SUM,6-
6ph L

Moore-Hudson House; see Hudson Summer House

Sturdivant-Moore-Hartley House
Centenary & Main Sts.
HABS AL-745
HABS ALA,24-SUM,4-
8ph L

Summerfield College,Boys' Dormitory; see Boys' Methodist College

Summerfield College,Dr. Hudson Building (Centenary Institute,Dr. Hudson Building)
College St.
HABS AL-742
HABS ALA,24-SUM,2C-
3ph L

Summerfield College,Dr. Jackson Building (Centenary Institute,Dr. Jackson Building)
Main & College Sts.
HABS AL-743
HABS ALA,24-SUM,2D-
2ph L

Summerfield College,Main Building
(Centenary Institute,Main Building; Methodist Orphans' Home)
Main & College Sts.
HABS AL-741
HABS ALA,24-SUM,2A-
2ph L

Summerfield College,Music Building
(Centenary Institute,Music Building)
Main & College Sts.
HABS AL-740
HABS ALA,24-SUM,2B-
5dr/3ph/2pg/fr L

Swift-Moore-Cottingham House; see Moore House

ELMORE COUNTY

ELMORE VIC.

Fitzpatrick,Gov. Benjamin,House (Oak Grove)
State Rt. 14 Vic.
HABS AL-697
HABS ALA,26-ELMO,1-
17ph L

Oak Grove; see Fitzpatrick,Gov. Benjamin,House

ROBINSON SPRINGS

Methodist Church (Robinson Springs United Methodist Church)
State Rt. 143
HABS AL-682
HABS ALA,26-ROBSP,1-
7ph L

Methodist Parsonage,Old
State Rt. 143
HABS AL-698
HABS ALA,26-ROBSP,2-
2ph L

Robinson Springs United Methodist Church; see Methodist Church

TALLASSEE

Tallassee Mills
1844 Old Mill Rd.
HABS AL-956
12dr/fr H

WETUMPKA

Airey,J. Bruce,House (Seaman-Airey House)
1202 W. Tuskeena St.
HABS AL-659
HABS ALA,26-WETU,10-
9ph L

Baptist Church (First Baptist Church)
205 W. Bridge St.
HABS AL-657
HABS ALA,266-WETU,9-
7ph L

Bateman,Florence Golson,House; see Bates-Jesse House

Bates-Jesse House (Northrup-Bateman House; Bateman,Florence Golson,House; Bates-Jesse-Ensken House)
311 Government St.
HABS AL-660
HABS ALA,26-WETU,3-
12ph L

Bates-Jesse-Ensken House; see Bates-Jesse House

Bradford House (Bradford-Stowe House)
401 W. Main St.
HABS AL-664
HABS ALA,26-WETU,7-
6ph L

Bradford-Stowe House; see Bradford House

Cantelow,Laura,House (207 West Tuskeena Street (House); Fitzpatrick,Kelly,Birthplace)
HABS AL-663
HABS ALA,26-WETU,6-
3ph L

First Baptist Church; see Baptist Church

Fitzpatrick,Kelly House (Trimble-Fitzpatrick House)
Autauga St.
HABS AL-658
HABS ALA,26-WETU,2-
14ph/2pg/fr L

Fitzpatrick,Kelly,Birthplace; see Cantelow,Laura,House

McQueen-McCullars House; see Tavern,Old

Methodist Church; see Wetumpka Methodist Church

Northrup-Bateman House; see Bates-Jesse House

Presbyterian Church; see Wetumpka Presbyterian Church

Seaman-Airey House; see Airey,J. Bruce,House

Smoot,E. L.,House
705 Mansion St.
HABS AL-661
HABS ALA,26-WETU,4-
10ph L

Tavern,Old (McQueen-McCullars House)
Broad & W. Bridge Sts.
HABS AL-662
HABS ALA,26-WETU,5-
6ph L

Trimble-Fitzpatrick House; see Fitzpatrick,Kelly House

207 West Tuskeena Street (House); see Cantelow,Laura,House

Wetumpka Methodist Church (Methodist Church)
306 W. Tuskeena St.
HABS AL-655
HABS ALA,26-WETU,1-
6ph L

Wetumpka Presbyterian Church (Presbyterian Church)
W. Bridge & N. Bridge Sts.
HABS AL-656
HABS ALA,26-WETU,8-
10ph/2pg L

WETUMPKA VIC.

Bullard-Brannon-Owen House; see Bullard,John,House

Bullard,John,House (Bullard-Brannon-Owen House; Sugarberry Hill; Henderson House; Tennessee Place)
Harrogate Springs Rd. Vic.
HABS AL-665
HABS ALA,26-WETU.V,1-
8ph/2pg/fr L

Henderson House; see Bullard,John,House

Sugarberry Hill; see Bullard,John,House

Tennessee Place; see Bullard,John,House

FAYETTE COUNTY

FAYETTE VIC.

McCaleb-Hollingsworth Mill (McCaleb's Old Mill)
(See FAYETTE CO.,HERRICK for documentation)
HABS AL-390
HABS ALA,29-HER,1-
L

McCaleb's Old Mill; see McCaleb-Hollingsworth Mill

HERRICK

McCaleb 's Old Mill; see McCaleb-Hollingsworth House

McCaleb-Hollingsworth House (McCaleb 's Old Mill)
Mill Creek
HABS AL-390
HABS ALA,29-HER,1-
4ph L

GREENE COUNTY

BOLIGEE

Beth Salem Presbyterian Church
County Rd. 1
HABS AL-282
HABS ALA,32-BOLI,1-
2ph/1pg L

BOLIGEE VIC.

Boligee Hill (Myrtlewood; Hays House)
(See GREENE CO.,EUTAW VIC. for documentation)
HABS AL-209
HABS ALA,32-EUTA.V,1-
15ph/1pg L

Gould House; see Hill of Howth

Hays House; see Boligee Hill

Hill of Howth (McKee-Gould House; Gould House)
County Rd. 19
HABS AL-208
HABS ALA,32-BOLI.V,1-
9ph/2pg L

McKee-Gould House; see Hill of Howth

Myrtlewood; see Boligee Hill

Weston (House,Smokehouse & Schoolhouse)
U.S. Rt. 11 & County Rd. 19 Vic.
HABS AL-272
HABS ALA,32-BOLI.V,2-
7ph L

CLINTON

George Washington Lodge Number 24; see Masonic Temple

Masonic Temple (George Washington Lodge Number 24; Store)
St. Rts. 14 & 39
HABS AL-229
HABS ALA,32-CLINT,1-
4ph/1pg L

Store; see Masonic Temple

ERIE

George Washington Lodge Number 24; see Masonic Temple

Masonic Temple (George Washington Lodge Number 24; Store)
(See GREENE CO.,CLINTON for documentation)
HABS AL-229
HABS ALA,32-CLINT,1-
4ph/1pg L

Store; see Masonic Temple

EUTAW

Alexander-Webb House; see Webb-Alexander House

Anthony,David Rinehart,House; see Wynne House

Banks,J. O.,House & Smokehouse (Shawver-Coleman-Banks House & Smokehouse)
Springfield Ave. & Pickens St.
HABS AL-246
HABS ALA,32-EUTA,8-
8ph/1pg/fr L

Clark-Malone House
243 Wilson St.
HABS AL-240
HABS ALA,32-EUTA,14-
4ph/1pg L

Clark-Smith House; see Smith,A. W.,House

Dunlap,C. W.,House
(Wilson-Herndon-Dunlap House)
237 Wilson Ave.
HABS AL-270
HABS ALA,32-EUTA,12-
7ph L

Eutaw Female Academy (Eutaw Female College; Mesopotamia Female Seminary; Mesopotamia Academy; Miles College,Dormitory)
Main St. & Wilson Ave. (moved from original site)
HABS AL-243
HABS ALA,32-EUTA,5- & 5A-
8ph/1pg L

Eutaw Female College; see Eutaw Female Academy

First Presbyterian Church
Main St. & Wilson Ave.
HABS AL-252
HABS ALA,32-EUTA,10-
10ph/1pg L

Greene County Courthouse
Main & Boligee Sts.,Prairie & Monroe Aves.
HABS AL-218
HABS ALA,32-EUTA,2-
8ph/2pg/fr L

Greene County Courthouse,Probate Judge's Office
Courthouse Sq.
HABS AL-218-A
HABS ALA,32-EUTA,15-
2ph L

Kirksey,Dr. H. A.,House; see Kirkwood

Kirkwood (Kirksey,Dr. H. A.,House)
Mesopotomia St. & Kirkwood Dr.,
HABS AL-210
HABS ALA,32-EUTA,1-
8ph/2pg L

Law Office,Old
Main St.
HABS AL-273
HABS ALA,32-EUTA,13-
2ph L

Mesopotamia Academy; see Eutaw Female Academy

Mesopotamia Female Seminary; see Eutaw Female Academy

Miles College,Dormitory; see Eutaw Female Academy

Perkins-Spencer House
(Spencer-Perkins House)
Spencer St.
HABS AL-241
HABS ALA,32-EUTA,3-
6ph/1pg L

Reese-Lucius House
242 Wilson Ave.
HABS AL-242
HABS ALA,32-EUTA,4-
5ph/1pg L

Shawver-Coleman-Banks House & Smokehouse; see Banks,J. O.,House & Smokehouse

Smith,A. W.,House (Clark-Smith House)
220 Main St.
HABS AL-251
HABS ALA,32-EUTA,9-
11ph/1pg L

Spencer-Perkins House; see Perkins-Spencer House

Webb-Alexander House
(Alexander-Webb House)
309 Main St.
HABS AL-245
HABS ALA,32-EUTA,7-
4ph/1pg L

White-McGiffert House & Office
Mesopotamia St.
HABS AL-269
HABS ALA,32-EUTA,11-
10ph L

Wilson-Herndon-Dunlap House; see Dunlap,C. W.,House

Winn House; see Wynne House

Wynne House (Anthony,David Rinehart,House; Winn House)
307 Wilson Ave.
HABS AL-244
HABS ALA,32-EUTA,6-
4ph/1pg L

EUTAW VIC.

Boligee Hill (Myrtlewood; Hays House)
Near U.S. Hwy 11
HABS AL-209
HABS ALA,32-EUTA.V,1-
15ph/1pg L

Hays House; see Boligee Hill

Myrtlewood; see Boligee Hill

FORKLAND

Brewer,H. B.,House
(Lewis-Parker-Gilmore House)
County Rd. 4
HABS AL-258
HABS ALA,32-FORK,7-
4ph L

Camp Chapel; see Methodist Church

Episcopal Church (St. John's Episcopal Church; St. John's-in-the-Prairies)
County Rd. 4 (moved from original location)
HABS AL-255
HABS ALA,32-FORK,1-
4ph L

Glover,Virginia,House
County Rds. 19 & 4
HABS AL-253
HABS ALA,32-FORK,5-
7ph L

Glover,William,House; see Tavern,The

Inn,Old; see Tavern,The

Levy-Glover Store (Store)
County Rds. 19 & 4
HABS AL-254
HABS ALA,32-FORK,6-
5ph L

Lewis-Parker-Gilmore House; see Brewer,H. B.,House

Methodist Church (Camp Chapel)
County Rd. 19 (Moved to Andalusia Vic.,AL)
HABS AL-256
HABS ALA,32-FORK,2-
4ph L

Methodist Parsonage
County Rd. 4
HABS AL-256-A
HABS ALA,32-FORK,3-
4ph L

St. John's Episcopal Church; see Episcopal Church

St. John's-in-the-Prairies; see Episcopal Church

Store; see Levy-Glover Store

Tavern,The (Glover,William,House; Inn,Old)
County Rd. 19
HABS AL-259
HABS ALA,32-FORK,4-
11ph L

FORKLAND VIC.

Fair Hill; see Perrin-Willis House

Glen Alpine; see McAlpine House

Glover-Legare House; see Rosemount

McAlpine House (Glen Alpine)
(See GREENE CO.,WATSONIA for documentation)
HABS AL-281
HABS ALA,32-WATSO,3-
1ph L

Perrin-Willis House (Fair Hill)
(See GREENE CO.,WATSONIA for documentation)
HABS AL-280
HABS ALA,32-WATSO,2-
3ph L

Rosemount (Glover-Legare House)
County Rd. 19
HABS AL-212
HABS ALA,32-FORK.V,1-
16dr/19ph/2pg L

Strawberry Hill Plantation (Walton,William,House)
U.S. Rt. 43
HABS AL-271
HABS ALA,32-FORK.V,2-
11ph/3pg L

Thornhill Plantation (Thornton Plantation House)
(See GREENE CO.,WATSONIA for documentation)
HABS AL-238
HABS ALA,32-WATSO,1-
16dr/37ph/2pg L

Thornton Plantation House; see Thornhill Plantation

Walton,William,House; see Strawberry Hill Plantation

WATSONIA

Fair Hill; see Perrin-Willis House

Glen Alpine; see McAlpine House

McAlpine House (Glen Alpine)
F.A.S. 1306
HABS AL-281
HABS ALA,32-WATSO,3-
1ph L

Perrin-Willis House (Fair Hill)
County Rd. 19
HABS AL-280
HABS ALA,32-WATSO,2-
3ph L

Thornhill Plantation (Thornton Plantation House)
County Rd. 19
HABS AL-238
HABS ALA,32-WATSO,1-
16dr/37ph/2pg L

Thornton Plantation House; see Thornhill Plantation

HALE COUNTY

AKRON VIC.

Tanglewood
HABS AL-177
HABS ALA,33-AKRO.V,1-
1dr/fr L

GALLION

Gracey-Spencer Mansion & Outbuildings; see Waldwic,House & Outbuildings

Spencer House & Outbuildings; see Waldwic,House & Outbuildings

Waldwic,House & Outbuildings (Gracey-Spencer Mansion & Outbuildings; Spencer House & Outbuildings)
State Rt. 69
HABS AL-260
HABS ALA,33-GALI,1-
11ph L

GREENSBORO

Carson,Doctor,House; see Seay,Gov. Thomas,House

Derrick House (Drake-Northrup House; Stickney-Northrup House)
603 E. Main St.
HABS AL-250
HABS ALA,33-GREBO,13-
12ph L

Drake-Northrup House; see Derrick House

Erwin,Cadwallader,House; see Glencairn

Gayle-Hobson-Tunstall House
1801 W. Main St.
HABS AL-232
HABS ALA,33-GREBO,3-
10ph/1pg L

Gayle-Locke House
University Ave. (College St.)
HABS AL-278
HABS ALA,33-GREBO,15-
7ph L

Gayle,Gov.,House; see Southern University,Chancellor's House

Glencairn (Erwin,Cadwallader,House)
Tuscaloosa St.
HABS AL-266
HABS ALA,33-GREBO,7-
12ph/2pg L

Greenwood; see Pickens,W. C.,House

Hannah,Dr. Robert C.,House
Church & South Sts.
HABS AL-275
HABS ALA,33-GREBO,8-
4ph L

Hobson,Adm. Richmond Pearson,House; see Magnolia Grove

Jackson House (Jackson-Locke House)
Demopolis St.
HABS AL-287
HABS ALA,33-GREBO,10-
5ph L

Jackson-Locke House; see Jackson House

Japonica Path; see Knight House

Johndston-Torbert House; see Torbert,Judge W. E.,House

Knight House (Norris-Smaw House; Japonica Path; Smaw House; Withers,Louise,House)
512 Main St.
HABS AL-220
HABS ALA,33-GREBO,2-
5ph/1pg L

Lewis-Murphy-Stewart House; see Webb House

Magnolia Grove (Hobson,Adm. Richmond Pearson,House)
1002 Hobson St.
HABS AL-219
HABS ALA,33-GREBO,1-
8dr/14ph/6pg/fr L

Magnolia Hall; see McCrary-Otts House

McCrary-Otts House (Magnolia Hall; Otts,J. W.,House)
805 Otts St.
HABS AL-265
HABS ALA,33-GREBO,6-
8dr/21ph/1pg/fr L

Methodist Hospital; see Southern University,Chancellor's House

Moore,Col. Sydenham,House; see Pickens,W. C.,House

Multa Flora; see Webb House

Norris-Smaw House; see Knight House

Otts,J. W.,House; see McCrary-Otts House

Otts,Lee,House; see Shackelford-McCrary-Otts House

Pickens,W. C.,House (Greenwood; Moore,Col. Sydenham,House; Rothenberg,E. G.,House)
2201 Main St.
HABS AL-235
HABS ALA,33-GREBO,5-
1ph L

Rothenberg,E. G.,House; see Pickens,W. C.,House

Seay,Gov. Thomas,House (Vaughn,J. A.,House; Carson,Doctor,House)
E. Main & Whelan Sts.
HABS AL-234
HABS ALA,33-GREBO,4-
9ph/1pg L

Shackelford-McCrary-Otts House (Otts,Lee,House)
901 Centreville St.
HABS AL-274
HABS ALA,33-GREBO,14-
5ph/2pg L

Smaw House; see Knight House

Southern University,Chancellor's House (Methodist Hospital; Gayle,Gov.,House)
College St.
HABS AL-277
HABS ALA,33-GREBO,12-
12ph L

Southern University,Old
University Ave. (College St.)
HABS AL-221
HABS ALA,33-GREBO,11-
15ph/2pg L

Stickney-Northrup House; see Derrick House

Torbert,Judge W. E.,House
(Johndston-Torbert House)
1101 South St.
HABS AL-286
HABS ALA,33-GREBO,9-
12ph L

Vaughn,J. A.,House; see Seay,Gov. Thomas,House

Webb House (Multa Flora; Lewis-Murphy-Stewart House)
520 Main St.
HABS AL-289
HABS ALA,33-GREBO,16-
14ph/2pg L

Withers,Louise,House; see Knight House

GREENSBORO VIC.

Cedarwood (Stickney,Joseph Blodgett,House)
HABS AL-843
HABS ALA,33-GREBO.V,1-
6dr L

Stickney,Joseph Blodgett,House; see Cedarwood

Tinker House (Columns)
HABS AL-220-A
HABS ALA,33-GREBO,2A-
3ph/1pg L

MOUNDVILLE VIC.

Cedarwood (Stickney,Joseph Blodgett,House)
(See HALE CO.,GREENSBORO VIC. for documentation)
HABS AL-843
HABS DLC/ADE-1983(HABS):92
6dr L

Stickney,Joseph Blodgett,House; see Cedarwood

Whatley,J. W.,House (Woodland)
State Rt. 69
HABS AL-279
HABS ALA,33-MOUND.V,1-
6ph L

Woodland; see Whatley,J. W.,House

NEWBERN

Baptist Church
State Rt. 61
HABS AL-237
HABS ALA,33-NEWB,2-
3ph/1pg L

Presbyterian Church
State Rt. 61
HABS AL-288
HABS ALA,33-NEWB,3-
4ph/2pg L

Walthalia; see Walthall House

Walthall House (Walthalia)
State Rt. 61
HABS AL-215
HABS ALA,33-NEWB,1-
7ph/2pg L

PRAIRIEVILLE

Episcopal Church (St. Andrew's Episcopal Church)
U. S. Rt. 80
HABS AL-291
HABS ALA,33-PRARV,1-
8ph L

St. Andrew's Episcopal Church; see Episcopal Church

SAWYERVILLE VIC.

Pickens,Gov. Samuel,House (Umbria; Sledge House)
State Rt. 14
HABS AL-236
HABS ALA,33-SAWV.V,1-
9dr/30ph L

Sledge House; see Pickens,Gov. Samuel,House

Umbria; see Pickens,Gov. Samuel,House

HENRY COUNTY

ABBEVILLE

Oates-Danzey House
W. Washington & Trawick Sts.
HABS AL-523
HABS ALA,34-ABVI,1-
6ph L

COLUMBIA

Dunwoody,S. M., House
Abbeville Hwy.
HABS AL-579
HABS ALA,35-COLUM,3-
3ph L

HALEBURG VIC.

Fluker,Col. Baldwin M.,House
(See HENRY CO.,SHORTERVILLE for documentation)
HABS AL-566
HABS ALA,34-SHORV,1-
2ph L

SHORTERVILLE

Chitley House
River Rd. (County Rd. 97)
HABS AL-575
HABS ALA,34-SHORV,2-
4ph L

Fluker,Col. Baldwin M.,House
Abbie Ridge Rd.
HABS AL-566
HABS ALA,34-SHORV,1-
2ph L

Irwin-McAllister House
Ft. Gaines Hwy.
HABS AL-524
HABS ALA,34-SHORV.V,1-
7ph L

Smith,Bartlett,House
(See HENRY CO.,SHORTERVILLE VIC. for documtatn.)
HABS AL-544
HABS ALA,34-SHORV.V,
11ph L

SHORTERVILLE VIC.

Smith,Bartlett,House
River Rd. (County Rd. 97)
HABS AL-544
HABS ALA,34-SHORV.V,
11ph L

HOUSTON COUNTY

COLUMBIA

Bowden,Sam,Hotel; see Bowden,Tom,House

Bowden,Tom,House (Bowden,Sam,Hotel)
Greenwood St.
HABS AL-580
HABS ALA,35-COLUM,4-
1ph L

McGriff,T. P.,House; see Taylor,J. B.,House

Taylor-McGriff House; see Taylor,J. B.,House

Taylor,J. B.,House (McGriff,T. P.,House; Taylor-McGriff House)
Washington St.
HABS AL-565
HABS ALA,35-COLUM,2-
3ph L

Teague-Regell House
South & Washington Sts.
HABS AL-567
HABS ALA,35-COLUM,1-
2ph L

FORKLAND VIC.

Dunwoody,S. M.,House
(See HENRY CO.,COLUMBIA for documentation)
HABS AL-579
L

Documentation: **ct** color transparencies **dr** measured drawings **fr** field records **pc** photograph captions **pg** pages of text **ph** photographs

GORDON

Britt-Williams-Borders House
Greenwood St.
HABS AL-568
HABS ALA,35-GORD,1-
1ph L

GORDON VIC.

Nunnley-Bowden House
State Rt. 95
HABS AL-569
HABS ALA,35-GORD.V,1-
3ph L

JACKSON COUNTY

BRIDGEPORT VIC.

Bridgeport Swing Span Bridge
Spanning Tennessee River
HAER AL-8
HAER ALA,36-BRIPO.V,1-
18ph/12pg/4pc L

JEFFERSON COUNTY

BESSEMER

Addison Elementery School; see Muscoda,School for Blacks

Bessemer Hall of History Museum; see Southern Railway Depot

Birmingham Industrial District; see Muscoda

Birmingham Industrial District; see Muscoda,Black Worker Houses

Birmingham Industrial District; see Muscoda,Independent Baptist Church

Birmingham Industrial District; see Muscoda,Mine Headquarters

Birmingham Industrial District; see Muscoda,President's House

Birmingham Industrial District; see Muscoda,School

Birmingham Industrial District; see Muscoda,School for Blacks

Birmingham Industrial District; see Muscoda,Starlight Baptist Church

Birmingham Industrial District; see Muscoda,Superintendent's House

Birmingham Industrial District; see Muscoda,Worker Houses

Birmingham Industrial District; see Pullman Standard Company Plant

Birmingham Industrial District; see Royster,F.S.,Guano Co.

Birmingham Industrial District; see Southern Railway Depot

Birmingham Industrial District; see U.S. Pipe Plant

Muscoda (Muscoda Village; Birmingham Industrial District)
HABS AL-953
H

Muscoda Village; see Muscoda

Muscoda,Black Worker Houses
(Birmingham Industrial District)
Morgan Rd.
HABS AL-953-E
H

Muscoda,Independent Baptist Church
(Birmingham Industrial District)
Ave. G
HABS AL-953-D
H

Muscoda,Mine Headquarters
(Birmingham Industrial District)
E. of St. Rt. 150,on S. slope of Red Mt.
HABS AL-953-H
H

Muscoda,President's House
(Birmingham Industrial District)
1405 Minnesota Ave.
HABS AL-953-A
H

Muscoda,School (Birmingham Industrial District)
HABS AL-953-G
H

Muscoda,School for Blacks (Addison Elementery School; Birmingham Industrial District)
413 Morgan Rd.
HABS AL-953-F
H

Muscoda,Starlight Baptist Church
(Birmingham Industrial District)
St. Rt. 150 at Morgan Rd.
HABS AL-953-I
H

Muscoda,Superintendent's House
(Birmingham Industrial District)
Mineesota Ave.
HABS AL-953-B
H

Muscoda,Worker Houses (Birmingham Industrial District)
1500 Block Minnesota Ave.
HABS AL-953-C
H

Pullman Standard Company Plant
(Trinity Industries Plant; Birmingham Industrial District)
401 N. Twenty-fourth St.
HAER AL-31
H

Royster,F.S.,Guano Co. (Birmingham Industrial District)
Thirty-second St.
HAER AL-33
H

Southern Railway Depot (Bessemer Hall of History Museum; Birmingham Industrial District)
1905 Alabama Ave.
HABS AL-923
H

Trinity Industries Plant; see Pullman Standard Company Plant

U.S. Pipe & Foundry Company Plant; see U.S. Pipe Plant

U.S. Pipe Plant (U.S. Pipe & Foundry Company Plant; Birmingham Industrial District)
2123 St. Louis Ave. at I-20,59
HAER AL-32
H

BIRMINGHAM

American Cast Iron Pipe Company Plant (Birmingham Industrial District)
1501 Thirty-first Ave. N.
HAER AL-35
H

Arlington (Mudd-Munger House; Munger House)
331 Cotton Ave.,SW
HABS AL-424
HABS ALA,37-BIRM,1-
23ph/2pg L

Birmingham District National Heritage Corridor; see Hardie-Tynes Manufacturing Company

Birmingham Industrial District; see American Cast Iron Pipe Company Plant

Birmingham Industrial District; see Hardie-Tynes Manufacturing Co.,Ait Compressor Hous

Birmingham Industrial District; see Hardie-Tynes Manufacturing Co.,Bath House

Birmingham Industrial District; see Hardie-Tynes Manufacturing Co.,Crane

Birmingham Industrial District; see Hardie-Tynes Manufacturing Co.,Erection Shop

Birmingham Industrial District; see Hardie-Tynes Manufacturing Co.,Fabrication Shop

Birmingham Industrial District; see Hardie-Tynes Manufacturing Co.,Foundry

Birmingham Industrial District; see Hardie-Tynes Manufacturing Co.,Machine Shop

Birmingham Industrial District; see Hardie-Tynes Manufacturing Co.,Main Office

Birmingham Industrial District; see Hardie-Tynes Manufacturing Co.,Paint Storage Shed

Birmingham Industrial District; see Hardie-Tynes Manufacturing Co.,Pattern Shop

Birmingham Industrial District; see Hardie-Tynes Manufacturing Co.,Pattern Storage

Birmingham Industrial District; see Hardie-Tynes Manufacturing Co.,Power House

Birmingham Industrial District; see Hardie-Tynes Manufacturing Co.,Sand Blasting Shed

Birmingham Industrial District; see Hardie-Tynes Manufacturing Co.,Shed

Birmingham Industrial District; see Hardie-Tynes Manufacturing Co.,Smith Shop

Birmingham Industrial District; see Heart of Dixie Railroad,Rolling Stock

Birmingham Industrial District; see Heaviest Corner on Earth (Commercial)

Birmingham Industrial District; see Ingram,Kelly Park

Birmingham Industrial District; see Linn Park

Birmingham Industrial District; see Pratt Coal & Coke Company,Convict Cemetery

Birmingham Industrial District; see Pratt Mines,Fraternal Cemetery

Birmingham Industrial District; see Swann & Company Research Laboratory

Birmingham Inustrial District; see Wade Sand & Gravel Company,Quarry

1700 Block Fourth Avenue N. (Streetscapes) (Fourth Ave. Nghbrhd.-Birmingham Industrial Dist.)
HABS AL-931
H

Brown,A.B.,House (Smithfield Nghbrhd.-Birmingham Industrial District
310 Fourth Terrace
HABS AL-930
H

Capitol Park; see Linn Park

Central Park; see Linn Park

Fourth Ave. Nghbrhd.-Birmingham Industrial Dist.; see 1700 Block Fourth Avenue N. (Streetscapes)

Hardie-Tynes Manufacturing Co.,Ait Compressor Hous (Birmingham Industrial District)
800 Twenty-eighth St.,N.
HAER AL-13-K
H

Hardie-Tynes Manufacturing Co.,Bath House (Birmingham Industrial District)
800 Twenty-eighth St.,N.
HAER AL-13-L
H

Hardie-Tynes Manufacturing Co.,Crane (Birmingham Industrial District)
800 Twenty-Eighth St.,N.
HAER AL-13-P
H

Hardie-Tynes Manufacturing Co.,Erection Shop (Birmingham Industrial District)
800 Twenty-eighth St.,N.
HAER AL-13-E
H

Hardie-Tynes Manufacturing Co.,Fabrication Shop (Birmingham Industrial District)
800 Twenty-eighth St.,N.
HAER AL-13-G
H

Hardie-Tynes Manufacturing Co.,Foundry (Birmingham Industrial District)
800 Twenty-eight St.,N.
HAER AL-13-F
H

Hardie-Tynes Manufacturing Co.,Machine Shop (Birmingham Industrial District)
800 Twenty-eigth St.,N.
HAER AL-13-B
H

Hardie-Tynes Manufacturing Co.,Main Office (Birmingham Industrial District)
800 Twenty-eighth St.,N.
HAER AL-13-J
H

Hardie-Tynes Manufacturing Co.,Paint Storage Shed (Birmingham Industrial District)
800 Twenty-eigth St.,N.
HAER AL-13-M
H

Hardie-Tynes Manufacturing Co.,Pattern Shop (Birmingham Industrial District)
800 Twenty-eighth St.,N.
HAER AL-13-H
H

Hardie-Tynes Manufacturing Co.,Pattern Storage (Birmingham Industrial District)
800 Twenty-eighth St.,N.
HAER AL-13-I
H

Hardie-Tynes Manufacturing Co.,Power House (Birmingham Industrial District)
800 Twenty-eighth St.,N.
HAER AL-13-D
H

Hardie-Tynes Manufacturing Co.,Sand Blasting Shed (Birmingham Industrial District)
800 Twenty-eighth St.,N.
HAER AL-13-N
H

Hardie-Tynes Manufacturing Co.,Shed (Birmingham Industrial District)
800 Twenty-eighth St.,N.
HAER AL-13-O
H

Hardie-Tynes Manufacturing Co.,Smith Shop (Birmingham Industrial District)
800 Twenty-eighth St.,N
HAER AL-13-C
H

Hardie-Tynes Manufacturing Company (Birmingham District National Heritage Corridor)
800 Twenty-eighth St.,N.
HAER AL-13
H

Heart of Dixie Railroad,Rolling Stock (Birmingham Industrial District)
1800 Block Powell Ave.
HAER AL-41-A
H

Heaviest Corner on Earth (Commercial) (Birmingham Industrial District)
First Ave. N. & Twentieth St. N.
HABS AL-927
H

Ingram,Kelly Park (West Park; Birmingham Industrial District)
Bounded by Seventh & Eighth Aves.,16th & 17th Sts.
HABS AL-951
H

Linn Park (Capitol Park; Central Park; Wilson,Woodrow,Park; Birmingham Industrial District)
Bounded by Park Pl.,8th Ave.,Short 20th & 21st Sts
HABS AL-926
H

Mudd-Munger House; see Arlington

Munger House; see Arlington

Pratt Coal & Coke Company,Convict Cemetery (Tennessee Coal & Iron Company,Convict Cemetery; U.S. Steel Pratt Mines,Convict Cemetery; Birmingham Industrial District)
Bounded by 1st St.,Ave. G,3rd Pl. & Birm. S'n. RR.
HABS AL-955
H

Pratt Mines,Fraternal Cemetery (Birmingham Industrial District)
Crest of Sheridan Rd.,Irish Hill
HABS AL-929
H

President's House; see Woodward House

219 Second Street (House) (Thomas Neighborhood-Birmingham Industrial District
HABS AL-928
H

Documentation: **ct** color transparencies **dr** measured drawings **fr** field records **pc** photograph captions **pg** pages of text **ph** photographs

Sloss Furnaces; see Sloss-Sheffield Steel & Iron Company,Furnaces

Sloss-Sheffield Steel & Iron Company,Furnaces (Sloss Furnaces)
First Ave. North Viaduct at Thirty-second St.
HAER AL-3
HAER ALA,73-BIRM,4-
20dr/125ph/37pg/10pc/fr L

Smith House; see Walker House

Smithfield Nghbrhd.-Birmingham Industrial District; see Brown,A.B.,House

Swann & Company Research Laboratory (Birmingham Industrial District)
205 Thirty-second St. S.
HABS AL-925
H

Tennessee Coal & Iron Company,Convict Cemetery; see Pratt Coal & Coke Company,Convict Cemetery

Thomas Neighborhood-Birmingham Industrial District; see 219 Second Street (House)

U.S. Steel Pratt Mines,Convict Cemetery; see Pratt Coal & Coke Company,Convict Cemetery

UAB-Birmingham Industrial District; see Woodward House

Wade Sand & Gravel Company,Quarry (Birmingham Inustrial District)
St. Hwy. 78
HAER AL-34-A
H

Walker House (Smith House; Walker-Smith House)
300 Center St.
HABS AL-425
HABS ALA,37-BIRM,2-
10ph/2pg L

Walker-Smith House; see Walker House

West Park; see Ingram,Kelly Park

Wilson,Woodrow,Park; see Linn Park

Woodward House (President's House; UAB-Birmingham Industrial District)
4101 Altamont Rd.
HABS AL-924
H

Worthington,Benjamin Pinckney,House
Sixth Ave South
HABS AL-426
HABS ALA,37-BIRM,3-
12ph L

BIRMINGHAM VIC.

Bayview Camp; see Bayview,Town of

Bayview,Town of (Bayview Camp; Tennessee Coal & Iron Company Town; Birmingham Industrial District)
Off Birmingport Rd. (St. Hwy. 269)
HABS AL-932
H

Birmingham Industrial District; see Bayview,Town of

Birmingham Industrial District; see Miller Electric Generating Plant

Miller Electric Generating Plant (Miller Steam Plant; Birmingham Industrial District)
Warrior River
HAER AL-36
H

Miller Steam Plant; see Miller Electric Generating Plant

Tennessee Coal & Iron Company Town; see Bayview,Town of

BROOKSIDE

Birmingham Industrial District; see Brookside Coal Mine

Birmingham Industrial District; see Brookside Coal Mine,Beehive Coke Ovens

Birmingham Industrial District; see Brookside Coal Mine,Tipple (Foundation)

Birmingham Industrial District; see Brookside Coal Mine,Washed Coal Stor. Bins (Fndtn)

Birmingham Industrial District; see Brookside Coal Mine,Washer & Crusher (Foundations)

Brookside Coal Mine (Sloss-Sheffield Steel & Iron Company Coal Mine; Birmingham Industrial District)
Mount Olive Rd.N. of Five Mile Creek Bridge
HAER AL-17
H

Brookside Coal Mine,Beehive Coke Ovens (Birmingham Industrial District)
Mount Olive Rd.,N. of Five Mile Creek Bridge
HAER AL-17-A
H

Brookside Coal Mine,Tipple (Foundation) (Birmingham Industrial District)
Mount Olive Rd.,N. of Five Mile Creek Bridge
HAER AL-17-C
H

Brookside Coal Mine,Washed Coal Stor. Bins (Fndtn) (Birmingham Industrial District)
Mount Olive Rd.,N. of Five Mile Creek Bridge
HAER AL-17-D
H

Brookside Coal Mine,Washer & Crusher (Foundations) (Birmingham Industrial District)
Mount Olive Rd.,N. of Five Mile Creek Bridge
HAER AL-17-B
H

Sloss-Sheffield Steel & Iron Company Coal Mine; see Brookside Coal Mine

FAIRFIELD

Birmingham Industrial District; see Fairfield #5 Furnace & Klopper Coke Plant

Birmingham Industrial District; see Fairfield,Town of

Fairfield #5 Furnace & Klopper Coke Plant (Birmingham Industrial District)
HAER AL-20
HAER ALA,2-TENSA,2-
H

Fairfield,Town of (Birmingham Industrial District)
HABS AL-933
H

FAIRFIELD VIC.

Birmingham Industrial District; see U.S.X. Fairfield Works

U.S. Steel Fairfield Works; see U.S.X. Fairfield Works

U.S.X. Fairfield Works (U.S. Steel Fairfield Works; Birmingham Industrial District)
N. of Valley Rd.,W. of Ensley-Pleasant Grove Rd.
HAER AL-37
H

IRONDALE

Birmingham Industrial District; see Norfolk & Southern Steam Locomotive No. 1218

Birmingham Industrial District; see Norfolk & Southern Steam Locomotive No. 611

Birmingham Industrial District; see Norris Steam Restoration Shop

Norfolk & Southern Steam Locomotive No. 1218 (Norfolk & Western Steam Locomotive No. 1218; Birmingham Industrial District)
Norris Yards,E. of Ruffner Rd.
HAER AL-39
H

Norfolk & Southern Steam Locomotive No. 611 (Norfolk & Western Steam Locomotive No. 611; Birmingham Industrial District)
Norris Yards,E. of Ruffner Rd.
HAER AL-38
H

Norfolk & Southern Steam Restoration Shop; see Norris Steam Restoration Shop

Norfolk & Western Steam Locomotive No. 1218; see Norfolk & Southern Steam Locomotive No. 1218

Norfolk & Western Steam Locomotive No. 611; see Norfolk & Southern Steam Locomotive No. 611

Norfolk & Western Steam Restoration Shop; see Norris Steam Restoration Shop

Norris Steam Restoration Shop (Norfolk & Southern Steam Restoration Shop; Norfolk & Western Steam Restoration Shop; Birmingham Industrial District)
Norris Yards,E. of Ruffner Rd.
HAER AL-40
H

ISHKOUDA

Birmingham Industrial District; see Ishkouda,Worker Houses

Ishkouda,Worker Houses (Tennessee Coal & Iron Company,Worker Houses; Birmingham Industrial District)
Ishkouda Rd.
HABS AL-934
H

Tennessee Coal & Iron Company,Worker Houses; see Ishkouda,Worker Houses

TARRANT

ABC Coke Plant (Birmingham Industrial District)
HAER AL-19
HAER ALA,2-TENSA,2-
H

Birmingham Industrial District; see ABC Coke Plant

THOMAS

Birmingham Industrial District; see Republic Steel Comm. & Worker Hsg.,Baptist Church

Birmingham Industrial District; see Republic Steel Comm. & Worker Hsg.,Gable Front Hse

Birmingham Industrial District; see Republic Steel Comm. & Worker Hsg.,Pyramid Cottage

Birmingham Industrial District; see Republic Steel Comm. & Worker Hsg.,Shot Gun House

Birmingham Industrial District; see Republic Steel Community & Worker Housing

Birmingham Industrial District; see St. Mark's Catholic Church

Birmingham Industrial District; see Thomas Baptist Church

Birmingham Industrial District; see Thomas By-Product Coke Works

Birmingham Industrial District; see Thomas By-Product Coke Works,Foreman' Office

Birmingham Industrial District; see Thomas By-Product Coke Works,Gatehoue & Weigh Sta.

Birmingham Industrial District; see Thomas By-Product Coke Works,Main Office

Birmingham Industrial District; see Thomas By-Product Coke Works,Power Plant

Birmingham Industrial District; see Thomas By-Product Coke Works,Pump House

Birmingham Industrial District; see Thomas By-Product Coke Works,Restrooms

Birmingham Industrial District; see Thomas By-Product Coke Works,Storage

Birmingham Industrial District; see Thomas By-Product Coke Works,Track Hooper & Wrkshp

Birmingham Industrial District; see Thomas By-Products Coke Works,Quenching Station

Birmngham Industrial District; see Thomas By-Product Coke Works,Bath House

Republic Steel Comm. & Worker Hsg.,Baptist Church (Birmingham Industrial District)
First & Pennsylvania
HAER AL-15-D
H

Republic Steel Comm. & Worker Hsg.,Gable Front Hse (Birmingham Industrial District)
214 Second Street
HAER AL-15-A
H

Republic Steel Comm. & Worker Hsg.,Pyramid Cottage (Birmingham Industrial District)
303 Third St.
HAER AL-15-C
H

Republic Steel Comm. & Worker Hsg.,Shot Gun House (Birmingham Industrial District)
355 Third St.
HAER AL-15-B
H

Republic Steel Community & Worker Housing (Birmingham Industrial District)
HAER AL-15
H

St. Mark's Catholic Church (Birmingham Industrial District)
1040 Tenth Ave. W.
HABS AL-935
H

Thomas Baptist Church (Thomas Prebyterian Church; Birmingham Industrial District)
FirstSt. & Pennsylvania Ave.
HABS AL-936
H

Thomas By-Product Coke Works (Birmingham Industrial District)
1200 Tenth St. W.
HAER AL-14
H

Thomas By-Product Coke Works,Bath House (Birmngham Industrial District)
1200 Tenth St. W.
HAER AL-14-A
H

Thomas By-Product Coke Works,Foreman' Office (Birmingham Industrial District)
1200 Tenth St. W.
HAER AL-14-C
H

Thomas By-Product Coke Works,Gatehoue & Weigh Sta. (Birmingham Industrial District)
1200 Tenth St. W.
HAER AL-14-B
H

Thomas By-Product Coke Works,Main Office (Birmingham Industrial District)
1200 Tenth St. W.
HAER AL-14-D
H

Thomas By-Product Coke Works,Power Plant (Birmingham Industrial District)
1200 Tenth St. W.
HAER AL-14-E
H

Thomas By-Product Coke Works,Pump House (Birmingham Industrial District)
1200 Tenth St. W.
HAER AL-14-F
H

Thomas By-Product Coke Works,Restrooms (Birmingham Industrial District)
1200 Tenth St. W.
HAER AL-14-J
H

Thomas By-Product Coke Works,Storage (Birmingham Industrial District)
1200 Tenth St. W.
HAER AL-14-H
H

Thomas By-Product Coke Works,Track Hooper & Wrkshp (Birmingham Industrial District)
1200 Tenth St. W.
HAER AL-14-I
H

Thomas By-Products Coke Works,Quenching Station (Birmingham Industrial District)
1200 Tenth St. W.
HAER AL-14-G
H

Thomas Prebyterian Church; see Thomas Baptist Church

WOODWARD

Woodward Coal & Iron Company Furnace; see Woodward Iron Company

Woodward Iron Company (Woodward Coal & Iron Company Furnace)
Opossum Creek Vic.
HAER AL-4
HAER ALA,37-WOOD,1-
14ph/1pg/1pc L

LAMAR COUNTY

CREWS DEPOT

Bankhead-Crews House; see Bankhead,George,House

Bankhead,George,House (Bankhead-Crews House)
Old Military Rd.
HABS AL-397
HABS ALA,38-CREWD,1-
3ph L

SULLIGENT

Bankhead,James Greer,House (Forest Home)
U.S. Rt. 278
HABS AL-391
HABS ALA,38-SUL,1-
7ph L

Forest Home; see Bankhead,James Greer,House

LAUDERDALE COUNTY

CENTER STAR VIC.

Cunningham House (first); see Taylor-Cunningham House (first)

Cunningham House (second); see Taylor-Cunningham House (second)

Cunningham,Jonathan B.,House; see Taylor-Cunningham House (second)

Taylor-Cunningham House (first) (Cunningham House (first))
(See LAUDERDALE CO.,ROGERSVILLE VIC. for documtn.)
HABS AL-377-A
HABS ALA,39-ROG.V,2-
10ph L

Taylor-Cunningham House (second) (Cunningham House (second); Cunningham,Jonathan B.,House)
(See LAUDERDALE CO.,ROGERSVILLE VIC. for documtn.)
HABS AL-377-B
HABS ALA,39-ROG.V,3-
5ph/1pg L

FLORENCE

Ashcraft House (Irvine,James Bennington,House)
461 N. Pine St.
HABS AL-358
HABS ALA,39-FLO,5-
8ph/1pg L

Coulter-McFarland House; see McFarland,Mary,House

Courtview (Foster-Rogers House; Rogers Hall)
505 N. Court St.,Univ. of N. Alabama Campus
HABS AL-329
HABS ALA,39-FLO,2-
17dr/32ph/3pg/fr L

First Presbyterian Church
E. Mobile St.
HABS AL-328
HABS ALA,39-FLO,7-
2ph/3pg/1pc L

Foster-Rogers House; see Courtview

Hawkins-Sample House (Sample,Mattie,House)
219 Hermitage Dr.
HABS AL-326
HABS ALA,39-FLO,1-
5ph/1pg L

Irvine House (Simpson-Irvine House)
459 N. Court St.
HABS AL-332
HABS ALA,39-FLO,3-
10ph/7pg/1pc L

Irvine,James Bennington,House; see Ashcraft House

Lambeth House (Pope's Tavern)
203 Hermitage Dr.
HABS AL-334
HABS ALA,39-FLO,4-
6ph/1pg L

Mapleton; see McFarland,Mary,House

McFarland,Mary,House (Mapleton; Coulter-McFarland House)
420 S. Pine St.
HABS AL-376
HABS ALA,39-FLO,6-
4ph L

Patton-Perry House; see Perry House

Patton,Gov. Robert,House; see Sweetwater

Perry House (Patton-Perry House)
N. Pine & Tuscaloosa Sts.
HABS AL-359
HABS ALA,39-FLO,9-
6ph/2pg L

Pope's Tavern; see Lambeth House

Rogers Hall; see Courtview

Sample,Mattie,House; see Hawkins-Sample House

Simpson-Irvine House; see Irvine House

Simpson,John,House; see Simpson,Will,House

Simpson,Will,House (Simpson,John,House)
112 S. Pine St.
HABS AL-330
HABS ALA,39-FLO,8-
2ph/2pg L

Sweetwater (Patton,Gov. Robert,House)
Sweetwater Ave. & Florence Blvd.
HABS AL-333
HABS ALA,39-FLO.V,2-
12ph L

FLORENCE VIC.

Forks of Cypress,The (Jackson Plantation House)
Jackson Rd. Vic.
HABS AL-375
HABS ALA,39-FLO.V,3-
24dr/27ph/2pg L

Hood,James,House (Woodlawn; Woodland)
County Rd. 14 & Savannah Hwy.
HABS AL-331
HABS ALA,39-FLO.V,1-
16ph/2pg L

Jackson Plantation House; see Forks of Cypress,The

Woodland; see Hood,James,House

Woodlawn; see Hood,James,House

ROGERSVILLE VIC.

Weaver,Adam,Log House
U. S. Hwy. 72
HABS AL-374
HABS ALA,39-ROG.V,1-
11ph/1pg L

ROGERSVILLE VIC.

Cunningham House (first); see Taylor-Cunningham House (first)

Cunningham House (second); see Taylor-Cunningham House (second)

Cunningham,Jonathan B.,House; see Taylor-Cunningham House (second)

Taylor-Cunningham House (first)
(Cunningham House (first))
Bellevue Rd.
HABS AL-377-A
HABS ALA,39-ROG.V,2-
10ph L

Taylor-Cunningham House (second)
(Cunningham House (second);
Cunningham,Jonathan B.,House)
Bellevue Rd.
HABS AL-377-B
HABS ALA,39-ROG.V,3-
5ph/1pg L

LAWRENCE COUNTY

COURTLAND

Baker-Campbell House; see Campbell House

Campbell House (Baker-Campbell House; Tennessee Street (House))
State Hwy. 20
HABS AL-383
HABS ALA,40-CORT,1-
4dr/4ph/fr L

Tennessee Street (House); see Campbell House

COURTLAND VIC.

Bride's Hill
County Rd. 43
HABS AL-865
HABS ALA,40-COURT.V,2-
1ph/1pg/1pc L

Rocky Hill (Saunders,Col. James Edmonds,House)
State Hwy. 20
HABS AL-311
HABS ALA,40-CORT.V,1-
8ph/2pg L

Saunders,Col. James Edmonds,House; see Rocky Hill

MOULTON

Lawrence County Courthouse
Courthouse Square
HABS AL-310
HABS ALA,40-MOULT,1-
13dr/10ph/3pg/1pc/fr L

TOWN CREEK VIC.

Goode,Freeman,House; see Saunders-Goode-Hall House

Hall House; see Saunders-Goode-Hall House

Saunders-Goode-Hall House (Hall House; Goode,Freeman,House)
State Hwy. 101
HABS AL-324
HABS ALA,40-TOWC.V,1-
38ph/2pg/fr L

WHEELER STATION

Home Sweet Home; see Wheeler,Gen. Joseph,House

Pond Spring; see Wheeler,Gen. Joseph,House

Wheeler,Gen. Joseph,House (Home Sweet Home; Pond Spring)
State Hwy. 20
HABS AL-347
HABS ALA,40-WHEL,1-
11dr/17ph/3pg/fr L

Wheeler,Gen. Joseph,House (Later House)
State Hwy. 20
HABS AL-347-A
HABS ALA,40-WHEL,2-
15ph L

LEE COUNTY

AUBURN

Cauthen House (Perry-Cauthen House)
E. Drake Ave.
HABS AL-551
HABS ALA,41-AUB,4-
8ph L

Drake-Samford House
449 N. Gay St.
HABS AL-503
HABS ALA,41-AUB,1-
2ph L

Holliday-Carey House
(Kidd-Holliday-Carey House)
360 N. College St.
HABS AL-540
HABS ALA,41-AUB,2-
6dr/9ph/2pg/fr L

Jones Hotel; see McElhaney House

Kidd-Holliday-Carey House; see Holliday-Carey House

McElhaney Hotel; see McElhaney House

McElhaney House (McElhaney Hotel; Jones Hotel)
135 N. College St.
HABS AL-550
HABS ALA,41-AUB,3-
14ph L

Meadows House
342 N. College St.
HABS AL-582
HABS ALA,41-AUB,5-
8ph L

Perry-Cauthen House; see Cauthen House

Scott-Yarbrough House
101 Debardeleben St.
HABS AL-893
HABS DLC/PP-1992:AL-3
3dr/fr L

AUBURN VIC.

Casey Homestead; see Frazier-Brown House

Frazier-Brown House (Noble Hall; Casey Homestead)
Shelton Mill Rd.
HABS AL-502
HABS ALA,41-AUB.V,2-
3dr/4ph/4pg/fr L

Moore-Whatley House
Moore's Mill Rd.
HABS AL-501
HABS ALA,41-AUB.V,1-
3dr/2ph/2pg/fr L

Noble Hall; see Frazier-Brown House

CHEWACLA

Chewacla Limeworks
Limekiln Rd.
HABS AL-509
HABS ALA,41-CHEWA,1-
9ph L

GOLD HILL

Ellington,James,House (Gold Hill)
Oak Bowery Rd. Vic.
HABS AL-581
HABS ALA,41-GOLD,1-
15ph L

Gold Hill; see Ellington,James,House

LOACHAPOKA

Baptist Church
Stage Rd.
HABS AL-512
HABS ALA,41-LOCA,1-
2dr/2ph/2pg/fr L

LOACHAPOKA VIC.

Hammack Plantation House
Waverly Rd.
HABS AL-513
HABS ALA,41-LOCA.V,1-
3dr/2ph/2pg/fr L

MOUNT JEFFERSON

Methodist Church (abandoned) (Mount Jefferson Methodist Church)
U.S. Rt. 431
HABS AL-505
HABS ALA,41-MOUJ,1- & 2-
1ph L

Mount Jefferson Methodist Church; see Methodist Church (abandoned)

Tucker-Fincher House
(Wheat-Tucker-Fincher House)
U.S. Rt. 431
HABS AL-878
HABS ALA,41-MOUJ,1-
11ph L

Wheat-Tucker-Fincher House; see Tucker-Fincher House

NOTASULGA VIC.

Le Sueur's Mill
Ropes Creek
HABS AL-537
HABS ALA,44-NOTA.V,1-
2ph L

OPELIKA

Kilgore House
411 Geneva St.
HABS AL-891
HABS 1991(HABS):33
9dr/14pg/fr L

McNamee-Torbert House
410 Geneva St.
HABS AL-892
HABS 1992(HABS):AL-1
12dr/fr L

OPELIKA VIC.

Chewacla Limeworks
(See LEE CO.,CHEWACLA for documentation)
HABS AL-509
HABS ALA,41-CHEWA,1-
9ph L

Methodist Church (abandoned) (Mount Jefferson Methodist Church)
(See LEE CO.,MOUNT JEFFERSON for documentation)
HABS AL-505
HABS ALA,41-MOUJ,1- & 2-
1ph L

Moffitt's Mill
County Rd. 12
HABS AL-507
HABS ALA,41- ,1-
1dr/3ph/1pg/fr L

Mount Jefferson Methodist Church; see Methodist Church (abandoned)

Spring Villa
County Rd. 36 (Spring Villa Rd.)
HABS AL-508
HABS ALA,41- ,2-
3dr/4ph/3pg/fr L

Tucker-Fincher House
(Wheat-Tucker-Fincher House)
(See LEE CO.,MOUNT JEFFERSON for documentation)
HABS AL-878
HABS ALA,41-MOUJ,1-
11ph L

Wheat-Tucker-Fincher House; see Tucker-Fincher House

LIMESTONE COUNTY

ATHENS

Athens Agricultural School Building; see Donnell,Father Robert,House

Athens College,Founder's Hall (Athens College,Main Building; Athens Female College,Main Building)
Beaty St.
HABS AL-301
HABS ALA,42-ATH,1-
10dr/2ph/2pg/fr L

Athens College,Main Building; see Athens College,Founder's Hall

Athens Female College,Main Building; see Athens College,Founder's Hall

Beaty-Mason House (Mason,J. G. & Mary,House)
211 S. Beaty St.
HABS AL-306
HABS ALA,42-ATH,4-
8dr/9ph/2pg L

Cedars,Thee"
E. Pryor St.
HABS AL-368
HABS ALA,42-ATH,12-
10ph L

Coman Hall; see Jones-Coman-Westmoreland House

Donnell,Father Robert,House (Athens Agricultural School Building)
601 S. Clinton St.
HABS AL-367
HABS ALA,42-ATH,7-
8ph L

Houston,Gov. George S.,House
101 Houston St.
HABS AL-341
HABS ALA,42-ATH,6-
6ph/2pg L

Jones-Coman-Westmoreland House
(Westmoreland House; Coman Hall)
517 S. Clinton St.
HABS AL-338
HABS ALA,42-ATH,11-
10ph/2pg L

Mason,J. G. & Mary,House; see Beaty-Mason House

Masonic Hall,Old
Monroe & E. Hobbs Sts.
HABS AL-305
HABS ALA,42-ATH,3-
4dr/1ph/2pg/fr L

Pettus House (Sloss-Pettus House)
N. Beaty & Hobbs Sts.
HABS AL-340
HABS ALA,42-ATH,5-
5ph L

Pryor,Frances Snow,House & Office
405 N. Jefferson St.
HABS AL-304
HABS ALA,42-ATH,2-
6dr/4ph/2pg/fr L

Richardson,Dr. R. H.,House
401 S. Clinton St.
HABS AL-370
HABS ALA,42-ATH,8-
6ph L

Sloss-Pettus House; see Pettus House

Vasser House; see Vining-Wood-Vasser House

Vining-Wood-Vasser House (Vasser House)
301 E. Washington St.
HABS AL-379
HABS ALA,42-ATH,10-
4ph L

Walker,Judge William Harrison,House
309 E. Clinton St.
HABS AL-371
HABS ALA,42,-ATH,9-
11ph L

Westmoreland House; see Jones-Coman-Westmoreland House

ATHENS VIC.

Cotton Hill; see Rowe,Jack,House

Rowe,Jack,House (Cotton Hill)
Brown's Ferry Rd. Vicinity
HABS AL-343
HABS ALA,42-ATH.V,1-
4ph/2pg L

BELLE MINA

Belle Mina; see Bibb,Gov. Thomas,House

Bibb,Gov. Thomas,House (Belle Mina)
County Rd. 71
HABS AL-303
HABS ALA,42-BELMI,1-
7dr/7ph/2pg/fr L

MOORESVILLE

Cotton Hill (Rowe,Jack,House)
(See LIMESTONE CO.,ATHENS VIC. for documentation)
HABS AL-343
HABS ALA,42-ATH.V,1-
L

High Street (Old Tavern)
HABS AL-308
HABS ALA,42-MOVI,2-
2dr/4ph/2pg/fr L

Hundley House (Hundley-Minor House)
Market St.
HABS AL-369
HABS ALA,42-MOVI,3-
4ph L

Hundley-Minor House; see Hundley House

Peebles-Zeitler-McCrary House; see Zeitler,Henry,House

Rowe,Jack,House; see Cotton Hill

Zeitler,Henry,House
(Peebles-Zeitler-McCrary House)
High St.
HABS AL-302
HABS ALA,42-MOVI,1-
6ph L

Locations: **H** HABS/HAER, National Park Service **L** Library of Congress

LOWNDES COUNTY

BENTON

Masonic Hall
Second & Church Sts.
HABS AL-756
HABS ALA,43-BENT,1-
2ph L

BURKVILLE VIC.

Graves,David,House
County Hwy. 40 at County Hwy. 37
HABS AL-885
HABS ALA,43-BURK.V,2-
6ph/10pg/1pc/fr L

Haigler,Josiah,Plantation Commissary (Loftin Grocery)
County Hwy. 37 North of U. S. Hwy. 80
HABS AL-884-B
HABS ALA,43-BURK.V,3C-
7ph/6pg/1pc/fr L

Haigler,Josiah,Plantation House
County Hwy. 37 North of U. S. Hwy. 80
HABS AL-884
HABS ALA,43-BURK.V,3A-
22ph/11pg/1pc/fr L

Haigler,Josiah,Plantation House,New
County Hwy. 37 North of U. S. Hwy. 80
HABS AL-884-A
HABS ALA,43-BURK.V,3B-
4ph/6pg/1pc/fr L

Loftin Grocery; see Haigler,Josiah,Plantation Commissary

Magnolia Crest; see Stone-McCarty House

Magnolia Crest; see Stone,Warren,House

McCary Tenant House
U. S. Rt. 80 near Berry Lake Rd.
HABS AL-888
HABS ALA,43-BURK.V,4-
7ph/5pg/1pc/fr L

McQueen,John,House (Queensdale)
U. S. Hwy. 80 west of Hwy. 37
HABS AL-887
HABS ALA,43-BURK.V,5-
5pg/fr L

McQueen,John,Servant's House
U. S. Hwy. 80 East of Berry Lake Rd.
HABS AL-887-A
HABS ALA,43-BURK.V,5A-
2ph/4pg/1pc L

Queensdale; see McQueen,John,House

Stone-McCarty House (Magnolia Crest)
County Rd. 40
HABS AL-652
HABS ALA,43-BURK,1-
4ph L

Stone,Warren,House (Magnolia Crest)
County Hwy. 40 west of County Hwy. 37
HABS AL-889
HABS ALA,43-BURK.V,6-
5ph/11pg/1pc/fr L

Young-Nall House
County Hwy. 40 at Lake Berry Rd.
HABS AL-886
HABS ALA,43-BURK.V,7-
15ph/10pg/1pc/fr L

HAYNEVILLE

Lowndes County Courthouse
Washington St. at Town Square
HABS AL-880
HABS ALA,43-HAYVI,1-
1dr/6ph/1pg/1pc L

LOWNDESBORO

Boxwood; see Reese,Mary,House

Cottage,The; see Lewis,Dixon H.,House

Episcopal Church; see St. Paul's Episcopal Church

Gordon,F. J.,House; see Williams-Bragg House

Hagood House; see Haygood House

Haygood House (Hagood House; Meadowlawn; Thomas-Hagood House)
State Hwy. 97 (County Rd. 29)
HABS AL-678
HABS ALA,43-LOWB,6-
18ph L

Homestead,Old; see Lewis,Francis,House

Howard House (Lewis-Cilley-Howard House)
State Hwy. 97 (County Rd. 29)
HABS AL-679
HABS ALA,43-LOWB,7-
2ph L

James,E. L.,House; see Lewis,Dixon H.,House

Lewis-Cilley-Howard House; see Howard House

Lewis-Hall-James House; see Lewis,Dixon H.,House

Lewis-Jones House; see Lewis,Dixon H.,House

Lewis,Dixon H.,House (Cottage,The; James,E. L.,House; Lewis-Jones House; Lewis-Hall-James House)
State Hwy. 97 (County Rd. 29)
HABS AL-670
HABS ALA,43-LOWB,11-
7ph L

Lewis,Francis,House (Homestead,Old)
State Hwy. 97 (County Rd. 29)
HABS AL-671
HABS ALA,43-LOWB,2-
3ph L

Lowndesboro Female Institute,President's House; see Reese,Mary,House

Meadowlawn; see Haygood House

Meadows-Powell House; see Powell House

Methodist Church,Old (Negro Methodist Church; St. James United Methodist Church)
State Hwy. 97 (County Rd. 29)
HABS AL-651
HABS ALA,43-LOWB,1-
4ph L

Mockingbird Place; see Powell House

Negro Methodist Church; see Methodist Church,Old

Powell House (Mockingbird Place; Meadows-Powell House)
State Hwy. 97 (County Rd. 29)
HABS AL-681
HABS ALA,43-LOWB,9-
5ph L

Presbyterian Church
State Hwy. 97 (County Rd. 29)
HABS AL-687
HABS ALA,43-LOWB,10-
4ph L

Red Church,The; see St. Paul's Episcopal Church

Reese,Mary,House (Boxwood; Lowndesboro Female Institute,President's House)
State Hwy. 97 (County Rd. 29)
HABS AL-677
HABS ALA,43-LOWB,5-
10ph L

St. James United Methodist Church; see Methodist Church,Old

St. Paul's Episcopal Church (Episcopal Church; Red Church,The)
State Hwy. 97 (County Rd. 29)
HABS AL-674
HABS ALA,43-LOWB,12-
9ph L

Thomas-Hagood House; see Haygood House

Tyson,Archibald,House
State Hwy. 97 (County Rd. 29)
HABS AL-672
HABS ALA,43-LOWB,3-
15ph L

Williams-Bragg House (Gordon,F. J.,House)
State Hwy. 97 (County Rd. 29)
HABS AL-673
HABS ALA,43-LOWB,4-
7ph L

LOWNDESBORO VIC.

Dicksonia; see Turner-Dickson House

Meadows,A. W.,House; see Wooten-Meadows House

Rosewood; see Wooten-Meadows House

Turner-Dickson House (Dicksonia)
State Hwy. 97 (County Rd. 29)
HABS AL-676
HABS ALA,43-LOWB.V,1-
12ph/2pg/fr L

Wooten-Meadows House (Rosewood; Meadows,A. W.,House)
State Hwy. 97 (County Rd. 29)
HABS AL-680
HABS ALA,43-LOWB,8-
8ph L

MACON COUNTY

TUSKEGEE

Callaway,C. J.,House; see Hunter-Callaway House

Carr,W. B.,House (301 Maple Street (House); Martin House)
HABS AL-536
HABS ALA,44-TUSG,2-
11ph L

Carver Museum (Tuskegee Institute National Historic Site)
Old Montgomery Rd. ,Tuskegee Institute Campus
HABS AL-876
HABS ALA,44-TUSG,9-
11dr/1ct/fr L

Cobb House (Foster-Cobb-Laslie House)
504 E. Main St.
HABS AL-541
HABS ALA,44-TUSG,3-
6dr/5ph/2pg/fr L

Dowdell,Rev. Lewis Flournoy,House; see Rush-Thornton House

Foster-Cobb-Laslie House; see Cobb House

Grey Columns (Varner-Alexander House; Tuskegee National Historic Site)
Old Montgomery Rd.
HABS AL-543
HABS ALA,44-TUSG,5-
18dr/12ph/2pg/1ct/fr L

Harris-Wadsworth House
615 W. Main St.
HABS AL-533
HABS ALA,44-TUSG,1-
8ph L

Hunter-Callaway House (Callaway,C. J.,House)
811 N. Maple St.
HABS AL-559
HABS ALA,44-TUSG,6-
7ph L

Johnston-Abercrombie-Lamar House; see Lamar,G. Y.,House

Lamar,G. Y.,House (Johnston-Abercrombie-Lamar House; Vason,Doctor,House)
U. S. Hwy. 29 (State Hwy. 15)
HABS AL-532
HABS ALA,44-TUSG.V,1-
8ph L

301 Maple Street (House); see Carr,W. B.,House

Martin House; see Carr,W. B.,House

Oaks,The (Washington,Booker T. ,House; Tuskegee Institute National Historic Site)
Old Montgomery Rd. ,Tuskegee Institute Campus
HABS AL-877
HABS ALA,44-TUSG,10-
11dr/fr L

Rockefeller Hall Bath House
Tuskegee University Campus
HABS AL-894
HABS DLC/PP-1992:AL-2
6dr/fr L

Rush-Thornton House (Thornton House; Dowdell,Rev. Lewis Flournoy,House)
U. S. Hwy. 29
HABS AL-585
HABS ALA,44-TUSG,7-
8ph L

Tate-Thompson House; see Thompson,G. C.,House

Thompson,G. C.,House (Tate-Thompson House)
302 N. Main St.
HABS AL-542
HABS ALA,44-TUSG,4-
3dr/16ph/4pg L

Thornton House; see Rush-Thornton House

Tuskegee Institute National Historic Site; see Carver Museum

Tuskegee Institute National Historic Site; see Oaks,The

Tuskegee National Historic Site; see Grey Columns

Varner-Alexander House; see Grey Columns

Vason,Doctor,House; see Lamar,G. Y.,House

Washington,Booker T. ,House; see Oaks,The

TUSKEGEE VIC.

Alexander-Hurt-Whatley House (Hurt,Judge W. H.,House)
County Rd. 10 (Old Columbus Hwy.)
HABS AL-560
HABS ALA,44-TUSG.V,3-
11dr/8ph/2pg/fr L

Cox House; see Plantation House,Frame

Hurt,Judge W. H.,House; see Alexander-Hurt-Whatley House

Plantation House,Frame (Cox House; Stagecoach Inn)
County Rd. 26
HABS AL-534
HABS ALA,44-TUSG.V,2-
5ph L

Stagecoach Inn; see Plantation House,Frame

MADISON COUNTY

HUNTSVILLE

Beirne House; see Bibb-Bradley-Beirne House

Bibb-Bradley-Beirne House (Beirne House; Bibb-Newman House; Bibb,Gov. Thomas,House)
303 Williams St.
HABS AL-403
HABS ALA,45-HUVI,1-
5dr/8ph/3pg/fr L

Bibb-Newman House; see Bibb-Bradley-Beirne House

Bibb,Gov. Thomas,House; see Bibb-Bradley-Beirne House

Boswell-McClung House (Boswell,C. S.,House; McClung-Watkins House)
415 McClung St.
HABS AL-478
HABS ALA,45-HUVI,16-
12ph L

Boswell,C. S.,House; see Boswell-McClung House

Brandon-Read-Burritt House; see Burritt House

Burritt House (Brandon-Read-Burritt House)
303 Eustis Ave.
HABS AL-474
HABS ALA,45-HUVI,11-
10ph/2pg L

Cabiness House (Roach-Cabiness House)
603 Randolph St.
HABS AL-431
HABS ALA,45-HUVI,9-
12dr/6ph/2pg/fr L

Chase,Henry B.,House (McDowell-Chase House)
517 Adams Ave.
HABS AL-409
HABS ALA,45-HUVI,6-
5ph/2pg L

Clarke-Fackler House; see Pynchon House

Clay,J. Withers,House (Huntsville Female Seminary,Steward's House; Lewis-Clay-Anderson House)
513 Eustis Ave.
HABS AL-408
HABS L,45-HUVI,5-
6ph/2pg L

Cox-White House; see White,Thomas W.,House

Dillworth,W. P.,House; see Robinson-Dillworth House

Fearn-Garth House
517 Franklin St.
HABS AL-414
HABS ALA,45-HUVI,7-
9dr/12ph/3pg/fr L

First National Bank (Huntsville Branch,State Bank of Alabama)
Jefferson St. & Fountain Rd.
HABS AL-405
HABS ALA,45-HUVI,3-
5dr/9ph/4pg/fr L

Greenlawn (Otie House)
U. S. Hwy. 431 (Memorial Pkwy.)
HABS AL-476
HABS ALA,45-HUVI.V,5-
10ph L

Hamlet House (Windham,William,House)
413 E. Holmes St.
HABS AL-413
HABS ALA,45-HUVI,15-
7ph L

Horton-McCracken House; see McCracken House

Huntsville Branch,State Bank of Alabama; see First National Bank

Huntsville Female Seminary,Steward's House; see Clay,J. Withers,House

Lewis-Clay-Anderson House; see Clay,J. Withers,House

Madison County Courthouse
Courthouse Square
HABS AL-437
HABS ALA,45-HUVI,10-
6dr/3ph/3pg L

Mastin,Gus,House (Meridian Pike (House))
HABS AL-436
HABS ALA,45-HUVI.V,4-
8ph L

McClung-Watkins House; see Boswell-McClung House

McCracken House (Horton-McCracken House)
Meridian Pike
HABS AL-410
HABS ALA,45-HUVI.V,2-
5ph/3pg L

McDowell-Chase House; see Chase,Henry B.,House

Meridian Pike (House); see Mastin,Gus,House

Morgan-Neal House; see Neal House

Neal House (Morgan-Neal House)
558 Franklin St.
HABS AL-412
HABS ALA,45-HUVI,14-
8ph/2pg L

Oaklawn; see Robinson-Dillworth House

Oaks Place (Steele-Fowler House)
808 Maysville Rd.
HABS AL-402
HABS ALA,45-HUVI.V,1-
4dr/11ph/5pg/fr L

Otie House; see Greenlawn

Perkins-Orgain-Winston House (Scruggs House)
401 Lincoln St.
HABS AL-473
HABS ALA,45-HUVI,13-
6ph/2pg L

Pope-Spragins House (Pope,Col. Leroy,House; Poplar Grove)
407 Echols Ave.
HABS AL-406
HABS ALA,45-HUVI,4-
3dr/13ph/2pg/fr L

Pope,Col. Leroy,House; see Pope-Spragins House

Poplar Grove; see Pope-Spragins House

Pynchon House (Clarke-Fackler House)
518 Adams Ave.
HABS AL-430
HABS ALA,45-HUVI,8-
4dr/8ph/3pg/fr L

Redstone Arsenal
HAER AL-9
HAER ALA,45-HUVI.V,6-
67pg/fr L

Roach-Cabiness House; see Cabiness House

Robinson-Dillworth House (Dillworth,W. P.,House; Robinson,John,House; Oaklawn)
2709 Meridian Pike
HABS AL-411
HABS ALA,45-HUVI.V,3-
8dr/11ph/3pg L

Robinson,John,House; see Robinson-Dillworth House

Scruggs House; see Perkins-Orgain-Winston House

Steele-Fowler House; see Oaks Place

Wade,David,House
Bob Wade Ln.
HABS AL-477
HABS ALA,45- ,1-
12ph L

Weeden,Miss Howard,House
300 Gates Ave.
HABS AL-404
HABS ALA,45-HUVI,2-
3dr/10ph/3pg/fr L

White,Thomas W.,House (Cox-White House)
461 Eustis Ave.
HABS AL-475
HABS ALA,45-HUVI,12-
8ph L

Windham,William,House; see Hamlet House

HUNTSVILLE VIC.

Redstone Arsenal,Building 7102; see Redstone Arsenal,Fire Station No. 3

Redstone Arsenal,Building 8012; see Redstone Arsenal,Harris Residence

Redstone Arsenal,Fire Station No. 3 (Redstone Arsenal,Building 7102)
Redstone Rd. bet. Post & Line Rds.
HABS AL-883-A
HABS ALA,45-HUVI.V,6/7102-
6ph/3pg/1pc L

Redstone Arsenal,Harris Residence (Redstone Arsenal,Building 8012)
Off Buxtia Rd. bet. Shields & McAlpine Rds.
HABS AL-883-B
HABS ALA,45-HUVI.V,6/8012-
6ph/2pg/1pc L

NEW MARKET

Five Oaks (Laxon,W. L. Jr.,House)
Winchester Pike
HABS AL-407
HABS ALA,45-NEWM.V,1-
11ph L

Laxon,W. L. Jr.,House; see Five Oaks

MARENGO COUNTY

DAYTON

Bruce House; see Walton-Bruce House

Jones,Leroy King,House; see Magnolia Grove

Magnolia Grove (Jones,Leroy King,House)
State Hwy. 25
HABS AL-153
HABS ALA,46-DAYT,2-
16ph L

Methodist Church
State Hwy. 25
HABS AL-149
HABS ALA,46-DAYT,1-
15ph L

Walton-Bruce House (Bruce House)
State Hwy. 25
HABS AL-140
HABS ALA,46-DAYT,3-
6ph L

DEMOPOLIS

Bluff Hall (Lyon-Smith House)
407 N. Commissioners Ave.
HABS AL-213
HABS ALA,46-DEMO,3-
18ph/3pg/1pc L

Gaineswood (Whitfield-Kirven House)
805 S. Cedar St.
HABS AL-211
HABS ALA,46-DEMO,1-
25dr/67ph/4pg/2pc L

Glover Family Mausoleum
Riverview Cemetery
HABS AL-212-A
HABS ALA,46-DEMO,2-
4dr/12ph L

Lyon Hall; see Lyon House

Lyon House (Lyon Hall; Lyon-Lamar House)
102 S. Main St.
HABS AL-239
HABS ALA,46-DEMO,4-
6ph/2pg L

Lyon-Lamar House; see Lyon House

Lyon-Smith House; see Bluff Hall

Whitfield-Kirven House; see Gaineswood

DIXON MILLS VIC.

Pearson House (Wright-Pearson House)
County Rd. 6
HABS AL-145
HABS ALA,46-MAR,1-
7ph L

Wright-Pearson House; see Pearson House

FAUNSDALE VIC.

Cedar Grove (Walker,Charles,House)
Uniontown Rd.
HABS AL-200
HABS ALA,46-FAUN.V,1-
33ph L

Norwood Plantation
County Rd. 54
HABS AL-261
HABS ALA,46-FAUN.V,2-
4ph L

Walker,Charles,House; see Cedar Grove

JEFFERSON

Grant,Basil,House; see Grant,Charles Brasfiels,House

Grant,Charles Brasfiels,House (Grant,Basil,House)
State Hwy. 28
HABS AL-144
HABS ALA,46-JEF,2-
8ph L

JEFFERSON VIC.

Allen,W. G.,House (Evergreen)
State Hwy. 28
HABS AL-142
HABS ALA,46-JEF,1-
8ph L

Evergreen; see Allen,W. G.,House

LINDEN

Baptist Church; see Marengo County Courthouse,Old

Marengo County Courthouse,Old (Baptist Church)
Cahaba Ave. & Mobile St.
HABS AL-143
HABS ALA,46-LIND,1-
9ph L

MARION COUNTY

BEXAR

Apothecary (Moorman,Dr. A. L.,Office)
County Rd. 13
HABS AL-389
HABS ALA,47-BEX,1-
4ph L

Moorman,Dr. A. L.,Office; see Apothecary

MOBILE COUNTY

CHASTANG

Chestang,Zeno,House
U. S. Hwy. 43,Chestang Landing
HABS AL-187
HABS ALA,49-CHAST,1-
5ph L

CITRONELLE

Jones House; see Pullman House

Pullman Hotel; see Pullman House

Pullman House (Pullman Hotel; Jones House)
104 Center St.
HABS AL-163
HABS ALA,49-CIT,1-
8ph/2pg L

DAUPHIN ISLAND

Fort Gaines
Pelican Point
HABS AL-102
HABS ALA,49-DAUPI,1-
16ph/3pg/1pc/fr L

Fort Gaines,Bake Ovens
HABS AL-102-C
1ph L

Fort Gaines,Barracks
HABS AL-102-B
2ph L

Fort Gaines,Officers' Quarters & Barracks
HABS AL-102-A
4ph L

Fort Gaines,Smithy
HABS AL-102-D
1ph L

DAWES

Vogtner Farm (House & Smokehouse)
Jeff Hamilton Rd. Vic.
HABS AL-188
HABS ALA,49-DAW,1-
8ph L

MOBILE

Anderson,Decatur C.,House; see 251 North Conception Street (House)

Ashalnd (Ruins); see Wilson,Augusta Evans,House (Ruins)

Atkinson,Octavia,House (Cunningham-Atkinson House)
(See BULLOCK CO.,PEACHBURG VIC. for documtatn.)
HABS AL-539
L

Ayers House (Private School; Robert,Madame Paul,House)
57 S. Hamilton St.
HABS AL-49
HABS ALA,49-MOBI,5-
5dr/4ph/2pg/fr L

Azalea Grove (Dawson,John C.,House; McKeon House; Palmetto Hall)
55 S. McGregor Ave.
HABS AL-54
HABS ALA,49-SPRIHI,4-
21ph/2pg L

Barker,P. D.,House (109 Saint Anthony Street (House); Spanish Dwelling,The; Creole House)
HABS AL-21-D
HABS ALA,49-MOBI,75-
1ph L

Barnwell-Mitchell House; see Kennedy,Joshua,House

Barton Academy
Government St.
HABS AL-32
HABS ALA,49-MOBI,34-
6dr/23ph/3pg/fr L

Bates-Henderson House; see Henderson,Doctor,House

Batre-Bernheimer-Saad House (Batre-Saad House; Bernheimer House)
155 Monroe St.
HABS AL-801
HABS ALA,49-MOBI,134-
3ph/1pg/1pc L

Batre-Hamilton House; see Broun,W. M.,House

Batre-Saad House; see Batre-Bernheimer-Saad House

Battle-Ross House (Ironwork); see Ross,William H.,House (Ironwork)

Beal-Gaillard House; see Gaillard,S. P.,House

Beck House; see Goelet-Randlette-Beck House

Beehive Church (Franklin Street Methodist Episcopal Church; Franklin Street Baptist Church)
Franklin & Saint Michael Sts.
HABS AL-26
HABS ALA,49-MOBI,28-
17ph/3pg L

Bernheimer House; see Batre-Bernheimer-Saad House

Bestor,Daniel Perrin Jr.,House (Ironwork)
208 Government St.
HABS AL-9-X
HABS ALA,49-MOBI,135-
2ph L

Bishop's House & Gates; see Ketchum,William H.,House & Gates (Ironwork)

Bloodgood's Row
306,308 & 310 Monroe St.
HABS AL-818
HABS ALA,49-MOBI,76-
3ph/1pc L

Bowers,Lloyd,Double House; see Huger-Douglas Houses

Bragg-Mitchell House; see Bragg,Judge John,House

Bragg,Judge John,House
(Bragg-Mitchell House)
1906 Spring Hill Ave.
HABS AL-30
HABS ALA,49-MOBI,32-
34ph/2pg L

Briarwood (Sewall,Judge Kiah B.,House)
Dauphin Way & Mobile St.
HABS AL-69
HABS ALA,49-MOBI,66-
25ph/2pg L

Brisk & Jacobson Store (Daniels,Elgin & Company)
51 Dauphin St.
HABS AL-790
HABS ALA,49-MOBI,122-
3ph/6pg L

Brooks House (Ironwork) (108 North Conception Street (House,Ironwork))
HABS AL-7-B
HABS ALA,49-MOBI,6-
1dr/2ph L

Broun,W. M.,House (Batre-Hamilton House)
(See MOBILE CO.,SPRING HILL for documentation)
HABS AL-58
HABS ALA,49-SPRIHI,5-
4ph/2pg L

Brown Place; see Bunker,Robert S.,House

Brown,Milton S.,House
108 S. Conception St.
HABS AL-78
HABS ALA,49-MOBI,74-
2ph L

Bunker-DuMont House; see DuMont House

Bunker,Robert S.,House (Moreland House; Brown Place)
157 Monroe St. (moved to 201 S. Warren St.)
HABS AL-802
HABS ALA,49-MOBI,93-
6ph/1pg/1pc L

Burgess-Maschmeyer House
1209 Government St.
HABS AL-847
HABS ALA,49-MOBI,216-
17ph/2pc L

Burgess-Maschmeyer House,Carriage House
1207 Government St.
HABS AL-847-A
HABS ALA,49-MOBI,216A-
1ph/1pc L

Bush-Mohr House (Ironwork); see Mohr,Dr. Charles,House (Ironwork)

Butt-Kling House (Iron Gate) (Kling House)
254 N. Jackson St.
HABS AL-7-WG
HABS ALA,49-MOBI,87A-
2ph L

Calef House (Staples,N. A.,House; Calef-Staples House)
1614 Old Shell Rd.
HABS AL-51
HABS ALA,49-MOBI,52-
4dr/23ph/9pg L

Calef-Staples House; see Calef House

Calvert-Webster House
265 N. Conception St.
HABS AL-55
HABS ALA,49-MOBI,55-
21ph/2pg L

Carolina Hill; see Dawson,William A.,House

Carriage Block
Government St.
HABS AL-36-A
HABS ALA,49-MOBI,37A-
1ph/fr L

Carriage Block,Iron Hitching Posts & Lamp Posts
Various Mobile locations
HABS AL-36
HABS ALA,49-MOBI,37-
2dr/19ph/2pg L

Cathedral of the Immaculate Conception
S. Claiborne St.
HABS AL-35
HABS ALA,49-MOBI,36-
35ph/4pg L

Catholic High School; see McGill Institute

Chamberlain-Rapier Double House; see Girard Double House

Chandler,Daniel,House; see McGill Institute

Christ Episcopal Church
Church & Saint Emanuel Sts.
HABS AL-31
HABS AL,49-MOBI,33-
6dr/29ph/2pg/fr L

6 Church Street (Commercial Building,Doorway)
HABS AL-66-A
HABS ALA,49-MOBI,186-
1ph L

301 Church Street (House) (Three Sisters House)
HABS AL-24
HABS ALA,49-MOBI,26-
1dr/4ph/2pg L

405 Church Street (House); see Church Street Block Study

Church Street Block Study
(Ravesies,Frederick P.,House; Delamier House; Hamilton-Gaillard House; 405 Church Street (House))
401-407 Church St.
HABS AL-803
HABS ALA,49-MOBI,191-
4ph/1pc L

Church Street Cemetery (Ironwork)
(Mobile Cemetery,Old (Ironwork))
Church & Bayou Sts.
HABS AL-845
HABS ALA,49-MOBI,9-
1dr/6ph L

City Hall; see Southern Market & Municipal Building

City Hospital,Old (Mobile City Hospital)
900-950 Saint Anthony St.
HABS AL-13
HABS ALA,14-MOBI,14-
5dr/11ph/3pg L

Clarke House; see Smith-Clarke House

Clarke Houses; see Robinson,Cornelius,Twin Houses

Clitherall House; see Horst,Henry,House

Cluis-Rubira House; see Cluis,Frederick V.,House

Cluis,Frederick V.,House (Cluis-Rubira House)
156 Saint Anthony St.
HABS AL-804
HABS ALA,49-MOBI,200-
8ph/1pc L

Coley Building; see Townsend-Foreman Building

Commercial Building; see Pollock Building

Conti House; see Rider House

308-310 Conti Street (Double House)
(Durand House)
HABS AL-59
HABS ALA,49-MOBI,58-
13ph/2pg/1pc L

Convent of the Visitation (Visitation Convent)
2300 Spring Hill Ave.
HABS AL-73
HABS ALA,49-MOBI,70-
7ph L

Convent of the Visitation,East Wing; see Convent of the Visitation,Section A

Convent of the Visitation,Gates & Wall
Spring Hill Ave.
HABS AL-73-A
HABS ALA,49-MOBI,70C-
5ph L

Convent of the Visitation,Section A (Convent of the Visitation,East Wing)
Spring Hill Ave.
HABS AL-73-B
HABS VA,49-,MOBI,70A-
11ph L

Convent of the Visitation,Section B (Convent of the Visitation,South Wing)
Spring Hill Ave.
HABS AL-73-C
HABS ALA,49-MOBI,70B-
15ph L

Convent of the Visitation,South Wing; see Convent of the Visitation,Section B

Convent of the Visitation,Water Wheel
Spring Hill Ave.
HABS AL-73-D
HABS ALA,49-MOBI,70D-
1ph L

Cotton Warehouse,Old; see Magnolia Cotton Warehouse

Cox-Deasy House
1115 Palmetto St.
HABS AL-846
HABS ALA,49-MOBI,217-
2ph/1pc L

Craft,John,House & Servants' Quarters; see Sanford-Staylor House & Servants' Quarters

Creole House; see Barker,P. D.,House

Creole House; see Hammond-Willoughby House

Creole House; see 256 Saint Louis Street (House)

Creole House; see Tarloon House

Cunningham-Atkinson House; see Atkinson,Octavia,House

Daniels,Elgin & Company; see Brisk & Jacobson Store

Dargan-Waring House; see Waring House

Dargan-Waring House,Gates; see Waring House,Gates

Dargan-Waring House,Privy; see Waring House,Privy

Dargan-Waring House,Slave Quarters; see Waring House,Slave Quarters

Dargan-Waring House,Stables; see Waring House,Stables

Dargan-Wraing House,Lodge; see Waring House,Texas

12 Dauphin Street (Commercial Building)
HABS AL-61-C
HABS ALA,49-MOBI,154-
1ph L

2 Dauphin Street (Commercial Building)
HABS AL-61-B
HABS ALA,49-MOBI,153-
1ph L

56 Dauphin Street (Commercial Building)
HABS AL-61-D
HABS ALA,49-MOBI,155-
1ph L

715 Dauphin Street (Commercial Building)
HABS AL-61-A
HABS ALA,49-MOBI,156-
1ph L

Dawson,James,Creole House; see Tarloon House

Dawson,John C.,House; see Azalea Grove

Dawson,William A.,House (Carolina Hill; Perdue House)
(See MOBILE CO.,SPRING HILL for documentation)
HABS AL-10
HABS ALA,49-SPRIHI,2-
6dr/9ph/3pg/fr L

Delamier House; see Church Street Block Study

Denniston House & Slave Quarters; see Oakleigh,House & Slave Quarters

Double House,French-type; see Girard Double House

Double House,French-type; see Reingard Double House

Douglas-Huger Houses; see Huger-Douglas Houses

DuMont House (Bunker-DuMont House; Noble,Annie B.,House)
157 Church St.
HABS AL-28
HABS ALA,49-MOBI,30-
17ph/2pg L

Durand House; see 308-310 Conti Street (Double House)

Elkus,Isaac,House (Ironwork); see 50 South Franklin Street (House,Ironwork)

Ellis-Lyons House; see Lyons House

Emanuel,Jonathan,House (Shrine House)
251 Government St.
HABS AL-3
HABS ALA,49-MOBI,3-
9dr/7ph/2pg/fr L

Eslava House; see Marshall-Eslava-Sledge House

Eslava,Miguel Jr.,House; see McMahon,J. J.,House

Exchange Alley (Commercial Building,Doorways)
HABS AL-66
HABS ALA,49-MOBI,188-
1ph L

Finch House (Ironwork); see 301 North Joachim Street (House,Ironwork)

Finnigan,Capt. Owen,House (Ironwork)
752 Government St.
HABS AL-9-Z
HABS ALA,49-MOBI,79-
1ph L

Foote,Charles K.,House (Ironwork); see Trammell House (Ironwork)

Ford House; see Hall House

Forsyth,John,House; see Tardy-Thorp House

Fort Conde,Charlotte House; see Kirkbride,Jonathan,House

Four Sisters House; see Tardy-Thorp House

Franklin Street Baptist Church; see Beehive Church

Franklin Street Methodist Episcopal Church; see Beehive Church

Frascatti
Conception St.
HABS AL-71
HABS ALA,49-MOBI,68-
12ph/2pg L

French Creole House; see McMahon,J. J.,House

French Creole,House; see 652 Saint Francis Street (House)

Gaillard,S. P.,House (Beal-Gaillard House)
(See MOBILE CO.,SPRING HILL for documentation)
HABS AL-107
HABS ALA,49-SPRIHI,6-
6ph L

Garconniere; see Waring House,Texas

Gas Lamps; see Lampposts

Gates-Daves House
1570-1572 Dauphin St.
HABS AL-799
HABS ALA,49-MOBI,131-
3ph/6pg L

Gazzam,Audley H.,House & Servants' Quarters
1255 Government St.
HABS AL-53
HABS ALA,49-MOBI,54-
49ph/2pg L

Gee-Barrow,House; see Gee,Gideon,House

Gee,Gideon,House (Gee-Barrow,House)
253 Monroe St. (moved to 251 Saint Anthony St.)
HABS AL-825
HABS ALA,49-MOBI,132-
1ph/4pg L

George,Elizabeth,House (Ironwork)
159 Monroe St.
HABS AL-9-K
HABS ALA,49-MOBI,80-
1ph L

Georgia Cottage; see Hardaway-Evans-Wilson-Sledge House

Gibbons-Torry House,Gate & Privy
(Torry,C. J.,House,Gate & Privy)
60 S. Conception St.
HABS AL-43
HABS ALA,49-MOBI,44-
27ph/2pg L

Gibbs House; see Wilson-Gibbs House

Gilmore-Gaines-Quigley House (Ironwork); see Quigley,Albert,House (Ironwork)

Girard Double House (Double House,French-type; Chamberlain-Rapier Double House)
56-58 S. Conception St.
HABS AL-12
HABS ALA,49-MOBI,13-
1dr/10ph/3pg/fr L

Gliddon,John S.,House
400 Saint Anthony St.
HABS AL-18
HABS ALA,49-MOBI,19- & 19A-
3dr/16ph/2pg/fr L

Goelet-Randlette-Beck House (Beck House; Randlette House; Randlette-Beck-Bedlin House)
1005 Augusta St.
HABS AL-855
HABS ALA,49-MOBI,218-
7ph/1pc L

Goldsby,J. W.,House & Iron Fence
452 Government St.
HABS AL-9-W
HABS ALA,49-MOBI,136-
2ph L

Goldsmith,Meyer,House
(Griffin-Goldsmith House)
408 Conti St.
HABS AL-76
HABS ALA,49-MOBI,203-
4ph/2pg L

Gonzales,Margaret,House (Ironwork)
(352 State Street (House,Ironwork))
HABS AL-9-E
HABS ALA,49-MOBI,82-
1ph L

Gordon House; see Tacon-Gordon House

Government St. Methodist Episcopal Church,South (Government Street United Methodist Church)
901 Government St.
HABS AL-853
HABS ALA,49-MOBI,219-
10ph/1pc L

110 Government Street (Commercial Building)
HABS AL-62-D
HABS ALA,49-MOBI,159-
1ph L

112-114 Government Street (Commercial Building)
HABS AL-62-E
HABS ALA,49-MOBI,160-
1ph L

158 Government Street (Commercial Building)
HABS AL-62-H
HABS ALA,49-MOBI,158-
1ph L

51-69 Government Street (Commercial Building)
HABS AL-62-G
HABS ALA,49-MOBI,162-
1ph L

66 Government Street (Commercial Building)
HABS AL-62-F
HABS ALA,49-MOBI,158-
1ph L

67-69 Government Street (Commercial Building)
HABS AL-67
HABS ALA,49-MOBI,64- & 64A-
35ph/2pg/fr L

71-93 Government Street (Commercial Building)
HABS AL-66-D
HABS ALA,49-MOBI,189-
1ph L

9 Government Street (Commercial Building)
HABS AL-62-A
HABS ALA,49-MOBI,157-
1ph L

453 Government Street (Iron Gate & Fence)
HABS AL-7-XXV
HABS ALA,49-MOBI,106A-
1ph L

201 Government Street (Iron Gate)
(moved to Spring Hill Ave. & Riviere du Chin Rd.)
HABS AL-9-BA-7
HABS ALA,49-MOBI,195A-
1ph L

605 Government Street (Iron Gate)
HABS AL-8-U
HABS ALA,49-MOBI,107A-
1ph L

250 Government Street (Ironwork)
HABS AL-7-D
HABS ALA,49-MOBI,8-
1dr/1ph/fr L

Government Street Presbyterian Church
Government & Jackson Sts.
HABS AL-1
HABS ALA,49-MOBI,1-
5dr/14ph/3pg/fr L

Government Street United Methodist Church; see Government St. Methodist Episcopal Church,South

Griffin-Goldsmith House; see Goldsmith,Meyer,House

Guesnard-Craft House
Jackson & Conti Sts.
HABS AL-806
HABS ALA,49-MOBI,203-
3ph/1pc L

Gulf City Hotel; see Southern Hotel

Gulf,Mobile & Ohio R.R.,Passenger Terminal
Beauregard St. & Telegraph Rd.
HABS AL-796
HABS ALA,49-MOBI,128-
2ph/1pg/1pc/1ct L

Hall House (Ford House; Hall-Ford House)
165 Saint Emanuel St.
HABS AL-46
HABS ALA,49-MOBI,47-
5dr/7ph/2pg/fr L

Hall-Ford House; see Hall House

Hall-Horst House; see Horst,Henry,House

Hamilton-Gaillard House; see Church Street Block Study

Hammond-Willoughby House (Creole House)
Saint Michael & Hamilton Sts.
HABS AL-44
HABS ALA,49-MOBI,45-
10ph/2pg L

Hanlein House; see 652 Saint Francis Street (House)

Hannah Houses; see Robinson,Cornelius,Twin Houses

Hardaway-Evans-Wilson-Sledge House
(Georgia Cottage)
2564 Spring Hill Ave.
HABS AL-826
HABS ALA,49-MOBI,133-
7ph/6pg L

Hazard-Semmes House; see Semmes,Judge Oliver J.,House

Hellen-Croom House
1001 Augusta St.
HABS AL-808
HABS ALA,49-MOBI,204-
4ph/1pc L

Henderson,Doctor,House (Bates-Henderson House)
12 N. Jackson St.
HABS AL-22-A
HABS ALA,49-MOBI,84-
1ph L

Hitching Posts,Iron
Various Mobile locations
HABS AL-36-B
HABS ALA,49-MOBI,37B-
1dr/15ph/fr L

Home Industry Foundry (Hunley Building)
250 N. Water St.
HABS AL-809
HABS ALA,49-MOBI,205-
2ph/1pc L

Horst,Henry,House (Hall-Horst House; Clitherall House)
110 Saint Emanuel St.
HABS AL-23
HABS ALA,49-MOBI,25-
15ph/2pg L

Horst,Martin,House
407 Conti St.
HABS AL-776
HABS ALA,49-MOBI,112-
8dr/9pg/fr L

Horta-Semmes House & Fence (Semmes,Adm. Raphael,House & Fence)
802 Government St.
HABS AL-56
HABS ALA,49-MOBI,56- & 56A-
9dr/31ph/2pg/fr L

Huger-Douglas Houses (Bowers,Lloyd,Double House; Douglas-Huger Houses)
109-111 S. Conception St.
HABS AL-60
HABS ALA,49-MOBI,49A-
5dr/10ph/2pg L

Huger,Charles L.,House (Ironwork)
154 S. Conception St.
HABS AL-9-BA-5
HABS ALA,49-MOBI,85-
2ph L

Hunley Building; see Home Industry Foundry

Iron Lace; see Richards,Charles G.,House

Jacobson House; see 351 Saint Michael Street (House)

James,Thomas S.,Double House; see Ottenstein,Augustine,House

Jordan House; see Rider House

Kennedy,Joshua,House (Barnwell-Mitchell House)
607 Government St.
HABS AL-800
HABS ALA,49-MOBI,206-
6ph/1pc L

Ketchum,Dr. George,House; see Silver-Ketchum House

Ketchum,William H.,House & Gates (Ironwork) (Bishop's House & Gates)
400 Government St.
HABS AL-9-U
HABS ALA,49-MOBI,137,137A- & 137B-
7ph L

Kilduff-Ray House
200 George St.
HABS AL-849
HABS ALA,49-MOBI,220-
6ph/1pc L

Kirkbride,Jonathan,House (Fort Conde,Charlotte House)
104 Theatre St.
HABS AL-14
HABS ALA,49-MOBI,15-
3dr/22ph/3pg/1pc L

Kling House; see Butt-Kling House (Iron Gate)

Kruse-Pinkerton House
300 Chatham St.
HABS AL-850
HABS ALA,49-MOBI,221-
5ph/1pc L

LaClede Hotel
150-160 Government St.
HABS AL-811
HABS ALA,49-MOBI,208-
4ph/1pc L

Lampposts (Street Lamps; Gas Lamps)
Various Mobile locations
HABS AL-36-C
HABS ALA,49-MOBI,37C-
1dr/4ph/2pg L

Larrouil House; see Larrouil-Arresijac House

Larrouil-Arresijac House (Larrouil House)
252 S. Claiborne St.
HABS AL-812
HABS ALA,49-MOBI,207-
3ph/1pc L

LeLoupe House; see Weldon-LeLoupe House

LeVert,Madame,House & Office
151 & 153 Government St.
HABS AL-29
HABS ALA,49-MOBI,31-
9dr/4ph/2pg L

Lodge,The; see Waring House,Texas

Lott,William,House
160 Rapier St.
HABS AL-851
HABS ALA,49-MOBI,222-
9ph/1pc L

Ludlow House
1113 Church St.
HABS AL-41
HABS ALA,49-MOBI,42-
17ph/1pg L

Lyons House (Ellis-Lyons House)
168 S. Royal St.
HABS AL-40
HABS ALA,49-MOBI,41-
3ph/2pg L

Lyons,Patrick,House (Ironwork)
300 State St.
HABS AL-9-S
HABS ALA,49-MOBI,88-
3ph L

Macy-Adams House (Macy,Robert C. ,House)
1569 Dauphin St.
HABS AL-813
HABS ALA,49-MOBI,209-
4ph/1pc L

Macy,Robert C. ,House; see Macy-Adams House

Magnolia Cemetery (Ironwork)
Virginia St.
HABS AL-7-JP
HABS ALA,49-MOBI,89-
37ph L

Magnolia Cotton Warehouse (Cotton Warehouse,Old; Warrant Warehouse Company)
Lipscomb & Magnolia Sts.
HABS AL-74
HABS ALA,49-MOBI,71-
3ph L

Marine Hospital & Gates; see U. S. Marine Hospital & Gates

Marshall-Eslava-Sledge House (Eslava House)
152 Tuthill Ln.
HABS AL-6
HABS ALA,49-SPRIHI,1-
8dr/15ph/2pg/fr L

Marx,Isaac,House (Tuthill House)
113 Church St. (moved to 307 University Blvd.)
HABS AL-778
HABS ALA,49-MOBI,114-
5dr/7pg/fr L

Mastin,Dr. Claude,House; see Phillipi-Mastin House

Maybrick House; see McGill Institute

McDowell,Withers,Company; see 50-52 North Commercial Street (Commercial Bldg.)

McGill Institute (Chandler,Daniel,House; Maybrick House; Catholic High School)
252 Government St.
HABS AL-77
HABS ALA,49-MOBI,73-
1dr/3ph L

McGowin-Creary House
1151 Government St.
HABS AL-852
HABS ALA,49-MOBI,223-
16ph/1pc L

McKeon House; see Azalea Grove

McMahon,J. J.,House (Eslava,Miguel Jr.,House; French Creole House)
456 Saint Francis St.
HABS AL-21-A
HABS ALA,49-MOBI,23-
16ph/2pg L

McMillan House (Ironwork)
256 N. Joachim St.
HABS AL-9-B
HABS ALA,49-MOBI,91-
5ph L

McMillan,Richard,House; see Richards,Charles G.,House

Middle Bay Light; see Mobile Light Number 6639

Middleton-Boulo House; see Middleton-Creole House

Middleton-Creole House (Middleton-Boulo House)
13 N. Cedar St.
HABS AL-42
HABS ALA,49-MOBI,43-
3ph/1pg L

Miller-O'Donnell House (Miller,James P.,House)
1102 S. Broad St.
HABS AL-814
HABS ALA,49-MOBI,210-
2ph/1pc L

Miller,James P.,House; see Miller-O'Donnell House

Mobile & Ohio Railroad Office Building
409 N. Royal St.
HABS AL-794
HABS ALA,49-MOBI,126-
1dr/4ph/8pg L

Mobile Cemetery,Old (Ironwork); see Church Street Cemetery (Ironwork)

Mobile City Hospital; see City Hospital,Old

Mobile Light Number 6639 (Middle Bay Light)
Mobile Bay
HABS AL-780
HABS ALA,49-MOBI,116-
5dr/5pg/fr L

Mohr,Dr. Charles,House (Ironwork) (Bush-Mohr House (Ironwork))
254 Saint Anthony St.
HABS AL-9-J
HABS ALA,49-MOBI,92-
4ph L

350 Monroe Street (House,Ironwork)
HABS AL-7-X
HABS ALA,49-MOBI,108-
2ph L

Moreland House; see Bunker,Robert S.,House

Noble,Annie B.,House; see DuMont House

104 North Commerce Street (Commercial Building)
HABS AL-63-J
HABS ALA,49-MOBI,146-
1ph L

114 North Commerce Street (Commercial Building)
HABS AL-63-K
HABS ALA,49-MOBI,147-
1ph L

117 North Commerce Street (Commercial Building)
HABS AL-63-L
HABS ALA,49-MOBI,148-
1ph L

15 North Commerce Street (Commercial Building)
HABS AL-63-D
HABS ALA,49-MOBI,143-
1ph L

150 North Commerce Street (Commercial Building)
HABS AL-63-M
HABS ALA,49-MOBI,149-
1ph L

16 North Commerce Street (Commercial Building)
HABS AL-63-G
HABS ALA,49-MOBI,144-
1ph L

7 North Commerce Street (Commercial Building)
HABS AL-791
HABS ALA,49-MOBI,140-
9ph/6pg L

8 North Commerce Street (Commercial Building)
HABS AL-63-A
HABS ALA,49-MOBI,141-
1ph L

9 North Commerce Street (Commercial Building)
HABS AL-63-F
HABS ALA,49-MOBI,142-
1ph L

50-52 North Commercial Street (Commercial Bldg.) (McDowell,Withers,Company)
HABS AL-784
HABS ALA,49-MOBI,145-
9dr/8pg L

203 North Conception Street (Commercial Building)
HABS AL-8-C
HABS ALA,49-MOBI,10-
1dr/1ph/fr L

251 North Conception Street (House) (Anderson,Decatur C.,House)
HABS AL-52
HABS ALA,49-MOBI,53-
14ph/2pg L

108 North Conception Street (House,Ironwork); see Brooks House (Ironwork)

8 North Hamilton Street (House) (Riley,James,House)
HABS AL-50
HABS ALA,49-MOBI,51-
11ph/2pg L

8-10 North Jackson Street (Double House); see Reingard Double House

256 North Jackson Street (House,Ironwork) (Riley,Tom,House (Ironwork))
HABS AL-9-Q
HABS ALA,49-MOBI,139-
2ph L

301 North Joachim Street (House,Ironwork) (Finch House (Ironwork))
HABS AL-9-F
HABS ALA,49-MOBI,78-
1ph L

364 North Royal Street (Commercial Building)
HABS AL-793
HABS ALA,49-MOBI,215-
3ph/1pg/1pc L

106 North Water Street (Commercial Building)
HABS AL-65-E
HABS ALA,49-MOBI,181-
1ph L

108 North Water Street (Commercial Building)
HABS AL-65-C
HABS ALA,49-MOBI,182-
1ph L

110 North Water Street (Commercial Building)
HABS AL-65-D
HABS ALA,49-MOBI,183-
1ph L

112 North Water Street (Commercial Building)
HABS AL-65-B
HABS ALA,49-MOBI,184-
1ph L

116 North Water Street (Commercial Building)
HABS AL-65-A
HABS ALA,49-MOBI,185-
1ph L

19-21 North Water Street (Commercial Building)
HABS AL-65-F
HABS ALA,49-MOBI,179-
1ph L

3 North Water Street (Commercial Building)
HABS AL-795
HABS ALA,49-MOBI,172-
2ph/3pg L

4 North Water Street (Commercial Building)
HABS AL-65-N
HABS ALA,49-MOBI,178-
1ph L

55 North Water Street (Commercial Building) (Partin Paper Company)
HABS AL-65-M
HABS ALA,49-MOBI,180-
1ph L

Number 5 Fire Station; see Washington Fire Engine Company Number 8

Oakleigh,House & Slave Quarters
(Denniston House & Slave Quarters)
350 Oakleigh Place
HABS AL-47
HABS ALA,49-MOBI,48-
13dr/27ph/3pg/1pc/3ct L

Odd Fellows Hall; see Second American Theater

Otis-Allen House
1050 Palmetto St.
HABS AL-854
HABS ALA,49-MOBI,224-
3ph/1pc L

Ottenstein,Augustine,House
(James,Thomas S.,Double House)
207-209 N. Jackson St.
HABS AL-27
HABS ALA,49-MOBI,29-
13dr/31ph/3pg/fr L

Palmetto Hall; see Azalea Grove

Parmly,Dr. Ludolph,Houses
303-305-307 Conception St.
HABS AL-815
HABS ALA,49-MOBI,5-
1dr/7ph/1pc L

Partin Paper Company; see 55 North Water Street (Commercial Building)

Perdue House; see Dawson,William A.,House

Phillipi-Mastin House (Mastin,Dr. Claude,House; Pinto,Antoine,House)
53 N. Jackson St.
HABS AL-816
HABS ALA,49-MOBI,211-
2ph/1pc L

Phoenix Fire Company Number 6
154 S. Franklin St. (moved to 203 S. Claiborne St)
HABS AL-7-Z
HABS ALA,49-MOBI,94-
2ph L

Pinto,Antoine,House; see Phillipi-Mastin House

Planters & Merchants Insurance Company
60 Saint Michael St.
HABS AL-777
HABS ALA,49-MOBI,113-
4dr/6pg/fr L

Pollock Building (Commercial Building)
51 S. Royal St.
HABS AL-48
HABS ALA,49-MOBI,49-
4ph/2pg L

Pomeroy Family Tomb
Magnolia Cemetery,Virginia St.
HABS AL-785
HABS ALA,49-MOBI,119-
4dr/2ph/4pg/1pc/fr L

Portier,Bishop Michael,House
307 Conti St.
HABS AL-37
HABS ALA,49-MOBI,38-
10dr/25ph/3pg/1pc L

Private School; see Ayers House

Protestant Orphans' Asylum
911 Dauphin St.
HABS AL-33
HABS ALA,49-MOBI,35-
5ph/2pg L

Quigley Twin House (Ironwork)
258 Congress St.
HABS AL-9-D
HABS ALA,49-MOBI,104-
1ph L

Quigley,Albert,House (Ironwork)
(Gilmore-Gaines-Quigley House (Ironwork))
751 Government St.
HABS AL-9-C
HABS ALA,49-MOBI,95-
10ph/1pg/1pc L

Randlette House; see Goelet-Randlette-Beck House

Randlette-Beck-Bedlin House; see Goelet-Randlette-Beck House

Ravesies,Frederick P.,House; see Church Street Block Study

Redwood,R. H.,House (Ironwork)
260 Saint Louis St.
HABS AL-9-T
HABS ALA,49-MOBI,138-
1ph L

Reingard Double House (8-10 North Jackson Street (Double House); Double House,French-type)
(Moved from Blakely,AL)
HABS AL-25
HABS ALA,49-MOBI,27-
1dr/10ph/2pg/fr L

Revault-Maupin-Shawhan House (Ironwork); see Revault-Shawhan House (Ironwork)

Revault-Shawhan House (Ironwork)
(Shawhan,Narcissa M.,House (Ironwork); Revault-Maupin-Shawhan House (Ironwork))
254 N. Conception St.
HABS AL-9-G
HABS ALA,49-MOBI,97-
1ph L

Richards,Charles G.,House
(McMillan,Richard,House; Iron Lace)
256 Joachim St.
HABS AL-810
HABS ALA,49-MOBI,192-
6ph/1pc L

Rider House (Conti House; Jordan House)
303 Conti St.
HABS AL-38
HABS ALA,49-MOBI,39-
10dr/7ph/2pg/fr L

Riley,James,House; see 8 North Hamilton Street (House)

Riley,Tom,House (Ironwork); see 256 North Jackson Street (House,Ironwork)

Robert,Madame Paul,House; see Ayers House

Roberts,James F.,Houses; see Robinson,Cornelius,Twin Houses

Robinson,Cornelius,Twin Houses
(Clarke Houses; Hannah Houses; Roberts,James F.,Houses)
157-159 N. Conception St.
HABS AL-807
HABS ALA,49-MOBI,77-
4ph/1pc L

Ross,William H.,House (Ironwork)
(Battle-Ross House (Ironwork))
602 Government St.
HABS AL-9-V
HABS ALA,49-MOBI,96-
2ph L

109 Saint Anthony Street (House); see Barker,P. D.,House

Saint Anthony Street (Iron Fence)
HABS AL-9-A
HABS ALA,49-MOBI,196A-
1ph L

652 Saint Francis Street (House)
(Hanlein House; French Creole,House)
HABS AL-21-B
HABS ALA,49-MOBI,83-
1ph L

256 Saint Francis Street (House,Ironwork)
HABS AL-7-R
HABS ALA,49-MOBI,109-
1ph L

251 Saint Joseph Street (Iron Fence & Gate)
HABS AL-8-TC
HABS ALA,49-MOBI,110A-
1ph L

253 Saint Joseph Street (Iron Gate)
HABS AL-8-TM
HABS ALA,49-MOBI,111A-
1ph L

256 Saint Louis Street (House) (Creole House)
HABS AL-45
HABS ALA,49-MOBI,46-
3ph/1pg L

154 Saint Louis Street (House,Iron Gate)
HABS AL-9-BB
HABS ALA,49-MOBI,11A-
1dr/3ph/1pg/fr L

155 Saint Louis Street (House,Iron Gate)
HABS AL-7-C
HABS ALA,49-MOBI,7A-
1dr/2ph/fr L

Saint Michael Street (Alley)
HABS AL-64-H
HABS ALA,49-MOBI,171-
3ph L

10 Saint Michael Street (Commercial Building)
HABS AL-64-B
HABS ALA,49-MOBI,165-
1ph L

56-58 Saint Michael Street (Commercial Building)
HABS AL-64-C
HABS ALA,49-MOBI,166-
1ph L

57 Saint Michael Street (Commercial Building)
HABS AL-64-D
HABS ALA,49-MOBI,167-
1ph L

67 Saint Michael Street (Commercial Building)
HABS AL-64-E
HABS ALA,49-MOBI,168-
1ph L

7 Saint Michael Street (Commercial Building)
HABS AL-792
HABS ALA,49-MOBI,164-
3ph/7pg L

78 Saint Michael Street (Commercial Building)
HABS AL-64-G
HABS ALA,49-MOBI,170-
1ph L

74-76 Saint Michael Street (Commercial Buildings)
HABS AL-64-F
HABS ALA,49-MOBI,169-
1ph L

351 Saint Michael Street (House) (Jacobson House; Vanroy-Barnwell House)
HABS AL-39
HABS ALA,49-MOBI,129-
9ph/1pg L

Sanford-Staylor House & Servants' Quarters (Staylor,William,House & Servants' Quarters; Craft,John,House & Servants' Quarters)
451-453 Saint William St.
HABS AL-22
HABS ALA,49-MOBI,24- & 24A-
30ph/2pg/fr L

Sanford-Thompson House (Thompson House)
1621 Spring Hill Ave.
HABS AL-817
HABS ALA,49-MOBI,212-
5ph/1pc L

Schieffelin-Sledge House (Gate & Fence) (Sledge House (Gate & Fence))
54 S. Jackson St.
HABS AL-72
HABS ALA,49-MOBI,69-
7ph L

Schley-Rutherford House
1263 Selma St.
HABS AL-857
HABS ALA,49-MOBI,225-
8ph/1pc L

Seamen's Bethel
75 Church St. (moved to 307 University Blvd.)
HABS AL-779
HABS ALA,49-MOBI,115-
5dr/5pg/fr L

Second American Theater (Odd Fellows Hall)
17 S. Royal St.
HABS AL-16
HABS ALA,49-MOBI,17-
1ph L

Semmes,Adm. Raphael,House & Fence; see Horta-Semmes House & Fence

Semmes,Judge Oliver J.,House (Hazard-Semmes House; Zimlich,Andrew,House)
2828 Dauphin Way
HABS AL-57
HABS ALA,49-MOBI,204-
19ph/2pg L

Sewall,Judge Kiah B.,House; see Briarwood

Shawhan,Narcissa M.,House (Ironwork); see Revault-Shawhan House (Ironwork)

Shippers Exchange Saloon
50 S. Commerce St.
HABS AL-789
HABS ALA,49-MOBI,121-
6ph/5pg L

Shrine House; see Emanuel,Jonathan,House

Silver-Ketchum House (Ketchum,Dr. George,House)
257 Saint Francis St.
HABS AL-798
HABS ALA,49-MOBI,130-
8ph/8pg L

Slatter Family Tomb
Magnolia Cemetery,Virginia St.
HABS AL-860
HABS ALA,49-MOBI,226-
11ph/1pc/2ct L

Sledge House (Gate & Fence); see Schieffelin-Sledge House (Gate & Fence)

Smith-Clarke House (Clarke House)
161 Saint Anthony St.
HABS AL-15
1dr/8ph/1pg L

Smith,Sidney,House (Iron Gate & Balcony)
203 Government St.
HABS AL-9-BA-8
HABS ALA,49-MOBI,197-
1ph L

12 South Commerce Street (Commercial Building)
HABS AL-63-E
HABS ALA,49-MOBI,150-
1ph L

55 South Commerce Street (Commercial Building)
HABS AL-63-B
HABS ALA,49-MOBI,151-
1ph L

58 South Commerce Street (Commercial Building)
HABS AL-63-C
HABS ALA,49-MOBI,152-
1ph L

207 South Conception Street (House)
HABS AL-8-SR
HABS ALA,49-MOBI,101-
1ph L

215 South Conception Street (Iron Fence & Gate)
HABS AL-8-X
HABS ALA,49-MOBI,102A-
1ph L

456 South Conception Street (Iron Fence & Gate)
(moved to 1802 Old Govt. & 3333 Riviere du Chin)
HABS AL-8-CX
HABS ALA,49-MOBI,103A-
1ph L

50 South Franklin Street (House,Ironwork) (Elkus,Isaac,House (Ironwork))
HABS AL-7-Y
HABS ALA,49-MOBI,105-
1ph L

204 South Joachim Street (House)
HABS AL-786
HABS ALA,49-MOBI,119-
3dr/2ph/6pg/fr L

208 South Joachim Street (House)
HABS AL-787
HABS ALA,49-MOBI,120-
6dr/3ph/7pg/fr L

23 South Royal Street (Commercial Building)
HABS AL-66-E
HABS ALA,49-MOBI,190-
1ph L

12 South Water Street (Commercial Building)
HABS AL-65-G
HABS ALA,49-MOBI,174-
2ph L

16 South Water Street (Commercial Building)
HABS AL-65-P
HABS ALA,49-MOBI,175-
1ph L

4 South Water Street (Commercial Building)
HABS AL-65-H
HABS ALA,49 MOBI,173-
1ph L

54 South Water Street (Commercial Building)
HABS AL-65-R
HABS ALA,49-MOBI,176-
1ph L

64 South Water Street (Commercial Building)
HABS AL-65-J
HABS ALA,49-MOBI,177-
3ph L

Southern Hotel (Gulf City Hotel)
53-65 Water St.
HABS AL-11
HABS ALA,49-MOBI,12-
7dr/27ph/2pg/fr L

Southern Market & Municipal Building (City Hall)
107-115 S. Royal St.
HABS AL-5
HABS ALA,49-MOBI,4-
15dr/55ph/37pg/3pc/fr L

Spanish Dwelling,The; see Barker,P. D.,House

Spring Hill College
(See MOBILE CO.,SPRING HILL for documentation)
HABS AL-34
HABS ALA,49-SPRIHI,3-
5dr/46ph/6pg L

Spring Hill College,Administration Building; see Spring Hill College,Main Building

Spring Hill College,First Building; see Spring Hill College,Original Building

Spring Hill College,Infirmary
Old Shell Rd.
HABS AL-34-C
HABS ALA,49-SPRIHI,3C-
1ph L

Spring Hill College,Main Building
(Spring Hill College,Administration Building)
Old Shell Rd.
HABS AL-34-B
HABS ALA,49-SPRIHI,3B-
5dr/41ph/fr L

Spring Hill College,Original Building
(Spring Hill College,First Building)
Old Shell Rd.
HABS AL-34-A
HABS ALA,49-SPRIHI,3A-
2ph L

Spring Hill College,Sodality Chapel
Old Shell Rd.
HABS AL-34-D
1ph L

Staples,N. A.,House; see Calef House

304 State Street (House,Ironwork)
(Tate House (Ironwork))
HABS AL-9-P
HABS ALA,49-MOBI,98-
1ph L

350 State Street (House,Ironwork)
(Walsh House)
HABS AL-9-N
HABS ALA,49-MOBI,100-
1ph L

352 State Street (House,Ironwork); see Gonzales,Margaret,House (Ironwork)

Staylor,William,House & Servants' Quarters; see Sanford-Staylor House & Servants' Quarters

Street Lamps; see Lampposts

Tacon-Gordon House (Gordon House)
1216 Government St.
HABS AL-848
HABS ALA,49-MOBI.227-
20ph/2pc L

Tardy-Thorp House (Four Sisters House; Tardy,Balthasar,House; Forsyth,John,House)
112 S. Conception St.
HABS AL-17
HABS ALA,49-MOBI,18-
3ph/2pg L

Tardy,Balthasar,House; see Tardy-Thorp House

Tarloon House (Dawson,James,Creole House; Creole House)
101 N. Hamilton St.
HABS AL-21
HABS ALA,49-MOBI,22-
1ph/1pg L

Tate House (Ironwork); see 304 State Street (House,Ironwork)

Texas House; see Waring House,Texas

Thompson House; see Sanford-Thompson House

Three Sisters House; see 301 Church Street (House)

Torry,C. J.,House,Gate & Privy; see Gibbons-Torry House,Gate & Privy

Toulmin,Gen. Theopolis,House
(See MOBILE CO.,TOULMINVILLE for documentation)
HABS AL-106
HABS ALA,49-TOUL,1-ı83(HABS):131°
30ph/2pg/2pc L

Townsend-Foreman Building (Coley Building)
56 Saint Francis St.
HABS AL-805
HABS ALA,49-MOBI,213-
3ph/1pc L

Trammell House (Ironwork)
(Foote,Charles K.,House (Ironwork))
255 N. Conception St.
HABS AL-9-H
HABS ALA,49-MOBI,99-
2ph L

Trinity Episcopal Church
Jackson St. (moved to 1900 Dauphin St.)
HABS AL-879
1ph L

Tuthill House; see Marx,Isaac,House

U. S. Marine Hospital & Gates (Marine Hospital & Gates)
800 Saint Anthony St.
HABS AL-781
HABS ALA,49-MOBI,90- & 90A-
5dr/7ph/8pg L

U. S. Post Office Building
Saint Joseph & Saint Michael Sts.
HABS AL-797
HABS ALA,49-MOBI,129-
3ph/5pg L

U.S. Custom House & Post Office
Royal & Saint Francis Sts.
HABS AL-830
HABS ALA,49-MOBI,228-
24ph/1pg/2pc/fr L

Vanroy-Barnwell House; see 351 Saint Michael Street (House)

Vincent-Walsh House
(Walsh,Richard,House)
1664 Spring Hill Ave.
HABS AL-70
HABS ALA,49-MOBI,67-
2ph/2pg L

Visitation Convent; see Convent of the Visitation

Walsh House; see 350 State Street (House,Ironwork)

Walsh,Richard,House; see Vincent-Walsh House

Waring House (Dargan-Waring House)
351 Government St.
HABS AL-19
HABS ALA,49-MOBI,20-
6dr/10ph/2pg/fr L

Waring House,Gates (Dargan-Waring House,Gates)
351 Government St.
HABS AL-19-A
HABS ALA,49-MOBI,20A-
1dr/3ph L

Waring House,Privy (Dargan-Waring House,Privy)
351 Government St.
HABS AL-19-C
1dr/2ph L

Waring House,Slave Quarters
(Dargan-Waring House,Slave Quarters)
351 Government St. (now S. Claiborne St.)
HABS AL-19-B
HABS ALA,49-MOBI,20C-
2dr/3ph L

Waring House,Stables (Dargan-Waring House,Stables)
108 S. Claiborne St.
HABS AL-19-E
HABS ALA,49-MOBI,20D-
1dr/3ph L

Waring House,Texas (Dargan-Wraing House,Lodge; Garconniere; Lodge,The; Texas House)
110 S. Claiborne St.
HABS AL-19-D
HABS ALA,49-MOBI,20B-
4dr/9ph L

Warrant Warehouse Company; see Magnolia Cotton Warehouse

Washington Fire Engine Company Number 8 (Number 5 Fire Station)
7 N. Lawrence St.
HABS AL-2
HABS ALA,49-MOBI,2-
2dr/11ph/2pg/fr L

Weldon-LeLoupe House (LeLoupe House; Weldon,John,House)
107 Saint Emanuel St.
HABS AL-20
HABS ALA,49-MOBI,21-
5ph/2pg L

Weldon,John,House; see Weldon-LeLoupe House

Wilson-Gibbs House (Gibbs House)
1012 Palmetto St.
HABS AL-856
HABS ALA,49-MOBI,229-
8ph/1pc/2ct L

Wilson,Augusta Evans,House (Ruins) (Ashalnd (Ruins))
Lanier Ave.
HABS AL-68
HABS ALA,49-MOBI,65-
4ph/2pg L

Worker's House
457 Eslava St.
HABS AL-821
HABS ALA,49-MOBI,214
3ph/1pc L

Zimlich,Andrew,House; see Semmes,Judge Oliver J.,House

MON LOUIS ISLAND

Boat Repair Yard,Old
Fowl River
HABS AL-189
HABS ALA,49- ,1-
4ph L

MOUNT VERNON

Barracks Building; see Mount Vernon Arsenal,Barracks Building

Beasley House; see Cooper-Beasley House

Center Building; see Mount Vernon Arsenal,Center Building

Cooper-Beasley House (Beasley House)
County Rd. 96 (Old Saint Stephens Rd.)
HABS AL-117
HABS ALA,49-MOUV,2-
4ph/2pg L

Curry,L. B.,House (Rogers-Curry House)
County Rd. 96 (Old Saint Stephens Rd.)
HABS AL-124
HABS ALA,49-MOUV,3-
3ph L

Fall,Nelias,House
County Rd. 96 (Old Saint Stephens Rd.)
HABS AL-162
HABS ALA,49-MOUV,5-
4ph/1pg L

Mount Vernon Arsenal,Old Barn; see Mount Vernon Arsenal,Stables

Mount Vernon Arsenal (Mount Vernon Barracks)
County Rd. 96 (Old Saint Stephens Rd.)
HABS AL-105
HABS ALA,49-MOUV,1-
47ph/2pg/5pc L

Mount Vernon Arsenal,Administration Building
Old Saint Stephens Rd. (County Rd. 96)
HABS AL-105-C
HABS ALA,49-MOUV,1-
5ph L

Mount Vernon Arsenal,Barracks Building (Mount Vernon Arsenal,Subaltern's Quarters; Barracks Building)
Old Saint Stephens Rd. (County Rd. 96)
HABS AL-105-E
HABS ALA,49-MOUV,1E-
4ph L

Mount Vernon Arsenal,Center Building (Center Building)
Old Saint Stephens Rd. (County Rd. 96)
HABS AL-105-G
HABS ALA,49-MOUV,1G-
3ph/1pc L

Mount Vernon Arsenal,Gates
Old Saint Stephens Rd. (County Rd. 96)
HABS AL-105-A
HABS ALA,49-MOUV,1-
4ph L

Mount Vernon Arsenal,Hospital Building
HABS AL-105-N
HABS ALA,49-MOUV,1N-
1ph/1pc L

Mount Vernon Arsenal,Inner Wall
Old Saint Stephens Rd. (County Rd. 96)
HABS AL-105-B
HABS ALA,49-MOUV,1-
6ph L

Mount Vernon Arsenal,Laboratory & Office (Mount Vernon Arsenal,Old Officers' Qtrs.)
Old Saint Stephens Rd. (County Rd. 96)
HABS AL-105-H
HABS ALA,49-MOUV,1-
2ph L

Mount Vernon Arsenal,Officers' Quarters; see Mount Vernon Arsenal,Workshop

Mount Vernon Arsenal,Old Barracks Building (Old Barracks Building)
Old Saint Stephens Rd. (County Rd. 96)
HABS AL-105-D
HABS ALA,49-MOUV,1D-
6ph/1pc L

Mount Vernon Arsenal,Old Mess Hall
Old Saint Stephens Rd. (County Rd. 96)
HABS AL-105-M
HABS ALA,49-MOUV,1-
1ph L

Mount Vernon Arsenal,Old Officers' Qtrs.; see Mount Vernon Arsenal,Laboratory & Office

Mount Vernon Arsenal,Paymaster's Office
Old Saint Stephens Rd. (County Rd. 96)
HABS AL-105-J
HABS ALA,49-MOUV,1-
8ph L

Mount Vernon Arsenal,Stables (Mount Vernon Arsenal,Old Barn)
Old Saint Stephens Rd. (County Rd. 96)
HABS AL-105-K
HABS ALA,49-MOUV,1-
2ph L

Mount Vernon Arsenal,Subaltern's Quarters; see Mount Vernon Arsenal,Barracks Building

Mount Vernon Arsenal,Workshop (Mount Vernon Arsenal,Officers' Quarters)
Old Saint Stephens Rd. (County Rd. 96)
HABS AL-105-F
HABS ALA,49-MOUV,1-
2ph L

Mount Vernon Arsenal,Workshop & Old Officers Qtrs.
Old Saint Stephens Rd. (County Rd. 96)
HABS AL-105-L
HABS ALA,49-MOUV,1-
2ph L

Mount Vernon Barracks; see Mount Vernon Arsenal

Old Barracks Building; see Mount Vernon Arsenal,Old Barracks Building

Rogers-Curry House; see Curry,L. B.,House

Schoolhouse,Indian
County Rd. 96 (Old Saint Stephens Rd.)
HABS AL-125
HABS ALA,49-MOUV,4-
3ph L

SPRING HILL

Batre-Hamilton House; see Broun,W. M.,House

Beal-Gaillard House; see Gaillard,S. P.,House

Broun,W. M.,House (Batre-Hamilton House)
320 Avalon St.
HABS AL-58
HABS ALA,49-SPRIHI,5-
4ph/2pg L

Carolina Hill; see Dawson,William A.,House

Dawson,William A.,House (Carolina Hill; Perdue House)
76 S. McGregor Ave.
HABS AL-10
HABS ALA,49-SPRIHI,2-
6dr/9ph/3pg/fr L

Eslava House; see Marshall-Eslava-Sledge House

Gaillard,S. P.,House (Beal-Gaillard House)
111 Myrtlewood Ln.
HABS AL-107
HABS ALA,49-SPRIHI,6-
6ph L

Marshall-Eslava-Sledge House (Eslava House)
(See MOBILE CO.,MOBILE for documentation)
HABS AL-6
HABS ALA,49-SPRIHI,1-
8dr/15ph/2pg/fr L

Perdue House; see Dawson,William A.,House

Spring Hill College
Old Shell Rd.
HABS AL-34
HABS ALA,49-SPRIHI,3-
5dr/46ph/6pg L

TOULMINVILLE

Toulmin,Gen. Theopolis,House
307 University Blvd. (Moved to Mobile,AL)
HABS AL-106
HABS ALA,49-TOUL,1-
30ph/2pg/2pc L

MONROE COUNTY

BURNT CORN VIC.

Watkins House
State Hwy. 30
HABS AL-112
HABS ALA,18- ,1-
3ph/2pg L

CLAIBORNE

Deer's Store
U.S. Hwy. 84 (State Hwy. 12)
HABS AL-104
HABS ALA,50-CLAB,1-
1dr/3ph/2pg L

Dellet,James,House
U. S. Hwy. 84 (State Hwy. 12)
HABS AL-121
HABS ALA,50-CLAB,2-
3ph/1pg/fr L

Masonic Hall (Masonic Temple)
(See MONROE CO.,PERDUE HILL for documnetation)
HABS AL-103
HABS ALA,50-PERHI,1-
2dr/5ph/1pg/fr L

Masonic Temple; see Masonic Hall

Travis,William B. ,House
HABS AL-882
HABS ALA,50-CLAB,3-
1dr/1pg L

FRANKLIN VIC.

Gin House (Mule Gin,Old)
State Hwy. 41 (moved from AL,Goode Plantation)
HABS AL-141
HABS ALA,50-FRANK.V,1-
4ph L

Mule Gin,Old; see Gin House

MONROEVILLE VIC.

Andrews,W. T.,House (Pioneer House)
State Hwy. 21-47
HABS AL-122
HABS ALA,50-MONRO.V,1-
1ph L

Pioneer House; see Andrews,W. T.,House

MOUNT PLEASANT

Ferrell,Judge,House
Old Federal Rd. (Chrysler Vic.)
HABS AL-114
HABS ALA,50-MOUPL,1-
1ph L

PERDUE HILL

Daniels,John,House; see House,Old Frame

House,Old Frame (Daniels,John,House)
U. S. Hwy. 84 (State Hwy. 12)
HABS AL-123
HABS ALA,50-PERHI,2-
1ph L

Masonic Hall (Masonic Temple)
U.S. Hwy. 84 (moved from AL,Claiborne)
HABS AL-103
HABS ALA,50-PERHI,1-
2dr/5ph/1pg/fr L

Masonic Temple; see Masonic Hall

MONTGOMERY COUNTY

MONTGOMERY

Alabama State Capitol (First Confederate Capitol)
Dexter Ave.
HABS AL-601
HABS ALA,51-MONG,1-
8dr/11ph/11pg L

Arrington House; see Bibb-Goldthwaithe-Arrington House

Ball,Charles P.,House; see Seibels-Ball-Lanier House

Barnes School for Boys; see Figh-Pickett House

Bibb-Goldthwaithe-Arrington House (Arrington House)
203 Church St.
HABS AL-611
HABS ALA,51-MONG,11-
25ph/2pg L

Branch,E. W.,House; see Ray-Branch House

Davis,Jefferson,House; see First White House of the Confederacy

Elks Club; see Murphy,John,House

Figh-Pickett House (Barnes School for Boys; Pickett House)
14 Clayton St.
HABS AL-626
HABS ALA,51-MONG,20-
7ph L

First Confederate Capitol; see Alabama State Capitol

First White House of the Confederacy (Davis,Jefferson,House)
625 Washington St. (moved from Bibb & Lee Sts.)
HABS AL-624
HABS ALA,51-MONG,13-
7dr/6ph/5pg L

Fitzpatrick-Saffold House (Saffold House)
442 S. McDonough St.
HABS AL-617
HABS ALA,51-MONG,12-
6dr/12ph/2pg L

Garrett-Hatchett House (Hatchett House)
313 Catoma St.
HABS AL-630
HABS ALA,51-MONG,14-
6dr/7ph/3pg L

Gerald-Bethea House (St. Mary's of Loretta Academy; Loretta Academy)
203 S. Lawrence St.
HABS AL-604
HABS ALA,51-MONG,4-
4dr/9ph/2pg L

Gilmer-Shorter-Lomax House (Lomax House)
235 S. Court St.
HABS AL-607
HABS ALA,51-MONG,7-
11ph/2pg L

Graves,Gov. Bibb,House; see Taylor-Ponder-Graves House

Harris-Smith House (Smith House)
Church & Catoma Sts.
HABS AL-610
HABS ALA,51-MONG,10-
18ph L

Hatchett House; see Garrett-Hatchett House

Hilliard-Nicrosi-Diffly House (Hilliard,Henry,House)
Jackson St.
HABS AL-613
2pg L

Hilliard,Henry,House; see Hilliard-Nicrosi-Diffly House

Housman House; see Oliver-Housman House

Kenneworth-Moffatt House (Moffatt House)
405 S. Hull St.
HABS AL-614
HABS ALA,51-MONG,19-
8ph L

Lomax House; see Gilmer-Shorter-Lomax House

Loretta Academy; see Gerald-Bethea House

Louisville & Nashville RR:Union Station Train Shed
Water St. ,opposite Lee St.
HAER AL-1
HAER ALA,51-MONG,23A-
18ph/3pg/3pc/fr L

McBryde-Screws-Tyson House (Tyson,John C.,House)
423 Mildred St.
HABS AL-608
HABS ALA,51-MONG,8-
14ph L

Moffatt House; see Kenneworth-Moffatt House

Murphy,John,House (Elks Club)
22 Bibb St.
HABS AL-603
HABS ALA,51-MONG,3-
3dr/18ph/3pg/fr L

Oliver-Housman House (Housman House)
Wilkerson & Montgomery Sts.
HABS AL-635
HABS ALA,51-MONG,15-
3dr/3ph/3pg/fr L

Owens-Teague House (Teague House)
440 S. Perry St.
HABS AL-606
HABS ALA,51-MONG,6-
3dr/18ph/2pg/fr L

Pickett House; see Figh-Pickett House

Pollard,Col. Charles Teed,House (Mansion)
117 Jefferson St.
HABS AL-605
HABS ALA,51-MONG,5-
6dr/24ph/2pg/fr L

Ray House; see Ray-Branch House

Ray-Branch House (Branch,E. W.,House; Ray House)
730 S. Court St.
HABS AL-609
HABS ALA,51-MONG,9-
1ph L

Saffold House; see Fitzpatrick-Saffold House

Sayre-Troy House (Troy House)
Adams & Jefferson St.
HABS AL-641
HABS ALA,51-MONG,21-
11ph/2pg L

Seibels-Ball-Lanier House (Ball,Charles P.,House)
407 Adams Ave.
HABS AL-612
HABS ALA,51-MONG,17-
8ph/3pg L

Smith House; see Harris-Smith House

St. John's Episcopal Church
113 Madison Ave.
HABS AL-643
HABS ALA,51-MONG,22-
2ph/2pg L

St. Mary's of Loretta Academy; see Gerald-Bethea House

Stone-Young Plantation House; see Stone-Young-Baggett House

Stone-Young-Baggett House (Stone-Young Plantation House)
County Rd. 54 (Old Selma Rd.)
HABS AL-650
HABS ALA,51-MONG.V,1-
9dr/33ph/2pg/fr L

Taylor-Ponder-Graves House (Graves,Gov. Bibb,House)
511 S. McDonough St.
HABS AL-644
HABS ALA,51-MONG,16-
11ph L

Teague House; see Owens-Teague House

Troy House; see Sayre-Troy House

Tyson,John C.,House; see McBryde-Screws-Tyson House

Union Station
Water St.
HAER AL-2
HAER ALA,51-MONG,24-
10ph/1pg/1pc L

Winter Building
2 Dexter Ave.
HABS AL-602
HABS ALA,51-MONG,2-
2dr/1ph/2pg/fr L

MORGAN COUNTY

DECATUR

Hinds House; see Rhea-Burleson-McEntire House

McEntire House; see Rhea-Burleson-McEntire House

Rhea-Burleson-McEntire House (McEntire House; Hinds House)
120 Sycamore St.
HABS AL-364
HABS ALA,52-DECA,2-
12ph L

State Bank Building, Old; see State Bank of Alabama,Decatur Branch

State Bank of Alabama,Decatur Branch (State Bank Building, Old)
Bank St. & Wilson Ave.
HABS AL-348
HABS ALA,52-DECA,1-
8dr/6ph/3pg/1pc/fr L

SOMERVILLE

Morgan County Courthouse,Old
Bluff City Rd.
HABS AL-861
HABS ALA,52-SOMVI,1-
1ph/1pg/1pc L

Rather-Rice-Gilchrist House
Bluff City Rd. Vic.
HABS AL-864
HABS ALA,52-SOMVI,2-
4ph/1pg/1pc L

PERRY COUNTY

MARION

Edwards,W. H.,House
Edwards Rd.
HABS AL-824
HABS ALA,53-MARI.V,3-
6ph L

Elmcrest; see Moore,Judge John,House

Ford House & Kitchen; see Lowrey-Ford House & Kitchen

Hanna,Doctor,House; see Whitsett-Hurt-Hanna House

King,Judge Porter,House
1001 Washington St.
HABS AL-772
HABS ALA,53-MARI,5-
8ph/1pg L

Lowrey-Ford House & Kitchen (Ford House & Kitchen)
Washington St. (County Rd. 45)
HABS AL-822
HABS ALA,53-MARI.V,1-
11ph L

Marion Female Seminary (Perry County High School,Old)
Monroe & Centreville Sts.
HABS AL-771
HABS ALA,53-MARI,4-
4ph/1pg L

Moore,Gov. Andrew Barry,House
State Hwy. 14
HABS AL-767
HABS ALA,53-MARI,2-
1ph/1pg L

Moore,Judge John,House (Elmcrest)
H. G. Williams Circle
HABS AL-770
HABS ALA,53-MARI,3-
7ph/1pg L

Perry County Courthouse,Old
Washington,Pickens,Jefferson & Green Sts.
HABS AL-766
HABS ALA,53-MARI,1-
12dr/24ph/1pg L

Perry County High School,Old; see Marion Female Seminary

Siloam Baptist Church
Washington & Early Sts.
HABS AL-774
HABS ALA,53-MARI,7-
4ph/1pg L

Whitsett-Hurt-Hanna House (Hanna,Doctor,House)
110 W. Lafayette St.
HABS AL-773
HABS ALA,53-MARI,6-
5ph/1pg L

MARION VIC.

Carlisle Hall; see Kenworthy Hall

Carlisle,Edwin Kenworth,House; see Kenworthy Hall

Coke-Crenshaw House; see Jones-Cocke-Crenshaw House

Jones-Cocke-Crenshaw House (Tuthill House; Coke-Crenshaw House)
Washington St. (County Rd. 45)
HABS AL-823
HABS ALA,53-MARI.V,2-
13ph L

Kenworthy Hall (Carlisle Hall; Carlisle,Edwin Kenworth,House)
State Hwy. 14 (Greensboro Rd.)
HABS AL-765
HABS ALA,53-MARI.V,5-
25ph/2pg L

Osborne-Jones House
County Rd. 45 (Washington St.)
HABS AL-788
HABS ALA,53-MARI.V,4-
9ph L

Tuthill House; see Jones-Cocke-Crenshaw House

UNIONTOWN

Davidson House; see Westwood

Masonic Hall
Water Ave. & North St.
HABS AL-768
HABS ALA,53-UNITO,3-
2ph L

Pitts' Folly,House & Outbuildings
State Hwy. 21
HABS AL-267
HABS ALA,53-UNITO,1-
23ph/2pg L

Westwood (Davidson House)
Water Ave. (State Hwy. 61)
HABS AL-769
HABS ALA,53-UNITO,2-
9ph L

PICKENS COUNTY

ALICEVILLE

Hughes,Benjamin,House & Outbuildings; see Ingleside,House & Outbuildings

Ingleside,House & Outbuildings (Hughes,Benjamin,House & Outbuildings)
Second St. (State Hwy. 14)
HABS AL-395
HABS ALA,54-ALIC,1-
11ph L

ALICEVILLE VIC.

Hughes,Dr. William,House & Outbuildings
Hughes Creek Vic.
HABS AL-396
HABS ALA,54-ALIC.V,1-
19ph L

CARROLLTON

First United Methodist Church; see Methodist Episcopal Church

Methodist Episcopal Church (First United Methodist Church)
Tuscaloosa St. (State Hwy. 86)
HABS AL-394
HABS ALA,54-CARL,3-
10ph L

Pettus,Edmund Winston,House
State Rd. 17
HABS AL-372
HABS ALA,54-CARL,1-
4ph L

Phoenix Hotel
Phoenix St.
HABS AL-393
HABS ALA,54-CARL,2-
15ph L

MEMPHIS

Boykin,Will,House
State Rt. 32 & County Rt. 1 Vic.
HABS AL-870
HABS ALA,54-MEM,1-
4dr/8ph/8pg/1pc/fr L

Charity House
State Rt. 32 & County Rt. 1 Vic.
HABS AL-871
HABS ALA,54-MEM,2-
4dr/10ph/8pg/1pc/fr L

Charity House,Outbuilding
State Rt. 32 & Co. Rt. 1
HABS AL-871-A
1ph/1pc L

Charity House,Outhouse
State Rt. 32 & Co. Rt. 1 Vic.
HABS AL-871-B
1ph/1pc L

Memphis,Town of
HABS AL-869
HABS ALA,54-MEM,3-
7ph/35pg/1pc L

PICKENSVILLE

Baptist Church
Bonner Mill Rd.
HABS AL-342
HABS ALA,54-PICK,2-
5ph L

Ferguson-Long House (Long,Gus,House)
Chopitoulas St. (State Hwy. 14)
HABS AL-386
HABS ALA,54-PICK,4-
8ph L

Long,Gus,House; see Ferguson-Long House

Methodist Church
Ferguson St.
HABS AL-387
HABS ALA,54-PICK,5-
6ph L

Peterson Building; see Store

Sander's House; see Saunders,Henry Williams,House

Saunders,Henry Williams,House (Williams,Henry,House; Sander's House)
Bonner Mill Rd. & Ferguson St.
HABS AL-392
HABS ALA,54-PICK,6-
9ph L

Store (Peterson Building)
State Hwys. 14 & 86
HABS AL-309
HABS ALA,54-PICK,1-
8ph L

Wilkins,Doctor,House
State Hwys. 14 & 86 Vic.
HABS AL-378
HABS ALA,54-PICK,3-
9ph L

Williams,Henry,House; see Saunders,Henry Williams,House

TOMBIGBEE VALLEY VIC

Bridges of the Upper Tombigbee River Valley
HAER AL-7
HAER ALA,54-TOMVA.V,1-
14ph/1pg/3pc L

PIKE COUNTY

ORION

Alabama College,Old; see Orion Male & Female Institute

Baptist Church
U. S. Hwy. 231
HABS AL-562
HABS ALA,55-ORIO,1-
5ph L

Chancey House; see Hanchey-Pennington House

Chancey,John,House
(See BULLOCK CO.,HIGH RIDGE VIC. for documtatn.)
HABS AL-572
HABS ALA,6-HIRI.V,2-
2ph L

Hanchey-Pennington House (Chancey House; Pennington House)
U. S. Hwy. 231
HABS AL-563
HABS ALA,55-ORIO,2-
3ph L

Henderson House; see McCullough-Henderson House

McCullough-Henderson House
(Henderson House)
U. S. Hwy. 231
HABS AL-596
HABS ALA,55-ORIO,4-
3ph L

Orion Academy; see Orion Male & Female Institute

Orion Male & Female Institute
(Alabama College,Old; Orion Academy)
U. S. Hwy. 231
HABS AL-574
HABS ALA,55-ORIO,3-
2ph L

Pennington House; see Hanchey-Pennington House

Siler,Solomon,House
U. S. Hwy. 231
HABS AL-597
HABS ALA,55-ORIO,5-
15ph L

ORION VIC.

Berry House (Berry-Braswell House; Braswell,E. B.,House)
(See PIKE CO.,HIGH RIDGE VIC. for documentation)
HABS AL-595
HABS ALA,6-HIRI,1-
5ph L

Berry-Braswell House; see Berry House

Braswell,E. B.,House; see Berry House

RUSSELL COUNTY

COTTONTON

Cotton Gin & Well Sweep (Mule Cotton Gin; Well Sweep)
Cliatt Plantation,State Rt. 165
HABS AL-552
HABS ALA,57-COT.V,1-
3dr/7ph/2pg/fr L

Mule Cotton Gin; see Cotton Gin & Well Sweep

Well Sweep; see Cotton Gin & Well Sweep

CRAWFORD

Tuskabatchee Masonic Lodge Number 863
U. S. Hwy. 80 & County Rd. 79
HABS AL-515
HABS ALA,57-CRAWF,1-
6ph L

FORT MITCHELL

Crowell-Alexander House; see Crowell-Cantey-Alexander House

Crowell-Cantey-Alexander House
(Crowell,Col. John,House; Crowell-Alexander House)
State Rd. 165
HABS AL-578
HABS ALA,57-FOMI,1-
15ph L

Crowell,Col. John,House; see Crowell-Cantey-Alexander House

Johnson,Enoch,House; see Post Office,Old

Post Office,Old (Johnson,Enoch,House)
HABS AL-594
HABS ALA,57-FOMI,2-
4ph L

GLENVILLE

Elmoreland; see Mitchell,Col. Americus,House

Glenville Plantation; see Mitchell,Col. Americus,House

Mitchell,Col. Americus,House
(Elmoreland; Glenville Plantation)
U.S. Hwy. 431
HABS AL-570
HABS ALA,57-GLENV,1-
15dr/28ph/2pg/fr L

PITTSVIEW VIC.

Elmoreland; see Mitchell,Col. Americus,House

Glennville Plantation; see Mitchell,Col. Americus,House

Mitchell,Col. Americus,House
(Elmoreland; Glennville Plantation)
(See RUSSELL CO.,GLENVILLE for documentation)
HABS AL-570
HABS ALA,57-GLENV,1-
15dr/28ph/2pg/fr L

Quarles,W. T.,House; see Richardson-Quarles-Comer House

Richardson-Quarles-Comer House
(Quarles,W. T.,House)
U. S. Hwy. 431 Vic.
HABS AL-514
HABS ALA,57-PITV.V,1-
5ph L

SEALE

Dudley's Hotel
Railroad & Main Sts.
HABS AL-531
HABS ALA,57-SEAL,1-
3ph L

SEALE VIC.

Bass-Perry House (Magnolia Green; Mott,J. F. ,House; Perry-Mott House)
U. S. Hwy. 431
HABS AL-588
HABS ALA,57-SEAL.V,1-
20ph L

Magnolia Green; see Bass-Perry House

Mott,J. F. ,House; see Bass-Perry House

Perry-Mott House; see Bass-Perry House

VILULA

Birds' Nest,The (Martin House; Vilula Tea Garden,The)
U.S. Rt. 43
HABS AL-545
HABS ALA,57-VILU,1-
10ph L

Martin House; see Birds' Nest,The

Vilula Tea Garden,The; see Birds' Nest,The

SHELBY COUNTY

CALERA

Birmingham Industrial District; see Wilton Depot

Heart of Dixie Railroad Museum; see Wilton Depot

Southern Railway Depot; see Wilton Depot

Wilton Depot (Southern Railway Depot; Heart of Dixie Railroad Museum; Birmingham Industrial District)
Ninth St.
HABS AL-937
H

COLUMBIA

Columbiana Cemetery-Birmingham Industrial District; see Ware Grave Plot

Ware Grave Plot (Columbiana Cemetery-Birmingham Industrial District
Shelby County Rd. 25
HABS AL-954
H

HARPERSVILLE VIC.

Chancellor,William,House
Chancellor Crossroads
HABS AL-435
HABS ALA,61- ,1-
2ph/1pg L

Eastis House; see Rock House,The

Rock House,The (Eastis House)
U.S. Rt. 280 (State Rt. 38)
HABS AL-447
HABS ALA,59-HARP.V,1-
3ph/1pg L

HELENA

Birmingham Industrial District; see Gould,Billy,Coal Mine & Coke Ovens

Gould,Billy,Coal Mine & Coke Ovens (Birmingham Industrial District)
Confluence of Cahaba River & Buck Creek
HAER AL-16
5ph/1pc H

HELENA VIC.

Cotton Press (Remains) (Mule Cotton Press (Remains))
Dunham Plantation,County Rd. 17
HABS AL-422
HABS ALA,59-HEL.V,1-
2dr/fr L

Mule Cotton Press (Remains); see Cotton Press (Remains)

MONTEVALLO

Alabama Girls Industrial School,East Building; see Main Hall

Alabama Women's College,Reynolds Hall; see Montevallo Male Institute

Birmingham Industrial District; see Main Street (Commercial Streetscapes)

King,Edmund,House (University of Montevallo,Guest House)
Highland & Bloch Sts.
HABS AL-438
HABS ALA,59-MONVA,2-
4ph/2pg/fr L

Main Hall (Alabama Girls Industrial School,East Building; U. of Montevallo-Birmingham Industrial District)
HABS AL-938
H

Main Street (Commercial Streetscapes) (Birmingham Industrial District)
HABS AL-939
H

Montevallo Male Institute (University of Montevallo,Reynolds Hall; Alabama Women's College,Reynolds Hall)
Highland St.
HABS AL-427
HABS ALA,59-MONVA,1A-
1ph/3pg/fr L

U. of Montevallo-Birmingham Industrial District; see Main Hall

University of Montevallo,Guest House; see King,Edmund,House

University of Montevallo,Reynolds Hall; see Montevallo Male Institute

SHELBY

Birmingham Industrial District; see Shelby Iron Works

Birmingham Industrial District; see Shelby Iron Works,Iron Master's House

Shelby Iron Works (Birmingham Industrial District)
County Rd. 42
HAER AL-42
H

Shelby Iron Works,Iron Master's House (Ware,Horace,House; Birmingham Industrial District)
County Rd. 42
HAER AL-42-A
H

Ware,Horace,House; see Shelby Iron Works,Iron Master's House

SUMTER COUNTY

BREWERSVILLE

Brewersville Methodist Church
St. Rt. 28
HABS AL-295
HABS ALA,60-BREWV,2-
9ph L

Henson House
(See SUMTER CO.,COATOPA for documentation)
HABS AL-293
HABS ALA,60-BREWV,2-
5ph L

Patton-Scales House (Patton,Joe,House)
St. Rt. 28
HABS AL-292
HABS ALA,60-BREWV,1-
5ph L

Patton,Joe,House; see Patton-Scales House

COATOPA

Henson House
St. Rt. 28
HABS AL-293
HABS ALA,60-COATO,1-
5ph L

COATOPA VIC.

Brewersville Methodist Church
(See SUMTER CO.,BREWERSVILLE for documentation)
HABS AL-295
HABS ALA,60-BREWV,2-
9ph L

Lee Haven
(See SUMTER CO.,LIVINGSTON for documentation)
HABS AL-290
HABS ALA,60-LIV,6-
10ph/2pg L

Patton-Scales House (Patton,Joe,House)
(See SUMTER CO.,BREWERSVILLE for documentation)
HABS AL-292
HABS ALA,60-BREWV,1-
5ph L

Patton,Joe,House; see Patton-Scales House

LIVINGSTON

Arrington-Chapman House (Livingston Hotel; Inn,Old)
207 W. Main St.
HABS AL-285
HABS ALA,60-LIV,5-
7ph L

Episcopal Church; see St. James' Episcopal Church

Harris-Ennis-White House (White,T. V.,House)
W. Main St.
HABS AL-264
HABS ALA,60-LIV,3-
5ph L

Inn,Old; see Arrington-Chapman House

Lakewood (Parker,J. L.,House)
U.S. Hwy. 11 (Washington St.)
HABS AL-284
HABS ALA,60-LIV,4-
13ph L

Lee Haven
County Rd. 21
HABS AL-290
HABS ALA,60-LIV,6-
10ph/2pg L

Little,W. G.,House
W. Main & Spring Sts.
HABS AL-262
HABS ALA,60-LIV,1-
6ph L

Livingston Hotel; see Arrington-Chapman House

McMahon House; see Pleasant Ridge

Parker,J. L.,House; see Lakewood

Pleasant Ridge (McMahon House)
100 W. Main St.
HABS AL-263
HABS ALA,60-LIV,2-
8ph L

Sherard,John H.,House (Southerland,R. H.,House)
State Rd. 28
HABS AL-283
HABS ALA,60-LIV.V,2-
16ph L

Southerland,R. H.,House; see Sherard,John H.,House

St. James' Episcopal Church (Episcopal Church)
Spring & Monroe Sts.
HABS AL-294
HABS ALA,60-LIV,7-
6ph L

White,T. V.,House; see Harris-Ennis-White House

LIVINGSTON VIC.

Lee,Col. J. M.,House; see Oak Manor

Oak Manor (Lee,Col. J. M.,House)
State Rd. 28
HABS AL-257
HABS ALA,60-LIV.V,1-
26ph L

TALLADEGA COUNTY

ALPINE

Alpine (Welch,Nathaniel,House & Outbuildings)
County Rd. 46
HABS AL-433
HABS ALA,61-ALP,1-
14ph L

Welch,Nathaniel,House & Outbuildings; see Alpine

ALPINE VIC.

Carlton-Autrey House; see Jenkins-Carlton-Autrey House

Jenkins-Carlton-Autrey House (Carlton-Autrey House)
(See CRENSHAW CO.,MOUNT IDA VIC. for documtatn.)
HABS AL-449
HABS ALA,21-MOUTI.V,1-
9ph L

Lawler House (Orange Vale; Lawler-Whiting-Bliss House; Whitney House)
(See TALLADEGA CO.,TALLADEGA VIC. for documtatn.)
HABS AL-443
HABS ALA,61- ,2-
16ph/1pg L

Lawler-Whiting-Bliss House; see Lawler House

Mallory House; see Sellwood

Morriss-Holmes House (Morriss,John,House)
(See TALLADEGA CO.,WINTERBORO for documentation)
HABS AL-459
HABS ALA,61-WINT,1-
5ph L

Morriss,John,House; see Morriss-Holmes House

Mount Ida (Reynolds House; Rendalia)
(See TALLADEGA CO.,SYLACAUGA VIC. for documtatn.)
HABS AL-442
HABS ALA,61-SYLA.V,3-
17ph/2pg L

Orange Vale; see Lawler House

Rendalia; see Mount Ida

Reynolds House; see Mount Ida

Riser House; see Wewoka

Riser House,Grist Mill; see Wewoka,Grist Mill

Sellwood (Mallory House)
(See TALLADEGA CO.,SYLACAUGA for documtatn.)
HABS AL-448
HABS ALA,61-SYLA.V,4-
9ph L

Wewoka (Riser House)
(See TALLADEGA CO.,SYLACAUGA VIC. for documtatn.)
HABS AL-429
HABS ALA,61-SYLA.V,2-
14ph L

Wewoka,Grist Mill (Riser House,Grist Mill)
(See TALLADEGA CO.,SYLACAUGA VIC. for documtatn.)
HABS AL-429-N
HABS ALA,61-SYLA.V,2B-
1ph L

Whitney House; see Lawler House

EASTABOGA VIC.

Covered Bridge (Peg Bridge,The Old)
Spanning Choccolocco Creek on County Rd. 93
HABS AL-445
HABS ALA,61-EAST.V,1-
7ph L

Peg Bridge,The Old; see Covered Bridge

MUNFORD

Academy,Old; see Spence House

Spence House (Academy,Old)
State Rd. 21
HABS AL-463
HABS ALA,61-MUNF,1-
4ph L

SYLACAUGA

Fluker,Baldwin,House
Talladega Hwy.
HABS AL-454
HABS ALA,61-SYLA,2-
5ph/1pg L

SYLACAUGA VIC.

Bledsoe-Cook House (Cook House)
State Rd. 21
HABS AL-439
HABS ALA,61-SYLA,1-
4ph/1pg L

Bledsoe-Kelly House; see Mountain Spring

Cook House; see Bledsoe-Cook House

Gantts' Quarry
Quarry Rd.
HAER AL-6
HAER ALA,61-SYLA.V,5-
9ph/1pg/1pc L

Kelly House; see Mountain Spring

Mallory House; see Sellwood

Mount Ida (Reynolds House; Rendalia)
County Rd. 11
HABS AL-442
HABS ALA,61-SYLA.V,3-
17ph/2pg L

Mountain Spring (Bledsoe-Kelly House; Kelly House)
State Rd. 21
HABS AL 428
HABS ALA,61-SYLA.V,1-
7ph L

Rendalia; see Mount Ida

Reynolds House; see Mount Ida

Riser House; see Wewoka

Riser House,Grist Mill; see Wewoka,Grist Mill

Sellwood (Mallory House)
St. Rt. 76
HABS AL-448
HABS ALA,61-SYLA.V,4-
9ph L

Wewoka (Riser House)
Riser Mill Rd.
HABS AL-429
HABS ALA,61-SYLA.V,2-
14ph L

Wewoka,Grist Mill (Riser House,Grist Mill)
Riser Mill Rd.
HABS AL-429-N
HABS ALA,61-SYLA.V,2B-
1ph L

TALLADEGA

Alabama Institute for Deaf & Blind; see East Alabama Masonic Female Institute

Cedarwood; see King Plantation

Chambers House (Huey-Stone-Chambers House)
301 N. East St.
HABS AL-457
HABS ALA,61-TALA,4-
13ph/1pg L

East Alabama Masonic Female Institute (Alabama Institute for Deaf & Blind; Manning Hall; Masonic Female Institute)
205 E. South St.
HABS AL-446
HABS ALA,61-TALA,1-
12dr/28ph/1pg L

Huey-Stone-Chambers House; see Chambers House

Isbell-Hicks House; see Isbell,James,House

Isbell,James,House (Isbell-Hicks House; Usrey Funeral Home)
108 E. North St.
HABS AL-455
HABS ALA,61-TALA,2-
11ph/1pg L

King Plantation (Cedarwood)
Frank St.
HABS AL-462
HABS ALA,61-TYALA.V,3-
7ph L

Manning Hall; see East Alabama Masonic Female Institute

Masonic Female Institute; see East Alabama Masonic Female Institute

Plowman-Elliott House; see Plowman,T. L. ,House

Plowman,T. L. ,House (Plowman-Elliott House)
511 S. East St.
HABS AL-456
HABS ALA,61-TALA,3-
11ph/1pg L

Talladega College,Swayne Hall
HABS AL-764
HABS ALA,61-TALA,5A-
10ph/2pg/1pc L

Usrey Funeral Home; see Isbell,James,House

TALLADEGA VIC.

Burt House (Curry-Burt-Smelley House; Curry House)
State Rd. 21
HABS AL-472
HABS ALA,61-TALA.V,4-
4ph L

Curry House; see Burt House

Curry-Burt-Smelley House; see Burt House

Hardie-Lewis House; see Thornhill

Lawler House (Orange Vale; Lawler-Whiting-Bliss House; Whitney House)
County Rd. 11
HABS AL-443
HABS ALA,61- ,2-
16ph/1pg L

Lawler-Whiting-Bliss House; see Lawler House

Mardis House (Mardis-Batchelor House)
U.S. Hwy. 231
HABS AL-460
HABS ALA,61-TALA.V,2-
5ph L

Mardis-Batchelor House; see Mardis House

Marker of Jackson Trace
U.S. Hwy. 231
HABS AL-460-A
HABS ALA,61-TALA.V,2C-
1ph L

Orange Vale; see Lawler House

Thornhill (Hardie-Lewis House; Welch,Tom,House)
State Rd. 21
HABS AL-441
HABS ALA,61-TALA.V,1-
7ph/2pg L

Welch,Tom,House; see Thornhill

Whitney House; see Lawler House

WINTERBORO

Morriss-Holmes House
(Morriss,John,House)
St. Rt. 76
HABS AL-459
HABS ALA,61-WINT,1-
5ph L

Morriss,John,House; see Morriss-Holmes House

TALLAPOOSA COUNTY

DADEVILLE

Dennis Hotel; see United States Hotel

Lane House (Mitchell-Lane House; Little Huntington)
311 W. Columbus St.
HABS AL-510
HABS ALA,62-DADV,1-
14ph L

Little Huntington; see Lane House

Mitchell-Lane House; see Lane House

Post Office & Hotel; see United States Hotel

United States Hotel (Dennis Hotel; Post Office & Hotel)
N. Broadnax & E. Green Sts.
HABS AL-511
HABS ALA,62-DADV,2-
11ph L

DADEVILLE VIC.

Black House; see Black-Gilling House

Black-Gilling House (Gregory House; Black House)
(See TALLAPOOSA CO.,DUDLEYVILLE VIC. for documtn.)
HABS AL-548
HABS ALA,62-DUDV.V,1-
L

Gardner,William A.,House
Lafayette Hwy. (County Rd. 75)
HABS AL-529
HABS ALA,62-DADV.V,1-
11ph L

Gregory House; see Black-Gilling House

DUDLEYVILLE VIC.

Balck-Gilling House (Gregory Housc; Black House)
County Rd. 44
HABS AL-548
HABS ALA,62-DUDV.V,1-
9ph L

Black House; see Balck-Gilling House

Gregory House; see Balck-Gilling House

TUSCALOOSA COUNTY

BUCKSVILLE

Tannehill Furnace (Ruins)
Mud Creek Vic.
HABS AL-276
HABS ALA,63-BUCK.V,1-
7ph L

HOLT

Birmingham Industrial District; see Empire Coke Plant

Birmingham Industrial District; see Holt Lock & Dam

Empire Coke Plant (Birmingham Industrial District)
HAER AL-21
HAER ALA,2-TENSA,2-
H

Holt Lock & Dam (Birmingham Industrial District)
HAER AL-22
HAER ALA,2-TENSA,2-
H

NORTHPORT

Birmingham Industrial District; see Jemison,Robert,Plantation

Birmingham Industrial District; see Main Street (Commercial Streetscapes)

Bryce Hospital; see Jemison,Robert,Plantation

Cherokee; see Jemison,Robert,Plantation

Jemison,Robert,Plantation (Cherokee; Bryce Hospital; Birmingham Industrial District)
Byler Rd.
HABS AL-941
H

Main Street (Commercial Streetscapes) (Birmingham Industrial District)
HABS AL-940
H

TUSCALOOSA

Alabama Museum of Natural History; see Smith Hall

Alabama State Capitol,Old (Capitol,Old)
Broad St.
HABS AL-867
HABS ALA,63-TUSLO,21-
4ph/1pg/1pc L

Battle-Friedman House (Battle,Alfred,House)
Greensboro Ave.
HABS AL-226
HABS ALA,63-TUSLO,13-
13ph/1pg L

Battle,Alfred,House; see Battle-Friedman House

Birmingham Industrial District; see Tuscaloosa,Downtown (Streetscapes)

Birmingham Industrial District; see University of Alabama,Guard Tower

Birmingham Industrial District; see Warrior River Lock No. 3 Wall

Capitol,Old; see Alabama State Capitol,Old

Christ Episcopal Church
605 Twenty-fifth Ave.
HABS AL-249
HABS ALA,63-TUSLO,20-
10ph/2pg/1pc L

Cochrane,Judge William C.,House (Stillman Institute)
3600 Fifteenth St.
HABS AL-217
HABS ALA,63-TUSLO,8-
7ph/1pg L

Collier-Whitt-Boone House (Collier,Governor,House)
905 Twenty-first Ave.
HABS AL-268
HABS ALA,63-TUSLO,19-
12ph L

Collier,Governor,House; see Collier-Whitt-Boone House

Deal,Doctor,House; see Dearing-Bagby House

Dearing House; see Dearing-Swaim House

Dearing-Bagby House (Deal,Doctor,House; Governor's Mansion; University Club)
421 Queen City Ave.
HABS AL-230
HABS ALA,63-TUSLO,16-
10ph/2pg L

Dearing-Swaim House (Spence House; Dearing House)
2111 Fourteenth St.
HABS AL-228
HABS ALA,63-TUSLO,15-
9ph/1pg L

Drish,Dr. John R.,House
2300 Seventeenth St.
HABS AL-201
HABS ALA,63-TUSLO,1-
5dr/9ph/3pg/1pc/fr L

Duffies Tavern (Tavern,Old)
2800 Twenty-eighth Ave.
HABS AL-224
HABS ALA,63-TUSLO,11-
11ph/2pg L

Eddins House (Price-Eddins-Rosenau House)
919 Greensboro Ave.
HABS AL-204
HABS ALA,63-TUSLO,4-
3dr/9ph/4pg/fr L

Foster House; see Foster-Shirley House

Foster-Shirley House (Foster House)
1600 Dearing Place
HABS AL-216
HABS ALA,63-TUSLO,7-
10ph/1pg L

Geological Survey of Alabama; see Smith Hall

Gluck House (Martin-Comegys-Cluck House)
2021 Seventh St.
HABS AL-225
HABS ALA,63-TUSLO,12-
3dr/9ph/2pg/fr L

Gorgas House; see University of Alabama,Gorgas House

Governor's Mansion; see Dearing-Bagby House

Guild,Dr. Lafayette,House; see Ormond-Litte House

Janus Place; see Scott-Moody House

Jemison-Van de Graaf-Burchfield House (Jemison,Sen. Robert,House)
1305 Greensboro Ave.
HABS AL-205
HABS ALA,63-TUSLO,5-
6ph/2pg L

Jemison,Sen. Robert,House; see Jemison-Van de Graaf-Burchfield House

Martin-Comegys-Cluck House; see Gluck House

Martin-Marlowe House; see Martin-Randolph-Marlowe House

Martin-Randolph-Marlowe House (Martin-Marlowe House)
816 Twenty-second Ave.
HABS AL-223
HABS ALA,63-TUSLO,10-
10ph/1pg L

Masonic Club House; see Prince,Thomas,House

Moody House; see Scott-Moody House

Ormond-Litte House (Guild,Dr. Lafayette,House)
325 Queen City Ave.
HABS AL-202
HABS ALA,63-TUSLO,2-
5dr/11ph/2pg/fr L

Peck,Samuel M.,House (Snow-Peck House)
Eighteenth St. & Thirtieth Ave.
HABS AL-222
HABS ALA,63-TUSLO,9-
11ph/2pg L

Presbyterian School; see Snow,E. N. C.,House

Price-Eddins-Rosenau House; see Eddins House

Prince,Thomas,House (Students' Masonic Building; Masonic Club House)
University Blvd.
HABS AL-248
HABS ALA,63-TUSLO,18-
9ph/2pg L

Scott-Moody House (Janus Place; Moody House; Scott,David,House)
1925 Eighth St.
HABS AL-227
HABS ALA,63-TUSLO,14-
9ph/1pg L

Scott,David,House; see Scott-Moody House

Smith Hall (Alabama Museum of Natural History; Geological Survey of Alabama; Univ. of Alabama-Birmingham Industrial District)
Capstone Dr. at Sixth Ave.
HABS AL-952
H

Snow-Peck House; see Peck,Samuel M.,House

Snow,E. N. C.,House (Wesleyan Female Academy; Presbyterian School)
2414 Eighth St.
HABS AL-206
HABS ALA,63-TUSLO,6-
13ph/2pg L

Spence House; see Dearing-Swaim House

Stillman Institute; see Cochrane,Judge William C.,House

Students' Masonic Building; see Prince,Thomas,House

Tavern,Old; see Duffies Tavern

Tuscaloosa,Downtown (Streetscapes) (Birmingham Industrial District)
2300 Block University Blvd.
HABS AL-943
H

Univ. of Alabama-Birmingham Industrial District; see Smith Hall

University Club; see Dearing-Bagby House

University of Alabama,Gorgas House (Gorgas House)
Ninth Ave. & Capstone Dr.
HABS AL-203
HABS ALA,63-TUSLO,3A-
4dr/9ph/3pg/fr L

University of Alabama,Guard Tower (Birmingham Industrial District)
Capstone Dr.
HABS AL-942
H

University of Alabama,Observatory
Stadium Dr. & Fifth St.
HABS AL-231
HABS ALA,63-TUSLO,3C-
3ph/2pg L

University of Alabama,President's House
University Blvd.
HABS AL-207
HABS ALA,63-TUSLO,3B-
16dr/47ph/2pg L

University Park Fishing Pier; see Warrior River Lock No. 3 Wall

Warrior River Lock No. 13 Wall; see Warrior River Lock No. 3 Wall

Warrior River Lock No. 3 Wall (Warrior River Lock No. 13 Wall; University Park Fishing Pier; Birmingham Industrial District)
River Rd. at University Park
HAER AL-43
H

Wesleyan Female Academy; see Snow,E. N. C.,House

TUSCALOOSA VIC.

Birmingham Industrial District; see Tuscaloosa Bridge

Tuscaloosa Bridge (Birmingham Industrial District)
HAER AL-23
HAER ALA,2-TENSA,2-
H

WALKER COUNTY

CORDOVA

Alabama State Docks (Cordova Docks; Birmingham Industrial District)
Warrior River
HABS AL-946
H

Birmingham Industrial District; see Alabama State Docks

Birmingham Industrial District; see Main Street (Streetscapes)

Cordova Docks; see Alabama State Docks

Main Street (Streetscapes) (Birmingham Industrial District)
HABS AL-944
H

CORDOVA VIC.

Birmingham Industrial District; see Sardis Baptist Church

Sardis Baptist Church (Birmingham Industrial District)
Sanders' Ferry,Wilson's Crossing,Warrior River
HABS AL-945
H

DORA

Birmingham Industrial District; see Dora Jail (Ruins)

Birmingham Industrial District; see Dora,Town of

Birmingham Industrial District; see Frisco Tunnel

Birmingham Industrial District; see Old Methodist Church

Dora Jail (Ruins) (Birmingham Industrial District)
HABS AL-896
HABS ALA,2-TENSA,2-
H

Dora,Town of (Birmingham Industrial District)
County Rd. 81
HABS AL-947
H

Frisco Tunnel (Birmingham Industrial District)
Walker Co. Rd. 81
HAER AL-24
HAER ALA,2-TENSA,2-
H

Old Methodist Church (Birmingham Industrial District)
Walker Co. Rd. 81
HABS AL-895
HABS ALA,2-TENSA,2-
H

JASPER

Birmingham Industrial District; see Temple Emanu El

Temple Emanu El (Birmingham Industrial District)
1501 Fifth Ave. N.
HABS AL-948
H

OAKMAN

Birmingham Industrial District; see Corry House

Birmingham Industrial District; see Stevenson House

Corry House (Old York; Museum of Southern Folklife; Birmingham Industrial District)
St. Hwy. 69
HABS AL-949
H

Museum of Southern Folklife; see Corry House

Old York; see Corry House

Stevenson House (Birmingham Industrial District)
U.S. Hwy. 69
HABS AL-950
H

TOWNLEY

Birmingham Industrial District; see Cedrum Mine

Cedrum Mine (Drummond Coal Co. Mine; Birmingham Industrial District)
County Rd. 124,S. of U.S. Hwy. 78
HAER AL-44
H

Drummond Coal Co. Mine; see Cedrum Mine

TOWNLEY VIC.

Birmingham Industrial District; see Boshell's Mill

Birmingham Industrial District; see Boshell's Mill,Grist Mill

Birmingham Industrial District; see Boshell's Mill,Saw Mill

Birmingham Industrial District; see Boshell's Mill,Water Turbine

Boshell's Mill (Birmingham Industrial District)
Lost Creek at Alabama Rte. 124,1.7 mi. S of Rt. 78
HAER AL-18
H

Boshell's Mill,Grist Mill (Birmingham Industrial District)
Bank of Lost Creek at St. Rt. 124,S. of U.S. 78
HAER AL-18-C
H

Boshell's Mill,Saw Mill (Birmingham Industrial District)
Bank of Lost Creek at St. Rt. 124, S. of U.S. 78
HAER AL-18-B
H

Boshell's Mill,Water Turbine (Birmingham Industrial District)
Across Lost Creek at St. Rt. 124,S. od U.S. 78
HAER AL-18-A
H

WASHINGTON COUNTY

MCINTOSH

Andrews Chapel
U. S. Hwy. 43 (State Hwy. 13)
HABS AL-866
HABS ALA,65-MCIN,1-
1dr L

ST. STEPHENS

Masonic Lodge; see Washington County Courthouse,Old

Masonic Temple; see Washington County Courthouse,Old

Washington County Courthouse,Old (Masonic Lodge; Masonic Temple)
County Rd. 34
HABS AL-111
HABS ALA,65-SAST,1-
3ph/2pg/fr L

WILCOX COUNTY

ALLENTON

Fitzgerald House; see Tavern,Old

Grace-Chestnut House; see Grace,Joshua B.,House & Outbuildings

Grace,Joshua B.,House & Outbuildings (Grace-Chestnut House)
County Rd. 24
HABS AL-190
HABS ALA,66-ALTO,1-
6ph/1pg L

Tavern,Old (Fitzgerald House)
County Rd. 24
HABS AL-191
HABS ALA,66-ALTO,2-
8ph/1pg L

CAMDEN

Bagby House (Bagby-Liddell House)
Broad St.
HABS AL-133
HABS ALA,66-CAM,4-
13ph L

Bagby-Liddell House; see Bagby House

Baptist Church
Broad St. (State Rd. 28)
HABS AL-169
HABS ALA,66-CAM,9-
6ph L

Beck,Franklin King,House
312 Clifton St.
HABS AL-132
HABS ALA,66-CAM,3-
11ph L

Black Store Number 2; see Broad Street (Store)

Black,Doctor,Store Number 1; see Bloch,Dr. Morris,Store Number 1

Bloch House; see Block House

Bloch,Dr. Morris,Store Number 1 (Water Street (Store); Black,Doctor,Store Number 1)
HABS AL-175-A
HABS ALA,66-CAM,17-
3ph L

Block House (Bloch House; 101 Hill Street (House))
HABS AL-171
HABS ALA,66-CAM,11-
6ph L

Broad Street (Store) (Black Store Number 2; McMillan Store)
HABS AL-175-C
HABS ALA,66-CAM,19-
3ph L

Broad Street (Store) (Sperlin,R. L.,Store)
HABS AL-175-B
HABS ALA,66-CAM,18-
3ph L

Camden High School; see Female Academy,Old

Coster House (Kester,Henry,House)
Broad & Hill Sts.
HABS AL-184
HABS ALA,66-CAM,23-
2ph L

Dale Lodge Number 25; see Masonic Temple

Dunn-Bonner House; see Dunn,Thomas,House

Dunn,Thomas,House (Dunn-Bonner House)
Broad St.
HABS AL-176
HABS ALA,66-CAM,20-
2ph/1pg L

Episcopal Church; see St. Mary's Episcopal Church

Fail-McIntosh House; see McIntosh House

Female Academy,Old (Wilcox Female Institute; Camden High School)
Broad St. (State Rt. 28)
HABS AL-170
HABS ALA,66-CAM,10-
8ph L

Handley-Felts House; see Hanley House

Hanley House (Handley-Felts House)
209 Caldwell St.
HABS AL-128
HABS ALA,66-CAM,1-
5ph/1pg L

Harris House; see McDowell House

101 Hill Street (House); see Block House

Jones Law Office; see Law Office

Jones-Liddell House; see Jones,Eustis,House

Jones-McIntosh House; see Jones,Gen. R. C.,House

Jones,Eustis,House (Jones-Liddell House)
Broad St.
HABS AL-178
HABS ALA,66-CAM,25-
2ph L

Jones,Gen. R. C.,House (Jones-McIntosh House)
Broad St.
HABS AL-180
HABS ALA,66-CAM,23-
11ph/1pg L

Kester,Henry,House; see Coster House

Kilpatrick,Col. John Young,House & Outbuildings
Bridgeport Rd. (County Rd. 37)
HABS AL-168
HABS ALA,66-CAM.V,3-
7ph L

Documentation: **ct** color transparencies **dr** measured drawings **fr** field records
pc photograph captions **pg** pages of text **ph** photographs

Law Office (Jones Law Office)
Court & Water Sts.
HABS AL-173-C
HABS ALA,66-CAM,15-
3ph L

Law Office (Miller,Gov. Benjamin M.,Law Office)
Planters & Water Sts.
HABS AL-173-A
HABS ALA,66-CAM,13-
4ph L

Law Office (Moore,Dr. W. W.,Office)
Court St.
HABS AL-173-B
HABS ALA,66-CAM,14-
3ph L

Law Office; see Newspaper Plant,Old

Liberty Hall; see McDowell House

Masonic Lodge Number 25; see Masonic Temple

Masonic Temple (Masonic Lodge Number 25; Dale Lodge Number 25)
Broad St. (State Rd. 28)
HABS AL-131
HABS ALA,66-CAM,2-
13ph L

Matheson-Moore-McLeod House; see Moore,S. D.,House

McDowell House (Liberty Hall; Harris House)
State Rd. 221
HABS AL-164
HABS ALA,66-CAM.V,8-
10ph L

McIntosh House (Fail-McIntosh House)
Fail St.
HABS AL-151
HABS ALA,66-CAM,8-
12ph/1pg L

McMillan House (McMillan-Moore-Gibbs House)
Broad St. (State Rd. 28)
HABS AL-182
HABS ALA,66-CAM,22-
2ph/1pg L

McMillan Store; see Broad Street (Store)

McMillan-Moore-Gibbs House; see McMillan House

McWilliams House (Sterrett-McWilliams House)
400 Clifton St.
HABS AL-134
HABS ALA,66-CAM,5-
19ph L

Miller,Gov. Benjamin M.,Law Office; see Law Office

Moore,Dr. W. W.,Office; see Law Office

Moore,S. D.,House (Matheson-Moore-McLeod House)
310 Broad St.
HABS AL-127
HABS ALA,66-CAM,24-
2ph/2pg L

Newson House (Newson-Sharp House)
State Rd. 10
HABS AL-113
HABS ALA,66-CAM.V,1-
2ph/1pg L

Newson-Sharp House; see Newson House

Newspaper Plant,Old (Law Office)
Planters St.
HABS AL-174
HABS ALA,66-CAM,16-
3ph L

Presbyterian Church
Broad St. (State Rd. 28)
HABS AL-185
HABS ALA,66-CAM,26-
3ph/2pg L

Sperlin,R. L.,Store; see Broad Street (Store)

St. Mary's Episcopal Church (Episcopal Church)
302 Clifton St.
HABS AL-135
HABS ALA,66-CAM,6-
4ph L

Sterrett-McWilliams House; see McWilliams House

Water Street (Store); see Bloch,Dr. Morris,Store Number 1

Wilcox County Courthouse
Broad,Claiborne,Court & Water Sts.
HABS AL-172
HABS ALA,66-CAM,12-
17ph L

Wilcox Female Institute; see Female Academy,Old

Wilcox Hotel
Broad St. (State Rt. 28)
HABS AL-136
HABS ALA,66-CAM,7-
14ph L

CAMDEN VIC.

Burford House
County Rd. 33 Vic.
HABS AL-129
HABS ALA,66-CAM.V,5-
19ph L

Capell House
(See WILCOX CO.,CAPELL for documentation)
HABS AL-166
HABS ALA,66-CAP,1-
8ph L

Clifton Ferry Landing & Store (Cook Store)
Clifton Ferry Access Rd.
HABS AL-167-A
HABS ALA,66-CAM.V,12-
5ph L

Clifton House
Clifton Ferry Access Rd.
HABS AL-167
HABS ALA,66-CAM.V,10-
2ph L

Cook Store; see Clifton Ferry Landing & Store

Countryside; see Tait,Robert,Plantation

Dawson,Col. E. N.,House
County Rd. 31
HABS AL-126
HABS ALA,66-CAM.V,2-
2ph/1pg L

Dry Forks Plantation (Tait,James Charles,House)
County Rd. 12
HABS AL-137
HABS ALA,66-CAM.V,6-
19ph L

Ervin House; see Tait,Robert,Plantation

Miller-Smith House (Miller,Dr. George,House)
St. Rt. 28
HABS AL-179
HABS ALA,66-CAM.V,4-
2ph/1pg L

Miller,Dr. George,House; see Miller-Smith House

Star,P. E.,House; see Tait,Felix,Plantation

Tait-Ervin House; see Tait,Robert,Plantation

Tait-Starr House; see Tait,Felix,Plantation

Tait,Felix,Plantation (Tait-Starr House; White Columns; Star,P. E.,House)
County Rd. 23
HABS AL-138
HABS ALA,66-CAM.V,7-
13ph L

Tait,James Charles,House; see Dry Forks Plantation

Tait,Robert,Plantation (Tait-Ervin House; Ervin House; Countryside)
County Rd. 33
HABS AL-139
HABS ALA,66-CAM.V,8-
11ph L

White Columns; see Tait,Felix,Plantation

CANTON BEND

Bethea-Strother House (Bethea,Ervett,House)
State Rd. 28
HABS AL-186
HABS ALA,66-CANB,1-
12ph/1pg L

Bethea,Ervett,House; see Bethea-Strother House

Henderson,William,Store (Strother Store)
State Rd. 28
HABS AL-194
HABS ALA,66-CANB,2-
4ph/1pg L

Miller-Smith House (Miller,Dr. George,House)
(See WILCOX CO.,CAMDEN VIC. for documentation)
HABS AL-179
HABS ALA,66-CAM.V,4-
2ph/1pg L

Miller,Dr. George,House; see Miller-Smith House

Strother Store; see Henderson,William,Store

CANTON BEND VIC.

Matthews-Tait House; see Tait,Frank,House

Matthews,William T.,House; see Tait,Frank,House

Tait,Frank,House (Matthews-Tait House; Youpon; Matthews,William T.,House)
County Rd. 19
HABS AL-130
HABS ALA,66-CANB.V,1-
16ph L

Youpon; see Tait,Frank,House

CAPELL

Capell House
St. Rt. 41
HABS AL-166
HABS ALA,66-CAP,1-
8ph L

CLIFTON FERRY

Clifton Ferry Landing & Store (Cook Store)
(See WILCOX CO.,CAMDEN VIC. for documentation)
HABS AL-167-A
HABS ALA,66-CAM.V,12-
5ph L

Clifton House
(See WILCOX CO.,CAMDEN VIC. for documentation)
HABS AL-167
HABS ALA,66-CAM.V,10-
2ph L

Cook Store; see Clifton Ferry Landing & Store

COY VIC.

Dry Forks Plantation (Tait,James Charles,House)
(See WILCOX CO.,CAMDEN VIC. for documentation)
HABS AL-137
HABS ALA,66-CAM.V,6-
19ph L

Tait,James Charles,House; see Dry Forks Plantation

MILLERS FERRY

Henderson House & Smokehouse; see Sellers-Henderson House & Smokehouse

Sellers House & Smokehouse; see Sellers-Henderson House & Smokehouse

Sellers-Henderson House & Smokehouse (Henderson House & Smokehouse; Sellers House & Smokehouse)
State Rt. 28
HABS AL-147
HABS ALA,66-MILF,1-
4ph/1pg L

MILLERS FERRY VIC.

Matthews House & Plantation Store; see Rosemary,House & Plantation Store

Matthews-Cade House & Plantation Store; see Rosemary,House & Plantation Store

Rosemary,House & Plantation Store (Matthews House & Plantation Store; Matthews-Cade House & Plantation Store)
State Rt. 28 Vic.
HABS AL-150
HABS ALA,66-MILF.V,1-
11ph/1pg L

OAK HILL

Fox-Harris-Jones House (Fox,Dr. Daniel J.,House)
State Rd. 21
HABS AL-148
HABS ALA,66-OAK,2-
9ph/1pg L

Fox,Dr. Daniel J.,House; see Fox-Harris-Jones House

Ramsey House; see Ramsey-Jones-Bonner House

Ramsey-Jones-Bonner House (Ramsey House)
State Rt. 10
HABS AL-108
HABS ALA,66-OAK,1-
8ph/1pg L

PINE APPLE

Hawthorne,Col. Joseph R.,House
Broad St. (County Rd. 59)
HABS AL-119
HABS ALA,66-PINA,1-
18ph/1pg L

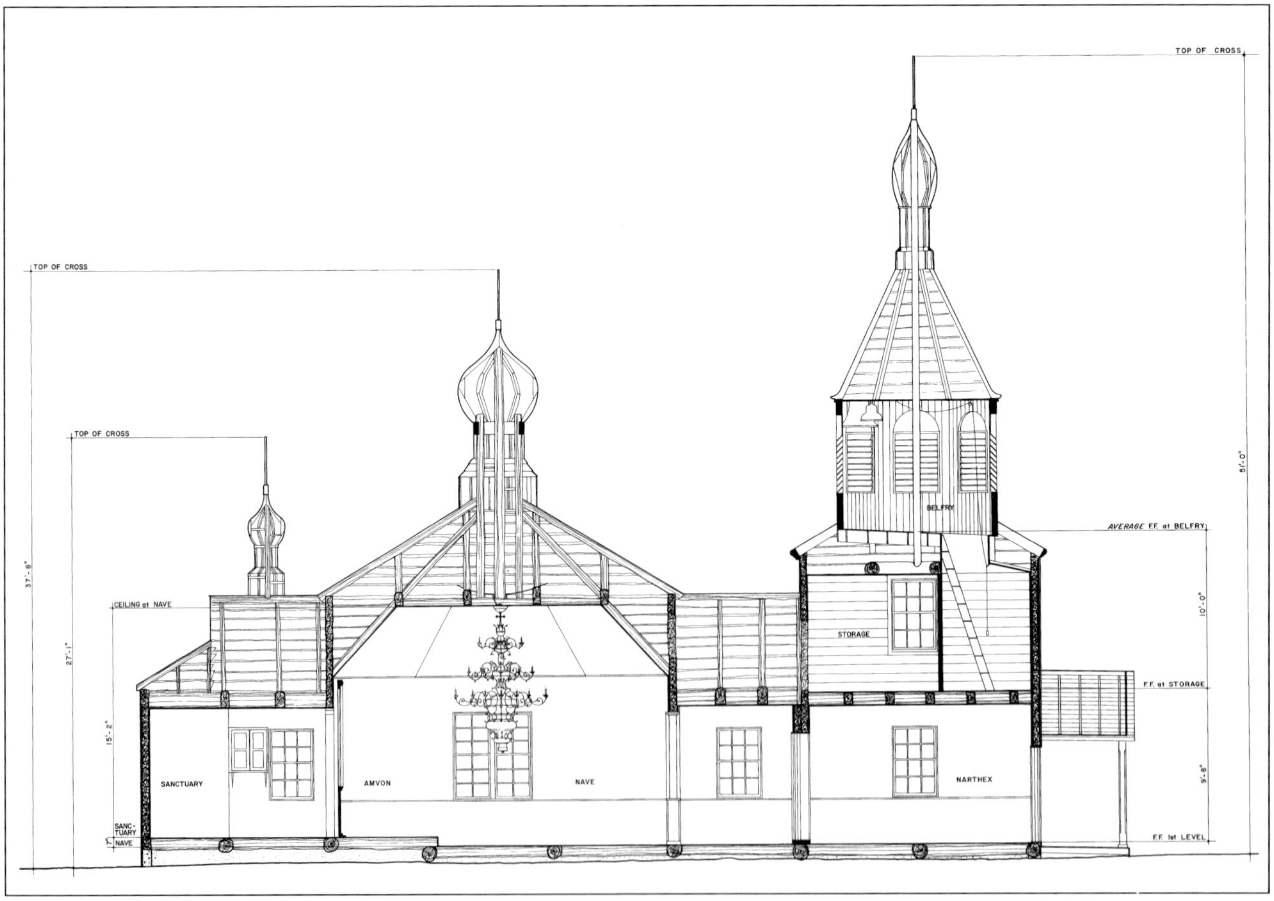

Totem Bight Community House (Mud Bight Village), Ketchikan vicinity, Gateway Borough, Alaska. West side and front. Photograph taken August 1970 (HABS AK,10-KECH.V,1-1).

Holy Assumption Russian Orthodox Church, Kenai, Kenai Peninsula, Alaska. Section A-A. Measured drawing delineated by K. Martin, 1986 (HABS AK 39-A, sheet 4 of 5).

Alaska

ALEUTIAN ISLANDS COUNTY

AKUTAN

Village of Akutan
HABS AK-96
H

COLD BAY

Fort Randall (Navy Town)
HABS AK-46
HABS AK,1-COLBA,1-
1pg L

Fort Randall,Latrine & Bath (Navy Town,Latrine & Bath)
NE of intersection of California Blvd. & Nurse Dr.
HABS AK-46-B
HABS AK,1-COLBA,1-B-
1ph/2pg/1pc L

Fort Randall,Neuro-Psychiatric Ward (Navy Town,Neuro-Psychiatric Ward)
NE of intersection of California Blvd & Nurse Dr.
HABS AK-46-A
HABS AK,1-COLBA,1-A-
8ph/2pg/1pc L

Fort Randall,Theater (Navy Town,Theater)
N of Jackson Lake on California Blvd.
HABS AK-46-C
HABS AK,1-COLBA,1-C-
1ph/2pg/1pc L

Navy Town; see Fort Randall

Navy Town,Latrine & Bath; see Fort Randall,Latrine & Bath

Navy Town,Neuro-Psychiatric Ward; see Fort Randall,Neuro-Psychiatric Ward

Navy Town,Theater; see Fort Randall,Theater

NIKOLSKI

Village of Nikolski
HABS AK-95
H

PRIBILOF ISLANDS

Sealing Plant
St. George Island
HAER AK-25
HAER 1992(HAER):AK-1
7ph/1pc L

ST. GEORGE

Russian-American Architecture Project; see St. George Russ. Orth. Church,Priest's House

Russian-American Architecture Project; see St. George Russian Orthodox Church

St. George Russ. Orth. Church,Priest's House (Russian-American Architecture Project)
St. George Island,Pribilof Islands
HABS AK-50-A
HABS DLC/PP-1993:AK-3
2ph/1pc L

St. George Russian Orthodox Church (Russian-American Architecture Project)
Pribilof Islands
HABS AK-50
HABS DLC/PP-1993:AK-3
10ph/7pg/1pc/6ct L

St. George,Village of
HABS AK-63
4ph/1pc H

ST. PAUL

Russian-American Architecture Project; see Ss. Peter & Paul Russian Orthodox Church

Ss. Peter & Paul Russian Orthodox Church (Russian-American Architecture Project)
St. Paul Island,Pribilof Islands
HABS AK-51
HABS DLC/PP-1993:AK-3
17ph/11pg/1pc/3ct L

St. Paul,City of
Pribilof Islands
HABS AK-62
9ph/1pc H

UNALASKA

Church of the Holy Ascension; see Holy Ascension Russian Orthodox Church

Holy Ascension Orthodox Church; see Holy Ascension Russian Orthodox Church

Holy Ascension Russian Orth Church & Bishop's Hse (Russian-American Architecture Project)
Unalaska Island
HABS AK-37
HABS AK,1-UNAK,1-;1993:AK-3
1ph/2pg/1pc L

Holy Ascension Russian Orth Church,Bishop's House (Russian-American Architecture Project)
Unalaska Island
HABS AK-37-B
HABS AK,1-UNAK,1-B-;1993:AK-3
3ph/2pg/2pc L

Holy Ascension Russian Orthodox Church (Holy Ascension Orthodox Church; Church of the Holy Ascension; Russian-American Architecture Project)
Unalaska Island
HABS AK-37-A
HABS AK,1-UNAK,1-A-;1993:AK-3
26ph/11pg/3pc L

Russian-American Architecture Project; see Holy Ascension Russian Orth Church & Bishop's Hse

Russian-American Architecture Project; see Holy Ascension Russian Orth Church,Bishop's House

Russian-American Architecture Project; see Holy Ascension Russian Orthodox Church

UNALASKA ISLAND

Administration Building; see Naval Operating Base Dutch Harbor & Fort Mears

Anti-Aircraft Training Center & Shop; see Naval Operating Base Dutch Harbor & Fort Mears

Bachelor Officers Quarters (Building No. 534); see Naval Operating Base Dutch Harbor & Fort Mears

Beer Hall (Building No. 502); see Naval Operating Base Dutch Harbor & Fort Mears

C. P. O. Quarters No. 1; see Naval Operating Base Dutch Harbor & Fort Mears

Civilian Contractor s Barracks; see Naval Operating Base Dutch Harbor & Fort Mears

Headquarters Area Recreation Hall & Theater; see Naval Operating Base Dutch Harbor & Fort Mears

Hill 400 Fixed Defense Battery Command Post; see Naval Operating Base Dutch Harbor & Fort Mears

Humpy Cove Magazine; see Naval Operating Base Dutch Harbor & Fort Mears

Humpy Cove Quonset Huts; see Naval Operating Base Dutch Harbor & Fort Mears

Iliuliuk Sub. Base Marine Railway Ship Repair Shed; see Naval Operating Base Dutch Harbor & Fort Mears

Joint Command Post; see Naval Operating Base Dutch Harbor & Fort Mears

Margaret Bay Cantonment Barracks; see Naval Operating Base Dutch Harbor & Fort Mears

Margaret Bay Cantonment Mess Hall; see Naval Operating Base Dutch Harbor & Fort Mears

Margaret Bay Cantonment Post Office (Bldg No. 759); see Naval Operating Base Dutch Harbor & Fort Mears

Margaret Bay Cantonment Theater; see Naval Operating Base Dutch Harbor & Fort Mears

Marine Barracks (Building No. 530); see Naval Operating Base Dutch Harbor & Fort Mears

Morris Cove Quonset Huts; see Naval Operating Base Dutch Harbor & Fort Mears

Mount Ballyhoo Garrison Barracks; see Naval Operating Base Dutch Harbor & Fort Mears

Naval Operating Base Dutch Harbor & Fort Mears
HABS AK-34
HABS 1989(HABS):1
7dr/5ph/45pg/1pc/1ct/fr L

Naval Operating Base Dutch Harbor & Fort Mears
HABS AK-34-A
HABS 1989(HABS):1
4dr/5ph/1pg/1pc/fr L

Naval Operating Base Dutch Harbor & Fort Mears
HABS AK-34-B
HABS 1989(HABS):1
3dr/3ph/1pg/1pc/fr L

Naval Operating Base Dutch Harbor & Fort Mears (Administration Building)
HABS AK-34-F
HABS 1989(HABS):1
4dr/14ph/1pg/1pc/3ct/fr L

Naval Operating Base Dutch Harbor & Fort Mears (Anti-Aircraft Training Center & Shop)
HABS AK-34-BB
HABS 1989(HABS):1
5ph/1pg/1pc/fr L

Naval Operating Base Dutch Harbor & Fort Mears (Bachelor Officers Quarters (Building No. 534))
HABS AK-34-I
HABS 1989(HABS):1
4dr/5ph/1pg/1pc/fr L

Naval Operating Base Dutch Harbor & Fort Mears (Beer Hall (Building No. 502))
HABS AK-34-G
HABS 1989(HABS):1
1dr/5ph/1pg/1pc/fr L

Naval Operating Base Dutch Harbor & Fort Mears (Civilian Contractor s Barracks)
HABS AK-34-M
HABS 1989(HABS):1
2dr/3ph/1pg/1pc/fr L

Naval Operating Base Dutch Harbor & Fort Mears (Headquarters Area Recreation Hall & Theater)
HABS AK-34-Z
HABS 1989(HABS):1
6ph/1pg/1pc/fr L

Naval Operating Base Dutch Harbor & Fort Mears (Hill 400 Fixed Defense Battery Command Post)
HABS AK-34-W
HABS 1989(HABS):1
1dr/2ph/1pg/1pc/3ct/fr L

Naval Operating Base Dutch Harbor & Fort Mears (Humpy Cove Magazine)
HABS AK-34-LL
HABS 1989(HABS):1
2ph/1pg/1pc L

Naval Operating Base Dutch Harbor & Fort Mears (Humpy Cove Quonset Huts)
HABS AK-34-KK
HABS 1989(HABS):1
1ph/1pg/1pc L

Naval Operating Base Dutch Harbor & Fort Mears (Iliuliuk Sub. Base Marine Railway Ship Repair Shed
HABS AK-34-FF
HABS 1989(HABS):1
6ph/1pg/1pc L

Naval Operating Base Dutch Harbor & Fort Mears (Joint Command Post)
HABS AK-34-E
HABS 1989(HABS):1
3dr/5ph/1pg/1pc/fr L

Naval Operating Base Dutch Harbor & Fort Mears (Margaret Bay Cantonment Barracks)
HABS AK-34-P
HABS 1989(HABS):1
2dr/8ph/1pg/1pc/fr L

Naval Operating Base Dutch Harbor & Fort Mears (Margaret Bay Cantonment Mess Hall)
HABS AK-34-AA
HABS 1989(HABS):1
1ph/1pg/1pc L

Naval Operating Base Dutch Harbor & Fort Mears (Margaret Bay Cantonment Post Office (Bldg No. 759)
HABS AK-34-R
HABS 1989(HABS):1
1dr/4ph/1pg/1pc/fr L

Naval Operating Base Dutch Harbor & Fort Mears (Margaret Bay Cantonment Theater)
HABS AK-34-Q
HABS 1989(HABS):1
2dr/2ph/1pg/1pc/fr L

Naval Operating Base Dutch Harbor & Fort Mears (Marine Barracks (Building No. 530))
HABS AK-34-K
HABS 1989(HABS):1
4dr/8ph/1pg/1pc/fr L

Naval Operating Base Dutch Harbor & Fort Mears (Morris Cove Quonset Huts)
HABS AK-34-JJ
HABS 1989(HABS):1
2ph/1pg/1pc/1ct L

Naval Operating Base Dutch Harbor & Fort Mears (Mount Ballyhoo Garrison Barracks)
HABS AK-34-T
HABS 1989(HABS):1
2dr/5ph/1pg/1pc/3ct/fr L

Naval Operating Base Dutch Harbor & Fort Mears (Naval Radio Station Apartment Building; C. P. O. Quarters No. 1)
HABS AK-34-N
HABS 1989(HABS):1
3dr/6ph/1pg/1pc/1ct/fr L

Naval Operating Base Dutch Harbor & Fort Mears (Naval Radio Station Powerhouse (Building No. 615); Radio Transmitter Building)
HABS AK-34-O
HABS 1989(HABS):1
1dr/3ph/1pg/1pc/1ct/fr L

Naval Operating Base Dutch Harbor & Fort Mears (Pacific Hut)
HABS AK-34-J
HABS 1989(HABS):1
1dr/5ph/1pg/1pc/2ct/fr L

Naval Operating Base Dutch Harbor & Fort Mears (Pillbox)
HABS AK-34-S
HABS 1989(HABS):1
1dr/1pg/fr L

Naval Operating Base Dutch Harbor & Fort Mears (Powerhouse (Building No. 409))
HABS AK-34-H
HABS 1989(HABS):1
5dr/5ph/1pg/1pc/fr L

Naval Operating Base Dutch Harbor & Fort Mears (Pyramid Valley Hospital Area)
HABS AK-34-Y
HABS 1989(HABS):1
1dr/14ph/1pg/1pc/1ct/fr L

Naval Operating Base Dutch Harbor & Fort Mears (Seaplane Ramp)
HABS AK-34-MM
HABS 1989(HABS):1
3ph/1pc L

Naval Operating Base Dutch Harbor & Fort Mears (Stockade)
HABS AK-34-X
HABS 1989(HABS):1
1dr/4ph/1pg/1pc/1ct/fr L

Naval Operating Base Dutch Harbor & Fort Mears (Torpedo Assembly Complex)
HABS AK-34-D
HABS 1989(HABS):1
3dr/7ph/1pg/1pc L

Naval Operating Base Dutch Harbor & Fort Mears (Torpedo Bombsight & Utility Shop)
HABS AK-34-C
HABS 1989(HABS):1
4dr/6ph/1pg/1pc/fr L

Naval Operating Base Dutch Harbor & Fort Mears (Ulakta Head Fixed Defense Battery Command Post No1
HABS AK-34-V
HABS 1989(HABS):1
1dr/3ph/1pg/1pc/1ct/fr L

Naval Operating Base Dutch Harbor & Fort Mears (Ulakta Head Fixed Defense Battery Command Post No2
HABS AK-34-CC
HABS 1989(HABS):1
2ph/1pg/1pc L

Naval Operating Base Dutch Harbor & Fort Mears (Ulakta Head Fixed Defense Installation Magazine)
HABS AK-34-DD
HABS 1989(HABS):1
3ph/1pg/1pc L

Naval Operating Base Dutch Harbor & Fort Mears (Ulakta Head Fixed Defense Installation Magazine)
HABS AK-34-U
HABS 1989(HABS):1
1dr/3ph/1pg/1pc L

Naval Operating Base Dutch Harbor & Fort Mears (Ulakta Head Fixed Defense Panama Gun Mounts)
HABS AK-34-EE
HABS 1989(HABS):1
3ph/1pg/1pc L

Naval Operating Base Dutch Harbor & Fort Mears (Unalaska Valley Cantonment Cabana Colony)
HABS AK-34-II
HABS 1989(HABS):1
5ph/1pg/1pc/5ct L

Naval Operating Base Dutch Harbor & Fort Mears (Warehouse (Building No. 518))
HABS AK-34-L
HABS 1989(HABS):1
2dr/8ph/1pg/1pc/fr L

Naval Radio Station Apartment Building; see Naval Operating Base Dutch Harbor & Fort Mears

Naval Radio Station Powerhouse (Building No. 615); see Naval Operating Base Dutch Harbor & Fort Mears

Pacific Hut; see Naval Operating Base Dutch Harbor & Fort Mears

Pillbox; see Naval Operating Base Dutch Harbor & Fort Mears

Powerhouse (Building No. 409); see Naval Operating Base Dutch Harbor & Fort Mears

Pyramid Valley Hospital Area; see Naval Operating Base Dutch Harbor & Fort Mears

Radio Transmitter Building; see Naval Operating Base Dutch Harbor & Fort Mears

Seaplane Ramp; see Naval Operating Base Dutch Harbor & Fort Mears

Stockade; see Naval Operating Base Dutch Harbor & Fort Mears

Torpedo Assembly Complex; see Naval Operating Base Dutch Harbor & Fort Mears

Torpedo Bombsight & Utility Shop; see Naval Operating Base Dutch Harbor & Fort Mears

Ulakta Head Fixed Defense Battery Command Post No1; see Naval Operating Base Dutch Harbor & Fort Mears

Ulakta Head Fixed Defense Battery Command Post No2; see Naval Operating Base Dutch Harbor & Fort Mears

Ulakta Head Fixed Defense Installation Magazine; see Naval Operating Base Dutch Harbor & Fort Mears

Ulakta Head Fixed Defense Panama Gun Mounts; see Naval Operating Base Dutch Harbor & Fort Mears

Unalaska Valley Cantonment Cabana Colony; see Naval Operating Base Dutch Harbor & Fort Mears

Warehouse (Building No. 518); see Naval Operating Base Dutch Harbor & Fort Mears

ANCHORAGE COUNTY

ANCHORAGE

Alaska Center for the Performing Arts
621 W. Sixth Ave.
HABS AK-169
1ph/1pc L

Alaska Methodist University,Campus Center (Alaska Pacific University,Atwood Center)
University Dr.
HABS AK-168-A
2ph/1pc L

Alaska Pacific University,Atwood Center; see Alaska Methodist University,Campus Center

Alaska Railroad Depot
411 First Ave.
HABS AK-171
1ph/1pc L

Anchorage Museum of History & Art
121 W. Seventh Ave.
HABS AK-170
1ph/1pc L

Anchorage Police Department Building
4501 S. Bragaw
HABS AK-177
1ph/1pc L

Anchorage,City of
HABS AK-179
2ph/1pc L

Anderson,Oscar,House
420 M St.
HABS AK-173
5ph/1pc L

Animal Control Center
4711 S. Bragaw
HABS AK-160
2ph/1pc L

BP Exploration Building
Seward Hwy. & Benson Blvd.
HABS AK-178
1ph/1pc L

CIRI Building
2525 C St.
HABS AK-174
1ph/1pc L

Club 25; see Wendler Building

David,Leopold,House
605 W. Second Ave.
HABS AK-167
1ph/1pc L

Fifth Avenue Mall
Fifth Ave. & C St.
HABS AK-161
2ph/1pc L

Fourth Avenue Theatre (Lathrop Building; Lathrop's Showhouse)
630 West Fourth Ave.
HABS AK-28
HABS AK,2-ANCH,1-
7ph/1pg/2pc/1ct L

Garden of Eatin'
2502 McKae Rd.
HABS AK-163
1ph/1pc L

KENI Radio Building
1777 Forest Park Dr.
HABS AK-176
2ph/1pc L

Kimball Building
500-504 W. Fifth Ave.
HABS AK-162
1ph/1pc L

Lathrop Building; see Fourth Avenue Theatre

Lathrop's Showhouse; see Fourth Avenue Theatre

Loussac,Z.J.,Public Library
3600 Denali St.
HABS AK-159
1ph/1pc L

Loxtave House
821 Brown St.
HABS AK-165
2ph/1pc L

Nike Hercules Missile Battery,Summit Site
Anchorage Alaska
HAER AK-18
2dr/26pg H

Potter Section House
Mile 115.3 Seward Hwy.
HABS AK-164
2ph/1pc L

Rabbit Creek White Alice Site
Anchorage Alaska
HAER AK-23
50pg H

Rabbit Creek White Alice Site,Radio Relay Station
HAER AK-23-A
HAER DLC/PP-1993:AK-1
12ph/1pc L

St. Mary's Episcopal Church
4502 Cassin Dr.
HABS AK-175
3ph/1pc L

U.S. Post Office & Courthouse
605 W. Fourth Ave.
HABS AK-166
1ph/1pc L

Visitor Information Center
Fourth Ave. & F St.
HABS AK-172
2ph/1pc L

Wendler Building (Club 25)
400 D St.
HABS AK-158
1ph/1pc L

EKLUTNA

St. Nicholas Russian Orthodox Churches,New Church
HABS AK-94-B
2ph/1pc H

St. Nicholas Russian Orthodox Churches,Old Church
HABS AK-94-A
7ph/5pg/1pc H

PORTAGE

Iditarod National Historic Trail; see Iditarod Trail,Portage Shelter Cabin

Iditarod Trail,Portage Shelter Cabin
(Iditarod National Historic Trail)
HABS AK-5-C
HABS AK,9-SEW,2-C-
4dr/4ph/1pc/2ct/fr L

ST. PAUL

Russian-American Architecture Project; see Ss. Peter and Paul Russ. Orth. Ch.,Priest's House

Ss. Peter and Paul Russ. Orth. Ch.,Priest's House (Russian-American Architecture Project)
St. Paul Island,Pribilof Islands
HABS AK-51-A
HABS DLC/PP-1993:AK-3
1ph/1pc L

BETHEL COUNTY

CHUATHBALUK

St. Sergius of Radonezh Russian Orthodox Church
HABS AK-90
10ph/4pg/1pc L

LIME VILLAGE

Ss. Constatine and Helen Russian Orthodox Church
HABS AK-89
8ph/3pg/1pc L

LOWER KALSKAG

St. Seraphim Russian Orthodox Churches,New Church
HABS AK-92-B
6ph/3pg/1pc L

St. Seraphim Russian Orthodox Churches,Old Church
HABS AK-92-A
8ph/3pg/1pc L

NAPASKIAK

St. Jacob Russian Orthodox Church
HABS AK-80
7ph/1pc H

St. Jacob Russian Orthodox Church,Churchyard
HABS AK-80-A
4ph/1pg/1pc H

Village of Napaskiak
HABS AK-71
H

BRISTOL BAY COUNTY

KING SALMON

Eskimo Pit House
HABS AK-98
H

KING SALMON VIC.

Fure's,Roy,Trapping Cabin
Katmai National Park and Preserve
HABS AK-18
HABS 1991(HABS):27;1993:AK-3
4dr/6ph/1pc L

KING SOLMON VIC.

Russian Orthodox Church
HABS AK-86
11ph/3pg/1pc L

NAKNEK

St. John the Baptist Russian Orthodox Church
HABS AK-85
10ph/3pg/1pc L

SOUTH NAKNEK

Elevation of the Holy Cross Russian Orthodox Churc
HABS AK-82
5ph/3pg/1pc L

DILLINGHAM COUNTY

CHIGNIK LAKE

St. Nicholas Russian Orthodox Churches,New Church
HABS AK-68-B
3ph/1pg/1pc H

St. Nicholas Russian Orthodox Churches,Old Church
HABS AK-68-A
2ph/1pg/1pc H

EKUK

St. Nicholas Russian Orthodox Church
HABS AK-88
9ph/3pg/1pc L

IGIUGIG

St. Nicholas Russian Orthodox Churches
HABS AK-81
2ph/3pg/1pc L

St. Nicholas Russian Orthodox Churches,New Church
HABS AK-81-B
1ph/1pc L

St. Nicholas Russian Orthodox Churches,Old Church
HABS AK-81-A
3ph/1pc L

NONDALTON

St. Nicholas Russian Orthodox Church
HABS AK-84
8ph/4pg/1pc L

PEDRO BAY

St. Nicholas Russian Orthodox Church
HABS AK-87
4ph/3pg/1pc L

FAIRBANKS NORTH STAR COUNTY

CHATANIKA VIC.

Davidson Ditch Waste Water Weir
Mile 63 of Alaska's Steese Hwy.
HAER AK-5
HAER AK,6-CHAT.V,1-
4ph/1pg/1pc L

ESTER

Cripple Creek,Assay Office-Superintendent's Office
HABS AK-126-D
1ph/1pc L

Cripple Creek,Bunkhouses
HABS AK-126-B
1ph/1pc L

Cripple Creek,Mess Hall
HABS AL-126-A
4ph/1pc L

Cripple Creek,Wanigan
HABS AK-126-C
1ph/1pc L

FAIRBANKS

Immaculate Conception Roman Catholic Church
115 N. Cushman St.
HABS AK-128
4ph/1pc L

Joy Elementary School
24 Margaret St.
HABS AK-131
2ph/1pc L

Lacey Street Theatre
Second Ave. & Lacey St.
HABS AK-129
2ph/1pc L

Ladd Field
Fort Wainwright
HABS AK-36
HABS 1989(HABS):1
1dr L

Ladd Field,Bachelor Officer Quarters (Ladd Field,Building No. 1045; Ladd Field,Murphy Hall)
Fort Wainwright
HABS AK-36-G
HABS 1989(HABS):1
1ph/1pc L

Ladd Field,Birchwood Hangar (Ladd Field,Building No. 2085)
Fort Wainwright
HABS AK-36-B
HABS 1989(HABS):1
2dr/5ph/1pg/1pc L

Ladd Field,Birchwood Hangar (Ladd Field,Building No. 3005)
Fort Wainwright
HABS AK-36-N
HABS 1989(HABS):1
2ph/1pc L

Ladd Field,Birchwood Hangar (Ladd Field,Building No. 3008)
Fort Wainwright
HABS AK-36-M
HABS 1989(HABS):1
1ph/1pc L

Ladd Field,Building No. 1; see Ladd Field,Commanding Officer Quarters

Ladd Field,Building No. 1021; see Ladd Field,Nurses Quarters

Ladd Field,Building No. 1034; see Ladd Field,Chapel

Ladd Field,Building No. 1045; see Ladd Field,Bachelor Officer Quarters

Ladd Field,Building No. 1049; see Ladd Field,Twelve Apartments-NCO

Ladd Field,Building No. 1542; see Ladd Field,Kodiak T-Hangar

Ladd Field,Building No. 1555; see Ladd Field,Hospital

Ladd Field,Building No. 1557; see Ladd Field,Hangar No. 1

Ladd Field,Building No. 1561; see Ladd Field,Power Plant

Ladd Field,Building No. 1562; see Ladd Field,Community Building

Ladd Field,Building No. 2085; see Ladd Field,Birchwood Hangar

Ladd Field,Building No. 3005; see Ladd Field,Birchwood Hangar

Ladd Field,Building No. 3008; see Ladd Field,Birchwood Hangar

Ladd Field,Chapel (Ladd Field,Building No. 1034)
Fort Wainwright
HABS AK-36-A
HABS 1989(HABS):1
1ph/1pc L

Ladd Field,Commanding Officer Quarters (Ladd Field,Building No. 1)
Fort Wainwright
HABS AK-36-H
HABS 1989(HABS):1
1ph/1pc L

Ladd Field,Community Building (Ladd Field,Building No. 1562; Ladd Field,Fluge Hall)
Fort Wainwright
HABS AK-36-K
HABS 1989(HABS):1
1dr/3ph/1pg/1pc L

Ladd Field,Fluge Hall; see Ladd Field,Community Building

Ladd Field,Hangar No. 1 (Ladd Field,Building No. 1557)
Fort Wainwright
HABS AK-36-E
HABS 1989(HABS):1
2dr/15ph/1pg/1pc L

Ladd Field,Hospital (Ladd Field,Building No. 1555; LaddField,Post Exchange)
Fort Wainwright
HABS AK-36-F
HABS 1989(HABS):1
3ph/1pc L

Ladd Field,Kodiak T-Hangar (Ladd Field,Building No. 1542)
Fort Wainwright
HABS AK-36-C
HABS 1989(HABS):1
4dr/9ph/1pg/1pc/fr L

Ladd Field,Murphy Hall; see Ladd Field,Bachelor Officer Quarters

Ladd Field,Nurses Quarters (Ladd Field,Building No. 1021)
Fort Wainwright
HABS AK-36-D
HABS 1989(HABS):1
1dr/2ph/1pg/1pc L

Ladd Field,Power Plant (Ladd Field,Building No. 1561)
Fort Wainwright
HABS AK-36-L
HABS 1989(HABS):1
2dr/8ph/1pg/1pc L

Ladd Field,Radio Station
Fort Wainwright
HABS AK-36-I
HABS 1989(HABS):1
5ph/1pg/1pc L

Ladd Field,Twelve Apartments-NCO (Ladd Field,Building No. 1049)
Fort Wainwright
HABS AK-36-J
HABS 1989(HABS):1
1ph/1pc L

LaddField,Post Exchange; see Ladd Field,Hospital

Launch Control Bldg.; see Nike Hercules Missile Battery,Tare Site

Launching Structure; see Nike Hercules Missile Battery,Tare Site

Log Building
Cushman St.
HABS AK-135
2ph/1pc L

Masonic Temple
809 First Ave.
HABS AK-134
2ph/1pc L

Nike Hercules Missile Battery,Tare Site
HAER AK-20
1dr H

Nike Hercules Missile Battery,Tare Site (Launch Control Bldg.)
HAER AK-20-A
2dr H

Nike Hercules Missile Battery,Tare Site (Launching Structure)
HAER AK-20-B
2dr H

St. Matthew's Episcopal Church
1022 First Ave.
HABS AK-133
1ph/1pc L

Thomas,George C.,Memorial Library
901 First Ave.
HABS AK-136
1ph/1pc L

U.S. Post Office and Courthouse
Cushman St.,between Second & Third Aves.
HABS AK-130
3ph/1pc L

U.S.O. Recreation Center
First Ave btwn Lacey & Cushman Sts.
HABS AK-49
HABS 1990 (HABS):1
3dr L

University of Alaska Museum
Yukon and Sheenjnk
HABS AK-127
6ph/1pc L

Wickersham House
Alaskaland
HABS AK-132
4ph/1pc L

FOX

Bunkhouse; see Fairbanks Exploration Co.,Goldstream Drede No. 8,

Fairbanks Exploration Co.,Goldstream Drede No. 8, (Bunkhouse)
HABS AK-137-A
3ph/1pc L

Fairbanks Exploration Co.,Goldstream Dredge No. 8
HABS AK-137
1ph/1pc L

PETERSBURG

Forest Service Office & Garage; see Petersburg Office & Garage

Petersburg Office & Garage (Forest Service Office & Garage)
107 Fram St.
HABS AK-21
HABS AK,22-PETBU,1-
4ph/13pg/1pc/fr L

HAINES COUNTY

HAINES VIC.

Dalton Trail Post (Pleasant Camp)
Mile 40,Haines Hwy.
HABS AK-4
HABS AK,7-HAIN.V,1-
34ph/6pg/2pc/fr L

Pleasant Camp; see Dalton Trail Post

JUNEAU COUNTY

JUNEAU

Alaska's Governor's Mansion
716 Calhoun Ave.
HABS AK-112
4ph/1pc L

Downtown (Commercial Buildings)
Franklin and Front Streets
HABS AK-115
5ph/1pc L

Juneau Public Library
292 Marine Way
HABS AK-113
3ph/1pc L

Juneau,City of
HABS AK-116
1ph/1pc L

Kennedy Street (Houses)
400-500 Blocks
HABS AK-114
2ph/1pc L

St. Nicholas Russian Orthodox Church
HABS AK-59
12ph/1pc/2ct H

St. Nicholas Russian Orthodox Church,Priest's Hse.
Juneau
HABS AK-59-A
1ph/1pc H

Wickersham House
213 Seventh St.
HABS AK-111
6ph/1pc L

KENAI PENINSULA COUNTY

ENGLISH BAY

New Church; see SS. Sergius & Herman Russian Orthodox Churches,

Old Church; see SS. Sergius & Herman Russian Orthodox Churches,

SS. Sergius & Herman Russian Orthodox Churches, (New Church)
HABS AK-91-B
3ph/1pc L

SS. Sergius & Herman Russian Orthodox Churches, (Old Church)
HABS AK-91-A
5ph/4pg/1pc L

Ss. Sergius and Herman Russian Orthodox Churches
HABS AK-91
2ph/1pc L

HOPE

Hope,Village of
HABS AK-8
HABS AK,9-HOPE,1-
11ph/1pc/5ct L

KENAI

Holy Assumption R.O. Church,Chapel of St. Nicholas (Russian-American Architecture Project)
Mission & Overland Sts.
HABS AK-39-B
HABS AK,9-KEN,1-B-;1993:AK-3
3dr/3ph/2pg/1pc/fr L

Holy Assumption Russian Orth Church,Rectory (Russian-American Architecture Project)
Mission & Overland Sts.
HABS AK-39-C
HABS AK,9-KEN,1-C-;1993:AK-3
2dr/1ph/1pc/fr L

Holy Assumption Russian Orthodox Church
Misson & Overland Sts.
HABS AK-39-A
HABS AK,9-KEN,1-A-;1993:AK-3
5dr/7ph/7pg/1pc/fr L

Holy Assumption Russian Orthodox Church Complex
HABS AK-39
HABS AK,9-KEN,1-
1dr/fr L

Russian-American Architecture Project; see Holy Assumption R.O. Church,Chapel of St. Nicholas

Russian-American Architecture Project; see Holy Assumption Russian Orth Church,Rectory

NINILCHIK

Holy Transfig. of Our Lord Russian Orthodox Church
HABS AK-93
13ph/5pg/1pc L

Village of Ninilchik
HABS AK-97
2ph/1pc H

SEWARD

Alaska Railroad Depot
HABS AK-45-E
HABS AK,9-SEW,1-E-
4ph/1pc L

Fourth Avenue (Commercial Buildings)
HABS AK-45-A
HABS AK,9-SEW,1-A-
2ph/1pc L

St. Peter's Episcopal Church
Second Ave. & Adams St.
HABS AK-45-C
HABS AK,9-SEW,1-C-
1ph/1pc L

Third Avenue (House)
HABS AK-45-B
HABS AK,9-SEW,1-B-
1ph/1pc L

Van Gilder Hotel
HABS AK-45-D
HABS AK,9-SEW,1-D-
1ph/1pc L

SEWARD TO NOME

Iditarod National Historic Trail; see Iditarod Trail Shelter Cabins

Iditarod Trail Shelter Cabins (Iditarod National Historic Trail)
Iditarod National Historic Trail
HABS AK-5
HABS AK,9-SEW,3-
1dr/fr L

KETCHIKAN GATEWAY COUNTY

KETCHIKAN

Dolly's House
24 Creek St.
HABS AK-119
2ph/1pc L

Front Street (Commercial Buildings)
200-300 Blocks
HABS AK-117
3ph/1pc L

Ketchikan,City of
HABS AK-120
9ph/1pc L

U. S. Coast Guard Headquarters Building
HABS AK-17
HABS AK,10-KETCH,1-
8ph/1pc L

Walker,Norman R.,House
541 Pine St.
HABS AK-118
3ph/1pc L

KETCHIKAN VIC.

Totem Bight Community House
N. Tongass Hwy.
HABS AK-3
HABS AK,10-KETCH.V,1-
1ph/1pg/1pc L

SAXMAN

Totem Park
HABS AK-121
2ph/1pc L

Totem Park,Tribal Building
HABS AK-121-A
3ph/1pc L

KOBUK

NOATAK VICINITY

Shelter Cabin No. 1 & 2
Cape Krusenstern National Monument
HABS AK-13
HABS AK,11-NOAT.V,1-
1dr L

KODIAK ISLAND COUNTY

AFOGNAK

Nat. of the Holy Theotokos Rus. Orth. Church,Pries
Afognak Island
HABS AK-55-A
HABS DLC/PP-1993:AK-3
1ph/1pc L

Nat. of the Holy Theotokos Rus. Orth.,Church,Bldgs
Afognak Island
HABS AK-55-B
HABS DLC/PP-1993:AK-3
2ph/1pc L

Nat. of the Holy Theotokos Russian Orthodox Church
HABS AK-55
HABS DLC/PP-1993:AK-3
13ph/5pg/1pc/1ct L

AKHIOK

Protection of the Holy Thestokos Rus. Orth. Church
Kodiak Island
HABS AK-54
HABS DLC/PP-1993:AK-3
14ph/5pg/1pc/4ct L

KODIAK

Advanced Undersea Weapons Shop Bldg.; see U.S. Coast Guard Station, Weapons Shop Bldg.

Aircraft Engine Test Building; see Kodiak Naval Operating Base,Aircraft Engine Bldg

Coast Guard Station (Kodiak Naval Operating Base)
Womens Bay,St. Paul Harbor
HABS AK-48
HABS 1990(HABS):1
4ph/1pc L

Erskine House; see Russian-American Company Magazin

Holy Resurrection Russian Orthodox Church
Mission Rd. & Kashevaroff St.
HABS AK-57
4ph/6pg/1pc L

Kodiak Naval Operating Base; see Coast Guard Station

Kodiak Naval Operating Base,Aircraft Engine Bldg (Aircraft Engine Test Building; Kodiak Naval Operating Base,Bldg No. 17)
5th St. & Tom Styles Rd.,U.S. Coast Guard Station
HABS AK-47-B
HABS AK,12-KODI,2-B-
4ph/2pg/1pc L

Kodiak Naval Operating Base,Bldg No. 17; see Kodiak Naval Operating Base,Aircraft Engine Bldg

Kodiak Naval Operating Base,Navy Barracks(Civilian
U.S. Coast Guard Station
HABS AK-47-A
HABS AK,12-KODI,2-A-
3ph/2pg/1pc L

Kodiak Naval Operating Base: Aircraft Maint. Bldg.; see U.S. Coast Guard Station: Hanger II

Kodiak Naval Operating Base: Fuel Pier; see U.S. Coast Guard Station: Fuel Pier

Kodiak Naval Operating Base: Marginal Wharf; see U.S. Coast Guard Station: Marginal Wharf

Russian-American Company Magazin (Erskine House)
101 Marine Way E.
HABS AK-2
HABS AK,12-KODI,1-;1993:AK-3
7dr/18ph/7pg/2pc L

U.S. Coast Guard Station, Crash Boat House
U.S. Coast Guard Station
HABS AK-48-B
HABS AK,12-KODI,3-B-
2ph/2pg/1pc L

U.S. Coast Guard Station, Weapons Shop Bldg. (Advanced Undersea Weapons Shop Bldg.)
U.S. Coast Guard Station
HABS AK-48-A
HABS AK,12-KODI,3-B-
2ph/2pg/1pc L

U.S. Coast Guard Station: Fuel Pier (Kodiak Naval Operating Base: Fuel Pier)
Womens Bay,St. Paul Harbor
HABS AK-48-D
HABS 1990 (HABS):1
8ph/1pg/1pc L

U.S. Coast Guard Station: Hanger II (Kodiak Naval Operating Base: Aircraft Maint. Bldg.
U.S. Coast Guard Support Center
HABS AK-48-E
HABS 1990 (HABS):1
7ph/1pg/1pc L

U.S. Coast Guard Station: Marginal Wharf (Kodiak Naval Operating Base: Marginal Wharf)
Women's Bay,off Nyman Peninsula
HABS AK-48-C
HABS 1990 (HABS):1
10ph/1pg/1pc L

MONK'S LAGOON

Russian-American Architecture Project; see SS. Sergius & Herman of Valaam R.O. Chpl.,Father G

Russian-American Architecture Project; see SS. Sergius & Herman of Valaam R.O. Chpl.,Well Hse

Russian-American Architecture Project; see SS. Sergius & Herman of Valaam Russ. Orth. Chapel

SS. Sergius & Herman of Valaam R.O. Chpl.,Father G (Russian-American Architecture Project)
Spruce Island
HABS AK-52-A
HABS DLC/PP-1993:AK-3
3ph/1pg/1pc L

SS. Sergius & Herman of Valaam R.O. Chpl.,Father G (Russian-American Architecture Project)
Spruce Island
HABS AK-52-B
HABS DLC/PP-1993:AK-3
4ph/1pg/1pc L

SS. Sergius & Herman of Valaam R.O. Chpl.,Well Hse (Russian-American Architecture Project)
Spruce Island
HABS AK-52-C
HABS DLC/PP-1993:AK-3
1ph/1pc L

SS. Sergius & Herman of Valaam Russ. Orth. Chapel (Russian-American Architecture Project)
Spruce Island
HABS AK-52
HABS DLC/PP-1993:AK-3
11ph/6pg/1pc/1ct L

OLD HARBOR

Three Saints Russian Orthodox Church
Kodiak Island
HABS AK-53
HABS DLC/PP-1993:AK-3
14ph/4pg/1pc/1ct L

OUZINKIE

Nativity of Our Lord Russian Orthodox Church
Spruce Island
HABS AK-56
HABS DLC/PP-1993:AK-3
16ph/5pg/1pc/3ct L

MATANUSKA-SUSITNA COUNTY

CHICKEN VIC.

Mulvane Dredge; see Wade,Jack,Dredge

Wade,Jack,Dredge (Mulvane Dredge)
Milepost 86,Taylor Hwy.
HAER AK-12
HAER AK,19-CHIC.V,1-
22ph/1pg/1pc/1ct L

KNIK

Iditarod National Historic Trail; see Iditarod Trail,Knik Cabin

Iditarod National Historic Trail; see Iditarod Trail,Knik Hall

Iditarod Trail,Knik Cabin (Iditarod National Historic Trail)
HABS AK-5-G
HABS AK,9-SEW,2-G-
2ph/1pc L

Iditarod Trail,Knik Hall (Iditarod National Historic Trail)
HABS AK-5-F
HABS AK,9-SEW,2-F-
5ph/1pc L

PALMER

Colony Village,Wireck Barn
Alaska State Fairgrounds,Glen Hwy.
HABS AK-141-A
1ph/1pc L

United Protestant Church (Presbyterian)
S. Denail St. and E. Elmwood Ave.
HABS AK-139
2ph/1pc L

United Protestant Church (Presbyterian),Rectory
S. Denali St. & E. Elmwood Ave.
HABS AK-139-A
1ph/1pc L

PALMER VIC.

Agricultural Experiment Station,Kodiak Cottage
Matanuska Trunk Rd.
HABS AK-138-A
9dr/2ph/1pc L

Bailey-Estelle Farm
Glenn Hwy. & Marsh Rd.
HABS AK-142
1ph/1pc L

Farm
Glenn Hwy. & Scott Rd.
HABS AK-143
1ph/1pc L

Independence Mine
HAER AK-8
HAER AK,13-PALM.V,1-
4ph/1pc L

Rebarchek Farm
Rebarcheck Rd.
HABS AL-140
5ph/1pc L

SKWENTNA

Iditarod National Historic Trail; see Iditarod Trail,Skwentna Crossing Shelter Cabin

Iditarod Trail,Skwentna Crossing Shelter Cabin (Iditarod National Historic Trail)
Iditarod National Historic Trail
HABS AK-5-A
HABS AK,9-SEW,2-A-
2dr/7ph/1pc/fr L

SUMMIT

Iditarod National Historic Trail; see Iditarod Trail,Summit Shelter Cabin

Iditarod Trail,Summit Shelter Cabin (Iditarod National Historic Trail)
HABS AK-5-I
HABS AK,9-SEW,2-I-
1ph/1pc L

SUTTON

Buffalo Coal Mine
Wishbone Hill,SE end,near Moose Creek
HAER AK-22
HAER 1989(HAER):1
8pg/fr L

Buffalo Coal Mine,Vulcan Cable Hoist
Wishbone Hill,SE end,near Mose Creek
HAER AK-22-A
HAER 1989(HAER):1
6ph/1pc L

Eska Coal Mine
Wishbone Hill
HAER AK-19
HAER 1989(HAER):1
17pg/fr L

Eska Coal Mine,Faquhar Drive Unit
Wishbone Hill
HAER AK-19-A
HAER 1989(HAER):1
3ph/1pc L

Eska Coal Mine,Jeffery Fan/Blower Unit
Wishbone Hill
HAER AK-19-B
HAER 1989(HAER):1
5ph/1pc L

Eska Coal Mine,McNally Dryer Unit
Wishbone Hill
HAER AK-19-C
HAER 1989(HAER):1
2ph/1pc L

Eska Coal Mine,Roof Parts
Wishbone Hill
HAER AK-19-D
HAER 1989(HAER):1
1ph/1pc L

NOME COUNTY

CAPE NOME

Iditarod National Historic Trail; see Iditarod Trail,Cape Nome Roadhouse

Iditarod Trail,Cape Nome Roadhouse (Iditarod National Historic Trail)
HABS AK-5-M
HABS AK,9-SEW,2-M-
4ph/1pc/1ct L

GOLOVIN

Iditarod National Historic Trail; see Iditarod Trail,Dexter Roadhouse

Iditarod Trail,Dexter Roadhouse (Iditarod National Historic Trail)
HABS AK-5-J
HABS AK,9-SEW,2-M-
3ph/1pc L

MOSES POINT

Iditarod National Historic Trail; see Iditarod Trail,Moses Point Shelter Cabin

Iditarod Trail,Moses Point Shelter Cabin (Iditarod National Historic Trail)
HABS AK-5-H
HABS AK,9-SEW,2-H-
4ph/1pc L

NOME

Hammon Consolidated Gold Fields
HAER AK-3
HAER AK,14-NOME,1-
20ph/2pc/1ct L

Iditarod National Historic Trail; see Iditarod Trail,St. Joseph's Roman Catholic Church

Iditarod Trail,St. Joseph's Roman Catholic Church (St. Joseph's Roman Catholic Church; Iditarod National Historic Trail)
(Moved from Fourth & Steadman)
HABS AK-5-N
HABS AK,9-SEW,2-N-;1990(HABS):1
8dr/1ph/1pc L

Nome,City of
HABS AK-6
HABS AK,14-NOME,2-
34ph/2pc/3ct L

St. Joseph's Roman Catholic Church; see Iditarod Trail,St. Joseph's Roman Catholic Church

NOME VIC.

Council City & Solomon River RR,Locomotives
Nome Vicinity
HAER AK-16
HAER AK,14-NOME.V,1-
4ph/1pc/4ct L

Solomon River Gold Dredge
HAER AK-2
HAER AK,14-NOME.V,2-
9ph/1pc/1ct L

PORT SAFETY

Iditarod National Historic Trail; see Iditarod Trail,Safety Roadhouse

Iditarod Trail,Safety Roadhouse (Iditarod National Historic Trail)
Iditarod National Historic Trail
HABS AK-5-L
HABS AK,9-SEW,2-L-
4ph/1pc L

SOLOMON

Iditarod National Historic Trail; see Iditarod Trail,Solomon Roadhouse

Iditarod Trail,Solomon Roadhouse (Iditarod National Historic Trail)
HABS AK-5-K
HABS AK,9-SEW,2-K-
4ph/1pc L

NORTH SLOPE COUNTY

BARROW

Alaska Court System Building
Agvik & Kiogak Sts.
HABS AK-145
1ph/1pc L

Arctic Slope Regional Corporation Office Building
Agvik & Kiogak Sts.
HABS AK-146
2ph/1pc L

Brower House
Building 3129,Browerville
HABS AK-147
3ph/1pc L

Point Barrow Refuge Station
Building 3220,Browerville
HABS AK-150
5ph/1pc L

St. Patrick's Roman Catholic Church
HABS AK-144
1ph/1pc L

Stuaqpak
Agvik St.
HABS AK-148
1ph/1pc L

Utkeagvik Presbyterian Church,Manse
Building 1268, Momegana St.
HABS AK-149-A
2ph/1pc L

BARROW VIC.

Naval Arctic Research Lab,Quonset Huts (Ukpeagvik Industrial Center-NARL,Quonset Huts)
Approx. 5 miles NE of Barrow
HABS AK-184-A
1ph/1pc L

Ukpeagvik Industrial Center-NARL,Quonset Huts; see Naval Arctic Research Lab,Quonset Huts

POINT HOPE

Cemetery
HABS AK-182
2ph/1pc L

Ooyatohna,Nanny,House
Tigara Village
HABS AK-183
7ph/1pc L

Town Hall
HABS AK-181
1ph/1pc L

PRUDHOE BAY

BP Facilities,Base Operations Center
HABS AK-125-A
7ph/1pc L

Prudhoe Bay,Town of
HABS AK-180
1ph/1pc L

PRUDHOE BAY VIC.

BP Facilities,Endicott Site
HABS AK-124
5ph/1pc L

BP Facilities,Endicott Site,Base Operations Center
HABS AK-124-A
4ph/1pc L

SITKA COUNTY

SITKA

Alaska Native Brotherhood Hall,Sitka Camp No. 1
Katlian St.
HABS AK-109
3ph/1pc L

Building No. 29; see Russian-American County Building

Jackson,Sheldon College
Lincoln St.
HABS AK-105
1ph/1pc L

Jackson,Sheldon Museum
Lincoln St.
HABS AK-106
4ph/1pc L

Jackson,Sheldon,College,Allen,Richard H.,Mem. Hall
Lincoln St.
HABS AK-105-A
2ph/1pc L

Jackson,Sheldon,College,Sage Memorial Building
Lincoln St.
HABS AK-105-C
1ph/1pc L

Jackson,Sheldon,College,Whitmore Hall
Lincoln St.
HABS AK-105-B
1ph/1pc L

Model Cottage
105 Mutlakatla St.
HABS AK-110
2ph/1pc L

Naval Operating Base
Japonski Island
HABS AK-107
3ph/1pc L

Pioneer's Home
Katliae Ave and Lincoln St.
HABS AK-104
1ph/1pc L

Russian Bishop's House
Lincoln and Monastery Sts.
HABS AK-64
28ph/2pc/3ct H

Russian Bishop's House,Priest's House
Lincoln and Monastery Sts.
HABS AK-64-B
1ph/1pc H

Russian Bishop's House,School
Lincoln & Monastery Sts.
HABS AK-64-A
1ph/1pc H

Russian-American Architecture Project; see St. Michael's Cathedral

Russian-American Company Building No. 29
202-206 Lincoln St.
HABS AK-108
2ph/1pc L

Russian-American County Building (Building No. 29)
HABS AK-99
H

Sitka,City of
HABS AK-185
4ph/1pc L

St. Michael's Cathedral
(Russian-American Architecture Project)
Lincoln St.
HABS AK-1
HABS AK,17-SITKA,1-;1993:AK-3
6dr/24ph/7pg/3pc/4ct/fr L

SKAGWAY-YAKUTAT-ANGOON COUNTY

ANGOON

St. John the Baptist Russian Orthodox Church
Angoon
HABS AK-61
10ph/1pc/3ct H

HOONAH

St. Nicholas Russian Orthodox Church
HABS AK-60
12ph/1pc/1ct H

SKAGWAY

Skagway,City of
HABS AK-15
HABS AK,18-SKAG,1-;87(HABS):50
77ph/3pc/22ct L

SKAGWAY VIC.

Canyon City,Building S3
Skagway,Alaska
HABS AK-30-A
HABS 1991(HABS):27
1dr L

Canyon City,Dyea-Klondike Transportation Co. Boile
Skagway,Alaska
HABS AK-30-B
HABS 1991(HABS):27
1dr L

Dyea,Town of
HABS AK-16
HABS AK,18-SKAG.V,1-
7ph/1pc/4ct L

Sheep Camp,Building S4
Skagway,Alaska
HABS AK-29-A
HABS 1991(HABS):27
1dr L

Sheep Camp,Building S5
Skagway,Alaska
HABS AK-29-B
HABS 1991(HABS):27
1dr L

Sheep Camp,Building S7
Skagway,Alaska
HABS AK-29-C
HABS 1991(HABS):27
1dr L

Sheep Camp,Building S8
Skagway,Alaska
HABS AK-29-D
HABS 1991(HABS):27
1dr L

SOUTHEAST FAIRBANKS COUNTY

DELTA JUNCTION VIC.

Valdez-Fairbanks Trail,Black Rapids Roadhouse
HABS AK-11-C
HABS AK,19-FOGRE,1-C-
1ph/1pc L

Valdez-Fairbanks Trail,Rika's Roadhouse
HABS AK-11-B
HABS AK,19-FOGRE,1-B-
2ph/1pc L

FORT GREELY

Valdez-Fairbanks Trail Roadhouses
HABS AK-11
HABS AK,19-FOGRE,1-
1dr/2ct/fr L

Valdez-Fairbanks Trail,Sullivan Roadhouse
HABS AK-11-A
HABS AK,19-FOGRE,1-A-
3dr/18ph/4pg/1pc/fr L

VALDEZ-CORDOVA COUNTY

CHISANA

Blacksmith's Shop; see Chisana,Town of

Chisana,Town of (Blacksmith's Shop; Wrangell-St. Elias National Park & Preserve)
HABS AK-9-H
HABS AK,20-CHIS,2-H-
1ph/1pc/3ct L

Chisana,Town of (Herst,Earl,Cabin; Wrangell-St. Elias National Park & Preserve)
HABS AK-9-E
HABS AK,20-CHIS,2-E-
4ph/1pc L

Chisana,Town of (McNutt,Ray,Cookhouse; Wrangell-St. Elias National Park & Preserve)
HABS AK-9-P
HABS AK,20-CHIS,2-P-
1ph/1pc L

Chisana,Town of (McNutt,Ray,Storage Shed; Wrangell-St. Elias National Park & Preserve)
HABS AK-9-Q
HABS AK,20-CHIS,2-Q-
1ph/1pc L

Chisana,Town of (Nelson,N. P. ,Cabin,First; Wrangell-St. Elias National Park & Preserve)
HABS AK-9-I
HABS AK,20-CHIS,2-I-
7ph/1pc L

Chisana,Town of (Post Office,Old; Wrangell-St. Elias National Park & Preserve)
HABS AK-9-F
HABS AK,20-CHIS,1-F-
1ph/1pc L

Chisana,Town of (U. S. Commissioner's Court; Wrangell-St. Elias National Park & Preserve)
HABS AK-9-A
HABS AK,20-CHIS,2-A-;1989(HABS):1
3dr/5ph/1pc/2ct/fr L

Chisana,Town of (U. S. Commissioner's Residence; Wrangell-St. Elias National Park & Preserve)
HABS AK-9-B
HABS AK,20-CHIS,2-B-;1989(HABS):1
3dr/4ph/1pc/fr L

Chisana,Town of (Women's Jail; Wrangell-St. Elias National Park & Preserve)
HABS AK-9-C
HABS K,20-CHIS,2-C-;1989(HABS):1
1dr/7ph/1pc/2ct/fr L

Chisana,Town of (Wrangell-St. Elias National Park & Preserve)
HABS AK-9
HABS AK,20-CHIS,2-; 1989(HABS):1
1dr/3ph/1pc/2ct/fr L

Herst,Earl,Cabin; see Chisana,Town of

McNutt,Ray,Cookhouse; see Chisana,Town of

McNutt,Ray,Storage Shed; see Chisana,Town of

Nelson,N. P. ,Cabin,First; see Chisana,Town of

Post Office,Old; see Chisana,Town of

Thorall,Ivan,Steam Powered Sawmill
HAER AK-17
HAER AK,20-CHIS,1-
4ph/1pg/1pc L

U. S. Commissioner's Court; see Chisana,Town of

U. S. Commissioner's Residence; see Chisana,Town of

Women's Jail; see Chisana,Town of

Wrangell-St. Elias National Park & Preserve; see Chisana,Town of

CHISANA VIC.

Chisana Trail Cabins (Wrangell-St. Elias National Park & Preserve)
HABS AK-10
HABS AK,20-CHIS.V,1-
1dr L

Chisana Trail,Solo Mountain Shelter Cabin (Wrangell-St. Elias National Park & Preserve)
HABS AK-10-A
HABS AK,20-CHIS.V,1-A-
1dr/9ph/1pc/fr L

Wrangell-St. Elias National Park & Preserve; see Chisana Trail Cabins

Wrangell-St. Elias National Park & Preserve; see Chisana Trail,Solo Mountain Shelter Cabin

CHITINA

Chitina,Town of
HABS AK-12
HABS AK,20-CHIT,1-
4ph/1pc/1ct L

CHITINA VIC.

Copper River & Northwestern RR,Gilahina Bridge (Gilahina Trestle; Gilahina Bridge)
Mile 28.5,McCarthy Rd. (Wrangell-St. Elias N.P.)
HAER AK-15
HAER AK,20-CHIT.V,1-
5ph/1pg/1pc/1ct L

Gilahina Bridge; see Copper River & Northwestern RR,Gilahina Bridge

Gilahina Trestle; see Copper River & Northwestern RR,Gilahina Bridge

Kuskalana Bridge (Wrangell-St. Elias National Park & Preserve)
Mile 146 of Copper River & Northwestern Road
HAER AK-4
HAER AK,20-CHIT.V,2-
9ph/1pc/4ct L

Wrangell-St. Elias National Park & Preserve; see Kuskalana Bridge

CORDOVA

Alaskan Hotel
600 First St.
HABS AK-155
1ph/1pc L

Cordova High School
Browning Ave.
HABS AK-153
1ph/1pc L

Cordova,City of
HABS AK-152
3ph/1pc L

Morpac Cannery
Ocean Dock Rd.
HABS AK-154
4ph/1pc L

St. George's Episcopal Church
Lake Ave.,between First & Second Sts.
HABS AK-156
2ph/1pc L

U.S. Post Office & Courthouse
Second St.
HABS AK-157
2ph/1pc L

CORDOVA VIC.

Boswell Bay Alascom Site; see Boswell Bay White Alice Site

Boswell Bay White Alice Site (Boswell Bay Alascom Site; Chugach National Forest)
HAER AK-21
HAER DLC/PP-1993:AK-1
1ph/15pg/1pc L

Boswell Bay White Alice Site,Dormitory
Chugach Nat'l Forest
HAER AK-21-D
HAER 1991(HAER):28
5ph/1pc L

Boswell Bay White Alice Site,Fire Control Bldg.
Chugach Nat'l Forest
HAER AK-21-C
HAER 1991(HAER):28
1ph/1pc L

Boswell Bay White Alice Site,Radio Relay Bldg.
Chugach Nat'l Forest
HAER AK-21-B
HAER 1991(HAER):28
15ph/1pc L

Boswell Bay White Alice Site,Tropospheric Antennas
Chugach Nat'l Forest
HAER AK-21-A
HAER 1991(HAER):28
3ph/1pc L

Boswell Bay White Alice Site,Warehouse
Chugach Nat'l Forest
HAER AK-21-E
HAER 1991(HAER):28
2ph/1pc L

Chugach National Forest; see Boswell Bay White Alice Site

Copper River & Northwest RR,Million Dollar Bridge (Million Dollar Bridge; Glacier Bridge)
Spanning Copper River at Miles Glacier
HAER AK-10
HAER AK,20-CORD.V,1-
17ph/1pg/1pc/7ct L

Glacier Bridge; see Copper River & Northwest RR,Million Dollar Bridge

Million Dollar Bridge; see Copper River & Northwest RR,Million Dollar Bridge

CORDOVA-MCCARTHY

St. Michael the Archangel Russian Orthodox Church
HABS AK-58
9ph/1pc/1ct H

GAKONA

Gakona Lodge & Trading Post
Mile 205, Glenn Hwy.
HABS AK-27
HABS AK,20-GAK,1-
5ph/1pg/1pc L

GAKONA VIC.

Sourdough Lodge
Mile 147.5, Richardson Highway
HABS AK-26
HABS AK,20-GAK.V,1-
11ph/2pg/1pc L

MCCARTHY

Kennecott Copper Corporation; see Kennecott Mines

Kennecott Mines (Kennecott Copper Corporation)
On Copper River & Northwestern RR
HAER AK-1
HAER AK,20-MCAR,1-
15dr/144ph/62pg/9pc/19ct/fr L

MCCARTHY VIC.

Green Butte Copper Co.
McCarthy Creek 12 mi NE
McCarthy(Wrangell-St.Elias
HAER AK-9
HAER AK,20-MCAR.V,1-
6ph/1pg/1pc/2ct L

Green Butte Copper Co.,Bathhouse
McCarthy Creek 12 mi NE
McCarthy(Wrangell-St. Elia
HAER AK-9-B
HAER AK,20-MCAR.V,2-B-
1ph/1pg/1pc L

Green Butte Copper Co.,Bunkhouse
McCarthy Creek 12 mi NE
McCarthy(Wrangell-St.Elias
HAER AK-9-C
HAER AK,20-MCAR.V,1-C-
3ph/1pg/1pc L

Green Butte Copper Co.,Bunkhouse (Upper camp)
McCarthy Creek 12 mi NE
McCarthy(Wrangell-St.Elias
HAER AK-9-J
HAER AK,20-MCAR.V,1-J-
7ph/1pg/1pc/1ct L

Green Butte Copper Co.,Covered Stairway
McCarthy Creek 12 mi NE
McCarthy(Wrangell-St.Elias
HAER AK-9-I
HAER AK,20-MCAR.V,1-I-
2ph/1pg/1pc/1ct L

Green Butte Copper Co.,Manager's House
McCarthy Creek 12 mi NE
McCarthy(Wrangell-St.Elias
HAER AK-9-A
HAER AK,20-MCAR.V,1-A-
2ph/1pg/1pc L

Green Butte Copper Co.,Portal Shed
McCarthy Creek 12 mi NE
McCarthy(Wrangell-St.Elias
HAER AK-9-H
HAER AK,20-MCAR.V,1-H-
6ph/1pg/1pc/3ct L

Green Butte Copper Co.,Stables
McCarthy Creek 12 mi NE
McCarthy(Wrangell-St.Elias
HAER AK-9-D
HAER AK,20-MCAR.V,1-D-
8ph/1pg/1pc L

Green Butte Copper Co.,Tin Shed
McCarthy Creek 12 mi NE
McCarthy(Wrangell-St.Elias
HAER AK-9-E
HAER AK,20-MCAR.V,1-E-
1ph/1pg/1pc L

Green Butte Copper Co.,Tram Terminous
McCarthy Creek 12 mi NE
McCarthy(Wrangell-St.Elias
HAER AK-9-F
HAER AK,20-MCAR.V,1-F-
1ph/1pg/1pc L

Green Butte Copper Co.,Warehouse
McCarthy Creek 12 mi NE
McCarthy(Wrangell-St.Elias
HAER AK-9-G
HAER AK,20-MCAR.V,1-G-
3ph/1pg/1pc L

Nizina Bridge
Mile 8,Nizina Rd. (Wrangell-St. Elias Nat'l Park)
HAER AK-14
HAER AK,20-MCAR.V,2-
6ph/1pg/1pc L

WRANGELL-PETERSBURG COUNTY

PETERSBURG

Petersburg,Town of
HABS AK-123
4ph/1pc L

Sons of Norway Hall
Indian St.
HABS AK-122
6ph/1pc L

WRANGELL

Chief Shakes House
Shakes Island
HABS AK-101
7ph/1pc L

Front Street (Commercial Buildings)
HABS AK-103
1ph/1pc L

U.S. Post Office & Customs House
Church St.
HABS AK-100
3ph/1pc L

Wrangell Museum; see Wrangell Public School

Wrangell Public School (Wrangell Museum)
126 Second St.
HABS AK-102
2ph/1pc L

YUKON-KOYUKUK COUNTY

BETTLES VIC.

Gates of the Arctic National Park; see Yale,Charlie,Cabins

Knorr,Vincent,Cabin
Gates of the Arctic National Park & Preserve
HABS AK-19
HABS AK,23-BET.V,2-
2dr/6ph/1pg/1pc/fr L

Postlethwaite-Jones Cabin
Nolan, on Smith Creek
HABS AK-24
HABS AK,23-BET.V,3-
5ph/1pg/1pc L

Wilcox,A.D.,Drift Mine
Linda Creek near Dalton Hwy.
HAER AK-7
HAER AK,23-BET.V,1-
1ph/1pg/1pc L

Wilcox,A.D.,Drift Mine,Boiler Cabin
Linda Creek near Dalton Hwy.
HAER AK-7-A
HAER AK,23-BET.V,1-A-
4ph/1pc L

Wilcox,A.D.,Drift Mine,Headframe
Linda Creek near Dalton Hwy.
HAER AK-7-B
HAER AK,23-BET.V,1-B-
1ph/1pc L

Wilcox,A.D.,Drift Mine,Residential Cabin
Linda Creek near Dalton Hwy.
HAER AK-7-C
HAER AK,23-BET.V,1-C-
4ph/1pc L

Yale,Charlie,Cabins (Gates of the Arctic National Park)
Glacier River near Nolan,Gates of the Arctic N.P.
HABS AK-20
HABS AK,23-BET.V,4-
2ph/1pg/1pc L

Yale,Charlie,Main Cabin
Glacier River near Nolan,Gates of the Arctic N.P.
HABS AK-20-A
HABS AK,23-BET.V,4-A-
7ph/1pc L

Yale,Charlie,Work Cabin
Glacier River near Nolan,Gates of the Arctic N.P.
HABS AK-20-B
HABS AK,23-BET.V,4-B-
3ph/1pc L

CIRCLE VIC.

McGregor,George, Cabin
Yukon River near Coal Creek,Yukon-Charley Natl Pre
HABS AK-43
HABS AK,23-CIRC.V,1-
2dr/4ph/6pg/1pc/fr L

Slaven,Frank,Roadhouse
Yukon River at Coal Creek,Yukon-Charley Natl Pres.
HABS AK-42
HABS AK,23-CIRC.V,2-
5dr/9ph/9pg/1pc/1ct/fr L

Slaven,Frank,Roadhouse,Shed
Yukon River at Coal Creek,Yukon-Charley Natl Pres.
HABS AK-42-A
HABS AK,23-CIRC.V,2-A-
1dr/fr L

Woodchopper Roadhouse
Yukon River, Yukon-Charley Natl Preserve
HABS AK-44
HABS AK,23-CIRC.V,3-
2dr/3ph/8pg/1pc/fr L

COLDFOOT

Minano,James,Cabin
Slate Creek at Koyukuk River,Bettles Vic.
HABS AK-23
HABS AK,23-COLFO,1-
7ph/5pg/1pc L

Schoolhouse
(See YUKON-KOYUKUK,WISEMAN for documentation)
HABS AK-25-A
HABS AK,23-WISMA,1-A-
1ph/1pg/1pc L

EAGLE

Amundsen Cabin
A Street
HABS AK-7-H
HABS AK,19-EGL,1-H-
1ph/1pg/1pc L

Church & Parish House
HABS AK-7-I
HABS AK,19-EGL,1-I-
4ph/1pg/1pc L

City Hall
C Street
HABS AK-7-G
HABS AK,19-EGL,1-G-
5ph/1pg/1pc L

Courthouse
First Avenue
HABS AK-7-E
HABS AK,19-EGL,1-E-
5ph/1pg/1pc L

Custom House (Noncommissioned Officers Quarters)
Front St. (Moved from Fort Egbert)
HABS AK-7-C
HABS AK,19-EGL,1-C-
5ph/1pg/1pc L

Eagle,Town of
South bank of the Yukon River at Mission Creek
HABS AK-7
HABS AK,19-EGL,1-
5ph/2pg/1pc/1ct L

Eagle,Town of,Cabin
Lot 5,Block 20 (Facing onto Second St.)
HABS AK-7-J
HABS 1990 (HABS):1
8ph/5pg/1pc L

Noncommissioned Officers Quarters; see Custom House

Northern Commercial Company Store
220 Front St.
HABS AK-7-B
HABS AK,19-EGL,1-B-
6ph/1pg/1pc/2ct L

Northern Commercial Company Warehouse
220 Front St.
HABS AK-7-A
HABS AK,19-EGL,1-A-
6ph/1pg/1pc L

Taylor Building
B St.
HABS AK-7-D
HABS AK,19-EGL,1-D-
2ph/1pg/1pc L

Wellhouse
First Ave.
HABS AK-7-F
HABS AK,19-EGL,1-F-
5ph/1pg/1pc L

EAGLE VIC.

Biederman,Ed,Fish Camp
Yukon River,Yukon-Charley Rivers Natl Preserve
HABS AK-40
HABS AK,19-EGL.V,2-
1dr/5pg/fr L

Biederman,Ed,Fish Camp,Boat
Yukon River,Yukon-Charley Rivers Natl Preserve
HABS AK-40-E
HABS AK,19-EGL.V,2-E-
2ph/1pc L

Biederman,Ed,Fish Camp,Bunkhouse
Yukon River,Yukon-Charley Rivers Natl Preserve
HABS AK-40-B
HABS AK,19-EGL.V,2-B-
1dr/3ph/1pc/fr L

Biederman,Ed,Fish Camp,Cache
Yukon River,Yukon-Charley Rivers Natl Preserve
HABS AK-40-C
HABS AK,19-EGL.V,2-C-
1dr/2ph/1pc/fr L

Biederman,Ed,Fish Camp,Greenhouse
Yukon River,Yukon-Charley Rivers Natl Preserve
HABS AK-40-D
HABS AK,19-EGL.V,2-D-
1ph/1pc L

Biederman,Ed,Fish Camp,Main Cabin
Yukon River,Yukon-Charley Rivers Natl Prescrve
HABS AK-40-A
HABS AK,19-EGL.V,2-A-
2dr/5ph/1pc/fr L

Custom House (Noncommissioned Officers Quarters)
Fort Egbert (Moved to Front Street,Eagle,Alaska)
HABS AK-7-C
HABS AK,19-EGL,1-C-
5ph/1pg/1pc L

Fort Egbert
Yukon River at Mission Creek
HABS AK-14
HABS AK,19-EGL.V,1-
1pg L

Fort Egbert, Firehouse; see Fort Egbert, Waterwagon Shed

Fort Egbert, Granary
Yukon River at Mission Creek
HABS AK-14-C
HABS AK,19-EGL.V,1-C-
3ph/1pg/1pc L

Fort Egbert, Heater House; see Fort Egbert, Waterwagon Shed

Fort Egbert, Mule Barn (Fort Egbert, Quartermaster s Stables)
Yukon River at Mission Creek
HABS AK-14-A
HABS AK,19-EGL.V,1-A-
10ph/1pg/1pc L

Fort Egbert, Quartermaster s Stables; see Fort Egbert, Mule Barn

Fort Egbert, Quartermaster Warehouse
Yukon River at Mission Creek
HABS AK-14-E
HABS AK,19-EGL.V,1-E-
2ph/1pg/1pc L

Fort Egbert, Waterwagon Shed (Fort Egbert, Heater House; Fort Egbert, Firehouse)
Yukon River at Mission Creek
HABS AK-14-D
HABS AK,19-EGL.V,1-D-
3ph/1pg/1pc L

Fort Egbert,Noncommissioned Officers Qtrs
Yukon River at Mission Creek
HABS AK-14-B
HABS AK,19-EGL.V,1-B-
9ph/1pg/1pc L

Gold Placers Incorporated
Near Coal Creek & Yukon River (Yukon-Charley N.P.)
HAER AK-11
HAER AK,19-EGL.V,4-
1pg L

Gold Placers Incorporated,Dredge
Near Coal Creek & Yukon River (Yukon-Charley N.P.)
HAER AK-11-A
HAER AK,19-EGL.V,4-A-
14ph/1pc/2ct L

Gold Placers Incorporated,Mess Hall
Near Coal Creek & Yukon River (Yukon-Charley N.P.)
HAER AK-11-C
HAER AK,19-EGL.V,4-C-
1ph/1pc L

Gold Placers Incorporated,Warehouse
Near Coal Creek & Yukon River (Yukon-Charley N.P.)
HAER AK-11-B
HAER AK,19-EGL.V,4-B-
2ph/1pc L

Gold Placers Incorporated,Worker Qtrs.
Near Coal Creek & Yukon River (Yukon-Charley N.P.)
HAER AK-11-D
HAER AK,19-EGL.V,4-D-
1ph/1pc L

Noncommissioned Officers Quarters; see Custom House

Taylor,James,Cabin
Opposite 4th of July Creek,Yukon River
HABS AK-41
HABS AK,19-EGL.V,3-
1dr/8pg/fr L

Taylor,James,Cabin,Dog Barn
Opposite 4th of July Creek,Yukon River
HABS AK-41-B
HABS AK,19-EGL.V,3-B-
1dr/4ph/1pc/fr L

Taylor,James,Cabin,Dog Corrals
Opposite 4th of July Creek,Yukon River
HABS AK-41-C
HABS AK,19-EGL.V,3-C-
1ph/1pc L

Taylor,James,Cabin,Shed
Opposite 4th of July Creek,Yukon River
HABS AK-41-A
HABS AK,19-EGL.V,3-A-
1dr/3ph/1pc/fr L

Taylor,James,Cabin,Shop
Opposite 4th of July Creek,Yukon River
HABS AK-41-D
HABS AK,19-EGL.V,3-D-
1dr/3ph/1pc/fr L

LOWER KALSKAG

St. Seraphim Russian Orthodox Churches
HABS AK-92
12ph/3pg/1pc H

MCKINLEY STATION

Cabin No. 4; see Pearson Cabin

Igloo Creek Cabin No. 25; see Mount McKinley Patrol, Igloo Creek Cabin No. 25

Mount McKinley Headquarters
Denali Natl Park & Preserve
HABS AK-35
HABS AK,23-MCKIN,1-
1ph/2pg/1pc/1ct L

Mount McKinley Hqtrs,Administration Bldg (Mount McKinley Hqtrs,Ranger Dormitory; Mount McKinley Hqtrs,Bldg No. 21)
Denali Natl Park & Preserve
HABS AK-35-C
HABS AK,23-MCKIN,1-C-
3dr/3ph/1pg/1pc L

Mount McKinley Hqtrs,Administration Bldg,First; see Mount McKinley Hqtrs,Employee Residence

Mount McKinley Hqtrs,Barn (Mount McKinley Hqtrs,Carpenter's Shop; Mount McKinley Hqtrs,Bldg. No. 106)
Denali Natl Park & Preserve
HABS AK-35-J
HABS AK,23-MCKIN,1-J-
2dr/2ph/1pg/1pc L

Mount McKinley Hqtrs,Bldg No. 101; see Mount McKinley Hqtrs,Warehouse

Mount McKinley Hqtrs,Bldg No. 102; see Mount McKinley Hqtrs,Garage & Repair Shop

Mount McKinley Hqtrs,Bldg No. 103; see Mount McKinley Hqtrs,Ranger Cache & Garage

Mount McKinley Hqtrs,Bldg No. 105; see Mount McKinley Hqtrs,Dog Feed Cache & Sled Storage

Mount McKinley Hqtrs,Bldg No. 12; see Mount McKinley Hqtrs,Employee Residence

Mount McKinley Hqtrs,Bldg No. 13; see Mount McKinley Hqtrs,Employee Residence

Mount McKinley Hqtrs,Bldg No. 21; see Mount McKinley Hqtrs,Administration Bldg

Mount McKinley Hqtrs,Bldg No. 22; see Mount McKinley Hqtrs,Employee Residence

Mount McKinley Hqtrs,Bldg. No. 10; see Mount McKinley Hqtrs,Electric Light Plant

Mount McKinley Hqtrs,Bldg. No. 106; see Mount McKinley Hqtrs,Barn

Mount McKinley Hqtrs,Bldg. No. 107; see Mount McKinley Hqtrs,Boiler House

Mount McKinley Hqtrs,Bldg. No. 111; see Mount McKinley Hqtrs,Employee Residence

Mount McKinley Hqtrs,Bldg. No. 112; see Mount McKinley Hqtrs,Comfort Station

Mount McKinley Hqtrs,Bldg. No. 23; see Mount McKinley Hqtrs,Superintendent's Residence

Mount McKinley Hqtrs,Boiler House (Mount McKinley Hqtrs,Plumbing Shop; Mount McKinley Hqtrs,Bldg. No. 107)
Denali Natl Park & Preserve
HABS AK-35-K
HABS AK,23-MCKIN,1-K-
2dr/1ph/1pg/1pc L

Mount McKinley Hqtrs,Carpenter's Shop; see Mount McKinley Hqtrs,Barn

Mount McKinley Hqtrs,Comfort Station (Mount McKinley Hqtrs,Residence; Mount McKinley Hqtrs,Bldg. No. 112)
Denali Natl Park & Preserve
HABS AK-35-N
HABS AK,23-MCKIN,1-N-
1dr/1ph/1pg/1pc L

Mount McKinley Hqtrs,Dog Feed Cache & Sled Storage (Mount McKinley Hqtrs,Bldg No. 105)
Denali Natl Park & Preserve
HABS AK-35-I
HABS AK,23-MCKIN,1-I-
3dr/5ph/1pg/1pc L

Mount McKinley Hqtrs,Electric Light Plant (Mount McKinley Hqtrs,Ranger Office; Mount McKinley Hqtrs,Bldg. No. 10)
Denali Nat'l Park
HABS AK-35-L
HABS AK,23-MCKIN,1-L-
1dr/3ph/1pg/1pc L

Mount McKinley Hqtrs,Employee Residence (Mount McKinley Hqtrs,Administration Bldg,First; Mount McKinley Hqtrs,Bldg No. 22)
Denali Natl Park & Preserve
HABS AK-35-D
HABS AK,23-MCKIN,1-D-
2dr/2ph/1pg/1pc L

Mount McKinley Hqtrs,Employee Residence (Mount McKinley Hqtrs,Bldg No. 12)
Denali Natl Park & Preserve
HABS AK-35-B
HABS AK,23-MCKIN,1-B-
3dr/1ph/1pg/1pc L

Mount McKinley Hqtrs,Employee Residence (Mount McKinley Hqtrs,Bldg No. 13)
Denali Natl Park & Preserve
HABS AK-35-A
HABS AK,23-MCKIN,1-A-
2dr/1ph/1pg/1pc L

Mount McKinley Hqtrs,Employee Residence (Mount McKinley Hqtrs,Superintendent's Garage; Mount McKinley Hqtrs,Bldg. No. 111)
Denali Natl Park & Preserve
HABS AK-35-M
HABS AK,23-MCKIN,1-M-
1dr/1ph/1pg/1pc L

Mount McKinley Hqtrs,Garage & Repair Shop (Mount McKinley Hqtrs,Bldg No. 102)
Denali Natl Park & Preserve
HABS AK-35-G
HABS AK,23-MCKIN,1-G-
2dr/1ph/1pg/1pc L

Mount McKinley Hqtrs,Plumbing Shop; see Mount McKinley Hqtrs,Boiler House

Mount McKinley Hqtrs,Ranger Cache & Garage (Mount McKinley Hqtrs,Bldg No. 103)
Denali Natl Park & Preserve
HABS AK-35-H
HABS AK,23-MCKIN,1-H-
2dr/2ph/1pg/1pc L

Mount McKinley Hqtrs,Ranger Dormitory; see Mount McKinley Hqtrs,Administration Bldg

Mount McKinley Hqtrs,Ranger Office; see Mount McKinley Hqtrs,Electric Light Plant

Mount McKinley Hqtrs,Residence; see Mount McKinley Hqtrs,Comfort Station

Mount McKinley Hqtrs,Superintendent's Garage; see Mount McKinley Hqtrs,Employee Residence

Mount McKinley Hqtrs,Superintendent's Residence (Mount McKinley Hqtrs,Bldg. No. 23)
Denali Natl Park & Preserve
HABS AK-35-E
HABS AK,23-MCKIN,1-E-
3dr/3ph/1pg/1pc L

Mount McKinley Hqtrs,Warehouse (Mount McKinley Hqtrs,Bldg No. 101)
Denali Natl Park & Preserve
HABS AK-35-F
HABS AK,23-MCKIN,1-F-
2dr/3ph/1pg/1pc L

Mount McKinley Patrol Cabins
Denali National Park & Preserve
HABS AK-32
HABS AK,23-MCKIN,2-
1pg L

Mount McKinley Patrol Cabins, Cabin No. 4; see Pearson Cabin

Mount McKinley Patrol, Igloo Creek Cabin No. 25 (Igloo Creek Cabin No. 25)
Naer Igloo Creek,mile 34.1,Denali Nat'l Park
HABS AK-32-A
HABS AK,23-MCKIN,2-A-
3ph/1pg/1pc L

Mount McKinley Patrol, Upper East Fork Cabin No.29
E. Fork Toklat River,mile 43,Denali Nat'l Park
HABS AK-32-B
HABS AK,23-MCKIN,2-B-
1ph/1pg/1pc L

Mount McKinley Ranger Station,Bldg No. 14; see Wonder Lake Ranger Station

Pearson Cabin (Mount McKinley Patrol Cabins, Cabin No. 4; Toklat Ranger Station; Cabin No. 4)
near Toklat River,Denali National Park & Preserve
HABS AK-33
HABS AK,23-MCKIN,3-
3dr/9ph/1pg/1pc/fr L

Toklat Ranger Station; see Pearson Cabin

Wonder Lake Ranger Station (Mount McKinley Ranger Station,Bldg No. 14)
Denali Natl Park & Preserve
HABS AK-31
HABS AK,23-MCKIN,4-
2dr/5ph/1pg/1pc L

NIKOLAI

Presentation of Our Lord Russian Orthodox Church
HABS AK-83
12ph/3pg/1pc L

NIKOLAI VIC.

Iditarod National Historic Trail; see Iditarod Trail,Rhon River Shelter Cabin

Iditarod Trail,Rhon River Shelter Cabin (Iditarod National Historic Trail)
Iditarod National Historic Trail
HABS AK-5-B
HABS AK,9-SEW,2-B-
2dr/6ph/1pc/fr L

WISEMAN

Heppenstall-Green Cabin
Koyukuk River at Wiseman Creek,Bettles Vic.
HABS AK-25-F
HABS AK,23-WISMA,1-F-
5ph/1pg/1pc L

Knorr,Vincent,Homestead
Koyukuk River at Wiseman Creek,Bettles Vic.
HABS AK-25-G
HABS AK,23-WISMA,1-G-
8ph/1pg/1pc L

Larson,Gus,Cabin
Koyukuk River at Wiseman Creek,Bettles Vic.
HABS AK-25-E
HABS AK,23-WISMA,1-E-
6ph/1pg/1pc L

Northern Commercial Company Store
Koyukuk River at Wiseman Creek,Bettles Vic.
HABS AK-25-C
HABS AK,23-WISMA,1-C-
7ph/1pg/1pc L

Pioneers of Alaska Igloo No. 8 (Siverly & Bowker Saloon)
Koyukuk River at Wiseman Creek,Bettles Vic.
HABS AK-25-B
HABS AK,23-WISMA,1-B-
5ph/1pg/1pc L

Schoolhouse
Koyukuk River,Bettles Vic. (moved from Coldfoot)
HABS AK-25-A
HABS AK,23-WISMA,1-A-
1ph/1pg/1pc L

Siverly & Bowker Saloon; see Pioneers of Alaska Igloo No. 8

Ulen,Dow,Cabin & Wind Generator
Koyukuk River at Wiseman Creek,Bettles Vic.
HABS AK-25-D
HABS AK,23-WISMA,1-D-
8ph/1pg/1pc L

Wiseman,Town of
Koyukuk River at Wiseman Creek,Bettles Vic.
HABS AK-25
HABS AK,23-WISMA,1-
7ph/3pg L H

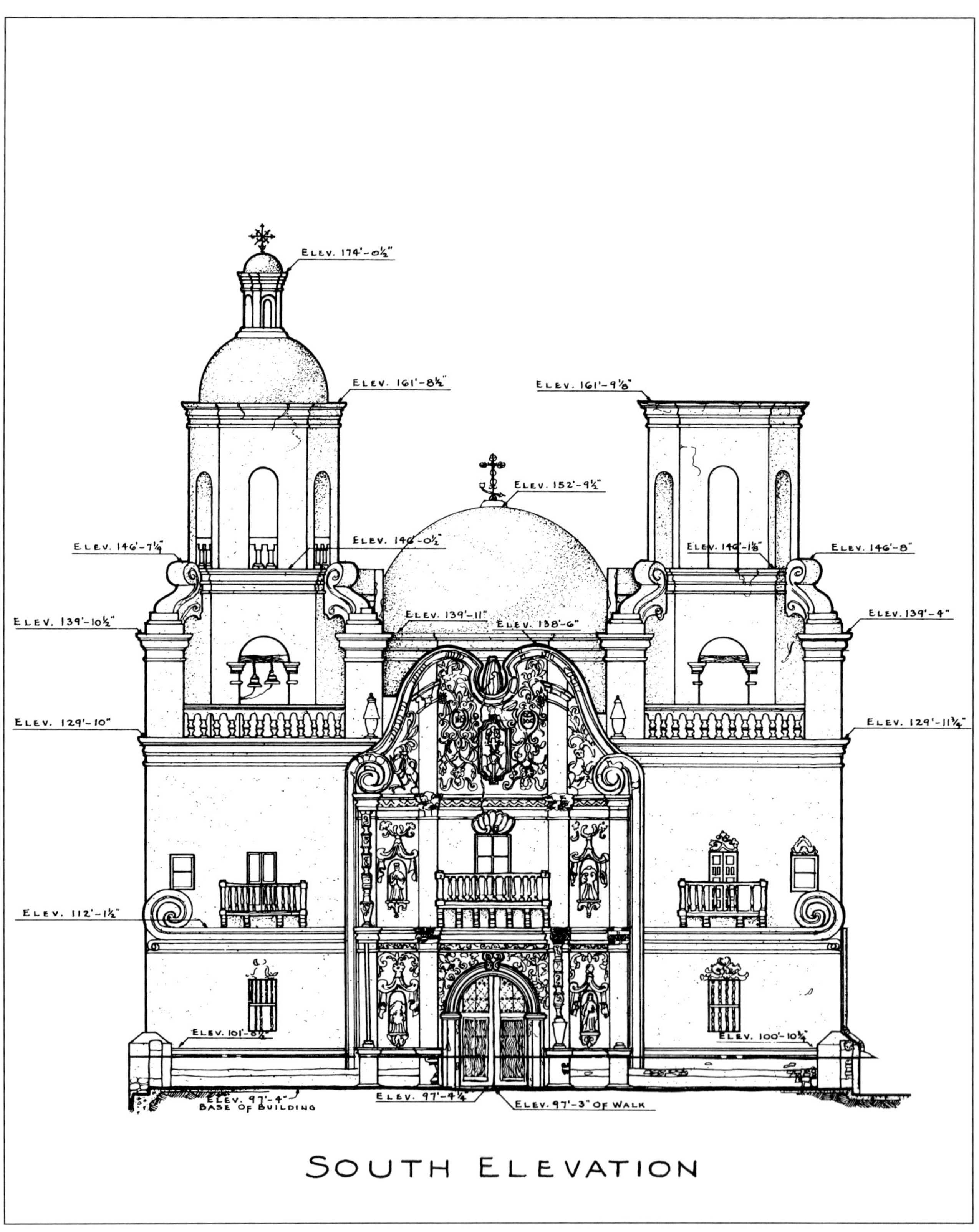

Mission San Xavier del Bac, Tucson vicinity, Pima County, Arizona. South elevation. Measured drawing delineated by William M. Collier, Jr. and Louis Williams, 1940 (HABS ARIZ-13, sheet 8 of 41; negative number LC-USZA1-873).

Arizona

APACHE COUNTY

CHINLE VIC.

Antelope House Ruin (Canyon De Chelly)
Canyon Del Muerto
HABS AZ-157
HABS DLC/PP-1992:AZ-5
1ph/1pc L

Canyon De Chelly; see Antelope House Ruin

Canyon De Chelly; see White House Ruin

Canyon de Chelly National Monument; see Mummy Cave

Mummy Cave (Canyon de Chelly National Monument)
Navajo Indian Reservation
HABS AZ-72
HABS ARIZ,1-CHIN.V,1-
(DLC/PP-1992:AZ-5)
4dr/1ph/1pc/fr L

White House Ruin (Canyon De Chelly)
Navajo Indian Reservation
HABS AZ-156
HABS DLC/PP-1992:AZ-5
2ph/1pc/fr L

GANADO

Hubbell Trading Post (Hubbell Trading Post National Historic Site)
HABS AZ-137
HABS ARIZ,1-GANA,1-
8dr/fr L

Hubbell Trading Post National Historic Site; see Hubbell Trading Post

Hubbell Trading Post National Historic Site; see Hubbell Trading Post,Bread Oven

Hubbell Trading Post National Historic Site; see Hubbell Trading Post,Bunkhouse

Hubbell Trading Post National Historic Site; see Hubbell Trading Post,Gazebo

Hubbell Trading Post National Historic Site; see Hubbell Trading Post,Guest Hogan

Hubbell Trading Post National Historic Site; see Hubbell Trading Post,Navajo Day School

Hubbell Trading Post National Historic Site; see Hubbell Trading Post,Root Cellar

Hubbell Trading Post National Historic Site; see Hubbell Trading Post,Storage Building

Hubbell Trading Post National Historic Site; see Hubbell,J. L. Trading Post,House

Hubbell Trading Post National Historic Site; see Hubbell,J. L.,Trading Post,HB-1

Hubbell Trading Post National Historic Site; see Hubbell,J. L.,Trading Post,Two-Story Barn

Hubbell Trading Post National Historic Site; see Hubbell,J. L.,Trading Post,Unfinished Shed

Hubbell Trading Post,Bread Oven (Hubbell Trading Post National Historic Site)
HABS AZ-137-A
HABS ARIZ,1-GANA-1F-
3dr/fr L

Hubbell Trading Post,Bunkhouse (Hubbell Trading Post National Historic Site)
HABS AZ-64
HABS ARIZ,1-GANA,1E-
4dr/fr L

Hubbell Trading Post,Comfort Station; see Hubbell Trading Post,Storage Building

Hubbell Trading Post,Gazebo (Hubbell Trading Post National Historic Site)
HABS AZ-137-C
HABS ARIZ,1-GANA,1G-
1dr/fr L

Hubbell Trading Post,Guest Hogan (Hubbell Trading Post National Historic Site)
HABS AZ-137-D
HABS ARIZ,1-GANA,1H-
3dr/fr L

Hubbell Trading Post,Navajo Day School (Hubbell Trading Post,Visitor Contact Center; Hubbell Trading Post National Historic Site)
HABS AZ-137-E
HABS ARIZ,1-GANA,1I-
6dr/fr L

Hubbell Trading Post,Root Cellar (Hubbell Trading Post National Historic Site)
HABS AZ-137-F
HABS ARIZ,1-GANA,1J
1dr/fr L

Hubbell Trading Post,Storage Building (Hubbell Trading Post,Comfort Station; Hubbell Trading Post National Historic Site)
HABS AZ-137-G
HABS ARIZ,1-GANA,1K-
2dr/fr L

Hubbell Trading Post,Visitor Contact Center; see Hubbell Trading Post,Navajo Day School

Hubbell,J. L. Trading Post,House (Hubbell Trading Post National Historic Site)
State Rt. 3 (Navajo Indian Reservation)
HABS AZ-60
HABS ARIZ,1-GANA,1B-
8dr L

Hubbell,J. L.,Trading Post,HB-1 (Hubbell Trading Post National Historic Site)
State Rt. 3 (Navajo Indian Reservation)
HABS AZ-59
HABS ARIZ,1-GANA,1A-
7dr L

Hubbell,J. L.,Trading Post,Two-Story Barn (Hubbell Trading Post National Historic Site)
State Rt. 3 (Navajo Indian Reservation)
HABS AZ-61
HABS ARIZ,1-GANA,1C-
7dr L

Hubbell,J. L.,Trading Post,Unfinished Shed (Hubbell Trading Post National Historic Site)
State Rt. 3 (Navajo Indian Reservation)
HABS AZ-62
HABS ARIZ,1-GANA,1D-
4dr L

HOLBROOK VIC.

Rio Puerco Bridge
Mainline Rd. Spanning Rio Puerco,Petrified Forest
HAER AZ-13
HAER 1991(HAER):18
29ph/22pg/3pc L

NAVAJO VIC.

Painted Desert Inn (Petrified Forest National Park)
HABS AZ-161
12dr H

Petrified Forest National Park; see Painted Desert Inn

TEEC NOS POS VIC.

Beesh Ligaii Bighan (Silver Structure; Feature 9)
W-NW of St. Hwy. 506 and Indian Hwy. 63 Junction
HAER AZ-32
HAER DLC/PP-1993:AZ-2
6ph/16pg/1pc/fr L

Feature 9; see Beesh Ligaii Bighan

Silver Structure; see Beesh Ligaii Bighan

COCHISE COUNTY

BOWIE VIC.

Fort Bowie (Ruins) (Fort Bowie National Historic Site)
HABS AZ-63
HABS ARIZ,2-BOWI.V,1- & 1A-
1dr/3ph/fr L

Fort Bowie National Historic Site; see Fort Bowie (Ruins)

Fort Bowie National Historic Site; see Fort Bowie,Cavalry Barracks

Fort Bowie National Historic Site; see Fort Bowie,Commanding Officer's Quarters

Fort Bowie National Historic Site; see Fort Bowie,Corrals

Fort Bowie National Historic Site; see Fort Bowie,Guardhouse

Fort Bowie National Historic Site; see Fort Bowie,Infantry Barracks

Fort Bowie National Historic Site; see Fort Bowie,Magazine

Fort Bowie National Historic Site; see Fort Bowie,New Hospital

Fort Bowie National Historic Site; see Fort Bowie,Schoolhouse

Fort Bowie National Historic Site; see Fort Bowie,Sutler's Store

Fort Bowie,Cavalry Barracks (Fort Bowie National Historic Site)
HABS AZ-63-A
HABS ARIZ,2-BOWI.V,1C-
5dr L

Fort Bowie,Commanding Officer's Quarters (Fort Bowie National Historic Site)
HABS AZ-63-D
HABS ARIZ,2-BOWI.V,1F-
2dr L

Fort Bowie,Corrals (Fort Bowie National Historic Site)
HABS AZ-63-B
HABS ARIZ,2-BOWI.V,1D-
1dr L

Fort Bowie,Guardhouse (Fort Bowie National Historic Site)
HABS AZ-63-E
HABS ARIZ,2-BOWI.V,1G-
1dr L

Fort Bowie,Infantry Barracks (Fort Bowie National Historic Site)
HABS AZ-63-C
HABS ARIZ,2-BOWI.V,1E-
1dr L

Fort Bowie,Magazine (Fort Bowie National Historic Site)
HABS AZ-63-I
HABS ARIZ,2-BOWI.V,1L-
1dr L

Fort Bowie,New Hospital (Fort Bowie National Historic Site)
HABS AZ-63-G
HABS ARIZ,2-BOWIV,1I-
3dr L

Fort Bowie,Schoolhouse (Fort Bowie National Historic Site)
HABS AZ-63-F
HABS ARIZ,2-BOWI.V,1H-
1dr L

Fort Bowie,Sutler's Store (Fort Bowie National Historic Site)
HABS AZ-63-H
HABS ARIZ,2-BOWI.V,1J-
4dr L

FAIRBANK

Fairbank Commercial Company Building
HABS AZ-76
HABS ARIZ,2-FAIRB,2-
1ph L

Fairbank Hotel
HABS AZ-75
HABS ARIZ,2-FAIRB,1-
5ph L

FAIRBANK VIC.

San Pablo de Quiburi Mission (Ruins); see Santa Ana de Quiburi Mission (Ruins)

Santa Ana de Quiburi Mission (Ruins) (San Pablo de Quiburi Mission (Ruins))
San Pedro River Vic.
HABS AZ-16
HABS ARIZ,2-FAIRB.V,1-
2ph/1pg/fr L

TOMBSTONE

Allen Street (Commercial Building)
HABS AZ-78
HABS ARIZ,2-TOMB,14-
1ph L

Allen Street (Commercial Building) (Shop Number 2)
HABS AZ-9-B
HABS ARIZ,2-TOMB,16-
1dr/1ph/1pg/fr L

Allen Street (Commercial Building) (Shop Number 3)
HABS AZ-9
HABS ARIZ,2-TOMB,17-
1dr/1ph/1pg/fr L

Allen Street (Commercial Building,Door) (Shop Number 1 (Door))
HABS AZ-9-A
HABS ARIZ,2-TOMB,15-
1dr/1ph/fr L

Bird Cage Theatre
Allen St.
HABS AZ-10
HABS ARIZ,2-TOMB,18-
3dr/2ph/2pg/fr L

Can Can Saloon
Fourth & Allen Sts.
HABS AZ-82
HABS ARIZ,2-TOMB,2-
1ph L

Cashman,Nellie,House
Toughnut & Sixth Sts.
HABS AZ-80
HABS ARIZ,2-TOMB,3-
1ph L

City Hall
Fremont St.
HABS AZ-86
HABS ARIZ,2-TOMB,4-
1ph L

City Hall,Old
Fremont St.
HABS AZ-48
HABS ARIZ,2-TOMB,5-
2ph L

Cochise County Courthouse
Toughnut & Third Sts.
HABS AZ-83
HABS ARIZ,2-TOMB,6-
5ph L

Crystal Palace Saloon
Allen & Fifth Sts.
HABS AZ-7
HABS ARIZ,2-TOMB,1-
1dr/4ph/2pg/fr L

Episcopal Church
Third & Safford Sts.
HABS AZ-84
HABS ARIZ,2-TOMB,7-
1ph L

Fifth Street (Commercial Building)
HABS AZ-79
HABS ARIZ,2-TOMB,12-
1ph L

Fire Station
Toughnut St.
HABS AZ-85
HABS ARIZ,2-TOMB,8-
1ph L

Fremont Street (Commercial Buildings,Ruins)
HABS AZ-49
HABS ARIZ,2-TOMB,19-
1ph L

Rose Tree Inn
Toughnut & Fourth Sts.
HABS AZ-81
HABS ARIZ,2-TOMB,9-
1ph L

Shop Number 1 (Door); see Allen Street (Commercial Building,Door)

Shop Number 2; see Allen Street (Commercial Building)

Shop Number 3; see Allen Street (Commercial Building)

Documentation: **ct** color transparencies **dr** measured drawings **fr** field records **pc** photograph captions **pg** pages of text **ph** photographs

South Third Street (Fence,Fenceposts & Gate)
HABS AZ-77
HABS ARIZ,2-TOMB,10A-
1ph L

Third & Allen Streets (Bank)
HABS AZ-87
HABS ARIZ,2-TOMB,11-
5ph/fr L

WILLCOX

House & Fence
HABS AZ-55
HABS ARIZ,2-WILCO,1-
2ph L

COCONINO COUNTY

COCONINO VIC.

Grand Canyon Power Plant
HAER AZ-2
HAER ARIZ,3-COCO.V,1-
13ph/1pc L

FLAGSTAFF VIC.

Big House Ruin; see Wupatki,Wukoki Ruin

Wupatki, Citadel Ruin
U.S. Highway 89, Loop Rd.
HABS AZ-152-C
HABS DLC/PP-1992:AZ-5
1ph/1pc L

Wupatki,Wukoki Ruin (Big House Ruin)
U.S. Highway 89, Loop Rd.
HABS AZ-152-B
HABS DLC/PP-1992:AZ-5
1ph/1pc L

Wupatki,Wupatki Ruin
U.S. Highway 89, Loop Rd.
HABS AZ-152-A
HABS DLC/PP-1992:AZ-5
3ph/1pc L

FLASGSTAFF VIC.

Wupatki,Ball Court
U.S. Highway 89, Loop Rd.
HABS AZ-152-D
HABS DLC/PP-1992:AZ-5
3ph/1pc L

GRAND CANYON N. P.

El Tovar Hotel (Grand Canyon National Park)
HABS AZ-74
HABS ARIZ,3-GRACAN,1-
7ph/1pc L

Grand Canyon National Park; see El Tovar Hotel

Kaibab Trail Suspension Bridge
Spanning Colorado River
HAER AZ-1
HAER ARIZ,3-GRACAN,3-
30ph/13pg/2pc L

Railroad Depot
HABS AZ-11
HABS ARIZ,3-GRACAN,2-
13ph/1pc L

Water Disposal System; see Water Reclamation Plant

Water Reclamation Plant (Water Reuse System; Water Disposal System)
Grand Canyon Natl Park
HAER AZ-3
HAER ARIZ,3-GRACAN,4-
44ph/14pg/3pc L

Water Reuse System; see Water Reclamation Plant

PAGE VIC.

Glen Canyon National Recreation Area; see Lee's Ferry

Glen Canyon National Recreation Area; see Lee's Ferry,Chicken House

Glen Canyon National Recreation Area; see Lee's Ferry,Fort

Glen Canyon National Recreation Area; see Lee's Ferry,Old Spencer Cabin

Glen Canyon National Recreation Area; see Lee's Ferry,Post Office

Glen Canyon National Recreation Area; see Lee's Ferry,Root Cellar

Lee's Ferry (Glen Canyon National Recreation Area)
U.S. Rt. Alt. 89
HABS AZ-58
HABS ARIZ,3-PAG.V,1-
1dr L

Lee's Ferry,Chicken House (Glen Canyon National Recreation Area)
U.S. Rt. Alt. 89
HABS AZ-58-C
HABS ARIZ,3-PAG.V,1C-
1dr L

Lee's Ferry,Fort (Glen Canyon National Recreation Area)
U.S. Rt. Alt. 89
HABS AZ-58-A
HABS ARIZ,3-PAG.V,1A-
3dr/fr L

Lee's Ferry,Old Spencer Cabin (Lee's Ferry,Silt Cabin; Spencer Building; Glen Canyon National Recreation Area)
U.S. Rt. Alt. 89
HABS AZ-58-E
HABS ARIZ,3-PAG.V,1E-
3dr L

Lee's Ferry,Post Office (Glen Canyon National Recreation Area)
U.S. Rt. Alt. 89
HABS AZ-58-B
HABS ARIZ,3-PAG.V,1B-
3dr L

Lee's Ferry,Root Cellar (Glen Canyon National Recreation Area)
U.S. Rt. Alt. 89
HABS AZ-58-D
HABS ARIZ,3-PAG.V,1D-
1dr L

Lee's Ferry,Silt Cabin; see Lee's Ferry,Old Spencer Cabin

Spencer Building; see Lee's Ferry,Old Spencer Cabin

WALPI

Pueblo of the First Mesa; see Pueblo of Walpi

Pueblo of Walpi (Pueblo of the First Mesa)
Hopi Reservation
HABS AZ-69
4dr H

GILA COUNTY

ROOSEVELT VIC.

Roosevelt Power Canal & Diversion Dam
Parallels the Salt River
HAER AZ-4
HAER ARIZ,4-ROOS.V,1-
82ph/82pg/7pc L

GRAHAM COUNTY

SAFFORD VIC.

Columbine Ranger Station (Columbine Work Station)
Coronado Nt'l Forest,Milepoet 143, St. Hwy. 336
HABS AZ-160
2ph/3pc H

Columbine Ranger Station,Garage (Columbine Work Station,Garage)
Coronado Nat'l Forest, Milepost 1343, St. Hwy. 366
HABS AZ-160-B
6ph/10pg/1pc H

Columbine Ranger Station,Residence (Columbine Work Station,Residence)
Coronado Nat'l Forest, Milepost 143, St. Hwy. 366
HABS AZ-160-A
10ph/10pg/1pc H

Columbine Work Station; see Columbine Ranger Station

Columbine Work Station,Garage; see Columbine Ranger Station,Garage

Columbine Work Station,Residence; see Columbine Ranger Station,Residence

MARICOPA COUNTY

CAVECREEK

Dome in the Desert
Grapevine Rd.
HABS AZ-148
HABS 1991(HABS):36
4dr/fr L

PHOENIX

Anderson House
505 N. Seventh St.
HABS AZ-30
HABS ARIZ,7-PHEN,1-
2ph L

Arizona Biltmore,Bathhouse & Cabanas
NE Corner,Twentyfourth St. & Missouri Ave.
HABS AZ-149-A
HABS DLC/PP-1992:AZ-4
51ph/10pg/3pc L

Arizona State Capitol Building
1700 W. Washington St.
HABS AZ-112
HABS ARIZ,7-PHEN,12-
4ph/1pc/4ct L

County/City Administration Building
Washington St.
HABS AZ-71
HABS ARIZ,7-PHEN,11-
4ph/3pg/1pc L

725 East Washington Street (House)
HABS AZ-35
HABS ARIZ,7-PHEN,10-
1ph L

Evans House
Washington St. & Eleventh Ave.
HABS AZ-31
HABS ARIZ,7-PHEN,2-
3ph L

Ford Hotel
Washington St. & Second Ave.
HABS AZ-32
HABS ARIZ,7-PHEN,3-
1ph L

Messinger House
Wood St. & Ninth Ave.
HABS AZ-36
HABS ARIZ,7-PHEN,4-
1ph L

606 1/2-608 Monroe Street (House)
HABS AZ-38
HABS ARIZ,7-PHEN,9-
1ph L

3320 North Central Avenue (House)
HABS AZ-33
HABS ARIZ,7-PHEN,7-
1ph L

3502 North Central Avenue (House)
HABS AZ-34
HABS ARIZ,7-PHEN,8-
1ph L

Old Crosscut Canal
No. Side of Salt River
HAER AZ-21
HAER DLC/PP-1993:AZ-2
36ph/17pg/4pc L

Pauson,Rose,House (Ruins) (Shiprock)
Thirty-Second St.
HABS AZ-143
HABS ARIZ,7-PHEN,13-
9ph/3pg/1pc/fr L

Rosens House
139 N. Sixth St.
HABS AZ-37
HABS ARIZ,7-PHEN,5-
1ph L

San Francisco Canal
Between 40th & Weir & 36th St. & Roeser Rd.
HAER AZ-8
HAER ARIZ,7-PHEN,14-
12ph/40pg/2pc L

Shiprock; see Pauson,Rose,House (Ruins)

Stroud Building
31-33 N. Central Ave.
HABS AZ-147
HABS DLC/PP-1992:AZ-4
24ph/21pg/5pc/fr L

Sweatnan House
Adams St. & Eighteenth Ave.
HABS AZ-39
HABS ARIZ,7-PHEN,6-
2ph L

PHOENIX VIC.

Arizona Canal
No. of the Salt River
HAER AZ-19
HAER DLC/PP-1992:AZ-3
62ph/70pg/6pc L

Bartlett Dam
Verde River
HAER AZ-25
HAER 1991(HAER):18
70ph/90pg/7pc L

Horse Mesa Dam
Salt River,65 mi. East of Phoenix
HAER AZ-15
HAER 1992(HAER):AZ-1
65ph/1pg/5pc L

Mormon Flat Dam
On Salt Riv.,Eastern Maricopa Co.,E. of Phoenix
HAER AZ-14
HAER 1992(HAER):AZ-1
61ph/156pg/6pc L

Pleasant Dam; see Waddell Dam

Waddell Dam (Pleasant Dam)
on the Agua Fria River,35 mi. NW of Phoenix
HAER AZ-11
HAER DLC/PP-1992:AZ-2
153ph/131pg/13pc L

SCOTTSDALE

City Hall
Civil Center
HABS AZ-141
HABS ARIZ,7-SCOT,1-
8ph/4pg/1pc L

TEMPE

Arizona Eastern Railroad Bridge
(Southern Pacific Railroad Bridge)
Spanning Salt River
HAER AZ-18
HAER 1991(HABS):17
8ph/21pg/1pc/fr L

Ash Avenue Bridge (Temple Bridge; Old Tempe Bridge; Salt River Bridge)
Spanning Salt River at Foot of Ash Avenue
HAER AZ-29
HAER 1991(HAER):18
50ph/33pg/6pc/fr L

Cross Cut Hydro Plant
North Side of Salt River
HAER AZ-30
HAER 1991(HAER):18
29ph/17pg/4pc L

Crosscut Steam Plant
N. side Salt River near Mill Ave. & Washington St.
HAER AZ-20
HAER DLC/PP-1993:AZ-2
34ph/38pg/3pc L

Crosscut Steam Plant,Ancillary Hydro Unit
N. side Salt River near Mill Ave. & Washington St.
HAER AZ-20-A
HAER DLC/PP-1993:AZ-2
3ph/1pc L

Crosscut Steam Plant,Indian Bend Pond & Pump Ditch
N. side Salt River near Mill Ave. & Washington St.
HAER AZ-20-B
HAER DLC/PP-1993:AZ-2
14ph/2pc L

Highline Canal and Pumping Station
So. side of Salt River btwn. Tempe,Phoenix & Mesa
HAER AZ-23
30ph/1pg/3pc L

Old Tempe Bridge; see Ash Avenue Bridge

Salt River Bridge; see Ash Avenue Bridge

Southern Pacific Railroad Bridge; see Arizona Eastern Railroad Bridge

Documentation: **ct** color transparencies **dr** measured drawings **fr** field records
pc photograph captions **pg** pages of text **ph** photographs

Tempe Canal
South Side Salt River in Tempe,Mesa & Phoenix
HAER AZ-16
HAER 1991(HABS):17
23ph/73pg/4pc L

Tempe Municipal Building
31 E. Fifth St.
HABS AZ-142
HABS ARIZ,7-TEMP,1-
5ph/13pg/1pc L

Temple Bridge; see Ash Avenue Bridge

Western Canal
So. side of Salt River btwn. Tempe,Phoenix & Mesa
HAER AZ-22
HAER 1992(HAER):AZ-1
22ph/25pg/3pc L

TEMPE & PHOENIX

Grand Canal
North side of Salt River
HAER AZ-17
HAER 1991(HAER):18
36ph/25pg/4pc L

WICKENBURG

Center Street (House)
HABS AZ-52
HABS ARIZ,7-WICK,1-
1ph L

South Flont Street (House)
HABS AZ-53
HABS ARIZ,7-WICK,3-
1ph L

South Flont Street (House)
HABS AZ-54
HABS ARIZ,7-WICK,2-
1ph L

MOHAVE COUNTY

MOCCASIN VIC.

Pipe Spring Fort (Pipe Spring National Monument; Windsor Castle)
HABS AZ-18
HABS ARIZ,8-MOC.V,1-
14dr/11ph/4pg/fr L

Pipe Spring National Monument; see Pipe Spring Fort

Windsor Castle; see Pipe Spring Fort

NAVAJO COUNTY

HOLBROOK

Holbrook Bridge
Spanning Little Colorado River
HAER AZ-9
HAER 1991(HAER):18
21ph/2pg/2pc L

KAYENTA VIC.

Cliff Dwelling of Keet Seel (Navajo National Monument)
Navajo Reservation
HABS AZ-70
HABS ARIZ,9-KAYT.V,1-
3dr L

Navajo National Monument; see Cliff Dwelling of Keet Seel

SHOWLOW VIC.

Cedar Canyon Bridge
Spanning Cedar Canyon at Hwy. 60
HAER AZ-26
HAER DLC/PP-1993:AZ-2
22ph/1pg/3pc L

Corduroy Creek Bridge
Spanning Corduroy Creek at Hwy. 60
HAER AZ-27
HAER DLC/PP-1993:AZ-2
29ph/22pg/3pc L

PIMA COUNTY

AJO VIC.

Bates Well,Corral
Growler Wash
HABS AZ-155-C
HABS DLC/PP-1992:AZ-5
1ph/1pc L

Bates Well,Cowhand House
Growler Wash
HABS AZ-155-A
HABS DLC/PP-1992:AZ-5
2ph/1pc L

Bates Well,Jacal
Growler Wash
HABS AZ-155-B
HABS DLC/PP-1992:AZ-5
1ph/1pc L

Hocker Well,Jacal (Organ Pipe Cactus National Monument)
HABS AZ-154-A
HABS DLC/PP-1992:AZ-5
2ph/1pc L

Organ Pipe Cactus National Monument; see Hocker Well,Jacal

ARIVACA

Arivaca Ranch
HABS AZ-88
HABS ARIZ,10-ARIV,2-
3ph L

Double House
HABS AZ-20
HABS ARIZ,10-ARIV,5-
1ph L

House
HABS AZ-21
HABS ARIZ,10-ARIV,3-
1ph L

House
HABS AZ-22
HABS ARIZ,10-ARIV,4-
1ph L

House & Addition
HABS AZ-23
HABS ARIZ,10-ARIV,6-
1ph L

Houses
HABS AZ-24
HABS ARIZ,10-ARIV,7-
1ph L

Santa Gertrudes de Arivaca Mission (Ruins)
HABS AZ-8
HABS ARIZ,10-ARIV,1-
1dr/2ph/1pg/fr L

LUKEVILLE VIC.

Gachado Well,Adobe House
Camino de Dos Republicas
HABS AZ-153-A
HABS DLC/PP-1992:AZ-5
1ph/1pc L

TOHONO O'ODHAM RESV.

San Xavier Hall
San Xavier Rd.
HABS AZ-150
HABS DLC/PP-1992:AZ-2
4dr L

TUCSON

Adobe Brick Kilns (Ruins)
HABS AZ-90
HABS ARIZ,10-TUCSO,7-
2ph L

Ahloy House; see Barrio Libre

Aragon,Albert,House
402 Second St.
HABS AZ-89
HABS ARIZ,10-TUCSO,5-
1ph L

Aros House; see Barrio Libre

Barrio Historico; see Barrio Libre

Barrio Libre (Barrio Historico; 519-527 South Convent Avenue (Apartments))
HABS AZ-73-10
HABS ARIZ,10-TUCSO,30/10-
2dr/2ph/3pg/1pc/2ct L

Barrio Libre (Barrio Historico; 440-446 South Convent Avenue (House))
HABS AZ-73-11
HABS ARIZ,10-TUCSO,30/11-
2dr/5ph/6pg/1pc/fr L

Barrio Libre (Barrio Historico; 500-502 South Convent Avenue (House))
HABS AZ-73-12
HABS ARIZ,10-TUCSO,30/12-
2dr/1ph/5pg/1pc/fr L

Barrio Libre (Barrio Historico; 510-512 South Convent Avenue (House))
HABS AZ-73-13
HABS ARIZ,10-TUCSO,30/13-
2dr/3ph/5pg/1pc/fr L

Barrio Libre (Barrio Historico; 168 1/2 West Kennedy Street (House,Addition); Bustamante,Antonio,Addition)
HABS AZ-73-14
HABS ARIZ,10-TUCSO,30/14-
2dr/3ph/1pg/1pc/1ct/fr L

Barrio Libre (Barrio Historico; 29-33 West Kennedy Street (House))
HABS AZ-73-20
HABS ARIZ,10-TUCSO,30/20-
1ph/1pc L

Barrio Libre (Barrio Historico; 74 West Kennedy Street (House))
HABS AZ-73-21
HABS ARIZ,10-TUCSO,30/21-
2dr/1ph/1pc L

Barrio Libre (Barrio Historico; 147 West Kennedy Street (House))
HABS AZ-73-22
HABS ARIZ,10-TUCSO,30/22-
2dr/1ph/3pg/1pc L

Barrio Libre (Barrio Historico; 477 South Meyer Avenue (House); 155-159 West Kennedy Street (House))
HABS AZ-73-23
HABS ARIZ,10-TUCSO,30/23-
2dr/1ph/3pg/1pc L

Barrio Libre (Barrio Historico; 530-576 South Eighth Avenue (House))
HABS AZ-73-24
HABS ARIZ,10-TUCSO,30/24-
2dr/2ph/5pg/1pc L

Barrio Libre (Barrio Historico; 363 South Meyer Avenue (House))
HABS AZ-73-27
HABS ARIZ,10-TUCSO,30/27-
2dr/1ph/1pc L

Barrio Libre (Barrio Historico; 527-529 South Meyer Avenue (House))
HABS AZ-73-28
HABS ARIZ,10-TUCSO,30/28-
2dr/3ph/5pg/1pc/fr L

Barrio Libre (Barrio Historico; 609-619 South Meyer Avenue (Apartments))
HABS AZ-73-30
HABS ARIZ,10-TUCSO,30/30-
2dr/1ph/3pg/1pc L

Barrio Libre (Barrio Historico; 486-490 South Meyer Avenue (Building); Lucky's Market)
HABS AZ-73-31
HABS ARIZ,10-TUCSO,30/31-
1dr/3ph/3pg/1pc/2ct L

Barrio Libre (Barrio Historico; 488-498 South Meyer Avenue (Apartments))
HABS AZ-73-32
HABS ARIZ,10-TUCSO,30/32-
2ph/3pg/1pc/2ct L

Barrio Libre (Barrio Historico; 508-518 South Meyer Avenue (Apartments))
HABS AZ-73-33
HABS ARIZ,10-TUCSO,30/33-
3ph/3pg/1pc/1ct L

Barrio Libre (Barrio Historico; 520-526 South Meyer Avenue (Apartments))
HABS AZ-73-34
HABS ARIZ,10-TUSC,30/34-
1ph/3pg/1pc L

Barrio Libre (Barrio Historico; 558-564 South Meyer Avenue (Apartments))
HABS AZ-73-35
HABS ARIZ,10-TUCS,30/35-
1ph/4pg/1pc/1ct L

Barrio Libre (Barrio Historico; 614 South Meyer Avenue (Building))
HABS AZ-73-36
HABS ARIZ,10-TUCSO,30/36-
1ph/3pg/1pc L

Barrio Libre (Barrio Historico; 209-219 West Seventeenth Street (Apartments))
HABS AZ-73-43
HABS ARIZ,10-TUCSO,30/43-
1ph/3pg/1pc L

Barrio Libre (Barrio Historico; 139 West Simpson Street (Building))
HABS AZ-73-44
HABS ARIZ,10-TUCSO,30/44-
1ph/1pc L

Barrio Libre (Barrio Historico; 141-147 West Simpson Street (Building))
HABS AZ-73-45
HABS ARIZ,10-TUCSO,30/45-
1ph/1pc L

Barrio Libre (Barrio Historico; 400 West Simpson Street (Commercial Building); Elysian Grove Market)
HABS AZ-73-46
HABS ARIZ,10-TUCSO,30/46-
1ph/1pc L

Barrio Libre (Barrio Historico; 367-371 South Meyer Avenue (House))
HABS AZ-73-51
HABS ARIZ,10-TUCSO,30/51-
3pg/fr L

Barrio Libre (Barrio Historico; 471-473 South Convent Avenue (House))
HABS AZ-73-52
HABS ARIZ,10-TUCSO,30/52-
1ph/3pg/1pc L

Barrio Libre (Barrio Historico; 447-451 South Main Avenue (House))
HABS AZ-73-53
HABS ARIZ,10-TUCSO,30/53
4dr/2ph/6pg/1pc/fr L

Barrio Libre (Barrio Historico; 441-447 South Convent Avenue (House))
HABS AZ-73-7
HABS ARIZ,10-TUCSO,30/7-
2dr/1ph/3pg/1pc L

Barrio Libre (Barrio Historico; 451 South Convent Avenue (House))
HABS AZ-73-8
HABS ARIZ,10-TUCSO,30/8-
2dr/1ph/3pg/1pc L

Barrio Libre (Barrio Historico; 479 & 481 South Convent Avenue (House))
HABS AZ-73-9
HABS ARIZ,10-TUCSO,30/9
1dr/2ph/3pg/1pc/1ct L

Barrio Libre (Barrio Historico; Prince Chapel,African M. E. Church)
S. Convent Ave. & W. Seventeenth St.
HABS AZ-73-40
HABS ARIZ,10-TUCSO,30/40-
2dr/1ph/3pg/1pc L

Barrio Libre (Barrio Historico; Wishing Shrine)
S. Main Ave.
HABS AZ-73-50
HABS ARIZ,10-TUCSO,30/50-
2ph/1pc/2ct L

Barrio Libre (Barrio Historico)
W. Kennedy,& W. 17th Sts.,Meyer & Convent Aves.
HABS AZ-73
HABS ARIZ,10-TUCSO,30-
32dr/13ph/18pg/2pc/fr L

Barrio Libre (Barrio Historico; Rubio House)
140 W. Kennedy St.
HABS AZ-73-42
HABS ARIZ,10-TUCSO,30/42-
2dr/2ph/5pg/1pc/fr L

Barrio Libre (Barrio Historico; Aros House)
145 W. Kennedy St.
HABS AZ-73-2
HABS ARIZ,10-TUCSO,30/2-
2dr/1ph/3pg/1pc L

Barrio Libre (Barrio Historico; Preciado House)
148-150 W. Kennedy St.
HABS AZ-73-39
HABS ARIZ,10-TUCSO,30/39-
2dr/3ph/6pg/1pc/1ct/fr L

Barrio Libre (Barrio Historico; Terrazas House)
418 S. Convent Ave.
HABS AZ-73-47
HABS ARIZ,10-TUCSO,30/47-
2ph/3pg/1pc L

Barrio Libre (Barrio Historico; Valencia House)
432-436 S. Convent Ave.
HABS AZ-73-48
HABS ARIZ,10-TUCSO,30/48-
2dr/4ph/7pg/1pc/fr L

Barrio Libre (Barrio Historico; Bojorquez House)
459 S. Convent Ave.
HABS AZ-73-4
HABS ARIZ,10-TUCSO,30/4-
2dr/1ph/3pg/1pc L

Documentation: **ct** color transparencies **dr** measured drawings **fr** field records
pc photograph captions **pg** pages of text **ph** photographs

Barrio Libre (Barrio Historico; Romero House)
469-471 S. Convent Ave.
HABS AZ-73-41
HABS ARIZ,10-TUCSO,30/41-
1ph/3pg/1pc L

Barrio Libre (Barrio Historico; Escalante House)
482-484 S. Convent Ave.
HABS AZ-73-16
HABS ARIZ,10-TUCSO,30/16-
2dr/1ph/5pg/1pc/fr L

Barrio Libre (Barrio Historico; Diaz House)
483 S. Convent Ave.
HABS AZ-73-15
HABS ARIZ,10-TUCSO,30/15-
1ph/3pg/1pc/2ct L

Barrio Libre (Barrio Historico; Bustamante,Antonio,House)
485-489 S. Meyer Ave. & 186 W. Kennedy St.
HABS AZ-73-5
HABS ARIZ,10-TUCSO,30/5-
3dr/2ph/8pg/1pc/1ct/fr L

Barrio Libre (Barrio Historico; Ahloy House)
492-494 S. Convent Ave.
HABS AZ-73-1
HABS ARIZ,10-TUCSO,30/1-
2dr/1ph/3pg/1pc/fr L

Barrio Libre (Barrio Historico; Garcia House)
496-498 S. Convent Ave.
HABS AZ-73-19
HABS ARIZ,10-TUCSO,30/19-
2dr/2ph/5pg/1pc/1ct/fr L

Barrio Libre (Barrio Historico; Munoz House)
499-501 S. Meyer Ave.
HABS AZ-73-37
HABS ARIZ,10-TUCSO,30/37-
2dr/1ph/6pg/1pc L

Barrio Libre (Barrio Historico; Villa House)
504-506 S. Convent Ave.
HABS AZ-73-49
HABS ARIZ,10-TUCSO,30/49-
2dr/1ph/6pg/1pc/fr L

Barrio Libre (Barrio Historico; Bustamante,Ramon,House)
505 S. Meyer Ave.
HABS AZ-73-6
HABS ARIZ,10-TUCSO,30/6-
2dr/3ph/6pg/1pc/fr L

Barrio Libre (Barrio Historico; Fimbres House Number 1)
509-513 S. Meyer Ave.
HABS AZ-73-17
HABS ARIZ,10-TUCSO,30/17-
2dr/1ph/5pg/1pc/fr L

Barrio Libre (Barrio Historico; Lopez House)
517 S. Convent Ave.
HABS AZ-73-26
HABS ARIZ,10-TUCSO,30/26-
2dr/1ph/2pg/1pc/1ct L

Barrio Libre (Barrio Historico; Fimbres House Number 2)
521-525 S. Meyer Ave.
HABS AZ-73-18
HABS ARIZ,10-TUCSO,30/18-
2dr/1ph/4pg/1pc/fr L

Barrio Libre (Barrio Historico; Wherehouse,The)
551-557 S. Meyer Ave.
HABS AZ-73-29
HABS ARIZ,10-TUCSO,30/29-
2dr/3ph/7pg/1pc/2ct/fr L

Barrio Libre (Barrio Historico; Bernal House)
571 S. Meyer Ave.
HABS AZ-73-3
HABS ARIZ,10-TUCSO,30/3-
2dr/1ph/5pg/1pc/1ct/fr L

Barrio Libre (Barrio Historico; Palafox House)
575-585 S. Meyer Ave.
HABS AZ-73-38
HABS ARIZ,10-TUCSO,30/38-
4dr/4ph/6pg/1pc/fr L

Barrio Libre (Barrio Historico; Lee Lung Sing Market)
600 S. Meyer Ave.
HABS AZ-73-25
HABS ARIZ,10-TUCSO,30/25-
2dr/1ph/3pg/1pc/1ct L

Bechtold House
Fifth & Main Sts.
HABS AZ-92
HABS ARIZ,10-TUCSO,6-
1ph L

Bernal House; see Barrio Libre

Bojorquez House; see Barrio Libre

Building No. 4; see Tucson Plant Material Center,Machinery Shed

Bustamante,Antonio,Addition; see Barrio Libre

Bustamante,Antonio,House; see Barrio Libre

Bustamante,Ramon,House; see Barrio Libre

Carrillo,Leopoldo,House (Priests' House)
1005 Mission Ave.
HABS AZ-5
HABS ARIZ,10-TUCSO,1-
5dr/5ph/1pg/fr L

Church of San Augustine
HABS AZ-15
HABS ARIZ,10-TUCSO,4-
2ph/1pg L

Courthouse Plaza (Row Houses)
HABS AZ-131
HABS ARIZ,10-TUCSO,19-
3ph L

Desert Botanical Laboratory Complex
Tumamoc Hill
HABS AZ-138
HABS ARIZ,10-TUCSO,31-
2dr/1ph/34pg/1pc/fr L

Desert Botanical Laboratory,Chemistry Building
Tumamoc Hill
HABS AZ-138-C
HABS ARIZ,10-TUCSO,31C-
2dr/3ph/fr L

Desert Botanical Laboratory,Forest Service Bldg.
Tumamoc Hill
HABS AZ-138-D
HABS ARIZ,10-TUCSO,31D-
2dr/3ph/fr L

Desert Botanical Laboratory,Main Laboratory Bldg.
Tumamoc Hill
HABS AZ-138-A
HABS ARIZ,10-TUCSO,31A-
4dr/6ph/fr L

Desert Botanical Laboratory,Shop Building
Tumamoc Hill
HABS AZ-138-B
HABS ARIZ,10-TUCSO,31B-
2dr/4ph/fr L

Diaz House; see Barrio Libre

47 East Alameda Street (House)
HABS AZ-93
HABS ARIZ,10-TUCSO,15-
5ph L

Elysian Grove Market; see Barrio Libre

Escalante House; see Barrio Libre

Feldman House
First Ave. & Second St.
HABS AZ-94
HABS ARIZ,10-TUCSO,8-
1ph L

Fickett,Fred W.,House
105 W. Franklin St.
HABS AZ-95
HABS ARIZ,10-TUCSO,9-
2ph L

Fimbres House Number 1; see Barrio Libre

Fimbres House Number 2; see Barrio Libre

Garcia House; see Barrio Libre

Hoff House
W. Franklin St.
HABS AZ-96
HABS ARIZ,10-TUCSO,10-
1ph L

House,Adobe
Paseo Redondo
HABS AZ-91
HABS ARIZ,10-TUCSO,29-
1ph L

Lee Lung Sing Market; see Barrio Libre

Lopez House; see Barrio Libre

Lucky's Market; see Barrio Libre

45-51 Mittenburg Street (House)
HABS AZ-97
HABS ARIZ,10-TUCSO,25-
1ph L

Munoz House; see Barrio Libre

299 North Court Street (House)
HABS AZ-98
HABS ARIZ,10-TUCSO,18-
1ph L

293 North Meyer Street (House)
HABS AZ-99
HABS ARIZ,10-TUCSO,23-
1ph L

124 North Stone Street (House)
HABS AZ-100
HABS ARIZ,10-TUCSO,28-
1ph L

Odermott,Dr.,House
304 N. Church St.
HABS AZ-102
HABS ARIZ,10-TUCSO,11-
1ph L

Palafox House; see Barrio Libre

385 Perry Street (House)
HABS AZ-101
HABS ARIZ,10-TUCSO,26-
1ph L

Police Station
S. Main St.
HABS AZ-50
HABS ARIZ,10-TUCSO,12-
1ph L

Preciado House; see Barrio Libre

Priests' House; see Carrillo,Leopoldo,House

Prince Chapel,African M. E. Church; see Barrio Libre

Robinson,Ballantyne,House
Military Plaza (141 S. Fifth Ave.)
HABS AZ-6
HABS ARIZ,10-TUCSO,2-
6dr/6ph/1pg/fr L

Romero House; see Barrio Libre

Rubio House; see Barrio Libre

San Cosme del Tucson Mission (Ruins)
Menlo Park
HABS AZ-12
HABS ARIZ,10-TUCSO,3-
4ph/5pg L

519-527 South Convent Avenue (Apartments); see Barrio Libre

440-446 South Convent Avenue (House); see Barrio Libre

441-447 South Convent Avenue (House); see Barrio Libre

451 South Convent Avenue (House); see Barrio Libre

471-473 South Convent Avenue (House); see Barrio Libre

479 & 481 South Convent Avenue (House); see Barrio Libre

500-502 South Convent Avenue (House); see Barrio Libre

510-512 South Convent Avenue (House); see Barrio Libre

68 South Convent Street (House)
HABS AZ-103
HABS ARIZ,10-TUCSO,17-
1ph L

530-576 South Eighth Avenue (House); see Barrio Libre

447-451 South Main Avenue (House); see Barrio Libre

212 South Main Street (House)
HABS AZ-105
HABS ARIZ,10-TUCSO,20-
1ph L

315 South Main Street (House)
HABS AZ-104
HABS ARIZ,10-TUCSO,21-
4ph L

820 South Main Street (House)
HABS AZ-106
HABS ARIZ,10-TUCSO,22-
1ph L

488-498 South Meyer Avenue (Apartments); see Barrio Libre

508-518 South Meyer Avenue (Apartments); see Barrio Libre

520-526 South Meyer Avenue (Apartments); see Barrio Libre

558-564 South Meyer Avenue (Apartments); see Barrio Libre

609-619 South Meyer Avenue (Apartments); see Barrio Libre

486-490 South Meyer Avenue (Building); see Barrio Libre

614 South Meyer Avenue (Building); see Barrio Libre

363 South Meyer Avenue (House); see Barrio Libre

367-371 South Meyer Avenue (House); see Barrio Libre

477 South Meyer Avenue (House); see Barrio Libre

527-529 South Meyer Avenue (House); see Barrio Libre

443 South Meyer Street (House,Doorway)
HABS AZ-107
HABS ARIZ,10-TUCSO,24-
1ph L

421 South Sixth Avenue (House)
HABS AZ-108
HABS ARIZ,10-TUCSO,27-
2ph L

St. John the Evangelist Church
3522 S. Seventh Ave.
HABS AZ-51
HABS ARIZ,10-TUCSO,13-
1ph L

Terrazas House; see Barrio Libre

Tucson Plant Material Center
3241 N. Romero Rd.
HABS AZ-159
3ph/9pg/1pc H

Tucson Plant Material Center,Machinery Shed (Building No. 4)
3241 N. Romero Rd.
HABS AZ-159-A
10ph/4pg/2pc H

University of Arizona,Old Main
University of Arizona Campus
HABS AZ-110
HABS ARIZ,10-TUCSO,14A-
3ph L

Valencia House; see Barrio Libre

Villa House; see Barrio Libre

195 West Alameda Street (House)
HABS AZ-109
HABS ARIZ,10-TUCSO,16-
2ph L

147 West Kennedy Street (House); see Barrio Libre

155-159 West Kennedy Street (House); see Barrio Libre

29-33 West Kennedy Street (House); see Barrio Libre

74 West Kennedy Street (House); see Barrio Libre

168 1/2 West Kennedy Street (House,Addition); see Barrio Libre

209-219 West Seventeenth Street (Apartments); see Barrio Libre

139 West Simpson Street (Building); see Barrio Libre

141-147 West Simpson Street (Building); see Barrio Libre

400 West Simpson Street (Commercial Building); see Barrio Libre

Wherehouse,The; see Barrio Libre

Wishing Shrine; see Barrio Libre

TUCSON VIC.

Fort Lowell
Fort Lowell Rd. Vic.
HABS AZ-17
HABS ARIZ,10-TUCSO.V,2-
7dr/9ph/8pg/fr L

Fort Lowell,Officers' Quarters
Fort Lowell Rd. Vic.
HABS AZ-17-A
HABS ARIZ,10-TUCSO.V,2-
6dr/3ph/fr L

Fort Lowell,Post Hospital (Ruins)
Fort Lowell Rd. Vic.
HABS AZ-17-C
HABS ARIZ,10-TUCSO.V,2-
5ph/2pg L

Fort Lowell,Summer Kitchen
Fort Lowell Rd. Vic.
HABS AZ-17-B
HABS ARIZ,10-TUCSO.V,2-
1dr/1ph/fr L

Indian Mission Village of Bac,House Number 1
HABS AZ-111-A
HABS ARIZ,10-TUCSO.V,4-
2ph L

Indian Mission Village of Bac,House Number 2
HABS AZ-111-B
HABS ARIZ,10-TUCSO.V,5-
1ph L

Indian Mission Village of Bac,House Number 3
HABS AZ-111-C
HABS ARIZ,10-TUCSO.V,6-
1ph L

Indian Mission Village of Bac,House Number 4
HABS AZ-111-D
HABS ARIZ,10-TUCSO.V,7-
1ph L

Indian Mission Village of Bac,House Number 5
HABS AZ-111-E
HABS ARIZ,10-TUCSO.V,8-
1ph L

Indian Mission Village of Bac,House Number 6
HABS AZ-111-F
HABS ARIZ,10-TUCSO.V,9-
1ph L

Leon Ranch House
Silver Bell Rd.
HABS AZ-4
HABS ARIZ,10-TUCSO.V,1-
4dr/1ph/fr L

San Xavier del Bac Mission
Mission Rd.
HABS AZ-13
HABS ARIZ,10-TUCSO.V,3-
41dr/207ph/8pg/fr L

PINAL COUNTY

COOLIDGE VIC.

Casa Grande (Ruins) (Casa Grande National Monument)
HABS AZ-14
HABS ARIZ,11-COOL.V,1-
2ph/3pg L

Casa Grande National Monument; see Casa Grande (Ruins)

FLORENCE

Collingwood Hotel,Old; see Post Office,Adobe

Collingwood House
HABS AZ-115
HABS ARIZ,11-FLOR,3-
1ph L

Convent,Old; see Ranch House,Adobe

House
Church Vic.
HABS AZ-120
HABS ARIZ,11-FLOR,7-
1ph L

House
Courthouse Vic.
HABS AZ-116
HABS ARIZ,11-FLOR,9-
1ph L

House
High School Vic.
HABS AZ-118
HABS ARIZ,11-FLOR,8-
1ph L

Land Office
HABS AZ-27
HABS ARIZ,11-FLOR,5-
1ph L

Main Street (House)
HABS AZ-114
HABS ARIZ,11-FLOR,6-
2ph L

Pinal County Courthouse
HABS AZ-130
HABS ARIZ,11-FLOR,4-
1ph L

Post Office,Adobe (Collingwood Hotel,Old)
HABS AZ-119
HABS ARIZ,11-FLOR,1-
2ph L

Ranch House,Adobe (Convent,Old)
HABS AZ-117
HABS ARIZ,11-FLOR,2-
1ph L

PERIDOT VIC.

Coolidge Dam
Gila River
HAER AZ-7
HAER ARIZ,11-PERI.V,1-;DLC/PP-1993:AZ-2
154ph/139pg/10pc L

POSTON VIC.

Blacksmith's Ramada
Gila River Vic.
HABS AZ-113
HABS ARIZ,11-POST.V,1-
2ph L

Double House,Indian
Gila River Vic.
HABS AZ-121
HABS ARIZ,11-POST.V,2-
4ph L

Farmhouse Group,Indian
Gila River Vic.
HABS AZ-123
HABS ARIZ,11-POST.V,3-
1ph L

Farmhouse,Indian Wattle-and-Daub
Gila River Vic.
HABS AZ-122
HABS ARIZ,11-POST.V,4-
2ph L

Farmhouse,Indian Wattle-and-Daub (with Ramada)
Gila River Vic.
HABS AZ-124
HABS ARIZ,11-POST.V,5-
2ph L

SACATON

House,Indian
Vah Ki Vic.
HABS AZ-43
HABS ARIZ,11-SAC,2-
1ph L

SACATON VIC.

Farmhouse,Indian Framed Adobe
HABS AZ-42
HABS ARIZ,11-SAC.V,1-
1ph L

House,Indian
HABS AZ-44
HABS ARIZ,11-SAC.V,2-
1ph L

House,Indian,with Bow Roof
HABS AZ-45
HABS ARIZ,11-SAC.V,3-
2ph L

House,Indian,with Shelter
HABS AZ-46
HABS ARIZ,11-SAC.V,4-
1ph L

House,Indian,with Veranda
HABS AZ-47
HABS ARIZ,11-SAC.V,5-
2ph L

SANTA CRUZ COUNTY

NOGALES VIC.

Kitchen,Pete,Ranch House
Portrero Creek Vic.
HABS AZ-125
HABS ARIZ,12-NOGAL.V,3-
4ph L

San Cayetano de Calabasas (Mission,Ruins)
Santa Cruz River Vic.
HABS AZ-2
HABS ARIZ,12-NOGAL.V,2-
3dr/4ph/1pg/fr L

San Gabriel de Guevavi (Mission,Ruins) (San Miguel de Guevavi (Mission,Ruins); San Rafael de Guevavi (Mission,Ruins); Santos Angeles (Mission,Ruins))
Santa Cruz River Vic.
HABS AZ-1
HABS ARIZ,12-NOGAL.V,1-
2dr/6ph/1pg/fr L

San Miguel de Guevavi (Mission,Ruins); see San Gabriel de Guevavi (Mission,Ruins)

San Rafael de Guevavi (Mission,Ruins); see San Gabriel de Guevavi (Mission,Ruins)

Santos Angeles (Mission,Ruins); see San Gabriel de Guevavi (Mission,Ruins)

PATAGONIA

Commercial Hotel
State Rt. 82 Vic.
HABS AZ-127
HABS ARIZ,12-PAT,1-
1ph L

PATAGONIA VIC.

Fort Crittenden (Ruins)
HABS AZ-126
HABS ARIZ,12-PAT.V,1-
1ph L

TUBAC

House,Mexican
HABS AZ-128
HABS ARIZ,12-TUBA,2-
1ph L

Santa Gertrudes de Tubac (Church)
HABS AZ-129
HABS ARIZ,12-TUBA,1-
2ph L

TUBAC VIC.

San Jose de Tumacacori (Mission,Ruins) (Tumacacori National Monument)
HABS AZ-3
HABS ARIZ,12-TUBA.V,1-
44dr/18ph/4pg/fr L

Tumacacori National Monument; see San Jose de Tumacacori (Mission,Ruins)

YAVAPAI COUNTY

CAMP VERDE

Camp Verde,Officer's House
HABS AZ-25
HABS ARIZ,13-CAMV,1A-
2ph L

Camp Verde,Officer's House
HABS AZ-26
HABS ARIZ,13-CAMV,1B-
1ph L

CAMP VERDE VIC.

Montezuma Castle (Montezuma Castle National Monument)
Off I-17
HABS AZ-151
HABS DLC/PP-1992:AZ-5
1ph/1pc L

Montezuma Castle National Monument; see Montezuma Castle

CAVE CREEK VIC.

Red Point Sheep Bridge; see Verde River Sheep Bridge

Verde River Sheep Bridge (Red Point Sheep Bridge)
Spanning Verde River (Tonto National Forest)
HAER AZ-10
HAER 1990(HAER):1
4dr/42ph/41pg/5pc/fr L

CROWN KING VIC.

Horsethief Basin Resort (Prescott National Forest)
Seven mi. SE of Crown King
HABS AZ-158
13ph/26pg/2pc H

Horsethief Basin Resort,Cabin No. 1 (Prescott National Forest)
Seven miles SE of Crown King
HABS AZ-158-A
4ph/1pc H

Horsethief Basin Resort,Cabin No. 10 (Prescott National Forest)
Seven miles SE of Crown King
HABS AZ-158-J
4ph/1pc H

Horsethief Basin Resort,Cabin No. 2 (Prescott National Forest)
Seven miles SE of Crown King
HABS AZ-158-B
2ph/1pc H

Horsethief Basin Resort,Cabin No. 3 (Prescott National Forest)
Seven miles SE of Crown King
HABS AZ-158-C
3ph/1pc H

Horsethief Basin Resort,Cabin no. 4 (Prescott National Forest)
Seven miles SE of Crown King
HABS AZ-158-D
3ph/1pc H

Horsethief Basin Resort,Cabin No. 5 (Prescott National Forest)
Seven miles SE of Crown King
HABS AZ-158-E
4ph/1pc H

Horsethief Basin Resort,Cabin No. 6 (Prescott National Forest)
Seven miles SE of Crown King
HABS AZ-158-F
4ph/1pc H

Horsethief Basin Resort,Cabin No. 7 (Prescott National Forest)
Seven miles SE of Crown King
HABS AZ-158-G)
3ph/1pc H

Horsethief Basin Resort,Cabin No. 8 (Prescott National Forest)
Seven miles SE of Crown King
HABS AZ-158-H
2ph/1pc H

Horsethief Basin Resort,Cabin No. 9 (Prescott National Forest)
Seven miles SE of Crown King
HABS AZ-158-I
8ph/1pc H

Horsethief Basin Resort,General Store (Prescott National Forest)
Seven miles SE of Crown King
HABS AZ-158-K
5ph/1pc H

Prescott National Forest; see Horsethief Basin Resort

Prescott National Forest; see Horsethief Basin Resort,Cabin No. 1

Prescott National Forest; see Horsethief Basin Resort,Cabin No. 10

Prescott National Forest; see Horsethief Basin Resort,Cabin No. 2

Prescott National Forest; see Horsethief Basin Resort,Cabin No. 3

Prescott National Forest; see Horsethief Basin Resort,Cabin no. 4

Prescott National Forest; see Horsethief Basin Resort,Cabin No. 5

Prescott National Forest; see Horsethief Basin Resort,Cabin No. 6

Prescott National Forest; see Horsethief Basin Resort,Cabin No. 7

Prescott National Forest; see Horsethief Basin Resort,Cabin No. 8

Prescott National Forest; see Horsethief Basin Resort,Cabin No. 9

Prescott National Forest; see Horsethief Basin Resort,General Store

PRESCOTT

Capitol,Old (Governor's Mansion)
W. Gurley St.
HABS AZ-40
HABS ARIZ,13-PRESC,1-
5ph/1pc L

Governor's Mansion; see Capitol,Old

PRESCOTT VIC.

Miller,S. C.,House
Miller's Valley
HABS AZ-41
HABS ARIZ,13-PRESC.V,1-
2ph L

Documentation: **ct** color transparencies **dr** measured drawings **fr** field records
pc photograph captions **pg** pages of text **ph** photographs

YUMA COUNTY

YUMA

Yuma Proving Ground
HAER AZ-5
HAER ARIZ,14-YUMA,1-
38pg/fr L

Bathhouse Row, Fordyce Bathhouse, Hot Springs, Garland County, Arkansas. Entrance foyer, first floor, from south. Photograph by Jack E. Boucher, June 1984 (HABS ARK,26-HOSP,1D-17).

Arkansas

BAXTER COUNTY

COTTER

Cotter Bridge (Ruthven,R. M.,Bridge)
Spanning White River at U.S. Hwy. 62
HAER AR-15
HAER DLC/PP-1992:AR-2
19ph/49pg/2pc L

Ruthven,R. M.,Bridge; see Cotter Bridge

NORFOLK

North Fork Bridge
Spans North Fork of White River at St. Hwy. 5
HAER AR-10
HAER DLC/PP-1992:AR-2
11ph/19pg/1pc L

BENTON COUNTY

GRAVETTE VIC.

Gravette-Decatur Bridge; see Spavinaw Creek Bridge

Spavinaw Creek Bridge
(Gravette-Decatur Bridge)
Spans Spavinaw Creek at Benton Co. Rd. 29
HAER AR-29
HAER DLC/PP-1992:AR-2
10ph/12pg/1pc L

HEALING SPRINGS VIC.

Osage Creek Bridge
HAER AR-30
HAER DLC/PP-1992:AR-2
8ph/2pg/1pc L

PEA RIDGE VIC.

Elkhorn Tavern
Telegraph Rd.
HABS AR-23
HABS AR,4-PEARI.V,1-
(DLC/PP-1992:AR-5)
11dr/12ph/2pc/fr L

SILOAN SPRINGS

Illinois River Bridge (Midway Bridge)
Spanning Illinois River at Benton Co. Rd. 3
HAER AR-28
HAER DLC/PP-1992:AR-2
9ph/22pg/1pc L

Midway Bridge; see Illinois River Bridge

WAR EAGLE

War Eagle Bridge
Spanning War Eagle Creek at Benton Co. Rd. No. 98
HAER AR-50
HAER DLC/PP-1992:AR-2
11ph/12pg/1pc L

CALHOUN COUNTY

CALION

Ouachita River Bridge
Spanning Ouachita River at U.S. Hwy. 167
HAER AR-19
HAER DLC/PP-1992:AR-2
4ph/26pg/1pc L

CALION VIC.

Ouachita River Lock & Dam No. 8
Ouachita River at River Mile 282.8
HAER AR-1
HAER AR,7-CAL.V,1-
49ph/6pg/3pc L

CARROLL COUNTY

BEAVER

Beaver Bridge
Spanning White River at St. Hwy. No. 187
HAER AR-53
HAER DLC/PP-1992:AR-2
7ph/2pg/1pc L

EUREKA SPRINGS

Mattock,F. L. ,Building (Weaver Building)
60 S. Main St.
HABS AR-33
HABS AR,8-EURSP,1-
23ph/1pg/1pc L

Weaver Building; see Mattock,F. L. ,Building

EUREKA SPRINGS VIC.

Mulladay Hollow Bridge
Spanning Mulladay Hollow Creek at County Rd. No.61
HAER AR-43
HAER DLC/PP-1992:AR-2
7ph/3pg/1pc L

OSAGE VIC.

Chaney Log House
Hwy. 68,N side
HABS AR-38
HABS AR,8-OSA.V,1-
7dr/fr L

CHICOT COUNTY

LAKE VILLAGE

Johnson,Lycurgus,House
State Hwy. 142
HABS AR-31
HABS AR,9-LAKVI,1-
11dr/fr L

CLARK COUNTY

OLD ROME VIC.

Little Missouri River Bridge
Spanning Little Missouri River at Co. Rd. No. 179
HAER AR-44
HAER DLC/PP-1992:AR-2
7ph/2pg/1pc L

CLEBURNE COUNTY

HEBER SPRINGS

Swinging Bridge; see Winkley Bridge

Winkley Bridge (Swinging Bridge)
Spanning Little Red River adj. to St. Hwy. No. 110
HAER AR-48
HAER DLC/PP-1992:AR-2
13ph/16pg/1pc L

CONWAY COUNTY

PETIT JEAN STATE PRK

Cedar Creek Bridge
Spanning Cedar Creek adjacent to St. Hwy. 154
HAER AR-31
HAER DLC/PP-1992:AR-2
7ph/11pg/1pc L

SPRINGFIELD

Springfield-Des Arc Bridge
Spans N. Brnch. Cadron Crk. at Springf.-Des Arc Rd
HAER AR-32
HAER DLC/PP-1992:AR-2
3dr/12ph/14pg/1pc/fr L

CRAIGHEAD COUNTY

LAKE CITY

St. Francis River Bridge
HAER AR-18
HAER DLC/PP-1992:AR-2
6ph/32pg/1pc L

CRAWFORD COUNTY

COVE CITY

Lee Creek Bridge
Spanning Lee Creek at State Hwy. No. 220
HAER AR-45
HAER DLC/PP-1992:AR-2
8ph/8pg/1pc/fr L

NATURAL DAM

Lee Creek Bridge (No. 1)
Spanning Lee Creek at St. Hwy. 59
HAER AR-24
HAER DLC/PP-1992:AR-2
6ph/11pg/1pc L

VAN BUREN

Drennen,Col. John,House
HABS AR-21
HABS ARK,17-VANB,1-
1ph/fr L

GARLAND COUNTY

FOUNTAIN LAKE VIC.

South Fork Bridge
Spans S. Fork of Saline Riv.,adj. to St. Hwy. 128
HAER AR-27
HAER DLC/PP-1992:AR-2
1dr/7ph/15pg/1pc/fr L

HOT SPRINGS

Bathhouse Row & Grand Promedade
(Hot Springs National Park)
Central Ave.
HABS AR-28
HABS AR,26-HOSP,1-
2dr/5ph/3pg/1pc/1ct/fr L

Bathhouse Row,Buckstaff Bathhouse
(Hot Springs National Park)
Central Ave.
HABS AR-28-G
HABS AR,26-HOSP,1G-
1dr/6ph/1pc/1ct/fr L

Bathhouse Row,Fordyce Bathhouse
(Hot Springs National Park)
Central Ave.
HABS AR-28-D
HABS AR,26-HOSP,1D-
1dr/32ph/2pc/8ct/fr L

Bathhouse Row,Hale Bathhouse (Hot Springs National Park)
Central Ave.
HABS AR-28-B
HABS AR,26-HOSP,1B-
2dr/17ph/3pg/1pc/1ct/fr L

Bathhouse Row,Lamar Bathhouse (Hot Springs National Park)
Central Ave.
HABS AR-28-H
HABS AR,36-HOSP,1H-
1dr/9ph/1pc/fr L

Bathhouse Row,Maurice Bathhouse
(Hot Springs National Park)
Central Ave.
HABS AR-28-C
HABS AR,26-HOSP,1C-
3dr/38ph/2pc/6ct/fr L

Bathhouse Row,Ozark Bathhouse (Hot Springs National Park)
Central Ave.
HABS AR-28-F
HABS AR,26-HOSP,1F-
1dr/9ph/1pc/1ct/fr L

Bathhouse Row,Quapaw Bathhouse
(Hot Springs National Park)
Central Ave.
HABS AR-28-E
HABS AR,26-HOSP,1E-
2dr/16ph/1pc/8ct/fr L

Bathhouse Row,Superior Bathhouse
(Hot Springs National Park)
Central Ave.
HABS AR-28-A
HABS AR,26-HOSP,1A-
2dr/15ph/1pc/fr L

Bathhouse Row,Visitor's Center (Hot Springs National Park)
Central Ave.
HABS AR-28-I
HABS AR,26-HOSP.1I-
1dr/8ph/1pc L

Hot Springs Nat. Pk. Bathhouse Row: Buckstaff Bath
State HWY 7,1 Mile North of U.S. HWY 70
HAER AR-4-G
10ph/4pg/1pc/fr L

Hot Springs Nat. Pk. Bathhouse Row: Fordyce Bath
State Hwy. 7,1 mile north of U.S. Hwy. 70
HAER AR-4-D
HAER 1991(HAER):29
15ph/4pg/1pc/fr L

Hot Springs Nat. Pk. Bathhouse Row: Hale Bathhouse
State Hwy. 7,1 mile north of U.S. Hwy. 70
HAER AR-4-B
HAER 1991(HAER):29
2ph/3pg/1pc/fr L

Hot Springs Nat. Pk. Bathhouse Row: Lamar Bath
State Hwy. 7,1 mile north of U.S. Hwy. 70
HAER AR-4-H
HAER 1991(HAER):29
10ph/4pg/1pc/fr L

Hot Springs Nat. Pk. Bathhouse Row: Maurice Bath
State Hwy. 7,1 mile north of U.S. Hwy. 70
HAER AR-4-C
HAER 1991(HAER):29
11ph/4pg/1pc/fr L

Hot Springs Nat. Pk. Bathhouse Row: Mech. & Piping
State Hwy. 7,1 mile north of U.S. Hwy. 70
HAER AR-4
HAER 1991(HAER):29
46pg L

Hot Springs Nat. Pk. Bathhouse Row: Ozark Bath
State Hwy. 7,1 mile north of U.S. Hwy. 70
HAER AR-4-F
HAER 1991(HAER):29
7ph/4pg/1pc/fr L

Hot Springs Nat. Pk. Bathhouse Row: Quapaw Bath
State Hwy. 7,1 mile north of U.S. Hwy. 70
HAER AR-4-E
HAER 1991(HAER):29
7ph/4pg/1pc/fr L

Hot Springs Nat. Pk. Bathhouse Row: Superior Bath
State Hwy. 7,1 mile north of U.S. Hwy. 70
HAER AR-4-A
HAER 1991(HAER):29
5ph/4pg/1pc/fr L

Hot Springs Nat. Pk. Bathhouse Row: Visitor's Ctr
State Hwy. 7,1 mile north of U.S. Hwy. 70
HAER AR-4-I
HAER 1991(HAER):29
5ph/1pc L

Hot Springs National Park; see Bathhouse Row & Grand Promedade

Hot Springs National Park; see Bathhouse Row,Buckstaff Bathhouse

Hot Springs National Park; see Bathhouse Row,Fordyce Bathhouse

Hot Springs National Park; see Bathhouse Row,Hale Bathhouse

Hot Springs National Park; see Bathhouse Row,Lamar Bathhouse

Hot Springs National Park; see Bathhouse Row,Maurice Bathhouse

Hot Springs National Park; see Bathhouse Row,Ozark Bathhouse

Hot Springs National Park; see Bathhouse Row,Quapaw Bathhouse

Hot Springs National Park; see Bathhouse Row,Superior Bathhouse

Hot Springs National Park; see Bathhouse Row,Visitor's Center

Pythian Bathhouse & Hotel
415 Malvern Ave.
HABS AR-29
HABS AR,26-HOSP,2-
5dr/3ph/1pc/fr L

HOT SPRINGS VIC.

Hot Springs National Park; see Ricks Estate,Boathouse

Hot Springs National Park; see Ricks Estate,Electric Power Generating Mill (Ruin)

Hot Springs National Park; see Ricks Estate,Stone Bridge

Ricks Estate,Boathouse (Hot Springs National Park)
Ricks Pond,Ricks Rd.
HABS AR-34-C
HABS AR,26-HOSP.V,1C-
2ph/1pc L

Ricks Estate,Electric Power Generating Mill (Ruin) (Hot Springs National Park)
Stone Bridge Rd.
HABS AR-34-A
HABS AR,26-HOSP.V,1A-
10ph/1pc L

Ricks Estate,Stone Bridge (Hot Springs National Park)
Ricks Pond,Ricks Rd.
HABS AR-34-B
HABS AR,26-HOSP.V,1B-
3ph/1pc L

GREENE COUNTY

PARAGOULD

Eight Mile Creek Bridge
Spanning Eight Mile Creek at U.S. Hwy. 49
HAER AR-17
HAER DLC/PP-1992:AR-2
10ph/6pg/1pc L

HEMPSTEAD COUNTY

BLEVINS

Log Cabin Tavern
State Hwy.
HABS AR-32-10
HABS ARK,29-BLEV,1-
3dr/2ph/6pg/fr L

WASHINGTON

Baptist Church
State Hwy. 4
HABS AR-32-5
HABS ARK,29-WASH,3-
6dr/2ph/2pg/fr L

Confederate State Capitol (Courthouse & State House,Old)
Old Military Rd.
HABS AR-32-3
HABS ARK,29-WASH,1-
9dr/2ph/2pg/fr L

Courthouse & State House,Old; see Confederate State Capitol

Jones,Dan W. ,House
HABS AR-32-7
HABS ARK,29-WASH,5-
7dr/2ph/1pg/fr L

Royston,Grandison D. ,House
State Hwy. 4
HABS AR-32-11
HABS ARK,29-WASH,6-
7dr/2ph/2pg/fr L

Stuart,A. O. ,House
HABS AR-32-6
HABS ARK,29-WASH,4-
5dr/2ph/2pg L

Tavern,Old
Military Rd.
HABS AR-32-4
HABS ARK,29-WASH,2-
5dr/2ph/1pg/fr L

Thomas,John T. ,House
Old Military Rd.
HABS AR-32-8
HABS ARK,29-WASH.V,1-
6dr/3ph/2pg/fr L

WASHINGTON VIC.

Holt,Milton T. ,House
Old Military Rd.
HABS AR-32-9
HABS ARK,29- ,1-
6dr/2ph/2pg/fr L

HOT SPRING COUNTY

MALVERN

Rockport Bridge
Spanning Ouachita River at Old St. Hwy. No. 84
HAER AR-47
HAER DLC/PP-1992:AR-2
10ph/31pg/1pc L

HOWARD COUNTY

CENTER POINT

Clardy-Lee House
State Hwy. 26
HABS AR-26
HABS AR,31-CEPO,1-
10dr/fr L

JACKSON COUNTY

NEWPORT

Newport Bridge
Spanning White River at St. Hwy. 14
HAER AR-12
HAER DLC/PP-1992:AR-2
7ph/38pg/1pc L

JEFFERSON COUNTY

PINE BLUFF

Pine Bluff Arsenal
HAER AR-2
HAER AR,35-PIBLU,1-
55pg/fr L

JOHNSON COUNTY

CLARKSVILLE VIC.

Stage Coach Inn,Old
HABS AR-17
HABS ARK,36-CLARK.V,1-
4ph L

FT. DOUGLAS

Big Piney Creek Bridge (Ft. Douglas Bridge)
Spanning Big Piney Creek at State Hwy. 123
HAER AR-22
HAER DLC/PP-1992:AR-2
10ph/9pg/1pc L

Ft. Douglas Bridge; see Big Piney Creek Bridge

LAWRENCE COUNTY

IMBODEN

Imboden Bridge; see St. Louis - San Francisco Bridge

St. Louis - San Francisco Bridge (Imboden Bridge)
Spanning Spring River at U.S. Hwy 62
HAER AR-26
HAER DLC/PP-1992:AR-2
9ph/15pg/1pc L

WALNUT RIDGE

Cache River Bridge
Spanning Cache River at U.S. Hwy. 412
HAER AR-25
HAER DLC/PP-1992:AR-2
7ph/12pg/1pc L

MILLER COUNTY

GARLAND CITY

Red River Bridge
Spanning Red River at U.S. Hwy. 82
HAER AR-14
HAER DLC/PP-1992:AR-2
6ph/31pg/1pc L

MISSISSIPPI COUNTY

WILSON

Wilson Cabin
HABS AR-22
HABS ARK,47-WILSO,1-
2ph L

MONROE COUNTY

CLARENDON

Clarendon Bridge
Spanning White River at U. S. Hwy. 79
HAER AR-49
HAER DLC/PP-1992:AR-2
9ph/28pg/1pc L

Monroe County Jail,Old
Main & Kendall Sts.
HABS AR-35
HABS AR,48-CLAR,1-
8dr/fr L

NEVADA COUNTY

ROSSTON

Carolina Church; see Carolina United Methodist Church

Carolina United Methodist Church (Carolina Church)
Washington Post Rd.
HABS AR-30
HABS AR,50-ROSS,1-
7dr/fr L

NEWTON COUNTY

HARRISON VIC.

Harp Creek Bridge
Spans Harp Creek at State Hwy. 7
HAER AR-9
HAER DLC/PP-1992:AR-2
8ph/9pg/1pc L

PONCA

Boxley Grist Mill
Boxley Vic. on AR Hwy. 43,Buffaloe Nat'l River
HAER AR-3
HAER AR,51-PON,1-
20dr/fr L

PRUITT

Buffalo River Bridge (Pruitt Bridge)
Spanning Buffalo River at State Hwy. 7
HAER AR-23
HAER DLC/PP-1992:AR-2
9ph/9pg/1pc L

Pruitt Bridge; see Buffalo River Bridge

PERRY COUNTY

PERRY VIC.

Cypress Creek Bridge
Spanning Cypress Creek at Co. Rd. 64
HAER AR-33
HAER DLC/PP-1992:AR-2
5ph/2pg/1pc L

POLK COUNTY

CAMP PIONEER VIC.

Mountain Fork Bridge
Spanning Mountain Fork Creek at Co. Rd. 38
HAER AR-34
HAER DLC/PP-1992:AR-2
8ph/2pg/1pc L

PRAIRIE COUNTY

DE VALLS BLUFF

De Valls Bluff Bridge; see White River Bridge

White River Bridge (De Valls Bluff Bridge)
Spanning White River at U.S. Hwy. 70
HAER AR-21
HAER DLC/PP-1992:AR-2
11ph/20pg/1pc L

PULASKI COUNTY

Arkansas,Historical Map
HABS AR-27
HABS ARK, -
1dr L

LITTLE ROCK

Cantrell Road Bridge; see Lincoln Avenue Viaduct

Conrad House
1410 Bragg St.
HABS AR-24
HABS AR,60-LIRO,7-
6ph/1pc L

Crittenden,Robert,House; see Henderliter Place,The

Curran Hall (Walter-Curran-Bell House)
615 E. Capitol St.
HABS AR-36
HABS AR,60-LIRO,8-
9dr/fr L

Henderliter Place,The (Crittenden,Robert,House)
Second & Cumberland Sts.
HABS AR-32-2
HABS ARK,60-LIRO,2-
7dr/2ph/1pg/fr L

Lincoln Avenue Viaduct (Cantrell Road Bridge)
Spn. Union Pac. RR btwn Baring Crs. Brdg&Union Sta
HAER AR-6
HAER DLC/PP-1992:AR-2
7ph/20pg/1pc L

Little Rock City Hall
Broadway & Markham
HABS AR-14
HABS ARK,60-LIRO,6-
10ph/3pg/1pc L

McHenry House
Hwy. 70 Vic.
HABS AR-13
HABS ARK,60- ,1-
11dr/6ph/3pg/fr L

Pike,Albert,House
411 E. Seventh St.
HABS AR-20
HABS ARK,60-LIRO,5-
1ph L

Second Street Bridge
Spanning Union Pacific RR lines
HAER AR-41
HAER DLC/PP-1992:AR-2
11ph/11pg/1pc L

State Capitol Building,Old
Markham & Center Sts.
HABS AR-32-1
HABS ARK,60-LIRO,1-
27dr/7ph/3pg/1pc/fr L

Trapmall Hall
423 E. Capitol Ave.
HABS AR-19
HABS ARK,60-LIRO,4-
1ph L

U. S. Arsenal Building
City Park
HABS AR-32-12
HABS ARK,60-LIRO,3-
12dr/2ph/2pg/fr L

Walter-Curran-Bell House; see Curran Hall

NORTH LITTLE ROCK

Administration Building of City of Argentia; see North Little Rock City Hall

Edgemere Street Bridge
Spanning Lake No. 3 adjacent branch at Edgemere St
HAER AR-40
HAER DLC/PP-1992:AR-2
4ph/3pg/1pc L

Fort Logan H. Roots Military Post,Building No. 1 (Veterans' Administration Hospital; Fort Logan H. Roots,Enlisted Men's Barracks)
Scenic Hill Dr.
HABS AR-25-A
HABS AR,60-NOLI,2A-
10ph/7pg/1pc L

Fort Logan H. Roots,Enlisted Men's Barracks; see Fort Logan H. Roots Military Post,Building No. 1

Fourteenth Street Bridge
Spanning Missouri Pacific RR at Fourteenth St.
HAER AR-42
HAER DLC/PP-1992:AR-2
5ph/2pg/1pc L

Lake No. 1 Bridge
Spanning Lake No. 1 at Avondale Rd.
HAER AR-39
HAER DLC/PP-1992:AR-2
4ph/3pg/1pc L

Lakeshore Drive Bridge
Spanning Lake No. 3 adjacent branch at Lakeshore D
HAER AR-52
HAER DLC/PP-1992:AR-2
6ph/3pg/1pc L

North Little Rock City Hall (Administration Building of City of Argentia)
Third & Main
HABS AR-15
HABS ARK,60-NOLI,1-
8ph/4pg/1pc L

Veterans' Administration Hospital; see Fort Logan H. Roots Military Post,Building No. 1

RANDOLPH COUNTY

POCAHONTAS

Black River Bridge
Spanning the Black River at U.S. Hwy. 67
HAER AR-8
HAER DLC/PP-1992:AR-2
5ph/23pg/1pc L

SALINE COUNTY

BENTON

Old River Bridge
Spanning Saline Riv. at Old Military Rd.(River Rd)
HAER AR-46
HAER DLC/PP-1992:AR-2
5ph/17pg/1pc L

Saline River Bridge
County Hwy. 365 across Saline River
HAER AR-7
HAER DLC/PP-1992:AR-2
6ph/11pg/1pc L

SEBASTIAN COUNTY

FORT SMITH

Federal Court Building (Fort Smith National Historic Site)
S. Third St. & Rogers Ave.
HABS AR-40
HABS DLC/PP-1992:AR-5
2ph/1pc L

Fort Smith National Historic Site; see Federal Court Building

Fort Smith National Historic Site; see Fort Smith,Barracks-Courthouse-Jail

Fort Smith National Historic Site; see Fort Smith,Commissary Building

Fort Smith,Barracks-Courthouse-Jail (Welfare Association Building; Red Cross Building; Fort Smith National Historic Site)
S. Third St. & Rogers Ave.
HABS AR-41
HABS DLC/PP-1992:AR-5
2ph/1pc L

Fort Smith,Commissary Building (Fort Smith National Historic Site)
100 S. Garrison Ave.
HABS AR-16
HABS ARK,66-FOSM,1A-
8dr/7ph/2pg/fr L

Red Cross Building; see Fort Smith,Barracks-Courthouse-Jail

Welfare Association Building; see Fort Smith,Barracks-Courthouse-Jail

JENNY LIND VIC.

Jenny Lind Bridge
Spanning Vache Grasse Creek trib. at Co. Rd. No. 8
HAER AR-54
HAER DLC/PP-1992:AR-2
2ph/2pg/1pc L

MILLTOWN

Milltown Bridge
Spanning Vache Grasse Creek trib. at Co. Rd. No.77
HAER AR-55
HAER DLC/PP-1992:AR-2
6ph/2pg/1pc L

SEVIER COUNTY

LOCKESBURG VIC.

Little Cossatot River Bridge
Spanning Little Cossatot River at Co. Rd. No. 139
HAER AR-35
HAER DLC/PP-1992:AR-2
6ph/3pg/1pc L

ST. FRANCIS COUNTY

FORREST CITY

St. Francis River Bridge
Spanning St. Francis River at U.S. Hwy. 70
HAER AR-20
HAER DLC/PP-1992:AR-2
11ph/18pg/1pc L

WASHINGTON COUNTY

FAYETTEVILLE

Fayetteville Natl Cemetery,Superintendent's Lodge
700 Government Ave.
HABS AR-39-A
HABS AR,72-FAYVI,1A-
8ph/1pc L

Wyman Bridge
Spanning the W. fork of the White River
HAER AR-38
HAER DLC/PP-1992:AR-2
3dr/12ph/7pg/1pc/fr L

FAYETTVILLE VIC.

Yell,Archibald,House
HABS AR-18
HABS ARK,72-FAYVI.V,1-
2ph L

JOHNSON

Johnson Mill (Truesdale's Mill)
Johnson Rd.
HABS AR-37
HABS AR,72-JOHN,1-
10dr/fr L

Truesdale's Mill; see Johnson Mill

WHITE COUNTY

JUDSONIA

Judsonia Bridge
HAER AR-51
HAER DLC/PP-1992:AR-2
3dr/11ph/12pg/1pc/fr L

WOODRUFF COUNTY

AUGUSTA

Augusta Bridge
Spanning White River at Hwy. 64
HAER AR-13
HAER DLC/PP-1992:AR-2
6ph/25pg/1pc L

YELL COUNTY

BELLEVILLE VIC.

Spring Lake Bridge
Spanning Bob Barnes Branch at Co. Rd. No. 36D
HAER AR-36
HAER DLC/PP-1992:AR-2
7ph/2pg/1pc L

OLA VIC.

Achmun Creek Bridge
HAER AR-37
HAER DLC/PP-1992:AR-2
5ph/2pg/1pc L

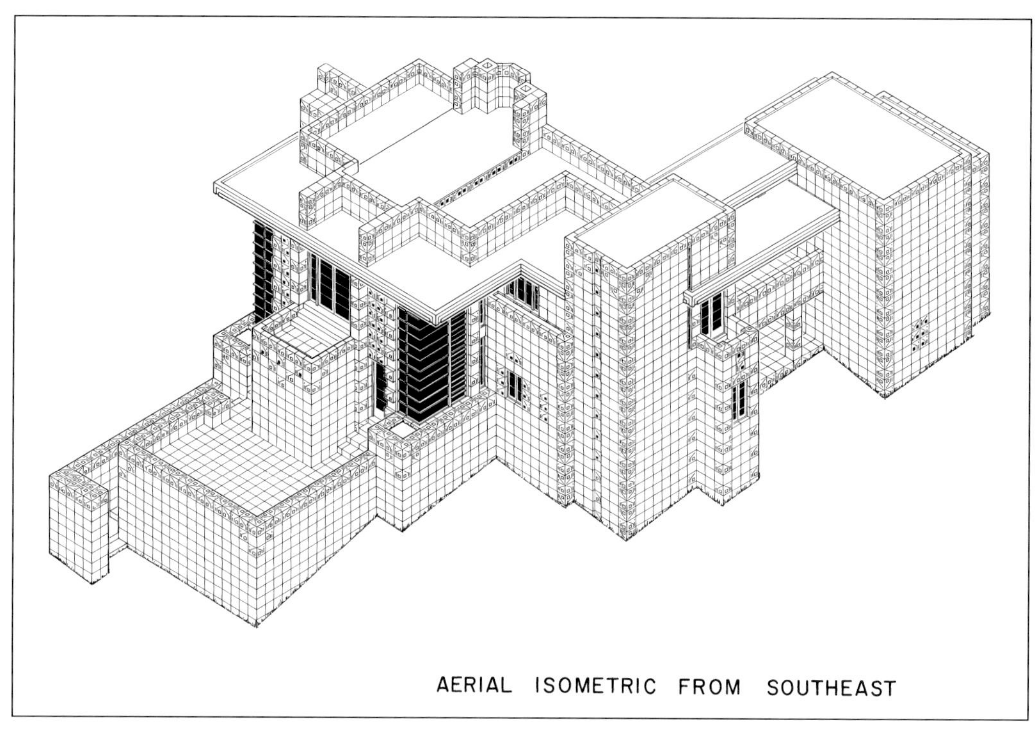

Freeman House, 1962 Glencoe Way, Los Angeles, Los Angeles County, California. Aerial isometric from southeast. Measured drawing delineated by Jeffrey B. Lentz, 1969 (HABS CA-1989; sheet 2 of 7; negative number LC-USZA1-1271).

Lost Horse Gold Mill, Joshua Tree National Monument, Twenty-Nine Palms vicinity, San Bernardino County, California. View of cams and weights of the stamp mill, a machine that pulverizes the ore to release the gold from the ore body. Photograph by Jet Lowe, 1992 (photo number HAER CA-128-12).

California

SAN JUAN CAPISTRANO

Mission San Juan Capistrano
Olive St. & Hwy. 101
HABS CA-331
HABS CAL,30-SAJUC,1-
1dr/2ph/2pg/fr L

ALAMEDA COUNTY

ALAMEDA

Union Iron Works Turbine Machine Shop
2200 Webster St.
HAER CA-43
HAER CAL,1-ALAM,2-
18ph/29pg/2pc/fr L

BERKELEY

Berkeley City Hall (City Hall,Old)
2134 Grove St.
HABS CA-417
HABS CAL,1-BERK,2-
4ph/7pg/1pc L

City Hall,Old; see Berkeley City Hall

Davis-Byrne Building
2134-2140 Dwight Way
HABS CA-2314
HABS DLC/PP-1992:CA-4
16ph/15pg/2pc L

Peralta Hall (St. Joseph's Academy)
HABS CA-1655
HABS CAL,1-BERK,1-
1ph L

St. Joseph's Academy; see Peralta Hall

CASTRO VALLEY

Crow Creek Bridge
Spanning Crow Creek on Grove Way
HAER CA-19
HAER CAL,1-CAVA,1-
8ph/5pg/1pc L

FREMONT

Champion House
1357 Mowry Ave.
HABS CA-2288
HABS 1991(HABS):5
5ph/8pg/1pc L

Champion House,Barn
1357 Mowry Ave.
HABS CA-2288-A
HABS 1991(HABS):5
3ph/1pc L

Mission San Jose Guadalupe
Mission & Washington Blvds.
HABS CA-1132
HABS CAL,1-FREMO,1-
22ph/17pg L

Santos Farm
1481 Mowry Ave.
HABS CA-2289
HABS 1991(HABS):5
6ph/9pg/1pc L

Santos Farm,Barn
1481 Mowry Ave.
HABS CA-2289-B
HABS 1991(HABS):5
3ph/1pc L

Santos Farm,House
1481 Mowry Ave.
HABS CA-2289-A
HABS 1991(HABS):5
6ph/1pc L

Santos Farm,Quonset Hut
1481 Mowry Ave.
HABS CA-2289-C
HABS 1991(HABS):5
1ph/1pc L

FREMONT (NILES)

Rancho Arroya de la Alameda Adobe (Vallejo,Jose de Jesus,Adobe)
Niles Blvd. & Nursery Ave.
HABS CA-1194
HABS CAL,1-NIL,1-
2ph L

Vallejo Flour Mill
Niles Canyon
HABS CA-1660
HABS CAL,1-NIL,2-
2ph L

Vallejo,Jose de Jesus,Adobe; see Rancho Arroya de la Alameda Adobe

FREMONT(WARM SPRING)

Cohen,A. A. ,House (Rancho Agua Caliente; Hidden Valley Ranch)
State Hwy. 9
HABS CA-1656
HABS CAL,1-WARM,1-
1ph L

Hidden Valley Ranch; see Cohen,A. A. ,House

Higuera,Abelardo,Adobe
Wabana St.
HABS CA-1666
HABS CAL,1-WARM,3-
3ph L

Higuera,Fulgencio,Adobe (Rancho Agua Caliente)
HABS CA-1665
HABS CAL,1-WARM,2-
3ph L

Indian Cemetery
Washington Blvd.
HABS CA-1658
HABS CAL,1-FREMO,2-
1ph L

Rancho Agua Caliente; see Cohen,A. A. ,House

Rancho Agua Caliente; see Higuera,Fulgencio,Adobe

HAYWARD

Brewery
HABS CA-1325
HABS CAL,1-HAY,1-
1ph L

LIVERMORE VIC.

Carroll Overhead Bridge
Altamont Pass Road
HAER CA-52
HAER CAL-1-LIVMO.V,1-
20ph/8pg/2pc L

OAKLAND

Breuner,John and Company Building
1515 Clay St.
HABS CA-2296
25ph/12pg/4pc H

Building No. 161; see Oakland Army Base,Transit Shed

716 Castro Street (House)
HABS CA-2058
HABS CAL,1-OAK,8-
6ph L

Fourth Church of Christ,Scientist
1330 Lakeshore Ave.
HABS CA-2272
HABS 1989(HABS):2
20ph/26pg/2pc L

Galinda Hotel
Eighth & Franklin Sts.
HABS CA-1898
HABS CAL,1-OAK,11-
2ph/1pg/1pc L

Greek Orthodox Church of the Assumption
920 Bush St.
HABS CA-2055
HABS CAL,1-OAK,6-
10ph/3pg L

Mahoney,Thomas,House
69 Eighth St.
HABS CA-2056
HABS CAL,1-OAK,5-
2ph L

Mills College; see Mills Hall

Mills Hall (Mills College)
5000 MacArthur Blvd.
HABS CA-2340
16ph/12pg/3pc H

Moss,J. Mora,House
Broadway & MacArthur Blvd.
HABS CA-1897
HABS CAL,1-OAK,2-
12dr/7ph/11pg/fr L

Oakland Army Base,Transit Shed (Building No. 161)
E. of Dunkirk St. & S. of Burma Rd.
HAER CA-125-A
HAER DLC/PP-1993:CA-2
35ph/13pg/3pc L

Oakland City Hall
Fourteenth & Washington Sts.
HABS CA-419
HABS CAL,1-OAK,10-
5ph/1pg/1pc/fr L

Pacific Telephone & Telegraph Co. (Building)
1519 Franklin St.
HABS CA-2317
32ph/48pg/3pc H

Paramount Theatre
2025 Broadway
HABS CA-1976
HABS CAL,1-OAK,9-
39ph/56pg/4pc/5ct L

Pardee,Gov. ,House
672 Eleventh St.
HABS CA-1899
HABS CAL,1-OAK,3-
8ph/7pg L

Quinn,William H. ,House
1425 Castro St.
HABS CA-2057
HABS CAL,1-OAK,4-
4ph L

Southern Pacific Ferry Slips; see Southern Pacific Mole & Pier

Southern Pacific Mole & Pier (Southern Pacific Ferry Slips)
Seventh St.
HABS CA-1888
HABS CAL,1-OAK,1-
19ph/11pg L

White,James,House
702 Eleventh St.
HABS CA-2054
HABS CAL,1-OAK,7-
6ph/2pg L

PLEASANTON

Kottinger,John W. ,Adobe
Ray St.
HABS CA-1859
HABS CAL,1-PLEAS,1-
1ph L

SAN LEANDRO

Estudillo House
1291 Carpenter St.
HABS CA-1662
HABS CAL,1-SANLE,1-
2ph L

Peralta,Ignacio,House
561 Lafayette
HABS CA-1896
HABS CAL,1-SANLE,2-
10ph/8pg L

TRACY VIC.

Mountain House
Mountain House & Livermore Altamont Pass Rds.
HABS CA-1199
HABS CAL,1-TRAC.V,1-
1ph L

UNION CITY

Apple Schmidt House; see Smith,Henry C. ,House

Smith,Henry C. ,House (Apple Schmidt House)
HABS CA-1659
HABS CAL,1-UNCI,1-
1ph L

AMADOR COUNTY

AMADOR CITY

Amador Hotel
Hwy. 49
HABS CA-1346
HABS CAL,3-AMCI,1-
1ph L

Commercial Buildings
Hwy. 49
HABS CA-1349
HABS CAL,3-AMCI,3-
1ph L

House,Brick (Mine House Hotel)
Hwy. 49
HABS CA-1350
HABS CAL,3-AMCI,4-
1ph L

Imperial Hotel
Hwy. 49
HABS CA-1348
HABS CAL,3-AMCI,2-
1ph L

Mine House Hotel; see House,Brick

BUENA VISTA

Buena Vista Stone Store
Lancha Plana & Jackson-Stockton Rds.
HABS CA-1508
HABS CAL,3-BUEVI,1-
1ph L

BUTTE CITY

Benoist-Ginocchio Store (Walls)
Hwy. 49
HABS CA-1506
HABS CAL,3-BUTCI,1-
1ph L

DRYTOWN

Drytown Hall
HABS CA-1155
HABS CAL,3-DRYTO,1-
1ph L

Masonic Temple
HABS CA-1515
HABS CAL,3-DRYTO,2-
1ph L

FIDDLETOWN

St. Charles Hotel
HABS CA-1154
HABS CAL,3-FIDTO,1-
1ph L

JACKSON

Brown,Armstead C. ,House (House,Brick)
HABS CA-1277
HABS CAL,3-JACSO,3-
2ph L

Hotel
Marcucci & Broadway
HABS CA-1283
HABS CAL,3-JACSO,1-
2ph L

House,Brick; see Brown,Armstead C. ,House

National Hotel
Main & Waxer Sts.
HABS CA-1520
HABS CAL,3-JACSO,7-
1ph L

Native Daughters of the Golden West Building
HABS CA-1509
HABS CAL,3-JACSO,5-
1ph L

Serbian Church
HABS CA-1870
HABS CAL,3-JACSO,2-
1ph L

Toll House
HABS CA-1519
HABS CAL,3-JACSO,6-
1ph L

Wells Fargo Express Office
HABS CA-1156
HABS CAL,3-JACSO,4-
1ph L

JACKSON GATE

Chichizola Store
Jackson Gate Rd.
HABS CA-1513
HABS CAL,3-JAKGA,1-
1ph L

MICHIGAN BAR

Heath's Store
HABS CA-1516
HABS CAL,3-MICH,1-
1ph L

OLETA

Barn,Frame
HABS CA-1352
HABS CAL,3-OLET,1-
1ph L

PINE GROVE

House,First
HABS CA-1514
HABS CAL,3-PIGRO,1-
1ph L

PLYMOUTH

House
HABS CA-1351
HABS CAL,3-PLYM,1-
1ph L

ROUND TOP

Kirkwood Inn & Round Top Post Office
U. S. Hwy. 88
HABS CA-1197
HABS CAL,3-ROUNT,1-
1ph L

VOLCANO

Adams Express Company Building
Main & Consolation Sts.
HABS CA-1518
HABS CAL,3-VOLC,8-
2ph L

Cannon,"Old Abe"
HABS CA-1507
HABS CAL,3-VOLC,6-
1ph L

Cigar Emporium; see Store,Stone

Cobblestone Art Gallery; see Store,Stone

Main Street (Commercial Buildings,Stone Walls)
HABS CA-1504
HABS CAL,3-VOLC,5-
2ph L

Masonic & I. O. O. F. Building
Main St.
HABS CA-1345
HABS CAL,3-VOLC,2-
3ph L

Sibley's Brewery; see Wine Shop

St. George Hotel
Main & National Sts.
HABS CA-1285
HABS CAL,3-VOLC,1-
6ph L

Store,Stone (Cigar Emporium; Cobblestone Art Gallery)
Main St.
HABS CA-1505
HABS CAL,3-VOLC,3-
2ph L

Volcano,General View
HABS CA-1510
HABS CAL,3-VOLC,4-
1ph L

Wine Shop (Sibley's Brewery)
HABS CA-1517
HABS CAL,3-VOLC,7-
1ph L

BUTTE COUNTY

BIDWELL BAR

Suspension Bridge & Stone Toll House
Curry-Bidwell Bar State Park
HABS CA-1476
HAER CA-34
HABS/HAER CAL,4-ORO.V,1-
1ph L

CENTERVILLE

Centerville Hydroelectric System
Butte Creek
HAER CA-127
HAER DLC/PP-1993:CA-3
1ph/1pc L

Centerville Hydroelectric System,Powerhouse
Butte Creek
HAER CA-127-A
HAER DLC/PP-1993:CA-3
22ph/8pg/3pc L

Centerville Hydroelectric Sytstem,Switch House
HAER CA-127-B
HAER DLC/PP-1993:CA-3
1ph/1pc L

CHEROKEE

Brewery (Ruins)
HABS CA-1702
HABS CAL,4-CHER,2-
1ph L

Wells Fargo & Company Vault (Ruins)
HABS CA-1680
HABS CAL,4-CHER,1-
1ph L

CHICO

Bidwell Mansion
525 Esplanade St.
HABS CA-1317
HABS CAL,4-CHIC,1-
10dr/9pg/fr L

OROVILLE VIC.

Bidwell Bar Suspension Bridge
Spanning Lake Oroville
HABS CA-1476
HAER CA-34
HABS/HAER CAL,4-ORO.V,1-
13ph/1pg/1pc/3ct L

CALAVERAS COUNTY

ALBANY FLAT

Romaggi,James,Fandango House
Hwy. 49
HABS CA-1204
HABS CAL,5-ALB,1-
4ph/fr L

ALTAVILLE

Gravestones
North Branch Cemetery
HABS CA-1487
HABS CAL,5-ALTA,2-
2ph L

Pache,P. F. & Company (Commercial Building); see Prince & Garibaldi Store

Prince & Garibaldi Store (Pache,P. F. & Company (Commercial Building))
Hwys. 4 & 49
HABS CA-1205
HABS CAL,5-ALTA,1-
2ph/fr L

ANGELS CAMP

Angels Camp,General View
Main Street
HABS CA-1499
HABS CAL,5-ANGEL,2-
3ph L

Fox House
HABS CA-1493
HABS CAL,5-ANGEL,7-
1ph L

Hotel Angels
Main St.
HABS CA-1547
HABS CAL,5-ANGEL,1-
1ph L

House
Hwy. 49
HABS CA-1275
HABS CAL,5-ANGEL,3-
1ph L

House,Stone (Pierano,Joseph,House & Store)
HABS CA-1276
HABS CAL,5-ANGEL,4-
1ph L

Pierano,Joseph,House & Store; see House,Stone

Scribner's Store
HABS CA-1491
HABS CAL,5-ANGEL,5-
1ph L

Utica Mine
HABS CA-1492
HABS CAL,5-ANGEL,6-
1ph/fr L

ANGELS CAMP VIC.

Burch,John,House
HABS CA-1278
HABS CAL,5-ANGEL.V,1-
1ph L

CAMPO SECO

Eperson,Robert,Building
Main St.
HABS CA-1115
HABS CAL,5-CAMP,1-
1ph/fr L

Messenger,Capt. ,House
Comanche Reservoir
HABS CA-1206
HABS CAL,5-CAMP,2-
1ph L

CARSON HILL

House
HABS CA-1273
HABS CAL,5-CARHI,1-
1ph L

Oneta Brothers General Merchandise (Stores,Frame & Stone)
HABS CA-1490
HABS CAL,5-CARHI,2-
1ph L

Stores,Frame & Stone; see Oneta Brothers General Merchandise

CLEAR VIEW

House,First; see Noce,John,House

Noce,John,House (Whiskey Slide; House,First)
HABS CA-1489
HABS CAL,5-WHISK,1-
1ph/fr L

Whiskey Slide; see Noce,John,House

COPPEROPOLIS

Congregational Church (I. O. O. F. Hall)
HABS CA-1123
HABS CAL,5-COP,1-
1ph L

I. O. O. F. Hall; see Congregational Church

Madam Felix-Hodson Mining District; see Royal Consolidated Gold Mine & Mills,Royal Mill

Royal Consolidated Gold Mine & Mills,Royal Mill (Madam Felix-Hodson Mining District)
4,0 Air Miles NW of Copperopolis
HAER CA-81-B
2dr/3ph/1pc H

COPPEROPOLIS VIC

Madam Felix-Hodson Dist. Gold Mines and Mills (Madam Felix-Hodson Mining District)
Southern Edge Salt Spring Valley
HAER CA-76
HAER 1991(HAER):2
1dr/19pg L

Madam Felix-Hodson Mining District; see Madam Felix-Hodson Dist. Gold Mines and Mills

COPPEROPOLIS VIC.

Brown Mill; see Defiance Mill

Defiance Mill (Brown Mill; Madam Felix-Hodson District Gold Mines & Mills)
Southern Edge of Salt Spring Valley
HAER CA-76-D
HAER 1991(HAER):2
1ph/1pc L

Empire Mill (Madam Felix-Hodson District Gold Mines & Mills)
Southern Edge of Salt Spring Valley
HAER CA-76-B
HAER 1991(HAER):2
1ph/1pc L

Gold Knoll Mill (Madam Felix-Hodson District Gold Mines & Mills)
Southern Edge of Salt Spring Valley
HAER CA-76-E
HAER 1991(HAER):2
1ph/1pc L

Madam Felix-Hodson District Gold Mines & Mills; see Defiance Mill

Madam Felix-Hodson District Gold Mines & Mills; see Empire Mill

Madam Felix-Hodson District Gold Mines & Mills; see Gold Knoll Mill

Madam Felix-Hodson District Gold Mines & Mills; see Wilbur-Womble Mill

Madam Felix-Hodson District Gold Mines and Mill; see Pine Log Mill

Madam Felix-Hodson Mining District; see Mountain King Gold Mine & Mill

Madam Felix-Hodson Mining District; see Royal Consolidated Gold Mine & Mills,Hoisting Work

Madam Felix-Hodson Mining District; see Royal Consolidated Mine and Mills

Mountain King Gold Mine & Mill (Madam Felix-Hodson Mining District)
4.3 Air mi. NW of Copperopolis
HAER CA-77
HAER 1991(HAER):2
3dr/3ph/11pg/1pc L

Pine Log Mill (Madam Felix-Hodson District Gold Mines and Mill)
Southern Edge of Salt Spring Valley
HAER CA-76-A
HAER 1991(HAER):2
1ph/1pc L

Royal Consolidated Gold Mine & Mills,Hoisting Work (Madam Felix-Hodson Mining District)
4.0 Air Mi. NW of Copperopolis
HAER CA-81-A
HAER 1991(HAER):2
1dr/1ph/1pg/1pc L

Royal Consolidated Mine and Mills (Madam Felix-Hodson Mining District)
4.0 Air mi. NW of Copperopolis
HAER CA-81
HAER 1991(HAER):2
1dr/27pg L

Stage Station
Tullock Reservoir
HABS CA-1480
HABS CAL,5-COP.V,1-
1ph L

Wilbur-Womble Mill (Madam Felix-Hodson District Gold Mines & Mills)
Southern Edge Of Salt Spring Valley
HAER CA-76-C
HAER 1991(HAER):2
2ph/1pc L

ELDORADOTOWN

Raggio Adobe
HABS CA-1587
HABS CAL,5-ELDO,2-
1ph L

Rodesino Adobe
HABS CA-1586
HABS CAL,5-ELDO,1-
1ph L

FELIX

Felix Post Office & School (Stage Stop,Old; Tower Ranch)
HABS CA-1118
HABS CAL,5-FELI,1-
8dr/1ph/2pg/fr L

Pedroli Ranch House (Williams,Andrew,Ranch)
HABS CA-1208
HABS CAL,5-FELI,4-
1ph L

Stage Stop,Old; see Felix Post Office & School

Tower Ranch; see Felix Post Office & School

Tower Ranch Barn
HABS CA-1207
HABS CAL,5-FELI,2A-
1ph L

Tower Ranch House
HABS CA-1117
HABS CAL,5-FELI,2-
2ph L

Williams,Andrew,Ranch; see Pedroli Ranch House

FELIX VIC.

House (Ruins); see Stone Creek Settlement (Ruins)

Mine Building (Williams,Andrew,Ranch)
HABS CA-1209
HABS CAL,5-FELI,5-
1ph L

Stone Creek Settlement (Ruins) (House (Ruins))
Salt Springs Valley
HABS CA-1122
HABS CAL,5-FELI,3-
1ph L

Williams,Andrew,Ranch; see Mine Building

FOURTH CROSSING

Foreman's Ranch Hotel; see Reddick,John,House

Reddick,John,House (Foreman's Ranch Hotel)
Hwy. 49
HABS CA-1129
HABS CAL,5-FOUR,1-
4ph/fr L

GLENCOE

Store,Frame
HABS CA-1488
HABS CAL,5-GLENC,1-
1ph L

HAPPY VALLEY

Building,Stone (North Star Mine Building)
HABS CA-1497
HABS CAL,5-HAPVA,1-
1ph L

North Star Mine Building; see Building,Stone

JESUS MARIA

Commercial Buildings & Houses,Frame
HABS CA-1483
HABS CAL,5-JESU,1-
1ph L

MELONES VIC.

Barn
HABS CA-1274
HABS CAL,5-MELO.V,1-
1ph L

MOKELUMNE HILL

Brewery (Ruins); see Stone Ruins

Calaveras County Branch Library; see Store & Post Office

Church,Frame (Congregational Church)
HABS CA-2338
HABS CAL,5-MOKHI,1-
1ph L

Congregational Church; see Church,Frame

I. O. O. F. Hall
Main St.
HABS CA-1281
HABS CAL,5-MOKHI,4-
2ph/fr L

Leger Hotel
Main St.
HABS CA-1874
HABS CAL,5-MOKHI,5-
1ph L

Stone Ruins (Brewery (Ruins))
HABS CA-1280
HABS CAI 5 MOKHI,3-
1ph L

Store (Ruins)
HABS CA-1279
HABS CAL,5-MOKHI,2-
1ph L

Store & Post Office (Calaveras County Branch Library)
Main St.
HABS CA-1875
HABS CAL,5-MOKHI,6-
1ph L

MURPHY'S

Compere,Victorene,Store
Main St.
HABS CA-1108
HABS CAL,5-MURPH,1-
4ph/fr L

Michaelson Store (Michelson,Albert,House)
Main St.
HABS CA-1211
HABS CAL,5-MURPH,5-
1ph L

Michelson,Albert,House; see Michaelson Store

Mitchler Hotel (Murphy's Hotel)
Main St.
HABS CA-1109
HABS CAL,5-MURPH,2-
4ph L

Murphy's Hotel; see Mitchler Hotel

Old Timers Museum; see Traver's,Peter L. ,Store & Wells Fargo Bldg.

School
HABS CA-1110
HABS CAL,5-MURPH,3-
1ph L

St. Patrick's Catholic Church
HABS CA-1112
HABS CAL,5-MURPH,4-
1ph L

Traver's,Peter L. ,Store & Wells Fargo Bldg. (Old Timers Museum)
HABS CA-1485
HABS CAL,5-MURPH,6-
1ph L

PILOT HILL

Bayley,A. J. ,Road House
HABS CA-1383
HABS CAL,9-PILHI,2-
5ph/1pg L

POVERTY FLAT

Commercial Building,Stone (Ruins)
HABS CA-1479
HABS CAL,5-POV,1-
2ph L

ROARING CAMP

Roaring Camp Buildings,Frame
HABS CA-1484
HABS CAL,5-ROAR,1-
1ph L

SAN ANDREAS

Aqostini Building; see Banque,J. ,Store

Banque,J. ,Store (Aqostini Building)
Main St.
HABS CA-1210
HABS CAL,5-SAND,2-
2ph/fr L

Calaveras Bar; see Friedburger Building

Friedburger Building (Calaveras Bar)
HABS CA-1478
HABS CAL,5-SAND,3-
1ph L

I. O. O. F. Hall
Main St.
HABS CA-1496
HABS CAL,5-SAND,8-
1ph/fr L

Metropolitan Hotel
HABS CA-1495
HABS CAL,5-SAND,7-
3ph L

San Andreas,General View
Main St.
HABS CA-1494
HABS CAL,5-SAND,1-
2ph L

Store,Adobe
HABS CA-1481
HABS CAL,5-SAND,4-
1ph L

Theatre,Old
HABS CA-1482
HABS CAL,5-SAND,5-
1ph L

COLUSA COUNTY

COLUSA

Colusa Bridge
Spanning Sacramento River
HAER CA-7
HAER CAL,6-COLU,3-
26ph/5pg/3pc L

Colusa County Courthouse
HABS CA-1806
HABS CAL,6-COLU,1-
1ph L

Hall of Records & County Jail
HABS CA-1807
HABS CAL,6-COLU,2-
1ph L

CONTRA COSTA COUNTY

ALAMO

Henry Hotel (Wolf Store)
Mt. Diablo Rd. & Hwy. 21
HABS CA-1657
HABS CAL,7-ALAMO,1-
1ph L

Wolf Store; see Henry Hotel

BRENTWOOD VIC.

Los Medanos Rancho; see Marsh,John,House

Marsh,John,House (Los Medanos Rancho)
Marsh Creek Rd.
HABS CA-1500
HABS CAL,7-BRENT.V,1-
5ph/10pg L

CONCORD

Pacneco,Fernando,Adobe
3119 Grant St.
HABS CA-173
HABS CAL,7-CONC,1-
3ph L

Pancheco,Salvio,Adobe
2030 Adobe St.
HABS CA-1847
HABS CAL,7-CONC,2-
2ph L

DANVILLE VIC.

O'Neill,Eugene,House (Tao House; O'Neill,Eugene,National Historic Site)
Kuss Rd.
HABS CA-2078
HABS CAL,7-DAN.V,1-
66ph/47pg/5pc/fr L

O'Neill,Eugene,House,Chicken Coop (Tao House,Chicken Coop; O'Neill,Eugene,National Historic Site)
Kuss Rd.
HABS CA-2078-A
HABS CAL,7-DAN.V,1-A-
1ph/1pg/1pc L

O'Neill,Eugene,House,Freshwater Tanks (Tao House,Freshwater Tanks; O'Neill,Eugene,National Historic Site)
Kuss Rd.
HABS CA-2078-H
HABS CAL,7-DAN.V,1-H-
2ph/1pc L

O'Neill,Eugene,House,New Barn (Tao House,New Barn; O'Neill,Eugene,National Historic Site)
Kuss Rd.
HABS CA-2078-E
HABS CAL,7-DAN.V,1-E-
4ph/1pc L

O'Neill,Eugene,House,Old Barn (Tao House,Old Barn; O'Neill,Eugene,National Historic Site)
Kuss Rd.
HABS CA-2078-B
HABS CAL,7-DAN.V,1-B-
4ph/1pg/1pc L

O'Neill,Eugene,House,Pool Equipment House (Tao House,Pool Equipment House; O'Neill,Eugene,National Historic Site)
Kuss Rd.
HABS CA-2078-D
HABS CAL,7-DAN.V,1-D-
1ph/1pg/1pc L

O'Neill,Eugene,House,Post O'Neill Residence (Tao House,Post O'Neill Residence; O'Neill,Eugene,National Historic Site)
Kuss Rd.
HABS CA-2078-F
HABS CAL,7-DAN.V,1-F-
2ph/1pc L

O'Neill,Eugene,House,Shop & Incinerator (Tao House,Shop & Incinerator; O'Neill,Eugene,National Historic Site)
HABS CA-2078-G
HABS CAL,7-DAN.V,1-G-
2ph/1pg/1pc L

O'Neill,Eugene,House,Swimming Pool Bathhouse (Tao House,Swimming Pool Bathhouse; O'Neill,Eugene,National Historic Site)
Kuss Rd.
HABS CA-2078-C
HABS CAL,7-DAN.V,1-C-
5ph/1pg/1pc L

O'Neill,Eugene,National Historic Site; see O'Neill,Eugene,House

O'Neill,Eugene,National Historic Site; see O'Neill,Eugene,House,Chicken Coop

O'Neill,Eugene,National Historic Site; see O'Neill,Eugene,House,Freshwater Tanks

O'Neill,Eugene,National Historic Site; see O'Neill,Eugene,House,New Barn

O'Neill,Eugene,National Historic Site; see O'Neill,Eugene,House,Old Barn

O'Neill,Eugene,National Historic Site; see O'Neill,Eugene,House,Pool Equipment House

O'Neill,Eugene,National Historic Site; see O'Neill,Eugene,House,Post O'Neill Residence

O'Neill,Eugene,National Historic Site; see O'Neill,Eugene,House,Shop & Incinerator

O'Neill,Eugene,National Historic Site; see O'Neill,Eugene,House,Swimming Pool Bathhouse

Tao House; see O'Neill,Eugene,House

Tao House,Chicken Coop; see O'Neill,Eugene,House,Chicken Coop

Tao House,Freshwater Tanks; see O'Neill,Eugene,House,Freshwater Tanks

Tao House,New Barn; see O'Neill,Eugene,House,New Barn

Tao House,Old Barn; see O'Neill,Eugene,House,Old Barn

Tao House,Pool Equipment House; see O'Neill,Eugene,House,Pool Equipment House

Tao House,Post O'Neill Residence; see O'Neill,Eugene,House,Post O'Neill Residence

Tao House,Shop & Incinerator; see O'Neill,Eugene,House,Shop & Incinerator

Tao House,Swimming Pool Bathhouse; see O'Neill,Eugene,House,Swimming Pool Bathhouse

MARTINEZ

Martinez,Vicente,Adobe
Pleasant Hill & Franklin Canyon Rds.
HABS CA-1913
HABS CAL,7-MART,2-
3dr/2ph/4pg L

Muir,John,House (Muir,John,National Historic Site; Strentzel,John,House)
Alhambra Blvd.
HABS CA-1890
HABS CAL,7-MART,1-
13dr/14ph/8pg L

Muir,John,National Historic Site; see Muir,John,House

Strentzel,John,House; see Muir,John,House

MORAGA VALLEY

Moraqa,Jose Joaquin,Adobe
HABS CA-1860
HABS CAL,7-MORAG,1-
2ph L

RICHMOND

119 Contra Costa Street (House); see Point Richmond Historic District

125 Contra Costa Street (House); see Point Richmond Historic District

25 Contra Costa Street (House); see Point Richmond Historic District

35 Contra Costa Street (House); see Point Richmond Historic District

425 Hillside Street (House); see Point Richmond Historic District

Point Richmond Historic District
Hillside & Contra Costa Sts.
HABS CA-2210
HABS CAL,7-RICH,1-
2ph/1pc L

Point Richmond Historic District (119 Contra Costa Street (House))
HABS CA-2210-D
HABS CAL,7-RICH,1-D-
1ph/2pg/1pc L

Point Richmond Historic District (125 Contra Costa Street (House))
HABS CA-2210-E
HABS CAL,7-RICH,1-E-
2ph/2pg/1pc L

Point Richmond Historic District (25 Contra Costa Street (House))
HABS CA-2210-B
HABS CAL,7-RICH,1-B-
1ph/2pg/1pc L

Point Richmond Historic District (35 Contra Costa Street (House))
HABS CA-2210-C
HABS CAL,7-RICH,1-C-
1ph/2pg/1pc L

Point Richmond Historic District (425 Hillside Street (House))
HABS CA-2210-A
HABS CAL,7-RICH,1-A-
1ph/2pg/1pc L

Santa Fe Railroad Depot
101 Garrad Blvd.
HABS CA-2342
6ph/2pg/1pc H

SAN PABLO

Castro-Alvarado Adobe (Racho San Pablo)
2748 San Pablo Ave.
HABS CA-1654
HABS CAL,7-SANPA,1-
1ph L

Racho San Pablo; see Castro-Alvarado Adobe

DEL NORTE COUNTY

CRESCENT CITY VIC.

Hiouchi Bridge; see Smith River Bridge

Smith River Bridge (Hiouchi Bridge)
CA State Hwy. 199 Spanning Smith River
HAER CA-75
HAER 1991(HAER):2
27ph/7pg/2pc L

SMITH RIVER

Rowdy Creek Bridge
Spanning Rowdy Creek at Fred Haight Dr.
HAER CA-68
HAER DLC/PP-1993:CA-3
29ph/3pg/3pc L

EL DORADO COUNTY

COLOMA

Barn
HABS CA-1377
HABS CAL,9-COLO,3A-
1ph L

Chinese Store (Ruins) (Wilder,Jonas,Store)
Main St.
HABS CA-1380
HABS CAL,9-COLO,5-
1ph L

House
HABS CA-1378
HABS CAL,9-COLO,4-
1ph L

Marshall,James W. ,Cabin
Marshall Monument Rd.
HABS CA-1309
HABS CAL,9-COLO,2-
3ph/fr L

Meyer House; see Sierra Nevada Hotel

Meyer's Dance Hall & Saloon
Shingle Spring Rd.
HABS CA-1381
HABS CAL,9-COLO,6-
2ph L

Orleans Hotel; see Post Office

Post Office (Orleans Hotel)
Main St.
HABS CA-1376
HABS CAL,9-COLO,1-
1ph L

Sierra Nevada Hotel (Meyer House)
HABS CA-1503
HABS CAL,9-COLO,7-
1ph L

Wilder,Jonas,Store; see Chinese Store (Ruins)

COLOMA VIC.

Meyer Hotel; see Sutter's Sawmill

Sutter's Sawmill (Meyer Hotel)
Marshall Gold Discovery State Historic Park
HABS CA-1301
HABS CAL,9-COLO.V,1-
5ph L

EL DORADO

Commercial Buildings,False Front
HABS CA-1355
HABS CAL,9-ELDO,1-
1ph L

Main Street (Store,Ruins)
HABS CA-1367
HABS CAL,9-ELDO,2-
1ph L

KELSEY

Allen's,Tom,Saloon; see Marshall,James W. ,House

Marshall,James W. ,Blacksmith Shop
HABS CA-1696
HABS CAL,9-KEL,2-
1ph L

Marshall,James W. ,House (Allen's,Tom,Saloon)
HABS CA-1308
HABS CAL,9-KEL,1-
1ph/fr L

KYBURZ

Kyburz Hotel (Yarnold's,Dick,Toll House; Mountain Retreat)
U. S. Hwy. 50
HABS CA-1708
HABS CAL,9-KYBUR,1-
1ph L

Mountain Retreat; see Kyburz Hotel

Yarnold's,Dick,Toll House; see Kyburz Hotel

MILLERTON

Fort Miller Blockhouse
Lake Millerton
HABS CA-1324
HABS CAL,10-MILL,1A-
1ph L

NASHVILLE

Barn,Log
HABS CA-1354
HABS CAL,9-NASHV,1-
1ph L

House
HABS CA-1353
HABS CAL,9-NASHV,2-
1ph L

PILOT HILL

Hotel
HABS CA-1382
HABS CAL,9-PILHI,1-
1ph L

PLACERVILLE

Bedford Inn
HABS CA-1364
HABS CAL,9-PLACVI,2-
1ph L

Bedford Street (House)
HABS CA-1370
HABS CAL,9-PLACVI,3-
2ph L

Bedford Street (House)
HABS CA-1375
HABS CAL,9-PLACVI,13-
1ph L

2934 Bedford Street (House)
HABS CA-1371
HABS CAL,9-PLACVI,4-
1ph L

50 Benham Street (House)
HABS CA-1368
HABS CAL,9-PLACVI,11-
2ph L

Building Adjoining Community Church
Main St.
HABS CA-1366
HABS CAL,9-PLACVI,10-
1ph L

California Automobile Association Building; see Main Street (Commercial Buildings)

Coloma Road (House)
HABS CA-1374
HABS CAL,9-PLACVI,5-
1ph L

Community Church; see El Dorado County Federated Church

El Dorado County Courthouse (Ruins)
Main St.
HABS CA-1675
HABS CAL,9-PLACVI,16-
1ph L

El Dorado County Federated Church
(Community Church)
Main St.
HABS CA-1365
HABS CAL,9-PLACVI,9-
1ph L

House,Brick & Stone
HABS CA-1373
HABS CAL,9-PLACVI,7-
1ph L

Main Street (Commercial Buildings)
HABS CA-1673
HABS CAL,9-PLACVI,15-
1ph L

Main Street (Commercial Buildings)
(California Automobile Association Building)
HABS CA-1362
HABS CAL,9-PLACVI,1-
2ph L

136 Main Street (House)
HABS CA-1372
HABS CAL,9-PLACVI,6-
1ph L

Pony Express Courier Bldg. ,(Strong Box & Cradle)
HABS CA-1707
HABS CAL,9-PLACVI,14-
2ph L

Thompson,Judge,House
32 Cedar Ravine
HABS CA-1369
HABS CAL,9-PLACVI,12-
1ph L

Zeisz,J. ,Building
HABS CA-1363
HABS CAL,9-PLACVI,8-
2ph L

PLACERVILLE VIC.

Chili Bar Bridge (South Fork American River Bridge)
Spanning S. Fork of American River at St. Hwy. 193
HAER CA-137
23ph/36pg/2pc H

South Fork American River Bridge; see Chili Bar Bridge

SHINGLE SPRINGS

Phelps Store
U. S. Hwy. 50
HABS CA-1357
HABS CAL,9-SHINGSP,1-
1ph L

STRAWBERRY

Strawberry House
Placerville Rd.
HABS CA-1682
HABS CAL,9-STRAW,1-
3ph L

TRAGEDY SPRINGS

Carved Tree Marker
HABS CA-1502
HABS CAL,9-TRAG,1-
1ph L

FRESNO COUNTY

BIG PINE

Shelter Cabin
Muir Pass
HABS CA-2336
HABS DLC/PP-1992:CA-5
1ph/1pc L

HUME

Hume Lake Dam
Sequioa National Forest
HAER CA-16
HAER CAL,10-HUME,1-
4dr/22ph/25pg/3pc/fr L

MILLERTON

Fort Miller
Lake Millerton
HABS CA-170
HABS CAL,10-MILL,1-
2ph L

Fort Miller Bakery
Lake Millerton
HABS CA-1329
HABS CAL,10-MILL,1E-
1ph L

Fort Miller Ford
Lake Millerton
HABS CA-1330
HABS CAL,10-MILL,1F-
1ph L

Fort Miller Hospital
Lake Millerton
HABS CA-1327
HABS CAL,10-MILL,1C-
1ph L

Fort Miller Mess Hall
Lake Millerton
HABS CA-1328
HABS CAL,10-MILL,1D-
2ph L

Fort Miller Officer's Quarters
Lake Millerton
HABS CA-1326
HABS CAL,10-MILL,1B-
2ph L

MILLERTON VIC.

Camp Barbour Blockhouse
HABS CA-1306
HABS CAL,10-MILL.V,1-
1ph L

GLENN COUNTY

HAMILTON CITY VIC.

Gianella Bridge (Gianelli Bridge)
State Hwy. 32,spanning Sacramento River
HAER CA-44
HAER CAL,11-HAMCI.V,1-
42ph/34pg/4pc L

Gianelli Bridge; see Gianella Bridge

WILLOWS

Glenn County Courthouse
526 Sycamore St.
HABS CA-1804
HABS CAL,11-WILL,1-
1ph L

HUMBOLDT COUNTY

ALTON VIC.

Alton Bridge; see Van Duzen River Bridge

Van Duzen River Bridge (Alton Bridge)
Spanning Van Duzen River at CA St. Hwy. 101
HAER CA-129
HAER DLC/PP-1993:CA-2
26ph/7pg/2pc L

ARCATA

Fourteenth & J Streets (House)
HABS CA-1457
HABS CAL,12-ARCA,1-
1ph L

Nixon House
1022 Tenth St.
HABS CA-1458
HABS CAL,12-ARCA,2-
2ph L

BRIDGEVILLE

Bridgeville,General View
HABS CA-1456
HABS CAL,12-BRIGVI,1-
1ph L

CARLOTTA VIC.

Upper Blue Slide Bridge,Bridge Number 4-94; see Van Duzen Bridge

Van Duzen Bridge (Upper Blue Slide Bridge,Bridge Number 4-94)
State Hwy. 36,spanning Van Duzen River
HAER CA-9
HAER CAL,12-CARL.V,1-
10ph/15pg/1pc L

EUREKA

Carson House (Ingomar Club)
143 M. St.
HABS CA-1911
HABS CAL,12-EVR,6- ι1991(HABS):5°
1dr/28ph/7pg/fr L

Fort Humboldt
HABS CA-1643
HABS CAL,12-EVR,5-
2ph L

314 H Street (House)
HABS CA-1461
HABS CAL,12-EVR,1-
3ph L

Hanna House; see Hustes House

Hustes House (Hanna House)
916 Second St.
HABS CA-1462
HABS CAL,12-EVR,2-
1ph L

Ingomar Club; see Carson House

Lindsay House
HABS CA-1459
HABS CAL,12-EVR,3-
1ph L

Stokes House
HABS CA-1460
HABS CAL,12-EVR,4-
3ph L

FERNDALE VIC.

Salt River Bridge (Valley Flower Bridge)
Spanning Salt River at Dillon Rd.
HAER CA-126
HAER DLC/PP-1993:CA-2
20ph/9pg/3pc L

Valley Flower Bridge; see Salt River Bridge

GARBERVILLE VIC.

Moody Bridge
Spanning South Fork Eel River
HAER CA-4
HAER CAL,12-GARB.V,1-
26ph/14pg/3pc L

HONEYDEW

Honeydew Creek Bridge
Wilder Ridge Rd.
HAER CA-22
HAER CAL,12-HOND,1-
14ph/10pg/1pc/fr L

MAD RIVER

Erickson Ranch House
HABS CA-1454
HABS CAL,12- ,1-
2ph L

Erickson Ranch Log Cabin
HABS CA-1455
HABS CAL,12- ,2-
1ph L

IMPERIAL COUNTY

WINTERHAVEN

Fort Yuma Old Barracks (Fort Yuma, Bldg. 210)
Yuma Indian Reservation
HABS CA-414
HABS CAL,13-WINT,1C-
3dr/fr L

Fort Yuma Old Indian Girls' Dormitory (Fort Yuma, Bldg. No. 209)
Yuma Indian Reservation
HABS CA-416
HABS CAL,13-WINT,2-
2dr/fr L

Fort Yuma Old Officers' Kitchen Cottage (Fort Yuma, Bldg. 208)
Yuma Indian Reservation
HABS CA-413
HABS CAL,13-WINT,1B-
3dr/fr L

Fort Yuma Old Officers' Quarters
Yuma Indian Reservaiton
HABS CA-412
HABS CAL,13-WINT,1A-
3dr/fr L

Fort Yuma, Bldg. No. 209; see Fort Yuma Old Indian Girls' Dormitory

Fort Yuma, Bldg. 208; see Fort Yuma Old Officers' Kitchen Cottage

Fort Yuma, Bldg. 210; see Fort Yuma Old Barracks

INYO COUNTY

DEATH VALLEY

Death Valley Ranch,Barn (Stables)
Death Valley National Monument
HABS CA-2257-D
HABS DLC/PP-1992:CA-2
6dr/30ph/12pg/2pc/fr L

Death Valley Ranch,Chimes Tower
Death Valley National Monument
HABS CA-2257-F
HABS DLC/PP-1992:CA-2
2dr/48ph/8pg/3pc/fr L

Death Valley Ranch,Cookhouse
Death Valley National Monument
HABS CA-2257-L
HABS DLC/PP-1992:CA-2
1dr/13ph/1pc/fr L

Death Valley Ranch,Entrance Gates & Dungeon Apt.
Death Valley National Monument
HABS CA-2257-H
HABS DLC/PP-1992:CA-2
2dr/5ph/5pg/1pc/fr L

Death Valley Ranch,Garage,Long Shed,Bunkhouse
Death Valley National Monument
HABS CA-2257-C
HABS DLC/PP-1992:CA-2
3dr/17ph/9pg/1pc/fr L

Death Valley Ranch,Guesthouse (Hacienda)
Death Valley National Monument
HABS CA-2257-B
HABS DLC/PP-1992:CA-2
4dr/27ph/8pg/2pc/fr L

Death Valley Ranch,Main House
Death Valley National Monument
HABS CA-2257-A
HABS DLC/PP-1992:CA-2
17dr/113ph/13pg/6pc/fr L

Death Valley Ranch,Power House
Death Valley National Monument
HABS CA-2257-E
HABS DLC/PP-1992:CA-2
3dr/32ph/9pg/2pc/fr L

Death Valley Ranch,Scotty's Castle
Death Valley National Monument
HABS CA-2257
HABS DLC/PP-1992:CA-2
6dr/5ph/63pg/1pc/fr L

Death Valley Ranch,Scotty's Original Castle
Death Valley National Monument
HABS CA-2257-M
HABS DLC/PP-1992:CA-2
1dr/4ph/1pc/fr L

Death Valley Ranch,Service Station,Gas Tank House
Death Valley National Monument
HABS CA-2257-G
HABS DLC/PP-1992:CA-2
1dr/8pg/fr L

Death Valley Ranch,Solar Heater
HABS CA-2257-K
HABS DLC/PP-1992:CA-2
3ph/5pg/1pc L

Death Valley Ranch,Swimming Pool
HABS CA-2257-I
HABS DLC/PP-1992:CA-2
4ph/5pg/1pc L

Death Valley Ranch,Wishing Well
Death Valley National Monument
HABS CA-2257-N
HABS DLC/PP-1992:CA-2
1dr/3ph/1pc/fr L

Death Valley,Gravel Plant,Bunker
HABS CA-2257-J
HABS DLC/PP-1992:CA-2
5ph/4pg/1pc L

Death Valley,Lower Grapevine Ranch
HABS CA-2286
HABS DLC/PP-1992:CA-2
1dr/7pg/fr L

Death Valley,Lower Grapevine Ranch,Blacksm. Forge
HABS CA-2286-C
HABS DLC/PP-1992:CA-2
1ph/1pc L

Death Valley,Lower Grapevine Ranch,Changing House
HABS CA-2286-E
HABS DLC/PP-1992:CA-2
4ph/1pc L

Death Valley,Lower Grapevine Ranch,Corral
HABS CA-2286-D
HABS DLC/PP-1992:CA-2
1ph/1pc L

Death Valley,Lower Grapevine Ranch,Garage
Death Valley National Monument
HABS CA-2286-B
HABS DLC/PP-1992:CA-2
1dr/1ph/1pc/fr L

Death Valley,Lower Grapevine Ranch,House
Death Valley National Monument
HABS CA-2286-A
HABS DLC/PP-1992:CA-2
3dr/6ph/1pc/fr L

KEELER

Main Street (Commercial Buildings)
HABS CA-1678
HABS CAL,14-KEEL,1-
1ph L

KERN COUNTY

LEBEC VIC.

Fort Tejon
Hwy. 99
HABS CA-39
HABS CAL,15-LEBEC.V,1-
1dr/2pg/fr L

Fort Tejon Barracks Number One
Hwy. 99
HABS CA-39-A
HABS CAL,15-LEBEC.V,1A-
2dr/3ph L

Fort Tejon Barracks Number Two
Hwy. 99
HABS CA-39-B
HABS CAL,15-LEBEC.V,1B-
2ph L

Fort Tejon Officers' Quarters
Hwy. 99
HABS CA-39-C
HABS CAL,15-LEBEC.V,1C-
3dr/3ph L

Fort Tejon Smokehouse
Hwy. 99
HABS CA-39-E
HABS CAL,15-LEBEC.V,1E-
1dr/1ph L

Fort Tejon Soldiers' Quarters
Hwy. 99
HABS CA-39-D
HABS CAL,15-LEBEC.V,1D-
2dr/2ph L

LAKE COUNTY

CLEAR LAKE

Cache Creek Bridge
Spanning Cache Creek,Dam Rd. vic.
HAER CA-49
HAER CAL,17-CLEAR,1-
15ph/7pg/1pc L

LASSEN COUNTY

HERLONG

Sierra Army Depot
HAER CA-25
HAER CAL,18-HERL,1-
39pg/fr L

SUSANVILLE VIC.

Fort Defiance (Roop's Fort)
HABS CA-1310
HABS CAL,18-SUSA.V,1-
2ph L

Roop's Fort; see Fort Defiance

LOS ANGELES COUNTY

ALHAMBRA

Alhambra Fire Station No. 4 (Fire Station No. 74)
2505 W. Norwood Pl.
HABS CA-2292
HABS 1991(HABS):5
9ph/2pg/1pc L

Fire Station No. 74; see Alhambra Fire Station No. 4

BALDWIN PARK

Baldwin Park City Hall; see Central School

Central School (Baldwin Park City Hall)
14403 E. Pacific Ave.
HABS CA-2016
HABS CAL,19-BALPK,1-
15ph L

BELL

Casa del Rancho San Antonio (Lugo,Vicente,House)
6360 E. Gage
HABS CA-36
HABS CAL,19-BEL,1-
4dr/3ph/1pg/fr L

Lugo,Vicente,House; see Casa del Rancho San Antonio

BEVERLY HILLS

Doheny Mansion (Greystone)
501 Doheny Rd.
HABS CA-2193
HABS CAL,19-BEVHI,1-
11ph/1pg/1pc L

Green Acres; see Lloyd,Harold,Estate

Greystone; see Doheny Mansion

Lloyd,Harold,Estate (Green Acres)
HABS CA-2192
HABS CAL,19-BEVHI,2-
20ph/1pg/2pc L

CALABASAS

Leonis,Miguel,Adobe
23537 Calabasas Rd.
HABS CA-342
HABS CAL,19-CALA,1-
5ph/12pg L

CALABASAS VIC.

Los Virgenes Rancho; see Reyes House

Reyes House (Los Virgenes Rancho)
State Hwy. 101
HABS CA-329
HABS CAL,19- ,1-
3dr/3ph/1pg L

CLAREMONT

Pitzer Psychological Services; see Pitzer Ranch,Pitzer-Peairs House

Pitzer Ranch
Bounded by Base Line Rd., Paoua and Towne Aves.
HABS CA-2267
HABS 1992(HABS):CA-1
12ph/19pg/2pc L

Pitzer Ranch, Garage
4353 Towne Ave.
HABS CA-2267-B
HABS 1992(HABS):CA-1
3ph/3pg/1pc L

Pitzer Ranch,Barn
100 ft. W. of Padua Ave. on Base Line Rd.
HABS CA-2267-I
HABS 1992(HABS):CA-1
5ph/4pg/1pc L

Pitzer Ranch,Foreman's Residence
926 E. Base Line Rd.
HABS CA-2267-D
HABS 1992(HABS):CA-1
5ph/5pg/1pc L

Pitzer Ranch,Pitzer-Peairs House
(Pitzer Psychological Services)
4353 Towne Ave.
HABS CA-2267-A
HABS 1992(HABS):CA-1
5ph/12pg/1pc L

Pitzer Ranch,Pumphouse
240 ft. W. of Padua Ave. at Base Line Rd.
HABS CA-2267-E
HABS 1992(HABS):CA-1
2ph/4pg/1pc L

Pitzer Ranch,Reservoir
SW Corner of Base Line Rod. and Padua Ave.
HABS CA-2267-J
HABS 1992(HABS):CA-1
4ph/3pg/1pc L

Pitzer Ranch,Rock Wall
4353 Towne Ave.
HABS CA-2267-C
HABS 1992(HABS):CA-1
11ph/3pg/1pc L

Pitzer Ranch,Shed
130 ft. W. of Padua Ave. on Base Line Rd.
HABS CA-2267-H
HABS 1992(HABS):CA-1
2ph/2pg/1pc L

Pitzer Ranch,Tenant House
150 ft. W. of Padua Ave. at Baseline Rd.
HABS CA-2267-G
HABS 1992(HABS):CA-1
3ph/2pg/1pc L

Pitzer Ranch,Water Tower
210 ft. W. of Padua Ave. at Base Line Rd.
HABS CA-2267-F-1
HABS 1992(HABS):CA-1
3ph/1pg/1pc L

ELIZABETH LAKE VIC.

Gorman,Maj. ,Stage Station
San Francisquito Rd.
HABS CA-330
HABS CAL,19-ELIZ.V,1-
4dr/3ph/1pg/fr L

GLENDALE

Casa Adobe de San Rafael
(Sanchez,Thomas,House)
1340 Dorothy Dr.
HABS CA-323
HABS CAL,19-GLEND,1-
3dr/5ph/1pg/fr L

Sanchez,Thomas,House; see Casa Adobe de San Rafael

INGLEWOOD

Academy Theater
3141 W. Manchester Blvd.
HABS CA-2020
HABS CAL,19-INGWO,2-
2ph/1pc L

Casa del Rancho Aguaja de la Centinela
7634 Midfield Rd.
HABS CA-312
HABS CAL,19-INGWO,1-
4dr/5ph/1pg/fr L

Freeman,Daniel,House
HABS CA-2115
HABS CAL,19-INGWO,3-
9ph/1pg/1pc L

LITTLEROCK VIC.

Littlerock Dam
Littlerock Creek
HAER CA-8
HAER CAL,19-LITRO.V,1-
19ph/53pg/2pc/1ct L

LONG BEACH

Casa de los Alamitos (Nieto,Don Manuel,House)
E. Anaheim Rd.
HABS CA-310
HABS CAL,19-LONGB,1-
4dr/1pg/fr L

Casa de los Cerritos (Temple,Don Juan,House)
4600 American Ave.
HABS CA-37-12
HABS CAL,19-LONGBN,1-
5dr/12ph/1pg/fr L

Ford Motor Co. Long Beach Ass. Plant,Assembly Bldg
700 Henry Ford Ave.
HAER CA-82-A
HAER DLC/PP-1992:CA-3
126ph/15pg/11pc/fr L

Ford Motor Co. Long Beach Assembly Plant,Crane
700 Henry Ford Ave.
HAER CA-82-C
HAER DLC/PP-1992:CA-3
6ph/5pg/1pc L

Ford Motor Co. Long Beach Assembly Plant,Oil House
700 Henry Ford Ave.
HAER CA-82-B
HAER DLC/PP-1992:CA-3
8ph/5pg/2pc L

Ford Motor Co. Long Beach Assembly Plant,Shed A
700 Henry Ford Ave.
HAER CA-82-D
HAER DLC/PP-1992:CA-3
2ph/6pg/1pc L

Ford Motor Co. Long Beach Assembly Plant,Sheds C&D
700 Henry Ford Ave.
HAER CA-82-E
HAER DLC/PP-1992:CA-3
3ph/6pg/1pc L

Ford Motor Company Long Beach Assembly Plant
700 Henry Ford Ave.
HAER CA-82
HAER DLC/PP-1992:CA-3
100pg/fr L

Nieto,Don Manuel,House; see Casa de los Alamitos

Temple,Don Juan,House; see Casa de los Cerritos

LOS ANGELES

"Angels Flight"
Third & Hill Sts.
HABS CA-337
HABS CAL,19-LOSAN,13-
5ph/6pg L

Apartments
462 S. Cochran Ave. & 5515-5525 W. Sixth St.
HABS CA-2042
HABS CAL,19-LOSAN,49-
1ph/1pc L

Barker Brothers Building
800 W. Seventh St.
HABS CA-2156
HABS CAL,19-LOSAN,54-
4ph/8pg/1pc L

Barn,Adobe; see El Escorpion Rancho

Barnsdall Park
4800 Hollywood Blvd.
HABS CA-1938
HABS CAL,19-LOSAN,55-
5dr/1pg/fr L

Barnsdall Park Residence A (Studio Residence A)
4800 Hollywood Blvd.
HABS CA-357
HABS CAL,19-LOSAN,29-
6ph/9pg L

Barnsdall,Aline,House; see Hollyhock House

Bolton Hall (Tujunga City Hall)
10110 Commerce Ave.
HABS CA-340
HABS CAL,19-TUJUN,1-
4ph/6pg L

Bradbury Building
304 S. Broadway
HABS CA-334
HABS CAL,19-LOSAN,11-
12dr/12ph/7pg/1pc/fr L

Broadway Department Store; see Coulter's Department Store

Bullocks-Wilshire Department Store
3050 Wilshire Blvd.
HABS CA-1941
HABS CAL,19-LOSAN,56-
1dr/9pg/fr L

Bunker Hill District
Temple,Fifth,Hill, & Fiqueroa Sts.
HABS CA-344
HABS CAL,19-LOSAN,17-
1ph/8pg L

Carl's Market; see Union Market

Casa Avila (Francisco,Don,Adobe)
14 Olvera St.
HABS CA-37-2
HABS CAL,19-LOSAN,2-
3dr/2ph/1pg/fr L

Casa Pelanconi
(Covacichi,Guiseppe,Building)
33-35 Olvera St.
HABS CA-37-3
HABS CAL,19-LOSAN,3-
5dr/2ph/1pg/fr L

Cathedral of St. Vibiana
Second & Main Sts.
HABS CA-343
HABS CAL,19-LOSAN,16-
4ph/11pg L

Coca-Cola Bottling Company
1334 S. Central Ave.
HABS CA-2022
HABS CAL,19-LOSAN,31-
2ph/1pc L

Coulter's Department Store (Broadway Department Store)
5600 Wilshire Blvd.
HABS CA-2023
HABS CAL,19-LOSAN,32-
2ph/1pc L

Covacichi,Guiseppe,Building; see Casa Pelanconi

Dark Room,The
5370 Wilshire Blvd.
HABS CA-2024
HABS CAL,19-LOSAN,33-
1ph/1pc L

Diamond Bar Ranch; see Vejar,Ricardo,Casa de

Dodge,Walter Luther,House
950 N. Kings Rd. ,West Hollywood District
HABS CA-355
HABS CAL,19-LOSAN,27-
9dr/34ph/9pg/1pc/fr L

Dominguez-Wilshire Building; see Hiss Tower

Drum Barracks Officers' Quarters
(Wilmington Federal Army Post Officers' Quarters)
1053-1955 Cary Ave.
HABS CA-353
HABS CAL,19-WILM,1A-
12ph/11pg L

523 East Third Street (House)
HABS CA-350
HABS CAL.19-LOSAN,18-
1ph/2pg L

Eastern Outfitting Company
849-851 S. Broadway
HABS CA-2025
HABS CAL,19-LOSAN,34-
2ph/1pc L

Edison Building
601 W. Fifth St.
HABS CA-2151
HABS CAL,19-LOSAN,57-
4ph/8pg/1pc L

El Alisal (Lummis,Charles,House)
200 East Ave.
HABS CA-339
HABS CAL,19-LOSAN,15-
5ph/13pg L

El Escorpion Rancho (Barn,Adobe)
400 Muirfield Rd.
HABS CA-326
HABS CAL,19-OWMO,1A-
4dr/3ph/1pg/fr L

Ennis House
2607 Glendower Ave.
HABS CA-1942
HABS CAL,19-LOSAN,58-
1dr/4pg L

Federal Title Building
437 S. Hill St.
HABS CA-2153
HABS CAL,19-LOSAN,59-
4ph/8pg/1pc L

Fifth Street Retaining Wall
Fifth St. btwn. Grand & Flower Sts.
HABS CA-2150
HABS CAL,19-LOSAN,60-
3ph/8pg/1pc L

Fire Station No. 28
644 S. Figueroa St.
HABS CA-2155
HABS CAL,19-LOSAN,61-
3ph/7pg/1pc L

First Masonic Temple; see Masonic Temple Number 42 F. & A. M.

Francisco,Don,Adobe; see Casa Avila

Freeman,Samuel,House
1962 Glencoe Way
HABS CA-1989
HABS CAL,19-LOSAN,62-
7dr/1pg/fr L

Friday Morning Club
938-940 S. Figueroa St.
HABS CA-2157
HABS CAL,19-LOSAN,63-
2ph/9pg/1pc L

Garnier Block
415 N. Los Angeles St.
HABS CA-321
HABS CAL,19-LOSAN,10-
1ph/6pg L

Goodyear Rubber Company
6701 S. Central Ave.
HAER CA-13
HAER CAL,19-LOSAN,52-
61ph/38pg/3pc/fr L

Hiss Tower (Dominguez-Wilshire Building)
5400-5420 Wilshire Blvd.
HABS CA-2027
HABS CAL,19-LOSAN,36-
1ph/1pc L

Documentation: **ct** color transparencies **dr** measured drawings **fr** field records
pc photograph captions **pg** pages of text **ph** photographs

Hollyhock House
(Barnsdall,Aline,House)
4800 Hollywood Blvd.
HABS CA-356
HABS CAL,19-LOSAN,28-
13ph/13pg L

Iglesia de Nuestra Senora la Reina de los Angeles; see Plaza Church

Jefferson,Thomas,High School
1319 E. Forty-First St.
HABS CA-2026
HABS CAL,19-LOSAN,35-
2ph/1pc L

KEHE Radio Studios
133-141 N. Vermont Ave.
HABS CA-2028
HABS CAL,19-LOSAN,37-
1ph/1pc L

LA Union Passenger Terminal,Mail,Bag. Express Bldg (LA Union Passenger Terminal,Utility Bldg; LA Union Passenger Terminal,Railway Expr. Agn.Bldg
800 N. Alameda St.
HABS CA-2158-B
HABS CAL,19-LOSAN,64-B-
54ph/3pg/4pc L

LA Union Passenger Terminal,Maintenance Dept. Bldg
800 N. Alameda St.
HABS CA-2158-D
HABS CAL,19-LOSAN,64-D-
3ph/1pc L

LA Union Passenger Terminal,Parking Lot
800 N. Alameda St.
HABS CA-2158-C
HABS CAL,19-LOSAN,64-C-
12ph/1pc L

LA Union Passenger Terminal,Railway Expr. Agn.Bldg; see LA Union Passenger Terminal,Mail,Bag. Express Bldg

LA Union Passenger Terminal,Utility Bldg; see LA Union Passenger Terminal,Mail,Bag. Express Bldg

Leimert Park Theater
3341 W. Forty-Third Pl.
HABS CA-2029
HABS CAL,19-LOSAN,38-
1ph/1pc L

Los Angeles City Hall
200 N. Spring St.
HABS CA-2159
HABS CAL,19-LOSAN,51-
16ph/8pg/1pc/fr L

Los Angeles Public Library
630 W. Fifth St.
HABS CA-1937
HABS CAL,19-LOSAN,65-
11dr/21ph/8pg/2pc/fr L

Los Angeles Union Passenger Terminal (Union Station)
800 N. Alameda St.
HABS CA-2158
HABS CAL,19-LOSAN,64-
7pg/fr L

Los Angeles Union Passenger Terminal,Tracks & Shed (Union Station)
800 N. Alameda St.
HABS CA-2158-A
HABS CAL,19-LOSAN,64-A-;1991(HABS):5
60ph/15pg/6pc L

Lovell (Health) House
4616 Dundee Dr.
HABS CA-1936
HABS CAL,19-LOSAN,66-
9dr/9pg/fr L

Lugo,Don Vicente,Casa de (St. Vincent's College)
516-522 1/2 N. Los Angeles St.
HABS CA-319
HABS CAL,19-LOSAN,7-
1dr/1ph/1pg/fr L

Lummis,Charles,House; see El Alisal

Masonic Temple Number 42 F. & A. M. (First Masonic Temple)
416 1/2 N. Main St.
HABS CA-32
HABS CAL,19-LOSAN,4-
1dr/1ph/1pg/fr L

May Company Department Store
6067 Wilshire Blvd.
HABS CA-2031
HABS CAL,19-LOSAN,39-
1ph/1pc L

Medical Square
2200 W. Third St.
HABS CA-2032
HABS CAL,19-LOSAN,40-
4ph/1pc L

Merced Theatre
420-422 N. Main St.
HABS CA-327
HABS CAL,19-LOSAN,8-
3dr/1ph/1pg/fr L

Merle Norman Building
2525 Main St.
HABS CA-2043
HABS CAL,19-LOSAN,50-
2ph/1pc L

Pan Pacific Auditorium
1600 Beverly Blvd.
HABS CA-2033
HABS CAL,19-LOSAN,41-
5ph/1pc L

Pico Hotel (Pico House,Old)
430 N. Main St.
HABS CA-317
HABS CAL,19-LOSAN,6-
8dr/1ph/1pg/fr L

Pico House,Old; see Pico Hotel

Plaza Church (Iglesia de Nuestra Senora la Reina de los Angeles)
535 N. Main St.
HABS CA-37-1
HABS CAL,19-LOSAN,1-
16dr/2ph/2pg/fr L

Plaza Fire House
126 Plaza St.
HABS CA-338
HABS CAL,19-LOSAN,14-
6ph/8pg L

Rancho La Brea Adobe
6301 W. Third St.
HABS CA-354
HABS CAL,19-LOSAN,26-
7ph/14pg L

Rancho Rincon de los Bueyes; see Rocha,Antonio Jose,House

Rees & Wirsching Building
223-227 N. Los Angeles St.
HABS CA-318
HABS CAL,19-LOSAN,9-
1ph/5pg L

Richfield Oil Building
555 S. Flower St.
HABS CA-1987
HABS CAL,19-LOSAN,67-
17dr/59ph/7pg/4pc L

Rocha,Antonio Jose,House (Rancho Rincon de los Bueyes)
Cadillac & Shenandoah Sts.
HABS CA-311
HABS CAL,19-LOSAN,5-
3dr/2ph/1pg/fr L

Sawtelle Veterans' Admin. Ctr. Domiciliary No. Six
Wilshire & Sawtelle
HABS CA-336
HABS CAL,19-LOSAN,12B-
2ph/8pg L

Sawtelle Veterans' Administration Center Chapels
Wilshire & Sawtelle Blvds.
HABS CA-335
HABS CAL,19-LOSAN,12A-
5ph/7pg L

Schindler,Rudolph M. ,House
833 N. Kings Rd.
HABS CA-1939
HABS CAL,19-LOSAN,68-
6dr/5pg L

Security First National Bank Building
5207-5209 Wilshire Blvd.
HABS CA-2039
HABS CAL,19-LOSAN,46-
3ph/1pc L

Selig Commercial Building
269-273 Western Ave.
HABS CA-2041
HABS CAL,19-LOSAN,48-
2ph/1pc L

Skinner House
1530 Easterly Terrace
HABS CA-2035
HABS CAL,19-LOSAN,42-
2ph L

Smith,Nelson K. ,House
191 S. Hudson Ave.
HABS CA-2036
HABS CAL,19-LOSAN,43-
4ph/1pc L

221 South Bunker Hill Avenue (House)
HABS CA-348
HABS CAL,19-LOSAN,22-
1ph/2pg L

237-241 South Bunker Hill Avenue (House)
HABS CA-347
HABS CAL,19-LOSAN,21-
1ph/2pg L

238 South Bunker Hill Avenue (House)
HABS CA-352
HABS CAL,19-LOSAN,23-
1ph/2pg L

251 South Bunker Hill Avenue (House)
HABS CA-351
HABS CAL,19-LOSAN,24-
1ph/2pg L

245 South Grand Avenue (House)
HABS CA-349
HABS CAL,19-LOSAN,25-
1ph/2pg L

221 South Olive Street (House)
HABS CA-346
HABS CAL,19-LOSAN,20-
1ph/2pg L

Sowden House
5121 Franklin Ave.
HABS CA-1940
HABS CAL,19-LOSAN,69-
8dr/18ph/6pg/1pc/fr L

St. Vincent's College; see Lugo,Don Vicente,Casa de

Storer House
8161 Hollywood Blvd.
HABS CA-1944
HABS CAL,19-LOSAN,70-
7dr/2pg L

Story, W. P. ,Building,(Garage Entrance)
610 S. Broadway
HABS CA-2040
HABS CAL,19-LOSAN,47-
5ph/1pc L

Studio Residence A; see Barnsdall Park Residence A

Subway Terminal Building
415-417 S. Hill St.
HABS CA-2154
HABS CAL,19-LOSAN,71-
3ph/9pg/1pc L

Sunset Towers Apartments
8358 Sunset Blvd.
HABS CA-2037
HABS CAL,19-LOSAN,44-
2ph/1pc L

Title Guarantee & Trust Building
401 W. Fifth St.
HABS CA-2152
HABS CAL,19-LOSAN,72-
5ph/9pg/1pc L

Tujunga City Hall; see Bolton Hall

Union Market (Carl's Market)
1530-1536 W. Sixth St.
HABS CA-2021
HABS CAL,19-LOSAN,30-
1ph L

Union Station; see Los Angeles Union Passenger Terminal

Union Station; see Los Angeles Union Passenger Terminal,Tracks & Shed

Val D'Amour Apartments
854 Oxford Ave.
HABS CA-2038
HABS CAL,19-LOSAN,45-
2ph/1pc L

Vejar,Ricardo,Casa de (Diamond Bar Ranch)
Valley Blvd.
HABS CA-37-10
HABS CAL,19-SPAD,1-
3dr/2ph/1pg/fr L

Venice Canals
Community of Venice
HAER CA-124
HAER DLC/PP-1993:CA-2
65ph/23pg/8pc L

Watts Towers of Simon Rodia
176 E. One-hundred-and-seventh St.
HABS CA-2119
HABS CAL,19-LOSAN,73-
2ph/1pc/7ct L

605 West Third Street (House)
HABS CA-345
HABS CAL,19-LOSAN,19-
1ph/2pg L

Wilmington Federal Army Post Officers' Quarters; see Drum Barracks Officers' Quarters

Zanja No. 3: Brick Culvert
Alameda St. between Temple & Aliso Sts.
HAER CA-50
HAER CAL,19-LOSAN,53-
1dr/14ph/51pg/1pc/fr L

LYNWOOD

Lynwood Pacific Electric Railway Depot
11453 Long Beach Blvd.
HABS CA-2074
HABS CAL,19-LYN,1-
10ph/3pg/1pc L

PACIFIC PALISADES

Rogers,Will,Ranch
14253 Sunset Blvd.
HABS CA-2273
HABS 1991(HABS):5
2dr L

Rogers,Will,Ranch,Guest House
14253 Sunset Blvd.
HABS CA-2273-B
HABS 1991(HABS):5
1dr/1pg/fr L

Rogers,Will,Ranch,Main House
14253 Sunset Blvd.
HABS CA-2273-A
HABS 1991(HABS):5
3dr/2pg/fr L

Rogers,Will,Ranch,Stables
14253 Sunset Blvd.
HABS CA-2273-C
HABS 1991(HABS):5
3dr/1pg/fr L

PASADENA

Busch,Max,House
160 S. San Rafael St.
HABS CA-2191
HABS CAL,19-PASA,4-
5ph/1pc L

Colorado Street Bridge
Spanning the Arroyo Seco at Colorado Blvd.
HAER CA-58
HAER 1991(HAER):2
13ph/34pg/2pc/fr L

El Molino Viejo
1120 Old Mill Rd.
HABS CA-34
HABS CAL,19-PASA,1-
6dr/4ph/1pg/fr L

Gamble,David B.,House; see Gamble,House,The

Gamble,House,The (Gamble,David B.,House)
4 Westmoreland Pl.
HABS CA-1981
HABS CAL,19-PASA,5-
11dr/4pg L

Huntington Hotel
1401 S. Oak Knoll Ave.
HABS CA-2251
HABS DLC/PP-1992:CA-3
15dr/20ph/99pg/2pc/fr L

Irwin,Theodore,House
240 N. Grand Ave.
HABS CA-1985
HABS CAL,19-PASA,6-
14dr/5pg/fr L

McCornack Army Hospital; see Vista del Arroyo Hotel Complex

McCornack Army Hospital,Bldg No. 16; see Vista del Arroyo Hotel Complex,Bungalow H

McCornack Army Hospital,Building No. 15; see Vista del Arroyo Hotel Complex,Bungalow G

McCornack Army Hospital,Building No. 2; see Vista del Arroyo Hotel Complex,Bungalow No. 5

McCornack Army Hospital,Building No. 3; see Vista Del Arroyo Hotel Complex,Arroyo Vista

Miltimore House
1301 Chelton Way
HABS CA-1988
HABS CAL,19-PASA,7-
6dr/8pg/fr L

Neighborhood Church
S. Pasadena Ave. & W. California Blvd.
HABS CA-2116
HABS CAL.19-PASA,8-
13ph/1pc L

Pasadena City Hall
100 N. Garfield Ave.
HABS CA-420
HABS CAL,19-PASA,2-
8ph/10pg/1pc/fr L

Prospect Boulevard Bridge
Prospect Blvd. spanning Seco St.
HAER CA-23
HAER CAL,19-PASA,3-
37ph/8pg/2pc L

Tilt,J. E. ,House
455 Bradford St.
HABS CA-2190
HABS CAL,19-PASA,9-
9ph/1pc L

Vista del Arroyo Hotel Comp.,Hinds & Conner Bungal (Vista del Arroyo Hotel Complex,Bungalow No. 7; Vista del Arroyo Hotel Complex,Apts. No. 248-250)
125 S. Grand Ave.
HABS CA-2184-H
9ph/13pg/1pc H

Vista del Arroyo Hotel Comp.,Stowell & Proust Bung (Vista del Arroyo Hotel Complex,Bungalow No. 6; Vista del Arroyo Hotel Complex,Apts. No. 133-139)
125 S. Grand Ave.
HABS CA-2184-G
5ph/11pg/1pc H

Vista del Arroyo Hotel Complex (McCornack Army Hospital)
125 S. Grand Ave.
HABS CA-2184
HABS CAL,19-PASA,10-
4ph/1pg/1pc L

Vista del Arroyo Hotel Complex,Apts. No. 115-122; see Vista del Arroyo Hotel Complex,Hamilton Bungalow

Vista del Arroyo Hotel Complex,Apts. No. 123-132; see Vista del Arroyo Hotel Complex,Bungalow No. 3

Vista del Arroyo Hotel Complex,Apts. No. 133-139; see Vista del Arroyo Hotel Comp.,Stowell & Proust Bung

Vista del Arroyo Hotel Complex,Apts. No. 161-175; see Vista del Arroyo Hotel Complex,Bungalow A

Vista del Arroyo Hotel Complex,Apts. No. 248-250; see Vista del Arroyo Hotel Comp.,Hinds & Conner Bungal

Vista Del Arroyo Hotel Complex,Arroyo Vista (McCornack Army Hospital,Building No. 3)
125 S. Grand Ave.
HABS CA-2184-B
HABS CAL,19-PASA,10-B-
5ph/5pg/1pc L

Vista del Arroyo Hotel Complex,Bungalow A (Vista del Arroyo Hotel Complex,Bungalow No. 8; Vista del Arroyo Hotel Complex,Apts. No. 161-175)
125 S. Grand Ave.
HABS CA-2184-I
10ph/16pg/1pc H

Vista del Arroyo Hotel Complex,Bungalow G (McCornack Army Hospital,Building No. 15)
125 S. Grand Ave.
HABS CA-2184-D
HABS CAL,19-PASA,10-D-
5ph/2pg/1pc L

Vista del Arroyo Hotel Complex,Bungalow H (McCornack Army Hospital,Bldg No. 16)
125 S. Grand Ave.
HABS CA-2184-C
HABS CAL,19-PASA,10-C-
3ph/3pg/1pc L

Vista del Arroyo Hotel Complex,Bungalow No. 3 (Vista del Arroyo Hotel Complex,Apts. No. 123-132)
125 S. Grand Ave.
HABS CA-2184-F
7ph/17pg/1pc H

Vista del Arroyo Hotel Complex,Bungalow No. 4; see Vista del Arroyo Hotel Complex,Hamilton Bungalow

Vista del Arroyo Hotel Complex,Bungalow No. 5 (McCornack Army Hospital,Building No. 2)
125 S. Grand Ave.
HABS CA-2184-A
HABS CAL,19-PASA,10-A-
3ph/2pg/1pc L

Vista del Arroyo Hotel Complex,Bungalow No. 6; see Vista del Arroyo Hotel Comp.,Stowell & Proust Bung

Vista del Arroyo Hotel Complex,Bungalow No. 7; see Vista del Arroyo Hotel Comp.,Hinds & Conner Bungal

Vista del Arroyo Hotel Complex,Bungalow No. 8; see Vista del Arroyo Hotel Complex,Bungalow A

Vista del Arroyo Hotel Complex,Hamilton Bungalow (Vista del Arroyo Hotel Complex,Bungalow No. 4; Vista del Arroyo Hotel Complex,Apts. No. 115-122)
125 S. Grand Ave.
HABS CA-2184-E
6ph/17pg/1pc H

POMONA

Palomares,Yqnaclo,Casa de
1569 N. Park Ave.
HABS CA-37-25
HABS CAL,19-POMO,1-
4dr/3ph/1pg/fr L

SAN DIMAS VIC.

Carrion,Saturnino,Casa de
Mountain Meadows Rd.
HABS CA-315
HABS CAL,19-SAND.V,1-
4dr/2ph/1pg/fr L

SAN FERNANDO

Celis,Eulogio de,House; see Pico,Andres,House

Harrington,M. R. ,House; see Pico,Andres,House

Lopez,Geronimo,Casa de
1102 Pico St.
HABS CA-341
HABS CAL,19-SANF,3-
4ph/7pg L

Mission San Fernando Rey de Espana Church
1551 San Fernando Rd.
HABS CA-325-B
HABS CAL,19-SANF,2B-
8dr/7ph/1pg/1pc L

Mission San Fernando Rey de Espana Fountains
15151 San Fernando Rd.
HABS CA-325-C
HABS CAL,19-SANF,2C-
2ph L

Mission San Fernando Rey de Espana Monastery
15151 San Fernando Rd.
HABS CA-37-5
HABS CAL,19-SANF,2A-
7dr/7ph/1pg/2pc L

Pico,Andres,House (Celis,Eulogio de,House; Harrington,M. R. ,House)
10940 Sepulveda Blvd.
HABS CA-324
HABS CAL,19-SANF,1-
8dr/4ph/1pg/fr L

SAN GABRIEL

Casa Viejo de Lopez
330 N. Santa Anita Ave.
HABS CA-316
HABS CAL,19-SANGA,3-
4dr/1ph/1pg/fr L

Grape Vine Adobe; see Padillo Adobe

Las Tunas Rancho; see Purcell House

Mission San Gabriel Arcangel
W. Mission Dr. & Junipero Serra St.
HABS CA-37-8
HABS CAL,19-SANGA,1-
12dr/12ph/3pg/fr L

Mission San Gabriel Arcangel Industrial Shop Ruins
W. Mission Dr. & Junipero Serra St.
HABS CA-37-8-A
HABS CAL,19-SANGA,1A-
7dr/9ph/fr L

Mission San Gabriel Arcangel Mill
W. Mission Dr. & Junipero Serra St.
HABS CA-37-8-B
HABS CAL,19-PASA,1-
12ph L

Padillo Adobe (Grape Vine Adobe)
Mission Dr.
HABS CA-328
HABS CAL,19-SANGA,4-
3dr/2ph/1pg/fr L

Purcell House (Las Tunas Rancho)
308 Mission
HABS CA-35
HABS CAL,19-SANGA,2-
3dr/3ph/1pg/fr L

SAN MARINO

Blanco,Miquel,Casa de
2625 Huntington Dr.
HABS CA-322
HABS CAL,19-SANMA,1-
6dr/4ph/1pg/fr L

SAN PEDRO

American Trona Corporation; see Fort MacArthur,Raw Salt Storage & Processing Bldgs

Fort MacArthur (500 Varas Square)
Pacific Ave.
HABS CA-2206
HABS CAL,19-SANPE,2-
4dr/53ph/21pg/5pc/fr L

Fort MacArthur,Raw Salt Storage & Processing Bldgs (American Trona Corporation)
Pacific Ave.
HAER CA-21
HAER CAL,19-SANPE,1-
4dr/7ph/10pg/1pc L

500 Varas Square; see Fort MacArthur

SANTA CATALINA ISL.

Mount Ada; see Wrigley,William,House

Wrigley,William,House (Mount Ada)
HABS CA-2189
HABS CAL,19-SANCA,1-
13ph/1pg/1pc/fr L

SANTA MONICA

West,Horatio,Court Apartments
140 Hollister St.
HABS CA-1984
HABS CAL,19-SANMO,1-
11dr/6ph/5pg/1pc/fr L

SIERRA MADRE VIC.

Shortcut Ranger Station,Angeles National Forest; see West Fork Ranger Station

West Fork Ranger Station (Shortcut Ranger Station,Angeles National Forest)
Rincon-Red Box Rd.
HABS CA-2202
HABS CAL,19-SIMA.V,1-
12ph/3pg/1pc L

SOUTH PASADENA

Adobe Flores; see Perez,Jose,Casa de

Oakland Avenue Waiting Station
Oakland Ave. at Fair Oaks Ave.
HABS CA-2290
HABS 1991(HABS):5
5dr/fr L

Perez,Jose,Casa de (Adobe Flores)
1804 Foothill Blvd.
HABS CA-33
HABS CAL,19-PASAS,1-
5dr/6ph/1pg/fr L

SYLMAR VIC.

LA-94-C; see Los Pinetos Nike Missile Site

LA-94-L; see Los Pinetos Nike Missile Site

Los Pinetos Nike Missile Site (LA-94-L; LA-94-C)
Santa Clara Rd.,Los Angeles National Forest
HAER CA-56
HAER 1992(HAER):CA-1
26ph/65pg/3pc L

Mt. Gleason Nike Missile Site
Angeles National Forest, S. of Soledad Canyon
HAER CA-57
HAER 1992(HAER):CA-1
71ph/71pg/6pc L

TERMINAL ISLAND

Double-Compound Steam Engine,"Sierra Nevada" (Ferryboat "Feather River"; Ferryboat "Edward T. Jeffrey")
Seaplane Anchorage vic.
HAER CA-24
HAER CAL,19-TERMIS,1-
15ph/13pg/1pc/fr L

Ferryboat "Edward T. Jeffrey"; see Double-Compound Steam Engine,"Sierra Nevada"

Ferryboat "Feather River"; see Double-Compound Steam Engine,"Sierra Nevada"

WHITTIER

Hacienda del Rancho Paso; see Pico,Pio,Casa de

Pico,Pio,Casa de (Hacienda del Rancho Paso)
Whittier Blvd. & Guirado St.
HABS CA-37-24
HABS CAL,19-WHIT,1-
6dr/7ph/1pg/fr L

Whittier Theatre
11602-11612 E. Whittier Blvd.
HABS CA-2291
HABS 1992(HABS):CA-1
53ph/23pg/4pc/fr L

MARIN COUNTY

ANGEL ISLAND

Fort McDowell
Angel Island
HABS CA-1841
HABS CAL,21-ANGEL,1-
1ph L

BOLINAS

Booth, F. E. Company Pier (Point Reyes National Seashore)
Point Reyes National Seashore
HABS CA-2073
HABS CAL,21-BOLI,1-
15ph/2pg/1pc L

Point Reyes National Seashore; see Booth, F. E. Company Pier

LAGUNITAS VIC.

Shafter Bridge
Spanning Lagunitas Creek on Sir Francis Drake Blvd
HAER CA-10
HAER CAL,21-LAG.V,1-
4ph/16pg/1pc L

OLEMA VIC.

Lime Kiln
State Hwy. 1
HABS CA-1437
HABS CAL,21-OLEM.V,1-
5ph L

POINT REYES

Point Reyes Lighthouse
Point Reyes National Seashore
HABS CA-2250
HABS CAL,21-POREY,1-
5dr/10ph/1pc L

SAN RAFAEL

Marin County Courthouse
Fourth St. between A & Court Sts.
HABS CA-1955
HABS CAL,21-SANRA,2-
8dr/7ph/5pg/1pc/fr L

Mission San Rafael Archangel
HABS CA-1131
HABS CAL,21-SANRA,1-
10ph L

SAUSALITO

Steam Schooner "Wapama"
San Francisco Maritime National Historical Park
HAER CA-67
HAER DLC/PP-1992:CA-3
38ph/1pg/3pc L

SAUSALITO VICINITY

Fort Cronkhite,Anit-Aircraft Battery No. 1
Wolf Ridge
HAER CA-134-1
2ph/18pg/1pc H

Fort Cronkhite,Anti-Arcft.Bat.No.1,Battery Offices
Wolf Ridge
HAER CA-134-1-C
2ph/1pc H

Fort Cronkhite,Anti-Arcft.Bat.No.1,Buried Quonset, (Hutmet)
Wolf Ridge
HAER CA-134-1-D
2ph/1pc H

Fort Cronkhite,Anti-Arcft.Bat.No.1,Concrete Foot., (Generator Pad)
Wolf Road
HAER CA-134-1-G
1ph/1pc H

Fort Cronkhite,Anti-Arcft.Bat.No.1,Director Pit
Wolf Ridge
HAER CA-134-1-B
2ph/1pc H

Fort Cronkhite,Anti-Arcft.Bat.No.1,Hutmet Anteroom
Wolf Ridge
HAER CA-134-1-E
2ph/1pc H

Fort Cronkhite,Anti-Arcrft.Bat.No.1,Height Finder
Wolf Ridge
HAER CA-134-1-A
2ph/1pc H

Generator Pad; see Fort Cronkhite,Anti-Arcft.Bat.No.1,Concrete Foot.,

Hutmet; see Fort Cronkhite,Anti-Arcft.Bat.No.1,Buried Quonset,

SAUSALITO VICINTIY

Fort Cronkhite,Anti-Arcft.Bat.No.1,DayRoom/MessHal
Wolf Ridge
HAER CA-134-1-F
1ph/1pc H

MARIPOSA COUNTY

AGUA FRIA

Agua Fria,General View
HABS CA-154
HABS CAL,22-AGUA,1-
1ph L

BAGBY

Bagby,General View (Benton Hills)
HABS CA-1703
HABS CA,22-BAG,1-
1ph L

Benton Hills; see Bagby,General View

Railroad Station (Yosemite National Park)
Yosemite National Park
HABS CA-1650
HABS CAL,22-BAG,2-
3dr/fr L

Yosemite National Park; see Railroad Station

BEAR VALLEY

Bear House Hotel; see Oso House Hotel

Fremont Cottage
HABS CA-1861
HABS CAL,22-BEAR,3-
1ph L

Oso House Hotel (Bear House Hotel)
HABS CA-1106
HABS CAL,22-BEAR,1-
2ph L

Wells Fargo Building
HABS CA-1704
HABS CAL,22-BEAR,2-
1ph L

COULTERVILLE

Bruschi Building (Bruschi Warehouse)
Main St.
HABS CA-1531
HABS CAL,22-COULT,3-
1ph L

Bruschi Stores
Main St.
HABS CA-1532
HABS CAL,22-COULT,4-
1ph L

Bruschi Warehouse; see Bruschi Building

Coulter's Hotel & Wagoner's Store
Main St.
HABS CA-1533
HABS CAL,22-COULT,5-
1ph L

Coulterville,General Views
Main St.
HABS CA-1336
HABS CAL,22-COULT,1-
2ph L

CURRY VILLAGE

Curry,Foster,Cabin (Yosemite National Park)
HABS CA-2181
HABS CAL,22-CURVI,1-
7ph/2pg/1pc L

Yosemite National Park; see Curry,Foster,Cabin

FORESTA VIC.

Meyer,George,Barn No. 1 (Yosemite National Park)
Old Coulterville Rd.
HABS CA-2182-A
HABS CAL,22-FOR.V,1-A-
6ph/2pg/1pc L

Meyer,George,Barn No. 2 (Yosemite National Park)
Old Coulterville Rd.
HABS CA-2182-B
HABS CAL,22-FOR.V,1-B-
7ph/2pg/1pc L

Yosemite National Park; see Meyer,George,Barn No. 1

Yosemite National Park; see Meyer,George,Barn No. 2

HORNITOS

Fandango Dance Hall
HABS CA-1530
HABS CAL,22-HORNI,9-
1ph L

Ghirardelli's Store (Ruins)
HABS CA-1526
HABS CAL,22-HORNI,8-
1ph L

Hornitos Hotel
HABS CA-1102
HABS CAL,22-HORNI,7-
2ph L

House,Adobe
HABS CA-1101
HABS CAL,22-HORNI,6-
1ph L

Jail
HABS CA-1522
HABS CAL,22-HORNI,4-
1ph L

Masonic Hall
HABS CA-1523
HABS CAL,22-HORNI,5-
1ph L

Native Sons of the Golden West Building (Wells Fargo Building)
HABS CA-1521
HABS CAL,22-HORNI,3-
1ph L

Plaza
HABS CA-1103
HABS CAL,22-HORNI,1-
1ph L

Principal Street & Plaza
HABS CA-1104
HABS CAL,22-HORNI,2-
1ph L

Wells Fargo Building; see Native Sons of the Golden West Building

INDIAN GULCH

Solari Hotel
HABS CA-1525
HABS CAL,22-INDI,1-
1ph L

MARIPOSA

Fremont's Store & Assay Office
HABS CA-1528
HABS CAL,22-MARI,2-
1ph L

Gazette Building
Mariposa County Fairgrounds
HABS CA-1534
HABS CAL,22-MARI,3-
1ph L

Mariposa County Courthouse
HABS CA-1105
HABS CAL,22-MARI,1-
2ph L

MORMAN BAR

Chinese Adobe Building
HABS CA-1529
HABS CAL,22-MORM,1-
1ph L

MOUNT BULLION

Marre Store
HABS CA-1527
HABS CAL,22-MOUB,1-
1ph L

MOUNT OPHIR

Trabucco Store (Ruins)
HABS CA-1524
HABS CAL,22-MOUTO,1-
1ph L

WAWONA

Chinquapin Service Station & Lunch Room
Glacier Point Rd. & State Hwy. 41
HABS CA-2299
HABS DLC/PP-1992:CA-4
13ph/9pg/1pc L

Wawona Hotel Complex
Yosemite Nat'l Park
HABS CA-1805
HABS CAL,22-WAWO,1-
6ph/29pg/1pc/fr L

Wawona Hotel Complex,Annex Building
Yosemite Nat'l Park
HABS CA-1805-G
HABS CAL,22-WAWO,1-G-
4dr/5ph/1pc/fr L

Wawona Hotel Complex,Clark Cottage; see Wawona Hotel Complex,Long White

Wawona Hotel Complex,Hotel
Yosemite Nat'l Park
HABS CA-1805-B
HABS CAL,22-WAWO,1-B-
10dr/10ph/1pc/fr L

Wawona Hotel Complex,Little Brown (Wawona Hotel Complex,Moore Cottage)
Yosemite Nat'l Park
HABS CA-1805-E
HABS CAL,22-WAWO,1-E-
5dr/3ph/1pc/fr L

Wawona Hotel Complex,Little White (Wawona Hotel Complex,Manager's Cottage)
Yosemite Nat'l Park
HABS CA-1805-C
HABS CAL,22-WAWO,1-C-
1dr/2ph/1pc/fr L

Wawona Hotel Complex,Long Brown (Wawona Hotel Complex,Washburn Cottage)
Yosemite Nat'l Park
HABS CA-1805-F
HABS CAL,22-WAWO,1-F-
7dr/2ph/1pc/fr L

Wawona Hotel Complex,Long White (Wawona Hotel Complex,Clark Cottage)
Yosemite Nat'l Park
HABS CA-1805-A
HABS CAL,22-WAWO,1-A-
6dr/2ph/1pc/fr L

Wawona Hotel Complex,Manager's Cottage; see Wawona Hotel Complex,Little White

Wawona Hotel Complex,Moore Cottage; see Wawona Hotel Complex,Little Brown

Wawona Hotel Complex,Thomas Hill Studio
Yosemite Nat'l Park
HABS CA-1805-D
HABS CAL,22-WAWO,1-D-
5dr/3ph/1pc/fr L

Wawona Hotel Complex,Washburn Cottage; see Wawona Hotel Complex,Long Brown

YOSEMITE NAT'L PARK

Cascades Power Plant; see Yosemite Hydroelectric Power Plant

Yosemite Hydroelectric Power Plant (Cascades Power Plant)
Hwys. 120 & 140,Yosemite National Park
HAER CA-20
HAER 1991(HAER):2
1dr/47ph/36pg/5pc L

YOSEMITE NATL. PARK

Cedar Cottage
HABS CA-1645
HABS CAL,22-YOSEM,2-
5dr L

Sentinel Hotel (Yosemite National Park)
HABS CA-1644
HABS CAL,22-YOSEM,1-
7dr/1ph/1pc L

Yosemite Chapel
HABS CA-1649
HABS CAL,22-YOSEM,3-
5dr L

Yosemite National Park; see Sentinel Hotel

YOSEMITE VILLAGE

Degnan,John,House (Yosemite National Park)
Southside Dr.
HABS CA-2178
HABS CAL,22-YOSVI,1-
6ph/1pg/1pc L

Degnan,John,House,Bakery (Yosemite National Park)
Southside Dr.
HABS CA-2178-B
HABS CAL,22-YOSVI,1-B-
5ph/1pg/1pc L

Degnan,John,House,Garage (Yosemite National Park)
Southside Dr.
HABS CA-2178-A
HABS CAL,22-YOSVI,1-A-
3ph/1pc L

Pohono Indian Studio (Yosemite National Park)
HABS CA-2180
HABS CAL,22-YOSVI,2-
5ph/2pg/1pc L

Superintendent's Residence (Yosemite National Park)
HABS CA-2179
HABS CAL,22-YOSVI,3-
11ph/3pg/1pc L

Superintendent's Residence,Garage (Yosemite National Park)
HABS CA-2179-A
HABS CAL,22-YOSVI,3-A-
3ph/2pg/1pc L

Yosemite National Park; see Degnan,John,House

Yosemite National Park; see Degnan,John,House,Bakery

Yosemite National Park; see Degnan,John,House,Garage

Yosemite National Park; see Pohono Indian Studio

Yosemite National Park; see Superintendent's Residence

Yosemite National Park; see Superintendent's Residence,Garage

MENDOCINO COUNTY

ALBION

Albion,General View
Albion River Vic.
HABS CA-1468
HABS CAL,23-ALB,1-
2ph L

Lumber Mill
Albion River
HABS CA-1469
HABS CAL,23-ALB,2-
1ph L

ELK

Elk,General View
HABS CA-1471
HABS CAL,23-ELK,1-
1ph L

FORT BRAGG VIC.

School
HABS CA-1465
HABS CAL,23-FOBRA.V,1-
1ph L

MENDOCINO

Bank of America; see Bank of Commerce

Bank of Commerce (Bank of America)
45100 Main St.
HABS CA-2243
HABS CAL,23-MENCI,25-
3ph/1pg/1pc L

Connemara House,Water Tower
Little Lake Rd.
HABS CA-2241
HABS CAL,23-MENCI,3-
3ph/1pc L

Denslow-Maxwell House
600 Kasten St.
HABS CA-2237
HABS CAL,23-MENCI,4-
3ph/1pg/1pc/1ct L

Ford House
735 Main St.,Mendocino Headlands State Park
HABS CA-2232
HABS CAL,23-MENCI,5-
2ph/1pg/1pc/1ct L

Fraga House,Water Tower (Frago House,Water Tower)
45040 Calpella St.
HABS CA-2231
HABS CAL,23-MENCI,6-
2ph/1pg/1pc L

Frago House,Water Tower; see Fraga House,Water Tower

Gallery Fair; see Odd Fellows Hall

Golgert House
Ukiah St.
HABS CA-2239
HABS CAL,23-MENCI,7-
2ph/1pg/1pc/fr L

Gorden,Henry,House (Gorden,Lupy,House; Gordon,Henry,House)
10521 School St.
HABS CA-2233
HABS CAL,23-MENCI,8-
2ph/1pg/1pc L

Gorden,Lupy,House; see Gorden,Henry,House

Gordon,Henry,House; see Gorden,Henry,House

Grindle,Joshua,House
44800 Little Lake Rd.
HABS CA-2230
HABS CAL,23-MENCI,9-
3ph/3pg/1pc L

Hills,Spencer,House
44900 Little Lake Rd.
HABS CA-2234
HABS CAL,23-MENCI,10-
3ph/3pg/1pc L

Jarvis-Nichols Building
45080 Main St.
HABS CA-2245
HABS CAL,23-MENCI,11-
3ph/1pg/1pc L

Johnson's,J. D. ,Store
449 Lansing St.
HABS CA-2240
HABS CAL,23-MENCI,12-
2ph/1pc/1ct L

Joss House
45160 Albion St.
HABS CA-2235
HABS CAL,23-MENCI,13-
2ph/1pg/1pc/2ct L

Kelley House
45007 Albion St.
HABS CA-2247
HABS CAL,23-MENCI,14-
3ph/1pg/1pc L

Kelley Rental Building (Medina Bidg.)
45040 Main St.
HABS CA-2248
HABS CAL,23-MENCI,15-
2ph/1pg/1pc L

Lansing House & Water Tower
44900 Main St.
HABS CA-2236
HABS CAL,23-MENCI,16-
4ph/1pg/1pc L

Lansing Street (Commercial Buildings) (Main Street (Commercial Buildings))
Lansing St.
HABS CA-1467
HABS CAL,23-MENCI,1-
2ph/1pc L

Lemos' Saloon
45170 Main St.
HABS CA-2246
HABS CAL,23-MENCI,17-
3ph/1pg/1pc L

Lisbon House; see Lisbon-Paoli Hotel

Lisbon-Paoli Hotel (Lisbon House)
45121 Ukiah St.
HABS CA-2242
HABS CAL,23-MENCI,18-
2ph/1pg/1pc L

MacCallum House
45020 Albion St.
HABS CA-2238
HABS CAL,23-MENCI,19-
2ph/1pg/1pc L

Main Street (Commercial Buildings); see Lansing Street (Commercial Buildings)

Masonic Temple
Lansing & Ukiah Sts.
HABS CA-1801
HABS CAL,23-MENCI,20-
10ph/1pc L

Medina Bidg.; see Kelley Rental Building

Mendocino Presbyterian Church
44831 Main St.
HABS CA-2229
HABS CAL,23-MENCI,21-
2ph/1pg/1pc/1ct/fr L

Mendocino,Town of
HABS CA-2249
HABS CAL,23-MENCI,22-
2ph/1pc/2ct L

Odd Fellows Hall (Gallery Fair)
45101 Ukiah St.
HABS CA-2244
HABS CAL,23-MENCI,23-
2ph/1pg/1pc/1ct L

Ukiah Street (Houses)
Ukiah St. between Howard & Lansing
HABS CA-1466
HABS CAL,23-MENCI,2-
2ph/1pc L

Water Tower
Main St. (West End)
HABS CA-2228
HABS CAL,23-MENCI,24-
2ph/1pc L

NAVARO RIVER

Fishing Resort
HABS CA-1470
HABS CAL,23- ,1-
1ph L

UKIAH VIC.

Cape Horn Dam; see Van Arsdale Dam

John Days Dam; see Van Arsdale Dam

Van Arsdale Dam (Cape Horn Dam; John Days Dam)
South Fork of the Eel River
HAER CA-53
HAER 1990 (HAER):2
12ph/5pg/1pc/fr L

WESTPORT

Residence Street (Houses)
HABS CA-1464
HABS CAL,23-WESPO,2-
1ph L

Westport,General View
HABS CA-1463
HABS CAL,23-WESPO,1-
1ph L

MERCED COUNTY

LOS BANOS VIC.

San Luis Gonzaga Adobe
State Hwy. 152
HABS CA-1891
HABS CAL,24- ,1-
3dr/8ph/6pg/fr L

MODOC COUNTY

NEWELL

Tule Lake Project Jail (Tule Lake Relocation/Segregation Center Jail)
Post Mile 44.85,State Rte. 139
HABS CA-2279
HABS 1991(HABS):5
28ph/7pg/3pc L

Tule Lake Relocation/Segregation Center Jail; see Tule Lake Project Jail

MONO COUNTY

BODIE

Bodie Bank
Bodie State Historic Park
HABS CA-1926
HABS CAL,26-BODI,7-
3ph/1pc/fr L

Bodie Jail
Bodie State Historic Park
HABS CA-1925
HABS CAL,26-BODI,8-
4ph/1pg/1pc/fr L

Bodie Railroad Station
Bodie State Historic Park
HABS CA-1928
HABS CAL,26-BODI,9-
2ph/1pc/fr L

Bodie Schoolhouse
Green & Mono Sts.
HABS CA-1934
HABS CAL,26-BODI,10-
2ph/1pc L

Bodie,General View
Bodie State Historic Park
HABS CA-1918
HABS CAL,26-BODI,1-
14ph/7pg L

Boone Store
Main & Green Sts.
HABS CA-1932
HABS CAL,26-BODI,11-
1ph/1pc L

Cain,D. V. ,House
Green & Fuller Sts.
HABS CA-1921
HABS CA,26-BODI,4-
9dr/2ph/4pg/fr L

Cain,J. S. ,House
Bodie State Historic Park
HABS CA-1920
HABS CAL,26-BODI,3-
9dr/5ph/4pg/fr L

Johl House
Main St.
HABS CA-1922
HABS CAL,26-BODI,5-
6dr/1ph/5pg/fr L

Methodist Church
Green & Fuller Sts.
HABS CA-1924
HABS CAL,26-BODI,6-
5dr/3ph/3pg/fr L

Miners' Union Hall
Main St.
HABS CA-1919
HABS CAL,26-BODI,2-
5dr/3ph/3pg/fr L

Murphy House
Prospect & Union St.
HABS CA-1935
HABS CAL,26-BODI,12-
1ph/1pc L

Parr House
Main St.
HABS CA-1931
HABS CAL,26-BODI,13-
1ph/1pc L

U. S. Land Office Building (Wheaton & Hollis Hotel & Bodie Store)
Main & Green Sts.
HABS CA-1933
HABS CAL,26-BODI,14-
2ph/1pc L

Wheaton & Hollis Hotel & Bodie Store; see U. S. Land Office Building

MONTEREY COUNTY

CARMEL

Mission San Carlos Borromeo del Carmelo
Rio Rd. & Lausen Dr.
HABS CA-136
HABS CAL,27-CARM,1-
67ph L

Tor House
26304 Ocean View Ave.
HABS CA-138
HABS CAL,27-CARM,2-
7pg L

CHUALAR VIC.

Salinas River Bridge
Spanning Salinas River on Chualar River Rd.
HAER CA-70
HAER 1990 (HAER):2
14ph/6pg/2pc L

JOLON VIC.

Mission San Antonio de Padua
Hunter Liggett Military Reservation
HABS CA-38-3
HABS CAL,27-JOLO.V,1-
17dr/56ph/1pg L

Roth Ranch
HABS CA-1433
HABS CAL,27-JOLO.V,2-
4ph L

MONTEREY

Abrego,Don Jose,Casa
Abrego & Webster Sts.
HABS CA-139
HABS CAL,27-MONT,16-
4ph L

Alvarado-La Porte Adobe (Wall)
Alvarado & Pearl
HABS CA-1646
HABS CAL,27-MONT,37-
1ph L

Alvarado,Casa
570 Dutra St.
HABS CA-135
HABS CAL,27-MONT,15-
4ph L

Amesti,Jose,Casa
516 Polk St.
HABS CA-143
HABS CAL,27-MONT,20-
10dr/7ph/6pg/fr L

Bonifacio,Casa (Gonzales,Jose Rafael,House; Rose,Sherman,Cottage)
785 Mesa Rd. (moved from Alvarado St.)
HABS CA-153
HABS CAL,27-MONT,30-
5ph L

Boronda,Don Manuel de,Casa
Boronda St.
HABS CA-1821
HABS CAL,27-MONT,39-
3ph L

Brown-Underwood Adobe
Pacific & Madison Sts.
HABS CA-129
HABS CAL,27-MONT,10-
1ph L

Bushton,Capt. William,House
(House,First Frame)
Munras & Webster Sts.
HABS CA-1535
HABS CAL,27-MONT,36-
8ph L

Casa de la Torre; see Federal Court,First

Casa de la Torre; see Torre,Jose,Casa

Casa del Oro (House of Gold)
Scott & Oliver Sts.
HABS CA-132
HABS CAL,27-MONT,13-
2ph L

Casa Verde (Stoddard House)
HABS CA-146
HABS CA,27-MONT,23-
1ph L

Castro,Gen. Jose,Headquarters
Tyler & Pearl Sts.
HABS CA-142
HABS CAL,27-MONT,19-
1ph L

Colton Hall & Jail
Pacific St.
HABS CA-130
HABS CAL,27-MONT,11-
9dr/15ph/7pg/fr L

Convent of St. Catherine at Monterey
Main & Franklin Sts.
HABS CA-1169
HABS CAL,27-MONT,32-
1ph L

Cooper House (Stone Wall)
508 Munras St.
HABS CA-1647
HABS CAL,27-MONT,6A-
1ph L

Cooper,Capt. John,House (Molera House)
508 Muras St.
HABS CA-125
HABS CAL,27-MONT,6-
2ph L

Custom House
Custom House Plaza
HABS CA-133
HABS CAL,27-MONT,14-
10dr/15ph/10pg/fr L

Diaz Store; see Escolle Store

Dickenson,Duncan,House (House,First Brick)
351 Decatur St.
HABS CA-145
HABS CAL,27-MONT,22-
1ph L

Doud,Frances,House
177 Van Buren St.
HABS CA-1648
HABS CAL,27-MONT,38-
1ph L

El Cuartel (Mexican Army Barracks)
HABS CA-1168
HABS CA,27-MONT,31-
1ph L

Escolle House; see Stokes House

Escolle Store (Diaz Store)
Munras & Polk Sts.
HABS CA-1184
HABS CAL,27-MONT,33-
1ph L

Federal Court,First (Casa de la Torre; Gree Adobe,The)
599 Polk St.
HABS CA-122
HABS CAL,27-MONT,3-
2ph L

Finch-Fleischer House
410 Monroe St.
HABS CA-1893
HABS CAL,27-MONT,41-
6ph/7pg L

First Theatre in California
Scott & Pacific Sts.
HABS CA-131
HABS CA,27-MONT,12-
8ph/fr L

Fremont,Gen. ,House
539 Hartnell St.
HABS CA-121
HABS CAL,27-MONT,2-
1ph L

French Consulate,First
404 Camino El Estero (moved from Fremont St.)
HABS CA-1202
HABS CAL,27-MONT,35-
1ph L

French Hotel; see Stevenson,Robert Louis,House

Garcia,Francisco,House
(Molera,Andrew J. ,House)
Van Buren & Jackson Sts.
HABS CA-148
HABS CAL,27-MONT,25-
12ph/fr L

Gonzales,Jose Rafael,House; see Bonifacio,Casa

Gordon,Samuel,House
(Roach,Phillip,House)
526 Pierce St.
HABS CA-150
HABS CA,27-MONT,27-
1ph L

Gree Adobe,The; see Federal Court,First

Gutierrez,Don Joaquin,House
590 Calle Princeipal
HABS CA-1201
HABS CAL,27-MONT,34-
1ph L

Hall of Records; see House of the Four Winds

House of Gold; see Casa del Oro

House of the Four Winds (La Casa de Los Ventanos; Hall of Records)
540 Calle Principal
HABS CA-126
HABS CAL,27-MONT,7-
3ph L

House,First Brick; see Dickenson,Duncan,House

House,First Frame; see Bushton,Capt. William,House

Hovden Cannery
886 Cannery Row
HAER CA-11
HAER CAL,27-MONT,44-
55ph/28pg/6pc/fr L

Jimeno,Don Manuel,Adobe
Main St.
HABS CA-1895
HABS CAL,27-MONT,43-
1ph L

La Casa de Los Ventanos; see House of the Four Winds

Lara-Soto House; see Soto,Jesus,Casa

Larkin House
464 Calle Principal
HABS CA-128
HABS CAL,27-MONT,9-
15dr/13ph/6pg/fr L

Merritt House
386 Pacific St.
HABS CA-147
HABS CAL,27-MONT,24-
1ph L

Mexican Army Barracks; see El Cuartel

Molera House; see Cooper,Capt. John,House

Molera,Andrew J. ,House; see Garcia,Francisco,House

Oliver House; see Torre,Jose,Casa

Pacheco,Don Francisco,Casa
Abrego & Webster Sts.
HABS CA-140
HABS CAL,27-MONT,17-
2ph L

Pacific House
200-222 Calle Principal
HABS CA-124
HABS CAL,27-MONT,5-
2ph L

Roach,Phillip,House; see Gordon,Samuel,House

Rose,Sherman,Cottage; see Bonifacio,Casa

Royal Presidio Chapel of San Carlos Boromeo (San Carlos Church)
550 Church St.
HABS CA-38-6
HABS CAL,27-MONT,1-
28dr/24ph/1pg L

Sambert,Adolpho,Casa
HABS CA-1536
HABS CAL,27-MONT,45-
1ph/1pc L

San Carlos Church; see Royal Presidio Chapel of San Carlos Boromeo

Serrano,Casa
412 Pacific St.
HABS CA-152
HABS CA,27-MONT,29-
3ph L

Sherman-Halleck Quarters; see Sherman,Gen. ,Quarters

Sherman,Gen. ,Quarters
(Sherman-Halleck Quarters)
464 Calle Principal
HABS CA-127
HABS CAL,27-MONT,8-
3ph L

Soberanes Adobe
336 Pacific St.
HABS CA-1892
HABS CAL,27-MONT,40-
15ph/6pg L

Soto,Jesus,Casa (Lara-Soto House)
460 Pierce St.
HABS CA-151
HABS CAL,27-MONT,28-
1ph L

Stevenson,Robert Louis,House (French Hotel)
530 Houston St.
HABS CA-141
HABS CAL,27-MONT,18-
7ph L

Stoddard House; see Casa Verde

Stokes House (Escolle House)
500 Hartnell St.
HABS CA-123
HABS CAL,27-MONT,4-
1ph L

Torre,Jose,Casa (Oliver House; Casa de la Torre)
502 Pierce St.
HABS CA-149
HABS CAL,27-MONT,26-
1ph L

U. S. Post Office
497 Alvarado St.
HABS CA-1203
HABS CAL,27-MONT,46-
1ph/1pc L

Washington Hotel
Washington & Pearl Sts.
HABS CA-1894
HABS CAL,27-MONT,42-
1ph L

Whaling Station
391 Decatur St.
HABS CA-144
HABS CAL,27-MONT,21-
2ph L

MONTEREY VIC.

Lighthouse
Point Pinos
HABS CA-1264
HABS CAL,27-MONT.V,1-
2ph L

SALINAS

El Colegio de San Jose,Academic Building (Hartnell College)
Rancho El Alisal
HABS CA-1171
HABS CAL,27-SALI.V,2A-
1ph L

El Colegio de San Jose,Dormitory (Hartnell College)
Rancho El Alisal
HABS CA-1172
HABS CAL,27-SALI.V,2B-
2ph L

Hartnell College; see El Colegio de San Jose,Academic Building

Hartnell College; see El Colegio de San Jose,Dormitory

SALINAS VIC.

Sherwood Ranch (Sobranes,Feliciano & Mariano,Ranch)
Natividad Rd.
HABS CA-1121
HABS CAL,27-SALI.V,1-
25dr/19ph/9pg/fr L

Sobranes,Feliciano & Mariano,Ranch; see Sherwood Ranch

SOLEDAD

Mission Nuestra Senora de la Soledad
HABS CA-1130
HABS CAL,27-SOL.V,1-
64ph/fr L

NAPA COUNTY

CALISTOGA VIC.

Bale's,Dr. Edward Turner,Grist Mill
Hwy. 29
HABS CA-166
HABS CAL,28-CAL.V,1-
4ph L

NAPA

Behlow Building
Second & Brown Sts.
HABS CA-1982
HABS CAL,28-NAPA,1-
8dr L

Migliavacca Building
First & Brown Sts.
HABS CA-1983
HABS CAL,28-NAPA,2-
6dr L

NEVADA COUNTY

BRIDGEPORT

Bridgeport Covered Bridge
HAER CA-41
HAER CAL,29-BRIGPO,1-
8ph/1pg/1pc/4ct L

Covered Bridge
Pleasant Valley Rd. & Yuba River
HABS CA-1401
HABS CAL,29-BRIGPO,1-
1ph L

GRASS VALLEY

Farmhouse,Frame; see Taylor-Barker House

Finney-Watt House (Watt House)
506 Linden St.
HABS CA-1391
HABS CAL,29-GRAVA,1-
2ph L

Iron Stove
HABS CA-1667
HABS CAL,29-GRAVA,5-
1ph L

Montez,Lola,House
248 Mill St.
HABS CA-1642
HABS CAL,29-GRAVA,4-
2ph L

Morateur's Hotel & Store
Mill St.
HABS CA-1539
HABS CAL,29-GRAVA,3-
1ph L

Mount St. Mary's Academy
Church & Chapel St.
HABS CA-1799
HABS CAL,29-GRAVA,7-
2ph L

Stores A & B,Brick
Mill St.
HABS CA-1692
HABS CAL,29-GRAVA,6-
1ph L

Taylor-Barker House
(Farmhouse,Frame)
653 Linden St.
HABS CA-1392
HABS CAL,29-GRAVA.V,1-
2ph L

Thomas House
220 N. School St.
HABS CA-1393
HABS CAL,29-GRAVA,2-
1ph L

Watt House; see Finney-Watt House

NEVADA CITY

Broad & North Pine Streets (Store)
HABS CA-1394
HABS CAL,29-NEVCI,2-
1ph L

Commercial Buildings
HABS CA-1538
HABS CAL,29-NEVCI,4-
1ph L

Fire House Number 2
Broad St.
HABS CA-1395
HABS CAL,29-NEVCI,3-
1ph/1pc L

Nevada City,General View
HABS CA-1802
HABS CAL,29-NEVCI,1-
1ph L

Nevada County Courthouse
HABS CA-1803
HABS CAL,29-NEVCI,5-
1ph/1pc L

NEVADA CITY VIC.

Purdon Crossing Bridge
HAER CA-40
HAER CAL,29-NEVCI.V,1-
11ph/1pg/1pc L

NORTH BLOOMFIELD

Houses,Frame
HABS CA-1537
HABS CAL,29-BLOOMN,1-
1ph L

NORTH SAN JUAN VIC.

Freeman's Crossing Bridge (Middle Yuba Bridge)
Spanning Middle Fork of Yuba River
HAER CA-131
HAER DLC/PP-1993:CA-3
25ph/8pg/2pc L

Middle Yuba Bridge; see Freeman's Crossing Bridge

RED DOG

Wells Fargo Building
HABS CA-1717
HABS CAL,29-RED,1-
1ph L

ROUGH AND READY

Rough and Ready Hotel
HABS CA-1540
HABS CAL,29-ROUGH,1-
1ph L

SAN JUAN

Capwell & Furth Store (Store,Brick)
Main St.
HABS CA-1397
HABS CAL,29-SANJUN,2-
2ph L

House
HABS CA-1396
HABS CAL,29-SANJUN,5-
1ph L

Main Street (Brick Buildings)
HABS CA-1398
HABS CAL,29-SANJUN,3-
1ph L

Main Street (Frame Buildings)
HABS CA-1697
HABS CAL,29-SANJUN,4-
1ph L

Masonic Hall & Wells Fargo Building
Main St.
HABS CA-1698
HABS CAL,29-SANJUN,6-
1ph L

Methodist Episcopal Church
Flume St.
HABS CA-1399
HABS CAL,29-SANJUN,1-
1ph L

Store,Brick; see Capwell & Furth Store

SWEETLAND

Hotel & Store
HABS CA-1400
HABS CAL,29-SWELA,1-
1ph L

ORANGE COUNTY

ANAHEIM

German House,Old; see Sheffield House

Pioneer House of the Mother Colony
414 N. West St. (moved from N. Los Angeles St.)
HABS CA-320
HABS CAL,30-ANHI,2-
2dr/2ph/1pg/fr L

Sheffield House (German House,Old)
506 Los Angeles St.
HABS CA-37
HABS CAL,30-ANHI,1-
10dr/5ph/1pg/fr L

HUNTINGTON BEACH

Huntington Beach Municipal Pier
Pacific Coast Hwy at Main St.
HAER CA-80
HAER DLC/PP-1993:CA-2
168ph/16pg/18pc L

IRVINE

Irvine Ranch,Agric. Headqrts.,Boyd Tenant House
SE of Intersect. of San Diego & Santa Ana Frwys.
HABS CA-2275-B
HABS 1992(HABS):CA-1
19ph/11pg/2pc L

Irvine Ranch,Agric. Headqrts.,Carillo Tenant House
SW of Intersect. of San Diego & Santa Ana Frwys.
HABS CA-2275-A
HABS 1992(HAS):CA-1
29ph/11pg/2pc L

LAGUNA BEACH VIC.

Dos Rocas; see Smithcliffs (House)

Howardscliffs; see Smithcliffs (House)

Smithcliffs (House) (Howardscliffs; Dos Rocas)
10010 N. Coast Hwy.
HABS CA-2298
HABS 1992(HABS):CA-1
19ph/11pg/3pc L

NEWPORT BEACH

Lovell Beach House
1242 W. Ocean Front
HABS CA-1986
HABS CAL,30-NEWBE,1-
10dr/10ph/5pg/1pc/fr L

SAN JUAN CAPISTRANO

Mission San Juan Capistrano,Barracks; see Mission San Juan Capistrano,Guest House

Mission San Juan Capistrano,Fountains
Olive St. & Hwy. 101
HABS CA-331-C
HABS CAL,30-SAJUC,1C-
1ph L

Mission San Juan Capistrano,Guest House (Mission San Juan Capistrano,Barracks)
Olive St. & Hwy. 101
HABS CA-331-F
HABS CAL,30-SAJUC,1F-
4dr/4ph L

Mission San Juan Capistrano,Industrial Shops
Olive St. & Hwy. 101
HABS CA-331-G
HABS CAL,30-SAJUC,1G-
2dr/7ph L

Mission San Juan Capistrano,Living Quarters
Olive St. & Hwy. 101
HABS CA-331-E
HABS CAL,30-SAJUC,1E-
7dr/5ph L

Mission San Juan Capistrano,Serra's Church
Olive St. & Hwy. 101
HABS CA-331-B
HABS CAL,30-SAJUC,1B-
9dr/9ph L

Mission San Juan Capistrano,Stone Church
Olive St. & Hwy. 101
HABS CA-331-A
HABS CAL,30-SAJUC,1A-
9dr/24ph L

Misson San Juan Capistrano,Padres' Campanerio
Olive St. & Hwy. 101
HABS CA-331-D
HABS CAL,30-SAJUC,1D-
8dr/9ph L

SANTA ANA

North Broadway Park District (2312 North Broadway Street (House))
HABS CA-2167-J
HABS CAL,30-SANA,1-J-
1ph/2pg/1pc L

North Broadway Park District (2314 North Broadway Street (House))
HABS CA-2167-I
HABS CAL,30-SANA,1-I-
1ph/2pg/1pc L

North Broadway Park District (2320 North Broadway Street (House))
HABS CA-2167-H
HABS CAL,30-SANA,1-H-
1ph/2pg/1pc L

North Broadway Park District (2324 North Broadway Street (House))
HABS CA-2167-G
HABS CAL,30-SANA,1-G-
1ph/2pg/1pc L

North Broadway Park District (2328 North Broadway Street (House))
HABS CA-2167-F
HABS CAL,30-SANA,1-F-
1ph/2pg/1pc L

North Broadway Park District (2330 North Broadway Street (House))
HABS CA-2167-E
HABS CAL,30-SANA,1-E-
1ph/2pg/1pc L

North Broadway Park District (2336 North Broadway Street (House))
HABS CA-2167-D
HABS CAL,30-SANA,1-D-
1ph/2pg/1pc L

North Broadway Park District (2338 North Broadway Street (House))
HABS CA-2167-C
HABS CAL,30-SANA,1-C-
1ph/2pg/1pc L

North Broadway Park District (2342 North Broadway Street (House))
HABS CA-2167-B
HABS CAL,30-SANA,1-B-
1ph/2pg/1pc L

North Broadway Park District (2344 North Broadway Street (House))
HABS CA-2167-A
HABS CAL,30-SANA,1-A-
1ph/2pg/1pc L

North Broadway Park District
(2312-2344 North Broadway Street (Houses))
HABS CA-2167
HABS CAL,30-SANA,1-
1ph/3pg/1pc L

2312 North Broadway Street (House); see North Broadway Park District

2314 North Broadway Street (House); see North Broadway Park District

2320 North Broadway Street (House); see North Broadway Park District

2324 North Broadway Street (House); see North Broadway Park District

2328 North Broadway Street (House); see North Broadway Park District

2330 North Broadway Street (House); see North Broadway Park District

2336 North Broadway Street (House); see North Broadway Park District

2338 North Broadway Street (House); see North Broadway Park District

2342 North Broadway Street (House); see North Broadway Park District

2344 North Broadway Street (House); see North Broadway Park District

2312-2344 North Broadway Street (Houses); see North Broadway Park District

PLACER COUNTY

AUBURN

Auburn,Chinese Section,General View
HABS CA-1388
HABS CAL,31-AUB,1-
1ph L

Auburn,General View
HABS CA-1385
HABS CAL,31-AUB,2-
2ph L

City Hall,Old Town (Ruins)
HABS CA-1390
HABS CAL,31-AUB,7-
2ph L

Commercial Buildings
HABS CA-1387
HABS CAL,31-AUB,3-
1ph L

Fire House & Commercial Buildings
Grass Valley & Sacramento Rds.
HABS CA-1384
HABS CAL,31-AUB,5-
1ph L

Lincoln Way & Maple Street (Commercial Building)
HABS CA-1386
HABS CAL,31-AUB,4-
1ph L

Stone,Henry,House
Nevada St.
HABS CA-1389
HABS CAL,31-AUB,6-
1ph L

CLIPPER GAP

Central Pacific RR:Clipper Gap Tunnel
HAER CA-30
HAER CAL,31-CLIPGA,1-
1ph/1pc L

PLUMAS COUNTY

PLUMAS

Tobin Highway Bridge
HAER CA-36
HAER CAL,32-PLUM,1-
3ph/1pc L

RIVERSIDE COUNTY

INDIO VIC.

Historic Mining Initiative Recording Project; see Lost Horse Gold Mill

Lost Horse Gold Mill (Historic Mining Initiative Recording Project)
Joshua Tree National Monument
HAER CA-128
H

PRADO VIC.

Bandini,Don Juan,House; see Cota House

Cota House (Bandini,Don Juan,House)
HABS CA-332
HABS CAL,33-PRAD.V,1-
3dr/4ph/1pg/fr L

RIVERSIDE

First Christian Church Parsonage
3575 Vine St.
HABS CA-2302
HABS DLC/PP-1992:CA-4
11ph/6pg/1pc L

SACRAMENTO COUNTY

FOLSOM

Assay Office; see Wells Fargo & Company Building

House
HABS CA-1361
HABS CAL,34-FOLSO,4-
1ph L

Methodist Episcopal Church
HABS CA-1359
HABS CAL,34-FOLSO,3-
1ph L

Trinity Episcopal Church
HABS CA-1360
HABS CAL,34-FOLSO,1-
1ph L

Wells Fargo & Company Building
(Assay Office)
HABS CA-1358
HABS CAL,34-FOLSO,2-
2ph L

ISLETON

Sacramento River Bridge
Spanning Sacramento River S. of Locke
HAER CA-55
HAER CAL,34-ISLE,1-
1ph/1pc/3ct L

LOCKE

Al's Place; see Town of Locke,Restaurant

Chong,Yuen,Market; see Town of Locke,Yuen Chong Market

Christian Center; see Town of Locke,Christian Center

Loy,Dai,Gambling Museum; see Town of Locke,Dai Loy Gambling Museum

Shoong,Joe,Chinese School; see Town of Locke,Joe Shoong Chinese School

Star Theatre; see Town of Locke,Star Theatre

Tenderloin-Twelve Club; see Town of Locke,Commercial Building

Town of Locke
HABS CA-2071
HABS CAL,34-LOCKE,1-
18dr/18ph/32pg/1pc/fr L

Town of Locke,Boat House
River Rd.
HABS CA-2071-AA
HABS CAL,34-LOCKE,1/27-
7ph/3pg/1pc L

Town of Locke,Christian Center
(Christian Center)
Key St.
HABS CA-2071-CC
HABS CAL,34-LOCKE,1/29-
4ph/4pg/1pc L

Town of Locke,Commercial Building
13927 River Rd.
HABS CA-2071-B
HABS CAL,34-LOCKE,1/2-
7ph/4pg/1pc L

Town of Locke,Commercial Building
13931 River Rd.
HABS CA-2071-C
HABS CAL,34-LOCKE,1/3-
3ph/4pg/1pc L

Town of Locke,Commercial Building
13943 River Rd.
HABS CA-2071-E
HABS CAL,34-LOCKE,1/5-
8ph/4pg/1pc L

Town of Locke,Commercial Building
13947 River Rd.
HABS CA-2071-F
HABS CAL,34-LOCKE,1/6-
4ph/4pg/1pc L

Town of Locke,Commercial Building
13955 River Rd.
HABS CA-2071-H
HABS CAL,34-LOCKE,1/8-
4ph/5pg/1pc L

Town of Locke,Commercial Building
13959 Main St.
HABS CA-2071-Y
HABS CAL,34-LOCKE,1/25-
3ph/4pg/1pc L

Town of Locke,Commercial Building
13963 River Rd.
HABS CA-2071-I
HABS CAL,34-LOCKE,1/9-
6ph/5pg/1pc L

Town of Locke,Commercial Building
(Tenderloin-Twelve Club)
13952 Main St.
HABS CA-2071-K
HABS CAL,34-LOCKE,1/11-
3ph/4pg/1pc L

Town of Locke,Commercial-Residential Structure
13935 Main St.
HABS CA-2071-S
HABS CAL,34-LOCKE,1/19-
6ph/3pg/1pc L

Town of Locke,Dai Loy Gambling Museum (Loy,Dai,Gambling Museum)
13951 Main St.
HABS CA-2071-W
HABS CAL,34-LOCKE,1/23-
17ph/4pg/1pc L

Town of Locke,House
Key St.
HABS CA-2071-BB
HABS CAL,34-LOCKE,1/28-
2ph/3pg/1pc L

Town of Locke,House
Main & Levee Rds.
HABS CA-2071-Z
HABS CAL,34-LOCKE,1/26-
2ph/3pg/1pc L

Town of Locke,House
13915 Main St.
HABS CA-2071-N
HABS CAL,34-LOCKE,1/14-
2ph/3pg/1pc L

Town of Locke,House
13919 Main St.
HABS CA-2071-O
HABS CAL,34-LOCKE,1/15-
3ph/4pg/1pc L

Town of Locke,House
13927 Main St.
HABS CA-2071-Q
HABS CAL,34-LOCKE,1/17-
2ph/4pg/1pc L

Town of Locke,House
13936 Main St.
HABS CA-2071-L
HABS CAL,34-LOCKE,1/12-
8ph/4pg/1pc L

Town of Locke,Jan Ying Association
(Ying,Jan,Association)
13947 Main St.
HABS CA-2071-V
HABS CAL,34-LOCKE,1/22-
7ph/5pg/1pc L

Town of Locke,Joe Shoong Chinese School (Shoong,Joe,Chinese School)
13920 Main St.
HABS CA-2071-M
HABS CAL,34-LOCKE,1/13-
6ph/3pg/1pc L

Town of Locke,Residential Building
River & Levee Rds.
HABS CA-2071-G
HABS CAL,34-LOCKE,1/7-
4ph/5pg/1pc L

Town of Locke,Residential Building
13931 Main St.
HABS CA-2071-R
HABS CAL,34-LOCKE,1/18-
2ph/4pg/1pc L

Town of Locke,Residential Building
13939 Main St.
HABS CA-2071-T
HABS CAL,34-LOCKE,1/20-
4ph/4pg/1pc L

Town of Locke,Residential Structure
13955 Main St.
HABS CA-2071-X
HABS CAL,34-LOCKE,1/24-
3ph/4pg/1pc L

Town of Locke,Restaurant (Al's Place)
13943 Main St.
HABS CA-2071-U
HABS CAL,34-LOCKE,1/21-
4ph/4pg/1pc L

Town of Locke,Star Theatre (Star Theatre)
13939 River Rd.
HABS CA-2071-D
HABS CAL,34-LOCKE,1/4-
6ph/5pg/1pc L

Town of Locke,The Tules (Tules,The)
River Rd.
HABS CA-2071-J
HABS CAL,34-LOCKE,1/10-
5ph/4pg/1pc L

Town of Locke,Warehouse (Warehouse)
13923 Main St.
HABS CA-2071-P
HABS CAL,34-LOCKE,1/16-
4ph/3pg/1pc L

Town of Locke,Yuen Chong Market
(Chong,Yuen,Market)
13923 River Rd.
HABS CA-2071-A
HABS CAL,34-LOCKE,1/1-
4ph/4pg/1pc L

Tules,The; see Town of Locke,The Tules

Warehouse; see Town of Locke,Warehouse

Ying,Jan,Association; see Town of Locke,Jan Ying Association

SACRAMENTO

Adams & Company Building
1014 Second St.
HABS CA-1883
HABS CAL,34-SAC,17-
6dr/5ph/6pg/fr L

Apollo Building
228-230 K St.
HABS CA-1716
HABS CAL,34-SAC,16-
3dr/2ph/4pg/fr L

Archives Building; see California State Printing Office

Aschenauer Building
1022 Third St.
HABS CA-1715
HABS CAL,34-SAC,15-
3dr/2ph/4pg/fr L

Bank Exchange Building
1030 Second St.
HABS CA-186
HABS CAL,34-SAC,50-
2ph/1pg/1pc L

Bee Building
1016-1020 Third St.
HABS CA-1714
HABS CAL,34-SAC,14-
4dr/1ph/3pg/fr L

Benicia Cemetery; see Sacramento Army Depot

Big Four Building
220-226 K St.
HABS CA-1170
HABS CAL,34-SAC,6-
7dr/11ph/5pg/fr L

Blake-Waters Assay Office
222 J St.
HABS CA-1711
HABS CAL,34-SAC,11-
2dr/2ph/3pg/fr L

Booth Building
1019-1021 Front St.
HABS CA-182
HABS CAL,34-SAC,51-
2ph/1pg/1pc L

Brannon Building
106-110 J & Front Sts.
HABS CA-181
HABS CAL,34-SAC,52-
3ph/1pg/1pc L

California Governor's Mansion; see Gallatin,Albert,House

California State Printing Office (Archives Building)
1020 O St.
HABS CA-2301
HABS DLC/PP-1992:CA-4
7ph/18pg/1pc L

Cavert Building
1207 Front St.
HABS CA-1254
HABS CAL,34-SAC,53-
2ph/1pg/1pc L

Cienfugo Building
1119 Second St.
HABS CA-1256
HABS CAL,34-SAC,23-
1ph/1pc L

City Market
118 J St.
HABS CA-199
HABS CAL,34-SAC,45-
2ph/1pg/1pc L

Collicott Drug Store (Haines Building)
129 J St.
HABS CA-171
HABS CAL,34-SAC,24-
1ph/1pg/1pc L

Cornwall,P. B. ,Building (Smith Building)
1011-1013 Second St.
HABS CA-1257
HABS CAL,34-SAC,47-
2ph/4pg/1pc L

Crocker Art Gallery
216 O St.
HABS CA-1885
HABS CAL,34-SAC,20-
8dr/20ph/13pg L

Democratic State Journal Building
Second & K Sts.
HABS CA-1251
HABS CAL,34-SAC,26-
2ph/1pg/1pc L

Diana Saloon
205 J St.
HABS CA-1706
HABS CAL,34-SAC,8-
3dr/4ph/4pg/fr L

Dingley Spice Mill
115 I St.
HABS CA-167
HABS CAL,34-SAC,54-
3ph/2pg/1pc L

Ebner's Hotel
116 K St.
HABS CA-1252
HABS CAL,34-SAC,27-
2ph/1pg/1pc L

Eureka Swimming Baths
908-910 Second St.
HABS CA-177
HABS CAL,34-SAC,28-
2ph/1pg/1pc L

Fashion Saloon
209 J St.
HABS CA-1261
HABS CAL,34-SAC,29-
6pg L

Figg,E. P. ,Building
224 J St.
HABS CA-1713
HABS CAL,34-SAC,13-
3dr/2ph/5pg/fr L

Fratt,Francis William,Building
1103-1109 Second St.
HABS CA-1255
HABS CAL,34-SAC,25-
3ph/4pg/1pc L

Gallatin,Albert,House (California Governor's Mansion)
1527 H St.
HABS CA-1886
HABS CAL,34-SAC,19-ı1991(HABS):5°
9dr/21ph/5pg/1pc/fr L H

Gregory-Barnes Store
126 J St.
HABS CA-197
HABS CAL,34-SAC,30-
2ph/2pg/1pc L

Haines Building; see Collicott Drug Store

Halls,Luhrs & Company Building
912-916 Second St.
HABS CA-176
HABS CAL,34-SAC,31-
2ph/2pg/1pc L

Hastings,B.F. ,Bank Building
128-132 J St.
HABS CA-1884
HABS CAL,34-SAC,18-
6ph/5pg L

Heywood Building
1001-1009 Second St.
HABS CA-1258
HABS CAL,34-SAC,22-
2ph/1pg L

Howard House
109-111 K St.
HABS CA-184
HABS CAL,34-SAC,32-
2ph/1pg/1pc L

J Street (Commercial Buildings)
HABS CA-1683
HABS CAL,34-SAC,7-
1ph/1pg L

125 K Street (House); see Union Hotel (Annex)

Lady Adams Building
113-115 K St.
HABS CA-190
HABS CAL,34-SAC,4-
6dr/2ph/1pg L

Latham Building
221-225 J St.
HABS CA-1710
HABS CAL,34-SAC,10-
4dr/3ph/4pg L

Leggett Ale House
1023 Front St.
HABS CA-183
HABS CAL,34-SAC,33-
2ph/1pg/1pc L

Lincoln School
418 P St.
HABS CA-2188
HABS CAL,34-SAC,55-
32ph/13pg/2pc L

M Street Bridge; see Sacramento River Bridge

Mechanics Exchange Hotel
116-122 I St.
HABS CA-178
HABS CAL,34-SAC,34-
4ph/3pg/1pc L

Morse Building
1025-1031 Second St.
HABS CA-1259
HABS CAL,34-SAC,46-
4ph/6pg/1pc L

Our House Saloon
926 Second St.
HABS CA-175
HABS CAL,34-SAC,35-
1ph/1pg/1pc L

1025 P Street Building; see Strub Building

Pioneer Hall & Bakery
120-124 J St.
HABS CA-198
HABS CAL,34-SAC,36-
2ph/1pg/1pc L

Pioneer Telegraph Building
1015 Second St.
HABS CA-191
HABS CAL,34-SAC,5-
5dr/2ph/1pg L

Rialto Building
225-230 J St.
HABS CA-192
HABS CAL,34-SAC,56-
5dr L

Rivett-Fuller Building
128 K St.
HABS CA-1250
HABS CAL,34-SAC,37-
3ph/1pg/1pc L

Sacramento Army Depot (Benicia Cemetery)
Fruitridge Rd.
HAER CA-27
HAER CAL,34-SAC,49-
35pg/fr L

Sacramento City Hall
915 I St.
HABS CA-418
HABS CAL,34-SAC,48-
7ph/10pg/1pc L

Sacramento Engine Company No. 3
1112 Second St.
HABS CA-1249
HABS CAL,34-SAC,38-
2ph/5pg/1pc L

Sacramento River Bridge (Tower Bridge; M Street Bridge)
CA State Hwy 275
HAER CA-73
HAER DLC/PP-1993:CA-3
108ph/9pg/9pc L

Sacramento,General View
HABS CA-1671
HABS CAL,34-SAC,3-
2ph L

Sacramento,General View,1865
HABS CA-1677
HABS CAL,34-MICH,1-
1ph L

Sacramento,Historic View,1850 Flood
HABS CA-1705
HABS CAL,34-SAC,1-
1ph L

Sacramento,Historic View,1852 Fire
HABS CA-1669
HABS CAL,34-SAC,2-
1ph L

Sazerac Building
131 J St.
HABS CA-172
HABS CAL,34-SAC,39-
2ph/1pg/1pc L

Smith Building; see Cornwall,P. B. ,Building

Stanford Brothers Store
1203 Front St.
HABS CA-1253
HABS CAL,34-SAC,40-
3ph/7pg/1pc L

Stanford-Lathrop Memorial Home; see Stanford,Leland,House

Stanford,Leland,House
(Stanford-Lathrop Memorial Home)
800 N St.
HABS CA-1709
HABS CAL,34-SAC,9-
9dr/17ph/19pg/fr L

Stein Building
218 J St.
HABS CA-1712
HABS CAL,34-SAC,12-
3dr/1ph/4pg L

Strub Building (1025 P Street Building)
HABS CA-2300
HABS DLC/PP-1992:CA-4
5ph/24pg/1pc L

Sutter's Fort
L & Twenty-Seventh Sts.
HABS CA-1294
HABS CAL,34-SAC,57-
25ph/2pg L

Tower Bridge; see Sacramento River Bridge

U. S. Post Office,Old
K & Seventh Sts.
HABS CA-1914
HABS CAL,34-SAC,21-
9ph/5pg L

Union Hotel
1024-1028 Second St.
HABS CA-187
HABS CAL,34-SAC,41-
1ph/5pg/1pc L

Union Hotel (Annex) (125 K Street (House))
HABS CA-185
HABS CAL,34-SAC,41A-
2ph/1pg/1pc L

Vernon-Brannan House
112-114 J St.
HABS CA-179
HABS CAL,34-SAC,43-
3ph/1pg/1pc L

Wormser,I. & S. ,Building
128 J St.
HABS CA-196
HABS CAL,34-SAC,44-
2ph/2pg/1pc L

WEST SACRAMENTO

M Street Bridge; see Sacramento River Bridge

Sacramento River Bridge (Tower Bridge; M Street Bridge)
(See SACRAMENTO COUNTY,SACRAMENTO for documtatn.)
HAER CA-73
HAER DLC/PP-1993:CA-3
108ph/9pg/9pc L

Tower Bridge; see Sacramento River Bridge

SAN BENITO COUNTY

SAN JUAN BAUTISTA

Anza,Juan de,House
Third & Franklin Sts.
HABS CA-38-5
HABS CAL,35-SAJUB,2-
3dr/2ph L

Castro,Gen. Jose,House
Mission Plaza
HABS CA-1120
HABS CAL,35-SAJUB,3-
5ph/1pc/fr L

Mexican Barracks; see Plaza Hotel

Mission San Juan Bautista
Second St.
HABS CA-38-4
HABS CAL,35-SAJUB,1-
38dr/4ph/1pg L

Mission San Juan Bautista,Church
Second St.
HABS CA-38-4-A
HABS CAL,35-SAJUB,1A-
7ph L

Mission San Juan Bautista,Garden
Second St.
HABS CA-38-4-C
HABS CAL,35-SAJUB,1C-
1ph L

Mission San Juan Bautista,Monastery
Second St.
HABS CA-38-4-B
HABS CAL,35-SAJUB,1B-
8ph L

Mission San Juan Bautista,Rectory
Second St.
HABS CA-38-4-D
HABS CAL,35-SAJUB,1D-
1ph L

Plaza Hotel (Mexican Barracks)
Second St.
HABS CA-1954
HABS CAL,35-SAJUB,4-
11dr/1ph L

Zanetta House
San Juan Bautista State Historical Park
HABS CA-1501
HABS CAL,35-SAJUB,5-
1ph/1pc L

SAN BERNARDINO COUNTY

CHINO VIC.

Slaughter House (Yorba,Antonio,House)
Prado Rd.
HABS CA-333
HABS CAL,36-CHINO.V,1-
2ph/1pg/fr L

Yorba,Antonio,House; see Slaughter House

ONTARIO

First Nazarene Church of Ontario
(Gallery Theatre)
126 East C. Street
HABS CA-2343
3dr/1ph/4pg/12pc H

First Nazarene Church of Ontaro,Parsonage
126 East C St.
HABS CA-2343-A
1dr/2ph/1pg/1pc H

Gallery Theatre; see First Nazarene Church of Ontario

REDLANDS VIC.

Santa Ana Riv. Hydro.Sys.,SAR-2 Forebay & Penstock
San Bernardino National Forest
HAER CA-130-P
4ph/1pc H

Santa Ana Riv.Hydro.Sys.,Abandoned Tunnel
San Bernardino National Forest
HAER CA-130-R
6ph/1pc H

Santa Ana Riv.Hydro.Sys.,Aqueduct
San Bernardino National Forest
HAER CA-130-T
1ph/1pc H

Santa Ana Riv.Hydro.Sys.,Bear Creek Dam & Con.Pool
San Bernardino National Forest
HAER CA-130-B
4ph/1pc H

Santa Ana Riv.Hydro.Sys.,Dom.Wat.Spl.Treat.House
San Bernardino National Forest
HAER CA-130-H
1ph/1pc H

Santa Ana Riv.Hydro.Sys.,Flume&Tunnel blw Fish Scr
San Bernardino National Forest
HAER CA-130-E
3ph/1pc H

Santa Ana Riv.Hydro.Sys.,Flumes&Tunnels blw Sandbo
San Bernardino National Forest
HAER CA-130-G
10ph/2pc H

Santa Ana Riv.Hydro.Sys.,Pipeline to Fish Screen
San Bernardino National Park
HAER CA-130-C
3ph/1pc H

Santa Ana Riv.Hydro.Sys.,Revolving Fish Screen
San Bernardino National Forest
HAER CA-130-D
3ph/1pc H

Santa Ana Riv.Hydro.Sys.,Sandbox at Breakneck Cree
San Bernardino National Forest
HAER CA-130-F
7ph/2pc H

Santa Ana Riv.Hydro.Sys.,Sandbox,SAR-1 Bypass
San Bernardino National Forest
HAER CA-130-N
1ph/1pc H

Santa Ana Riv.Hydro.Sys.,Sandbox,SAR-3 Flowline
San Bernardino National Forest
HAER CA-130-S
5ph/1pc H

Santa Ana Riv.Hydro.Sys.,Santa Ana Riv.Div.Dam
San Bernardino National Forest
HAER CA-130-A
5ph/1pc H

Santa Ana Riv.Hydro.Sys.,SAR-1 Forebay & Penstock
San Bernardino National Forest
HAER CA-130-I
5ph/1pc H

Santa Ana Riv.Hydro.Sys.,SAR-1 Machine Shop
San Bernardino National Forest
HAER CA-130-L
6ph/2pc H

Santa Ana Riv.Hydro.Sys.,SAR-1 Powder Magazine
San Bernardino National Forest
HAER CA-130-M
1ph/1pc H

Santa Ana Riv.Hydro.Sys.,SAR-1 Powerhouse
San Bernardino National Forest
HAER CA-130-J
61ph/6pc H

Santa Ana Riv.Hydro.Sys.,SAR-1 Stable
San Bernardino National Forest
HAER CA-130-K
13ph/2pc H

Santa Ana Riv.Hydro.Sys.,SAR-2 Intake
San Bernardino National Forest
HAER CA-130-O
2ph/1pc H

Santa Ana Riv.Hydro.Sys.,SAR-2 Powerhouse
San Bernardino National Forest
HAER CA-130-Q
53ph/6pc H

Santa Ana Riv.Hydro.Sys.,SAR-3 Forebay & Penstock
San Bernardino National Forest
HAER CA-130-V
4ph/1pc H

Santa Ana Riv.Hydro.Sys.,SAR-3 Powerhouse
San Bernardino National Forest
HAER CA-130-W
34ph/4pc H

Santa Ana Riv.Hydro.Sys.,Transmission Lines
San Bernardino National Forest
HAER CA-130-X
6ph/2pc H

Santa Ana Riv.Hydro.Sys.,Warm Springs Canyon/SAR-3
San Bernardino National Forest
HAER CA-130-U
11ph/2pc H

Santa Ana River Hydroelectric System
San Bernardino National Forest
HAER CA-130
56ph/182pg/8pc H

SAN BERNARDINO

San Bernardino City Hall
300 N. "D" St.
HABS CA-433
HABS CAL,36-SANBER,1-
5ph/4pg/1pc L

TWENTY-NINE PALMS V.

Desert Queen Ranch,Main Ranch House (Joshua Tree National Monument)
HABS CA-2347-A
2ph/1pc H

Documentation: **ct** color transparencies **dr** measured drawings **fr** field records
pc photograph captions **pg** pages of text **ph** photographs

Joshua Tree National Monument; see Desert Queen Ranch,Main Ranch House

SAN DIEGO COUNTY

CARLSBAD VIC.

Rancho Agua Hedionda,Casa del
HABS CA-410
HABS CAL,37-CARL.V,1-
4dr/6ph/2pg/fr L

CORONADO

Graham Memorial Presbyterian Church
95 C Ave.
HABS CA-2195
HABS CAL,37-CORO,2-
1ph/4pg/1pc L

Hotel Del Coronado
1500 Orange Ave.
HABS CA-1958
HABS CAL,37-CORO,1-
8dr/36ph/18pg/2pc/fr L

ESCONDIDO

Calfame Packing Plant; see Escondido Orange Association Packing House

Escondido Orange Association Packing House (Calfame Packing Plant)
1155 W. Mission Ave.
HAER CA-69
HAER 1992(HAER):CA-1
20ph/35pg/2pc L

JULIAN

Julian Library; see Witch Creek Schoolhouse

Witch Creek Schoolhouse (Julian Library)
Fourth & Washington Sts.
HABS CA-1972
HABS CAL,37-JUL,1-
1ph/5pg/1pc L

LA JOLLA

Bishop's School,The
7607 La Jolla Blvd.
HABS CA-1968
HABS CAL,37-LAJOL,2-
8ph/2pg/1pc/1ct L

La Jolla Women's Club
715 Silverado St.
HABS CA-1957
HABS CAL,37-LAJOL,1-
5dr/14ph/15pg/fr L

Pueblo Ribera Court
230 Granvilla St.
HABS CA-1943
HABS CAL,37-LAJOL,3-
11ph/6pg/1pc L

Red Rest & Red Roost (Neptune) Cottages
1179 & 1187 Coast Blvd.
HABS CA-1973
HABS CAL,37-LAJOL,4-
6ph/7pg/1pc/fr L

NATIONAL CITY

Brick Row; see Kimball Block Rowhouses

Granger Music Hall
1700 E. Fourth St.
HABS CA-1998
HABS CAL,37-NATC,2-
3dr/9ph/8pg/1pc/fr L

Kimball Block Rowhouses (Brick Row)
A Ave. W side,btwn. Ninth & Tenth Sts.
HABS CA-1969
HABS CAL,37-NATC,3-
7ph/4pg/1pc/1ct/fr L

Kimball,Frank,House
21 W. Plaza Blvd.
HABS CA-2166
HABS CAL,37-NATC,4-
4ph/9pg/1pc L

St. Matthew's Episcopal Church
521 E. Eighth St.
HABS CA-1959
HABS CAL,37-NATC,1-
5dr/13ph/8pg/fr L

OAK GROVE

Butterfield Stage Station
HABS CA-49
HABS CAL,37-OAK,1-
6ph/1pg/1pc/fr L

OCEANSIDE

Mission San Luis Rey de Francia
Mission Rd.
HABS CA-42
HABS CAL,37-OCSI.V,1-
25dr/24ph/1pg/fr L

Rancho Santa Margarita y Los Flores,Casa del
U. S. Hwy. 101
HABS CA-48
HABS CAL,37-OCSI.V,2-
14ph/1pg L

PALA

Asistencia of San Antonio de Pala
Mission Rd.
HABS CA-44
HABS CAL,37-PALA,1-
7dr/14ph/2pg/fr L

POINT LOMA

Point Loma Lighthouse No. 355 (Point Loma Lighthouse,Old)
Cabrillo National Monument
HABS CA-41
HABS CAL,37-POLO,1-
19dr/16ph/13pg/fr L

Point Loma Lighthouse,Old; see Point Loma Lighthouse No. 355

RANCHO PENASQUITOS

Johnson-Taylor Ranch House (Rancho Penasquitos)
Black Mountain Rd. vic.
HABS CA-2072
HABS CAL,37-RANPE,1-
3dr/3ph/8pg/1pc/fr L

Johnson-Taylor Ranch,Barn (Rancho Penasquitos,Barn)
Black Mountain Rd. vic.
HABS CA-2072-A
HABS CAL,37-RANPE,1-A-
2ph/1pc L

Rancho Penasquitos; see Johnson-Taylor Ranch House

Rancho Penasquitos,Barn; see Johnson-Taylor Ranch,Barn

RANCHO SANTA FE

Baker-Megrew Rowhouse (Cottage C)
6122 Paseo Delicias
HABS CA-2312
2dr/4ph/11pg/1pc H

Bingham,Samuel,House
6427 La Valle Plateada
HABS CA-2321
3ph/1pc H

Christiancy Apartments
La Granada & Paseo Delicias
HABS CA-2324
1ph/1pc H

Cottage A; see Spurr-Clotfelter Rowhouse

Cottage B; see Nelson,Sidney and Ruth,Rowhouse

Cottage C; see Baker-Megrew Rowhouse

Cottage D; see Moore,Glenn & Ida May,Rowhouse

Country Friends Store
6030 El Tordo
HABS CA-2329
2ph/1pc H

El Tordo Apartments
6116 El Tordo
HABS CA-2328
2ph/1pc H

Garage Block Building
6033 Paseo Delicias
HABS CA-2327
5ph/1pc H

House
La Granda & Via de Santa Fe
HABS CA-2322
2ph/1pc H

Joers-Ketchum Rowhouse
6108 Paseo Delicias
HABS CA-2309
2dr/6ph/8pg/1pc H

Joers-Ketchum Store
6014-6016 La Granada
HABS CA-2308
1dr/12ph/9pg/1pc H

Joers,F. W.,House
6135 La Flecha
HABS CA-2326
4ph/1pc H

La Flecha House
6036 La Flecha
HABS CA-2304
1dr/5ph/17pg/1pc H

La Morada (The Inn at Rancho Santa Fe)
5951 Lineade Cielo
HABS CA-2307
1dr/13ph/13pg/1pc H

Moore,Glenn & Ida May,Rowhouse (Cottage D)
6126 Paseo Delicias
HABS CA-2303
2dr/13ph/16pg/1pc H

Nelson,Sidney and Ruth,Rowhouse (Cottage B)
6118 Paseo Delicias
HABS CA-2311
2dr/4ph/11pg/1pc H

Osuna,Juan,House
Via de la Valle
HABS CA-2333
3ph/1pc H

Osuna,Leandro,House
Via de Santa Fe
HABS CA-2332
4ph/1pc H

Rancho Santa Fe
HABS CA-2315
1dr/9ph/41pg/1pc H

Rancho Santa Fe Civic Center
HABS CA-2305
2dr/10ph/1pc H

Rancho Santa Fe Garden Club
La Granada & Avenida de Acacias
HABS CA-2325
2ph/1pc H

Rancho Santa Fe School (Second)
6024 Paseo Delicias
HABS CA-2318
6ph/1pc H

Rancho Santa Fe School (Third)
17022 Avenida de Acacias
HABS CA-2330
1ph/1pc H

Santa Fe Irrigation District Offices
Linea del Cielo
HABS CA-2323
4ph/1pc H

Santa Fe Land Improvement Co. Administration Bldg.
6009 Paseo Delicias
HABS CA-2306-B
6ph/7pg/1pc H

Santa Fe Land Improvement Co. Headquarters Bldg.
6015 Paseo Delicias
HABS CA-2306-C
7ph/12pg/1pc H

Santa Fe Land Improvement Co. Office Building
16915 Avenida de Acacias
HABS CA-2306-A
4ph/9pg/1pc H

Santa Fe Land Improvement Company Office Block
Paseo Delicias
HABS CA-2306
1dr H

Spurr-Clotfelter Rowhouse (Cottage A)
6112 Paseo Delicias
HABS CA-2310
2dr/4ph/12pg/1pc H

Stoltzfus-Humphries House
6855 La Valle Plateada
HABS CA-2319
15ph/1pc H

Studio Shop and Tea Room
6106 Paseo Delicias
HABS CA-2316
7pg/1pc H

The Inn at Rancho Santa Fe; see La Morada

Whitsitt House
5860 Lago Linda
HABS CA-2331
2ph/1pc H

SAN DIEGO

Albatross Cottages
3353,3367,3407 & 3415 Albatross St.
HABS CA-2165
HABS CAL,37-SANDI,15-
3ph/3pg/1pc L

Albatross Cottages,Lee Cottage No. 1
3367 Albatross St.
HABS CA-2165-B
HABS CAL,37-SANDI,15-B-
5ph/1pc L

Albatross Cottages,Lee Cottage No. 2
3353 Albatross St.
HABS CA-2165-A
HABS CAL,37-SANDI,15-A-
6ph/1pc L

Albatross Cottages,Teats Cottage No. 1
3415 Albatross St.
HABS CA-2165-D
HABS CAL,37-SANDI,15-D-
3ph/1pc L

Albatross Cottages,Teats Cottage No. 2
3407 Albatross St.
HABS CA-2165-C
HABS CAL,37-SANDI,15-C-
4ph/1pc L

Aztec Brewery; see Savage Tire Factory

Aztec Brewing Company; see Savage Tire Factory

Aztec Brewing Company; see Savage Tire Factory,Factory Building

Aztec Brewing Company; see Savage Tire Factory,Office Building

Aztec Brewing Company; see Savage Tire Factory,Original Brick Warehouse

Aztec Brewing Company; see Savage Tire Factory,Rathskeller

Aztec Brewing Company; see Savage Tire Factory,2201-2299 Warehouse

Aztec Brewing Company,Factory Building; see Savage Tire Factory,Factory Building

Aztec Brewing Company,Office Building; see Savage Tire Factory,Office Building

Aztec Brewing Company,Original Brick Warehouse; see Savage Tire Factory,Original Brick Warehouse

Aztec Brewing Company,Rathskeller; see Savage Tire Factory,Rathskeller

Aztec Brewing Company,2201-2299 Warehouse; see Savage Tire Factory,2201-2299 Warehouse

Aztec Brewing Company,2341-2399 Warehouse; see Savage Tire Factory,2341-2399 Warehouse

Backesto Block
Fifth Ave. & Market St.
HABS CA-427
HABS CAL,37-SANDI,3-
1ph/4pg L

Balboa Park,Botanical Garden
Balboa Park,El Prado Area
HABS CA-1963-B
HABS CAL,37-SANDI,16-B-
5ph/1pc L

Balboa Park,California Tower
Balboa Park,El Prado Area
HABS CA-1963-A
HABS CAL,37-SANDI,16-A-
2ph/3pg/1pc/fr L

Bank of Commerce Building
835 Fifth Ave.
HABS CA-1961
HABS CAL,37-SANDI,11-
1dr/3ph/6pg/fr L

Cossitt,Mary,House
3526 Seventh Ave.
HABS CA-2163
HABS CAL,37-SANDI,17-
7ph/6pg/1pc L

Davis,William Heath,House
227 Eleventh Ave.
HABS CA-423
HABS CAL,37-SANDI,2-
6dr/11ph/4pg/1pc/fr L

Fort Rosecrans,Argonaut Hall (Naval Submarine Base,YMCA Service Club; Naval Submarine Base,Building No. 138)
Point Loma
HABS CA-2255-C
HABS 1992(HABS):CA-1
1ph/1pc L

Fort Rosecrans,Barracks (Naval Submarine Base,Building No. 137)
Point Loma
HABS CA-2255-B
HABS 1992(HABSD):CA-1
1ph/1pc L

Fort Rosecrans,Barracks (Naval Submarine Base,Building No. 139)
Point Loma
HABS CA-2255-D
HABS 1992(HABS):CA-1
1ph/1pc L

Fort Rosecrans,Mining Casemate (Naval Submarine Base,Building No. 167)
Point Loma
HABS CA-2255-A
HABS 1992(HABS):CA-1
28ph/17pg/2pc L

Fort Rosecrans,Post Exchange (Naval Submarine Base,Office Building; Naval Submarine Base,Building No. 158)
Point Loma
HABS CA-2255-E
HABS 1992(HABS):CA-1
1ph/1pc L

Fraternal Spirtualist Church; see Temple Beth Israel

Frost Lumber Company; see Maier Brewing Company Warehouse

Ft. Rosecrans (Naval Submarine Base)
Point Loma
HABS CA-2255
HABS 1992(HABS):CA-1
2ph/7pg/1pc L

Grand Hotel (Horton Hotel)
332 F St.
HABS CA-1974
HABS CAL,37-SANDI,18-
2dr/2ph/6pg/1pc/fr L

Greely Building; see Nesmith-Greely Building

Horton Hotel; see Grand Hotel

I. O. O. F. Building
526 Market St.
HABS CA-429
HABS CAL,37-SANDI,5-
1ph/8pg L

Klauber,Melville,House
3060 Sixth Ave.
HABS CA-1962
HABS CAL,37-SANDI,12-
2dr/21ph/10pg L

Lee,Alice,House
3578 Seventh Ave.
HABS CA-2161
HABS CAL,37-SANDI,19-
1ph/1pg/1pc L

Long-Waterman House
2408 First Ave.
HABS CA-1964
HABS CAL,37-SANDI,20-
8dr/8ph/6pg/1pc/1ct/fr L

Maier Brewing Company Warehouse (Frost Lumber Company)
505 W. Market St.
HABS CA-2270
HABS 1992(HABS):CA-1
9ph/9pg/1pc L

Marston,Arthur,House
3575 Seventh Ave.
HABS CA-2164
HABS CAL,37-SANDI,21-
6ph/1pg/1pc/fr L

Marston,George W. ,House
3525 Seventh Ave.
HABS CA-1960
HABS CAL,37-SANDI,10-
5dr/14ph/11pg/fr L

McGurck Block
Fifth & Market Sts.
HABS CA-428
HABS CAL,37-SANDI,4-
1ph/3pg L

Mission San Diego de Alcala
Misson Valley Rd.
HABS CA-321
HABS CAL,37-SANDI,1-
24dr/10ph/1pg L

Naval Submarine Base; see Ft. Rosecrans

Naval Submarine Base,Building No. 137; see Fort Rosecrans,Barracks

Naval Submarine Base,Building No. 138; see Fort Rosecrans,Argonaut Hall

Naval Submarine Base,Building No. 139; see Fort Rosecrans,Barracks

Naval Submarine Base,Building No. 158; see Fort Rosecrans,Post Exchange

Naval Submarine Base,Building No. 167; see Fort Rosecrans,Mining Casemate

Naval Submarine Base,Office Building; see Fort Rosecrans,Post Exchange

Naval Submarine Base,YMCA Service Club; see Fort Rosecrans,Argonaut Hall

Nesmith-Greely Building (Greely Building)
825 Fifth Ave.
HABS CA-1971
HABS CAL,37-SANDI,13-
1dr/1ph/5pg L

Santa Fe Railroad Station
1050 Kettner Blvd.
HABS CA-1965
HABS CAL,37-SANDI,22-
15ph/10pg/1pc/fr L

Savage Tire Factory (Aztec Brewery)
2201-2399 Main St.
HAER CA-79
HAER 1992(HAER):CA-1
1ph/24pg/1pc L

Savage Tire Factory (Aztec Brewing Company)
2201-2399 Main St.
HAER CA-79-F
H

Savage Tire Factory,Factory Building (Aztec Brewing Company)
2201-2399 Main St.
HAER CA-79-D
HAER 1991(HAER):2
18ph/2pc H

Savage Tire Factory,Factory Building (Aztec Brewing Company,Factory Building)
Main St.
HAER CA-79-D
HAER 1991(HAER):2
18ph/2pc L

Savage Tire Factory,Office Building (Aztec Brewing Company)
2201-2399 Main St.
HAER CA-79-B
HAER 1991(HAER):2
13ph/1pc H

Savage Tire Factory,Office Building (Aztec Brewing Company,Office Building)
Main St.
HAER CA-79-B
HAER 1991(HAER):2
13ph/1pc L

Savage Tire Factory,Original Brick Warehouse (Aztec Brewing Company)
2201-2399 Main St.
HAER CA-79-E
HAER 1991(HAER):2
8ph/1pc H

Savage Tire Factory,Original Brick Warehouse (Aztec Brewing Company,Original Brick Warehouse)
Main St.
HAER CA-79-E
HAER 1991(HAER):2
8ph/1pc L

Savage Tire Factory,Rathskeller (Aztec Brewing Company)
2201-2399 Main St.
HAER CA-79-C
HAER 1991(HAER):2
2ph/1pc H

Savage Tire Factory,Rathskeller (Aztec Brewing Company,Rathskeller)
Main St.
HAER CA-79-C
HAER 1991(HAER):2
2ph/1pc L

Savage Tire Factory,2201-2299 Warehouse (Aztec Brewing Company)
2201-2399 Main St.
HAER CA-79-A
HAER 1991(HAER):2
7ph/1pc H

Savage Tire Factory,2201-2299 Warehouse (Aztec Brewing Company,2201-2299 Warehouse)
Main St.
HAER CA-79-A
HAER 1991(HAER):2
7ph/1pc L

Savage Tire Factory,2341-2399 Warehouse (Aztec Brewing Company,2341-2399 Warehouse)
Main St.
HAER CA-79-F
HAER 1991(HAER):2
3ph/1pc L

Shepard,Jesse,House; see Villa Montezuma

Sherman-Gilbert House
Heritage Park
HABS CA-1967
HABS CAL,37-SANDI,23-
3ph/3pg/1pc L

Spreckels Building & Theater
123 Broadway
HABS CA-1966
HABS CAL,37-SANDI,24-
9ph/5pg/2pc/fr L

Stingaree Bordello
303-324 Island St.
HABS CA-2214
HABS CAL,37-SANDI,25-
11ph/14pg/1pc L

Teats,Katherine,House
3560 Seventh Ave.
HABS CA-2162
HABS CAL,37-SANDI,26-
5ph/6pg/1pc L

Temple Beth Israel (Fraternal Spirtualist Church)
1502 Second Ave.
HABS CA-1999
HABS CAL,37-SANDI,14-
5dr/6ph/8pg/1pc/1ct/fr L

U.S. Naval Hospital
Park Blvd.,Balboa Park
HABS CA-1548
HABS CAL,37-SANDI,27-
6dr/83ph/78pg/6pc/fr L

U.S. Naval Hospital,Administration Bldg. (U.S. Naval Hospital,Bldg. No. 1)
Park Blvd,Balboa Park
HABS CA-1548-A
HABS CAL,37-SANDI,27-A-
27ph/9pg/2pc L

U.S. Naval Hospital,Bldg. No. 1; see U.S. Naval Hospital,Administration Bldg.

U.S. Naval Hospital,Bldg. No. 10; see U.S. Naval Hospital,Ward D

U.S. Naval Hospital,Bldg. No. 11; see U.S. Naval Hospital,Service Bldg.

U.S. Naval Hospital,Bldg. No. 13; see U.S. Naval Hospital,Incinerator Bldg.

U.S. Naval Hospital,Bldg. No. 14; see U.S. Naval Hospital,Laboratory & Outpatient Bldg.

U.S. Naval Hospital,Bldg. No. 15; see U.S. Naval Hospital,North Ward

U.S. Naval Hospital,Bldg. No. 17; see U.S. Naval Hospital,Guinea Pig & Rabbit House

U.S. Naval Hospital,Bldg. No. 2; see U.S. Naval Hospital,Ward A

U.S. Naval Hospital,Bldg. No. 20; see U.S. Naval Hospital,Contagious Ward

U.S. Naval Hospital,Bldg. No. 21; see U.S. Naval Hospital,Corps Barracks

U.S. Naval Hospital,Bldg. No. 22; see U.S. Naval Hospital,Sick Officers Qtrs.

U.S. Naval Hospital,Bldg. No. 23; see U.S. Naval Hospital,Gate House

U.S. Naval Hospital,Bldg. No. 36; see U.S. Naval Hospital,South Ward

U.S. Naval Hospital,Bldg. No. 37; see U.S. Naval Hospital,Medical Storehouse

U.S. Naval Hospital,Bldg. No. 38; see U.S. Naval Hospital,Sick Officers & Outpatient Bld

U.S. Naval Hospital,Bldg. No. 4; see U.S. Naval Hospital,Subsistence Bldg.

U.S. Naval Hospital,Bldg. No. 49; see U.S. Naval Hospital,North Crosswalk

U.S. Naval Hospital,Bldg. No. 5; see U.S. Naval Hospital,Ward B

U.S. Naval Hospital,Bldg. No. 6; see U.S. Naval Hospital,Power House

U.S. Naval Hospital,Bldg. No. 81; see U.S. Naval Hospital,Executive Officer's Qtrs.

U.S. Naval Hospital,Bldg. No. 82; see U.S. Naval Hospital,Surgeon's Qtrs.

U.S. Naval Hospital,Bldg. No. 83; see U.S. Naval Hospital,Double Qtrs.

U.S. Naval Hospital,Bldg. No. 9; see U.S. Naval Hospital,Ward C

U.S. Naval Hospital,Bldg.No. 4; see U.S. Naval Hospital,Operating Bldg.

U.S. Naval Hospital,Contagious Ward (U.S. Naval Hospital,Bldg. No. 20)
Park Blvd.,Balboa Park
HABS CA-1548-N
HABS CAL,37-SANDI,27-N-
25ph/2pg/2pc L

U.S. Naval Hospital,Corps Barracks (U.S. Naval Hospital,Bldg. No. 21)
Park Blvd.,Balboa Park
HABS CA-1548-O
HABS CAL,37-SANDI,27-O-
25ph/3pg/2pc L

U.S. Naval Hospital,Double Qtrs. (U.S. Naval Hospital,Bldg. No. 83; U.S. Naval Hospital,Qtrs. D & E)
Park Blvd.,Balboa Park
HABS CA-1548-S
HABS CAL,37-SANDI,27-S-
15ph/2pg/2pc L

U.S. Naval Hospital,Executive Officer's Qtrs. (U.S. Naval Hospital,Bldg. No. 81; U.S. Naval Hospital,Qtrs. B)
Park Blvd.,Balboa Park
HABS CA-1548-Q
HABS CAL,37-SANDI,27-Q-
13ph/7pg/1pc L

U.S. Naval Hospital,Gate House (U.S. Naval Hospital,Bldg. No. 23)
Park Blvd.,Balboa Park
HABS CA-1548-T
HABS CAL,37-SANDI,27-T-
6ph/2pg/1pc L

U.S. Naval Hospital,Guinea Pig & Rabbit House (U.S. Naval Hospital,Bldg. No. 17)
Park Blvd.,Balboa Park
HABS CA-1548-L
HABS CAL,37-SANDI,27-L-
3ph/1pg/1pc L

U.S. Naval Hospital,Incinerator Bldg. (U.S. Naval Hospital,Bldg. No. 13)
Park Blvd.,Balboa Park
HABS CA-1548-M
HABS CAL,37-SANDI,27-M-
8ph/2pg/1pc L

U.S. Naval Hospital,Laboratory & Outpatient Bldg. (U.S. Naval Hospital,Bldg. No. 14)
Park Blvd.,Balboa Park
HABS CA-1548-J
HABS CAL,37-SANDI,27-J-
13ph/3pg/1pc L

U.S. Naval Hospital,Medical Storehouse (U.S. Naval Hospital,Bldg. No. 37)
Park Blvd.,Balboa Park
HABS CA-1548-V
HABS CAL,37-SANDI,27-V-
5ph/3pg/1pc L

U.S. Naval Hospital,North Crosswalk (U.S. Naval Hospital,Bldg. No. 49)
Park Blvd.,Balboa Park
HABS CA-1548-X
HABS CAL,37-SANDI,27-X-
2ph/3pg/1pc L

U.S. Naval Hospital,North Ward (U.S. Naval Hospital,Bldg. No. 15)
Park Blvd.,Balboa Park
HABS CA-1548-K
HABS CAL,37-SANDI,27-K-
15ph/3pg/2pc L

U.S. Naval Hospital,Operating Bldg. (U.S. Naval Hospital,Bldg.No. 4)
Park Blvd.,Balboa Park
HABS CA-1548-C
HABS CAL,37-SANDI,27-C-
5ph/3pg/1pc L

U.S. Naval Hospital,Power House (U.S. Naval Hospital,Bldg. No. 6)
Park Blvd.,Balboa Park
HABS CA-1548-F
HABS CAL,37-SANDI,27-F-
5ph/2pg/1pc L

U.S. Naval Hospital,Qtrs. B; see U.S. Naval Hospital,Executive Officer's Qtrs.

U.S. Naval Hospital,Qtrs. C; see U.S. Naval Hospital,Surgeon's Qtrs.

U.S. Naval Hospital,Qtrs. D & E; see U.S. Naval Hospital,Double Qtrs.

U.S. Naval Hospital,Service Bldg. (U.S. Naval Hospital,Bldg. No. 11)
Park Blvd.,Balboa Park
HABS CA-1548-I
HABS CAL,37-SANDI,27-I-
15ph/3pg/2pc L

U.S. Naval Hospital,Sick Officers & Outpatient Bld (U.S. Naval Hospital,Bldg. No. 38)
Park Blvd.,Balboa Park
HABS CA-1548-W
HABS CAL,37-SANDI,27-W-
4ph/2pg/1pc L

U.S. Naval Hospital,Sick Officers Qtrs. (U.S. Naval Hospital,Bldg. No. 22)
Park Blvd.,Balboa Park
HABS CA-1548-P
HABS CAL,37-SANDI,27-P-
9ph/2pg/1pc L

U.S. Naval Hospital,South Ward (U.S. Naval Hospital,Bldg. No. 36)
Park Blvd.,Balboa Park
HABS CA-1548-U
HABS CAL,37-SANDI,27-U-
10ph/2pg/1pc L

U.S. Naval Hospital,Subsistence Bldg. (U.S. Naval Hospital,Bldg. No. 4)
Park Blvd.,Balboa Park
HABS CA-1548-D
HABS CAL,37-SANDI,27-D-
14ph/3pg/2pc L

U.S. Naval Hospital,Surgeon's Qtrs. (U.S. Naval Hospital,Bldg. No. 82; U.S. Naval Hospital,Qtrs. C)
Park Blvd.,Balboa Park
HABS CA-1548-R
HABS CAL,37-SANDI,27-R-
10ph/2pg/1pc L

U.S. Naval Hospital,Ward A (U.S. Naval Hospital,Bldg. No. 2)
Park Blvd.,Balboa Park
HABS CA-1548-B
HABS CAL,37-SANDI,27-B-
13ph/3pg/2pc L

U.S. Naval Hospital,Ward B (U.S. Naval Hospital,Bldg. No. 5)
Park Blvd.,Balboa Park
HABS CA-1548-E
HABS CAL,37-SANDI,27-E-
13ph/3pg/1pc L

U.S. Naval Hospital,Ward C (U.S. Naval Hospital,Bldg. No. 9)
Park Blvd.,Balboa Park
HABS CA-1548-G
HABS CAL,37-SANDI,27-G-
17ph/2pg/2pc L

U.S. Naval Hospital,Ward D (U.S. Naval Hospital,Bldg. No. 10)
Park Blvd.,Balboa Park
HABS CA-1548-H
HABS CAL,37-SANDI,27-H-
11ph/3pg/1pc L

Villa Montezuma (Shepard,Jesse,House)
1925 K St.
HABS CA-432
HABS CAL,37-SANDI,6-
8dr/11ph/7pg/fr L

Whaley House
2482 San Diego Ave.
HABS CA-422
HABS CAL,37-OLTO,5-
9ph/11pg L

SAN DIEGO (OLD TOWN)

Bandera,Casa de la; see Machado,Casa de

Bandini,Don Juan,Home
Mason & Calhoun Sts.
HABS CA-46
HABS CAL,37-OLTO,2-
4dr/4ph/1pg/fr L

Derby,George,House (Pendleton,George,House)
4017 Harney St.
HABS CA-430
HABS CAL,37-OLTO,6-
6ph/5pg L

Estudillo,Jose Antonio,House (Ramona's Marriage Place)
Mason St. & San Diego Ave.
HABS CA-45
HABS CAL,37-OLTO,1-
6dr/7ph/2pg L

Lopez,La Casa de
Twiggs St.
HABS CA-47
HABS CAL,37-OLTO,3-
2dr/3ph/1pg/fr L

Machado,Casa de (Bandera,Casa de la)
2745 San Diego Ave.
HABS CA-411
HABS CAL,37-OLTO,4-
4ph/1pg/fr L

Pendleton,George,House; see Derby,George,House

Ramona's Marriage Place; see Estudillo,Jose Antonio,House

SAN LUIS REY (VISTA)

Rancho Guajome,La Casa de
HABS CA-43
HABS CAL,37-VIST.V,1-
11dr/14ph/1pg/fr L

SPRING VALLEY

Bancroft House
9050 Memory Lane
HABS CA-431
HABS CAL,37-SPRIV,1-
4ph/6pg L

WARNER SPRINGS

Kimbie-Wilson House
HABS CA-426
HABS CAL,37-WARN,1-
4ph/1pc/fr L

WARNER SPRINGS VIC.

Warner Ranch,Barn,Trading Post
HABS CA-425
HABS CAL,37-WARN.V,1-B-
3dr/2ph/4pg/fr L

Warner Ranch,Ranch House
HABS CA-424
HABS CAL,37-WARN.V,1-
4dr/3ph/10pg L

SAN FRANCISCO COUNTY

SAN FRANCISCO

Abandoned Ships,Historic View,1849-1850
Yerba Beuna Cove
HABS CA-1557
HABS CAL,38-SANFRA,85-
1ph L

Adelphian Apartments (Jordan Hotel)
820 O'Farrel St.
HABS CA-2344
10ph/7pg/1pc H

Admission Day Celebration,Historic View,1850 (San Francisco,Historic View,1850)
Montgomery & California Sts.
HABS CA-1159
HABS CAL,38-SANFRA,87-
1ph L

Alcatraz Island,Military Chapel
Alcatraz Island,San Francisco Bay
HABS CA-1792-J
HABS CAL,38-ALCA,1-J-
5ph/1pc L

Alcatraz Island,Power Plant
Alcatraz Island,San Francisco Bay
HABS CA-1792-E
HABS CAL,38-ALCA,1-E-
7ph/1pc/2ct L

Alcatraz Island,Warehouse/Bakery
Alcatraz Island,San Francisco Bay
HABS CA-1792-F
HABS CAL,38-ALCA,1-F-
3ph/1pc/2ct L

Alcatraz,Bldg. 64
Alcatraz Island,San Francisco Bay
HABS CA-1792-G
HABS CAL,38-ALCA,1-G-
4ph/1pc/1ct L

Alcatraz,Cell House
Alcatraz Island,San Francisco Bay
HABS CA-1792-A
HABS CAL,38-ALCA,1-A-
29ph/2pc/7ct L

Alcatraz,China Alley
Alcatraz Island,San Francisco Bay
HABS CA-1792-H
HABS CAL,38-ALCA,1-H-
3ph/1pc/1ct L

Alcatraz,Guard Tower
Alcatraz Island,San Francisco Bay
HABS CA-1792-I
HABS CAL,38-ALCA,1-I-
2ph/1pc/1ct L

Alcatraz,Industries Bldg.
Alcatraz Island,San Francisco Bay
HABS CA-1792-C
HABS CAL,38-ALCA,1-C-
4ph/1pc L

Alcatraz,Laundry Bldg.
Alcatraz Island,San Francisco Bay
HABS CA-1792-D
HABS CAL,38-ALCA,1-D-
7ph/1pc L

Alcatraz,Military Buildings
Alcatraz Island
HABS CA-1792
HABS CAL,38-ALCA,1-
1ph L

Alcatraz,Officer's Club
Alcatraz Island,San Francisco Bay
HABS CA-1792-L
HABS CAL,38-ALCA,1-L-
4ph/1pc/1ct L

Alcatraz,Sally Port
Alcatraz Island,San Francisco Bay
HABS CA-1792-K
HABS CAL,38-ALCA,1-K-
5ph/1pc/1ct L

Alcatraz,Warden's House
Alcatraz Island,San Francisco Bay
HABS CA-1792-B
HABS CAL,38-ALCA,1-B-
7ph/1pc/1ct L

Alvord Lake Bridge
HAER CA-33
HAER CAL,38-SANFRA,138-
4ph/1pg/1pc L

Anderson-Christofani Shipyard
Innes Ave. & Griffith St.
HAER CA-14
HAER CAL,38-SANFRA,139-
18ph/1pg/1pc L

Anglo & London Paris National Bank
(Anglo California National Bank; Crocker Bank)
One Sansome St.
HABS CA-2185
HABS CAL,38-SANFRA,144-
33ph/10pg/2pc L

Anglo California National Bank; see Anglo & London Paris National Bank

Appraiser's Building (Custom House,Old)
Sansome St.
HABS CA-1231
HABS CAL,38-SANFRA,24-
1ph L

Bank Building
California & Liedesdorff Sts.
HABS CA-1728
HABS CAL,38-SANFRA,46-
10ph/4pg L

Battery Street,Historic View
HABS CA-1723
HABS CAL,38-SANFRA,109-
1ph L

Blackstone House
Blackstone Court
HABS CA-1224
HABS CAL,38-SANFRA,20-
2ph L

Blake,Moffitt & Towne Building
41 First St.
HABS CA-2204
HABS CAL,38-SANFRA,145-
7ph/17pg/1pc L

Blumenthal Building; see Grace Building

Bolton & Barron Building
Montgomery & Merchant Sts.
HABS CA-1232
HABS CAL,38-SANFRA,25-
1ph L

Booth,Edwin,House
35 Calhoun St.
HABS CA-1242
HABS CAL,38-SANFRA,33-
1ph L

Bourn,William,House
2550 Webster St.
HABS CA-2219
HABS CAL,38-SANFRA,146-
1ph/1pc L

Broderick Engine Company Number 1,Historic View
Sacramento & Kearny Sts.
HABS CA-1166
HABS CAL,38-SANFRA,15-
1ph L

Building Quarters Number 17; see Fort Mason,Barracks

Buildings Numbers 1020,1022,1024,1026; see Letterman General Hospital,Nurses' Quarters

California & Sansome Streets,Historic View,1872
HABS CA-1167
HABS CAL,38-SANFRA,101-
1ph L

City Hall
Civic Center
HABS CA-1881
HABS CAL,38-SANFRA,71-
13ph/12pg/1pc L

City of Paris Dry Goods Company
(Spring Valley Water Company Building)
Geary & Stockton Sts.
HABS CA-2019
HABS CAL,38-SANFRA,135-
45dr/79ph/30pg/5pc/fr L

Clay Street Bank,Historic View
35 Clay St.
HABS CA-1744
HABS CAL,38-SANFRA,56-
1ph L

Cliff House Fire,Historic View
Point Lobos
HABS CA-1736
HABS CAL,38-SANFRA,50-
1ph L

Crocker Bank; see Anglo & London Paris National Bank

Cunningham's Wharf,Historic View
Commercial St.
HABS CA-1743
HABS CAL,38-SANFRA,55-
1ph L

Custom House,Old; see Appraiser's Building

Dakin,Capt. ,House
Taylor & Vallejo Sts.
HABS CA-1240
HABS CAL,38-SANFRA,32-
2ph L

Eagle Cafe (McComrick Steamship Office)
2566 Powell St. (moved to Pier 39)
HABS CA-2046
HABS CAL,38-SANFRA,132-
7ph/3pg L

Engine 15 Firehouse
California St.
HABS CA-1882
HABS CAL,38-SANFRA,72-
10dr/9ph/4pg/fr L

Express Building,Historic View
California & Montgomery Sts.
HABS CA-1769
HABS CAL,38-SANFRA,64-
4ph L

Ferry Building
Embarcadero & Market St.
HABS CA-1910
HABS CAL,38-SANFRA,78-
3ph/10pg L

Fleischhacker Pool & Bath House
Sloat Blvd. & Great Hwy.
HABS CA-2075
HABS CAL,38-SANFRA,136-
26ph/20pg/2pc/fr L

Flood,James Clair,Mansion (Pacific Union Club)
1000 California St.
HABS CA-1230
HABS CAL,38-SANFRA,23-
3ph L

Folsom & Second Streets,Historic View
HABS CA-1718
HABS CAL,38-SANFRA,95-
1ph L

Fort Gunnybags,Historic View; see Sacramento Block,Historic View

Fort Mason
Van Ness,Bay & Laguna Sts.
HABS CA-1119
HABS CAL,38-SANFRA,9-
6ph L

Fort Mason NCO Quarters,Number 12
HABS CA-1178
HABS CAL,38-SANFRA,9E-
1ph L

Fort Mason,Barracks (Building Quarters Number 17)
HABS CA-1179
HABS CAL,38-SANFRA,9I-
2ph L

Fort Mason,Barracks Number 19
HABS CA-1181
HABS CAL,38-SANFRA,9J-
2ph L

Fort Mason,N C O Quarters Number 13
HABS CA-1177
HABS CAL,38-SANFRA,9F-
1ph L

Fort Mason,Officer's Club (Fort Mason,Quarters Number 1)
HABS CA-1877
HABS CAL,38-SANFRA-9-A-
2ph/fr L

Fort Mason,Quarters Number 1; see Fort Mason,Officer's Club

Fort Mason,Quarters Number 2
HABS CA-1878
HABS CAL,38-SANFRA,9-B-
3ph/fr L

Fort Mason,Quarters Number 3
HABS CA-1879
HABS CAL,38-SANFRA,9-C-
1ph/fr L

Fort Mason,Quarters Number 4
HABS CA-1880
HABS CAL,38-SANFRA,9-D-
2ph/fr L

Fort Mason,W O & N C O Quarters Number 14
HABS CA-1176
HABS CAL,38,SANFRA,9G-
1ph L

Fort Mason,W O Quarters Number 16
HABS CA-1180
HABS CAL,38-SANFRA,9H-
1ph L

Fort Point (Fort Point National Historic Site; Fort Winfield Scott)
U. S. Hwy. 101
HABS CA-1239
HABS CAL,38-SANFRA,4-
45ph/1pg/2pc/4ct L

Fort Point National Historic Site; see Fort Point

Fort Winfield Scott; see Fort Point

Fortman House
Gougn & Eddy Sts.
HABS CA-1161
HABS CAL,38-SANFRA,11-
1ph L

Fremont Hotel,Historic View
Telegraph Hill
HABS CA-1726
HABS CAL,38-SANFRA,44-
1ph L

Fremont House,Historic View
Black Point
HABS CA-1175
HABS CAL,38-SANFRA,16-
1ph L

Golden Gate Bridge
Spanning mouth of San Francisco Bay
HAER CA-31
HAER CAL,38-SANFRA,140-
41ph/1pg/3pc/15ct L

Golden Gate Park,Conservatory
Golden Gate Park
HABS CA-2227
HABS CAL,38-SANFRA,147-
11ph/1pc/1ct L

Grace Building (Blumenthal Building)
87 Third St.
HABS CA-2208
HABS CAL,38-SANFRA,148-
5ph/1pg/1pc L

Haas-Lilienthal House
2007 Franklin St.
HABS CA-1160
HABS CAL,38-SANFRA,10-
8ph/12pg/1pc/4ct L

Hallidie Building
130 Sutter St.
HABS CA-2221
HABS CAL,38-SANFRA,149-
1ph/1pc L

Hibernia Bank
1 Jones St.
HABS CA-2224
HABS CAL,38-SANFRA,150-
5ph/1pc L

Hibernia Savings & Loan Soc. Bldgs. ,Historic View
Montgomery & Post Sts.
HABS CA-1735
HABS CAL,38-SANFRA,49-
2ph L

Hindu Society (Vedanta Society)
2963 Webster St.
HABS CA-1286
HABS CAL,38-SANFRA,151-
3ph/1pc L

Holbrook Building
58 Sutter St.
HABS CA-2186
HABS CAL,38-SANFRA,152-
16ph/8pg/2pc L

Holy Cross Parish Hall
Eddy St. (moved from Market & Second Sts.)
HABS CA-1908
HABS CAL,38-SANFRA,76-
3ph/8pg L

Hotaling Building
451 Jackson St.
HABS CA-1475
HABS CAL,38-SANFRA,37-
3ph/8pg L

Humphrey House
986 Chestnut St.
HABS CA-155
HABS CAL,38-SANFRA,7-
5ph/fr L

Jackson Square (Commercial Building)
415-431 Jackson St.
HABS CA-1903
HABS CAL,38-SANFRA,154-
1ph/1pc L

Jackson Square (Commercial Building)
441 Jackson St.
HABS CA-1902
HABS CAL,38-SANFRA,156-
1ph/1pc L

Jackson Square (Commercial Building)
445 Jackson St.
HABS CA-1901
HABS CAL,38-SANRA,155-
2ph/1pc L

Jackson Square (Commercial Building)
463-473 Jackson St.
HABS CA-1900
HABS CAL,38-SANFRA,153-
2ph/1pc L

Jackson Street (Commercial Buildings)
Jackson St. btwn. Montgomery & Sansome Sts.
HABS CA-1473
HABS CAL,38-SANFRA,3-
2ph L

Jordan Hotel; see Adelphian Apartments

King,James,of William Banking House,Historic View
Montgomery & Commercial Sts.
HABS CA-1822
HABS CAL,38-SANFRA,68-
2ph L

Leese,Jacob,House,Historic View
Grant Ave.
HABS CA-1869
HABS CAL,38-SANFRA,70-
1ph L

Letterman General Hospital,Nurses' Quarters (Thompson Hall; Buildings Numbers 1020,1022,1024,1026)
Girard Rd. & Lincoln Blvd.,Presidio of San Fran.
HABS CA-2269
HABS 1992(HABS):CA-1
34ph/11pg/3pc/fr L

Lick House,Historic View
Montgomery & Sutter Sts.
HABS CA-1727
HABS CAL,38-SANFRA,45-
1ph L

Lincoln School,Historic View
Fifth St.
HABS CA-1868
HABS CAL,38-SANFRA,69-
1ph L

Maguires Music Hall,Historic View
Pine St.
HABS CA-1724
HABS CAL,38-SANFRA,43-
1ph L

Maritime Museum
Beach St. ,W of Polk St.
HABS CA-2225
HABS CAL,38-SANFRA,157-
7ph/1pc L

Market Street,Historic View
HABS CA-1722
HABS CAL,38-SANFRA,114-
1ph L

Market Street,Historic View
HABS CA-1796
HABS CAL,38-SANFRA,113-
1ph L

Masonic Hall,Old,Historic View
Montgomery St.
HABS CA-1747
HABS CAL,38-SANFRA,52-
1ph L

Masonic Temple Center,Historic View
Post & Montgomery Sts.
HABS CA-1739
HABS CAL,38-SANFRA,51-
1ph L

McComrick Steamship Office; see Eagle Cafe

McCoy Label Company; see U. S. Sub-Treasury & Mint

Medical-Dental Building
450 Sutter St.
HABS CA-2226
HABS CAL,38-SANFRA,158-
9ph/1pc L

Mercantile Library Building,Historic View
Bush & Sansome Sts.
HABS CA-1163
HABS CAL,38-SANFRA,13-
1ph L

Metroplitan Theater,Historic View
Montgomery & Jackson Sts.
HABS CA-1745
HABS CAL,38-SANFRA,57-
1ph L

Mexican Custom House,Historic View
Portsmouth Sq.
HABS CA-1293
HABS CAL,38-SANFRA,35-
3ph L

Mills Building
220 Montgomery St.
HABS CA-2223
HABS CAL,38-SANFRA,159-
7ph/1pc L

Miners' Exchange Bank,Historic View; see Wright's Historic View

Mission Delores; see Mission San Francisco de Asis

Mission San Francisco de Asis (Mission Delores)
Mission & Sixteenth Sts.
HABS CA-113
HABS CAL,38-SANFRA,1-
39dr/35ph/9pg/fr L

Montgomery & Post Streets,Historic View
HABS CA-1823
HABS CAL,38-SANFRA,98-
1ph L

Montgomery Block
28 Montgomery St.
HABS CA-1228
HABS CAL,38-SANFRA,6-
13dr/12ph/7pg/fr L

Montgomery Street (Commercial Building)
HABS CA-1474
HABS CAL,38-SANFRA,124-
1ph L

802 Montgomery Street (Commerical Building)
HABS CA-1472
HABS CAL,38-SANFRA,125-
1ph L

Montgomery Street,Historic View
HABS CA-1165
HABS CAL,38-SANFRA,116-
1ph L

Montgomery Street,Historic View
HABS CA-1797
HABS CAL,38-SANFRA,123-
3ph L

Morris,V. C. ,Store
140 Maiden Lane
HABS CA-2216
HABS CAL,38-SANFRA,160-
9ph/1pc L

Nevada National Bank,Historic View
Montgomery & Pine Sts.
HABS CA-1164
HABS CAL,38-SANFRA,14-
1ph L

Niantic Hotel,Historic View
Clay & Sansome Sts.
HABS CA-1719
HABS CAL,38-SANFRA,40-
1ph L

North Beach,Historic View,1865
HABS CA-1733
HABS CAL,38-SANFRA,99-
1ph L

North Point Pier Bulkhead Buildings
Embarcadero,Kearney & Powell Sts.
HABS CA-2047
HABS CAL,38-SANFRA,134-
27ph/3pg L

O'Brien House
1045 Green St.
HABS CA-1236
HABS CAL,38-SANFRA,29-
1ph L

Oakland-San Francisco Bay Bridge
HAER CA-32
HAER CAL,38-SANFRA,141-
53ph/3pc L

Occidental Hotel,Historic View
Montgomery & Bush Sts.
HABS CA-1162
HABS CAL,38-SANFRA,12-
1ph L

Octagon House
2645 Gough St.
HABS CA-1223
HABS CAL,38-SANFRA,19-
10ph/8pg L

Ortman-Shumate House
1901 Scott St.
HABS CA-2220
HABS CAL,38-SANFRA,161-
1ph/1pc L

Pacific Union Club; see Flood,James Clair,Mansion

Palace of Fine Arts
Baker St.
HABS CA-1909
HABS CAL,38-SANFRA,77-
13ph/13pg/1pc/3ct L

Palmer,Silas,House
Van Ness & Washington Sts.
HABS CA-1289
HABS CAL,38-SANFRA,34-
1ph L

Parrott's Granite Block,Historic View
California & Montgomery Sts.
HABS CA-1770
HABS CAL,38-SANFRA,65-
2ph L

Phelps House
329 Divisadero St.
HABS CA-1904
HABS CAL,38-SANFRA,73-
7ph/7pg L

Pier 16 & Bulkhead Building
Howard St.
HAER CA-5
HAER CAL,38-SANFRA,142-
27ph/59pg/2pc L

Pier 42 Bulkhead Building
Pier 42,Embarcadero
HABS CA-2287
HABS 1991(HABS):5
15ph/3pg/2pc L

Polk-Williams House
1013 Vallejo St.
HABS CA-2217
HABS CAL,38-SANFRA,162-
1ph/1pc L

Portmouth Square,Historic View
HABS CA-1555
HABS CAL,38-SANFRA,38-
5ph L

Portmouth Square,Historic View
HABS CA-1725
HABS CAL,38-SANFRA,88-
1ph L

Post Office,First,Historic View
Stockton & Washington Sts.
HABS CA-1791
HABS CAL,38-SANFRA,67-
1ph L

Post Office,Old,Historic View
Kearney & Clay Sts.
HABS CA-1751
HABS CAL,38-SANFRA,60-
1ph L

Post Office,Second,Historic View
Clay & Pike Sts.
HABS CA-1225
HABS CAL,38-SANFRA,21-
1ph L

Powell Street
HABS CA-1790
HABS CAL,38-SANFRA,163-
1ph/1pc L

Presidio of San Francisco
U. S. 101 & I-480
HABS CA-1114
HABS CAL,38-SANFRA,8-
8ph L

Presidio,Barracks
U. S. 101 & I-480
HABS CA-1173
HABS CAL,38-SANFRA,8G-
4ph/1pc/2ct L

Presidio,Chapel of Our Lady
Moraga Ave.
HABS CA-1217
HABS CAL,38-SANFRA,8F-
6ph/1pc L

Presidio,Commandancia
(Presidio,Officer's Club)
Moraga Ave.
HABS CA-1100
HABS CAL,38-SANFRA,8A-
7ph L

Presidio,Gen. Pershing's House
Moraga Ave.
HABS CA-1215
HABS CAL,38-SANFRA,8D-
2ph L

Presidio,Gun Emplacements
U. S. 101 & I-480
HABS CA-1212
HABS CAL,38-SANFRA,8H-
6ph/1pc L

Presidio,Officer's Club; see Presidio,Commandancia

Presidio,Officers' Quarters
Funston Ave.
HABS CA-1214
HABS CAL,38-SANFRA,8C-
3ph/1pc L

Presidio,Old Station Hospital
(Presidio,Post Hospital)
Funston Ave. & Lincoln Blvd.
HABS CA-1216
HABS
CAL,38-SANFRA,8E-;1992(HABS):CA-1°
10dr/4ph/1pc/1ct/fr L

Presidio,Post Hospital; see Presidio,Old Station Hospital

Presidio,Powder Magazine
Graham St.
HABS CA-1213
HABS CAL,38-SANFRA,8B-
2ph L

Presidio,Stables
U. S. 101 & I-480
HABS CA-1174
HABS CAL,38-SANFRA,8I-
1ph/1pc L

Railroad House,Historic View
48 Commercial St.
HABS CA-1720
HABS CAL,38-SANFRA,41-
1ph L

Reservoir Keeper's House
Bay & Hyde Sts.
HABS CA-1234
HABS CAL,38-SANFRA,27-
1ph L

Roos Brothers Store,Historic View
Post & Kearny Sts.
HABS CA-1721
HABS CAL,38-SANFRA,42-
1ph L

Russ Building,Historic View
Montgomery & Pine Sts.
HABS CA-1754
HABS CAL,38-SANFRA,62-
1ph L

Russian Hill (Houses),Historic View
Green St.
HABS CA-1737
HABS CAL,38-SANFRA,112-
2ph L

Sacramento Block,Historic View (Fort Gunnybags,Historic View)
Sacramento St. & Battery St.
HABS CA-1746
HABS CAL,38-SANFRA,58-
3ph L

3397-3399 Sacramento Street (House)
HABS CA-2044
HABS CAL,38-SANFRA,133-
8ph L

Sacramento Street,Historic View
HABS CA-1780
HABS CAL,38-SANFRA,104-
1ph L

Sacramento Street,Historic View
HABS CA-2199
1ph L

Sailors' Home,Historic View; see U. S. Marine Hospital,Historic View

San Francisco & San Jose Railroad Building
Montgomery & Post Sts.
HABS CA-1729
HABS CAL,38-SANFRA,47-
1ph L

San Francisco Cable Rlwy:Cable Car Powerhse & Barn (United Railroads of San Francisco)
1201 Mason St.
HAER CA-12-A
HAER CAL,38-SANFRA,137-A-
5dr L

San Francisco Civic Center,Civic Auditorium
Civic Center
HABS CA-2222-C
HABS CAL,38-SANFRA,71-C-
1ph/1pc L

San Francisco Civic Center,Library
Civic Center
HABS CA-2222-A
HABS CAL,38-SANFRA,71-A-
1ph/1pc L

San Francisco Civic Center,Opera House
Civic Center
HABS CA-2222-B
HABS CAL,38-SANFRA,71-B-
1ph/1pc L

San Francisco Civic Center,State Building
Civic Center
HABS CA-2222-D
HABS CAL,38-SANFRA,71-D-
1ph/1pc L

San Francisco Daily Morning Call,Historic View
Clay & Montgomery Sts.
HABS CA-1753
HABS CAL,38-SANFRA,61-
1ph L

San Francisco Fire Dept. ,Pumping Station Number 2
Van Ness Ave. at Bay
HAER CA-1
HAER CAL,38-SANFRA,143-
51ph/12pg/3pc/1ct L

San Francisco Maritime National Historical Park; see Ship BALCLUTHA

San Francisco,Historic View,1837
HABS CA-1866
HABS CAL,38-SANFRA,79-
1ph L

San Francisco,Historic View,1846
HABS CA-1732
HABS CAL,38-SANFRA,80-
1ph L

San Francisco,Historic View,1848
HABS CA-1760
HABS CAL,38-SANFRA,81-
1ph L

San Francisco,Historic View,1849
HABS CA-1758
HABS CAL,38-SANFRA,84-
1ph L

San Francisco,Historic View,1849
HABS CA-1759
HABS CAL,38-SANFRA,83-
1ph L

San Francisco,Historic View,1849
HABS CA-1782
HABS CAL,38-SANFRA,82-
1ph L

San Francisco,Historic View,1850
HABS CA-1776
HABS CAL,38-SANFRA,86-
1ph L

San Francisco,Historic View,1850; see Admission Day Celebration,Historic View,1850

San Francisco,Historic View,1851
HABS CA-1756
HABS CAL,38-SANFRA,89-
1ph L

San Francisco,Historic View,1851 Fire
HABS CA-1730
HABS CAL,38-SANFRA,90-
1ph L

San Francisco,Historic View,1852 Plat Map
HABS CA-1222
HABS CAL,38-SANFRA,91-
1ph L

San Francisco,Historic View,1853
HABS CA-1761
HABS CAL,38-SANFRA,93-
1ph L

San Francisco,Historic View,1853 Plat Map
HABS CA-1221
HABS CAL,38-SANFRA,92-
2ph L

San Francisco,Historic View,1856
HABS CA-1762
HABS CAL,38-SANFRA,94-
2ph L

San Francisco,Historic View,1856
HABS CA-1814
HABS CAL,38-SANFRA,96-
1ph L

San Francisco,Historic View,1859 Plat Map
HABS CA-1220
HABS CAL,38-SANFRA,97-
2ph L

San Francisco,Historic View,1868
HABS CA-1734
HABS CAL,38-SANFRA,100-
1ph L

San Francisco,Historic View,1875
HABS CA-1767
HABS CAL,38-SANFRA,102-
1ph L

San Francisco,Historic View,1880
HABS CA-1781
HABS CAL,38-SANFRA,103-
1ph L

San Francisco,Historic View,1906
HABS CA-1764
HABS CAL,38-SANFRA,106-
6ph L

San Francisco,Historic View,1906 Fire
HABS CA-1798
HABS CAL,38-SANFRA,105-
2ph L

San Francisco,Historic View,1906 Fire
HABS CA-1817
HABS CAL,38-SANFRA,110-
1ph L

San Francisco,Historic View,1906 Fire
HABS CA-1818
HABS CAL,38-SANFRA,108-
1ph L

San Francisco,Historic View,1906 Fire
HABS CA-1819
HABS CAL,38-SANFRA,107-
1ph L

San Francisco,Historic View,1906 Fire
California & Sansome Sts.
HABS CA-1820
HABS CAL,38-SANFRA,111-
1ph L

San Francisco,Historic View,1906 Fire
Market St.
HABS CA-1778
HABS CAL,38-SANFRA,115-
1ph L

Sansome Street,Historic View,1850
HABS CA-1227
HABS CAL,38-SANFRA,128-
1ph L

Schooner C.A. THAYER
HAER CA-61
31ph/2pc/fr H

Scow Schooner ALMA
HAER CA-60
13ph/1pc/fr H

Sea Wall Warehouse
1501 Sansome St.
HABS CA-2194
HABS CAL,38-SANFRA,164-
6ph/1pc L

Sheldon Building
9-15 First St.
HABS CA-2203
HABS CAL,38-SANFRA,165-
9ph/19pg/1pc L

Ship BALCLUTHA (Ship STAR OF ALASKA; Ship PACIFIC QUEEN; San Francisco Maritime National Historical Park)
2905 Hyde Street Pier
HAER CA-54
69dr/142ph/189pg/9pc/fr L

Ship PACIFIC QUEEN; see Ship BALCLUTHA

Ship STAR OF ALASKA; see Ship BALCLUTHA

Spreckels Mansion
2080 Washington St.
HABS CA-1906
HABS CAL,38-SANFRA,74-
2ph/10pg L

Spring Valley Water Company Building; see City of Paris Dry Goods Company

St. Francis Church,Historic View
610 Vallejo St.
HABS CA-1219
HABS CAL,38-SANFRA,18-
3ph L

St. Mary's Church
660 California St.
HABS CA-1237
HABS CAL,38-SANFRA,30-
12ph L

St. Patrick's Church
756 Mission St.
HABS CA-1233
HABS CAL,38-SANFRA,26-
4ph L

St. Rose's Church
N. Brannan & Fifth Sts.
HABS CA-1311
HABS CAL,38-SANFRA,36-
3ph L

Steam Tug "Eppleton Hall"
San Francisco Maritime Nat. Hst. Park,Hyde St.Pier
HAER CA-63
HAER DLC/PP-1992:CA-3
20ph/1pg/2pc L

Stevenson-Osbourne House
Hyde & Lombard Sts.
HABS CA-1229
HABS CAL,38-SANFRA,22-
4ph L

Stockton Street,Historic View
HABS CA-1815
HABS CAL,38-SANFRA,129-
1ph L

Sutro,Adolph,House
Pt. Lobos & Forty-Eighth Ave.
HABS CA-1238
HABS CAL,38-SANFRA,31-
10ph L

Telegraph Hill (House)
1301 Montgomery St.
HABS CA-1241
HABS CAL,38-SANFRA,126-
1ph L

Telegraph Hill (Houses)
Alta St.
HABS CA-1243
HABS CAL,38-SANFRA,118-
1ph L

Telegraph Hill (Houses)
Filbert St.
HABS CA-1246
HABS CAL,38-SANFRA,119-
1ph L

Telegraph Hill (Houses)
Montgomery & Union Sts.
HABS CA-1245
HABS CAL,38-SANFRA,122-
1ph L

Telegraph Hill (Houses)
Napier La.
HABS CA-1244
HABS CAL,38-SANFRA,120-
1ph L

Telegraph Hill (Houses)
Union St.
HABS CA-1226
HABS CAL,38-SANFRA,127-
2ph L

Telegraph Hill,Historic View
HABS CA-1247
HABS CAL,38-SANFRA,117-
3ph L

Telegraph Hill,Historic View
Greenwich St.
HABS CA-1248
HABS CAL,38-SANFRA,121-
1ph L

Thompson Hall; see Letterman General Hospital,Nurses' Quarters

Trocadero Inn
Twenty-second Ave.
HABS CA-119
HABS CAL,38-SANFRA,2-
12dr/9ph/2pg/fr L

Tug HERCULES
HAER CA-62
32ph/2pc/fr H

U. S. Branch Mint
Mission & Fifth Sts.
HABS CA-160
HABS CAL,38-SANFRA,5-
22dr/33ph/3pg/fr L

U. S. Custom House,Old,Historic View
Battery & Washington Sts.
HABS CA-1556
HABS CAL,38-SANFRA,39-
1ph L

U. S. Marine Hospital,Historic View
(Sailors' Home,Historic View)
Spear & Harrison Sts.
HABS CA-1741
HABS CAL,38-SANFRA,54-
1ph L

U. S. Sub-Treasury & Mint (McCoy Label Company)
608 Commercial St.
HABS CA-1218
HABS CAL,38-SANFRA,17-
4ph L

Union Depot & Ferry House,Historic View
Market St.
HABS CA-1749
HABS CAL,38-SANFRA,59-
1ph L

United Railroads of San Francisco; see San Francisco Cable Rlwy:Cable Car Powerhse & Barn

2213-2217 Van Ness Avenue,Historic View,(Houses)
HABS CA-1235
HABS CAL,38-SANFRA,28-
1ph L

Vedanta Society; see Hindu Society

Warner's Cobweb Palace,Historic View
HABS CA-1740
HABS CAL,38-SANFRA,53-
2ph L

Wells Fargo & Company Building,Historic View
114 Montgomery St.
HABS CA-1768
HABS CAL,38-SANFRA,63-
1ph L

Wells Fargo Bank,Historic View
Sansome & California Sts.
HABS CA-1771
HABS CAL,38-SANFRA,66-
1ph L

Westerfeld House
1198 Fulton St.
HABS CA-2218
HABS CAL,38-SANFRA,166-
2ph/1pc L

Whittier Mansion
2090 Jackson St.
HABS CA-1907
HABS CAL,38-SANFRA,75-
16ph/19pg L

Wright's Historic View (Miners' Exchange Bank,Historic View)
Montgomery & Jackson Sts.
HABS CA-1731
HABS CAL,38-SANFRA,48-
1ph L

Yerba Buena Island,Naval Buildings
HABS CA-1793
HABS CAL,38-SANFRA,131-
4ph L

Yerba Buena Lighthouse Buildings
Yerba Buena Island
HABS CA-1554
HABS CAL,38-SANFRA,130-
1ph L

SAN FRANCISCO

San Francisco Cable Railway
Washington & Mason Sts.
HAER CA-12
HAER CAL,38-SANFRA,137-
8dr/65ph/114pg/15pc/fr L

SAN JOAQUIN COUNTY

ALBA

Farmhouse
HABS CA-12
HABS CAL,39-ALBA,1-
2ph L

CORRAL HOLLOW

House,Frame
HABS CA-1619
HABS CAL,39-COHO,1-
1ph/1pc L

Outbuilding
HABS CA-1613
HABS CAL,39-COHO,1-A-
1ph/1pc L

ESCALON

Jones House
HABS CA-117
HABS CAL,39-ESCA,1-
3ph L

FRENCH CAMP

Noble,Col. ,House
HABS CA-1617
HABS CAL,39-FRECA,1-
1ph/1pc L

LATHROP

Main Street (Commercial Buildings)
HABS CA-1595
HABS CAL,39-LATH,2-
1ph/1pc L

Sharpe Army Depot
HAER CA-26
HAER CAL,39-LATH,1-
35pg/fr L

LOCKEFORD

Harmony Grove Methodist Church
Lockeford Rd.
HABS CA-1614
HABS CAL,39-LOCFO,1-
1ph/1pc L

LODI

Commercial Buildings
HABS CA-1598
HABS CAL,39-LODI,1-
1ph/1pc L

STOCKTON

"Green Dragon"; see Columbia House

Avon Theatre
Main & California Sts.
HABS CA-1593
HABS CAL,39-STOCK,2-
1ph/1pc L

Barnhart House
Magnolia & Hunter Sts.
HABS CA-1621
HABS CAL,39-STOCK,3-
1ph/1pc L

Budd,Gov. James H. ,Mansion
HABS CA-1627
HABS CAL,39-STOCK,4-
1ph/1pc L

Carson House
HABS CA-1612
HABS CAL,39-STOCK,5-
1ph/1pc L

Christian Church
HABS CA-1615
HABS CAL,39-STOCK,6-
1ph/1pc L

Clark,Dr. Asa,House
Oak & Hunter Sts.
HABS CA-1581
HABS CAL,39-STOCK,7-
1ph/1pc L

Columbia House ("Green Dragon")
Channel & San Joaquin Sts.
HABS CA-1580
HABS CAL,39-STOCK,8-
1ph/1pc L

Commercial Hotel
Main St. ,200 Block
HABS CA-1629
HABS CAL,39-STOCK,9-
1ph/1pc L

Creanor,Judge,House
Fremont & Commercial Sts.
HABS CA-1616
HABS CAL,39-STOCK,10-
1ph/1pc L

Eureka Firehouse
HABS CA-1638
HABS CAL,39-STOCK,11-
2ph/1pc L

First Baptist Church
HABS CA-1583
HABS CAL,39-STOCK,12-
1ph/1pc L

Forty Ninth Drug Store; see Holden Store

Globe Iron Works
HABS CA-1605
HABS CAL,39-STOCK,13-
1ph/1pc L

Hart & Thrift Building
HABS CA-1600
HABS CAL,39-STOCK,14-
1ph/1pc L

Hazelton Library; see Stewart,Frank,Library

Holden Store (Forty Ninth Drug Store)
El Dorado & Main Sts.
HABS CA-1634
HABS CAL,39-STOCK,15-
1ph/1pc L

I. O. O. F. Building
El Dorado & Main Sts.
HABS CA-1625
HABS CAL,39-STOCK,16-
1ph/1pc L

Keyes House
California & Market Sts.
HABS CA-1609
HABS CAL,39-STOCK,17-
1ph/1pc L

Mansion House
HABS CA-1603
HABS CAL,39-STOCK,18-
1ph/1pc L

Masonic Temple & R. P. Parker Store
Hunter St.
HABS CA-1604
HABS CAL,39-STOCK,19-
1ph/1pc L

McKee Block (Sterling Corner)
Main & Hunter Sts.
HABS CA-1602
HABS CAL,39-STOCK,20-
1ph/1pc L

Philadephia House
HABS CA-1607
HABS CAL,39-STOCK,21-
1ph/1pc L

San Joaquin County Courthouse
HABS CA-1632
HABS CAL,39-STOCK,22-
2ph/1pc L

San Joaquin County Courthouse
Main & Hunter Sts.
HABS CA-1639
HABS CAL,39-STOCK,23-
1ph/1pc L

San Joaquin Firehouse
Weber Ave. & California St.
HABS CA-1640
HABS CAL,39-STOCK,24-
1ph/1pc L

Simpson,Andrew,House
Oak & El Dorado Sts.
HABS CA-1626
HABS CAL,39-STOCK,25-
1ph/1pc L

Smith,Capt. ,House
HABS CA-1618
HABS CAL,39-STOCK,26-
1ph/1pc L

Sperry Corn Elevator Complex
Weber Ave. (N. side),W. of Edison St.
HAER CA-47
HAER CAL,39-STOCK,1-
32ph/9pg/2pc L

St. Mary's Cathedral Church
HABS CA-1624
HABS CAL,39-STOCK,27-
1ph/1pc L

Sterling Corner; see McKee Block

Stewart,Frank,Library (Hazelton Library)
Market & Hunter Sts.
HABS CA-1631
HABS CAL,39-STOCK,28-
1ph/1pc L

Stockton,Historic View
HABS CA-1601
HABS CAL,39-STOCK,29-
17ph/1pc L

Terry,Judge Daniel S. ,House
Fremont & Center Sts.
HABS CA-1582
HABS CAL,39-STOCK,30-
1ph/1pc L

Trahearne,Washington,House
El Dorado & Park Sts.
HABS CA-1596
HABS CAL,39-STOCK,31-
1ph/1pc L

Weber,Capt. Charles M. ,House
HABS CA-1641
HABS CAL,39-STOCK,32-
3ph/1pc L

STOCKTON VIC.

Tone,Jack,House
Jack Tone Rd.
HABS CA-1620
HABS CAL,39-STOCK.V,1-
1ph/1pc L

WOODBRIDGE

Arizona State Home for Insane
HABS CA-1636
HABS CAL,39-WOBRI,1-
2ph/1pc L

I. O. O. F. Building
HABS CA-1590
HABS CAL,39-WOBRI,2-
1ph/1pc L

Woodbridge College
HABS CA-1635
HABS CAL,39-WOBRI,3-
1ph/1pc L

Woods Hotel
HABS CA-1610
HABS CAL,39-WOBRI,4-
1ph/1pc L

Woods,Jeremiah,Cottage
HABS CA-1611
HABS CAL,39-WOBRI,5-
1ph/1pc L

SAN LUIS OBISPO COUNTY

NIPOMO VIC.

Dana,William G. ,House
Guadalupe Rd.
HABS CA-23
HABS CAL,40-NIPO.V,1-
7dr/8ph/1pg/fr L

SAN LUIS OBISPO

Mission San Luis Obispo de Tolosa
782 Monterey St.
HABS CA-210
HABS CAL,40-SANLO,1-
15dr/14ph/2pg/fr L

Mission San Luis Obispo de Tolosa,Monastery
782 Monterey St.
HABS CA-210-A
HABS CAL,40-SANLO,1A-
4dr/4ph L

SAN MIGUEL VIC.

Caledonia Inn
Hwy. 101
HABS CA-1300
HABS CAL,40-SANMI.V,2-
2ph/1pc L

Mission San Miguel Arcangel
Hwy. 101
HABS CA-38-2
HABS CAL,40-SANMI.V,1-
36dr/36ph/1pg/3pc/fr L

SANTA MARGARITA VIC.

Mission Chapel of Santa Margarita; see Santa Margarita Asistencia

Santa Margarita Asistencia (Mission Chapel of Santa Margarita)
HABS CA-1182
HABS CAL,40-SANMAR.V,1-
19ph/2pc L

SAN MATEO COUNTY

ATHERTON

Linden Towers Gates
Middlefield Rd. at James La.
HABS CA-2118
HABS CAL,41-ATH,1-
9ph/1pg/1pc/1ct L

Watkins-Cartan Carriage House
25 Isabella Ave.
HABS CA-1990-A
HABS CAL,41-ATH,2-A-
1dr/fr L

Watkins-Cartan House
25 Isabella Ave.
HABS CA-1990
HABS CAL,41-ATH,2-
7dr/4ph/1pg/1pc/1ct/fr L

BELMONT

Ralston Hall (Ralston-Sharon House)
Ralston Ave.
HABS CA-1674
HABS CAL,41-BELM,1-
19ph/10pg/1pc/1ct L

Ralston-Sharon House; see Ralston Hall

BURLINGAME

Southern Pacific Railroad Station
Burlingame Ave. & California Dr.
HABS CA-2120
HABS CAL,41-BURL,1-
19ph/2pg/1pc L

HALF MOON BAY

Community Methodist Church
Johnston & Miramontes Sts.
HABS CA-2121
HABS CAL,41-HAMOB,1-
8ph/1pg/1pc/2ct L

Johnston,James,House
Higgins Rd.
HABS CA-2122
HABS CAL,41-HAMOB,2-
15ph/1pg/1pc L

Johnston,William,House
306 Higgins Rd.
HABS CA-2123
HABS CAL,41-HAMOB,3-
4ph/1pg/1pc L

Pilarcitos Livery Stable; see Vasquez,Pablo,Stable

Vasquez,Pablo,House
270 N. Main St.
HABS CA-2124
HABS CAL,41-HAMOB,4-
4ph/1pg/1pc L

Vasquez,Pablo,Stable (Pilarcitos Livery Stable)
200 N. Main St.
HABS CA-2124-A
HABS CAL,41-HAMOB,4-A-
3ph/1pg/1pc L

HILLSBOROUGH

Carolans
565 Remillard Dr.
HABS CA-2196
HABS CAL,41-HILBO,1-
11ph/1pg/1pc L

Clark House (House-on-Hill)
HABS CA-2126
HABS CAL,41-HILBO,2-
15ph/2pg/1pc L

Grant-Blyth House; see Villa Rose

House-on-Hill; see Clark House

Strawberry Hill; see Villa Rose

Villa Rose (Grant-Blyth House; Strawberry Hill)
Redington Rd.
HABS CA-2125
HABS CAL,41-HILBO,3-
12ph/1pg/1pc/1ct L

MENLO PARK

Atalaya (Meyer,J. Henry,House)
2212 Santa Cruz Ave.
HABS CA-2127
HABS CAL,41-MENPA,1-
2ph/1pg/1pc L

Church of the Nativity
210 Oak Grove Ave.
HABS CA-1995
HABS CAL,41-MENPA,2-
4dr/20ph/1pg/1pc/3ct/fr L

Meyer,J. Henry,House; see Atalaya

Payne-Douglass House
Valparaiso Ave.
HABS CA-2128
HABS CAL,41-MENPA,3-
9ph/6pg/1pc L

San Francisco & San Jose Railroad Station
1100 Merrill St.
HABS CA-1994
HABS CAL,41-MENPA,4-
4dr/11ph/1pg/1pc/1ct/fr L

MILLBRAE

Southern Pacific Depot
21 E. Millbrae Ave.
HABS CA-2059
HABS CAL,41-MILB,1-
11ph/1pc L

PESCADERO

Congregational Church
San Gregorio St.
HABS CA-163
HABS CAL,41-PESC,2-
7ph/1pg/1pc L

Garretson Schoolhouse
2307 Pescadero Rd.
HABS CA-2132
HABS CAL,41-PESC,3-
2ph/1pg/1pc L

Graham,Issac,House (White House)
Cabrillo Hwy.
HABS CA-2130
HABS CAL,41-PESC,4-
6ph/1pg/1pc L

I. O. O. F. Hall
110 San Gregorio St.
HABS CA-2134
HABS CAL,41-PESC,5-
2ph/1pg/1pc L

McCormick,James,House
San Gregorio St.
HABS CA-2131
HABS CAL,41-PESC,6-
4ph/1pg/1pc L

Methodist Episcopal Church
108 San Gregorio St.
HABS CA-162
HABS CAL,41-PESC,7-
11ph/1pg/1pc L

Moore,Thomas W. ,House
114 San Gregorio St.
HABS CA-2136
HABS CAL,41-PESC,8-
2ph/1pg/1pc L

108-114 San Gregorio Street (Buildings)
HABS CA-1996
HABS CAL,41-PESC,1-
1dr/2ph/1pc/fr L

St. Anthony's Roman Catholic Church
North St.
HABS CA-2133
HABS CAL,41-PESC,9-
10ph/1pg/1pc L

Weeks,Bartlett V. ,House
172 Goulson St.
HABS CA-2137
HABS CAL,41-PESC,10-
4ph/1pg/1pc L

Weeks,Braddock,House
Pescadero Rd.
HABS CA-2138
HABS CAL,41-PESC,11-
7ph/1pg/1pc L

Wells Fargo Building
HABS CA-1701
HABS CAL,41-PESC,12-
1ph/1pc L

White House; see Graham,Issac,House

Woodhams House
112 San Gregorio St.
HABS CA-2135
HABS CAL,41-PESC,13-
4ph/1pg/1pc L

PESCADERO VIC.

Ano Nuevo Ranch House; see Steele Brothers Dairies

Barn; see Steele Brothers Dairies

Cascade Ranch Dairy Building; see Steele Brothers Dairies

Cascade Ranch House; see Steele Brothers Dairies

Cloverdale Ranch Barn; see Steele Brothers Dairies

Dickerman Barn; see Steele Brothers Dairies

House; see Steele Brothers Dairies

Pigeon Point Lighthouse
State Hwy. 1
HABS CA-1997
HABS CAL,41-PESC.V,1-
5dr/19ph/1pg/2pc/3ct/fr L

Pigeon Point Lighthouse,Workshop
HABS CA-1997-A
HABS CAL,41-PESC.V,1-A-
1dr/fr L

Ramsey-Steele House; see Steele Brothers Dairies

Steele Brothers Dairies
Cabrillo Hwy.
HABS CA-2129
HABS CAL,41-PESC.V,2-
3pg L

Steele Brothers Dairies (Ano Nuevo Ranch House; Steele,Horace,House)
Ano Nuevo State Preserve
HABS CA-2129-F
HABS CAL,41-PESC.V,2-F-
2ph/1pc L

Steele Brothers Dairies (Barn)
HABS CA-2129-G
HABS CAL,41-PESC.V,2-G-
2ph/1pc L

Steele Brothers Dairies (Cascade Ranch Dairy Building)
HABS CA-2129-A
HABS CAL,41-PESC.V,2-A-
5ph/1pc L

Steele Brothers Dairies (Cascade Ranch House; Steele,Rensselaer,House)
HABS CA-2129-B
HABS CAL,41-PESC.V,2-B-
3ph/1pc L

Steele Brothers Dairies (Cloverdale Ranch Barn)
HABS CA-2129-C
HABS CAL,41-PESC.V,2-C-
12ph/1pc L

Steele Brothers Dairies (Dickerman Barn)
HABS CA-2129-E
HABS CAL,41-PESC.V,2-E-
7ph/1pc L

Steele Brothers Dairies (House)
HABS CA-2129-H
HABS CAL,41-PESC.V,2-H-
2ph/1pc L

Steele Brothers Dairies (House)
HABS CA-2129-I
HABS CAL,41-PESC.V,2-I-
2ph/1pc L

Steele Brothers Dairies (Ramsey-Steele House)
HABS CA-2129-D
HABS CAL,41-PESC.V,2-D-
7ph/1pc/1ct L

Steele,Horace,House; see Steele Brothers Dairies

Steele,Rensselaer,House; see Steele Brothers Dairies

PORTOLA VALLEY

Buelna's Roadhouse
3915 Alpine Rd.
HABS CA-2139
HABS CAL,41-PORVA,1-
5ph/1pg/1pc L

Our Lady of the Wayside Roman Catholic Church
930 Portola Rd.
HABS CA-2140
HABS CAL,41-PORVA,2-
12ph/1pg/1pc L

Portola Valley School
775 Portola Rd.
HABS CA-1992
HABS CAL,41-PORVA,3-
4dr/4ph/3pg/1pc/fr L

REDWOOD CITY

Bank of San Mateo County
2000-2002 Broadway
HABS CA-1991
HABS CAL,41-REDWO,1-
7dr/11ph/3pg/1pc/fr L

Diller-Chamberlain Store
726 Main St.
HABS CA-2141
HABS CAL,41-REDWO,2-
3ph/4pg/1pc L

Fitzpatrick Building
2010 Broadway
HABS CA-2142
HABS CAL,41-REDWO,3-
8ph/1pg/1pc L

San Mateo County Courthouse
Middlefield,Hamilton,Broadway & Marshall Sts.
HABS CA-2143
HABS CAL,41-REDWO,4-
7ph/4pg/1pc/6ct L

SAN CARLOS

Southern Pacific Depot
559 El Camino Real
HABS CA-2278
HABS 1992(HABS):CA-1
50ph/9pg/5pc L

SAN GREGORIO

San Gregorio House
San Gregorio Rd.
HABS CA-1993
HABS CAL,41-SANGR,1-
2dr/14ph/1pg/1pc/fr L

SAN MATEO

St. Matthew's Episcopal Church
El Camino Real & Baldwin St.
HABS CA-2144
HABS CAL,41-SANMA,1-
13ph/1pg/1pc L

SAN PEDRO VALLEY

Sanchez,Francisco,Adobe
Linda Mar Blvd. & Adobe Dr.
HABS CA-156
HABS CAL,41- ,1-
8dr/10ph/5pg/fr L

WOODSIDE

Bourn-Roth Estate; see Filoli

Filoli (Bourn-Roth Estate)
Canada Rd.
HABS CA-2117
HABS CAL,41-WOOD,1-
21ph/3pg/1pc L

Fleishhacker House; see Green Gables

Green Gables (Fleishhacker House)
329 Albion Ave.
HABS CA-2147
HABS CAL,41-WOOD,2-
51ph/1pg/3pc/5ct L

La Questa Wine Cellar
240 La Questa Rd.
HABS CA-2145
HABS CAL,41-WOOD,3-
3ph/1pg/1pc L

Woodside Store
Kings Mountain Rd.
HABS CA-2146
HABS CAL,41-WOOD,4-
11ph/1pg/1pc/1ct L

SANTA BARBARA COUNTY

BUELLTON

Cuesta,La Casa de Eduardo de la
Hwy. 101
HABS CA-27
HABS CAL,42-BUEL.V,1-
3dr/2ph/1pg/fr L

BUELLTON VIC.

Cuesta,La Case de Cota de la
Lompoc Rd.
HABS CA-28
HABS CAL,42-BUEL.V,2-
3dr/2ph/1pg/fr L

GUADALUPE

Guadalupe Rancho Adobes
114 & 120 Third Ave.
HABS CA-29
HABS CAL,42-GUAD,1-
6dr/1ph/1pg/1pc/fr L

Guadalupe Rancho Adobes,Adobe Number 1
114 Third Ave.
HABS CA-29-A
HABS CAL,42-GUAD,1A-
2ph/fr L

GUADLUPE

Guadalupe Rancho Adobes,Adobe Number 2
120 Third Ave.
HABS CA-29-B
HABS CAL,42-GUAD,1B-
3ph L

LOMPOC

Azimuth Alignment Shed; see Vandenberg Air Force Base,Space Launch Complex 3,

Entry Control Point; see Vandenberg Air Force Base,Space Launch Complex 3,

Launch Operations Building; see Vandenberg Air Force Base,Space Launch Complex 3,

Launch Pad 3 East; see Vandenberg Air Force Base,Space Launch Complex 3,

Launch Pad 3 West; see Vandenberg Air Force Base,Space Launch Complex 3,

Meteorological Shed and Tower; see Vandenberg Air Force Base,Space Launch Complex 3,

Pyrotechnic Shed; see Vandenberg Air Force Base,Space Launch Complex 3,

Sewage Treatment Plant; see Vandenberg Air Force Base,Space Launch Complex 3,

SLC-3 Air Force Building; see Vandenberg Air Force Base,Space Launch Complex 3,

Storage Shed; see Vandenberg Air Force Base,Space Launch Complex 3,

Technical Support Building; see Vandenberg Air Force Base,Space Launch Complex 3,

Traffic Check House; see Vandenberg Air Force Base,Space Launch Complex 3,

Vandenberg Air Force Base,Sp.Lnch.Cmp.3,Bldg. 756; see Vandenberg Air Force Base,Space Launch Complex 3,

Vandenberg Air Force Base,Sp.Lnch.Cmp.3,Bldg. 757; see Vandenberg Air Force Base,Space Launch Complex 3,

Vandenberg Air Force Base,Sp.Lnch.Cmp.3,Bldg. 759; see Vandenberg Air Force Base,Space Launch Complex 3,

Vandenberg Air Force Base,Sp.Lnch.Cmp.3,Bldg. 761; see Vandenberg Air Force Base,Space Launch Complex 3,

Vandenberg Air Force Base,Sp.Lnch.Cmp.3,Bldg. 762,; see Vandenberg Air Force Base,Space Launch Complex 3,

Vandenberg Air Force Base,Sp.Lnch.Cmp.3,Bldg. 763; see Vandenberg Air Force Base,Space Launch Complex 3,

Vandenberg Air Force Base,Sp.Lnch.Cmp.3,Bldg. 766; see Vandenberg Air Force Base,Space Launch Complex 3,

Vandenberg Air Force Base,Sp.Lnch.Cmp.3,Bldg. 768; see Vandenberg Air Force Base,Space Launch Complex 3,

Vandenberg Air Force Base,Sp.Lnch.Cmp.3,Bldg. 769; see Vandenberg Air Force Base,Space Launch Complex 3,

Vandenberg Air Force Base,Sp.Lnch.Cmp.3,Bldg. 773; see Vandenberg Air Force Base,Space Launch Complex 3,

Vandenberg Air Force Base,Sp.Lnch.Cmp.3,Bldg. 775; see Vandenberg Air Force Base,Space Launch Complex 3,

Vandenberg Air Force Base,Sp.Lnch.Cmp.3,Bldg. 776; see Vandenberg Air Force Base,Space Launch Complex 3,

Vandenberg Air Force Base,Sp.Lnch.Cpm.3,Blockhouse; see Vandenberg Air Force Base,Space Launch Complex 3,

Vandenberg Air Force Base,Space Launch Complex 3
Napa & Alden Rds.
HAER CA-133-1
15ph/164pg/2pc L

Vandenberg Air Force Base,Space Launch Complex 3, (Azimuth Alignment Shed; Vandenberg Air Force Base,Sp.Lnch.Cmp.3,Bldg. 775)
Napa & Alden Rds.
HAER CA-133-1-N
2ph/1pc L

Vandenberg Air Force Base,Space Launch Complex 3, (Entry Control Point; Vandenberg Air Force Base,Sp.Lnch.Cmp.3,Bldg. 768)
Napa & Alden Rds.
HAER CA-133-1-J
5ph/1pc L

Vandenberg Air Force Base,Space Launch Complex 3, (Launch Operations Building; Vandenberg Air Force Base,Sp.Lnch.Cpm.3,Blockhouse Vandenberg Air Force Base,Sp.Lnch.Cmp.3,Bldg. 763)
Napa & Alden Rds.
HAER CA-133-1-A
120ph/11pc L

Vandenberg Air Force Base,Space Launch Complex 3, (Launch Pad 3 East)
Napa & Alden Rds.
HAER CA-133-1-B
278ph/23pc L

Vandenberg Air Force Base,Space Launch Complex 3, (Launch Pad 3 West)
Napa & Alden Rds.
HAER CA-133-1-C
183ph/16pc L

Vandenberg Air Force Base,Space Launch Complex 3, (Meteorological Shed and Tower; Vandenberg Air Force Base,Sp.Lnch.Cmp.3,Bldg. 756)
Napa & Alden Rds.
HAER CA-133-1-G
5ph/1pc L

Vandenberg Air Force Base,Space Launch Complex 3, (Pyrotechnic Shed; Vandenberg Air Force Base,Sp.Lnch.Cmp.3,Bldg. 757)
Napa & Alden Rds.
HAER CA-133-1-M
6ph/1pc L

Vandenberg Air Force Base,Space Launch Complex 3, (Sewage Treatment Plant; Vandenberg Air Force Base,Sp.Lnch.Cmp.3,Bldg. 769)
Napa & Alden Rds.
HAER CA-133-1-I
1ph/1pc L

Vandenberg Air Force Base,Space Launch Complex 3, (SLC-3 Air Force Building; Vandenberg Air Force Base,Sp.Lnch.Cmp.3,Bldg. 761)
Napa & Alden Rds.
HAER CA-133-1-F
4ph/1pc L

Vandenberg Air Force Base,Space Launch Complex 3, (Storage Shed; Vandenberg Air Force Base,Sp.Lnch.Cmp.3,Bldg. 773)
Napa & Alden Rds.
HAER CA-133-1-K
2ph/1pc L

Vandenberg Air Force Base,Space Launch Complex 3, (Storage Shed; Vandenberg Air Force Base,Sp.Lnch.Cmp.3,Bldg. 776)
Napa & Alden Rds.
HAER CA-133-1-L
4ph/1pc L

Vandenberg Air Force Base,Space Launch Complex 3, (Technical Support Building; Vandenberg Air Force Base,Sp.Lnch.Cmp.3,Bldg. 762, 762A)
Napa & Alden Rds.
HAER CA-133-1-E
8ph/1pc L

Vandenberg Air Force Base,Space Launch Complex 3, (Traffic Check House; Vandenberg Air Force Base,Sp.Lnch.Cmp.3,Bldg. 759)
Napa & Alden Rds.
HAER CA-133-1-H
1ph/1pc L

Vandenberg Air Force Base,Space Launch Complex 3, (Vehicle Support Building; Vandenberg Air Force Base,Sp.Lnch.Cmp.3,Bldg. 766)
Napa & Alden Rds.
HAER CA-133-1-D
21ph/3pc L

Vehicle Support Building; see Vandenberg Air Force Base,Space Launch Complex 3,

762A; see Vandenberg Air Force Base,Space Launch Complex 3,

LOMPOC VIC.

Mission La Purisima Conception
HABS CA-211
HABS CAL,42-LOMP.V,1-
6ph/2pg L

Point Arguello Coast Guard Rescue Station
HAER CA-6
HAER CAL,42-LOMP.V,2-
3dr/33ph/55pg/3pc L

San Antonio Creek Bridge
State Hwy. 1
HAER CA-18
HAER CAL,42-LOMP.V,3-
12ph/7pg/1pc L

MONTECITO

Ortega House
29 Sheffield Dr.
HABS CA-314
HABS CAL,42-MONT,1-
5dr/4ph/1pg/fr L

SANTA BARBARA

Adobe,Historic
715 Santa Barbara St.
HABS CA-249
HABS CAL,42-SANBA,18-
1ph/1pc L

710 Anacapa St. (House)
710 Anacapa St.
HABS CA-2258
HABS CAL,42-SANBA,17-
1ph/1pg/1pc L

Andria's Restaurant; see Larco Building

Birabent Adobe
820 Santa Barbara St.
HABS CA-247
HABS CAL,42-SANBA,19-
1ph/1pc L

Caneda Adobe
121 E. Canon Perdido St.
HABS CA-242
HABS CAL,42-SANBA,12-
4ph/5pg L

Carillo,La Casa de Joaquin
11 E. Carrillo St.
HABS CA-25
HABS CAL,42-SANBA,6-
4dr/8ph/1pg/1pc/fr L

Covarrubias Adobe
715 Santa Barbara St.
HABS CA-26
HABS CAL,42-SANBA,7-
3dr/7ph/1pg/1pc/fr L

East de la Guerra Street (Commercial Building)
HABS CA-245
HABS CAL,42-SANBA,20-
1ph/1pc L

El Cuartel
122 E. Canon Perdido St.
HABS CA-37-36
HABS CAL,42-SANBA,3-
3dr/6ph/1pg/1pc/fr L

Fernald,Charles,House
412 W. Montecito St. (moved fr. 422 Santa Barbara)
HABS CA-240
HABS CAL,42-SANBA,10-
12ph/9pg L

Guerra,La Casa de la
11-19 E. de la Guerra St.
HABS CA-313
HABS CAL,42-SANBA,8-
6dr/7ph/12pg/fr L

Hayman,Albert,Cottage
212 Palm Ave.
HABS CA-2212
HABS CAL,42-SANBA,21-
6ph/2pg/1pc L

Hunt-Stambach House
404 W. Montecito St. (moved from Victoria St.)
HABS CA-241
HABS CAL,42-SANBA,11-
8ph/7pg L

Knox Brick House
914 Anacape St.
HABS CA-244
HABS CAL,42-SANBA,14-
4ph/7pg L

Larco Building (Andria's Restaurant)
214 State St.
HABS CA-2213
HABS CAL,42-SANBA,22-
11ph/5pg/1pc L

Miranda House
806 Anacapa St.
HABS CA-37-35
HABS CAL,42-SANBA,2-
4dr/1ph/1pg/fr L

Mission Santa Barbara
Laguna St. & Mission Canyon Rd.
HABS CA-21
HABS CAL,42-SANBA,5-
30dr/11ph/2pg L

Orena,Gaspar,House
E. de la Guerra St.
HABS CA-246
HABS CAL,42-SANBA,23-
3ph/1pc L

Pico,Buena Ventura,Adobe
920 Anacapa St.
HABS CA-243
HABS CAL,42-SANBA,13-
2ph/6pg L

San Roque Canyon Bridge
State Hwy. 192
HAER CA-17
HAER CAL,42-SANBA,15-
22ph/4pg/2pc L

Stewart's De-Rooting,Plumbing & Supply; see Young,T.J.,Cottage

Trussel House
327 Castillo St.
HABS CA-248
HABS CAL,42-SANBA,24-
1ph/1pc L

Trussell-Winchester Adobe
412 W. Montecito St.
HABS CA-239
HABS CAL,42-SANBA,9-
5ph/7pg L

Vhay,Mrs. A. L. M. ,House
835 Leguna St.
HABS CA-37-37
HABS CAL,42-SANBA,4-
4dr/10ph/1pg/fr L

326 West Ortega St. (House)
326 W. Ortega St.
HABS CA-2259
HABS CAL,42-SANBA,16-
1ph/1pg/1pc L

Wood,V.E.,Auto Building
315 State St.
HABS CA-2215
HABS CAL,42-SANBA,25-
15ph/5pg/2pc L

Yorbe-Abadie House
de la Guerra Plaza
HABS CA-37-33
HABS CAL,42-SANBA,1-
4dr/2ph/1pg/fr L

Young,T.J.,Cottage (Stewart's De-Rooting,Plumbing & Supply)
208 Palm Ave.
HABS CA-2211
HABS CAL,42-SANBA,26-
6ph/2pg/1pc L

SOLVANG

Mission Santa Ynez
State Hwy. 150
HABS CA-24
HABS CAL,42-SOLV,1-
11dr/5ph/2pg/fr L

Mission Santa Ynez,Church
State Hwy. 150
HABS CA-24-A
HABS CAL,42-SOLV,1A-
8ph L

Mission Santa Ynez,Monastery
State Hwy. 150
HABS CA-24-B
HABS CAL,42-SOLV,1B-
5ph L

Mission Santa Ynez,Tannery
State Hwy. 150
HABS CA-24-C
HABS CAL,42-SOLV,1C-
2ph L

SANTA CLARA COUNTY

ALAMEDA

Alameda City Hall
2329 Santa Clara Ave.
HABS CA-415
HABS CAL,1-ALAM,1-
5ph/27pg/1pc L

CAMPBELL

Campbell Union Grammar School
11 E. Campbell Ave.
HABS CA-2207
HABS CAL,43-CAMP,1-
33ph/15pg/2pc L

Le Fevre House
1444 Moore
HABS CA-2281
HABS 1992(HABS):CA-1
27ph/5pg/2pc L

Le Fevre House,Barn
1444 Moore
HABS CA-2281-A
HABS 1992(HABS):CA-1
9ph/1pc L

COYOTE

Laguna Seca Rancho (Rancho del Refugio de la Laguna Seca)
Hwy. 101
HABS CA-2003
HABS CAL,43-COYO,1-
7dr/10ph/8pg/1pc/fr L

Laguna Seca Rancho,Barn
U. S. Hwy. 101
HABS CA-2003-B
HABS CAL,43-COYO,1B-
2dr/2ph L

Laguna Seca Rancho,Office
U. S. Hwy. 101
HABS CA-2003-C
HABS CAL,43-COYO,1-
1dr/fr L

Laguna Seca Rancho,Stone Building
U. S. Hwy. 101
HABS CA-2003-A
HABS CAL,43-COYO,1A-
3dr/5ph L

Rancho del Refugio de la Laguna Seca; see Laguna Seca Rancho

COYOTE VIC.

Stevens Ranch Complex
State Rt. 101
HABS CA-2018
HABS CAL,43-COYO.V,1-
24ph/9pg/2pc L

Twin Oaks Dairy
Metcalfe Rd.
HABS CA-2017
HABS CAL,43-COYO.V,2-
23ph/8pg/2pc L

CUPERTINO

Collins School (Cupertino de Oro Club)
20441 Homestead Ave.
HABS CA-2091
HABS CAL,43-CUP,4-
6ph/1pg/1pc L

Cupertino de Oro Club; see Collins School

Maryknoll Seminary
23000 Cristo Rey Dr.
HABS CA-2092
HABS CAL,43-CUP,3-
3ph/1pg/1pc L

Older House; see Woodhills

Picchetti Winery
13100 Montebello Rd.
HABS CA-2012
HABS CAL,43-CUP,2-
4dr/6ph/7pg/1pc/1ct/fr L

Woodhills (Older House)
Prospect Rd.
HABS CA-2007
HABS CAL,43-CUP,1-
5dr/17ph/15pg/2pc/1ct/fr L

GILROY

Christian Church (Latin American Assemblies of God)
160 Fifth St.
HABS CA-2060
HABS CAL,43-GIL,5-
3dr/4ph/10pg/1pc/fr L

Eschenburg-Silva Cow Barn
3665 Pacheco Pass Rd.
HABS CA-2096
HABS CAL,43-GIL,4-
4dr/5ph/6pg/1pc/fr L

Gilroy Free Public Library (Gilroy Historical Museum)
195 Fifth St.
HABS CA-2093
HABS CAL,43-GIL,3-
4ph/1pg/1pc L

Gilroy Historical Museum; see Gilroy Free Public Library

Hoenck House
9480 Murray Ave.
HABS CA-2095
HABS CAL,43-GIL,7-
8ph/6pg/1pc L

Latin American Assemblies of God; see Christian Church

Lilly's Auto Camp
8877 Monterey Hwy.
HABS CA-2094
HABS CAL,43-GIL,2-
2dr/6ph/9pg/1pc/fr L

Live Oak Creamery
88 Martin St.
HABS CA-2065
HABS CAL,43-GIL,8-
3dr/7ph/9pg/1pc/fr L

Willson House
1980 Pacheco Rd.
HABS CA-2097
HABS CAL,43-GIL,1-
10ph/5pg/1pc L

GILROY VIC.

Llagas Creek Bridge
Spanning Llagas Creek,Gilman Rd. at Holsclaw Rd.
HAER CA-45
HAER CAL,43-GIL.V,1-
7ph/5pg/1pc L

Norris,Frank,Memorial
Redwood Retreat Rd.
HABS CA-1544
HABS CAL,43-GIL.V,2-
1ph/1pc L

Stevenson,Robert Louis,Ranch House
Redwood Retreat Rd.
HABS CA-1545
HABS CAL,43-GIL.V,3-
1ph/1pc L

LOS ALTOS

Christ Episcopal Church (Foothills Congregational Church)
461 Orange Ave.
HABS CA-2013
HABS CAL,43-LOSALT,1-
1dr/14ph/8pg/2pc L

Foothills Congregational Church; see Christ Episcopal Church

LOS ALTOS HILLS

Lynn,Martha,Tank House
12899 Viscano Pl.
HABS CA-2066
HABS CAL,43-LOSAHI,1-
1dr/4ph/4pg/1pc/fr L

LOS GATOS

Forbes Mill Addition
Church & E. Main Sts.
HABS CA-2062
HABS CAL,43-LOSGA,1-
2dr/8ph/5pg/1pc/fr L

Young's Home in the Heart of the Hills; see Yung See San Fong (House)

Yung See San Fong (House) (Young's Home in the Heart of the Hills)
16660 Cypress Way
HABS CA-2070
HABS CAL,43-LOSGA,2-
6dr/12ph/15pg/1pc/fr L

MILPITAS VIC.

Alviso,Jose Maria,Adobe
HABS CA-1663
HABS CAL,43-MIL.V,1-
2ph/1pc L

Higuera,Jose,Adobe
Rancho Higuera Rd.
HABS CA-1664
HABS CAL,43-MIL.V,2-13
2ph/1pc L

MONTA VISTA VIC.

Woelffel Cannery
10120 Imperial Ave.
HABS CA-2099
HABS CAL,43-MONVI.V,1-
11ph/4pg/1pc L

MORGAN HILL

Fountain Oaks
15835 Carey Ave.
HABS CA-2100
HABS CAL,43-MORHI,2-
9ph/13pg/1pc L

Fountain Oaks,Guest House
15835 Carey Ave.
HABS CA-2100-A
HABS CAL,43-MORHI,2A-
6ph/5pg/1pc L

Morgan Hill House; see Villa Miramonte

Villa Miramonte (Morgan Hill House)
17860 N. Monterey Rd.
HABS CA-2101
HABS CAL,43-MORHI,3-
6ph/1pc L

MORGAN HILL VIC.

Machado School
Sycamore Ave.
HABS CA-2102
HABS CAL,43-MORHI.V,1-
8ph/1pc L

Malaguerra Winery
Burnett Rd.
HABS CA-2004
HABS CAL,43-MORHI.V,2-
3dr/5ph/9pg/1pc/fr L

NEW ALMADEN

Adobe House
Almaden Rd.
HABS CA-1623
HABS CAL,43-ALMA,6-
1ph/1pc L

Almaden Club House; see Casa Grande

Almaden Club House; see Casa Grande,Pagoda

Almaden Mine,Office & Shop Buildings; see New Almaden Quicksilver Mine

Carson House
21570 Almaden Rd.
HABS CA-115
HABS CAL,43-ALMA,2-
11dr/10ph/2pg/1pc/fr L

Casa Grande (Almaden Club House)
21350 Almaden Rd.
HABS CA-1116
HABS CAL,43-ALMA,4-
10ph/12pg/1pc L

Casa Grande,Pagoda (Almaden Club House)
21350 Almaden Rd.
HABS CA-1116-A
HABS CAL,43-ALMA,4-A-
1ph/1pc L

El Adobe Viejo
Almaden Rd.
HABS CA-1622
HABS CAL,43-ALMA,3-
1ph L

Guadalupe Mine,Church & Schoolhouse
Guadalupe Mine
HABS CA-157
HABS CAL,43-ALMA,7-
3ph/1pc L

Guadalupe Mine,Miners' Cabins
Guadalupe Mine
HABS CA-120
HABS CAL,43-ALMA,8-:13
1ph/1pc L

Laird Adobe
Almaden Rd.
HABS CA-134
HABS CAL,43-ALMA,9-:13
1ph/1pc L

Mine Hill School
New Almaden Quicksilver Mine County Park
HABS CA-1125
HABS CAL,43-ALMA,5-
3dr/6ph/9pg/1pc/fr L

New Almaden Quicksilver Mine (Almaden Mine,Office & Shop Buildings)
New Almaden Quicksilver Mine County Park
HABS CA-114
HABS CAL,43-ALMA,1-
16dr/16ph/13pg/2pc/fr L

Shannon Farmhouse
14475 Shannon Rd.
HABS CA-1124
HABS CAL,43-ALMA,10- 3
1ph/1pc L

West,Dr. ,House
HABS CA-1183
HABS CAL,43-ALMA,11-
1ph/1pc L

PALO ALTO

Channing Market; see Emperger Grocer

Documentation: **ct** color transparencies **dr** measured drawings **fr** field records
pc photograph captions **pg** pages of text **ph** photographs

Courtyard Building
533-539 Ramona Street
HABS CA-2098
6ph/1pc/fr L

de Lemos,Pedro,Building; see 520-526 Ramona Street (Commercial Building)

Emperger Grocer (Channing Market)
532 Channing Ave.
HABS CA-2103
HABS CAL,43-PALAL,1-
2dr/3ph/13pg/1pc/fr L

General Petroleum Gasoline Station; see Violet Ray Gasoline Station

Kennedy,John G. ,House
423 Chaucer St.
HABS CA-2076
HABS CAL,43-PALAL,3-
15ph/6pg/2pc L

520-526 Ramona Street (Commercial Building) (de Lemos,Pedro,Building)
520-526 Ramona St.
HABS CA-2067
HABS CAL,43-PALAL,4-
5dr/6ph/14pg/1pc/1ct/fr L

Violet Ray Gasoline Station (General Petroleum Gasoline Station)
799 Alma St.
HABS CA-2069
HABS CAL,43-PALAL,5-
2dr/5ph/7pg/1pc/fr L

PALTO ALTO

Veterans Building; see Y. W. C. A. Hostess House

Y. W. C. A. Hostess House (Veterans Building)
University Ave.
HABS CA-1670
HABS CAL,43-PALAL,6-
2ph/1pc L

SAN FELIPE VIC.

Pacheco Creek Bridge
San Felipe Rd. ,spanning Pacheco Creek
HAER CA-46
HAER CAL,43-SANFE.V,1-
12ph/4pg/1pc L

SAN JOSE

Allen,Horace,Gasoline Station
505 E. San Carlos St.
HABS CA-2105
HABS CAL,43-SANJOS,6-
3dr/6ph/9pg/1pc/fr L

Baker,Rev. George B. ,House; see Blanchard House

Blanchard House (Baker,Rev. George B. ,House)
HABS CA-1787
HABS CAL,43-SANJOS,13-
1ph/1pc L

1147 Chapman Street (House)
HABS CA-2109
HABS CAL,43-SANJOS,11-
4ph/1pc L

Col,Peter E. ,House
1163 Martin Ave.
HABS CA-2008
HABS CAL,43-SANJOS,2-
5dr/7ph/7pg/1pc/fr L

College Park Association of Friends' Meetinghouse (Friends' Meetinghouse)
1041 Morse St.
HABS CA-2061
HABS CAL,43-SANJOS,3-
2dr/3ph/9pg/1pc/fr L

Friends' Meetinghouse; see College Park Association of Friends' Meetinghouse

Gates,Howard B. ,House
62 S. Thirteenth St.
HABS CA-2077
HABS CAL,43-SANJOS,7-
10dr/13ph/18pg/1pc/fr L

Greenawalt,David, Farm (Greenawalt,David,Tank House)
14611 Almaden Expwy.
HABS CA-2009
HABS CAL,43-SANJOS,10-
4dr/5ph/6pg/1pc/fr L

Greenawalt,David,Farm,Tank House
14611 Almaden Expwy.
HABS CA-2009-A
HABS CAL,43-SANJOS,10A-
3dr/1ph/1pc L

Greenawalt,David,Tank House; see Greenawalt,David, Farm

Hanchett Residence Park
1225-1257 Martin Ave.
HABS CA-2010
HABS CAL,43-SANJOS,8-
4dr/6ph/14pg/1pc/fr L

Horn,Emily,House
2341 N. First St.
HABS CA-2108
HABS CAL,43-SANJOS,4-
6ph/6pg/1pc L

Hutton,Warner,House
13495 Sousa Lane
HABS CA-2280
HABS 1991(HABS):5
36ph/5pg/3pc L

Kennedy,James P. ,House
Stockton Ranch
HABS CA-1789
HABS CAL,43-SANJOS,14-
1ph/1pc L

Kirk-Farrington House
1615 Dry Creek Rd.
HABS CA-2090
HABS CAL,43-SANJOS,15-
7dr L

Lick Observatory
Mt. Hamilton
HABS CA-2110
HABS CAL,43-SANJOS,5-
5ph/1pg/1pc/fr L

Masonic Temple
262-272 S. First St.
HABS CA-2045
HABS CAL,43-SANJOS,1-
4ph L

O'Brien Court
1076-1092 O'Brien Court
HABS CA-2106
HABS CAL,43-SANJOS,12-
3dr/8ph/14pg/1pc/fr L

Pina House
3260 Alameda St.
HABS CA-1846
HABS CAL,43-SANJOS,16-
1ph/1pc L

Winchester House (Winchester Mystery House)
525 S. Winchester Blvd.
HABS CA-2107
HABS CAL,43-SANJOS,9-
10ph/2pg/1pc/3ct L

Winchester Mystery House; see Winchester House

SAN MARTIN

Krohn,John,Tank House
13000 Foothill Ave.
HABS CA-2111
HABS CAL,43-SANMA,1-
3dr/6ph/7pg/1pc/fr L

SANTA CLARA

Harrison Street Block (Houses)
1009-1091 Harrison St.
HABS CA-2063
HABS CAL,43-SANCLA,2-
4dr/8ph/19pg/1pc/fr L

Landrum,Andrew,House
1217 Santa Clara St.
HABS CA-2064
HABS CAL,43-SANCLA,1-
3dr/5ph/7pg/1pc/fr L

Larder House
1065 Alviso St.
HABS CA-2112
HABS CAL,43-SANCLA,3-
2ph/1pc L

Mission Santa Clara de Asis
Franklin & Grant Sts.
HABS CA-1133
HABS CAL,43-SANCLA,5-
34ph/3pc/fr L

Santa Clara Verein
1082 Alviso St.
HABS CA-2068
HABS CAL,43-SANCLA,4-;1992(HABS):CA-1°
2dr/17ph/9pg/3pc/fr L

SANTA CLARA VIC.

Lick,James,Mill
Montague Rd.
HABS CA-2011
HABS CAL,43-SANCLA.V,1-
6dr/13ph/12pg/1pc/fr L

Lick,James,Mill,Granary
Montague Rd.
HABS CA-2011-B
HABS CAL,43-SANCLA.V,1B-
3dr/2ph L

Lick,James,Mill,House
Montague Rd.
HABS CA-2011-A
HABS CAL,43-SANCLA.V,1A-
10ph/1pc L

Lick,James,Mill,Office
Montague Rd.
HABS CA-2011-C
HABS CAL,43-SANCLA.V,1C-
2ph/1pc L

SARATOGA

Casa Tierra
15231 Quito Rd.
HABS CA-2113
HABS CAL,43-SARA,1-
11ph/5pg/1pc/2ct L

Dyer,H. P. ,House
16055 Sanborn Rd.
HABS CA-2050
HABS CAL,43-SARA,4-
8ph/4pg/1pc L

Saratoga Foothill Club
20399 Park Pl.
HABS CA-2014
HABS CAL,43-SARA,2-
10dr/7ph/10pg/1pc/fr L

Welch-Hurst
15800 Sanborn Rd.
HABS CA-2006
HABS CAL,43-SARA,5-
5dr/6ph/8pg/1pc/1ct/fr L

SARATOGA VIC.

Phelan,James Duval,House; see Villa Montalvo

Villa Montalvo (Phelan,James Duval,House)
Montalvo Rd.
HABS CA-2048
HABS CAL,43-SARA.V,1-
9ph/10pg/1pc/1ct L

STANFORD

Coutts,Peter,Library; see Frenchman's Library

Dunn-Bacon House
565 Mayfield Ave.
HABS CA-2175
HABS CAL,43-STANF,1-
4ph/1pc L

Durand-Kirkman House; see Durand,Dr. W. F. ,House

Durand,Dr. W. F. ,House
(Durand-Kirkman House)
623 Cabrillo Ave.
HABS CA-2176
HABS CAL,43-STANF,2-
6ph/1pc L

Escondite Cottage
Escondido Rd.
HABS CA-2168
HABS CAL,43-STANF,3-
5ph/1pc L

Frenchman's Library
(Coutts,Peter,Library)
860 Escondido Rd.
HABS CA-2169
HABS CAL,43-STANF,4-
6ph/1pc L

Frenchman's Tower
Old Page Mill Rd.
HABS CA-2170
HABS CAL,43-STANF,5-
3ph/1pc L

Griffin-Drell House
570 Alvarado Rd.
HABS CA-2173
HABS CAL,43-STANF,6-
3ph/1pc L

Hoover,Lou Henry,House
San Juan Hill
HABS CA-2177
HABS CAL,43-STANF,7-
20ph/2pc/4ct L

Palo Alto Winery
Welch Rd. at Quarry Rd.
HABS CA-2171
HABS CAL,43-STANF,8-
7ph/1pc L

Salvatierra Street House
Salvatierra St.
HABS CA-2174
HABS CAL,43-STANF,9-
4ph/1pc L

Stanford University Memorial Church
Stanford University Campus
HABS CA-2172-A
HABS CAL,43-STANF,10-A-
18ph/1pc/4ct L

Stanford University Quadrangle
Stanford University Campus
HABS CA-2172
HABS CAL,43-STANF,10-3
26ph/2pc/2ct L

SANTA CRUZ COUNTY

GLEN CANYON

Covered Bridge
HABS CA-1551
HABS CAL,44-GLECA,1-
1ph/1pc L

SANTA CRUZ

Mission Santa Cruz
Emmet & School Sts.
HABS CA-1552
HABS CAL,44-SACRU,1-
20ph/2pc L

Santa Cruz,Town of
HABS CA-1550
HABS CAL,44-SACRU,2-
3ph/1pc L

Wilder Ranch
1401 Coast Rd.
HABS CA-2274
HABS 1991(HABS):5
3dr/fr L

Wilder Ranch,Cow Barn
1401 Coast Rd.
HABS CA-2274-B
HABS 1991(HABS):5
1dr/6pg/fr L

Wilder Ranch,Granary
1401 Coast Rd.
HABS CA-2274-D
HABS 1991(HABS):5
5pg/fr L

Wilder Ranch,Horse Barn
1401 Coast Rd.
HABS CA-2274-A
HABS 1991(HABS):5
2dr/10pg/fr L

Wilder Ranch,Shops/Bunkhouse
1401 Coast Rd.
HABS CA-2274-C
HABS 1991(HABS):5
1dr/7pg/fr L

SOQUEL

Congregational Church
HABS CA-1192
HABS CAL,44-SOQ,1-
3ph/1pc L

SHASTA COUNTY

LASSEN PEAK

Building Number 1; see Lassen Volcanic National Park

Building Number 178; see Lassen Volcanic National Park

Building Number 21; see Lassen Volcanic National Park

Building Number 284; see Lassen Volcanic National Park

Building Number 287; see Lassen Volcanic National Park

Building Number 37; see Lassen Volcanic National Park

Building Number 41; see Lassen Volcanic National Park

Building Number 43; see Lassen Volcanic National Park

Building Number 44; see Lassen Volcanic National Park

Building Number 49; see Lassen Volcanic National Park

Building Number 50; see Lassen Volcanic National Park

Building Number 58; see Lassen Volcanic National Park

Comfort Station; see Lassen Volcanic National Park

Lassen Volcanic National Park (Comfort Station; Building Number 44)
HABS CA-2114-G
HABS CAL,45-LASS,1-G-
8ph/1pc L

Lassen Volcanic National Park (Loomis Museum; Building Number 43)
HABS CA-2114-F
HABS CAL,45-LASS,1-F-
9ph/1pc L

Lassen Volcanic National Park (Loomis Seismograph Station; Building Number 178)
HABS CA-2114-K
HABS CAL,45-LASS,1-K-
6ph/1pc L

Lassen Volcanic National Park (Lost Creek Flume)
HABS CA-2114-A
HABS CAL,45-LASS,1-A-
9ph/1pc L

Lassen Volcanic National Park (Manzanita Ranger Residence; Building Number 49)
HABS CA-2114-H
HABS CAL,45-LASS,1-H-
8ph/1pc L

Lassen Volcanic National Park (Manzinita Kiosk; Building Number 50)
HABS CA-2114-I
HABS CAL,45-LASS,1-I-
5ph/1pc L

Lassen Volcanic National Park (Naturalist's Residence; Building Number 41)
HABS CA-2114-E
HABS CAL,45-LASS,1-E-
8ph/2pc L

Lassen Volcanic National Park (Park Headquarters; Building Number 1)
HABS CA-2114-B
HABS CAL,45-LASS,1-B-
10ph/1pc L

Lassen Volcanic National Park (Service Station; Building Number 21)
HABS CA-2114-C
HABS CAL,45-LASS,1-C-
6ph/1pc L

Lassen Volcanic National Park (Summit Lake Ranger Station; Building Number 37)
HABS CA-2114-D
HABS CAL,45-LASS,1-D-
8ph/1pc L

Lassen Volcanic National Park (Warner Valley Cook's Cabin; Building Number 287)
HABS CA-2114-M
HABS CAL,45-LASS,1-M-
6ph/1pc L

Lassen Volcanic National Park (Warner Valley Hay Barn; Building Number 284)
HABS CA-2114-L
HABS CAL,45-LASS,1-L-
8ph/1pc L

Lassen Volcanic National Park (Warner Valley Ranger Residence; Building Number 58)
HABS CA-2114-J
HABS CAL,45-LASS,1-J-
8ph/1pc L

Loomis Museum; see Lassen Volcanic National Park

Loomis Seismograph Station; see Lassen Volcanic National Park

Lost Creek Flume; see Lassen Volcanic National Park

Manzanita Ranger Residence; see Lassen Volcanic National Park

Manzinita Kiosk; see Lassen Volcanic National Park

Naturalist's Residence; see Lassen Volcanic National Park

Park Headquarters; see Lassen Volcanic National Park

Service Station; see Lassen Volcanic National Park

Summit Lake Ranger Station; see Lassen Volcanic National Park

Warner Valley Cook's Cabin; see Lassen Volcanic National Park

Warner Valley Hay Barn; see Lassen Volcanic National Park

Warner Valley Ranger Residence; see Lassen Volcanic National Park

REDDING

City Hall
1313 Market St.
HABS CA-2252
HABS CAL,45-RED,1-
3ph/5pg/1pc/fr L

SHASTA

Bystle House
Trinity & High Sts.
HABS CA-1445
HABS CAL,45-SHAST,6-
1ph L

Foster House
HABS CA-1443
HABS CAL,45-SHAST,4-
2ph L

Main Street (Commercial Buildings)
HABS CA-1305
HABS CAL,45-SHAST,1-
4ph/1pc L

Masonic Hall & Store (Western Star Lodge Number 2)
HABS CA-1303
HABS CAL,45-SHAST,3-
3ph/1pc L

Shasta County Courthouse (Ruins)
HABS CA-1297
HABS CAL,45-SHAST,2-
8ph/1pg/1pc L

Shurtleff,Dr. ,House
HABS CA-1444
HABS CAL,45-SHAST,5-
3ph L

Western Star Lodge Number 2; see Masonic Hall & Store

SHINGLETOWN VIC.

Pacific Power Company Rock Wall; see Rock Wall

Rock Wall (Pacific Power Company Rock Wall)
N. side of Battle Creek Canyon
HAER CA-135
12ph/17pg/2pc L

SIERRA COUNTY

DOWNIEVILLE

Catholic Church
Sierra City Rd.
HABS CA-1405
HABS CAL,46-DOWNV,2-
1ph L

Courthouse,House
HABS CA-1417
HABS CAL,46-DOWNV,5-
1ph L

Courthouse,Old (Pioneer Museum Building)
HABS CA-1687
HABS CAL,46-DOWNV,15-
1ph/1pc L

Downie,Maj. ,House
HABS CA-1407
HABS CAL,46-DOWNV,6-
2ph L

Downieville Courthouse
HABS CA-1402
HABS CAL,46-DOWNV,4-
1ph L

Downieville,General View
HABS CA-1291
HABS CAL,46-DOWNV,1-
5ph/1pc L

Elmwood Cottage; see Sierra City Road (Houses)

I. O. O. F. Hall
HABS CA-1403
HABS CAL,46-DOWNV,14-
1ph L

Main Street (Commercial Buildings)
HABS CA-1290
HABS CAL,46-DOWNV,12-
6ph/1pc L

Main Street (Commercial Buildings)
HABS CA-1290
HABS CAL,46-DOWNV,12-
6ph/1pc L

Miner's Drug Store; see Wells Fargo Building

Pioneer Museum Building; see Courthouse,Old

Sierra City Road (Church)
HABS CA-1404
HABS CAL,46-DOWNV,3-
1ph L

Sierra City Road (Frame Houses & Church)
HABS CA-1410
HABS CAL,46-DOWNV,3-
1ph L

Sierra City Road (Frame Houses & Church)
HABS CA-1410
HABS CAL,46-DOWNV,13-
1ph L

Sierra City Road (House)
HABS CA-1412
HABS CAL,46-DOWNV,10-
1ph L

Sierra City Road (House)
HABS CA-1414
HABS CAL,46-DOWNV,11-
1ph L

Sierra City Road (Houses) (Elmwood Cottage)
HABS CA-1408
HABS CAL,46-DOWNV,8-
1ph L

St. Charles Hotel
HABS CA-1406
HABS CAL,46-DOWNV,7-
3ph L

Wells Fargo Building (Miner's Drug Store)
HABS CA-1292
HABS CAL,46-DOWNV,16-
1ph/1pc L

DOWNIEVILLE VIC.

Hydraulic Mine
HABS CA-1420
HABS CAL,46-DOWNV.V,1-
1ph L

GOODYEAR'S BAR

Goodyear's Bar,General View
HABS CA-1679
HABS CAL,46-GOYBA,1-
1ph/1pc L

SIERRA CITY

Bush,August C. ,Building; see Wells Fargo and Company Building

Main Street (Commercial Buildings)
HABS CA-1422
HABS CAL,96-SIRCI,4-
1ph L

Main Street (Commercial Buildings)
HABS CA-1477
HABS CAL,46-SIRCI,6-
1ph L

Main Street (House)
HABS CA-1423
HABS CAL,46-SIRCI,3-
1ph L

Main Street (House)
HABS CA-1425
HABS CAL,46-SIRCI,1-
1ph L

Main Street (House)
HABS CA-2337
HABS CAL,46-SIRCI,2-
1ph L

Mine,Old
HABS CA-1421
HABS CAL,46-SIRCI,5-
2ph L

Wells Fargo and Company Building (Bush,August C. ,Building)
HABS CA-1426
HABS CAL,46-SIRCI,7-
3ph L

SIERRAVILLE

Sierraville,General View
HABS CA-1676
HABS CAL,46-SIRVI,8-
1ph/1pc L

SISKIYOU COUNTY

CALLAHAN

Callahan Ranch Hotel & Farrington Hotel
HABS CA-1189
HABS CAL,47-CALL,1-
1ph/1pg/1pc L

SAWYER'S BAR

Store Buildings
HABS CA-1191
HABS CAL,47-SAWBA,1-
1ph/1pc L

SAWYERS BAR

Catholic Church
HABS CA-1190
HABS CAL,47-SAWBA,2-
1ph/1pc L

SOLANO COUNTY

BENICIA

Benicia Arsenal
Benicia Industrial Park
HABS CA-1773
HABS CAL,48-BENI,4-
1dr/10ph/1pc/fr L

Benicia Arsenal,Barracks
HABS CA-1774
HABS CAL,48-BENI,4A-
1dr/7ph/1pc L

Benicia Arsenal,Barracks (Building Number 45)
HABS CA-1826
HABS CAL,48-BENI,4B-
4ph/5pg/1pc L

Benicia Arsenal,Building Number 1; see Benicia Arsenal,Hospital

Benicia Arsenal,Building Number 39; see Benicia Arsenal,Guard and Engine House

Benicia Arsenal,Building Number 74
HABS CA-1775
HABS CAL,48-BENI,4I-
1ph/1pc L

Benicia Arsenal,Buildings Number 33,34,35; see Benicia Arsenal,Enlisted Men's Quarters

Benicia Arsenal,Commanding Officer's Quarters (Quarters Number 1,Building Number 28)
HABS CA-1843
HABS CAL,48-BENI,4C-
9ph/4pg/1pc L

Benicia Arsenal,Dock
HABS CA-1834
HABS CAL,48-BENI,4D-
1ph/1pc L

Benicia Arsenal,Duplex Officer's Quarters (Officer's Quarters No. 3 & 4,Buildings No. 25 & 26
HABS CA-1947
HABS CAL,48-BENI,4E-
5ph/2pg/1pc L

Benicia Arsenal,Enlisted Men's Quarters (Benicia Arsenal,Buildings Number 33,34,35)
HABS CA-1949
HABS CAL,48-BENI,4F-
3ph/1pg/1pc L

Benicia Arsenal,Guard and Engine House (Benicia Arsenal,Building Number 39)
HABS CA-1832
HABS CAL,48-BENI,4G-
6ph/6pg/1pc L

Benicia Arsenal,Gun Yard
HABS CA-1842
HABS CAL,48-BENI,4H-
1ph/1pc L

Benicia Arsenal,Hospital (Benicia Arsenal,Building Number 1)
HABS CA-1945
HABS CAL,48-BENI,4J-
5ph/6pg/1pc L

Benicia Arsenal,Lieutenant's Quarters (Officer's Quarters Number 2,Building Number 27)
HABS CA-1825
HABS CAL,48-BENI,4K-
1ph/2pg/1pc L

Benicia Arsenal,Main Gateway
HABS CA-1844
HABS CAL,48-BENI,4L-
2ph/1pc L

Benicia Arsenal,Office Building (Building Number 47)
M St. Vic.
HABS CA-1827
HABS CAL,48-BENI,4M-
3ph/1pg/1pc L

Benicia Arsenal,Powder Magazine No. 5 (Bldg. No.14 (Benicia-Martinez Bridge Maintenance Yard)
Junction of Interstate Hwys. 680 and 780
HABS CA-1839
HABS CAL,48,BENI,4-O1992(HABS):CA-1°
21ph/5pg/4pc L

Benicia Arsenal,Powder Magazine Number 2 (Building Number 10)
HABS CA-1948
HABS CAL,48-BENI,4N-
5dr/10ph/6pg/1pc/fr L

Benicia Arsenal,Shop Buildings (Buildings Numbers 55,56,57)
Tyler St. ,Benicia Industrial Park
HABS CA-1833
HABS CAL,48-BENI,4P-
15ph/8pg/2pc L

Benicia Arsenal,Shops Storehouse (Building Number 49)
HABS CA-1838
HABS CAL,48-BENI,4Q-
3ph/2pg/1pc L

Benicia Arsenal,Stables (Building Number 51)
HABS CA-1979
HABS CAL,48-BENI,4R-
1ph/1pc L

Benicia Arsenal,Storehouse (Building Number 48)
HABS CA-1978
HABS CAL,48,BENI,4-U-
1ph/1pc L

Benicia Arsenal,Storehouse (Clocktower Building,Number 29)
Comandant's Lane,Benicia Industrial Park
HABS CA-1828
HABS CAL,48,BEN1,4-S-
6dr/17ph/12pg/2pc/fr L

Benicia Arsenal,Storehouses and Engine House (Camel Barns; Bldgs. Nos. 7,8,9)
HABS CA-1946
HABS CAL,48-BENI,4T-
4dr/8ph/9pg/1pc/fr L

Benicia State Capitol (California State Capitol)
First & G Sts.
HABS CA-1188
HABS CAL,48-BENI,2-
5dr/12ph/15pg/1pc/fr L

Benicia-Martinez Bridge Maintenance Yard; see Benicia Arsenal,Powder Magazine No. 5 (Bldg. No.14

Benicia,City of (General Views)
HABS CA-2079
HABS CAL,48-BENI,5-
46ph/3pc/fr L

Bldgs. Nos. 7,8,9; see Benicia Arsenal,Storehouses and Engine House

Building Number 10; see Benicia Arsenal,Powder Magazine Number 2

Building Number 45; see Benicia Arsenal,Barracks

Building Number 47; see Benicia Arsenal,Office Building

Building Number 48; see Benicia Arsenal,Storehouse

Building Number 49; see Benicia Arsenal,Shops Storehouse

Building Number 51; see Benicia Arsenal,Stables

Buildings Numbers 55,56,57; see Benicia Arsenal,Shop Buildings

California Hotel (California House)
First & H Sts.
HABS CA-1187
HABS CAL,48-BENI,1-
1ph L

California House; see California Hotel

California State Capitol; see Benicia State Capitol

Camel Barns; see Benicia Arsenal,Storehouses and Engine House

Carr House
165 E. D St.
HABS CA-2052
HABS CAL,48-BENI,6-
7dr/4ph/7pg/1pc/fr L

City Hotel (Golden Horseshoe)
415 First St.
HABS CA-2080
HABS CAL,48-BENI,9-
3ph/1pg/1pc L

Clocktower Building,Number 29; see Benicia Arsenal,Storehouse

Crooks House
285 W. G St.
HABS CA-2081
HABS CAL,48-BENI,7-
11ph/9pg/1pc L

Fairview Hotel (Washington House Hotel)
333 First St.
HABS CA-2088
HABS CAL,48-BENI,10-
1ph/1pg/1pc L

Fischer-Hanlon House
G St. between First and W. Second Sts.
HABS CA-1889
HABS CAL,48-BENI,11-
3ph/1pg/1pc L

Fish House; see Riddell Fish House

Frisbie-Walsh House
235 E. L St.
HABS CA-2087
HABS CAL,48-BENI,12-
5ph/1pg/1pc L

Golden Horseshoe; see City Hotel

Masonic Temple
110 W. J St.
HABS CA-1887
HABS CAL,48-BENI,13-
5ph/6pg/1pc L

Officer's Quarters No. 3 & 4,Buildings No. 25 & 26; see Benicia Arsenal,Duplex Officer's Quarters

Officer's Quarters Number 2,Building Number 27; see Benicia Arsenal,Lieutenant's Quarters

Quarters Number 1,Building Number 28; see Benicia Arsenal,Commanding Officer's Quarters

Riddell Fish House (Fish House)
245 W. K St.
HABS CA-2082
HABS CAL,48-BENI,8-
21ph/8pg/2pc L

Solano House; see Union Hotel

Southern Pacific Passenger Depot
SE First & A Sts. (moved from CA,Banta)
HABS CA-2085
HABS CAL,48-BENI,17-
3ph/1pg/1pc L

St. Catherine's Academy
Solano Square
HABS CA-1542
HABS CAL,48-BENI,3-
1ph L

St. Dominic's Catholic Church
475 E. I St.
HABS CA-2083
HABS CAL,48-BENI,14-
9ph/1pg/1pc L

St. Paul's Episcopal Church
120 E. J St.
HABS CA-2053
HABS CAL,48-BENI,15A-
6dr/13ph/14pg/2pc/fr L

St. Paul's Episcopal Church,Rectory
122 E. J St. (moved from CT,Torrington)
HABS CA-2084
HABS CAL,48-BENI,15B-
2ph/1pg/1pc L

Union Hotel (Solano House)
401-05 First St.
HABS CA-2086
HABS CAL,48-BENI,18-
3ph/1pg/1pc/fr L

Von Pfister,Semple,Store
D St. Vic.
HABS CA-1912
HABS CAL,48-BENI,16-
1ph/1pg/1pc L

Washington House Hotel; see Fairview Hotel

Wingfield,Bishop J. H. D. ,House
36 Wingfield Way
HABS CA-2089
HABS CAL,48-BENI,19-
5ph/1pg/1pc L

FAIRFIELD

Fairfield City Hall
1000 Webster St.
HABS CA-421
HABS CAL,48-FAIR,1-
6ph/6pg/1pc L

MARE ISLAND

Commandant's Office and Administration Building; see Mare Island Naval Shipyard

Mare Island Naval Shipyard (Commandant's Office and Administration Building)
HABS CA-1824
HABS CAL,48-MARI,1A-
1ph L

Mare Island Naval Shipyard (Naval Buildings,Old)
HABS CA-1543
HAER CA-3
HABS/HAER CAL,48-MARI,1-
14dr/42ph/10pg/3pc L

Mare Island Naval Shipyard,Building 47
HABS CA-1543-E
HABS CAL,48-MARI,1E-
1ph/1pg/1pc L

Mare Island Naval Shipyard,Magazine A-1
HABS CA-1543-B
HABS CAL,48-MARI,1B-
4ph/1pg/1pc L

Mare Island Naval Shipyard,Smithy,Bldg. No. 46
HABS CA-1543-D
HABS CAL,48-MARI,1D-
2ph/1pg/1pc L

Mare Island Naval Shipyard,St. Peter's Chapel
HABS CA-1543-C
HABS CAL,48-MARI,1C-
4ph/1pg/1pc/2ct L

Naval Buildings,Old; see Mare Island Naval Shipyard

VACAVILLE

Pena Adobe
Pena Adobe Rd.
HABS CA-1198
HABS CAL,48-VACA,1-
5dr/4ph/1pg/1pc/fr L

VALLEJO

Mare Island Naval Shipyard,Building No. 99A; see Mare Island Naval Shipyard,Fire House Annex

Mare Island Naval Shipyard,Building 99; see Mare Island Naval Shipyard,Firehouse

Mare Island Naval Shipyard,Central Fire Station; see Mare Island Naval Shipyard,Fire House Annex

Mare Island Naval Shipyard,Central Fire Station; see Mare Island Naval Shipyard,Firehouse

Mare Island Naval Shipyard,Fire House Annex (Mare Island Naval Shipyard,Building No. 99A; Mare Island Naval Shipyard,Central Fire Station)
HABS CA-2295
HABS 1992(HABS):CA-1
10ph/14pg/2pc L

Mare Island Naval Shipyard,Firehouse (Mare Island Naval Shipyard,Building 99; Mare Island Naval Shipyard,Central Fire Station)
HABS CA-2294
HABS 1992(HABS):CA-1
34ph/15pg/3pc L

SONOMA COUNTY

FORT ROSS

Block House; see Fort Ross

Fort Ross
HABS CA-1312
HABS CAL,49-FORO,1-
8ph/1pc L

Fort Ross (Block House)
HABS CA-1314
HABS CAL,49-FORO,1C-
1ph L

Fort Ross,Commandant's House; see Fort Ross,Russian Barracks

Fort Ross,Russian Barracks (Fort Ross,Commandant's House)
HABS CA-1315
HABS CAL,49-FORO,1B-
5ph/1pc L

Fort Ross,Russian Chapel
HABS CA-38-10
HABS CAL,49-FORO,1A-
6dr/17ph/1pc L

PETALUMA

Eldredge,Bernard E. ,Farm; see Schlake Ranch

Eldredge,Bernard E. ,Farm,Blacksmith Shop; see Schlake Ranch,Blacksmith Shop

Eldredge,Bernard E. ,Farm,Chickenhouse; see Schlake Ranch,Colony Chickenhouse

Eldredge,Bernard E. ,Farm,Farmhouse; see Schlake Ranch,Farmhouse

Eldredge,Bernard E. ,Farm,Garage; see Schlake Ranch,Garage

Eldredge,Bernard E. ,Farm,New Barn; see Schlake Ranch,New Barn

Eldredge,Bernard E. ,Farm,Old Barn; see Schlake Ranch,Old Barn

Eldredge,Bernard E. ,Farm,Poultry Complex; see Schlake Ranch,Poultry Complex

Eldredge,Bernard E. ,Farm,Pumphouse; see Schlake Ranch,Pumphouse

Eldredge,Bernard E. ,Farm,Shiplap Outbuilding; see Schlake Ranch,Shiplap Outbuilding

Eldredge,Bernard E. ,Farm,Smokehouse & Dairy House; see Schlake Ranch,Smokehouse & Dairy House

Eldredge,Bernard E. ,Farm,Water Tower; see Schlake Ranch,Water Tower

Jurgensen Ranch; see Schlake Ranch

Jurgensen Ranch,Blacksmith Shop; see Schlake Ranch,Blacksmith Shop

Jurgensen Ranch,Colony Chickenhouse; see Schlake Ranch,Colony Chickenhouse

Jurgensen Ranch,Farmhouse; see Schlake Ranch,Farmhouse

Jurgensen Ranch,Garage; see Schlake Ranch,Garage

Jurgensen Ranch,New Barn; see Schlake Ranch,New Barn

Jurgensen Ranch,Old Barn; see Schlake Ranch,Old Barn

Jurgensen Ranch,Poultry Complex; see Schlake Ranch,Poultry Complex

Jurgensen Ranch,Pumphouse; see Schlake Ranch,Pumphouse

Jurgensen Ranch,Shiplap Outbuilding; see Schlake Ranch,Shiplap Outbuilding

Jurgensen Ranch,Smokehouse & Dairy House; see Schlake Ranch,Smokehouse & Dairy House

Jurgensen Ranch,Water Tower; see Schlake Ranch,Water Tower

Schlake Ranch (Jurgensen Ranch; Eldredge,Bernard E. ,Farm)
2300 E. Washington St.
HABS CA-2205
HABS CAL,49-PET,1-
1ph/1pc/fr L

Schlake Ranch,Blacksmith Shop (Jurgensen Ranch,Blacksmith Shop; Eldredge,Bernard E. ,Farm,Blacksmith Shop)
2300 E. Washington St.
HABS CA-2205-H
HABS CAL,49-PET,1-H-
2ph/1pc L

Schlake Ranch,Colony Chickenhouse (Jurgensen Ranch,Colony Chickenhouse; Eldredge,Bernard E. ,Farm,Chickenhouse)
2300 E. Washington St.
HABS CA-2205-E
HABS CAL,49-PET,1-E-
1ph/1pc L

Schlake Ranch,Farmhouse (Jurgensen Ranch,Farmhouse; Eldredge,Bernard E. ,Farm,Farmhouse)
2300 E. Washington St.
HABS CA-2205-A
HABS CAL,49-PET,1-A-
7ph/1pg/1pc L

Schlake Ranch,Garage (Jurgensen Ranch,Garage; Eldredge,Bernard E. ,Farm,Garage)
2300 E. Washington St.
HABS CA-2205-K
HABS CAL,49-PET,1-K-
1ph/1pc L

Schlake Ranch,New Barn (Jurgensen Ranch,New Barn; Eldredge,Bernard E. ,Farm,New Barn)
2300 E. Washington St.
HABS CA-2205-F
HABS CAL,49-PET,1-F-
4ph/1pg/1pc L

Schlake Ranch,Old Barn (Jurgensen Ranch,Old Barn; Eldredge,Bernard E. ,Farm,Old Barn)
2300 Washington St.
HABS CA-2205-D
HABS CAL,49-PET,1-D-
3ph/1pg/1pc L

Schlake Ranch,Poultry Complex (Jurgensen Ranch,Poultry Complex; Eldredge,Bernard E. ,Farm,Poultry Complex)
2300 E. Washington St.
HABS CA-2205-G
HABS CAL,49-PET,1-G-
1ph/1pc L

Schlake Ranch,Pumphouse (Jurgensen Ranch,Pumphouse; Eldredge,Bernard E. ,Farm,Pumphouse)
2300 E. Washington St.
HABS CA-2205-J
HABS CAL,49-PET,1-J-
1ph/1pc L

Schlake Ranch,Shiplap Outbuilding (Jurgensen Ranch,Shiplap Outbuilding; Eldredge,Bernard E. ,Farm,Shiplap Outbuilding)
2300 E. Washington St.
HABS CA-2205-C
HABS CAL,49-PET,1-C-
1ph/1pc L

Schlake Ranch,Smokehouse & Dairy House (Jurgensen Ranch,Smokehouse & Dairy House; Eldredge,Bernard E. ,Farm,Smokehouse & Dairy House
2300 E. Washington St.
HABS CA-2205-I
HABS CAL,49-PET,1-I-
1ph/1pc L

Schlake Ranch,Water Tower (Jurgensen Ranch,Water Tower; Eldredge,Bernard E. ,Farm,Water Tower)
2300 E. Washington St.
HABS CA-2205-B
HABS CAL,49-PET,1-B-
1ph/1pc L

PETALUMA VIC.

Adobe
NE of Petaluma on Pacific Duck Farm
HABS CA-38-9
HABS CAL,49-PET.V,2-
1dr/1ph L

Vallejo,Adobe
HABS CA-38-1
HABS CAL,49-PETY.V,1-
9dr/10ph L

SABASTOPOL

Gold Ridge Farm (Luther Burbank Experiment Farm)
7777 Bodega Ave.
HABS CA-2254
HABS 992(HABS):CA-1
23ph/34pg/3pc/fr L

Luther Burbank Experiment Farm; see Gold Ridge Farm

SANTA ROSA

Burbank,Luther,House
200 Santa Rosa Ave.
HABS CA-2201
HABS CAL,49-SANRO,4-
5dr/4ph/10pg/1pc/fr L

Burbank,Luther,House,Gardens
200 Santa Rosa Ave.
HABS CA-2201-B
HABS CAL,49-SANRO,4-B-
7dr/29pg/fr L

Burbank,Luther,House,Greenhouse
200 Santa Rosa Ave.
HABS CA-2201-A
HABS CAL,49-SANRO,4-A-
5dr/4ph/1pg/1pc/fr L

Carrillo Adobe
HABS CA-1442
HABS CAL,49-SANRO,1-
3dr/7ph/4pg/fr L

Santa Rosa Post Office and Federal Building
401 Fifth St. (moved to Seventh St.)
HABS CA-2051
HABS CAL,49-SANRO,3-
23ph/9pg L

SANTA ROSA VIC.

Fountain Grove,Barn
Mendocino Ave. & US Highway 101
HABS CA-1915
HABS CAL,49-SANRO,2-
5dr/8ph/1pg/fr L

Fountain Grove,Hop Kilns
HABS CA-1651
HABS CAL,49-SANRO,2-A-
3ph/1pc L

Fountain Grove,House
Highway 101
HABS CA-1917
HABS CAL,49-SANRO,2-B-
7ph/1pg/1pc L

Fountain Grove,Winery
HABS CA-1916
HABS CAL,49-SANRA,2-C-
1ph/1pg/1pc L

Fountain Grove,Winery (Champagne Storage Building)
HABS CA-1916-B
HABS CAL,49-SANRO,2-E-
1ph/1pc L

Fountain Grove,Winery (Vat Buildings)
HABS CA-1916-A
HABS CAL,49-SANRO,2-D-
2ph/1pc L

SONOMA

Alder Adobe; see Ray House

Blue Wing Inn (Sonoma House)
HABS CA-1438
HABS CAL,49-SONO,3-
2ph/fr L

Lachryma Montis; see Vallejo,Gen. ,House

Mexican Army Barracks; see Sonoma Barracks

Mission San Francisco Solano De Sonoma
First & Spain Sts.
HABS CA-1138
HABS CA;,49-SONO,2-
30ph/1pg/3pc L

Ray House (Alder Adobe; Ray-Adler House)
HABS CA-1439
HABS CAL,49-SONO,4-
1ph L

Ray-Adler House; see Ray House

Sonoma Barracks (Mexican Army Barracks)
Spain & First Sts.
HABS CA-1560
HABS CAL,49-SONO,9-
1ph/1pg/1pc L

Sonoma House; see Blue Wing Inn

Sonoma Plaza,Bear Flag Flagstaff
HABS CA-1436
HABS CAL,49-SONO,7-
1ph L

Temelec Hall
20750 Arnold Ave.
HABS CA-1563
HABS CAL,49-SONO,8-
21ph/10pg L

Vallejo Chalet
HABS CA-1441
HABS CAL,49-SONO,6-
1ph/fr L

Vallejo,Gen. ,House (Lachryma Montis)
N. Third St. W.
HABS CA-1440
HABS CAL,49-SONO,5-
6dr/4ph/7pg/fr L

STANISLAUS COUNTY

KNIGHTS FERRY

(HAER Number assigned WRO 6/14/88); see Covered Bridge

Covered Bridge ((HAER Number assigned WRO 6/14/88))
Tulloch Mill,Stanislaus River
HABS CA-158
HAER CA-65
HABS/HAER CAL,50-KNITF,3-
3ph L

Dent House
Ellen St.
HABS CA-1193
HABS CAL,50-KNITF,7-
2ph L

Fire House
HABS CA-161
HABS CAL,50-KNITF,4-
1ph L

Jail
Main St.
HABS CA-164
HABS CAL,50-KNITF,5-
1ph L

Knights Ferry,General View
HABS CA-169
HABS CAL,50-KNITF,8-
1ph L

Miller House
Sonora Hwy.
HABS CA-18
HABS CAL,50-KNITF,1-
3dr/3ph L

Schell House
HABS CA-118
HABS CAL,50-KNITF,6-
1ph L

Tulloch Mill
Stanislaus River
HABS CA-137
HABS CAL,50-KNITF,2-
9dr/12ph/fr L

Tulloch Mill,Crib Dam
HABS CA-168
HABS CAL,50-KNITF,2B-
1ph L

Tulloch Mill,Warehouse
HABS CA-165
HABS CAL,50-KNITF,2A-
2dr/4ph L

RIVERBANK

Riverbank Army Ammunition Plant
HAER CA-28
HAER CAL,50-RIVBA,1-
45pg/fr L

TEHAMA COUNTY

RED BLUFF VIC.

Battle Creek Hydroelectric System (Coleman Power House; Inskip Power House; South Power House; Volta Power House)
Battle Creek & Tributaries
HAER CA-2
HAER CAL,52-REDBLU.V,1-
20dr/174ph/181pg/14pc/fr L

Coleman Power House; see Battle Creek Hydroelectric System

Inskip Power House; see Battle Creek Hydroelectric System

South Power House; see Battle Creek Hydroelectric System

Volta Power House; see Battle Creek Hydroelectric System

TRINITY COUNTY

CARRVILLE

Gold Dredge
HABS CA-1186
HABS CAL,53-CARR,1-
1ph/1pc L

SALYER VIC.

South Fork Trinity River Bridge
State Hwy 299 spanning S Fork Trinity River
HAER CA-29
HAER CAL,53-SALY.V,1-;1991(HAER):2
61ph/5pg/6pc/2ct L

WEAVERVILLE

Blacksmith Shop
HABS CA-1185
HABS CAL,53-WEAVI,10-
1ph/1pc L

Brewery,Old
Main st.
HABS CA-1449
HABS CAL,53-WEAVI,2-
1ph L

Chinese Joss House
State Historical Park
HABS CA-1452
HABS CAL,53-WEAVI,6-
11dr/5ph/19pg L

Cole,John,Building; see I. O. O. F. Lodge Number 55 Hall

Fire Engine,Old
HABS CA-1453
HABS CAL,53-WEAVI,9-
1ph/1pc L

I. O. O. F. Lodge Number 55 Hall (Cole,John,Building)
HABS CA-1448
HABS CAL,53-WEAVI,3-
2ph L

Jumper House
HABS CA-1451
HABS CAL,53-WEAVI,8-
2ph L

Native Sons of the Golden West Building
HABS CA-1668
HABS CAL,53-WEAVI,11-
1ph/1pg/1pc L

Store
HABS CA-1450
HABS CAL,53-WEAVI,4-
3ph L

Trinity County Courthouse
Main & Court Sts.
HABS CA-1447
HABS CAL,53-WEAVI,7-
1ph L

Weaverville,General View
HABS CA-2197
HABS CAL,53-WEAVI,1-
3ph L

TULARE COUNTY

GIANT FOREST VILLAGE

Cabin No. 53; see Camp Kaweah Historic District

Cafeteria; see Camp Kaweah Historic District

Camp Kaweah Historic District (Cabin No. 53; Sequoia National Park)
HABS CA-2148-G
HABS CAL,54-GIFO,1-G-
2ph/1pc/fr L

Camp Kaweah Historic District (Cafeteria; Sequoia National Park)
HABS CA-2148-A
HABS CAL,54-GIFO,1-A-
5ph/1pc/fr L

Camp Kaweah Historic District (Comfort Station; Sequoia National Park)
HABS CA-2148-C
HABS CAL,54-GIFO,1-C-
4ph/1pg/1pc/fr L

Camp Kaweah Historic District (Curio Shop; Sequoia National Park)
HABS CA-2148-D
HABS CAL,54-GIFO,1-D-
3ph/1pc/fr L

Camp Kaweah Historic District (Giant Forest Market; Sequoia National Park)
HABS CA-2148-B
HABS CAL,54-GIFO,1-B-
8ph/1pg/1pc/fr L

Camp Kaweah Historic District (National Park Service Residence No. 55; Sequoia National Park)
HABS CA-2148-E
HABS CAL,54-GIFO,1-E-
7ph/1pc/fr L

Camp Kaweah Historic District (Office-Warehouse; Sequoia National Park)
HABS CA-2148-F
HABS CAL,54-GIFO,1-F-
4ph/1pg/1pc/fr L

Comfort Station; see Camp Kaweah Historic District

Curio Shop; see Camp Kaweah Historic District

Giant Forest Market; see Camp Kaweah Historic District

National Park Service Residence No. 55; see Camp Kaweah Historic District

Office-Warehouse; see Camp Kaweah Historic District

Sequoia National Park; see Camp Kaweah Historic District

SPRINGVILLE VIC.

Bridge No. 46-10; see Tule River Hydroelectric Complex,Tule River Bridge

Tule River Hydroelectric Complex
CA Hwy. 190 at N. Fork of Mid. Fork of Tule Riv.
HAER CA-48
11ph/11pg/2pc L

Tule River Hydroelectric Complex,Tule River Bridge (Bridge No. 46-10)
Spanning the N. Fork of Mid.Fork of Tule River
HAER CA-48-A
18ph/4pg/2pc L

THREE RIVERS VIC.

Amphitheater; see Giant Forest Lodge Historic District

Cabin A; see Giant Forest Lodge Historic District

Cabin B; see Giant Forest Lodge Historic District

Cabin H; see Giant Forest Lodge Historic District

Cabin No. 22; see Giant Forest Lodge Historic District

Cabin No. 27-28; see Giant Forest Lodge Historic District

Cabin No. 5; see Giant Forest Lodge Historic District

Cabin No. 6; see Giant Forest Lodge Historic District

Cabin No. 7; see Giant Forest Lodge Historic District

Cabin No. 8; see Giant Forest Lodge Historic District

General Office Building; see Giant Forest Lodge Historic District

Giant Forest Lodge Historic District (Amphitheater; Sequoia National Park)
HABS CA-193-B
HABS CAL,54-THRIV.V,1-B-
2ph/1pc/fr L

Giant Forest Lodge Historic District (Cabin A; Sequoia National Park)
HABS CA-193-D
HABS CAL,54-THRIV.V,1-D-
6ph/1pg/1pc/fr L

Giant Forest Lodge Historic District (Cabin B; Sequoia National Park)
HABS CA-193-E
HABS CAL,54-THRIV.V,1-E-
3ph/1pg/1pc/fr L

Giant Forest Lodge Historic District (Cabin H; Sequoia National Park)
HABS CA-193-F
HABS CAL,54-THRIV.V,1-F-
3ph/1pg/1pc/fr L

Giant Forest Lodge Historic District (Cabin No. 22; Sequoia National Park)
HABS CA-193-K
HABS CAL,54-THRIV.V,1-K-
5ph/1pc/fr L

Giant Forest Lodge Historic District (Cabin No. 27-28; Sequoia National Park)
HABS CA-193-L
HABS CAL,54-THRIV.V,1-L-
4ph/1pc L

Giant Forest Lodge Historic District (Cabin No. 5; Sequoia National Park)
HABS CA-193-G
HABS CAL,54-THRIV.V,1-G-
1ph/1pc/fr L

Giant Forest Lodge Historic District (Cabin No. 6; Sequoia National Park)
HABS CA-193-H
HABS CAL,54-THRIV.V,1-H-
1ph/1pc/fr L

Giant Forest Lodge Historic District (Cabin No. 7; Sequoia National Park)
HABS CA-193-I
HABS CAL,54-THRIV.V,1-I-
1ph/1pc/fr L

Giant Forest Lodge Historic District (Cabin No. 8; Sequoia National Park)
HABS CA-193-J
HABS CAL,54-THRIV.V,1-J-
2ph/1pc/fr L

Giant Forest Lodge Historic District (General Office Building; Sequoia National Park)
HABS CA-193-C
HABS CAL,54-THRIV.V,1-C-
4ph/1pg/1pc/fr L

Giant Forest Lodge Historic District (Registration Building; Sequoia National Park)
HABS CA-193-A
HABS CAL,54-THRIV.V,1-A-
7ph/1pg/1pc/fr L

Registration Building; see Giant Forest Lodge Historic District

Sequoia National Park; see Giant Forest Lodge Historic District

TULARE

Kern St. (Commercial Buildings)
HABS CA-1794
HABS CAL,54-TULA,1-
1ph/1pc L

TUOLUMNE COUNTY

BIG OAK FLAT

I. O. O. F. Hall
HABS CA-1578
HABS CAL,55-BOF,1-
1ph/1pc L

CHINESE CAMP

Bruschi Store
HABS CA-1569
HABS CAL,55-CHICA,1-
1ph/1pc L

COLUMBIA

Building,Brick
HABS CA-1695
HABS CAL,55-COLUM,9-
1ph L

City Hotel
Main St. (Columbia State Historical Park)
HABS CA-1146
HABS CAL,55-COLUM,4-
2ph L

Columbia,General View
Columbia State Historical Park
HABS CA-1873
HABS CAL,55-COLUM,10-
2ph/1pc L

Grave Stones,Mountain View Cemetery
Bigler St.
HABS CA-37-11-A
HABS CAL,55-COLUM,1-
1ph L

Grave Stones,St. Anne's Cemetery
HABS CA-38-11-B
HABS CAL,55-COLUM,2A-
1ph L

I. O. O. F. Building
State & Broadway Sts. (Columbia State Hist. Park)
HABS CA-1693
HABS CAL,55-COLUM,11-
2ph/1pg/1pc L

Livery Stable
HABS CA-1872
HABS CAL,55-COLUM,12-
4ph/1pc L

Main Street (Commercial Building)
Columbia State Historical Park
HABS CA-1147
HABS CAL,55-COLUM,8-
1ph L

Main Street (Commercial Buildings)
HABS CA-1299
HABS CAL,55-COLUM,13-
3ph/1pc L

Mills,D. O. ,Bank; see Mills,D. O. ,Building

Mills,D. O. ,Building (Mills,D. O. ,Bank)
HABS CA-1573
HABS CAL,55-COLUM,14-
1ph/1pc L

Pioneer Saloon
HABS CA-1145
HABS CAL,55-COLUM,7-
3ph L

Solari's Building
Columbia State Historical Park
HABS CA-1144
HABS CAL,55-COLUM,6-
4ph L

Springfield Brewery; see Tuolumne Engine House No. 1 & Springfield Brewery

St. Anne's Church
Church St.
HABS CA-1142
HABS CAL,55-COLUM,2-
5dr/7ph L

Sun Lun Sing Store
N. Main St. (Columbia State Historical Park)
HABS CA-2000
HABS CAL,55-COLUM,15-
3ph/1pc L

Trading Post,Old
Main & State Sts.
HABS CA-1143
HABS CAL,55-COLUM,5-
2ph/1pc L

Tuolumne Engine House No. 1 & Springfield Brewery (Springfield Brewery)
Columbia State Historical Park
HABS CA-1871
HABS CAL,55-COLUM,16-
3ph/1pg/1pc L

Wells Fargo and Company Building
Main & Washington Sts. (Columbia State Hist. Park)
HABS CA-174
HABS CAL,33-COLUM,3-
11dr/1ph/fr L

DARDANELLE VIC.

Dardanelle Bridge; see Middle Fork Stanislaus River Bridge

Middle Fork Stanislaus River Bridge (Dardanelle Bridge)
Spans Middle Fork Stanislaus River at St. Hwy. 108
HAER CA-72
HAER DLC/PP-1993:CA-2
20ph/5pg/2pc L

DRAGON GULCH

Gilman,Tom,Cabin
HABS CA-1200
HABS CAL,55-DRAGU,1-
1ph/1pc L

GROVELAND VIC.

Harte,Bret,House (Tennessee's Cabin)
HABS CA-1568
HABS CAL,55-GROLA.V,1-
1ph/1pc L

North Mountain Lookout
Stanislaus National Forest
HABS CA-2271
HABS DLC/PP-1992:CA-2
15ph/25pg/1pc L

Tennessee's Cabin; see Harte,Bret,House

JACKASS HILL

Gillis Cabin; see Twain,Mark,Cabin

Twain,Mark,Cabin (Gillis Cabin)
HABS CA-1296
HABS CAL,55-JACHI,1-
4ph/1pg/1pc L

MONTEZUMA

Hotel and Store
HABS CA-1574
HABS CAL,55-MONT,1-
1ph L

PRIESTS

Priest's Hotel
HABS CA-1572
HABS CAL,55-PRI,1-
1ph/1pc L

QUARTZ MOUNTAIN

Quartz Mountain,General View
HABS CA-1196
HABS CAL,55-QUAMO,1-
1ph/1pc L

SHAW'S FLAT

Mississippi House & Post Office
Shaw Flat & Mt. Beow Rds.
HABS CA-1579
HABS CAL,55-SHAF,1-
1ph/1pg/1pc L

SONORA

Cady House
Dodge and Norlin Sts.
HABS CA-116
HABS CAL,55-SONO,2-
6dr/5ph/1pg/fr L

City Hotel
HABS CA-1566
HABS CAL,55-SONO,20-
1ph/1pc L

Commercial Building (Iron Doors)
HABS CA-1699
HABS CAL,55-SONO,15-
2ph/1pc L

Dodge & Stuart Streets (House)
HABS CA-1139
HABS CAL,55-SONO,10-
1ph L

Dorsey House
HABS CA-1134
HABS CAL,55-SONO,3-
2ph L

Gem Cafe; see Store Building

Grave Stones,Jewish Cemetery
Yaney Ave. between Vigilance and Seco Sts.
HABS CA-38-11-A
HABS CAL,55-SONO,1-
1ph L

Gunn,Dr. Lewis,Adobe; see Italia Hotel

House,Second
Dodge and Stewart Sts.
HABS CA-1140
HABS CAL,55-SONO,11-
1ph L

Italia Hotel (Gunn,Dr. Lewis,Adobe)
Washington St.
HABS CA-1135
HABS CAL,55-SONO,4-
1ph L

Jewish Cemetery
Yaney Ave.
HABS CA-38-7
HABS CAL,55-SONO,1-
4dr/7ph L

Leonard,Thomas,House
HABS CA-1512
HABS CAL,55-SONO,12-
1ph L

McCormick House
HABS CA-1111
HABS CAL,55-SONO,7-
3ph L

Methodist Church
HABS CA-1567
HABS CAL,55-SONO,16-
1ph/1pc L

Post Office,First
HABS CA-1575
HABS CAL,55-SONO,13-
1ph L

Sonora,General View
HABS CA-1195
HABS CAL,55-SONO,17-
3ph/1pc L

St. James Episcopal Church
Washington & Theall Sts.
HABS CA-1141
HABS CAL,55-SONO,5-
2ph L

St. Patrick's Church
Dodge & Norlin Sts.
HABS CA-189
HABS CAL,55-SONO,6-
2ph L

Stockton Record Building
HABS CA-1690
HABS CAL,55-SONO,18-
1ph/1pc L

Store Building (Gem Cafe)
Washington St.
HABS CA-1688
HABS CAL,55-SONO,14-
1ph L

Sugg House (Sugg-McDonald House)
37 Theall St.
HABS CA-1137
HABS CAL,55-SONO,9-
1ph L

Sugg-McDonald House; see Sugg House

Union Democrat Building
HABS CA-1691
HABS CAL,55-SONO,19-
2ph/1pc L

1100 Washington Street (House)
HABS CA-1136
HABS CAL,55-SONO,8-
1ph L

SONORA VIC.

Dam,Stone
HABS CA-188
HABS CAL,55-SONO.V,1-
2ph L

Kiln,Lime
HABS CA-195
HABS CAL,55-SONO.V,2-
1ph L

SPRINGFIELD

House
HABS CA-1148
HABS CAL,55-SPRIF,2-
1ph L

Methodist Church; see School

School (Methodist Church)
Horseshoe Bend and Springfield Rd.
HABS CA-1149
HABS CAL,55-SPRIF,1-
3ph L

STENT

Stent,General View
HABS CA-1577
HABS CAL,55-STENT,1-
1ph/1pc L

TUOLUMNE MEADOWS

Tuolumne Meadows Ranger Station
(Yosemite National Park)
Tioga Pass Rd.
HABS CA-2183
HABS CAL,22-TUME,1-
6ph/2pg/1pc L

Yosemite National Park; see Tuolumne Meadows Ranger Station

TUTTLETOWN

Swerer's Store
HABS CA-1272
HABS CAL,55-TUTTO,1-
2ph/1pg/1pc L

Tuttletown Hotel
HABS CA-1571
HABS CAL,55-TUTTO,2-
2ph/1pc L

TUTTLETOWN VIC.

Farmhouse
HABS CA-1271
HABS CAL,55-TUTTO.V,1-
1ph L

WOODS CROSSING

Farm Buildings
HABS CA-1570
HABS CAL,55- ,1-
1ph/1pc L

VENTURA COUNTY

PIRU VIC.

Camulos,Del Rancho,La Casa
State Hwy. 12
HABS CA-38
HABS CAL,56-PIRU.V,1-
16dr/17ph/1pg/fr L

VENTURA

Mission San Buenaventura
E. Main St. & S. Figueroa St.
HABS CA-22
HABS CAL,56-VENT,1-
10dr/7ph/2pg L

VENTURA VIC.

Anacapa Island Light Station
East Anacapa Island
HABS CA-2335
H

Anacapa Island Light Station,House
East Anacapa Island
HABS CA-2335-A
HABS DLC/PP-1992:CA-4
1ph/1pc L

Anacapa Island Light Station,Light Tower (Fog Horn House)
East Anacapa Island
HABS CA-2335-B
HABS DLC/PP-1992:CA-4
1ph/1pc L

Fog Horn House; see Anacapa Island Light Station,Light Tower

YOLO COUNTY

WOODLAND

Southern Pacific Depot
450 East St. at Lincoln Ave.
HABS CA-2297
HABS 1992(HABS):CA-1
4ph/6pg/1pc L

YUBA COUNTY

BEAR RIVER

Bear River Hotel & Wells Fargo Office
HABS CA-1689
HABS CAL,58-BERIV,1-
1ph/1pc L

BROWN'S VALLEY VIC.

Oregon House (Stage Station,Old)
HABS CA-1428
HABS CAL,58-BROVA,1-
1ph L

Stage Station,Old; see Oregon House

DOBBINS

Hotel
HABS CA-1427
HABS CAL,58-DOB,1-
2ph L

DOBBINS VIC.

Freeman's Crossing Bridge (Middle Yuba Bridge)
See documents under NEVADA CO.,NORTH SAN JUAN VIC.
HAER CA-131
HAER DLC/PP-1993:CA-3
25ph/8pg/2pc L

Middle Yuba Bridge; see Freeman's Crossing Bridge

MARYSVILLE

Aaron,Mary,Museum; see Miller-Aaron House

C Street (House)
HABS CA-1431
HABS CAL,58-MARVI,4-
1ph L

C Street (House)
HABS CA-1432
HABS CAL,58-MARVI,5-
1ph L

C Street & Sixth Street (Houses)
HABS CA-1430
HABS CAL,58-MARVI,3-
1ph L

D Street (Commerical Buildings)
HABS CA-1808
HABS CAL,58-MARVI,6-
1ph/1pc L

Marysville Grammar School
HABS CA-1812
HABS CAL,58-MARVI,7-
1ph/1pg/1pc L

Marysville High School
HABS CA-1811
HABS CAL,58-MARVI,8-
1ph/1pg/1pc L

Miller-Aaron House
(Aaron,Mary,Museum)
704 D St.
HABS CA-1113
HABS CAL,58-MARVI,1-
1ph/4pg L

Presbyterian Church
Fifth & D Sts.
HABS CA-1429
HABS CAL,58-MARVI,2-
1ph L

Yuba County Courthouse
Sixth & D Sts.
HABS CA-1810
HABS CAL,58-MARVI,9-
1ph/1pg/1pc L

Yuba County Hall of Records
HABS CA-1813
HABS CAL,58-MARVI,10-
1ph/1pc L

SMARTSVILLE

O'Brian,James,House
O'Brian Rd.
HABS CA-1809
HABS CAL,58-SMAVI,1-
1ph/1pg/1pc L

TIMBUCTOO

Main Street (Commercial Buildings)
HABS CA-1546
HABS CAL,58-TIMTO,1-
2ph/1pc L

Wells Fargo Express Office Building
N. Hwy. 20
HABS CA-1295
HABS CAL,58-TIMTO,2-
2ph/1pg/1pc L

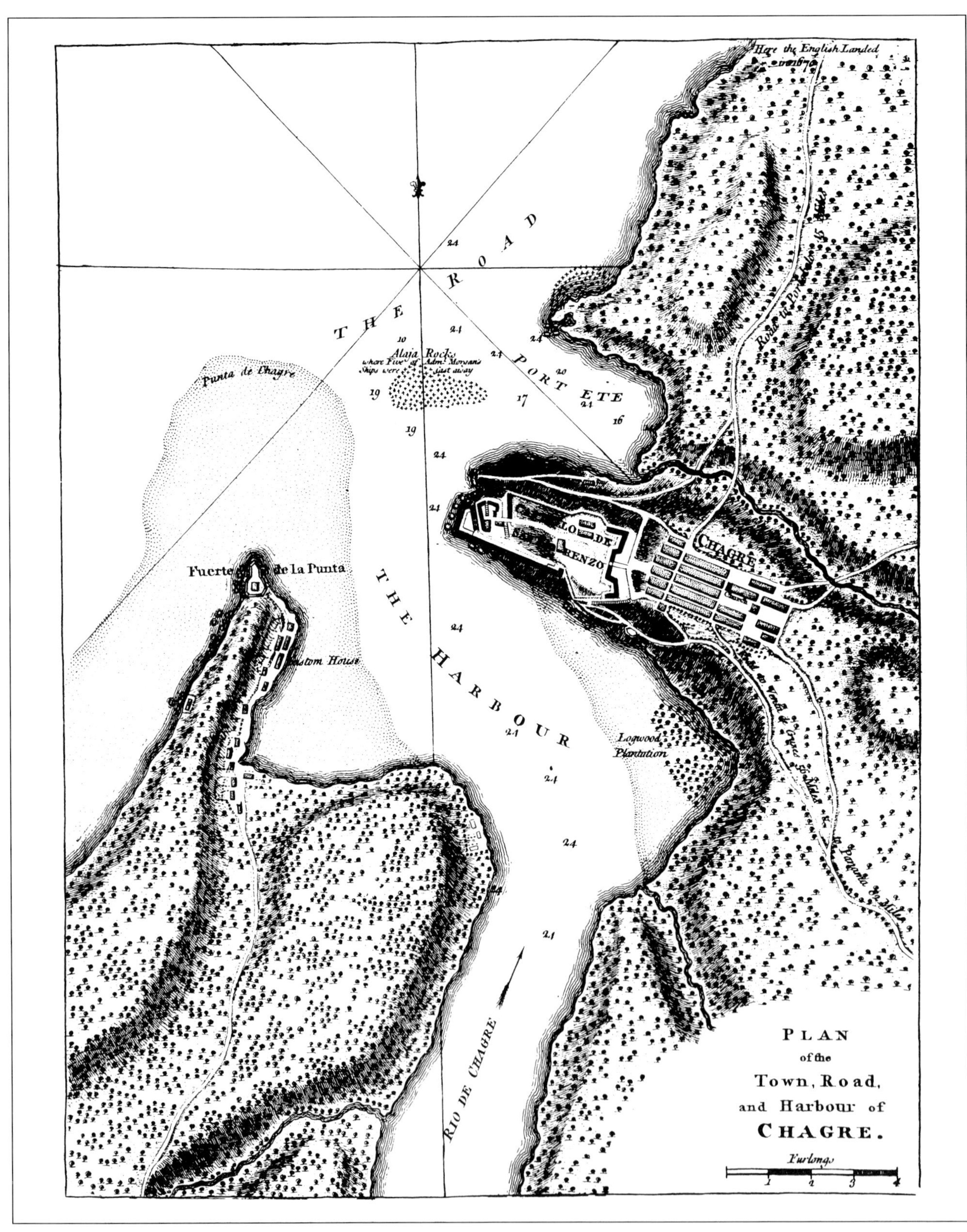

Fort San Lorenzo, Panama Canal Zone. Plan of the town road and harbour of Chagre. Drawing from 1940's (HABS CZ-1, sheet 2 of 4).

Canal Zone

CANAL ZONE

COLON VIC.

Fort San Lorenzo
Chagres River
HABS CZ-1
4dr L

Ritter Ranch Barn, Dolores vicinity, Montezuma County, Colorado. Interior, second floor, west side. Photograph by Jet Lowe, September 1981 (HABS COLO,42-DOL.V,4A-10)

Colorado

ADAMS COUNTY

AURORA

Windler Farm
Vic. of E. 48th Ave. & Picadilly Rd.
HABS CO-84
HABS 1989(HABS):3
11ph/16pg/1pc L

Windler Farm,Farmhouse
Vic. of E. 48th Ave. & Picadilly Rd.
HABS CO-84-A
HABS 1989(HABS):3
6ph/1pc L

BRIGHTON VIC.

Baseline Bridge
Spanning S. Platte River on County Rd. 168
HAER CO-44
HAER COLO,1-BRIG.V,1-
7ph/2pg/1pc L

Brantner Ditch
South Platte River
HAER CO-47
HAER 1990 (HAER):3
7ph/13pg/1pc L

Burlington Ditch
S. Platte Rvr. Drain. Area,Water Dist. No. 2,Di.2
HAER CO-45
HAER 1990 (HAER):3
9ph/17pg/2pc/fr L

O'Brian Canal
S. Platte Rvr. Drain. Area NE of Denver
HAER CO-46
HAER 1990 (HAER):3
7ph/14pg/2pc/fr L

COMMERCE CITY

Rocky Mountain Arsenal
HAER CO-21
HAER COLO,1-CIMCI,1-
51pg/fr L

DENVER VIC.

Doherty Ditch; see Highline Extension Canal

Farrel Farm (Larson Farm)
7381 N. Washington St.
HABS CO-59
HABS COLO,1-DENV.V,1-
1dr/5ph/11pg/1pc L

Farrel Farm,Barn (Larson Farm,Barn)
7381 N. Washington St.
HABS CO-59-F
HABS COLO,1-DENV.V,1F-
2ph/2pc L

Farrel Farm,Bunkhouse (Larson Farm,Bunkhouse)
7381 N. Washington St.
HABS CO-59-C
HABS COLO,1-DENV.V,1C-
1ph/1pc L

Farrel Farm,Coal Shed (Larson Farm,Coal Shed)
7381 N. Washington St.
HABS CO-59-B
HABS COLO,1-DENV.V,1B-
1ph/1pc L

Farrel Farm,Farmhouse (Larson Farm,Farmhouse)
7381 N. Washington St.
HABS CO-59-A
HABS COLO,1-DENV.V,1A-
7ph/1pc L

Farrel Farm,Garage (Larson Farm,Garage)
7381 N. Washington St.
HABS CO-59-E
HABS COLO,1-DENV.V,1E-
1ph/1pc L

Farrel Farm,Garage,New (Larson Farm,Garage,New)
7381 N. Washington St.
HABS CO-59-H
HABS COLO,1-DENV.V,1H-
1ph L

Farrel Farm,House,New (Larson Farm,House,New)
7381 N. Washington St.
HABS CO-59-G
HABS COLO,1-DENV.V,1G-
1ph L

Farrel Farm,Ice House (Larson Farm,Ice House)
7381 N. Washington St.
HABS CO-59-D
HABS COLO.1-DENV.V,1D-
1ph/1pc L

Farrel Farm,Silos (Larson Farm,Silos)
7381 N. Washington St.
HABS CO-59-I
HABS COLO,1-DENV.V,1I-
1ph/1pc L

Highline Extension Canal (Doherty Ditch)
HAER CO-67
HAER DLC/PP-1993:CO-3
2dr/23ph/19pg/2pc L

Larson Farm; see Farrel Farm

Larson Farm,Barn; see Farrel Farm,Barn

Larson Farm,Bunkhouse; see Farrel Farm,Bunkhouse

Larson Farm,Coal Shed; see Farrel Farm,Coal Shed

Larson Farm,Farmhouse; see Farrel Farm,Farmhouse

Larson Farm,Garage; see Farrel Farm,Garage

Larson Farm,Garage,New; see Farrel Farm,Garage,New

Larson Farm,House,New; see Farrel Farm,House,New

Larson Farm,Ice House; see Farrel Farm,Ice House

Larson Farm,Silos; see Farrel Farm,Silos

WATKINS VIC.

Box Elder Road
Btw. 104th & 112th Aves., Hudson & Watkins Rds.
HAER CO-65
1dr/6ph/14pg/1pc H

ARAPAHOE COUNTY

LITTLETON

Bemis,Fred A. ,Farmhouse (Littleton Historical Museum,Bemis Farmhouse)
6028 S. Gallop St. (Moved from Original Site)
HABS CO-88
HABS 1991(HABS):18
6dr L

Littleton Center for Cultural Arts; see Littleton Town Hall

Littleton Denver & Rio Grande Western Depot
2199 West Littleton Blvd.
HABS CO-46
HABS COLO,3-LIT,2-
17ph/10pg/1pc L

Littleton Historical Museum,Bemis Farmhouse; see Bemis,Fred A. ,Farmhouse

Littleton Town Hall (Littleton Center for Cultural Arts)
2450 W. Main St.
HABS CO-34
HABS COLO,3-LIT,1-
2ph/3pg/1pc L

BENT COUNTY

LA JUNTA

Bent's Old Fort National Historic Site; see Fort Bent,Old

Fort Bent,Old (Bent's Old Fort National Historic Site)
HABS CO-22
HABS COLO,6-LAJUNT,1-
4dr L

BOULDER COUNTY

BOULDER

Howard Ditch
East Boulder Community Park
HAER CO-64
HAER 1991(HAER):7
7ph/6pg/1pc L

CHAFFEE COUNTY

BUENA VISTA VIC.

Four Mile Bridge
Spanning Arkansas River
HAER CO-35
HAER COLO,8-BUENA.V,1-
8ph/2pg/1pc L

IRON CITY

Murphy,Mary,Mining Complex,Boarding House
HAER CO-26-B
HAER 1991(HAER):7
3ph/1pc L

Murphy,Mary,Mining Complex,Iron City Cemetery
HAER CO-26-G
HAER 1991(HAER):7
4ph/1pc L

Murphy,Mary,Mining Complex,Mill and Tailings
HAER CO-26-E
HAER 1991(HAER):7
2ph/1pc L

Murphy,Mary,Mining Complex,Mine Ore and Bin Chute
HAER CO-26-F
HAER 1991(HAER):7
2ph/1pc L

Murphy,Mary,Mining Complex,Mine Shaft House
HAER CO-26-C
HAER 1991(HAER):7
4ph/1pc L

Murphy,Mary,Mining Complex,Sluice
HAER CO-26-D
HAER 1991(HAER):7
2ph/1pc L

Murphy,Mary,Mining Complex,Superintendent's House
HAER CO-26-A
HAER 1991(HAER):7
2ph/1pc L

NATHROP VIC.

Chalk Creek Bridge; see Hortense Bridge

Hortense Bridge (Chalk Creek Bridge)
Spanning Chalk Creek on State Hwy 162
HAER CO-49
HAER COLO,8-NATH.V,1-
10ph/10pg/1pc L

ROMLEY

Denver South Park & Pacific RR Bridge
Spanning Chalk Creek,near Mt. Princeton Hot Spring
HAER CO-25
HAER 1991(HAER):7
2ph/1pc L

Denver South Park & Pacific RR Truss Bridge
HAER CO-24
HAER 1990 (HAER):3
2ph/1pc L

Romley,Town of
HABS CO-73
HABS 1989(HABS):3
2ph/1pc L

ST. ELMO

Paramount Mine
HAER CO-23
HAER 1991(HAER):7
8ph/1pc L

St. Elmo Historic District
HABS CO-72
5dr/12ph/50pg/1pc/fr H

CLEAR CREEK COUNTY

GEORGETOWN

Hamill House Complex
Argentine & Third Sts.
HABS CO-60
HABS COLO,10-GEO,1-
1dr L

Hamill House Complex,Carriage House
Argentine & Third Sts.
HABS CO-60-C
HABS COLO,10-GEO,1C-
6dr/1pg L

Hamill House Complex,House
Argentine & Third Sts.
HABS CO-60-A
HABS COLO,10-GEO,1A-
1pg L

Hamill House Complex,Office Building
Argentine & Third Sts.
HABS CO-60-B
HABS COLO,10-GEO,1B-
11dr/1pg L

IDAHO SPRINGS VIC.

Mount Evans Crest House
S.R. 5,Mt. Evans summit,Arapaho Nat'l Forest
HABS CO-81
HABS COLO,10-IDASP.V,1A-
16ph/14pg/1pc/fr L

SILVER PLUME

Silver Plume School
Main St.
HABS CO-23
HABS COLO,10-SILV,1-
3dr/1pg L

CROWLEY COUNTY

MANZANOLA VIC.

Clifton Bridge; see Manzanola Bridge

Manzanola Bridge (Clifton Bridge)
State Hwy. 207,spanning Arkansas River
HAER CO-20
HAER COLO,13-MANZ.V,1-
12ph/3pg/1pc L

DELTA COUNTY

DELTA

Delta Bridge
Spanning Gunnison River on U. S. 50
HAER CO-62
HAER 1991(HAER):7
18ph/3pg/1pc L

DELTA VIC.

Roubideau Bridge
Spanning the Gunnison River at County Rd. G50R
HAER CO-70
HAER DLC/PP-1993:CO-2
17ph/3pg/1pc L

HOTCHKISS VIC.

Hotchkiss Bridge
Spanning North Fork River on County Road 3400
HAER CO-40
HAER COLO,15-HOTCH,V,1-
9ph/2pg/1pc L

DENVER COUNTY

DENVER

Acme Upholstery Supply Company; see West Wazee Street Warehouse District

Arapahoe & 17th Streets (Commercial Buildings); see Skyline Urban Renewal Area

1622-1632 Arapahoe Street (Commercial Buildings); see Skyline Urban Renewal Area

Baker, W. Brown Building (Skyline Urban Renewal Area)
1319 Larimer St.
HABS CO-106
HABS COLO,16-DENV,30-
1ph/1pc L

Barclay Block (Skyline Urban Renewal Area)
1755 Larimer St.
HABS CO-118
HABS COLO,16-DENV,42-
2ph/1pc L

Batione Block (Skyline Urban Renewal Area)
1720 Larimer St.
HABS CO-117
HABS COLO,16-DENV,41-
1ph/1pc L

1650 Blake Street (Commercial Building)
HABS CO-31
HABS COLO,16-DENV,5-
1ph/1pg/1pc/fr L

Brecht Candy Company; see West Wazee Street Warehouse District

Broadway Bridge
Spanning Cherry Creek on Broadway at Speer Blvd.
HAER CO-48
HAER COLO,16-DENV,46-
9ph/8pg/1pc L

Carson Crockery; see West Wazee Street Warehouse District

Carson's,Inc.; see West Wazee Street Warehouse District

Central Presbyterian Church
1660 Sherman St.
HABS CO-41
HABS COLO,16-DENV,9-
20ph/6pg/1pc L

Cherry Creek Railroad Bridge
Spanning Cherry Creek, north of Delgany St.
HAER CO-58
HAER 1990 (HAER):3
8ph/5pg/1pc L

City & County Building
Civic Center
HABS CO-68
HABS COLO,16-DENV,7-
15ph/7pg/1pc/fr L

Clayton Block (Skyline Urban Renewal Area)
Lawrence & Seventeenth Sts.
HABS CO-102
HABS COLO,16-DENV,26-
1ph/1pc L

Colorada & Southern Railway Denver Roundhouse Com.
Seventh St.,East of the S. Platte River
HAER CO-56
HAER 1991(HAER):7
1dr/27ph/12pg/2pc L

Colorado Casket Company; see West Wazee Street Warehouse District

Colorado Historic Bridges Survey
HAER CO-30
HAER COLO,16-DENV,47-
210pg L

Columbia Hotel (Skyline Urban Renewal Area)
Market & Seventeenth Sts.
HABS CO-121
HABS COLO,16-DENV,45-
1ph/1pc L

CORY HOTEL; see PLYMOUTH PLACE

Curtis-Clarke Block (Skyline Urban Renewal Area)
1634 Larimer St.
HABS CO-113
HABS COLO,16-DENV,37-
2ph/1pc L

Daniel's & Fisher's Store (Skyline Urban Renewal Area)
Lawrence & Sixteenth Sts.
HABS CO-100
HABS COLO,16-DENV,24-
1ph/1pc L

Davis,Fred Furniture Mart & Railroad Building (Skyline Urban Renewal Area)
1501 Larimer St.
HABS CO-108
HABS COLO,16-DENV,32-
1ph/1pc L

Delaware Street Tramway Power Sub-Station (Denver Mint Tramway Pressroom)
1448 Delaware St.
HAER CO-12
HAER COLO,16-DENV,49-
17ph/17pg/2pc L

Delgany Street Railroad Bridge
Spanning Cherry Creek at Delgany St.
HAER CO-57
HAER 1990 (HAER):3
10ph/6pg/1pc L

Denver City Cable Railway Company (Skyline Urban Renewal Area)
Lawrence & Eighteenth Sts.
HABS CO-105
HABS COLO,16-DENV,29-
3ph/1pc L

Denver Dry Goods Company Warehouse; see West Wazee Street Warehouse District

Denver Mint Tramway Pressroom; see Delaware Street Tramway Power Sub-Station

Denver-Delgany Sanitation Main; see Thirty-first Street Overflow Structure

Desks,Inc.; see West Wazee Street Warehouse District

Empire Building
430 Sixteenth St.
HABS CO-87
HABS 1991(HABS):18
29ph/24pg/4pc L

Essex Building (Skyline Urban Renewal Area)
Lawrence & Sixteenth Sts.
HABS CO-98
HABS COLO,16-DENV,22-
1ph/1pc L

Fourteenth Street Viaduct
14th St. at Wazee St.
HAER CO-52
HAER 1989(HAER):2
16ph/3pg/1pc L

Gem Hotel & Theater (Skyline Urban Renewal Area)
1746 Curtis St.
HABS CO-120
HABS COLO,16-DENV,44-
1ph/1pc L

General Novelty Store (Skyline Urban Renewal Area)
1734 Lawrence St.
HABS CO-104
HABS COLO,16-DENV,28-
1ph/1pc L

Glenarm Branch,Denver Young Men's Christian Assoc. (Glenarm Recreation Center)
501 Twenty-eighth St.
HABS CO-45
HABS COLO,16-DENV,10A-
9ph/16pg/1pc L

Glenarm Recreation Center; see Glenarm Branch,Denver Young Men's Christian Assoc.

Globeville Community House (Globeville Youth Center; Globeville Recreation Center)
4496 Grant St.
HABS CO-51
HABS COLO,16-DENV,11-
9ph/12pg/1pc L

Globeville Recreation Center; see Globeville Community House

Globeville Youth Center; see Globeville Community House

Golden Eagle Department Store (Skyline Urban Renewal Area)
Lawrence & Sixteenth Sts.
HABS CO-99
HABS COLO,16-DENV,23-
1ph/1pc L

Goodblock Building (Skyline Urban Renewal Area)
Larimer & Sixteenth Sts.
HABS CO-110
HABS COLO,16-DENV,34-
2ph/1pc L

Granite Hotel (Skyline Urban Renewal Area)
Larimer & Fifteenth Sts.
HABS CO-107
HABS COLO,16-DENV,31-
1ph/1pc L

Great Northern Hotel (Skyline Urban Renewal Area)
1612 Larimer St.
HABS CO-112
HABS COLO,16-DENV,36-
1ph/1pc L

Groff-Collins & W.S. Chessman Buildings (Skyline Urban Renewal Area)
Larimer & Seventeenth Sts.
HABS CO-114
HABS COLO,16-DENV,38-
2ph/1pc L

Hotel Metropole & Broadway Theater
1756 Broadway St.
HABS CO-64
HABS COLO,16-DENV,12-
6ph/18pg/1pc L

Interstate Trust Building (Skyline Urban Renewal Area)
Lawrence & Sixteenth Sts.
HABS CO-101
HABS COLO,16-DENV,25-
1ph/1pc L

Kacey Fine Furniture; see West Wazee Street Warehouse District

Larimer Square; see Skyline Urban Renewal Area

1516-1520 Larimer Street (Commercial Building) (Skyline Urban Renewal Area)
HABS CO-109
HABS COLO,16-DENV,33-
1ph/1pc L

1701 Larimer Street (Commercial Building) (Skyline Urban Renewal Area)
HABS CO-115
HABS COLO,16-DENV,39-
1ph/1pc L

1851 Larimer Street (Skyline Urban Renewal Area)
HABS CO-119
HABS COLO,16-DENV,43-
1ph/1pc L

Lawrence & 15th Streets (Commercial Building) (Skyline Urban Renewal Area)
HABS CO-97
HABS COLO,16-DENV,21
2ph/1pc L

1611 Market Street (Commercial Building)
HABS CO-30
HABS COLO,16-DENV,4-
2ph/1pg/1pc/fr L

1615-1617 Market Street (Commercial Building)
HABS CO-28
HABS COLO,16-DENV,2-
2ph/1pg/1pc/fr L

1623 Market Street (Commercial Building)
HABS CO-29
HABS COLO,16-DENV,3-
1ph/1pg/1pc/fr L

Meir,Golda,House
1606-1608 Julian St. (moved to 1301 S. Lipan St.)
HABS CO-82
HABS COLO,16-DENV,13-
7ph/1pg/1pc/fr L

Midwest Steel & Iron Works Company
25 Larimer St.
HAER CO-19
HAER COLO,16-DENV,53-
16ph/26pg/1pc/fr L

Milwakee Brewery Company; see Tivoli-Union Brewery,West Denver Turnhalle

Milwaukee Brewery Company; see Tivoli-Union Brewery

Moffat Station
2101 Fifteenth St.
HABS CO-83
HABS 1991(HABS):18
4dr/8ph/18pg/1pc/fr L H

Molina Plow Company; see West Wazee Street Warehouse District

Moore,J. M. ,Estate Warehouse; see West Wazee Street Warehouse District

National Hotel (Skyline Urban Renewal Area)
1713 Larimer St.
HABS CO-116
HABS COLO,16-DENV,40-
1ph/1pc L

National Radium Institute
500 S. Santa Fe Dr.
HAER CO-42
HAER COLO,16-DENV,52-
8ph/13pg/1pc L

Nineteenth Street Bridge
Spanning South Platte River on Nineteenth St.
HAER CO-59
HAER 1990 (HAER):3
2dr/9ph/10pg/1pc/fr L

PLYMOUTH PLACE (CORY HOTEL)
1560-1572 BROADWAY
HABS CO-24
HABS COLO,16-DENV,1-
11dr/7ph/12pg/fr L

Schleier,George,Carriage House
1655 Grant St.
HABS CO-40-A
HABS COLO,16-DENV,14A-
2ph/1pc L

Schleier,George,Mansion
1665 Grant St.
HABS CO-40
HABS COLO,16-DENV,14-
51ph/8pg/2pc L

Skyline Urban Renewal Area
HABS CO-50
HABS COLO,16-DENV,17-
1ph/1pc L

Skyline Urban Renewal Area
(Arapahoe & 17th Streets (Commercial Buildings))
Arapahoe & 17th Streets
HABS CO-50-C
HABS COLO,16-DENV,20-
1ph/1pc L

Skyline Urban Renewal Area
(1622-1632 Arapahoe Street (Commercial Buildings))
1622-1632 Arapahoe Street
HABS CO-50-B
HABS COLO,16-DENV,19-
1ph/2pc L

Skyline Urban Renewal Area; see Baker, W. Brown Building

Skyline Urban Renewal Area; see Barclay Block

Skyline Urban Renewal Area; see Batione Block

Skyline Urban Renewal Area; see Clayton Block

Skyline Urban Renewal Area; see Columbia Hotel

Skyline Urban Renewal Area; see Curtis-Clarke Block

Skyline Urban Renewal Area; see Daniel's & Fisher's Store

Skyline Urban Renewal Area; see Davis,Fred Furniture Mart & Railroad Building

Skyline Urban Renewal Area; see Denver City Cable Railway Company

Skyline Urban Renewal Area; see Essex Building

Skyline Urban Renewal Area; see Gem Hotel & Theater

Skyline Urban Renewal Area; see General Novelty Store

Skyline Urban Renewal Area; see Golden Eagle Department Store

Skyline Urban Renewal Area; see Goodblock Building

Skyline Urban Renewal Area; see Granite Hotel

Skyline Urban Renewal Area; see Great Northern Hotel

Skyline Urban Renewal Area; see Groff-Collins & W.S. Chessman Buildings

Skyline Urban Renewal Area; see Interstate Trust Building

Skyline Urban Renewal Area (Larimer Square)
1400 Block,Larimer St.
HABS CO-50-A
HABS COLO,16-DENV,18-
2ph/1pc L

Skyline Urban Renewal Area; see 1516-1520 Larimer Street (Commercial Building)

Skyline Urban Renewal Area; see 1701 Larimer Street (Commercial Building)

Skyline Urban Renewal Area; see 1851 Larimer Street

Skyline Urban Renewal Area; see Lawrence & 15th Streets (Commercial Building)

Skyline Urban Renewal Area; see National Hotel

Skyline Urban Renewal Area; see Tabor, H.A.W. Block

Skyline Urban Renewal Area; see Western Novelty Company

Tabor, H.A.W. Block (Skyline Urban Renewal Area)
Larimer & Sixteenth Sts.
HABS CO-111
HABS COLO,16-DENV,35-
2ph/1pc L

Tears-McFarlane Garage
1200 Williams St.
HABS CO-27
HABS COLO,16-DENV,6-
7ph/1pg/1pc L

Thirsty's; see 901 Wazee Street (Commercial Building)

Thirty-first Street Overflow Structure (Denver-Delgany Sanitation Main)
Thirty-first St.
HAER CO-18
HAER COLO,16-DENV,51-
18ph/7pg/1pc L

Tivoli-Union Brewery (Milwaukee Brewery Company)
1320-1348 Tenth St.
HABS CO-26
HAER CO-1
HABS/HAER COLO,16-DENV,15-
25ph/3pg/2pc L

Tivoli-Union Brewery,West Denver Turnhalle (Milwakee Brewery Company)
Thirty-first St.
HABS CO-26-A
HABS COLO,16-DENV,15-
6ph/1pc L

Twentieth Street Viaduct
Spans Platte Riv. Valley btwn 33rd Ave. & Blake St
HAER CO-51
HAER DLC/PP-1993:CO-3
2dr/20ph/4pg/2pc L

Union Pacific Railroad Warehouse
1711-1735 Nineteenth Street
HABS CO-128
15ph/8pg/1pc H

1123 Wazee Street (Commercial Building); see West Wazee Street Warehouse District

1143 Wazee Street (Commercial Building); see West Wazee Street Warehouse District

1225-1233 Wazee Street (Commercial Building); see West Wazee Street Warehouse District

901 Wazee Street (Commercial Building) (Thirsty's)
HABS CO-69
HABS COLO,16-DENV,8-
2ph/2pg/1pc L

West Wazee Street Warehouse District
1100-1300 blocks of Wazee St.
HABS CO-70
HABS COLO,16-DENV,16-
4ph/11pg/1pc L

West Wazee Street Warehouse District (Brecht Candy Company; Acme Upholstery Supply Company)
1333 Wazee St.
HABS CO-70-I
HABS COLO,16-DENV,16I-
2ph/2pg/1pc L

West Wazee Street Warehouse District (Carson Crockery; Carson's,Inc.)
1301 Wazee St.
HABS CO-70-H
HABS COLO,16-DENV,16H-
1ph/2pg/1pc L

West Wazee Street Warehouse District (Colorado Casket Company)
1213-1221 Wazee St.
HABS CO-70-E
HABS COLO,16-DENV,16E-
1ph/2pg/1pc L

West Wazee Street Warehouse District (Denver Dry Goods Company Warehouse; Kacey Fine Furniture)
1201-1209 Wazee St.
HABS CO-70-D
HABS COLO,16-DENV,16D-
1ph/2pg/1pc L

West Wazee Street Warehouse District (Molina Plow Company; Desks,Inc.)
1127 Wazee St.
HABS CO-70-B
HABS COLO,16-DENV,16B-
1ph/2pg/1pc L

West Wazee Street Warehouse District (Moore,J. M. ,Estate Warehouse)
1235-1245 Wazee St.
HABS CO-70-G
HABS COLO,16-DENV,16G-
1ph/2pg/1pc L

West Wazee Street Warehouse District (1123 Wazee Street (Commercial Building))
HABS CO-70-A
HABS COLO,16-DENV,16A-
1ph/2pg/1pc L

West Wazee Street Warehouse District (1143 Wazee Street (Commercial Building))
HABS CO-70-C
HABS COLO,16-DENV,16C-
1ph/2pg/1pc L

West Wazee Street Warehouse District (1225-1233 Wazee Street (Commercial Building))
HABS CO-70-F
HABS COLO,16-DENV,16F-
1ph/2pg/1pc L

Western Novelty Company (Skyline Urban Renewal Area)
1725-1731 Lawrence St.
HABS CO-103
HABS COLO,16-DENV,27-
3ph/1pc L

DENVER VIC.

South Platte Canyon Road Bridge
HAER CO-7
1dr/fr H

Wells Fargo Butterfield Stage Station
HABS CO-36-C-2
HABS COLO,16-DENV.V,1-
9dr/1pg/fr L

DOUGLAS COUNTY

SEDALIA VIC. (CHR)

Cheese Ranch
161 Holman Way
HABS CO-48
HABS COLO,18-SED.V,2-
27ph/8pg/2pc L

Highlands Ranch
161 Holman Way
HABS CO-47
HABS COLO,18-SED.V,1-
50ph/11pg/3pc/fr L

EAGLE COUNTY

WOLCOTT

Bocco House (Wolcott Stage Station)
NW Junction-U. S. Hwy. 6 & 131
HABS CO-33
HABS COLO,19-WOLC,1-
3dr/8ph/1pg/1pc L

Wolcott Stage Station; see Bocco House

GARFIELD COUNTY

BATTLEMENT MESA

Battlement Mesa School
HABS CO-42
HABS COLO,23-BATME,1-
8ph/3pg/1pc L

McGuirk-Nordstrom House
HABS CO-44
HABS COLO,23-BATME,2-
4ph/1pg/1pc L

Spencer House
HABS CO-43
HABS COLO,23-BATME,3-
5ph/1pg/1pc L

GLENWOOD SPRINGS

Hot Springs Lodge
HABS CO-52
HABS COLO,23-GLENS,1-
2ph/1pc L

Shoshone Hydroelectric Plant Complex
60111 U. S. Hwy. 6
HAER CO-5
HAER COLO,23-GLENS.V,1-
38ph/21pg/4pc/fr L

RIFLE VIC.

Havemeyer-Willcox Canal System
HAER CO-3
HAER COLO,23-RIF.V,1-
8dr/15ph/26pg/2pc L

GILPIN COUNTY

BLACK HAWK

Gregory Tailings (Ruins)
State Highways 269 & 119
HAER CO-39
HAER COLO,24-BHAWK,1-
12ph/4pg/1pc L

Lace House,The
161 Main St.
HABS CO-122
HABS DLC/PP-1992:CO-3
7dr/7ph/11pg/1pc/fr L H

CENTRAL CITY

Opera House
HABS CO-36-C-3
HABS COLO,24-CENCI,1-
11ph/fr L

Teller House
HABS CO-36-C-4
HABS COLO,24-CENCI,2-
3ph L

GRAND COUNTY

GRAND LAKE VIC.

Rocky Mountain National Park Roads & Bridges
(See LARIMER COUNTY,ESTES PARK VIC. for documtn.)
HAER CO-78
L

PARSHALL VIC.

Horseshoe Ranger Station
15 mi. S. of Parshall
HABS CO-62
HABS 1991(HABS):18
4dr/10ph/7pg/1pc L

GUNNISON COUNTY

GUNNISON VIC.

Cooper 2BR Ranch,Barn (Curecanti National Recreation Area; Curecanti Recreation Area)
HABS CO-25-A
HABS COLO,26-GUNS.V,1A-
3ph L

Cooper 2BR Ranch,Bunkhouse
Curecanti Recreation Area
HABS CO-25-B
HABS COLO,26-GUNS.V,1B-
1ph L

Curecanti National Recreation Area; see Cooper 2BR Ranch,Barn

Curecanti Recreation Area; see Cooper 2BR Ranch,Barn

JEFFERSON COUNTY

ARVADA

Graves,William,House
5250 Marshall St.
HABS CO-85
HABS 1989(HABS):3
7ph/1pg/1pc L

LAKEWOOD

Peterson House (Ticen House)
Morrison Rd. ,Bear Creek Lake Park
HABS CO-66
HABS COLO,23-LAKWD,2-
7ph/7pg/1pc L

Ticen House; see Peterson House

MORRISON VIC.

Lime Kiln Near Morrison
Junction of Hwy. 8 & Rooney Rd.
HAER CO-11
HAER COLO,30-MORR.V,2-
10ph/16pg/1pc L

Rooney Ranch
Rooney Rd. & W. Alameda Pkwy.
HABS CO-65
HABS COLO,30-MORR.V,1-
1dr/4ph/28pg/2pc L

Rooney Ranch,Barn
HABS CO-65-B
HABS COLO,30-MORR.V,1B-
6ph/2pc L

Rooney Ranch,Basement House
HABS CO-65-G
HABS COLO,30-MORR.V,1G-
1ph/1pc L

Rooney Ranch,Blacksmith Shop
HABS CO-65-E
HABS COLO,30-MORR.V,1E-
2ph/1pc L

Rooney Ranch,Duplex
HABS CO-65-H
HABS COLO,30-MORR.V,1H-
2ph/1pc L

Rooney Ranch,Garage No. 1
HABS CO-65-F
HABS COLO,30-MORR.V,1F-
3ph/1pc L

Rooney Ranch,Garage No. 2
HABS CO-65-I
HABS COLO,30-MORR.V,1I-
1ph/1pc L

Rooney Ranch,Garage No. 3
HABS CO-65-K
HABS COLO,30-MORR.V,1K-
1ph/1pc L

Rooney Ranch,Granary
HABS CO-65-D
HABS COLO,30-MORR.V,1D-
3ph/1pc L

Rooney Ranch,Inspiration Tree Picnic Area
HABS CO-65-Q
HABS COLO,30-MORR.V,1O-
1ph/1pc L

Rooney Ranch,Main House
HABS CO-65-A
HABS COLO,30-MORR.V,1A-
9ph/1pc L

Rooney Ranch,Rooney,Alex,House
HABS CO-65-O
HABS COLO,30-MORR.V,1N-
2ph/1pc L

Rooney Ranch,Rooney,Eileen,House
HABS CO-65-L
HABS COLO,30-MORR.V,1L-
1ph/1pc L

Rooney Ranch,Rooney,Grandma,House
HABS CO-65-J
HABS COLO,30-MORR.V,1J-
1ph/1pc L

Rooney Ranch,Spring House
HABS CO-65-C
HABS COLO,30-MORR.V,1C-
1ph/1pc L

Rooney Ranch,Vesey,James,House
HABS CO-65-N
HABS COLO,30-MORR.V,1M-
1ph/1pc L

MOUNT VERNON

Steele,Gov. ,House
HABS CO-36-C-1
HABS COLO,30- ,1-
6dr/1pg/fr L

WATERTON VIC.

Denver & Rio Grande Rockwork
East of S. Platte
HAER CO-14
HAER COLO,30-WATER.V,1-
7ph/1pg/1pc L

Keystone Bridge (Mill Gulch Bridge)
Spanning S. Platte River
HAER CO-9
HAER COLO,30-WATER.V,2-
10ph/1pg L

Mill Gulch Bridge; see Keystone Bridge

LA PLATA COUNTY

BONDAD VIC.

Twin Rock Irrigation Ditch (Twin Rocks Ditch)
Westbank of Animas River,East of U.S. Highway 550
HAER CO-68
HAER DLC/PP-1992:CO-5
18ph/18pg/2pc L

Twin Rocks Ditch; see Twin Rock Irrigation Ditch

DURANGO

San Juan & New York Mining &Smelting:Smelter Stack
State Route 160
HAER CO-38
HAER COLO,33-DUR,1A-
8ph/10pg/1pc L

San Juan & New York Smelter,Superintendent's House
State Rt. 160
HAER CO-38-A
HAER COLO,33-DUR,1B-
3ph/9pg/1pc L

TACOMA VIC.

Aspaas Dam (Tacoma Project)
HAER CO-16
HAER COLO,33-TAC.V,2-
13ph/6pg L

Power Flume No. 1 (Tacoma Project)
HAER CO-17
HAER COLO,33-TAC.V,3-
20ph/6pg/2pc L

Tacoma Project; see Aspaas Dam

Tacoma Project; see Power Flume No. 1

Tacoma Project; see Terminal Dam

Terminal Dam (Tacoma Project)
HAER CO-15
HAER COLO,33-TAC.V,4-
22ph/6pg/2pc L

LAKE COUNTY

WATERTON VIC.

Deansbury Bridge
Spanning South Platte River
HAER CO-13
HAER COLO,30-WATER.V,3-
7ph/1pg/1pc L

LARIMER COUNTY

ESTES PARK VIC.

Rocky Mountain National Park; see White,William Allen,Cabins

White,William Allen,Cabins (Rocky Mountain National Park)
HABS CO-63
HABS COLO,35-ESPK.V,2-
6dr L

White,William Allen,Cabins-Lower Sleeping Cabin
HABS CO-63-C
HABS COLO,35-ESPK.V,2C-
1dr L

White,William Allen,Cabins-Main Cabin
HABS CO-63-A
HABS COLO,35-ESPK.V,2A-
2dr L

White,William Allen,Cabins-Upper Sleeping Cabin
HABS CO-63-B
HABS COLO,35-ESPK.V,2B-
1dr L

White,William Allen,Cabins-Work Cabin
HABS CO-63-D
HABS COLO,35-ESPK.V,2D-
1dr L

FORT COLLINS

740 Martinez Street (House)
HABS CO-67
HABS COLO,35-FTCOL,1-
6ph/2pg/1pc L

LAS ANIMAS COUNTY

SEGUNDO

Penitente Morada
HABS CO-58
HABS COLO,36-SEGU.V,1-
2ph L

TIJERAS

Santa Nina de Atoche
Tijeras Plaza
HABS CO-54
HABS COLO,36-TIJER,1-
1ph L

TRINIDAD

Benitez,Frederico,House
612 E. Main St.
HABS CO-55
HABS COLO,36-TRIN,1-
3ph L

Commercial Street Bridge
Spanning Purgatoire River on Commercial St.
HAER CO-53
HAER 1990 (HAER):3
12ph/2pg/1pc L

Linden Avenue Bridge (Main Street Bridge)
Spanning Purgatoire River on Linden Ave.
HAER CO-54
HAER 1990 (HAER):3
14ph/2pg/1pc L

Main Street Bridge; see Linden Avenue Bridge

Trinidad Foundry & Machine Company
Goddard Ave.
HAER CO-6
HAER COLO,36-TRIN,2-
1dr/1ph/29pg/2pc L

Trinidad Foundry & Machine Company,Foundry
Goddard Ave.
HAER CO-6-C
HAER COLO,36-TRIN,2C-
6ph L

Trinidad Foundry & Machine Company,Machine Shop
Goddard Ave.
HAER CO-6-D
HAER COLO,36-TRIN,2D-
4ph/1pc L

Trinidad Foundry & Machine Company,Office
Goddard Ave.
HAER CO-6-A
HAER COLO,36-TRIN,2A-
5ph/1pc L

Trinidad Foundry & Machine Company,Pattern Shop
Goddard Ave.
HAER CO-6-B
HAER COLO,36-TRIN,2B-
5ph/1pc L

WESTON VIC.

Guadaloupe Mission Church
Medina Plaza
HABS CO-57
HABS COLO,36-WEST.V,2-
1ph L

Vigil Plaza,Church
HABS CO-56
HABS COLO,36-WEST.V,1-
4ph L

MESA COUNTY

GRAND JUNCTION

Black Bridge
Spanning Gunnison River
HAER CO-30-G
HAER 1989(HAER):2
8ph/2pg/1pc L

Fifth Street Bridge
U.S. 50 at Colorado River
HAER CO-41
HAER COLO,39-GRAJU,1-
17ph/2pg/1pc L

MONTEZUMA COUNTY

CORTEZ VIC.

Cliff Palace (Mesa Verde National Park)
HABS CO-130
HABS DLC/PP-1992:CO-5
1ph/1pc L

Mesa Verde National Park; see Cliff Palace

DOLORES VIC.

Concrete Diversion Dam; see Montezuma Valley Irrigation Company System

Dolores River Area Survey (Ranches)
HABS CO-35
HABS COLO,42-DOL.V,1-
6dr/24pg/fr L

Earthen Diversion Dam; see Montezuma Valley Irrigation Company System

Gate Keeper's Residence; see Montezuma Valley Irrigation Company System

Gauging Station; see Montezuma Valley Irrigation Company System

Kuhlman-Periman Ranch
County Rt. 28
HABS CO-39
HABS COLO,42-DOL.V,2-
7dr/3ph/14pg/2pc/fr L

Kuhlman-Periman Ranch,Barn
County Rt. 28
HABS CO-39-A
HABS COLO,42-DOL.V,2A-
3dr/3ph/1pc/fr L

Kuhlman-Periman Ranch,Chicken House
HABS CO-39-B
HABS COLO,42-DOL.V,2B-
1dr/4ph/1pc/fr L

Kuhlman-Periman Ranch,Garage
HABS CO-39-D
HABS COLO,42-DOL.V,2D-
1dr/1ph/1pc/fr L

Kuhlman-Periman Ranch,Privy & Hog Shed
County Route 28
HABS CO-39-E
HABS COLO,42-DOL.V,2E-
1dr/1ph/1pc/fr L

Kuhlman-Periman Ranch,Stock Loading Chute
County Route 28
HABS CO-39-F
HABS COLO,42-DOL.V,2F-
1ph/1pc L

Kuhlman-Periman Ranch,Workshop
County Route 28
HABS CO-39-C
HABS COLO,42-DOL.V,2C-
1dr/2ph/1pc/fr L

Lift Gate; see Montezuma Valley Irrigation Company System

McPhee Dam Site; see Montezuma Valley Irrigation Company System

Montezuma Valley Irrigation Company System
HAER CO-4
HAER COLO,42-DOL.V,5-
7ph/24pg/2pc/fr L

Montezuma Valley Irrigation Company System (Concrete Diversion Dam)
HAER CO-4-G
HAER COLO,42-DOL.V,5G-
3ph/1pc L

Montezuma Valley Irrigation Company System (Earthen Diversion Dam)
HAER CO-4-F
HAER COLO,42-DOL.V,5F-
1ph/1pc L

Montezuma Valley Irrigation Company System (Gate Keeper's Residence)
HAER CO-4-H
HAER COLO,42-DOL.V,5H-
3ph/1pc L

Montezuma Valley Irrigation Company System (Gauging Station)
HAER CO-4-C
HAER COLO,42-DOL.V,5C-
1ph/1pc L

Montezuma Valley Irrigation Company System (Lift Gate)
HAER CO-4-E
HAER COLO,42-DOL.V,5E-
2ph/1pc L

Montezuma Valley Irrigation Company System (McPhee Dam Site)
HAER CO-4-I
HAER COLO,42-DOL.V,5I-
5ph/1pc L

Montezuma Valley Irrigation Company System (Tunnel)
HAER CO-4-A
HAER COLO,42-DOL.V,5A-
9ph/1pc L

Montezuma Valley Irrigation Company System (Tunnel Diversion Site)
HAER CO-4-B
HAER COLO,42-DOL.V,5B-
1ph/1pc L

Montezuma Valley Irrigation Company System (Wooden Tainter Gates)
HAER CO-4-D
HAER COLO,42-DOL.V,5D-
2ph/1pc L

Reynolds Ranch
County Rt. 27
HABS CO-37
HABS COLO,42-DOL.V,3-
4dr/9ph/5pg/1pc/fr L

Ritter Ranch
Old Dolores Hwy.
HABS CO-38
HABS COLO,42-DOL.V,4-
6dr/3ph/15pg/1pc/fr L

Ritter Ranch,Barn
HABS CO-38-A
HABS COLO,42-DOL.V,4A-
3dr/16ph/1pc/fr L

Ritter Ranch,Bunk House
HABS CO-38-J
HABS COLO,42-DOL.V,4J-
1ph/1pc/fr L

Ritter Ranch,Chicken House
HABS CO-38-D
HABS COLO,42-DOL.V,4D-
2ph/1pc/fr L

Ritter Ranch,Garage
HABS CO-38-H
HABS COLO,42-DOL.V,4H-
2ph/1pc/fr L

Ritter Ranch,Guest House
HABS CO-38-B
HABS COLO,42-DOL.V,4B-
1dr/2ph/1pc/fr L

Ritter Ranch,Implement Shed
HABS CO-38-E
HABS COLO,42-DOL.V,4E-
1ph/1pc/fr L

Ritter Ranch,Potato Shed
HABS CO-38-C
HABS COLO,42-DOL.V,4C-
1dr/4ph/2pc/fr L

Ritter Ranch,Privy
HABS CO-38-G
HABS COLO,42-DOL.V,4G-
1ph/1pc/fr L

Ritter Ranch,Smokehouse
HABS CO-38-F
HABS COLO,42-DOL.V,4F-
1ph/1pc/fr L

Ritter Ranch,Storage Shed
HABS CO-38-I
HABS COLO,42-DOL.V,4I-
1ph/1pc/fr L

Tunnel; see Montezuma Valley Irrigation Company System

Tunnel Diversion Site; see Montezuma Valley Irrigation Company System

Wooden Tainter Gates; see Montezuma Valley Irrigation Company System

MCPHEE

McPhee,Town of
McPhee Rd
HABS CO-36
HABS COLO,42-MCPHE,1-
1dr/13ph/35pg/1pc/fr L

MESA VERDE N. P.

Nusbaum,Aileen,Hospital; see Spruce Tree Terrace

Spruce Tree Terrace (Nusbaum,Aileen,Hospital)
Chapin Mesa
HABS CO-71
HABS COLO,42-MEVPK,2-
14ph/1pg/1pc L

OTERO COUNTY

LA JUNTA

Rizzuto Building; see Woodruff Block

Woodruff Block (Rizzuto Building)
22-24 W. First St.
HABS CO-75
HABS COLO,45-LAJUN,1-
11ph/1pg/1pc L

SWINK VIC.

Swink Bridge
Spanning Arkansas River (County Rd. 24.5)
HAER CO-37
HAER COLO,45-SWINK.V,1-
12ph/2pg/1pc L

PITKIN COUNTY

ASPEN

Aspen Lumber Company Building
100 W. Cooper St.
HABS CO-61
HABS COLO,49-ASP,2- ı1991(HABS):18°
5dr/12ph/4pg/1pc/fr L

PUEBLO COUNTY

BOONE VIC.

Nepesta Bridge
Spanning Arkansas River on County Rd. 613
HAER CO-55
HAER 1990 (HAER):3
10ph/2pg/1pc L

PUEBLO VIC.

Pueblo Depot Activity
15 Miles east of Pueblo
HAER CO-22
HAER COLO,51-PUEB.V,1-
57pg/fr L

RIO BLANCO COUNTY

RANGELY VIC.

Uintah Railway,Whiskey Creek Trestle (Whiskey Creek Trestle)
Baxter Pass Rd. & Whiskey Creek Rd.
HAER CO-10
HAER COLO,52-RANGY.V,2-
4ph/9pg/1pc L

Whiskey Creek Trestle; see Uintah Railway,Whiskey Creek Trestle

RIO GRANDE COUNTY

DEL NORTE VIC.

State Bridge
Spanning Rio Grande River
HAER CO-36
HAER COLO,53-DELN.V,1-
14ph/2pg/1pc L

ROUTT COUNTY

STEAMBOAT SPRINGS VI

Bridge over Elk River; see Four Mile Bridge

Four Mile Bridge (Bridge over Elk River)
Spanning Elk River on County Rd. 42
HAER CO-60
HAER 1989(HAER):2
11ph/2pg/1pc L

SAN JUAN COUNTY

SILVERTON

Art Emporium; see Silverton Historic District

Blacksmith Shop; see Silverton Historic District

City Hall; see Silverton Historic District

Courthouse; see Silverton Historic District

E. Thirteenth & Green Sts. (Commercial Building); see Silverton Historic District

False Front Structure; see Silverton Historic District

Gingerbread House; see Silverton Historic District

Grand Imperial Hotel; see Silverton Historic District

815 Green St. (House); see Silverton Historic District

964 Green St. (House); see Silverton Historic District

Hardware Store; see Silverton Historic District

House; see Silverton Historic District

Jail; see Silverton Historic District

Livery; see Silverton Historic District

Masonic Lodge; see Silverton Historic District

Pickle Barrel Restaurant; see Silverton Historic District

1067 Reese St. (House); see Silverton Historic District

Saloon Museum; see Silverton Historic District

Silverton & Northern Passenger Station; see Silverton Historic District

Silverton Historic District
HABS CO-53
HABS COLO,56-SILTN,1-
21ph/1pg/2pc/fr L

Silverton Historic District (Art Emporium)
1228 Green St.
HABS CO-53-E
HABS COLO,56-SILTN,6-
1ph/1pc L

Silverton Historic District (Blacksmith Shop)
Blair St.
HABS CO-53-T
HABS COLO,56-SILTN,21-
1ph/1pc L

Silverton Historic District (City Hall)
E. Fourteenth & Green Sts.
HABS CO-53-J
HABS COLO,56-SILTN,11-
2ph/1pc L

Silverton Historic District (Courthouse)
W. Fifteenth & Green Sts.
HABS CO-53-L
HABS COLO,56-SILTN,13-
1ph/1pc L

Silverton Historic District (E. Thirteenth & Green Sts. (Commercial Building))
E. Thirteenh & Green Sts.
HABS CO-53-H
HABS COLO,56-SILTN,9-
1ph/1pc L

Silverton Historic District (False Front Structure)
W. Fourteenth St.
HABS CO-53-Q
HABS COLO,56-SILTN,18-
1ph/1pc L

Silverton Historic District (Gingerbread House)
Snowden St.
HABS CO-53-P
HABS COLO,56-SILTN,17-
1ph/1pc L

Silverton Historic District (Grand Imperial Hotel)
W. Twelfth & Green Sts.
HABS CO-53-D
HABS COLO,56-SILTN,5-
2ph/1pc L

Silverton Historic District (815 Green St. (House))
HABS CO-53-A
HABS COLO,56-SILTN,2-
1ph/1pc L

Silverton Historic District (964 Green St. (House))
964 Green St.
HABS CO-53-B
HABS COLO,56-SILTN,3-
1ph/1pc L

Silverton Historic District (Hardware Store)
1321 Blair St.
HABS CO-53-S
HABS COLO,56-SILTN,20-
1ph/1pc L

Silverton Historic District (House)
Rt. 110
HABS CO-53-V
HABS COLO,56-SILTN,23-
1ph/1pc L

Silverton Historic District (Jail)
W. Fifteenth & Green Sts.
HABS CO-53-K
HABS COLO,56-SILTN,12-
1ph/1pc L

Silverton Historic District (Livery)
HABS CO-53-F
HABS COLO,56-SILTN,7-
1ph/1pc L

Silverton Historic District (Masonic Lodge)
W. Thirteenth & Reese Sts.
HABS CO-53-O
HABS COLO,56-SILTN,16-
1ph/1pc L

Silverton Historic District (Pickle Barrel Restaurant)
E. Thirteenth & Green Sts.
HABS CO-53-G
HABS COLO,56-SILTN,8-
2ph/1pc L

Silverton Historic District (1067 Reese St. (House))
HABS CO-53-M
HABS COLO,56-SILTN,14-
1ph/1pc L

Silverton Historic District (Saloon Museum)
Blair St.
HABS CO-53-U
HABS COLO,56-SILTN,22-
1ph/1pc L

Silverton Historic District (Silverton & Northern Passenger Station)
HABS CO-53-W
HABS COLO,56-SILTN,24-
2ph/1pc L

Silverton Historic District (Stable)
Blair St.
HABS CO-53-R
HABS COLO,56-SILTN,19-
1ph/1pc L

Silverton Historic District (Two-Entry Livery)
1112 E. Green St.
HABS CO-53-C
HABS COLO,56-SILTN,4-
1ph/1pc L

Silverton Historic District (United Church of Silverton)
Eleventh & Reese Sts.
HABS CO-53-N
HABS COLO,56-SILTN,15-
2ph/1pc L

Silverton Historic District (Wyman Block)
W. Fourteenth & Green Sts.
HABS CO-53-I
HABS COLO,56-SILTN,10-
1ph/1pc L

Stable; see Silverton Historic District

Two-Entry Livery; see Silverton Historic District

United Church of Silverton; see Silverton Historic District

Wyman Block; see Silverton Historic District

SAN MIGUEL COUNTY

AMES VIC.

Ames Hydroelectric Plant (Telluride Power Company,Power Station)
HAER CO-2
HAER COLO,57-AMES.V,2A-
10ph/1pg/1pc/fr L

Telluride Power Company,Power Station; see Ames Hydroelectric Plant

SUMMIT COUNTY

KOKOMO

Masonic Temple
HABS CO-21
HABS COLO,59-KOKO,1-
1ph L

WELD COUNTY

GREELEY

Lincoln Schools (Structure Number 2)
Eleventh St. & Fourth Ave.
HABS CO-32
HABS COLO,62-GREEL,1A-
9ph/2pg/1pc L

First Church of Christ, Congregational (Meetinghouse), Farmington, Hartford County, Connecticut. Exterior view. Photograph by Jack E. Boucher, 1976 (HABS CONN,2-FARM,2-8)

Connecticut

FAIRFIELD COUNTY

Merritt Parkway,(S.bound) Maintenance Garage
Abutting N. side of Merritt Pkwy.
HAER CT-135
HAER DLC/PP-1993:CT-5
4ph/4pg/1pc/fr L

BRIDGEPORT

Armstrong Mill Historic District
(3-31/2 Armstrong Place (House))
HABS CT-344
HABS CONN,1-BRIGPO,3-
3ph/1pc/fr L

3-31/2 Armstrong Place (House); see Armstrong Mill Historic District

Barna House; see Knapp,George S. ,House

Engine House No. 5
274 Middle St.
HABS CT-360
HABS CONN,1-BRIGPO,4-
9ph/2pg/1pc L

Knapp,George S. ,House (Barna House)
2414 North Ave.
HABS CT-343
HABS CONN,1-BRIGPO,2-
11ph/1pc L

Victorian Cottage
Boston Post Rd.
HABS CT-106
HABS CONN,1-BRIGPO,1-
1ph/1pg L

COS COB

Bush-Holley House
39 Strickland Rd.
HABS CT-279
HABS CONN,1-COSCOB,1
18dr/17ph/11pg L

DANBURY

Patch Street Bridge
Spanning Kohanza Brook on Patch St.
HAER CT-30
HAER CONN,1-DA,2-
20ph/20pg/2pc L

DARIEN

Clock-Turner House
1830 Boston Post Rd.
HABS CT-17
HABS CONN,1-DAR,2-
8dr/2ph/2pg L

Hubbard House; see Parsons,Lt. William,House

Mather,Deacon Joseph,House; see Mather,Stephen Tyng,House

Mather,Stephen Tyng,House
(Mather,Deacon Joseph,House)
19 Stephen Mather Rd.
HABS CT-289
HABS CONN,1-DAR,3-
18ph/9pg L

Parsons,Lt. William,House (Hubbard House)
(See MA,HAMPSHIRE CO.,NORTHAMPTON for documentn.)
HABS MA-188
L

EASTON

Dillon,Jane,House
Rock House Rd.
HABS CT-73
HABS CONN,1-EATO,2-
11dr/7ph/3pg L

Trup,Rudolph,House
Rock House Rd.
HABS CT-72
HABS CONN,1-EATO,1-
14dr/2ph/2pg L

FAIRFIELD

Bronson,Frederic,Windmill
3015 Bronson Rd.
HABS CT-325
HABS CONN,1-FAIRF,14-
2dr/11ph/1pg/1pc L

Burr,Thaddeus,Homestead
491 Old Post Rd.
HABS CT-3-17
HABS CONN,1-FAIRF,1-
12dr/5ph/5pg L

Congregational Parsonage; see Sherman,Judge Roger M. ,House

Fairfield Academy,Old
Boston Post Rd.
HABS CT-28
HABS CONN,1-FAIRF,2-
9dr/5ph/3pg L

Grasmere Avenue Bridge
Spanning Railroad at Grasmere Ave.
HAER CT-15
HAER CONN,1-FAIRF,13-
11ph/1pc L

Merritt Parkway,(N.bound) Fairfield Service Statn.
Abutting S. side of Merritt Pkwy.
HAER CT-136
HAER DLC/PP-1993:CT-5
3ph/2pg/1pc/fr L

Merritt Parkway,(S.bound) Fairfield Service Statn.
Abbutting N. side of Merritt Pkwy.
HAER CT-137
HAER DLC/PP-1993:CT-5
2ph/2pg/1pc/fr L

Merritt Parkway,Black Rock Trnpk./Rt. 58 Bridge
Spanning Black Rock Trnpk.
HAER CT-111
HAER DLC/PP-1993:CT-5
2ph/6pg/1pc/fr L

Merritt Parkway,Bridge No. 744 (Sport Hill Road Bridge)
Spanning Merritt Pkwy. at Rt. 59
HAER CT-55
HAER DLC/PP-1993:CT-5
17ph/10pg/3pc/fr L

Merritt Parkway,Burr Street Bridge
Spanning Merritt Pkwy.
HAER CT-110
HAER DLC/PP-1993:CT-5
4ph/6pg/1pc/fr L

Merritt Parkway,Congress Street Bridge
Spanning Merritt Pkwy.
HAER CT-108
HAER DLC/PP-1993:CT-5
2ph/6pg/1pc/fr L

Merritt Parkway,Cricker Brook Culvert
Spanning Cricker Brook
HAER CT-112
HAER DLC/PP-1993:CT-5
5pg/fr L

Merritt Parkway,Cross Highway Bridge
Spanning Cross Hwy.
HAER CT-105
HAER LC/PP-1993:CT-5
1ph/7pg/1pc/fr L

Merritt Parkway,Hillside Road Bridge
Spanning Hillside Rd.
HAER CT-109
HAER DLC/PP-1993:CT-5
2ph/6pg/1pc/fr L

Merritt Parkway,Merwins Lane Bridge
HAER CT-106
HAER DLC/PP-1993:CT-5
5ph/7pg/1pc/fr L

Merritt Parkway,Mill River Bridge
Spanning Mill River
HAER CT-114
HAER DLC/PP-1993:CT-5
6pg/fr L

Merritt Parkway,Morehouse Highway Bridge
Spanning Merritt Pkwy.
HAER CT-113
HAER DLC/PP-1993:CT-5
1ph/7pg/1pc/fr L

Merritt Parkway,Redding Road Bridge
Spanning Merritt Pkwy.
HAER CT-107
HAER DLC/PP-1993:CT-5
4ph/7pg/1pc/fr L

Ogden,David,House
1520 Bronson Rd.
HABS CT-56
HABS CONN,1-FAIRF,10-
10dr/18ph/3pg L

Powder House
Center St.
HABS CT-40
HABS CONN,1-FAIRF,3-
1dr/1ph/2pg L

Sherman,Judge Roger M. ,House (Congregational Parsonage)
500 Old Post Rd.
HABS CT-60
HABS CONN,1-FAIRF,4-
13dr/5ph/4pg L

Sherwood,Hull,House
762 Mill Hill Rd.
HABS CT-58
HABS CONN,1-FAIRF,8-
11dr/16ph/3pg L

Sport Hill Road Bridge; see Merritt Parkway,Bridge No. 744

Sturges,Benjamin,House (Trubee-Knapp House)
Rowland Rd.
HABS CT-54
HABS CONN,1-FAIRF,9-
9dr/7ph/3pg L

Trubee-Knapp House; see Sturges,Benjamin,House

GREENWICH

Mead,Abraham D. ,House (Oliver D. Mead,House)
Field Pt. Park Vic.
HABS CT-38
HABS CONN,1-GREWI.V,1-
8dr/4ph/3pg L

Merritt Parkway
HAER CT-63
HAER DLC/PP-1993:CT-5
21dr/119ph/159pg/8pc/fr L

Merritt Parkway,East Branch Byram River Bridge
Spanning E. branch of Byram River
HAER CT-67
HAER DLC/PP-1993:CT-5
5pg/fr L

Merritt Parkway,Glenville Water Co. & Brook Bridge
Spanning Glenville Water Co. & brook
HAER CT-66
HAER DLC/PP-1993:CT-5
1ph/6pg/1pc/fr L

Merritt Parkway,Greenwich (N.bound) Service Statn.
Abutting S. side of Merritt Pkwy.
HAER CT-131
HAER DLC/PP-1993:CT-5
2ph/2pg/1pc/fr L

Merritt Parkway,Greenwich (S.bound) Service Statn.
Abutting N. side of Merritt Pkwy.
HAER CT-132
HAER DLC/PP-1993:CT-5
2ph/2pg/1pc L

Merritt Parkway,Lake Avenue Bridge
Spanning Merritt Pkwy.
HAER CT-69
HAER DLC/PP-1993:CT-5
5ph/7pg/1pc/fr L

Merritt Parkway,North Street Bridge
Spanning Merritt Pkwy.
HAER CT-70
HAER DLC/PP-1993:CT-5
2ph/6pg/1pc/fr L

Merritt Parkway,Riversville Rd. (E. Branch) Bridge
Spanning Riversville Rd. & E. branch of Byram Riv.
HAER CT-65
HAER DLC/PP-1993:CT-5
1ph/6pg/1pc/fr L

Merritt Parkway,Round Hill Road Bridge
Spanning Merritt Pkwy.
HAER CT-68
HAER DLC/PP-1993:CT-5
4ph/6pg/1pc/fr L

Merritt Parkway,Stanwich Road Bridge
Spanning Merritt Pkwy.
HAER CT-72
HAER DLC/PP-1993:CT-5
5ph/6pg/1pc/fr L

Merritt Parkway,Taconic Road Bridge
Spanning Taconic Rd.
HAER CT-71
HAER DLC/PP-1993:CT-5
2ph/6pg/1pc/fr L

Merritt Parkway,West Branch Byram River Bridge
Spanning W. branch of Byram River
HAER CT-64
HAER DLC/PP-1993:CT-5
2ph/5pg/1pc/fr L

Oliver D. Mead,House; see Mead,Abraham D. ,House

Riverside Avenue Bridge
Riverside Ave. over NE Corridor RR right-of-way
HAER CT-13
HAER CONN,1-GREWI,1-
11ph/2pg/1pc/2ct L

NEW CANAAN

Merritt Parkway,(N.bound) New Canaan Service Sta.
Abutting S. side of Merritt Pkwy.
HAER CT-133
HAER DLC/PP-1993:CT-5
1ph/2pg/1pc/fr L

Merritt Parkway,(S.bound) New Canaan Service Sta.
Abutting N. side of Merritt Pkwy.
HAER CT-134
HAER DLC/PP-1993:CT-5
1ph/2pg/1pc/fr L

Merritt Parkway,Bridge No. 711; see Merritt Parkway,Lapham Avenue Bridge

Merritt Parkway,Darien Road/Rt. 29 Bridge; see Merritt Parkway,South Avenue/Rt. 124 Bridge

Merritt Parkway,Lapham Avenue Bridge (Merritt Parkway,Bridge No. 711)
Spanning Merritt Pkwy. at St. Rt. 165
HAER CT-38
HAER DLC/PP-1993:CT-5
16ph/7pg/2pc/fr L

Merritt Parkway,Marvin River Road Bridge (Merritt Parkway,Weed Avenue Bridge)
Spanning Merritt Pkwy.
HAER CT-86
HAER DLC/PP-1993:CT-5
2ph/6pg/1pc/fr L

Merritt Parkway,Metro North Railroad Bridge (Merritt Parkway,NY,New Haven & Harford RR Bridge)
Spanning Merritt Pkwy.
HAER CT-83
HAER DLC/PP-1993:CT-5
3ph/6pg/1pc/fr L

Merritt Parkway,NY,New Haven & Harford RR Bridge; see Merritt Parkway,Metro North Railroad Bridge

Merritt Parkway,Old Stamford Rd./Rt. 106 Bridge (Merritt Parkway,Stamford Avenue Bridge)
Spanning Old Stamford Rd./Rt. 106
HAER CT-82
HAER DLC/PP-1993:CT-5
6pg/fr L

Merritt Parkway,Ponus Ridge Road Bridge
Spanning Merritt Pkwy.
HAER CT-81
HAER DLC/PP-1993:CT-5
2ph/6pg/1pc/fr L

Merritt Parkway,South Avenue/Rt. 124 Bridge (Merritt Parkway,Darien Road/Rt. 29 Bridge)
Spanning Merritt Pkwy.
HAER CT-84
HAER DLC/PP-1993:CT-5
4ph/6pg/1pc/fr L

Merritt Parkway,Stamford Avenue Bridge; see Merritt Parkway,Old Stamford Rd./Rt. 106 Bridge

Merritt Parkway,Weed Avenue Bridge; see Merritt Parkway,Marvin River Road Bridge

Merritt Parkway,White Oak Shade Road Bridge
Spanning Merritt Pkwy.
HAER CT-85
HAER DLC/PP-1993:CT-5
6ph/7pg/1pc/fr L

Rogers,John,Studio
10 Cherry St.
HABS CT-351
HABS CONN,1-NECA,1-
5ph/1pg/1pc L

NEW CANAAN VIC.

Fauntleroy House
Ponus Ridge
HABS CT-43
HABS CONN,1-NECA.V,1-
9dr/2ph/2pg L

NORTH GREENWICH

Field-Carpenter House
Old Bedford Rd.
HABS CT-352
HABS CONN,1-GREWIN,1-
6dr/10pg/fr L

NORWALK

Lockwood-Mathews House
Veterans' Memorial Park, SE
HABS CT-265
HABS CONN,1-NOWA,2-
36ph/16pg/1pc/fr L

Merritt Parkway,Chestnut Hill Road/Route 53 Bridge
Spanning Chestnut Hill Rd./Rt.53
HAER CT-97
HAER DLC/PP-1993:CT-5
1ph/5pg/1pc/fr L

Merritt Parkway,Comstock Hill Road Bridge
Spanning Merritt Pkwy.
HAER CT-88
HAER DLC/PP-1993:CT-5
6ph/6pg/1pc/fr L

Merritt Parkway,East Rocks Road Bridge
Spanning Merritt Pkwy.
HAER CT-95
HAER DLC/PP-1993:CT-5
2ph/6pg/1pc/fr L

Merritt Parkway,Grumman Avenue Bridge
Spanning Merritt Pkwy.
HAER CT-96
HAER DLC/PP-1993:CT-5
6ph/6pg/1pc/fr L

Merritt Parkway,Main Avenue/Route 7 Bridge
Spanning Main Ave./Rt. 7
HAER CT-93
HAER DLC/PP-1993:CT-5
2ph/6pg/1pc/fr L

Merritt Parkway,Metro North Railroad Bridge (Merritt Parkway,Winnipank Railroad Bridge)
Spanning Metro North Railroad
HAER CT-91
HAER DLC/PP-1993:CT-5
1ph/5pg/1pc/fr L

Merritt Parkway,New Canaan Road/Route 123 Bridge
Spanning New Canaan Rd./Rt. 123
HAER CT-87
HAER DLC/PP-1993:CT-5
3ph/6pg/1pc/fr L

Merritt Parkway,Norwalk River Bridge
Spanning Norwalk River
HAER CT-92
HAER DLC/PP-1993:CT-5
1ph/5pg/1pc/fr L

Merritt Parkway,Perry Avenue Bridge
Spanning Perry Ave.
HAER CT-90
HAER DLC/PP-1993:CT-5
1ph/5pg/1pc/fr L

Merritt Parkway,Silvermine Avenue Bridge
Spanning Silvermine Ave.
HAER CT-89
HAER DLC/PP-1993:CT-5
2ph/6pg/1pc/fr L

Merritt Parkway,Silvermine River Bridge
Spanning Silvermine River
HAER CT-121
HAER DLC/PP-1993:CT-5
5pg/fr L

Merritt Parkway,West Rocks Road Bridge
Spanning Merritt Pkwy.
HAER CT-94
HAER DLC/PP-1993:CT-5
3ph/6pg/1pc/fr L

Merritt Parkway,Winnipank Railroad Bridge; see Merritt Parkway,Metro North Railroad Bridge

Sherman,Taylor,House
89 Main St.
HABS CT-77
HABS CONN,1-NOWA,1-
13dr/4ph/2pg/fr L

REDDING

Bartlett,Rev. Nathaniel,Parsonage; see Sanford,Jonathan B. ,House

Sanford,Jonathan B. ,House
(Bartlett,Rev. Nathaniel,Parsonage)
Georgetown Rd.
HABS CT-74
HABS CONN,1-RED,1-
12dr/4ph/3pg/fr L

RIDGEFIELD

Hawley,Rev. Thomas,House
Main St. & Branchville Rd.
HABS CT-46
HABS CONN,1-RIDG,2-
9dr/2ph L

Remington,Frederick,House
HABS CT-353
HABS CONN,1-RIDG,3-
5ph/1pc L

SILVERMINE

Buttery Sawmill
Silvermine Brook
HABS CT-63
HABS CONN,1-SILM,1-
8dr/4ph/3pg L

SOUTH NORWALK

South Main Street,Block 43 (Commercial Buildings)
S. Main & Washington Sts.
HABS CT-349
HABS CONN,1-NOWAS,1-
6dr/13ph/1pc/fr L

SOUTHPORT

Bulkley,Capt. Ward,House
298 Harbor Rd.
HABS CT-330
HABS CONN,1-SOUPO,32-
1ph L

Bulkley,Moses,House
176 Main St.
HABS CT-299
HABS CONN,1-SOUPO,12-
3ph/4pg L

Bulkley,William,House
824 Harbor Rd.
HABS CT-309
HABS CONN,1-SOUPO,20-
4ph/5pg L

Connecticut Bank,Mill River Branch
227 Main St.
HABS CT-319
HABS CONN,1-SOUPO,27-
3ph/6pg/fr L

Jelliff,C. O. ,Company
354 Pequot Rd.
HABS CT-291
HABS CONN,1-SOUPO,5-
1ph/3pg L

Jelliff,Francis,House
212 Center St.
HABS CT-290
HABS CONN,1-SOUPO,4-
5dr/10ph L

Jennings,Nehemiah,Block
668-70 Main St.
HABS CT-294
HABS CONN,1-SOUPO,7-
1ph L

Meeker,Wakeman B. ,House
25 Westway Rd.
HABS CT-318
HABS CONN,1-SOUPO,40-
6ph/5pg L

New York,New Haven & Hartford RR Freight House
Station St.
HABS CT-292
HABS CONN,1-SOUPO,6-
2ph L

New York,New Haven & Hartford RR Station
Railroad Pl.
HABS CT-293
HABS CONN,1-SOUPO,41-
5ph/4pg L

Nichols,Allen,House
494 Harbor Rd.
HABS CT-336
HABS CONN,1-SOUPO,37-
1ph L

Osborn,John,House
Kings Highway
HABS CT-20
HABS CONN,1-SOUPO,1-
8dr/4ph/2pg L

Pequot Library
720 Pequot Rd.
HABS CT-314
HABS CONN,1-SOUPO,23-
3dr/13ph/11pg L

Pequot School
214 Main St.
HABS CT-320
HABS CONN,1-SOUPO,28-
1ph/3pg L

Perry,Austin,House
712 Harbor Rd.
HABS CT-300
HABS CONN,1-SOUPO,15-
4ph/6pg L

Perry,Charles,House
564 Harbor Rd.
HABS CT-306
HABS CONN,1-SOUPO,18-
4ph/8pg L

Perry,Francis D. ,House (Trinity Church Rectory)
678 Pequot Rd.
HABS CT-317
HABS CONN,1-SOUPO,26-
8ph/5pg/fr L

Perry,Gurdon,House
780 Harbor Rd.
HABS CT-328
HABS CONN,1-SOUPO,31-
7ph L

Perry,Henry,House
45 Westway Rd.
HABS CT-305
HABS CONN,1-SOUPO,17-
4ph/5pg L

Perry,John Hoyt,House
134 Center St.
HABS CT-334
HABS CONN,1-SOUPO,35-
2ph L

Perry,Oliver H. ,House
750 Harbor Rd.
HABS CT-302
HABS CONN,1-SOUPO,14-
7ph/7pg L

Pike,Julius,House
62 Center St.
HABS CT-337
HABS CONN,1-SOUPO,38-
9ph L

Pomeroy,Benjamin,Carriage House
658 Pequot Rd.
HABS CT-310
HABS CONN,1-SOUPO,11A-
1ph/3pg L

Pomeroy,Benjamin,House
658 Pequot Rd.
HABS CT-298
HABS CONN,1-SOUPO,11-
9ph/6pg L

Sheffield,Paschal,House
104 Old South Rd.
HABS CT-303
HABS CONN,1-SOUPO,16-
7ph/4pg L

Sherwood-Banks House
98 Banks Pl.
HABS CT-316
HABS CONN,1-SOUPO,25-
8ph/fr L

Sherwood,Oliver T. ,House
683 Pequot Rd.
HABS CT-295
HABS CONN,1-SOUPO,8-
2ph/6pg L

Sherwood,Simon C. ,House
67 Westway Rd.
HABS CT-296
HABS CONN,1-SOUPO,9-
2ph/6pg L

Southport Congregational Church
523 Pequot Rd.
HABS CT-311
HABS CONN,1-SOUPO,21-
5ph/7pg L

Southport Harbor,Mill River
Southport Harbor
HABS CT-331
HABS CONN,1-SOUPO,33-
6ph L

Southport Savings Bank
226 Main St.
HABS CT-315
HABS CONN,1-SOUPO,24-
6dr/8ph/17pg/fr L

46 Station Street (House)
HABS CT-327
HABS CONN,1-SOUPO,30-
1ph L

Sturges,Barnabas,House
534 Harbor Rd.
HABS CT-332
HABS CONN,1-SOUPO,34-
2ph L

Sturges,Henry,House
608 Harbor Rd.
HABS CT-335
HABS CONN,1-SOUPO,36-
5ph L

Thorp,Capt. Walter,House
198 Oxford Rd.
HABS CT-307
HABS CONN,1-SOUPO,19-
1ph/5pg L

Trinity Church (P. E.)
651 Pequot Rd.
HABS CT-312
HABS CONN,1-SOUPO,22-
9dr/58ph/26pg/fr L

Trinity Church Rectory; see
Perry,Francis D. ,House

Trinity Parish Chapel (P. E.)
651 Pequot Rd.
HABS CT-313
HABS CONN,1-SOUPO,22A-
2dr/5ph/7pg/fr L

Wakeman Memorial
648 Harbor Rd.
HABS CT-321
HABS CONN,1-SOUPO,29-
1ph/3pg L

Wakeman,Capt. William Webb,House
478 Harbor Rd.(formerly 137 Rose Hill Rd.)
HABS CT-301
HABS CONN,1-SOUPO,13-
12ph/6pg L

Wakeman,Zalmon,House
418 Harbor Rd.
HABS CT-297
HABS CONN,1-SOUPO,10-
9ph/6pg L

Waugh House
249 Old South Rd.
HABS CT-338
HABS CONN,1-SOUPO,39-
5ph L

STAMFORD

Knap,Samuel,House
Oxen Walk,984 Stillwater Rd.
HABS CT-354
HABS CONN,1-STAMF,4-
6ph/1pg/1pc L

Merritt Parkway,Guinea Road Bridge
(Merritt Parkway,Rocky Craig Road Bridge)
Spanning Merritt Pkwy.
HAER CT-73
HAER DLC/PP-1993:CT-5
4ph/5pg/1pc/fr L

Merritt Parkway,High Ridge Road/Route 137 Bridge
Spanning High Ridge Rd./Rt. 137
HAER CT-79
HAER DLC/PP-1993:CT-5
2ph/6pg/1pc/fr L

Merritt Parkway,Long Ridge Road/Route 104 Bridge
Spanning Long Ridge Rd./Rt. 104
HAER CT-76
HAER DLC/PP-1993:CT-5
1ph/5pg/1pc/fr L

Merritt Parkway,Mianus River Culvert
Spanning Mianus River
HAER CT-74
HAER DLC/PP-1993:CT-5
5pg/fr L

Merritt Parkway,Newfield Avenue Bridge
Spanning Merritt Pkwy.
HAER CT-80
HAER DLC/PP-1993:CT-5
3ph/5pg/1pc/fr L

Merritt Parkway,Rippowam River Bridge
Spanning Rippowam River
HAER CT-78
HAER DLC/PP-1993:CT-5
3ph/5pg/1pc/fr L

Merritt Parkway,Riverbank Road Bridge
Spanning Merritt Pkwy.
HAER CT-75
HAER DLC/PP-1993:CT-5
2ph/6pg/1pc/fr L

Merritt Parkway,Rocky Craig Road Bridge; see Merritt Parkway,Guinea Road Bridge

Merritt Parkway,Wire Mille Road Bridge
Spanning Merritt Pkwy.
HAER CT-77
HAER DLC/PP-1993:CT-5
4ph/5pg/1pc/fr L

New York,New Haven & Hartford RR,Stamford Station (Stamford Station)
44 Station Place
HAER CT-9
HAER CONN,1-STAMF,1-
15ph/24pg/1pc L

New York,New Haven & Hartford RR:Auto.Signaliz.Sys (NY,NH & Hartford RR:Automatic Signalization System
Long Is. Sound shoreline btwn Stamford & New Haven
HAER CT-8
HAER CONN,1-STAMF,2-
45ph/29pg/3pc L

NY,NH & Hartford RR:Automatic Signalization System; see New York,New Haven & Hartford RR:Auto.Signaliz.Sys

Stamford Station; see New York,New Haven & Hartford RR,Stamford Station

Stamford Street Railroad,Trolley Barn & Office
35 Station Place
HAER CT-10
HAER CONN,1-STAMF,3-
5ph/23pg/1pc L

STANWICH VIC.

Blockhouse; see Stone House

Ingersoll House; see Stone House

Stone House (Ingersoll House; Blockhouse)
Farms Rd.
HABS CT-37
HABS CONN,1-STAN.V,1-
9dr/4ph L

STRATFORD

Christ Church
Main St.
HABS CT-355
HABS CONN,1-STRAT,18-
11ph/1pc L

Cranston House; see McEwen House

Curtis,Freeman L. ,House
3355 Main St.
HABS CT-12
HABS CONN,1-STRAT,2-
7dr/6ph/2pg L

McEwen House (Cranston House)
HABS CT-215
HABS CONN,1-STRAT,5-
1ph L

Merritt Parkway,Cutspring Road Bridge
Spanning Cutspring Rd.
HAER CT-127
HAER DLC/PP-1993:CT-5
1ph/6pg/1pc/fr L

Merritt Parkway,Huntington Road Bridge
HAER CT-126
HAER DLC/PP-1993:CT-5
1ph/6pg/1pc/fr L

Merritt Parkway,James Farm Road Bridge
Spanning Merritt Pkwy.
HAER CT-129
HAER DLC/PP-1993:CT-5
4ph/6pg/1pc/fr L

Merritt Parkway,Main Street/Route 110 Bridge
Spanning Main St./Rt. 110
HAER CT-130
HAER DLC/PP-1993:CT-5
4ph/6pg/1pc/fr L

Merritt Parkway,Pumpkin Brook Culvert
Spanning Pumpkin Brook
HAER CT-128
HAER DLC/PP-1993:CT-5
5pg/fr L

Merritt Parkway,Toll Booth
Boothe Memorial Park
HAER CT-138
HAER DLC/PP-1993:CT-5
1ph/1pc/fr L

Moses-Wheeler House
East Main St.
HABS CT-239
HABS CONN,1-STRAT,16-
5dr/fr L

Perry-Fairchild Homestead
1128 W. Broad St.
HABS CT-65
HABS CONN,1-STRAT,4-
9dr/4ph/2pg/fr L

Plant House,Old
HABS CT-216
HABS CONN,1-STRAT,6-
2ph L

Stratford Army Engine Plant
550 South Main St.
HAER CT-14
HAER CONN,1-STRAT,17-
59pg/fr L

Walker,Gen. Joseph,House
2175 Elm St.
HABS CT-66
HABS CONN,1-STRAT,1-
10dr/7ph/6pg L

TRUMBULL

Kaatz Icehouse
255 Whitney Ave.
HAER CT-6
HAER CONN,1-TRUM,2-
12ph/2pg/1pc/fr L

Merritt Parkway,Frenchtown Road Bridge
Spanning Merritt Pkwy.
HAER CT-119
HAER DLC/PP-1993:CT-5
4ph/6pg/1pc/fr L

Merritt Parkway,Huntington Turnpike/Rt. 108 Bridge
Spanning Merritt Pakwy.
HAER CT-124
HAER DLC/PP-1993:CT-5
6pg/fr L

Merritt Parkway,Madison Avenue Bridge
Spanning Merritt Pkwy.
HAER CT-117
HAER DLC/PP-1993:CT-5
3ph/6pg/1pc/fr L

Merritt Parkway,Main Street/Route 25 Bridge
Spanning Merritt Pkwy.
HAER CT-118
HAER DLC/PP-1993:CT-5
3ph/5pg/1pc/fr L

Merritt Parkway,Nichols-Shelton Road Bridge
Spanning Merritt Pkwy.
HAER CT-125
HAER DLC/PP-1993:CT-5
1ph/5pg/1pc/fr L

Merritt Parkway,Park Avenue Bridge
HAER CT-115
HAER DLC/PP-1993:CT-5
1ph/6pg/1pc/fr L

Merritt Parkway,Pequonnock River Bridge
Spanning Pequonnock River
HAER CT-57
HAER DLC/PP-1993:CT-5
9ph/9pg/2pc/fr L

Merritt Parkway,Plattsville Road Bridge
Spanning Merritt Pkwy.
HAER CT-116
HAER DLC/PP-1993:CT-5
3ph/6pg/1pc/fr L

Merritt Parkway,Reservoir Road Bridge
Spanning Reservoir Rd.
HAER CT-120
HAER DLC/PP-1993:CT-5
1ph/5pg/1pc/fr L

Merritt Parkway,Rocky Hill Road Bridge
Spanning Merritt Pkwy.
HAER CT-56
HAER DLC/PP-1993:CT-5
2ph/5pg/1pc/fr L

Merritt Parkway,Unity Road Bridge
Spanning Unity Rd.
HAER CT-123
HAER DLC/PP-1993:CT-5
1ph/6pg/1pc/fr L

Merritt Parkway,White Plains Road/Route 127 Bridge
Spanning White Plains Rd./Rt. 127
HAER CT-122
HAER DLC/PP-1993:CT-5
1ph/5pg/1pc/fr L

WESTPORT

Beachside Avenue Bridge
HAER CT-5
HAER CONN,1-WESPO,6-
15ph/3pg/2pc L

Dunn House
Myrtle Ave.
HABS CT-440
HABS CONN,1-WESPO,1-
7dr/4ph/2pg L

First Congregational Church of Saugatuck
HABS CT-123
HABS CONN,1-WESPO,4-
1ph L

Jessup House
HABS CT-214
HABS CONN,1-WESPO,2-
2ph L

Merritt Parkway,Bayberry Lane Bridge
Spanning Bayberry Ln.
HAER CT-104
HAER DLC/PP-1993:CT-5
2ph/5pg/1pc/fr L

Merritt Parkway,Bridge No. 727; see Merritt Parkway,Wilton Road Bridge

Merritt Parkway,Clinton Ave./N. Clinton Ave. Bridg
Spanning Merritt Pkwy.
HAER CT-100
HAER DLC/PP-1993:CT-5
2ph/7pg/1pc/fr L

Merritt Parkway,Easton Road/Route 136 Bridge
Spanning Easton Rd./Rt. 136
HAER CT-102
HAER DLC/PP-1993:CT-5
3ph/6pg/1pc/fr L

Merritt Parkway,Newton Turnpike Bridge
Spanning Merritt Pkwy.
HAER CT-98
HAER DLC/PP-1993:CT-5
1ph/6pg/1pc/fr L

Merritt Parkway,North Avenue Bridge
Spanning Merritt Pkwy.
HAER CT-103
HAER DLC/PP-1993:CT-5
3ph/5pg/1pc/fr L

Merritt Parkway,Saugatuck River Bridge
Spanning Saugatuck River
HAER CT-99
HAER DLC/PP-1993:CT-5
11ph/6pg/1pc/fr L

Merritt Parkway,Weston Road/Route 57 Bridge
Spanning Weston Rd./Rt. 57
HAER CT-101
HAER DLC/PP-1993:CT-5
1ph/6pg/1pc/fr L

Merritt Parkway,Wilton Road Bridge (Merritt Parkway,Bridge No. 727)
Spanning Wilton Rd./Rt. 33
HAER CT-39
HAER DLC/PP-1993:CT-5
17ph/7pg/3pc/fr L

Prince, William Meade,House (Raymond,Lewis,House)
St. John Place
HABS CT-69
HABS CONN,1-WESPO,3-
9dr/4ph/2pg/fr L

Raymond,Lewis,House; see Prince, William Meade,House

WILTON

Congregational Church
HABS CT-194
HABS CONN,1-WILT,3-
1ph L

Lambert,David,House
Danbury Post Rd.
HABS CT-29
HABS CONN,1-WILT,1-
8dr/4ph/2pg L

Lambert,David,Servants House
Danbury Post Rd.
HABS CT-30
HABS CONN,1-WILT,1-A-
3dr/2ph/2pg L

Wilton Town Hall
HABS CT-31
HABS CONN,1-WILT,2-
6dr/2ph/2pg L

HARTFORD COUNTY

BRISTOL

Curtis,Dr. William M.,House
23-25 High Street
HABS CT-430
HABS DLC/PP-1993:CT-5
21ph/5pg/3pc L

EAST GRANBY

Thompson Farmhouse
HABS CT-197
HABS CONN,2-GRANBE,1-
2ph L

EAST HARTFORD

535 Main Street (House)
535 Main St.
HABS CT-415
HABS 1991(HABS):6
15ph/4pg/1pc L

Minister's Hotel; see Pitkin,Squire Elisha,House

Pitkin,Squire Elisha,House (Minister's Hotel)
Roberts Lane
HABS CT-18
HABS CONN,2-HARFE,1-
5ph/2pg L

EAST HARTLAND

Congregational Church
HABS CT-195
HABS CONN,2-HARLA,1-
1ph L

EAST WINDSOR HILL

Watson-Bancroft House
Main St.
HABS CT-219
HABS CONN,2-WINHIE,4-
4ph L

Woods House
HABS CT-218
HABS CONN,2-WINHIE,3-
1ph L

FARMINGTON

Bridge No. 475
Spans The Pequabuck River on U.S. Rt. 6
HAER CT-48
11ph/6pg/2pc H

Cowles,Maj. Gen. Solomon,House
Main St.
HABS CT-3-6
HABS CONN,2-FARM,6-
11dr/16ph/4pg L

Deming House
HABS CT-115
HABS CONN,2-FARM,7-
1ph/1pg L

First Church of Christ Congregational Church (Meetinghouse)
HABS CT-224
HABS CONN,2-FARM,2-
2ph/3pg/1pc/2ct L

Gleason House
23 Main St.
HABS CT-389
HABS CONN,2-FARM,8-
1ph L

Meetinghouse; see First Church of Christ Congregational Church

Stanley-Whitman House
37 High St.
HABS CT-356
HABS CONN,2-FARM,9-
5ph/1pg/1pc L

GLASTONBURY

Welles,Gideon,House
Main & Hebron Sts.
HABS CT-39
HABS CONN,2-GLASB,1-
5ph/2pg L

HARTFORD

Armsmear; see Colt,Samuel,House

Barnard,Henry,House
118 Main St.
HABS CT-358
HABS CONN,2-HARF,11-
4ph/1pg/1pc L

Catlin House; see Sigourney,Lydia,House

Colt,Samuel,House (Armsmear)
80 Wethersfield Ave.
HABS CT-357
HABS CONN,2-HARF,12-
3ph/1pg/1pc L

22-24 Congress Street (House)
HABS CT-339
HABS CONN,2-HARF,5-
3ph/1pc L

Corning Building
100 Pearl St.
HABS CT-396
HABS CONN,2-HARF,13-
5ph/24pg/1pc L

42 Dean Street (House)
HABS CT-341
HABS CONN,2-HARF,7-
3ph/1pc L

50 Dean Street (House)
HABS CT-340
HABS CONN,2-HARF,6-
4ph/1pc L

Grey House
833 Park St. (rear)
HABS CT-350
HABS CONN,2-HARF,14-
3ph/1pg/1pc L

Mechanics Savings Bank Building
80 Pearl St.
HABS CT-395
HABS CONN,2-HARF,15-
16ph/11pg/2pc L

12-20 Morris Street (Apartments)
HABS CT-342
HABS CONN,2-HARF,8-
4ph/1pc L

704 Park Street (Commercial Building)
HABS CT-427
HABS DLC/PP-1992:CT-4
4ph/2pg/1pc L

83-85 Sigourney Street (Commercial Buildings)
HABS CT-393
HABS CONN,2-HARF,10-
4ph/1pg/1pc L

286-288 Sigourney Street Residence
(Moved to 195 Sargeant St.)
HABS CT-346
HABS CONN,2-HARF,9-
3ph/1pc L

Sigourney,Lydia,House (Catlin House)
15 Hurlburt St.
HABS CT-24
HABS CONN,2-HARF,2-
15dr/2ph/3pg L

State House,Old
(Statehouse,Connecticut)
Main St. & Central Row
HABS CT-3-3
HABS CONN,2-HARF,1-
18dr/12ph/4pg/1pc L

Statehouse,Connecticut; see State House,Old

Twain,Mark,House; see Twain,Mark,Memorial

Twain,Mark,Memorial
(Twain,Mark,House)
531 Farmington Ave.
HABS CT-359
HABS CONN,2-HARF,16-
6ph/1pg/1pc L

NEW BRITAIN

New Britain City Hall; see Russell & Erwin Building

Russell & Erwin Building (Russwin Hotel; New Britain City Hall)
27 W. Main St.
HABS CT-2
HABS CONN,2-NEBRI,1-
8ph/8pg L

Russwin Hotel; see Russell & Erwin Building

PLAINVILLE

81-83 East Main Street (House)
HABS CT-367
HABS CONN,2-PLA,1-
3ph/2pg/1pc L

85 East Main Street (House)
HABS CT-368
HABS CONN,2-PLA,2-
4ph/2pg/1pc L

ROCKY HILL

Academy Hall
HABS CT-230
HABS CONN,2-ROHI,11-
6dr L

Deming,Capt. Asa,House
Rocky Hill (moved to MA,Wellesley)
HABS CT-13
HABS CONN,2-ROHI,3-
18dr/7ph/2pg L

Rocky Hill Congregational Church
Church & Main Sts.
HABS CT-64
HABS CONN,2-ROHI,5-
18dr/10ph/3pg L

SCANTIC

House (Doorways)
HABS CT-196
HABS CONN,2-SCANT,1-
1ph L

SOUTH GLASTONBURY

Welles-Shipman House
Station St.
HABS CT-57
HABS CONN,2-GLASBS,1-
17dr/6ph/3pg L

SUFFIELD

Bissell,Harvey,House
240 Main St.
HABS CT-81
HABS CONN,2-SUFI,5-
17dr/3ph/3pg L

Burbank-Hatheway Barns & Carriage House
Main St.
HABS CT-266
HABS CONN,2-SUFI,7A-
1ph/1pg L

Burbank-Hatheway House
Main St.
HABS CT-240
HABS CONN,2-SUFI,7-
15ph/4pg L

Burbank-Hatheway Summer or Well House
Main St.
HABS CT-267
HABS CONN,2-SUFI,7B-
1ph/1pg L

King,Lt. William,Place
N. Main St.
HABS CT-61
HABS CONN,2-SUFI,1-
15dr/8ph/3pg L

SUFFIELD CENTER

Gay,Rev. Ebenezer,Manse
Rt. 75
HABS CT-59
HABS CONN,2-SUFI,2-
21dr/3ph/3pg L

WEST HARTFORD

1013 Farmington Avenue (House)
HABS CT-429
HABS DLC/PP-1992:CT-4
16ph/3pg/2pc L

Webster,Noah,Birthplace; see Webster,Noah,House

Webster,Noah,House
(Webster,Noah,Birthplace)
227 S. Main St.
HABS CT-16
HABS CONN,2-HARFW,1-
5ph/1pg/1pc L

WEST SUFFIELD

Sheldon,Capt. Jonathan,House
Sheldon St.
HABS CT-85
HABS CONN,2-SUFIW,1-
20dr/3ph/3pg L

WETHERSFIELD

Belden,Simeon,House
HABS CT-129
HABS CONN,2-WETH,1-
3ph L

Congregational Church,Old; see First Church of Christ

Deming,Peter,House
HABS CT-110
HABS CONN,2-WETH,7-
1ph/1pg L

First Church of Christ (Congregational Church,Old)
HABS CT-128
HABS CONN,2-WETH,2-
3ph L

Fish House; see Warehouse,Old

Hospitality Hall; see Webb,Joseph,House

Warehouse,Old (Fish House)
HABS CT-127
HABS CONN,2-WETH,9-
2ph L

Webb,Joseph,House
(Webb,Joseph,Tavern; Hospitality Hall)
HABS CT-114
HABS CONN,2-WETH,8-
1ph/1pg L

Webb,Joseph,Tavern; see Webb,Joseph,House

Williams House,Older
HABS CT-390
HABS CONN,2-WETH,6-
1ph L

WINDSOR

Bridge No. 452; see Palisado Avenue Bridge

Chaffee,Hezekiah,House
108 Palisado Ave.
HABS CT-34
HABS CONN,2-WIND,3-
15dr/7ph/2pg L

Ellsworth,Jonathan,House
HABS CT-391
HABS CONN,2-WIND,4-
1ph L

Fyler,Lt. Walter,House
HABS CT-112
HABS CONN,2-WIND,6-
1ph/1pg L

Hartford & New Haven Railroad:Depot
35 Central St.
HAER CT-23-A
HAER CONN,2-WIND,7-A-
15ph/10pg/1pc L

Hartford & New Haven Railroad:Freight Depot
40 Central St.
HAER CT-23-B
HAER CONN,2-WIND,7-B-
8ph/10pg/1pc L

Palisado Avenue Bridge (Bridge No. 452)
Spanning Farmington River at St. Rt. 159
HAER CT-31
21ph/5pg/2pc H

WINDSOR HILL

Moore,Samuel,House
Main St.
HABS CT-42
HABS CONN,2-WINHIE,5-
15dr/5ph/2pg L

WINDSOR LOCKS

Bridge No. 1360; see Bridge Street Bridge

Bridge Street Bridge (Bridge No. 1360)
Spanning Connecticut River on CT State Rt. 140
HAER CT-34
HAER 1990 (HAER):4
14ph/5pg/1pc H

LITCHFIELD COUNTY

BARKHAMSTED

Mallory Tavern
HABS CT-199
HABS CONN,3-BARK,1-
3ph L

COLEBROOK

General Store
HABS CT-201
HABS CONN,3-COLB,1-
1ph L

Phelphs,Capt. Arah,Inn (Red Lion Inn)
HABS CT-200
HABS CONN,3-COLB.V,1-
7ph L

Red Lion Inn; see Phelphs,Capt. Arah,Inn

Rockwell,Capt. Samuel,House
HABS CT-202
HABS CONN,3-COLB,2-
1ph L

Rockwell,Martin,House
Colebrook Green
HABS CT-203
HABS CONN,3-COLB,3-
1ph L

CORNWALL

Congregational Church
HABS CT-188
HABS CONN,3-CORWA,1-
3ph L

EAST CANAAN

Congregational Church
HABS CT-189
HABS CONN,3-CANAE,1-
1ph L

FALLS VILLAGE

Hosford House
Beebe Hill Rd.
HABS CT-222
HABS CONN,3-FALVI,3-
1ph L

Matthews,Col. ,House
HABS CT-179
HABS CONN,3-FALVI,2-
2ph L

Robbins House
HABS CT-178
HABS CONN,3-FALVI,1-
3ph L

GAYLORDSVILLE

Gaylord House
HABS CT-176
HABS CONN,3-GAYLV,1-
1ph L

GOSHEN

Birds Eye Norton House
HABS CT-147
HABS CONN,3-GOSH,1-
5ph L

HARWINTON

Congregational Church
HABS CT-158
HABS CONN,3-HARWI,1-
2ph L

House on Center Green
HABS CT-221
HABS CONN,3-HARWI,3-
1ph L

Messenger House
HABS CT-159
HABS CONN,3-HARWI,2-
1ph L

KENT

Bacon House; see Mills House

Bog Hollow Bridge (Bridge No. 1594)
Spanning the Housatonic River on CT State Rt. 341
HAER CT-33
HAER 1991(HAER):20
15ph/4pg/1pc L

Bridge No. 1594; see Bog Hollow Bridge

Flanders Arms; see Hall,Lawrence K. ,House

Hall,Lawrence K. ,House (Flanders Arms)
HABS CT-186
HABS CONN,3-KENT,5-
4ph L

House
HABS CT-187
HABS CONN,3-KENT,6-
1ph L

Mills House (Bacon House)
HABS CT-183
HABS CONN,3-KENT,2-
5ph L

Roberts House
HABS CT-185
HABS CONN,3-KENT,4-
4ph L

Tolman House
HABS CT-184
HABS CONN,3-KENT,3-
1ph L

LAKEVILLE

Holly House
HABS CT-141
HABS CONN,3-LAKVI,1-
11ph L

LITCHFIELD

First Congregational Church
HABS CT-177
HABS CONN,3-LIT,13-
8ph L

Gould House; see Sheldon,Elisha,House

Law School
South St.
HABS CT-381
HABS CONN,3-LIT,8-
1ph L

Phelps' Tavern
East St.
HABS CT-79
HABS CONN,3-LIT,12-
2ph/3pg L

Seymour,Ozias,Homestead (St. Michael's Episcopal Rectory)
South St.
HABS CT-384
HABS CONN,3-LIT,9-
1ph L

Sheldon Tavern; see Sheldon,Elisha,House

Sheldon,Elisha,House (Sheldon Tavern; Gould House)
HABS CT-220
HABS CONN,3-LIT,7-
2ph L

St. Michael's Episcopal Rectory; see Seymour,Ozias,Homestead

Welch,Gerret P. ,House
HABS CT-382
HABS CONN,3-LIT,11-
1ph L

Welch,Maj. David,House
HABS CT-383
HABS CONN,3-LIT,10-
1ph L

NEW MILFORD

Boardman's Lenticular Bridge
Spanning Housatonic River on Boardman's Rd.
HAER CT-16
HAER CONN,3-NEMI,1-
12ph/1pg/1pc L

Brige No. 556; see Gaylordsville Bridge

Gaylordsville Bridge (Brige No. 556)
Spanning Housatonic River at U.S. Hwy. 7
HAER CT-32
22ph/6pg/2pc H

Lover's Leap Lenticular Bridge
Spanning Housatonic River on Pumpkin Hill Rd.
HAER CT-17
HAER CONN,3-NEMI,2-
11ph/1pg/1pc/1ct L

NEW PRESTON

Congregational Church
HABS CT-236
HABS CONN,3-NEPRET,1-
4dr L

NORFOLK

First Congregational Church
Norfolk Green Vic.
HABS CT-193
HABS CONN,3-NORF,1-
1ph L

NORTH CANAAN

Herman House
HABS CT-126
HABS CONN,3-CANAN,1-
1ph L

NORTH CORNWALL

"Long House"
HABS CT-157
HABS CONN,3-CORWA.V,3-
1ph L

Adelphi Institute
HABS CT-156
HABS CONN,3-CORWA.V,2-
1ph L

Church
HABS CT-155
HABS CONN,3-CORWA.V,1-
5ph L

NORTH WOODBURY

Store at the Four Corners
HABS CT-175
HABS CONN,3-WOON,1-
1ph L

SHARON

House
Sharon Green Vic.
HABS CT-152
HABS CONN,3-SHAR,4-
1ph L

King,George,House
HABS CT-149
HABS CONN,3-SHAR,1-
1ph L

Prindle,Charles,House
HABS CT-150
HABS CONN,3-SHAR,2-
1ph L

Shop & Post Office,Old
Sharon Green Vic.
HABS CT-151
HABS CONN,3-SHAR,3-
1ph L

SOUTH CANAAN

Congregational Church
HABS CT-190
HABS CONN,3-CANAS,1-
7ph L

House Opposite Church
HABS CT-191
HABS CONN,3-CANAS,2-
1ph L

Hunt House (Doorway)
HABS CT-192
HABS CONN,3-CANAS,3-
1ph L

THOMASTON

Frost Bridge Road Bridge
Spanning the Naugatuck River
HAER CT-35
HAER 1989(HAER):3
13ph/7pg/1pc L

TORRINGTON

St. Paul's Episcopal Church,Rectory
(See CA,SOLANO CO.,BENICIA for documentation)
HABS CA-2084
HABS CAL,48-BENI,15B-
2ph/1pg/1pc L

WATERTOWN

First Congregational Church
HABS CT-223
HABS CONN,3-WAT,1-
2ph L

Green & De Forest Streets (House)
HABS CT-173
HABS CONN,3-WAT,2-
1ph L

WEST GOSHEN

Academy,Old (Library)
HABS CT-148
HABS CONN,3-GOSHWI,1-
1ph L

Library; see Academy,Old

WINCHESTER CENTER

Bronson House (Sherwood,George,House)
Winchester Center Green Vic.
HABS CT-154
HABS CONN,3-WI,2-
3ph L

Greek Doric Church; see Winchester Center Congregational Church

Sherwood,George,House; see Bronson House

Winchester Center Congregational Church (Greek Doric Church)
Winchester Center Green Vic.
HABS CT-153
HABS CONN,3-WI,1-
1ph L

WINSTED

Historical Society; see Rockwell,Solomon,House

Rockwell,Solomon,House (Historical Society)
Prospect St.
HABS CT-142
HABS CONN,3-WIN,2-
20ph L

Winsted Post Office
328 Main St. (U.S. Rt. 44)
HABS CT-428
HABS DLC/PP-1993:CT-5
3ph/11pg/1pc L

WOODBURY

Curtiss House
HABS CT-226
HABS CONN,3-WOO,6-
1ph L

Glebe House
Hollow Rd.
HABS CT-324
HABS CONN,3-WOO,1-
9dr L

King Solomon's Lodge (Masonic Temple)
State Rt. 202
HABS CT-44
HABS CONN,3-WOO,4-
9dr/3ph L

Masonic Temple; see King Solomon's Lodge

Minor,Joseph,House
HABS CT-227
HABS CONN,3-WOO,7-
1ph L

North Congregational Church
Town Square Vic.
HABS CT-174
HABS CONN,3-WOO,10-
2ph L

St. Paul's Church
HABS CT-113
HABS CONN,3-WOO,9-
1ph/1pg L

Thompson House
HABS CT-228
HABS CONN,3-WOO,8-
1ph L

Webb,Dr. ,House
HABS CT-377
HABS CONN,3-WOO,5-
1ph L

WOODBURY VIC.

Minor,Samuel,House
W. side of Flanders Rd.
HABS CT-322
HABS CONN,3-WOO.V,1-
7dr L

MIDDLESEX COUNTY

CHESTER

Clark-Holmes Cottage
HABS CT-139
HABS CONN,4-CHET,3-
1ph L

Mitchell,Abram,House (Pratt,Dr. Ambrose,House)
HABS CT-138
HABS CONN,4-CHET,2-
10ph L

Pratt,Dr. Ambrose,House; see Mitchell,Abram,House

Warner,Jonathan,House
Middlesex Turnpike
HABS CT-137
HABS CONN,4-CHET,1-
5ph L

CLINTON

Stanton,Adam,House (Stanton,John A. ,Memorial)
HABS CT-102
HABS CONN,4-CLIT,1-
2ph L

Stanton,John A. ,Memorial; see Stanton,Adam,House

DURHAM

Lyman,Thomas,House
HABS CT-233
HABS CONN,4-DUR,1-
12dr L

EAST HADDAM

Champion,Gen. Epaphroditus,House (Terraces,The)
HABS CT-130
HABS CONN,4-HADE,1-
9ph L

Hale,Nathan,Schoolhouse
Nathan Hale Park (moved from Village Green)
HABS CT-131
HABS CONN,4-HADE,2-
1ph L

Terraces,The; see Champion,Gen. Epaphroditus,House

EAST HAMPTON

Bevin Brothers Bell Shops
Bevin Ct.
HAER CT-12
HAER CONN,4-HAMPE,1-
13ph/2pg/1pc L

ESSEX

Dauntless Club; see Hayden,Uriah,House

Documentation: **ct** color transparencies **dr** measured drawings **fr** field records **pc** photograph captions **pg** pages of text **ph** photographs

Hayden,Uriah,House (Ship Tavern,Old; Dauntless Club)
HABS CT-133
HABS CONN,4-ESSEX,4-
1ph L

House,Long Yellow
26 West Ave.
HABS CT-135
HABS CONN,4-ESSEX,2-
1ph L

Pratt House
HABS CT-134
HABS CONN,4-ESSEX,5-
2ph L

Ship Tavern,Old; see Hayden,Uriah,House

Starkey House
Main St.
HABS CT-441
HABS CONN,4-ESSEX,6-
1ph L

KILLINGWORTH

Healy,Kent,House
Chestnut Hill Rd.
HABS CT-232
HABS CONN,4-KILWO,2-
8dr L

North Congregational Church
HABS CT-105
HABS CONN,4-KILWO,1-
1ph/1pg L

MIDDLEFIELD

Talcott,Stephen,House
HABS CT-235
HABS CONN,4-MIDFI,1-
7dr L

MIDDLETOWN

Alsop,Richard,House
301 High St.
HABS CT-3-4
HABS CONN,4-MIDTO,3-
7dr/13ph/3pg L

Exchange Block (Mansion House Block)
108-150 Main St.
HABS CT-326
HABS CONN,4-MIDTO,8-
23ph/16pg/2pc L

Hall,William,House; see Metro South Historic District

Mansion House Block; see Exchange Block

Metro South Historic District (Hall,William,House)
171 Main St.
HABS CT-237-A
HABS CONN,4-MIDTO,12-A-
3ph/1pg/1pc/fr L

Metro South Historic District (Middlesex Theater)
109-111 College St.
HABS CT-237-B
HABS CONN,4-MIDTO,12-B-
7ph/1pg/1pc/fr L

Middlesex Theater; see Metro South Historic District

Russell House
HABS CT-407
HABS CONN,4-MIDTO,5-
1ph L

Russell,Samuel,House
350 High St.
HABS CT-388
HABS CONN,4-MIDTO,6-
1ph/1pg L

Russell,T. Mcdonough,House
High & Washington Sts.
HABS CT-387
HABS CONN,4-MIDTO,7-
1ph/1pg L

MOODUS

Hurd House
HABS CT-132
HABS CONN,4-MOOD,1-
2ph L

NORTH PLAIN

Baker,Nathaniel,House
HABS CT-41
HABS CONN,4-NOPLA,1-
10dr/2ph L

OLD SAYBROOK

Cornfield Point Farm; see Hart,Samuel,Farmhouse

Eliot,Dr. Augustus,House (Eliot,Dr. Samuel,House)
500 Main St.
HABS CT-364
HABS CONN,4-SAYBO,6-
4ph/19pg/1pc L

Eliot,Dr. Samuel,House; see Eliot,Dr. Augustus,House

Hart,Gen. William,House
350 Main St.
HABS CT-366
HABS CONN,4-SAYBO,7-
2ph/16pg/1pc/fr L

Hart,Samuel,Farmhouse (Neck Farm; Cornfield Point Farm; Jarvis Farm)
Moore Park,Forest Glen
HABS CT-365
HABS CONN,4-SAYBO,8-
3pg L

Jarvis Farm; see Hart,Samuel,Farmhouse

Neck Farm; see Hart,Samuel,Farmhouse

Pratt,Timothy,House
325 Main St.
HABS CT-370
HABS CONN,4-SAYBO,9-
1ph/4pg/1pc L

St. Mary's-By-The-Sea (Chapel)
Borough of Fenwick
HABS CT-371
HABS CONN,4-SAYBO,10-
1pg L

PORTLAND

Hall,Samuel,House
478 Main St.
HABS CT-51
HABS CONN,4-PORT,1-
12dr/8ph/2pg L

NEW HAVEN COUNTY

BETHANY

Wheeler-Beecher House
Amity Rd.
HABS CT-68
HABS CONN,5-BETH,1-
25dr/5ph/3pg L

BRANFORD

Academy (Masonic Lodge)
HABS CT-19
HABS CONN,5-BRA,1-
5dr/4ph/2pg L

Harrison-Linsley House
New Haven Turpike
HABS CT-111
HABS CONN,5-BRA,2-
2ph L

Masonic Lodge; see Academy

CHESHIRE

Beach Tavern (Franklin,Ben,Inn; Roxbury School)
Main St.
HABS CT-32
HABS CONN,5-CHESH,1-
18dr/5ph/3pg L

Field,Azabah,House
Main St.
HABS CT-36
HABS CONN,5-CHESH,2-
9dr/2ph/2pg L

Franklin,Ben,Inn; see Beach Tavern

Hitchcock,Col. Rufus,House (Phillips,A. W. ,House)
46 Church Dr.
HABS CT-385
HABS CONN,5-CHESH,4-
1ph L

Holt,Benjamin,Hall; see Peck,Levi,House

Peck,Levi,House (Holt,Benjamin,Hall)
HABS CT-386
HABS CONN,5-CHESH,3-
1ph L

Phillips,A. W. ,House; see Hitchcock,Col. Rufus,House

Roxbury School; see Beach Tavern

DERBY

Derby Hydroelectric Project; see Ousatonic Water Power Company: Dam & Canals

Ousatonic Water Power Company: Dam & Canals (Derby Hydroelectric Project)
CT Routes 34 & 108, 1 mi.N. of Derby-Shelton Brdg.
HAER CT-36
HAER 1991(HAER):20
31ph/16pg/4pc L

EAST HAVEN

Atwater House; see Hemingway Tavern,Old

Church,Old Stone (Congregational)
3 High St.
HABS CT-104
HABS CONN,5-HAVE,1-
1ph/1pg L

Hemingway Tavern,Old
(Hemingway,Samuel,Tavern; Atwater House)
262 Main St.
HABS CT-11
HABS CONN,5-HAVE,2-
13dr/5ph/5pg L

Hemingway,Samuel,Tavern; see Hemingway Tavern,Old

Hotchkiss,Joseph,House
N. High St.
HABS CT-21
HABS CONN,5-HAVE,3-
7dr/2ph/2pg L

Smith,Jim,House; see Thompson,Stephen,House

Thompson,Stephen,House
(Smith,Jim,House)
298 Hemingway Ave.
HABS CT-78
HABS CONN,5-HAVE,4-
1ph/2pg L

GUILFORD

Acadian House
Union St.
HABS CT-15
HABS CONN,5-GUIL,12-
9dr/4ph/3pg L

Kingsworth,Henry,House; see Starr,Comfort,House

Leete-Griswold House
Petticoat Lane
HABS CT-234
HABS CONN,5-GUIL,26-
7dr L

Starr,Comfort,House
(Kingsworth,Henry,House)
138 State St.
HABS CT-82
HABS CONN,5-GUIL,18-
14dr/3ph/3pg L

HAMDEN

Ford,Moses,House
152 Waite St.
HABS CT-52
HABS CONN,5-HAM,2-
14dr/8ph/2pg L

Grace Episcopal Church
Dixwell Ave.
HABS CT-67
HABS CONN,5-HAM,1-
17dr/3ph/3pg L

Whitney,Eli,Armory Site
W. of Whitney Ave. ,Armory St. Vic.
HAER CT-2
HAER CONN,5-HAM,3-
1dr/26ph/116pg L

Whitney,Eli,Armory:Barn
Whitney Ave.
HAER CT-2-A
HAER CONN,5-HAM,3A-
7dr/16ph/7pg/fr L

Whitney,Eli,Armory:Boarding House
Whitney Ave.
HAER CT-2-D
HAER CONN,5-HAM,3D-
1dr/2ph/1pg/fr L

Whitney,Eli,Armory:Forge Building
Mill River
HAER CT-2-B
HAER CONN,5-HAM,3B-
1dr/8ph/1pg L

Whitney,Eli,Armory:Fuel Storage Shed
Mill River
HAER CT-2-C
HAER CONN,5-HAM,3C-
2dr/2ph/1pg/fr L

MADISON

Field,David,House
HABS CT-33
HABS CONN,5-MAD,3-
4ph/2pg L

Graves,Deacon John,House (Redfield House; Tuxas Farms)
HABS CT-122
HABS CONN,5-MAD,1-
1ph L

Redfield House; see Graves,Deacon John,House

Tuxas Farms; see Graves,Deacon John,House

MERIDEN

Andrews Homestead
Rt. 6A West
HABS CT-323
HABS CONN,5-MER,1-
10dr L

MILFORD

Ford,Col. Stephen,House
W. Main St.
HABS CT-14
HABS CONN,5-MILF,2-
15dr/5ph/2pg L

W. Main Street Bridge
Spanning Wepawaug River
HAER CT-45
16ph/6pg/3pc H

MONTOWESE

Beach,Benjamin,House (Button House)
U. S. Rt. 5
HABS CT-50
HABS CONN,5-MONTO,1-
12dr/4ph/3pg L

Button House; see Beach,Benjamin,House

NAUGATUCK

Naugatuck Rubber Factories Complex
(U. S. Rubber)
Bounded by Cedar,Water,Church,Elm Sts. & Amtrak RW
HAER CT-21
HAER CONN,5-NAUG,1-
76pg/fr L

U. S. Rubber; see Naugatuck Rubber Factories Complex

NEW HAVEN

Atwater-Ciampolini House
321 Whitney Ave.
HABS CT-282
HABS CONN,5-NEWHA,31-
8ph/6pg L

Bassett,John E. & Company (Hardware Store)
754 Chapel St.
HABS CT-283
HABS CONN,5-NEWHA,32-
3ph/7pg L

Benjamin,Everard,House (Bigelow,H. B. ,House)
232 Bradley St.
HABS CT-286
HABS CONN,5-NEWHA,34-
5ph/7pg L

Bigelow,H. B. ,House; see Benjamin,Everard,House

Bishop,Timothy,House
Elm St.
HABS CT-276
HABS CONN,5-NEWHA,27-
5dr/5ph/7pg L

Bristol,Willis,House
584 Chapel St.
HABS CT-274
HABS CONN,5-NEWHA,26-
6dr/12ph/8pg L

Center Church; see First Church of Christ,Congregational

Chandler-Bacon House (New Haven Coffee House)
247 Church St.
HABS CT-75
HABS CONN,5-NEWHA,9-
20dr/5ph/3pg L

Chapel Street Swing Bridge (State Bridge No. 3807)
Spanning Mill River on Chapel St.
HAER CT-42
HAER 1989(HAER):3
35ph/8pg/5pc L

Collins House; see Townshend House

Connecticut Agriculture Experiment Station (Osborne Library)
123 Huntington St.
HABS CT-372
HABS CONN,5-NEWHA,40-
2ph/1pc L

Cook,John,House (Ballroom)
35 Elm St.
HABS CT-270
HABS CONN,5-NEWHA,13-
5dr/2ph/5pg L

50-58 Crown Street (Commercial Building)
HABS CT-418
HABS DLC/PP-1993:CT-5
3ph/6pg/1pc L

51-55 Crown Street (Commercial Building)
HABS CT-419
HABS DLC/PP-1993:CT-5
1ph/5pg/1pc L

Dana,James Dwight,House
24 Hillhouse Ave.
HABS CT-273
HABS CONN,5-NEWHA,25-
6dr/9ph/7pg L

Davies,John M. ,House
393 Prospect St.
HABS CT-284
HABS CONN,5-NEWHA,33-
10ph/7pg L

Dawson and Douglass Building
294 State Street
HABS CT-421
HABS DLC/PP-1993:CT-5
4ph/8pg/1pc L

Ensign,Wooster A.,& Son Hardware Store
75 Orange Street
HABS CT-422
HABS DLC/PP-1993:CT-5
4ph/5pg/1pc L

Exchange Building
121-127 Church St.,855-871 Chapel St.
HABS CT-412
16ph/3pg/2pc H

Field Building
40-44 Crown Street
HABS CT-417
HABS DLC/PP-1993:CT-5
3ph/6pg/1pc L

First Church of Christ,Congregational (Center Church)
Temple St.
HABS CT-109
HABS CONN,5-NEWHA,1-
5dr/3ph/21pg L

First Telephone Exchange Building (Metropolitan Building)
741 Chapel St.
HABS CT-373
HABS CONN,5-NEWHA,41-
1ph/1pc L

Free Public Library; see Ives Memorial Library

Grove Street Cemetery Entrance
227 Grove St.
HABS CT-275
HABS CONN,5-NEWHA,3-
4dr/2ph/6pg L

Hardware Store; see Bassett,John E. & Company

Hillhouse Mansion; see Sachem's Wood

Hyland-Fiske-Wildman House
Boston St.
HABS CT-117
HABS CONN,5-GUIL,19-
5dr/2ph L

Ives Memorial Library (Free Public Library)
133 Elm St.
HABS CT-414
HABS DLC/PP-1993:CT-5
50ph/29pg/3pc L

Marsh,Othniel C. ,House
360 Prospect St.
HABS CT-374
HABS CONN,5-NEWHA,42-
4ph/1pg/1pc L

Metropolitan Building; see First Telephone Exchange Building

Morris,John,House (Pardee,William S. ,House)
Lighthouse Rd. & Morris Ave.
HABS CT-27
HABS CONN,5-NEWHA,8-
17dr/10ph/4pg L

New Haven City Hall & Courthouse
Church St.
HABS CT-281
HABS CONN,5-NEWHA,30-
12dr/10ph/12pg L

New Haven Coffee House; see Chandler-Bacon House

North Church,Old; see United Church

Northeast Corridor; see Northeast Railroad Corridor

Northeast Railroad Corridor (Northeast Corridor)
Amtrak Rt. btwn. NY/CT & CT/RI State Lines
HAER CT-11
HAER CONN,5-NEWHA,37-
125ph/8pc/fr L

Norton,John Pitkin,House
52 Hillhouse Ave.
HABS CT-287
HABS CONN,5-NEWHA,35-
12ph/6pg L

Osborne Library; see Connecticut Agriculture Experiment Station

Pardee,William S. ,House; see Morris,John,House

Pinto,William,House (Whitney,Eli,House)
275 Orange St.
HABS CT-277
HABS CONN,5-NEWHA,28-
4dr/4ph/7pg L

Powell Building
155-157 Church St.
HABS CT-363
HABS CONN,5-NEWHA,43-
15ph/18pg/1pc L

Sachem Street Barn
HABS CT-229
HABS CONN,5-NEWHA,24-
3dr L

Sachem's Wood (Hillhouse Mansion)
Hillhouse Ave.
HABS CT-116
HABS CONN.5-NEWHA,12-
1ph/1pg L

Skinner-Trowbridge House
46 Hillhouse Ave.
HABS CT-272
HABS CONN,5-NEWHA,15-
7dr/7ph/8pg L

Smith,Widow,House
1706 Quinnipiac Ave.
HABS CT-84
HABS CONN,5-NEWHA,10-
19dr/3ph/3pg L

State Bridge No. 3807; see Chapel Street Swing Bridge

Third Congregational Soc. ,Church of the Redeemer (Trinity Evangelical Lutheran Church)
292 Orange St.
HABS CT-278
HABS CONN,5-NEWHA,29-
2dr/6ph/7pg L

Townsend City Savings Bank
793 Chapel St.
HABS CT-288
HABS CONN,5-NEWHA,36-
4ph/6pg L

Townshend House (Collins House)
35 Hillhouse Ave.
HABS CT-107
HABS CONN,5-NEWHA,11-
1ph/1pg L

Trinity Evangelical Lutheran Church; see Third Congregational Soc. ,Church of the Redeemer

United Church (North Church,Old)
Elm & Temple Sts.
HABS CT-3-1
HABS CONN,5-NEWHA,2-
13dr/5ph/7pg L

Water Street Bridge
US Rt. 1 spanning Metro-North Commuter RR
HAER CT-29
HAER CONN,5-NEWHA,38-
13ph/10pg/1pc L

Webster,Noah,House
Temple & Grove Sts. (moved to MI,Dearborn)
HABS CT-3-16
HABS CONN,5-NEWHA,7-
4dr/1ph/10pg L

Wheeler,E.S.,& Company Building
26-28 Crown Street
HABS CT-423
HABS DLC/PP-1993:CT-5
5ph/7pg/1pc L

Whitney,Eli,House; see Pinto,William,House

Winchester Repeat. Arms Co:Tract K Shooting Range (Winchester Research:Ballistics Lab. Test Range)
125 Munson St. (rear section)
HAER CT-28
HAER CONN,5-NEWHA,39-
8ph/13pg/1pc L

Winchester Research:Ballistics Lab. Test Range; see Winchester Repeat. Arms Co:Tract K Shooting Range

WOODWARD,REV. JOHN,HOUSE
409 FORBES AVE.
HABS CT-271
HABS CONN,5-NEWHA,14-
8dr/3ph/20pg L

Yale University,Connecticut Hall
HABS CT-3-5
HABS CONN,5-NEWHA,6A-
15dr/2ph/8pg L

Yale University,Dwight Hall
69 High St.
HABS CT-285
HABS CIBBM5-NEWHA,6B-
13ph/8pg L

NORTH BRANFORD

Tolman House (Ruins)
HABS CT-140
HABS CONN,5-BRAN,1-
5ph L

NORTH BRANFORD VIC.

Baldwin,George,House
(Russell,Lydia,House)
State Rt. 80
HABS CT-48
HABS CONN,5-BRAN.V,1-
6dr/3ph/2pg L

Russell,Lydia,House; see Baldwin,George,House

NORTH GUILFORD

North Guilford Congregational Church
HABS CT-231
HABS CONN,5-GUILN,1-
6dr L

NORTHFORD CENTER

Parsonage,Old; see Williams,Rev. Warham,House

Williams,Rev. Warham,House
(Parsonage,Old)
HABS CT-53
HABS CONN,5-NORF,2-
19dr/14ph/3pg L

SOUTHBURY

Bullet Hill School
U. S. Rts. 6 & 202
HABS CT-45
HABS CONN,5-SOUB,7-
13dr/5ph L

STRAITSVILLE

Collins Tavern
HABS CT-379
HABS CONN,5-STRATV,1-
1ph L

WALLINGFORD

Beach,Moses Yale,House
86 N. Main St.
HABS CT-269
HABS CONN,5-WALF,6-
5dr/14ph/4pg/1pc/fr L

Royce,Nehemiah,House
N. Main St.
HABS CT-238
HABS CONN,5-WALF,4-
2dr L

Toelles Road Bridge
Spanning Quinnipiac River
HAER CT-20
HAER CONN,5-WALF,5-
6ph/2pg/1pc L

WATERBURY

10-12 Bank Street (Commercial Building)
HABS CT-398
HABS CONN,5-WATB,3-
1ph/1pg/1pc L

14-20 Bank Street (Commercial Building) (Henry's Hotel)
HABS CT-399
HABS CONN,5-WATB,4-
3ph/1pg/1pc L

2-8 Bank Street (Commercial Building) (Bauby's Corner)
HABS CT-397
HABS CONN,5-WATB,5-
2ph/1pg/1pc L

22-30 Bank Street (Commercial Building)
HABS CT-400
HABS CONN,5-WATB,6-
2ph/1pg/1pc L

Bauby's Corner; see 2-8 Bank Street (Commercial Building)

Drescher's Cafe
16 Harrison Ave.
HABS CT-401
HABS CONN,5-WATB,7-
4ph/1pg/1pc/fr L

Ells Building
17-21 W. Main St.
HABS CT-404
HABS CONN,5-WATB,8-
2ph/1pg/1pc L

Franklin House; see Griggs Building

Griggs Building (Franklin House; Rex Hotel)
221-227 Bank St.
HABS CT-410
HABS 1991(HABS):6
14ph/22pg/1pc L

Henry's Hotel; see 14-20 Bank Street (Commercial Building)

Hotchkiss Block (Irving Block)
11 E. Main St.
HABS CT-345
HABS CONN,5-WATB,1-
14ph/4pg/2pc L

Jacques,John J. ,Building
11-15 W. Main St.
HABS CT-403
HABS CONN,5-WATB,9-
1ph/1pg/1pc L

Lewis Building
25-31 W. Main St.
HABS CT-405
HABS CONN,5-WATB,10-
3ph/1pg/1pc L

241 Lincoln Street (House)
HABS CT-431
HABS DLC/PP-1993:CT-5
4ph/1pc L

Morrow Building; see Republican Building

Pritchard Building
207-211 Bank St.
HABS CT-408
HABS 1991(HABS):6
7ph/17pg/1pc L

Republican Building (Morrow Building)
229-231 Bank St.
HABS CT-411
HABS 1991(HABS):6
9ph/21pg/1pc L

Rex Hotel; see Griggs Building

16-32 Spring Street (Commercial Building)
HABS CT-424
HABS DLC/PP-1992:CT-5
18ph/1pg/3pc L

36-38 Spring Street (Commercial Building)
HABS CT-425
HABS DLC/PP-1992:CT-5
12ph/2pg/2pc L

Turner,E. T. ,Building
17-19 Harrison Ave.
HABS CT-402
HABS CONN,5-WATB,11-
1ph/1pg/1pc L

Washington Avenue Lenticular Truss Bridge
Spanning Mad River
HAER CT-18
HAER CONN,5-WATB,2-
6ph/1pg/1pc L

Whittemore Building
214-219 Bank St.
HABS CT-409
HABS 1991(HABS):6
6ph/19pg/1pc L

WEST HAVEN

Painter,Thomas,House (Smith,Capt. Samuel,House)
255 Main St.
HABS CT-62
HABS CONN,5-HAVW,2-
18dr/5ph/3pg L

Smith,Capt. Samuel,House; see Painter,Thomas,House

Ward-Heitmann House
277 Elm St.
HABS CT-22
HABS CONN,5-HAVW,1-
13dr/7ph L

WHITNEYVILLE

Whitneyville Congregational Church
HABS CT-108
HABS CONN,5-WHITV,1-
1ph L

WOODBRIDGE

Clark Tavern
Litchfield Turnpike
HABS CT-76
HABS CONN,5-WOOD,1-
12dr/6ph/3pg L

NEW LONDON COUNTY

COLCHESTER

Champion,Col. Henry,House
HABS CT-143
HABS CONN,6-WESCH,1-
10ph L

Double Intersection Warren Truss Bridge
Spanning Blackledge River
HAER CT-7
HAER CONN,6-COLCH,4-
12ph/2pg/1pc L

Felton House on Green
HABS CT-146
HABS CONN,6-COLCH,3-
1ph L

Hayward House on Green
HABS CT-144
HABS CONN,6-COLCH,1-
1ph L

Williams House on Green
HABS CT-145
HABS CONN,6-COLCH,2-
1ph L

EAST LYME

Lee,Thomas,House
HABS CT-121
HABS CONN,6-LYME,4-
1ph L

New York,New Haven & Hartford RR:Niantic Bridge (Niantic Bridge; Northeast Corridor Project)
Spanning Niantic River btwn. East Lyme & Waterford
HAER CT-27
HAER CONN,6-LYME,5-
19ph/10pg/1pc L

Niantic Bridge; see New York,New Haven & Hartford RR:Niantic Bridge

Niantic River Swing Bridge
Spanning Niantic River btwn East Lyme & Waterford
HAER CT-22
HAER CONN,6-LYME,6-
16ph/6pg/2pc L

Northeast Corridor Project; see New York,New Haven & Hartford RR:Niantic Bridge

FITCHVILLE

Bozrah Town Hall
HABS CT-243
HABS CONN,6-FITCH,1-
2ph/3pg L

GROTON

Building 70; see U.S. Nav. Sub. Base,New London Sub.Escape Trng.Tnk

Mystic River Bridge; see New York,New Haven & Hartford RR:Mystic River Brid

New York,New Haven & Hartford RR:Mystic River Brid (Mystic River Bridge; Northeast Corridor Project)
Spanning Mystic River btwn. Groton & Stonington
HAER CT-26
HAER CONN,6-GROT,1-
14ph/9pg/1pc L

Northeast Corridor Project; see New York,New Haven & Hartford RR:Mystic River Brid

U.S. Nav. Sub. Base,New London Sub.Escape Trng.Tnk (Building 70)
Albacore and Darter Rds.
HAER CT-37-A
53ph/30pg/5pc H

HADLYME

Selden,Col. Samuel,Homestead
Selden's Neck
HABS CT-70
HABS CONN,6-HADLY,2-
22dr/6ph/3pg L

HAMBURG COVE

Brockway House,Old; see Johnson,Capt. ,House

Johnson,Capt. ,House (Brockway House,Old)
Hamburg Cove
HABS CT-55
HABS CONN,6-HAMB,1-
15dr/5ph/4pg L

LEBANON

Trumbull,Gov. Jonathan,House (moved from Town St. & Colchester Rd.)
HABS CT-180
HABS CONN,6-LEBA,1-
2ph L

Trumbull,Gov. Jonathan,War Office
HABS CT-181
HABS CONN,6-LEBA,2-
5ph L

LYME

Cottage
HABS CT-380
HABS CONN,6-LYM,1-
1ph L

NEW LONDON

Captains Row
HABS CT-406
HABS CONN,6-NEWLO,10-
1ph L

Chappell,F. H. , & Co.; see Thames Tow Boat Company

County Courthouse
State & Huntington Sts.
HABS CT-3-2
HABS CONN,6-NEWLO,2-
9dr/5ph/2pg L

Groton Bridge; see New York,New Haven & Hartford RR:Groton Bridge

Hempstead,Stephen,House
HABS CT-208
HABS CONN,6-NEWLO,7-
1ph L

Huguenot House
HABS CT-209
HABS CONN,6-NEWLO,3-
1ph L

Latimer,Jonathan,House
HABS CT-211
HABS CONN,6-NEWLO,9-
1ph L

New London Railroad Station (Union Railroad Station)
State St. Vic.
HABS CT-347
HABS CONN,6-NEWLO,14-
15ph/1pg/2pc L

New York,New Haven & Hartford RR:Groton Bridge (Groton Bridge; Thames River Bridge; Northeast Corridor Project)
Spanning Thames River btwn. New London & Groton
HAER CT-25
HAER CONN,6-NEWLO,11-
24ph/9pg/2pc L

New York,New Haven & Hartford RR:Shaw's Cove Bridg (Shaw's Cove Bridge; Northeast Corridor Project)
Spanning Shaw's Cove
HAER CT-24
HAER CONN,6-NEWLO,12-
13ph/8pg/1pc L

Northeast Corridor Project; see New York,New Haven & Hartford RR:Groton Bridge

Northeast Corridor Project; see New York,New Haven & Hartford RR:Shaw's Cove Bridg

Shaw,Capt. Nathaniel,Mansion
11 Blinman St.
HABS CT-210
HABS CONN,6-NEWLO,8-
2ph L

Shaw's Cove Bridge; see New York,New Haven & Hartford RR:Shaw's Cove Bridg

Thames River Bridge; see New York,New Haven & Hartford RR:Groton Bridge

Thames Shipyard; see Thames Tow Boat Company

Thames Shipyard,Headhouse; see Thames Tow Boat Company,Headhouse

Thames Shipyard,Ships Cradle No. 3; see Thames Tow Boat Company,Ships Cradle No. 3

Thames Tow Boat Company (Thames Shipyard; Chappell,F. H. , & Co.)
HAER CT-1
HAER CONN,6-NEWLO,13-
1dr/91ph/10pg/5pc/fr L

Thames Tow Boat Company,Headhouse (Thames Shipyard,Headhouse)
Uncasville
HAER CT-1-A
HAER CONN,6-NEWLO,13-A-
3dr/fr L

Thames Tow Boat Company,Ships Cradle No. 3 (Thames Shipyard,Ships Cradle No. 3)
Uncasville
HAER CT-1-B
HAER CONN,6-NEWLO,13-B-
1dr/fr L

Town Mill,Old
Mill St.
HABS CT-3-18
HABS CONN,6-NEWLO,1-
6dr/5ph/2pg L

Union Railroad Station; see New London Railroad Station

NORTH STONINGTON

House
Post Office Vic.
HABS CT-124
HABS CONN,6-STONIN,2-
3ph L

Main St. (House,Front entrance)
HABS CT-125
HABS CONN,6-STONIN,3-
1ph L

NORWICH

Christ Church Rectory
118 Washington St.
HABS CT-261
HABS CONN,6-NOR,14-
2ph/3pg L

Converse,Col. ,Barn
185 Washington St.
HABS CT-263
HABS CONN,6-NOR,13A-
1ph/1pg L

Converse,Col. ,House
185 Washington St.
HABS CT-260
HABS CONN,6-NOR,13-
9ph/4pg L

Dewitt,Capt. Jacob,House (Sigourney,Lydia Huntley,School)
189 Broadway St.
HABS CT-249
HABS CONN,6-NOR,2-
4ph/3pg L

Donahue-Wood House
24 Maple St.
HABS CT-256
HABS CONN,6-NOR,9-
2ph/3pg L

Elks Club; see Slater,John Fox,House

Ely House
231 Broadway
HABS CT-225
HABS CONN,6-NOR,8-
4ph/3pg L

Huntington,Eliza,Memorial Home
99 Washington St.
HABS CT-259
HABS CONN,6-NOR,12-
3ph/3pg L

Indian Leap Pedestrian Bridge
HAER CT-4
HAER CONN,6-NOR,18-
14ph/20pg/2pc L

Johnson,John,House
171 Broadway
HABS CT-258
HABS CONN,6-NOR,11-
3ph/3pg L

Learned-Aiken House
157 Washington St.
HABS CT-253
HABS CONN,6-NOR,6-
1ph/3pg L

Norwich City Hall (Norwich City Hall & Courthouse)
Union Square
HABS CT-1
HABS CONN,6-NOR,17-
3ph/3pg/1pc L

Norwich City Hall & Courthouse; see Norwich City Hall

Osgood,Charles,House
151 Washington St.
HABS CT-254
HABS CONN,6-NOR,7-
3ph/3pg L

Perkins,Hezekiah,House
185 Broadway
HABS CT-262
HABS CONN,6-NOR,15-
4ph/3pg L

Shannon,James B. ,Mausoleum
St. Mary's Cemetery
HABS CT-264
HABS CONN,6-NOR,16A-
2ph/2pg L

Sigourney,Lydia Huntley,School; see Dewitt,Capt. Jacob,House

Slater,John Fox,House (Elks Club)
352 E. Main St.
HABS CT-252
HABS CONN,6-NOR,5-
7ph/3pg L

Slater,John Fox,Memorial Museum
108 Crescent St.
HABS CT-251
HABS CONN,6-NOR,4-
11ph/4pg L

Trinity Episcopal Church
HABS CT-375
HABS CONN,6-NOR,19-
4dr L

Washington Street Historic District
HABS CT-348
HABS CONN,6-NOR,20-
170ph/22pg/9pc L

Whiting,Capt. ,House (Y. M. C. A.)
337 E. Main St.
HABS CT-250
HABS CONN,6-NOR,3-
1ph/2pg L

Woodhull House
167 Broadway
HABS CT-257
HABS CONN,6-NOR,10-
6ph/3pg L

Y. M. C. A.; see Whiting,Capt. ,House

NORWICH VIC.

Merritt Parkway,Visitor's Center
HAER CT-139
HAER DLC/PP-1993:CT-5
2ph/1pc L

NORWICHTOWN

Baldwin,Ebenezer,House,Old
HABS CT-3-19
HABS CONN,6-NORT,3-
10dr/2ph/2pg L

Bradford-Huntington House
16 Huntingtown Lane
HABS CT-247
HABS CONN,6-NORT,5-
15ph/5pg L

Carpenter,Gardner,House
55 E. Town St.
HABS CT-244
HABS CONN,6-NORT,8-
5ph/3pg L

Carpenter,Joseph,Silversmith Shop
71 E. Town St.
HABS CT-248
HABS CONN,6-NORT,15-
8ph/4pg L

Charlton,Capt. Richard,Cottage
12 Mediterranean Lane
HABS CT-246
HABS CONN,6-NORT,17-
7ph/3pg L

Leffingwell,Thomas,Inn
348 Washington St.
HABS CT-245
HABS CONN,6-NORT,16-
10ph/12pg L

OLD LYME

Mather,Samuel,House (Parsonage,The)
HABS CT-118
HABS CONN,6-LYMO,3-
2ph L

Parsonage,The; see
Mather,Samuel,House

Sill,John,House
Lyme St.
HABS CT-268
HABS CONN,6-LYMO,10
12dr/fr L

PAWCATUCK

Noyes,Capt. Thomas,House
Old Pequot Trail
HABS CT-101
HABS CONN,6-PAWC,1-
20dr/8ph L

PRESTON CITY

Church,Old
HABS CT-206
HABS CONN,6-PRET,3-
1ph L

House Opposite the Church
HABS CT-207
HABS CONN,6-PRET,4-
2ph L

STONINGTON

Stanton,Robert,House
HABS CT-26
HABS CONN,6-STONI,4-
14dr/5ph/2pg L

TAFTVILLE

Ponemah Mills
Main St.
HABS CT-242
HABS CONN,6-TAFT,2-
9ph/5pg L

Ponemah Mills Workers' Houses
Shetucket & Norwich Aves.
HABS CT-241
HABS CONN,6-TAFT,1-
3ph/4pg L

TOLLAND COUNTY

BOLTON (CENTER)

White,Asa,Tavern
HABS CT-47
HABS CONN,7-BOLT,1-
10dr/4ph L

W. STAFFORD SPRINGS

Bradway,Charles P. ,Machine Works
State Rt. 190,intersection Cooper Lane Rd. Vic.
HABS CT-280
HABS CONN,7-STAF.V,1-
9dr L

WINDHAM COUNTY

BROOKLYN

First Ecclesiastical Society; see
Unitarian Church

Putnam,Gen. Israel,Privy
HABS CT-103
HABS CONN,8-BROOK,2-
1dr/2ph L

Town Hall (Windham County Courthouse)
HABS CT-120
HABS CONN,8-BROOK,3-
3ph L

Trinity Episcopal Church
HABS CT-205
HABS CONN,8-BROOK,5-
2ph L

Unitarian Church (First Ecclesiastical Society)
HABS CT-119
HABS CONN,8-BROOK,1-
4ph L

Well House,Old
Maplehurst Farm
HABS CT-204
HABS CONN,8-BROOK,4A-
1ph L

Windham County Courthouse; see
Town Hall

CANTERBURY

Crandall,Prudence,School for Negro Girls; see Payne,Elisha,House

First Congregational Church
HABS CT-162
HABS CONN,8-CANBU,3-
2ph L

House (Palladian Window)
HABS CT-161
HABS CONN,8-CANBU,2-
1ph L

Kinney,David,House (Maple Lane Farm)
Black Hill Rd.
HABS CT-170
HABS CONN,8-CANBU.V,1-
2ph L

Maple Lane Farm; see
Kinney,David,House

Payne,Elisha,House
(Crandall,Prudence,School for Negro Girls)
HABS CT-163
HABS CONN,8-CANBU,1-
4ph/1pg L

Turnpike House (Doorway)
Rt. 14
HABS CT-164
HABS CONN,8-CANBU,4-
1ph L

HAMPTON

Ahern House
HABS CT-378
HABS CONN,8-HAMP,1-
1ph L

PHOENIXVILLE

Phoenix Mill
N. bank of Still River
HAER CT-3
HAER CONN,8-PHOE,1-
7dr/21ph/5pg/1pc/fr L

PLAINFIELD

Academy,Old
HABS CT-171
HABS CONN,8-PLAIF,5-
1ph L

Cleveland House
Bradford Hill
HABS CT-169
HABS CONN,8-PLAIF,4-
3ph L

First Congregational Church
HABS CT-172
HABS CONN,8-PLAIF,1-
1ph L

Main Street (Houses)
HABS CT-168
HABS CONN,8-PLAIF,3-
1ph L

PUTNAM

305 Church Street (House); see Putnam Manufacturing Company Workers' Houses

313 Church Street (House); see Putnam Manufacturing Company Workers' Houses

317 Church Street (House); see Putnam Manufacturing Company Workers' Houses

305-317 Church Street (Houses); see Putnam Manufacturing Company Workers' Houses

Putnam Manufacturing Company Workers' Houses (305 Church Street (House))
HABS CT-361-A
HABS CONN,8-PUT,1-A-
7ph/2pg/1pc L

Putnam Manufacturing Company Workers' Houses (313 Church Street (House))
HABS CT-361-B
HABS CONN,8-PUT,1-B-
7ph/2pg/1pc L

Putnam Manufacturing Company Workers' Houses (317 Church Street (House))
HABS CT-361-C
HABS CONN,8-PUT,1-C-
4ph/2pg/1pc L

Putnam Manufacturing Company Workers' Houses (305-317 Church Street (Houses))
HABS CT-361
HABS CONN,8-PUT,1-
7pg L

SOUTH CANTERBURY

Baldwin,Capt. ,House
HABS CT-182
HABS CONN,8-CANBUS,2-
1ph L

Clark,Capt. John Benjamin,House
HABS CT-160
HABS CONN,8-CANBUS,1-
4ph L

STERLING HILL

Douglass House
HABS CT-165
HABS CONN,8-STER,1-
1ph L

Dunay Homestead (Doorway)
HABS CT-167
HABS CONN,8-STER,3-
1ph L

Gallup,A. J. ,House
HABS CT-166
HABS CONN,8-STER,2-
5ph L

WILLIMANTIC

House,Stone
HABS CT-392
HABS CONN,8-WILM,1-
1ph L

WOODSTOCK

Bowen House
HABS CT-376
HABS CONN,8-WOOD,1-
54ph/3pc L

Documentation: **ct** color transparencies **dr** measured drawings **fr** field records
pc photograph captions **pg** pages of text **ph** photographs

The Old Arsenal, New Castle, New Castle County, Delaware. View from southwest. Photograph by W.S. Stewart, November 23, 1936 (HABS DEL,2-NEWCA,41-1).

Delaware

KENT COUNTY

BLACKISTON VIC.

Blackiston,Benjamin,House (Deer Park)
County Rd. 131
HABS DE-223
HABS DEL,1-BLAC.V,1-
5dr/fr L

Deer Park; see
Blackiston,Benjamin,House

CAMDEN

Camden Friends Meetinghouse
(Quaker Meetinghouse)
E. Camden-Wyoming Ave.
HABS DE-5
HABS DEL,1-CAM,2-
1ph/1pg L

Hunn House; see Spruce Acres

Jenkins,Hunn House; see Spruce Acres

Quaker Meetinghouse; see Camden
Friends Meetinghouse

Spruce Acres (Hunn House;
Jenkins,Hunn House)
110 N. Main St.
HABS DE-4
HABS DEL,1-CAM,1-
1ph/1pg L

CAMDEN VIC.

Brecknock
U. S. Rt. 13
HABS DE-178
HABS DEL,1-CAM,3-
22ph/12pg/2pc/2ct L

Great Geneva
Rt. 10
HABS DE-139
HABS DEL,1-CAM.V,1-
2ph/2pg L

CLAYTON VIC.

Hoffecker House (Hoffecker-Lockwood
House)
State Rt. 6
HABS DE-140
HABS DEL,1-CLAYT,1-
1ph/2pg L

Hoffecker-Lockwood House; see
Hoffecker House

DOVER

Bradford-Loockerman House
(Loockerman,Vincent,House;
Lookerman,Nicholas,House)
419 S. State St.
HABS DE-142
HABS DEL,1-DOV,4-
4ph/2pg L

Christ Church (Episcopal) (Old Christ
Church)
Water & S. State Sts.
HABS DE-73
HABS DEL,1-DOV,2-
3ph/1pg L

Crawford House; see Ridgely,Dr.
Henry,House

**Delaware Agricultural Museum,Pratt
Smokehouse;** see Pratt Smokehouse

Delaware State House (State House,Old)
East side of the Green
HABS DE-199
HABS DEL,1-DOV,8-
9ph/1pg/1pc/1ct L

Governor's House; see Woodburn

Greenwold (Hayes,Manlove,Jr. ,House)
625 S. State St.
HABS DE-198
HABS DEL,1-DOV,11-
15ph/1pg/1pc L

Hayes,Manlove,Jr. ,House; see
Greenwold

Hillyard,Charles,House; see Woodburn

Loockerman,Vincent,House; see
Bradford-Loockerman House

Lookerman,Nicholas,House; see
Bradford-Loockerman House

Old Christ Church; see Christ Church
(Episcopal)

Parke-Ridgely House (Ridgely House)
7 The Green
HABS DE-144
HABS DEL,1-DOV,5-
8ph/2pg/1pc L

Pratt Smokehouse (Delaware
Agricultural Museum,Pratt Smokehouse)
U. S. Rt. 13
HABS DE-245-A
HABS DEL,1-DOV,9-A-
4dr/1pg/fr L

Richardson & Robbins Cannery
Kings Hwy.
HAER DE-3
HAER DEL,1-DOV,7-
27ph/14pg L

Ridgely House; see Parke-Ridgely House

Ridgely,Dr. Henry,House (Crawford
House)
6 S. State St.
HABS DE-177
HABS DEL,1-DOV,10-
18ph/1pg/2pc/3ct L

Rose Cottage
102 S. State St.
HABS DE-176
HABS DEL,1-DOV,12-
13ph/1pg/2pc L

State House,Old; see Delaware State
House

Woodburn (Hillyard,Charles,House;
Governor's House)
Kings Hwy.
HABS DE-146
HABS DEL,1-DOV,6-
5ph/2pg L

DOVER VIC.

Cedar Tree Lane Farm (Maple Lane
Farm)
Rt. 8,Rt. 9 vic.
HABS DE-74
HABS DEL,1-DOV.V,2-
2ph/1pg/1pc L

Dickinson,John,Feed Barn
Kitts Hummock Rd.
HABS DE-17-A
HABS DEL.1-DOV.V,1-A-
12ph/5pg/1pc L

Dickinson,John,Mansion
(Dickinson,Samuel,House)
Kitts Hummock Rd.
HABS DE-17
HABS DEL,1-DOV.V,1-
14ph/1pg/1pc/5ct L

Dickinson,Samuel,House; see
Dickinson,John,Mansion

Kingston-Upon-Hull (Town Point)
Kitts Hummock Rd.
HABS DE-175
HABS DEL,1-DOV.V,3-
6dr/12ph/12pg/1pc/fr L

Maple Lane Farm; see Cedar Tree Lane
Farm

Town Point; see Kingston-Upon-Hull

FREDERICA

Dill, John, Store (Wootten Store)
2 Market St.
HABS DE-174
HABS DEL,1-FRED,1-
3ph/7pg/1pc L

Wootten Store; see Dill, John, Store

FREDERICA VIC.

Barratt's Chapel,Old (Methodist)
Rt. 113
HABS DE-16
HABS DEL,1-FRED.V,2-
2ph/1pg/1pc L

Douglass House; see Mordington

Mordington (Douglass House)
Canterbury-Milford Rd.
HABS DE-6
HABS DEL,1-FRED.V,1-
4ph/3pg L

HARRINGTON VIC.

Baynard House
Lewis Rd. (moved to MD-Chesapeake City Vic.)
HABS DE-159
HABS DEL,1-HAR.V,1-
2dr/6ph/6pg/fr L

Vogl House
State Rd. 277
HABS DE-173
HABS DEL,1-HAR.V,2-
22ph/1pg/2pc/1ct L

KENTON VIC.

Aspendale (Numbers,Charles,House)
Rt. 300 (Downs Chapel)
HABS DE-143
HABS DEL,1-KENT.V,1-
11dr/27ph/15pg/2pc/2ct/fr L

Numbers,Charles,House; see Aspendale

LEIPSIC

Mansion,Ruth,House
Main St.
HABS DE-130
HABS DEL,1-LEIP,1-
2ph/1pg L

Naudain,Andrew,House; see Snowland (Interiors)

Snowland (Interiors)
(Naudain,Andrew,House)
Rt. 42
HABS DE-145
HABS DEL,1-LEIP,2-
2ph/2pg L

LEIPSIC VIC.

Wheel of Fortune (House)
State Rt. 9
HABS DE-76
HABS DEL,1-LEIP.V,4-
4ph/3pg/1pc L

York Seat Farm
Rt. 9,Little Creek Vic.
HABS DE-75
HABS DEL,1-LEIP.V,3-
3ph/1pg/1pc L

LITTLE CREEK

Octagonal School House (Pleasant Hill Academy)
Rt. 9
HABS DE-18
HABS DEL,1-LEIP.V,1-
1ph/1pg L

Pleasant Hill Academy; see Octagonal School House

LITTLE CREEK VIC.

Little Creek Friends Meetinghouse
(Quaker Meetinghouse)
State Rd. 340
HABS DE-19
HABS DEL,1-LEIP.V,2-
1ph/1pg L

Port Mahon Lighthouse
State Rt. 89 at mouth of Mahon River
HABS DE-214
HABS DEL,1-LITCRE.V,1-
4dr/10ph/13pg/1pc/fr L

Quaker Meetinghouse; see Little Creek Friends Meetinghouse

MAGNOLIA

Lindale,John B. ,Farm,Barn
24 S. Main St.
HABS DE-172-C
HABS DEL,1-MAG,1-C-
1ph/1pc L

Lindale,John B. ,Farm,Office
24 S. Main St.
HABS DE-172-A
HABS DEL,1-MAG,1-A-
3ph/1pc L

Lindale,John B. ,Farm,Small Barn
24 S. Main St.
HABS DE-172-D
HABS DEL,1-MAG,1-D-
1ph/1pc L

Lindale,John B. ,Farm,Water Tower
24 S. Main St.
HABS DE-172-B
HABS DEL,1-MAG,1-B-
1ph/1pc L

Lindale,John B. ,Farm,Well House
24 S. Main St.
HABS DE-172-E
HABS DEL,1-MAG,1-E-
1ph/1pc L

Lindale,John B.,House & Farm
24 S. Main St.
HABS DE-172
HABS DEL,1-MAG,1-
4dr/12ph/12pg/1pc/5ct/fr L

Lowber,Matthew,House
N. Main St.
HABS DE-182
HABS DEL,1-MAG,2-
7dr/9ph/12pg/1pc/fr L

MILFORD

Thorne,Parson,Mansion
501 NW Front St.
HABS DE-197
HABS DEL,1-MILF,2-
18ph/1pg/1pc/1ct L

MILFORD VIC.

J. H. Wilkerson & Sons Brick Works
Front St. (Rd. 409)
HAER DE-5
HAER DEL,1-MILF,1-
3dr/35ph/12pg/fr L

SMYRNA

Benson,Benjamin,House (Hoffecker,W. O. ,House)
123 W. Commerce St.
HABS DE-126
HABS DEL,1-SMYR,6-
1ph/1pg L

Clayton House,Old; see Spruance,Enoch,House

Cummins-Stockley House (Stockley House)
215 N. Main St.
HABS DE-124
HABS DEL,1-SMYR,4-
2ph/1pg/1pc L

England,John,House; see Woodlawn

Hoffecker,W. O. ,House; see Benson,Benjamin,House

Morris-Cummins House; see Woodlawn

Mustard,Peterson,House; see Pope-Mustard Mansion

Odd Fellows Cemetery Gate
Rt. 13 N. of Rt. 12
HABS DE-237
HABS DEL,1-SMYR,8-
5ph/1pg/1pc L

Pierce,Abraham,House (Spruance House)
12 E. Commerce St.
HABS DE-123
HABS DEL,1-SMYR,3-
2ph/1pg L

Pope-Mustard Mansion
(Mustard,Peterson,House)
204 W. Mount Vernon St.
HABS DE-125
HABS DEL,1-SMYR,5-
1ph/1pg L

Spruance House; see Pierce,Abraham,House

Spruance,Enoch,House (Clayton House,Old)
117 E. Commerce St.
HABS DE-122
HABS DEL,1-SMYR,2-
4ph/1pg/1pc L

Stockley House; see Cummins-Stockley House

Woodlawn (Morris-Cummins House; England,John,House)
Rt. 13,State Rd. 12 vic.
HABS DE-141
HABS DEL,1-SMYR,7-
6ph/2pg/1pc L

SMYRNA VIC.

Belmont Hall (Collins,Thomas,House)
Rt. 13
HABS DE-147
HABS DEL,1-SMYR.V,3-
12ph/4pg L

Collins,Thomas,House; see Belmont Hall

Davis-Boyer House
Duck Creek Pkwy.
HABS DE-128
HABS DEL,1-DUCK,2-
1ph/1pg L

Lindens,The (Short House)
Rt. 13 A
HABS DE-127
HABS DEL,1-DUCK,1-
1ph/1pg L

Short House; see Lindens,The

NEW CASTLE COUNTY

ARMSTRONG CORNER VIC

Achmester,Frame Granary
Rd. 429,Rt. 896 vic.
HABS DE-221-C
HABS DEL,2-ARCO.V,1-C-
5ph/1pg/1pc L

Achmester,Log Granary
Rd. 429,Rt. 896 vic.
HABS DE-221-B
HABS DEL,2-ARCO.V,1-B-
2dr/2ph/1pg/1pc/fr L

Achmester,Main House
(Mansfield,Richard,House; Nowland House)
Rd. 429,Rt. 896 vic.
HABS DE-221-A
HABS DEL,2-ARCO.V,1-A-
2ph/2pg L

Achmester,Smokehouse
Rd. 429 (St. Georges Hundred)
HABS DE-221-D
HABS DEL,2-ARCO.V,1-D-
3dr/1pg/fr L

Mansfield,Richard,House; see Achmester,Main House

Nowland House; see Achmester,Main House

ASHLAND

Ashland Covered Bridge (Barley Mill Road Covered Bridge)
Red Clay Creek-Barley Mill Rd.
HABS DE-162
HABS DEL,2-YORK.V,1-
3ph/3pg L

Barley Mill Road Covered Bridge; see Ashland Covered Bridge

BIDDLES CORNER

Vandergrift-Biddle House
Jct. US Rte. 13 & County Rd.2, St. Georges Hundred
HABS DE-224
HABS DEL,2-BIDCO,1-
8dr/fr L

BIDDLES CORNER VIC.

Liston Range Rear Light
County Rd. 2
HAER DE-10
HAER DEL,2-BIDCO.V,1-
2dr/10ph/11pg/fr L

Mondamon Farm Barrack
Rt. 2,near Rt. 13
HABS DE-225
HABS DEL,2-BIDCO.V,2-
2ph/1pg L

Retirement Barn
(Vandegrift,Christopher,Barn)
U. S. Rt. 13,near Rt.2
HABS DE-219
HABS DEL,2-BIDCO.V,3-
1dr/3ph/1pg/1pc/fr L

Vandegrift,Christopher,Barn; see Retirement Barn

CENTERVILLE VIC.

Center Meeting House
Center Meeting Rd.
HABS DE-53
HABS DEL,2-CENV.V,1-
1ph/1pg L

CHRISTIANA

Shannon Hotel
1 E. Main St.
HABS DE-190
HABS DEL,2-CHRIS,1-
4dr/8ph/8pg/1pc/fr L

CHRISTIANA VIC.

Foster,Alexander,Grist Mill
Smalley's Dam Rd.
HABS DE-59
HABS DEL,2-CHRIS.V,1-
1ph/1pg L

CLAYMONT VIC.

Lodge House,Old
Rt. 13
HABS DE-50
HABS DEL,2-HOLO.V,1-
1ph/1pg L

COLLINS BEACH VIC.

Collins-Johnson House; see Collins-Sharp House

Collins-Sharp House (Vogel House; Collins-Johnson House)
State Rd. 493 (moved to DE,Odessa)
HABS DE-179
HABS DEL,2-COLBE.V,1-
11ph/1pc L

Vogel House; see Collins-Sharp House

CORNER KETCH

Eastburn Farmhouse; see House,Rural Farmhouse

House,Rural Farmhouse (Eastburn Farmhouse)
Pleasant Hill Rd.
HABS DE-166
HABS DEL,2-CORNK,1-
3ph/4pg L

CORNER KETCH VIC.

Corner Ketch Barn (Thompson Barn; Fongeni)
Rt. 290
HABS DE-205
HABS DEL,2-CORNK.V,3-
8ph/1pg/1pc L

Fongeni; see Corner Ketch Barn

Mill Creek Friends Meetinghouse
Landenburg-Wilmington Rd.
HABS DE-161
HABS DEL,2-CORNK.V,1-
7ph/4pg L

Thompson Barn; see Corner Ketch Barn

CRISTIANA VIC.

Boyce House; see Hale-Byrnes House

Bread & Cheese Island House; see Hale-Byrnes House

Hale-Byrnes House (Boyce House; Bread & Cheese Island House)
Rt. 7
HABS DE-60
HABS DEL,2-CHRIS.V,2-
1ph/1pg L

GLASGOW

Pencader Presbyterian Church
Rt. 896
HABS DE-58
HABS DEL,2-GLASG,1-
1ph/1pg L

GLASGOW VIC.

Black,Samuel H. ,Farm; see La Grange Granary

La Grange Granary (Black,Samuel H. ,Farm)
U. S. Rt. 40 near Rt. 896
HABS DE-216
HABS DEL,2-GLASG.V,1-
1ph/1pg L

GRANOGUE VIC.

Smith's Bridge (Smith's Covered Bridge)
Brandywine Creek at Smith Bridge Rd.
HABS DE-1
HABS DEL,2-BEAVA,1-
3dr/3ph/2pg/fr L

Smith's Covered Bridge; see Smith's Bridge

GREENVILLE VIC.

Birkenhead Mill; see DuPont Powder Mill

DuPont Powder Mill (Eleutherian Mills; Birkenhead Mill; Lynch,Charles,Mill)
Brandywine River (Hagley Museum)
HABS DE-2
HABS DEL,2-HAG,1-
4dr/3ph/2pg/1pc/fr L

Eleutherian Mills; see DuPont Powder Mill

Lynch,Charles,Mill; see DuPont Powder Mill

HOCKESSIN VIC.

Mendenhall Mill
Mill Creek Rd.
HABS DE-167
HABS DEL,2-HOCK.V,2-
3ph/5pg L

North Star Schoolhouse (Public School Number Thirty)
North Star & Henderson Rds.
HABS DE-163
HABS DEL,2-HOCK.V,1-
3ph/3pg L

Public School Number Thirty; see North Star Schoolhouse

KIRKWOOD VIC.

McCoy House
U. S. Rt. 13 vic. at St. Georges
HABS DE-191
HABS DEL,2-KIRWO.V,1-
6pg L

MARSHALLTON

Greenbank Mill
Greenbank Rd.
HABS DE-164
HABS DEL,2-MARSH.V,1-
12ph/6pg L

MARSHALLTON VIC.

Harlan Grist Mill
Mermaid-Stoney Batter Rd.
HABS DE-68
HABS DEL,2-MARSH.V,2-
1ph/1pg L

MCCONOUGH VIC.

Monterey,Main House
State Rd. 423,E. of Rt. 13
HABS DE-207-A
HABS DEL,2-MCDO.V,1-A-
13ph/1pc L

MCDONOUGH VIC.

Monterey
State Rd. 423,E. of Rt. 13
HABS DE-207
HABS DEL,2-MCD0.V,1-
2pg L

Monterey,Icehouse
State Rd. 423,E. of Rt. 13
HABS DE-207-E
HABS DEL,2-MCDO.V,1-E-
1ph/1pc L

Monterey,Lumber House
State Rd. 423,E. of Rt. 13
HABS DE-207-D
HABS DEL,2-MCDO.V,1-D-
1ph/1pc L

Monterey,Privy
State Rd. 423,E. of Rt. 13
HABS DE-207-B
HABS DEL,2-MCDO.V,1-B-
3ph/1pc L

Monterey,Smokehouse
State Rd. 423,.7 mi. E. of Route 13
HABS DE-207-C
HABS 1991(HABS):25
3dr/1ph/1pg/1pc/fr L

MIDDLETOWN VIC.

Brady,George,House; see Greenlawn,Main House

Brady,William & George,House,Carriage Barn; see Greenlawn,Carriage Barn

Brady,William,Farm Manager's House; see Greenlawn,Tenant House

Brady,William,House; see Greenlawn,Main House

Cochran Grange
U. S. Rt. 301,near junction of Rts. 301 & 71
HABS DE-208
HABS DEL,2-MIDTO.V,3-
2ph/1pg L

Cochran Grange,Bank Barn
U. S. Rt. 301,near junction of Rts. 301 & 71
HABS DE-208-B
HABS DEL,2-MIDTO.V,3-B-
3dr/7ph/1pg/1pc/fr L

Cochran Grange,Granary
U. S. Rt. 301,near junction of Rts. 301 & 71
HABS DE-208-D
HABS DEL,2-MIDTO.V,3-D-
1dr/3ph/1pg/1pc/fr L

Cochran Grange,Main House
U. S. Rt. 301, W. of Middletown & Rt. 71
HABS DE-208-A
HABS DEL,2-MIDTO.V,3-A-
7ph/2pg/1pc L

Cochran Grange,Threshing Barn
U. S. Rt. 301,near junction of Rts. 301 & 71
HABS DE-208-C
HABS DEL,2-MIDTO.V,3-C-
2dr/2ph/1pg/1pc/fr L

Davis,Outten,House; see Greenlawn,Main House

Greenlawn,Carriage Barn (Brady,William & George,House,Carriage Barn)
Rt. 896
HABS DE-215-C
HABS DEL,2-MIDTO.V,4-C-
6dr/4ph/1pg/1pc/fr L

Greenlawn,Main House (Davis,Outten,House; Brady,William,House; Brady,George,House)
Rt. 896
HABS DE-215-A
HABS DEL,2-MIDTO.V,4-A-
10ph/2pg/1pc L

Greenlawn,Tenant House (Brady,William,Farm Manager's House)
Rt. 896
HABS DE-215-B
HABS DEL,2-MIDTO.V,4-B-
1ph/1pg/1pc L

Hedgelawn
U. S. Route 301
HABS DE-189
HABS DEL,2-MIDTO.V,5-
11ph/1pg/1pc/2ct L

Hedgelawn-Kohl Smokehouse; see Hedgelawn,Smokehouse

Hedgelawn,Crib Barn & Granary
Rt. 301 & Rt. 10
HABS DE-189-A
HABS DEL,2-MIDTO.V,5-A-
5dr/1pg/fr L

Hedgelawn,Smokehouse (Hedgelawn-Kohl Smokehouse)
State Rt. 299 (St. Georges Hundred)
HABS DE-189-B
HABS DEL,2-MIDTO.V,5-B-
4dr/1pg/fr L

Naudain House (Naudain,Arnold S. ,House; Schee House)
Rt. 896
HABS DE-148
HABS DEL,2-MIDTO.V,2-
2ph/1pg L

Naudain,Arnold S. ,House; see Naudain House

Noxontown Mill
Noxontown Rd. (County Rd. 38)
HAER DE-9
HAER DEL,2-MIDTO,1-
5dr/24ph/12pg/fr L

Rothwell Farm,Barn
Rt. 458 near Rt. 42
HABS DE-227
HABS DEL,2-MIDTO.V,6-
6ph/1pg/1pc L

Schee House; see Naudain House

St. Anne's Church,Old; see St. Anne's Episcopal Church

St. Anne's Episcopal Church (St. Anne's Church,Old)
Route 896
HABS DE-72
HABS DEL,2-MIDTO.V,1-
2ph/2pg L

MILLTOWN VIC.

Delaware Log House; see Robinson-Murray House

Murray House; see Robinson-Murray House

Robinson-Murray House (Murray House; Delaware Log House)
Limestone Rd.
HABS DE-169
HABS DEL,2-MILTO.V,1-
10ph/3pg L

MINQUADALE

Lobdell,George,House (Minquadale Home for the Aged)
U. S. Rt. 13,Wilmington vic.
HABS DE-222
HABS DEL,2-MINQ,1-
12ph/3pg/1pc L

Minquadale Home for the Aged; see Lobdell,George,House

MT. CUBA VIC.

Cleremont
4400 Lancaster Pike, Christiana Hundred
HABS DE-242
HABS DEL,2-MCUB.V,1-
6ph/1pg/1pc L

MT. PLEASANT VIC.

Jones Farm; see Wheatland Farm Complex

Wheatland Farm Complex (Jones Farm)
Rd. 432 near Rd. 435
HABS DE-220
HABS DEL,2-MOPLE.V,1-
1ph/1pg/1pc L

NAAMAN

Block House; see Robinson,Thomas Jr. ,Kitchen Dependency

Naaman's House; see Robinson,Col. Thomas,House

Robinson House; see Robinson,Col. Thomas,House

Robinson,Col. Thomas,House (Robinson House; Naaman's House)
Naaman's Rd. at Philadelphia Pike (Rt.13)
HABS DE-52
HABS DEL,2-NAMA,2-
1ph/1pg L

Robinson,Thomas Jr. ,Kitchen Dependency (Block House)
Naaman's Rd. at Philadelphia Pike
HABS DE-51
HABS DEL,2-NAMA,1-
2ph/1pg L

NEW CASTLE

Academy Building,Old
The Green
HABS DE-78
HABS DEL,2-NEWCA,14-
4ph/1pg L

Alexander,Archibald,House
26-28 Third St.
HABS DE-105
HABS DEL,2-NEWCA,36-
2ph/1pg L

Amstel House
2 E. Fourth St.
HABS DE-9-3
HABS DEL,2-NEWCA,10-
6dr/7ph/5pg/fr L

Arsenal,The
The Green
HABS DE-133
HABS DEL,2-NEWCA,41-
1ph/1pg L

Aull House (Double Wooden Laird House)
49-51 The Strand
HABS DE-86
HABS DEL,2-NEWCA,18-
2ph/1pg L

Bedford,Gunning,House
6 The Strand
HABS DE-99-B
HABS DEL,2-NEWCA,32-
1pg L

Booth,James,House & Office
216 Delaware St.
HABS DE-88
HABS DEL,2-NEWCA,25-
7ph/1pg L

Cloud's Row
117-125 Delaware St.
HABS DE-83
HABS DEL,2-NEWCA,24-
1ph/1pg L

Colby House (Rosemont House)
110 Delaware St.
HABS DE-82
HABS DEL,2-NEWCA,23-
4ph/1pg/1pc L

Couper,Samuel,House
14 The Strand
HABS DE-112
HABS DEL,2-NEWCA,37-
9ph/2pg L

Deemer House; see Lesley-Travers Mansion

Dorsey House
8 E. Third St.
HABS DE-109
HABS DEL,2-NEWCA,8-
1ph/1pg L

Double Wooden Laird House; see Aull House

Dutch House,Old
32 E. Third St.
HABS DE-93
HABS DEL,2-NEWCA,26-
2ph/1pg/1pc L

Farmers Bank,Old
4 The Strand
HABS DE-99-A
HABS DEL,2-NEWCA,31-
1ph/1pg L

Foster,James W. ,House
159 E. Third St.
HABS DE-120
HABS DEL,2-NEWCA,39-
1ph/1pg L

Gemmill House (Wiley,John,House)
18 E. Third St.
HABS DE-110
HABS DEL,2-NEWCA,22-
2ph/1pg L

Glebe Farm; see Glebe House

Glebe House (Glebe Farm)
Sixth St. East of Rt. 9
HABS DE-134
HABS DEL,2-NEWCA,42-
1ph/1pg L

Immanuel Church (Episcopal)
The Green
HABS DE-79
HABS DEL,2-NEWCA,3-
5ph/3pg L

Immanuel Church Parish House; see Thomas,Charles,House

Jefferson Hotel,Old (Strand Hotel,The; Jefferson House)
Delaware St. & The Strand
HABS DE-98
HABS DEL,2-NEWCA,30-
1ph/1pg L

Jefferson House; see Jefferson Hotel,Old

Johns,Chancellor Kensey,House; see Johns,Kensey,Sr. ,House

Johns,Kensey,Jr. ,House
Delaware & Fourth Sts.
HABS DE-119
HABS DEL,2-NEWCA,12-
3ph/1pg L

Johns,Kensey,Sr. ,House
(Johns,Chancellor Kensey,House)
2 E. Third St.
HABS DE-9-6
HABS DEL,2-NEWCA,5-
12dr/6ph/2pg/fr L

King,William M. ,House
100 The Strand
HABS DE-95
HABS DEL,2-NEWCA,28-
1ph/1pg L

Lesley-Travers Mansion (Deemer House)
112 W. Sixth St.
HABS DE-181
HABS DEL,2-NEWCA,45-
22ph/4pg/2pc/6ct L

McCullough's Row; see 27-33 The Strand,Row Houses

McIntire House (McWilliams,R. ,House)
8 The Strand
HABS DE-99-C
HABS DEL,2-NEWCA,33-
1pg L

McWilliams,R. ,House; see McIntire House

Mercer,Hugh,House; see Willis,Rodney,House

New Castle & Frenchtown Railroad
HAER DE-18
HAER DEL,2-NEWCA,44-
5dr/9ph/28pg/fr L

New Castle Courthouse,Old
Delaware St.
HABS DE-80
HABS DEL,2-NEWCA,1-
4ph/2pg L

New Castle Presbyterian Church; see Presbyterian Church,Old

New Castle-Frenchtown Railroad Ticket Office
Washington Ave. Crossing (moved to Delaware St.)
HABS DE-104
HABS DEL,2-NEWCA,35-
1ph/1pg L

Penn,William,House
206 Delaware St.
HABS DE-101
HABS DEL,2-NEWCA,34-
3ph/1pg L

Presbyterian Church,Old (New Castle Presbyterian Church)
Second St. btwn. Harmony & Delaware Sts.
HABS DE-84
HABS DEL,2-NEWCA,4-
3ph/2pg/1pc L

Read,George,II,House
42 The Strand
HABS DE-81
HABS DEL,2-NEWCA,9-
3ph/1pg/1pc L

Rodney,George,House & Office
16 Third St.
HABS DE-118
HABS DEL,2-NEWCA,38-
1ph/1pg L

Rosemont House; see Colby House

Strand Hotel,The; see Jefferson Hotel,Old

27-33 The Strand,Row Houses
(McCullough's Row)
HABS DE-97
HABS DEL,2-NEWCA,29-
1ph/1pg L

Thomas,Charles,House (Immanuel Church Parish House)
The Strand & Harmony St.
HABS DE-87
HABS DEL,2-NEWCA,13-
5ph/1pg L

Tile House
54 The Strand
HABS DE-138
HABS DEL,2-NEWCA,43-
1ph L

Town Hall
Second & Delaware Sts.
HABS DE-9-4
HABS DEL,2-NEWCA,2-
5dr/4ph/2pg/1pc L

Van Dyke,Kensey Johns,House
300 Delaware St.
HABS DE-92
HABS DEL,2-NEWCA,7-
2ph/1pg L

Van Dyke,Nicholas Jr. ,House
400 Delaware St.
HABS DE-9-5
HABS DEL,2-NEWCA,11-
8dr/3ph/3pg/fr L

Van Leuvenigh House
2 The Strand West
HABS DE-121
HABS DEL,2-NEWCA,40-
1ph/1pg L

Wiley,John,House; see Gemmill House

Willis,Rodney,House
(Mercer,Hugh,House)
126 Harmony St.
HABS DE-94
HABS DEL,2-NEWCA,27-
1ph/1pg L

NEW CASTLE VIC.

Buttonwoods,The (Mansion House)
Forrester Ave.
HABS DE-71
HABS DEL,2-NEWCA.V,3-
5ph/1pg L

Eves Place,Old
Delaware Memorial Bridge Vic.
HABS DE-70
HABS DEL,2-NEWCA.V,2-
1ph/1pg L

Grantham House
229 Grantham Lane
HABS DE-107
HABS DEL,2-NEWCA.V,7-
5ph/1pg L

Hermitage,The
Rt. 273
HABS DE-106
HABS DEL,2-NEWCA.V,6-
4ph/1pg L

Mansion House; see Buttonwoods,The

Maple Shade Mansion
Delaware River
HABS DE-135
HABS DEL,2-NEWCA.V,9-
1ph/1pg L

Monk Barns (Tenant House)
Rt. 9
HABS DE-85
HABS DEL,2-NEWCA.V,4-
1ph/1pg L

Porter,Alexander,Mansion Farm
Rt. 9
HABS DE-108
HABS DEL,2-NEWCA.V,8-
1ph/1pg L

Regency House; see Swanwyck

Stoneham; see Stonum

Stonum (Stoneham)
Ninth & Washington Sts.
HABS DE-91
HABS DEL,2-NEWCA.V,5-
6ph/1pg L

Swanwick; see Swanwyck

Swanwick Manor; see Swanwyck

Swanwyck (Swanwick; Swanwick Manor; Regency House)
65 Landers Lane
HABS DE-48
HABS DEL,2-NEWCA.V,1-
6ph/1pg/1pc L

Tenant House; see Monk Barns

NEWARK

Alumni House; see Old College Historic District

Carpenter Log House; see Robinson House

Documentation: **ct** color transparencies **dr** measured drawings **fr** field records
pc photograph captions **pg** pages of text **ph** photographs

Curtis Paper Mill (Millford Mills; Nonantum Mills)
Rt. 72
HAER DE-1
HAER DEL,2-NEWARK,1-
19ph/10pg L

Granite Mansion Pumphouse; see Granite Mansion Smokehouse

Granite Mansion Smokehouse (Granite Mansion Springhouse; Granite Mansion Pumphouse)
292 W. Main St.
HABS DE-243-A
HABS DEL,2-NEWARK,2-A-
3dr/1pg L

Granite Mansion Springhouse; see Granite Mansion Smokehouse

Millford Mills; see Curtis Paper Mill

Nonantum Mills; see Curtis Paper Mill

Old College; see Old College Historic District

Old College Historic District (Alumni House)
Main & College Sts.
HABS DE-212-B
HABS 1984(HABS):117.5
1ph L

Old College Historic District (Old College)
W. Main St. at S. College
HABS DE-212-A
HABS DEL,2-NEWARK,3-A-
11ph/2pc L

Robinson House (Carpenter Log House)
Walter S. Carpenter State Park, Pleasant Hill Road
HABS DE-241
HABS DEL,2-NEWARK,4-
6ph/2pg/1pc L

NEWARK VIC.

Aikens Tavern Historic District
U. S. 40 & DE-896
HABS DE-210
HABS DEL,2-NEWARK.V,4-
1ph/1pc L

Cooch House; see Cooch,Thomas,House

Cooch,Thomas,House (Cooch House)
961 Old Baltimore Pike
HABS DE-57
HABS DEL,2-COOBR,1-
2ph/1pg L

Eastburn-Jeanes Limekilns
State Rt. 72
HABS DE-165
HAER DE-2
HABS / HAER DEL,2-CORNK.V,2-
2dr/5ph/15pg/1pc/fr L

England-Eastburn House; see England,John,House

England,John,House (England-Eastburn House; Red Mill Farm)
81 Red Mill Rd.
HABS DE-137
HABS DEL,2-NEWARK.V,3-
5ph/8pg L

Ferguson,Robert,House
636 Chestnut Hill Rd.
HABS DE-69
HABS DEL,2-NEWARK.V,5-
12ph/3pg/1pc/fr L

Red Mill Farm; see England,John,House

Welsh Tract Baptist Church
Welsh Tract Church Rd.
HABS DE-56
HABS DEL,2-COOBR.V,1-
4dr/1ph/1pg/fr L

White Clay Creek Presbyterian Church
Robert Kirkwood Hwy. & Polly Drummond Hill Rd.
HABS DE-160
HABS DEL,2-NEWARK.V,1-
5ph/4pg L

Wilson,Alexander,Agricultural Works Complex
County Route 4, Pencader Hundred
HABS DE-209
HABS DEL,2-NEWARK.V,6-
13dr/27ph/19pg/2pc/fr L

NEWPORT

Galloway House
Johns & Ayre Sts.
HABS DE-132
HABS DEL,2-NEWPO,2-
3ph/1pg L

Myers House (Parkin-Myers House)
Market & Johns Sts.
HABS DE-47
HABS DEL,2-NEWPO,1-
1ph/1pg L

Parkin-Myers House; see Myers House

ODESSA

Appoquinimink Friends Meetinghouse; see Odessa Friends Meetinghouse

Brick Hotel,The (Odessa Inn,Old)
Main St.
HABS DE-113
HABS DEL,2-OD,4-
2ph/1pg L

Corbit-Sharp House
(Corbit,William,House)
Main St.
HABS DE-90
HABS DEL,2-OD,3-
7ph/1pg L

Corbit-Sharp Smokehouse
(Corbit,William,Smokehouse)
State Rt. 299 (St. Georges Hundred)
HABS DE-90-A
HABS DEL,2-OD,3-A-
2dr/1pg/fr L

Corbit,William,House; see Corbit-Sharp House

Corbit,William,Smokehouse; see Corbit-Sharp Smokehouse

Heller House (Wilson,David,House)
Rt. 299
HABS DE-114
HABS DEL,2-OD,5-
3ph/1pg L

High Street (Houses); see Odessa Historic District

Main Street (Houses); see Odessa Historic District

Odessa Friends Meetinghouse
(Appoquinimink Friends Meetinghouse)
Rt. 299
HABS DE-115
HABS DEL,2-OD,1-
1ph/1pg L

Odessa Historic District (High Street (Houses))
HABS DE-111-C
HABS DEL,2-OD,6-C-
2ph/1pc L

Odessa Historic District (Main Street (Houses))
Appoquinimink Creek,High,Main & Fourth Sts.
HABS DE-111-A
HABS DEL,2-OD,6-A-
2ph/1pc L

Odessa Historic District (Third Street (Houses))
HABS DE-111-B
HABS DEL,2-OD,6-B-
2ph/1pc L

Odessa Inn,Old; see Brick Hotel,The

Third Street (Houses); see Odessa Historic District

Wilson-Warner House
(Wilson,David,House)
Main St.
HABS DE-89
HABS DEL,2-OD,2-
4ph/1pg L

Wilson,David,House; see Heller House

Wilson,David,House; see Wilson-Warner House

ODESSA VIC.

Cleaver,Ike, Muskrat Shed
Thomas Corner Road near Appoquinimink Creek
HABS DE-247
HABS DEL,2-OD.V,2-
6dr/1pg/fr L

Delcross Farm; see Woodlawn

Delcross Farm, Barn; see Woodlawn,Barn

Delcross Farm, Carriage Barn & Stable; see Woodlawn,Carriage Barn & Stable

Delcross Farm, Crib Barn & Granary; see Woodlawn,Crib Barn & Granary

Delcross Farm, East Cart Shed; see Woodlawn,East Cart Shed

Delcross Farm, House; see Woodlawn,House

Delcross Farm, West Cart Shed; see Woodlawn,West Cart Shed

Drawyers Presbyterian Church,Old
Rt. 13
HABS DE-3
HABS DEL,2-OD.V,1-
14dr/6ph/2pg/fr L

Oakland Plantation,Smokehouse
Intersection of Rts. 428 & 429 (St. Georges Hund.)
HABS DE-246-A
HABS 1991(HABS):25
4dr/1pg/fr L

Vail,A. M. ,Cartshed
Rt. 438
HABS DE-234
HABS DEL,2-OD.V,3-
1ph/1pg/1pc L

Wiliams, Jonathan K., Farm, Carriage Barn & Stable; see Woodlawn,Carriage Barn & Stable

Williams, Jonathan K., Farm, Barn; see Woodlawn,Barn

Williams, Jonathan K., Farm, Crib Barn & Granary; see Woodlawn,Crib Barn & Granary

Williams, Jonathan K., Farm, East Cart Shed; see Woodlawn,East Cart Shed

Williams, Jonathan K., Farm, House; see Woodlawn,House

Williams, Jonathan K., Farm, West Cart Shed; see Woodlawn,West Cart Shed

Williams,Jonathon K. ,Farm; see Woodlawn

Woodlawn (Delcross Farm; Williams,Jonathon K. ,Farm)
County Rt. 429, St. Georges Hundred
HABS DE-229
HABS DEL,2-OD.V,4-
1pg L

Woodlawn,Barn (Delcross Farm, Barn; Williams, Jonathan K., Farm, Barn)
County Rt. 429, St. Georges Hundred
HABS DE-229-B
HABS DEL,2-OD.V,4-B-
6dr/6ph/1pg/1pc/fr L

Woodlawn,Carriage Barn & Stable (Delcross Farm, Carriage Barn & Stable; Wiliams, Jonathan K., Farm, Carriage Barn & Stable
County Rt. 429, St. Georges Hundred
HABS DE-229-C
HABS DEL,2-OD.V,4-C-
2dr/1pg/fr L

Woodlawn,Crib Barn & Granary (Delcross Farm, Crib Barn & Granary; Williams, Jonathan K., Farm, Crib Barn & Granary)
County Rt. 429, St. Georges Hundred
HABS DE-229-D
HABS DEL,2-OD.V,4-D-
3dr/1pg/fr L

Woodlawn,East Cart Shed (Delcross Farm, East Cart Shed; Williams, Jonathan K., Farm, East Cart Shed)
County Rt. 429, St. Georges Hundred
HABS DE-229-E
HABS DEL,2-OD.V,4-E-
1pg L

Woodlawn,House (Delcross Farm, House; Williams, Jonathan K., Farm, House)
County Rt. 429, St. Georges Hundred
HABS DE-229-A
HABS DEL,2-OD.V,4-A-
1pg L

Woodlawn,West Cart Shed (Delcross Farm, West Cart Shed; Williams, Jonathan K., Farm, West Cart Shed)
County Rt. 429, St. Georges Hundred
HABS DE-229-F
HABS DEL,2-OD.V,4-F-
1pg L

OGLETOWN VIC.

England's,John,Grist Mill
81 Red Mill Rd.
HABS DE-136
HABS DEL,2-NEWARK.V,2-
1ph/1pg L

PEA PATCH ISLAND

Fort Delaware
HABS DE-194
HABS DEL,2-PEPIS,1-
37ph/1pg/2pc L

Fort Delaware,Torpedo House
HABS DE-194-A
HABS DEL,2-PEPIS,1-A-
1ph/1pc L

PORT PENN VIC.

Ashton,Robert,House (Carey House)
Rd. 418, W. of Rt. 2
HABS DE-240
HABS DEL,2-POPEN.V,1-
8ph/2pg/1pc/fr L

Carey House; see Ashton,Robert,House

PRICE'S CORNER VIC.

Bird,Thomas,House
(moved to DE,Wilmington)
HABS DE-131
HABS DEL,2-PRICO,1-
2ph/1pg/1pc L

PRICES CORNER VIC.

Bower,Paul E.,Jr.,House; see Williams,Andrew Jackson,House

Connor,John M.,House; see Elliot,William,House

Elliot,William,House (Connor,John M.,House)
2206 Newport Gap Pike (State Rt. 41)
HABS DE-248
HABS 1991(HABS):25
5ph/1pg/1pc/fr H

Williams,Andrew Jackson,House (Bower,Paul E.,Jr.,House)
2200 Newport Gap Pike (State Rt. 41)
HABS DE-249
HABS 1991(HABS):25
3ph/1pg/1pc/fr H

ROCKLAND

Kirk's Mill,Old
Brandywine Creek at Rd. 232
HABS DE-64
HABS DEL,2-ROCLA,2-
1ph/1pg L

Mill House Row
Rockland Road
HABS DE-63
HABS DEL,2-ROCLA,1-
1ph/1pg L

ROCKLAND VIC.

Black Gates (Gate Lodges)
Rockland Rd.
HABS DE-62
HABS DEL,2-ROCLA.V,1-
2ph/1pg L

Gate Lodges; see Black Gates

SMYRNA VIC.

Allee House (McClements Farm)
Adjoining Bombay Hook Wildlife Refuge
HABS DE-180
HABS DEL,2-SMYR.V,1-
8ph/1pc L

Allee House,Smokehouse (McClements Farm,Smokehouse)
Adjoining Bombay Hook Wildlife Refuge
HABS DE-180-A
HABS DEL,2-SMYR.V,1-A-
1ph/1pc L

McClements Farm; see Allee House

McClements Farm,Smokehouse; see Allee House,Smokehouse

Store,Brick (Store,Brick,Farm)
Rt. 488,E of Rd. 489
HABS DE-218
HABS DEL,2-SMYR.V,2-
2dr/4ph/1pg/1pc/fr L

Store,Brick,Farm; see Store,Brick

STANTON

St. James Protestant Episcopal Church
St. James Church Rd. & Old Capital Trail
HABS DE-55
HABS DEL,2-STA,1-
8ph/6pg L

Stanton-Tatnall-Byrnes House
201 Old Mill Lane
HABS DE-168
HABS DEL,2-STA,2-
6ph/5pg L

SUMMIT BRIDGE VIC.

Biggs,B. T. ,Farm,Stable (Westview Farm,Stable)
Rt. 435,near Rt.433
HABS DE-226
HABS DEL,2-SUBR.V,1-
1ph/1pg/1pc L

Westview Farm,Stable; see Biggs,B. T. ,Farm,Stable

TAYLOR'S BRIDGE

Reedy Island Range Rear Light
Rt. 9
HAER DE-11
HAER DEL,2-TAYBR,1-
2dr/6ph/6pg/fr L

TAYLOR'S BRIDGE VIC.

Huguenot House (Naudain,Elias S. ,House)
Rt. 9
HABS DE-77
HABS DEL,2-TAYBR.V,1-
6ph/3pg L

Naudain,Elias S. ,House; see Huguenot House

THOMAS LANDING VIC.

Thomas Landing Barn
Terminus Rt. 440 (Thomas Landing)
HABS DE-228
HABS DEL,2-THOLA.V,1-
3ph/1pg/1pc L

TOWNSEND

Townsend Water Tower
Lattomus Avenue
HAER DE-24
5ph/5pg/1pc L

TYBOUTS CORNER VIC.

Buena Vista
U. S. Rt. 13, S. of U. S. Rt. 40
HABS DE-206
HABS DEL,1-TYCO.V,1-
11ph/2pg/1pc L

Couper Bank Barn (Lester Barn)
Rd. 381 near U. S. Rt. 13
HABS DE-217
HABS DEL,2-TYCO.V,2-
5dr/4ph/1pg/1pc/fr L

Lester Barn; see Couper Bank Barn

Tybout,G. Z. ,Barn
Rt. 381 near Rt. 13
HABS DE-230
HABS DEL,2-TYCO.V,3-
2ph/1pg/1pc L

WILMINGTON

(Documentation filed under Price's Corner Vic.); see Bird,Thomas,House

Asbury Methodist Episcopal Church
Third & Walnut Sts.
HABS DE-39
HABS DEL,2-WILM,26-
1ph/1pg L

Augustine Bridge
Brandywine River,Augustine Cutoff
HAER DE-20
HAER DEL,2-WILM,39-
5dr/49ph/3pg/4pc L

Banning House
809 S. Broom St.
HABS DE-43
HABS DEL,2-WILM,30-
1ph/1pg L

Bird,Thomas,House ((Documentation filed under Price's Corner Vic.))
Fort Christina Park (moved from DE,Price's Corner)
HABS DE-131
HABS 1985(HABS):114
2ph/1pg/1pc L

Brandywine Academy
5 Vandever Ave.
HABS DE-9-1
HABS DEL,2-WILM,8-
2dr/3ph/2pg/1pc L

Brandywine Pumping Station
Sixteenth & Market Sts.
HAER DE-19
HAER DEL,2-WILM,38-
3ph/6pg L

Brick Arch Viaduct; see Pennsylvania Railroad Improvements

Bush,Samuel,House
211 N. Walnut St.
HABS DE-38
HABS DEL,2-WILM,25-
1ph/1pg L

Canby,Samuel,House
1401 N. Market St.
HABS DE-11
HABS DEL,2-WILM,6-
14dr/13ph/2pg/fr L

Cathedral Church of St. John
Concord Ave. & N. Market St.
HABS DE-204
HABS DEL,2-WILM,46-
6ph/1pg/1pc L

City/County Building (Wilmington Public Building)
1000 King St.
HABS DE-102
HABS DEL,2-WILM,41-
3ph/6pg/1pc L

City/County Building,New
800 French St.
HABS DE-103
HABS DEL,2-WILM,42-
6ph/4pg/1pc/fr L

Coxe,Thomas A. ,Houses
107-109 E. Sixth St. (moved to Market St.)
HABS DE-42
HABS DEL,2-WILM,29-
1ph/1pg L

Customs House,Old
King at Sixth St.
HABS DE-188
HABS DEL,2-WILM,47-
19ph/1pg/1pc L

Delaware Avenue Historic District
Delaware Ave. btwn. N. Harrison & N. Broom Sts.
HABS DE-117
HABS DEL,2-WILM,48-
3ph/1pc L

Derrickson House
1801 N. Market St.
HABS DE-34
HABS DEL,2-WILM,21-
1ph/1pg L

Dingee,Jacob,House
(Gray,Joseph,House)
105 E. Seventh St.(moved to 500 Block N. Market St
HABS DE-24
HABS DEL,2-WILM,12-
2ph/1pg L

Dingee,Obadiah,House (Lloyd House)
107 E. Seventh St. (moved to Market St.)
HABS DE-23
HABS DEL,2-WILM,11-
1ph/1pg L

DuPont,Charles I. ,House
Main St. ,Henry Clay Village
HABS DE-66
HABS DEL,2-HENC,3-
2ph/1pg/1pc L

Febiger,Christian,House; see Tatnall,Edward T. ,House

First Presbyterian Church,Old
S. Park Drive at West St.,moved from 10th & Market
HABS DE-202
HABS DEL,2-WILM,49-
3ph/1pg/1pc L

228 French Street (House)
228 French St.
HABS DE-233
HABS DEL,2-WILM,45-
1ph/3pg/1pc L

German Hall
205 E. Sixth St.
HABS DE-41
HABS DEL,2-WILM,28-
1ph/1pg L

Gibbons House
1311 N. Market St.
HABS DE-27
HABS DEL,2-WILM,2-
2ph/1pg L

Grand Opera House; see Masonic Hall & Grand Theater

Gray,Joseph,House; see Dingee,Jacob,House

Harlan & Hollingsworth Company Factory
100 S. West St.
HAER DE-8
HAER DEL,2-WILM,32-
27ph/15pg L

Holy Trinity Church (Swedes Church,Old)
Seventh & Church St.
HABS DE-9-2
HABS DEL,2-WILM,1-
7dr/8ph/5pg L

House of Burgesses; see Town Hall,Old

202 King Street (Commercial Building); see King Street,200 Block

204 King Street (Commercial Building); see King Street,200 Block

206-208 King Street (Commercial Building); see King Street,200 Block

210 King Street (Commercial Building); see King Street,200 Block

212 King Street (Commercial Building); see King Street,200 Block

214 King Street (Commercial Building); see King Street,200 Block

216 King Street (Commercial Building); see King Street,200 Block

218 King Street (Commercial Building); see King Street,200 Block

220 King Street (Commercial Building); see King Street,200 Block

226-230 King Street (Commercial Building); see King Street,200 Block

232 King Street (Commercial Building); see King Street,200 Block

234 King Street (Commercial Building); see King Street,200 Block

236 King Street (Commercial Building); see King Street,200 Block

200-236 King Street (Commercial Buildings); see King Street,200 Block

King Street,200 Block (202 King Street (Commercial Building))
202 King Street
HABS DE-129-M
HABS DEL,2-WILM,50-M-
2ph/1pg/1pc L

King Street,200 Block (204 King Street (Commercial Building))
204 King Street
HABS DE-129-L
HABS DEL,2-WILM,50-L-
1ph/1pg/1pc L

King Street,200 Block (206-208 King Street (Commercial Building))
206-208 King Street
HABS DE-129-K
HABS DEL,2-WILM,50-K-
1ph/1pg/1pc L

King Street,200 Block (210 King Street (Commercial Building))
210 King Street
HABS DE-129-J
HABS DEL,2-WILM,50-J-
2ph/1pg/1pc L

King Street,200 Block (212 King Street (Commercial Building))
212 King Street
HABS DE-129-I
HABS DEL,2-WILM,50-I-
1pg L

King Street,200 Block (214 King Street (Commercial Building))
214 King Street
HABS DE-129-H
HABS DEL,2-WILM,50-H-
1ph/1pg/1pc L

King Street,200 Block (216 King Street (Commercial Building))
216 King Street
HABS DE-129-G
HABS DEL,2-WILM,50-G-
4ph/1pg/1pc L

King Street,200 Block (218 King Street (Commercial Building))
218 King Street
HABS DE-129-F
HABS DEL,2-WILM,50-F-
1pg L

King Street,200 Block (220 King Street (Commercial Building))
220 King Street
HABS DE-129-E
HABS DEL,2-WILM,50-E-
1ph/1pg/1pc L

King Street,200 Block (226-230 King Street (Commercial Building))
226-230 King Street
HABS DE-129-D
HABS DEL,2-WILM,50-D-
2ph/1pg/1pc L

King Street,200 Block (232 King Street (Commercial Building))
232 King Street
HABS DE-129-C
HABS DEL,2-WILM,50-C-
1ph/1pg/1pc L

King Street,200 Block (234 King Street (Commercial Building))
234 King Street
HABS DE-129-B
HABS DEL,2-WILM,50-B-
2ph/1pg/1pc L

King Street,200 Block (236 King Street (Commercial Building))
236 King Street
HABS DE-129-A
HABS DEL,2-WILM,50-A-
1ph/1pg/1pc L

King Street,200 Block (200-236 King Street (Commercial Buildings))
200-236 King Street
HABS DE-129
HABS DEL,2-WILM,50-
4ph/18pg/1pc L

Latimer House; see Latimeria

Latimer,Henry,House; see Woodstock

Latimeria (Latimer House)
Newport Pike (Maryland Ave.)
HABS DE-44
HABS DEL,2-WILM,31-
2ph/1pg L

Lea,William,House
1901 N. Market St.
HABS DE-31
HABS DEL,2-WILM,18-
2ph/1pg/1pc L

Lloyd House; see Dingee,Obadiah,House

Lobdell Car Wheel Company
Christina Ave.
HAER DE-15
HAER DEL,2-WILM,35-
14ph/16pg L

Marot,John,House
1203 & 1205 N. Market St.
HABS DE-29
HABS DEL,2-WILM,16-
1ph/1pg L

Masonic Hall & Grand Theater (Grand Opera House)
818 N. Market St.
HABS DE-170
HABS DEL,2-WILM,51-
6ph/2pg/1pc L

Mendenhall,Capt. Thomas,House
Front & Walnut Sts.
HABS DE-21
HABS DEL,2-WILM,9-
1ph/1pg L

Newlin,Ann,Houses
108 & 110 E. Fifth St.
HABS DE-36
HABS DEL,2-WILM,23-
1ph/1pg L

Newlin,Samuel,Houses
423-425 French St.
HABS DE-37
HABS DEL,2-WILM,24-
1ph/1pg L

Northeast Corridor; see Northeast Railroad Corridor

Northeast Railroad Corridor
(Northeast Corridor)
Amtrak Rt. btwn. MD/DE & DE/PA State Lines
HAER DE-21
HAER DEL,2-WILM,43-
17ph/3pc/fr L

Palmer House
1322 King St.
HABS DE-25
HABS DEL,2-WILM,13-
1ph/1pg L

Peirce,Robert,House
201-203 N. Walnut
HABS DE-22
HABS DEL,2-WILM,10-
1ph/1pg L

Pennsylvania Central Wilmington Shop; see Pennsylvania Railroad Improvements

Pennsylvania Railroad Improvements
Vandever St. & Baltimore & Ohio Railroad Vic.
HAER DE-12
HAER DEL,2-WILM,33-
2ph/34pg L

Pennsylvania Railroad Improvements
(Brick Arch Viaduct)
Liberty St. to Baltimore & Ohio Railroad
HAER DE-12-B
HAER DEL,2-WILM,33B-
3ph L

Pennsylvania Railroad Improvements
(Pennsylvania Railroad Office Building)
French St. at Christiana River
HAER DE-12-E
HAER DEL,2-WILM,33E-
2ph L

Pennsylvania Railroad Improvements
(Repair Shop; Wilmington Yards & Shop; Pennsylvania Central Wilmington Shop)
Vandever & Bowers Sts.
HAER DE-12-A
HAER DEL,2-WILM,33A-
18ph L

Pennsylvania Railroad Improvements
(Swing Bridge)
Penn. R. R. over Brandywine River
HAER DE-12-C
HAER DEL,2-WILM,33C-
8ph L

Pennsylvania Railroad Improvements
(Wilmington Train Station)
Front & French Sts.
HAER DE-12-D
HAER DEL,2-WILM,33D-
5ph L

Pennsylvania Railroad Office Building; see Pennsylvania Railroad Improvements

Phillips-Thompson Building
200-206 E. Fourth St.
HABS DE-213
HABS DEL,2-WILM,52-
23ph/25pg/2pc L

Price,Joseph,House
1301 N. Market St.
HABS DE-28
HABS DEL,2-WILM,15-
6dr/4ph/1pg/fr L

Repair Shop; see Pennsylvania Railroad Improvements

Rhoads,J. E. & Sons
2100 W. Eleventh St.
HAER DE-17
HAER DEL,2-WILM,37-
8ph/11pg L

Rockford Village
Rockford & Ivy Rds.
HABS DE-187
HABS DEL,2-WILM,53-
40ph/2pc L

Rockford Water Tower
Rockford Park
HAER DE-16
HAER DEL,2-WILM,36-
9ph/3pg L

Sharp,Jacob,House
213 Lombard St.
HABS DE-40
HABS DEL,2-WILM,27-
1ph/1pg L

Smith,William,House
1905 N. Market St.
HABS DE-30
HABS DEL,2-WILM,17-
1ph/1pg L

12 Spring Alley (Commercial Building)
HABS DE-201
HABS DEL,2-WILM,44-
5ph/1pg/1pc L

Starr,Jacob,House (Van Kirk,Michael,House)
1310 N. King St.
HABS DE-26
HABS DEL,2-WILM,14-
6dr/6ph/1pg/fr L

Strauss,Emma,House
625 French St.
HABS DE-35
HABS DEL,2-WILM,22-
1ph/1pg L

Swedes Church,Old; see Holy Trinity Church

Swing Bridge; see Pennsylvania Railroad Improvements

Tatnall,Edward T. ,House
(Febiger,Christian,House)
1807 N. Market St.
HABS DE-32
HABS DEL,2-WILM,19-
1ph/1pg L

Tatnall,Joseph,House
1803 N. Market St.
HABS DE-33
HABS DEL,2-WILM,20-
2ph/1pg/1pc L

Town Hall,Old (House of Burgesses)
512 Market St.
HABS DE-96
HABS DEL,2-WILM,41-
13ph/10pg/2pc L

Van Kirk,Michael,House; see Starr,Jacob,House

Welde,William,House
102 N. Walnut St.
HABS DE-20
HABS DEL,2-WILM,7-
1ph/1pg L

Wilmington & Northern Railroad:Repair Shop
Beech St.
HAER DE-13
HAER DEL,2-WILM,34-
4dr/12ph/12pg/fr L

Wilmington Friends Meetinghouse
4th & West Sts.
HABS DE-203
HABS DEL,2-WILM,3-
12ph/2pg/1pc L

Wilmington Public Building; see City/County Building

Wilmington Train Station; see Pennsylvania Railroad Improvements

Wilmington Yards & Shop; see Pennsylvania Railroad Improvements

Woodstock (Woodstock-Latimer House; Latimer,Henry,House)
102 Middleboro Rd. in Banning Park
HABS DE-54
HABS DEL,2-RICHP,3-
4ph/1pg L

Woodstock-Latimer House; see Woodstock

WILMINGTON VIC.

Bell Tower Mill; see Walker's Mill

Brick Mill House; see Richardson,John,House

First Bank of the U. S. Iron Gates; see Winterthur Museum Iron Gates

Glynrich; see Richardson,John,House

Glynrich; see Richardson,Richard,House

Heald Street Bridge
Spanning Conrail RR on S. Heald St. (U.S. Rt. 13)
HAER DE-27
42ph/6pg/4pc H

Jacquett,Peter,House; see Long Hook Farm

Kent Manor Inn; see Long Hook Farm

Long Hook Farm (Jacquett,Peter,House; Kent Manor Inn)
1051 S. Market St.
HABS DE-61
HABS DEL,2-WILM.V,2-
3ph/2pg/1pc L

Mill House Row; see Walker's Bank

Richardson,John,House (Brick Mill House; Glynrich)
15 Race St.,Richardson Park
HABS DE-45
HABS DEL,2-RICHP,1-
15ph/2pg/1pc L

Richardson,Richard,House (Glynrich)
Maryland Ave. (Rt. 4)
HABS DE-46
HABS DEL,2-RICHP,2-
3ph/1pg L

Rockwood
(Shipley-Bringhurst-Hargraves Mansion)
610 Shipley Rd.
HABS DE-186
HABS DEL,2-WILM.V,3-
21ph/2pg/1pc L

Shipley-Bringhurst-Hargraves Mansion; see Rockwood

Tussey House
Philadelphia Pike
HABS DE-49
HABS DEL,2-WILM.V,1-
1ph/1pg L

Walker's Bank (Mill House Row)
Rising Sun Lane
HABS DE-67
HABS DEL,2-HENC,2-
1ph/1pg L

Walker's Mill (Bell Tower Mill)
Rising Sun Lane
HABS DE-65
HABS DEL,2-HENC,1-
1ph/1pg L

West Brandywine Grange
4008 Concord Pike
HABS DE-236
HABS DEL,2-WILM.V,4-
13ph/3pg/1pc L

Winterthur Museum Iron Gates (First Bank of the U. S. Iron Gates)
Rt. 52
HABS DE-193
HABS DEL,2-WILM.V,4-
9ph/1pc L

YORKLYN

Garrett Snuff Mill
Rt. 82
HAER DE-14
HAER DEL,2-YORK,1-
41ph/26pg/fr L

SUSSEX COUNTY

BETHEL

Dowd House; see Ship-Carpenter's House

Robins House; see Ship Carpenter's House

Ship Carpenter's House (Robins House)
Main St.
HABS DE-151
HABS DEL,3-BETH,2-
3ph/2pg L

Ship-Carpenter's House (Dowd House)
Main St.
HABS DE-150
HABS DEL,3-BETH,1-
2ph/1pg L

BRIDGEVILLE

Sudler,Dr. John R. ,House
N. Main St.
HABS DE-184
HABS DEL,3-BRIVI,1-
5dr/11ph/8pg/1pc/2ct/fr L

CLARKSVILLE VIC.

Blackwater Presbyterian Church
State Rd. 54
HABS DE-200
HABS DEL,3-CLAVI.V,1-
10ph/1pg/1pc/3ct L

COOL SPRING VIC.

Fisher House; see White Meadow Farm

Martin House; see White Meadow Farm

White Meadow Farm (Fisher House; Martin House)
State Rds. 290 & 262 (moved to DE,Lewes)
HABS DE-157
HABS DEL,3-COOL,1-
12ph/2pg/1pc L

DAGSBORO

Prince George's Chapel
Rt. 26
HABS DE-158
HABS DEL,3-DAG,1-
4ph/2pg/1pc L

GEORGETOWN

Judges,The (House)
104 W. Market St.
HABS DE-154
HABS DEL,3-GEOTO,1-
1ph/2pg L

Judges,The,Law Office
100 W. Market St.
HABS DE-155
HABS DEL,3-GEOTO,2-
1ph/1pg L

GREENWOOD VIC.

Locust Grove (Richards House)
State Rds. 34 & 32
HABS DE-171
HABS DEL,3-GREW.V,1-
10ph/1pc L

Richards House; see Locust Grove

LAUREL

Collins House; see Rosemont

Mitchell,Gov. Nathaniel,House; see Rosemont

Rosemont (Collins House; Mitchell,Gov. Nathaniel,House)
121 Delaware Ave.
HABS DE-7
HABS DEL,3-LAU,1-
1ph/1pg L

LAUREL VIC.

Christ Church,Old (Lightwood,Old; Christ Episcopal Church)
State Rds. 465 & 465-A
HABS DE-8
HABS DEL,3-LAU.V,1-
12dr/5ph/2pg/fr L

Christ Episcopal Church; see Christ Church,Old

Lightwood,Old; see Christ Church,Old

Whaley Homestead
Rt. 24
HABS DE-9
HABS DEL,3-LAU.V,2-
1ph/1pg L

LEWES

Coleman House
422 Kings Hwy.
HABS DE-15
HABS DEL,3-LEW,6-
2ph/1pg L

Documentation filed under Cool Spring Vic. ,DE; see White Meadow Farm

Fisher House; see White Meadow Farm

Hall,Col. David,House
107 Kings Hwy.
HABS DE-149
HABS DEL,3-LEW,7-
2ph/1pg L

Hocker,H. W. ,Manufacturing Company Factory (Hocker,H. W. ,Paste Brush Factory)
224 Front St.
HAER DE-7
HAER DEL,3-LEW,8-
1dr/9ph/9pg/fr L

Hocker,H. W. ,Paste Brush Factory; see Hocker,H. W. ,Manufacturing Company Factory

Martin House; see White Meadow Farm

Maull Homestead; see
Maull,Thomas,House

Maull,Thomas,House
(Paynter,Samuel,House; Maull
Homestead)
542 Pilot Town Rd.
HABS DE-13
HABS DEL,3-LEW,4-
5ph/3pg/1pc L

Metcalf House
202 W. Third St.
HABS DE-12
HABS DEL,3-LEW,3-
2ph/1pg L

Paynter,Samuel,House; see
Maull,Thomas,House

Skellenger House
Pilot Town Rd.
HABS DE-14
HABS DEL,3-LEW,5-
1ph/1pg L

White Meadow Farm (Fisher House;
Martin House; Documentation filed under
Cool Spring Vic. ,DE)
Kings Hwy. (moved from DE,Cool Spring
vic.)
HABS DE-157
HABS DEL,3-COOL,1-
12ph/2pg/1pc L

MILFORD

Causey House
2 Causey Ave.
HABS DE-183
HABS DEL,3-MILF,2-
10ph/1pg/1pc L

Church Street Bridge; see Railroad
Avenue Bridge

Milford Ice & Coal Company
18 Maple Ave.
HAER DE-4
HAER DEL,3-MILF,3-
3dr/29ph/12pg/fr L

Railroad Avenue Bridge (Church Street
Bridge)
See documentation under KENT
CO.,MILFORD
HAER DE-36
L

MILFORD VIC.

Potter Mansion
Rts. 201 & 202 vic.
HABS DE-235
HABS DEL,3-MILF.V,1-
3ph/1pg/1pc L

MILLSBORO

**Houston-White Company Mill &
Basket Factory**
Main St. & Railroad Ave.
HAER DE-6
HAER DEL,3-MILB,1-
5dr/48ph/18pg/fr L

OAK ORCHARD VIC.

White House Farm
Long Neck Rd. vic. at Indian River Bay
HABS DE-10
HABS DEL,3-OKOR.V,1-
1ph/1pg L

REHOBETH BEACH

Rehoboth Avenue Bridge
State Rt. 1A (Rehoboth Ave)over Lewes &
Reh. Canal
HAER DE-22
HAER DEL,3-REHOB,2-
37ph/6pg/2pc L

REHOBETH BEACH VIC.

Homestead,The; see Marsh,Peter,House

Marsh,Peter,House (Homestead,The)
10 Dodd's Lane
HABS DE-152
HABS DEL,3-REHOB,1-
5ph/2pg L

SEAFORD VIC.

Cannon's Savannah (Maston House)
Atlanta-Seaford Rd.
HABS DE-192
HABS DEL,3-SEFO.V,1-
5ph/8pg/1pc L

Maston House; see Cannon's Savannah

Ross,Gov. William H. ,House
State Rt. 543
HABS DE-196
HABS DEL,3-SEFO.V,2-
19ph/1pg/1pc/1ct L

WOODLAND

Cannon Hall (Cannon,Jacob,House)
Rd. 79 at Woodland Ferry
HABS DE-156
HABS DEL,3-WOOD,2-
2ph/2pg/1pc L

Cannon,Jacob,House; see Cannon Hall

WOODLAND VIC.

Walnut Landing (House)
State Rd. 79
HABS DE-153
HABS DEL,3-WOOD,1-
3ph/2pg L

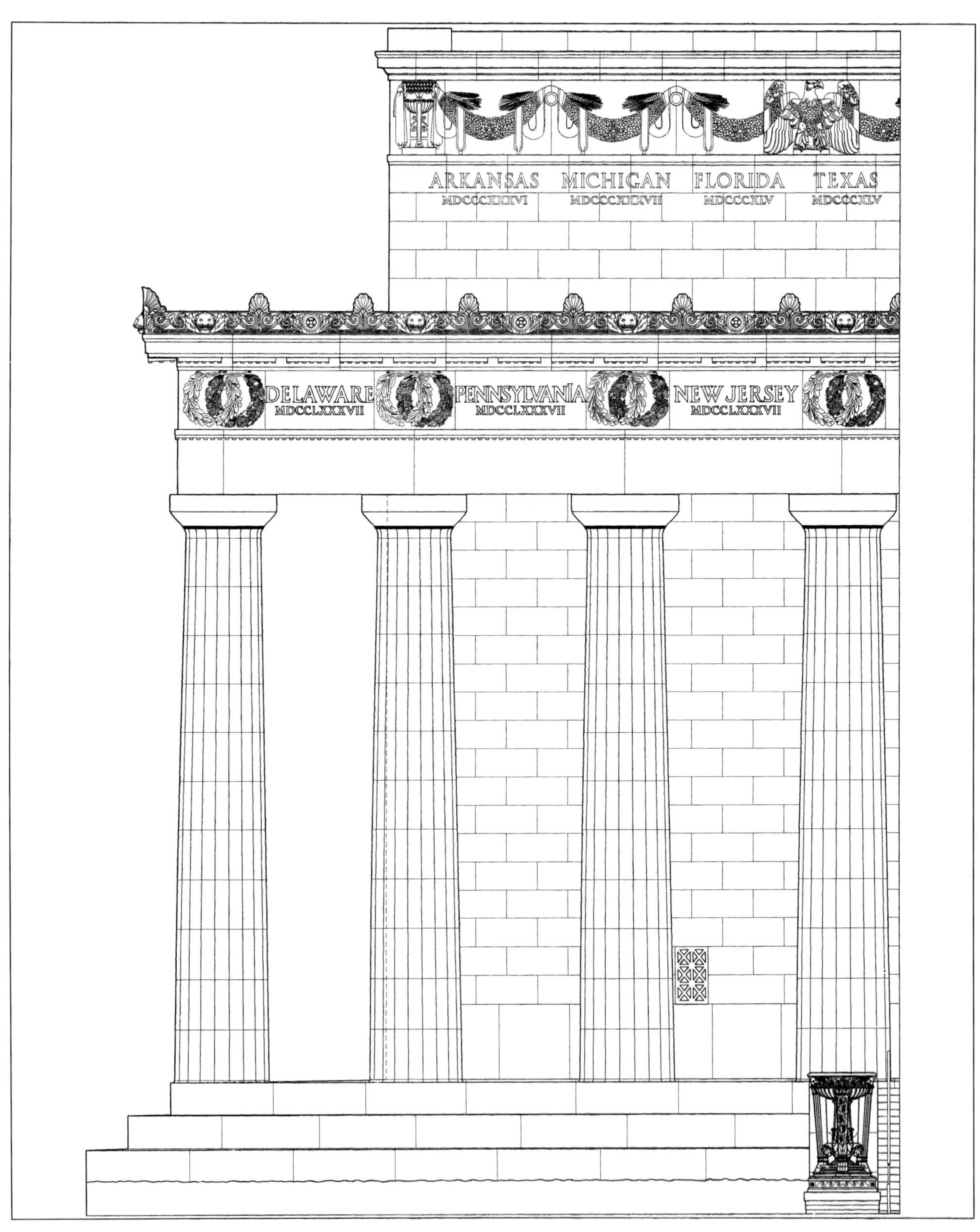

Lincoln Memorial, Washington, D.C. East elevation detail. CAD drawing by Ellyn P. Goldkind, Shelley M. Homeyer, Dana L. Lockett, Mellonee Rheams, Mark Schara, Jose Raul Vasquez, and Crystal Willingham, 1993 (HABS DC-3, sheet 23 of 28).

District Of Columbia

ARLINGTON

Arlington Memorial Bridge: Boundary Channel Ext. (Boundary Channel Extension)
Span. Mt. Vernon Mem. Hwy. & Boundary Channel
HAER DC-7-B
HAER 1990 (HAER):5
4ph/5pg/1pc L

Boundary Channel Extension; see Arlington Memorial Bridge: Boundary Channel Ext.

DISTRICT OF COLUMBIA

WASHINGTON

224 A St.,N.E. (House)
Capitol Hill Historic District
HABS DC-555
HABS DC,WASH,558-
1dr L

Abner,Edward,Building (Playland Adult Bookstore)
413-415 Ninth St. ,NW
HABS DC-522
HABS DC,WASH,281-
6ph/11pg/1pc L

Adams Building
816 F St. ,NW
HABS DC-214
HABS DC,WASH,171-
4ph/15pg/1pc L

Adams House
1801 Park Rd.
HABS DC-469
HABS DC,WASH,383-
2pg/fr L

Adams Memorial (Grief)
Section E,Rock Creek Cemetery
HABS DC-280
HABS DC,WASH,384-
6ph/1pg/1pc L

Adams-Mason House (Georgetown)
1072 Thomas Jefferson St. NW
HABS DC-161
HABS DC,GEO,94-
10ph/11pg/1pc L H

Adas Israel Synagogue
Third & G Sts. NW (moved from Sixth & G Sts. NW)
HABS DC-173
HABS DC,WASH,385-
5dr/5ph/7pg/1pc/fr L

Aged Woman's Home; see Female Union Benevolent Society

All Souls Church
Sixteenth & Harvard Sts. NW
HABS DC-542
HABS DC,WASH,386-
1dr L

Alla-Scala Restaurant; see 425-429 Eleventh Street (Commercial Building)

Am-Chi Restaurant; see 421 Eleventh Street (Commercial Building)

Ambassador Hotel
Fourteenth & K Sts. NW
HABS DC-371
HABS DC,WASH,387-
4ph/1pc L

American Bank Building
1315-1317 F St. NW
HABS DC-305
HABS DC,WASH,388-
1ph/1pg/1pc L

American Institute of Architects Headquarters; see Octagon House

American Institute of Architects Library; see Octagon House,Stable

American Mosaic Company Building
912 I St. NW
HABS DC-387
HABS DC,WASH,254
9ph/3pg/1pc L

American National Red Cross National Headquarters; see Red Cross Building

American University,Ohio Hall of Government (McKinley-Ohio Hall of Government)
Massachusetts & Nebraska Aves.
HABS DC-458
HABS DC,WASH,389-
41pg L

American University,The College of History (Hurst Hall)
Massachusetts & Nebraska Aves. NW at Ward Circle
HABS DC-399
HABS DC,WASH,390-
44pg/fr L

Anderson,Larz,House (Society of the Cincinnati Headquarters)
2118 Massachusetts Ave. NW
HABS DC-255
HABS DC,WASH,198-
15ph/28pg/1pc L

Antique House,Old; see 817 Market Space NW (Commercial Building)

Antonio's Spanish-Italian Cafeteria & Takeout; see 633 D St. ,NW (Commercial Building)

Apartment Building (Chinese Legation)
Nineteenth & Vernon Sts. NW
HABS DC-425
HABS DC,WASH,391-
2ph/1pc L

Apex Liquor Store; see Central National Bank Building

Argyle Terrace; see Miller House

Arlington Memorial Bridge (Memorial Bridge)
Spanning Potomac River btwn Lin. Mem. & Arl. Cemt.
HAER DC-7
HAER 1990 (HAER):5
19ph/8pg/2pc L

Arlington Memorial Bridge: Boundary Channel Ext. (Boundary Channel Extension)
Span. Mt. Vernon Mem. Hwy. & Boundary Channel
HAER DC-7-B
HAER 1990 (HAER):5
4ph/5pg/1pc L

Arlington Memorial Bridge: Watergate & Bridge Plz. (Watergate & Bridge Plaza)
Adjacent to Arlington Mem. Bridge & Lincoln Mem.
HAER DC-7-A
HAER 1990 (HAER):5
3ph/5pg/1pc L

Army Medical Museum & Library
Seventh St. & Independence Ave. SW
HABS DC-306
HABS DC,WASH,392-
9ph/1pg/1pc L

Army War College (National War College)
Fort Lesley J. McNair
HABS DC-277
HABS DC,WASH,393-
11ph/2pg/1pc/2ct L

Artifactory; see 641 Indiana Ave. , NW (Commercial Building)

Arts Club of Washington; see Caldwell,Timothy,House

Ascension & St. Agnes Church
1217 Massachusetts Ave. NW
HABS DC-448
HABS DC,WASH,394-
1ph/1pc L

Atlantic Building
930 F St.,NW
HABS DC-569-A
HABS DLC/PP-1992:DC-3
20dr/13ph/1pg/1pc/fr L

Atlantic Coastline Building
601 Pennsylvania Ave. NW
HABS DC-394
HABS DC,WASH,324-
3ph/3pg/2pc L

Atlas Building; see Warder Building

Auditors Complex,Annex Building 2
Independence Ave,Fifteenth St SW,Fourteenth St SW
HABS DC-524-B
HABS DC,WASH,395B-
13ph/2pg/1pc L

Auditors Complex,Annex Buildings
Independence Ave,Fourteenth St SW,Fifteenth St SW
HABS DC-524
HABS DC,WASH,395-
4ph/16pg/1pc L

Auditors Complex,Annex Buildings 1 & 1-A
Independence Ave.,Fifteenth St SW,Fourteenth St SW
HABS DC-524-A
HABS DC,WASH,395A-
6ph/2pg/1pc L

Australian Emmbassy; see Wilkins House

1000 B Street SW (House)
HABS DC-15
HABS DC,WASH,126-
3dr/2ph L

Babcock,Orville E. ,House (2024-2026 G Street NW (Row Houses))
HABS DC-403
HABS DC,WASH,396-
5ph/1pg/1pc/fr L

Bacon House; see Ringgold-Carroll House

Bag Mart; see 414-416 Seventh St. ,NW (Commercial Building)

Bag Mart; see 432 Seventh St. ,NW (Commercial Building)

Baker Building
1320-1322 F St.
HABS DC-379
HABS DC,WASH,247-
2ph/6pg/1pc L

Bank of Columbia (Georgetown Town Hall; DC Engine Company Number Five Firehouse; National Firefighting Museum)
3210 M St. NW
HABS DC-119
HABS DC,GEO,78-
6dr/1ph/5pg/fr L

Barber Shop
3251 M St. NW
HABS DC-121
HABS DC,GEO,80-
2ph/6pg L

Barney Neighborhood House; see Duncanson-Cranch House

Barney,A. Clifford,House; see Hughes,Charles Evans,House

Barney,Alice Pike,Studio House
2306 Massachusetts Ave. NW
HABS DC-256
HABS DC,WASH,199-
3ph/3pg/1pc L

Barney's Restaurant; see Brown's Marble Hotel

Barrett,James I. ,House
1400 Twenty-ninth St. NW
HABS DC-180
HABS DC,GEO,103-
2ph/11pg L

Bartholdi Fountain
Independence Ave. & C St. SW
HABS DC-533
HABS DC,WASH,397-
3ph/1pc/4ct L

Bassin's Restaurant; see Loughran Building

Baum,H. & Son
616-618 E St. ,NW
HABS DC-610
HABS DC,WASH,351-
1ph/9pg/1pc L

Beale,Joseph,House (Embassy of the Arab Republic of Egypt)
2301 Massachusetts Ave. NW
HABS DC-257
HABS DC,WASH,200-
14ph/16pg L

Beall's Express Building
1522 Wisconsin Ave. NW
HABS DC-80
HABS DC,GEO,56-
1ph L

Bebb House (Octagonal House)
1830 Phelps Pl. NW
HABS DC-13
HABS DC,WASH,124-
2dr L

Becker's Leather Goods Store; see 1314 F Street NW (Commercial Building)

Bell,Alexander Graham,Association for the Deaf; see Volta Bureau

Bellevue; see Dumbarton House

Berry,Philip T. ,House
1402 Thirty-first St. NW
HABS DC-253
HABS DC,GEO,121-
4ph/14pg L

Bethune,Mary McLeod,Carriage House; see 1318 Vermont Ave.,NW,Carriage House

Bibb House; see Bronaugh-Bibb-Libby House

Bicentennial Building
600 E St. ,NW
HABS DC-599
HABS DC,WASH,339-
20pg L

Big Flipper; see Ferree Building

Birch Funeral Home
3034 M St. NW
HABS DC-142
HABS DC,GEO,85-
3ph/9pg L

Birch,W. Taylor,House
3099 Q St. NW
HABS DC-187
HABS DC,GEO,110-
9ph/11pg L

Blair House (Lovell,Joseph,House)
1651 Pennsylvania Ave. NW
HABS DC-45
HABS DC,WASH,27-
3ph/7pg/1pc/2ct L

Bliss,Dr. A. C. ,House
1218 Sixteenth St. NW
HABS DC-398
HABS DC,WASH,364-
2ph/1pg/2ct L

Bluffs Footbridge (Rock Creek & Potomac Parkway Project 1992)
HAER DC-33
H

Bodisco House (Smith,Clement,House)
3322 O St. NW
HABS DC-174
HABS DC,GEO,38-
3ph/1pg/1pc L

Bomford's Mill (Wilkins-Rogers Milling Company)
Potomac & Grace Sts.
HABS DC-143
HABS DC,GEO,86-
18ph/15pg L

Boston Buffet Lunch; see Ferree Building

Boston,Isaaz,House; see Howard Road Historic District

Boulder Bridge
Beach Drive Spanning Rock Creek
HAER DC-12
HAER 1989(HAER):4
4ph/7pg/1pc L

Boundary Channel Extension; see Arlington Memorial Bridge: Boundary Channel Ext.

Boundary Footbridge (Rock Creek & Potomac Parkway Project 1992)
HAER DC-34
H

Boundary Street; see Florida Avenue

Bowen,Anthony,YMCA Building; see Twelfth Street YMCA Building

Bowie House (Sevier House)
3124 Q St. NW
HABS DC-60
HABS DC,GEO,12-
2ph L

Boyce & Lewis Shoes; see 437-441 Seventh Street NW (Commercial Building)

Documentation: **ct** color transparencies **dr** measured drawings **fr** field records **pc** photograph captions **pg** pages of text **ph** photographs

Brady,Mathew B. ,Studio
625 Pennsylvania Ave. NW
HABS DC-295
HABS DC,WASH,325-
13pg L

Brickyard Hill House
3134 South St. NW
HABS DC-158
HABS DC,GEO,92-
8ph/13pg L

Bridge over Boundary Channel (Mount Vernon Memorial Hwy:Boundary Channel Bridge)
Spanning Channel Between Potomac R. & Boundary Ch.
HAER DC-19
HAER 1989(HAER):4
4ph/7pg/1pc L

Broadmoor,The,Apartment Building
3601 Connecticut Ave.
HABS DC-556
HABS DC,WASH,398-
2ph/1pg/1pc L

Brodt's Hat Factory
423 Eleventh St.
HABS DC-480
HABS DC,WASH,264-
1ph/12pg/1pc L

Bronaugh-Bibb-Libby House (Bibb House)
1409 Thirty-fifth St. NW
HABS DC-209
HABS DC,GEO,145-
1ph/12pg L

Brown House
1404 Thirty-fifth St. NW
HABS DC-191
HABS DC,GEO,127-
1ph/12pg L

Brown House; see Goszler-Meem-Brown House

Brown's Marble Hotel (Indian Queen Hotel; Metropolitan Hotel; Barney's Restaurant)
621 Pennsylvania Ave. NW
HABS DC-322
HABS DC,WASH,326-
3ph/4pg/1pc L

Brownley Building
1300-1304 F St. NW
HABS DC-381
HABS DC,WASH,244-
7ph/5pg/1pc L

Bruce,Blanche K. ,House
909 M St. NW
HABS DC-370
HABS DC,WASH,399-
9ph/1pg/1pc/1ct L

Buehler House; see Sullivan House

Building 137; see Navy Yard,General Foundry

Building 167; see Navy Yard,Boilermakers Shop

Bulfinch-Capitol Gatepost (U.S. Capitol Gatepost)
Constitution Ave. & Seventh St.,N.W.(SW Corner)
HABS DC-719
HABS DLC/PP-1993:DC-5
1dr/fr L

Bulfnch Capitol Gatehouses; see U.S. Capitol Gatehouses

3110 Bumbarton Avenue,NW (House) (Georgetown)
HABS DC-735
1ph/1pc H

Bunche,Ralph J. ,House
1510 Jackson St. NE
HABS DC-360
HABS DC,WASH,232-
14ph/7pg/2pc L

Burke Park; see Gompers,Samuel A.,Park & Reservation 68

Burling,Edward,Jr. ,House (Georgetown)
1339 Twenty-ninth St. NW
HABS DC-465
HABS DC,GEO,148-
1ph/3pg/1pc L H

Busch Building
710 E St. ,NW
HABS DC-575
HABS DC,WASH,289-
15ph/10pg/1pc L

Bussard-Newman House
1311 Thirty-fifth St. NW
HABS DC-196
HABS DC,GEO,132-
1ph/10pg L

607-609 C Street (Commercial Building) (McDonald's)
HABS DC-515
HABS DC,WASH,315-
1ph/3pg/1pc L

458 C Street NW
HABS DC-374
HABS DC,WASH,240-
6ph/3pg/1pc L

Cairo Hotel
1615 Q St. NW
HABS DC-307
HABS DC,WASH,400-
4ph/1pg/1pc L

Caldwell,Elias B. ,House,Doorway & Int. Archway
206 Pennsylvania Ave. SE
HABS DC-137
HABS DC,WASH,7-
2ph/1pc L

Caldwell,Timothy,House (Arts Club of Washington)
2017 I St. NW
HABS DC-84
HABS DC,WASH,22-
11dr/12ph/14pg/1pc/2ct L

Calvert Street Bridge
(Ellington,Duke,Memorial Bridge; Rock Creek & Potomac Parkway Project 1992)
HAER DC-23
H

Camaroon Chancery; see Hauge,Christian,House

Cameron House; see Tayloe,Benjamin Ogle,House

Canadian Chancery; see Moore,Clarence,House

Canal Street at Independence Avenue (Row House); see Southeast Area Survey

Canal Warehouse
3222 M St. NW
HABS DC-144
HABS DC,GEO,87-
4ph/5pg L

Cannon House Office Building
First St. & Independence Ave. SE
HABS DC-2
HABS 1983(HABS):176
1ph/1pc/2ct L

Capital Garage
1320 New York Ave. NW
HABS DC-279
HABS DC,WASH,402-
5ph/1pg/1pc L

Capital Souvenirs; see 320 Eighth Street NW (Commercial Building)

Capital Traction Company Powerhouse
3142 K St. NW
HABS DC-145
HABS DC,GEO,88-
12ph/18pg L

Capital Traction Company Union Station
3600 M St. NW
HABS DC-125
HABS DC,GEO,84-
15ph/15pg L

Capitol Hill Historic District
HABS DC-550
HABS DC,WASH,553-
1dr L

Capitol Hill Historic District
Capitol Hill (Map)
HABS DC-621
HABS 1991(HABS):28
1dr L

Capitol Hill Historic District; see 630-656 East Capitol Street

Capitol Hill Historic District; see 114-154 Eleventh Street,SE (Houses)

Capitol Hill Historic District; see 16 Fifth Street,N.E. (House)

Capitol Hill Historic District; see 1206-1242 Pennsylvania Avenue,Southeast (Houses)

Careleton,Joseph,House
1052-54 Potomac St. NW
HABS DC-146
HABS DC,GEO,89-
4ph/7pg L

Carleton Chambers (Apartment Hotel); see Hay-Adams Hotel

Carpel's Liquor Store; see 1001 D Street (Commercial Building)

Carriage House
1313 Thirty-first St. NW
HABS DC-250
HABS DC,GEO,119-
2ph/8pg L

Carroll House; see Duddington Mansion

101 & 122-124 Carroll Street (House); see Southeast Area Survey

Carthage,The,Apartment Building
2301 Connecticut Ave.
HABS DC-557
HABS DC,WASH,405-
1ph/1pg/1pc L

Cary,Mary Ann Shadd,House
1421 W St. NW
HABS DC-368
HABS DC,WASH,403-
1ph/1pg/1pc L

Castle,The; see Smithsonian Institution Building

Cedar Hill; see Douglass,Frederick,House

Central Armature Works
625-27 D St.,NW
HABS DC-611
HABS DC,WASH,352-
ıDLC/PP-1992:DC-4°
3ph/10pg/2pc L

Central Armature Works; see 629 D Street NW (Commercial Building)

Central National Bank Building (Apex Liquor Store; St. Marc Hotel)
631 Pennsylvania Ave. NW
HABS DC-229
HABS DC,WASH,186-
3ph/17pg/1pc L

Central Public Library; see Washington Public Library

Central Union Mission
624 Indiana Ave. NW
HABS DC-511
HABS DC,WASH,313-
3ph/3pg/1pc L

3219 Cherry Hill Lane,NW (House) (Georgetown)
HABS DC-737
1ph/1pc H

Chesapeake & Ohio Canal National Historic Park; see Chesapeake & Ohio Canal,Georgetown Section

Chesapeake & Ohio Canal,Georgetown Section (Chesapeake & Ohio Canal National Historic Park)
E. & W. parallel to M St. NW
HABS DC-147
HABS DC,GEO,25- ı1991(HABS):28°
17ph/15pg/fr L

Chesapeake,The,Apartment Building
4607 Connecticut Ave.
HABS DC-562
HABS DC,WASH,404-
1ph/1pg/1pc L

Chinatown
H St. NW,600-800 Blocks & Seventh St. ,700 Block
HABS DC-456
HABS DC,WASH,548-
9ph/1pc L

Chinese Chancery; see Fahnestock,Gibson,House

Chinese Community Church
1011 L St. NW
HABS DC-281
HABS DC,WASH,406-
2ph/1pg/1pc L

Chinese Legation; see Apartment Building

Christ Church
620 G St. SE
HABS DC-48
HABS DC,WASH,139-
10dr/4ph/3pg/1pc L

Christ Church (Episcopal)
3116 O St. NW
HABS DC-243
HABS DC,GEO,113-
10ph/20pg L

Christian Science Building; see Gray,Justice Horace,House

Church of the Covenant (National Presbyterian Church)
Eighteenth & N Sts. NW
HABS DC-140
HABS DC,WASH,407-
9ph/1pg/1pc L

City Hall,Old; see District of Columbia City Hall

City Post Office
HABS DC-570
HABS DLC/PP-1993:DC-3
177ph/148pg/16pc L

City Tavern
3206-3208 M St. NW
HABS DC-81
HABS DC,GEO,57-
18ph/4pg L

Cloud,Abner,House
Intersection of Canal Rd. & Reservoir Rd. NW
HABS DC-99
HABS DC,WASH,167-
22dr/3ph/4pg/fr L

Cole,Annie A. ,House
1400-1402 Massachusetts Ave. NW
HABS DC-450
HABS DC,WASH,408-
1ph/1pg/1pc L

Columbia Historical Society; see Heurich,Christian,Mansion

Columbia Inst. for Deaf & Dumb,Professor's House; see Gallaudet College,Professor's House

Columbia Inst. for the Deaf & Dumb,President's Hse; see Gallaudet College,President's House

Columbia Institute for the Deaf & Dumb; see Galludet College

Columbia Institute for the Deaf & Dumb,College Hal; see Galludet College,College Hall

Columbia Institute for the Deaf & Dumb,Gate House; see Gallaudet College,Gate House

Columbia Institute for the Deaf & Dumb,Gym; see Gallaudet College,Gymnasium

Columbia Railway Company Car Barns (Trinidad Cable Car Barns)
Fifteenth St. & Benning Rd. NE
HABS DC-297
HABS DC,WASH,409-
9ph/1pg/1pc L

Commandant's House; see U. S. Marine Corps Commandant's House

Concordia German Evangelical Church; see Concordia United Church of Christ

Concordia United Church of Christ (Concordia German Evangelical Church)
1920 G St. NW
HABS DC-396
HABS DC,WASH,410-
1ph/1pg/1pc L

Congressional Cemetary (Latrobe Cenotaphs)
Eighteenth & E Sts. SE
HABS DC-424
HABS DC,WASH,255-
2dr/fr L

Connecticut Avenue
HABS DC-698
H

2101 Connecticut Avenue (Apartment Building)
HABS DC-560
HABS DC,WASH,370-
1ph/1pg/1pc L

2929 Connecticut Avenue (Apartment Building)
HABS DC-561
HABS DC,WASH,372-
1ph/1pg/1pc L

Documentation: **ct** color transparencies **dr** measured drawings **fr** field records
pc photograph captions **pg** pages of text **ph** photographs

4701 Connecticut Avenue (Apartment Building)
HABS DC-563
HABS DC,WASH,377-
2ph/1pg/1pc L

4801 Connecticut Avenue (Apartment Building)
HABS DC-564
HABS DC,WASH,378-
1ph/1pg/1pc L

Connecticut Avenue Bridge (Rock Creek & Potomac Parkway Project 1992)
Spanning Klingle Valley
HAER DC-27
H

Connecticut Avenue Bridge; see Taft,William H. ,Memorial Bridge

1800 Connecticut Avenue,N.W. (House)
Corner of Florida Ave.
HABS DC-558
HABS DC,WASH,367-
1ph/1pg/1pc L

Convention Center Site,District of Columbia (H Street,900 & 1000 Block; Ninth Street,800 & 900 Block; Eleventh Street,800 Block; New York Avenue,900 & 1000 Block)
I St. ,900 & 1000 Block,Tenth St.,800 & 900 Block
HABS DC-384
HABS DC,WASH,252-
66ph/4pg/5pc L

Cooke's Row,Villa No. 3
3013 Q St. NW
HABS DC-182
HABS DC,GEO,105-
5ph/15pg L

Corcoran Art Gallery (U.S. Court of Claims; Smithsonian Institution,Renwick Gallery)
Seventeenth St. & Pennsylvania Ave. NW
HABS DC-49
HABS DC,WASH,140-
3dr/30ph/24pg/2pc/fr L

Corcoran,Thomas,House
3119 M St. NW
HABS DC-34
HABS DC,GEO,47-
1ph L

Cordova Apartments (President Madison Apartments)
1908 Florida Ave. NW
HABS DC-422
HABS DC,WASH,411-
3ph/1pc L

Corson & Gruman Company; see Ray's Warehouse & Office

Cosmopolitan Theatre; see Earle Theatre

Cosmos Club; see Townsend House

Cosmos Club (Old); see Cutts,Richard,House

Cowing,John C. ,House
Museum of American History,Smithsonian Institution
HABS DC-473
HABS DC,WASH,412-
3dr/fr L

Cox,Col. John,House
3339 N St. NW
HABS DC-150
HABS DC,GEO,37-
3ph L

Cramphin,Thomas,Building
3209-3211 M St. NW
HABS DC-118
HABS DC,GEO,77-
2ph/7pg L

Crandall's Theater,Rendezvous Adult Magazines&Film; see Riley Building,Rendezvous Adult Magazines & Films

Crandall's Theater,Sunny's Surplus; see Riley Building,Sunny's Surplus

Crandell,Germond,Building
401-407 Seventh St. NW
HABS DC-224
HABS DC,WASH,181-
10ph/29pg/2pc L

Crawford-Cassin House
3017 O St. NW
HABS DC-184
HABS DC,GEO,107-
6ph/13pg L

Cullinan Building (Union Clothing and Furniture)
415 Seventh St. ,NW
HABS DC-225
HABS DC,WASH,182-
7ph/18pg/1pc L

Culver,Fredrick B. ,House
809 E St. NW
HABS DC-220
HABS DC,WASH,177-
4ph/5pg L

Cutts,Richard,House
(Madison,Dolley,House; Cosmos Club (Old))
1518 H St. NW
HABS DC-58
HABS DC,WASH,32-
3ph/5pg/2pc L

Czechoslovakian Embassy; see Hauge,Christian,House

633 D St. ,NW (Commercial Building)
(Antonio's Spanish-Italian Cafeteria & Takeout)
HABS DC-612
HABS DC,WASH,353-
1ph/10pg/1pc L

635 & 637 D St. ,NW (Commercial Building)
HABS DC-613
HABS DC,WASH,354-
1ph/9pg/1pc L

639 D St. ,NW (Commercial Building)
HABS DC-603
HABS DC,WASH,355-
1ph/8pg/1pc L

641 D St. ,NW (Commercial Building)
(Leon's & Resenblatt's)
HABS DC-602
HABS DC,WASH,342-
8pg L

645 D St. ,NW (Commercial Building)
(Lincoln Inn Restaurant)
HABS DC-614
HABS DC,WASH,356-
1ph/7pg/1pc L

709 D St. ,NW (Commercial Building)
(Union Hardware Decorator Center)
HABS DC-584
HABS DC,WASH,298-
1ph/8pg/1pc L

713 D St. ,NW (Commercial Building)
(D. C. Souvenirs)
HABS DC-579
HABS DC,WASH,293-
2ph/9pg/1pc L

629 D St. ,NW (Rear) (Warehouse)
HABS DC-616
HABS DC,WASH,360-
6pg L

631 D St. ,NW (Rear) (Warehouse)
HABS DC-615
HABS DC,WASH,359-
7pg L

1001 D Street (Commercial Building)
(Carpel's Liquor Store; Fotomat)
1001 D St.
HABS DC-488
HABS DC,WASH,270-
2ph/2pg/1pc L

1003 D Street (Commercial Building)
(Souvenir World)
HABS DC-489
HABS DC,WASH,271-
2pg L

1005-1007 D Street (Commercial Building) (Kaufman,D. J. ,Store & Blimpie Restaurant)
HABS DC-490
HABS DC,WASH,272-
1ph/4pg/1pc/fr L

1015 D Street (Commercial Building)
(Price Is Right Store; New Life Yogurt Store)
HABS DC-492
HABS DC,WASH,274-
1ph/3pg/1pc/fr L

629 D Street NW (Commercial Building) (Central Armature Works)
HABS DC-308
HABS DLC/PP-1992:DC-4
3ph/16pg/3pc L

22 D Street SE (House)
HABS DC-17
HABS DC,WASH,127-
3ph L

626 D Street,NW (Commercial Building) (Leonard's Lunchh)
HABS DC-595
HABS DC,WASH,310-
1ph/7pg/1pc L

D. C. Central Public Library,Old
499 Pennsylvania Ave. NW
HABS DC-372
HABS DC,WASH,241
1ph/2pg/1pc L

D. C. Souvenirs; see 713 D St. ,NW (Commercial Building)

D. C. Space; see 443 Seventh Street,NW (Commercial Building)

Daly,Carroll,House
1306 Thirty-fifth St. NW
HABS DC-205
HABS DC,GEO,141-
1ph/8pg L

Dash's Designer; see 1308 F Street NW (Commercial Building)

Dashiell,George W. ,Building
1203 Pennsylvania Ave. NW
HABS DC-432
HABS DC,WASH,225-
5ph/9pg/1pc L

Davidson,John,House
1220 Wisconsin Ave. NW
HABS DC-102
HABS DC,GEO,62-
2ph/5pg L

Davis,James Y. ,Sons Building
1201 Pennsylvania Ave. & 408 Twelfth St. NW
HABS DC-312
HABS DC,WASH,222-
10ph/12pg/1pc L

DC Engine Company Number Five Firehouse; see Bank of Columbia

De La Roche-Jewell Tenant House
1320 Thirtieth St. NW
HABS DC-179
HABS DC,GEO,102-
2ph/9pg L

Decatur House (National Trust for Historic Preservation)
748 Jackson Pl. NW
HABS DC-16
HABS DC,WASH,28-
31dr/43ph/2pg/2pc/2ct/fr L

Decatur-Gunther House (Williams,John S. ,House; Hood House)
2812 N St. NW
HABS DC-29
HABS DC,GEO,43-
28dr/15ph/5pg L

Delano,Frederic,House (Residence of the Ambassador of Ireland)
2244 S St. NW
HABS DC-419
HABS DC,WASH,413-
1ph/1pg/1pc L

Delaware Avenue
HABS DC-699
H

3023 Dent Place,NW (House) (Georgetown)
HABS DC-732
1ph/1pc H

Devil's Cahir Footbridge (Lyon's Mill Footbridge; Rock Creek & Potomac Parkway Project 1992)
HAER DC-35
H

Devore-Chase House
2000 Twenty-fourth St. NW
HABS DC-288
HABS DC,WASH,197-
9ph/10pg L

District Building
Fourteenth & E Sts. NW (SE Corner)
HABS DC-314
HABS D.C.WASH,256-
6ph/6pg L

District of Columbia City Hall (City Hall,Old; District of Columbia Superior Court)
451 Indiana Ave. NW
HABS DC-41
HABS D.C.WASH,136-
15ph/1pg/1pc/fr L

District of Columbia Superior Court; see District of Columbia City Hall

Dix,General John A. ,House
456 C St. NW
HABS DC-373
HABS DC,WASH,239-
8ph/3pg/1pc L

Dodge,Francis,Warehouse
1006 Wisconsin Ave. NW
HABS DC-436
HABS DC,GEO,60-
4ph/9pg L

Dodge,Robert P. ,House
1534 Twenty-eighth St. NW
HABS DC-246
HABS DC,GEO,116-
9ph/16pg L

Douglas Records; see 425 Seventh St. ,NW (Commercial Building)

Douglass,Frederick,House (Cedar Hill; Van Hook,John,House)
1411 W St. SE
HABS DC-97
HABS DC,WASH,166-
8dr/11ph/6pg/6ct/fr L

Dresden,The,Apartment Building
2126 Connecticut Ave.
HABS DC-565
HABS DC,WASH,414-
1ph/1pg/1pc L

Duddington Mansion (Carroll House)
First & Second & E & F Sts. SE
HABS DC-8
HABS DC,WASH,122-
2dr/6ph/5pg L

3015 Dumbarton Avenue NW (House)
HABS DC-183
HABS DC,GEO,106-
2ph/12pg L

3037 Dumbarton Avenue,NW (House) (Georgetown)
HABS DC-733
1ph/1pc H

3127 Dumbarton Avenue,NW (House) (Georgetown)
HABS DC-736
1ph/1pc H

Dumbarton House (Bellevue; Rittenhouse Place; National Headquarters of Colonial Dames of America
2715 Q St. NW (moved from Q St. above Rock Creek)
HABS DC-434
HABS DC,GEO,9-
3ph/1pg/1pc/fr L

3128 Dumbarton Street,Northwest (House) (Georgetown Historic District)
HABS DC-636
HABS 1991(HABS):28
1dr/1ph/1pc/fr L

3130 Dumbarton Street,Northwest (House) (Georgetown Historic District)
HABS DC-634
HABS 1991(HABS):28
1dr/fr L

Dunbar,Elizabeth A. ,House
1425 Thirty-fourth St. NW
HABS DC-460
HABS DC,GEO,149-
3pg L

Duncanson-Cranch House (Barney Neighborhood House)
468-470 N St. SW
HABS DC-128
HABS DC,WASH,118-
4ph/1pg/1pc L

Duncanson,William,House; see Maples,The

DuPont Circle (Reservations 59,60,61; Pacific Circle)
HABS DC-669
H

Dutch Boy Delicatessen; see 639 Indiana Ave. ,NW (Commercial Building)

Duvall Foundry
1050 Thirtieth St. NW
HABS DC-154
HABS DC,GEO,91-
4ph/12pg/fr L

624 E St. ,NW (Commercial Building) (Independence Federal Savings & Trust)
HABS DC-609
HABS DC,WASH,350-
1ph/9pg/1pc L

626 E St. ,NW (Commercial Building)
HABS DC-601
HABS DC,WASH,341-
10pg L

Documentation: **ct** color transparencies **dr** measured drawings **fr** field records **pc** photograph captions **pg** pages of text **ph** photographs

1216 E Street NW (Commercial Building & Garage)
HABS DC-354
1ph/7pg/1pc L

1200 E Street NW (Commercial Building) (Service Station and Garage)
HABS DC-420
HABS DC,WASH,223-
2ph/5pg/1pc L

625 E Street NW (Commercial Building)
HABS DC-228
HABS DC,WASH,185-
1ph L

1208-1214 E Street NW (Garage)
HABS DC-426
HABS DC,WASH,224-
1ph/3pg/1pc L

2029 E Street NW (House)
HABS DC-136
HABS DC,WASH,15-
3ph/1pc L

514 E Street NW (House)
HABS DC-236
HABS DC,WASH,193-
1ph L

515 E. Capitol St.,S.E. (House)
Capitol Hill Historic District
HABS DC-554
HABS DC,WASH,557-
1dr L

619 E. Capitol St.,S.E. (House)
Capitol Hill Historic District
HABS DC-552
HABS DC,WASH,555-
1dr L

Eagle House; see Mountz,John,House

Earle Theatre (Cosmopolitan Theatre; Warner Theatre)
Thirteenth & E Sts.,NW
HABS DC-639
HABS DLC/PP-1993:DC-5
111ph/64pg/9pc L

Easby House
D St. NW
HABS DC-7
HABS DC,WASH,39-
2dr/4ph L

500 East Capitol Street (House)
HABS DC-331
HABS DC,WASH,379-
2ph/1pg/1pc L

630-656 East Capitol Street (Capitol Hill Historic District)
HABS DC-655
HABS 1992(HABS):DC-1
4dr/fr L

1124 East Capitol Street,S.E. (House)
1124 E. Capitol St.,SE
HABS DC-626
HABS 1991(HABS):28
1dr/fr L

317 East Capitol Street,S.E. (House)
317 E. Capitol St.,SE
HABS DC-622
HABS 1991(HABS):28
1dr/fr L

602 East Capitol Street,S.E. (House)
602 E. Capitol St.,SE
HABS DC-624
HABS 1991(HABS):28
1dr/fr L

913 East Capitol Street,S.E. (House)
913 E. Capitol St.,SE
HABS DC-623
HABS 1991(HABS):28
1dr/fr L

East Potomac Park (Reservation 333)
HABS DC-692
H

Eastern Market
Seventh St. SE
HABS DC-291
HABS DC,WASH,415-
12ph/1pg/1pc L

Eastern Market Metro Station
(Resrevations 44,44A,45,46,47,47A,48,49)
HABS DC-670
H

308-310 Eighth St. NW (Commercial Building)
HABS DC-309
HABS DC,WASH,374-
1ph/1pg/1pc L

Eighth Street
HABS DC-718
H

408 Eighth Street (Commercial Building) (National Art and Frame Company)
HABS DC-517
HABS DC,WASH,286-
3ph/8pg/1pc L

320 Eighth Street NW (Commercial Building)
HABS DC-237
HABS DC,WASH,194-
1ph L

320 Eighth Street NW (Commercial Building) (Capital Souvenirs)
HABS DC-498
HABS DC,WASH,375-
1ph/2pg/1pc L

322 Eighth Street NW (Commercial Building) (Piccolo's)
HABS DC-499
HABS DC,WASH,376-
5ph/2pg/1pc L

405 Eleventh Street (Commercial Building) (Universal Newstand)
HABS DC-475
HABS DC,WASH,259-
2pg L

407 Eleventh Street (Commercial Building) (Kung Fu Restaurant)
HABS DC-476
HABS DC,WASH,260-
2pg L

409 Eleventh Street (Commercial Building) (Tanen's)
HABS DC-477
HABS DC,WASH,261-
2pg L

421 Eleventh Street (Commercial Building) (Am-Chi Restaurant)
HABS DC-479
HABS DC,WASH,263-
1ph/10pg/1pc L

425-429 Eleventh Street (Commercial Building) (Alla-Scala Restaurant)
HABS DC-481
HABS DC,WASH,275-
1ph/13pg/1pc L

415-417 Eleventh Street (Commercial Buildings) (Staley's Hong Kong Exchange & Regency Liquors)
HABS DC-478
HABS DC,WASH,262-
1ph/2pg/1pc L

132-144 & 900-905 Eleventh Street (Row Houses); see Southeast Area Survey

304-306 Eleventh Street SW,(Double House)
HABS DC-56
HABS DC,WASH,146-
2ph L

114-154 Eleventh Street,SE (Houses)
(Capitol Hill Historic District)
HABS DC-653
HABS 1991(HABS):28
3dr/fr L

Eleventh Street,800 Block; see Convention Center Site,District of Columbia

Elks Lodge; see Washington Lodge Number 15,B. P. O. E.

Ellington,Duke,Memorial Bridge; see Calvert Street Bridge

Embassy Chevron; see Embassy Gulf Sevice Center

Embassy Gulf Sevice Center (Embassy Chevron; Rock Creek & Potomac Parkway Project 1992)
2200 P St.
HABS DC-664
H

Embassy of Greece Annex; see Sheridan,Irene,House

Embassy of Luxembourg; see Stewart,Alexander,House

Embassy of Poland (Polish Embassy)
2640 Sixteenth St. NW
HABS DC-538
HABS DC,WASH,416-
1dr L

Embassy of the Arab Republic of Egypt; see Beale,Joseph,House

Embassy of the Fed. Repub. of Camaroon Chancery; see Hauge,Christian,House

Embassy of the Union of Soviet Socialist Republics; see Pullman House

Engine Company Number Fifteen,Firehouse
2100 Fourteenth St. SE
HABS DC-92
HABS DC,WASH,162-
1ph L

Engine Company Number Four,Firehouse
931 R St. NW
HABS DC-87
HABS DC,WASH,156-
1ph L

Engine Company Number Nine,Firehouse
1624 U St. NW
HABS DC-89
HABS DC,WASH,159-
1ph L

Engine Company Number One,Firehouse
1643 K St. NW
HABS DC-86
HABS DC,WASH,155-
1ph L

Engine Company Number Seventeen,Firehouse
1227 Monroe St. NE
HABS DC-93
HABS DC,WASH,163-
2ph L

Engine Company Number Six,Firehouse
438 Massachusetts Ave. NW
HABS DC-88
HABS DC,WASH,158-
1ph L

Engine Company Number Ten,Firehouse
1341 Maryland Ave. NE
HABS DC-90
HABS DC,WASH,160-
1ph L

Engine Company Number Twelve,Firehouse
1626 N. Capitol St.
HABS DC-91
HABS DC,WASH,161-
1ph L

Engine Company Number Twenty-one,Firehouse
1763 Lanier Place NW
HABS DC-94
HABS DC,WASH,164-
1ph L

Engine Company Number Twenty-Two,Firehouse
5760 Georgia Ave. NW
HABS DC-95
HABS DC,WASH,165-
1ph L

Engine Company Number Two,Firehouse
719 Twelfth St. NW
HABS DC-350
HABS DC,WASH,417-
2ph/1pg/1pc L

Estes Mill (Ruins)
Rock Creek Park
HABS DC-40
HABS DC,WASH,135-
1ph L

Evening Star Building
Eleventh St. & Pennsylvania Ave.
HABS DC-316
HABS DC,WASH,418-
1ph/1pg/1pc L

Everett,Edward H. ,House (Turkish Embassy)
1606 Twenty-third St. NW
HABS DC-258
HABS DC,WASH,201-
10ph/21pg L

Evermay
1623 Twenty-eighth St. NW
HABS DC-61
HABS DC,GEO,49-
2ph L

Executive Mansion,The; see White House,The

1002,1006 Eye Street (House); see Southeast Area Survey

Eye Street NW (House)
HABS DC-131
HABS DC,WASH,117-
1ph L

Eynon Building
3407 M St. NW
HABS DC-124
HABS DC,GEO,83-
3ph/6pg L

920-930 F St.,NW (Commercial Buildings)
HABS DC-569
HABS DLC/PP-1992:DC-3
1dr/9ph/1pc/fr L

1925 F Street Club; see Steedman-Ray House

1308 F Street NW (Commercial Building) (Dash's Designer)
HABS DC-380
HABS DC,WASH,248-
2ph/5pg/1pc L

1310 F Street NW (Commercial Building) (Raleigh's Haberdasher)
HABS DC-377
HABS DC,WASH,245-
3ph/6pg/1pc L

1314 F Street NW (Commercial Building) (Becker's Leather Goods Store)
HABS DC-376
HABS DC,WASH,246-
5ph/6pg/1pc L

812 F Street NW (Commercial Building)
812 F St. (previously recorded as 814 F St. ,NW)
HABS DC-213
HABS DC,WASH,170-
4ph/13pg/1pc L

818 F Street NW (Commercial Building)
HABS DC-215
HABS DC,WASH,172-
3ph/13pg/1pc L

1901 F Street NW (Row House)
HABS DC-327
HABS DC,WASH,368-
12ph/2pg/1pc L

1903-1911 F Street NW (Row Houses)
HABS DC-328
HABS DC,WASH,479-
9ph/1pg/1pc L

F Street NW,600 Block
HABS DC-444
HABS DC,WASH,476-
2ph/1pc L

F Street NW,600 Block (Commercial Buildings)
HABS DC-335
HABS DC,WASH,477-
3ph/1pg/1pc L

920-926 F Street,NW (Commercial Buildings) (Schwartz Building)
HABS DC-569-B
HABS DLC/PP-1992:DC-3
5dr/12ph/2pg/1pc/fr L

F. W. Woolworth Companyu (National Sales; Kinney Shoes)
406-410 Seventh St. ,NW
HABS DC-583
HABS DC,WASH,297-
1ph/9pg/1pc L

F&W Grand; see Jenifer Building (Commercial Building)

Fahnestock,Gibson,House (Republic of China Chancery; Chinese Chancery)
2311 Massachusetts Ave. NW
HABS DC-259
HABS DC,WASH,202-
5ph/14pg/1pc L

Fairbanks,Henry Parker,House; see Wilson,Woodrow,House

Famous Shoes; see 409-411 Seventh St. ,NW (Commercial Building)

Fantasy Books; see 410-412 Tenth Street (Commercial Building)

Farragut Square (Reservation 12)
HABS DC-671
H

Federal Triangle Building
315 9th St. NW,corner of 9th & D Sts. NW (sqr.408)
HABS DC-500
HABS DC,WASH,419-
2ph/2pg/1pc L

Female Union Benevolent Society (Lutz,John,House; Aged Woman's Home)
1255 Wisconsin Ave. NW
HABS DC-105
HABS DC,GEO,65-
3ph/7pg L

Fenwick,Teresa,House (Parrot,Thomas,House)
3512 P St. NW
HABS DC-83
HABS DC,GEO,58-
10dr/19ph/14pg L

Ferree Building (Boston Buffet Lunch; Big Flipper; Golden Fry)
417 Ninth St. ,NW
HABS DC-521
HABS DC,WASH,283-
9ph/12pg/1pc L

Field,Mrs. Marshall,House (Inter-American Defense Board Headquarters; Pink Palace)
2600 Sixteenth St. NW
HABS DC-537
HABS DC,WASH,420-
1dr L

Fields Building
614 Indiana Ave. NW
HABS DC-510
HABS DC,WASH,316-
1ph/2pg/1pc L

16 Fifth Street,N.E. (House) (Capitol Hill Historic District)
HABS DC-551
HABS DC,WASH,554-
1dr L

Findley House
3606 N St. NW
HABS DC-192
HABS DC,GEO,128-
1ph/8pg L

Finley,David E. ,House
3318 O St. NW
HABS DC-461
HABS DC,GEO,150-
9pg L

Firemen's Insurance Company Building
303 Seventh St. NW
HABS DC-235
HABS DC,WASH,192-
3ph/14pg/1pc L

First Baptist Church of Georgetown
Twenty-Seventh St. NW
HABS DC-241
HABS DC,GEO,111-
4ph/13pg L

214 First Street (House); see Southeast Area Survey

Fitzhugh,Emma S. ,House (Philippine Embassy)
2253 R St. NW
HABS DC-260
HABS DC,WASH,203-
7ph/2pg/1pc L

Florida Avenue (Boundary Street)
HABS DC-700
H

Florida House; see Manning,Edwin C. ,House

Folger Park (Reservation 16)
HABS DC-672
H

Ford Motor Company Building
451-455 Pennsylvania Ave. NW
HABS DC-375
HABS DC,WASH,238-
17ph/7pg/1pc/fr L

Ford's Theater (Ford's Theater National Historic Park)
511 Eleventh St. NW
HABS DC-82
HABS DC,WASH,421-
2dr/4ph/8pg/1pc L

Ford's Theater National Historic Park; see Ford's Theater

Forrest-Marbury House
3350 M St. NW
HABS DC-68
HABS DC,GEO,55-
8ph/2pg L

Fotomat; see 1001 D Street (Commercial Building)

501-511 Fourteenth Street NW (Commercial Building) (Locker Room,The)
HABS DC-356
HABS DC,WASH,229-
1ph/3pg/1pc L

Foxhall,Henry,House (McKenny House)
3123 Dumbarton Ave.
HABS DC-66
HABS DC,GEO,54-
2ph L

Franklin Park (Reservation 9)
HABS DC-673
H

Franklin School
Thirteenth & K Sts. NW
HABS DC-289
HABS DC,WASH,422-
22ph/1pg/1pc L

Fraser,George,House (Scott-Thorpe House; Golden Parrot Restaurant; Golden Booeymonger Restaurant)
R & Twentieth Sts.
HABS DC-318
HABS DC,WASH,423-
1ph/1pg/1pc L

French House; see Oak Hill

French,Benjamin Brown,School
545 Seventh St. SE
HABS DC-467
HABS DC,WASH,424-
2ph/1pc L

Friendship House; see Maples,The

Frisco's; see Stone,William J. ,Building

600-602 & 1100 G Street (House); see Southeast Area Survey

1908-1916 G Street NW (Row Houses)
HABS DC-404
HABS DC,WASH,480-
9ph/1pc L

2024-2026 G Street NW (Row Houses); see Babcock,Orville E. ,House

613-631 G Street SW (Framehouses)
HABS DC-53
3ph L

G Street,NW,1200 Block (Comm. Bldgs.) , No. 1201
HABS DC-333-A
HABS DC,WASH,425-
1ph/1pg/1pc L

G Street,NW,1200 Block (Comm. Bldgs.) ,No. 1204
HABS DC-333-B
HABS DC,WASH,426-
1ph/1pc L

G Street,NW,1200 Block (Comm. Bldgs.) ,No. 1239
HABS DC-333-C
HABS DC,WASH,427-
1ph/1pg/1pc L

Gallaudet College,Gate House (Columbia Institute for the Deaf & Dumb,Gate House)
Seventh & Florida Ave. NE
HABS DC-667
HABS DC,WASH,428D-
2ph/1pc L

Gallaudet College,Gymnasium (Columbia Institute for the Deaf & Dumb,Gym)
Seventh & Florida Ave.,N.E.
HABS DC-640
HABS DC,WASH,428E-
8ph/1pc L

Gallaudet College,President's House (Columbia Inst. for the Deaf & Dumb,President's Hse
Seventh St. & Florida Ave. NE
HABS DC-303
HABS DC,WASH,428C-
16ph/1pc L

Gallaudet College,Professor's House (Columbia Inst. for Deaf & Dumb,Professor's House)
Seventh & Florida Ave.,NE
HABS DC-641
HABS DC,WASH,428F-
2ph/1pc L

Galludet College (Columbia Institute for the Deaf & Dumb)
Seventh & Florida Ave. NE
HABS DC-300
HABS DC,WASH,428-
12ph/1pc L

Galludet College,Chapel Hall
Seventh & Florida Ave. NE
HABS DC-301
HABS DC,WASH,428A-
12ph/1pc L

Galludet College,College Hall (Columbia Institute for the Deaf & Dumb,College Hal
Seventh & Florida Ave. NE
HABS DC-302
HABS DC,WASH,428B-
12ph/1pc L

Galt & Brother Jewelers (Medco Discount Center)
1107 Pennsylvania Ave. NW
HABS DC-546
HABS DC,WASH,547-
14ph/1pc L

Gantt-Williams House; see Owens,Isaac,House (Doorway)

Garfield Park (Resrvation 17)
HABS DC-674
H

Gazebo
3233 N St. NW
HABS DC-155
HABS DC,GEO,36A-
1ph L

George & Company; see 427 & 429 Seventh St. ,NW (Commercial Building)

Georgetown; see Adams-Mason House

Georgetown; see 3110 Bumbarton Avenue,NW (House)

Georgetown; see Burling,Edward,Jr. ,House

Georgetown; see 3219 Cherry Hill Lane,NW (House)

Georgetown; see 3023 Dent Place,NW (House)

Georgetown; see 3037 Dumbarton Avenue,NW (House)

Georgetown; see 3127 Dumbarton Avenue,NW (House)

Georgetown; see McCleery House

Georgetown; see 3041 N St.,NW (House)

Georgetown; see 2823 N Street,NW (House)

Georgetown; see 3254 N Street,NW (House)

Georgetown; see 3626 N Street,NW (House)

Georgetown; see 3632 N Street,NW (House)

Georgetown; see 3122 O Street,NW (House)

Georgetown; see 3132 O Street,NW (House)

Georgetown; see 3314 O Street,NW (House)

Georgetown; see 3517 O Street,NW (House)

Georgetown; see 3615 O Street,NW (House)

Georgetown; see 2803 P Street,NW (House)

Georgetown; see 2811 P Street,NW (House)

Georgetown; see 3022 P Street,NW (House)

Georgetown; see 3042 P Street,NW (House)

Georgetown; see 3116 P Street,NW (House)

Georgetown; see 2704 Poplar Street,NW (House)

Georgetown; see 3611 Prospect Street,NW (House)

Georgetown; see 3106 Q Street,NW (House)

Georgetown; see 3308 R Street,NW (House)

Georgetown; see 3216 Reservoir Road,NW (House)

Georgetown; see 1219 Thirthieth Street,NW (House)

Georgetown; see 1029 Thirtieth Street,NW (House)

Georgetown; see 1248 Thirtieth Street,NW (House)

Georgetown; see 1530 Thirtieth Street,NW (House)

Georgetown; see 1322 Thirty-fifth Street,NW (House)

Georgetown; see 1545 Thirty-fifth Street,NW (House)

Georgetown; see 1680 Thirty-first Street,NW (House)

Georgetown; see 1238 Thirty-fourth Street,NW (House)

Georgetown; see 1406 Thirty-fourth Street,NW (House)

Georgetown; see 1514 Thirty-fourth Street,NW (House)

Georgetown; see 1603 Thirty-fourth Street,NW (House)

Georgetown; see 1304 Thirty-sixth Street,NW (House)

Georgetown; see 1420 Thirty-sixth Street,NW (House)

Georgetown; see 1520 Thirty-third Street,NW (House)

Georgetown; see 1617 Twebty-ninth Street,NW (House)

Georgetown; see 1314 Twenty-eighth Street,NW (House)

Georgetown; see 1348 Twenty-eighth Street,NW (House)

Georgetown; see 1521 Twenty-ninth Street,NW (HOUSE)

Georgetown; see 1529 Twenty-ninth Street,NW (House)

Georgetown; see 1539 Twenty-ninth Street,NW (House)

Georgetown; see 1350 Twenty-seventh Street,NW (House)

Georgetown; see 1417 Twenty-seventh Street,NW (House)

Georgetown; see 3215 Volta Street,NW (House)

Georgetown Club,The; see 1530 Wisconsin Avenue NW (House)

Georgetown Historic District; see 3128 Dumbarton Street,Northwest (House)

Georgetown Historic District; see 3130 Dumbarton Street,Northwest (House)

Georgetown Historic District; see Georgetown Historic District-Facades

Georgetown Historic District; see 3334 N Street,N. W. (House)

Georgetown Historic District; see 3111 N Street,Northwest

Georgetown Historic District; see 3328 N Street,Northwest

Georgetown Historic District; see 3300 O Street,Northwest (House)

Georgetown Historic District; see 3006 P Street,Northwest (House)

Georgetown Historic District; see 3040 P Street,Northwest (House)

Georgetown Historic District; see 3234 Prospect Street,N.W. (House)

Georgetown Historic District; see 3320 Prospect Street,Northwest (House)

Georgetown Historic District; see 1408 Thirty-Fifth Street,N. W. (House)

Georgetown Historic District; see 1209 Thirty-Fifth Street,Northwest (House)

Georgetown Historic District; see 1422 Thirty-Third Street,Northwest (House)

Georgetown Historic District; see 1352 Twenty-Eighth Street,Northwest (House)

Georgetown Historic District; see 1537 Twenty-Eighth Street,Northwest (House)

Georgetown Historic District-Facades (Georgetown Historic District)
HABS DC-620
HABS 1991(HABS):28
2dr L

Georgetown Market,The
3276 M St. NW
HABS DC-123
HABS DC,GEO,82-
3ph/7pg L

Georgetown Town Hall; see Bank of Columbia

Georgetown University,Healy Building
Thirty-seventh & O Sts. NW
HABS DC-248
HABS DC,GEO,118-
41ph/41pg L

Georgetown University,North Building,Old
Thirty-Seventh & O Sts. NW
HABS DC-170
HABS DC,GEO,20A-
5ph/1pg/1pc L

Georgetown Visitation Convent
1500 Thirty-fifth St. NW
HABS DC-211
HABS DC,GEO,147-
1ph/14pg L

Georgia Avenue; see Potomac Avenue

German Hi-Fi; see Hume Building

Gilman's,Z. D.,Drug Store (Weiss,Mark,Camera Center)
627 Pennsylvania Ave. NW
HABS DC-129
HABS DC,WASH,327-
9ph/10pg/1pc L

Girl Scout Teahouse (Hains Point Teahouse87); Hains Point Inn)
East Potomac Park
HABS DC-549
HABS DC,WASH,430-
25ph/16pg/2pc L

Glover,Charles C.,Bridge; see Massachusetts Avenue Bridge

Godey Lime Kilns (Ruins)
Junction of Rock Creek & Potomac Pkwy.
HABS DC-441
HABS DC,WASH,168-
3dr/5ph/4pg/1pc L

Golden Booeymonger Restaurant; see Fraser,George,House

Golden Bull Restaurant
308 Sixth St. NW
HABS DC-514
HABS D,WASH,321-
1ph/2pg/1pc L

Golden Fry; see Ferree Building

Golden Parrot Restaurant; see Fraser,George,House

Gompers,Samuel A.,Park & Reservation 68 (Reservations 68,68A,69,69A; Burke Park)
HABS DC-675
H

Goszler-Manogue House
1307 Thirty-fifth St. NW
HABS DC-193
HABS DC,GEO,129-
1ph/12pg L

Goszler-Meem-Brown House (Brown House)
3412 O St. NW
HABS DC-204
HABS DC,GEO,140-
1ph/8pg L

Grace Protestant Episcopal Church
1041 Wisconsin Ave. NW
HABS DC-440
HABS DC,GEO,61-
6dr/7ph/15pg/fr L

Grant Road Bridge
Spanning Broad Branch Creek on Grant Road
HAER DC-17
HAER 1989(HAER):4
4ph/4pg/1pc L

Gray,Justice Horace,House (Christian Science Building)
1601 Eye St. NW
HABS DC-79
HABS DC,WASH,154-
1ph L

Greyhound Bus Terminal
New York Ave. & Eleventh St. NW
HABS DC-402
HABS DC,WASH,431-
2ph/1pg/1pc L

Grief; see Adams Memorial

Grimke,Charlotte Forten,House
1608 R St. NW
HABS DC-366
HABS DC,WASH,432-
1ph/1pg/1pc L

Gunston Hall School for Girls
1904 T St. NW
HABS DC-416
HABS DC,WASH,433-
1ph/1pg/1pc L

Gutman-Wise Building
3140 M St. NW
HABS DC-117
HABS DC,GEO,76-
2ph/6pg L

1003 H Street NW (House)
HABS DC-132
HABS DC,WASH,18-
3ph L

H Street,900 & 1000 Block; see Convention Center Site,District of Columbia

HAER:4 dr,9 ph,1 da;HABS:22 ph,17 da.; see Potomac Aqueduct

Hains Point Inn; see Girl Scout Teahouse

Hains Point Teahouse87); see Girl Scout Teahouse

Halcyon House (Stoddert,Benjamin,House)
3400 Prospect St. NW
HABS DC-69
HABS DC,GEO,13-
4ph/26pg L

Hall,John Stoddert,House
2808 N St. NW
HABS DC-156
HABS DC,GEO,34-
3ph L

Halliday,Henrietta M. ,House (Irish Chancery)
2234 Massachusetts Ave. NW
HABS DC-261
HABS DC,WASH,204-
9ph/21pg L

Hamburgh House
412 Twentieth St. NW
HABS DC-10-6
HABS DC,WASH,120-
1dr/3ph/2pg/fr L

Hammel's Restaurant
416 Tenth St.
HABS DC-485
HABS DC,WASH,267-
1ph/2pg/1pc L

Harnedy Row Houses
3617-21 Prospect St. NW
HABS DC-206
HABS DC,GEO,142-
1ph/6pg L

Harrison,Jane Stone,Building
1205 Pennsylvania Ave. NW
HABS DC-429
HABS DC,WASH,226-
8ph/6pg/1pc L

Hauge,Christian,House (Czechoslovakian Embassy; Embassy of the Fed. Repub. of Camaroon Chancery; Camaroon Chancery)
2349 Massachusetts Ave. NW
HABS DC-262
HABS DC,WASH,205-
16ph/17pg L

Hay-Adams Hotel (Carleton Chambers (Apartment Hotel))
800 Sixteenth St. NW
HABS DC-534
HABS DC,WASH,434-
2dr L

Hayman,David & Company; see 625 Indiana Avenue NW (Commercial Building)

Hedges,Nicholas,House
1069 Thomas Jefferson St. NW
HABS DC-160
HABS DC,GEO,93-
18ph/11pg L

Henry,Patrick,Building
601 D St. ,NW
HABS DC-598
HABS DC,WASH,338-
52pg L

Herman's World of Sporting Goods; see Oppenheimer,Simon, & Brother Building

Herron-Moxley House
1503 Thirty-fifth St. NW
HABS DC-195
HABS DC,GEO,131-
1ph/9pg L

Heurich,Christian,Mansion (Columbia Historical Society)
1307 New Hampshire Ave. NW
HABS DC-292
HABS DC,WASH,435-
1dr/15ph/1pg/1pc L

Hewlings,T.B.A.,Villa; see Ingleside

Hi-Boy Restaurant; see 435 Seventh St. ,NW (Commercial Building)

Hickory House; see Perry Building

High Street Bridge (Wisconsin Avenue Bridge)
Wisconsin Ave. NW,Spanning C & O Canal
HABS DC-30
HABS DC,GEO,25-
2dr L

Hillyer Place
Between Q & R & 20th & 21st Sts. NW
HABS DC-294
HABS DC,WASH,549-
7ph/1pg/1pc L

Holt,Dr. Henry C. ,House; see Jackson Hill

Holy Trinity Parish
Thirty-sixth St. btw. N & O Sts. NW
HABS DC-201
HABS DC,GEO,137-
4ph/22pg L

Honeymoon House; see Law,Thomas,House

Hood House; see Decatur-Gunther House

Hooe,James C. ,House
2230 Massachusetts Ave. NW
HABS DC-263
HABS DC,WASH,206-
5ph/2pg L

Hooper,Robert King,House; see Lindens,The

Hospital for Sick Children
1731 Bunker Hill Rd. NE
HABS DC-642
32ph/18pg/2pc H

Hotel Washington
Fifteenth St. & Pennsylvania Ave. NW
HABS DC-317
HABS DC,WASH,436-
1ph/1pg/1pc L

House Where Lincoln Died; see Peterson House

Howard Road Historic District
Howard Rd. ,blocks 1000-1100
HABS DC-395
HABS DC,WASH,437-
18pg L

Howard Road Historic District
(Boston,Isaaz,House)
1004 Howard Rd.
HABS DC-395-B
HABS DC,WASH,439-
4ph/2pg/1pc L

Howard Road Historic District
(Lucas,Samuel H. ,House No. 1)
1023 Howard Rd.
HABS DC-395-H
HABS DC,WASH,445-
9ph/2pg/1pc L

Howard Road Historic District
(Lucas,Samuel H. ,House No. 2)
1018 Howard Rd.
HABS DC-395-G
HABS DC,WASH,444-
5ph/2pg/1pc L

Howard Road Historic District
(Lucas,Samuel H. ,House No. 3)
1014 Howard Rd.
HABS DC-395-E
HABS DC,WASH,442-
3ph/2pg/1pc L

Howard Road Historic District
(Miller,Henry F. ,Apartment Building)
1101-1107 Howard Rd.
HABS DC-395-J
HABS DC,WASH,447-
4ph/2pg/1pc L

Howard Road Historic District
(Phillips,Sylvia L. ,House)
1009 Howard Rd.
HABS DC-395-C
HABS DC,WASH,440-
8ph/2pg/1pc L

Howard Road Historic District
(Sharp,Lloyd,House)
1010 Howard Rd.
HABS DC-395-D
HABS DC,WASH,441-
4ph/2pg/1pc L

Howard Road Historic District
(Smith,Samuel,House)
1027 Howard Rd.
HABS DC-395-I
HABS DC,WASH,446-
3ph/2pg/1pc L

Howard Road Historic District
(Smoot,Minnie B. ,Apartment Building; Wilson,J. Finley,Memorial Lodge No. 13)
1015 Howard Rd.
HABS DC-395-F
HABS DC,WASH,443-
7ph/3pg/1pc L

Howard Road Historic District
(Sparks,Thomas,House)
1003 Howard Rd.
HABS DC-395-A
HABS DC,WASH,438-
4ph/2pg/1pc L

Howard Road Historic District
(Willis,William E. ,House)
1119 Howard Rd.
HABS DC-395-K
HABS DC,WASH,448-
4ph/2pg/1pc L

Howard University, Howard Hall; see Howard,Gen. Oliver O. ,House

Howard University,Founders Library
2400 Sixth St. NW
HABS DC-364
HABS DC,WASH,236-
30ph/10pg/2pc L

Howard,Gen. Oliver O. ,House (Howard University, Howard Hall)
607 Howard Pl. NW
HABS DC-284
HABS DC,WASH,236B-
2ph/1pg/1pc L

Hub Annex; see Polkinhorn Building

Hub Furniture Store; see 309-319 Seventh St. ,NW (Commercial Building)

Hughes,Charles Evans,House
(Barney,A. Clifford,House; Union of Burma Chancery)
2223 R St. NW
HABS DC-278
HABS DC,WASH,449-
3ph/1pg/1pc L

Humble Service Station
Twenty-sixth St. & Pennsylvania Ave. NW
HABS DC-319
HABS DCWASH,450-
1ph/1pg/1pc L

Hume Building (German Hi-Fi)
807 Market Space NW,Square 408,Lot 802
HABS DC-452
HABS DC,WASH,179-
3ph/2pg/1pc L

Hurley,John,House
3619 O St. NW
HABS DC-200
HABS DC,GEO,136-
1ph/6pg L

Hurst Hall; see American University,The College of History

2000-2042 I Street (Commercial Buildings) (Red Lion Row)
HABS DC-400
HABS DC,WASH,552-
11ph/1pc L

2000-2042 I Street NW (Commercial Bldgs) ,No. 2030 (Red Lion Row; 2030 I Street NW (House))
2030 I St. NW
HABS DC-400-A
HABS DC,WASH,552A-
6ph/1pc/fr L

2030 I Street NW (House); see 2000-2042 I Street NW (Commercial Bldgs) ,No. 2030

I Street NW,1900 Block (Houses)
HABS DC-337
HABS DC,WASH,451-
3ph/1pc L

Immaculate Conception Church
1515 Eighth St. NW
HABS DC-285
HABS DC,WASH,452-
2ph/1pg/1pc L

Independence Federal Savings & Trust; see 624 E St. ,NW (Commercial Building)

Independent Order of Odd Fellows Building (IOOR Temple)
419-423 Seventh St. ,NW
HABS DC-604
HABS DC,WASH,344-
1ph/12pg/1pc L

Indian Queen Hotel; see Brown's Marble Hotel

641 Indiana Ave. , NW (Commercial Building) (Artifactory)
HABS DC-593
HABS DC,WASH,309-
1ph/8pg/1pc L

633 Indiana Ave. ,NW (Commercial Building) (People's Drugstore; PEPCO)
HABS DC-591
HABS DC,WASH,305-
21pg L

639 Indiana Ave. ,NW (Commercial Building) (Dutch Boy Delicatessen)
HABS DC-589
HABS DC,WASH,303-
1ph/9pg/1pc L

643 Indiana Ave. ,NW (Commercial Building) (Marv's Restaurant)
HABS DC-588
HABS DC,WASH,302-
13pg L

Indiana Avenue (Louisiana Avenue)
HABS DC-713
H

600 Indiana Avenue NW (Commercial Building)
HABS DC-506
HABS DC,WASH,320-
3ph/2pg/1pc L

608 Indiana Avenue NW (Commercial Building)
HABS DC-507
HABS DC,WASH,319-
2ph/3pg/1pc L

610 Indiana Avenue NW (Commercial Building)
HABS DC-508
HABS DC,WASH,318-
1ph/3pg/1pc L

612 Indiana Avenue NW (Commercial Building)
HABS DC-509
HABS DC,WASH,317-
2ph/2pg/1pc L

625 Indiana Avenue NW (Commercial Building) (Hayman,David & Company)
HABS DC-230
HABS DC,WASH,187-
2ph/10pg/1pc L

Indonesian Embassy; see Walsh-Mclean House

Ingleside (Hewlings,T.B.A.,Villa; Stoddard Baptist Home)
1818 Newton St. NW
HABS DC-502
HABS DC,WASH,44-
10ph/9pg/1pc L

Inlet Bridge; see Tidal Reservoir Inlet Bridge

Inter-American Defense Board Headquarters; see Field,Mrs. Marshall,House

IOOR Temple; see Independent Order of Odd Fellows Building

Iowa Circle; see Logan Circle

Irish Chancery; see Halliday,Henrietta M. ,House

Irving's Camera Shop; see Thorn Building

Islamic Center,The; see Mosque

Jackson (Public) School
R St. & Avon Pl. NW
HABS DC-244
HABS DC,GEO,114-
9ph/10pg L

Jackson Hill (Holt,Dr. Henry C. ,House; National Zoological Park Adminstration Building)
Adams Mill Rd. Vic.
HABS DC-21
HABS DC,WASH,128-
6ph/3pg/1pc L

Jackson,Albert,House
1694 Thirty-first St. NW
HABS DC-181
HABS DC,GEO,104-
4ph/6pg L

Japanese Embassy
2516 Massachusetts Ave. NW
HABS DC-264
HABS DC,WASH,207-
3ph/2pg L

Jefferson Building; see Library of Congress

Jefferson Memorial
East Potomac Park
HABS DC-4
HABS DC,WASH,453-
1ph/1pg/1pc L

1063 Jefferson Street NW (House)
HABS DC-159
HABS DC,GEO,39-
1ph L

Jenifer Building (Commercial Building) (F&W Grand)
400-404 Seventh St.,NW
HABS DC-233
HABS DC,WASH,190-
3ph/19pg/1pc L

Jewell,Capt. Theodore,House
2135 R St. NW
HABS DC-417
HABS DC,WASH,454-
2ph/1pg/1pc/1ct L

Johnson,Capt. Joseph,House
49 T St. SW,Buzzards Point
HABS DC-10-3
HABS DC,WASH,100-
2dr/4ph/4pg L

Joyce Road Bridge; see Old Military Road Bridge

Judiciary Building
601 Indiana Ave. ,NW
HABS DC-596
HABS DC,WASH,306-
12pg L

Judiciary Square (Reservation 7)
HABS DC-690
H

K Street
HABS DC-714
H

808-810,812-814, & 1016 K Street (House); see Southeast Area Survey

K Street Bridge (Rock Creek & Potomac Parkway Project 1992)
Rock Creek Pkwy.
HAER DC-20
H

Kane,Daniel,House
1419 Thirty-sixth St. NW
HABS DC-197
HABS DC,GEO,133-
1ph/9pg L

Kann,S. , & Sons (Kann's Department Store)
Market Space,between Seventh and Eighth Sts. NW
HABS DC-365
HABS DC,WASH,336-
9ph/2pg/1pc/fr L

Kann's Department Store; see Kann,S. , & Sons

Kaufman,D. J. ,Store & Blimpie Restaurant; see 1005-1007 D Street (Commercial Building)

Keep Building
801-805 Market Space
HABS DC-320
HABS DC,WASH,481-
1ph/1pg/1pc L

Keith-Albee Building
Fifteenth & G Sts. NW
HABS DC-423
HABS DC,WASH,455-
8ph/18pg/1pc/fr L

Kelly House
1239 Thirty-seventh St. NW
HABS DC-203
HABS DC,GEO,139-
1ph/1pg L

Kennedy-Warren,The,Apartment Building
3133 Connecticut Ave.
HABS DC-566
HABS DC,WASH,456-
1ph/1pg/1pc L

Kentucky Avenue
HABS DC-701
H

Key,Francis Scott,House
3518 M St. NW
HABS DC-23
HABS DC,GEO,42-
8dr/4ph/fr L

Key,Philip Barton,House; see Woodley

King House
528 Seventeenth St. NW
HABS DC-57
HABS DC,WASH,37-
1ph/1pg L

Kinney Shoes; see F. W. Woolworth Companyu

Klingle House; see Linnean Hill

Knowles,William,House
1228 Thirtieth St. NW
HABS DC-163
HABS DC,GEO,33-
4ph/11pg L

Kraemer,Charles,House
1841 Park Rd. NW
HABS DC-283
HABS DC,WASH,457-
2ph/1pg/1pc L

Kung Fu Restaurant; see 407 Eleventh Street (Commercial Building)

817-819 L Street (House); see Southeast Area Survey

L'Enfant-McMillan Plan of Wash.,DC
HABS DC-668
H

La Touraine; see Orienta Coffee Building

Lafayette Park (Reservaion 10)
HABS DC-676
H

Lansburgh,Julius,Furniture Company; see Masonic Temple

Lansburgh's Department Store
E & Eighth Sts. NW
HABS DC-355
HABS DC,WASH,288-
6ph/18pg/2pc/fr L

Lansburgh's Department Store
420-426 Seventh St. ,NW
HABS DC-576
HABS DC,WASH,290-
6ph/16pg/1pc L

Lansburgh's Storage Building
413 Eighth St. ,NW
HABS DC-586
HABS DC,WASH,300-
9pg L

Lansburgh's Warehouse
410 Eight St. ,NW
HABS DC-518
HABS DC,WASH,279-
1ph/16pg/1pc L

Latrobe Cenotaphs; see Congressional Cemetary

Laughlin,Ambassador & Mrs. Irwin Boyle,House; see Meridian House

Law,Thomas,House (Honeymoon House; Tiber Island Center for Cultural & Community Act.)
1252 Sixth St. SW
HABS DC-20
HABS DC,WASH,13-
7dr/5ph/1pg/2pc L

Layhman,Christopher,House; see Stone House,Old

Le Droit Building
800-812 F St. NW
HABS DC-212
HABS DC,WASH,169-
9ph/22pg/1pc L

Le Droit Park
Second & Seventh Sts. & Florida Ave. & Elm St. NW
HABS DC-287
HABS DC,WASH,458-
2pg/1pc L

Le Droit Park (1901 Sixth Street NW (House))
HABS DC-287-A
HABS DC,WASH,458A-
2ph/1pc L

Le Droit Park (201 T Street NW (House))
HABS DC-287-G
HABS DC,WASH,458G-
7ph/1pc L

Le Droit Park (1908 Third Street NW (House))
HABS DC-287-B
HABS DC,WASH,458B-
1ph/1pc L

Le Droit Park (1922 Third Street NW (House))
HABS DC-287-C
HABS DC,WASH,458C-
1ph/1pc L

Le Droit Park (314 U Street NW (Carriage House))
HABS DC-287-D
HABS DC,WASH,458D-
1ph/1pc L

Le Droit Park (316 U Street NW (House))
HABS DC-287-E
HABS DC,WASH,458E-
1ph/1pc L

Le Droit Park (603-605 U Street NW (Houses))
HABS DC-287-F
HABS DC,WASH,458F-
1ph/1pc L

Lee,Thomas Simm,House; see 3001-3009 M Street NW (Row Houses)

Lemon Building
1729 New York Ave. NW
HABS DC-338
HABS DC,WASH,459-
4ph/2pg/1pc/fr L

Lenthall Houses
612-614 Nineteenth St. NW-moved to 606-610 21st St
HABS DC-438
HABS DC,WASH,43-
43ph/1pg/2pc/fr L

Leon's & Resenblatt's; see 641 D St. ,NW (Commercial Building)

Leonard's Lunchh; see 626 D Street,NW (Commercial Building)

Lerner Shops; see 414-416 Seventh St. ,NW (Commercial Building)

Lewis,Edward Simon,House (Washington-Lewis House)
456 N St. SW
HABS DC-26
HABS DC,WASH,129-
3dr/5ph/1pg/1pc L

Library of Congress (Jefferson Building)
First St. & Independence Ave. SE
HABS DC-351
HABS DC,WASH,461A-
25ph/2pg/2pc/1ct L

Lihault House (Simms House)
3610 O St. NW
HABS DC-207
HABS DC,GEO,143-
1ph/9pg L

Lincoln Inn Restaurant; see 645 D St. ,NW (Commercial Building)

Lincoln Memorial
W. Potomac Park
HABS DC-3
HABS DC,WASH,462-
3ph/1pg/1pc/2ct L

Lincoln Park (Reservation 14)
HABS DC-677
H

Documentation: **ct** color transparencies **dr** measured drawings **fr** field records
pc photograph captions **pg** pages of text **ph** photographs

Lindens,The (Hooper,Robert King,House)
2401 Kalorama Ave. (moved from MA,Danvers)
HABS MA-2-33
HABS MASS,5-DAV,2-
29dr/22ph/fr L

Lingen,Gen. James,House; see Prospect House

Linnean Hill (Pierce,Joshua,House; Klingle House)
3545 Williamsburg Lane NW
HABS DC-168
HABS DC,WASH,123-
11dr/10ph L

Litchfield,Grace Denio,House
2010 Massachusetts Ave. NW
HABS DC-321
HABS DC,WASH,463-
9ph/1pg/1pc L

Litwin,L. ,& Son; see McCutcheon Building

Lock Keeper's House (Toll Keepers Lodge)
Seventeenth St. & Constitution Ave. NW
HABS DC-36
HABS DC,WASH,12-
5ph L

Locker Room,The; see 501-511 Fourteenth Street NW (Commercial Building)

Loeb Company Store; see Merchants & Mechanics Savings Bank

Loew's Palace Theatre
1306 F Street
HABS DC-378
HABS DC,WASH,249-
6ph/7pg/1pc L

Logan Circle (Logan Circle Area Survey; Iowa Circle)
Vermont Ave. ,Rhode Island Ave. ,& Thirteenth St.
HABS DC-339
HABS 1985(HABS):69
9ph/1pc L

1 & 2 Logan Circle (House) (Logan Circle Area Survey)
HABS DC-339-A
2ph/8pg/1pc L

4 Logan Circle (House) (Logan Circle Area Survey)
HABS DC-339-B
2ph/1pc L

Logan Circle Area Survey; see Logan Circle

Logan Circle Area Survey; see 1 & 2 Logan Circle (House)

Logan Circle Area Survey; see 4 Logan Circle (House)

Logan Circle Area Survey; see 1205-1215 Rhode Island Avenue NW (Houses)

Logan Circle Area Survey; see 1300-1322 Rhode Island Avenue NW (Houses)

Logan Circle Area Survey; see 1301-1313 Rhode Island Avenue NW (Houses)

Logan Circle Area Survey; see 1500 Thirteenth Street NW (House)

Logan Circle Area Survey; see 1502 Thirteenth Street NW (House)

Logan Circle Area Survey; see 1500-1514 Thirteenth Street NW (Houses)

Logan Circle Area Survey; see 1314 Vermont Avenue NW (House)

Logan Circle Area Survey; see 1501-1523 Vermont Avenue NW (Houses)

Longden House
1555 Thirty-fifth St. NW
HABS DC-194
HABS DC,GEO,130-
1ph/8pg L

Loughran Building (Bassin's Restaurant)
1347 E St. NW
HABS DC-389
HABS DC,WASH,230-
2ph/3pg/2pc L

Louis Cocktail Lounge; see 305 Ninth Street NW (Commercial Building)

Louisiana Avenue; see Indiana Avenue

Lovell,Joseph,House; see Blair House

Lucas,Samuel H. ,House No. 1; see Howard Road Historic District

Lucas,Samuel H. ,House No. 2; see Howard Road Historic District

Lucas,Samuel H. ,House No. 3; see Howard Road Historic District

Luther Place Memorial Church
1226 Vermont Ave. NW
HABS DC-446
HABS DC,WASH,482-
1ph/1pg/1pc L

Lutz,John,House; see Female Union Benevolent Society

Lyon's Mill Footbridge; see Devil's Cahir Footbridge

M Street Bridge (Rock Creek & Potomac Parkway Project, 1992)
HAER DC-37
H

2919 M Street NW (House)
HABS DC-64
HABS DC,GEO,50-
1ph L

2922 M Street NW (House)
HABS DC-112
HABS DC,GEO,72-
2ph/5pg L

3111-3113 M Street NW (House)
HABS DC-32
HABS DC,GEO,45-
1ph L

3115-17 M Street NW (House)
HABS DC-33
HABS DC,GEO,46-
7dr/2ph/2pg L

3001-3009 M Street NW (Row Houses) (Lee,Thomas Simm,House)
HABS DC-65
HABS DC,GEO,5-
5dr/3ph L

Mackall House,Old; see Mackall Square

Mackall Square (Mackall House,Old)
1633 Twenty-ninth St.
HABS DC-164
HABS DC,GEO,8-
4ph L

Madison,Dolley,House; see Cutts,Richard,House

Mahorney-Harrington House
1423 Thirty-Sixth St. NW
HABS DC-188
HABS DC,GEO,124-
1ph/9pg L

Mahorney-O'Brien House
3522 P St. NW
HABS DC-198
HABS DC,GEO,134-
1ph/9pg L

Malcolm X Park; see Meridian Hill Park

Mall (Reservations 3,4,5,6)
HABS DC-678
H

Mankins,William,House
1411 Thirty-fifth St. NW
HABS DC-190
HABS DC,GEO,126-
1ph/11pg L

Manning,Edwin C. ,House (Florida House)
200 E. Capitol St. NE
HABS DC-330
HABS DC,WASH,483-
2ph/7pg/1pc/fr L

Maple Square; see Maples,The

Maples,The (Duncanson,William,House; Maple Square; Friendship House)
630 South Carolina Ave. SE
HABS DC-10-5
HABS DC,WASH,14-
5dr/16ph/4pg/1pc L

Marceron,William,Building
1335 Wisconsin Ave. NW
HABS DC-107
HABS DC,GEO,67-
5ph/5pg L

Marcey-Payne Building
1321 1/2-1325 1/2 Wisconsin Ave. NW
HABS DC-106
HABS DC,GEO,66-
5ph/9pg L

Maret School; see Woodley

Marine Barracks; see U. S. Marine Corps Commandant's House

Marion Park (Reservation 18)
HABS DC-679
H

809 Market Space NW (Commercial Building)
HABS DC-222
HABS DC,WASH,179-
4ph/4pg/1pc L

811 Market Space NW (Commercial Building) (Souvenirs)
Square 408,Lot 803
HABS DC-232
HABS DC,WASH,189-
3ph/1pg L

813-815 Market Space NW (Commercial Building) (National Permanent Federal Savings)
Square 408,Lots 804 & 15
HABS DC-453
HABS DC,WASH,381-
1ph/2pg/1pc L

817 Market Space NW (Commercial Building) (Antique House,Old)
Square 408,Lot 817
HABS DC-454
HABS DC,WASH,382-
3ph/2pg/1pc L

Market Square (Reservations 34,35,36,36A)
HABS DC-691
H

Marlatt,Dr. Charles L. ,House
Sixteenth & Church Sts. NW
HABS DC-541
HABS DC,WASH,484-
2dr L

Marv's Restaurant; see 643 Indiana Ave. ,NW (Commercial Building)

Maryland Avenue
HABS DC-702
H

Mason,Gen. John,House
Analostan Island or Theodore Roosevelt Island
HABS DC-28
HABS DC,WASH,131
16dr/73ph/27pg L

Mason,John Thomson,House (Quality Hill; Worthington House)
3425 Prospect St. NW
HABS DC-167
HABS DC,GEO,11-
7ph/18pg/1pc L

Masonic Hall; see Masonic Temple

Masonic Temple (Masonic Hall; Lansburgh,Julius,Furniture Company)
F & Ninth Sts. NW
HABS DC-218
HABS DC,WASH,175-
5ph/6pg/1pc L

Masonic Temple,Old (Naval Lodge Number Four)
Virginia Ave. & Fifth St. SE
HABS DC-437
HABS DC,WASH,148-
4ph L

Massachusetts Avenue
HABS DC-703
H

Massachusetts Avenue Bridge (Glover,Charles C.,Bridge; Rock Creek & Potomac Parkway Project 1992)
HAER DC-22
H

1780 Massachusetts Avenue NW (House)
HABS DC-238
HABS DC,WASH,366-
1ph/1pc L

1730 Massachusetts Avenue,NW (House)
HABS DC-462
HABS DC,WASH,550-
2pg L

Maury,John,House
302 C St. NW
HABS DC-10-4
HABS DC,WASH,119-
5dr/1ph/2pg/fr L

Mayor-Smallwood House
324-326 Virginia Ave.
HABS DC-439
HABS DC,WASH,79-
3ph L

McCarthy-Sullivan House
3623 O St. NW
HABS DC-199
HABS DC,GEO,135-
1ph/4pg L

McCleery House (Georgetown)
1068 Thirtieth St. NW
HABS DC-162
HABS DC,GEO,95-
11ph/11pg/1pc L H

McCormick Apartments (National Trust for Historic Preservation Hq.)
1785 Massachusetts Ave. NW
HABS DC-265
HABS DC,WASH,208-
5ph/17pg L

McCutcheon Building (Litwin,L. ,& Son)
637 Indiana Ave.
HABS DC-413
HABS DC,WASH,308-
3dr/1ph/10pg/1pc/fr L

McDonald's; see 607-609 C Street (Commercial Building)

McKenny House; see Foxhall,Henry,House

McKinley-Ohio Hall of Government; see American University,Ohio Hall of Government

McLean,John R. ,House
1500 I St. NW
HABS DC-24
HABS DC,WASH,133-
25ph/1pg L

McPherson Square (Reservation 11)
HABS DC-680
H

Medco Discount Center; see Galt & Brother Jewelers

Meigs,Gen. Montgomery,House
1239 Vermont Ave. NW
HABS DC-50
HABS DC,WASH,141-
4ph/1pg L

Memorial Bridge; see Arlington Memorial Bridge

Memorial Continental Hall (National Society of the DAR Headquarters & Museum)
Seventeenth St. between C & D Sts. NW
HABS DC-282
HABS DC,WASH,485-
2ph/1pg/1pc L

Merchants & Mechanics Savings Bank (Loeb Company Store)
Seventh & G Sts. NW
HABS DC-239
HABS DC,WASH,195-
1ph L

Meridian Hill Park (Malcolm X Park)
Bounded by 15th,16th,Euclid & W Sts.,N.W.
HABS DC-532
HABS DC,WASH,486-
25dr/51ph/68pg/4pc/8ct/fr L

Meridian House (Laughlin,Ambassador & Mrs. Irwin Boyle,House)
1630 Crescent Place NW
HABS DC-540
HABS DC,WASH,487-
1dr L

Methodist Episcopal Church,South (Mount Vernon Place United Methodist Church)
900 Massachusetts Ave. NW
HABS DC-451
HABS DC,WASH,488-
1ph/1pc L

Methodist Episcopal Parsonage House
1221 Twenty-eighth St. NW
HABS DC-176
HABS DC,GEO,99-
3ph/11pg L

Metropolitan Hotel; see Brown's Marble Hotel

Metropolitan A. M. E. Church
1518 M St. NW
HABS DC-352
HABS DCWASH,489-
2ph/1pg/1pc L

Documentation: **ct** color transparencies **dr** measured drawings **fr** field records **pc** photograph captions **pg** pages of text **ph** photographs

Michler Place
F St. btw. Seventeenth & Eighteenth Sts. NW
HABS DC-340
HABS DC,WASH,490-
2ph/13pg/1pc L

Milkhouse Ford (Rock Creek & Potomac Parkway Project 1992)
HAER DC-25
H

Miller House (Argyle Terrace)
2201 Massachusetts Ave. NW
HABS DC-275
HABS DC,WASH,217-
6ph/19pg L

Miller,Benjamin,House
1524 Twenty-eighth St. NW
HABS DC-247
HABS DC,GEO,117-
3ph/14pg L

Miller,Henry F. ,Apartment Building; see Howard Road Historic District

Monument Grounds (Reservation 2)
HABS DC-681
H

Moore,Clarence,House (Canadian Chancery)
1746 Massachusetts Ave. NW
HABS DC-267
HABS DC,WASH,210-
13ph/21pg L

Moore,Frederick L. ,House
168 Thirty-first St. NW
HABS DC-464
HABS DC,GEO,151-
4pg L

Moran,Francis B. ,House (Pakistani Chancery)
2315 Massachusetts Ave. NW
HABS DC-268
HABS DC,WASH,211-
7ph/3pg L

Morrison Paper Company (Stein's Dry Cleaning & Shoe Repair)
1009 D St.
HABS DC-491
HABS DC,WASH,273-
1ph/2pg/1pc L

Morrow Drive Bridge (Rock Creek & Potomac Parkway Project 1992)
HAER DC-30
H

Morton's; see 314-316 Seventh Street NW (Commercial Building)

Mosque (Islamic Center,The)
2551 Massachusetts Ave. NW
HABS DC-286
HABS DC,WASH,491-
3ph/1pg/1pc L

Motion Picture Association; see Tuckerman,Lucius,House

Mount Vernon Apartments
922-924 Ninth St. NW
HABS DC-385
HABS DC,WASH,251-
6ph/1pg/1pc L

Mount Vernon Memorial Hwy:Boundary Channel Bridge; see Bridge over Boundary Channel

Mount Vernon Place United Methodist Church; see Methodist Episcopal Church,South

Mount Vernon Square (Reservations 8,70,71,175,176)
HABS DC-682
H

Mount Vernon Theatre
918 Ninth St. NW
HABS DC-254
HABS DC,WASH,219-
2dr/5ph/15pg L

Mount Zion United Methodist Church
1334 Twenty-ninth St. NW
HABS DC-242
HABS DC,GEO,112-
5ph/16pg L

Mountz,John,House (Eagle House)
3016 M St. NW
HABS DC-18
HABS DC,GEO,30-
4dr/3ph L

Mulliken-Spragins Tenant House
Nat'l Museum of American History,Smithsonian Inst.
HABS DC-390
HABS DC,WASH,492-
3dr/8ph/1pc/fr L

Munsey Building
1327-1329 E St. NW
HABS DC-358
HABS DC,WASH,237-
6dr/14ph/15pg/2pc/fr L

Museum Building; see Smithsonian Institute,Arts & Industries Building

3041 N St.,NW (House) (Georgetown)
HABS DC-734
1ph/1pc H

2817 N Street NW (House)
HABS DC-157
HABS DC,GEO,35-
2ph L

3334 N Street,N. W. (House) (Georgetown Historic District)
HABS DC-660
HABS DLC/PP-1993:DC-1
1dr/fr L

3014 N Street,N.W. (House)
3014 N St.,NW
HABS DC-630
HABS 1991(HABS):28
1dr/fr L

3320 N Street,N.W.(House)
3320 N St.,NW
HABS DC-633
HABS 1991(HABS):28
1dr/fr L

3111 N Street,Northwest (Georgetown Historic District)
HABS DC-646
HABS 1991(HABS):28
1dr/fr L

3328 N Street,Northwest (Georgetown Historic District)
HABS DC-647
HABS 1991(HABS):28
1dr/fr L

2823 N Street,NW (House) (Georgetown)
HABS DC-731
1ph/1pc H

3254 N Street,NW (House) (Georgetown)
HABS DC-728
1ph/1pc H

3626 N Street,NW (House) (Georgetown)
HABS DC-738
1ph/1pc H

3632 N Street,NW (House) (Georgetown)
HABS DC-739
2ph/1pc H

National Archives
Constitution Ave. NW
HABS DC-296
HABS DC,WASH,493-
3ph/1pg/1pc/2ct L

National Art and Frame Company; see 408 Eighth Street (Commercial Building)

National Bank of Washington (National Bank of Washington,Washington Branch)
301 Seventh St. NW
HABS DC-223
HABS DC,WASH,180-
6ph/10pg L

National Bank of Washington,Georgetown Branch; see Potomac Savings Bank

National Bank of Washington,Washington Branch; see National Bank of Washington

National Building Museum; see Pension Building

National Firefighting Museum; see Bank of Columbia

National Headquarters of Colonial Dames of America; see Dumbarton House

National Metropolitan Bank Building
613 Fifteenth St. NW
HABS DC-431
HABS DC,WASH,494-
14ph/1pg/1pc L

National Museum of American Art; see Patent Office Building

National Permanent Federal Savings; see 813-815 Market Space NW (Commercial Building)

National Portrait Gallery; see Patent Office Building

National Presbyterian Church; see Church of the Covenant

National Sales; see F. W. Woolworth Companyu

National Society of the DAR Headquarters & Museum; see Memorial Continental Hall

National Trust for Historic Preservation; see Decatur House

National Trust for Historic Preservation Hq.; see McCormick Apartments

National Union Building
918 F St. NW
HABS DC-463
HABS DC,WASH,495-
8pg L

National War College; see Army War College

National Zoological Park Adminstration Building; see Jackson Hill

Naval Hospital,Old
921 Pennsylvania Ave. SE
HABS DC-468
HABS DC,WASH,496-
2ph/1pc L

Naval Lodge Number Four; see Masonic Temple,Old

Naval Observatory,Old (U. S. Navy Bureau Med. & Surg. ,Potomac Annex)
Twenty-Third & E Sts. NW
HABS DC-341
HABS DC,WASH,497A-
2ph/1pg/1pc L

Navy Yard
Bounded by M,Eleventh SE,Anacostia River,First SE
HABS DC-442
HABS DC,WASH,74C- ι1991(HABS):28°
6pg/fr L

Navy Yard Main Gate
Eighth & M Sts. SE
HABS DC-100
HABS DC,WASH,74-
7ph/4pg/2ct L

Navy Yard Quarters B (Second Officer's House)
E. Side of Drill Field,Washington Navy Yard
HABS DC-101
HABS DC,WASH,74B-
8dr/8ph/4pg L

Navy Yard,Boilermakers Shop (Building 167)
Navy Yard Annex
HABS DC-442-B
HABS DC,WASH,74E-
24ph/3pg/1pc L

Navy Yard,Building 36; see Navy Yard,Ordnance Building

Navy Yard,Commandant's House (Quarters A)
Eighth & M Sts. SE
HABS DC-12
HABS DC,WASH,74A-
2dr/9ph/9pg/1pc/fr L

Navy Yard,General Foundry (Building 137)
Navy Yard Annex
HABS DC-442-A
HABS DC,WASH,74D-
34ph/3pg/2pc L

Navy Yard,Ordnance Building (Navy Yard,Building 36)
Intersection of Paulding and Kennon Streets
HABS DC-422-C
HABS DLC/PP-1993:DC-5
36ph/10pg/5pc L

New Hampshire Avenue
HABS DC-704
H

New Jersey Avenue
HABS DC-715
H

New Life Yogurt Store; see 1015 D Street (Commercial Building)

New York Avenue
HABS DC-716
H

New York Avenue,900 & 1000 Block; see Convention Center Site,District of Columbia

1810-1820 Nineteenth St. NW (Row Houses)
HABS DC-415
HABS DC,WASH,478-
4ph/1pg/1pc L

Nineteenth Street Baptist Church
Nineteenth & I Sts. (demolished)
HABS DC-357
HABS DC,WASH,499-
4ph/2pg/1pc L

305 Ninth Street NW (Commercial Building) (Louis Cocktail Lounge)
Square 408,Lot 815
HABS DC-455
HABS DC,WASH,373-
1ph/1pg/1pc L

616 Ninth Street NW (Commercial Building)
HABS DC-234
HABS DC,WASH,191-
1ph L

618 Ninth Street NW (Commercial Building)
HABS DC-231
HABS DC,WASH,188-
1ph L

Ninth Street NW, 500 Block (Commercial Buildings)
HABS DC-445
HABS DC,WASH,500-
1ph/1pc L

28 Ninth Street,N.E. (House)
28 Ninth St.,NE
HABS DC-627
HABS 1991(HABS):28
1dr/fr L

Ninth Street,800 & 900 Block; see Convention Center Site,District of Columbia

Nordlinger Building
3128 M St. NW
HABS DC-116
HABS DC,GEO,75-
2ph/5pg L

North Carolina Avenue
HABS DC-705
H

156-158 North Carolina Avenue (Houses); see Southeast Area Survey

Northeast Corridor; see Northeast Railroad Corridor

Northeast Railroad Corridor (Northeast Corridor)
Amtrak Rt. btwn. Union Station & DC/MD State Line
HAER DC-3
HAER DC,WASH,559-
7ph/2pc/fr L

Northern Market (O Street Market)
Seventh & O Sts. NW
HABS DC-342
HABS DC,WASH,498-
3ph/1pg/1pc L

O Street Market; see Northern Market

3121 O Street,Northwest (House)
Georgetown Historic District
HABS DC-649
HABS 1991(HABS):28
1dr/fr L

3300 O Street,Northwest (House) (Georgetown Historic District)
HABS DC-638
HABS 1991(HABS):28
1dr/fr L

3122 O Street,NW (House) (Georgetown)
HABS DC-748
1ph/1pc H

3132 O Street,NW (House) (Georgetown)
HABS DC-749
1ph/1pc H

3314 O Street,NW (House) (Georgetown)
HABS DC-750
1ph/1pc H

3517 O Street,NW (House) (Georgetown)
HABS DC-751
1ph/1pc H

3615 O Street,NW (House) (Georgetown)
HABS DC-752
1ph/1pc H

Oak Hill (French House)
Connecticut Ave.
HABS DC-42
HABS DC,WASH,137-
1ph L

Oak Hill Cemetery,Chapel
3001 R St. NW
HABS DC-172
HABS DC,GEO,41B-
14dr/7ph/9pg L

Oak Hill Cemetery,Gatehouse
3001 R St. NW
HABS DC-249
HABS DC,GEO,41C-
4ph/16pg L

Occidental Hotel & Restaurant
1411 Pennsylvania Ave. NW
HABS DC-325
HABS DC,WASH,243-
3ph/5pg/1pc L

Occidental Restaurant (Owen House)
1413 Pennsylvania Ave. NW
HABS DC-382
HABS DC,WASH,242-
2ph/5pg/1pc L

Octagon House (Tayloe,Col. John,House; American Institute of Architects Headquarters)
1799 New York Ave. NW
HABS DC-25
HABS DC,WASH,8-;1993:DC-3
175ph/1pg/12pc L

Octagon House,Stable
(Tayloe,John,House,Stable; American Institute of Architects Library)
1799 New York Ave. NW
HABS DC-336
HABS DC,WASH,8B-
3ph/3pg/fr L

Octagonal House; see Bebb House

Old Ebbitt Grill
1427 F St. NW
HABS DC-315
HABS DC,WASH,501-
13ph/1pg/1pc L

Old Executive Office Building; see State,War & Navy Building

Old Harvard Street Bridge (Rock Creek & Potomac Parkway Project 1992)
HAER DC-26
H

Old Military Road Bridge (Joyce Road Bridge)
Joyce Road Spanning Rock Creek
HAER DC-18
HAER 1989(HAER):4
4ph/5pg/1pc L

Oppenheimer,Simon, & Brother Building (Herman's World of Sporting Goods)
800 E St. ,NW
HABS DC-519
HABS DC,WASH,280-
4ph/13pg/1pc L

Orienta Coffee Building (La Touraine)
300 Sixth St. NW
HABS DC-512
HABS DC,WASH,322-
3ph/3pg/1pc L

Owen House; see Occidental Restaurant

Owens,Isaac,House (Doorway)
(Gantt-Williams House)
2806 N St. NW
HABS DC-62
HABS DC,GEO,51-
1ph L

P Street Bridge; see Rock Creek & Potomac Parkway Bridge near P Street

2918 P Street,N.W. (House)
2918 P St.,NW
HABS DC-631
HABS 1991(HABS):28
1dr/fr L

3019 P Street,N.W. (House)
3019 P St.,NW
HABS DC-629
HABS 1991(HABS):28
1dr/fr L

3006 P Street,Northwest (House)
(Georgetown Historic District)
HABS DC-645
HABS 1991(HABS):28
1dr/fr L

3040 P Street,Northwest (House)
(Georgetown Historic District)
HABS DC-648
HABS 1991(HABS):28
1dr/fr L

2803 P Street,NW (House) (Georgetown)
HABS DC-754
1ph/1pc H

2811 P Street,NW (House) (Georgetown)
HABS DC-753
1ph/1pc H

3022 P Street,NW (House) (Georgetown)
HABS DC-756
1ph/1pc H

3042 P Street,NW (House) (Georgetown)
3042 P Street,NW
HABS DC-743
1ph/1pc H

3116 P Street,NW (House) (Georgetown)
HABS DC-757
1ph/1pc H

Pacific Circle; see DuPont Circle

Pakistani Chancery; see Moran,Francis B. ,House

Park & Shop Shopping Center
3507-3523 Connecticut Ave. NW btwn Ordway & Porter
HABS DC-548
HABS DC,WASH,502-
5ph/3pg/1pc L

Parrot,Thomas,House; see Fenwick,Teresa,House

Patent Office Building (U. S. Civil Service Commission; National Portrait Gallery; National Museum of American Art)
Seventh,Ninth,F & G Sts. NW
HABS DC-130
HABS DLC/ADE-1983(HABS):134
37ph/2pg/2pc/4ct L H

Patterson House (Washington Club)
15 Dupont Circle NW
HABS DC-270
HABS DC,WASH,212-183(HAER):84
7ph/19pg L

Patterson,Edgar,House
1241 Thirtieth St. NW
HABS DC-177
HABS DC,GEO,100-
3ph/10pg L

Pendleton & Robinson Law Offices
306 Sixth St. NW
HABS DC-513
HABS DC,WASH,314-
1ph/1pg/1pc L

Penn Camera Exchange
414 Tenth St.
HABS DC-486
HABS DC,WASH,268-
1ph/2pg/1pc L

1922-1932 Pennsylvania Ave. NW (Commercial Bldg.)
HABS DC-334
HABS DC,WASH,369-
4ph/1pg/1pc L

1922 Pennsylvania Ave. NW (Commercial Building)
HABS DC-334-A
HABS DC,WASH,369A-
3ph L

1924-1926 Pennsylvania Ave.,NW (Commercial Bldg.)
HABS DC-334-B
HABS DC,WASH,369B-
1ph L

1928-1932 Pennsylvania Ave.,NW (Commercial Bldg.)
HABS DC-334-C
HABS DC,WASH,369C-
2ph L

Pennsylvania Avenue
HABS DC-706
H

Pennsylvania Avenue Bridge (Rock Creek & Potomac Parkway Project)
HAER DC-21
H

2411 Pennsylvania Avenue NW (House)
HABS DC-27
HABS DC,WASH,23-
2dr/4ph L

Pennsylvania Avenue NW,900 Block
HABS DC-304
HABS DC,WASH,504-
8ph/1pc L

1002 Pennsylvania Avenue SE (House)
HABS DC-466
HABS DC,WASH,361-
2ph/1pc L

1206-1242 Pennsylvania Avenue,Southeast (Houses) (Capitol Hill Historic District)
HABS DC-654
HABS 1991(HABS):28
3dr/fr L

Pension Building (National Building Museum)
440 G St. NW
HABS DC-76
HABS DC,WASH,152-
1dr/53ph/2pg/4pc/8ct/fr L

People's Drugstore; see 633 Indiana Ave. ,NW (Commercial Building)

PEPCO; see 633 Indiana Ave. ,NW (Commercial Building)

PEPCO Power Station
922 I St. NW
HABS DC-388
HABS DC,WASH,250-
14ph/3pg/1pc L

Perry Building (Hickory House)
819-821 Market Space NW,Square 408,Corner Lot 805
HABS DC-221
HABS DC,WASH,178-
6ph/8pg/1pc L

Pershing Park (Reservation 617)
HABS DC-695
H

Pershing Square & National Square; see Square 226 & Reservations 32 & 33

Pershing Square & Shepherd & Pulaski Parks; see Square 226 & Reservations 32 & 33

Peruvian Embassy; see Wilkins House

Peter Houses
2618-2620 K St. NW
HABS DC-70
HABS DC,WASH,41-
5ph/2pg L

Peterson House (House Where Lincoln Died)
516 Tenth St. NW
HABS DC-165
HABS DC,WASH,505-
5dr/4ph/1pc/1ct/fr L

Philippine Embassy; see Fitzhugh,Emma S. ,House

Phillips Collection,The; see Phillips,Duncan,House

Phillips,Duncan,House (Phillips Collection,The)
1600-1614 Twenty-first St. NW
HABS DC-447
HABS DC,WASH,506-
1ph/1pg/1pc L

Phillips,Sylvia L. ,House; see Howard Road Historic District

Piccolo's; see 322 Eighth Street NW (Commercial Building)

Pierce Mill (Rock Creek Park)
Tilden St. & Beach Dr. NW
HABS DC-22
HABS DC-WASH,109-;DLC/PP-1993:DC-1
22dr/22ph/10pg/fr L

Pierce Mill Bridge (Rock Creek & Potomac Parkway Project 1992)
HAER DC-28
H

Pierce,Isaac,House
711 Sixth St. SE
HABS DC-14
HABS DC,WASH,125-
6dr/3ph L

Pierce,Joshua,House; see Linnean Hill

Pinehurst Bridge
Beach Drive,Spanning Pinehurst Branch Creek,NW
HAER DC-15
HAER 1989(HAER):4
3ph/5pg/1pc L

Pink Palace; see Field,Mrs. Marshall,House

Playland Adult Bookstore; see Abner,Edward,Building

PMI Parking Garage
403-407 Ninth St. ,NW
HABS DC-523
HABS DC,WASH,282-
4ph/13pg/1pc L

Polish Embassy; see Embassy of Poland

Polkinhorn Building (Hub Annex)
638 D Street NW
HABS DC-568
HABS DC,WASH,311-
3ph/14pg/1pc L

2704 Poplar Street,NW (House) (Georgetown)
2704 Poplar Street,NW
HABS DC-741
2ph/1pc H

Post Office Building,Old; see U. S. Post Office Department

Potomac Aqueduct (HAER:4 dr,9 ph,1 da;HABS:22 ph,17 da.)
Spanning the Potomac River
HABS DC-166
HAER DC-4
HABS/HAER DC,GEO,1-
4dr/31ph/18pg/1pc L

Potomac Avenue (Georgia Avenue)
HABS DC-707
H

Potomac Electric Power Company
422 Eighth St. ,NW
HABS DC-573
HABS DC,WASH,278-
9pg L

Potomac Electric Power Company Substation
405 Eighth St. ,NW NW
HABS DC-577
HABS DC,WASH,291-
1ph/7pg/1pc L

Potomac Lodge Number Five
1058 Thomas Jefferson St. NW (Georgetown)
HABS DC-153
HABS DC,GEO,152-
1ph/12pg/1pc L

Potomac Realty Company,House No. 10
1128 Sixteenth St. NW
HABS DC-535
HABS DC,WASH,507-
1dr L

Potomac Savings Bank (National Bank of Washington,Georgetown Branch)
1200 Wisconsin Ave. NW
HABS DC-323
HABS DC,GEO,123-
1ph/4pg L

1008 Potomac Street (House); see Southeast Area Survey

1016-1018 Potomac Street (House); see Southeast Area Survey

1061-1063 Potomac Street NW,Double House
HABS DC-152
HABS DC,GEO,40-
1ph L

Powhatan Hotel (Smith,Roger,Hotel)
Pennsylvania Ave. & Eighteenth St. NW
HABS DC-545
HABS DC,WASH,508-
4ph/1pg/1pc L

President Madison Apartments; see Cordova Apartments

Price Is Right Store; see 1015 D Street (Commercial Building)

Prospect House (Lingen,Gen. James,House)
3508 Prospect St. NW
HABS DC-210
1ph/17pg L

3234 Prospect Street,N.W. (House) (Georgetown Historic District)
HABS DC-662
HABS DLC/PP-1993:DC-1
1dr L

3320 Prospect Street,Northwest (House) (Georgetown Historic District)
HABS DC-651
HABS 1991(HABS):28
1dr/fr L

3611 Prospect Street,NW (House) (Georgetown)
3611 Prospect Street,NW
HABS DC-747
1ph/1pc H

Public Sale; see 431 & 433 Seventh St. ,NW (Commercial Building)

Pullman House (Embassy of the Union of Soviet Socialist Republics
1119-1125 Sixteenth St. NW
HABS DC-269
HABS DC,WASH,509-
17ph/1pg/1pc/1ct L

Q Street Bridge (Rock Creek & Potomac Parkway Project, 1992)
HAER DC-38
H

Q Street NW,1700 Block (Row Houses)
HABS DC-345
HABS DC,WASH,510-
5ph/1pg/1pc L

3106 Q Street,NW (House) (Georgetown)
3106 Q Street,NW
HABS DC-773
HABS MO,96-SALU,105E-
1ph/1pc H

Quality Hill; see Mason,John Thomson,House

Quarters A; see Navy Yard,Commandant's House

3308 R Street,NW (House) (Georgetown)
3308 R Street,NW
HABS DC-774
HABS MO,96-SALU,105E-
1ph/1pc H

Raleigh's Haberdasher; see 1310 F Street NW (Commercial Building)

Rapids Footbridge
Spanning Rock Creek .7 Mi. S. of Joyce Rd. NW
HAER DC-14
HAER 1989(HAER):4
5ph/5pg/1pc L

Rawlins Park (Reservation 13)
HABS DC-683
H

Ray,Alexander,House; see Steedman-Ray House

Ray's Warehouse & Office (Corson & Gruman Company)
3260-3262 K St. NW
HABS DC-148
HABS DC,GEO,90-
5ph/13pg L

Reckert House
3232 M St. NW
HABS DC-120
HABS DC,GEO,79-
1ph/5pg L

Red Cross Building (American National Red Cross National Headquarters)
Seventeenth & E Sts. NW
HABS DC-347
HABS DC,WASH,511-
8ph/1pg/1pc/1ct L

Red Lion Row; see 2000-2042 I Street (Commercial Buildings)

Red Lion Row; see 2000-2042 I Street NW (Commercial Bldgs) ,No. 2030

Reintzel,Anthony,Building
3258 M St. NW
HABS DC-122
HABS DC,GEO,81-
6pg L

Republic of China Chancery; see Fahnestock,Gibson,House

Reservaion 10; see Lafayette Park

Reservation 1; see White House Grounds

Reservation 11; see McPherson Square

Reservation 12; see Farragut Square

Reservation 13; see Rawlins Park

Reservation 14; see Lincoln Park

Reservation 15; see Stanton Square

Reservation 16; see Folger Park

Reservation 18; see Marion Park

Reservation 2; see Monument Grounds

Reservation 332; see West Potomac Park

Reservation 333; see East Potomac Park

Reservation 334; see Union Plaza

Reservation 360; see Rock Creek & Potomac Parkway

Reservation 617; see Pershing Park

Reservation 7; see Judiciary Square

Reservation 9; see Franklin Park

Reservations 25,26,27; see Washington Circle

Reservations 3,4,5,6; see Mall

Reservations 32,33; see Western Plaza

Reservations 34,35,36,36A; see Market Square

Reservations 38,38A,39 & 41,41A,40 & 42,43; see Seward Square

Reservations 59,60,61; see DuPont Circle

Reservations 62,62A,62B,63,64,64A,64B; see Scott Circle

Reservations 65,66,161,162; see Thomas Circle

Reservations 68,68A,69,69A; see Gompers,Samuel A.,Park & Reservation 68

Reservations 8,70,71,175,176; see Mount Vernon Square

4437 Reservoir Road NW (House)
HABS DC-126
HABS DC,WASH,130-
4ph L

3216 Reservoir Road,NW (House) (Georgetown)
3216 Reservoir Road,NW
HABS DC-745
1ph/1pc H

Residence of the Ambassador of Ireland; see Delano,Frederic,House

Resrevations 44,44A,45,46,47,47A,48,49; see Eastern Market Metro Station

Resrvation 17; see Garfield Park

Rhode Island Avenue
HABS DC-708
H

1115 Rhode Island Avenue NW (House)
HABS DC-470
HABS DC,WASH,363-
1ph/1pc L

1205-1215 Rhode Island Avenue NW (Houses) (Logan Circle Area Survey)
HABS DC-526
HABS DC,WASH,467-
2ph/1pc L

1300-1322 Rhode Island Avenue NW (Houses) (Logan Circle Area Survey)
HABS DC-527
HABS DC,WASH,468-
5ph/1pc L

1301-1313 Rhode Island Avenue NW (Houses) (Logan Circle Area Survey)
HABS DC-528
HABS DC,WASH,469-
4ph/1pc L

Rhodes Tavern
601-603 Fifteenth St. & 1431 F St. NW
HABS DC-326
HABS DC,WASH,512-
5dr/10ph/1pg/2pc L

Richards,Zalmon,House
1301 Corcoran St. NW
HABS DC-343
HABS DC,WASH,513-
2ph/1pg/1pc L

Riggs National Bank
1503-1505 Pennsylvania Ave. NW
HABS DC-543
HABS DC,WASH,514-
9pg/fr L

Riggs National Bank,Seventh & D Street Office
318 Seventh St. NW
HABS DC-496
HABS DC,WASH,332-
2ph/6pg/1pc L

Riggs National Bank,Washington Loan & Trust Branch; see Washington Loan & Trust Company

Riggs National Bank,17th & G Branch; see Washington Loan & Trust Company,West End Branch

Riggs-Riley House
3038 N St. NW
HABS DC-46
HABS DC,GEO,48-
12dr/1ph/1pg L

Riley Building,Rendezvous Adult Magazines & Films (Crandall's Theater,Rendezvous Adult Magazines&Film
437 Ninth St. ,NW
HABS DC-520-B
HABS DC,WASH,284-
3ph/9pg/1pc L

Riley Building,Sunny's Surplus (Crandall's Theater,Sunny's Surplus)
816 E St. ,NW
HABS DC-520-A
HABS DC,WASH,285-
3ph/11pg/1pc L

Riley Springs Footbridge (Rock Creek & Potomac Parkway Project 1992)
HAER DC-32
H

Ringgold-Carroll House (Bacon House)
1801 F St. NW
HABS DC-391
HABS DC,WASH,34-
60ph/4pc L

Rittenhouse Place; see Dumbarton House

Robertson,Thomas,House
3116-3118 M St. NW
HABS DC-115
HABS DC,GEO,74-
1ph/6pg L

Rock Creek & Potomac Parkway (Reservation 360)
HABS DC-697
H

Rock Creek & Potomac Parkway (Reservation 360) (Rock Creek & Potomac Parkway Project 1992)
HABS DC-663
H

Rock Creek & Potomac Parkway Bridge near P Street (P Street Bridge)
HAER DC-11
6ph/5pg/1pc L

Rock Creek & Potomac Parkway Project; see Pennsylvania Avenue Bridge

Rock Creek & Potomac Parkway Project 1992; see Bluffs Footbridge

Rock Creek & Potomac Parkway Project 1992; see Boundary Footbridge

Rock Creek & Potomac Parkway Project 1992; see Calvert Street Bridge

Rock Creek & Potomac Parkway Project 1992; see Connecticut Avenue Bridge

Rock Creek & Potomac Parkway Project 1992; see Devil's Cahir Footbridge

Rock Creek & Potomac Parkway Project 1992; see Embassy Gulf Sevice Center

Rock Creek & Potomac Parkway Project 1992; see K Street Bridge

Rock Creek & Potomac Parkway Project 1992; see Massachusetts Avenue Bridge

Rock Creek & Potomac Parkway Project 1992; see Milkhouse Ford

Rock Creek & Potomac Parkway Project 1992; see Morrow Drive Bridge

Rock Creek & Potomac Parkway Project 1992; see Old Harvard Street Bridge

Rock Creek & Potomac Parkway Project 1992; see Pierce Mill Bridge

Rock Creek & Potomac Parkway Project 1992; see Riley Springs Footbridge

Rock Creek & Potomac Parkway Project 1992; see Rock Creek & Potomac Parkway (Reservation 360)

Rock Creek & Potomac Parkway Project 1992; see Rolling Meadow Footbridge

Rock Creek & Potomac Parkway Project 1992; see Shoreham Hill Footbridge

Rock Creek & Potomac Parkway Project 1992; see Sixteenth Street Bridge

Rock Creek & Potomac Parkway Project 1992; see Watergate Exxon

Rock Creek & Potomac Parkway Project 1992; see Woodley Lane Bridge Abutment

Rock Creek & Potomac Parkway Project, 1992; see M Street Bridge

Rock Creek & Potomac Parkway Project, 1992; see Q Street Bridge

Rock Creek Park; see Pierce Mill

Rolling Meadow Footbridge (Rock Creek & Potomac Parkway Project 1992)
HAER DC-31
H

Ross & Getty Building
3005-3011 M St. NW
HABS DC-113
HABS DC,GEO,5A-
5ph/7pg/1pc L

Ross Drive Bridge
Ross Dr. Spanning Rock Creek .6 Mi. S. of Joyce Rd
HAER DC-13
HAER 1989(HAER):4
5ph/5pg/1pc L

Ross,Andrew,Tenant House I
1208 Thirtieth St. NW
HABS DC-435
HABS DC,GEO,97-
3ph/12pg L

Ross,Andrew,Tenant House II
1210 Thirtieth St. NW
HABS DC-175
HABS DC,GEO,98-
5ph/11pg L

Ruppert,Anton,House
New York Ave.
HABS DC-6
HABS DC,WASH,121-
4dr/8ph/6pg/fr L

S. S. Kresge Company
712 E St. ,NW
HABS DC-580
HABS DC,ASH,294-
5ph/20pg/1pc L

Sarbov Parking Garage
624 D St. ,NW
HABS DC-592
HABS DC,WASH,307-
17pg L

Saunders,Capt. Henry,House:Virginia Room
Nat'l Museum of American History,Smithsonian Inst.
HABS DC-525-A
HABS DC,WASH,515A-
4dr/fr L

Schwartz Building; see 920-926 F Street,NW (Commercial Buildings)

Scott Circle (Reservations 62,62A,62B,63,64,64A,64B)
HABS DC-684
H

Scott-Thorpe House; see Fraser,George,House

Scottish Rite Temple,Prince Hall Affiliation
1633 Eleventh St. NW
HABS DC-346
HABS DC,WASH,516-
4ph/1pg/1pc L

Second Officer's House; see Navy Yard Quarters B

215 Second Street (House); see Southeast Area Survey

Service Station and Garage; see 1200 E Street NW (Commercial Building)

Seven Buildings
1901-1913 Pennsylvania Ave. NW
HABS DC-59
HABS DC,WASH,25-
5ph/1pg L

Seventh & G Streets (School); see Southeast Area Survey

Documentation: **ct** color transparencies **dr** measured drawings **fr** field records
pc photograph captions **pg** pages of text **ph** photographs

309-319 Seventh St. ,NW (Commercial Building) (Hub Furniture Store)
HABS DC-590
HABS DC,WASH,304-
2ph/12pg/1pc L

310 Seventh St. ,NW (Commercial Building)
HABS DC-587
HABS DC,WASH,335-
4pg L

409-411 Seventh St. ,NW (Commercial Building) (Famous Shoes)
HABS DC-617
HABS DC,WASH,357-
8pg L

414-416 Seventh St. ,NW (Commercial Building) (Lerner Shops; Bag Mart)
HABS DC-582
HABS DC,WASH,296-
1ph/11pg/1pc L

425 Seventh St. ,NW (Commercial Building) (Douglas Records)
HABS DC-605
HABS DC,WASH,345-
1ph/9pg/1pc L

427 & 429 Seventh St. ,NW (Commercial Building) (George & Company)
HABS DC-606
HABS DC,WASH,346-
1ph/11pg/1pc L

431 & 433 Seventh St. ,NW (Commercial Building) (Public Sale)
HABS DC-607
HABS DC,WASH,347-
1ph/10pg/1pc L

432 Seventh St. ,NW (Commercial Building) (Bag Mart)
HABS DC-581
HABS DC,WASH,295-
1ph/6pg/1pc L

435 Seventh St. ,NW (Commercial Building) (Hi-Boy Restaurant)
HABS DC-608
HABS DC,WASH,348-
2ph/7pg/1pc L

312 Seventh Street NW (Commercial Building)
HABS DC-494
HABS DC,WASH,334-
2ph/5pg/1pc L

314-316 Seventh Street NW (Commercial Building) (Morton's)
HABS DC-495
HABS DC,WASH,333-
1ph/3pg/1pc L

437-441 Seventh Street NW (Commercial Building) (Boyce & Lewis Shoes)
HABS DC-497
HABS DC,WASH,349-
1ph/11pg/1pc L

700 Seventh Street NW (Commercial Building)
HABS DC-443
HABS DC,WASH,380-
1ph/1pc L

1005-1023 Seventh Street NW (Commercial Buildings)
HABS DC-85
HABS DC,WASH,362-
4ph/1pg/1pc L

Seventh Street NW,500 Block (Commercial Buildings)
HABS DC-313
HABS DC,WASH,517-
2ph/1pc L

443 Seventh Street,NW (Commercial Building) (D. C. Space)
HABS DC-600
HABS DC,WASH,340-
ıDLC/PP-1992:DC-4°
6ph/11pg/2pc L

541 Seventh Street,S.E. (House)
541 Seventh St.,SE
HABS DC-625
HABS 1991(HABS):28
1dr/fr L

Sevier House; see Bowie House

Seward Square (Reservations 38,38A,39 & 41,41A,40 & 42,43)
HABS DC-685
H

Sharp,Lloyd,House; see Howard Road Historic District

Sheridan,Irene,House (Embassy of Greece Annex)
2211 Massachusetts Ave. NW
HABS DC-418
HABS DC,WASH,518-
1ph/1pc/1ct L

Shields,Susan Hart,House
1401 Sixteenth St. NW
HABS DC-536
HABS DC,WASH,519-
1dr L

Shoreham Hill Bridge
Rock Creek & Potomac Pkwy,Spanning Rock Creek
HAER DC-10
HAER 1989(HAER):4
3ph/7pg/1pc L

Shoreham Hill Footbridge (Rock Creek & Potomac Parkway Project 1992)
HAER DC-36
H

Simms House; see Lihault House

Sims House
2803 M St. NW
HABS DC-111
HABS DC,GEO,71-
1ph/5pg L

Sixteenth Street
HABS DC-717
H

Sixteenth Street Bridge (Rock Creek & Potomac Parkway Project 1992)
HAER DC-29
H

1218 Sixteenth Street NW (House)
HABS DC-151
HABS DC,WASH,364-
2ph/1pc L

Sixth & G Streets SW (House)
HABS DC-54
HABS DC,WASH,144-
2ph L

119 Sixth St.,N.E. (House)
Capitol Hill Historic District
HABS DC-553
HABS DC,WASH,555-
1dr/1pc L

507 Sixth Street NW (Apartment House)
HABS DC-227
HABS DC,WASH,184-
1ph/1pg L

1901 Sixth Street NW (House); see Le Droit Park

513 Sixth Street NW (House)
HABS DC-226
HABS DC,WASH,183-
5ph/7pg L

601-613 Sixth Street SW (Row Houses)
HABS DC-55
HABS DC,WASH,145-
2ph L

Smith Row (Smith,Col. James,Row Houses)
3255-3263 N St. NW
HABS DC-67
HABS DC,GEO,53-
3ph/1pg/1pc L

Smith-Morton Row House
3034 P St. NW
HABS DC-185
HABS DC,GEO,108-
5ph/12pg L

Smith,Clement,House; see Bodisco House

Smith,Col. James,Row Houses; see Smith Row

Smith,Roger,Hotel; see Powhatan Hotel

Smith,Samuel,House; see Howard Road Historic District

Smithsonian Institute,Arts & Industries Building (Museum Building)
900 Jefferson Dr. SW
HABS DC-298
HABS DC,WASH,520A-
12ph/6pg/1pc/4ct L

Smithsonian Institution Building (Castle,The; Smithsonian Institution Building,Old)
Jefferson Dr. btwn. Ninth & Twelfth Sts. SW
HABS DC-141
HABS DC,WASH,520B-
27dr/127ph/6pg/10pc/1ct/fr L

Smithsonian Institution Building,Old; see Smithsonian Institution Building

Smithsonian Institution,Renwick Gallery; see Corcoran Art Gallery

Smoot,Minnie B. ,Apartment Building; see Howard Road Historic District

Society of the Cincinnati Headquarters; see Anderson,Larz,House

Soldiers Home,Old; see U. S. Soldiers Home

Soldiers Home,Old,Anderson Cottage; see U. S. Soldiers Home,Corn Rigs

Soldiers Home,Old,Bandstand; see U.S. Soldiers Home,Bandstand

Soldiers Home,Old,Brick House with Mansard Roof; see U.S. Soldiers Home,Brick House with Mansard Roof

Soldiers Home,Old,Chapel; see U. S. Soldiers Home,Chapel

Soldiers Home,Old,Corn Rigs; see U. S. Soldiers Home,Corn Rigs

Soldiers Home,Old,Grant Building; see U. S. Soldiers Home,Grant Building

Soldiers Home,Old,Quarters 1; see U. S. Soldiers Home,Quarters 1

Soldiers Home,Old,Quarters 2; see U. S. Soldiers Home,Quarters 2

Soldiers Home,Old,Scott Building; see U. S. Soldiers Home,Scott Building

Soldiers Home,Old,Sherman Building,South; see U. S. Soldiers Home,Scott Building

Soldiers Home,Old,Stanley Hall; see U. S. Soldiers Home,Stanley Hall

Soldiers Home,Old,Stone Gatehouse; see U.S. Soldiers Home,Stone Gatehouse

Soldiers Home,Old,Stone House with Mansard Roof; see U.S. Soldiers Home,Stone House with Mansard Roof

Soldiers Home,Old,Street Furniture; see U.S. Soldiers Home,Street Furniture

Soldiers Home,Old,Stuccoed Gable-Roof House; see U.S. Soldiers Home,Stuccoed Gable-Roof House

Soldiers Home,Old,Stuccoed Gatehouse; see U.S. Soldiers Home,Stuccoed Gatehouse

Soldiers Home,Old,Watertower; see U.S. Soldiers Home,Watertower

South Carolina Avenue
HABS DC-709
H

South Waterside Drive Overpass
Southbound Access Ramp From Mass. Ave.
HAER DC-16
HAER 1989(HAER):4
7ph/9pg/1pc L

Southeast Area Survey (101 & 122-124 Carroll Street (House); 1008 Potomac Street (House); Canal Street at Independence Avenue (Row House); 1016-1018 Potomac Street (House))
HABS DC-71
HABS DC,WASH,147-
10ph L

Southeast Area Survey (132-144 & 900-905 Eleventh Street (Row Houses); 215 Second Street (House); Seventh & G Streets (School); 214 First Street (House)) Sixth & G Streets (Synagogue)
HABS DC-74
HABS DC,WASH,151-
6ph L

Southeast Area Survey (600-602 & 1100 G Street (House); 1002,1006 Eye Street (House); 808-810,812-814, & 1016 K Street (House); 817-819 L Street (House))
HABS DC-73
HABS DC,WASH,150-
10ph L

Southeast Area Survey (330 & 706-708 Virginia Avenue (Houses); 306-308,324-326 Virginia Avenue (Houses); 156-158 North Carolina Avenue (Houses))
HABS DC-72
HABS DC,WASH,149-
8ph L

Souvenir World; see 1003 D Street (Commercial Building)

Souvenirs; see 811 Market Space NW (Commercial Building)

Sparks,Thomas,House; see Howard Road Historic District

Square 226 & Reservations 32 & 33 (Pershing Square & National Square; Pershing Square & Shepherd & Pulaski Parks)
Pennsylvania Ave. NW,btwn. Thirteenth & Fifteenth
HABS DC-474
HABS DC,WASH,330-
2dr/12pg L

Square 348 (Commercial Buildings)
Tenth,Eleventh,D & E Sts.
HABS DC-493
HABS DC,WASH,257-
3ph/1pg/1pc L

Square 406 (Commercial Buildings)
Eighth,Ninth,E & F Sts. ,NW
HABS DC-572
HABS DC,WSH,276-
2ph/17pg/1pc L

Square 407 (Commercial Buildings)
Eighth,Ninth,D & E Sts. ,NW
HABS DC-516
HABS DC,WASH,277-
3ph/24pg/1pc L

Square 431 (Commercial Building)
Seventh,Eighth,D & E Sts. ,NW
HABS DC-574
HABS DC,WASH,287-
3ph/25pg/1pc L

Square 432 (Commercial Buildings)
Seventh,Eighth,D,Sts. & Pennsylvania Ave.,N.W.
HABS DC-484
HABS DC,WASH,331-
1ph/13pg/1pc L

Square 457 (Commercial Buildings)
D,E,Sixth,& Seventh Sts. ,NW
HABS DC-597
HABS DC,WASH,337-
2ph/27pg/1pc/fr L

Square 458 (Commercial Buildings)
Sixth,Seventh,D Sts. ,& Indiana Ave. ,NW
HABS DC-618
HABS DC,WASH,301-
2ph/20pg/1pc L

Square 459 (Commercial Building)
Indiana Ave. btwn. Sixth & Seventh Sts.
HABS DC-505
HABS DC,WASH,312-
1ph/8pg/1pc L

Square 460 (Commercial Buildings)
Pennsylvania Ave. btwn. Sixth & Seventh Sts.
HABS DC-501
HABS DC,WASH,323-
5pg L

Square 491 (Commercial Buildings)
Sixth,C Sts. ,& Pennsylvania Ave. & Marshall Pl.
HABS DC-619
HABS DC,WASH,329-
8pg L

St. Elizabeth's Hospital, B Building (No. 75)
2700 Martin Luther King Jr. Ave. SE
HABS DC-349-A
HABS DC,WASH,221A-
8ph/1pc L

St. Elizabeth's Hospital,C Building (No. 73)
2700 Martin Luther King Jr. Ave. SE
HABS DC-349-B
HABS DC,WASH,221B-
9ph/1pc L

St. Elizabeth's Hospital,I Building (No. 95)
2700 Martin Luther King Jr. Ave. SE
HABS DC-349-C
HABS DC,WASH,221C-
6ph/1pc L

St. Elizabeth's Hospital,J Building (No. 60)
2700 Martin Luther King Jr. Ave. SE
HABS DC-349-D
HABS DC,WASH,221D-
6ph/1pc L

St. Elizabeth's Hospital,K Building (No.66)
2700 Martin Luther King Jr. Ave. SE
HABS DC-349-E
HABS DC,WASH,221E-
8ph/1pc L

St. Elizabeth's Hospital,L Building (No. 64)
2700 Martin Luther King Jr. Ave. SE
HABS DC-349-F
HABS DC,WASH,221F-
8ph/1pc L

St. Elizabeth's Hospital,M Building (No.72)
2700 Martin Luther King Jr. Ave. SE
HABS DC-349-G
HABS DC,WASH,221G-
7ph/1pc L

St. Elizabeth's Hospital,N Building (No. 94)
2700 Martin Luther King Jr. Ave. SE
HABS DC-349-H
HABS DC,WASH,221H-
6ph/1pc L

St. Elizabeth's Hospital,P Building (No. 100)
2700 Martin Luther King Jr. Ave. SE
HABS DC-349-I
HABS DC,WASH,221I-
8ph/1pc L

St. Elizabeth's Hospital,Q Building (No.68)
2700 Martin Luther King Jr. Ave. SE
HABS DC-349-J
HABS DC,WASH,221J-
7ph/1pc L

St. Elizabeth's Hospital,R Building (No. 89)
2700 Martin Luther King Jr. Ave. SE
HABS DC-349-K
HABS DC,WASH,221K-
8ph/1pc L

St. John's Church
Sixteenth & H Sts. NW
HABS DC-19
HABS DC,WASH,29- ı1991(HABS):28°
13dr/25ph/31pg/2ct/fr L

St. John's Church,Ashburton House
(St. John's Church,Buckingham House; St. John's Church,St. John's Rectory)
16th & H Sts. NW
HABS DC-19-A
HABS DC,WASH,29B-
1ph/1pc L

St. John's Church,Buckingham House; see St. John's Church,Ashburton House

St. John's Church,St. John's Rectory; see St. John's Church,Ashburton House

St. Luke's Episcopal Church
Fifteenth & Church Sts. NW
HABS DC-359
HABS DC,WASH,231-
11ph/8pg/1pc L

St. Marc Hotel; see Central National Bank Building

St. Paul's Episcopal Church
Rock Creek Parish
HABS DC-47
HABS DC,WASH,19-
11dr L

Staley's Hong Kong Exchange & Regency Liquors; see 415-417 Eleventh Street (Commercial Buildings)

Stanley,Arthur C. ,House
2370 Massachusetts Ave. NW
HABS DC-271
HABS DC,WASH,213-
6ph/2pg L

Stanton Square (Reservation 15)
HABS DC-686
H

Star Parking Garage
1006 E St.
HABS DC-483
HABS DC,WASH,266-
1ph/2pg/1pc L

State,War & Navy Building (Old Executive Office Building)
Pennsylvania Ave. & Seventeeth St. NW
HABS DC-290
HABS DC,WASH,521-
10ph/1pg/1pc L

Steedman-Ray House
(Ray,Alexander,House; 1925 F Street Club)
1925 F St. NW
HABS DC-44
HABS DC,WASH,138-
5dr/3ph/26pg/1pc/fr L

Stein's Dry Cleaning & Shoe Repair; see Morrison Paper Company

Stewart,Alexander,House (Embassy of Luxembourg)
2200 Massachusetts Ave. NW
HABS DC-272
HABS DC,WASH,214-
9ph/13pg L

Stoddard Baptist Home; see Ingleside

Stoddert,Benjamin,House; see Halcyon House

Stohlman's Confectionary
1254 Wisconsin Ave. NW
HABS DC-104
HABS DC,GEO,64-
5ph/5pg L

Stone House,Old
(Layhman,Christopher,House)
3051 M St. NW
HABS DC-10-2
HABS DC,GEO,3-
3dr/7ph/4pg/1pc L

Stone,William J. ,Building (Frisco's)
1345 E St. NW
HABS DC-430
HABS DC,WASH,228-
1ph/1pc L

Street Furniture,Georgetown
Georgetown Vicinity
HABS DC-252
HABS DC,GEO,120-
14ph/7pg L

Sulgrave Club; see Wadsworth,Herbert,House

Sullivan House (Buehler House)
3617 O St. NW
HABS DC-189
HABS DC,GEO,125-
1ph/6pg L

Sullivan,Jeremiah,Building
1331 Thirty-fifth St. NW
HABS DC-202
HABS DC,GEO,138-
1ph/6pg L

201 T Street NW (House); see Le Droit Park

Taft,William H. ,Memorial Bridge
(Connecticut Avenue Bridge)
Connecticut Ave. ,spng Rock Creek,Rock Creek Park
HAER DC-6
HAER DC,WASH,560-
8ph/1pg/1pc L

Tanen's; see 409 Eleventh Street (Commercial Building)

Tayloe,Benjamin Ogle,House (Cameron House)
25 Madison Pl. NW
HABS DC-51
HABS DC,WASH,31-
1ph/1pg L

Tayloe,Col. John,House; see Octagon House

Tayloe,John,House,Stable; see Octagon House,Stable

Temperance Fountain
Pennsylvania Ave. & Seventh St. NW
HABS DC-240
HABS DC,WASH,196-
1ph L

Tennessee Avenue
HABS DC-710
H

410-412 Tenth Street (Commercial Building) (Fantasy Books)
HABS DC-487
HABS DC,WASH,269-
1ph/2pg/1pc L

420 Tenth Street,Southeast (House)
Capitol Hill Historic District
HABS DC-628
HABS 1991(HABS):28
4dr/fr L

Terrell,Mary Church,House
326 T St. NW
HABS DC-367
HABS DC,WASH,522-
3ph/1pg/2pc L

1908 Third Street NW (House); see Le Droit Park

1922 Third Street NW (House); see Le Droit Park

1500 Thirteenth Street NW (House) (Logan Circle Area Survey)
HABS DC-529-A
HABS DC,WASH,473-
4ph/1pc L

1502 Thirteenth Street NW (House) (Logan Circle Area Survey)
HABS DC-529-B
HABS DC,WASH,475-
5ph/1pc L

1500-1514 Thirteenth Street NW (Houses) (Logan Circle Area Survey)
HABS DC-529
HABS DC,WASH,474-
2ph/1pc L

1219 Thirthieth Street,NW (House) (Georgetown)
HABS DC-766
1ph/1pc H

2618 Thirtieth Street NW (House)
HABS DC-299
HABS DC,WASH,371-
6ph/1pg/1pc L

1330 Thirtieth Street,N.W. (House)
1330 Thirtieth St.,NW
HABS DC-632
HABS 1991(HABS):28
1dr/fr L

1029 Thirtieth Street,NW (House) (Georgetown)
HABS DC-765
1ph/1pc H

1248 Thirtieth Street,NW (House) (Georgetown)
HABS DC-767
1ph/1pc H

1530 Thirtieth Street,NW (House) (Georgetown)
HABS DC-768
1ph/1pc H

1408 Thirty-Fifth Street,N. W. (House) (Georgetown Historic District)
HABS DC-661
HABS DLC/PP-1993:DC-1
1dr/fr L

1209 Thirty-Fifth Street,Northwest (House) (Georgetown Historic District)
HABS DC-635
HABS 1991(HABS):28
1dr/fr L

1322 Thirty-fifth Street,NW (House) (Georgetown)
HABS DC-722
1ph/1pc H

1545 Thirty-fifth Street,NW (House) (Georgetown)
HABS DC-727
1ph/1pc H

1680 Thirty-first Street,NW (House) (Georgetown)
HABS DC-769
3ph/1pc H

1238 Thirty-fourth Street,NW (House) (Georgetown)
HABS DC-720
1ph/1pc H

1406 Thirty-fourth Street,NW (House) (Georgetown)
HABS DC-724
1ph/1pc H

1514 Thirty-fourth Street,NW (House) (Georgetown)
HABS DC-726
1ph/1pc H

1603 Thirty-fourth Street,NW (House) (Georgetown)
HABS DC-730
1ph/1pc H

1304 Thirty-sixth Street,NW (House) (Georgetown)
HABS DC-721
1ph/1pc H

1420 Thirty-sixth Street,NW (House) (Georgetown)
HABS DC-725
1ph/1pc H

1422 Thirty-Third Street,Northwest (House) (Georgetown Historic District)
HABS DC-637
HABS 1991(HABS):28
1dr/fr L

1520 Thirty-third Street,NW (House) (Georgetown)
1502 Thirty-third Street,NW
HABS DC-771
HABS MO,96-SALU,105E-
1ph/1pc H

Thomas Building
M St. & Thomas Circle
HABS DC-449
HABS DC,WASH,523-
1ph/1pc L

Thomas Circle (Reservations 65,66,161,162)
HABS DC-687
H

Thomas Circle (Houses)
HABS DC-459
HABS DC,WASH,460-
4ph/1pc L

Thomson,Strong John,Elementary School
1024 Twelfth St. NW
HABS DC-414
HABS DC,WASH,525-
5pg L

Thorn Building (Irving's Camera Shop)
417 Seventh St. NW
HABS DC-471
HABS DC,WASH,358-
1ph/10pg/1pc L

Thoron,Ward,House; see Williamson,William,House (Doorway)

Tiber Island Center for Cultural & Community Act.; see Law,Thomas,House

Tidal Basin; see Tidal Reservoir

Tidal Basin Inlet Bridge; see Tidal Reservoir Inlet Bridge

Tidal Basin Outlet Bridge; see Tidal Reservoir Outlet

Tidal Reservoir (Tidal Basin)
Between the Potomac River & the Washington Channel
HAER DC-9
HAER 1989(HAER):4
4pg L

Tidal Reservoir Inlet Bridge (Inlet Bridge; Tidal Basin Inlet Bridge)
Ohio Dr,SW,Spanning the Inlet of the Tidal Basin
HAER DC-9-A
HAER 1989(HAER):4
7ph/9pg/1pc L

Tidal Reservoir Outlet (Tidal Reservoir Outlet Bridge; Tidal Basin Outlet Bridge)
HAER DC-9-B
HAER 1989(HAER):4
4ph/5pg/1pc L

Tidal Reservoir Outlet Bridge; see Tidal Reservoir Outlet

Toll Keepers Lodge; see Lock Keeper's House

Townsend House (Cosmos Club)
2121 Massachusetts Ave. NW
HABS DC-273
HABS DC,WASH,215-
11ph/32pg L

Trans-Lux Theatre
Fourteenth St. btw. H St. & New York Ave.
HABS DC-393
HABS DC,WASH,526-
4ph/1pg/1pc L

Trinidad Cable Car Barns; see Columbia Railway Company Car Barns

Truck Company Number Four,Firehouse
219 M St. NW
HABS DC-96
HABS DC,WASH,157
2ph L

True Reformer Building
1200 U St. NW
HABS DC-362
HABS DC,WASH,234-
14ph/9pg/1pc L

Tuckerman,Lucius,House (Motion Picture Association)
1600 I St. NW
HABS DC-78
HABS DC,WASH,153-
8ph/5pg/1pc L

Documentation: **ct** color transparencies **dr** measured drawings **fr** field records **pc** photograph captions **pg** pages of text **ph** photographs

Tudor Place
1644 Thirty-first St. NW
HABS DC-171
HABS DC,GEO,2-
73ph/5pg/7pc/fr L

Turkish Embassy; see Everett,Edward H. ,House

1617 Twebty-ninth Street,NW (House) (Georgetown)
HABS DC-764
1ph/1pc H

Twelfth Street YMCA Building (Bowen,Anthony,YMCA Building)
1816 Twelfth St. NW
HABS DC-361
HABS DC,WASH,233-
23ph/9pg/2pc L

723-725 Twentieth Street (House)
HABS DC-127
HABS DC,WASH,132-
1ph L

1222 Twenty-eighth St. NW (Cottage)
HABS DC-149
HABS DC,GEO,32-
2ph L

1352 Twenty-Eighth Street,Northwest (House) (Georgetown Historic District)
HABS DC-650
HABS 1991(HABS):28
1dr/fr L

1537 Twenty-Eighth Street,Northwest (House) (Georgetown Historic District)
HABS DC-652
HABS 1991(HABS):28
1dr/fr L

1314 Twenty-eighth Street,NW (House) (Georgetown)
HABS DC-759
1ph/1pc H

1348 Twenty-eighth Street,NW (House) (Georgetown)
HABS DC-760
1ph/1pc H

Twenty-first Street NW (1400 Block) (Houses)
HABS DC-472
HABS DC,WASH,527-
1ph L

1521 Twenty-ninth Street,NW (HOUSE) (Georgetown)
HABS DC-761
1ph/1pc H

1529 Twenty-ninth Street,NW (House) (Georgetown)
HABS DC-762
1ph/1pc H

1539 Twenty-ninth Street,NW (House) (Georgetown)
HABS DC-763
1ph/1pc H

1350 Twenty-seventh Street,NW (House) (Georgetown)
HABS DC-723
1ph/1pc H

1417 Twenty-seventh Street,NW (House) (Georgetown)
HABS DC-758
1ph/1pc H

Tyler,Grafton,Double House
1314 Thirtieth St. NW
HABS DC-178
HABS DC,GEO,101-
6ph/13pg L

314 U Street NW (Carriage House); see Le Droit Park

316 U Street NW (House); see Le Droit Park

603-605 U Street NW (Houses); see Le Droit Park

1312 U Street,SE (House)
HABS DC-408
HABS DC,WASH,365-
1ph/1pc L

U. S. Capitol
Intersection of N. ,S. , & E. Capitol Sts.
HABS DC-38
HABS DC,WASH,1-
20ph/1pg/1pc/8ct L

U. S. Capitol-Light Standards
Capitol Grounds,E. of Capitol
HABS DC-77
HABS DC,WASH,1D-
2ph L

U. S. Capitol-Shelter
Capitol Grounds,NE of Capitol
HABS DC-75
HABS DC,WASH,1C-
3ph L

U. S. Capitol,Gateposts
Nineteenth St. & Constitution (moved from Capitol)
HABS DC-35
HABS DC,WASH,1A-
1dr/11ph/1pc L

U. S. Civil Service Commission; see Patent Office Building

U. S. Customhouse & Post Office (U. S. Post Office,Georgetown Station)
1221 Thirty-first St. NW
HABS DC-138
HABS DC,GEO,31-
11dr/17ph/21pg L

U. S. Department of the Interior
Eighteenth & C Sts. NW
HABS DC-410
HABS DC,WASH,528-
175ph/1pg/12pc L

U. S. Department of the Treasury
Fifteenth St. & Pennsylvania Ave. NW
HABS DC-348
HABS DC,WASH,529-
7dr/25ph/2pg/2pc/fr L

U. S. Gen. Serv. Admin. ,Central Heating Plant
C & D Sts. between 12 & 13th Sts. SW
HABS DC-383
HABS DC,WASH,530A-
20ph/1pg/2pc L

U. S. General Post Office (U. S. Tariff Commission Building)
Btw. Seventh, Eighth,E & F Sts. NW
HABS DC-219
HABS DC,WASH,176-
28ph/19pg L

U. S. Marine Corps Commandant's House (Commandant's House; Marine Barracks)
801 G St. SE
HABS DC-134
HABS DC,WASH,531-
5ph/1pg/1pc/2ct L

U. S. Navy & Munitions Buildings
Constitution Ave. between 17th & 21st
HABS DC-324
HABS DC,WASH,532-
10ph/2pg/1pc L

U. S. Navy Bureau Med. & Surg. ,Potomac Annex; see Naval Observatory,Old

U. S. Post Office Department (Post Office Building,Old)
1100 Pennsylvania Ave. NW
HABS DC-135
HABS DC,WASH,533A-
19ph/3pg/2pc L

U. S. Post Office,Georgetown Station; see U. S. Customhouse & Post Office

U. S. Soldiers Home (Soldiers Home,Old)
Rock Creek Church Rd. & Upshur St. NW
HABS DC-353
HABS DC,WASH,534-
20ph/1pg/1pc/3ct L

U. S. Soldiers Home,Anderson Cottage; see U. S. Soldiers Home,Corn Rigs

U. S. Soldiers Home,Chapel (Soldiers Home,Old,Chapel)
Rock Creek Church Rd. & Upshur St. NW
HABS DC-353-G
HABS DC,WASH,534G-
7ph/1pg/1pc L

U. S. Soldiers Home,Corn Rigs (U. S. Soldiers Home,Anderson Cottage; Soldiers Home,Old,Corn Rigs; Soldiers Home,Old,Anderson Cottage)
Rock Creek Church Rd. & Upshur St. NW
HABS DC-353-D
HABS DC,WASH,534D-
6ph/1pg/1pc L

U. S. Soldiers Home,Grant Building (Soldiers Home,Old,Grant Building)
Rock Creek Church Rd. & Upshur St.
HABS DC-353-F
HABS DC,WASH,534F-
6ph/1pg/1pc L

U. S. Soldiers Home,Quarters 1 (Soldiers Home,Old,Quarters 1)
Rock Creek Church Rd. & Upshur St. NW
HABS DC-353-A
HABS DC,WASH,534A-
3ph/1pg/1pc L

U. S. Soldiers Home,Quarters 2 (Soldiers Home,Old,Quarters 2)
Rock Creek Church Rd. & Upshur St. NW
HABS DC-353-B
HABS DC,WASH,534B-
3ph/1pg/1pc L

U. S. Soldiers Home,Scott Building (U. S. Soldiers Home,Sherman Building,South; Soldiers Home,Old,Scott Building; Soldiers Home,Old,Sherman Building,South)
Rock Creek Church Rd. & Upshur St. NW
HABS DC-353-C
HABS DC,WASH,534C-
33ph/1pg/2pc L

U. S. Soldiers Home,Sherman Building,South; see U. S. Soldiers Home,Scott Building

U. S. Soldiers Home,Stanley Hall (Soldiers Home,Old,Stanley Hall)
Rock Creek Church Rd. & Upshur St. NW
HABS DC-353-E
HABS DC,WASH,534E-
6ph/1pg/1pc/1ct L

U. S. Storage Company
418 Tenth St. NW
HABS DC-311
HABS DC,WASH,258-
2ph/13pg/1pc L

U. S. Supreme Court
First & E. Capitol Sts. NE
HABS DC-1
HABS DC,WASH,535-
2ph/1pg/1pc L

U. S. Tariff Commission Building; see U. S. General Post Office

U.S. Capitol Gatehouses (Bulfnch Capitol Gatehouses)
15th & 17th Sts. at Constitution Ave.
HABS DC-31
HABS DC,WASH,1-B-;DLC/PP-1993:DC-5
12dr/12ph/14pg/1pc/fr L

U.S. Capitol Gatepost; see Bulfinch-Capitol Gatepost

U.S. Court of Claims; see Corcoran Art Gallery

U.S. Soldiers Home,Bandstand (Soldiers Home,Old,Bandstand)
Rock Creek Church Rd. at Upshur St.
HABS DC-353-N
HABS DC,WASH,534N-
3ph/1pc L

U.S. Soldiers Home,Brick House with Mansard Roof (Soldiers Home,Old,Brick House with Mansard Roof)
Rock Creek Church Rd. at Upshur St.
HABS DC-353-J
HABS DC,WASH,534J-
2ph/1pc L

U.S. Soldiers Home,Stone Gatehouse (Soldiers Home,Old,Stone Gatehouse)
Rock Creek Church Rd. at Upshur St.
HABS DC-353-H
HABS DC,WASH,534H-
2ph/1pc L

U.S. Soldiers Home,Stone House with Mansard Roof (Soldiers Home,Old,Stone House with Mansard Roof)
Rock Creek Church Rd. at Upshur St.
HABS DC-353-K
HABS DC,WASH,534K-
4ph/1pc L

U.S. Soldiers Home,Street Furniture (Soldiers Home,Old,Street Furniture)
Rock Creek Church Rd. at Upshur St.
HABS DC-353-P
HABS DC,WASH,534P-
1ph/1pc L

U.S. Soldiers Home,Stuccoed Gable-Roof House (Soldiers Home,Old,Stuccoed Gable-Roof House)
Rock Creek Church Rd. at Upshur St.
HABS DC-353-L
HABS DC,WASH,534L-
2ph/1pc L

U.S. Soldiers Home,Stuccoed Gable-Roof House (Soldiers Home,Old,Stuccoed Gable-Roof House)
Rock Creek Church Rd. at Upshur St.
HABS DC-353-M
HABS DC,WASH,534M-
2ph/1pc L

U.S. Soldiers Home,Stuccoed Gatehouse (Soldiers Home,Old,Stuccoed Gatehouse)
Rock Creek Church Rd. at Upshur St.
HABS DC-353-I
2ph/1pc L

U.S. Soldiers Home,Watertower (Soldiers Home,Old,Watertower)
Rock Creek Church Rd. at Upshur St.
HABS DC-353-O
HABS DC,WASH,534O-
2ph/1pc L

Unification Church; see Washington Chapel,Church of Jesus Christ of L.D.S.

Union Clothing and Furniture; see Cullinan Building

Union Hardware Company
711 D St. ,NW
HABS DC-585
HABS DC,WASH,299-
1ph/3pg/1pc L

Union Hardware Decorator Center; see 709 D St. ,NW (Commercial Building)

Union of Burma Chancery; see Hughes,Charles Evans,House

Union Plaza (Reservation 334)
HABS DC-694
H

Union Station
50 Massachusetts Ave. NE
HABS DC-139
HABS DC,WASH,536- ;1991(HABS):28°
29ph/1pg/2pc/6ct/fr L

Union Station Steam Plant; see Washington Terminal Company Power Plant

United Clay Products Co. ,New York Ave. Brickyard
2801 New York Ave. NE
HAER DC-2
HAER DC,WASH,561-
8ph/23pg/1pc L

Universal Newstand; see 405 Eleventh Street (Commercial Building)

Van Hook,John,House; see Douglass,Frederick,House

Van Ness Mausoleum
Thirtieth & R Sts. ,Oak Hill Cemetary
HABS DC-169
HABS DC,GEO,41A-
2ph L

1318 Vermont Ave.,NW,Carriage House (Bethune,Mary McLeod,Carriage House)
1318 Vermont Ave.,NW
HABS DC-775-A
1dr/1ph H

Vermont Avenue
HABS DC-711
H

1314 Vermont Avenue NW (House) (Logan Circle Area Survey)
HABS DC-530-A
HABS DC,WASH,471-
1ph/1pc L

1501-1523 Vermont Avenue NW (Houses) (Logan Circle Area Survey)
HABS DC-531
HABS DC,WASH,472-
4ph/1pc L

Vienna Hat Company & Dart Drug Store
431-437 Eleventh St.
HABS DC-482
HABS DC,WASH,265-
2ph/13pg/1pc L

Vigilant Firehouse
1066 Wisconsin Ave. NW
HABS DC-98
HABS DC,GEO,59-
4dr/4ph/4pg L

Virginia Avenue
HABS DC-712
H

306-308,324-326 Virginia Avenue (Houses); see Southeast Area Survey

Documentation: **ct** color transparencies **dr** measured drawings **fr** field records
pc photograph captions **pg** pages of text **ph** photographs

330 & 706-708 Virginia Avenue (Houses); see Southeast Area Survey

Volta Bureau (Bell,Alexander Graham,Association for the Deaf)
1537 Thirty-fifth St. NW
HABS DC-245
HABS SC,GEO,115-
12ph/13pg L

3215 Volta Street,NW (House) (Georgetown)
3215 Volta Street,NW
HABS DC-772
HABS MO,96-SALU,105E-
1ph/1pc H

Wadsworth,Herbert,House (Sulgrave Club)
1801 Massachusetts Ave. NW
HABS DC-274
HABS DC,WASH,216-
9ph/2pg L

Waffle Shop
619 Pennsylvania Ave. NW
HABS DC-503
HABS DC,WASH,328-
1ph/1pg/1pc L

Walker,David,House
932 Twenty-seventh St. NW
HABS DC-9
HABS DC,WASH,42-
4dr/3ph/fr L

Walsh-Mclean House (Indonesian Embassy)
2020 Massachusetts Ave. NW
HABS DC-266
HABS DC,WASH,209-
11ph/24pg L

Warder Building (Atlas Building)
527 Ninth St. NW
HABS DC-216
HABS DC,WASH,173-
4ph/19pg/1pc L

Wardman Building
K St. NW,1400 Block
HABS DC-409
HABS DC,WASH,537-
4ph/1pc L

Warner Theatre; see Earle Theatre

Warren,Bates,Apartment Building
2029 Connecticut Ave. NW
HABS DC-559
HABS DC,WASH,538-
1ph/1pg L

Washington Chapel,Church of Jesus Christ of L.D.S. (Unification Church)
2810 Sixteenth St. NW
HABS DC-539
HABS DC,WASH,539-
1dr L

Washington Circle (Reservations 25,26,27)
HABS DC-688
H

Washington Club; see Patterson House

Washington Loan & Trust Company (Riggs National Bank,Washington Loan & Trust Branch
F & Ninth Sts.
HABS DC-217
HABS DC,WASH,174-
5ph/8pg L

Washington Loan & Trust Company,West End Branch (Riggs National Bank,17th & G Branch)
Seventeenth & G Sts. NW
HABS DC-344
HABS DC,WASH,540-
14dr/8ph/1pg/1pc/fr L

Washington Lodge Number 15,B. P. O. E. (Elks Lodge)
919 H St. NW
HABS DC-386
HABS DC,WASH,253-
12ph/17pg/1pc/fr L

Washington Monument
Fifteenth St. btw. Independence & Constitution NW
HABS DC-428
HAER DC-5
HABS/HAER DC,WASH,2-
1dr/7ph/1pg/1pc L

Washington Public Library (Central Public Library)
Eighth & K Sts. NW,Mount Vernon Sq.
HABS DC-457
HABS DC,WASH,551-
11ph/29pg/2pc L

Washington Terminal Company Power Plant (Union Station Steam Plant)
First Ave. NE
HAER DC-1
HAER DC,WASH,562-
5ph/1pg/1pc L

Washington-Lewis House; see Lewis,Edward Simon,House

Watergate & Bridge Plaza; see Arlington Memorial Bridge: Watergate & Bridge Plz.

Watergate Exxon (Rock Creek & Potomac Parkway Project 1992)
2708 Virginia Ave.,NW
HABS DC-665
H

Weiss,Mark,Camera Center; see Gilman's,Z. D.,Drug Store

West Georgetown School
1640 Wisconsin Ave. NW
HABS DC-110
HABS DC,GEO,70-
7ph/8pg L

West Potomac Park (Reservation 332)
HABS DC-693
H

West Washington Hotel
1238 Wisconsin Ave. NW
HABS DC-103
HABS DC,GEO,63-
2ph/7pg/1pc L

Western Plaza (Reservations 32,33)
HABS DC-696
H

Westory Building
605 Fourteenth St. NE
HABS DC-329
HABS DC,WASH,541-
1ph/1pg/1pc L

Wheat Row
1315-1321 Fourth St. SW
HABS DC-10
HABS DC,WASH,17-
5dr/5ph/1pg/1pc L

Wheat Row,1315 Fourth Street SW
HABS DC-10-A
HABS DC,WASH,17A-
1ph L

Wheat Row,1321 Fourth Street SW
HABS DC-10-B
HABS DC,WASH,17B-
1ph L

Wheatley Row House
1018 Twenty-ninth St. NW
HABS DC-666
HABS DC,GEO,96-
6ph/13pg L

Wheatley Town House
3043 N St. NW
HABS DC-186
HABS DC,GEO,109-
6ph/11pg L

Wheatley,Francis,House
3060-3066 M St. NW
HABS DC-114
HABS DC,GEO,73-
3ph/9pg L

White House Grounds (Reservation 1)
HABS DC-689
H

White House National Historic Park; see White House,The

White House,The (Executive Mansion,The; White House National Historic Park)
1600 Pennsylvania Ave.,NW
HABS DC-37
HABS DC,WASH,134-
41dr/600ph/2pg/33pc/1ct L

Whitelaw Apartment House
1839 Thirteenth St. NW
HABS DC-363
HABS DC,WASH,235-
14ph/10pg/1pc L

Wilkins House (Australian Emmbassy; Peruvian Embassy)
1700 Massachusetts Ave. NW
HABS DC-276
HABS DC,WASH,218-
10ph/18pg L

Wilkins-Rogers Milling Company; see Bomford's Mill

Willard Hotel,The New
1401-1409 Pennsylvania Ave. NW
HABS DC-293
HABS DC,WASH,542-
23ph/28pg/2pc/2ct L

Williams,John S. ,House; see Decatur-Gunther House

Williamson,William,House (Doorway) (Thoron,Ward,House)
2900 N St. NW
HABS DC-63
HABS DC,GEO,52-
1ph L

Willis,William E. ,House; see Howard Road Historic District

Wilson,J. Finley,Memorial Lodge No. 13; see Howard Road Historic District

Wilson,Woodrow,House
(Fairbanks,Henry Parker,House)
2340 S St. NW
HABS DC-133
HABS DC,WASH,220-
13dr/37ph/54pg/3pc/1ct/fr L

Winder Building
Seventeenth & F Sts. ,NW
HABS DC-392
HABS DC,WASH,543-
13dr/16ph/1pg/1pc/fr L

Wisconsin Avenue Bridge; see High Street Bridge

1527-1529 Wisconsin Avenue NW (House)
HABS DC-108
HABS DC,GEO,68-
3ph/8pg L

1530 Wisconsin Avenue NW (House)
(Georgetown Club,The)
HABS DC-109
HABS DC,GEO,69-
2ph/8pg L

Wood-Deming Houses
2017-2019 Connecticut Ave. NW
HABS DC-427
HABS DC,WASH,544-
1ph/1pg/1pc L

Woodley (Key,Philip Barton,House; Maret School)
3000 Cathedral Ave.
HABS DC-52
HABS DC,WASH,142-
6ph/2pg L

Woodley Lane Bridge Abutment (Rock Creek & Potomac Parkway Project 1992)
HAER DC-24
H

Woodson,Carter G. ,House
1538 Ninth St. NW
HABS DC-369
HABS DC,WASH,545-
3ph/1pg/1pc L

Woodward & Lothrop Department Store
G & 11th Sts. NW
HABS DC-310
HABS DC,WASH,546-
1ph/1pc L

Worthington House; see Mason,John Thomson,House

Zepp Row House
1407 Thirty-seventh St. NW
HABS DC-208
HABS DC,GEO,144-
2ph/6pg L

Mobile Launcher One, Kennedy Space Center, Titusville vicinity, Brevard County, Florida. Aerial view of mobile launcher. Photograph by NASA, 1983 (HAER FLA,5-TIVI.V,1-3).

Florida

PENSACOLA

(Bldg. 18); see U. S. Naval Air Station,Marine Barracks

U. S. Naval Air Station,Marine Barracks ((Bldg. 18))
HABS FL-246
HABS FLA,17-PENSA,72-
3ph/1pc L

ALACHUA COUNTY

CROSS CREEK

Rawlings,Marjorie Kinnan,House
State Rt. 325 Vic.
HABS FL-165
HABS FLA,1-CROCR,1-
6ph/5pg/1pc L

GAINESVILLE

Bailey,Maj. James B.,House
1121 NW Sixth St.
HABS FL-121
HABS FLA,1-GAINV,1-
11dr/3pg L

Bauknight Building
SW First Ave. & S. Main St.
HABS FL-273
HABS FLA,1-GAINV,2-
3dr L

Gulf Oil Company Service Station
SE First Ave. & SE Second St.
HABS FL-275
HABS FLA,1-GAINV,3-
5dr L

Masonic Temple, Lodge F.&A.M. No. 41
215 North Main St.
HABS FL-368
HABS 1988(HABS):5
16dr/fr L

Odd Fellows Home
SE Second St. & SE Eighth St.
HABS FL-285
HABS FLA,1-GAINV,4-
5dr L

ISLAND GROVE

Crosby House (Dupree,W.H. House)
St. Rd. 200-A
HABS FL-369
HABS FLA,1-IGRO,1-
8dr/fr L

Dupree,W.H. House; see Crosby House

BRADFORD COUNTY

STARKE

Bradford County Courthouse
W. Call St.
HABS FL-286
HABS FLA,4-STARKE,1-
4dr L

BREVARD COUNTY

TITUSVILLE VIC.

Mobile Launcher One
Kennedy Space Ctr.
HAER FL-4
HAER FLA,5-TIVI.V,1-
46ph/4pg/4pc L

BROWARD COUNTY

FORT LAUDERDALE

Bartlett,Frederic Clay,Art Studio & Tower; see Bonnet House,Art Studio & Tower

Bartlett,Frederic Clay,Boat House; see Bonnet House,Boat House

Bartlett,Frederic Clay,Greenhouse,Museum & Bam.Bar; see Bonnet House,Greenhouse,Shell Museum & Bamboo Bar

Bartlett,Frederic Clay,House; see Bonnet House

Bartlett,Frederic Clay,Music Studio & Guest Wing; see Bonnet House,Music Studio & Guest Wing

Bonnet House (Bartlett,Frederic Clay,House)
900 N. Birch Rd.
HABS FL-366
HABS FLA.6-FOLAU,1-
6dr/fr L

Bonnet House,Art Studio & Tower (Bartlett,Frederic Clay,Art Studio & Tower)
900 N. Birch Rd.
HABS FL-366-A
HABS FLA,6-FOLAU,1A-
3dr/fr L

Bonnet House,Boat House (Bartlett,Frederic Clay,Boat House)
900 N. Birch Rd.
HABS FL-366-B
HABS FLA,6-FOLAU,1B-
2dr/fr L

Bonnet House,Greenhouse,Shell Museum & Bamboo Bar (Bartlett,Frederic Clay,Greenhouse,Museum & Bam.Bar
900 N. Birch Rd.
HABS FL-366-C
HABS FLA,6-FOLAU,1C-
2dr/fr L

Bonnet House,Music Studio & Guest Wing (Bartlett,Frederic Clay,Music Studio & Guest Wing)
900 N. Birch Rd.
HABS FL-366-D
HABS FLA,6-FOLAU,1D-
3dr/fr L

DADE COUNTY

CORAL GABLES

Coral Gables (Entrances,Streets,Gates, & Squares)
HABS FL-335
HABS FLA,13-CORGA,5-
15ph/2pc/fr L

Coral Gables City Hall
405 Biltmore Way
HABS FL-361
HABS FLA,13-CORGA,1-
9ph/10pg/1pc/fr L

Coral Gables Police & Fire Station (Municipal Building)
2801 Salzedo St.
HABS FL-332
HABS FLA,13-CORGA,2-
3dr L

Granada Plaza
HABS FL-333
HABS FLA,13-CORGA,3-
4dr/1ph/1pc L

Merrick Manor; see Merrick,Rev. Solomon G. ,House

Merrick,Rev. Solomon G. ,House (Merrick Manor)
907 Coral Way
HABS FL-334
HABS FLA,13-CORGA,4-
3dr L

Municipal Building; see Coral Gables Police & Fire Station

KEY BISCAYNE

Princeton Railroad Station
Crandon Park Zoo
HABS FL-365
HABS FLA,13-KYBI,1-
5dr/fr L

MIAMI

Amsterdam Palace Apartments; see Miami Beach Art Deco Historic District

Azora Apartments; see Miami Beach Art Deco Historic District

Bancroft Hotel and Apartments; see Miami Beach Art Deco Historic District

Barbizon Apartment Hotel; see Miami Beach Art Deco Historic District

Barnacle,The; see Munroe,Ralph M. ,House

Beach Plaza Hotel; see Miami Beach Art Deco Historic District

Beachway Apartments; see Miami Beach Art Deco Historic District

Beacon Hotel; see Miami Beach Art Deco Historic District

Berkeley Shore Hotel and Apartments; see Miami Beach Art Deco Historic District

Black,Sarah Elizabeth (Maud),House
10400 Old Cutler Rd.
HABS FL-336
HABS FLA,13-MIAM,3-
2dr/2ph/11pg/1pc/fr L

Breakwater Hotel; see Miami Beach Art Deco Historic District

Cardozo Hotel; see Miami Beach Art Deco Historic District

Century Hotel; see Miami Beach Art Deco Historic District

Collins Park Hotel; see Miami Beach Art Deco Historic District

Colony Hotel; see Miami Beach Art Deco Historic District

El Dorado Apartments; see Miami Beach Art Deco Historic District

Fort Dallas,Barracks
Lummas Park
HABS FL-15-6
HABS FLA,13-MIAM,1A-
5dr/2ph/5pg L

Governor Hotel; see Miami Beach Art Deco Historic District

Jackson,Dr. James M. ,Office & Surgery
190 SE Twelfth Terrace
HABS FL-337
HABS FLA,13-MIAM,4-
3dr L

Lincoln Road Mall; see Miami Beach Art Deco Historic District

Luigi's Restaurant; see Miami Beach Art Deco Historic District

Marina Building; see Pan American Airways System Terminal Building

Medco Discount; see Miami Beach Art Deco Historic District

Miami Beach Art Deco Historic District
HABS FL-322
HABS FLA,13-MIAM,5-
81ph/4pc/2ct L

Miami Beach Art Deco Historic District (Amsterdam Palace Apartments)
1116 Ocean Drive
HABS FL-322-A
HABS FLA,13-MIAM,6-
3ph/1pc L

Miami Beach Art Deco Historic District (Azora Apartments)
828 Collins Ave.
HABS FL-322-B
HABS FLA,13-MIAM,7-
1ph/1pc L

Miami Beach Art Deco Historic District (Bancroft Hotel and Apartments)
1501 Collins Ave.
HABS FL-322-C
HABS FLA,13-MIAM,8-
2ph/1pc L

Miami Beach Art Deco Historic District (Barbizon Apartment Hotel)
600 Block of Ocean Drive
HABS FL-322-D
HABS FLA,13-MIAM,9-
1ph/1pc L

Miami Beach Art Deco Historic District (Beach Plaza Hotel)
1401 Collins Ave.
HABS FL-322-E
HABS FLA,13-MIAM,10-
1ph/1pc L

Miami Beach Art Deco Historic District (Beachway Apartments)
701 Fourteenth St.
HABS FL-322-F
HABS FLA,13-MIAM,11-
1ph/1pc L

Miami Beach Art Deco Historic District (Beacon Hotel)
720 Ocean Dr.
HABS FL-322-G
HABS FLA,13-MIAM,12-
1ph/1pc L

Miami Beach Art Deco Historic District (Berkeley Shore Hotel and Apartments)
1610 Collins Ave.
HABS FL-322-H
HABS FLA,13-MIAM,13-
2ph/1pc L

Miami Beach Art Deco Historic District (Breakwater Hotel)
940 Ocean Dr.
HABS FL-322-I
HABS FLA,13-MIAM,14-
2ph/1pc L

Miami Beach Art Deco Historic District (Cardozo Hotel)
1300 Ocean Dr.
HABS FL-322-J
HABS FLA,13-MIAM,15-
8ph/1pc/1ct L

Miami Beach Art Deco Historic District (Century Hotel)
140 Ocean Dr.
HABS FL-322-K
HABS FLA,13-MAIM,16-
1ph/1pc L

Miami Beach Art Deco Historic District (Collins Park Hotel)
2000 Park Ave.
HABS FL-322-L
HABS FLA,13-MIAM,17-
4ph/1pc L

Miami Beach Art Deco Historic District (Colony Hotel)
736 Ocean Dr.
HABS FL-322-M
HABS FLA,13-MIAM,18-
2ph/1pc/1ct L

Miami Beach Art Deco Historic District (El Dorado Apartments)
1040 Lenox Ave.
HABS FL-322-N
HABS FLA,13-MIAM,19-
2ph/1pc L

Miami Beach Art Deco Historic District (Governor Hotel)
435 Twenty-first St.
HABS FL-322-O
HABS FLA,13-MIAM,20-
3ph/1pc L

Miami Beach Art Deco Historic District (Lincoln Road Mall)
HABS FL-322-P
HABS FLA,13-MIAM,21-
10ph/1pc L

Miami Beach Art Deco Historic District (Luigi's Restaurant)
900 Block of Lincoln Road Mall
HABS FL-322-Q
HABS FLA,13-,MIAM,22-
4ph/1pc L

Miami Beach Art Deco Historic District (Medco Discount)
744 Lincoln Road Mall
HABS FL-322-R
HABS FLA,13-MIAM,23-
2ph/1pc L

Miami Beach Art Deco Historic District (New Yorker Hotel)
1611 Collins Ave.
HABS FL-322-S
HABS FLA,13-MIAM,24-
3ph/1pc L

Miami Beach Art Deco Historic District (Park Central Hotel)
640 Ocean Dr.
HABS FL-322-T
HABS FLA,13-MIAM,25-
3ph/1pc L

Miami Beach Art Deco Historic District (Senator Hotel Apartments)
1201 Collins Ave.
HABS FL-322-V
HABS FLA,13-MIAM,27-
7ph/1pc L

Miami Beach Art Deco Historic District (St. Moritz Hotel-Motel)
1565 Collins Ave.
HABS FL-322-U
HABS FLA,13-MIAM,26-
2ph/1pc L

Miami Beach Art Deco Historic District (1015 Thirteenth Street)
HABS FL-322-W
HABS FLA,13-MIAM,28-
2ph/1pc L

Miami Beach Art Deco Historic District (763 Thirteenth Street)
HABS FL-322-X
HABS FLA,13-MIAM,29-
3ph/1pc L

Miami Beach Art Deco Historic District (Tiffany Hotel)
801 Collins Ave.
HABS FL-322-Y
HABS FLA,13-MIAM,30-
4ph/1pc L

Miami Beach Art Deco Historic District (Victor Hotel)
1144 Ocean Dr.
HABS FL-322-Z
HABS FLA,13-MIAM,31-
8ph/1pc L

Miami City Hall; see Pan American Airways System Terminal Building

Munroe,Ralph M. ,Boathouse
3485 Main Hwy. (Coconut Grove)
HABS FL-261-A
HABS FLA,13-MIAM,32A-
3dr/6ph/1pc L

Munroe,Ralph M. ,House (Barnacle,The)
3485 Main Hwy. ,Coconut Grove
HABS FL-261
HABS FLA,12-MIAM,32-
8dr/11ph/5pg/1pc/fr L

Munroe,Ralph M. ,House,Three Sisters Cottage
HABS FL-261-B
HABS FLA,13-MIAM,32B-
1ph/1pc L

New Yorker Hotel; see Miami Beach Art Deco Historic District

Pan American Airways System Terminal Building (Miami City Hall; Marina Building)
3500 Pan American Dr.
HABS FL-363
HABS FLA,13-MIAM,2-
9ph/11pg/1pc/fr L

Park Central Hotel; see Miami Beach Art Deco Historic District

Plymouth Congregational Church
Devon Rd.
HABS FL-339
HABS FLA,13-MIAM,33-
3dr L

Senator Hotel Apartments; see Miami Beach Art Deco Historic District

St. Moritz Hotel-Motel; see Miami Beach Art Deco Historic District

1015 Thirteenth Street; see Miami Beach Art Deco Historic District

763 Thirteenth Street; see Miami Beach Art Deco Historic District

Tiffany Hotel; see Miami Beach Art Deco Historic District

Victor Hotel; see Miami Beach Art Deco Historic District

DUVAL COUNTY

FORT GEORGE ISLAND

Jai,Anna,House (Slave Quarters & Driver's Cabin)
HABS FL-15-1
HABS FLA,16-FOGEO.V,1-
7dr/3ph/9pg L

JACKSONVILLE

Adams Building
517-527 W. Bay St.
HABS FL-341
HABS FLA,16-JACK,4-
5pg L

Ahaveth Chesed Synogogue (Orinetal Greek Orthodox Church)
723 Laura St.
HABS FL-350
HABS FLA,16-JACK,5-
4dr/6pg/fr L

Brewster Hospital & Nurse Training School; see 915 West Monroe Street (Commercial Building)

Daniel,Dr. Richard P. ,House
1120 Hubbard St.
HABS FL-342
HABS FLA,16-JACK,6-
5dr/9pg/fr L

Doty,Clarence T.,Carriage House
510 Lomax St.
HABS FL-343-A
HABS FLA,16-JACK,7A-
1dr/fr L

Doty,Clarence T.,Residence
510 Lomax St.
HABS FL-343
HABS FLA,16-JACK,7-
5dr/8pg/fr L

El Modelo Building
501-513 W. Bay St.
HABS FL-345
HABS FLA,16-JACK,8-
7pg L

LaVilla Boarding House,New York Inn
830 Houston St.
HABS FL-346-A
HABS FLA,16-JACK,9A-
10pg L

LaVilla Boarding House,Turkish Harem
832-834 Houston St.
HABS FL-346-B
HABS FLA,16-JACK,9B-
12pg L

LaVilla Boarding House,836 Houston St.(residential
836 Houston St.
HABS FL-346-C
HABS FLA,16-JACK,9C-
11pg L

LaVilla Boarding Houses
830-836 Houston St.
HABS FL-346
HABS FLA,16-JACK,9-
3dr/fr L

Love-McGinnis House
2063 Oak St.
HABS FL-347
HABS FLA,16-JACK,10-
9pg L

Morocco Temple
219 Newnan St.
HABS FL-349
HABS FLA,16-JACK,11-
9pg L

Orinetal Greek Orthodox Church; see Ahaveth Chesed Synogogue

Riverside Baptist Church
2650 Park St.
HABS FL-351
HABS FLA,16-JACK,12-
11pg L

St. Andrew's Parish Episcopal Church
317 Florida Ave.
HABS FL-352
HABS FLA,16-JACK,13-
7pg/fr L

St. James Building
117 W. Duval St.
HABS FL-353
HABS FLA,16-JACK,14-
10pg L

Union Terminal
1034-1076 W. Bay St.
HABS FL-344
HABS FLA,16-JACK,15A-
9pg L

915 West Monroe Street (Commercial Building) (Brewster Hospital & Nurse Training School)
HABS FL-348
HABS FLA,16-JACK,3-
8pg L

811 West Union Street (Cottage)
HABS FL-354
HABS FLA,16-JACK,2-
3pg L

ST. JOHNS BLUFF

Spanish-American War Fort
HABS FL-15-2
HABS FLA,16- ,1-
5dr/3ph/6pg L

ESCAMBIA COUNTY

PENSACOLA

(Quarters 1); see U. S. Naval Air Station,Commandant's Quarters

Axelson,Birger,House
314 S. Florida Blanca St.
HABS FL-321
HABS FLA,17-PENSA,58-
1ph/1pc L

Axelson,Gustave,House
318 South Florida Blanca St.
HABS FL-320
HABS FLA,17-PENSA,57-
2ph/1pc L

Barkley House
410 S. Florida Blanca St.
HABS FL-148
HABS FLA,17-PENSA,7-
6dr/7ph/7pg L

Barn,The
101 W. Jackson St.
HABS FL-295
HABS FLA,17-PENSA,32-
1ph/1pc L

Bateria de San Antonio (Fort San Carlos)
San Carlos & Hovey Rds.
HABS FL-144
HABS FLA,17-PENSA,3-
9dr/15ph/9pg L

Bear Block (Penko Building)
404 S. Palafax St.
HABS FL-201
HABS FLA,17-PENSA,15-
7ph/7pg L

Bldg. 26; see U. S. Naval Air Station,Foundry

Boysen-Perry House (Scottish Rite Temple; Perry House)
N. Palafax & E. Wright Sts.
HABS FL-149
HABS FLA,17-PENSA,8-
7ph/3pg/1pc L

Building No. 27; see U. S. Naval Air Station,Coal Shed

Building No. 34; see U. S. Naval Air Station,Commandant's Offices

Charbonier,Antonio,House
335 E. Intendencia St.
HABS FL-308
HABS FLA,17-PENSA,45-
1ph/1pc L

Christ Church
18 W. Wright St.
HABS FL-288
HABS FLA,17-PENSA,25-
4ph/1pc L

Christ Episcopal Church (Pensacola Historical Museum)
405 S. Adams St.
HABS FL-146
HABS FLA,17-PENSA,5-
8ph/3pg L

Christie House
323 E. Romana St.
HABS FL-310
HABS FLA,17-PENSA,47-
1ph/1pc L

Dorr House,The
305 S. Adams St.
HABS FL-209
HABS FLA,17-PENSA,21-
7ph/7pg/1pc L

411 East Government Street (House)
Seville Square Vic.
HABS FL-306
HABS FLA,17-PENSA,43-
1ph/1pc L

501 East Government Street (House)
Seville Square Vic.
HABS FL-307
HABS FLA,17-PENSA,44-
1ph/1pc L

310 East Government Street (Law Offices)
Seville Square Vic.
HABS FL-305
HABS FLA,17-PENSA,42-
1ph/1pc L

240 East Intendencia Street (Offices)
Seville Square Vic.
HABS FL-309
HABS FLA,17-PENSA,46-
1ph/1pc L

421 East Zaragoza Street (House)
HABS FL-314
HABS FLA,17-PENSA,51-
1ph/1pc L

433 East Zaragoza Street (House)
HABS FL-311
HABS FLA,17-PENSA,48-
1ph/1pc L

437 East Zaragoza Street (House)
HABS FL-312
HABS FLA,17-PENSA,49-
1ph/1pc L

Fordham House
417 E. Zaragoza St.
HABS FL-315
HABS FLA,17-PENSA,52-
1ph/1pc L

Fort Barrancas
San Carlos & Hovey Rds. Vic.
HABS FL-143
HABS FLA,17-PENSA,2-
3dr/26ph/10pg/1pc/1ct/fr L

Fort Redoubt,U. S. Naval Air Station
HABS FL-145
HABS FLA,17-PENSA,4-
5ph/2pg L

Fort San Carlos; see Bateria de San Antonio

Hispanic Museum; see West Florida Museum of History

Information Center
(Pensacola-Escambia Development Comm. ,Offices of)
801 N. Palafax St.
HABS FL-302
HABS FLA,17-PENSA,39-
1ph/1pc L

Julee Cottage
214 W. Zaragoza St.
HABS FL-198
HABS FLA,17-PENSA,12-
4dr/5ph/5pg L

Lambert House
412 E. Zaragoza St.
HABS FL-259
HABS FLA,17-PENSA,24-
6dr/5ph/7pg L

Lavalle,Charles,House
203 E. Church St. (moved from 111 W Government St)
HABS FL-199
HABS FLA,17-PENSA,13-
6dr/8ph/6pg/1pc L

Lee,William Franklin,House
420 S. Alcaniz St.
HABS FL-317
HABS FLA,17-PENSA,54-
2ph/1pc L

Louisville & Nashville Railroad,Marine Terminal
207 E. Main St.
HABS FL-211
HABS FLA,17-PENSA,23-
10ph/6pg/1pc L

McClelland House
304 E. Government St.
HABS FL-303
HABS FLA,17-PENSA,40-
1ph/1pc L

McKenzie Oerting & Company Building
601 S. Palafax St.
HABS FL-206
HABS FLA,17-PENSA,-18
6ph/5pg L

Merritt-Rule House (Rule House)
619 N. Baylen St.
HABS FL-296
HABS FLA,17-PENSA,33-
1ph/1pc L

Moreno Cottage
211 E. Zaragoza St.
HABS FL-204
HABS FLA,17-PENSA,17-
3ph/5pg L

Moreno,Theodore,House
300 E. Government St.
HABS FL-202
HABS FLA,17-PENSA,16-
4dr/8ph/6pg/1pc/1ct L

1300 North Baylon Street (House)
HABS FL-299
HABS FLA,17-PENSA,36-
1ph/1pc L

904 North Baylon Street (House)
HABS FL-301
HABS FLA,17-PENSA,38-
1ph/1pc L

919 North Baylon Street (House)
HABS FL-298
HABS FLA,17-PENSA,35-
1ph/1pc L

Octagon,The; see U. S. Naval Air Station, Chapel & Armory

Ordnance Workshop; see U. S. Naval Air Station,General Warehouse

Payne House
1125 N. Spring St.
HABS FL-300
HABS FLA,17-PENSA,37-
1ph/1pc L

Penko Building; see Bear Block

Pensacola Athletic Club (Rafford Hall)
Baylon & Belmont Sts.
HABS FL-282
HABS FLA,17-PENSA,59-
3dr L

Pensacola Historical Museum; see Christ Episcopal Church

Pensacola Lighthouse
San Carlos Rd.
HABS FL-147
HABS FLA,17-PENSA,6-
3dr/13ph/22pg/2ct/fr L

Pensacola-Escambia Development Comm. ,Offices of; see Information Center

Perry House; see Boysen-Perry House

Perry,Mary Thackeray,House
434 E. Zaragoza St.
HABS FL-203
HABS FLA,17-PENSA,10-
4dr/8ph/6pg/1pc L

Piermont-Marple House
18 W. Larva St.
HABS FL-294
HABS FLA,17-PENSA,31-
1ph/1pc L

Piney Woods (Sawmill)
Main & Barracks Sts.
HABS FL-316
HABS FLA,17-PENSA,53-
1ph/1pc L

Plaza Ferdinand VII
Palafax,Government,Jefferson, & Zaragoza Sts.
HABS FL-207
HABS FLA,17-PENSA,19-
5ph/3pg L

Public Works Center; see U. S. Naval Air Station,Ship Carpenter's Workshop

Quarters Number 8; see U. S. Naval Air Station,Captain's Quarters

Quarters 41; see U. S. Naval Air Station,Senior Officers' Quarters

Quarters 5; see U. S. Naval Air Station,Senior Officers' Quarters

Quina,Desiderio,House
206 S. Alcaniz St.
HABS FL-196
HABS FLA,17-PENSA,9-
7dr/8ph/7pg/1pc L

Rafford Hall; see Pensacola Athletic Club

Rule House; see Merritt-Rule House

Sawmill; see Piney Woods

Scottish Rite Temple; see Boysen-Perry House

Seville Square
Adams,Government,Alcaniz & Zaragoza Sts.
HABS FL-208
HABS FLA,17-PENSA,20-
3ph/3pg L

Smith House
300 S. Alcaniz St.
HABS FL-319
HABS FLA,17-PENSA,56-
1ph/1pc L

St. Michael's Creole Benevolent Association
410 E. Government St.
HABS FL-210
HABS FLA,17-PENSA,22-
4ph/5pg/1pc/2ct L

Steamboat House
308 E. Government St.
HABS FL-304
HABS FLA,17-PENSA,41-
2ph/1pc L

Turner,Charles H. ,House
823 N. Baylen St.
HABS FL-297
HABS FLA,17-PENSA,34-
1ph/1pc L

U. S. Naval Air Sta. ,U. S. Schools of Photography
HABS FL-257
HABS FLA,17-PENSA,60-
7ph/1pc/2ct L

U. S. Naval Air Station, Chapel & Armory (Octagon,The)
Central Ave.
HABS FL-238
HABS FLA,17-PENSA,61-
4dr/7ph/10pg/1pc L

U. S. Naval Air Station,Aircraft Repair Shop
HABS FL-250
HABS FLA,17-PENSA,62-
5ph/1pc L

U. S. Naval Air Station,Bower's Store
HABS FL-245
HABS FLA,17-PENSA,63-
3ph/1pc L

U. S. Naval Air Station,Brig,Building 8
HABS FL-243
HABS FLA,17-PENSA,64-
2ph/7pg/1pc/fr L

U. S. Naval Air Station,Buildings 144 & 238
HAER FL-1
HAER FLA,17-PENSA,89-
7ph/2pg/1pc L

U. S. Naval Air Station,Captain's Quarters (Quarters Number 8)
HABS FL-219
HABS FLA,17-PENSA,65-
5dr/6ph/10pg/1pc/fr L

U. S. Naval Air Station,Carriage House
HABS FL-216
HABS FLA,17-PENSA,66-
5ph/1pc L

U. S. Naval Air Station,Coal Shed (Building No. 27)
HABS FL-247
HABS FLA,17-PENSA,67-
3ph/1pc L

U. S. Naval Air Station,Commandant's Offices (Building No. 34)
HABS FL-214
HABS FLA,17-PENSA,68-
6dr/7ph/12pg/1pc/2ct/fr L

U. S. Naval Air Station,Commandant's Quarters ((Quarters 1))
HABS FL-215
HABS FLA,17-PENSA,69-
11dr/10ph/18pg/1pc/fr L

U. S. Naval Air Station,Foundry (Bldg. 26)
HABS FL-248
HABS FLA,17-PENSA,70-
1ph/1pc L

U. S. Naval Air Station,General Warehouse (Ordnance Workshop)
West Ave.
HABS FL-213
HABS FLA,17-PENSA,71-
6dr/7ph/9pg/1pc/3ct/fr L

U. S. Naval Air Station,Navy Hospital Wall,Early
HABS FL-258
HABS FLA,17-PENSA,73-
6ph/1pc L

U. S. Naval Air Station,Navy Yard Gate
South & West Aves.
HABS FL-142
HABS FLA,17-PENSA,1
2dr/4ph/6pg L

U. S. Naval Air Station,Plant Maintenance Shop
HABS FL-241
HABS FLA,17-PENSA,74-
7ph/8pg/1pc/fr L

U. S. Naval Air Station,Power Plant
HABS FL-249
HABS FLA,17-PENSA,75-
13ph/1pc L

U. S. Naval Air Station,Quarters Number 34
HABS FL-251
HABS FLA,17-PENSA,76-
1ph/1pc L

U. S. Naval Air Station,Quarters Number 35
HABS FL-252
HABS FLA,17-PENSA,77-
2ph/1pc L

U. S. Naval Air Station,Quarters Number 39
HABS FL-253
HABS FLA,17-PENSA,78-
1ph/1pc L

U. S. Naval Air Station,Quarters Number 43
HABS FL-254
HABS FLA,17-PENSA,79-
3ph/1pc L

U. S. Naval Air Station,Quarters Number 47
HABS FL-256
HABS FLA,17-PENSA,81-
3ph/1pc L

U. S. Naval Air Station,Quarters Number46
HABS FL-255
HABS FLA,17-PENSA,80-
9ph/1pc L

U. S. Naval Air Station,Seaplane Hangar
HABS FL-242
HABS FLA,17-PENSA,82-
5ph/6pg/1pc L

U. S. Naval Air Station,Senior Officers' Quarters (Quarters 41)
HABS FL-239
HABS FLA,17-PENSA,83-
6ph/7pg/1pc/fr L

U. S. Naval Air Station,Senior Officers' Quarters (Quarters 5)
HABS FL-244
HABS FLA,17-PENSA,84-
2ph/8pg/1pc/fr L

U. S. Naval Air Station,Ship Carpenter's Workshop (Public Works Center)
HABS FL-236
HABS FLA,17-PENSA,85-
3dr/3ph/8pg/1pc/fr L

U. S. Naval Air Station,Stable
HABS FL-218
HABS FLA,17-PENSA,86-
3ph/1pc L

U. S. Naval Air Station,Storehouse Building
HABS FL-237
HABS FLA,17-PENSA,87-
5ph/11pg/1pc L

U. S. Naval Air Station,Wet Basin
HABS FL-240
HABS FLA,17-PENSA,88-
2dr/7ph/8pg/1pc/fr L

Walton,Dorothy,House
221 E. Zaragoza St. (moved from 137 W. Romana St.)
HABS FL-205
HABS FLA,17-PENSA,11-
4dr/3ph/6pg L

Warehouse
E. Main St.
HABS FL-313
HABS FLA,17-PENSA,50-
1ph/1pc L

Weis,C. A. Jr. ,House
312 W. Blount St.
HABS FL-290
HABS FLA,17-PENSA,27-
1ph/1pc L

West Florida Museum of History (Hispanic Museum)
200 E. Zaragoza St.
HABS FL-318
HABS FLA,17-PENSA,55-
2ph/1pc/2ct L

14 West Gadsden Street (House)
N. Hill Vic.
HABS FL-293
HABS FLA,17-PENSA,30-
2ph/1pc L

284 West Gonzalez Street (House)
N. Hill Vic.
HABS FL-292
HABS FLA,17-PENSA,29-
1ph/1pc L

123 West Lloyd Street (House)
N. Hill Vic.
HABS FL-291
HABS FLA,17-PENSA,28-
1ph/1pc L

Wright,Isaac,House
431 E. Zaragoza St.
HABS FL-200
HABS FLA,17-PENSA,14-
3dr/4ph/6pg L

Yniestra House
1200 N. Palafax St.
HABS FL-289
HABS FLA,17-PENSA,26-
1ph/1pc L

FLAGLER COUNTY

ST. AUGUSTINE VIC.

Cherokee Grove
Mantanzas River Vic.
HABS FL-235
HABS FLA,18-SAUG.V,1-
6dr L

FRANKLIN COUNTY

APALACHICOLA

Raney House,The (Raney,David G. ,House)
Market & F Sts.
HABS FL-150
HABS FLA,19-APA,1-
5dr/5ph/3pg L

Raney,David G. ,House; see Raney House,The

Trinity Episcopal Church
Gorrie Square
HABS FL-151
HABS FLA,19-APA,2-
10ph/6pg L

GADSDEN COUNTY

QUINCY

Bruce,William & Hector,House
U. S. Hwy. 90 (Chattahoochee Hwy.)
HABS FL-152
HABS FLA,20-QUI,1-
3ph/3pg L

White,Judge P. W. ,House
212 N. Madison St.
HABS FL-153
HABS FLA,20,QUI,2-
4ph/3pg L

HAMILTON COUNTY

WHITE SPRINGS

Bath House
Spring St.
HABS FL-277
HABS FLA,24-WHISP,1-
5dr L

HILLSBOROUGH COUNTY

TAMPA

Seddon Island Scherzer Rolling Lift Bridge
Spanning Garrison Channel fm Tampa to Sedden Isla.
HAER FL-3
HAER FLA,29-TAMP,21-
24ph/11pg/2pc L

Sulphur Springs Arcade; see Sulphur Springs Hotel

Sulphur Springs Hotel (Sulphur Springs Arcade)
8122 N. Nebraska Ave.
HABS FL-355
HABS FLA,29-TAMP,2-
1ph/4pg/1pc L

Tampa Bay Hotel (University of Tampa)
401 W. Kennedy Blvd.
HABS FL-362
HABS FLA,29-TAMP,3A-
13dr/fr L

Tampa City Hall
315 E. Kennedy Blvd.
HABS FL-338
HABS FLA,29-TAMP,1-
16ph/10pg/1pc/fr L

University of Tampa; see Tampa Bay Hotel

TAMPA,YBOR CITY

see 1402 North Nineteenth Street (Commercial)

Centrol Espanol
1500 Block of Seventh Ave.
HABS FL-331
HABS FLA,29-TAMP,8-
2ph/1pc L

Cherokee Club (El Pasaje)
1318 Ninth Ave.
HABS FL-271
HABS FLA,29-TAMP,9-
7dr/12ph/11pg/1pc/fr L

del Rio,Antonio,Building (Llano Building)
1514,1516,1518 E. Eighth Ave.
HABS FL-265
HABS FLA,29-TAMP,21-
3dr/3ph/7pg/1pc/1ct/fr L

1822 East Fourteenth Street (House)
HABS FL-326
HABS FLA,29-TAMP,6-
4ph/1pc L

1504 East Ninth Avenue (Commercial Building)
HABS FL-325
HABS FLA,29-TAMP,5-
2ph/1pc L

El Dorado Hotel (Scaglione Hotel)
1804 Fourteenth St.
HABS FL-264
HABS FLA,29-TAMP,10-
3dr/8pg/fr L

El Pasaje; see Cherokee Club

Gutierrez Building
1603 E. Seventh Ave.
HABS FL-263
HABS FLA,29-TAMP,11-
3dr/3ph/10pg/1pc/fr L

Leibovitz,M. ,Building
1818 E. Seventh Ave.
HABS FL-266
HABS FLA,29-TAMP,12-
1dr/7pg/fr L

Llano Building; see del Rio,Antonio,Building

Marcos,B. F. ,Building
1610 E. Seventh Ave.
HABS FL-267
HABS FLA,29-TAMP,13-
2dr/2ph/6pg/1pc/1ct/fr L

Mayo,F. ,Building
1518 E. Seventh Ave.
HABS FL-268
HABS FLA,29-TAMP,14-
1dr/1ph/6pg/1pc/fr L

1913 North Howard Street (Commercial)
HABS FL-330
HABS FLA,29-TAMP,7-
3ph/1pc L

1402 North Nineteenth Street (Commercial) (.)
HABS FL-327
HABS FLA,29-TAMP,4-
3ph/1pc L

Scaglione Hotel; see El Dorado Hotel

Scozzari Brothers Building
1901 E. Seventh Ave.
HABS FL-269
HABS FLA,29-TAMP,15-
2dr/3ph/8pg/1pc/fr L

Simovitz Building
2113 W. Main St.
HABS FL-328
HABS FLA,29-TAMP,16-
2ph/1pc L

Tampa Ironwork
HABS FL-272
HABS FLA,29-TAMP,17-
3dr/2pg/fr L

Warren Building
2117 W. Main St.
HABS FL-329
HABS FLA,29-TAMP,18-
3ph/1pc L

Ybor Cigar Factory
1916 N. Fourteenth St.
HABS FL-270
HABS FLA,29-TAMP,19-
13dr/32ph/22pg/3pc/4ct/fr L

Ybor City,Tampa (Site Plan)
HABS FL-217
HABS FLA,29-TAMP,20-
1dr L

JACKSON COUNTY

MARIANNA

Ely,Francis R. ,House
242 W. Lafayette St.
HABS FL-154
HABS FLA,32-MARI,1-
8ph/5pg L

JEFFERSON COUNTY

CAPPS

May,Asa,House
U. S. Rt. 19
HABS FL-284
HABS FLA,33-CAPPS,1-
8dr L

MONTICELLO

Monticello Presbyterian Church
Dogwood & Waukeenia Sts.
HABS FL-155
HABS FLA,33-MONT,1-
4ph/3pg L

Wirick-Simmons House
Jefferson & Pearl Sts.
HABS FL-156
HABS FLA,33-MONT,2-
12dr/4ph/3pg L

LEON COUNTY

TALLAHASSEE

Bank of Florida
Calhoun & Appalachia Pky. (moved from Adams St.)
HABS FL-159
HABS FLA,37-TALA,4-
6dr/3ph/3pg L

Bethel Baptist Church
224 North Blvd.
HABS FL-287
HABS FLA,37-TALA,8-
4dr L

Butler,Robert,House
3502 Old Bainbridge Rd.
HABS FL-157
HABS FLA,37-TALA,2-
5ph/3pg L

Call Mansion
HABS FL-18
HABS FLA,37-TALA,1-
2ph/1pg L

Chaires,Benjamin,House; see Columns,The

Columns,The (Chaires,Benjamin,House)
Park & Adams Sts.
HABS FL-158
HABS FLA,37-TALA,3-
6ph/3pg L

First Presbyterian Church
Adams & Park Sts.
HABS FL-162
HABS FLA,37-TALA,7-
6ph/4pg L

Kirksey,James,House
325 N. Calhoun St.
HABS FL-161
HABS FLA,37-TALA,6-
9ph/3pg L

Randall,Thomas,House
434 North Calhoun St.
HABS FL-160
HABS FLA,37-TALA,5-
5ph/3pg L

TALLAHASSEE VIC.

Goodwood Plantation
HABS FL-19
HABS FLA,37-TALA.V,1-
4dr/2ph/1pg L

Goodwood Plantation,Girl's Cottage
HABS FL-19-A
HABS DLC/PP-1993:FL-1
7dr/fr L

Goodwood Plantation,Old Kitchen
HABS FL-19-B
HABS DLC/PP-1993:FL-1
8dr/fr L

MADISON COUNTY

MADISON

Wardlaw-Smith House
Washington St.
HABS FL-163
HABS FLA,40-MAD,1-
13dr/8ph/3pg L

MANATEE COUNTY

ELLENTON

Gamble Mansion
Manatee River Vic.
HABS FL-112
HABS FLA,41-ELTO,1-
10dr/2ph/1pg L

MONROE COUNTY

DRY TORTUGAS ISLANDS

Fort Jefferson (Fort Jefferson National Monument)
Garden Key
HABS FL-44
HABS FLA,44- ,1-
44ph/11pg/2pc L

Fort Jefferson Nat. Mon. ,Enlisted Men's Barr. I; see Fort Jefferson,Enlisted Men's Barracks I

Fort Jefferson Nat. Mon. ,Enlisted Men's Barr. II; see Fort Jefferson,Enlisted Men's Barracks II

Fort Jefferson National Mon. ,Powder Magazine A; see Fort Jefferson,Powder Magazine A

Fort Jefferson National Mon. ,Powder Magazine B; see Fort Jefferson,Powder Magazine B

Fort Jefferson National Monument; see Fort Jefferson

Fort Jefferson National Monument,Hot Shot Furnace; see Fort Jefferson,Hot Shot Furnace

Fort Jefferson,Enlisted Men's Barracks I (Fort Jefferson Nat. Mon. ,Enlisted Men's Barr. I)
Garden Key
HABS FL-44-A
HABS FLA,44- ,1F-
2ph/1pc L

Fort Jefferson,Enlisted Men's Barracks II (Fort Jefferson Nat. Mon. ,Enlisted Men's Barr. II)
Garden Key
HABS FL-44-B
HABS FLA,44- ,1G-
1ph/1pc L

Fort Jefferson,Hot Shot Furnace (Fort Jefferson National Monument,Hot Shot Furnace)
Garden Key
HABS FL-44-E
HABS FLA,44- ,1J-
1ph/1pc L

Fort Jefferson,Powder Magazine A (Fort Jefferson National Mon. ,Powder Magazine A)
Garden Key
HABS FL-44-C
HABS FLA,44- ,1H-
1ph/1pc L

Fort Jefferson,Powder Magazine B (Fort Jefferson National Mon. ,Powder Magazine B)
Garden Key
HABS FL-44-D
HABS FLA,44- .1I-
1ph/1pc L

KEY WEST

Audubon House; see Geiger,John,House

Bartlum,Capt. John,House
730 Eaton St.
HABS FL-185
HABS FLA,44-KEY,18-
4ph/4pg/1pc/fr L

Convent of Mary Immaculate
600 Truman Ave.
HABS FL-184
HABS FLA,44-KEY,23-
9ph/6pg L

El Patio Apartments; see Gato,Eduardo H. ,House

Fort Taylor
Whitehead Spit Vic.
HABS FL-283
HABS FLA,44-KEY,2-
22ph/4pg/2pc/fr L

Gato,Eduardo H. ,House (Mercedes Hospital; El Patio Apartments)
1209 Virginia St.
HABS FL-186
HABS FLA,44-KEY,5-
5ph/5pg/1pc L

Geiger,John,House (Audubon House)
205 Whitehead St.
HABS FL-177
HABS FLA,44-KEY,10-
6dr/7ph/6pg/1pc/fr L

Kemp,Richard Moore,House
601 Caroline St.
HABS FL-180
HABS FLA,44-KEY,7-
7dr/8ph/5pg/1pc/fr L

Key West Post Office (U. S. Custom House; U. S. Courthouse & Lighthouse Quarters; Post Office & Customs House,Old)
Front St.
HABS FL-187
HABS FLA,44-KEY,3-
19ph/8pg/2pc L

Lowe,Capt. John Jr. ,House
620 Southard St.
HABS FL-181
HABS FLA,44-KEY-21-
8dr/13ph/1pc/fr L

Mallory Steamship Company Ticket Office; see Southern Express Company

Memorial to the U. S. Battleship Maine
Key West Cemetery
HABS FL-191
HABS FLA,44-KEY,15-
2pg L

Mercedes Hospital; see Gato,Eduardo H. ,House

Perky Bat Tower
Airport Rd.
HABS FL-193
HABS FLA,44-KEY,6-
3ph/4pg/1pc L

Porter,Commodore,Apartments; see Webb-Porter House

Porter,Dr. Joseph Y. ,II,House; see Webb-Porter House

Post Office & Customs House,Old; see Key West Post Office

Roberts,Capt. Richard,House
408 William St.
HABS FL-178
HABS FLA,44-KEY,9-
8dr/7ph/5pg/1pc/fr L

Roberts,George Francis Bartlum,House
412 William St.
HABS FL-183
HABS FLA,44-KEY,19-
5dr/2ph/6pg/1pc/fr L

Roberts,Samuel,House
1025 Fleming St.
HABS FL-182
HABS FLA,44-KEY,20-
5dr/4ph/6pg/1pc/fr L

Sand Key Lighthouse
Sand Key
HABS FL-189
HABS FLA,44-KEY,17-
8ph/5pg/1pc L

Southern Express Company (Mallory Steamship Company Ticket Office)
Mallory Square
HABS FL-174
HABS FLA,44-KEY,13-
4dr/4ph/6pg/1pc L

Tift & Company, Ships Chandlery & Icehouse
Mallory Square
HABS FL-176
HABS FLA,44-KEY,8-
4dr/4ph/8pg/1pc/fr L

Tift-Hemingway House
907 Whitehead St.
HABS FL-179
HABS FLA,44-KEY,11-
7dr/12ph/8pg/1pc/fr L

U. S. Courthouse & Lighthouse Quarters; see Key West Post Office

U. S. Custom House; see Key West Post Office

U. S. Marine Hospital
Emma St.
HABS FL-194
HABS FLA,44-KEY,22-
4ph/5pg/1pc L

U. S. Navy Coal Depot & Storehouse
Front & Whitehead Sts.
HABS FL-190
HABS FLA,44-KEY,16-
8ph/7pg/1pc L

Wall & Company Warehouse
Wall & Exchange Sts.
HABS FL-175
HABS FLA,44-KEY,12-
3dr/4ph/5pg/1pc/fr L

Watlington,Capt. Francis,House
322 Duval St.
HABS FL-192
HABS FLA,44-KEY,14-
6ph/5pg/1pc L

Webb-Porter House (Porter,Dr. Joseph Y. ,II,House; Porter,Commodore,Apartments)
429 Caroline St.
HABS FL-188
HABS FLA,44-KEY,4-
4ph/5pg L

West Indian Type House
HABS FL-120
HABS FLA,44-KEY,1-
1ph L

KNIGHT KEY

Knight Key Bridge; see Seven Mile Bridge

Moser Channel Bridge; see Seven Mile Bridge

Pacet Channel Viaduct; see Seven Mile Bridge

Pigeon Key Bridge; see Seven Mile Bridge

Seven Mile Bridge (Knight Key Bridge; Pigeon Key Bridge; Moser Channel Bridge; Pacet Channel Viaduct)
Linking Florida Keys
HAER FL-2
HAER FLA,44-KNIKE,1-
81ph/42pg/7pc L

NASSAU COUNTY

FERNANDINA BEACH

Fernandina Depot,Old
100 Atlantic Ave.
HABS FL-280
HABS FLA,45-FERB,1-
6dr/8pg/fr L

First Presbyterian Church
19 N. Sixth St.
HABS FL-278
HABS FLA,45-FERB,2-
5dr/7pg/fr L

Florida House
20 & 23 S. Third St.
HABS FL-356
HABS FLA,45-FERB,3-
7pg L

Lesesne House
415 Atlantic Ave.
HABS FL-357
HABS FLA,45-FERB,4-
7pg L

Lewis,C.W.,House
27 S. Seventh St.
HABS FL-279
HABS FLA,45-FERB,5-
6dr/13pg/fr L

Nassau County Courthouse
Atlantic Ave. & Fifth St.
HABS FL-358
HABS FLA,45-FERB,6-
23ph/5pg/2pc L

St. Peter's Parish (Episcopal Church)
Eighth St. & Atlantic Ave.
HABS FL-281
HABS FLA,45-FERB,7-
6dr/24pg/fr L

U. S. Post Office,Custom House & Courthouse
400 Atlantic Ave.
HABS FL-359
HABS FLA,45-FERB,8-
4pg L

Villa Las Palmas
315 Alachua Ave.
HABS FL-360
HABS FLA,45-FERB,9-
6pg L

ORANGE COUNTY

MAITLAND

Maitland Art Center
231 W. Packwood Ave.
HABS FL-364
HABS FLA,48-MAIT,1-
26dr/fr L

ORLANDO

Atlantic Coastline Railroad Station
(Orlando Train Station)
1402 Sligh Blvd.
HABS FL-260
HABS FLA,48-ORL,1-
6dr L

Orlando Train Station; see Atlantic Coastline Railroad Station

PALM BEACH COUNTY

MANALAPAN

Vanderbilt,Harold S. ,House
1100 S. Ocean Blvd.
HABS FL-234
HABS FLA,50-MANAL,1-
13pg L

PALM BEACH

Banyans,The; see Brelsford House

Bethesda-By-The-Sea
549 N. Lake Trail
HABS FL-222
HABS FLA,50-PALM,2-
7ph/8pg/1pc L

Bingham-Blossom House
1250 S. Ocean Blvd.
HABS FL-221
HABS FLA,50-PALM,13-
9ph/12pg/1pc/1ct L

Bolton,Chester C. ,House (Casa Apava)
1300 Ocean Blvd.
HABS FL-232
HABS FLA,50-PALM,14-
17ph/16pg/1pc/2ct L

Breakers Hotel,Cottage (Spray,The)
S. County Rd.
HABS FL-223
HABS FLA,50-PALM,9A-
6ph/6pg/1pc L

Breakers Hotel,The
S. County Rd.
HABS FL-228
HABS FLA,50-PALM,9-
33ph/25pg/2pc/1ct L

Brelsford House (Banyans,The)
1 S. Lake Trail
HABS FL-225
HABS FLA,50-PALM,10-
10ph/8pg/1pc L

Casa Apava; see Bolton,Chester C. ,House

Casa Della Porta; see McAneeny-Howerdd House

Duck's Nest; see Maddock,Henry,House

Everglades Club
HABS FL-226
HABS FLA,50-PALM,12-
20ph/11pg/2pc/2ct L

Flagler,Henry M. ,Mansion (Whitehall)
Whitehall Way
HABS FL-224
HABS FLA,50-PALM,11-
2dr/24ph/32pg/2pc/1ct L

Maddock,Henry,House (Duck's Nest)
561 N. Lake Trail
HABS FL-220
HABS FLA,50-PALM,7-
5ph/8pg/1pc L

Mar-A-Lago
1100 S. Ocean Blvd.
HABS FL-195
HABS FLA,50-PALM,1-
111ph/36pg L

McAneeny-Howerdd House (Casa Della Porta)
195 Via Del Mar
HABS FL-231
HABS FLA,50-PALM,8-
26ph/18pg/2pc/1ct L

Paramount Theatre
Sunrise Ave. & N. County Rd.
HABS FL-230
HABS FLA,50-PALM,5-
15ph/16pg/1pc/1ct L

Rasmussen-Donahue House
780 S. Ocean Blvd.
HABS FL-229
HABS FLA,50-PALM,4-
1ph/10pg/1pc L

Seaboard Airline Railway Station
(Seaboard Coast Line Railroad Passenger Station)
Datura St. & Tamarind Ave.
HABS FL-233
HABS FLA,50-PALM,3-
15ph/8pg/1pc L

Seaboard Coast Line Railroad Passenger Station; see Seaboard Airline Railway Station

Singer,Paris,Apartment
HABS FL-227
HABS FLA,50-PALM,12A-
2ph/5pg/2pc L

Spray,The; see Breakers Hotel,Cottage

Whitehall; see Flagler,Henry M. ,Mansion

PINELLAS COUNTY

ST. PETERSBURG BEACH

Don ce Sar Hotel
3400 Gulf Blvd.
HABS FL-324
HABS FLA,52-SPEBE,1-
2ph/1pc/3ct L

POLK COUNTY

AUBURDALE

Patterson,Dr. John,House
Northeast Ariana Estates
HABS FL-197
HABS FLA,53-AUB,1-
8dr L

LAKELAND

Florida Southern College
McDonald & Johnson Aves.
HABS FL-323
HABS FLA,53-LAKE,1-
53ph/21pg/4pc/fr L

Florida Southern College,Annie Pfeiffer Chapel
McDonald & Johnson Aves.
HABS FL-323-A
HABS FLA,53-LAKE,1A-
11ph/1pc/5ct/fr L

Florida Southern College,Auditorium-Music Building
(Florida Southern College,Branscomb Memorial Audit.
McDonald & Johnson Aves.
HABS FL-323-H
HABS FLA,53-LAKE,1H-
4ph/1pc/fr L

Florida Southern College,Branscomb Memorial Audit.; see Florida Southern College,Auditorium-Music Building

Florida Southern College,Buckner Building; see Florida Southern College,Roux, E. T. ,Library

Florida Southern College,Cosmography Building; see Florida Southern College,Polk Science Building

Florida Southern College,Danforth,Wm. H. ,Chapel
McDonald & Johnson Aves.
HABS FL-323-B
HABS FLA,53-LAKE,1B-
3ph/1pc/1ct/fr L

Florida Southern College,Esplanade (walkway)
McDonald & Johnson Aves.
HABS FL-323-E
HABS FLA,53-LAKE,1E-
4ph/1pc/fr L

Florida Southern College,Industrial Arts Building; see Florida Southern College,Ordway,Lucius,Arts Bldg.

Florida Southern College,Ordway,Lucius,Arts Bldg.
(Florida Southern College,Industrial Arts Building)
McDonald & Johnson Aves.
HABS FL-323-G
HABS FLA,53-LAKE,1G-
7ph/1pc/fr L

Florida Southern College,Polk Science Building (Florida Southern College,Cosmography Building)
McDonald & Johnson Aves.
HABS FL-323-F
HABS FLA,53-LAKE,1F-
10ph/1pc/fr L

Florida Southern College,Roux, E. T. ,Library (Florida Southern College,Buckner Building)
HABS FL-323-D
HABS FLA,53-LAKE,1D-
6ph/1pc/1ct/fr L

Florida Southern College,Watson,Emile E,Admin Bldg
McDonald & Johnson Aves.
HABS FL-323-C
HABS FLA,53-LAKE,1C-
9ph/1pc/1ct/fr L

SEMINOLE COUNTY

ALTAMONTE SPRINGS

Inside-Outside House; see Pierce,Capt. ,House

Pierce,Capt. ,House (Inside-Outside House)
Boston Ave.
HABS FL-274
HABS FLA,59-ALTSP,1-
7dr L

ST. JOHNS COUNTY

RATTLESNAKE ISLAND

Fort Matanzas (Fort Matanzas National Monument)
HABS FL-15-5
HABS FLA,55- ,1-
12dr/19ph/3pg/1pc L

Fort Matanzas National Monument; see Fort Matanzas

ST. AUGUSTINE

Alcazar Hotel (Lightner Museum of Hobbies)
75 King St.
HABS FL-168
HABS FLA,55-SAUG,43-
8ph/5pg/1pc L

Arrivas,Don Raimundo,House
44 S. George St.
HABS FL-122
HABS FLA,55-SAUG,23-
10dr/20ph/18pg/fr L

Cannonball House; see Tovar,Don Joseph,House

Canova-DeMedicis House
46 Bridge St.
HABS FL-127
HABS FLA,55-SAUG,26-
5dr/2ph/5pg L

Casa Monica (Cordova Hotel)
King & Cordova Sts.
HABS FL-169
HABS FLA,55-SAUG,44-
4ph/2pg/1pc L

Castillo de San Marcos (Spanish Castle San Marcos; 1ort Marion)
1 Castillo Dr.
HABS FL-17
HABS FLA,55-SAUG,1-
20dr/41ph/1pg/2pc/fr L

Cathedral Rectory,The
Saint George & Cathedral Sts.
HABS FL-379
HABS FLA,55-SAUG,2-
16dr/1ph/5pg L

City Gate
Orange St.
HABS FL-15-3
HABS FLA,55-SAUG,9-
17dr/1ph/2pg L

City Library (Spanish House; Segui-Smith House)
Auiles St. & Artillery Lane
HABS FL-13
HABS FLA,55-SAUG,3-
6dr/3ph/3pg L

Cordova Hotel; see Casa Monica

De Mesa-Sanchez House (Spanish Inn,Old)
43 Saint George St.
HABS FL-135
HABS FLA,55-SAUG,33-
4dr/8ph/5pg L

Fatio House; see Ximenez-Fatio House

Fernandez-Llambias House
31 Saint Francis St.
HABS FL-171
HABS FLA,55-SAUG,42-
2ph/9pg L

Flagler Memorial Presbyterian Church
Valencia & Sevilla Sts.
HABS FL-170
HABS FLA,55-SAUG,41-
8ph/8pg L

Flagler Memorial Presbyterian Church,Parsonage
39 Sevilla St.
HABS FL-172
HABS FLA,55-SAUG,13-
5ph/4pg L

Flaglev College; see Hotel Ponce de Leon

Fornells,Don Pedro,House
62 Spanish St.
HABS FL-137
HABS FLA,55-SAUG,35-
7dr/2ph/8pg L

Garcia-Dummitt House
279 Saint George St.
HABS FL-129
HABS FLA,55-SAUG,28-
4dr/2ph/4pg L

Gonzalez-Alvarez House; see Oldest House,The

Gothic Style House
HABS FL-139
HABS FLA,55-SAUG,22-
1ph L

Grace Methodist Church (Grace Methodist Episcopal Church)
Carrera & Cordova Sts.
HABS FL-167
HABS FLA,55-SAUG,40-
4ph/9pg L

Grace Methodist Episcopal Church; see Grace Methodist Church

Horruytiner,Don Pedro,House
214 Saint George St.
HABS FL-130
HABS FLA,55-SAUG,29-
9dr/5ph/7pg L

Hotel Ponce de Leon (Flaglev College)
King,Valencia,Sevilla & Cordova Sts.
HABS FL-173
HABS FLA,55-SAUG,45-
13ph/4pg/1pc L

Huertas-Canova House (Prince Murat House)
250 Saint George St.
HABS FL-14
HABS FLA,55-SAUG,7-
7dr/5ph/5pg L

Lightner Museum of Hobbies; see Alcazar Hotel

Long-Sanchez House
43 Marine St.
HABS FL-132
HABS FLA,55-SAUG,30-
9dr/5ph/4pg L

Marin,Francisco,House
47 Marine St.
HABS FL-166
HABS FLA,55-SAUG,39-
1ph/4pg L

1ort Marion; see Castillo de San Marcos

Minorcan Chapel
39 Saint George St.
HABS FL-134
HABS FLA,55-SAUG,32-
5dr/2ph/18pg L

O'Reilly,Don Miguelde,House
32 Auiles St.
HABS FL-123
HABS FLA,55-SAUG,16-
3dr/8ph/7pg L

Oldest House,The (Gonzalez-Alvarez House)
14 Saint Francis St.
HABS FL-138
HABS FLA,55-SAUG,11-ı1991(HABS):24°
21dr/14ph/fr L

Ortega-MacMillan House
224 Saint George St.
HABS FL-124
HABS FLA,55-SAUG,24-
3dr/10ph/18pg L

Papy,Gaspar,House
36 Aviles St.
HABS FL-164
HABS FLA,55-SAUG,38-
1ph/6pg L

Paredes,Don Juan,House
54 Saint George St.
HABS FL-136
HABS FLA,55-SAUG,34-
1ph/7pg L

Perez-Sanchez House
101 Charlotte St.
HABS FL-128
HABS FLA,55-SAUG,27-
4dr/6ph/6pg L

Poujoud-Slater House; see Poujoud,Augustus,House

Poujoud,Augustus,House (Poujoud-Slater House)
105-107 Saint George St.
HABS FL-125
HABS FLA,55-SAUG,4-
4dr/5ph/8pg L

Prince Murat House; see Huertas-Canova House

Public Market
Charlotte St.
HABS FL-131
HABS FLA,55-SAUG,20-
3dr/1ph/9pg L

Rodriguez-Avero-Sanchez House
52 Saint George St.
HABS FL-126
HABS FLA,55-SAUG,25-
3dr/7ph/15pg L

Schoolhouse,Old
14 Saint George St.
HABS FL-115
HABS FLA,55-SAUG,8-
6dr/1ph/2pg L

Segui-Smith House; see City Library

Solana,Don Manuel,House
20 Charlotte St.
HABS FL-133
HABS FLA,55-SAUG,31-
5dr/2ph/4pg L

Spanish Castle San Marcos; see Castillo de San Marcos

Spanish House; see City Library

Spanish Inn,Old; see De Mesa-Sanchez House

Spanish Treasury,Old (Women's Exchange)
143 Saint George & Treasury Sts.
HABS FL-119
HABS FLA,55-SAUG,17-
14dr/6ph/2pg L

Tovar,Don Joseph,House (Cannonball House)
22 Saint Francis St.
HABS FL-140
HABS FLA,55-SAUG,36-
17dr/3ph/6pg/fr L

Triay,Antonio J. ,House
42 Spanish St.
HABS FL-141
HABS FLA,55-SAUG,37-
4dr/2ph/10pg L

Trinity Church (Episcopal)
Saint George & King Sts.
HABS FL-110
HABS FLA,55-SAUG,10-
6dr/1ph L

Women's Exchange; see Spanish Treasury,Old

Ximenez-Fatio House (Fatio House)
22 Auiles St.
HABS FL-116
HABS FLA,55-SAUG,12-
12dr/6ph/11pg L

TAYLOR COUNTY

HAMPTON SPRINGS VIC.

Whiddon Log Cabin
U. S. Rt. 98
HABS FL-276
HABS FLA,62-HAMPS.V,1-
8dr L

VOLUSIA COUNTY

NEW SMYRNA

Mission Atocuimi de Jororo
HABS FL-15-4
HABS FLA,64-NESM.V,1-
3dr/5ph/2pg L

Rankin House, Columbus, Muscogee County, Georgia. Details of entrance and ironwork. Photograph by L.D. Andrew, May 23, 1936 (HABS GA,108-COLM,4-1).

Georgia

BALDWIN COUNTY

MILLEDGEVILLE

Cedars,The
Columbia St.
HABS GA-191
HABS GA,5-MILG,7-
4ph/1pg L

Charlton-Wilkinson Impact Area; see 620 North Wilkinson Street (House)

Charlton-Wilkinson Impact Area; see 630 North Wilkinson Street (House)

Charlton-Wilkinson Impact Area; see 636 North Wilkinson Street (House)

Charlton-Wilkinson Impact Area; see 605 Simmons Avenue (House)

Conn House
Wilkinson & Green Sts.
HABS GA-132
HABS GA,5-MILG,2-
1ph/1pg L

Governor's Mansion,Old
Clark & Green Sts.
HABS GA-156
HABS GA,5-MILG,1-
10ph/3pg/1pc L

Homestead,The; see Williams-Ferguson House

Hotel,Old; see Stetson-Sanford House

Milledgeville State Hospital,Central Building
HABS GA-1156
HABS GA,5-MILG,9-
1ph/1pg L

620 North Wilkinson Street (House)
(Charlton-Wilkinson Impact Area)
HABS GA-2248
HABS DLC/PP-1993:GA-5
9ph/5pg/1pc L

630 North Wilkinson Street (House)
(Charlton-Wilkinson Impact Area)
HABS GA-2249
HABS DLC/PP-1993:GA-5
8ph/5pg/1pc L

636 North Wilkinson Street (House)
(Charlton-Wilkinson Impact Area)
HABS GA-2250
HABS DLC/PP-1993:GA-5
7ph/5pg/1pc L

605 Simmons Avenue (House)
(Charlton-Wilkinson Impact Area)
HABS GA-2247
HABS DLC/PP-1993:GA-5
9ph/5pg/1pc L

State Capitol,Old
HABS GA-137
HABS GA,5-MILG,6-
4ph/1pg L

Stetson-Sanford House (Hotel,Old)
Wilkinson & Hancock Sts.
HABS GA-136
HABS GA,5-MILG,5-
6ph/2pg L

Williams-Ferguson House (Homestead,The)
Liberty & Washington Sts.
HABS GA-134
HABS GA,5-MILG,4-
4ph/1pg/1pc L

Williams-Orme-Crawford House
211 Liberty St.
HABS GA-133
HABS GA,5-MILG,3-
8ph/1pg L

MILLEDGEVILLE VIC.

Boykin Hall (Whitaker House; Hinton Hall)
HABS GA-170
HABS GA,5-   ,2-
12ph/2pg L

Hinton Hall; see Boykin Hall

Johnson-Ennis,Gov. ,House (Rockwell House)
HABS GA-135
HABS GA,5-MILG.V,2-
3ph/1pg L

Lockerly House; see Tucker,Daniel R. ,House

Mitchell-McComb House; see Mount Nebo House

Mount Nebo House (Mitchell-McComb House)
Rt. 22
HABS GA-14-4
HABS GA,5-   ,1-
4dr/4ph/3pg L

Polhill-Baugh House
St. Hwy. 243
HABS GA-1154
HABS GA,5-MILG.V,4-
1ph/1pc L

Rockwell House; see Johnson-Ennis,Gov. ,House

Tucker-Hollinshead-Hatcher House; see Tucker,Daniel R. ,House

Tucker,Daniel R. ,House (Lockerly House; Tucker-Hollinshead-Hatcher House)
HABS GA-1151
HABS GA,5-MILG.V,3-
1ph/1pg L

Westover
Old Eaton Rd.
HABS GA-14-31
HABS GA,5-MILG.V,1-
5dr/9ph/3pg/fr L

Whitaker House; see Boykin Hall

MILLEGEVILLE

Bell,Col. Frank,House
HABS GA-192
HABS GA,5-MILG,8-
1ph/1pg L

BANKS COUNTY

HOMER VIC.

Wood,John C.,Homeplace
U.S. 441
HABS GA-2246
HABS DLC/PP-1993:GA-5
2ph/7pg/1pc L

Wood,John C.,Homeplace,House
U.S. 441
HABS GA-2246-A
HABS DLC/PP-1993:GA-5
9ph/1pc L

Wood,John C.,Homeplace,Store
U.S. 441
HABS GA-2246-B
HABS DLC/PP-1993:GA-5
2ph/1pc L

BARROW COUNTY

HOSCHTON VIC.

Cochran Log House
HABS GA-14-23
HABS GA,7-   ,1-
2dr/2ph/1pg L

BARTOW COUNTY

ADAIRSVILLE VIC.

GDOT Bridge No. 015/00316/x/00051N; see Woody Allen Road Bridge

Woody Allen Road Bridge (GDOT Bridge No. 015/00316/x/00051N)
Spanning Oothalooga Creek at County Rd. 316
HAER GA-66
HAER GA,8-ADVI,1-
6ph/1pg/1pc L

CARTERSVILLE VIC.

Bartow County Road 343 Bridge; see Dowhait's Bridge

Dowhait's Bridge (Bartow County Road 343 Bridge; GDOT Bridge No. 015/00343/X/00116.S)
Bartow County Rd. 343,spanning Etowah River
HAER GA-56
HAER GA,8-CARVI.V,1-
6ph/1pg/1pc L

GDOT Bridge No. 015/00343/X/00116.S; see Dowhait's Bridge

BEN HILL COUNTY

FITZGERALD

Fans & Stoves of Fitzgerald,Inc.; see McDonald,A. J., Homeplace

McDonald,A. J., Homeplace (Fans & Stoves of Fitzgerald,Inc.)
103 W. Roanoke Drive
HABS GA-2183
HABS 1989(HABS):5
11ph/3pg/1pc L

BIBB COUNTY

MACON

Andrews House
110 Third St.
HABS GA-141
HABS GA,11-MACO,3-
4ph/1pg L

Baber House (Clinic Hospital; Lamar-Cobb House)
Walnut St.
HABS GA-190
HABS GA,11-MACO,12-
9ph/6pg L

Bibb County Academy; see Callaway House

Birdsey House (Coleman-Solomon-Speer House)
Vineville Ave.
HABS GA-165
HABS GA,11-MACO,8-
1ph/1pg L

Callaway House (Macon Hospital; Bibb County Academy)
Pine St.
HABS GA-189
HABS GA,11-MACO,11-
1ph/2pg L

Canning House (Holt,Asa,House)
854-56 Mulberry St.
HABS GA-142
HABS GA,11-MACO,4-
1ph/1pg L

Chapman-Green House; see Poe House

Christ Church Rectory,Old
211 Walnut St.
HABS GA-1100
HABS GA,11-MACO,14-
1ph/1pg L

Clinic Hospital; see Baber House

Coleman House (Cowles-Coleman-O'Neal House; Overlook)
HABS GA-1124
HABS GA,11-MACO,15-
1ph/2pg L

Coleman-Solomon-Speer House; see Birdsey House

Cowles-Coleman-O'Neal House; see Coleman House

Cowles,Jerry,House (Jones-Walker-Scottish Rite-Masons-Sams House)
4596 Rivoli Dr. (moved from 519 Walnut St.)
HABS GA-14-27
HABS GA,11-MACO,1-
3dr/6ph/2pg/fr L

Emerson & Holmes Building
556 Mulberry St.
HABS GA-195
HABS GA,11-MACO,13-
5ph/1pg L

First Presbyterian Church
682-690 Mulberry St.
HABS GA-274
HABS GA,11-MACO,16-
1ph/1pc L

Holt-Peeler House (Holt,Thaddeus Goode,House)
HABS GA-144
HABS GA,11-MACO,6-
1ph/1pg L

Holt,Asa,House; see Canning House

Holt,Thaddeus Goode,House; see Holt-Peeler House

Johnston-Hay House
934 Georgia Ave.
HABS GA-275
HABS GA,11-MACO,17-
2ph/1pc L

Jones-Walker-Scottish Rite-Masons-Sams House; see Cowles,Jerry,House

Lamar-Cobb House; see Baber House

Macon Hospital; see Callaway House

Overlook; see Coleman House

Poe House (Chapman-Green House)
Washington Ave. & Poplar St.
HABS GA-139
HABS GA,11-MACO,2-
5ph/1pg L

Raines-Jones-Miller-Carmichael House; see Raines,Cadwalader,House

Raines,Cadwalader,House (Raines-Jones-Miller-Carmichael House)
1183 Georgia Ave.
HABS GA-145
HABS GA,11-MACO,7-
3ph/1pg L

Slade Houses (State Bank,Old)
453 Walnut St.
HABS GA-168
HABS GA,11-MACO,9-
4ph/2pg L

Small,Ralph,House
115 Rogers Ave.
HABS GA-143
HABS GA,11-MACO,5-
1ph/1pg L

State Bank,Old; see Slade Houses

BURKE COUNTY

WAYNESBORO

Munnerlyn House (Waynesboro Inn,The)
HABS GA-2120
HABS GA,17-WANBO,1-
1ph/2pg L

Waynesboro Inn,The; see Munnerlyn House

CAMDEN COUNTY

CUMBERLAND ISLAND

Carnegie Family Mansion; see Dungeness

Dungeness (Carnegie Family Mansion)
HABS GA-2160
HABS GA,20-CUMBI,1-
6ph/3pg L

Greene,Gen. Nathaniel,Cottage
HABS GA-2161
HABS GA,20-CUMBI,2-
4ph/2pg L

Plantation Office
HABS GA-1220
HABS DLC/ADE-1983(HABS):100
3dr L

ST. MARY'S

Orange Hall
HABS GA-14-16
HABS GA,20-SAMA,1-
12dr/5ph/3pg L

ST. MARY'S VIC.

Santa Maria Mission (Ruins)
HABS GA-14-18
HABS GA,20-SAMA.V,1-
2dr/6ph/3pg L

WOODBINE VIC.

Refuge Plantation
Satilla River
HABS GA-248
HABS GA,20-WOBI.V,1-
3ph/1pg L

CHATHAM COUNTY

SAVANNAH

918 Abercorn Street (House); see Savannah Victorian Historic District

Alee Temple (House); see Mercer-Wilder House

Alee Temple,Carriage House; see Mercer-Wilder House,Carriage House

Anderson-Leslie House (Leslie House)
4 W. Oglethorpe St.
HABS GA-1173
HABS GA,26-SAV,63-
5ph/1pg/1pc L

Anderson-Preston House
14 E. Oglethorpe St.
HABS GA-1212
HABS GA,26-SAV,64-
4ph/1pg/1pc L

Arnold House,Old
128 State St.
HABS GA-289
HABS GA,26-SAV,37-
2ph/1pg L

Ash,John,House
114-116 W. Hull St.
HABS GA-1211
HABS GA,26-SAV,65-
5ph/1pg/1pc L

Bank and Newspaper Office; see Newspaper Office

Battersby-Hartridge-Anderson House
119 E. Charlton St.
HABS GA-254
HABS GHA,26-SAV,28-
1ph/1pg L

Bay St. Viaduct; see Central of Georgia RR,Bay St. Viaduct

Bonticou,Timothy,Double House
419-421 E. Broughton Ln (moved to 418-420 State St
HABS GA-1176
HABS GA,26-SAV,66-
6dr/4ph/1pg/1pc/fr L

312 & 314 Broughton Street (Houses)
HABS GA-240
HABS GA,26-SAV,25-
2ph/1pg L

Bulloch-Stoddard-Cumming House; see Cunningham House (Portico)

Central of GA RR,Savannah Repair Shops & Term. Fac
W. Broad,Jones,W. Boundary & Hull Sts.
HAER GA-1
HAER GA,26-SAV,55-
17dr/133ph/146pg/7pc/fr L

Central of Georgia Railroad,Dooley Yard Viaduct; see Central of Georgia RR,1860 Brick Arch Viaduct

Central of Georgia Railroad,Mainline Viaduct; see Central of Georgia RR,1853 Brick Arch Viaduct

Central of Georgia RR,Bay St. Viaduct
(Bay St. Viaduct; GDOT Bridge #051-0025-A-00138N)
U.S. 17 & Bay St.,spanning Central of Georgia RR
HAER GA-70
HAER 1989(HAER):5
12ph/2pg/1pc L

Central of Georgia RR,Bridges
HABS GA-213
HABS GA,26-SAV,17-& 18-
1pg L

Central of Georgia RR,Cotton Yard Gates
W. Broad St.
HAER GA-51
HAER GA,26-SAV,59-
8ph/1pc L

Central of Georgia RR,Down Freight Warehouse
233 W. Broad St. (at rear of Red Building)
HAER GA-52-A
HAER GA,26-SAV,58B-
9ph/1pc L

Central of Georgia RR,Gray (Administration) Bldg.
227 W. Broad St.
HABS GA-2168
HAER GA-53
HABS/HAER GA,26-SAV,57A-
19ph/1pg/1pc L

Central of Georgia RR,Passen. Station & Train Shed
Railroad Ave. & W. Broad St.
HABS GA-2167
HAER GA-2
HABS/HAER GA,26-SAV,56-
5dr/44ph/11pg/3pc/fr L

Central of Georgia RR,Red (Admin.) Building (Red Building)
233 W. Broad Street
HAER GA-52
HAER GA,26-SAV,58A-
7ph/1pc L

Central of Georgia RR,Up Freight Warehouse
227 W. Broad St. (at rear of Gray Building)
HAER GA-53-A
HAER GA,26-SAV,57B-
14ph/1pc L

Central of Georgia RR,1853 Brick Arch Viaduct (Central of Georgia Railroad,Mainline Viaduct)
Spanning W. Boundary St. & Savannah-Ogeechee Canal
HABS GA-213-A
HAER GA-3
HABS/HAER GA,26-SAV,17-
1dr/12ph/1pc/fr L

Central of Georgia RR,1860 Brick Arch Viaduct (Central of Georgia Railroad,Dooley Yard Viaduct)
Spanning W. Boundary St. & Savannah-Ogeechee Canal
HABS GA-213-B
HAER GA-4
HABS/HAER GA,26-SAV,18-
1dr/11ph/2pc/fr L

Chamber of Commerce; see Savannah Cotton Exchange

Champion-McAlpin-Fowlkes House
230 Barnard St.
HABS GA-288
HABS GA,26-SAV,36-
9ph/2pg L

Charlton,Dr. ,House
220 E. Ogelthorpe
HABS GA-286
HABS GA,26-SAV,34-
1ph/1pg L

Chippewa Square Monument
(Oglethorpe,Gen. James,Statue)
HABS GA-1179
HABS GA,26-SAV,4-
3ph/1pg/1pc L

Christ Church (Episcopal)
28 Bull St.
HABS GA-236
HABS GA,26-SAV,2-
8ph/4pg/1pc L

Clark,William,House (Doorway)
107 Oglethorpe St.
HABS GA-214
HABS GA,26-SAV,19-
2ph/1pg L

Cluskey,Charles B. ,Embankment Stores
E. Bay St.
HABS GA-1180
HABS GA,26-SAV,67-
3dr/3ph/1pg/1pc/fr L

Cunningham House (Portico)
(Bulloch-Stoddard-Cumming House)
101 E. Oglethorpe St.
HABS GA-257
HABS GA,26-SAV,30-
1ph/1pg L

Custom House
Bay & Bull Sts.
HABS GA-215
HABS GA,26-SAV,20-
2ph/1pg L

Davenport,Isaiah,House
324 E. State St.
HABS GA-14-8
HABS GA,26-SAV,6-
5dr/11ph/6pg/1pc/fr L

Denis,Richard,Houses
25-27 Lincoln St.
HABS GA-2143
HABS GA,26-SAV,50-
1ph/2pg L

Dent House; see Williams,Stephen B. ,House

1002 Drayton Street (House); see Savannah Victorian Historic District

818 Drayton Street (House); see Savannah Victorian Historic District

313 East Bolton Street (House); see Savannah Victorian Historic District

321 East Bolton Street (House); see Savannah Victorian Historic District

103 East Duffy Lane (House); see Savannah Victorian Historic District

201-203 East Duffy Street (House); see Savannah Victorian Historic District

404-410 East Duffy Street (House); see Savannah Victorian Historic District

525-527-529 East Gwinnett Lane (House); see Savannah Victorian Historic District

118 & 124 East Harris Street (House)
HABS GA-24
HABS GA,26-SAV,12-
1ph/1pg L

224 East Henry Street (House); see Savannah Victorian Historic District

301-303 East Henry Street (House); see Savannah Victorian Historic District

521 East Henry Street (House); see Savannah Victorian Historic District

115 East Park Avenue (House); see Savannah Victorian Historic District

103-109 East President Street (Houses)
HABS GA-1215
HABS GA,26-SAV,62-
5ph/1pg/1pc L

300-306 East Waldburg Street (House); see Savannah Victorian Historic District

414-416 East Waldburg Street (House); see Savannah Victorian Historic District

203 East York Street (House, Iron Balustrade)
HABS GA-287
HABS GA,26-SAV,35-
1ph/1pg L

Eppinger-Lane House
211 W. Perry St. (moved to 404 E. Bryan St.)
HABS GA-1214
HABS GA,26-SAV,68-
5ph/1pg/1pc L

Factor's Warehouse
River St. W.
HABS GA-2144
HABS GA,26-SAV,51-
1ph/1pg L

First African Baptist Church
Bryant,Montgomery & Saint Julian Sts.
HABS GA-276
HABS GA,26-SAV,33-
2ph/1pg L

First Baptist Church
223 Bull St.
HABS GA-1182
HABS GA,26-SAV,69-
6ph/1pg/1pc L

Fort Savannah; see Fort Wayne

Fort Wayne (Fort Savannah)
E. Bay St. Vic.
HABS GA-23
HABS GA,26-SAV,11-
1ph/1pg L

Frogtown District (Savannah Repair Shops)
Bounded by Jones,I-66 Ramp, & W. Boundary Sts.
HABS GA-196
HABS GA,26-SAV,54-
5ph/1pc L

GDOT Bridge #051-0025-A-00138N; see Central of Georgia RR,Bay St. Viaduct

Gibbons Block
Congress,Saint Julian,Barnard,Whitaker Sts.
HABS GA-2130
HABS GA,26-SAV,40-
3ph/1pg L

Green-Meldrim House (Sherman's Headquarters; Green,Charles,House)
327 Bull St.
HABS GA-222
HABS GA,26-SAV,22-
21dr/21ph/2pg/1pc/fr L

Green,Charles,House; see Green-Meldrim House

Greene,Nathanael,Monument
Johnson Square
HABS GA-1183
HABS GA,26-SAV,70-
3ph/1pg/1pc L

Habersham House (Pink House)
Reynolds Sq. Vic.
HABS GA-238
HABS GA,26-SAV,24-
7ph/2pg L

Hamilton-Turner House; see Hamilton,Samuel P. ,House

Hamilton-Turner House,Carriage House; see Hamilton,Samuel P. ,House,Carriage House

Hamilton,Samuel P. ,House (Hamilton-Turner House)
330 Abercorn St.
HABS GA-1201
HABS GA,26-SAV,71-
5ph/1pg/1pc L

Hamilton,Samuel P. ,House,Carriage House (Hamilton-Turner House,Carriage House)
330 Abercorn St.
HABS GA-1201-A
HABS GA,26-SAV,71A-
3ph/1pc L

Hampton Lillibridge House,No. 1
507 E. Julian St. (moved from 310 E. Bryan St.)
HABS GA-1185
HABS GA,26-SAV,72-
4dr/4ph/1pg/1pc/fr L

Hampton Lillibridge House,No. 2
312 E. Bryan St. (demolished)
HABS GA-1186
HABS GA,26-SAV,73-
2dr/4ph/1pc/fr L

Helmly Building; see Savannah Historic District

Houston-Screven House (Johnston House)
HABS GA-246
HABS GA,26-SAV,26-
3ph/1pg L

Independent Presbyterian Church
Bull & Oglethorpe Sts.
HABS GA-237
HABS GA,26-SAV,3-
9ph/3pg/1pc L

Johnston House; see Houston-Screven House

Le Page House (Entrance)
112 W. Hull St.
HABS GA-259
HABS GA,26-SAV,32-
2ph/1pg L

Leslie House; see Anderson-Leslie House

Low House
329 Abercorn St.
HABS GA-210
HABS GA,26-SAV,14-
5ph/1pg L

Low,Juliette G. ,House; see Wayne-Gordon House

Lufborrow-Ravennel House
McDonough & Floyd Sts.
HABS GA-2139
HABS GA,26-SAV,47-
1ph/1pg L

Mackay House
125 E. Congress St.
HABS GA-2138
HABS GA,26-SAV,46-
22ph/1pg L

Marshall,Mary,Houses
127-129 Abercorn St.
HABS GA-1200
HABS GA,26-SAV,74-
5ph/1pg/1pc L

Marshall,Mary,Houses,Carriage House
127-129 Abercorn St.
HABS GA-1200-A
HABS GA,26-SAV,74A-
3ph L

McDonough Row; see Troup Trust

Documentation: **ct** color transparencies **dr** measured drawings **fr** field records **pc** photograph captions **pg** pages of text **ph** photographs

McIntosh,Gen. Lachlan,House
110 E. Oglethorpe
HABS GA-22
HABS GA,26-SAV,8-
1ph/1pg L

Mercer-Wilder House (Alee Temple (House))
429 Bull St.
HABS GA-1189
HABS GA,26-SAV,75-
6ph/1pg/1pc L

Mercer-Wilder House,Carriage House (Alee Temple,Carriage House)
429 Bull St.
HABS GA-1189-A
HABS GA,26-SAV,75A-
3ph L

Mickve Israel Synagogue
428 Bull St.
HABS GA-1190
HABS GA,26-SAV,76-
6ph/1pg/1pc L

Minis House
204 Hull St.
HABS GA-14-28
HABS GA,26-SAV,9-
4dr/5ph/2pg L

Minis,Abram,House (Red Cross Building)
204 E. Jones St.
HABS GA-281
HABS GA,26-SAV,77-
5ph/1pg/1pc L

Minis,Abram,House,Carriage House (Red Cross Building,Carriage House)
204 E. Jones St.
HABS GA-281-A
HABS GA,26-SAV,77A-
3ph L

Newspaper Office (Bank and Newspaper Office)
19 E. Bay St.
HABS GA-2131
HABS GA,26-SAV,41-
1ph/1pg L

Oglethorpe,Gen. James,Statue; see Chippewa Square Monument

Pink House; see Habersham House

Red Building; see Central of Georgia RR,Red (Admin.) Building

Red Cross Building; see Minis,Abram,House

Red Cross Building,Carriage House; see Minis,Abram,House,Carriage House

Reid Servants' & Carriage House
118 E. State St. (rear lot)
HABS GA-2137
HABS GA,26-SAV,45A-
3ph/1pg L

Remshart,William,Row Houses
104,106,108,110 W. Jones St.
HABS GA-1191
HABS GA,26-SAV,78-
8dr/5ph/1pg/1pc/fr L

Remshart,William,Row Houses; see 108 W. Jones St. (House)

Richardson-Maxwell-Owen-Thomas House
124 Abercorn St.
HABS GA-14-9
HABS GA,26-SAV,7-
8dr/20ph/2pg L

Roberts,Hiram,House (Sturges,Oliver,House; Sturges-Roberts House)
27 Abercorn St.
HABS GA-25
HABS GA,26-SAV,13-
3ph/1pg L

Row Houses
101-129 Gordon St.
HABS GA-2145
HABS GA,26-SAV,52-
3ph L

Savannah City Hall
Bay & Bull Sts.
HABS GA-2165
HABS GA,26-SAV,61-
42ph/11pg/1pc/fr L

Savannah Cotton Exchange (Chamber of Commerce)
100 E. Bay St.
HABS GA-1194
HABS GA,26-SAV,79-
5ph/1pg/1pc L

Savannah Historic District (Helmly Building)
127-131 Whitaker St.
HABS GA-1203-B
HABS GA,26-SAV,88-
6ph/1pg/1pc L

Savannah Historic District (Whitfield Building; Union Society Building)
121-125 Whitaker St.
HABS GA-1203-A
HABS GA,26-SAV,87-
7ph/1pg/1pc L

Savannah Repair Shops; see Frogtown District

Savannah Victorian Historic District
(918 Abercorn Street (House))
HABS GA-1169-M
HABS GA,26-SAV,53M-
2dr/3ph/4pg/1pc/fr L

Savannah Victorian Historic District
(1002 Drayton Street (House))
HABS GA-1169-P
HABS GA,26-SAV,53P-
1dr/8ph/5pg/1pc/fr L

Savannah Victorian Historic District
(818 Drayton Street (House))
HABS GA-1169-J
HABS GA,26-SAV,53J-
2dr/1ph/3pg/1pc/fr L

Savannah Victorian Historic District
(313 East Bolton Street (House))
HABS GA-1169-K
HABS GA,26-SAV,53K-
1dr/2ph/4pg/1pc/fr L

Savannah Victorian Historic District
(321 East Bolton Street (House))
HABS GA-1169-L
HABS GA,26-SAV,53L-
1dr/8ph/5pg/1pc/fr L

Savannah Victorian Historic District
(103 East Duffy Lane (House))
HABS GA-1169-R
HABS GA,26-SAV,53R-
1dr/4pg/fr L

Savannah Victorian Historic District
(201-203 East Duffy Street (House))
HABS GA-1169-S
HABS GA,26-SAV,53S-
2dr/5ph/5pg/1pc/fr L

Savannah Victorian Historic District
(404-410 East Duffy Street (House))
HABS GA-1169-T
HABS GA,26-SAV,53T-
2dr/3ph/4pg/1pc/fr L

Savannah Victorian Historic District
(525-527-529 East Gwinnett Lane (House))
HABS GA-1169-I
HABS GA,26-SAV,53I-
1dr/4pg/1pc/fr L

Savannah Victorian Historic District
(224 East Henry Street (House))
HABS GA-1169-U
HABS GA,26-SAV,53U-
1dr/3ph/6pg/1pc/fr L

Savannah Victorian Historic District
(301-303 East Henry Street (House))
HABS GA-1169-V
HABS GA,26-SAV,53V-
1dr/3ph/4pg/1pc/fr L

Savannah Victorian Historic District
(521 East Henry Street (House))
HABS GA-1169-W
HABS GA,26-SAV,53W-
1dr/2ph/4pg/1pc/fr L

Savannah Victorian Historic District
(115 East Park Avenue (House))
HABS GA-1169-Q
HABS GA,26-SAV,53Q-
1dr/1ph/4pg/1pc/fr L

Savannah Victorian Historic District
(300-306 East Waldburg Street (House))
HABS GA-1169-N
HABS GA,26-SAV,53N-
2dr/3ph/4pg/1pc/fr L

Savannah Victorian Historic District
(414-416 East Waldburg Street (House))
HABS GA-1169-O
HABS GA,26-SAV,53O-
2dr/5ph/4pg/1pc/fr L

Savannah Victorian Historic District
(213 West Bolton Street (House))
HABS GA-1169-B
HABS GA,26-SAV,53B-
1dr/2ph/6pg/fr L

Savannah Victorian Historic District
(217-219 West Bolton Street (House))
HABS GA-1169-C
HABS GA,26-SAV,53C-
1dr/5ph/4pg/1pc/fr L

Savannah Victorian Historic District (107 West Duffy Street (House))
HABS GA-1169-F
HABS GA,26-SAV,53F-
4dr/12ph/5pg/1pc/fr L

Savannah Victorian Historic District (301-305 West Duffy Street (House))
HABS GA-1169-G
HABS GA,26-SAV,53G-
1dr/1ph/5pg/1pc L

Savannah Victorian Historic District (215 West Gwinnett Street (House))
HABS GA-1169-A
HABS GA,26-SAV,53A-
2dr/5ph/6pg/1pc/fr L

Savannah Victorian Historic District (210-212 West Henry Street (House))
HABS GA-1169-H
HABS GA,26-SAV,53H-
1dr/2ph/5pg/1pc/fr L

Savannah Victorian Historic District (119 West Park Avenue (House))
HABS GA-1169-E
HABS GA,26-SAV,53E-
1dr/3ph/5pg/1pc/fr L

Savannah Victorian Historic District (207 West Waldburg Street (House))
HABS GA-1169-D
HABS GA,26-SAV,53D-
1dr/1ph/4pg/1pc/fr L

Savannah Victorian Historict District
Gwinnett,E. Broad,W. Broad St. & Anderson La.
HABS GA-1169
HABS GA,26-SAV,53-
1dr/254ph/27pg/14pc/18ct/fr L

Scarborough,William,House
41 W. Broad St.
HABS GA-2127
HABS GA,26-SAV,39-
22dr/11ph/4pg/1pc/fr L

Sherman's Headquarters; see Green-Meldrim House

Sisters of Mercy; see St. Vincent's Academy

Smets House (Iron Balcony)
Jones & Bull Sts.
HABS GA-258
HABS GA,26-SAV,31-
1ph/1pg L

Smith's,Archibald,Factor's Building (Van Schaick Warehouse)
202-206 E. Bay St.
HABS GA-1195
HABS GA,26-SAV,80-
1pg/fr L

Sorrel-Weed House
6 W. Harris St.
HABS GA-2140
HABS GA,26-SAV,48-
15ph/3pg L

Spencer-Woodbridge House
22 Habersham St.
HABS GA-2133
HABS GA,26-SAV,42-
4ph/1pg L

St. John's Episcopal Church
329 Bull St.
HABS GA-1192
HABS GA,26-SAV,60-
1ph/1pc L

St. Vincent's Academy (Sisters of Mercy)
207 E. Liberty St.
HABS GA-1193
HABS GA,26-SAV,81-
5ph/1pg/1pc L

Sturges-Roberts House; see Roberts,Hiram,House

Sturges,Oliver,House; see Roberts,Hiram,House

Taylor,William,Store
204 W. Bay St.
HABS GA-1196
HABS GA,26-SAV,82-
4dr/7ph/3pg/1pc L

Telfair Academy of Arts & Sciences
HABS GA-217
HABS GA,26-SAV,21-
4ph/1pg L

Tenement Houses
421-423 E. York St.
HABS GA-2134
HABS GA,26-SAV,43-
1ph/1pg L

Tobias House
18 W. Harris St.
HABS GA-256
HABS GA,26-SAV,29-
2ph/1pg L

Trinity Church
Saint James Sq.
HABS GA-212
HABS GA,26-SAV,16-
1ph/1pg L

Troup Trust (McDonough Row)
410-424 E. Macon St.
HABS GA-1197
HABS GA,26-SAV,83-
5ph/1pg/1pc L

U. S. Bank,Old Branch
HABS GA-291
HABS GA,26-SAV,38-
1ph/1pg L

Union Society Building; see Savannah Historic District

Van Schaick Warehouse; see Smith's,Archibald,Factor's Building

108 W. Jones St. (House)
(Remshart,William,Row Houses)
HABS GA-1191-A
4ph/1pc L

Waring House
127 Oglethorpe St.
HABS GA-2142
HABS GA,26-SAV,49-
4ph/1pg L

Wayne-Gordon House (Low,Juliette G. ,House)
10 E. Oglethorpe St.
HABS GA-211
HABS GA,26-SAV,15-
9ph/2pg L

213 West Bolton Street (House); see Savannah Victorian Historic District

217-219 West Bolton Street (House); see Savannah Victorian Historic District

107 West Duffy Street (House); see Savannah Victorian Historic District

301-305 West Duffy Street (House); see Savannah Victorian Historic District

215 West Gwinnett Street (House); see Savannah Victorian Historic District

210-212 West Henry Street (House); see Savannah Victorian Historic District

115 West Oglethorpe Street (House, Doorway)
HABS GA-249
HABS GA,26-SAV,27-
1ph/1pg L

119 West Park Avenue (House); see Savannah Victorian Historic District

207 West Waldburg Street (House); see Savannah Victorian Historic District

Wetter House
425 Oglethorpe St.
HABS GA-2136
HABS GA,26-SAV,44-
7ph/2pg L

Whitfield Building; see Savannah Historic District

Williams,Stephen B. ,House (Dent House)
128 W. Liberty St.
HABS GA-1210
HABS GA,26-SAV,84-
5ph/1pg/1pc L

Williams,William,House
18 E. Oglethorpe St.
HABS GA-1213
HABS GA,26-SAV,85-
5ph/1pg/1pc L

SAVANNAH VIC.

Cockspur Lighthouse (Fort Pulaski National Monument)
Cockspur Island
HABS GA-2265
H

Fort Pulaski (Fort Pulaski National Monument)
Cockspur Island
HABS GA-2158
HABS GA,26-SAV.V,2-(DLC/PP-1992:GA-5)
19ph/2pc L

Fort Pulaski National Monument; see Cockspur Lighthouse

Fort Pulaski National Monument; see Fort Pulaski

Fort Wymberly; see Wormsloe

Harbor Beacon,Old
Harbor
HABS GA-232
HABS GA,26-SAV,23-
1ph/1pg L

Hermitage (McAlpin Plantation)
Savannah River vic.
HABS GA-225
HABS GA,26-SAV.V,1-
3dr/5ph/2pg L

McAlpin Plantation; see Hermitage

Wild Heron Plantation
Little Ogeechee River Vic.
HABS GA-253
HABS GA,26-SAV.V,3-
3ph/3pg/1pc L

Wormsloe (Fort Wymberly)
Isle of Hope,Savannah Vic.
HABS GA-2126
HABS GA,26-ILHO,1-
6ph/2pg L

CLARKE COUNTY

ATHENS

Camak House
279 Meigs St.
HABS GA-14-67
HABS GA,30-ATH,3-
4dr/2ph/2pg L

Cobb Institute,Girls' Dormitory (Cobb,Lucy,Institute)
220 N. Milledge Ave.
HABS GA-1120
HABS GA,30-ATH,11- 1983(HABS):22°
5ph/1pg/1pc L

Cobb,Lucy,Institute; see Cobb Institute,Girls' Dormitory

Cobb,T. R. R. ,House (McKinley-Lumpkin House)
194 Prince Ave.
HABS GA-1116
HABS GA,30-ATH,10-1983(HABS):22°
5ph/1pg L

Crane,Ross,House (S. A. E. Chapter House)
Pulaski & Washington Sts.
HABS GA-1111
HABS GA,30-ATH,5-
5ph/1pg L

Dearing House
HABS GA-1133
HABS GA,30-ATH,16-
3ph/1pg L

Delta Tau Delta House; see Lumpkin,Joseph Henry,House

First Presbyterian Church
HABS GA-1165
HABS GA,30-ATH,20-
1ph L

Golding-Gerdine House
129 Dougherty St.
HABS GA-1130
HABS GA,30-ATH,15-
1ph/1pg L

Grady,Henry,House; see Taylor,Gen. R. D. B. ,House

Grant-Hill-White-Bradshaw House (Hill,Benjamin J. ,House; University of Georgia,President's House)
570 Prince Ave.
HABS GA-120
HABS GA,30-ATH,4D
3ph/2pg/1pc L

Hamilton-Hunnicutt House
325 Milledge Ave.
HABS GA-1128
HABS GA,30-ATH,13-
1ph/1pg L

Hayes,Charles,House
1720 S. Lumpkin St.
HABS GA-2101
HABS GA,30-ATH,23-
1ph/1pc L

Hill,Benjamin J. ,House; see Grant-Hill-White-Bradshaw House

Hodgson House
87 Oconee St.
HABS GA-1160
HABS GA,30-ATH,18-
2ph L

Hotel
480 Broad St.
HABS GA-1122
HABS GA,30-ATH,12-
1ph/1pg L

Lumpkin,Joseph Henry,House (Delta Tau Delta House)
248 Prince St.
HABS GA-1115
HABS GA,30-ATH,9-
2ph/2pg L

1234 Lumpkins Street (House)
HABS GA-1166
HABS GA,30-ATH,21-
1ph L

Lyle House (Lyle-Hunnicutt House)
320 Lumpkin St.
HABS GA-1129
HABS GA,30-ATH,14-
1ph/1pg L

Lyle-Hunnicutt House; see Lyle House

McKinley-Lumpkin House; see Cobb,T. R. R. ,House

Merk House
735 Prince Ave.
HABS GA-2102
HABS GA,30-ATH,24-
1ph/1pc L

225 Milledge Avenue (House)
HABS GA-1163
HABS GA,30-ATH,19-
1ph L

897 Milledge Avenue (House)
HABS GA-1167
HABS GA,30-ATH,22-
1ph L

Nicholson House
224 Thomas St.
HABS GA-1134
HABS GA,30-ATH,17-
1ph/1pg L

Parr House
227 Bloomfield St.
HABS GA-2103
HABS GA,30-ATH,25
1ph/1pc L

Phi Kappa Literary Society Hall; see University of Georgia,Phi Kappa Hall

Presbyterian Manse; see Reed House

Reed House (Presbyterian Manse)
185 Hull St.
HABS GA-1112
HABS GA,30-ATH,6-
1ph/1pg L

S. A. E. Chapter House; see Crane,Ross,House

Sledge,James,House
749 Cobb St.
HABS GA-2104
HABS GA,30-ATH,26-
2ph/1pc L

Taylor Monument
Oconee Hills Cemetery
HABS GA-2105
HABS GA-30-ATH,27-
1pc L

Taylor-Grady House; see Taylor,Gen. R. D. B. ,House

Taylor,Gen. R. D. B. ,House (Grady,Henry,House; Taylor-Grady House)
634 Prince Ave.
HABS GA-1114
HABS GA,30-ATH,8-
5ph/1pg/1pc L

Thomas-Carithers House (University of Georgia,Alpha Gamma Delta)
530 Milledge Ave.
HABS GA-1131
HABS GA,30-ATH,4E-
1ph/1pc L

Thomas,Stevens,House
347 Hancock St. (moved from Pulaski St.)
HABS GA-1113
HABS GA,30-ATH,7-
1ph/1pg L

University of Georgia,Alpha Gamma Delta; see Thomas-Carithers House

University of Georgia,Chapel
HABS GA-1164
HABS GA,30-ATH,4C-
1ph L

University of Georgia,Demosthenian Hall
HABS GA-14-87
HABS GA,30-ATH,4A-
5dr/7ph/1pg L

University of Georgia,Phi Kappa Hall (Phi Kappa Literary Society Hall)
Broad & Jackson Sts.
HABS GA-1117
HABS GA,30-ATH,4B-
2ph/1pg L

University of Georgia,President's House; see Grant-Hill-White-Bradshaw House

University of Georgia,Sigma Phi Epsilon; see White,H. C. ,House

Upson House
1000 Prince Ave.
HABS GA-14-66
HABS GA,30-ATH,2-
4dr/4ph/2pg L

White,H. C. ,House (University of Georgia,Sigma Phi Epsilon)
327 S. Milledge Ave.
HABS GA-2106
HABS GA,30-ATH,4F-
1ph/1pc L

ATHENS VIC.

Tallassee Shoals Hydroelectric Facility
Middle Oconee River
HAER GA-59
HAER GA,30-ATH.V,1-
14ph/5pg/1pc L

COBB COUNTY

ATLANTA VIC.

Covered Bridge
Spanning Soap Creek
HABS GA-185
HABS GA,34- ,1-
1ph/1pg L

KENNESAW

Kennesaw Mountain National Battlefield Park; see Kolb House

Kolb House (Kennesaw Mountain National Battlefield Park)
Powder Springs Rd.
HABS GA-299
HABS GA,34-KENN,1A-
(DLC/PP-1992:GA-5)
36ph/1pg/4pc L

MARIETTA

Bostwick-Fraser-Couper House; see Fraser-Couper House

Fraser-Couper House
(Bostwick-Fraser-Couper House)
HABS GA-1107
HABS GA,34-MARI,1-
2ph/1pg L

COFFEE COUNTY

JACKSONVILLE VIC.

GDOT Bridge No. 069/00031/2864.N; see Millhollin,J. H. ,Memorial Bridge

Jacksonville Ferry Bridge; see Millhollin,J. H. ,Memorial Bridge

Millhollin,J. H. ,Memorial Bridge
(Jacksonville Ferry Bridge; GDOT Bridge No. 069/00031/2864.N)
Spanning Ocmulgee River at Blackshear Rd.
HAER GA-57
HAER GA,35-JACVI.V,1-
10ph/6pg/1pc L

COWETA COUNTY

NEWNAN VIC.

"Hale Nui"; see Blount House

Blount House (Gordon-Banks House; "Hale Nui")
(moved from GA,Haddock Vic.)
HABS GA-1125
HABS GA,85-HAD.V,1-
22ph/3pg L

Gordon-Banks House; see Blount House

CRAWFORD COUNTY

KNOXVILLE

Crawford County Courthouse
HABS GA-151
HABS GA,40-KNOX,1-
3ph/1pg L

DADE COUNTY

RISING FAWN VIC.

County Road 130 Bridge
Spanning Gulf Creek
HAER GA-45
HAER GA,42-RIFA.V,1-
5ph/2pg/1pc L

DE KALB COUNTY

PANOLA VIC.

Latimer-Felton House
Atlanta Vic.
HABS GA-1106
HABS GA,45-PANO.V,1-
2dr/1ph/2pg L

SCOTTDALE

Scottdale Mills Complex
E. Ponce de Leon Ave. Vic.
HAER GA-63
1pg/fr H

Scottdale Mills Complex,Administrative Building
E. Ponce de Leon Ave. Vic.
HAER GA-63-B
1ph H

Scottdale Mills Complex,Ancillary Building
E. Ponce de Leon Ave. Vic.
HAER GA-63-C
1ph H

Scottdale Mills Complex,Employee Entrance Building
E. Ponce de Leon Ave. Vic.
HAER GA-63-D
1ph H

Scottdale Mills Complex,Mill Houses
Patterson Ave.
HAER GA-63-F
1ph H

Scottdale Mills Complex,Scottdale School (Scottdale School/25/86))
E. Ponce de Leon Ave. Vic.
HAER GA-63-A
2ph/1pg/fr H

Scottdale Mills,Teachers' House & Health Clinic
E. Ponce de Leon Ave. Vic.
HAER GA-63-E
1ph/1pg H

Scottdale School/25/86); see Scottdale Mills Complex,Scottdale School

EFFINGHAM COUNTY

RINCON

Jerusalem Church (Lutheran Meetinghouse; Salzburger Church)
HABS GA-242
HABS GA,52-RIN,1-
4ph/2pg L

Lutheran Meetinghouse; see Jerusalem Church

Salzburger Church; see Jerusalem Church

ELBERT COUNTY

ELBERTON VIC.

Pearle Cotton Mill & Dam
Elbert Co. Rd. 245
HAER GA-42
HAER GA,53-ELBE.V,1-
5dr/27ph/25pg/3pc/6ct/fr L

HEARDMONT VIC.

Blackwell Bridge
Heardmont Vic. ,County Rd. 244
HAER GA-41
HAER GA,53-HEAR.V,1-
2dr/10ph/2pg/1pc/fr L

Dye-White Farm
County Rd. 244
HABS GA-31
HABS GA,53-HEAR.V,1-
1dr/18ph/12pg/1pc L

MIDDLETON

Eureka; see Grogan House

Grogan House (Eureka)
NW Side County Rd.
HABS GA-33
HABS GA,53-MIDTO,1-
6dr/19ph/13pg/1pc L

PEARL VIC.

Allen,Williams,House (Beverly Plantation)
County Rd. 245
HABS GA-34
HABS GA,53-PEAR.V1-
1dr/20pg L

Beverly Plantation; see Allen,Williams,House

RUCKERSVILLE

Anderson,W. Frank,Farm
County Rd. 239
HABS GA-35
HABS GA,53-RUCK.V,3-
1dr/10ph/9pg/1pc L

RUCKERSVILLE VIC.

Alexander-Cleveland Farm
County Rd. 238
HABS GA-30
HABS GA,53-RUCK.V,1-
6dr/29ph/15pg/2pc/4ct L

RUCKERVILLE VIC.

Anderson,Reuben J.,Farm
County Rd. 239 Vic.
HABS GA-32
HABS GA,53-RUCK.V,2-
1dr/17ph/10pg/1pc L

SAVANNAH

Smith-McGee Bridge
Georgia Rt. 181
HAER GA-39
HAER GA,74-HART.V,2-
10ph/2pg L

SAVANNAH VIC.

Georgia-Carolina Memorial Bridge
State Hwy. 72
HAER GA-38
HAER GA,53-ELBE.V,2-
11ph/3pg L

FANNIN COUNTY

DIAL

Fannin County Road 222 Bridge
(GDOT Bridge #111/00810/00184N)
Spanning Toccoa River
HAER GA-58
HAER GA,56-DIAL,1-
5ph/2pg/1pc L

GDOT Bridge #111/00810/00184N; see Fannin County Road 222 Bridge

MINERAL BLUFF

Georgia DOT Bridge #111-00060P-00020N
Georgia State Rt. 60 spur spanning Hempton Creek
HAER GA-82
7ph/3pg/1pc H

FLOYD COUNTY

MOUNT BERRY

Berry Schools Historic District (Landscape)
HABS GA-2170
HABS GA,58-MOBE,1-
11ph/8pg/1pc/fr L

ROME

"Thornwood"
Shorter College Vic.
HABS GA-152
HABS GA,58-ROM,1-
3ph/1pg L

Second Avenue Bridge
Spanning Oostanaula on State Rt. 101 (Second Ave.)
HAER GA-54
HAER GA,58-ROM,2-
11ph/1pg/1pc L

FULTON COUNTY

ATLANTA

Ansley Building; see Atlanta Fixtures Building

Atlanta City Hall
68 Mitchell St. SW.
HABS GA-2166
HABS GA,61-ATLA,7-
7ph/4pg/1pc L

Atlanta Fixtures Building (Ansley Building; Steele Building)
102-106 Pryor St.
HABS GA-1204
HABS GA,61-ATLA,9-
1dr/20ph/19pg/1pc/fr L

Atlanta Public Library; see Carnegie Library of Atlanta

Atlanta University,Fountain Hall; see Atlanta University,Stone Hall

Atlanta University,Stone Hall (Atlanta University,Fountain Hall)
Morris Brown College Campus
HABS GA-1172
HABS GA,61-ATLA,10A-
11ph/1pg/1pc/2ct L

472-550 Auburn Ave. & 39 Boulevard Ave.; see King,Martin Luther Jr.,Nat. Hist. Site (Facades)

514 Auburn Avenue (Duplex); see King,Martin Luther Jr.,National Historic Site

526 Auburn Avenue (House); see King,Martin Luther Jr., National Historic Site

Auburn Avenue and Boulevard (General View) (King,Martin Luther,Jr.,Historic District)
HABS GA-2214
HABS GA,61-ATLA,46-
1ph/1pc L

126-255 Auburn Avenue(Commercial Buildings); see Sweet Auburn Historic District,Street Facades

Boyce,Benorsey House (King,Martin Luther,Jr.,Historic District)
78 Howell Street
HABS GA-2212
HABS GA,61-ATLA,45-
2ph/1pc L

Brown-Hayes Department Store; see King,Martin Luther Jr.,National Historic Site

Cabbagetown District (Johnson House)
HABS GA-1121-A
HABS GA,61-ATLA,11A-
1ph L

Cabbagetown District (General Views)
Boulevard,Pearl St. ,Memorial Dr. , & RR tracks
HABS GA-1121
HABS GA,61-ATLA,11-
3ph/1pc L

Carnegie Library of Atlanta (Atlanta Public Library)
126 Carnegie Way
HABS GA-1216
HABS GA,61-ATLA,12-
21ph/1pg/2pc L

Ebenezer Baptist Church; see King,Martin Luther Jr.,National Historic Site

39 Eleventh Street (House)
HABS GA-36
HABS GA,61-ATLA,8-
7dr/fr L

Equitable Building (Trust Company of Georgia)
25 Pryor St. NE
HABS GA-2107
HABS GA,61-ATLA,13-
14ph/1pg/1pc L

Fox Theater
Ponce de Leon Ave. & Peachtree St.
HABS GA-2108
HABS GA,61-ATLA,2-
2ph L

Georgia State Capitol
Capitol Square
HABS GA-2109
HABS GA,61-ATLA,3-
1ph/1pc L

Harris,Joel Chandler,House
1050 Gordon St.
HABS GA-2182
HABS GA,61-ATLA,14-
12ph/1pg/1pc L

Herndon & Atlantic Life Building; see Sweet Auburn Historic District

Hope,John,Homes, Building B-1
338 Spelman Lane (Originally Leonard Street)
HABS GA-2253-B
HABS DLC/PP-1993:GA-5
6ph/6pg/1pc L

Hope,John,Homes, Building B-8
337 Northside Drive
HABS GA-2253-A
HABS DLC/PP-1993:GA-5
6ph/6pg/1pc L

House behind 937 Railroad Ave.; see Johnsontown Historic District

House,Burned; see Johnsontown Historic District

Howell Street (General View)
(King,Martin Luther,Jr. , Historic District)
HABS GA-2213
HABS GA,61-ATLA,47-
1ph/1pc L

91 Howell Street (House) (King,Martin Luther,Jr.,Historic District)
HABS GA-2211
HABS GA,61-ATLA,44-
1ph/1pc L

Johnson House; see Cabbagetown District

Johnsontown Historic District
HABS GA-38
HABS GA,61-ATLA,15-
5ph/1pc L

Johnsontown Historic District (House behind 937 Railroad Ave.)
HABS GA-38-D
HABS GA,61-ATLA,19-
1ph/1pg/1pc L

Johnsontown Historic District
(House,Burned)
3344 Oak Valley Rd. (directly N of)
HABS GA-38-AA
HABS GA,61-ATLA,42-
1ph/1pg/1pc L

Johnsontown Historic District (3331 Oak Valley Road (House))
HABS GA-38-L
HABS GA,61-ATLA,27-
1ph/1pg/1pc L

Johnsontown Historic District (3335 Oak Valley Road (House))
HABS GA-38-M
HABS GA,61-ATLA,28-
1ph/1pg/1pc L

Johnsontown Historic District (3339 Oak Valley Road (House))
HABS GA-38-N
HABS GA,61-ATLA,29-
1ph/1pg/1pc L

Johnsontown Historic District (3344 Oak Valley Road (House))
HABS GA-38-O
HABS GA,61-ATLA,30-
1ph/1pg/1pc L

Johnsontown Historic District (3345 Oak Valley Road (House))
HABS GA-38-P
HABS GA,61-ATLA,31-
2ph/1pg/1pc L

Johnsontown Historic District (3351 Oak Valley Road (House))
HABS GA-38-Q
HABS GA,61-ATLA,32-
1ph/1pg/1pc L

Johnsontown Historic District (3353 Oak Valley Road (House))
HABS GA-38-R
HABS GA,61-ATLA,33-
1ph/1pg/1pc L

Johnsontown Historic District (3355 Oak Valley Road (House))
HABS GA-38-S
HABS GA,61-ATLA,34-
1ph/1pg/1pc L

Johnsontown Historic District (3357 Oak Valley Road (House))
HABS GA-38-T
HABS GA,61-ATLA,35-
1ph/1pg/1pc L

Johnsontown Historic District (3361 Oak Valley Road (House))
HABS GA-38-Z
HABS GA,61-ATLA,41-
1ph/1pg/1pc L

Johnsontown Historic District (3363 Oak Valley Road (House))
HABS GA-38-U
HABS GA,61-ATLA,36-
1ph/1pg/1pc L

Johnsontown Historic District (3371 Oak Valley Road (House))
HABS GA-38-V
HABS GA,61-ATLA,37-
1ph/1pg/1pc L

Johnsontown Historic District (3379 Oak Valley Road (House))
HABS GA-38-W
HABS GA,61-ATLA,38-
1ph/1pg/1pc L

Johnsontown Historic District (3383 Oak Valley Road (House))
HABS GA-38-X
HABS GA,61-ATLA,39-
1ph/1pg/1pc L

Johnsontown Historic District (933 Railroad Avenue (House))
HABS GA-38-A
HABS GA,61-ATLA,16-
1ph/1pg/1pc L

Johnsontown Historic District (934 Railroad Avenue (House))
HABS GA-38-B
HABS GA,61-ATLA,17-
1ph/1pg/1pc L

Johnsontown Historic District (937 Railroad Avenue (House))
HABS GA-38-C
HABS GA,61-ATLA,18-
1ph/1pg/1pc L

Johnsontown Historic District (938 Railroad Avenue (House))
HABS GA-38-E
HABS GA,61-ATLA,20-
1ph/1pg/1pc L

Johnsontown Historic District (943 Railroad Avenue (House))
HABS GA-38-F
HABS GA,61-ATLA,21-
1ph/1pg/1pc L

Johnsontown Historic District (945 Railroad Avenue (House))
HABS GA-38-G
HABS GA,61-ATLA,22-
1ph/1pg/1pc L

Johnsontown Historic District (959 Railroad Avenue (House))
HABS GA-38-H
HABS GA,61-ATLA,23-
1ph/1pg/1pc L

Johnsontown Historic District (961 Railroad Avenue (House))
HABS GA-38-I
HABS GA,61-ATLA,2-
1ph/1pg/1pc L

Johnsontown Historic District (971 Railroad Avenue (House))
HABS GA-38-K
HABS GA,61-ATLA,26-
1ph/1pg/1pc L

Johnsontown Historic District (Wolfe & Wright Avenues (House))
HABS GA-38-Y
HABS GA,61-ATLA,40-
1ph/1pg/1pc L

Johnsontown Historic District (Zion Hill Baptist Church)
Railroad Ave.
HABS GA-38-J
HABS GA,61-ATLA,25-
1ph/1pg/1pc L

King,Martin Luther Jr., National Historic Site (526 Auburn Avenue (House))
526 Auburn Ave.
HABS GA-2169-C
HABS GA,61-ATLA,51-
6dr/fr L

King,Martin Luther Jr.,Nat. Hist. Site (Facades) (472-550 Auburn Ave. & 39 Boulevard Ave.)
472-550 Auburn Ave. & 39 Boulevard Ave.
HABS GA-2169-A
HABS GA,61-ATLA,49-
13dr/fr L

King,Martin Luther Jr.,National Historic Site (514 Auburn Avenue (Duplex))
514 Auburn Ave.
HABS GA-2169-B
HABS GA,61-ATLA,50-
7dr/fr L

King,Martin Luther Jr.,National Historic Site (Brown-Hayes Department Store)
461-467 Edgewood Ave. NE
HABS GA-2169-E
HABS GA,61-ATLA,53-
7dr/fr L

King,Martin Luther Jr.,National Historic Site (Ebenezer Baptist Church)
407 Auburn Ave. NE
HABS GA-2169-F
HABS GA,61-ATLA,54-
14dr/2ph/1pc/fr L

King,Martin Luther Jr.,National Historic Site (Smith-Charleston House)
509 Auburn Ave. NE
HABS GA-2169-D
HABS GA,61-ATLA,52-
4dr/fr L

King,Martin Luther,Jr. , Historic District; see Howell Street (General View)

King,Martin Luther,Jr. ,Birth Home
501 Auburn Ave.
HABS GA-1171
HABS GA,61-ATLA,48-
9ph/1pg/1pc/3ct L

King,Martin Luther,Jr.,Historic District; see Auburn Avenue and Boulevard (General View)

King,Martin Luther,Jr.,Historic District; see Boyce,Benorsey House

King,Martin Luther,Jr.,Historic District; see 91 Howell Street (House)

Marietta Road Bridge
Marietta Rd.,Spanning Inman Railroad Yards
HAER GA-44
HAER GA,61-ATLA,6-
22ph/1pg/1pc L

3331 Oak Valley Road (House); see Johnsontown Historic District

3335 Oak Valley Road (House); see Johnsontown Historic District

3339 Oak Valley Road (House); see Johnsontown Historic District

3344 Oak Valley Road (House); see Johnsontown Historic District

3345 Oak Valley Road (House); see Johnsontown Historic District

3351 Oak Valley Road (House); see Johnsontown Historic District

3353 Oak Valley Road (House); see Johnsontown Historic District

3355 Oak Valley Road (House); see Johnsontown Historic District

3357 Oak Valley Road (House); see Johnsontown Historic District

3361 Oak Valley Road (House); see Johnsontown Historic District

3363 Oak Valley Road (House); see Johnsontown Historic District

3371 Oak Valley Road (House); see Johnsontown Historic District

3379 Oak Valley Road (House); see Johnsontown Historic District

3383 Oak Valley Road (House); see Johnsontown Historic District

Odd Fellows Building & Auditorium; see Sweet Auburn Historic District

Peters,Edward,House
179 Ponce de Leon Ave.
HABS GA-1221
HABS GA,61-ATLA,4-
1ph/1pc L

933 Railroad Avenue (House); see Johnsontown Historic District

934 Railroad Avenue (House); see Johnsontown Historic District

937 Railroad Avenue (House); see Johnsontown Historic District

938 Railroad Avenue (House); see Johnsontown Historic District

943 Railroad Avenue (House); see Johnsontown Historic District

945 Railroad Avenue (House); see Johnsontown Historic District

959 Railroad Avenue (House); see Johnsontown Historic District

961 Railroad Avenue (House); see Johnsontown Historic District

971 Railroad Avenue (House); see Johnsontown Historic District

Smith-Charleston House; see King,Martin Luther Jr.,National Historic Site

Steele Building; see Atlanta Fixtures Building

Swan House
3099 Andrews Dr. NW
HABS GA-2111
HABS GA,61-ATLA,5-
3ph/1pc L

Sweet Auburn Historic District
Auburn Ave. ,Courtlant St. ,I-85
HABS GA-1170
HABS GA,61-ATLA,1-
36dr/64ph/61pg L

Sweet Auburn Historic District (Herndon & Atlantic Life Building)
229-243 Auburn Ave.
HABS GA-1170-A
HABS GA,61-ATLA,1A-
9dr/7ph/1pc/1ct L

Sweet Auburn Historic District (Odd Fellows Building & Auditorium)
228-250 Auburn Ave.
HABS GA-1170-B
HABS GA,61-ATLA,1B-
9dr/17ph/2pg/2pc/6ct L

Sweet Auburn Historic District,Street Facades (126-255 Auburn Avenue(Commercial Buildings))
HABS GA-1170-C
HABS GA,61-ATLA,1C-
18dr/96ph/6pg/3pc/fr L

Trust Company of Georgia; see Equitable Building

Wolfe & Wright Avenues (House); see Johnsontown Historic District

Zion Hill Baptist Church; see Johnsontown Historic District

COLLEGE PARK

Ben's Antiques; see College Park City Hall,Old

Bits & Pieces Antiques; see 3816 East Main Street (Commercial Building)

College Park City Hall,Old (Ben's Antiques)
3814 E. Main St.
HABS GA-2178
HABS GA,61-COPK,3-
10ph/4pg/1pc L

3810 East Main Street (Commercial Building) (Sarah's Antiques)
HABS GA-2177
HABS GA,61-COPK,2-
4ph/3pg/1pc L

3816 East Main Street (Commercial Building) (Bits & Pieces Antiques)
HABS GA-2179
HABS GA,61-COPK,4-
4ph/4pg/1pc L

3818 East Main Street (Commercial Building)
HABS GA-2180
HABS GA,6-COPK,5-
8ph/4pg/1pc L

Sarah's Antiques
3806-3808 E. Main St.
HABS GA-2176
HABS GA,61-COPK,1-
11ph/4pg/1pc L

Sarah's Antiques; see 3810 East Main Street (Commercial Building)

FAIRBURN

Campbell County Courthouse at Fairburn
45 E. Broad St.
HABS GA-187
HABS GA,61-FAIRB,1-
1ph/1pc L

FAIRBURN VIC.

Beaver House at Campbellton
HABS GA-1155
HABS GA,61-FAIRB.V,2-
1ph/1pg L

Campbell County Courthouse at Campbellton,Old
HABS GA-154
HABS GA,61-FAIRB.V,1-
1ph/1pg L

ROSWELL

Barrington Hall
HABS GA-1105
HABS GA,61-ROSW,5-
1ph/2pg L

Bulloch Hall
HABS GA-14-13
HABS GA,61-ROSW,1-
3dr/5ph/2pg L

Holly Hill; see Lewis Place

Lewis Place (Holly Hill)
HABS GA-1104
HABS GA,61-ROSW,4-
1ph/2pg L

Methodist Church,Old
HABS GA-193
HABS GA,61-ROSW,2-
1ph/1pg L

Mimosa Hall (Phoenix Hall)
HABS GA-1102
HABS GA,61-ROSW,3-
4ph/2pg L

Phoenix Hall; see Mimosa Hall

GLYNN COUNTY

BROADFIELD VIC.

"Altama"
N. Main Brunswick Hwy.
HABS GA-235
HABS GA,64- ,2-
1ph/1pg L

Elizafield Plantation Sugar Mill Building; see Santo Domingo Mission (Ruins)

Santo Domingo Mission (Ruins) (Elizafield Plantation Sugar Mill Building)
Altamaha River
HABS GA-2118
HABS GA,64- ,1-
1dr/5ph/2pg L

JEKYLL ISLAND

Horton House (Remains)
Main Rd.
HABS GA-2150
HABS GA,64-JEKI,1-
3dr/5ph/5pg L

Rockefeller Cottage
331 Riverview Drive
HABS GA-2164
HABS GA,64-JEKI,2-
3dr L

ST. SIMONS ISLAND

Cannons Point,Kitchen Building (Ruins) (Fort Frederica National Monument)
Cannons Point
HABS GA-2159
HABS GA,64-CANPO,1-
1ph L

Couper's Point,"Rest" House (Ruins) (Fort Frederica National Monument)
Couper's Point
HABS GA-255
HABS GA,64-SASI,4-
1ph/2pg L

Fort Frederica National Monument; see Cannons Point,Kitchen Building (Ruins)

Fort Frederica National Monument; see Couper's Point,"Rest" House (Ruins)

Fort Frederica National Monument; see Fort Frederica,Barracks (Ruins)

Fort Frederica National Monument; see Fort Frederica,Callwell,John,House (Ruins)

Fort Frederica National Monument; see Fort Frederica,duBignon House (Ruins)

Fort Frederica National Monument; see Fort Frederica,Foundation in Northeast Bastion

Fort Frederica National Monument; see Fort Frederica,Hawkins-Davison Houses (Ruins)

Fort Frederica National Monument; see Fort Frederica,Houston House Storage Bins (Ruins)

Fort Frederica National Monument; see Fort Frederica,Humbe House (Ruins)

Fort Frederica National Monument; see Fort Frederica,King's Magazine (Ruins)

Fort Frederica National Monument; see Fort Frederica,Levally,John,House (Ruins)

Fort Frederica National Monument; see Fort Frederica,Mackay,Capt. John,House (Ruins)

Fort Frederica National Monument; see Fort Frederica,Moore,Francis,House (Ruins)

Fort Frederica National Monument; see Fort Frederica,Retreat Plantation,House (Ruins)

Fort Frederica National Monument; see Fort Frederica,South Storehouse (Ruins)

Fort Frederica National Monument; see Fort Frederica,Welch House (Ruins)

Fort Frederica,Barracks (Ruins) (Fort Frederica National Monument)
HABS GA-2146
HABS GA,64-FRED,1-
7dr/18ph/2pg L

Fort Frederica,Callwell,John,House (Ruins) (Fort Frederica National Monument)
Lot No. 3,North Ward
HABS GA-2147
HABS GA,64-FRED,5-
3dr/12ph/4pg L

Fort Frederica,duBignon House (Ruins) (Fort Frederica National Monument)
Lot No. 7,South Ward
HABS GA-2152
HABS GA,64-FRED,9-
2dr/9ph/3pg L

Fort Frederica,Foundation in Northeast Bastion (Fort Frederica National Monument)
HABS GA-2157
HABS GA,64-FRED,3-
1ph L

Fort Frederica,Hawkins-Davison Houses (Ruins) (Fort Frederica National Monument)
Lots No. 1 & 2,South Ward
HABS GA-2149
HABS GA,64-FRED,7-
3dr/9ph/5pg L

Fort Frederica,Houston House Storage Bins (Ruins) (Fort Frederica National Monument)
Lot No. 3,South Ward
HABS GA-2155
HABS GA,64-FRED,12-
2ph/2pg L

Fort Frederica,Humbe House (Ruins) (Fort Frederica National Monument)
Lot No. 8,South Ward
HABS GA-2153
HABS GA,64-FRED,10-
2ph/2pg L

Fort Frederica,King's Magazine (Ruins) (Fort Frederica National Monument)
HABS GA-2162
HABS GA,64-FRED,4-
2dr/11ph/4pg L

Fort Frederica,Levally,John,House (Ruins) (Fort Frederica National Monument)
Lot No. 9,South Ward
HABS GA-2154
HABS GA,64-FRED,11-
1dr/3ph/2pg L

Fort Frederica,Mackay,Capt. John,House (Ruins) (Fort Frederica National Monument)
Lot No. 6,North Ward
HABS GA-2148
HABS GA,64-FRED,6-
3dr/9ph/2pg/fr L

Fort Frederica,Moore,Francis,House (Ruins) (Fort Frederica National Monument)
Lot No. 20,North Ward
HABS GA-2163
HABS GA,64-FRED,13-
3dr L

Fort Frederica,Retreat Plantation,House (Ruins) (Fort Frederica National Monument; Orange Grove)
HABS GA-220
HABS GA,64-SASI,2-
4ph/4pg L

Fort Frederica,South Storehouse (Ruins) (Fort Frederica National Monument)
HABS GA-2156
HABS GA,64-FRED,2-
2dr/2ph/2pg L

Fort Frederica,Welch House (Ruins) (Fort Frederica National Monument)
Lot No. 5,South Ward
HABS GA-2151
HABS GA,64-FRED,8-
3dr/8ph/2pg L

Hamilton Plantation
HABS GA-219
HABS GA,64-SASI,2B-1
2ph L

Orange Grove; see Fort Frederica,Retreat Plantation,House (Ruins)

Slave Hospital
HABS GA-21
HABS GA,,123-AUG,56/8
3ph L

GORDON COUNTY

CASH VIC.

GDOT Bridge No. 129/00228/x/00074.E; see Lutens Bridge

Lutens Bridge (GDOT Bridge No. 129/00228/x/00074.E)
County Road 228, Spanning Pine Log Creek
HAER GA-68
HAER GA,65-FAIR.V,1-
4ph/2pg/1pc L

FAIRMOUNT VIC.

GDOT Bridge No. 120/00220/x/00420 N; see Gordon County Road 220 Bridge

Gordon County Road 220 Bridge (GDOT Bridge No. 120/00220/x/00420 N)
Spanning Pine Log Creek on County Rd. 220
HAER GA-65
HAER GA,65-FAIR.V,1-
5ph/1pg/1pc L

NEW TOWN VIC.

GDOT Bridge No. 129/00024/x/00152N; see Gordon County Road No. 24 Bridge

Gordon County Road No. 24 Bridge (GDOT Bridge No. 129/00024/x/00152N)
Spanning New Town Creek at County Rd. 24
HAER GA-69
HAER GA,65-NEWTO.V,1-
5ph/2pg/1pc L

RANGER VIC.

Moss-Kelly House
Lick Creek Rd. near Redbud Creek
HABS GA-1218
HABS GA,65-RANG.V,1-
6dr/fr L

GWINNETT COUNTY

SNELLSVILLE VIC.

Holmes,Benjamin,Farm
1458 Dogwood Rd.
HABS GA-2236
HABS DLC/PP-1993:GA-5
11ph/13pg/1pc L

SNELLVILLE VIC.

Holmes,Benjamin,Farm,Smokehouse
1458 Dogwood Road
HABS GA-2236-A
HABS DLC/PP-1993:GA-5
2ph/1pg/1pc L

HABERSHAM COUNTY

CLARKSVILLE

West-Jackson Barn
111 N. Washington St.
HABS GA-1206-A
HABS GA,69-CLAVI,1B-
1ph/1pc L

West-Jackson Garage
111 N. Washington St.
HABS GA-1206-B
HABS GA,69-CLAVI,1A-
1ph/1pc L

West-Jackson House
111 N. Washington St.
HABS GA-1206
HABS GA,69-CLAVI,1-
10ph/1pg/1pc L

HALL COUNTY

GAINESVILLE

Chamblee Building; see Odd Fellows Hall

Odd Fellows Hall (Chamblee Building)
Sycamore & Summitt Sts.
HABS GA-1168
HABS GA,70-GAIN,1-
5ph/5pg/1pc/fr L

HANCOCK COUNTY

SHOALS VIC.

Cheely,Thomas,House
County Rd. S-1098
HABS GA-1119
HABS GA,71-SHOL.V,1-
2ph/1pc L

SPARTA

Hancock County Courthouse
Town Square
HABS GA-228
HABS GA,71-SPART,4-
1ph/1pc L

Little,Judge,House
Main St.
HABS GA-188
HABS GA,71-SPART,3-
4ph/1pg L

Sayre-Shivers House (Turner House)
Broad & Robins Sts.
HABS GA-179
HABS GA,71-SPART,1-
8ph/2pg L

Terrell-Stone House (Terrell,Dr. William,House)
HABS GA-186
HABS GA,71-SPART,2-
6ph/3pg L

Terrell,Dr. William,House; see Terrell-Stone House

Turner House; see Sayre-Shivers House

HARALSON COUNTY

TALLAPOOSA VIC.

Haralson County Bridge
County Rd. 189,spanning Tallapoosa River
HAER GA-50
HAER GA,72-TALL.V,1-
9ph/1pg/1pc L

HARRIS COUNTY

ATLANTA

Hope,John,Homes (Public Housing)
Bounded by Larkin, Dora, Spelman Streets and Lane
HABS GA-2253
HABS DLC/PP-1993:GA-5
7ph/36pg/1pc L

ELLERSLIE VIC.

Georgia DOT Bridge #145-00315-017.37E
St. Rt. 315 spanning Southern Railroad
HAER GA-79
5ph/3pg/1pc L

WHITESVILLE VIC.

Davidson,John,House
HABS GA-1144
HABS GA,73-WHIT.V,1-
2ph/1pg L

HART COUNTY

HARTWELL VIC.

Hart County Bridge
State Rt. 181,spanning Savannah River
HAER GA-49
HAER GA,74-HART.V,1-
10ph/1pg/1pc L

HENRY COUNTY

MC DONOUGH

Lowe-Turner House
88 Keys Ferry St.
HABS GA-270
HABS GA,79-MCDO,1-
14ph/2pg/1pc L

Lowe-Turner House,Outbuilding
88 Keys Ferry St.
HABS GA-270-A
HABS GA,79-MCDO,1A-
1ph/1pc L

IRWIN COUNTY

IRWINVILLE VIC.

Georgia DOT Bridge No. 155-00032-001.54E
Spanning Sand Creek at St. Rt. 32
HAER GA-81
6ph/3pg/1pc H

JACKSON COUNTY

JEFFERSON

Bell House; see Etheridge-Stanton House

Bell-Maddox House
HABS GA-11
HABS GA,79-JEF,1-
1ph/1pg L

Curry Creek Bridge (GDOT Bridge No. 157/00015/012.80N)
Spanning Curry Creek at St. Rt. 15
HAER GA-67
HAER GA,79-JEF,6-
9ph/1pg/1pc L

Etheridge-Stanton House (Bell House)
186 Lee St.
HABS GA-184
HABS GA,79-JEF,5-
2ph/1pg L

GDOT Bridge No. 157/00015/012.80N; see Curry Creek Bridge

Harrison Hotel
HABS GA-157
HABS GA,79-JEF,4-
1ph/1pg L

Pendergrass Store
HABS GA-16
HABS GA,79-JEF,2-
2ph/1pg L

Presbyterian Church
HABS GA-17
HABS GA,79-JEF,3-
1ph/1pg L

JEFFERSON COUNTY

LOUISVILLE

GDOT Bridge #081/00255/X/00059; see Jefferson County Road 255 Bridge

Jefferson County Road 255 Bridge (GDOT Bridge #081/00255/X/00059)
Spanning Rocky Comfort Creek
HAER GA-60
HAER GA,82-LOUVI,2-
7ph/1pg/1pc L

Slave Market
Public Sq.
HABS GA-14-2
HABS GA,82-LOUVI,1-
1dr/2ph/3pg L

JONES COUNTY

CLINTON

Jade-Barron House; see Mitchell-Barron House

Johnson House
HABS GA-1123
HABS GA,85-CLIN,3-
6ph/1pg L

Lowther Hall
HABS GA-14-59
HABS GA,85-CLIN,1-
7dr/13ph/2pg L

Mitchell-Barron House (Jade-Barron House)
Washington & Madison Sts.
HABS GA-155
HABS GA,85-CLIN,2-
17ph/1pg/1pc L

HADDOCK VIC.

"Hale Nui"; see Blount House

Blount House (Gordon-Banks House; "Hale Nui")
(moved to GA,Newnan Vic.)
HABS GA-1125
HABS GA,85-HAD.V,1-
22ph/3pg L

Gordon-Banks House; see Blount House

LAURENS COUNTY

MONTROSE VIC.

White Hall
Georgia Hwy. 26
HABS GA-159
HABS GA,88-MONT,V.1-
2ph/1pc L

LIBERTY COUNTY

MIDWAY

Midway Congregational Church
HABS GA-14-44
HABS GA,909-MID,1-
2dr/4ph/3pg L

LUMPKIN COUNTY

DAHLENEGA

Hotel,Old
Main Sq.
HABS GA-180
HABS GA,94-DAHL,1-
1ph/1pg L

Lumpkin County Courthouse
HABS GA-181
HABS GA,94-DAHL,2-
1ph/1pg L

MACON COUNTY

MARSHALLVILLE

Frederick-Wade House
HABS GA-146
HABS GA,97-MARSH,1-
1ph/1pg L

McCaskill-Rumph House
HABS GA-149
HABS GA,97-MARSH,3-
1ph/1pg L

Slappey House
HABS GA-147
HABS GA,97-MARSH,2-
1ph/1pg L

MARSHALLVILLE VIC.

Bryan Place; see Stage Coach Inn

Felton,Billy,Place
HABS GA-169
HABS GA,97-MARSH.V,3-
1ph/1pg L

Rumph House
HABS GA-160
HABS GA,97-MARSH.V,2-
3ph/1pg L

Stage Coach Inn (Bryan Place)
HABS GA-148
HABS GA,97-MARSH.V,1-
2ph/1pg L

MADISON COUNTY

CARLTON VIC.

Broad River Highway Bridge
State Rt. 72,spanning Broad River
HAER GA-47
HAER GA,98-CARL.V,1-
5ph/1pg/1pc L

MCDUFFIE COUNTY

COBBHAM

Few,Ignatius,House
HABS GA-1153
HABS GA,95-COB,1-
2ph/1pg L

THOMSON VIC.

Rock House,Old
Stephen Hunter Rd.
HABS GA-277
HABS GA,95-THOM.V.1-
1ph/1pc L

MCINTOSH COUNTY

DARIEN

Ashantilly Plantation
HABS GA-282
HABS GA,96-DARI.V,2-
10ph/2pg L

DARIEN VIC.

Cabin
HABS GA-283
HABS GA,96-DARI.V,3-
2ph/1pg L

Epping House
HABS GA-234
HABS GA,96-RIDG,1-
3ph/1pg L

Tolomato Mission (Ruins)
HABS GA-271
HABS GA,96-DARI.V,1-
8ph/4pg L

SAPELO ISLAND

Spanish Fort (Ruins)
HABS GA-2129
HABS GA,96-SAPI,1-
1ph/3pg L

MERIWETHER COUNTY

WARM SPRINGS

Roosevelt's Little White House
Georgia Hwy. 85-W
HABS GA-279
HABS GA,100-WASP,1-
1ph/1pc L

MILLER COUNTY

COLQUITT VIC.

Georgia DOT Bridge #201-00091-01541N
Spanning Big Drain Creek at State Rt. 91
HAER GA-78
6ph/3pg/1pc H

MORGAN COUNTY

MADISON

Box Wood; see Kolb-Pou-Newton House

Kolb-Pou-Newton House (Box Wood)
218 S. Second St.
HABS GA-183
HABS GA,106-MAD,2-
4ph/1pg L

Thurleston
455 Dixie Hwy.
HABS GA-182
HABS GA,106-MAD,1-
2ph/1pg L

MURRAY COUNTY

SPRING PLACE

Vann,Chief James Clement,House
U. S. Rt. 76 & State Rt. 255
HABS GA-174
HABS GA,107-SPLA,1-
7dr/21ph/5pg L

MUSCOGEE COUNTY

BIBB CITY

Bibb Company (Columbus Plant)
Thirty-eighth St. & First Ave. (Columbus vic.)
HAER GA-12
HAER GA,108-COLM,27-
1dr/34ph/28pg L

COLUMBUS

Alexander-McGehee-Woodall House
1543 Second Ave.
HABS GA-153
HABS GA,108-COLM,9-
2ph/1pg L

Bank of Columbus
1048 Broadway
HABS GA-292
HABS GA,108-COLM,28-
1ph/1pc L

Bradley,W. C. ,Company
Front Ave.
HAER GA-35
HAER GA,108-COLM,23-
9ph/1pc/fr L

Cargill House (Lion House)
1316 Third Ave.
HABS GA-1132
HABS GA,108-COLM,11-
5ph/1pg L

City Mills Company
Eighteenth St. & First Ave.
HAER GA-25
HAER GA,108-COLM,19-
3dr/36ph/33pg/fr L

Columbus Iron Works
Front Ave. between Eighth & Tenth Sts.
HAER GA-28
HAER GA,108-COLM,22-
46ph/26pg/fr L

Columbus Manufacturing Company
Thirty-second St. & First Ave.
HAER GA-29
HAER GA,108-COLM,26-
7ph/6pg L

Columbus Railroad Company:Power Station
Eighteenth St. on Chattahoochee River
HAER GA-27
HAER GA,108-COLM,18-
8ph/19pg L

Cook-Thomas House
HABS GA-111
HABS GA,108-COLM,3-
1ph/1pg L

Crawford-Jenkins Boarding House; see Crawford,Judge,House

Crawford,Judge,House
(Crawford-Jenkins Boarding House)
Thirteenth St.
HABS GA-1142
HABS GA,108-COLM,14-
1ph/1pg L

Dinglewood
1429 Dinglewood Dr.
HABS GA-293
HABS GA,108-COLM,30-
2ph/1pc L

Downing House (Ironwork)
815 Broadway
HABS GA-1141
HABS GA,108-COLM,13-
3ph/1pg L

Eagle & Phenix Mills
Front St. (1200-1300 Blocks)
HAER GA-30
HAER GA,108-COLM,17-
4dr/68ph/65pg/fr L

Elks' Home; see Fontaine Home

Elms (Estes-Bowers Place)
1846 Buena Vista Rd.
HABS GA-1103
HABS GA,108-COLM,1-
2ph/2pg L

Empire Mills Company
Front Ave. between Eighth & Tenth Sts.
HAER GA-31
HAER GA,108-COLM,24-
3ph/1pc L

Estes-Bowers Place; see Elms

Fontaine Home (Elks' Home)
1044 Front Ave.
HABS GA-140
HABS GA,108-COLM,8-
8ph/1pg L

Front Avenue Industrial District
Front Ave. between Eighth & Fourteenth Sts.
HAER GA-33
HAER GA,108-COLM,20-
13dr/fr L

Garrard-Slade House; see St. Elmo

Griffin-Mott House
Mott St. & Front Ave.
HABS GA-163
HABS GA,108-COLM,10-
2ph/1pg L

Hydroelectric Power Development North Highlands
Thirty-eighth St. on Chattahoochee River
HAER GA-26
HAER GA,108-COLM,25-
5ph/14pg L

Lion House; see Cargill House

Loeb,Sol,Company; see Loeb,Sol,Warehouse

Loeb,Sol,Warehouse (Loeb,Sol,Company)
900 Front Ave.
HAER GA-24
HAER GA,108-COLM,21-
2ph/4pg L

May's Folly
527 First Ave.
HABS GA-294
HABS GA,108-COLM,29-
2ph/1pc L

Muscogee Manufacturing Company
(Muscogee Mills)
Front Ave.
HABS GA-110
HAER GA-23
HABS/HAER GA,108-COLM,2-
2dr/24ph/14pg/fr L

Muscogee Mills; see Muscogee Manufacturing Company

Pease Home
908 Broadway
HABS GA-1135
HABS GA,108-COLM,12-
4ph/1pg L

Rankin House (Doorway & Interior)
1440 Second Ave.
HABS GA-112
HABS GA,108-COLM,4-
2ph/1pg L

Redd House
HABS GA-138
HABS GA,108-COLM,7-
1ph/1pg L

Seaboard Airline Railway,Freight Depot
Front Ave. ,1200-1300 Blocks
HAER GA-21
HAER HAER GA,108-COLM,15-
15ph/4pg/fr L

Springer Opera House
105 Tenth St.
HABS GA-295
HABS GA,108-COLM,31-
2ph/1pc L

St. Elmo (Garrard-Slade House)
2810 Saint Elmo Dr.
HABS GA-129
HABS GA,108-COLM,6-
2dr/7ph/2pg L

Swift Mansion
HABS GA-114
HABS GA,108-COLM,5-
2ph/1pg L

Water Power Development at Falls of Chattahoochee
Chattahoochee River
HAER GA-22
HAER GA,108-COLM,16-
2dr/23ph/42pg L

COLUMBUS VIC.

Bass Place (Slave Cabins)
HABS GA-1150
HABS GA,108-COLM.V,2-
2ph/1pg L

Gunby House
HABS GA-119
HABS GA,108-COLM.V,1-
2ph/2pg L

NEWTON COUNTY

COVINGTON

Alcovy Road Bridge (County Road 73 Bridge; GDOT Bridge #217/00073/X/000.01W)
Spanning Alcovy River
HAER GA-62
HAER GA,109-COVI,4-
10ph/1pg/1pc L

Carr Hill
W. Hill St.
HABS GA-126
HABS GA,109-COVI,2-
5ph/2pg L

County Road 73 Bridge; see Alcovy Road Bridge

Downs House
HABS GA-124
HABS GA,109-COVI,1-
2ph/2pg L

GDOT Bridge #217/00073/X/000.01W; see Alcovy Road Bridge

Spense-Harris House
HABS GA-130
HABS GA,109-COVI,3-
1ph/1pg L

Documentation: **ct** color transparencies **dr** measured drawings **fr** field records
pc photograph captions **pg** pages of text **ph** photographs

COVINGTON VIC.

Salem Camp Ground
HABS GA-128
HABS GA,109-COVI.V,1-
4ph/1pg L

OXFORD

Emory Church,Old
HABS GA-125
HABS GA,109-OXFO,1-
1ph/1pg L

Emory College,Few Literary Society Hall
HABS GA-198
HABS GA,109-OXFO,2B-
2ph/1pg L

Emory College,Phi Gamma Literary Society Hall
HABS GA-197
HABS GA,109-OXFO,2A-
1ph/1pg L

OCONEE COUNTY

WATKINSVILLE

Eagle Tavern
Macon Rd.
HABS GA-1127
HABS GA,110-WATV,1-
1ph/1pg L

OGLETHORPE COUNTY

ARNOLDSVILLE VIC.

Daniels Place,Old
HABS GA-1109
HABS GA,111-ARNV.V,1-
5ph/1pg L

LEXINGTON

Cox-Chedel-Johnston House
HABS GA-175
HABS GA,111-LEX,4-
2ph/1pg L

Cox-Steward-Knox Place (Pigeon House & Farm Bell)
HABS GA-172
HABS GA,111-LEX,3-
2ph/1pg L

Gilmer House
HABS GA-178
HABS GA,111-LEX,6-
3ph/2pg L

Oglethorpe County Courthouse
Town Square
HABS GA-194
HABS GA,111-LEX,7-
1ph/1pc L

Platt,Judge,House
HABS GA-18
HABS GA,111-LEX,1-
3ph/1pg L

Saims-Bacon House
HABS GA-171
HABS GA,111-LEX,2-
1ph/1pg L

Willingham-Wadkins House
HABS GA-176
HABS GA,111-LEX,5-
1ph/1pg L

PEACH COUNTY

FORT VALLEY

Vinson House
Woolfolk Road, North of U.S. 341/S. R. 7
HABS GA-2233
HABS DLC/PP-1993:GA-5
11ph/4pg/1pc L

PIKE COUNTY

BARNESVILLE VIC.

Gachette House
HABS GA-14-121
HABS GA,116- ,1-
3dr/2ph/2pg L

PUTNAM COUNTY

EATONTON

Paschal-Sammons House
Maple Ave.
HABS GA-27
HABS GA,119-EAT,1-
1ph/1pc L

Putnam County Courthouse
Town Square
HABS GA-28
HABS GA,119-EAT,2-
1ph/1pc L

EATONTON VIC.

Rock Eagle Mound
Rock Eagle State Park,U.S. Rt. 441
HABS GA-29
HABS GA,119-EAT.V,1-
1ph/1pc L

RICHMOND COUNTY

AUGUSTA

Academy of Richmond County,Old (Young Men's Library Assoc. & Augusta Museum)
540 Telfair St.
HABS GA-229
HABS GA,123-AUG,14-
1ph/2pg L

American Foundry; see Hight & MacMurphy Foundry

American Foundry; see Pendleton & Boardman Foundry

Augusta Canal
HAER GA-5
HAER GA,123-AUG,41-
8dr/47ph/26pg/fr L

Augusta Canal Industrial District
HAER GA-36
HAER GA,123-AUG,48-
2ph/1pc L

Augusta Lumber Company; see Augusta Machine Works

Augusta Machine Works (Augusta Lumber Company)
Jackson,Adams, & Campbell Sts. ,Augusta Canal
HAER GA-14
HAER GA,123-AUG,45-
4ph/11pg L

Augusta Railway Company:West Power Station
Fifteenth & Greene Sts. ,Augusta Canal
HAER GA-20
HAER GA,123-AUG,43-
1ph/7pg L

Augusta Water Works
Goodrich St. extension,Augusta Canal
HAER GA-16
HAER GA,123-AUG,42-
7ph/20pg L

Azalea Cottage
2236 Walton Way
HABS GA-272
HABS GA,123-AUG,28-
2ph/1pg L

Bennoch House
119 Eighth St.
HABS GA-230
HABS GA,123-AUG,15-
1ph/2pg L

Blanche Mill; see Globe Mill

Broad Street Stores (South Side)
Broad,Fifth & Sixth Sts.
HABS GA-273
HABS GA,123-AUG,30-
5ph/1pg L

Campbell Building
102-124 Eighth St.
HABS GA-2181
HABS GA,123-AUG,62-
15ph/5pg/1pc L

Chafee House
914 Milledge Rd.
HABS GA-26
HABS GA,123-AUG,7-
13ph/2pg L

Chew-Dearing-Battey House
428 Washington St.
HABS GA-260
HABS GA,123-AUG,20-
2ph/1pg L

Clanton-Vason-Coleman House
503 Greene St.
HABS GA-224
HABS GA,123-AUG,1-
9ph/1pg L

Confederate States Powder Works Chimney
Goodrich St.
HABS GA-1101
HABS GA,123-AUG,54A-
1ph/1pc L

Crescent Grain & Feed Mill (Southern Milling Company)
1015 Twiggs Rd.
HAER GA-11
HAER GA,123-AUG,55-
3ph/6pg L

Cunningham's Flour Mill
Augusta Canal
HAER GA-17
HAER GA,123-AUG,52-
1ph/5pg L

Daniels,Zachary,House
448 Greene St.
HABS GA-2112
HABS GA,123-AVG,56/8-
1ph/1pc L

Dartmouth Spinning Company (Sutherland Mill)
510 Cottage St. ,Augusta Canal
HAER GA-6
HAER GA,123-AUG,51-
4ph/8pg L

Edwards,Tommy,Car Company
114 Sixth St.
HABS GA-2174
HABS GA,123-AUG,63-
6ph/3pg/1pc L

Enterprise Manufacturing Company
1450 Greene St. ,Augusta Canal
HAER GA-13
HAER GA,123-AUG,44-
5dr/14ph/14pg/fr L

First Presbyterian Church
642 Telfair St.
HABS GA-2113
HABS GA,123-AUG,159-
1ph/1pc L

Fruitlands
HABS GA-252
HABS GA,123-AUG,19-
2ph/1pg L

Georgia Iron Works
620-640 Twelfth St. ,Augusta Canal
HAER GA-7
HAER GA,123-AUG,47-
5ph/20pg L

Globe Mill (Blanche Mill)
Twelfth & Thirteenth Sts. ,2 & 3 levels Aug. Canal
HAER GA-9
HAER GA,123-AUG,49-
10ph/4pg L

Gordon Military Store & Pawnshop
593-595 Broad St.
HABS GA-2175
HABS GA,123-AUG,64-
8ph/3pg/1pc L

Government House,Old; see Murphey House

467 Greene Street (House,Ironwork)
HABS GA-263
HABS GA,123-AUG,22-
2ph/1pg L

Greene Street Historic District
Greene St. ,Gordon Hwy. to Augusta Canal Bridge
HABS GA-269
HABS GA,123-AUG,56-
83ph/6pg/7pc/fr L

Harper-Cohen House
2150 Battle Row
HABS GA-221
HABS GA,123-AUG,9-
1ph/1pg L

High Gate (Nesbitt House)
820 Milledge Rd.
HABS GA-266
HABS GA,123-AUG,25-
1ph/2pg L

Hight & MacMurphy Foundry (Lombard Ironworks & Supply Company; American Foundry)
636 Eleventh St.
HAER GA-10
HAER GA,123-AUG,50A
7ph/9pg L

Ike's Cottage
2604 Washington Rd.
HABS GA-2114
HABS GA,123-AUG,60-
1ph/1pc L

Jail
Watkins & Elbert St.
HABS GA-264
HABS GA,123-AUG,23-
1ph/1pg L

Kilpatrick House
Forrest Hills Rd. (moved from Greene St.)
HABS GA-233
HABS GA,123-AUG,16-
6ph/1pg L

King,John P. ,Manufacturing Company
1701 Goodrich St. ,Augusta Canal
HAER GA-15
HAER GA,123-AUG,46-
3dr/29ph/23pg/fr L

Lombard Iron Works & Supply Company; see Pendleton & Boardman Foundry

Lombard Ironworks & Supply Company; see Hight & MacMurphy Foundry

Mackay's Trading Post; see White House

Meadow Garden
(Walton,George,Cottage)
Nelson St.
HABS GA-2100
HABS GA,123-AUG,35-
6ph/2pg L

Medical College,Old
598 Telfair St.
HABS GA-14-70
HABS GA,123-AUG,11-
14dr/4ph/2pg L

Montrose; see Reid-Jones-Carpenter House

Murphey House (Government House,Old)
Telfair St.
HABS GA-268
HABS GA,123-AUG,27-
5ph/2pg L

Nesbitt House; see High Gate

Oertel House
638 Greene St.
HABS GA-297
HABS GA,123-AUG,29-
9ph/1pg L

Paragon Mill
Augusta Canal
HAER GA-8
HAER GA,123-AUG,57-
7pg L

Pendleton & Boardman Foundry (Lombard Iron Works & Supply Company; American Foundry)
636 Eleventh St.
HAER GA-10-A
HAER GA,123-AUG,50B-
1dr/1ph/4pg L

Phinizy Residence
519 Greene St.
HABS GA-223
HABS GA,123-AUG,10-
3ph/2pg L

Platt-Fleming-Welker-d'Antignac House
453 Greene St.
HABS GA-262
HABS GA,123-AUG,21-
2ph/1pg L

Reid-Jones-Carpenter House (Montrose)
2249 Walton Way
HABS GA-227
HABS GA,123-AUG,13-
6ph/1pg L

Richmond County Courthouse
HABS GA-239
HABS GA,123-AUG,17-
4ph/1pg L

Russell & Simmons Factory
Goodrich St. ,Augusta Canal
HAER GA-34
HAER GA,123-AUG,58-
2ph/7pg L

Sacred Heart Church (Catholic)
Greene & Thirteenth Sts.
HABS GA-2115
HABS GA,123-AVG,56/61
1ph/1pc L

Documentation: **ct** color transparencies **dr** measured drawings **fr** field records
pc photograph captions **pg** pages of text **ph** photographs

Shamrock Mill Site
HAER GA-18
HAER GA,123-AUG,53-
3pg L

Sibley Manufacturing Co.
Goodrich St.
HABS GA-2116
HABS GA,123,-AUG,54-
1ph L

Sibley Manufacturing Company
1717 Goodrich St. ,Augusta Canal
HAER GA-19
HAER GA,123-AUG,54-
7dr/22ph/26pg/fr L

Southern Milling Company; see Crescent Grain & Feed Mill

St. Paul's Church (Episcopal)
605 Reynolds St.
HABS GA-241
HABS GA,123-AUG,3A-
1ph/2pg L

St. Paul's Parish Cemetery Gate & Gravestones
605 Reynolds St.
HABS GA-231
HABS GA,123-AUG,3B-
5ph/1pg L

Sutherland Mill; see Dartmouth Spinning Company

U. S. Arsenal
Walton Way Vic.
HABS GA-251
HABS GA,123-AUG,18-
6ph/3pg L

Walton,George,Cottage; see Meadow Garden

Ware-Sibley-Clark House
506 Telfair St.
HABS GA-2128
HABS GA,123-AUG,36-
8dr/17ph/3pg L

261 Watkins Street (House)
HABS GA-265
HABS GA,123-AUG,40-
1ph/1pg L

White House (Mackay's Trading Post)
1822 Broad St.
HABS GA-14-7
HABS GA,123-AUG,8-
8dr/5ph/3pg L

White,Mayor,House
2234 Walton Way
HABS GA-226
HABS GA,123-AUG,12-
1ph/1pg L

Wilson,Woodrow,Boyhood Home
419 Seventh St.
HABS GA-2117
HABS GA,123-AUG.61-
1ph/1pc L

Women's Club
825 Greene St.
HABS GA-267
HABS GA,123-AUG,26-
4ph/1pg L

Young Men's Library Assoc. & Augusta Museum; see Academy of Richmond County,Old

AUGUSTA VIC.

Glassock House
Old Savannah Rd.
HABS GA-250
HABS GA,123-AUG.V,2-
2ph/1pg L

Harper House
Wrightsboro Rd.
HABS GA-14-69
HABS GA,123-AUG.V,1-
11dr/4ph/2pg/fr L

SPALDING COUNTY

GRIFFEN

Drewry House (Eason-Drewry House)
303 N. Thirteenth St.
HABS GA-1147
HABS GA,128-GRIF,2-
1ph/1pg L

Eason-Drewry House; see Drewry House

Nichols,J. P. ,House
225 N. Thirteenth St.
HABS GA-1146
HABS GA,128-GRIF,1-
1ph/1pg L

GRIFFIN

Bailey-Tebeault House
Meriwether St.
HABS GA-1148
HABS GA,128-GRIF,3-
4ph/1pg L

Collins,Jack,Texaco Station
223 W. Taylor St.
HABS GA-2173
HABS GA,128-GRIF,5-
7ph/3pg/1pc L

Gibson,Rev. Obediah C. ,House
W. Tinsley St.
HABS GA-1149
HABS GA,128-GRIF,4-
1ph/1pg L

STEPHENS COUNTY

TOCCOA VIC.

Jarrett Manor; see Travelers Rest

Travelers Rest (Jarrett Manor)
HABS GA-14-5
HABS GA,129-TOCO.V,1-
4dr/3ph/3pg/fr L

SUMTER COUNTY

PLAINS

Carter Peanut Warehouse Complex
HABS GA-2202
HABS 1990 (HABS):2
3ph/11pg/1pc/fr L

Carter,Billy,Service Station
(Jennings,Mill,Service Station)
216 W. Church St.
HABS GA-243
HABS 1990 (HABS):2
4ph/8pg/2pc/fr L

Carter,Hugh,Antique Store; see Oliver-McDonald Company

Carter,Hugh,Worm Farm Office; see Plains Bank

Carter,Jimmy,Dura Apartment,No. 9A; see Plains Public Housing, No. 9A

Carter,Jimmy,House
209 Woodland Dr.
HABS GA-244
HABS 1990 (HABS):2
6ph/10pg/1pc L

Carter,Jimmy,Interim House; see Rylander,Matthew Edmund,House

Carter,Lillian & Earl,House
Georgia Rt. 280 btwn Walters & Thomas Sts.
HABS GA-2207
HABS 1990 (HABS):2
4ph/7pg/1pc L

Carter,Rosalynn,Childhood Home
(Crawford,W. H.,House)
219 S. Bond St.
HABS GA-2203
HABS 1990 (HABS):2
7ph/8pg/1pc/1ct/fr L

Crawford,W. H.,House; see Carter,Rosalynn,Childhood Home

Dean,Ross,Funeral Home
Main Street btwn Bond & Hudson Sts.
HABS GA-2215
HABS 1990 (HABS):2
1ph/5pg/1pc L

Forrester General Store
Hudson & Main Sts.
HABS GA-2214
HABS 1990 (HABS):2
1ph/5pg/1pc/fr L

Jennings,Mill,Service Station; see Carter,Billy,Service Station

Lunsford-French-Timmerman General Store (Turner's Hardware Store)
Main Street
HABS GA-2217
HABS 1990 (HABS):2
1ph/6pg/1pc L

Maranatha Baptist Church
Georgia Hwy. 49 near Hospital St.
HABS GA-2208
HABS 1990 (HABS):2
4ph/7pg/1pc/fr L

Oliver-French Company
Main Street
HABS GA-2219
HABS 1990 (HABS):2
1ph/6pg/1pc/1ct/fr L

Oliver-French-Shields Company
Main Street
HABS GA-2220
HABS 1990 (HABS):2
1ph/6pg/1pc L

Oliver-McDonald Company
(Carter,Hugh,Antique Store)
Main Street
HABS GA-2221
HABS 1990 (HABS):2
1ph/6pg/1pc L

Plains Bank (Carter,Hugh,Worm Farm Office)
Main Street
HABS GA-2218
HABS 1990 (HABS):2
1ph/6pg/1pc/fr L

Plains Baptist Church
Bond & Paschal Sts.
HABS GA-2212
HABS 1990 (HABS):2
5ph/8pg/1pc/2ct/fr L

Plains Convalescent Home; see Wise Sanatorium No. 2

Plains Depot
Hudson & Main Sts.
HABS GA-2209
HABS 1990 (HABS):2
5dr/10ph/9pg/1pc/fr L

Plains High School; see Plains School

Plains High School,Gymnasium; see Plains School,Gymnasium

Plains Methodist Church
Hwy. 280 across from Thomas St.
HABS GA-2211
HABS 1990 (HABS):2
4ph/8pg/1pc/fr L

Plains Public Housing, No. 9A
(Carter,Jimmy,Dura Apartment,No. 9A)
Paschal & Thomas Sts.
HABS GA-2210
HABS 1990 (HABS):2
1dr/3ph/7pg/1pc/fr L

Plains School (Plains High School)
Bond Street (opposite Paschal St.)
HABS GA-2206
HABS 1990 (HABS):2
6dr/25ph/14pg/2pc/fr L

Plains School,Gymnasium (Plains High School,Gymnasium)
Bond Street (opposite Paschal St.)
HABS GA-2206-A
HABS 1990 (HABS):2
13ph/1pc/fr L

Pond House
Fish Pond Road (near Old Plains Hwy.)
HABS GA-2204
HABS 1990 (HABS):2
6ph/7pg/1pc L

Rylander,Matthew Edmund,House
(Carter,Jimmy,Interim House)
Old Plains Hwy. (near Hwy. 280)
HABS GA-2205
HABS 1990 (HABS):2
12ph/13pg/1pc/fr L

Turner's Hardware Store; see Lunsford-French-Timmerman General Store

Wellons,A. C.,Building; see Wise Sanatorium No. 1

Wise Sanatorium No. 1 (Wellons,A. C.,Building)
Main Street
HABS GA-2216
HABS 1990 (HABS):2
2ph/8pg/1pc/1ct/fr L

Wise Sanatorium No. 2 (Plains Convalescent Home)
Hospital Street
HABS GA-2213
HABS 1990 (HABS):2
14ph/12pg/1pc/fr L

PLAINS & PLAINS VIC.

Carter,Jimmy,National Historic Site & Presv. Dist.
HABS GA-2230
HABS 1990 (HABS):2
1dr/1ct L

PLAINS VIC.

Carter,Jimmy,Boyhood Home
(Plexico,J.F.,House)
Old Plains Hwy.
HABS GA-245
HABS 1990 (HABS):2
4dr/10ph/12pg/2pc/fr L

Carter,Jimmy,Boyhood Home,Tenant House
Old Plains Hwy. (Lebanon Cemetary Rd.)
HABS GA-245-B
HABS 1990 (HABS):2
5ph/1pc L

Plexico,J.F.,House; see Carter,Jimmy,Boyhood Home

TALBOT COUNTY

TALBOTTON

Episcopal Church
HABS GA-1139
HABS GA,132-TALB,5-
3ph/1pg L

Hill-Leonard House
HABS GA-1108
HABS GA,132-TALB,1-
3ph/1pg L

Leonard,Dr. ,House
Macon Rd.
HABS GA-1118
HABS GA,132-TALB,2-
4ph/2pg L

Maxwell House
HABS GA-1140
HABS GA,132-TALB,6-
1ph/1pg L

Methodist Church
HABS GA-1126
HABS GA,132-TALB,3-
2ph/1pg L

Straus Le Vert Memorial Hall
HABS GA-1136
HABS GA,132-TALB,4-
1ph/1pg L

TALIAFERRO COUNTY

CRAWFORDVILLE

Liberty Hall (Stephens,Alexander,House)
HABS GA-158
HABS GA,133-CRAWV,1-
4ph/1pg L

Stephens,Alexander,House; see Liberty Hall

THOMAS COUNTY

THOMASVILLE

Thomas County Courthouse
Broad St.
HABS GA-216
HABS GA,138-THOVI,1-
8dr/6pg L

TIFT COUNTY

TIFTON

Tifton Bridge
U. S. Rt. 82/State Rt. 50 over Seaboard Coastln.RR
HAER GA-48
HAER GA,139-TIFT,1-
9ph/1pg/1pc L

TOWNS COUNTY

HIAWASSEE VIC.

Headen Bridge (Kelly Bridge)
County Rd. 87,spanning Hiawassee River
HAER GA-46
HAER GA,141-HIAW.V,1-
5ph/2pg/1pc L

Kelly Bridge; see Headen Bridge

Documentation: **ct** color transparencies **dr** measured drawings **fr** field records
pc photograph captions **pg** pages of text **ph** photographs

TROUP COUNTY

LA GRANGE

Beall-Dallis House
206 Broad St.
HABS GA-117
HABS GA,143-LAGR,4-
1ph/1pg L

Culberson House
207 Broad St.
HABS GA-116
HABS GA,143-LAGR,3-
2ph/1pg L

Edwards House,Old
203 Broad St.
HABS GA-118
HABS GA,143-LAGR,5-
2ph/1pg L

Huntley House
302 Broad St.
HABS GA-122
HABS GA,143-LAGR,7-
1ph/1pg L

Oaks,The; see Todd Place

Render House
Hines St.
HABS GA-14-62
HABS GA,143-LAGR,1-
5dr/2ph/2pg L

Todd Place (Oaks,The)
1103 Vernon St.
HABS GA-14-99
HABS GA,143-LAGR,2-
9dr/3ph/3pg/fr L

LA GRANGE VIC.

Boddie House
Greenville Rd.
HABS GA-1143
HABS GA,143- ,1-
12ph/1pg L

Cameron House (Mantel)
HABS GA-121
HABS GA,143-LAGR,6-
1ph/1pg L

LAGRANGE

119 Burr Street (House)
HABS GA-2187
HABS 1989(HABS):5
3ph/1pg/1pc L

326 Daniel Street (House)
HABS GA-2188
HABS 1989(HABS):5
3ph/1pg/1pc L

306 Dix Street (House)
HABS GA-2189
HABS 1989(HABS):5
4ph/1pg/1pc L

308 Dix Street (House)
HABS GA-2190
HABS 1989(HABS):5
4ph/1pg/1pc L

310 Dix Street (House)
HABS GA-2191
HABS 1989(HABS):5
3ph/1pg/1pc L

314 Dix Street (House)
HABS GA-2192
HABS 1989(HABS):5
3ph/1pg/1pc L

400 1/2 Dix Street (House)
HABS GA-2193
HABS 1989(HABS):5
4ph/1pg/1pc L

503 Dix Street (House)
HABS GA-2194
HABS 1989(HABS):5
4ph/1pg/1pc L

505 Dix Street (House)
HABS GA-2195
HABS 1989(HABS):5
4ph/1pg/1pc L

507 Dix Street (House)
HABS GA-2196
HABS 1989(HABS):5
4ph/1pg/1pc L

513 Dix Street (House)
HABS GA-2197
HABS 1989(HABS):5
4ph/1pg/1pc L

Herndon-Glanton-Reeves House
524 Greenville St.
HABS GA-2186
HABS 1989(HABS):5
15ph/4pg/1pc L

WEST POINT

Booker House
Chattahoochee River Vic.
HABS GA-161
HABS GA,143-WESP,1-
1ph/1pg L

UNION COUNTY

BLAIRSVILLE VIC.

Smith Bridge
Spanning Nottely River on Dooley Rd (County Rd 83)
HAER GA-55
HAER GA,146-BLAIR.V,1-
6ph/1pg/1pc L

WALKER COUNTY

LA FAYETTE

Marsh-Warthen House
HABS GA-150
HABS GA,148-LAFA,1-
3ph/1pg L

ROCK SPRING.

Carter's Quarters
Old Federal Rd.
HABS GA-173
HABS GA,148-ROSP,1-
6ph/3pg L

WALTON COUNTY

BETWEEN

Briscoe Store; see Upshaw-Briscoe Store

Upshaw-Briscoe Store (Briscoe Store)
U. S. Rt. 78 & County Rd. 56 (New Hope Church Rd.)
HABS GA-1208
HABS GA,149-BET,2-
7ph/1pg/1pc L

Upshaw,James Berrien,Homeplace
U. S. Rt. 78 & County Rd. 56 (New Hope Church Rd.)
HABS GA-1209
HABS GA,149-BET,1-
4ph/1pg/1pc L

HIGH SHOALS

Casulon Plantation
HABS GA-1110
HABS GA,149-HISHO,1-
8ph/1pg L

MONROE

Birscoe-Selman House
HABS GA-1137
HABS GA,149-MONRO,1-
3ph/1pg L

Davis House (Davis-Edwards House)
238 N. Broad St.
HABS GA-1138
HABS GA,149-MONRO,2-
2ph/1pg/1pc L

Davis-Edwards House; see Davis House

WASHINGTON COUNTY

DAVIDSBORO VIC.

Jordan Cabin (Jordan-Pierson Plantation)
Georgia Hwy. 231
HABS GA-164
HABS GA,152-DAV.V,1-
1ph/1pc L

Jordan-Pierson Plantation; see Jordan Cabin

WARTHEN VIC.

Harrison House
Georgia Hwy. 15 vic.
HABS GA-2121
HABS GA,152-WAR.V,1-
1ph/1pc L

WHEELER COUNTY

GLENWOOD VIC.

Mitchell Plantation (Overseer's Cabin)
Oconee River
HABS GA-290
HABS GA,155-GLEN.V,1-
2pg L

WHITE COUNTY

CLEVELAND

Mauney Homestead
State Rt. 129
HABS GA-1219
HABS GA,156-CLEV,1-
2dr/8ph/1pg L

NACOOCHEE VALLEY

Crescent Hill Baptist Church
Georgia Hwy. 17
HABS GA-162
HABS GA,156-NAVA,1-
1ph/1pc L

Nichols-Hardman House
Georgia Hwy. 17 & Georgia Hwy. 75
HABS GA-167
HABS GA,156-NAVA,2-
1ph/1pg/1pc L

Nichols-Hardman House,Gazebo
Georgia Hwy. 17 & Georgia Hwy. 75
HABS GA-167-A
HABS GA,156-NAVA,2A-
2ph L

WILKES COUNTY

WASHINGTON

Barnett Tupper McRae House; see Bennett House

Bennett House (Barnett Tupper McRae House)
Robert Toombs Ave.
HABS GA-1158
HABS GA,159-WASH,5-
2ph L

Gilbert-Alexander-Wright House
312 N. Alexander Ave.
HABS GA-1145
HABS GA,159-WASH,4-
5ph/2pg L

New Haywood
201 W. Robert Toombs Ave.
HABS GA-2122
HABS GA,159-WASH,6-
1ph/1pc L

Presbyterian Church
HABS GA-115
HABS GA,159-WASH,3-
4ph/1pg L

Toombs,Robert,House
320 E. Robert Toombs Ave.
HABS GA-13
HABS GA,159-WASH,1-
2ph/2pg L

Wingfield-Cade-Saunders House
120 Tignall Rd.
HABS GA-19
HABS GA,159-WASH,2-
4ph/1pg L

WASHINGTON VIC.

Daniel,James C. ,House
Bartram Trace Rd.
HABS GA-2123
HABS GA,159-WASH.V,1-
2ph/1pc L

WILKINSON COUNTY

TOOMSBORO VIC.

Jackson House
Georgia Hwy. 112
HABS GA-278
HABS GA,160-TOOM-V,1-
1ph/1pc L

Orote Airfield, Apra Harbor Naval Reservation, Orote Point, Guam. View showing center of runway, looking west. Photograph by K.W. Scott, August 1986 (HAER GU,1-OROPT,1-5).

Guam

GUAM COUNTY

OROTE POINT

Orote Point Airfield
Apra Harbor Naval Reservation
HAER GU-1
HAER 1988(HAER):20
6ph/6pg/1pc/fr L

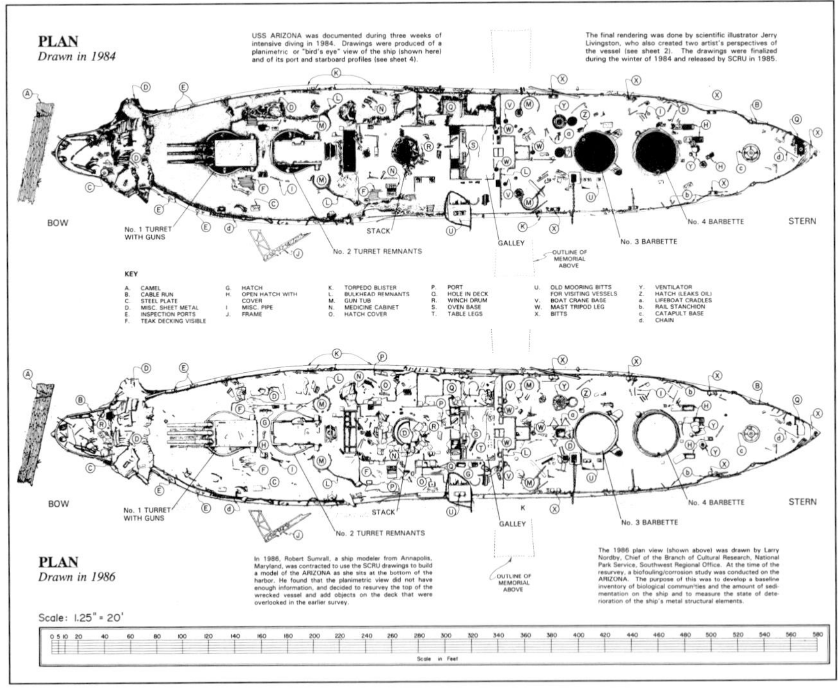

St. Philomena Roman Catholic Church, Churchyard, Kalaupapa Leprosy Settlement, Kalawao, Molokai Island, Hawaii. General view from churchyard from northwest to coast. Photograph by Jack E. Boucher, July 1991 (accession number 1992(HABS):HI-4; photo HABS HI-69-A-1).

USS Arizona (BB-39), submerged off Ford Island, Pearl Harbor, Honolulu County, Hawaii. Captioned measured drawing of the 1984 and 1986 planimetric views of the top deck. The 1986 plan adds objects on the deck that were not originally recorded during the 1984 project. Delineated by Larry V. Nordby, Jerry L. Livingston, 1984; Larry V. Nordby, 1986. Drawings photographically reproduced and spliced onto the HAER sheet by Robbyn Jackson, 1991 (HAER HI-13, sheet 3 of 4).

Hawaii

HAWAII COUNTY

HILO

Wailoa Bridge
Spanning Wailoa River at Kamehameha Ave.
HAER HI-4
HAER HI,1-HILO,1-
37ph/3pg/2pc L

KAILUA-KONA

Hulihee Palace
Alii Dr.
HABS HI-49
HABS HI,1-KAIKO,1-
8dr/2ph/8pg/1pc/fr L

Mokuaikaua Congregational Church
Alli Dr.
HABS HI-50
HABS HI,1-KAIKO,2-
2ph/5pg/1pc L

KOHALA

Bliss-Bond House; see Bond House

Bond House (Bliss-Bond House; Iole)
State Rt. 27 vic.
HABS HI-48
HABS HI,1-KOHAL,1-
7dr/2ph/7pg/1pc/fr L

Iole; see Bond House

PUAKO

Hoku Loa Church
Puako Rd.
HABS HI-12
HABS HI,1-PUAKO,1-
4dr/4ph/1pc/fr L

HONOLULU COUNTY

HONOLULU

Academy of Fine Arts (Honolulu Academy of Arts)
900 S. Beretania St.
HABS HI-27
HABS HI,2-HONLU,2-
18ph/1pc L

Aliiolani Hale (Judiciary Building)
463 King St.
HABS HI-18
HABS HI,2-HONLU,3-
12dr/22ph/22pg/1pc/fr L

Bank of Bishop & Co. Building; see Merchant & Nuuanu Sts.,Bank of Bishop & Co. Bldg.

Bishop Estate Building; see Merchant & Nuuanu Streets,Bishop Estate Building

Bishop Museum,Bishop Hall
Likelike Hwy.
HABS HI-25
HABS HI,2-HONLU,5-
2ph/1pc L

Bishop Museum,Main Building
Likelike Hwy.
HABS HI-26
HABS HI,2-HONLU,4-
11ph/1pc L

Chamberlain House (Mission Group)
King & Kawaiahao Sts.
HABS HI-4
HABS HI,2-HONLU,6-
7dr/15ph/1pc/fr L

Courthouse,Old
Queen St. between Fort & Bishop Sts.
HABS HI-5
HABS HI,2-HONLU,7-
8dr/7ph/1pc/fr L

Dillingham,Walter F.,House; see La Pietra

Foster,T.R.,Building; see Merchant & Nuuanu Streets,T.R. Foster Building

Governor's House; see Washington Place

Halekoa; see Iolani Barracks

Honolulu Academy of Arts; see Academy of Fine Arts

Honolulu Police Station; see Merchant & Nuuanu Streets,Honolulu Police Station

Iolani Bandstand (Palace Bandstand)
King & Richards Sts.
HABS HI-2
HABS HI,2-HONLU,9-
3dr/8ph/5pg/1pc/fr L

Iolani Barracks (Halekoa)
Richards & Hotel Sts.
HABS HI-3
HABS HI,2-HONLU,10-
6dr/17ph/1pc L

Iolani Palace
King & Richards Sts.
HABS HI-1
HABS HI,2-HONLU,8-
22dr/57ph/1pg/3pc/fr L

Izumo Taisha Kyo; see Kukui Shrine

Judd Building; see Merchant & Nuuanu Streets,Judd Building

Judiciary Building; see Aliiolani Hale

Kamehameha V Post Office; see Post Office,Old

Kamehameha V Summer House
Moanalua Gardens
HABS HI-16
HABS HI,2-HONLU,11-
6ph/1pc L

Kapuaiwa Building
426 S. Queen St.
HABS HI-24
HABS HI,2-HONLU,12-
3ph/1pc L

Kawaiahao Church
Punchbowl & King Sts.
HABS HI-14
HABS HI,2-HONLU,13-
10dr/19ph/14pg/1pc/fr L

Kukui Shrine (Izumo Taisha Kyo)
College Walk
HABS HI-29
HABS HI,2-HONLU,14-
5ph/1pc L

La Pietra (Dillingham,Walter F.,House)
Poni Moi Rd. ,Diamond Head
HABS HI-30
HABS HI,2-HONLU,15-
16ph/5pg/1pc L

Lunalilo's Tomb
Punchbowl & King Sts. (Kawaiahao Churchyard)
HABS HI-15
HABS HI,2-HONLU,16-
6dr/9ph/14pg/1pc/fr L

Melcher's Building
51-55 Merchant St.
HABS HI-34
HABS HI,2-HONLU,17-
1ph/8pg/1pc L

Merchant & Nuuanu Streets,Bishop Estate Building (Bishop Estate Building)
77 Merchant St.
HABS HI-55-H
HABS HI,2-HONLU,18-H-
7pg/fr L

Merchant & Nuuanu Streets,Honolulu Police Station (Honolulu Police Station)
842 Bethel St.
HABS HI-55-K
HABS HI,2-HONLU,18-K-
9pg/fr L

Merchant & Nuuanu Streets,Irwin Block (Merchant & Nuuanu Streets,Nippu Jiji Building; Nippu Jiji Building)
912-928 Nuuanu St.
HABS HI-55-M
HABS HI,2-HONLU,18-H-
7pg/fr L

Merchant & Nuuanu Streets,J.T. Waterhouse Bldg. (Waterhouse,J.T.,Building)
14 Merchant St.
HABS HI-55-C
HABS HI,2-HONLU,18-C-
7pg/fr L

Merchant & Nuuanu Streets,Judd Building (Judd Building)
111 Merchant St.
HABS HI-55-G
HABS HI,2-HONLU,18-G-
9pg/fr L

Merchant & Nuuanu Streets,Nippu Jiji Building; see Merchant & Nuuanu Streets,Irwin Block

Merchant & Nuuanu Streets,Royal Saloon (Royal Saloon)
901 Nuuanu St.,2 Merchant St.
HABS HI-55-B
HABS HI,2-HONLU,18-B-
8pg/fr L

Merchant & Nuuanu Streets,Strangenwald Building (Strangenwald Building)
115 Merchant St.
HABS HI-55-F
HABS HI,2-HONLU,28-F-
6pg/fr L

Merchant & Nuuanu Streets,T.R. Foster Building (Foster,T.R.,Building)
902 Nuuanu St.
HABS HI-55-L
HABS HI,2-HONLU,18-L-
6pg/fr L

Merchant & Nuuanu Streets,Wing Wo Tai & Co. Bldg. (Wing Wo Tai & Company Building)
923 Nuuanu St.
HABS HI-55-A
HABS HI,2-HONLU,18-A-
8pg/fr L

Merchant & Nuuanu Sts. Commercial Bldgs.
Island of Oahu
HABS HI-55
HABS HI,2-HONLU,18-
14dr/8pg/fr L

Merchant & Nuuanu Sts.,Bank of Bishop & Co. Bldg. (Bank of Bishop & Co. Building)
65 Merchant St.
HABS HI-55-I
HABS HI,2-HONLU,18-I-
9pg/fr L

Merchant & Nuuanu Sts.,Yokohama Specie Bank Bldg. (Yokohama Specie Bank Building)
24-32 Merchant St.
HABS HI-55-D
HABS HI,2-HONLU,18-D-
11pg/fr L

Mission Frame House (Mission Group)
King & Kawaiahao Sts.
HABS HI-21
HABS HI,2-HONLU,19-
7dr/14ph/16pg/1pc/fr L

Mission Group; see Chamberlain House

Mission Group; see Mission Frame House

Mission Group; see Mission Printing Office

Mission Group; see Schoolhouse,Adobe

Mission Printing Office (Mission Group)
King & Kawaiahao Sts.
HABS HI-20
HABS HI,2-HONLU,20-
3dr/6ph/10pg/1pc/fr L

Nippu Jiji Building; see Merchant & Nuuanu Streets,Irwin Block

Our Lady of Peace Cathedral
1183 Fort St.
HABS HI-28
HABS HI,2-HONLU,21-
8dr/13ph/8pg/1pc/fr L

Palace Bandstand; see Iolani Bandstand

Post Office,Old (Kamehameha V Post Office)
Merchant & Bethel Sts.
HABS HI-7
HABS HI,2-HONLU,22-
10dr/7ph/15pg/1pc/fr L

Punahou School,School Hall
1601 Punahou St.
HABS HI-22
HABS HI,2-HONLU,23-
3ph/4pg/1pc L

Queen Emma's Summer Palace
2913 Pali Hwy.
HABS HI-17
HABS HI,2-HONLU,24-
6dr/6ph/15pg/1pc/fr L

Royal Mausoleum
2261 Nuuanu Ave.
HABS HI-23
HABS HI,2-HONLU,25-
4ph/6pg/1pc L

Royal Saloon; see Merchant & Nuuanu Streets,Royal Saloon

Schoolhouse,Adobe (Mission Group)
Kawaiahao St. at Mission Lane
HABS HI-19
HABS HI,2-HONLU,26-
6ph/5pg/1pc L

Spalding,Philip,House
Makiki Heights Dr.
HABS HI-31
HABS HI,2-HONLU,27-
11ph/1pc L

Strangenwald Building; see Merchant & Nuuanu Streets,Strangenwald Building

Washington Place (Governor's House)
Beretania & Miller Sts.
HABS HI-6
HABS HI,2-HONLU,28-
10dr/23ph/14pg/1pc/fr L

Waterhouse,J.T.,Building; see Merchant & Nuuanu Streets,J.T. Waterhouse Bldg.

Wing Wo Tai & Company Building; see Merchant & Nuuanu Streets,Wing Wo Tai & Co. Bldg.

Yokohama Specie Bank Building; see Merchant & Nuuanu Sts.,Yokohama Specie Bank Bldg.

PEARL HARBOR

BB-39; see USS Arizona

Bldg. No. 186; see U.S. Naval Base,Pearl Harbor,Bachelor Offcr. Qrts.

Building No. 238; see U.S. Nav. Base,Pearl Harbor,Bach. Offrs. Qs. Mess

Building No. 239; see U.S. Nav. Base,Pearl Harbor,Bach. Offrs. Qs. Mess

Building No. 26; see U.S. Naval Base,Pearl Harbor,Appld. Instrctn. Bldg

Building No. 468A; see U.S. Nav. Base,Pearl Harbor,Admin. Bldg.

Building No. 469; see U.S. Nav. Base,Pearl Harbor,Electronics Shop

Building No. 499; see U.S. Nav. Base,Pearl Harb.,Fleet Acct. & Disp. Ctr

Building No. 85; see U.S. Nav. Base,Pearl Har.,Hale Alii Housing Garage

Headquarters,Commanders,WWII,CINCPACFLT
Marai St.
HABS HI-32
HABS HI,2-PEHA,1-
8ph/1pc L

Pearl Harbor Naval Shipyard,Bldg. No. 58
Pearl Harbor Shipyd.,S. Crnr. of Ave. G & Sixth St
HAER HI-6
HAER DLC/PP-1992:HI-2
4ph/2pg/1pc L

Shipping/Transfer Building No. 47; see U.S. Nav. Base,Pearl Harbor,Amo. Handling Facility

Shipping/Transfer Building No. 48; see U.S. Nav. Base,Pearl Harbor,Amo. Handling Facility

Special Weapons Building No. 989; see U.S. Naval Base,Pearl Harbor,Storage Facility

Special Weapons Building No. 990; see U.S. Naval Base,Pearl Harbor,Overhaul Facility

Special Weapons Buillding No. 1026; see U.S. Naval Base,Pearl Harbor,Storage Facility

U. S. Naval Base,Pearl Harbor
Naval Base Pearl Harbor
HABS HI-60
fr H

Documentation: **ct** color transparencies **dr** measured drawings **fr** field records **pc** photograph captions **pg** pages of text **ph** photographs

U.S. Nav. Base,Pearl Har.,Hale Alii Housing Garage (U.S. Nav. Base,Pearl Harbor,Naval Public Works Ctr Building No. 85)
Hale Alii Ave. & Ave. "D"
HABS HI-134
2ph/3pg/2pc H

U.S. Nav. Base,Pearl Har.,Nav. Magaz. Lualualei Br; see U.S. Nav. Base,Pearl Harbor,Amo. Handling Facility

U.S. Nav. Base,Pearl Harb.,Fleet Acct. & Disp. Ctr (U.S. Nav. Base,Pearl Harb.,Pacific Detachment; Building No. 499)
178 Main St.
HABS HI-131
HABS DLC/PP-1993:HI-2
6ph/5pg/3pc L

U.S. Nav. Base,Pearl Harb.,Pacific Detachment; see U.S. Nav. Base,Pearl Harb.,Fleet Acct. & Disp. Ctr

U.S. Nav. Base,Pearl Harbor,Admin. Bldg. (U.S. Nav. Base,Pearl Harbor,Nav. Sub. Base; Building No. 468A)
Kuahua Peninsula,W. of Jarvis St.
HABS HI-136
1ph/2pg/2pc H

U.S. Nav. Base,Pearl Harbor,Amo. Handling Facility (U.S. Nav. Base,Pearl Har.,Nav. Magaz. Lualualei Br Shipping/Transfer Building No. 48)
West Loch along First St. at W1 Pier
HABS HI-143
3ph/3pg/2pc H

U.S. Nav. Base,Pearl Harbor,Amo. Handling Facility (U.S. Nav. Base,Pearl Har.,Nav. Magaz. Lualualei Br Shipping/Transfer Building No. 47)
West Loch along First St. at W3 Pier
HABS HI-142
2ph/3pg/2pc H

U.S. Nav. Base,Pearl Harbor,Bach. Offrs. Qs. Mess (U.S. Nav. Base,Pearl Harbor,Naval Station; Building No. 239)
Ford Island
HABS HI-62-A
1ph/3pg/2pc H

U.S. Nav. Base,Pearl Harbor,Bach. Offrs. Qs. Mess (U.S. Naval Base,Pearl Harbor,Naval Station; Building No. 238)
Ford Island
HABS HI-62
3ph/3pg/2pc H

U.S. Nav. Base,Pearl Harbor,Berthing Wharf S378 (U.S. Nav. Base,Pearl Harbor,Naval Station; Warf No. F-5)
Beckoning Point,SE of Cowpens St.,Ford Island
HAER HI-9
8ph/4pg/2pc L

U.S. Nav. Base,Pearl Harbor,Electronics Shop (U.S. Nav. Base,Pearl Harbor,Nav. Sub. Base; Building No. 469)
Kuahua Peninsula,W. of Jarvis St.
HABS HI-138
3ph/2pg/2pc H

U.S. Nav. Base,Pearl Harbor,Nav. Sub. Base; see U.S. Nav. Base,Pearl Harbor,Admin. Bldg.

U.S. Nav. Base,Pearl Harbor,Nav. Sub. Base; see U.S. Nav. Base,Pearl Harbor,Electronics Shop

U.S. Nav. Base,Pearl Harbor,Naval Public Works Ctr; see U.S. Nav. Base,Pearl Har.,Hale Alii Housing Garage

U.S. Nav. Base,Pearl Harbor,Naval Station; see U.S. Nav. Base,Pearl Harbor,Bach. Offrs. Qs. Mess

U.S. Nav. Base,Pearl Harbor,Naval Station; see U.S. Nav. Base,Pearl Harbor,Berthing Wharf S378

U.S. Nav. Base,Pearl Harbor,Naval Station; see U.S. Nav. Base,Pearl Harbor,Sm. Craft Berthing Wha

U.S. Nav. Base,Pearl Harbor,Sm. Craft Berthing Wha (U.S. Nav. Base,Pearl Harbor,Naval Station; Wharf S35)
Beckoning Point,northeast side of Waipio Peninsula
HAER HI-18
3ph/3pg/2pc L

U.S. Nav. Base,Pearl Harbor,Small Berthing Wharf (U.S. Naval Base, Pearl Harbor, Naval Station; Wharf S374 & Wharf F-3 1/2)
Ford Island
HAER HI-14
6ph/3pg/2pc L

U.S. Naval Base, Pearl Harbor
HAER HI-16
fr H

U.S. Naval Base, Pearl Harbor, Naval Station; see U.S. Nav. Base,Pearl Harbor,Small Berthing Wharf

U.S. Naval Base,Pearl Harbor,Appld. Instrctn. Bldg (U.S. Naval Base,Pearl Harbor,Naval Station; Building No. 26)
Swan St.,near Lexington Blvd. & Gannet St.
HABS HI-132
2ph/3pg/2pc H

U.S. Naval Base,Pearl Harbor,Bachelor Offcr. Qrts. (U.S. Naval Base,Pearl Harbor,Naval Station; Bldg. No. 186)
Ford Island
HABS HI-61
6ph/3pg/2pc H

U.S. Naval Base,Pearl Harbor,Drydock No. 4 (U.S. Naval Base,Pearl Harbor,Naval Shipyard)
W. of St. Rt. 92,W. of Nimitz Gate
HAER HI-15
6ph/2pg/1pc L

U.S. Naval Base,Pearl Harbor,Hangar 6
South End of Ford Island
HAER HI-5
HAER HI,2-HONLU,1-
21ph/9pg/2pc L

U.S. Naval Base,Pearl Harbor,Naval Shipyard; see U.S. Naval Base,Pearl Harbor,Drydock No. 4

U.S. Naval Base,Pearl Harbor,Naval Station; see U.S. Nav. Base,Pearl Harbor,Bach. Offrs. Qs. Mess

U.S. Naval Base,Pearl Harbor,Naval Station; see U.S. Naval Base,Pearl Harbor,Appld. Instrctn. Bldg

U.S. Naval Base,Pearl Harbor,Naval Station; see U.S. Naval Base,Pearl Harbor,Bachelor Offcr. Qrts.

U.S. Naval Base,Pearl Harbor,Naval Submarine Base; see U.S. Naval Base,Pearl Harbor,Overhaul Facility

U.S. Naval Base,Pearl Harbor,Naval Submarine Base; see U.S. Naval Base,Pearl Harbor,Storage Facility

U.S. Naval Base,Pearl Harbor,Nvl. Shpyrd.,Bldg. 1E
Pearl Harbor Naval Base
HABS HI-65
HABS DLC/PP-1992:HI-4
7ph/6pg/1pc L

U.S. Naval Base,Pearl Harbor,Overhaul Facility (U.S. Naval Base,Pearl Harbor,Naval Submarine Base; Special Weapons Building No. 990)
Gilmore Street at Magazine Loch
HABS HI-147
4ph/3pg/2pc H

U.S. Naval Base,Pearl Harbor,Storage Facility (U.S. Naval Base,Pearl Harbor,Naval Submarine Base; Special Weapons Buillding No. 1026)
Gilmore Street at Magazine Loch
HABS HI-149
4ph/3pg/2pc H

U.S. Naval Base,Pearl Harbor,Storage Facility (U.S. Naval Base,Pearl Harbor,Naval Submarine Base; Special Weapons Building No. 989)
Hunter Street at Magazine Loch
HABS HI-148
3ph/3pg/2pc H

USS Arizona (BB-39)
Submerged,off Ford Island,Pearl Harbor
HAER HI-13
4dr H

USS Utah
Submerged,off Ford Island,Pearl Harbor
HAER HI-12
H

Warf No. F-5; see U.S. Nav. Base,Pearl Harbor,Berthing Wharf S378

Wharf S35; see U.S. Nav. Base,Pearl Harbor,Sm. Craft Berthing Wha

Wharf S374 & Wharf F-3 1/2; see U.S. Nav. Base,Pearl Harbor,Small Berthing Wharf

WAHIAWA

Dole,James,House
Dole Rd.
HABS HI-33
HABS HI,2-WAHWA,1-
6ph/1pc L

WAIANAE

U.S. Naval Base,Pearl Harbor,Anten. Towers S109-11; see U.S. Naval Base,Pearl Harbor,Lualualei Radio Trans

U.S. Naval Base,Pearl Harbor,Lualualei Radio Trans (U.S. Naval Base,Pearl Harbor,Nav. Comp. & Telecom. U.S. Naval Base,Pearl Harbor,Anten. Towers S109-11 (See HONOLULU COUNTY,PEARL HARBOR for documentn.)
HABS HI-152
HABS DC,GEO,42-
L

U.S. Naval Base,Pearl Harbor,Nav. Comp. & Telecom.; see U.S. Naval Base,Pearl Harbor,Lualualei Radio Trans

KALAWAO

KALAUPAPA

A.J.A. Buddhist Hall (Benevolent Society Hall; Building No. 308; Kalaupapa Leprosy Settlement)
Moloka'i
HABS HI-82
HABS DLC/PP-1992:HI-4
3ph/1pc L

Abandoned Store (Building No. 260; Kalaupapa Leprosy Settlement)
Kamehameha St.,Moloka'i Island
HABS HI-86
HABS DLC/PP-1992:HI-4
2ph/1pc L

Administrative Building No. 270 (Kalaupapa Leprosy Settlement,Administrative Center
Moloka'i Island
HABS HI-96
HABS DLC/PP-1992:HI-4
1ph/1pc L

Bay View Home,Board Batten (Building No. 10A; Kalaupapa Leprosy Settlement)
Moloka'i Island
HABS HI-85-H
HABS DLC/PP-1992:HI-4
2ph/1pc L

Bay View Home,Building No. 8 (Kalaupapa Leprosy Settlement)
Moloka'i Island
HABS HI-85-J
HABS DLC/PP-1992:HI-4
3ph/1pc L

Bay View Home,Kitchen & Dining Area (Building No. 5; Kalaupapa Leprosy Settlement)
Moloka'i Island
HABS HI-85-D
HABS DLC/PP-1992:HI-4
5ph/1pc L

Bay View Home,Kitchen,Old (Building No. 6; Kalaupapa Leprosy Settlement)
Moloka'i Island
HABS HI-85-E
HABS DLC/PP-1992:HI-4
20ph/2pc L

Bay View Home,Quonset Residence (Building No. 10; Kalaupapa Leprosy Settlement)
Moloka'i Island
HABS HI-85-I
HABS DLC/PP-1992:HI-4
2ph/1pc L

Bay View Home,Residence No. 1 (Kalaupapa Leprosy Settlement)
Moloka'i Island
HABS HI-85-A
HABS DLC/PP-1992:HI-4
3ph/1pc L

Bay View Home,Residence No. 11 (Kalaupapa Leprosy Settlement)
Moloka'i Island
HABS HI-85-G
HABS DLC/PP-1992:HI-4
1ph/1pc L

Bay View Home,Residence No. 2 (Kalaupapa Leprosy Settlement)
Moloka'i Island
HABS HI-85-B
HABS DLC/PP-1992:HI-4
3ph/1pc L

Bay View Home,Residence No. 3 (Kalaupapa Leprosy Settlement)
Moloka'i Island
HABS HI-85-C
HABS DLC/PP-1992:HI-4
4ph/1pc L

Bay View Home,Residence No. 64 (Kalaupapa Leprosy Settlement)
Moloka'i Island
HABS HI-85-F
HABS DLC/PP-1992:HI-4
2ph/1pc L

Benevolent Society Hall; see A.J.A. Buddhist Hall

Bishop Home,Bake Oven (Kalaupapa Leprosy Settlement)
Moloka'i Island
HABS HI-83-C
HABS DLC/PP-1992:HI-4
3ph/1pc L

Bishop Home,Sisters' Convent (Building No. 15; Kalaupapa Leprosy Settlement)
Moloka'i Island
HABS HI-83-B
HABS DLC/PP-1992:HI-4
3ph/1pc L

Bishop Home,St. Elizabeth Chapel (Kalaupapa Leprosy Settlement)
Moloka'i Island
HABS HI-83-A
HABS DLC/PP-1992:HI-4
3ph/1pc L

Building No 264; see Carpenter Shop

Building No. 1A; see Staff Row,Guest Cottage

Building No. 10; see Bay View Home,Quonset Residence

Building No. 10; see Staff Row,Doctor's House

Building No. 10A; see Bay View Home,Board Batten

Building No. 12; see McVeigh Home,Apartment Building

Building No. 14; see Staff Row,Administrative Residence

Building No. 15; see Bishop Home,Sisters' Convent

Building No. 16; see Staff Row,Electrician's Residence

Building No. 23; see McVeigh Home,Recreation Hall

Building No. 24; see McVeigh Home,Pool Hall

Building No. 256; see Latter Day Saints Rectory

Building No. 257A; see Latter Day Saints Parish Hall

Building No. 258A; see Motor Pool Gas Station

Building No. 259; see Motor Pool Garage

Building No. 260; see Abandoned Store

Building No. 262; see Crematory

Building No. 263; see Plumbing Warehouse

Building No. 263-A; see Lumber Warehouse

Building No. 265; see Maintenance Shop

Building No. 267-8; see Butcher Shop & Freezer

Building No. 27; see McVeigh Home,Card Room

Building No. 271; see Food Warehouse

Building No. 272; see Patient Store

Building No. 273; see Gas Station

Building No. 278; see Visitor Quarters,Visitor-Patient Meeting Hall

Building No. 283; see Fumigation Hall

Building No. 288; see Mission House Drew

Building No. 300; see Paschoal Craft Building

Building No. 301; see Fire Station

Building No. 302-3; see Jail & Police Station

Building No. 308; see A.J.A. Buddhist Hall

Building No. 5; see Bay View Home,Kitchen & Dining Area

Building No. 5; see Staff Row,Central Kitchen

Building No. 522; see Visitor Quarters,Telephone Sub-Station

Building No. 523; see Visitor Quarters,Patient Restrooms

Building No. 6; see Bay View Home,Kitchen,Old

Building No. 6; see Staff Row,Freezer Shelter

Building No. 62; see Rea's Store & Bar

Building No. 630; see Slaughterhouse

Building No. 65-296; see Mother Marianne Library

Building No. 7; see Outpatient Clinic

Building No. 8; see Staff Row,Dentist House

Buildng No. 1; see Staff Row,Corner Residence

Butcher Shop & Freezer (Building No. 267-8; Kalaupapa Leprosy Settlement,Industrial Center)
Moloka'i Island
HABS HI-91
HABS DLC/PP-1992:HI-4
2ph/1pc L

Carpenter Shop (Building No 264; Kalaupapa Leprosy Settlement,Industrial Center)
Moloka'i Island
HABS HI-93
HABS DLC/PP-1992:HI-4
1ph/1pc L

Cemetery,Airport Road (Kalaupapa Leprosy Settlement)
Moloka'i Island
HABS HI-128
HABS DLC/PP-1992:HI-4
8ph/1pc L

Church of Jesus Christ of Latter Day Saint's,The; see Latter Day Saints Mormon Church

Copes Monument (Kalaupapa Leprosy Settlement,Bishop Home)
Moloka'i Island
HABS HI-127
HABS DLC/PP-1992:HI-4
1ph/1pc L

Crematory (Building No. 262; Kalaupapa Leprosy Settlement,Industrial Center)
Moloka'i Island
HABS HI-121
HABS DLC/PP-1992:HI-4
1ph/1pc L

Damien Monument (Kalaupapa Leprosy Settlement,Bishop Home)
Moloka'i Island
HABS HI-126
HABS DLC/PP-1992:HI-4
1ph/1pc L

Fire Station (Building No. 301; Kalaupapa Leprosy Settlement)
Moloka'i Island
HABS HI-78
HABS DLC/PP-1992:HI-4
3ph/1pc L

Food Warehouse (Building No. 271; Kalaupapa Leprosy Settlement,Industrial Center)
Moloka'i Island
HABS HI-122
HABS DLC/PP-1992:HI-4
2ph/1pc L

Fumigation Hall (Building No. 283; Kalaupapa Leprosy Settlement)
Moloka'i Island
HABS HI-75
HABS DLC/PP-1992:HI-4
6ph/1pc L

Gas Station (Building No. 273; Kalaupapa Leprosy Settlement,Administrative Center
Moloka'i Island
HABS HI-94
HABS DLC/PP-1992:HI-4
1ph/1pc L

Jail & Police Station (Building No. 302-3; Kalaupapa Leprosy Settlement,Administrative Center
Moloka'i Island
HABS HI-84
HABS DLC/PP-1992:HI-4
3ph/1pc L

Kalaupapa Leprosy Settlement; see A.J.A. Buddhist Hall

Kalaupapa Leprosy Settlement; see Abandoned Store

Kalaupapa Leprosy Settlement; see Bay View Home,Board Batten

Kalaupapa Leprosy Settlement; see Bay View Home,Building No. 8

Kalaupapa Leprosy Settlement; see Bay View Home,Kitchen & Dining Area

Kalaupapa Leprosy Settlement; see Bay View Home,Kitchen,Old

Kalaupapa Leprosy Settlement; see Bay View Home,Quonset Residence

Kalaupapa Leprosy Settlement; see Bay View Home,Residence No. 1

Kalaupapa Leprosy Settlement; see Bay View Home,Residence No. 11

Kalaupapa Leprosy Settlement; see Bay View Home,Residence No. 2

Kalaupapa Leprosy Settlement; see Bay View Home,Residence No. 3

Kalaupapa Leprosy Settlement; see Bay View Home,Residence No. 64

Kalaupapa Leprosy Settlement; see Bishop Home,Bake Oven

Kalaupapa Leprosy Settlement; see Bishop Home,Sisters' Convent

Kalaupapa Leprosy Settlement; see Bishop Home,St. Elizabeth Chapel

Kalaupapa Leprosy Settlement; see Cemetery,Airport Road

Kalaupapa Leprosy Settlement; see Fire Station

Kalaupapa Leprosy Settlement; see Fumigation Hall

Kalaupapa Leprosy Settlement; see Kalaupapa Social Hall

Kalaupapa Leprosy Settlement; see Latter Day Saints Mormon Church

Kalaupapa Leprosy Settlement; see Latter Day Saints Parish Hall

Kalaupapa Leprosy Settlement; see Latter Day Saints Rectory

Kalaupapa Leprosy Settlement; see McVeigh Home,Apartment Building

Kalaupapa Leprosy Settlement; see McVeigh Home,Card Room

Kalaupapa Leprosy Settlement; see McVeigh Home,Cottage No. 1

Kalaupapa Leprosy Settlement; see McVeigh Home,Cottage No. 13

Kalaupapa Leprosy Settlement; see McVeigh Home,Cottage No. 15

Kalaupapa Leprosy Settlement; see McVeigh Home,Cottage No. 2

Kalaupapa Leprosy Settlement; see McVeigh Home,Dormitory

Kalaupapa Leprosy Settlement; see McVeigh Home,Pool Hall

Kalaupapa Leprosy Settlement; see McVeigh Home,Recreation Hall

Kalaupapa Leprosy Settlement; see Mother Marianne Library

Kalaupapa Leprosy Settlement; see Motor Pool Garage

Kalaupapa Leprosy Settlement; see Motor Pool Gas Station

Kalaupapa Leprosy Settlement; see Outpatient Clinic

Kalaupapa Leprosy Settlement; see Paschoal Craft Building

Kalaupapa Leprosy Settlement; see Rea's Store & Bar

Kalaupapa Leprosy Settlement; see Rea's Store & Bar,Restroom

Kalaupapa Leprosy Settlement; see Residence,Building No. 114

Kalaupapa Leprosy Settlement; see Residence,Building No. 115

Kalaupapa Leprosy Settlement; see Residence,Building No. 116

Kalaupapa Leprosy Settlement; see Residence,Building No. 118

Kalaupapa Leprosy Settlement; see Residence,Building No. 119

Kalaupapa Leprosy Settlement; see Residence,Building No. 281

Kalaupapa Leprosy Settlement; see Residence,Building No. 53

Kalaupapa Leprosy Settlement; see Residence,Building No. 56

Kalaupapa Leprosy Settlement; see Residence,Building No. 62-117

Kalaupapa Leprosy Settlement; see Residence,Building No. 71R-61

Kalaupapa Leprosy Settlement; see Slaughterhouse

Kalaupapa Leprosy Settlement; see Staff Row,Administrative Residence

Kalaupapa Leprosy Settlement; see Staff Row,Central Kitchen

Kalaupapa Leprosy Settlement; see Staff Row,Corner Residence

Kalaupapa Leprosy Settlement; see Staff Row,Dentist House

Kalaupapa Leprosy Settlement; see Staff Row,Doctor's House

Kalaupapa Leprosy Settlement; see Staff Row,Electrician's Residence

Kalaupapa Leprosy Settlement; see Staff Row,Freezer Shelter

Kalaupapa Leprosy Settlement; see Staff Row,Garage

Kalaupapa Leprosy Settlement; see Staff Row,Guest Cottage

Kalaupapa Leprosy Settlement; see Town of Kalaupapa

Kalaupapa Leprosy Settlement; see Visitor Quarters,Building No. 274

Kalaupapa Leprosy Settlement; see Visitor Quarters,Building No. 277

Kalaupapa Leprosy Settlement; see Visitor Quarters,Patient Restrooms

Kalaupapa Leprosy Settlement; see Visitor Quarters,Telephone Sub-Station

Kalaupapa Leprosy Settlement; see Visitor Quarters,Visitor-Patient Meeting Hall

Kalaupapa Leprosy Settlement,Administrative Center; see Administrative Building No. 270

Kalaupapa Leprosy Settlement,Administrative Center; see Gas Station

Kalaupapa Leprosy Settlement,Administrative Center; see Jail & Police Station

Kalaupapa Leprosy Settlement,Administrative Center; see Patient Store

Kalaupapa Leprosy Settlement,Administrative Center; see Post Office & Courthouse

Kalaupapa Leprosy Settlement,Bishop Home; see Copes Monument

Kalaupapa Leprosy Settlement,Bishop Home; see Damien Monument

Kalaupapa Leprosy Settlement,Calvinist Mission; see Kanaana Hou Calvinist Church

Kalaupapa Leprosy Settlement,Calvinist Mission; see Mission House Drew

Kalaupapa Leprosy Settlement,Catholic Mission; see St. Francis Catholic Church

Kalaupapa Leprosy Settlement,Catholic Mission; see St. Francis Church Library

Kalaupapa Leprosy Settlement,Industrial Center; see Butcher Shop & Freezer

Kalaupapa Leprosy Settlement,Industrial Center; see Carpenter Shop

Kalaupapa Leprosy Settlement,Industrial Center; see Crematory

Kalaupapa Leprosy Settlement,Industrial Center; see Food Warehouse

Kalaupapa Leprosy Settlement,Industrial Center; see Lumber Warehouse

Kalaupapa Leprosy Settlement,Industrial Center; see Maintenance Shop

Kalaupapa Leprosy Settlement,Industrial Center; see Plumbing Warehouse

Kalaupapa Social Hall (Paschoal Community Hall; Kalaupapa Leprosy Settlement)
Moloka'i Island
HABS HI-67
HABS DLC/PP-1992:HI-4,-5
7dr/35ph/29pg/3pc L

Kanaana Hou Calvinist Church (Kalaupapa Leprosy Settlement,Calvinist Mission)
Moloka'i Island
HABS HI-123
HABS DLC/PP-1992:HI-4
11ph/1pc L

Latter Day Saints Mormon Church (Church of Jesus Christ of Latter Day Saint's,The; Kalaupapa Leprosy Settlement)
Moloka'i Island
HABS HI-116
HABS DLC/PP-1992:HI-4
2ph/1pc L

Latter Day Saints Parish Hall (Building No. 257A; Kalaupapa Leprosy Settlement)
Kamehameha St.,Moloka'i Island
HABS HI-115
HABS DLC/PP-1992:HI-4
2ph/1pc L

Latter Day Saints Rectory (Building No. 256; Kalaupapa Leprosy Settlement)
Kamehameha St.,Moloka'i Island
HABS HI-130
HABS DLC/PP-1992:HI-4
1ph/1pc L

Lumber Warehouse (Building No. 263-A; Kalaupapa Leprosy Settlement,Industrial Center)
Moloka'i Island
HABS HI-120
HABS DLC/PP-1992:HI-4
2ph/1pc L

Maintenance Shop (Building No. 265; Kalaupapa Leprosy Settlement,Industrial Center)
Moloka'i Island
HABS HI-92
HABS DLC/PP-1992:HI-4
1ph/1pc L

McVeigh Home,Apartment Building (Building No. 12; Kalaupapa Leprosy Settlement)
Moloka'i Island
HABS HI-95-D
HABS DLC/PP-1992:HI-4
2ph/1pc L

McVeigh Home,Card Room (Building No. 27; Kalaupapa Leprosy Settlement)
Moloka'i Island
HABS HI-95-G
HABS DLC/PP-1992:HI-4
1ph/1pc L

McVeigh Home,Cottage No. 1 (Kalaupapa Leprosy Settlement)
Moloka'i Island
HABS HI-95-B
HABS DLC/PP-1992:HI-4
1ph/1pc L

McVeigh Home,Cottage No. 13 (Kalaupapa Leprosy Settlement)
Moloka'i Island
HABS HI-95-H
HABS DLC/PP-1992:HI-4
2ph/1pc L

McVeigh Home,Cottage No. 15 (Kalaupapa Leprosy Settlement)
Moloka'i Island
HABS HI-95-I
HABS DLC/PP-1992:HI-4
1ph/1pc L

McVeigh Home,Cottage No. 2 (Kalaupapa Leprosy Settlement)
Moloka'i Island
HABS HI-95-C
HABS DLC/PP-1992:HI-4
1ph/1pc L

McVeigh Home,Dormitory (Kalaupapa Leprosy Settlement)
Moloka'i Island
HABS HI-95-A
HABS DLC/PP-1992:HI-4
3ph/1pc L

McVeigh Home,Pool Hall (Building No. 24; Kalaupapa Leprosy Settlement)
Moloka'i Island
HABS HI-95-F
HABS DLC/PP-1992:HI-4
1ph/1pc L

McVeigh Home,Recreation Hall (Building No. 23; Kalaupapa Leprosy Settlement)
Moloka'i Island
HABS HI-95-E
HABS DLC/PP-1992:HI-4
2ph/1pc L

Mission House Drew (Building No. 288; Kalaupapa Leprosy Settlement,Calvinist Mission)
Moloka'i Island
HABS HI-118
HABS DLC/PP-1992:HI-4
4ph/1pc L

Mother Marianne Library (Building No. 65-296; Kalaupapa Leprosy Settlement)
Moloka'i Island
HABS HI-101
HABS DLC/PP-1992:HI-4
1ph/1pc L

Motor Pool Garage (Building No. 259; Kalaupapa Leprosy Settlement)
Moloka'i Island
HABS HI-111
HABS DLC/PP-1992:HI-4
1ph/1pc L

Motor Pool Gas Station (Building No. 258A; Kalaupapa Leprosy Settlement)
Moloka'i Island
HABS HI-110
HABS DLC/PP-1992:HI-4
1ph/1pc L

Outpatient Clinic (Building No. 7; Kalaupapa Leprosy Settlement)
Moloka'i Island
HABS HI-117
HABS DLC/PP-1992:HI-4
2ph/1pc L

Paschoal Community Hall; see Kalaupapa Social Hall

Paschoal Craft Building (Building No. 300; Kalaupapa Leprosy Settlement)
Moloka'i Island
HABS HI-72
HABS DLC/PP-1992:HI-4
3ph/1pc L

Patient Store (Building No. 272; Kalaupapa Leprosy Settlement,Administrative Center
Moloka'i Island
HABS HI-76
HABS DLC/PP-1992:HI-4
4ph/1pc L

Plumbing Warehouse (Building No. 263; Kalaupapa Leprosy Settlement,Industrial Center)
Moloka'i Island
HABS HI-119
HABS DLC/PP-1992:HI-4
1ph/1pc L

Post Office & Courthouse (Kalaupapa Leprosy Settlement,Administrative Center
Moloka'i Island
HABS HI-77
HABS DLC/PP-1992:HI-4
3ph/1pc L

Rea's Store & Bar (Building No. 62; Kalaupapa Leprosy Settlement)
Moloka'i Island
HABS HI-124
HABS DLC/PP-1992:HI-4
2ph/1pc L

Rea's Store & Bar,Restroom (Kalaupapa Leprosy Settlement)
Moloka'i Island
HABS HI-124-A
HABS DLC/PP-1992:HI-4
1ph/1pc L

Residence,Building No. 114 (Kalaupapa Leprosy Settlement)
Goodhue St.,Moloka'i Island
HABS HI-107
HABS DLC/PP-1992:HI-4
3ph/1pc L

Residence,Building No. 115 (Kalaupapa Leprosy Settlement)
Goodhue St.,Moloka'i Island
HABS HI-106
HABS DLC/PP-1992:HI-4
1ph/1pc L

Residence,Building No. 116 (Kalaupapa Leprosy Settlement)
Goodhue St.,Moloka'i Island
HABS HI-108
HABS DLC/PP-1992:HI-4
2ph/1pc L

Residence,Building No. 118 (Kalaupapa Leprosy Settlement)
Goodhue St.,Moloka'i Island
HABS HI-105
HABS DLC/PP-1992:HI-4
2ph/1pc L

Residence,Building No. 119 (Kalaupapa Leprosy Settlement)
School St.,Moloka'i Island
HABS HI-109
HABS DLC/PP-1992:HI-4
3ph/1pc L

Residence,Building No. 281 (Kalaupapa Leprosy Settlement)
Puahi St.,Moloka'i Island
HABS HI-87
HABS DLC/PP-1992:HI-4
2ph/1pc L

Residence,Building No. 53 (Kalaupapa Leprosy Settlement)
Kilohana St.,Moloka'i Island
HABS HI-112
HABS DLC/PP-1992:HI-4
1ph/1pc L

Residence,Building No. 56 (Kalaupapa Leprosy Settlement)
Kamehameha St.,Moloka'i Island
HABS HI-79
HABS DLC/PP-1992:HI-4
2ph/1pc L

Residence,Building No. 62-117 (Kalaupapa Leprosy Settlement)
Moloka'i Island
HABS HI-100
HABS DLC/PP-1992:HI-4
1ph/1pc L

Residence,Building No. 71R-61 (Kalaupapa Leprosy Settlement)
Moloka'i Island
HABS HI-98
HABS DLC/PP-1992:HI-4
1ph/1pc L

Slaughterhouse (Building No. 630; Kalaupapa Leprosy Settlement)
Moloka'i Island
HABS HI-97
HABS DLC/PP-1992:HI-4
1ph/1pc L

St. Francis Catholic Church (Kalaupapa Leprosy Settlement,Catholic Mission)
Moloka'i Island
HABS HI-80
HABS DLC/PP-1992:HI-4
21ph/2pc L

St. Francis Church Library (Kalaupapa Leprosy Settlement,Catholic Mission)
Moloka'i Island
HABS HI-81
HABS DLC/PP-1992:HI-4
1ph/1pc L

Staff Row,Administrative Residence (Building No. 14; Kalaupapa Leprosy Settlement)
Moloka'i Island
HABS HI-88-G
HABS DLC/PP-1992:HI-4
3ph/1pc L

Staff Row,Central Kitchen (Building No. 5; Kalaupapa Leprosy Settlement)
Moloka'i Island
HABS HI-88-A
HABS DLC/PP-1992:HI-4
3ph/1pc L

Staff Row,Corner Residence (Buildng No. 1; Kalaupapa Leprosy Settlement)
Moloka'i Island
HABS HI-88-B
HABS DLC/PP-1992:HI-4
3ph/1pc L

Staff Row,Dentist House (Building No. 8; Kalaupapa Leprosy Settlement)
Moloka'i Island
HABS HI-88-F
HABS DLC/PP-1992:HI-4
2ph/1pc L

Staff Row,Doctor's House (Building No. 10; Kalaupapa Leprosy Settlement)
Moloka'i Island
HABS HI-88-H
HABS DLC/PP-1992:HI-4
4ph/1pc L

Staff Row,Electrician's Residence (Building No. 16; Kalaupapa Leprosy Settlement)
Moloka'i Island
HABS HI-88-D
HABS DLC/PP-1992:HI-4
2ph/1pc L

Staff Row,Freezer Shelter (Building No. 6; Kalaupapa Leprosy Settlement)
Moloka'i Island
HABS HI-88-E
HABS DLC/PP-1992:HI-4
1ph/1pc L

Staff Row,Garage (Kalaupapa Leprosy Settlement)
Moloka'i Island
HABS HI-88-C
HABS DLC/PP-1992:HI-4
1ph/1pc L

Staff Row,Guest Cottage (Building No. 1A; Kalaupapa Leprosy Settlement)
Moloka'i Island
HABS HI-88-I
HABS DLC/PP-1992:HI-4
3ph/1pc L

Town of Kalaupapa (Kalaupapa Leprosy Settlement)
HABS HI-66
HABS DLC/PP-1992:HI-4
2ph/1pc L

Visitor Quarters,Building No. 274 (Kalaupapa Leprosy Settlement)
Moloka'i Island
HABS HI-71-C
HABS DLC/PP-1992:HI-4
2ph/1pc L

Visitor Quarters,Building No. 277 (Wilcox Memorial Building; Kalaupapa Leprosy Settlement)
Moloka'i Island
HABS HI-71-B
HABS DLC/PP-1992:HI-4
2ph/1pc L

Visitor Quarters,Patient Restrooms (Building No. 523; Kalaupapa Leprosy Settlement)
Moloka'i Island
HABS HI-71-D
HABS DLC/PP-1992:HI-4
1ph/1pc L

Visitor Quarters,Telephone Sub-Station (Building No. 522; Kalaupapa Leprosy Settlement)
Moloka'i Island
HABS HI-71-E
HABS DLC/PP-1992:HI-4
2ph/1pc L

Visitor Quarters,Visitor-Patient Meeting Hall (Building No. 278; Kalaupapa Leprosy Settlement)
Moloka'i Island
HABS HI-71-A
HABS DLC/PP-1992:HI-4
4ph/1pc L

Wilcox Memorial Building; see Visitor Quarters,Building No. 277

KALAUPAPA VIC.

Airport Terminal (Building No. 703; Kalaupapa Leprosy Settlement)
Airport Rd.,Moloka'i Island
HABS HI-104
HABS DLC/PP-1992:HI-4
1ph/1pc L

Beach House,Building No. 695 (Kalaupapa Leprosy Settlement)
Airport Rd.,Moloka'i Island
HABS HI-102
HABS DLC/PP-1992:HI-4
1ph/1pc L

Beach House,Building No. 699 (Kalaupapa Leprosy Settlement)
Airport Rd.,Moloka'i Island
HABS HI-103
HABS DLC/PP-1992:HI-4
3ph/1pc L

Building No. 687; see Public Restroom

Building No. 703; see Airport Terminal

Kalaupapa Leprosy Settlement; see Airport Terminal

Kalaupapa Leprosy Settlement; see Beach House,Building No. 695

Kalaupapa Leprosy Settlement; see Beach House,Building No. 699

Kalaupapa Leprosy Settlement; see Lion's Pavilion

Kalaupapa Leprosy Settlement; see Moloka'i Light Station

Kalaupapa Leprosy Settlement; see Moloka'i Light Station,Generator Shed

Kalaupapa Leprosy Settlement; see Moloka'i Light Station,Lighthouse

Kalaupapa Leprosy Settlement; see Moloka'i Light Station,Residence No. 1

Kalaupapa Leprosy Settlement; see Moloka'i Light Station,Residence No. 2

Kalaupapa Leprosy Settlement; see Moloka'i Light Station,Storage Vault

Kalaupapa Leprosy Settlement; see Molokai Light Station,Watertank

Kalaupapa Leprosy Settlement; see Public Restroom

Lion's Pavilion (Ocean View Pavilion; Kalaupapa Leprosy Settlement)
Airport Rd.,Moloka'i Island
HABS HI-113
HABS DLC/PP-1992:HI-4
1ph/1pc L

Moloka'i Light Station (Kalaupapa Leprosy Settlement)
Makanalua,Moloka'i Island
HABS HI-99
HABS DLC/PP-1992:HI-4
1ph/1pc L

Moloka'i Light Station,Generator Shed (Kalaupapa Leprosy Settlement)
Makanalua,Moloka'i Island
HABS HI-99-E
HABS DLC/PP-1992:HI-4
2ph/1pc L

Moloka'i Light Station,Lighthouse (Kalaupapa Leprosy Settlement)
Makanalua,Moloka'i Island
HABS HI-99-A
HABS DLC/PP-1992:HI-4
5ph/1pc L

Moloka'i Light Station,Residence No. 1 (Kalaupapa Leprosy Settlement)
Makanalua,Moloka'i Island
HABS HI-99-B
HABS DLC/PP-1992:HI-4
2ph/1pc L

Moloka'i Light Station,Residence No. 2 (Kalaupapa Leprosy Settlement)
Makanalua,Moloka'i Island
HABS HI-99-F
HABS DLC/PP-1992:HI-4
2ph/1pc L

Moloka'i Light Station,Storage Vault (Kalaupapa Leprosy Settlement)
Makanalua,Moloka'i Island
HABS HI-99-C
HABS DLC/PP-1992:HI-4
1ph/1pc L

Molokai Light Station,Watertank (Kalaupapa Leprosy Settlement)
Makanalua,Moloka'i Island
HABS HI-99-D
HABS DLC/PP-1992:HI-4
1ph/1pc L

Ocean View Pavilion; see Lion's Pavilion

Public Restroom (Building No. 687; Kalaupapa Leprosy Settlement)
Airport Rd.,acr. from Lion's Pavilion,Moloka'i Is.
HABS HI-114
HABS DLC/PP-1992:HI-4
1ph/1pc L

KALAWAO

Baldwin Home Kitchen Ruins (Kalaupapa Leprosy Settlement,Kalawao Settlement)
W. of St. Philomena Church,Moloka'i Island
HABS HI-90
HABS DLC/PP-1992:HI-4
3ph/1pc L

Building No. 635; see Rock Crusher

Church of the Healing Spring; see Siloama Protestant Church

Father Damien's Church; see St. Philomena Roman Catholic Church

Kalaupapa Leprosy Settlement; see Rock Crusher

Kalaupapa Leprosy Settlement,Kalawao Settlement; see Baldwin Home Kitchen Ruins

Kalaupapa Leprosy Settlement,Kalawao Settlement; see Siloama Church,Restrooms

Kalaupapa Leprosy Settlement,Kalawao Settlement; see Siloama Protestant Church

Kalaupapa Leprosy Settlement,Kalawao Settlement; see St. Philomena Roman Catholic Church

Kalaupapa Leprosy Settlement,Kalawao Settlement; see St. Philomena Roman Catholic Church,Churchyard

Rock Crusher (Building No. 635; Kalaupapa Leprosy Settlement)
At ruins of Baldwin Home For Boys,Moloka'i Island
HABS HI-89
HABS DLC/PP-1992:HI-4
4ph/1pc L

Siloama Church,Restrooms (Kalaupapa Leprosy Settlement,Kalawao Settlement)
Moloka'i Island
HABS HI-70-A
HABS DLC/PP-1992:HI-4
1ph/1pc L

Siloama Protestant Church (Church of the Healing Spring; Kalaupapa Leprosy Settlement,Kalawao Settlement)
Moloka'i Island
HABS HI-70
HABS DLC/PP-1992:HI-4
9ph/1pc L

St. Philomena Roman Catholic Church (Father Damien's Church; Kalaupapa Leprosy Settlement,Kalawao Settlement)
Moloka'i Island
HABS HI-69
HABS DLC/PP-1992:HI-4
28ph/2pc L

St. Philomena Roman Catholic Church,Churchyard (Kalaupapa Leprosy Settlement,Kalawao Settlement)
Moloka'i Island
HABS HI-69-A
HABS DLC/PP-1992:HI-4
3ph/1pc L

KAUAI COUNTY

HANALEI

Hanalei Pier
Hanalei Bay off Weke Road
HAER HI-17
HAER DLC/PP-1993:HI-2
24ph/3pg/2pc L

Haraguchi Rice Mill
Hanalei River
HAER HI-3
HAER HI,4-HANLI,1-
4dr/12ph/1pc/fr L

Mahamoku (Wilcox,Mabel I.,Hanalei Beach House)
5344 Weke Rd.
HABS HI-58
HABS HI,4-HANLI,2-
6dr/fr L

Waioli Church (Waioli Hui'ia Social Hall)
Island of Kauai
HABS HI-52
HABS HI,4-HANLI,3-
4dr/6ph/3pg/1pc L

Waioli Hui'ia Social Hall; see Waioli Church

Waioli Mission House
Kauai Belt Hwy.
HABS HI-53
HABS HI,4-HANLI,4-
8dr/5ph/3pg/1pc L

Wilcox,Mabel I.,Hanalei Beach House; see Mahamoku

HANAMAULU

Lihue Plantation Home One
Kuhio Hwy.
HABS HI-59-A
HABS HI,4-HANMU,1-A-
1dr/fr L

Lihue Plantation Home Two
Kuhio Hwy.
HABS HI-59-B
HABS HI,4-HANMU,1-B-
2dr/fr L

Lihue Plantation House
Kuhio Hwy.
HABS HI-59
HABS HI,4-HANMU,1-
1dr/fr L

LIHUE

Grove Farm,G.N. Wilcox House (Wilcox,G.N.,House)
Nawiliwili Rd. (St. Rte. 58)
HABS HI-56
HABS HI,4-LIHU,1-
5dr/33ph/2pc/fr L

Wilcox,G.N.,House; see Grove Farm,G.N. Wilcox House

MAUI COUNTY

KAUNAKAKAI (MOLOKAI)

Kamoi Theater
Ala Malama Ave. & Kamoi St.
HABS HI-57
HABS 1989(HABS):6
12ph/28pg/1pc L

KUALAPUU (MOLOKAI IS

Meyer,R. W. ,Sugar Mill,1878
State Rt. 47
HAER HI-1
HAER HI,5-KALPU,1-
7dr/35ph/52pg/7pc/fr L

LAHAINA

Baldwin House
Front & Dickenson Sts.
HABS HI-43
HABS HI,5-LAHA,1-
12ph/1pc L

Chee Kung Tong Society Headquarters
858 Front St.
HABS HI-40
HABS HI,5-LAHA,2-
7ph/1pc L

Court & Custom House; see Maui Courthouse,Old

Hale Aloha Church
600 Laukini St.
HABS HI-10
HABS HI,5-LAHA,3-
6dr/5ph/3pg/1pc/fr L

Hale Pa'i (Printing Shop)
On grounds of Lahainaluna Seminary
HABS HI-8
HABS HI,5-LAHA,11-
5dr/6ph/4pg/1pc/fr L

Hale Paahao (Prison)
Wainee & Prison Rds.
HABS HI-37
HABS HI,5-LAHA,4-
9ph/1pc L

Master's Reading Room
Dickenson & Front Sts.
HABS HI-13
HABS HI,5-LAHA,5-
5dr/3ph/1pc/fr L

Maui Courthouse,Old (Court & Custom House)
Wharf & Canal Sts.
HABS HI-9
HABS HI,5-LAHA,6-
8dr/6ph/1pg/1pc/fr L

Pioneer Hotel
Front & Hotel Sts.
HABS HI-41
HABS HI,5-LAHA,7-
10ph/1pc L

Pioneer Mill,Office
Lahainaluna Rd. & Mill St.
HABS HI-39
HABS HI,5-LAHA,8-
3ph/1pc L

Pioneer Mill,Time Clock
Lahainaluna Rd.
HABS HI-38
HABS HI,5-LAHA,9-
2ph/1pc L

U. S. Marine Hospital
1038 Front St.
HABS HI-11
HABS HI,5-LAHA,10-
5dr/2ph/4pg/1pc/fr L

OLOWALU

Olowalu Church (Ruins)
HABS HI-35
HABS HI,5-OLOW,1-
5ph/1pc L

PAIA

Hamakuapoko Mill (Ruins)
Puunee Sugar Mill Vic.
HABS HI-44
HABS HI,5-PAIA,1-
6ph/1pc L

PUKOO VIC. (MOLOKAI)

Kaluaaha Congregational Church
State Rt. 45
HABS HI-51
HABS HI,5-PUKO.V,1-
7dr/2ph/7pg/1pc/fr L

SPRECKELSVILLE

Spreckels Sugar Mill
HABS HI-54
HABS HI,5-SPRK,1-
2ph/1pc L

ULUPALAKUA

Ulupalakua Ranch,Guest House
HABS HI-47-A
HABS HI,5-ULUP,1-A-
2ph/1pc L

Ulupalakua Ranch,Jail
HABS HI-47-B
HABS HI,5-ULUP,1-B-
2ph/1pc L

Ulupalakua Ranch,Main House
HABS HI-47
HABS HI,5-ULUP,1-
8ph/1pc L

WAIAKOA

Holy Ghost Roman Catholic Church
HABS HI-45
HABS HI,5-WAIKO,1-
10ph/1pc L

WAILUKU

Alexander,William & Mary,House (Parsonage)
HABS HI-46
HABS HI,5-WAILU,1-
1ph/1pc L

Bailey House (Wailuku Mission)
Iao Valley Rd.
HABS HI-42
HABS HI,5-WAILU,2-
6ph/1pc L

Kaahumanu Church
S. High St.
HABS HI-36
HABS HI,5-WAILU,3-
4ph/1pc L

Parsonage; see Alexander,William & Mary,House

Wailuku Mission; see Bailey House

Documentation: **ct** color transparencies **dr** measured drawings **fr** field records
pc photograph captions **pg** pages of text **ph** photographs

American Falls Water, Power, & Light Company, American Falls, Power County, Idaho. Island plant: view northeast. Photograph by Melville Studio, 1976 (HAER ID,39-AMFA,1-25).

Post Office Block (Boise Basin Museum), Idaho City, Boise County, Idaho. East (front) elevation. Photograph by Duane Garrett, 1976 (HABS ID,8-IDCI,10-1).

Idaho

ADA COUNTY

BOISE

(Alexander's store); see Alexander's Building

Ada Theatre (Egyptian Theatre)
700 Main St.
HABS ID-3
HABS ID,1-BOISE,8-
21ph/17pg/2pc L

Alexander's Building ((Alexander's store))
826 Main St.
HABS ID-4
HABS ID,1-BOISE,1-
12ph/4pg/1pc L

609 Ash Street (House); see Lee Street Historic District

611 Ash Street (House); see Lee Street Historic District

611 Ash Street,Garage; see Lee Street Historic District

Boise City National Bank (Simplot Building)
805 W. Idaho St.
HABS ID-23
HABS ID,1-BOISE,7-
9ph/10pg/1pc/fr L

Boise Fruit & Produce Bldg.; see Smith,O.W. Building Complex

Boise Ice & Produce Company (Idaho Fish & Poultry Company; South Eighth Street Historic District)
504 S. Ninth St.
HABS ID-72
HABS 1992(HABS):ID-1
4ph/2pg/1pc L

Boise Project, Boise Project Office (Boise Project, Central Snake Project Office)
HAER ID-17-C
45ph/26pg/4pc H

Boise Project, Central Snake Project Office; see Boise Project, Boise Project Office

Brady,Gov. ,Mansion
140 Main St.
HABS ID-28
HABS ID,1-BOISE,9-
11ph/1pc L

Christ Chapel
Broadway & Campus Dr.
HABS ID-25
HABS ID,1-BOISE,10-
6ph/1pc L

Churchill's Restaurant; see Turnverein Hall

Congregation Beth Israel Synagogue
1102 State St.
HABS ID-26
HABS ID,1-BOISE,11-
6ph/1pc L

Davis Warehouse (Peasley Transfer & Storage Company; Idaho Fish & Poultry Company; Heller Sales Company; South Eighth Street Historic District)
418 S. Ninth St.
HABS ID-70
HABS 1992(HABS):ID-1
4ph/2pg/1pc L

Eastman Building; see Overland Building

Egyptian Theatre; see Ada Theatre

Falk-Bloch Mercantile Company (Falk's ID Department Store)
100 N. Eighth St.
HABS ID-18
HABS ID,1-BOISE,3-
12ph/19pg/2pc L

Falk's ID Department Store; see Falk-Bloch Mercantile Company

Fidelity Building; see Montandon Building

Fort Boise,Commanding Officer's Quarters (Veteran's Administration Center)
HABS ID-27
HABS ID,1-BOISE,12A-
7ph/1pc L

Heller Sales Company; see Davis Warehouse

Idaho Building
216 N. Eighth St.
HABS ID-21
HABS ID,1-BOISE,6-
7ph/4pg/1pc/fr L

Idaho Candy Company Warehouse (South Eighth Street Historic District)
500 S. Eighth St.
HABS ID-73
HABS 1992(HABS):ID-1
4ph/2pg/1pc L

Idaho Fish & Poultry Company; see Boise Ice & Produce Company

Idaho Fish & Poultry Company; see Davis Warehouse

Idaho Milling & Elevator Company (South Eighth Street Historic District)
416 S. Eighth St.
HABS ID-68
HABS 1992(HABS):ID-1
2ph/2pg/1pc L

Idanha Hotel
928 Main St.
HABS ID-29
HABS ID,1-BOISE,13-
14ph/10pg/1pc L

Jake's Restaurant; see Turnverein Hall

Lee Street Historic District
609-611 Ash St.
HABS ID-24
HABS ID,1-BOISE,14-
1ph/3pg/1pc L

Lee Street Historic District (609 Ash Street (House))
HABS ID-24-A
HABS ID,1-BOISE,14A-
4ph L

Lee Street Historic District (611 Ash Street (House))
HABS ID-24-B
HABS ID,1-BOISE,14B-
4ph L

Lee Street Historic District (611 Ash Street,Garage)
HABS ID-24-C
HABS ID,1-BOISE,14C-
1ph L

Montandon Building (Fidelity Building)
722 W. Idaho St.
HABS ID-19
HABS ID,1-BOISE,4-
6ph/7pg/1pc/fr L

Moore-Cunningham House
1109 Warm Springs Ave.
HABS ID-30
HABS ID,1-BOISE,17-
17ph/1pc L

Overland Building (Eastman Building)
101-109 N. Eighth St.
HABS ID-17
HABS ID,1-BOISE,2-
8ph/7pg/1pc/fr L

Peasley Transfer & Storage Company; see Davis Warehouse

Simplot Building; see Boise City National Bank

Smith,O.W. Building Complex (Boise Fruit & Produce Bldg.; South Eighth Street Historic District)
501-503 S. Eighth St.
HABS ID-71
HABS 1992(HABS):ID-1
3ph/2pg/1pc L

Smith,O.W.,Building Complex (South Eighth Street Historic District)
417 S. Eighth St.
HABS ID-69
HABS 1992(HABS):ID-1
2ph/2pg/1pc L

South Eighth Street Historic District; see Boise Ice & Produce Company

South Eighth Street Historic District; see Davis Warehouse

South Eighth Street Historic District; see Idaho Candy Company Warehouse

South Eighth Street Historic District; see Idaho Milling & Elevator Company

South Eighth Street Historic District; see Smith,O.W. Building Complex

South Eighth Street Historic District; see Smith,O.W.,Building Complex

St. Alphonsus Hospital
508 N. Fifth St.
HABS ID-31
HABS ID,1-BOISE,18-
8ph/1pc L

Turnverein Hall (Churchill's Restaurant; Jake's Restaurant)
100 S. Sixth St.
HABS ID-32
HABS ID,1-BOISE,19-
6ph/1pc L

U. S. Assay Office
210 Main St.
HABS ID-10
HABS ID,1-BOISE,20-
7dr/6ph/8pg/1pc/fr L

Union Block
710-720 W. Idaho St.
HABS ID-20
HABS ID,1-BOISE,5-
10ph/15pg/2pc/fr L

Union Pacific Railroad Depot
1701 Eastover Terrace
HABS ID-33
HABS ID,1-BOISE,21A-
12ph/1pc L

Veteran's Administration Center; see Fort Boise,Commanding Officer's Quarters

BOISE VIC.

Boise Project,Boise River Diversion Dam
Across Boise River
HAER ID-17-A
HAER DLC/PP-1993:ID-2
43ph/5pc L

KUNA

Swan Falls Village,Clubhouse 011
Snake River
HABS ID-105-I
HABS DLC/PP-1993:ID-1
8ph/1pc L

Swan Falls Village,Cottage 362
Snake River
HABS ID-105-F
HABS DLC/PP-1993:ID-1
4ph/1pc L

Swan Falls Village,Garage 393
Snake River
HABS ID-105-H
HABS DLC/PP-1993:ID-1
2ph/1pc L

KUNA VIC.

Cottage 231; see Swan Falls Village,Superintendent's Cottage

Swan Falls Village
Snake River
HABS ID-105
HABS DLC/PP-1993:ID-1
24ph/43pg/5pc L

Swan Falls Village,Cottage 101
Snake River
HABS ID-105-A
HABS DLC/PP-1993:ID-1
10ph/1pc L

Swan Falls Village,Cottage 181
Snake River
HABS ID-105-B
HABS DLC/PP-1993:ID-1
4ph/1pc L

Swan Falls Village,Cottage 191
Snake River
HABS ID-105-C
HABS DLC/PP-1993:ID-1
11ph/2pc L

Swan Falls Village,Cottage 361
Snake River
HABS ID-105-E
HABS DLC/PP-1993:ID-1
10ph/1pc L

Swan Falls Village,Cottage 363
Snake River
HABS ID-105-G
HABS DLC/PP-1993:ID-1
4ph/1pc L

Swan Falls Village,Superintendent's Cottage (Cottage 231)
Snake River
HABS ID-105-D
HABS DLC/PP-1993:ID-1
14ph/2pc L

BANNOCK COUNTY

MCCAMMON

McCammon Bridge; see McCammon Overhead and River Crossing Bridge

McCammon Overhead and River Crossing Bridge (McCammon Bridge)
Interstate 15,Business,3.3 mile post
HAER ID-19
13ph/11pg/1pc L

POCATELLO

Pocatello Railroad YMCA Building
N. Arthur Ave. Vic.
HABS ID-104
HABS 1991(HABS):14
17ph L

BEAR LAKE COUNTY

MONTPELIER VIC.

Dingle Station Bridge; see East Dingle Bridge

East Dingle Bridge (Dingle Station Bridge)
Spanning Bear River on Hunter Mill Rd.
HAER ID-13
HAER 1989(HAER):6
7ph/8pg/1pc L

BINGHAM COUNTY

SHELLEY VIC.

Snake River Valley Irrigation District
East Side of Snake River (River Mile 796)
HAER ID-10
HAER ID,6-SHEL.V,1-
15ph/20pg/2pc L

WOODVILLE VIC.

Woodville Canal Company
W. side of Snake River (River Mile 796)
HAER ID-9
HAER ID,6-WOVI.V,1-
10ph/17pg/1pc L

BLAINE COUNTY

STANLEY VIC.

Peavy Cabins
Block A, Lot 1, Pettit Lake Summer Home Area
HABS ID-107
3ph/18pg/1pc H

Peavy Cabins,Bunkhouse; see Peavy Cabins,Cabin 3

Peavy Cabins,Bunkhouse; see Peavy Cabins,Cabin 4

Peavy Cabins,Cabin 1 (Peavy Cabins,Kitchen/Dining Room)
Block A, Lot 1, Pettit Lake Summer Home Area
HABS ID-107-A
5ph/1pc H

Peavy Cabins,Cabin 2 (Peavy Cabins,Multi-purpose Cabin)
Block A, Lot 1, Pettit Lake Summer Home Area
HABS ID-107-B
4ph/1pc H

Peavy Cabins,Cabin 3 (Peavy Cabins,Bunkhouse; Peavy Cabins,Hooneymoon Hut)
Block A, Lot 1, Pettit Lake Summer Home Area
HABS ID-107-C
4ph/1pc H

Peavy Cabins,Cabin 4 (Peavy Cabins,Bunkhouse; Peavy Cabins,Ram Pasture)
Block A, Lot 1, Pettit Lake Summer Home Area
HABS ID-107-D
2ph/1pc H

Peavy Cabins,Hooneymoon Hut; see Peavy Cabins,Cabin 3

Peavy Cabins,Kitchen/Dining Room; see Peavy Cabins,Cabin 1

Peavy Cabins,Multi-purpose Cabin; see Peavy Cabins,Cabin 2

Peavy Cabins,Ram Pasture; see Peavy Cabins,Cabin 4

BOISE COUNTY

GARDEN VALLEY

Building No. 1125,Boise National Forest; see Garden Valley Work Station,Large Bungalow

Building No. 1126,Boise National Forest; see Garden Valley Work Station,Small House

Garden Valley Work Station,Large Bungalow (Building No. 1125,Boise National Forest)
HABS ID-57
HABS ID,8-GARVA,2A-
1dr/8ph/1pc/fr L

Garden Valley Work Station,Small House (Building No. 1126,Boise National Forest)
HABS ID-58
HABS ID,8-GARVA,2B-
1dr/5ph/1pc/fr L

IDAHO CITY

Boise Basin Mercantile Company Block
Main & Commercial Sts.
HABS ID-13
HABS ID,8-IDCI,8-
6dr/8ph/11pg/1pc/fr L

Boise Basin Museum; see Post Office Block

Boise County Courthouse
Main & Wall Sts.
HABS ID-11
HABS ID,8-IDCI,6-
7dr/8ph/8pg/1pc/fr L

City Hall; see Idaho City Schoolhouse

Galbraith House
Montgomery St.
HABS ID-7
HABS ID,8-IDCI,3-
7dr/6ph/4pg/1pc/fr L

Idaho City Schoolhouse (City Hall)
School & Main Sts.
HABS ID-6
HABS ID,8-IDCI,2-
7dr/6ph/5pg/1pc/fr L

Idaho World Building
Main & Commercial Sts.
HABS ID-9
HABS ID,8-IDCI,5-
5dr/5ph/6pg/fr L

Masonic Temple,Idaho Lodge Number 1
Wall St.
HABS ID-5
HABS ID,8-IDCI,1-
7dr/10ph/6pg/2pc/fr L

Miners' Exchange Block
Main & Wall Sts.
HABS ID-14
HABS ID,8-IDCI,9-
5dr/12ph/9pg/2pc/fr L

Pioneer Lodge Number 1
E. Commercial St.
HABS ID-8
HABS ID,8-IDCI,4-
5dr/7ph/7pg/1pc/fr L

Post Office Block (Boise Basin Museum)
Wall & Montgomery Sts.
HABS ID-15
HABS ID,8-IDCI,10-
8ph/7pg/1pc/fr L

St. Joseph's Roman Catholic Church
High & Wallula Sts.
HABS ID-12
HABS ID,8-IDCI,7-
4dr/10ph/6pg/1pc/fr L

IDAHO CITY VIC.

Boise National Forest (site plan)
HABS ID-66
HABS ID,8-IDCI.V,1-
1dr L

Building No. 1311,Boise National Forest; see Cottonwood Work Station,Garage

Building No. 1319,Boise National Forest; see Cottonwood Work Station,Cellar

Building No. 1515,Boise National Forest; see Cottonwood Work Station,Tool Shed

Cottonwood Work Station,Cellar (Building No. 1319,Boise National Forest)
HABS ID-50
HABS ID,8-IDCI.V,2A-
1dr/2ph/1pc/fr L

Cottonwood Work Station,Garage (Building No. 1311,Boise National Forest)
HABS ID-51
HABS ID,8-IDCI.V,2B-
1dr/3ph/1pc/fr L

Cottonwood Work Station,Tool Shed (Building No. 1515,Boise National Forest)
HABS ID-52
HABS ID,8-IDCI.V,2C-
1dr/2ph/1pc/fr L

LOWMAN VIC.

Beaver Creek Work Station,Log Cabin (Building No. 1107,Boise National Forest)
HABS ID-56
HABS ID,8-LOW.V,2A-
1dr/4ph/1pc/fr L

Building No. 1107,Boise National Forest; see Beaver Creek Work Station,Log Cabin

BONNER COUNTY

OLDTOWN

Oldtown Bridge
Spanning Pend Oreille River,U. S. Hwy. 2
HAER ID-7
HAER ID,9-OLDTO,1-
12ph/3pg/1pc L

BOUNDARY COUNTY

BONNER'S FERRY

Bonner's Ferry Bridge
Spanning the Kootenai River
HAER ID-5
HAER ID,11-BONFE,1-
16ph/25pg/1pc L

EASTPORT

U.S. Border Inspctn. Stn.,Customs Officers Residn.
W. side of State Rte. 95
HABS ID-101-A
HABS DLC/PP-1992:ID-5
7ph/9pg/1pc L

U.S. Border Inspctn. Stn.,Immigation Officers Res.
W. side of State Rte. 95
HABS ID-101-B
HABS DLC/PP-1992:ID-5
3ph/9pg/1pc L

United States Border Inspection Station
W. side of State Rte. 95
HABS ID-101
HABS DLC/PP-1992:ID-5
21ph/13pg/3pc L

CANYON COUNTY

NAMPA VIC.

Boise Project,Deer Flat Embankments
Lake Lowell
HAER ID-17-B
82ph/115pg/9pc H

CASSIA COUNTY

BURLEY

Bonneville Power Administration Burley Substation (Burley Substation)
1221 Albion Ave.
HAER ID-22
HAER DLC/PP-1993:ID-3
13ph/19pg/2pc L

Burley Substation; see Bonneville Power Administration Burley Substation

ELMORE COUNTY

ATLANTA

Atlanta Guard Station,Icehouse (Building No. 1445,Boise National Forest)
HABS ID-55
HABS ID,20-ATLA,2A-
1dr/2ph/1pc/fr L

Building No. 1445,Boise National Forest; see Atlanta Guard Station,Icehouse

ATLANTA VIC.

Building No. 1179,Boise National Forest; see Dutch Creek Work Station,Bunkhouse

Building No. 1606,Boise National Forest; see Dutch Creek Work Station,Kitchen

Dutch Creek Work Station,Bunkhouse (Building No. 1179,Boise National Forest)
HABS ID-62
HABS ID,20-ATLA.V,2A-
1dr/5ph/1pc/fr L

Dutch Creek Work Station,Kitchen (Building No. 1606,Boise National Forest)
HABS ID-63
HABS ID,20-ATLA.V,2B-
1dr/5ph/fr L

FRANKLIN COUNTY

THATCHER VIC.

Thatcher Bridge
Spanning Bear River
HAER ID-4
HAER ID,21-THAT.V,1-
9ph/5pg/1pc L

FREMONT COUNTY

ASHTON

Fall River Bridge
Spanning Fall River on CCC Camp Rd.
HAER ID-6
HAER ID,22-ASHT,1-
11ph/3pg/1pc L

ISLAND PARK

Buffalo Guard Station (Buffalo Ranger Station,Targhee National Forest; Island Park Ranger Station)
U. S. Hwy. 20/191 at Buffalo River
HABS ID-65
HABS ID,22-ILPA,2-
3ph/13pg/1pc L

Buffalo Guard Station,Garage (Building No. 1306-A,Targhee National Forest)
U. S. Hwy. 20/191 at Buffalo River
HABS ID-65-F
HABS ID,22-ILPA,2F-
1pg/1pc L

Buffalo Guard Station,Garage (Building No. 1308,Targhee National Forest)
U. S. Hwy. 20/191 at Buffalo River
HABS ID-65-C
HABS ID,22-ILPA,2C-
6ph/3pg/1pc L

Buffalo Guard Station,Office (Building No. 1201,Targhee National Forest)
U. S. Hwy. 20/191 at Buffalo River
HABS ID-65-A
HABS ID,22-ILPA,2A-
11ph/3pg/1pc L

Buffalo Guard Station,Pumphouse (Building No. 1306-A,Targhee National Forest)
U. S. Hwy. 20/191 at Buffalo River
HABS ID-65-E
HABS ID,22-ILPA,2E-
3ph/3pg/1pc L

Buffalo Guard Station,Residence (Building No. 1101,Targhee National Forest)
U. S. Hwy. 20/191 at Buffalo River
HABS ID-65-B
HABS ID,22-ILPA,2B-
12ph/3pg/1pc L

Buffalo Guard Station,Residence (Building No. 1102,Targhee National Forest)
U. S. Hwy. 20/191 at Buffalo River
HABS ID-65-D
HABS ID,22-ILPA,2D-
17ph/3pg/1pc L

Buffalo Ranger Station,Targhee National Forest; see Buffalo Guard Station

Building No. 1101,Targhee National Forest; see Buffalo Guard Station,Residence

Building No. 1102,Targhee National Forest; see Buffalo Guard Station,Residence

Building No. 1201,Targhee National Forest; see Buffalo Guard Station,Office

Building No. 1306-A,Targhee National Forest; see Buffalo Guard Station,Garage

Building No. 1306-A,Targhee National Forest; see Buffalo Guard Station,Pumphouse

Building No. 1308,Targhee National Forest; see Buffalo Guard Station,Garage

Island Park Ranger Station; see Buffalo Guard Station

ISLAND PARK VIC.

Burland Summer Home Complex (Capitolo-Rinetti Summer Home Complex)
E. side of State Hwy. 84
HABS ID-100
HABS DLC/PP-1992:ID-5
1ph/8pg/1pc/fr L

Burland Summer Home Complex,Guest Cabin (Capitolo-Rinetti Summer Home Complex,Guest Cabin)
HABS ID-100-B
HABS DLC/PP-1992:ID-5
4ph/11pg/1pc/fr L

Burland Summer Home Complex,Outbuilding (Capitolo-Rinetti Summer Home Complex,Outbuilding)
State Hwy. 84
HABS ID-100-C
HABS DLC/PP-1992:ID-5
1ph/6pg/1pc L

Burland Summer Home Complex,Summer House (Capitolo-Rinetti Summer Home Complex,Summer House)
State Hwy. 84
HABS ID-100-A
HABS DLC/PP-1992:IA-5
5ph/11pg/1pc/fr L

Capitolo-Rinetti Summer Home Complex; see Burland Summer Home Complex

Capitolo-Rinetti Summer Home Complex,Guest Cabin; see Burland Summer Home Complex,Guest Cabin

Capitolo-Rinetti Summer Home Complex,Outbuilding; see Burland Summer Home Complex,Outbuilding

Capitolo-Rinetti Summer Home Complex,Summer House; see Burland Summer Home Complex,Summer House

GEM COUNTY

MONTOUR

Adams,George,House (Thornton,John,House)
S. Broadway St. ,W side
HABS ID-44
HABS ID,23-MONT,1-
9ph/10pg/1pc/fr L

Amyx-Cox Barn; see Amyx,Fred,Barn

Amyx,Fred,Barn (Amyx-Cox Barn; Pole Barn)
N. Broadway,W. side
HABS ID-40
HABS ID,23-MONT,2-
6ph/6pg/1pc/fr L

Amyx,Lois,Barn; see Plowman Sawmill

Broadway Livery
N. Broadway St. Vic.
HABS ID-38
HABS ID,23-MONT,3-
1dr/2ph/12pg/1pc/fr L

Broadway Livery,Cox,Lloyd,House
N. Broadway St. Vic.
HABS ID-38-A
HABS ID,23-MONT,3A-
4dr/10ph/fr L

Broadway Livery,Cox,Lloyd,Livery Feed Barn
N. Broadway St. Vic.
HABS ID-38-B
HABS ID,23-MONT,3B-
3dr/9ph/fr L

Farmers' & Stockgrowers' Bank
Broadway & Main Sts.
HABS ID-39
HABS ID,23-MONT,4-
6ph/8pg/1pc/fr L

Freeman,Ray,Barn; see Scott,James,Barn

Hill,Dolores,House; see Idaho Northern Railroad,House

Idaho Northern Railroad,House
(Hill,Dolores,House)
Broadway & Main Sts.
HABS ID-45
HABS ID,23-MONT,5A-
7ph/9pg/1pc/fr L

Idaho Northern Railroad,Tool Shed
(Union Pacific Railroad,Tool Shed)
N. Broadway St. ,W side
HABS ID-46
HABS ID,23-MONT,5B-
4ph/6pg/1pc/fr L

Methodist Episcopal Church of Montour
S. Walnut St. ,east side of
HABS ID-36
HABS ID,23-MONT,6-
4dr/12ph/7pg/1pc/fr L

Montour School
S. Broadway St. ,east side of
HABS ID-37
HABS ID,23-MONT,7-
9dr/12ph/8pg/1pc/fr L

Plowman Sawmill (Amyx,Lois,Barn)
Payette River,N bank
HABS ID-47
HABS ID,23-MONT,8-
8ph/11pg/1pc/fr L

Pole Barn; see Amyx,Fred,Barn

Pugh,Harvey A. ,House
(Saxton,William,House)
N. Broadway St. ,E side
HABS ID-41
HABS ID,23-MONT,9-
7ph/16pg/1pc/fr L

Pugh,Harvey A. ,House,Elevator,Mill & Warehouse
(Saxton,William,House,Elevator,Mill & Warehouse)
N. Broadway St. ,E side
HABS ID-41-A
HABS ID,23-MONT,9A-
7ph/fr L

Saxton,William,House; see Pugh,Harvey A. ,House

Saxton,William,House,Elevator,Mill & Warehouse; see Pugh,Harvey A. ,House,Elevator,Mill & Warehouse

Scott,James,Barn (Freeman,Ray,Barn)
E. Main St. ,S side
HABS ID-43
HABS ID,23-MONT,10A-
4ph/7pg/1pc/fr L

Sheldrew,Victor,House
S. Broadway St. ,W side
HABS ID-42
HABS ID,23-MONT,11-
9ph/7pg/1pc/fr L

Thornton,John,House; see Adams,George,House

Union Pacific Railroad,Tool Shed; see Idaho Northern Railroad,Tool Shed

MONTOUR VIC.

Amos,Joe,Barn (York,Richard,Barn)
HABS ID-48
HABS ID,23-MONT.V,1A-
6ph/7pg/1pc/fr L

Mitchell,Marsh & Ireton Ranch
HABS ID-35
HABS ID,23-MONT.V,2-
2dr/2ph/22pg/3pc/fr L

Mitchell,Marsh & Ireton Ranch,Barn
HABS ID-35-C
HABS ID,23-MONT.V,2C-
2dr/22ph/fr L

Mitchell,Marsh & Ireton Ranch,Cellar
HABS ID-35-B
HABS ID,23-MONT.V,2B-
3dr/9ph/fr L

Mitchell,Marsh & Ireton Ranch,House
HABS ID-35-A
HABS ID,23-MONT.V,2A-
5dr/9ph/fr L

Montour,Idaho (site map)
HABS ID-49
HABS ID,23-MONT.V,3-
1dr/1pg L

York,Richard,Barn; see Amos,Joe,Barn

OLA VIC.

Building No. 1627,Boise National Forest; see Third Fork Guard Station,Log Storage Shed

Third Fork Guard Station,Log Storage Shed (Building No. 1627,Boise National Forest)
HABS ID-59
HABS ID,23-OLA.V,2A-
1dr/2ph/1pc/fr L

IDAHO COUNTY

ELK CITY VIC.

Nez Perce National Forest; see Red River Ranger Station

Nez Perce National Forest; see Red River Ranger Station,Cookhouse

Nez Perce National Forest; see Red River Ranger Station,Garage

Nez Perce National Forest; see Red River Ranger Station,Office

Nez Perce National Forest; see Red River Ranger Station,Woodshed

Red River Ranger Station (Nez Perce National Forest)
HABS ID-74
HABS DLC/PP-1992:ID-4
2pg/fr L

Red River Ranger Station,Cookhouse
(Nez Perce National Forest)
HABS ID-74-B
HABS DLC/PP-1992:ID-4
1pg L

Red River Ranger Station,Garage (Nez Perce National Forest)
HABS ID-74-C
HABS DLC/PP-1992:ID-4
1pg L

Red River Ranger Station,Office (Nez Perce National Forest)
HABS ID-74-A
HABS DLC/PP-1992:ID-4
1pg L

Red River Ranger Station,Woodshed
(Nez Perce National Forest)
HABS ID-74-D
HABS DLC/PP-1992:ID-4
1pg L

KAMIAH VIC.

Cowley,Henry T. ,House
(McBeth,Sue,Cabin)
State Rt. 9
HABS ID-2
HABS ID,25-KAMI.V,1-
3dr/fr L

McBeth,Sue,Cabin; see Cowley,Henry T. ,House

JEFFERSON COUNTY

HEISE VIC.

Bldg. No. 1205; see Heise Ranger Station Office

Heise Ranger Station Office (Bldg. No. 1205)
.25 mi. S. of Hsise-Kelly Canyon Rd.
Targhee N.F.
HABS ID-67
HABS ID,26-HEIS.V,2A-
12ph/4pg/1pc L

JEROME COUNTY

MURTAUGH VIC.

Murtaugh Bridge
HAER ID-1
HAER 10,27-MURT.V,1-
8ph/7pg/1pc L

TWIN FALLS VIC.

Milner Dam & Main Canal: Twin Falls Canal Company
On Snake River, 11 mi. W. of city of Burley, Idaho
HAER ID-15
HAER 1991(HAER):1
198ph/66pg/26pc L

KOOTENAI COUNTY

CATALDO VIC.

Sacred Heart Mission
Interstate 90 & Interchange 39
HABS ID-1
HABS ID,28-CATAL.V,1-
10dr/13ph/8pg L

COEUR D'ALENE

Kootenai County Courthouse
501 Government Way
HABS ID-102
HABS 1989(HABS):8
9ph/5pg/1pc L

LEMHI COUNTY

LEADORE VIC.

Birch Creek Charcoal Kilns; see Warren King Charcoal Kilns

Warren King Charcoal Kilns (Birch Creek Charcoal Kilns)
5 miles west of Idaho Hwy. 28,Targhee Nat. Forest
HAER ID-11
HAER 1991(HAER):1
11ph/20pg/2pc L

SALMON

Salmon City Hall & Library
200 Main St.
HABS ID-98
HABS 1989(HABS):8
5ph/9pg/1pc L

SALMON VIC.

(Feature 1); see Gold Dust Mine,Mill and Camp Complex,Cabin

(Feature 10); see Gold Dust Mine,Mill,and Camp Complex,Bunkhouse

(Feature 12); see Gold Dust Mine,Mill,and Camp Complex,Shed

(feature 15); see Gold Dust Mine,Mill,and Camp Complex,Log Building

(Feature 16); see Leesburg Townsite,Laundry-Springhouse-Storage

(Feature 17); see Gold Dust Mine,Mill,and Camp Complex,Tram

(Feature 18); see Gold Dust Mine,Mill,and Camp Complex,Mill

(Feature 19); see Gold Dust Mine,Mill,and Camp Complex,Hoist House

(Feature 20); see Leesburg Townsite,Butcher Shop-Workshop

(Feature 4); see Gold Dust Mine,Mill,and Camp Complex,Cabin

(Feature 9); see Leesburg Townsite,Butcher Shop-Freight Depot

Bonanza Hydraulic Mining Site
Swamp Gulch
HAER ID-23
HAER DLC/PP-1993:ID-3
24pg L

Bonanza Hydraulic Mining Site,Ditch
Swamp Gulch
HAER ID-23-B
HAER DLC/PP-1993:ID-3
1ph/1pc L

Bonanza Hydraulic Mining Site,Flume & Pressure Box
Swamp Gulch
HAER ID-23-C
HAER DLC/PP-1993:ID-3
2ph/1pc L

Bonanza Hydraulic Mining Site,Gate
Swamp Gulch
HAER ID-23-D
HAER DLC/PP-1993:ID-3
1ph/1pc L

Bonanza Hydraulic Mining Site,Main Storage Rsrvr.
Swamp Gulch
HAER ID-23-A
HAER DLC/PP-1993:ID-3
3ph/1pc L

Bonanza Hydraulic Mining Site,Placer Pit
Swamp Gulch
HAER ID-23-E
HAER DLC/PP-1993:ID-3
2ph/1pc L

Bonanza Hydraulic Mining Site,Sawmill Site
Swamp Gulch
HAER ID-23-G
HAER DLC/PP-1993:ID-3
2ph/1pc L

Bonanza Hydraulic Mining Site,Sluice Box
Swamp Gulch
HAER ID-23-F
HAER DLC/PP-1993:ID-3
3ph/1pc L

Gold Dust Mine,Mill & Camp Complex
Wards Gulch
HAER ID-24
HAER DLC/PP-1993:ID-3
7ph/28pg/1pc L

Gold Dust Mine,Mill and Camp Complex,Cabin ((Feature 1))
Wards Gulch
HAER ID-24-A
HAER DLC/PP-1993:ID-3
1ph/1pc L

Gold Dust Mine,Mill,and Camp Complex,Bunkhouse ((Feature 10))
Wards Gulch
HAER ID-24-C
HAER DLC/PP-1993:ID-3
1ph/1pc L

Gold Dust Mine,Mill,and Camp Complex,Cabin ((Feature 4))
Wards Gulch
HAER ID-24-B
HAER DLC/PP-1993:ID-3
1ph/1pc L

Gold Dust Mine,Mill,and Camp Complex,Hoist House ((Feature 19))
Wards Gulch
HAER ID-24-H
HAER DLC/PP-1993:ID-3
3ph/1pc L

Gold Dust Mine,Mill,and Camp Complex,Log Building ((feature 15))
Wards Gulch
HAER ID-24-E
HAER DLC/PP-1993:ID-3
1ph/1pc L

Gold Dust Mine,Mill,and Camp Complex,Mill ((Feature 18))
Wards Gulch
HAER ID-24-G
HAER DLC/PP-1993:ID-3
4ph/1pc L

Gold Dust Mine,Mill,and Camp Complex,Shed ((Feature 12))
Ward Gulch
HAER ID-24-D
HAER DLC/PP-1993:ID-3
1ph/1pc L

Gold Dust Mine,Mill,and Camp Complex,Tram ((Feature 17))
Wards Gulch
HAER ID-24-F
HAER DLC/PP-1993:ID-3
1ph/1pc L

Leesburg Mining District
HAER ID-25
25pg H

Leesburg Townsite
Napias Creek
HABS ID-106
HABS DLC/PP-1993:ID-3
1dr/13ph/43pg/2pc L

Leesburg Townsite,Barn (Feature 23)
Napias Creek
HABS ID-106-S
HABS DLC/PP-1993:ID-3
1ph/1pc L

Leesburg Townsite,Boarding House (Feature 18)
Napias Creek
HABS ID-106-O
HABS DLC/PP-1993:ID-3
2ph/1pc L

Leesburg Townsite,Butch Shop/Freight Depot (Leesburg Townsite,Feature 9)
Napias Creek
HABS ID-106-F
3ph/1pc H

Leesburg Townsite,Butcher Shop-Freight Depot ((Feature 9))
Napias Creek
HABS ID-106-F
HABS DLC/PP-1993:ID-3
3ph/1pc L

Leesburg Townsite,Butcher Shop-Workshop ((Feature 20))
Napias Creek
HABS ID-106-Q
HABS DLC/PP-1993:ID-3
4ph/1pc L

Leesburg Townsite,Cabin (Feature 13)
Napias Creek
HABS ID-106-J
HABS DLC/PP-1993:ID-3
3ph/1pc L

Leesburg Townsite,Cabin (Feature 14)
Napias Creek
HABS ID-106-K
HABS DLC/PP-1993:ID-3
4ph/1pc L

Leesburg Townsite,Cemetary
Napias Creek
HABS ID-106-V
HABS DLC/PP-1993:ID-3
6ph/1pc L

Leesburg Townsite,Chickenhouse (Feature 21)
Napias Creek
HABS ID-106-R
HABS DLC/PP-1993:ID-3
3ph/1pc L

Leesburg Townsite,Chinese Roasting Pit
Napias Creek
HABS ID-106-W
HABS DLC/PP-1993:ID-3
1ph/1pc L

Leesburg Townsite,Ditches
Napias Creek
HABS ID-106-X
HABS DLC/PP-1993:ID-3
5ph/1pc L

Leesburg Townsite,Dugout Ruin (Leesburg Townsite,Feature 5)
Napias Creek
HABS ID-106-D
1ph/1pc H

Leesburg Townsite,Dugout Ruin (Feature 5)
Napias Creek
HABS ID-106-D
HABS DLC/PP-1993:ID-3
1ph/1pc L

Leesburg Townsite,Feature 10; see Leesburg Townsite,House

Leesburg Townsite,Feature 11; see Leesburg Townsite,Root Cellar

Leesburg Townsite,Feature 5; see Leesburg Townsite,Dugout Ruin

Leesburg Townsite,Feature 9; see Leesburg Townsite,Butch Shop/Freight Depot

Leesburg Townsite,Hotel & Post Office (Feature 17)
Napias Creek
HABS ID-106-N
HABS DLC/PP-1993:ID-3
5ph/1pc L

Leesburg Townsite,House (Leesburg Townsite,Feature 10)
Napias Creek
HABS ID-106-G
4ph/1pc H

Leesburg Townsite,House (Feature 1)
Napias Creek
HABS ID-106-A
HABS DLC/PP-1993:ID-3
4ph/1pc L

Leesburg Townsite,House (Feature 10)
Napias Creek
HABS ID-106-G
HABS DLC/PP-1993:ID-3
4ph/1pc L

Leesburg Townsite,House (Feature 15)
Napias Creek
HABS ID-106-L
HABS DLC/PP-1993:ID-3
1ph/1pc L

Leesburg Townsite,Laundry-Springhouse-Storage ((Feature 16))
Napias Creek
HABS ID-106-M
HABS DLC/PP-1993:ID-3
2ph/1pc L

Leesburg Townsite,Privy (Feature 19)
Napias Creek
HABS ID-106-P
HABS DLC/PP-1993:ID-3
1ph/1pc L

Leesburg Townsite,Privy (Feature 8)
Napias Creek
HABS ID-106-E
HABS DLC/PP-1993:ID-3
1ph/1pc L

Leesburg Townsite,Root Cellar (Leesburg Townsite,Feature 11)
Napias Creek
HABS ID-106-H
2ph/1pc H

Leesburg Townsite,Root Cellar (Feature 11)
Napias Creek
HABS ID-106-H
HABS DLC/PP-1993:ID-3
2ph/1pc L

Leesburg Townsite,Root Cellar (Feature 24)
Napias Creek
HABS ID-106-T
HABS DLC/PP-1993:ID-3
2ph/1pc L

Leesburg Townsite,Ruin (Feature 25)
Napias Creek
HABS ID-106-U
HABS DLC/PP-1993:ID-3
1ph/1pc L

Leesburg Townsite,Schoolhouse (Feature 12)
Napias Creek
HABS ID-106-I
HABS DLC/PP-1993:ID-3
5ph/1pc L

Leesburg Townsite,Stable (Feature 2)
Napias Creek
HABS ID-106-B
HABS DLC/PP-1993:ID-3
3ph/1pc L

Leesburg Townsite,Stage Office (Feature 3)
Napias Creek
HABS ID-106-C
HABS DLC/P-1993:ID-3
2ph/1pc L

MINIDOKA COUNTY

PAUL

Conner's Cafe; see 8 East Idaho St. (Commercial Bldg.)

1 East Idaho St. (Commercial Bldg.)
(Feeders Grain Bldg.)
HABS ID-79
HABS 1989(HABS):8
8ph/2pg/1pc L

8 East Idaho St. (Commercial Bldg.)
(Mr. Lucky's; Conner's Cafe)
HABS ID-80
HABS 1989(HABS):8
7ph/2pg/1pc L

Feeders Grain Bldg.; see 1 East Idaho St. (Commercial Bldg.)

Mr. Lucky's; see 8 East Idaho St. (Commercial Bldg.)

NEZ PERCE COUNTY

SPALDING

Agency Employee House (Crawford House; Nez Perce National Historical Park)
HABS ID-34
HABS ID,35-SPALD,2-
8ph/1pg/1pc L

Crawford House; see Agency Employee House

Nez Perce Agency-Agency Log Building (Nez Perce National Historical Park)
S. bank of Clearwater River
HABS ID-76
3ph/1pg/1pc L

Nez Perce Agency-Agent's Residence (Nez Perce National Historical Park)
W. of Bridge spanning Lapwai Creek,N. of railroad
HABS ID-77
2ph/1pg/1pc L

Nez Perce National Historical Park; see Agency Employee House

Nez Perce National Historical Park; see Nez Perce Agency-Agency Log Building

Nez Perce National Historical Park; see Nez Perce Agency-Agent's Residence

Nez Perce National Historical Park; see Poor Coyote's Cabin

Nez Perce National Historical Park; see Watson's Store

Poor Coyote's Cabin (Nez Perce National Historical Park)
Beneath U.S. Hwy. 95
HABS ID-75
5ph/5pg/1pc L

Watson's Store (Nez Perce National Historical Park)
S. of railroad,W. of Lapwai Creek
HABS ID-78
5ph/1pg/1pc L

OWYHEE COUNTY

BRUNEAU VALLEY VIC.

Bridge No. 993370; see Hot Springs Bridge

Hot Springs Bridge (Bridge No. 993370)
Spanning Bruneau River,Hot Springs Rd.
HAER ID-12
HAER ID,37-BRUN.V,1-
16ph/8pg/2pc L

KUNA VIC.

Swan Falls Dam
Snake River
HAER ID-20
HAER 1991(HAER):1
110ph/72pg/12pc/fr L

Swan Falls Dam,A-Frame Crane Gantry
Snake River
HAER ID-20
HAER 1991(HAER):1
2ph/1pc L

Swan Falls Dam,Blacksmith Shop and Annex
Snake River
HAER ID-20-A
HAER 1991(HAER):1
15ph/2pc L

Swan Falls Dam,Building No. 133; see Swan Falls Dam,Carpenter Shop

Swan Falls Dam,Building No. 134; see Swan Falls Dam,Wood Shop

Swan Falls Dam,Building No. 135; see Swan Falls Dam,Material Shed

Swan Falls Dam,Carpenter Shop (Swan Falls Dam,Building No. 133)
Snake River
HAER ID-20-F
HAER 1991(HAER):1
4ph/1pc L

Swan Falls Dam,Garage
Snake River
HAER ID-20-I
HAER 1991(HAER):1
2ph/1pc L

Swan Falls Dam,House
Snake River
HAER ID-20-J
HAER 1991(HAER):1
2ph/1pc L

Swan Falls Dam,Material Shed (Swan Falls Dam,Building No. 135)
Snake River
HAER ID-20-C
HAER 1991(HAER):1
3ph/1pc L

Swan Falls Dam,Raw Stock Storage Crib
Snake River
HAER ID-20-E
HAER 1991(HAER):1
1ph/1pc L

Swan Falls Dam,Restroom
Snake River
HAER ID-20-B
HAER 1991(HAER):1
1ph/1pc L

Swan Falls Dam,Storage Shed A
Snake River
HAER ID-20-D
HAER 1991(HAER):1
2ph/1pc L

Swan Falls Dam,Storage Shed B
Snake River
HAER ID-20-H
HAER 1991(HAER):1
2ph/1pc L

Swan Falls Dam,Wood Shop (Swan Falls Dam,Building No. 134)
Snake River
HAER ID-20-G
HAER 1991(HAER):1
4ph/1pc L

POWER COUNTY

AMERICAN FALLS

American Falls P. L. & W. Co. ,Island Power Plant
Snake River, below American Falls Dam
HAER ID-2
HAER ID,39-AMFA,1-
3dr/55ph/4pg/3pc/fr L

SHOSHONE COUNTY

AVERY

Avery Ranger Station
Saint Joe National Forest
HABS ID-16
HABS ID,40-AVERY,1-
13pg/fr L

WALLACE

Beiswinger,Carl and Annie,House
22 Westside
HABS ID-95
HABS 1991(HABS):14
3ph/8pg/1pc L

Beiswinger,Carl,House
18 Westside
HABS ID-94
HABS 1991(HABS):14
3ph/7pg/1pc L

Cornelius,George,House; see Olson,Henry and Olga,House

6 Hemlock (House)
6 Hemlock
HABS ID-90
HABS 1991(HABS):14
3ph/8pg/1pc L

8 Hemlock (House)
8 Hemlock
HABS ID-91
HABS 1991(HABS):14
3ph/7pg/1pc L

9 Hemlock (House)
9 Hemlock
HABS ID-85
HABS 1991(HABS):14
4ph/6pg/1pc L

2 Hemlock House)
2 Hemlock
HABS ID-89
HABS 1991(HABS):14
3ph/7pg/1pc L

Johnson,Leonard A.,House
8 Spruce St.
HABS ID-92
HABS 1991(HABS):14
4ph/8pg/1pc L

Olson,Henry and Olga,House
(Cornelius,George,House)
71 Tamarack
HABS ID-87
HABS 1991(HABS):14
5ph/7pg/1pc L

Reich,Leo,E.,House
1 Hemlock
HABS ID-84
HABS 1991(HABS):14
4ph/6pg/1pc L

61 River Street (House)
61 River St.
HABS ID-93
HABS 1991(HABS):14
4ph/8pg/1pc L

Smith,Henry,House
12 Westside
HABS ID-82
HABS 1991(HABS):14
3ph/6pg/1pc L

5 Spruce Street (House)
5 Spruce Street
HABS ID-86
HABS 1991(HABS):14
3ph/6pg/1pc L

Vallard,Diserie,House
24 Westside
HABS ID-96
HABS 1991(HABS):14
3ph/8pg/1pc L

11 Westside (House)
11 Westside
HABS ID-88
HABS 1991(HABS):14
3ph/7pg/1pc L

15 Westside (House)
15 Westside
HABS ID-83
HABS 1991(HABS):14
3ph/6pg/1pc L

28 Westside (House)
28 Westside
HABS ID-97
HABS 1991(HABS):14
4ph/6pg/1pc L

7 Westside (House)
7 Westside
HABS ID-81
HABS 1991(HABS):14
4ph/8pg/1pc L

TWIN FALLS COUNTY

TWIN FALLS

Perrine Bridge; see Twin Falls-Jerome Bridge

Rock Creek Bridge (Singing Bridge)
HAER ID-21
12ph/6pg/1pc H

Singing Bridge; see Rock Creek Bridge

Twin Falls-Jerome Bridge (Perrine Bridge)
U. S. Hwy. 93 Spanning Snake River
HAER ID-3
HAER ID,42-TWIFA,1-
39ph/10pg/2pc L

VALLEY COUNTY

CASCADE VIC.

Building No. 1103,Boise National Forest; see Crawford Guard Station,Frame Barracks

Building No. 2172,Boise National Forest; see Crawford Guard Station,Barn

Crawford Guard Station,Barn
(Building No. 2172,Boise National Forest)
HABS ID-53
HABS ID,43-CASC.V,2A-
3dr/11ph/1pc/fr L

Crawford Guard Station,Frame Barracks (Building No. 1103,Boise National Forest)
HABS ID-54
HABS ID,43-CASC.V,2B-
1dr/2ph/1pc/fr L

SMITHS FERRY VIC.

Building No. 1132,Boise National Forest; see High Valley Work Station,Small Bungalow

Building No. 1408,Boise National Forest; see High Valley Work Station,Log Warehouse

High Valley Work Station,Log Warehouse (Building No. 1408,Boise National Forest)
HABS ID-61
HABS ID,43-SMIF.V,2B-
1dr/2ph/1pc/fr L

High Valley Work Station,Small Bungalow (Building No. 1132,Boise National Forest)
HABS ID-60
HABS ID,43-SMIF.V,2A-
1dr/7ph/1pc/fr L

WARM LAKE VIC.

Building No. 1139,Boise National Forest; see Landmark Ranger Station,Ranger House

Landmark Ranger Station,Ranger House (Building No. 1139,Boise National Forest)
HABS ID-64
HABS ID,43-WALAK.V,2A-
1dr/7ph/1pc/fr L

WASHINGTON COUNTY

CAMBRIDGE VIC.

Burton Road Bridge
Spanning Little Weiser River
HAER ID-8
HAER ID,44-CAMB.V,1-
18ph/5pg/2pc L

MIDVALE

Midvale Bridge
Bridge St. Spanning Weiser River
HAER ID-14
HAER 1991(HAER):1
26ph/6pg/1pc L

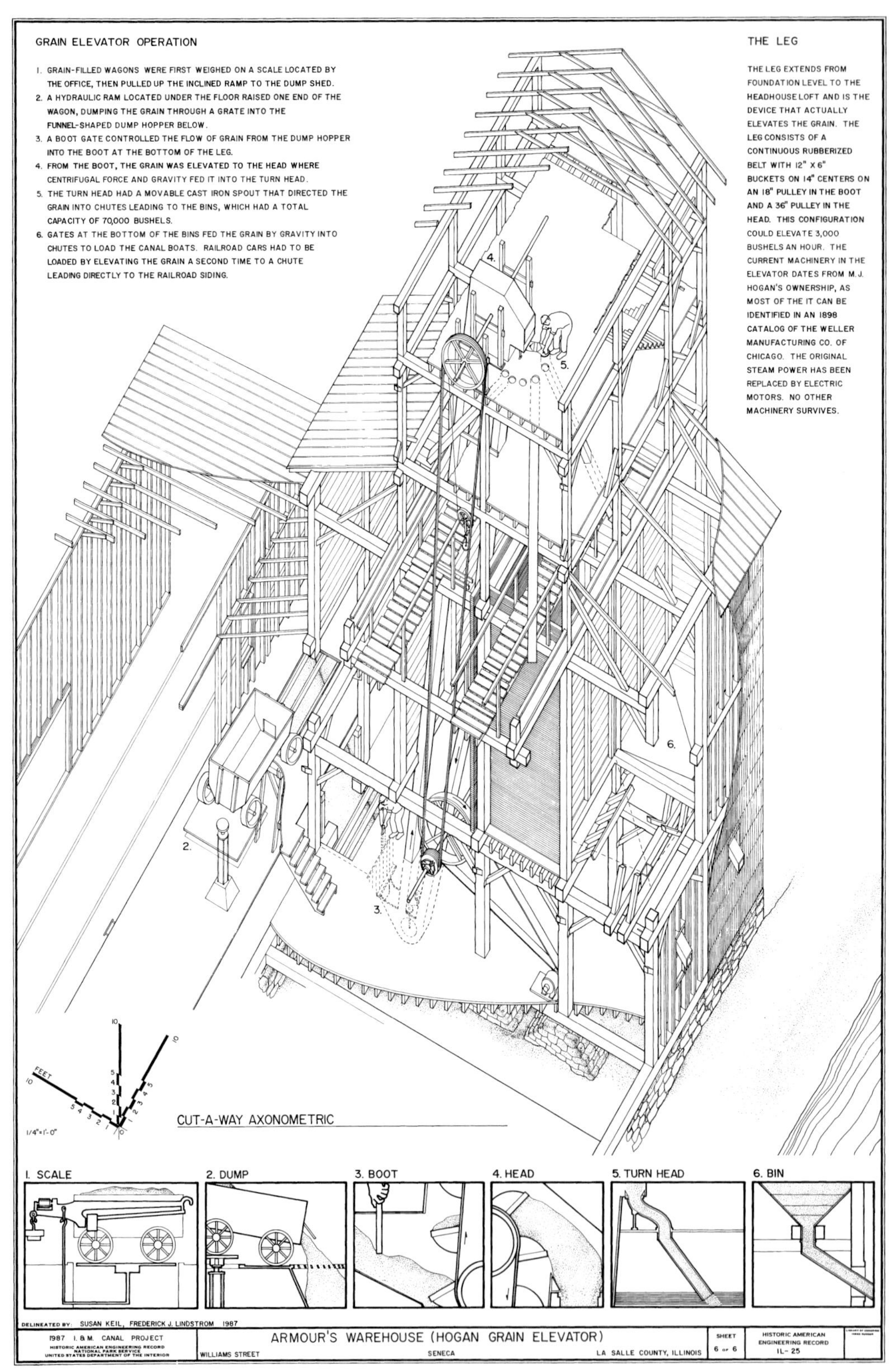

Armour's Warehouse (Hogan Grain Elevator), Seneca, LaSalle County, Illinois. Cut-away axonometric measured drawing delineated by Susan Keil, Frederick J. Lindstrom, 1987 (HAER IL-25, sheet 6 of 6; accession number 1992(HAER):IL-2).

Illinois

CHICAGO

(Burlington Northern)/Union Stockyards & Transit C; see Penn.(Conrail)/ Chicago & Northern Pacific

"Eight Track" Bascule Bridges; see Penn.(Conrail)/ Chicago & Northern Pacific

I & M Canal Nat'l Heritage Corridor; see Penn.(Conrail)/ Chicago & Northern Pacific

Penn.(Conrail)/ Chicago & Northern Pacific ((Burlington Northern)/Union Stockyards & Transit C "Eight Track" Bascule Bridges; I & M Canal Nat'l Heritage Corridor)
HAER IL-99
H

ADAMS COUNTY

FALL CREEK VIC.

Fall Creek Bridge Spanning Fall Creek Gorge
Fall Creek Station
HABS IL-267
HABS ILL,1-FALC.V,1-
1dr/2ph/2pg L

PAYSON

Congregational Church
Park Drive & State Rt. 96
HABS IL-265
HABS ILL,1-PAYSO,1-
3dr/3ph/3pg L

Congregational Church Parsonage
HABS IL-266
HABS ILL.1-PAYSO,2
3dr/5ph L

QUINCY

Chicago,Burlington & Quincy RR:Freight Office
Second & Broadway Sts.
HAER IL-10
HAER ILL,1-QUI,3A-
10ph/3pg/1pc L

Francis Hall (Quincy College)
1800 College Ave.
HABS IL-1181
29ph/16pg/2pc H

Knoyer Farmhouse
HABS IL-246
HABS ILL,1-QUI,1-
3ph/2pc/fr L

Miss. River 9-Ft. Channel Proj.,Lock & Dam No. 21
Upper Mississippi River
HAER IL-30
HAER 1991(HAER):14
27ph/15pg/2pc L

Quincy College; see Francis Hall

Washington Park (Buildings)
Maine,Fourth,Hampshire, & Fifth Sts.
HABS IL-1122
HABS ILL,1-QUI,4-
18dr/fr L

Woods,Governor John,House
425 S. Twelfth St.
HABS IL-188
HABS ILL,1-QUI,2-
6ph/1pg/1pc/fr L

ALEXANDER COUNTY

CAIRO

Langan,Peter T. ,House
HABS IL-218
HABS ILL,2-CARO,1-
5ph/2pg/fr L

Store Building
509 Commercial Ave.
HABS IL-25-21
HABS ILL,2-CARO,2-
3dr/1ph/2pg/fr L

THEBES

Thebes Courthouse
HABS IL-25-17
HABS ILL,2-THEB,1-
7dr/2ph/4pg/fr L

BOONE COUNTY

BELVIDERE

Dunton House
807 McKinley Ave.
HABS IL-171
HABS ILL,4-BELV,2-
1dr/12ph/1pg/fr L

Hildrup,Jesse,House
1215 N. State St.
HABS IL-160
HABS ILL,4-BELV,1-
2dr/9ph/2pg/fr L

Palmer House
327 W. Lincoln Ave.
HABS IL-185
HABS ILL,4-BELV,4-
8ph/1pc/fr L

Wheeler House
222 W. Locust St.
HABS IL-172
HABS ILL,4-BELV,3-
1dr/6ph/1pg/fr L

BELVIDERE VIC.

Newton Farmhouse
Belvidere-Kirkland Rd.
HABS IL-159
HABS ILL,4- ,1-
1dr/8ph/1pg/fr L

CHERRY VALLEY

Hale House
State Rt. 5
HABS IL-161
HABS ILL,4-CHVA.V,1-
4ph/1pc/fr L

BROWN COUNTY

ELGIN

Hinsdell,A. B. ,House
443 E. Chicago St.
HABS IL-26-10
HABS ILL,45-ELG,1-
4dr/3ph/2pg/fr L

BUREAU COUNTY

DEPUE

Hassler Tavern
U. S. Rt. 6
HABS IL-142
HABS ILL,6-DEPU,V.1-
2dr/3ph/3pg/fr L

LAMOILLE VIC.

Smith Farmhouse
U. S. Rt. 34
HABS IL-146
HABS ILL,6-LAMO.V,1-
1dr/5ph/2pg/fr L

CARROLL COUNTY

MT. CARROLL

Main & Market Streets (Structures)
Courthouse Sq.,Main,Market,Center,Clay & Broadway
HABS IL-1148
HABS ILL,8-MTCAR,1-
15dr/fr L

SAVANNA

Savanna Army Depot
HAER IL-19
HAER ILL,8-SAV.V,1-
53pg/fr L

CASS COUNTY

BEARDSTOWN

Billings,Horace,House
Lafayette & Third Sts.
HABS IL-26-28
HABS ILL,9-BEATO,1-
2dr/3ph/2pg/fr L

Cass County Courthouse,Old (City Hall)
HABS IL-284
HABS ILL,9-BEATO,3-
5ph/4pg/1pc L

City Hall; see Cass County Courthouse,Old

Commercial Buildings
HABS IL-285
HABS ILL,9-BEATO,4-
1ph/1pg/1pc/fr L

Sturtevant,Christopher C. ,House
301 Washington St.
HABS IL-26-29
HABS ILL,9-BEATO,2-
6dr/10ph/1pg/1pc/fr L

VIRGINIA VIC.

Allandale (Cunningham,Andrew,Farm)
HABS IL-261
HABS ILL,9-VIRG.V,1-
4dr/5ph/4pg L

Cunningham,Andrew,Farm; see Allandale

CHAMPAIGN COUNTY

HOMER VIC.

Covered Wooden Bridge
Spanning Salt Fork River,State Rt. 49
HABS IL-25-19
HABS ILL,10-HOM.V,1-
3dr/1ph/5pg/fr L

PENFIELD

Penfield Elevators
Front St.
HABS IL-1133
HABS ILL,10-PEN,1-
1dr/fr L

Penfield Elevators,East Elevator
Front St.
HABS IL-1133-B
HABS ILL,10-PEN,1B-
8dr/fr L

Penfield Elevators,West Penfield
Front St.
HABS IL-1133-A
HABS ILL,10-PEN,1A-
4dr/fr L

RANTOUL VIC.

Chanute Air Force Base; see Red Cross Complex: Main Building (Building 391)

Red Cross Complex: Main Building (Building 391) (Chanute Air Force Base)
SW corner Borman & Eagle Sts.
HABS IL-1161)
10dr H

URBANA VIC.

Blackberry School
1725 North & 1700 East (country rds.)
HABS IL-1162
HABS DLC/PP-1993:IL-1
4dr/fr L

Phillips Farmhouse
1725 North & 1700 East (country rds.)
HABS IL-1163
HABS DLC/PP-1993:IL-1
4dr/fr L

CLINTON COUNTY

CARLYLE

Suspension Bridge
Spanning Kaskaskia River
HABS IL-225
HABS ILL,14-CARL,1-
2dr/3ph/3pg/fr L

COLES COUNTY

OAKLAND

Public Square (Buildings)
N. Walnut,W. Montgomery,N. Pike, & W. Main Sts.
HABS IL-252
HABS ILL,15-OAK,1-
20dr/fr L

COOK COUNTY

Chicago River Bascule Bridge, Monroe St. (I & M Canal Nat'l Heritage Corridor)
HAER IL-53
HAER ILL,81-ROCIL,3/1-
H

Chicago River Bascule Bridge, Wabash Ave. (I & M Canal Nat'l Heritage Corridor)
HAER IL-48
HAER ILL,81-ROCIL,3/1-
H

I & M Canal Nat'l Heritage Corridor; see Chicago River Bascule Bridge, Monroe St.

I & M Canal Nat'l Heritage Corridor; see Chicago River Bascule Bridge, Wabash Ave.

BLUE ISLAND VIC.

Calumet-Sag Channel Bridges (Ill. & Mich. Canal National Heritage Corridor)
Caulmet-Sag Channel
HAER IL-121
7ph H

Ill. & Mich. Canal National Heritage Corridor; see Calumet-Sag Channel Bridges

BROOKFIELD

Brookfield Kindergarten
3601 Forest Ave.
HABS IL-1087
HABS ILL,16-BROOK,1-
5dr/4ph/6pg L

CHICAGO

Abbott,Robert S. ,House
4742 Martin Luther King Dr.
HABS IL-1092
HABS ILL,16-CHIG,97-
1ph/1pc L

Aiken Institute; see Second Baptist Church

Aldine Square (De Sable Square)
Vincennes Ave.
HABS IL-153
HABS ILL,16-CHIG,5-
1dr/11ph/2pg/fr L

Aldine Square,Smith House (Enterprise Institute)
HABS IL-153-A
HABS ILL,16-CHIG,5A-
4ph L

American College of Surgeons; see Nickerson,Samuel M. ,House

Armco-Ferro-Mayflower House (Century of Progress Architectural District)
(See IN,PORTER CO.,BEVERLY SHORES for documentn.)
HABS IN-244
L

AT & SF RR: Grain Elevator (I & M Canal Nat'l Heritage Corridor)
On AT & SF slip
HAER IL-75
H

Atchison,Topeka & Santa Fe RR Bridge; see Chicago & Alton (Illinois Central Gulf) RR Bridge

Atchison,Topeka,& Sant Fe RR Bridge (I & M Canal Nat'l Heritage Corridor)
Across Sanitary & Ship Canal,E. of Harlem Ave.
HAER IL-39
HAER ILL,81-ROCIL,3/1-
15ph H

Documentation: **ct** color transparencies **dr** measured drawings **fr** field records
pc photograph captions **pg** pages of text **ph** photographs

Auditorium Annex (Pick-Congress Hotel)
504 S. Michigan Ave.
HABS IL-1012
HABS ILL,16-CHIG,39A-
4ph/3pg L

Auditorium Building (Roosevelt University)
430 S. Michigan Ave.
HABS IL-1007
HABS ILL,16-CHIG,39-
61dr/111ph/86pg/9pc/fr L

Ayer Building (McClurg Building; Crown Building)
218 S. Wabash Ave.
HABS IL-1025
HABS ILL,16-CHIG,27-
2ph/3pg L

Ayer,Edward E. ,House
2 E. Banks St.
HABS IL-1035
HABS ILL,16-CHIG,37-
5ph/10pg L

Bach,Emil,House
7415 N. Sheridan Rd.
HABS IL-1088
HABS ILL,16-CHIG,83-
6dr/3ph/7pg L

Baltimore & Ohio RR,Chicago Terminal RR Bascule Br (I & M Canal Nat'l Heritage Corridor)
HAER IL-67
H

Bay State Building & Kranz Building; see Springer Block

Belt RR of Chicago Bridge; see Chicago & Western Indiana RR Bridge

Boulevard Recording Studios,Inc.; see Chicago Historical Society

Cable Building
57 E. Jackson Blvd.
HABS IL-1003
HABS ILL,16-CHIG,8-
5dr/5pg L

Cahokia Courthouse
Jackson Park (moved from IL CAHOKIA)
HABS IL-26-31-A
HABS ILL,16-CHIG,3-
1dr/9ph/4pg/1pc L

Carpenter,Judge,House(Cast Iron Balcony Railing); see Chicago Ironwork

Carson,Pirie,Scott & Company Department Store; see Schlesinger & Mayer Department Store

Casey Building
173-177 N. Wells St.
HABS IL-1038
HABS ILL,16-CHIG,41-
2ph/5pg L

Cast Iron Fence; see Chicago Ironwork

Cast Iron Fence & Gate; see Chicago Ironwork

Cast Iron Fence & Railing; see Chicago Ironwork

Cast Iron Fence Railing; see Chicago Ironwork

Cast Iron Gate; see Chicago Ironwork

Cast Iron Gate; see DeKoven,John House

Cast Iron Gate & Fence; see Chicago Ironwork

Cast Iron Gatepost & Fence; see Chicago Ironwork

Cast Iron House & Gate; see Chicago Ironwork

Cast Iron Porch Railing & Fence; see Chicago Ironwork

Cast Iron Stair Railing; see Chicago Ironwork

Cast Iron Stair Railing; see 1021 S. Wabash Avenue

Cast Iron Stair Railing & Fence; see Chicago Ironwork

Central Cold Storage Warehouse; see Sibley,Hiram,Warehouse

Century of Preogress Architectural District; see Cypress Log Cabin,Cabin

Century of Progress Architectural District; see Armco-Ferro-Mayflower House

Century of Progress Architectural District; see Cypress Log Cabin,Guest House

Century of Progress Architectural District; see Florida Tropical House

Century of Progress Architectural District; see Wieboldt-Rostone House

Cermak Rd.: Chicago River Bridge (I & M Canal Nat'l Heritage Corridor)
HAER IL-50
HAER ILL,81-ROCIL,3/1-
33ph H

Chapin & Gore Building
63 E. Adams St.
HABS IL-1039
HABS ILL,16-CHIG,42-
3dr/3ph/1pc L

Charnley,James,House
1365 N. Astor St.
HABS IL-1009
HABS ILL,16-CHIG,12-
7dr/6ph/6pg L

Chicago & Alton (Illinois Central Gulf) RR Bridge (Chicago,Madison & Northern RR Bridge; Atchison,Topeka & Santa Fe RR Bridge; I & M Canal Nat'l Heritage Corridor)
HAER IL-104
H

Chicago & West. Indiana RR:Dearborn Sta. Trainshed (Polk Street Station)
47 W. Polk St.
HAER IL-6
HAER ILL,16-CHIG,104A-
14ph/2pg/1pc L

Chicago & Western Indiana RR Bridge (Belt RR of Chicago Bridge; I & M Canal Nat'l Heritage Corridor)
HAER IL-79
H

Chicago Board of Health; see Chicago Criminal Courts Building

Chicago City Hall (City Hall-County Building)
121 N. LaSalle St.
HABS IL-1128
HABS ILL,16-CHIG,94-
58ph/32pg/4pc L

Chicago Criminal Courts Building (Chicago Board of Health)
54 W. Hubbard St.
HABS IL-1036
HABS ILL,16-CHIG,38-
3ph/5pg L

Chicago Historical Society (Boulevard Recording Studios,Inc.)
632 N. Dearborn St.
HABS IL-1010
HABS ILL,16-CHIG,13-
2ph/4pg L

Chicago Home for Girls; see Pontiac Building

Chicago Ironwork
HABS IL-155
HABS ILL,16-CHIG,7-
2dr/2pg/fr L

Chicago Ironwork (Carpenter,Judge,House(Cast Iron Balcony Railing))
945 N. Dearborn St.
HABS IL-155-B
HABS ILL,16-CHIG,7B2-
3ph L

Chicago Ironwork (Cast Iron Fence)
613 N. Wabash Ave.
HABS IL-155-S
HABS ILL,16-CHIG,7E1-
1ph L

Chicago Ironwork (Cast Iron Fence)
650 Rush St.
HABS IL-155-N
HABS ILL,16-CHIG,7D1-
1ph L

Chicago Ironwork (Cast Iron Fence)
711 N. Rush St.
HABS IL-155-Q
HABS ILL,16-CHIG,7D4-
1ph L

Chicago Ironwork (Cast Iron Fence)
720 N. Rush St.
HABS IL-155-R
HABS ILL,16-CHIG,7D5-
1ph L

Chicago Ironwork (Cast Iron Fence & Gate)
Huron & Wabash Aves.
HABS IL-155-L
HABS ILL,16-CHIG,7E3-
1ph L

Chicago Ironwork (Cast Iron Fence & Gate)
701 Rush St.
HABS IL-155-P
HABS ILL,16-CHIG,7D3-
1ph L

Chicago Ironwork (Cast Iron Fence & Railing)
1133 W. Washington Blvd.
HABS IL-155-U
HABS ILL,16-CHIG,7A3-
1ph L

Chicago Ironwork (Cast Iron Fence Railing)
1000 N. Dearborn St.
HABS IL-155-C
HABS ILL,16-CHIG,7B3-
1ph L

Chicago Ironwork (Cast Iron Fence Railing)
1153 N. Dearborn St.
HABS IL-155-E
HABS ILL,16-CHIG,7B5-
1ph L

Chicago Ironwork (Cast Iron Gate)
1362 N. Dearborn St.
HABS IL-155-K
HABS ILL,16-CHIG,7B11-
1ph L

Chicago Ironwork (Cast Iron Gate & Fence)
1210 N. Dearborn St.
HABS IL-155-H
HABS ILL,L6-CHIG,7B8-
2ph L

Chicago Ironwork (Cast Iron Gate & Fence)
1339 N. Dearborn St.
HABS IL-155-J
HABS ILL,16-CHIG,7B10-
1ph L

Chicago Ironwork (Cast Iron Gate & Fence)
675 Rush St.
HABS IL-155-O
HABS ILL,16-CHIG,7D2-
2ph L

Chicago Ironwork (Cast Iron Gatepost & Fence)
1156 N. Dearborn St.
HABS IL-155-F
HABS ILL,16-CHIG,7B6-
1ph L

Chicago Ironwork (Cast Iron House & Gate; Strong,William M. ,Estate)
1352 W. Washington Blvd.
HABS IL-155-W
HABS ILL,16-CHIG,7A1-
5ph/fr L

Chicago Ironwork (Cast Iron Porch Railing & Fence)
1237 N. Dearborn St.
HABS IL-155-I
HABS ILL,16-CHIG,7B9-
5ph L

Chicago Ironwork (Cast Iron Stair Railing)
1149 W. Washington Blvd.
HABS IL-155-V
HABS ILL,16-CHIG,7A2-
1ph L

Chicago Ironwork (Cast Iron Stair Railing)
66 W. Oak St.
HABS IL-155-M
HABS ILL,16-CHIG,7C-
1ph L

Chicago Ironwork (Cast Iron Stair Railing)
923 N. Dearborn St.
HABS IL-155-A
HABS ILL,16-CHIG,7B1-
1ph L

Chicago Ironwork (Cast Iron Stair Railing & Fence)
1159 N. Dearborn St.
HABS IL-155-G
HABS ILL,16-CHIG,7B7-
1ph L

Chicago Ironwork; see DeKoven,John House

Chicago Ironwork Survey; see 1021 S. Wabash Avenue

Chicago Midway Airport,South Terminal; see Midway Airport,South Terminal

Chicago Public Library
Michigan,Washington,Randolph Sts. & N. Garland Ct.
HABS IL-1011
HABS ILL,16-CHIG,14-
5ph/5pg L

Chicago River Bascule Bridge, Adams St.; see W. Adams St.: Chicago River Bridge

Chicago River Bascule Bridge, Clark St. (I & M Canal Nat'l Heritage Corridor)
HAER IL-64
HAER ILL,81-ROCIL,3/1-
H

Chicago River Bascule Bridge, Franklin St. (I & M Canal Nat'l Heritage Corridor)
HAER IL-65
H

Chicago River Bascule Bridge, Jackson Blvd.
HAER IL-55
HAER ILL,81-ROCIL,3/1-
H

Chicago River Bascule Bridge, LaSalle St. (I & M Canal Nat'l Heritage Corridor)
HAER IL-66
H

Chicago River Bascule Bridge, Michigan Ave. (I & M Canal Nat'l Heritage Corridor)
HAER IL-37
HAER ILL,81-ROCIL,3/1-
H

Chicago River Bascule Bridge, Outer Drive (I & M Canal Nat'l Heritage Corridor)
HAER IL-54
HAER ILL,81-ROCIL,3/1-
H

Chicago River Bascule Bridge, Wells St. (I & M Nat'l Heritage Corridor)
HAER IL-52
HAER ILL,81-ROCIL,3/1-
H

Chicago River Bascule Bridge,Michigan Ave. (I & M Canal Nat'l Heritage Corridor)
HAER IL-37
H

Chicago River Bascule Bridge,Washington St. Bridge (I & M Canal Nat'l Heritage Corridor)
Across Chicago R. & Chicago,Milwaukee,& St.Paul RR
HAER IL-38
HAER ILL,81-ROCIL,3/1-
H

Chicago School of Architecture Foundation; see Glessner,John J. ,House

Chicago Stock Exchange Building
30 N. LaSalle St.
HABS IL-1034
HABS ILL,16-CHIG,36-
9dr/13ph/9pg/2pc/fr L

Chicago Water Tower
800 N. Michigan Ave.
HABS IL-1041
HABS ILL,16-CHIG,43-
1ph/7pg L

Chicago,Madison & Northern RR Bridge; see Chicago & Alton (Illinois Central Gulf) RR Bridge

City Club of Chicago
(Marshall,John,Law School)
315 S. Plymouth Ct.
HABS IL-1080
HABS ILL,16-CHIG,78-
2ph/5pg L

City Hall-County Building; see Chicago City Hall

City Hall-County Building,Sixth
LaSalle,Washington,Clark & Randolph Sts.
HABS IL-1127
HABS ILL,16-CHIG,93-
1ph/1pc L

Documentation: **ct** color transparencies **dr** measured drawings **fr** field records **pc** photograph captions **pg** pages of text **ph** photographs

City Hall,Third
Randolph St.
HABS IL-1126
HABS ILL,16-CHIG,92-
1ph/1pc L

Clarke,Henry,House
(Clarke,Widow,House)
4526 S. Wabash Ave. (moved from Michigan Ave.)
HABS IL-135
HABS ILL,16-CHIG,4-
6dr/4ph/3pg/1pc/fr L

Clarke,Widow,House; see Clarke,Henry,House

Cleveland,Grover,Elementary School
3850 N. Albany St.
HABS IL-1079
HABS ILL,16-CHIG,77-
2ph/3pg L

Coleman Funeral Home; see Krause Music Store

Columbian Exposition Store Buildings
E. Fifty-Seventh Blvd. & Stony Island Ave.
HABS IL-1062
HABS ILL,16-CHIG,63A-
1ph/6pg L

Commonwealth Edison Co.,Fisk St. Generating Statio; see Commonwealth Elec.Co.,Fisk St. Elec.Generating Sta

Commonwealth Elec.Co.,Fisk St. Elec.Generating Sta (Commonwealth Edison Co.,Fisk St. Generating Statio I & M Canal National Heritage Corridor)
1111 W. Cermak Ave.
HAER IL-105
20ph/5pg/2pc L

Commonwlth Edison Co.,Crawford Elec. Genratng Sta. (I & M Canal National Heritage Corridor)
3501 S. Pulaski Rd.
HAER IL-114
12ph/3pg/1pc L

Crown Building; see Ayer Building

Cypress Log Cabin,Cabin (Century of Preogress Architectural District)
(See IN,PORTER CO.,BEVERLY SHORES for documentn.)
HABS IN-241-A
L

Cypress Log Cabin,Guest House (Century of Progress Architectural District)
(See IN,PORTER CO.,BEVERLY SHORES for documentn.)
HABS IN-241-B
L

De Sable Square; see Aldine Square

DeKoven,John House (Chicago Ironwork; Cast Iron Gate)
1150 N. Dearborn St.
HABS IL-155-D
1dr/4ph/8pg/1pc/fr L

DeKoven,Reginald,House
104 E. Bellevue Place
HABS IL-1042
HABS ILL,16-CHIG,44-
4dr/4ph/10pg L

Dewes,Francis J. ,House (Swedish Engineers' Society)
503 W. Wrightwood Ave
HABS IL-1043
HABS ILL,16-CHIG,45-
8ph/12pg L

Edison Shop (Hung-Fa Restaurant)
229 S. Wabash Ave.
HABS IL-1044
HABS ILL,16-CHIG,46-
1ph/7pg L

Elevator "A"; see Illinois Central RR:Grain Elevator "A"

Enterprise Institute; see Aldine Square,Smith House

Fair Store (Montgomery Ward Store)
126-144 S. State St.
HABS IL-1060
HABS ILL,16-CHIG,62-
3ph/8pg L

Federal Building; see U. S. Post Office,Customs House & Sub-Treasury

Fine Arts Building; see Studebaker Building

First Congregational Church of Austin (Our Lady of Lebanon-Roman Catholic Church)
5701 Midway Park
HABS IL-1067
HABS ILL,16-CHIG,68-
4dr/5ph/5pg L

First Regiment Infantry Armory
1552 S. Michigan Ave.
HABS IL-1069
HABS ILL,16-CHIG,69-
6ph/7pg/1pc L

Fisher Building
343 Dearborn St.
HABS IL-1082
HABS ILL,16-CHIG,80-
7ph/8pg L

Florida House; see Florida Tropical House

Florida Tropical House (Florida House; Century of Progress Architectural District)
(See IN,PORTER CO.,BEVERLY SHORES for documentn.)
HABS IN-242
L

Fortnightly Club of Chicago; see Lathrop,Bryan,House

Francis Apartments
4304 S. Forestville Ave.
HABS IL-1076
HABS ILL,16-CHIG,74-
5ph/4pg L

Fuller Park Community Building
S. Princeton Ave. & Forty-Fifth St.
HABS IL-1083
HABS ILL,16-CHIG,81-
6ph/3pg L

Gage Building; see Gage,Keith & Ascher Buildings

Gage,Keith & Ascher Buildings
(McCormick,Stanley R. ,Building; Gage Building)
18 & 30 S. Michigan Ave.
HABS IL-1065
HABS ILL,16-CHIG,66-
5ph/15pg/2pc/fr L

Garden City Warehouse
320 W. Jackson Blvd.
HABS IL-1013
HABS ILL,16-CHIG,15-
1dr/2ph/8pg/fr L

Garrick Theatre; see Schiller Building

Getty Tomb
Graceland Cemetery,N. Clark & W. Irving Park Rd.
HABS IL-1045
HABS ILL,16-CHIG,47-
6ph/5pg L

Giles Building
423-429 S. Wabash Ave.
HABS IL-1014
HABS ILL,16-CHIG,16-
2ph/4pg L

Glessner,John J. ,House (Chicago School of Architecture Foundation)
1800 S. Prairie Ave.
HABS IL-1015
HABS ILL,16-CHIG,17-
6dr/17ph/25pg/1pc/fr L

Government Building; see U. S. Post Office,Customs House & Sub-Treasury

Graham Foundation for Studies in Fine Arts; see Madlener,Albert F. ,House

Grain Elevator "A"; see Illinois Central RR:Grain Elevator "A"

Granada Theatre
6425-6441 N. Sheridan Rd.
HABS IL-1156
HABS DLC/PP-1992:IL-4
31ph/14pg/2pc L

Grand Central Station
201 W. Harrison St. (Cnr W. Harrison & S. Wells) W
HABS IL-1016
HABS ILL,16-CHIG,18-
4dr/6ph/13pg/1pc/fr L

Halsted,Ann,Townhouses
1826-1834 Lincoln Park Ave. W.
HABS IL-1096
HABS ILL,16-CHIG,85-
4dr/2ph/11pg/fr L

Hammond Library
44 N. Ashland Ave.
HABS IL-1017
HABS ILL,16-CHIG,19-
3ph/4pg L

Heath,Ira A. ,House
3132 S. Prairie Ave.
HABS IL-1066
HABS ILL,16-CHIG,67-
3dr/3ph/8pg/fr L

Heller,Isidore,House
5132 S. Woodlawn Ave.
HABS IL-1046
HABS ILL,16-CHIG,48-
4dr/7ph/6pg/fr L

Holy Family Church (Roman Catholic)
1104-1114 W. Roosevelt Rd.
HABS IL-1048
HABS ILL,16-CHIG,50-
4ph/11pg L

Holy Trinity Russian & Greek Orthodox Church (Holy Trinity Russian Orth. ,Greek Cath. Church)
1121 N. Leavitt St.
HABS IL-1071
HABS ILL,16-CHIG,71-
3dr/6ph/11pg/fr L

Holy Trinity Russian Orth. ,Greek Cath. Church; see Holy Trinity Russian & Greek Orthodox Church

Hotel Florence
11111 S. Forrestville Ave.
HABS IL-1018
HABS ILL,16-CHIG,20-
5dr/21ph/13pg/3pc/1ct/fr L

Hull House; see Hull,Charles J. ,House

Hull House,Dining Room; see Hull,Charles J. ,House,Dining Room Wing

Hull,Charles J. ,House (Hull House)
800 S. Halsted St.
HABS IL-1110
HABS ILL,16-CHIG,98-
10pg/fr L

Hull,Charles J. ,House,Dining Room Wing (Hull House,Dining Room)
800 S. Halsted St.
HABS IL-1110-A
HABS ILL,16-CHIG,98A-
5pg L

Hung-Fa Restaurant; see Edison Shop

I & M Canal Nat'l Heritage Corridor; see AT & SF RR: Grain Elevator

I & M Canal Nat'l Heritage Corridor; see Atchison,Topeka,& Sant Fe RR Bridge

I & M Canal Nat'l Heritage Corridor; see Baltimore & Ohio RR,Chicago Terminal RR Bascule Br

I & M Canal Nat'l Heritage Corridor; see Cermak Rd.: Chicago River Bridge

I & M Canal Nat'l Heritage Corridor; see Chicago & Alton (Illinois Central Gulf) RR Bridge

I & M Canal Nat'l Heritage Corridor; see Chicago & Western Indiana RR Bridge

I & M Canal Nat'l Heritage Corridor; see Chicago River Bascule Bridge, Clark St.

I & M Canal Nat'l Heritage Corridor; see Chicago River Bascule Bridge, Franklin St.

I & M Canal Nat'l Heritage Corridor; see Chicago River Bascule Bridge, LaSalle St.

I & M Canal Nat'l Heritage Corridor; see Chicago River Bascule Bridge, Michigan Ave.

I & M Canal Nat'l Heritage Corridor; see Chicago River Bascule Bridge, Outer Drive

I & M Canal Nat'l Heritage Corridor; see Chicago River Bascule Bridge,Michigan Ave.

I & M Canal Nat'l Heritage Corridor; see Chicago River Bascule Bridge,Washington St. Bridge

I & M Canal Nat'l Heritage Corridor; see W. Adams St.: Chicago River Bridge

I & M Canal Nat'l Heritage Corridor; see Western Ave: Sanitary & Ship Canal Bridge

I & M Canal National Heritage Corridor; see Commonwealth Elec.Co.,Fisk St. Elec.Generating Sta

I & M Canal National Heritage Corridor; see Commonwlth Edison Co.,Crawford Elec. Genratng Sta.

I & M Nat'l Heritage Corridor; see Chicago River Bascule Bridge, Wells St.

Illinois Central Railroad Station
Michigan & Roosevelt Sts.
HABS IL-1106
HABS ILL,16-CHIG,99A-
7ph/1pc L

Illinois Central RR:Grain Elevator "A" (Elevator "A"; Grain Elevator "A")
South Water St.
HAER IL-15
HAER ILL,16-CHIG,99B-
7ph/1pg/1pc/fr L

Immaculata High School (Roman Catholic)
640 W. Irving Park Rd.
HABS IL-1074
HABS ILL,16-CHIG,73-
2ph/2pg L

Irving Apartments (Newberry Library)
Oak & State Sts.
HABS IL-1081
HABS ILL,16-CHIG,79-
3ph/1pc L

Jewelers' Building
15-19 S. Wabash Ave.
HABS IL-1049
HABS ILL,16-CHIG,51-
3dr/10ph/7pg/1pc/fr L

Jones School
607 S. Plymouth Court
HABS IL-1019
HABS ILL,16-CHIG,21-
2ph/4pg L

Kehilath Anshe Ma'ariv Synagogue (Pilgrim Baptist Church)
3301 S. Indiana Ave.
HABS IL-1054
HABS ILL,16-CHIG,56-
5dr/9ph/8pg L

Kenna,John Francis,Apartments
2214 E. Sixty-Ninth St.
HABS IL-1094
HABS ILL,16-CHIG,84-
6dr/3ph/8pg/fr L

Kimball,W. W. ,House
1801 S. Prairie Ave.
HABS IL-1077
HABS ILL,16-CHIG,75-
3ph/5pg L

Krause Music Store (Coleman Funeral Home)
4611 N. Lincoln Ave.
HABS IL-1073
HABS ILL,16-CHIG,72-
1ph/9pg L

Lake Street Elevated Railway:Interlocking Tower
Pulaski Rd.
HAER IL-3
HAER ILL,16-CHIG,105A-
4ph/1pg/1pc L

Lakeside Press (Triangle Publications Building; Plymouth Polk Building; R & R Donnelly Building)
731 Plymouth Ct.
HABS IL-1020
HABS ILL,16-CHIG,22-
1ph/3pg L

Lakeview Pumping Station
Clarendon & Montrose Aves.
HAER IL-4
HAER ILL,16-CHIG,106-
113ph/15pg/6pc L

Lathrop,Bryan,House (Fortnightly Club of Chicago)
120 E. Bellevue Place
HABS IL-1037
HABS ILL,16-CHIG,40-
4ph/6pg L

Leiter I Building
200-208 W. Monroe St.
HABS IL-1021
HABS ILL,16-CHIG,23-
6dr/2ph/4pg L

Leiter II Building (Sears,Roebuck & Company Building)
S. State & E. Congress Sts.
HABS IL-1022
HABS ILL,16-CHIG,24-
3ph/3pg L

Madlener,Albert F. ,House (Graham Foundation for Studies in Fine Arts)
4 W. Burton Place
HABS IL-1023
HABS ILL,16-CHIG,25-
9dr/9ph/4pg/fr L

Magerstadt,Ernest J. ,House
4930 S. Greenwood Ave.
HABS IL-1024
HABS ILL,16-CHIG,26-
4dr/8ph/20pg L

Malcolm Building
662 N. Clark St.
HABS IL-1050
HABS ILL,16-CHIG,52-
2ph/4pg L

Manhattan Building
431 S. Dearborn St.
HABS IL-1051
HABS ILL,16-CHIG,53-
3ph/7pg L

Marquette Building
140 S. Dearborn St.
HABS IL-1070
HABS ILL,16-CHIG,70-
3dr/10ph/17pg/1pc/fr L

Marshall,John,Law School; see City Club of Chicago

McClurg Building; see Ayer Building

McCormick,Stanley R. ,Building; see Gage,Keith & Ascher Buildings

Meyer Building
301-311 W. VanBuren St.
HABS IL-1026
HABS ILL,16-CHIG,28-
2ph/5pg L

Midway Airport,South Terminal (Chicago Midway Airport,South Terminal)
Cicero Ave. ,btwn. Fifty-fifth & Sixty-third Sts.
HABS IL-305
HABS ILL,16-CHIG,100A-
4pg L

Monadnock Block
53 W. Jackson Blvd.
HABS IL-1027
HABS ILL,16-CHIG,88-
4ph/7pg L

Montgomery Ward Store; see Fair Store

Morningstar-Paisley Company; see Schoenhofen Brewing Company,Powerhouse

Newberry Library; see Irving Apartments

Nickerson,Samuel M. ,House (American College of Surgeons)
40 E. Erie St.
HABS IL-1052
HABS ILL,16-CHIG,54-
6dr/8ph/17pg L

1359-1363 North Paulina Street (Apartment Bldgs.)
HABS IL-1118
HABS ILL,16-CHIG,96-
3ph/1pc L

1359 North Paulina Street (Apartment Building)
HABS IL-1118-A
HABS ILL,16-CHIG,96A-
1dr/1ph/1pg/1pc L

1361 North Paulina Street (Apartment Building)
HABS IL-1118-B
HABS ILL,16-CHIG,96B-
1dr/4ph/1pg/1pc L

1363 North Paulina Street (Apartment Building)
HABS IL-1118-C
HABS ILL,16-CHIG,96C-
1dr/3ph/1pg L

Northwestern Elevated Railroad:Interlocking Tower
Wilson Ave.
HAER IL-2
HAER ILL,16-CHIG,107A-
4ph/1pg/1pc L

Occidental Building
107-111 N. Wacker Dr.
HABS IL-1028
HABS ILL,16-CHIG,29-
3ph/6pg L

Old Colony Building
407 S. Dearborn St.
HABS IL-1053
HABS ILL,16-CHIG,55-
3dr/15ph/13pg/1pc/fr L

Our Lady of Lebanon-Roman Catholic Church; see First Congregational Church of Austin

Palace Hotel (St. Regis Hotel)
516 N. Clark St.
HABS IL-1057
HABS ILL,16-CHIG,59-
2ph/5pg L

Phelps-Dodge-Palmer Building
200 W. Adams St.
HABS IL-1124
HABS ILL,16-CHIG,101-
1dr/41ph/16pg/5pc/fr L

Pick-Congress Hotel; see Auditorium Annex

Pilgrim Baptist Church; see Kehilath Anshe Ma'ariv Synagogue

Plaza Hotel
1553 N. Clark St.
HABS IL-1055
HABS ILL,16-CHIG,57-
3ph/6pg L

Plymouth Polk Building; see Lakeside Press

Polk Street Station; see Chicago & West. Indiana RR:Dearborn Sta. Trainshed

Pontiac Building (Chicago Home for Girls)
542 S. Dearborn St.
HABS IL-1102
HABS ILL,16-CHIG,86-
6dr/2ph/5pg L

Pullman Company Administration Building & Shops
1101 S. Cottage Grove Ave.
HABS IL-1091
HABS ILL,16-CHIG,90-
11ph/19pg/4ct L

Pullman Industrial Complex
One Hundred Eleventh St. & Cottage Grove Ave. Vic.
HAER IL-5
HAER ILL,16-CHIG,102-
7dr/15ph/182pg/1pc L

Pullman Industrial Complex,Worker's Housing
111 Street & Cottage Grove Ave. vic.
HABS IL-173
HABS ILL,16-CHIG,102A-
8ph/1pc L

R & R Donnelly Building; see Lakeside Press

Reliance Building
32 N. State St.
HABS IL-1029
HABS ILL,16-CHIG,30-
4dr/6ph/11pg/1pc/fr L

Republic Building (Strong Building)
209 S. State St.
HABS IL-1004
HABS ILL,16-CHIG,9-
8dr/71ph/3pg L

Robie,Frederick C. ,House
5757 Woodlawn Ave.
HABS IL-1005
HABS ILL,16-CHIG,33-
25dr/9ph/17pg/fr L

Rookery Building
209 S. LaSalle St.
HABS IL-1030
HABS ILL,16-CHIG,31-
8dr/24ph/11pg/2pc/fr L

Roosevelt University; see Auditorium Building

Rostone House; see Wieboldt-Rostone House

1021 S. Wabash Avenue (Chicago Ironwork Survey; Cast Iron Stair Railing)
1021 S. Wabash Ave.
HABS IL-155-T
HABS ILL,16-CHIG,7E2-,DLC/ADE=83(HABS):53
2ph/1pc L

Schiller Building (Garrick Theatre)
64 W. Randolph St.
HABS IL-1058
HABS ILL,16-CHIG,60-
11dr/8ph/12pg L

Schlesinger & Mayer Department Store (Carson,Pirie,Scott & Company Department Store)
S. State & E. Madison Sts.
HABS IL-1064
HABS ILL,16-CHIG,65-
4dr/4ph/10pg L

Schoenhofen Brewing Company,Powerhouse
(Morningstar-Paisley Company)
1770 Canalport Ave.
HABS IL-1059
HABS ILL,16-CHIG,61-
4ph/5pg L

Schoenhofen,Peter,Brewery Complex
W. Eighteenth St. & Canalport Ave.
HAER IL-12
HAER ILL,16-CHIG,61-
24ph/46pg/3pc L

Scoville Building
619-631 W. Washington St.
HABS IL-1114
8dr/9ph/2pg/1pc L

Sears,Roebuck & Company Building; see Leiter II Building

Second Baptist Church (Aiken Institute)
Morgan & Monroe Sts.
HABS IL-26-2
HABS ILL,16-CHIG,2-
6dr/7ph/2pg/fr L

Shedd Park Recreation Building
S. Twenty-Third St. & Lawndale Ave.
HABS IL-1107
HABS ILL,16-CHIG,87-
4dr L

Sheldon,Daniel H. ,House
723 W. Congress St.
HABS IL-26-1
HABS ILL,16-CHIG,1-
3dr/2ph/1pg/fr L

Shreve Building
100-104 W. Lake St.
HABS IL-1031
HABS ILL,16-CHIG,32-
1ph/4pg L

Sibley,Hiram,Warehouse (Central Cold Storage Warehouse)
315-331 N. Clark St.
HABS IL-1047
HABS ILL,16-CHIG,49-
8ph/7pg L

1017 South Wabash Avenue
HABS IL-184
HABS ILL,16-CHIG,95-
3ph/1pc L

Springer Block (Bay State Building & Kranz Building)
126-146 N. State St.
HABS IL-1008
HABS ILL,16-CHIG,11-
2ph/6pg L

St. Gabriel's Church (Roman Catholic)
4522 S. Wallace St.
HABS IL-1032
HABS ILL,16-CHIG,34-
5ph/5pg L

St. Ignatius College (St. Ignatius High School)
1076 Roosevelt Rd.
HABS IL-1056
HABS ILL,16-CHIG,58-
1ph/7pg L

St. Ignatius High School; see St. Ignatius College

St. Patrick's Church
Adams & Desplaines Sts.
HABS IL-1033
HABS ILL,16-CHIG,35-
4dr/7ph/11pg/1pc/fr L

St. Regis Hotel; see Palace Hotel

Steffens,Oscar,House
7631 N. Sheridan Rd.
HABS IL-1063
HABS ILL,16-CHIG,64-
6dr/4pg L

Strong Building; see Republic Building

Strong,William M. ,Estate; see Chicago Ironwork

Studebaker Building (Fine Arts Building)
410 S. Michigan Ave.
HABS IL-1078
HABS ILL,16-CHIG,76-
1ph/1pc L

Sullivan,Albert W. ,House
4575 Lake Park Ave.
HABS IL-1006
HABS ILL,16-CHIG,10-
2ph/4pg L

Swedish Engineers' Society; see Dewes,Francis J. ,House

Tenement Building "E"
Langley Ave.
HABS IL-1111
HABS ILL,16-CHIG,102B-
4dr/fr L

Triangle Publications Building; see Lakeside Press

U. S. Courthouse; see U. S. Post Office,Customs House & Sub-Treasury

U. S. Marine Hospital (U. S. Public Health Clinic)
4141 N. Clarendon Ave.
HABS IL-1084
HABS ILL,16-CHIG,82-
1ph/5pg L

U. S. Post Office,Customs House & Sub-Treasury (Government Building; Federal Building; U. S. Courthouse)
218 S. Dearborn St.
HABS IL-1040
HABS ILL,16-CHIG,89-
5ph/13pg L

U. S. Public Health Clinic; see U. S. Marine Hospital

Underwriters' Laboratories
207-231 E. Ohio St.
HABS IL-1116
HABS ILL,16-CHIG,103-
60ph/31pg/6pc/fr L

Union Elevated Railroad:Adams Street Station
Wabash Ave.
HAER IL-1-C
HAER ILL,16-CHIG,108C-
4ph/1pg/1pc L

Union Elevated Railroad:Clark Street Station
Lake St.
HAER IL-1-E
HAER ILL,16-CHIG,108E-
5ph/1pg/1pc L

Union Elevated Railroad:Quincy Street Station
Wells St.
HAER IL-1-A
HAER ILL,16-CHIG,108A-
1ph/1pg/1pc L

Union Elevated Railroad:Randolf Street Station
Wells St.
HAER IL-1-F
HAER ILL,16-CHIG,108F-
5ph/1pg/1pc L

Union Elevated Railroad:Randolph Street Station
Wabash Ave.
HAER IL-1-D
HAER ILL,16-CHIG,108D-
4ph/1pg/1pc L

Union Elevated Railroad:State Street Station
Van Buren St.
HAER IL-1-B
HAER ILL,16-CHIG,108B-
7ph/1pg/1pc L

Union Elevated Railroad:Union Loop
Wells,Van Buren,Lake Sts. & Wabash Ave.
HAER IL-1
HAER ILL,16-CHIG,108-
19ph/4pg/2pc L

W. Adams St.: Chicago River Bridge (Chicago River Bascule Bridge, Adams St.; I & M Canal Nat'l Heritage Corridor)
HAER IL-51
HAER ILL,81-ROCIL,3/1-
H

Wentworth,John,Farm House
HABS IL-156
HABS ILL,16-SUM,1-
2dr/7ph L

Western Ave: Sanitary & Ship Canal Bridge (I & M Canal Nat'l Heritage Corridor)
HAER IL-40
HAER ILL,81-ROCIL,3/1-
36ph H

Wieboldt-Rostone House (Rostone House; Century of Progress Architectural District)
(See IN,PORTER CO.,BEVERLY SHORES for documentn.)
HABS IN-240
L

EVANSTON

Carter,Frederick B. ,Jr. ,House
1024 Judson St.
HABS IL-1086
HABS ILL,16-EVAN,2-
5dr/3ph/5pg L

Comstock,Hurd,House II
1631 Ashland Ave.
HABS IL-1089
HABS ILL,16-EVAN,3-
7dr/2ph/10pg L

Long,John T. ,House (Shadrach Bond Mantel)
922 Sheridan Rd.
HABS IL-26-31
HABS ILL,16-EVAN,1-
1dr/2ph/2pg L

Shadrach Bond Mantel
929 Sheridan Rd. (moved from IL Kaskaskia)
HABS IL-26-31-B
HABS ILL,16-EVAN,1-
fr L

Willard,Frances E. ,House (Women's Christian Temperence Union)
1730 Chicago Ave.
HABS IL-1095
HABS ILL,16-EVAN,4-
5dr/2ph/13pg/fr L

Women's Christian Temperence Union; see Willard,Frances E. ,House

GLENCOE

Albright,Julius,House
Hohfelder Rd.
HABS IL-134
HABS ILL,16-GLENC,1-
1dr/5ph/3pg/fr L

Glasner,W. A. ,House
850 Sheridan Rd.
HABS IL-1098
HABS ILL,16-GLENC,2-
4dr L

KENILWORTH

Kenilworth Club
10 Kenilworth Ave.
HABS IL-1090
HABS ILL,16-KENILL,1-
6dr/4ph/8pg/fr L

LEMONT

Illinois Pure Aluminum Company
109 Holmes St.
HAER IL-45
HAER ILL,81-ROCIL,3/1-
14ph/2pg/2pc L

Lemont,Town of
HABS IL-311
HABS 1990 (HABS):4
241pg/fr L

OAK PARK

Eastbrook,T. S. ,House
200 N. Scoville St.
HABS IL-1085
HABS ILL,16-OAKPA,2-
4dr/3ph/4pg/fr L

Lamar Theatre; see Oak Park Theatre

McCready,Edward W. ,House
231 N. Euclid St.
HABS IL-1075
HABS ILL,16-OAKPA,1-
5dr/3ph/5pg L

Oak Park Theatre (Lamar Theatre)
116-120 S. Marion St.
HABS IL-1149
HABS ILL,16-OAKPA,4-
5ph/2pg/1pc/fr L

Unitarian-Universalist Church; see Unity Temple

Unity Temple (Unitarian-Universalist Church)
875 Lake St.
HABS IL-1093
HABS ILL,16-OAKPA,3-
7dr/5ph/12pg/3ct L

Wright,Frank Lloyd,House & Studio
428 Forest Ave. & 951 Chicago Ave.
HABS IL-1099
HABS ILL,16-OAKPA,5-
7ph/16pg/1pc L

RIVER FOREST

Drummond,William E. ,House
559 Edgewood Place
HABS IL-1072
HABS ILL,16-RIVFO,2-
5dr/3ph/4pg L

Winslow,William H. ,House
Auvergne Place
HABS IL-1061
HABS ILL,16-RIVFO,1-
5dr/13ph/17pg L

RIVERSIDE

Babson Stable & Service Building
283 Gatesby Ln.
HABS IL-1068
HABS ILL,16-RIVSI,1A-
7dr/7ph/6pg/fr L

Coonley,Avery,House
300 Scottswood Rd.
HABS IL-1100
HABS ILL,16-RIVSI,2-
6ph/1pc L

SUMMIT

Summit,Town of
HABS IL-319
HABS 1989(HABS):9
126pg/fr L

WILMETTE

Baker,Ralph S. ,House
1226 Ashland Ave.
HABS IL-1097
HABS ILL,16-WILM,1-
6dr/3ph/5pg L

Bersbach,Alfred,House
1120 Michigan Ave.
HABS IL-1103
HABS ILL,16-WILM,2-
2ph/4pg L

Roemer House
2739 Old Glenview Rd.
HABS IL-1152
HABS 1991(HABS):17
13ph/6pg/1pc L

DOUGLAS COUNTY

GENOA VIC.

Perkins Farmhouse
Rt. 22
HABS IL-26-30
HABS ILL,19-GENO.V,1-
2dr/2ph/1pg/fr L

DU PAGE COUNTY

ADDISON

Heideman Windmill
Rt. 5
HABS IL-26-4
HABS ILL,22-ADI.V,1-
4dr/2ph/1pg/fr L

BLOOMINGDALE VIC.

Laudon-Bender Farmhouse
HABS IL-26-7
HABS ILL,22-BLOOM.V,1-
2dr/2ph/1pg/fr L

ELMHURST

Henderson,F. B. ,House
301 S. Kenilworth Ave.
HABS IL-137
HABS ILL,22-ELM,2-
3ph/1pc L

ELMURST

Emery House
218 Arlington St.
HABS IL-1101
HABS ILL,22-ELM,1-
7dr L

FULLERBURG VIC.

Graue Water Mill
York Rd.
HABS IL-26-6
HABS ILL,22-FULB.V,1-
3dr/3ph/2pg/fr L

FULLERSBURG

Ogden Avenue (House)
HABS IL-170
HABS ILL,22-FULB,2-
1ph L

Tavern,Old
Ogden Ave.
HABS IL-170
HABS ILL,22-FULB,1-
2dr/7ph/2pg/fr L

Toll House,Old
HABS IL-170-A
HABS ILL,22-FULB,2A-
1ph/fr L

NADERVILLE

Hobson Law Office
215 W. Main St.
HABS IL-26-33
HABS ILL,22-NAPVI,2-
4dr/4ph/1pg/fr L

NAPERVILLE

First Baptist Church
34 Washington Ave.
HABS IL-136
HABS ILL,22-NAPVI,3-
2dr/3ph/3pg/fr L

Pre-Emption House
Chicago Ave. & Main St.
HABS IL-26-5
HABS ILL,22-NAPVI,1-
6dr/3ph/2pg/fr L

NAPERVILLE VIC.

Hobson Grist Mill (Hobson Mill (Monument & Millstones))
DuPage County Pioneer Park
HABS IL-154-A
HABS ILL,22-NAPVI.V,2,2A-
2ph L

Hobson House
HABS IL-154
HABS ILL,22-NAPVI.V,1-
3dr/11ph/2pg/fr L

Hobson Mill (Monument & Millstones); see Hobson Grist Mill

WARRENVILLE

Warren,Col. ,House
Warrenville Rd.
HABS IL-26-8
HABS ILL,22-WARVI,1-
5dr/3ph/2pg L

Warrenville Methodist Church
HABS IL-26-32
HABS ILL,22-WARVI,2-
1dr/2ph/1pg/fr L

EDGAR COUNTY

PARIS

Austin,A. B. ,House
501 Jefferson Ave.
HABS IL-280
HABS ILL,23-PAR,1-
3dr/5ph/2pg/fr L

EDWARDS COUNTY

ALBION

French,George,House
State Rt. 130
HABS IL-25-1
HABS ILL,24-ALBI,1-
5dr/2ph/2pg/fr L

Thompson,Frank B. ,House
State Rt. 130
HABS IL-25-2
HABS ILL,24-ALBI,2-
7dr/5ph/3pg/1pc/fr L

FORD COUNTY

PAXTON

Middlecoff (J. P.)-Baier House
440 E. Pells St.
HABS IL-1120
HABS ILL,27-PAX,1-
10dr/fr L

Paxton Water Tower
Centre & Market Sts.
HABS IL-1121
HABS ILL,27-PAX,2-
4dr L

FULTON COUNTY

LEWISTON

Walker,Maj. Newton,House
Main St.
HABS IL-283
HABS ILL,29-LEWTO,1-
2dr/4ph/2pg L

LONDON MILLS VIC.

Indian Ford Bridge
HAER IL-13
HAER ILL,29-LONMI.V,1-
8ph/3pg/1pc L

GALLATIN COUNTY

NEW HAVEN

Sheridan Tavern
33 Mill St.
HABS IL-25-5
HABS ILL,30-NEHA,1-
4dr/3ph/2pg/fr L

SHAWNEETOWN

Bank in Illinois,First; see Marshall,John,House

Marshall,John,House (Bank in Illinois,First)
HABS IL-25-3
HABS ILL,30-SHAWT,1-
3dr/2ph/4pg/fr L

State Bank,Old
Main St. & Rt. 13
HABS IL-25-4
HABS ILL,30-SHAWT,2-
6dr/5ph/3pg/fr L

GRUNDY COUNTY

MINNOKA

Chicago,Ottawa,& Peoria Interurban RR:Minnoka Sta.; see Illinois Traction System: Minnoka Pass. Station

I & M Canal Nat'l Heritage Corridor; see Illinois Traction System: Minnoka Pass. Station

Illinois Traction System: Minnoka Pass. Station (Chicago,Ottawa,& Peoria Interurban RR:Minnoka Sta. I & M Canal Nat'l Heritage Corridor)
HAER IL-84
H

MINOOKA VIC.

Rutherford Barn
E. Hansel Rd.
HABS IL-1151
HABS DLC/PP-1992:IL-5
4dr/12pg/fr L

MORRIS

Chicago,Ottawa & Peoria Interurban RR:Morris Sta.; see Illinois Traction System:Morris Passenger Station

Chicago,Rock Isl. & Pacific RR Morris Pass. Depot (I & M Canal Nat'l Heritage Corridor)
HAER IL-80
H

Chicago,Rock Isl. & Pacific RR: I & M Canal Bridge; see Rock Island RR: I & M Canal Bridge,Morris Spur

Documentation: **ct** color transparencies **dr** measured drawings **fr** field records
pc photograph captions **pg** pages of text **ph** photographs

Farmer's Square Deal Cooperative: Grain Elevator (I & M Canal Nat'l Heritage Corridor)
HAER IL-88
H

Gebhard Brewery (I & M Canal Nat'l Heritage Corridor)
HAER IL-69
20ph H

I & M Canal Nat'l Heritage Corridor; see Chicago,Rock Isl. & Pacific RR Morris Pass. Depot

I & M Canal Nat'l Heritage Corridor; see Farmer's Square Deal Cooperative: Grain Elevator

I & M Canal Nat'l Heritage Corridor; see Gebhard Brewery

I & M Canal Nat'l Heritage Corridor; see Illinois Traction System:Morris Passenger Station

I & M Canal Nat'l Heritage Corridor; see Morris Grain Co.: Elevator

I & M Canal Nat'l Heritage Corridor; see Rock Island RR: I & M Canal Bridge,Morris Spur

Illinois Traction System:Morris Passenger Station (Chicago,Ottawa & Peoria Interurban RR:Morris Sta.; I & M Canal Nat'l Heritage Corridor)
HAER IL-85
H

Morris Grain Co.: Elevator (I & M Canal Nat'l Heritage Corridor)
HAER IL-89
H

Morris,Town of
HABS IL-310
HABS 1990 (HABS):4
694pg/fr L

Rock Island RR: I & M Canal Bridge,Morris Spur (Chicago,Rock Isl. & Pacific RR: I & M Canal Bridge I & M Canal Nat'l Heritage Corridor)
HAER IL-81
H

MORRIS VIC.

Aux Sable Creek Aqueduct (I & M Canal Nat'l Heritage Corridor)
HAER IL-47
HAER ILL,81-ROCIL,3/1-
6ph H

Aux Sable Lift Lock & Locktender's House; see Lift Lock No. 8 & Spillway

I & M Canal Nat'l Heritage Corridor; see Aux Sable Creek Aqueduct

I & M Canal Nat'l Heritage Corridor; see Lift Lock No. 8 & Spillway

Lift Lock No. 8 & Spillway (Aux Sable Lift Lock & Locktender's House; I & M Canal Nat'l Heritage Corridor)
HAER IL-77
H

HANCOCK COUNTY

NAUVOO

Ashby,Snow,House
HABS IL-1145
HABS ILL,34-NAU,13-
1ph/1pc L

Babbitt,Almon W. ,House
Main & Kimball Sts.
HABS IL-26-25
HABS ILL,34-NAU,2-
6dr/8ph/2pg L

Bangham House
Mulhollen & Seventeenth Sts.
HABS IL-255
HABS ILL,34-NAU,10-
1ph L

Baumert House
Mulhollen & Fifteenth Sts.
HABS IL-26-27
HABS ILL,34-NAU,4-
3dr/2ph/1pg/fr L

Blacksmith Shop
HABS IL-1141
HABS ILL,34-NAU,14-
1ph/1pc L

Browning,Jonathan,House
Main St.
HABS IL-245
HABS ILL,34-NAU,6-
2dr/6ph/1pg/1pc/fr L

Building,Stone
HABS IL-1144
HABS ILL,34-NAU,15-
1ph/1pc L

Gross,Cooper,House
Knight & Sixteenth Sts.
HABS IL-254
HABS ILL,34-NAU,9-
1ph L

House,Brick
HABS IL-1143
HABS ILL,34-NAU,17-
1ph/1pc L

House,Brick
HABS IL-1146
HABS ILL,34-NAU,16-
1ph/1pc L

Kaufman,Adam,House
Corlis & Sidney Sts.
HABS IL-257
HABS ILL,34-NAU,12-
1ph L

Kimball,Heber C. ,House
Ninth & Munson Sts.
HABS IL-244
HABS ILL,34-NAU,5-
3dr/5ph/2pg/1pc/fr L

Mansion House (Smith,Joseph,House)
Main & Water Sts.
HABS IL-26-24
HABS ILL,34-NAU,1-
5dr/9ph/2pg/1pc L

Mix,P. ,House
Kimball & Twenty-First Sts.
HABS IL-256
HABS ILL,34-NAU,11-
1ph L

Mormon Tabernacle
HABS IL-1138
HABS ILL,34-NAU,18-
1ph/1pc L

Newspaper Office & Print Shop
HABS IL-1142
HABS ILL,34-NAU,19-
2ph/1pc/3ct L

Scovill Bakery
HABS IL-1137
HABS ILL,34-NAU,20-
1ph/1pc L

Seventies Hall
HABS IL-1140
HABS ILL,34-NAU,21-
2ph/1pc L

Smith,Joseph,House
HABS IL-253
HABS ILL,34-NAU,8-
2ph/1pc/1ct L

Smith,Joseph,House; see Mansion House

Smith,Lucy Mack, & Jos. Bates Noble House
HABS IL-1139
HABS ILL,34-NAU,22-
1ph/1pc L

Winery
HABS IL-1136
HABS ILL,34-NAU,23-
1ph/1pc L

Woodruff,Wilford,House
Tenth & Hotchkiss Sts.
HABS IL-26-26
HABS ILL,34-NAU,3-
5dr/4ph/2pg/fr L

Young,Brigham,House
Granger & Kimball Sts.
HABS IL-250
HABS ILL,34-NAU,7-
1dr/7ph/2pg/1pc L

WARSAW

Adams House & Adjoining Building; see Main Street,Historic View

202 Main Street (Commercial Building)
HABS IL-249-B
HABS ILL,34-WAR,2A-
1dr/1ph L

222 Main Street (Commercial Building)
HABS IL-249-D
HABS ILL,34-WAR,2B-
1dr/1ph L

421 Main Street (Commercial Building)
HABS IL-249-F
HABS ILL,34-WAR,3A-
1ph L

202-230 Main Street (Commercial Buildings)
HABS IL-249-C
HABS ILL,34-WAR,2-
5ph/3pg L

407-413,421-429 Main Street (Commercial Buildings)
HABS IL-249-E
HABS ILL,34-WAR,3-
2ph L

Main Street,Historic View
HABS IL-249
HABS ILL,34-WAR,1-
1ph L

Main Street,Historic View (Adams House & Adjoining Building)
HABS IL-249-A
HABS ILL,34-WAR,1A-
1ph L

Mussetter House
950 Webster St.
HABS IL-251
HABS ILL,34-WAR,4-
2ph L

HENDERSON COUNTY

BIGGSVILLE VIC.

Citizen's Bridge; see MacArthur Bridge

MacArthur Bridge (Citizen's Bridge)
Span. Mississippi Rvr. on Hwy. 34 btwn IL & IA
HAER IA-21
HAER 1990 (HAER):6
73ph/48pg/6pc L

GLADSTONE

Miss. River 9-Ft. Channel Proj.,Lock & Dam No. 18
Upper Mississippi River
HAER IL-29
HAER 1991(HAER):14
18ph/15pg/2pc L

OQUAWKA

Henderson County Courthouse
Fourth & Warren Sts.
HABS IL-240
HABS ILL,36-OQUA,1-
7dr/11ph/3pg/fr L

Knowles House
Fourth St.
HABS IL-241
HABS ILL,36-OQUA,2-
2dr/3ph/1pg/fr L

OQUAWKA VIC.

Eames Covered Bridge
Spanning Henderson Creek
HABS IL-243
HABS ILL,36-OQUA.V,2-
2dr/5ph/2pg/fr L

Jack's Mill,Covered Bridge
Spanning Henderson Creek
HABS IL-242
HABS ILL,36-OQUA.V,1-
2dr/5ph/2pg/fr L

HENRY COUNTY

BISHOP HILL

House,Brick
HABS IL-258
HABS ILL,37-BISH,23-
3ph/1pc/fr L

House,Brick
HABS IL-259
HABS ILL,37-BISH,24-
1ph/1pc L

Jansonist Colony
HABS IL-169
HABS ILL,37-BISH, -
4pg/fr L

Jansonist Colony,Administration Building
Johnson & Main Sts.
HABS IL-169-R
HABS ILL,37-BISH,17-
6ph/1pc L

Jansonist Colony,Apartment House
Main & Johnson Sts.
HABS IL-169-I
HABS DLC/ADE183:54, 84:145°
4ph/2pc L

Jansonist Colony,Apartment House,Old
Main St.
HABS IL-169-A
HABS ILL,37-BISH,2-
5ph/2pc L

Jansonist Colony,Apartments,Big Brick
Park St.
HABS IL-169-B
HABS ILL,37-BISH,5-
2pg L

Jansonist Colony,Bandstand
Bishop Hill Park
HABS IL-169-X
HABS ILL,37-BISH,22-
1ph/1pc L

Jansonist Colony,Bjorklund Hotel
HABS IL-169-C
HABS ILL,37-BISH,10-
5ph/1pg/2pc L

Jansonist Colony,Blacksmith & Carpenter Shops
Bishop Hill & Christina Sts.
HABS IL-169-D
HABS ILL,37-BISH,6-
3ph/1pg/1pc L

Jansonist Colony,Carriage & Wagon Shop
Bishop Hill St.
HABS IL-169-E
HABS ILL,37-BISH,7-
3ph/1pg/2pc/fr L

Jansonist Colony,Colony Bakery & Brewery,Old
HABS IL-169-F
HABS ILL,37-BISH,4-
1pg L

Jansonist Colony,Colony Hospital
Olson St.
HABS IL-169-H
HABS ILL,37-BISH,14-
4ph/2pg L

Jansonist Colony,Colony School
Main & Olson Sts.
HABS IL-169-J
HABS ILL,37-BISH,11-
3ph/1pg/1pc L

Jansonist Colony,Colony Store & Post Office
Main & Bishop Hill Sts.
HABS IL-169-K
HABS ILL,37-BISH,3-
1dr/5ph/1pg/3pc/fr L

Jansonist Colony,Cooperative Store
Main & Christina Sts.
HABS IL-169-L
HABS ILL,37-BISH,13-
1dr/fr L

Jansonist Colony,Dairy Bldg (Butter & Cheese Fac.)
Ericson St.
HABS IL-169-M
HABS ILL,37-BISH,9-
1ph/1pg/1pc L

Jansonist Colony,Jacobson,Jacob,House
Bishop Hill St.
HABS IL-169-O
HABS ILL,37-BISH,15-
5ph/1pc L

Jansonist Colony,Krans House
Christina St.
HABS IL-169-T
HABS ILL,37-BISH,18-
1ph/1pc L

Jansonist Colony,Krusbo
Park St.
HABS IL-169-U
HABS ILL,37-BISH,19-
1ph/1pc L

Jansonist Colony,Meat Storage Building
Maiden La.
HABS IL-169-L
HABS ILL,37-BISH,23-
3ph/1pc L

Jansonist Colony,Old Colony Church
Bishop Hill & Maiden Lane Sts.
HABS IL-169-G
HABS ILL,37-BISH,8-
10ph/2pg/2pc/fr L

Jansonist Colony,Olson Barn
Park St.
HABS IL-169-Q
HABS ILL,37-BISH,16-
7ph/1pc L

Jansonist Colony,Poppy Barn
Bishop Hill St.
HABS IL-169-V
HABS ILL,37-BISH,20-
1ph/1pc L

Jansonist Colony,Steeple Building
Main & Bishop Hill Sts.
HABS IL-169-N
HABS ILL,37-BISH,1-
6dr/17ph/4pg/4pc/fr L

Jansonist Colony,Street Scene
HABS IL-169-P
HABS ILL,37-BISH,12-
1ph/1pg/1pc L

Jansonist Colony,Swanson House
Bishop Hill St.
HABS IL-169-W
HABS ILL,37-BISH,21-
2ph/1pc L

BISHOP HILL VIC.

Jansonist Colony,Grain Elevator
2 mi. E of Bishop Hill
HABS IL-169-Y
HABS ILL,37-BISH.V,1-
1ph/1pc L

IROQUOIS COUNTY

DELRAY

Delray Bridge (Spring Creek Bridge)
Spanning Spring Creek
HAER IL-35
HAER 1989(HAER):7
12ph/8pg/1pc L

Spring Creek Bridge; see Delray Bridge

ONARGA VIC.

Larch Farm; see Pinkerton,Allan,House

Pinkerton,Allan,House (Larch Farm)
HABS IL-263
HABS ILL,38-ONAR.V,1-
3dr/11ph/4pg/fr L

JACKSON COUNTY

CARBONDALE VIC.

Log Cabin
HABS IL-25-16
HABS ILL,39-CARB.V,1-
2dr/2ph/2pg L

JEFFERSON COUNTY

MOUNT VERNON

Appellate Court Building
Fourteenth & Main Sts.
HABS IL-25-14
HABS ILL,41-MOVER,1-
4dr/4ph/4pg L

JO DAVIESS COUNTY

GALENA

Barrows-Coatsworth Building
122 Main St.
HABS IL-1112
HABS ILL,43-GALA,32-
6ph/4pg L

Biesman House
Bouthiller St.,U.S. Grant Home St. Hist. Site
HABS IL-1158-B
HABS 1992(HABS):IL-1
9dr/fr L

Buden House
HABS IL-197
HABS ILL,43-GALA,29-
1ph L

Calderwood,Celia,House
N. Bench St.
HABS IL-178
HABS ILL,43-GALA,19-
1ph/1pg/1pc L

Clarey House
HABS IL-198
HABS ILL,43-GALA,30-
1ph L

Cottage,Brick
408 S. Dodge St.
HABS IL-151
HABS ILL,43-GALA,12-
1dr/2ph/2pg/fr L

Custom House & Post Office
HABS IL-306
HABS ILL,43-GALA,33-
3ph/1pc L

Doorways of Galena,Ryan House
HABS IL-178
HABS ILL,43-GALA, -
16ph/3pg/1pc L

Doorways,Dowling,John,House
Main & Diagonal Sts.
HABS IL-178-A
HABS ILL,43-GALA,27-
1ph/1pg L

Doorways,First Methodist Church
Bench St.
HABS IL-178-C
HABS ILL,43-GALA,23-
1ph/1pg/1pc L

Doorways,Grimm,Heike,House
608 S. Bench St.
HABS IL-178-D
HABS ILL,43-GALA,18-
1ph L

Doorways,Harmony Lodge of Odd Fellows
Bench St.
HABS IL-178-E
HABS ILL,43-GALA,22-
1ph/1pc L

Doorways,Hempstead,Charles,House
611 S. Bench St.
HABS IL-178-F
HABS ILL,43-GALA,16-
1ph/1pg L

Doorways,House,Red Brick
Elk & Prospect Sts.
HABS IL-178-B
HABS ILL,43-GALA,25-
1ph/1pg/1pc L

Doorways,Klingel,Peter,House
Bench St.
HABS IL-178-G
HABS ILL,43-GALA,20-
1ph/1pg/1pc L

Doorways,Maxiener,Elizabeth,Cottage
104 S. Bench St.
HABS IL-178-H
HABS ILL,43-GALA,14-
1dr/2ph L

Doorways,Porter House
110 N. Bench St.
HABS IL-178-I
HABS ILL,43-GALA,15-
1dr/1ph/1pg L

Doorways,Ryan House
Bench St.
HABS IL-178-J
HABS ILL,42-GALA,24-
2ph L

Doorways,Sisters of Mercy Convent
226 N. Bench St.
HABS IL-178-K
HABS ILL,43-GALA,17-
1dr/1ph/1pg L

Doorways,Telford Shop
Bench St.
HABS IL-178-L
HABS ILL,43-GALA,21-
1ph/1pg/1pc L

Doorways,Warehouse
S. Main St.
HABS IL-178-M
HABS ILL,43-GALA,26-
1ph/1pg/1pc L

Dowling,John,House
120 N. Bench St.
HABS IL-26-14
HABS ILL,43-GALA,4-
7dr/4ph/1pg/fr L

Dowling,Nicholas,Building
Diagonal & Main Sts.
HABS IL-26-17
HABS ILL,43-GALA,6-
4dr/4ph/1pg/fr L

Felt,S. M. ,House (Staircase)
Prospect St.
HABS IL-26-16
HABS ILL,43-GALA,5-
4dr/3ph/1pg/fr L

First Presbyterian Church
Bench St.
HABS IL-177
HABS ILL,43-GALA,34-
11ph/1pc/fr L

Grace Episcopal Church
S. Prospect St.
HABS IL-150
HABS ILL,43-GALA,11-
5dr/14ph/2pg/fr L

Grant House,First
121 S. High St.
HABS IL-26-12
HABS ILL,43-GALA,2-
2dr/4ph/1pg/fr L

Grant,U.S. Home St.His. Site: Biesman & Nolan Hses
Bouthiller St.
HABS IL-1158
HABS 1992(HABS):IL-1
2dr/fr L

Hoge,Joseph,House
512 Park Ave.
HABS IL-26-11
HABS ILL,43-GALA,1-
5dr/7ph/1pg/fr L

Hunkins House
HABS IL-199
HABS ILL,43-GALA,31-
1ph L

Marine Hospital
HABS IL-307
HABS ILL,43-GALA,35-
3ph/1pc L

Market House,Old (Town Hall)
N. Commerce & Troy Sts.
HABS IL-149
HABS ILL,43-GALA,10-
8dr/12ph/3pg/fr L

Mississippi House (Hotel)
S. Main St.
HABS IL-152
HABS ILL,43-GALA,13-
2dr/2ph/2pg L

Nolan House
Bouthiller St.,U.S. Grant Home St. Hist. Site
HABS IL-1158-A
HABS 1992(HABS):IL-1
7dr/fr L

Smith,Gen. ,House
South & Bench Sts.
HABS IL-26-13
HABS ILL,43-GALA,3-
6dr/6ph/1pg/fr L

Specht House
HABS IL-196
HABS ILL,43-GALA,28-
3ph L

Stahl,Frederick,House
605 S. Bench St.
HABS IL-26-18
HABS ILL,43-GALA,7-
4dr/4ph/1pg/fr L

Telford House
Park Ave.
HABS IL-26-20
HABS ILL,43-GALA,9-
4dr/4ph/1pg/fr L

Town Hall; see Market House,Old

Washburne,Sen. Elihu B. ,House
908 Third St.
HABS IL-26-19
HABS ILL,43-GALA,8-
5dr/6ph/2pg/1pc L

GALENA VIC.

Chetlain,Louis,House
HABS IL-26-15
HABS ILL,43-GALA,V.1-
3dr/3ph/1pg/fr L

Roberts,James M. ,House
Rt. 5
HABS IL-26-21
HABS ILL,43-GALA.V,2-
6dr/3ph/2pg/fr L

KANE COUNTY

AURORA

Chicago,Burlington & Quincy RR:Roundhouse & Shops
Broadway & Spring Sts.
HAER IL-8
HAER ILL,45-AUR,1-
131ph/119pg/9pc/3ct/fr L

BATAVIA

Burke House
Washington St.
HABS IL-163
HABS ILL,45-BATA,1-
2dr/10ph/1pg/fr L

United Methodist Church of Batavia
8 N. Batavia Ave.
HABS IL-1135
HABS ILL,45-BATA,2-
8dr L

FAYVILLE

Keating House
U. S. Hwy. 430
HABS IL-165
HABS ILL,45-FAYV,1-
2dr/12ph/1pg/fr L

GENEVA

Unitarian Church,Old
Second & James Sts.
HABS IL-164
HABS ILL,45-GEVA,2-
1dr/3ph/2pg/fr L

Wells,Capt. ,House
S. Third St.
HABS IL-138
HABS ILL,45-GEVA,1-
3dr/4ph/2pg/fr L

GENEVA VIC.

Bristol Farmhouse
River Rd.
HABS IL-26-22
HABS ILL,45-GEVA.V,1-
3dr/3ph/1pg/fr L

ST. CHARLES

Jucket House
110 Third St.
HABS IL-162
HABS ILL,45-SAICH,2-
1dr/7ph/1pg/fr L

Lewis,Dr. Jas. K. ,House
19 S. Fifth St.
HABS IL-26-9
HABS ILL,45-SAICH,1-
5dr/2ph/1pg/fr L

KENDALL COUNTY

LISBON

Congregational Church
HABS IL-148
HABS ILL,47-LISB,1-
3dr/2ph/3pg/fr L

PLANO VIC.

Farnsworth,Edith,House
Fox River Rd. & Milbrook Rd.
HABS IL-1105
HABS ILL,47-PLAN.V,1-
10ph/8pg/1pc L

KNOX COUNTY

GALESBURG

Sandburg,Carl,Cottage
331 East Third St.
HABS IL-1159
HABS 1992(HABS):IL-1
7dr/fr L

KNOXVILLE

County Jail
115 Market St.
HABS IL-248-B
HABS ILL,48-KNOV,3-
5ph L

Hall of Records
Main St.
HABS IL-248-A
HABS ILL,48-KNOV,2-
2ph/fr L

Knox County Courthouse,Old
Main St.
HABS IL-248
HABS ILL,48-KNOV,1-
8dr/19ph/2pg/fr L

LONDON MILLS

London Mills Bridge
Spanning Spoon River
HAER IL-11
HAER ILL,48-LONMI,1-
10ph/3pg/1pc/fr L

LA SALLE COUNTY

LA SALLE

I & M Canal Nat'l Heritage Corridor; see Illinois Central Gulf RR Bridge

I & M Canal Nat'l Heritage Corridor; see Shippingsport Bridge

Illinois Central Gulf RR Bridge (I & M Canal Nat'l Heritage Corridor)
HAER IL-49
HAER ILL,81-ROCIL,3/1-
21ph H

Shippingsport Bridge (I & M Canal Nat'l Heritage Corridor)
State Rte. 51 crossing the Illinois River
HAER IL-56
HAER ILL,81-ROCIL,3/1-
48ph H

LASALLE

I & M Canal Nat'l Heritage Corridor; see LaSalle Passenger Depot

I & M Canal Nat'l Heritage Corridor; see Lift Lock No. 15

I & M Canal Nat'l Heritage Corridor; see Rock Island RR: LaSalle Freight Depot

Illinois Central Railroad
N. of First St.,E. of Union St.
HAER IL-23
fr H

Illinois Central Railroad,Freight Depot (LaSalle Freight Depot)
N. of First St.,E. of Union St.
HAER IL-23-A
3dr/9ph/3pg/1pc/fr L

Illinois Central Railroad,Freight Depot II
N. of First St.,E. of Union St.
HAER IL-23-B
6ph/1pc L

Illinois Central Railroad,Passenger Depot
N. of First St.,E. of Union St.
HAER IL-23-C
1ph/1pc L

Illinois Central Railroad,Passenger Depot II
N. of First Street,E. of Union St.
HAER IL-23-D
10ph/2pc L

Illinois Central Railroad,Sand Tank
N. of First St.,E. of Union St.
HAER IL-23-E
1ph/1pc L

LaSalle Freight Depot; see Illinois Central Railroad,Freight Depot

LaSalle Passenger Depot (I & M Canal Nat'l Heritage Corridor)
HAER IL-70
18ph H

Lasalle,Town of
HABS IL-313
HABS 1990 (HABS):4
341pg/fr L

Lift Lock No. 15 (I & M Canal Nat'l Heritage Corridor)
HAER IL-72
H

Rock Island RR: LaSalle Freight Depot (I & M Canal Nat'l Heritage Corridor)
Canal St. E. of Creve Coeur St.
HAER IL-74
H

MARSEILLES

Chicago,Rock Isl. & Pacific RR: Marseilles Depot (I & M Canal Nat'l Heritage Corridor)
HAER IL-98
H

I & M Canal Nat'l Heritage Corridor; see Chicago,Rock Isl. & Pacific RR: Marseilles Depot

I & M Canal Nat'l Heritage Corridor; see Illinois Power Co: Marseilles Hydro-Electric Plant

I & M Canal Nat'l Heritage Corridor; see J. Harrington & Co.: Grain Elevator & Office

I & M Canal Nat'l Heritage Corridor; see Marseille Nabisco Bridge

I & M Canal Nat'l Heritage Corridor; see National Biscuit Co.: Marseilles Factory

Illinois Power Co: Marseilles Hydro-Electric Plant (Illinois Traction System Hydro-Electric Plant; I & M Canal Nat'l Heritage Corridor)
HAER IL-93
H

Illinois Traction System Hydro-Electric Plant; see Illinois Power Co: Marseilles Hydro-Electric Plant

J. Harrington & Co.: Grain Elevator & Office (M & M Grain & Farm Supply Co.: Grain Elevator; I & M Canal Nat'l Heritage Corridor)
HAER IL-96
H

M & M Grain & Farm Supply Co.: Grain Elevator; see J. Harrington & Co.: Grain Elevator & Office

Marseille Nabisco Bridge (I & M Canal Nat'l Heritage Corridor)
HAER IL-97
H

Marseilles,Town of
HABS IL-317
HABS 1990 (HABS):4
128pg/fr L

Nabisco Main Carton Factory; see National Biscuit Co.: Marseilles Factory

National Biscuit Co.: Marseilles Factory (Nabisco Main Carton Factory; I & M Canal Nat'l Heritage Corridor)
HAER IL-68
30ph H

MENDOTA

Clark,Warren,House; see Octagon House

Octagon House (Clark,Warren,House)
HABS IL-180
HABS ILL,50-MEND,1-
3ph/2pg/fr L

OTTAWA

Chicago, Rock Isl. & Pac. RR: Ottawa Passenger Sta (I & M Canal Nat'l Heritage Corridor)
Columbus St. btwn. E. Marquette & Joliet Sts.
HAER IL-62
HAER ILL,81-ROCIL,3/1-
12ph H

Chicago,Burlington & Quincy RR Bridge (I & M Canal Nat'l Heritage Corridor)
HAER IL-71
H

Chicago,Burlington & Qunicy RR: Ottawa Pass. Sta. (I & M Canal Nat'l Heritage Corridor)
Corner of Walnut & Main Sts.
HAER IL-73
H

Fox River Aqueduct (I & M Canal Nat'l Heritage Corridor)
HAER IL-46
HAER ILL,81-ROCIL,3/1-
3ph H

Hossack,John,House
210 Prospect Ave.
HABS IL-141
HABS ILL,50-OTWA,1-
3dr/5ph/3pg/1pc/fr L

I & M Canal Nat'l Heritage Corridor; see Chicago, Rock Isl. & Pac. RR: Ottawa Passenger Sta

I & M Canal Nat'l Heritage Corridor; see Chicago,Burlington & Quincy RR Bridge

I & M Canal Nat'l Heritage Corridor; see Chicago,Burlington & Qunicy RR: Ottawa Pass. Sta.

I & M Canal Nat'l Heritage Corridor; see Fox River Aqueduct

I & M Canal Nat'l Heritage Corridor; see Illinois Traction System: Fox River Bridge

I & M Canal Nat'l Heritage Corridor; see King & Hamilton Agricultural Implement Mfg. Co.

I & M Canal Nat'l Heritage Corridor; see Ottawa Toll House

Illinois Traction System: Fox River Bridge (I & M Canal Nat'l Heritage Corridor)
HAER IL-82
H

King & Hamilton Agricultural Implement Mfg. Co. (I & M Canal Nat'l Heritage Corridor)
HAER IL-76
H

Ottawa Toll House (I & M Canal Nat'l Heritage Corridor)
HAER IL-100
H

Ottawa,Town of
HABS IL-316
HABS 1990 (HABS):4
679pg/fr L

OTTAWA VIC.

Mill "C" Complex (Ottawa Silica Company)
S. of Dee Bennet Rd., near Illinois River
HAER IL-24
1dr/3ph/3pg/1pc/fr L

Mill "C" Complex,Sand Draining & Drying Building
S. of Dee Bennet Rd.,near Illinois River
HAER IL-24-B
3dr/3ph/1pc L

Mill "C" Complex,Sand Sorting Building
S. of Dee Bennet Rd.,near Illinois River
HAER IL-24-A
7dr/16ph/2pc L

Ottawa Silica Company; see Mill "C" Complex

PERU

I & M Canal Nat'l Heritage Corridor; see Star Union Beer Co.: Brewery & Bottling Works

I & M Canal Nat'l Heritage Corridor; see Western Clock Co. (Westclox)

Peru,Town of
HABS IL-312
HABS 1989(HABS):9;1993:IL-3
4ph/531pg/1pc/fr L

Star Union Beer Co.: Brewery & Bottling Works (I & M Canal Nat'l Heritage Corridor)
HAER IL-86
H

Western Clock Co. (Westclox) (I & M Canal Nat'l Heritage Corridor)
HAER IL-83
H

SENECA

Armour's Warehouse (Hogan Grain Elevator)
Williams St.
HAER IL-25
HAER DLC/PP-1993:IL-2
6dr/3ph/16pg/1pc/fr L

Armour's Warehouse,Corn Crib (Hogan Grain Elevator,Corn Crib)
Williams St.
HAER IL-25-A
fr H

Chicago,Rock Isl & Pacific:Seneca Passenger Depot (I & M Canal Nat'l Heritage Corridor)
HAER IL-44
HAER ILL,81-ROCIL,3/1-
6ph H

Hogan Grain Elevator; see Armour's Warehouse

Hogan Grain Elevator,Corn Crib; see Armour's Warehouse,Corn Crib

I & M Canal Nat'l Heritage Corridor; see Chicago,Rock Isl & Pacific:Seneca Passenger Depot

Seneca,Town of
HABS IL-318
HABS 1989(HABS):9
103pg/fr L

UTICA

Chicago,Rock Isl. & Pacific RR: Utica Pass. Depot (I & M Canal Nat'l Heritage Corridor)
HAER IL-94
H

I & M Canal Nat'l Heritage Corridor; see Chicago,Rock Isl. & Pacific RR: Utica Pass. Depot

I & M Canal Nat'l Heritage Corridor; see Nash,Wright & Company:Grain Elevator (ca.1892)

Nash,Wright & Company:Grain Elevator (ca.1892) (Utica Elevator Co.: Grain Elevator; I & M Canal Nat'l Heritage Corridor)
HAER IL-95
H

Utica Elevator Co.: Grain Elevator; see Nash,Wright & Company:Grain Elevator (ca.1892)

Utica,Town of
HABS IL-315-A
71pg/fr L

UTICA VIC.

Halfway House; see Spring Valley House

Spring Valley House (Halfway House)
Dee Bennett Rd.
HABS IL-1150
HABS DLC/PP-1992:IL-5;1993:IL-3
8dr/1ph/15pg/1pc/fr L

Utica Township
HABS IL-315
HABS 1989(HABS):9
122pg/fr L

LAKE COUNTY

FORT SHERIDAN

Artillery Barracks,Building Number 84; see Fort Sheridan Historic District

Bachelor Officers Quarters,Open Mess,Building 31; see Fort Sheridan Historic District

Bakery,Building Number 34; see Fort Sheridan Historic District

Blacksmith Shop,Building Number 77; see Fort Sheridan Historic District

Captains's Quarters,Building Number 12; see Fort Sheridan Historic District

Cavalry Stable,Building Number 43; see Fort Sheridan Historic District

Cold Storage House,Building Number 100; see Fort Sheridan Historic District

Company Kitchens,Building Number 108; see Fort Sheridan Historic District

Dead House,Building Number 87; see Fort Sheridan Historic District

Fire Station,Building Number 79; see Fort Sheridan Historic District

Forage Storehouse,Building Number 39; see Fort Sheridan Historic District

Fort Sheridan Historic District
Chicago Vic.
HABS IL-1113
HABS ILL,49-FTSH,1-
7ph/26pg/2pc/fr L

Fort Sheridan Historic District (Artillery Barracks,Building Number 84)
Leonard Wood Ave.
HABS IL-1113-25
HABS ILL,49-FTSH,1/25-
6ph/5pg/1pc L

Fort Sheridan Historic District (Bachelor Officers Quarters,Open Mess,Building 31)
Leonard Wood Ave.
HABS IL-1113-6
HABS ILL,49-FTSH,1/6-
11ph/7pg/1pc/1ct L

Fort Sheridan Historic District (Bakery,Building Number 34)
Lyster Rd.
HABS IL-1113-8
HABS ILL,49-FTSH,1/8-
3ph/5pg/1pc L

Fort Sheridan Historic District (Blacksmith Shop,Building Number 77)
Thorpe Rd.
HABS IL-1113-22
HABS ILL,49-FTSH,1/22-
3ph/4pg/1pc L

Fort Sheridan Historic District (Captains's Quarters,Building Number 12)
149 Logan Loop
HABS IL-1113-3
HABS ILL,49-FTSH,1/3-
12ph/7pg/1pc/1ct L

Fort Sheridan Historic District (Cavalry Stable,Building Number 43)
Thorpe & Chapman Rds.
HABS IL-1113-14
HABS ILL,49-FTSH,1/14-
6ph/5pg/1pc/1ct L

Fort Sheridan Historic District (Cold Storage House,Building Number 100)
Lyster Rd.
HABS IL-1113-30
HABS ILL,49-FTSH,1/30-
2ph/4pg/1pc L

Fort Sheridan Historic District (Company Kitchens,Building Number 108)
Whistler Rd.
HABS IL-1113-31
HABS ILL,49-FTSH,1/31-
3ph/5pg/1pc L

Fort Sheridan Historic District (Dead House,Building Number 87)
Bradley Loop
HABS IL-1113-26
HABS ILL,49-FTSH,1/26-
2ph/4pg/1pc L

Fort Sheridan Historic District (Fire Station,Building Number 79)
Whistler & Ronan Rds.
HABS IL-1113-24
HABS ILL,49-FTSH,1/24-
4ph/4pg/1pc L

Fort Sheridan Historic District (Forage Storehouse,Building Number 39)
Thorpe Rd.
HABS IL-1113-13
HABS ILL,49-FTSH,1/13-
6ph/6pg/1pc/1ct L

Fort Sheridan Historic District (Guardhouse,Building Number 33)
Lyster Rd.
HABS IL-1113-7
HABS ILL,49-FTSH,1/7-
16ph/7pg/1pc/1ct L

Fort Sheridan Historic District (Gun Shed,Building Number 89)
Ronan Rd.
HABS IL-1113-27
HABS ILL,49-FTSH,1/27-
4ph/4pg/1pc/1ct L

Fort Sheridan Historic District (Infantry Barracks,Building Number 48)
Leonard Wood Ave.
HABS IL-1113-17
HABS ILL,49-FTSH,1/17-
12ph/7pg L

Fort Sheridan Historic District (Infantry Drill Hall,Building Number 60)
Whistler & Ronan Rds.
HABS IL-1113-21
HABS ILL,49-FTSH,1/21-
7ph/5pg/1pc/1ct L

Fort Sheridan Historic District (Lieutenant's Quarters,Building Number 22)
165 Scott Loop
HABS IL-1113-4
HABS ILL,49-FTSH,1/4-
11ph/7pg/1pc L

Fort Sheridan Historic District (Lieutenant's Quarters,Building Number 92)
3711 Leonard Wood Ave.
HABS IL-1113-29
HABS ILL,49-FTSH,1/29-
3ph/6pg/1pc L

Fort Sheridan Historic District (Magazine,Building Number 57A)
Bartlett Ravine Rd.
HABS IL-1113-19
HABS ILL,49-FTSH,1/19-
2ph/4pg/1pc L

Fort Sheridan Historic District (Mess Hall & Heating Plant,Building Number 47)
Whistler Rd.
HABS IL-1113-16
HABS ILL,49-FTSH,1/16-
7ph/6pg/1pc/1ct L

Fort Sheridan Historic District (Non-Commissioned Officer's Quarters,Building 46)
Ronan & Lyster Rds.
HABS IL-1113-15
HABS ILL,49-FTSH,1/15-
3ph/6pg/1pc/1ct L

Fort Sheridan Historic District (Non-Commissioned Officer's Quarters,Building 91)
3612 Lyster Rd.
HABS IL-1113-28
HABS ILL,49-FTSH,1/28-
4ph/5pg/1pc/1ct L

Fort Sheridan Historic District (Ordnance Storehouse,Building Number 59)
3588 Lyster Rd.
HABS IL-1113-20
HABS ILL,49-FTSH,1/20-
3ph/5pg/1pc L

Fort Sheridan Historic District (Post Commandant's Quarters,Building Number 9)
111 Logan Loop
HABS IL-1113-2
HABS ILL,49-FTSH,1/2-
13ph/8pg/1pc/1ct L

Fort Sheridan Historic District (Post Hospital,Building Number 1; Lovell Hospital)
Bradley Loop
HABS IL-1113-1
HABS ILL,49-FTSH,1/1-
9ph/7pg/1pc L

Fort Sheridan Historic District (Pumping Station,Building Number 29)
Nicholson Rd.
HABS IL-1113-5
HABS ILL,49-FTSH,1/5-
4ph/5pg/1pc L

Fort Sheridan Historic District (Quarter Master Stable Guardhouse,Building 37)
Lyster Rd.
HABS IL-1113-11
HABS ILL,49-FTSH,1/11-
3ph/5pg/1pc L

Fort Sheridan Historic District (Quartermaster Stable,Building Number 38)
Lyster Rd.
HABS IL-1113-12
HABS ILL,49-FTSH,1/12-
8ph/6pg/1pc/1ct L

Fort Sheridan Historic District (Quartermaster,Commissary Storehouse,Building 35)
Lyster Rd.
HABS IL-1113-9
HABS ILL,49-FTSH,1/9-
6ph/6pg/1pc L

Fort Sheridan Historic District (Saddlers' & Stable Sargeants Building,Number 78)
Ronan Rd.
HABS IL-1113-23
HABS ILL,49-FTSH,1/23-
3ph/5pg/1pc L

Fort Sheridan Historic District (Water Tower,Building Number 49)
Leonard Wood Ave.
HABS IL-1113-18
HABS ILL,49-FTSH,1/18-
19ph/8pg/2pc/2ct L

Fort Sheridan Historic District (Workshops,Building Number 36)
Lyster Rd.
HABS IL-1113-10
HABS ILL,49-FTSH,1/10-
6ph/5pg/1pc/1ct L

Guardhouse,Building Number 33; see Fort Sheridan Historic District

Gun Shed,Building Number 89; see Fort Sheridan Historic District

Infantry Barracks,Building Number 48; see Fort Sheridan Historic District

Infantry Drill Hall,Building Number 60; see Fort Sheridan Historic District

Lieutenant's Quarters,Building Number 22; see Fort Sheridan Historic District

Lieutenant's Quarters,Building Number 92; see Fort Sheridan Historic District

Lovell Hospital; see Fort Sheridan Historic District

Magazine,Building Number 57A; see Fort Sheridan Historic District

Mess Hall & Heating Plant,Building Number 47; see Fort Sheridan Historic District

Non-Commissioned Officer's Quarters,Building 46; see Fort Sheridan Historic District

Non-Commissioned Officer's Quarters,Building 91; see Fort Sheridan Historic District

Ordnance Storehouse,Building Number 59; see Fort Sheridan Historic District

Post Commandant's Quarters,Building Number 9; see Fort Sheridan Historic District

Post Hospital,Building Number 1; see Fort Sheridan Historic District

Pumping Station,Building Number 29; see Fort Sheridan Historic District

Quarter Master Stable Guardhouse,Building 37; see Fort Sheridan Historic District

Quartermaster Stable,Building Number 38; see Fort Sheridan Historic District

Quartermaster,Commissary Storehouse,Building 35; see Fort Sheridan Historic District

Saddlers' & Stable Sargeants Building,Number 78; see Fort Sheridan Historic District

Water Tower,Building Number 49; see Fort Sheridan Historic District

Workshops,Building Number 36; see Fort Sheridan Historic District

HALFDAY

Tavern
HABS IL-139
HABS ILL,49-HAFDA,1-
1dr/2ph/3pg/fr L

HIGHLAND PARK

Casino Building
Ravina Park
HABS IL-1147
HABS 1991(HABS(:17
7dr/10ph/4pg/1pc/fr L

MUNDELEIN

Marsh's Settlement,Schoolhouse
Rt. 176
HABS IL-140
HABS ILL,49-MUND,1-
1dr/2ph/3pg/fr L

WAUKEGAN

Swartout House
414 Sheridan Rd.
HABS IL-26-3
HABS ILL,49-WAUK,1-
4dr/3ph/1pg/fr L

WAUKEGAN VIC.

Lighthouse
HABS IL-176
HABS ILL,49-WAUK,2-
1ph L

LEE COUNTY

LEE CENTER

Adams,Dr. ,Office
Old Dixon-Chicago Pike
HABS IL-167
HABS ILL,52-LEEC,2-
1dr/10ph/2pg L

Four Bottle Tavern
Old Dixon-Chicago Pike
HABS IL-166
HABS ILL,52-LEEC,1-
2dr/7ph/1pg/fr L

SUBLETTE

Baptist Parsonage,Old
Snyder & Virginia Sts.
HABS IL-168
HABS ILL,52-SUB,1-
2dr/8ph/1pg/fr L

LIVINGSTON COUNTY

SAUNEMIN VIC.

Vieley Bridge
Spanning N. Fork Vermillion River at Twp. Rd. 220D
HAER IL-22
HAER ILL,53-SAUN.V,1-
14ph/6pg/1pc L

MACON COUNTY

DECATUR

Macon County Courthouse,First
Fairview Park (moved from Main St.)
HABS IL-222
HABS ILL,58-DECA,1-
2dr/2ph/3pg/fr L

MACOUPIN COUNTY

CARLINVILLE

Macoupin County Courthouse
HABS IL-1183
HABS DLC/PP-1993:IL-1
19dr/fr L

MADISON COUNTY

ALTON

Academic Hall,Old; see Shurtleff College,Loomis Hall

Alton Bridge
Spanning Mississippi River between IL & MO
HAER IL-21
HAER 1989(HAER):7
44ph/3pc L

Shurtleff College,Loomis Hall (Academic Hall,Old)
HABS IL-25-20
HABS ILL,60-ALT,1A-
7dr/1ph/3pg/fr L

Upper Miss. Riv. 9-Ft. Chnl. Proj.,Lock & Dam 26
HAER IL-31
HAER DLC/PP-1992:IL-3
81ph/10pg/6pc L

ALTON VIC.

Upper Miss. Riv. 9-Ft. Chnl. Proj.,Lock & Dam 26R
HAER IL-32
HAER DLC/PP-1992:IL-3
59ph/8pg/5pc L

EDWARDSVILLE

Wabash Hotel,Old
Main & Union Sts.
HABS IL-236
HABS ILL,60-EDVI,1-
3dr/1ph/3pg/fr L

Warren,Hooper,Print Shop
HABS IL-238
HABS ILL,6--EDVI,2-
1ph/3pg L

EDWARDSVILLE VIC.

Paddock,Galus,Farm (Windmill)
Springfield Rd.
HABS IL-237
HABS ILL,60- ,1A-
3dr/2ph/2pg/fr L

Windmill; see Paddock,Galus,Farm

GODFREY

Godfrey Congregational Church
State Rt. 111
HABS IL-25-10
HABS ILL,60-GODF,2-
9dr/6ph/7pg/1pc/fr L

Godfrey Homestead
Delhi Rd.
HABS IL-25-9
HABS ILL,6-GODF,1-
6dr/3ph/2pg/fr L

GRANITE CITY

St. Louis Area Support Center
HAER IL-17
HAER ILL,60-GRACI,1-
29pg/fr L

Upper Miss. Riv. 9-Ft. Chnl. Proj.,Lock & Dam 27
HAER IL-33
HAER DLC/PP-1992:IL-3
92ph/10pg/7pc L

MCHENRY COUNTY

MARENGO

Rogers,Anson,House & Farm Buildings
U. S. Rt. 20
HABS IL-144
HABS ILL,56-MARGO,2-
3dr/6ph/3pg/fr L

Thompson Store
109 W. Grant Hwy.
HABS IL-143
HABS ILL,56-MARGO,1-
2dr/3ph/2pg/fr L

WOODSTOCK VIC.

Kennedy Farmhouse
Rt. 14
HABS IL-182
HABS ILL,56-WOOD.V,1-
2dr/13ph/1pc/fr L

MCLEAN COUNTY

BLOOMINGTON

Davis,David,Mansion
Monroe & Davis Sts.
HABS IL-302
HABS ILL,57-BLOOM,2-
7dr/8ph/4pg/fr L

Major's Hall
117 E. Front St.
HABS IL-239
HABS ILL,57-BLOOM,1-
2dr/1ph/5pg/fr L

NORMAL

Fell,Jesse,House
502 Irving (moved from Broadway & Irving Sts.)
HABS IL-262
HABS ILL,57-NORM,1-
2dr/3ph/4pg/fr L

MENARD COUNTY

PETERSBURG

Mick Cottage & Summer Kitchens
(Ogg-Scott House)
423 N. Seventh St.
HABS IL-1115
HABS ILL,65-PETE,2-
11ph/2pg/1pc L

Ogg-Scott House; see Mick Cottage & Summer Kitchens

MERCER COUNTY

KEITHSBURG

Keithsburg Bridge (Wycoff Bridge; Watts Bridge)
Sixteenth Street Spanning Pope Creek
HAER IL-34
HAER 1991(HAER):14
10ph/11pg/1pc L

Watts Bridge; see Keithsburg Bridge

Wycoff Bridge; see Keithsburg Bridge

NEW BOSTON

Miss. River 9-Ft. Channel Proj.,Lock & Dam No. 17
Upper Mississippi River
HAER IL-28
HAER 1991(HAER):14
78ph/14pg/5pc L

MONROE COUNTY

COLUMBIA

Buck Tavern (Grosse Inn)
401 Main St.
HABS IL-232-3
HABS ILL,67-COLUM,3-
2dr/4ph/2pg/1pc/fr L

808 East Main Street (House)
HABS IL-232-6
HABS ILL,67-COLUM,6A-
4dr/2ph/1pg L

810 East Main Street (House)
HABS IL-232-7
HABS ILL,67-COLUM,6B-
3dr/1ph/1pg L

812 East Main Street (House)
HABS IL-232-8
HABS ILL,67-COLUM,6C-
4dr/2ph/1pg L

Grosse Inn; see Buck Tavern

Grosse,Emelie,House (Gundlach House)
HABS IL-232-1
HABS ILL,67-COLUM,1-
3dr/13ph/2pg/1pc/fr L

Gundlach House; see Grosse,Emelie,House

Habermehl,Jacob,House (Pig's Eye House)
Second & Pine Sts.
HABS IL-232-4
HABS ILL,67-COLUM,4-
1ph/1pg/fr L

House,Brick
HABS IL-189
HABS ILL,67-COLUM,10-
1ph/1pc L

House,Brick
HABS IL-190
HABS ILL,67-COLUM,11-
1ph/1pc L

House,Brick
HABS IL-191
HABS ILL,67-COLUM,12-
1ph/1pc L

House,Brick
HABS IL-220
HABS ILL,67-COLUM,9-
1ph/1pc/fr L

House,Brick
HABS IL-260
HABS ILL,67-COLUM,8-
1ph/1pc L

House,Stone
HABS IL-187
HABS ILL,67-COLUM,13-
1ph/1pc L

Ichmiller,Mary,House
803 E. Main St.
HABS IL-232-9
HABS ILL,67-COLUM,7-
3ph/2pg/1pc/fr L

808-812 Main Street (Houses)
HABS IL-232
HABS ILL,67-COLUM,6-
3ph L

Otto,Emil,House
Main St.
HABS IL-232-2
HABS ILL,67-COLUM,2-
2dr/3ph/2pg/1pc/fr L

Pig's Eye House; see Habermehl,Jacob,House

Schneider,Ed J. ,House
123 E. Main St.
HABS IL-232-5
HABS ILL,67-COLUM,5-
2dr/1ph/1pg L

Street Scene
HABS IL-186
HABS ILL,67-COLUM,14-
1ph/1pc L

WATERLOO

House,Brick
HABS IL-193
HABS ILL,67-WALO,1-
2ph/1pc L

House,Frame
HABS IL-219
HABS ILL,67-WALO,2-
2ph/1pc/fr L

House,Stone
HABS IL-194
HABS ILL,67-WALO,3-
1ph/1pc L

House,Stone
HABS IL-195
HABS ILL,67-WALO,4-
1ph/1pc L

WATERLOO VIC.

Fort Lemen; see Lemen,James,House

Lemen,James,House (Fort Lemen)
State Hwy. 3
HABS IL-230
HABS ILL,67-WALO.V,1-
2dr/3ph/3pg L

MORGAN COUNTY

JACKSONVILLE

"Prairie College"; see Illinois College,Beecher Hall

Clay,Porter,House (Sanders House)
1019 W. State St.
HABS IL-226
HABS ILL,69-JACVI,3-
11dr/4ph/5pg/fr L

Duncan,Gov. Joseph,House
4 Duncan Pl.
HABS IL-25-8
HABS ILL,69-JACVI,1-
11dr/4ph/7pg/fr L

Illinois College,Beecher Hall ("Prairie College")
HABS IL-25-11
HABS ILL,69-JACVI,2A-
11dr/4ph/15pg L

Sanders House; see Clay,Porter,House

OGLE COUNTY

GRAND DETOUR

Paine,Horace,House
Walker & Illinois Sts.
HABS IL-175
HABS ILL,71-GRAD,3-
2dr/9ph/1pg/1pc/fr L

Pankhurst House
HABS IL-183
HABS ILL,71-GRAD,2-
6ph L

St. Peter's Episcopal Church
Rock & Main Sts.
HABS IL-174
HABS ILL,71-GRAD,1-
1dr/8ph/3pg/fr L

PEORIA COUNTY

JUBILEE

Jubilee College
HABS IL-235
HABS ILL,72-JUB,1-
6dr/12ph/10pg/fr L

MOSSVILLE

Methodist Episcopal Church (Presbyterian Church)
HABS IL-282
HABS ILL,72-MOSVI,1-
2dr/4ph/2pg/fr L

Presbyterian Church; see Methodist Episcopal Church

PEORIA

Bohanan House (West Bluff Historic District "Beer Baron Row")
509 W. High St.
HABS IL-1174
HABS DLC/PP-1992:IL-3
1dr/fr L

Bourland House (West Bluff Historic District "Beer Baron Row")
519 W. High St.
HABS IL-1178
HABS DLC/PP-1992:IL-3
1dr/fr L

Easton House (West Bluff Historic District "Beer Baron Row")
1125 Main St.
HABS IL-1166
HABS DLC/PP-1992:IL-3
1dr/fr L

Francis,J. H.,House (West Bluff Historic District "Beer Baron Row")
429 W. High St.
HABS IL-1170
HABS DLC/PP-1992;IL-3
1dr/fr L

Francis,W.,House (West Bluff Historic District "Beer Baron Row")
600 W. High St.
HABS IL-1180
HABS DLC/PP-1992;IL-3
1dr/fr L

Giant Oak Park (West Bluff Historic District "Beer Baron Row")
420 W. High St.
HABS IL-1169
HABS DLC/PP-1992;IL-3
1dr/fr L

Hale Memorial Methodist-Episcopal Church (West Bluff Historic District "Beer Baron Row")
HABS IL-1165
HABS DLC/PP-1992;IL-3
8dr/fr L

Hardin House (West Bluff Historic District "Beer Baron Row")
511 W. High St.
HABS IL-1176
HABS DLC/PP-1992;IL-3
1dr/fr L

Peoria City Hall
419 Fulton St.
HABS IL-1129
HABS ILL,72-PEOR,1-
15ph/9pg/2pc L

443 W. High St. (West Bluff Historic District "Beer Baron Row")
HABS IL-1173
HABS DLC/PP-1992:IL-3
2dr/fr L

510 W. High St. (West Bluff Historic District "Beer Baron Row")
HABS IL-1175
HABS DLC/PP-1992:IL-3
1dr/fr L

West Bluff Historic District "Beer Baron Row"; see Bohanan House

West Bluff Historic District "Beer Baron Row"; see Bourland House

West Bluff Historic District "Beer Baron Row"; see Easton House

West Bluff Historic District "Beer Baron Row"; see Francis,J. H.,House

West Bluff Historic District "Beer Baron Row"; see Francis,W.,House

West Bluff Historic District "Beer Baron Row"; see Giant Oak Park

West Bluff Historic District "Beer Baron Row"; see Hale Memorial Methodist-Episcopal Church

West Bluff Historic District "Beer Baron Row"; see Hardin House

West Bluff Historic District "Beer Baron Row"; see 443 W. High St.

West Bluff Historic District "Beer Baron Row"; see 510 W. High St.

West Bluff Historic District "Beer Baron Row"; see West Bluff:High Street

West Bluff Historic District "Beer Baron Row"; see 423 West High Street

West Bluff Historic District "Beer Baron Row"; see 437 West High Street

West Bluff Historic District "Beer Baron Row"; see 438 West High Street

West Bluff Historic District "Beer Baron Row"; see 518 West High Street

West Bluff Historic District "Beer Baron Row"; see 524 West High Street

West Bluff Historic District "Beer Baron Row"; see West High Street,House

West Bluff:High Street (West Bluff Historic District "Beer Baron Row")
High St.
HABS IL-1164
HABS DLC/PP-1992;IL-3
2dr/fr L

423 West High Street (West Bluff Historic District "Beer Baron Row")
HABS IL-1167
HABS DLC/PP-1992:IL-3
1dr/fr L H

437 West High Street (West Bluff Historic District "Beer Baron Row")
HABS IL-1171
HABS DLC/PP-1992:IL-3
2dr/fr L

438 West High Street (West Bluff Historic District "Beer Baron Row")
HABS IL-1172
HABS DLC/PP-1992:IL-3
1dr/fr L

518 West High Street (West Bluff Historic District "Beer Baron Row")
HABS IL-1177
HABS DLC/PP-1992:IL-3
1dr/fr L

524 West High Street (West Bluff Historic District "Beer Baron Row")
HABS IL-1179
HABS DLC/PP-1992:IL-3
1dr/fr L

West High Street,House (West Bluff Historic District "Beer Baron Row")
HABS IL-1168
HABS DLC/PP-1992;IL-3
1dr/fr L

PIATT COUNTY

BEMENT

Bryant House
116 Wilson St.
HABS IL-223
HABS ILL,74-BEM,1-
2dr/3ph/5pg/fr L

BEMENT VIC.

Lincoln-Douglas Road Marker
HABS IL-1117
HABS ILL,74-BEM.V,1-
1ph L

MONTICELLO

Hammerschmidt,Louis,House
817 Charter St.
HABS IL-25-12
HABS ILL,74-MONCEL,1-
4dr/1ph/1pg/fr L

WHITE HEATH VIC.

Caldwell Elevator
State Rd. 10
HABS IL-1134
HABS ILL,74-WHEA.V,1-
9dr/fr L

PIKE COUNTY

BARRY

Gray,Burton,House
835 Rodgers St.
HABS IL-1131
HABS ILL,75-BAR,3-
4ph/4pg/1pc L

809 Rodgers Street (House)
HABS IL-1130
HABS ILL,75-BAR,2-
2ph/1pg/1pc L

865 Rodgers Street (House)
HABS IL-1132
HABS ILL,75-BAR,1-
2ph/1pg/1pc L

EAST HANNIBAL

Twain,Mark,Memorial Bridge
(See MISSOURI,PIKE COUNTY,HANNIBAL for documents.)
HAER MO-77
HAER DC,GEO,42-
L

PITTSFIELD

Worthington House
Franklin & W. Washington Sts.
HABS IL-264
HABS ILL,75-PITFI,1-
3dr/5ph/4pg/fr L

PULASKI COUNTY

CAIRO

Cairo Bridge
Spanning Ohio River
HAER IL-36
HAER ILL,77-CAIRO,1-
3ph/1pc L

RANDOLPH COUNTY

EDEN VIC.

Bannister,Oliver,House
HABS IL-297
HABS ILL,79-ED.V,1-
2ph L

FORT GAGE

Fort Kaskaskia (Ruins)
HABS IL-287
HABS ILL,79-FORGA,2-
2ph L

Menard,Pierre,House
County HWY. 6
HABS IL-286
HABS ILL,79-FORGA,1-
ι1991(HABS):17°
1dr/8ph/4pg/1pc/fr L

KASKASKIA

Shandrach Bond Mantel
(moved to IL Evanston 929 Sheridan Rd.)
HABS IL-26-31-B
HABS ILL,16-EVAN,1-
fr L

PRAIRIE DU ROCHER

Fort de Chartres
HABS IL-304
HABS ILL,79-PRARO.V,1-
4ph/1pc L

Fort de Chartres
Fort de Chartres State Park
HABS IL-309
HABS ILL,79-PRARO.V,1-
7ph L

Fort de Chartres,Powder Magazine
HABS IL-1157
1ph/1pc L

Fort de Chartres,Powder Magazine
Fort de Chartres State Park
HABS IL-288
HABS ILL,79-PRARO.V,1A-
4ph/1pc L

Fort de Chartres:East Barracks Foundation
Fort de Chartres State Park
HABS IL-299
HABS ILL,79-PRARO.V,1C-
1ph L

Fort de Chartres:Foundation of Officers' Quarters
Fort de Chartres State Park
HABS IL-289
HABS ILL,79-PRARO.V,1B-
1ph L

Fort de Chartres:Foundation-Commandant's Quarters
Fort de Chartres State Park
HABS IL-301
HABS ILL,79-PRARO.V,1E-
1ph L

Fort de Chartres:West Barracks Foundation
Fort de Chartres State Park
HABS IL-300
HABS ILL,79-PRARO.V,1D-
1ph L

French (Creole) House
Market St.
HABS IL-234
HABS ILL,79-PRARO,1-
4dr/1ph/2pg/fr L

REDBUD

Schuck House
HABS IL-294
HABS ILL,79-REDBU,1-
3ph L

SPARTA VIC.

Fulton House
HABS IL-293
HABS ILL,79-SPART.V,2-
1ph L

Glen,Amos,House
HABS IL-292
HABS ILL,79-SPART.V,1-
2ph L

TILDEN VIC.

Boyd,Sammuel,House
HABS IL-298
HABS ILL,79-TILD.V,1-
3ph L

ROCK ISLAND COUNTY

ROCK ISLAND

Bridge Spanning Mississippi River
HABS IL-1002
HABS ILL,81-ROCIL,4-
1ph L

Davenport,Col. ,House; see Rock Island Arsenal,Building No. 346

Fort Armstrong
HABS IL-1000
HABS ILL,81-ROCIL,2-
4ph/1pg L

Miss. River 9-Ft. Channel Proj.,Lock & Dam No. 15
Upper Mississipi River (Arsenal Island)
HAER IL-27
HAER 1991(HAER):14
52ph/16pg/4pc L

Rock Island Arsenal
HABS IL-1001
HAER IL-20
HABS/HAER ILL,81-ROCIL,3-
4dr/3ph/29pg/2pc/fr L

Rock Island Arsenal,A-C Connection; see Rock Island Arsenal,Building No. 103

Rock Island Arsenal,Artillery Wheel Stock Dry Kiln; see Rock Island Arsenal,Building No. 139

Rock Island Arsenal,B-D Connection; see Rock Island Arsenal,Building No. 61

Rock Island Arsenal,Barracks,Ameta Building; see Rock Island Arsenal,Building No. 90

Rock Island Arsenal,Building No. 1
(Rock Island Arsenal,Commanding Officer's Quarters)
Gillespie Ave. between Terr
HABS IL-1001-E
HABS ILL,81-ROCIL,3/1-
35ph/27pg/3pc L

Rock Island Arsenal,Building No. 102
(Rock Island Arsenal,Shop A)
Rodman Ave. between Gillespie Ave. & First St.
HAER IL-20-F
HAER ILL,81-ROCIL,3/102-
14ph/13pg/2pc L

Rock Island Arsenal,Building No. 103
(Rock Island Arsenal,A-C Connection)
Rodman Ave. & First St.
HAER IL-20-S
HAER ILL,81-ROCIL,3/103-
3ph/9pg/1pc L

Rock Island Arsenal,Building No. 104
(Rock Island Arsenal,Shop C)
Rodman Ave. between First & Second Sts.
HAER IL-20-G
HAER ILL,81-ROCIL,3/104-
6ph/14pg/1pc L

Rock Island Arsenal,Building No. 105
(Rock Island Arsenal,Shop C,Boiler House)
South Ave. between Gillespie Ave. & Second St.
HAER IL-20-K
HAER ILL,81-ROCIL,3/105-
8ph/11pg/1pc L

Rock Island Arsenal,Building No. 106
(Rock Island Arsenal,Shop E)
Rodman Ave. between Second & Third Sts.
HAER IL-20-H
HAER ILL,81-ROCIL,3/106-
18ph/15pg/2pc L

Rock Island Arsenal,Building No. 108
(Rock Island Arsenal,Shop G)
Rodman Ave. between Third & Fourth Sts.
HAER IL-20-I
HAER ILL,81-ROCIL,3/108-
6ph/15pg/1pc L

Rock Island Arsenal,Building No. 109
(Rock Island Arsenal,G-I Connection)
Rodman Ave. & Fourth St.
HAER IL-20-T
HAER ILL,81-ROCIL,3/109-
5ph/9pg/1pc L

Rock Island Arsenal,Building No. 110
(Rock Island Arsenal,Shop I)
Rodman Ave. between Fourth St. & East Ave.
HAER IL-20-J
HAER ILL,81-ROCIL,3/110-
7ph/15pg/1pc L

Rock Island Arsenal,Building No. 131
(Rock Island Arsenal,Storehouse A)
South Ave. between Gillespie Ave. & Second St.
HAER IL-20-BB
HAER ILL,81-ROCIL,3/131-
22ph/10pg/2pc L

Rock Island Arsenal,Building No. 133
(Rock Island Arsenal,Incinerator Building)
Gillespie Ave. between South Ave. & Ramsey St.
HAER IL-20-Y
HAER ILL,81-ROCIL,3/133-
4ph/9pg/1pc L

Rock Island Arsenal,Building No. 138
(Rock Island Arsenal,Lumber Shed)
Second Ave. between South Ave. & Ramsey St.
HAER IL-20-N
HAER ILL,81-ROCIL,3/138-
11ph/8pg/1pc L

Rock Island Arsenal,Building No. 139
(Rock Island Arsenal,Artillery Wheel Stock Dry Kiln
Second St. between Ramsey St. & South Ave.
HAER IL-20-W
HAER ILL,81-ROCIL,3/139-
5ph/9pg/1pc L

Rock Island Arsenal,Building No. 140
(Rock Island Arsenal,Gun Stock Dry Kiln)
Second St. between Ramsey St. & South Ave.
HAER IL-20-X
HAER ILL,81-ROCIL,3/140-
7ph/10pg/1pc L

Rock Island Arsenal,Building No. 160
(Rock Island Arsenal,Powerhouse; Rock Island Arsenal,Hydroelectric Plant)
Sylvan Drive
HAER IL-20-CC
HAER ILL,81-ROCIL,3/160-
24ph/13pg/2pc L

Rock Island Arsenal,Building No. 2
(Rock Island Arsenal,Subaltern Officer's Quarters)
Terrace Drive between Gillespie Ave. & East Ave.
HABS IL-1001-F
HABS ILL,81-ROCIL,3/2-
15ph/14pg/2pc L

Rock Island Arsenal,Building No. 210
(Rock Island Arsenal,Shop R,Recuperator Building)
Rodman Ave. & Gronen St.
HAER IL-20-Z
HAER ILL,81-ROCIL,3/210-
9ph/9pg/1pc L

Rock Island Arsenal,Building No. 220
(Rock Island Arsenal,Shop M,Field & Seige Building)
Rodman Ave. between Flager & Gronen Sts.
HAER IL-20-AA
HAER ILL,81-ROCIL,3/220-
13ph/12pg/2pc L

Rock Island Arsenal,Building No. 225
(Rock Island Arsenal,Post Building; Rock Island Arsenal,Fire Engine & Main Guard House
Rodman Ave. between Flagler St. & Gillespie Ave.
HABS IL-1001-B
HABS ILL,81-ROCIL,3/225-
15ph/13pg/2pc L

Rock Island Arsenal,Building No. 250
(Rock Island,Artillery Ammunition Assembling Plant)
Gillespie Ave. between Ramsey St. & South Ave.
HAER IL-20-U
HAER ILL,81-ROCIL,3/250-
14ph/12pg/2pc L

Rock Island Arsenal,Building No. 251
(Rock Island Arsenal,TNT Building)
Gillespie Ave. & Ramsey St.
HAER IL-20-V
HAER ILL,81-ROCIL,3/251-
6ph/9pg/1pc L

Rock Island Arsenal,Building No. 280
(Rock Island Arsenal,Magazine)
Sylvan Drive
HAER IL-20-O
HAER ILL,81-ROCIL,3/280-
6ph/8pg/1pc L

Rock Island Arsenal,Building No. 3
(Rock Island Arsenal,Subaltern Officer's Quarters)
Terrace Drive between Gillespie & East Aves.
HABS IL-1001-G
HABS ILL,81-ROCIL,3/3-
17ph/13pg/2pc L

Rock Island Arsenal,Building No. 321
(Rock Island Arsenal,Guard House)
Rodman Ave. & Rock Island Ave.
HABS IL-1001-D
HABS ILL,81-ROCIL,3/321-
6ph/8pg/1pc L

Rock Island Arsenal,Building No. 346
(Davenport,Col. ,House)
Davenport Drive,Arsenal Grounds
HABS IL-158
HABS ILL,81-ROCIL,1-
4dr/27ph/12pg/1pc/fr L

Rock Island Arsenal,Building No. 360
(Rock Island Arsenal,Headquarters)
Gillespie Av. between Rodman Ave. & North Ave.
HABS IL-1001-C
HABS ILL,81-ROCIL,3/360-
20ph/14pg/2pc L

Rock Island Arsenal,Building No. 4
(Rock Island Arsenal,Subaltern Officer's Quarters)
Terrace Ave. between Gillespie & East Aves.
HABS IL-1001-H
HABS ILL,81-ROCIL,3/4-
13ph/13pg/2pc L

Rock Island Arsenal,Building No. 53
(Rock Island Arsenal,Water Pumping Reservoir)
North Ave. N. of Midpoint
HAER IL-20-M
HAER ILL,81-ROCIL,3/53-
5ph/10pg/1pc L

Rock Island Arsenal,Building No. 56
(Rock Island Arsenal,Storehouse K)
North Ave. & East Ave.
HAER IL-20-L
HAER ILL,81-ROCIL,3/56-
11ph/11pg/1pc L

Rock Island Arsenal,Building No. 60
(Rock Island Arsenal,Shop B)
Rodman Ave. between Gillespie Ave. & First St.
HAER IL-20-A
HAER ILL,81-ROCIL,3/60-
8ph/18pg/1pc L

Rock Island Arsenal,Building No. 61
(Rock Island Arsenal,B-D Connection)
Rodman Ave. & First St.
HAER IL-20-Q
HAER ILL,81-ROCIL,3/61-
3ph/9pg/1pc L

Rock Island Arsenal,Building No. 62
(Rock Island Arsenal,Shop D)
Rodman Ave. between First & Second Sts.
HAER IL-20-B
HAER ILL,81-ROCIL,3/62-
7ph/14pg/1pc L

Rock Island Arsenal,Building No. 64
(Rock Island Arsenal,Shop F)
Rodman Ave. between Second & Third Sts.
HAER IL-20-C
HAER ILL,81-ROCIL,3/64-
20ph/16pg/2pc L

Rock Island Arsenal,Building No. 66
(Rock Island Arsenal,Shop H)
Rodman Ave. between Third & Fourth Sts.
HAER IL-20-D
HAER ILL,81-ROCIL,3/66-
18ph/15pg/2pc L

Rock Island Arsenal,Building No. 67
(Rock Island Arsenal,H-K Connection)
Rodman Ave. & Fourth St.
HAER IL-20-R
HAER ILL,81-ROCIL,3/67-
5ph/9pg/1pc L

Rock Island Arsenal,Building No. 68
(Rock Island Arsenal,Shop K)
Rodman Ave. between Fourth St. & East Ave.
HAER IL-20-E
HAER ILL,81-ROCIL,3/68-
9ph/15pg/1pc L

Rock Island Arsenal,Building No. 90
(Rock Island Arsenal,Barracks,Ameta Building)
East Ave. between North Ave. & King Drive
HABS IL-1001-A
HABS ILL,81-ROCIL,3/90-
16ph/12pg/2pc L

Rock Island Arsenal,Commanding Officer's Quarters; see Rock Island Arsenal,Building No. 1

Rock Island Arsenal,Fire Engine & Main Guard House; see Rock Island Arsenal,Building No. 225

Rock Island Arsenal,G-I Connection; see Rock Island Arsenal,Building No. 109

Rock Island Arsenal,Government Bridge; see Rock Island Arsenal,Rock Island Bridge

Rock Island Arsenal,Guard House; see Rock Island Arsenal,Building No. 321

Rock Island Arsenal,Gun Stock Dry Kiln; see Rock Island Arsenal,Building No. 140

Rock Island Arsenal,H-K Connection; see Rock Island Arsenal,Building No. 67

Rock Island Arsenal,Headquarters; see Rock Island Arsenal,Building No. 360

Rock Island Arsenal,Hydroelectric Plant; see Rock Island Arsenal,Building No. 160

Rock Island Arsenal,Incinerator Building; see Rock Island Arsenal,Building No. 133

Rock Island Arsenal,Lumber Shed; see Rock Island Arsenal,Building No. 138

Rock Island Arsenal,Magazine; see Rock Island Arsenal,Building No. 280

Rock Island Arsenal,Post Building; see Rock Island Arsenal,Building No. 225

Rock Island Arsenal,Powerhouse; see Rock Island Arsenal,Building No. 160

Rock Island Arsenal,Rock Island Bridge (Rock Island Arsenal,Government Bridge)
Fort Armstrong Ave.
HAER IL-20-P
HAER ILL,81-ROCIL,3A-
26ph/16pg/2pc L

Rock Island Arsenal,Shop A; see Rock Island Arsenal,Building No. 102

Rock Island Arsenal,Shop B; see Rock Island Arsenal,Building No. 60

Rock Island Arsenal,Shop C; see Rock Island Arsenal,Building No. 104

Rock Island Arsenal,Shop C,Boiler House; see Rock Island Arsenal,Building No. 105

Rock Island Arsenal,Shop D; see Rock Island Arsenal,Building No. 62

Rock Island Arsenal,Shop E; see Rock Island Arsenal,Building No. 106

Rock Island Arsenal,Shop F; see Rock Island Arsenal,Building No. 64

Rock Island Arsenal,Shop G; see Rock Island Arsenal,Building No. 108

Rock Island Arsenal,Shop H; see Rock Island Arsenal,Building No. 66

Rock Island Arsenal,Shop I; see Rock Island Arsenal,Building No. 110

Rock Island Arsenal,Shop K; see Rock Island Arsenal,Building No. 68

Rock Island Arsenal,Shop M,Field & Seige Building; see Rock Island Arsenal,Building No. 220

Rock Island Arsenal,Shop R,Recuperator Building; see Rock Island Arsenal,Building No. 210

Rock Island Arsenal,Storehouse A; see Rock Island Arsenal,Building No. 131

Rock Island Arsenal,Storehouse K; see Rock Island Arsenal,Building No. 56

Rock Island Arsenal,Subaltern Officer's Quarters; see Rock Island Arsenal,Building No. 2

Rock Island Arsenal,Subaltern Officer's Quarters; see Rock Island Arsenal,Building No. 3

Rock Island Arsenal,Subaltern Officer's Quarters; see Rock Island Arsenal,Building No. 4

Rock Island Arsenal,TNT Building; see Rock Island Arsenal,Building No. 251

Rock Island Arsenal,Water Pumping Reservoir; see Rock Island Arsenal,Building No. 53

Rock Island,Artillery Ammunition Assembling Plant; see Rock Island Arsenal,Building No. 250

SANGAMON COUNTY

PLEASANT PLAINS

Fink,Dr. F. C. ,House
State Rt. 125
HABS IL-269
HABS ILL,84-PLEP.V,1-
4dr/6ph/3pg/fr L

SPRINGFIELD

Lincoln Home National Historic Site; see Lincoln Home Site,Arnold House

Lincoln Home National Historic Site; see Lincoln Home Site,Dean House

Lincoln Home National Historic Site; see Lincoln Home Site,Dubois House

Lincoln Home National Historic Site; see Lincoln Home Site,Miller House

Lincoln Home National Historic Site; see Lincoln Home Site,Sprigg House

Lincoln Home Site,Aitkin Barn
519 S. 8th St.(alley),Lincoln Home NHS
HABS IL-1123-L
HABS ILL,84-SPRIF,2L-
1dr/fr L

Lincoln Home Site,Arnold House
(Lincoln Home National Historic Site)
810 E. Jackson Ave.
HABS IL-1123-A
HABS ILL,84-SPRIF,2A-
3dr/fr L

Lincoln Home Site,Beedle House
8th St. between Jackson St. & Capitol Ave.
HABS IL-1123-H
HABS ILL,84-SPRIF,2H-
4dr/fr L

Lincoln Home Site,Chronology Drawings:1839-1986 (Lincoln Home Site,Lincoln,Abraham,Cottage; Lincoln Home Site,Dresser,Rev. Charles,House)
Jackson & 8th Sts.,Lincoln Home NHS
HABS IL-1123-K
HABS ILL,84-SPRIF,2K-
6dr/fr L

Lincoln Home Site,Dean House
(Lincoln Home National Historic Site)
419 S. Eighth St.
HABS IL-1123-E
HABS ILL,84-SPRIF,2E-
4dr/fr L

Lincoln Home Site,Dresser,Rev. Charles,House; see Lincoln Home Site,Chronology Drawings:1839-1986

Lincoln Home Site,Dubois House
(Lincoln Home National Historic Site)
519 S. Eighth St.
HABS IL-1123-C
HABS ILL,84-SPRIF,2C-
4dr/fr L

Lincoln Home Site,Lincoln,Abraham,Cottage; see Lincoln Home Site,Chronology Drawings:1839-1986

Lincoln Home Site,Lyon House
8th St. between Jackson St. & Capitol Ave.
HABS IL-1123-I
HABS ILL,84-SPRIF,2I-
3dr/fr L

Lincoln Home Site,Miller House
(Lincoln Home National Historic Site)
511 S. Eighth St.
HABS IL-1123-B
HABS ILL,84-SPRIF,2B-
4dr/fr L

Lincoln Home Site,S. Eighth St. (Houses)
South 8th St.,Lincoln Home NHS
HABS IL-1123-J
HABS ILL,84-SPRIF,2J-
12dr/fr L

Lincoln Home Site,Shutt House
Edwards & 8th Sts.
HABS IL-1123-F
HABS ILL,84-SPRIF,2F-
5dr/fr L

Lincoln Home Site,Site Plan
8th St.
HABS IL-1123
HABS ILL,84-SPRIF,2-
1dr/fr L

Lincoln Home Site,Sprigg House
(Lincoln Home National Historic Site)
507 S. Eighth St.
HABS IL-1123-D
HABS ILL,84-SPRIF,2D-
4dr/fr L

Lincoln Home Site,Stuve Carriage House
7th & Edwards St.(rear),Lincoln Home NHS
HABS IL-1123-G
HABS ILL,84-SPRIF,2G-
3dr/fr L

Sangamon County Courthouse; see State House,Old

State House,Old (Sangamon County Courthouse; Third State Capitol)
HABS IL-224
HABS ILL,82-SPRIF,1-
7dr/5ph/7pg/fr L

Third State Capitol; see State House,Old

SCOTT COUNTY

WINCHESTER

Presbyterian Church
W. Cherry & N. Mechanic Sts.
HABS IL-25-15
HABS ILL,86-WINCH,1-
6dr/4ph/3pg/fr L

ST. CLAIR COUNTY

BELLEVILLE

Hinckley House; see Lincoln Hotel

Lincoln Hotel (Hinckley House)
N. High & E. "A" Sts.
HABS IL-229
HABS ILL,82-BELVI,1-
5dr/2ph/3pg L

CAHOKIA

Cakohia Courthouse
(moved to IL Chicago Jackson Park)
HABS IL-26-31-A
HABS ILL,82-CAHO,4-
1dr/9ph/4pg L

Church of the Holy Family
State Rt. 157
HABS IL-25-6
HABS ILL,82-CAHO,1-
9dr/11ph/6pg/1pc/fr L

Jarrot,Nicholas,Mansion
State Rt. 157
HABS IL-25-7
HABS ILL,82-CAHO,2-
16dr/2ph/9pg/fr L

Priest's House
State Rt. 157
HABS IL-25-13
HABS ILL,82-CAHO,3-
4dr/1ph/2pg/fr L

EAST ST. LOUIS

Eads Bridge (St. Louis Bridge; Illinois and St. Louis Bridge)
See record under MISSOURI, ST. LOUIS, ST. LOUIS
HABS MO-1190
HAER MO-12
HABS/HAER MO,96-SALU,77-
38ph/2pg/3pc/2ct L

Illinois and St. Louis Bridge; see Eads Bridge

St. Louis Bridge; see Eads Bridge

LEBANON

McKendree College,Chapel
College Square
HABS IL-228
HABS ILL,82-LEBA,1B-
6dr/3ph/2pg/fr L

McKendree College,Old Main Building
College Square
HABS IL-227
HABS ILL,82-LEBA,1A-
3dr/3ph/2pg/fr L

Mermaid House
114 E. Saint Louis St.
HABS IL-231
HABS ILL,82-LEBA,2-
2dr/3ph/2pg/fr L

NEW BADEN VIC.

Griffen House
HABS IL-296
HABS ILL,82- ,1-
5ph L

STARK COUNTY

TOULON

Hall,Dr. ,House & Office
301 Franklin St.
HABS IL-247
HABS ILL,88-TOUL,1,2-
2dr/12ph/2pg/fr L

STEPHENSON COUNTY

FREEPORT VIC.

Pecatonica River Bridge
Spanning Pecatonica River at Winnesheik Rd.
HAER IL-9
HAER ILL,89-FREP.V,1-
10ph/6pg/1pc L

LENA VIC.

Octagon House,Stone
HABS IL-179
HABS ILL,89-LENA,1-
9ph/1pc/fr L

TAZEWELL COUNTY

MACKINAW

Pendergast Inn
Market & Monroe Sts.
HABS IL-268
HABS ILL,90-MACK,1-
3dr/2ph/3pg/fr L

TREMONT

Jones-Menard House
HABS IL-281
HABS ILL,90-TREMO,1-
4dr/5ph/3pg/fr L

UNION COUNTY

ANNA

Stinson Memorial Public Library
Main & High Sts.
HABS IL-1108
HABS ILL,91-ANNA,1-
4dr L

JONESBORO

Jail Building,Old
First & Mississippi Sts.
HABS IL-233
HABS ILL,91-JONBO,1-
2dr/2ph/2pg/fr L

WARREN COUNTY

LITTLE YORK VIC.

Campbell Bridge (Little York Bridge)
Spanning Cedar Creek at Sumner Twp. Rd. 22
HAER IL-109
10ph/12pg/1pc L

Little York Bridge; see Campbell Bridge

MONMOUTH

Johnson House
300 E. Archer Ave.
HABS IL-26-23
HABS ILL,94-MONMO,1-
3dr/3ph/1pg L

WHITESIDE COUNTY

FULTON VIC.

Miss. River 9-Ft. Channel Proj.,Lock & Dam No. 13
Upper Mississippi River
HAER IL-26
HAER 1991(HAER):14
14ph/16pg/2pc L

WILL COUNTY

CHANNAHON

Channahon Locktender's House (Lift Lock No. 6) (I & M Canal Nat'l Heritage Corridor)
HAER IL-102
H

DuPage River Dam (I & M Nat'l Heritage Corridor)
HAER IL-43
HAER ILL,81-ROCIL,3/1-
3ph H

I & M Canal Nat'l Heritage Corridor; see Channahon Locktender's House (Lift Lock No. 6)

I & M Canal Nat'l Heritage Corridor; see Lift Lock No. 6

I & M Canal Nat'l Heritage Corridor; see Lift Lock No. 7 & Waste Gate

I & M Nat'l Heritage Corridor; see DuPage River Dam

Lift Lock No. 6 (I & M Canal Nat'l Heritage Corridor)
HAER IL-101
H

Lift Lock No. 7 & Waste Gate (I & M Canal Nat'l Heritage Corridor)
E. Side of DuPage Riv.
HAER IL-42
HAER ILL,81-ROCIL,3/1-
6ph H

CHANNAHON VIC.

Illinois & Michigan Canal,Locks & Lockhouse
HABS IL-157
HABS ILL,99-CHA.V,1A-
2dr/9ph/2pg/fr L

FRANKFORT VIC.

Baumgartner Creamery
U.S. Rte. 45
HABS IL-1160
HABS DLC/PP-1992:IL-5
7ph/21pg/1pc L

JOLIET

AT & SF RR: I & M Canal Bridge (I & M Canal Nat'l Heritage Corridor)
Crossing the I & M Canal at Des Plaines River
HAER IL-59
HAER ILL,81-ROCIL,3/1-
15ph H

City of Joliet: Union Station (I & M Canal Nat'l Heritage Corridor)
50 E. Jefferson St.
HAER IL-63
HAER ILL,81-ROCIL,3/1-
24ph H

Elgin,Joliet & Eastern RR Station (Fitzgerald's Furniture; I & M Canal Nat'l Heritage Corridor)
HAER IL-87
H

Fitzgerald's Furniture; see Elgin,Joliet & Eastern RR Station

I & M Canal Nat'l Heritage Corridor; see AT & SF RR: I & M Canal Bridge

I & M Canal Nat'l Heritage Corridor; see City of Joliet: Union Station

I & M Canal Nat'l Heritage Corridor; see Elgin,Joliet & Eastern RR Station

I & M Canal Nat'l Heritage Corridor; see Jefferson St.: Des Plaines River Bridge

I & M Canal Nat'l Heritage Corridor; see Joliet Iron & Steel Company: Joliet Iron Works

I & M Canal Nat'l Heritage Corridor; see RI RR: Des Plaines River Bridge

I & M Canal Nat'l Heritage Corridor; see SF RR: Joliet Freight Depot

Jefferson St.: Des Plaines River Bridge (I & M Canal Nat'l Heritage Corridor)
HAER IL-58
HAER ILL,81-ROCIL,3/1-
9ph H

Joliet Army Ammunition Plant
HAER IL-18
HAER ILL,99-JOL.V,1-
63pg/fr L

Joliet Iron & Steel Company: Joliet Iron Works (U.S. Steel Corp.: Joliet Works; I & M Canal Nat'l Heritage Corridor)
303 Mound Rd.
HAER IL-57
HAER ILL,81-ROCIL,3/1-
27ph H

Joliet,Town of
HABS IL-320
HABS 1990 (HABS):4
442pg/fr L

RI RR: Des Plaines River Bridge (I & M Canal Nat'l Heritage Corridor)
HAER IL-60
HAER ILL,81-ROCIL,3/1-
42ph H

SF RR: Joliet Freight Depot (I & M Canal Nat'l Heritage Corridor)
Cass & Scott Sts.
HAER IL-61
HAER ILL,81-ROCIL,3/1-
6ph H

U.S. Steel Corp.: Joliet Works; see Joliet Iron & Steel Company: Joliet Iron Works

LOCKPORT

Central High School
Lockport Historic District
HAER IL-16-H
HAER ILL,99-LOCK,7-
3ph/1pc L

Chicago Sanitary & Ship Canal:Butterfly Dam; see Lockport Historic District

Chicago Sanitary & Ship Canal:Swing Bridge; see Lockport Historic District

Fitzpatrick House
W. Boundry of Lockport,20 mi. SW of Chicago
HABS IL-1153
HABS 1991(HABS):17
15dr/fr L

Fitzpatrick House,Horse Barn
HABS IL-1153-A
HABS 1991(HABS):17
2dr/fr L

Funeral Parlor
Lockport Historic District
HAER IL-16-F
HAER ILL,99-LOCK,5-
2ph/1pc L

Hyland Building
Lockport Historic District
HAER IL-16-I
HAER ILL,99-LOCK,8-
6ph/1pc L

I & M Canal Nat'l Heritage Corridor; see Lockport DuPage Farmer's Elev. Co.: Corn Cob Incin

I & M Canal Nat'l Heritage Corridor; see Lockport DuPage Farmer's Elevator Co.: Grain Elev.

Illinois & Michigan Canal; see Lockport Historic District

Lockport DuPage Farmer's Elev. Co.: Corn Cob Incin (I & M Canal Nat'l Heritage Corridor)
HAER IL-91
H

Lockport DuPage Farmer's Elevator Co.: Grain Elev. (I & M Canal Nat'l Heritage Corridor)
HAER IL-90
H

Lockport Historic District
Bounded by Eighth,Hamilton,Eleventh & IL & MI Cana
HAER IL-16
HAER ILL,99-LOCK,1-
28ph/80pg/3pc/2ct L

Lockport Historic District (Chicago Sanitary & Ship Canal:Butterfly Dam)
HAER IL-16-C
HAER ILL,99-LOCK,3A-
6ph/1pg/1pc/1ct L

Lockport Historic District (Chicago Sanitary & Ship Canal:Swing Bridge)
Sixteenth St.
HAER IL-16-D
HAER ILL,99-LOCK,3B-
6ph/1pg/3pc/2ct L

Lockport Historic District (Illinois & Michigan Canal)
HAER IL-16-A
HAER ILL,99-LOCK,2-
9ph/1pg/1pc/2ct L

Lockport Historic District (Stone Arch Bridge)
Spanning Des Plaines River at Ninth St.
HAER IL-16-B
HAER ILL,99-LOCK,9-
2ph/1pg/1pc L

Norton and Company Warehouse
Lockport Historic District
HAER IL-16-G
HAER ILL,99-LOCK,6-
7ph/6pg/1pc L

Stone Arch Bridge; see Lockport Historic District

Train Station
Lockport Historic District
HAER IL-16-E
HAER ILL,99-LOCK,4-
1ph/1pc L

Documentation: **ct** color transparencies **dr** measured drawings **fr** field records
pc photograph captions **pg** pages of text **ph** photographs

MARSEILLES

I & M Canal Nat'l Heritage Corridor; see Lift Lock 10

Lift Lock 10 (I & M Canal Nat'l Heritage Corridor)
HAER IL-92
H

PLAINSFIELD

Green,Dennison,House
Main St.
HABS IL-147
HABS ILL,99-PLAFI,1-
2dr/3ph/3pg/fr L

ROCKDALE

Chicago,Ottawa,& Peoria Interurban RR: Rockdale Pa; see Illinois Traction System: Rockdale Passenger Sta.

I & M Canal Nat'l Heritage Corridor; see Illinois Traction System: Rockdale Passenger Sta.

Illinois Traction System: Rockdale Passenger Sta. (Chicago,Ottawa,& Peoria Interurban RR: Rockdale Pa I & M Canal Nat'l Heritage Corridor)
HAER IL-78
H

ROCKDALE VIV.

Chicago,Rock Isl. & Pacific RR: I & M Canal Bridge (I & M Canal Nat'l Heritage Corridor)
HAER IL-103
H

I & M Canal Nat'l Heritage Corridor; see Chicago,Rock Isl. & Pacific RR: I & M Canal Bridge

ROMEOVILLE

I & M Canal Nat'l Heritage Corridor; see Romeo Rd.: Chicago Drainage Canal Bridge

Romeo Rd.: Chicago Drainage Canal Bridge (I & M Canal Nat'l Heritage Corridor)
Across Sanitary & Ship Canal
HAER IL-41
HAER ILL,81-ROCIL,3/1-
21ph H

WILLIAMSON COUNTY

MARION

Attendents Quarters; see V.A. Medical Center,Building 13

Boiler House; see V.A. Medical Center,Building 14

Dining Hall Building; see V.A. Medical Center,Building 2

Garage Building; see V.A. Medical Center,Building 15

Hospital Building; see V.A. Medical Center,Building 1

Nurses Quarters; see V.A. Medical Center,Building 8

V.A. Medical Center,Building 1 (Hospital Building)
Old State Rt. 13 W.
HABS IL-1155-A
HABS DLC/PP-1992:IL-5
23ph/2pg/4pc/fr L

V.A. Medical Center,Building 13 (Attendents Quarters)
Old State Rt. 13 W
HABS IL-1155-D
HABS DLC/PP-1992:IL-5
4ph/2pg/2pc/fr L

V.A. Medical Center,Building 14 (Boiler House)
Old State Rt. 13 W.
HABS IL-1155-E
HABS DLC/PP-1992:IL-5
1ph/1pg/1pc/fr L

V.A. Medical Center,Building 15 (Garage Building)
Old State Rt. 13 W.
HABS IL-1155-F
HABS DLC/PP-1992:IL-5
1ph/1pg/1pc/fr L

V.A. Medical Center,Building 2 (Dining Hall Building)
Old State Rt. 13 W
HABS IL-1155-B
HABS DLC/PP-1992:IL-5
4ph/2pg/2pc/fr L

V.A. Medical Center,Building 8 (Nurses Quarters)
Old State Rt. 13 W
HABS IL-1155-C
HABS DLC/PP-1992:IL-5
4ph/2pg/2pc/fr L

Veterans Administration Medical Center
Old State Rt. 13 W
HABS IL-1155
HABS DLC/PP-1992:IL-5
5ph/17pg/2pc/fr L

WINNEBAGO COUNTY

ROCKFORD

Luce House
HABS IL-181
HABS ILL,101-ROCFO,1-
10ph/1pg/fr L

The Limestones; see Ticknor & Dickerman s & Winnebago National Bank

Ticknor & Dickerman s & Winnebago National Bank (The Limestones)
118-120 S. Main St.
HABS IL-1154
HABS 1991(HABS):14
10ph/20pg/1pc L

ROCKFORD VIC.

Brown,Mowry,House
State Rt. 2,Owen Twp.
HABS IL-303
HABS ILL,101-ROCFO.V,1-
15ph/14pg/1pc L

ROCKTON

First Congregational Church
Union St.
HABS IL-145
HABS ILL,101-ROCT,1-
5dr/2ph/2pg/fr L

Charles L. Shrewsbury House, Madison, Jefferson County, Indiana. General view circular stair, first floor from north. Photograph by Jack E. Boucher, September 1971 (HABS IN,39-MAD,1-11).

Indiana

ADAMS COUNTY

DECATUR

Art Deco Building,Small
Thirteenth & Adams Sts.
HABS IN-168
HABS IND,1-DECA,1-
5dr L

GENEVA

Ceylon Covered Bridge
County Rd. 900 S. ,Spanning Wabash River
HAER IN-57
HAER IND,1-GENE,1-
6dr L

ALLEN COUNTY

FORT WAYNE

Aboite Township School No. 5
Center & Homestead Rds.
HABS IN-155
HABS IND,2-FOWA,3-
5dr L

City Light & Power
1950 N. Clinton St.
HABS IN-251
12dr H

Ewing,William G. ,House
Berry & Ewing Sts.
HABS IN-24-10
HABS IND,2-FOWA,2-
17dr/4ph/2pg/fr L

Swinney House
Swinney Park & Jefferson St.
HABS IN-24-6
HABS IND,2-FOWA,1-
10dr/3ph/2pg/fr L

PLEASANT TOWNSHIP

Pleasant Township School
Smith & Ferguson Rds.
HABS IN-78
HABS IND,2-PLETO,1-
7dr L

BARTHOLOMEW COUNTY

COLUMBUS

Cerealine Manufacturing Company,Mill A
Jackson & Brown Sts.
HAER IN-34
HAER IND,3-COLU,2A-
2dr/5ph/4pg/1pc/fr L

Reeves Pulley Company (Reliance Electric Company Division)
Seventh & Wilson Sts.
HAER IN-15
HAER IND,3-COLU,3-
1dr/14ph/6pg/1pc/fr L

Reliance Electric Company Division; see Reeves Pulley Company

Zaharako's Ice Cream Parlor
329 Washington St.
HABS IN-77
HABS IND,3-COLU,1-
8ph/1pg/1pc/2ct L

BLACKFORD COUNTY

HARTFORD CITY

Hartford City Public Library
314 N. High St.
HABS IN-169
HABS IND,5-HARCI,1-
9dr L

CARROLL COUNTY

CUTLER

Adams Mill Covered Bridge
County Rd. 50 E. Spanning Wildcat Creek
HAER IN-29
HAER IND,8-CUT,1-
5dr/3pg L

CASS COUNTY

LOGANSPORT

Logansport State Hospital,Women's Infirmary (Northern Indiana Hospital for the Insane; Longcliff Hospital)
R. R. 2
HABS IN-202
HABS IND,9-LOGPO,1A-
7dr/fr L

Longcliff Hospital; see Logansport State Hospital,Women's Infirmary

Northern Indiana Hospital for the Insane; see Logansport State Hospital,Women's Infirmary

YOUNG AMERICA VIC.

Attica Bridge (Cass County Bridge 158)
Spanning Deer Creek on County Road 500 East
HAER IN-60
15ph/4pg/2pc L

Cass County Bridge 158; see Attica Bridge

CLARK COUNTY

CHARLESTOWN

Indiana Army Ammunition Plant
HAER IN-55
HAER IND,10-CHAR,1-
72pg/fr L

JEFFERSONVILLE

Grisamore House
111-113 W. Chestnut
HABS IN-24-18
HABS IND,10-JEFVI,1-
6dr/2ph/2pg/fr L

CLAY COUNTY

CLAY CITY VIC.

Feederdam Bridge
State Rt. 59,spanning Eel River
HAER IN-21
HAER IND,11-CLACI.V,1-
13ph/1pc L

CRAWFORD COUNTY

ALTON VIC.

Mill Creek Bridge (Modified Pratt Truss Bridge)
Mill Creek
HAER IN-23
HAER IND,13-ALT.V,1-
9ph/2pg/1pc L

Modified Pratt Truss Bridge; see Mill Creek Bridge

HUTSONVILLE

Hutsonville Bridge
Spanning Wabash River on State Rt. 154
HAER IN-59
HAER 1989(HAER):8
75ph/52pg/4pc L

DAVIESS COUNTY

WASHINGTON

Baltimore & Ohio Railroad,Repair Shop; see Ohio & Mississippi Railroad,Repair Shops,West Shop

Baltimore & Ohio Railroad,Repair Shops; see Ohio & Miss. RR,Rpr. Shops,Turntable & Roundhouse

Baltimore & Ohio Railroad,Repair Shops; see Ohio & Mississippi Railroad, Repair Shops

Baltimore & Ohio Railroad,Repair Shops; see Ohio & Mississippi Railroad,Repair Shops,East Shop

Baltimore & Ohio Railroad,Repair Shops; see Ohio & Mississippi RR,Repair Shops,Office Bldg.

Baltimore & Ohio Railroad,Repair Shops; see Ohio & Mississippi RR,Repair Shops,Power House

Baltimore & Ohio Railroad,Repair Shops; see Ohio & Mississippi RR,Repair Shops,Stencil Shop

Ohio & Miss. RR,Rpr. Shops,Turntable & Roundhouse (Baltimore & Ohio Railroad,Repair Shops; U. S. Railway Equipment Company)
Van Trees & Seventeenth Sts.
HAER IN-5-F
4ph H

Ohio & Mississippi Railroad, Repair Shops (Baltimore & Ohio Railroad,Repair Shops; U. S. Railway Equipment Company)
Van Trees & Seventeenth Sts.
HAER IN-5
HAER IND,14-WASH,1-
7dr/34ph/2pc/fr L

Ohio & Mississippi Railroad,Repair Shops,East Shop (Baltimore & Ohio Railroad,Repair Shops; U. S. Railway Equipment Company)
Van Trees & Seventeenth Sts.
HAER IN-5-B
6ph H

Ohio & Mississippi Railroad,Repair Shops,West Shop (Baltimore & Ohio Railroad,Repair Shop)
Van Trees & Seventeenth Sts.
HAER IN-5-G
4ph H

Ohio & Mississippi RR,Repair Shops,Office Bldg. (Baltimore & Ohio Railroad,Repair Shops; U. S. Railway Equipment Company)
Van Trees & Seventeenth Sts.
HAER IN-5-C
4ph H

Ohio & Mississippi RR,Repair Shops,Power House (Baltimore & Ohio Railroad,Repair Shops; U. S. Railway Equipment Company)
Van Trees & Seventeenth Sts.
HAER IN-5-D
3ph H

Ohio & Mississippi RR,Repair Shops,Stencil Shop (Baltimore & Ohio Railroad,Repair Shops; U. S. Railway Equipment Company)
Van Trees & Seventeenth Sts.
HAER IN-5-E
3ph H

U. S. Railway Equipment Company; see Ohio & Miss. RR,Rpr. Shops,Turntable & Roundhouse

U. S. Railway Equipment Company; see Ohio & Mississippi Railroad, Repair Shops

U. S. Railway Equipment Company; see Ohio & Mississippi Railroad,Repair Shops,East Shop

U. S. Railway Equipment Company; see Ohio & Mississippi RR,Repair Shops,Office Bldg.

U. S. Railway Equipment Company; see Ohio & Mississippi RR,Repair Shops,Power House

U. S. Railway Equipment Company; see Ohio & Mississippi RR,Repair Shops,Stencil Shop

DE KALB COUNTY

BUTLER

Butler Masonic Lodge (Parkison Building)
100 S. Broadway
HABS IN-200
HABS IND,17-BUT,1-
3ph/5pg/1pc L

Parkison Building; see Butler Masonic Lodge

DEARBORN COUNTY

AURORA

Holman-Hamilton House; see Veraestau

Holman-Hamilton House,Carriage House & Stable; see Veraestau,Carriage House & Stable

Veraestau (Holman-Hamilton House)
Holman Hill Rd.
HABS IN-184
HABS IND,15-AUR,1-
6dr/15ph/6pg/1pc L

Veraestau,Carriage House & Stable (Holman-Hamilton House,Carriage House & Stable)
Holman Hill Rd.
HABS IN-184-A
HABS IND,15-AUR,1A-
3dr/3ph/1pc L

DECATUR COUNTY

GREENSBURG VIC.

Barn,Brick
State Rt. 3
HAER IN-43
HAER IND,16-GREBU.V,1-
4ph L

DELAWARE COUNTY

HARRISON TWP.

Beechgrove Church
County Rd. 700 North
HABS IN-179
HABS IND,18-HARTO,1-
8dr L

MUNCIE

Ball State University,Administration Building
University & McKinley Aves.
HABS IN-150
HABS IND,18-MUNCI,3A-
9dr L

Federal Building (U. S. Post Office,Old)
Charles & High Sts.
HABS IN-180
HABS IND,18-MUNCI,4-
4dr L

Hathaway House
1001 West Riverside Ave.
HABS IN-188
HABS IND,18-MUNCI,5-
7dr L

Sample,Judge Karl,House
621 E. Main St.
HABS IN-182
HABS IND,18-MUNCI,6-
2dr L

615 South Hagadorn Street (Office Building)
HABS IN-165
HABS IND.18-MUNCI,1-
5dr L

Swain,C. W. ,Building
120 N. High St.
HABS IN-174
HABS IND,18-MUNCI,7-
6dr L

U. S. Post Office,Old; see Federal Building

Union Station
630 S. High St.
HABS IN-166
HABS IND,18-MUNCI,8-
6dr L

620 West Howard Street (Building)
HABS IN-185
HABS IND,18-MUNCI,2-
1dr L

Wilkinson House
3100 W. University Ave.
HABS IN-181
HABS IN,18-MUNCI,9-
3dr L

MUNCIE VIC.

Garner,Job,House
County Rds. 400 N & 700 W
HABS IN-154
HABS IND,18-MUNCI.V,1-
6dr L

YORKTOWN

Delaware County Bridge No. 131
County Rt. 750 Spanning White River
HAER IN-47
HAER IND,18-YORK.V,2-
3dr L

YORKTOWN VIC.

Hofherr Round Barn
County Rd. 650 West
HABS IN-186
HABS IND,18-YORK.V,1A-
5dr L

ELKHART COUNTY

ELKHART

Public School No. 10
Hammond Ave.
HABS IN-173
HABS IND,20-ELK,5-
7dr L

105 South Main Street (Commercial Building)
HABS IN-205
HABS IND,20-ELK,1-
3ph/5pg/1pc L

107 South Main Street (Commercial Building)
HABS IN-206
HABS IND,20-ELK,2-
4ph/4pg/1pc L

113-115 West Jackson St. (Commercial Bldg.)
HABS IN-208
HABS IND,20-ELK,4-
6ph/8pg/1pc L

111 West Jackson Street (Commercial Bldg.)
HABS IN-207
HABS IND,20-ELK,3-
4ph/4pg/1pc L

FAYETTE COUNTY

CONNERSVILLE

Ansted-Higgins Spring Company
Mount & Sixteenth Sts.
HAER IN-9
HAER IND,21-CONVI,2-
2ph/3pg/1pc/fr L

Auburn Automobile Company; see Lexington Motor Company

Canal House
111 E. Fourth St.
HABS IN-107
HABS IND,21-CONVI,1-
9dr/9ph/8pg/fr L

Central Manufacturing Company
Eighteenth St.
HAER IN-10
HAER IND,21-CONVI,3-
3ph/3pg/1pc L

Connersville Blower Company
Columbia Ave. & Mount St.
HAER IN-13
HAER IND,21-CONVI,4-
2ph/2pg/1pc/fr L

Connersville Furniture Company
Illinois Ave.
HAER IN-12
HAER IND,21-CONVI,5-
4ph/3pg/1pc/fr L

Connersville Industrial Park
Eleventh & Twenty-first Sts.
HAER IN-7
HAER IND,21-CONVI,6-
1dr/1ph/5pg/1pc L

Lexington Motor Company (Auburn Automobile Company)
Eighteenth St. & Columbia Ave.
HAER IN-11
HAER IND,21-CONVI,7-
4dr/24ph/6pg/2pc/fr L

McFarlan Carriage Company (McFarlan Motor Car Company)
Mount St.
HAER IN-8
HAER IND,21-CONVI,8-
1ph/5pg/1pc/fr L

McFarlan Motor Car Company; see McFarlan Carriage Company

Munk & Roberts Furniture Company
Western Ave.
HAER IN-14
HAER IND,21-CONVI,9-
3dr/1ph/3pg/1pc/fr L

Roots,P. H. & F. M. ,Company
Eastern Avenue
HAER IN-3
HAER IND,21-CONVI,10-
6dr/35ph/10pg/2pc/fr L

CONNERSVILLE VIC.

Gray House
County Rd.
HABS IN-108
HABS IND,21-CONVI.V,1-
6dr/10ph/6pg/97ct/fr L

WATERLOO VIC.

McDivitt Round Barn; see Ranck Round Barn

Ranck Round Barn (McDivitt Round Barn)
Fayette-Wayne County Line Rd.
HABS IN-106
HABS IND,21-WATLO.V,1A-
8ph/1pg/1pc/2ct L

FLOYD COUNTY

NEW ALBANY

Smith,Isaac P. ,House
513 E. Main St.
HABS IN-151
HABS IND,22-NEWAL,1-
9dr/7pg L

FOUNTAIN COUNTY

RIVERSIDE VIC.

Riverside-Independence Bridge
Spanning Wabash River at County Rd. 500
HAER IN-67
HAER DLC/PP-1993:IN-2
24ph/8pg/3pc L

FRANKLIN COUNTY

FAIRFIELD

Logan Cabin
State Rt. 101
HABS IN-24-19
HABS IND,24-FARF,1-
8dr/4ph/1pg/fr L

METAMORA

Whitewater Canal Aqueduct
Duck Creek
HABS IN-24-20
HABS IND,24,METMO,1-
4dr/4ph/1pg/fr L

FULTON COUNTY

ROCHESTER VIC.

Modified Pratt Through-truss Bridge; see Tippecanoe River Bridge

Tippecanoe River Bridge (Modified Pratt Through-truss Bridge)
State Rt. 25 & Tippecanoe River
HAER IN-25
HAER IND,25-ROCH.V,1-
16ph/1pg/1pc L

GRANT COUNTY

MARION

Swayzee-Erlewine-Love House
223 North Adams St.
HABS IN-178
HABS IND,27-MAR,1-
10dr L

MATTHEWS

Cumberland Covered Bridge
County Rd. 990 E. Spanning Mississinewa River
HAER IN-50
HAER IND,27-MATH,1-
6dr/3pg L

HAMILTON COUNTY

NOBLESVILLE

Doan House
30 Connor Lane
HABS IN-96
HABS IND,29-NOBL,1-
3dr/12ph/fr L

NOBLESVILLE VIC.

Conner,William,House
Hwy. 234
HABS IN-46
HABS IND,29-NOBL.V,4-
4ph L

Conner,William,Loom House
State Hwy. 234
HABS IN-47
HABS IND,29-NOBL.V,5-
1ph L

Conner,William,Prairie Farm
State Hwy. 234
HABS IN-40
HABS IND,29-NOBL.V,1-
1ph/4pg L

Conner,William,Still House
State Hwy. 234
HABS IN-45
HABS IND,29-NOBL.V,3-
1ph L

Conner,William,Trading Post
State Hwy. 234
HABS IN-44
HABS IND,29-NOBL.V,2-
3ph L

Hamilton County Bridge #218
Greenfield Pike,spanning Stoney Creek
HAER IN-52
HAER IND,29-NOBL.V,6-
16ph/14pg/1pc L

HANCOCK COUNTY

MCCORDSVILLE VIC.

Kingen Round Barn; see Littleton Round Barn

Littleton Round Barn (Kingen Round Barn)
500 West,600 North Rd.
HABS IN-159
HABS IND,30-MCOVI.V,1A-
5dr/fr L

WILKINSON

Octagon House
HABS IN-172
HABS IND,30-WILK,1-
4dr L

HARRISON COUNTY

CORYDON

State Capitol,First
HABS IN-26
HABS IND,31-CORY,1-
13dr/6ph L

HENRY COUNTY

KNIGHTSTOWN

Knightstown Academy
Carey St.
HABS IN-198
HABS IND,33-KNITO,1-
12dr/fr L

MOORELAND VIC.

Wilbur Wright Birthplace; see Wilbur Wright State Memorial

Wilbur Wright State Memorial (Wilbur Wright Birthplace)
County Rd. 750 East
HABS IN-167
HABS IND,33-MOOR.V,1-
4dr L

HOWARD COUNTY

KOKOMO

Vermont Covered Bridge
Deffenbaugh St. Spanning Kokomo Creek
HAER IN-30
HAER IND,34-KOKO,1-
5dr/3pg L

HUNTINGTON COUNTY

HUNTINGTON

Richardville,Chief,House
U. S. Rt. 24
HABS IN-157
HABS IND,35-HUNT,1-
10dr/9pg/fr L

JACKSON COUNTY

MEDORA

Medora Covered Bridge
State Rt. 235 Spanning E. Fork White River
HAER IN-45
HAER IND,36-MED,1-
6dr L

MEDORA VIC.

Hall,George,Barn
Rural Rt. 1
HABS IN-183
HABS IND,35-MED.V,1A-
6dr L

SEYMOUR

Bells Ford Covered Bridge
State Rt. 258 Spanning E. Fork White River
HAER IN-46
HAER IND,36-SEYM,1-
6dr L

JEFFERSON COUNTY

MADISON

American Tobacco Company Prizery; see Tobacco Prizing House

Ben Schroeder Saddle Tree Company (Madison Historic District)
106 Milton St.
HAER IN-26
HAER IND,39-MAD,43-
3dr/28ph/12pg/2pc/fr L H

Bierck-Heuse Commercial Block; see 223-229 East Main Street

200 Block Main St. (Commercial Bldgs.)
HABS IN-230
HABS IND,39-MAD,47-
4ph/1pc L

300 Block Main St. (Commercial Bldgs.)
HABS IN-231
HABS IND,39-MAD,48-
1ph/1pc L

Documentation: **ct** color transparencies **dr** measured drawings **fr** field records
pc photograph captions **pg** pages of text **ph** photographs

Bruning Carriage House
722 W. Main St. ,rear (moved to 719 W. Main,rear)
HABS IN-122
HABS IND,39-MAD,32A-
1ph/7pg/1pc L

Carriage House and Stables
(McKim,R.,Company Storage; Madison Historic District)
120 Elm St.
HAER IN-76
3dr H

Christ Episcopal Church
506 Mulberry St.
HABS IN-123
HABS IND,39-MAD,33-
2ph/10pg/1pc/1ct L

Colby-Jefferson House
302 Elm St.
HABS IN-124
HABS IND,39-MAD,34-
4ph/11pg/1pc/3ct L

Collins,Andrew,Building; see 201-215 West Main Street

Costigan,Francis,House
408 W. Third St.
HABS IN-87
HABS IND,39-MAD,11-
6dr/10ph/7pg/1pc/1ct/fr L

Davidson & Driggs Building; see 201-215 West Main Street

Devenish-Haigh House
108 E. Third
HABS IN-125
HABS IND,39-MAD,35-
1ph/7pg/1pc/1ct L

Eagle Cotton Mill
108 St. Michael's Ave.
HABS IN-94
HABS IND,39-MAD,13-
1ph/6pg L

102-104 1/2 East Main Street (Commercial Building) (Foster Building)
HABS IN-86
HABS IND,39-MAD,10-
3dr/8ph/4pg/fr L

217-229 East Main Street (Commercial Buildings)
HABS IN-134
HABS IND,39-MAD,27-
2dr/1ph/1pc/20ct L

710-714 East Main Street (Row Houses)
HABS IN-133
HABS IND,39-MAD,31-
7dr/4ph/10pg/1pc/1ct/fr L

217-219 East Main Street (Masonic Lodge)
217-219 E. Main St.
HABS IN-134-A
HABS IND,39-MAD,28-
1ph/9pg/1pc/fr L

221 East Main Street (Hunt Building)
221 E. Main St.
HABS IN-134-B
HABS IND,39-MAD,29-
6pg/fr L

223-229 East Main Street (Bierck-Heuse Commercial Block)
223-229 E. Main St.
HABS IN-134-C
HABS IND,39-MAD,30-
1ph/8pg/1pc/fr L

Eckert,John,House
510 W. Second St.
HABS IN-126
HABS IND,39-MAD,18-
3dr/1ph/7pg/1pc/2ct/fr L

Fair Play Fire Engine & Hose Company No. 1
405 E. Main St.
HABS IN-90
HABS IND,39-MAD,16-
4dr/4ph/9pg/1pc/3ct/fr L

First Baptist Church
416 Vine St.
HABS IN-127
HABS IND,39-MAD,19-
4dr/10pg/2ct/fr L

First Presbyterian Church
202 Broadway
HABS IN-95
HABS IND,39-MAD,36-
11pg L

Foster Building; see 102-104 1/2 East Main Street (Commercial Building)

Frevart-Schnaitter House
740 W. Main St.
HABS IN-91
HABS IND,39-MAD,12-
2ph/3pg L

Hubbard Block; see 201-215 West Main Street

Hubbard Building; see 201-215 West Main Street

Hunt Building; see 221 East Main Street

Hutchings,Dr. William Davies,Office
718 W. Third St.
HABS IN-81
HABS IND,39-MAD,5-
5dr/4ph/7pg/2ct/fr L

Jefferson County Courthouse
Jefferson & Main Sts.
HABS IN-153
HABS IND,39-MAD,37-
3ph/1pc/1ct L

Jefferson County Jail & Sheriff's House
Courthouse Square
HABS IN-84
HABS IND,39-MAD,9-
10dr/9ph/13pg/fr L

Jefferson Proving Ground
HAER IN-54
HAER IND,39-MAD,44-
44pg/fr L

Lanier,James E. D. ,House
511 W. First St.
HABS IN-23
HABS IND,39-MAD,4-
15dr/13ph/6pg/4ct L

Madison & Indianapolis Railroad,Madison Incline (Madison Cut)
W. Main St.
HAER IN-19
HAER IND,39-MAD,45A-
2ph/1pc/fr L

Madison Cut; see Madison & Indianapolis Railroad,Madison Incline

Madison Historic District; see Ben Schroeder Saddle Tree Company

Madison Historic District; see Carriage House and Stables

Madison Historic District; see Tobacco Prizing House

Madison,Town of
HABS IN-88
HABS IND,39-MAD,41-
35ph/2pc/6ct L

Main Street (Commercial Buildings)
HABS IN-42
HABS IND,39-MAD,46-
6ph/1pc/2ct L

Major Apron Works; see Tobacco Prizing House

Masonic Lodge; see 217-219 East Main Street

McKim,R.,Company Storage; see Carriage House and Stables

McNaughton House
(Sanders-McNaughton)
416 E. Second St.
HABS IN-89
HABS IND,39-MAD,15-
2ph/6pg L

Miller Wagon Manufacturing Shop
805-809 Walnut St.
HABS IN-128
HABS IND,39-MAD,38-
13pg L

Mulberry Street Block (Commercial Buildings)
301-315 Mulberry St.
HABS IN-83
HABS IND,39-MAD,7-
6dr/5ph/13pg/fr L

Mulvey,John,Building; see 201-215 West Main Street

Pitt. ,Cinn. ,Chicago & St. Louis Railway Co. Sta.
614 W. First St.
HABS IN-93
HABS IND,39-MAD,14-
1ph/4pg L

Robinson-Schofield House
221 W. Second St.
HABS IN-82
HABS IND,39-MAD,6-
8dr/4ph/9pg/2ct/fr L

Locations: **H** HABS/HAER, National Park Service **L** Library of Congress

Sanders-McNaughton; see McNaughton House

Second Presbyterian Church
500 West St.
HABS IN-24-15
HABS IND,39-MAD,3-
8dr/4ph/1pg/1ct/fr L

Shrewsbury,Charles L. ,House
301 W. First St.
HABS IN-8
HABS IND,39-MAD,1-
16dr/17ph/6pg/1pc/1ct L

Shuh,Jacob,House
718 W. Main St.
HABS IN-92
HABS IND,39-MAD,17-
8dr/2ph/10pg/1pc/1ct/fr L

St. Mary's Roman Catholic Church & School
413 E. Second St.
HABS IN-164
HABS IND,39-MAD,39-
3ph/1pc L

St. Michael's Catholic Church
519 E. Third St.
HABS IN-129
HABS IND,39-MAD,8A-
5ph/12pg/1pc/1ct L

St. Michael's Rectory
519 E. Third St.
HABS IN-85
HABS IND,39-MAD,8-
7dr/6ph/7pg/fr L

Sullivan,Jeremiah,House
304 W. Second St.
HABS IN-9
HABS IND,39-MAD,2-
10dr/16ph/1pg/1pc/5ct L

Talbott,Richard,House
301 W. Second St.
HABS IN-130
HABS IND,39-MAD,20-
6dr/2ph/10pg/1pc/1ct/fr L

Tobacco Prizing House (American Tobacco Company Prizery; Major Apron Works; Trow Flour Mill Cooperage; Madison Historic District)
116 Elm St.
HAER IN-75
3dr H

Trow Flour Mill Cooperage; see Tobacco Prizing House

Walnut Street Fire Company No. 4
808 Walnut St.
HABS IN-131
HABS IND,39-MAD,40-
1ph/9pg/1pc/1ct L

Washington Fire Company No. 2
104 W. Third St.
HABS IN-132
HABS IND,39-MAD,42-
2ph/7pg/1pc/1ct L

201-215 West Main Street (Commercial Buildings)
HABS IN-135
HABS IND,39-MAD,21-
2dr/fr L

201-215 West Main Street (Collins,Andrew,Building)
215 W. Main St.
HABS IN-135-E
HABS IND,39-MAD,26-
7pg/fr L

201-215 West Main Street (Davidson & Driggs Building)
213 W. Main St.
HABS IN-135-D
HABS IND,39-MAD,25-
6pg/fr L

201-215 West Main Street (Hubbard Block)
201-207 W. Main St.
HABS IN-135-A
HABS IND,39-MAD,22-
8pg/fr L

201-215 West Main Street (Hubbard Building)
209 W. Main St.
HABS IN-135-B
HABS IND,39-MAD,23-
6pg/fr L

201-215 West Main Street (Mulvey,John,Building)
211 W. Main St.
HABS IN-135-C
HABS IND,39-MAD,24-
7pg/fr L

MADISON VIC.

Bachman House
Lonesome Hollow
HABS IN-121
HABS IND,39-MAD.V,1-
7dr/8pg/fr L

JENNINGS COUNTY

VERNON

Madison & Indianapolis Railroad,Vernon Overpass
Gains St. & Pike St.
HAER IN-20
HAER IND,48-VERNO,1A-
5ph L

JOHNSON COUNTY

FRANKLIN

Johnson County Courthouse
5 Jefferson St.
HABS IN-229
HABS 1992(HABS):IN-1
13dr/1pg/fr L

KNOX COUNTY

VINCENNES

Brouillette House
509 N. First St.
HABS IN-160
HABS IND,42-VINC,3-
7ph/1pg/1pc L

Clark,George Rogers Memorial
DuBoise St. and Second St.
HABS IN-234
HABS DLC/PP-1992:IN-4
2ph/1pc L

College of Vincennes; see St. Francis Xavier Cathedral

Grouseland; see Harrison,William Henry,House

Harrison,William Henry,House (Grouseland)
Park & Scott Sts.
HABS IN-24-17
HABS IND,42-VINC,2-
9dr/6ph/24pg/2ct/fr L

St. Francis Xavier Cathedral (College of Vincennes)
Vigo St.
HABS IN-24-7
HABS IND,42-VINC,1-
22dr/3ph/2pg L

St. Francis Xavier Cathedral,Library
Vigo St.
HABS IN-24-7-B
HABS IND,42-VINC,1B-
1ph L

St. Francis Xavier Cathedral,Priests' House
Vigo St.
HABS IN-24-7-C
HABS IND,42-VINC,1C-
1ph L

St. Francix Xavier Cathedral,St. Rose Chapel
Second St.
HABS IN-24-7-A
HABS IND,42-VINC,1A-
5dr/1ph L

LA PORTE COUNTY

MICHIGAN CITY

Michigan City Lighthouse
Washington Park
HABS IN-99
HABS IND,46-MICI,1-
9dr/5pg L

NEW CARLISLE

Brown-Augustine House
U. S. Hwy. 20
HABS IN-21
HABS IND,46- ,1-
10dr L

PINOLA

Ames-Paton House
HABS IN-34
HABS IND,46-PINO,1-
3dr/8ph/3pg L

LAGRANGE COUNTY

MONGO

O'Ferrell,John,Store
County Rd. 400N
HABS IN-148
HABS IND,44-MONG,1-
4dr/4pg L

LAKE COUNTY

GARY

City Hall; see Gary Municipal Building

Gary Land Company Building
Gateway Park,4th Ave. & Penn St(moved fr Broadway)
HABS IN-196
HABS IND,45-GARY,2-
6ph/10pg/1pc L

Gary Municipal Building (City Hall)
401 Broadway
HABS IN-197
HABS IND,49-GARY,1-
8ph/10pg/1pc/fr L

ST. JOHN

Pioneer Church
Burr St.
HABS IN-175
HABS IND,45-SJOH,1-
3dr L

LAWRENCE COUNTY

MITCHELL

Riley School
Seventh & College Sts.
HABS IN-147
HABS IND,47-MITCH,1-
6ph/1pc L

MADISON COUNTY

ANDERSON

Anderson Carriage Manufacturing Company
Twenty-fifth & Walton Sts.
HAER IN-37
HAER IND,48-AND,2-
7ph/5pg/1pc/fr L

Buckeye Manufacturing Company
Columbia Ave.
HAER IN-35
HAER IND,48-AND,3-
1dr/15ph/5pg/1pc/fr L

Courthouse Square Row Buildings,Facade Study
Ninth St.
HABS IN-187
HABS IND,48-AND,1-
4dr L

DeTamble Motors Factory; see Speed Changing Pulley Company Factory

Nyberg Automobile Company; see Rider-Lewis Motor Car Company

Rider-Lewis Motor Car Company
(Nyberg Automobile Company)
W. Second St. & Sycamore
HAER IN-38
HAER IND,48-AND,4-
1dr/13ph/5pg/1pc/fr L

Speed Changing Pulley Company Factory (DeTamble Motors Factory; Spring Air Bedding)
Thirty-second St.
HAER IN-36
HAER IND,48-AND,5-
1dr/9ph/8pg/1pc/fr L

Spring Air Bedding; see Speed Changing Pulley Company Factory

PENDLETON VIC.

Fussell,Solomon,House
State Rt. 38
HABS IN-163
HABS IND,48-PEN.V,1-
6dr/1pg L

MARION COUNTY

INDIANAPOLIS

Allison,James A. ,Mansion (Riverdale; Marian College Library)
3200 Coldspring Rd.
HABS IN-68
HABS IND,49-IND,23-
12ph/6pg L

Arsenal Technical High School; see U. S. Arsenal,Arsenal Building

Athenaeum,The; see Das Deutsche Haus

Ayres,L. S. ,Company,Warehouse Annex; see Elliott's Block

Bates-Hendricks House
1526 S. New Jersey St.
HABS IN-64
HABS IND,49-IND,19-
2ph/15pg L

Brownsville Covered Bridge (Wagon Bridge)
Eagle Creek Park (moved from IN,Brownsville)
HAER IN-27
HAER IND,81-BROVI,1-
5dr/16ph/4pg/1pc L

Christ Church (Episcopal)
N. Meridian & E. Wabash Sts.
HABS IN-24-3
HABS IND,49-IND,2-
18dr/3ph/5pg/fr L

Cole Motor Car Company Factory
(Service Supply Company,Inc.)
730 E. Washington St.
HABS IN-71
HABS IND,49-IND,26-
1ph/5pg L

Cornelius Printing Company; see Elliott's Block

Crown Hill Cemetery,Chapel & Vault
Thirty-fourth St.
HABS IN-58
HABS IND,49-IND,13B-
10ph/7pg L

Crown Hill Cemetery,Gateway
3402 Blvd. Place
HABS IN-57
HABS IND,49-IND,13A-
6ph/5pg L

Crown Hill Cemetery,Office Building
3402 Blvd. Place
HABS IN-56
HABS IND,49-IND,13C-
7dr/7ph/13pg L

Das Deutsche Haus (Athenaeum,The)
401 E. Michigan St.
HABS IN-63
HABS IND,49-IND,18-
21ph/12pg L

Despa House
538 Lockerbie St.
HABS IN-55
HABS IND,49-IND,12-
8dr/7pg L

Duesenberg Automobile Company Factory
W. Washington & Harding Sts.
HABS IN-70
HABS IND,49-IND,25-
7ph L

Duesenberg Automobile Company Factory,Building #1
1501 W. Washington St.
HABS IN-70-A
HABS IND,49-IND,25A-
3dr/15ph/15pg/1pc/fr L

Elliott's Block (Ayres,L. S. ,Company,Warehouse Annex; Cornelius Printing Company)
14-22 W. Maryland St.
HABS IN-60
HABS IND,49-IND,15-
2dr/3ph/9pg L

Harrison,Benjamin,House
1230 N. Delaware St.
HABS IN-53
HABS IND,49-IND,10-
8dr/10ph/11pg L

Holler,George & Netty,House
324 N. Park Ave.
HABS IN-49
HABS IND,49-IND,6-
11dr/5ph/7pg L

House of Crane Building
124 South Meridian St.
HABS IN-228
13ph/7pg/1pc H

House of the Twin Chimneys (West,John,House)
7607 Allisonville Rd.
HABS IN-36
HABS IND,49-IND,5-
4dr/7ph/3pg L

Indiana Central Canal,Indianapolis Division
Parallel to West St.
HAER IN-32
HAER IND,49-IND,35A-
25ph/42pg/2pc/fr L

Indiana National Bank Building
3 Virginia Ave.
HABS IN-62
HABS IND,49-IND,17-
14ph/11pg L

Indiana State Central Hospital for the Insane (Pathological Department Building)
3000 W. Washington St.
HABS IN-69
HABS IND,49-IND,24-
2ph/8pg L

Indiana State Museum; see Indianapolis City Hall

Indiana Theatre
134 W. Washington St.
HABS IN-101
HABS IND,49-IND,29-
49ph/50pg L

Indianapolis City Hall (Indiana State Museum)
202 N. Alabama
HABS IN-156
HABS IND,49-IND,30-
8ph/21pg/1pc/fr L

Indianapolis City Market (Market House)
222 E. Market St.
HABS IN-59
HAER IN-6
HABS/HAER IND,49-IND,14-
6dr/22ph/11pg/2ct/fr L

Indianapolis News Mechanical Building
30 W. Court St.
HABS IN-222
HABS DLC/PP-1993:IN-3
6ph/9pg/1pc L

Indianapolis Public Library
2822 E. Washington St.
HABS IN-171
HABS IND,49-IND,31-
6dr L

Journal Building
46-48 Monument Circle
HABS IN-213
8ph/23pg/1pc H

Lockefield Garden Apartments
900 Indiana Ave.
HABS IN-194
HABS IND,49-IND,32-
105ph/7pg/4pc L

Macy House
408 N. Delaware St.
HABS IN-24-2
HABS IND,49-IND,1-
11dr/1ph/2pg L

Maennerchor Building
102 W. Michigan St.
HABS IN-100
HABS IND,49-IND,33-
13ph/7pg/2pc/fr L

Marian College Library; see Allison,James A. ,Mansion

Market House; see Indianapolis City Market

Morris-Butler House
1204 N. Park Ave.
HABS IN-52
HABS IND,49-IND,9-
9dr/13ph/18pg L

Nickum,John R. ,House; see Riley,James Whitcomb,House

Occidental Building (Commercial Building)
41-47 W. Washington St.
HABS IN-211
HABS DLC/PP-1992:IN-5
8ph/16pg/1pc L

Pathological Department Building; see Indiana State Central Hospital for the Insane

Prosser House
1454 E. Tenth St.
HABS IN-35
HABS IND,49-IND,4-
5dr/6ph/3pg L

Riley,James Whitcomb,House (Nickum,John R. ,House)
528 Lockerbie St.
HABS IN-51
HABS IND,49-IND,8-
8dr/16ph/13pg L

Riverdale; see Allison,James A. ,Mansion

Roosevelt Building
9 N. Illinois St.
HABS IN-215
HABS DLC/PP-1993:IN-3
12ph/17pg/1pc L

Rost Jewelry Company Building
25 North Illinois St.
HABS IN-216
8ph/15pg/1pc H

Schnull's Block (Commercial Building)
102-108 S. Meridian St.
HABS IN-210
HABS 1991(HABS):16
13pg L

Service Supply Company,Inc.; see Cole Motor Car Company Factory

Soldiers' & Sailors' Monument
Monument Plaza
HABS IN-61
HABS IND,49-IND,16-
15ph/20pg L

Sommers,Richard W. ,House (Tudor Hall)
3650 Coldspring Rd.
HABS IN-73
HABS IND,49-IND,28-
2ph L

122 South Meridian Street
HABS IN-227
11ph/6pg/1pc H

Star Service Shop
130 N. Illinois St.
HABS IN-72
HABS IND49-IND27-
1ph/3pg L

Staub,Joseph W. ,House
342 N. College Ave.
HABS IN-50
HABS IND,49-IND,7-
10dr/5ph/10pg L

Tudor Hall; see Sommers,Richard W. ,House

U. S. Arsenal,Arsenal Building (Arsenal Technical High School)
1500 E. Michigan St.
HABS IN-66
HABS IND,49-IND,21-
3ph/10pg L

Union Station
Jackson Place & Illinois St.
HABS IN-65
HABS IND,49-IND,20-
15ph/13pg L

Vinton-Pierce House
1415 N. Meridian St.
HABS IN-24
HABS IND,49-IND,3-
12dr L

Wagon Bridge; see Brownsville Covered Bridge

Webber House
621 Lockerbie St.
HABS IN-54
HABS IND,49-IND,11-
8dr/9pg L

West,John,House; see House of the Twin Chimneys

White,Joseph,House
441 South Park
HABS IN-176
HABS IND,49-IND,34-
9dr L

Woodruff Place
East,West, & Middle Drives
HABS IN-67
HABS IND,49-IND,22-
14ph/6pg L

MARSHALL COUNTY

INDIANAPOLIS

Malott Building
118 S. Meridian St.
HABS IN-226
8ph/6pg/1pc H

MONROE COUNTY

BLOOMINGTON

Wylie House
Second & Lincoln Sts.
HABS IN-41
HABS IND,53-BLOOM,1-
5ph/4pg L

MONTGOMERY COUNTY

ALAMO VIC.

Deer's Mill Covered Bridge
State Rt. 234 Spanning Sugar Creek
HAER IN-28
HAER IND,54-ALA.V,1-
5dr/3pg L

CRAWFORDSVILLE

Montgomery County Jail
Washington & Spring Sts.
HAER IN-17
HAER IND,54-CRAVI,1-
23ph/4pg/2pc/fr L

Yount Woolen Mill
State Rt. 32
HAER IN-18
HAER IND,54-CRAVI.V,1-
7ph/1pg/fr L

OHIO COUNTY

AURORA VIC.

Laughery Creek Bridge
Spanning Laughery Creek
HAER IN-16
HAER IND,15-AUR.V,1-
6dr/15ph/13pg/1pc/fr L

ORANGE COUNTY

PAOLI

Gospel Street Bridge (Pratt Truss Bridge)
S. Gospel St. ,spanning Lick Creek
HAER IN-24
HAER IND,59-PAOL,2-
11ph/1pg/1pc L

Orange County Courthouse
State Rts. 156 & 37
HABS IN-29
HABS IND,59-PAOL,1-
4ph L

Pratt Truss Bridge; see Gospel Street Bridge

WEST BADEN

Northwood Institute; see West Baden Springs Hotel

West Baden Springs Hotel (Northwood Institute)
State Rt. 56
HAER IN-2
HAER IND,59-BADW,1-
8dr/51ph/3pc/9ct/fr L

OWEN COUNTY

GOSPORT

Gosport Covered Bridge
White River
HAER IN-39
HAER IND,60-GOSP,1-
1ph/3pg/1pc/fr L

Gosport Passenger & Freight Company; see New Albany & Salem Railroad

New Albany & Salem Railroad (Gosport Passenger & Freight Company)
North St.
HAER IN-4
HAER IND,60-GOSP,2A-
3dr/5ph/5pg/1pc/1ct/fr L

PARKE COUNTY

BLOOMINGDALE

Jackson Covered Bridge
Spanning Sugar Creek
HAER IN-48
HAER IND,61-BLOMD.V,1-
5dr L

MANSFIELD

Mansfield Covered Bridge
Spanning Big Raccoon Creek
HAER IN-44
HAER IND,61-MANS,1-
4dr L

MONTEZUMA

Leatherwood Station Covered Bridge
Spanning Leatherwood Creek
HAER IN-40
HAER IND,61-MONT,1-
15ph/8pg/2pc L

TURKEY RUN ST. PARK

Narrows Covered Bridge
County Rd. 280 E. Spanning Sugar Creek
HAER IN-49
HAER IND,61-TURPA,2-
5dr L

PERRY COUNTY

CANNELTON

Cannelton Cotton Mill (Indiana Cotton Mills)
Front & Fourth Sts.
HAER IN-1
HAER IND,62-CANN,2-
8dr/42ph/11pg/3pc/8ct/fr L

Cannelton Cotton Mill,Superintendent's House
Front & Washington Sts.
HAER IN-1-A
HAER IND,62-CANN,2A-
3ph/1pc/fr L

Cannelton Cotton Mill,Worker's Housing (A) (Indiana Cotton Mills)
Fourth St.
HAER IN-1-B
HAER IND,62-CANN,2B-
2ph/1pc L

Cannelton Cotton Mills,Worker's Housing (B) (Indiana Cotton Mills)
Fifth St.
HAER IN-1-C
HAER IND,62-CANN,2C-
4ph/1pc L

Heck,Jacob,Building
HABS IN-162
HABS IND,62-CANN,1-
3ph/1pc L

Indiana Cotton Mills; see Cannelton Cotton Mill

Indiana Cotton Mills; see Cannelton Cotton Mill,Worker's Housing (A)

Indiana Cotton Mills; see Cannelton Cotton Mills,Worker's Housing (B)

PORTER COUNTY

CHESTERTON VIC.

Augsburg Swensk Skola (Burstrom Chapel)
Oak Hill Rd.
HABS IN-48
HABS IND,64-CHEST.V,1-
3dr/4ph/3pg L

Burstrom Chapel; see Augsburg Swensk Skola

POSEY COUNTY

NEW HARMONY

Granary; see Rappite Fort

Laboratory,New; see Owen,Dr. David Dale,House

Owen,Dr. David Dale,House (Laboratory,New)
Church St. (State Hwy. 66)
HABS IN-24-4
HABS IND,65-NEHAR,1-
8dr/4ph/2pg/fr L

Owens,D. P. House
Church & Main Sts.
HABS IN-161
HABS IND,65-NEHAR,12-
2ph/1pc L

Poet's House (Rappite House)
Granary & West Sts.
HABS IN-37
HABS IND,65-NEHAR,8-
5dr/5ph/3pg L

Rappite Brick House
South St.
HABS IN-22
HABS IND,65-NEHAR,3-
1ph L

Rappite Community House No. 2
Main St.
HABS IN-5
HABS IND,65-NEHAR,2-
9dr/5ph/2pg L

Rappite Community House No. 2 Annex; see Rappite Dye House

Rappite Community House No. 3; see Rappite Tavern

Rappite Community House No. 4
Church St.
HABS IN-32
HABS IND,65-NEHAR,5-
6ph L

Rappite Dye House (Rappite Community House No. 2 Annex)
Main & Granary Sts.
HABS IN-38
HABS IND,65-NEHAR,9-
4dr/5ph/3pg L

Rappite Fort (Granary)
Granary St.
HABS IN-31
HABS IND,65-NEHAR,4-
1ph L

Rappite House
Granary St.
HABS IN-43
HABS IND,65-NEHAR,11-
4ph/1pg L

Rappite House; see Poet's House

Rappite Tavern (Rappite Community House No. 3)
Church St.
HABS IN-39
HABS IND,65-NEHAR,10-
3dr/2ph/3pg L

Schnee House
Lot 67,Owens Add.
HABS IN-30
HABS IND,65-NEHAR,6-
4ph/fr L

Vondegrift House
Lot 69,Owens Add.
HABS IN-33
HABS IND,65-NEHAR,7-
3ph L

RANDOLPH COUNTY

RIDGEVILLE

Pennsylvania Railroad,Ridgeville Switching Station
East Rd.
HABS IN-158
HABS IND,68-RIDVI,1A-
6dr L

UNION CITY

Union City Railroad Depot
North Howard St.
HABS IN-189
HABS IND,68-UNCI,1A-
3dr L

RIPLEY COUNTY

MORRIS

Nobbe,Marie K. ,House
State Rd. 46
HABS IN-149
HABS IND,69-MORI,1-
8dr L

VERSAILLES

Busching Covered Bridge
Covered Bridge Rd. Spanning Laughery Creek
HAER IN-33
HAER IND,69-VERS,1-
3dr/3pg L

RUSH COUNTY

RUSHVILLE

Melodeon Hall
132-138 W. Second St.
HABS IN-97
HABS IND,70-RUVI,1-
5ph/4pg/1pc/2ct L

RUSHVILLE VIC.

Kennedy Covered Bridge
State Rt. 44,spanning Flat Rock River
HABS IN-24-1
HABS IND,70-RUVI.V,1-
7dr/1pg/fr L

SHELBY COUNTY

SHELBYVILLE

Major,Charles,School
102 E. Franklin St.
HABS IN-201
HABS IND,73-SHEVI,1-
12ph/21pg/1pc/fr L

ST. JOSEPH COUNTY

MISHAWAKA

Kamm Building
111 N. Main St.
HABS IN-139
HABS IND,71-MISH,1C-
12ph L

Mishawaka Trust & Savings Company
N. Main St. & Lincolnway W.
HABS IN-137
HABS IND,71-MISH,1A-
27ph L

115 N. Main St. (Commercial Building)
HABS IN-141
HABS IND,71-MISH,1E-
4ph L

107-109 North Main Street (Commercial Building)
HABS IN-138
HABS IND,71-MISH,1B-
6ph L

113 North Main Street (Commercial Building)
HABS IN-140
HABS IND,71-MISH,1D-
4ph L

Documentation: **ct** color transparencies **dr** measured drawings **fr** field records
pc photograph captions **pg** pages of text **ph** photographs

117-119 North Main Street (Commercial Building)
HABS IN-142
HABS IND,71-MISH,1F-
5ph L

121-125 North Main Street (Commercial Building)
HABS IN-143
HABS IND,71-MISH,1H-
12ph L

North Main Street,100 Block
HABS IN-136
HABS IND,71-MISH,1-
9ph L

111 West First Street (Commercial Building)
HABS IN-144
HABS IND,71-MISH,1G-
8ph/8pg L

SOUTH BEND

Court House,Old
114 S.Lafayette Blvd. (moved from Main St.)
HABS IN-24-12
HABS IND,71-SOUB,1-
12dr/3ph/2pg/1ct/fr L

STEUBEN COUNTY

ANGOLA VIC.

Power's Church
County Rd. 800E
HABS IN-193
HABS IND,76-ANG.V,1-
4dr/fr L

SWITZERLAND COUNTY

PATRIOT VIC.

Merit-Tandy Farmstead
RR 1,Box 225
HABS IN-195
HABS IND,78-PAT.V,1-
6dr/13ph/23pg/1pc L

Merit-Tandy Farmstead,Barn
RR 1,Box 225
HABS IN-195-B
HABS IND,78-PAT.V,1B-
4ph L

Merit-Tandy Farmstead,Ice Storage House
RR 1,Box 225
HABS IN-195-A
HABS IND,78-PAT.V,1A-
1ph L

VEVAY

DuFour,John Francis,House; see Ferry House

Ferry House (DuFour,John Francis,House; Graham House)
Ohio River Vic.
HABS IN-24-16
HABS IND,78-VEVA,1-
3dr/3ph/2pg/fr L

Graham House; see Ferry House

Methodist Episcopal Church,Ruter Chapel
Main & Union Sts.
HABS IN-27
HABS IND,78-VEVA,2-
6dr L

Privy (six-sided)
Courthouse Vic.
HABS IN-80
HABS IND,78-VEVA,4-
2ph/1pg L

Schneck,U. P. ,House
630 Market St.
HABS IN-28
HABS IND,78-VEVA,3-
10dr L

TIPPECANOE COUNTY

CLARKS HILL VIC.

Shirley's Restaurant
U. S. Hwy. 52 & State Rd. 28
HABS IN-177
HABS IND,79-CLAHI.V,1-
5dr L

LAFAYETTE

Lafayette Street Railway Powerhouse
2 South St.
HAER IN-41
HAER IND,79-LAFY,2A-
24ph/30pg/2pc L

Ward,James,House
1116 Columbia St.
HABS IN-192
HABS IND,79-LAFY,1-
5dr/fr L

UNION COUNTY

BROWNSVILLE

Brownsville Covered Bridge (Wagon Bridge)
Spanning Whitewater River (moved to Indianapolis)
HAER IN-27
HAER IND,81-BROVI,1-
5dr/16ph/4pg/1pc L

Wagon Bridge; see Brownsville Covered Bridge

DUNLAPSVILLE

Dunlapsville Covered Bridge
Roseburg Rd. Spanning E. Fork Whitewater River
HAER IN-31
HAER IND,81-DUNVI,1-
6dr/3pg L

VANDERBURGH COUNTY

EVANSVILLE

Carpenter,Willard,House
413 Carpenter St.
HABS IN-24-11
HABS IND,82-EVA,1-
15dr/2ph/1pg L

VERMILLION COUNTY

NEWPORT

Newport Army Ammunition Plant
HAER IN-53
HAER IND,83-NEWP,1-
53pg/fr L

VIGO COUNTY

TERRE HAUTE

Wabash River Bridge
Spanning Wabash River at U.S. Hwy. 40
HAER IN-64
30ph/6pg/3pc H

WABASH COUNTY

NORTH MANCHESTER

North Manchester Public Library
Main St.
HABS IN-152
HABS IND,85-MANO,1-
6dr L

WARREN COUNTY

INDEPENDENCE VIC.

Riverside-Independence Bridge
See Fountain Co.,Riverside Vic. for documentation
HAER IN-67
HAER DLC/PP-1993:IN-2
24ph/8pg/3pc L

WARRICK COUNTY

NEWBURGH

House,Old Stone; see Roberts,Gaines Hardy,House

Roberts,Gaines Hardy,House (House,Old Stone)
Wonderland Route
HABS IN-24-13
HABS IND,87-NEBU.V,1-
8dr/1ph/2pg L

WASHINGTON COUNTY

SALEM

Hay,John,Birthplace (Morrison,John J.,House)
College Ave.
HABS IN-25
HABS IND,88-SAL,1-
4dr L

Morrison,John J.,House; see Hay,John,Birthplace

WAYNE COUNTY

CAMBRIDGE CITY

Conklin,Benjamin,House
302 E. Main St.
HABS IN-98
HABS IND,89-CAMB,1-
10dr/13ph/8pg/1ct/fr L

Hotel Kirby; see Vinton House Inn

Vinton House Inn (Hotel Kirby)
National Rd. (U. S. Rt. 40)
HABS IN-191
HABS IND,89-CAMB,2-
2dr/fr L

CENTERVILLE

Julian,Jacob,House (Morton,Oliver P. ,House)
313 W. Main St.
HABS IN-102
HABS IND,89-CENVI,1-
6ph/5pg/1pc L

Lantz House
214 W. Main St.
HABS IN-103
HABS IND,89-CENVI,2-
8dr/11ph/7pg/1pc/2ct/fr L

Mansion House
214 E. Main St.
HABS IN-104
HABS IND,89-CENVI,3-
8dr/9ph/7pg/1pc/1ct/fr L

Masonic Hall; see Wayne County Warden's House

Morton,Oliver P. ,House; see Julian,Jacob,House

Wayne County Warden's House (Masonic Hall)
E. Main St. & Fifth St.
HABS IN-105
HABS IND,89-CENVI,4-
8ph/7pg/1pc/1ct L

FOUNTAIN CITY

Coffin,Levi,House
Main Cross & Mill Sts.
HABS IN-79
HABS IND,89-FOUCI,1-
10dr L

MILTON

Justice House
109 Seminary St.
HABS IN-190
HABS IND,89-MILT,1-
1dr L

MILTON VIC.

Daniels House
State Rt. 1
HABS IN-117
HABS IND,89-MILT.V,2-
14ph/1pc/3ct L

Daniels House,Outbuilding
State Rt. 1
HABS IN-117-A
HABS IND,89-MILT.V,2A-
1ph L

Kinsey,Isaac,House
502 E. Sarver Rd.
HABS IN-109
HABS IND,89-MILT.V,1-
9dr/22ph/9pg/6ct/fr L

MOUNT AUBURN

Huddleston House
E. Main St. (U. S. Rt. 40)
HABS IN-110
HABS 1985(HABS):19
8dr/12ph/6pg/1pc/2ct/fr L

PENNVILLE

Coffee Pot Restaurant
U. S. Rt. 40
HABS IN-120
HABS IND,89-PENVI,1-
2ph/1pc L

RICHMOND

Adams House
Liberty Ave.
HABS IN-111
HABS IND,89-RICH,10-
9ph/3pg/1pc L

Bethel African Methodist Episcopal Church
200 Sixth St.
HABS IN-112
HABS IND,89-RICH,8-
7ph/9pg/1ct L

City Market House
S. Sixty & A Sts.
HABS IN-24-14
HABS IND,89-RICH,1-
3dr/3ph/2pg/fr L

Earlham College Observatory
National Rd.
HABS IN-113
HABS IND,89-RICH,2-
3ph/5pg L

Harrison,Thomas,House
514 W. Main St.
HABS IN-146
HABS IND,89-RICH,9-
7dr/20ph/7pg/fr L

Hicksite Friends Meetinghouse (Wayne County Museum)
1150 N. A St.
HABS IN-119
HABS IND,89-RICH,5-
1ph/4pg/2ct L

Knights of Columbus Building; see Starr Historic District

Lynde House; see Starr Historic District

203-205 North Eleventh Street (House); see Starr Historic District

210 North Eleventh Street (House); see Starr Historic District

215 North Eleventh Street (House); see Starr Historic District

222 North Tenth Street (House); see Starr Historic District

224 North Twelfth Street (House); see Starr Historic District

312 North Twelfth Street (House); see Starr Historic District

322 North Twelfth Street (House); see Starr Historic District

Raukopf House
240 S. Third St.
HABS IN-118
HABS IND,89-RICH,6-
4ph/5pg L

Scott,Andrew,House
126 N. Tenth St.
HABS IN-145
HABS IND,89-RICH,4-
13ph/6pg/1ct L

Starr Historic District
HABS IN-114
HABS IND,89-RICH,7-
6ph/1ct L

Starr Historic District (Knights of Columbus Building)
204 N. Tenth St.
HABS IN-114-K
HABS IND,89-RICH,7K-
8ph/1ct L

Starr Historic District (Lynde House)
308 N. Twelfth St.
HABS IN-114-F
HABS IND,89-RICH,7F-
1ph L

Starr Historic District (203-205 North Eleventh Street (House))
HABS IN-114-B
HABS IND,89-RICH,7B-
1ph L

Starr Historic District (210 North Eleventh Street (House))
HABS IN-114-C
HABS IND,89-RICH,7C-
1ph L

Starr Historic District (215 North Eleventh Street (House))
HABS IN-114-D
HABS IND,89-RICH,7D-
1ph L

Starr Historic District (222 North Tenth Street (House))
HABS IN-114-L
HABS IND,89-RICH,7L-
7ph/1pc L

Starr Historic District (224 North Twelfth Street (House))
HABS IN-114-E
HABS IND,89-RICH,7E
1ph L

Starr Historic District (312 North Twelfth Street (House))
HABS IN-114-G
1ph L

Starr Historic District (322 North Twelfth Street (House))
HABS IN-114-H
HABS IND,89-RICH,7H-
1ph L

Starr Historic District
(Starr,Elizabeth,House)
326 N. Tenth St.
HABS IN-114-A
HABS IND,89-RICH,7A-
1ph L

Starr Historic District (207 Thirteenth Street (House))
HABS IN-114-I
HABS IND,89-RICH,7I
1ph L

Starr Historic District (227 Thirteenth Street (House))
HABS IN-114-J
HABS IND,89-RICH,7J-
1ph L

Starr Piano Factory & Richmond Gas Company
G St. Bridge & Main St. Bridge
HAER IN-42
HAER IND,89-RICH,13-
6ph/5pg/1pc L

Starr,Elizabeth,House; see Starr Historic District

207 Thirteenth Street (House); see Starr Historic District

227 Thirteenth Street (House); see Starr Historic District

Wayne County Courthouse
Courthouse Square
HABS IN-115
HABS IND,89-RICH,3-
29ph/9pg/2ct L

Wayne County Museum; see Hicksite Friends Meetinghouse

Workers' Cottages
Bound by South Second,Eleventh,A, & E Sts.
HABS IN-116
HABS IND,89-RICH,12-
2dr/17ph/6pg/1pc/fr L

WELLS COUNTY

VERA CRUZ VIC.

Double Intersection Pratt (Whipple) Truss Bridge; see Wabash River Bridge

Wabash River Bridge (Double Intersection Pratt (Whipple) Truss Bridge)
State Rt. 316 & Wabash River
HAER IN-22
HAER IND,90-VECRU.V,1-
21ph/1pc/fr L

Woodbury County Courthouse, Sioux City, Woodbury County, Iowa. Interior, rotunda, general view from the east. Photograph by Jack E. Boucher, November 1976 (HABS IOWA,97-SIOCI,3-17).

Iowa

ALLAMAKEE COUNTY

WAUKON

Almquist,P. J. ,House
16 Second St. NW
HABS IA-151
HABS IOWA,3-WAUK,1-
16ph/4pg/1pc L

AUDUBON COUNTY

AUDUBON

Audubon Public Library
401 North Park Place
HABS IA-166
19ph/8pg/4pc H

BENTON COUNTY

VINTON

Iowa Braille & Sight Saving School; see Iowa Institution for the Education of the Blind

Iowa Institution for the Education of the Blind (Iowa Braille & Sight Saving School)
HABS IA-63
HABS IOWA,6-VINT,1-
8ph/23pg/1pc L

BLACK HAWK COUNTY

WATERLOO

Cedar Park Restroom; see Waterloo Water Works,Well House 4

House
HABS IA-101
HABS IOWA,7-WATLO,1-
2ph/1pg/1pc L

Russell,Rensselaer,House
520 W. Third St.
HABS IA-64
HABS IOWA,7-WATLO,2-
4ph/15pg/1pc L

Waterloo Water Works,Well House 4 (Cedar Park Restroom)
Fairview & Lafayette Ave.
HABS IA-125
HABS IOWA,7-WATLO,3-
5dr/9ph/1pg/1pc/fr L

BOONE COUNTY

BOONE

City Hall
Eighth & Allen Sts.
HABS IA-105
HABS IOWA,8-BOONE,1-
1ph/3pg/1pc L

BREMER COUNTY

WAVERLY VIC.

Dix's Bridge; see Waverly Junction Bridge

Waverly Junction Bridge (Dix's Bridge)
Spanning Shell Rock River at Country Rd.
HAER IA-38
HAER DLC/PP-1993:IA-2
18ph/9pg/2pc L

BUCHANAN COUNTY

INDEPENDENCE

Iowa Hospital for the Insane (State Mental Health Institute)
State Rt. 248
HABS IA-54
HABS IOWA,10-INDEP,1-
4ph/15pg/1pc L

State Mental Health Institute; see Iowa Hospital for the Insane

QUASQUETON

Cedar Rock; see Walter,Lowell,House

Walter,Lowell,House (Cedar Rock)
Rt. W-38 Vic.
HABS IA-130
HABS IOWA,10-QUAS,1-
9pg L

BUTLER COUNTY

GREENE

Shell Rock River Bridge; see Traer Street Bridge

Traer Street Bridge (Shell Rock River Bridge)
Spanning Shell Rock River at Traer St.
HAER IA-9
HAER IOWA,12-GREENE,1-
20ph/13pg/2pc L

CEDAR COUNTY

SPRINGDALE VIC.

Brown,John,House; see Maxson,William,House

Maxson,William,House (Brown,John,House)
State Hwy. No. 1
HABS IA-30-16
HABS IOWA,16-SPRING.V,1-
8dr/8ph L

WEST BRANCH

Friends Meetinghouse; see Quaker Meetinghouse

Herbert Hoover National Historic Site; see Hoover,Herbert,Birthplace House

Hoover,Herbert,Birthplace House (Hoover,Jesse,House; Herbert Hoover National Historic Site)
Penn & Downey Sts.
HABS IA-21
HABS IOWA,16-WEBRA,1-
4dr/9ph/1pg/1pc L

Hoover,Jesse,House; see Hoover,Herbert,Birthplace House

Quaker Meetinghouse (Friends Meetinghouse)
Downey St. ,Wapsinono Creek Vic.
HABS IA-25
HABS IOWA,16-WEBRA,2-
10dr/7ph/1pc L

CERRO GORDO COUNTY

MASON CITY

Bijou Theatre; see Zoller Block

City Fire Department Headquarters
19 First St. SW
HABS IA-126
HABS IOWA,17-MASCIT,5-
7dr/14ph/6pg/1pc L

City National Bank (Van Duyn's Clothing Store)
4 S. Federal Ave.
HABS IA-79
HABS IOWA,17-MASCIT,3-
1ph/1pg/1pc L

Knights of Columbus Building
202-204 S. Federal Ave.
HABS IA-127
HABS IOWA,17-MASCIT,6-
10dr/16ph/9pg/1pc L

McFarlane,W. T. ,Building
123 S. Federal Ave.
HABS IA-128
HABS IOWA,17-MASCIT,7-
7ph/2pg/1pc L

Melson,Joshua G. ,House
56 River Heights Dr.
HABS IA-95
HABS IOWA,17-MASCIT,1-
3ph/1pg/1pc L

Park Inn Hotel
15 W. State St.
HABS IA-80
HABS IOWA,17-MASCIT,2-
1ph/1pg/1pc L

Rule,Arthur L. ,House
11 S. Rock Glen
HABS IA-57
HABS IOWA,17-MASCIT,8-
3ph/2pg/1pc L

Taylor Bridge
Spanning Winnebago River, U. S. Rt. 18
HAER IA-11
HAER IOWA,17-MASCIT,4-
9ph/7pg/1pc L

Van Duyn's Clothing Store; see City National Bank

Zoller Block (Bijou Theatre)
119-121 S. Federal Ave.
HABS IA-129
HABS IOWA,17-MASCIT,9-
4ph/3pg/1pc L

CHEROKEE COUNTY

CHEROKEE

Hospital for the Insane,Main Building (State Mental Health Institute,Main Building)
W. Main St. Vic.
HABS IA-51
HABS IOWA,18-CHER,1-
7ph/18pg/1pc L

State Mental Health Institute,Main Building; see Hospital for the Insane,Main Building

CHICKASAW COUNTY

NASHUA VIC.

Church in the Vale,Little Brown (First Congregational Church)
State Rt. 346
HABS IA-20
HABS IOWA,19-NASH.V,1-
9dr/4ph/1pg/1pc L

First Congregational Church; see Church in the Vale,Little Brown

CLAYTON COUNTY

ELKADER

Water Mill,Old,Turkey River
N. Main St.
HABS IA-30-37
HABS IOWA,22-ELK,1-
1ph L

GUTTENBURG

Upper Miss. River 9-Foot Channel,Lock & Dam No. 10
HAER IA-22
HAER IOWA,22-GUTBU,1-
114ph/11pg/8pc L

CLINTON COUNTY

CLINTON

Clinton County Courthouse
Courthouse Square
HABS IA-100
HABS IOWA,23-CLINT,3-
7ph/1pc L

United States Post Office
S. Fifth Ave & S. Third St.
HABS IA-112
HABS IOWA,23-CLINT,4-
3ph/1pc L

Van Allen,John D. , & Son,Store (Von Mauer,Petersen Harned,Store)
Fifth Ave. S & S. Second St.
HABS IA-22
HABS IOWA,23-CLINT,1-
8dr/4ph/1pc/2ct L

Von Mauer,Petersen Harned,Store; see Van Allen,John D. , & Son,Store

Young,W. J. ,Machine Shop
S. Tenth St. & Second Ave.
HAER IA-14
HAER IOWA,23-CLINT,2-
14dr/17ph/7pg/1pc/fr L

CRAWFORD COUNTY

DOW CITY

Dow,Simeon E. ,House
S. Prince St.
HABS IA-70
HABS IOWA,24-DOWCIT,1-
2ph/1pg/1pc L

DAVIS COUNTY

BLOOMFIELD VIC.

Russell,Henry L. ,House
Rt. 6,(West Grove Twp.)
HABS IA-137
HABS IOWA,26-BLOFI,1-
3dr/6ph/18pg/1pc L

DES MOINES COUNTY

BURLINGTON

Burlington Bridge
HAER IA-20
HAER IOWA,29-BURL,5-
46ph/3pc L

Carpenter,G. B. P. ,House
100 Block of Polk Sts. (Prospect Point)
HABS IA-108
HABS IOWA,29-BURL,4-
1ph/2pg/1pc L

Hedge Hill (Hedge,Thomas,House)
609 Fifth St.
HABS IA-85
HABS IOWA,29-BURL,3-
1ph/1pg L

Hedge,Thomas,House; see Hedge Hill

House,First Brick in Iowa; see Rorer,Judge David,House

Mason,Judge Charles,House
931 N. Sixth St.
HABS IA-30-3
HABS IOWA,29-BURL,1-
7dr/3ph/1pg/1pc L

Rorer,Judge David,House (House,First Brick in Iowa)
N. Fourth & Columbia Sts.
HABS IA-30-24
HABS IOWA,29-BURL,2-
1ph L

Sixth Street Viaduct
Spanning Burlington Northern RR and Valley St.
HAER IA-36
HAER DLC/PP-1993:IA-2
28ph/19pg/3pc L

BURLINGTON VIC.

Citizen's Bridge; see MacArthur Bridge

MacArthur Bridge (Citizen's Bridge)
Span. Mississippi Rvr. on Hwy. 34 btwn IA & IL
HAER IA-21
HAER 1990 (HAER):6
73ph/48pg/6pc L

MIDDLETOWN

Iowa Army Ammunition Plant
HAER IA-13
HAER IOWA,29-MIDTO,1-
73pg/fr L

DICKINSON COUNTY

OKOBOJI VIC.

Okoboji Bridge
HAER IA-40
H

Documentation: **ct** color transparencies **dr** measured drawings **fr** field records
pc photograph captions **pg** pages of text **ph** photographs

SPIRIT LAKE

Gardner,Rowland,Log Cabin
(Sharp,Abbie Gardner,Log Cabin)
Monument St. ,Arnolds Park Vic.
HABS IA-30-40
HABS IOWA,30-SPIRLA,1-
1ph L

Sharp,Abbie Gardner,Log Cabin; see Gardner,Rowland,Log Cabin

DUBUQUE COUNTY

DUBUQUE

Archbishop's Residence; see Stout,F. D. ,House

Comm & Indstl Bldgs, Halpin Block
53-55 Locust St.
HABS IA-160-AZ
HABS DLC/PP-1992:IA-5
6ph/3pg/1pc L

Comm & Indstl Bldgs,Ambrose Gleed Malthouse
75 S. Locust St.
HABS IA-160-E
HABS DLC/PP-1992:IA-5
2ph/3pg/1pc L

Comm & Indstl Bldgs,American House Hotel
400-414 Central Ave.
HABS IA-160-P
HABS DLC/PP-1992:IA-5
5dr/19ph/3pg/2pc L

Comm & Indstl Bldgs,Armour & Co Meat Packing Plant
298 Iowa St.
HABS IA-160-K
HABS DLC/PP-1992:IA-5
4ph/2pg/1pc L

Comm & Indstl Bldgs,Becker-Hazelton Co. Warehouse
280 Iowa St.
HABS IA-160-L
HABS DLC/PP-1992:IA-5
12ph/3pg/1pc L

Comm & Indstl Bldgs,Bell Block
470 Central Ave.
HABS IA-160-S
HABS DLC/PP-1992:IA-5
6ph/3pg/1pc L

Comm & Indstl Bldgs,Bennett House Hotel
84 Main St.
HABS IA-160-BB
HABS DLC/PP-1992:IA-5
5ph/2pg/1pc L

Comm & Indstl Bldgs,Bishop's Block
90 Main St.
HABS IA-160-BA
HABS DLC/PP-1992:IA-5
42ph/4pg/3pc L

Comm & Indstl Bldgs,Bowman & Haley Garage
450 Central Ave.
HABS IA-160-R
HABS DLC/PP-1992:IA-5
2ph/2pg/1pc L

Comm & Indstl Bldgs,Bush,Robison & Co, Warehouse
HABS IA-160-BG
HABS DLC/PP-1992:IA-5
2ph/2pg/1pc L

Comm & Indstl Bldgs,C,B & Nthrn RR Passenger Depot
100 E. Third St.
HABS IA-160-Z
HABS DLC/PP-1992:IA-5
3ph/3pg/1pc L

Comm & Indstl Bldgs,C,M & SP RR Passenger Depot
Central Ave.
HABS IA-160-O
HABS DLC/PP-1992:IA-5
2ph/2pg/1pc L

Comm & Indstl Bldgs,C,M & SP RR,Freight Depot
Sixth & White Sts.
HABS IA-160-AA
HABS DLC/PP-1992:IA-5
2dr/16ph/2pg/2pc L

Comm & Indstl Bldgs,Carr Ryder & Adams,Fcty Annex
Tenth & Jackson Sts.
HABS IA-160-AN
HABS DLC/PP-1992:IA-5
8ph/2pg/1pc L

Comm & Indstl Bldgs,Carr,Ryder & Adams Co. Factory
Tenth & Jackson Sts.
HABS IA-160-AM
HABS DLC/PP-1992:IA-5
13ph/2pg/1pc L

Comm & Indstl Bldgs,Carr,Ryder & Adams Co. Pwrhse.
Tenth & Jackson Sts.
HABS IA-160-AF
HABS DLC/PP-1992:IA-5
10ph/3pg/1pc L

Comm & Indstl Bldgs,Carr,Ryder & Adams Co,Warehse
Eleventh & Washington St.
HABS IA-160-AP
HABS DLC/PP-1992:IA-5
8ph/2pg/1pc L

Comm & Indstl Bldgs,Carr,Ryder & Adams,Lumber Whss
Eleventh & Pine Sts.
HABS IA-160-AX
HABS DLC/PP-1992:IA-5
1dr/11ph/2pg/1pc L

Comm & Indstl Bldgs,Carr,Ryder & Adams,Office Bldg
1098 Jackson St.
HABS IA-160-AO
HABS DLC/PP-1992:IA-5
3ph/2pg/1pc L

Comm & Indstl Bldgs,Dubuque Ice Harbor
HABS IA-160-AQ
HABS DLC/PP-1992:IA-5
10ph/2pg/1pc L

Comm & Indstl Bldgs,Dubuque Linseed Oil Paint,Fcty
901 Jackson St.
HABS IA-160-AE
HABS DLC/PP-1992:IA-5
1ph/2pg/1pc L

Comm & Indstl Bldgs,Dubuque Oat Meal Mill Pwrhse.
Seventh & Washington Sts.
HABS IA-160-AU
HABS DLC/PP-1992:IA-5
1dr/10ph/3pg/1pc L

Comm & Indstl Bldgs,Dubuque Paper Co. Warehouse
280 Iowa St.
HABS IA-160-N
HABS DLC/PP-1992:IA-5
1dr/17ph/2pg/2pc L

Comm & Indstl Bldgs,Dubuque Seed Co. Warehouse
169-171 Iowa St.
HABS IA-160-I
HABS DLC/PP-1992:IA-5
3dr/18ph/3pg/2pc L

Comm & Indstl Bldgs,Dubuque Water Co. Pumphouse
Eighth & PineSts.
HABS IA-160-AV
HABS DLC/PP-1992:IA-5
4ph/2pg/1pc L

Comm & Indstl Bldgs,Ede's Robe Tanning Co.,Factory
41 Main Street
HABS IA-160-BN
HABS DLC/PP-1992:IA-5
4ph/3pg/1pc L

Comm & Indstl Bldgs,Farley & Loetscher Mfg.
585 White St.
HABS IA-160-V
HABS DLC/PP-1992:IA-5
3ph/2pg/1pc L

Comm & Indstl Bldgs,Farley & Loetscher Mfg,Annex
Seventh & Jackson Sts.
HABS IA-160-AG
HABS DLC/PP-1992:IA-5
13ph/2pg/1pc L

Comm & Indstl Bldgs,Farley & Loetscher Mfg,Fcty I
810 Jackson St.
HABS IA-160-AD
HABS DLC/PP-1992:IA-5
9ph/2pg/1pc L

Comm & Indstl Bldgs,Farley & Loetscher Mfg,Fcty II
750 White St.
HABS IA-160-AC
HABS DLC/PP-1992:IA-5
5ph/2pg/1pc L

Comm & Indstl Bldgs,Farley & Loetscher Mfg,Lumber
Eighth & Washington Sts.
HABS IA-160-AH
HABS DLC/PP-1992:IA-5
11ph/2pg/1pc L

Comm & Indstl Bldgs,Farley & Loetscher Mfg,Pwrhse
Eighth & Jackson Sts.
HABS IA-160-AI
HABS DLC/PP-1992:IA-5
1ph/2pg/1pc L

Comm & Indstl Bldgs,Flatiron Park
Main,Jones & Shields Sts.
HABS IA-160-BR
HABS DLC/PP-1992:IA-5
2ph/1pg/1pc L

Comm & Indstl Bldgs,Fluckiger Motor Co. Showroom
484 Central Ave.
HABS IA-160-T
HABS DLC/PP-1992:IA-5
3ph/2pg/1pc L

Comm & Indstl Bldgs,Herancourt Furniture Co. Fcty.
1100 Elm St.
HABS IA-160-AW
HABS DLC/PP-1992:IA-5
6ph/3pg/1pc L

Comm & Indstl Bldgs,IL Central RR Freight Depot
First & Iowa Sts.
HABS IA-160-G
HABS DLC/PP-1992:IA-5
18ph/3pg/2pc L

Comm & Indstl Bldgs,IL Central RR Passenger Depot
Iowa & Jones Sts.
HABS IA-160-A
HABS DLC/PP-1992:IA-5
1dr/21ph/3pg/2pc L

Comm & Indstl Bldgs,Intl Harvester Co Showrm,Offic
10 S. Main St.
HABS IA-160-B
HABS DLC/PP-1992:IA-5
19ph/3pg/2pc L

Comm & Indstl Bldgs,Intl Harvester Co Truck Showrm
8 S. Main St.
HABS IA-160-D
HABS DLC/PP-1992:IA-5
5ph/2pg/1pc L

Comm & Indstl Bldgs,Iowa Iron Works Blacksmith Shp
Ninth & Washington Sts.
HABS IA-160-AR
HABS DLC/PP-1992:IA-5
4ph/3pg/1pc L

Comm & Indstl Bldgs,Jackson Vinegar Co. Warehouse
64 Main St.
HABS IA-160-BF
HABS DLC/PP-1992:IA-5
5ph/2pg/1pc L

Comm & Indstl Bldgs,James Beach & Sons Co Fcty & W
57 S. Locust St.
HABS IA-160-F
HABS DLC/PP-1992:IA-5
21ph/4pg/2pc L

Comm & Indstl Bldgs,Joseph Motor Sales Co. Showrm.
99 Main St.
HABS IA-160-BP
HABS DLC/PP-1992:IA-5
3ph/2pg/1pc L

Comm & Indstl Bldgs,Karigan's Restaurant
401-405 Central Ave.
HABS IA-160-J
HABS DLC/PP-1992:IA-5
2ph/2pg/1pc L

Comm & Indstl Bldgs,Kassler Motor Co. Showroom
Fifth & White St.
HABS IA-160-X
HABS DLC/PP-1992:IA-5
3ph/2pg/1pc L

Comm & Indstl Bldgs,Key City Elec St RR,Pwrhse & S
Eighth & Washington Sts.
HABS IA-160-AT
HABS DLC/PP-1992:IA-5
12ph/4pg/1pc L

Comm & Indstl Bldgs,Key City Gas Co. Warehouse
10 Bluff St.
HABS IA-160-AY
HABS DLC/PP-1992:IA-5
4ph/2pg/1pc L

Comm & Indstl Bldgs,Key City Iron Works Foundry
898 Jackson St.
HABS IA-160-AK
HABS DLC/PP-1992:IA-5
9ph/2pg/1pc L

Comm & Indstl Bldgs,Klauer Mfg. Co. Factory
301 Ninth St.
HABS IA-160-AS
HABS DLC/PP-1992:IA-5
6ph/3pg/1pc L

Comm & Indstl Bldgs,Kretschner Mfg Co,Fcty & Whse
220 E. Ninth St.
HABS IA-160-AL
HABS DLC/PP-1992:IA-5
8ph/3pg/1pc L

Comm & Indstl Bldgs,M.M. Walker Co., Warehouse
40 Main St.
HABS IA-160-BJ
HABS DLC/PP-1992:IA-5
19ph/3pg/2pc L

Comm & Indstl Bldgs,Maizewood Insulation Co Fcty
275 Salina St.
HABS IA-160-C
HABS DLC/PP-1992:IA-5
7ph/3pg/1pc L

Comm & Indstl Bldgs,McFadden Coffee & Spice Co Fc
145 First St.
HABS IA-160-H
HABS DLC/PP-1992:IA-5
1dr/14ph/3pg/1pc L

Comm & Indstl Bldgs,Midland Labs.,Fcty & Warehse
210 Jones St.
HABS IA-160-BM
HABS DLC/PP-1992:IA-5
2ph/2pg/1pc L

Comm & Indstl Bldgs,Peter Even & Son Auto Co,Showr
65 Main St.
HABS IA-160-BO
HABS DLC/PP-1992:IA-5
3ph/2pg/1pc L

Comm & Indstl Bldgs,Reo Sales Co. Showroom
420 Central Ave.
HABS IA-160-Q
HABS DLC/PP-1992:IA-5
3ph/2pg/1pc L

Comm & Indstl Bldgs,Schroeder-Kleine Grocer Co,Whs
44-48 Main St.
HABS IA-160-BI
HABS DLC/PP-1992:IA-5
6ph/3pg/1pc L

Comm & Indstl Bldgs,Swift & Co. Meat Processing Pl
698 White St.
HABS IA-160-AB
HABS DLC/PP-1992:IA-5
2ph/2pg/1pc L

Comm & Indstl Bldgs,Thomas J. Mulgrew Co,Offc Bldg
30 Main St.
HABS IA-160-BK
HABS DLC/PP-1992:IA-5
4ph/2pg/1pc L

Comm & Indstl Bldgs,Trausch Baking Co. Bakery
25 Main St.
HABS IA-160-BL
HABS DLC/PP-1992:IA-5
3ph/2pg/1pc L

Comm & Indstl Bldgs,Wieneke-Hoerr Co. Factory
850 Jackson St.
HABS IA-160-AJ
HABS DLC/PP-1992:IA-5
3ph/2pg/1pc L

Comm & Indstl Bldgs,240-250 First Street
HABS IA-160-BS
HABS DLC/PP-1992:IA-5
4ph/2pg/1pc L

Comm & Indstl Bldgs,260 Iowa Street
HABS IA-160-M
HABS DLC/PP-1992:IA-5
3ph/2pg/1pc L

Comm & Indstl Bldgs,465 White Street
HABS IA-160-Y
HABS DLC/PP-1992:IA-5
1ph/1pg/1pc L

Comm & Indstl Bldgs,504 Central Avenue
HABS IA-160-U
HABS DLC/PP-1992:IA-5
5ph/2pg/1pc L

Comm & Indstl Bldgs,549-553 White Street
HABS IA-160-W
HABS DLC/PP-1992:IA-5
3ph/2pg/1pc L

Comm & Indstl Bldgs,56 Main Street
HABS IA-160-BH
HABS DLC/PP-1992:IA-5
2ph/2pg/1pc L

Comm & Indstl Bldgs,76 Main Street
HABS IA-160-BD
HABS DLC/PP-1992:IA-5
2ph/2pg/1pc L

Comm & Indstl Bldgs,80 Main Street
HABS IA-160-BC
HABS DLC/PP-1992:IA-5
3ph/2pg/1pc L

Dubuque & Wisconsin Bridge; see Eagle Point Bridge

Dubuque City Hall
50 W. Thirteenth St.
HABS IA-71
HABS IOWA,31-DUBU,4-
6ph/1pc L

Dubuque Commercial and Industrial Buildings
HABS IA-160
HABS DLC/PP-1992:IA-5
1dr/74ph/14pg/7pc L

Dubuque County Courthouse
720 Central Ave.
HABS IA-109
HABS IOWA,31-DUBU,5-
9ph/1pc L

Dubuque County Jail
36 E. Eighth St.
HABS IA-72
HABS IOWA,31-DUBU,6-
10ph/1pc L

Eagle Point Bridge (Dubuque & Wisconsin Bridge)
HAER IA-2
HAER IOWA,31-DUBU,3-
81ph/39pg/6pc L

Egelhof-Casper Funeral Home; see Stout,Fannie,House

Five Flags Theater; see Majestic Theater

Hamm,Mathais,House
2241 Lincoln Ave.
HABS IA-73
HABS IOWA,31-DUBU,7-
17ph/1pc/4ct L

Langworthy,Edward,House
1095 W. Third St.
HABS IA-30-14
HABS IOWA,31-DUBU,2-
6dr/12ph/1pc/2ct L

Majestic Theater (Orpheum Theater; Five Flags Theater)
405 Main St.
HABS IA-124
HABS IOWA,31-DUBU,8-
12ph/1pc/5ct L

Miss. River 9-Ft. Channel Proj.,Lock & Dam No. 11
Upper Mississippi River
HAER IA-23
HAER 1991(HAER):25
50ph/16pg/3pc L

Miss. River 9-Ft. Channel Proj.,Lock & Dams 11-22
Upper Mississippi River
HAER IA-33
HAER 1991(HAER):25
103pg L

Orpheum Theater; see Majestic Theater

Shot Tower
Commercial & E. Fourth Sts.
HABS IA-30-8
HABS IOWA,31-DUBU,1-
1dr/3ph/1pc/4ct L

Stout,F. D. ,House (Archbishop's Residence)
1105 Locust St.
HABS IA-110
HABS IOWA,31-DUBU,9-
6ph/1pc/8ct L

Stout,Fannie,House (Egelhof-Casper Funeral Home)
1145 Locust St.
HABS IA-111
HABS IOWA,31-DUBU,10-
15ph/1pc L

Workingmen's Houses
Locust,S. Locust and Dodge Sts. and Southern Ave.
HABS IA-159
HABS DLC/PP-1992:IA-5
38ph/14pg/3pc L

Workingmen's Houses,Berg,Adam P.,House
770 Dodge St.
HABS IA-159-AX
HABS DLC/PP-1992:IA-5
1dr/8ph/2pg/1pc L

Workingmen's Houses,Brennan,Mary,House
367 S. Locust St.
HABS IA-159-L
HABS DLC/PP-1992:IA-5
2ph/2pg/1pc L

Workingmen's Houses,Burke,Patrick,House
205 S. Locust St.
HABS IA-159-A
HABS DLC/PP-1992:IA-5
1dr/8ph/2pg/1pc L

Workingmen's Houses,Burns,David,House
670 Dodge St.
HABS IA-159-AU
HABS DLC/PP-1992:IA-5
3ph/2pg/1pc L

Workingmen's Houses,Byrne,John,House
666 Dodge St.
HABS IA-159-AT
HABS DLC/PP-1992:IA-5
5ph/2pg/1pc L

Workingmen's Houses,Cane,Michael,House
391 Southern Ave.
HABS IA-159-AG
HABS DLC/PP-1992:IA-5
2ph/2pg/1pc L

Workingmen's Houses,Clancy,Watthew,House
794 Dodge St.
HABS IA-159-AZ
HABS DLC/PP-1992:IA-5
2ph/2pg/1pc L

Workingmen's Houses,Colford,Alexander C.,House
384 Southern Ave.
HABS IA-159-AJ
HABS DLC/PP-1992:IA-5
2ph/2pg/1pc L

Workingmen's Houses,Colford,Peter,House
283 Southern Ave.
HABS IA-159-X
HABS DLC/PP-1992:IA-5
3ph/2pg/1pc L

Workingmen's Houses,Coughlin,William,House
860 Dodge St.
HABS IA-159-BJ
HABS DLC/PP-1992:IA-5
3ph/2pg/1pc L

Workingmen's Houses,Coyne,John,House
357 Southern Ave.
HABS IA-159-AC
HABS DLC/PP-1992:IA-5
1dr/8ph/2pg/1pc L

Workingmen's Houses,Crowley,Jeremiah,House
388 Southern Ave.
HABS IA-159-AI
HABS DLC/PP-1992:IA-5
3ph/2pg/1pc L

Workingmen's Houses,Donahue,Harry J.,House
106 Southern Ave.
HABS IA-159-S
HABS DLC/PP-1992:IA-5
4ph/2pg/1pc L

Workingmen's Houses,Donahue,John H.,House
98 Southern Ave.
HABS IA-159-R
HABS DLC/PP-1992:IA-5
5ph/2pg/1pc L

Workingmen's Houses,Doyle,Eliza,House
376 Southern Ave.
HABS IA-159-AK
HABS DLC/PP-1992:IA-5
2ph/2pg/1pc L

Workingmen's Houses,Dumphy,Martin,House
387 Southern Ave.
HABS IA-159-AF
HABS DLC/PP-1992:IA-5
7ph/2pg/1pc L

Workingmen's Houses,Fenton,Michael,House
375 S. Locust St.
HABS IA-159-M
HABS DLC/PP-1992:IA-5
1dr/5ph/2pg/1pc L

Workingmen's Houses,Flynn,Michael,House
321 S. Locust St.
HABS IA-159-G
HABS DLC/PP-1992:IA-5
2ph/2pg/1pc L

Workingmen's Houses,Hipman,William P.,House I
804 Dodge St.
HABS IA-159-BA
HABS DLC/PP-1992:IA-5
2ph/2pg/1pc L

Workingmen's Houses,Hipman,William P.,House II
816 Dodge St.
HABS IA-159-BD
HABS DLC/PP-1992:IA-5
2ph/2pg/1pc L

Workingmen's Houses,Kelly,John H.,House
274 Southern Ave.
HABS IA-159-W
HABS DLC/PP-1992:IA-5
5dr/14ph/6pg/1pc L

Workingmen's Houses,Kelly,Joseph,House
311 Southern Ave.
HABS IA-159-Y
HABS DLC/PP-1992:IA-5
3ph/2pg/1pc L

Workingmen's Houses,Kelly,Timothy,House
364 Southern Ave.
HABS IA-159-AN
HABS DLC/PP-1992:IA-5
3ph/2pg/1pc L

Workingmen's Houses,Kelly,William H.,House
329 Sothern Ave.
HABS IA-159-AA
HABS DLC/PP-1992:IA-5
2ph/2pg/1pc L

Workingmen's Houses,Kennedy,Patrick,House
289 S. Locust St.
HABS IA-159-F
HABS DLC/PP-1992:IA-5
3ph/2pg/1pc L

Workingmen's Houses,Lahr,John,House
229 S. Locust St.
HABS IA-159-D
HABS DLC/PP-1992:IA-5
3ph/2pg/1pc L

Workingmen's Houses,Mahoney,Jeremiah,House
263 Southern Ave.
HABS IA-159-V
HABS DLC/PP-1992:IA-5
1dr/8ph/2pg/1pc L

Workingmen's Houses,Mahony,Michael,House
235 S. Locust St.
HABS IA-159-E
HABS DLC/PP-1992:IA-5
1dr/7ph/2pg/1pc L

Workingmen's Houses,Martin,James,House
844 Dodge St.
HABS IA-159-BI
HABS DLC/PP-1992:IA-5
1dr/8ph/2pg/1pc L

Workingmen's Houses,McGee,John,House
251 Southern Ave.
HABS IA-159-T
HABS DLC/PP-1992:IA-5
3ph/2pg/1pc L

Workingmen's Houses,McNulty,John,House
824 Dodge St.
HABS IA-159-BF
HABS DLC/PP-1992:IA-5
3ph/2pg/1pc L

Workingmen's Houses,McQueen,Ann,House
650 Dodge St.
HABS IA-159-AR
HABS DLC/PP-1992:IA-5
1dr/7ph/2pg/1pc L

Workingmen's Houses,Mehan,Bridget,House
359 S. Locust St.
HABS IA-159-K
HABS DLC/PP-1992:IA-5
2ph/2pg/1pc L

Workingmen's Houses,Morris,Ann,House
358 Southern Ave.
HABS IA-159-BK
HABS DLC/PP-1992:IA-5
5ph/2pg/1pc L

Workingmen's Houses,O'Toole,Charles,House
654 Dodge St.
HABS IA-159-AS
HABS DLC/PP-1992:IA-5
2ph/2pg/1pc L

Workingmen's Houses,Powers,Dennis,House
345 S. Locust St.
HABS IA-159-J
HABS DLC/PP-1992:IA-5
2ph/2pg/1pc L

Workingmen's Houses,Purcell,Phillip M.,House
393 Southern Ave.
HABS IA-159-AH
HABS DLC/PP-1992:IA-5
2ph/2pg/1pc L

Workingmen's Houses,Rooney,James,House
354 Southern Ave.
HABS IA-159-AB
HABS DLC/PP-1992:IA-5
3ph/2pg/1pc L

Workingmen's Houses,Rooney,Thomas,House
368 Southern Ave.
HABS IA-159-AM
HABS DLC/PP-1992:IA-5
4ph/2pg/1pc L

Workingmen's Houses,Rooney,William,House
314 Southern Ave.
HABS IA-159-Z
HABS DLC/PP-1992:IA-5
3ph/2pg/1pc L

Workingmen's Houses,Scarry,Patrick,House
636 Dodge St.
HABS IA-159-AP
HABS DLC/PP-1992:IA-5
4ph/2pg/1pc L

Workingmen's Houses,Scollard,Johanna,House
215 S. Locust St.
HABS IA-159-B
HABS DLC/PP-1992:IA-5
2ph/2pg/1pc L

Workingmen's Houses,Spark,George R.,House
381 Southern Ave.
HABS IA-159-AE
HABS DLC/PP-1992:IA-5
1ph/2pg/1pc L

Workingmen's Houses,Strain,James P.,House
821 Dodge St.
HABS IA-159-BE
HABS DLC/PP-1992:IA-5
4ph/2pg/1pc L

Workingmen's Houses,Sullivan,Daniel J.,House
830 Dodge St.
HABS IA-159-BH
HABS DLC/PP-1992:IA-5
3ph/2pg/1pc L

Workingmen's Houses,Sullivan,Michael,House
383 S. Locust St.
HABS IA-159-N
HABS DLC/PP-1992:IA-5
5dr/11ph/7pg/1pc L

Workingmen's Houses,Sutton,Nicholas,N.,House
9 Locust St.
HABS IA-159-BP
HABS DLC/PP-1992:IA-5
3ph/2pg/1pc L

Workingmen's Houses,Theno,Frank,House
809 Dodge St.
HABS IA-159-BB
HABS DLC/PP-1992:IA-5
3ph/2pg/1pc L

Workingmen's Houses,Thornton,Nicholas,House
365 Southern Ave.
HABS IA-159-AD
HABS DLC/PP-1992:IA-5
1dr/12ph/3pg/1pc L

Workingmen's Houses,Tracy,Margaret,House
682 Dodge St.
HABS IA-159-AW
HABS DLC/PP-1992:IA-5
2ph/2pg/1pc L

Workingmen's Houses,Walsh,Ann,House
642 Dodge St.
HABS IA-159-AQ
HABS DLC/PP-1992:IA-5
2ph/2pg/1pc L

Workingmen's Houses,Welsh,James,House
616 Dodge St.
HABS IA-159-AO
HABS DLC/PP-1992:IA-5
1dr/7ph/2pg/1pc L

Workingmen's Houses,Wilson,Catherine,House
678 Dodge St.
HABS IA-159-AV
HABS DLC/PP-1992:IA-5
2ph/2pg/1pc L

Workingmen's Houses,19 Locust Street
HABS IA-159-BO
HABS DLC/PP-1992:IA-5
2ph/2pg/1pc L

Workingmen's Houses,225 South Locust Street
HABS IA-159-C
HABS DLC/PP-1992:IA-5
2ph/2pg/1pc L

Workingmen's Houses,257 Southern Avenue
HABS IA-159-U
HABS DLC/PP-1992:IA-5
2ph/2pg/1pc L

Workingmen's Houses,27-29 Locust Street
HABS IA-159-BN
HABS DLC/PP-1992:IA-5
2ph/2pg/1pc L

Workingmen's Houses,31-35 Locust Street
HABS IA-159-BM
HABS DLC/PP-1992:IA-5
2ph/2pg/1pc L

Workingmen's Houses,329 South Locust Street
HABS IA-159-H
HABS DLC/PP-1992:IA-5
1dr/5ph/2pg/1pc L

Workingmen's Houses,337 South Locust Street
HABS IA-159-I
HABS DLC/PP-1992:IA-5
2ph/2pg/1pc L

Workingmen's Houses,37-39 Locust Street
HABS IA-159-BL
HABS DLC/PP-1992:IA-5
5ph/2pg/1pc L

Workingmen's Houses,372 Southern Avenue
HABS IA-159-AL
HABS DLC/PP-1992:IA-5
2ph/2pg/1pc L

Workingmen's Houses,70 Southern Avenue
HABS IA-159-O
HABS DLC/PP-1992:IA-5
2ph/2pg/1pc L

Workingmen's Houses,784 Dodge Street
HABS IA-159-AY
HABS DLC/PP-1992:IA-5
2ph/2pg/1pc L

Workingmen's Houses,810 Dodge Street
HABS IA-159-BC
HABS DLC/PP-1992:IA-5
1ph/2pg/1pc L

Workingmen's Houses,827 Dodge Street
HABS IA-159-BG
HABS DLC/PP-1992:IA-5
2ph/2pg/1pc L

Workingmen's Houses,89 Southern Avenue
HABS IA-159-P
HABS DLC/PP-1992:IA-5
3ph/2pg/1pc L

Workingmen's Houses,95 Southern Avenue
HABS IA-159-Q
HABS DLC/PP-1992:IA-5
4ph/2pg/1pc L

DUBUQUE VIC.

Dubuque,Julien,Monument (Grave)
Mississippi River Vic. ,Julien Dubuque Dr.
HABS IA-30-9
HABS IOWA,31-DUBU.V,1-
1dr/3ph/1pc L

HOLY CROSS VIC.

Pin Oak Tavern (Western Hotel)
U. S. Rt. 52
HABS IA-30-10
HABS IOWA,31-HOLCRO.V,1-
2dr/1ph/fr L

Western Hotel; see Pin Oak Tavern

FAYETTE COUNTY

CLERMONT VIC.

Larrabee,Gov. William,House; see Montauk

Montauk (Larrabee,Gov. William,House)
U. S. Rt. 18
HABS IA-66
HABS IOWA,33-CLER.V,1-
5ph/1pg/1pc L

FRANKLIN COUNTY

HAMPTON

Franklin County Courthouse II
Courthouse Square
HABS IA-120
HABS IOWA,35-HAMP,1-
1ph/7pg/1pc L

FREMONT COUNTY

RIVERTON VIC.

Nebraska City Bridge
Span. Missouri Rvr. near Hwy. 2 btwn Iowa & Neb.
HAER NE-2
HAER 1990 (HAER):6
3dr/59ph/509pg/4pc L

HAMILTON COUNTY

WEBSTER CITY

Kendall Young Library
1202 Wilson St.
HABS IA-102
HABS IOWA,40-WEBCIT,1-
1ph/1pg/1pc L

HARRISON COUNTY

MISSOURI VALLEY VIC.

Blair Bridge; see Lincoln,Abraham,Memorial Bridge

Lincoln,Abraham,Memorial Bridge (Blair Bridge)
Span. Missouri Rvr. btwn IA & NE
HAER NE-1
HAER 1990 (HAER):6
37ph/52pg/3pc L

HENRY COUNTY

JACKSON TWP.

Boyleston Bridge
Spanning Skunk River
HAER IA-5
HAER IOWA,44-JACTOS,1-
24ph/12pg/2pc L

MOUNT PLEASANT

Iowa Insane Hospital (State Mental Health Institute)
U. S. Rt. 218
HABS IA-58
HABS IOWA,44-MOPLE,1-
6ph/33pg/1pc L

Iowa Wesleyan College,Main Building,Old (Mount Pleasant Collegiate Institute,Main Bldg,Old)
Broad St.
HABS IA-59
HABS IOWA,44-MOPLE,2-
2ph/10pg/1pc L

Iowa Wesleyan College,Pioneer Hall (Mount Pleasant Collegiate Institute,Pioneer Hall)
Broad St.
HABS IA-60
HABS IOWA,44-MOPLE,3-
3ph/10pg/1pc L

Mount Pleasant Collegiate Institute,Main Bldg,Old; see Iowa Wesleyan College,Main Building,Old

Mount Pleasant Collegiate Institute,Pioneer Hall; see Iowa Wesleyan College,Pioneer Hall

State Mental Health Institute; see Iowa Insane Hospital

HOWARD COUNTY

LIME SPRINGS VIC.

Davis Bridge
Spanning Upper Iowa River at County Rd. 16
HAER IA-35
HAER DLC/PP-1993:IA-3
18ph/13pg/2pc L

PROTIVIN

Chyle,Frank,Jr.,Barn
Main St.
HABS IA-163-B
HABS 1989(HABS):7
1ph/1pc L

Chyle,Frank,Jr.,Granary
Main St.
HABS IA-163-D
HABS 1989(HABS):7
1ph/1pc L

Chyle,Frank,Jr.,House
Main Street
HABS IA-163
HABS 1989(HABS):7
6ph/11pg/1pc L

Chyle,Frank,Jr.,Milkhouse
Main St.
HABS IA-163-C
HABS 1990 (HABS):3
1ph/1pc L

Chyle,Frank,Jr.,Summer Kitchen
Main St.
HABS IA-163-A
HABS 1990 (HABS):3
1ph/1pc L

HUMBOLDT COUNTY

HUMBOLDT

Johnson Building
532 Sumner Ave.
HABS IA-156
HABS IOWA,46-HUMB,1-
8ph/10pg/1pc L

IOWA COUNTY

AMANA

Amana Colonies
State Rts. 223 & 149 & U. S. Rt. 6
HABS IA-99
HABS IOWA,48-AMA,7-
10ph/1pc/4ct L

Amana Colonies,General Store & Offices
State Rt. 220
HABS IA-44
HABS IOWA,48-AMA,3-
2ph/1pg/1pc L

Haas,John,House (Ox Yoke Inn)
State Rt. 220
HABS IA-46
HABS IOWA,48-AMA,4-
2ph/1pg/1pc L

Lauer Meetinghouse
State Rt. 220 Vic.
HABS IA-30-18
HABS IOWA,48-AMA,1-
1ph L

Main Meetinghouse
State Rt. 220 Vic.
HABS IA-84
HABS IOWA,48-AMA,6-
1ph/1pg/1pc L

Moershal,W. F. ,House
State Rt. 220
HABS IA-47
HABS IOWA,48-AMA,5-
2ph/1pg/1pc L

Ox Yoke Inn; see Haas,John,House

Pitz Meetinghouse
State Rt. 220 Vic.
HABS IA-30-43
HABS IOWA,48-AMA,2-
1ph L

AMANA VIC.

West Amana Flour Mill
HABS IA-30-45
HABS IOWA,48-AMA.V,1-
1ph L

JACKSON COUNTY

BELLEVUE

Miss. River 9-Ft. Channel Proj.,Lock & Dam No. 12
Upper Mississippi River
HAER IA-24
HAER 1991(HAER):25
23ph/14pg/2pc L

MAQUOKETA VIC.

Cottonville Bridge
County Rd. D-61 at Farmer's Creek
HAER IA-31
HAER DLC/PP-1992:IA-5
1dr/12ph/15pg/1pc L

MONMOUTH TOWNSHIP

Bear Creek Bridge; see Mill Rock Bridge

Mill Rock Bridge (Bear Creek Bridge)
Spanning Big Bear Creek
HAER IA-7
HAER IOWA,49-MONMO,1-
16ph/6pg/2pc L

ST. DONATUS

Frank,Stephen,House
Davenport Rd.
HABS IA-30-17
HABS IOWA,49-SAIDO,1-
2dr/2ph L

JASPER COUNTY

MONROE

Kling,H. A. ,House
416 N. Monroe St.
HABS IA-30-33
HABS IOWA,50-MONRO,1-
3ph L

NEWTON

Marsh Rainbow Arch Bridge
West Eighth St. North
HAER IA-4
HAER IOWA,50-NEWT,1-
39ph/34pg/2pc L

VANDALIA

Pulver,Ferdinand Daniel,House
County Rd. F-70 Vic.
HABS IA-30-1
HABS IOWA,50-VANDA,1-
9dr/5ph/fr L

JEFFERSON COUNTY

FAIRFIELD

Clarke,James Frederic,House
500 S. Main St.
HABS IA-23
HABS IOWA,51-FAIRF,2-
4dr/6ph/15pg/1pc L

Parsons College,Ewing Hall
HABS IA-30-23
HABS IOWA,51-FAIRF,1A-
1ph L

JOHNSON COUNTY

IOWA CITY

Benton Street Bridge
Spanning the Iowa River at Benton St.
HAER IA-30
HAER DLC/PP-1992:IA-5
46ph/71pg/4pc/fr L

Capitol,Old (First State Capitol; Third Territorial Capitol)
Clinton St. & Iowa Ave.
HABS IA-30-29
HABS IOWA,52-IOWCI,2-
1ph L

Capitol,Temporary (Second Territorial Capitol)
HABS IA-30-28
HABS IOWA,52-IOWCI,1-
1ph L

First State Capitol; see Capitol,Old

Lucas,Gov. Robert,House (Plum Grove)
1030 Carroll Ave.
HABS IA-30-41
HABS IOWA,52-IOWCI,3-
1ph/1pc L

Plum Grove; see Lucas,Gov. Robert,House

Third Territorial Capitol; see Capitol,Old

SOLON VIC.

Sutliff Bridge; see Sutliff's Ferry Bridge

Sutliff's Ferry Bridge (Sutliff Bridge)
Spanning Cedar River (Cedar Twp.)
HAER IA-6
HAER IOWA,52-SOLON.V,1-
35ph/41pg/3pc L

JONES COUNTY

CLAY TOWNSHIP

Jones County Bowstring Bridge; see Supple Ford Bridge

Supple Ford Bridge (Jones County Bowstring Bridge)
Spanning S. Fork of Maquoketa River
HAER IA-32
10ph/10pg/1pc L

LEE COUNTY

FORT MADISON

Lee County Courthouse
701 Ave. F
HABS IA-76
HABS IOWA,56-FTMAD,1-
1ph/1pg/1pc L

KEOKUK

House,Brick
HABS IA-157
HABS IOWA,56-KEOK,2-
1ph/1pc L

Keokuk & Hamilton Bridge
Spanning Mississippi River
HAER IA-3
HAER IOWA,56-KEOK,1-
101ph/57pg/8pc L

Miss. River 9-Ft. Channel Proj.,Lock & Dam No. 19
Upper Mississippi River
HAER IA-27
HAER 1991(HAER):25
79ph/17pg/5pc L

LINN COUNTY

CEDAR RAPIDS

Hamilton,James E. ,House
2345 Linden Ave.
HABS IA-86
HABS IOWA,57-CEDRA,1-
1ph/1pc L

LYON COUNTY

ROCK RAPIDS VIC.

Bridge,Reinforced Concrete Arch
(Melan Bridge)
Spanning Dry Creek
HAER IA-15
HAER IOWA,59-ROCRA.V,1-
1pg L

Melan Bridge; see Bridge,Reinforced Concrete Arch

MADISON COUNTY

BEVINGTON

Bevington Bridge
Spanning the Middle River at Warren St.
HAER IA-37
18ph/10pg/2pc L

WINTERSET

Clark,Caleb,House
814 S. Eighth St.
HABS IA-65
HABS IOWA,61-WINSE,1-
3ph/1pg/1pc L

Madison County Courthouse
Courthouse Square
HABS IA-83
HABS IOWA,61-WINSE,2-
5ph/15pg/1pc L

Tidrick,M. R. ,House
122 S. Fourth Ave.
HABS IA-139
HABS IOWA,61-WINSE,3-
4ph/1pg/1pc L

Vawter,J. G. ,House
First Ave. & South St.
HABS IA-138
HABS IOWA,61-WINSE,4-
4ph/1pg/1pc L

MAHASKA COUNTY

OSKALOOSA

Belvidere Saloon & Rock Island Brewery Company (Iowa Penn Central Regional Shopping Center)
307-309 High Ave. W.
HABS IA-176
3ph/1pg/1pc L

Green,J. H., & Co. Building (Rivola Theatre; Iowa Penn Central Regional Shoping Center)
202 High Ave. W.
HABS IA-167
22ph/7pg/2pc L

Gruwell,C. B. & Company,Building (Iowa Penn Central Regional Shopping Center)
206 High Ave. W.
HABS IA-168
1ph/1pg/1pc L

Hetherington Confectionery & Ice Cream Shop (Iowa Penn Central Regional Shopping Center)
319 High Ave. W.
HABS IA-173
1ph/1pg/1pc L

Hoffman,Phillip,House (Iowa Penn Central Regional Shopping Center)
309 High Ave. W.
HABS IA-185
3ph/1pg/1pc L

Holt & Son Grocery Store (Iowa Penn Central Regional Shopping Center)
313 High Ave. W.
HABS IA-175
2ph/1pg/1pc L

Holt Commercial Building (Iowa Penn Central Regional Shopping Center)
215 High Ave. W.
HABS IA-181
3ph/1pg/1pc L

Hoopes & BeDillion Restaurant (Iowa Penn Central Regional Shopping Center)
315 High Ave. W.
HABS IA-174
1ph/1pg/1pc L

Howar,C. E.,Cigars & Freeland Ice Cream Parlor (Iowa Penn Central Regional Shopping Center)
203-205 High Ave. W.
HABS IA-183
1ph/1pg/1pc L

Iowa Penn Cantral Regional Shopping Center; see Mattison's,W.,Groceries & Provisions

Iowa Penn Central Regional Shoping Center; see Green,J. H., & Co. Building

Iowa Penn Central Regional Shopping Center; see Belvidere Saloon & Rock Island Brewery Company

Iowa Penn Central Regional Shopping Center; see Gruwell,C. B. & Company,Building

Iowa Penn Central Regional Shopping Center; see Hetherington Confectionery & Ice Cream Shop

Iowa Penn Central Regional Shopping Center; see Hoffman,Phillip,House

Iowa Penn Central Regional Shopping Center; see Holt & Son Grocery Store

Iowa Penn Central Regional Shopping Center; see Holt Commercial Building

Iowa Penn Central Regional Shopping Center; see Hoopes & BeDillion Restaurant

Iowa Penn Central Regional Shopping Center; see Howar,C. E.,Cigars & Freeland Ice Cream Parlor

Iowa Penn Central Regional Shopping Center; see McCall's, F.W., Marble Shop

Iowa Penn Central Regional Shopping Center; see McGregor's Furniture House

Iowa Penn Central Regional Shopping Center; see Oller,J.W.,Groceries

Iowa Penn Central Regional Shopping Center; see Oskaloosa Implement Company

Iowa Penn Central Regional Shopping Center; see Roenspiess,L. P., Cigar Manufacturing

Iowa Penn Central Regional Shopping Center; see Salvation Army Barracks

Iowa Penn Central Regional Shopping Center; see Swearengen,L. A., Meat Market

Iowa Penn Central Regional Shopping Center; see Waggoner,John,House

Iowa Penn Central Regional Shopping Center; see Wilkins,S. J. & Company,Building

Kalbach & Son Building (Kalbach Lumber Company)
S. "B" St. & First Ave. W.
HABS IA-186
7ph/8pg/1pc L

Kalbach Lumber Company; see Kalbach & Son Building

Mattison's,W.,Groceries & Provisions (Iowa Penn Cantral Regional Shopping Center)
211 High Ave. West
HABS IA-182
2ph/1pg/1pc L

McCall's, F.W., Marble Shop (Iowa Penn Central Regional Shopping Center)
214 High Ave. W.
HABS IA-169
3ph/4pg/1pc L

McGregor's Furniture House (Iowa Penn Central Regional Shopping Center)
301-305 High Ave. W.
HABS IA-177
3ph/1pg/1pc L

Oller,J.W.,Groceries (Iowa Penn Central Regional Shopping Center)
321 High Ave. W.
HABS IA-172
3ph/1pg/1pc L

Oskaloosa Implement Company (Iowa Penn Central Regional Shopping Center)
221 High Ave. W.
HABS IA-178
2ph/1pg/1pc L

Oskaloosa,Town of
Bounded by High Ave. W., High Ave. N., S. "B" St.
HABS IA-147
7pg L

Rivola Theatre; see Green,J. H., & Co. Building

Roenspiess,L. P., Cigar Manufacturing (Iowa Penn Central Regional Shopping Center)
219 High Ave. W.
HABS IA-179
2ph/1pg/1pc L

Salvation Army Barracks (Iowa Penn Central Regional Shopping Center)
302-304 High Ave. W.
HABS IA-170
2ph/1pg/1pc L

Swearengen,L. A., Meat Market (Iowa Penn Central Regional Shopping Center)
323 High Ave. W.
HABS IA-171
2ph/1pg/1pc L

Waggoner,John,House (Iowa Penn Central Regional Shopping Center)
301 First Ave. W.
HABS IA-184
5ph/1pg/1pc L

Wilkins,S. J. & Company,Building (Iowa Penn Central Regional Shopping Center)
217 High Ave. W.
HABS IA-180
3ph/1pg/1pc L

OSKALOOSA VIC.

Nelson,Daniel,Barn
Glendale Rd.
HABS IA-81-A
HABS IOWA,62-OSK.V,1A-
2ph/1pc L

Nelson,Daniel,Farm
Glendale Rd.
HABS IA-81
HABS IOWA,62-OSK.V,1-
6ph/1pg/1pc L

MARION COUNTY

KNOXVILLE VIC.

Reichard,John,House
State Rt. 92 vic.
HABS IA-55
HABS IOWA,63-KNOX.V,1-
7dr/28ph/23pg/2pc/fr L

PELLA

Central College,Temporary Quarters
1107 W. Washington St.
HABS IA-96
HABS IOWA,63-PEL,2-
2ph/1pg/1pc L

Earp,Wyatt,House; see Van Spankeren House

Roelofsz,Dr. Joost,House (Viersen House)
1008-10 Main St. (Reformation Ave.)
HABS IA-30-32
HABS IOWA,63-PEL,1-
2ph/2pg L

Van Spankeren House
(Earp,Wyatt,House)
507 E. Franklin St.
HABS IA-97
HABS IOWA,63-PEL,3-
3ph/1pg/1pc L

Viersen House; see Roelofsz,Dr. Joost,House

MARSHALL COUNTY

BANGOR VIC.

Honey Creek Bridge
Spanning Honey Creek at One-Hundred Fifth St.
HAER IA-39
HAER DLC/PP-1993:IA-2
15ph/13pg/1pc L

MARIETTA

Hicksite Friends Meetinghouse
County Rd. E-29
HABS IA-30-13
HABS IOWA,64-MARI,1-
1ph L

MARSHALLTOWN

First Church of Christ (Scientist)
W. Main & N. Fifth St.
HABS IA-94
HABS IOWA,64-MARS,1-
2ph/1pg/1pc L

Marshall County Courthouse
Square by Center,Main & Church Sts. & First Ave.
HABS IA-78
HABS IOWA,64-MARS,2-
1ph/1pg/1pc L

Rainbow Arch Bridge; see South Third Avenue Bridge

South Third Avenue Bridge (Rainbow Arch Bridge)
HAER IA-8
HAER IOWA,64-MARS,3-
8ph/13pg/1pc L

MARSHALLTOWN VIC.

Rock Valley Bridge
Spanning N. Timber Creek on Old U.S. Hwy. 30
HAER IA-29
HAER 1990 (HAER):6
12ph/26pg/1pc L

MONTGOMERY COUNTY

RED OAK

Montgomery County Courthouse
Courthouse Square
HABS IA-98
HABS IOWA,69-REDO,1-
2ph/1pg/1pc L

MUSCATINE COUNTY

MUSCATINE

Clark,Alexander,Houses
307-309 Chestnut St.
HABS IA-107
HABS IOWA,7-MUSCA,1-
8ph/15pg/1pc/fr L

Hershey Memorial Hospital
(Hershey,Benjamin,Memorial Convalescent Home)
1810 Mulberry Ave.
HABS IA-142
HABS IOWA,70-MUSCA,2-
21ph/1pg/2pc L

Hershey,Benjamin,Memorial Convalescent Home; see Hershey Memorial Hospital

MUSCATINE VIC.

Miss. River 9-Ft. Channel Proj.,Lock & Dam No. 16
Upper Mississippi River
HAER IA-26
HAER 1991(HAER):25
21ph/13pg/2pc L

PAGE COUNTY

CLARINDA

Iowa Hospital for the Insane,Main Building (State Mental Health Institute, Main Building)
W. Main St. Vic.
HABS IA-52
HABS IOWA,73-CLAR,1-
8ph/39pg/1pc L

State Mental Health Institute, Main Building; see Iowa Hospital for the Insane,Main Building

POLK COUNTY

DES MOINES

Allen-Hubbell House; see Terrace Hill

Bachelor Officers Quarters; see Ft. Des Moines Hist. Comp., Bldg. 46

Bankers' Trust Building; see Equitable Life Assurance Company Building

Brinsmaid,S. S. ,House
Grand Ave. & Thirty-sixth St.
HABS IA-67
HABS IOWA,77-DESMO,15-
6ph/1pg/2pc L

Butler,Earl,House (Open Bible College)
2633 S. Fluer Dr.
HABS IA-89
HABS IOWA,77-DESMO,11-
1ph/1pg/1pc L

Capitol,Temporary (Second State Capitol)
Site of Soldiers & Sailors Monument
HABS IA-30
HABS IOWA,77-DESMO,2-
1ph L

Cavalry Band Stable; see Ft. Des Moines Hist. Comp.,Bldg. 87

Cavalry Drill Hall; see Ft. Des Moines Hist. Comp., Bldg. 47

Cromer,Frederick,House
1053 Ninth Street
HABS IA-135
HABS IOWA,77-DESMO,16-
10ph/6pg/1pc L

den Hartog House
2210 Army Post Road
HABS IA-144
HABS IOWA,77-DESMO,23-
15ph/1pg/1pc L

Des Moines Art Center
Greenwood Park
HABS IA-140
HABS IOWA,77-DESMO,17-
6ph/23pg/1pc L

Des Moines City Hall; see Municipal Building

Double Field Officers' Quarters; see Ft. Des Moines Hist. Comp., Bldgs. 14,15

East Locust Street Commercial District
521-529 E. Locust St.
HABS IA-143
HABS IOWA,77-DESMO,18-
3ph/4pg/1pc L

East Locust Street Commercial District (Garton Bakery & Confectionery)
523 E. Locust St.
HABS IA-143-B
HABS IOWA,77-DESMO,18-B-
1dr/8ph/1pg/1pc L

East Locust Street Commercial District (Nielsen,Gehrke, & Hansen Clothing Store; Garfield Clothing Store)
525-529 E. Locust St.
HABS IA-143-C
HABS IOWA,77-DESMO,18-C-
11ph/1pg/1pc L

East Locust Street Commercial District (Wheeler,C. F. ,Grocery; Woolworth,F. W. ,Building)
521 E. Locust St.
HABS IA-143-A
HABS IOWA,77-DESMO,18-A-
1ph/1pg/1pc L

Electrical Substation; see Ft. Des Moines Hist. Comp.,Bldg. 149

Equitable Life Assurance Company Building (Bankers' Trust Building)
605 Locust St.
HABS IA-68
HABS IOWA,77-DESMO,12
18ph/4pg/2pc L

Field Offices' Quarters; see Ft. Des Moines Hist Comp.,Bldg. 7

Fleming Building
Walnut & Sixth Sts.
HABS IA-90
HABS IOWA,77-DESMO,8-
1ph/1pg/1pc L

Fort Des Moines (Log); see House in Des Moines,First

Ft. Des Moines Hist Comp.,Bldg. 7
(Field Offices' Quarters)
HABS IA-121-A
HABS DLC/PP-1993:IA-1
6ph/3pg/1pc L

Ft. Des Moines Hist. Comp.
HABS IA-121
HABS DLC/PP-1993:IA-1
6dr/25ph/53pg/2pc L

Ft. Des Moines Hist. Comp., Bldg. 46
(Bachelor Officers Quarters)
HABS IA-121-C
HABS DLC/PP-1993:IA-1
9ph/4pg/1pc L

Ft. Des Moines Hist. Comp., Bldg. 47
(Cavalry Drill Hall)
HABS IA-121-D
HABS DLC/PP-1993:IA-1
7ph/2pg/1pc L

Ft. Des Moines Hist. Comp., Bldgs. 14,15 (Double Field Officers' Quarters)
HABS IA-121-B
HABS DLC/PP-1993:IA-1
4ph/3pg/1pc L

Ft. Des Moines Hist. Comp.,Bldg. 122
(Quartermaster Workshop)
HABS IA-121-W
HABS DLC/PP-1993:IA-1
3ph/2pg/1pc L

Ft. Des Moines Hist. Comp.,Bldg. 123 (Q.M. Stable)
HABS IA-121-X
HABS DLC/PP-1993:IA-1
4ph/3pg/1pc L

Ft. Des Moines Hist. Comp.,Bldg. 126 (Q.M. Stable)
HABS IA-121-Y
HABS DLC/PP-1993:IA-1
4ph/2pg/1pc L

Ft. Des Moines Hist. Comp.,Bldg. 127 (Q.M. Stable)
HABS IA-121-Z
HABS DLC/PP-1993:IA-1
5ph/2pg/1pc L

Ft. Des Moines Hist. Comp.,Bldg. 135
(Granary)
HABS IA-121-AA
HABS DLC/PP-1993:IA-1
4ph/2pg/1pc L

Ft. Des Moines Hist. Comp.,Bldg. 137
(Quartermaster and Subsistence Office Storehouse)
HABS IA-121-BB
HABS DLC/PP-1993:IA-1
3ph/3pg/1pc L

Ft. Des Moines Hist. Comp.,Bldg. 138
(Quartermaster Storehouse)
HABS IA-121-CC
HABS DLC/PP-1993:IA-1
4ph/2pg/1pc L

Ft. Des Moines Hist. Comp.,Bldg. 149
(Electrical Substation)
HABS IA-121-DD
HABS DLC/PP-1993:IA-1
2ph/1pg/1pc L

Ft. Des Moines Hist. Comp.,Bldg. 152
(Mounted Guard Shelter)
HABS IA-121-EE
HABS DLC/PP-1993:IA-1
4ph/1pg/1pc L

Ft. Des Moines Hist. Comp.,Bldg. 49
(Post Chapel)
HABS IA-121-E
HABS DLC/PP-1993:IA-1
10ph/3pg/1pc L

Ft. Des Moines Hist. Comp.,Bldg. 55,56 (Dbl. Barr.
HABS IA-121-F
HABS DLC/PP-1993:IA-1
9ph/4pg/1pc L

Ft. Des Moines Hist. Comp.,Bldg. 58 (Barracks)
HABS IA-121-G
HABS DLC/PP-1993:IA-1
7ph/4pg/1pc L

Ft. Des Moines Hist. Comp.,Bldg. 59,60 (Dbl. Barr.
HABS IA-121-H
HABS DLC/PP-1993:IA-1
6ph/4pg/1pc L

Ft. Des Moines Hist. Comp.,Bldg. 61,62 (Dbl. Barr.
HABS IA-121-I
HABS DLC/PP-1993:IA-1
5ph/4pg/1pc L

Ft. Des Moines Hist. Comp.,Bldg. 63,64 (Dbl. Barr.
HABS IA-121-J
HABS DLC/PP-1993:IA-1
7ph/3pg/1pc L

Ft. Des Moines Hist. Comp.,Bldg. 65,66 (Dbl. Barr.
HABS IA-121-K
HABS DLC/PP-1993:IA-1
5ph/4pg/1pc L

Ft. Des Moines Hist. Comp.,Bldg. 68 (Cav. Stable)
HABS IA-121-L
HABS DLC/PP-1993:IA-1
2ph/2pg/1pc L

Ft. Des Moines Hist. Comp.,Bldg. 69 (Stable Guard)
HABS IA-121-M
HABS DLC/PP-1993:IA-1
1ph/1pg/1pc L

Ft. Des Moines Hist. Comp.,Bldg. 70 (Cav. Stable)
HABS IA-121-N
HABS DLC/PP-1993:IA-1
1ph/2pg/1pc L

Ft. Des Moines Hist. Comp.,Bldg. 71 (Cav. Stable)
HABS IA-121-O
HABS DLC/PP-1993:IA-1
2ph/2pg/1pc L

Ft. Des Moines Hist. Comp.,Bldg. 72 (Stable Guard)
HABS IA-121-P
HABS DLC/PP-1993:IA-1
1ph/2pg/1pc L

Ft. Des Moines Hist. Comp.,Bldg. 73 (Cav. Stable)
HABS IA-121-Q
HABS DLC/PP-1993:IA-1
2ph/2pg/1pc L

Ft. Des Moines Hist. Comp.,Bldg. 75 (Stable Guard)
HABS IA-121-R
HABS DLC/PP-1993:IA-1
4ph/1pg/1pc L

Ft. Des Moines Hist. Comp.,Bldg. 81 (Cav. Stable)
HABS IA-121-S
HABS DLC/PP-1993:IA-1
2ph/2pg/1pc L

Ft. Des Moines Hist. Comp.,Bldg. 83 (Cav. Stable)
HABS IA-121-T
HABS DLC/PP-1993:IA-1
2ph/2pg/1pc L

Ft. Des Moines Hist. Comp.,Bldg. 86 (Cav. Stable)
HABS IA-121-U
HABS DLC/PP-1993:IA-1
5ph/2pg/1pc L

Ft. Des Moines Hist. Comp.,Bldg. 87
(Cavalry Band Stable)
HABS IA-121-V
HABS DLC/PP-1993:IA-1
5ph/2pg/1pc L

Garfield Clothing Store; see East Locust Street Commercial District

Garton Bakery & Confectionery; see East Locust Street Commercial District

Governor's Mansion; see Terrace Hill

Governor's Mansion,Old; see Witmer,W. W. ,House

Granary; see Ft. Des Moines Hist. Comp.,Bldg. 135

Granger,Barlow,House
Pioneer Park
HABS IA-30-15
HABS IOWA,77-DESMO,1-
10dr/6ph/fr L

House in Des Moines,First (Fort Des Moines (Log))
HABS IA-30-34
HABS IOWA,77-DESMO,3-
1ph L

House,Bungalow
1506 Thompson Ave.
HABS IA-91
HABS IOWA,77-DESMO,10-
1ph/1pg/1pc L

Iowa Girls High School Athletic Association; see Witmer,W. W. ,House

Kurtz,L. H. ,Company; see 131-133 Second Avenue (Commercial Building)

Lumbard,M. A. ,House
1059 Ninth St.
HABS IA-136
HABS IOWA,77-DESMO,19-
11ph/6pg/1pc L

Mounted Guard Shelter; see Ft. Des Moines Hist. Comp.,Bldg. 152

Municipal Building (Des Moines City Hall)
E. First & Locust Sts.
HABS IA-152
HABS IOWA,77-DESMO,13-
8ph/18pg/1pc/fr L

Nielsen,Gehrke, & Hansen Clothing Store; see East Locust Street Commercial District

Open Bible College; see Butler,Earl,House

Polk County Courthouse
Fifth & Court Sts. ,Courthouse Square
HABS IA-93
HABS IOWA,77-DESMO,9-
5ph/1pg/1pc L

Post Chapel; see Ft. Des Moines Hist. Comp.,Bldg. 49

Post Office Building,First
HABS IA-30-35
HABS IOWA,77-DESMO,4-
1ph L

Quartermaster and Subsistence Office Storehouse; see Ft. Des Moines Hist. Comp.,Bldg. 137

Quartermaster Storehouse; see Ft. Des Moines Hist. Comp.,Bldg. 138

Quartermaster Workshop; see Ft. Des Moines Hist. Comp.,Bldg. 122

Rollins,Ralph,House (Tudor Style House)
HABS IA-92
HABS IOWA,77-DESMO,6-
1ph/1pg/1pc L

Sakulin,Barney,Log House (Restoration)
Old Fort Des Moines
HABS IA-106
HABS IOWA,77-DESMO,20-
8dr L

131-133 Second Avenue (Commercial Building) (Kurtz,L. H. ,Company)
HABS IA-149
HABS IOWA,77-DESMO,14-
7ph/3pg/1pc L

Terrace Hill (Allen-Hubbell House; Governor's Mansion)
2300 Grand Ave.
HABS IA-69
HABS IOWA,77-DESMO,7-
1ph/1pg/1pc L

Tudor Style House; see Rollins,Ralph,House

U. S. Courthouse & Post Office
Fifth St. & Court Ave.
HABS IA-36
HABS IOWA,77-DESMO,21-
11ph/15pg/1pc L

Wheeler,C. F. ,Grocery; see East Locust Street Commercial District

Windsor Purity Candy Company
125-129 Second Ave.
HABS IA-148
HABS IOWA,77-DESMO,22-
8ph/6pg/1pc L

Witmer,W. W. ,House (Iowa Girls High School Athletic Association; Governor's Mansion,Old)
2900 Grand Ave.
HABS IA-104
HABS IOWA,77-DESMO,5-
1ph/1pg/1pc L

Woolworth,F. W. ,Building; see East Locust Street Commercial District

VALLEY JUNCTION VIC.

Clegg House
State Hwy. 90,W. Des Moines Vic.
HABS IA-30-7
HABS IOWA,77-VALJ.V,1-
9dr/2ph L

POTTAWATTAMIE COUNTY

COUNCIL BLUFFS

Dodge,Gen. Grenville M. ,House
605 S. Third St.
HABS IA-30-5
HABS IOWA,78,COUB,1-
3dr/10ph/8pg/1pc/fr L

Iowa Institute for Education of the Deaf & Dumb (Iowa State School for the Deaf)
South Ave. & State Rt. 92 Vic.
HABS IA-53
HABS IOWA,78-COUB,5-
2ph/17pg/1pc L

Iowa State School for the Deaf; see Iowa Institute for Education of the Deaf & Dumb

Pottawattamie County Courthouse
Pearl St. & Fifth Ave.
HABS IA-87
HABS IOWA,78-COUB,4-
4ph/1pg/1pc L

Pottawattamie County Jail
226 Pearl St.
HABS IA-88
HABS IOWA,78-COUB,3-
2ph/1pg/1pc L

Sutherland,D. B. ,House
HABS IA-103
HABS IOWA,78-COUB,6-
1ph/1pg/1pc L

Union Pacific Station (Transfer Depot & Hotel)
Twenty-first St.
HABS IA-30-6
HABS IOWA,78-COUB,2-
10dr/6ph/fr L

POWESHIEK COUNTY

GRINELL

Merchants' National Bank (Poweshiek County National Bank)
Fourth Ave. & Broad St.
HABS IA-77
HABS IOWA,79-GRIN,1-;DLC/PP-1992:IA-2
10dr/4ph/1pg/1pc/fr L

Poweshiek County National Bank; see Merchants' National Bank

SCOTT COUNTY

DAVENPORT

Bergfeld,Fritz,Block (Kistenmacher Drug Store)
321-323 W. Second St.
HABS IA-133
HABS IOWA,82-DAVPO,2-
4ph/2pg/1pc L

Del Rich Loan Building; see Schmidt,George M. ,Block

Dessaint,Louis C. ,House; see Palmer Mansion

Fickie Mansion; see Parker,J. Monroe,House

Grace Episcopal Cathedral (Trinity Episcopal Cathedral)
1121 Main St.
HABS IA-114
HABS IOWA,82-DAVPO,4-
14ph/12pg/2pc/2ct L

Kistenmacher Drug Store; see Bergfeld,Fritz,Block

Palmer Mansion (Dessaint,Louis C. ,House)
808 Brady St.
HABS IA-165
HABS 1991(HABS):12
13dr L

Parker,J. Monroe,House (Fickie Mansion)
Main & Twelfth Sts.
HABS IA-113
HABS IOWA,82-DAVPO,5-
14ph/1pc/2ct L

Schmidt,George M. ,Block (Del Rich Loan Building)
301-303 W. Second Street
HABS IA-131
HABS IOWA,82-DAVPO,6-
4ph/2pg/1pc L

Trinity Episcopal Cathedral; see Grace Episcopal Cathedral

305-307 West Second Street (Commercial Block)
HABS IA-132
HABS IOWA,82-DAVPO,1-
3ph/2pg/1pc L

325-327 West Second Street (Commercial Building)
HABS IA-134
HABS IOWA,82-DAVPO,3-
2ph/2pg/1pc L

LE CLAIRE

Cody,Isaac,House
1034 N. Cody St. (moved to Cody,WY)
HABS IA-56
HABS IOWA,82-LECLA,1-
1ph/1pg/1pc L

LE CLAIRE VIC.

Miss. River 9-Ft. Channel Proj.,Lock & Dam No. 14
Upper Mississippi River
HAER IA-25
HAER 1991(HAER):25
54ph/17pg/4pc L

STORY COUNTY

AMES

Dairy Industry Building
Iowa State University campus
HABS IA-164
HABS 1991(HABS):12
51ph/36pg/5pc L

Iowa State University,College Building (Iowa State University,Main Building,Old)
Morrill Rd. ,site of Beardshear Hall
HABS IA-116
HABS IOWA,85-AMES,1-
4ph/43pg/1pc L

Iowa State University,Farm House
Knoll Rd. Vic.
HABS IA-123
HABS IOWA,85-AMES,2-
6ph/32pg/1pc L

Iowa State University,Main Building,Old; see Iowa State University,College Building

Iowa State University,Morrill Hall
Morrill Rd.
HABS IA-50
HABS IOWA,85-AMES,3-
8ph/23pg/1pc L

GILBERT VIC.

Methodist Episcopal Church of Milford Township (Pleasant Grove Community Church)
County Rd. E-23
HABS IA-119
HABS IOWA,85-GIL.V,1-
4ph/12pg/1pc L

Pleasant Grove Community Church; see Methodist Episcopal Church of Milford Township

SHELDAHL

First Evangelical Lutheran Church (Sheldahl Norwegian Lutheran Church)
County Rd. R-38 & NW 166 Ave.
HABS IA-62
HABS IOWA,85-SHEL,1-
3dr/4ph/10pg/1pc L

Sheldahl Norwegian Lutheran Church; see First Evangelical Lutheran Church

UNION COUNTY

CRESTON

Chicago,Burlington & Quincy RR, West (Creston Municipal Complex)
116 W. Adams
HABS IA-150
HABS IOWA,88-CREST,1-
23ph/4pg/1pc/fr L

Creston Municipal Complex; see Chicago,Burlington & Quincy RR, West

VAN BUREN COUNTY

BENTONSPORT

Hancock,John,House
Third & Walnut Sts.
HABS IA-30-19
HABS IOWA,89-BENPO,1-
9dr/5ph/fr L

KEOSAUQUA

Pearson,Benjamin Franklin,House
Dodge St.
HABS IA-30-27
HABS IOWA,89-KESAU,1-
2ph L

WAPELLO COUNTY

AGENCY CITY

Agency House,Old
HABS IA-30-31
HABS IOWA,90-AGENCI,1-
1ph L

FLORES VIC.

Mars Hill Baptist Church
HABS IA-74
HABS IOWA,90-FLOR.V,1-
3ph/1pg/1pc L

OTTUMWA

Morrell,John & Company Meat Packing Plant,Bldg.27B
316 South Iowa Street
HAER IA-34-B
12ph/1pc H

Morrell,John & Company Meat Packing Plant,Bldg.49
316 South Iowa Street
HAER IA-34-A
12ph/1pc H

Morrell,John,& Company Meat Packing Plant
316 South Iowa Street
HAER IA-34
2dr/8ph/39pg/1pc L

Morrell,John,& Company Meat Packing Plant,Bldg.15
316 S. Iowa St.
HAER IA-34-C
15ph/2pc L

WARREN COUNTY

CARLISLE VIC.

Covered Bridge (Owens Covered Bridge)
Spanning North River (moved to Lake Easter Park)
HABS IA-30-2
HABS IOWA,91-CARL.V,1-
4dr/2ph/fr L

Owens Covered Bridge; see Covered Bridge

WEBSTER COUNTY

FORT DODGE

Butler,J. B. ,House
327 S. Twelfth St.
HABS IA-75
HABS IOWA,94-FTDO,1-
1ph/1pg/1pc L

Hawkeye Avenue Bridge; see Open Spandrel Bridge

Open Spandrel Bridge (Hawkeye Avenue Bridge)
Hawkeye Ave. ,spanning Des Moines River
HAER IA-17
HAER IOWA,94-FTDO,2-
17ph/27pg/2pc L

Swain-Vincent House
824 Third Ave. ,South
HABS IA-38
HABS IOWA,94-FTDO,3-
5ph/14pg/1pc L

WINNESHIEK COUNTY

DECORAH

Bucknell,W. S. ,House
210-13 Winnebago St.
HABS IA-30-4
HABS IOWA,96-DECOR,1-
5dr/2ph/fr L

City Stone Mill (Painter-Bernatz Mill)
200 N. Mill St.
HABS IA-30-11
HABS IOWA,96-DECOR,2-
3dr/2ph/fr L

Painter-Bernatz Mill; see City Stone Mill

DECORAH VIC.

Freeport Bridge
Spanning Upper Iowa River
HAER IA-19
HAER IOWA,96-DECOR.V,1-
3dr/38ph/1pg/3pc L

FESTINA VIC.

St. Anthony's Chapel (The Little Church)
Old Mission Vic.
HABS IA-30-12
HABS IOWA,96-FESTI.V,1-
2dr/1ph/fr L

The Little Church; see St. Anthony's Chapel

FRANKVILLE VIC.

Perry & Allen Patent Bowstring Truss Bridge
Spanning unnamed tributary of Yellow River
HAER IA-10
HAER IOWA,96-FRANK.V,1-
13ph/1pc/fr L H

KENDALLVILLE VIC.

Lower Plymouth Rock Bridge
Spanning Upper Iowa River
HAER IA-18
HAER IOWA,96-KEND.V,1-
26ph/80pg/3pc L

WOODBURY COUNTY

SIOUX CITY

Bekins Building; see Chicago & North Western Railway Co.,Freight House

Chicago & North Western Railway Co.,Freight House (Bekins Building)
Third and Jackson Sts.
HABS IA-187
HABS IOWA,97-SIOCI,2-
8ph/8pg/1pc L

Combination Bridge; see Pacific Shortline Bridge

Pacific Shortline Bridge (Combination Bridge)
U. S. Route 20,spanning Missouri River
HAER IA-1
HAER IOWA,97-SIOCI,1-
5dr/100ph/59pg/8pc/fr L

Woodbury County Courthouse
Seventh & Douglas Sts.
HABS IA-82
HABS IOWA,97-SIOCI,3-
22ph/1pg/1pc/2ct L

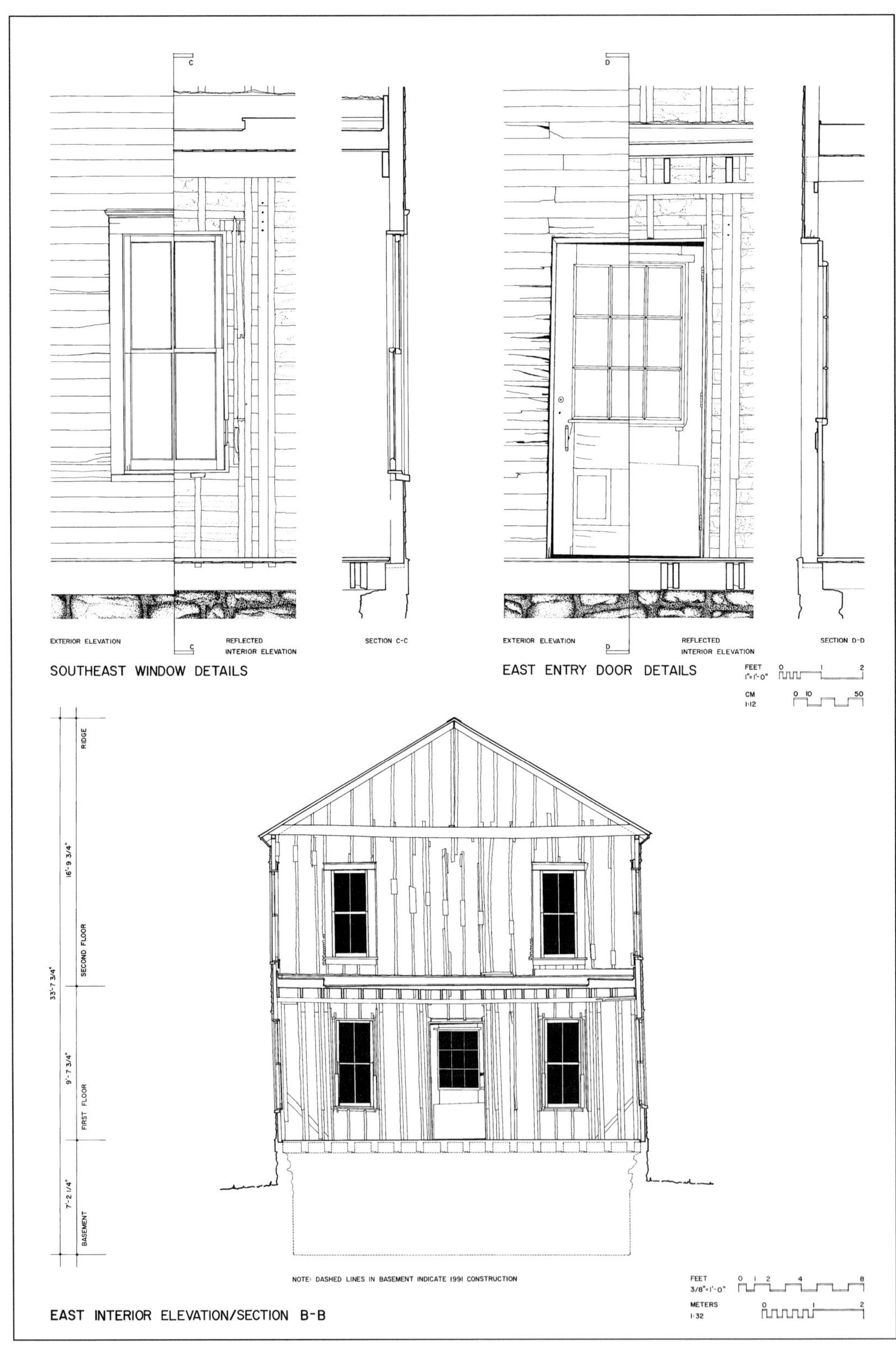

Constitution Hall, LeCompton, Douglas County, Kansas. Southeast window details, east entry door details; east interior elevation / section B-B. Measured drawing delineated by Edward T. Schmitz, Keri J.Winslow, Steven W. Harrington, and David W. Haase-Devine, 1992. Winner of the 1993 Charles E. Peterson Prize (HABS KS-64, sheet 8 of 8).

Kansas

DICKINSON COUNTY

ABILENE

Eisenhower House
201 SE Fourth (moved from original site)
HABS KS-4
HABS KANS,21-ABI,1-
10dr/13ph L

ENTERPRISE

Enterprise Parker Truss Bridge
Spanning Smoky Hill River on K-43 Hwy.
HAER KS-5
HAER KANS,21-ENPRI,1-
24ph/8pg/1pc L

HOPE VIC.

Kandt-Domann Farmstead
State Rt. 3
HABS KS-42
HABS KANS,21-HOPE.V,1-
1dr/10ph/2pg/1pc/fr L

Kandt-Domann Farmstead,Barn
State Rt. 3
HABS KS-42-B
HABS KANS,21-HOPE.V,1-B-
4dr/16ph/1pc/fr L

Kandt-Domann Farmstead,Frame Out Building
State Rt. 3
HABS KS-42-F
HABS KANS,21-HOPE.V,1-F-
3ph/1pc L

Kandt-Domann Farmstead,Garage No. 1
State Rt. 3
HABS KS-42-I
HABS KANS,21-HOPE.V,1-I-
3ph/1pc L

Kandt-Domann Farmstead,Garage No. 2
State Rt. 3
HABS KS-42-J
HABS KANS,21-HOPE.V,1-J-
1ph/1pc L

Kandt-Domann Farmstead,Granary
State Rt. 3
HABS KS-42-E
HABS KANS,21-HOPE.V,1-E-
4ph/1pc L

Kandt-Domann Farmstead,Machine Shed
State Rt. 3
HABS KS-42-G
HABS KANS,21-HOPE.V,1-G-
5ph/1pc L

Kandt-Domann Farmstead,Multipurpose Stone Building
State Rt. 3
HABS KS-42-C
HABS KANS,21-HOPE.V,1-C-
3dr/22ph/1pc/fr L

Kandt-Domann Farmstead,Smokehouse
State Rt. 3
HABS KS-42-H
HABS KANS,21-HOPE.V,1-H-
2ph/1pc L

Kandt-Domann Farmstead,Stone House
State Rt. 3
HABS KS-42-A
HABS KANS,21-HOPE.V,1-A-
4dr/21ph/1pc/fr L

Kandt-Domann Farmstead,Wash House
State Rt. 3
HABS KS-42-D
HABS KANS,21-HOPE.V,1-D-
2dr/13ph/1pc/fr L

DONIPHAN COUNTY

HIGHLAND

Highland Junior College,Irvin Hall
Highland Junior College Campus
HABS KS-9
HABS KANS,22-HILA,1-
3ph/4pg L

DOUGLAS COUNTY

BALDWIN

Baker University,Old Castle
513 Fifth St. ,Baker University Campus
HABS KS-5
HABS KANS,23-BALD,1-
4ph/5pg L

CLINTON VIC.

Barber Schoolhouse
Rt. 442
HABS KS-37
HABS KANS,23-CLINT.V,1-
3dr/5ph/1pc L

LAWRENCE

Babcock Carriage House
Given Court
HABS KS-31
HABS KANS,23-LAWR,3-
6dr L

Beach,Olive,House
603 Ohio
HABS KS-32
HABS KANS,23-LAWR,4-
21dr L

Bell,George,House; see Pais,Dorothy,House

District School
Seventh & Lincoln Sts.
HABS KS-33
HABS KANS,23-LAWR,5-
7dr L

Lawrence Bible Chapel
1001 Kentucky St.
HABS KS-35
HABS KANS,23-LAWR,6-
7dr L

Lawrence City Hall; see Watkins,J. B. ,Land Company

Morrow House
1408 Kentucky St.
HABS KS-43
HABS KANS,23-LAWR,7-
14dr L

National Bank Building; see Watkins,J. B. ,Land Company

Pais,Dorothy,House (Bell,George,House)
1008 Ohio St.
HABS KS-34
HABS KANS,23-LAWR,8-
6dr L

Steen,Elizabeth D.,House
1225 Vermont Ave.
HABS KS-44
HABS KANS,23-LAWR,9-
10dr L

Thacher,Solon O.,House
1613 Tennessee Ave.
HABS KS-45
HABS KANS,23-LAWR,10-
5dr L

Trinity Episcopal Parish House
1009 Vermont St.
HABS KS-10
HABS KANS,23-LAWR,1-
4ph/4pg L

Watkins,Elizabeth M. ,Community Museum; see Watkins,J. B. ,Land Company

Watkins,J. B. ,Land Company (National Bank Building; Lawrence City Hall; Watkins,Elizabeth M. ,Community Museum)
1047 Massachusetts St.
HABS KS-50
HABS KANS,23-LAWR,2-
19ph/14pg/1pc/fr L

Zimmerman House
304 Indiana St.
HABS KS-46
HABS KANS,23-LAWR,11-
17dr L

LECOMPTON

Constitution Hall
315 Elmore St.
HABS KS-64
8dr/fr H

STULL VIC.

Deister Farmstead
Rt. 442
HABS KS-36
HABS KANS,23-STUL.V,1-
18dr/1ph/1pg/1pc L

Deister Farmstead,Boxcar Shed
Rt. 442
HABS KS-36-G
HABS KANS,23-STUL.V,1-G-
4ph/1pc L

Deister Farmstead,Garage-Granary
HABS KS-36-H
HABS KANS,23-STUL.V,1-H-
4ph/1pc L

Deister Farmstead,House
Rt. 442
HABS KS-36-A
HABS KANS,23-STUL.V,1-A-
8ph/1pc L

Deister Farmstead,New Chickenhouse
Rt. 442
HABS KS-36-I
HABS KANS,23-STUL.V,1-I-
4ph/1pc L

Deister Farmstead,Outhouse
Rt. 442
HABS KS-36-J
HABS KANS,23-STUL.V,1-J-
4ph/1pc L

Deister Farmstead,Pole Barn
Rt. 442
HABS KS-36-F
HABS KANS,23-STUL.V,1-F-
4ph/1pc L

Deister Farmstead,Smoke-Chickenhouse
Rt. 442
HABS KS-36-C
HABS KANS,23-STUL.V,1-C-
3ph/1pc L

Deister Farmstead,Stone Barn
Rt. 442
HABS KS-36-B
HABS KANS,23-STUL.V,1-B-
9ph/1pc L

Deister Farmstead,Wash-Utility Shed
Rt. 442
HABS KS-36-D
HABS KANS,23-STUL.V,1-D-
3ph/1pc L

Deister Farmstead,Wood Barn
HABS KS-36-E
HABS KANS,23-STUL.V,1-E-
4ph/1pc L

VINLAND

Presbyterian Church
HABS KS-47
HABS KANS,23-VIN,1-
11dr L

ELLIS COUNTY

CATHERINE

Catherine,Town of
HABS KS-38
HABS KANS,26-CAT,1-
4ph/2pg/1pc/fr L

HAYS

Old Fort Hays,Blockhouse
HABS KS-58-A
HABS DLC/PP-1993:KS-1
6dr/fr L

Old Fort Hays,Guardhouse
HABS KS-58-B
HABS DLC/PP-1993:KS-1
4dr/fr L

Old Fort Hays,Officer's Quarters No. 2
HABS KS-58-D
HABS DLC/PP-1993:KS-1
5dr/fr L

Old Fort Hays,Officer's Quarters No. 3
HABS KS-58-C
HABS DLC/PP-1993:KS-1
5dr/fr L

MUNJOR

Munjor,Town of
HABS KS-39
HABS KANS,26-MUNJ,1-
4ph/2pg/1pc/fr L

SCHOENCHEN

St. Anthony's Catholic Church; see St. Antonius Kirche

St. Antonius Kirche (St. Anthony's Catholic Church)
HABS KS-40
HABS KANS,26-SCHO,1-
1ph/1pg/1pc L

GRAHAM COUNTY

NICODEMUS

A.M.E. Church
Adams & 3rd Sts.
HABS KS-49-I
HABS KANS,33-NICO,1-I-
6ph/6pg/1pc/fr L

American Legion Hall; see Fairview School

Dabney,Carrie,House
Hill City Township
HABS KS-49-A
HABS KANS,33-NICO,1-A-
6ph/1pc/fr L

District No. 1 School
Madison & 4th Sts.
HABS KS-49-O
HABS KANS,33-NICO,1-O-
3dr/6ph/2pg/1pc/fr L

Edwards,John,House
HABS KS-49-Y
HABS KANS,33-NICO,1-Y-
6ph/1pc/fr L

Fairview School (American Legion Hall)
Washington & 2nd Sts.
HABS KS-49-C
HABS KANS,33-NICO,1-C-
3ph/2pg/1pc/fr L

First Baptist Church,Old
4th & Washington Sts.
HABS KS-49-K
HABS KANS,33-NICO,1-K-
9dr/8ph/6pg/1pc/fr L

First Baptist Parsonage
4th & Washington St.
HABS KS-49-L
HABS KANS,33-NICO,1-L-
5ph/2pg/1pc/fr L

Fletcher-Switzer House
Washington & 2nd Sts.
HABS KS-49-G
HABS KANS,33-NICO,1-G-
9dr/5ph/1pc/fr L

Lacey,Tim,House (Ruin)
Block 35
HABS KS-49-Q
HABS KANS,33-NICO,1-Q-
3ph/2pg/1pc/fr L

Mount Olive Church
South St.
HABS KS-49-V
HABS KANS,33-NICO,1-V-
6ph/1pc/fr L

Mount Olive School
South St.
HABS KS-49-W
HABS KANS,33-NICO,1-W-
4ph/1pc/fr L

Nicodemus Historic District
HABS KS-49
HABS KANS,33-NICO,1-
5dr/10ph/2pg/1pc/fr L

Nicodemus Township Hall
Washington & 2nd Sts.
HABS KS-49-B
HABS KANS,33-NICO,1-B-
6ph/2pg/1pc/fr L

Sayers,Calvin,House
Madison St.
HABS KS-49-P
HABS KANS,33-NICO,1-P-
7ph/2pg/1pc/fr L

Scruggs,Jerry,House
Adams & 2nd St.
HABS KS-49-D
HABS KANS,33-NICO,1-D-
4ph/2pg/1pc/fr L

Scruggs,Jerry,House
Seventh St.
HABS KS-49-X
HABS KANS,33-NICO,1-X-
3ph/1pc/fr L

Stewart,Dr.,House
Washington St.
HABS KS-49-N
HABS KANS,33-NICO,1-N-
5ph/2pg/1pc/fr L

Switzer Bunkhouse
Washington & 3rd Sts.
HABS KS-49-F
HABS KANS,33-NICO,1-F-
3ph/1pc/fr L

Vanduvall,Alexander G.,House
HABS KS-49-S
HABS KANS,33-NICO,1-S-
4ph/1pc/fr L

Vaughn,Clementine,House
HABS KS-49-R
HABS KANS,33-NICO,1-R-
4ph/2pg/1pc/fr L

Wellington,Lloyd,House
Adams & 2nd Sts.
HABS KS-49-E
HABS KANS,33-NICO,1-E-
4ph/2pg/1pc/fr L

Williams,Ace,House
4th St.
HABS KS-49-J
HABS KANS,33-NICO,1-J-
2ph/2pg/1pc/fr L

Williams,Charles,House
South Ave. & 4th St.
HABS KS-49-M
HABS KANS,33-NICO,1-M-
4ph/2pg/1pc/fr L

Williams,Emma,House
HABS KS-49-U
HABS KANS,33-NICO,1-U-
2ph/1pc/fr L

Williams,Henry,House
HABS KS-49-T
HABS KANS,33-NICO,1-T-
8ph/1pc/fr L

Wilson's,Joe,Post Office
South Ave. & 3rd St.
HABS KS-49-H
HABS KANS,33-NICO,1-H-
2ph/2pg/1pc/fr L

JEFFERSON COUNTY

MERIDEN VIC.

Meriden Rock Creek Bridge
Spanning Rock Creek
HAER KS-2
HAER KANS,44-MERI.V,1-
13ph/6pg/1pc L

OSKALOOSA

Jefferson County Courthouse
Town Sq.
HABS KS-19
HABS KANS,44-OSKA,1-
7ph/4pg L

VALLEY FALLS VIC.

Half-Mound Bridge
Spanning Delaware River
HAER KS-1
HAER KANS,44-VAFA.V,1-
11ph/3pg/1pc L

JOHNSON COUNTY

DE SOTO

Sunflower Army Ammunition Plant
HAER KS-3
HAER KANS,46-DESOT,1-
63pg/fr L

KANSAS CITY VIC.

Manual Training Schl. for Indian Children,E. Bldg.; see Shawnee Methodist Mission,East Building

Manual Training Schl. for Indian Children,N. Bldg.; see Shawnee Methodist Mission,North Building

Manual Training Schl. for Indian Children,W. Bldg.; see Shawnee Methodist Mission,West Building

Shawnee Methodist Mission,East Building (Manual Training Schl. for Indian Children,E. Bldg.
Fifty-third St. & Mission Rd.
HABS KS-3
HABS KANS,46- ,1B-
3ph/1pg L

Shawnee Methodist Mission,North Building (Manual Training Schl. for Indian Children,N. Bldg.
Fifty-third St. & Mission Rd.
HABS KS-2
HABS KANS,46- ,1C-
8ph/1pg L

Shawnee Methodist Mission,West Building (Manual Training Schl. for Indian Children,W. Bldg.
Fifty-third St. & Mission Rd.
HABS KS-1
HABS KANS,46- ,1A-
7ph/1pg L

OVERLAND PARK

Building,Old Stone
11920 W. Ninety-fifth St.
HABS KS-48
HABS KANS,46-OVPA,1-
9dr L

LABETTE COUNTY

PARSONS

Kansas Army Ammunition Plant
HAER KS-4
HAER KANS,50-PARS,1-
77pg/fr L

LEAVENWORTH COUNTY

FORT LEAVENWORTH

Fort Leavenworth,Officers' Quarters; see Fort Leavenworth,The Rookery

Fort Leavenworth,The Rookery (Fort Leavenworth,Officers' Quarters)
12-14 Sumner Place
HABS KS-7
HABS KANS,52-FOLEV,2-
4ph/4pg L

20-22 Sumner Place (House)
HABS KS-8
HABS KANS,52-FOLEV,3-
8ph/5pg L

LEAVENWORTH

Fort Leavenworth
Metropolitan Ave. & Seventh St.
HABS KS-53
HABS KANS,52-LEAV,1-
22ph/17pg/2pc/fr L

Fort Leavenworth,Building No. 1
1 Scott Ave.
HABS KS-53-K
HABS KANS,52-LEAV,1-K-
7ph/26pg/1pc L

Fort Leavenworth,Building No. 12
32-34 Sumner Place
HABS KS-53-P
HABS KANS,52-LEAV,1-P-
8ph/19pg/1pc L

Fort Leavenworth,Building No. 16
24 Sumner Place
HABS KS-53-E
HABS KANS,52-LEAV,1-E-
8ph/19pg/1pc L

Fort Leavenworth,Building No. 17
20-22 Sumner Place
HABS KS-53-N
HABS KANS,52-LEAV,1-N-
12ph/27pg/1pc L

Fort Leavenworth,Building No. 18
16-18 Sumner Place
HABS KS-53-I
HABS KANS,52-LEAV,1-I-
8ph/23pg/1pc L

Fort Leavenworth,Building No. 184
629-631 Grant Ave.
HABS KS-53-L
HABS KANS,52-LEAV,1-L-
7ph/14pg/1pc L

Fort Leavenworth,Building No. 19
(Rookery,The)
12-14 Sumner Place
HABS KS-53-M
HABS KANS,52-LEAV,1-M-
10ph/46pg/1pc L

Fort Leavenworth,Building No. 21
(Syracuse Houses 8/1/85))
4-6 Sumner Place
HABS KS-53-B
HABS KANS,52-LEAV,1-B-
9ph/22pg/1pc L

Fort Leavenworth,Building No. 357
20-22 Riverside Ave.
HABS KS-53-A
HABS KANS,52-LEAV,1-A-
14ph/24pg/1pc L

Fort Leavenworth,Building No. 37
630-632 Thomas Ave.
HABS KS-53-O
HABS KANS,52-LEAV,1-O-
10ph/15pg/1pc L

Fort Leavenworth,Building No. 41
622 Thomas Ave.
HABS KS-53-J
HABS KANS,52-LEAV,1-J-
6ph/16pg/1pc L

Fort Leavenworth,Building No. 433
10-12 Riverside Ave.
HABS KS-53-G
HABS KANS,52-LEAV,1-G-
8ph/21pg/1pc L

Fort Leavenworth,Building No. 436
5 Riverside Ave.
HABS KS-53-F
HABS KANS,52-LEAV,1-F-
6ph/18pg/1pc L

Fort Leavenworth,Building No. 5
611 Scott Ave.
HABS KS-53-C
HABS KANS,52-LEAV,1-C-
8ph/24pg/1pc L

Fort Leavenworth,Building No. 6
624 Scott Ave.
HABS KS-53-H
HABS KANS,52-LEAV,1-H-
7ph/15pg/1pc L

Fort Leavenworth,Building No. 7
620 Scott Ave.
HABS KS-53-D
HABS KANS,52-LEAV,1-D-
7ph/23pg/1pc L

Leavenworth Bridge
Spanning Missouri River
HAER KS-6
HAER KANS,52-LEAV,4-
47ph/3pc L

Rookery,The; see Fort Leavenworth,Building No. 19

Syracuse Houses 8/1/85); see Fort Leavenworth,Building No. 21

SPRINGDALE VIC.

Covered Bridge
Spanning Stranger Creek
HABS KS-13
HABS KANS,52-SPRI.V,1-
6ph/3pg L

LYON COUNTY

MILLER VIC.

Mickel House
HABS KS-16
HABS KANS,56-MIL.V,1-
3ph/3pg L

MCPHERSON COUNTY

INMAN VIC.

Bethel Sanctuary
HABS KS-66
6dr/fr H

MIAMI COUNTY

OSAWATOMIE

Adair,Samuel,Cabin
John Brown Mem. Park (moved from original site)
HABS KS-18
HABS KANS,61-OSA,1-
4ph/4pg L

PAOLA

Paola Free Library
101 E. Peoria St.
HABS KS-52
HABS KANS,61-PAOLA,1-
7ph/6pg/1pc L

MONTGOMERY COUNTY

COFFEYVILLE

Parker Bridge
Spanning Verdigris River 1.5 miles SE Coffeyville
HAER KS-7
HAER 1990 (HAER):7
22ph/10pg/2pc L

MORRIS COUNTY

COUNCIL GROVE

Last Chance Store
Chautauqa & Main Sts.
HABS KS-6
HABS KANS,64-COUGR,1-
3ph/4pg L

NEMAHA COUNTY

ALBANY

Albany Schoolhouse
HABS KS-20
HABS KANS,66-ALB,1-
8ph/5pg L

OSBORNE COUNTY

BLOOMINGTON

Stone Smokehouse
HABS KS-51
HABS KANS,71-BLOOM,1-
6ph/1pg/1pc L

PAWNEE COUNTY

LARNED

Fort Larned National Historic Site; see Fort Larned, Barracks (West)

Fort Larned, Barracks (West) (Fort Larned, Infantry Barracks; Fort Larned National Historic Site)
HABS KS-21
HABS KANS,73-LARN,1-
5dr/12ph L

Fort Larned, Infantry Barracks; see Fort Larned, Barracks (West)

Fort Larned,Bakery & Mess Hall
HABS KS-24
HABS KANS,73-LARN,4-
4dr/5ph L

Fort Larned,Barracks (East) (Barn)
(Fort Larned,Cavalry Barracks (Barn))
HABS KS-22
HABS KANS,73-LARN,2-
5dr/8ph L

Fort Larned,Blacksmith & Wheelwright Shop
HABS KS-23
HABS KANS,73-LARN,3-
4dr/6ph L

Fort Larned,Cavalry Barracks (Barn); see Fort Larned,Barracks (East) (Barn)

Fort Larned,Commanding Officer's Quarters
HABS KS-28
HABS KANS,73-LARN,8-
7dr/6ph L

Documentation: **ct** color transparencies **dr** measured drawings **fr** field records
pc photograph captions **pg** pages of text **ph** photographs

Fort Larned,Commissary Storehouse & Stables
HABS KS-25
HABS KANS,73-LARN,5-
4dr/8ph L

Fort Larned,Officers' Quarters (North)
HABS KS-29
HABS KANS,73-LARN,9-
6dr/3ph L

Fort Larned,Officers' Quarters (South)
HABS KS-27
HABS KANS,73-LARN,7-
6dr/11ph L

Fort Larned,Quartermaster Storehouse
HABS KS-26
HABS KANS,73-LARN,6-
5dr/6ph L

RILEY COUNTY

FORT RILEY

First Territorial Capitol of Kansas
(Fort Riley)
Fort Riley Military Reserve
HABS KS-15
HABS KANS,81-FORIL,1-
6dr/14ph/4pg/fr L

Fort Riley
HABS KS-54
HABS KANS,81-FORIL,2-
25ph/28pg/2pc/fr L

Fort Riley; see First Territorial Capitol of Kansas

Fort Riley,Building No. 100
100 Schofield Circle
HABS KS-54-J
HABS KANS,81-FORIL,2-J-
9ph/22pg/1pc L

Fort Riley,Building No. 107
107 Reed Ave.
HABS KS-54-L
HABS KANS,81-FORIL,2-L-
7ph/15pg/1pc L

Fort Riley,Building No. 117
117 Lower Brick Row
HABS KS-54-K
HABS KANS,81-FORIL,2-K-
5ph/15pg/1pc L

Fort Riley,Building No. 12
12 Forsythe Ave.
HABS KS-54-D
HABS KANS,81-FORIL,2-D-
8ph/16pg/1pc L

Fort Riley,Building No. 122
122 Lower Brick Row
HABS KS-54-M
HABS KANS,81-FORIL,2-M-
7ph/11pg/1pc L

Fort Riley,Building No. 123
123 Huebner Rd.
HABS KS-54-B
HABS KANS,81-FORIL,2-B-
9ph/16pg/1pc L

Fort Riley,Building No. 16
16 Forsythe Ave.
HABS KS-54-G
HABS KANS,81-FORIL,2-G-
8ph/18pg/1pc L

Fort Riley,Building No. 162
162 Schofield Circle
HABS KS-54-I
HABS KANS,81-FORIL,2-I-
9ph/11pg/1pc L

Fort Riley,Building No. 174
HABS KS-54-N
HABS KANS,81-FORIL,2-N-
8ph/10pg/1pc L

Fort Riley,Building No. 2
HABS KS-54-E
HABS KANS,81-FORIL,2-E-
9ph/20pg/1pc L

Fort Riley,Building No. 219
219 Huebner Rd.
HABS KS-54-O
HABS KANS,81-FORIL,2-O-
5ph/12pg/1pc L

Fort Riley,Building No. 234
234 Lower Brick Row
HABS KS-54-P
HABS KANS,81-FORIL,2-P-
6ph/12pg/1pc L

Fort Riley,Building No. 24
24 Sheridan Ave.
HABS KS-54-A
HABS KANS,81-FORIL,2-A-
10ph/15pg/1pc L

Fort Riley,Building No. 25
25 Sheridan Ave.
HABS KS-54-C
HABS KANS,81-FORIL,2-C-
8ph/19pg/1pc L

Fort Riley,Building No. 373
373 Stone Court
HABS KS-54-Q
HABS KANS,81-FORIL,2-Q-
5ph/12pg/1pc L

Fort Riley,Building No. 4
4 Barry Ave.
HABS KS-54-H
HABS KANS,81-FORIL,2-H-
8ph/12pg/1pc L

Fort Riley,Building No. 73
73 Holbrook Ave.
HABS KS-54-F
HABS KANS,81-FORIL,2-F-
8ph/15pg/1pc L

MANHATTAN

Goodnow,Isaac,House
2301 Claflin Rd.
HABS KS-11
HABS KANS,81-MAN,1-
4ph/5pg L

Woman's Club,The
900 Poyntz
HABS KS-68
8dr/fr H

RUSH COUNTY

LIEBENTHAL

Liebenthal,Town of
HABS KS-41
HABS KANS,83-LIEB,1-
5ph/2pg/1pc/fr L

SHAWNEE COUNTY

SILVER LAKE VIC.

Indian Agency House
U. S. Rt. 1
HABS KS-12
HABS KANS,89-SILV.V,1-
3ph/7pg L

SHERIDAN COUNTY

STUDLEY

Cottonwood Ranch
Rt. 24
HABS KS-60
HABS DLC/PP-1993:KS-1
9dr/4ph/1pc/fr L

STUDLEY VIC.

Cottonwood Ranch,Wash House
Rt. 24
HABS KS-60-A
HABS DLC/PP-1993:KS-1
1dr/fr L

Cottonwwod Ranch,Outbuildings
Rt. 24
HABS KS-60-B
HABS DLC/PP-1993:KS-1
1dr/fr L

WABAUNSEE COUNTY

WABAUNSEE

Beecher "Bible & Rifle" Church
HABS KS-14
HABS KANS,99-WABAU,1-
6dr/8ph/4pg/fr L

WASHINGTON COUNTY

HANOVER

Hollenberg Pony Express Station
Rt. 243
HABS KS-59
HABS DLC/PP-1993:KS-1
10dr/17ph/1pc/fr L

WYANDOTTE COUNTY

MUNCIE

Grinter,Moses,House
1420 S. Seventy-eighth St.
HABS KS-17
HABS KANS,105,MUNC,1-
8ph/4pg L

Shaker Centre Family Dwelling House (Third) (Shaker Church Family House), Pleasant Hill, Mercer County, Kentucky. First floor, stair hall. Photograph by Jack E. Boucher, 1963 (HABS KY,84-SHAKT,2-21).

Kentucky

BELL COUNTY

PINEVILLE

Freight Depot Bridge; see Pine Street Bridge

KY Route 2014 Bridge
Spanning Cumberland River on KY Rt. 2014
HAER KY-24
HAER 1989(HAER):9
12ph/2pg/1pc L

Pine Street Bridge (Freight Depot Bridge)
Pine St. (State Rt. 66) ,spanning Cumberland River
HAER KY-12
HAER KY,7-PINVI,1-
12ph/14pg/1pc L

BOONE COUNTY

BURLINGTON VIC.

Piatt's Landing (Winfield Cottage)
Upper East Bend Bottoms
HABS KY-138
HABS KY,8-BURL.V,1A-
11dr/10ph/7pg/1pc/fr L

Winfield Cottage; see Piatt's Landing

BOURBON COUNTY

PARIS

Cane Ridge Meetinghouse
Little Rock Rd.
HABS KY-20-8
HABS KY,9-CANRI,1-
8dr/5ph/3pg/fr L

Drenan,Tom,House; see Grange,The

Garrard,Gov. James,House; see Mount Lebanon

Grange,The (Drenan,Tom,House)
Maysville Pike (U. S. Rt. 68)
HABS KY-32
HABS KY,9-MILBU.V,1-
11ph/3pg L

Johnson's Inn,Old
Georgetown Pike
HABS KY-31
HABS KY,9-PAR.V,2-
6ph/2pg L

Mount Lebanon (Garrard,Gov. James,House)
Peacock Rd.
HABS KY-30
HABS KY,9-PAR.V,1-
12ph/3pg L

BOYLE COUNTY

DANVILLE

Adams House; see Crow's Inn

Barbee House; see Crow's Inn

Boyle County Courthouse
HABS KY-38
HABS KY,11-DANV,7-
1ph L

Centre College,Old
HABS KY-34
HABS KY,11-DANV,3-
3ph L

Clark Station
Stanford Pike
HABS KY-42
HABS KY,11-DANV,10-
2ph L

Cragfont; see Wilson Station

Crow's Inn (Adams House; Barbee House)
Stanford Rd.
HABS KY-36
HABS KY,11-DANV,5-
2ph L

Davenport Tavern
W. Main St.
HABS KY-39
HABS KY,11-DANV,8-
1ph/1pg L

Jacobs Hall,Kentucky School for the Deaf
South Third St.
HABS KY-207
HABS KY,11-DANV,11A-
4ph/1pg/1pc L

McDowell,Dr. Ephraim,Apothecary Shop
123 S. Second St.
HABS KY-33-A
HABS KY,11-DANV,2-
1ph L

McDowell,Dr. Ephraim,House
125 S. Second St.
HABS KY-33
HABS KY,11-DANV,1-
14ph/1pc/fr L

McIlvoy Building
W. Main St.
HABS KY-40
HABS KY,11-DANV,9-
1ph/1pg L

Mound Cottage
HABS KY-35
HABS KY,11-DANV,4-
2ph L

Mount Airy
410 E. Main St.
HABS KY-37
HABS KY,11-DANV,6-
2ph L

Wilson Station (Cragfont)
HABS KY-41
HABS KY,11-DANV.V,1-
3ph L

DANVILLE VIC.

Crow,William,House
HABS KY-43
HABS KY,11-DANV.V,2-
3ph L

BRACKEN COUNTY

MILFORD VIC.

KY 539 Bridge; see North Fork Bridge

North Fork Bridge (KY 539 Bridge)
Spanning North Fork of Licking River
HAER KY-2
HAER KY,12-MILF.V,1-
15ph/4pg/1pc L

CHRISTIAN COUNTY

HOPKINSVILLE VIC.

Kentucky Route 124 Bridge; see Suger Creek Bridge

Suger Creek Bridge (Kentucky Route 124 Bridge)
Spanning Suger Creek
HAER KY-7
HAER KY,24-HOPVI.V,1-
9ph/2pg/1pc L

DAVIESS COUNTY

OWENSBORO VIC.

Daviess County Bridge; see Kentucky Route 762 Bridge

Kentucky Route 762 Bridge (Daviess County Bridge)
Spanning South Fork of Panther Creek
HAER KY-8
HAER KY,30-OWENB.B,1-
11ph/2pg/1pc L

EDMONSON COUNTY

MAMMOTH CAVE

Mammoth Cave Saltpeter Works
Mammoth Cave National Park
HAER KY-18
HAER 1989(HAER):9
12dr/20ph/37pg/2pc/fr L

FAYETTE COUNTY

LEXINGTON

Ali Haggin,James Ben,Barn
4160 Paris Pike (U. S. 27/68)
HABS KY-171
HABS KY,34-LEX,11A-
7dr/fr L

Bodley House (Pindell House)
200 N. Market St.
HABS KY-53
HABS KY,34-LEX,2-
3ph/1pg L

Botherum (Johnson House)
341 Madison Pl.
HABS KY-54
HABS KY,34-LEX,3-
4ph/1pg L

Bradford,John,House
193 N. Mill St.
HABS KY-55
HABS KY,34-LEX,4-
1ph L

Bruen,Joseph,House; see Ingelside

Bryan Station (Rogers,Joseph,House)
Bryan Station Pike
HABS KY-161
HABS KY,34-LEX.V,1-
7pg L

Buckner House; see Rose Hill

Gratz,Benjamin,House; see Mount Hope

Hopemont (Morgan,Gen. John Hunt,House; Hunt-Morgan House)
201 N. Mill St.
HABS KY-60
HABS KY,34-LEX,8-
8dr/2ph/1pg/fr L

Hunt-Morgan House; see Hopemont

Hunt,Francis Key,House; see Loudoun

Ingelside (Bruen,Joseph,House)
Gibson Ave.
HABS KY-57
HABS KY,34-LEX,6-
6ph/2pg L

Johnson House; see Botherum

Loudoun (Hunt,Francis Key,House)
Bryan Ave.
HABS KY-58
HABS KY,34-LEX,7-
10ph/1pg/fr L

Morgan,Gen. John Hunt,House; see Hopemont

Morrison College,Transylvania University (Morrison,Old)
W. Third St.,between Upper St. & Broadway
HABS KY-61
HABS KY,34-LEX,9A-
5ph/2pg/1pc L

Morrison,Old; see Morrison College,Transylvania University

Mount Hope (Gratz,Benjamin,House)
231 N. Mill St.
HABS KY-56
HABS KY,34-LEX,5-
2ph/1pg L

Pindell House; see Bodley House

Rogers,Joseph,House; see Bryan Station

Rose Hill (Buckner House)
461 N. Limestone St.
HABS KY-20-16
HABS KY,34-LEX,1-
22dr/12ph/3pg/fr L

Talbert,William,House
215 N. Mill St.
HABS KY-102
HABS KY,34-LEX,12-
10ph/4pg/1pc L

University of Kentucky,Carnegie Library
HABS KY-158
HABS KY,34-LEX,13A-
6ph/8pg/1pc L

University of Kentucky,Patterson House
HABS KY-157
HABS KY,34-LEX,13B-
1ph/5pg/1pc L

University of Kentucky,White Hall
HABS KY-156
HABS KY,34-LEX,13C-
1ph/7pg/1pc L

535 West Short Street (Old Doorway)
(moved from 655 Price Ave.)
HABS KY-62
HABS KY,34-LEX,10-
1ph L

LEXINGTON (VIC.)

Lexington-Blue Grass Depot
HAER KY-11
HAER KY,34-LEX.V,4-
44pg/fr L

LEXINGTON VIC.

Ashland (Clay,Henry,House)
Richmond Rd.,2 mi. SE of Lexington
HABS KY-172
HABS KY,34-LEX.V,3-
8ph/2pc L

Ashland,Gardener's Cottage
(Clay,Henry,House,Gardener's Cottage)
Richmond Road,2 mi. SE of Lexington
HABS KY-172-A
HABS KY,34-LEX.V,3A-
1ph/1pc L

Ashland,Ice Houses
(Clay,Henry,House,Ice Houses)
Richmond Road 2 mi. SE of Lexington
HABS KY-172-D
HABS KY,34-LEX.V,3D-
1ph/1pc L

Ashland,Privy & Wash House
(Clay,Henry,House,Privy & Wash House)
Richmond Road 2 mi. SE of Lexington
HABS KY-172-C
HABS K,34-LEX.V,3C-
1ph/1pc L

Ashland,Smokehouse
(Clay,Henry,House,Smokehouse)
Richmond Road,2 mi. SE of Lexington
HABS KY-172-B
HABS KY,34-LEX.V,3B-
1ph/1pc L

Clay,Henry,House; see Ashland

Clay,Henry,House,Gardener's Cottage; see Ashland,Gardener's Cottage

Clay,Henry,House,Ice Houses; see Ashland,Ice Houses

Clay,Henry,House,Privy & Wash House; see Ashland,Privy & Wash House

Clay,Henry,House,Smokehouse; see Ashland,Smokehouse

Eothan; see Malvern Hill

Malvern Hill (Eothan)
Georgetown Rd.
HABS KY-59
HABS KY,34-LEX.V,2-
3ph/1pg L

FRANKLIN COUNTY

FRANKFORT

Brown,Orlando,House
202 Wilkinson St.
HABS KY-45
HABS KY,37-FRAFO,3-
1ph L

Church of the Good Shepherd
HABS KY-46
HABS KY,37-FRAFO,4-
1ph L

Liberty Hall
Main & Wilkinson Sts.
HABS KY-20-2
HABS KY,37-FRAFO,2-
15dr/36ph/3pg/2pc/fr L

State House,Old
Broadway,bounded by Madison,Clinton & Lewis Sts.
HABS KY-20-1
HABS KY,37-FRAFO,1-
23dr/19ph/4pg/2pc/fr L

Ziegler,Rev. J. R. ,House
509 Shelby St.
HABS KY-103
HABS KY,37-FRAFO,5-
14dr L

FRANKFORT VIC.

Kentucky Route 1005 Bridge; see Red Bridge

Red Bridge (Kentucky Route 1005 Bridge)
Spanning North Benson Creek
HAER KY-13
HAER KY,37-FRAFO.V,1-
13ph/3pg/1pc L

GRANT COUNTY

HOLBROOK VIC.

KY 1993 Bridge; see Starnes Bridge

Starnes Bridge (KY 1993 Bridge)
Spanning Eagle Creek
HAER KY-3
HAER KY,41-HOLB.V,1-
15ph/4pg/1pc L

GREEN COUNTY

GREENSBURG

Courthouse,Old
Main St.
HABS KY-20-4
HABS KY,44-GREBU,1-
5dr/3ph/2pg L

HARLAN COUNTY

LOYALL

Kentucky Rt. 840 Bridge
Spanning Cumberland River
HAER KY-14
HAER 1989(HAER):9
11ph/2pg/1pc L

HARRISON COUNTY

CYNTHIANA

Covered Bridge,Wood
Licking River,S. Fork
HABS KY-20-20
HABS KY,49-CYNTH,1-
4dr/2ph/2pg/fr L

HART COUNTY

MUNFORDVILLE VIC.

Buckner,Gen. Bolivar,House; see Glen Lily

Glen Lily (Buckner,Gen. Bolivar,House)
HABS KY-75
HABS KY,50-MUNFO.V,1-
9ph L

HENDERSON COUNTY

GENEVA VIC.

Anderson Place; see Indian Valley

Indian Valley (Anderson Place)
HABS KY-29
HABS KY,51- ,1-
2ph/2pg L

HENDERSON

Henderson County Courthouse
First & Main Sts.
HABS KY-20-18
HABS KY,51-HEND,1-
9dr/5ph/2pg/fr L

Lockett,Beulah & Eva,House
Elm & Jefferson Sts.
HABS KY-28
HABS KY,51-HEND,4-
10ph/2pg L

Powell,Gov. Lazarus,House
HABS KY-27
HABS KY,51-HEND,3-
8ph/2pg L

St. Paul's Episcopal Church
Third & Main Sts.
HABS KY-26
HABS KY,51-HEND,2-
9ph/2pg L

JEFFERSON COUNTY

BUECHEL VIC.

Hikes Place
Rt. 7
HABS KY-70
HABS KY,56-BUECH.V,1-
7ph L

LOUISVILLE

(Commercial Bldg.); see Kentucky Theater

Atherton Building
466 River City Mall
HABS KY-137
HABS KY,56-LOUVI,28-
6dr/18ph/6pg/2pc/fr L

Bainbridge Row; see Palmer,Dr. ,House

Bank of Louisville Building
322 W. Main St.
HABS KY-20-3
HABS KY,56-LOUVI,1-
4dr/9ph/2pg/1pc/fr L

Bates,Levin,House; see Johnson,Jacob,House

Berkeley Hotel; see Rossmore Apartment House

Big Four Bridge
Spanning Ohio River
HAER KY-10
HAER KY,56-LOUVI,71-
13ph/1pg/1pc L

Board of Trade Building; see Lithgow Building

Brennan House; see Ronald-Brennan House

Bullitt House; see Oxmoor

Cave Hill Cemetery
701 Baxter Ave.
HABS KY-142
HABS KY,56-LOUVI,11-
5pg L

Cave Hill Cemetery,Ben Smith Mausoleum
Cave Hill Cemetery
HABS KY-122
HABS KY,56-LOUV1,11C-
3dr/5ph/2pg/fr L

Cave Hill Cemetery,Rustic Shelter House
Cave Hill Cemetery
HABS KY-123
HABS KY,56-LOUV1,11B-
6dr/3ph/1pg/1pc/fr L

Cave Hill Cemetery,Salve-Bullett Mausoleum
Cave Hill Cemetery
HABS KY-121
HABS KY,56-LOUV1,11A-
4dr/3ph/3pg/1pc/fr L

Churchill Downs
700 Central Ave.
HABS KY-210
HABS KY.56-LOUV1,29-
7ph/1pc L

City Hall
601 W. Jefferson St.
HABS KY-143
HABS KY,56-LOUV1,16-
8ph/8pg/1pc/3ct L

Clark,George M. ,House; see Spring Station

Conrad,Theophilus,Home (Hughes,Rose Anna,Presbyterian Home)
1402 St. James Court
HABS KY-144
HABS KY,56-LOUV1,23-
14ph/9pg/1pc/4ct L

1005 East Liberty Street (House); see Phoenix Hill Historic District

709 East Madison Street (House); see Phoenix Hill Historic District

728 East Madison Street (House); see Phoenix Hill Historic District

730 East Madison Street (House); see Phoenix Hill Historic District

732 East Madison Street (House); see Phoenix Hill Historic District

734 East Madison Street (House); see Phoenix Hill Historic District

736 East Madison Street (House); see Phoenix Hill Historic District

738 East Madison Street (House); see Phoenix Hill Historic District

817 East Madison Street (House); see Phoenix Hill Historic District

823 East Madison Street (House); see Phoenix Hill Historic District

825 East Madison Street (House); see Phoenix Hill Historic District

827 East Madison Street (House); see Phoenix Hill Historic District

828 East Madison Street (House); see Phoenix Hill Historic District

835 East Madison Street (House); see Phoenix Hill Historic District

837 East Madison Street (House); see Phoenix Hill Historic District

912 East Madison Street (House); see Phoenix Hill Historic District

916 East Madison Street (House); see Phoenix Hill Historic District

918 East Madison Street (House); see Phoenix Hill Historic District

922 East Madison Street (House); see Phoenix Hill Historic District

914 East Marshall Street (Commercial Building); see Phoenix Hill Historic District

924 East Marshall Street (House); see Phoenix Hill Historic District

926 East Marshall Street (House); see Phoenix Hill Historic District

940 East Marshall Street (House); see Phoenix Hill Historic District

903 East Muhammad Ali Boulevard (Comm./Res. Bldg.); see Phoenix Hill Historic District

905 East Muhammad Ali Boulevard (Comm./Res. Bldg.); see Phoenix Hill Historic District

736 East Muhammad Ali Boulevard (House); see Phoenix Hill Historic District

816-818 East Muhammad Ali Boulevard (House); see Phoenix Hill Historic District

826 East Muhammad Ali Boulevard (House); see Phoenix Hill Historic District

836 East Muhammad Ali Boulevard (House); see Phoenix Hill Historic District

903 East Walnut Street (Comm./Residential Bldg.); see Phoenix Hill Historic District

905 East Walnut Street (Comm./Residential Bldg.); see Phoenix Hill Historic District

736 East Walnut Street (House); see Phoenix Hill Historic District

816-818 East Walnut Street (House); see Phoenix Hill Historic District

826 East Walnut Street (House); see Phoenix Hill Historic District

836 East Walnut Street (House); see Phoenix Hill Historic District

Franklin Building (Liberty Bank)
658-660 S. Fourth Ave.
HABS KY-176
HABS KY,56-LOUVI,30-
6ph/3pg/2pc L

Gas Station
HABS KY-154
HABS KY,56-LOUVI.20-
2ph/1pc/2ct L

Hart Block (Hildebrand Block)
728 W. Main St.
HABS KY-120
HABS KY,56-LOUV1,10G
3dr/5ph/3pg/1pc/4ct/fr L

Hildebrand Block; see Hart Block

Hughes,Rose Anna,Presbyterian Home; see Conrad,Theophilus,Home

Jefferson County Community College; see Louisville Presbyterian Theological Seminary

Jefferson County Courthouse
531 W. Jefferson St.
HABS KY-117
HABS KY,56-LOUV1,19-
7dr/5ph/12pg/2ct/fr L

Johnson,Jacob,House
(Bates,Levin,House)
7300 Bardstown Rd.
HABS KY-179
HABS KY,56-LOUVI,31-
20ph/14pg/1pc L

Kentucky School for the Blind
1867 Frankfort Ave.
HABS KY-20-19
HABS KY,56-LOUVI,2-
16dr/15ph/3pg/fr L

Kentucky Theater ((Commercial Bldg.))
649-651 S. Fourth St.
HABS KY-159
HABS KY,56-LOUVI,32-
16ph/7pg/1pc L

Kuntz Shotgun House
1401 E. Washington St.
HABS KY-152
HABS KY,56-LOUVI,13-
4dr/6ph/1pg/1pc/2ct/fr L

Liberty Bank; see Franklin Building

Lithgow Building (Board of Trade Building)
301 W. Main St.
HABS KY-141
HABS KY,56-LOUV1,10H-
8ph/8pg/1pc L

Loew's Theater (United Artists Theater; Penthouse Theater)
625 S. Fourth St.
HABS KY-134
HABS KY,56-LOUVI,17-
51ph/5pg/3pc L

Louisville & Nashville Railroad,Union Station (Union Station)
1000 W. Broadway
HABS KY-152
HABS KY,56-LOUVI,23-
12ph/7pg/1pc/2ct L

Louisville Medical College (University of Louisville,Medical School)
101 W. Chestnut St.
HABS KY-145
HABS KY,56-LOUVI,15-
10ph/4pg/1pc/2ct L

Louisville Presbyterian Theological Seminary (Jefferson County Community College)
109 E. Broadway
HABS KY-146
HABS KY,56-LOUVI,14-
8ph/9pg/1pc/5ct L

Louisville Water Company Pumping Stations
Zorn Ave. & River Rd.
HAER KY-9
HAER KY,56-LOUVI,72-
21ph/2pg/2pc/6ct L

Main Street,600 & 700 Block (Buildings)
HABS KY-147
HABS KY,56-LOUVI,10-
63ph/7pg/4ct L

Ohio Falls Dye & Finishing Works Building; see Phoenix Hill Historic District

Oxmoor (Bullitt House)
Shelbyville Pike
HABS KY-67
HABS KY,56-LOUVI.V,3-
4ph L

Palmer,Dr. ,House (Bainbridge Row)
721 W. Jefferson St.
HABS KY-63
HABS KY,56-LOUVI,4-
3ph L

Parrish Implement Company; see Phoenix Hill Historic District

Penthouse Theater; see Loew's Theater

Phoenix Cafeteria
644-646 S. Fourth Ave.
HABS KY-174
HABS KY,56-LOUVI,33-
5ph/2pg/2pc L

Phoenix Hill Historic District
HABS KY-163
HABS KY,56-LOUVI,34-
9ph/1pc L

Phoenix Hill Historic District (1005 East Liberty Street (House))
HABS KY-163-GG
HABS KY,56-LOUVI,67-
3ph/1pg/1pc L

Phoenix Hill Historic District (709 East Madison Street (House))
HABS KY-163-A
HABS KY,56-LOUVI,35-
1ph/1pg/1pc L

Phoenix Hill Historic District (728 East Madison Street (House))
HABS KY-163-B
HABS KY,56-LOUVI,36-
2ph/1pg/1pc L

Phoenix Hill Historic District (730 East Madison Street (House))
HABS KY-163-C
HABS KY,56-LOUVI,37-
3ph/1pg/1pc L

Phoenix Hill Historic District (732 East Madison Street (House))
HABS KY-163-D
HABS KY,56-LOUVI,38-
1ph/1pg/1pc L

Phoenix Hill Historic District (734 East Madison Street (House))
HABS KY-163-E
HABS KY,56-LOUVI,39-
2ph/1pg/1pc L

Phoenix Hill Historic District (736 East Madison Street (House))
HABS KY-163-F
HABS KY,56-LOUVI,40-
1ph/1pg/1pc L

Phoenix Hill Historic District (738 East Madison Street (House))
HABS KY-163-G
HABS KY,56-LOUVI,41-
1ph/1pg/1pc L

Phoenix Hill Historic District (817 East Madison Street (House))
HABS KY-163-H
HABS KY,56-LOUVI,42-
1ph/1pg/1pc L

Phoenix Hill Historic District (823 East Madison Street (House))
HABS KY-163-I
HABS KY,56-LOUVI,43-
1ph/1pg/1pc L

Phoenix Hill Historic District (825 East Madison Street (House))
HABS KY-163-J
HABS KY,56-LOUVI,44-
1ph/1pg/1pc L

Phoenix Hill Historic District (827 East Madison Street (House))
HABS KY-163-K
HABS KY,56-LOUVI,45-
1ph/1pg/1pc L

Phoenix Hill Historic District (828 East Madison Street (House))
HABS KY-163-L
HABS KY,56-LOUVI,46-
3ph/1pg/1pc L

Phoenix Hill Historic District (835 East Madison Street (House))
HABS KY-163-M
HABS KY,56-LOUVI,47-
1ph/1pg/1pc L

Phoenix Hill Historic District (837 East Madison Street (House))
HABS KY-163-N
HABS KY,56-LOUVI,48-
1ph/1pg/1pc L

Phoenix Hill Historic District (912 East Madison Street (House))
HABS KY-163-O
HABS KY,56-LOUVI,49-
2ph/1pg/1pc L

Phoenix Hill Historic District (916 East Madison Street (House))
HABS KY-163-P
HABS KY,56-LOUVI,50-
2ph/1pg/1pc L

Phoenix Hill Historic District (918 East Madison Street (House))
HABS KY-163-Q
HABS KY,56-LOUVI,51-
2ph/1pg/1pc L

Phoenix Hill Historic District (922 East Madison Street (House))
HABS KY-163-R
HABS KY,56-LOUVI,52-
2ph/1pg/1pc L

Phoenix Hill Historic District (914 East Marshall Street (Commercial Building); Parrish Implement Company)
HABS KY-163-S
HABS KY,56-LOUVI,53-
2ph/1pg/1pc L

Phoenix Hill Historic District (924 East Marshall Street (House))
HABS KY-163-T
HABS KY,56-LOUVI,54-
2ph/1pg/1pc L

Phoenix Hill Historic District (926 East Marshall Street (House))
HABS KY-163-U
HABS KY,56-LOUVI,55-
2ph/1pg/1pc L

Phoenix Hill Historic District (940 East Marshall Street (House))
HABS KY-163-V
HABS KY,56-LOUVI,56-
2ph/1pg/1pc L

Phoenix Hill Historic District (903 East Muhammad Ali Boulevard (Comm./Res. Bldg.) 903 East Walnut Street (Comm./Residential Bldg.))
HABS KY-163-AA
HABS KY,56-LOUVI,61-
1ph/1pg/1pc L

Phoenix Hill Historic District (905 East Muhammad Ali Boulevard (Comm./Res. Bldg.) 905 East Walnut Street (Comm./Residential Bldg.))
HABS KY-163-BB
HABS KY,56-LOUVI,62-
1ph/1pg/1pc L

Phoenix Hill Historic District (736 East Muhammad Ali Boulevard (House); 736 East Walnut Street (House))
HABS KY-163-W
HABS KY,56-LOUVI,57-
1ph/1pg/1pc L

Phoenix Hill Historic District (816-818 East Muhammad Ali Boulevard (House); 816-818 East Walnut Street (House))
HABS KY-163-X
HABS KY,56-LOUVI,58-
1ph/1pg/1pc L

Phoenix Hill Historic District (826 East Muhammad Ali Boulevard (House); 826 East Walnut Street (House))
HABS KY-163-Y
HABS KY,56-LOUVI,59-
2ph/1pg/1pc L

Phoenix Hill Historic District (836 East Muhammad Ali Boulevard (House); 836 East Walnut Street (House))
HABS KY-163-Z
HABS KY,56-LOUVI,60-
1ph/1pg/1pc L

Phoenix Hill Historic District (Ohio Falls Dye & Finishing Works Building) 731-733 E. Madison St.
HABS KY-163-HH
HABS KY,56-LOUVI,68-
7ph/2pg/1pc L

Phoenix Hill Historic District (509 South Shelby Street (House))
HABS KY-163-CC
HABS KY,56-LOUVI,63-
1ph/1pg/1pc L

Phoenix Hill Historic District (519 South Shelby Street (house))
HABS KY-163-DD
HABS KY,56-LOUVI,64-
1ph/1pg/1pc L

Phoenix Hill Historic District (536-538 South Shelby Street (House))
HABS KY-163-EE
HABS KY,56-LOUVI,65-
1ph/1pg/1pc L

Phoenix Hill Historic District (540 South Shelby Street (House))
HABS KY-163-FF
HABS KY,56-LOUVI,66-
1ph/1pg/1pc L

Republic Building
427 W. Muhammed Ali Blvd.
HABS KY-140
HABS KY,56-LOUVI,69-
6dr/20ph/5pg/2pc/fr L

Roman Catholic Cathedral of the Assumption
435 S. Fifth St.
HABS KY-64
HABS KY,56-LOUVI,5-
1ph/fr L

Ronald-Brennan House (Brennan House)
631 S. Fifth St.
HABS KY-118
HABS KY,56-LOUV1,9-
6dr/30ph/10pg/2pc/2ct/fr L

Rossmore Apartment House (Berkeley Hotel)
664 S. Fourth Ave.
HABS KY-150
HABS KY,56-LOUVI,70-
2dr/10ph/8pg/2pc/fr L

Seelbach Hotel
500 S. Fourth St.
HABS KY-148
HABS KY,56-LOUVI,25-
16ph/6pg/1pc L

508 South Campbell Street (House)
HABS KY-180
HABS KY,56-LOUVI,26-
3ph/1pg/1pc L

642 South Fourth Avenue (Commercial Building)
HABS KY-175
HABS KY,56-LOUVI,27-
5ph/1pg/2pc L

509 South Shelby Street (House); see Phoenix Hill Historic District

519 South Shelby Street (house); see Phoenix Hill Historic District

536-538 South Shelby Street (House); see Phoenix Hill Historic District

540 South Shelby Street (House); see Phoenix Hill Historic District

Spring Bank Farm
7506 Old Shepherdsville Rd.
HABS KY-149
HABS KY,56-LOUV1,7-
12ph/5pg/1pc/2ct L

Spring Station (Clark,George M. ,House)
Lexington Rd. & Cannon's Lane
HABS KY-23
HABS KY,56-LOUVI,3-
10ph/2pg L

Trinity Methodist Episcopal Church
Third & Guthrie Sts.
HABS KY-65
HABS KY,56-LOUVI,6-
1ph L

Tyler Block
319 W. Jefferson St.
HABS KY-151
HABS KY,56-LOUV1,18-
2ph/4pg L

Union Station; see Louisville & Nashville Railroad,Union Station

United Artists Theater; see Loew's Theater

University of Louisville,Medical School; see Louisville Medical College

Vienna Restaurant
133-135 S. Fourth St.
HABS KY-153
HABS KY,56-LOUVI,24-
8ph/5pg/1pc/7ct L

LOUISVILLE VIC.

Croghan House (Locust Grove)
561 Blankenbaker Lane
HABS KY-66
HABS KY,56-LOUVI.V,2-
9ph/2pc L

Farmington (Speed,John,House)
3033 Bardstown Rd.
HABS KY-24
HABS KY,56-LOUVI.V,1-
8dr/29ph/10pg/2pc/4ct/fr L

Locust Grove; see Croghan House

Speed,John,House; see Farmington

ST. MATTHEWS

Humphrey,Judge Churchill,House; see Ridgeway

Ridgeway (Humphrey,Judge Churchill,House)
4095 Massey Ave.
HABS KY-68
HABS KY,56-SAMA,2-
9dr/25ph/8pg/1pc/fr L

Springfield; see Taylor,Zachary,House

Taylor,Zachary,House (Springfield)
5608 Apache Rd. (formerly Blakenbaker La.)
HABS KY-69
HABS KY,56-SAMA,1-
18ph/6pg/2pc L

JOHNSON COUNTY

FISHTRAP VIC.

Fishtrap United Baptist Church
Paint Creek
HABS KY-135
HABS KY,58-FISHT.V,1-
6ph/3pg L

KENTON COUNTY

COVINGTON

Beard, Daniel Carter, House
322 East Third St.
HABS KY-164
HABS KY,59-COV,1-
19ph/1pg/2pc L

Champion Ice Manufacturing & Cold Storage Co. (City Ice & Fuel Co.)
40 E. Second St.
HAER KY-26
HAER 1989(HAER):9
26ph/15pg/2pc L

City Ice & Fuel Co.; see Champion Ice Manufacturing & Cold Storage Co.

COVINGTON VIC.

Covington & Cincinnati Suspension Bridge
Spanning Ohio River,Covington,KY-Cincinnati,OH
HAER KY-20
HAER KY,59-COV.V,1-
4ph/1pg/1pc L

LUDLOW

Closson House,Old (Masonic Temple)
Closson Court & Ringold Sts.
HABS KY-20-13
HABS KY,59-LUDLO,1-
6dr/4ph/2pg L

Elmwood Hall
246 Forest Ave.
HABS KY-22
HABS KY,59-LUDLO,2-
19dr/5ph/3pg L

Masonic Temple; see Closson House,Old

LARUE COUNTY

HODGENVILLE

Abraham Lincoln Birthplace National Historic Site; see Creel Cabin

Creel Cabin (Abraham Lincoln Birthplace National Historic Site)
HABS KY-96
HABS KY,62-HODGV,2-
3ph L

Lincoln,Abraham,Birthplace (Lincoln,Abraham,Birthplace National Historic Site)
HABS KY-95
HABS KY,62-HODV,1-
3ph L

Lincoln,Abraham,Birthplace National Historic Site; see Lincoln,Abraham,Birthplace

LEE COUNTY

BEATTYVILLE

Lee County Courthouse
Main St.
HABS KY-139
HABS KY,65-BETVI,1-
2dr/10ph/1pg/1pc L

LEWIS COUNTY

VANCEBURG VIC.

Bierly,John,House (Bierly,Maude,House)
State Rt. 8
HABS KY-168
HABS KY,68-VANC.V,1-
5ph/18pg/1pc L

Bierly,Maude,House; see Bierly,John,House

Bruce,Thomas J. ,Barn
State Rt. 8
HABS KY-166-A
HABS KY,68-VANC.V,2A-
1ph/1pc L

Bruce,Thomas J. ,House (Cook,Hazel,House)
State Rt. 8 (south side)
HABS KY-166
HABS KY,68-VANC.V,2-
6ph/17pg/1pc L

Carr,Fred,House (Kimble,Helen Rose,House)
State Rt. 8
HABS KY-165
HABS KY,68-VANC.V,3-
6ph/17pg/1pc L

Carrs Methodist Church; see Taylor,Peter,Chapel

Cook,Hazel,House; see Bruce,Thomas J. ,House

Kimble,Helen Rose,House; see Carr,Fred,House

Taylor,Peter,Chapel (Carrs Methodist Church)
State Rt. 8
HABS KY-167
HABS KY,68-VANC.V,4-
4ph/13pg/1pc L

LINCOLN COUNTY

STANFORD

Whitley,Col. William,House
Stanford-Crab Orchard Pike
HABS KY-20-7
HABS KY,69- ,1-
7dr/9ph/2pg L

LOGAN COUNTY

SOUTH UNION

Barn (Center Portion)
HABS KY-104
HABS KY,71-SOUN,8-
1ph/1pc L

Shaker Center Family Dairy; see Shaker Centre Family Preservatory

Shaker Centre Family Drying House
U. S. Rt. 68
HABS KY-109
HABS KY,71-SOUN,1-
5ph L

Shaker Centre Family Dwelling House
U. S. Rt. 68
HABS KY-105
HABS KY,71-SOUN,2-
52ph/1pc L

Shaker Centre Family Dwelling,Bell Tower
U. S. Rt. 68
HABS KY-105-A
HABS KY,71-SOUN,2A-
1ph/1pc L

Shaker Centre Family General View
U. S. Rt. 68
HABS KY-107
HABS KY,71-SOUN,3-
1ph L

Shaker Centre Family Ministry's Shop & Dwelling
U. S. Rt. 68
HABS KY-108
HABS KY,71-SOUN,6-
5ph/1pc L

Shaker Centre Family Preservatory (Shaker Center Family Dairy)
U. S. Rt. 68
HABS KY-106
HABS KY,71-SOUN,4-
2ph/1pc L

Shaker Centre Family Washhouse
U. S. Rt. 68
HABS KY-110
HABS KY,71-SOUN,5-
13ph/1pc L

Shaker Centre Family Well Structure
U. S. Rt. 68
HABS KY-155
HABS KY,71-SOUN,9-
1ph/1pc L

Shaker South Union Hotel; see Shaker South Union Tavern

Shaker South Union Tavern (Shaker South Union Hotel)
Rt. 73
HABS KY-111
HABS KY,71-SOUN,7-
2ph L

MADISON COUNTY

BEREA

Berea College,Lincoln Hall
Berea College
HABS KY-173
HABS KY,76-BER,1A-
5ph/2pg/2pc L

RICHMOND

Castlewood
U. S. Rt. 25
HABS KY-20-17
HABS KY,76-RICH.V,1-
19dr/5ph/2pg/1pc L

Woodlawn
HABS KY-98
HABS KY,76-RICH,1-
1ph L

WHITE HALL

Whitehall
Clay Ln.
HABS KY-101
HABS KY,76-WHAL,1-
12dr/8ph/1pc/fr L

WHITEHALL

Whitehall,Log Cabin
Clay Ln.
HABS KY-101-A
HABS KY,76-WHAL,1A-
1ph/fr L

Whitehall,Stone Outbuilding
Clay Ln.
HABS KY-101-B
HABS KY,76-WHAL.1B-
1ph/fr L

MARION COUNTY

BRADFORDSVILLE

Kentucky Route 49 Bridge
Spanning Rolling Fork River
HAER KY-17
HAER KY,78-BRADVI,1-
14ph/2pg/1pc L

LORETTO VIC.

Burk's Makers Mark Distillery, Bonded Warehouse A
3 mi. E. of Loretto
HAER KY-19-A
2ph/1pc L

Burk's Makers Mark Distillery,Bonded Warehouse D
3 mi. E. of Loretto
HAER KY-19-B
1ph/1pc L

Burk's Makers Mark Distillery,Quart House
3 mi. E. of Loretto
HAER KY-19-C
1ph/1pc L

Burks' Makers Mark Distillery
HAER KY-19
HAER KY,78-LOR.V,1
5ph/1pg/1pc L

MASON COUNTY

MAYSVILLE

Russell Theater
9 E. Third St.
HABS KY-160
HABS KY,81-MAYVI,1-
1ph/1pc/4ct L

WASHINGTON

Bank of Kentucky
Main St.
HABS KY-162
HABS KY,81-WASH,2-
1ph/10pg/1pc L

Collins-Davis House
Main St.
HABS KY-124
HABS KY,81-WASH,3-
5dr/6ph/10pg/1pc/1ct/fr L

Johnston,Albert Sidney,House; see Wilson,Nathaniel,House

Key,Marshall,House
(Taylor,Francis,House)
Main St.
HABS KY-127
HABS KY,81-WASH,4-
8dr/15ph/11pg/1pc/1ct/fr L

Key,Marshall,House,Outbuilding
Main St.
HABS KY-127-A
HABS KY,81-WASH,4A-
3dr/2ph/1pc/fr L

Main Street (Row Houses)
HABS KY-130
HABS KY,81-WASH,5-
4dr/15ph/9pg/1pc/fr L

Main Street (Stone House)
HABS KY-125
HABS KY,81-WASH,6-
6dr/5ph/9pg/1pc/fr L

Marshall,Thomas,House
U. S. Hwy. 68
HABS KY-20-14
HABS KY,81-WASH,1-
20dr/7ph/10pg/1pc/3ct/fr L

Methodist Episcopal Church South
Main St.
HABS KY-128
HABS KY,81-WASH,7-
3dr/4ph/6pg/1pc/1ct/fr L

Moose House; see Murphy-Lashbrooke House

Murphy-Lashbrooke House (Moose House)
Main St. & Berry Alley
HABS KY-129
HABS KY,81-WASH,8-
5dr/11ph/8pg/1pc/1ct/fr L

Taylor House & Store
Main & Williams Sts.
HABS KY-132
HABS KY,81-WASH,9-
3dr/6ph/6pg/1pc/1ct/fr L

Taylor,Francis,House; see Key,Marshall,House

Washington Hall
Main St.
HABS KY-131
HABS KY,81-WASH,10-
6dr/6ph/8pg/1pc/fr L

Washington Hall,Corn Crib
HABS KY-131-A
HABS KY,81-WASH,10A-
1dr/fr L

Washington Historic District
HABS KY-133
HABS KY,81-WASH,12-
2dr/13ph/1pc/fr L

Wilson,Nathaniel,House
(Johnston,Albert Sidney,House)
Harold St.
HABS KY-126
HABS KY,81-WASH,11-
10dr/8ph/8pg/1pc/fr L

MCCRACKEN COUNTY

PADUCAH

Paducah City Hall
S. Fifth St.
HABS KY-170
HABS KY,73-PAD,1-
4ph/9pg/1pc/fr L

MEADE COUNTY

BRANDENBURG

Doe Run Hotel (Water Power Mill,Old)
U. S. Rt. 60
HABS KY-25
HABS KY,82-BRAND.V,1-
5ph/2pg L

Water Power Mill,Old; see Doe Run Hotel

GRAHAMTON

Textile Mill & Storage Warehouse
U. S. Rt. 60
HABS KY-20-6
HABS KY,82-GRAMT,1-
15dr/3ph/3pg/fr L

WOLF CREEK

KY Route 228 Bridge
Spanning Wolf Creek on KY Rt. 228
HAER KY-21
HAER 1989(HAER):9
13ph/3pg/1pc L

MERCER COUNTY

HARRODSBURG

Aspen Hall
Beaumont Ave.
HABS KY-47
HABS KY,84-HARBU,1-
1ph L

Clay Hill
853 Beaumont Ave.
HABS KY-48
HABS KY,84-HARBU,2-
3ph L

Court View
360 N. Main St.
HABS KY-49
HABS KY,84-HARBU,3-
1ph L

Hart,Rebecca,Cabin
HABS KY-94
HABS KY,84-HARBU,6-
2ph L

Mansion,The
Pioneer Memorial State Park
HABS KY-50
HABS KY,84-HARBU,4-
6ph L

Mud Meetinghouse
Dry Branch Rd.
HABS KY-20-15
HABS KY,84-HARBU.V,1-
4dr/3ph/2pg L

Smith,Zachary,House
Hillcrest & S. Greenville Sts.
HABS KY-74
HABS KY,84-HARBU,5-
1ph L

Taylor,Samuel,House
Chatham Pike
HABS KY-52
HABS KY,84-HARBU.V,3-
10dr/12ph/2pg/fr L

HARRODSBURG VIC.

Marrs Log House
Chatham Pike
HABS KY-51
HABS KY,84-HARBU.V,2-
6ph/1pg L

PLEASANT HILL

Shaker Blacksmith's & Carpenter's Shop (Shaker Broom Factory)
Village Rd.
HABS KY-79
HABS KY,84-SHAKT,5-
2ph/1pc L

Shaker Broom Factory; see Shaker Blacksmith's & Carpenter's Shop

Shaker Centre Family Dwelling House (Shakertown Inn)
U.S. Rt 68
HABS KY-20-12
HABS KY,84-SHAKT,1-
9dr/20ph/2pg/2pc/fr L

Shaker Centre Family Dwelling House (First) (Shaker Farm Deacon's Shop; Shaker First House)
U.S. Rt. 68
HABS KY-77
HABS KY,84-SHAKT,3-
13ph/2pc L

Shaker Centre Family Dwelling House (Third) (Shaker Church Family House)
Village Rd.
HABS KY-76
HABS KY,84-SHAKT,2-
35ph/1pc/2ct L

Shaker Centre Family Tan Yard
Village Rd.
HABS KY-99
HABS KY,84-SHAKT,25-
1ph/1pc/2ct L

Shaker Centre Family Trustees' Office (Shaker Guest House)
U.S. Rt. 68
HABS KY-81
HABS KY,84-SHAKT,7-
23ph/2pc L

Shaker Centre Family Washhouse (Shaker Men's Shower House)
Village Rd.
HABS KY-93
HABS KY,84-SHAKT,19-
1ph L

Shaker Church Family House; see Shaker Centre Family Dwelling House (Third)

Shaker Coopers' Shop (Shaker North Workshop)
U.S. Rt. 68
HABS KY-83
HABS KY,84-SHAKT,9-
8ph/2pc L

Shaker Dr. Pennebaker House; see Shaker West Family Dwelling House (First)

Shaker East Family Brethrens' Shop (Shaker South Workshop; Trustee's Office)
U.S. Rt. 68
HABS KY-82
HABS KY,84-SHAKT,8-
12ph/2pc L

Shaker East Family Broom Shop (Shaker Outbuilding)
Village Rd.
HABS KY-92
HABS KY,84-SHAKT,18-
1ph L

Shaker East Family Dwelling House
U.S. Rt. 68
HABS KY-212
HABS KY,84-SHAKT,26-
3ph/1pc L

Shaker East Family Sisters' Shop (Shaker Silkworm House)
U.S. Rt. 68
HABS KY-89
HABS KY,84-SHAKT,15-
9ph/2pc/2ct L

Shaker East Family Wash House
U.S. Rt. 68
HABS KY-88
HABS KY,84-SHAKT,14-
7ph/2pc L

Shaker Farm Deacon's Shop; see Shaker Centre Family Dwelling House (First)

Shaker First House; see Shaker Centre Family Dwelling House (First)

Shaker Guest House; see Shaker Centre Family Trustees' Office

Shaker Meetinghouse (Shakertown Baptist Church)
U.S. Rt. 68
HABS KY-78
HABS KY,84-SHAKT,4-
11ph/2pc L

Shaker Men's Shower House; see Shaker Centre Family Washhouse

Shaker Ministry Shop,First (Shaker Ministry's Old Yellow Frame Shop)
U.S. Rt. 68
HABS KY-113
HABS KY,84-SHAKT,24-
5ph/1pc L

Shaker Ministry's Old Yellow Frame Shop; see Shaker Ministry Shop,First

Shaker Ministry's Shop (Second)
U.S. Rt. 68
HABS KY-114
HABS KY,84-SHAKT,23-
4ph/2pc L

Shaker North Family Dwelling House
U.S. Rt. 68
HABS KY-169
HABS KY,84-SHAKT,27-
6ph/2pc/1ct L

Shaker North Family Home; see Shaker West Family Sisters' Shop

Shaker North Workshop; see Shaker Coopers' Shop

Shaker Old Stone Shop; see Shaker West Family Dwelling House (First)

Shaker Outbuilding; see Shaker East Family Broom Shop

Shaker Pennebaker School for Girls; see Shaker West Family Dwelling House (Second)

Shaker Silkworm House; see Shaker East Family Sisters' Shop

Shaker Smoke House
HABS KY-86
HABS KY,84-SHAKT,12-
1ph L

Shaker South Workshop; see Shaker East Family Brethrens' Shop

Shaker Water Tower Building
U.S. Rt. 68
HABS KY-84
HABS KY,84-SHAKT,10-
5dr/4ph/1pc/fr L

Shaker West Family Barn
Village Rd.
HABS KY-87
HABS KY,84-SHAKT,13-
1ph L

Shaker West Family Drying House
Village Rd.
HABS KY-112
HABS ,Y,84-SHAKT,22-
1ph L

Shaker West Family Dwelling House (First) (Shaker Dr. Pennebaker House; Shaker Old Stone Shop)
U.S. Rt. 68
HABS KY-90
HABS KY,84-SHAKT,16-
9ph/2pc L

Shaker West Family Dwelling House (Second) (Shaker Pennebaker School for Girls)
U.S. Rt. 68
HABS KY-91
HABS KY,84-SHAKT,17-
14ph/2pc L

Shaker West Family Preserve House
Village Rd.
HABS KY-85
HABS KY,84-SHAKT,11-
2ph L

Shaker West Family Privy
Village Rd.
HABS KY-115
HABS KY,84-SHAKT,21-
1ph L

Shaker West Family Sisters' Shop (Shaker North Family Home)
U.S. Rt. 68
HABS KY-80
HABS KY,84-SHAKT,6-
6ph/2pc L

Shaker West Family Washhouse
U.S. Rt. 68
HABS KY-116
HABS KY,84-SHAKT,20-
3ph/2pc L

Shakertown Baptist Church; see Shaker Meetinghouse

Shakertown Inn; see Shaker Centre Family Dwelling House

Trustee's Office; see Shaker East Family Brethrens' Shop

PLEASANT VILLAGE

Shaker Post Office
U.S. RT. 68
HABS KY-213
HABS KY,84-SHAKT,28-
1ph/1pc L

TALMAGE

McAfee House
HABS KY-71
HABS KY,84-TALM,1-
3dr/3ph/2pg/fr L

NELSON COUNTY

BARDSTOWN

Beckham House; see Wickland

St. Joseph's Cathedral
HABS KY-20-9
HABS KY,90-BARTO,2-
10dr/5ph/4pg/fr L

Wickland (Beckham House)
U. S. Rt. 55
HABS KY-20-5
HABS KY,90-BARTO,1-
13dr/9ph/2pg/fr L

BARDSTOWN VIC.

Federal Hill; see My Old Kentucky Home

My Old Kentucky Home (Federal Hill)
HABS KY-44
HABS KY,90-BARTO.V,1-
4ph L

St. Thomas Catholic Church
U. S. Rt. 31 E.
HABS KY-100
HABS KY,90-BARTO.V,2-
7dr/4pg L

CHAPLIN VIC.

KY Route 1754 Bridge
Spanning Chaplin River on Kentucky Rt. 1754
HAER KY-22
HAER 1989(HAER):9
15ph/3pg/1pc L

PENDLETON COUNTY

BUTLER

Covered Bridge,Wood
Spanning Licking River
HABS KY-20-11
HABS KY,96-BUT,1-
5dr/2ph/2pg/fr L

PIKE COUNTY

PIKEVILLE

U. S. 23 Middle Bridge
Spanning Levisa Fork
HAER KY-5
HAER KY,98-PIKVI,1-
16ph/4pg/1pc L

PIKEVILLE VIC.

Boldman Bridge (KY 1384 Suspension Bridge)
Spanning Levisa Fork
HAER KY-4
HAER KY,98-PIKVI.V,1-
12ph/2pg/1pc L

KY 1384 Suspension Bridge; see Boldman Bridge

POWELL COUNTY

STANTON

Powell County Courthouse
Washington & Court Sts.
HABS KY-136
HABS KY,99-STAN,1-
6dr/16ph/1pc L

SCOTT COUNTY

GEORGETOWN

Cantrill #3 House,Mary Cecil
121 N. Mulberry St.
HABS KY-223
HABS DLC/PP-1993:KY-5
3ph/6pg/1pc L

Cantrill,Mary Cecil,No. 2 House
117 N. Mulberry St.
HABS KY-222
HABS DLC/PP-1993:KY-5
8ph/7pg/1pc L

Cantrill,Mary Cecil,No. 6 House
107-108 Post Office Alley
HABS KY-219
HABS DLC/PP-1993:KY-5
5ph/6pg/1pc L

Cantrill,Mary Cecil,No. 7 House
109 Post Office Alley
HABS KY-220
HABS DLC/PP-1993:KY-5
3ph/6pg/1pc L

Haywood,J.W. & Maggie,House
135 North Mulberry St.
HABS KY-225
HABS DLC/PP-1993:KY-5
4ph/6pg/1pc L

Thomas,House,Manlius
125 N. Mulberry St.
HABS KY-224
HABS DLC/PP-1993:KY-5
11ph/6pg/1pc L

SHELBY COUNTY

SAMPSONVILLE

Whitney M. Young Jr. Job Corps Training Center; see Young,Whitney M.,Jr.,Birthplace

Young,Whitney M.,Jr.,Birthplace (Whitney M. Young Jr. Job Corps Training Center)
U.S. Rt. 60
HABS KY-211
HABS KY,106-SIMVI,1-
3ph/1pc L

SHELBYVILLE

Cross Keys Tavern
U. S. Rt. 60
HABS KY-20-21
HABS KY,106-SHELB.V,1-
6dr/9ph/2pg/fr L

SHELBYVILLE VIC.

Inn,Old Stone
U. S. Rt. 60
HABS KY-72
HABS KY,106-SHELB.V,2-
2ph L

Threlkeld,Thomas,House (Weakley House)
Benson Pike
HABS KY-204
HABS KY,106-SHELB.V,3-
12dr/9ph/3pg/1pc/fr L

Weakley House; see Threlkeld,Thomas,House

SPENCER COUNTY

TAYLORSVILLE VIC.

Carrithers-Cochran House
Carrithers Lane
HABS KY-181
HABS KY,108-TAYVI.V,1-
7ph/5pg/1pc L

WARREN COUNTY

BOWLING GREEN

Porter,O. D. ,Building
227 E. Main St.
HABS KY-182
HABS KY,114-BOGR,1-
5ph/1pg/1pc L

WASHINGTON COUNTY

SPRINGFIELD

Washington County Courthouse
HABS KY-73
HABS KY,115-SPRIF,1-
1ph L

WEBSTER COUNTY

DIXON VIC.

Mitchell-Griggs Road Bridge
Spannning Caney Fork on Mitchell-Griggs Rd.
HAER KY-6
HAER KY,117-DIX.V,1-
7ph/3pg/1pc L

WHITLEY COUNTY

WILLIAMSBURG

Kentucky Route 296 Bridge; see Williamsburg Bridge

Williamsburg Bridge (Kentucky Route 296 Bridge)
Spanning Cumberland River
HAER KY-16
HAER KY,118-WILBU,1-
11ph/3pg/1pc L

WILLIAMSBURG VIC.

KY Rt. 478 Bridge
Spanning Jellico Creek
HAER KY-23
HAER 1989(HAER):9
12ph/2pg/1pc L

WOODFORD COUNTY

PISGAH

Pisgah Presbyterian Church & Academy
Pisgah-Georgetown Pike
HABS KY-20-10
HABS KY,120-PISG.V,1-AND V,2-
5dr/5ph/3pg/fr L

TROY VIC.

Guyn,William,House
Mundy's Landing & Pauls Mill Rds.
HABS KY-97
HABS KY,120-TROY.V,1-
11ph/3pg L

Guyn's Mill Complex
Mundy's Landing & Pauls Mill Rds.
HAER KY-1
HAER KY,120TROY.V,2-
5pg L

Guyn's Mill Complex,Blacksmith Shop
Mundy's Landing & Pauls Mill Rds.
HAER KY-1-C
HAER KY,120-TROY.V,2C-
4ph/1pc L

Guyn's Mill Complex,Grist Mill
Mundy's Landing & Pauls Mill Rds.
HAER KY-1-A
HAER KY,120-TROY.V,2A-
30ph/2pc L

Guyn's Mill Complex,Saw Mill
Mundy's Landing & Pauls Mill Rds.
HAER KY-1-B
HAER KY,120-TROY.V,2B-
18ph/2pc L

Le Prêtre Mansion, New Orleans, Orleans Parish, Louisiana. Cast iron column; column capital. Measured drawing delineated by U.J. Theriot and A.B. Cruise, April 18, 1940 (HABS LA-53, sheet 21 of 26; negative number LC-USZA3-5)

Louisiana

ASCENSION PARISH

BURNSIDE

Burnside Plantation (Houmas,The)
State Hwy. 1
HABS LA-26
HABS LA,3-BURSI,1-
7dr/13ph/3pg/fr L

Houmas,The; see Burnside Plantation

GEISMAR VIC.

Ashland Belle Helene Plantation (Ashland Plantation)
Hwy. 75
HABS LA-80
HABS LA,3-GEIM.V,1-;1991(HABS):31
9dr/9ph/2pg/fr L

Ashland Plantation; see Ashland Belle Helene Plantation

ASSUMPTION PARISH

NAPOLEONVILLE VIC.

Woodlawn Plantation
State Hwy. 77
HABS LA-20
HABS LA,4-NAPO.V,1-
20dr/13ph/5pg/fr L

CADDO PARISH

SHREVEPORT

McNeil Street Pumping Station
McNeil St. & Cross Bayou
HAER LA-2
HAER LA,9-SHREV,2-
10dr/106ph/180pg/15pc/4ct/fr L

U. S. Post Office & Courthouse
Marshall & Texas Sts.
HABS LA-1125
HABS LA,9-SHREV,1-
11dr/23ph L

EAST BATON ROUGE PARISH

BATON ROUGE

Blum House
630 Louisiana Ave.
HABS LA-1126
HABS LA,17-BATRO,1-
4dr/13ph/9pg/1pc/fr L

Columbia Theatre (Paramount Theatre)
215 Riverside Mall
HABS LA-1133
HABS LA,17-BATRO,7-
4dr/16ph/19pg/1pc/4ct/fr L

Fire Station Number 1; see Laurel Street Station

825-827 Frisco Street (House); see Suburb Gracie

855-865 Frisco Street (House); see Suburb Gracie

1360 Gayso Street (House); see Suburb Gracie

1660 Gracie Street (House); see Suburb Gracie

Grand Theatre
133 S. Twelfth St.
HABS LA-1128
HABS LA,17-BATRO,3-
5ph/7pg/1pc L

Knox Cottage
1029 America St.
HABS LA-1129
HABS LA,17-BATRO,4-
4dr/7ph/8pg/1pc/fr L

Lakes,The; see Suburb Gracie

Laurel Street Station (Fire Station Number 1)
1801 Laurel St.
HABS LA-1127
HABS LA,17-BATRO,2-
6dr/11ph/11pg/1ct/fr L

Louisana State Capitol (Old State Capitol)
N. Blvd. ,Saint Philip,America & Front Sts.
HABS LA-1132
HABS LA,17-BATRO,6-
27ph/11pg/2pc/5ct L

Louisiana State Prison Store (Warden's House)
703 Laurel St.
HABS LA-1140
HABS LA,17-BATRO,15-
15ph/8pg/1pc/3ct L

LSU Livestock Judging Pavilion (Building No. 23)
Louisiana State University, Tower Drive
HABS LA-1207-A
HABS 1991(HABS):31
14dr/fr L

Magnolia Mound
2161 Nicholson Dr.
HABS LA-1130
HABS LA,17-BATRO,14-
ı1991(HABS):31°
19dr/16ph/16pg/2pc/6ct/fr L

Old Arsenal Museum; see U.S. Arsenal Powder Magazine

Old Spanish Arsenal; see U.S. Arsenal Powder Magazine

Old State Capitol; see Louisana State Capitol

Paramount Theatre; see Columbia Theatre

Pentagon Barracks; see U. S. Barracks

Planter's Cabin
7815 Highland Rd.
HABS LA-1135
HABS LA,17-BATRO,9-
2dr/12ph/7pg/1pc/2ct/fr L

Post Office (Post Office,Old)
355 N. Blvd.
HABS LA-1131
HABS LA,17-BATRO,5-
11ph/9pg/1pc/1ct L

Post Office,Old; see Post Office

Santa Maria Plantation
Perkins Rd.
HABS LA-1137
HABS LA,17-BATRO,11-
19ph/8pg/2pc/1ct L

St. James Episcopal Church
208 N. Fourth St.
HABS LA-1136
HABS LA,17-BATRO,10-
15ph/6pg/1pc/2ct L

Suburb Gracie (825-827 Frisco Street (House))
HABS LA-1138-A
HABS LA,17-BATRO,12A-
3ph/2pc/1ct L

Suburb Gracie (855-865 Frisco Street (House))
HABS LA-1138-B
HABS LA,17-BATRO,12B-
4ph/2pc L

Suburb Gracie (1360 Gayso Street (House))
HABS LA-1138-C
HABS LA,17-BATRO,12C-
4ph/2pc L

Suburb Gracie (1660 Gracie Street (House))
HABS LA-1138-D
HABS LA,17-BATRO,12D-
3ph/2pc L

Suburb Gracie (Lakes,The)
North,N. Seventeenth,N. Thirteenth & Fuqua Sts.
HABS LA-1138
HABS LA,17-BATRO,12-
5dr/9pg/2pc/fr L

Tessier Building
342,346,348 Lafayette St.
HABS LA-1139
HABS LA,17-BATRO,13-
10ph/8pg/1ct L

U. S. Barracks (Pentagon Barracks)
Riverside Mall,Capitol Ave. ,Front St.
HABS LA-1134
HABS LA,17-BATRO,8-
13ph/6pg/2ct L

U.S. Arsenal Powder Magazine (Old Spanish Arsenal; Old Arsenal Museum)
East Garden, State Capitol Grounds
HABS LA-1215
HABS 1991(HABS):31
8dr/fr L

Warden's House; see Louisiana State Prison Store

Willow Grove Plantation
18367 Perkins Rd.
HABS LA-1238
6dr/fr H

EAST FELICIANA PARISH

CLINTON

Braeme House
State Hwy. 36
HABS LA-40
HABS LA,19-CLINT,3-
14dr/9ph/4pg/fr L

Clinton Courthouse
Saint Helena St.
HABS LA-30
HABS LA,19-CLINT,1-
14dr/4ph/3pg/fr L

Lawyers' Row
Saint Helena St. & Liberty Rd.
HABS LA-31
HABS LA,19-CLINT,2-
2dr/3ph/1pg/fr L

IBERIA PARISH

AVERY ISLAND

Akzo Salt Company Town; see Salt Mine Village

Avery Island Salt Works
Akzo Salt Inc., Avery Island
HAER LA-9
HAER DLC/PP-1992:LA-4
20dr/106ph/28pg/6pc/fr L

McIlhenny Company Town; see Tango Village

Salt Mine Village (Akzo Salt Company Town)
HABS LA-1220
HABS DLC/PP-1992:LA-2
ιDLC/PP-1992:LA-4°
1dr/5ph/1pc/fr L

Salt Mine Village,Baptist Church
HABS LA-1220-A
HABS DLC/PP-1992:LA-2
1dr L

Salt Mine Village,Bradford Club
HABS LA-1220-C
HABS DLC/PP-1992:LA-2
3dr L

Salt Mine Village,Company Store
HABS LA-1220-B
HABS DLC/PP-1992:LA-2
3dr L

Salt Mine Village,Salt Workers' Houses No. 6
HABS LA-1220-I
HABS DLC/PP-1992:LA-2
1dr L

Salt Mine Village,Salt Workers' Houses,No. 1
HABS LA-1220-D
HABS DLC/PP-1992:LA-2
1dr L

Salt Mine Village,Salt Workers' Houses,No. 2
HABS LA-1220-E
HABS DLC/PP-1992:LA-2
1dr L

Salt Mine Village,Salt Workers' Houses,No. 3
HABS LA-1220-F
HABS DLC/PP-1992:LA-2
1dr L

Salt Mine Village,Salt Workers' Houses,No. 4
HABS LA-1220-G
HABS DLC/PP-1992:LA-2
1dr L

Salt Mine Village,Salt Workers' Houses,No. 5
HABS LA-1220-H
HABS DLC/PP-1992:LA-2
1dr L

Tango Village (McIlhenny Company Town)
HABS LA-1219
HABS DLC/PP-1992:LA-2
2dr/fr L

Tango Village,Tabasco Deli Company Store
HABS LA-1219-A
HABS DLC/PP-1992:LA-2
2dr L

Tango Village,Tabasco Workers' Houses,No. 1
HABS LA-1219-B
HABS DLC/PP-1992:LA-2
1dr L

Tango Village,Tabasco Workers' Houses,No. 2
HABS LA-1219-C
HABS DLC/PP-1992:LA-2
1dr L

Tango Village,Tabasco Workers' Houses,No. 3
HABS LA-1219-D
HABS DLC/PP-1992:LA-2
1dr L

NEW IBERIA

Shadows on the Teche
(Weeks,David,House)
Main & Weeks Sts.
HABS LA-75
HABS LA,23-NEWIB,1-
17dr/11ph/6pg L

Weeks,David,House; see Shadows on the Teche

IBERVILLE PARISH

IBERVILLE VIC.

Kroll House
Moved from St. John the Baptist Parish
HABS LA-1179
HABS 1991(HABS):31
5dr L

PLAQUEMINE

Iberville Parish Courthouse
(Plaquemine City Hall)
209 Main St.
HABS LA-1208
HABS 1991(HABS):31
8dr/fr L

Plaquemine City Hall; see Iberville Parish Courthouse

Variety Plantation
State Hwy. 3066,Bayou Plaquemine
HABS LA-1141
HABS LA,24-PLAQ,1-
11dr L

ST. GABRIEL

St. Gabriel Church,Old
St. Hwy. 75
HABS LA-1237
9dr/fr H

SUNSHINE VIC.

Bagatelle Plantation
(moved from St. James Parish)
HABS LA-1142
HABS LA,47- ,1-
10dr/20ph/7pg/2pc/fr L

WHITE CASTLE VIC.

Belle Grove
HABS LA-36
HABS LA,24-WHICA.V,1-
36dr/21ph/22pg/fr L

JEFFERSON PARISH

METAIRIE

New Orleans Sewerage & Water Board; see Pumping Station No. 6

Pumping Station No. 6 (New Orleans Sewerage & Water Board)
See Orleans Parish,New Orleans for documentation
HABS LA-1235
L

NEW ORLEANS

Petit Desert; see Seven Oaks Plantation

Seven Oaks Plantation (Petit Desert)
HABS LA-1158
HABS LA,26-WESWE,1-
13ph/10pg/1pc L

LAFAYETTE PARISH

LAFAYETTE

Bank of Lafayette (City Hall,Old)
217 W. Main St.
HABS LA-1154
HABS LA,28-LAFY,1-
10ph/5pg/1pc L

City Hall,Old; see Bank of Lafayette

Lafayette City Hall; see Sears Department Store

Sears Department Store (Lafayette City Hall)
705 W. University Ave.
HABS LA-1157
HABS LA,28-LAFY,2-
12ph/4pg/1pc L

LAFOURCHE PARISH

LAROSE VIC.

M/V "Fox"; see Motorized Sailing Vessel "Fox"

Motorized Sailing Vessel "Fox" (M/V "Fox")
Bayou Lafourche (beached on E. Bank of)
HAER LA-5
HAER LA,29-LAR,1-
15ph/36pg/1pc/fr L

THIBODAUX

Laurel Valley Sugar Plantation
State Rt. 308
HAER LA-1
HAER LA,29-THIB,1-
2dr/17ph/23pg/3pc/fr L

Laurel Valley Sugar Plantation:"Big" House
State Rt. 308
HAER LA-1-E
HAER LA-29-THIB,1E-
3dr/9ph/1pc/fr L

Laurel Valley Sugar Plantation:Boarding House
State Rt. 308
HAER LA-1-F
HAER LA,29-THIB,1F-
2dr/6ph/2pc/1ct/fr L

Laurel Valley Sugar Plantation:Corn Crib
State Rt. 308
HAER LA-1-D
HAER LA,29-THIB,1D-
2dr/3ph/8pg/1pc/1ct/fr L

Laurel Valley Sugar Plantation:Double Creole Qtrs.
State Rt. 308
HAER LA-1-H
HAER LA,29-THIB,1H-
1dr/10ph/2pc L

Laurel Valley Sugar Plantation:Drainage Plant
State Rt. 308
HAER LA-1-C
HAER LA,29-THIB,1C-
2dr/5ph/29pg/2pc/fr L

Laurel Valley Sugar Plantation:Engineer's House
State Rt. 308
HAER LA-1-G
HAER LA,29-THIB,1G-
1dr/1ph/1pc/fr L

Laurel Valley Sugar Plantation:General Store
State Rt. 308
HAER LA-1-K
HAER LA,29-THIB,1K-
1dr/2ph/1pc/fr L

Laurel Valley Sugar Plantation:Railroad (Melodia Switch)
State Rt. 308
HAER LA-1-B
HAER LA,29-THIB,1B-
1ph/27pg/1pc L

Laurel Valley Sugar Plantation:School House
State Rt. 308
HAER LA-1-L
HAER LA,29-THIB,1L-
1dr/2ph/1pc/2ct L

Laurel Valley Sugar Plantation:Shotgun Quarters
State Rt. 308
HAER LA-1-J
HAER LA,29-THIB,1J-
1dr/5ph/1pc/4ct L

Laurel Valley Sugar Plantation:Sugar Mill
State Rt. 308
HAER LA-1-A
HAER LA,29-THIB,LA-
6dr/14ph/77pg/2pc/2ct/fr L

Melodia Switch; see Laurel Valley Sugar Plantation:Railroad

LINCOLN PARISH

DUBACH VIC.

Autrey and Nolan Houses
Rte. 151
HABS LA-1217
HABS DLC/PP-1992:LA-2
1dr L

Autrey House
Rte. 151
HABS LA-1217-A
HABS DLC/PP-1992:LA-2
8dr/fr L

Nolan House
HABS LA-1217-B
HABS DLC/PP-1992:LA-2
8dr/fr L

NATCHITOCHES PARISH

BERMUDA

Bermuda Plantation (Prudhomme Family)
Cane River
HABS LA-2-2
HABS LA,35-BERM,1-
3ph L

Oakland Plantation
LA Rt. 494
HABS LA-1192
HABS 1991(HABS):31
32dr/fr L

Oakland Plantation,Barn
Rt. 494
HABS LA-1192-J
HABS 1991(HABS):31
4dr/fr L

Oakland Plantation,Carpenter's Shop
Rt. 494
HABS LA-1192-B
HABS 1991(HABS):31
1dr/fr L

Oakland Plantation,Carriage House
Rt. 494
HABS LA-1192-L
HABS 1991(HABS):31
3dr/fr L

Oakland Plantation,Chicken Coop
Rt. 494
HABS LA-1192-D
HABS 1991(HABS):31
2dr/fr L

Oakland Plantation,Cook's House
Rt. 494
HABS LA-1192-A
HABS 1991(HABS):31
3dr/fr L

Oakland Plantation,Corral Shed
Rt. 494
HABS LA-1192-N
HABS 1991(HABS):31
1dr/fr L

Oakland Plantation,Doctor's House
Rt. 494
HABS LA-1192-P
HABS 1991(HABS):31
4dr/fr L

Oakland Plantation,Fattening Pen
Rt. 494
HABS LA-1192-G
HABS 1991(HABS):31
1dr/fr L

Oakland Plantation,North Pigennier
Rt. 494
HABS LA-1192-I
HABS 1991(HABS):31
2dr/fr L

Oakland Plantation,Overseer's House
Rt. 494
HABS LA-1192-Q
HABS 1991(HABS):31
3dr/fr L

Oakland Plantation,Plantation Store & Post Office
Rt. 494
HABS LA-1192-O
HABS 1991(HABS):31
5dr/fr L

Oakland Plantation,Setting Pen
Rt. 494
HABS LA-1192-C
HABS 1991(HABS):1
1dr/fr L

Oakland Plantation,Slave Quarter
Rt. 494
HABS LA-1192-M
HABS 1991(HABS):31
3dr/fr L

Oakland Plantation,South Pigeonnier
Rt. 494
HABS LA-1192-K
HABS 1991(HABS):31
2dr/fr L

Oakland Plantation,Stables
Rt.494
HABS LA-1192-H
HABS 1991(HABS):31
4dr/fr L

Oakland Plantation,Storage Shed
Rt. 494
HABS LA-1192-E
HABS 1991(HABS):31
1dr/fr L

Oakland Plantation,Wash House
Rt. 494
HABS LA-1192-F
HABS 1991(HABS):31
1dr/fr L

MELROSE

African House; see Melrose Plantation,African House

Melrose Plantation (Yucca Plantation)
State Rt. 119
HABS LA-2-69
HABS LA,35-MELRO,1-
4ph/3pg/1pc L

Melrose Plantation,African House
(Yucca Plantation,African House; African House)
State Rt. 119
HABS LA-2-69-B
HABS LA,35-MELRO,1B-
3dr/3ph/4pg/1pc L

Melrose Plantation,Slave Hospital
(Yucca Plantation,Slave Hospital; Slave Hospital; Yucca House)
State Rt. 119
HABS LA-2-69-A
HABS LA,35-MELRO,1A-
2ph/2pg/1pc L

Slave Hospital; see Melrose Plantation,Slave Hospital

Yucca House; see Melrose Plantation,Slave Hospital

Yucca Plantation; see Melrose Plantation

Yucca Plantation,African House; see Melrose Plantation,African House

Yucca Plantation,Slave Hospital; see Melrose Plantation,Slave Hospital

NATCHITOCHES

Balcony Building
120 Washington St.
HABS LA-2-3
HABS LA,35-NATCH,1-
1ph L

Church of the Immaculate Conception
HABS LA-2-4
HABS LA,35-NATCH,2-
1ph L

Duplex Columns
312 Jefferson St.
HABS LA-2-5
HABS LA,35-NATCH,3-
1ph L

Episcopal Church (Trinity Church)
HABS LA-2-6
HABS LA,35-NATCH,4-
1ph L

Lemee House
308-309 Jefferson St.
HABS LA-2-193
HABS LA,35-NATCH,6-
7dr/9ph/2pg/fr L

Magnolia Plantation,Blacksmith Shop
LA Rte. 119
HABS LA-1193-D
HABS 1991(HABS):31
4dr/fr L

Magnolia Plantation,Corn Crib
LA Rte. 119
HABS LA-1193-G
HABS 1991(HABS):31
1dr L

Magnolia Plantation,Cotton Gin Press
LA Rte. 119
HABS LA-1193-A
HABS 1991(HABS):31
6dr/fr L

Magnolia Plantation,Magnolia Store
LA Rte. 119
HABS LA-1193-H
HABS 1991(HABS):31
2dr L

Magnolia Plantation,Overseer's House
LA Rte. 119
HABS LA-1193-C
HABS 1991(HABS):31
6dr/fr L

Magnolia Plantation,Pigeonnier & Fattening Pen
LA Rte. 119
HABS LA-1193-E
HABS 1991(HABS):31
1dr/fr L

Magnolia Plantation,Privy
LA Rte. 119
HABS LA-1193-F
HABS 1991(HABS):31
1dr/fr L

Magnolia Plantation,Slave Quarters
LA Rte. 119
HABS LA-1193-B
HABS 1991(HABS):31
2dr/fr L

Northwestern State University,Women's Gymnasium
U.S. Hwy. 6
HABS LA-1209-A
HABS 1991(HABS):31
8dr/fr L

Prudhomme-Hughes Building
HABS LA-2-7
HABS LA,35-NATCH,5-
2ph L

Tauzin House
HABS LA-2-8
HABS LA,35-NATCH.V,1-
1ph L

Trinity Church; see Episcopal Church

NATCHITOCHES VIC.

Magnolia Plantation
LA Rt. 119
HABS LA-1193
HABS 1991(HABS):31
4dr/fr L

ORLEANS PARISH

NEW ORLEANS

"Court of the Lions"; see Vieux Carre Squares

"Tivoli"; see Fernandez-Tissot House

Antoine's Annex; see Vieux Carre Squares

Antoine's Restaurant; see Vieux Carre Squares

Antoine's Restaurant (Service Building); see Vieux Carre Squares

Archbishopric
1114 Chartres St.
HABS LA-18-2
HABS LA,36-NEWOR,2-
31dr/29ph/4pg/fr L

Documentation: **ct** color transparencies **dr** measured drawings **fr** field records
pc photograph captions **pg** pages of text **ph** photographs

Arsenal
615 Saint Peter St.
HABS LA-18-6
HABS LA,36-NEWOR,6-
6dr/7ph/16pg/fr L

Baker d'Acquin's House; see Vieux Carre Squares

Bank of the United States
339 Royal St.
HABS LA-1159
HABS 1984(HABS):293
fr L

Beauregard House
1113 Chartres St.
HABS LA-18-1
HABS LA,36-NEWOR,1-
16dr/14ph/14pg/fr L

Boimare-Schloeman Building; see Vieux Carre Squares

Bosque House
617-619 Chartres St.
HABS LA-81
HABS LA,36-NEWOR,19-
16dr/fr L

Bosworth-Hammond House
1126 Washington Ave.
HABS LA-1143
HABS LA,36-NEWOR,73-
7ph/1pc L

701 Bourbon Street (Commercial Building)
HABS LA-1144
HABS LA,36-NEWOR,71-
6ph/1pc L

941 Bourbon Street (Cottage) (Lafayette's Blacksmith Shop)
HABS LA-24
HABS LA,36-NEWOR,13-
6dr/4ph/4pg/fr L

Brevard,Albert Hamilton,House
1239 First St.
HABS LA-1118
HABS LA,36-NEWOR,66-
6dr/6ph/6pg L

Burgundy & St. Roch Streets (Gas Station); see Faubourg Marigny District

Cabildo,The (City Hall; Casa Capitular)
711 Chartres St.
HABS LA-18-4
HABS LA,36-NEWOR,4-
29dr/28ph/10pg/1pc/fr L

Cafe Toulousin; see Vieux Carre Squares

Calaboose Building; see Louisiana State Museum Building

Casa Capitular; see Cabildo,The

Casa Flinard; see Nichols,Valery,House

Castillon House
Decatur & Saint Peter Sts.
HABS LA-191
HABS LA,36-NEWOR,24-
57pg L

Central Congregational Church
S. Liberty & Cleveland Ave.
HABS LA-22
HABS LA,36-NEWOR,11-
6dr/4ph/3pg L

Chartres Street (Buildings)
HABS LA-1146
HABS LA,36-NEWOR,74-
7ph/1pc L

Chesneau Mansion (Lafitte Bank)
533 St. Louis St.,Vieux Carre Historic District
HABS LA-1190
HABS 1991(HABS):31
11dr/fr L

Church of the Immaculate Conception
132 Baronne St.
HABS LA-1147
HABS LA,36-NEWOR,75-
1ph/1pg/1pc L

City Hall; see Cabildo,The

City Hall (Gallier Hall; Municipal Hall)
545 Saint Charles St.
HABS LA-193
HABS LA,36-NEWOR,21-
8ph/12pg/fr L

Coffini Cottage; see Vieux Carre Squares

Convent of Notre Dame (St. Joseph's Orphan Asylum)
835 Josephine St.
HABS LA-1102
HABS LA,36-NEWOR,50-
3ph/1pg L

Convent of the Holy Family
Orleans St.
HABS LA-1124
HABS LA,36-NEWOR,76-
3dr L

Counting House of William Nott & Company; see Vieux Carre Squares

Dabney,Lavinia C. ,House
2265 Saint Charles Ave.
HABS LA-1113
HABS LA,36-NEWOR,61-
8ph/5pg L

1113-1115 Dauphine Street (House)
HABS LA-1172
HABS 1984(HABS):293
fr L

2519 Dauphine Street (House); see Faubourg Marigny District

631-633 Dauphine Street (House)
HABS LA-1173
HABS 1984(HABS):293
fr L

deArmas,Felix,House,Site of; see Vieux Carre Squares

1107-1133 Decatur Street (Commercial Buildings); see Ursuline's Row Houses

Dujarreau-Rouquette House
413 Royal St.
HABS LA-1170
HABS 1984(HABS):293
fr L

Duncan,Albert House
2010-2010 1/2 Louisiana Ave.
HABS LA-1223
7ph/5pg/1pc H

Duplantier Family Tomb
N. Claiborne St.
HABS LA-1107
HABS LA,36-NEWOR,55-
6dr/2ph/2pg L

Faubourg Marigny District (Burgundy & St. Roch Streets (Gas Station))
HABS LA-27-G
HABS LA,36-NEWOR,77G-
1ph/1pc L

Faubourg Marigny District (2519 Dauphine Street (House))
HABS LA-27-D
HABS LA,36-NEWOR,77D-
1ph/1pc L

Faubourg Marigny District (Kerlerec & Pauger Streets (General View))
HABS LA-27-H
HABS LA,36-NEWOR,77H-
1ph/1pc L

Faubourg Marigny District (Laundry (Cardau Drugs))
Spain & Burgundy Sts.
HABS LA-27-C
HABS LA,36-NEWOR,77C-
1ph/1pc L

Faubourg Marigny District (1451 Pauger Street (House))
HABS LA-27-F
HABS LA,36-NEWOR,77F-
1ph/1pc L

Faubourg Marigny District (1463 Pauger Street (House))
HABS LA-27-E
HABS LA,36-NEWOR,77E-
1ph/1pc L

Faubourg Marigny District (2447-2449 Royal Street (House))
HABS LA-27-A
HABS LA,36-NEWOR,77A-
3ph/1pc L

Faubourg Marigny District (Spain & Burgundy Streets (General View))
HABS LA-27-B
HABS LA,36-NEWOR,77B-
1ph/1pc L

Federal Jail; see U. S. Branch Mint

Fernandez-Tissot House ("Tivoli")
1400 Moss St.
HABS LA-1117
HABS LA,36-NEWOR,65-
4dr/1ph/6pg L

Ferrera Tenement House II
3421-3423 Danneel St.
HABS LA-1227
9ph/5pg/1pc H

Ferrera Tenement House 1
3417-3419 Danneel St.
HABS LA-1226
3ph/5pg/1pc H

First Presbyterian Church
South St.
HABS LA-1103
HABS LA,36-NEWOR,51-
2ph/1pg L

Fouche House
619 Bourbon St.
HABS LA-1148
HABS LA,36-NEWOR,78-
5dr/1ph/12pg/1pc/fr L

Fourth Street (General View); see Irish Channel Historic District

Frostall,Edmund J. ,House
920 Saint Louis St.
HABS LA-1114
HABS LA,36-NEWOR,62-
2ph/8pg L

Gaillard House
915-917 Saint Ann St.
HABS LA-69
HABS LA,36-NEWOR,79-
5ph/1pc L

Gallier Hall; see City Hall

Gallier House
1132 Royal St.
HABS LA-1211
HABS 1991(HABS):31
27dr/fr L

Gally House
536 Chartres St.
HABS LA-29
HABS LA,36-NEWOR,14-
24dr/18ph/5pg/fr L

Gaudet House
Chestnut & Josephine Sts.
HABS LA-1149
HABS LA,36-NEWOR,80-
17ph/2pc L

George,Sieur,House; see Skyscraper,First

Girod House
500-506 Chartres St.
HABS LA-18-9
HABS LA,36-NEWOR,8-
32dr/19ph/23pg/fr L

524 Governor Nichols Street (House)
HABS LA-1150
HABS LA,36-NEWOR,2E-
5ph L

Grailhe Family Tomb
N. Claiborne St.
HABS LA-1108
HABS LA,36-NEWOR,56-
5dr/4ph/2pg L

Grandchamp's Pharmacie; see Vieux Carre Squares

Grinnan-Henderson-Reilly House; see Grinnan,Robert A. ,House

Grinnan,Robert A. ,House
(Grinnan-Henderson-Reilly House)
2221 Prytania St.
HABS LA-1120
HABS LA,36-NEWOR,23-
6dr/10ph/12pg L

Grinnan,Robert A. ,House (Garconniere)
2221 Prytania St.
HABS LA-1121
HABS LA,36-NEWOR,23A-
2ph/1pc L

Hearn,Lafcadio,Domicile; see Vieux Carre Squares

Herman-Grima House
820 Saint Louis St.
HABS LA-1122
HABS LA,36-NEWOR,68-
6ph/5pg L

Herman-Grima House (Garconniere & Kitchen)
820 Saint Louis St.
HABS LA-1123
HABS LA,36-NEWOR,69-
2ph L

Holy Rosary Convent; see Michel-Pitot House

Irish Channel Historic District (Fourth Street (General View))
HABS LA-28-A
HABS LA,36-NEWOR,82A-
3ph/1pc L

Irish Channel Historic District
(Rousseau Street)
HABS LA-28-B
HABS LA,36-NEWOR,82B-
1ph/1pc L

Jackson House; see Louisiana State Museum Building

Jorda,Jayme,House,Site of; see Vieux Carre Squares

Jourdan Property,Site of; see Vieux Carre Squares

Kerlerec & Pauger Streets (General View); see Faubourg Marigny District

Kohn-Anglade House; see Vieux Carre Squares

Kohn-Anglade House (Dependencies); see Vieux Carre Squares

Lacoste,Jean,Cottage; see Vieux Carre Squares

Lafayette's Blacksmith Shop; see 941 Bourbon Street (Cottage)

Lafitte Bank; see Chesneau Mansion

Lanoix,Louis,House
514-516-518 Toulouse St.
HABS LA-1115
HABS LA,36-NEWOR,63-
8dr/1ph/7pg/fr L

LaRionda Cottage
1218-1220 Burgundy St.
HABS LA-192
HABS LA,36-NEWOR,20-
12dr/3ph/2pg/fr L

Latour & Laclotte's Atelier
625-627 Dauphine St.
HABS LA-1151
HABS LA,36-NEWOR,83-
4dr/1ph/1pc/fr L

Laundry (Cardau Drugs); see Faubourg Marigny District

Lear,Alton House
2016-2018 Louisiana Ave.
HABS LA-1224
7ph/5pg/1pc H

Lemonnier House; see Skyscraper,First

Lombard Manor House
HABS LA-1197
HABS 1991(HABS):31
16dr/fr L

Louisiana State Bank
403 Royal St.
HABS LA-18-8
HABS LA,36-NEWOR,7-
18dr/9ph/12pg/fr L

Louisiana State Museum Building
(Calaboose Building)
616 Orleans Alley
HABS LA-18-10-A
HABS LA,36-NEWOR,9B-
2ph L

Louisiana State Museum Building
(Jackson House)
Saint Peter St. & Cabildo Ave.
HABS LA-18-10-B
HABS LA,36-NEWOR,9A-
3ph L

Louisiana State Museum Buildings
HABS LA-18-10
HABS LA,36-NEWOR,9-
12dr/5ph/3pg/fr L

Louisiana Sugar Exchange
N. Front & Bienville Sts.
HABS LA-1110
HABS LA,36-NEWOR,58-
3ph/3pg L

Madame John's Legacy
632 Dumaine St.
HABS LA-39
HABS LA,36-NEWOR,16-
4dr/5ph/5pg L

Marine Hospital
HABS LA-1153
HABS LA,36-NEWOR,84-
12ph/2pg L

Meilleur House; see Vieux Carre Squares

Merieult House; see Vieux Carre Squares

Merieult Stables; see Vieux Carre Squares

Documentation: **ct** color transparencies **dr** measured drawings **fr** field records
pc photograph captions **pg** pages of text **ph** photographs

Michel-Pitot House (Holy Rosary Convent)
1370 Moss St. (moved to 1440 Moss St.)
HABS LA-1116
HABS LA,36-NEWOR,64-
6dr/1ph/8pg L

Municipal Hall; see City Hall

New Orleans Sewerage & Water Board; see Pumping Station No. 6

Nichols,Valery,House (Casa Flinard)
723 Toulouse St.
HABS LA-33
HABS LA,36-NEWOR,15-
18dr/19ph/8pg/fr L

Nolte,Vincent,House; see Vieux Carre Squares

Olivier,David,House (Olivier,David,Plantation)
4111 Chartres St.
HABS LA-70
HABS LA,36-NEWOR,49-
4dr/8ph/5pg L

Olivier,David,Plantation; see Olivier,David,House

Orleans Ball Room
717 Orleans St.
HABS LA-1155
HABS LA,36-NEWOR,85-
6dr/4ph/12pg/1pc/fr L

Our Lady of Guadaloupe Roman Catholic Church; see St. Anthony's Chapel

1436 Pauger Street (Cottage)
HABS LA-23
HABS LA,36-NEWOR,12-
6dr/4ph/4pg/fr L

1451 Pauger Street (House); see Faubourg Marigny District

1463 Pauger Street (House); see Faubourg Marigny District

Pension de Boulanger,Site of; see Vieux Carre Squares

Peychaud House (Service Wing); see Vieux Carre Squares

Pitot House
HABS LA-1229
HABS DLC/PP-1993:LA-1
13dr/fr L

Planter's Association Office; see Vieux Carre Squares

Poeyfarre House; see Vieux Carre Squares

Poeyfarre Houses; see Vieux Carre Squares

Presbytere
Jackson Square
HABS LA-18-5
HABS LA,36-NEWOR,5-
22dr/15ph/12pg/fr L

Pretre Mansion,Le
716 Dauphine St.
HABS LA-53
HABS LA,36-NEWOR,18-
26dr/13ph/6pg/fr L

Pumping Station No. 6 (New Orleans Sewerage & Water Board)
Orpheum Ave. & Hyacinth St.
HABS LA-1235
9dr H

Ramsey,James,Commercial Building; see Vieux Carre Squares

Robinson-Jordan House
1415 Third St.
HABS LA-1156
HABS LA,36-NEWOR,86-
8ph/1pg/1pc L

Roche,Widow,House; see Vieux Carre Squares

Rouselle House
202-2014 Louisiana Ave.
HABS LA-1225
6ph/5pg/1pc H

Rousseau Street; see Irish Channel Historic District

Rouzan Residence; see Vieux Carre Squares

Royal House Hotel; see Vieux Carre Squares

Royal Street (Commercial Buildings)
HABS LA-176
HABS LA,36-NEWOR,87-
15ph/2pc L

2447-2449 Royal Street (House); see Faubourg Marigny District

600 Royal Street (House)
HABS LA-1175
HABS 1984(HABS):293
fr L

San Antoine Mortuary Chapel; see St. Anthony's Chapel

Second District,Square Number 62; see Vieux Carre Squares

Short,Col. Robert Henry,House
1448 Fourth St.
HABS LA-1112
HABS LA,36-NEWOR,60-
6ph/6pg L

Skyscraper,First (George,Sieur,House; Lemonnier House)
HABS LA-21
HABS LA,36-NEWOR,10-
20dr/15ph/17pg/fr L

618 South Street (House)
HABS LA-1171
HABS 1984(HABS):293
fr L

Spain & Burgundy Streets (General View); see Faubourg Marigny District

Spanish Comandancia; see Vieux Carre Squares

Spanish Custom House
1300 Moss St.
HABS LA-18-3
HABS LA,36-NEWOR,3-
12dr/14ph/7pg/fr L

St. Anthony's Chapel (Our Lady of Guadaloupe Roman Catholic Church; San Antoine Mortuary Chapel)
411 N. Ramparti St.
HABS LA-1104
HABS LA,36-NEWOR,52-
3ph/1pg L

St. John the Baptist Church
1117-1139 Dryades St.
HABS LA-1105
HABS LA,36-NEWOR,53-
1ph/1pg L

St. Joseph's Orphan Asylum; see Convent of Notre Dame

St. Mary's Assumption Church
2030 Constance St.
HABS LA-1106
HABS LA,36-NEWOR,54-
1ph/2pg L

St. Patrick's Roman Catholic Church
724 Camp St.
HABS LA-1111
HABS LA,36-NEWOR,59-
13ph/5pg L

514-516 St. Philip Street (House)
HABS LA-1174
HABS 1984(HABS):293
fr L

931 St. Philip Street (House)
HABS LA-160
HABS LA,36-NEWOR,72-
1ph/1pc L

Taney,C. H. ,House
908 Saint Louis St.
HABS LA-1160
HABS LA,36-NEWOR,88-
6ph/1pc L

1617-1619 Teche Street (House)
HABS LA-25
HABS LA,36-NEWOR,70-
4ph/1pg/1pc/fr L

Troxler-Psayla Cottage
919 Saint Philip St.
HABS LA-196
HABS LA,36-NEWOR,22-
4dr L

U. S. Branch Mint (Federal Jail)
400 Esplanade Ave.
HABS LA-1119
HABS LA,36-NEWOR,67-
11ph/17pg L

U. S. Custom House
423 Canal St.
HABS LA-1109
HABS LA,36-NEWOR,57-
14ph/7pg L

Ursuline's Row Houses (1107-1133 Decatur Street (Commercial Buildings))
HABS LA-1101-41
HABS LA,36-NEWOR,2D-
5ph L

Vieux Carre Squares (Antoine's Annex)
719-723-725 Saint Louis St.
HABS LA-1100-A
HABS LA,36-NEWOR,41-
30pg L

Vieux Carre Squares (Antoine's Restaurant; Ramsey,James,Commercial Building)
713-717 Saint Louis St.
HABS LA-1100-B
HABS LA,36-NEWOR,40-
12pg L

Vieux Carre Squares (Baker d'Acquin's House)
720-724 Toulouse St.
HABS LA-1100-D
HABS LA,36-NEWOR,45-
17pg L

Vieux Carre Squares (Boimare-Schloeman Building)
509-511 Royal St.
HABS LA-1100-E
HABS LA,36-NEWOR,28-
9pg L

Vieux Carre Squares (Cafe Toulousin)
732 Toulouse St.
HABS LA-1100-F
HABS LA,36-NEWOR,47-
9pg L

Vieux Carre Squares (Coffini Cottage)
726-728 Toulouse St.
HABS LA-1100-G
HABS LA,36-NEWOR,46-
16pg L

Vieux Carre Squares (Counting House of William Nott & Company; Antoine's Restaurant (Service Building); Spanish Comandancia)
519 Royal St.
HABS LA-1100-H
HABS LA,36-NEWOR,30-
31pg L

Vieux Carre Squares (deArmas,Felix,House,Site of)
513 Royal St.
HABS LA-1100-C
HABS LA,36-NEWOR,29-
3pg L

Vieux Carre Squares (Grandchamp's Pharmacie)
501 Royal St.
HABS LA-1100-I
HABS LA,36-NEWOR,26-
14pg L

Vieux Carre Squares (Jorda,Jayme,House,Site of)
521-523 Royal St.
HABS LA-1100-J
HABS LA,36-NEWOR,31-
20pg L

Vieux Carre Squares (Jourdan Property,Site of)
500 Bourbon St.
HABS LA-1100-K
HABS LA,36-NEWOR,34-
23pg L

Vieux Carre Squares (Kohn-Anglade House; Hearn,Lafcadio,Domicile)
516 Bourbon St.
HABS LA-1100-L
HABS LA,36-NEWOR,36-
16pg L

Vieux Carre Squares (Kohn-Anglade House (Dependencies))
508 Bourbon St.
HABS LA-1100-M
HABS LA,36-NEWOR,35-
1pg L

Vieux Carre Squares (Lacoste,Jean,Cottage)
526 Bourbon St.
HABS LA-1100-N
HABS LA,36-NEWOR,38-
25pg L

Vieux Carre Squares (Meilleur House)
511-515 Bourbon St.
HABS LA-1100-X
HABS LA,36-NEWOR,89-
5dr/1ph/1pc/fr L

Vieux Carre Squares (Merieult House)
527-533 Royal St.
HABS LA-1100-O
HABS LA,36-NEWOR,32-
35pg L

Vieux Carre Squares (Merieult Stables; Royal House Hotel)
718 Toulouse St.
HABS LA-1100-P
HABS LA,36-NEWOR,44-
17pg L

Vieux Carre Squares (Nolte,Vincent,House; "Court of the Lions")
535-541 Royal St. & 708 Toulouse St.
HABS LA-1100-Q
HABS LA,36-NEWOR,33-
20pg/fr L

Vieux Carre Squares (Pension de Boulanger,Site of)
727-733 Saint Louis St.
HABS LA-1100-R
HABS LA,36-NEWOR,42-
10pg L

Vieux Carre Squares (Peychaud House (Service Wing))
727 Toulouse St.
HABS LA-41
HABS LA,36-NEWOR,17-
5dr L

Vieux Carre Squares (Planter's Association Office)
714 Toulouse St.
HABS LA-1100-S
HABS LA,36-NEWOR,43-
4pg L

Vieux Carre Squares (Poeyfarre House)
532 Bourbon St.
HABS LA-1100-T
HABS LA,36-NEWOR,39-
9pg L

Vieux Carre Squares (Poeyfarre Houses)
734-740 Toulouse St. & 540 Bourbon St.
HABS LA-1100-U
HABS LA,36-NEWOR,48-
11pg L

Vieux Carre Squares (Roche,Widow,House)
HABS LA-1100-V
HABS LA,36-NEWOR,27-
16pg L

Vieux Carre Squares (Rouzan Residence)
522 Bourbon St.
HABS LA-1100-W
HABS LA,36-NEWOR,37-
5pg L

Vieux Carre Squares (Second District,Square Number 62)
Royal,Bourbon,Saint Louis, & Toulouse Sts.
HABS LA-1100
HABS LA,36-NEWOR,25-
2dr/14pg L

Villa Meilleur
1418 Governor Nichols St.
HABS LA-1216
HABS 1992(HABS):LA-1
45dr/fr L

NEW ORLEANS VIC.

Bayou St. John Hotel (Ruins); see Spanish Fort (Ruins)

Fort St. John (Ruins); see Spanish Fort (Ruins)

Spanish Fort (Ruins) (Fort St. John (Ruins); Bayou St. John Hotel (Ruins))
Bayou Saint John at Lake Pontchartrain
HABS LA-18-25
HABS LA,36-NEWOR.V,1-
5dr/27ph/14pg/fr L

OUACHITA PARISH

MONROE

Cooley,G.B.,House
1011 S. Grand Street
HABS LA-1230
HABS DLC/PP-1993:LA-1
7dr/fr L

Layton Castle
1133 S. Grand
HABS LA-1231
HABS DLC/PP-1993:LA-1
9dr/fr L

Documentation: **ct** color transparencies **dr** measured drawings **fr** field records
pc photograph captions **pg** pages of text **ph** photographs

PLAQUEMINES PARISH

Frank's Island Lighthouse
North East Pass,Mississippi River
HABS LA-19
HABS LA,38- ,1-
1dr/7ph/6pg L

POINTE COUPEE PARISH

BATCHELOR

Lakeside Plantation,Pigeonniers
HABS LA-1180-A
HABS 1991(HABS):31
4dr L

LAKELAND

Alma Sugarcane Plantation
HABS LA-1239
18dr/fr H

NEW ROADS

Labatut Plantation
4 mi. N. of New Roads on River Rd. Facing Miss. R.
HABS LA-1205
HABS 1991(HABS):31
3dr/fr L

Labatut Plantation, Main House
4 mi. N. of New Roads on River R. facing Miss. R.
HABS LA-1205-A
HABS 1991(HABS):31
20dr/fr L

Pleasant View Farms
HABS LA-152
HABS LA,39-NEWRO,1-
2ph/1pc L

NEW ROADS VIC.

Le Veau House
Chenal vic.
HABS LA-95
HABS LA,39-NEWRO.V,3-
3ph/1pc L

Parlange Plantation
State Hwy. 93
HABS LA-34
HABS LA,39-NEWRO.V,1-;DLC/PP-1993:LA-2
21dr/15ph/5pg/fr L

Riche,Fannie,Plantation
State Hwy. 30
HABS LA-35
HABS LA,39-NEWRO.V,2-
21dr/11ph/7pg/fr L

Riche,Fannie,Plantation
(Riche,Fannie,Plantation,Negro Cabin)
State Hwy. 30
HABS LA-35-A
HABS LA,39-NEWRO.V,2A-
2dr/4ph L

Riche,Fannie,Plantation,Negro Cabin; see Riche,Fannie,Plantation

OSCAR VIC.

Austerlitz Plantation
St. Hwy. 1
HABS LA-1228
HABS 1991(HABS):31;DLC/PP-1993:LA-1
9dr/fr L

Riverlake Plantation
HABS LA-1187
HABS 1991(HABS):31
19dr/fr L

Riverlake Plantation,Pigeonnier One
HABS LA-1187-A
HABS 1991(HABS):31
1dr L

Riverlake Plantation,Pigeonnier Two
HABS LA-1187-B
HABS 1991(HABS):31
3dr L

Riverlake Plantation,Sugar Mill
HABS LA-146
HABS LA,39-OSC.V,1-
2ph/1pc L

RAPIDES PARISH

ALEXANDRIA

O'Shee House
1606 Fourth St.
HABS LA-1177
HABS LA,40-ALEX,1-
12ph/18pg/1pc L

ALEXANDRIA VIC.

Bailey's Dam
Red River
HAER LA-6
HAER 1987(HAER):28
21ph/12pg/2pc L

Baillio,Peter,House (Kent)
Bayou Rapids
HABS LA-2-1
HABS LA,40-ALEX.V,1-
2ph L

Kent; see Baillio,Peter,House

CHAMBERS VIC.

Rosalie Plantation
HABS LA-1232
2dr H

Rosalie Plantation,Sugarhouse
Rosalie Plantation
HABS LA-1232-A
HABS DLC/PP-1993:LA-1
2dr/fr L

FRANKLIN

Sterling Sugar Mill
Parish Rd. 28 (Sterling Rd.)
HABS LA-1210
HABS 1992(HABS):LA-1
12dr/fr L

LECOMPTE VIC.

Meeker Sugar Cooperative
U.S. Hwy 71
HABS LA-1191
HABS 1991(HABS):31
2dr/fr L

Meeker Sugar Cooperative,Administrative Office
U.S. Hwy 71
HABS LA-1191-E
HABS 1991(HABS):31
2dr/fr L

Meeker Sugar Cooperative,Chemist's Office
U.S. Hwy 71
HABS LA-1191-D
HABS 1991(HABS):31
1dr/fr L

Meeker Sugar Cooperative,Sugar Mill
U.S. Hwy 71
HABS LA-1191-A
HABS 1991(HABS):31
5dr/fr L

Meeker Sugar Cooperative,Syrup Canning Bldg.
U.S. Hwy 71
HABS LA-1191-B
HABS 1991(HABS):31
1dr/fr L

Meeker Sugar Cooperative,Warehouse & Privy
U.S. Hwy 71
HABS LA-1191-C, LA-1191-F
HABS 1991(HABS):31
3dr L

LONGLEAF

Cromwell Lumber Mill
U. S. Hwy. 165
HABS LA-1233
HABS DLC/PP-1993:LA-1
15dr/fr L

ST. BERNARD PARISH

MISSISSIPPI RIVER

Beauregard,Rene,House
HABS LA-18-7
HABS LA,44-CHALM,1-
9dr/11ph/5pg/fr L

ST. CHARLES PARISH

DESTREHAN

Destrehan Plantation
River Rd.
HABS LA-1212
HABS 1992(HABS):LA-1
37dr/fr L

Destrehan Plantation, Garconierres
River Rd.
HABS LA-1212-A
HABS 1992(HABS):LA-1
1dr L

HAHNVILLE

Homeplace Plantation
River Rd.
HABS LA-155
HABS LA,45-HAHNV,1-
12dr/20ph/3pg/fr L

Lehmann,Dr. ,House
HABS LA-194
HABS LA,45-HAHNV,2-
1ph L

HANHVILLE

Zeringue House
Hanhville Triangle
HABS LA-1181
HABS 1991(HABS):31
13dr L

SAINT ROSE

Ormond Plantation
State Hwy. 1
HABS LA-18-13
HABS LA,45-DEST.V,1-
14dr/12ph/7pg/fr L

SAINT ROSE VIC.

Barbarra Plantation (Garconniere)
(Rose Plantation)
HABS LA-18-12
HABS LA,45-SAIRO.V,1-
12dr/10ph/5pg/fr L

Rose Plantation; see Barbarra Plantation (Garconniere)

ST. JAMES PARISH

???

Bagatelle Plantation
East River Rd. (moved to Iberville Parish)
HABS LA-1142
HABS LA,47- ,1-
10dr/20ph/7pg/2pc/fr L

Bagatelle Plantation,North Kitchen Support Bldg.
E. River Rd. (moved to Iberville Parish)
HABS LA-1142-B
HABS LA,47- ,1B-
1ph/1pc L

Bagatelle Plantation,South Kitchen Support Bldg.
E. River Rd. (moved to Iberville Parish)
HABS LA-1142-A
HABS LA,47- ,1A-
3ph/1pc L

Bagatelle Plantation,South Slave Cabin
E. River Rd. (moved to Iberville Parish)
HABS LA-1142-C
HABS LA,47- ,1C-
4ph/1pc L

Bagatelle Plantation,Stables
E. River Rd. (moved to Iberville Parish)
HABS LA-1142-D
HABS LA,47- ,1D-
1ph/1pc L

CONVENT VIC.

Uncle Sam Plantation
HABS LA-74
HABS LA,47-CONV.V,1-
17dr/30ph/3pg/fr L

ST. JAMES

Crescent Farm Plantation
SW of River Rd.
HABS LA-1195
HABS 1991(HABS):31
1dr L

Graugnard Farms Plantation
HABS LA-1202
HABS 1991(HABS):31
13dr/fr L

Hymel House
SW of River Rd. on Crescent Farm Plantation
HABS LA-1200
HABS 1991(HABS):31
10dr/fr L

Robicheaux House
SW of River Rd. on Crescent Farm Plantation
HABS LA-1199
HABS 1991(HABS):31
5dr/fr L

UNION VIC.

Academy,The
HABS LA-1161
HABS LA,47-UNI.V,1-
3ph L

VACHERIE

Laura Plantation
River Rd.
HABS LA-1213
HABS 1992(HABS):LA-1
17dr/fr L

Laura Plantation,Main House
River Rd.
HABS LA-1213-A
HABS DLC/PP-1992:LA-2
15dr L

Laura Plantation,Second House
River Rd.
HABS LA-1213-B
HABS DLC/PP-1992:LA-2
7dr L

ST. JOHN THE BAPTIST PARISH

Angelina Plantation (Dove Cote & Doll House)
State Hwy. 1
HABS LA-18-14
HABS LA,48-MOTAI.V,1-
8dr/5ph/5pg/fr L

EDGARD

Columbia Plantation
HABS LA-1204
HABS 1991(HABS):31
13dr/fr L

Kroll Plantation
HABS LA-1198
HABS 1991(HABS):31
9dr/fr L

LA PLACE

Lougue Plantation; see Montegut Plantation

Montegut Plantation (Lougue Plantation)
HABS LA-1189
HABS 1991(HABS):31
9dr L

LUCY

Glendale Plantation
HABS LA-150
HABS LA,48-LUCY,1- ı1991(HABS):31°
26dr/3ph/fr L

RESERVE VIC.

Evergreen Plantation
HABS LA-1236
37dr/fr H

WALLACE

Whitney Plantation
LA Rt. 18
HABS LA-1194
HABS 1992(HABS):LA-1
6dr L

Whitney Plantation Outbuildings
LA Rt. 18
HABS LA-1194-A
13dr H

ST. LANDRY PARISH

GRAND COTEAU

Convent of the Sacred Heart
HABS LA-54
HABS LA,49-GRANC,1-
1ph L

Petetin's Store
HABS LA-86
HABS LA,49-GRANC,2-
1ph L

Documentation: **ct** color transparencies **dr** measured drawings **fr** field records
pc photograph captions **pg** pages of text **ph** photographs

KROTZ SPRINGS

Atchafalaya River Bridge; see Krotz Springs Bridge

Krotz Springs Bridge (U. S. Route 190 Bridge; Atchafalaya River Bridge)
Spanning Atchafalaya River
HAER LA-7
HAER LA,49-KROSP,1-
34ph/9pg/2pc L

U. S. Route 190 Bridge; see Krotz Springs Bridge

OPELOUSAS

Dupre,Governor Jacques,Gravesite
Opelousas Cemetery
HABS LA-1196
HABS 1991(HABS):31
4dr L

Dupre,Governor Jacques,House
Adjacent to Jct. LA Hwy. 10 & U.S. Hwy. 167
HABS LA-1201
HABS 1991(HABS):31
10dr/fr L

Hebrard House
304 Bellevue St.
HABS LA-83
HABS LA,49-OPEL,1-
1ph L

OPELOUSAS VIC.

Lastrapes House
HABS LA-89
HABS LA,49-OPEL.V,1-
6dr/13ph/1pg/fr L

Live Oak Plantation House (Powers Place,Old)
Betwen Opelousas & Washington,Louisiana
HABS LA-1188
HABS 1991(HABS):31
12dr L

Powers Place,Old; see Live Oak Plantation House

SUNSET VIC.

Chretien Point Plantation
HABS LA-64
HABS LA,49-SUN.V,1-
9dr/21ph/6pg/fr L

WASHINGTON

Hinckley House
De Jean St.
HABS LA-1162
HABS LA,49-WASH,2-
4dr L

Immaculate Conception Catholic Church
Moundville St.
HABS LA-1163
HABS LA,49-WASH,3-
7dr L

Lyons Warehouse
Water & Main Sts.
HABS LA-1164
HABS LA,49-WASH,4-
6dr L

Magnolia Ridge
De Jean St.
HABS LA-1165
HABS LA,49-WASH,5-
4dr L

Nicholson House
Corso St.
HABS LA-1166
HABS LA,49-WASH,6-
3dr L

Pierrel,A. S. ,House
De Jean St.
HABS LA-1167
HABS LA,49-WASH,7-
5dr L

Schmit Hotel
HABS LA-195
HABS LA,49-WASH,1-
1ph L

Schulze House
Water St.
HABS LA-1168
HABS LA,49-WASH,8-
4dr L

Wartelle Plantation
HABS LA-1203
HABS 1991(HABS):31
18dr/fr L

Wolff,J. ,House
Main St.
HABS LA-1169
HABS LA,49-WASH,9-
6dr L

ST. MARTIN PARISH

RUTH

Bayou Teche Bridge
Spanning Bayou Teche
HAER LA-8
HAER LA,50-RUTH,1-
11ph/9pg/1pc L

ST. MARTINVILLE

Fontenette House
Intersection of Main & Hamilton Sts.
HABS LA-1182
HABS 1991(HABS):31
6dr L

Foti Townhouse
132 S. Main St.
HABS LA-1184
HABS 1991(HABS):31
2dr L

Gary Building (Tertrou-Broussard Store)
214-216 S. Main St.
HABS LA-1183
HABS 1991(HABS):31
1dr L

Martin House
HABS LA-1185
HABS 1991(HABS):31
11dr/fr L

Tertrou-Broussard Store; see Gary Building

ST. MARTINVILLE VIC.

St. John Plantation
State Hwy. 347
HABS LA-1186
HABS 1991(HABS):31
1dr L

St. John Plantation,Creole Cottage One
State Hwy. 347
HABS LA-1186-A
HABS 1991(HABS):31
3dr L

St. John Plantation,Creole Cottage Two
State HWY. 347
HABS LA-1186-B
HABS 1991(HABS):31
3dr L

WEBSTER PARISH

DOYLINE

Louisiana Army Ammunition Plant
HAER LA-3
HAER LA,60-DOY,1-
50pg/fr L

WEST FELICIANA PARISH

BAINS

Greenwood Plantation (Ventress)
HABS LA-16
HABS LA,63-BAI,1-
4dr L

Ventress; see Greenwood Plantation

SAINT FRANCISVILLE

Afton Villa
Hwy. 61
HABS LA-58
HABS LA,63-SAIFR.V,1-
4ph/1pg L

Rosedown Plantation
HABS LA-1101
HABS LA,63-SAIFR,1-
18ph/3pg L

WEYANOKE

St. Mary's Episcopal Church
Ner LA Hwy. 66
HABS LA-1218
10dr/fr L

WEYANOKE VIC.

Live Oak Plantation House
Between Weyanoke & Bains
HABS LA-17
HABS LA,63-WEY.V,1-
14dr/10ph/3pg/fr L

Portland Breakwater Lighthouse, South Portland, Cumberland County, Maine. West (door) elevation. Photograph by Gerda Peterich, September 1962 (HABS ME,3-PORTS,1-2).

Maine

ANDROSCOGGIN COUNTY

LEWISTON

Lewiston City Hall
Pine & Park Sts.
HABS ME-174
HABS ME,1-LEW,1-
6ph/6pg/1pc/fr L

CUMBERLAND COUNTY

BAILEY ISLAND

Bailey Island Bridge
HAER ME-5
HAER ME,3-BAILI,1-
16ph/1pg/1pc/3ct L

BRUNSWICK

Bowdoin College,Massachusetts Hall
Bath St.
HABS ME-109
HABS ME,3-BRU,1-
5dr/10ph/6pg L

CAPE ELIZABETH

Brown-Donahue House (Brown,C. A. ,House; Donahue,Helen,House)
Delano Park
HABS ME-119
HABS ME,3-CAPEL,1-
6dr/7ph/7pg/fr L

Brown,C. A. ,House; see Brown-Donahue House

Donahue,Helen,House; see Brown-Donahue House

Portland Head Light
Portland Head,E. of Shore Rd.
HABS ME-123
HABS ME,3-CAPEL,2-
3dr/14ph/7pg/fr L

FALMOUTH VIC.

Merrill,James,House
Falmouth Rd.
HABS ME-115
HABS ME,3-FAL.V,1-
7ph/5pg L

HARPSWELL

Harpswell Neck Road Meetinghouse (Harpswell Neck Road Townhouse)
State Rt. 123
HABS ME-58
HABS ME,3-HARP,1-
13dr/8ph/2pg/fr L

Harpswell Neck Road Townhouse; see Harpswell Neck Road Meetinghouse

PORTLAND

Bailey,Deacon John,House
1235 Congress St.
HABS ME-4
HABS ME,3-PORT,9-
10dr/8ph/2pg/fr L

Bethel Building; see Mariners' Church

Children's Hospital; see Storer-Mussey House

Churchill House; see Ingraham-Preble-Churchill House

Clapp,Charles Q.,House (School of Fine & Applied Art; Portland Art School)
97 Spring St.
HABS ME-62
HABS ME,3-PORT,19-
12dr/4ph/5pg/1pc/fr L

First Parish Church (Unitarian)
425 Congress St.
HABS ME-6
HABS ME,3-PORT,3-
18dr/3ph/6pg/fr L

Fort Gorges
Hog Island Ledge,Portland Harbor
HABS ME-134
HABS ME,3-PORT,20-
2dr/23ph/5pg/2pc/fr L

Hunnewell-Shepley House; see Shepley House

Ingraham-Preble-Churchill House (Churchill House)
51 State St.
HABS ME-35
HABS ME,3-PORT,2-
5ph/2pg L

Longfellow,Henry W. ,House; see Wadsworth-Longfellow House

Mariners' Church (Bethel Building)
Fore St.
HABS ME-135
HABS ME,3-PORT,21-
4ph/5pg/1pc L

McLellan-Sweat House (McLellan,Hugh,House; Sweat,Lorenzo de Medici,House)
111 High St.
HABS ME-121
HABS ME,3-PORT,6-
5dr/10ph/9pg/1pc/fr L

McLellan,Hugh,House; see McLellan-Sweat House

Mechanics' Hall
159 Congress St.
HABS ME-129
HABS ME,3-PORT,16-
3ph L

Morse-Libby House (Victoria Mansion)
109 Danforth St.
HABS ME-53
HABS ME,3-PORT,15-
2dr/17ph/fr L

Munjoy Hill Observatory; see Portland Observatory

Mussey,John,House; see Storer-Mussey House

Park Street Block
Park,Spring & Gray Sts.
HABS ME-118
HABS ME,3-PORT,23
4dr/5ph/5pg/1pc/fr L

Portland Art School; see Clapp,Charles Q.,House

Portland Club; see Shepley House

Portland Merchants' Exchange
Middle St.
HABS ME-133
HABS ME,3-PORT,18-
2ph L

Portland Observatory (Munjoy Hill Observatory)
138 Congress St.
HABS ME-1
HABS ME,3-PORT,7-
4dr/1ph/1pg L

School of Fine & Applied Art; see Clapp,Charles Q.,House

Shepley House (Hunnewell-Shepley House; Portland Club)
156 State St.
HABS ME-127
HABS ME,3-PORT,24-
5ph/1pg/1pc L

Stevens,John Calvin,House
52 Bowdoin St.
HABS ME-137
HABS ME,3-PORT,17-
11ph/8pg L

Storer-Mussey House (Children's Hospital; Mussey,John,House)
91 Danforth St. NW
HABS ME-31
HABS ME,3-PORT,1-
15ph/2pg/fr L

Sweat,Lorenzo de Medici,House; see McLellan-Sweat House

U. S. Customs House
312 Fore St.
HABS ME-138
HABS ME,3-PORT,25-
24ph/6pg/2pc L

U. S. Post Office & Courthouse,Old
169 Middle St.
HABS ME-120
HABS ME,3-PORT,11-
11ph/8pg L

Union Wharf Building (19-22)
Commercial St.
HABS ME-114
HABS ME,3-PORT,10-
5dr/3ph/6pg/fr L

Victoria Mansion; see Morse-Libby House

Wadsworth-Longfellow House (Longfellow,Henry W. ,House)
487 Congress St.
HABS ME-2
HABS ME,3-PORT,8-
13dr/9ph/3pg/fr L

Woodman Building
140 Middle St.
HABS ME-136
HABS ME,3-PORT,26-
12ph/7pg/1pc L

SABBATHDAY LAKE

Shaker Church Family Barns
Sabbathday Lake,State Rt. 26
HABS ME-167
HABS ME,3-SAB,2-
2ph L

Shaker Church Family Boys' Shop
Sabbathday Lake,State Rt. 26
HABS ME-166
HABS ME,3-SAB,3-
1ph L

Shaker Church Family General View
Sabbathday Lake,State Rt. 26
HABS ME-165
HABS ME,3-SAB,4-
1ph L

Shaker Church Family Washhouse
Sabbathday Lake,State Rt. 26
HABS ME-164
HABS ME,3-SAB,5-
1ph L

Shaker Community Meetinghouse
Sabbathday Lake,State Rt. 26
HABS ME-107
HABS ME,3-SAB,1-
6dr/19ph/5pg/fr L

Shaker Ministry's Shop
Sabbathday Lake,State Rt. 26
HABS ME-163
HABS ME,3-SAB,6-
3ph L

SOUTH PORTLAND

Clipper Ship Snow Squall Bow
Spring Point Museum,Southern Maine Tech. College
HAER ME-7
10dr H

Portland Breakwater Lighthouse
Portland Harbor
HABS ME-112
HABS ME,3-PORTS,1-
3dr/7ph/10pg L

SOUTH WINDHAM VIC.

Babbs Bridge; see Covered Bridge

Covered Bridge (Babbs Bridge)
Harry Cane Rd. spanning Presumpscot River
HABS ME-61
HABS ME,3-WINDS.V,1-
3dr/fr L

STROUDWATER

Means,Capt. James,House
2 Waldo St.
HABS ME-5
HABS ME,3-STROWA,2-
13dr/8ph/2pg L

Tate,George,House
1270 Westbrook St.
HABS ME-3
HABS ME,3-STROWA,1-
14dr/19ph/2pg/fr L

WINDHAM CENTER VIC.

Hanson,Ezekiel,House (Stencils)
Albion Rd.
HABS ME-69
HABS ME,3-WIND.V,1-
9dr/fr L

HANCOCK COUNTY

BAKER ISLAND

Acadia National Park; see Baker Island Light,Lightkeeper's House

Baker Island Light,Lightkeeper's House (Acadia National Park)
HABS ME-172
HABS ME,5-BAKIS,1-
6dr/fr L

Gilley,Elisha,House
HABS ME-171
HABS ME,5-BAKIS,2-
7dr/fr L

BAR HARBOR VIC.

Sieur de Monts Springhouse
Rt. 3 & Park Rd.
HABS ME-173
HABS ME,5-BAHA.V,1-
3dr L

CASTINE

Fort Pentagoet
Perkins St.
HABS ME-13
HABS ME,5-CAST,1-
1ph L

ELLSWORTH

Black,Col. John,House (Woodlawn)
W. Main St. (State Rt. 172)
HABS ME-25
HABS ME,5-ELWO,1-
19ph/3pg/1pc/3ct L

Black,Col. John,House,Carriage House (Woodlawn,Carriage House)
W. Main St. (State Rt. 172)
HABS ME-25-B
HABS ME,5-ELWO,1-B-
1ph/1pc L

Black,Col. John,House,Stables & Carriage House (Woodlawn,Stables & Carriage House)
W. Main St. (State Rt. 172)
HABS ME-25-A
HABS ME,5-ELWO,1-A-
2ph/1pc L

City Library; see Jordan,Benjamin,House

Jordan,Benjamin,House (City Library)
46 State St.
HABS ME-24
HABS ME,5-ELWO,2-
4ph/2pg L

Woodlawn; see Black,Col. John,House

Woodlawn,Carriage House; see Black,Col. John,House,Carriage House

Woodlawn,Stables & Carriage House; see Black,Col. John,House,Stables & Carriage House

LITTLE CRANBERRY IS.

Blue Duck Ships Store
Harborside on Hadlock Cove,Isleford
HABS ME-170
HABS ME,5-LICRIS,1-
6dr/fr L

SOUTHWEST HARBOR VIC

Carroll House
State Rt. 102
HABS ME-169
HABS ME,5-SOUHA.V,1-
6dr/fr L

KENNEBEC COUNTY

AUGUSTA

Fort Western,Main Building
Bowman St.
HABS ME-56
HABS ME,6-AUG,1-
17dr/13ph/3pg/fr L

Maine State House
State & Capitol Sts.
HABS ME-130
HABS ME,6-AUG,2-
4dr/50ph/11pg/5pc/fr L

GARDINER

Christ Church (Episcopal)
1 Dresden Ave.
HABS ME-143
HABS ME,6-GARD,2-
11ph/8pg L

Oaklands
Dresden St. at Kennebec River
HABS ME-113
HABS ME,6-GARD,1-
3dr/14ph/9pg/fr L

HALLOWELL

Bodwell,Gov. Joseph R. ,House
15 Middle St.
HABS ME-160
HABS ME,6-HAL,8-
14ph/6pg L

Building,Granite-Fronted; see Sewall Warehouse

Emporium,The
154 Water St.
HABS ME-156
HABS ME,6-HAL,7-
5ph/5pg L

Gage Block (106-114 Second Street (Row House))
HABS ME-145
HABS ME,6-HAL,1-
2ph/7pg L

Hallowell Mill
HAER ME-2
HAER ME,6-HAL,9-
7ph/2pg/1pc L

Hubbard Free Library
115 Second St.
HABS ME-158
HABS ME,6-HAL,3-
12ph/8pg L

Hubbard,Gov. John,Homestead
52 Winthrop St.
HABS ME-144
HABS ME,6-HAL,5-
23ph/10pg L

106-114 Second Street (Row House); see Gage Block

Sewall Warehouse
(Building,Granite-Fronted)
156 Water St.
HABS ME-150
HABS ME,6-HAL,6-
4ph/8pg L

St. Matthew's Church (Episcopal)
20 Union St.
HABS ME-146
HABS ME,6-HAL,2-
8ph/6pg L

Thing,Capt. Abraham,House
159 Second St.
HABS ME-147
HABS ME,6-HAL,4-
13ph/7pg L

MONMOUTH

Cumston Hall
Main St.
HABS ME-161
HABS ME,6-MON,1-
15ph/5pg L

WINSLOW

Fort Halifax,Blockhouse
U. S. Rt. 201
HABS ME-55
HABS ME,6-WINLO,1-
13dr/2ph/3pg L

KNOX COUNTY

CAMDEN

Cushing,Capt. ,House
31 Chestnut St.
HABS ME-88
HABS ME,7-CAM,1-
3ph/3pg/1pc/fr L

ROCKLAND

Farnsworth,William A. ,Homestead
21 Elm St.
HABS ME-77
HABS ME,7-ROCLA,1-
2dr/9ph/8pg/1pc/fr L

Grand Army Hotel
Limerock & Union Sts.
HABS ME-67
HABS ME,7-ROCLA,4-
1ph/2pg/1pc/fr L

Snow,I. ,House
9 Water St.
HABS ME-96
HABS ME,7-ROCLA,2-
3ph/4pg/1pc/fr L

U. S. Customhouse & Post Office Building
17 School St.
HABS ME-139
HABS ME,7-ROCLA,3-
22ph/7pg L

ROCKLAND VIC.

Saddleback Ledge Lighthouse
Penobscot Bay
HABS ME-79
HABS ME,7-ROCLA.V,1-
3dr/4ph/9pg/1pc/fr L

ROCKPORT

Hanson-Cramer House
Sea St. (moved from Pascal's Ave.)
HABS ME-78
HABS ME,7-ROCPO,1-
2dr/7ph/4pg/fr L

Shepard, H. L. ,Company,Lime Kiln
Rockport Harbor
HABS ME-95
HABS ME,7-ROCPO,2-
4ph/3pg/1pc/fr L

Tyler,Coburn,House Fence
Union St. (Old Camden Rd.)
HABS ME-100
HABS ME,7-ROCPO,3-
1ph/1pg L

ROCKPORT VIC.

McCobb-Dodge House; see Spite House

Spite House (McCobb-Dodge House)
Calderwood Rd. (moved from ME,Phippsburg)
HABS ME-75
HABS ME,7-ROCPO.V,1-
7dr/6ph/4pg/fr L

THOMASTON

North Parish Meetinghouse
St. George Rd. (State Rt. 131)
HABS ME-105
HABS ME,7-THOM,1-
5ph/5pg/1pc/fr L

Ruggles,Judge John,House
29 Main St.
HABS ME-106
HABS ME,7-THOM,2-
5ph/5pg/1pc/fr L

WARREN

Cobb,Miles,Farmhouse
Main St. & State Rt. 131 at Hinchley's Corner
HABS ME-76
HABS ME,7-WAR,1-
2dr/5ph/3pg/fr L

LINCOLN COUNTY

ALNA

Alna District School
State Rt. 218
HABS ME-33
HABS ME,8-ALNA,2-
1dr/1ph/2pg/fr L

Alna Meetinghouse
State Rt. 218
HABS ME-34
HABS ME,8-ALNA,1-
12dr/7ph/2pg/fr L

Jones-Hilton House
HABS ME-178
HABS ME,8-ALNA,3-
2ph/1pc L

BRISTOL VIC.

School House,Old Stone
State Rt. 130
HABS ME-47
HABS ME,8-BRIST.V,1-
4dr/2ph/2pg/fr L

CEDAR GROVE

Bowman-Carney House
State Rt. 128
HABS ME-45
HABS ME,8-CEGRO,2-
15dr/11ph/2pg/fr L

Pownalborough Courthouse
State Rt. 128
HABS ME-42
HABS ME,8-CEGRO,1-
19dr/10ph/1pg/fr L

DAMARISCOTTA

Cottrill,Matthew,House
Main St. (U. S. Rt. 1A)
HABS ME-93
HABS ME,8-DAMAR,1-
3ph/3pg L

Damariscotta Baptist Church
Main St. (U. S. Rt. 1A) & Bristol Rd.
HABS ME-66
HABS ME,8-DAMAR,2-
3ph/2pg/1pc/fr L

Day,Deacon Daniel,House
Bristol Rd. (State Rt. 129)
HABS ME-80
HABS ME,8-DAMARM,2-
6dr/5ph/3pg L

DAMARISCOTTA MILLS

St. Patrick's Roman Catholic Church
State Rt. 215
HABS ME-84
HABS ME,8-DAMARM,3-
2dr/4ph/4pg/fr L

DARMARISCOTTA MILLS

Kavanaugh,James,House
State Rt. 215 at Damariscotta Lake
HABS ME-22
HABS ME,8-DAMARM,1-
6dr/9ph/5pg/fr L

EDGECOMB

Antoinette,Marie,House; see Decker-Clough House

Clough House; see Decker-Clough House

Decker-Clough House (Clough House; Antoinette,Marie,House)
State Rt. 27 (moved from Squam Island)
HABS ME-54
HABS ME,8-EDCO,2-
1ph/2pg L

HEAD TIDE

Clark,Capt. ,House (Spring House)
HABS ME-176
HABS ME,8-HETI,1-
2ph/1pg/1pc L

Head Tide Church
HABS ME-179
HABS ME,8-HETI,2-
12ph/1pg/1pc L

Jewett,Rev. ,Jeremiah,House
HABS ME-175
HABS ME,8-HETI,3-
1ph/1pg/1pc L

Robinson,Edwin Arlington,House
HABS ME-177
HABS ME,8-HETI,4-
2ph/1pg/1pc L

Spring House; see Clark,Capt. ,House

JEFFERSON VIC.

Cattle Pound
State Rt. 126
HABS ME-60
HABS ME,8-JEF.V,1-
1dr/2ph/2pg/fr L

NEWCASTLE

Glidden,William T. ,Austin Block
Main St. (U. S. Rt. 1) & River Rd. (State Rt. 215)
HABS ME-81
HABS ME,8-NEWC,1-
3dr/3ph/3pg/fr L

NEWCASTLE VIC.

Perkins House
Main St.
HABS ME-83
HABS ME,8-NEWC,2-
2dr/5ph/3pg/fr L

NORTH EDGECOMB

Fort Edgecomb,Blockhouse
Davis Island
HABS ME-52
HABS ME,8-EDCON,1-
12dr/1ph/2pg/fr L

WALDOBORO VIC.

German Lutheran Church
State Rt. 32
HABS ME-44
HABS ME,8-WABO,1-
18dr/2ph/3pg/fr L

WALPOLE VIC.

Walpole Meetinghouse
State Rt. 129
HABS ME-50
HABS ME,8-WALP,1-
19dr/8ph/2pg/fr L

WESTPORT ISLAND

Antoinette,Marie,House; see Decker-Clough House

Clough House; see Decker-Clough House

Decker-Clough House (Clough House; Antoinette,Marie,House)
(moved to Sheepscot River & State Rt. 27)
HABS ME-54
HABS ME,8-EDCO,2-
1ph/2pg L

WISCASSET

Academy,Old
Warren & Hodge Sts.
HABS ME-48
HABS ME,8-WISC,4-
9dr/3ph/1pg/fr L

Clark-Wood House
High St.
HABS ME-87
HABS ME,8-WISC,9-
1ph/2pg L

Hodge,Henry,House
Hodge & Main Sts.
HABS ME-49
HABS ME,8-WISC,5-
19dr/12ph/2pg/fr L

Lee,Judge Silas,House
High St.
HABS ME-101
HABS ME,8-WISC,12-
2ph/5pg/1pc/fr L

Lincoln County Courthouse
High St.
HABS ME-97
HABS ME,8-WISC,11-
5ph/6pg/1pc/fr L

Lincoln County Jail,Old
Federal St. (State Rt. 218)
HABS ME-82
HABS ME,8-WISC,7-
3dr/2ph/3pg/fr L

Nickels-Sortwell House (Sortwell House)
Main & Federal Sts.
HABS ME-102
HABS ME,8-WISC,13-
4ph/5pg/1pc/fr L

Page,Samuel,House
Lee St.
HABS ME-91
HABS ME,8-WISC,10-
2ph/4pg/1pc/fr L

Powder House,Old
Churchill St.
HABS ME-70
HABS ME,8-WISC,6-
3dr/fr L

Scott,Capt. George,House
Federal St. (State Rt. 218)
HABS ME-85
HABS ME,8-WISC,8-
2dr/1ph/3pg/fr L

Sortwell House; see Nickels-Sortwell House

OXFORD COUNTY

ANDOVER

Lovejoy Bridge
HAER ME-4
HAER ME,9-AND,1-
3ph/1pg/1pc L

PARIS

Hamlin Memorial Library; see Oxford Country Jail,Old

Hubbard House
Village Green
HABS ME-39
HABS ME,9-PARHI,5-
3ph/2pg L

Kimball House; see Rawson-Kimball House

Mallow House
Village Green
HABS ME-40
HABS ME,9-PARHI,2-
3ph/1pg L

Oxford Country Jail,Old (Hamlin Memorial Library)
Village Green
HABS ME-37
HABS ME,9-PARHI,3-
2dr/10ph/2pg/fr L

Parris,Gov. Albion K. ,Law Office
Village Green
HABS ME-38
HABS ME,9-PARHI,4-
1ph/1pg L

Rawson-Kimball House (Kimball House)
Village Green
HABS ME-41
HABS ME,9-PARHI,1-
3ph/1pg L

PORTER

Porter Meetinghouse
Mill Brook
HABS ME-51
HABS ME,9-PORT,1-
11dr/4ph/2pg L

SAGADAHOC COUNTY

BATH

Central Church (Congregational)
804 Washington St.
HABS ME-148
HABS ME,12-BATH,8-
13ph/8pg L

Church Block
44 Front St.
HABS ME-157
HABS ME,12-BATH,6-
9ph/5pg L

Grace Episcopal Church
Oak & Middle Sts.
HABS ME-110
HABS ME,12-BATH,1-
2dr/5ph/3pg/fr L

Patten,George F. ,House
118 Front St.
HABS ME-141
HABS ME,12-BATH,7-
10ph/8pg L

Percy & Small Shipyard
263 Washington St.
HAER ME-1
HAER ME,12-BATH,10-
20ph/6pg/1pc L

Richardson,Capt. John G. ,House
964 Washington St.
HABS ME-140
HABS ME,12-BATH,2-
11ph/7pg L

Swedenborgian Church
876 Middle St.
HABS ME-151
HABS ME,12-BATH,3-
9ph/6pg L

Tallman,Henry,House
982 High St.
HABS ME-152
HABS ME,12-BATH,9-
13ph/7pg L

U. S. Custom House & Post Office
25 Front St.
HABS ME-153
HABS ME,12-BATH,4-
11ph/8pg L

Winter Street Church (Congregational)
880 Washington St.
HABS ME-154
HABS ME,12-BATH,5-
19ph/9pg L

PHIPPSBURG

McCobb-Dodge House; see Spite House

McCobb-Hill-Minott House
Parker Head Rd.
HABS ME-117
HABS ME,12-PHIP,1-
5dr/9ph/5pg/fr L

Spite House (McCobb-Dodge House) (moved to ME,Rockport Vic. ,Calderwood Rd.)
HABS ME-75
HABS ME,7-ROCPO.V,1-
7dr/6ph/4pg/fr L

PHIPPSBURG VIC.

Drummond Cemetery Wall
State Rts. 209 & 216
HABS ME-63
HABS ME,12-PHIP.V,1-
2dr L

Phippsburg Congregational Church
Gun Hill at Kennebec River
HABS ME-108
HABS ME,12-PHIP.V,2-
2dr/6ph/3pg/fr L

RICHMOND

Richmond-Dresden Union Methodist Church
Pleasant St.
HABS ME-155
HABS ME,12-RICH,3-
7ph/6pg L

Southard,Thomas Jefferson,Block
25 Front St.
HABS ME-159
HABS ME,12-RICH,4-
12ph/8pg L

Southard,Thomas Jefferson,House
17 Church St.
HABS ME-149
HABS ME,12-RICH,2-
13ph/9pg L

Stearns,Capt. David,House
3 Gardiner St.
HABS ME-142
HABS ME,12-RICH,1-
6ph/7pg L

ROBINHOOD

Riggs Cottage; see Riggs,Benjamin,House

Riggs Store Building
Riggs Cove
HABS ME-29
HABS ME,12-ROB,5-
1ph/fr L

Riggs Wharf Buildings
Riggs Cove
HABS ME-30
HABS ME,12-ROB,6-
1ph L

Riggs,Benjamin,House (Riggs Cottage)
Riggs Cove
HABS ME-46
HABS ME,12-ROB,1-
19dr/3ph/2pg/fr L

Riggs,James,House
State Rt. 127
HABS ME-27
HABS ME,12-ROB,2-
2ph L

Riggs,Moses,House
Riggs Cove
HABS ME-28
HABS ME,12-ROB,4-
2ph L

Riggs,Warner,Gravestone
Riggs Family Cemetery,Riggs Cove
HABS ME-59
HABS ME,12-ROB,7-
1dr L

TOPSHAM

Holden,Capt. Daniel,House
24 Elm St.
HABS ME-116
HABS ME,12-TOP,1-
3dr/9ph/7pg/fr L

TOPSHAM VIC.

Hunter,John,Tavern
Topsham-Bowdoinham Rd. (State Rt. 24)
HABS ME-111
HABS ME,12-TOP.V,1-
7dr/8ph/5pg/fr L

SOMERSET COUNTY

NEW PORTLAND

New Portland Suspension Bridge (Wire Bridge)
Spanning Carrabasset River
HAER ME-3
HAER ME,13-NEWPO,1-
14ph/2pg/1pc/1ct L

Wire Bridge; see New Portland Suspension Bridge

WALDO COUNTY

BELFAST

Anderson,Gov. Hugh J. ,House; see Bishop-Anderson House

Avery-Stevens House (Stevens House)
38 Church St.
HABS ME-16
HABS ME,14-BELF,1-
8ph/1pg L

Belfast National Bank
Main & Beaver Sts.
HABS ME-103
HABS ME,14-BELF,13-
4ph/5pg/1pc/fr L

Bishop-Anderson House (Anderson,Gov. Hugh J. ,House)
Church & Anderson Sts.
HABS ME-23
HABS ME,14-BELF,7-
1ph/1pg L

Black Horse Tavern
Searsport Ave. (U. S. Rt. 1)
HABS ME-18
HABS ME,14-BELF,3-
4ph/1pg L

Burrill,William H. ,House
13 Church St.
HABS ME-89
HABS ME,14-BELF,9-
1ph/3pg L

Field,Benjamin,House; see Field,Bohan Prentice,House

Field,Bohan Prentice,House
(Field,Benjamin,House)
139 High St.
HABS ME-19
HABS ME,14-BELF,4-
2ph/1pg L

First Church (Congregational Unitarian)
Church & Spring Sts.
HABS ME-86
HABS ME,14-BELF,8-
1dr/10ph/5pg/2pc/2ct/fr L

Johnson House; see Johnson-Pratt House

Johnson-Pratt House (Johnson House; Johnson,Ralph,House)
100 High St.
HABS ME-20
HABS ME,14-BELF,5-
2dr/1ph/4pg/fr L

Johnson,Judge Alfred W. ,House; see Whittier,Thomas,House

Johnson,Ralph,House; see Johnson-Pratt House

Kimball-Salmon House (Salmon House)
46 Church St.
HABS ME-17
HABS ME,14-BELF,2-
2ph/1pg L

Masonic Temple
Main & High (U. S. Rt. 1A) Sts.
HABS ME-104
HABS ME,14-BELF,14-
4ph/3pg L

Perry House
Searsport Ave. (U. S. Rt. 1)
HABS ME-65
HABS ME,14-BELF,15-
1ph/2pg/1pc/fr L

Salmon House; see Kimball-Salmon House

Shute,Captain William,House
10 Waldo Ave. (State Rt. 137)
HABS ME-99
HABS ME,14-BELF,12-
2ph/3pg L

Stevens House; see Avery-Stevens House

Treadwell,Charles,House
26 Northport Ave. (moved from Miller & High Sts.)
HABS ME-94
HABS ME,14-BELF,11-
4ph/1pg L

White,James P. ,House
1 Church St.
HABS ME-92
HABS ME,14-BELF,10-
7ph/5pg/1pc/fr L

Whittier,Thomas,House (Johnson,Judge Alfred W. ,House)
76 Church St.
HABS ME-21
HABS ME,14-BELF,6-
1ph/1pg L

BELFAST VIC.

Miller,Joseph,House
Marsh Rd.
HABS ME-90
HABS ME,14-BELF.V,1-
1ph/2pg L

LINCOLNVILLE

Bayshore Union Church
U. S. Rt. 1
HABS ME-98
HABS ME,14-LINC,1-
2ph/3pg L

SEARSPORT

Ward House
U. S. Rt. 1
HABS ME-73
HABS ME,14-SEARP,1-
1ph L

WASHINGTON COUNTY

COLUMBIA FALLS

Ruggles,Judge Thomas,House
Pleasant River Bridge Vic.
HABS ME-26
HABS ME,15-COLUF,1-
15ph/3pg/1pc L

MACHIAS

Burnham Tavern (Mason's Arms)
High St.
HABS ME-64
HABS ME,15-MACH,1-
11ph/2pg L

Mason's Arms; see Burnham Tavern

ST. CROIX ISLAND

St. Croix Island National Monument; see St. Croix Island National Monument,Barn

St. Croix Island National Monument; see St. Croix Isle. Nat'l Monument,Lighthouse & Res.

St. Croix Island National Monument,Barn (St. Croix Island National Monument)
HABS ME-168-D
HABS ME,15-SACRI,1-D-
2dr/fr L

Documentation: **ct** color transparencies **dr** measured drawings **fr** field records
pc photograph captions **pg** pages of text **ph** photographs

St. Croix Island National Monument,Boathouse
HABS ME-168-E
HABS ME,15-SACRI,1-E-
3dr/fr L

St. Croix Island National Monument,Fog Bell Tower
HABS ME-168-B
HABS ME,15-SACRI,1-B-
3dr/fr L

St. Croix Island National Monument,Oil House
HABS ME-168-C
HABS ME,15-SACRI,1-C-
1dr/fr L

St. Croix Isle. Nat'l Monument,Lighthouse & Res. (St. Croix Island National Monument)
HABS ME-168-A
HABS ME,15-SACRI,1-A-
9dr/fr L

YORK COUNTY

ALFRED

Holmes-Sayward House (Sayward House)
U. S. Rt. 202 (State Rt. 4)
HABS ME-32
HABS ME,16-ALF,1-
17dr/9ph/2pg/1pc L

Sayward House; see Holmes-Sayward House

BIDDEFORD

Cutts,Col. Thomas,House
(moved to ME,Saco,Glen Haven Circle)
HABS ME-7
HABS ME,16-SACO,2-
14dr/8ph/2pg/fr L

Haley,Benjamin,House
Pool Rd. (State Rt. 208)
HABS ME-36
HABS ME,16-BIDPO,1-
3ph/2pg L

Lafayette House (Spring,Capt. Seth,Inn)
14 Elm St.
HABS ME-8
HABS ME,16-BID,2-
2dr/2ph/1pg/fr L

Spring,Capt. Seth,Inn; see Lafayette House

BOON ISLAND

Boon Island Light Tower
HABS ME-122
HABS ME,16-BOONI,1-
6ph/4pg L

KENNEBUNK

Bourne House; see Parsons-Bourne House

Bourne,George W. ,House (Wedding Cake House)
104 Summer St. (State Rt. 35)
HABS ME-74
HABS ME,16-KEN,6-
17ph/8pg/1pc/fr L

Bourne,George W. ,House (Fence) (Wedding Cake House (Fence))
104 Summer St. (State Rt. 35)
HABS ME-71
HABS ME,16-KEN,6C-
4dr L

Brick Store Museum; see Lord,William,Building

First Parish Church (Unitarian)
U. S. Rt. 1 & State Rt. 35
HABS ME-124
HABS ME,16-KEN,1-
3dr/13ph/9pg/2pc/fr L

Kimball,James,House
2 Summer St.
HABS ME-14
HABS ME,16-KEN,4-
16dr/5ph/2pg/fr L

Lord,William,Building (Brick Store Museum)
117 Main St.
HABS ME-132
HABS ME,16-KEN,7-
5ph/5pg/1pc L

Mousam House (Paneling)
U. S. Rt. 1
HABS ME-68
HABS ME,16-KEN,3-
1dr/fr L

Parsons-Bourne House (Bourne House)
Bourne St.
HABS ME-15
HABS ME,16-KEN,5-
10ph/2pg L

Wedding Cake House; see Bourne,George W. ,House

Wedding Cake House (Fence); see Bourne,George W. ,House (Fence)

KENNEBUNKPORT

Kennebunk River Club
Ocean Ave.
HABS ME-125
HABS ME,16-KENP,5-
3dr/5ph/4pg/1pc/fr L

Larabee-Carl,House
North St.
HABS ME-72
HABS ME,16-KENP,4-
3dr L

Perkins Grist Mill
Mill Pond,North St. vic.
HABS ME-126
HABS ME,16-KENP,6-
4dr/8ph/4pg/1pc/fr L

South Congregational Church
Temple St. between Kennebunk River & Maine St.
HABS ME-162
HABS ME,16-KENP,2-
6ph/2pg/1pc/fr L

KITTERY POINT

Gerrish Warehouse
Pepperrell Cove,State Rt. 103 vic.
HABS ME-131
HABS ME,16-KITPO,16-
3dr/4ph/4pg/1pc/fr L

Pepperrell,William,House
State Rt. 103
HABS ME-128
HABS ME,16-KITPO,4-
10dr/15ph/12pg/1pc/fr L

OGUNQUIT

Perkins,Isaiah,House
Shore Rd.
HABS ME-57
HABS ME,16-OGU,1-
9dr/fr L

SACO

Cutts,Col. Thomas,House
Glen Haven Circle (moved from Factory Island)
HABS ME-7
HABS ME,16-SACO,2-
14dr/8ph/2pg/fr L

SCOTLAND

Maxwell,Alexander,Garrison House; see McIntire-Garrison House

McIntire-Garrison House
(Maxwell,Alexander,Garrison House)
S. Berwick Rd. (State Rt. 91)
HABS ME-9
HABS ME,16-BERN.V,1-
13dr/6ph/3pg/fr L

WELLS

Jefferds' Tavern
Harraseekit Rd. (moved to ME,York,U. S. Rt. 1A)
HABS ME-43
HABS ME,16-WEL,3-
15dr/10ph/2pg/fr L

Storer-Garrison House
U. S. Rt. 1
HABS ME-12
HABS ME,16-WEL,2-
2ph/2pg L

YORK

Jefferds' Tavern
U. S. Rt. 1A (moved from ME,Wells Vic.)
HABS ME-43
HABS ME,16-WEL,3-
15dr/10ph/2pg/fr L

Junkins Garrison House
S. Berwick Rd. (State Rt. 91)
HABS ME-11
HABS ME,16-BERN.V,2-
1ph L

King's Prison; see York County Gaol,Old

York County Gaol,Old (King's Prison; York Village)
4 Lindsay Rd.
HABS ME-10
HABS ME,16-YORK.V,1-
7dr/11ph/16pg L

York Village; see York County Gaol,Old

Documentation: **ct** color transparencies **dr** measured drawings **fr** field records
pc photograph captions **pg** pages of text **ph** photographs

Chase-Lloyd House (Samuel Chase House), Annapolis, Anne Arundel County, Maryland. Front elevation. Photograph by Charles E. Peterson, May 1942 (HABS MD,2-ANNA,2-10)

Maryland

HAGERSTOWN VIC.

Herman Farm,Wash House
N. side of Showalter Rd.,E. of I-81
HABS MD-993-C
HABS DLC/PP-1993:MD-5
4ph/4pg/1pc L

ALLEGANY COUNTY

CUMBERLAND

Baltimore & Ohio Railroad,Cumberland Shops
S. of Williams St.
HAER MD-2
1ph H

Baltimore & Ohio RR,Queen City Hotel & Station (Queen City Hotel & Station)
W. Side of Park St. ,Opposite Ann St.
HAER MD-4
HAER MD,1/CUMB,1-
2dr/36ph/3pg/2pc/fr L

Baltimore & Ohio RR:Bolt & Forge Shop (Bolt & Forge Shop)
Spring St.
HAER MD-2-B
HAER MD,1/CUMB,2B-
6dr/10ph/1pg/1pc/fr L

Baltimore & Ohio RR:Rail Rolling Mill (Rail Rolling Mill)
Elm St. & Locust Alley
HAER MD-2-A
HAER MD,1-CUMB,ZA-
4dr/9ph/2pg/1pc/fr L

Bolt & Forge Shop; see Baltimore & Ohio RR:Bolt & Forge Shop

Chesapeake & Ohio Canal National Historical Park; see Chesapeake & Ohio Canal,Lockhouse 75

Chesapeake & Ohio Canal,Lockhouse 75 (Chesapeake & Ohio Canal National Historical Park)
State Rt. 51 & Patterson Ck.
HAER MD-26
HAER MD,1-CUMB,3-
1dr/fr L

Queen City Hotel & Station; see Baltimore & Ohio RR,Queen City Hotel & Station

Rail Rolling Mill; see Baltimore & Ohio RR:Rail Rolling Mill

CUMBERLAND VIC.

Chesapeake & Ohio Canal National Historical Park; see Chesapeake & Ohio Canal,Evitts Creek Aqueduct

Chesapeake & Ohio Canal National Historical Park; see Chesapeake & Ohio Canal,Lock Tender's Hse,Lock 75

Chesapeake & Ohio Canal National Historical Park; see Chesapeake & Ohio Canal,Lock 75

Chesapeake & Ohio Canal National Historical Park; see Chesapeake & Ohio Canal,Lockhouse at Lock 74

Chesapeake & Ohio Canal,Aqueduct 11; see Chesapeake & Ohio Canal,Evitts Creek Aqueduct

Chesapeake & Ohio Canal,Evitts Creek Aqueduct (Chesapeake & Ohio Canal,Aqueduct 11; Chesapeake & Ohio Canal National Historical Park)
HABS MD-824
HABS MD,1-CUMB.V,2-
3ph/1pc L

Chesapeake & Ohio Canal,Lock Tender's Hse,Lock 75 (Chesapeake & Ohio Canal National Historical Park)
HABS MD-823
HABS MD,1-CUMB.V,4-
5dr/fr L

Chesapeake & Ohio Canal,Lock 74
State Rt. 51
HABS MD-821
1ph L

Chesapeake & Ohio Canal,Lock 75 (Chesapeake & Ohio Canal National Historical Park)
HABS MD-822
HABS MD,1-CUMB.V,3-
1ph/1pc L

Chesapeake & Ohio Canal,Lockhouse at Lock 74 (Chesapeake & Ohio Canal National Historical Park)
HABS MD-820
HABS MD,1-CUMB.V,5-95
fr L

Cumberland & Penn. R. R. ,Wills Creek Bridge (Wills Creek Bridge)
Spanning Wills Ck. 587 ft. W. of Eckhart Junction
HAER MD-5
HAER MD,1-CUMB.V,1-
5ph/1pg/1pc L

Wills Creek Bridge; see Cumberland & Penn. R. R. ,Wills Creek Bridge

FROSTBURG

Krause,Charles R. ,House
41 W. Main St.
HABS MD-908
HABS MD,1-FROSB,1-
6ph/3pg/1pc L

Price,Dr. James Marshall,House
39 W. Main St.
HABS MD-907
HABS MD,1-FROSB,2-
15ph/3pg/1pc L

HANCOCK VIC.

Chesapeake & Ohio Canal National Historical Park; see Chesapeake & Ohio Canal,Sideling Creek Aqueduct

Chesapeake & Ohio Canal,Sideling Creek Aqueduct (Chesapeake & Ohio Canal National Historical Park)
Lock 56 vic.
HABS MD-806
HABS MD,1-HAN.V,1-
3ph/1pc L

MIDLAND

Ocean Mine No. 1,Powerhouse & Ventilation Fan
St. Rt. 36
HAER MD-73
21ph/16pg/1pc H

OLD TOWN VIC.

Chesapeake & Ohio Canal National Historical Park; see Chesapeake & Ohio Canal,Busey Cabin

Chesapeake & Ohio Canal,Busey Cabin (Chesapeake & Ohio Canal,Construc. Office,Lock 60; Chesapeake & Ohio Canal National Historical Park)
HABS MD-805
HABS MD,1-OLDTO.V,2-
3ph/1pc/fr L

Chesapeake & Ohio Canal,Construc. Office,Lock 60; see Chesapeake & Ohio Canal,Busey Cabin

OLDTOWN

Bridge at Lock 68; see C & O Canal:Iron Bridge at Lock No. 68

C & O Canal:Iron Bridge at Lock No. 68 (Bridge at Lock 68)
Mile 164.82 of the C & O Canal Natl Park
HAER MD-70
HAER 1989(HAER):11
5ph/4pg/1pc L

Chesapeake & Ohio Canal National Historical Park; see Chesapeake & Ohio Canal,Lockhouse at Lock 68

Chesapeake & Ohio Canal National Historical Park; see Chesapeake & Ohio Canal,Lockhouse at Lock 70

Chesapeake & Ohio Canal,Lockhouse at Lock 68 (Chesapeake & Ohio Canal,Lockhouse,Crabtree's Lock; Chesapeake & Ohio Canal National Historical Park)
HABS MD-814
HABS MD,1-OLDTO.V,6-
4ph/1pc L

Chesapeake & Ohio Canal,Lockhouse at Lock 70 (Chesapeake & Ohio Canal,Lockhouse at Old Town Lock Chesapeake & Ohio Canal National Historical Park)
HABS MD-815
HABS MD,1-OLDTO,1-
3ph/1pc/fr L

Chesapeake & Ohio Canal,Lockhouse at Old Town Lock; see Chesapeake & Ohio Canal,Lockhouse at Lock 70

Chesapeake & Ohio Canal,Lockhouse,Crabtree's Lock; see Chesapeake & Ohio Canal,Lockhouse at Lock 68

OLDTOWN VIC.

Chesapeake & Ohio Canal National Historical Park; see Chesapeake & Ohio Canal,Carpenter Shop at Lock 66

Chesapeake & Ohio Canal National Historical Park; see Chesapeake & Ohio Canal,Lock 71

Chesapeake & Ohio Canal National Historical Park; see Chesapeake & Ohio Canal,Lock 72

Chesapeake & Ohio Canal National Historical Park; see Chesapeake & Ohio Canal,Lockhouse at Lock 71

Chesapeake & Ohio Canal National Historical Park; see Chesapeake & Ohio Canal,Lockhouse at Lock 72

Chesapeake & Ohio Canal National Historical Park; see Chesapeake & Ohio Canal,Paw-Paw Tunnel

Chesapeake & Ohio Canal National Historical Park; see Chesapeake & Ohio Canal,Section House

Chesapeake & Ohio Canal National Historical Park; see Chesapeake & Ohio Canal,Town Creek Aqueduct

Chesapeake & Ohio Canal,Aqueduct No. 10; see Chesapeake & Ohio Canal,Town Creek Aqueduct

Chesapeake & Ohio Canal,Carpenter Shop at Lock 66 (Chesapeake & Ohio Canal,Woodwork Shop; Chesapeake & Ohio Canal National Historical Park)
HABS MD-809
HABS MD,1-OLDTO.V,3-
7ph/1pc/fr L

Chesapeake & Ohio Canal,Lock 71 (Chesapeake & Ohio Canal National Historical Park)
HABS MD-816
HABS MD,1-OLDTO.V,7-
1ph/1pc L

Chesapeake & Ohio Canal,Lock 72 (Chesapeake & Ohio Canal,The Narrows; Chesapeake & Ohio Canal National Historical Park)
HABS MD-819
HABS MD,1-OLDTO.V,9-
2ph/1pc L

Chesapeake & Ohio Canal,Lockhouse at Lock 71 (Chesapeake & Ohio Canal National Historical Park)
HABS MD-817
HABS MD,1-OLDTO.V,8-
3ph/1pc/fr L

Chesapeake & Ohio Canal,Lockhouse at Lock 72 (Chesapeake & Ohio Canal,Lockhouse at The Narrows; Chesapeake & Ohio Canal National Historical Park)
HABS MD-818
HABS MD,1-OLDTO.V,10-
3ph/1pc/fr L

Chesapeake & Ohio Canal,Lockhouse at The Narrows; see Chesapeake & Ohio Canal,Lockhouse at Lock 72

Chesapeake & Ohio Canal,Paw-Paw Tunnel (Chesapeake & Ohio Canal National Historical Park)
HABS MD-810
HABS MD,1-OLDTO.V,4-
7ph/1pc L

Chesapeake & Ohio Canal,Section House (Chesapeake & Ohio Canal National Historical Park)
Lock 66 vic.
HABS MD-807
HABS MD,1-OLDTO.V,5-
3ph/1pc L

Chesapeake & Ohio Canal,The Narrows; see Chesapeake & Ohio Canal,Lock 72

Chesapeake & Ohio Canal,Town Creek Aqueduct (Chesapeake & Ohio Canal National Historical Park; Chesapeake & Ohio Canal,Aqueduct No. 10)
Spanning Town Creek
HABS MD-813
HAER MD-31
HABS/HAER MD,1-OLDTO.V,1-
2dr/3ph/1pc/fr L

Chesapeake & Ohio Canal,Woodwork Shop; see Chesapeake & Ohio Canal,Carpenter Shop at Lock 66

PAPW PAW VIC.

Chesapeake & Ohio Canal,Lift Lock 66 (Chesapeake & Ohio National Historical Park)
State Rt. 51
HAER MD-30-C
HAER MD,1-PAW.V,1C-
2dr/fr L

Chesapeake & Ohio National Historical Park; see Chesapeake & Ohio Canal,Lift Lock 66

PAW PAW VIC.

Chesapeake & Ohio Canal National Historical Park; see Chesapeake & Ohio Canal,Lock 64 2/3

Chesapeake & Ohio Canal National Historical Park; see Chesapeake & Ohio Canal,Locks 63 1/3, 64 2/3, & 66

Chesapeake & Ohio Canal,Lock 64 2/3 (Chesapeake & Ohio Canal National Historical Park)
State Rt. 51 Vic.
HAER MD-30-B
HAER MD,1-PAW.V,1B-
1dr/fr L

Chesapeake & Ohio Canal,Locks 63 1/3, 64 2/3, & 66 (Chesapeake & Ohio Canal National Historical Park)
State Rt. 51
HAER MD-30
HAER MD,1-PAW.V,1-
1dr/fr L

PAW PAW VIC. (WV)

Chesapeake & Ohio Canal National Historical Park; see Chesapeake & Ohio Canal,Lock 63 1/3

Chesapeake & Ohio Canal,Lock 63 1/3 (Chesapeake & Ohio Canal National Historical Park)
State Rt. 51 Vic.
HAER MD-30-A
HAER MD,1-PAW.V,1A-
1dr/fr L

WESTERNPORT

Waverly Street Bridge (WesternPort Bowstring Arch-Truss Bridge)
Spanning George's Creek,Westernport,MD
HAER MD-83
HAER DLC/PP-1992:MD-3
8dr/11ph/12pg/1pc/fr L

WesternPort Bowstring Arch-Truss Bridge; see Waverly Street Bridge

ANNE ARUNDEL COUNTY

House
HABS MD-890
HABS MD,2- ,4-
1ph L

ANNAPOLIS

Academic Group; see U. S. Naval Academy;Mahan,Maury & Sampson Halls

Acton (Hammond's Plains; Murray Hill)
1 Acton Pl.
HABS MD-296
HABS MD,2-ANNA,20
4dr/1ph/5pg/1pc/fr L

Acton,Springhouse
HABS MD-296-A
HABS MD,2-ANNA,20A-
1ph/1pg/1pc L

Adams-Kilty House; see Adams,William,House

Adams,William,House (Adams-Kilty House)
131 Charles St.
HABS MD-264
HABS MD,2-ANNA,47-
4ph/10pg L

Annapolis,Town Plan
HABS MD-1076
1dr H

Baer's Clothing Store; see Williams,James,House

Barber,George & John,Store
77-79 Main St.
HABS MD-266
HABS MD,2-ANNA,48-
5dr/3ph/6pg/1pc/fr L

Bladen's Folly; see St. John's College,McDowell Hall

Blue Ball Tavern; see Davis House

Brice,James,House
42 East St.
HABS MD-247
HABS MD,2-ANNA,7-
15ph/11pg L

Brice,John II,House (Jennings House)
195 Prince George St.
HABS MD-282
HABS MD,2-ANNA,14-
1ph/5pg/1pc L

Brice,John III,House; see Dorsey,Maj. Edward, House

Brooksby-Shaw House (Shaw,John,House)
21 State Circle
HABS MD-250
HABS MD,2-ANNA,10-
4ph/2pg L

Bryce,Frances,Boarding House
18 West St.
HABS MD-265
HABS MD,2-ANNA,49-
3ph/2pg/1pc L

Buchanan House; see U. S. Naval Academy,Superintendent's Quarters

Building,Three House Brick; see Ridout,John,Tenant Houses

Callahan,John,House; see Pinckney,William,House

Carroll,Charles,House
Duke of Gloucester St. & Spa Creek
HABS MD-293
HABS MD,2-ANNA,24-
2ph L

Carroll,Charles,The Barrister,House; see Davis House

Carroll,Charles,The Settler,House
139 Market St.
HABS MD-285
HABS MD,2-ANNA,30-
4ph/1pc L

Carvel House; see Scott,Dr. Upton,House

Carvell Hall Hotel; see Paca,William,House

Cathedral of the Navy; see U. S. Naval Academy,Academy Chapel

Chase House,Annex
235 King George St.
HABS MD-244
HABS MD,2-ANNA,3-
1ph L

Chase-Lloyd House (Chase,Samuel,House)
22 Maryland Ave. & King George St.
HABS MD-243
HABS MD,2-ANNA,2
7dr/20ph/20pg/fr L

Chase,Samuel,House; see Chase-Lloyd House

City Ballroom or Assembly Room(s) (Municipal Building)
150 Duke of Gloucester St.
HABS MD-41
HABS MD,2-ANNA,43-
6ph/7pg/1pc/fr L

Creagh,Patrick,House; see Smith,Aunt Lucy,House

Custom House,Old; see Inn,Old

Davis House (Tydings House; Carroll,Charles,The Barrister,House; Blue Ball Tavern)
King George St. (moved from Main & Conduit Sts.)
HABS MD-258
HABS MD,2-ANNA,33-
8ph/2pg/1pc L

Dockside Restaurant; see Williams,James,House

Donaldson-Steuart House; see King William's School

Dorsey,Maj. Edward, House (Brice,John III,House; Marchand House)
211 Prince George St.
HABS MD-107
HABS MD,2-ANNA,34-
1ph L

Franklin Store
206 Main St. & Chancery Lane
HABS MD-281
HABS MD,2-ANNA,50-
1ph/1pc L

Franklin,James Shaw,Law Office
17 State Circle at Chancery Lane
HABS MD-280
HABS MD,2-ANNA,51-
1ph/3pg/1pc L

Ghiselin Boarding House
28 West St.
HABS MD-268
HABS MD,2-ANNA,53-
1ph/1pg/1pc L

Ghiselin Boarding House
30 West St.
HABS MD-269
HABS MD,2-ANNA,52-
1ph/1pc L

Government House; see Governor's Mansion

Governor's Mansion (Government House)
State Circle at School St.
HABS MD-146
HABS MD,2-ANNA,38-
1ph/1pg L

Grammer,Frederick,House; see Inn,Old

Great Hall; see St. John's College,McDowell Hall

Green,Jonas,House
124 Charles St.
HABS MD-259
HABS MD,2-ANNA,35-
9ph/4pg/1pc L

Hammond-Harwood House
19 Maryland Ave. & King George St.
HABS MD-251
HABS MD,2-ANNA,18-
17ph/14pg/1pc/1ct L

Hammond's Plains; see Acton

Holland-Hohne House
45 Fleet St.
HABS MD-262
HABS MD,2-ANNA,54-
5dr/2ph/1pg/1pc/fr L

Hopkins,Walton H. ,House (Walton,Dr. Thomas O. ,House)
15 Maryland Ave.
HABS MD-276
HABS MD,2-ANNA,55-
6ph/8pg/1pc L

Hutton,Samuel,House & No. 32 Cornhill Street; see Nos. 30 & 32 Cornhill Street

Inn,Old (Custom House,Old; Grammer,Frederick,House)
Main & Green Sts.
HABS MD-257
HABS MD,2-ANNA,32-
2ph/1pc L

Inn,Old (Middleton's Tavern; Marx House)
Dock & Randall Sts.
HABS MD-256
HABS MD,2-ANNA,28-
2ph/1pg/1pc L

Jennings House; see Brice,John II,House

Johnson,Reverdy,House
Saint John's College (moved from 9 Northwest St.)
HABS MD-273
HABS MD,2-ANNA,56-
3ph/2pg/1pc L

Kentish Inn; see King William's School

Key House; see Scott,Dr. Upton,House

King William's School
(Workman,Anthony,Inn; Donaldson-Steuart House; Kentish Inn)
10 Francis St.
HABS MD-260
HABS MD,2-ANNA,39-
7ph/2pg/1pc L

Lloyd-Dulany House
162 Conduit St.
HABS MD-277
HABS 1983(HABS):136
5ph/1pg/1pc L

Lockerman-Tilton House
9-11 Maryland Ave.
HABS MD-287
HABS MD,2-ANNA,5-
4ph/1pg/1pc L

160-166 Main Street (Building)
HABS MD-270
HABS MD,2-ANNA,44-
1ph/1pc L

Mann's Hotel Row Houses
150-160 Conduit St.
HABS MD-289
HABS MD,2-ANNA,57-
2ph/1pc L

Marchand House; see Dorsey,Maj. Edward, House

Market House
Market Space,Main & Dock Sts.
HABS MD-234
HABS MD,2-ANNA,58-
4dr L

Marx House; see Inn,Old

Maryland State House
State Circle
HABS MD-245
HABS MD,2-ANNA,4
48dr/101ph/2pg/7pc/24ct/fr L

Middleton's Tavern; see Inn,Old

Midshipman's Quarters; see U. S. Naval Academy,Bancroft Hall

Monroe,James,Dry Goods Store
140 Main St.
HABS MD-261
HABS MD,2-ANNA,59-
7dr/3ph/5pg/1pc/fr L

Moss House; see Sands,John,House

Municipal Building; see City Ballroom or Assembly Room(s)

Murray Hill; see Acton

Naval Academy Alumni Association House; see Ogle,Gov. Samuel,House

19-21 Northwest Street (Houses)
HABS MD-290
HABS MD,2-ANNA,45-
1ph/1pg L

Nos. 30 & 32 Cornhill Street
(Hutton,Samuel,House & No. 32 Cornhill Street)
HABS MD-1079
1dr/fr H

Ogle Hall; see Ogle,Gov. Samuel,House

Ogle,Gov. Samuel,House (Ogle Hall; Naval Academy Alumni Association House; Stevenson,Dr. William,House)
33 College Ave.
HABS MD-242
HABS MD,2-ANNA,1-
3ph/2pg/1pc/fr L

Paca,William,House (Carvell Hall Hotel)
186 Prince George St.
HABS MD-253
HABS MD,2-ANNA,23-
6ph/3pg/1pc L

Pinckney-Callahan House; see Pinckney,William,House

Pinckney,William,House
(Pinckney-Callahan House; Callahan,John,House)
164 Conduit St. (moved from Bladen St.)
HABS MD-255
HABS MD,2-ANNA,26-
2ph/2pg/1pc L

Pinkney Street (Houses); see Taylor Street (Frame Houses)

Pinkney Street Warehouse; see Tobacco Prize House

Randall,Alexander,Double House
88-90 State Circle
HABS MD-272
HABS MD,2-ANNA,60-
6ph/5pg/1pc L

Reynold's Tavern
4 Church Circle at Franklin St.
HABS MD-248
HABS MD,2-ANNA,8
9dr/5ph/23pg/1pc/fr L

Reynold's Tavern,Smokehouse
Church Circle at Franklin St.
HABS MD-248-A
HABS MD,2-ANNA,8A-
1dr/1ph/1pg/1pc/fr L

Ridout,John,House
120 Duke of Gloucester St.
HABS MD-91
HABS MD,2-ANNA,19-
11ph/5pg/1pc L

Ridout,John,Tenant Houses
(Building,Three House Brick)
110,112,114 Duke of Gloucester St.
HABS MD-252
HABS MD,2-ANNA,22-
7ph/7pg/1pc L

Rutland,Thomas,House
(Stewart,Peggy,House)
207 Hanover St.
HABS MD-278
HABS MD,2-ANNA,15-
3ph/4pg/1pc L

Sands,John,House (Moss House)
130 Prince George St.
HABS MD-254
HABS MD,2-ANNA,25-
4ph/1pg/1pc L

Scott,Dr. Upton,House (Carvel House; Key House)
4 Shipwright St.
HABS MD-246
HABS MD,2-ANNA,6
5dr/13ph/17pg/1pc L

Scott,Upton,Stable
4 Shipwright St.
HABS MD-246-A
HABS MD,2-ANNA,61-
3dr/3ph/4pg/1pc/fr L

Sharpe,Gov. Horatio,House; see Whitehall

Shaw House; see Slicer-Shiplap House

Shaw,John,House; see Brooksby-Shaw House

Slicer-Shiplap House (Shaw House; Smith,Edward,House)
18 Pinkney St.
HABS MD-249
HABS MD,2-ANNA,9-
6dr/8ph/6pg/1pc/fr L

Smith,Aunt Lucy,House
(Creagh,Patrick,House)
160 Prince George St.
HABS MD-295
HABS MD,2-ANNA,13-
1ph/4pg L

Smith,Edward,House; see Slicer-Shiplap House

St. John's College,Brick Double House
(St. John's College,Faculty Residence; St. John's College,Paca-Carroll Hall)
Saint John's St.
HABS MD-292
HABS MD,2-ANNA,41-
1ph/4pg L

St. John's College,Chase-Stone House
235 King George St.
HABS MD-236
HABS MD,2-ANNA,61-
2pg L

St. John's College,Faculty Residence; see St. John's College,Brick Double House

St. John's College,Humphreys Hall
College Ave.
HABS MD-274
HABS MD,2-ANNA,62-
2ph/2pg/1pc L

Documentation: **ct** color transparencies **dr** measured drawings **fr** field records
pc photograph captions **pg** pages of text **ph** photographs

St. John's College,McDowell Hall
(Great Hall; Bladen's Folly)
College Ave.
HABS MD-291
HABS MD,2-ANNA,40A-
3ph/2pg L

St. John's College,Paca-Carroll Hall; see St. John's College,Brick Double House

St. John's College,Pinkney Hall
College Ave.
HABS MD-275
HABS MD,2-ANNA,63-
3ph/5pg/1pc L

Stevenson,Dr. William,House; see Ogle,Gov. Samuel,House

Stewart,Peggy,House; see Rutland,Thomas,House

Taylor Street (Frame Houses) (Pinkney Street (Houses))
HABS MD-271
HABS MD,2-ANNA,42-
2ph/1pg/1pc L

Tobacco Prize House (Pinkney Street Warehouse)
14 Pinkney St.
HABS MD-283
HABS MD,2-ANNA,64-
1ph/1pg/1pc L

Treasury Building,Old
State Circle
HABS MD-10
HABS MD,2-ANNA,37-
7dr/5ph/5pg/1pc L

Tydings House; see Davis House

U. S. Naval Academy
HABS MD-329
HABS MD,2-ANNA,65/1-
1dr/6ph/9pg/1pc/fr L

U. S. Naval Academy;Mahan,Maury & Sampson Halls (Academic Group)
HABS MD-329-6
HABS MD,2-ANNA,65/6-
26ph/20pg/2pc/2ct/fr L

U. S. Naval Academy,Academy Chapel (Cathedral of the Navy)
HABS MD-329-1
24ph/18pg/2pc/fr L

U. S. Naval Academy,Bancroft Hall (Midshipman's Quarters)
HABS MD-329-2
HABS MD,2-ANNA,65/2-
37ph/21pg/2pc/2ct/fr L

U. S. Naval Academy,Deferrization Plant,Bldg. 104C
Parker Rd.
HABS MD-329-11
HABS MD,2-ANNA,65/11-
5ph/3pg/1pc L

U. S. Naval Academy,Griffin Hall,Building 110
Parker and Decatur Rds.
HABS MD-329-9
HABS MD,2-ANNA,65/9-
13ph/7pg/1pc L

U. S. Naval Academy,Isherwood Hall,Building 104
Parker Rd.
HABS MD-329-7
HABS MD,2-ANNA,65/7
39ph/9pg/3pc L

U. S. Naval Academy,Isherwood Shop,Building 104A
Parker Rd.
HABS MD-329-8
HABS MD,2-ANNA,65/8-
11ph/6pg/1pc L

U. S. Naval Academy,MacDonough & Dahlgren Halls
HABS MD-329-3 & 4
HABS MD,2-ANNA,65/3-,MD,2-ANNA,65/4-
34ph/15pg/2pc/fr L

U. S. Naval Academy,Melville Hall,Building 116
Parker Rd.
HABS MD-329-10
HABS MD,2-ANNA,65/10-
8ph/5pg/1pc L

U. S. Naval Academy,Superintendent's Quarters (Buchanan House)
HABS MD-329-5
15ph/10pg/1pc/fr L

Walton,Dr. Thomas O. ,House; see Hopkins,Walton H. ,House

31-33 West Street (Commercial Building)
HABS MD-267
HABS MD,2-ANNA,46-
1ph/1pg/1pc/fr L

Whitehall (Sharpe,Gov. Horatio,House)
Saint Margaret's Rd.
HABS MD-294
HABS MD,2
6ph/5pg L

Williams,James,House (Dockside Restaurant; Baer's Clothing Store)
22 Market Space
HABS MD-279
HABS MD,2-ANNA,66-
2ph/5pg/1pc L

Workman,Anthony,Inn; see King William's School

ANNAPOLIS VIC.

Cheston House; see Ridge,The

Hawthorne Ridge; see Ridge,The

Ridge,The (Cheston House; Hawthorne Ridge)
Lankford Rd.
HABS MD-147
HABS MD,2- ,6-
1ph L

BUTLER VIC.

Foxhall Farm; see McCeney,Dr. ,House

McCeney,Dr. ,House (Foxhall Farm)
Polling House Rd.
HABS MD-123
HABS MD,2-HARWO.V,2-
1ph L

COLLINSVILLE VIC.

Locust Grove
Chew's Inn Vic.
HABS MD-121
HABS MD,2- ,3-
1ph L

CROWNSVILLE VIC.

Rising Sun Tavern
(Worthington,Charles,Tavern)
Generals Hwy. (State Rt. 178)
HABS MD-845
HABS MD,2-CROWN.V,2-
3ph L

Worthington,Charles,Tavern; see Rising Sun Tavern

CUMBERSTONE

Cedar Park (Galloway House; Ewen Upon Ewenton)
Cumberstone Rd. on West River
HABS MD-847
HABS MD,2-CUMB.V,1-
18ph/1pg/1pc L

Ewen Upon Ewenton; see Cedar Park

Galloway House; see Cedar Park

CUMBERSTONE VIC.

Castle,The (Worthington House; Larkin's Hundred)
Mill Swamp Rd.
HABS MD-152
HABS MD,2-CUMB.V,3-
1ph L

Ivy Neck
Rhode & West Rivers
HABS MD-844
HABS MD,2-CUMB.V,2-
3ph L

Larkin's Hundred; see Castle,The

Worthington House; see Castle,The

DAVIDSONVILLE VIC.

1556 Aberdeen Street (Old House near Doden) (Bridge Hill)
HABS MD-153
HABS MD,2-DAVI.V,6-
1ph L

All Hallows Church
All Hallows Church Rd. & State Rt. 2
HABS MD-37
HABS MD,2-DAVI.V,1-
4dr/11ph/1pg/fr L

Bamford,Warren,House; see Friend's Choice

Bridge Hill; see 1556 Aberdeen Street (Old House near Doden)

Friend's Choice (Linden Grove; White Chimneys; Bamford,Warren,House)
Queen Anne Bridge Rd.
HABS MD-100
HABS MD,2-DAVI.V,2-
3ph L

Hopkins-Iglehart House; see Mount Airy

Idlewilde; see Townsend House

Iglehart,James Alexis,House; see Mount Airy

Linden Grove; see Friend's Choice

Mount Airy (Iglehart,James Alexis,House; Hopkins-Iglehart House)
Mount Airy Rd. ,State Rt. 424 Vic.
HABS MD-102
HABS MD,2-DAVI.V,4-
3ph/1pg L

Oakland
Ferry Rd.
HABS MD-101
HABS MD,2-DAVI.V,3-
2ph L

Townsend House (Idlewilde; Townsend-Mackall Place)
Davidsonville Rd. (State Rt. 424)
HABS MD-103
HABS MD,2-DAVI.V,5-
2ph L

Townsend-Mackall Place; see Townsend House

White Chimneys; see Friend's Choice

FAIRHAVEN VIC.

Folly Farm (Larkin's Hill Farm; Larkin's Hills)
Mill Swamp Rd.
HABS MD-263
HABS MD,2-FAIR.V,1-
1ph L

Larkin's Hill Farm; see Folly Farm

Larkin's Hills; see Folly Farm

FRIENDSHIP VIC.

Carr,Dr. Benjamin,House; see Trenton Hall

Harrison,Richard,House; see Holly Hill

Holland's Hills; see Holly Hill

Holly Hill (Rose Valley; Holland's Hills; Harrison,Richard,House)
Friendship Rd. (State Rt. 261)
HABS MD-284
HABS MD,2-FREN.V,1-
9dr/16ph/2pg/1pc L

Rose Valley; see Holly Hill

Trenton Hall (Carr,Dr. Benjamin,House)
SW of Friendship Rd. (State Rt. 261)
HABS MD-155
HABS MD,2-FREN.V,2-
1ph L

GALESVILLE VIC.

Galloway Place,Old; see Tulip Hill

Galloway,Samuel,House; see Tulip Hill

Tulip Hill (Galloway Place,Old; Galloway,Samuel,House)
Cumberstone Rd.
HABS MD-286
HABS MD,2-GAL.V,1-
8ph L

GAMBRILLS VIC.

Anne Arundel County Free School; see First Free School

First Free School (Anne Arundel County Free School; Maryland Free School)
Rutland Rd. Vic.
HABS MD-106
HABS MD,2-GAMB,1-
3dr/2ph L

Maryland Free School; see First Free School

HARWOOD VIC.

Bassford-Gardner House (Mount Pleasant)
HABS MD-144
HABS MD,2-HARWO.V,3-
3ph/1pg L

Mount Pleasant; see Bassford-Gardner House

Rawlings Tavern
State Rt. 2
HABS MD-112
HABS MD,2-HARWO.V,1-
2ph L

LOTHIAN

Hall,Sally,House; see Lothian

Lothian (Hall,Sally,House; Thomas,Phillip)
Marlboro Rd. (State Rt. 408)
HABS MD-312
HABS MD,2-LOTH,1-
1dr/2ph/1pg/1pc L

Thomas,Phillip; see Lothian

PINDELL

Neff,Benjamin C. ,House (Portland Manor)
Brooks Wood Rd.
HABS MD-130
HABS MD,2-PIND,1-
1ph L

Portland Manor; see Neff,Benjamin C. ,House

RIVIERA BEACH VIC.

Seven Foot Knoll Lighthouse
Mouth of Patapsco River
HAER MD-54
HAER 1991(HAER):13
37ph/8pg/1pc L

ROBINSON VIC.

Old Annapolis Boulevard (Stone House)
HABS MD-288
HABS MD,2-ROB.V,1-
1ph L

ROUND BAY VIC.

Belvoir (Scotts Plantation)
Generals Hwy. (State Rt. 178)
HABS MD-846
HABS MD,2-CROWN.V,1-
3ph L

Scotts Plantation; see Belvoir

SOUTH RIVER VIC.

Almshouse at London Town (Town Hall,Old; London Town Publik House)
London Town Rd.
HABS MD-29
HABS MD,2-SORI.V,3-
10ph/1pg L

Hopkins,Cadwalleder Edwards,House
Bell Branch Rd.
HABS MD-118
HABS MD,2-SORI.V,5-
1ph L

London Town Publik House; see Almshouse at London Town

Shadow Point; see Solomons Island Road (Frame House)

Solomons Island Road (Frame House) (Shadow Point)
HABS MD-298
HABS MD,2-SORI,1-
1ph L

South River Club
Solomons Island Rd. (State Rt. 2) Vic.
HABS MD-843
HABS MD,2-SORI.V,4-
1ph L

Town Hall,Old; see Almshouse at London Town

TRACY'S LANDING VIC.

Herring Creek Episcopal Church; see St. James Parish Episcopal Church

St. James Parish Episcopal Church (Herring Creek Episcopal Church)
Solomons Island Rd. (State Rt. 2)
HABS MD-850
HABS MD,2-TRALA.V,1-
1ph L

Documentation: **ct** color transparencies **dr** measured drawings **fr** field records
pc photograph captions **pg** pages of text **ph** photographs

BALTIMORE (CITY)

(Norton Tin Plate and Can Company); see American Can Company

Abel,A. S.,Building
Baltimore & Eutaw Sts.
HAER MD-66
HAER MD,4-BALT,124-
2ph/1pc L

Abell House; see North Charles Street (House,Cast-Iron Porches)

Aged Men's Home
1400 W. Lexington St.
HABS MD-182
HABS MD,4-BALT,110-
4ph/4pg L

Aged Women's Home
1400 W. Lexington St.
HABS MD-183
HABS MD,4-BALT,111-
9ph/8pg L

Albemarle & Granby Streets (Brick House)
HABS MD-360
HABS MD,4-BALT,61-
1ph L

102 Albermarle Street (Double House)
HABS MD-348
HABS MD,4-BALT,60-
1ph L

Aliceanna & South Dallas Streets (Brick Row House)
HABS MD-401
HABS MD,4-BALT,86-
1ph L

American Brewery; see Wiessner Brewery

American Can Company ((Norton Tin Plate and Can Company))
North of Harbor,Along Boston and Hudon Streets
HAER MD-63
HAER MD,4-BALT,125-
59ph/31pg/10pc L

Archbishop's House (Roman Catholic Episcopal Residence)
408 N. Charles St.
HABS MD-400
HABS MD,4-BALT,38-
1ph L

Arthur's Bakery; see North Eutaw Street,Arthur's Bakery

Ashland Avenue,100 Block (Brick Row Houses)
HABS MD-402
HABS MD,4-BALT,87-
1ph L

Athenaeum Club
(Howard,William,House)
Charles & Franklin Sts.
HABS MD-68
HABS MD,4-BALT,30-
1ph L

B. & O. Railroad,Camden Station,Warehse. Off. Bldg
Camden St.
HABS MD-326-A
HABS MD,4-BALT,126A-
6dr L

Backus,Dr. John,House; see First Presbyterian Church Manse

Baltimore & Ohio Railroad,Carrollton Viaduct (Carrollton Viaduct)
Over Gwynn's Falls near Carroll Park
HAER MD-9
HAER MD,4BALT,129-8
5ph/2pg/1pc L

Baltimore & Ohio Railroad,Howard Street Tunnel (Howard Street Tunnel)
1300 Mt. Royal Ave.
HAER MD-11
HAER MD,4-BALT,130-
6ph/2pg/1pc L

Baltimore & Ohio Railroad,Locust Pt. Tobacco Ware. (Locust Point Tobacco Warehouse)
Fort Ave. ,NE side
HAER MD-20
HAER MD,4-BALT,131-
4ph/1pg/1pc L

Baltimore & Ohio Railroad,Mount Clare Station
500 Block W. Pratt St.
HABS MD-852
HABS MD,4-BALT,51-
1ph L

Baltimore & Ohio Railroad,Mount Royal Station
Cathedral St. & Mt. Royal Ave.
HABS MD-193
HAER MD-10
HABS/HAER MD,4-BALT,119ι1984(HAER):128°
8ph/8pg/1pc L

Baltimore & Ohio Railroad,Tobacco Warehouse (Henderson's Wharf)
1000-1001 Fell St.
HAER MD-51
HAER MD,4-BALT,132-
27ph/4pg/2pc L

Baltimore & Ohio RR,Mount Clare Passenger Car Shop (Mount Clare Passenger Car Shop)
Pratt St. between Carey & Poppleton Sts.
HAER MD-6
HAER MD,4-BALT,127-
3dr/18ph/3pg/2pc/fr L

Baltimore & Ohio RR,Mount Clare Shops (Mount Clare Shops)
S. Side of Pratt St. between Carey & Poppleton
HAER MD-6-A
HAER MD,4-BALT,127A-
66ph/3pg/4pc L

Baltimore & Ohio RR:Mount Royal Trainshed (Mount Royal Station Trainshed)
1400 Cathedral St.
HAER MD-29
HAER MD,4-BALT,128-
7ph/4pg/1pc/fr L

Baltimore & 0hio Railroad,Camden Station (Camden Station)
Camden St. between Howard & Eutaw Sts.
HABS MD-326
HAER MD-7
HABS/HAER MD,4-BALT,126-
9dr/21ph/3pg/3pc/fr L

Baltimore City Hall; see City Hall,Baltimore,The

Baltimore City Jail
801 Van Buren & E. Madison Sts.
HABS MD-184
HABS MD,4-BALT,112-
10ph/14pg L

Baltimore City Jail Gateway & Warden's House
400 E. Madison St.
HABS MD-184-A
HABS MD,4-BALT,112A-
4ph L

Baltimore Federal Savings & Loan Association; see Merchant's National Bank

Bartlett-Hayward Industrial Complex (Hayward & Friend; Bartlett,Robbins & Company; Koppers Company,Bartlett-Hayward Division)
200 Scott St.
HAER MD-42
HAER MD,4-BALT,133-
19ph/10pg/1pc L

Bartlett,Robbins & Company; see Bartlett-Hayward Industrial Complex

Battle Monument
Calvert St.
HABS MD-185
HABS MD,4-BALT,113-
5ph/11pg L

Belmont (d'Annenous,Chevalier Chas. F. A. Le P.,House)
North & Harford Aves.
HABS MD-339
HABS MD,4-BALT,39-
4ph L

228-230 Bradford Street (Commercial Buildings)
HABS MD-911
HABS MD,4-BALT,154-
2ph/1pg/1pc L

Broadway & East Lombard Streets (House); see Cast-Iron Porches

Brown's Wharf Warehouse
935 Fell St.,Fells Pt.
HAER MD-61
HAER MD,4-BALT,134-
4ph/1pc/2ct L

Calvert & Lexington Streets (House)
HABS MD-64
HABS MD,4-BALT,26-
1ph L

Calvert & Lexington Streets (House)
NE Corner
HABS MD-67
HABS MD,4-BALT,29-
1ph L

Calvert Station; see North Central Railroad,Baltimore Freight House

Camden Station; see Baltimore & Ohio Railroad,Camden Station

Campbell-Edwards House
406 Diamond St.
HABS MD-972
HABS DLC/PP-1992:MD-5
4ph/3pg/1pc L

Carroll Mansion; see Caton House

Carroll,Charles Jr. ,Mansion; see Homewood

Carrollton Viaduct; see Baltimore & Ohio Railroad,Carrollton Viaduct

Cast-Iron Balcony (Exeter & Watson Streets (House))
HABS MD-365
HABS MD,4-BALT,71-
1ph L

Cast-Iron Porches (Broadway & East Lombard Streets (House))
HABS MD-374
HABS MD,4-BALT,65-
1ph L

504-520 Cathedral Street (Houses)
HABS MD-376
HABS MD,4-BALT,90-
1ph L

505-517 Cathedral Street (Houses)
HABS MD-375
HABS MD,4-BALT,89-
1ph L

600-610 Cathedral Street (Houses)
HABS MD-377
HABS MD,4-BALT,92-
1ph L

607-609 Cathedral Street (Houses)
HABS MD-352
HABS MD,4-BALT,91-
1ph L

800-810 Cathedral Street (Row Houses)
Madison Ave.
HABS MD-379
HABS MD,4-BALT,93-
1ph L

Caton House (Carroll Mansion; Caton-Carroll House; Wilson,Henry,House)
Lombard & S. Front Sts.
HABS MD-5
HABS MD,4-BALT,14-
14dr/12ph/6pg L

Caton-Carroll House; see Caton House

Central Police Building,Old; see Police Department Headquarters

Charles & Fayette Streets (Church)
HABS MD-66
HABS MD,4-BALT,28-
1ph L

Chestnut,William,House
Baltimore St.
HABS MD-345
HABS MD,4-BALT,42-
1ph L

City Hall,Baltimore,The (Baltimore City Hall)
Holliday St.
HABS MD-46
HABS MD,4-BALT,123-
25ph/28pg/2pc L

Clipper Mill Worker Housing
Clipper Mill Road
HAER MD-65
HAER MD,4-BALT,135-
1ph/1pc L

Colored School No. 9 (Public School No. 104; Elliott,Robert Brown,School)
1431 N. Carey St.
HABS MD-235
HABS MD,4-BALT,169-
4ph/7pg/1pc L

Commercial & Farmers Bank; see Howard & Redwood Streets (Commercial Building)

Courtland Street (Houses)
St. Paul Place
HABS MD-65
HABS MD,4-BALT,27-
1ph L

Cromwell,Oliver,School; see Public School No. 74

204-212 Cross Street (Houses); see 1022-1036 Sharp Street & 1017-1031 Plum Alley (Hse

d'Annenous,Chevalier Chas. F. A. Le P.,House; see Belmont

Damon House,Old (Stewart,David,House; Upton; Damon-Stewart House)
811 W. Lanvale St.
HABS MD-347
HABS MD,4-BALT,44-
2ph L

Damon-Stewart House; see Damon House,Old

Druid Mill (Textile)
Union Ave. at Ash St.,Woodberry
HAER MD-59
HAER MD,4-BALT,16-
3ph/1pc L

1426-1446 East Baltimore Street (Commercial Bldgs)
HABS MD-904
HABS MD,4-BALT,153-
4ph/4pg/1pc L

1426-1446 East Baltimore Street (Commercial Bldgs) (1426-1428 East Baltimore Street)
HABS MD-904-A
HABS MD,4-BALT,153A-
2pg L

1426-1446 East Baltimore Street (Commercial Bldgs) (1430 East Baltimore Street)
HABS MD-904-B
HABS MD,4-BALT,153B-
1pg L

1426-1446 East Baltimore Street (Commercial Bldgs) (1432 East Baltimore Street)
HABS MD-904-C
HABS MD,4-BALT,153C-
2pg L

1426-1446 East Baltimore Street (Commercial Bldgs) (1434 East Baltimore Street)
HABS MD-904-D
HABS MD,4-BALT,153D-
2pg L

1426-1446 East Baltimore Street (Commercial Bldgs) (1436 East Baltimore Street)
HABS MD-904-E
HABS MD,4-BALT,153E-
2pg L

1426-1446 East Baltimore Street (Commercial Bldgs) (1438 East Baltimore Street)
HABS MD-904-F
HABS MD,4-BALT,153F-
2pg L

1426-1446 East Baltimore Street (Commercial Bldgs) (1440 East Baltimore Street)
HABS MD-904-G
HABS MD,4-BALT,153G-
2pg L

1426-1446 East Baltimore Street (Commercial Bldgs) (1442 East Baltimore Street)
HABS MD-904-H
HABS MD,4-BALT,153H-
2pg L

1426-1446 East Baltimore Street (Commercial Bldgs) (1444 East Baltimore Street)
HABS MD-904-I
HABS MD,4-BALT,153I-
2pg L

1426-1446 East Baltimore Street (Commercial Bldgs) (1446 East Baltimore Street)
HABS MD-904-J
HABS MD,4-BALT,153J-
2pg L

1012 East Baltimore Street (House)
HABS MD-361
HABS MD,4-BALT,62-
2ph L

1426-1428 East Baltimore Street; see 1426-1446 East Baltimore Street (Commercial Bldgs)

1430 East Baltimore Street; see 1426-1446 East Baltimore Street (Commercial Bldgs)

1432 East Baltimore Street; see 1426-1446 East Baltimore Street (Commercial Bldgs)

1434 East Baltimore Street; see 1426-1446 East Baltimore Street (Commercial Bldgs)

1436 East Baltimore Street; see 1426-1446 East Baltimore Street (Commercial Bldgs)

1438 East Baltimore Street; see 1426-1446 East Baltimore Street (Commercial Bldgs)

1440 East Baltimore Street; see 1426-1446 East Baltimore Street (Commercial Bldgs)

1442 East Baltimore Street; see 1426-1446 East Baltimore Street (Commercial Bldgs)

1444 East Baltimore Street; see 1426-1446 East Baltimore Street (Commercial Bldgs)

1446 East Baltimore Street; see 1426-1446 East Baltimore Street (Commercial Bldgs)

601-607 East Chase Street (Houses)
HABS MD-317
HABS MD,4-BALT,122-
6ph/1pc/fr L

East Indian Restaurant; see 113 South Broadway Street (Second Story Porch)

East Lombard & South Front Streets (Brick House)
opposite Caton House
HABS MD-343
HABS MD,4-BALT,76-
1ph L

304 East Lombard Street (Commercial Building)
HABS MD-919
HABS MD,4-BALT,155-
3ph/2pg/1pc L

12 East Pleasant Street (Brick House)
HABS MD-373
HABS MD,4-BALT,81-
2ph L

11 East Pleasant Street (House)
HABS MD-43-B
HABS MD,4-BALT,150A-
5ph L

11 1/2 East Pleasant Street (House)
HABS MD-43-C
HABS MD,4-BALT,8-
4ph L

15 East Pleasant Street (House) (Smith,Dr. James,House)
HABS MD-43-D
HABS MD,4-BALT,7-
8ph L

9 East Pleasant Street (House)
HABS MD-43-A
HABS MD,4-BALT,10-
2ph L

Eigenbrot Brewery
Calverton & Baltimore Sts.
HAER MD-64
HAER MD,4-BALT,137-
3ph/1pc L

Elliott,Robert Brown,School; see Colored School No. 9

Eutaw Place Baptist Church
Dolphin & Eutaw Sts.
HABS MD-194
HABS MD,4-BALT,120-
2ph/11pg L

Exeter & Watson Streets (House); see Cast-Iron Balcony

Fell House; see 1621 Thames Street (House)

Fell's Point Theatre; see 814 South Broadway (Brick Building)

Firehouse,Engine Company No. 6 (Independent Fire Company)
416 Gay St.
HABS MD-353
HABS MD,4-BALT,168-
3dr/2pg/fr L

Firehouse,Engine Company Number 15
Lombard St. & Howard St.
HABS MD-854
HABS MD,4-BALT,166-
1pg L

Firehouse,Engine Company Number 8
323 Mulberry St.
HABS MD-354
HABS MD,4-BALT,167-
1pg L

First Baptist Church (Round Top Church)
Sharp & Lombard Sts.
HABS MD-75
HABS MD,4-BALT,37-
1ph L

First Presbyterian Church
Guilford Ave. & Fayette St.
HABS MD-73
HABS MD,4-BALT,35-
1ph L

First Presbyterian Church
Madison St. & Park Ave.
HABS MD-195
HABS MD,4-BALT,121-
6ph/18pg L

First Presbyterian Church Manse (Backus,Dr. John,House)
210 W. Madison St.
HABS MD-195-A
HABS MD,4-BALT,121A-
5ph L

First Unitarian Church (Unitarian Church)
Franklin & Charles Sts.
HABS MD-229
HABS MD,4-BALT,58-
12ph L

Flag House (Pickersgill,Mary Young,House)
844 E. Pratt & Albemarle Sts.
HABS MD-356
HABS MD,4-BALT,45-
1ph L

1522 Fleet Street (House-Interior Stairway)
HABS MD-366
HABS MD,4-BALT,72-
1ph L

Forbes Houses; see 1626-1628 Thames Street (Row Houses)

Foreign Market; see 814 South Broadway (Brick Building)

Forrest & E. Monument Sts. (Row of Brick Houses)
HABS MD-404
HABS MD,4-BALT,94-
1ph L

Fort McHenry National Monument & Historic Shrine; see Fort McHenry,Commanding Officer's Office & Qtrs.

Fort McHenry National Monument & Historic Shrine; see Fort McHenry,Powder Magazine

Fort McHenry National Monument & Historic Shrine (Fort Whetstone)
Whetstone Point at Fort Ave.
HABS MD-63
HABS MD,4-BALT,5-
11dr/32ph/77pg L

Fort McHenry,Building A; see Fort McHenry,Commanding Officer's Office & Qtrs.

Fort McHenry,Building C; see Fort McHenry,Officers' Quarters

Fort McHenry,Commanding Officer's Office & Qtrs. (Fort McHenry,Building A; Fort McHenry National Monument & Historic Shrine)
Whetstone Point at Fort Ave.
HABS MD-196
HABS MD,4-BALT,5A-
6ph L

Fort McHenry,Flag Pole Base
E. Fort Ave.
HABS MD-204
HABS MD,4-BALT,5F-
1dr L

Fort McHenry,Officers' Quarters (Fort McHenry,Building C)
Whetstone Point at Fort Ave.
HABS MD-198
HABS MD,4-BALT,5C-
4ph L

Fort McHenry,Powder Magazine (Fort McHenry National Monument & Historic Shrine)
Fort Ave. at Whetstone Point
HABS MD-197
HABS MD,4-BALT,5B-
6dr/5ph/15pg/fr L

Fort McHenry,Soldiers' Barracks No. 1,Building D
Fort Ave. at Whetstone Point
HABS MD-199
HABS MD,4-BALT,5D-
8dr/8ph/16pg/fr L

Fort McHenry,Soldiers' Barracks No. 2,Building E
Fort Ave. at Whetstone Point
HABS MD-200
HABS MD,4-BALT,5E-
8dr/11ph/15pg L

Fort Whetstone; see Fort McHenry National Monument & Historic Shrine

Franklin Square (Twin Houses)
100 Block N. Calhoun St. ,W. side
HABS MD-412
HABS MD,4-BALT,66-
1ph L

Franklin Street Presbyterian Church
Franklin & Cathedral Sts.
HABS MD-187
HABS MD,4-BALT,114-
6ph/9pg L

Garrett Racing Stables (Montebello Estate Stables)
HABS MD-357
HABS MD,4-BALT,50A-
4ph L

Garrett-Jacobs House
7,9,11,13 W. Mount Vernon Place
HABS MD-188
HABS MD,4-BALT,115-
14ph/18pg L

German Evangelical Reformed Church; see Otterbein United Brethren Church

Gilman,Daniel C. ,House
614 Park Ave.
HABS MD-358
HABS MD,4-BALT,46-
2ph L

Gladding,Harry,House; see 1 West Mount Vernon Place (House)

Hammond-Crane House
404 Diamond St.
HABS MD-971
HABS DLC/PP-1992:MD-5
7ph/3pg/1pc L

Harper,Robert Goodloe,Dairy & Springhouse (Oaklands Springhouse) (moved to Baltimore Museum of Art,Charles St.)
HABS MD-394
HABS MD,4-BALT,53A-
2ph L

Harper,Robert Goodloe,House
Cathedral St.
HABS MD-359
HABS MD,4-BALT,47-
1ph L

Hayward & Friend; see Bartlett-Hayward Industrial Complex

Henderson's Wharf; see Baltimore & Ohio Railroad,Tobacco Warehouse

145 Henrietta Street (House); see 129-169 Henrietta Street (Houses & Commercial Bldg

129-169 Henrietta Street (Houses & Commercial Bldg (145 Henrietta Street (House); 1021 Peach Alley (House); Sharp-Leadenhall Area Survey)
HABS MD-924-A
HABS MD,4-BALT,152A-
1dr L

129-169 Henrietta Street (Hses. & Comm. Bldgs.) (Sharp-Leadenhall Area Survey)
HABS MD-924
HABS MD,4-BALT,152-
1dr L

Hochschild-Kohn Annex; see West Lexington Street,Murphy Building

Hochschild-Kohn Annex; see West Lexington Street,No. 308 (Commercial Bldg.)

Hochschild-Kohn Annex; see West Lexington Street,No. 310 (Commercial Bldg.)

Hollingsworth-Steel House
931 Fell St.
HABS MD-189
HABS MD,4-BALT,116-
4ph/8pg L

Homewood (Carroll,Charles Jr. ,Mansion)
N. Charles & Thirty-fourth Sts.
HABS MD-35
HABS MD,4-BALT,1-
17ph/5pg L

House
HABS MD-811
HABS MD,4-BALT,179-
1ph/1pc L

Houses adjoining Caton House
802-804 E. Lombard St.
HABS MD-350
HABS MD,4-BALT,75-
1ph L

Howard & Redwood Streets (Commercial Building) (Commercial & Farmers Bank)
HABS MD-395
HABS MD,4-BALT,43-
2ph L

Howard Street Tunnel; see Baltimore & Ohio Railroad,Howard Street Tunnel

Howard,William,House; see Athenaeum Club

Independent Fire Company; see Firehouse,Engine Company No. 6

Jencks,Francis,House; see 1 West Mount Vernon Place (House)

Kerr-Jenkins Warehouse
Philpot St. (1400 block),Fells Pt.
HAER MD-62
HAER MD,4-BALT,138-
9ph/1pc L

2701 Keyworth Avenue (Rowhouse)
HABS MD-995
HABS DLC/PP-1993:MD-5
4ph/3pg/1pc L

2703 Keyworth Avenue (Rowhouse)
HABS MD-996
HABS DLC/PP-1993:MD-5
5ph/3pg/1pc L

2705 Keyworth Avenue (Rowhouse)
HABS MD-997
HABS DLC/PP-1993:MD-5
2pg/1pc L

2707 Keyworth Avenue (Rowhouse)
HABS MD-998
HABS DLC/PP-1993:MD-5
1ph/2pg/1pc L

Koppers Company,Bartlett-Hayward Division; see Bartlett-Hayward Industrial Complex

Latrobe,J. H. B. ,House
Courtland (St. Paul Place) & Lexington Sts.
HABS MD-72
HABS MD,4-BALT,34-
1ph L

Lee & South Charles Street (Brick Row Houses)
HABS MD-380
HABS MD,4-BALT,96-
1ph L

Levering Coffee Warehouse
Philpot St. (1400 block)
HAER MD-60
HAER MD,4-BALT,139-
2ph/1pc L

Lexington Market Addition; see 123-125 North Paca Street (Commercial Buildings)

Lexington Market Addition; see 407-431 West Lexington Street (Commercial Bldgs.)

Lloyd Street Synagogue
Lloyd & Watson Sts.
HABS MD-190
HABS MD,4-BALT,117-
4ph/8pg L

Locust Point Tobacco Warehouse; see Baltimore & Ohio Railroad,Locust Pt. Tobacco Ware.

Lorman House
Charles & Lexington Sts.
HABS MD-69
HABS MD,4-BALT,31-
1ph L

Madison Avenue & Preston Street (Brick House)
HABS MD-369
HABS MD,4-BALT,77-
1ph L

McKim Free School
1120 E. Baltimore St.
HABS MD-305
HABS MD,4-BALT,49-
8dr/1ph L

McKim House
Park Ave. & Center St.
HABS MD-390
HABS MD,4-BALT,48-
1ph L

Meadow Mill (Textile)
Union Ave. & Seneca St.,Woodberry
HAER MD-56
HAER MD,4-BALT,140-
2ph/1pc L

Mechanics Hall; see Watchman Fire Company Firehouse

Mercantile Trust & Deposit Company
Redwood & Calvert Sts.
HABS MD-191
HABS MD,4-BALT,118-
2ph/8pg L

Merchant's National Bank (Baltimore Federal Savings & Loan Association)
301 Water St.
HABS MD-920
HABS MD,4-BALT,170-
10ph/1pg/1pc L

Merchants' Shot Tower; see Phoenix Shot Tower

Minor Basilica,Assumption of the Virgin Mary; see Roman Catholic Cathedral of Baltimore

Montebello Estate Stables; see Garrett Racing Stables

36 Montgomery Street (House)
HABS MD-370
HABS MD,4-BALT,78-
9dr/2ph L

Morton,George C. ,House; see 107 West Monument Street (House)

Mount Clare
Bayard & S. Monroe Sts. ,Carroll Park
HABS MD-192
HABS MD,4-BALT,3-
7ph/17pg L

Mount Clare Passenger Car Shop; see Baltimore & Ohio RR,Mount Clare Passenger Car Shop

Mount Clare Shops; see Baltimore & Ohio RR,Mount Clare Shops

Mount Royal Station Trainshed; see Baltimore & Ohio RR:Mount Royal Trainshed

Mount Vernon Club; see Randall,Blanchard,House

Mount Vernon Mills,Mill No. 1 (Textile)
Falls Rd. & Chestnut St.
HAER MD-58-A
HAER MD,4-BALT,141A-
2ph/1pc/2ct L

Mount Vernon Mills,Mill No. 2 (Textile)
Falls RD. & Chestnut St.
HAER MD-58-B
HAER MD,4-BALT,141B-
2ph/1pc L

Mount Washington Mills
Falls Rd. & Cotton Ave.
HAER MD-57
HAER MD,4-BALT,142-
5ph/1pc/1ct L

Municipal Museum; see Peale,Rembrandt,Museum

Murphy Building; see West Lexington Street,Murphy Building

National Union Bank Building
Fayette & Charles Sts.
HABS MD-393
HABS MD,4-BALT,52-
5ph L

606-628 North Calvert Street (Houses); see Waterloo Row

608 North Calvert Street (Row House)
(Waterloo Row)
HABS MD-7-E
HABS MD,4-BALT,16E-
6ph L

612 North Calvert Street (Row House)
(Waterloo Row)
HABS MD-7-D
HABS MD,4-BALT,16D-
1ph L

616 North Calvert Street (Row House)
(Waterloo Row)
HABS MD-7-C
HABS MD,4-BALT,16C-
1ph L

622 North Calvert Street (Row House)
(Waterloo Row)
HABS MD-7-A
HABS MD,4-BALT,16A-
4ph L

620 North Calvert Street (Stable)
(Waterloo Row)
HABS MD-7-B
HABS MD,4-BALT,16B-
1ph L

North Central Railroad,Baltimore Freight House (Calvert Station)
Guilford & Centre Sts.
HAER MD-38
HAER MD,4-BALT,143-
7ph/1pg/2pc L

North Charles Street (House,Cast-Iron Porches) (Schapiro,John D. ,House; Peabody Conservatory of Music; Abell House)
609 Washington Place (N. Charles St.)
HABS MD-363
HABS MD,4-BALT,68-
1ph L

417 North Charles Street (Town House)
HABS MD-411
HABS MD,4-BALT,67-
1ph L

North Eutaw Street,Arthur's Bakery
(Arthur's Bakery)
223 N. Eutaw St.
HABS MD-40-A
HABS MD,4-BALT,171A-
10dr/21ph/4pg/2pc L

North Eutaw Street,No. 201 (Commercial Building)
HABS MD-40-B
HABS MD,4-BALT,171B-
3ph/1pg/1pc L

North Eutaw Street,No. 203-205 (Commercial Bldg.)
HABS MD-40-C
HABS MD,4-BALT,171C-
2ph/1pg/1pc L

North Eutaw Street,No. 207-209 (Commercial Bldgs)
HABS MD-40-D
HABS MD,4-BALT,171D-
2ph/1pg/1pc L

North Eutaw Street,No. 211 (Commercial Building)
HABS MD-40-E
HABS MD,4-BALT,171E-
2ph/2pg/1pc L

North Eutaw Street,No. 221 (Commercial Building)
HABS MD-40-F
HABS MD,4-BALT,171F-
2ph/1pg/1pc L

North Eutaw Street,200 Block (Commercial Bldgs.)
HABS MD-40
HABS MD,4-BALT,171-
2dr/1ph/5pg/1pc L

608-614 North Paca Street (Brick Row Houses)
HABS MD-405
HABS MD,4-BALT,99-
1ph L

123 North Paca Street (Commercial Building); see 123-125 North Paca Street (Commercial Buildings)

125 North Paca Street (Commercial Building); see 123-125 North Paca Street (Commercial Buildings)

123-125 North Paca Street (Commercial Buildings) (Lexington Market Addition; 123 North Paca Street (Commercial Building))
HABS MD-917-A
HABS MD,4-BALT,151A-
1ph/1pg/1pc L

123-125 North Paca Street (Commercial Buildings) (Lexington Market Addition; 125 North Paca Street (Commercial Building))
HABS MD-917-B
HABS MD,4-BALT,151B-
1ph/1pg/1pc L

508-522 North Paca Street (Houses)
HABS MD-382
HABS MD,4-BALT,98-
1ph L

420-422 North Washington Street (Houses)
HABS MD-905
HABS MD,4-BALT,158-
2ph/3pg/1pc L

Northeast Corridor; see Northeast Railroad Corridor

Northeast Corridor Project; see Union Junction Interlocking Tower

Northeast Railroad Corridor (Northeast Corridor)
Amtrak Rt. btwn. DC/MD & MD/DE State Lines
HAER MD-45
HAER MD,4-BALT,147-
60ph/6pc/fr L

Oaklands Springhouse; see Harper,Robert Goodloe,Dairy & Springhouse

1734-1736 Orleans Street (Double House)
HABS MD-18
HABS MD,4-BALT,21-
9dr/1ph/2pg L

Otterbein United Brethren Church (German Evangelical Reformed Church)
122 W. Conway St.
HABS MD-396
HABS MD,4-BALT,54-
4ph L

P. W. & B. Railroad,President Street Station (Pennsylvania RR,President Street Station)
President & Fleet St.
HABS MD-31
HAER MD-8
HABS/HAER MD,4-BALT,25-
4dr/8ph/5pg/fr L H

405-411 Park Avenue (Double Houses)
E. side between Mulberry & Franklin Sts.
HABS MD-351
HABS MD,4-BALT,80-
1ph L

Park Avenue (House Fronts)
400 Block (E. side)
HABS MD-383
HABS MD,4-BALT,100-
1ph L

Park Avenue (House Fronts)
400 Block & W. Centre St. (W. side)
HABS MD-384
HABS MD,4-BALT,101-
1ph L

833-837 Park Avenue (Houses)
HABS MD-385
HABS MD,4-BALT,102-
1ph L

Pascault Row
651-665 W. Lexington St.
HABS MD-397
HABS MD,4-BALT,84-
4ph/1pg/1pc/fr L

Peabody Conservatory of Music; see North Charles Street (House,Cast-Iron Porches)

1021 Peach Alley (House); see 129-169 Henrietta Street (Houses & Commercial Bldg

Peale,Rembrandt,Museum (Municipal Museum; Peale's Baltimore Museum & Gallery of Fine Arts)
225 N. Holliday St.
HABS MD-398
HABS MD,4-BALT,55-
6ph L

Peale's Baltimore Museum & Gallery of Fine Arts; see Peale,Rembrandt,Museum

Pennsylvania Railroad,Calvert Station
Calvert & Franklin Sts.
HABS MD-342
HABS MD,4-BALT,40-
4ph L

Pennsylvania Railroad:Canton Coal Pier
Clinton St. at Keith Ave. (Canton Ave.)
HAER MD-34
HAER MD,4-BALT,144-
44ph/2pg/3pc L

Pennsylvania RR,President Street Station; see P. W. & B. Railroad,President Street Station

Phoenix Shot Tower (Merchants' Shot Tower)
Front & Fayette Sts.
HABS MD-21
HABS MD,4-BALT,22-
2dr/4ph/8pg/fr L

Pickersgill,Mary Young,House; see Flag House

Pine Street,400 Block (Brick Houses)
HABS MD-386
HABS MD,4-BALT,103-
1ph L

Pleasant Street (Houses)
9,11,11 1/2,15 E. Pleasant St.
HABS MD-43
HABS MD,4-BALT,6-
1ph/4pg L

1023 Plum Alley (House); see 1022-1036 Sharp Street & 1017-1031 Plum Alley (Hse

1017-1031 Plum Alley (Houses); see 1022-1036 Sharp Street & 1017-1031 Plum Alley (Hse

Police Department Headquarters (Central Police Building,Old)
100 Fallsway
HABS MD-909
HABS MD,4-BALT,172-
34ph/14pg L

Poppleton (Houses)
W. Lexington,N. Schroeder,Vine, & N. Carlton Sts.
HABS MD-886
HABS MD,4-BALT,173-
8pg/fr L

Pratt & Paca Streets (Brick Building)
HABS MD-341
HABS MD,4-BALT,82-
1ph L

Public School No. 104; see Colored School No. 9

Public School No. 74 (Cromwell,Oliver,School)
220 Homewood Ave.
HABS MD-233
HABS MD,4-BALT,174-
5ph/8pg/1pc L

Purity Creamery Building; see 407-431 West Lexington Street (Commercial Bldgs.)

Randall,Blanchard,House (Tiffany-Fisher House; Mount Vernon Club)
8 W. Mount Vernon Place
HABS MD-371
HABS MD,4-BALT,56-;1988(HABS):118
1ph/fr L

Residence Row (8-18 West Hamilton Street (Houses))
HABS MD-399
HABS MD,4-BALT,95-
2ph L

Roman Catholic Cathedral of Baltimore (Minor Basilica,Assumption of the Virgin Mary)
Cathedral St.
HABS MD-186
HABS MD,4-BALT,41-
4ph/4pg L

Roman Catholic Episcopal Residence; see Archbishop's House

Round Top Church; see First Baptist Church

Saint Paul & Saratoga Streets (House)
HABS MD-70
HABS MD,4-BALT,32-
1ph L

Sanders House; see 520-522 South Chapel Street (Double House)

Schapiro,John D. ,House; see North Charles Street (House,Cast-Iron Porches)

Seven Store Fronts & Residences; see 635-647 West Pratt Street (Commercial Buildings)

1628-1630-1632 Shakespeare Street (Brick Houses)
HABS MD-387
HABS MD,4-BALT,105-
1ph L

Shakespeare Street,1600 Block (Brick Cottage)
HABS MD-346
HABS MD,4-BALT,83-
1ph L

1028 Sharp Street (House); see 1022-1036 Sharp Street & 1017-1031 Plum Alley (Hse

921 Sharp Street (House); see 901-947 Sharp Street (Houses & Commercial Bldgs.)

901-947 Sharp Street (Houses & Commercial Bldgs.) (921 Sharp Street (House); Sharp-Leadenhall Area Survey)
HABS MD-925-A
HABS MD,4-BALT,165A-
1dr L

901-947 Sharp Street (Houses & Commercial Bldgs.) (Sharp-Leadenhall Area Survey)
HABS MD-925
HABS MD,4-BALT,165-
1dr L

1001-1045 Sharp Street (Houses & Commercial Bldgs) (1023-1025 Sharp Street (Houses); Sharp-Leadenhall Area Survey)
HABS MD-926-A
HABS MD,4-BALT,149A-
1dr L

1001-1045 Sharp Street (Houses & Commercial Bldgs) (Sharp-Leadenhall Area Survey)
HABS MD-926
HABS MD,4-BALT,149-
1dr L

1023-1025 Sharp Street (Houses); see 1001-1045 Sharp Street (Houses & Commercial Bldgs)

1022-1036 Sharp Street & 1017-1031 Plum Alley (Hse (1017-1031 Plum Alley (Houses); 204-212 Cross Street (Houses); Sharp-Leadenhall Area Survey)
HABS MD-927
HABS MD,4-BALT,150-
1dr L

1022-1036 Sharp Street & 1017-1031 Plum Alley (Hse (1028 Sharp Street (House); 1023 Plum Alley (House); Sharp-Leadenhall Area Survey)
HABS MD-927-A
HABS 1985(HABS):119
1dr L

Sharp-Leadenhall Area Survey; see 129-169 Henrietta Street (Houses & Commercial Bldg

Sharp-Leadenhall Area Survey; see 129-169 Henrietta Street (Hses. & Comm. Bldgs.)

Sharp-Leadenhall Area Survey; see 901-947 Sharp Street (Houses & Commercial Bldgs.)

Sharp-Leadenhall Area Survey; see 1001-1045 Sharp Street (Houses & Commercial Bldgs)

Sharp-Leadenhall Area Survey; see 1022-1036 Sharp Street & 1017-1031 Plum Alley (Hse

Smith,Dr. James,House; see 15 East Pleasant Street (House)

Somerset Street,400 Block (Houses)
HABS MD-858
HABS MD,4-BALT,106-
1ph L

812 South Ann Street (House)
HABS MD-853
HABS MD,4-BALT,164-
8dr L

814 South Broadway (Brick Building) (Fell's Point Theatre; Foreign Market)
HABS MD-340
HABS MD,4-BALT,64-
1ph L

122-128 South Broadway (Brick Row Houses)
HABS MD-403
HABS MD,4-BALT,88-
1ph L

113 South Broadway Street (Second Story Porch) (East Indian Restaurant)
HABS MD-362
HABS MD,4-BALT,63-
1ph L

520-522 South Chapel Street (Double House) (Sanders House)
Fell's Point
HABS MD-4
HABS MD,4-BALT,13-
3dr/3ph/2pg/fr L

248-250 South Exeter Street (Double House)
HABS MD-349
HABS MD,4-BALT,70-
1ph L

104 South Exeter Street (House-Mantel)
HABS MD-364
HABS MD,4-BALT,69-
1ph L

832 South Hanover Street (Store Front)
HABS MD-6
HABS MD,4-BALT,15-
2dr/1ph/2pg/fr L

104-106 South Paca Street (Double Houses)
HABS MD-17
HABS MD,4-BALT,20-
5dr/1ph/2pg/fr L

37 South Street (Commercial Building)
HABS MD-918
HABS MD,4-BALT,156-
4ph/2pg/1pc L

St. Francis Xavier Roman Catholic Church
Calvert & Pleasant Sts.
HABS MD-30
HABS MD,4-BALT,24-
1ph/1pg L

St. James Catholic Church & Rectory
1225 E. Eager St.
HABS MD-969
HABS MD,4-BALT,175-
19ph/14pg/1pc L

St. Mary's Seminary
600 N. Paca St.
HABS MD-47
HABS MD,4-BALT,18-
47ph/12pg/6pc/fr L

St. Mary's Seminary Chapel
N. Paca St. & Druid Hill Ave.
HABS MD-13
HABS MD,4-BALT,18A-
17dr/25ph/9pg/fr L

St. Mary's Seminary,Mother Seton's House
600 N. Paca St.
HABS MD-391
HABS MD,4-BALT,18B-
6ph L

St. Paul's Rectory
24 W. Saratoga & Cathedral Sts.
HABS MD-409
HABS MD,4-BALT,4-
1ph L

Standard Distillers Products,Inc. ,Building
306-310 E. Lombard St.
HABS MD-897
HABS MD,4-BALT,176-
2dr/12ph/2pg/1pc L

Steele-Taggart House; see Taggart-Steele House

Stewart,David,House; see Damon House,Old

Strouse Building
Paca & Lombard Sts.
HAER MD-67
HAER MD,4-BALT,148-
4ph/1pc L

Sugar House (Refinery)
Aliceanna & Chester Sts.
HABS MD-11
HABS MD,4-BALT,17-
6dr/5ph/3pg/fr L

Swan-Frick House
W. Franklin St.
HABS MD-74
HABS MD,4-BALT,36-
1ph L

Taggart-Steele House (Steele-Taggart House)
Cathedral & Madison Sts.
HABS MD-410
HABS MD,4-BALT,57-
1ph L

1621 Thames Street (House) (Van Bidder House; Fell House)
Fell's Point
HABS MD-22
HABS MD,4-BALT,23-
11dr/15ph/5pg/fr L

1626-1628 Thames Street (Row Houses) (Forbes Houses)
HABS MD-406
HABS MD,4-BALT,107-
1ph L

Thomas-Jenks House; see 1 West Mount Vernon Place (House)

Tiffany-Fisher House; see Randall,Blanchard,House

U. S. Appraisers Stores,Old (U. S. Public Store Number 1)
Gay & Lombard Sts.
HABS MD-3
HABS MD,4-BALT,12-
6dr/12ph/3pg L

U. S. Public Store Number 1; see U. S. Appraisers Stores,Old

Union Junction Interlocking Tower (Northeast Corridor Project)
Bounded by Federal,Guilford,Royal, & Calvert Sts.
HAER MD-50
HAER MD,4-BALT,145-
6ph/14pg/1pc L

Unitarian Church; see First Unitarian Church

University of Maryland,Davidge Hall; see University of Maryland,Medical Building

University of Maryland,Medical Building (University of Maryland,Davidge Hall)
Greene & Lombard Sts.
HABS MD-304
HABS MD,4-BALT,59B-
11dr/2ph L

Upton; see Damon House,Old

Van Bidder House; see 1621 Thames Street (House)

341 W. Franklin Street (House-Exterior Stairway)
HABS MD-367
HABS MD,4-BALT,73-
1ph L

Washington Monument
Mount Vernon Place & Washington Place
HABS MD-71
HABS MD,4-BALT,33-
4ph L

Watchman Fire Company Firehouse (Mechanics Hall)
Montgomery St.
HABS MD-851
HABS MD,4-BALT,177-
1pg L

Waterloo Row (606-628 North Calvert Street (Houses))
HABS MD-7
HABS MD,4-BALT,16-
8dr/2ph/5pg/fr L

Waterloo Row; see 608 North Calvert Street (Row House)

Waterloo Row; see 612 North Calvert Street (Row House)

Waterloo Row; see 616 North Calvert Street (Row House)

Waterloo Row; see 622 North Calvert Street (Row House)

Waterloo Row; see 620 North Calvert Street (Stable)

922-924-926 Watson Street (Row Houses)
HABS MD-408
HABS MD,4-BALT,108-
1ph L

Waverly Terrace
N. Carey St. & Franklin Square
HABS MD-414
HABS MD,4-BALT,85-
3ph L

743-759 West Baltimore Street (Commercial Bldg.) (748-762 West Redwood Street (Houses); 642-652 West Conway Street (Houses))
HABS MD-928
HABS MD,4-BALT,162-
1dr L

646 West Conway Street (House) (819 West Lombard Street (House))
HABS MD-932
HABS MD,4-BALT,159-
1dr L

642-652 West Conway Street (Houses); see 743-759 West Baltimore Street (Commercial Bldg.)

741 West Fayette Street (House)
HABS MD-931
HABS MD,4-LT,161-
1dr L

704-714 & 733-743 West Fayette Street (Houses) (815-819 West Lombard Street (Houses))
HABS MD-929
HABS MD,4-BALT,160-
1dr L

8-18 West Hamilton Street (Houses); see Residence Row

837-843 West Lexington Street (Brick Houses)
HABS MD-381
HABS MD,4-BALT,97-
1ph L

419-421 West Lexington Street (Commercial Bldg.); see 407-431 West Lexington Street (Commercial Bldgs.)

423-425 West Lexington Street (Commercial Bldg.); see 407-431 West Lexington Street (Commercial Bldgs.)

407-431 West Lexington Street (Commercial Bldgs.) (Lexington Market Addition; 407 West Lexington Street (Commercial Building))
HABS MD-916-A
HABS MD,4-BALT,157A-
1ph/1pg/1pc L

407-431 West Lexington Street (Commercial Bldgs.) (Lexington Market Addition; 409 West Lexington Street (Commercial Building))
HABS MD-916-B
HABS MD,4-BALT,157B-
2ph/1pg/1pc L

407-431 West Lexington Street (Commercial Bldgs.) (Lexington Market Addition; 411 West Lexington Street (Commercial Building))
HABS MD-916-C
HABS MD,4-BALT,157C-
1ph/1pg/1pc L

407-431 West Lexington Street (Commercial Bldgs.) (Lexington Market Addition; 413 West Lexington Street (Commercial Building))
HABS MD-916-D
HABS MD,4-BALT,157D-
1ph/1pg/1pc L

407-431 West Lexington Street (Commercial Bldgs.) (Lexington Market Addition; 415 West Lexington Street (Commercial Building))
HABS MD-916-E
HABS MD,4-BALT,157E-
1ph/1pg/1pc L

407-431 West Lexington Street (Commercial Bldgs.) (Lexington Market Addition; 419-421 West Lexington Street (Commercial Bldg.))
HABS MD-916-F
HABS MD,4-BALT,157F-
1ph/1pg/1pc L

407-431 West Lexington Street (Commercial Bldgs.) (Lexington Market Addition; 423-425 West Lexington Street (Commercial Bldg.))
HABS MD-916-G
HABS MD,4-BALT,157G-
1ph/1pg/1pc L

407-431 West Lexington Street (Commercial Bldgs.) (Lexington Market Addition; Purity Creamery Building)
427-431 W. Lexington St.
HABS MD-916-H
HABS MD,4-BALT,157H-
4ph/1pg/1pc L

407 West Lexington Street (Commercial Building); see 407-431 West Lexington Street (Commercial Bldgs.)

409 West Lexington Street (Commercial Building); see 407-431 West Lexington Street (Commercial Bldgs.)

411 West Lexington Street (Commercial Building); see 407-431 West Lexington Street (Commercial Bldgs.)

413 West Lexington Street (Commercial Building); see 407-431 West Lexington Street (Commercial Bldgs.)

415 West Lexington Street (Commercial Building); see 407-431 West Lexington Street (Commercial Bldgs.)

742 West Lexington Street (House)
HABS MD-368
HABS MD,4-BALT,74-
1ph L

West Lexington Street,Murphy Building (Murphy Building; Hochschild-Kohn Annex)
320-322 W. Lexington St.
HABS MD-77-A
HABS MD,4-BALT,178A-
1dr/12ph/3pg/1pc/fr L

West Lexington Street,No. 308 (Commercial Bldg.) (Hochschild-Kohn Annex)
308 W. Lexington St.
HABS MD-77-H
HABS MD,4-BALT78H-
4ph/4pg/1pc L

West Lexington Street,No. 310 (Commercial Bldg.) (Hochschild-Kohn Annex)
310 W. Lexington St.
HABS MD-77-I
HABS MD,4-BALT,178I-
3ph/4pg/1pc L

West Lexington Street,No. 312 (Commercial Bldg.)
HABS MD-77-B
HABS MD,4-BALT,178B-
1ph/1pg/1pc/fr L

West Lexington Street,No. 314 (Commercial Bldg.)
HABS MD-77-C
HABS MD,4-BALT,178C-
2ph/2pg/1pc/fr L

West Lexington Street,No. 316-318 (Commer. Bldg.)
HABS MD-77-D
HABS MD,4-BALT,178D-
2ph/2pg/1pc/fr L

West Lexington Street,No. 324 (Commercial Bldg.)
HABS MD-77-E
HABS MD,4-BALT,178E-
1ph/1pg/1pc/fr L

West Lexington Street,No. 326 (Commercial Bldg.)
HABS MD-77-F
HABS MD,4-BALT,178F-
1ph/1pg/1pc/fr L

West Lexington Street,No. 328-330 (Commer. Bldg.)
HABS MD-77-G
HABS MD,4-BALT,178G-
3ph/2pg/1pc/fr L

West Lexington Street,300 Block (Commercial Bldgs)
HABS MD-77
HABS MD,4-BALT,178-
1dr/1ph/1pg/1pc/fr L

819 West Lombard Street (House); see 646 West Conway Street (House)

815-819 West Lombard Street (Houses); see 704-714 & 733-743 West Fayette Street (Houses)

107 West Monument Street (House) (Morton,George C. ,House)
HABS MD-1
HABS MD,4-BALT,11-
14dr/6ph/3pg/fr L

1 West Mount Vernon Place (House) (Jencks,Francis,House; Thomas-Jenks House; Gladding,Harry,House)
HABS MD-372
HABS MD,4-BALT,79-
3ph L

635-647 West Pratt Street (Commercial Buildings) (Seven Store Fronts & Residences)
HABS MD-16
HABS MD,4-BALT,19-
5dr/2ph/2pg/fr L

23-47 West Preston Street (Brick Row Houses)
HABS MD-407
HABS MD,4-BALT,104-
1ph L

756 West Redwood Street (House)
HABS MD-930
HABS MD,4-BALT,163-
1dr L

748-762 West Redwood Street (Houses); see 743-759 West Baltimore Street (Commercial Bldg.)

Wiessner Brewery (American Brewery)
1700 N. Gay St.
HAER MD-25
HAER MD,4-BALT,146-
20ph/5pg/3pc/fr L

Wilmot Street,800 Block (Houses)
HABS MD-389
HABS MD,4-BALT,109-
1ph L

Wilson,Henry,House; see Caton House

BALTIMORE COUNTY

BALTIMORE VIC.

Bridge No. 2; see Matthews Bridge

Gaugh,Harry Dorsey,House; see Perry Hall

Linden
Belair Rd. (U. S. Rt. 1)
HABS MD-848
HABS MD,3- ,3-
4ph L

Mann's Hill Bridge; see Matthews Bridge

Matthews Bridge (Mann's Hill Bridge; Bridge No. 2)
Spanning Loch Raven Reservoir on Dulaney Valley Rd
HAER MD-68
HAER MD,4-BALT.V,1-
11ph/1pg/1pc/fr L

Perry Hall (Gaugh,Harry Dorsey,House)
Perry Hall Rd. ,U. S. Rt. 1 Vic.
HABS MD-842
HABS MD,3-PERHA,1-
3ph L

CHASE VIC.

Aberdeen Proving Ground (Edgewood Arsenal)
(See HARFORD CO.,ABERDEEN for documentation)
HABS MD-1071
HAER MD-47
HABS/HAER MD,13-ABER,1-
106pg/fr L

Edgewood Arsenal; see Aberdeen Proving Ground

COCKEYSVILLE

(Doc. filed under Bladensburg,Prince Georges Co.); see Ross,Dr. David,House

Loveton
York Rd.
HABS MD-855
HABS MD,3-COCK,1-
8dr L

Ross House; see Ross,Dr. David,House

Ross,Dr. David,House (Ross House; (Doc. filed under Bladensburg,Prince Georges Co.)
Preserva. Hill,Western Run Rd (moved fr Bladensbrg
HABS MD-120
HABS MD,17-BLAD,2-
9dr/7ph/1pg/2pc L

COCKEYSVILLE VIC.

Balama Farms; see York Road (Stone House)

Hayfields Farm Buildings (Merryman,John,Farm Buildings)
Worthington Valley
HABS MD-15
HABS MD,3-COCK.V,1-
8dr/23ph/5pg/fr L

Merryman,John,Farm Buildings; see Hayfields Farm Buildings

York Road (Stone House) (Balama Farms)
Marble Hill Vic.
HABS MD-835
HABS MD,3-MARB.V,1-
1ph L

FORK VIC.

Pork Forest
Harford Rd. (State Rt. 197)
HABS MD-832
HABS MD,3-FORK.V,1-
5ph L

FRANKLINVILLE VIC.

Orwell
Franklinville Rd.
HABS MD-28
HABS MD,3-UPFA.V,1-
3ph/3pg L

HEREFORD VIC.

Barn,Stone & Brick; see Ednor & York Rds. (Stone Barn)

Ednor & York Rds. (Stone Barn) (Barn,Stone & Brick; Gorsuch,John M. ,Farm Barn; Glencoe Gardens)
HABS MD-61
HABS MD,3- ,2-
4ph L

Glencoe Gardens; see Ednor & York Rds. (Stone Barn)

Gorsuch,John M. ,Farm Barn; see Ednor & York Rds. (Stone Barn)

ILCHESTER

Mill Houses
River Rd.
HABS MD-830
HABS MD,3- ,5-
1ph L

Mill,Old
River Rd.
HABS MD-831
HABS MD,3- 4-
1ph L

ILCHESTER VIC.

Baltimore & Ohio Railroad,Patterson Viaduct (Patterson Viaduct)
W. Bank of Patapsco River,near Ilchester Bridge
HABS MD-878
HAER MD-12
HABS/HAER MD,3- ,6
3ph/1pc L

Patterson Viaduct; see Baltimore & Ohio Railroad,Patterson Viaduct

KINGSVILLE

Kingsville Inn (Interiors) (Lassahn,E. F. ,Funeral Parlor)
11750 Belair Rd. (U. S. Rt. 1)
HABS MD-833
HABS MD,3-KINVI,2-
2ph L

Lassahn,E. F. ,Funeral Parlor; see Kingsville Inn (Interiors)

KINGSVILLE VIC.

Bellevue Farm,Milk House (Milk House,Old)
Silver Spring Rd.
HABS MD-34
HABS MD,3-KINVI.V,1A-
3ph/2pg L

Irish Lane (House) (7221 New Cut Road (House))
HABS MD-834
HABS MD,3-KINVI.V,2-
1ph L

Milk House,Old; see Bellevue Farm,Milk House

7221 New Cut Road (House); see Irish Lane (House)

LONG GREEN

Prospect Hill (Ringgold House)
Kanes Rd.
HABS MD-325
HABS MD,3-LONGR,1-
6ph L

Ringgold House; see Prospect Hill

MONKTON VIC.

My Lady's Manor; see St. James' Church

St. James' Church (My Lady's Manor)
Monkton Rd.
HABS MD-836
HABS MD,3-MONK.V,1-
2ph L

OELLA

Mill Houses
929-947 Oella Ave.
HABS MD-839
HABS MD,3-0EL,2-
1ph L

Mill,Old
Oella Ave.
HABS MD-837
HABS MD,3-OEL,1-
1ph L

OWINGS MILL

Cooperage Shop,Old
Reisterstown Rd.
HABS MD-840
HABS MD,3-OWMI,1-
1ph L

Groff's Mill; see Mill Building

Mill Building (Groff's Mill; Owings Mill)
Bonita Ave.
HABS MD-841
HABS MD,3-OWMI,2-
2ph L

Owings Mill; see Mill Building

OWINGS MILLS VIC.

Blendon Estate (Caves Valley Historic District)
11747 Park Heights Ave.
HABS MD-994
HABS DLC/PP-1992:MD-5
1ph/9pg/1pc L

Blendon Estate,Barn (Caves Valley Historic District)
11747 Park Heights Ave.
HABS MD-994-B
HABS DLC/PP-1992:MD-5
16ph/11pg/2pc L

Blendon Estate,Tenant House (Caves Valley Historic District)
11747 Park Heights Ave.
HABS MD-994-A
HABS DLC/PP-1992:MD-5
11ph/11pg/2pc L

Caves Valley Historic District; see Blendon Estate

Caves Valley Historic District; see Blendon Estate,Barn

Caves Valley Historic District; see Blendon Estate,Tenant House

PARKTON VIC.

Halfway House; see Weisburg Inn

Weisburg Inn (Halfway House)
York & Weisburg Rds.
HABS MD-332
HABS MD,3-PARK.V,1-
2ph L

PHOENIX VIC.

Phillpot House (Rockford)
Phillpot Rd.
HABS MD-333
HABS MD,3-PHEN,1-
4ph L

Rockford; see Phillpot House

PIKESVILLE

U. S. Arsenal
Reisterstown Rd.
HABS MD-14
HABS MD,3-PIKV,1-
14dr/20ph/8pg/fr L

RANDALLSTOWN VIC.

Branton (Wyatt Place; Residence,Old)
Liberty Rd.
HABS MD-334
HABS MD,3-RAND.V,1-
1ph L

Residence,Old; see Branton

Wyatt Place; see Branton

REISTERSTOWN VIC.

Craddock House; see Ten Mile House

Ten Mile House (Craddock House)
Reisterstown Rd.
HABS MD-335
HABS MD,3-REIST.V,1-
2ph L

SUNNYBROOK

King's Tavern (Interior)
HABS MD-849
HABS MD,3-SUNB,1-
1ph L

SWEET AIR

Boyce,Roger,House; see Sweet Air

Clynmalira Manor; see Sweet Air

Sweet Air (Clynmalira Manor; Boyce,Roger,House)
Manor Rd. & State Rt. 145
HABS MD-337
HABS MD,3-SWETA,1-
5ph L

TOWSON

Baltimore County Courthouse
Washington Ave.
HABS MD-338
HABS MD,3-TOW,1-
1ph L

Hampton (Hampton Farm; Hampton National Historic Site)
535 Hampton Lane; 537 1/2 St. Francis Rd.
HABS MD-226
HABS MD,3-TOW.V,1-
3dr L

Hampton Farm; see Hampton

Hampton Mansion (Hampton National Historic Site)
535 Hampton Lane
HABS MD-226-A
HABS MD,3-TOW.V,1A-
18dr/25ph/24pg/fr L

Hampton National Historic Site; see Hampton

Hampton National Historic Site; see Hampton Mansion

Hampton National Historic Site; see Hampton,Carpenter-Blacksmith Shop

Hampton National Historic Site; see Hampton,Corn Crib

Hampton National Historic Site; see Hampton,Cow Barn

Hampton National Historic Site; see Hampton,Dairy

Hampton National Historic Site; see Hampton,Greenhouse Number One

Hampton National Historic Site; see Hampton,Icehouse

Hampton National Historic Site; see Hampton,Long Barn-Granary

Hampton National Historic Site; see Hampton,Mule Barn

Hampton National Historic Site; see Hampton,Overseer's House

Hampton National Historic Site; see Hampton,Quarters One

Hampton National Historic Site; see Hampton,Quarters Three

Hampton National Historic Site; see Hampton,Quarters Two

Hampton National Historic Site; see Hampton,Stable Number One

Hampton National Historic Site; see Hampton,Stable Number Two

Hampton,Blacksmith Shop; see Hampton,Carpenter-Blacksmith Shop

Hampton,Burial Vault
535 Hampton Lane
HABS MD-226-W
HABS MD,3-TOW.V,1Y-
6pg L

Hampton,Carpenter-Blacksmith Shop (Hampton,Blacksmith Shop; Hampton National Historic Site)
537 1/2 St. Francis Rd.
HABS MD-226-I
HABS MD,3-TOW.V,1V-
1dr/1ph/4pg/fr L

Hampton,Carriage House
535 Hampton Lane
HABS MD-226-P
HABS MD,3-TOW.V,1H-
5pg L

Hampton,Corn Crib (Hampton National Historic Site)
537 1/2 St. Francis Rd.
HABS MD-226-N
HABS MD,3-TOW.V,1W-
1dr/1ph/4pg/fr L

Hampton,Cow Barn (Hampton National Historic Site)
537 1/2 St. Francis Rd.
HABS MD-226-H
HABS MD,3-TOW.V,1U-
2dr/3ph/5pg/fr L

Hampton,Dairy (Hampton National Historic Site)
537 1/2 St. Francis Rd.
HABS MD-226-F
HABS MD,3-TOW.V,1S-
3dr/3ph/5pg/fr L

Hampton,Farmhouse; see Hampton,Overseer's House

Hampton,Gardener's House
535 Hampton Lane
HABS MD-226-V
HABS MD,3-TOW.V,1K-
9pg L

Hampton,Granary; see Hampton,Long Barn-Granary

Hampton,Greenhouse Number One (Hampton National Historic Site)
535 Hampton Lane
HABS MD-226-D
HABS MD,3-TOW.V,1I-
1dr/1ph/5pg/fr L

Hampton,Greenhouse Number Two
535 Hampton Lane
HABS MD-226-U
HABS MD,3-TOW.V,1J-
5pg L

Hampton,Icehouse (Hampton National Historic Site)
535 Hampton Lane
HABS MD-226-E
HABS MD,3-TOW.V,1T-
2dr/2ph/4pg/fr L

Hampton,Long Barn-Granary (Hampton,Granary; Hampton National Historic Site)
537 1/2 Saint Francis Rd.
HABS MD-226-G
HABS MD,3-TOW.V,1-;83:160;86:38
1dr/10ph/4pg/1pc/fr L

Hampton,Mule Barn (Hampton National Historic Site)
537 1/2 St. Francis Rd.
HABS MD-226-O
HABS MD,3-TOW.V,1X-ι1983(HABS):160°
1dr/1ph/4pg/fr L

Hampton,Orangery
535 Hampton Lane
HABS MD-226-R
HABS MD,3-TOW.V,1C-
1ph/5pg L

Hampton,Overseer's House (Hampton,Farmhouse; Hampton National Historic Site)
537 1/2 St. Francis Rd.
HABS MD-226-J
HABS MD,3-TOW.V,1N-
3dr/4ph/8pg/fr L

Hampton,Privy
535 Hampton Lane
HABS MD-226-Q
HABS MD,3-TOW.V,1E-
5pg L

Hampton,Quarters One (Hampton National Historic Site)
537 1/2 St. Francis Rd.
HABS MD-226-K
HABS MD,3-TOW.V,1P-ı1983(HABS):160°
1dr/4pg/fr L

Hampton,Quarters Three (Hampton National Historic Site)
537 1/2 St. Francis Rd.
HABS MD-226-M
HABS MD,3-TOW.V,1R-
1dr/1ph/5pg/fr L

Hampton,Quarters Two (Hampton National Historic Site)
537 1/2 St. Francis Rd.
HABS MD-226-L
HABS MD,3-TOW.V,1Q-ı1983(HABS):160°
1dr/1ph/5pg/fr L

Hampton,Smokehouse
535 Hampton Lane
HABS MD-226-T
HABS MD,3-TOW.V,1G-
4pg L

Hampton,Stable Number One (Hampton National Historic Site)
535 Hampton Lane
HABS MD-226-B
HABS MD,3-TOW.V,1L-
6dr/2ph/7pg/fr L

Hampton,Stable Number Two (Hampton National Historic Site)
535 Hampton Lane
HABS MD-226-C
HABS MD,3-TOW.V,1M-
6dr/6pg/fr L

Hampton,Woodshed
535 Hampton Lane
HABS MD-226-S
HABS MD,3-TOW.V,1F-
5pg L

WOODLAWN

6720 Dogwood Road (House)
6720 Dogwood Rd.
HABS MD-992
HABS 1991(HABS):30
3dr/fr L

CALVERT COUNTY

ADELINA

Berry; see Taney Place

Hance,Benjamin,House; see Taney Place

Taney Place (Berry; Hance,Benjamin,House)
State Rt. 508
HABS MD-138
HABS MD,5-PRIFK.V,1-
3ph L

BARSTOW VIC.

Cedar Hill (Gant House)
German Chapel Rd.
HABS MD-173
HABS MD,5-SOL.V,1-
1ph L

Gant House; see Cedar Hill

CHANEYVILLE VIC.

Caucaud,David,House; see Talbot,Dr. Russell,House

Hampton; see Talbot,Dr. Russell,House

Talbot,Dr. Russell,House (Hampton; Caucaud,David,House)
Flint Hill Rd.
HABS MD-145
HABS MD,5- ,3-
1ph L

DARE'S WHARF VIC.

Dare House
Dare's Rd. (State Rt. 402)
HABS MD-124
HABS MD,5- ,2-
1ph L

HUNTINGTOWN VIC.

Huntingfields; see Stanforth,John,House

Lowery; see Stanforth,John,House

Lyon House; see Stanforth,John,House

Stanforth,John,House (Huntingfields; Lowery; Lyon House)
Lowery Rd. Vic.
HABS MD-105
HABS MD,5-HUNT,1-
3ph L

LITTLE COVE POINT

Clark,Capt. ,House; see Eltonhead Manor

Eltonhead Manor (Clark,Capt. ,House; Little Cove Point Road (Old House))
HABS MD-2
HABS MD,5- ,1-
3dr/6ph/4pg L

Little Cove Point Road (Old House); see Eltonhead Manor

LOWER MARLBORO

Wilson House
(moved from MD,Upper Marlboro)
HABS MD-126
HABS MD,17-MARBU,2-
2ph L

LOWER MARLBORO VIC.

Building,Small
State Rt. 262
HABS MD-131
HABS MD,5-MARL.V,2-
2ph L

Graeme,Charles,House; see Graeme,Malcolm,House

Graeme,Malcolm,House (Patuxent Manor; Graeme,Charles,House)
State Rt. 262 Vic.
HABS MD-122
HABS MD,5-MARL.V,1-
2ph L

Patuxent Manor; see Graeme,Malcolm,House

LUSBY VIC.

Arminger's Bar; see Solomons Island Road (Farmhouse)

Breedon-Day Farm; see Day-Breedon House & Farm Buildings

Charles' Gift (House on Calvert Cliffs; Preston's Cliff)
State Rts. 2 & 4
HABS MD-416
HABS MD,5-LUSB.V,6-
2dr/14ph/1pc L

Christ Church Parish; see Middleham Protestant Episcopal Chapel

Corn Crib on the Cliffs; see House,Old Frame,& Log Corn Crib

Day-Breedon House & Farm Buildings (Morgan Hill Farm Buildings; Day,Robert,House; Breedon-Day Farm)
Sollers Rd.
HABS MD-175
HABS MD,5-SOL.V,2
4dr/8ph/1pc L

Day-Breedon House & Farm Buildings,Corn Crib
Sollers Rd.
HABS MD-175-B
HABS MD,5-SOL.V,28-
1ph/1pc L

Day-Breedon House & Farm Buildings,Tobacco House
Sollers Rd.
HABS MD-175-A
HABS MD,5-SOL.V,2A-
3ph/1pc L

Day,Robert,House; see Day-Breedon House & Farm Buildings

Documentation: **ct** color transparencies **dr** measured drawings **fr** field records
pc photograph captions **pg** pages of text **ph** photographs

Goldstein House (Parran's Park; Lusby (House))
State Rts. 2 & 4
HABS MD-162
HABS MD,5-LUSB.V,3-
1ph L

House on Calvert Cliffs; see Charles' Gift

House,Old Frame,& Log Corn Crib (Corn Crib on the Cliffs)
Calvert Cliffs
HABS MD-415
HABS MD,5-LUSB.V,4-
4ph L

Lusby (Frame House); see Solomons Island Road (Farmhouse)

Lusby (House); see Goldstein House

Middleham Protestant Episcopal Chapel (Christ Church Parish)
Solomons Island Rd. (State Rts. 2 & 4)
HABS MD-418
HABS MD,5-LUSB.V,1-
1ph L

Morgan Hill Farm Buildings; see Day-Breedon House & Farm Buildings

Parran's Park; see Goldstein House

Preston-on-the-Patuxent (Preston,Richard,House)
Turner Rd.
HABS MD-419
HABS MD,5-SOL.V,4-
5ph L

Preston,Richard,House; see Preston-on-the-Patuxent

Preston's Cliff; see Charles' Gift

Solomons Island Road (Farmhouse) (Arminger's Bar; Lusby (Frame House))
State Rts. 2 & 4
HABS MD-133
HABS MD,5-LUSB.V,2-
1ph L

Solomons Island Road (Frame House)
HABS MD-889
HABS MD,5-LUSB.V,5-
1ph L

MACKALL

Mackall House (Mackall's Hill)
St. Leonard Creek
HABS MD-129
HABS MD,5-MACK,1-
1ph L

Mackall's Hill; see Mackall House

OWINGS VIC.

Maidstone
HABS MD-895
HABS MD,5-OWI.V,1-
2dr L

PRINCE FREDERICK VIC

Kitts Marsh Farm,Tobacco Barn; see Tobacco Barn

Tobacco Barn (Kitts Marsh Farm,Tobacco Barn)
Patuxent River,State Rt. 508
HABS MD-420
HABS MD,5-PRIFK.V,2-
1ph L

SOLLERS VIC.

Cage,The; see Parrott's Cage

Parran,Thomas,House; see Parrott's Cage

Parrott,William,House; see Parrott's Cage

Parrott's Cage (Parran,Thomas,House; Cage,The; Parrott,William,House)
Cage Rd.
HABS MD-174
HABS MD,5-SOL.V,3-
2ph L

SOLOMONS

Bugeye "Louise Travers"
Intersection Rts. 2 & 4,Solomons,MD
HAER MD-55
HAER 1991(HAER):13
13dr/25ph/10pg/2pc/fr L

SOLOMONS ISLAND VIC.

Tobacco Barn
Prince Frederick Vic.
HABS MD-421
HABS MD,5-SOLO.V,1-
1ph L

STOAKLEY

Solomons Island Road (Tobacco Barn)
State Rts. 2 & 4
HABS MD-422
HABS MD,5-PRIFK.V,3-
1ph L

SUNDERLAND VIC.

All Saints' Protestant Episcopal Church
State Rts. 2 & 4
HABS MD-423
HABS MD,5-SUND.V,1-
1ph L

CAROLINE COUNTY

BETHLEHEM

White Marsh Farm (White Marshes)
State Rt. 328
HABS MD-424
HABS MD,6-BETH.V,1-
3ph L

White Marshes; see White Marsh Farm

DENTON

28 Third Street (House)
HABS MD-882
HABS MD,6-DENT,1-
1ph/4pg/1pc L

FEDERALSBURG

Federalsburg Windmill
Oak Grove Rd.
HABS MD-425
HABS MD,6-FEDBU,1-
1ph L

RIDGELY

510 Central (Commercial Bldg) (Lane & Lang's Hardware; Rampmeyer's,Lucy,Store)
HABS MD-970
HABS MD,6-RIDG,1-
8ph/3pg/2pc L

Lane & Lang's Hardware; see 510 Central (Commercial Bldg)

Rampmeyer's,Lucy,Store; see 510 Central (Commercial Bldg)

WILLISTON LANDING

Philips Range; see Williston Road (Brick House)

Potter Hall; see Williston Road (Brick House)

Store,Old
HABS MD-427
HABS MD,6-WIL,2-
1ph L

Williston Road (Brick House) (Potter Hall; Philips Range)
Choptank River Vic.
HABS MD-426
HABS MD,6-WIL,1-
2ph L

CARROLL COUNTY

KEYMAR VIC.

Keymar Bridge
Spanning Little Pipe Creek
HABS MD-20
HABS MD,7-KEYM.V,1-
1dr/2ph/1pg/fr L

SYKESVILLE

Baltimore & Ohio Railroad,Sykesville Station (Sykesville Station)
W. Side of Main St.
HAER MD-19
HAER MD,7-SYK,1-
1ph/1pc L

Sykesville Station; see Baltimore & Ohio Railroad,Sykesville Station

WESTMINSTER

19-21 Union Street (House)
HABS MD-921
HABS MD,7-WEMIN,1-
4ph/1pg/1pc L

29 1/2 Union Street (House)
HABS MD-923
HABS MD,7-WEMIN,3-
3ph/1pg/1pc L

27-29 Union Street (Houses)
HABS MD-922
HABS MD,7-WEMIN,2-
3ph/1pg/1pc L

Union Street District
Union St. btwn. Pennsylvania Ave. & W. Main St.
HABS MD-898
HABS MD,7-WEMIN,4-
5pg L

Westminster Rescue Mission
Railroad Ave. & Winters St.
HABS MD-933
HABS MD,7-WEMIN,5-
4ph/3pg/1pc L

CECIL COUNTY

BLUE BALL

Blue Ball Tavern (Job,Andrew,House)
State Rt. 273 & Blue Ball Rd. (State Rt. 545)
HABS MD-428
HABS MD,8-BLUBA,1-
1ph L

Job,Andrew,House; see Blue Ball Tavern

BOHEMIA RIVER

Bohemia (MacGregory Delight; Milligan Hall; Milligan,George,House)
HABS MD-23
HABS MD,8- ,1-
10ph/1pg L

MacGregory Delight; see Bohemia

Milligan Hall; see Bohemia

Milligan,George,House; see Bohemia

CALVERT VIC.

Meetinghouse,Brick
Calvert & Bayview Rds.
HABS MD-429
HABS MD,8-CALV.V,1-
2ph L

CECILTON

House,Old Frame
U. S. Rt. 213 & State Rt. 282
HABS MD-430
HABS MD,8-CECI,1-
1ph L

CECILTON VIC.

Anchorage,The; see Fredericktown Road (Brick Farmhouse)

Fredericktown Road (Brick Farmhouse) (Anchorage,The)
U. S. Rt. 213
HABS MD-431
HABS MD,8-CECI.V,2-
1ph L

Greenfield Castle & Outbuildings
U. S. Rt. 213
HABS MD-432
HABS MD,8-CECI.V,1-
2ph L

CHARLESTOWN

Bladen Street (Frame House with Gambrel Roof)
HABS MD-435
HABS MD,8-CHART,3-
3ph L

Indian Queen & Adjacent Houses (Indian Queen Tavern; Red Lyon Inn's Indian Queen Hotel)
Market St.
HABS MD-436
HABS MD,8-CHART,1-
1ph L

Indian Queen Tavern; see Indian Queen & Adjacent Houses

Market Street (Brick House)
Indian Queen Vic.
HABS MD-434
HABS MD,8-CHART,2-
1ph L

Red Lyon Inn's Indian Queen Hotel; see Indian Queen & Adjacent Houses

CHESAPEAKE CITY

Chesapeake & Delaware Canal:Pump House
C & D Canal,south side of
HAER MD-39
HAER MD,8-CHESCI,1-
5dr/21pg/fr L

CONONINGO VIC.

Success
U. S. Rt. 222
HABS MD-437
HABS MD,8-CONO.V,1-
2ph L

EARLEVILLE VIC.

Bellevue (Frisby's Prime Choice)
State Rt. 282
HABS MD-438
HABS MD,8-EARL.V,1-
1ph L

Frisby's Prime Choice; see Bellevue

Grove Neck; see Rich Neck Farm

Mt Harmon Plantation at World's End
HABS MD-861
HABS MD,8-EARL.V,2-
24ph/1pg/2pc/2ct L

Mt Harmon Plantation at World's End,Kitchen
HABS MD-861-A
HABS MD,8-EARL.V,2A-
4ph/1pc L

Mt Harmon Plantatn at Worlds End,Tobacco Prize Hse
HABS MD-861-B
HABS MD,8-EARL.V,2B-
3ph/1pc L

Rich Neck Farm (Grove Neck)
Grove Neck Rd. Vic.
HABS MD-457
HABS MD,8- ,2-
1ph L

ELK MILLS

Elk Mills (Building)
State Rt. 277 Vic.
HABS MD-439
HABS MD,8,ELKMI,1-
2ph L

Mill Houses (Mill Village,Row Houses)
State Rt. 277
HABS MD-440
HABS MD8,ELKMI,2-
1ph L

Mill Village,Row Houses; see Mill Houses

ELK MILLS VIC.

House,Old Stone,with Frame Addition
State Rt. 316
HABS MD-441
HABS MD,8-ELKMI.V,1-
1ph L

ELKTON

American Legion Cecil Post 15; see Partridge Hill

Cast-Iron Grapevine Porch (226 Main Street (House))
HABS MD-449
HABS MD,8-ELKO,10-
1ph L

Elkton House; see 222 Main Street (Brick House)

Elkton Landing (Stone House)
Landing Lane
HABS MD-444
HABS MD,8-ELKTO,12-
2ph L

Fountain Inn
HABS MD-442
HABS MD,8-ELKTO,1-
3ph L

Hollingsworth Tavern
205 Main St.
HABS MD-443
HABS MD,8-ELKTO,2-
1ph L

Hollingsworth,Col. Henry,House; see Partridge Hill

222 Main Street (Brick House) (Elkton House)
HABS MD-447
HABS MD,8-ELKO,4-
1ph L

Main Street (House) (Mitchell,Dr. Abraham,House)
E. of North St.
HABS MD-446
HABS MD,8-ELKO,8-
2ph L

142 Main Street (House) (Wedding Chapel)
HABS MD-450
HABS MD,8-ELKO,11-
1ph L

205 Main Street (House)
HABS MD-448
HABS MD,8-ELKO,9-
1ph L

226 Main Street (House); see Cast-Iron Grapevine Porch

Main Street (House-Entrance Doorway)
E. of Bow St.
HABS MD-445
HABS MD,8-ELKO,7-
1ph L

Mitchell,Dr. Abraham,House; see Main Street (House)

Partridge Hill (Hollingsworth,Col. Henry,House; American Legion Cecil Post 15)
129 Main St.
HABS MD-452
HABS MD,8-ELKTO,3-
7ph L

Pearce Store; see South Main Street (Brick House)

South Main Street (Brick House) (Pearce Store)
HABS MD-453
HABS MD,8-ELKTO,5-
1ph L

Wedding Chapel; see 142 Main Street (House)

West Main & North Bridge Streets (Brick House)
HABS MD-451
HABS MD,8-ELKO,6-
1ph L

ELKTON VIC.

Brentwood; see West Williams Road (Brick Farmhouse)

Cecil County Center & Red Cross; see Holly Hall

Frenchtown Landing House
Frenchtown Rd.
HABS MD-454
HABS MD,8,ELKTOV.1-
2ph L

Holly Hall (Cecil County Center & Red Cross; Sewell,Gen. James,House)
U. S. Rt. 213
HABS MD-455
HABS MD,8-ELKTO.V,2-
5ph L

Sewell,Gen. James,House; see Holly Hall

West Williams Road (Brick Farmhouse) (Brentwood)
HABS MD-456
HABS MD,8-ELKTO.V,3-
1ph L

LANGFORD VIC.

Farmhouse,Brick (Stephney Farm)
HABS MD-458
HABS MD,8- ,3-
1ph L

Stephney Farm; see Farmhouse,Brick

NORTH EAST

Green Hill,Slave Quarters & Woodhouse (Russell,Thomas,House)
State Rt. 7
HABS MD-459
HABS MD,8-NOREA,3A-
1ph L

House,Frame
HABS MD-460
HABS MD,8-NOREA,4-
1ph L

Inn,Old
HABS MD-461
HABS MD,8-NOREA,2-
5ph L

Russell,Thomas,House; see Green Hill,Slave Quarters & Woodhouse

St. Mary's Protestant Episcopal Church
State Rt. 272
HABS MD-462
HABS MD,8-NOREA,1-
3ph L

PERRYVILLE VIC.

Principio Furnace
Port Rd. (State Rt. 7)
HABS MD-467
HABS MD,8-PRINF,1-
3ph L

PORT DEPOSIT

184-186 Conowingo Road (Row Houses); see Main Street (Block of Houses)

Main Street (Block of Houses) (184-186 Conowingo Road (Row Houses))
U. S. Rt. 222
HABS MD-465
HABS MD.8.PODEP,4-
1ph L

58 Main Street (Houses)
Conowingo Rd. (U. S. Rt. 222)
HABS MD-464
HABS MD,8-PODEP,3-
1ph L

Main Street (Stone House)
Conowingo Rd. (U. S. Rt. 222)
HABS MD-463
HABS MD,8-PODEP,2-
1ph L

Tome,Jacob,Mansion
U. S. Rt. 222
HABS MD-466
HABS MD,8-PODEP,1-
1ph L

ST. AUGUSTINE

Great House Farm; see Great House Plantation

Great House Plantation (Great House Farm)
Mitton Rd.
HABS MD-468
HABS MD,8-SAUG,1-
8ph/1pg L

WARWICK

Old Bohemia; see St. Francis Xavier Roman Catholic Church

St. Francis Xavier Roman Catholic Church (Old Bohemia)
Warwick & Church Rds.
HABS MD-241
HABS MD,8-WAR,1-
7dr/12ph/3pg L

CHARLES COUNTY

BLOSSOM POINT

Ballast House
La Plata Vic.
HABS MD-318
HABS MD,9-BLOPT,1-
7dr/10ph/9pg/1pc/fr L

BRYANS ROAD VIC.

Marshall Hall
State Rt. 227 at Potomac River
HABS MD-891
HABS MD,9-BRYRO.V,1-
6dr L

LA PLATA VIC.

Habre de Venture (Stone,Thomas,House; Stone,Thomas,National Historic Site)
Rose Hill Rd.
HABS MD-470
HABS MD,9-PORTO.V,3-
14dr/5ph/fr L

Habre de Venture,Corn Crib (Stone,Thomas,House,Corn Crib; Stone,Thomas,National Historic Site)
Rose Hill Rd.
HABS MD-470-B
HABS MD,9-PORTO.V,3B-
3dr/fr L

Habre de Venture,Main Barn (Stone,Thomas,House,Main Barn; Stone,Thomas,National Historic Site)
Rose Hill Rd.
HABS MD-470-A
HABS MD,9-PORTO.V,3A-
5dr/fr L

Habre de Venture,Tenant House (Stone,Thomas,House,Tenant House; Stone,Thomas,National Historic Site)
Rose Hill Rd.
HABS MD-470-C
HABS MD,9-PORTO.V,3C-
2dr/fr L

Habre de Venture,Wagon House (Stone,Thomas,House,Wagon House; Stone,Thomas,National Historic Site)
Rose Hill Rd.
HABS MD-470-D
HABS MD,9-PORTO.V,3D-
1dr/fr L

Locust Grove
HABS MD-240
HABS MD,9-LAPLA.V,2-
11dr L

Stone,Thomas,House; see Habre de Venture

Stone,Thomas,House,Corn Crib; see Habre de Venture,Corn Crib

Stone,Thomas,House,Main Barn; see Habre de Venture,Main Barn

Stone,Thomas,House,Tenant House; see Habre de Venture,Tenant House

Stone,Thomas,House,Wagon House; see Habre de Venture,Wagon House

Stone,Thomas,National Historic Site; see Habre de Venture

Stone,Thomas,National Historic Site; see Habre de Venture,Corn Crib

Stone,Thomas,National Historic Site; see Habre de Venture,Main Barn

Stone,Thomas,National Historic Site; see Habre de Venture,Tenant House

Stone,Thomas,National Historic Site; see Habre de Venture,Wagon House

MARBURY VIC.

Mattawoman; see Smallwood's Retreat

Smallwood,Gen. William,House; see Smallwood's Retreat

Smallwood's Retreat (Mattawoman; Smallwood,Gen. William,House)
State Rts. 224 & 484
HABS MD-38
HABS MD,9-MARB.V,1-
7dr/12ph/1pg/fr L

MORGANTOWN

Harris,Morgan,House; see Waverly

Waverly (Harris,Morgan,House)
State Rt. 229 Vic.
HABS MD-177
HABS MD,9-WAY.V,1-
2ph L

NEWPORT VIC.

Sarum
State Rt. 234 Vic.
HABS MD-860
HABS MD,9-NEPO.V,1-
20ph/1pg/1pc L

PORT TOBACCO

Chapel Point Road (Gambrel Roof House) (Stagg Hall; Parnham-Padgett House)
HABS MD-469
HABS MD,9-PORTO,1-
1ph L

Parnham-Padgett House; see Chapel Point Road (Gambrel Roof House)

Stagg Hall; see Chapel Point Road (Gambrel Roof House)

PORT TOBACCO VIC.

Brown,Dr. Gustavus,House; see Rose Hill

Rose Hill (Brown,Dr. Gustavus,House)
Rose Hill Rd.
HABS MD-58
HABS MD,9-PORTO.V,1-
5ph/1pg L

WALDORE

Bolton
HABS MD-893
HABS MD,9-WALD,1-
1dr L

DORCHESTER COUNTY

CAMBRIDGE VIC.

Farm Group
E. New Market Vic.
HABS MD-471
HABS MD,10-CAMB.V,2-
1ph L

Green Farm; see House, Brick end frame,with Gambrel roof

House, Brick end frame,with Gambrel roof (Green Farm)
U. S. Rt. 50 Vic.
HABS MD-474
HABS MD,10-CAMB.V,4-
2ph L

House,Frame
E. New Market Vic.
HABS MD-473
HABS MD,10-CAMB.V,3-
1ph L

House,Haunted (Shoal Creek House)
U. S. Rt. 50 Vic.
HABS MD-472
HABS MD,10-CAMB.V,1-
1ph L

Shoal Creek House; see House,Haunted

CHURCH CREEK

Trinity Episcopal Church,Old
Church Creek Rd. (State Rt. 16)
HABS MD-201
HABS MD,10-CHUCK,1-
1ph/2pg L

ELDORADO VIC.

Lee House; see Rehobeth

Rehobeth (Lee House)
Punkum Rd.
HABS MD-27
HABS MD,10-ELDO.V,1-
2ph/5pg L

NEW MARKET

Friendship Hall
State Rts. 16 & 14
HABS MD-475
HABS MD,10-NEMAE,2-
5ph L

House,Old,of the Hinges & Outbuildings
HABS MD-476
HABS MD,10-NEMAE,1-
4ph L

Rose Hill
HABS MD-859
HABS MD,10-NEMA,1-
5dr/9ph/1pc L

Rose Hill,Dependency
HABS MD-859-A
HABS MD,10-NEMA,1A-
1ph/1pc L

SECRETARY

Carthagena; see Sewall,Henry,House

My Lady Sewall's Manor House; see Sewall,Henry,House

Sewall,Henry,House (My Lady Sewall's Manor House; Carthagena; Tripp,Henry,House)
My Lady Sewall's Manor Rd. & State Rt. 14
HABS MD-60
HABS MD,10-SEC,1-
1ph/1pg L

Tripp,Henry,House; see Sewall,Henry,House

SECRETARY VIC.

Warwick Fort Manor House (Ruins)
Warwick Rd.
HABS MD-169
HABS MD,10-SEC.V,1-
1ph L

SHARPTOWN VIC.

Sharptown Bridge
Spanning Nanticoke River,State Rt. 313
HAER MD-52
HAER MD,10-SHATO.V,1-
31ph/3pg/3pc L

VIENNA

Nanticoke River (Frame House)
HABS MD-477
HABS MD,10-VIENA,1-
1ph L

FREDERICK COUNTY

BRUNSWICK

Chesapeake & Ohio Canal National Historical Park; see Chesapeake & Ohio Canal,Lock 30

Chesapeake & Ohio Canal,Lock 30 (Chesapeake & Ohio Canal National Historical Park)
HABS MD-754
HABS MD,11-BRUN,1-
1ph/1pc L

CATOCTIN VIC.

Catoctin Furnace,Stack Number 2 (Isabella)
U. S. Rt. 15
HABS MD-478
HABS MD,11-CATOC.V,1-
1ph L

Isabella; see Catoctin Furnace,Stack Number 2

CATOCTIN VILLAGE

Catoctin Manor (Iron Master's House)
U. S. Rt. 15
HABS MD-479
HABS MD,11-CATOC,1-
1ph L

Iron Master's House; see Catoctin Manor

Main Street (Cottages) (Stone Workers' Cottages)
State Rt. 806
HABS MD-480
HABS MD,11-CATOC,2-
2ph L

Stone Workers' Cottages; see Main Street (Cottages)

DICKERSON VIC.

Chesapeake & Ohio Canal National Historical Park; see Chesapeake & Ohio Canal,Monocacy Aqueduct

Chesapeake & Ohio Canal,Monocacy Aqueduct (Chesapeake & Ohio Canal National Historical Park)
42.2 Miles above Tidewater (above Lock 27)
HABS MD-19
HABS MD,11- ,3
2dr/16ph/3pg/1pc/fr L

Rock Hall & Slave Quarters
HABS MD-572
HABS MD,11- ,4-
6ph/fr L

FREDERICK

119-150 All Saints Street (Houses)
HABS MD-481
HABS MD,11-FRED,14-
1ph L

All Saints' Chapel; see All Saints' Parish Episcopal Church

All Saints' Parish Episcopal Church (All Saints' Chapel)
Lee Court
HABS MD-490
HABS MD,11-FRED,3-
1ph L

Baltimore & Ohio Railroad,Frederick Station (Frederick Station)
SE Corner of Market & All Saints Sts.
HAER MD-18
HAER MD,11-FRED,20-
3ph/1pc L

Baltzell,Dr. John,House; see Loat's Female Orphan Home

Bentz Street (Houses)
HABS MD-484
HABS MD,11-FRED,15-
1ph L

314-322 Bentz Street (Houses)
HABS MD-483
HABS MD,11-FRED,16-
1ph L

Derange Street (Rusticated Wooden House) (West Patrick Street (House))
HABS MD-487
HABS MD,11-FRED,13-
1ph L

96-120 East Street (Houses)
HABS MD-485
HABS MD,11-FRED,17-
1ph L

Fifth Street (Double House)
HABS MD-482
HABS MD,11-FRED,12-
1ph L

Fourth Street (Row Cottages)
Fifth St.
HABS MD-494
HABS MD,11-FRED,19-
1ph L

Frederick Academy of the Visitation Convent; see St. John's Roman Catholic Church & Convent

Frederick County Historical Society; see Loat's Female Orphan Home

Frederick Station; see Baltimore & Ohio Railroad,Frederick Station

Hessian Barracks; see Revolutionary Barracks

Loat's Female Orphan Home (Frederick County Historical Society; Baltzell,Dr. John,House)
24 E. Church St.
HABS MD-489
HABS MD,11-FRED,9-
2ph L

407-411 North Market Street (Houses)
HABS MD-495
HABS MD,11-FRED,8-
1ph L

Revolutionary Barracks (Hessian Barracks)
242 S. Market St.
HABS MD-492
HABS MD,11-FRED,6-
2ph L

20-22 South Court Street (Houses)
HABS MD-896
HABS MD,11-FRED,21-
3pg/fr L

59-61 South Market Street (Commercial Building)
HABS MD-902
HABS MD,11-FRED,22-
19ph/10pg/1pc L

St. John's Roman Catholic Church & Convent (Frederick Academy of the Visitation Convent)
Second St.
HABS MD-496
HABS MD,11-FRED,10-
1ph/1pg L

Taney,Roger Brook,House
121 S. Benzt St.
HABS MD-497
HABS MD,11-FRED,11-
1ph L

Trail & Ross Houses
Courthouse Square
HABS MD-498
HABS MD,11-FRED,5-
1ph L

U. S. Post Office
201 E. Patrick St.
HABS MD-900
HABS MD,11-FRED,23-
11ph/7pg/1pc L

West Patrick Street (House); see Derange Street (Rusticated Wooden House)

324-344 West Patrick Street (Houses)
HABS MD-486
HABS MD,11-FRED,18-
1ph L

FREDERICK VIC.

Jug Bridge
Frederick Rd. spanning Monacacy River
HABS MD-488
HABS MD,11-FRED.V,5-
7ph L

Jug Bridge,Old Toll House
State Rt. 144
HABS MD-491
HABS MD,11-FRED.V,3-
3ph L

Monocacy Battle Centennial Monument
Urbana Pk.,Monocacy National Battefield
HABS MD-1059
HABS DLC/PP-1992:MD-4
3ph/1pc L

14th Regiment New Jersey Vol. Infantry Monument
Off Urbana Pk. near Railroad Bridge
HABS MD-1057
HABS DLC/PP-1992:MD-4
3ph/1pc L

67th,87th & 138th Regmts. Pennsylvania Vol. Monmt.
Araby Church Rd.,NW of Baker Balley Rd.
HABS MD-1056
HABS DLC/PP-1992:MD-4
4ph/1pc L

Rose Garden; see Rose Hill Manor

Rose Hill Manor (Rose Garden; Tasker's Chance)
1611 N. Market St.
HABS MD-493
HABS MD,11-FRED.V,10-
5ph L

Southern Soldiers Monument
Urbana Pk.,Monocacy National Battlefield
HABS MD-1058
HABS DLC/PP-1992:MD-4
3ph/1pc L

Springfield
W. of U. S. Rt. 15
HABS MD-499
HABS MD,11-FRED.V,11-
1ph L

Tasker's Chance; see Rose Hill Manor

Tenth Vermont Infantry Monument
Araby Church Rd. & Baker Valley Rd.
HABS MD-1055
HABS DLC/PP-1992:MD-4
3ph/1pc L

JEFFERSON

Jefferson Primary School
Lander Rd. at State Rt. 180
HABS MD-899
HABS MD,11-JEF,2-
8ph/4pg/1pc L

LANDER'S LANDING

Chesapeake & Ohio Canal National Historical Park; see Chesapeake & Ohio Canal,Lock 29

Chesapeake & Ohio Canal National Historical Park; see Chesapeake & Ohio Canal,Lockhouse at Lock 29

Chesapeake & Ohio Canal,Lock 29
(Chesapeake & Ohio Canal National Historical Park)
Catoctin Station Vic.
HABS MD-752
HABS MD,11-LAN,1-
2ph/1pc L

Chesapeake & Ohio Canal,Lockhouse at Lock 29 (Chesapeake & Ohio Canal National Historical Park)
HABS MD-751
HABS MD,11-LAN,2-
1ph/1pg/fr L

LIBERTY TOWN

Academy,Old
Liberty Rd. (State Rt. 26)
HABS MD-502
HABS MD,11-LIBTO,2-
1ph L

Coale,Richard,House; see Main Street (Brick House)

Jones-Sappington House
(Jones,Abraham,House; Sappington,Augustus,House)
Liberty Rd. (State Rt. 26)
HABS MD-501
HABS MD,11-LIBTO,1-
2ph L

Jones,Abraham,House; see Jones-Sappington House

Main Street (Brick House) (Sappington House; Coale,Richard,House)
Liberty & Green Valley Rds. (State Rts. 26 & 75)
HABS MD-500
HABS MD,11-LIBTO,5-
1ph L

Sappington Farmhouse
Liberty Rd. (State Rt. 26)
HABS MD-503
HABS MD,11-LIBTO,3-
1ph L

Sappington House; see Main Street (Brick House)

Sappington,Augustus,House; see Jones-Sappington House

Wagner,Mary,House
Liberty Rd. (State Rt. 26)
HABS MD-504
HABS MD,11-LIBTO,4-
1ph L

MIDDLETOWN

Stemble,Frederick,House
113-115 W. Main St.
HABS MD-331
HABS MD,11-MIDTO,1-
6dr/fr L

MIDDLETOWN VIC.

Poffenberger Road Bridge
Spanning Catoctin Creek
HAER MD-35
HAER MD,11-MIDTO.V,1-
13ph/1pg/1pc L

POINT OF ROCKS

Baltimore & Ohio Railroad,Point of Rocks Station
State Rt. 28 Vic.
HABS MD-506
HAER MD-14
HABS/HAER MD,11-PORO,1-
8dr/14ph/2pg/1pc/fr L

POINT OF ROCKS VIC.

Baltimore & Ohio Railroad,Point of Rocks Tunnel (Point of Rocks Tunnel)
HAER MD-15
HAER MD,11-PORO.V,1-
2ph/1pc L

Chesapeake & Ohio Canal National Historical Park; see Chesapeake & Ohio Canal,Catoctin Creek Aqueduct

Chesapeake & Ohio Canal National Historical Park; see Chesapeake & Ohio Canal,Lockhouse at Lock 28

Chesapeake & Ohio Canal,Catoctin Creek Aqueduct (Chesapeake & Ohio Canal National Historical Park)
HABS MD-753
HABS MD,11-PORO.V,2-
6ph/1pc L

Chesapeake & Ohio Canal,Lockhouse at Lock 28 (Chesapeake & Ohio Canal National Historical Park)
HABS MD-750
HABS MD,11-PORO.V,3-
3ph/1pc/fr L

Point of Rocks Tunnel; see Baltimore & Ohio Railroad,Point of Rocks Tunnel

ROCKY RIDGE VIC.

Old Mill Road Bridge
Spanning Owens Creek on Old Mill Rd.
HAER MD-36
HAER MD,11-ROCRI.V,1-
6ph/1pg/1pc/2ct L

UNION BRIDGE VIC.

Hopewell
Pearre Rd.
HABS MD-328
HABS MD,11-UBRI.V,1-
28ph/2pc/7ct L

URBANA

Amelung,John Frederick,House
Park Mills Rd.
HABS MD-32
HABS MD,11-URB,1-
2ph/1pg L

Boscobel; see Gambrill House

Clifton Farm (Worthington Farm; Riveside Farm)
Monocacy National Battlefield,off Baker Rd.
HABS MD-1052
HABS DLC/PP-1992:MD-4
6dr/25ph/49pg/2pc/fr L

Edgewood; see Gambrill House

Gambrill House (Edgewood; Boscobel)
Monocacy National Battlefield,Urbana Pk.
HABS MD-1051
HABS DLC/PP-1992:MD-4
17dr/37ph/37pg/3pc/fr L

Riveside Farm; see Clifton Farm

Worthington Farm; see Clifton Farm

GARRETT COUNTY

GRANSTVILLE VIC

Casselman River Bridge
National Rd. at Little Crossings
HABS MD-139
HABS MD,12-GRANT.V,1-
3ph L

HARFORD COUNTY

ABERDEEN

Aberdeen Prov. Ground: White Phosphorous Proc. Plt (Edgewood Arsenal: White Phosphorous Procing. Plt.)
N.W. Corner Hoadley & Magnolia Rds. in APG
HAER MD-47-A
HAER 1991(HAER):13
18ph/27pg/1pc L

Aberdeen Proving Ground (Edgewood Arsenal)
HABS MD-1071
HAER MD-47
HABS/HAER MD,13-ABER,1-
106pg/fr L

Edgewood Arsenal; see Aberdeen Proving Ground

Edgewood Arsenal: White Phosphorous Procing. Plt.; see Aberdeen Prov. Ground: White Phosphorous Proc. Plt

BEL AIR

Harford National Bank
HABS MD-320
HABS MD,13-BELA,2-
3dr L

Liriodendron
502 W. Gordon St.
HABS MD-327
HABS MD,13-BELA,3-
13ph/1pc L

Liriodendron,Barn
502 W. Gordon St.
HABS MD-327-A
HABS MD,13-BELA,3A-
11dr/38ph/2pc/fr L

Masonic Lodge
Wall St.
HABS MD-319
HABS MD,13-BELA,4-
8dr L

BEL AIR VIC.

Booth House (Tudor Hill; Booth,Junius Brutus,House; Tudor Hall)
Tudor Lane,RFD No. 1
HABS MD-510
HABS MD,13-BELA.V,2-
1ph L

Booth,Junius Brutus,House; see Booth House

Dallam House (Dallams,The; Webster House)
Wheel Rd.
HABS MD-507
HABS MD,13-BELA.V,3-
1ph L

Dallams,The; see Dallam House

Thomas Run House
Kalmia & Thomas Run Rds.
HABS MD-508
HABS MD,13-BELA.V,4-
2ph L

Tudor Hall; see Booth House

Tudor Hill; see Booth House

Webster House; see Dallam House

BELCAMP

Hall's Plains; see Sophia's Dairy

Simmon's Neglect; see Sophia's Dairy

Sophia's Dairy (Hall's Plains; Simmon's Neglect)
Pulaski Hwy. Vic.
HABS MD-8
HABS MD,13-BELCA,1-
15dr/9ph/3pg L

CHURCHVILLE VIC.

Archer,Dr. John,House; see Medical Hall

Medical Hall (Archer,Dr. John,House)
Medical Hall Rd.
HABS MD-33
HABS MD,13-CHURVI.V,1-
3ph/1pg L

Snake Fence,Old,& Log House
HABS MD-511
HABS MD,13-CHURVI.V,2-
1ph L

CRESWELL VIC.

Mount Adams; see Mount,The

Mount,The (Mount Adams; Webster's Mount; Webster,Capt. ,House; Webster,D. L. ,House)
Fountain Green Rd. (State Rt. 543)
HABS MD-512
HABS MD,13-CRES.V,1-
2ph L

Webster,Capt. ,House; see Mount,The

Webster,D. L. ,House; see Mount,The

Webster's Mount; see Mount,The

DARLINGTON

Kirk House
W. side Darlington Rd. (State Rt. 161)
HABS MD-513
HABS MD,13-DARL,1-
2ph L

DARLINGTON VIC.

Holloway House
Stafford Rd. (State Rt. 161)
HABS MD-515
HABS MD,13-DARL.V,2-
1ph L

Philip's Purchase; see Rigbie House

Prospect Academy; see Schoolhouse,Stone Hexagonal

Rigbie House (Philip's Purchase; Rigbie,Col. James,House)
Caselton Rd. (State Rt. 623)
HABS MD-24
HABS MD,13-DARL.V,1-
7ph/6pg L

Rigbie,Col. James,House; see Rigbie House

Schoolhouse,Stone Hexagonal (Prospect Academy)
3736 Green Spring Rd.
HABS MD-514
HABS MD,13-DARL.V,3-
1ph L

FALLSTON

Little Falls Friends' Meetinghouse; see Quaker Meetinghouse

Quaker Meetinghouse (Little Falls Friends' Meetinghouse)
E. side Mountain Rd.
HABS MD-516
HABS MD,13-FAL,1-
1ph L

FALLSTON VIC.

Bon Air (Delaporte,Capt. Francis,House)
Laurel Brook Rd.
HABS MD-42
HABS MD,13-FAL.V,1-
6ph/3pg L

Delaporte,Capt. Francis,House; see Bon Air

GLENVILLE

Paul,J. Gilman D. ,House (Proctor,Thomas,House)
Deths Rd.
HABS MD-517
HABS MD,13-GLENV,1-
2ph L

Proctor,Thomas,House; see Paul,J. Gilman D. ,House

HAVRE DE GRACE

Congress & Saint John's Streets (Old Ordinary) (Ordinary on Waterfront)
HABS MD-519
HABS MD,13-HAV,1-
2ph L

Ordinary on Waterfront; see Congress & Saint John's Streets (Old Ordinary)

Saint John's Street (Connected Frame Houses) (Swan's Inn)
Waterfront Vic.
HABS MD-518
HABS MD,13-HAV,2-
1ph L

Susquehanna River Bridge
Spanning Susquehanna River
HAER MD-46
HAER MD,13-HAV,4-
15ph/1pg/2pc L

Swan's Inn; see Saint John's Street (Connected Frame Houses)

HAVRE DE GRACE VIC.

Angel Hill
Sego St.
HABS MD-520
HABS MD,13-HAV.V,1-
2ph L

Post Road Bridge
State Rt. 7-A
HAER MD-44
HAER MD,13-HAV,3-
33ph/4pg/6pc L

Sion Hill School
2026 Level Rd.
HABS MD-521
HABS MD,13-HAV.V,2-
4ph L

HICKORY

St. Ignatius Catholic Church
533 E. Jarrettsville Rd.
HABS MD-522
HABS MD,13-HICK,1-
1ph L

JERUSALEM

Grist Mill; see Jerusalem Grist Mill

Jerusalem Grist Mill (Grist Mill; Little Gunpowder)
Jerusalem Rd. Vic. ,Little Gunpowder River
HABS MD-523
HABS MD,13-JERU,1-
1ph L

Little Gunpowder; see Jerusalem Grist Mill

JERUSALEM VIC.

Covered Bridge (Jericho Bridge)
Jericho Rd. spanning Little Gunpowder Falls
HABS MD-12
HABS MD,13-JERU.V,1-
2dr/2ph/1pg/fr L

Jericho Bridge; see Covered Bridge

Norris,Edward,House; see Olney

Olney (Shriver,J. Alexis,House; Norris,Edward,House)
Hollingsworth Rd.
HABS MD-509
HABS MD,13-JERU.V,2-
1ph L

Shriver,J. Alexis,House; see Olney

JOPPATOWNE

Old Joppa; see Rumsey,Benjamin,House

Rumsey,Benjamin,House (Old Joppa)
Bridge Dr.
HABS MD-9
HABS MD,13-JOP,1-
10dr/3ph/6pg L

LAPIDUM

Carter-Archec House; see Rock Run Mill,Outbuildings

Carter,John, House; see Rock Run Mill,Outbuildings

Rock Run Grist Mill; see Rock Run Water Mill

Rock Run Mill,Outbuildings (Rock Run Miller's House; Carter-Archec House; Carter,John, House)
Susquehanna State Park,Rock Run Rd.
HABS MD-524
HABS MD,13-LAP,2-
5ph L

Rock Run Miller's House; see Rock Run Mill,Outbuildings

Rock Run Water Mill (Rock Run Grist Mill)
Susquehanna State Park,Stafford Rd.
HABS MD-525
HABS MD,13-LAP,1-
3ph L

LAPIDUM VIC.

Land of Promise (Paul,Gilman,House)
Susquehanna State Park,235 Quaker Bottom Rd.
HABS MD-526
HABS MD,13-LAP.V,1-
1ph L

Paul,Gilman,House; see Land of Promise

LEVEL VIC.

Royal Exchange; see 3850 West Chapel Road (Brick House Number 2)

3844 West Chapel Road (Brick House Number l)
HABS MD-527
HABS MD,13-LEV.V,2-
1ph L

3850 West Chapel Road (Brick House Number 2) (Royal Exchange)
HABS MD-528
HABS MD,13-LEV.V,1-
1ph L

PERRYMAN

Spesutie Protestant Episcopal Church,Vestry
Perryman Rd. (State Rt. 159)
HABS MD-530
HABS MD,13-PERYM,2-
1ph L

Documentation: **ct** color transparencies **dr** measured drawings **fr** field records
pc photograph captions **pg** pages of text **ph** photographs

STOCKTON VIC.

Mountain Road (Farmhouse)
HABS MD-531
HABS MD,13- ,1-
1ph L

WATERVALE

Gorsuch Mansion; see Joesting Farm

Joesting Farm (Gorsuch Mansion; Winters Run Golf Course)
Tollgate Rd.
HABS MD-532
HABS MD,13-WATVA,1-
3ph L

Winters Run Golf Course; see Joesting Farm

WATERVALE VIC.

Joshua's Meadows; see 300 North Tollgate Road (Old Brick Cottage)

300 North Tollgate Road (Old Brick Cottage) (Joshua's Meadows)
HABS MD-533
HABS MD,13-WATVA.V,1-
1ph L

WILNA VIC.

Prospect
Hollingsworth Rd. Vic.
HABS MD-534
HABS MD,13-WIL.V,1-
1ph L

HOWARD COUNTY

BALTIMORE VIC.

Folly Quarter
HABS MD-148
HABS MD,14- ,1-
2ph L

ELKRIDGE

Baltimore & Ohio Railroad Bridge; see Baltimore & Ohio Railroad,Thomas Bridge

Baltimore & Ohio Railroad,Thomas Bridge (Baltimore & Ohio Railroad Bridge; Latrobe's Folly; Relay Viaduct; Thomas Viaduct)
Spanning Patapsco River
HABS MD-535
HAER MD-3
HABS/HAER MD,14-ELK,1
22ph/3pg/2pc L

Latrobe's Folly; see Baltimore & Ohio Railroad,Thomas Bridge

Relay Viaduct; see Baltimore & Ohio Railroad,Thomas Bridge

Thomas Viaduct; see Baltimore & Ohio Railroad,Thomas Bridge

ELLICOTT CITY

Baltimore & Ohio Railroad,Ellicott's Mills Station (Ellicott City Station)
S. Side of State Rt. 144
HAER MD-13
HAER MD,14-ELLCI,11-
9ph/1pc/fr L

Berg Alnwick; see Patapsco Heights Girls' School

Columbia Pike (Stone Houses with Frame Additions)
HABS MD-538
HABS MD,14-ELLCI,6-
1ph L

Columbia Pike (Stone Houses) (Tongue Row)
HABS MD-537
HABS MD,14-ELLCI,5-
1ph L

3801 Columbia Pike(Connected Stone & Frame Houses)
HABS MD-539
HABS MD,14-ELLCI,7-
1ph L

Ellicott City Station; see Baltimore & Ohio Railroad,Ellicott's Mills Station

Ellicott,William,House; see Mount Ida

Hilltop Theatre; see Patapsco Heights Girls' School

House,Log
Merryman Rd.
HABS MD-321
HABS MD,14-ELLCI,12-
4dr/fr L

Howard County Courthouse
Court Ave.
HABS MD-536
HABS MD,14-ELLCI,1-
1ph L

8133 Main Street (Shop Front)
HABS MD-544
HABS MD,14-ELLCI,9-
1ph L

8010-8046 Main Street (Stone House Facades) (Patapsco Hotel)
HABS MD-540
HABS MD,14-ELLCI,8-
1ph L

Maryland Women's War Relief Hospital; see Patapsco Heights Girls' School

Mill
Frederick Rd.
HABS MD-838
HABS MD,14-ELLCI,3
1ph L

Mill Houses
1209-1217 Oella Rd.
HABS MD-542
HABS MD,14-ELLCI,4-
2ph L

Mount Ida (Ellicott,William,House)
3691 Sarah's Lane
HABS MD-306
HABS MD,14-ELLCI,10-
13dr/8ph L

Patapsco Female Institute; see Patapsco Heights Girls' School

Patapsco Heights Girls' School (Patapsco Female Institute; Hilltop Theatre; Maryland Women's War Relief Hospital; Berg Alnwick)
Church Rd.
HABS MD-543
HABS MD,14-ELLCI,2-
1ph L

Patapsco Hotel; see 8010-8046 Main Street (Stone House Facades)

Tongue Row; see Columbia Pike (Stone Houses)

ELLICOTT CITY VIC.

Burleigh Manor
Centennial Lane
HABS MD-545
HABS MD,14-ELLCI.V,1-
5ph L

Doughoregan Manor
Manorhouse Rd.
HABS MD-230
HABS MD,14-ELLCI.V,2-
16ph L

Doughoregan Manor,Barn
Manorhouse Rd.
HABS MD-230-A
HABS MD,14-ELLCI.V,2H-
5ph L

ILCHESTER VIC.

Baltimore & Ohio Railroad,Ilchester Tunnel (Ilchester Tunnel)
E. side of Patapsco River
HAER MD-21
HAER MD,14-ILCH.V,1-
1ph/1pc L

Ilchester Tunnel; see Baltimore & Ohio Railroad,Ilchester Tunnel

SAVAGE

Baltimore & Ohio RR:Bollman Truss Bridge (Bollman's Iron Suspension & Trussed Bridge)
Spanning Little Patuxent River
HAER MD-1
HAER MD,14-SAV,1-
7dr/12ph/5pg/2pc/fr L

Bollman's Iron Suspension & Trussed Bridge; see Baltimore & Ohio RR:Bollman Truss Bridge

KENT COUNTY

Nicholson House; see 111 North Queen Street (House with Wood Porch)

111 North Queen Street (House with Wood Porch) (Nicholson House)
HABS MD-548
HABS MD,15-CHETO,7-
1ph L

CHESTERTOWN

Abbey,The; see Pearce House

Catlin House; see Pearce House

101 Church Street (Brick House) (Geddes-Piper House)
Queen & Lawyer Sts. Vic.
HABS MD-547
HABS MD,15-CHETO,5-
1ph L

Custom House,Old
101-103 Water St.
HABS MD-549
HABS MD,15-CHETO,1-
1ph L

Denton House; see Smyth-Letherbury House

Denton-Weeks House; see Smyth-Letherbury House

Geddes-Piper House; see 101 Church Street (Brick House)

Hubbard House; see Widehall

Pearce House (Abbey,The; Ringgold,Thomas,House; Catlin House)
106 Water St.
HABS MD-546
HABS MD,15-CHETO,3-
11ph L

Ringgold,Thomas,House; see Pearce House

River House; see Smyth-Letherbury House

Smyth-Letherbury House (River House; Denton House; 107 Water Street (House); Denton-Weeks House)
HABS MD-231
HABS MD,15-CHETO,6-
10dr/9ph/15pg L

107 Water Street (House); see Smyth-Letherbury House

White Swan Tavern
233 High St.
HABS MD-239
HABS MD,15-CHETO,8-
6dr L

Widehall (Hubbard House)
101 Water (Front) St.
HABS MD-550
HABS MD,15-CHETO,2-
10ph L

CHESTERTOWN VIC.

Airy Hill; see Wick's Place,Old

Godlington Manor
HABS MD-868
HABS MD,15-CHETO.V,2-
11dr/18ph/1pg/1pc L

Godlington Manor,Milkhouse
HABS MD-868-A
HABS MD,15-CHETO.V,2A-
1ph/1pc L

Rose Hill
HABS MD-869
HABS MD,15-CHETO.V,3
6ph/1pc L

Wick-Sterling House; see Wick's Place,Old

Wick's Place,Old (Airy Hill; Wick-Sterling House)
Airport Rd.
HABS MD-551
HABS MD,15-CHETO.V,1-
4ph L

CHESTERVILLE

Gooding,Aaron L. ,Store; see Spencer,Isaac,House

Salter House; see Spencer,Isaac,House

Spencer,Isaac,House (Gooding,Aaron L. ,Store; Salter House)
Morgnec Rd. (Rt. 447) & Rt. 290
HABS MD-316
HABS MD,15 CHESV 1-
12dr/26ph L

Town of Chesterville
Morgnec Rd. & Rt. 290
HABS MD-866
HABS MD,15-CHESV,2-
1ph/1pc L

Town of Chesterville,Chesterville Store
Morgnec Rd. & Rt. 290
HABS MD-866-A
HABS MD,15-CHESV,2A-
3dr/4ph/1pc L

Town of Chesterville,Hotel
Morgnec Rd. & Rt. 290
HABS MD-866-B
HABS MD,15-CHESV,2B-
1ph/1pc L

Town of Chesterville,Salter House
Morgnec Rd. & Rt. 290
HABS MD-866-C
HABS MD,15-CHESV,2C-
1ph/1pc L

FAIRLEE CREEK

Carvill Hall
HABS MD-867
HABS MD,15-FACR,1-
8dr/15ph/1pc L

GALENA

Cottage,Frame
U. S. Rt. 213
HABS MD-552
HABS MD,15-GAL,2-
1ph L

Stephens House
U. S. Rt. 213
HABS MD-553
HABS MD,15-GAL,1-
1ph L

GEORGETOWN

Knight,Kitty,House
U. S. Rt. 213
HABS MD-554
HABS MD,15-GEOTO,1-
2ph L

Valley Cottage; see Wallis House

Wallis House (Valley Cottage)
U. S. Rt. 213
HABS MD-555
HABS MD,15-GEOTO,2-
4ph L

LOCUST GROVE VIC.

Farmhouse near Shrewsbury Church (Merritt Farmhouse)
U. S. Rt. 213
HABS MD-558
HABS MD,15-LOGRO.V,1-
1ph L

Merritt Farmhouse; see Farmhouse near Shrewsbury Church

SANDY BOTTOM

St. Paul's Episcopal Church
Sandy Bottom Rd.
HABS MD-556
HABS MD,15-LANK.V,1-
2ph L

St. Paul's Episcopal Church,Vestry House
Sandy Bottom Rd.
HABS MD-557
HABS MD,15-LANK.V,2-
1ph L

STILL POND

Harper,George,Store
MD. Rt. 292 & Main St.
HABS MD-324
HABS MD,15-STIPO,1-
10dr/22ph/1pg/2pc L

MONTGOMERY COUNTY

C & O Canal National Historical Park; see Chesapeake & Ohio Canal,Bridges,Aqueducts,etc.

Chesapeake & Ohio Canal,Bridges,Aqueducts,etc. (C & O Canal National Historical Park)
HABS MD-57
HABS MD,16- ,2-
10dr/10ph/3pg/fr L

ASHTON

Brooke Manor; see Cherry Grove

Cherry Grove (Brooke Manor; Thomas,Richard,House)
17530 New Hampshire Ave. (State Rt. 650)
HABS MD-559
HABS MD,16-ASH,1-
5ph L

Thomas,Richard,House; see Cherry Grove

BEALLSVILLE

Charlene Manor (Griffith,Charles G. ,House)
State Rt. 28
HABS MD-560
HABS MD,16-BEALV,1-
2ph L

Griffith,Charles G. ,House; see Charlene Manor

BEALLSVILLE VIC.

Inverness
State Rt. 28
HABS MD-561
HABS MD,16-BEALV.V,1-
1ph L

BETHESDA

Quarters,Old (Slave Quarters)
Wisconsin Ave. & State Rt. 193
HABS MD-84
HABS MD,16-BETH,1-
1ph L

Slave Quarters; see Quarters,Old

BOYDS

Greenwood
HABS MD-541
HABS MD,16-BOYD,1-
1ph L

BRIGHTON

Brighton Grange Hall (St. Luke's Parish Hall)
263 Brighton Dam Road at New Hampshire Ave.
HABS MD-1018
HABS DLC/PP-1992:MD-4
16ph/2pg/2pc L

St. Luke's Parish Hall; see Brighton Grange Hall

BROOKEVILLE

Brookeville Academy
Georgia Ave. (State Rt. 97)
HABS MD-563
HABS MD,16-BROV,2-
2ph L

Stone Lodge (Valley House)
318 Market St. ,Brookeville Center
HABS MD-566
HABS MD,16-BROV,1-
2ph L

Valley House; see Stone Lodge

BROOKEVILLE VIC.

Brewer House; see Greenwood

Davis,Ephraim,House; see Greenwood

Day House; see Greenwood

Greenwood (Hygham; Davis,Ephraim,House; Day House; Brewer House)
1721 Georgia Ave. (State Rt. 27)
HABS MD-564
HABS MD,16-BROV.V,2-
5ph L

Hygham; see Greenwood

Locust Grove (Thomas,John,House; Riggs,John Hammond,House)
3415 Brookeville Rd.
HABS MD-565
HABS MD,16-BROV.V,3-
1ph L

Riggs,John Hammond,House; see Locust Grove

Thomas,John,House; see Locust Grove

BROOKMONT VIC.

Chesapeake & Ohio Canal,Lockhouse at Lock 5 (Chesapeake & Ohio Canal,Lockhouse,Williard's Lock)
George Washington Pkwy. Vic.
HABS MD-56-B
HABS MD,16- ,2A-
3dr L

Chesapeake & Ohio Canal,Lockhouse at Lock 6
HABS MD-56-A
HABS MD,16- ,3A-
3dr/1pg/fr L

Chesapeake & Ohio Canal,Lockhouse,Williard's Lock; see Chesapeake & Ohio Canal,Lockhouse at Lock 5

BURTONSVILLE

Burton House
Birmingham Dr.
HABS MD-132
HABS MD,16-BURT,1-
1ph L

CABIN JOHN

Cabin John Aqueduct Bridge
MacArthur Blvd. spanning Cabin John Creek
HABS MD-180
HAER MD-53
HABS/HAER MD,16-CABJO,1-ı87(HAER):45°
11ph/1pg/1pc/3ct L

CABIN JOHN VIC.

Chesapeake & Ohio Canal,Lock 12
HABS MD-57-F
HABS MD,16- ,10B-
3pg/fr L

Chesapeake & Ohio Canal,Lockhouse at Lock 10
HABS MD-56-F
HABS MD,16- ,7A-
2dr/fr L

Chesapeake & Ohio Canal,Lockhouse at Lock 11
HABS MD-56-G
HABS MD,16- ,8A-
2dr/fr L

Chesapeake & Ohio Canal,Lockhouse at Lock 12
HABS MD-56-H
HABS MD,16- ,10A-
1dr/fr L

Chesapeake & Ohio Canal,Lockhouse at Lock 13
HABS MD-56-I
HABS MD,16- ,11A-
3dr/fr L

Chesapeake & Ohio Canal,Lockhouse at Lock 14
HABS MD-56-J
HABS MD,16- ,12A-
1dr/fr L

Chesapeake & Ohio Canal,Lockhouse at Lock 8
George Washington Pkwy. Vic.
HABS MD-56-D
HABS MD,16- ,5A-
2dr/fr L

Chesapeake & Ohio Canal,Lockhouse at Lock 9
HABS MD-56-E
HABS MD,16- ,6-
2dr/fr L

Chesapeake & Ohio Canal,Milestone,Lock 11 Vic.
HABS MD-57-G
HABS MD,16- ,9-
1dr L

CHEVY CHASE VIC.

Hayes Manor (Williamson,Rev. Alexander,House)
4101 Manor Rd.
HABS MD-202
HABS MD,16-CHEV,1- ı1991(HABS):30°
13dr/31ph/14pg/fr L

Williamson,Rev. Alexander,House; see Hayes Manor

CLARKSBURG

Dowden's Ordinary
State Rt. 355 & Stringtown Rd.
HABS MD-76
HABS MD,16-CLARB,2-
1ph L

COLESVILLE

Miller's House
E. Randolph Rd.
HABS MD-567
HABS MD,16-COLVI.V,2-
2ph L

Valley Mill
E. Randolph Rd. (State Rt. 183)
HABS MD-568
HABS MD,16-COLVI.V,1-
3ph L

DARNESTOWN VIC.

Kelley,John T. ,House; see Pleasant Hills

Pleasant Hills (Kelley,John T. ,House)
14800 Fisher Ave. (State Rt. 107)
HABS MD-141
HABS MD,16-DART.V,1-
3ph L

DAWSONVILLE

Aix La Chapelle (Brewer,Dr. William,House; Randles' Farm)
Darnestown Rd. (State Rt. 28)
HABS MD-569
HABS MD,16-DAWV.V,2-
4ph L

Brewer,Dr. William,House; see Aix La Chapelle

Randles' Farm; see Aix La Chapelle

DAWSONVILLE VIC.

Darnall House
Whites Ferry Rd. (State Rt. 107)
HABS MD-570
HABS MD,16-DAWV.V,3-
7ph L

Dawson,Robert Dayne,House
15200 Sugarland Rd.
HABS MD-55
HABS MD,16-DAWV.V,1-
6dr/9ph/fr L

DICKERSON

Gott,Richard Sr. ,House; see Mount Carmel

Gutheim,Frederick A.,House; see Mount Ephraim

Gutheim,Frederick A.,Outbuilding; see Mount Ephraim,Outbuilding

Locust Grove; see Mount Carmel

Mount Carmel (Gott,Richard Sr. ,House; Locust Grove)
State Rt. 28
HABS MD-571
HABS MD,16-DICK,1-
3ph L

Mount Ephraim (Gutheim,Frederick A.,House)
23720 Mt. Ephraim Rd.
HABS MD-967
HABS MD,16-DICK,2-
8ph/20pg/1pc/1ct L

Mount Ephraim,Outbuilding (Gutheim,Frederick A.,Outbuilding)
23720 Mount Ephraim Road
HABS MD-967-A
HABS MD,16-DICK,2A
2ph/1pc L

DICKERSON VIC.

Chesapeake & Ohio Canal National Historical Park; see Chesapeake & Ohio Canal,Culvert 65

Chesapeake & Ohio Canal National Historical Park; see Chesapeake & Ohio Canal,Lock 26

Chesapeake & Ohio Canal National Historical Park; see Chesapeake & Ohio Canal,Lockhouse at Lock 26

Chesapeake & Ohio Canal National Historical Park; see Chesapeake & Ohio Canal,Lockhouse at Lock 27

Chesapeake & Ohio Canal National Historical Park; see Chesapeake & Ohio Canal,Waste Weir,Lock 27

Chesapeake & Ohio Canal,Concrete Drainway; see Chesapeake & Ohio Canal,Waste Weir,Lock 27

Chesapeake & Ohio Canal,Culvert 65 (Chesapeake & Ohio Canal National Historical Park)
Martinsburg Rd. Vic.
HAER MD-32
HAER MD,16-DICK.V,1-
2dr/fr L

Chesapeake & Ohio Canal,Lock 26 (Chesapeake & Ohio Canal,Wood's Lock; Chesapeake & Ohio Canal National Historical Park)
HABS MD-744
HABS MD,16-DICK.V,2-
2ph/1pc L

Chesapeake & Ohio Canal,Lockhouse at Lock 26 (Chesapeake & Ohio Canal,Lockhouse,Wood's Lock; Chesapeake & Ohio Canal National Historical Park)
Monocacy River Aqueduct Vic.
HABS MD-745
HABS MD16-DICK.V,3-
1ph/1pc L

Chesapeake & Ohio Canal,Lockhouse at Lock 27 (Chesapeake & Ohio Canal National Historical Park)
HABS MD-748
HABS MD,16-DICK.V,4-
4ph/1pc L

Chesapeake & Ohio Canal,Lockhouse,Wood's Lock; see Chesapeake & Ohio Canal,Lockhouse at Lock 26

Chesapeake & Ohio Canal,Waste Weir,Lock 27 (Chesapeake & Ohio Canal,Concrete Drainway; Chesapeake & Ohio Canal National Historical Park)
HABS MD-747
HABS MD,16-DICK.V,5-
2ph L

Chesapeake & Ohio Canal,Wood's Lock; see Chesapeake & Ohio Canal,Lock 26

EDNOR

Clifton
17107 New Hampshire Ave.
HABS MD-54
HABS MD,16-EDNO,1-
9dr/14ph/fr L

ETCHISON

Etchison Cabin (Warfield Log Cabin; Etchison,Martha,House)
3111 Damascus Rd. (State Rt. 108)
HABS MD-573
HABS MD,16-ETCH,1-
3ph L

Etchison,Martha,House; see Etchison Cabin

Warfield Log Cabin; see Etchison Cabin

GAITHERSBURG

Clopper's Mill,Miller's House; see Woodlands

Gaithersburg Latitude Observatory
100 De Sellum Ave.
HAER MD-78
HAER 1991(HAER):13
6dr L

Woodlands (Clopper's Mill,Miller's House)
State Rt. 117
HABS MD-575
HABS MD,16-GAITH.V,3-
1ph L

GAITHERSBURG VIC.

Baltimore & Ohio Railroad,Waring Viaduct (Waring Viaduct)
Spanning Great Seneca Creek .4 mile SW of US 270
HAER MD-22
HAER MD,16-GAITH.V,4-
3ph/1pc L

Elgar's Mill; see Muncaster Mill & Saw Mill

Magruder,Col. Zadok,House; see Mount Pleasant

Milton's Mill; see Muncaster Mill & Saw Mill

Mount Pleasant (Magruder,Col. Zadok,House)
State Rt. 355 & Shady Grove Rd.
HABS MD-574
HABS MD,16-GAITH.V,2-
3ph L

Muncaster Mill & Saw Mill (Elgar's Mill; Milton's Mill)
State Rt. 115
HABS MD-94
HABS MD,16-GAITH.V,1-
6ph L

Waring Viaduct; see Baltimore & Ohio Railroad,Waring Viaduct

GLEN ECHO

Barton,Clara,House
(Barton,Clara,National Historic Site)
5801 Oxford Rd.
HABS MD-300
HABS MD,16-GLENEC,2-
9dr/11ph/1pc/fr L

Barton,Clara,National Historic Site; see Barton,Clara,House

Crystal Pool; see Glen Echo Amusement Park,Crystal Swimming Pool

Glen Echo Amusement Park,Crystal Swimming Pool (Crystal Pool)
MacArthur Blvd. ,Glen Echo Park
HAER MD-43
HAER MD,16-GLENEC,1-
26ph/1pg/2pc L

GLEN ECHO VIC.

Bonfield's Service Station
6124 MacArthur Blvd.
HABS MD-965
HABS MD,16-GLENEC.V,1-
6ph/5pg/1pc L

Chesapeake & Ohio Canal,Lockhouse & Lock 7 (Lockhouse & Shafer's Lock; Chesapeake & Ohio Canal,Shafer's Lock & Lockhouse)
George Washington Pkwy. Vic.
HABS MD-56-C
HABS MD,16- ,4-
2dr L

Chesapeake & Ohio Canal,Shafer's Lock & Lockhouse; see Chesapeake & Ohio Canal,Lockhouse & Lock 7

Lockhouse & Shafer's Lock; see Chesapeake & Ohio Canal,Lockhouse & Lock 7

GREAT FALLS

C & O Canal National Historical Park; see Chesapeake & Ohio Canal,Great Falls Tavern

Chesapeake & Ohio Canal,Frame House Number 1
Lock 20 Vic.
HABS MD-56-M
HABS MD,16- ,22-
1dr/fr L

Chesapeake & Ohio Canal,Frame House Number 2
Lock 20 Vic.
HABS MD-56-N
HABS MD,16- ,23-
1dr/fr L

Chesapeake & Ohio Canal,Great Falls Tavern (Cromelin House; C & O Canal National Historical Park)
Lock 20,MacArthur Blvd. Vic.
HABS MD-56-R
HABS MD,16- ,20-
10dr/1ph/fr L

Chesapeake & Ohio Canal,Lock 20
(Chesapeake & Ohio Canal,Tavern Lock)
MacArthur Blvd.
HABS MD-57-E
HABS MD,16- ,19B-
1dr/3ph/fr L

Chesapeake & Ohio Canal,Lockhouse (Ruins) ,Lock 20
HABS MD-56-S
HABS MD,16- ,19A-
1ph L

Chesapeake & Ohio Canal,Log House
Lock 20 Vic.
HABS MD-56-0
HABS MD,16- ,24-
1dr/fr L

Chesapeake & Ohio Canal,Repair Shop at Lock 20
HABS MD-57-D
HABS MD,16- ,25-
3dr/fr L

Chesapeake & Ohio Canal,Tavern Lock; see Chesapeake & Ohio Canal,Lock 20

Cromelin House; see Chesapeake & Ohio Canal,Great Falls Tavern

GREAT FALLS VIC.

Chesapeake & Ohio Canal,Lockhouse at Lock 16
HABS MD-56-K
HABS MD,16- ,14-
2dr/fr L

Chesapeake & Ohio Canal,Lockhouse at Lock 21 (Chesapeake & Ohio Canal,Swain's House,Lock 21; Chesapeake & Ohio Canal,Lockhouse at Oak Springs; Swain's Lockhouse at Lock 21)
Swain's Lock Rd. ,State Rt. 190 Vic.
HABS MD-56-P
HABS MD,16- ,26A-
5dr/fr L

Chesapeake & Ohio Canal,Lockhouse at Oak Springs; see Chesapeake & Ohio Canal,Lockhouse at Lock 21

Chesapeake & Ohio Canal,Swain's House,Lock 21; see Chesapeake & Ohio Canal,Lockhouse at Lock 21

Swain's Lockhouse at Lock 21; see Chesapeake & Ohio Canal,Lockhouse at Lock 21

LAYTONSVILLE

Layton,John S. ,House
Sundown Rd. (State Rt. 420) & State Rt. 108
HABS MD-576
HABS MD,16-LATOV,1-
3ph L

LAYTONSVILLE VIC.

Four Chimney House; see Retirement

Ober,Robert,House; see Retirement

Retirement (Four Chimney House; Ober,Robert,House; Rolling Ridge)
7215 Sundown Rd. (State Rt. 420)
HABS MD-577
HABS MD,16-LATOV.V,1-
2ph L

Rolling Ridge; see Retirement

MARTINSBURG VIC.

C & O Canal:White's Ferry Iron Bridge (White's Ferry Bridge)
Mile 35.49 of the C & O Canal National Park
HAER MD-69
HAER 1989(HAER):11
4ph/4pg/1pc L

Chesapeake & Ohio Canal National Historical Park; see Chesapeake & Ohio Canal,Warehouse,White's Ferry

Chesapeake & Ohio Canal,Broad Run Aqueduct (Chesapeake & Ohio Canal,Culvert No. 44 1/2; Chesapeake & Ohio Canal,Broad Run Trunk)
Lock 25 Vic.
HABS MD-741
HABS MD,16-MARB.V,1-
4dr/6ph/1pc/fr L

Chesapeake & Ohio Canal,Broad Run Trunk; see Chesapeake & Ohio Canal,Broad Run Aqueduct

Chesapeake & Ohio Canal,Culvert No. 44 1/2; see Chesapeake & Ohio Canal,Broad Run Aqueduct

Chesapeake & Ohio Canal,Warehouse,(Ruins); see Chesapeake & Ohio Canal,Warehouse,White's Ferry

Chesapeake & Ohio Canal,Warehouse,White's Ferry
(Chesapeake & Ohio Canal,Warehouse,(Ruins); Chesapeake & Ohio Canal National Historical Park)
HABS MD-742
HABS MD,16-MARB.V,2-
3ph/1pc L

White's Ferry Bridge; see C & O Canal:White's Ferry Iron Bridge

NORWOOD

Thomas,Richard,House; see Woodlawn Manor

Woodlawn Manor (Thomas,Richard,House)
16501 Norwood Dr.
HABS MD-578
HABS MD,16-NORWO,1-
3ph L

NORWOOD VIC.

Llewellyn Fields
HABS MD-602
HABS MD,16-NORWO.V,1-
1ph L

Norwood
HABS MD-603
HABS MD,16-NORWO.V,2-
2ph L

OLNEY

Barnsley,James F. ,House; see House,Small (Chimney)

Brooke,Col. Richard,House; see Fairhill

Fairhill (Brooke,Col. Richard,House)
3201 Sandy Spring Rd. (State Rt. 108)
HABS MD-581
HABS MD,16-OLNEY,2-
2ph L

House,Small (Chimney) (Barnsley,James F. ,House)
State Rt. 97
HABS MD-582
HABS MD,16-OLNEY,3-
1ph L

Olney House
HABS MD-583
HABS MD,16-OLNEY,1-
2ph L

OLNEY VIC.

Belmont (Waters,Thomas,Place; Waters,William,House; Dorsey,Caleb,House)
Georgia Ave. (State Rt. 97) Vic.
HABS MD-579
HABS MD,16-OLNEY.V,2-
5ph L

Birdsall,William,House; see Rockland

Brooke,Basil,House; see Falling Green

Dorsey,Caleb,House; see Belmont

Falling Green (Brooke,Basil,House)
4501 Laytonsville Rd. (State Rt. 108)
HABS MD-580
HABS MD,16-OLNEY.V,1-
5ph L

Rockland (Birdsall,William,House)
2701 Laytonsville Rd. (State Rt. 108)
HABS MD-584
HABS MD,16-OLNEY.V,3-
1ph L

Waters,Thomas,Place; see Belmont

Waters,William,House; see Belmont

POOLESVILLE

House,Stone (Valhalla; Rosedale)
107 Fisher Ave.
HABS MD-585
HABS MD,16-POOV,8-
2ph L

Irvine Farm; see Milford,Dr. ,House

Kohloss Row; see Main Street (Houses)

Main Street (Houses) (Kohloss Row; Merchants Hotel)
Fisher Ave. & Jerusalem Rd. (State Rt. 109)
HABS MD-127
HABS MD,16-POOV,4-
1ph L

Merchants Hotel; see Main Street (Houses)

Milford,Dr. ,House (Poole's Hazard; Irvine Farm)
17610 Cattail Rd.
HABS MD-588
HABS MD,16-POOV,5-
1ph L

Poole,Dr. Sprig,House
HABS MD-591
HABS MD,16-POOV,2-
2ph L

Poole,Richard,House
HABS MD-590
HABS MD,16-POOV,6-
1ph L

Poole's Hazard; see Milford,Dr. ,House

Pyles House
HABS MD-592
HABS MD,16-POOV,7-
2ph L

Rosedale; see House,Stone

Stoney Castle
State Rt. 109 Vic.
HABS MD-119
HABS MD,16-POOV,3-
1ph L

Umstead House
HABS MD-593
HABS MD,16-POOV,9-
1ph L

Valhalla; see House,Stone

POOLESVILLE VIC.

Chiswell's Delight; see Grayhaven Manor

Chiswell's Inheritance; see Grayhaven Manor

Chiswell's Manor; see Grayhaven Manor

East Oaks Manor; see Little Oak Manor

Grayhaven Manor (Chiswell's Manor; Chiswell's Delight; Chiswell's Inheritance; Sara's Delight)
State Rt. 109 Vic.
HABS MD-136
HABS MD,16-POOV.V,1-
12ph L

Kilmain
Whites Ferry Rd. Vic.
HABS MD-586
HABS MD,16-POOV.V,2-
2ph L

Little Oak Manor (East Oaks Manor; Young,Henry,House)
21524 Whites Ferry Rd. (State Rt. 107)
HABS MD-587
HABS MD,16-POOV.V,3-
3ph L

Mount Pleasant
HABS MD-589
HABS MD,16-POOV.V,4-
3ph L

Sara's Delight; see Grayhaven Manor

Young,Henry,House; see Little Oak Manor

POTOMAC VIC.

Chesapeake & Ohio Canal National Historical Park; see Chesapeake & Ohio Canal,Lockhouse 18 (Ruins)

Chesapeake & Ohio Canal,Lockhouse 18 (Ruins) (Chesapeake & Ohio Canal National Historical Park)
Lock 18,MacArthur Blvd. Vic.
HAER MD-33
HAER MD,16-POTO.V,1-
2dr/fr L

Chesapeake & Ohio Canal,Stop Gate,Lock 16
HABS MD-57-I
HABS MD,16- ,15-
1ph/fr L

REDLAND

Flower Hill
HABS MD-594
HABS MD,16-RED,1-
2ph L

REDLAND VIC.

Magruder Place; see Ridge,The

Ridge,The (Magruder Place)
HABS MD-595
HABS MD,16-RED.V,1-
7ph L

RIVERSIDE

Chesapeake & Ohio Canal National Historical Park; see Chesapeake & Ohio Canal,Lockhouse at Lock 24

Chesapeake & Ohio Canal,Lockhouse at Lock 22 (Chesapeake & Ohio Canal,Lockhouse,Pennyfield Lock)
Pennyfield Lock Rd. ,State Rt. 190 Vic.
HABS MD-56-Q
HABS MD,16- ,27A-
3dr/fr L

Chesapeake & Ohio Canal,Lockhouse at Lock 24 (Chesapeake & Ohio Canal National Historical Park)
Tidewater Vic.
HABS MD-56-T
HABS MD,16- ,29A-
2dr/1ph L

Chesapeake & Ohio Canal,Lockhouse,Pennyfield Lock; see Chesapeake & Ohio Canal,Lockhouse at Lock 22

RIVERSIE

Chesapeake & Ohio Canal,Lock 24 (Chesapeake & Ohio Canal,Riley's Lock)
Riley's Lock Rd.
HABS MD-57-C
HABS MD,16- ,29-
2ph L

Chesapeake & Ohio Canal,Riley's Lock; see Chesapeake & Ohio Canal,Lock 24

ROCKVILLE

Baltimore & Ohio Railroad,Station & Freight House
98 Baltimore Rd.
HABS MD-238
HABS MDROCV2- I,2-
5dr/17ph/16pg/5ct/fr L

Beallmont (Dawson House)
103 W. Montgomery Ave.
HABS MD-596
HABS MD,16-ROCVI,1-
6ph L

Dawson House; see Beallmont

First National Bank of Maryland
4 Courthouse Sq.
HABS MD-915
HABS MD,16-ROCVI,3-
2ph/1pc L

Montgomery County Courthouse (1891)
Court House Sq.
HABS MD-912
HABS MD,16-ROCVI,4-
24ph/2pc/8ct L

Montgomery Courthouse,1931 Addition
Courthouse Sq.
HABS MD-913
HABS MD,16-ROCVI,5-
5ph/1pc L

U. S. Post Office,Courthouse Station
S. Washington St. & W. Montgomery Ave. on Cthse.Sq
HABS MD-914
HABS MD,16-ROCVI,6-
1ph/1pc L

SANDY SPRING

Auburn Barn
HABS MD-597
HABS MD,16-SANSP,2A-
1ph L

Avelon
HABS MD-598
HABS MD,16-SANSP,3-
1ph L

Cedars,The; see Farquhar House

Cloverly
HABS MD-599
HABS MD,16-SANSP,4-
3ph L

Farquhar House (Cedars,The)
1601 Sandy Spring Rd. (Rt. 108)
HABS MD-964
HABS MD,16-SANSP,6-
13ph/17pg/1pc L

Friends Meetinghouse
Meetinghouse Lane
HABS MD-600
HABS MD,16-SANSP,1-
1ph L

Harewood
HABS MD-601
HABS MD,16-SANSP,5-
2ph L

SENECA VIC.

Chesapeake & Ohio Canal National Historical Park; see Chesapeake & Ohio Canal,Lock 25

Chesapeake & Ohio Canal National Historical Park; see Chesapeake & Ohio Canal,Lockhouse at Lock 25

Chesapeake & Ohio Canal,Aqueduct Number 1 (Chesapeake & Ohio Canal,Seneca Creek Aqueduct)
Riley's Lock Rd. Vic. ,State Rt. 190
HABS MD-57-B
HABS MD,16- ,30-
2dr/3ph/fr L

Chesapeake & Ohio Canal,Edward's Ferry; see Chesapeake & Ohio Canal,Lock 25

Chesapeake & Ohio Canal,Lock 25 (Chesapeake & Ohio Canal,Edward's Ferry; Chesapeake & Ohio Canal National Historical Park)
HABS MD-739
HABS MD,16- ,31B-
1ph/1pc L

Chesapeake & Ohio Canal,Lockhouse at Lock 25 (Chesapeake & Ohio Canal,Lockhouse,Edward's Ferry; Chesapeake & Ohio Canal National Historical Park)
Edward's Ferry Rd.
HABS MD-738
HABS MD,16 ,31A
4ph/1pc L

Chesapeake & Ohio Canal,Lockhouse,Edward's Ferry; see Chesapeake & Ohio Canal,Lockhouse at Lock 25

Chesapeake & Ohio Canal,Seneca Creek Aqueduct; see Chesapeake & Ohio Canal,Aqueduct Number 1

Chesapeake & Ohio Canal,Swing Bridge,Lock 25
Edward's Ferry Rd. Vic.
HABS MD-57-A
HABS MD,16- ,31-
1dr L

Kiplinger,Austin,House; see Montevideo

Montevideo (Peter,John Parke Custis,House; Kiplinger,Austin,House)
Montevideo Rd.
HABS MD-125
HABS MD,16-SENCA.V,1-
5ph L

Peter,John Parke Custis,House; see Montevideo

River View
HABS MD-604
HABS MD,16-SENCA.V,2-
8ph L

Stone Cutting Building
Tschiffeley Mill Rd.
HABS MD-299
HABS MD,16-SENCA.V, -
2dr L

SILVER SPRING

Polychrome House No. One
9900 Colesville Rd. (U.S. Rt. 29)
HABS MD-1077
4dr/fr H

SOMERSET VIC.

Loughborough House; see Milton

Milton (Loughborough House)
River Rd.
HABS MD-10-1
HABS MD,16-SOM,1-
3dr/6ph/2pg/fr L

UNITY

Gaither-Brown House (Griffith,Henry II,House)
3801 Howard Chapel Rd.
HABS MD-113
HABS MD,16-UNI.V,2-
4ph L

Griffith,Henry II,House; see Gaither-Brown House

UNITY VIC.

Gaither,Samuel,Barn
3101 Mount Carmel Cemetery Rd.
HABS MD-108
HABS MD,16-UNI.V,1A-
2ph L

Gaither,Samuel,House (Rolling Acres)
3101 Mount Carmel Cemetery Rd.
HABS MD-96
HABS MD,16-UNI.V,1-
2ph L

Rolling Acres; see Gaither,Samuel,House

Tradelphia Mill Group
Tradelphia Lake Rd.
HABS MD-114
HABS MD,16-UNI.V,3-
5ph L

PRINCE GEORGE'S COUNTY

ACCOKEEK VIC.

Christ Church
Farmington Rd.
HABS MD-605
HABS MD,17-ACCO.V,1-
2ph L

ADELPHI

Blossum Point Research Facility,LaPlata,MD.; see Diamond,Harry,Laboratories/Blossum Point Res.Faci.

Diamond,Harry,Laboratories/Blossum Point Res.Faci. (Blossum Point Research Facility,LaPlata,MD.; Woodbridge Research Facility,Woodbridge,VA.)
2800 Powder Mill Rd.
HAER MD-48
HAER MD,17-ADEL,1-
47pg/fr L

Woodbridge Research Facility,Woodbridge,VA.; see Diamond,Harry,Laboratories/Blossum Point Res.Faci.

AQUASCO

Cabin,Small
HABS MD-606
HABS MD,17-AQUA,4-
1ph L

Grymes House
Aquasco Rd. (State Rt. 381)
HABS MD-607
HABS MD,17-AQUA,1-
1ph L

House,Plank
HABS MD-608
HABS MD,17-AQUA,2-
2ph L

Thomas House (Ruins)
HABS MD-880
HABS MD,17-AQUA,3-
4ph L

AQUASCO VIC.

Poplar Hill
Croom (State Rt. 382) & Aquasco Rds.
HABS MD-609
HABS MD,17-AQUA.V,1-
1ph L

Spring Hill
Aquasco Farm Rd.
HABS MD-610
HABS MD,17-AQUA.V,2-
2ph/1pg L

BADEN

St. Paul's Church
Baden-Westwood & Horsehead Rds.
HABS MD-110
HABS MD,17-BAD,1-
6ph L

BADEN VIC.

Anchovie Hills (Cross Place; Magruder,Alexander,House)
Croom Rd. (State Rt. 382)
HABS MD-613
HABS MD,17-BAD.V,1-
3ph/1pg L

Connick's Folly
Aquasco Rd. (State Rt. 381)
HABS MD-614
HABS MD,17-BAD.V,2-
1ph L

Cross Place; see Anchovie Hills

Horsehead Tavern
Horsehead & Brandywine (State Rt. 381) Rds.
HABS MD-612
HABS MD,17-BAD.V,3-
1ph L

Magruder,Alexander,House; see Anchovie Hills

BELTSVILLE

Abraham Hall
7612 Old Muirkirk Rd.
HABS MD-1043
5ph/1pc H

St. Joseph's Chapel
Ammendale Rd.
HABS MD-1022
10ph/1pc H

BLADENSBURG

Boatswick Hall
(Lowndes,Christopher,House)
3901 Forty-eighth & Quincy Sts.
HABS MD-615
HABS MD,17-BLAD,1-
3ph L

Cross House; see Parthenon Manor

Decatur Heights; see Parthenon Manor

Lowndes,Christopher,House; see Boatswick Hall

Lowndes,Christopher,House; see Parthenon Manor

Magruder House
Bladensburg Rd.
HABS MD-616
HABS MD,17-BLAD,3
5dr/1ph L

Parthenon Manor (Cross House; Decatur Heights; Lowndes,Christopher,House)
Edmonston Rd. (State Rt. 450 Vic.)
HABS MD-313
HABS MD,17-BLAD,4-
3dr/4ph L

Ross House; see Ross,Dr. David,House

Ross,Dr. David,House (Ross House)
Annapolis Rd. (moved to Cockeysville)
HABS MD-120
HABS MD,17-BLAD,2
9dr/7ph/1pg/2pc L

BLANDENSBURG

Indian Queen Tavern,Old; see Washington,George,House

Inn,Old; see Washington,George,House

Washington,George,House (Indian Queen Tavern,Old; Inn,Old)
Baltimore Ave. & Upshur St.
HABS MD-617
HABS MD,17-BLAD,5-
1ph L

BOWIE

Belair (Bowie City Hall; Ogle,Samuel,House)
Tulip Grove Dr. ,Belair-at-Bowie
HABS MD-87
HABS MD,17-COLTO.V,1-
12ph/1pg L

Bowie City Hall; see Belair

Goodloe,D. S. S.,House
13809 Jericho Park Rd.
HABS MD-1062
2ph/2pg/1pc H

Governor's Bridge (Patuxent Bridge)
HAER MD-85
1ph/2pg/1pc H

Ogle,Samuel,House; see Belair

Patuxent Bridge; see Governor's Bridge

BOWIE VIC.

Duckett,Thomas,House; see Melford

Gladswood
Patuxent Wild Life Center,State Rt. 197
HABS MD-618
HABS MD,17-BOWI.V,1-
6ph L

Melford (Duckett,Thomas,House; Slingluff House)
Crain Hwy. (U. S. Rt. 301)
HABS MD-627
HABS MD,17-COLTO.V,6-
2ph L

Slingluff House; see Melford

BUENA VISTA

Duvall,Benjamin,House; see Marietta

Marietta (Duvall,Benjamin,House)
5626 Bell Station Rd.
HABS MD-619
HABS MD,17-BUEVI,1-
2ph L

BUENA VISTA VIC.

Duckett House; see Forest Hill

Forest Hill (Duckett House)
4310 Enterprise Rd. (State Rt. 556)
HABS MD-624
HABS MD,17-COLTO,1-
2ph L

CHELTENHAM

Westwood
Westwood Dr.
HABS MD-621
HABS MD,17-CHELT,2-
3ph L

CHELTENHAM VIC.

Poplar Neck
U. S. Naval Research Station,Dangerfield Rd.
HABS MD-620
HABS MD,17-CHELT,1-
1ph L

CHEVERLY

Bellamy House,The
2819 Cheverly Ave.
HABS MD-1016
HABS 1992(HABS):MD-1
4dr/fr L

CLINTON VIC.

Griffin,Walter B. ,House; see Mudd,Dr. Sydney Emanuel,House

Mudd,Dr. Sydney Emanuel,House (Griffin,Walter B. ,House)
Grafton Lane & Colorado St.
HABS MD-622
HABS MD,17-CLINT.V,1-
1ph L

COLLEGE PARK

Inn,Old; see Rossburg House

Rossburg House (Inn,Old; University of Maryland,Faculty Club)
Baltimore Ave. (U. S. Rt. 1) Vic.
HABS MD-623
HABS MD,17-COLPA,1-
1ph L

University of Maryland,Faculty Club; see Rossburg House

COLLINGTON VIC.

Bowie,Walter,House; see Willow Grove

Darnell's Grove; see Willow Grove

Duckett,Baruch,House; see Fairview

Fairview (Duckett,Baruch,House)
4410 Church Rd.
HABS MD-86
HABS MD,17-COLTO.V,5-
5ph L

Holy Trinity Church
Annapolis Rd. (State Rt. 450)
HABS MD-625
HABS MD,17-COLTO.V,3-
1ph L

Locust Grove; see Willow Grove

Trinity Parish House (Trinity Rectory)
Annapolis Rd. (State Rt. 450)
HABS MD-626
HABS MD,17-COLTO.V,4-
1ph L

Trinity Rectory; see Trinity Parish House

Willow Grove (Bowie,Walter,House; Darnell's Grove; Locust Grove)
Annapolis Rd. (State Rt. 450)
HABS MD-628
HABS MD,17-COLTO.V,7-
3ph L

CONTEE

Oaklands (Snowden,Richard,House)
Contee Rd.
HABS MD-109
HABS MD,17-CONT,1-
7ph L

Snowden,Richard,House; see Oaklands

CROOM

St. Thomas' Church
St. Thomas' Church & Croom Rds.
HABS MD-631
HABS MD,17-CROM,1-
1ph L

CROOM VIC.

Bellefields (Sim,Col. Patrick,House; Sim's Delight)
3800 Duley Station Rd.
HABS MD-629
HABS MD,17-CROM.V,1-
3ph L

Claggett House; see Half Pone Farm

Half Pone Farm (Claggett House)
Patuxent River Park,Croom Airport Rd.
HABS MD-630
HABS MD,17-CROM.V,2-
4ph L

Sim,Col. Patrick,House; see Bellefields

Sim's Delight; see Bellefields

FORESTVILLE VIC.

Dunblane (Magruder,John,House)
Westphalia Rd.
HABS MD-633
HABS MD,17-FORVI.V,1-
5ph L

Magruder,John,House; see Dunblane

FORESTVILLE.

Cottage,The
Ardwick-Ardmore & Lottsford Vista Rds.
HABS MD-632
HABS MD,17-FORVI,1-
1ph L

FORT WASHINGTON VIC.

Hatton Mansion
HABS MD-111
HABS MD,17-FOWA.V,2-
7ph L

FRIENDLY VIC.

Battersea; see Harmony Hall

Broad Creek Church (St. John's Church)
9801 Old Oxon Hill Rd.
HABS MD-49
HABS MD,17-BROCK,1-
3ph/3pg L

Harmony Hall (Battersea)
10500 Livingstone Rd.
HABS MD-10-8
HABS MD,17-BROCK,3-
6dr/16ph/8pg/1pc/fr L

Lyles House (Want Water)
Livingston Rd.
HABS MD-10-7
HABS MD,17-BROCK,2-
5dr/8ph/6pg/1pc/fr L

St. John's Church; see Broad Creek Church

Want Water; see Lyles House

FT. WASH.FOREST VIC.

Fort Washington National Park; see Fort Washington,Powder Magazine Number 1

Fort Washington,Powder Magazine Number 1 (Fort Washington National Park)
HABS MD-307-F
HABS MD,17-FOWA,1- 1991(HABS):30
1dr/fr L

FT.WASH. FOREST VIC.

Fort Washington
Fort Washington Rd.
HABS MD-307
H

Fort Washington,Barracks
Fort Washington Rd.
HABS MD-307-C
HABS DLC/PP-1992:MD-4
1ph/1pc L

Fort Washington,Commandant's House
Fort Washington Rd.
HABS MD-307-E
HABS DLC/PP-1992:MD-4
5ph/1pc L

Fort Washington,Fort
Fort Washington Rd.
HABS MD-307-D
HABS DLC/PP-1992:MD-4
17ph/3pc L

Fort Washington,Main Gate (Sally Port)
Fort Washington Rd.
HABS MD-307-A
HABS DLC/PP-1992:MD-4
20ph/3pc L

Fort Washington,Officer's Quarters
Fort Washington Rd.
HABS MD-307-B
HABS DLC/PP-1992:MD-4
8ph/1pc L

Sally Port; see Fort Washington,Main Gate

HYATTSVILLE (WASO)

Hyattsville Hardware
5121 Baltimore Ave.
HABS MD-1042
5ph/1pc H

LANDOVER VIC.

Beall's Pleasure
(Stoddert,Benjamin,House)
Landover Rd. Vic.
HABS MD-635
HABS MD,17-LAND,1-
2ph L

Grovehurst
Brightseat Rd. & Hamlin St.
HABS MD-636
HABS MD,17-LAND.V,1-
3ph L

Stoddert,Benjamin,House; see Beall's Pleasure

LANGLEY PARK

Adelphi Mill (Riggs Mill; Adelphi Water Mill)
Adelphi Mill Recreation Center,State Rt. 212
HABS MD-93
HABS MD,17-CHIL.V,1-
9ph/fr L

Adelphi Mill,Miller's House (Riggs Mill,Cottage)
Adelphi Mill Recreation Center,State Rt. 212
HABS MD-93-A
HABS MD,17-CHIL.V,2-
1ph L

Adelphi Water Mill; see Adelphi Mill

Riggs Mill; see Adelphi Mill

Riggs Mill,Cottage; see Adelphi Mill,Miller's House

LARGO VIC.

Ellerslee; see Partnership

Friendship
Kolbies Corner,State Rts. 214 & 556
HABS MD-50
HABS MD,17-KOLB,1-
6dr/14ph/fr L

Hall House; see Partnership

Largo
Big Chimney Branch Rd.
HABS MD-637
HABS MD,17-LARG,1-
1ph L

Magruder House; see Mount Lubentia

Mount Lubentia (Magruder House)
601 Largo Rd. & Kettering Dr.
HABS MD-638
HABS MD,17-LARG.V,1-
20ph L

Northampton
Northampton Way
HABS MD-639
HABS MD,17-LARG.V,2-
4ph L

Oakhill
Lochton Dr. & Prenton St.
HABS MD-640
HABS MD,17-LARG.V,3-
4ph L

Partnership (Hall House; Ellerslee)
Central Ave. (State Rt. 214)
HABS MD-641
HABS MD,17-KOLB.V,1-
3ph L

LAUREL VIC.

Baltimore Road (House)
HABS MD-179
HABS MD,17-LAUR.V,4-
1ph L

Montpelier (Snowden-Long House; Snowden,Thomas,House)
Montpelier Dr. & State Rt. 197
HABS MD-140
HABS MD,17-LAUR.V,1-
21ph L

Rose Cottage; see Snowden Hill

Snow Hill (Snowden,Samuel,House)
Laurel-Bowie (State Rt. 197) & Contee Rds.
HABS MD-642
HABS MD,17-LAUR.V,2-
2ph L

Snowden Hill (Rose Cottage)
Patuxent Wildlife Research Center
HABS MD-643
HABS MD,17-LAUR.V,3-
1ph L

Snowden-Long House; see Montpelier

Snowden,Samuel,House; see Snow Hill

Snowden,Thomas,House; see Montpelier

LEELAND

St. Barnabas Church
HABS MD-128
HABS MD,17-LELD,1-
6ph L

LEELAND VIC.

Bowie,Robert,House; see Bowieville

Bowieville (Bowie,Robert,House)
2300 Church Rd.
HABS MD-644
HABS MD,17-LELD.V,1-
2ph L

Carter,Bernard Moore,House; see Goodwood

Goodwood (Carter,Bernard Moore,House)
HABS MD-664
HABS MD,17-LELD.V,2-
3ph L

MITCHELLVILLE

Holy Family Church
12010 Woodmore Rd.
HABS MD-1021
1pc H

White,Newton H.,Mansion
2708 Enterprise Rd.
HABS MD-1063
3ph/1pg/1pc H

MULLIKIN

Essington Hall (Interiors)
Old Mount Oak Rd.
HABS MD-648
HABS MD,17-MUL,1-
3ph L

MULLIKIN VIC.

Elverton Hall
HABS MD-647
HABS MD,17-MUL.V,1-
3ph L

NOTTINGHAM

Bowie,John Jr. ,House; see Mattaponi

Cedars,The (House,Small; Smith,John,House)
HABS MD-51
HABS MD,17-NOT,1-
8dr/5ph/2pg/fr L

Harmony Hall (Ruins)
Nottingham Rd.
HABS MD-650
HABS MD,17-NOT,2-
1ph L

House,Small; see Cedars,The

Mattaponi (Bowie,John Jr. ,House)
Mattaponi Rd.
HABS MD-651
HABS MD,17-CROM.V,3-
3ph L

Smith,John,House; see Cedars,The

OXON HILL

Bain,Dr. ,House; see Salubria

Oxon Hill Manor
6701 Oxon Hill Rd.
HABS MD-301
HABS MD,17-OXHI,1
28ph/13pg/1pc L

Oxon Hill Manor,Garage; see Oxon Hill Manor,Manager's Residence,Garage & Grnhs

Oxon Hill Manor,Greenhouse; see Oxon Hill Manor,Manager's Residence,Garage & Grnhs

Oxon Hill Manor,Grounds
6701 Oxon Hill Rd.
HABS MD-301-A
HABS MD,17-OXHI,1A-
6ph/1pc L

Oxon Hill Manor,Manager's Residence,Garage & Grnhs (Oxon Hill Manor,Garage; Oxon Hill Manor,Greenhouse)
6701 Oxon Hill Rd.
HABS MD-301-B
HABS MD,17-OXHI,1B-
3ph/1pc L

Oxon Hill Manor,Stable
6701 Oxon Hill Rd.
HABS MD-301-C
HABS MD,17-OXHI,1C-
2ph/1pc L

Salubria (Bain,Dr. ,House)
6900 Oxon Hill Rd. (State Rt. 414)
HABS MD-652
HABS MD,17-OXHI.V,1-
3ph L

St. Barnabus Church,Oxon Hill
HABS MD-1064
1ph/2pg/1pc H

OXON HILL VIC.

Barnaby Manor
Wheeler & Wheeler Hill Rds.
HABS MD-314
HABS MD,17-OXHI.V,2-
4dr/2ph/1pc L

PISCATAWAY

Brent House (Hardy Tavern)
Piscataway Rd. (State Rt. 223)
HABS MD-653
HABS MD,17-PISC,2-
1ph L

Claggetts' Tavern; see Piscataway Tavern

Hardy Tavern; see Brent House

Piscataway Tavern (Claggetts' Tavern)
Piscataway Rd. (State Rt. 223) Vic.
HABS MD-52
HABS MD,17-PISC,1-
4dr/6ph/fr L

PISCATAWAY VIC.

Belle Vue Farm; see Belview

Belview (Belle Vue Farm; Steed House)
3201 Steed Rd.
HABS MD-654
HABS MD,17-TIP.V,2-
1ph L

Hostetter House; see St. James

Marbury House; see Wyoming

St. James (Hostetter House; St. James Hill)
14200 Livingston Rd.
HABS MD-115
HABS MD,17-PISC.V,1-
3ph L

St. James Hill; see St. James

Steed House; see Belview

Wyoming (Marbury House)
330 Thrift St.
HABS MD-53
HABS MD,17-TIP.V,1-
4dr/4ph/fr L

RITCHIE

Berry,Zechariah,House; see Concord

Concord (Berry,Zechariah,House)
8000 Walker Mill Rd.
HABS MD-656
HABS MD,17-SEPL.V,1-
1ph L

RIVERDALE

Baltimore House (Riverdale; Calvert Mansion; de Stier,Baron,House)
4811 Riverdale Rd.
HABS MD-655
HABS MD,17-RIV,1-
6dr/3ph L H

Calvert Mansion; see Baltimore House

de Stier,Baron,House; see Baltimore House

Riverdale; see Baltimore House

Smith,Harry,House
4707 Oliver St.
HABS MD-1078
9dr/fr H

ROSARYVILLE

Darnall,Henry II,House; see Poplar Hill

Dower House; see Mount Airy

His Lordship's Kindness; see Poplar Hill

Mount Airy (Dower House)
HABS MD-117
HABS MD,17-ROSVI.V,2-
11ph L

Poplar Hill (Darnall,Henry II,House; His Lordship's Kindness)
His Lordship's Kindness Rd.
HABS MD-315
HABS MD,17-ROSVI.V,1
3dr/19ph/1pc L

SEAT PLEASANT

Chesapeake Beach RR Engine House
21 Yost Pl.
HAER MD-49
HAER MD,17-SEPL,2-
18ph/10pg/2pc L

SEAT PLEASANT VIC.

Berry,Zechariah,House; see Independence

Glenway (Hill,William H. ,House)
Rolling Ridge Dr.
HABS MD-657
HABS MD,17-SEPL.V,2-
1ph L

Hill,William H. ,House; see Glenway

Independence (Berry,Zechariah,House)
Seventy-seventh St.
HABS MD-658
HABS MD,17-SEPL.V,3-
1ph L

THOMAS BROOK VIC.

Gwynn Park (Gwynn,William H. ,House)
296 Dyson Rd.
HABS MD-659
HABS MD,17-T.B.V,1-
2ph L

Gwynn,William H. ,House; see Gwynn Park

TOWNSEND VIC.

Pheasant's Thicket
HABS MD-879
HABS MD,17-TOSE.V,1-
5ph/1pc L

UPPER MARLBORO

Billingsley (Weems House)
6900 Green Landing Rd.
HABS MD-660
HABS MD,17-MARBU.V,4-
1ph L

Buck,Harry,House (Hill-Buck House)
N. of Main St.
HABS MD-661
HABS MD,17-MARBU,3-
1ph L

Buck,Sarah,House
Main St. Vic.
HABS MD-662
HABS MD,17-MARBU,4-
1ph L

Compton-Bassett Chapel
Marlboro Pike (State Rt. 408)
HABS MD-135
HABS MD,17-MARBU.V,3A-
2ph L

Compton-Bassett House (Hill,Clement V,House)
Old Marlboro Pike (State Rt. 408)
HABS MD-134
HABS MD,17-MARBU.V,3-
4ph L

Content
14518 Church St.
HABS MD-663
HABS MD,17-MARBU,5-
1ph L

Crawford,David,House; see Sasscer's House

Diggs,Ignatius,House; see Melwood Park

Hill-Buck House; see Buck,Harry,House

Hill,Clement V,House; see Compton-Bassett House

Kingstead House; see Sasscer's House

Melwood Farms (Melwood House)
10200 Old Marlboro Pike (State Rt. 408)
HABS MD-670
HABS MD,17-MARBU.V,6-
2ph L

Melwood House; see Melwood Farms

Melwood Park (Diggs,Ignatius,House)
Old Marlboro Pike (State Rt. 408)
HABS MD-142
HABS MD,17-MARBU.V,2-
5ph L

Mount Pleasant
Mount Pleasant Rd.
HABS MD-665
HABS MD,17-MARBU.V,8-
3ph/1pg L

Overseer's House
5601 Old Crain Hwy.
HABS MD-645
HABS MD,17-MARBU,6-
1ph L

Sasscer's Green
1732 Crain Hwy. (U. S. Rt. 301)
HABS MD-666
HABS MD,17-MARBU.V,9-
1ph L

Sasscer's House (Crawford,David,House; Kingstead House)
5415 Old Crain Hwy. (U. S. Rt. 301)
HABS MD-667
HABS MD,17-MARBU,7-
2ph L

St. Mary's Beneficial Society Hall
14825 Pratt St.,at Main St.
HABS MD-1044
2ph/1pg/1pc H

Trinity Church (Episcopal)
14519 Church St.
HABS MD-1041
9ph/1pg/1pc H

Upper Marlboro Tavern
Main St.
HABS MD-137
HABS MD,17-MARBU,1-
9ph/1pc L

Weems House; see Billingsley

Wilson House
(moved to MD,Lower Marlboro)
HABS MD-126
HABS MD,17-MARBU,2-
2ph L

UPPER MARLBORO VIC.

Charleston; see Mount Calvert

Claggett,Thomas VI,House; see Weston

Cleremont
HABS MD-669
HABS MD,17-MARBU.V,5-
1ph L

Mount Calvert (Charleston)
Mount Calvert Rd.
HABS MD-176
HABS MD,17-MARBU.V,7-
5ph L

Weston (Claggett,Thomas VI,House)
Old Crain Hwy. Vic.
HABS MD-668
HABS MD,17-MARBU.V,1-
4ph L

Woodstock
Crain Hwy. (U. S. Rt. 301)
HABS MD-646
HABS MD,17-ROSVI.V,3-
1ph L

WOODMORE

Bermondsey (Hill,Charles,House)
Woodmore Rd.
HABS MD-671
HABS MD,17-WOOD.V,1-
2ph L

Duckett,Isaac,House; see Pleasant Prospect

Hill,Charles,House; see Bermondsey

Mullikin,James,House; see Mullikin's Delight

Mullikin's Delight
(Mullikin,James,House)
2307 Church Rd.
HABS MD-649
HABS MD,17-MUL.V,2-
3ph L

Pleasant Prospect (Duckett,Isaac,House)
13008 Woodmore Rd.
HABS MD-672
HABS MD,17-WOOD.V,2-
5ph L

QUEEN ANNE'S COUNTY

CENTREVILLE VIC.

Hollyday,James,House; see Readbourne

Peace & Plenty (Wright House)
U. S. Rt. 213
HABS MD-673
HABS MD,18-CENVI.V,2-
2ph L

Readbourne (Hollyday,James,House)
Land's End Rd. ,Wilmer Neck
HABS MD-99
HABS MD,18-CENVI.V,1-
9ph L

Walnut Grove (Wright House)
Wright Neck at Reid Creek
HABS MD-228
HABS MD,18-CENVI.V,3-
6dr L

Wright House; see Peace & Plenty

Wright House; see Walnut Grove

CHURCH HILL VIC.

Bishopton
HABS MD-894
HABS MD,18-CHUHI.V,2-
3dr L

HILLSBORO VIC.

Main Street (Brick House)
(Sellers,Francis,House)
HABS MD-675
HABS MD,18- ,4-
1ph L

Sellers,Francis,House; see Main Street (Brick House)

KENT ISLAND

Fisherman's House
HABS MD-678
HABS MD,18- ,3-
1ph L

QUEENSTOWN

Bowlingly
State Rt. 18 Vic.
HABS MD-892
HABS MD,18-QUETO,1-
31ph/1pg/2pc/40ct L

ROMANKOKE

Kent Fort Manor
Kent Point Rd.
HABS MD-681
HABS MD,18-ROMA.V,1-
1ph L

RUTHSBURG VIC.

Thomas House
State Rt. 304
HABS MD-25
HABS MD,18-ING.V,1-
1ph/3pg L

STEVENSVILLE

Kent Island (Brick House) (Steven's Adventure)
State Rt. 18 Vic.
HABS MD-674
HABS MD,18-CHEST.V,1-
1ph L

Steven's Adventure; see Kent Island (Brick House)

STEVENSVILLE VIC.

Carvel House
Kent Point Rd. Vic.
HABS MD-677
HABS MD,18- ,1-
1ph L

Friendship; see Stinton

House at Matapeake; see Stinton

Mattapex Farm; see Shippen Creek Road (Farm)

Shippen Creek Road (Farm) (Mattapex Farm)
HABS MD-680
HABS MD,18- ,2-
1ph L

Stinton (House at Matapeake; Friendship)
State Rt. 8
HABS MD-679
HABS MD,18-MAT,1-
6ph L

WYE MILLS

Clover Fields (Forman House; Hemsley,William,House; Hopewell)
Forman's Lodge Rd.
HABS MD-178
HABS MD,18-WYM.V,1-
17ph/1pc L

Forman House; see Clover Fields

Hemsley,William,House; see Clover Fields

Hopewell; see Clover Fields

SOMERSET COUNTY

CRISFIELD

Makepeace (Roach-Gunby House)
Johnson Creek Vic.
HABS MD-698
HABS MD,20-CRISF.V,1-
4dr/5ph/1pg L

Roach-Gunby House; see Makepeace

KINGSTON VIC.

Kingston Hall
Big Annemessex River Vic. ,W. of Marion Rd.
HABS MD-160
HABS MD,20-KING.V,1-
4ph L

Waters House
State Rt. 413 Vic.
HABS MD-161
HABS MD,20-KING.V,2-
1ph L

MANOKIN

Almodington (Elzey,Col. Arnold,House)
Deal Island Rd.
HABS MD-699
HABS MD,20- ,2-
3ph L

Elzey,Col. Arnold,House; see Almodington

MANOKIN VIC.

Sudler s Conclusion,Meat House and Barn (Sudler s Seclusion,Meat House and Barn)
N. W. of Manokin off Rte. 361
HABS MD-865-A
HABS MD,20-MANK.V,1A-
1ph/1pc L

Sudler s Seclusion,Meat House and Barn; see Sudler s Conclusion,Meat House and Barn

Sudler's Conclusion (Sudler's Seclusion)
Rt. 361 Vic. ,NW of Manokin
HABS MD-865
HABS MD,10-MANK.V,1-
7dr/8ph/1pg/1pc L

Sudler's Conclusion,Dependency (Sudler's Seclusion,Dependency)
N. W. of Manokin off Rte. 361
HABS MD-865-B
HABS MD,20-MANK.V,1B-
1ph/1pc L

Sudler's Seclusion; see Sudler's Conclusion

Sudler's Seclusion,Dependency; see Sudler's Conclusion,Dependency

PRINCESS ANNE

Church Street (House)
HABS MD-151
HABS MD,20-CRISF,1-
1ph L

Teackle Mansion (Teackle,Littleton Dennis,House)
Prince William & Mansion Sts.
HABS MD-164
HABS MD,20-PRINA,1-
1ph L

Teackle,Littleton Dennis,House; see Teackle Mansion

ST. MARY'S COUNTY

BUSHWOOD

Ocean Hall
HABS MD-323
HABS MD,19-BUWO,1-
9dr/17ph/1pc L

CHAPTICO VIC.

Bachelor's Hope
(Hammersley,William,House; Manor Lodge)
Manor Rd.
HABS MD-59
HABS MD,19-CLEM.V,1-
35ph/2pg/2pc/4ct L

Bachelor's Hope,Garage
(Hammersley,William,House,Garage; Manor Lodge,Garage)
Manor Rd.
HABS MD-59-A
HABS MD,19-CLEM.V,1A-
1ph/1pc L

Bachelor's Hope,Tobacco Shed
(Hammersley,William,House,Tobacco Shed; Manor Lodge,Tobacco Shed)
Manor Rd.
HABS MD-59-B
HABS MD,19-CLEM.V,1B-
1ph L

Hammersley,William,House; see Bachelor's Hope

Hammersley,William,House,Garage; see Bachelor's Hope,Garage

Hammersley,William,House,Tobacco Shed; see Bachelor's Hope,Tobacco Shed

Manor Lodge; see Bachelor's Hope

Manor Lodge,Garage; see Bachelor's Hope,Garage

Manor Lodge,Tobacco Shed; see Bachelor's Hope,Tobacco Shed

CHARLOTTE HALL

Charlotte Hall Military Academy; see Charlotte Hall School

Charlotte Hall Military Academy,Admin. Building; see Charlotte Hall School,Administration Building

Charlotte Hall School (Charlotte Hall Military Academy)
State Rts. 5 & 236
HABS MD-682
HABS MD,19-CHARHA,2-
1ph L

Charlotte Hall School,Administration Building (Charlotte Hall Military Academy,Admin. Building)
State Rts. 5 & 236
HABS MD-682-A
HABS MD,19-CHARHA,2A
12ph/1pg/1pc L

Hatch-Dent House (White House)
State Rts. 236 & 5
HABS MD-683
HABS MD,19-CHARHA,1-
4ph L

House,Frame
HABS MD-684
HABS MD,19-CHARHA,4-
1ph L

White House; see Hatch-Dent House

COMPTON VIC.

St. Francis Xavier Church
State Rt. 243 Vic.
HABS MD-322
HABS MD,19-COMP.V,1-
7dr/14ph/1pc/fr L

St. Francis Xavier Church,Manor House
State Rt. 243 vic.
HABS MD-322-A
HABS MD,19-COMP.V,1A-
4ph/1pc/fr L

DRAYDEN VIC.

Cherryfield; see Coad-Fenwick House

Coad-Fenwick House (Cherryfield; Porto Bello)
Cherryfield Point
HABS MD-685
HABS MD,19-DRAY.V,1-
1ph L

Porto Bello; see Coad-Fenwick House

GREAT MILLS

Allston,J. J. ,House; see Great Mills Road (House)

Great Mills Farmhouse; see Great Mills Road (House)

Great Mills Road (House) (Allston,J. J. ,House; Great Mills Farmhouse; Wolseley Manor)
Saint Mary's Creek Vic.
HABS MD-158
HABS MD,19-GREMI.V,1-
1ph L

Wolseley Manor; see Great Mills Road (House)

HOLLYWOOD VIC.

Bowles Separation; see Sotterly

Bowles,James,House; see Sotterly

Cornwaleys,Thomas,House; see Resurrection Manor

Industry
HABS MD-686
HABS MD,19-HOLWO.V,2-
2ph L

Resurrection Manor (Scotch Neck; Cornwaleys,Thomas,House)
Old Hwy.
HABS MD-36
HABS MD,19-HOLWO.V,1-
8dr/7ph/fr L

Scotch Neck; see Resurrection Manor

Sotterly (Bowles Separation; Bowles,James,House)
State Rt. 245 & Vista Rd. Vic.
HABS MD-181
HABS MD,19-HOLWO.V,3-
6dr/34ph/28pg/3pc L

Sotterly,Barn
State Rt. 245 & Vista Rd. Vic.
HABS MD-181-D
HABS MD,19-HOLWO.V,3D-
1ph L

Sotterly,Ceiling Detail
State Rt. 245 & Vista Rd. Vic.
HABS MD-181-E
HABS MD,19-HOLWO.V,3E-
1ph L

Sotterly,Gate Lodge
State Rt. 245 & Vista Rd. Vic.
HABS MD-181-B
HABS MD,19-HOLWO.V,3B-
1ph L

Sotterly,Necessary
State Rt. 245 & Vista Rd. Vic.
HABS MD-181-A
HABS MD,19-HOLWO.V,3A-
1ph L

Sotterly,Plans
State Rt. 245 & Vista Rd. Vic.
HABS MD-181-F
HABS MD,19-HOLWO.V,3F-
2ph L

Sotterly,Slave Quarters
State Rt. 245 & Vista Rd. Vic.
HABS MD-181-C
HABS MD,19-HOLWO.V,3C-
3ph/1pc L

LAUREL GROVE VIC.

Cremona
Sotterly Vic.
HABS MD-694
HABS MD,19-LAUR.V,1-
4ph L

Dela Brooke House
Patuxent River Vic.
HABS MD-695
HABS MD,19-LAUR.V,2-
1ph L

LEONARDTOWN

Key House; see Tudor Hall

Tudor Hall (Key House)
Tudor Rd.
HABS MD-687
HABS MD,19-LENTO,1-
3ph L

LEONARDTOWN VIC.

Nevitt's St. Anne
HABS MD-873
HABS MD,19-LENTO.V,2-
3dr/6ph/1pc L

St. Andrew's Episcopal Church
Saint Andrew's Church Rd.
HABS MD-45
HABS MD,19-LENTO.V,1-
2ph/7pg L

LEXINGTON PARK

Halfhead Folly; see Long Lane Farm

Jarboe,Lt. Col. John,House; see Long Lane Farm

Long Lane Farm (Jarboe,Lt. Col. John,House; Halfhead Folly)
State Rt. 712 Vic.
HABS MD-159
HABS MD,19-JARB.V,1-
11ph/1pc L

LEXINGTON PARK VIC.

Cedar Point Lighthouse
Cedar Point at Patuxent River & Chesapeake Bay
HABS MD-906
HABS MD,19-LEXP.V,1-
18ph/7pg/2pc L

MADDOX VIC.

Mill Point House
State Rt. 238 Vic.
HABS MD-104
HABS MD,19-MAD.V,1-
3ph L

MILLSTONE LANDING

Catholic Church
Patuxent Naval Air Test Center
HABS MD-876
HABS MD,19-MIL.V,3-
1ph L

MILLSTONE LANDING VI

Calvert House; see Mattapany

Documentation: **ct** color transparencies **dr** measured drawings **fr** field records
pc photograph captions **pg** pages of text **ph** photographs

Mattapany (Calvert House)
Patuxent River Vic.
HABS MD-688
HABS MD,19-MIL.V,1-
4ph L

Susquehanna (Susquehanna Point)
HABS MD-689
HABS MD,19-MIL.V,2-
3ph L

Susquehanna Point; see Susquehanna

MORGANZA

Little St. Thomas Barn
HABS MD-870
HABS MD,19-MORG,1-
3ph/1pc L

NEW MARKET VIC.

Barber,S. F. ,House
HABS MD-872
HABS MD,19-NEMA.V,2-
6ph/1pc L

Farmhouse
HABS MD-871
HABS MD,19-NEMA.V,1-
2ph/1pc L

OAKVILLE VIC.

Sandgates on Cat Creek
East of Oakville on St. Rte. 472
HABS MD-874
HABS MD,19-OKVI.V,1-
5dr/3ph/2pg/1pc L

RIDGE

Calvert,William,House; see Calvert's Rest

Calvert's Rest (Calvert,William,House; Scotland)
Curley Rd.
HABS MD-168
HABS MD,19-SCOT.V,1-
7ph/1pc L

Scotland; see Calvert's Rest

RIDGE VIC.

Bard's Field
HABS MD-875
HABS MD,19-RID.V,1-
7ph/1pc L

ST. INIGOES VIC.

Jesuit Manor Farm,Old Tobacco Barn
HABS MD-167
HABS MD,19-SAIGO.V,2A-
4ph L

St. Ignatius Roman Catholic Church
Webster Field Rd.
HABS MD-166
HABS MD,19-SAIGO.V,1-
1ph L

ST. MARY'S CITY

Trinity Protestant Episcopal Church
HABS MD-690
HABS MD,19-SAMA,1-
1ph L

ST. MARY'S CITY VIC.

Clocker,Daniel,House; see Clocker's Fancy

Clocker's Fancy (Clocker,Daniel,House)
HABS MD-691
HABS MD,19-SAMA.V,2-
2ph L

Cornwallis Manor; see Cross Manor

Cross Manor (Cornwallis Manor)
HABS MD-692
HABS MD,19-SAMA.V,3-
3ph L

Farmhouse,Brick
HABS MD-877
HABS MD,19-SAMA.V,4-
1ph L

ST. MARY'S VIC.

McKay House; see West St. Mary's Manor

West St. Mary's Manor (McKay House)
W. Saint Mary's Manor Rd.
HABS MD-97
HABS MD,19-SAMA.V,1-
5ph/1pg L

VALLEY LEE

St. George's Church
HABS MD-696
HABS MD,19-VALE,1-
2ph L

VALLEY LEE VIC.

House,Frame
HABS MD-697
HABS MD,19-VALE.V,2-
1ph L

Mulberry Fields
State Rt. 244
HABS MD-83
HABS MD,19-VALE.V,1-
13ph L

TALBOT COUNTY

EASTON

House,Brick
Higgins or Locust St. ,S. of August St.
HABS MD-702
HABS MD,21-EATO,4-
1ph L

Myrtle Grove (House)
Goldsborough Neck Rd.
HABS MD-336
HABS MD,21-EATO,10-
5pg L

North Washington Street (Brick Row Houses)
HABS MD-704
HABS MD,21-EATO,6-
4ph L

Quaker Meetinghouse (Third Haven Meetinghouse,Old)
Washington St.
HABS MD-703
HABS MD,21-EATO.V,1-
3ph L

107-109 S. Washington Street (Brick Double Houses)
HABS MD-701
HABS MD,21-EATO,5-
1ph L

18 South West Street (House)
HABS MD-302
HABS MD,21-EATO,8-
8dr L

20 South West Street (House)
HABS MD-303
HABS MD,21-EATO,9-
6dr L

Third Haven Meetinghouse,Old; see Quaker Meetinghouse

Washington Street (Brick Row Houses)
Opposite Courthouse
HABS MD-705
HABS MD,21-EATO,7-
2ph L

EASTON VIC.

Bartlett-Dixon House; see Old Bloomfield

Dover Ferry Farm
Dover Rd. (State Rt. 331)
HABS MD-700
HABS MD,21- ,2-
1ph L

Goldsborough,Robert,House; see Pleasant Valley

Hollyday,Henry,House; see Ratcliffe Manor

Locust Grove
Villa Rd.
HABS MD-308
HABS MD,21-EATO.V,7-
2dr/4ph/3pg L

Old Bloomfield (Bartlett-Dixon House)
Bloomfield Rd.
HABS MD-143
HABS MD,21-EATO.V,6-
2ph L

Orchard Knob; see Troth's Fortune

Pleasant Valley (Goldsborough,Robert,House)
Gross Coate Rd.
HABS MD-92
HABS MD,21-EATO.V,4-
2ph L

Ratcliffe Manor (Hollyday,Henry,House)
Easton Pkwy. (State Rt. 322) Vic.
HABS MD-89
HABS MD,21-EATO.V,3-
13ph L

Troth,William,House; see Troth's Fortune

Troth's Fortune (Orchard Knob; Troth,William,House)
Dover Rd. (State Rt. 331)
HABS MD-98
HABS MD,21-EATO.V,5
1ph/5pg L

MATTHEWS VIC.

Beaver Neck Farm; see Cottage,Brick

Cottage,Brick (Beaver Neck Farm)
Easton-Denton Rd. (State Rt. 328)
HABS MD-710
HABS MD,21- ,5-
1ph L

MC DANIEL VIC.

Indian Range Barn
State Rt. 33
HABS MD-310
HABS MD,21-MCDAN.V,1-
1dr L

OXFORD VIC.

Bingham House; see Jena

Gibson,Jacob,House; see Jena

Jena (Jenna; Bingham House; Gibson,Jacob,House)
Oxford Rd. (State Rt. 333)
HABS MD-163
HABS MD,21-OXFO.V,1-
1ph L

Jenna; see Jena

Otwell
Otwell Rd.
HABS MD-706
HABS MD,21-OXFO.V,2-
3ph/1pc L

QUEEN ANNE

House,Gambrel Roof
HABS MD-887
HABS MD,21-QUENA,1-
2ph L

Tavern,Old
HABS MD-708
HABS MD,21-QUENA,2-
1ph L

ST. MICHAELS

Skipjack E.C. Collier; see Two-Sail Bateau E.C. Collier

Two-Sail Bateau E.C. Collier (Skipjack E.C. Collier)
Chesapeake Bay Maritime Museum,Mills St.
HAER MD-77
HAER 1991(HAER):13
8dr/53ph/17pg/3pc/fr L

ST. MICHAELS VIC.

Hope House
Bruffs Island Rd. Vic.
HABS MD-154
HABS MD,21-SAIMI.V,2-
2ph L

TRAPPE

Dickinson House
Maple & S. Main Sts.
HABS MD-709
HABS MD,21-TRAP,1-
1ph L

TUNIS MILLS VIC.

Fair View (Skinner House)
HABS MD-26
HABS MD,21-SAIMI.V,1-
3ph/2pg L

Lloyd,Edward IV,House; see Wye House,Mansion

Skinner House; see Fair View

Wye House,Captain's House
Bruffs Island Rd.
HABS MD-88-D
HABS MD,21-EATO.V,2B-
8ph L

Wye House,Cemetery
Bruffs Island Rd.
HABS MD-88-F
HABS MD,21-EATON,2E-
3ph L

Wye House,Corn Crib
Bruffs Island Rd.
HABS MD-88-E
HABS MD,21-EATO.V,2D-
1ph L

Wye House,Mansion (Lloyd,Edward IV,House)
Bruffs Island Rd.
HABS MD-88-C
HABS MD,21-EATO.V,2-
19ph L

Wye House,Orangery
Bruffs Island Rd.
HABS MD-88-A
HABS MD,21-EATO.V,2A-
4dr/9ph L

Wye House,Smokehouse
Bruffs Island Rd.
HABS MD-88-B
HABS MD,21-EATO.V,2C-
2dr/4ph L

TUNIS MILLS VIC..

Wye Town Farm,Corn Crib
Maritime Museum (moved from MD,Tunis Mills)
HABS MD-309
HABS MD,21-TUMI.V,1-
1dr/2ph L

WYE MILLS

Creamery,The; see Store Building,Old

House near Wye Oak; see House,Old & Wye Oak

House,Old & Wye Oak (House near Wye Oak)
Old Wye Mills-Easton Rd. (State Rt. 662)
HABS MD-712
HABS MD,21-WYM,2-
1ph L

St. Luke's Church (Wye Church,Old)
Old Wye Mills-Easton Rd. (State Rt. 662)
HABS MD-711
HABS MD,21-WYM,1-
2ph L

Store Building,Old (Creamery,The)
State Rts. 662 & 404
HABS MD-713
HABS MD,21-WYM,3-
1ph L

Wye Church,Old; see St. Luke's Church

WASHINGTON COUNTY

ANTIETAM VIC.

Chesapeake & Ohio Canal National Historical Park; see Chesapeake & Ohio Canal,Antietam Creek Aqueduct

Chesapeake & Ohio Canal National Historical Park; see Chesapeake & Ohio Canal,Culvert above Lock 37

Chesapeake & Ohio Canal National Historical Park; see Chesapeake & Ohio Canal,Lock Tender's Hse,Lock 37

Chesapeake & Ohio Canal National Historical Park; see Chesapeake & Ohio Canal,Lock 37

Chesapeake & Ohio Canal National Historical Park; see Chesapeake & Ohio Canal,Waste Weir,Lock No. 37

Chesapeake & Ohio Canal,Antietam Creek Aqueduct (Chesapeake & Ohio Canal,Aqueduct 4; Chesapeake & Ohio Canal National Historical Park)
Canal Rd.
HABS MD-205
HABS MD,22-ANTI.V,3-
4dr/4ph/1pc/fr L

Chesapeake & Ohio Canal,Aqueduct 4; see Chesapeake & Ohio Canal,Antietam Creek Aqueduct

Documentation: **ct** color transparencies **dr** measured drawings **fr** field records
pc photograph captions **pg** pages of text **ph** photographs

Chesapeake & Ohio Canal,Culvert; see Chesapeake & Ohio Canal,Culvert above Lock 37

Chesapeake & Ohio Canal,Culvert above Lock 37 (Chesapeake & Ohio Canal,Culvert; Chesapeake & Ohio Canal National Historical Park)
HABS MD-206
HABS MD,22-ANTI.V,4-
1dr/fr L

Chesapeake & Ohio Canal,Lock Tender's Hse,Lock 37 (Chesapeake & Ohio Canal,Lock Tender's Hse,Mtn Lock Chesapeake & Ohio Canal National Historical Park)
HABS MD-208
HABS MD,22-ANTI.V,6-
9dr/4ph/1pc/fr L

Chesapeake & Ohio Canal,Lock Tender's Hse,Mtn Lock; see Chesapeake & Ohio Canal,Lock Tender's Hse,Lock 37

Chesapeake & Ohio Canal,Lock 37 (Chesapeake & Ohio Canal,Mountain Lock; Chesapeake & Ohio Canal National Historical Park)
HABS MD-207
HABS MD,22-ANTI.V,5-
1dr/1ph/1pc/fr L

Chesapeake & Ohio Canal,Mountain Lock; see Chesapeake & Ohio Canal,Lock 37

Chesapeake & Ohio Canal,Waste Weir,Lock No. 37 (Chesapeake & Ohio Canal National Historical Park)
HABS MD-209
HABS MD,22-ANTI.V,7-
1dr/fr L

Roulette Farm Group
HABS MD-85
HABS MD,22-ANTI.V,1-
3ph L

BIG SPRING VIC.

C & O Canal:McCoy's Ferry Road Culvert (McCoy's Ferry Road Culvert; McCoy's Ferry Road Tunnel; Culvert No. 142)
Mile 110.42 of the C & O Canal Natl Park
HAER MD-71
HAER 1989(HAER):11
2ph/7pg/1pc L

C & O Canal:Prather's Neck Road Culvert (Prather's Neck Road Culvert; Prather's Neck Road Tunnel; Culvert No. 139)
Mile 108.74 of the C & O Canal Natl Park
HAER MD-72
HAER 1989(HAER):11
3ph/7pg/1pc L

Culvert No. 139; see C & O Canal:Prather's Neck Road Culvert

Culvert No. 142; see C & O Canal:McCoy's Ferry Road Culvert

McCoy's Ferry Road Culvert; see C & O Canal:McCoy's Ferry Road Culvert

McCoy's Ferry Road Tunnel; see C & O Canal:McCoy's Ferry Road Culvert

Prather's Neck Road Culvert; see C & O Canal:Prather's Neck Road Culvert

Prather's Neck Road Tunnel; see C & O Canal:Prather's Neck Road Culvert

CLEARSPRING VIC.

Chesapeake & Ohio Canal National Historical Park; see Chesapeake & Ohio Canal,Mule Barn

Chesapeake & Ohio Canal,Mule Barn (Chesapeake & Ohio Canal National Historical Park)
Four Lock Rd.
HAER MD-28
HAER MD,22-CLESP.V,1-
3dr/fr L

FORT FREDERICK VIC.

C & O Canal,Lock 50,Fourth of Four Locks; see Chesapeake & Ohio Canal,Lock 50

C&O Canal,Lock Tender's House,Fourth of Four Locks; see Ches. & Ohio Canal,Lock Tender's House at Lock 50

Ches. & Oh. Can.,Lock Tender's Hse at "Four Locks"; see Ches. & Ohio Canal,Lock Tender's House at Lock 48

Ches. & Ohio Canal,Lock Tender's House at Lock 48 (Ches. & Oh. Can.,Lock Tender's Hse at "Four Locks" Chesapeake & Ohio Canal National Historical Park)
108.9 Miles above Tidewater
HABS MD-215
HABS MD,22-FOFR.V,1-
7dr/3ph/1pc/fr L

Ches. & Ohio Canal,Lock Tender's House at Lock 50 (C&O Canal,Lock Tender's House,Fourth of Four Locks Chesapeake & Ohio Canal National Historical Park)
108.9 Miles above Tidewater
HABS MD-216
HABS MD,22-FOFR.V,2-
3dr/3ph/1pc/fr L

Chesapeake & Ohio Canal National Historicak Park; see Chesapeake & Ohio Canal,Lockhouse at Lock 46

Chesapeake & Ohio Canal National Historical Park; see Ches. & Ohio Canal,Lock Tender's House at Lock 48

Chesapeake & Ohio Canal National Historical Park; see Ches. & Ohio Canal,Lock Tender's House at Lock 50

Chesapeake & Ohio Canal National Historical Park; see Chesapeake & Ohio Canal,Culvert 39

Chesapeake & Ohio Canal National Historical Park; see Chesapeake & Ohio Canal,Dam 5

Chesapeake & Ohio Canal National Historical Park; see Chesapeake & Ohio Canal,Feeder Lock at Dam 5

Chesapeake & Ohio Canal National Historical Park; see Chesapeake & Ohio Canal,Lock 46

Chesapeake & Ohio Canal National Historical Park; see Chesapeake & Ohio Canal,Lock 47

Chesapeake & Ohio Canal National Historical Park; see Chesapeake & Ohio Canal,Lock 48

Chesapeake & Ohio Canal National Historical Park; see Chesapeake & Ohio Canal,Lock 49

Chesapeake & Ohio Canal National Historical Park; see Chesapeake & Ohio Canal,Lock 50

Chesapeake & Ohio Canal National Historical Park; see Chesapeake & Ohio Canal,Lockhouse at Dam 5

Chesapeake & Ohio Canal National Historical Park; see Chesapeake & Ohio Canal,Waste Weir 18

Chesapeake & Ohio Canal,Culvert above Lift Lock 48; see Chesapeake & Ohio Canal,Culvert 39

Chesapeake & Ohio Canal,Culvert 39 (Chesapeake & Ohio Canal,Culvert above Lift Lock 48 Chesapeake & Ohio Canal,Neck Road Culvert; Chesapeake & Ohio Canal,Prather's Neck; Chesapeake & Ohio Canal National Historical Park)
HABS MD-218
HABS MD,22-FOFR.V,3-
1dr/fr L

Chesapeake & Ohio Canal,Dam 5 (Chesapeake & Ohio Canal National Historical Park)
HABS MD-789
HABS MD,22-FOFR.V,4-
1ph/1pc L

Chesapeake & Ohio Canal,Feeder Lock at Dam 5 (Chesapeake & Ohio Canal,Guard Lock at Dam 5; Chesapeake & Ohio Canal,Inlet Lock at Dam 5; Chesapeake & Ohio Canal National Historical Park)
HABS MD-788
HABS MD,22-FOFR.V,5-
3ph/1pc L

Chesapeake & Ohio Canal,First of the Four Locks; see Chesapeake & Ohio Canal,Lock 47

Chesapeake & Ohio Canal,Guard Lock at Dam 5; see Chesapeake & Ohio Canal,Feeder Lock at Dam 5

Chesapeake & Ohio Canal,Inlet Lock at Dam 5; see Chesapeake & Ohio Canal,Feeder Lock at Dam 5

Chesapeake & Ohio Canal,Lock 46 (Chesapeake & Ohio Canal National Historical Park)
HABS MD-793
HABS MD,22-FOFR.V,6-
1ph/1pc L

Chesapeake & Ohio Canal,Lock 47 (Chesapeake & Ohio Canal,First of the Four Locks; Chesapeake & Ohio Canal National Historical Park)
HABS MD-211
HABS MD,22-FOFR.V,7-
2dr/fr L

Chesapeake & Ohio Canal,Lock 48 (Chesapeake & Ohio Canal National Historical Park)
HABS MD-212
HABS MD,22-FOFR.V,8-
1dr/fr L

Chesapeake & Ohio Canal,Lock 49 (Chesapeake & Ohio Canal,Third of the Four Locks; Chesapeake & Ohio Canal National Historical Park)
HABS MD-213
HABS MD,22-FOFR.V,9-
2dr/fr L

Chesapeake & Ohio Canal,Lock 50 (C & O Canal,Lock 50,Fourth of Four Locks; Chesapeake & Ohio Canal National Historical Park)
HABS MD-214
HABS MD,22-FOFR.10-
2dr/fr L

Chesapeake & Ohio Canal,Lockhouse at Dam 5 (Chesapeake & Ohio Canal National Historical Park)
HABS MD-790
HABS MD,22-FOFR.V,11-
1ph/1pc L

Chesapeake & Ohio Canal,Lockhouse at Lock 46 (Chesapeake & Ohio Canal National Historicak Park)
HABS MD-792
HABS MD,22-FOFR.V,12-
2ph/1pc L

Chesapeake & Ohio Canal,Neck Road Culvert; see Chesapeake & Ohio Canal,Culvert 39

Chesapeake & Ohio Canal,Prather's Neck; see Chesapeake & Ohio Canal,Culvert 39

Chesapeake & Ohio Canal,Roving Bridge,Lock 46 (Chesapeake & 0hio Canal National Historical Park)
Dam 5 Vic.
HABS MD-217
HABS MD,22-FOFR.V,13-
2dr/fr L

Chesapeake & Ohio Canal,Third of the Four Locks; see Chesapeake & Ohio Canal,Lock 49

Chesapeake & Ohio Canal,Waste Weir above Lock 50; see Chesapeake & Ohio Canal,Waste Weir 18

Chesapeake & Ohio Canal,Waste Weir 18 (Chesapeake & Ohio Canal,Waste Weir above Lock 50; Chesapeake & Ohio Canal National Historical Park)
HABS MD-219
HABS MD,22-FOFR.V,14-
1dr/fr L

Chesapeake & 0hio Canal National Historical Park; see Chesapeake & Ohio Canal,Roving Bridge,Lock 46

HAGERSTOWN

Hager,Jonathan,House (Foundation)
HABS MD-39
HABS MD,22-HAGTO,2-
6dr/17ph/27pg L

Hagerstown Bank
HABS MD-44
HABS MD,22-HAGTO,1-
1ph/4pg L

25-27 North Potomac Street (Commercial Building)
HABS MD-888
HABS MD,22-HAGTO,3-
5ph/3pg/1pc L

HAGERSTOWN VIC.

Bridge Spanning Conocheague Creek (National Road,Wilson Bridge; Wilson's Bridge)
Old Rt. 40,7 miles W. of Hagerstown
HABS MD-139-A
HAER MD-41
HABS/HAER MD,22-HAGTO.V,2
2dr/19ph/17pg/2pc/fr L

Fort Frederick
HABS MD-95
HABS MD,22-HAGTO.V,1-
1ph L

Herman Farm (Schindel Farm)
N. side of Showalter Rd.,E. of I-81
HABS MD-993
HABS DLC/PP-1993:MD-5
2ph/11pg/1pc L

Herman Farm,Barn
N. side of Showalter Rd.,E. of I-81
HABS MD-993-B
HABS DLC/PP-1993:MD-5
14ph/14pg/2pc L

Herman Farm,House
N. side of Showalter Rd.,E. of I-81
HABS MD-993-A
HABS DLC/PP-1993:MD-5
30ph/17pg/2pc L

National Road,Wilson Bridge; see Bridge Spanning Conocheague Creek

Schindel Farm; see Herman Farm

Wilson's Bridge; see Bridge Spanning Conocheague Creek

HANCOCK VIC.

C & O Canal,Second Culvert Between Locks 55 & 56; see Chesapeake & Ohio Canal,Culvert 200

C. & O. Canal,First Culvert Between Locks 55 & 56; see Chesapeake & Ohio Canal,Culvert 199

Chesapeake & Ohio Canal National Historical Park; see Chesapeake & Ohio Canal,Culvert 199

Chesapeake & Ohio Canal National Historical Park; see Chesapeake & Ohio Canal,Culvert 200

Chesapeake & Ohio Canal National Historical Park; see Chesapeake & Ohio Canal,Feeder Lock,Lock 55

Chesapeake & Ohio Canal National Historical Park; see Chesapeake & Ohio Canal,Lock 54

Chesapeake & Ohio Canal National Historical Park; see Chesapeake & Ohio Canal,Lock 55

Chesapeake & Ohio Canal National Historical Park; see Chesapeake & Ohio Canal,Lock 56

Chesapeake & Ohio Canal National Historical Park; see Chesapeake & Ohio Canal,Lockhouse at Lock 54

Chesapeake & Ohio Canal National Historical Park; see Chesapeake & Ohio Canal,Lockhouse at Lock 56

Chesapeake & Ohio Canal,Culvert 199 (C. & O. Canal,First Culvert Between Locks 55 & 56; Chesapeake & Ohio Canal National Historical Park)
HABS MD-800
HABS MD,22-HAN.V,1-
4ph/1pc L

Chesapeake & Ohio Canal,Culvert 200 (C & O Canal,Second Culvert Between Locks 55 & 56; Chesapeake & Ohio Canal National Historical Park)
HABS MD-801
HABS MD,22-HAN.V,2-
1ph/1pc L

Chesapeake & Ohio Canal,Feeder Lock,Lock 55 (Chesapeake & Ohio Canal National Historical Park)
HABS MD-881
HABS MD,22-HAN.V,3-
2ph/1pc L

Chesapeake & Ohio Canal,Lock 54 (Chesapeake & Ohio Canal National Historical Park)
Deneen Rd.
HABS MD-796
HABS MD,22-HAN.V,4-
1ph/1pc L

Chesapeake & Ohio Canal,Lock 55 (Chesapeake & Ohio Canal National Historical Park)
Dam 6
HABS MD-799
HABS MD,22-HAN.V,5-
3ph/1pc L

Chesapeake & Ohio Canal,Lock 56 (Chesapeake & Ohio Canal,Pearre Lock; Chesapeake & Ohio Canal National Historical Park)
Ziegler Rd.
HABS MD-802
HABS MD,22-HAN.V,6-
2ph/1pc L

Chesapeake & Ohio Canal,Lockhouse at Lock 54 (Chesapeake & Ohio Canal National Historical Park)
Deneen Rd.
HABS MD-797
HABS MD,22-HAN.V,7-
2ph/1pc L

Chesapeake & Ohio Canal,Lockhouse at Lock 56 (Chesapeake & Ohio Canal,Lockhouse at Pearre Lock; Chesapeake & Ohio Canal National Historical Park)
Ziegler Rd.
HABS MD-803
HABS MD,22-HAN.V,8-
3ph/1pc/fr L

Chesapeake & Ohio Canal,Lockhouse at Pearre Lock; see Chesapeake & Ohio Canal,Lockhouse at Lock 56

Chesapeake & Ohio Canal,Pearre Lock; see Chesapeake & Ohio Canal,Lock 56

HARPERS FERRY VIC.

Baltimore & Ohio Railroad,Harpers Ferry Tunnel (Harpers Ferry Tunnel)
N. Bank of Potomac River Opposite Harpers Ferry
HAER MD-17
HAER MD,22-HARF.V,2-
1ph/1pc L

Baltimore & Ohio RR,Harpers Ferry Bridge Piers (Harpers Ferry Bridge Piers)
Junction of Potomac & Shenandoah Rivers
HAER MD-16
HAER MD,22-HARF.V,1-
5ph/1pc L

Chesapeake & Ohio Canal National Historical Park; see Chesapeake & Ohio Canal,Dry Dock at Lock 35

Chesapeake & Ohio Canal National Historical Park; see Chesapeake & Ohio Canal,Feeder Lock Above Lock 35

Chesapeake & Ohio Canal National Historical Park; see Chesapeake & Ohio Canal,Lock Tender's Hse,Lock 35

Chesapeake & Ohio Canal National Historical Park; see Chesapeake & Ohio Canal,Lock 32

Chesapeake & Ohio Canal National Historical Park; see Chesapeake & Ohio Canal,Lock 33 Complex

Chesapeake & Ohio Canal National Historical Park; see Chesapeake & Ohio Canal,Lock 34

Chesapeake & Ohio Canal National Historical Park; see Chesapeake & Ohio Canal,Lock 35

Chesapeake & Ohio Canal National Historical Park; see Chesapeake & Ohio Canal,Lock 36

Chesapeake & Ohio Canal National Historical Park; see Chesapeake & Ohio Canal,Lockhouse at Feeder Lock

Chesapeake & Ohio Canal National Historical Park; see Chesapeake & Ohio Canal,Salty Dog Tavern

Chesapeake & Ohio Canal National Historical Park; see Chesapeake & Ohio Canal,Shenandoah River Lock

Chesapeake & Ohio Canal National Historical Park; see Chesapeake & Ohio Canal,Structures at Dam 3

Chesapeake & Ohio Canal National Historical Park; see Chesapeake & Ohio Canal,Typical Lock Gate

Chesapeake & Ohio Canal,Dry Dock at Lock 35 (Chesapeake & Ohio Canal National Historical Park)
HABS MD-885
HABS MD,22-HARF.V,6-
1dr/4ph/1pc L

Chesapeake & Ohio Canal,Feeder Lock Above Lock 35 (Chesapeake & Ohio Canal National Historical Park)
Dam 3 Vic.
HABS MD-883
HABS MD,22-HARF.V,7-
1dr/4ph/1pc L

Chesapeake & Ohio Canal,Goodheart's Lock; see Chesapeake & Ohio Canal,Lock 34

Chesapeake & Ohio Canal,Lock Tender's Hse,Lock 35 (Chesapeake & Ohio Canal National Historical Park)
HABS MD-774
HABS MD,22-HARF.V,11-
1dr L

Chesapeake & Ohio Canal,Lock 32 (Chesapeake & Ohio Canal National Historical Park)
HABS MD-759
HAER MD-27-A
HABS/HAER MD,22-HARF.V,3A-
1dr/1ph/1pc/fr L

Chesapeake & Ohio Canal,Lock 33 Complex (Chesapeake & Ohio Canal National Historical Park)
HABS MD-762
HAER MD-27
HABS/HAER MD,22-HARF.V,3-
2dr/5ph/1pc/fr L

Chesapeake & Ohio Canal,Lock 34 (Chesapeake & Ohio Canal,Goodheart's Lock; Chesapeake & Ohio Canal National Historical Park)
Harpers Ferry Rd.
HABS MD-766
HABS MD,22-HARF.V,8-
4ph/1pc L

Chesapeake & Ohio Canal,Lock 35 (Chesapeake & Ohio Canal National Historical Park)
HABS MD-773
HABS MD,22-HARF.V,9-
2dr/4ph/1pc/fr L

Chesapeake & Ohio Canal,Lock 36 (Chesapeake & Ohio Canal National Historical Park)
HABS MD-775
HABS MD,22-HARF.V,10-
1dr/4ph/1pc/fr L

Chesapeake & Ohio Canal,Lockhouse at Feeder Lock (Chesapeake & Ohio Canal National Historical Park)
Dam 3
HABS MD-768
HABS MD,22-HARF.V,12-
2dr/4ph/1pc L

Chesapeake & Ohio Canal,Outlet above Lock 32; see Chesapeake & Ohio Canal,Shenandoah River Lock

Chesapeake & Ohio Canal,Salty Dog Tavern (Chesapeake & Ohio Canal National Historical Park)
Lock 33 Vic.
HAER MD-27-C
HAER MD,22-HARF.V,3C-
1dr/fr L

Chesapeake & Ohio Canal,Shenandoah River Lock (Chesapeake & Ohio Canal,Outlet above Lock 32; Chesapeake & Ohio Canal National Historical Park)
HABS MD-760
HABS D,22-HARF.V,4-
1ph/1pc L

Chesapeake & Ohio Canal,Structures at Dam 3 (Chesapeake & Ohio Canal National Historical Park)
HABS MD-761
HABS MD,22-HARF.V,13-
2dr/fr L

Chesapeake & Ohio Canal,Typical Lock Gate (Chesapeake & Ohio Canal National Historical Park)
HABS MD-767
HABS MD,22-HARF.V,5-
1dr L

Harpers Ferry Bridge Piers; see Baltimore & Ohio RR,Harpers Ferry Bridge Piers

Harpers Ferry Tunnel; see Baltimore & Ohio Railroad,Harpers Ferry Tunnel

KEEDYSVILLE VIC.

Antietam Bridge; see Baltimore & Ohio Railroad,Long Bridge

Baltimore & Ohio Railroad,Long Bridge (Antietam Bridge)
HAER MD-37
HAER MD,22-KEED.V,1-
5ph/1pg/1pc L

SAMPLES MANOR VIC.

Brown,John,Farm; see Kennedy Farm

Kennedy Farm (Brown,John,Farm)
Chestnut Grove Rd.
HABS MD-227
HABS MD,22-SAMAN.V,1-
8dr/12ph/3pg/1pc/fr L

SHARPSBURG

Antietam National Batlefield; see Poffenberg Farm,House

Antietam National Cemetery
Boonsboro Pike (State Rt. 34)
HABS MD-936
HABS MD,22-SHARP,1-;DLC/PP-1993:MD-2
1dr/11ph/1pc/fr L

Antietam National Cemetery,Entrance Gates
Boonsboro Pike (State Rt. 34)
HABS MD-936-B
HABS MD,22-SHARP,1B-
2dr/fr L

Antietam National Cemetery,Lodge House
Boonsboro Pike (State Rt. 34)
HABS MD-936-A
HABS MD,22-SHARP,1A-
8dr/fr L

Hoffman,Farm,Main House
Keedysville Rd.,Antietam National Battlefield Park
HABS MD-961-A
HABS 1992(HABS):MD-1
1ph/1pc L

Middlekauf Farm,Barn
HABS MD-949-B
HABS 1992(HABS):MD-1
1ph/1pc L

Middlekauf Farm,Brick-Stone House
HABS MD-949-A
HABS 1992(HABS):MD-1
1ph/1pc L

Middlekauf Farm,Main House
HABS MD-949
HABS 1992(HABS):MD-1
5ph/2pg/1pc L

Middlekauf Farm,Spring House
HABS MD-949-C
HABS 1992(HABS):MD-1
1ph/1pc L

Mumma Farm,Barn
Smoketown Rd.
HABS MD-950-B
HABS 1991(HABS):30
8dr/1ph/1pc/fr L

Mumma Farm,Outbuildings
Smoketown Rd.
HABS MD-950-E
HABS 1991(HABS):30
3ph/1pc/fr L

Mumma Farm,Springhouse
Smoketown Rd.
HABS MD-950-C
HABS 1991(HABS):30
2dr/2ph/1pc/fr L

Neikirk Farm,Barn
Mansfield Rd.
HABS MD-952-A
HABS 1992(HABS):MD-1
1ph/1pc L

Neikirk Farm,House
Mansfield Rd.
HABS MD-952
HABS 1992(HABS):MD-1
2ph/1pg/1pc L

Newcomer Farm,Barn
Boonsboro Pike near Middle Bridge
HABS MD-941-A
HABS 1992(HABS):MD-1
4ph/1pc L

Otto Farm
Burnside Bridge Rd.
HABS MD-943
HABS 1991(HABS):30
1dr L

Otto Farm,House
Burnside Bridge Rd.
HABS MD-943-A
HABS 1991(HABS):30
4dr/14ph/1pg/1pc/fr L

Poffenberg Farm,House (Antietam National Batlefield)
HABS MD-130-A
HABS DLC/PP-1992:MD-5
3ph/1pc L

Poffenberger,Joseph,Farm,Dependency
Hagerstown Pike (MD Rt. 65),Antietam Nat. Bat. Pk.
HABS MD-966-B
HABS 1992(HABS):MD-1
1ph/1pc L

Sherrick,Joseph,Farm,Smoke House
Burnside Bridge Rd.
HABS MD-935-D
HABS 1992(HABS):MD-1
4ph/1pc L

Snavely's Ford House
HABS MD-963
HABS 1992(HABS):MD-1
1ph/2pg/1pc L

SHARPSBURG VIC.

Antietam National Battlefield
Antietam National Battlefield Park
HABS MD-934
HABS 1992(HABS):MD-1;DLC/PP-1993:MD-2
110ph/8pc L

Antietam National Battlefield; see Dunkard (Church of the Brethren) Church

Burnside Bridge
Historic Burnside Bridge Rd.,Antietam Nat'l Battle
HABS MD-937
HABS MD,22-SHARP.V,4-
3dr/fr L

Chesapeake & Ohio Canal National Historical Park; see Chesapeake & Ohio Canal,Feeder Lock above Dam 4

Chesapeake & Ohio Canal National Historical Park; see Chesapeake & Ohio Canal,Stop Lock at Dam 4

Chesapeake & Ohio Canal,Culvert above Lock 39; see Chesapeake & Ohio Canal,Culvert 100

Chesapeake & Ohio Canal,Culvert 100 (Chesapeake & Ohio Canal,Culvert above Lock 39)
Canal Rd. ,State Rt. 34 Vic.
HABS MD-221
HABS MD,22-SHARP.V,5-
1dr/fr L

Chesapeake & Ohio Canal,Feeder Lock above Dam 4 (Chesapeake & Ohio Canal,Guard Lock above Dam 4; Chesapeake & Ohio Canal,Inlet Lock above Dam 4; Chesapeake & Ohio Canal National Historical Park)
HABS MD-222
HABS MD,22-SHARP.V,2-
1dr/fr L

Chesapeake & Ohio Canal,Frame Section House; see Chesapeake & Ohio Canal,Section House,Lock 39

Chesapeake & Ohio Canal,Guard Lock above Dam 4; see Chesapeake & Ohio Canal,Feeder Lock above Dam 4

Chesapeake & Ohio Canal,Inlet Lock above Dam 4; see Chesapeake & Ohio Canal,Feeder Lock above Dam 4

Chesapeake & Ohio Canal,Section House,Lock 39 (Chesapeake & Ohio Canal,Frame Section House; Chesapeake & Ohio National Historical Park)
HABS MD-220
HABS MD,22-SHARP.V,6-
2dr/fr L

Chesapeake & Ohio Canal,Stop Lock at Dam 4 (Chesapeake & Ohio Canal National Historical Park)
HABS MD-223
HABS MD,22-SHARP.V,7-
4dr/fr L

Chesapeake & Ohio National Historical Park; see Chesapeake & Ohio Canal,Section House,Lock 39

Cost House (Hitt House)
Keedysville Rd.,Antietam National Battlefield Park
HABS MD-957
HABS 1992(HABS):MD-1
1ph/2pg/1pc L

Dunkard (Church of the Brethren) Church (Dunker Church; Antietam National Battlefield)
Hagerstown & Smoketown Rds.
HABS MD-203
HABS MD,22-SHARP.V,1-(DLC/PP-1992:MD-5)
6dr/8ph/1pc/fr L

Dunker Church; see Dunkard (Church of the Brethren) Church

Farm Complex Number 3
Antietam National Battlefield Park
HABS MD-940
HABS 1992(HABS):MD-1
2ph/1pc L

Farm Complex Number 3,Barn
Antietam National Battlefield Park
HABS MD-940-A
HABS 1992(HABS):MD-1
2ph/1pc L

Farm Complex Number 8
E. of Harpers Ferry Rd.
HABS MD-945
HABS 1992(HABS):MD-1
2ph/1pc L

Grove Farm,Barn
Antietam National Battlefield Park
HABS MD-954-A
HABS 1992(HABS):MD-1
1ph/1pc L

Grove Farm,Dependency
Antietam National Battlefield Park
HABS MD-954-B
HABS 1992(HABS):MD-1
1ph/1pc L

Grove Farm,House
Antietam National Battlefield Park
HABS MD-954
HABS 1992(HABS):MD-1
2ph/1pc L

Hitt House; see Cost House

Hitt House; see Pry,Samuel,House

Hitt Mill; see Pry,Samuel,Mill

Hoffman,Farm,House
Keedysville Rd.,Antietam National Battlefield Park
HABS MD-961
HABS 1992(HABS):MD-1
4ph/2pg/1pc L

Kefauver House; see Poffenberger,Samuel,House

Lines,Farm,Barn
Smoketown Rd.,Antietam National Battlefield Park
HABS MD-960-A
HABS 1992(HABS):MD-1
1ph/1pc L

Lines,Farm,House
Smoketown Rd.,Antietam National Battlefield Park
HABS MD-960
HABS 1992(HABS):MD-1
1ph/1pg/1pc L

Major General Jesse L. Reno Monument
Fox's Gap,South Mt.,E. of Rte. 67,S. of Rte. 40
HABS MD-1066
3ph/1pc H

Miller,D.R. Farm,Barn
Hagerstown Pike,Antietam National Battlefield Pk.
HABS MD-948-A
HABS 1992(HABS):MD-1
1ph/1pc L

Miller,D.R. Farm,House
Hagerstown Pike,Antietam National Battlefield Pk.
HABS MD-948
HABS 1992(HABS):D-1
1ph/1pg/1pc L

Miller,M. Farm,House
Antietam National Battlefield Park
HABS MD-951
HABS 1992(HABS):MD
2ph/2pg/1pc L

Mount Pleasant; see Newcomer Farm,House

Mumma Farm
Smoketown Rd.
HABS MD-950
HABS 1991(HABS):30
1dr/3ph/2pg/1pc/fr L

Mumma Farm,House
Smoketown Rd.
HABS MD-950-A
HABS 1991(HABS):30
5dr/18ph/2pc/fr L

Mumma Farm,Smokehouse
Smoketown Rd.
HABS MD-950-D
HABS 1991(HABS):30
1dr/fr L

National Road Tollhouse
Antietam National Battlefield Site
HABS MD-939
HABS 1992(HABS):MD-1
2ph/1pg/1pc L

Newcomer Farm,House (Mount Pleasant)
Boonsboro Pike near Middle Bridge
HABS MD-941
HABS 1992(HABS):MD-1
2ph/1pg/1pc L

Piper Farm,Barn
HABS MD-946-A
HABS 1992(HABS):MD-1
2ph/1pc L

Piper Farm,House
HABS MD-946
HABS 1992(HABS):MD-1
6ph/2pg/1pc L

Poffenberger,A.,Barn
Antietam National Battlefield Park
HABS MD-90-A
HABS 1992(HABS):MD-1
5ph/2pc L

Poffenberger,A.,Loghouse
Antietam National Battlefield Park
HABS MD-90
HABS MD,22-ANTI.V,2-ı1992(HABS):MD-1°
7ph/1pc L

Poffenberger,Joseph,Farm,Barn
Hagerstown Pike (MD Rt. 65),Antietam Nat. Bat. Pk.
HABS MD-966-A
HABS 1992(HABS):MD-1
3ph/1pc L

Poffenberger,Joseph,Farm,House
Hagerstown Pike (MD Rt. 65),Antietam Nat. Bat. Pk.
HABS MD-966
HABS 1992(HABS):MD-1
6ph/1pg/1pc L

Poffenberger,Samuel,House (Kefauver House)
Antietam National Battlefield Park
HABS MD-964
HABS 1992(HABS):MD-1
2ph/2pg/1pc L

Pry,Philip,Farm
Boonsboro Pike (SR 34),Antietam Nat'l Battlefield
HABS MD-864
HABS MD,22-SHARP.V,8-
11dr/fr L

Pry,Philip,Farm,Barn
Boonsboro Pike (SR 34),Antietam Nat'l Battlefield
HABS MD-864-A
HABS MD,22-SHARP.V,8A-ı1992(HABS):MD-1°
9dr/2ph/1pc/fr L

Pry,Philip,Farm,Outbuildings (Pry,Philip,Farm,Root Cellar; Pry,Philip,Farm,Spring House)
Boonsboro Pike (SR 34),Antietam Nat'l Battlefield
HABS MD-864-B
HABS MD,22-SHARP.V,8B-
1dr/fr L

Pry,Philip,Farm,Root Cellar; see Pry,Philip,Farm,Outbuildings

Pry,Philip,Farm,Spring House; see Pry,Philip,Farm,Outbuildings

Pry,Samuel,House (Hitt House)
Keedysville Rd.,Antietam National Battlefield Park
HABS MD-958
HABS 1992(HABS):MD-1
1ph/1pg/1pc L

Pry,Samuel,Mill (Hitt Mill)
Keedysville Rd.,Antietam National Battlefield Park
HABS MD-958-A
HABS 1992(HABS):MD-1
2ph/2pg/1pc L

Reel Barn
Landing Rd.
HABS MD-962-A
HABS 1992(HABS):MD-1
1ph/1pc L

Reel Farm,House
Landing Rd.,Antietam National Battlefield Park
HABS MD-962
HABS 1992(HABS):MD-1
1ph/1pc L

Remsberg House
Rte. 65
HABS MD-947
HABS 19929H(HABS):MD-1
2ph/1pc L

Rohrbach,Henry,Farm,Barn
E. of Burnside Bridge Rd.
HABS MD-944-A
HABS 1992(HABS):MD-1
6ph/1pc L

Rohrbach,Henry,Farm,House
E. of Burnside Bridge Rd.
HABS MD-944
HABS 1992(HABS):MD-1
2ph/2pg/1pc L

Rohrbach,Henry,Farm,Outbuildings
E. of Burnside Bridge Rd.
HABS MD-944-C
HABS 1992(HABS):MD-
2ph/1pc L

Rohrbach,Henry,Farm,Springhouse
E. of Burnside Bridge Rd.
HABS MD-944-B
HABS 1992(HABS):MD-1
1ph/1pc L

Roulette Farm Group (House)
HABS MD-85
HABS DLC/PP-1992;MD-3
4ph/2pg/1pc L

Roulette Farm Group,Barn
Antietam National Battlefield Park
HABS MD-85-A
HABS DLC/PP-1992;MD-3
3ph/1pc L

Roulette Farm Group,Slave Quarters
Antietam National Battlefield Park
HABS MD-85-B
HABS DLC/PP-1992;MD-3
1ph/1pc L

Sherrick House,Corn Crib
Burnside Bridge Road (Rural Rt. 1)
HABS MD-935-C
HABS MD,22-SHARP.V,3C-
1dr/fr L

Sherrick House,Summer Kitchen
Burnside Bridge Rd. (Rural Rt. 1)
HABS MD-935-B
HABS MD,22-SHARP.V,3B-
1dr/fr L

Sherrick,Joseph,Farm
Burnside Bridge Rd. (Rural Rt. 1)
HABS MD-935
HABS MD,22-SHARP.V,3-
3dr/fr L

Sherrick,Joseph,Farm,House
Burnside Bridge Rd. (Rural Rt. 1)
HABS MD-935-A
HABS MD,22-SHARP.V,3A-
7dr/fr L

Smith House
Keedysville Rd. Near Upper Bridge
HABS MD-955
HABS 1991(HABS):MD-1
3ph/1pc L

Stone House
Burnside Bridge Rd.,Antietam National Battlef. Pk.
HABS MD-942
HABS 1992(HABS):MD-1
3ph/1pg/1pc L

Stone House,Mill
Burnside Bridge Rd.,Antietam National Battlef. Pk.
HABS MD-942-A
HABS 1992(HABS):MD-1
1ph/1pc L

Upper Bridge
Keedysville Rd.
HABS MD-959
HABS 1992(HABS):MD-1
2ph/1pc L

WEVERTON VIC.

C. & O. Canal National Historical Park; see Chesapeake & Ohio Canal,Locktender's Hse. ,Lock 36

Chesapeake & Ohio Canal National Historical Park; see Chesapeake & Ohio Canal,Israel Creek Aqueduct

Chesapeake & Ohio Canal National Historical Park; see Chesapeake & Ohio Canal,Lock 31

Chesapeake & Ohio Canal National Historical Park; see Chesapeake & Ohio Canal,Lockhouse at Lock 31

Chesapeake & Ohio Canal National Historical Park; see Chesapeake & Ohio Canal,Waste Weir,Lock 31

Chesapeake & Ohio Canal,Israel Creek Aqueduct (Chesapeake & Ohio Canal,Israel Creek Culvert; Chesapeake & Ohio Canal National Historical Park)
Lock 31 Vic.
HABS MD-758
HABS D,22-WEV.V,1-
2ph/1pc L

Chesapeake & Ohio Canal,Israel Creek Culvert; see Chesapeake & Ohio Canal,Israel Creek Aqueduct

Chesapeake & Ohio Canal,Lock 31
(Chesapeake & Ohio Canal National Historical Park)
U. S. Rt. 340 Vic.
HABS MD-755
HABS MD,22-WEV.V,2-
2ph/1pc L

Chesapeake & Ohio Canal,Lockhouse at Lock 31 (Chesapeake & Ohio Canal National Historical Park)
HABS MD-756
HABS MD,22-WEV.V,3-
4ph/1pc/fr L

Chesapeake & Ohio Canal,Locktender's Hse. ,Lock 36 (C. & O. Canal National Historical Park)
Dam 3 Vic.
HABS MD-884
HABS MD,22-WEV.V,4-
2dr/2ph/1pc/fr L

Chesapeake & Ohio Canal,Waste Weir,Lock 31 (Chesapeake & Ohio Canal National Historical Park)
U.S. Rt. 340 Vic.
HABS MD-757
HABS MD,22-WEV.V,5-
2ph/1pc L

WILLIAMPSORT VIC.

Chesapeake & Ohio Canal National Historical Park; see Chesapeake & Ohio Canal,Conococheague Creek Aquedu

Chesapeake & Ohio Canal,Aqueduct 5; see Chesapeake & Ohio Canal,Conococheague Creek Aquedu

Chesapeake & Ohio Canal,Conococheague Creek Aquedu (Chesapeake & Ohio Canal,Aqueduct 5; Chesapeake & Ohio Canal National Historical Park)
99.8 Miles above Tidewater
HABS MD-224
HABS MD,22-WILPO.V,2-
2dr/10ph/1pc/fr L

WILLIAMSPORT

Chesapeake & Ohio Canal Lift Bridge; see Potomac Edison Company:Ches. & Ohio Canal Bridge

Potomac Edison Company:Ches. & Ohio Canal Bridge (Chesapeake & Ohio Canal Lift Bridge)
Spanning C & O Canal S. of U. S. 11
HAER MD-23
HAER MD,22-WILPOL,1-
1ph/1pc/fr L

Salisbury Street Bridge
Spanning C&O Canal (Milepost 99.65) & WM Railroad
HAER MD-24
HAER MD,22-WILPO,2-
2dr/1ph/1pg/1pc/fr L

Documentation: **ct** color transparencies **dr** measured drawings **fr** field records
pc photograph captions **pg** pages of text **ph** photographs

WILLIAMSPORT VIC.

Chesapeake & Ohio Canal National Historical Park; see Chesapeake & Ohio Canal,Charles Mill

Chesapeake & Ohio Canal National Historical Park; see Chesapeake & Ohio Canal,Lock 44

CHesapeake & Ohio Canal National Historical Park; see Chesapeake & Ohio Canal,Lockhouse at Lock 44

Chesapeake & Ohio Canal,Charles Mill (Chesapeake & Ohio Canal,Middlekauff's Mill; Chesapeake & Ohio Canal National Historical Park)
Locks 44 & 45 Vic.
HABS MD-210
HABS MD,22-WILPO,V,5-
4dr/2ph/1pc/fr L

Chesapeake & Ohio Canal,Lock 44 (Chesapeake & Ohio Canal,Williamsport Lock; Chesapeake & Ohio Canal National Historical Park)
Canal St.
HABS MD-785
HABS MD,22-WILPO.V,4-
3ph L

Chesapeake & Ohio Canal,Lockhouse at Lock 44 (Chesapeake & Ohio Canal,Lockhouse,Wmsport. Lock; CHesapeake & Ohio Canal National Historical Park)
Canal St.
HABS MD-786
HABS MD,22-WILPO.V,3-
3ph/1pc/fr L

Chesapeake & Ohio Canal,Lockhouse,Wmsport. Lock; see Chesapeake & Ohio Canal,Lockhouse at Lock 44

Chesapeake & Ohio Canal,Middlekauff's Mill; see Chesapeake & Ohio Canal,Charles Mill

Chesapeake & Ohio Canal,Stop Gate at Dam 4; see Chesapeake & Ohio Canal,Stop Lock at Dam 4

Chesapeake & Ohio Canal,Stop Lock at Dam 4 (Chesapeake & Ohio Canal,Stop Gate at Dam 4; Chesapeake & Ohio Canal,Winch House at Dam 4)
Dam 4 Rd.
HABS MD-57-H
HABS MD,22-WILPO.V,1-
2dr/fr L

Chesapeake & Ohio Canal,Williamsport Lock; see Chesapeake & Ohio Canal,Lock 44

Chesapeake & Ohio Canal,Winch House at Dam 4; see Chesapeake & Ohio Canal,Stop Lock at Dam 4

WICOMICO COUNTY

ALLEN VIC.

Bound's Lott
HABS MD-862
HABS MD,23-ALL.V,1-
7dr/11ph/1pc L

HEBRON VIC.

Chapel of Ease of Stephen Parish; see Spring Hill Church

Spring Hill Church (St. Paul's Episcopal Church; Chapel of Ease of Stephen Parish)
U. S. Rt. 50
HABS MD-715
HABS MD,23-HEBRO.V,1-
1ph L

St. Paul's Episcopal Church; see Spring Hill Church

SALISBURY

Poplar Hill Mansion
117 Elizabeth St.
HABS MD-716
HABS MD,23-SALB,1-
1ph L

WORCESTER COUNTY

BEAVERDAM VIC.

Schoolfield Farm, House
Hillman Rd.
HABS MD-225
HABS MD,24-BEAV.V,1-
2dr/11ph/3pg L

BERLIN

Burleigh Cottage; see Burley Cottage

Burley Cottage (Burleigh Cottage)
Main St.
HABS MD-149
HABS MD,24-BERL,1-
1ph L

BERLIN VIC.

Carey,Edward Lee,House; see Fassit House

Fassett,William,House; see Henry's Grove

Fassit House (Carey,Edward Lee,House)
Lewis Store Rd. (State Rt. 376)
HABS MD-170
HABS MD,24- ,2-
4ph L

Genesar (Genezir)
State Rt. 611
IIABS MD-330
HABS MD,24-BERL.V,2-
13dr/39ph/6pg/2pc/fr L

Genezir; see Genesar

Henry,Julie,House; see Henry's Grove

Henry's Grove (Henry,Julie,House; Fassett,William,House)
Fassett Point,Stephen Decatur Memorial Rd. Vic.
HABS MD-150
HABS MD,24-BERL.V,3-
3ph L

House,Gambrel (Ruins)
Sinapuxent Neck
HABS MD-171
HABS MD,24- ,4-
2ph L

GIRDLETREE

Hall House (Olney,W. T. ,House)
Cherrix Rd.
HABS MD-62
HABS MD,24-GIRD,1-
1ph/1pg L

Olney,W. T. ,House; see Hall House

GIRDLETREE VIC.

Barnes,Benjamin,House
Stockton Rd. (State Rt. 12)
HABS MD-156
HABS MD,24-SNOHI.V,1-
4ph L

Simperton
Watermelon Point,Bayside Rd.
HABS MD-157
HABS MD,24- ,3-
3ph/1pg L

POCOMOKE CITY VIC.

Bishop Farm
McMaster Rd.
HABS MD-311
HABS MD,24-POCI.V,1-
4dr L

McKay,Sydney,House
HABS MD-863
HABS MD,24-POCI.V,2-
3dr/3ph/1pc L

POKOMOKE CITY

201-215 Bonneville Avenue (Houses)
HABS MD-910
HABS MD,24-POCI,1-
7ph/4pg/1pc L

SNOW HILL LANDING

Devereaux House; see Mount Ephraim

Mount Ephraim (Devereaux House)
Bayside Rd. ,Chincoteague Bay Vic.
HABS MD-165
HABS MD,24-PUBLA.V,1-
3ph/1pg L

SNOW HILL VIC.

Dover
Public Landing Rd. (State Rt. 365)
HABS MD-172
HABS MD,24-   ,1-
2ph   L

Nassawango Iron Furnace
Furnace Rd., 1.2 miles west of Md. Rte. 12
HAER MD-76
HAER 1991(HAER):13
12dr/4ph/1pc/fr   L

Documentation: **ct** color transparencies **dr** measured drawings **fr** field records **pc** photograph captions **pg** pages of text **ph** photographs

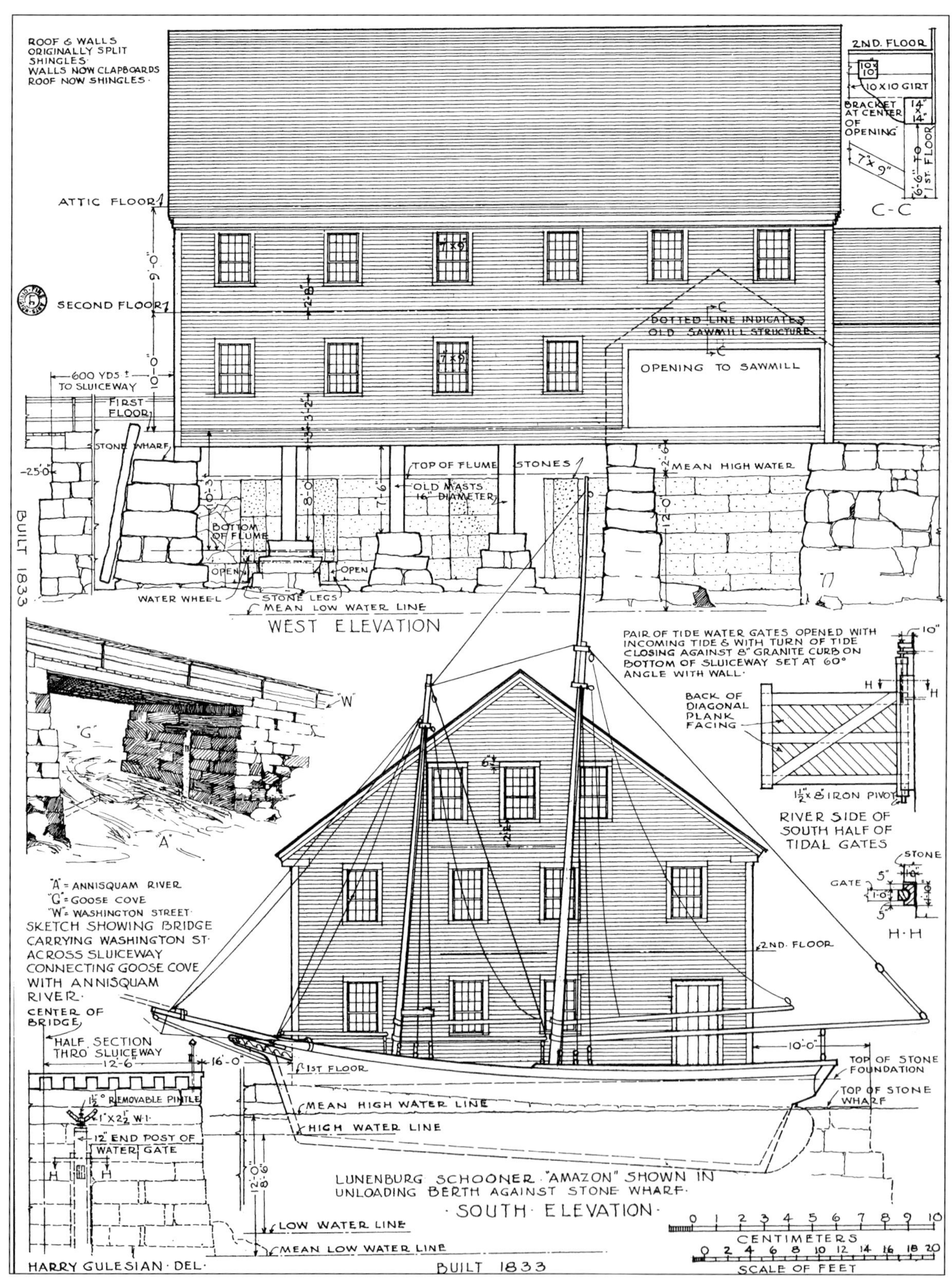

William Hodgkins Tide Mill, Annisquam, Essex County, Massachusetts. West elevation [of sawmill]; south elevation [with outline of schooner "Amazon"]. Measured drawing delineated by Harry Gulesian, 1940 (HABS MA-2-92, sheet 2 of 3).

Massachusetts

Massachusetts Historic Bridges
HAER MA-123
50pg H

BOSTON HARBOR

Deer Island Pumping Station,Barn (Deer Island Pumping Station,Boat Locker)
Deer Island,Southwest Quadrant
HABS MA-1244
HABS 1991(HABS):15
10ph/35pg/2pc L

Deer Island Pumping Station,Boat Locker; see Deer Island Pumping Station,Barn

BARNSTABLE COUNTY

BARNSTABLE

Crocker Tavern
Main St.
HABS MA-694
HABS MASS,1-BAR,2-
6dr/3ph/3pg/1pc/fr L

Gorham,Isaac,House
HABS MA-425
HABS MASS,1-BAR,1-
5ph L

Jail,Old
State Rt. 6A & Old Jail Ln.
HABS MA-976
HABS MASS,1-BAR,3-
11ph/1pc L

Lombard Farm,Barns (Poorhouse Barns)
Prospect St. (State Rt. 149)
HABS MA-964
HABS MASS,1-BAR,5-
1dr/2ph/3pg/1pc L

Lombard Farm,House (Poorhouse)
Prospect St. (State Rt. 149)
HABS MA-963
HABS MASS,1-BAR,4-
8dr/5ph/7pg/1pc/fr L

Poorhouse; see Lombard Farm,House

Poorhouse Barns; see Lombard Farm,Barns

West Parish Congregational Church (West Parish Meeting House)
State Rt. 149
HABS MA-779
HABS MASS,1-BAR,6-
1ph/3pg/1pc L

West Parish Meeting House; see West Parish Congregational Church

BOURNE

Camp Edwards
HABS MA-1249
HABS DLC/PP-1992:MA-4
19ph/7pg/1pc L

Camp Edwards,Building T-1209 (Major Generals' Quarters)
HABS MA-1249-A
HABS DLC/PP-1992:MA-4
3ph/9pg/1pc L

Camp Edwards,Building T-1222 (Storehouse & Company Administration)
HABS MA-1249-B
HABS DLC/PP-1992:MA-4
1ph/10pg/1pc L

Camp Edwards,Building T-1229 (Storehouse & Company Administration,Double)
HABS MA-1249-C
HABS DLC/PP-1992:MA-4
5ph/9pg/1pc L

Camp Edwards,Building T-1233 (Recreation Building)
HABS MA-1249-D
HABS DLC/PP-1992:MA-4
1ph/10pg/1pc L

Camp Edwards,Building T-1240 (Officers' Mess (118-Man))
HABS MA-1249-E
HABS DLC/PP-1992:MA-4
2ph/9pg/1pc L

Camp Edwards,Building T-1242 (Enlisted Men's Mess)
HABS MA-1249-F
HABS DLC/PP-1992:MA-4
2ph/10pg/1pc L

Camp Edwards,Building T-1267 (Day Room)
HABS MA-1249-G
HABS DLC/PP-1992:MA-4
4ph/9pg/1pc L

Camp Edwards,Building T-1310 (Enlisted Men's Barracks)
HABS MA-1249-H
HABS DLC/PP-1992:MA-4
4ph/10pg/1pc L

Camp Edwards,Building T-1369 (Motor Repair Shop)
HABS MA-1249-I
HABS DLC/PP-1992:MA-4
3ph/9pg/1pc L

Camp Edwards,Building T-3599 (Motor Shed)
HABS MA-1249-J
HABS DLC/PP-1992:MA-4
1ph/9pg/1pc L

Day Room; see Camp Edwards,Building T-1267

Enlisted Men's Barracks; see Camp Edwards,Building T-1310

Enlisted Men's Mess; see Camp Edwards,Building T-1242

Major Generals' Quarters; see Camp Edwards,Building T-1209

Motor Repair Shop; see Camp Edwards,Building T-1369

Motor Shed; see Camp Edwards,Building T-3599

Officers' Mess (118-Man); see Camp Edwards,Building T-1240

Recreation Building; see Camp Edwards,Building T-1233

Storehouse & Company Administration; see Camp Edwards,Building T-1222

Storehouse & Company Administration,Double; see Camp Edwards,Building T-1229

BREWSTER

Brewster Mill (House)
HABS MA-439
HABS MASS,1-BREW,3-
3ph L

Cobb,Capt. Elijah,House
Lower Rd.
HABS MA-732
HABS MASS,1-BREW,4-
1ph/3pg/1pc L

Dillingham,Isaac,House
State Rt. 6A
HABS MA-733
HABS MASS,1-BREW,5-
2ph/2pg/1pc L

Stony Brook Mill (Water Mill,Old)
Old Coach Rd.
HABS MA-179
HABS MASS,1-BREWW,1-
3dr/3ph/1pg/1pc L

Water Mill,Old; see Stony Brook Mill

Winslow House
HABS MA-344
HABS MASS,1-BREW,2-
5ph L

BUZZARDS BAY

Cape Cod Canal Lift Bridge
Spanning Cape Cod Canal
HAER MA-66
HAER 1990 (HAER):8
11ph/1pc L

CHATHAM

Atwood,Joseph,House
Atwood St.
HABS MA-161
HABS MASS,1-CHAT,2-
7dr/6ph L

Chatham Windmill
Atwood St.
HABS MA-2-61
HABS MASS,1-CHAT,3-
5dr/1ph L

Congregational Church
Old Harbor Rd. & Main St.
HABS MA-428
HABS MASS,1-CHAT,5-
1ph L

Howes,Capt. Solomon,House
Queen Anne Rd.
HABS MA-2-62
HABS MASS,1-CHAT,1-
4dr/1ph L

Kimball-Ryder House
HABS MA-427
HABS MASS,1-CHAT,4-
1ph L

CHATHAM VIC.

Monomoy Point Light Station
Approx. 3500 ft. NE Powder Hole Pond,Monomoy NWR
HAER MA-62
HAER 1991(HAER):22
18ph/26pg/3pc L

CHATHAMPORT

Ryder,Christopher,House
Ryder's Cove Vic.
HABS MA-118
HABS MASS,1-CHATPO,1-
15dr/6ph L

DENNIS

Howes-Jorgenson House
State Rt. 6A
HABS MA-731
HABS MASS,1-DEN,1-
1ph/2pg/1pc L

EAST SANDWICH

Nye House
King's Hwy.(U. S. Rt. 6)
HABS MA-206
HABS MASS,1-SANDE,1-
2dr/1ph L

EASTHAM

Cape Cod Windmill (Eastham Windmill)
Samoset Rd. (moved from MA,Truro)
HABS MA-2-21
HABS MASS,1-EAST,1-
5dr/7ph/1pc L

Doane-Chase House; see Doane,Sylvanus,House

Doane,Isaiah,House
Nauset Rd.
HABS MA-1267
HABS MASS,1-EAST,4-
1ph/1pc L

Doane,John,House
Nauset Rd.
HABS MA-1127
HABS MASS,1-EAST,5-
1ph/1pc L

Doane,Noah,House
Nauset Rd.
HABS MA-1126
HABS MASS,1-EAST,6-
2ph/1pc L

Doane,Randall,House
Nauset Rd.
HABS MA-734
HABS MASS,1-EAST,7-
1ph/2pg/1pc L

Doane,Simeon,House
Nauset Rd.
HABS MA-735
HABS MASS,1-EAST,8-
1ph/2pg/1pc L

Doane,Sylvanus,House (Doane-Chase House)
Nauset Rd.
HABS MA-712
HABS MASS,1-EAST,9-
5dr/5ph/5pg/1pc/fr L

Eastham Windmill; see Cape Cod Windmill

Higgins House
HABS MA-433
HABS MASS,1-EAST,3-
1ph L

Knowles,Seth,House
Fort Hill Rd.
HABS MA-1128
HABS MASS,1-EAST,10-
2ph/1pc L

Knowles,Sylvanus,House
Fort Hill Rd.
HABS MA-1129
HABS MASS,1-EAST,11-
1ph/1pc L

Penniman,Capt. Edward,Barn
Fort Hill Rd.
HABS MA-699
HABS MASS,1-EAST,13-
4dr/3ph/2pg/1pc/fr L

Penniman,Capt. Edward,House
Fort Hill Rd.
HABS MA-693
HABS MASS,1-EAST,12-
9dr/11ph/4pg/1pc/fr L

Prence,Gov. Thomas,House
King's Hwy. (U.S. Rt. 6)
HABS MA-2-79
HABS MASS,1-EAST,2-
1dr/1ph L

Swift,Nathaniel,House
U. S. Rt. 6
HABS MA-736
HABS MASS,1-EAST,14-
1ph/3pg/1pc L

FALMOUTH

Conent House
65 Palmer Ave.
HABS MA-977
HABS MASS,1-FAL,1-
7ph/1pc L

Marine Biological Lab.,Carpenter Shop & Boat House
99 Water St.
HABS MA-1251-B
7ph/8pg/2pc H

Marine Biological Lab.,Garage & Store House Bldg.
103 Water St.
HABS MA-1251-C
5ph/2pg/2pc H

Marine Biological Lab.,Shipping & Scuba Building
101 Water St.
HABS MA-1251-D
3ph/2pg/2pc H

Marine Biological Lab.,Supply Building
111 Water St.
HABS MA-1251-A
9ph/8pg/2pc H

Marine Biological Laboratory
Albatross & North Sts. btw. Water St. & Eel Pond
HABS MA-1251
1ph/16pg/1pc H

MASHPEE

Indian Church,Old
HABS MA-978
HABS MASS,1-MASH,1-
10ph/1pc L

NORTH CHATHAM

Nelson,Col. John,House; see Sampson,Jennie,House

Sampson,Jennie,House (Nelson,Col. John,House)
Cotchpinicutt Rd. (moved from MA,Lakeville)
HABS MA-297
HABS MASS,12-LAKVI,2-
6ph/fr L

ORLEANS

French Cable Station
Cove Rd. & MA Rt. 28
HAER MA-67
HAER 1990 (HAER):8
5ph/1pc L

PROVINCETOWN

Church of the Redeemer (Universalist Church)
236 Commercial St.
HABS MA-737
HABS MASS,1-PTOWN,1-
6ph/3pg/1pc L

Pilgrim Monument
Bradford St.
HABS MA-738
HABS MASS,1-PTOWN,2-
1ph/1pc L

Universalist Church; see Church of the Redeemer

SANDWICH

Hoxie House
State Rt. 130
HABS MA-739
HABS MASS,1-SAND,1-
2ph/2pg/1pc L

SOUTH ORLEANS

Kendrick,Jonathan,House
State Highway
HABS MA-119
HABS MASS,1-ORLS,1-
6dr/1ph L

TRURO

Adams,Zenas,House
N. Pamet Rd.
HABS MA-740
HABS MASS,1-TRU,1-
5ph/4pg/1pc L

Atkins,Jonah,House (Kahn,E. J. ,House)
S. Pamet Rd.
HABS MA-707
HABS MASS,1-TRU,2-
3dr/8ph/4pg/1pc/fr L

Bog House,The
N. Pamet Rd.
HABS MA-1116
HABS MASS,1-TRU,3-
1ph/1pc L

Cape Cod Windmill (Eastham Windmill) (moved from MA,Plymouth)
HABS MA-2-21
HABS MASS,1-EAST,1-
5dr/7ph L

Cappers House; see Rich,Elisha,House

Cobb,Elisha,House (Collinson House)
Prince Valley Rd.
HABS MA-705
HABS MASS,1-TRU,4-
3dr/3ph/5pg/1pc/fr L

Cobb,Elisha,Summer Kitchen (Collinson Summer Kitchen)
Prince Valley Rd.
HABS MA-706
HABS MASS,1-TRU,5-
1dr/1ph/1pg/1pc/fr L

Cole,Joseph S. ,House
Prince Valley Rd.
HABS MA-741
HABS MASS,1-TRU,6-
1ph/4pg/1pc L

Collins,Benjamin,House
S. Pamet Rd.
HABS MA-711
HABS MASS,1-TRU,7-
4dr/6ph/4pg/1pc/fr L

Collins,Jonathan,House
S. Pamet Rd.
HABS MA-742
HABS MASS,1-TRU,8-
3ph/3pg/1pc L

Collinson House; see Cobb,Elisha,House

Collinson Summer Kitchen; see Cobb,Elisha,Summer Kitchen

Dyer,Benjamin,Barn
N. Pamet Rd.
HABS MA-698
HABS MASS,1-TRU,10-
2dr/2pg/fr L

Dyer,Benjamin,House
N. Pamet Rd.
HABS MA-743
HABS MASS,1-TRU,9-
2ph/2pg/1pc L

Dyer,Ebenezer,House
Higgins Hollow Rd.
HABS MA-744
HABS MASS,1-TRU,11-
2ph/3pg/1pc L

Dyer,Joshua,Housc
N. Pamet Rd.
HABS MA-700
HABS MASS,1-TRU,12-
3dr/3ph/4pg/1pc/fr L

Dyer,Nathaniel,House
N. Pamet Rd.
HABS MA-713
HABS MASS,1-TRU,13-
3dr/5ph/4pg/1pc/fr L

Dyer,Thomas,House
Longnook Rd.
HABS MA-745
HABS MASS,1-TRU,14-
3ph/4pg/1pc L

Eastham Windmill; see Cape Cod Windmill

First Congregational Church
Truro Center
HABS MA-746
HABS MASS,1-TRU,15-
2ph/2pg/1pc L

Freeman,Edmund,House
Truro Rd.
HABS MA-702
HABS MASS,1-TRU,16-
5dr/4ph/3pg/1pc/fr L

Freeman,Edmund,Woodhouse
Truro Rd.
HABS MA-701
HABS MASS,1-TRU,17-
2dr/1ph/2pg/1pc/fr L

Harding,Ephraim,House
S. Pamet Rd.
HABS MA-714
HABS MASS,1-TRU,18-
3dr/5ph/4pg/1pc/fr L

Harding,Lot,House
N. Pamet Rd.
HABS MA-715
HABS MASS,1-TRU,19-
5dr/7ph/4pg/1pc/fr L

Higgins,Daniel P. ,Barn
Higgins Hollow Rd.
HABS MA-696
HABS MASS,1-TRU,21-
3dr/2ph/2pg/1pc/fr L

Higgins,Daniel P. ,House
Higgins Hollow Rd.
HABS MA-747
HABS MASS,1-TRU,20-
4ph/2pg/1pc L

Higgins,Jedediah,House
Higgins Hollow Rd.
HABS MA-748
HABS MASS,1-TRU,22-
6ph/3pg/1pc L

Highland Hotel
Old King's Hwy. & Highland Rd.
HABS MA-749
HABS MASS,1-TRU,23-
1ph/1pg/1pc L

Highland Light; see Highland Lighthouse

Highland Lighthouse (Highland Light)
Highland Rd.
HABS MA-750
HABS MASS,1-TRU,24-
1ph/4pg/1pc L

Hopkins,Thomas,House
Holsbery Lane
HABS MA-751
HABS MASS,1-TRU,25-
3ph/3pg/1pc L

Kahn,E. J. ,House; see Atkins,Jonah,House

Kelley,Benjamin S.,House
Higgins Hollow Rd.
HABS MA-716
HABS MASS,1-TRU,26-
4dr/3ph/4pg/1pc/fr L

Knowles,Paul,House
S. Pamet Rd.
HABS MA-752
HABS MASS,1-TRU,27-
1ph/1pc L

Mayo,John,House
Old County Rd. Vic.
HABS MA-1117
HABS MASS,1-TRU,28-
1ph/1pc L

Mayo,Nehemiah,House
Old County & Depot Rds.
HABS MA-753
HABS MASS,1-TRU,29-
4ph/2pg/1pc L

Mayo,Sally,House
Holsberry Ln.
HABS MA-1118
HABS MASS,1-TRU,30-
1ph/1pc L

Newcomb,William T. ,House
Pump Log Point
HABS MA-754
HABS MASS,1-TRU,31-
6ph/5pg/1pc L

Paine-Atkins House
Longnook Rd.
HABS MA-757
HABS MASS,1-TRU,34-
6ph/6pg/1pc L

Paine,Richard,House
Longnook & Higgins Hollow Rds.
HABS MA-755
HABS MASS,1-TRU,32-
5ph/3pg/1pc L

Paine,Samuel,House (Woolley House)
Longnook & Higgins Hollow Rds.
HABS MA-756
HABS MASS,1-TRU,33-
6dr/5ph/5pg/1pc L

Rich-Cobb House
Prince Valley Rd.
HABS MA-766
HABS MASS,1-TRU,47-
6ph/3pg/1pc L

Rich-Higgins House
Longnook Rd.
HABS MA-718
HABS MASS,1-TRU,48-
4dr/13ph/6pg/1pc/fr L

Rich,Atwood,House
Ryder Beach Rd.
HABS MA-719
HABS MASS,1-TRU,35-
4dr/4ph/5pg/1pc/fr L

Rich,Capt. Zoheth,House
Longnook & Higgins Hollow Rds.
HABS MA-758
HABS MASS,1-TRU,36-
3ph/4pg/1pc L

Rich,Elisha,House (Cappers House)
Ryder Beach Rd.
HABS MA-710
HABS MASS,1-TRU,37-
4dr/4ph/4pg/1pc/fr L

Rich,Ephraim,House
Pump Log Point
HABS MA-717
HABS MASS,1-TRU,38-
3dr/8ph/5pg/1pc/fr L

Rich,Isaac,House
S. Pamet Rd.
HABS MA-759
HABS MASS,1-TRU,39-
3ph/4pg/1pc L

Rich,John C. ,House
Old County Rd. Vic.
HABS MA-1119
HABS MASS,1-TRU,40-
1ph/1pc L

Rich,Joseph,House
S. Pamet Rd.
HABS MA-760
HABS MASS,1-TRU,41-
3ph/1pc L

Rich,Richard,House
S. Pamet Rd.
HABS MA-761
HABS MASS,1-TRU,42-
5ph/4pg/1pc L

Rich,Shebnah,House
Longnook Rd.
HABS MA-764
HABS MASS,1-TRU,43-
7ph/5pg/1pc L

Rich,Thomas Jr. ,House
Old County Rd.
HABS MA-763
HABS MASS,1-TRU,44-
3ph/3pg/1pc L

Rich,Thomas,House
Old County Rd.
HABS MA-762
HABS MASS,1-TRU,45-
4ph/5pg/1pc L

Rich,Warren,House
Ryder's Beach Rd. Vic.
HABS MA-765
HABS MASS,1-TRU,46-
3ph/1pg/1pc L

Small,Isaac,House
Old King's Hwy. & Highland Rd.
HABS MA-695
HABS MASS,1-TRU,49-
4dr/12ph/6pg/1pc/fr L

Small,Thomas K. ,House
Highland Rd. & Old King's Hwy.
HABS MA-767
HABS MASS,1-TRU,50-
1ph/5pg/1pc L

Snow,Ambrose,House & Cobbler Shop
N. Pamet Rd.
HABS MA-768
HABS MASS,1-TRU,51-
5ph/3pg/1pc L

Snow,Ambrose,Privy
N. Pamet Rd.
HABS MA-697
HABS MASS,1-TRU,52-
2dr/1ph/1pg/1pc/fr L

Snow,Ephraim,House
N. Pamet Rd.
HABS MA-720
HABS MASS,1-TRU,53-
4dr/5ph/5pg/1pc/fr L

Snow,Joshua,House
N. Pamet Rd.
HABS MA-769
HABS MASS,1-TRU,54-
6ph/2pg/1pc L

Snow,Joshua,Woodhouse
N. Pamet Rd.
HABS MA-769-A
HABS MASS,1-TRU,54A-
1ph/1pc L

Snow,Stephen,House
S. Pamet Rd.
HABS MA-770
HABS MASS,1-TRU,55-
5ph/1pc L

Snow,William P. ,House
S. Pamet Rd.
HABS MA-771
HABS MASS,1-TRU,56-
4ph/3pg/1pc L

Stocker,David,House
Holsberry Ln.
HABS MA-1120
HABS MASS,1-TRU,57-
1ph/1pc L

Wilson House
S. Pamet Rd.
HABS MA-1130
fr H

Woolley House; see Paine,Samuel,House

WELLFLEET

Atwood-Higgins House
Bound Brook Island Rd.
HABS MA-1087
HABS MASS,1-WEL,4-
14dr/13ph/6pg/1pc/fr L

Atwood,Ebenezer L.,House
Bound Brook Island Rd.
HABS MA-708
HABS MASS,1-WEL,2-
2dr/6ph/4pg/1pc/fr L

Atwood,Joel,House
Bound Brook Island Rd.
HABS MA-772
HABS MASS,1-WEL,3-
1ph/4pg/1pc L

Baker,David,House
Bound Brook Island Rd.
HABS MA-709
HABS MASS,1-WEL,5-
3dr/5ph/4pg/1pc/fr L

Freeman,Joseph,House
Old Truro Rd.
HABS MA-773
HABS MASS,1-WEL,6-
1ph/3pg/1pc L

Gormley,Charles,House
Herring Pond Rd.
HABS MA-774
HABS MASS,1-WEL,7-
1ph/3pg/1pc L

Grey,Henry,House
Pamet Point Rd.
HABS MA-1089
HABS MASS,1-WEL,8-
1ph/1pc L

Higgins,Elnathan,House
Pamet Point Rd.
HABS MA-775
HABS MASS,1-WEL,9-
1ph/3pg/1pc L

Higgins,George K. ,Barn
Bound Brook Island Rd.
HABS MA-1122
HABS MASS,1-WEL,10-
1ph/1pc L

Higgins,Josiah,House
Gull & Higgins Ponds Vic.
HABS MA-776
HABS MASS,1-WEL,11-
1ph/2pg/1pc L

Newcomb,John,House (Wellfleet Oysterman House)
Williams Pond
HABS MA-704
HABS 1984(HABS):275
2dr/3ph/2pg/1pc/fr L

Rich,Samuel,House
Bound Brook Island Rd. Vic.
HABS MA-1123
HABS MASS,1-WEL,13-
1ph/1pc L

Rowell House
Gull Pond Rd.
HABS MA-777
HABS MASS,1-WEL,14-
3dr/2ph/3pg/1pc/fr L

Ryder-Paine House
Pamet Point Rd.
HABS MA-1124
HABS MASS,1-WEL,15-
1ph/1pc L

Wellfleet Oysterman House; see Newcomb,John,House

Williams,Justin,House
Pamet Point Rd.
HABS MA-703
HABS MASS,1-WEL,16-
4dr/5ph/2pg/1pc/fr L

Young,B. S. ,House
U. S. Rt. 6
HABS MA-778
HABS MASS,1-WEL,17-
1ph/2pg/1pc L

WEST CHATHAM

Buck House
Barn Hill Rd.
HABS MA-2-8
HABS MASS,1-CHATW,1-
5dr/1ph L

Harding,Enoch,Salt Works
Buck's Creek
HABS MA-172
HABS MASS,1-CHATW,2-
4dr/3ph L

YARMOUTH

Kelly,Elizabeth,House
HABS MA-296
HABS MASS,1-YARM,1-
2ph L

BERKSHIRE COUNTY

ADAMS

Quaker Meetinghouse; see Society of Friends Meetinghouse

Society of Friends Meetinghouse (Quaker Meetinghouse)
West Rd. & Maple St.
HABS MA-2-44
HABS MASS,2-ADAM,1-
4dr/1ph L

CLARKSBURG

Musterfield House
Middle Rd.
HABS MA-2-25
HABS MASS,2-CLAR,1-
6dr/1ph L

DALTON

Crane & Company,Inc.; see Crane Paper Mill,Government Mill

Crane & Company,Inc.; see Crane Paper Mill,Pioneer Museum

Crane Paper Mill,Government Mill (Crane & Company,Inc.)
30 South St.
HABS MA-1240
HABS 1989(HABS):10
1ph/1pc L

Crane Paper Mill,Pioneer Museum (Crane & Company,Inc.)
30 South St.
HABS MA-1240-A
HABS 1989(HABS):10
4ph/1pc L

EGREMONT

Egremont Academy; see Town Hall

Town Hall (Egremont Academy)
State Rts. 41 & 17
HABS MA-220
HABS MASS,2-EGMO,1-
6dr/2ph L

GREAT BARRINGTON

Bryant,William Cullen,House; see Dwight,Gen. Joseph,House

Dwight,Gen. Joseph,House (Bryant,William Cullen,House)
U. S. Rt. 7 & State Rt. 23
HABS MA-360
HABS MASS,2-GREBA,1-
10ph L

HANCOCK

Shaker Building Number 4; see Shaker Ministry's Washhouse

Shaker Church Family (General Views)
U. S. Rt. 20
HABS MA-721
HABS MASS,2-HANC,6-
5ph L

Shaker Church Family Brethren's Shop
U. S. Rt. 20
HABS MA-722
HABS MASS,2-HANC,1-
11ph/3pg L

Shaker Church Family Concrete Barn
U. S. Rt. 20
HABS MA-1082
HABS MASS,2-HANC,2-
2ph L

Shaker Church Family Dairy & Weave Shop (Shaker Church Family Sisters' Shop (second))
U. S. Rt. 20
HABS MA-726
HABS MASS,2-HANC,3-
9dr/10ph/3pg L

Shaker Church Family Frame Barn (Shaker Ministry's Barn & Wagon Shed)
U. S. Rt. 20
HABS MA-1083
HABS MASS,2-HANC,5-
1ph L

Shaker Church Family Icehouse
U. S. Rt. 20
HABS MA-1084
HABS MASS,2-HANC,7-
3ph L

Shaker Church Family Main Dwelling House
U. S. Rt. 20
HABS MA-723
HABS MASS,2-HANC,4-
50ph L

Shaker Church Family Poultry House
U. S. Rt. 20
HABS MA-1093
HABS MASS,2-HANC,8-
1ph L

Shaker Church Family Round Barn
U. S. Rt. 20
HABS MA-674
HABS MASS,2-HANC,9-
2dr/22ph/2pg L

Shaker Church Family Seed Shop
U. S. Rt. 20
HABS MA-1095
HABS MASS,2-HANC,10-
1ph L

Shaker Church Family Sisters' Shop (first)
U. S. Rt. 20
HABS MA-1094
HABS MASS,2-HANC,11-
2ph L

Shaker Church Family Sisters' Shop (second); see Shaker Church Family Dairy & Weave Shop

Shaker Church Family Tannery
U. S. Rt. 20
HABS MA-727
HABS MASS,2-HANC,12-
12ph/2pg L

Shaker Church Family Trustees' Office
U. S. Rt. 20
HABS MA-728
HABS MASS,2-HANC,13-
3ph L

Shaker Church Family Washhouse & Machine Shop
U. S. Rt. 20
HABS MA-730
HABS MASS,2-HANC,14-
9dr/23ph/3pg L

Shaker Meetinghouse (first)
U. S. Rt. 20
HABS MA-692
HABS MASS,2-HANC,15-
2ph L

Shaker Meetinghouse (second)
U. S. Rt. 20
HABS MA-724
HABS MASS,2-HANC,16-
20ph/3pg L

Shaker Ministry's Barn & Wagon Shed; see Shaker Church Family Frame Barn

Shaker Ministry's Shop
U. S. Rt. 20
HABS MA-725
HABS MASS,2-HANC,17-
4ph L

Shaker Ministry's Washhouse (Shaker Building Number 4)
U. S. Rt. 20
HABS MA-729
HABS MASS,2-HANC,18-
4ph L

HINSDALE

Hinsdale Library
Maple Street
HABS MA-1235
HABS 1990 (HABS):5
7ph/1pg/1pc L

LANESBOROUGH

First Baptist Church
HABS MA-463
HABS MASS,2-LANBO,2-
1ph L

Registry of Deeds Building
HABS MA-372
HABS MASS,2-LANBO,1-
2ph/fr L

St. Lukes Episcopal Church
N. Main St. (Rt. 7)
HABS MA-1241
HABS 1989(HABS):10
10ph/1pg/1pc L

LEE

Golden Hill Road Bridge; see Tuttle Bridge

Shea's Crossing; see Tuttle Bridge

Tuttle Bridge (Golden Hill Road Bridge; Shea's Crossing)
Spanning the Housatonic River on Golden Hill Rd.
HAER MA-105
HAER DLC/PP-1992:MA-4
11ph/15pg/1pc/fr L

LENOX

Lenox Academy
75 Main St.
HABS MA-1239
HABS 1989(HABS):10
4ph/1pg/1pc L

NEW MARLBOROUGH

Harmon,Lieutenant,House
HABS MA-386
HABS MASS,2-NEMAR,1-
1ph L

NORTH ADAMS

Baker Bridge; see Blackinton Bridge

Blackinton Bridge (Galvin Road Bridge; Baker Bridge)
Spanning the Hoosic River on Galvin Rd.
HAER MA-109
HAER DLC/PP-1992:MA-4
10ph/19pg/1pc/fr L

Galvin Road Bridge; see Blackinton Bridge

PITTSFIELD

Arrowhead (Bush-Melville House)
780 Holmes Rd.
HABS MA-2-23
HABS MASS,2-PITFI,1-
3dr/3ph/fr L

Brattle,William Jr.,House
626 Williams St.
HABS MA-2-54
HABS MASS,2-PITFI,4-
6dr/4ph L

Bulfinch Church
North St. & Maplewood Ave. (moved from Park Row)
HABS MA-2-24
HABS MASS,2-PITFI,2-
11dr/6ph L

Bush-Melville House; see Arrowhead

Colt-Pingree House
HABS MA-477
HABS MASS,2-PITFI,6-
1ph L

First Bank Building
800 East St. (moved from original Pittsfield site)
HABS MA-2-46
HABS MASS,2-PITFI,3-
1dr/1ph L

Peace Party House
East St. & Wendell Ave.
HABS MA-478
HABS MASS,2-PITFI,7-
1ph L

Pittsfield City Hall (U. S. Post Office)
66 Allen St.
HABS MA-1173
HABS MASS,2-PITFI,8-
3ph/2pg/1pc/fr L

U. S. Post Office; see Pittsfield City Hall

West Part School
West & Churchill Sts.
HABS MA-2-89
HABS MASS,2-PITFI,5-
1dr/1ph L

RICHMOND

Peirson House
HABS MA-396
HABS MASS,2-RICH,1-
3ph L

SHEFFIELD

Ashley,Col. John,House
Cooper Rd. Vic.
HABS MA-401
HABS MASS,2-SHEFF,5-
9ph L

Ashley,Gen. John,House (Doorway)
HABS MA-400
HABS MASS,2-SHEFF,4-
1ph L

Congregational Church
HABS MA-892
HABS MASS,2-SHEFF,1-
2ph/1pc L

Hall,Parker L.,Law Office
State Rt. 7
HABS MA-233
HABS MASS,2-SHEFF,3-
1dr/1ph L

SOUTH LEE

Merrell's Tavern
Main St.
HABS MA-622
HABS MASS,2-LEES,1-
5dr L

SOUTH WILLIAMSTOWN

Deming,Titus,House
New Ashford Rd.
HABS MA-106
HABS MASS,2-WILLS,1-
6dr/7ph L

STOCKBRIDGE

Butler Bridge (Lester Bridge)
Spans Housatonic R. on Butler Rd.(N. Glendale Rd.)
HAER MA-115
HAER DLC/PP-1992:MA-4
4dr/13ph/12pg/1pc/fr L

Congregational Church
Stockbridge Common
HABS MA-894
HABS MASS,2-STOCK,1-
1ph/1pc L

Hampden County Memorial Bridge
Spanning the Connecticut River on Memorial Dr.
HAER MA-114
HAER DLC/PP-1992:MA-4
13ph/14pg/1pc L

Hopkins,Mark,House
HABS MA-408
HABS MASS,2-STOCK,4-
1ph L

Housatonic National Bank
HABS MA-895
HABS MASS,2-STOCK,5-
1ph/1pc L

Lester Bridge; see Butler Bridge

Yale-Duryea Mills
E. Main St.
HABS MA-107
HABS MASS,2-STOCK,3-
2dr/6ph L

TYRINGHAM

Shaker Damm; see Tyringham Shaker Settlement,Dam

Tyringham Shaker Settlement,Barn & Garage
Jerusalem Rd.
HABS MA-1238-B
HABS 1989(HABS):10
1ph/1pc L

Tyringham Shaker Settlement,Building No. 21
Jerusalem Rd.
HABS MA-1238-E
HABS 1989(HABS):10
2ph/1pc L

Tyringham Shaker Settlement,Building No. 24
Jerusalem Rd.
HABS MA-1238-D
HABS 1989(HABS):10
2ph/1pc L

Tyringham Shaker Settlement,Building No. 26
Jerusalem Rd.
HABS MA-1238-C
HABS 1989(HABS):10
3ph/1pc L

Tyringham Shaker Settlement,Dam (Shaker Damm)
Jerusalem Rd.
HAER MA-86
HAER 1989(HAER):10
5ph/1pg/1pc L

Tyringham Shaker Settlement,Main House & Office
Jerusalem Rd.
HABS MA-1238
HABS 1989(HABS):10
6ph/1pc L

Tyringham Shaker Settlement,Ox Barn
Jerusalem Rd.
HABS MA-1238-A
HABS 1989(HABS):10
10ph/1pg/1pc L

WEST STOCKBRIDGE

Bank Building,Old (House,Greek Temple)
HABS MA-496
HABS MASS,2-STOCKW,4-
1ph L

Engine House (Ruins)
Mill St.
HABS MA-149
HABS MASS,2-STOCKW,1-
1dr/1ph L

House,Greek Temple; see Bank Building,Old

Marble House
HABS MA-415
HABS MASS,2-STOCKW,2-
1ph L

Marble Mill
HABS MA-416
HABS MASS,2-STOCKW,3-
1ph L

WILLIAMSTOWN

Smedley,Nehemiah,House
State Rt. 2
HABS MA-2-18
HABS MASS,2-WILL,5-
7dr/2ph L

Williams College,President's House
Williams College Campus
HABS MA-1164
HABS MASS,2-WILL,1-
3ph/1pc L

Williamstown Railroad Station
N. Hoosac Rd. & Cole Ave.
HABS MA-1080
HABS MASS,2-WILL,6-
7dr/9ph/5pg/1pc/fr L

WINDSOR

Coleman Bridge (Windsor Bush Road Bridge)
Sp. Phelps Brook,on Windsor Bush Rd.,Windsor St.F.
HAER MA-119
HAER DLC/PP-1992:MA-4
4dr/10ph/22pg/1pc/fr L

Windsor Bush Road Bridge; see Coleman Bridge

BRISTOL COUNTY

ACOAXET

Richmond-Manchester House
Howland Rd.
HABS MA-160
HABS MASS,3-ACO,1-
6dr/2ph L

ATTLEBORO

Robinson,Joel,House
HABS MA-437
HABS MASS,3-ATBO,3-
1ph L

Thatcher House
HABS MA-339
HABS MASS,3-ATBO,2-
4ph L

Well Sweep
HABS MA-438
HABS MASS,3-ATBO,4A-
1ph L

ATTLEBORO VIC.

Daggett,John,House
480 N. Main St.
HABS MA-174
HABS MASS,3-ATBO,1-
6dr/2ph L

ATTLEBORO-PLAINVILLE

Angle Tree Stone
Town Line
HABS MA-181
HABS MASS,3-ATBON.V,2-
5dr/2ph/fr L

DARTMOUTH

Apponagansett Meetinghouse
HABS MA-441
HABS MASS,3-DART,1-
3ph L

DIGHTON

Baylies,Maj. Hadijah,House
HABS MA-431
HABS MASS,3-DIT,2-
1ph L

Brick,The (Church)
HABS MA-355
HABS MASS,3-DIT,1-
1ph L

Coram House
HABS MA-432
HABS MASS,3-DIT,3-
2ph L

Delare Cottage
HABS MA-446
HABS MASS,3-DIT,6-
2ph L

Ellery House
HABS MA-444
HABS MASS,3-DIT,4-
1ph L

Tulip Tree House
HABS MA-445
HABS MASS,3-DIT,5-
3ph L

EAST TAUNTON

Dean,Nathan,House
Old Colony Rd.
HABS MA-143
HABS MASS,3-TAUTE,1-
16dr/12ph L

EASTON

Milestones P,Q,R & S
Bay St.
HABS MA-128
HABS MASS,3-EATO,1-
4ph L

FAIRHAVEN

Academy,Old
Main St.
HABS MA-690
HABS MASS,3-FAIR,12-
4ph/4pg L

Bennett,Capt. Thomas,House
199 Main St.
HABS MA-608
HABS MASS,3-FAIR,11-
15dr L

Fish,Reuben,House
William & Union Sts.
HABS MA-136
HABS MASS,3-FAIR,10-
8dr L

FALL RIVER

Academy Building (Borden Block; Academy of Music)
68-114 South Main St.
HABS MA-1000
HABS MASS,3-FALL,9-
7dr/23ph/17pg/2pc L

Academy of Music; see Academy Building

American Print Works,No. 6 Mill; see Metacomet Mill

Borden Block; see Academy Building

Borden,Richard,Manufacturing Co.,Number 1 Mill
Rodman St. & Plymouth Ave.
HABS MA-984
HABS MASS,3-FALL,6-
3dr/19ph/7pg/fr L

Charlton Mill
Howe & Crawford Sts.
HABS MA-986
HABS MASS,3-FALL,8-
2dr/14ph/6pg L

Davol Mills
Rodman St. & Plymouth Ave.
HABS MA-985
HABS MASS,3-FALL,7-
2dr/15ph/7pg L

Durfee Mills
Plymouth Ave. & Pleasant St.
HABS MA-982
HABS MASS,3-FALL,4-
7dr/29ph/9pg L

Metacomet Mill (American Print Works,No. 6 Mill)
Davol & Anawan Sts.
HABS MA-983
HABS MASS,3-FALL,5-
5dr/19ph/7pg/1pc/fr L

Union Mills
Pleasant St. & Hwy. I-195,Interchange No. 12
HABS MA-981
HABS MASS,3-FALL,3-
7dr/17ph/8pg L

FREETOWN

Barnaby,James,House
N. Main St.
HABS MA-2-27
HABS MASS,3-FRETO,1-
8dr/5ph L

NEW BEDFORD

Baker Oil Works; see Delano,George, & Sons,Oil Works

Congregational Church (First Unitarian Church)
Union & Eighth Sts.
HABS MA-681
HABS MASS,3-NEBED,15-
9ph/6pg L

Custom House
Second & William Sts.
HABS MA-682
HABS MASS,3-NEBED,16-
6ph/7pg L

Delano,George, & Sons,Oil Works (Baker Oil Works; Gabell Building)
South and S. Second Sts.
HAER MA-10
HAER MASS,3-NEBED,25-
11ph/4pg/1pc/fr L

First Unitarian Church; see Congregational Church

Friends Meetinghouse
Spring St.
HABS MA-467
HABS MASS,3-NEBED,8-
3ph/2pg L

Gabell Building; see Delano,George, & Sons,Oil Works

Grinell,Joseph,Mansion (St. John's Roman Catholic Convent & Academy)
379 County St.
HABS MA-675
HABS MASS,3-NEBED,9-
4ph/5pg L

Harrison,John,Building
23 Centre St.
HABS MA-686
HABS MASS,3-NEBED,20-
1ph/2pg L

Institution for Savings (Third District Courthouse)
Second & Williams Sts
HABS MA-684
HABS MASS,3-NEBED,18-
2ph/4pg L

Merchants & Mechanics Bank Building
56-62 North Water St.
HABS MA-683
HABS MASS,3-NEBED,17-
4ph/5pg L

New Bedford-Fairhaven Middle Bridge
Spanning the Acushnet River on U.S. Hwy. 6
HAER MA-101
HAER DLC/PP-1992:MA-4
18ph/21pg/1pc/fr L

North Front Street & Rose Alley (Warehouse)
HABS MA-688
HABS MASS,3-NEBED,22-
2ph/4pg L

Rodman,Samuel Jr.,House
Spring & County Sts.
HABS MA-466
HABS MASS,3-NEBED,7-
1ph/1pg L

Rodman,William R.,House
388 County St.
HABS MA-676
HABS MASS,3-NEBED,10-
4ph/6pg L

Rotch,William J.,House
19 Irving St. (moved from 103 Orchard St.)
HABS MA-678
HABS MASS,3-NEBED,12-
9ph/17pg L

Rotch,William Jr.,House
15 Johnny Cake Hill
HABS MA-679
HABS MASS,3-NEBED,13-
3ph/4pg L

Russell,Charles,Building
Union & Water Sts.
HABS MA-687
HABS MASS,3-NEBED,21-
1ph/2pg L

Seaman's Bethel
Johnny Cake Hill
HABS MA-680
HABS MASS,3-NEBED,14-
2ph/2pg L

St. John's Roman Catholic Convent & Academy; see Grinell,Joseph,Mansion

Taber,Henry,House
115 Orchard St.
HABS MA-677
HABS MASS,3-NEBED,11-
5ph/3pg L

Tallman,William,Warehouse
106 N. Front St.
HABS MA-685
HABS MASS,3-NEBED,19-
3ph/3pg L

Third District Courthouse; see Institution for Savings

Union and Front Streets (Warehouse)
HABS MA-689
HABS MASS,3-NEBED,23-
1ph/2pg L

Wamsutta Mill
Achushnet Ave.
HABS MA-987
HABS MASS,3-NEBED,24-
8ph L

NORTH ATTLEBORO

Daggett,Handel,House
HABS MA-390
HABS MASS,3-ATBON,1-
4ph L

Ellis,Jabez,House
HABS MA-391
HABS MASS,3-ATBON,2-
4ph L

Mann,Dr. Bezaleel,House
HABS MA-392
HABS MASS,3-ATBON,3-
4ph L

Powder House
Mount Hope St.,Oldtown
HABS MA-148
HABS MASS,3-OLTO,1-
1dr/1ph/fr L

NORTH ATTLEBORO VIC.

Congregational Church
Old Post Rd.
HABS MA-189
HABS MASS,3-OLTO,3-
23dr/6ph L

Stanley-Mathewson House
Old Post Rd.
HABS MA-170
HABS MASS,3-ATBON.V,1-
8dr/2ph/fr L

Stearns,Capt. John,House
Old Post Rd.,Oldtown
HABS MA-165
HABS MASS,3-OLTO,2-
12dr/5ph/fr L

NORTH DIGHTON

Clouston,Capt. John,House
Somerset Ave.
HABS MA-164
HABS MASS,3-DITN,1-
5dr/3ph L

NORTH EASTON

Ames,Oliver,Free Library
53 Main St.
HABS MA-1220
HABS 1989(HABS):10
15ph/1pg/1pc L

New York,New Haven & Hartford Railroad Station; see Old Colony Railroad Station

Old Colony Railroad Station (New York,New Haven & Hartford Railroad Station)
HABS MA-663
HABS MASS,3-EATON,1-
4ph/3pg L

NORTON

Avery,Rev. Joseph,House
Main St.
HABS MA-244
HABS MASS,3-NORT,1-
7dr/4ph L

Clark House; see Norton Cotton Mill House

Clark,Rev. Pitt,House
Mansfield Ave.
HABS MA-257
HABS MASS,3-NORT,2-
12dr/8ph L

Devoe House; see Norton Cotton Mill House

Milestones T & U
Bay St.
HABS MA-128
HABS MASS,3-NORT,4-
2ph L

Newcomb,Jonathan,House
HABS MA-393
HABS MASS,3-NORT,3-
7ph L

Norton Cotton Mill House (Clark House)
200 E. Main St.
HABS MA-997
HABS MASS,3-NORT,5-
6ph/1pc L

Norton Cotton Mill House (Devoe House)
338 E. Main St. (moved from 198 E. Main St.)
HABS MA-998
HABS MASS,3-NORT,6-
3ph/1pc L

NORTON VIC.

Canoe River Mill
HAER MA-15
HAER MASS,3-NORT.V,1-
5ph/1pg/1pc L

REHOBOTH

Carpenter,Col.Thomas,House
HABS MA-394
HABS MASS,3-REHOB,1-
4ph/fr L

SEEKONK

Martin,Lieut. Gov. Simeon,Blacksmith Shop
County St.
HABS MA-235
HABS MASS,3-SEKO,3-
4dr L

Martin,Lieut. Gov. Simeon,House
County St.
HABS MA-2-90
HABS MASS,3-SEKO,1-
20dr/6ph L

Martin,Sylvanus,Barn
County St.
HABS MA-234
HABS MASS,3-SEKO,2-
3dr/fr L

Martin,Sylvanus,House
HABS MA-1209
HABS MASS,3-SEKO,2A-
1ph/1pc L

SOMERSET

Bowers,Jarathmael,House
55 Main St.
HABS MA-2-17
HABS MASS,3-SOM,1-
21dr/8ph L

Pettis,Henry,House
Main St. & Pierce Rd.
HABS MA-2-52
HABS MASS,3-SOM,2-
10dr/2ph L

SOUTH SOMERSET

Brayton,John,Homestead
Brayton Ave.
HABS MA-2-43
HABS MASS,3-SOMS,1-
9dr/2ph L

SOUTH WESTPORT

Waite-Potter House
Sanford Rd.
HABS MA-2-65
HABS MASS,3-WESPOS,1-
2dr/1ph L

SWANSEA

Luther,Joseph G.,Store
Luther's Corner
HABS MA-134
HABS MASS,3-SWAN,2-
3dr/8ph L

Tavern,Old
U. S. Rt. 6 & Milford Rd.
HABS MA-105
HABS MASS,3-SWAN,1-
11dr/2ph/fr L

TAUNTON

Milk Bottle Dairy Bar & Restaurant
Rt. 138
HABS MA-1221
HABS 1989(HABS):10
2ph/1pc L

Taunton State Hospital
Danforth St.
HABS MA-1219
HABS 1989(HABS):10
11ph/1pg/1pc L

DUKES COUNTY

TISBURY

Gray,Lucy,House
Indian Hill Rd.
HABS MA-2-88
HABS MASS,4-TISB,1-
4dr/3ph L

VINEYARD HAVEN

Alabamiam; see Pilot Schooner "Alabama"

Pilot Schooner "Alabama" (Alabamiam)
Moored in harbor at Vineyard Haven
HAER MA-64
HAER DLC/PP-1992:MA-3
12dr/39ph/56pg/5pc/fr L

ESSEX COUNTY

AMESBURY

Chain Bridge; see Essex-Merrimac Bridge

Essex-Merrimac Bridge (Chain Bridge)
Spans Merrimack Riv. btwn. Newburyport & Deer Isld
HAER MA-93
HAER DLC/PP-1992:MA-4
12ph/18pg/1pc/fr L

Powder House
HABS MA-338
HABS MASS,5-AMB,2-
1ph L

Powow River Bridge
Spanning the Powow River on Main St.
HAER MA-92
HAER DLC/PP-1992:MA-4
9ph/12pg/1pc/fr L

Rocky Hill Meetinghouse
Elm St. & Portsmouth Rd.
HABS MA-250
HABS MASS,5-AMB,1-
29dr/25ph L

ANDOVER

Abbot,Benjamin,Farmhouse
Andover St. & Argilla Rd.
HABS MA-2-9
HABS MASS,5-ANDO,1-
12dr/4ph/fr L

ANNISQUAM

Customs House,Old
River Rd.
HABS MA-2-12
HABS MASS,5-ANNI,1-
2dr/2ph L

Hodgkins,William,Tide Mill
Washington St.
HABS MA-2-92
HABS MASS,5-ANNI,2-
3dr/9ph L

Lobster Cove
HABS MA-115
HABS MASS,5-ANNI,3-
6dr L

BEVERLY

Balch,John,House
448 Cabot St.
HABS MA-584
HABS MASS,5-BEV,6-
2ph L

Cabot,John,House & Garden
117 Cabot St.
HABS MA-282
HABS MASS,5-BEV,4-
5dr/3ph/fr L

First Baptist Church (Pulpit)
HABS MA-619
HABS MASS,5-BEV,9-
1dr L

Foster Warehouse
HABS MA-260
HABS MASS,5-BEV,1-
3ph/fr L

Foster,George B.,House & Fence
21 Bartlett St.
HABS MA-267
HABS MASS,5-BEV,3-
1dr/3ph/fr L

Kilham,Austin D.,House (Garden)
8 Thorndike St.
HABS MA-266
HABS MASS,5-BEV,2-
4dr/2ph L

Pierce,Benjamin,House
305 Cabot St.
HABS MA-606
HABS MASS,5-BEV,8-
12dr L

Powder House
Powder House Hill
HABS MA-583
HABS MASS,5-BEV,5-
1ph L

Second Church
HABS MA-585
HABS MASS,5-BEV,7-
1ph L

United Shoe Machine Company
134 McKay Street
HAER MA-71
HAER 1990 (HAER):8
6ph/1pc L

BOXFORD

Goodridge,Benjamin,House; see Gould,Daniel,House

Goodridge,Benjamin,Shoemaker's Shop; see Shoemaker's Shop

Gould,Daniel,House
(Goodridge,Benjamin,House)
Georgetown Rd.
HABS MA-2-30
HABS MASS,5-BOX,3-
10dr/1ph L

Saw,Grist & Knife Mill Group
Middleton Rd.
HABS MA-2-15
HABS MASS,5-BOX,2-
5dr/6ph L

Shoemaker's Shop
(Goodridge,Benjamin,Shoemaker's Shop)
Georgetown Rd.
HABS MA-2-58
HABS MASS,5-BOX,4-
1dr/1ph L

DANVERS

Derby Summer House
Glen Magna Estate (moved from MA,Peabody)
HABS MA-783
HABS MASS,5-DAV,11-
10ph/1pg/1pc L

Fowler,Samuel,House
166 High St.
HABS MA-586
HABS MASS,5-DAV,10-
1ph L

Gage,General,House; see Lindens,The (House & Garden)

Holten,Judge Samuel,House
171 Holten St.
HABS MA-152
HABS MASS,5-DAV,3-
10dr/7ph/fr L

Hooper,King,House & Garden; see Lindens,The (House & Garden)

Jacobs,George,House
Margin St.
HABS MA-243
HABS MASS,5-DAV,7-
6dr/19ph L

Lindens,The (House & Garden)
(Hooper,King,House & Garden; Gage,General,House)
Sylvan St. (moved to Washington,D.C.)
HABS MA-2-33
HABS MASS,5-DAV,2-
29dr/22ph/fr L

Nurse,Rebecca,House & Garden
149 Pine St.
HABS MA-239
HABS MASS,5-DAV,1-
2dr/2ph L

Oak Knoll (House & Garden)
Summer St.
HABS MA-205
HABS MASS,5-DAV,6-
3dr/2ph/fr L

Porter,Elias Endicott,House & Farm Gates
Locust St.
HABS MA-289
HABS MASS,5-DAV,8-
1dr/3ph/fr L

Putnam,Gen. Israel,Birthplace; see Putnam,Gen. Israel,House

Putnam,Gen. Israel,Birthplace (Garden); see Putnam,Gen. Israel,House (Garden)

Putnam,Gen. Israel,House
(Putnam,Gen. Israel,Birthplace)
431 Maple St.
HABS MA-153
HABS MASS,5-DAV,4-
11dr/2ph/fr L

Putnam,Gen. Israel,House (Garden)
(Putnam,Gen. Israel,Birthplace (Garden))
431 Maple St.
HABS MA-153-A
HABS MASS,5-DAV,4A-
2dr/fr L

Warren,Betsy K.,Garden
124 High St.
HABS MA-290
HABS MASS,5-DAV,9-
5dr L

ESSEX

Essex Town Hall
Martin St.
HABS MA-1222
HABS 1989(HABS):10
9ph/1pg/1pc L

GEORGETOWN

Brockelbank,Capt. Samuel,House (Fence); see White Horse Tavern (Fence)

36 East Main Street (House & Fence)
HABS MA-449
HABS MASS,5-GEOT0,5-
2ph L

Nelson,Capt. Bill,House (Fence)
8 Elm St.
HABS MA-254
HABS MASS,5-GEOTO,4A-
1dr/2ph L

White Horse Tavern (Fence)
(Brockelbank,Capt. Samuel,House (Fence))
108 E. Main St.
HABS MA-253
HABS MASS,5-GEOTO,2-
1dr/1ph/fr L

GLOUCESTER

Annisquam Bridge (Bridgewater Street Bridge)
Spanning Lobster Cove btwn Washington & River Sts.
HAER MA-61
HAER MASS,5-GLO,4-
16ph/14pg/2pc L

Bridgewater Street Bridge; see Annisquam Bridge

First Universalist Church (Independent Christian Church)
Middle St.
HABS MA-451
HABS MASS,5-GLO,1-
16ph L

Independent Christian Church; see First Universalist Church

Schoolhouse
HABS MA-453
HABS MASS,5-GLO,2-
2ph L

HAMILTON-IPSWICH

Warner's Bridge
Mill Rd.,spanning Ipswich River
HABS MA-251
HABS MASS,5-HAM,1-
1dr/4ph L

HAVERHILL

Duston Garrison House
(Duston,Thomas,House)
Hillsdale Ave.
HABS MA-273
HABS MASS,5-HAV,8-
4ph L

Duston,Thomas,House; see Duston Garrison House

Merrimac Bridge (Rocks Bridge)
Spanning the Merrimac River on Bridge St.
HAER MA-103
HAER DLC/PP-1992:MA-4
10ph/22pg/1pc/fr L

Rocks Bridge; see Merrimac Bridge

IPSWICH

Appleton,William,House
(Choate,Sally,House)
HABS MA-607
HABS MASS,5-IPSWI,20-
5dr L

Caldwell,Waldo,House (Interiors)
High St.
HABS MA-462
HABS MASS,5-IPSWI,6-
6ph L

Choate Bridge
State Rt. 1A,spanning Ipswich River
HABS MA-2-69
HAER MA-81
HABS/HAER MASS,5-IPSWI,8-ı91(HAER):22;88(HABS):83°
21ph/13pg/4pc L

Choate,Sally,House; see Appleton,William,House

Clam Box Restaurant
High St. & Mile Lane (Rt. 1-A)
HABS MA-1245
HABS 1989(HABS):10
3ph/1pg/1pc L

Congregational Parsonage (Fencepost)
19 N. Main St.
HABS MA-255
HABS MASS,5-IPSWI,10-
1dr/fr L

Dane,Dr. Philemon,House & Fence
41 S. Main St.
HABS MA-256
HABS MASS,5-IPSWI,11-
2dr/3ph/fr L

Heard,John,Estate
State Rt. 1A
HABS MA-321
HABS MASS,5-IPSWI,12-
3ph/fr L

Howard-Emerson House
Turkey Shore Rd.
HABS MA-423
HABS MASS,5-IPSWI,7-
3ph L

Kimball,John,House
75 High St.
HABS MA-177
HABS MASS,5-IPSWI,9-
5dr/10ph L

Milestone TT; see Twenty-five-mile Stone

Morton-Corbett-House
8 East St.
HABS MA-457
HABS MASS,5-IPSWI,16-
3ph L

40 North Main Street (House)
HABS MA-461
HABS MASS,5-IPSWI,18-
2ph L

Post Office,Old
HABS MA-456
HABS MASS,5-IPSWI,15-
2ph L

Proctor House
Jeffrey's Neck Rd. (moved from original location)
HABS MA-322
HABS MASS,5-IPSWI,13-
12ph L

Renault-Foster House
Water St.
HABS MA-633
HABS MASS,5-IPSWI,21-
3dr L

Saltonstall-Whipple House; see Whipple,John,House

Treadwell House
HABS MA-368
HABS MASS,5-IPSWI,14-
1ph/fr L

Twenty-five-mile Stone (Milestone TT)
Bay Rd.
HABS MA-128
HABS MASS,5-IPSWI,19-
1ph L

Wade,Col. Nathaniel,House
HABS MA-458
HABS MASS,5-IPSWI,17-
2ph L

Whipple,John,House
(Saltonstall-Whipple House)
53 S. Main St.
HABS MA-460
HABS MASS,5-IPSWI,5-
1ph L

LAWRENCE

30-32 Atlantic Block (Atlantic Boardinghouse; Peter's,Bill,Cafe)
401-403 Canal St. & 2 Amesbury St.
HABS MA-505
HABS MASS,5-LAWR,4-
5dr/12ph/46pg/1pc L

Atlantic Boardinghouse; see 30-32 Atlantic Block

Duck Bridge (Union Street Bridge)
Spanning the Merrimack River on Union St.
HAER MA-104
HAER DLC/PP-1992:MA-4
14ph/11pg/1pc L

Everett Mills; see Lawrence Machine Shop

Lawrence Machine Shop (Everett Mills)
Union & Canal Sts.
HABS MA-988
HABS MASS,5-LAWR,1-
5dr/15ph/6pg/fr L

Moseley Truss Bridge; see Upper Pacific Mills Bridge

Pemberton Mill
Union St. vic.
HABS MA-989
HABS MASS,5-LAWR,2-
4dr/12ph/5pg L

Peter's,Bill,Cafe; see 30-32 Atlantic Block

Union Street Bridge; see Duck Bridge

Upper Pacific Mills Bridge (Moseley Truss Bridge)
Moved to Merrimack College,North Andover,MA
HAER MA-72
HAER 1990 (HAER):8
2dr/15ph/27pg/2pc/fr L

Washington Mills,Gatehouse
North Canal
HABS MA-990
HABS MASS,5-LAWR,3-
2ph/3pg L

LYNN

Lynn Realty Company,Building Number 28; see Lynn Realty Company,Building Number 3

Lynn Realty Company,Building Number 3 (Lynn Realty Company,Building Number 28)
696 Washington St.
HABS MA-1001
HABS MASS,5-LYN,1A-
7ph/2pg/1pc L

Lynn Realty Company,Building Number 8
274 Broad St.
HABS MA-1002
HABS MASS,5-LYN,1B-
8ph/4pg/1pc L

Saugus River Drawbridge
(See Essex,Saugus for Documentation)
HAER MA-84
L

MANCHESTER

Forster,Maj. Israel,House
State Rt. 127
HABS MA-373
HABS MASS,5-MANCH,3-
15ph/fr L

Lee,Ma'm,Cottage
39 Forest St.
HABS MA-323
HABS MASS,5-MANCH,2-
7dr/6ph/fr L

Orthodox Congregational Church
Central & Church Sts.
HABS MA-268
HABS MASS,5-MANCH,1-
12ph/fr L

MARBLEHEAD

Artillery House,Old; see Gun House,Old

Boardman House (Waters,William,House & Bakery)
Washington St.
HABS MA-2-31
HABS MASS,5-MARB,4-
12dr/10ph/fr L

Gun House,Old (Artillery House,Old)
45 Elm St.
HABS MA-186
HABS MASS,5-MARB,52-
3dr/2ph L

Hooper,King,House; see Hooper,Robert,House

Hooper,Robert,House
(Hooper,King,House)
8 Hooper St.
HABS MA-249
HABS MASS,5-MARB,53-
27dr/32ph L

Jayne,Peter,House
37 Mugford St.
HABS MA-374
HABS MASS,5-MARB,54-
10ph L

Lee,Jeremiah,House
161 Washington St.
HABS MA-859
HABS MASS,5-MARB,55-
4ph/1pg/1pc L

Powder House
Green St.
HABS MA-2-67
HABS MASS,5-MARB,5-
1dr/1ph L

Town House
Market Square
HABS MA-2-6
HABS MASS,5-MARB,3-
6dr/2ph/fr L

Trevett,Capt. Samuel,House
65 Washington St.
HABS MA-104
HABS MASS,5-MARB,6-
14dr/9ph L

Waters,William,House & Bakery; see Boardman House

MIDDLETON

Bradstreet House
HABS MA-587
HABS MASS,5-MID,1-
2ph L

NEWBURY

Coffin,Tristram,House (Coffyn House)
14 High Rd.
HABS MA-472
HABS MASS,5-NEWB,1-
1ph L

Coffyn House; see Coffin,Tristram,House

Jackman-Willett House
(Jackman,Richard,House)
Lower Green Vic. (moved from original site)
HABS MA-471
HABS MASS,5-NEWB,5-
1ph L

Jackman,Richard,House; see Jackman-Willett House

Knight-Short House
(Knight,Nathaniel,House; Short House)
6 High St.
HABS MA-468
HABS MASS,5-NEWB,3-
2ph L

Knight,Nathaniel,House; see Knight-Short House

Milestone
Boston Rd. Vic.
HABS MA-1179
HABS MASS,5-NEWB,7-
1ph/1pc L

Milestone
Lower Rd.
HABS MA-1180
HABS MASS,5-NEWB,8-
1ph/1pc L

Milestones UU,VV,WW,XX,YY & ZZ
Various Newbury locations
HABS MA-128
HABS MASS,5-NEWB,6-
6ph L

Short House; see Knight-Short House

Toppan,Dr. Peter,House
HABS MA-469
HABS MASS,5-NEWB,2-
1ph L

NEWBURY OLD TOWN

Blue Anchor Tavern; see Swett-Ilsley House

Swett-Ilsley House (Blue Anchor Tavern)
4-6 High St.
HABS MA-470
HABS MASS,5-NEWB,4-
6dr/2ph/fr L

NEWBURYPORT

Cushing,John N.,House & Garden
98 High St.
HABS MA-213
HABS MASS,5-NEWBP,10-
7dr/6ph/fr L

Gaol,Gaoler's House & Barn
Auburn & Vernon Sts.
HABS MA-121
HABS MASS,5-NEWBP,19-
12dr/8ph/fr L

Globe Steam Mills
Federal St.
HABS MA-295
HABS MASS,5-NEWBP,25-
15dr/4ph/fr L

Hennessey House
2 Summer St.
HABS MA-2-82
HABS MASS,5-NEWBP,11-
4dr/1ph/1pg/fr L

Highway Cut-off Demolition Area
Summer,Winter,High & Merrimac Sts.
HABS MA-117
HABS MASS,5-NEWBP,18-
6dr/10ph/fr L

Marden House
32 Summer St.
HABS MA-2-87
HABS MASS,5-NEWBP,13-
6dr/6ph/fr L

Meetinghouse of First Religious Society
Pleasant St.
HABS MA-623
HABS MASS,5-NEWBP,7-
1dr/4ph L

Moulton,Joseph,House & Garden
89-91 High St.
HABS MA-216
HABS MASS,5-NEWBP,23-
6dr/5ph/fr L

Pierce-Knapp-Perry House & Garden
(Pierce,Benjamin,House & Garden)
47 High St.
HABS MA-236
HABS MASS,5-NEWBP,24-
9dr/3ph/fr L

Pierce,Benjamin,House & Garden; see Pierce-Knapp-Perry House & Garden

Regan House
7 Birch St.
HABS MA-110
HABS MASS,5-NEWBP,17-
3dr/2ph/fr L

Semple House
176 High St.
HABS MA-2-93
HABS MASS,5-NEWBP,14-
6dr/fr L

Stocker-Wheelwright Garden
(Wheelwright,William,Garden; Stocker,Ebenezer,Garden)
75 High St.
HABS MA-209
HABS MASS,5-NEWBP,22-
6dr/fr L

Stocker,Ebenezer,Garden; see Stocker-Wheelwright Garden

Stockman House
5 Birch St.
HABS MA-2-95
HABS MASS,5-NEWBP,15-
2dr/3ph/fr L

Stockman,Charles,House
31-33 Winter St.
HABS MA-140
HABS MASS,5-NEWBP,21-
5dr/6ph/fr L

Stonecutting Shop
2 Summer St.
HABS MA-2-97
HABS MASS,5-NEWBP,16-
1dr/2ph/fr L

Thibault House
8 Summer St.
HABS MA-123
HABS MASS,5-NEWBP,20-
5dr/1ph/fr L

Thurlow House
43 Winter St.
HABS MA-2-83
HABS MASS,5-NEWBP,12-
3dr/3ph/fr L

Wheelwright-Richardson House & Garden; see Wheelwright,Abraham,House & Garden

Wheelwright,Abraham,House & Garden (Wheelwright-Richardson House & Garden)
77 High St.
HABS MA-780
HABS MASS,5-NEWBP,5-
8ph L

Wheelwright,William,Garden; see Stocker-Wheelwright Garden

NORTH ANDOVER

Bradstreet,Gov. Simon,House
(Parson-Barnard House)
159 Osgood St.
HABS MA-2-63
HABS MASS,5-ANDON,1-
12dr/6ph L

Kittredge,Dr. Thomas,House & Fence
114 Academy Rd.
HABS MA-475
HABS MASS,5-ANDON,4-
3ph L

Moseley Truss Bridge; see Upper Pacific Mills Bridge

Parson-Barnard House; see Bradstreet,Gov. Simon,House

Town Scales House
Andover St.
HABS MA-2-100
HABS MASS,5-ANDON,3-
1dr/1ph L

Upper Pacific Mills Bridge (Moseley Truss Bridge)
Moved from North Canal,Lawrence,MA
HAER MA-72
HAER 1990(HAER):8;DLC/PP-1993:MA-1
2dr/15ph/27pg/2pc/fr L

PEABODY

Derby Summer House
Derby,Elias,Farm (moved to MA,Danvers)
HABS MA-783
HABS MASS,5-DAV,11-
10ph/1pg/1pc L

ROCKPORT

Bradley's Wharf (Motif Number One)
Bearskin Neck
HABS MA-227
HABS MASS,5-ROCPO,1-
2dr/fr L

Motif Number One; see Bradley's Wharf

ROWLEY

Billings,Elizabeth,House & Fence
Main St.
HABS MA-277
HABS MASS,5-ROWL,1-
3dr/2ph/fr L

Milestone BBB; see Twenty-seven-mile Stone

Twenty-seven-mile Stone (Milestone BBB)
Newburyport Turnpike
HABS MA-128
HABS MASS,5-ROWL,2-
1ph L

SALEM

Andrew-Safford House & Garden (Andrew,John,House & Garden)
13 Washington Sq.
HABS MA-281-A
HABS MASS,5-SAL,9-
4dr/6ph/fr L

Andrew-Safford Stable; see Andrew,John,Stable

Andrew,John,House & Garden; see Andrew-Safford House & Garden

Andrew,John,Stable (Andrew-Safford Stable)
13 Washington Square
HABS MA-281
HABS MASS,5-SAL,9-
6dr/2ph L

Baldwin-Lyman,House (Fence)
92 Washington Sq.
HABS MA-485
HABS MASS,5-SAL,39A-
3ph/fr L

Boardman-Bowen House (Fence)
1 Boardman St.
HABS MA-490
HABS MASS,5-SAL,43-
2ph L

Bowker,Joel,Garden (Crombie,Benjamin,Garden)
9 Crombie St.
HABS MA-262
HABS MASS,5-SAL,27-
2dr/fr L

Brooks House
260 Lafayette St.
HABS MA-796
HABS MASS,5-SAL,47-
2ph/1pg/1pc L

Cook-Oliver House
142 Federal St.
HABS MA-333
HABS MASS,5-SAL,34-
25ph/fr L

Corwin,Jonathan,House (Witch House,The Old)
310 Essex St.
HABS MA-398
HABS MASS,5-SAL,13-
2ph/fr L

Crombie,Benjamin,Garden; see Bowker,Joel,Garden

Crowninshield Warehouse
India St.
HABS MA-259
HABS MASS,5-SAL,26-
4dr/2ph/fr L

Crowninshield-Devereaux House
74 Washington Sq.
HABS MA-582
HABS MASS,5-SAL,45-
2ph L

Custom House & Public Stores (Salem Maritime National Historic Site)
178 Derby St.
HABS MA-799
HABS MASS,5-SAL,48-
16dr/14ph/1pg/1pc/fr L

Custom House & Public Stores,Scale House (Salem Maritime National Historic Site)
178 Derby St.
HABS MA-799-A
HABS MASS,5-SAL,48A-
2dr/1ph/5pg/1pc/fr L

Daland,Benjamin,Garden; see Robinson,John,Garden

Daland,Benjamin,Stable; see Robinson,John,Stable

Daniel,Stephen,House
Daniels & Essex Sts.
HABS MA-116
HABS MASS,5-SAL,20-
16dr/12ph L

Derby House (Salem Maritime National Historic Site)
168 Derby St.
HABS MA-269
HABS MASS,5-SAL,30-
17dr/14ph/17pg/1pc/fr L

Dodge-Shreve House
29 Chestnut St.
HABS MA-795
HABS MASS,5-SAL,11-
2ph/1pg/1pc L

Dodge,Pickering,House & Garden
40 Dearborn St.
HABS MA-184
HABS MASS,5-SAL,21-
4dr/4ph/fr L

East India Marine Hall (Peabody Museum)
161 Essex St.
HABS MA-798
HABS MASS,5-SAL,49-
6ph/1pg/1pc L

Finnegan,Doctor,House (Fencepost)
HABS MA-487
HABS MASS,5-SAL,41A-
1ph/fr L

First Universalist Meetinghouse
HABS MA-399
HABS MASS,5-SAL,35-
8ph L

Forrester-Peabody House & Garden
29 Washington Sq.
HABS MA-264
HABS MASS,5-SAL,18-
3dr/4ph/fr L

Forrester's Warehouse (Salem Maritime National Historic Site)
187 Derby St. (Central Wharf)
HABS MA-572
HABS MASS,5-SAL,5-
4dr/fr L

Gardner-White-Pingree House & Garden
128 Essex St.
HABS MA-271
HABS MASS,5-SAL,2-
1dr/2ph/fr L

Hamilton Hall
7 Cambridge St.
HABS MA-483
HABS MASS,5-SAL,37-
3ph L

Hawkes,Gen. Benjamin,House
4 Custom House Place
HABS MA-270
HABS MASS,5-SAL,31-
2dr/15ph/1pc/fr L

Hawthorne,Nathaniel,Birthplace
27 Union St.
HABS MA-581
HABS MASS,5-SAL,44-
1ph L

Hodges-Peele-West Summerhouse
(Hodges,Capt. Jonathan,Summerhouse)
12 Chestnut St.
HABS MA-265
HABS MASS,5-SAL,29A-
1dr/1ph/fr L

Hodges-Webb-Meek House
81 Essex St.
HABS MA-797
HABS MASS,5-SAL,50-
3ph/1pc L

Hodges,Capt. Jonathan,Summerhouse; see Hodges-Peele-West Summerhouse

House of the Seven Gables
(Turner,John,House; Turner-Ingersoll House)
54 Turner St.
HABS MA-629
HABS MASS,5-SAL,16-
4ph/1pg/1pc L

Lindall-Barnard-Andrews House (Fence)
393 Essex St.
HABS MA-484
HABS MASS,5-SAL,38A-
2ph/fr L

Lindall-Gibbs-Osgood Garden
314 Essex St.
HABS MA-263
HABS MASS,5-SAL,28-
2dr L

Loring-Emmerton House & Fence
Essex St.
HABS MA-480
HABS MASS,5-SAL,7-
6ph L

Manning,Robert,Garden
33 Dearborn St.
HABS MA-187
HABS MASS,5-SAL,22-
4dr/fr L

Narbonne Barn
71 Essex St.
HABS MA-802-A
HABS MASS,5-SAL,51A-
3ph/1pc L

Narbonne House
71 Essex St.
HABS MA-802
HABS 1984(HABS):194
4dr/22ph/1pg/2pc/fr L

Oliver Primary School
HABS MA-329
HABS MASS,5-SAL,33-
5ph/fr L

Peabody Museum; see East India Marine Hall

Phillips House & Fence
36 Chestnut St.
HABS MA-488
HABS MASS,5-SAL,42-
4ph L

Phippen,Doctor,House & Fence
Chestnut St.
HABS MA-486
HABS MASS,5-SAL,40-
3ph/fr L

Pickering House & Fence
30 Chestnut St.
HABS MA-482
HABS MASS,5-SAL,36-
1ph L

Pickering,John,House & Garden
18 Broad St.
HABS MA-212
HABS MASS,5-SAL,24-
6dr/1ph/fr L

Pickman,Benjamin,House
165 Essex St.
HABS MA-332
HABS MASS,5-SAL,3-
7ph/fr L

Pierce-Nichols House & Garden; see Pierce,Jerathmeel,House & Garden

Pierce,Jerathmeel,House & Garden
(Pierce-Nichols House & Garden)
80 Federal St.
HABS MA-224
HABS MASS,5-SAL,15-
9dr/7ph/fr L

Public Library; see Waters-Bertram House

Robinson,John,Garden
(Daland,Benjamin,Garden)
18 Summer St.
HABS MA-208-A
HABS MASS,5-SAL,23A-
3dr/fr L

Robinson,John,Stable
(Daland,Benjamin,Stable)
18 Summer St.
HABS MA-208
HABS MASS,5-SAL,23D-
8dr/3ph L

Ropes Memorial
318 Essex St.
HABS MA-481
HABS MASS,5-SAL,6-
1ph L

Rum Shop (Salem Maritime National Historic Site)
Derby St. & Palfrey Court
HABS MA-801
HABS MASS,5-SAL,52-
(DLC/PP-1992:MA-5)
2dr/2ph/1pg/2pc/fr L

Salem City Hall
93 Washington St.
HABS MA-1
HABS MASS,5-SAL,46-
6ph/4pg/1pc/fr L

Salem Maritime National Historic Site; see Custom House & Public Stores

Salem Maritime National Historic Site; see Custom House & Public Stores,Scale House

Salem Maritime National Historic Site; see Derby House

Salem Maritime National Historic Site; see Forrester's Warehouse

Salem Maritime National Historic Site; see Rum Shop

Saltonstall,Leverett,Garden
(Saunders,Thomas,Garden)
41 Chestnut St.
HABS MA-228
HABS MASS,5-SAL,25-
4dr/2ph/fr L

Saunders,Thomas,Garden; see Saltonstall,Leverett,Garden

Ship Chandler's Shop
Federal & North Sts.
HABS MA-291
HABS MASS,5-SAL,32-
7dr/2ph/fr L

Turner-Ingersoll House; see House of the Seven Gables

Turner,John,House; see House of the Seven Gables

Ward,Joshua,House (Washington House)
148 Washington St.
HABS MA-2-57
HABS MASS,5-SAL,19-
11dr/19ph L

Washington House; see Ward,Joshua,House

Water-Bertram House,Fountain
370 Essex St.
HABS MA-803-A
HABS MASS,5-SAL,53A-
1ph/1pc L

Waters-Bertram House (Public Library)
370 Essex St.
HABS MA-803
HABS MASS,5-SAL,53-
1ph/1pg/1pc L

Witch House,The Old; see Corwin,Jonathan,House

SAUGUS

B + M Eastern Route Bridge 9.55; see Saugus River Drawbridge

Boardman House; see Scotch House

Saugus River Drawbridge (B + M Eastern Route Bridge 9.55)
B + M Eastern Route Bridge 9.55
HAER MA-84
45ph/8pg/4pc H

Scotch House (Boardman House)
7 Howard St.
HABS MA-492
HABS MASS,5-SAUG,1-
1dr/2ph L

SWAMPSCOTT

Boston & Maine Railroad:Essex Street Bridge (Eastern Division Bridge No. 22)
Spanning the Boston & Maine Railroad on Essex St.
HAER MA-116
HAER DLC/PP-1992:MA-4
4ph/7pg/1pc/fr L

Eastern Division Bridge No. 22; see Boston & Maine Railroad:Essex Street Bridge

Humphrey,John,House
99 Paradise Rd.
HABS MA-580
HABS MASS,5-SWAM,1-
1ph L

TOPSFIELD

Andrews House
HABS MA-621
HABS MASS,5-TOP,4-
3dr L

Capen,Parson Joseph,House
1 Howlett St.
HABS MA-214
HABS MASS,5-TOP,1-
3dr/6ph/1pg L

Elmwood Mansion
HABS MA-524
HABS MASS,5-TOP,3-
2ph L

WENHAM

Milestones QQ,RR & SS
Bay Rd.
HABS MA-128
HABS MASS,5-WEN,2-
3ph L

FRANKLIN COUNTY

ASHFIELD

Congregational Meetinghouse; see Town Hall

St. John's Episcopal Church
Main St. & Baptist Corner Rd.
HABS MA-648
HABS MASS,6-ASH,2-
5ph/3pg L

Town Hall (Congregational Meetinghouse)
Main St.
HABS MA-436
HABS MASS,6-ASH,1-
6ph/4pg L

BERNARDSTON

Connecticut River RR: Fall River Viaduct
Spanning Fall River
HAER MA-74
HAER 1990 (HAER):8
1ph/1pc L

BUCKLAND

Griswold,Maj. Joseph,House; see Lyon,Mary,House

Lyon,Mary,House (Griswold,Maj. Joseph,House)
Upper St.
HABS MA-108
HABS MASS,6-BUCLA,1-
7dr/4ph L

CHESTER

North Chester Village Bridge (Smith Road Bridge)
Spanning Westfield River on Smith Rd.
HAER MA-97
HAER DLC/PP-1992:MA-4
8ph/10pg/1pc/fr L

Smith Road Bridge; see North Chester Village Bridge

CONWAY

Herrick,Joe,House (Old) (Parsons,Joel,House)
Poland Rd.
HABS MA-2-99
HABS MASS,6-CON,1-
7dr/3ph L

Parsons,Joel,House; see Herrick,Joe,House (Old)

DEERFIELD

Brick Church; see First Church of Deerfield

First Church of Deerfield (Brick Church)
Old Deerfield St.
HABS MA-639
HABS MASS,6-DEER,11-
9dr/10ph/6pg/1pc/fr L

Frary-Barnard House
Old Deerfield St.
HABS MA-628
HABS MASS,6-DEER,14-
2ph/1pg L

DEERFIELD VIC.

Allen House (Fuller Studio)
Bars Rd.
HABS MA-658
HABS MASS,6-DEER.V,2-
7ph/4pg L

Fuller Studio; see Allen House

Locke-Fuller House
Bars Rd.
HABS MA-645
HABS MASS,6-DEER.V,1-
4dr/4ph/4pg L

DEERFIELD VILLAGE

Barnard-Willard House; see Manse,The Old

Dickinson,Capt. Thomas,House
Old Deerfield St.
HABS MA-641
HABS MASS,6-DEER,5-
5dr/5ph/4pg/fr L

Dickinson,David,House (Smith House)
Old Deerfield St.
HABS MA-640
HABS MASS,6-DEER,21-
8dr/5ph/3pg/fr L

First Deerfield Academy; see Memorial Hall

Indian House,Old (Fragments); see Sheldon,John,House (Fragments)

Lyman,Augustus,House (Williams,Bishop John,Birthplace)
Old Deerfield St.
HABS MA-625
HABS MASS,6-DEER,20-
1ph/2pg L

Manse,The Old (Barnard-Willard House)
Old Deerfield St.
HABS MA-626
HABS MASS,6-DEER,6-
1ph/1pg L

Memorial Hall (First Deerfield Academy)
Memorial Rd.
HABS MA-646
HABS MASS,6-DEER,18-
4dr/5ph/5pg/fr L

Nims,Godfrey,House
Old Deerfield St. & Memorial Rd.
HABS MA-647
HABS MASS,6-DEER,15-
5dr/5ph/4pg/fr L

Ray,Benjamin,House
Old Deerfield St.
HABS MA-624
HABS MASS,6-DEER,19-
1ph/2pg L

Sheldon,John,House (Fragments) (Indian House,Old (Fragments))
Memorial Hall Museum
HABS MA-649
HABS MASS,6-DEER,22-
2dr/3ph/18pg L

Smith House; see Dickinson,David,House

Stebbins,Joseph,House
Old Deerfield St.
HABS MA-652
HABS MASS,6-DEER,1-
6ph/3pg L

Wells-Thorn House
Old Deerfield St. & Memorial Rd.
HABS MA-653
HABS MASS,6-DEER,10-
4ph/3pg L

Williams,Bishop John,Birthplace; see Lyman,Augustus,House

Williams,Parson John,House
Albany Rd.
HABS MA-627
HABS MASS,6-DEER,3-
5dr/6ph/4pg/fr L

EAST NORTHFIELD

Alexander,Simeon,House
188 Main St.
HABS MA-662
HABS MASS,6-NORTHE,2-
5ph/3pg L

Colton,Capt. Richard,House
Main St.
HABS MA-660
HABS MASS,6-NORTHE,1-
4ph/2pg L

ERVING

French King Bridge
Spanning Connecticut River on State Hwy. 2
HAER MA-100
HAER DLC/PP-1992:MA-4
12ph/37pg/1pc/fr L

GREENFIELD

Coleman-Hollister House
Bank Row
HABS MA-2-19
HABS MASS,6-GREF,1-
20dr/10ph L

Gould-Potter House
486 Main St.
HABS MA-642
HABS MASS,6-GREF,3-
3dr/7ph/4pg/fr L

Greenfield Public Library; see Leavitt-Hovey House

Leavitt-Hovey House (Greenfield Public Library)
402 Main St.
HABS MA-656
HABS MASS,6-GREF,4-
4ph/3pg L

Newton,Rev. Roger,House
Newton Place (moved from original location)
HABS MA-2-94
HABS MASS,6-GREF,2-
8dr/2ph L

GREENFIELD VIC.

McHard House
U. S. Rt. 5
HABS MA-2-45
HABS MASS,6-GREF.V,2-
1dr/1ph/fr L

MILLVILLE

Blackstone Canal Lock No. 24
East of MA 122
HAER MA-78
HAER 1990 (HAER):8
6ph/1pc L

MONTAGUE

Cabot Station Elec. Generating Plant,Gantry Crane
Montague City Rd.,Turners Falls Vic.
HAER MA-79
HAER 1989(HAER):10
24ph/7pg/3pc L

Eleventh Street Bridge
Spanning the Turners Fall Canal on Eleventh St.
HAER MA-107
HAER DLC/PP-1992:MA-4
8ph/27pg/1pc/fr L

MONTAGUE CITY

Covered Bridge
Spanning Connecticut River
HABS MA-101
HABS MASS,6-MONT,1-
4dr/3ph L

NEW SALEM

Allen,Samuel C.,House
S. Main St.
HABS MA-846
HABS MASS,6-NESAL,1-
5ph/1pc L

NORTHFIELD

Hall-Spring House
89 Main St.
HABS MA-643
HABS MASS,6-NORTH,2-
6ph/3pg L

Lane,Capt. Samuel,House
33 Main St.
HABS MA-661
HABS MASS,6-NORTH,6-
5ph/3pg L

Mattoon,Isaac,House
26 Main St.
HABS MA-659
HABS MASS,6-NORTH,5-
5ph/3pg L

Pomery,William,House
Main St.
HABS MA-654
HABS MASS,6-NORTH,3-
5ph/3pg L

Schell Memorial Bridge
Spanning Connecticut River on East Northfield Rd.
HAER MA-111
HAER DLC/PP-1992:MA-4
8ph/41pg/1pc/fr L

Stratton House
HABS MA-476
HABS MASS,6-NORTH,1-
2ph L

White-Field House
Main & Maple Sts.
HABS MA-655
HABS MASS,6-NORTH,4-
6ph/3pg L

NORTHFIELD VIC.

Chalet Schell
HABS MA-1134
HABS MASS,6-NORTH.V,1-
7ph/1pc L

RIVERSIDE

Red House,The Old
French King Hwy. (Riverside)
HABS MA-2-60
HABS MASS,6-RIVSI,1-
5dr/4ph L

SHELBURNE

Arms House
Shelburne-Colrain Rd.
HABS MA-493
HABS MASS,6-SHELB,1-
2ph L

Bardwell,Daniel P.,Ash House
Bardwell's Ferry Rd.
HABS MA-691
HABS MASS,6-SHELB,3-
1ph L

Bardwell,Daniel P.,House
Bardwell's Ferry Rd.
HABS MA-657
HABS MASS,6-SHELB,2-
10ph/4pg L

Bardwell's Ferry Bridge
Spanning Deerfield River on Bardwell's Ferry Rd.
HAER MA-98
HAER DLC/PP-1992:MA-4
6dr/19ph/29pg/2pc/fr L

Shelburne Falls Bridge
Spanning the Deerfield River on Bridge St.
HAER MA-96
HAER DLC/PP-1992:MA-4
12ph/24pg/1pc/fr L

SOUTH DEERFIELD

Wapping School
Greenfield Rd.
HABS MA-2-81
HABS MASS,6-DEERS,2-
1dr/1ph L

WEST NORTHFIELD

Belding,Elijah E.,House
Mt. Hermon Station Rd.
HABS MA-635
HABS MASS,6-NORTHW,1-
5ph/3pg L

HAMPDEN COUNTY

AGAWAM

Allen House
HABS MA-1125
HABS MASS,7-AGAM,4-
2ph/2pg/1pc L

Colton-Cooley House; see Cooley,Isaac,House

Cooley,Isaac,House (Colton-Cooley House; King,Martin,Inn)
740 Elm St.
HABS MA-2-51
HABS MASS,7-AGAM,2-
8dr/2ph L

King,Martin,Inn; see Cooley,Isaac,House

Leonard,Capt. Charles,House
663 Main St.
HABS MA-2-50
HABS MASS,7-AGAM,1-
14dr/3ph/fr L

Tobacco Barn
663 Main St.
HABS MA-151
HABS MASS,7-AGAM,3-
1dr/1ph L

BLANDFORD

First Congregational Church (Old White Church)
North St.
HABS MA-1237
HABS 1989(HABS):10
9ph/1pg/1pc L

Old White Church; see First Congregational Church

BRIMFIELD

Chamberlain House
HABS MA-311
HABS MASS,7-BRIMF,1-
4ph/1pc/fr L

CHESTER

Bascom,Rev. Aaron,House
Middlefield Rd.
HABS MA-112
HABS MASS,7-CHES,1-
6dr/7ph L

CHICOPEE

Chicopee City Hall (City Hall,Old)
Market Square
HABS MA-201
HABS MASS,7-CHICO,1-
6ph/4pg/1pc L

City Hall,Old; see Chicopee City Hall

GRANVILLE

Curtis Tavern
State Rt. 57
HABS MA-221
HABS MASS,7-GRANV,1-
5ph/1pc/fr L

Scott House
State Rt. 57
HABS MA-1135
HABS MASS,7-GRANV,2-
2ph/1pc L

HOLYOKE

Holyoke Bridge
Spng Connecticut Riv,btn Holyoke & S. Hadley Falls
HAER MA-18
HAER MASS,7-HOLYO,1-
2dr/27ph/20pg/3pc L

LONGMEADOW

Colton,Capt. Gideon,House
1028 Longmeadow St.
HABS MA-2-36
HABS MASS,7-LONGM,1-
13dr/8ph L

Field,Col. Alexander,House
280 Longmeadow St.
HABS MA-173
HABS MASS,7-LONGM,2-
14dr/9ph/fr L

LUDLOW-WILBRAHAM

Covered Bridge
Spanning Chicopee River
HABS MA-497
HABS MASS,7-LUDLO.V,1-
2ph L

NORTH BROOKFIELD

Potter,Capt. John,House
(moved to MA,West Springfield)
HABS MA-852
HABS MASS,7-SPRIFW,3-
13ph/1pg/1pc L

PALMER

Boston and Albany Railroad Station
HABS MA-664
HABS MASS,7-PALM,1-
4ph/3pg L

Day & Night Diner
456 N. Main St.
HABS MA-1231
HABS 1989(HABS):10
10ph/1pg/1pc L

RUSSELL

Woronoco Bridge
Spanning the Westfield River on Bridge St.
HAER MA-113
HAER DLC/PP-1992:MA-4
9ph/10pg/1pc/fr L

SPRINGFIELD

Alexander House
HABS MA-406
HABS MASS,7-SPRIF,1-
17ph L

Boston Road (Milestone)
HABS MA-407
HABS MASS,7-SPRIF,2-
1ph L

Church of the Unity
207 State St.
HABS MA-637
HABS MASS,7-SPRIF,3-
6ph/8pg L

Daigle Apartment House; see Outing Park

Hollywood; see Outing Park

Janisheffski Apartment House; see Outing Park

Laboeuf Apartment House; see Outing Park

Mills-Stebbins House
3 Crescent Hill
HABS MA-973
HABS MASS,7-SPRIF,5-
11dr/23ph/2pc/fr L

Moineau Building; see Outing Park

Morin Apartment House; see Outing Park

Outing Park (Daigle Apartment House)
60 Saratoga St.
HABS MA-1136-C
HABS MASS,7-SPRIF,6C-
2ph/7pg/1pc L

Outing Park (Hollywood)
Bounded by Adams,Richelieu,Marble, & Main Sts.
HABS MA-1136
HABS MASS,7-SPRIF,6-
10ph/15pg/1pc L

Outing Park (Janisheffski Apartment House)
70 Saratoga St.
HABS MA-1136-D
HABS MASS,7-SPRIF,6D-
3ph/8pg/1pc L

Outing Park (Laboeuf Apartment House)
102-104 Oswego St.
HABS MA-1136-H
HABS MASS,7-SPRIF,6H-
3ph/8pg/1pc L

Outing Park (Moineau Building)
693-697 Main St. & 16 Saratoga St.
HABS MA-1136-A
HABS MASS,7-SPRIF,6A-
7ph/8pg/1pc L

Outing Park (Morin Apartment House)
54 Saratoga St.
HABS MA-1136-B
HABS MASS,7-SPRIF,6B-
2ph/7pg/1pc L

Outing Park (Pawlowicz Apartment House)
78 Saratoga St.
HABS MA-1136-E
HABS MASS,7-SPRIF,6E-
3ph/8pg/1pc L

Outing Park (Prefontaine Apartment House)
257 Dwight St. extension & 55 Saratoga St.
HABS MA-1136-G
HABS MASS,7-SPRIF,6G-
3ph/8pg/1pc L

Outing Park (Provost Apartment House)
47 Richelieu St.
HABS MA-1136-I
HABS MASS,7-SPRIF,6I-
3ph/8pg/1pc L

Outing Park (Sullivan Apartment House)
82-84 Saratoga St.
HABS MA-1136-F
HABS MASS,7-SPRIF,6F-
4ph/8pg/1pc L

Pawlowicz Apartment House; see Outing Park

Prefontaine Apartment House; see Outing Park

Provost Apartment House; see Outing Park

Springfield City Hall; see Springfield Municipal Group

Springfield Municipal Group (Springfield City Hall)
36 Court St.
HABS MA-1172
HABS MASS,7-SPRIF,4-
9ph/4pg/1pc/fr L

Sullivan Apartment House; see Outing Park

WEST BROOKFIELD

Gilbert,Levi & Peletiah,House
(moved to MA,West Springfield)
HABS MA-850
HABS MASS,7-SPRIFW,4-
3ph/1pc L

WEST SPRINGFIELD

Atkinson,John,Tavern
Exposition Grounds (moved from MA,Prescott)
HABS MA-844
HABS MASS,7-SPRIFW,5-
3ph/1pc L

Chesterfield Blacksmith Shop
Exposition Grounds (moved from NH,Chester)
HABS NH-41
HABS NH,3-CHEST,1-
L

Day,Josiah,House
Park Street Museum
HABS MA-634
HABS MASS,7-SPRIFW,2-
4dr/fr L

Eddy,Zachariah,Law Office
Exposition Grounds (moved from MA,Middleboro)
HABS MA-851
HABS MASS,7-SPRIFW,6-
1ph/1pc L

Gilbert,Levi & Peletiah,House
Exposition Grounds (moved from MA,W. Brookfield)
HABS MA-850
HABS MASS,7-SPRIFW,4-
3ph/1pc L

Meetinghouse
HABS MA-630
HABS MASS,7-SPRIFW,
1ph L

Potter,Capt. John,House
Exposition Grounds (moved from MA,N. Brookfield)
HABS MA-852
HABS MASS,7-SPRIFW,3-
13ph/1pg/1pc L

Salisbury Meetinghouse
Exposition Grounds (moved from NH,Salisbury)
HABS MA-843
HABS MASS,7-SPRIFW,7-
1ph/1pc L

Schoolhouse,Little Red
Eastern States Exposition Grounds
HABS MA-293
HABS MASS,7-SPRIFW,8-
1ph/1pc L

WESTFIELD

Arnold House
140 Franklin St.
HABS MA-2-35
HABS MASS,7-WESFI,1-
3dr/1ph L

Fowler,Albert,Tobacco Barn; see Tobacco Barn

Tobacco Barn (Fowler,Albert,Tobacco Barn)
South St. Ext.
HABS MA-103
HABS MASS,7-WESFI,2-
1dr/1ph/fr L

HAMPSHIRE COUNTY

AMHERST

Amherst College,Lawrence Observatory (The Octagn; The Woods Cabinet)
Rt. 116
HABS MA-1233
HABS 1989(HABS):10
6ph/1pg/1pc L

Boltwood-Stockbridge House
University of Massachusetts Campus
HABS MA-636
HABS MASS,8-AM,1-
4ph/4pg L

Strong,Nehemiah,House
67 Amity St.
HABS MA-650
HABS MASS,8-AM,2-
5ph/3pg L

The Octagn; see Amherst College,Lawrence Observatory

The Woods Cabinet; see Amherst College,Lawrence Observatory

CUMMINGTON

Bryant,William Cullen,Homestead
HABS MA-1260
5dr/15pg H

EASTHAMPTON

Easthampton Town Hall
43 Main St.
HABS MA-1232
HABS 1989(HABS):10
7ph/1pg/1pc L

GRANBY

Aldrich Mill
54 Aldrich St.
HABS MA-1229
HABS 1989(HABS):10
8ph/1pg/1pc L

HADLEY

Huntington House
(Porter-Phelps-Huntington House)
State Rt. 47
HABS MA-361
HABS MASS,8-HAD,7-
10ph/fr L

Keefe,John,Tobacco Barns; see Tobacco Barns

Porter Store,Old
Old Hadley St.
HABS MA-158
HABS MASS,8-HAD,6-
3dr/1ph L

Porter-Phelps-Huntington House; see Huntington House

Porter,Samuel,House
West St.
HABS MA-2-53
HABS MASS,8-HAD,3-
11dr/5ph L

Tobacco Barns (Keefe,John,Tobacco Barns)
Old Hadley St.
HABS MA-113
HABS MASS,8-HAD,5-
1dr/1ph/fr L

HATFIELD

Billings,Cornelia,House
HABS MA-454
HABS MASS,8-HAT,4-
2ph L

Billings,Lieut. David,House
77 Main St.
HABS MA-166
HABS MASS,8-HAT,3-
11dr/3ph/fr L

Morton House (Partridge,Cotton,House)
Bridge Ln. & Lower Main St.
HABS MA-2-73
HABS MASS,8-HAT,1-
6dr/2ph/fr L

Partridge,Cotton,House; see Morton House

NORTHAMPTON

Allen House
HABS MA-474
HABS MASS,8-NORTH,3-
2ph L

Bay State Bridge (Clement Street Bridge)
Spanning the Mill River on Clement St.
HAER MA-110
HAER DLC/PP-1992:MA-4
3ph/9pg/1pc/fr L

Boston & Maine RR:Northampton Lattice Truss Bridge
HAER MA-55
HAER MASS,8-NORTH,6-
16ph/1pg/1pc/8ct L

Clement Street Bridge; see Bay State Bridge

Damons,Isaac,House
46 Bridge St.
HABS MA-638
HABS MASS,8-NORTH,4-
5ph/4pg L

Hubbard House; see Parsons,Lt. William House

Hunt-Brewster House
18 Old South St.
HABS MA-644
HABS MASS,8-NORTH,5-
5ph/3pg L

Parsons,Lt. William House (Hubbard House)
392 Bridge St. (moved to CT,Darien)
HABS MA-188
HABS MASS,8-NORTH,2-
17dr/3pg/fr L

PELHAM

Charcoal Kilns
Valley Rd.
HABS MA-2-72
HABS MASS,8-PEL,1-
1dr/4ph L

PRESCOTT

Atkinson,John,Tavern
(moved to MA,Springfield Vic.)
HABS MA-844
HABS MASS,7-SPRIFW,5-
3ph/1pc L

Enfield Road (Schoolhouse)
HABS MA-2-98
HABS MASS,8-PRESC,1-
2dr/1ph L

Schoolhouse,Old Red
Cooleyville Rd.
HABS MA-193
HABS MASS,8-PRESC,2-
2dr/2ph/fr L

SOUTH HADLEY

Woodbridge,Col. Ruggles,House
26 Woodbridge St.
HABS MA-180
HABS MASS,8-HADS,1-
18dr/8ph/fr L

Wright House
96 College St.
HABS MA-182
HABS MASS,8-HADS,2-
8dr/3ph/fr L

WESTHAMPTON

Hunt,Capt. Jared,House
HABS MA-413
HABS MASS,8-WESHA,1-
4ph/fr L

WILLIAMSBURG

Greek Revival House; see Josiah Hayden House

Josiah Hayden House (Greek Revival House)
127 Main St.
HABS MA-1234
HABS 1989(HABS):10
11ph/1pg/1pc L

WORTHINGTON

Woodbridge,Jonathan,House
Four Corners
HABS MA-124
HABS MASS,8-WORTH,1-
21dr/fr L

MIDDLESEX COUNTY

ACTON

Faulkner House
High St.
HABS MA-543
HABS MASS,9-ACT,1-
5ph L

ARLINGTON

Calvary Methodist Episcopal Church,Tower
Mass. Ave. (moved from Boylston Market,Boston)
HABS MA-589
HABS MA,9-ARL,3-
1ph L

Russell,Jason,House
7 Jason St. (moved from original site)
HABS MA-588
HABS MASS,9-ARL,2-
1ph L

Schwamb Mill
17 Mill Lane
HAER MA-12
HAER MASS,9-ARL,4-
10dr/38ph/42pg/fr L

ARLINGTON HEIGHTS

Milestone
Paul Revere Rd.
HABS MA-1181
HABS MASS,9-ARL,5-
1ph/1pc L

ASHBY

Fitch,John,House; see Kendall,Asa,House

Kendall,Asa,House (Fitch,John,House)
South Rd.
HABS MA-230
HABS MASS,9-ASHBY,1-
9dr/1ph/fr L

ASHLAND

Frankland,Sir Henry,Garden
Old Bay Path
HABS MA-202
HABS MASS,9-ASHLA,1-
1dr/fr L

AUBURNDALE

Boston and Albany Railroad Station
HABS MA-665
HABS MASS,9-AUB,1-
5ph/3pg L

BEDFORD

Meetinghouse of First Parish (Unitarian)
HABS MA-538
HABS MASS,9-BED,1-
4ph L

Penniman-Stearns House (Stearns House)
State Rt. 62
HABS MA-592
HABS MASS,9-BED,2-
5ph L

Pollard Tavern
Great Rd.
HABS MA-142
HABS MASS,9-BED,5-
10dr/2ph/fr L

Stearns House; see Penniman-Stearns House

BEDFORD VIC.

Garrison House,Old
Bedford Springs
HABS MA-539
HABS MASS,9-BED,6-
1ph L

BELMONT

Boston & Maine Railroad:Clark Street Bridge
Spanning Boston & Maine Railroad on Clark St.
HAER MA-94
HAER DLC/:1992:MA-4
5ph/8pg/1pc L

BILLERICA

Allen Tavern
HABS MA-528
HABS MASS,9-BIL,5-
1ph L

Bowers,Dr. William,House
HABS MA-530
HABS MASS,9-BIL,3-
2ph L

First Parish Unitarian Church
HABS MA-529
HABS MASS,9-BIL,2-
2ph L

Locke,Hon. Joseph,House
HABS MA-531
HABS MASS,9-BIL,6-
1ph L

Manning,Ensign Samuel,Manse
Chelmsford Rd.
HABS MA-532
HABS MASS,9-BIL,1-
2ph L

Schoolhouse,Little Red
HABS MA-591
HABS MASS,9-BIL,7-
1ph L

BURLINGTON

Winn,William H.,House
New Bridge Ave. & Winn St.
HABS MA-199
HABS MASS,9-BURL,1-
10dr/7ph/fr L

Wyman,Francis,House
Francis Wyman Rd.
HABS MA-298
HABS MASS,9-BURL,2-
11dr/5ph/fr L

CAMBRIDGE

Abbot,Edwin H.,House (Longy School of Music)
1 Follen St.
HABS MA-1037
HABS MASS,9-CAMB,39-
11ph/7pg/1pc L

22 Appian Way (House)
HABS MA-782
HABS MASS,9-CAMB,24-
1ph L

Baldwin,Maria,House
196 Prospect St.
HABS MA-1086
HABS MASS,9-CAMB,40-
2ph/4pg/1pc L

Batchelder,Francis,House
467 Cambridge St.
HABS MA-884
HABS MASS,9-CAMB,41-
6ph/1pg/1pc L

Bates,Moses,House
69 Thorndike St.
HABS MA-876
HABS MASS,9-CAMB,42-
3ph/1pg/1pc L

Brattle,Gen. William,House
42 Brattle St.
HABS MA-274
HABS MASS,9-CAMB,9-
8ph L

Cambridge City Hall
795 Massachusetts Ave.
HABS MA-1038
HABS MASS,9-CAMB,35-
6ph/5pg/1pc L

Cambridge Junior College; see Kelley,Stillman F.,House

1667 Cambridge Street (Apartment House)
HABS MA-879
HABS MASS,9-CAMB,37-
7ph/1pg/1pc L

Carey,Arthur Astor,House
28 Fayerweather St.
HABS MA-1039
HABS MASS,9-CAMB,15-
6ph/9pg L

Christ Church
Garden St.
HABS MA-2-3
HABS MASS,9-CAMB,4-
8dr/4ph/1pc L

Coburn,Sara,House
7 Dana St.
HABS MA-871
HABS MASS,9-CAMB,43-
4ph/1pg/1pc L

Deane,Ezra,House
21-23 Fayette St.
HABS MA-864
HABS MASS,9-CAMB,44-
5ph/1pg/1pc L

Dodge,Edward S.,House
70 Sparks St.
HABS MA-1015
HABS MASS,9-CAMB,16-
12ph/7pg L

Dunster,The (Harvard University,Dudley Hall)
Dunster St.
HABS MA-818
HABS MASS,9-CAMB,45-
3ph/3pg/1pc L

Eight-mile Stones (Milestones JJ,KK)
Mass. Ave. & Garden St.
HABS MA-128
HABS MASS,9-CAMB,12-
2dr/2ph L

Episcopal Theo. School,St. John's Memorial Chapel
99 Brattle St.
HABS MA-1016
HABS MASS,9-CAMB,46-
2ph/8pg/1pc L

Episcopal Theological School,Burnham Hall (Episcopal Theological School,Old Refectory)
99 Brattle St.
HABS MA-1137
HABS MASS,9-CAMB,47-
4pg L

Episcopal Theological School,Lawrence Hall
99 Brattle St.
HABS MA-1177
HABS MASS,9-CAMB,48-
6pg L

Episcopal Theological School,Old Refectory; see Episcopal Theological School,Burnham Hall

Episcopal Theological School,Quadrangle
99 Brattle St.
HABS MA-1079
HABS MASS,9-CAMB,49-
2ph/1pc L

Episcopal Theological School,Reed Hall
99 Brattle St.
HABS MA-863
HABS MASS,9-CAMB,50-
2ph/6pg/1pc L

First Baptist Church
5 Magazine St.
HABS MA-1017
HABS MASS,9-CAMB,51-
6ph/10pg/1pc L

First Evangelical Congregational Church (Prospect Congregational Church; Prospect Street Church)
99 Prospect St.
HABS MA-1030
HABS MASS,9-CAMB,17-
6ph/9pg L

Fiske,John,House
22 Berkeley St.
HABS MA-1018
HABS MASS,9-CAMB,18-
6ph/9pg L

Flagstaff Park
Mass. Ave. & Kirkland St.
HABS MA-999
HABS MASS,9-CAMB,34-
16ph/5pg/2pc/fr L

Ford Motor Company Assembly Plant
640 Memorial Dr.
HAER MA-30
HAER MASS,9-CAMB,36-
1ph/1pg/1pc L

Fort Washington
Waverly St.
HABS MA-2-48
HABS MASS,9-CAMB,5-
3dr/2ph L

Garden House (Gray,Asa,House)
88 Garden St.
HABS MA-1019
HABS MASS,9-CAMB,52-
6ph/9pg/1pc L

Gray,Asa,House; see Garden House

Greenough House
42 Quincy St.
HABS MA-1020
HABS MASS,9-CAMB,19-
5ph/7pg L

Guyot-Horsford House & Stable
27 Craigie St.
HABS MA-1021
HABS MASS,9-CAMB,20-
4ph/7pg L

Harvard College,Holden Chapel
Harvard Yard
HABS MA-2-1
HABS MASS,9-CAMB,3C-
5dr/2ph L

Harvard College,Hollis Hall
Harvard Yard
HABS MA-2-2
HABS MASS,9-CAMB,3D-
10dr/3ph L

Harvard University,Dudley Hall; see Dunster,The

Harvard University,Lawrence Hall
3 Kirkland St.
HABS MA-1022
HABS MASS,9-CAMB,21-
3ph/8pg L

Higginson,Stephen Jr.,House
7 Kirkland St.
HABS MA-840
HABS MASS,9-CAMB,22-
6ph L

Higginson,Thomas Wentworth,House
29 Buckingham St.
HABS MA-1023
HABS MASS,9-CAMB,23-
5ph/6pg L

Houghton,Amory,House
61 Otis St.
HABS MA-865
HABS MASS,9-CAMB,53-
3ph/1pg/1pc L

Hoyt,Benjamin,House
134 Otis St.
HABS MA-866
HABS MASS,9-CAMB,54-
1ph/1pg/1pc L

Hyatt,Alpheus,House
19 Francis Ave.
HABS MA-883
HABS MASS,9-CAMB,55-
6ph/1pg/1pc L

Ireland,Abraham,Gravestone (Stone LL)
Mass. Ave. & Garden St.
HABS MA-128
HABS MASS,9-CAMB,11-
1ph L

James,William,House
95 Irving St.
HABS MA-1024
HABS MASS,9-CAMB,25-
3ph/7pg L

Kelley,Stillman F.,House (Cambridge Junior College)
49 Washington Ave.
HABS MA-1025
HABS MASS,9-CAMB,26-
9ph/7pg L

Longfellow House & Garden; see Vassall-Craigie-Longfellow House & Garden

Longfellow National Historic Site; see Vassall-Craigie-Longfellow House & Garden

Longy School of Music; see Abbot,Edwin H.,House

MacKay,Frances M.,House
10 Follen St.
HABS MA-1026
HABS MASS,9-CAMB,27-
6ph/9pg L

Mass. Institute of Tech.,Kresge Auditorium
Massachusetts Ave. at Amherst St.
HABS MA-1217
HABS 1989(HABS):10
6ph/1pg/1pc L

Melendy,Henry,House
81 Washington Ave.
HABS MA-1027
HABS MASS,9-CAMB,28-
4ph/7pg L

Middlesex County Jailer's House
50 Thorndike St.
HABS MA-873
HABS MASS,9-CAMB,56-
2ph/1pg/1pc L

Middlesex County Registry of Deeds
Third & Cambridge Sts.
HABS MA-877
HABS MASS,9-CAMB,57-
5ph/1pc L

Middlesex County Superior Court Building
Third,Otis & Thorndike Sts.
HABS MA-1028
HABS MASS,9-CAMB,58-
6ph/8pg/1pc L

Milestones JJ,KK; see Eight-mile Stones

MIT,Ashdown House; see Riverbank Court

Mount Auburn Cemetery,Bigelow Chapel
580 Mount Auburn St.
HABS MA-1216-A
HABS 1989(HABS):10
8ph/1pg/1pc L

Mount Auburn Cemetery,Main Gate
580 Mount Auburn St.
HABS MA-1216
HABS 1989(HABS):10
13ph/1pg/1pc L

Mount Auburn Cemetery,Sphinx
580 Mount Auburn St.
HABS MA-1216-B
HABS 1989(HABS):10
3ph/1pg/1pc L

Norton-Johnson-Burleigh House
85 Brattle St.
HABS MA-886
HABS MASS,9-CAMB,59-
6ph/1pg/1pc L

Parsons-Warner House (Parsons,Sabra,House; Radcliffe College,Warner House)
63 Garden St.
HABS MA-1029
HABS MASS,9-CAMB,29-
4ph/8pg L

Parsons,Sabra,House; see Parsons-Warner House

Prospect Congregational Church; see First Evangelical Congregational Church

Documentation: **ct** color transparencies **dr** measured drawings **fr** field records
pc photograph captions **pg** pages of text **ph** photographs

Prospect Street Church; see First Evangelical Congregational Church

Radcliffe College,Warner House; see Parsons-Warner House

Riverbank Court (MIT,Ashdown House)
305 Memorial Drive
HABS MA-1031
HABS MASS,9-CAMB,30-
5ph/9pg L

Saunders,Charles,House
1627 Massachusetts Ave.
HABS MA-870
HABS MASS,9-CAMB,60-
8ph/1pg/1pc L

Sewall,Stephen,House
13 DeWolfe St.
HABS MA-618
HABS MASS,9-CAMB,13-
2dr L

84-92 Spring Street (Row Houses)
HABS MA-867
HABS MASS,9-CAMB,38-
3ph/1pg/1pc L

St. James Church
1991 Massachusetts Ave.
HABS MA-1032
HABS MASS,9-CAMB,31-
3ph/8pg L

Stevens-Hovey House
(Stevens,Atherton,House)
75 Winter St.
HABS MA-885
HABS MASS,9-CAMB,61-
4ph/1pg/1pc L

Stevens,Atherton,House; see Stevens-Hovey House

Stone LL; see Ireland,Abraham,Gravestone

Stoughton,Mary Fiske,House
90 Brattle St.
HABS MA-1033
HABS MASS,9-CAMB,62-
10ph/8pg/1pc L

Taylor,Charles,House & Stable
1105 Massachusetts Ave.
HABS MA-1034
HABS MASS,9-CAMB,32-
3ph/7pg L

Thorpe,Annie Longfellow,House
115 Brattle St.
HABS MA-875
HABS MASS,9-CAMB,63-
8ph/1pg/1pc L

Treadwell-Sparks House
48 Quincy St. (moved to 21 Kirkland St.)
HABS MA-869
HABS MASS,9-CAMB,64-
5ph/1pg/1pc L

Valentine-Fuller House & Garden
125 Prospect St.
HABS MA-283
HABS MASS,9-CAMB,10-
1dr/10ph/10pg L

Van Brunt,Henry,House
167 Brattle St.
HABS MA-874
HABS MASS,9-CAMB,65-
4ph/1pg/1pc L

Vassall-Craigie-Longfellow House & Garden (Longfellow House & Garden; Longfellow National Historic Site)
105 Brattle St.
HABS MA-169
HABS MASS,9-CAMB,1-
ı1991(HABS):15°
25dr/26ph/fr L

Watson,Daniel,House
5 Russell St.
HABS MA-868
HABS MASS,9-CAMB,66-
3ph/1pg/1pc L

Welch-Ross House
24 Craigie St.
HABS MA-1035
HABS MASS,9-CAMB,33-
5ph/9pg L

Whittemore,George Washington,House
329 Harvard St.
HABS MA-881
HABS MASS,9-CAMB,14-
11ph/11pg L

Wood-Boyd House
33 Linnaean St.
HABS MA-880
HABS MASS,9-CAMB,67-
3ph/1pg/1pc L

Wyeth-Allyn House
5 Berkeley St.
HABS MA-1036
HABS MASS,9-CAMB,68-
3ph/8pg/1pc L

CARLISLE

Unitarian Church
HABS MA-537
HABS MASS,9-CARL,1-
1ph L

CHELMSFORD

First Congregational Church
HABS MA-601
HABS MASS,9-CHELM,2-
1ph L

Fiske House
Littleton St. & Billerica Rd.
HABS MA-318
HABS MASS,9-CHELM,6-
7ph L

CONCORD

Alcott House; see Orchard House

Ball,Caleb,House; see Wayside,The

Bank Building,Old
Main St.
HABS MA-2-4
HABS MASS,9-CON,8-
5dr/1ph L

Brooks,Samuel,House (Minute Man National Historical Park)
North Great Rd. (State Rt. 2A)
HABS MA-819
HABS MASS,9-CON,12-
7dr/4ph/4pg/1pc/fr L

Brown,Reuben,House; see Bulkeley,Peter,House

Bulkeley,Peter,House
(Brown,Reuben,House)
27 Lexington Rd.
HABS MA-791
HABS MASS,9-CON,13-
5ph/4pg/1pc L

Bullet-Hole House; see Jones,Elisha,House

Buttrick,Maj. John,Carriage House
Minute Man National Historic Park
HABS MA-1146-A
HABS MASS,9-CON,14A-
2ph/1pc L

Buttrick,Maj. John,House
Liberty St.,Minute Man Nat'l Historical Park
HABS MA-1146
HABS MASS,9-CON,14-
3dr/10ph/1pc/fr L

Emerson,Rev. William,House; see Manse,Old

Hunt-Hosmer Barn (Minute Man National Historical Park)
Lowell Rd.
HABS MA-821
HABS MASS,9-CON,16-
5dr/3ph/3pg/1pc/fr L

Hunt-Hosmer House
Lowell Rd.
HABS MA-820
HABS MASS,9-CON,15-
3ph/3pg/1pc L

Jones-Keyes House; see Jones,Elisha,House

Jones,Elisha,House (Bullet-Hole House; Jones-Keyes House; Minute Man National Historical Park)
26 Monument St.
HABS MA-555
HABS
MASS,9-CON,11-(DLC/PP-1992:MA-5)
8ph/2pc L

Manse,Old (Emerson,Rev. William,House; Minute Man National Historical Park)
Monument St.
HABS MA-554
HABS MASS,9-CON,3-
7ph/4pg/1pc L

Meriam House (Minute Man National Historical Park)
Meriam's Corner
HABS MA-822
HABS MASS,9-CON,17-
1ph/1pc L

Minute Man National Historical Park; see Brooks,Samuel,House

Minute Man National Historical Park; see Hunt-Hosmer Barn

Minute Man National Historical Park; see Jones,Elisha,House

Minute Man National Historical Park; see Manse,Old

Minute Man National Historical Park; see Meriam House

Minute Man National Historical Park; see Stowe,Widow,House

Minute Man National Historical Park; see Taylor,Daniel,House

Minute Man National Historical Park; see Wayside,The

Orchard House (Alcott House)
Lexington Rd.
HABS MA-552
HABS MASS,9-CON,4-
1ph L

Stowe,Nathaniel,House; see Stowe,Widow,House

Stowe,Widow,House
(Stowe,Nathaniel,House; Minute Man National Historical Park)
Lexington Rd.
HABS MA-794
HABS MASS,9-CON,18-(DLC/PP-1992:MA-5)
4ph/2pc L

Taylor,Daniel,House (Minute Man National Historical Park)
663 Lexington Rd.
HABS MA-792
HABS MASS,9-CON,19-(DLC/PP-1992:MA-5)
10dr/8ph/3pc/fr L

Wayside,The (Ball,Caleb,House; Whitney,Samuel,House; Minute Man National Historical Park)
Lexington Rd.
HABS MA-551
HABS MASS,9-CON,9-
7dr/30ph/4pg/2pc/fr L

Whitney,Samuel,House; see Wayside,The

Wright Tavern
2 Lexington Rd.
HABS MA-553
HABS MASS,9-CON,10-
6dr/11ph/1pc/fr L

EAST LEXINGTON

Building,Stone (Cary Memorial Library)
1874 Massachusetts Ave.
HABS MA-605
HABS MASS,9-LEXE,2-
2ph L

Cary Memorial Library; see Building,Stone

Follen Church (Unitarian) (Octagon Church)
HABS MA-590
HABS MASS,9-LEXE,1-
1ph L

Octagon Church; see Follen Church (Unitarian)

FRAMINGHAM

Boston and Albany Railroad Station
Waverly St.
HABS MA-666
HABS MASS,9-FRAM,10-
5ph/3pg L

Eames,Jonathan,House (House,Old Red)
Union Ave.
HABS MA-324
HABS MASS,9-FRAM,6-
3ph/fr L

First Baptist Church & Carriage Shed
HABS MA-320
HABS MASS,9-FRAM,5-
3ph L

Framingham Academy
Vernon & Grove Sts.
HABS MA-2-16
HABS MASS,9-FRAM,1-
3dr/1ph L

Gates House & Elm
Gates St.
HABS MA-286
HABS MASS,9-FRAM,4-
1ph L

House,Old Red; see Eames,Jonathan,House

Howe-Gregory House
Wayside Inn Rd.
HABS MA-238
HABS MASS,9-FRAM,2-
3ph/fr L

Kellogg House
Kellogg St.
HABS MA-359
HABS MASS,9-FRAM,7-
5ph/fr L

Milestone
Worcester Turnpike
HABS MA-1182
HABS MASS,9-FRAM,11-
1ph/1pc L

Milestones PP & XXX
HABS MA-128
HABS MASS,9-FRAM,9-
2ph L

Nixon,Col. Thomas,House
881 Edmands Rd.
HABS MA-247
HABS MASS,9-FRAM,3-
1ph/fr L

Pike-Haven-Foster House
Grove & Belknap Sts.
HABS MA-616
HABS MASS,9-FRAM,8-
7dr/3ph L

GROTON

Groton School
HABS MA-1148
HABS MASS,9-GROT,4-
1ph/1pc L

Milestone
Main St.
HABS MA-1183
HABS MASS,9-GROT,5-
1ph/1pc L

Milestone
Main St.
HABS MA-1184
HABS MASS,9-GROT,6-
1ph/1pc L

Prescott,Dr. Oliver,Milestones
Farmers Row & Main St.
HABS MA-203
HABS MASS,9-GROT,2-
7dr/6ph/fr L

Robbins,Andrew,House
HABS MA-603
HABS MASS,9-GROT,3-
2ph L

HOLLISTON

Boston & Worcester RR:Bogastow Brook Viaduct
Spanning Bogastow Brook at Woodland Ave.
HAER MA-48
HAER MASS,9-HOLST,1-
2ph/1pg/1pc L

Goodwill Shoe Company Factory
(Williams,Arthur A. ,Shoe Factory)
26-28 Water St.
HAER MA-51
HAER MASS,9-HOLST,2-
1ph/1pg/1pc L

Williams,Arthur A. ,Shoe Factory; see Goodwill Shoe Company Factory

HOPKINTON

Framingham Moto Parts; see Hopkinton Supply Company Building

Hopkinton Supply Company Building
(Framingham Moto Parts)
26-28 Main St. (corner of Wolcott St.)
HABS MA-1227
HABS 1989(HABS):10
6ph/1pg/1pc L

LAWRENCE

South Canal Bridge
South Broadway Vic.
HAER MA-11
5ph/fr H

LEXINGTON

Buckman Tavern
Bedford St.
HABS MA-547
HABS MASS,9-LEX,1-
9dr/3ph/1pc/fr L

Fiske,Ebenezer,House Site (Minute Man National Historical Park)
Massachusetts Ave.
HABS MA-1149
HABS MASS,9-LEX,17-
1dr L

Hancock-Clarke House
35 Hancock St.
HABS MA-549
HABS MASS,9-LEX,2-
7dr/4ph/1pc/fr L

Hargrove Barn
Massachusetts Ave.,Minute Man Nat'l Historic Park
HABS MA-1150
HABS MASS,9-LEX,19-
1dr/4ph/1pc/fr L

Harrington,Jonathan Jr.,House
Elm & Bedford Sts.
HABS MA-548
HABS MASS,9-LEX,6-
1ph L

Lexington & West Cambridge RR:Lexington Depot
Depot Sq.
HAER MA-21
HAER MASS,9-LEX,16-
3ph/2pg/1pc L

Minute Man National Historical Park; see Fiske,Ebenezer,House Site

Minute Man National Historical Park; see Whittemore,Jacob,House

Munroe Tavern
1332 Massachusetts Ave.
HABS MA-550
HABS MASS,9-LEX,3-
7dr/3ph/1pc/fr L

Muzzey,John,House; see Whittemore,Jacob,House

Robbins-Stone House
699 Massachusetts Ave.
HABS MA-609
HABS MASS,9-LEX,14-
5dr L

Town Office Building
1625 Massachusetts Ave.
HABS MA-1174
HABS MASS,9-LEX,15-
4ph/19pg/1pc L

Whittemore,Jacob,House (Muzzey,John,House; Minute Man National Historical Park)
621 Marrett St.
HABS MA-823
HABS MASS,9-LEX,20-
9dr/4ph/4pg/1pc/fr L

LINCOLN

Brooks-Conary House; see Brooks,Daniel,House

Brooks,Daniel,House (Brooks-Conary House)
Brooks Rd.
HABS MA-824
HABS MASS,9-LIN,3-
3dr/2ph/1pc/fr L

Brooks,Job,House
Minuteman National Historical Park
HABS MA-1264
HABS DLC/PP-1992:MA-5
2ph/1pc L

Brooks,Joshua,House (Minute Man National Historical Park)
North Great Rd. (State Rt. 2A)
HABS MA-825
HABS MASS,9-LIN,4-
(DLC/PP-1992:MA-5)
11dr/9ph/4pg/2pc/fr L

Brooks,Noah,Tavern (Hartwell-Rogers House; Brooks,Thomas,Farm; Minute Man National Historical Park)
North Great Rd. (State Rt. 2A)
HABS MA-826
HABS MASS,9-LIN,5-
8dr/7ph/4pg/1pc/fr L

Brooks,Thomas,Farm; see Brooks,Noah,Tavern

Brown-Carley House; see Brown,Nathan,House

Brown,Nathan,House (Brown-Carley House)
Tower Rd.
HABS MA-827
HABS MASS,9-LIN,6-
4dr/2ph/1pc/fr L

Gropius House (Storrow House)
68 Baker Bridge Rd.
HABS MA-1228
HABS 1990 (HABS):5
42ph/1pg/2pc L

Hartwell Tavern (Hartwell,Ephraim,House; Minute Man National Historical Park)
Virginia Rd.
HABS MA-829
HABS MASS,9-LIN,7-
(DLC/PP-1992:MA-5)
11dr/13ph/5pg/2pc/fr L

Hartwell-Rogers House; see Brooks,Noah,Tavern

Hartwell,Ephraim,House; see Hartwell Tavern

Hartwell,Sergeant Samuel,House (Minute Man National Historical Park)
Virginia Rd.,Minute Man Nat'l Historic Park
HABS MA-828
HABS MASS,9-LIN,8-
(DLC/PP-1992:MA-5)
7dr/10ph/3pg/3pc/fr L

Knowles Barn (Nelson Barn; Minute Man National Historical Park)
Old Concord Rd.
HABS MA-793
HABS MASS,9-LIN,10-
3ph/1pc L

Milestone WWW; see Sixteen-mile Stone

Minute Man National Historical Park; see Brooks,Joshua,House

Minute Man National Historical Park; see Brooks,Noah,Tavern

Minute Man National Historical Park; see Hartwell Tavern

Minute Man National Historical Park; see Hartwell,Sergeant Samuel,House

Minute Man National Historical Park; see Knowles Barn

Minute Man National Historical Park; see Nelson,John,House

Minute Man National Historical Park; see Nelson,Josiah,House Site

Minute Man National Historical Park; see Nelson,Thomas Jr.,House

Nelson Barn; see Knowles Barn

Nelson,John,Barn
Great North Rd. (State Rt. 2A),Minute Man NHP
HABS MA-831
HABS MASS,9-LIN,12-
3dr/10ph/2pc/fr L

Nelson,John,House (Minute Man National Historical Park)
North Great Rd. (State Rt. 2A)
HABS MA-830
HABS MASS,9-LIN,11-
6dr/6ph/3pg/1pc/fr L

Nelson,Josiah,House Site (Minute Man National Historical Park)
Nelson Rd.
HABS MA-832
HABS MASS,9-LIN,13-
1dr L

Nelson,Thomas Jr.,House (Minute Man National Historical Park)
Nelson Rd.
HABS MA-1263
HABS DLC/PP-1992:MA-5
1ph/1pc L

Sixteen-mile Stone (Milestone WWW)
HABS MA-128
HABS MASS,9-LIN,2-
1ph L

Smith,Captain William,House
Virginia Rd.,Minute Man Nat'l Historical Park
HABS MA-833
HABS MASS,9-LIN,14-
8dr/9ph/2pc/fr L

Storrow House; see Gropius House

LOWELL

Aiken Street Bridge (Oulette Bridge)
Spanning the Merrimack River on Aiken St.
HAER MA-106
HAER DLC/PP-1992:MA-4
11ph/23pg/1pc L

Boott & Massachusetts Cotton Mills Agents' House
63-67 Kirk St.
HABS MA-996
HABS MASS9-LOW,17-
7ph/4pg/1pc/fr L

Boott Cotton Mills
John St. at Merrimack River
HAER MA-16
HAER MASS,9-LOW,7-
100dr/62ph/99pg/3pc/5ct/fr L

Bowers,Jarathmael,House & Barns
HABS MA-525
HABS MASS,9-LOW,4-
3ph L

Brick Block
Dutton St.
HABS MA-1151
HABS MASS,9-LOW,18-
10ph/2pg/1pc/fr L

City Hall,Old; see Town Hall,Old

Eastern Canal
Bridge & Armory Sts. Vic.
HAER MA-7
HAER MASS,9-LOW,14-
5ph/1pg/1pc L

Eastern Canal,Boott Dam
HAER MA-7-A
HAER MASS,9-LOW,14A-
3ph/1pg/1pc L

Eastern Canal,Boott Penstock
Between Eastern & Merrimack Canals
HAER MA-7-B
HAER MASS,9-LOW,14B-
2ph/1pg/1pc L

Hamilton Canal
Jackson St. Vic.
HAER MA-4
HAER MASS,9-LOW,11-
4ph/1pg/1pc L

Hamilton Canal,Guard Gates
HAER MA-4-A
HAER MASS,9-LOW,11A-
6ph/1pg/1pc L

Hamilton Canal,Wasteway Gatehouse
HAER MA-4-B
HAER MASS,9-LOW,11B-
1ph/1pg/1pc L

Lawrence Canal,Lawrence Dam
Lawrence & Merrimack Canals
HAER MA-6-A
HAER MASS,9-LOW,13A-
3ph/1pg/1pc L

Lowell Canal System
Merrimack & Concord Rivers
HAER MA-1
HAER MASS,9-LOW,8-
2dr/32ph/150pg/3pc L

Lowell Canal System,Pawtucket Dam
Merrimack River,above Pawtucket Falls
HAER MA-1-A
HAER MASS,9-LOW,8A-
13ph/1pg/1pc L

Lowell City Hall
407 Merrimack St.
HABS MA-1152
HABS MASS,9-LOW,6-
10ph/26pg/1pc/1ct/fr L

Massachusetts Mills
95 Bridge St.
HAER MA-89
2ph/9pg/2pc L

Massachusetts Mills,Cloth Room/Section 15
95 Bridge St.
HAER MA-89-A
18ph/18pg/3pc L

Merrimack Canal
HAER MA-3
HAER MASS,9-LOW,10-
5ph/1pg/1pc L

Merrimack Canal,Merrimack Dam
HAER MA-3-A
HAER MASS,9-LOW,10A-
5ph/1pg/1pc L

Merrimack Canal,Rolling Dam
HAER MA-3-B
HAER MASS,9-LOW,10B-
1ph/1pg/1pc L

Middlesex Canal,Canal Office
Middlesex Village
HABS MA-380-A
HABS MASS,9- ,9-
1ph L

Moody Street Feeder
Moody St. Vic.
HAER MA-9
HAER MASS,9-LOW,16-
2ph/1pg/1pc L

Moody Street Feeder,Gatehouse
Moody Street Feeder & Merrimack Canal
HAER MA-9-A
HAER MASS,9-LOW,16A-
6ph/4pg/1pc L

New Block
Dutton St.
HABS MA-1153
HABS MASS,9-LOW,19-
7ph/2pg/1pc/fr L

Northern Canal
Pawtucket & Ford Sts. Vic.
HAER MA-8
HAER MASS,9-LOW,15-
7ph/1pg/1pc L

Northern Canal,Great River Wall
HAER MA-8-B
HAER MASS,9-LOW,15B-
14ph/1pg/2pc L

Northern Canal,Pawtucket Gatehouse
Northern Canal & Merrimack River
HAER MA-8-A
HAER MASS,9-LOW,15A-
1dr/16ph/1pg/2pc L

Northern Canal,Waste Gates
HAER MA-8-C
HAER MASS,9-LOW,15C-
5dr/8ph/1pg/1pc/fr L

Oulette Bridge; see Aiken Street Bridge

Pawtucket Canal
Pawtucket Falls Vic.
HAER MA-2
HAER MASS,9-LOW,9-
3ph/1pg/1pc L

Pawtucket Canal,Guard Locks
HAER MA-2-A
HAER MASS,9-LOW,9A-
3dr/40ph/1pg/4pc/fr L

Pawtucket Canal,Lower Locks
HAER MA-2-C
HAER MASS,9-LOW,9C-
6dr/15ph/1pg/2pc/fr L

Pawtucket Canal,Swamp Locks
Pawtucket & Merrimack Canals
HAER MA-2-B
HAER MASS,9-LOW,9B-
6dr/20ph/2pg/2pc/fr L

Tenement House
Chelmsford Glass Works
HABS MA-327
HABS MASS,9-LOW,3-
1ph/fr L

Town Hall,Old (City Hall,Old)
226-232 Merrimack St.
HABS MA-995
HABS MASS,9-LOW,20-
5dr/2pg/fr L

Western Canal
Pawtucket & Merrimack Canals Vic.
HAER MA-5
HAER MASS,9-LOW,12-
3ph/1pg/1pc L

Western Canal,Guard Gates
Western & Northern Canals
HAER MA-5-C
HAER MASS,9-LOW,12C-
4ph/1pg/1pc L

Western Canal,Hickey Hall Dam
HAER MA-5-A
HAER MASS,9-LOW,12A-
5ph/1pg/1pc L

Western Canal,Tremont Gatehouse
Western & Lawrence Canals
HAER MA-5-B
HAER MASS,9-LOW,12B-
4ph/1pg/1pc L

Whistler,James Abbott McNeill,Birthplace
243 Worthen St.
HABS MA-526
HABS MASS,9-LOW,5-
1ph L

LOWELL-SOMERVILLE

Middlesex Canal
From Merrimack River to Boston Harbor
HABS MA-380
HABS MASS,9- ,2-10-
12ph L

MALDEN

City Hall,Old; see Malden Town Hall

Five-mile Stone (Milestone AAA)
Newburyport Turnpike
HABS MA-128
HABS MASS,9-MALD,1-
1ph L

Malden Town Hall (City Hall,Old)
Main & Pleasant Sts.
HABS MA-979
HABS MASS,9-MALD,2-
15ph/5pg/1pc/fr L

Milestone AAA; see Five-mile Stone

MEDFORD

Blanchard,George,House
18 Bradbury Ave.
HABS MA-2-5
HABS MASS,9-MED,7-
7dr/31ph/2pc/fr L

Hall,Andrew,House
45 High St.
HABS MA-159
HABS MASS,9-MED,9-
1dr/1ph L

Hall,Benjamin Jr.,House
57 High St.
HABS MA-2-56
HABS MASS,9-MED,8-
24dr/4ph/fr L

Hall,Ebenezer,House
49 High St.
HABS MA-261
HABS MASS,9-MED,6-
10dr L

Lawrence Farmhouse
353 Lawrence Rd.
HABS MA-246
HABS MASS,9-MED,12-
14dr L

Magoun,Thatcher,House
117 High St.
HABS MA-194
HABS MASS,9-MED,10-
11dr/5ph L

Middlesex Canal,Stone Bridge
HABS MA-380-B
HABS MASS,9- ,10-
1ph L

Milestone
Andover & Medford Turnpike
HABS MA-1185
HABS MASS,9-MED,13-
1ph/1pc L

Osgood,Rev. David,House
141 High St.
HABS MA-111
HABS MASS,9-MED,4-
17dr/4ph/fr L

Royal,Col. Isaac,House (Forecourt Fence) (Usher-Royall House (Forecourt Fence))
Main St.
HABS MA-130-A
HABS MASS,9-MED,1C-
1dr/1ph/fr L

Royall,Col. Isaac,Garden House (Usher-Royall Garden House)
Main St. Vic.
HABS MA-129
HABS MASS,9-MED,1A-
4dr/3ph/fr L

Royall,Col. Isaac,House (Usher-Royall House)
Main St. ,between George & Royall Sts.
HABS MA-577
HABS MASS,9-MED,1-
11ph/1pc L

Royall,Col. Isaac,Slave Quarters (Usher-Royall Slave Quarters)
15 George St.
HABS MA-130
HABS MASS,9-MED,1B-
11dr/6ph/fr L

Sawyer,Nathan,Cottage
306 Riverside Ave.
HABS MA-219
HABS MASS,9-MED,11-
6dr/3ph L

Usher-Royall Garden House; see Royall,Col. Isaac,Garden House

Usher-Royall House; see Royall,Col. Isaac,House

Usher-Royall House (Forecourt Fence); see Royal,Col. Isaac,House (Forecourt Fence)

Usher-Royall Slave Quarters; see Royall,Col. Isaac,Slave Quarters

MELROSE

Lynde,Ensign Thomas,House
HABS MA-464
HABS MASS,9-MELRO,1-
3ph L

Milestone
Main & Foster Sts.
HABS MA-1186
HABS MASS,9-MELRO,3-
1ph/1pc L

Upham,Phineas,House
253 Upham St.
HABS MA-489
HABS MASS,9-MELRO,2-
10dr/2ph L

NATICK

Boston & Albany Railroad:Marion Street Bridge
Spanning the Boston & Albany RR on Marion St.
HAER MA-108
HAER DLC/PP-1992:MA-4
11ph/10pg/1pc L

Wilson,Henry,Shoe Shop
W. Central & Mill Sts.
HABS MA-176
HABS MASS,9-NAT,1-
1dr/4ph/fr L

NEWTON

Boston & Albany Railroad Station
1897 Washington St.
HABS MA-667
HABS MASS,9-NEWT,13-
3ph/3pg L

Crehore Paper Mill
375 Elliot St.
HABS MA-545
HABS MASS,9-NEWT,12-
1ph L

Jackson,Timothy,House & Garden
527 Washington St.
HABS MA-139
HABS MASS,9-NEWT,1-
13dr/12ph/fr L

Kenrick House
302 Waverly Ave.
HABS MA-387
HABS MASS,9-NEWT,4-
10ph L

Mill House Number 1
Chestnut St.
HABS MA-388-A
HABS MASS,9-NEWT,5-
4ph/fr L

Mill House Number 2
Chestnut St.
HABS MA-388-B
HABS MASS,9-NEWT,6-
2ph/fr L

Mill House Number 3
Sullivan Ave.
HABS MA-388-C
HABS MASS,9-NEWT,7-
3ph/fr L

Mill House Number 4
Chestnut St.
HABS MA-388-D
HABS MASS,9-NEWT,8-
2ph/fr L

Mill House Number 5
Chestnut St.
HABS MA-388-E
HABS MASS,9-NEWT,9-
2ph/fr L

Silver Lake Cordage Company
308 Nevada St.
HAER MA-33
HAER MASS,9-NEWT,14-
2ph/1pg/1pc/2ct L

St. Mary's Episcopal Church
HABS MA-389
HABS MASS,9-NEWT,11-
9ph/fr L

Sudbury River Aqueduct,Echo Bridge
Spanning Charles River at Upper Newton Falls
HAER MA-39
HAER MASS,9-NEWT,15-
4ph/1pg/1pc/1ct L

Three Mill Houses
Chestnut St. & Sullivan Ave.
HABS MA-388
HABS MASS,9-NEWT,10-
1ph/fr L

Woodward,John,House
238 Woodward St.
HABS MA-146
HABS MASS,9-NEWT,2-
11dr/9ph/fr L

Wyman-Tower House
401 Woodward St.
HABS MA-147
HABS MASS,9-NEWT,3-
14dr/2ph/fr L

NEWTON CENTRE

Weeks,John Wingate,Junior High School
Hereward & Rowena Sts.
HABS MA-1121
HABS MASS,9-NEWTC,1-
17ph/12pg/1pc L

NORTH BILLERICA

Middlesex Canal
HABS MA-380-C
HABS MASS,9- ,2-
1ph L

NORTH PEPPERELL

District School Number 4
North & Prescott Sts.
HABS MA-222
HABS MASS,9-PEPN,1-
3dr/fr L

NORTH READING

Crosby,Guy M. Jr.,House
HABS MA-523
HABS MASS,9-READN,1-
2ph L

NORTH WOBURN

Bartlett-Wheeler House
(Bartlett,Joseph,House)
827 Main St.
HABS MA-276
HABS MASS,9-WOBN,3-
15ph L

Bartlett,Joseph,House; see Bartlett-Wheeler House

Middlesex Canal
School St.
HABS MA-380-D
HABS MASS,9- ,4-
1ph L

Rumford,Count,Birthplace (House & Garden) (Thompson,Benjamin,House & Garden)
90 Elm St.
HABS MA-240
HABS MASS,9-WOBN,1-
2dr/4ph L

Thompson,Benjamin,House & Garden; see Rumford,Count,Birthplace (House & Garden)

PEPPERELL

Jewett,Nehemiah,Bridge
Groton St.,spanning Nashua River
HABS MA-225
HABS MASS,9-PEP,1-
4dr/2ph/fr L

Prescott,Col. William,House
HABS MA-604
HABS MASS,9-PEP,2-
2ph L

READING

Bryant,Abram Jr.,House; see Parker Tavern

Parker Tavern (Bryant,Abram Jr.,House)
Washington St.
HABS MA-522
HABS MASS,9-READ,1-
2ph L

SHERBORN

Leland,Deacon William,House
HABS MA-402
HABS MASS,9-SHERB,1-
4ph/fr L

SHIRLEY

First Parish Meetinghouse
HABS MA-540
HABS MASS,9-SHIR,1-
4ph L

Pound,Stone
HABS MA-541
HABS MASS,9-SHIR,2-
2ph L

SOMERVILLE

Lee,Maj. Gen.,Headquarters; see Tufts,Oliver,House

Mystic River Drawbridge No. 7
Spanning Mystic Riv. at Boston & ME RR Eastern Rt.
HAER MA-88
HAER DLC/PP-1993:MA-3
36ph/36pg/3pc L

Powder House,Old
Broadway & College Ave.
HABS MA-178
HABS MASS,9-SOMV,1-
1dr/2ph/fr L

Round House
HABS MA-501
HABS MASS,9-SOMV,4-
3ph L

Tufts,Francis,House
HABS MA-403
HABS MASS,9-SOMV,2-
3ph L

Tufts,Oliver,House (Lee,Maj. Gen.,Headquarters)
78 Sycamore St. (moved from original site)
HABS MA-404
HABS MASS,9-SOMV,3-
1ph L

SOUTH PEPPERELL VIC.

Coburn's Tavern
State Rt. 119
HABS MA-226
HABS MASS,9-PEP.V,1-
16dr/fr L

SOUTH SUDBURY

Howe's Tavern; see Wayside Inn

Red Horse Tavern; see Wayside Inn

Wayside Inn (Howe's Tavern; Red Horse Tavern)
Old Boston Post Rd. (U. S. Rt. 20)
HABS MA-632
HABS MASS,9-SUDS,1-
2ph L

STONEHAM

First Congregational Church
HABS MA-593
HABS MASS,9-STO,2-
1ph L

Green,Jonathan,House
HABS MA-527
HABS MASS,9-STO,1-
1ph L

TOWNSEND

Conant House
HABS MA-536
HABS MASS,9-TOW,4-
3ph L

Documentation: **ct** color transparencies **dr** measured drawings **fr** field records
pc photograph captions **pg** pages of text **ph** photographs

Methodist Episcopal Church
HABS MA-533
HABS MASS,9-TOW,1-
3ph L

Spaulding Cooperage Shop
HABS MA-535
HABS MASS,9-TOW,3-
2ph L

Spaulding Grist Mill
HABS MA-534
HABS MASS,9-TOW,2-
2ph L

TYNGSBOROUGH

Brinley-O'Neill House
HABS MA-409
HABS MASS,9-TYNG,2-
6ph/fr L

School Number 2
HABS MA-602
HABS MASS,9-TYNG,4-
1ph L

Tyng House
HABS MA-410
HABS MASS,9-TYNG,3-
8ph/fr L

WAKEFIELD

Hartshorne,Col. James,House
41 Church St.
HABS MA-521
HABS MASS,9-WAK,1-
4ph L

WALTHAM

Boston Manufacturing Company
144-190 Moody St.
HAER MA-54
HAER MASS,9-WALTH,4-
70ph/14pg/6pc L

Central Massachusetts Railroad:Linden St. Bridge
Spanning Linden St.
HAER MA-46
HAER MASS,9-WALTH,5-
2ph/1pg/1pc/3ct L

Gore,Gov. Christopher,Coach House & Stable
HABS MA-834
HABS MASS,9-WALTH,7-
7ph/1pc L

Gore,Gov. Christopher,Garden
Gore St.
HABS MA-210-A
HABS MASS,9-WALTH,2A-
7dr/3ph L

Gore,Gov. Christopher,Mansion
Gore St.
HABS MA-210
HABS MASS,9-WALTH,2-
31dr L

Lyman,Theodore,House (Garden & Summerhouse); see Vale,The (Garden & Summerhouse)

Mill,Stone
South St.
HABS MA-502
HABS MASS,9-WALTH,3-
6ph L

Vale,The (Garden & Summerhouse)
(Lyman,Theodore,House (Garden & Summerhouse))
Beaver St.
HABS MA-204
HABS MASS,9-WALTH,1-
15dr/3ph/fr L

Waltham Watch Company
221-257 Crescent St.
HAER MA-31
HAER MASS,9-WALTH,6-
1ph/1pg/1pc L

WATERTOWN

Bemis,John,House
425 Main St.
HABS MA-131
HABS MASS,9-WATO,1-
11dr/3ph L

Brown,Abraham,House
562 Main St.
HABS MA-781
HABS MASS,9-WATO,4-
2ph L

Caldwell,Daniel,House
126 Main St.
HABS MA-132
HABS MASS,9-WATO,2-
6dr/4ph L

Conant House
HABS MA-494
HABS MASS,9-WATO,3-
2ph L

U. S. Army Materials & Mechan. Resrch Ctr,Bldg 111; see Watertown Arsenal,Building No. 111

U. S. Army Materials & Mechan. Resrch Ctr,Bldg 114; see Watertown Arsenal,Building No. 114

U. S. Army Materials & Mechan. Resrch Ctr,Bldg 116; see Watertown Arsenal,Building No. 116

U. S. Army Materials & Mechan. Resrch Ctr,Bldg 121; see Watertown Arsenal,Building No. 121

U. S. Army Materials & Mechan. Resrch Ctr,Bldg 152; see Watertown Arsenal,Building No. 152

U. S. Army Materials & Mechan. Resrch Ctr,Bldg 211; see Watertown Arsenal,Building No. 211

U. S. Army Materials & Mechan. Resrch Ctr,Bldg 212; see Watertown Arsenal,Building No. 212

U. S. Army Materials & Mechan. Resrch Ctr,Bldg 311; see Watertown Arsenal,Building No. 311

U. S. Army Materials & Mechan. Resrch Ctr,Bldg 312; see Watertown Arsenal,Building No. 312

U. S. Army Materials & Mechan. Resrch Ctr,Bldg 313; see Watertown Arsenal,Building No. 313

U. S. Army Materials & Mechan. Resrch Ctr,Bldg 34; see Watertown Arsenal,Building No. 34

U. S. Army Materials & Mechan. Resrch Ctr,Bldg 36; see Watertown Arsenal,Building No. 36

U. S. Army Materials & Mechan. Resrch Ctr,Bldg 37; see Watertown Arsenal,Building No. 37

U. S. Army Materials & Mechan. Resrch Ctr,Bldg 43; see Watertown Arsenal,Building No. 43

U. S. Army Materials & Mechan. Resrch Ctr,Bldg 51; see Watertown Arsenal,Building No. 51

U. S. Army Materials & Mechan. Resrch Ctr,Bldg 71; see Watertown Arsenal,Building No. 71

U. S. Army Materials & Mechan. Resrch Ctr,Bldg 72; see Watertown Arsenal,Building No. 72

U. S. Army Materials & Mechanics Research Center; see Watertown Arsenal

Watertown Arsenal (U. S. Army Materials & Mechanics Research Center)
HAER MA-20
HAER MASS,9-WATO,5-
191pg/fr L

Watertown Arsenal,Building No. 111
(Watertown Arsenal,Commanding Officer's Quarters; U. S. Army Materials & Mechan. Resrch Ctr,Bldg 111
Arsenal St.
HAER MA-20-D
HAER MASS,9-WATO,5D-
1ph/1pc L

Watertown Arsenal,Building No. 114
(U. S. Army Materials & Mechan. Resrch Ctr,Bldg 114
HAER MA-20-L
HAER MASS,9-WATO,5L-
7ph/1pc L

Watertown Arsenal,Building No. 116
(U. S. Army Materials & Mechan. Resrch Ctr,Bldg 116
HAER MA-20-M
HAER MASS,9-WATO,5M-
2ph/1pc L

Watertown Arsenal,Building No. 121
(U. S. Army Materials & Mechan. Resrch Ctr,Bldg 121
HAER MA-20-N
HAER MASS,9-WATO,5N-
2ph/1pc L

Watertown Arsenal,Building No. 152 (U. S. Army Materials & Mechan. Resrch Ctr,Bldg 152
HAER MA-20-O
HAER MASS,9-WATO,5"O"-
9ph/1pc L

Watertown Arsenal,Building No. 211 (U. S. Army Materials & Mechan. Resrch Ctr,Bldg 211
HAER MA-20-P
HAER MASS,9-WATO,5P-
1ph/1pc L

Watertown Arsenal,Building No. 212 (U. S. Army Materials & Mechan. Resrch Ctr,Bldg 212
HAER MA-20-Q
HAER MASS,9-WATO,5Q-
4ph/1pc L

Watertown Arsenal,Building No. 311 (Watertown Arsenal,Sea Coast Gun & Carriage Shop; U. S. Army Materials & Mechan. Resrch Ctr,Bldg 311
HAER MA-20-E
HAER MASS,9-WATO,5E-
3ph/1pc L

Watertown Arsenal,Building No. 312 (Watertown Arsenal,Erecting Shop; U. S. Army Materials & Mechan. Resrch Ctr,Bldg 312
HAER MA-20-F
HAER MASS,9-WATO,5F-
3ph/1pc L

Watertown Arsenal,Building No. 313 (Watertown Arsenal,Carriage & Machine Shop; U. S. Army Materials & Mechan. Resrch Ctr,Bldg 313
HAER MA-20-G
HAER MASS,9-WATO,5G-
4ph/1pc L

Watertown Arsenal,Building No. 34 (U. S. Army Materials & Mechan. Resrch Ctr,Bldg 34)
Arsenal St.
HAER MA-20-H
HAER MASS,9-WATO,5H-
3ph/1pc L

Watertown Arsenal,Building No. 36 (Watertown Arsenal,Gun Carriage Storehouse; U. S. Army Materials & Mechan. Resrch Ctr,Bldg 36)
Arsenal St.
HAER MA-20-A
HAER MASS,9-WATO,5A-
1ph/1pc L

Watertown Arsenal,Building No. 37 (Watertown Arsenal,Timber Storehouse; U. S. Army Materials & Mechan. Resrch Ctr,Bldg 37)
Arsenal St.
HAER MA-20-B
HAER MASS,9-WATO,5B-
7ph/1pc L

Watertown Arsenal,Building No. 43 (Watertown Arsenal,Smith Shop; U. S. Army Materials & Mechan. Resrch Ctr,Bldg 43)
Arsenal St.
HAER MA-20-C
HAER MASS,9-WATO,5C-
5ph/1pc L

Watertown Arsenal,Building No. 51 (U. S. Army Materials & Mechan. Resrch Ctr,Bldg 51)
HAER MA-20-I
HAER MASS,9-WATO,5"I"-
7ph/1pc L

Watertown Arsenal,Building No. 71 (U. S. Army Materials & Mechan. Resrch Ctr,Bldg 71)
HAER MA-20-J
HAER MASS,9-WATO,5J-
1ph/1pc L

Watertown Arsenal,Building No. 72 (U. S. Army Materials & Mechan. Resrch Ctr,Bldg 72)
HAER MA-20-K
HAER MASS,9-WATO,5K-
2ph/1pc L

Watertown Arsenal,Building Number 141 (Watertown Arsenal,Guardhouse; Watertown Redevelopment Authority Building)
463 Arsenal St.
HABS MA-1009
HABS MASS,9-WATO,6-
12ph/2pg/1pc L

Watertown Arsenal,Carriage & Machine Shop; see Watertown Arsenal,Building No. 313

Watertown Arsenal,Commanding Officer's Quarters; see Watertown Arsenal,Building No. 111

Watertown Arsenal,Erecting Shop; see Watertown Arsenal,Building No. 312

Watertown Arsenal,Guardhouse; see Watertown Arsenal,Building Number 141

Watertown Arsenal,Gun Carriage Storehouse; see Watertown Arsenal,Building No. 36

Watertown Arsenal,Sea Coast Gun & Carriage Shop; see Watertown Arsenal,Building No. 311

Watertown Arsenal,Smith Shop; see Watertown Arsenal,Building No. 43

Watertown Arsenal,Timber Storehouse; see Watertown Arsenal,Building No. 37

Watertown Redevelopment Authority Building; see Watertown Arsenal,Building Number 141

WAYLAND

Milestones MM,NN & OO
Various Wayland locations
HABS MA-128
HABS MASS,9-WAYL,2-
3ph L

Town Bridge,Old
Spanning Sudbury River
HABS MA-2-75
HABS MASS,9-WAYL,1-
1dr/1ph/fr L

WEST MEDFORD

Brooks Farmhouse (Brooks,Capt. Caleb,House)
24 Woburn St.
HABS MA-229
HABS MASS,9-MEDW,2-
6dr/2ph L

Brooks,Capt. Caleb,House; see Brooks Farmhouse

Brooks,Jonathan,House
Woburn & High Sts.
HABS MA-144
HABS MASS,9-MEDW,1-
9dr/7ph/fr L

WESTON

Fiske,Isaac,Law Office (Lawyer's Office)
Central Ave.
HABS MA-2-34
HABS MASS,9-WESTO,1-
3dr/1ph/fr L

Golden Ball Tavern
662 Central Ave.
HABS MA-414
HABS MASS,9-WESTO,2-
7ph/fr L

Lamson House
HABS MA-495
HABS MASS,9-WESTO,3-
2ph L

Lawyer's Office; see Fiske,Isaac,Law Office

WILMINGTON

Middlesex Canal,Lock-keeper's House
Gillis Lock,Shawsheen Ave.
HABS MA-380-F
HABS MASS,9- ,8-
1ph L

Middlesex Canal,Lubber Brook Aqueduct
HABS MA-380-G
HABS MASS,9- ,5-
2ph L

Middlesex Canal,Maple Meadow Brook Aqueduct
HABS MA-380-H
HABS MASS,9- ,6-
1ph L

Documentation: **ct** color transparencies **dr** measured drawings **fr** field records **pc** photograph captions **pg** pages of text **ph** photographs

Middlesex Canal,Nichols Lock
Nichols St.
HABS MA-380-I
HABS MASS,9- ,3-
1ph L

WILMINGTON-BILLERICA

Middlesex Canal,Shawsheen Aqueduct
HABS MA-380-E
HABS MASS,9- ,7-
3ph L

WOBURN

B. P. Station; see Beacon Oil Company Gas Station

Baldwin,Col. Loammi,Mansion
Elm St.
HABS MA-419
HABS MASS,9-WOBN,2-
13ph/fr L

Beacon Oil Company Gas Station (B. P. Station)
107 Winn St.
HABS MA-1223
HABS 1989(HABS):10
5ph/1pg/1pc L

Horn Pond Tavern
HABS MA-578
HABS MASS,9-WOB,1-
1ph L

Milestone
Montrale Ave. Bridge Vic.
HABS MA-1187
HABS MASS,9-WOB,2-
1ph/1pc L

NANTUCKET COUNTY

NANTUCKET

Academy Lane (Houses)
HABS MA-1262
HABS DLC/PP-1993:MA-1
25dr/26pg/fr L

African Society Baptist Church
York St.
HABS MA-909
HABS MASS,10-NANT,32-
3dr/2ph/4pg/fr L

Ayers,Lawrence,House; see Orange & Union Streets Neighborhood Study

Barker,Francis,House; see Orange & Union Streets Neighborhood Study

Barnard-Pease House; see 19 Hussey Street (House)

Barnard,John,House
84 Main St.
HABS MA-1105
HABS MASS,10-NANT,77-
10dr L

Barrett,John Wendell,House (Wallace Hall)
72 Main St.
HABS MA-915
HABS MASS,10-NANT,36-
7ph/4pg L

Baxter,Capt. Reuben,House; see India Street Neighborhood Study

Beard,John,House; see Orange & Union Streets Neighborhood Study

Beard,Matthew,House; see Orange & Union Streets Neighborhood Study

Beebe,Nathan,House; see Orange & Union Streets Neighborhood Study

Big Shop,The; see Folger,Charles & Hiram,Shop

Blackburn,Elizabeth,House; see Orange & Union Streets Neighborhood Study

Breakers,The
HABS MA-970
HABS MASS,10-NANT,78-
6ph/1pc L

Brock,Major,House; see India Street Neighborhood Study

Bunker-Chace House; see India Street Neighborhood Study

Bunker,Andrew,House; see India Street Neighborhood Study

Bunker,Joshua,House; see Orange & Union Streets Neighborhood Study

Bunker,Reuben R.,House
Academy Hill
HABS MA-916
HABS MASS,10-NANT,37-
3ph/3pg L

Bunker,Tristram,House
3 Bear St.
HABS MA-900
HABS MASS,10-NANT,24-
6dr/6ph/6pg/fr L

Candle Factory; see Starbuck,Joseph,House

Carroll House; see India Street Neighborhood Study

Cary,Capt. Nathaniel,House; see Orange & Union Streets Neighborhood Study

Cary,Edward,House
117 Main St.
HABS MA-855
HABS MASS,10-NANT,20-
5ph/3pg L

Centre Street United Methodist Church
Centre & Main Sts.
HABS MA-1007
HABS MASS,10-NANT,74-
8dr/15ph/6pg/fr L

Chase,Abel,House; see Orange & Union Streets Neighborhood Study

Chase,Isaac,House; see Orange & Union Streets Neighborhood Study

Clapp,Timothy G.,House; see Orange & Union Streets Neighborhood Study

Codd,James,House; see Orange & Union Streets Neighborhood Study

Coffin School
4 Winter St.
HABS MA-1248
11dr/14pg/fr L

Coffin-Athearn Stores
2 Union St.
HABS MA-906
HABS MASS,10-NANT,29-
3dr/2ph/6pg/fr L

Coffin-Chapin House
9 Pine St.
HABS MA-1157
HABS MASS,10-NANT,79-
10dr L

Coffin-Gardner House
33 Milk St.
HABS MA-854
HABS MASS,10-NANT,19-
12dr/5ph/5pg/fr L

Coffin,Daniel,House; see India Street Neighborhood Study

Coffin,Henry,House
75 Main St.
HABS MA-811
HABS MASS,10-NANT,13-
11dr/16ph/9pg/fr L

Coffin,Jared,House; see Moor's End

Coffin,Jared,House (Ocean House)
29 Broad St.
HABS MA-918
HABS MASS,10-NANT,39-
6ph/4pg L

Coffin,Jethro,House (Oldest House)
Sunset Hill
HABS MA-919
HABS MASS,10-NANT,40-
22ph/6pg L

Coffin,Joshua,House
52 Centre St.
HABS MA-920
HABS MASS,10-NANT,72-
11dr/12ph/10pg/fr L

Coffin,Maj. Josiah,House
60 Cliff Rd.
HABS MA-911
HABS MASS,10-NANT,33-
9dr/10ph/7pg/fr L

Coffin,Thaddeus,House
89 Main St.
HABS MA-921
HABS MASS,10-NANT,41-
7ph/4pg/1pc L

Coggeshall,Benjamin,House; see Orange & Union Streets Neighborhood Study

Coggeshall,Peleg,House; see Orange & Union Streets Neighborhood Study

Coleman,Elihu,House
Hawthorne Ln.
HABS MA-2-86
HABS MASS,10-NANT,4-
10dr/8ph/8pg L

Coleman,Richard,House; see Orange & Union Streets Neighborhood Study

2nd Congregational Meetinghouse Society Church; see Orange & Union Streets Neighborhood Study

Daggett,Margaret Gardner,House
(Sevenfires)
111 Main St.
HABS MA-922
HABS MASS,10-NANT,42-
5ph/3pg L

Dexioma
Broadway,Siasconset
HABS MA-1206
7dr H

Dickie House; see McCleave-Dickie House

Dunham House; see India Street Neighborhood Study

East Mill; see Windmill,Old

Easton-Joy House (Joy,Obed,House)
4 N. Water St.
HABS MA-957
HABS MASS,10-NANT,67-
5ph/3pg/1pc L

Easton-Wood House; see Wood,Charles,House

Eighteen-Hundred House
4 Mill St.
HABS MA-1102
HABS MASS,10-NANT,80-
8dr L

Ewer,Silvanus,House; see Orange & Union Streets Neighborhood Study

First Baptist Church
1 Summer St.
HABS MA-1252
HABS DLC/PP-1992:MA-2
8dr/8pg/fr L

First Congregational Church
62 Centre St.
HABS MA-902
HABS MASS,10-NANT,26-
8dr/19ph/6pg/fr L

First Congregational Church (North Vestry)
Beacon Hill
HABS MA-903
HABS MASS,10-NANT,27-
6dr/8ph/6pg/fr L

Fish Shanties
Old South Wharf
HABS MA-853
HABS MASS,10-NANT,18-
9ph/2pg L

Folger,Charles & Hiram,Shop (Big Shop,The)
35 Milk St.
HABS MA-923
HABS MASS,10-NANT,43-
2ph/4pg L

Folger,Peter,House
51 Centre St.
HABS MA-924
HABS MASS,10-NANT,44-
3ph/3pg L

Folger,Philip H. ,Block
56 & 58 Main St.
HABS MA-949
HABS MASS,10-NANT,61-
14dr/10ph/6pg L H

Folger,Robert,House; see India Street Neighborhood Study

Folger,Seth,House; see Orange & Union Streets Neighborhood Study

Gaol,Old
Vestal St. (moved from original site)
HABS MA-120
HABS MASS,10-NANT,5-
9dr/1ph L H

Gardner,Barnabas,House
153 Main St.
HABS MA-925
HABS MASS,10-NANT,45-
2ph/3pg L

Gardner,Benjamin,Store; see Holmes & Wyer Carpenters' Shop

Gardner,George,House
8 Pine St.
HABS MA-858
HABS MASS,10-NANT,21-
2ph/3pg L

Gardner,Grindell,House
30 Hussey St.
HABS MA-927
HABS MASS,10-NANT,46-
2ph/3pg L

Gardner,Richard Jr.,House
32 W. Chester St.
HABS MA-839
HABS MASS,10-NANT,17-
8ph/4pg L

Gardner,Richard,House
139 Main St.
HABS MA-955
HABS MASS,10-NANT,65-
10ph/4pg/1pc L

Gardner,Sally Beard,House; see Orange & Union Streets Neighborhood Study

Gardner,Silas,House
21 Milk St.
HABS MA-928
HABS MASS,10-NANT,47-
2ph/4pg L

Gardner,Solomon & Paul,House; see Orange & Union Streets Neighborhood Study

Gorham.Josiah,House; see Orange & Union Streets Neighborhood Study

Great Point Lighthouse
Great Point
HABS MA-1006
HABS MASS,10-NANT,73-
6dr/10ph/5pg/fr L

Green,Elisha,House; see Orange & Union Streets Neighborhood Study

Hadwen & Barney Candle House
(Whaling Museum)
Broad & South Sts.
HABS MA-907
HABS MASS,10-NANT,30-
9dr/3ph/6pg/fr L

Hadwen-Wright House
94 Main St.
HABS MA-905
HABS MASS,10-NANT,28-
10dr/15ph/9pg/fr L

Hadwen,William,House (Satler Memorial)
96 Main St.
HABS MA-929
HABS MASS,10-NANT,48-
12dr/7ph/10pg L

Heart's Ease
Center St. ,Siasconset
HABS MA-1204
7dr H

Holland House; see India Street Neighborhood Study

Holmes & Wyer Carpenters' Shop
(Gardner,Benjamin,Store)
Straight Wharf
HABS MA-913
HABS MASS,10-NANT,34-
8dr/4ph/5pg/fr L

19 Hussey Street (House)
(Barnard-Pease House)
HABS MA-195
HABS MASS,10-NANT,10-
15dr/2ph L H

Hussey,Charles F.,House; see India Street Neighborhood Study

Hussey,Christopher,House
12 Orange St.
HABS MA-1101
HABS MASS,10-NANT,81-
8dr L

Hussey,Christopher,House; see Orange & Union Streets Neighborhood Study

Hussey,Eliab,House; see India Street Neighborhood Study

Hussey,Zaccheus,House; see India Street Neighborhood Study

India House; see India Street Neighborhood Study

Documentation: **ct** color transparencies **dr** measured drawings **fr** field records
pc photograph captions **pg** pages of text **ph** photographs

India Street Neighborhood Study
15-45 India St.
HABS MA-1013
HABS MASS,10-NANT,75-
7dr/12ph/8pg/fr L

India Street Neighborhood Study
(Baxter,Capt. Reuben,House)
23 India St.
HABS MA-1051
HABS MASS,10-NANT,75L-
1ph/3pg/fr L

India Street Neighborhood Study
(Bunker,Andrew,House; Bunker-Chace House)
41 India St.
HABS MA-1042
HABS MASS,10-NANT,75C-
10dr/2ph/5pg/fr L H

India Street Neighborhood Study
(Coffin,Daniel,House)
25 India St.
HABS MA-1050
HABS MASS,10-NANT,75K-
3ph/5pg/fr L

India Street Neighborhood Study
(Folger,Robert,House)
27 India St.
HABS MA-1049
HABS MASS,10-NANT,75J-
2ph/5pg/fr L

India Street Neighborhood Study
(Hussey,Charles F.,House; India House)
37 India St.
HABS MA-1044
HABS MASS,10-NANT,75E-
1ph/5pg/fr L

India Street Neighborhood Study
(Hussey,Eliab,House; Dunham House)
31 India St.
HABS MA-1047
HABS MASS,10-NANT,75H-
1ph/5pg/fr L

India Street Neighborhood Study
(Hussey,Zaccheus,House)
19 India St.
HABS MA-1053
HABS MASS,10-NANT,75N-
3ph/3pg/fr L

India Street Neighborhood Study
(Lawrence,George,House; Snow House)
35 India St.
HABS MA-1045
HABS MASS,10-NANT,75F-
1ph/3pg/fr L

India Street Neighborhood Study
(Macy,Gorham,House; Holland House)
39 India St.
HABS MA-1043
HABS MASS,10-NANT,75D-
1ph/3pg/fr L

India Street Neighborhood Study
(Nye,Meletiah,House; Carroll House)
43 India St.
HABS MA-1041
HABS MASS,10-NANT,75B-
3ph/3pg/fr L

India Street Neighborhood Study
(Russell,John,House; Brock,Major,House)
33 India St.
HABS MA-1046
HABS MASS,10-NANT,75G-
5ph/5pg/fr L

India Street Neighborhood Study
(Stubbs,Capt. William,House)
15 India St.
HABS MA-1055
HABS MASS,10-NANT,75Q-
1ph/3pg/fr L

India Street Neighborhood Study
(Swain,John Howland,House)
21 India St.
HABS MA-1052
HABS MASS,10-NANT,75M-
1ph/3pg/fr L

India Street Neighborhood Study
(Swift,Benjamin,House)
29 India St.
HABS MA-1048
HABS MASS,10-NANT,75I-
9ph/6pg/fr L

India Street Neighborhood Study
(Taber,Rescom,House; Joy,Captain,House)
45 India St.
HABS MA-1040
HABS MASS,75-NANT,75A-
1ph/5pg/fr L

India Street Neighborhood Study
(Wood,Obediah,House)
17 India St.
HABS MA-1054
HABS MASS,10-NANT,75P-
1ph/3pg/fr L

Jones,Capt. Silas,House
5 Orange St.
HABS MA-956
HABS MASS,10-NANT,66-
6ph/3pg L

Joy,Captain,House; see India Street Neighborhood Study

Joy,Obed,House; see Easton-Joy House

Joy,Reuben,House; see Macy,Zaccheus,House

Lawrence,George,House; see India Street Neighborhood Study

Leaded-Glass Fixed Window from a Nantucket House
Fair St. Museum
HABS MA-856
1dr H

Lower Main Street,South Side (Buildings)
12 & 14 Main St.
HABS MA-954
HABS MASS,10-NANT,82-
1ph/5pg L

Macy,Francis,House
77 Main St.
HABS MA-931
HABS MASS,10-NANT,50-
7ph/3pg L

Macy,Gorham,House; see India Street Neighborhood Study

Macy,Job,House
11 Mill St.
HABS MA-932
HABS MASS,10-NANT,51-
8dr/7ph/7pg/fr L

Macy,Nathaniel,House
12 Liberty St.
HABS MA-1003
HABS MASS,10-NANT,71-
11dr/10ph/9pg/fr L

Macy,Thomas,Warehouse
Straight Wharf
HABS MA-914
HABS MASS,10-NANT,35-
8dr/2ph/5pg L

Macy,William F.,House; see Orange & Union Streets Neighborhood Study

Macy,Zaccheus,House
(Joy,Reuben,House)
107 Main St.
HABS MA-934
HABS MASS,10-NANT,52-
5ph/4pg L

17-57 Main Street (Commercial Buildings)
HABS MA-952
HABS MASS,10-NANT,64-
7ph/4pg L

Main Street,South Side (Buildings)
18-54 Main St.
HABS MA-950
HABS MASS,10-NANT,62-
12ph/2pg L

Masonic Lodge; see Union Lodge,F. & A. M.

McCleave-Dickie House (Dickie House)
1 Weymouth St.
HABS MA-1099
HABS MASS,10-NANT,83-
9dr L

Meridian Stones
(Mitchell,William,Meridian Stones)
Main & Fair Sts.
HABS MA-183
HABS MASS,10-NANT,9-
2dr/fr L

Methodist Church
Centre St. at Liberty St.
HABS MA-1207
10dr H

Mitchell,Frederick,House
69 Main St.
HABS MA-936
HABS MASS,10-NANT,53-
13ph/4pg L

Mitchell,Maria,House; see Swain-Mitchell House

Mitchell,William,Meridian Stones; see Meridian Stones

Mooers,Lucinda,Homestead; see Orange & Union Streets Neighborhood Study

Moor's End (Coffin,Jared,House)
19 Pleasant St.
HABS MA-917
HABS MASS,10-NANT,38-
12ph/3pg L

Myrick,Andrew,House; see Orange & Union Streets Neighborhood Study

Nantucket Atheneum
Lower India & Federal Sts.
HABS MA-812
HABS MASS,10-NANT,14-
10dr/9ph/7pg/fr L

Nantucket Historical Study (General Views)
HABS MA-1178
HABS MASS,10-NANT,84-
190ph/9pc L

Nantucket Island,Aerial Views
HABS MA-1155
2ph H

Nantucket Lodge No. 66,I. O. O. F.
(Sherburne Hall; Petticoat Row)
7-21 Centre St.
HABS MA-908
HABS MASS,10-NANT,31-
6dr/3ph/7pg/fr L

Nantucket Looms,The
16 Main St.
HABS MA-951
HABS MASS,10-NANT,63-
3ph/2pg L

Nichols,William,House; see Orange & Union Streets Neighborhood Study

Nicholson-True House
38 India St.
HABS MA-1110
9dr H

Nye,Meletiah,House; see India Street Neighborhood Study

Ocean House; see Coffin,Jared,House

Oldest House; see Coffin,Jethro,House

Orange & Union Streets Neighborhood Study
8-31 Orange St. ,9-21 Union St. ,Stone Alley
HABS MA-1014
HABS MASS,10-NANT,76-
12dr/43ph/11pg/fr L H

Orange & Union Streets Neighborhood Study
(Barker,Francis,House)
13 Union St.
HABS MA-1058
HABS MASS,10-NANT,76C-
2ph/5pg/fr L

Orange & Union Streets Neighborhood Study
(Beard,John,House; Mooers,Lucinda,Homestead)
20 Orange St.
HABS MA-1069
HABS MASS,10-NANT,76O-
2ph/5pg/fr L

Orange & Union Streets Neighborhood Study
(Beard,Matthew,House; Gardner,Sally Beard,House)
18 Orange St.
HABS MA-1068
HABS MASS,10-NANT,76N-
2ph/3pg/fr L

Orange & Union Streets Neighborhood Study
(Beebe,Nathan,House)
11 Union St.
HABS MA-1057
HABS MASS,10-NANT,76B-
4ph/3pg/fr L

Orange & Union Streets Neighborhood Study
(Bunker,Joshua,House; Snelling,Rev. Samuel,House)
25 Orange St.
HABS MA-1071
HABS MASS,10-NANT,76V-
1ph/5pg/fr L

Orange & Union Streets Neighborhood Study
(Chase,Isaac,House; Chase,Abel,House)
14 1/2 Orange St.
HABS MA-1066
HABS MASS,10-NANT,76L-
4ph/5pg/fr L

Orange & Union Streets Neighborhood Study
(Coggeshall,Benjamin,House)
8 Orange St.
HABS MA-1062
HABS MASS,10-NANT,76H-
1ph/3pg/fr L

Orange & Union Streets Neighborhood Study
(Coggeshall,Peleg,House; Cary,Capt. Nathaniel,House)
10 Orange St.
HABS MA-1063
HABS MASS,10-NANT,76I-
2ph/5pg/fr L

Orange & Union Streets Neighborhood Study
(Coleman,Richard,House)
21 Union St.
HABS MA-904
HABS MASS,10-NANT,76G-
9dr/10ph/8pg/fr L

Orange & Union Streets Neighborhood Study (2nd Congregational Meetinghouse Society Church; Unitarian Church)
Orange St.
HABS MA-838
HABS MASS,10-NANT,76S-
7dr/7ph/8pg/fr L

Orange & Union Streets Neighborhood Study
(Ewer,Silvanus,House)
19 Union St.
HABS MA-1061
HABS MASS,10-NANT,76F-
2ph/3pg/fr L

Orange & Union Streets Neighborhood Study
(Folger,Seth,House)
26 Orange St.
HABS MA-1072
HABS MASS,10-NANT,76Q-
1ph/2pg/fr L

Orange & Union Streets Neighborhood Study (Gardner,Solomon & Paul,House)
1 & 3 Stone Alley
HABS MA-1076
HABS MASS,10-NANT,76Y-
8dr/2ph/6pg/fr L H

Orange & Union Streets Neighborhood Study
(Gorham.Josiah,House; Blackburn,Elizabeth,House)
29 Orange St.
HABS MA-1074
HABS MASS,10-NANT,76W-
2ph/4pg/fr L

Orange & Union Streets Neighborhood Study
(Green,Elisha,House)
9 Union St.
HABS MA-1056
HABS MASS,10-NANT,76A-
2ph/3pg/fr L

Orange & Union Streets Neighborhood Study
(Hussey,Christopher,House)
12 Orange St.
HABS MA-1064
HABS MASS,10-NANT,76J-
1ph/5pg/fr L

Orange & Union Streets Neighborhood Study (Macy,William F.,House)
31 Orange St.
HABS MA-1075
HABS MASS,10-NANT,76X-
2ph/2pg/fr L

Orange & Union Streets Neighborhood Study
(Myrick,Andrew,House)
16 Orange St.
HABS MA-1067
HABS MASS,10-NANT,76M-
1ph/3pg/fr L

Orange & Union Streets Neighborhood Study
(Nichols,William,House; Clapp,Timothy G.,House)
HABS MA-1059
HABS MASS,10-NANT,76D-
1ph/5pg/fr L

Documentation: **ct** color transparencies **dr** measured drawings **fr** field records
pc photograph captions **pg** pages of text **ph** photographs

Orange & Union Streets Neighborhood Study
(Pierce,Easton,Russell,Bunker & Gardner Houses; Orange Street Block)
15,17,19,21 & 23 Orange St.
HABS MA-947
HABS MASS,10-NANT,76U-
8dr/18ph/7pg/fr L

Orange & Union Streets Neighborhood Study
(Pinkham,Henry,House; Ayers,Lawrence,House)
13 Orange St.
HABS MA-1065
HABS MASS,10-NANT,76T-
2ph/3pg/fr L

Orange & Union Streets Neighborhood Study
(Starbuck,Levi,House; Codd,James,House)
14 Orange St.
HABS MA-912
HABS MASS,10-NANT,76K-
10dr/2ph/7pg/fr L

Orange & Union Streets Neighborhood Study (Tupper-Folger House; Tupper,Benjamin,House)
28 Orange St.
HABS MA-1073
HABS MASS,10-NANT,76R-
2ph/3pg/fr L

Orange & Union Streets Neighborhood Study (Upton,George B.,House)
2 Stone Alley
HABS MA-1077
HABS MASS,10-NANT,76Z-
2ph/4pg/fr L

Orange & Union Streets Neighborhood Study
(West,Joseph,House)
17 Union St.
HABS MA-1060
HABS MASS,10-NANT,76E-
2ph/3pg/fr L

Orange & Union Streets Neighborhood Study
(Woodbury,Nathaniel,House)
22 Orange St.
HABS MA-1070
HABS MASS,10-NANT,76P-
2ph/3pg/fr L

Orange Street Block; see Orange & Union Streets Neighborhood Study

Pacific Club; see Rotch,William,Warehouse

Pacific National Bank
Main,Centre & Liberty Sts.
HABS MA-938
HABS MASS,10-NANT,54-
4ph/3pg L

Parliament House
10 Pine St.
HABS MA-1201
10dr H

Petticoat Row; see Nantucket Lodge No. 66,I. O. O. F.

Pierce,Easton,Russell,Bunker & Gardner Houses; see Orange & Union Streets Neighborhood Study

Pinkham,Henry,House; see Orange & Union Streets Neighborhood Study

Raymond-Coleman House
53 Orange St.
HABS MA-837
HABS MASS,10-NANT,16-
3ph/3pg L

Rotch,William,Warehouse (Pacific Club)
Main & South Water Sts.
HABS MA-836
HABS MASS,10-NANT,15-
11dr/10ph/8pg/fr L H

Russell,John,House; see India Street Neighborhood Study

Sandanwede (Stiefel House)
79 Hulbert Ave.
HABS MA-968
HABS MASS,10-NANT,70-
4dr/11ph/6pg L

Sanford,Frederick C.,Garden
Federal,Broad & Water Sts.
HABS MA-162
HABS MASS,10-NANT,7A-
5dr/fr L

Satler Memorial; see Hadwen,William,House

Sea Cliff Inn
31 Cliff Rd.
HABS MA-967
HABS MASS,10-NANT,69-
18ph/6pg L

Sevenfires; see Daggett,Margaret Gardner,House

Sherburne Hall; see Nantucket Lodge No. 66,I. O. O. F.

Siasconset Neighborhood Study
Broadway,Shell,New,Center & Front Sts. & Pump Sq.
HABS MA-1208
30dr H

Siasconset Union Chapel
New St. ,Siasconset
HABS MA-1205
12dr H

Snelling,Rev. Samuel,House; see Orange & Union Streets Neighborhood Study

Snow House; see India Street Neighborhood Study

Society of Friends Meetinghouse
Fair St.
HABS MA-966
HABS MASS,10-NANT,68-
6dr/5ph/5pg L

Star of the Sea Youth Hostel
Western Ave.
HABS MA-1100
HABS MASS,10-NANT,85-
11dr L

Starbuck-Newhouse House
15 Liberty St.
HABS MA-1103
HABS MASS,10-NANT,86-
10dr L

Starbuck,Christopher,House
105 Main St.
HABS MA-939
HABS MASS,10-NANT,55-
12dr/4ph/3pg L H

Starbuck,Joseph,House (Candle Factory)
4 New Dollar Ln.
HABS MA-940
HABS MASS,10-NANT,56-
9ph/4pg L

Starbuck,Joseph,Houses (Three Bricks,The)
93,95, & 97 Main St.
HABS MA-941
HABS MASS,10-NANT,57-
8ph/5pg L

Starbuck,Levi,House; see Orange & Union Streets Neighborhood Study

Starbuck,Thomas,Homestead
11 Milk St.
HABS MA-942
HABS MASS,10-NANT,12-
3ph/3pg L

Steamboat Wharf
Steamboat Wharf
HABS MA-1203
6dr H

Stiefel House; see Sandanwede

Stubbs,Capt. William,House; see India Street Neighborhood Study

Swain House
3 Weymouth St.
HABS MA-1098
HABS MASS,10-NANT,87-
5dr L

Swain-Macy House (Valentine-Swain House)
99 Main St.
HABS MA-944
HABS MASS,10-NANT,59-
13ph/7pg L

Swain-Mitchell House
(Mitchell,Maria,House)
1 Vestal St.
HABS MA-901
HABS MASS,10-NANT,25-
10dr/8ph/8pg L

Swain,John Howland,House; see India Street Neighborhood Study

Swift,Benjamin,House; see India Street Neighborhood Study

Swift,Henry,House (Garden)
91 Main St.
HABS MA-167
HABS MASS,10-NANT,8A-
2dr/fr L

Taber,Rescom,House; see India Street Neighborhood Study

Tashama Farm
Surfside Rd.
HABS MA-943
HABS MASS,10-NANT,58-
3ph/3pg L

Three Bricks,The; see Starbuck,Joseph,Houses

Tupper-Folger House; see Orange & Union Streets Neighborhood Study

Tupper,Benjamin,House; see Orange & Union Streets Neighborhood Study

U.S. Lifesaving Station
Surfside
HABS MA-930
HABS MASS,10-NANT,49-
3ph/3pg/fr L

Union Lodge,F. & A. M. (Masonic Lodge)
63 Main St.
HABS MA-899
HABS MASS,10-NANT,23-
6dr/5ph/7pg/fr L

Unitarian Church; see Orange & Union Streets Neighborhood Study

Upton,George B.,House; see Orange & Union Streets Neighborhood Study

Valentine-Swain House; see Swain-Macy House

Wallace Hall; see Barrett,John Wendell,House

Wellington-Merrill House
27 Hulbert Ave.
HABS MA-1104
HABS MASS,10-NANT,88-
10dr L

West,Joseph,House; see Orange & Union Streets Neighborhood Study

Whaling Museum; see Hadwen & Barney Candle House

Windmill,Old (East Mill)
N. Mill & S. Mill Sts.
HABS MA-141
HABS MASS,10-NANT,6-
5dr/3ph L

Wood,Charles,House (Easton-Wood House)
1 North Water St.
HABS MA-898
HABS MASS,10-NANT,22-
5dr/4ph/6pg L

Wood,Obediah,House; see India Street Neighborhood Study

Woodbury,Nathaniel,House; see Orange & Union Streets Neighborhood Study

Worth-Gardner House
3 Academy La.
HABS MA-1253
HABS DLC/PP-1992:MA-2
15dr/11pg/fr L

Wyer,Robert,House
33 Orange St.
HABS MA-946
HABS MASS,10-NANT,60-
3ph/3pg L

Yard Fences and Porch Newels
Nantucket County
HABS MA-614
HABS MASS,10- ,1-
1dr L

SIASCONSET

Auld Lang Syne; see Coffin,Micah,House

Baxter,Capt. William,House; see Shanunga

Cary,Betsey,Cottage; see Shanunga

Coffin,Micah,House (Auld Lang Syne; Coleman,Capt. Henry,House)
Broadway
HABS MA-857
HABS MASS,10-SCON,2-
2dr/2ph/4pg L

Coleman,Capt. Henry,House; see Coffin,Micah,House

Shanunga (Cary,Betsey,Cottage; Baxter,Capt. William,House)
Mitchell St. (moved from original location)
HABS MA-610
HABS MASS,10-SCON,1-
2dr/3ph/5pg L

NORFOLK COUNTY

BRAINTREE

Milestone J; see Twelve-mile Stone

Twelve-mile Stone (Milestone J)
Commercial St.
HABS MA-128
HABS MASS,11-BRAI,2-
1ph L

BROOKLINE

Boston Water Works:Fisher Hill Reservoir & Gatehse
Fisher Ave.
HAER MA-50
HAER MASS,11-BROK,3-
1ph/1pg/1pc L

Cochituate Aqueduct,Brookline Reservoir Gatehouse
Boylston & Warren Sts.
HAER MA-32
HAER MASS,11-BROK,4-
2ph/1pg/1pc L

Fairsted (Olmsted,Frederick Law,National Historic Site)
99 Warren Street
HABS MA-1168
HABS MASS,11-BROK,6-
13dr/14ph/1pg/1pc/fr L

John F. Kennedy National Historic Site; see Kennedy,John Fitzgerald,Birthplace

Kennedy,John Fitzgerald,Birthplace (John F. Kennedy National Historic Site)
83 Beals St.
HABS MA-897
HABS MASS,11-BROK,7-
7dr/25ph/1pg/2pc L

Lynch-O'Gorman House
41 Mason Terrace
HABS MA-959
HABS MASS,11-BROK,8-
10ph/1pc L

Milestones GG & OOO
Various Brookline locations
HABS MA-128
HABS MASS,11-BROK,2-
2dr/2ph L

Olmsted,Frederick Law,National Historic Site; see Fairsted

Reservoir Car House; see West End Street Railway:Cleveland Circle Car House

West End Street Railway:Cleveland Circle Car House (Reservoir Car House)
Chestnut Hill Ave. & Beacon St. vic.
HAER MA-43
HAER MASS,11-BROK,5-
1ph/1pg/1pc L

CANTON

Boston & Providence RR:Canton Viaduct
Neponset St. at E. branch of Neponset River
HAER MA-27
HAER MASS,11-CANT,2-
2ph/2pg/1pc/1ct L

Milestones L,M,N & O
Washington St.
HABS MA-128
HABS MASS,11-CANT,1-
4ph L

COHASSET

Cushing-Nichols House
HABS MA-350
HABS MASS,11-COHA,4-
3ph/fr L

First Parish Meetinghouse
Cohasset Common
HABS MA-349
HABS MASS,11-COHA,1-
5ph/fr L

Fitch House
HABS MA-598
HABS MASS,11,COHA,6-
1ph L

Hobart,Rev. Nehemiah,House
HABS MA-351
HABS MASS,11-COHA,5-
10ph/fr L

Shaw-Souther House
Highland Ave.
HABS MA-231
HABS MASS,11-COHA,3-
16dr L

DEDHAM

Allin Congregational Church
High St.
HABS MA-568
HABS MASS,11-DED,6-
1ph L

Barrows Woolen Mill; see Norfolk Manufacturing Co. Cotton Mill

Dedham Inn; see Richards,Edward M.,House

Fairbanks,Jonathan,House
511 East St.
HABS MA-223
HABS MASS,11-DED,1-
24dr/25ph/1pg/2pc L

Fisher-Whiting House
218 Cedar St.
HABS MA-114
HABS MASS,11-DED,3-
9dr/7ph/fr L

Haven,Samuel,House
669 High St.
HABS MA-567
HABS MASS,11-DED,5-
2ph L

Lovell,John M.,House; see Richards,Edward M.,House

Norfolk Manufacturing Co. Cotton Mill (Barrows Woolen Mill; United Waste Co.)
90 Milton St.
HAER MA-80
HAER MASS,11-DED,7-
20ph/1pg/2pc/3ct L

Powder House
162 Ames St.
HABS MA-2-66
HABS MASS,11-DED,2-
1dr/1ph/fr L

Richards,Edward M.,House
(Lovell,John M.,House; Dedham Inn)
Highland Ave.
HABS MA-258
HABS MASS,11-DED,4-
6dr/1ph/4pg/fr L

Spring Street Bridge (Vine Rock Bridge)
Spanning Charles Rvie between Dedham & Boston
HAER MA-95
HAER DLC/PP-1992:MA-4
4ph/8pg/1pc L

United Waste Co.; see Norfolk Manufacturing Co. Cotton Mill

Vine Rock Bridge; see Spring Street Bridge

DOVER

Caryl Parsonage
Dedham St.
HABS MA-357
HABS MASS,11-DOV,1-
11ph L

Chickering House
HABS MA-566
HABS MASS,11-DOV,3-
1ph L

First Parish Meetinghouse
Springdale Ave.
HABS MA-565
HABS MASS,11-DOV,2-
1ph L

Wentworth,Col. Paul,House
(moved from NH,Salmon Falls)
HABS NH-35
HABS NH,9-SALFA,1-
41dr/154ph/12pg/fr L

FRANKLIN

Schoolhouse,Little Red Brick
HABS MA-450
HABS MASS,11-FRANK,1-
2ph L

MEDFIELD

Clark,Seth,House; see Peak House,The

Peak House,The (Clark,Seth,House)
Main St.
HABS MA-2-77
HABS MASS,11-MED,1-
2dr/2ph/fr L

MILTON

"Suffolk Resolves House"; see Vose,Daniel,House

Belcher,Gov. Jonathan,House & Garden
401 Adams St.
HABS MA-196
HABS MASS,11-MILT,6-
9dr/4ph/fr L

Davenport,Isaac,House
HABS MA-465
HABS MASS,11-MILT,8-
1ph L

Forbes Museum; see Forbes,Capt. Robert Bennett,House

Forbes,Capt. Robert Bennett,House
(Forbes Museum)
215 Adams St.
HABS MA-975
HABS MASS,11-MILT,11-
8ph/1pc L

Holbrook,Dr. Amos,Garden
203 Adams St.
HABS MA-232
HABS MASS,11-MILT,7-
4dr/fr L

Howe,Joseph N.,House
597 Randolph Ave.
HABS MA-138
HABS MASS,11-MILT,4-
6dr/2ph/fr L

Hutchinson,Gov. Thomas,House (Wing)
195 Adams St.
HABS MA-168
HABS MASS,11-MILT,5-
6dr/2ph/fr L

Hutchinson,Gov. Thomas,House & Garden
195 Adams St.
HABS MA-168-A
HABS MASS,11-MILT,5-
4dr/1ph/fr L

Milestones C,F,G,K,FFF & JJJ
Various Milton locations
HABS MA-128
HABS MASS,11-MILT,9-
3dr/9ph L

Powder House
781 Canton Ave.
HABS MA-2-66-A
HABS MASS,11-MILT,3-
1dr/1ph/fr L

Shepard-Hinckley House
264 Brook Rd.
HABS MA-613
HABS MASS,11-MILT,10-
7dr L

Vose,Daniel,House ("Suffolk Resolves House")
1370 Canton Ave. (moved from 38 Adams St.)
HABS MA-2-13
HABS MASS,11-MILT,2-
6dr/3ph L

NATICK

Natick Research & Development Laboratories
HAER MA-52
HAER MASS,9-NAT,2-
38pg/fr L

PLAINVILLE

Slack,Benjamin,House
South St.
HABS MA-155
HABS MASS,11-PLANV,1-
7dr/1ph/fr L

QUINCY

Apprentice School; see General Dynamics Corporation Shipyard,

Jainer & Sheet Metal Shops; see General Dynamics Corporation Shipyard,

McMylar Crane; see General Dynamics Corporation Shipyard,

Outfitting Pier 2; see General Dynamics Corporation Shipyard,

Outfitting Pier 3; see General Dynamics Corporation Shipyard,

XYZ Crane & Towers; see General Dynamics Corporation Shipyard,

Adams Garden; see Adams Mansion,Flower Garden

Adams Mansion (Vassal House; Adams National Historic Site)
135 Adams St.
HABS MA-615
HABS MASS,11-QUI,5-(DLC/PP-1992:MA-5)
26dr/38ph/7pg/3pc/fr L

Adams Mansion,Carriagehouse-Stable (Adams National Historic Site; Vassall House,Carriagehouse-Stable; House,Old,Carriagehouse-Stable)
135 Adams St.
HABS MA-504
HABS MASS,11-QUI,5B-
2ph/1pc/fr L

Adams Mansion,Doghouse (Adams National Historic Site; Vassal-Adams House,Doghouse; House,Old,Doghouse)
135 Adams St.
HABS MA-994
HABS MASS,11-QUI,5C-
1dr/fr L

Adams Mansion,Flower Garden (Adams National Historic Site,Flower Garden; Vassal-Adams House,Flower Garden; House,Old-Flower Garden; Adams Garden)
135 Adams St.
HABS MA-215
HABS MASS,11-QUI,5A-
14dr L

Adams Mansion,Stone Library (Adams National Historic Site)
135 Adams St.
HABS MA-841
HABS MASS,11-QUI,5D-(DLC/PP-1992:MA-5)
7dr/8ph/2pc/fr L

Adams Mansion,Woodshed (Adams National Historic Site; Vassal House,Woodshed; House,Old,Woodshed)
135 Adams St.
HABS MA-842
HABS MASS,11-QUI,5E-
3dr/2ph/1pc/fr L

Adams National Historic Site; see Adams Mansion

Adams National Historic Site; see Adams Mansion,Carriagehouse-Stable

Adams National Historic Site; see Adams Mansion,Doghouse

Adams National Historic Site; see Adams Mansion,Stone Library

Adams National Historic Site; see Adams Mansion,Woodshed

Adams National Historic Site,Flower Garden; see Adams Mansion,Flower Garden

Adams,John Quincy,Birthplace
141 Franklin St.
HABS MA-597
HABS MASS,11-QUI,7-
3dr/7ph/4pg/1pc/fr L

Adams,John,Birthplace
133 Franklin St.
HABS MA-596
HABS MASS,11-QUI,6-
4dr/11ph/2pg/1pc/fr L

Blue Bell Tavern; see Railroad House,Old

Church of the Presidents; see Stone Temple

General Dynamics Corp. Shipyard, Structure No. 33S; see General Dynamics Corporation Shipyard,

General Dynamics Corp. Shipyard,Structure No. 21S; see General Dynamics Corporation Shipyard,

General Dynamics Corp. Shipyard,Structure No. 22S; see General Dynamics Corporation Shipyard,Dravo Cranes

General Dynamics Corporation Shipyard
97 E. Howard St. at Fore River
HAER MA-26
HAER MASS,11-QUI,10-
5ph/23pg/3pc L

General Dynamics Corporation Shipyard, (Apprentice School; General Dynamics Corporation Shipyard, Bldg. 41)
97 East Howard Street
HAER MA-26-B
16ph/7pg/3pc H

General Dynamics Corporation Shipyard, (Jainer & Sheet Metal Shops; General Dynamics Corporation Shipyard, Bldg. No. 9
97 East Howard Street
HAER MA-26-A
25ph/7pg/4pc H

General Dynamics Corporation Shipyard, (McMylar Crane; General Dynamics Corp. Shipyard, Structure No. 33S
97 East Howard street
HAER MA-26-G
25ph/7pg/4pc H

General Dynamics Corporation Shipyard, (Outfitting Pier 2; General Dynamics Corporation Shipyard, Pier 25)
97 East Howard Street
HAER MA-26-C
14ph/6pg/3pc H

General Dynamics Corporation Shipyard, (Outfitting Pier 3; General Dynamics Corporation Shipyard, Pier 35)
97 East Howard Street
HAER MA-26-D
6ph/6pg/2pc H

General Dynamics Corporation Shipyard, (XYZ Crane & Towers; General Dynamics Corp. Shipyard,Structure No. 21S)
97 East Howard Street
HAER MA-26-E
16ph/6pg/3pc H

General Dynamics Corporation Shipyard, Bldg. No. 9; see General Dynamics Corporation Shipyard,

General Dynamics Corporation Shipyard, Bldg. 41; see General Dynamics Corporation Shipyard,

General Dynamics Corporation Shipyard, Pier 25; see General Dynamics Corporation Shipyard,

General Dynamics Corporation Shipyard, Pier 35; see General Dynamics Corporation Shipyard,

General Dynamics Corporation Shipyard,Dravo Cranes (General Dynamics Corp. Shipyard,Structure No. 22S)
97 East Howard Street
HAER MA-26-F
18ph/6pg/3pc H

Granite Railway
Pine Hill Quarry to Neponset River
HABS MA-150
HABS MASS,11-QUI,4-
6dr/9ph/fr L

House,Old-Flower Garden; see Adams Mansion,Flower Garden

House,Old,Carriagehouse-Stable; see Adams Mansion,Carriagehouse-Stable

House,Old,Doghouse; see Adams Mansion,Doghouse

House,Old,Woodshed; see Adams Mansion,Woodshed

Milestones H,I,CCC,DDD & EEE
Various Quincy locations
HABS MA-128
HABS MASS,11-QUI,9-
3dr/5ph L

Quincy,Col. Josiah,House
20 Muirhead St.
HABS MA-2-42
HABS MASS,11-QUI,3-
13dr/8ph/fr L

Railroad House,Old (Blue Bell Tavern)
Granite Railway
HABS MA-150-A
HABS MASS,11-QUI,4C-
1dr/1ph L

Souther Tide Mill Dam
HAER MA-57
5ph/15pg/1pc H

Stone Temple (Unitarian Church; Church of the Presidents)
1266 Hancock St.
HABS MA-599
HABS MASS,11-QUI,8-
2ph L

Unitarian Church; see Stone Temple

Vassal House; see Adams Mansion

Vassal House,Woodshed; see Adams Mansion,Woodshed

Vassal-Adams House,Doghouse; see Adams Mansion,Doghouse

Vassal-Adams House,Flower Garden; see Adams Mansion,Flower Garden

Vassall House,Carriagehouse-Stable; see Adams Mansion,Carriagehouse-Stable

RANDOLPH

Milestone GGG; see Twelve-mile Stone

Twelve-mile Stone (Milestone GGG)
Old St.
HABS MA-128
HABS MASS,11-RAND,4-
1ph L

SHARON

Cobb's Tavern
36 Bay St.
HABS MA-336
HABS MASS,11-SHAR,1-
9ph/16pg L

STOUGHTON

Atherton,Samuel,House
449 Central St.
HABS MA-200
HABS MASS,11-STOU,2-
7dr/2ph L

Boston & Providence Railroad,Stoughton Station
53 Wyman St.
HAER MA-28
HAER MASS,11-STOU,3-
1ph/1pg/1pc L

New Haven Railroad Station
Wyman St.
HABS MA-972
HABS MASS,11-STOU,5-
7ph/1pg/1pc L

Stoughton Water Works:Pumping Station
Central St. ,1700 Block
HAER MA-45
HAER MASS,11-STOU,4-
1ph/1pg/1pc L

Washington Hotel
710 Turnpike St.
HABS MA-171
HABS MASS,11-STOU,1-
10dr/5ph L

WALPOLE

Fales,L. F. ,Machine Company
East & Elm Sts.
HAER MA-49
HAER MASS,11-WALP,2-
1ph/1pg/1pc L

Gilmore,W. K. ,Grain Elevator
East St.
HAER MA-44
HAER MASS,11-WALP,3-
1ph/1pg/1pc L

Milestone CC; see Twenty-mile Stone

Twenty-mile Stone (Milestone CC)
Town Hall Vic.
HABS MA-128
HABS MASS,11-WALP,1-
1ph L

WELLESLEY

Blossom Street Bridge; see Boston & Albany Railroad:Weston Road Bridge

Boston & Albany Railroad:Kingsbury Street Bridge
Spanning the Boston & Albany RR on Kingsbury St.
HAER MA-117
HAER DLC/PP-1992:MA-4
5ph/10pg/1pc L

Boston & Albany Railroad:Weston Road Bridge (Blossom Street Bridge)
Spanning the Boston & Albany RR on Weston Rd.
HAER MA-118
HAER DLC/PP-1992:MA-4
10ph/10pg/1pc L

Boston and Albany Railroad Station
HABS MA-668
HABS MASS,11-WEL,3-
3ph/3pg L

Cheney Bridge
HAER MA-85
2ph H

Deming,Capt. Asa,House
(moved from CT,Rocky Hill)
HABS CT-13
HABS CONN,2-ROHI,3-
18dr/7ph/2pg L

Ellis Stone Barn
Boylston St.
HABS MA-145
HABS MASS,11-WEL,1-
2dr/3ph/fr L

Hunnewell Cottage (The Cottage)
848 Washington St.
HABS MA-1226
HABS 1989(HABS):10
15ph/1pg/1pc L

The Cottage; see Hunnewell Cottage

Town Hall of Wellesley
525 Washington St.
HABS MA-1230
HABS 1989(HABS):10
15ph/1pg/1pc L

Ware,Ruben,Mill
HABS MA-546
HABS MASS,11-WEL,2-
1ph L

WESTWOOD

Town Pound
Grove St.
HABS MA-2-32
HABS MASS,11-WESWO,1-
1dr/1ph/fr L

WEYMOUTH

Adams,Abigail (Smith),House
450 Bridge St.
HABS MA-417
HABS MASS,11-WEYMO,2-
1ph/fr L

Edison Elec. Illum. Co. ,Chas. L. Edgar Station
Bridge St. at Fore River
HAER MA-34
HAER MASS,11-WEYMO,6-
3ph/1pg/1pc L

First Church
HABS MA-594
HABS MASS,11-WEYMO,3-
1ph L

Fogg,John S. ,Shoe Factory
4-10 Union St. ,Columbian Square
HAER MA-42
HAER MASS,11-WEYMO,4-
2ph/2pg/1pc L

Fore River Bridge
Rt. 3A,spanning Fore River
HAER MA-36
HAER MASS,11-WEYMO,5-
4ph/1pg/1pc L

Wildes,Capt. William,House
872 Commercial St.
HABS MA-248
HABS MASS,11-WEYMO,1-
13ph/fr L

WRENTHAM

Fisher,David,House (Gray Door Inn)
HABS MA-420
HABS MASS,11-WRENTH,1-
4ph/fr L

Gray Door Inn; see Fisher,David,House

Guild-Kollock House
HABS MA-421
HABS MASS,11-WRENTH,2-
9ph/fr L

PLYMOUTH COUNTY

BRIDGEWATER

Andrews House (Pratt,Betty,House)
38 Walnut St.
HABS MA-2-91
HABS MASS,12-BRIG,1-
5dr/7ph L

Haywood House
HABS MA-343
HABS MASS,12-BRIG,2-
2ph L

Pratt,Betty,House; see Andrews House

BROCKTON

Brockton City Hall
45 School St.
HABS MA-1158
HABS MASS,12-BROCK,1-
12ph/8pg/1pc/fr L

DUXBURY

King Caesar House
King Caesar Rd.,Powder Point
HABS MA-326
HABS MASS,12-DUX,3-
5ph L

U.S. Frigate Constitution,Cannon
HABS MA-2-84-B
HABS MASS,12-DUX,2-
1ph L

GREENBUSH

Old Oaken Bucket House
Old Oaken Bucket Rd.
HABS MA-2-41
HABS MASS,12-GREBU,2-
6dr/2ph/fr L

Stedman-Russell-Stockbridge Grist Mill; see Stedman,Isaac,Grist Mill

Stedman,Isaac,Grist Mill
(Stedman-Russell-Stockbridge Grist Mill)
County Way
HABS MA-2-14
HABS MASS,12-GREBU,1-
3dr/2ph/fr L

HALIFAX

Fence
HABS MA-328
HABS MASS,12-HAL,4A-
1ph L

Standish,Shadrach,House
Monponsett St.
HABS MA-2-70
HABS MASS,12-HAL,3-
3dr/4ph L

Wood,Timothy,House
HABS MA-362
HABS MASS,12-HAL,5-
11ph L

HANOVER CENTER

Stetson,Samuel,House
Hanover St.
HABS MA-611
HABS MASS,12-HANO,3-
6dr L

HINGHAM

Beal,John,House
HABS MA-364
HABS MASS,12-HING,9-
4ph/fr L

Cushing House
S. Pleasant St.
HABS MA-2-85
HABS MASS,12-HING,6-
12dr/9ph/fr L

First Parish Meetinghouse; see Old Ship Church

Garrison House,Old; see Lincoln,Perez,House

Lincoln,Gen. Benjamin,House
HABS MA-363
HABS MASS,12-HING,8-
13ph/fr L

Lincoln,Perez,House (Garrison House,Old)
123 North St. (moved from original location)
HABS MA-600
HABS MASS,12-HING,12-
5ph L

Lincoln,Samuel,Cottage
182 North St.
HABS MA-620
HABS MASS,12-HING,13-
2dr L

Loring,Thomas,House
HABS MA-366
HABS MASS,12-HING,10-
3ph/fr L

Old Ship Church (First Parish Meetinghouse)
88 Main St.
HABS MA-595
HABS MASS,12-HING,5-
11dr/21ph/2pg/1pc/fr L

Pilgrim Cottage
HABS MA-455
HABS MASS,12-HING,11-
1ph L

Shute,Daniel,House
Main & S. Pleasant Sts.
HABS MA-197
HABS MASS,12-HING,7-
21dr/15ph L

Wilder,Jabez,House
Main St.
HABS MA-137
HABS MASS,12-HING,1-
13dr/10ph L

KINGSTON

Bradford,Maj. John,House (Jones River Village Club)
Maple St. & Landing Rd.
HABS MA-2-78
HABS MASS,12-KING,1-
6dr/7ph L

Holmes House
HABS MA-369
HABS MASS,12-KING,3-
3ph L

Jones River Village Club; see Bradford,Maj. John,House

Sever,Squire William,House & Garden
2 Linden St.
HABS MA-135
HABS MASS,12-KING,2-
25dr/19ph/fr L

Willet,Capt. Thomas,House
HABS MA-370
HABS MASS,12-KING,4-
9ph/fr L

LAKEVILLE

Nelson,Col. John,House; see Sampson,Jennie,House

Sampson,Jennie,House (Nelson,Col. John,House)
Main St. (moved to MA,North Chatham)
HABS MA-297
HABS MASS,12-LAKVI,2-
6ph/fr L

Ward,George,House
Crooked Ln.
HABS MA-2-20
HABS MASS,12-LAKVI,1-
6dr/2ph L

MARION

First Universalist Church
Pleasant & Main Sts.
HABS MA-241
HABS MASS,12-MAR,2-
7dr L

MARSHFIELD

Hatch,Walter,House
HABS MA-375
HABS MASS,12-MARSF,1-
5ph/fr L

Thomas,Anthony,House
HABS MA-376
HABS MASS,12-MARSF,2-
4ph/fr L

Weatherbee,George H.,House
HABS MA-377
HABS MASS,12-MARSF,3-
10ph/fr L

Winslow House
HABS MA-815
HABS MASS,12-MARSF,4-
5ph L

MARSHFIELD HILLS

Clift House
Spring St.
HABS MA-207
HABS MASS,12-MARSH,1-
19dr/1ph L

MIDDLEBORO

Eddy,Zachariah,Law Office
(moved to MA,West Springfield)
HABS MA-851
HABS MASS,7-SPRIFW,6-
1ph/1pc L

MIDDLEBOROUGH

Central Methodist Church
Cherry St.
HABS MA-2-68
HABS MASS,12-MIDBO,8-
2dr/1ph L

First Congregational Church,Carriage Sheds
Plympton St.
HABS MA-2-39
HABS MASS,12-MIDBO,4-
1dr/8ph L

Mill Houses
20 & 22 Jackson St.
HABS MA-379-A
HABS MASS,12-MIDBO,12-
1ph/fr L

Mill Houses
24,26 & 28 Jackson St.
HABS MA-379-B
HABS MASS,12-MIDBO,13-
4ph/fr L

Mill Houses
30 Jackson St.
HABS MA-379-C
HABS MASS,12-MIDBO,14-
3ph/fr L

Mill Houses
32 & 34 Jackson St.
HABS MA-379-D
HABS MAS,12-MIDBO,15-
1ph/fr L

Mill Houses
36 & 38 Jackson St.
HABS MA-379-E
HABS MASS,12-MIDBO,16-
1ph L

Peirce,Col. P. H.,Store
N. Main St.
HABS MA-2-7
HABS MASS,12-MIDBO,1-
9dr/10ph L

Peirce,L. T.,Store
N. Main & Jackson Sts.
HABS MA-2-28
HABS MASS,12-MIDBO,2-
2dr/1ph L

Robinson,E.,Store
N. Main & Jackson Sts.
HABS MA-2-29
HABS MASS,12-MIDBO,3-
1dr/1ph L

Sampson,Deborah,House
280 Wareham St.
HABS MA-2-49
HABS MASS,12-MIDBO,6-
1dr/1ph L

Sproat House
HABS MA-378
HABS MASS,12-MIDBO,11-
9ph/fr L

Tavern Inn,Old
Wareham St. (State Rt. 28)
HABS MA-2-40
HABS MASS,12-MIDBO,5-
4dr/8ph L

Thompson,Venus,House
Thompson St.
HABS MA-2-64
HABS MASS,12-MIDBO,7-
3dr/1ph L

Wood,Judge,Office
123 S. Main St.
HABS MA-198
HABS MASS,12-MIDBO,9-
2dr/2ph/fr L

Wood,Silas,House
HABS MA-331
HABS MASS,12-MIDBO,10-
3ph L

NORTH CARVER

Sturtevant House
N. Carver Green
HABS MA-2-96
HABS MASS,12-CARVN,1-
2dr/2ph L

NORTH HINGHAM

New North Meetinghouse
North & Lincoln Sts.
HABS MA-422
HABS MASS,12-HINGN,1-
3ph/fr L

NORTH PEMBROKE

Society of Friends Meetinghouse
Schoosett St. (Rts. 139 & 53)
HABS MA-2-59
HABS MASS,12-PEMBN,1-ı1989(HABS):10°
7dr/14ph/1pg/1pc/fr L

NORWELL

Bryant-Cushing House
Cornet Stetson Rd.
HABS MA-109
HABS MASS,12-NOR,1-
12dr/9ph/fr L

PLYMOUTH

Cape Cod Windmill (Eastham Windmill)
(moved to MA,Truro)
HABS MA-2-21
HABS MASS,1-EAST,1-
5dr/7ph L

Eastham Windmill; see Cape Cod Windmill

Lord House (Garden); see Warren,David,House (Garden)

Warren,David,House (Garden) (Lord House (Garden))
24 North St.
HABS MA-185
HABS MASS,12-PLYM,23A-
2dr/fr L

SCITUATE

Lawson Water Tower
First Parish Rd.
HABS MA-1218
HABS 1989(HABS):10
13ph/1pg/1pc L

SCITUATE VIC.

Lighthouse & Keeper's House
Cedar Point Scituate Harbor
HABS MA-2-22
HABS MASS,12-SCIT.V,1-
5dr/2ph/fr L

WAREHAM

Fearing-Warr House
(Fearing,Israel,House)
14 Elm St.
HABS MA-102
HABS MASS,12-WARH,1-
16dr/5ph L

Fearing,Israel,House; see Fearing-Warr House

Tremont Nail Works
21 Elm St.
HAER MA-77
HAER 1990 (HAER):8
9ph/1pc L

SUFFOLK COUNTY

BOSTON

"Gothic,The" (Apartment House)
47 Allen St.
HABS MA-669
HABS MASS,13-BOST,63-
4ph/2pg L

Abolition Church (Boston African American National Historic Site)
8 Smith Court
HABS MA-2-74
HABS MASS,13-BOST,42-
3dr/12ph/2pg/1pc/fr L

American Brewing Company
325 Heath St.
HAER MA-29
HAER MASS,13-BOST,73-
2ph/1pg/1pc L

Amory-Ticknor House
9 Park St.
HABS MA-175
HABS MASS,13-BOST,15-
19dr/13ph L

Locations: **H** HABS/HAER, National Park Service **L** Library of Congress

Appleton,Nathan,House (Women's City Club)
40 Beacon St.
HABS MA-813
HABS MASS,13-BOST,94-
2dr/2ph/1pc/fr L

Argyle Building (Sheffield,The)
390 Massachusetts Ave.
HABS MA-1111
HABS MASS,13-BOST,95-
3ph/1pg/1pc L

Arlington Street Church
Arlington & Boylston Sts.
HABS MA-817
HABS MASS,13-BOST,34-
7ph/1pc L

B. F. Keith Memorial Theatre (Opera House)
539 Washington St.
HABS MA-1078
HABS MASS,13-BOST,69-
40ph/62pg/3pc L

Back Bay Station
145 Dartmouth St.
HABS MA-1107
HABS MASS,13-BOST,96-
15ph/4pg/1pc L

Blake,James,House
735 Columbia Rd.
HABS MA-560
HABS MASS,13-DORCH,5-
8ph/1pg/1pc L

Boston & Maine RR:Charles River Bridges
Charles River,North Station vic.
HAER MA-22
HAER MASS,13-BOST,74-
2ph/2pg/1pc L

Boston African American National Historic Site; see Abolition Church

Boston City Hall (City Hall,New)
One City Hall Sq.
HABS MA-1176
HABS MASS,13-BOST,71-
12ph/11pg/1pc/fr L

Boston City Hall (City Hall,Old)
41-45 School St.
HABS MA-860
HABS MASS,13-BOST,70-
24ph/15pg/2pc L

Boston Elevated Railway,Elevated Mainline (Metro. Bay Trans. Authority,Orange Line)
Washington St.
HAER MA-14
85ph/319pg/11pc L

Boston National Historic Park; see Revere,Paul,House

Boston National Historical Park; see Dorchester Heights Monument

Boston Public Garden, Suspension Bridge
Boston Public Garden
HAER MA-76
HAER 1990 (HAER):8
6ph/1pc L

Boston Townhouse,Second; see Massachusetts State House,Old

Boston Water Wks:Chestnut Hill High Serv Pump Stat
2450 Beacon St.
HAER MA-24
HAER MASS,13-BOST,75-
5ph/2pg/1pc/1ct L

Boston Water Works,Leavitt Pumping Engine (Chestnut Hill High Service Pump. Sta. Engine No. 3
2450 Beacon St.
HAER MA-24-A
HAER MASS,13-BOST,75A-
3ph/5pg/1pc L

Boston Water Works,Worthington Pump (Chestnut Hill High Service Pump. Sta. Engine No. 4
2450 Beacon St.
HAER MA-24-B
HAER MASS,13-BOST,75B-
3ph/1pg/1pc L

Boston Water Works:Roxbury Standpipe
Fort Ave. ,Highland Park
HAER MA-25
HAER MASS,13-BOST,76-
1ph/2pg/1pc/1ct L

Boundary Marker,Boston & Roxbury
2 Nawn St.
HABS MA-1192
HABS MASS,13-BOST,97-
1ph/1pc L

Boundary Stone TTT-Boston Stone; see Boundary Stones QQQ,RRR,SSS, & TTT

Boundary Stones QQQ,RRR,SSS, & TTT (Boundary Stone TTT-Boston Stone)
Various Boston locations
HABS MA-128
HABS MASS,13-BOST,46-
3dr/4ph L

Butler School
River St.,Hyde Park
HABS MA-564
HABS MASS,13-BOST,59-
1ph L

Cambridge Bridge; see Longfellow Bridge

Capen House; see Union Oyster House (Restaurant)

Charles Street Meetinghouse; see Church of Third Baptist Society

Charlestown Navy Yard,Buildings 58 & 60; see Charlestown Navy Yard,Ropewalk & Tar House

Charlestown Navy Yard,Ropewalk & Tar House (Charlestown Navy Yard,Buildings 58 & 60)
HABS MA-1247-A
HABS 1991(HABS):15
14dr/fr L

Chestnut Hill High Service Pump. Sta. Engine No. 3; see Boston Water Works,Leavitt Pumping Engine

Chestnut Hill High Service Pump. Sta. Engine No. 4; see Boston Water Works,Worthington Pump

Christ Church (Old North Church)
193 Salem St.
HABS MA-500
HABS MASS,13-BOST,5-
2ph L

Church of Third Baptist Society (Charles Street Meetinghouse)
Charles St.
HABS MA-544
HABS MASS,13-BOST,58-
1ph L

City Hall,New; see Boston City Hall

City Hall,Old; see Boston City Hall

Clap,Bela & Caleb,House
44-46 Temple St.
HABS MA-2-80
HABS MASS,13-BOST,43-
10dr/4ph/fr L

Clough-Langdon House (Clough,Ebenezer,House)
21 Unity St.
HABS MA-342
HABS MASS,13-BOST,8-
8dr/12ph/4pg/fr L

Clough-Langdon House; see Langdon House

Clough,Ebenezer,House; see Clough-Langdon House

Codman Building
30-48 Hanover St.
HABS MA-784
HABS MASS,13-BOST,98-
3ph/1pc L

Congress Street Bascule Bridge
Spanning Fort Point Channel at Congress St.
HAER MA-38
HAER MASS,13-BOST,77-
DLC/PP-1992:MA-4
41ph/19pg/5pc L

Cornhill District (Houses)
Scollay Sq. & Brattle St.
HABS MA-790
HABS MASS,13-BOST,99-
5ph/1pc L

Cradle of Liberty; see Faneuil Hall

Customs House
State St. at India St.
HABS MA-789
HABS MASS,13-BOST,100-
1ph/1pg/1pc L

Documentation: **ct** color transparencies **dr** measured drawings **fr** field records
pc photograph captions **pg** pages of text **ph** photographs

Dorchester Heights Monument (Boston National Historical Park)
Thomas Park
HABS MA-1171
HABS MASS,13-BOST,101-
7dr/19ph/4pg/3pc/fr L

East Boston Pumping Station
Chelsea St. at Chelsea Creek
HAER MA-65
HAER MASS,13-BOST,78-
16ph/2pg/1pc L

Edison-Spencer-Grafton Block
254-264 Columbus Ave.
HABS MA-1114
HABS MASS,13-BOST,102-
3ph/1pg/1pc L

15 Elm Street (Building)
HABS MA-788
HABS MASS,13-BOST,88-
1ph/2pg/1pc L

Faneuil Hall (Cradle of Liberty)
Dock Square
HABS MA-163
HABS MASS,13-BOST,2-ı1989(HABS):10
4dr/15ph/3pg/2pc L

Fort Independence
Castle Island
HABS MA-570
HABS MASS,13-BOST,37-
6ph L

Fort Winthrop,Citadel
Governor's Island
HABS MA-617
HABS MASS,13-BOST,62-
13dr L

Franklin Park Zoo,Elephant House
Seaver St.
HABS MA-1097
HABS MASS,13-BOST,68B-
8ph L

Franklin Park Zoo,Feline House
Seaver St.
HABS MA-1096
HABS MASS,13-BOST,68A-
8ph L

Franklin Place & Tontine Crescent
Franklin St.
HABS MA-612
HABS MASS,13-BOST,61-
1dr L

Franklin,Benjamin,Birthplace Site
17 Milk St.
HABS MA-1161
HABS MASS,13-BOST,103-
2ph/1pc L

91 Green Street (House)
HABS MA-671
HABS MASS,13-BOST,65-
5ph/2pg L

Hancock House
Beacon St.
HABS MA-1159
HABS MASS,13-BOST,104-
7ph/1pc L

Hancock,Ebenezer,House; see Marshall-Hancock House

Hancock,Ebenezer,House (Mantels); see Marshall-Hancock House (Mantels)

Harvard Bridge
Spanning Charles River at Massachusetts Ave.
HAER MA-53
HAER MASS,13-BOST,79-
58ph/62pg/4pc L

Hollis Street Church
Hollis St.
HABS MA-156
HABS MASS,13-BOST,48-
5dr/4ph L

Hollis Street Theater
Hollis St.
HABS MA-157
HABS MASS,13-BOST,49-
6dr/8ph L

Hotel Glendon
18-28 Cazenove St.
HABS MA-1108
HABS MASS,13-BOST,105-
3ph/7pg/1pc L

India Wharf Stores
306-308 Atlantic Ave.
HABS MA-2-76
HABS MASS,13-BOST,6-
5dr/7ph/fr L

Iron Standard & Gate
Tremont Place
HABS MA-2-11-A
HABS MASS,13-BOST,39-
1dr/2ph L

John Widdicomb Company Furniture Store; see Mott Iron Works Building

King's Chapel
Tremont St.
HABS MA-1160
HABS MASS,13-BOST,55-
1ph/1pc L

Langdon House (Clough-Langdon House)
21 Unity St.
HABS MA-342-A
7dr L

Longfellow Bridge (Cambridge Bridge)
Spanning Charles River at Main St.
HAER MA-47
HAER MASS,13-BOST,80-
4ph/2pg/1pc L

M.I.T.,Rogers Building
491 Boylston St.
HABS MA-252
HABS MASS,13-BOST,56-
23dr/15ph/fr L

72 Marlborough St.,Residential Hydraulic Elevator (Wheeler-Donelan House,Hydraulic Elevator)
HAER MA-56
HAER MASS,13-BOST,72-
16ph/13pg/2pc L

72 Marlborough Street (House)
HABS MA-1210
HABS 1989(HABS):10
11ph/7pg/1pc L

Marshall House (Inn) (Mantels); see Marshall-Hancock House (Mantels)

Marshall Inn; see Marshall-Hancock House

Marshall-Hancock House
(Hancock,Ebenezer,House; Marshall Inn)
10 Marshall St.
HABS MA-2-55
HABS MASS,13-BOST,41-
6dr/3ph L

Marshall-Hancock House (Mantels)
(Hancock,Ebenezer,House (Mantels); Marshall House (Inn) (Mantels))
10 Marshall St.
HABS MA-2-55-A
HABS MASS,13-BOST,41A-
1dr L

Mass. Charitable Mechanics Assoc.,Exhibition Hall
Huntington Ave. & West Newton St.
HABS MA-672
HABS MASS,13-BOST,66-
6ph/4pg L

Mass. General Hospital,Bulfinch Building
Fruit St.
HABS MA-556
HABS MASS,13-BOST,7-
3ph L

391-393 Massachusetts Ave. (Apartments)
HABS MA-1112
HABS MASS,13-BOST,93-
2ph/1pg/1pc L

Massachusetts State House,Gates & Steps
Beacon St.
HABS MA-245
HABS MASS,13-BOST,1-
10dr/6ph/fr L

Massachusetts State House,Old (Boston Townhouse,Second)
206 Washington St. (corner of State St.)
HABS MA-1246
HABS 1989(HABS):10
19ph/5pg/1pc L

Mayhew School
Poplar & Chambers Sts.
HABS MA-673
HABS MASS,13-BOST,67-
8ph/2pg L

47 McLean Street (House)
HABS MA-670
HABS MASS,13-BOST,64-
7ph/3pg L

Metro Water BD:Chestnut Hill Low Serv. Pump Statio
Beacon St.
HAER MA-23
HAER MASS,13-BOST,81-
1ph/2pg/1pc L

Metro. Bay Trans. Authority,Orange Line; see Boston Elevated Railway,Elevated Mainline

Milestone
Opposite 1040 Adams St.
HABS MA-1191
HABS MASS,13-BOST,109-
1ph/1pc L

Milestone
Public Alley No. 102,near Marshall St.
HABS MA-1189
HABS MASS,13-BOST,107-
1ph/1pc L

Milestone
Tremont St.
HABS MA-1193
HABS MASS,13-BOST,106-
1ph/1pc L

Milestone
150 Harvard Ave.
HABS MA-1190
HABS MASS,13-BOST,108-
1ph/1pc L

Mott Iron Works Building (John Widdicomb Company Furniture Store)
90-92 Berkeley St.
HABS MA-1113
HABS MASS,13-BOST,110-
2ph/1pg/1pc L

Nell,William C. ,House
3 Smith Ct.
HABS MA-1088
HABS MASS,13-BOST,126-
2ph/4pg/1pc L

New England Merchants Bank Building
State & Congress Sts.
HABS MA-1162
HABS MASS,13-BOST,111-
3ph/1pc L

Nickerson,George A. ,House
303 Commonwealth Ave.
HABS MA-961
HABS MASS,13-BOST,112-
9ph/4pg/1pc L

North Market Building
N. Market St.
HABS MA-1169
1dr L

Northeast Corridor; see Northeast Railroad Corridor

Northeast Corridor Project; see South Station Tower No. 1 & Interlocking System

Northeast Railroad Corridor (Northeast Corridor)
Amtrak Rt. btwn. RI/MA State Line & South Station
HAER MA-19
HAER MASS,13-BOST,83-
30ph/3pc/fr L

Northern Avenue Swing Bridge
Spanning Fort Point Channel at Northern Ave.
HAER MA-37
HAER MASS,13-BOST,84-
3ph/1pg/1pc L

NY,NH & Hartford RR,Fort Point Channel Bridge (Scherzer Rolling Lift Bridge)
Spanning Fort Point Channell
HAER MA-35
HAER MASS,13-BOST,82-
8ph/1pg/1pc/2ct L

Old North Church; see Christ Church

Old South Church; see Old South Meetinghouse

Old South Meetinghouse (Old South Church)
Washington & Milk Sts.
HABS MA-960
HABS MASS,13-BOST,54-
15dr/43ph/3pc L

Opera House; see B. F. Keith Memorial Theatre

Otis,Harrison Gray,House (first) (Society For the Preservation of N. E. Antiquities)
141 Cambridge St.
HABS MA-845
HABS MASS,13-BOST,113-
3ph/1pg/1pc L

Otis,Harrison Gray,House (second)
85 Mount Vernon St.
HABS MA-962
HABS MASS,13-BOST,114-
9dr/20ph/7pg/1pc/fr L

Painters' Arms
Hanover St.
HABS MA-128
HABS MASS,13-BOST,60-
1ph L

Park Street Church
Tremont & Park Sts.
HABS MA-631
HABS MASS,13-BOST,50-
1ph L

Parker,Daniel P.,House (Women's City Club)
39 Beacon St.
HABS MA-814
HABS MASS,13-BOST,115-
7ph/1pc L

Parkman House (Tuckerman-Parkman House)
33 Beacon St.
HABS MA-965
HABS MASS,13-BOST,116-
10ph/6pg/1pc L

Parkman Market
Cambridge & N. Grove Sts.
HABS MA-2-47
HABS MASS,13-BOST,40-
6dr/2ph L

Pierce-Hichborn House; see Pierce,Moses,House

Pierce,Moses,House (Pierce-Hichborn House)
29 North Square
HABS MA-499
HABS MASS,13-BOST,57-
2ph L

Pierce,Thomas,House
Adams & Minot Sts.
HABS MA-561
HABS MASS,13-DORCH,6-
1ph/fr L

Police Station No. 10
1170 Columbus Ave.
HABS MA-1115
HABS MASS,13-BOST,117-
7ph/4pg/1pc L

Province House,The; see Sergeant,Peter,House

Quincy Market
S. Market St.
HABS MA-1166
HABS MASS,13-BOST,118-
ı1989(HABS):10°
3dr/12ph/3pg/1pc/2ct/fr L

Reed,Reuben,Building
7-9 Elm St.
HABS MA-785
HABS MASS,13-BOST,119-
3ph/1pc L

Revere,Paul,House (Boston National Historic Park)
19 North Square
HABS MA-491
HABS MASS,13-BOST,26-
5dr/8ph/1pc/2ct/fr L

Roxbury Gas Light Company,Gasholder
8 Gerard St. at Massachusetts Ave.
HAER MA-40
HAER MASS,13-BOST,85-
1ph/1pg/1pc L

Savage House
30 Dock Square
HABS MA-503
HABS MASS,13-BOST,22-
2dr L

Scherzer Rolling Lift Bridge; see NY,NH & Hartford RR,Fort Point Channel Bridge

Sears' Block
72 Cornhill St.
HABS MA-786
HABS MASS,13-BOST,120-
5ph/2pc L

Sears' Convex Block (Sears' Crescent)
50-56 Cornhill St.
HABS MA-787
HABS MASS,13-BOST,121-
4ph/1pc L

Sears' Crescent; see Sears' Convex Block

Sergeant,Peter,House (Province House,The)
Washington St.
HABS MA-816
HABS MASS,13-BOST,38-
1ph L

Sheffield,The; see Argyle Building

Shirley-Eustis House
(Shirley,Governor,Mansion)
33 Shirley St.
HABS MA-275
HABS MASS,13-ROX,9-
14dr/27ph/2pc L

Shirley,Governor,Mansion; see Shirley-Eustis House

Society For the Preservation of N. E. Antiquities; see Otis,Harrison Gray,House (first)

South Market
37 S. Market Street
HABS MA-1170
1dr L

South Station Tower No. 1 & Interlocking System (Northeast Corridor Project)
Dewey Sq.
HAER MA-58
HAER MASS,13-BOST,86-
20ph/18pg/2pc L

18-20 St. Charles St. (Houses)
HABS MA-1109
HABS MASS,13-BOST,89-
2ph/10pg/1pc L

St. Patrick's Church,Old
Northampton St.
HABS MA-154
HABS MASS,13-BOST,47-
11dr/1ph L

Steps between Brattle & Cornhill
HABS MA-1138
HABS MASS,13-BOST,122-
1ph/1pc L

Structural Studies of Seven Massachusetts Bridges
HAER MA-127
30pg H

Summer Street Retractile Bridge
Spanning Port Point Channel at Summer St.
HAER MA-41
HAER MASS,13-BOST,87-
2ph/1pg/1pc L

Tool House
Copp's Hill Burial Ground
HABS MA-498
HABS MASS,13-BOST,20A-
4ph L

Transcript Building
Washington & Milk Sts.
HABS MA-1139
HABS MASS,13-BOST,123-
1ph/1pc L

Trinity Episcopal Church
Copley Square
HABS MA-1215
HABS 1989(HABS):10
36ph/4pg/2pc L

Tuckerman-Parkman House; see Parkman House

Union Oyster House (Restaurant)
(Capen House)
41-43 Union St.
HABS MA-127
HABS MASS,13-BOST,45-
3dr/1ph/fr L

Warehouse
68 Broad St.
HABS MA-125
HABS MASS,13-BOST,44-
3dr/1ph L

Washington & Franklin Streets (Building)
HABS MA-1140
HABS MASS,13-BOST,124-
2ph/1pc L

199 Washington Street (Building)
HABS MA-1141
HABS MASS,13-BOST,90-
3ph/1pc L

258 Washington Street (Building)
HABS MA-1142
HABS MASS,13-BOST,92-
1ph/1pc L

245 West Canton Street (House)
HABS MA-1175
HABS MASS,13-BOST,91-
1ph/4pg/1pc L

West Church
131 Cambridge St.
HABS MA-279
HABS MASS,13-BOST,4-
14ph/1pc L

Wheeler-Donelan House,Hydraulic Elevator; see 72 Marlborough St.,Residential Hydraulic Elevator

Whiting Building
Washington St.
HABS MA-1143
HABS MASS,13-BOST,125-
1ph/1pc L

Women's City Club; see Appleton,Nathan,House

Women's City Club; see Parker,Daniel P.,House

Wrought Iron Archway & Steps
Province & Bosworth Sts.
HABS MA-2-11-B
HABS MASS,13-BOST,38A-
2dr/2ph L

BOSTON VIC.

Milestones
Various Boston vicinity locations
HABS MA-128
HABS MASS,13-BOST.V,1-
28dr L

BRIGHTON

Milestones HH & II
Harvard St.
HABS MA-128
HABS MASS,13-BRI,2-
1dr/2ph L

CHARLESTOWN

Adams,Major,House
HABS MA-352
HABS MASS,13-CHAR,10-
5ph L

Andrews-Getchell House
21 Cordis Ave.
HABS MA-191
HABS MASS,13-CHAR,5-
16dr/4ph L

11 Devens Street (House)
HABS MA-348
HABS MASS,13-CHAR,9-
6ph L

Devens,Gen. Charles,House
30 Union St.
HABS MA-346
HABS MASS,13-CHAR,7-
2ph L

Everett,Edward,House
16 Harvard St.
HABS MA-347
HABS MASS,13-CHAR,8-
5ph L

Hyde-Lincoln House
32 Cordis Ave.
HABS MA-299
HABS MASS,13-CHAR,6-
10dr/7ph L

Hyde-Worthen House
(Hyde,George,House)
69 Rutherford Ave.
HABS MA-192
HABS MASS,13-CHAR,1-
7dr/7ph L

Hyde,George,House; see Hyde-Worthen House

U. S. Frigate "Constitution",Cannon
(moved to NY,Schoharie)
HABS MA-2-84-C
HABS NY,48-SCHO,5-
1ph L

U.S. Frigate Constitution,Commodore's Quarters
U. S. Navy Yard
HABS MA-2-84-A
HABS MASS,13-CHAR,3-
2dr/3ph/fr L

U.S. Navy Yard,Commandant's House
Chelsea St.
HABS MA-2-10
HABS MASS,13-CHAR,2-
7dr/2ph/fr L

CHELSEA

Captains' Row
Marginal & Shurtleff Sts.
HABS MA-2-37
HABS MASS,13-CHEL,1-
3ph/fr L

Cary-Bellingham Mansion
34 Parker St.
HABS MA-576
HABS MASS,13-CHEL,4-
2ph L

Octagon House; see Tucker,Bevis,House

Tucker,Bevis,House (Octagon House)
HABS MA-579
HABS MASS,13-CHEL,5-
1ph L

Way-Ireland-Pratt House
481 Washington Ave.
HABS MA-211
HABS MASS,13-CHEL,3-
14dr L

DORCHESTER

Bird-Sawyer House
(Bird,Thomas,House)
41 Humphreys St.
HABS MA-278
HABS MASS,13-DORCH,3-
12dr/14ph/fr L

Bird,Thomas,House; see Bird-Sawyer House

Clap,Roger,House
199 Boston St. (moved from 25 Willow Court)
HABS MA-190
HABS MASS,13-DORCH,2-
30dr L

Clapp,William,House
195 Boston St.
HABS MA-447
HABS MASS,13-DORCH,4-
2ph L

First Parish Church (Unitarian)
Church & Parish Sts.
HABS MA-569
HABS MASS,13-DORCH,9-
2ph L

Lyceum Hall
Meetinghouse Hill
HABS MA-571
HABS MASS,13-DORCH,10-
1ph L

Milestones A,B,E,HHH,III & PPP
Various Dorchester locations
HABS MA-128
HABS MASS,13-DORCH,11-
5dr/6ph L

Pierce,Robert,House
24 Oakton Ave.
HABS MA-562
HABS MASS,13-DORCH,7-
10dr/15ph/4pg/1pc/fr L

Second Church
Washington & Center Sts.
HABS MA-563
HABS MASS,13-DORCH,8-
3ph L

Trotter,William Monroe,House
97 Sawyer Ave.
HABS MA-1165
HABS MASS,13-DORCH,12-
1ph/5pg/1pc L

JAMAICA PLAIN

Loring-Greenough House & Garden
12 South St.
HABS MA-272
HABS MASS,13-JAMP,1-
2dr/2ph/fr L

REVERE VIC.

Bennett-Slade-Parsons House
(Bennett,Samuel,House; Rumney Hall)
50 Marshall St.
HABS MA-218
HABS MASS,13-REV.V,1-
11dr/fr L

Bennett,Samuel,House; see Bennett-Slade-Parsons House

Rumney Hall; see Bennett-Slade-Parsons House

ROXBURY

Curtis House
HABS MA-479
HABS MASS,13-ROX,5-
4ph L

Dillaway-Thomas House
Eliot Square
HABS MA-558
HABS MASS,13-ROX,2-
2ph L

First Church
Eliot Square
HABS MA-557
HABS MASS,13-ROX,1-
4ph L

Hale,Edward Everett,House
39 Highland St.
HABS MA-559
HABS MASS,13-ROX,6-
1ph L

Hayden,Judge,House & Garden
281 Heath St.
HABS MA-294
HABS MASS,13-ROX,4-
1dr/3ph/fr L

Milestones D,Y,Z,AA,BB,FF & NN
Various Roxbury locations
HABS MA-128
HABS MASS,13-ROX,8-
7dr/7ph L

Milestones V,W & X; see Parting Stone,The

Parting Stone,The (Milestones V,W & X)
Roxbury & Center Sts.
HABS MA-128
HABS MASS,13-ROX,7-
2dr/3ph L

Puddingstone Building,Old
199 Ruggles St.
HABS MA-126
HABS MASS,13-ROX,3-
1dr/3ph/fr L

SOUTH BOSTON

St. Augustine Chapel
St. Augustine Cemetery,Dorchester St.
HABS MA-2-26
HABS MASS,13-BOSTS,1-
6dr/1ph/fr L

WINTHROP

Winthrop,Deane,House
40 Shirley St.
HABS MA-575
HABS MASS,13-WINTH,1-
2ph L

WORCESTER COUNTY

ATHOL

Meetinghouse
HABS MA-893
HABS MASS,14-ATH,1-
2ph/1pc L

AUBURN

Chapin,Thaddeus,House
HABS MA-340
HABS MASS,14-AUB,1-
2ph/fr L

BLACKSTONE

Building,Old Stone
HABS MA-459
HABS MASS,14-BLACK,1-
2ph L

BOLTON

Milestone YYY; see Thirty-one-mile Stone

Thirty-one-mile Stone (Milestone YYY)
HABS MA-128
HABS MASS,14-BOLT,1-
1ph L

BROOKFIELD

Banister House
HABS MA-345
HABS MASS,14-BROK,2-
12ph/fr L

Crosby,Col. J.,House
Main St.
HABS MA-133
HABS MASS,14-BROK,1-
12dr/8ph L

Milestone
Rt. 9
HABS MA-1194
HABS MASS,14-BROK,3-
1ph/1pc L

CHARLTON

Bob's Yankee Diner
Rt. 20
HABS MA-1242
HABS 1989(HABS):10
10ph/1pc L

Old Nort Charlton Inn; see Rider Tavern

Rider Tavern (Old Nort Charlton Inn)
Stafford St. (opposite Northside Rd.)
HABS MA-1224
HABS 1990 (HABS):5
20ph/1pg/1pc L

Towne,Gen. Salem,House
Old County Rd. (moved to MA,Sturbridge)
HABS MA-2-38
HABS MASS,14-CHAR,1-
16dr/8ph L

EAST BROOKFIELD

Milestone
Rt. 9
HABS MA-1195
HABS MASS,14-BROKE,1-
1ph/1pc L

FITCHBURG

Cushing Flour & Grain Mill
Laurel St. Bridge Vic.
HABS MA-896
HABS MASS,14-FIT,1-
2ph/1pc L

Rollstone Street Bridge,Lower
Spanning the Nashua River on Rollstone St.
HAER MA-102
HAER DLC/PP-1992:MA-4
11ph/19pg/1pc/fr L

GRAFTON

Wyman-Gordon Company,Grafton Plant
244 Worcester St.
HAER MA-82
HAER MASS,14-GRAF,1-
3ph/1pc/1ct L

Wyman-Gordon Company,Grafton Plant,18000 Ton Press
244 Worcester St.
HAER MA-82-B
HAER MASS,14-GRAF,1B-
6ph/1pc L

Wyman-Gordon Company,Grafton Plant,2000 Ton Press
244 Worcester St.
HAER MA-82-A
HAER MASS,14-GRAF,1A-
2ph/1pc L

Wyman-Gordon Company,Grafton Plant,50000 Ton Press
244 Worcester St.
HAER MA-82-C
HAER MASS,14-GRAF,1C-
13ph/1pg/1pc/2ct L

HARVARD

"Fruitlands"
Fruitlands Museum,Prospect Hill Rd.
HABS MA-1005
HABS MASS,14-HARV,18-
9dr/3pg/1ct/fr L

Ireland,Shadrach,House; see Shaker Church Family Square House

Shaker Church Family Barn (Ruins)
Shaker Rd. Vic.
HABS MA-861
HABS MASS,14-HARV,2-
2dr/4ph L

Shaker Church Family Dwelling House (second) (Shaker Church Family Second House)
Shaker Rd.
HABS MA-810
HABS MASS,14-HARV,12-
8dr/6ph/2pg L

Shaker Church Family Herb Drying House
Shaker Rd.
HABS MA-1091
HABS MASS,14-HARV,3-
4dr L

Shaker Church Family Office Building; see Shaker Church Family Trustees' Office (second)

Shaker Church Family Second House; see Shaker Church Family Dwelling House (second)

Shaker Church Family Square House (Ireland,Shadrach,House)
Shaker Rd.
HABS MA-804
HABS MASS,14-HARV,6-
8dr/7ph/2pg L

Shaker Church Family Tailors' Shop
Shaker Rd.
HABS MA-805
HABS MASS,14-HARV,7-
2ph/2pg L

Shaker Church Family Trustees' Office (second) (Shaker Church Family Office Building)
Shaker Rd.
HABS MA-809
HABS MASS,14-HARV,11-
10ph/2pg L

Shaker Family Church,General Views
Shaker Rd.
HABS MA-862
HABS MASS,14-HARV,1-
1ph/fr L

Shaker Holy Hill Outdoor Worship Area
Shaker Rd.
HABS MA-1092
HABS MASS,14-HARV,4-
2dr L

Shaker House
Fruitlands Museum,Prospect Hill Rd.
HABS MA-1004
HABS MASS,14-HARV,19-
5dr/3pg/fr L

Shaker Meetinghouse
Shaker Rd.
HABS MA-806
HABS MASS,14-HARV,8-
8dr/10ph/2pg L

Shaker Ministry's House; see Shaker Ministry's Shop

Shaker Ministry's Shop (Shaker Ministry's House)
Shaker Rd.
HABS MA-807
HABS MASS,14-HARV,9-
4dr/8ph/1pg L

Shaker North Family Dwelling House
Shaker Rd.
HABS MA-1090
HABS MASS,14-HARV,5-
7dr L

Shaker South Family Applesauce Shop; see Shaker South Family Shop Number 1

Shaker South Family Barn
S. Shaker Rd.
HABS MA-808
HABS MASS,14-HARV,10-
4dr/17ph/1pg L

Shaker South Family Dwelling House
S. Shaker Rd.
HABS MA-888
HABS MASS,14-HARV,13-
8dr/25ph L

Shaker South Family Laundry; see Shaker South Family Washhouse

Shaker South Family Privy
S. Shaker Rd.
HABS MA-1085
HABS MASS,14-HARV,17-
2ph L

Shaker South Family Shop Number 1 (Shaker South Family Applesauce Shop)
S. Shaker Rd.
HABS MA-890
HABS MASS,14-HARV,15-
4ph L

Shaker South Family Shop Number 2
S. Shaker Rd.
HABS MA-891
HABS MASS,14-HARV,16-
4ph L

Shaker South Family Washhouse (Shaker South Family Laundry)
S. Shaker Rd.
HABS MA-889
HABS MASS,14-HARV,14-
12ph L

HOLDEN

Alden Research Laboratory,Rotating Boom (Worcester Polytechnic Institute,Rotating Boom)
HAER MA-60-A
HAER MASS,14-HOLD,4A-
3ph/1pg/1pc L

Alden Research Laboratory,Venturi Meter; see Venturi Meter

Venturi Meter (Worcester Polytechnic Institute,Venturi Meter; Alden Research Laboratory,Venturi Meter)
HAER MA-60-B
HAER MASS,14-HOLD,4B-
1ph/1pg/1pc L

Worcester Polytechnic Institute,Rotating Boom; see Alden Research Laboratory,Rotating Boom

Worcester Polytechnic Institute,Venturi Meter; see Venturi Meter

LANCASTER

First Parish Church (The Fifth Meetinghouse; Lancaster Meetinghouse)
Town Green,Thayer Drive
HABS MA-542
HABS MASS,14-LANC,1-ı1989(HABS):10°
17ph/1pg/1pc L

First Parish Church,Stables
Town Green,Thayer Drive
HABS MA-542-A
HABS 1989(HABS):10
4ph/1pc L

Lancaster Meetinghouse; see First Parish Church

The Fifth Meetinghouse; see First Parish Church

LANCASTER VIC.

Atherton Bridge (Bolton Road Bridge)
Spanning Nashua River on Bolton Rd.
HAER MA-17
HAER MASS,14-LANC.V,1-
DLC/PP-1992:MA-4
3dr/21ph/23pg/2pc/fr L

Bolton Road Bridge; see Atherton Bridge

Ponakin Road Bridge
Spanning Nashua River on Ponakin Rd.
HAER MA-13
HAER MASS,14-LANC.V,2-
DLC/PP-1992:MA-4
6dr/19ph/24pg/2pc/fr L

LEICESTER

Milestone
Rt. 9
HABS MA-1196
HABS MASS,14-LEIC,3-
1ph/1pc L

Milestone
Rt. 9 at Collier's Corner
HABS MA-1197
HABS MASS,14-LEIC,2-
1ph/1pc L

MENDON

First Parish Church (Unitarian) & Carriage Shed
Maple & Elm Sts.
HABS MA-242
HABS MASS,14-MEND,1-
20dr/7ph L

Milestones DD & EE
Hastings St.
HABS MA-128
HABS MASS,14-MEND,2-
2ph L

MILFORD

Milestone VVV; see Thirty-four-mile Stone

Thirty-four-mile Stone (Milestone VVV)
HABS MA-128
HABS MASS,14-MILF,1-
1ph L

MILLVILLE

Covered Bridge
HABS MA-440
HABS MASS,14-MILV,1-
4ph L

MILLVILLE VIC.

Chestnut Hill Meetinghouse (South Parish Meetinghouse)
Chestnut St.
HABS MA-122
HABS MASS,14-MILV.V,1-
20dr/12ph/fr L

South Parish Meetinghouse; see Chestnut Hill Meetinghouse

NORTH UXBRIDGE

Crown & Eagle Mills (Uxbridge Cotton Mills)
123 Hartford Ave. E
HABS MA-991
HABS MASS,14-UXN,1-
3dr/66ph/6pg/2pc/fr L

Uxbridge Cotton Mills; see Crown & Eagle Mills

NORTHBRIDGE

Old Brick Mill; see Whittinsville Brick Mill

Whitinsville Brick Mill,Forge
56 Douglas Rd.
HABS MA-1225-A
HABS 1989(HABS):10
1ph/1pc L

Whittinsville Brick Mill (Old Brick Mill)
56 Douglas Rd.
HABS MA-1225
HABS 1989(HABS):10
6ph/1pg/1pc L

OAKHAM

Adams,Eli,House
HABS MA-284
HABS MASS,14-OAK,1-
16ph L

Lincoln House
HABS MA-285
HABS MASS,14-OAK,2-
3ph L

Saw Mill,Old
HABS MA-287
HABS MASS,14-OAK,3-
9ph L

OXFORD

Bartlett's Bridge
Spanning the French River on Clara Barton Rd.
HAER MA-112
HAER DLC/PP-1992:MA-4
4ph/14pg/1pc L

RUTLAND

Putnam,Gen. Rufus,House
Main St.
HABS MA-2-71
HABS MASS,14-RUT,1-
15dr/7ph L

SPENCER

Milestone
State Rt. 9 (Boston Post Rd.)
HABS MA-1202
HABS MASS,14-SPEN,1-
1ph/1pc L

STERLING

Campground Road Bridge; see Hastings Bridge

Hastings Bridge (Campground Road Bridge)
Boston & Maine RR at Campground Rd.
HAER MA-83
18ph/8pg/2pc H

STURBRIDGE

Towne,Gen. Salem,House
Sturbridge Village (moved from MA,Charlton)
HABS MA-2-38
HABS MASS,14-CHAR,1-
16dr/8ph L

Documentation: **ct** color transparencies **dr** measured drawings **fr** field records
pc photograph captions **pg** pages of text **ph** photographs

Wight,Oliver,House
State Rt. 131
HABS MA-217
HABS MASS,14-STURB,1-
15dr/5ph L

TEMPLETON

Federated Church; see First Parish Congregational Church

First Parish Congregational Church (Federated Church)
Templeton Common
HABS MA-848
HABS MASS,14-TEMP,1-
2ph/1pc L

House of 1763
HABS MA-1167
HABS MASS,14-TEMP,2-
1ph/1pc L

Lee,Col. Artemus,House
Templeton Common
HABS MA-849
HABS MASS,14-TEMP,3-
1ph/1pc L

Stile,John W. ,House
Templeton Common
HABS MA-847
HABS MASS,14-TEMP,4-
1ph/1pc L

UXBRIDGE

Masonic Building & Courthouse
HABS MA-411
HABS MASS,14-UXBRI,1-
4ph L

Wheelock,Lieut. Simeon,House
N. Main St.
HABS MA-412
HABS MASS,14-UXBRI,2-
6ph L

WEBSTER

North Village Bridge
Spanning the French River on N. Main St.
HAER MA-99
HAER DLC/PP-1992:MA-4
4dr/15ph/17pg/1pc/fr L

North Village Schoolhouse
N. Main St.,.125 m. S. of Dlater St.
HABS MA-1211
HABS MASS,14-WEB,1-
7ph/8pg/1pc L

Slater,George B.,Carriage House
216 N. Main St.
HABS MA-1212
HABS 1991(HABS):15
9ph/5pg/1pc L

WEST BROOKFIELD

Milestone
East End of Town Common
HABS MA-1200
HABS MASS,14-BROKW,2-
1ph/1pc L

Milestone
Foster Hill Rd.
HABS MA-1199
HABS MASS,14-BROKW,1-
1ph/1pc L

WESTBORO

Milestone
Worcester Turnpike
HABS MA-1198
HABS MASS,14-WEBO,1-
1ph/1pc L

WILKINSONVILLE

Dudley,D. T. & Son Company
Providence Rd.
HABS MA-1144
HABS MASS,14-WILK,1-
1dr L

Dudley,D. T. ,& Son Company,Machine Shop & Powerhs
Providence Rd.
HABS MA-1144-B
HABS MASS,14-WILK,1B-
2dr L

Dudley,D. T., & Son Company,Main Shop
Providence Rd.
HABS MA-1144-A
HABS MASS,14-WILK,1A-
4dr L

WORCESTER

Higgins Armory (Higgins,John Woodman,Armory Museum)
100 Barber Ave.
HABS MA-1236
HABS 1989(HABS):10
16ph/1pg/1pc L

Higgins,John Woodman,Armory Museum; see Higgins Armory

S. B. Watson Cottage (Wheeler Cottage)
297 Belmont St.
HABS MA-1213
HABS 1991(HABS):15
5ph/5pg/1pc L

Salisbury,Stephen,Mansion (first)
40 Highland St.
HABS MA-573
HABS MASS,14-WORC,1-
1ph L

Salisbury,Stephen,Mansion (second)
HABS MA-574
HABS MASS,14-WORC,2-
2ph L

Wheeler Cottage; see S. B. Watson Cottage

Worcester Cons. Street Railway,Admin. Building (Worcester Cons. Street Railway,Car Barn)
99-109 Main St.
HABS MA-1106
HABS MASS,14-WORC,3-
9ph/2pg/1pc/fr L

Worcester Cons. Street Railway,Car Barn; see Worcester Cons. Street Railway,Admin. Building

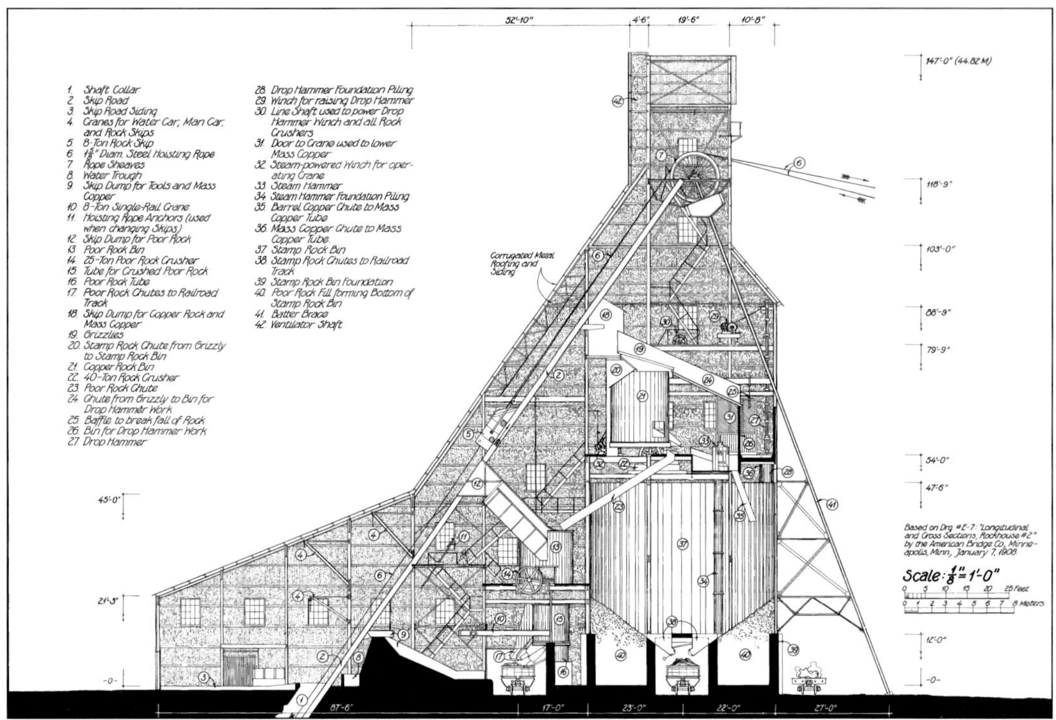

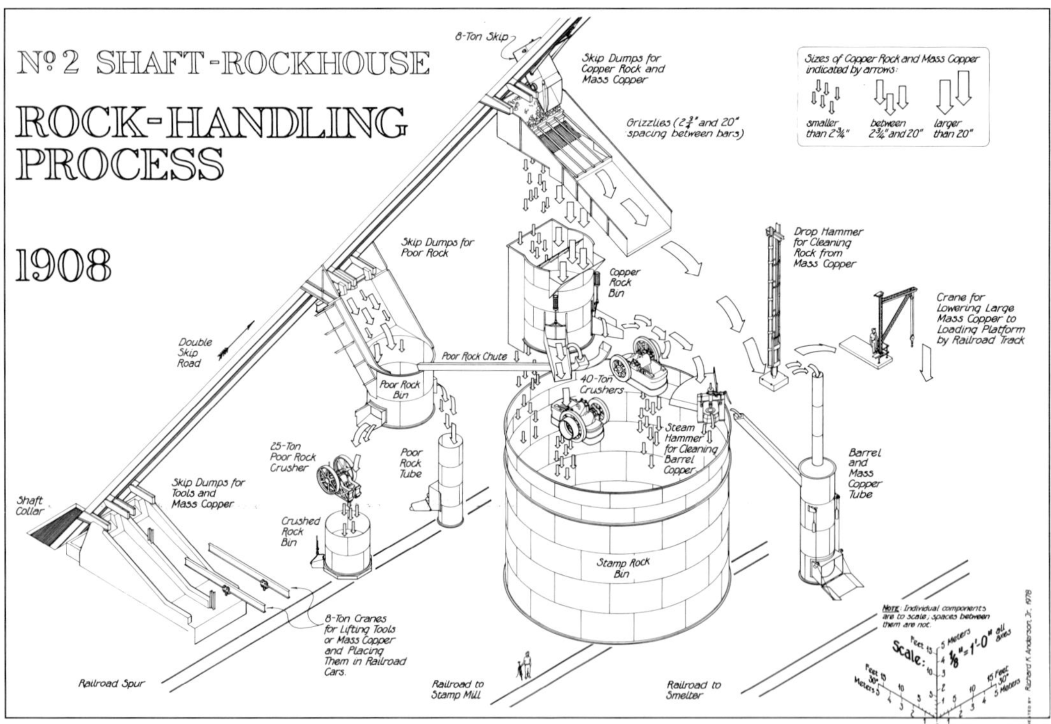

Quincy Mining Company: No. 2 Shaft-Rockhouse (1908), Hancock, Houghton County, Michigan. Measured drawing delineated by Durward W. Potter, Jr., 1978; Richard K. Anderson, Jr., 1979 (HAER MI-2, sheet 19 of 34).

Quincy Mining Company: No. 2 Shaft-Rockhouse (1908), Hancock, Houghton County, Michigan. Rock-handling process (1908). Measured drawing delineated by Richard K. Anderson, Jr., 1978 (HAER MI-2, sheet 18 of 34).

Michigan

LELAND

Cottage Row
HABS MI-382
H

Post Office
HABS MI-384
H

ALGER COUNTY

EAST MUNISING

Becker Barn (Pictured Rocks National Lakeshore)
HABS MI-307
HABS MICH,2-MUNIE,1-
3pg/fr L

Pictured Rocks National Lakeshore; see Becker Barn

GRAND ISLAND

Hotel Williams
Murray Bay
HABS MI-258
HABS MICH,2-GRAIL,1-
1ph/2pg/1pc L

Hotel Williams,Log Building No. 1
Murray Bay
HABS MI-258-C
HABS MICH,2-GRAIL,1C-
4ph/3pg/1pc L

Hotel Williams,Log Building No. 2
Murray Bay
HABS MI-258-D
HABS MICH,2-GRAIL,1D-
4ph/3pg/1pc L

Hotel Williams,Log Building No. 4
Murray Bay
HABS MI-258-E
HABS MICH,2-GRAIL,1E-
2ph/3pg/1pc L

Hotel Williams,Log Building No. 5
Murray Bay
HABS MI-258-F
HABS MICH,2-GRAIL,1F-
2ph/3pg/1pc L

Hotel Williams,Log Building No. 8 (Stone Quarry Cottage)
Murray Bay
HABS MI-258-G
HABS MICH,2-GRAIL,1G-
3ph/2pg/1pc L

Hotel Williams,Williams House (Williams Hotel Annex)
Murray Bay
HABS MI-258-A
HABS MICH,2-GRAIL,1A-
1ph/3pg/1pc L

Hotel Williams,Williams Log House
Murray Bay
HABS MI-258-B
HABS MICH,2-GRAIL,1B-
2ph/2pg/1pc L

Stone Quarry Cottage; see Hotel Williams,Log Building No. 8

Williams Hotel Annex; see Hotel Williams,Williams House

GRAND MARAIS VIC

Au Sable Light Station
Southern Shore of Lake Superior
HABS MI-317
HABS 1991(HABS):26
7dr/fr L

GRAND MARAIS VIC.

Au Sable Light Station, Boathouse
Southern Shore of Lake Superior
HABS MI-317-C
HABS 1991(HABS):26
1dr/fr L

Au Sable Light Station,Dwelling
Southern Shore of Lake Superior
HABS MI-317-A
3dr H

Au Sable Light Station,Fog Signals
Southern Shore of Lake Superior
HABS MI-317-B
HABS 1991(HABS):26
1dr/fr H

ALLEGAN COUNTY

HAMILTON VIC.

Thirty-Sixth Street Bridge
Spanning Rabbit River
HAER MI-18
HAER MICH,3-HAM.V,1-
7ph/3pg/1pc L

BARRY COUNTY

HASTINGS VIC.

McCann Road Bridge
Spanning Thornapple River,Section 31,Irving Twp.
HAER MI-17
HAER MICH,8-HAST.V,1-
7ph/3pg/1pc L

BAY COUNTY

BAY CITY

Bay City City Hall
301 Washington Ave.
HABS MI-218
HABS MICH,9-BAYCI,1-
6ph/6pg/1pc L

BERRIEN COUNTY

BENTON VIC.

State Route M-139 Bridge
Spanning Ox Creek
HAER MI-46
HAER DLC/PP-1993:MI-2
23ph/13pg/4pc L

NILES

Paine Bank
212 W. Third St.
HABS MI-220
HABS MICH,11-NIL,1-
9dr L

CALHOUN COUNTY

BATTLE CREEK

Michigan Central Railroad Station (New York Central Railroad Station)
Capitol Ave.
HABS MI-234
HABS MICH,3-BATCR,1-
5ph/1pg/1pc L

New York Central Railroad Station; see Michigan Central Railroad Station

Post,C. W. ,Office Building
63-65 W. Michigan Ave.
HABS MI-313
HABS MICH,3-BATCR,2-
4dr/27ph/14pg/2pc L

BATTLECREEK VIC.

County Park Bridge; see F Drive N. Bridge

F Drive N. Bridge (County Park Bridge)
Spanning Kalamazoo River
HAER MI-33
14ph/4pg/1pc H

MARSHALL

Allcott,Sidney S. ,House
302 W. Mansion St.
HABS MI-239
HABS MICH,13-MARSH,7-
3ph/5pg/1pc L

Baker,Abner,House
318 W. Mansion St.
HABS MI-236
HABS MICH,13-MARSH,8-
5dr/5ph/5pg/1pc/fr L

Baker,Abner,House,Carriage House
318 W. Mansion St.
HABS MI-236-A
HABS MICH,13-MARSH,8A-
1ph/2pg/1pc/fr L

Benedict-Joy House
224 N. Kalamazoo Ave.
HABS MI-240
HABS MICH,13-MARSH,9-
2ph/3pg/1pc L

Brewer,Chauncey,House (Oakhill)
410 N. Eagle St.
HABS MI-244
HABS MICH,13-MARSH,10-
3ph/3pg/1pc L

Brooks,Craig Wright,House
High & Mansion Sts.
HABS MI-27-20
HABS MICH,13-MARSH,3-
7dr/3ph/2pg/1pc/fr L

Brooks,Harold Craig,House
(Fitch,Jabez,House)
N. Kalamazoo Ave. & Prospect St.
HABS MI-27-18
HABS MICH,13-MARSH,1-
12dr/5ph/4pg/1pc/fr L

Capitol Hill School (Fourth Ward School)
602 Washington St.
HABS MI-227
HABS MICH,13-MARSH,11-
5dr/2ph/5pg/1pc/fr L

East Michigan Avenue (Commercial Building)
HABS MI-245
HABS MICH,13-MARSH,12-
1ph/1pg/1pc L

117 East Michigan Avenue (Commercial Building)
HABS MI-247
HABS MICH,13-MARCH,5-
1ph/1pg/1pc L

Fitch,Jabez,House; see Brooks,Harold Craig,House

Fourth Ward School; see Capitol Hill School

Honolulu House; see Pratt,Abner,House

Marshall Tavern
Michigan Ave. & Eagle St.
HABS MI-27-19
HABS MICH,13-MARSH,2-
10dr/1ph/2pg/fr L

Oakhill; see Brewer,Chauncey,House

Pratt,Abner,House (Honolulu House)
107 N. Kalamazoo Ave.
HABS MI-228
HABS MICH,13-MARSH,13-
8dr/8ph/15pg/1pc/fr L

106 West Michigan Avenue (Commercial Building)
HABS MI-249
HABS MICH,13-MARSH,4-
1ph/1pg/1pc L

136 West Michigan Avenue (Commercial Building)
HABS MI-248
HABS MICH,13-MARSH,6-
1ph/1pg/1pc L

CHIPPEWA COUNTY

SAULT STE. MARIE

Hydroelectric Plant & Canal; see Michigan Lake Superior Power Company

Michigan Lake Superior Power Company (Hydroelectric Plant & Canal)
Portage St.
HAER MI-1
HAER MICH,17-SAUMA,1-
8dr/141ph/236pg/19pc/2ct L

Spruce Street Bridge
E. Spruce St. ,500 Block,spanning Power Canal
HAER MI-5
HAER MICH,17-SAUMA,2-
21ph/4pg/2pc L

CLINTON COUNTY

OVID

Congregational Church (United Church)
N. Main & E. Pearl Sts.
HABS MI-250
HABS MICH,19-OVID,1-
3ph/1pg/1pc L

United Church; see Congregational Church

EATON COUNTY

CHARLOTTE

Eaton County Courthouse
W. Lawrence Ave.
HABS MI-229
HABS MICH,23-CHAR,1-
6ph/1pg/1pc L

EATON RAPIDS

Gallery,John & William,Mill (Horner's Original Mill)
Canal & N. Main Sts.
HABS MI-226
HABS MICH,23-EATRA,1-
8dr/5ph/1pc/fr L

Horner's Original Mill; see Gallery,John & William,Mill

West Knight Street Bridge
Spanning Spring Brook (west of Knight St.)
HAER MI-7
HAER MICH,23-EATRA,2-
11ph/12pg/1pc L

EATON TOWNSHIP

Petrieville Road Bridge
Spanning Grand River
HAER MI-14
HAER MICH,23-EATON,1-
8ph/3pg/1pc L

VERMONTVILLE

First Congregational Chapel
N. Main & W. Main Sts.
HABS MI-225
HABS MICH,23-VERVI,1-
5dr/4ph/1pg/1pc/fr L

First Congregational Church
S. Main & W. Main Sts.
HABS MI-224
HABS MICH,23-VERVI,2-
7dr/5ph/11pg/1pc/fr L

GRATIOT COUNTY

ST. LOUIS VIC.

Cheesman Road Bridge
Spanning Pine Bridge
HAER MI-21
HAER 1989(HAER):12
11ph/2pg/1pc L

SUMNER VIC.

Ferris Road Bridge
Spanning Pine River
HAER MI-20
9ph/3pg/3pc H

HILLSDALE COUNTY

CAMDEN

Cambria Road Bridge
Spanning St. Joseph River
HAER MI-43
14ph/3pg/1pc H

LITCHFIELD VIC.

Cronk Road Bridge
Spanning St. Joseph River
HAER MI-22
11ph/3pg/1pc H

HOUGHTON COUNTY

BEACON HILL

Redridge Steel Dam
Salmon Trout River
HAER MI-10
HAER MICH,31-BEHIL,1-
1ph/3pg/1pc L

Redridge Timber Crib Dam
Salmon Trout River
HAER MI-11
HAER MICH,31-BEHIL,2-
1ph/2pg/1pc L

HANCOCK

Quincy Mining Company
HAER MI-2
HAER MICH,31-HANC,1-
34dr/278ph/679pg/28pc/13ct/fr L

INGHAM COUNTY

LANSING

Diamond Reo Motor Plant
2100 S. Washington St.
HAER MI-4
HAER MICH,33-LAN,1-
20ph/8pg/2pc L

Hermann House
520 North Capitol Avenue
HABS MI-237
HABS MICH,33-LAN,2-
10dr/fr L

Michigan State Capitol
Capitol St.
HABS MI-230
26ph/25pg H

Olds,Ransom E. ,House
720 Washington Ave. & Main St.
HABS MI-231
HABS MICH,33-LAN,3-
6ph/1pg/1pc L

MASON VIC.

516 Hogsback Road (House)
HABS MI-223
HABS MICH,33-MAS.V,1-
5dr/4ph/1pg/1pc/fr L

WILLIAMSTON TWP.

St. Katherine's Episcopal Chapel
4650 Meridian Rd.
HABS MI-232
HABS MICH,33-WILTO,1-
6dr/4ph/12pg/fr L

IONIA COUNTY

IONIA

Hall,Frederick,House
126 E. Main St.
HABS MI-238
HABS MICH,34-ION,1-
7ph/14pg/1pc L

JACKSON COUNTY

GRASS LAKE

Soper Residence (Village Farm)
971 Michigan Ave. (U. S. Rt. 12)
HABS MI-111
HABS MICH,38-GRALA.V,1-
8dr/4ph/1pg/fr L

Village Farm; see Soper Residence

GRASS LAKE VIC.

Smith,Hiram,House & Barn
Michigan & Wolf Lake Rds.
HABS MI-113
HABS MICH,38-GRALA,1-
4dr/4ph/1pg L

Smith,Sidney T. ,House
Michigan Ave. (U. S. Rt. 12)
HABS MI-115
HABS MICH,38-GRALA.V,2-
7dr/3ph/2pg/fr L

KALAMAZOO COUNTY

KALAMAZOO

Kalamazoo State Hospital
Oakland Dr.
HABS MI-251
HABS MICH,39-KALAM,1-
6ph/1pg/1pc L

Mosel Avenue Bridge
Spanning the Kalamazoo River on Mosel Ave.
HAER MI-37
HAER DLC/PP-1992:MI-2
33ph/5pg/2pc L

Mosel Avenue Grade Separation
Spanning Riverview Dr.
HAER MI-36
HAER 1992(HAER):MI-1
26ph/5pg/1pc L

OSHTEMO VIC.

"O" Avenue Bridge; see Morton's Highway Crossing

Bridge 154.23; see Morton's Highway Crossing

Morton's Highway Crossing ("O" Avenue Bridge; Bridge 154.23)
Spanning Amtrak on "O" Avenue
HAER MI-44
13ph/8pg/1pc H

KENT COUNTY

EAST GRAND RAPIDS

Lovett-Barnard House
2211 Lake Dr. ,SE.
HABS MI-259
HABS MICH,41-GRARAE,1-
5dr/2ph/4pg/1pc L

GRAND RAPIDS

Amberg,David M. ,House
573 College Ave.
HABS MI-242
HABS MICH,41-GRARA,7-
5ph/1pg/1pc L

Bridge Street Bridge
Spanning Grand River,Michigan & Bridge Sts.
HAER MI-27
HAER MICH,41-GRARA,10-
25ph/11pg/3pc L

Dikeman,Aaron B. ,House
302 Fulton St. SE
HABS MI-24
HABS MICH,41-GRALA,6-
6dr/5ph/1pg/fr L

Grand Rapids Art Gallery; see Pike,Abraham,House

Grand Rapids City Hall
35 Lyon St. NW
HABS MI-243
HABS MICH,41-GRARA,8-
5ph/1pg/1pc L

Hatch,Damon,House
445 Cherry St. SE
HABS MI-23
HABS MICH,41-GRARA,5-
6dr/4ph/1pg/fr L

May,Meyer S. ,House
450 Madison Ave.
HABS MI-241
HABS MICH,41-GRARA,9-
4ph/1pg/1pc L

Noble,Boardman,House
671 Front Ave. NW
HABS MI-22
HABS MICH,41-GRARA,4-
5dr/5ph/1pg/fr L

Pearl Street Bridge
Spanning Grand River at Pearl St.
HAER MI-8
HAER MICH,41-GRARA,11-
7ph/7pg/1pc L

Pike,Abraham,House (Grand Rapids Art Gallery)
230 E. Fulton St. SE
HABS MI-27-10
HABS MICH,41-GRARA,1-
7dr/2ph/1pg/1pc/fr L

Sanford,Samuel,House
540 Cherry St.
HABS MI-21
HABS MICH,41-GRARA,3-
6dr/4ph/1pg/fr L

Turner,Eliphalet H. ,House
731 Front Ave. NW
HABS MI-27-12
HABS MICH,41-GRARA,2-
9dr/5ph/2pg/1pc/fr L

KEWEENAW COUNTY

HOUGHTON VIC.

Isle Royale National Park; see Rock Harbor Lodge Guest House

Rock Harbor Lodge Guest House (Isle Royale National Park)
Rock Harbor
HABS MI-246
HABS MICH,42-HOU.V,2A-
8ph/5pg/1pc L

ISLE ROYALE

Rock Harbor Lighthouse
HABS MI-386
H

MENAGERIE ISLAND

Isle Royale Light Station
HABS MI-387
H

PASSAGE ISLAND

Passage Island Light Station
HABS MI-385
H

ROCK OF AGES

Rock of Ages Lighthouse
HABS MI-388
H

LEELANAU COUNTY

EMPIRE VIC.

Sleeping Bear Dunes National Lakeshore
HABS MI-385
2dr H

GLEN ARBOR

Assigned to Wenchel (9/1/87); see Glen Haven Historic District

Blacksmith Shop (Glen Haven Historic District)
Sleeping Bear Dunes National Lakeshore,Rte. 209
HABS MI-380
2dr H

Day,D.H.,Farm (Glen Haven Historic District)
Sleeping Bear Dunes National Lakeshore,Rte. 209
HABS MI-375
3dr/2ph/1pc H

Day,D.H.,Garage (Glen Haven Historic District)
Sleeping Bear Dunes National Lakeshore,Rte. 209
HABS MI-379
1dr H

Day,Robert,House (Glen Haven Historic District)
Sleeping Bear Dunes National Lakeshore,Rte. 209
HABS MI-377
1dr H

Eckert House
Port Oneida,Sleeping Bear Dunes National Lakeshore
HABS MI-383
HABS 1992(HABS):MI-1
1ph/1pc L

Glen Haven Cannery (Glen Haven Historic District)
Sleeping Bear Dunes National Lakeshore
HABS MI-376
2dr/1ph/1pc H

Glen Haven Historic District (Assigned to Wenchel (9/1/87))
Sleeping Bear Dunes National Lakeshore,Rte. 209
HABS MI-256
4dr/1ph/1pc H

Glen Haven Historic District; see Blacksmith Shop

Glen Haven Historic District; see Day,D.H.,Farm

Glen Haven Historic District; see Day,D.H.,Garage

Glen Haven Historic District; see Day,Robert,House

Glen Haven Historic District; see Glen Haven Cannery

Glen Haven Historic District; see Restroom Building & Signal Tower

Glen Haven Historic District; see Sleeping Bear Inn

Glen Haven Historic District; see Sleeping Bear Inn,Garage/Dorm

Kelderhouse Cemetary; see Port Oneida Cemetary

Lawr Farm,House
Port Oneida,Sleeping Bear Dunes National Lakeshore
HABS MI-365-A
HABS 1992(HABS):MI-1
1ph/1pc L

Mason Farm,House
Port Oneida,Sleeping Bear Dunes National Lakeshore
HABS MI-364-A
HABS 1992(HABS):MI-1
1ph/1pc L

Miller Farm,Barn
Port Oneida,Sleeping Bear Dunes National Lakeshore
HABS MI-358-A
HABS 1992(HABS):MI-1
1ph/1pc L

Miller,Fred,Farm (Sleeping Bear Dunes National Lakeshore)
Thorsen Rd.
HABS MI-396
1ph/1pc H

North Unity School
Port Oneida,Sleeping Bear Dunes National Lakeshore
HABS MI-350
HABS 1992(HABS):MI-1
1ph/1pc L

Olsen,Howard,Farm (Sleeping Bear Dunes National Lakeshore)
Kelderhouse Rd.
HABS MI-395
HABS ALA,49-MOBI,11A-
2ph/1pc H

Olson,Charles,Farm,House
Port Oneida,Sleeping Bear Dunes National Lakeshore
HABS MI-354-A
1dr/1ph/1pc L

Port Oneida Cemetary (Kelderhouse Cemetary)
Port Oneida,Sleeping Bear Dunes National Lakeshore
HABS MI-357
HABS 1992(HABS):MI-1
1ph/1pc L

Port Oneida Community Center
Port Oneida,Sleeping Bear Dunes National Lakeshore
HABS MI-353
HABS 1992(HABS):MI-1
1ph/1pc L

Port Oneida Community Center,Privy
Port Oneida,Sleeping Bear Dunes National Lakeshore
HABS MI-353-A
HABS 1992(HABS):MI-1
1ph/1pc L

Restroom Building & Signal Tower (Glen Haven Historic District)
Sleeping Bear Dunes National Lakeshore,Rte. 209
HABS MI-378
1dr H

Sleeping Bear Dunes National Lakeshore; see Miller,Fred,Farm

Sleeping Bear Dunes National Lakeshore; see Olsen,Howard,Farm

Sleeping Bear Inn (Glen Haven Historic District)
Sleeping Bear Dunes National Lakeshore,Rte. 209
HABS MI-381
5dr/8ph H

Sleeping Bear Inn,Garage/Dorm (Glen Haven Historic District)
Sleeping Bear Dunes National Lakeshore,Rte. 209
HABS MI-381-A
1dr/1ph/1pc H

U.S. Lighthouse Reservation,Fog Signal Building
Sleeping Bear Dunes Nat. Lakeshore,S. Manitou Isl.
HABS MI-336-C
1ph/1pc H

U.S. Lighthouse Reservation,Oil Storage Shed
Sleeping Bear Dunes Nat. Lakesh.,S. Manitou Island
HABS MI-336-B
1ph/1pc H

GLEN ARBOR VIC.

Barratt Farm,Barn
Port Oneida,Sleeping Bear Dunes National Lakeshore
HABS MI-359-A
HABS 1992(HABS):MI-1
1ph/1pc L

Basch Centennial Farm,House
Port Oneida,Sleeping Bear Dunes National Lakeshore
HABS MI-362-A
HABS 1992(HABS):MI-1
1ph/1pc L

Basch,Martin,Farm,House
Port Oneida,Sleeping Bear Dunes National Lakeshore
HABS MI-355-A
HABS 1992(HABS):MI-1
3ph/1pc L

Burfield Farm
Port Oneida,Sleeping Bear Dunes National Lakeshore
HABS MI-363
HABS 1992(HABS):MI-1
1ph/1pc L

Klett Farm
Port Oneida,Sleeping Bear Dunes National Lakeshore
HABS MI-352
HABS 1992(HABS):MI-1
1ph/1pc L

Klett Farm,House
Port Oneida,Sleeping Bear Dunes National Lakeshore
HABS MI-352-A
HABS 1992(HABS):MI-1
1ph/1pc L

Thorsen Farm,Barn
Port Oneida,Sleeping Bear Dunes National Lakeshore
HABS MI-351-B
HABS 1992(HABS):MI-1
1ph/1pc L

Thorsen Farm,House
Port Oneida,Sleeping Bear Dunes National Lakeshore
HABS MI-351-A
HABS 1992(HABS):MI-1
1ph/1pc L

U. S. Lighthouse Reservation
South Manitou Island
HABS MI-336
2dr/fr H

U. S. Lighthouse Reservation,Quarters & Light
South Manitou Island
HABS MI-337
7dr/fr H

Watkins Farm,Barn
Port Oneida,Sleeping Bear Dunes National Lakeshore
HABS MI-356-A
HABS 1992(HABS):MI-1
1ph/1pc L

Weaver Farm,House
Port Oneida,Sleeping Bear Dunes National Lakeshore
HABS MI-360-A
HABS 1992(HABS):MI-1
1ph/1pc L

LELAND

Burdick House (Cottage Row)
Sleeping Bear Dunes Nat. Lakesh.,N. Manitou Island
HABS MI-366
1dr/1ph/1pc H

Cottage Row; see Burdick House

Cottage Row; see Degan House

Cottage Row; see Fiske House

Cottage Row; see Hollister House

Cottage Row; see Londergan Cottage

Cottage Row; see Monte Carlo

Cottage Row; see Summer Hotel

Cottage Row; see Tree House

Cottage Row; see Wing House

Degan House (Cottage Row)
Sleeping Bear Dunes Nat. Lakesh.,N. Manitou Island
HABS MI-367
2dr/1ph/1pc H

Fiske House (Cottage Row)
Sleeping Bear Dunes Nat. Lakesh.,N. Manitou Island
HABS MI-368
1dr/1ph/1pc H

Hollister House (Cottage Row)
Sleeping Bear Dunes Nat. Lakesh.,N. Manitou Island
HABS MI-369
1dr/1ph/1pc H

Londergan Cottage (Cottage Row)
Sleeping Bear Dunes Nat. Lakesh.,N. Manitou Island
HABS MI-370
1dr/1ph/1pc H

Monte Carlo (Cottage Row)
Sleeping Bear Dunes Nat. Lakesh.,N. Manitou Island
HABS MI-371
1dr/1ph/1pc H

Summer Hotel (Cottage Row)
Sleeping Bear Dunes Nat. Lakesh.,N. Manitou Island
HABS MI-372
1dr/2ph/1pc H

Tree House (Cottage Row)
Sleeping Bear Dunes Nat. Lakesh.,N. Manitou Island
HABS MI-373
1dr/1ph/1pc H

U.S. Lifesaving Station,Boathouse
Sleeping Bear Dunes Nat. Lakeshore,N. Manitou Isl.
HABS MI-338-B
2dr/1ph/1pc H

U.S. Lifesaving Station,Crew's Quarters
Sleeping Bear Dunes Nat. Lakeshore,N. Manitou Isl.
HABS MI-338-A
4dr/1ph/1pc H

Wing House (Cottage Row)
Sleeping Bear Dunes Nat. Lakesh.,N. Manitou Island
HABS MI-374
1dr/1ph/1pc H

LELAND VIC.

U. S. Lighthouse Reservation,Station & Boathouse
North Manitou Island
HABS MI-338
6dr/fr H

PORT ONEIDA

Hayms Farm (Schmidt,John,Farm; HS-35-123)
Basch Rd.
HABS MI-394
1ph H

HS-35-123; see Hayms Farm

HS-35-183; see Kelderhouse Farm

Kelderhouse Farm (HS-35-183)
Port Oneida Rd.
HABS MI-393
1ph H

Schmidt,John,Farm; see Hayms Farm

LENAWEE COUNTY

ADRIAN

Civil War Monument (Latrobe Column)
Monument Park
HABS MI-233
HABS MICH,46-ADRI,1A-
1dr/5ph/8pg/2pc/fr L

Latrobe Column; see Civil War Monument

TECUMSEH

Anderson,Elijah,House
401 Chicago Blvd. & N. Union St.
HABS MI-27-16
HABS MICH,46-TECUM,1-
10dr/2ph/2pg/fr L

LIVINGSTON COUNTY

BRIGHTON

Appleton,John D. ,House
325 S. Grand River Ave.
HABS MI-235
HABS MICH,47-GRIG,1-
6dr/4ph/6pg/1pc/fr L

RUSHTON

Olds,Alonzo,House
10084 Rushton Rd.
HABS MI-15
HABS MICH,47-RUSH,1-
7dr/3ph/1pg/fr L

MACKINAC COUNTY

MACKINAC ISLAND

American Fur Company Buildings
HABS MI-215
HABS MICH,49-MACKI,3-
21dr/3ph/5pg/fr L

Biddle,Edward,House
HABS MI-216
HABS MICH,49-MACKI,4-
6dr/4ph/2pg/fr L

Fort Mackinac,E. Blockhouse
HABS MI-213-B
HABS MICH,49-MACKI,1B-
3dr/2ph/1pg/fr L

Fort Mackinac,Guardhouse
HABS MI-28
HABS MICH,49-MACKI,1G-
2dr/2ph/1pg L

Fort Mackinac,N. Blockhouse
HABS MI-213-C
HABS MICH,49-MACKI,1A-
1dr/2ph/1pg L

Fort Mackinac,Officers Stone Quarters
HABS MI-25
HABS MICH,49-MACKI,1D-
8dr/4ph/3pg/fr L

Fort Mackinac,Officers Wood Quarters
HABS MI-26
HABS MICH,49-MACKI,1E-
3dr/2ph/2pg/fr L

Fort Mackinac,Post Headquarters
HABS MI-29
HABS MICH,49-MACKI,1H-
2dr/1ph/1pg/fr L

Fort Mackinac,Post Hospital
HABS MI-27
HABS MICH,49-MACKI,1F-
5dr/3ph/2pg/fr L

Fort Mackinac,Ramparts & Sally Ports
HABS MI-213-A
HABS MICH,49-MACKI,1-
4dr/6ph/2pg/fr L

Fort Mackinac,West Blockhouse
HABS MI-213-D
HABS MICH,49-MACKI,1C-
2dr/1ph/1pg/fr L

Grand Hotel
Grand Hotel Ave.
HABS MI-298
HABS MICH,49-MACKI,5-
5ph/1pg/1pc L

Mission Church,Old
HABS MI-214
HABS MICH,49-MACKI,2-
8dr/3ph/3pg/fr L

MACOMB COUNTY

WARREN

Detroit Arsenal (Detroit Tank Plant; Pontiac Storage Facility; Keweenaw Field Station)
6501 E. Eleven Mile Rd.
HAER MI-12
HAER MICH,50-WAR,1-
26ph/61pg/3pc/fr L

Detroit Tank Plant; see Detroit Arsenal

Keweenaw Field Station; see Detroit Arsenal

Pontiac Storage Facility; see Detroit Arsenal

MARQUETTE COUNTY

CHAMPION VIC.

White Deer Lake Camp
Cyrus H. McCormick Experimental Forest
HABS MI-30
HABS MICH,52-CHAM.V,1-
4pg/fr L

White Deer Lake Camp,Beaver Cabin
Cyrus H. McCormick Experimental Forest
HABS MI-30-A
HABS MICH,52-CHAM.V,1A-
14ph/1pg/1pc L

White Deer Lake Camp,Birch Cabin
Cyrus H. McCormick Experimental Forest
HABS MI-30-B
HABS MICH,52-CHAM.V,1B-
13ph/1pg/1pc L

White Deer Lake Camp,Chimney Cabin
Cyrus H. McCormick Experimental Forest
HABS MI-30-C
HABS MICH,52-CHAM.V,1C-
45ph/2pg/3pc L

White Deer Lake Camp,Library Cabin
Cyrus H. McCormick Experimental Forest
HABS MI-30-D
HABS MICH,52-CHAM.V,1D-
21ph/1pg/2pc L

White Deer Lake Camp,Living Room Cabin
Cyrus H. McCormick Experimental Forest
HABS MI-30-E
HABS MICH,52-CHAM.V,1E-
21ph/1pg L

ISHPEMING

Cliff Shaft Mine Head Frame (Shaft House,Reinforced-Concrete)
HAER MI-3
HAER MICH,52-ISH,1-
1ph/1pg/1pc L

Shaft House,Reinforced-Concrete; see Cliff Shaft Mine Head Frame

MONROE COUNTY

MONROE

McClelland,Gov. Robert B. ,House
47 E. Elm St.
HABS MI-17
HABS MICH,58-MONRO,1-
14dr/2ph/2pg/fr L

Monroe Street Bridge (State M-50,M-125 Bridge)
Spanning the River Raisin at Monroe St.
HAER MI-35
HAER 1991(HAER):8
26ph/17pg/4pc L

Nims,Rudolph,House
206 W. Noble St.
HABS MI-18
HABS MICH,58-MONRO,2-
9dr/2ph/2pg/fr L

State M-50,M-125 Bridge; see Monroe Street Bridge

MUSKEGON COUNTY

MUSKEGON

Lake Shore Drive Bridge; see Lake Street Bridge

Lake Street Bridge (Lake Shore Drive Bridge; Ruddiman Creek Bridge)
Spanning Ruddiman Creek at Lake Shore Drive
HAER MI-15
HAER MICH,61-MUSK,1-
27ph/6pg/2pc L

Ruddiman Creek Bridge; see Lake Street Bridge

NORTON SHORES

Antisdale,William S.,Memorial State Reward Bridge (Henry Street Bridge)
Spanning Mona Lake at Henry St.
HAER MI-26
HAER 1991(HAER):8
15ph/5pg/1pc L

Henry Street Bridge; see Antisdale,William S.,Memorial State Reward Bridge

OTTAWA COUNTY

SPRINGLAKE

Interurban Station
N. side of M104,E. of Grand Haven Bridge
HABS MI-342
15ph/4pg/2pc H

PRESQUE ISLE COUNTY

PRESQUE ISLE

Presque Isle Light Station
Off SR 405,At N. end Grand Lake Road
HAER MI-30
HAER 1992(HAER):MI-1
11ph/6pg/1pc L

SAGINAW COUNTY

FRANKENMUTH VIC.

Black Bridge; see Dehmel Road Bridge

Dehmel Road Bridge (Black Bridge)
Spanning Cass River
HAER MI-28
HAER MICH,73-FRANK.V,1-
9pg/fr L

SHIAWASSEE COUNTY

BANCROFT VIC.

Cole Road Bridge; see Knaggs Bridge

Knaggs Bridge (Cole Road Bridge)
Spanning the Shiawassee River on Cole Rd.
HAER MI-29
HAER 1989(HAER):12
12ph/7pg/1pc L

ST. CLAIR COUNTY

PORT HURON

American Plaza; see Blue Water Bridge Plaza

Blue Water Bridge Plaza (U.S. Customs/Toll Plaza; U.S. Plaza; American Plaza)
410 Elmwood St.
HAER MI-16
HAER MICH,74-POHU,1-
43ph/35pg/8pc L

U.S. Customs/Toll Plaza; see Blue Water Bridge Plaza

U.S. Plaza; see Blue Water Bridge Plaza

WASHTENAW COUNTY

ANN ARBOR

Anderson House
2301 Packard Rd.
HABS MI-27-22
HABS MICH,81-ANAR,3-
9dr/2ph/2pg/fr L

Brown,Anson,Commercial Building (Exchange & Ingalls Blocks)
1003-1005 Broadway
HABS MI-110
HABS MICH,81-ANAR,4-
2dr/1ph/2pg L

Colonial Inn
HABS MI-297
HABS MICH,81-ANAR,6-
4dr L

Covert,Norman B. ,House
1500 Dexter Ave.
HABS MI-118
HABS MICH,81-ANAR,5-
2dr/2ph/fr L

DeForest Barn
Dixboro & Geddes Rds.
HABS MI-301
HABS MICH,81-ANAR,7A-
3dr L

Exchange & Ingalls Blocks; see Brown,Anson,Commercial Building

Hall,Dr. Richard Neville,House
1330 Hill St.
HABS MI-305
HABS MICH,81-ANAR,8-
3dr L

Hoover House
2015 Washtenaw
HABS MI-303
HABS MICH,81-ANAR,9-
4dr L

Lloyd House
1734 Washtenaw
HABS MI-304
HABS MICH,81-ANAR,10-
4dr L

Perry House (Perry House,The Old)
1317 Pontiac St.
HABS MI-306
HABS MICH,81-ANAR,11-
4dr L

Perry House,The Old; see Perry House

Sinclair House
1223 Pontiac St.
HABS MI-27-3
HABS MICH,81-ANAR,2-
7dr/3ph/2pg/fr L

Ticknor,Dr. Benajah,House
2781 Packard St.
HABS MI-19
HABS MICH,81-ANAR.V,1-
9dr/5ph/1pg/fr L

University Observatory,Old; see University of Michigan,Detroit Observatory

University of Michigan,Detroit Observatory (University Observatory,Old)
Observatory & Ann Sts.
HABS MI-302
HABS MICH,81-ANAR,12A-
7dr/3pg L

Wilson,Judge R. S. ,House
E. Ann & N. Division Sts.
HABS MI-27-2
HABS MICH,81-ANAR,1-
8dr/3ph/2pg/fr L

DEXTER

Dexter,Judge Samuel W. ,House
W. Huron St.
HABS MI-116
HABS MICH,81-DEX,1-
4dr/8ph/2pg/fr L

DEXTER VIC.

Dexter,Judge Samuel,Country House
8401 Ann Arbor St.
HABS MI-27-21
HABS MICH,81-DEX.V,1-
17dr/7ph/3pg/fr L

DIXBORO

Methodist Episcopal Church
Plymouth Rd.
HABS MI-16
HABS MICH,81-DIXBO,1-
5dr/3ph/1pg/fr L

SHARONVILLE VIC.

Porter,Squire Michael,House
Jacob & Kendall Rds.
HABS MI-114
HABS MICH,81-SHAR.V,1-
8dr/4ph/2pg/fr L

YPSILANTI

Ballard House
125 N. Huron St.
HABS MI-27-23
HABS MICH,81-YPSI,1-
12dr/2ph/2pg/fr L

Ballard,Arden H. ,House (Ladies Literary Club)
218 N. Washington St.
HABS MI-14
HABS MICH,81-YPSI,2-
7dr/7ph/1pg/fr L

Ladies Literary Club; see Ballard,Arden H. ,House

U. S. Post Office
HABS MI-296
HABS MICH,81-YPSI,3-
3dr L

WAYNE COUNTY

CANTON TOWNSHIP

Moore,Alfred,House
W. Warren & Ridge Rds.
HABS MI-112
HABS MICH,82- ,1-
9dr/4ph/1pg/fr L

Yost,William,House
6020 Sheldon Rd.
HABS MI-117
HABS MICH,82- ,2-
4dr/3ph/1pg/fr L

DEARBORN

Detroit Arsenal
Michigan Ave. & Monroe Blvd.
HABS MI-27-7
HABS MICH,82-DERB,1-
11dr/7ph/4pg L

Detroit Arsenal,Officers' Quarters
21950 Michigan Ave.
HABS MI-27-7-A
HABS MICH,82-DERB,1A-
7dr/3ph L

Detroit Arsenal,Smith's & Carpenter's Shops
Garrison Ave.
HABS MI-27-7-B
HABS MICH,82-DERB,1C-
1dr/2ph/fr L

Detroit Arsenal,Sutler's Shop
Garrison Ave. & Monroe Blvd.
HABS MI-27-7-C
HABS MICH,82-DERB,1B-
2dr/2ph/fr L

DETROIT

Adair Street Warehouse; see Buhl Sons Company Complex

Aluminum Castings Company; see Poletown Historic District

Aluminum Manufacturers,Inc.; see Poletown Historic District

Basso Building
7338 Woodward Ave.
HABS MI-274
HABS MICH,82-DETRO,19-
18ph/14pg/2pc L

Beaver Realty Company; see Jones,James M. ,House

Bohn Aluminum and Brass Corporation; see Poletown Historic District

Buckland-Van Wald Bldg; see Reid,William, & Company Bldg

Buhl Sons Company Complex (Adair Street Warehouse)
120-234 Adair St.
HAER MI-13
HAER MICH,82-DETRO,45-
27ph/12pg/2pc L

Bull Dog Electric Company; see Poletown Historic District

Chene Street Commercial District; see Poletown Historic District

Christ Episcopal Church
976 E. Jefferson Ave.
HABS MI-260
HABS MICH,82-DETRO,5-
1ph L

City Hall,Old
Woodward Ave. & Cadillac Sq.
HABS MI-221
HABS MICH,82-DETRO,6-
4ph/1pg/1pc L

Customs House
Griswold & Larned Sts.
HABS MI-222
HABS MICH,82-DETRO,7-
19ph/1pg/2pc L

D. W. G. Cigar Corporation; see Poletown Historic District

D. W. Hacker Company,The; see Poletown Historic District

Dennison Book Keeping Service; see Poletown Historic District

Detroit & Cleveland Navigation Company Warehouse
Wayne St.
HABS MI-119
HABS MICH,82-DETRO,15-
7dr/25ph/3pg L

Detroit Edison Hart Substation
11736 E. Vernor
HAER MI-25
HAER MICH,82-DETRO,43A-
22ph/14pg/3pc/fr L

Detroit Steel Products Company Plant; see Poletown Historic District

1491 East Congress Street (House)
HABS MI-266
HABS MICH,82-DETRO,14-
1ph L

404 East Ferry Avenue (House)
(Fairview Sanitarium)
HABS MI-312
HABS MICH,82-DETRO,18-
4ph/2pg/1pc L

East Ferry Avenue Historic District
E. Ferry Ave. btwn. Woodward & Beaubien Aves.
HABS MI-311
HABS MICH,82-DETRO,20-
18pg L

976-78 East Woodbridge Street (Double House)
HABS MI-263
HABS MICH,82-DETRO,13-
1ph L

Fairview Sanitarium; see 404 East Ferry Avenue (House)

First Bank in Detroit
Jefferson Ave. & Randolph St.
HABS MI-264
HABS MICH,82-DETRO,8-
1ph L

Fisher Body Company Plant No. 12; see Poletown Historic District

Fisher Building
3011 W. Grand Blvd.
HABS MI-309
HABS MICH,82-DETRO,21-
6ph/1pg/1pc L

Fort Street Presbyterian Church
Fort & Third Sts.
HABS MI-265
HABS MICH,82-DETRO,9-
1ph L

Fort Wayne
W. Jefferson & Livernois Aves.
HABS MI-27-4
HABS MICH,82-DETRO,2-
14dr/6ph/4pg L

Fort Wayne,Old Barracks
W. Jefferson Ave.
HABS MI-27-4-A
HABS MICH,82-DETRO,2B-
10dr/1ph/fr L

Fort Wayne,Powder House
W. Jefferson Ave.
HABS MI-27-4-B
HABS MICH,82-DETRO,2C-
2dr/1ph/fr L

Fort Wayne,Sally Ports
W. Jefferson Ave.
HABS MI-27-4-C
HABS MICH,82-DETRO,2A-
1dr/4ph/fr L

General Aluminum and Brass Casting Works; see Poletown Historic District

General Motors Building
3044 W. Grand Blvd.
HABS MI-20
HABS MICH,82-DETRO,22-
5ph/1pg/1pc L

Grand Riviera Theatre
9222 Grand River Ave.
HABS MI-270
HABS MICH,82-DETRO,16-
6dr/28ph/24pg L

Graylawn Apartments; see Poletown Historic District

Guarantee Trust & Loan Company,Ltd.; see Poletown Historic District

Guardian Building; see Union Trust Building

Hackett,Lee J. ,Company; see Poletown Historic District

Helms Corporation; see Poletown Historic District

Hervey Park Elementary School; see Poletown Historic District

Hupp Motor Car Company; see Poletown Historic District

Immaculate Conception Catholic Church; see Poletown Historic District

Industrial Women's Service Center; see Poletown Historic District

Jones,James M. ,House (Beaver Realty Company)
1460 E. Jefferson Ave.
HABS MI-13
HABS MICH,82-DETRO,4-
7dr/1ph/1pg L

Majeske,Joseph F. ,School; see Poletown Historic District

Mariner's Church
Woodward Ave. 6 Woodbridge St.
HABS MI-11
HABS MICH,82-DETRO,3-
15dr/6ph/3pg/fr L

Mercantile Building
554 W. Jefferson Ave.
HABS MI-267
HABS MICH,82-DETRO,10-
1ph L

Messiah Evangelical Lutheran Church; see United Auto Workers (U.A.W.) Hall,Local No. 7

Metropolitan Building
25-107 John R St.
HABS MI-261
HABS MICH,82-DETRO,23-
21ph/14pg/3pc L

Mid-West Paper Products Company; see Poletown Historic District

100-102 Monroe Avenue (Commercial Building)
HABS MI-330
4ph/10pg/2pc H

16-30 Monroe Avenue (Commercial Building)
HABS MI-321
8ph/14pg/2pc H

32-42 Monroe Avenue (Commercial Building)
HABS MI-322
7ph/13pg/2pc H

52-54 Monroe Avenue (Commercial Building)
HABS MI-324
2ph/4pg/2pc H

58 Monroe Avenue (Commercial Building)
HABS MI-325
4ph/4pg/2pc H

62 Monroe Avenue (Commercial Building)
HABS MI-326
2ph/4pg/2pc H

66-68 Monroe Avenue (Commercial Building)
HABS MI-327
3ph/4pg/2pc H

70-72 Monroe Avenue (Commercial Building)
HABS MI-328
2ph/4pg/2pc H

74-78 Monroe Avenue (Commercial Building)
HABS MI-329
12ph/10pg/2pc H

104-106 Monroe Street (Commercial Building)
HABS MI-331
2ph/8pg/2pc H

Murphy Ironworks,Office Building (Stoker,Riley,Co.,Office Building)
101 Walker St.
HABS MI-319
HABS DLC/PP-1993:MI-5
42ph/21pg/3pc L

Mutual Electric and Machine Company; see Poletown Historic District

National Can Company; see Poletown Historic District

New Center Building
7430 Second Ave.
HABS MI-310
HABS MICH,82-DETRO,24-
5ph/1pg/1pc L

Olympia Arena (Olympia Stadium)
5920 Grand River Ave.
HABS MI-252
HABS MICH,82-DETRO,25-
16ph/12pg/2pc L

Olympia Stadium; see Olympia Arena

Orchestra Hall (Paradise Theatre)
3711 Woodward Ave.
HABS MI-271
HABS MICH,82-DETRO,17-
22ph/23pg L

Paradise Theatre; see Orchestra Hall

Parke-Davis Industrial Site (Stroh River Place Complex)
Bounded by MacDougall & Joseph Campau Aves.
HAER MI-19
HAER MICH,82-DETRO,44-
20ph/3pc L

Poletown Historic District (Bohn Aluminum and Brass Corporation; National Can Company; General Aluminum and Brass Casting Works; Helms Corporation)
2512 E. Grand Blvd.
HABS MI-275-3
HABS MICH,82-DETRO,29-
2ph/6pg/1pc L

Poletown Historic District (Bull Dog Electric Company; Aluminum Castings Company; Aluminum Manufacturers,Inc.; Mutual Electric and Machine Company)
7500 Joseph Campau Ave.
HABS MI-275-2
HABS MICH,82-DETRO,28-
5ph/4pg/1pc L

Poletown Historic District (Chene Street Commercial District)
Chene St. btwn. Interstate 94 & Grand Blvd.
HABS MI-275-15
HABS 1985(HABS):150
11ph/8pg/1pc L

Poletown Historic District (Detroit Steel Products Company Plant; Mid-West Paper Products Company)
7610 Joseph Campau Ave.
HABS MI-275-1
HABS MICH,82-DETRO,27-
6ph/5pg/1pc L

Poletown Historic District (Fisher Body Company Plant No. 12; Hackett,Lee J. ,Company)
1961 E. Milwaukee Ave.
HABS MI-275-12
HABS MICH,82-DETRO,38A-
7ph/5pg/1pc L

Poletown Historic District (Graylawn Apartments)
Chene St. Commercial District
HABS MI-275-13
4ph/1pc L

Poletown Historic District (Guarantee Trust & Loan Company,Ltd.; Dennison Book Keeping Service)
2126 E. Canal Blvd.
HABS MI-275-4
HABS MICH,82-DETRO,30-
1ph/5pg/1pc L

Poletown Historic District (Hervey Park Elementary School)
3010 E. Milwaukee Ave.
HABS MI-275-14
HABS MICH,82-DETRO,39-
3ph/9pg/1pc L

Poletown Historic District (Hupp Motor Car Company)
Milwaukee Ave. & Mt. Elliott Ave.
HABS MI-275-11
HABS MICH,82-DETRO,37-
7ph/7pg/1pc L

Poletown Historic District (Immaculate Conception Catholic Church)
3414 Trombly Ave.
HABS MI-275-6
HABS MICH,82-DETRO,32-
18ph/7pg/1pc L

Poletown Historic District (Industrial Women's Service Center)
2431 E. Grand Blvd.
HABS MI-275-10
HABS MICH,82-DETRO,36-
2ph/5pg/1pc L

Poletown Historic District (Majeske,Joseph F. ,School)
2139 Trombly Ave.
HABS MI-275-8
HABS MICH,82-DETRO,34-
4ph/10pg/1pc L

Poletown Historic District (Schwartz,Benard,Cigar Corporation; D. W. G. Cigar Corporation; D. W. Hacker Company,The)
2180 E. Milwaukee Ave.
HABS MI-275-9
HABS MICH,82-DETRO,35-
2ph/7pg/1pc L

Poletown Historic District (St. Hyacinth Roman Catholic Church & School)
3151 Farnsworth
HABS MI-275-7
HABS MICH,82-DETRO,33-
1ph/3pg/1pc L

Poletown Historic District (St. Nicholas Greek Catholic Church; Temple of Faith Missionary Baptist Church)
2390 E. Grand Blvd.
HABS MI-275-5
HABS MICH,82-DETRO,31-
7ph/4pg/1pc L

Poletown Historic District (Zabawski Building)
Chene St. Commercial District
HABS MI-275-16
2ph/1pc L

Reid,William, & Company Bldg (Buckland-Van Wald Bldg)
426-430 W. Larned St.
HABS MI-314
HABS MICH,82-DETRO,41-
14ph/10pg/1pc/fr L

Schwartz,Benard,Cigar Corporation; see Poletown Historic District

Seitz,Henry,Building (Wardwell House)
16109 E. Jefferson Ave. ,Grosse Pointe Park
HABS MI-12
HABS MICH,82-GROSP,1-
5dr/3ph/1pg L

Sibley House
976 E. Jefferson Ave.
HABS MI-269
HABS MICH,82-DETRO,12-
1ph L

St. Hyacinth Roman Catholic Church & School; see Poletown Historic District

St. John's Episcopal Church
Woodward Ave. & Vernor Hwy.
HABS MI-268
HABS MICH,82-DETRO,11-
1ph L

St. Nicholas Greek Catholic Church; see Poletown Historic District

Stoker,Riley,Co.,Office Building; see Murphy Ironworks,Office Building

Stroh River Place Complex; see Parke-Davis Industrial Site

Sts. Peter & Paul's Jesuit Church
E. Jefferson Ave. & Saint Antoine St.
HABS MI-27-1
HABS MICH,82-DETRO,1-
11dr/3ph/4pg/fr L

Temple of Faith Missionary Baptist Church; see Poletown Historic District

Union Trust Building (Guardian Building)
500 Griswold St.
HABS MI-273
HABS MICH,82-DETRO,42-
15ph/1pg/1pc L

United Auto Workers (U.A.W.) Hall,Local No. 7 (Messiah Evangelical Lutheran Church)
1551 Hart St.
HABS MI-316
18ph/17pg/3pc H

Wardwell House; see Seitz,Henry,Building

Zabawski Building; see Poletown Historic District

DETROIT & DEARBORN

Dix Bascule Bridge
Spanning the Rouge River at Dix Ave.
HAER MI-32
HAER 1991(HAER):8
13ph/18pg/2pc L

HAMTRAMCK

Dodge Brothers Motor Car Company Plant (Dodge Main)
Btwn. Joseph Campau & Conant Aves.
HAER MI-6
HAER MICH,82-HAMT,1-
313ph/46pg/11pc L

Dodge Main; see Dodge Brothers Motor Car Company Plant

James C. Burbank House (Livingston GriggsHouse), St. Paul, Ramsey County, Minnesota. Stairhall, stair, details of balusters. Photograph by Jack E. Boucher, November 1960 (HABS MINN, 62SAIPA,13-7)

Minnesota

AITKIN COUNTY

SANDY LAKE

Sandy Lake Dam,Tender's Residence
Junction of Mississippi and Sandy Rivers
HABS MN-126
HABS DLC/PP-1992:MN-5
11ph/11pg/1pc L

ANOKA COUNTY

ANOKA

Woodbury House
Main St. & Second Ave.
HABS MN-29-13
HABS MINN,2-ANOK,1-
2dr/1pg/fr L

BECKER COUNTY

DETROIT LAKES

Detroit Lakes Public Library
1000 Washington Ave.
HABS MN-102
HABS DLC/PP-1992:MN-2
11ph/1pc L

BELTRAMI COUNTY

SAUM VIC.

Saum School
Co. Hwy. 23
HABS MN-104
HABS DLC/PP-1992:MN-2
3ph/1pc L

Saum School,Old
County Hwy. 23
HABS MN-104-A
HABS DLC/PP-1992:MN-2
3ph/1pc L

BIG STONE COUNTY

ARTICHOKE

Artichoke Township Hall; see District 13 School

District 13 School (Artichoke Township Hall)
Co. Rd. 25
HABS MN-120
HABS DLC/PP-1992:MN-2
1ph/1pc L

BLUE EARTH COUNTY

SKYLINE VIC.

Kern Truss Bridge
Township Rd. over LeSueur River
HAER MN-45
HAER DLC/PP-1992:MN-2
9ph/1pc L

ST. CLAIR

Indian Agency House
HABS MN-29-43
HABS MINN,7-SAICLA,1-
4dr/2ph/1pg/fr L

BROWN COUNTY

NEW ULM

August Schell Brewing Company
Twentieth St. South
HAER MN-40
HAER DLC/PP-1992:MN-2
11ph/1pc L

August Schell Brewing Company,Schell Residence
Twentieth St. South
HAER MN-40-A
HAER DLC/PP-1992:MN-2
2ph/1pc L

August Schell Brewing Company,Worker's Cottage
Twentieth St. South
HAER MN-40-B
HAER DLC/PP-1992:MN-2
1ph/1pc L

Berndt,Julius,House
HABS MN-1-6
HABS MINN,8-NEWUL,1-
1ph L

Hermann Monument
Hermann Heights Park
HABS MN-96
HABS DLC/PP-1992:MN-2
4ph/1pc L

CARLTON COUNTY

CLOQUET

Lindholm Oil Company Service Station
202 Cloquet Ave.
HABS MN-118
HABS DLC/PP-1992:MN-2
6ph/1pc L

CLOQUET VIC.

St. Joseph & Mary Church
Mission Rd.
HABS MN-106
HABS DLC/PP-1992:MN-2
3ph/1pc L

SAWYER

Church,Log
HABS MN-29-28
HABS MINN,9-SAW,1-
3dr/2ph/2pg/fr L

SILVER BROOK TWP.

Jay Cooke State Park,Pedestrian Suspension Bridge
MN Hwy. 210,crossing St. Louis River
HAER MN-53
HAER DLC/PP-1992:MN-2
4ph/1pc L

CARVER COUNTY

WATERTOWN

Lewis Avenue Historic District; see 108 Lewis Avenue North,House

Lewis Avenue Historic District; see 112 Lewis Avenue North,House

200 Lewis Avenue North (House)
(Lewis Avenue North Historic District)
HABS MN-130
11ph/14pg/1pc H

Lewis Avenue North Historic District; see 200 Lewis Avenue North (House)

108 Lewis Avenue North,House (Lewis Avenue Historic District)
108 Lewis Avenue North
HABS MN-129
4ph/5pg/1pc H

112 Lewis Avenue North,House (Lewis Avenue Historic District)
112 Lewis Avenue North
HABS MN-128
4ph/5pg/1pc H

CHIPPEWA COUNTY

MONTEVIDEO

Wilkins,Daniel,Log House
Smith Park
HABS MN-1-1
HABS MINN,12-MONT,1-
3ph/1pg L

WATSON

Watson Farmer's Elevator
U.S. Hwy. 59
HAER MN-49
HAER DLC/PP-1992:MN-2
3ph/1pc L

WATSON VIC.

Lac Qui Parle Mission Church (Ruins)
HABS MN-1-2
HABS MINN,12-WAT.V,1-
1ph/2pg L

CHISAGO COUNTY

CENTER CITY

Center City Hist. Dist.,Swedish Evang Luth. Church (Chisago Lake Church)
Summit Ave.
HABS MN-117-C
HABS DLC/PP-1992:MN-2
1ph/1pc L

Center City Historic District,100 Summit Avenue
HABS MN-117-A
HABS DLC/PP-1992:MN-2
1ph/1pc L

Center City Historic District,120-144 Summit Ave.
HABS MN-117
HABS DLC/PP-1992:MN-2
2ph/1pc L

Center City Historic District,220 Summit Avenue
HABS MN-117-B
HABS DLC/PP-1992:MN-2
1ph/1pc L

Chisago Lake Church; see Center City Hist. Dist.,Swedish Evang Luth. Church

TAYLORS FALLS

Branch Street Library
HABS MN-29-17
HABS MINN,13-TAYFA,3-
3dr/2ph/2pg/fr L

First Methodist Church
Government St.
HABS MN-29-15
HABS MINN,13-TAYFA,1-
4dr/2ph/1pg/fr L

Folsom,W. H. C. ,House
HABS MN-29-16
HABS MINN,13-TAYFA,2-
6dr/4ph/2pg/fr L

CLAY COUNTY

MOORHEAD

Hearl,Melvin E.,Post No. 21; see Moorhead American Legion Building

Moorhead American Legion Building
(Hearl,Melvin E.,Post No. 21)
700 First Ave. N.
HABS MN-127
HABS DLC/PP-1992:MN-2
4dr/fr L

CLEARWATER COUNTY

LAKE ITASCA VIC.

Itasca State Park,Forest Inn
Off Hwy. No. 11
HABS MN-114
HABS DLC/PP-1992:MN-2
1ph/1pc L

Itasca State Park,Old Headwaters Building
HABS MN-114-A
HABS DLC/PP-1992:MN-2
2ph/1pc L

Itasca State Park,Old Timer's Cabin
HABS MN-114-B
HABS DLC/PP-1992:MN-2
3ph/1pc L

COOK COUNTY

GRAND MARAIS

Grand Portage National Monument,Buildings Complex
Off Hwy. 16,NE tip of Lake Superior
HABS MN-76
HABS 1991(HABS):8
13ph/1pg/1pc L

Grand Portage National Monument,Warehouse
Off Hwy. 16,NE tip of Lake Superior
HABS MN-76-A
HABS 1991(HABS):8
2ph/1pc L

COTTONWOOD COUNTY

JEFFERS VIC.

Jeffers Petroglyphs
Delton Township
HABS MN-109
HABS DLC/PP-1992:MN-2
5ph/1pc L

DAKOTA COUNTY

MENDOTA

Faribault House
Minnesota River Vic.
HABS MN-29-7
HABS MINN,19-MEND,2-
2dr/2ph/3pg L

St. Peter's Catholic Church
HABS MN-29-4
HABS MINN,19-MEND,1-
3dr/1ph/1pg/fr L

FILLMORE COUNTY

RUSHFORD

Bridge No. 4900
Spanning the Root River at Trunk Highway 16
HAER MN-55
38ph/7pg/3pc L

GOODHUE COUNTY

FRONTENAC

St. Hubert's Lodge
Garrard Ave.
HABS MN-29-34
HABS MINN,25-FRONT,1-
6dr/8ph/3pg/fr L

RED WING VIC.

Locks & Dams No. 3 through 10; see Upper Mississippi River 9 foot Channel Proj. Hist.

Upper Miss. River 9-Foot Channel Lock & Dam No. 3
HAER MN-21
HAER MINN,25-REW.V,2-
98ph/11pg/7pc L

Upper Mississippi River 9 foot Channel Proj. Hist. (Locks & Dams No. 3 through 10)
Mississippi River btwn Minneapolis & Guttenberg,IA
HAER MN-20
HAER MINN,25-REW.V,1-
48pg L

GRANT COUNTY

HERMAN

Herman Grain Elevators,Farmer's Elevator Company
MN Hwys. 9 & 27
HAER MN-51-A
HAER DLC/PP-1992:MN-2
1ph/1pc L

Herman Grain Elevators,Herman Market Company
MN Hwys. 9 & 27
HAER MN-51
HAER DLC/PP-1992:MN-2
1ph/1pc L

Herman Grain Elevators,South Elevator
MN Hwys. 9 & 27
HAER MN-51-B
HAER DLC/PP-1992:MN-2
1ph/1pc L

HENNEPIN COUNTY

BLOOMINGTON

Pond House
Nicollet Ave.
HABS MN-29-22
HABS MINN,27-BLOMT,1-
3dr/3ph/1pg/fr L

EDEN PRARIE

Glen Lake Sanitarium
See documentation under
MN,HENNEPIN CO.,MINNETONKA
HABS MN-133
HABS MINN,2-ANOK,1-
L

EXCELSIOR

Trinity Chapel (Episcopal)
Second & Center Sts.
HABS MN-29-6
HABS MINN,27-EXCEL,1-
6dr/2ph/1pg/fr L

HENNEPIN

Minnesota Veterans Home Complex,Domiciliary No. 3
5101 Minnehaha Ave. S.
HABS MN-74-C
HABS DLC/PP-1993:MN-1
7pg L

MINNEAPOLIS

Bremer,Frederika,Intermediate School
1214 Lowry Ave. N
HABS MN-33
HABS MINN,27-MINAP,12-
61ph/16pg/4pc/fr L

Broadway Bridge (Twentieth Avenue North Bridge)
Broadway St. ,spanning Mississippi River
HAER MN-2
HAER MINN,27-MINAP,10-
58ph/31pg/3pc L

Building No. 10; see Minnesota Veterans Home Complex,Admin. Building

Building No. 13; see Minnesota Veterans Home Complex,Laundry Building

Building No. 14; see Minnesota Veterans' Home Complex,Power House

Building No. 7; see Minnesota Veterans Home Complex,Dining Hall

Chicago,Milwaukee,St. Paul & Pacific RR,Freighthse
201-211 Third Ave. So.
HABS MN-91
HABS 1991(HABS):8
17ph/3pg/2pc L

Church of Minneapolis (New Church Society)
905 Fifth Ave.
HABS MN-29-9
HABS MINN,27-MINAP,5-
5dr/2ph/1pg/fr L

City Hall-Courthouse; see Municipal Building

Como-Harriet Streetcar Line & Trolley,Car No. 265
Forty-second St. West at Queen Avenue
HAER MN-42
7ph/1pc L

Ferry Farm; see Stevens,Col. J. H. ,House

Godfrey,Ard,House
Ortman St.
HABS MN-29-2
HABS MINN,27-MINAP,2-
3dr/2ph/1pg/fr L

Guaranty Loan Building; see Metropolitan Building

Hennepin Avenue Bridge; see Steel Arch Bridge

Lake Street-Marshall Avenue Bridge
Spanning the Mississippi River
HAER MN-6
HAER 1989(HAER):13
47ph/24pg/3pc/fr L

127 Main Street SE (Building)
HABS MN-29-8
HABS MINN,27-MINAP,4-
3dr/1ph/1pg/fr L

425 Marshall Ave. (Commercial Building)
HABS MN-29-11
HABS MINN,27-MINAP,7-
3dr/2ph/2pg/fr L

Metropolitan Building (Guaranty Loan Building)
308 Second Ave. South
HABS MN-49
HABS MINN,27-MINAP,13-
6ph/1pg L

Minneapolis Warehouse Dist.,200-204 Washington N.
HABS MN-110-H
HABS DLC/PP-1992:MN-2
1ph/1pc L

Minneapolis Warehouse Dist.,8th Ave. & Washington
HABS MN-110-R
HABS DLC/PP-1992:MN-2
1ph/1pc L

Minneapolis Warehouse District,Acme Electronics
Third Ave. N.
HABS MN-110-D
HABS DLC/PP-1992:MN-2
1ph/1pc L

Minneapolis Warehouse District,Berman Buckskin Co.
Hennepin Ave. at N. First St.
HABS MN-110-V
HABS DLC/PP-1992:MN-2
1ph/1pc L

Minneapolis Warehouse District,Butler Square
HABS MN-110-F
HABS DLC/PP-1992:MN-2
1ph/1pc L

Minneapolis Warehouse District,Colonial Warehouse
200 Third Ave. N.
HABS MN-110-W
HABS DLC/PP-1992:MN-2
3ph/1pc L

Minneapolis Warehouse District,Commercial Building
256 First Ave. N.
HABS MN-110-I
HABS DLC/PP-1992:MN-2
1ph/1pc L

Minneapolis Warehouse District,Creamette Co. Bldg.
N. First St.
HABS MN-110-X
HABS DLC/PP-1992:MN-2
1ph/1pc L

Minneapolis Warehouse District,Falk Paper Company
N. Third St. at Seventh Ave.
HABS MN-110-O
HABS DLC/PP-1992:MN-2
3ph/1pc L

Minneapolis Warehouse District,Ford Center
HABS MN-110-L
HABS DLC/PP-1992:MN-2
1ph/1pc L

Minneapolis Warehouse District,Itasca Warehouse
N. First St.
HABS MN-110-Y
HABS DLC/PP-1992:MN-2
1ph/1pc L

Minneapolis Warehouse District,Kickernick Building
First Ave. N.
HABS MN-110-E
HABS DLC/PP-1992:MN-2
1ph/1pc L

Minneapolis Warehouse District,Lindsay Building
400 N. First St.
HABS MN-110-S
HABS DLC/PP-1992:MN-2
1ph/1pc L

Minneapolis Warehouse District,Litin Paper Co.
Seventh Ave.
HABS MN-110-N
HABS DLC/PP-1992:MN-2
1ph/1pc L

Minneapolis Warehouse District,Lumber Exchange Bld
HABS MN-110-B
HABS DLC/PP-1992:MN-2
1ph/1pc L

Minneapolis Warehouse District,Magnum Fire Corp.
614 N. First St.
HABS MN-110-AA
HABS DLC/PP-1992:MN-2
1ph/1pc L

Minneapolis Warehouse District,Masonic Temple
Hennepin Ave.
HABS MN-110-AB
HABS DLC/PP-1992:MN-2
2ph/1pc L

Minneapolis Warehouse District,Minnesota Opera Co.
614-624 N. First St.
HABS MN-110-Z
HABS DLC/PP-1992:MN-2
1ph/1pc L

Minneapolis Warehouse District,Safe Storage Bldg.
N. First Ave. & N. First St.
HABS MN-110-U
HABS DLC/PP-1992:MN-2
1ph/1pc L

Minneapolis Warehouse District,Seymour Block
N. Second Ave. between N. First & Second Sts.
HABS MN-110-P
HABS DLC/PP-1992:MN-2
1ph/1pc L

Minneapolis Warehouse District,Whitney Building
200 N. Second St.
HABS MN-110-T
HABS DLC/PP-1992:MN-2
1ph/1pc L

Minneapolis Warehouse District,24 Third Ave. North
HABS MN-110-J
HABS DLC/PP-1992:MN-2
1ph/1pc L

Minneapolis Warehouse District,250 North 3rd Ave.
HABS MN-110-K
HABS DLC/PP-1992:MN-2
1ph/1pc L

Minneapolis Warehouse District,300 1st Ave. North
HABS MN-110-A
HABS DLC/PP-1992:MN-2
2ph/1pc L

Minneapolis Warehouse District,300-314 3rd Ave.
HABS MN-110-C
HABS DLC/PP-1992:MN-2
2ph/1pc L

Minneapolis Warehouse District,5th St. & 3rd Ave N
HABS MN-110-G
HABS DLC/PP-1992:MN-2
1ph/1pc L

Minneapolis Warehouse District,701 North Third St.
HABS MN-110-M
HABS DLC/PP-1992:MN-2
1ph/1pc L

Minneapolis Warehse Dist.,International Harvester
700 N. Washington Ave.
HABS MN-110-Q
HABS DLC/PP-1992:MN-2
3ph/1pc L

Minnesota Veterans Home Complex,Admin. Building (Building No. 10)
5101 Minnehaha Ave. S.
HABS MN-74-H
HABS DLC/PP-1993:MN-1
11dr/2ph/7pg/1pc L

Minnesota Veterans Home Complex,Dining Hall (Building No. 7)
5101 Minnehaha Ave. S.
HABS MN-74-F
HABS DLC/PP-1993:MN-1
1ph/8pg/1pc L

Minnesota Veterans Home Complex,Domiciliary No. 1
5101 Minnehaha Ave. S.
HABS MN-74-A
HABS DLC/PP-1993:MN-1
1ph/7pg/1pc L

Minnesota Veterans Home Complex,Domiciliary No. 2
5101 Minnehaha Ave. S.
HABS MN-74-B
HABS DLC/PP-1993:MN-1
1ph/8pg/1pc L

Minnesota Veterans Home Complex,Domiciliary No. 6
5101 Minnehaha Ave. S.
HABS MN-74-E
HABS DLC/PP-1993:MN-1
1ph/8pg/1pc L

Minnesota Veterans Home Complex,Domiciliary No. 9
5101 Minnehaha Ave. S.
HABS MN-74-G
HABS DLC/PP-1993:MN-1
1ph/11pg/1pc L

Minnesota Veterans Home Complex,Domiciliary,No. 4
5101 Minnehaha Ave. S.
HABS MN-74-D
HABS DLC/PP-1993:MN-1
1ph/7pg/1pc L

Minnesota Veterans Home Complex,Laundry Building (Building No. 13)
5101 Minnehaha Ave. S.
HABS MN-74-I
HABS DLC/PP-1993:MN-1
1ph/8pg/1pc L

Minnesota Veterans Home Complex,Paint Shop & Garag
5101 Minnehaha Ave. S.
HABS MN-74-L
HABS DLC/PP-1992:MN-1
1ph/6pg/1pc L

Minnesota Veterans Home Complex,Steel Bridge
5101 Minnehaha Ave. S.
HABS MN-74-N
HABS DLC/PP-1993:MN-1
1ph/5pg/1pc L

Minnesota Veterans Home Complex,Storage Building
5101 Minnehaha Ave. S.
HABS MN-74-J
HABS DLC/PP-1993:MN-1
1ph/8pg/1pc L

Minnesota Veterans Home Complex,Ten Stall Garage
5101 Minnehaha Ave. S.
HABS MN-74-M
HABS DLC/PP-1993:MN-1
1ph/5pg/1pc L

Minnesota Veterans' Home Complex,Power House (Building No. 14)
5101 Minnehaha Ave. S.
HABS MN-74-K
HABS DLC/PP-1993:MN-1
1ph/10pg/1pc L

Municipal Building (City Hall-Courthouse)
350 S. Fifth St.
HABS MN-30
HABS MINN,27-MINAP,9-
25ph/79pg/1pc/fr L

New Church Society; see Church of Minneapolis

Nicollet Hotel
235 Hennepin Ave.
HABS MN-122
17ph/21pg/2pc H

Our Lady of Lourdes Church
21 Prince St. SE
HABS MN-29-10
HABS MINN,27-MINAP,6-
8dr/3ph/1pg/fr L

Pillsbury Milling Complex
Main & Second Sts.,SE between Third & Fifth Sts.
HABS MN-29-5
HABS MINN,2-ANOK,1-;DLC/PP-1993:MN-1
1ph/3pg/1pc L

Pillsbury Milling Complex,Bran House
116 SE Third Ave.
HABS MN-29-5-B
HABS
1991(HABS):8;DLC/PP-1993:MN-1
1ph/3pg/1pc L

Pillsbury Milling Complex,Cleaning House
315-335 Main St.,SE
HABS MN-29-5-F
HABS
1991(HABS):8;DLC/PP-1993:MN-1
1ph/6pg/1pc L

Pillsbury Milling Complex,Concrete Elevators
Second St.,SE between SE Third and Fifth Aves.
HABS MN-29-5-D
HABS
1991(HABS):8;DLC/PP-1993:MN-1
1ph/6pg/1pc L

Pillsbury Milling Complex,Machine Shop
300-310 Second St.,SE
HABS MN-29-5-C
HABS
1991(HABS):8;DLC/PP-1993:MN-1
1ph/9pg/1pc L

Pillsbury Milling Complex,Pillsbury "A" Mill
116 Third Ave.
HABS MN-29-5-A
HABS
MINN,27-MINAP,3-;1991(HABS):8;DLC/PP-1993:MN-1
22dr/23ph/8pg/3pc/fr L

Pillsbury Milling Complex,South "A" Mill
335 Main St.,SE
HABS MN-29-5-G
HABS
1991(HABS):8;DLC/PP-1993:MN-1
1ph/10pg/1pc L

Pillsbury Milling Complex,Tile Elevator
Main St.,SE between SE Third & Fifth Aves.
HABS MN-29-5-E
HABS
1991(HABS):8;DLC/PP-1993:MN-1
1ph/5pg/1pc L

Pillsbury Milling Complex,Warehouse No. 2
129 Fifth Ave.,SE
HABS MN-29-5-H
HABS
1991(HABS):8;DLC/PP-1993:MN-1
1ph/9pg/1pc L

Pioneer Steel Elevator
2547 Fifth St. NE
HAER MN-50
HAER DLC/PP-1992:MN-2
2ph/1pc L

Steel Arch Bridge (Hennepin Avenue Bridge)
Hennepin Ave. spanning W channel of Mississippi R.
HAER MN-18
HAER MINN,27-MNAP,11-
43ph/34pg/3pc L

Stevens,Col. J. H. ,House (Ferry Farm)
Minnehaha Park (moved from Ferry Farm,Miss. River)
HABS MN-29-1
HABS MINN,27-MINAP,1-
2dr/2ph/1pg/fr L

Twentieth Avenue North Bridge; see Broadway Bridge

Washburn-Crosby Milling Company; see Washburn-Crosby Milling Complex

Washburn-Crosby Milling Complex (Washburn-Crosby Milling Company)
701-729 First St.,south of Portland Ave.
HABS MN-69
HABS DLC/PP-1993:MN-1
22ph/4pg/2pc L

Washburn-Crosby Milling Complex,East Engine House
S. First St between Portland & Eighth Ave.
HABS MN-69-D
HABS DLC/PP-1993:MN-1
1ph/8pg/1pc L

Washburn-Crosby Milling Complex,Feed Elevator
715 S. First St.
HABS MN-69-G
HABS DLC/PP-1993:MN-1
1ph/7pg/1pc L

Washburn-Crosby Milling Complex,Humboldt Mill
710-714 S. Second St.
HABS MN-69-H
HABS DLC/PP-1993:MN-1
1ph/6pg/1pc L

Washburn-Crosby Milling Complex,Mill Office
701 S. First St.
HABS MN-69-B
HABS DLC/PP-1993:MN-1
1ph/7pg/1pc L

Washburn-Crosby Milling Complex,No. 1 Elevator
711-729 S. First St.
HABS MN-69-F
HABS DLC/PP-1993:MN-1
1ph/10pg/1pc L

Washburn-Crosby Milling Complex,Utility Building
630 S. Second St.
HABS MN-69-J
HABS DLC/PP-1993:MN-1
1ph/5pg/1pc L

Washburn-Crosby Milling Complex,Washburn 'A' Mill
701-709 S. First & Second Sts.
HABS MN-69-A
HABS DLC/PP-1993:MN-1
18dr/1ph/9pg/1pc L

Washburn-Crosby Milling Complex,West Engine House
701-709 S. First St.
HABS MN-69-C
HABS DLC/PP-1993:MN-1
1ph/5pg/1pc L

Washburn-Crosby Milling Complex,Wheat House
708 S. Second St.
HABS MN-69-I
1ph/5pg/1pc L

Washburn-Crosby Milling Complex,Wheel House
711-719 S. First St.
HABS MN-69-E
HABS DLC/PP-1993:MN-1
1ph/7pg/1pc L

West House
200 Second St. SE
HABS MN-29-14
HABS MINN,27-MINAP,8-
6dr/2ph/1pg/fr L

MINNEAPOLIS VIC.

Fort Snelling Complex,Administration Building
Taylor Ave.
HABS MN-56-L
HABS 1989(HABS):11
9dr/31ph/2pc/fr L

Fort Snelling complex,Building No. 226
Minnehaha Ave.,Fort Snelling Historic District
HABS MN-56-X
HABS 1991(HABS):8
3ph/3pg/1pc L

Fort Snelling Complex,Building No. 240
Minnehaha Ave., Fort Snelling Historic District
HABS MN-56-M
6ph/1pg/1pc L

Fort Snelling Complex,Building No. 241
Minnehaha Ave.,Fort Snelling Historic Distric
HABS MN-56-N
HABS 1991(HABS):8
4ph/1pg/1pc L

Fort Snelling Complex,Building No. 242
Minnehaha Avenue, Fort Snelling Historic District
HABS MN-56-O
HABS 1991(HABS):8
4ph/1pg/1pc L

Fort Snelling Complex,Building No. 243
Minnehaha Ave.,Fort Snelling Historic District
HABS MN-56-P
HABS 1991(HABS):8
3ph/1pg/1pc L

Fort Snelling Complex,Building No. 244
Minnehaha Avenue, Fort Snelling Historic District
HABS MN-56-Q
HABS 1991(HABS):8
4ph/1pg/1pc L

Fort Snelling Complex,Building No. 245
Minnehaha Avenue, Fort Snelling Historic District
HABS MN-56-R
HABS 1991(HABS):8
4ph/1pg/1pc L

Fort Snelling Complex,Building No. 246
Minnehaha Avenue, Fort Snelling Historic District
HABS MN-56-S
HABS 1991(HABS):8
4ph/1pg/1pc L

Fort Snelling Complex,Building No. 247
Minnehaha Avenue, Fort Snelling Historic District
HABS MN-56-T
HABS 1991(HABS):8
4ph/1pg/1pc L

Fort Snelling Complex,Building No. 248
Minnehaha Avenue, Fort Snelling Historic District
HABS MN-56-U
HABS 1991(HABS):8
4ph/1pg/1pc L

Fort Snelling Complex,Building No. 249
Minnehaha Ave.,Fort Snelling Historic District
HABS MN-56-V
HABS 1991(HABS):8
4ph/1pg/1pc L

Fort Snelling Complex,Building No. 253
Minnehaha Ave.,Fort Snelling Historic District
HABS MN-56-W
HABS 1991(HABS):8
7ph/1pg/1pc L

Fort Snelling Complex,Grandstand
HABS MN-56-E
HABS MINN,27-FOSNEL,2-E-
12ph/1pc/fr L

Fort Snelling Complex,Quarters Buildings 70-75
HABS MN-56-F-K
HABS MINN,2-FOSNEL,2-F through -K
19ph/1pg/2pc/fr L

Fort Snelling Complex,Stables
HABS MN-56-A-D
HABS MINN,27-FOSNEL,2-A through -D
21ph/1pg/2pc/fr L

Fort Snelling,Commandant's House
Bounded by Miss. Riv.,Airport,Minnehaha Prk.
HABS MN-77-B
HABS 1991(HABS):8
1ph/1pc L

Fort Snelling,Department of the Dakota
Bounded by Miss. Riv.,Airport,Minnehaha Prk.
HABS MN-88
5ph/1pg/1pc L

Fort Snelling,Dept. of the Dakota,Adm. Bldg. No.67
Taylor Ave.
HABS MN-88-A
HABS 1991(HABS):8
2ph/1pc L

Fort Snelling,Dept. of the Dakota,Barracks No. 101
Taylor Ave.
HABS MN-88-F
HABS 1991(HABS):8
3ph/1pc L

Fort Snelling,Dept. of the Dakota,Bat. Qtr. No.151
Leavenworth Ave.
HABS MN-88-E
HABS 1991(HABS):8
3ph/1pc L

Fort Snelling,Dept. of the Dakota,Bldg. No. 108 (Garage Building)
HABS MN-88-Q
HABS 1991(HABS):8
1ph/1pc L

Fort Snelling,Dept. of the Dakota,Bldg. No. 112 (Utility Building)
HABS MN-88-P
HABS 1991(HABS):8
2ph/1pc L

Fort Snelling,Dept. of the Dakota,Bldg. No. 17 (Veteran's Administration,Outpatient Clinic)
HABS MN-88-G
HABS 1991(HABS):8
1ph/1pc L

Fort Snelling,Dept. of the Dakota,Bldg. No. 18 (Veterans Administration,Outpatient Clinic)
HABS MN-88-H
HABS 1991(HABS):8
1ph/1pc L

Fort Snelling,Dept. of the Dakota,Bldg. No. 30 (Stables Building)
HABS MN-88-K
HABS 1991(HABS):8
1ph/1pc L

Fort Snelling,Dept. of the Dakota,Bldg. No. 53
Taylor Ave.
HABS MN-88-V
HABS 1991(HABS):8
1ph/1pc L

Fort Snelling,Dept. of the Dakota,Bldg. No. 54
Taylor Ave.
HABS MN-88-S
HABS 1991(HABS):8
1ph/1pc L

Fort Snelling,Dept. of the Dakota,Bldg. No. 55
Taylor Ave.
HABS MN-88-T
HABS 1991(HABS):8
1ph/1pc L

Fort Snelling,Dept. of the Dakota,Bldg. No. 56
Taylor Ave.
HABS MN-88-U
HABS 1991(HABS):8
1ph/1pc L

Fort Snelling,Dept. of the Dakota,Bldg. No. 57
Taylor Ave.
HABS MN-88-X
HABS 1991(HABS):8
1ph/1pc L

Fort Snelling,Dept. of the Dakota,Bldg. No. 62
Ramsey St.
HABS MN-88-J
HABS 1991(HABS):8
1ph/1pc L

Fort Snelling,Dept. of the Dakota,Bldg. No. 63
Off Ramsey St.
HABS MN-88-O
HABS 1991(HABS):8
1ph/1pc L

Fort Snelling,Dept. of the Dakota,Bldg. No. 64
Off Ramsey St.
HABS MN-88-M
HABS 1991(HABS):8
1ph/1pc L

Fort Snelling,Dept. of the Dakota,Bldg. No. 65
Off Taylor Ave.
HABS MN-88-R
HABS 1991(HABS):8
2ph/1pc L

Fort Snelling,Dept. of the Dakota,Bldg. No. 66
Off Taylor Ave.
HABS MN-88-W
HABS 1991(HABS):8
1ph/1pc L

Fort Snelling,Dept. of the Dakota,Bldg. No. 76
Ramsey St.
HABS MN-88-N
HABS 1991(HABS):8
2ph/1pc L

Fort Snelling,Dept. of the Dakota,Building No. 22 (Veterans Administration,Orthotic Prosthetic Lab)
HABS MN-88-L
HABS 1991(HABS):8
1ph/1pc L

Fort Snelling,Dept. of the Dakota,Memorial Chapel
Cloverleaf off W. Seventh St.,Rte. 5
HABS MN-88-I
HABS 1991(HABS):8
1ph/1pc L

Fort Snelling,Dept. of the Dakota,Quarters No. 152
Taylor Ave.
HABS MN-88-B
HABS 1991(HABS):8
4ph/1pc L

Fort Snelling,Dept. of the Dakota,Quarters No. 157
Leavenworth Ave.
HABS MN-88-D
HABS 1991(HABS):8
4ph/1pc L

Fort Snelling,Dept. of the Dakota,Quarters No. 159
Taylor Ave.
HABS MN-88-C
HABS 1991(HABS):8
3ph/1pc L

Fort Snelling,Gatehouse/Guardhouse
Bounded by Miss. Riv.,Airport,Minnehaha Prk.
HABS MN-77-A
HABS 1991(HABS):8
1ph/1pc L

Fort Snelling,Hexagon Tower
Bounded by Miss. Riv.,Airport,Minnehaha Prk.
HABS MN-29-12
HABS MINN,27-FOSNEL,1B-;1991(HABS):8
1dr/4ph/1pg/1pc/fr L

Fort Snelling,Officers' Quarters
Bounded by Miss. Riv.,Airport,Minnehaha Prk.
HABS MN-77-C
HABS 1991(HABS):
3ph/1pc L

Fort Snelling,Old Fort Area
Bounded by Miss. River,Airport,Minnehaha Prk.
HABS MN-77
HABS 1991(HABS):8
15ph/1pg/1pc L

Fort Snelling,Quarters Buildings 240-249,253
Minnehaha Ave.,Fort Snelling Historic Distric.
HABS MN-56-Y
HABS MINN,27-FOSNEL,2-;1991(HABS):8
4ph/6pg/1pc L

Fort Snelling,Round Tower
Bound by Miss. Riv.,Airport,Minnehaha Prk.
HABS MN-29-3
HABS MINN,27-FOSNEL,1A-;1991(HABS):8
1dr/3ph/1pg/1pc/fr L

Garage Building; see Fort Snelling,Dept. of the Dakota,Bldg. No. 108

Stables Building; see Fort Snelling,Dept. of the Dakota,Bldg. No. 30

Utility Building; see Fort Snelling,Dept. of the Dakota,Bldg. No. 112

Veteran's Administration,Outpatient Clinic; see Fort Snelling,Dept. of the Dakota,Bldg. No. 17

Veterans Administration,Orthotic Prosthetic Lab; see Fort Snelling,Dept. of the Dakota,Building No. 22

Veterans Administration,Outpatient Clinic; see Fort Snelling,Dept. of the Dakota,Bldg. No. 18

ST. LOUIS PARK

Peavy-Haglin Experimental Concrete Grain Elevator
SE Corner,Hwys. 7 & 100
HAER MN-25
HAER 1991(HAER):4
1ph/1pg/1pc L

HOUSTON COUNTY

HOUSTON VIC.

Miss. River 9-Foot Channel Project,Lock & Dam No.8
On Miss. Riv. near Vernon Co.,WI (see CCN WI0215)
HAER WI-49
L

LA CRESENT VIC.

Schech's Mill
Beaver Creek State Park
HAER MN-41
HAER DLC/PP-1992:MN-2
23ph/2pc L

ISANTI COUNTY

NORTH BRANCH VIC.

Dahl-Nordin House; see Nordin,John Mangus,House

Nordin,John Mangus,House
(Dahl-Nordin House)
County Rd. 48
HABS MN-55
HABS MINN,30-NOBRA,1-
7dr/3ph L

LAC QUI PARLE COUNTY

MADISON

Lac Qui Parle County Courthouse
600 Sixth St.
HABS MN-97
HABS DLC/PP-1992:MN-2
2ph/1pc L

Madison Carnegie Library
401 Sixth Ave.
HABS MN-98
HABS DLC/PP-1992:MN-2
1ph/1pc L

LAKE COUNTY

TWO HARBOR'S VIC.

Split Rock Lighthouse,Keeper's Cottages
Off Hwy. 61,38.0 Mi. NE of Duluth
HAER MN-43-A
HAER DLC/PP-1992:MN-2
1ph/1pc L

TWO HARBORS

Duluth & Iron Range Railway,Mallet Locomotive
D & IR Railroad Depot,Sixth St.
HAER MN-34
HAER 1991(HAER):4
3ph/1pg/1pc L

Duluth & Iron Range Railway,Ore Dock No. 6 (Duluth, Missabe & Iron Range Railway,Ore Dock No.6
Agate Bay
HAER MN-33
HAER 1991(HAER):4
2ph/1pg/1pc L

Duluth & Iron Range Railway,Three-spot Locomotive
D & IR Railroad Depot,Sixth St.
HAER MN-35
HAER 1991(HAER):4
2ph/1pg/1pc L

Duluth, Missabe & Iron Range Railway,Ore Dock No.6; see Duluth & Iron Range Railway,Ore Dock No. 6

Tug Boat "Edna G."
Agate Bay
HAER MN-26
HAER 1991(HAER):4
21ph/1pg/1pc L

TWO HARBORS VIC.

Split Rock Lighthouse
Off Hwy. 61,38.0 mi. NE of Duluth
HAER MN-43
HAER DLC/PP-1992:MN-2
8ph/1pc L

LE SUEUR COUNTY

ELYSIAN

Elysian Water Tower & Engine House
Frank St. NE
HAER MN-19
HAER 1989(HAER):13
12ph/8pg/1pc L

Elysian Water Tower,Pumphouse
Frank St. NE
HAER MN-19-A
HAER 1989(HAER):13
8ph/1pc L

LE SUEUR

Mayo House
HABS MN-29-44
HABS MINN,40-LESUR,1-
2ph/2pg/fr L

MAHNOMEN COUNTY

MAHNOMEN

Mahnomen City Drive-In Movie Theater
U.S. Hwy. 59 at MN Hwy. 200
HABS MN-121
HABS DLC/PP-1992:MN-2
1ph/1pc L

Mahnomen County Fairgrounds
Junction MN 200 & Co. Hwy. 137
HABS MN-103
HABS DLC/PP-1992:MN-2
6ph/1pc L

MILLE LACS COUNTY

VINELAND

Kathio Site Indian Burial Grounds
Along U.S. 169,SW shore of Mille Lacs Lake
HABS MN-78
HABS 1991(HABS):8
2ph/1pg/1pc L

MORRISON COUNTY

LITTLE FALLS

Kiewel Brewery
508 NE Seventh St.
HAER MN-1
HAER MINN,49-LITFA,1-
10ph/14pg/1pc L

Lindbergh,Charles A.,Sr.,House,Farm Mgr's. House
Lindbergh Dr.,SW,County Rd. 52
HABS MN-79-A
HABS 1991(HABS):8
2ph/1pc L

Lindbergh,Charles A.,Sr.,House,Ice House
Lindbergh Rd.,SW,County Rd. 52
HABS MN-79-B
HABS 1991(HABS):8
1ph/1pc L

LITTLE FALLS VIC.

Lindbergh House & Interpretive Center; see Lindbergh,Charles A.,Sr.,House

Lindbergh,Charles A.,Sr.,House (Lindbergh House & Interpretive Center)
Lindbergh Dr.,SW,County Rd. 52
HABS MN-79
HABS 1991(HABS):8
9ph/1pg/1pc L

NICOLLET COUNTY

FORT RIDGELEY

Fort Ridgeley,Commissary Building
HABS MN-1-5
HABS MINN,52-FORIG,1-B-
2ph L

Fort Ridgeley,Powder Magazine
HABS MN-1-4
HABS MINN,52-FORIG,1-A-
2ph L

OLMSTED COUNTY

ROCHESTER

Mayo Clinic,Plummer Building
110-115 Second Ave.
HABS MN-80
HABS 1991(HABS):8
17ph/1pg/1pc L

OTTER TAIL COUNTY

UNDERWOOD VIC.

Maine Roller Mill; see Phelps Mill

Phelps Mill (Maine Roller Mill)
Co. Hwy 45,N. confluence Lion Lk. & Ottertail Riv.
HAER MN-47
HAER DLC/PP-1992:MN-2
2ph/1pc L

PIPESTONE COUNTY

PIPESTONE

Pipestone Historic Dist.,Pipestone County Courthse
Third St.
HABS MN-115-E
HABS DLC/PP-1992:MN-2
1ph/1pc L

Pipestone Historic District
Main St. btwn. Third St. & Second Ave.
HABS MN-115
HABS DLC/PP-1992:MN-2
1ph/1pc L

Pipestone Historic District,A.F. & A.M. Building
HABS MN-115-B
HABS DLC/PP-1992:MN-2
1ph/1pc L

Pipestone Historic District,Bank-Calumet Hotel
HABS MN-115-C
HABS DLC/PP-1992:MN-2
2ph/1pc L

Pipestone Historic District,Moore Building
Main St.
HABS MN-115-A
HABS DLC/PP-1992:MN-2
1ph/1pc L

Pipestone Historic District,Old City Hall
Hiawatha St.
HABS MN-115-F
HABS DLC/PP-1992:MN-2
1ph/1pc L

Pipestone Historic District,Old Masonic Temple
Main St.
HABS MN-115-D
HABS DLC/PP-1992:MN-2
1ph/1pc L

PIPESTONE VIC.

Pipestone National Monument,Rock Quarry
Park Entrance Rd.,Twp. 106N.,Range 46W.
HAER MN-27
HAER 1991(HAER):4
7ph/1pg/1pc L

RAMSEY COUNTY

NEW BRIGHTON

Twin Cities Army Ammunition Plant
HAER MN-4
HAER MINN,62-NEBRI,1-
58pg/fr L

ST. PAUL

Allen,James D. ,Building (Aslesen Building)
379-381 Sibley St.
HABS MN-63
HABS 1991(HABS):8
2ph/4pg/1pc/fr L

Aslesen Building; see Allen,James D. ,Building

Assumption School,Old
Eighth & Exchange Sts.
HABS MN-29-31
HABS MINN,62-SAIPA,6-
3dr/2ph/1pg/fr L

Bishop Block (Sperry Office Furniture Company)
371-375 Sibley St.
HABS MN-62
HABS 1991(HABS):8
2ph/4pg/1pc/fr L

Burbank,James C. ,House (Livingston-Griggs House)
432 Summit Ave.
HABS MN-53
HABS MINN,62-SAIPA,13-
8ph/5pg/1pc/fr L

Church of the Assumption (Roman Catholic)
51 W. Ninth St.
HABS MN-45
HABS MINN,62-SAIPA,7-
5ph/7pg L

Church of the Good Shepherd (Episcopal Church,Old)
Twelfth & Cedar Sts.
HABS MN-29-26
HABS MINN,62-SAIPA,3-
6dr/2ph/1pg/fr L

Como Conservatory
HABS MN-99
HABS DLC/PP-1992:MN-2
10ph/1pc L

Custom House
Fifth & Wabasha Sts.
HABS MN-29-25
HABS MINN,62-SAIPA,2-
4dr/2ph/1pg/fr L

Episcopal Church,Old; see Church of the Good Shepherd

Fitzgerald,F. Scott,House (Summit Terrace)
599 Summit Ave.
HABS MN-83
HABS 1991(HABS):8
4ph/1pg/1pc L

German Presbyterian Bethlehem Church (Little Bethlehem Church)
311 Ramsey St.
HABS MN-57
HABS MINN,62-SAIPA,14-
3ph/1pg/1pc L

High Bridge; see Smith Avenue High Bridge

Hill,James J.,House
240 Summit Ave.
HABS MN-52
HABS MINN,62-SAIPA,15-;1991(HABS):8
48ph/2pg/2pc/fr L

Hill,James J.,House,Gatehouse
240 Summit Ave.
HABS MN-52-A
HABS 1991(HABS)
1ph/1pc L

Historic Hill District,Laurel Terrace; see Laurel Terrace

Hunt,Daniel H. ,House
2478 Territorial Rd.
HABS MN-58
HABS MINN,62-SAIPA,16-
2ph/1pc L

IFT Hanger; see Northwest Airways Hangar & Administration Bldg.

Jackson Street Shops
Jackson St. and Pennsylvania Ave.
HABS MN-67
HABS DLC/PP-1992:MN-5
3ph/11pg/1pc L

Jackson Street Shops,Blacksmith and Boiler Shop
Jackson St. and Pennsylvania Ave.
HABS MN-67-A
HABS DLC/PP-1992:MN-5
2ph/7pg/1pc L

Jackson Street Shops,Car Shop and Wood Shop
Jackson St. and Pennsylvania Ave.
HABS MN-67-G
HABS DLC/PP-1992:MN-5
4ph/5pg/1pc L

Jackson Street Shops,Chimney
Jackson St. and Pennsylvania Ave.
HABS MN-67-F
HABS DLC/PP-1992:MN-5
1ph/3pg/1pc L

Jackson Street Shops,Engine House
Jackson St. and Pennsylvania Ave.
HABS MN-67-K
HABS DLC/PP-1992:MN-5
2ph/8pg/1pc L

Jackson Street Shops,Machine Shop
Jackson St. and Pennsylvania Ave.
HABS MN-67-B
HABS DLC/PP-1992:MN-5
5ph/7pg/1pc L

Jackson Street Shops,Oil House
Jackson St. and Pennsylvania Ave.
HABS MN-67-D
HABS DLC/PP-1992:MN-5
2ph/7pg/1pc L

Jackson Street Shops,Paint Shop
45 E. Pennsylvania Ave.
HABS MN-67-H
HABS MINN,62-SAIPA,17-H-(DLC/PP-1992:MN-5)
5dr/1ph/7pg/1pc/fr L

Jackson Street Shops,Paint Spray Building
Jackson St. and Pennsylvania Ave.
HABS MN-67-I
HABS DLC/PP-1992:MN-5
2ph/5pg/1pc L

Jackson Street Shops,Pattern Shop
Jackson St. and Pennsylvania Ave.
HABS MN-67-E
HABS DLC/PP-1992:MN-5
2ph/4pg/1pc L

Jackson Street Shops,Pattern Storage Building
Jackson St. and Arch St.
HABS MN-67-L
HABS DLC/PP-1992:MN-5
3ph/4pg/1pc L

Jackson Street Shops,Power House
Jackson St. and Pennsylvania Ave.
HABS MN-67-J
HABS DLC/PP-1992:MN-5
2ph/7pg/1pc L

Jackson Street Shops,Storage Shed
Jackson St. and Pennsylvania Ave.
HABS MN-67-M
HABS DLC/PP-1992:MN-5
1ph/3pg/1pc L

Jackson Street Shops,Store House
Jackson St. and Pennsylvania Ave.
HABS MN-67-C
HABS DLC/PP-1992:MN-5
2ph/9pg/1pc L

Kellogg,Frank Billings,House
633 Fairmont Ave.
HABS MN-51
HABS MINN,62-SAIPA,18-;1991(HABS):8
12ph/2pg/2pc L

Laurel Terrace (Historic Hill District,Laurel Terrace; Riley's Row)
294-296 Laurel Ave.
HABS MN-61
HABS MINN,62-SAIPA,19-
3ph/1pg/1pc L

Little Bethlehem Church; see German Presbyterian Bethlehem Church

Livingston-Griggs House; see Burbank,James C. ,House

Log Chapel (Muskego Church)
HABS MN-29-24
HABS MINN,62-SAIPA,1-
3dr/3ph/1pg/fr L

Mansion House; see Ramsey,Alexander,House

Mattock School (Webster School)
Randolph St. & Snelling Ave.
HABS MN-29-27
HABS MINN,62-SAIPA,4-
4dr/2ph/1pg/fr L

McGrorty-Kittson House
603 Jackson St.
HABS MN-46
HABS MINN,62-SAIPA,8-
2ph/4pg L

Merriam Park Branch Library
1831 Marshall Ave.
HABS MN-123
HABS DLC/PP-1992:MN-5
26ph/19pg/2pc L

Mickey's Diner
36 W. Ninth St.
HABS MN-100
HABS DLC/PP-1992:MN-2
1ph/1pc L

Muskego Church; see Log Chapel

New York Life Insurance Company Building
Sixth & Minnesota Sts.
HABS MN-54
HABS MINN,62-SAIPA,20-
5ph/1pg/1pc L

Northwest Airways Hangar & Administration Bldg. (IFT Hanger)
590 Bayfield St.,St. Paul Downtown Airport(Holman)
HAER MN-37
HAER 1991(HAER):4
31ph/20pg/3pc L

Pilgram Baptist Church
732 Central Ave. West
HABS MN-112
HABS DLC/PP-1992:MN-2
2ph/1pc L

Postelethwait House
Twelfth St.
HABS MN-29-30
HABS MINN,62-SAIPA,5-
3dr/2ph/1pg/fr L

Ramsey,Alexander,House (Mansion House)
265 S. Exchange St.
HABS MN-48
HABS MINN,62-SAIPA,10-
16ph/27pg L

Ramsey,Justice Cornelius,House
252 W. Seventh St.
HABS MN-47
HABS MINN,62-SAIPA,9-
1ph/3pg L

Riley's Row; see Laurel Terrace

Smith Avenue High Bridge (High Bridge)
Smith Ave. btwn. Cherokee Ave. & Cliff St.
HAER MN-5
HAER MINN,62-SAIPA,12-
79ph/45pg/5pc/fr L

Spangenberg,Frederick,House
375 Mt. Curve Ave.
HABS MN-60
HABS MINN,62-SAIPA,21-
2ph/1pg/1pc L

Sperry Office Furniture Company; see Bishop Block

St. Paul City Hall & Ramsey County Courthouse
15 W. Kellogg Blvd.
HABS MN-32
HABS MINN,62-SAIPA,11-
39ph/13pg/3pc L

St. Paul's Women's City Club
305 St. Peter St.
HABS MN-101
HABS DLC/PP-1992:MN-2
6ph/1pc L

Summit Terrace; see Fitzgerald,F. Scott,House

Torre de San Miguel Bell Tower
Wood St.,"Torre de San Miguel"
HABS MN-111
HABS DLC/PP-1992:MN-2
1ph/1pc L

Waldman,Anton,House
445 Smith St.
HABS MN-59
HABS MINN,62-SAIPA,22-
1ph/1pc L

Webster School; see Mattock School

REDWOOD COUNTY

LAMBERTON

City Blacksmith Shop (Hanzlik's Blacksmith Shop)
Corner of Douglas St. & Second Ave.
HAER MN-46
HAER DLC/PP-1992:MN-2
10ph/1pc L

Hanzlik's Blacksmith Shop; see City Blacksmith Shop

SEAFORTH VIC.

Johnson Bridge
Spanning Redwood River
HAER MN-56
HAER DLC/PP-1993:MN-2
9ph/10pg/1pc L

RICE COUNTY

NERSTAND VIC.

Veblen,Thomas,Farmstead; see Veblen,Thorstein,Farmstead,House

Veblen,Thorstein,Farmstead,Barn
Section 12,Wheeling Twp.
HABS MN-82-A
HABS 1991(HABS):8
8ph/1pc L

Veblen,Thorstein,Farmstead,House (Veblen,Thomas,Farmstead)
Section 12,Wheeling Twp.
HABS MN-82
HABS 1991(HABS):8
3ph/1pg/1pc L

Veblen,Thorstein,Farmstead,Outbuildings
Section 12,Wheeling Twp.
HABS MN-82-B
HABS 1991(HABS):8
2ph/1pc L

NERSTRAND VIC.

Valley Grove Churches,New
Co. Rd. 29,1/4 mi. from MN Hwy. 246
HABS MN-119-A
HABS DLC/PP-1992:MN-2
4ph/1pc L

Valley Grove Churches,Old Church
Co. Rd. 29,1/4 mi. from MN Hwy. 246
HABS MN-119
HABS DLC/PP-1992:MN-2
5ph/1pc L

NORTHFIELD

Rolvaag,O.E.,House
311 Manitou St.
HABS MN-81
HABS 1991(HABS):8
4ph/1pg/1pc L

SHERBURNE COUNTY

ELK RIVER

Elk River Bridge (State Bridge 3093)
Spanning Elk River at Main Street
HAER MN-54
8ph/21pg/1pc L

State Bridge 3093; see Elk River Bridge

ELK RIVER VIC.

Kelley,Oliver Hudson,Homestead
15788 Kelley Farm Rd.,U.S. Hwy. 10
HABS MN-84
HABS 1991(HABS):8
7ph/1pg/1pc L

Kelley,Oliver Hudson,Homestead,Barn
15788 Kelley Farm Rd.,U.S. Hwy. 10
HABS MN-84-A
HABS 1991(HABS):8
2ph/1pc L

SANTIAGO

Fox,Herbert Maximilian,House
County Rd. 69
HABS MN-65
HABS MINN,71-SAGO,1-
22ph/4pg/2pc/fr L

ST. LOUIS COUNTY

BABBIT

Mesabi Iron Co. Mag. Con. Plt.,Concentrator Bldg. (Reserve Mining Company Test Plant)
HAER MN-38-D
HAER 1991(HAER):4
1ph/1pc L

Mesabi Iron Co. Magnetic Con. Plant,Boiler House (Reserve Mining Company Test Plant)
HAER MN-38-C
HAER 1991(HAER):4
2ph/1pc L

Mesabi Iron Co. Magnetic Con. Plt.,Pelletizer Bldg (Reserve Mining Company Test Plant)
HAER MN-38-B
HAER 1991(HAER):4
5ph/1pc L

Mesabi Iron Co. Magnetic Con. Plt.,Quonset Garage (Reserve Mining Company Test Plant)
HAER MN-38-E
HAER 1991(HAER):4
1ph/1pc L

Mesabi Iron Co.,Magnetic Concentration Plant (Reserve Mining Company Test Plant)
HAER MN-38
HAER 1991(HAER):4
5ph/1pg/1pc L

Mesabi Iron Company Con. Plant,Crusher Building (Reserve Mining Company Test Plant)
HAER MN-38-A
HAER 1991(HAER):4
3ph/1pc L

Reserve Mining Company Test Plant; see Mesabi Iron Co. Mag. Con. Plt.,Concentrator Bldg.

Reserve Mining Company Test Plant; see Mesabi Iron Co. Magnetic Con. Plant,Boiler House

Reserve Mining Company Test Plant; see Mesabi Iron Co. Magnetic Con. Plt.,Pelletizer Bldg

Reserve Mining Company Test Plant; see Mesabi Iron Co. Magnetic Con. Plt.,Quonset Garage

Reserve Mining Company Test Plant; see Mesabi Iron Co.,Magnetic Concentration Plant

Reserve Mining Company Test Plant; see Mesabi Iron Company Con. Plant,Crusher Building

Silver Bay/Rsv. Min.,Mag. Con. Plt.,Conveyor
HAER MN-28-A
3ph/1pc L

Silver Bay/Rsv. Min.,Mag. Con. Plt.,Dump Car Bldg.
HAER MN-28-E
3ph/1pc L

Silver Bay/Rsv. Min.,Mag. Con. Plt.,Filtration Plt
HAER MN-28-F
3ph/1pc L

Silver Bay/Rsv. Min.,Mag. Con. Plt.,Fine Cr. Bldg.
HAER MN-28-D
7ph/1pc L

Silver Bay/Rsv. Min.,Mag. Con. Plt.,Fine Cr. Silo
HAER MN-28-C
2ph/1pc L

Silver Bay/Rsv. Min.,Mag. Con. Plt.,Peletizer Bldg
HAER MN-28-G
8ph/1pc L

Silver Bay/Rsv. Min.,Mag. Con. Plt.,Power House
HAER MN-28-B
1ph/1pc L

BABITT

Silver Bay/Rsrv. Min.,Mag. Con. Plt.,Taconite Plt.
HAER MN-28
4ph/1pc L

DULUTH

City Hall
411 W. First St.
HABS MN-31
HABS MINN,69-DULU,5-
8ph/17pg/1pc/fr L

Drug Store,First
E. Superior St.
HABS MN-29-21
HABS MINN,69-DULU,3-
1dr/1ph/1pg/fr L

Duluth Aerial Lift Bridge
Lake Ave.,across the Duluth Ship Canal
HAER MN-44
HAER DLC/PP-1992:MN-2
8ph/1pc L

Endion Passenger Depot
1504 South St.
HAER MN-9
HAER MINN,69-DULU,6-
18ph/4pg/2pc L

Fire Hall,First
E. Second St.
HABS MN-29-20
HABS MINN,69-DULU,2-
2dr/1ph/1pg/fr L

Fire Tower
Rice Lake Rd.
HABS MN-29-39
HABS MINN,69- ,3-
1dr/1ph/1pg/fr L

Fitger Brewery Complex
600 E. Superior St.
HAER MN-3
HAER MINN,69-DULU,7-
11pg L

Fitger Brewery Complex,Stable & Garage
600 E. Superior St.
HAER MN-3-A
HAER MINN,69-DULU,7-A-
29ph/2pg/2pc L

Goodfellowship Building
1242 Eighty-eighth Ave.
HABS MN-64
HABS MINN,69-DULU,8-
32ph/3pg/2pc/fr L

Lighthouse,Old
Minnesota Point
HABS MN-29-23
HABS MINN,69-DULU,4-
1dr/2ph/1pg/fr L

Morgan Park Historic District,Company Store
Eighty-eighth Ave. & Edward St.
HABS MN-116-C
HABS DLC/PP-1992:MN-2
1ph/1pc L

Morgan Park Historic District,Protestant Church
Arbor St. & Eighty-eighth Ave.
HABS MN-116-D
HABS DLC/PP-1992:MN-2
1ph/1pc L

Morgan Park Historic District,85th Ave.
HABS MN-116
HABS DLC/PP-1992:MN-2
1ph/1pc L

Morgan Park Historic District,87th Ave.
HABS MN-116-A
HABS DLC/PP-1992:MN-2
2ph/1pc L

Morgan Park Historic District,88th Ave.
HABS MN-116-B
HABS DLC/PP-1992:MN-2
1ph/1pc L

Post Office,First
First Alley
HABS MN-29-19
HABS MINN,69-DULU,1-
1dr/2ph/1pg/fr L

DULUTH VIC.

Krazszawaski Log House
Gnesen Rd.
HABS MN-29-36
HABS MINN,69, ,2-
3dr/4ph/1pg/fr L

Quaeva Log House
Rice Lake Rd.
HABS MN-29-29
HABS MINN,69- ,1-
3dr/3ph/1pg/fr L

ELY VIC.

Burntside Lodge
Off County Rd. 88
HABS MN-105
HABS DLC/PP-1992:MN-2
6ph/1pc L

Burntside Lodge,Cabin No. 26
Off County Rd. 88
HABS MN-105-D
HABS DLC/PP-1992:MN-2
2ph/1pc L

Burntside Lodge,Cabin No. 27
HABS MN-105-C
HABS DLC/PP-1992:MN-2
4ph/1pc L

Burntside Lodge,Cabins No. 23 & 24
Off County Rd. 88
HABS MN-105-E
HABS DLC/PP-1992:MN-2
1ph/1pc L

Burntside Lodge,Cabins No. 4 & 9
Off County Rd. 88
HABS MN-105-F
HABS DLC/PP-1992:MN-2
1ph/1pc L

Burntside Lodge,Post
Off County Rd. 88
HABS MN-105-A
HABS DLC/PP-1992:MN-2
2ph/1pc L

Burntside Lodge,Stone Cottage
Off County Rd. 88
HABS MN-105-B
HABS DLC/PP-1992:MN-2
1ph/1pc L

Logging Camp
HABS MN-29-37
HABS MINN,69-ELY.V,1-
4dr/1pg/fr L

Shaft House; see Timber Headframe

Timber Headframe (Shaft House)
HABS MN-29-41
HABS MINN,69-ELY.V,2-
1dr/1pg/fr L

HIBBING VIC.

Hull-Rust Mahoning Open Pit Iron Mine
Third Ave. East
HAER MN-29
HAER 1991(HAER):4
10ph/1pg/1pc L

MOUNTAIN IRON VIC.

Mountain Iron Mine
N. of Mountain Iron village,Government Lots 3 & 4
HAER MN-31
HAER 1991(HAER):4
3ph/1pg/1pc L

TOWER VIC.

Soudan Iron Mine
Tower-Soudan State Park
HAER MN-30
HAER 1991(HAER):4
39ph/1pg/1pc L

STEARNS COUNTY

CHOKIO

Chokio Grain Elevators
MN Hwy. 28
HAER MN-52
HAER DLC/PP-1992:MN-2
6ph/1pc L

COLLEGEVILLE

St. Johns University,Abbey Church
St. Johns University
HABS MN-18
HABS DLC/PP-1992:MN-2
3ph/1pc L

ROCKVILLE

Clark & McCormack Quarry
(Coldspring Granite Co.,Rockville Quarry)
MN HWY 23 at Pine St.
HAER MN-48
HAER DLC/PP-1992:MN-2
14ph/1pc L

Clark and McCormack Quarry,House
MN Hwy. 23 at Pine St.
HAER MN-48-A
HAER DLC/PP-1992:MN-2
1ph/1pc L

Coldspring Granite Co.,Rockville Quarry; see Clark & McCormack Quarry

SAUK CENTRE

Lewis,Sinclair,Boyhood Home
812 Sinclair Lewis Ave.
HABS MN-86
HABS 1991(HABS):8
10ph/1pg/1pc L

Lewis,Sinclair,Boyhood Home,Barn
812 Sinclair Lewis Ave.
HABS MN-86-A
HABS 1991(HABS):8
1ph/1pc L

STEELE COUNTY

OWATONNA

National Farmers Bank of Owatonna
110 Cedar St., at corner of E. Broadway
HABS MN-85
HABS 1991(HABS):8
22ph/1pg/2pc/5ct L

TRAVERSE COUNTY

BROWN'S VALLEY

Brown,Joseph R. ,House
Sam Brown Mem. Park (moved from Dakota Territory)
HABS MN-1-3
HABS MINN,78-BROVA,1-
4ph/1pg L

WABASHA COUNTY

LAKE CITY

Brown's Hotel
Lake Pepin
HABS MN-29-40
HABS MINN,79-LACIT,1-
5dr/3ph/1pg/fr L

WABASHA

First Congregational Parsonage
305 W. Second St. (Wabasha Historic District)
HABS MN-66
HABS MINN,79-WAB,1-
7ph/5pg/1pc L

Livery Stable
Walnut Ave.(rear 305 W. Main St.)Wabasha Hist Dist
HABS MN-71
HABS MINN,79-WAB,2-
10ph/4pg/1pc L

McKenzie,Duncan,Livery Stable
306 W. Main St., Wabasha Historic District
HABS MN-72
HABS MINN,79-WAB,3-
6ph/4pg/1pc L

Replogle House
305 W. Main St. (Wabasha Historic District)
HABS MN-70
HABS MINN,79-WAB,4-
7ph/5pg/1pc L

WASHINGTON COUNTY

AFTON

Mackey House
Washington Ave.
HABS MN-29-38
HABS MINN,82-AFT,2-
5dr/3ph/1pg/fr L

Octagonal House
Washington Ave.
HABS MN-29-32
HABS MINN,82-AFT,1-
8dr/3ph/1pg/fr L

MARINE

Meeting Hall
HABS MN-29-18
HABS MINN,82-MARI,1-
3dr/2ph/1pg/fr L

STILLWATER VIC.

Bridge,Stone Highway
HABS MN-29-35
HABS MINN,82-STIWA,1-
1dr/2ph/1pg L

St. Croix Boom Site
3 Mis. N. of Stillwater,along St. Croix River
HAER MN-36
HAER 1991(HAER):4
5ph/1pg/1pc L

WILKIN COUNTY

KENT VIC.

Femco Fam,Granary
HABS MN-113-B
HABS DLC/PP-1992:MN-2
2ph/1pc L

Femco Farm
1/4 mi. off County Rd. 153
HABS MN-113
HABS DLC/PP-1992:MN-2
3ph/1pc L

Femco Farm,Corn Crib
HABS MN-113-E
HABS DLC/PP-1992:MN-2
1ph/1pc L

Femco Farm,Cow Barn
HABS MN-113-A
HABS DLC/PP-1992:MN-2
9ph/1pc L

Femco Farm,Fertilizer Bin
HABS MN-113-H
HABS DLC/PP-1992:MN-2
1ph/1pc L

Femco Farm,Hog Barn (Femco Farm,Machine Shed)
HABS MN-113-F
HABS DLC/PP-1992:MN-2
1ph/1pc L

Femco Farm,Machine Shed
HABS MN-113-G
HABS DLC/PP-1992:MN-2
1ph/1pc L

Femco Farm,Machine Shed; see Femco Farm,Hog Barn

Femco Farm,Milk House
HABS MN-113-I
HABS DLC/PP-1992:MN-2
1ph/1pc L

Femco Farm,Sheep Barn
HABS MN-113-D
HABS DLC/PP-1992:MN-2
2ph/1pc L

Femco Farm,Steel Grain Bin
HABS MN-113-C
HABS DLC/PP-1992:MN-2
1ph/1pc L

Femco Farm,Tractor
HABS MN-113-J
HABS DLC/PP-1992:MN-2
1ph/1pc L

WINONA COUNTY

DRESBACH VIC.

Upper Miss. River 9-Foot Channel,Lock & Dam No. 7
HAER MN-24
HAER MINN,85-DRES.V,1-
76ph/9pg/5pc L

MINNIESKA VIC.

Upper Miss. River 9-Foot Channel,Lock & Dam No. 5
HAER MN-22
HAER MINN,85-MIN.V,1-
92ph/11pg/6pc L

TROY VIC.

Troy Mill
Saratoga Township
HABS MN-29-33
HABS MINN,85-TROY.V,1-
2dr/2ph/1pg/fr L

WINONA

Winona Bridge
Spanning Mississippi River
HAER MN-8
HAER MINN,85-WIN,1-
58ph/4pc L

WINONA VIC.

Upper Miss. River 9-Foot Channel,Lock & Dam No. 5A
HAER MN-23
HAER MINN,85-WIN.V,1-
103ph/10pg/7pc L

WRIGHT COUNTY

COKATO

Bull,Henry C.,House
195 E. 3rd St.
HABS MN-89
HABS MINN,86-COKA,1-
8ph/4pg/1pc L

YELLOW MEDICINE COUNTY

GRANITE FALLS

Volstead,Andrew John,House
163 Ninth Ave.
HABS MN-87
HABS 1991(HABS):8
11ph/1pg/1pc L

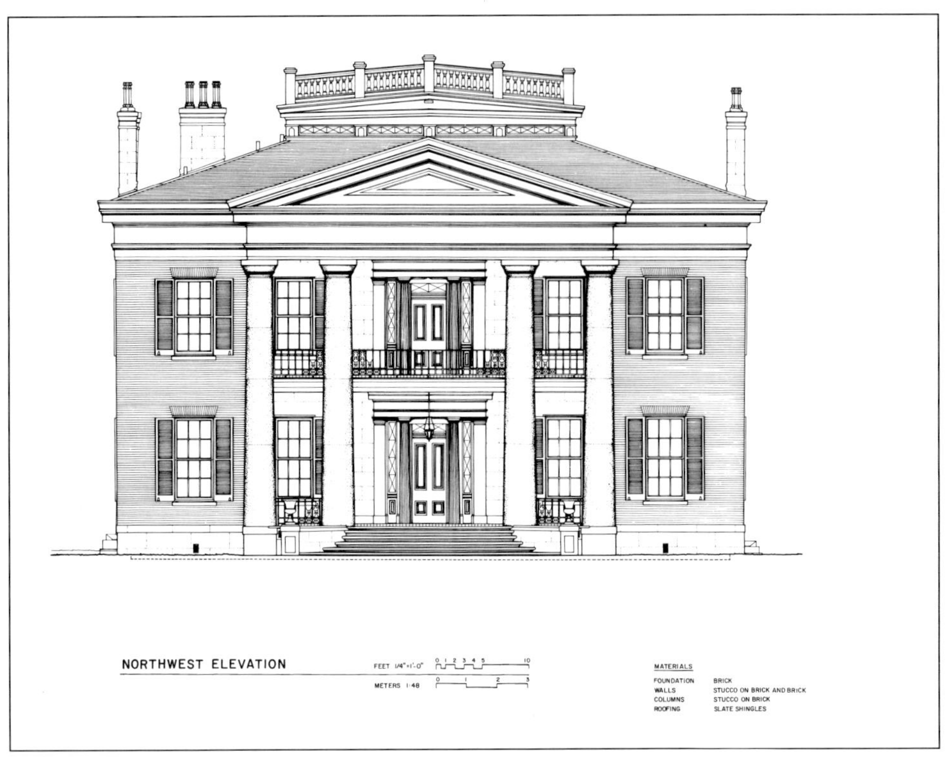

Melrose, Natchez, Adams County, Mississippi. Northwest elevation. Measured drawing delineated by Lawrence A. Weintraub, 1993 (HABS MS-61-A, sheet 10 of 22).

D'Evereux, Natchez, Adams County, Mississippi. Ornamental plaster and cast-iron details. Measured drawing delineated by Harry Weir and A.H. Town, February 1934 (HABS MS-17-6, sheet 7 of 7).

Mississippi

ADAMS COUNTY

KINGSTON

Greek Revival House (Church)
HABS MS-160
HABS MISS,1-KING,1-
1ph L

NATCHEZ

Airlie (Buckner House)
Myrtle St.
HABS MS-43
HABS MISS,1-NATCH,15-
2ph/1pg L

Arlington
Main St.
HABS MS-17-8
HABS MISS,1-NATCH,4-
10dr/2ph/6pg/fr L

Arrighi
219-221 Main St.
HABS MS-17-9
HABS MISS,1-NATCH,5-
1dr/1ph/5pg/fr L

Bahin House; see Williamsburg

Banker's House,Commercial Bank (Stowers,Luther,House)
107 S. Canal St.
HABS MS-196
HABS MISS,1-NATCH,25-
9ph/6pg/1pc L

Beltzhoover House; see Green Leaves

Bledsoe House; see Kings Tavern

Bontura House
Broadway & Market Sts.
HABS MS-161
HABS MISS,1-NATCH,22-
2ph L

Buckner House; see Airlie

Carpenter House; see Dunleith

Charity Hospital
HABS MS-148
HABS MISS,1-NATCH,18-
2ph/1pg L

Commercial Bank (First Church of Christ,Scientist)
206 Main St.
HABS MS-190
HABS MISS,1-NATCH,26-
8ph/3pg/1pc L

Connelly's Tavern; see Gilreath's Hill

Conti House (Holmes,Gov. ,House)
Wall St.
HABS MS-35
HABS MISS,1-NATCH,11-
3ph/1pg L

Dunleith (Carpenter House)
Homochito St.
HABS MS-2
HABS MISS,1-NATCH,8-
5ph/1pg/1pc L

Elward House
612 Washington St.
HABS MS-44
HABS MISS,1-NATCH,16-
8dr/2ph/1pg/fr L

Feltus House; see Linden

First Church of Christ,Scientist; see Commercial Bank

Gilreath's Hill (Connelly's Tavern)
Canal St.
HABS MS-17-4
HABS MISS,1-NATCH,2-
9dr/2ph/6pg/fr L

Green Leaves (Beltzhoover House)
303 Rankin St.
HABS MS-8
HABS MISS,1-NATCH,9-
5ph/1pg L

Holmes,Gov. ,House; see Conti House

Johnson & McCallum Houses
HABS MS-270
H

Johnson,William,Dependency
HABS MS-270-B
H

Johnson,William,House
HABS MS-270-A
H

Kings Tavern (Bledsoe House)
Jefferson St.
HABS MS-37
HABS MISS,1-NATCH,12-
1ph/1pg L

Lawyers' Row
State & Wall Sts.
HABS MS-10
HABS MISS,1-NATCH,10-
3ph/1pg L

Linden (Feltus House)
HABS MS-17-10
HABS MISS,1-NATCH,6-
6dr/4ph/5pg/fr L

Main Street & Broadway Building
100 Main St.
HABS MS-193
HABS MISS,1-NATCH,27-
2ph/3pg/1pc L

Mamye Banachi Home; see Williamsburg

Manse,The
Rankin St.
HABS MS-150
HABS MISS,1-NATCH,19-
3ph/1pg/fr L

311-313 Market Street (Parish House)
HABS MS-17-11
HABS MISS,1-NATCH,7-
3dr/2ph/5pg/fr L

Marschalk Printing Office
Wall & Franklin Sts.
HABS MS-40
HABS MISS,1-NATCH,13-
2ph/1pg L

McCallum,House
HABS MS-270-C
H

Molasses Flats (Postlewaite Building)
200 Main St.
HABS MS-192
HABS MISS,1-NATCH,28-
1ph/4pg/1pc L

Monmouth House
E. Franklin St. & Melrose Ave.
HABS MS-194
HABS MISS,1-NATCH,29-
12ph/7pg/1pc L

Natchez Bluffs & Under-the-Hill Historic District
Silver St. & adjacent area
HABS MS-212
HABS MISS,1-NATCH,30-
11ph/1pc L

Natchez City Map
HABS MS-17-12
HABS MISS,1-NATCH, -
1dr L

Postlewaite Building; see Molasses Flats

Railroad Terminal
200 Broadway St.
HABS MS-195
HABS MISS,1-NATCH,31-
1ph/3pg/1pc L

Rosalie
100 Orleans St.
HABS MS-17-1
HABS MISS,1-NATCH,1-
9dr/3ph/7pg/fr L

Slave Hospital
HABS MS-156
HABS MISS,1-NATCH,20-
1ph L

Spanish House,Old; see Washington & Wall Streets (House)

St. Catherine Street (House)
HABS MS-163
HABS MISS,1-NATCH,23-
1ph L

St. Mary's Cathedral
HABS MS-42
HABS MISS,1-NATCH,14-
2ph/1pg L

Stanton Hall
Pearl & High Sts.
HABS MS-157
HABS MISS,1-NATCH,21-
1ph L

Stowers,Luther,House; see Banker's House,Commercial Bank

Van Court House
510 Washington St.
HABS MS-17-7
HABS MISS,1-NATCH,3-
6dr/2ph/1pg/fr L

Washington & Wall Streets (House) (Spanish House,Old)
HABS MS-162
HABS MISS,1-NATCH,24-
2ph L

Williamsburg (Bahin House; Mamye Banachi Home)
821 Main St.
HABS MS-55
HABS MISS,1-NATCH,17-
5ph/6pg/1pc L

NATCHEZ VIC.

Auburn (Duncan,Stephen,House)
Auburn Blvd. Duncan Memorial Park
HABS MS-9
HABS MISS,1-NATCH.V,4-
7ph/1pg L

Bellevue; see Gloucester

Briars,The
HABS MS-41
HABS MISS,1-NATCH.V,6-
1ph/1pg L

D'Evereux
HABS MS-17-6
HABS MISS,1-NATCH.V,2-
7dr/1ph/5pg/fr L

Duncan,Stephen,House; see Auburn

Elmscourt
HABS MS-49
HABS MISS,1-NATCH.V,9-
1ph/1pg L

Gardens,The (McConchie's House)
Cemetery Rd.
HABS MS-36
HABS MISS,1-NATCH.V,5-
3ph/1pg L

Gloucester (Bellevue)
Lower Woodville Rd.
HABS MS-17-5
HABS MISS,1-NATCH.V,1-
6dr/4ph/5pg/1pc/fr L

Homewood
HABS MS-149
HABS MISS,1-NATCH.V,13-
7dr/10ph/1pg L

Hope Farm (Villa) (Miller,Balfour,House)
Auburn Ave. & Homochitto St.
HABS MS-46
HABS MISS,1-NATCH.V,7-
7dr/3ph/1pg/fr L

Longwood (Ward House; Nutt's Folly)
HABS MS-1
HABS MISS,1-NATCH.V,3-
4ph/1pg L

McConchie's House; see Gardens,The

Melrose
HABS MS-61
HABS MISS,1-NATCH.V,12-
2ph/1pg L

Melrose,Carriage House (Natchez National Historic Park)
1 Melrose-Montebello Parkway
HABS MS-61-L
3ph/1pc H

Miller,Balfour,House; see Hope Farm (Villa)

Natchez National Historic Park; see Melrose,Carriage House

Nutt's Folly; see Longwood

Saragosa
HABS MS-152
HABS MISS,1-NATCH.V,14-
3ph/1pg L

Slave Quarters & Ruins,Concord
HABS MS-51
HABS MISS,1-NATCH.V,10-
3ph/1pg L

Slave School
HABS MS-158
HABS MISS,1-NATCH.V,15-
2ph L

Springfield
U. S. Rt. 1
HABS MS-54
HABS MISS,1-NATCH,11-
10ph/1pg/1pc L

Ward House; see Longwood

Windy Hill Manor
Library Rd.
HABS MS-48
HABS MISS,1-NATCH.V,8-
5ph/1pg/fr L

WASHINGTON

Assembly Hall
State Rt. 61
HABS MS-39
HABS MISS,1-WASH,5-
3ph/1pc L

Jefferson College (Jefferson Military College)
North St.
HABS MS-4
HABS MISS,1-WASH,2-
23ph/5pg/2pc L

Jefferson College,Kitchen (Jefferson Military College,Kitchen)
North St.
HABS MS-4-A
HABS MISS,1-WASH,2-B-
8ph/1pc L

Jefferson College,President's House (Jefferson Military College,President's House)
North St.
HABS MS-5
HABS MISS,1-WASH,2-C-
3ph/1pg/1pc L

Jefferson College,Raymond Hall (Jefferson Military College,Raymond Hall)
North St.
HABS MS-4-B
HABS MISS,1-WSH,2-A-
2ph/1pc L

Jefferson Military College; see Jefferson College

Jefferson Military College,Kitchen; see Jefferson College,Kitchen

Jefferson Military College,President's House; see Jefferson College,President's House

Jefferson Military College,Raymond Hall; see Jefferson College,Raymond Hall

Meade,Cowles,House
HABS MS-7
HABS MISS,1-WASH,4-
5ph/1pg L

Methodist Church,Old
HABS MS-6
HABS MISS,1-WASH,3-
2ph/1pg L

Rawlings House
HABS MS-3
HABS MISS,1-WASH,1-
3ph/1pg L

Whitney House
North & College Sts.
HABS MS-165
HABS MISS,1-WASH,6-
4ph/1pc L

WASHINGTON VIC.

Brandon Hall
HABS MS-151
HABS MISS,1-WASH.V,1-
4ph/1pg L

Foster,James,House
Foster Mound Rd.
HABS MS-153
HABS MISS,1-WASH.V,2-
1ph/1pc L

Foster,William,House
Rand Rd.
HABS MS-45
HABS MISS,1-WASH.V,3-
1ph/1pc L

Propinquity
U. S. Hwy. 61 N.
HABS MS-199
HABS MISS,1-WASH.V,4-
7ph/4pg/1pc L

Selma
U. S. Hwy. 61 N.
HABS MS-198
HABS MISS,1-WASH.V,5-
4ph/4pg/1pc L

Sweet Auburn
U. S. Hwy. 84 & 98 E.
HABS MS-200
HABS MISS,1-WASH.V,6-
8ph/4pg/1pc L

Traveler's Rest
HABS MS-265
HABS MISS,1-WASH.V,7-
7ph/1pc L

ALCORN COUNTY

CORINTH

Alcorn County Jail
Taylor St. at Railroad tracks
HABS MS-233
HABS MISS,2-CORI,2-
2ph/1pc L

1022 Candler Place (House)
HABS MS-240
HABS MISS,2-CORI,1-
3ph/1pc L

Corinth Machinery Company
Fillmore St. & Gulf & Ohio Railroad
HABS MS-239
HABS MISS,2-CORI,3-
3ph/1pc L

Curlee House (Verandah House,The)
711 Jackson St.
HABS MS-238
HABS MISS,2-CORI,4-
7ph/1pc L

Curles Clothing Store; see Liddon Building

First Presbyterian Church
Fillmore St.
HABS MS-237
HABS MISS,2-CORI,5-
7ph/1pc L

Liddon Building (Curles Clothing Store)
405-409 Cruise St.
HABS MS-235
HABS MISS,2-CORI,7-
3ph/1pc L

McGlathery House
HABS MS-234
HABS MISS,2-CORI,8-
4ph/1pc L

Reubel,Abe,House
1109 Jackson St.
HABS MS-236
HABS MISS,2-CORI,9-
10ph/1pc/1ct L

Rowsoy House
HABS MS-241
HABS MISS,2-CORI,10-
2ph/1pc L

Smith,O. R. ,House
HABS MS-231
HABS MISS,2-CORI,11-
4ph/1pc L

Verandah House,The; see Curlee House

Wallace House
HABS MS-232
HABS MISS,2-CORI,12-
3ph/1pc L

Williams,Bailey,House
HABS MS-229
HABS MISS,2-CORI,13-
4ph/1pc L

Williams,H. I. ,House
HABS MS-242
HABS MISS,2-CORI,6-
2ph/1pc L

RIENZI

Courthouse of Old Tishomingo County; see Jacinto Courthouse

Jacinto Courthouse (Courthouse of Old Tishomingo County)
Court Square
HABS MS-230
HABS MISS,2-RIENZ,1-
12ph/1pc/3ct L

AMITE COUNTY

GLOSTER VIC.

Casselle House
HABS MS-62
HABS MISS,3-GLOST.V,2-
1ph/1pg L

GLOSTER VICINITY

Dixon House (Interior)
HABS MS-53
HABS MISS,3-GLOST.V,1-
1ph/1pg L

LIBERTY VIC.

Chaffin House & Barn
HABS MS-57
HABS MISS,3-LIB.V,1-
3ph/1pg L

BOLIVAR COUNTY

BENOIT

Burris House
HABS MS-140
HABS MISS,6-BENO,1-
2ph/1pg L

MOUND BAYOU

Montgomery,Isaiah Thornton,House
W. Main St.
HABS MS-197
HABS MISS,6-MOBA,1-
2ph/1pg/1pc L

CARROLL COUNTY

CARROLLTON VIC.

Cotesworth
HABS MS-111
HABS MISS,8-CARL.V,2-
2ph/1pg L

Malmaison
HABS MS-110
HABS MISS,8-CARL.V,1-
6ph/1pg L

VAIDEN VIC.

Vaiden,Dr. E. M. ,House
HABS MS-113
HABS MISS,8-VAID.V,1-
3ph/1pg L

CLAIBORNE COUNTY

ALCORN VIC.

Alcorn State University,Literary Society Building (Belles Lettres)
Alcorn State University Campus
HABS MS-201
HABS MISS,11-ALCO.V,1-
4ph/1pg/1pc L

Alcorn State University,Oakland Chapel
Alcorn State University Campus
HABS MS-202
HABS MISS,11-ALCO.V,2-
9ph/4pg/2pc L

Belles Lettres; see Alcorn State University,Literary Society Building

PORT GIBSON

Anchuka (Archer House)
HABS MS-28
HABS MISS,11-POGIB,7-
4ph/1pg L

Archer House; see Anchuka

Catholic Church (St. Joseph's Catholic Church)
HABS MS-155
HABS MISS,11-POGIB,8-
1ph L

Christian Chapel Church
Church & Orange Sts.
HABS MS-203
HABS MISS,11-POGIB,9-
2ph/1pg/1pc L

Disharoon,G. L. ,House
Church St.
HABS MS-21
HABS MISS,11-POGIB,1-
3ph/1pg L

Gage,R. D. ,House & Servants' House
HABS MS-24
HABS MISS,11-POGIB,4-A-
2ph/1pg L

Jean,Dan,House
HABS MS-22
HABS MISS,11-POGIB,2-
2ph/1pg L

Pope Building
625-627 Market St.
HABS MS-204
HABS MISS,11-POGIB,10-
3ph/1pg/1pc L

Port Gibson Bank
HABS MS-25
HABS MISS,11-POGIB,5-
2ph/1pg L

Presbyterian Church
HABS MS-23
HABS MISS,11-POGIB,3-
5ph/1pg L

Sacred Heart Roman Catholic Church (new location)
Grand Gulf Mil. Mon. Park (Moved from Rodney,MS)
HABS MS-208
HABS SEE SAME IN RODNEY,JEFFERSON COUNTY (MS0192)
L

Shreve House
HABS MS-27
HABS MISS,11-POGIB,6-
2ph/1pg L

St. Joseph's Catholic Church; see Catholic Church

Van Dorn House
Van Dorn Dr.
HABS MS-205
HABS MISS,11-POGIB,11-
4ph/3pg/1pc L

PORT GIBSON VIC.

Windson Plantation; see Windsor Castle Ruins

Windsor Castle Ruins (Windson Plantation)
HABS MS-26
HABS MISS,11-POGIB.V,1-
2ph/1pg L

CLAY COUNTY

WEST POINT

Cedar Oaks
Barton Ferry Rd.
HABS MS-182
HABS MISS,13-WESPO,1-
4dr/10ph/11pg/1pc/fr L

WEST POINT VIC.

Waverley (Waverly)
Waverley Rd.
HABS MS-87
HABS MISS,44-COLUM.V,2-
27ph/1pg/2pc/2ct L

Waverly; see Waverley

HANCOCK COUNTY

BAY ST. LOUIS

Mississippi Army Ammunition Plant
HAER MS-4
HAER MISS,23-BASLO,1-
37pg/fr L

HARRISON COUNTY

BILOXI

Fayard House,Old (Ruins)
HABS MS-13
HABS MISS,24-BILX,5-
3ph/1pg L

Filbrick (Philbrick House)
HABS MS-15
HABS MISS,24-BILX,4-
2ph/1pg L

Gillis House (Vance-Gillis House)
513 E. Beach Blvd. (moved to)
HABS MS-154
HABS MISS,24-BILX,6-
10dr/1ph/1pg/fr L

Keller House (Wood,Ralph,House)
E. Beach
HABS MS-14
HABS MISS,24-BILX,2-
2ph/1pg L

Philbrick House; see Filbrick

Reed,Pleasant,House
928 Elmer St.
HABS MS-186
HABS MISS,24-BILX,7-
2dr/1pg/fr L

Vance-Gillis House; see Gillis House

Wood,Ralph,House; see Keller House

BILOXI VIC.

Beauvoir (Davis,Jefferson,House)
HABS MS-12
HABS MISS,24-BILX.V,1-
7ph/1pg L

Davis,Jefferson,House; see Beauvoir

GULFPORT

Grass Lawn
720 E. Beach Blvd.
HABS MS-168
HABS MISS,24-GUPO,1-
8ph/1pg/1pc L

HINDS COUNTY

CLINTON

Mississippi College,Chapel (Provine Chapel)
HABS MS-30
HABS MISS,25-CLINT,1A-
1ph/1pg L

Moss House,Old (Ruins)
HABS MS-31
HABS MISS,25-CLINT,2-
1ph/1pg L

Provine Chapel; see Mississippi College,Chapel

EDWARDS VIC.

Coker House
Champion Hill
HABS MS-267
HABS MISS,25-EDWA.V,1-
11ph/1pg/1pc/1ct L

JACKSON

Bell,Joe,House
317 S. Congress St.
HABS MS-38
HABS MISS,25-JACK,1-
1ph/1pg L

Boyd House; see Oaks,The

Brame,Judge,House
HABS MS-80
HABS MISS,25-JACK,8-
1ph/1pg L

City Hall
HABS MS-147
HABS MISS,25-JACK,9-
2ph/1pg L

Governor's Mansion
316 E. Capitol St.
HABS MS-67
HABS MISS,25-JACK,6-
8dr/99ph/3pg/5pc/fr L

Julienne House
421 Yazoo St.
HABS MS-66
HABS MISS,25-JACK,5-
2ph/1pg L

Manship House
Northwest & Fortification Sts.
HABS MS-68
HABS MISS,25-JACK,7-
10dr/14ph/6pg/1pc/fr L

Oaks,The (Boyd House)
823 N. Jefferson St.
HABS MS-211
HABS MISS,25-JACK,12-
2ph/2pg/1pc L

Old State Capitol; see State Capitol,Old

Paramount Theater
115 E. Capitol St.
HABS MS-185
HABS MISS,25-JACK,10-
3ph/1pc L

Patton,John W. ,House
512 N. State St.
HABS MS-47
HABS MISS,25-JACK,2-
2ph/1pg L

Penney,J. C. (Building)
157 E. Capitol St.
HABS MS-184
HABS MISS,25-JACK,11-
5ph/1pg/1pc/fr L

Powers,Col. ,House
Amite St.
HABS MS-65
HABS MISS,25-JACK,4-
1ph/1pg L

State Capitol,New
Mississippi St. at Congress St.
HABS MS-191
HABS MISS,25-JACK,13-
3ph/2pg/1pc L

State Capitol,Old (Old State Capitol)
100 N. State St.
HABS MS-56
HABS MISS,25-JACK,3-
10ph/3pg/1pc L

RAYMOND

Hinds County Courthouse
HABS MS-32
HABS MISS,25-RAYM,1-
1ph/1pg L

RAYMOND VIC.

Peyton,John B. ,House (Waverly)
HABS MS-33
HABS MISS,25-RAYM.V,1-
1ph/1pg L

Waverly; see Peyton,John B. ,House

HOLMES COUNTY

LEXINGTON

Gwin House
HABS MS-109
HABS MISS,26-LEX,1-
1ph/1pg L

LEXINGTON VIC.

Burrwood
HABS MS-107
HABS MISS,26-LEX.V,1-
1ph/1pg L

Dale House
HABS MS-108
HABS MISS,26-LEX.V,2-
1ph/1pg L

JACKSON COUNTY

OCEAN SPRINGS

Sullivan,Louis H. ,Summer House
HABS MS-166
HABS MISS,30-OCSPRI,1-
3dr L

PASCAGOULA

Bellevue; see Pollack House

De La Pointe-Krebs House; see French Fort,Old

Delmas,Valentine,House
Front St.
HABS MS-17
HABS MISS,30-PASCA,2-
4ph/1pg L

French Fort,Old (De La Pointe-Krebs House; Spanish Fort,Old)
HABS MS-18
HABS MISS,30-PASCA,3-
10dr/25ph/2pg/fr L

La Frederick de St. Ferol House
HABS MS-16
HABS MISS,30-PASCA,1-
1ph/1pg L

Pollack House (Bellevue)
E. Beach Blvd.
HABS MS-20
HABS MISS,30-PASCA,5-
2ph/1pg L

Spanish Fort,Old; see French Fort,Old

Warren,Frank,House
E. Beach
HABS MS-19
HABS MISS,30-PASCA,4-
1ph/1pg L

JEFFERSON COUNTY

CANNONSBURG VIC.

Chamberlain House; see Mound Plantation

Mound Plantation (Mount Locust; Chamberlain House; Natchez Trace National Parkway)
Rt. 4,Box 166,Natchez Trace Nat'l Parkway
HABS MS-159
HABS MISS,32-CANBU.V,1-
13dr/18ph/12pg/1pc/fr L

Mount Locust; see Mound Plantation

Natchez Trace National Parkway; see Mound Plantation

CHURCH HILL

Christ Episcopal Church; see Church Hill Chapel

Church Hill Chapel (Christ Episcopal Church)
HABS MS-34
HABS MISS,32-CHUHI,1-
3ph/1pg L

RODNEY

Presbyterian Church
HABS MS-29
HABS MISS,32-ROD,1-
2ph/1pg L

Sacred Heart Roman Catholic Church (old location)
Spring Branch Creek (Moved to Port Gibson,MS)
HABS MS-208
HABS MISS,32-ROD,2-
5ph/4pg/1pc L

RODNEY VIC.

Laurel Hill Plantation House
Rodney & Red Licks Rds.
HABS MS-207
HABS MISS,32-ROD.V,1-
4ph/5pg L

LAFAYETTE COUNTY

OXFORD

Ammadelle
637 N. Lamar Blvd.
HABS MS-251
HABS MISS,36-OXFO,1-
7ph/1pc/2ct L

City Hall,Old; see Federal Building,Old

Faulkner,William,House; see Rowan Oak

Federal Building,Old (City Hall,Old)
On the Square at Jackson St.
HABS MS-256
HABS MISS,36-OXFO,2-
6ph/1pc L

Fiddler's Folly
520 N. Lamar
HABS MS-252
HABS MISS,36-OXFO,3-
7ph/1pc/1ct L

Freeland & Gafford Law Office (Sullivan Law Office,Old)
1013 Jackson Ave.
HABS MS-255
HABS MISS,36-OXFO,4-
3ph/1pc L

Isom Place
1003 Jefferson St.
HABS MS-254
HABS MISS,36-OXFO,5-
6ph/1pc L

Lafayette County Courthouse
Court House Square
HABS MS-268
HABS MISS,36-OXFO,6-
1ph/1pg/1pc L

Lamar,L. Q. C. ,House
616 N. Fourteenth St.
HABS MS-249
HABS MISS,36-OXFO,7-
3ph/1pc L

Neilson,J. E. ,Company; see Neilson's

Neilson's (Neilson,J. E. ,Company)
On the Square
HABS MS-247
HABS MISS,36-OXFO,8-
2ph/1pc L

Rowan Oak (Faulkner,William,House)
Old Taylor Rd.
HABS MS-248
HABS MISS,36-OXFO,9-
11ph/1pc/1ct L

Shadowlawn
712 S. Eleventh St.
HABS MS-253
HABS MISS,36-OXFO,10-
7ph/1pc L

St. Peter's Episcopal Church
113 S. Ninth St.
HABS MS-250
HABS MISS,36-OXFO,11-
4ph/2pc L

Sullivan Law Office,Old; see Freeland & Gafford Law Office

University of Mississippi,Bernard Observatory
University Circle
HABS MS-243
HABS MISS,36-OXFO,12-
12ph/1pc L

University of Mississippi,Geology Building
University Circle
HABS MS-245
HABS MISS,36-OXFO,13-
5ph/1pc/1ct L

University of Mississippi,Lyceum Building
University Circle
HABS MS-244
HABS MISS,36-OXFO,14-
4ph/1pc/1ct L

University of Mississippi,Skipworth House
508 University Ave.
HABS MS-246
HABS MISS,36-OXFO,15-
10ph/1pc L

LOWNDES COUNTY

CARMEN CHURCH VIC.

Gardner Farm; see Jeffries-Gardner Farm

Jeffries-Gardner Farm (Gardner Farm)
HABS MS-170
HABS MISS,44-CARCH.V,1-
1dr/18ph/12pg/2pc/fr L

Norwood-Williams House (Williams House)
HABS MS-171
HABS MISS,44-CARCH.V,2-
4ph/9pg/1pc/fr L

Williams House; see Norwood-Williams House

COLUMBUS

Banks House (White Arches)
HABS MS-104
HABS MISS,44-COLUM,15-
3ph/1pg L

Billups,John,House (Snowden)
HABS MS-91
HABS MISS,44-COLUM,9-
3ph/1pg L

Burris House (Riverview; McLaran-Humphreys House)
514 S. Second St.
HABS MS-83
HABS MISS,44-COLUM,3-
16ph/1pg/1pc/1ct L

Camellia Place (Lull-Moore House)
416 N. Seventh St.
HABS MS-258
HABS MISS,44-COLUM,17-
7ph/1pc L

Catholic Church (Church of the Annunciation)
808 S. Second Ave.
HABS MS-101
HABS MISS,44-COLUM,12-
7ph/1pg/1pc L

Cedars,The
HABS MS-84
HABS MISS,44-COLUM,4-
1ph/1pg L

Church of the Annunciation; see Catholic Church

Errolton; see Weaver House

Flynn House
HABS MS-85
HABS MISS,44-COLUM,5-
2ph/1pg L

Fort House; see Thermerlaine

Franklin Academy
HABS MS-89
HABS MISS,44-COLUM,8-
1ph/1pg L

Franklin Square; see Pratt House

Hardy,J. W. ,Estate (Whitehall)
HABS MS-93
HABS MISS,44-COLUM,11-
4ph/1pg L

Homewood
702 Main St.
HABS MS-262
HABS MISS,44-COLUM,18-
7ph/1pc L

Kinnebrew House (Temple Heights)
HABS MS-86
HABS MISS,44-COLUM,6-
2ph/1pg L

Lee,Gen. Steven D. ,House
HABS MS-105
HABS MISS,44-COLUM,16-
2ph/1pg L

Lindamood House
810 Highland Circle
HABS MS-259
HABS MISS,44-COLUM,19-
8ph/1pc L

Love,Amzi,House
305 S. Seventh St.
HABS MS-260
HABS MISS,44-COLUM,20-
6ph/1pc L

Lowndes County Courthouse
HABS MS-81
HABS MISS,44-COLUM,1-
1ph/1pg L

Lull-Moore House; see Camellia Place

Magahy House (Shadow Lawn)
HABS MS-92
HABS MISS,44-COLUM,10-
2ph/1pg L

McLaran-Humphreys House; see Burris House

Pratt House (Franklin Square)
HABS MS-102
HABS MISS,44-COLUM,13-
2ph/1pg L

Riverview; see Burris House

Rosedale
HABS MS-82
HABS MISS,44-COLUM,2-
2ph/1pg L

Shadow Lawn; see Magahy House

Snowden; see Billups,John,House

Temple Heights; see Kinnebrew House

Thermerlaine (Fort House)
510 N. Seventh St.
HABS MS-257
HABS MISS,44-COLUM,21-
8ph/1pc/2ct L

Thomas,Pratt,House; see Woodward House

Twelve Gables
220 S. Third St.
HABS MS-261
HABS MISS,44-COLUM,22-
4ph/1pc L

United States Post Office
524 Main St.
HABS MS-214
HABS MISS,44-COLUM,23-
6ph/1pg/1pc L

Weaver House (Errolton)
HABS MS-103
HABS MISS,44-COLUM,14-
2ph/1pg L

White Arches; see Banks House

Whitehall; see Hardy,J. W. ,Estate

Woodward House (Thomas,Pratt,House)
HABS MS-88
HABS MISS,44-COLUM,7-
1ph/1pg L

COLUMBUS VIC.

Belmont
Neilson Rd.
HABS MS-263
HABS MISS,44-COLUM.V,4-
4ph/1pc L

Cedar Ridge; see Cox House

Cox House (Cedar Ridge; Cox-Uithoven House)
Old Aberdeen Rd.
HABS MS-264
HABS MISS,44-COLUM.V,5-
8ph/1pc/2ct L

Cox-Uithoven House; see Cox House

Sanders House
HABS MS-106
HABS MISS,44-COLUM.V,1-
2ph/1pg L

STEENS VIC.

Covered Bridge,Old
HABS MS-90
HABS MISS,44-STEN.V,1-
2ph/1pg L

TOMBIGBEE VALLEY VIC

Bridges of the Upper Tombigbee River Valley
HAER MS-11
HAER MISS,44-COLUM.V,3
75ph/126pg/14pc L

MADISON COUNTY

MANNSDALE

Chapel of the Cross
HABS MS-17-3
HABS MISS,45-MAND,1-
6dr/1ph/4pg/fr L

MARION COUNTY

COLUMBIA (SOUTH)

Ford House
HABS MS-11
HABS MISS,46-COLUM.V,1-
4ph/1pg L

MARSHALL COUNTY

HOLLY SPRINGS

Airliewood
109 Salem Ave.
HABS MS-219
HABS MISS,47-HOLSP,1-
9ph/1pc L

Cedarhurst
103 Salem Ave.
HABS MS-224
HABS MISS,47-HOLSP,2-
6ph/2pc L

Christ Episcopal Church
Randolph St. & Van Dorn Ave.
HABS MS-223
HABS MISS,47-HOLSP,3-
9ph/1pc/1ct L

Depot,The
274 Van Dorn Ave.
HABS MS-222
HABS MISS,47-HOLSP,4-
5ph/1pc/1ct L

Gray Gables
142 College Ave.
HABS MS-221
HABS MISS,47-HOLSP,5-
8ph/1pc L

Montrose
110 Salem Ave.
HABS MS-226
HABS MISS,47-HOLSP,6-
9ph/1pc L

Oakleigh
91 Salem Ave.
HABS MS-220
HABS MISS,47-HOLSP,7-
9ph/2pc L

Polk-Cochran Place (Tuckahoe)
9 Craft St.
HABS MS-217
HABS MISS,47-HOLSP,8-
6ph/1pc L

St. Joseph's Catholic Church
E. College Ave.
HABS MS-216
HABS MISS,47-HOLSP,9-
4ph/1pc L

Tallaloosa
HABS MS-227
HABS MISS,47-HOLSP,10-
10ph/1pc/1ct L

Tuckahoe; see Polk-Cochran Place

Wakefield
104 Salem Ave.
HABS MS-225
HABS MISS,47-HOLSP,11-
5ph/1pc L

Walter Place
331 Chulahoma Ave.
HABS MS-218
HABS MISS,47-HOLSP,12-
13ph/2pc L

White Pillars
234 Maury St.
HABS MS-228
HABS MISS,47-HOLSP,13-
2ph/1pc L

MONROE COUNTY

ABERDEEN

Aberdeen Station (Frisco Railway Depot)
U. S. Rt. 45
HABS MS-169
HABS MISS,48-ABDE,12-
4dr/10ph/14pg/1pc/fr L

Barrett House
HABS MS-75
HABS MISS,48-ABDE,7-
2ph/1pg L

Bradford Place
HABS MS-79
HABS MISS,48-ABDE,11-
2ph/1pg L

Castle,The
HABS MS-76
HABS MISS,48-ABDE,8-
2ph/1pg L

Davis,Col. ,House (Davis,Judge Reuben,House)
Commerce St.
HABS MS-74
HABS MISS,48-ABDE,6-
2ph/1pg L

Davis,Judge Reuben,House; see Davis,Col. ,House

French House
HABS MS-71
HABS MISS,48-ABDE,3-
2ph/1pg L

Frisco Railway Depot; see Aberdeen Station

Holiday Haven
Meridian St.
HABS MS-70
HABS MISS,48-ABDE,2-
2ph/1pg L

Howard House
423 High St.
HABS MS-69
HABS MISS,48-ABDE,1-
2ph/1pg L

Mann House
HABS MS-78
HABS MISS,48-ABDE,10-
1ph/1pg L

Martin's Bluff (Buildings & Dam Abutment) (Taylor's,Murff's & Pickle's Stores)
E. Bank of Tombigbee River
HABS MS-209
HABS MISS,48-ABDE,13-
13ph/1pc/fr L

Strong House
HABS MS-72
HABS MISSS,48-ABDE,4-
1ph/1pg L

Taylor's,Murff's & Pickle's Stores; see Martin's Bluff (Buildings & Dam Abutment)

Walker,W. B. ,House
HABS MS-73
HABS MISS,48-ABDE,5-
3ph/1pg L

Woods House
HABS MS-77
HABS MISS,48-ABDE,9-
2ph/1pg L

MONTGOMERY COUNTY

WINONA

Moore,Col. ,House
HABS MS-112
HABS MISS,49-WINO,1-
2ph/1pg L

NOXUBEE COUNTY

MACON

Cline House
HABS MS-97
HABS MISS,52-MACO,4-
3ph/1pg L

Harrison House
HABS MS-96
HABS MISS,52-MACO,3-
1ph/1pg L

Pleasants,J. J. ,House
HABS MS-94
HABS MISS,52-MACO,1-
2ph/1pg L

Richardson House
HABS MS-95
HABS MISS,52-MACO,2-
2ph/1pg L

Scales House
HABS MS-98
HABS MISS,52-MACO,5-
2ph/1pg L

Yates House
HABS MS-99
HABS MISS,52-MACO,6-
1ph/1pg L

MACON VIC.

Water Power Grist Mill,Old
HABS MS-100
HABS MISS,52-MACO.V,1-
2ph/1pg L

PRENTISS COUNTY

NEW SITE VICINITY

Searcy,Ezra,House
W. of Prentiss-Tishimingo County Line
HABS MS-172
HABS MISS,59-NESI.V,1-
8ph/14pg/1pc/fr L

TISHOMINGO COUNTY

DENNIS VIC.

Bay Springs Bridge
Spanning Mackey's Creek
HAER MS-3
HAER MISS,71-DEN.V,1-
2dr/1pg/fr L

TISHOMINGO VICINITY

Adams,R. G. ,House
Mackeys Creek Vic.
HABS MS-173
HABS MISS,71-TISH.V,1-
3dr/14ph/10pg/1pc/fr L

Allen Line Schoolteacher's House
Marietta & Jacinto Rd.
HABS MS-174
HABS MISS,71-TISH.V,2-
5ph/13pg/1pc/fr L

Butler Dogtrot
Old Natchez Trace
HABS MS-183
HABS MISS,71-TISH.V,3-
5dr/27ph/10pg/2pc/fr L

Butler,James T. ,House
Old Natchez Trace
HABS MS-175
HABS MISS,71-TISH.V,4-
8ph/11pg/1pc/fr L

Eaton,Billie,House
Old Natchez Trace
HABS MS-176
HABS MISS,71-TISH.V,5-
7ph/15pg/1pc/fr L

Eaton,John,House
Old Natchez Trace Vic.
HABS MS-177
HABS MISS,71-TISH.V,6-
3dr/10ph/9pg/1pc/fr L

Holley,Nancy Belle,House
Old Natchez Trace Vic.
HABS MS-178
HABS MISS,71-TISH.V,7-
8ph/11pg/1pc/fr L

Riddle,A. L. ,House
Old Natchez Trace Vic.
HABS MS-179
HABS MISS,71-TISH.V,8-
5ph/9pg/1pc/fr L

Riddle,M. V. ,Barn
Old Natchez Trace Vic.
HABS MS-180
HABS MISS,71-TISH.V,9-
2dr/13ph/8pg/1pc/fr L

Trimm,John R. ,Barn
Old Natchez Trace
HABS MS-181
HABS MISS,71-TISH.V,10-
2dr/5ph/7pg/1pc/fr L

WARREN COUNTY

BLAKELY

Blakely Gin
HABS MS-138
HABS MISS,75-BLAK,2-
3ph/1pg L

Blakely Plantation
HABS MS-137
HABS MISS,75-BLAK,1-
9ph/1pg L

BOVINA VICINITY

Illinois Central Gulf RR Bridge
Spanning Big Black River near Bovina
HAER MS-6
HAER MISS,75-BOVI.V,1-
5ph/1pc/1ct L

EDWARDS VIC.

Messinger House
HABS MS-135
HABS MISS,75- ,1-
2ph/1pg L

VICKSBURG

Balfour,Dr. William T. ,House
Crawford St.
HABS MS-116
HABS MISS,75-VICK,4-
3ph/1pg L

Bodley House; see Plain Gables

Booth,Duncan,House
HABS MS-132
HABS MISS,75-VICK.V,2-
3ph/1pg L

Bryan House; see Marshall,Rev. C. K. ,House

Canizaro House; see McRae Bank

Confederate Avenue Bridge (Vicksburg National Military Park)
Vicksburg Nat'l Military Park
HAER MS-12
HAER MISS,75-VICK,19-
8ph/1pg/1pc/1ct L

Cook,Col. Edwin Grey,House
1104 Harrison St.
HABS MS-126
HABS MISS,75-VICK,14-
2ph/1pg L

Floweree (Tuminello House)
2309 Pearl St.
HABS MS-167
HABS MISS,75-VICK,22-
14dr/9ph/1pc/fr L

Green,Duff,House
Locust & First East St.
HABS MS-120
HABS MISS,75-VICK,8-
1ph/1pg L

Hicks,Dr. John,House (Steigleman House)
Main St.
HABS MS-123
HABS MISS,75-VICK,11-
1ph/1pg L

Hotel Washington
Washington & China Sts.
HABS MS-187
HABS MISS,75-VICK,23-
1ph/1pg/1pc L

Hyland House
HABS MS-136
HABS MISS,75-VICK.V,5-
2ph/1pg L

Keystone Bridge Company Bridge
Fairground St. spanning Illinois Central RR Tracks
HAER MS-5
HAER MISS,75-VICK,20-
13ph/1pc L

Klein,John A. ,House
2200 Oak St.
HABS MS-129
HABS MISS,75-VICK,17-
2ph/1pg L

Lake,William A. ,House
Main St.
HABS MS-122
HABS MISS,75-VICK,10-
1ph/1pg L

Lane,John,House
Crawford St.
HABS MS-114
HABS MISS,75-VICK,2-
1ph/1pg L

Luckett Group
1116 Crawford St.
HABS MS-117
HABS MISS,75-VICK,5-
2ph/1pg L

Marshall,Rev. C. K. ,House (Bryan House)
1128 Grove St.
HABS MS-130
HABS MISS,75-VICK,18-
2ph/1pg L

Masonic Temple
Grove & Washington Sts.
HABS MS-188
HABS MISS,75-VICK,24-
5ph/2pg/1pc L

McNutt,Gov. A. G. ,House
Monroe & First East Sts.
HABS MS-121
HABS MISS,75-VICK,9-
1ph/1pg L

McRae Bank (Canizaro House; Planters Hall)
906 Monroe St.
HABS MS-118
HABS MISS,75-VICK,6-
1ph/1pg L

Pemberton's Headquarters
1018 Crawford St.
HABS MS-266
HABS MISS,75-VICK,25-
1ph/1pc L

Plain Gables (Bodley House)
805 Locust St.
HABS MS-127
HABS MISS,75-VICK,15-
1ph/1pg L

Planters Hall; see McRae Bank

Porterfield House; see Shamrock

Shamrock (Porterfield House)
Oak St.
HABS MS-17-2
HABS MISS,75-VICK,1-
9dr/1ph/6pg/fr L

Shannon,Marmaduke,House
701 Adams St.
HABS MS-124
HABS MISS,75-VICK,12-
2ph/1pg L

Shirley House; see Wexford Lodge

St. Francis Xavier Convent
Crawford St.
HABS MS-115
HABS MISS,75-VICK,3-
1ph/1pg L

St. Paul's Catholic Church Rectory
Crawford St.
HABS MS-189
HABS MISS,75-VICK,26-
3ph/3pg/1pc L

Steele,Esther R. ,House
1202 Adams St.
HABS MS-128
HABS MISS,75-VICK,16-
1ph/1pg L

Steigleman House; see Hicks,Dr. John,House

Tuminello House; see Floweree

U.S.S. Cairo Ironclad
Vicksburg National Military Park
HAER MS-7
HAER MISS,75-VICK,21-
9ph/1pc L

Vicksburg National Military Park; see Confederate Avenue Bridge

Warren County Courthouse
Grove St.
HABS MS-119
HABS MISS,75-VICK,7-
9dr/4ph/1pg L

Waterways Experiment Station,Hydraulics Laboratory
Halls Ferry Road,two miles south of I-20
HAER MS-2
HAER 1989(HAER):15
48ph/61pg/4pc/fr L

Wexford Lodge (Shirley House)
Vicksburg National Military Park
HABS MS-133
HABS MISS,75-VICK.V,3-
22ph/1pg/fr L

Wilson,Victor,House
1010 First East St.
HABS MS-125
HABS MISS,75-VICK,13-
1ph/1pg L

VICKSBURG VIC.

Ferguson House
HABS MS-134
HABS MISS,75-VICK.V,4-
1ph/1pg L

Fonsylvania; see Rummage House

Rummage House (Wale House; Fonsylvania)
HABS MS-131
HABS MISS,75-VICK.V,1-
2ph/1pg L

Wale House; see Rummage House

WASHINGTON COUNTY

CHATHAM VIC.

Everhope
HABS MS-145
HABS MISS,76-CHAT.V,1-
1ph/1pg L

FOOTE VIC.

Erwin House (Mount Holly Plantation)
HABS MS-146
HABS MISS,76-FOOT.V,1-
1ph/1pg L

Mount Holly Plantation; see Erwin House

GREENVILLE VIC.

Locust
HABS MS-142
HABS MISS,76-GRENV.V,2-
2ph/1pg L

GREENVILLE VICINITY

McAlester House; see Wildwood

Wildwood (McAlester House)
HABS MS-141
HABS MISS,76-GRENV.V,1-
2ph/1pg L

LONGWOOD

Longwood
HABS MS-144
HABS MISS,76-LONG,1-
1ph/1pg L

WAYSIDE

Belmont
HABS MS-143
HABS MISS,76-WAY,1-
3ph/1pg L

WILKINSON COUNTY

FORT ADAMS

Curry House
HABS MS-63
HABS MISS,79-FOAD,1-
1ph/1pg L

Murray House
HABS MS-64
HABS MISS,79-FOAD,2-
1ph/1pg L

FORT ADAMS VIC.

Desert Plantation; see Sample,Capt. Carmichael,House (Interior)

Sample,Capt. Carmichael,House (Interior) (Desert Plantation)
HABS MS-59
HABS MISS,79-FOAD.V,2-
1ph/1pg L

Wall,Evans,House
HABS MS-52
HABS MISS,79-FOAD.V,1-
7ph/1pg/fr L

WOODVILLE

Baptist Church
HABS MS-50
HABS MISS,79-WODVI,1-
1ph/1pg L

Lewis House
HABS MS-58
HABS MISS,79-WODVI,2-
5ph/1pg L

WOODVILLE VIC.

Saulsberry (Sheppard House)
HABS MS-60
HABS MISS,79-WODVI.V,1-
3ph/1pg L

Sheppard House; see Saulsberry

West Feliciana Railroad Right-of-Way
HAER MS-1
HAER MISS,79-WODVI.V,2-
19ph/9pg/2pc L

YALOBUSHA COUNTY

COFFEEVILLE

Coffeeville Hotel
Illinois Central & Gulf RR vic.
HABS MS-215
HABS MISS,81-COFVI,1-
12ph/8pg/1pc L

YAZOO COUNTY

YAZOO CITY VIC.

Bleak House
HABS MS-139
HABS MISS,82-YACI.V,1-
2ph/1pg L

St. Louis Union Station, St. Louis, St. Louis County, Missouri. Interior, north side of grand hall showing north entrance. Photograph by Jack E. Boucher, April or May 1986 (HABS MO,96-SALU,126-12).

Missouri

???

Piaget-van Ravenswaay Collection
HABS MO-1800
HABS MO,O- ,1-
19pg L

STE. GENEVIEVE

House,Brick
HABS MO-1619
HABS MO,97-SAIGEN,28-
1ph/1pg/1pc L

WEINGARTEN

Our Lady of Help Christians Church
HABS MO-1628
HABS MO,97-WEIN,1-
1ph/1pg/1pc/fr L

ZELL

St. Joseph's Church
HABS MO-1629
HABS MO,97-ZELL,1-
5ph/1pg/1pc/fr L

ADAIR COUNTY

BRASHEAR VIC.

Old Grade Road Bridge
Spanning Brashear Drainage Ditch (Salt River)
HAER MO-47
HAER 1989(HAER):14
12ph/3pg/1pc L

CONNELSVILLE VIC.

Nineveh Bridge
Spanning Old Channel of Chariton River
HAER MO-59
HAER 199HAER):9
12ph/5pg/1pc L

ATCHISON COUNTY

FAIRFAX VIC.

East Fork Little Tarkio Bridge
Spanning E. Fork of Little Tarkio River
HAER MO-54
HAER 1992(HAER):MD-1
12ph/4pg/1pc L

BARTON COUNTY

LIBERAL

Spook Hall
HABS MO-1300
HABS MO,6-LIB,1-
2ph/1pg/1pc L

BENTON COUNTY

???

Log Cabin
HABS MO-1263
HABS MO,8- ,1-
2ph/1pc L

South Pleasant Hill School
Old Rt. 83
HABS MO-1262
HABS MO,8- ,2-
1ph/1pc L

Union Baptist Church
HABS MO-1264
HABS MO,8- ,3-
2ph/1pc L

FAIRFIELD VIC.

Steel Truss Bridge
Spanning Osage River on State Hwy. 7
HAER MO-21
HAER MO,8-FAR.V,1-
1ph/1pc L

WARSAW

Middle Bridge
Spanning Osage River
HAER MO-3
HAER MO,8-WARS,1-
17ph/29pg/1pc L

Warsaw Bridge
Spanning S. Grand River
HAER MO-18
HAER MO,8-WARS,2-
3ph/1pc L

WARSAW VIC.

Bryan's Crossing Bridge
Spanning S. Grand River
HAER MO-19
HAER MO,8-WARS.V,8-
3ph/1pc L

Heath,Calloway G. ,House
Rt. 7 & Rt. KK Vic.
HABS MO-1248
HABS MO,8-WARS.V,2-
8dr/5ph/1pc L

House
Rt. KK
HABS MO-1238
HABS MO,8-WARS.V,3-
6ph/4pg/1pc L

House
Rt. O & Rt. 83 Vic.
HABS MO-1240
HABS MO,8-WARS.V,5-
8ph/6pg/1pc L

House
Rt. 7 & Rt. KK Vic.
HABS MO-1239
HABS MO,8-WARS.V,4-
4ph/5pg/1pc L

Kinkead,Samuel,House
S. Grand River & Little Tebo Creek Vic.
HABS MO-1221
HABS MO,8-WARS.V,1-
6dr/6ph/6pg/1pc L

Lynn House; see Smith,William F. ,House

Peal Bend School
Rt. KK & Valley View Vic.
HABS MO-1242
HABS MO,8-WARS.V,7-
5ph/6pg/1pc L

Smith,William F. ,House (Lynn House; Tract #1713)
Hogles Creek School Vic.
HABS MO-1241
HABS MO,8-WARS.V,6-
4ph/6pg/1pc L

Tract #1713; see Smith,William F. ,House

BOLLINGER COUNTY

LEOPOLD

Catholic Church
HABS MO-1301
HABS MO,9-LEOP,1-
1ph/1pc L

BOONE COUNTY

COLUMBIA

Boone County Courthouse,Old
HABS MO-1153
HABS MO,10-COLUM,1-
1ph/1pg L

Field,John,House (Price-Willis House)
East Broadway
HABS MO-1302
HABS MO,10-COLUM,4-
7ph/1pg/1pc/fr L

Price-Willis House; see Field,John,House

University of Missouri,First Building (Columns)
HABS MO-1155
HABS MO,10-COLUM,2-
2ph/1pg L

University of Missouri,Jefferson,Thomas,Tombstone
HABS MO-1154
HABS MO,10-COLUM,3-
2ph/1pg L

COLUMBIA VIC.

Greenwood
HABS MO-1151
HABS MO,10-COLUM.V,2-
7ph L

Shipley House
HABS MO-1149
HABS MO,10-COLUM.V,1-
2ph L

Woodside
HABS MO-1152
HABS MO,10-COLUM.V,3-
4ph L

ROCHEPORT

Campbell,Charlie,House
HABS MO-1303
HABS MO,10-ROCHE,1-
2ph/1pg/1pc L

Christian Church
HABS MO-1304
HABS MO,10-ROCHE,2-
1ph/1pg/1pc L

Rocheport Baptist Church (Rocheport Community Hall)
HABS MO-1305
HABS MO,10-ROCHE,3-
2ph/1pg/1pc L

Rocheport Community Hall; see Rocheport Baptist Church

Wilcox,George,House
Columbia & Main Sts.
HABS MO-1306
HABS MO,10-ROCHE,4-
5ph/1pg/1pc/fr L

BUCHANAN COUNTY

ST. JOSEPH

(Per P. Kissling change from 1408 Charles St.); see Mulvihill,John,Duplex

American National Bank; see German American Bank

Architect's Folly
610 S. Tenth St.
HABS MO-1842
HABS MO,11-SAJOE,2-
2ph/1pc/2ct L

Brittain-Richardson & Co. Bldg.
224 N. 4th St.
HABS MO-1859
HABS MO,11-SAJOE,3-
3ph/1pg/1pc L

Buchanan County Courthouse
Jules St. between 3rd & 4th Sts
HABS MO-1844
HABS MO,11-SAJOE,4-
6ph/1pg/1pc/1ct L

City Auditorium,Old
404-424 N. Fourth St.
HABS MO-1274
HABS MO,11-SAJOE,5-
24ph/6pg/2pc L

City Hall
Eleventh & Frederick Ave.
HABS MO-250
HABS MO,11-SAJOE,1-
12ph/3pg/1pc/fr L

907-911 Dewey St.
907-911 Dewey St.
HABS MO-1894
11ph/12pg/1pc H

Englehart-Winning & Co. Bldg.
212 N. 4th St.
HABS MO-1857
HABS MO,11-SAJOE,7-
2ph/1pg/1pc L

Englehart-Winning & Co. Bldg.
216-218 N. 4th St.
HABS MO-1858
HABS MO,11-SAJOE,6-
2ph/1pg/1pc/1ct L

First Federal Bank; see German American Bank

German American Bank (First Federal Bank; American National Bank)
624 Felix St.
HABS MO-1845
HABS MO,11-SAJOE,8-
6ph/3pg/1pc/1ct L

Gilbert,M.G.,House
217 S. Thirteenth St.
HABS MO-1887
8ph/7pg/1pc H

Grief,Joseph House
719-721 S. 10th St.
HABS MO-1880
HABS DLC/PP-1992:MO-5
6ph/9pg/1pc L

Hanna,F.R.,House
1101 Corby St.
HABS MO-1876
HABS DLC/PP-1992:MO-5
10ph/8pg/1pc L

James,Jesse,House
12th St. & Mitchell Ave.
HABS MO-1846
HABS MO,11-SAJOE,9-
1ph/1pg/1pc L

McDonald,R.L., & Co. Bldg.
202 N. 4th St.
HABS MO-1856
HABS MO,11,SAJOE,10-
4ph/1pg/1pc/1ct L

Missouri Theater Building
713-715 Edmond St.
HABS MO-1847
HABS MO,11-SAJOE,11-
10ph/3pg/1pc/2ct L

Missouri Valley Trust Company
4th & Felix Sts.
HABS MO-1848
HABS MO,11-SAJOE,12-
14ph/3pg/1pc/3ct L

Morris-Burnett Block
302-306 Edmond St.
HABS MO-1877
10ph/7pg/1pc H

Motter,Joshua,House
301 S. 10th St.
HABS MO-1843
HABS MO,11-SAJOE,13-
6ph/1pg/1pc/2ct L

Mulvihill,John,Duplex ((Per P. Kissling change from 1408 Charles St.))
1408-1410 Charles Street
HABS MO-1886
11ph/7pg/1pc H

701 North Twelfth Street (House)
HABS MO-1889
9ph/8pg/1pc H

703 North Twelfth Street (House)
703 North 12th St.
HABS MO-1890
8ph/9pg/1pc H

Ogden House
809 Hall St.
HABS MO-1849
HABS MO,11-SAJOE,14-
7ph/1pg/1pc/1ct L

Patee House Hotel
S. 12th & Penn Sts.
HABS MO-1850
HABS MO,11-SAJOE,15-
6ph/2pg/1pc/2ct L

Pike's Peak Stables; see Pony Express Stables

Pony Express Stables (Pike's Peak Stables)
914 Penn St.
HABS MO-1851
HABS MO,11-SAJOE,16-
3ph/1pg/1pc/1ct L

Robidoux Row
219-225 E. Poulin St.
HABS MO-1852
HABS MO,11-SAJOE,17-
4ph/1pg/1pc/1ct L

Schuster,Adam N.,House
703 Hall St.
HABS MO-1853
HABS MO,11-SAJOE,18-
19ph/1pg/1pc/3ct L

806-808 South Eleventh Street (House)
HABS MO-1881
HABS 1991(HABS):19;DLC/PP-1992:MO-5
8ph/9pg/1pc L

602-604 South Ninth Street (House)
HABS MO-1884
10ph/9pg/1pc H

618-20 South Ninth Street,Duplex
618-20 South Ninth Street
HABS MO-1885
11ph/9pg/1pc H

South Third & Charles Streets (Commercial Bldg.)
HABS MO-1860
HABS MO,11-SAJOE,19-
3ph/1pc L

St. Joseph Museum; see Tootle House

Tootle House (St. Joseph Museum)
Eleventh & Charles Sts.
HABS MO-1855
HABS MO,11-SAJOE,20-
5ph/1pg/1pc/1ct L

Tootle-Lemon & Company Bankers
NW corner 6th & Francis
HABS MO-1854
HABS MO,11-SAJOE,21-
3ph/1pg/1pc/1ct L

ST. JOSEPH VIC.

Saxton Road Bridge
Spanning Platte River,on Saxton-Easton Rd.
HAER MO-61
HAER DLC/PP-1992:MO-2
12ph/5pg/1pc L

BUTLER COUNTY

POPLAR BLUFF VIC.

Roxie Road Bridge
Spanning Cane Creek at County Rd. 450
HAER MO-70
10ph/8pg/1pc H

CALDWELL COUNTY

KINGSTON VIC.

Gould Farm Bridge
Spanning Shoal Creek, 5 mi. S. of U.S. Hwy. 36
HAER MO-51
HAER 1991(HAER):9
13ph/8pg/1pc L

CALLAWAY COUNTY

AUXVASSE

Bennett House
HABS MO-185
HABS MO,14-AUVA,1-
1ph/1pg L

AUXVASSE VIC.

Curd,Gen. ,Mansion
HABS MO-184
HABS MO,14-AUVA.V,2-
1ph/1pg L

Swan,John,House
HABS MO-183
HABS MO,14-AUVA.V,1-
1ph/1pg L

FULTON

Courthouse
HABS MO-176
HABS MO,14-FULT,6-
3ph/1pg L

Harris House
815 Court St.
HABS MO-173
HABS MO,14-FULT,3-
1ph/1pg L

Henderson,Judge James S. ,House
703 Market St.
HABS MO-172
HABS MO,14-FULT,2-
1ph/1pg L

Hockaday,Judge Irving,House
HABS MO-171
HABS MO,14-FULT,1-
2ph/1pg L

McCradie House
Bluff & Fifth Sts.
HABS MO-174
HABS MO,14-FULT,4-
1ph/1pg L

Nash-Hollman House
HABS MO-177
HABS MO,14-MOKA.V,1-
2ph/1pg L

Nesbeth Mansion
Old Fulton Rd.
HABS MO-175
HABS MO,14-FULT,5-
1ph/1pg L

JEFFERSON CITY VIC.

House,Log
State Rt. 63
HABS MO-1328
HABS MO,14-JEFCI.V,1-
2ph/1pg/1pc L

MOKANE

Ferguson,Swan,House
HABS MO-181
HABS MO,14-MOKA.V,3-
1ph/1pg L

Moore,John B. ,House
HABS MO-182
HABS MO,14-MOKA.V,4-
2ph/1pg L

Ratekin,LeGrand,House
HABS MO-179
HABS MO,14-MOKA.V,2-
1ph/1pg L

Rogers Log Cabin
HABS MO-178
HABS MO,14-MOKA,1-
1ph/1pg L

Smith,Thomas,House
HABS MO-180
HABS MO,14-MOKA,2-
1ph/1pg L

CAPE GIRARDEAU COUNTY

ALLENVILLE

Bridge,Covered
HABS MO-1325
HABS MO,16-ALLVI,1-
3ph/1pg/1pc/fr L

BUFORDVILLE

Bollinger Covered Bridge & Mill
HABS MO-1307
HABS MO,16-BUFVI,1-
4ph/1pg/1pc/fr L

CAPE GIRARDEAU

Ellis,Alfred P. ,House (Ranney-Walthen House)
HABS MO-1311
HABS MO,16-CAPGI,1-
8ph/1pg/1pc/fr L

Ranney-Walthen House; see Ellis,Alfred P. ,House

St. Vincent's Church
Main & William Sts.
HABS MO-1309
HABS MO,16-CAPGI,2-
2ph/1pg/1pc L

St. Vincent's College
201 Morgan Oak St.
HABS MO-1310
HABS MO,16-CAPGI,3-
2ph/1pg/1pc/fr L

Weber House
HABS MO-1308
HABS M16-CAPGI,4-
4ph/1pc/fr L

Wharf Buildings,Brick
HABS MO-1312
HABS MO,16-CAPGI,5-
4ph/1pg/1pc/fr L

JACKSON

Bodenstein House
HABS MO-1313
HABS MO,16-JACK,7-
1ph/1pg/1pc L

Criddle-Sander House
HABS MO-1317
HABS MO,16-JACK,1-
1ph/1pg/1pc/fr L

Daley's Tin Shop
HABS MO-1319
HABS MO,16-JACK,2-
1ph/1pg/1pc/fr L

Frizel-Welling House
(Grainger,Juliette,House)
HABS MO-1318
HABS MO,16-JACK,3-
4ph/1pg/1pc/fr L

Grainger,Juliette,House; see Frizel-Welling House

Kneibert House
Main & High Sts.
HABS MO-1315
HABS MO,16-JACK,4-
3ph/1pg/1pc/fr L

Koehler House
HABS MO-1320
HABS MO,16-JACK,5-
2ph/1pg/1pc L

Oliver House
HABS MO-1316
HABS MO,16-JACK,6-
1ph/1pg/1pc/fr L

JACKSON VIC.

Byrd,Stephen,House
HABS MO-1314
HABS MO,16-JACK.V,2-
1ph/1pg/1pc L

McKendree Chapel
HABS MO-1321
HABS MO,16-JACK.V,1-
2ph/1pg/1pc L

MILLERSVILLE

Masonic Hall Building
HABS MO-1326
HABS MO,16-MILVI,1-
1ph/1pg/1pc L

OLD APPLETON

Apple Creek Mill
HABS MO-1323
HABS MO,16-APPOL,1-
2ph/1pg/1pc/fr L

McClain,Alfred,House
HABS MO-1322
HABS MO,16-APPOL,3-
2ph/1pg/1pc L

Shourtz-Mclane House
(Wucher,Hugo,House)
HABS MO-1324
HABS MO,16-APPOL,2-
1ph/1pg/1pc/fr L

Wucher,Hugo,House; see Shourtz-Mclane House

CHARITON COUNTY

BRUNSWICK

Applegate House
HABS MO-1329
HABS MO,21-BRUNS,1-
3ph/1pc/fr L

Bragg House
HABS MO-1330
HABS MO,21-BRUNS,2-
5ph/1pc L

Heisel House
HABS MO-1331
HABS MO,21-BRUNS,3-
1ph/1pg/1pc L

Presbyterian Church
HABS MO-1332
HABS MO,21-BRUNS,4-
2ph/1pg/1pc/fr L

Staples House
HABS MO-1333
HABS MO,21-BRUNS,5-
2ph/1pg/1pc/fr L

CHRISTIAN COUNTY

NIXA VIC.

Blue Springs Bridge; see Howard Ford Bridge

Howard Ford Bridge (Blue Springs Bridge)
Spanning James River on Cart Rd. 143
HAER MO-52
HAER DLC/PP-1992:MO-2
16ph/18pg/1pc L

CLAY COUNTY

EXCELSIOR SPRINGS VI

Mount Vernon Church
Watkins Mill State Park
HABS MO-1185
HABS MO,24-EXPRI.V,2
8dr L

EXCELSIOR SRINGS VIC

Franklin School
Watkins Mill State Park
HABS MO-1180
HABS MO,24-EXPR.V,1-
7dr L

LAWSON VIC.

Watkins Mill
Highway MM
HAER MO-1
HAER MO,24-LAWS.V,1-
94ph/80pg/9pc/20ct L

PARADISE VIC.

Paradise Road Bridge
Spanning Little Platte River
HAER MO-7
HAER MO,24-PARA.V,1-
11ph/1pg/1pc L

SMITHVILLE VIC.

Poff,James,House
Paradise Rd.
HABS MO-1225
HABS MO,24-SMITV.V,2-
10ph/8pg L

Rollins,Sophia,House
Farm Rt. F. Vic.
HABS MO-1226
HABS MO,24-SMITV.V,3-
14ph/9pg L

Ross,Rueben,Barn
Clinton County Line Vic.
HABS MO-1223
HABS MO24-SMITV.V,1-ι86(HABS):124°
5dr/9ph/6pg/fr L

CLINTON COUNTY

TRIMBLE VIC.

Waddell "A" Truss Bridge
Spanning Lin Branch Creek
HAER MO-8
HAER MO,25-TRIM.V,1-
3dr/16ph/8pg/1pc/fr L

COLE COUNTY

JEFFERSON

Bald Hill Road Bridge; see Schneider's Ford Bridge

Schneider's Ford Bridge (Bald Hill Road Bridge)
Spanning Moreau River on Bald Hill Rd.
HAER MO-42
HAER 1989(HAER):14
11ph/5pg/1pc L

JEFFERSON CITY

Byrd-Haar House
614 West Main St.
HABS MO-1277
HABS MO,26-JEFCI,1-
8ph/6pg/1pc L

Cady Machine Shop; see Holt,Hiram,House

Cole County Jail
HABS MO-1334
HABS MO,26-JEFCI,2-
4ph/1pg/1pc/fr L

Commercial Building,Brick
HABS MO-1337
HABS MO,26-JEFCI,3-
1ph/1pg/1pc L

Governor's Mansion
100 Madison St.
HABS MO-1841
HABS MO,26-JEFCI,4-
12ph/3pg/1pc/1ct L

Documentation: **ct** color transparencies **dr** measured drawings **fr** field records
pc photograph captions **pg** pages of text **ph** photographs

Hagan House
501 Cherry St.
HABS MO-1200
HABS MO,26-JEFCI,5-
10ph/4pg/1pc L

Holt,Hiram,House (Cady Machine Shop)
428 W. Main St. (rear)
HABS MO-1255
HABS MO,26-JEFCI,6-
7ph/6pg/1pc L

House,Stone
Main St.
HABS MO-1338
HABS MO,26-JEFCI,7-
1ph/1pc L

Jefferson Street Bridge
Spanning the East Branch of Wears Creek
HAER MO-31
HAER 1989(HAER):14
7ph/3pg/1pc L

Jones-Wells House
626 W. Main St.
HABS MO-1256
HABS MO,26-JEFCI,9-
10ph/5pg/1pc L

Missouri State Capitol
High St. between Broadway & Jefferson Sts.
HABS MO-1840
HABS MO,26-JEFCI,10-
14ph/2pg/1pc/4ct L

Porth,Doctor,House
Main & Bolivar Sts.
HABS MO-1335
HABS MO,26-JEFCI,11-
2ph/1pg/1pc/fr L

Red-Franz House
620 West Main St.
HABS MO-1278
HABS MO,26-JEFCI,12-
10ph/5pg/1pc L

Ross House
W. McCarty & Walnut Sts.
HABS MO-1258
HABS MO,26-JEFCI,13-
9ph/5pg/1pc L

Schulte's Summer Kitchen
Walnut St. (Lots 295 & 296)
HABS MO-1257
HABS MO,26-JEFCI,14A-
7ph/5pg/1pc L

JEFFERSON CITY VIC.

Jefferson Landing Building (Lohman's Landing Building)
Water & Jefferson Sts.
HABS MO-1194
HABS MO,26-JEFCI,8-
2ph/2pg/1pc L

Lohman's Landing Building; see Jefferson Landing Building

TAOS

Dirckx House
HABS MO-1793
HABS MO,26-TAOS,1-
2ph/1pg/1pc L

Dirckx House,Chicken Coop
HABS MO-1793-A
HABS MO,26-TAOS,1A-
1ph/1pg/1pc L

St. Francis Xavier Roman Catholic Church
HABS MO-1791
HABS MO,26-TAOS,3-
1ph/1pg/1pc L

COOPER COUNTY

???

House,Log
HABS MO-1790
HABS MO,27.----,1-
1ph/1pg/1pc L

BLACKWATER VIC.

Roberts Bluff Bridge
.5 miles E of Blackwater
HAER MO-33
HAER MO,27-BLAC.V,1-
15ph/12pg/1pc L

BOONVILLE

Adelphai College
Vine & Fourth Sts.
HABS MO-1339
HABS MO,27-BOONV,2-
1ph/1pg/1pc/fr L

Beck's Bakery Shop
Main & Court Sts.
HABS MO-1342
HABS MO,27-BOONV,3-
1ph/1pg/1pc L

Boller House
HABS MO-1369
HABS MO,27-BOONV,4-
6ph/1pg/1pc/fr L

Boonville Female College
HABS MO-1343
HABS MO,27-BOONV,5-
1ph/1pg/1pc/fr L

Boonville,Town of
HABS MO-1374
HABS MO,27-BOONV,6-
5ph/1pg/1pc/fr L

Brant,Henry,House
714 Morgan St.
HABS MO-1344
HABS MO,27-BOONV,7-
4ph/1pg/1pc/fr L

Central National Bank
Main & Morgan Sts.
HABS MO-1345
HABS MO,27-BOONV,8-
1ph/1pg/1pc/fr L

Christ Episcopal Church
Vine & Fourth Sts.
HABS MO-1373
HABS MO,27-BOONV,9-
3ph/1pg/1pc/fr L

City Cemetery,Old
HABS MO-1372
HABS MO,27-BOONV,10-
1ph/1pg/1pc L

City Hotel,Old
High St.
HABS MO-1346
HABS MO,27-BOONV,11-
2ph/1pg/1pc/fr L

Commercial Hotel
HABS MO-1347
HABS MO,27-BOONV,12-
1ph/1pg/1pc/fr L

Crane House
S. Seventh St.
HABS MO-1348
HABS MO,27-BOONV,13-
4ph/1pg/1pc/fr L

Fifth & Morgan Streets (Commercial Buildings)
HABS MO-1788
HABS MO,27-ABOONV,14-
2ph/1pg/1pc L

Forest Hill; see Nelson,Thomas Withers,House

Gray Hotel
Morgan St.
HABS MO-1349
HABS MO,27-BOONV,15-
4ph/1pg/1pc/fr L

Hain House
Fourth & Chestnut Sts.
HABS MO-1350
HABS MO,27-BOONV,16-
7ph/1pg/1pc L

House,Brick
614 Sixth St.
HABS MO-1784
HABS MO,27-BOONV,17-
1ph/1pg/1pc L

Huber House
Spring St.
HABS MO-1352
HABS MO,27-BOONV,18-
1ph/1pg/1pc L

Kaiser Hotel; see Parks,Thomas,Building

Lionberger,David,House
Third & Spring Sts.
HABS MO-1354
HABS MO,27-BOONV,19-
2ph/1pg/1pc/fr L

Manger-Hoefer House
214 Seventh St.
HABS MO-1370
HABS MO,27-BOONV,20-
1ph/1pg/1pc L

McFarland House
Morgan & Seventh Sts.
HABS MO-1356
HABS MO,27-BOONV,21-
8ph/1pg/1pc L

McPherson,Captain Henry,House
HABS MO-1357
HABS MO,27-BOONV,22-
1ph/1pg/1pc/fr L

Meyer-Lionberger House
HABS MO-1358
HABS MO,27-BOONV,23-
2ph/1pg/1pc/fr L

Nelson,Thomas Withers,House (Forest Hill)
HABS MO-1359
HABS O,27-BOONV,24-
4ph/1pg/1pc/fr L

Parks,Thomas,Building (Kaiser Hotel)
Morgan St. between Fourth & Main Sts.
HABS MO-1340
HABS MO,27-BOONV,25-
2ph/1pg/1pc/fr L

Sahm House
HABS MO-1360
HABS MO,27-BOONV,26-
1ph/1pg/1pc/fr L

Speed House
Morgan & Third Sts.
HABS MO-1361
HABS MO,27-BOONV,27-
1ph/1pg/1pc L

St. Peter & Paul Roman Catholic Church
Seventh & Spring Sts.
HABS MO-1785
HABS MO,27-BOONV,28-
1ph/1pg/1pc L

Stahl House
HABS MO-1362
HABS MO,27-BOONV,29-
4ph/1pg/1pc/fr L

Summers House
HABS MO-1363
HABS MO,27-BOONV,30-
1ph/1pg/1pc/fr L

Thespian Hall
Fifth & Vine Sts.
HABS MO-233
HABS MO,27-BOONV,1-
20ph/3pg/2pc L

Thoma House
HABS MO-1364
HABS MO,27-BOONV,31-
1ph/1pg/1pc L

Thompkins,Judge Benjamin F. ,House
Locust St.
HABS MO-1365
HABS MO,27-BOONV,32-
2ph/1pg/1pc L

Walden House
Spring St.
HABS MO-1366
HABS MO,27-BOONV,33-
1ph/1pg/1pc/fr L

Walnut Grove Cemetery
HABS MO-1371
HABS MO,27-BOONV,34-
9ph/1pg/1pc/fr L

Wright House
Spring Street
HABS MO-1368
HABS MO,27-BOONV,35-
1ph/1pg/1pc L

BOONVILLE VIC.

Adams,William M. ,House
HABS MO-1382
HABS MO,27-BOONV.V,1-
9ph/1pg/1pc/fr L

Adams,William M. ,Slave Cabin
HABS MO-1382-A
HABS MO,27-BOONV.V,1A-
1ph/1pc L

Boonville Winery (Brewery,The Old)
HABS MO-1787
HABS MO,27-BOONV.V,2-
3ph/1pg/1pc L

Brewery,The Old; see Boonville Winery

Elliott House
HABS MO-1390
HABS MO,27-BOONV.V,14-
4ph/1pg/1pc L

Hayes House
HABS MO-1375
HABS MO,27-BOONV.V,3-
1ph/1pc L

Hickox,Benjamin F. ,House
HABS MO-1378
HABS MO,27-BOONV.V,4-
3ph/1pg/1pc/fr L

Holland House
HABS MO-1351
HABS MO,27-BOONV.V,5-
2ph/1pg/1pc/fr L

House,Log
HABS MO-1387
HABS MO,27-BOONV.V,15-
1ph/1pg/1pc L

Jones,Caleb,House
HABS MO-1384
HABS MO,27-BOONV.V,6-
2ph/1pg/1pc/fr L

Lionberger,Isaac,House
HABS MO-1377
HABS MO,27-BOONV.V,7-
4ph/1pg/1pc/fr L

Muir,William D. ,House
Jefferson City Rd.
HABS MO-1379
HABS MO,27-BOONV.V,8-
3ph/1pg/1pc/fr L

Potter,William,House
HABS MO-1380
HABS MO,27-BOONV.V,9-
2ph/1pg/1pc/fr L

Savage-Quarles House
HABS MO-1383
HABS MO,27-BOONV.V,10-
2ph/1pg/1pc/fr L

Schmidt,Herman,House
Rt. 2 (Overton Rd.)
HABS MO-1376
HABS MO,27-BOONV.V,11-
17ph/2pg/1pc L

Shoemaker House
State Rt. 5
HABS MO-1386
HABS MO,27-BOONV.V,13-
2ph/1pg/1pc/fr L

BOONVILLE VICINITY

Shed,Stone
HABS MO-1381
HABS MO,27-BOONV.V,12-
2ph/1pg/1pc L

BUNCETON VIC.

Leonard Farm; see Ravenswood Farm,Main House

Leonard Farm,Bull Barn; see Ravenswood Farm,Bull Barn

Leonard Farm,Mule Barn; see Ravenswood Farm,Mule Barn

Leonard Farm,Tally Ho Barn; see Ravenswood Farm,Tally Ho Barn

Leonard Farn,Kitchen; see Ravenswood Farm,Kitchen

Ravenswood Farm,Bull Barn (Leonard Farm,Bull Barn)
Rural Rte. 1
HABS MO-1839-B
HABS MO,27-BUNC.V,18-
2ph/1pc L

Ravenswood Farm,Kitchen (Leonard Farn,Kitchen)
Rural Rt. 1
HABS MO-1839-A
HABS MO,27-BUNC.V,1A-
2ph/1pc L

Ravenswood Farm,Main House (Leonard Farm)
Rural Route 1
HABS MO-1839
HABS MO,27-BUNC.V,1-
19ph/4pg/1pc/6ct L

Ravenswood Farm,Mule Barn (Leonard Farm,Mule Barn)
Rural Rte. 1
HABS MO-1839-C
HABS MO,27-BUNC.V,1C-
1ph/1pc L

Ravenswood Farm,Tally Ho Barn (Leonard Farm,Tally Ho Barn)
Rural Rte. 1
HABS MO-1839-D
HABS MO,27-BUNC.V,1D-
1ph/1pc L

COTTON

Cotton Bridge; see Dick's Mill Bridge

Dick's Mill Bridge (Cotton Bridge)
Spanning Moniteau Creek
HAER MO-43
HAER 1989(HAER):14
11ph/5pg/1pc L

LAMINE VIC.

Castleman,David,House
HABS MO-1388
HABS MO,27-LAMI.V,1-
4ph/1pg/1pc L

MacMahan,Thomas,House
HABS MO-1385
HABS MO,27-LAMI.V,2-
2ph/1pg/1pc/fr L

MacMahan,Thomas,House
HABS MO-1389
HABS MO,27-LAMI.V,3-
2ph/1pg/1pc L

NEW LEBANON

New Lebanon Presbyterian Church
HABS MO-1391
HABS MO,27-NELEB,1-
1ph/1pg/1pc/fr L

OVERTON VIC.

Givens Log House
HABS MO-1392
HABS MO,27-OVER.V,1-
1ph/1pg/1pc L

PISGAH

Maxey House
HABS MO-1393
HABS MO,27-PISG,1-
2ph/1pg/1pc L

PISGAH VIC.

Reavis,Andrew,House
HABS MO-1394
HABS MO,27-PISG.V,1-
2ph/1pg/1pc L

PLEASANT GREEN VIC.

Mount Nebo Baptist Church
HABS MO-1395
HABS MO,27-PLEGR.V,1-
1ph/1pg/1pc/fr L

SPEED VIC.

Pulley House
HABS MO-1396
HABS MO,27-SPEED.V,1-
1ph/1pg/1pc L

DAVIESS COUNTY

JAMESON VIC.

Lewis Mill Bridge
Spanning Grand River Btwn. Grand Ri. & Marion Twps
HAER MO-45
HAER 1989(HAER):14
13ph/10pg/1pc L

LOCK SPRINGS VIC.

Lock Springs Bridge
Spanning Grand River on Cart Rd. 127
HAER MO-46
HAER 1989(HAER):14
11ph/11pg/1pc L

DOUGLAS COUNTY

VANZANT VIC.

Clearwater Beach Bathhouse (Noblett Bathhouse; Noblett Lake Rec. Area,Mark Twain National Forest)
Clearwater Beach access road
HABS MO-1874
HABS DLC/PP-1993:MO-1
10ph/19pg/1pc L

Noblett Bathhouse; see Clearwater Beach Bathhouse

Noblett Lake Rec. Area,Mark Twain National Forest; see Clearwater Beach Bathhouse

FRANKLIN COUNTY

BEAUFORT VIC.

Voss Mill & Miller's House, Miller's House
HABS MO-1748-B
HABS MO,36-BEAU.V,1B-
3ph/1pc/fr L

Voss Mill & Miller's House, Voss Mill
Bourbeuse River
HABS MO-1748
HABS MO,36-BEAU.V,1-
3ph/2pg/1pc L

DETMOLD VIC.

Pelster House-Barn
Cedar Fork Rd.
HABS MO-244
HABS MO,36-DET.V,1-
18ph/6pg/1pc L

ETLAH

Big Berger Creek Bridge
Spanning Big Berger Creek on Route B
HAER MO-39
HAER 1989(HAER):14
12ph/7pg/1pc L

GERALD VIC.

Ebenezer Evangelical & Reformed Church
HABS MO-1749
HABS MO,36-GER.V,1-
2ph/1pg/1pc L

KRAKOW

St. Gertrude's Roman Catholic Church
HABS MO-1398
HABS MO,36-KRAK.1-
3ph/1pg/1pc L

KRAKOW VIC.

Filla,Andrew,Stone House
HABS MO-1397
HABS MO,36-KRAK.V,1-
2ph/1pg/1pc L

NEW HAVEN VIC.

House
HABS MO-1739
HABS MO,36-NEHAV.V,1-
2ph/1pg/1pc L

SULLIVAN

Harney,General William Selby,House
HABS MO-1399
HABS MO,36-SULL,1-
3ph/1pg/1pc L

WASHINGTON

Busch,Louisa,House
HABS MO-1400
HABS MO,36-WASH,2-
2ph/1pg/1pc L

Dickbrader,J. H. ,House
HABS MO-1401
HABS MO,36-WASH,3-
2ph/1pg/1pc L

Droege House
HABS MO-1404
HABS MO,36-WASH,7-
2ph/1pg/1pc L

Eitzen Building
200 Jefferson St.
HABS MO-1402
HABS MO,36-WASH,4-
2ph/1pg/1pc/fr L

Fricke,Barnard,House (Sigmund Store Building)
9 W. Second St.
HABS MO-1408
HABS MO,36-WASH,6-
1ph/1pg/1pc/fr L

Hirschl-Bendheim Corncob Pipe Factory
HABS MO-1803
HABS MO,36-WASH,1-
1ph/1pg/1pc L

House,Courtyard
HABS MO-1405
HABS MO,36-WASH,8-
1ph/1pc L

Kreuger Building
114-116 Jefferson St.
HABS MO-1740
HABS MO,36-WASH,9-
4ph/1pg/1pc L

Narup,Fred,House
Fourth & Elm Sts.
HABS MO-1406
HABS MO,36-WASH,10-
1ph/1pg/1pc/fr L

Reichard Building
Main & Jefferson Sts.
HABS MO-1407
HABS MO,36-WASH,11-
2ph/1pg/1pc/fr L

Ritter House
Fifth St.
HABS MO-1742
HABS MO,36-WASH,12-
1ph/1pg/1pc L

Schwarzer Zither Company
HABS MO-1802
HABS MO,36-WASH,13-
2ph/1pg/1pc L

Second Street (Commercial Building)
HABS MO-1744
HABS MO,36-WASH,5-
2ph/1pg/1pc L

Sigmund Store Building; see
Fricke,Barnard,House

Stumpe,William,Smokehouse
Second & Stafford Sts.
HABS MO-1745
HABS MO,36-WASH,14-
1ph/1pg/1pc L

Third & Jefferson Streets (Buildings)
HABS MO-1741
HABS MO,36-WASH,15-
1ph/1pg/1pc L

Trentmann,Louis,House
Fifth St.
HABS MO-1743
HABS MO,36-WASH,16-
1ph/1pg/1pc L

Washington,Town of
HABS MO-1410
HABS MO,36-WASH.1
3ph/1pc L

Wehrmann,Louis,House
Jefferson St.
HABS MO-1409
HABS MO,36-WASH,18-
2ph/1pg/1pc L

WASHINGTON VIC.

Brinker Barn
Hwy. 100
HABS MO-1747
HABS MO,36-WASH,V.1A-
2ph/1pg/1pc L

Busch House & Barn
HABS MO-1411
HABS MO,36-WASH.V,2-
2ph/1pc L

Kaiser Barn
Hwy. 100
HABS MO-1412
HABS MO,36-WASH.V,3A-
3ph/1pg/1pc L

Newport Presbyterian Church
HABS MO-1435
HABS MO,36-WASH.V,4-
1ph/1pg/1pc L

GASCONADE COUNTY

BAY

Bay Mercantile Company,Barn
County Rt. K
HABS MO-245-A
HABS MO,37-BAY,1A-
6dr/8ph/2pc/fr L

Bay Mercantile Company,Store & Residence
County Rt. K
HABS MO-245
HABS MO,37-BAY,1-
7dr/16ph/5pg/2pc/fr L

BAY VIC.

Brinkmann Farm
Hwy. 50
HABS MO-1762
HABS MO,37-BAY.V,1-
3ph/1pg/1pc L

BEAUFORT VIC.

Voss Mill
Bourbeuse River
HABS MO-1748-A
HABS MO,36-BEAU.V,1A-
3ph L

DRAKE VIC.

House
U.S. Rt. 50
HABS MO-1413
HABS MO,37-DRAK.V,1-
1ph/1pg/1pc L

Neese House
U. S. 50 W.
HABS MO-1414
HABS MO,37-DRAK.V,2-
4ph/1pg/1pc L

Ruskaup,Ben,House
U. S. 50 W.
HABS MO-1415
HABS MO,37-DRAK.V,3-
4ph/1pg/1pc/fr L

Ruskaup,Ben,Shed
U. S. 50 W.
HABS MO-1415-A
HABS MO,37-DRAK.V,3A-
1ph/1pc L

FREDERICKSBURG VIC.

Johnson House
HABS MO-1763
HABS MO,37-FRED.V,1-
2ph/1pg/1pc L

GASCONADE VIC.

Kotthoff-Weeks Farm
County Rt. J vic.
HABS MO-248
HABS MO,37-GASC.V,1-
1dr/1ph/10pg/1pc L

Kotthoff-Weeks Farm,Barn
County Rt. J vic.
HABS MO-248-C
HABS MO,37-GASC.V,1C-
6dr/21ph/1pc/fr L

Kotthoff-Weeks Farm,Smokehouse
County Rt. J vic.
HABS MO-248-B
HABS MO,37-GASC.V,1B-
1dr/2ph/1pc/fr L

Kotthoff-Weeks Farmhouse
County Rt. J vic.
HABS MO-248-A
HABS MO,37-GASC.V,1A-
7dr/9ph/1pc/fr L

HERMANN

Catholic Cemetery
HABS MO-1416
HABS MO,37-HERM,1-
2ph/1pg/1pc L

Commercial Building
HABS MO-1425
HABS MO,37-HERM,2-
2ph/1pg/1pc L

Concert Hall
206 E. First St.
HABS MO-1752
HABS MO,37-HERM,3-
1ph/1pg/1pc/2ct L

East Fourth Street (House)
HABS MO-1765
HABS MO,37-HERM,4-
1ph/1pg/1pc L

Eberlin,Michael,House
Rt. 100 SW.
HABS MO-1434
HABS MO,37-HERM,5-
6ph/1pg/1pc/fr L

Eitzen-Scharnhorst House
HABS MO-1422
HABS MO,37-HERM,6-
1ph/1pg/1pc L

Hermann Star Mills
238 E. First St.
HABS MO-252
HABS MO,37-HERM,7-
7dr/9ph/9pg/1pc/fr L

Hermann,Town of
HABS MO-1419
HABS MO,37-HERM,8-
11ph/1pc L

House
HABS MO-1428
HABS MO,37-HERM,10-
1ph/1pc L

House
HABS MO-1430
HABS MO,37-HERM,9-
1ph/1pg/1pc L

House,Brick
HABS MO-1421
HABS MO,37-HERM,11-
1ph/1pg/1pc L

House,Brick
HABS MO-1423
HABS MO,37-HERM,12-
1ph/1pg/1pc L

House,Brick
HABS MO-1424
HABS MO,37-HERM,13-
3ph/1pg/1pc L

House,Frame
First St.
HABS MO-1420
HABS MO,37-HERM,15-
1ph/1pg/1pc/fr L

House,Frame
W. Second St.
HABS MO-1426
HABS MO,37-HERM,14-
1ph/1pg/1pc L

Houses
HABS MO-1429
HABS MO,37-HERM,16-
2ph/1pg/1pc L

Klenk House
HABS MO-1432
HABS MO,37-HERM,17-
1ph/1pg/1pc L

Market House
Market St.
HABS MO-1754
HABS MO,37-HERM,18-
1ph/1pg/1pc L

Nasse,Dr. August,House & Double Building
HABS MO-1427
HABS MO,37-HERM,19-
4ph/1pg/1pc/fr L

Pommer-Gentner House
108 Market St.
HABS MO-253
HABS MO,37-HERM,20-
15ph/9pg/2pc L

Rotunda,The
Eitzen Park (Fairgrounds)
HABS MO-254
HABS MO,37-HERM,21-
6ph/5pg/1pc L

Smokehouse
HABS MO-1431
HABS MO,37-HERM,22-
1ph/1pg/1pc/fr L

Stone Hill Winery
401 W. Twelfth St.
HABS MO-255
HABS MO,37-HERM,23-
17dr/41ph/9pg/1pc/5ct L

Strehly,C. P. ,House
130 Second St.
HABS MO-256
HABS MO,37-HERM,24-
9dr/14ph/9pg/2pc/fr L

White House Hotel
232 E. Wharf St.
HABS MO-257
HABS MO,37-HERM,25-
13ph/6pg L

Wine Vault
HABS MO-1753
HABS MO,37-HERM,26-
1ph/1pc L

Zorn,Peter,Stable
HABS MO-1417
HABS MO,37-HERM,27A-
1ph/1pg/1pc/fr L

HERMANN VIC.

Fricke Wine Press Building
Cole Creek vic.
HABS MO-1760
HABS MO,37-HERM.V,1A-
2ph/1pg/1pc/fr L

Gaebler House
HABS MO-1755
HABS MO,37-HERM.V,2-
2ph/1pg/1pc L

Kemper,Christopher,House
Rt. 100 SW.
HABS MO-1756
HABS MO,37-HERM.V,3-
1ph/1pg/1pc L

Langendorfer House
Frene Creek Valley
HABS MO-1758
HABS MO,37-HERM.V,4-
4ph/2pg/1pc L

Oelschlager House
Hwy. 100
HABS MO-1759
HABS MO,37-HERM.V,5-
2ph/1pg/1pc L

Poeschel-Harrison House
HABS MO-1764
HABS MO,37-HERM.V,7-
2ph/1pg/1pc L

Poeschel,William,House
W. Tenth St. extension
HABS MO-258
HABS MO,37-HERM.V,6-
10ph/7pg/1pc L

Schramm,L. ,Barn
HABS MO-1433
HABS MO,37-HERM.V,8A-
2ph/1pg/1pc L

St. Johannis Kirche
County Rt. J
HABS MO-1767
HABS MO,37-HERM.V,9-
1ph/1pg/1pc/fr L

OWENSVILLE VIC.

Kramer-Witte Barn
County Rt. P
HABS MO-259
HABS MO,37-OWVI.V,1A-
8dr/12ph/5pg/1pc/fr L

GENTRY COUNTY

GENTRYVILLE

Grand River Bridge
Spanning Grand River,on County Rd. No. 459
HAER MO-60
HAER DLC/PP-1992:MO-2
10ph/5pg/1pc L

GREENE COUNTY

ASH GROVE VIC.

Clear Creek Bridge
Spanning Clear Creek on Farm Rd. 33
HAER MO-41
HAER 1989(HAER):14
12ph/14pg/1pc L

Leeper Ford Bridge
Spanning Big Sac River on Farm Rd. 34
HAER MO-62
HAER DLC/PP-1992:MO-2
13ph/17pg/1pc L

SPRINGFIELD

Cooper-Herman House; see
Walnut-Dollison Historic District

825 East Cherry Street (House); see
Walnut-Dollison Historic District

918 East McDaniel Street (House); see
Hampton Wedge Historic District

922 East McDaniel Street (House); see
Hampton Wedge Historic District

926 East McDaniel Street (House); see
Hampton Wedge Historic District

931 East McDaniel Street (House); see
Hampton Wedge Historic District

933 East McDaniel Street (House); see
Hampton Wedge Historic District

942 East McDaniel Street (House); see Hampton Wedge Historic District

948 East McDaniel Street (House); see Hampton Wedge Historic District

954 East McDaniel Street (House); see Hampton Wedge Historic District

737 East Walnut Street (House); see Walnut-Dollison Historic District

743 East Walnut Street (House); see Walnut-Dollison Historic District

815 East Walnut Street (House); see Walnut-Dollison Historic District

903 East Walnut Street (House); see Walnut-Dollison Historic District

Hackney,Garrett W. ,House; see Walnut-Dollison Historic District

Hamel,Albert A. ,House; see Walnut-Dollison Historic District

Hampton Wedge Historic District (918 East McDaniel Street (House))
HABS MO-1253-D
HABS MO,39-SPRIF,5-
2ph/1pg/1pc L

Hampton Wedge Historic District (922 East McDaniel Street (House))
HABS MO-1253-E
HABS MO,39-SPRIF,6-
1ph/1pg/1pc L

Hampton Wedge Historic District (926 East McDaniel Street (House))
HABS MO-1253-F
HABS MO,39-SPRIF,7-
1ph/1pg/1pc L

Hampton Wedge Historic District (931 East McDaniel Street (House))
HABS MO-1253-G
HABS MO,39-SPRIF,8-
1ph/1pg/1pc L

Hampton Wedge Historic District (933 East McDaniel Street (House))
HABS MO-1253-H
HABS MO,39-SPRIF,9-
1ph/1pg/1pc L

Hampton Wedge Historic District (942 East McDaniel Street (House))
HABS MO-1253-I
HABS MO,39-SPRIF,10-
1dr/4ph/6pg/1pc L

Hampton Wedge Historic District (948 East McDaniel Street (House))
HABS MO-1253-J
HABS MO,39-SPRIF,11-
1ph/1pg/1pc L

Hampton Wedge Historic District (954 East McDaniel Street (House))
HABS MO-1253-K
HABS MO,39-SPRIF,12-
1ph/1pg/1pc L

Hampton Wedge Historic District (225 South McAllister Avenue (House))
HABS MO-1253-A
HABS MO,39-SPRIF,2-
1ph/1pg/1pc L

Hampton Wedge Historic District (231 South McAllister Avenue (House))
HABS MO-1253-B
HABS MO,39-SPRIF,3-
1ph/1pg/1pc L

Hampton Wedge Historic District (237 South McAllister Avenue (House))
HABS MO-1253-C
HABS M0,39-SPRIF,4-
1dr/5ph/5pg/1pc/fr L

Hardrick House; see Walnut-Dollison Historic District

Horton,Harry G. ,House; see Walnut-Dollison Historic District

Jewell-Baldwin House; see Walnut-Dollison Historic District

Mack,James B. ,House; see Walnut-Dollison Historic District

Massey,Frank R. ,House; see Walnut-Dollison Historic District

McCray,Daniel,House; see Walnut-Dollison Historic District

McGregor,Arch D. ,House; see Walnut-Dollison Historic District

Roblee,Edward T. ,House; see Walnut-Dollison Historic District

Rose,Charles G. ,House; see Walnut-Dollison Historic District

Shockley Firestone Building
816 Saint Louis St.
HABS MO-1254
HABS MO,39-SPRIF,13-
3ph/1pg/1pc L

Smith,H. M. ,House; see Walnut-Dollison Historic District

221 South Dollison Avenue (House); see Walnut-Dollison Historic District

305 South Dollison Avenue (House); see Walnut-Dollison Historic District

308 South Dollison Avenue (House); see Walnut-Dollison Historic District

321 South Dollison Avenue (House); see Walnut-Dollison Historic District

324-326 South Dollison Avenue (House); see Walnut-Dollison Historic District

328-330 South Dollison Avenue (House); see Walnut-Dollison Historic District

424 South Dollison Avenue (House); see Walnut-Dollison Historic District

428 South Dollison Avenue (House); see Walnut-Dollison Historic District

510 South Dollison Avenue (House); see Walnut-Dollison Historic District

516 South Dollison Avenue (House); see Walnut-Dollison Historic District

521 South Dollison Avenue (House); see Walnut-Dollison Historic District

527 South Dollison Avenue (House); see Walnut-Dollison Historic District

535 South Dollison Avenue (House); see Walnut-Dollison Historic District

828 South Dollison Avenue (House); see Walnut-Dollison Historic District

225 South McAllister Avenue (House); see Hampton Wedge Historic District

231 South McAllister Avenue (House); see Hampton Wedge Historic District

237 South McAllister Avenue (House); see Hampton Wedge Historic District

Tabor House; see Walnut-Dollison Historic District

Walnut-Dollison Historic District
S. Dollison,E. Elm,E. Cherry & E. Walnut Sts.
HABS MO-1252
HABS MO,39-SPRIF,14-
2dr/9ph/11pg/1pc L

Walnut-Dollison Historic District (Cooper-Herman House)
929 E. Walnut St.
HABS MO-1252-HH
HABS MO,39-SPRIF,49-
1dr/8ph/8pg/1pc/fr L

Walnut-Dollison Historic District (825 East Cherry Street (House))
HABS MO-1252-U
HABS MO,39-SPRIF,36-
1ph/1pg/1pc L

Walnut-Dollison Historic District (737 East Walnut Street (House))
HABS MO-1252-W
HABS MO,39-SPRIF,38-
1ph/1pg/1pc L

Walnut-Dollison Historic District (743 East Walnut Street (House))
HABS MO-1252-X
HABS MO,39-SPRIF,39-
2ph/1pg/1pc L

Walnut-Dollison Historic District (815 East Walnut Street (House))
HABS MO-1252-Z
HABS MO,39-SPRIF,41
2ph/2pg/1pc L

Walnut-Dollison Historic District (903 East Walnut Street (House))
HABS MO-1252-EE
HABS MO,39-SPRIF,46-
2ph/1pg/1pc L

Walnut-Dollison Historic District
(Hackney,Garrett W. ,House)
819 E. Walnut St.
HABS MO-1252-AA
HABS MO,39-SPRIF,42-
1dr/7ph/8pg/1pc/fr L

Walnut-Dollison Historic District
(Hamel,Albert A. ,House)
900 E. Elm St.
HABS MO-1252-T
HABS MO,39-SPRIF,35-
1dr/4ph/6pg/1pc/fr L

Walnut-Dollison Historic District
(Hardrick House)
300-302 S. Dollison Ave.
HABS MO-1252-B
HABS MO,39-SPRIF,16-
2ph/2pg/1pc L

Walnut-Dollison Historic District
(Horton,Harry G. ,House)
320 S. Dollison Ave.
HABS MO-1252-F
HABS MO,39-SPRIF,20-
1ph/2pg/1pc L

Walnut-Dollison Historic District
(Jewell-Baldwin House)
913 E. Walnut St.
HABS MO-1252-FF
HABS MO,39-SPRIF,47-
1dr/13ph/8pg/1pc/fr L

Walnut-Dollison Historic District
(Mack,James B. ,House)
832 E. Elm St.
HABS MO-1252-R
HABS MO,39-SPRIF,33-
2ph/2pg/1pc L

Walnut-Dollison Historic District
(Massey,Frank R. ,House)
838 E. Walnut St.
HABS MO-1252-CC
HABS MO,92/AUG.3-
2ph/2pg/1pc L

Walnut-Dollison Historic District
(McCray,Daniel,House)
803 E. Walnut St.
HABS MO-1252-Y
HABS MO,39-SPRIF,40-
2ph/1pg/1pc L

Walnut-Dollison Historic District
(McGregor,Arch D. ,House)
839 E. Walnut St.
HABS MO-1252-DD
HABS MO,39-SPRIF,45-
3ph/2pg/1pc L

Walnut-Dollison Historic District
(Roblee,Edward T. ,House)
901 E. Cherry St.
HABS MO-1252-V
HABS MO,39-SPRIF,37-
1pg L

Walnut-Dollison Historic District
(Rose,Charles G. ,House)
919 E. Walnut St.
HABS MO-1252-GG
HABS MO,39-SPRIF,48-
1dr/7ph/6pg/1pc/fr L

Walnut-Dollison Historic District
(Smith,H. M. ,House)
809 E. Walnut St.
HABS MO-1252-II
HABS MO,39-SPRIF,50-
3ph/2pg/1pc L

Walnut-Dollison Historic District (221 South Dollison Avenue (House))
HABS MO-1252-A
HABS MO,39-SPRIF,15-
1ph/1pg/1pc L

Walnut-Dollison Historic District (305 South Dollison Avenue (House))
HABS MO-1252-C
HABS MO,39-SPRIF,17-
3ph/2pg/1pc L

Walnut-Dollison Historic District (308 South Dollison Avenue (House))
HABS MO-1252-D
HABS MO,39-SPRIF,18-
3ph/1pg/1pc L

Walnut-Dollison Historic District (321 South Dollison Avenue (House))
HABS MO-1252-G
HABS MO,39-SPRIF,21-
2ph/2pg/1pc L

Walnut-Dollison Historic District
(324-326 South Dollison Avenue (House))
HABS MO-1252-H
HABS MO,39-SPRIF,22-
1ph/1pg/1pc L

Walnut-Dollison Historic District
(328-330 South Dollison Avenue (House))
HABS MO-1252-I
HABS MO,39-SPRIF,23-
1ph/1pg/1pc L

Walnut-Dollison Historic District (424 South Dollison Avenue (House))
HABS MO-1252-J
HABS 1986(HABS):9
1ph/1pg/1pc L

Walnut-Dollison Historic District (428 South Dollison Avenue (House))
HABS MO-1252-K
HABS MO,39-SPRIF,25-
2ph/1pg/1pc L

Walnut-Dollison Historic District (510 South Dollison Avenue (House))
HABS MO-1252-L
HABS MO,39-SPRIF,26-
2ph/1pg/1pc L

Walnut-Dollison Historic District (516 South Dollison Avenue (House))
HABS MO-1252-N
HABS MO,39-SPRIF,29-
1ph/1pg/1pc L

Walnut-Dollison Historic District (521 South Dollison Avenue (House))
HABS MO-1252-O
HABS MO,39-SPRIF,30-
1ph/1pg/1pc L

Walnut-Dollison Historic District (527 South Dollison Avenue (House))
HABS MO-1252-P
HABS MO,39-SPRIF,31-
1ph/1pg/1pc L

Walnut-Dollison Historic District (535 South Dollison Avenue (House))
HABS MO-1252-Q
HABS MO,39-SPRIF,32-
2ph/1pg/1pc L

Walnut-Dollison Historic District (828 South Dollison Avenue (House))
HABS MO-1252-BB
HABS MO,39-SPRIF,43-
2ph/1pc L

Walnut-Dollison Historic District
(Tabor House)
315 S. Dollison Ave.
HABS MO-1252-E
HABS MO,39-SPRIF,19-
2ph/2pg/1pc L

Walnut-Dollison Historic District
(Watson,Gustavus A. ,House)
515 S. Dollison Ave.
HABS MO-1252-M
HABS MO,39-SPRIF,27-
2ph/2pg/1pc L

Walnut-Dollison Historic District
(Watson,Gustavus A. ,House)
836 E. Elm St.
HABS MO-1252-S
HABS MO,39-SPRIF,34-
4ph/2pg/1pc L

Watson,Gustavus A. ,House; see Walnut-Dollison Historic District

SPRINGFIELD VIC.

Bridge No. 2415
Spanning Wilson Creek at Farm Rd. 156
HAER MO-67
9ph/23pg/1pc H

James River Bridge
.6 Mi. N. of Greene-Christian County Line
HAER MO-44
HAER 1989(HAER):14
13ph/16pg/1pc L

Ray House (Wilson's Creek Battlefield National Park)
HABS MO-1201
HABS MO,39-SPRIF.V,1A-
5dr L

Wilson's Creek Battlefield National Park; see Ray House

HENRY COUNTY

CLINTON

Truman, Harry S., Dam & Reservoir Bldgs. Inventory
HABS MO-1287
HABS MO,42-CLINT,2-
2pg/fr L

CLINTON VIC.

Bethlehem Baptist Church
Rt. AA & 35 Vic.
HABS MO-1227
HABS MO,42-CLINT.V,2-
9ph/8pg/1pc L

Burkhart,Peter,Farm
Rt. EE
HABS MO-1228
HABS MO,42-CLINT.V,3-
7ph/8pg/1pc L

Chastain,Jeremiah,Farm
Tightwad Vic.
HABS MO-1230
HABS MO,42-CLINT.V,5-
6ph/6pg/1pc L

French,George,Farm
Rt. AA & 35 Vic.
HABS MO-1229
HABS MO,42-CLINT.V,4-
7ph/6pg/1pc L

House (Tract #2607 B)
HABS MO-1231
HABS MO,42-CLINT.V,6-
5ph/6pg/1pc L

Noble,Joseph,House
Rt. EE in LaDue
HABS MO-1249
HABS MO,42-CLINT.V,1-
6dr/5ph/1pc L

Tract #2607 B; see House

DEEPWATER

House
HABS MO-1275
HABS MO,42-DEEP,1-
1ph/1pc L

Second & Front Streets (House)
HABS MO-1265
HABS MO,42-DEEP,2-
2ph/1pc L

DEEPWATER VIC.

French,John,Barn
S. Grand River Vic.
HABS MO-1245-A
HABS MO,42-DEEP.V,5A-
5dr/5ph/1pc/fr L

French,John,Farm
S. Grand River
HABS MO-1245
HABS MO,42-DEEP.V,5-
4dr/8ph/9pg/1pc L

French,John,Outbuilding
S. Grand River Vic.
HABS MO-1245-B
HABS MO,42-DEEP.V,5B-
3ph/1pc L

Gaskill,Moses,House
Rt. W Vic.
HABS MO-1244
HABS MO,42-DEEP.V,4-
4dr/9ph/5pg/1pc L

House (Tract #11142)
Rd. E
HABS MO-1232
HABS MO,42-DEEP.V,1
7ph/7pg/2pc L

Lloyd,William C. ,House (Tract #11627)
Rd. E
HABS MO-1233
HABS MO,42-DEEP.V,2-
6ph/6pg/1pc L

Rickson House; see Stewart-Rickson House

Stewart-Rickson House (Rickson House)
Rd. E. Vic.
HABS MO-1234
HABS MO,42-DEEP.V,3-
7ph/6pg/1pc L

Tract #11142; see House

Tract #11627; see Lloyd,William C. ,House

GAINES VIC.

Surprise School Bridge
Spanning S. Grand River
HAER MO-4
HAER MO,42-GAIN.V,1-
1ph/1pc L

HICKORY COUNTY

???

Concrete Ford
Spanning Little Mill Creek
HABS MO-1267
HABS MO,43- ,1-
1ph/1pc L

Farm
HABS MO-1276
HABS MO,43- ,2-
1ph/1pc L

School
HABS MO-1269
HABS MO,43- ,3 -
2ph/1pc L

Silo
HABS MO-1268
HABS MO,43- ,4
2ph/1pc L

HERMITAGE

Jail
Courthouse Square
HABS MO-1266
HABS MO,43-HERMI,1-
1ph/1pc L

HERMITAGE VIC.

William's Bend Bridge
Spanning Pomme de Terre River
HAER MO-20
HAER MO-43-HERM.V, 1-
2ph/1pc L

HOWARD COUNTY

ARMSTRONG VIC.

Denny House
HABS MO-1445
HABS MO,45-ARM.V, 1-
1ph/1pg/1pc L

ESTILL VIC.

Estill,James R. ,House
HABS MO-1446
HABS MO,45-EST.V,1-
3ph/1pg/1pc/fr L

FAYETTE

Boon,Hampton,House
HABS MO-1438
HABS MO,45-FAY,1-
5ph/1pg/1pc L

Leonard,Judge Abiel,House
HABS MO-1439
HABS MO,45-FAY,2-
5ph/1pg/1pc/fr L

Leonard,Judge Abiel,Outbuildings
HABS MO-1439-A
HABS MO,45-FAY,2A-
2ph/1pg/1pc L

St. Mary's Episcopal Church
HABS MO-1436
HABS MO,45-FAY,3-
1ph/1pg/1pc L

Wright Building
Public Square
HABS MO-1437
HABS MO,45-FAY,4-
3ph/1pg/1pc L

FAYETTE VIC.

Condron,John,Outbuildings
HABS MO-1441
HABS MO,45-FAY.V,2A-
3ph/1pg/1pc/fr L

Hughes House
HABS MO-1440
HABS MO,45-FAY.V,3-
10ph/1pg/1pc/fr L

Jackson,Claiborne Fox,House
HABS MO-1444
HABS MO,45-FAY.V,4-
1ph/1pg/1pc L

Jackson,Stephen,House
U. S. Rt. 5
HABS MO-1443
HABS MO,45-FAY.V,5-
3ph/1pg/1pc/fr L

Kingsbury,Noah,House (Talbot,Dr. John,House)
HABS MO-1489
HABS MO,45-FAY.V,6-
1ph/1pg/1pc/fr L

Lilac Hill (Morrison House)
HABS MO-239
HABS MO,45-FAY.V,1-
19ph/1pg/1pc L

Morrison House; see Lilac Hill

Mount Moriah Church
HABS MO-1487
HABS MO,45-FAY.V,9-
1ph/1pg/1pc L

Spence House
HABS MO-1442
HABS MO,45-FAY.V,7-
3ph/1pg/1pc L

Talbot,Dr. John,House; see Kingsbury,Noah,House

Walcott House
Hwys. 3 & 5
HABS MO-1488
HABS MO,45-FAY.V,8-
1ph/1pg/1pc L

GLASGOW

Audsley House; see Layman,Monte,House

Audsley Undertaking Building
HABS MO-1461
HABS MO,45-GLASG,1-
1ph/1pg/1pc L

Bowen House
HABS MO-1463
HABS MO,45-GLASG,3-
3ph/1pg/1pc/fr L

Chicago & Alton Railway Bridge
HABS MO-1465
HABS MO,45-GLASG,4A-
1ph/1pg/1pc L

Glasgow City Hall
HABS MO-1466
HABS MO,45-GLASG,6-
2ph/1pg/1pc L

Glasgow Female Seminary Building
HABS MO-1469
HABS MO,45-GLASG,7-
1ph/1pg/1pc/fr L

Grisham House
HABS MO-1467
HABS MO,45-GLASG,8-
1ph/1pg/1pc/fr L

Heminway House
HABS MO-1470
HABS MO,45-GLASG,9-
1ph/1pg/1pc L

House,Frame
HABS MO-1468
HABS MO,45-GLASG,11-
1ph/1pc L

Layman,Monte,House (Audsley House)
HABS MO-1460
HABS MO,45-GLASG,12-
1ph/1pg/1pc L

Lewis Library
HABS MO-1471
HABS MO,45-GLASG,13-
6ph/1pg/1pc/fr L

Main Street (Commercial Buildings)
HABS MO-1472
HABS MO,45-GLASG,14-
2ph/1pc/fr L

Methodist Church
HABS MO-1473
HABS MO,45-GLASG,15-
1ph/1pg/1pc/fr L

Montague House
HABS MO-1474
HABS MO,45-GLASG,16-
6ph/1pg/1pc/fr L

Presbyterian Church
HABS MO-1476
HABS MO,45-GLASG,17-
1ph/1pg/1pc L

Pritchett School Institute
HABS MO-1477
HABS MO,45-GLASG,18-
1ph/1pg/1pc L

Renne House
HABS MO-1478
HABS MO,45-GLASG,19-
3ph/1pg/1pc L

Swinney,Captain W. D. ,House
HABS MO-1475
HABS MO,45-GLASG,20-
2ph/1pg/1pc/fr L

Vaughan,Doctor Isaac,House
HABS MO-1479
HABS MO,45-GLASG,21-
1ph/1pg/1pc L

Weinand House
HABS MO-1480
HABS MO,45-GLASG,10-
3ph/1pc L

GLASGOW VIC.

Clark,John B. ,House
HABS MO-1481
HABS HABS,MO,45-GLASG.V,10-
5ph/1pg/1pc L

Earickson-Harrison House
HABS MO-1482
HABS MO,45-GLASG,V,4-
5ph/1pg/1pc/fr L

Eddins House
HABS MO-1484
HABS MO,45-GLASG.V,5-
14ph/1pg/1pc/fr L

Harrison,John,House
HABS MO-1485
HABS MO,45-GLASG.V,6-
1ph/1pg/1pc L

Jackson,John,House
HABS MO-241
HABS MO,45-GLASG.V,2-
15ph/1pg/1pc/fr L

Lewis House
HABS MO-1486
HABS MO,45-GLASG.V,7-
1ph/1pg/1pc L

Sylvan Villa
Fayette Rd.
HABS MO-240
HABS MO,45-GLASG.V,1-
4ph/1pg L

Turner Barn
HABS MO-242-A
HABS MO,45-GLASG.V,3A-
1ph/1pg/1pc L

Turner,Talton,House
HABS MO-242
HABS MO,45-GLASG.V,3-
18ph/1pg/1pc/fr L

NEW FRANKLIN

Chilton House
Missouri Ave.
HABS MO-237
HABS MO,45-NEFRA,1-
10ph/1pg/1pc/fr L

NEW FRANKLIN VIC.

Boggs,Thomas C. ,House
HABS MO-1451
HABS MO,45-NEFRA.V,3-
2ph/1pg/1pc/fr L

Boonville Bridge
(See COOPER COUNTY,BOONVILLE for documentation)
HAER MO-80
L

Burckhardt,Nicholas S. ,House
HABS MO-243
HABS MO,45-NEFRA.V,2-
19ph/2pg/1pc/fr L

Callaway,Stephen,House
HABS MO-1452
HABS MO,45-NEFRA.V,4-
6ph/1pg/1pc/fr L

Carson,William,House
HABS MO-1490
HABS MO,45-NEFRA.V,12-
7ph/1pg/1pc/fr L

Carson,William,Outbuilding
HABS MO-1490-A
HABS MO,45-NEFRA.V,12A-
1ph/1pg/1pc L

Crews House
HABS MO-1494
HABS MO,45-NEFRA.V,13-
4ph/1pg/1pc/fr L

Franklin Academy
HABS MO-1449
HABS MO,45-NEFRA.V,14-
2ph/1pg/1pc/fr L

Herndon,John G. ,House
HABS MO-1453
HABS MO,45-NEFRA.V,5-
5ph/1pg/1pc L

Hickman,Thomas,House
HABS MO-1454
HABS MO,45-NEFRA.V,11-
6ph/1pg/1pc/fr L

Hocker House
HABS MO-1455
HABS MO,45-NEFRA.V,6-
12ph/1pg/1pc/fr L

Jordan House (Turner,Ephraim,House)
HABS MO-1456
HABS MO,45-NEFRA.V,7-
3ph/1pg/1pc L

Kingsbury House (Scott,William,House)
HABS MO-238
HABS MO,45-NEFRA.V,1-
12ph/1pg/1pc/fr L

Kinney's Folly; see Rivercene

Moore's Landing
HABS MO-1457
HABS MO,45-NEFRA.V,8-
4ph/1pg/1pc/fr L

Ray,James,House
HABS MO-1458
HABS MO,45-NEFRA.V,9-
3ph/1pg/1pc/fr L

Rivercene (Kinney's Folly)
HABS MO-1459
HABS MO,45-NEFRA.V,10-
4ph/1pg/1pc/fr L

Scott,William,House; see Kingsbury House

Turner,Ephraim,House; see Jordan House

PETERSBURG VIC.

Cooper Cemetery
HABS MO-1450
HABS MO,45-PET.V,1-
2ph/1pg/1pc L

JACKSON COUNTY

INDEPENDENCE

Adkins Cabin (Aiken Cabin)
107 W. Kansas Ave.
HABS MO-219
HABS MO,48-INDEP,1-
1ph/1pg L

Aiken Cabin; see Adkins Cabin

Haukenberry House; see Noland-Haukenberry House

Jackson County Courthouse
107-109 W. Kansas Ave.
HABS MO-220
HABS MO,48-INDEP,2-
1ph/1pg L

Lake City Army Ammunition Plant
HAER MO-22
HAER MO,48-INDEP,5-
63pg/fr L

Noland-Haukenberry House
(Noland,Joseph Tiford,House; Haukenberry House)
216 N. Delaware St.
HABS MO-1911
H

Noland,Joseph Tiford,House; see Noland-Haukenberry House

Truman,Harry S,House (Truman,Harry S,National Historic Site)
219 N. Delaware St.
HABS MO-1175
HABS MO,48-INDEP,3-
20ph/3pc/10ct L

Truman,Harry S,House,Carriage House (Truman,Harry S,National Historic Site)
219 N. Delaware St.
HABS MO-1175-A
HABS MO-48-INDEP,3A-
2ph/1pc L

Truman,Harry S,National Historic Site; see Truman,Harry S,House

Truman,Harry S,National Historic Site; see Truman,Harry S,House,Carriage House

Vaile,Harvey M.,Mansion
1500 N. Liberty St.
HABS MO-1861
HABS MO,48-INDEP,4-
14ph/2pg/1pc/2ct L

Wallace,Frank,House
601 W. Truman Rd.
HABS MO-1909
H

Wallace,George,House
605 W. Truman Rd.
HABS MO-1910
H

KANSAS CITY

A. S. B. Bridge; see Armour,Swift,Burlington Bridge

Armour,Swift,Burlington Bridge (A. S. B. Bridge)
HAER MO-2
HAER MO,48-KANCI,16-
92ph/16pg/6pc L

Bruner,Roland E.,House; see Mineral Hall

Bullene,Moore,Emery & Company Building (Emery,Bird & Thayer Building)
1016-1018 Grand Ave.
HABS MO-138
HABS MO8-KANCI,7-
29ph/5pg/2pc/fr L

Civic Auditorium; see Municipal Auditorium

Conklin House
1207 Pennsylvania Ave. (Quality Hill Hist. Dist.)
HABS MO-1872
HABS 1989(HABS):12
6ph/3pg/1pc L

Corinthian Hall; see Long,R.A.,House

Corrigan,Bernard,House
1200 W. 55th St.
HABS MO-1862
HABS MO,48-KANCI,6-
15ph/5pg/1pc/2ct L

Emery,Bird & Thayer Building; see Bullene,Moore,Emery & Company Building

First Presbyterian Church
Pennyslvania St. ,Westport Vic.
HABS MO-31-18
HABS MO,48-KANCI,2-
3dr/1ph/1pg L

Harris,John,House
4000 Baltimore Ave.
HABS MO-31-16
HABS MO,48-KANCI,1-
11dr/5ph/1pg/1pc L

Huston,William F.,House
1910 Woodland Ave.
HABS MO-1261
HABS 1989(HABS):12
5ph/4pg/1pc/fr L

Kansas City City Hall
414 E. Twelfth St.
HABS MO-266
HABS MO,48-KANCI,4-
21ph/3pg/1pc L

Kansas City General Hospital
2315 Locust
HABS MO-251
HABS MO,48-KANCI,8-
34ph/14pg/2pc L

Kansas City Museum of History & Science; see Long,R.A.,House

Long,R.A.,House (Corinthian Hall; Kansas City Museum of History & Science)
3218 Gladstone Blvd.
HABS MO-1863
HABS MO,48-KANCI,9-
14ph/4pg/1pc/1ct L

Majors,Alexander,House
8145 State Line
HABS MO-1801
HABS MO,48-KANCI,5-
2ph/1pg/1pc L

Miller Plaza
9-17 Miller Plaza including 3225 Main St.
HABS MO-1892
10ph/24pg/1pc H

Miller Plaza,12-14 Miller Plaza
HABS MO-1892-B
5ph/2pg/1pc H

Miller Plaza,16-18 Miller Plaza
HABS MO-1892-C
5ph/2pg/1pc H

Miller Plaza,20-22 Miller Plaza
HABS MO-1892-D
5ph/2pg/1pc H

Miller Plaza,23-25 Miller Plaza
HABS MO-1892-G
4ph/2pg/1pc H

Miller Plaza,31-33 Miller Plaza
HABS MO-1892-F
3ph/2pg/1pc H

Miller Plaza,3225 Main Street
HABS MO-1892-A
2ph/3pg/1pc H

Miller Plaza,35-37 Miller Plaza
HABS MO-1892-E
6ph/3pg/1pc H

Miller Plaza,9 Miller Plaza
HABS MO-1892-H
5ph/3pg/1pc H

Mineral Hall (Bruner,Roland E.,House; Ownby House)
4340 Oak St.
HABS MO-1864
HABS MO,48-KANCI,10-
4ph/2pg/1pc/1ct L

Municipal Auditorium (Civic Auditorium)
1310 Wyandotte St.
HABS MO-136
HABS MO,48-KANCI,11-
27ph/1pg/2pc/fr L

New York Life Insurance Building
20 W. North St.
HABS MO-18
HABS MO,48-KANCI,12-
20ph/10pg/2pc L

Ownby House; see Mineral Hall

4533-39 Roanoke Parkway,Apartment
4533-39 Roanoke Parkway
HABS MO-1891
8ph/11pg/1pc H

Rockford School
Raytown & Longview Rd.
HABS MO-1224
HABS MO,48-KANCI,3-
5dr/5ph/10pg/fr L

Rockhill Road Bridge
Spanning Brush Creek btw. Forty-eighth & Volker
HAER MO-58
HAER 1991(HAER):9
13ph/11pg/1pc L

Scarritt Building & Arcade
Ninth St. & Grand Ave. , & 819 Walnut St.
HABS MO-263
HABS MO,48-KANCI,13-
18ph/2pc/fr L

Standard Theatre
300 W. Twelfth St.
HABS MO-264
HABS MO,48-KANCI,14-
12ph/1pg/1pc/fr L

Warner Plaza
Both sides of Warner Plaza b/t Main & Warwick
HABS MO-1893
1dr/9ph/22pg/1pc/fr H

Warner Plaza,12 Warner Plaza
HABS MO-1893-C
5ph/2pg/1pc H

Warner Plaza,22 Warner Plaza
HABS MO-1893-D
5ph/3pg/1pc H

Warner Plaza,23 Warner Plaza
HABS MO-1893-J
5ph/3pg/1pc H

Warner Plaza,28 Warner Plaza
HABS MO-1893-E
5ph/3pg/1pc H

Warner Plaza,29 Warner Plaza
HABS MO-1893-I
5ph/2pg/1pc H

Warner Plaza,3245 Main Street
HABS MO-1893-A
4ph/4pg/1pc H

Warner Plaza,3251 Main Street
HABS MO-1893-L
4ph/4pg/1pc H

Warner Plaza,37 Warner Plaza
HABS MO-1893-H
5ph/3pg/1pc H

Warner Plaza,42 Warner Plaza
HABS MO-1893-F
6ph/4pg/1pc H

Warner Plaza,43 Warner Plaza
HABS MO-1893-G
6ph/4pg/1pc H

Warner Plaza,8 Warner Plaza
HABS MO-1893-B
3ph/2pg/1pc H

Warner Plaza,9 Warner Plaza
HABS MO-1893-K
6ph/2pg/1pc H

Wornall House
146 West 61 Terrace
HABS MO-267
HABS MO,48-KANCI,15-
6dr L

LEES SUMMIT

Farm Row; see Longview Farm,Workers' Cottages

Long,Robert A. ,House; see Longview Farm

Longview Farm (Long,Robert A. ,House)
Longview Rd.
HABS MO-1222
HABS MO,48-LESUM,1-
2dr/4ph/37pg/fr L

Longview Farm,Assistant Manager's House
HABS MO-1222-43
HABS MO,48-LESUM,1/43-
5dr/9ph/6pg/2ct/fr L

Longview Farm,Bandstand
Longview Rd.
HABS MO-1222-18
HABS MO,48-LESUM,1/18-
3ph L

Longview Farm,Boarding House (Longview Farm,Hotel)
HABS MO-1222-33
HABS MO,48-LESUM,1/33-
7dr/20ph/6pg/3ct/fr L

Longview Farm,Brood Mare Barn
Longview Rd.
HABS MO-1222-38
HABS MO,48-LESUM,1/38-
5ph L

Longview Farm,Brood Mare Manager's House
Longview Rd.
HABS MO-1222-39
HABS MO,48-LESUM,1/39-
3ph L

Longview Farm,Chapel
Longview Rd.
HABS MO-1222-6
HABS MO,48-LESUM,1/6-
12ph/2ct L

Longview Farm,Colt Barn
Longview Rd.
HABS MO-1222-34
HABS MO,48-LESUM,1/34-
1ph L

Longview Farm,Dairy Manager's House
Longview Rd.
HABS MO-1222-23
HABS MO,48-LESUM,1/23-
3ph L

Longview Farm,Duplex; see Longview Farm,Sunny Slope Farmhouse

Longview Farm,Entrance Gates
Longview Rd.
HABS MO-1222-5
HABS MO,48-LESUM,1/5-
2ph/1ct L

Longview Farm,Garage,Apartment & Powerhouse
HABS MO-1222-26
HABS MO,48-LESUM,1/26-
7dr/16ph/9pg/4ct L

Longview Farm,Gate Lodge Number 1
Longview Rd.
HABS MO-1222-46
HABS MO,48-LESUM,1/46-
10ph L

Longview Farm,Gate Lodge Number 2
HABS MO-1222-47
HABS MO,48-LESUM,1/47-
2dr/9ph/6pg/fr L

Longview Farm,General Manager's House
HABS MO-1222-42
HABS MO,48-LESUM,1/42-
5dr/9ph/7pg/fr L

Longview Farm,Grandstand & Clubhouse
Longview Rd.
HABS MO-1222-17
HABS MO,48-LESUM,1/17-
18ph L

Longview Farm,Greenhouse Manager's House
HABS MO-1222-27
HABS MO,48-LESUM,1/27-
2dr/6ph/5pg/1ct/fr L

Longview Farm,Greenhouses
HABS MO-1222-25
HABS MO,48-LESUM,1/25-
7dr/9ph/4pg/fr L

Longview Farm,Hog & Sale Barn
Longview Rd.
HABS MO-1222-35
HABS MO,48-LESUM,1/35-
1ph L

Longview Farm,Hog Manager's House
Longview Rd.
HABS MO-1222-36
HABS MO,48-LESUM,1/36-
7ph/1ct L

Longview Farm,Horse Trainer's House
Longview Rd.
HABS MO-1222-40
HABS MO,48-LESUM,1/40-
1ph L

Longview Farm,Hospital Barn
Longview Rd.
HABS MO-1222-9
HABS MO,48-LESUM,1/9-
4ph/1ct L

Longview Farm,Hotel; see Longview Farm,Boarding House

Longview Farm,Implement Shed
Longview Rd.
HABS MO-1222-30
HABS MO,48-LESUM,1/30-
7ph L

Longview Farm,Main Residence
Longview Rd.
HABS MO-1222-1
HABS MO,48-LESUM,1/1-
22ph/1ct L

Longview Farm,Manure Pit
Longview Rd.
HABS MO-1222-24
HABS MO,48-LESUM,1/24-
2ph L

Longview Farm,North Dairy Barn
Longview Rd.
HABS MO-1222-21
HABS MO,48-LESUM,1/21-
21ph/3ct/fr L

Longview Farm,Office
Longview Rd.
HABS MO-1222-8
HABS MO,48-LESUM,1/8-
10ph/fr L

Longview Farm,Paint,Carpentry & Blacksmith Shop
Longview Rd.
HABS MO-1222-31
HABS MO,48-LESUM,1/31-
14ph L

Longview Farm,Pump House
Longview Rd.
HABS MO-1222-11
HABS MO,48-LESUM,1/11-
3ph L

Longview Farm,Saddle Horse Barn
Longview Rd.
HABS MO-1222-16
HABS MO,48-LESUM,1/16-
1ph L

Longview Farm,Saddle Horse Manager's House
Longview Rd.
HABS MO-1222-19
HABS MO,48-LESUM,1/19-
3ph/fr L

Longview Farm,Show Horse Barn
Longview Rd.
HABS MO-1222-14
HABS MO,48-LESUM,1/14-
6dr/27ph/3pg/5ct/fr L

Longview Farm,South Dairy Barn-Milkhouse
Longview Rd.
HABS MO-1222-20
HABS MO,48-LESUM,1/20-
25ph/8ct L

Longview Farm,Stallion Barn
Longview Rd.
HABS MO-1222-15
HABS MO,48-LESUM,1/15-
3ph/1ct L

Longview Farm,Summer Camp
Longview Rd.
HABS MO-1222-13
HABS MO,48-LESUM,1/13-
1ph L

Longview Farm,Sunny Slope Farmhouse (Longview Farm,Duplex)
Longview Rd.
HABS MO-1222-44
HABS MO,48-LESUM,1/44-
6ph L

Longview Farm,Water Tank
Longview Rd.
HABS MO-1222-7
HABS MO,48-LESUM,1/7-
2ph/1ct L

Longview Farm,Well House
Longview Rd.
HABS MO-1222-3
HABS MO,48-LESUM,1/3-
3ph L

Longview Farm,Work Horse Barn
HABS MO-1222-29
HABS MO,48-LESUM,1/29-
10dr/27ph/6pg/4ct/fr L

Longview Farm,Worker's Residence
Longview Rd.
HABS MO-1222-45
HABS MO,48-LESUM,1/45-
2ph L

Longview Farm,Workers' Cottages (Farm Row)
HABS MO-1222-41
HABS MO,48-LESUM,1/41-
1dr/14ph/6pg/fr L

Longview Farms,Pergola
Longview Rd.
HABS MO-1222-4
HABS MO,48-LESUM,1/4-
7ph/4ct L

JASPER COUNTY

CARTHAGE VIC.

American Mill Bridge
Spanning Center Creek,intersection Rts. H & 71 vic
HAER MO-25
HAER HAER MO,49-CAR.V,1-
16ph/12pg/1pc L

JOPLIN

Connor Hotel,The
324 Main St.
HABS MO-1202
HABS MO,49-JOPL,1-
21ph/5pg L

JEFFERSON COUNTY

BARNHART

Cedars,The (O'Fallon House)
HABS MO-198
HABS MO,50-BARN,1-
2ph/1pg/1pc/fr L

Cedars,The,Slave Cabin (O'Fallon Slave Cabin)
HABS MO-198-A
HABS MO,50-BARN,1A-
2ph/1pg/1pc/fr L

Cedars,The,Smokehouse (O'Fallon Smokehouse)
HABS MO-198-B
HABS MO,50-BARN,1B-
1ph/1pc/fr L

O'Fallon House; see Cedars,The

O'Fallon Slave Cabin; see Cedars,The,Slave Cabin

Documentation: **ct** color transparencies **dr** measured drawings **fr** field records
pc photograph captions **pg** pages of text **ph** photographs

O'Fallon Smokehouse; see Cedars,The,Smokehouse

BARNHART VIC.

McQuire Antique Shop
U. S. Rt. 67
HABS MO-1492
HABS MO,50-BARN.V,1
1ph/1pc L

BECK

Pioneer Log House
HABS MO-194
HABS MO,50-BECK,1-
2ph/1pg L

CRYSTAL CITY VIC.

Kennett Castle; see Selma Hall

Selma Hall (Kennett Castle)
HABS MO-1493
HABS MO,50-CRYCI,1-
24ph/1pg/2pc/fr L

DANBY

Brook,Capt. ,Farm
Rt. 25
HABS MO-1101
HABS MO,50-DANB,1-
1ph/1pg L

GOLDMAN VIC.

Sandy Creek Bridge
HABS MO-1156
HABS MO,50-GOLD.V,1-
2ph/4pg L

HERCULANEUM

McMurray House
HABS MO-1100
HABS MO,50-HERC,1-
1ph/1pg L

KIMMSWICK

Hermann-Oheim House
Fourth & Market Sts.
HABS MO-1132
HABS MO,50-KIMWI,1-
6dr/13ph/3pg/1pc L

Windsor Harbor Road Bridge
Spanning Rock Creek on Windsor Harbor Rd.
HAER MO-63
14ph/5pg/1pc L

MORSE MILL VIC.

Klondike Road Bridge (Votaw Road Bridge)
Spanning Big River at Klondike Road
HAER MO-71
12ph/6pg/1pc L

Votaw Road Bridge; see Klondike Road Bridge

PEVELY

Moss,Milton,House
Pleasant Valley
HABS MO-197
HABS MO,50-PEV,3-
1ph/1pg L

Ziegler,Capt. ,House
HABS MO-195
HABS MO,50-PEV,1-
1ph/1pg L

PEVELY VIC.

Ashley House; see Greystone

Greystone (Ashley House)
HABS MO-1133
HABS MO,50-PEV.V,1-
12dr/15ph/1pg/1pc/fr L

Harrington Log Cabin
HABS MO-196
HABS MO,50-PEV,2-
13ph/2pg/1pc/fr L

VINELAND VIC.

Vineland Road Bridge; see Wilson Hollow Road Bridge

Wilson Hollow Road Bridge (Vineland Road Bridge)
Spanning Big River at Wilson Hollow Rd.
HAER MO-72
11ph/7pg/1pc L

LAFAYETTE COUNTY

DOVER

Christian Church
HABS MO-1496
HABS MO,54-DOV,1-
1ph/1pg/1pc L

House,Brick
HABS MO-1495
HABS MO,54-DOV,2-
1ph/1pg/1pc/fr L

Methodist Church
HABS MO-1497
HABS MO,54-DOV,3-
2ph/1pg/1pc L

LEXINGTON

Anderson House; see Anderson,Col. William Oliver,House

Anderson,Col. William Oliver,House (Anderson House)
Civil War Battle of Lexington State Park
HABS MO-224
HABS MO,54-LEX,1-
14dr/17ph/1pg/1pc/fr L

Bates House
HABS MO-1503
HABS MO,54-LEX,8-
2ph/1pc L

Battlefield Monument
HABS MO-1511
HABS MO,54-LEX,9-
1ph/1pg/1pc L

Carr-O'Malley House
Highland Ave.
HABS MO-236
HABS MO,54-LEX,7-
1ph L

Cemetery
HABS MO-1510
HABS MO,54-LEX,10-
11ph/1pg/1pc/fr L

Chadwick House; see McCausland,W. G. ,House

Childs House
HABS MO-1506
HABS MO,54-LEX,11-
1ph/1pc L

Christ Episcopal Church
Thirteenth & Franklin Sts.
HABS MO-235
HABS MO,54-LEX,6-
6ph/1pg/1pc/fr L

Cumberland Presbyterian Church
HABS MO-227
HABS MO,54-LEX,4-
1ph L

House
HABS MO-1508
HABS MO,54-LEX,12-
1ph/1pg/1pc L

House,Brick
HABS MO-1504
HABS MO,54-LEX,13-
1ph/1pg/1pc/fr L

House,Brick
HABS MO-1505
HABS MO,54-LEX,14-
1ph/1pc L

House,Frame
HABS MO-1507
HABS MO,54-LEX,15-
1ph/1pc L

Lafayette County Courthouse
HABS MO-228
HABS MO,54-LEX,5-
9ph/1pg/1pc/fr L

Masonic College Memorial
College Park
HABS MO-1515
HABS MO,54-LEX,16-
2ph/1pg/1pc L

McCausland,W. G. ,House (Chadwick House)
HABS MO-226
HABS MO,54-LEX,3-
6ph/1pc/fr L

Pioneer Mother Monument
HABS MO-1513
HABS MO,54-LEX,17-
1ph/1pg/1pc L

Pomeroy-Pristine House
1611 South St.
HABS MO-225
HABS MO,54-LEX,2-
9ph/1pg/1pc/fr L

Public Library & Historical Association
112 S. Thirteenth St.
HABS MO-1514
HABS MO,54-LEX,18-
2ph/1pg/1pc/fr L

Russell House
HABS MO-1509
HABS MO,54-LEX,19-
4ph/1pg/1pc/fr L

Russell,Majors,& Waddell Monument
College Park
HABS MO-1512
HABS MO,54-LEX,20-
1ph/1pg/1pc L

LEXINGTON VIC.

Aull House
HABS MO-234
HABS MO,54-LEX.V,2-
7ph/1pg/1pc/fr L

Aull Ice House
HABS MO-234-B
HABS MO,54-LEX.V,2B-
1ph/1pg/1pc L

Aull Outbuilding
HABS MO-234-A
HABS MO,54-LEX.V,2A-
1ph/1pg/1pc L

Catron,John,House
HABS MO-1517
HABS MO,54-LEX.V,3
5ph/1pg/1pc/fr L

Courthouse Gates
HABS MO-1516
HABS MO,54-LEX.V,4-
2ph/1pg/1pc L

Hicklin House
HABS MO-1518
HABS MO,54-LEX.V,5-
2ph/1pg/1pc/fr L

House
U. S. Rt. 24
HABS MO-1520
HABS MO,54-LEX.V,6-
1ph/1pg/1pc L

House,Frame
HABS MO-1519
HABS MO,54-LEX.V,7-
4ph/1pc L

Limerick's Folly (Linwood Lawn)
HABS MO-229
HABS MO,54-LEX.V,1-
13ph/1pg/1pc/fr L

Linwood Lawn; see Limerick's Folly

WAVERLY

Buford,Manville,House
HABS MO-1501
HABS MO,54-WAVE,1-
2ph/1pg/1pc L

Groves House
HABS MO-1502
HABS MO,54-WAVE,2-
2ph/1pg/1pc/fr L

House
HABS MO-1499
HABS MO,54-WAVE,3-
1ph/1pg/1pc L

Weber Hotel
HABS MO-1500
HABS MO,54-WAVE,4-
1ph/1pg/1pc L

LEWIS COUNTY

CANTON

Miss. River 9-Ft. Channel Proj.,Lock & Dam No. 20
Upper Mississippi River
HAER MO-34
HAER 1991(HAER):9
33ph/18pg/2pc L

LINCOLN COUNTY

CAP-AU-GRIS

Upper Miss. Riv. 9-Ft. Chnl. Proj.,Lock & Dam 25
HAER MO-37
HAER DLC/PP-1992:MO-3
93ph/9pg/7pc L

MOSCOW MILLS

Drover's Inn
HABS MO-156
HABS MO,57-MOSC,1-
1ph/1pg L

Ross,Shapley,House
HABS MO-1521
HABS MO,57-MOSC,2-
3ph/1pg/1pc/fr L

TROY

Worsham House
HABS MO-1522
HABS MO,57-TROY,1-
2ph/1pg/1pc/fr L

LINN COUNTY

LACLEDE

Harris-Lamme House; see Pershing,Gen. John J. ,Boyhood Home

Pershing,Gen. John J. ,Boyhood Home
(Harris-Lamme House)
State & Worlow Sts.
HABS MO-268
HABS MO,58-LACL,1-
7dr/6ph/1pc L

MADISON COUNTY

FREDERICKTOWN VIC.

Farmhouse,Frame
HABS MO-1810
HABS MO,62-FRETO.V,1-
1ph/1pc L

Springhouse
HABS MO-1523
HABS MO,62-FRETO.V,2-
2ph/1pg/1pc/fr L

MINE LA MOTTE

House,Brick
HABS MO-1524
HABS MO,62-MILAM,1-
1ph/1pg/1pc L

MARION COUNTY

HANNIBAL

Cardiff Hill
HABS MO-1529
HABS MO,64-HANIB,1-
7ph/1pc L

205-209 Center St. (Commercial Bldg.)
Mark Twain Historic District
HABS MO-1870
HABS 1989(HABS):12
2ph/1pc L

Clemens,J. M.,Law Office
(Twain,Mark,Father's Law Office)
Hill St.,Mark Twain Historic District
HABS MO-1869
HABS 1989(HABS):12
3ph/1pc L

Cruikshank,J.J. Jr.,Residence; see Rockcliffe Mansion

Digel Block (Commercial Buildings)
218-220-222 S. Main and 112 Lyon St.
HABS MO-1875
HABS 1991(HABS):19
11ph/7pg/1pc L

House of the Pilasters
N. Main & Hill Sts.,Mark Twain Historic District
HABS MO-1868
HABS 1989(HABS):12
2ph/1pc L

Mitchell-Anderson House
1008 Broadway
HABS MO-1115
HABS MO,64-HANIB,2-
9ph/4pg/1pc L

Documentation: **ct** color transparencies **dr** measured drawings **fr** field records **pc** photograph captions **pg** pages of text **ph** photographs

Mount Olivet Cemetery
HABS MO-1528
HABS MO,64-HANIB,3-
2ph/1pg/1pc L

Robinson Mortuary
1216-1218 Broadway
HABS MO-1251
HABS MO,64-HANIB,4-
11ph/5pg/1pc L

Rockcliffe Mansion (Cruikshank,J.J. Jr.,Residence)
1000 Bird St.
HABS MO-1866
HABS MO,65-HANIB,5-
23ph/2pg/2pc/3ct L

Schaffer's Smoke House
308 Broadway
HABS MO-1867
HABS MO,64-HANIB,6-
5ph/1pc L

Thatcher,Becky,House
211 Hill St.
HABS MO-1527
HABS MO,64-HANIB,7-
3ph/1pg/2pc L

Twain,Mark,Father's Law Office; see Clemens,J. M.,Law Office

Twain,Mark,House
206 Hill St. between N. Main & First Sts.
HABS MO-1526
HABS MO,64-HANIB,8-
11ph/1pg/2pc/1ct/fr L

HANNIBAL VIC.

Masterson,Robert,House
HABS MO-1865
HABS MO,64-HANIB.
20ph/4pg/2pc/2ct L

PALMYRA

House,Brick
HABS MO-1530
HABS MO,64-PALM,1-
1ph/1pg/1pc/fr L

Russell,John Warden,House
HABS MO-1531
HABS MO,64-PALM,2-
1ph/1pg/1pc/fr L

St. Paul's College
HABS MO-1532
HABS MO,64-PALM,3-
1pg/fr L

St. Paul's College,Dormitory
HABS MO-1532-B
HABS MO,64-PALM,3B-
2ph/1pg/1pc/fr L

St. Paul's College,President's House
HABS MO-1532-A
HABS MO,64-PALM,3A-
2ph/1pg/1pc/fr L

PHILADELPHIA VIC.

Ayers,Dr. ,House
HABS MO-1525
HABS MO,64-PHILA.V,1-
2ph/1pg/1pc/fr L

MERCER COUNTY

UNIVERSITY CITY

City Hall (Woman's Magazine Building)
6801 Delmar
HABS MO-249
HABS MO,95-UVCI,1-
13ph/9pg/1pc L

Woman's Magazine Building; see City Hall

MONITEAU COUNTY

BACON VIC.

Bacon Bridge
Spanning Moniteau Creek
HAER MO-32
HAER MO,68-JAME.V,1-
10ph/10pg/1pc L

ENON VIC.

Bruce,Louis,Farmstead Historic District; see Rock Enon Farm

Bruce,Louis,Farmstead Historic District; see Rock Enon Farm,House

Rock Enon Farm
(Bruce,Louis,Farmstead Historic District)
St. Rt. V
HABS MO-1915
3dr H

Rock Enon Farm,House
(Bruce,Louis,Farmstead Historic District)
St. Rt. V
HABS MO-1915-A
5dr H

TIPTON

Homfeldt House
HABS MO-1533
HABS MO,68-TIP.1-
1ph/1pg/1pc/fr L

Maclay House
HABS MO-1534
HABS MO,68-TIP,2-
1ph/1pg/1pc/fr L

MONROE COUNTY

FLORIDA

Scobee,James W. ,Farm
Salt River Vic.
HABS MO-1219
HABS MO,69-FLOR.V,1-
1dr/5ph/8pg/1pc/fr L

Violette,Merritt A. ,House
State Rt. 107 & County Rt. U Vic.
HABS MO-1205
HABS MO,69-FLOR,1-
5dr/7ph/9pg/1pc/fr L

GOSS

Eakin,Robert,Farm
County Rt. U Vic.
HABS MO-1206
HABS MO,69-GOSS.V,1-
1dr/5ph/8pg/1pc/fr L

Mappin,Matthew,House
County Rt. U & U. S. Rt. 24 Vic.
HABS MO-1207
HABS MO,69-GOSS.V,2-
5dr/8ph/15pg/2pc/2ct/fr L

Smith,Samuel H. ,House
Salt River Vic.
HABS MO-1208
HABS MO,69-GOSS.V,3-
3dr/7ph/17pg/1pc/fr L

NORTH FORK VIC.

Fields,Charles,Granary
County Rt. P
HABS MO-1210
HABS MO,69-NORFO.V,1-
1dr/7ph/7pg/1pc/fr L

PARIS VIC.

Johnson,Daniel,House
State Rt. 154
HABS MO-1211
HABS MO,69-PARIS.V,1-
2dr/8ph/8pg/1pc/fr L

SANTA FE VIC.

Monroe County Bridge; see Santa Fe Bridge

Santa Fe Bridge (Monroe County Bridge)
Spanning S. Fork of Salt River at County Rd. 24
HAER MO-68
18ph/13pg/2pc H

STOUTSVILLE

Slee,Hugh C. ,House
Hill & Walnut Sts.
HABS MO-1213
HABS MO,69-STOUT,2-
2dr/6ph/9pg/1pc/fr L

Stoutsville,Town of
HABS MO-1212
HABS MO,69-STOUT,1-
2dr L

STOUTSVILLE VIC.

Salt River Settlement
HABS MO-1203
HABS MO,69-STOUT.V,1-
1dr L

VICTOR

Calhoon,A. Owen,House
Paris-to-Louisiana Rd. Vic.
HABS MO-1215
HABS MO,69-VICT,2-
2dr/10ph/10pg/2pc L

Hattersley,William,Store
Paris-to-Louisiana Rd. Vic.
HABS MO-1216
HABS MO,69-VICT,3-
2dr/11ph/9pg/2pc/2ct/fr L

Meeter,Mitchell,Barn
State Rt. 154 Vic.
HABS MO-1218
HABS MO,69-VICT.V,2-
2dr/5ph/8pg/1pc/fr L

Sinclair,James M. ,Farm
State Rt. 154 & County Rt. Z Vic.
HABS MO-1220
HABS MO,69-VICT.V,3-
1dr/15ph/7pg/2pc/fr L

Victor,Village of,General View
HABS MO-1214
HABS MO,69-VICT,1-
1dr L

VICTOR VIC.

Crow,Basil,House
State Rt. 154
HABS MO-1217
HABS MO,69-VICT.V,1-
1dr/7ph/9pg/1pc/fr L

MONTGOMERY COUNTY

DANVILLE

Danville Female Academy,Chapel
HABS MO-1535
HABS MO,70-DANV,1-
2ph/1pg/1pc/fr L

Fulkerson Tavern
HABS MO-1538
HABS MO,70-DANV,2-
4ph/1pg/1pc/fr L

House
HABS MO-1536
HABS MO,70-DANV,3-
2ph/1pg/1pc L

See-Nunelly Tavern
HABS MO-1537
HABS MO,70-DANV,4-
3ph/1pg/1pc/fr L

DANVILLE VIC.

House,Frame
U. S. Rt. 40
HABS MO-1541
HABS MO,70-DANV.V,1-
1ph/1pg/1pc/fr L

STARKENBURG

Cemetery
HABS MO-1544
HABS MO,70-STABU.1-
1ph/1pc L

Log Chapel
State Rt. P
HABS MO-1543
HABS MO,70-STABU,2-
1ph/1pg/1pc L

St. Martin's Church
HABS MO-1542
HABS MO,70-STABU,3-
2ph/1pg/1pc L

MORGAN COUNTY

FLORENCE

Hummel Pottery Building
HABS MO-1548
HABS MO,71-FLORE,1-
3ph/1pc L

GRAVOIS MILLS

Watts Log Cabin
Grandad Spring
HABS MO-1782
HABS MO,71-GRAMI,1-
1ph/1pg/1pc L

VERSAILLES

Bank Barn
HABS MO-1547
HABS MO,71-VERS.V,1-
2ph/1pg/1pc L

Baumgartner Farm House
HABS MO-1545
HABS MO,71-VERS.V,2-
2ph/1pg/1pc/fr L

Baumgartner Farm,Barn
HABS MO-1545-A
HABS MO,71-VERS.V,2A-
3ph/1pg/1pc/fr L

Gingerich Bank Barn
HABS MO-1546
HABS MO,71-VERS.V,3-
3ph/1pg/1pc/fr L

NEW MADRID COUNTY

NEW MADRID

Weigle,Joseph,House
HABS MO-1549
HABS MO,72-NEMAD,1-
1ph/1pg/1pc/fr L

NEWTON COUNTY

DIAMOND VIC.

Carver,Moses,House (George Washington Carver National Monument)
HABS MO-1912
HABS DLC/PP-1992:MO-5
2ph/1pc L

George Washington Carver National Monument; see Carver,Moses,House

NEOSHO VIC.

Lime Kiln Road Bridge
Spanning Shoal Creek
HAER MO-5
HAER MO,73-NEO.V,1-
20ph/3pg/1pc L

RITCHEY VIC.

Clear Creek Bridge (Shoal Creek Bridge)
Spanning Clear Creek at County Rd. 312
HAER MO-69
9ph/9pg/1pc H

Shoal Creek Bridge; see Clear Creek Bridge

NODAWAY COUNTY

HOPKINS VIC.

Noakes Bridge
Spanning One Hundred And Two River,SW of Hopkins
HAER MO-55
HAER DLC/PP-1992:MO-2
12ph/6pg/1pc L

OSAGE COUNTY

LOOSE CREEK

Church of the Immaculate Conception
HABS MO-1798
HABS MO,76-LOCRE,1-
1ph/1pg/1pc L

RICHFOUNTAIN

Sacred Heart Roman Catholic Church
HABS MO-1797
HABS MO,76-RICHFO,1-
3ph/1pg/1pc L

WESTPHALIA

St. Joseph's Roman Catholic Church
Main St.
HABS MO-1794
HABS MO,76-WESPH,1-
5ph/2pg/1pc L

Westerman House
Main St.
HABS MO-1812
HABS MO,76-WESPH,2-
1ph/1pg/1pc L

WESTPHALIA VIC.

House,Stone
Rt. 63 N.
HABS MO-1550
HABS MO,76-WESPH.V,1-
6ph/1pg/1pc/fr L

Stake-and-Rider Fence
HABS MO-1796
HABS MO,76-WESPH.V,2-
1ph/1pg/1pc L

PERRY COUNTY

ALTENBURG

Concordia College Building
State Rt. A
HABS MO-1552
HABS MO,79-ALBU,1-
3ph/1pg/1pc/fr L

Krahmer House
HABS MO-1553
HABS MO,79-ALBU,2-
2ph/1pg/1pc/fr L

Trinity Lutheran Church
HABS MO-1554
HABS MO,79-ALBU,3-
3ph/1pg/1pc/fr L

ALTENBURG VIC.

Oehlert,Gottlieb,Barn
HABS MO-1555
HABS MO,79-ALBU.V,1A-
1ph/1pg/1pc/fr L

CROSSTOWN VIC.

Jones House
HABS MO-1556
HABS MO,79-CROS.V,1-
4ph/1pg/1pc L

PERRYVILLE

House,Stone
HABS MO-1557
HABS MO,79-PERVI,2-
1ph/1pg/1pc/fr L

House,Stone
HABS MO-1559
HABS MO,79-PERVI,1-
3ph/1pg/1pc/fr L

Roth,Emma,House
12 S. Spring St.
HABS MO-1279
HABS MO,79-PERVI,3-
6ph/1pg/1pc/fr L

St. Mary's Of The Barrens
HABS MO-1558
HABS MO,79-PERVI,4-
8ph/1pg/1pc/fr L

PERRYVILLE VIC.

Cheveaux Barn
HABS MO-1560-B
HABS MO,79-PERVI.V,1B-
1ph/1pg/1pc L

Cheveaux House
U. S. Rt. 61
HABS MO-1560
HABS MO,79-PERVI.V,1-
6ph/1pg/1pc/fr L

Cheveaux Shrine
HABS MO-1560-A
HABS MO,79-PERVI.V,1A-
2ph/1pg/1pc L

McCauley House
State Rt. 51
HABS MO-1561
HABS MO,79-PERVI.V,2-
2ph/1pg/1pc L

PETTIS COUNTY

LONGWOOD VIC.

Shelton's Ford Bridge; see Trickum Road Bridge

Trickum Bridge; see Trickum Road Bridge

Trickum Road Bridge (Trickum Bridge; Shelton's Ford Bridge)
Spanning Heath's Creek,W. of US Hwy. 65 at Rt. BB
HAER MO-64
HAER DLC/PP-1992:MO-2
7ph/8pg/1pc L

SEDALIA

Washington Avenue Bridge (Washington Avenue Viaduct)
Spanning Missouri Pacific RR tracks,Main & St. Lou
HAER MO-29
HAER MO,80-SEDAL,1-
17ph/18pg/1pc L

Washington Avenue Viaduct; see Washington Avenue Bridge

PIKE COUNTY

CLARKSVILLE

Upper Miss. Riv. 9-Ft. Chnl. Proj.,Lock &Dam 24-27
HAER MO-50
HAER DLC/PP-1992:MO-3
125pg L

Upper Miss. Rive. 9-Ft. Chnl. Proj.,Lock & Dam 24
HAER MO-36
HAER DLC/PP-1992:MO-3
44ph/9pg/3pc L

PLATTE COUNTY

HOOVER VIC.

George Washington Carver National Monument; see Noah's Arc Covered Bridge

Noah's Arc Covered Bridge (George Washington Carver National Monument)
County Rt. B over Little Platte River
HABS MO-270
HABS MO,83-HOOV.V,1-
22dr L

PLATTE CITY

Jenkins,Howell,House
HABS MO-1805
HABS MO,83-PLATCI,1-
3ph/1pg/1pc L

POLK COUNTY

BOLIVAR VIC.

Sunset Bridge
Spanning Pomme de Terre River
HAER MO-27
HAER MO,84-BOLI.V,1-
12ph/13pg/1pc L

PULASKI COUNTY

DIXON VIC.

Riddle Bridge
Spanning Gasconada River
HAER MO-28
HAER MO,85-DIXON.V,1-
17ph/14pg/1pc L

RALLS COUNTY

CENTER VIC.

Bell,Samuel F. ,House
County Rt. CC Vic.
HABS MO-1204
HABS MO,87-CENT.V,1-
5dr/15ph/9pg/1pc/fr L

HANNIBAL VIC.

Garth,John,House (Woodside Place)
New London GRavel Rd. (Rural Rt. 1)
HABS MO-1871
HABS MO,87-HANIB.V,1-
13ph/3pg/1pc/3ct L

Woodside Place; see Garth,John,House

JOANNA

Peterson,John,House
HABS MO-1209
HABS MO,87-JOANN.V,1-
1dr/7ph/9pg/1pc/fr L

NEW LONDON

Ralls County Courthouse
HABS MO-1562
HABS MO,87-NEWLO,1-
2ph/1pg/1pc/fr L

SAVERTON

Miss. River 9-Ft. Channel Proj.,Lock & Dam No. 22
Upper Mississippi River
HAER MO-35
HAER 1991(HAER):9
21ph/15pg/2pc L

RAY COUNTY

RAYVILLE VIC.

Crooked River Bridge
Spanning Crooked River south of Rt. FF
HAER MO-66
11ph/9pg/1pc H

RIPLEY COUNTY

DONIPHAN VIC.

Current River Bridge
Spanning the Current River at Doniphan
HAER MO-65
HAER DLC/PP-1992:MO-4
9ph/13pg/1pc L

SALINE COUNTY

ARROW ROCK

Arrow Rock Lutheran Church
HABS MO-1684
HABS MO,98-ARORO,6-
1ph/1pg/1pc/fr L

Bingham,George Caleb,House
Arrow Rock State Park
HABS MO-221
HABS MO,98-ARORO,1-
6ph/2pg/1pc/fr L

Bradford, Dr. J. W. ,House
HABS MO-1682
HABS MO,98-ARORO,7-
3ph/1pg/1pc/fr L

City Jail,Old
Arrow Rock State Park
HABS MO-232
HABS MO,98-ARORO,5-
2ph/1pg L

Digges House
HABS MO-1680
HABS MO,98-ARORO,8-
1ph/1pg/1pc L

Houston Tavern (Tavern,Old)
Arrow Rock State Park
HABS MO-222
HABS MO,98-ARORO,2-
16ph/3pg/1pc/fr L

Price House
HABS MO-230
HABS MO,98-ARORO,3-
7ph/1pg/1pc/fr L

Seminary Building,Old
HABS MO-231
HABS MO,98-ARORO,4-
5ph/1pg/1pc/fr L

Tavern,Old; see Houston Tavern

Thompson-McQuire House
HABS MO-1681
HABS MO,98-ARORO,9-
3ph/1pg/1pc L

Woods House
HABS MO-1683
HABS MO,98-ARORO,10-
1ph/1pg/1pc/fr L

ARROW ROCK VIC.

House
State Rt. 41
HABS MO-1688
HABS MO,98-ARORO.V,2-
3ph/1pg/1pc L

Locke-Hardeman House
HABS MO-1686
HABS MO,98-ARORO.V,3-
3ph/1pg/1pc/fr L

Orear-Blakey House
State Rt. 41
HABS MO-1685
HABS MO,98-ARORO.V,4-
2ph/1pg/1pc L

Sappington,William B. ,Cemetery
HABS MO-223-A
HABS MO,98-ARORO.V,1A-
4ph/1pc L

Sappington,William B. ,House
HABS MO-223
HABS MO,98-ARORO.V,1-
25ph/3pg/1pc/fr L

Thompson,R. L. ,House
HABS MO-1687
HABS MO,98-ARORO.V,5-
4ph/1pg/1pc L

MIAMI

Christian Church
HABS MO-1678
HABS MO,98-MIAMI,1-
1ph/1pg/1pc L

NELSON VIC.

Napton,Judge William B. ,House
HABS MO-1679
HABS MO,98-NEL.V,1-
3ph/1pg/1pc/fr L

SCOTT COUNTY

NEW HAMBURG

St. Lawrence Church
HABS MO-1689
HABS MO,101-NEHAM,1-
1ph/1pg/1pc L

SIKESTON

Grain Elevator
HABS MO-1691
HABS MO,101-SIKE,1-
1ph/1pc/fr L

SIKESTON VIC.

Cotton Gin
HABS MO-1690
HABS MO,101-SIKE.V,1-
1ph/1pc L

SHELBY COUNTY

BETHEL

Colony Dormitory
HABS MO-1147-B
HABS MO,103-BETH,1B-
1ph/1pg/1pc/fr L

Colony House,Brick
HABS MO-1147-C
HABS MO,103-BETH,1C-
1ph/1pg/1pc L

Colony House,Half-Timbered
HABS MO-1147-D
HABS MO,103-BETH,1D-
1ph/1pg/1pc/fr L

Colony Tannery
HABS MO-1147-A
HABS MO,103-BETH,1A-
8ph/1pg/1pc/fr L

Colony Wagon Factory
HABS MO-1147-F
HABS MO,103-BETH,1F-
1ph/1pg/1pc/fr L

BETHEL VIC.

Elim House (Keil,Dr. William,House)
HABS MO-1146
HABS MO,103-BETH.V,1-
8ph/1pg/1pc/fr L

Keil,Dr. William,House; see Elim House

Keil,John,Office
HABS MO-1697
HABS MO,103-BETH.V,2-
1ph/1pg/1pc/fr L

ST. CHARLES COUNTY

AUGUSTA

American Legion Park Bandstand
HABS MO-1773
HABS MO,92-AUG.1A-
1ph/1pg/1pc L

Ebenezer Evangelical Church
HABS MO-1576
HABS MO,92-AUG.2-
1ph/1pg/1pc L

Harold,Leonard,House
HABS MO-1772
HABS MO,92-AUG.3-
4ph/1pg/1pc L

House,Frame
HABS MO-1577
HABS MO,92-AUG,5-
1ph/1pg/1pc L

House,Frame
HABS MO-1578
HABS MO,92-AUG,4-
1ph/1pg/1pc/fr L

Laumeier,Charles,House
Rt. 1
HABS MO-1774
HABS MO,92-AUG,6-
7ph/1pg/1pc L

Mount Pleasant (Muench House)
HABS MO-1770
HABS MO,92-AUG,10-
3ph/1pg/1pc L

Mt. Pleasant Wine Company Buildings
HABS MO-1811
HABS MO,92-AUG,11-
2ph/1pg/1pc L

Muench House; see Mount Pleasant

Muhm House
HABS MO-1771
HABS MO,92-AUG,9-
1ph/1pg/1pc L

COTTLEVILLE

Edwards,Dr. ,House
HABS MO-1579
HABS MO,92-COT,1-
1ph/1pg/1pc L

House,Frame
HABS MO-1580
HABS MO,92-COT,2-
1ph/1pg/1pc L

Public School Building
HABS MO-1581
HABS MO,92-COT,3-
1ph/1pg/1pc L

St. John's Evangelical Church
HABS MO-1582
HABS MO,92-COT,4-
1ph/1pg/1pc L

COTTLEVILLE VIC.

Campbell,Capt. ,House
HABS MO-157
HABS MO,92-COT.V,1-
1ph/1pg L

Cottle Farm
HABS MO-1584
HABS MO,92-COT.V,2-
3ph/1pg/1pc L

Cottle Outbuilding
HABS MO-1584-A
HABS MO,92-COT.V,2A-
1ph/1pc L

Pitman House
HABS MO-1583
HABS MO,92-COT.V,3-
3ph/1pg/1pc/fr L

DARDENNE

Mascheny,Dr. ,House
HABS MO-158
HABS MO,92-DARD,1-
1ph/1pg L

DEFIANCE

Parson's House
HABS MO-188
HABS MO,92-DEFI,1-
1ph/1pg L

DEFIANCE VIC.

Boone,Nathan,House
Femme Osage Valley
HABS MO-159
HABS MO,92-DEFI.V,4-
6ph/2pg/1pc/fr L

Brien,Jonathan,House
HABS MO-160
HABS MO,92-DEFI.V,1-
2ph/1pg L

Fant,Buckner,House
HABS MO-189
HABS MO,92-DEFI.V,3-
1ph/1pg L

Hays,Daniel,Stone House
HABS MO-161
HABS MO,92-DEFI.V,2-
2ph/1pg L

FEMME OSAGE

Evangelical Church School
HABS MO-1587
HABS MO,92-FEMO,2-
1ph/1pg/1pc/fr L

Evangelical Parsonage; see Garlichs,Herman,House

Garlichs,Herman,House (Evangelical Parsonage)
HABS MO-1586
HABS MO,92-FEMO,3-
4ph/1pg/1pc/fr L

Log Cabin
HABS MO-1585
HABS MO,92-FEMO,4-
2ph/1pg/1pc L

FEMME OSAGE VIC.

Deubbert,Oscar,Farm
HABS MO-1588
HABS MO,92-FEMO.V,1-
2ph/1pg/1pc L

Deubbert,Oscar,Farm,Barn
HABS MO-1588-A
HABS MO,92-FEMO.V,1A-
1ph/1pc L

Fuchs House
Rt. 1
HABS MO-1589
HABS MO,92-FEMO.V,2-
1ph/1pg/1pc L

Fuchs Mill
HABS MO-1589-A
HABS MO,92-FEMO.V,2A-
3ph/1pg/1pc/fr L

House,Log
Hwy. 98
HABS MO-1777
HABS MO,92-FEMO.V,3-
1ph/1pg/1pc L

Schremm,Oscar,House
Femme Osage Valley
HABS MO-1590
HABS MO,92-FEMO.V,4-
2ph/1pg/1pc/fr L

FLINTHILL VIC.

Broadhead House
HABS MO-154
HABS MO,92-FLIHI.V,1-
1ph/1pg L

Hubbart,Josiah,House
HABS MO-155
HABS MO,92-FLIHI.V,2-
2ph/1pg L

GREEN BOTTOM

Flaugherty House
HABS MO-186
HABS MO,92- ,1-
1ph/1pg L

Green House
HABS MO-187
HABS MO,92- ,2-
2ph/1pg L

HARVESTER

Village Well
HABS MO-1591
HABS MO,92-HARV,1-
1ph/1pc/fr L

MATSON

Matson,Richard,House
HABS MO-1592
HABS MO,92-MAT,1-
5ph/1pg/1pc/fr L

MATSON VIC.

Boone,Daniel,Farm; see Matson,Abraham,House

Boone,Daniel,Springhouse; see Matson,Abraham,Springhouse

Matson,Abraham,House
(Boone,Daniel,Farm)
HABS MO-1593
HABS MO,92-MAT.V,1-
7ph/1pg/1pc/fr L

Matson,Abraham,Springhouse
(Boone,Daniel,Springhouse)
HABS MO-1593-A
HABS MO,92-MAT.V,1A-
3ph/1pc/fr L

O'FALLON

Zumwalt,Jacob,Log Cabin
HABS MO-153
HABS MO,92-OFAL,1-
1ph/1pg L

PORTAGE DES SIOUX

House,Frame
HABS MO-1597
HABS MO,92-PORT,2-
1ph/1pg/1pc L

Payne House
HABS MO-168
HABS MO,92-PORT,1-
1ph/1pg L

ST. CHARLES

Academy of the Sacred Heart; see Sacred Heart Convent

Academy of the Sacred Heart,Shrine; see Sacred Heart Convent,Shrine

Bruns House
Hwy. 94
HABS MO-1769
HABS MO,92-SAICH,14-
1ph/1pg/1pc L

Chambers House; see Virginia Hotel

Chanter House
HABS MO-192
HABS MO,92-SAICH,13-
1ph/1pg L

Colier Methodist Episcopal Church
617 S. Main St.
HABS MO-166
HABS MO,92-SAICH,7-
1ph/1pg L

Coontz House
906 S. Main St.
HABS MO-164
HABS MO,92-SAICH,5-
1ph/1pg L

Defiance Road Bridge (McCormick Bridge)
Spanning Femme Osage Creek on Defiance Rd.
HAER MO-57
HAER 1991(HAER):9
12ph/9pg/1pc L

Flaugherty-McNair House
724 Main St.
HABS MO-169
HABS MO,92-SAICH,9-
1ph/1pg L

Freese Farm
1500 Harvester Rd.
HABS MO-1776
HABS MO,92-SAICH,15-
1pg L

Freese Farm,Barn
1500 Harvester Rd.
HABS MO-1776-B
HABS MO,92-SAICH,15B-
3ph/1pg/1pc L

Freese Farm,Well House
1500 Harvester Rd.
HABS MO-1776-A
HABS MO,92-SAICH,15A-
1ph/1pg/1pc L

Frieden's Evangelical and Reformed Church
HABS MO-1594
HABS MO,92-SAICH,16-
3ph/1pg/1pc/fr L

Griffith,Daniel D. ,House
U. S. Rt. 40
HABS MO-152
HABS MO,92-SAICH.V,2-
11ph/1pg/1pc/fr L

House
HABS MO-1566
HABS MO,92-SAICH,17-
1ph/1pc/fr L

House,Brick
HABS MO-1564
HABS MO,92-SAICH,22-
1ph/1pg/1pc L

House,Brick
HABS MO-1571
HABS MO,92-SAICH,20-
1ph/1pg/1pc L

House,Brick
HABS MO-1572
HABS MO,92-SAICH,19-
1ph/1pg/1pc/fr L

House,Brick
HABS MO-1573
HABS MO,92-SAICH,18-
2ph/1pg/1pc/fr L

House,Brick
HABS MO-1574
HABS MO,92-SAICH,23-
1ph/1pg/1pc/fr L

House,Brick
Hwy. Rt. 40
HABS MO-1575
HABS MO,92-SAICH,21-
1ph/1pg/1pc L

House,Frame
HABS MO-1567
HABS MO,92-SAICH,24-
1ph/1pg/1pc/fr L

House,Frame
HABS MO-1568
HABS MO,92-SAICH,26-
1ph/1pc L

House,Frame
HABS MO-1569
HABS MO,92-SAICH,27-
1ph/1pg/1pc/fr L

House,Frame
HABS MO-1570
HABS MO,92-SAICH,25-
1ph/1pc L

Keebe,Timothy,House
Main & Pike Sts.
HABS MO-191
HABS MO,92-SAICH,12-
1ph/1pg L

Kuhlmann House
HABS MO-163
HABS MO,92-SAICH,4-
1ph/1pg L

McCormick Bridge; see Defiance Road Bridge

McElhiney Mansion
(Powell,Ludwell,House)
Sixth & Jefferson Sts.
HABS MO-167
HABS MO,92-SAICH,8-
4ph/1pg/1pc/fr L

Moore House
1017 S. Main St.
HABS MO-165
HABS MO,92-SAICH,6-
1ph/1pg L

Old Route 40 Bridge; see Old St.Charles Bridge

Old St.Charles Bridge (Old Route 40 Bridge)
On Rte. 115
HAER MO-30
HAER DLC/PP-1992:MO-2
22ph/39pg/2pc L

Powell,Ludwell,House; see McElhiney Mansion

Rock House
HABS MO-149
HABS MO,92-SAICH,3-
2ph/1pg L

Documentation: **ct** color transparencies **dr** measured drawings **fr** field records
pc photograph captions **pg** pages of text **ph** photographs

Sacred Heart Convent (Academy of the Sacred Heart)
619 N. Second St.
HABS MO-147
HABS MO,92-SAICH,2-
2ph/1pg/1pc/fr L

Sacred Heart Convent,Shrine (Academy of the Sacred Heart,Shrine)
619 North Second St.
HABS MO-147-A
HABS MO,92-SAICH,2A-
1ph/1pg/1pc L

Slave Cabin
HABS MO-170
HABS MO,92-SAICH,10-
1ph/1pg L

Slave House
HABS MO-151
HABS MO,92-SAICH,8A-
2ph/1pg L

St. Charles Courthouse
Second,Third,Jefferson,& Washington Sts.
HABS MO-1563
HABS MO,92-SAICH,28-
1ph/1pg/1pc/fr L

St. Charles Evangelical Church
HABS MO-1565
HABS MO,92-SAICH,29-
1ph/1pg/1pc L

State Legislative Assembly Hall,First
208-214 S. Main St.
HABS MO-148
HABS MO,92-SAICH,1-
2ph/1pg L

Virginia Hotel (Chambers House)
234 S. Main St.
HABS MO-190
HABS MO,92-SAICH,11-
1ph/1pg L

ST. CHARLES VIC.

Friedens Church School,Teacher's House
Hwy. 94
HABS MO-1768
HABS MO,92-SAICH.V,3A-
1ph/1pg/1pc L

House,Brick
HABS MO-1596
HABS MO,92-SAICH.V,4-
2ph/1pg/1pc/fr L

House,Frame
State Rt. 94
HABS MO-1595
HABS MO,92-SAICH.V,5-
1ph/1pg/1pc/fr L

House,Log
HABS MO-1778
HABS MO,92-SAICH.V,6-
1ph/1pg/1pc L

Potter House; see Shore House,Old

Shore House,Old (Potter House)
St. Charles Rd.
HABS MO-150
HABS MO,92-SAICH.V,1-
1ph/1pg L

ST. PETER'S VIC.

House,Brick
U. S. Rt. 40
HABS MO-1598
HABS MO,92-SPET.V,1-
2ph/1pg/1pc/fr L

House,Brick
U. S. Rt. 40
HABS MO-1599
HABS MO,92-SPET.V,2-
3ph/1pg/1pc/fr L

WELDON SPRINGS

Coonce,Jacob,Log Cabin
HABS MO-162
HABS MO,92-WELSP,1-
1ph/1pg L

WELDON SPRINGS VIC.

Howell,Thomas,House
HABS MO-1600
HABS MO,92-WELSP.V,1-
6ph/1pg/1pc/fr L

Howell,Thomas,Outbuilding
HABS MO-1600-A
HABS MO,92-WELSP.V,1A-
2ph/1pc L

ST. CLAIR COUNTY

LOWRY CITY VIC.

House
Rt. 22
HABS MO-1236
HABS MO,93-LOWCIT.V,2-
4ph/5pg/1pc L

House (Tract #1917)
HABS MO-1235
HABS MO,93-LOWCIT.V,1-
6ph/6pg/1pc L

Tract #1917; see House

OSCEOLA

Osage River Bridge
Spanning Osage River on State Hwy. M-13
HAER MO-17
HAER MO,93-OSCEO,1-
4ph/1pc L

Osceola Bridge
Spanning Osage River
HAER MO-16
HAER MO,93-0SCEO,2-
2ph/1pc L

OSCEOLA VIC.

Hooper,John M. ,House
HABS MO-1243
HABS MO,93-OSCEO.V,1-
7ph/6pg/1pc L

House
Hwy. 82
HABS MO-1272
HABS MO,93-OSCEO,V,2-
6ph/1pg/1pc L

ROSCOE

Barber Shop
Main St.
HABS MO-1270
HABS MO,93-ROSC,4-
1ph/1pc L

Commercial Block (Jones Drug Block)
Main & First Sts.
HABS MO-1246
HABS MO,93-ROSC,1-
6dr/13ph/7pg/1pc/fr L

Harness Shop
Main St.
HABS MO-1271
HABS MO,93-ROSC,5-
1ph/1pc L

Jones Drug Block; see Commercial Block

Roscoe Bridge
Spanning Osage River on State Hwy. E
HAER MO-15
HAER MO,93-ROSC,3-
2ph/1pc L

Weinlig Store
Main St.
HABS MO-1247
HABS MO,93-ROSC,2-
1dr/4ph/5pg/1pc/fr L

ROSCOE VIC.

House (Tract No. 6300)
.3 mi. N. of Rt. 82 2 mi. E of Roscoe
HABS MO-1237
HABS MO,93-ROSC.V,1
9ph/8pg/1pc/fr L

Tract No. 6300; see House

ST. FRANCOIS COUNTY

???

Springhouse
HABS MO-1601
HABS MO,94- ,1-
1ph/1pg/1pc L

BONNE TERRE VIC.

House,Frame
HABS MO-1604
HABS MO,94-BONT.V,1-
3ph/1pg/1pc L

House,Stone
HABS MO-1603
HABS MO,94-BONT.V,2-
2ph/1pg/1pc L

DESLOGE VICINITY

Cedar Falls Road Bridge
Spanning Flat River,E. of U.S. Hwy. 67
HAER MO-49
HAER 1991(HAER):9
12ph/4pg/1pc L

FARMINGTON

Brown,Tom V. House; see Murphy House

Bruett House
HABS MO-1605
HABS MO,94-FARM,1-
1ph/1pg/1pc/fr L

Cayce Plantation; see Hospital,Presbyterian Orphanage

Hospital,Presbyterian Orphanage
(Cayce Plantation)
HABS MO-1606
HABS MO,94-FARM,2-
1ph/1pg/1pc/fr L

Murphy House (Brown,Tom V. House)
HABS MO-1607
HABS MO,94-FARM,3-
1ph/1pg/1pc/fr L

Weber House
HABS MO-1608
HABS MO,94-FARM,4-
1ph/1pg/1pc L

FLAT RIVER VIC.

House,Stone
HABS MO-1609
HABS MO,94-FLATR.V,1-
1ph/1pg/1pc L

Lead Smelter
HABS MO-1602
HABS MO,94-FLATR.V,2-
3ph/1pc L

FRENCH VILLAGE

La Haint House
HABS MO-1610
HABS MO,94-FREVIL,1-
3ph/1pg/1pc L

ST. LOUIS (CITY)

Allen Street; see Soulard Neighborhood Historic District

Allen-Collier Building
7-11 N. First St.
HABS MO-1160
HABS MO,96-SALU,71-
7dr/3ph/1pg/1pc/fr L

Aloe Plaza Fountain
HABS MO-1654
HABS MO,96-SALU,82-
2ph/1pg/1pc L

Anheuser-Busch Brewery
Broadway & Pestalozzi
HABS MO-1613
HABS MO,96-SALU,83-
3ph/1pg/1pc L

Ann Street; see Soulard Neighborhood Historic District

Bacon House (Lace House)
1131 Morrison Ave.
HABS MO-110
HABS MO,96-SALU,22-
3ph/1pg L

Bain,George,House
2115 Park Ave.
HABS MO-1157-A
HABS MO,96-SALU,52-
2ph/2pg L

Bauer,J. L.,House (Kingsway Center Commercial Area)
4935 Page Blvd.
HABS MO-60-H
1pg L

Bellefontaine Cemetery
4947 W. Florissant Ave.
HABS MO-1637
HABS MO,96-SALU,84-
5ph/1pg/1pc L

Bellefontaine Cemetery,Adolphus & Ully Busch Tomb
4947 W. Florissant Ave.
HABS MO-1637-C
HABS MO,96-SALU,84C-
3ph/1pc/1ct L

Bellefontaine Cemetery,Wainwright Tomb
4947 W. Florissant Ave.
HABS MO-1637-A
HABS MO,96-SALU,84A-
9ph/1pg/2pc/1ct L

Bellefontaine Cemetery,William Clark Tomb
4947 W. Florissant Ave.
HABS MO-1637-B
HABS MO,96-SALU,84B-
3ph/1pc L

Berthold,Eugene,House
4482 Lindell Blvd.
HABS MO-1672
HABS MO,96-SALU,85-
1ph/1pc L

Bissell Street Water Tower; see Water Tower,Red

Bissell,Capt. Lewis,Mansion
Randall Pl.
HABS MO-16
HABS MO,96-SALU,19-
16dr/17ph/4pg/1pc L

Bloch House (Kingsway Center Commercial Area)
4921 Page Blvd.
HABS MO-60-D
HABS 1991(HABS):19
7ph/3pg/1pc L

Blossom House
Union Blvd. & Enright Ave.
HABS MO-31-4
HABS MO,96-SALU,4-
2dr/2ph/2pg/1pc/fr L

Blow,Henry,House
HABS MO-1655
HABS MO,96-SALU,86-
4ph/1pg/1pc/fr L

Booth-Papin Building
119-121 N. First St.
HABS MO-1162
HABS MO,96-SALU,73-
6dr L

Brant,Joshua,House
HABS MO-1808
HABS MO,96-SALV,87-
1ph/1pc L

Calvary Cemetery,Sherman Tomb
5239 W. Florissant Ave.
HABS MO-124-C
HABS MO,96-SALU,35C-
1ph/1pg/1pc L

Calvary Cemetery,Thomas Biddle Tomb
5239 W. Florissant Ave.
HABS MO-124-B
HABS MO,96-SALU,35B-
2ph/1pg/1pc L

Campbell,Robert,House
1508 Locust St.
HABS MO-12
HABS MO,96-SALU,15-
10dr/9ph/2pg/1pc L

Castleman-Mackay Mansion
HABS MO-1161-A
HABS MO,96-SALU,53-
8ph/3pg L

Cathedral,Old; see Church of St. Louis of France (Roman Catholic)

Cavender,Gen. John S. ,House
21 Benton Pl.
HABS MO-1162-A
HABS MO,96-SALU,54-
5ph/4pg L

Central West End Historic Complex; see Marshall,Dr. Milton C.,Building

Central West End Historic District
4200 Block of Westminster Place
HABS MO-1878
9pg H

Central West End Historic District; see Parker,George W.,House

Documentation: **ct** color transparencies **dr** measured drawings **fr** field records
pc photograph captions **pg** pages of text **ph** photographs

Chatillon-DeMenil House
3352 S. Thirteenth St.
HABS MO-14
HABS MO,96-SALU,17-
3ph/1pg L

211-213 Chestnut Street (Commercial Building); see St. Louis River Front

Chouteau Building
523-529 N. First St.
HABS MO-271
HABS MO,96-SALU,88-
4dr/fr L

Chouteau,Auguste,Gravestone
Calvary Cemetery
HABS MO-124-A
HABS MO,96-SALU,35-
1ph/1pg L

Christ Church Cathedral
Thirteenth & Locust Sts.
HABS MO-1630
HABS MO,96-SALU,89-
1ph/1pg/1pc L

Church of St. Louis of France (Roman Catholic) (Cathedral,Old)
Third & Walnut Sts.
HABS MO-31-1
HABS MO,96-SALU,1-
14dr/7ph/2pg/1pc/fr L

Church of St. Mary of Victory; see St. Mary's Roman Catholic Church

Church of the Messiah (Unitarian)
Garrison & Locust Sts.
HABS MO-1179
HABS MO,96-SALU,67-
1ph L

Civil Courts Building
Eleventh to Twelfth,Market to Chestnut Sts.
HABS MO-1806
HABS MO,96-SALU,90-
1ph/1pg/1pc/fr L

Clay,Col. Henry,House (Orchard Farm,Old)
5239 W. Florissant Ave.
HABS MO-118
HABS MO,96-SALU,29-
4ph/1pg/1pc L

Clemens,James S. ,House
HABS MO-1163-A
HABS MO,96-SALU,55-
8ph/3pg L

Climatron; see Missouri Botanical Garden,Climatron

College Church; see St. Francis Xavier's Church

Compton Hill Water Tower; see Reservoir Park,Compton Hill Water Tower

Cotton Belt Building
408 Pine
HABS MO-272
HABS MO,96-SALU,91-
9ph/1pc L

Cupples,Samuel,House
3673 W. Pine Blvd.
HABS MO-1833
HABS MO,96-SALU,92-
17ph/2pg/1pc/3ct L

Davis-Glaude House (Kingsway Center Commercial Area)
4931 Page Blvd.
HABS MO-60-G
HABS 1991(HABS):19
7ph/2pg/1pc L

DeBaliviere Station Garage
577 DeBaliviere
HAER MO-6
HAER MO,96-SALU,75-
34ph/27pg/2pc L

Demenil,George S. ,House
HABS MO-1667
HABS MO,96-SALU,94-
2ph/1pc L

DeMenil,Nicholas,House
Thirteenth & Cherokee Sts.
HABS MO-1668
HABS MO,96-SALU,93-
3ph/1pg/1pc/fr L

Eads Bridge
Washington St.,spanning Mississippi River
HABS MO-1190
HAER MO-12
HABS/HAER MO,96-SALU,77-
38ph/2pg/3pc/2ct L

Edison Brothers Bldg.,Trompe L'Oeil Mural
400 14th St.
HABS MO-1837
HABS MO,96-SALU,95-
1ph/2pg/1pc/1ct L

Eighteenth Street Bridge
HAER MO-10
HAER MO,96-SALU,76-
37ph/7pg/2pc L

Eliot House
4446 Westminster Place
HABS MO-1164-A
HABS MO,96-SALU,56-
2ph/1pg L

Euclid Realty Flat (Kingsway Center Commercial Area)
1307-1309 Euclid Ave.
HABS MO-60-I
HABS 1991(HABS):19
7ph/3pg/1pc L

Euclid Realty Flats (Kingsway Center Commercial Area)
4901-4911 Page Blvd.
HABS MO-60-A
HABS 1991(HABS):19
7ph/3pg/1pc L

Field,Eugene,House
634 S. Broadway
HABS MO-31-3
HABS MO,96-SALU,3-
4dr/4ph/2pg/1pc/fr L

Forest Park
Lindell Blvd. to Oakland Ave. ,Kings Hwy.
HABS MO-1662
HABS MO,96-SALU,96-
2ph/1pc/fr L

Forest Park,Art Museum
HABS MO-1662-B
HABS MO,96-SALU,96B-
1ph/1pg/1pc/fr L

Forest Park,Jefferson Memorial Building
HABS MO-1662-C
HABS MO,96-SALU,96C-
1ph/1pg/1pc/fr L

Forest Park,Jewel Box
HABS MO-1662-A
HABS MO,96-SALU,96A-
1ph/1pg/1pc/fr L

Gantt,Thomas,Building
219-221 Chestnut St.
HABS MO-1158
HABS MO,96-SALU,70-
9dr L

Gaty,Sam,Mansion
3408 N. Ninth St.
HABS MO-128
HABS MO,96-SALU,39-
1ph/1pg L

Geyer Street; see Soulard Neighborhood Historic District

Graham & Newman Building (Newman's Folly)
210-218-220 Olive St.
HABS MO-1177
HABS MO,96-SALU,65-
1ph L

Grant-Dent House
702 Fourth & Cerre Sts.
HABS MO-31-2
HABS MO,96-SALU,2-
4dr/4ph/1pg/1pc/fr L

Hall Building
309 Market St.
HABS MO-1142
HABS MO,96-SALU,51-
3ph/fr L

Hanlan Buck Stove Company Building
N. Third St.
HABS MO-1650
HABS MO,96-SALU,97-
1ph/1pg/1pc L

Hanpeter House (Kingsway Center Commercial Area)
1317 Euclid Ave.
HABS MO-60-J
HABS 1991(HABS):19
3ph/3pg/1pc L

Hehman House (Kingsway Center Commercial Area)
4929 Page Blvd.
HABS MO-60-F
HABS 1991(HABS):19
7ph/4pg/1pc L

Humphrey House (Kingsway Center Commercial Area)
1316 Aubert Ave.
HABS MO-60-U
HABS 1991(HABS):19
7ph/4pg/1pc L

Hussman House (Kingsway Center Commercial Area)
1345 (1) Euclid Ave.
HABS MO-60-M
HABS 1991(HABS):19
7ph/4pg/1pc L

Hynson House (Kingsway Center Commercial Area)
1314 Aubert
HABS MO-60-T
HABS 1991(HABS):19
7ph/4pg/1pc L

Jefferson National Expansion Memorial Arch (St. Louis Gateway Arch)
Mississippi River between Washington & Poplar Sts.
HAER MO-40
HAER MO,96-SALU,78-
34ph/2pc/9ct L

Johnson House
613 Market St.
HABS MO-1145
HABS MO,96-SALU,50-
4ph/3pg/1pc/fr L

Katharmon Chemical Building
First St.
HABS MO-1644
HABS MO,96-SALU,98-
1ph/1pg/1pc/fr L

Kingshighway Viaduct
Spanning Railroad Tracks at Kingshighway Blvd.
HAER MO-38
HAER 1989(HAER):14
17ph/9pg/2pc L

Kingsway Center Commercial Area; see Bauer,J. L.,House

Kingsway Center Commercial Area; see Bloch House

Kingsway Center Commercial Area; see Davis-Glaude House

Kingsway Center Commercial Area; see Euclid Realty Flat

Kingsway Center Commercial Area; see Euclid Realty Flats

Kingsway Center Commercial Area; see Hanpeter House

Kingsway Center Commercial Area; see Hehman House

Kingsway Center Commercial Area; see Humphrey House

Kingsway Center Commercial Area; see Hussman House

Kingsway Center Commercial Area; see Hynson House

Kingsway Center Commercial Area; see Kuhn-Le Faiure House

Kingsway Center Commercial Area; see Reinhardt House

Kingsway Center Commercial Area; see Schmitt,Fred,Building

Kingsway Center Commercial Area; see Schmitt,Fred,Stable

Kingsway Center Commercial Area; see Silva House

Kingsway Center Commercial Area; see Small House

Kingsway Center Commercial Area; see Small,J. P.,House

Kingsway Center Commercial Area; see Smith,James R.,House

Kingsway Center Commercial Area; see Vander Lippe House

Kingsway Center Commercial Area; see Wilkinson House

Kingway Center Commercial Area
Bounded by KingsHwy.,Dr. M.L.King Blvds,Euclid Ave
HABS MO-60
HABS 1991(HABS):19
1dr/8ph/13pg/1pc L

Kuhn-Le Faiure House (Kingsway Center Commercial Area)
4923 Page Blvd.
HABS MO-60-E
HABS 1991(HABS):19
7ph/3pg/1pc L

Kulage-Backer House
1413 S. Tenth St.
HABS MO-115
HABS MO,96-SALU,27-
1pg L

Kunkel,Charles,House
W. Pine St.
HABS MO-1657
HABS MO,96-SALU,99-
2ph/1pg/1pc L

Labadie Cottage
317 Poplar St.
HABS MO-127
HABS MO,96-SALU,38-
1ph/1pg L

Labadie House
517-19 S. Third St.
HABS MO-119
HABS MO,96-SALU,30-
5dr/1ph/1pg L

Lace House; see Bacon House

Lafayette Park,Statue of Thomas Hart Benton
HABS MO-1661
HABS MO,96-SALU,100-
2ph/1pg/1pc L

Lafayette Street; see Soulard Neighborhood Historic District

Levee & Steamboat
HABS MO-1663
HABS MO,96-SALU,101-
1ph/1pc/fr L

Lindemann-Kahre House
6700 Robbins Mill Rd.
HABS MO-1191
HABS MO,96-SALU,102-
5ph/1pc L

Lionberger,Isaac H. ,House
HABS MO-1165
HABS MO,96-SALU,57-
5ph/4pg L

Logan,Capt. Floyd,House
2825 Pine St.
HABS MO-1166
HABS MO,96-SALU,58-
4ph/3pg L

Mallinckrodt House
3524 N. Ninth St.
HABS MO-129
HABS MO,96-SALU,40-
1ph/1pg L

Marie & St. Joseph Church
8304 Minnesota Ave.
HABS MO-117
HABS MO,96-SALU,28-
1ph/1pg L

Marine Hospital
Marine Ave.
HABS MO-1136
HABS MO,96-SALU,45-
4ph/2pg L

Marshall,Dr. Milton C.,Building
(Central West End Historic Complex)
414-418 North Boyle Avenue
HABS MO-1898
4ph/5pg/1pc H

Matigny,Jean Baptiste,House
S. E. Corner of First & Walnut Sts.
HABS MO-1260
HABS MO,96-SALU,103-
1dr L

Maury House
HABS MO-19
HABS MO,96-SALU,21-
3ph/1pg L

McEwing-McManus House
3127 Laclede Ave.
HABS MO-1167
HABS MO,96-SALU,59-
4ph/3pg L

Meier,Adolphus,House
Ninth & Bremen Ave.
HABS MO-130
HABS MO,96-SALU,41-
1ph/1pg L

Merchant's Exchange
Third St. from Chestnut to Pine Sts.
HABS MO-1635
HABS MO,96-SALU,104-
5ph/1pg/1pc L

Merchants' Bank Building
First & Locust Sts.
HABS MO-1176
HABS MO,96-SALU,64-
3ph/fr L

Michael Building
207 N. First St.
HABS MO-1157
HABS MO,96-SALU,69-
6dr L

Missouri Botancial Garden,Henry Shaw House; see Shaw,Henry,House

Missouri Botanical Garden, Old Mausoleum; see Missouri Botanical Garden,Temple of Victory

Missouri Botanical Garden,Administration Building
2345 Tower Grove Ave.
HABS MO-1135-B
HABS MO,96-SALU,105B-
8dr/5ph/7pg/1pc/fr L

Missouri Botanical Garden,Cleveland Ave. Gatehouse
2345 Tower Grove Ave.
HABS MO-1135-F
HABS MO,96-SALU,105F-
6ph/7pg/1pc L

Missouri Botanical Garden,Climatron (Climatron)
2345 Tower Grove Ave.
HABS MO-1135-L
HABS MO,96-SALU,105L-
12ph/1pg/1pc L

Missouri Botanical Garden,Desert House
2345 Tower Grove Ave.
HABS MO-1135-K
HABS MO,96-SALU,105K-
2ph/1pc L

Missouri Botanical Garden,Flora Avenue Gate; see Missouri Botanical Garden,Old Main Gate

Missouri Botanical Garden,Henry Shaw Mausoleum
2345 Tower Grove Ave.
HABS MO-1135-E
HABS MO,96-SALU,105E-
3dr/11ph/7pg/2pc/2ct/fr L

Missouri Botanical Garden,Henry Shaw Townhouse
2345 Tower Grove Ave.
HABS MO-1135-A
HABS MO,96-SALU,105A-
10dr/31ph/12pg/3pc/fr L

Missouri Botanical Garden,Japanese Tea House
2345 Tower Grove Ave.
HABS MO-1135-I
HABS MO,96-SALU,105I-
5ph/1pc L

Missouri Botanical Garden,Linnaean House
2345 Tower Grove Ave.
HABS MO-1135-D
HABS MO,96-SALU,105D-
3dr/14ph/10pg/2pc/fr L

Missouri Botanical Garden,Mediterranean House
2345 Tower Grove Ave.
HABS MO-1135-J
HABS MO,96-SALU,105J-
2ph/1pc L

Missouri Botanical Garden,Museum
2345 Tower Grove Ave.
HABS MO-1135-C
HABS MO,96-SALU,105C-
4dr/14ph/10pg/1pc/fr L

Missouri Botanical Garden,Old Main Gate (Missouri Botanical Garden,Flora Avenue Gate)
2345 Tower Grove Ave.
HABS MO-1135-G
HABS MO,96-SALU,105G-
4ph/1pc L

Missouri Botanical Garden,Ridgway Center
2345 Tower Grove Ave.
HABS MO-1135-M
HABS MO,96-SALU,105M-
2ph/1pc L

Missouri Botanical Garden,Temple of Victory (Missouri Botanical Garden, Old Mausoleum)
2345 Tower Grove Ave.
HABS MO-1135-H
HABS MO,96-SALU,105H-
1ph/1pc L

Missouri Botantical Garden (Shaw's Garden)
2345 Tower Grove Ave.
HABS MO-1135
HABS MO,96-SALU,105-
24dr/31ph/20pg/3pc/4ct/fr L

Mitchell,Mary,House
Spring & Pine Sts.
HABS MO-1658
HABS MO,96-SALU,106-
3ph/1pg/1pc L

Municipal Auditorium
Fourteenth to Fifteenth,Market to Clark Sts.
HABS MO-1641
HABS ,96-SALU,107-
2ph/1pg/1pc/fr L

Musick's Ferry Rock House,Old
Hall Ferry Rd.
HABS MO-142
HABS MO,96-SALU,42-
1ph/1pg L

National Hotel,Old
Third & National Sts.
HABS MO-1647
HABS MO,96-SALU,108-
1ph/1pg/1pc L

Neighborhood Gardens
8th St. between Biddle & O'Fallon Sts.
HABS MO-1834
HABS MO,96-SALU,109-
8ph/5pg/2pc/2ct L

New National Hotel; see St. Louis River Front

Newman's Folly; see Graham & Newman Building

North First Street (Commercial Buildings)
HABS MO-1664
HABS MO,96-SALU,110-
1ph/1pg/1pc/fr L

North Grand Water Tower
N. Grand & 20th Streets
HABS MO-1671
HABS MO,96-SALU,111-
3ph/1pg/2pc/1ct L

119-121 North Main Street (Commercial Building); see St. Louis River Front

303 North Main Street (Commercial Building); see St. Louis River Front

305 North Main Street (Commercial Building); see St. Louis River Front

7-15 North Main Street (Commercial Building); see St. Louis River Front

Old Stone House; see Roy,Jean Baptiste,House

Orchard Farm,Old; see Clay,Col. Henry,House

Papin Building
113-115 N. First St.
HABS MO-1161
HABS MO,96-SALU,72-
5dr/1ph/1pg/1pc/fr L

Parker,George W.,House (Central West End Historic District)
4216 Westminster Place
HABS MO-1897
9ph/11pg/1pc H

Parochial School,First in St. Louis
HABS MO-112
HABS MO,96-SALU,24-
1ph/1pg L

6922 Pennsylvania Avenue (House)
HABS MO-1677
HABS MO,95-SALU.V,3-
1ph/1pg/1pc L

Peper Building
Raeder Place,La Clede's Landing
HABS MO-1831
HABS MO,96-SALU,112-
3ph/1pg/1pc/1ct L

Post Office & Customs House
Ninth & Locust,Eighth & Olive Sts.
HABS MO-1195
HABS MO,96-SALU,113-
13ph/8pg/1pc/fr L

Post Office & Customs House,Old
Third & Olive Sts.
HABS MO-1159
HABS MO,96-SALU,114-
2dr/2ph/1pg/1pc/fr L

Post Office Building,Old (Ruins)
22-26 N. Second St.
HABS MO-1139
HABS MO,96-SALU,48-
13dr/5ph L

Potter,Henry S. ,House
Cabanne & Goodfellow Sts.
HABS MO-1648
HABS MO,96-SALU,115-
3ph/1pg/1pc L

Reinhardt House (Kingsway Center Commercial Area)
1405 Euclid Ave.
HABS MO-60-Q
HABS 1991(HABS):19
7ph/4pg/1pc L

Reller,F. ,House
821 Destreham St.
HABS MO-126
HABS MO,96-SALU,37-
1ph/1pg L

Reservoir Park,Compton Hill Water Tower (Compton Hill Water Tower)
Reservoir Park,Grant & Russel Blvds. & Lafayette
HABS MO-1832-A
HABS MO,96-SALU,116A-
3ph/2pg/1pc/1ct L

Rice House; see St. Louis River Front

Rock House,Old
Wharf & Chestnut Sts.
HABS MO-31-5
HABS MO,96-SALU,5-
2dr/3ph/4pg/1pc/fr L

Row Houses,Stone
200 Stein St.
HABS MO-17
HABS MO,96-SALU,20-
2ph/2pg/1pc L

Roy,Jean Baptiste,House (Old Stone House)
615 S. Second St.
HABS MO-13
HABS MO,96-SALU,16-
9dr/5ph/3pg/1pc/fr L

Russell Street; see Soulard Neighborhood Historic District

S. Eighth Street; see Soulard Neighborhood Historic District

S. Eleventh Street; see Soulard Neighborhood Historic District

S. Ninth Street; see Soulard Neighborhood Historic District

S. Seventh Street; see Soulard Neighborhood Historic District

S. Tenth Street; see Soulard Neighborhood Historic District

S. Thirteenth Street; see Soulard Neighborhood Historic District

S. Twelfth Street; see Soulard Neighborhood Historic District

Schmitt,Fred,Building (Kingsway Center Commercial Area)
4913-4915 Page Blvd.
HABS MO-60-B
HABS 1991(HABS):19
6ph/3pg/1pc L

Schmitt,Fred,Stable (Kingsway Center Commercial Area)
Rear of 4913-4915 Page Blvd.
HABS MO-60-O
HABS 1991(HABS):19
5ph/3pg/1pc L

Scott's Hotel; see St. Louis River Front

Shaw,Henry,Commercial Building
N. First St.
HABS MO-1659
HABS MO,96-SALU,117-
1ph/1pg/1pc L

Shaw,Henry,House (Tower Grove; Missouri Botancial Garden,Henry Shaw House)
2345 Tower Grove Avenue
HABS MO-31-7
HABS MO,96-SALU,7-
7dr/29ph/1pg/3pc L

Shaw's Garden; see Missouri Botantical Garden

Shenandoah Street; see Soulard Neighborhood Historic District

Sherman,Gen. ,House
912 Garrison Ave.
HABS MO-125
HABS MO,96-SALU,36-
2ph/1pg L

Sherrick,George W. ,House
2618 S. Seventh St.
HABS MO-1168
HABS MO,96-SALU,60-
7ph/2pg L

Sidewalk Sewer Cover
HABS MO-1656
HABS MO,96-SALU,118-
1ph/1pc L

Sidney Street; see Soulard Neighborhood Historic District

Silva House (Kingsway Center Commercial Area)
1333 Euclid Ave.
HABS MO-60-K
HABS 1991(HABS):19
7ph/4pg/1pc L

Sisters of St. Joseph Convent
HABS MO-123
HABS MO,96-SALU,34-
1ph/1pg L

Small House (Kingsway Center Commercial Area)
1337 Euclid Ave.
HABS MO-60-L
HABS 1991(HABS):19
6ph/4pg/1pc L

Small,J. P.,House (Kingsway Center Commercial Area)
1413 Euclid Ave.
HABS MO-60-S
HABS 1991(HABS):19
7ph/4pg/1pc L

Smith,James R.,House (Kingsway Center Commercial Area)
1401 Euclid Ave.
HABS MO-60-P
HABS 1991(HABS):19
7ph/4pg/1pc L

Soldier's Memorial Building
Olive & Third Sts.
HABS MO-1639
HABS MO,96-SALU,119-
1ph/1pg/1pc L

Soulard Mansion
1249 S. Ninth St.
HABS MO-113
HABS MO,96-SALU,25-
1ph/1pg L

Soulard Neighborhood Historic District
HABS MO-275
HABS MO,96-SALU,120-
1pg/fr L

Soulard Neighborhood Historic District (Allen Street)
HABS MO-275-H
HABS MO,96-SALU,120H-
3ph/1pc L

Soulard Neighborhood Historic District (Ann Street)
HABS MO-275-I
HABS MO,96-SALU,120I-
1ph/1pc L

Soulard Neighborhood Historic District (Geyer Street)
HABS MO-275-J
HABS MO,96-SALU,120J-
2ph/1pc L

Soulard Neighborhood Historic District (Lafayette Street)
HABS MO-275-K
HABS MO,96-SALU,120K-
6ph/1pc L

Soulard Neighborhood Historic District (Russell Street)
HABS MO-275-L
HABS MO,96-SALU,120L-
2ph/1pc L

Soulard Neighborhood Historic District (S. Eighth Street)
HABS MO-275-B
HABS MO,96-SALU,120B-
9ph/1pc L

Soulard Neighborhood Historic District (S. Eleventh Street)
HABS MO-275-E
HABS MO,96-SALU,120E-
11ph/1pc L

Soulard Neighborhood Historic District (S. Ninth Street)
HABS MO-275-C
HABS MO,96-SALU,120C-
12ph/1pc L

Soulard Neighborhood Historic District (S. Seventh Street)
HABS MO-275-A
HABS MO,96-SALU,120A-
4ph/1pc L

Soulard Neighborhood Historic District (S. Tenth Street)
HABS MO-275-D
HABS MO,96-SALU,120D-
9ph/1pc L

Soulard Neighborhood Historic District (S. Thirteenth Street)
HABS MO-275-G
HABS MO,96-SALU,120G-
1ph/1pc L

Soulard Neighborhood Historic District (S. Twelfth Street)
HABS MO-275-F
HABS MO,96-SALU,120F-
13ph/1pc L

Soulard Neighborhood Historic District (Shenandoah Street)
HABS MO-275-M
HABS MO,96-SALU,120M-
1ph/1pc L

Soulard Neighborhood Historic District (Sidney Street)
HABS MO-275-N
HABS MO,96-SALU,120N-
4ph/1pc L

Soulard Neighborhood Historic District (Victor Street)
HABS MO-275-O
HABS MO,96-SALU,120O-
1ph/1pc L

Soulard Neighborhood Historic District (Withnell Street)
HABS MO-275-P
HABS MO,96-SALU,120P-
2ph/1pc L

South Main Street (Commercial Buildings)
HABS MO-1665
HABS MO,96-SALU,121-
1ph/1pg/1pc/fr L

South Thirteenth Street,3300 Block (Houses)
HABS MO-1632
HABS MO,96-SALU,122-
1ph/1pg/1pc/fr L

St. Francis Xavier's Church (College Church)
Grand & Lindell Sts.
HABS MO-1653
HABS MO,96-SALU,123-
1ph/1pg/1pc L

St. John's Catholic Church
HABS MO-121
HABS MO,96-SALU,32-
1ph/1pg L

St. Louis Army Ammunition Plant
4800 Goodfellow Blvd.
HAER MO-9
HAER MO,96-SALU,79-
43pg/fr L

St. Louis Arsenal,Building Number 3
Second & Arsenal Sts.
HABS MO-1158-A
HABS MO,96-SALU,23J-
2ph/2pg L

St. Louis Arsenal,Building Number 6
Second & Arsenal Sts.
HABS MO-1159-A
HABS MO,96-SALU,23K-
4ph/2pg L

St. Louis Arsenal,Old Barracks
Second & Arsenal Sts.
HABS MO-1160-A
HABS MO,96-SALU,23L-
2ph/2pg L

St. Louis Cathedral
4400 Lindell Blvd.
HABS MO-1643
HABS MO,96-SALU,124-
1ph/1pg/1pc L

St. Louis City Hall
Tucker Blvd. at Market St.
HABS MO-265
HABS MO,96-SALU,68-
14ph/21pg/2pc L

St. Louis Courthouse,Old
Fourth to Broadway,Market to Chestnut Sts.
HABS MO-31-8
HABS MO,96-SALU,8-
49dr/10ph/3pg/1pc L

St. Louis Gateway Arch; see Jefferson National Expansion Memorial Arch

St. Louis Public Library
Olive St. between 13th & 14th
HABS MO-1835
HABS MO,96-SALV,125-
4ph/1pg/1pc/1ct L

St. Louis River Front (211-213 Chestnut Street (Commercial Building))
HABS MO-11-C
HABS MO,96-SALU,9-
1ph L

St. Louis River Front (New National Hotel; Scott's Hotel; U. S. Hotel; Rice House)
300 Market St.
HABS MO-1131
HABS MO,96-SALU,43-
21dr/14ph/2pg L

St. Louis River Front (119-121 North Main Street (Commercial Building))
HABS MO-11-B
HABS MO,96-SALU,11-
1ph L

St. Louis River Front (303 North Main Street (Commercial Building))
HABS MO-11-D
HABS MO,96-SALU,12-
1ph L

St. Louis River Front (305 North Main Street (Commercial Building))
HABS MO-11-E
HABS MO,96-SALU,13-
1ph L

St. Louis River Front (7-15 North Main Street (Commercial Building))
HABS MO-11-A
HABS MO,96-SALU,10-
1ph L

St. Louis River Front (115 Valentine Street (Brick House))
115 Valentine St.
HABS MO-11-F
HABS MO,96-SALU,14-
1ph L

St. Louis Union Station
Market St. between 18th & 19th
HABS MO-1670
HABS MO,96-SALU,126-
16ph/1pg/2pc/2ct L

St. Louis Union Station Powerhouse
S. 18th St.,North of U.S. Hwy. 40
HAER MO-23
HAER MO,96-SALU,80-
30ph/12pg/2pc L

St. Louis Union Station Train Shed
1820 Market St.
HAER MO-24
HAER MO,96-SALU,81-
4ph/1pg/2pc L

St. Louis University,Administration Building
Grand & Pine Blvds.
HABS MO-1642
HABS MO,96-SALU,127-
1ph/1pg/1pc L

St. Mark's Episcopal Church
4714 Clifton St.
HABS MO-1652
HABS MO,96-SALU,128-
3ph/1pg/1pc L

St. Mary's Roman Catholic Church (Church of St. Mary of Victory)
748 S. Third St.
HABS MO-31-6
HABS MO,96-SALU,6-
8dr/1ph/1pg L

St. Nicholas Hotel; see Victoria Building

St. Patrick's Church
Sixth & Biddle Sts.
HABS MO-122
HABS MO,96-SALU,33-
3ph/1pg L

St. Vincent de Paul Church
HABS MO-114
HABS MO,96,SALU,26-
2ph/1pg L

Steinkauler,Guido,House
HABS MO-1169
HABS MO,96-SALU,61-
7ph/2pg L

Streetscape
HABS MO-1666
HABS MO,96-SALU,129-
1ph/1pc L

Temple Israel (Union Memorial African Methodist Episcopal Church)
Leffingwell & Pine Sts.
HABS MO-1170
HABS MO,96-SALU,62-
5ph/3pg L

Thieleman,John G. ,House
1825 S. Ninth St.
HABS MO-1171
HABS MO,96-SALU,63-
4ph/2pg L

Tower Gr. Pk.,Magnolia & Tower Grove Ave. Entrance; see Tower Grove Park,North Gate

Tower Grove; see Shaw,Henry,House

Tower Grove Park
4255 Arsenal St.
HABS MO-1137
HABS MO,96-SALU,46-
4dr/13ph/16pg/1pc/3ct/fr L

Tower Grove Park,Arsenal Street Gate; see Tower Grove Park,South Gate

Tower Grove Park,Bridges
4255 Arsenal St.
HABS MO-1137-T
HABS MO,96-SALU,46T-
2dr/2ph/5pg/1pc/fr L

Tower Grove Park,Children's Playground Summerhouse; see Tower Grove Park,Shelter Twenty-five

Tower Grove Park,Chinese Pavilion; see Tower Grove Park,Shelter Twenty-one

Tower Grove Park,East Gate Entrance (Tower Grove Park,Grand Boulevard Entrance)
4255 Arsenal St.
HABS MO-1137-A
HABS MO,96-SALU,46A-
1dr/13ph/5pg/1pc/fr L

Tower Grove Park,Grand Boulevard Entrance; see Tower Grove Park,East Gate Entrance

Tower Grove Park,Lily Pond Summerhouse; see Tower Grove Park,Shelter Twenty-eight

Tower Grove Park,Music Stand (Tower Grove Park,Structure Fifteen)
4255 Arsenal St.
HABS MO-1137-K
HABS MO,96-SALU,46K-
1dr/3ph/5pg/1pc/fr L

Tower Grove Park,North Gate (Tower Gr. Pk.,Magnolia & Tower Grove Ave. Entrance
4255 Arsenal St.
HABS MO-1137-C
HABS MO,96-SALU,46C-
1dr/2ph/6pg/1pc/fr L

Tower Grove Park,Picnic Shelter; see Tower Grove Park,Shelter Sixteen

Tower Grove Park,Planthouse Range (Tower Grove Park,Structures Two & Three)
4255 Arsenal St.
HABS MO-1137-U
HABS MO,96-SALU,46U-
4ph/6pg/1pc L

Tower Grove Park,Sailboat Pond
4255 Arsenal St.
HABS MO-1137-H
HABS MO,96-SALU,46H-
2dr/8ph/5pg/1pc/fr L

Tower Grove Park,Shelter Eighteen (Tower Grove Park,Well House)
4255 Arsenal St.
HABS MO-1137-N
HABS MO,96-SALU,46N-
1dr/1ph/4pg/1pc/fr L

Tower Grove Park,Shelter Eleven (Tower Grove Park,South Well)
4255 Arsenal St.
HABS MO-1137-J
HABS MO,96-SALU,46J-
1dr/1ph/4pg/1pc/fr L

Tower Grove Park,Shelter Seventeen
4255 Arsenal St.
HABS MO-1137-M
HABS MO,96-SALU,46M-
1dr/2ph/4pg/1pc/fr L

Tower Grove Park,Shelter Sixteen (Tower Grove Park,Picnic Shelter)
4255 Arsenal St.
HABS MO-1137-L
HABS MO,96-SALU,46L-
1dr/3ph/4pg/1pc/fr L

Tower Grove Park,Shelter Ten (Tower Grove Park,Turkish Pavilion)
4255 Arsenal St.
HABS MO-1137-I
HABS MO,96-SALU,46I-
1dr/5ph/4pg/1pc/fr L

Tower Grove Park,Shelter Twenty-eight (Tower Grove Park,Lily Pond Summerhouse)
4255 Arsenal St.
HABS MO-1137-S
HABS MO,96-SALU,46S-
1dr/3ph/4pg/1pc/fr L

Tower Grove Park,Shelter Twenty-five (Tower Grove Park,Children's Playground Summerhouse
4255 Arsenal St.
HABS MO-1137-R
HABS MO,96-SALU,46R-
1dr/4ph/4pg/1pc/fr L

Tower Grove Park,Shelter Twenty-one (Tower Grove Park,Chinese Pavilion)
4255 Arsenal St.
HABS MO-1137-P
HABS MO,96-SALU,46P-
1dr/3ph/3pg/1pc/fr L

Tower Grove Park,Shelter Twenty-two (Tower Grove Park,Sons of Rest Shelter)
4255 Arsenal St.
HABS MO-1137-Q
HABS MO,96-SALU,46Q-
1dr/5ph/4pg/1pc/fr L

Tower Grove Park,Shelters Nineteen & Twenty (Tower Grove Park,Wellhouses)
4255 Arsenal St.
HABS MO-1137-0
HABS MO,96-SALU,460-
1dr/3ph/4pg/1pc/fr L

Tower Grove Park,Sons of Rest Shelter; see Tower Grove Park,Shelter Twenty-two

Tower Grove Park,South Gate (Tower Grove Park,Arsenal Street Gate)
4255 Arsenal St.
HABS MO-1137-D
HABS MO,96-SALU,46D-
1dr/2ph/4pg/1pc/fr L

Tower Grove Park,South Gate Lodge (Tower Grove Park,Structure Twelve)
4255 Arsenal St.
HABS MO-1137-E
HABS MO,96-SALU,46E-
10dr/11ph/6pg/1pc/fr L

Tower Grove Park,South Well; see Tower Grove Park,Shelter Eleven

Tower Grove Park,Stone House & Stable Complex (Tower Grove Park,Structures Thirty-one X,Seven,Six
4255 Arsenal St.
HABS MO-1137-G
HABS MO,96-SALU,46G-
5ph/7pg/1pc L

Tower Grove Park,Structure Fifteen; see Tower Grove Park,Music Stand

Tower Grove Park,Structure Thirty-two X; see Tower Grove Park,West Gate House & Gate

Tower Grove Park,Structure Twelve; see Tower Grove Park,South Gate Lodge

Tower Grove Park,Structure Twenty-nine; see Tower Grove Park,Superintendent's House

Tower Grove Park,Structures Thirty-one X,Seven,Six; see Tower Grove Park,Stone House & Stable Complex

Tower Grove Park,Structures Two & Three; see Tower Grove Park,Planthouse Range

Tower Grove Park,Superintendent's House (Tower Grove Park,Structure Twenty-nine)
4255 Arsenal St.
HABS MO-1137-F
HABS MO,96-SALU,46F-
8dr/14ph/8pg/1pc/fr L

Tower Grove Park,Turkish Pavilion; see Tower Grove Park,Shelter Ten

Tower Grove Park,Well House; see Tower Grove Park,Shelter Eighteen

Tower Grove Park,Wellhouses; see Tower Grove Park,Shelters Nineteen & Twenty

Tower Grove Park,West Gate House & Gate (Tower Grove Park,Structure Thirty-two X)
4255 Arsenal St.
HABS MO-1137-B
HABS MO,96-SALU,46B-
2dr/4ph/7pg/1pc/fr L

Twenty-first Street Bridge
Spanning RR tracks at Twenty-first St.
HAER MO-11
HAER MO,96-SALU,74-
34ph/3pg/3pc L

U. S. Hotel; see St. Louis River Front

Union Memorial African Methodist Episcopal Church; see Temple Israel

United States Arsenal
Second & Arsenal Sts.
HABS MO-111
HABS MO,96-SALU,23-
10ph/3pg/1pc L

University Building
Sixteenth & Pine St.
HABS MO-120
HABS MO,96-SALU,31-
1ph/1pg L

115 Valentine Street (Brick House); see St. Louis River Front

Vander Lippe House (Kingsway Center Commercial Area)
1409 Euclid Ave.
HABS MO-60-R
HABS 1991(HABS):19
7ph/4pg/1pc L

Victor Street; see Soulard Neighborhood Historic District

Victoria Building (St. Nicholas Hotel)
Eighth & Locust Sts.
HABS MO-1138
HABS MO,96-SALU,47-
3ph/2pg L

Wainwright Building
Seventh & Chestnut Sts.
HABS MO-1140
HABS MO,96-SALU,49-
45ph/7pg/5pc/1ct/fr L

Walsh House
2721 Pine St.
HABS MO-15
HABS MO,96-SALU,18-
2ph/1pg L

Washington Terrace
Union Blvd.
HABS MO-274
HABS MO,96-SALU,130-
33ph/3pc/2ct L

Washington University,Brookings Hall
Skinker & Lindell Blvd.
HABS MO-1638
HABS MO,96-SALU,131-
1ph/1pg/1pc L

Water Tower,Red (Bissell Street Water Tower)
Blair & Bissell Sts.
HABS MO-1192
HABS MO,96-SALU,132-
6ph/1pg/2pc/1ct L

Whittemore,John,House
Garrison & Franklin Sts.
HABS MO-1178
HABS MO,96-SALU,66-
1ph L

Wilkinson House (Kingsway Center Commercial Area)
1347 Euclid Ave.
HABS MO-60-N
HABS 1991(HABS):19
6ph/4pg/1pc L

Withnell Street; see Soulard Neighborhood Historic District

Farrel House (Kingsway Center Commercial Area)
4917 Page Blvd.
HABS MO-60-C
HABS 1991(HABS):19
6ph/3pg/1pc L

Kingsway Center Commercial Area; see Farrel House

ST. LOUIS COUNTY

AFFTON

Benoist,Louis A. ,House; see Oakland

Benoist,Louis A. ,House,Servants' Quarters; see Oakland,Servants' Quarters

Oakland (Benoist,Louis A. ,House)
7801 Genesta St.
HABS MO-1182
HABS MO,95-AFT,1-
12dr/10ph/1pc L

Oakland,Servants' Quarters (Benoist,Louis A. ,House,Servants' Quarters)
7801 Genesta St.
HABS MO-1182-A
HABS MO,95-AFT,1A-
1ph/1pc L

AFFTON VIC.

Grant-Dent Country House (Whitehaven)
Grant Rd.
HABS MO-1150
HABS MO,95-AFT.V,1-
3dr/21ph/2pg L

Grant,Gen. ,Cabin; see Hardscrabble

Hardscrabble (Grant,Gen. ,Cabin)
Gravois Rd.
HABS MO-1134
HABS MO,95-AFT.V,2-
12ph/1pg L

Whitehaven; see Grant-Dent Country House

AFTON VIC.

Grant Road (Log Cabin)
HABS MO-1676
HABS MO,95-AFT.V,3-
1ph/1pc L

BELLEFONTAINE NEIGH.

Bissell,Gen. Daniel,House; see Franklinville Farms

Franklinville Farms (Bissell,Gen. Daniel,House)
10225 Bellefontaine Rd.
HABS MO-145
HABS MO,95-BELNEB,1-
15dr/3ph/2pg/1pc L

BELLEFONTAINE VIC.

Bellefontaine Church
Bellefontaine Rd.
HABS MO-1144
HABS MO,95-BELFO.V,1-
1ph/1pg L

BONFILS

Chouteau House
HABS MO-1674
HABS MO,95-BONFI,1-
1ph/1pg/1pc/fr L

CARONDELET

Marine Villa (Thul-Peters House)
3811 Kosciusko St.
HABS MO-1172
HABS MO,95-CARON,1-
8ph/2pg L

Thul-Peters House; see Marine Villa

CHESTERFIELD

Bates,Gov. Frederick,House; see Thornhill

Bonhomme Church,Old; see Bonhomme Presbyterian Church

Bonhomme Presbyterian Church (Bonhomme Church,Old; Stone Church,Old)
White & Conway Rds.
HABS MO-137
HABS MO,95-CHEST,2-
8dr/5ph/1pg/1pc L

Stone Church,Old; see Bonhomme Presbyterian Church

Stuart Log Cabin
HABS MO-144
HABS MO,95-CHEST.V,1-
2ph/1pg L

Thornhill (Bates,Gov. Frederick,House)
Arrowhead Lane
HABS MO-131
HABS MO,95-CHEST,1-
4dr/10ph/1pg/1pc L

CLAYTON

Hanley,Martin F. ,House
7600 Westmoreland Dr.
HABS MO-1193
HABS MO,95-CLAYT,1-
12dr/4pg/fr L

CRESTWOOD

Long,William,Log House
9385 Pardee Rd.
HABS MO-1186
HABS MO,95-CREST,2-
4dr/7ph/1pc L

Sappington,Thomas,House
Sappington Rd.
HABS MO-1173
HABS MO,95-CREST,1-
9ph/4pg/1pc L

ELLISVILLE

Ferris,Capt. Harvey,House
1362 Manchester Rd.
HABS MO-1184
HABS MO,95-ELLIS,1-
9dr/9ph/1pc L

FLORISSANT

Archambault House
603 St. Denis St.
HABS MO-1822
HABS MO,95-FLORI,5-
1ph/1pg/1pc L

Aubuchon,Baptiste G. ,House
450 Rue St. Jacques
HABS MO-1821
HABS MO,95-FLORI,6-
1ph/1pg/1pc L

Casa Alvarez
289 Rue St. Denis
HABS MO-1815
HABS MO,95-FLORI,7-
7ph/1pg/1pc L

Fort Bellefontaine
Bellefontaine Farms
HABS MO-146
HABS MO,95-FLORI,4-
2ph/1pg L

Fort Bellefontaine,Powder Magazine
HABS MO-146-A
HABS MO,95-FLORI,4-
3ph/2pg L

House,Brick
HABS MO-1824
HABS MO,95-FLORI,8-
1ph/1pg/1pc L

House,Brick
300 Washington St.
HABS MO-1823
HABS MO,95-FLORI,9-
2ph/1pg/1pc L

House,Frame
HABS MO-1827
HABS MO,95-FLORI,14-
4ph/1pg/1pc L

House,Frame
HABS MO-1828
HABS MO,95-FLORI,11-
1ph/1pg/1pc L

House,Frame
HABS MO-1829
HABS MO,95-FLORI,13-
1ph/1pg/1pc L

House,Frame
1191 Saint Michael St.
HABS MO-1818
HABS MO,95-FLORI,12-
2ph/1pg/1pc L

House,Frame
905 Lafayette
HABS MO-1826
HABS MO,95-FLORI,10-
1ph/1pg/1pc L

Myers,John B. ,Barn
180 W. Dunn Rd.
HABS MO-1183-A
HABS MO,95-FLORI,15A-
1ph/1pc L

Myers,John B. ,House
180 W. Dunn Rd.
HABS MO-1183
HABS MO,95-FLORI,15-
10dr/7ph/1pc L

Sisters of Loretto Convent
HABS MO-139
HABS MO,95-FLORI,1-
5ph/2pg/1pc/fr L

St. Ferdinand Church
W. End Of St. Francis St.
HABS MO-140
HABS MO,95-FLORI,2-
5ph/2pg/1pc L

St. Stanislaus Seminary
700 Howderschell Rd.
HABS MO-141
HABS MO,95-FLORI,3-
6ph/1pg/1pc L

Store & Residence,Brick
HABS MO-1819
HABS MO,95-FLORI,16-
2ph/1pg/1pc L

Store & Residence,Brick
100-1-2 Rue St. Louis at Jefferson
HABS MO-1825
HABS MO,95-FLORI,18-
1ph/1pg/1pc L

Store & Residence,Brick
599 St. Denis St.
HABS MO-1820
HABS MO,95-FLORI,17-
1ph/1pg/1pc L

FLORISSANT VIC.

Mullanphy House; see Taille de Noyer

Taille de Noyer (Mullanphy House)
400 Taille de Noyer
HABS MO-1143
HABS MO,95-FLORI.V,2-
10dr/6ph/3pg L

GLENDALE

Armstrong House
700 E. Collins Ave.
HABS MO-143
HABS MO,95-GLEND,1-
2ph/1pg L

GUMBO VIC.

Rupple Log Cabin
HABS MO-1675
HABS MO,95-GUM.V,1-
2ph/1pg/1pc L

KIRKWOOD

Eliot Unitarian Chapel; see Grace Episcopal Church

Grace Episcopal Church (Eliot Unitarian Chapel)
N. Taylor & Argonne Sts.
HABS MO-1187
HABS MO,95-KIRK,1-
1ph/1pg/1pc L

Missouri-Pacific Railroad Station
HABS MO-1188
HABS MO,95-KIRK,2-
3ph/1pc L

Mudd's Grove
302 W. Argonne Dr.
HABS MO-1189
HABS MO,95-KIRK,3-
5ph/1pg/1pc L

MAPLEWOOD

Bartold Grove
Manchester & Hanley Sts.
HABS MO-193
HABS MO,95-MAPWO,1-
2ph/1pg L

NORTHWOODS

Minoma
6617 Hazel Ave.
HABS MO-1830
HABS MO,95-NORWO,1-
6ph/1pg/1pc L

OVERLAND

Ferguson Log Cabin
3631 Brown Rd.
HABS MO-132
HABS MO,95-OVLA,1-
3ph/1pg/1pc L

McKibben House
HABS MO-133
HABS MO,95-OVLA,2-
1ph/1pg L

Powers Mansion
National Bridge & Brown Rds.
HABS MO-134
HABS MO,95-OVLA,3-
1ph/1pg L

PATTONVILLE

Fee Fee Church
Fee Fee Rd.
HABS MO-135
HABS MO,95-PATVI,1-
2ph/1pg L

ST. LOUIS VIC.

Bellefontaine Bridge
HAER MO-26
HAER MO,95-SALU.V,1-
31ph/2pc L

Jefferson Barracks
Jefferson Barracks Historical Park
HABS MO-1809
HABS MO,95-SALU.V,2-
9ph/1pg/1pc L

Jefferson Barracks,Laborers' House
Jefferson Barracks Historical Park
HABS MO-1809-B
HABS MO,95-SALU.V,2B-
12ph/2pc L

Jefferson Barracks,Powder Magazine,Brick & Stone
Jefferson Barracks Historical Park
HABS MO-1809-D
HABS MO,95-SALU.V,2D-
1ph/1pc L

Jefferson Barracks,Powder Magazine,Stone
Jefferson Barracks Historical Park
HABS MO-1809-C
HABS MO,95-SALU.V,2C-
3ph/1pc L

Jefferson Barracks,Stable
Jefferson Barracks Historical Park
HABS MO-1809-A
HABS MO,95-SALU.V,2A-
6ph/1pc L

WEBSTER GROVES

Griffen,Peers,House
224 College Ave.
HABS MO-1181
HABS MO,95-WEBGRO,1-
10dr/4ph/1pc L

WELLSTON

O'Brien,Dr. ,House
1232 Sutter Ave.
HABS MO-116
HABS MO,95-WEL,1-
2ph/1pg L

STE. GENEVIEVE COUNTY

BLOOMDALE

Lee,Capt. ,House
Starr Rt.
HABS MO-1102
HABS MO,97-BLOOM,1-
1ph/1pg L

BLOOMSDALE

Brooks House
State Rt. 25
HABS MO-1612
HABS MO,97-BLOOM,3-
1ph/1pg/1pc L

Drury House
HABS MO-1103
HABS MO,97-BLOOM,2-
1ph/1pg L

St. Philomena's Church
HABS MO-1611
HABS MO,97-BLOOM,4-
2ph/1pg/1pc L

STE. GENEVIEVE

Amoureaux House
St. Mary's Rd.
HABS MO-1113
HABS MO,97-SAIGEN,13-
10dr/21ph/2pg/2pc/1ct/fr L

Baptiste,Jean,House; see Valle,Jean Baptiste,House

Beauvais,Joseph V.,House
20 S. Main St.
HABS MO-1121
HABS MO,97-SAIGEN,20-
ι1991(HABS):19°
8dr/12ph/8pg/2pc/1ct/fr L

Beauvais,Vital St. Gemme,House II
St. Mary's Rd.
HABS MO-1284
HABS MO,97-SAIGEN,36-
ι1991(HABS):19°
5dr/2ph/5pg/1pc/fr L

Bequet-Ribault House (Ribeau House)
St. Mary's Rd.
HABS MO-1114
HABS MO,97-SAIGEN,14-
ι1991(HABS):19°
9dr/17ph/8pg/2pc/1ct/fr L

Bogy's House
HABS MO-1123
HABS MO,97-SAIGEN,22-
1ph/1pg L

Bolduc,Louis,House
123 S. Main St.
HABS MO-1105
HABS MO,97-SAIGEN,6-
ι1991(HABS):19°
15dr/35ph/8pg/2pc/3ct/fr L

Church of Ste. Genevieve
Dubourg Pl.
HABS MO-1621
HABS MO,97-SAIGEN,25-
10ph/1pg/1pc/fr L

Convent of the Sisters of St. Joseph
Dubourg Place
HABS MO-1618
HABS MO,97-SAIGEN,26-
3ph/1pg/1pc/fr L

Courthouse,First; see Price,John,House

DeLuziere,Pierre Delassus,House
U.S. Rt. 61
HABS MO-1283
HABS MO,97-SAIGEN.V,5-
ι1991(HABS):19°
5dr/13ph/6pg/1pc/1ct/fr L

Detchmendy House
Main & Market Sts.
HABS MO-1110
HABS MO,97-SAIGEN,10-
1ph/1pg L

Dorlac,Pierre,House; see Valle,Jean Baptiste,House II

Dufour House
Merchant St.
HABS MO-1119
HABS MO,97-SAIGEN,18-
2ph/1pg/1pc/fr L

First Parochial School; see Pratte Warehouse

Green Tree Tavern; see Janis,Nicolas,House

House
HABS MO-1617
HABS MO,97-SAIGEN,27-
1ph/1pg/1pc L

House,First Brick,West of Mississippi River; see Price,John,House

Indian Trading Post
Second & Merchant Sts.
HABS MO-31-13
HABS MO07-SAIGEN,4-
2dr/9ph/1pg/1pc/fr L

Jacques Dubreuil Guibourd House
Fourth & Merchant Sts.
HABS MO-1109
HABS MO,97-SAIGEN,9-
28ph/2pg/3pc/1ct/fr L

Janis-Ziegler House; see Janis,Nicolas,House

Janis,Nicolas,House (Janis-Ziegler House; Green Tree Tavern)
244 Old St. Mary's Rd.
HABS MO-1104
HABS MO,97-SAIGEN,5-
ι1991(HABS):19°
9dr/19ph/9pg/2pc/1ct/fr L

La Haye House
704 La Porte St.
HABS MO-1838
HABS MO,97-SAIGEN,29-
3ph/1pc L

Lasource-Durand House
St. Mary's Rd. behind Bequet-Ribault House
HABS MO-1281
HABS MO,97-SAIGEN,30-
ı1991(HABS):19°
9dr/6ph/6pg/1pc/fr L

Le Compte,Henry,House
HABS MO-1125
HABS MO,97-SAIGEN,23-
2ph/2pg/1pc/fr L

Linden House
116 S. Main St.
HABS MO-1174
HABS MO,97-SAIGEN,35-
1dr/1ph/1pc L

Linn,Sen. Lewis F. House
Merchant St.
HABS MO-1117
HABS MO,97-SAIGEN,16-
2ph/1pg/1pc/fr L

Loretto Convent,Old (Meillieur House)
Main St.
HABS MO-1111
HABS MO,97-SAIGEN,11-
1ph/1pg L

Meillieur House; see Loretto Convent,Old

Millard,Josiah,House (Valle, Francois B.,House; Wilder House)
1007 N. Main St.
HABS MO-1122
HABS MO,97-SAIGEN,21-
16ph/2pg/2pc/1ct/fr L

Misplait,Basil,House
Old St. Mary's Rd.
HABS MO-1616
HABS MO,97-SAIGEN,31-
4ph/1pg/1pc L

Philipson-Valle House; see Valle,Felix & Odile Pratt,House

Philipson-Valle Slave Quarters; see Valle,Felix & Odile Pratt,Slave Quarters

Post Office,Old
HABS MO-1112
HABS MO,97-SAIGEN,12-
1ph/1pg L

Pratte Warehouse (First Parochial School)
HABS MO-1108
HABS MO,97-SAIGEN,8-
7ph/2pg/1pc/fr L

Pratte,Joseph,House
HABS MO-1124
HABS MO,97-SAIMA,1-
1ph/1pg L

Price,John,House (Courthouse,First; House,First Brick,West of Mississippi River)
Third & Market Sts.
HABS MO-1107
HABS MO,97-SAIGEN,7-
5ph/2pg/2pc/1ct L

Ribeau House; see Bequet-Ribault House

Rozier Bank
Second & Merchant Sts.
HABS MO-1116
HABS MO,97-SAIGEN,15-
1ph/1pg L

Rozier House
St. Mary's Rd.
HABS MO-1280
HABS 1991(HABS):19
3dr/5pg/fr L

Second & Gabourie Streets (Old Stone House)
Corner of Second & Gabourie Sts.
HABS MO-31-12
HABS MO,97-SAIGEN,3-
2dr/6ph/1pg/1pc/1ct L

Seraphin,Joseph,House
74 Seraphin St.
HABS MO-1282
HABS MO,97-SAIGEN,31-
ı1991(HABS):19°
2dr/3ph/5pg/1pc/fr L

Shaw,Dr. Benjamin,House
Merchant & Second Sts.
HABS MO-1120
HABS MO,97-SAIGEN,19-
4ph/1pg/1pc/fr L

Ste. Genevieve Academy
Fifth & Washington Sts.
HABS MO-1118
HABS MO,97-SAIGEN,17-
6ph/2pg/2pc/1ct/fr L

Ste. Genevieve Cemetery
Fifth St.
HABS MO-1130
HABS MO,97-SAIGEN,24-
1ph/1pg L

Ste. Genevieve Hotel,Slave Quarters
HABS MO-1620
HABS MO,97-SAIGEN,33-
1ph/1pc L

Valle, Francois B.,House; see Millard,Josiah,House

Valle,Felix & Odile Pratt,House (Philipson-Valle House)
Merchant & Second Sts.
HABS MO-31-11
HABS MO,97-SAIGEN,2-
7dr/15ph/1pg/2pc/1ct/fr L

Valle,Felix & Odile Pratt,Slave Quarters (Philipson-Valle Slave Quarters)
SE corner of Merchant & Second Sts.
HABS MO-31-11-A
HABS MO,97-SAIGEN,2A-
3ph/1pc L

Valle,Jean Baptiste,Barn
HABS MO-31-10-A
HABS MO,97-SAIGEN,1A-
2ph/1pc L

Valle,Jean Baptiste,House (Baptiste,Jean,House)
99 S. Main St. (NW corner of Main & Market Sts.)
HABS MO-31-10
HABS MO,97-SAIGEN,1-
8dr/25ph/7pg/2pc/2ct/fr L

Valle,Jean Baptiste,House II (Dorlac,Pierre,House)
St. Mary's Rd.
HABS MO-1285
HABS MO,97-SAIGEN,34-
ı1991(HABS):19°
5dr/8ph/6pg/1pc/fr L

Wilder House; see Millard,Josiah,House

STE. GENEVIEVE VIC.

House
HABS MO-1624
HABS MO,97-SAIGEN.V,1-
1ph/1pg/1pc L

House
HABS MO-1625
HABS MO,97-SAIGEN.V,2-
1ph/1pg/1pc L

House,Log
HABS MO-1626
HABS MO,97-SAIGEN.V,3-
1ph/1pg/1pc L

Lee House
State Rt. 25
HABS MO-1623
HABS MO,97-BLOOM.V,1-
1ph/1pg/1pc L

Petrequin Legrave House; see St. Gemme,Captain,House

St. Gemme,Captain,House (Petrequin Legrave House)
Maple St.
HABS MO-1627
HABS MO,97-SAIGEN.V,4-
10ph/1pg/1pc/fr L

STODDARD COUNTY

DEXTER VIC.

Evans Pottery (Simmemon Pottery)
HABS MO-1698
HABS MO,104-DEXT.V,1-
3ph/1pg/1pc/fr L

Simmemon Pottery; see Evans Pottery

STONE COUNTY

Lampe Tower Site; see Wilderness Tower Site

Mark Twain National Forest; see Wilderness Tower Site

Wilderness Tower Site (Lampe Tower Site; Mark Twain National Forest)
East of Missouri Highways 13 and 86
HABS MO-1913
HAER LAMPE VIC.
24ph/19pg/3pc/fr H

JAMESVILLE VIC.

Hootentown Bridge
County Rt. 133,Spanning James River
HAER MO-48
HAER 1992(HAER):MD-1
11ph/15pg/1pc L

WARREN COUNTY

???

Loutre Island Old Brick Church
HABS MO-1539
HABS MO,110- ,3
7ph/1pg/1pc/fr L

Talbot House
Loutre Island
HABS MO-1780
HABS MO,110- ,2-
2ph/1pg/1pc L

Wagon Shed
HABS MO-1781
HABS MO,110- ,1-
1ph/1pg/1pc L

DUTZOW VIC.

Borgman,Herman,Mill
HABS MO-1700
HABS MO,110-DUTZ.V,1-
2ph/1pg/1pc/fr L

Muench,Frederick,Farm
HABS MO-1699
HABS MO,110-DUTZ.V,2-
2ph/1pg/1pc/fr L

Muench,Frederick,Farm,Outbuilding
HABS MO-1699-B
HABS MO,110-DUTZ.V,2B-
1ph/1pc/fr L

DUZOW VIC.

Muench,Frederick,Farm,Barn
HABS MO-1699-A
HABS MO,110-DUTZ.V,2A-
5ph/1pc/fr L

MARTHASVILLE

Deere,John,Blacksmith Shop
HABS MO-1707
HABS MO,110-MARVI,1-
4ph/1pc/fr L

German Evangelical Church
Boone's Lick Rd. & Thurmann
HABS MO-1706
HABS MO,110-MARVI,2-
2ph/1pg/1pc L

Grabs,Augustus Ferdinand,House
HABS MO-1708
HABS MO,110-MARVI,3-
4ph/1pg/1pc/fr L

MARTHASVILLE VIC.

Barn
HABS MO-1713
HABS MO,110-MARVI.V,8-
1ph/1pg/1pc/fr L

Bierbaum Farmhouse
Dutzow R. F. D.
HABS MO-1779
HABS MO,110-MARVI.V,9-
2ph/1pg/1pc L

Bryan-Boone Cemetery
HABS MO-1710
HABS MO,110-MARVI.V,1-
1ph/1pc L

Building,Stone
HABS MO-1715
HABS MO,110-MARVI.V,10-
1ph/1pc/fr L

Callaway,Flanders,House
Hwy. Rt. 47
HABS MO-1711
HABS MO,110-MARVI.V,2-
4ph/1pg/1pc/fr L

Goll,Charles,House
HABS MO-1712
HABS MO,110-MARVI.V,3-
2ph/1pc/fr L

Goll,Charles,Summer Kitchen
HABS MO-1712-A
HABS MO,110-MARVI.V,3A-
1ph/fr L

Knapheide,Henry,House
HABS MO-1738
HABS MO,110-MARVI.V,5-
2ph/1pg/1pc/fr L

Marthasville College Building
HABS MO-1701
HABS MO,110-MARVI.V,11-
1ph/1pg/1pc/fr L

Marthasville Seminary Printing Shop
HABS MO-1702
HABS MO,110-MARVI.V,12-
1ph/1pg/1pc/fr L

Schuster,Jacob,Farm,Log Cabin Crib
Rt. 95
HABS MO-1714
HABS MO,110-MARVI.V,6-
2ph/1pg/1pc L

Wyatt House
HABS MO-1709
HABS MO,110-MARVI.V,7-
1ph/1pg/1pc L

WARRENTON

House
HABS MO-1705
HABS MO,110-WARTO.1-
1ph/1pg/1pc/fr L

WARRENTON VIC.

House
State Rt. 47
HABS MO-1704
HABS MO,110-WARTO.V,1-
1ph/1pg/1pc/fr L

Schuetzenfest Hall
Boone's Lick Rd.
HABS MO-1703
HABS MO,110-WARTO.V,2-
3ph/1pg/1pc/fr L

WASHINGTON COUNTY

CALEDONIA

Bellevue Collegiate Institute
HABS MO-1722
HABS MO,111-CALDO,1-
1ph/1pg/1pc/fr L

Eversole,William G. ,House
HABS MO-1721
HABS MO,111-CALDO,2-
4ph/1pg/1pc/fr L

Presbyterian Church
HABS MO-1720
HABS MO,111-CALDO,3-
2ph/1pg/1pc/fr L

Relfe,Dr. James Hugh,House
HABS MO-1723
HABS MO,111-CALDO,4-
1ph/1pg/1pc/fr L

Thompson,Jane,House
HABS MO-1719
HABS MO,111-CALDO,5-
8ph/1pg/1pc/fr L

Thompson,Jane,Slave Cabin
HABS MO-1719-A
HABS MO,111-CALDO,5A-
2ph/1pc/fr L

CALEDONIA VIC.

Russell,Alexander,House
State Rt. 21
HABS MO-1717
HABS MO,111-CALDO.V,1-
2ph/1pg/1pc/fr L

Woods,William,House
HABS MO-1718
HABS MO,111-CALDO.V,2-
7ph/1pg/1pc/fr L

Woods,William,Springhouse
HABS MO-1718-A
HABS MO,111-CALDO.V,2A-
5ph/1pg/1pc/fr L

CANNON CREEK

Cannon Creek Mine Smelter
HABS MO-1716
HABS MO,111-CANCR,1-
2ph/1pc L

OLD MINES

Allen House; see Murphy House

Baptist Church
HABS MO-1727
HABS MO,111-OLMI,3-
2ph/1pg/1pc/fr L

Coleman House
HABS MO-1726
HABS MO,111-OLMI,4-
2ph/1pg/1pc/fr L

House,Frame
HABS MO-1725
HABS MO,111-OLMI,5-
3ph/1pg/1pc/fr L

La Marque House
HABS MO-1728
HABS MO,111-OLMI,6-
4ph/1pg/1pc/fr L

Murphy House (Allen House)
HABS MO-199
HABS MO,111-0LMI,1-
6ph/1pg/1pc/fr L

Parish House
HABS MO-1724
HABS MO,111-OLMI,7-
1ph/1pg/1pc/fr L

St. Joachim's Church
HABS MO-1129
HABS MO,111,OLMI,2-
8ph/2pg/1pc/fr L

OLD MINES VIC.

Houses
State Hwy. 21
HABS MO-1807
HABS MO,111-OLMI.V,1-
1ph/1pg/1pc L

PIEDMONT VIC.

Stokely,Joseph,Log House
HABS MO-1737
HABS MO,112-PIED.V,1-
2ph/1pg/1pc/fr L

POTOSI

Austin,Moses,House
HABS MO-1735
HABS MO,111-POTO,1-
2ph/1pg/1pc/fr L

County Clerk's Office
HABS MO-1733
HABS MO,111-POTO,2-
1ph/1pc/fr L

Eversole House
HABS MO-1734
HABS MO,111-POTO,3-
1ph/1pg/1pc/fr L

Perry-McGready House
HABS MO-1736
HABS MO,111-POTO,6-
16ph/1pg/1pc/fr L

Perry-Stratton House
HABS MO-1731
HABS MO,111-POTO,7-
3ph/1pg/1pc/fr L

Perry,Clarence,House
HABS MO-1730
HABS MO,111-POTO,4-
1ph/1pg/1pc/fr L

Perry,William,House
HABS MO-1732
HABS MO,111-POTO,5-
1ph/1pg/1pc/fr L

Presbyterian Church
HABS MO-1729
HABS M0,111-POTO,8-
4ph/1pg/1pc/fr L

Valle,Basile,House
HABS MO-1540
HABS MO,111-POTO,9-
5ph/1pg/1pc/fr L

RACOLA

Bequette Log House
HABS MO-1126
HABS MO,111,RACO,1-
1ph/1pg L

Loomes San Soucie Log Cabin
HABS MO-1128
HABS MO,111-RACO,3-
1ph/1pg L

Lucas Log Cabin
HABS MO-1127
HABS MO,111,RACO,2-
1ph/1pg L

Anaconda Reduction Department, Anaconda vicinity, Deer Lodge County, Montana. View of the foundry department breaker house. Photograph by Jet Lowe, 1979 (HAER MONT,12-ANAC.V,1-4).

Montana

BEAVERHEAD COUNTY

BANNACK

Beaverhead County Courthouse
Main St.
HABS MT-5
HABS MONT,1-BRAN,2-
9dr/12ph/6pg/fr L

Methodist Church
Main St.
HABS MT-6
HABS MONT,1-BRAN,3-
5dr/2ph/5pg/fr L

School and Masonic Temple
Main St.
HABS MT-4
HABS MONT,1-BRAN,1-
7dr/3ph/6pg/fr L

BIG HORN COUNTY

CUSTER BATTLEFIELD

Custer Battlefield National Monument; see Superintendent's Lodge

Superintendent's Lodge (Custer Battlefield National Monument)
HABS MT-7
HABS MONT,2-CUST,1-
12dr/4ph/6pg/fr L

HARDIN

Hardin City Hall; see Hardin City Water Works

Hardin City Water Works (Hardin City Hall)
101 E. 4th St.
HABS MT-71
HABS MONT,2-HARD,1-
37ph/18pg/3pc L

BLAINE COUNTY

COBURG

Milk River Bridge at Coberg
Spanning Milk River
HAER MT-4
HAER MONT,3-COBU,1-
8ph/1pg/1pc/9ct L

FORT BELKNAP

Fort Belknap Indian Agency,Building No. 15; see Fort Belknap Indian Agency,Employees Club

Fort Belknap Indian Agency,Building No. 28; see Fort Belknap Indian Agency,House

Fort Belknap Indian Agency,Employees Club (Fort Belknap Indian Agency,Building No. 15)
HABS MT-80-A
HABS 1991(HABS):2
5ph/20pg/1pc L

Fort Belknap Indian Agency,House (Fort Belknap Indian Agency,Building No. 28)
HABS MT-80-B
HABS 1991(HABS):2
3ph/1pc L

BROADWATER COUNTY

LOMBARD VIC.

Lombard Coke Ovens,Stone Foundation
Missouri River near Toston Dam Reservoir
HAER MT-54-C
HAER 1990 (HAER):9
1ph/1pc L

RADERSBURG VIC.

Vermont Marble Quarry,Abandoned Mine Site
Limestone Hills, 2.25 mi. NE of Radersburg
HAER MT-11
HAER MONT,4-RADBU.V,1-
4ph/6pg/1pc L

TOSTON VIC.

Lombard Coke Ovens
N. Bank of Missouri River near Toston Dam Reservo.
HAER MT-54
HAER 1990 (HAER):9
8ph/21pg/1pc L

Lombard Coke Ovens,Caretaker's Cabin
Missouri River near Toston Dam Reservoir
HAER MT-54-B
HAER 1990 (HAER):9
2ph/1pc L

Lombard Coke Ovens,Tipple
Missouri River near Toston Dam Reservoir
HAER MT-54-A
HAER 1990 (HAER):9
2ph/1pc L

CARBON COUNTY

FORT SMITH VIC.

Bighorn Canyon National Recreation Area; see Hillsboro Ranch

Cedarvale; see Hillsboro Ranch

Hillsboro Ranch (Cedarvale; Bighorn Canyon National Recreation Area)
HABS MT-43
HABS MONT,5-FOSMI.V,1-
5dr L

FROMBERG VIC.

Fromberg Bridge
Spanning Clark's Fork of Yellowstone River
HAER MT-7
HAER MONT,5-FROBE.V,1-
5ph/2pg/1pc/2ct L

JOLIET

Rock Creek Bridge
Spans Rock Creek at County Rd.,S. end of Main St.
HAER MT-56
HAER DLC/PP-1993:MT-3
7ph/5pg/1pc L

RED LODGE VIC.

Foster Gulch Mine
Bear Creek 1 mi. SW of Town of Bear Creek
HAER MT-31
HAER MONT,5-RELO.V,1-
4ph/1pg/1pc L

Foster Gulch Mine,Boiler Housing
Bear Creek 1 mi. SW of Town of Bear Creek
HAER MT-31-B
HAER MONT,5-RELO.V,1-B-
1ph/1pc L

Foster Gulch Mine,Change House
Bear Creek 1 mi. SW of Town of Bear Creek
HAER MT-31-D
HAER MONT,5-RELO.V,1-D-
1ph/1pc L

Foster Gulch Mine,Coal Bin
Bear Creek 1 mi. SW of Town of Bear Creek
HAER MT-31-F
HAER MONT,5-RELO.V,1-F-
1ph/1pc L

Foster Gulch Mine,Electric Power Station Ruins
Bear Creek 1 mi. SW of Town of Bear Creek
HAER MT-31-E
HAER MONT,5-RELO.V,1-E-
1ph/1pc L

Foster Gulch Mine,Fan Housing
Bear Creek 1 mi. SW of Town of Bear Creek
HAER MT-31-G
HAER MONT,5-RELO.V,1-G-
1ph/1pc L

Foster Gulch Mine,Machine Shop
Bear Creek 1 mi. SW of Town of Bear Creek
HAER MT-31-C
HAER MONT,5-RELO.V,1-C-
2ph/1pc L

Foster Gulch Mine,Tipple (ruins)
Bear Creek 1 mi. SW of Town of Bear Creek
HAER MT-31-A
HAER MONT,5-RELO.V,1-A-
1ph/1pc L

Smith Mine
Bear Creek 1.5 mi. W of Town of Bear Creek
HAER MT-32
HAER MONT,5-RELO.V,2-
3ph/30pg/1pc L

Smith Mine,Blacksmith/Mine Car Repair Bldg.
Bear Creek 1.5 mi. W of Town of Bear Creek
HAER MT-32-D
HAER MONT,5-RELO.V,2-D-
1ph/1pc L

Smith Mine,Boilers (ruins)
Bear Creek 1.5 mi. W of Town of Bear Creek
HAER MT-32-F
HAER MONT,5-RELO.V,2-F-
1ph/1pc L

Smith Mine,Electric Transfer Bldg.
Bear Creek 1.5 mi. W of Town of Bear Creek
HAER MT-32-E
HAER MONT,5-RELO.V,2-E-
1ph/1pc L

Smith Mine,Machine Shop/Maintenance Bldg.
Bear Creek 1.5 mi. W of Town of Bear Creek
HAER MT-32-C
HAER MONT,5-RELO.V,2-C-
1ph/1pc L

Smith Mine,Processing Plant
Bear Creek 1.5 mi. W of Town of Bear Creek
HAER MT-32-A
HAER MONT,5-RELO.V,2-A-
3ph/1pc L

Smith Mine,Tipple
Bear Creek 1.5 mi. W of Town of Bear Creek
HAER MT-32-B
HAER MONT,5-RELO.V,2-B-
2ph/1pc L

CASCADE COUNTY

GREAT FALLS

108 Central (Commercial Building)
(Park Hotel Annex)
108 Central Ave.
HABS MT-36
HABS MONT,7-GREFA,1-
12ph/5pg/1pc L

Park Hotel Annex; see 108 Central (Commercial Building)

Rolland Apartments
216-218 2nd Avenue North
HABS MT-74
HABS 1989(HABS):13
9ph/4pg/1pc L

Sparling Hotel
3rd St. North
HABS MT-75
HABS 1989(HABS):13
9ph/5pg/1pc L

Tenth Street Bridge
Spanning Missouri River
HAER MT-8
HAER MONT,7-GREFA,2-;DLC/PP-1993:MT-2
13ph/14pg/2pc/fr L

STOCKETT VIC.

Giffen Mine
3 Mi. SW of Stockett (Sec. 14,22,23 T18N R4E)
HAER MT-30
HAER 1989(HAER):16
1ph/14pg/1pc L

Giffen Mine,Fan Housing
3 mi. SW of Stockett (Sec. 14,22,23; T18N R4E)
HAER MT-30-B
HAER 1989(HAER):16
1ph/1pc L

Giffen Mine,Mine Shop
3 mi. SW of Stockett (Sec. 14,22,23; T18N R4E)
HAER MT-30-C
HAER 1989(HAER):16
1ph/1pc L

Giffen Mine,Tipple
3 mi. SW of Stockett (Sec. 14,22,23; T18N R4E)
HAER MT-30-A
HAER 1989(HAER):16
3ph/1pc L

CHOUTEAU COUNTY

FORT BENTON

Fort Benton Bridge
Spanning the Missouri River
HAER MT-9
HAER MONT,8-FOBE,1-
19ph/3pg/2pc/2ct L

FORT BENTON VIC.

Great Northern Railroad Bed
From Big Sandy to Verona
HAER MT-53
HAER 1989(HAER):16
8ph/13pg/1pc/3ct L

CUSTER COUNTY

MILES CITY

Fort Keogh,Livestock & Range Research Station
3 mi. west of Miles City on U.S. HWY. 10
HABS MT-76-C
HABS 1991(HABS):2
3ph/12pg/1pc L

Fort Keogh,Officers Quarters A
3 mi west of Miles City on U.S. HWY. 10
HABS MT-76-A
HABS 1991(HABS):2
20ph/2pc L

Fort Keogh,Officers Quarters B
3 mi. west of Miles City on U.S. HWY. 10
HABS MT-76-B
HABS 1991(HABS):2
13ph/1pc L

Miles,Gen. ,House
Hwy. 10
HABS MT-8
HABS MONT,9-MILCI,1-
9dr/3ph/4pg L

Tongue River Bridge
Spanning Tongue River
HAER MT-16
HAER MONT,9-MILCI,2-
11ph/1pg/1pc/2ct L

MILES CITY VIC.

Fort Keogh Bridge
Spanning the Yellowstone River
HAER MT-13
HAER MONT,9-MILCI.V,1-
17ph/2pg/2pc/4ct L

Kinsey Bridge
Spanning Yellowstone River
HAER MT-14
HAER MONT,9-MILCI.V,2-
3ph/2pg/1pc L

Paragon Bridge
Spanning the Yellowstone River
HAER MT-15
HAER MONT,9-MILCI.V,3-
15ph/2pg/1pc/1ct L

DEER LODGE COUNTY

ANACONDA

Anaconda City Hall; see Anaconda Historic District

Anaconda Historic District
Park & Commercial Sts. ,Main St. vic.
HABS MT-53
HABS MONT,12-ANAC,1-
13ph/1pg/2pc L

Anaconda Historic District (Anaconda City Hall)
E. Commercial & Cedar Aves.
HABS MT-53-T
HABS MONT,12-ANAC,1-T-
1ph/1pg/1pc L

Anaconda Historic District (Anaconda Junior High School)
Forth & Main Sts.
HABS MT-53-L
HABS MONT,12-ANAC,1-L-
1ph/1pg/1pc L

Anaconda Historic District (Anaconda Leader Building)
121 Main St.
HABS MT-53-F
HABS MONT,12-ANAC,1-F-
1ph/1pg/1pc L

Anaconda Historic District (Anaconda Standard Building)
219-221 Main St.
HABS MT-53-J
HABS MONT,12-ANAC,1-J-
1ph/1pg/1pc L

Anaconda Historic District (Ancient Order of Hibernians Hall)
321-323 E. Commercial St.
HABS MT-53-U
HABS MONT,12-ANAC,1-U-;
1989(HABS):13
2dr/14ph/9pg/2pc L

Anaconda Historic District (Barich Block)
416-420 Park St.
HABS MT-53-O
HABS MONT,12-ANAC,1-O-
1ph/1pg/1pc L

Anaconda Historic District (Benevolent & Protective Order of Elks Building)
217 Main St.
HABS MT-53-I
HABS MONT,12-ANAC,1-I-
1ph/1pg/1pc L

Anaconda Historic District (Butte,Anaconda & Pacific RR,General Offices)
300 W. Commercial Ave.
HABS MT-53-P
HABS MONT,12-ANAC,1-P-
1ph/1pg/1pc L

Anaconda Historic District (Club Moderne)
801 E. Park Ave.
HABS MT-53-A
HABS MONT,12-ANAC,1-A-
5ph/1pg/1pc L

Anaconda Historic District (Daly Bank Building)
123 Main St.
HABS MT-53-G
HABS MONT,12-ANAC,1-G-
1ph/1pg/1pc L

Anaconda Historic District (Daly,Marcus,Hotel)
200-208 Main St.
HABS MT-53-H
HABS MONT,12-ANAC,1-H-
1ph/1pg/1pc L

Anaconda Historic District (Davidson Block)
200 E. Park Ave.
HABS MT-53-N
HABS MONT,12-ANAC,1-N-
1ph/1pg/1pc L

Anaconda Historic District (Deer Lodge County Courthouse)
Main St. ,s. end
HABS MT-53-C
HABS MONT,12-ANAC,1-C-
1ph/1pg/1pc L

Anaconda Historic District (Durston Building)
Main St. & E. Park Ave.
HABS MT-53-M
HABS MONT,12-ANAC,1-M-
2ph/1pg/1pc L

Anaconda Historic District (225-229 East Commercial Avenue)
HABS MT-53-R
HABS MONT,12-ANAC,1-R-
1ph/1pg/1pc L

Anaconda Historic District (319 East Commercial Avenue)
HABS MT-53-S
HABS MONT,12-ANAC,1-S-
1ph/1pg/1pc L

Anaconda Historic District (Electric Light Building)
101-103 Main St.
HABS MT-53-D
HABS MONT,12-ANAC,1-D-
1ph/1pg/1pc L

Anaconda Historic District (Hearst Free Library)
Forth & Main Sts.
HABS MT-53-K
HABS MONT,12-ANAC,1-K-
1ph/1pg/1pc L

Anaconda Historic District (Mahie Block)
124 E. Commercial Ave.
HABS MT-53-Q
HABS MONT,12-ANAC,1-Q-
2ph/1pg/1pc L

Anaconda Historic District (Petritz Building)
115-119 Main St.
HABS MT-53-E
HABS MONT,12-ANAC,1-E-
1ph/1pg/1pc L

Anaconda Historic District (Washoe Theater)
305 Main St.
HABS MT-53-B
HABS MONT,12-ANAC,1-B-
11ph/1pg/1pc L

Anaconda Junior High School; see Anaconda Historic District

Anaconda Leader Building; see Anaconda Historic District

Anaconda Standard Building; see Anaconda Historic District

Ancient Order of Hibernians Hall; see Anaconda Historic District

Barich Block; see Anaconda Historic District

Benevolent & Protective Order of Elks Building; see Anaconda Historic District

Butte,Anaconda & Pacific RR,General Offices; see Anaconda Historic District

Club Moderne; see Anaconda Historic District

Daly Bank Building; see Anaconda Historic District

Daly,Marcus,Hotel; see Anaconda Historic District

Daly,Marcus,Hotel; see Montana Hotel

Davidson Block; see Anaconda Historic District

Deer Lodge County Courthouse; see Anaconda Historic District

Durston Building; see Anaconda Historic District

225-229 East Commercial Avenue; see Anaconda Historic District

319 East Commercial Avenue; see Anaconda Historic District

Electric Light Building; see Anaconda Historic District

Hearst Free Library; see Anaconda Historic District

Mahie Block; see Anaconda Historic District

Montana Hotel (Daly,Marcus,Hotel)
Park St. & S. Main
HABS MT-33
HABS MONT,12-ANAC,2-
12ph/8pg/1pc L

Petritz Building; see Anaconda Historic District

Washoe Theater; see Anaconda Historic District

ANACONDA VIC.

Anaconda Reduction Department
HAER MT-37
HAER MONT,12-ANAC.V,1-
8ph/3pg/1pc L

FERGUS COUNTY

DANVERS VIC.

Deerfield Bridge
Spanning Judith River
HAER MT-17
HAER MONT,14-DAN.V,1-
1ph/1pg/1pc L

Sample's Crossing Bridge
Spanning Judith River
HAER MT-19
HAER MONT,14-DAN.V,2-
1ph/2pg/1pc L

MOORE VIC.

Judith River Bridge
Spanning Judith River
HAER MT-18
HAER MONT,14-MOR.V,1-
5ph/1pg/1pc/1ct L

FLATHEAD COUNTY

CORAM VIC.

Coram Bridge
Spanning Flathead River
HAER MT-20
HAER MONT,15-COR.V,1-
11ph/1pg/1pc L

KALISPELL

Flathead Lake Cherry Growers Association Warehouse
20 N. Main St.
HAER MT-6
HAER MONT,15-KALSP,1-
21ph/7pg/1pc/fr L

KALISPELL VIC.

Steel Bridge,Old
Spanning Flathead River
HAER MT-21
HAER MONT,15-KALSP.V,1-
10ph/2pg/1pc/2ct L

TRIPLE ARCH VIC.

Going to the Sun Road
Glacier National Park
HAER MT-67
HAER 1988(HAER):95,VOID 11/17/92
34ph/5pg/3pc H

WEST GLACIER

Avalanche Creek Bridge (Glacier National Park)
Spanning Avalanche Ck. at Going-to-the-Sun Rd.
HAER MT-73
HAER DLC/PP-1993:MT-1
1ph/5pg/1pc/fr L

Belton Bridge (Glacier National Park)
Spanning middle fork of Flathead Riv. at Going-to-
HAER MT-68
HAER DLC/PP-1993:MT-1
1ph/9pg/1pc/fr L

Common Drainage Culvert (Glacier National Park)
Beneath Going-to-the-Sun Rd.
HAER MT-69
HAER DLC/PP-1993:MT-1
5pg/fr L

Creek Culvert (Glacier National Park)
Spanning unnamed creek(near Logan Ck.) at Going-to
HAER MT-74
HAER DLC/PP-1993:MT-1
5pg/fr L

Glacier National Park; see Avalanche Creek Bridge

Glacier National Park; see Belton Bridge

Glacier National Park; see Common Drainage Culvert

Glacier National Park; see Creek Culvert

Glacier National Park; see Going-to-the-Sun Road

Glacier National Park; see Going-to-the-Sun Road System Bridges

Glacier National Park; see Going-to-the-Sun Road System Culverts

Glacier National Park; see Going-to-the-Sun Road System Details

Glacier National Park; see Granite Creek Culvert

Glacier National Park; see Haystack Creek Culvert

Glacier National Park; see Horse Trail Underpass

Glacier National Park; see Logan Creek Bridge

Glacier National Park; see Snyder Creek Bridge

Glacier National Park; see Sprague Creek Culvert

Glacier National Park; see Triple Arches

Glacier National Park; see West Side Tunnel

Going-to-the-Sun Road (Glacier National Park)
HAER MT-67
HAER DLC/PP-1993:MT-1
3dr/88ph/55pg/7pc/fr L

Going-to-the-Sun Road System Bridges (Glacier National Park)
HAER MT-67-A
HAER DLC/PP-1993:MT-1
1dr L

Going-to-the-Sun Road System Culverts (Glacier National Park)
HAER MT-67-B
HAER DLC/PP-1993:MT-1
2dr L

Going-to-the-Sun Road System Details (Glacier National Park)
HAER MT-67-C
HAER DLC/PP-1993:MT-1
1dr/fr L

Granite Creek Culvert (Glacier National Park)
Spanning Granite Ck. at Going-to-the-Sun Rd.
HAER MT-77
HAER DLC/PP-1993:MT-1
5pg L

Haystack Creek Culvert (Glacier National Park)
Spanning N. gulch of Haystack Ck. at Going-to-the-
HAER MT-78
HAER DLC/PP-1993:MT-1
1ph/5pg/1pc/fr L

Horse Trail Underpass (Glacier National Park)
Beneath Going-to-the-Sun Rd. NE of W. Glacier Entr
HAER MT-72
HAER DLC/PP-1993:MT-1
1ph/5pg/1pc/fr L

Logan Creek Bridge (Glacier National Park)
Spanning Logan Ck. at Going-to-the-Sun Rd.
HAER MT-75
HAER DLC/PP-1993:MT-1
1dr/1ph/5pg/1pc/fr L

Snyder Creek Bridge (Glacier National Park)
Spanning Snyder Ck. at Going-to-the-Sun Rd.
HAER MT-71
HAER DLC/PP-1993:MT-1
1ph/5pg/1pc/fr L

Sprague Creek Culvert (Glacier National Park)
Spanning Sprague Ck. at Going-to-the-Sun Rd.
HAER MT-70
HAER DLC/PP-1993:MT-1
1ph/5pg/1pc/fr L

Triple Arches (Glacier National Park)
Spanning rift on Pollock Mt. at Going-to-the-Sun R
HAER MT-79
HAER DLC/PP-1993:MT-1
1dr/1ph/5pg/1pc/fr L

West Side Tunnel (Glacier National Park)
On Going-to-the-Sun Rd. NE of W. Glacier Entrance
HAER MT-76
HAER DLC/PP-1993:MT-1
3ph/5pg/1pc L

GALLATIN COUNTY

BOZEMAN

City Hall & Opera House
Rouse Ave. & E. Main St.
HABS MT-18
HABS MONT,16-BOZ,1-
10dr/12ph/8pg L

Montana State University,Montana Hall
W. Garfield St.
HABS MT-25
HABS MONT,16-BOZ,2-
2ph/9pg/1pc L

Tracy,William H. ,House
5 W. Mendenhall St.
HABS MT-29
HABS MONT,16-BOZ,3-
3ph/6pg/1pc L

BOZEMAN VIC.

O'Brien,James,Homestead
(Spain,Clarkson Farmstead)
HABS MT-83
11pg/1pc H

O'Brien,James,Homestead,First Shed
(Spain,Clarkson Farmstead)
HABS MT-83-C
1ph H

O'Brien,James,Homestead,Garage
(Spain,Clarkson Farmstead)
HABS MT-83-B
2ph H

O'Brien,James,Homestead,Hay Barn
HABS MT-83-G
1ph H

O'Brien,James,Homestead,Residence
(Spain,Clarkson Farmstead)
HABS MT-83-A
4ph H

O'Brien,James,Homestead,Second Shed
HABS MT-83-E
1ph H

O'Brien,James,Homestead,Shed and Bunkhouse (Spain,Clarkson Farmstead)
HABS MT-83-D
2ph H

O'Brien,James,Homestead,Stock Barn
(Spain,Clarkson Farmstead)
HABS MT-83-F
1ph H

Spain,Clarkson Farmstead; see O'Brien,James,Homestead

Spain,Clarkson Farmstead; see O'Brien,James,Homestead,First Shed

Spain,Clarkson Farmstead; see O'Brien,James,Homestead,Garage

Spain,Clarkson Farmstead; see O'Brien,James,Homestead,Residence

Spain,Clarkson Farmstead; see O'Brien,James,Homestead,Shed and Bunkhouse

Spain,Clarkson Farmstead; see O'Brien,James,Homestead,Stock Barn

GLACIER COUNTY

BABB VIC.

St. Mary River Bridge & Siphon
Spanning St. Mary River
HAER MT-22
HAER MONT,18-BABB.V,1-
15ph/2pg/1pc/4ct L

EAST GLACIER PARK V.

Three Bears Lake and Dams
North of Marian Pass
HAER MT-88
14ph/6pg/2pc H

Three Bears Lake and Dams,East Dam
North of Marias Pass
HAER MT-88-A
6ph/1pc H

Three Bears Lake and Dams,Water Control Box
North of Marias Pass
HAER MT-88-C
11ph/1pc H

Three Bears Lake and Dams,West Dam
North of Marias Pass
HAER MT-88-B
5ph/1pc H

EAST GLACIER VIC.

Glacier National Park; see Lubec Ranger Station

Lubec Ranger Station (Glacier National Park)
HABS MT-42
HABS MONT,18-GLACE.V,1-
7dr L

ST. MARY

Baring Creek Bridge (Glacier National Park)
Spanning Baring Ck. at Going-to-the-Sun Rd.
HAER MT-82
HAER DLC/PP-1993:MT-1
3dr/2ph/5pg/1pc/fr L

Divide Creek Bridge (Glacier National Park)
Spanning Divide Ck. at Going-to-the-Sun Rd.
HAER MT-85
HAER DLC/PP-1993:MT-1
1ph/5pg/1pc L

East Side Tunnel (Glacier National Park)
Through Piegan Mt. at Going-to-the-Sun Rd.
HAER MT-80
HAER DLC/PP-1993:MT-1
1ph/5pg/1pc L

Glacier National Park; see Baring Creek Bridge

Glacier National Park; see Divide Creek Bridge

Glacier National Park; see East Side Tunnel

Glacier National Park; see Golden Stairs Retaining Wall

Glacier National Park; see Siyeh Creek Culvert

Glacier National Park; see St. Mary River Bridge

Golden Stairs Retaining Wall (Glacier National Park)
Beneath Going-to-the-Sun Rd. 43 miles NE of W. Gla
HAER MT-83
HAER DLC/PP-1993:MT-1
1ph/5pg/1pc L

Siyeh Creek Culvert (Glacier National Park)
Spanning Siyeh Ck. at Going-to-the-Sun Rd.
HAER MT-81
HAER DLC/PP-1993:MT-1
1ph/5pg/1pc/fr L

St. Mary River Bridge (Glacier National Park)
Spanning St. Mary Riv. at Going-to-the-Sun Rd.
HAER MT-84
HAER DLC/PP-1993:MT-1
1ph/6pg/1pc/fr L

GOLDEN VALLEY COUNTY

BARBER

Barber Bridge
Spanning Musselshell River
HAER MT-12
HAER MONT,19-BARB,1-
6ph/1pg/1pc L

GRANITE COUNTY

GOLDCREEK VIC.

Master Placer Mining Camp
HAER MT-39
HAER MONT,20-GOCRE.V,1-
1ph/2pg/1pc L

Pineau Placer Mining Camp
HAER MT-38
HAER MONT,20-GOCRE.V,2-
1ph/2pg/1pc L

Pineau Placer Mining Camp,Reservoir & Cabin
HAER MT-38-A
HAER MONT,20-GOCRE.V,2-A-
2ph/2pg/1pc L

GRANITE

Miners Union Hall
Main St.
HABS MT-15
HABS MONT,20-GRANI,1-
11dr/12ph/6pg/1pc/fr L

Superintendent's House
Magnolia Ave.
HABS MT-16
HABS MONT,20-GRANI,2-
6dr/2ph/4pg/1pc/fr L

HALL VIC.

Emmetsburg Cemetery Monument
HAER MT-48
HAER MONT,20-HALL.V,1-
1ph/2pg/1pc L

Sunrise Mine
HAER MT-50
HAER MONT,20-HALL.V,2-
1ph/2pg/1pc L

MAXVILLE VIC.

Copper State Mine
HAER MT-40
HAER MONT,20-MAX.V,1-
1ph/2pg/1pc L

Moonlight Mining Camp
HAER MT-46
HAER MONT,20-MAX.V,2-
1ph/2pg/1pc L

Royal Basin Mine & Mill Site
HAER MT-47
HAER MONT,20-MAX.V,3-
1ph/2pg/1pc L

HILL COUNTY

ROCKY BOY'S AGENCY

Rocky Boy's Agency Flour Mill
HAER MT-65
HAER 1989(HAER):16
9ph/14pg/1pc L

JEFFERSON COUNTY

???

Efraimson,Andrew,Homestead
HABS MT-40
HABS MONT,22- ,1-
3ph/4pg/1pc L

ELKHORN

Fraternity Hall
Main St.
HABS MT-9
HABS MONT,22-ELK,1-
5dr/3ph/5pg L

RADERSBURG VIC.

Zimmerman,Clara,Homestead
HABS MT-41
HABS MONT,22-RADBU.V,1-
3ph/4pg/1pc L

LEWIS AND CLARK COUNTY

AUGUSTA VIC.

Dearborn River High Bridge
Spanning Dearborn River
HAER MT-23
HAER MONT,25-AUG.V,1-
11ph/2pg/1pc/7ct L

CRAIG VIC.

Wolf Creek Bridge
Spanning Missouri River
HAER MT-24
HAER MONT,25-CRA.V,1-
6ph/1pg/1pc L

HELENA

Ashby,S. C. ,House
642 Dearborn St.
HABS MT-21
HABS MONT,25-HEL,2-
13ph/6pg/1pc L

Federal Reserve Bank of Minneapolis,Helena Branch
400 N. Park Avenue
HABS MT-72
HABS 1989(HABS):13
10ph/9pg/1pc L

Governors Mansion,Old
304 N. Ewing St.
HABS MT-31
HABS MONT,25-HEL.V,3-
2ph/5pg/1pc L

Great Northern Depot (Helena Great Northern Depot)
100-110 Neill Avenue
HAER MT-52
HAER 1990 (HAER):9
7ph/11pg/1pc L

Hauser,Samuel T. ,House
720 Madison Ave.
HABS MT-23
HABS MONT,25-HEL,4-
4ph/6pg/1pc L

Helena Great Northern Depot; see Great Northern Depot

Kluge House
540 W. Main St.
HABS MT-17
HABS MONT,25-HEL,V-
10dr/4ph/4pg/1pc/fr L

Kohrs,Conrad,House
804 Dearborn Ave.
HABS MT-32
HABS MONT,25-HEL,5-
3ph/6pg/1pc L

Lewis & Clark County Courthouse
Broadway
HABS MT-27
HABS MONT,25-HEL,6-
3ph/6pg/1pc L

Masonic Temple,Second
Broadway & Jackson Sts.
HABS MT-34
HABS MONT,25-HEL,7-
1ph/7pg/1pc L

Neill,J. S. M. ,House
725 Madison Ave.
HABS MT-22
HABS MONT,25-HEL,8-
3ph/5pg/1pc L

Power,T. C. ,Mansion
604 Harrison Ave.
HABS MT-28
HABS MONT,25-HEL,9-
3ph/7pg/1pc L

Seligman,A. J. ,House
802 Madison Ave.
HABS MT-24
HABS MONT,25-HEL,10-
2ph/6pg/1pc L

U. S. Assay Office
206 Broadway St.
HABS MT-26
HABS MONT,25-HEL,11-
6ph/7pg/1pc L

HELENA VIC.

Child,W. C. ,Ranch
State Hwy. 279
HABS MT-30
HABS MONT,25-HEL.V,1-
3ph/6pg/1pc L

Green Meadow Ranch
HABS MT-35
HABS MONT,25-HEL.V,2-
1ph/5pg/1pc L

York Bridge
F. A. S. Rt. 280
HAER MT-2
HAER MONT,25-HEL.V,3-
14ph/17pg/1pc L

LINCOLN COUNTY

FORTINE VIC.

Dahlberg,Swan J.,Farmstead
U.S. Hwy. 93
HABS MT-81
HABS 1991(HABS):2
9pg L

Dahlberg,Swan J.,Farmstead,Residence
(Dahlberg,Swan J.,Farmstead,Structure No. 9.)
U.S. Hwy. 93
HABS MT-81-A
HABS 1991(HABS):2
3ph/1pc L

Dahlberg,Swan J.,Farmstead,Structure No. 9.; see Dahlberg,Swan J.,Farmstead,Residence

FORTINE VICINITY

Dalberg,Swan J.,Farmstead,Bunkhouse & Granary
(Dalberg,Swan J.,Farmstead,Structure No. 1)
U.S. HWY. 93
HABS MT-81-C
HABS 1991(HABS):2
3ph/1pc L

Dalberg,Swan J.,Farmstead,Garage/Storage Shed
(Structure No. 7)
U.S. HWY. 93,Fortine Vic.
HABS MT-81-B
HABS 1991(HABS):2
3ph/1pc L

Dalberg,Swan J.,Farmstead,Structure No. 1; see Dalberg,Swan J.,Farmstead,Bunkhouse & Granary

Structure No. 7; see Dalberg,Swan J.,Farmstead,Garage/Storage Shed

TROY

Troy-Libby Highway
Between Troy & Libby
HAER MT-66
15ph/15pg/2pc H

MADISON COUNTY

NE ENNIS

Nunn Hydro Electric Plant
On the Madison River
HAER MT-87
16ph/7pg/2pc H

TWIN BRIDGES

Madison County Fairgrounds
U. S. Hwy. 41
HABS MT-52
HABS MONT,29-TWIB,1-
1dr L

Madison County Fairgrounds,Gazebo
HABS MT-52-B
HABS MONT,29-TWIB,1-B-
1dr L

Madison County Fairgrounds,Grandstand
HABS MT-52-G
HABS MONT,29-TWIB,1-G-
3dr L

Madison County Fairgrounds,Ground Keeper's House
HABS MT-52-A
HABS MONT,29-TWIB,1-A-
2dr L

Madison County Fairgrounds,Livestock Shed
HABS MT-52-E
HABS MONT,29-TWIB,1-E-
3dr L

Madison County Fairgrounds,Octagonal Pavilion
HABS MT-52-D
HABS MONT,29-TWIB,1-D-
5dr L

Madison County Fairgrounds,Square Building
HABS MT-52-C
HABS MONT,29-TWIB,1-C-
4dr L

Madison County Fairgrounds,Stock Barns One & Two
HABS MT-52-F
HABS MONT,29-TWIB,1-F-
2dr L

VIRGINIA CITY

Content Corner
Wallace & Jackson Sts.
HABS MT-2
HABS MONT,29-VIRG,2-
7dr/9ph/6pg L

Madison County Courthouse
Wallace St.
HABS MT-3
HABS MONT,29-VIRG,3-
20dr/8ph/6pg L

Sanders,Col. W. F. ,House
Idaho St.
HABS MT-1
HABS MONT,29-VIRG,1-
12dr/6ph/6pg L

MEAGHER COUNTY

WHITE SULPHUR SPRING

Camp Baker; see Fort Logan,Blockhouse

Fort Logan,Blockhouse (Camp Baker)
HABS MT-19
HABS MONT,30-WIT.V,1-
7dr/7ph/4pg/fr L

MINERAL COUNTY

ALBERTON VIC.

Fish Creek Bridge
Cyr-Iron Mountain Rd.
HAER MT-49
HAER 1991(HAER):3
7ph/13pg/1pc/fr L

ST. REGIS VIC.

Mullan Road Segment
HAER MT-45
HAER MONT,31-SAIREG.V,1-
1ph/2pg/1pc L

MISSOULA COUNTY

ALBERTON VIC.

Alberton Pictograph
HAER MT-44
HAER MONT,32-ALBER.V,1-
1ph/2pg/1pc L

FORT MISSOULA

Fort Missoula,Laundry Building
HABS MT-20
HABS MONT,32-MISS,3-
4ph/3pg/1pc/fr L

Fort Missoula,N. C. O. Living Quarters
HABS MT-14
HABS MONT,32-MISS,2-
6dr/5ph/5pg/fr L

Fort Missoula,Powder Magazine
HABS MT-13
HABS MONT,32-MISS,1-
4dr/3ph/3pg/fr L

LOLO VIC.

Traveler's Rest/Lolo Trail
HAER MT-42
HAER MONT,32-LOLO.V,1-
1ph/2pg/1pc L

MILLTOWN

Milltown Dam
Clark Fork River,6 miles upstream from Missoula
HAER MT-43
HAER 1990 (HAER):9
19ph/31pg/2pc L

Milltown Dam,Center House
Clark Fork River,6 miles upstream from Missoula
HAER MT-43-D
HAER 1990 (HAER):9
1ph/1pc L

Milltown Dam,East Side House
Clark Fork River,6 miles upstream from Missoula
HAER MT-43-E
HAER 1990 (HAER):9
1ph/1pc L

Milltown Dam,Powerhouse
Clark Fork River,6 miles upstream from Missoula
HAER MT-43-A
HAER 1990 (HAER):9
7ph/1pc L

Milltown Dam,Spillway
Clark Fork River,6 miles upstream from Missoula
HAER MT-43-B
HAER 1990 (HAER):9
5ph/1pc L

Milltown Dam,West Side House
Clark Fork River,6 miles upstream from Missoula
HAER MT-43-C
HAER 1990 (HAER):9
1ph/1pc L

MUSSELSHELL COUNTY

ROUNDUP VIC.

Roundup Bridge
Spanning Musselshell River
HAER MT-25
HAER MONT,33-ROUN.V,1-
11ph/2pg/1pc L

PARK COUNTY

LIVINGSTON VIC.

Pine Creek Bridge
Spanning Yellowstone River 10 mi. S. of Livingston
HAER MT-61
HAER 1991(HAER):3
14ph/10pg/1pc L

SPRINGDALE

Springdale Bridge
Federal Aid Secondary Rt. 563
HAER MT-10
HAER MONT,34-SPRIDA.V,1-
9ph/9pg/1pc L

POWELL COUNTY

AVON VIC.

Kimmerly Ditch & Flume
Avon vicinity
HAER MT-58
5ph/10pg/1pc L

Rice's Gas Station Complex
Kimmerly Lots S. of Avon,32 mi. W. of Helena
HABS MT-78
HABS 1991(HABS):2
4ph/6pg/1pc L

Rice's Gas Station Complex,Log House
Kimmerly Lots S. of Avon,32 mi. W. of Helena
HABS MT-78-B
HABS 1991(HABS):8
1pg L

Rice's Gas Station Complex,Motel
Kimmerly Lots,S. of Avon,32 mi. W. of Helena
HABS MT-78-A
HABS 1991(HABS):2
1ph/1pg/1pc L

Rice's Gas Station Complex,Privy
Kimmerly Lots South of Avon (32 mi. W. of Helena)
HABS MT-78-C
HABS 1991(HABS):2
1pg L

DEER LODGE

Grant-Kohrs Ranch Complex
(Grant-Kohrs Ranch National Historic Site)
Hwy. 10
HABS MT-39
HABS MONT,39-DELO,1-
15ph/2pg/1pc/1ct/fr L

Grant-Kohrs Ranch Complex,Bielenberg Barn
(Grant-Kohrs Ranch National Historic Site)
Hwy. 10
HABS MT-39-I
HABS MONT,39-DELO,1-I-
3ph/1pc L

Grant-Kohrs Ranch Complex,Brooder House (Grant-Kohrs Ranch National Historic Site)
Hwy. 10
HABS MT-39-P
HABS MONT,39-DELO,1-P-
2ph/1pc L

Grant-Kohrs Ranch Complex,Buggy Shed (Grant-Kohrs Ranch National Historic Site)
Hwy. 10
HABS MT-39-D
HABS MONT,39-DELO,1-D-
2ph/1pc L

Grant-Kohrs Ranch Complex,Bunkhouse (Grant-Kohrs Ranch National Historic Site)
Hwy. 10
HABS MT-39-B
HABS MONT,39-DELO,1-B-
11ph/1pc L

Grant-Kohrs Ranch Complex,Cattle Equipment (Grant-Kohrs Ranch National Historic Site)
Hwy. 10
HABS MT-39-W
HABS MONT,39-DELO,1-W-
4ph/1pc L

Grant-Kohrs Ranch Complex,Chicken House (Grant-Kohrs Ranch National Historic Site)
Hwy. 10
HABS MT-39-O
HABS MONT,39-DELO,1-O-
3ph/1pc L

Grant-Kohrs Ranch Complex,Cow Shed (Grant-Kohrs Ranch National Historic Site)
Hwy. 10
HABS MT-39-L
HABS MONT,39-DELO,1-L-
6ph/1pc L

Grant-Kohrs Ranch Complex,Dairy
(Grant-Kohrs Ranch National Historic Site)
Hwy. 10
HABS MT-39-N
HABS MONT,39-DELO,1-N-
6ph/1pc L

Grant-Kohrs Ranch Complex,Draft Horse Barn (Grant-Kohrs Ranch National Historic Site)
Hwy. 10
HABS MT-39-J
HABS MONT,39-DELO,1-J-
9ph/1pc L

Grant-Kohrs Ranch Complex,Feed Lots & Sheds (Grant-Kohrs Ranch National Historic Site)
Hwy. 10
HABS MT-39-M
HABS MONT,39-DELO,1-M-
9ph/1pc L

Grant-Kohrs Ranch Complex,Flumes
(Grant-Kohrs Ranch National Historic Site)
Hwy. 10
HABS MT-39-X
HABS MONT,39-DELO,1-X-
2ph/1pc L

Grant-Kohrs Ranch Complex,Garage/Blacksmith Shop
(Grant-Kohrs Ranch National Historic Site)
Hwy. 10
HABS MT-39-C
HABS MONT,39-DELO,1-C-
2ph/1pc L

Grant-Kohrs Ranch Complex,Granary No. 1 (Grant-Kohrs Ranch National Historic Site)
Hwy. 10
HABS MT-39-Q
HABS MONT,39-DELO,1-Q-
2ph/1pc L

Grant-Kohrs Ranch Complex,Granary No. 2 (Grant-Kohrs Ranch National Historic Site)
Hwy. 10
HABS MT-39-R
HABS MONT,39-DELO,1-R-
3ph/1pc L

Grant-Kohrs Ranch Complex,Ice House (Grant-Kohrs Ranch National Historic Site)
Hwy. 10
HABS MT-39-S
HABS MONT,39-DELO,1-S-
3ph/1pc L

Grant-Kohrs Ranch Complex,Leeds-Lion Barn (Grant-Kohrs Ranch National Historic Site)
Hwy. 10
HABS MT-39-F
HABS MONT,39-DELO,1-F-
2ph/1pc L

Grant-Kohrs Ranch Complex,Machine Shed (Grant-Kohrs Ranch National Historic Site)
Hwy. 10
HABS MT-39-T
HABS MONT,39-DELO,1-T-
2ph/1pc L

Grant-Kohrs Ranch Complex,Outhouses (Grant-Kohrs Ranch National Historic Site)
Hwy. 10
HABS MT-39-U
HABS MONT,39-DELO,1-U-
3ph/1pc L

Grant-Kohrs Ranch Complex,Ox Barn (Grant-Kohrs Ranch National Historic Site)
Hwy. 10
HABS MT-39-K
HABS MONT,39-DELO,1-K-
3ph/1pc L

Grant-Kohrs Ranch Complex,Ranch House (Grant-Kohrs Ranch National Historic Site)
Hwy. 10
HABS MT-39-A
HABS MONT,39-DELO,1-A-
23ph/2pc L

Grant-Kohrs Ranch Complex,Stallion Barn No. 1 (Grant-Kohrs Ranch Historic Site)
Hwy. 10
HABS MT-39-G
HABS MONT,39-DELO,1-G-
2ph/1pc L

Grant-Kohrs Ranch Complex,Stallion Barn No. 2 (Grant-Kohrs Ranch National Historic Site)
Hwy. 10
HABS MT-39-H
HABS MONT,39-DELO,1-H-
3ph/1pc L

Grant-Kohrs Ranch Complex,Stock Shelters (Grant-Kohrs Ranch National Historic Site)
Hwy. 10
HABS MT-39-V
HABS MONT,39-DELO,1-V-
4ph/1pc L

Grant-Kohrs Ranch Complex,Thoroughbred Barn (Grant-Kohrs Ranch National Historic Site)
Hwy. 10
HABS MT-39-E
HABS MONT,39-DELO,1-E-
4ph/1pc L

Grant-Kohrs Ranch Historic Site; see Grant-Kohrs Ranch Complex,Stallion Barn No. 1

Grant-Kohrs Ranch National Historic Site; see Grant-Kohrs Ranch Complex

Grant-Kohrs Ranch National Historic Site; see Grant-Kohrs Ranch Complex,Bielenberg Barn

Grant-Kohrs Ranch National Historic Site; see Grant-Kohrs Ranch Complex,Brooder House

Grant-Kohrs Ranch National Historic Site; see Grant-Kohrs Ranch Complex,Buggy Shed

Grant-Kohrs Ranch National Historic Site; see Grant-Kohrs Ranch Complex,Bunkhouse

Grant-Kohrs Ranch National Historic Site; see Grant-Kohrs Ranch Complex,Cattle Equipment

Grant-Kohrs Ranch National Historic Site; see Grant-Kohrs Ranch Complex,Chicken House

Grant-Kohrs Ranch National Historic Site; see Grant-Kohrs Ranch Complex,Cow Shed

Grant-Kohrs Ranch National Historic Site; see Grant-Kohrs Ranch Complex,Dairy

Grant-Kohrs Ranch National Historic Site; see Grant-Kohrs Ranch Complex,Draft Horse Barn

Grant-Kohrs Ranch National Historic Site; see Grant-Kohrs Ranch Complex,Feed Lots & Sheds

Grant-Kohrs Ranch National Historic Site; see Grant-Kohrs Ranch Complex,Flumes

Grant-Kohrs Ranch National Historic Site; see Grant-Kohrs Ranch Complex,Garage/Blacksmith Shop

Grant-Kohrs Ranch National Historic Site; see Grant-Kohrs Ranch Complex,Granary No. 1

Grant-Kohrs Ranch National Historic Site; see Grant-Kohrs Ranch Complex,Granary No. 2

Grant-Kohrs Ranch National Historic Site; see Grant-Kohrs Ranch Complex,Ice House

Grant-Kohrs Ranch National Historic Site; see Grant-Kohrs Ranch Complex,Leeds-Lion Barn

Grant-Kohrs Ranch National Historic Site; see Grant-Kohrs Ranch Complex,Machine Shed

Grant-Kohrs Ranch National Historic Site; see Grant-Kohrs Ranch Complex,Outhouses

Grant-Kohrs Ranch National Historic Site; see Grant-Kohrs Ranch Complex,Ox Barn

Grant-Kohrs Ranch National Historic Site; see Grant-Kohrs Ranch Complex,Ranch House

Grant-Kohrs Ranch National Historic Site; see Grant-Kohrs Ranch Complex,Stallion Barn No. 2

Grant-Kohrs Ranch National Historic Site; see Grant-Kohrs Ranch Complex,Stock Shelters

Grant-Kohrs Ranch National Historic Site; see Grant-Kohrs Ranch Complex,Thoroughbred Barn

DEER LODGE VIC.

Chicago,Milwaukee,St. Paul & Pacific RR Roundhouse
Kentucky Ave.
HAER MT-5
HAER MONT,39-DELO.V,1-
23ph/6pg/2pc L

GOLDCREEK VIC.

Mullan Road
Sec. 28;T9N,R10W,approx. 6 mi. SE of Goldcreek
HAER MT-41
HAER MONT,39-GOCRE.V,1-
3ph/2pg/1pc L

PRAIRIE COUNTY

TERRY VIC.

Calipso Bridge
Spanning Yellowstone River
HAER MT-26
HAER MONT,40-TER.V,1-
6ph/2pg/1pc/2ct L

RAVALLI COUNTY

CORVALLIS

Cowan House
1021 Main St.
HABS MT-73
HABS MONT,41-CORV,1-
6ph/7pg/1pc L

STEVENSVILLE

Fort Owen
U. S. Rt. 93
HABS MT-12
HABS MONT,41-STEV,3-
7dr/8ph/12pg/fr L

St. Mary's Mission (Roman Catholic)
HABS MT-10
HABS MONT,41-STEV,1-
15dr/12ph/6pg/fr L

St. Mary's Pharmacy
HABS MT-11
HABS MONT,41-STEV,2-
7dr/5ph/4pg/fr L

VICTOR VIC.

Victor Bridge
Spanning Bitterroot River
HAER MT-1
HAER MONT,41-VICT.V,1-
11ph/6pg/1pc L

RICHLAND COUNTY

NOHLY VIC.

Nohly Bridge; see Snowden Bridge

Snowden Bridge (Nohly Bridge)
Spanning Missouri River
HAER MT-27
HAER MONT,42-NOH.V,1-
21ph/2pg/2pc/4ct L

ROSEBUD COUNTY

COLSTRIP VIC.

Doc Tatlor Place,Barn
HABS MT-82-A
2ph H

Doc Taylor Place
HABS MT-82
3ph/8pg/1pc H

Doc Taylor Place,Cabin
HABS MT-82-B
7ph H

Doc Taylor Place,Windmill Ruins
HABS MT-82-C
1ph H

LAME DEER

U. S. Indian Service Laborer's Cottage
HABS MT-44
HABS MONT,44-LADE,1-
10ph/8pg/1pc L

SANDERS COUNTY

THOMPSON FALLS

Dry Channel Bridge
Spanning Clark Fork
HAER MT-29
HAER MONT,45-THOFA,1-
2ph/2pg/1pc L

Main Channel Bridge
Spanning Clark Fork
HAER MT-28
HAER MONT,45-THOFA,2-
11ph/2pg/1pc/4ct L

SILVER BOW COUNTY

BUTTE

Butte Historic District
Bounded by Copper,Arizona,Mercury & Continental St
HAER MT-35
HAER MONT,47-BUT,1-
80ph/7pg/8pc L

BUTTE VIC.

Anselmo Mine; see Butte Mineyards,Anselmo Mine

Badger State Mine; see Butte Mineyards,Badger State Mine

Belmont Mine; see Butte Mineyards,Belmont Mine

Berkeley Pit; see Butte Mineyards,Berkeley Pit

Butte Mineyards
HAER MT-36
HAER MONT,47-BUT.V,1-
5ph/1pg/1pc L

Butte Mineyards,Anselmo Mine (Anselmo Mine)
HAER MT-36-A
HAER MONT,47-BUT.V,1-A-
32ph/3pc L

Butte Mineyards,Badger State Mine (Badger State Mine)
HAER MT-36-I
HAER MONT,47-BUT.V,1-I-
12ph/1pc L

Butte Mineyards,Belmont Mine (Belmont Mine)
HAER MT-36-H
HAER MONT,47-BUT.V,1-H-
1ph/1pc L

Butte Mineyards,Berkeley Pit (Berkeley Pit)
HAER MT-36-D
HAER MONT,47-BUT.V,1-D-
3ph/1pc L

Butte Mineyards,Diamond Mine (Diamond Mine)
HAER MT-36-B
HAER MONT,47-BUT.V,1-B-
19ph/2pc L

Butte Mineyards,Kelley Mine (Kelley Mine)
HAER MT-36-E
HAER MONT,47-BUT.V,1-E-
6ph/1pc L

Butte Mineyards,Mountain Con Mine (Mountain Con Mine)
HAER MT-36-F
HAER MONT,47-BUT.V,1-F-
2ph/1pc L

Butte Mineyards,Original Mine (Original Mine)
HAER MT-36-G
HAER MONT,47-BUT.V,1-G-
1ph/1pc L

Butte Mineyards,Steward Mine; see Butte Mineyards,Stewart Mine

Butte Mineyards,Stewart Mine (Butte Mineyards,Steward Mine; Stewart Mine)
Intersection of Main & Woolman St.
HAER MT-36-C
HAER MONT,47-BUT.V,1-C-
23ph/24pg/2pc L

Diamond Mine; see Butte Mineyards,Diamond Mine

Kelley Mine; see Butte Mineyards,Kelley Mine

Mountain Con Mine; see Butte Mineyards,Mountain Con Mine

Original Mine; see Butte Mineyards,Original Mine

Stewart Mine; see Butte Mineyards,Stewart Mine

DIVIDE VIC.

Big Hole Pump Station
Old Hwy. 43
HAER MT-34
HAER MONT,47-DIVI.V,1-
14ph/3pg/1pc L

SWEET GRASS COUNTY

GREYCLIFF VIC.

Greycliff Bridge
Spanning the Yellowstone River,1/2 mi. E. Greyclif
HAER MT-62
HAER 1991(HAER):3
10ph/10pg/1pc L

VALLEY COUNTY

GLASGOW VIC.

Vandalia Bridge
Spanning Milk River,16 mi. W. of Glasgow
HAER MT-59
HAER 1991(HAER):3
12ph/9pg/1pc L

WIBAUX COUNTY

WIBAUX

Cannon-Davis House
Highway 7 South
HABS MT-77
HABS 1989(HABS):13
9ph/8pg/1pc L

YELLOWSTONE COUNTY

BILLINGS

Myaer Barn
2747 Old Hardin Rd.,Lockwood Flats area
HABS MT-69-B
5ph/1pc L

Myaer House
2747 Old Hardin Rd.,Lockwood Flats area
HABS MT-69-A
HABS 1991(HABS):2
6ph/6pg/1pc L

BILLINGS VIC.

Duck Creek Bridge
Spanning Yellowstone River on
Rte.329,SW of Billin
HAER MT-60
HAER 1991(HAER):3
14ph/10pg/2pc L

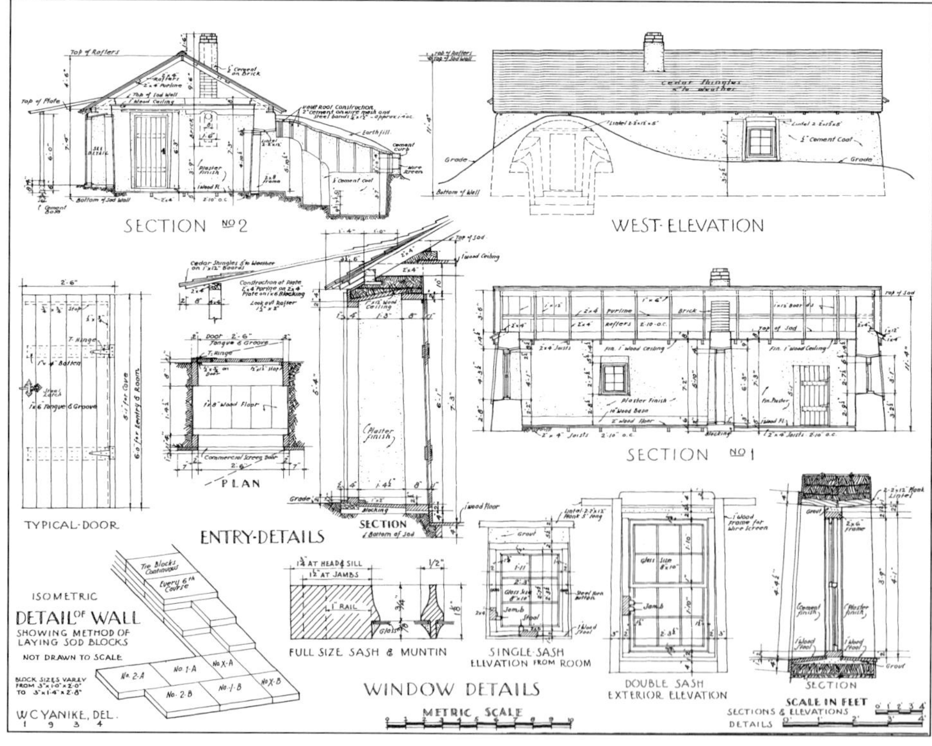

Swann's Drugstore (Niobrara Tribune), Niobrara, Knox County, Nebraska. Southwest elevation with awning. Photograph by Sam Amato, October 1977 (HABS NEB,54-NIOB,11-3).

Gustav Rohrich Sod House, Bellwood, Butler County, Nebraska. Sections, west elevation, entry details, window details. Measured drawing delineated by W.C. Yanike, March 1, 1934 (HABS NE-35-10, sheet 2 of 2; negative number LC-USZA3-34).

Nebraska

BUTLER COUNTY

BELLWOOD

Rohrich,Gustav,Sod House
HABS NE-35-10
HABS NEB,12-BELWO.V,1-
2dr/5ph/1pg/fr L

CASS COUNTY

PLATTSMOUTH VIC.

Plattsmouth Bridge
Spanning Missouri River
HAER NE-5
HAER NEB,13-PLATT.V,1-
7ph/1pc L

DAKOTA COUNTY

DAKOTA CITY

Lutheran Church
Fourteenth & Hickory Sts.
HABS NE-35-19
HABS NEB,22-DAKCI,1-
1dr/1ph/1pg/fr L

DOUGLAS COUNTY

FLORENCE

Mitchell House
Thirty-first & State Sts.
HABS NE-35-13
HABS NEB,28-FLOR,1-
5dr/2ph/1pg/fr L

MILLARD

Ehlers,Hans,Farm
F St.,Papillon 18 Damsite
HABS NE-42
HABS NEB,28-MILL.V,1-
1ph/7pg/1pc/fr L

Ehlers,Hans,Farm,Barn
F St.,Papillon Damsite
HABS NE-42-B
HABS NEB,28-MILL.V,1B-
2ph/1pc/fr L

Ehlers,Hans,Farm,Chickenhouse
F St.,Papillion 18 Damsite
HABS NE-42-G
HABS NEB,28-MILL.V,1G-
2ph/1pc/fr L

Ehlers,Hans,Farm,Corncrib
F St.,Papillion Damsite
HABS NE-42-E
HABS NEB,28-MILL.V,1E-
2ph/1pc/fr L

Ehlers,Hans,Farm,Hog Shed
F St.,Papillion Damsite
HABS NE-42-D
HABS NEB,28-MILL.V,1D-
2ph/1pc/fr L

Ehlers,Hans,Farm,Main House
F St.,Papillon Damsite
HABS NE-42-A
HABS NEB,28-MILL.V,1A-
4ph/1pc/fr L

Ehlers,Hans,Farm,Pumphouse
F St.,Papillion 18 Damsite
HABS NE-42-H
HABS NEB,28-MILL.V,1H-
1ph/1pc/fr L

Ehlers,Hans,Farm,Root Cellar
F St.,Papillion 18 Damsite
HABS NE-42-I
HABS NEB,28-MILL.V,1I-
1ph/1pc/fr L

Ehlers,Hans,Farm,Shed
F St.,Papillion Damsite
HABS NE-42-F
HABS NEB,28-MILL.V,1F-
2ph/1pc/fr L

Ehlers,Hans,Farm,Summer Kitchen
F St.,Papillion Damsite
HABS NE-42-C
HABS NEB,28-MILL.V,1C-
2ph/1pc/fr L

OMAHA

General Storehouse Building No. 21; see Omaha Quartermaster Depot Historic District

Nash Building
901-911 Douglas St. & 902-912 Farnam St.
HABS NE-36
HABS NEB,28-OMAH,1-
14ph/10pg/1pc L

Omaha Bridge
Spanning Missouri River
HAER NE-6
HAER NEB,28-OMAH,4-
5ph/1pc L

Omaha Quartermaster Depot; see Omaha Quartermaster Depot Historic District

Omaha Quartermaster Depot Historic District (Omaha Quartermaster Depot; General Storehouse Building No. 21)
Twenty-second & Woolworth Sts.
HABS NE-40-A
HABS 1984(HABS):153
10ph/15pg/fr L

Smith,M. E. ,Building
201 S. Tenth St.
HABS NE-35
HABS NEB,28-OMAH,3-
11ph/11pg L

GAGE COUNTY

BEATRICE

Freeman School (Homestead National Monument of America)
HABS NE-22
HABS NEB,34-BEAT.V,1A-
3dr L

Homestead National Monument of America; see Freeman School

Homestead National Monument of America; see Palmer-Epard Cabin

Palmer-Epard Cabin (Homestead National Monument of America)
HABS NE-21
HABS NEB,34-BEAT.V,1B-
1dr L

HALL COUNTY

GRAND ISLAND

Cornhusker Army Ammunition Plant
HAER NE-3
HAER NEB,40-GRIS.V,1-
57pg/fr L

KNOX COUNTY

CROFTON

Chambers-Mayberry House
(moved from NE,Niobrara,Oak & Fifth Ave.)
HABS NE-23
HABS NEB,54-NIOB,1-
4dr/8ph/10pg/1pc/fr L

NIOBRARA

American Legion Building (Dwight's,W. W. ,Jewelry Store)
Elm St.
HABS NE-24
HABS NEB,54-NIOB,2-
5dr/2ph/7pg/1pc/fr L

Bonesteel,H. E. ,Company; see Koster's Theatre

Chambers-Mayberry House
Oak & Fifth Ave. (moved to NE,Crofton)
HABS NE-23
HABS NEB,54-NIOB,1-
4dr/8ph/10pg/1pc/fr L

Dwight's,W. W. ,Jewelry Store; see American Legion Building

First Methodist Episcopal Church (Niobrara Public Library)
Fourth Ave.
HABS NE-25
HABS NEB,54-NIOB,3-
4dr/1ph/9pg/1pc/fr L

First Presbyterian Church of Niobrara
Sixth & Maple Sts.
HABS NE-26
HABS NEB,54-NIOB,4-
4dr/2ph/9pg/1pc L

Independent Order of Odd Fellows Lodge Number 82; see Knox County Courthouse

Knox County Courthouse (Independent Order of Odd Fellows Lodge Number 82)
Fourth Ave. & Elm St.
HABS NE-27
HABS NEB,54-NIOB,5-
5dr/3ph/13pg/1pc/fr L

Koster's Theatre (Niobrara,The; Bonesteel,H. E. ,Company; Olson's Market)
Elm St.
HABS NE-28
HABS NEB,54-NIOB,6-
4dr/6ph/15pg/1pc/fr L

Masonic Temple; see Niobrara Valley Bank

Niobrara Public Library; see First Methodist Episcopal Church

Niobrara Tribune; see Swann's Drugstore

Niobrara Valley Bank (Masonic Temple; Palen Block)
Elm St.
HABS NE-29
HABS NEB,54-NIOB,7-
5dr/11ph/25pg/1pc/fr L

Niobrara,The; see Koster's Theatre

Olson's Market; see Koster's Theatre

Opocensky,Frederick,House (Thierolf's Rest Home)
Sixth Ave.
HABS NE-30
HABS NEB,54-NIOB,8-
4dr/5ph/13pg/1pc/fr L

Palen Block; see Niobrara Valley Bank

St. Paul's Episcopal Church
Fourth Ave. (moved to NE,Santee,Ind. Reserv.)
HABS NE-31
HABS NEB,54-NIOB,9-
3dr/2ph/11pg/1pc/fr L

State Bank of Niobrara
Elm St.
HABS NE-32
HABS NEB,54-NIOB,10-
2dr/3ph/6pg/1pc/fr L

Swann's Drugstore (Niobrara Tribune)
Elm St.
HABS NE-33
HABS NEB,54-NIOB,11-
3dr/5ph/10pg/1pc/fr L

Thierolf's Rest Home; see Opocensky,Frederick,House

Zapadni Cesko-Bratreske Jednoty Hall Number 53
Fifth Ave.
HABS NE-34
HABS NEB,54-NIOB,12-
6dr/11ph/11pg/1pc/fr L

SANTEE

St. Paul's Episcopal Church
Santee Indian Reservation (moved from NE,Niobra)
HABS NE-31
HABS NEB,54-NIOB,9-
3dr/2ph/11pg/1pc/fr L

SANTEE RESERVATION

Chapel and Manse Congregational Mission (Parsonage,Santee Congregational Mission)
HABS NE-16
HABS NEB,54-SANT.V,2-
1dr/9ph/10pg L

Parsonage,Santee Congregational Mission; see Chapel and Manse Congregational Mission

SANTEE VIC.

Episcopal Church; see Episcopal Mission

Episcopal Mission (Episcopal Church)
HABS NE-20
HABS NEB,54-SANT.V,1-
5dr/8ph/1pg/fr L

LANCASTER COUNTY

LINCOLN

Bryan,William J. ,House
1625 D St.
HABS NE-35-8
HABS NEB,55-LINC,4-
11dr/2ph/1pg/fr L

Church of the Holy Trinity (Episcopal)
1200 J St.
HABS NE-35-6
HABS NEB,55-LINC,3-
20dr/5ph/1pg/fr L

City Hall,Old; see Lincoln City Hall

Eaton-Worster House
715 S. First St. (South Bottoms Historic District)
HABS NE-43-E
HABS 1987(HABS):55
2ph/9pg/1pc L

Goldstein-Kahem-Knaub House
701 S. First St. (South Bottoms Historic District)
HABS NE-43-A
HABS NEB,55-LINC,6A-
2ph/8pg/1pc L

Kennard,T. P. ,House
1627 H St.
HABS NE-35-4
HABS NEB,55-LINC,2-
10dr/2ph/1pg/fr L

Leavitt,Bert W. (House) (Veterans Administration Medical Ctr. Bldg. No. 20)
600 S. Seventieth St.
HABS NE-41-A
HABS 1991(HABS):23
4ph/7pg/1pc L

Lincoln City Hall (City Hall,Old; U. S. Post Office & Courthouse)
916 "O" St.
HABS NE-17
HABS NEB,55-LINC,5-
6ph/11pg/1pc/fr L

McKinley High School
1500 M St.
HABS NE-35-2
HABS NEB,55-LINC,1-
12dr/3ph/1pg/fr L

Popp-Fries House
705 S. First St. (South Bottoms Historic District)
HABS NE-43-B
HABS 1987(HABS):55
2ph/10pg/1pc L

Sharton,Henry,House
709 S. First St. (South Bottoms Historic District)
HABS NE-43-C
HABS NEB,55-LINC,6C-
4ph/7pg/1pc L

South Bottoms Historic District
701,705,709,711 & 715 S. First St.
HABS NE-43
HABS 1987(HABS):55
2ph/19pg/1pc L

U. S. Post Office & Courthouse; see Lincoln City Hall

U. S. Veterans Administration Medical Center
600 S. Seventieth St.
HABS NE-41
HABS NEB,55-LINC,7-
15ph/15pg/fr L

Veterans Administration Medical Ctr. Bldg. No. 20; see Leavitt,Bert W. (House)

Worster-Gert House
711 S. First St. (South Bottoms Historic District)
HABS NE-43-D
HABS NEB,55-LINC,6D-
2ph/7pg/1pc L

NEMAHA COUNTY

BROWNSVILLE

Cogswell,A. P. ,House
HABS NE-38
HABS NEB,64-BROVI,3-
2ph L

BROWNVILLE

Furnas,Gov. Robert W. ,House
Sixth St.
HABS NE-35-17
HABS NEB,64-BROVI,2-
3dr/2ph/1pg/fr L

Methodist Church
Fifth St.
HABS NE-35-15
HABS NEB,64-BROVI,1-
1dr/1ph/1pg/fr L

OTOE COUNTY

NEBRAKA CITY

Grant,S. L. ,House
Fourteenth St. & Third St.
HABS NE-35-3
HABS NEB,66-NEBCI,2-
7dr/1ph/1pg/fr L

NEBRASKA CITY

Otoe County Courthouse
Tenth & Central Ave.
HABS NE-35-1
HABS NEB,66-NEBCI,1-
9dr/2ph/1pg/fr L

St. Benedict Parish Church & School
Clay & Fifth Sts.
HABS NE-35-5
HABS NEB,66-NEBCI,3-
6dr/2ph/1pg/fr L

Wessell House
Nebraska Ave. & Eighth St.
HABS NE-35-11
HABS NEB,66-NEBCI,4-
7dr/1ph/1pg/fr L

NEBRASKA CITY VIC.

Nebraska City Bridge
Span. Missouri River near Hwy. 2 btwn Neb. & Iowa
HAER NE-2
HAER 1990 (HAER):11
3dr/59ph/509pg/4pc L

RICHARDSON COUNTY

HUMBOLDT

Nims,Reuel,Store
S. terminus of Parkview St.
HABS NE-37
HABS NEB,74-HUMB,1-
3dr/13ph/3pg/1pc L

RULO

Rulo Bridge
Spanning Missouri River
HAER NE-4
HAER NEB,74-RULO,1-
11ph/2pc L

SARPY COUNTY

BELLEVUE

Presbyterian Church
Franklin & Twentieth Sts.
HABS NE-35-7
HABS NEB,77-BELVU,1-
4dr/2ph/1pg/fr L

Town Hall
Main & Twenty-third Sts.
HABS NE-35-9
HABS NEB,77-BELVU,2-
7dr/1ph/1pg L

WASHINGTON COUNTY

BLAIR VIC.

Blair Bridge; see
Lincoln,Abraham,Memorial Bridge

Blair Crossing Bridge
Spanning Missouri River
HAER NE-7
HAER NEB,89-BLAIR.V,1-
5ph/1pc L

Lincoln,Abraham,Memorial Bridge
(Blair Bridge)
Span. Missouri Rvr. on Hwy. 30 btwn NE & IA
HAER NE-1
HAER 1990 (HAER):11
37ph/52pg/3pc L

Town of Virginia City, Storey County, Nevada. View from northwest. Photograph by William H. Knowles, April 1937 (HABS NEV,15-VIRG,1-8).

Liberty Fire House, Gold Hill, Storey County, Nevada. Exterior view. Photograph by Robert W. Kerrigan, March 1937 (HABS NEV,15-GOLD,1-1).

Nevada

CARSON CITY (CITY)

Chartz,Alfred,House
412 Nevada St.
HABS NV-13-15
HABS NEV,13-CARCI,14-
3ph/7pg L

Curry,Abraham,House
406 N. Nevada St.
HABS NV-13-13
HABS NEV,13-CARCI,12-
5ph/10pg L

Ferris,G. W. G. ,House
311 W. Third St.
HABS NV-13-14
HABS NEV,13-CARCI,13-
5ph/11pg L

First United Methodist Church
200 N. Division St.
HABS NV-13-10
HABS NEV,13-CARCI,9-
9ph/8pg L

King Street,General View,1880
HABS NV-13-20
HABS NEV,13-CARCI,2-
2ph L

Meder,Lew M. ,House
308 N. Nevada St.
HABS NV-13-27
HABS NEV,13-CARCI,21-
5dr/fr L

Nevada State Capitol
Plaza at Carson St.
HABS NV-13-5
HABS NEV,13-CARCI,4-
23ph/15pg L

Nevada State Orphanage
HABS NV-13-21
HABS NEV,13-CARCI,19-
1ph L

Nevada State Printing Office
S. Fall St.
HABS NV-13-9
HABS NEV,13-CARCI,8-
5ph/9pg L

Rinckel,Mathias,Mansion
102 N. Curry St.
HABS NV-13-17
HABS NEV,13-CARCI,16-
6ph/13pg L

Roberts,James D. ,House
1207 N. Carson St.
HABS NV-13-28
HABS NEV,13-CARCI,22-
5dr L

Second & Carson Streets,General View,1860-70
HABS NV-13-23
HABS NEV,13-CARCI,1-
2ph L

Smail House
512 N. Curry St.
HABS NV-13-16
HABS NEV,13-CARCI,15-
3ph/6pg L

Smaill,David,House
313 W. Ann St.
HABS NV-13-19
HABS NEV,13-CARCI,18-
5ph/7pg L

St. Peter's Episcopal Church
312 N. Division St.
HABS NV-13-11
HABS NEV,13-CARCI,10-
7dr/7ph/10pg/fr L

Stewart-Nye House
108 N. Minnesota St.
HABS NV-13-12
HABS NEV,13-CARCI,11-
4ph/11pg L

Sweeney,E. D. ,Building
102 S. Curry St.
HABS NV-13-6
HABS NEV,13-CARCI,5-
4ph/8pg L

Twain,Mark,House
Division & Spear Sts.
HABS NV-13-2
HABS NEV,13-CARCI,3-
1ph L

U. S. Post Office
N. Carson St.
HABS NV-13-8
HABS NEV,13-CARCI,7-
4ph/9pg L

United States Mint
Carson St.
HABS NV-13-22
HABS NEV,13-CARCI,20-
14ph/12pg L

Virginia & Truckee Railroad Shops
Between Plaza,Ann,Stewart & Sophia Sts.
HABS NV-13-7
HABS NEV,13-CARCI,6-
8dr/11ph/11pg/fr L

Yerington,Henry Marvin,House
512 N. Division St.
HABS NV-13-18
HABS NEV,13-CARU,17-
12ph/13pg L

CHURCHILL COUNTY

FALLON

Truckee-Carson Irrig. Dist. ,Blacksm. Sh./Iron Hse
Sixth & Taylor Sts.
HAER NV-6-H
HAER NEV,1-FALL,IH-
7ph/1pg/1pc L

Truckee-Carson Irrig. Dist. ,Car Repair Shop
Sixth & Taylor Sts.
HAER NV-6-E
HAER NEV,1-FALL,1E-
7ph/1pg/1pc L

Truckee-Carson Irrig. Dist. ,Car Supplies Storehse
Sixth & Taylor Sts.
HAER NV-6-I
HAER NEV,1-FALL,1I
5ph/1pg/1pc L

Truckee-Carson Irrig. Dist. ,Electrical Warehouse
Sixth & Taylor Sts.
HAER NV-6-F
HAER NEV,1-FALL,1F-
10ph/1pg/1pc L

Truckee-Carson Irrig. Dist. ,Tool Hse & Wagon Shed
Sixth & Taylor Sts.
HAER NV-6-C
HAER NEV,1-FALL,1C-
6ph/1pg/1pc L

Truckee-Carson Irrig. Dist. Fac. Yard,Machine Shop
Sixth & Taylor Sts.
HAER NV-6-G
HAER NEV,1-FALL,1G-
9ph/1pg/1pc L

Truckee-Carson Irrig. Dist. Fac. Yard,Shed
Sixth & Taylor Sts.
HAER NV-6-D
HAER NEV,1-FALL,1D-
5ph/1pg/1pc L

Truckee-Carson Irrig. Dist. Facility Yard
Sixth & Taylor Sts.
HAER NV-6
HAER 1987(HAER):25
13ph/17pg/1pc L

Truckee-Carson Irrig. Dist. Facility Yard,Saw Shed
Sixth & Taylor Sts.
HAER NV-6-J
HAER NEV,1-FALL,1J-
1ph/1pg/1pc L

Truckee-Carson Irrig. Dist. Yard,Watchman's Garage
Sixth & Taylor Sts.
HAER NV-6-A
HAER NEV,1-FALL,1A-
3ph/1pg/1pc L

Truckee-Carson Irrig. Dist. Yard,Watchman's House
Sixth & Taylor Sts.
HAER NV-6-B
HAER NEV,1-FALL,1B-
5ph/1pg/1pc L

FALLON VIC.

Boyer Ranch (Lamb Ranch)
U.S. Hwy 50, 44 miles E. of Fallon
HABS NV-20
HABS 1989(HABS):16
2ph/1pc L

Boyer Ranch,Gilbert's Root Cellar (Lamb Ranch,Gilbert's Root Cellar)
44 Mi. E. of Fallon,on U. S. Hwy 50
HABS NV-20-B
HABS 1989(HABS):16
8ph/4pg/1pc L

Boyer Ranch,Gilbert's Storeroom (Lamb Ranch,Gilbert's Storeroom)
44 Mi. E. of Fallon,on U. S. Hwy 50
HABS NV-20-A
HABS 1989(HABS):16
11ph/6pg/1pc L

Lamb Ranch; see Boyer Ranch

Lamb Ranch,Gilbert's Root Cellar; see Boyer Ranch,Gilbert's Root Cellar

Lamb Ranch,Gilbert's Storeroom; see Boyer Ranch,Gilbert's Storeroom

CLARK COUNTY

GLENDALE JUNCTION

Muddy River Bridge
Spanning Muddy River NE of I-15 & SR 168
HAER NV-7
HAER NEV,2-GLENJ,1-
15ph/7pg/2pc L

NORTH LAS VEGAS

Kiel Ranch
200 W. Carey Ave.
HABS NV-19
5ph/59pg/3pc/fr H

Kiel Ranch,Adobe Structure
200 W. Carey Ave.
HABS NV-19-B
4ph H

Kiel Ranch,Brown House
200 W. Carey Ave.
HABS NV-19-F
6ph H

Kiel Ranch,Cinderblock House
200 W. Carey Ave.
HABS NV-19-G
5ph H

Kiel Ranch,Doll House
200 W. Carey Ave.
HABS NV-19-E
3ph H

Kiel Ranch,Foreman's House
200 W. Carey Ave.
HABS NV-19-D
5ph H

Kiel Ranch,Livestock Shed
200 W. Carey Ave.
HABS NV-19-I
2ph H

Kiel Ranch,Park Mansion (Kiel Ranch,White House)
200 W. Carey Ave.
HABS NV-19-A
8ph H

Kiel Ranch,Remnant House
200 W. Carey Ave.
HABS NV-19-C
2ph H

Kiel Ranch,White House; see Kiel Ranch,Park Mansion

Kiel Ranch,Wooden Duplex
200 W. Carey Ave.
HABS NV-19-H
5ph H

DOUGLAS COUNTY

GENOA

Genoa,General View,1890
Genoa Vic.
HABS NV-3-12
HABS NEV,3-GENO,1-
1ph L

Log Cabin,First
HABS NV-3-11
HABS NEV,3-GENO,2-
1ph L

EUREKA COUNTY

EUREKA

Eureka County Courthouse
Main St.
HABS NV-6-6
HABS NEV,6-EUR,4-
1ph L

Eureka Sentinel Building
Monroe St.
HABS NV-6-7
HABS NEV,6-EUR,5-
1ph L

First Methodist Church (Hooper Garage)
Spring St.
HABS NV-6-1
HABS NEV,6-EUR,1-
1ph L

Hooper Garage; see First Methodist Church

Presbyterian Church
Edwards St.
HABS NV-6-5
HABS NEV,6-EUR,3-
1ph L

St. Brendan's Roman Catholic Church
O'Neal Ave.
HABS NV-6-4
HABS NEV,6-EUR,2-
1ph L

LINCOLN COUNTY

PIOCHE

Lincoln County Courthouse,Old
HABS NV-9-1
HABS NEV,9-PIOCH,1-
1ph L

LYON COUNTY

DAYTON

Bluestone Manufacturing Company
Main St. & Shady Ave.
HABS NV-13-30
HABS NEV,10-DAYT,1-
1dr/fr L

DAYTON VIC.

Sutro Tunnel Entrance
Comstock Mines Vic.
HABS NV-10-1
HABS NEV,10-DAYT.V,2-
1ph L

SILVER CITY

Donovan's Mill
HAER NV-3
HAER NEV,10-SILCI,1-
46ph/6pg/3pc/fr L

WEEKS VIC.

Fort Churchill (Ruins)
U. S. 95-A,Old Buckland Ranch
HABS NV-10-17
HABS NEV,10-CHURCH.V,1-
6ph L

MINERAL COUNTY

AURORA

Main Street,General View
HABS NV-11-17
HABS NEV,11-AURO,1-
1ph L

HAWTHORNE

Bank; see Hawthorne Naval Ammo. Depot,Babbitt Housing Area,

Bowling Center; see Hawthorne Naval Ammo. Depot,Babbitt Housing Area,

Building No. C191; see Hawthorne Naval Ammo. Depot,Babbitt Housing Area,

Building No. C192; see Hawthorne Naval Ammo. Depot,Babbitt Housing Area,

Building No. C194; see Hawthorne Naval Ammo. Depot,Babbitt Housing Area,

Building No. C195; see Hawthorne Naval Ammo. Depot,Babbitt Housing Area,

Building No. C198; see Hawthorne Naval Ammo. Depot,Babbitt Housing Area,

Building No. C357; see Hawthorne Naval Ammo. Depot,Babbitt Housing Area,

Building No. C425; see Hawthorne Naval Ammo. Depot,Babbitt Housing Area,

Building No. C427; see Hawthorne Naval Ammo. Depot,Babbitt Housing Area,

Building No. C428; see Hawthorne Naval Ammo. Depot,Babbitt Housing Area,

Drug Store/Union Hall; see Hawthorne Naval Ammo. Depot,Babbitt Housing Area,

Entertainment Shop; see Hawthorne Naval Ammo. Depot,Babbitt Housing Area,

Fountain; see Hawthorne Naval Ammo. Depot,Babbitt Housing Area,

Grocery Store/Meat Market; see Hawthorne Naval Ammo. Depot,Babbitt Housing Area,

Hawthorne Army Ammunition Plant
HAER NV-5
HAER NEV,11-HAWT,1-
70pg/fr L

Hawthorne Naval Ammo. Depot,Babbitt Housing Area
Hwy. 95
HABS NV-23
4ph/136pg/2pc/fr H

Hawthorne Naval Ammo. Depot,Babbitt Housing Area, (Bank; Building No. C191)
Hwy. 95
HABS NV-23-B
1ph/1pc H

Hawthorne Naval Ammo. Depot,Babbitt Housing Area, (Bowling Center; Building No. C357)
Hwy. 95
HABS NV-23-G
1ph/1pc H

Hawthorne Naval Ammo. Depot,Babbitt Housing Area, (Drug Store/Union Hall; Building No. C194)
Hwy. 95
HABS NV-23-E
1ph/1pc H

Hawthorne Naval Ammo. Depot,Babbitt Housing Area, (Entertainment Shop; Building No. C428)
Hwy. 95
HABS NV-23-K
1ph/1pc H

Hawthorne Naval Ammo. Depot,Babbitt Housing Area, (Fountain)
Hwy. 95
HABS NV-23-A
1ph/1pc H

Hawthorne Naval Ammo. Depot,Babbitt Housing Area, (Grocery Store/Meat Market; Building No. C198)
Hwy. 95
HABS NV-23-D
2ph/1pc H

Hawthorne Naval Ammo. Depot,Babbitt Housing Area, (Library; Building No. C425)
Hwy. 95
HABS NV-23-H
1ph/1pc H

Hawthorne Naval Ammo. Depot,Babbitt Housing Area, (Post Office/Barber Shop; Building No. C192)
Hwy. 95
HABS NV-23-C
1ph/1pc H

Hawthorne Naval Ammo. Depot,Babbitt Housing Area, (Recreation Hall; Building No. C427)
Hwy. 95
HABS NV-23-J
1ph/1pc H

Hawthorne Naval Ammo. Depot,Babbitt Housing Area, (Thrift Shop; Building No. C195)
Hwy. 95
HABS NV-23-F
1ph/1pc H

Hawthorne Naval Ammunition Depot,Bldg. No. 20; see Hawthorne Naval Ammunition Depot,Greenhouse

Hawthorne Naval Ammunition Depot,Greenhouse (Hawthorne Naval Ammunition Depot,Bldg. No. 20)
Personnel & Industrial Area
HABS NV-21-A
HABS DLC/PP-1993:NV-3
8ph/7pg/1pc L

Library; see Hawthorne Naval Ammo. Depot,Babbitt Housing Area,

Post Office/Barber Shop; see Hawthorne Naval Ammo. Depot,Babbitt Housing Area,

Recreation Hall; see Hawthorne Naval Ammo. Depot,Babbitt Housing Area,

Thrift Shop; see Hawthorne Naval Ammo. Depot,Babbitt Housing Area,

HAWTHRONE

Building No. C426; see Hawthorne Naval Ammo. Depot,Babbitt Housing Area,

Entertainment Shop; see Hawthorne Naval Ammo. Depot,Babbitt Housing Area,

Hawthorne Naval Ammo. Depot,Babbitt Housing Area, (Entertainment Shop; Building No. C426)
Hwy. 95
HABS NV-23-I
1ph/1pc H

NYE COUNTY

RHYOLITE VIC.

Bullfrog Mine
HAER NV-2
HAER NEV,12-RHYO.V,1-
81ph/65pg/4pc/fr L

TONOPAH

Mitzpah Mine
HAER NV-4
HAER NEV,12-TONO,1-
26ph/7pg/2pc L

PERSHING COUNTY

HUMBOLDT CITY

Bank (Ruins)
HABS NV-14-30
HABS NEV,14-HUMB,2-
2ph L

Humboldt City,General View,Ghost Town
HABS NV-14-29
HABS NEV,14-HUMB,1-
1ph L

STOREY COUNTY

GOLD HILL

Liberty Fire House
HABS NV-15-13
HABS NEV,15-GOLD,1-
2ph L

Miner's Union Hall
B St.
HABS NV-15-14
HABS NEV,15-GOLD,2-
4ph L

VIRGINIA

Fourth Ward School
S. C St. at Hwy. 17
HABS NV-15-21
HABS NEV,15-VIRG,8-
9dr/3ph/fr L

VIRGINIA CITY

"Evening Chronicle" Building
C St.
HABS NV-15-39
HABS NEV,15-VIRG,14-
1ph L

Bar,Old
C St.
HABS NV-15-33
HABS NEV,15-VIRG,10-
1ph L

Blaubelt Mansion
HABS NV-15-5
HABS NEV,15-VIRG,22-
2ph L

Brick Vaults,Office of Cons. Virginia Mining Co.
HABS NV-15-2
HABS NEV,15-VIRG,21-
1ph L

C Street Area Survey (Commercial Buildings)
HABS NV-15-1
HABS NEV,15-VIRG,2-
21ph L

Cemetery
HABS NV-15-79
HABS NEV,15-VIRG,35-
6ph L

Comstock House
C St.
HABS NV-15-35
HABS NEV,15-VIRG,11-
1ph L

Crystal Saloon
HABS NV-15-29
HABS NEV,15-VIRG,26-
4ph L

Episcopal Church
D St.
HABS NV-15-30
HABS NEV,15-VIRG,27-
2ph L

Fire House
HABS NV-15-87
HABS NEV,15-VIRG,43-
1ph L

Fire Station
HABS NV-15-88
HABS NEV,15-VIRG,44-
1ph L

First Street (Commercial Buildings)
HABS NV-15-78
HABS NEV,15-VIRG,34-
1ph L

Frederick House
D St.
HABS NV-15-26
HABS NEV,15-VIRG,25-
2ph L

Hall of Records
B St.
HABS NV-15-89
HABS NEV,15-VIRG,20-
2ph L

Hardware & General Store
C St.
HABS NV-15-8
HABS NEV,15-VIRG,5-
1ph L

Harness Shop
HABS NV-15-81
HABS NEV,15-VIRG,37-
1ph L

Hose House
HABS NV-15-82
HABS NEV,15-VIRG,38-
1ph L

House,Frame
HABS NV-15-58
HABS NEV,15-VIRG,33-
4ph L

Jail
HABS NV-15-54
HABS NEV,15-VIRG,32-
3ph L

King House
HABS NV-15-31
HABS NEV,15-VIRG,28-
8ph L

Knights of Pythias Hall
W. side B St.
HABS NV-15-11
HABS NEV,15-VIRG,18-
5dr/1ph/fr L

Masonic Hall
C St.
HABS NV-15-18
HABS NEV,15-VIRG,7-
1ph L

Mine,General View
HABS NV-15-86
HABS NEV,15-VIRG,42-
1ph L

Miners' Union Hall
W. side B St.
HABS NV-15-20
HABS NEV,15-VIRG,19-
5dr/2ph/fr L

Molinelli's Hotel
C St.
HABS NV-15-38
HABS NEV,15-VIRG,13-
1ph L

Norcross Mining Office
HABS NV-15-41
HABS NEV,15-VIRG,30-
3ph L

Palace Clothing Store Building
C St.
HABS NV-15-36
HABS NEV,15-VIRG,12-
1ph L

Piper's Opera House
B & Union Sts.
HABS NV-15-7
HABS NEV,15-VIRG,17-
7dr/8ph/fr L

Savage Mining Office
HABS NV-15-12
HABS NEV,15-VIRG,23-
2ph L

Shaft House,Active Mine
HABS NV-15-84
HABS NEV,15-VIRG,40-
1ph L

Shaft House,Consolidated CA & VA Mine
HABS NV-15-85
HABS NEV,15-VIRG,41-
1ph L

Silver Hotel
C St.
HABS NV-15-40
HABS NEV,15-VIRG,15-
1ph L

St. Mary's in the Mountains
HABS NV-15-52
HABS NEV,15-VIRG,31-
10ph/fr L

Store,Frame
HABS NV-15-80
HABS NEV,15-VIRG,36-
1ph L

Storey County Courthouse
HABS NV-15-19
HABS NEV,15-VIRG,24-
5ph L

Sutro Mansion
HABS NV-15-83
HABS NEV,15-VIRG,39-
1ph L

Twain,Mark,"Enterprise" Building
C St.
HABS NV-15-9
HABS NEV,15-VIRG,6-
1ph L

Union Brewery
HABS NV-15-37
HABS NEV,15-VIRG,29-
1ph L

Virginia City News Building
C St.
HABS NV-15-32
HABS NEV,15-VIRG,9-
1ph L

Virginia City Union Sunday School
C St.
HABS NV-15-4
HABS NEV,15-VIRG,4-
1ph L

Virginia City,General View Area Survey
HABS NV-15-77
HABS NEV,15-VIRG,1-
11ph L

Virginia Hotel
C St.
HABS NV-15-3
HABS NEV,15-VIRG,3-
1ph L

Wells Fargo Building
C St.
HABS NV-15-46
HABS NEV,15-VIRG,16-
9ph L

WASHOE COUNTY

RENO

Booth Street Bridge; see Riverside Bridge

Riverside Bridge (Booth Street Bridge)
Spanning the Truckee River at Booth St.
HAER NV-10
HAER DLC/PP-1992:NV-2
18ph/7pg/2pc L

University of Nevada (Site Plan)
Evans,Virginia & Ninth Sts.
HABS NV-18
1dr L

University of Nevada,Reno,Dairy Building (Veterinary Science Building)
North of East 9th St.
HABS NV-18-A
HABS 1989(HABS):16
20ph/9pg/2pc L

Veterinary Science Building; see University of Nevada,Reno,Dairy Building

VERDI

East Verdi Bridge
Rte425, Spanning Truckee River,W. of I-80 & SR-425
HAER NV-8
HAER 1991(HAER):6
20ph/11pg/2pc L

West Verdi Bridge
State Rt. 425,Spanning Truckee River
HAER NV-9
HAER 1991(HAER):6
24ph/2pg/2pc L

WHITE PINE COUNTY

BAKER VIC.

Lehman Caves National Monument; see Rhodes,C. T. ,Log Cabin

Rhodes,C. T. ,Log Cabin (Lehman Caves National Monument)
Lehman Caves entrance Vic.
HABS NV-17-1
HABS NEV,17- ,1-
2dr/7ph/3pg L

Augustus Saint-Gaudens National Historic Site, Little Studio, Cornish County, New Hampshire. Inside pergola. Photograph by Jack E. Boucher, August 1965 (HABS NH,10-CORN,1B-3)

Cornish-Windsor Covered Bridge across Connecticut River between Cornish, New Hampshire and Windsor,Vermont, Sullivan County, New Hampshire. General 3/4 elevation view, looking northwest, from New Hampshire side of river. Photograph by Jet Lowe, 1984 (HAER NH,10-CORN,2-2).

New Hampshire

WESTMINSTER

(SEE NH, Cheshire Co., Walpole for documentation); see Walpole, NH & Westminster, VT Bridge

Walpole, NH & Westminster, VT Bridge ((SEE NH, Cheshire Co., Walpole for documentation))
Spanning CT river btwn Westminster, VT & Walpole
HAER NH-13
H

CHESHIRE COUNTY

CHESTERFIELD

Blacksmith Shop
(moved to MA,Storrowtown,West Springfield)
HABS NH-41
HABS NH,3-CHEST,1-
2dr/3ph/fr L

HARRISVILLE

Cheshire Mill,Number One
Main & Grove Sts.
HABS NH-173
HABS NH,3-HAR,3-
4dr/22ph/4pg/fr L

Cheshire Mills Company Boarding House
Main St.
HABS NH-174
HABS NH,3-HAR,4-
3dr/6ph/4pg/fr L

Harris Mill
Main & Prospect Sts.
HABS NH-171
HABS NH,3-HAR,1-
4dr/11ph/6pg/fr L

Harris Mill Storehouse
Main & Prospect Sts.
HABS NH-172
HABS NH,3-HAR,2-
2dr/6ph/4pg/fr L

HINSDALE

Vernon Station Hydroelectric Facility
(See VT,WINDHAM CO.,VERNON for documentation)
HAER VT-24
L

STODDARD VIC.

Bridge,Stone
Route 9
HABS NH-32
HABS NH,3-STOD.V,1-
9ph L

WALPOLE

Allen,Gen. Amasa,House
Main St.
HABS NH-53
HABS NH,3-WALP,2-
3pg L

Bellows Falls Arch Bridge
Spanning Connecticut River
HAER NH-6
HAER NH,3-WALPN,1-
3dr/23ph/6pg/2pc/fr L

Bellows-Grant House
Main St.
HABS NH-60
HABS NH,3-WALP,5-
7ph/3pg L

Buffum House
Main & Middle Sts.
HABS NH-61
HABS NH,3-WALP,6-
11ph/3pg L

Hooper Golf Club; see Watkins',Alexander,Tavern

Howland House (Interior)
Westminster St.
HABS NH-59
HABS NH,3-WALP,4-
4ph/3pg L

Howland-Schofield House
Elm & Pleasant Sts.
HABS NH-65
HABS NH,3-WALP,10-
1ph/1pg L

Knapp House
Wentworth Rd.
HABS NH-52
HABS NH,3-WALP,1-
7ph/3pg L

Porter,Margaret,House
Main & Middle Sts.
HABS NH-63
HABS NH,3-WALP,8-
1ph/1pg L

Walpole Academy (Walpole Historical Society)
Main St.
HABS NH-62
HABS NH,3-WALP,7-
1ph/2pg L

Walpole Historical Society; see Walpole Academy

Walpole Village Bridge; see Walpole-Westminster Bridge

Walpole-Westminster Bridge (Walpole Village Bridge)
Spanning CT River btwn Walpole NH & Westminst. VT
HAER NH-13
HAER 1991(HAER):19
27ph/27pg/4pc L

Watkins',Alexander,Tavern (Hooper Golf Club)
Prospect Hill
HABS NH-64
HABS NH,3-WALP,9-
6ph/3pg L

Wing,Rodney,House
Westminster St.
HABS NH-58
HABS NH,3-WALP,3-
1ph/1pg L

WESTMORELAND

Park Hill Meetinghouse
State Route 63
HABS NH-57
HABS NH,3-PARK,1-
3ph/4pg/1ct L

COOS COUNTY

LANCASTER

Main Street Bridge
Spanning Israels River at (St. Rts. 2 & 3)
HAER NH-17
22ph/17pg/2pc H

GRAFTON COUNTY

BATH

Woods-Goodale Law Offices
U. S. Route 302
HABS NH-66
HABS NH,5-BATH,1-
2ph/3pg L

CAMPTON

Osgood Bridge
Spanning Beebe River,Perch Pond Rd.
HAER NH-10
HAER NH,5-CAMPHO,1-
23ph/16pg/2pc L

CAMPTON VIC.

Pioneer Cabin
HABS NH-36
HABS NH,5-CAMP.V,1-
12dr/24ph/1pg/fr L

EASTON

Merrill (Youngs) Mill (Youngs Mill)
HABS NH-43
HABS NH,5-EASTO,1-
9dr L

Youngs Mill; see Merrill (Youngs) Mill

ENFIELD VIC.

Shaker Church Family Cow Barn
State Route 4A
HABS NH-192
HABS NH,5-ENFI.V,1B-
3dr/13ph/9pg/1pc/2ct/fr L

Shaker Church Family Dwelling House (Shaker Great Stone House; Shaker Enfield Center Second Dwelling)
State Route 4A
HABS NH-75
HABS NH,5-ENFI.V,1A-
11dr/27ph/21pg/2pc/4ct/fr L

Shaker Church Family General Views
State Route 4A
HABS NH-190
HABS NH,5-ENFI.V,1-
1dr/1ph L

Shaker Church Family Laundry & Dairy
State Route 4A
HABS NH-193
HABS NH,5-ENFI.VC,1C-
6ph/1pc/4ct L

Shaker Church Family Machine Shop
State Route 4A
HABS NH-175
HABS NH,5-ENFI.V,1E-
2ph L

Shaker Enfield Center Second Dwelling; see Shaker Church Family Dwelling House

Shaker Great Stone House; see Shaker Church Family Dwelling House

Shaker Ministry's Shop
State Route 4A
HABS NH-194
HABS NH,5-ENFI.V,1D-
1ph/1pc L

HANOVER

Choate House (Ripley,Sylvanus,House)
27 N. Main St.
HABS NH-72
HABS NH,5-HANO,3-
1ph/3pg L

Dartmouth College,Reed hall
HABS NH-67
HABS NH,5-HANO,1A-
3ph/3pg L

Dartmouth College,Shattuck Observatory
HABS NH-69
HABS NH,5-HANO,1B-
1ph/3pg L

Dartmouth College,Thornton Hall
HABS NH-70
HABS NH,5-HANO,1C-
2ph/3pg L

Dartmouth College,Webster Cottage
27B Main St.
HABS NH-68
HABS NH,5-HANO,2-
2ph/3pg L

Dartmouth College,Wentworth Hall
HABS NH-71
HABS NH,5-HANO,1D-
2ph/3pg L

Delta Kappa Epsilon Fraternity House; see Storrs,Capt. Aaron,House

Ripley,Sylvanus,House; see Choate House

Storrs,Capt. Aaron,House (Delta Kappa Epsilon Fraternity House)
6 W. Wheelock St.
HABS NH-73
HABS NH,5-HANO,4-
1ph/3pg L

Woodward-Lord House
41 College St. (moved to N. Park St.)
HABS NH-74
HABS NH,5-HAN0,5-
1ph/3pg L

LYME

Lyme Congregational Church
The Green
HABS NH-77
HABS NH,5-LYM,1-
4ph/3pg L

Lyme Congregational Church,Horse Sheds
The Green
HABS NH-76
HABS NH,5-LYM,1A-
2ph/2pg L

LYME VIC.

Snow,Enos,Farm
River Rd.
HABS NH-78
HABS NH,5-LYM.V,1-
3ph/3pg L

Wittenborn-Wagner House
River Rd.
HABS NH-79
HABS NH,5-LYM.V,2-
4ph/2pg L

ORFORD

Covered Bridge
Spanning Connecticut River
HABS NH-29
HABS NH,5-ORF,2-
5dr/3ph/1pg/fr L

Orford Congregational Church
Main St.
HABS NH-210
HABS NH,5-ORF,4-
4ph/2pg/1pc/fr L

Wheeler House
Orford St.
HABS NH-80
HABS NH,5-ORF,3-
9dr/15ph/9pg/fr L

HILLSBOROUGH COUNTY

ANTRIM

Loomis House
HABS NH-49
HABS NH,6-ANT,1-
3dr L

HILLSBORO

Bridge,Stone
Routes 32 & 9
HABS NH-32-C
HABS NH,6-HILLO.V,2-
1ph/1pc L

Bridges,Stone-Map of Locations
HABS NH-32-A
HABS NH,6-Hillu.V,1
1dr/2pg/fr L

Carr Bridge,Old
Spanning Beard Creek
HABS NH-32-B
HABS NH,6-HILLO.V,1-
1dr/5ph/1pc L

Gleason Falls Bridge
Spanning Beard Brook
HABS NH-32-D
HABS NH,6-HILLO.V,2-
2dr/3ph/1pc L

Second New Hampshire Turnpike Bridge
Fullers Tannery
HABS NH-32-A
HABS NH,6-HILLO,1-
2dr/3ph/1pc L

HILLSBOROUGH

Dutton Twin Houses
Main St. (Rt. 202)
HABS NH-161
HABS NH,6-HILL,1-
3ph/4pg L

HILLSBOROUGH VIC.

Pierce Homestead
State Rt. 31
HABS NH-202
HABS NH,6-HILL.V,2-
6ph/5pg L

MANCHESTER

Amoskeag Counting Rooms,Cloth Rooms & Archway
Canal St.
HABS NH-114
HABS NH,6-MANCH,2/1A-
5dr/fr L

Amoskeag Manufacturing Company,Mill No. 9
Arms St.
HABS NH-111
HABS NH,6-MANCH,2/1B-
2dr/fr L

Amoskeag Manufacturing Company,Paper Mill
Canal St.
HABS NH-110
HABS NH,6-MANCH,2/2-
3dr L

Amoskeag Mills,River Dye House & Bleach House
Bridge St. at Merrimack River
HABS NH-115
HABS NH,6-MANCH,2/1C-
1dr/fr L

Amoskeag Millyard
Canal St.
HABS NH-109
HABS NH,6-MANCH,2-; 2A-; 2B-; 2C-; 2D-
4dr/121ph/18pg/fr L

Cavanaugh Brothers Sales Stable
58 W. Central St.
HABS NH-122
HABS NH,6-MANCH,5-
7ph/11pg L

Cohas Brook Bridge
Spanning Cohas Brook,Hwy. 28 (S. Willow St.)
HAER NH-9
HAER NH,6-MANCH,11-
17ph/17pg L

1143-1167 Elm Street (Commercial Buildings) (Ferretti Building)
HABS NH-199
HABS NH,6-MANCH,3-
5ph/3pg L

Ferretti Building; see 1143-1167 Elm Street (Commercial Buildings)

First Methodist Episcopal Church
Valley & Jewett Sts. (moved from NH,Derryville)
HABS NH-28
HABS NH,6-MANCH,1-
16dr/5ph/1pg L

Harrington-Smith Block (Opera House Block)
18-52 Hanover St.
HABS NH-209
HABS NH,6-MANCH,6-
19ph/35pg/1pc L

Kearns Block
15-17 Bridge St.
HABS NH-200
HABS NH,6-MANCH,7-
4ph/13pg L

Manchester Hotel; see Shea Block

Manchester Mills,Counting House
Commercial St.
HABS NH-119
HABS NH,6-MANCH,2/3D-
1dr/fr L

Manchester Mills,No. 1 Mill
Commercial St.
HABS NH-116
HABS NH,6-MANCH,2/3A-
5dr/fr L

Manchester Mills,No. 2 Mill
Commercial St.
HABS NH-117
HABS NH,6-MANCH,2/3B-
1dr/fr L

Manchester Mills,No. 3 Mill
Textile Ct.
HABS NH-118
HABS NH,6-MANCH,2/3C-
2dr/fr L

191-193 Merrimack Street (House)
HABS NH-206
HABS NH,6-MANCH,4-
7ph/9pg L

Mills 2,3, & 4; see Stark Mills,Mills Nos. 2,3, & 4

Monadnock-Upton Block
1140-1160 Elm St.
HABS NH-201
HABS NH,6-MANCH,8-
9ph/27pg/1pc L

Notre Dame Bridge
Spanning the Merrimack River on Bridge St.
HAER NH-14
57ph/30pg/5pc L

Opera House Block; see Harrington-Smith Block

Shea Block (Manchester Hotel)
50 W. Central St.
HABS NH-120
HABS NH,6-MANCH,9-
6ph/12pg L

Stark Mills,Mill No. 4,South Half
Canal St.
HABS NH-112
HABS NH,6-MANCH,2/4B-
4dr/fr L

Stark Mills,Mills Nos. 2,3, & 4 (Mills 2,3, & 4)
Canal St.
HABS NH-113
HABS NH,6-MANCH,2/4A-
4dr/fr L

Thorpe,T. L. ,Building
19 Traction St.
HABS NH-121
HABS NH,6-MANCH,10
9ph/10pg L

MARLBOROUGH

Stone,Solon W. ,House
15 Frost St.
HABS NH-211
HABS NH,3-MARLB,1-
15ph/3pg/1pc L

MERRIMACK COUNTY

BOSCAWEN

Bonney Tavern; see Penacook House

Penacook House (Bonney Tavern)
Daniel Webster Highway
HABS NH-25
HABS 1983(HABS):165
79ph/4pc/fr L

BOW MILLS VIC.

Nichols Saw Mill
HABS NH-31
HABS NH,7-BOWMIL.V-1-
20dr/1pg L

CANTERBURY

Shaker Church Family Barn & Granary
Shaker Village Rd.
HABS NH-177
HABS NH,7-CANT,1-
3ph L

Shaker Church Family Boys' House (Shaker Church Family Creamery)
Shaker Village Rd.
HABS NH-178
HABS NH,7-CANT,2-
1ph L

Shaker Church Family Brethen's Shop
Shaker Village Rd.
HABS NH-179
HABS NH,7-CANT,3-
2ph L

Shaker Church Family Broom & Carpenters' Shop
Shaker Village Rd.
HABS NH-191
HABS NH,7-CANT,14-
1ph L

Shaker Church Family Children's House; see Shaker Church Family East House

Shaker Church Family Creamery; see Shaker Church Family Boys' House

Shaker Church Family Dwelling House
Shaker Village Rd.
HABS NH-180
HABS NH,7-CANT,4-
12ph L

Shaker Church Family East House (Shaker Church Family Girls' House; Shaker Church Family Children's House)
Shaker Village Rd.
HABS NH-184
HABS NH 7 CANT 8-
2ph L

Shaker Church Family Enfield House (Shaker Church Family Trustees' Office)
Shaker Village Rd.
HABS NH-181
HABS NH,7-CANT,5-
4ph L

Shaker Church Family General View
Shaker Rd.
HABS NH-183
HABS NH 7, CANT,7-
3ph L

Shaker Church Family Girls' House; see Shaker Church Family East House

Shaker Church Family Schoolhouse
Shaker Village Rd.
HABS NH-188
HABS NH,7-CANT,12-
4ph L

Shaker Church Family Syrup Shop
Shaker Village Rd.
HABS NH-189
HABS NH,7-CANT,13-
2ph L

Shaker Church Family Trustees' Office; see Shaker Church Family Enfield House

Shaker Church Family Washhouse
Shaker Village Rd.
HABS NH-185
HABS NH,7-CANT,9-
2ph L

Shaker Meetinghouse
Shaker Village Rd.
HABS NH-186
HABS NH,7-CANT,10-
2ph L

Shaker Ministry's Shop
Shaker Village Rd.
HABS NH-187
HABS NH,7-CANT,11-
1ph L

CANTURBURY

Shaker Church Family Firehouse and Powerhouse
Shaker Village Rd.
HABS NH-182
HABS NH,7-CANT,6-
1ph L

CHICHESTER

Jenkins House
S. side of Dover Rd. (St. Rt. 4),W. of Main St.
HABS NH-217
HABS DLC/PP-1993:NH-5
10ph/10pg/1pc L

Prescott,Betsy,House
S. side of Dover Rd. (St. Rt. 4),W. of Main St.
HABS NH-218
HABS DLC/PP-1993:NH-5
10ph/11pg/1pc L

CONCORD

Centennial Block
57-62 N. Main St.
HABS NH-162
HABS NH,7-CON,2-
5ph/2pg L

Concord Gas Light Co:Oil Tank Storage Building
South Main St.
HAER NH-18-A
4ph/1pc L

Concord Gas Light Co:1922 Gasholder
South Main St.
HAER NH-18-B
HAER NH,7-CON,9B-
2ph/1pc L

Concord Gas Light Company
S. Main St.
HAER NH-18
7ph/1pc L

Concord Gas Light Company,Gasholder House
South Main St.
HAER NH-7
HAER NH,7-CON,9C-
3dr/16ph/24pg/2pc/fr L

Eagle Furniture Store; see Merchants' Exchange Block

Eagle Hotel Garage (Rogers Garage)
102 1/2 N. Main St.
HABS NH-208
HABS NH,7-CON,3A
4ph/3pg L

Merchants' Exchange Block (Eagle Furniture Store)
94-102 N. Main St.
HABS NH-207
HABS NH,7-CON,4-
1dr/6ph/5pg L

Merrimack County Bank
214 N. Main St.
HABS NH-164
HABS NH,7-CON,5-
4ph/5pg L

Rogers Garage; see Eagle Hotel Garage

Walker,Joseph,Cottage
278 N. Main St.
HABS NH-163
HABS NH,7-CON,6-
2ph/4pg L

Walker,Rev. Timothy,House
276 N. Main St.
HABS NH-166
HABS NH,7-CON,7-
6ph/6pg L

Warehouse
100-102 N. Main St. (rear)
HABS NH-165
HABS NH,7-CON,8-
1ph/4pg L

HENNIKER

Ocean-Born-Mary House
Rt. 202 vic.
HABS NH-160
HABS NH,7-HEN,2-
6ph/3pg L

HOPKINTON

Boulder Farm
Dunbarton Rd.
HABS NH-42
HABS NH,7-HOP,2-
17dr L

Contoocook Covered Bridge
Spanning Contoocook River
HABS NH-21
HABS NH,7-CONT,1-
6dr/1ph/5pg/fr L

HOPKINTON VIC.

Bridge,New; see Covered Bridge

Covered Bridge (Bridge,New; Henniker Bridge,New)
Spanning Contoocook River
HABS NH-30
HABS NH,7-HOP.V,2-
4dr/3ph/3pg/fr L

Henniker Bridge,New; see Covered Bridge

HOPKINTON VILLAGE

St. Andrew's Church (Episcopal)
Hopkinton Village
HABS NH-167
HABS NH,7-HOP,3-
2ph/5pg L

SALISBURY

Salisbury Meetinghouse
(moved to MA,Springfield Vic.)
HABS MA-843
HABS MASS,7-SPRIFW,7-
1ph/1pc L

SALISBURY HEIGHTS

Williams,Thomas & Eliphalet,House
Route 4, N. side
HABS NH-168
HABS NH,7-SALISB,1-
2ph/5pg L

WEBSTER

Corser Hill Meeting House (First Congregational Church)
HABS NH-169
HABS NH,7-WEBS,1-
4ph/5pg L

First Congregational Church; see Corser Hill Meeting House

Webster Meeting House
HABS NH-170
HABS NH,7-WEBS,2-
1ph/5pg L

WEST HENNIKER

House
S. side of Rt. 9
HABS NH-214
HABS NH,7-HENWE,2-
1ph/1pc L

WEST HENNIKER VILLAG

Wilcoxen House
Rt. 9
HABS NH-203
HABS NH,7-HENWE,1-
6ph/4pg L

ROCKINGHAM COUNTY

DERRYVILLE

First Methodist Episcopal Church
Mammoth & Huse Rds. (moved to NH,Manchester)
HABS NH-205
HABS NH,7-CONT,1-
16dr/5ph/1pg L

EXETER

Folsom,Simeon,House & Stores
Pleasant & High Sts.
HABS NH-8
HABS NH,8-EX,3-
15dr/3ph/13pg/fr L

Giddings Tavern
37 Park & Summers Sts.
HABS NH-2
HABS NH,8-EX,7-
25dr/9ph/11pg/fr L

Gilman Garrison
Water & Clifford Sts.
HABS NH-18
HABS NH,8-EX,2-
38dr/31ph/1pg/fr L

Liberty Emery House
41 Main St.
HABS NH-9
HABS NH,8-EX,8-
15dr/7ph/10pg/fr L

Powder House
HABS NH-13
HABS NH,8-EX,9-
2dr/2ph/1pg/fr L

GREENLAND

Weeks House
Greenland
HABS NH-40
HABS NH,8-GRELA,1-
6dr/9ph/fr L

HAMPTON

Moulton,Gen. Jonathan,House
Rt. 1 and Drakeside Rd.
HABS NH-50
HABS NH,8-HAMTO,1-
2ph L

HAMPTON FALLS

Cram,John,Farmstead
HABS NH-23
HABS NH,8-HAMTOF,1-
17dr/21ph/12pg L

Weare Saw & Grist Mill
HABS NH-44
HABS NH,8-HAMTOF 2-
20dr/34ph/3pg/fr L

KENSINGTON

Hardy,John,Small House
HABS NH-48
HABS NH,8-KENSI,2-
1dr L

Lovering Farmhouse
HABS NH-46
HABS NH,8-KENSI,1-
7dr L

NEWINGTON

Parsonage
HABS NH-19
HABS NH,8-NEWI,2-
16dr/14ph/1pg/fr L

NEWMARKET

Doe Garrison
Lamprey River & Great Bay
HABS NH-37
HABS NH,8-NEWM,1-
23dr/49ph/1pg/1pc/fr L

NORTHWOOD NARROWS

James Saw Mill
Narrows Brook
HABS NH-45
HABS NH,8-NORNA,1-
26dr/60ph/1pg/fr L

PORTSMOUTH

Abbott House (Marden,James,House)
82 Jefferson St.
HABS NH-81
HABS NH,8-PORT,140-
2ph L

Bailey,Daniel,House
139 Manning St.
HABS NH-82
HABS NH,8-PORT,143-
3ph L

Barnes,Capt. ,House
218 Islington St.
HABS NH-26
HABS NH,8-PORT,124-
65dr/29ph/11pg/fr L

Blunt,Capt. Robert,House
(Cotton,Leonard,House)
144 Washington St.
HABS NH-83
HABS NH,8-PORT,150-
2ph/3pg L

Boyd-Raynes House (Meserve,Col. Nathaniel,House)
Maplewood Ave.
HABS NH-5
HABS NH,8-PORT,26-
25dr/20ph/1pg/fr L

Boyd,Col. George,Tomb
Old North Cemetery
HABS NH-204
HABS NH,8-PORT,118-
3dr/3ph L

Chase,Reverend Stephen,House
358 Court St.
HABS NH-84
HABS NH,8-PORT,10-
10ph/3pg L

Clark,John,House
95 Jefferson St.
HABS NH-85
HABS NH,8-PORT,141-
7dr/7ph/1pg L

Cotton,Leonard,House; see Blunt,Capt. Robert,House

Cotton,Leonard,Tenant House; see Ingraham House

Cotton,Sarah,House; see Peacock House

Cotton,William,House; see Smalley Estate

Cullen House
186 Marcy St.
HABS NH-87
HABS NH,8-PORT,145-
1ph L

Custom House
Daniel & Penhallow Sts.
HABS NH-4
HABS NH,8-PORT,57-
14dr/5ph/8pg/1pc L

Custom House
State & Pleasant Streets
HABS NH-215
4ph/1pc L

33-35 Deer Street (House)
HABS NH-10
HABS NH,8-PORT,51-
8dr/5ph/9pg/fr L

Drisco House
65-67 Charles St.
HABS NH-88
HABS NH,8-PORT,131-
3ph/1pg L

Earl of Halifax Tavern; see Pitt,William,Tavern

Goodwin House (Sherburne,Capt. John,House)
55 Charles St.
HABS NH-89
HABS NH,8-PORT,130-
3ph L

Green House
167 Washington St.
HABS NH-90
HABS NH,8-PORT,149-
2ph L

Hill,Capt. John,House
61 Washington St.
HABS NH-86
HABS NH,8-PORT,147-
2ph/2pg L

Hough,Capt. Thomas,House
23-25 Liberty St.
HABS NH-91
HABS NH,8-PORT,142-
2ph/1pg L

Ingraham House (Cotton,Leonard,Tenant House)
72 Atkinson St.
HABS NH-94
HABS NH,8-PORT,126-
2ph L

Jackson,Dr. John,House; see Odiorne,Augustus,House

Jackson,Samuel House; see Ryder-Wood House

Jones,Joshua,House; see L-Shaped House

Kelly Property (Shapley Town House)
454-456 Court St.
HABS NH-95
HABS NH,8-PORT,135-
4ph L

L-Shaped House (Jones,Joshua,House)
90 Atkinson St.
HABS NH-93
HABS NH,8-PORT,128-
4ph L

Langdon,Gov. John,House
143 Pleasant St.
HABS NH-51
HABS NH,8-PORT,7-
5dr L

Lowd,Peter,House
43 Charles St.
HABS NH-96
HABS NH,8-PORT,129-
2ph/1pg L

Marden,James,House; see Abbott House

Meserve,Col. Nathaniel,House; see Boyd-Raynes House

Odiorne,Augustus,House (Jackson,Dr. John,House)
46 Jefferson St.
HABS NH-97
HABS NH,8-PORT,138-
3ph L

Peacock House (Cotton,Sarah,House)
Atkinson & Jefferson Sts.
HABS NH-99
HABS NH,8-PORT,125-
1ph L

Penhallow,Deacon,House
95 Newton St.
HABS NH-100
HABS NH,8-PORT,146-
6ph L

Pierce House
153 Washington St.
HABS NH-101
HABS NH,8-PORT,9-
2ph L

Pitt,William,Tavern (Earl of Halifax Tavern)
402-404 Court St.
HABS NH-102
HABS NH,8-PORT,133-
3ph/1pg L

Ryder-Wood House (Jackson,Samuel House)
16 Jefferson St.
HABS NH-103
HABS NH,8-PORT,137-
3ph/1pg L

Shapley Town House; see Kelly Property

Shapley,Reuben,House
420 Court St.
HABS NH-104
HABS NH,8-PORT,134-
2ph/2pg L

Sheafe Warehouse
Graves End St. (moved to Prescott Park)
HABS NH-7
HABS NH,8-PORT,119
5dr/4ph/1pg/fr L

Sherburne,Capt. John,House; see Goodwin House

Shore,Christian,House; see Woodbury,Gov. Levi,House

Smalley Estate (Cotton,William,House)
80 Atkinson St.
HABS NH-92
HABS NH,8-PORT,127-
2ph L

South Meeting House
Meeting House Hill,facing Marcy St.
HABS NH-105
HABS NH,8-PORT,76-
3ph/2pg L

State House,Old
Court St.
HABS NH-98
HABS NH,8-PORT,132-
4ph/1pg L

Sunday School House
111-113 Washington St.
HABS NH-106
HABS NH,8-PORT,148-
3ph/2pg L

Twin Houses (Winn-Yeaton Connected Houses)
66 & 74 Jefferson St.
HABS NH-107
HABS NH,8-PORT,139-
5ph L

Webster,Daniel,House
Hancock St.
HABS NH-108
HABS NH,8-PORT,136-
2ph/1pg L

Wentworth-Coolidge Mansion
Little Harbor Rd.
HABS NH-47
HABS NH,8-PORT,144-
2dr L

Wentworth,Col. Joshua,House
121 Hanover St. (moved to Hancock St.)
HABS NH-3
HABS NH,8-PORT,121-
25dr/13ph/1pg/fr L

Whidden,Michael,House
117 Deer St. (moved to High St.)
HABS NH-11
HABS NH,8-PORT,122-
9dr/4ph/13pg/fr L

Winn-Yeaton Connected Houses; see Twin Houses

Woodbury,Gov. Levi,House (Shore,Christian,House)
Woodbury Ave. & Boyd Rd.
HABS NH-20
HABS NH,8-PORT,123-
51dr/22ph/fr L

RAYMOND

Prescott Bridge
Spanning the Lamprey River on Prescott Road
HAER NH-16
HAER 1991(HAER):19
21ph/12pg/2pc L

ROCKINGHAM

Moody Parsonage
HABS NH-15
HABS NH,8-ROCK,1-
19dr/13ph/23pg/fr L

RYE

Seavey,Amos,House
Beach Blvd.
HABS NH-16
HABS NH,8-RY,1-
21dr/17ph/1pg/fr L

SANDOWN

Meetinghouse
Phillips Rd.
HABS NH-17
HABS NH,8-SAND,1-
42dr/18ph/1pg/fr L

STRATHAM

Winnicut Grist Mill
Winnicut River
HABS NH-24
HABS NH,8-STRAT,1-
23dr/11ph/10pg L

STRAFFORD COUNTY

DURHAM

Durham Falls Bridge
Spanning the Oyster River at State Rt. 108
HAER NH-15
32ph/17pg/2pc L

Smith,Ebenezer,House
20 Main St.
HABS NH-14
HABS NH,9-DUR,4-
38dr/6ph/16pg L

Sullivan,Gen. John,House
Newmarket Rd.
HABS NH-1
HABS NH,9-DUR,1-
15dr/12ph/1pg/fr L

Town Hall
Newmarket & Dover Rds.
HABS NH-6
HABS NH,9-DUR,2-
22dr/5ph/1pg/fr L

Town Pound
Route 108
HABS NH-12
HABS NH,9-DUR,3-
2dr/fr L

Woodman Garrison
Garrison Ave.
HABS NH-33
HABS NH,9-DUR,5-
6dr/66ph/2pg/fr L

DURHAM VIC.

Pendergast Garrison
Packer's Falls
HABS NH-22
HABS NH,9-DUR.V,1-
20dr/12ph/14pg L

SALMON FALLS

Wentworth,Col. Paul,House
Dover St. (moved to MA,Dover)
HABS NH-35
HABS NH,9-SALFA,1-
41dr/154ph/12pg/fr L

SOMERSWORTH

17-19 Market Street (Houses) (Mill Management Housing)
HABS NH-123
HABS NH,9-SOMER,1A-
10ph/18pg L

Mill Management Housing; see 17-19 Market Street (Houses)

SOMERSWORTH VIC.

Free Will Baptist Church
10 Green St.
HABS NH-213
HABS 1989(HABS):14
18ph/24pg/2pc L

SULLIVAN COUNTY

ACWORTH

Acworth Meetinghouse
Town Green
HABS NH-54
HABS NH,10-ACWO,1-
1ph/3pg L

Grout,Nathaniel,House
S. Acworth Rd.
HABS NH-55
HABS NH,10-ACWO,2-
1ph/3pg L

CHARLESTON

Vryling-Lovell House
S. Main St.
HABS NH-56
HABS NH,10-CHAR,2-
1ph/2pg L

CLAREMONT

Arpin House; see Houde,Emma,House

Bob's Finishing Shop; see River Street Historic District

City Hall/Opera House; see Claremont Village Industrial District

Claremont Rehabilitation Project; see Sullivan Machinery Company

Claremont Village Industrial District
HAER NH-1
HAER NH,10-CLAR,5-
4dr/48ph/2pg/7pc/fr L

Claremont Village Industrial District (City Hall/Opera House)
HAER NH-1-A
HAER NH,10-CLAR,18-
1ph/1pc L

Claremont Village Industrial District; see Monadnock Mills

Claremont Village Industrial District; see Monadnock Mills:Mill No. 1

Claremont Village Industrial District; see Monadnock Mills:Mill No. 2

Claremont Village Industrial District; see Monadnock Mills:Mill No. 3

Claremont Village Industrial District (Moody Hotel)
Tremont Square
HAER NH-1-B
HAER NH,10-CLAR,19-
1ph/1pc L

Claremont Village Industrial District; see River Street Historic District

4 Crescent Street Tenement; see Monadnock Mill Tenement

Dexter-Fitchburg House; see Dexter,David,House

Dexter,David,House (Dexter-Fitchburg House)
HABS NH-195
HABS NH,10-CLAR,1-
30ph/3pg L

Fluette,Adelard,House (LaPorte House)
71 Washington St.
HABS NH-197
HABS NH,10-CLAR,2-
7ph/5pg L

Houde,Emma,House (Arpin House)
77 Washington St.
HABS NH-198
HABS NH,10-CLAR,3-
7ph/5pg L

LaPorte House; see Fluette,Adelard,House

95 Main Street (House); see River Street Historic District

Monadnock Mill Tenement (4 Crescent Street Tenement)
1-18 Crescent St.
HABS NH-176
HABS NH,10-CLAR,4A-
11ph/4pg/1pc L

Monadnock Mills (Claremont Village Industrial District)
HAER NH-2
HAER NH,10-CLAR,6-
22ph/1pg/3pc/fr L

Monadnock Mills:Mill No. 1 (Claremont Village Industrial District)
13-17 Water St.
HAER NH-2-A
HAER NH,10-CLAR,6A
5dr/6ph/1pc/fr L

Monadnock Mills:Mill No. 2 (Claremont Village Industrial District)
HAER NH-2-B
HAER NH,10-CLAR,6B-
2ph/1pc/fr L

Monadnock Mills:Mill No. 3 (Claremont Village Industrial District)
HAER NH-2-C
HAER NH,10-CLAR,6C-
2ph/1pc/fr L

Moody Hotel; see Claremont Village Industrial District

36 River Street (House); see River Street Historic District

38 River Street (House); see River Street Historic District

40-42 River Street (House); see River Street Historic District

22-28 River Street (Houses); see River Street Historic District

8-20 River Street (Houses); see River Street Historic District

River Street Historic District (Bob's Finishing Shop; Claremont Village Industrial District)
30-32 River St.
HAER NH-5-C
HAER NH,10-CLAR,12-
3ph/1pc L

River Street Historic District (Claremont Village Industrial District)
River St. btwn. Union & Pearl Sts.
HAER NH-5
HAER NH,10-CLAR,9-
15dr/8ph/1pg/1pc L

River Street Historic District (95 Main Street (House); Claremont Village Industrial District)
HAER NH-5-G
HAER NH,10-CLAR,16-
8ph/1pc L

River Street Historic District (36 River Street (House); Claremont Village Industrial District)
HAER NH-5-D
HAER NH,10-CLAR,13-
6ph/1pc L

River Street Historic District (38 River Street (House); Claremont Village Industrial District)
HAER NH-5-E
HAER NH,10-CLAR,14-
6ph/1pc L

River Street Historic District (40-42 River Street (House); Claremont Village Industrial District)
HAER NH-5-F
HAER NH,10-CLAR,15-
7ph/1pc L

River Street Historic District (22-28 River Street (Houses); Claremont Village Industrial District)
HAER NH-5-B
HAER NH,10-CLAR,11-
4ph/1pc L

River Street Historic District (8-20 River Street (Houses); Claremont Village Industrial District)
HAER NH-5-A
HAER NH,10-CLAR,10-
5ph/1pc L

River Street Historic District (Workers' Cottage; Claremont Village Industrial District)
97 Main St.
HAER NH-5-H
HAER NH,10-CLAR,17-
5ph/1pc L

Sugar River Grist Mill & Saw Mill (Sugar River Mills)
159 Main St.
HAER NH-3
HAER NH,10-CLAR,8-
6dr/17ph/1pg/3pc/fr L

Sugar River Mills; see Sugar River Grist Mill & Saw Mill

Sullivan Machinery Company (Claremont Rehabilitation Project)
Main St. between Pearl & Water Sts.
HAER NH-4
HAER NH,10-CLAR,7-
1dr/49ph/32pg/7pc L

Workers' Cottage; see River Street Historic District

CORNISH

Aspet; see Saint-Gaudens,Augustus,National Historic Site

Caretaker's Cottage and Garage; see Saint-Gaudens,Augustus,National Historic Site

Cornish-Windsor Covered Bridge
Spanning Conn. River btwn Cornish,NH & Windsor,VT
HAER NH-8
HAER NH,10-CORN,2-
10ph/1pg L

Little Studio; see Saint-Gaudens,Augustus,National Historic Site

New Studio; see Saint-Gaudens,Augustus,National Historic Site

Ravine Studio; see Saint-Gaudens,Augustus,National Historic Site

Saint-Gaudens Tomb; see Saint-Gaudens,Augustus,National Historic Site

Saint-Gaudens,Augustus,National Historic Site (Aspet)
Saint Gaudens Rd. ,off State Rt. 12A
HABS NH-196-A
HABS NH,10-CORN,1A-
14ph L

Saint-Gaudens,Augustus,National Historic Site (Caretaker's Cottage and Garage)
Saint Gaudens Rd. ,off State Rt. 12A
HABS NH-196-F
HABS NH,10-CORN,1F,
3ph L

Saint-Gaudens,Augustus,National Historic Site (Little Studio)
Saint Gaudens Rd. ,off State Rt. 12A
HABS NH-196-B
HABS NH,10-CORN,1B-
5ph L

Saint-Gaudens,Augustus,National Historic Site (New Studio)
Saint Gaudens Rd. ,off State Rt. 12A
HABS NH-196-C
HABS NH,10-CORN,1C-
3ph L

Saint-Gaudens,Augustus,National Historic Site (Ravine Studio)
Saint Gaudens Rd. ,off State Rt. 12A
HABS NH-196-D
HABS NH,10-CORN,1D-
2dr/fr L

Saint-Gaudens,Augustus,National Historic Site (Stables)
Saint Gaudens Rd. ,off State Rt. 12A
HABS NH-196-G
HABS NH,10-CORN,1G-
4dr/4ph/fr L

Saint-Gaudens,Augustus,National Historic Site (Temple; Saint-Gaudens Tomb)
Saint Gaudens Rd. ,off State Rt. 12A
HABS NH-196-E
HABS NH,10-CORN,1E-
1ph L

Stables; see Saint-Gaudens,Augustus,National Historic Site

Temple; see Saint-Gaudens,Augustus,National Historic Site

GOSHEN

Baker-Booth Blacksmith Shop
Lear Hill Rd.,W. of Rt. 10
HABS NH-216
HABS DLC/PP-1993:NH-5
13ph/4pg/1pc L

NEWPORT

Breck,James,House
Main & Elm Sts. (SW corner)
HABS NH-212
HABS NH-10-NEWP,2-
5ph/1pg L

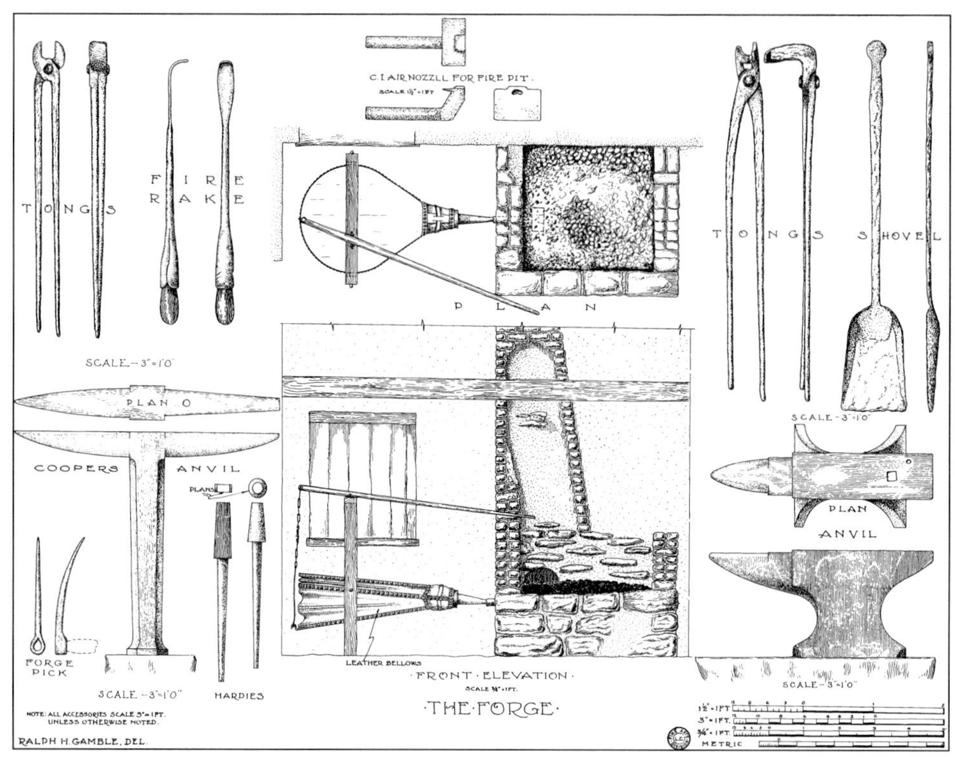

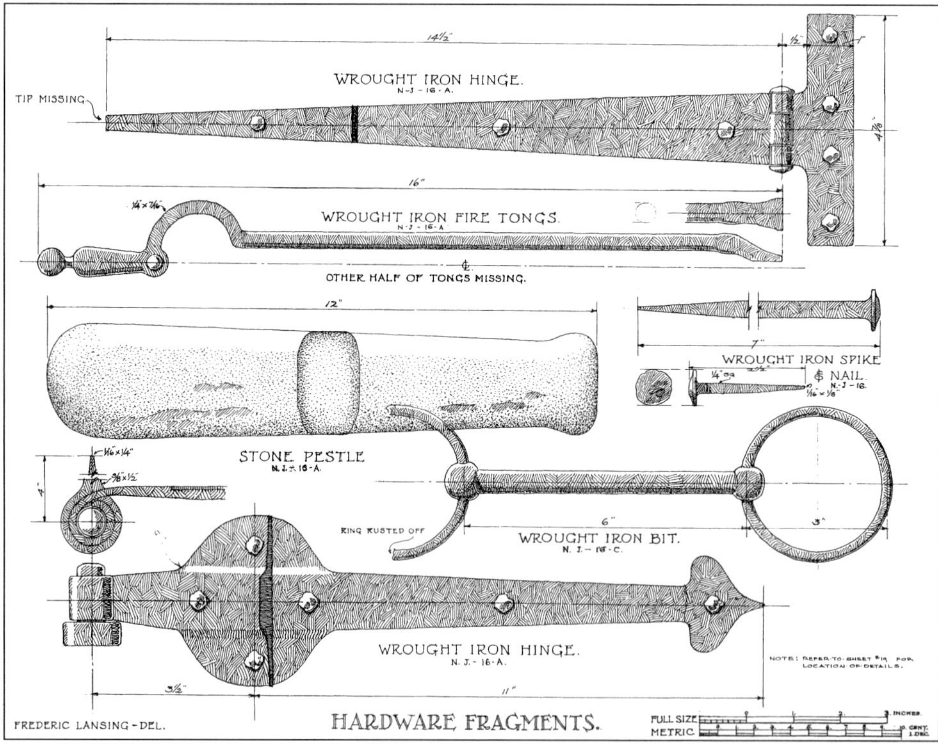

Reuben Matlack Blacksmith and Wheelwright Shop, Maple Shade, Burlington County, New Jersey. The forge. Measured drawing delineated by Ralph H. Gamble, 1936 (HABS NJ-264, sheet 7 of 10).

Samuel Demarest House, New Milford, Bergen County, New Jersey. Hardware fragments. Measured drawing delineated by Frederic Lansing, 1936 (HABS NJ-16, sheet 27 of 27).

New Jersey

ATLANTIC COUNTY

New Jersey Coastal Heritage Trail; see Tuckahoe River Bridge

Tuckahoe River Bridge (New Jersey Coastal Heritage Trail)
See same name under Cape May Co.,Tuckahoe Vic.
HAER NJ-89
L

ABSECON

Doughty,Daniel,House (New Jersey Coastal Heritage Trail)
46 Shore Rd.
HABS NJ-1125
1ph/1pc H

Methodist Meetinghouse
50 W. Church st.
HABS NJ-662
HABS NJ,1-ABSEC,1-
17dr/fr L

New Jersey Coastal Heritage Trail; see Doughty,Daniel,House

New Jersey Coastal Heritage Trail; see Pitney,Jonathan,House

Pitney,Jonathan,House (New Jersey Coastal Heritage Trail)
Shore Rd.
HABS NJ-1126
1ph/1pc H

ATLANTIC CITY

Absecon Lighthouse
Pacific Ave. ,btwn. Rhode Island & Vermont Aves.
HABS NJ-734
HABS NJ,1-ATCI,2-
4dr/1ph/2pg/1pc/fr L

All-War Memorial (New Jersey Coastal Heritage Trail)
Albany & Atlantic Aves.
HABS NJ-1128
2ph/1pc H

Atlantic City Boardwalk (New Jersey Coastal Heritage Trail)
Beachfront btw. Fredericksburg & Maine Aves.
HABS NJ-1161
H

Atlantic City Convention Hall (New Jersey Coastal Heritage Trail)
On the Boardwalk,W. of Mississippi Ave.
HABS NJ-1130
8ph/1pc H

Blenheim Hotel
Ohio Ave. & Boardwalk
HABS NJ-864
HABS NJ,1-ATCI,3-
14dr/173ph/19pg/9pc/22ct/fr L

Chalfonte Hotel
Pacific & North Carolina Aves.
HABS NJ-869
HABS NJ,1-ATCI,4-
19dr/88ph/30pg/6pc/fr L

Church of the Ascension (New Jersey Coastal Heritage Trail)
1601 Pacific Ave.
HABS NJ-1129
2ph/1pc H

City Hall
Atlantic & Tennessee Aves.
HABS NJ-815
HABS NJ,1-ATCI,5-
25ph/1pg/2pc L

Claridge Hotel and Casino (New Jersey Coastal Heritage Trail)
Indiana Ave. at the Boardwalk
HABS NJ-1170
1ph/1pc H

Dennis Hotel
Michigan Ave. & Boardwalk
HABS NJ-862
HABS NJ,1-ATCI,6-
16dr/127ph/14pg/7pc/11ct/fr L

Fire Station No. 4 (New Jersey Coastal Heritage Trail)
California & Atlantic Aves.
HABS NJ-1168
3ph/1pc H

Hoffman House,The (Holmhurst Hotel)
123-131 Pennsylvania Ave.
HABS NJ-925
HABS NJ,1-ATCI,7-
28ph/20pg/1pc L

Holmhurst Hotel; see Hoffman House,The

Marlborough Hotel
Boardwalk at Park Place
HABS NJ-863
HABS NJ,1-ATCI,8-
13dr/76ph/11pg/4pc/13ct L

Marlborough,Blenheim & Dennis Hotels(aerial views)
Btwn Park Place,Michigan Ave. & Boardwalk
HABS NJ-976
HABS NJ,1-ATCI,9-
70ph/5pc L

New Jersey Coastal Heritage Trail; see All-War Memorial

New Jersey Coastal Heritage Trail; see Atlantic City Boardwalk

New Jersey Coastal Heritage Trail; see Atlantic City Convention Hall

New Jersey Coastal Heritage Trail; see Church of the Ascension

New Jersey Coastal Heritage Trail; see Claridge Hotel and Casino

New Jersey Coastal Heritage Trail; see Fire Station No. 4

New Jersey Coastal Heritage Trail; see Wells Fargo Guard Services Building

Seaside Hotel
Pennsylvania Ave. & Boardwalk
HABS NJ-938
HABS NJ,1-ATCI,10-
6ph/2pg/1pc L

Shelburne Hotel
Michigan Ave. & the Boardwalk
HABS NJ-929
HABS NJ,1-ATCI,11-
6ph/6pg/1pc L

Steel Pier
Boardwalk at Virginia Ave.
HAER NJ-64
HAER NJ,1-ATCI,1-
11ph/3pg/1pc L

Sun Gallery Bridge
Spanning Ohio Ave.,Marlborough-Blenheim Hotels
HABS NJ-975
HABS NJ,1-ATCI,12-
15ph/1pc L

Wells Fargo Guard Services Building (New Jersey Coastal Heritage Trail)
210 N. Albany Ave.
HABS NJ-1127
1ph/1pc H

BRIGANTINE

Brigantine Inn (New Jersey Coastal Heritage Trail)
1400 Ocean Ave.
HABS NJ-1171
1ph/1pc H

New Jersey Coastal Heritage Trail; see Brigantine Inn

EGG HARBOR CITY VIC.

Lower Bank Road Bridge
Spanning Mullica River
HAER NJ-73
HAER DLC/PP-1993:NJ-3
33ph/16pg/3pc L

HEAD-OF-THE-RIVER

Head-of-the-River Methodist Episcopal Church
Etna Rd.
HABS NJ-274
HABS NJ,1- ,1-
9dr/2ph/4pg/fr L

LEEDS POINT

Japheth House; see Leeds,Japhet,House

Leeds,Japhet,House (Japheth House)
Moss Mill Rd.
HABS NJ-399
HABS NJ,1-LEEPO,1-
10dr/1ph/2pg/fr L

MARGATE CITY

Lucy; see Margate Elephant

Margate City,Town of (New Jersey Coastal Heritage Trail)
Absecon Island
HABS NJ-1064
2ph/1pc H

Margate Elephant (Lucy)
Atlantic Ave. & Decatur St.
HABS NJ-816
HABS NJ,1-MARGCI,1-
4dr/6ph/1pc L

New Jersey Coastal Heritage Trail; see Margate City,Town of

MAYS LANDING

Forge,Walter,Mansion
HABS NJ-288
HABS NJ,1-MAYLA.V,1-
14dr/2ph/4pg/fr L

Mays Landing Presbyterian Church
HABS NJ-516
HABS NJ,1-MAYLA,1-
12dr/3ph/3pg/6ct/fr L

PLEASANTVILLE

New Jersey Coastal Heritage Trail; see Studebaker Dealership

Studebaker Dealership (New Jersey Coastal Heritage Trail)
U.S. Hwy. 40
HABS NJ-1131
2ph/1pc H

PORT REPUBLIC

Clark,Adrial,House
Church Lane & Main Sts.
HABS NJ-645
HABS NJ,1-POREP,1-
12dr/4ph/4pg/fr L

Franklin Inn & Store
Mill Rd.
HABS NJ-663
HABS NJ,1-POREP,2-
17dr/23ph/4pg/fr L

Johnson,Joseph,House
New York Rd. ,Nacote Creek vic.
HABS NJ-728
HABS NJ,1-POREP,3-
7ph/3pg/1pc L

SMITHVILLE

New Jersey Coastal Heritage Trail; see Smithville Inn

Smith Homestead
1597 New York & Moss Hill Rds.
HABS NJ-280
HABS NJ,1-SMITH,1-
8dr/2ph/4pg/fr L

Smithville Inn (New Jersey Coastal Heritage Trail)
3 N. New York Rd.
HABS NJ-1172
1ph/1pc H

SOMERS POINT

Somers Mansion
Shore Rd. & Goll St.
HABS NJ-281
HABS NJ,1-SOMPO,1-
17dr/6ph/4pg/1ct/fr L

VENTNOR

New Jersey Coastal Heritage Trail; see 7223-27 Ventnor Avenue (Commercial)

New Jersey Coastal Heritage Trail; see Ventnor Twin Theater

7223-27 Ventnor Avenue (Commercial) (New Jersey Coastal Heritage Trail)
HABS NJ-1169
1ph/1pc H

Ventnor Twin Theater (New Jersey Coastal Heritage Trail)
5211 Ventnor Ave.
HABS NJ-1124
1ph/1pc H

BERGEN COUNTY

ALPINE

Cornwallis Headquarters
Palisade Interstate Park
HABS NJ-115
HABS NJ,2-ALP,1-
6dr/5ph/3pg/fr L

Huyler Dock House
Palisades Interstate Park
HABS NJ-167
HABS NJ,2-ALP,2-
7dr/2ph/3pg/fr L

BERGENFIELD

Kipp,Nicholas,House
221 N. Washington Ave.
HABS NJ-423
HABS NJ,2-BERG,1-
26dr/10ph/2pg/fr L

CLOSTER

De Clerque Farm Group
Piermont Rd.
HABS NJ-364
HABS NJ,2-CLOST,3-
24dr/8ph/3pg/fr L

Doremus,David D. ,House
Piermont Rd.
HABS NJ-361
HABS NJ,2-CLOST,1-
11dr/4ph/2pg/fr L

Durie,Nicholas,House
Schraalenburg Rd.
HABS NJ-472
HABS NJ,2-CLOST,4-
28dr/10ph/2pg/fr L

Parcel,Walter,House; see Van der Beck Slave House

Van der Beck Slave House (Parcel,Walter,House)
Piermont Rd.
HABS NJ-363
HABS NJ,2-CLOST,2A-
7dr/1ph/3pg/fr L

CRESSKILL

Huyler,Capt. John,Homestead
500 County Rd.
HABS NJ-168
HABS NJ,2-CRESK,1-
12dr/3ph/2pg/fr L

Westervelt,Benjamin P. ,House
County Rd.
HABS NJ-422
HABS NJ,2-CRESK,2-
19dr/4ph/4pg/fr L

DEMAREST

Bogert,Matthew P. ,Stone Well House
Orchard Rd.
HABS NJ-428
HABS NJ,2-DEMA,1-
1dr/1ph/2pg L

DUMONT

Demarest,Daniel,House
404 Washington Ave.
HABS NJ-657
HABS NJ,2-DUMO,4-
17dr/9ph/8pg/fr L

North Reformed Church of Schraalenburgh
Washington & Madison Aves.
HABS NJ-173
HABS NJ,2-DUMO,3-
22dr/5ph/2pg/fr L

North Reformed Church of Schraalenburgh Parsonage
191 Washington Ave.
HABS NJ-172
HABS NJ,2-DUMO,2-
16dr/7ph/2pg/fr L

Zabriskie-Christie House
10 Colonial Court
HABS NJ-5
HABS NJ,2-DUMO,1-
19dr/6ph/3pg/fr L

E. RUTHERFORD

Kip-Outwater,Richard,House
231 Hackensack St.
HABS NJ-700
HABS NJ,2-RUTHE,1-
20dr/8ph/6pg/fr L

EDGEWATER

Edgewater Ford Assembly Plant Complex
309 River Rd.
HAER NJ-53
HAER NJ,2-EDWA,1-
14ph/7pg/1pc L

Ford Motor Co. Edgewater Assem. Plant,Assem. Bldg.
309 River Rd.
HAER NJ-53-A
100ph/102pg/8pc H

Ford Motor Co. Edgewater Assem. Plant,Substation
309 River Rd.
HAER NJ-53-B
2ph/6pg/2pc H

Kellogg,Spencer, & Sons,Inc. ,Pier & Transit Shed
139-155 River Rd.
HAER NJ-48
HAER NJ,2-EDWA,2-
21ph/27pg/2pc L

EMERSON

Blauvelt House
Old Hook Rd.
HABS NJ-111
HABS NJ,2-EMSO,1-
11dr/5ph/2pg/fr L

ENGLEWOOD

Lydecker House
220 Grand Ave.
HABS NJ-162
HABS NJ,2-ENG,2-
7dr/5ph/2pg/fr L

Van Brunt,John,House
315 Grand Ave.
HABS NJ-392
HABS NJ,2-ENG,3-
16dr/8ph/2pg/fr L

Westervelt,Peter,House
290 Grand Ave.
HABS NJ-112
HABS NJ,2-ENG,1-
9dr/5ph/2pg/fr L

FAIR LAWN

Ackerman,Maria Ann,House; see Vanderbeck,Jacob,House

Alyea-Outwater House; see Lee,Maj. Henry,Headquarters

Hooper,Peter A. ,House
E. Fair Lawn Ave.
HABS NJ-174
HABS NJ,2-FAIR,2-
12dr/7ph/3pg/fr L

Lee,Maj. Henry,Headquarters (Alyea-Outwater House)
Wagaraw Rd.
HABS NJ-551
HABS NJ,2-FAIR,3-
20dr/3ph/6pg/fr L

Vanderbeck,Jacob,House (Ackerman,Maria Ann,House)
Dunker Hook Rd.
HABS NJ-563
HABS NJ,2-FAIR,4-
11dr/3ph/3pg/fr L

Vanderbeck,Jacob,House & Kitchen
Saddle River Rd. & Dunker Hook Lane
HABS NJ-45
HABS NJ,2-FAIR,1-
16dr/4ph/2pg/fr L

FORT LEE

Church of the Madonna
Church St.
HABS NJ-421
HABS NJ,2-FOLE,1-
13dr/3ph/2pg/fr L

George Washington Bridge
Spng Hudson River btwn Fort Lee,NJ & Manhattan,NY
HAER NY-129
HAER NY,31-NEYO,161-
63ph/1pg/4pc/8ct L

GLEN ROCK

Berdan House
Lincoln Ave.
HABS NJ-299
HABS NJ,2-GLEN,1-
11dr/3ph/2pg/fr L

HACKENSACK

Ackerman-Brinkerhoff House
184 Essex St.
HABS NJ-7
HABS NJ,2-HACK,2-
6dr/3ph/10pg/fr L

Brinkerhoff House
36 Essex St.
HABS NJ-622
HABS NJ,2-HACK,8-
3ph/3pg/1pc L

Demarest Homestead; see Van Giesen,George,House

First Reformed Church of Hackensack
Church & Court Sts.
HABS NJ-4
HABS NJ,2-HACK,1-
8dr/2ph/10pg/fr L

Hopper,John,House
249 Polifly Rd.
HABS NJ-352
HABS NJ,2-HACK,6-
21dr/6ph/3pg/fr L

Lozier,Nicholas,House (Westervelt House; Van Buskirk House)
393 Main St.
HABS NJ-177
HABS NJ,2-HACK,5-
9dr/1ph/4pg/fr L

Terheun House
450 River & Anderson Sts.
HABS NJ-8
HABS NJ,2-HACK,3-
5dr/5ph/2pg/fr L

Van Buskirk House; see Lozier,Nicholas,House

Van Giesen,George,House (Demarest Homestead)
Terrace Ave. & Essex St.
HABS NJ-680
HABS NJ,2-HACK,7-
17dr/6ph/6pg/fr L

Washington Mansion House Tavern (Zabriskie,Peter,House)
Main St. & Washington Pl.
HABS NJ-117
HABS NJ,2-HACK,4-
20dr/3ph/3pg/fr L

Westervelt House; see Lozier,Nicholas,House

Zabriskie,Peter,House; see Washington Mansion House Tavern

HILLSDALE

Demarest,Samuel G. ,House
Demarest Ave.
HABS NJ-500
HABS NJ,2-HILDA,1-
16dr/2ph/2pg/fr L

HOHOKUS

Hermitage, The, Smokehouse
335 N. Franklin Turnpike
HABS NJ-98-A
HABS NJ,2-HOHO,1-A-
1ph L

Hermitage,The (Provost,Col. Marc,House)
335 N. Franklin Turnpike
HABS NJ-98
HABS NJ,2-HOHO,1-
20dr/27ph/4pg/3pc/fr L

Provost,Col. Marc,House; see Hermitage,The

HOHOKUS TWP.

Van Horn,Abram,House
Valley Rd.
HABS NJ-114
HABS NJ,2-MAWA.V,1-
10dr/5ph/2pg/fr L

LEONIA

Vreeland House
125 Lakeview Ave.
HABS NJ-158
HABS NJ,2-LEO,1-
15dr/16ph/3pg/fr L

LYNDHURST

Van Winkle,Jacob W. ,House
316 Riverside Ave.
HABS NJ-477
HABS NJ,2-LYND,1-
16dr/5ph/3pg/fr L

MAYWOOD

Berdan,John D. ,House
465 Maywood Ave.
HABS NJ-640
HABS NJ,2-MAYWO,1-
24dr/6ph/4pg/fr L

Oldis-Brinckerhoff House
Maywood & Central Aves.
HABS NJ-697
HABS NJ,2-MAYWO,3-
16dr/5ph/5pg/fr L

Romine-Van Voorhis House; see Van Voorhis,Henry A. ,House

Van Voorhis,Henry A. ,House
(Romine-Van Voorhis House)
306 Maywood Ave.
HABS NJ-667
HABS NJ,2-MAYWO,2-
15dr/4ph/4pg/fr L

MIDLAND PARK

Baldwin,David,House
60 Lake Ave.
HABS NJ-420
HABS NJ,2-MIDPA,2-
18dr/11ph/2pg/fr L

Lozier-Wortendyke House
(Lozier,Cornelius,House)
Paterson Ave. & Goffle Rd.
HABS NJ-375
HABS NJ,2-MIDPA,1-
10dr/1ph/2pg/fr L

Lozier,Cornelius,House; see Lozier-Wortendyke House

MONTVALE BORO

Eckerson,Abram G. ,House
Chestnut Ridge Rd.
HABS NJ-175
HABS NJ,2-MONT,1-
17dr/6ph/2pg/fr L

NEW MILFORD

des Marest,David,House (Gurd House)
River Rd.
HABS NJ-11
HABS NJ,2-NEMIL,1-
8dr/6ph/5pg/fr L

des Marest,Samuel,House
River Rd.
HABS NJ-16
HABS NJ,2-NEMIL,2-
37dr/5ph/6pg/fr L

Gurd House; see des Marest,David,House

OAKLAND

Church of Ponds
Oakland & Franklin Lakes Rd.
HABS NJ-116
HABS NJ,2-OAKL,1-
10dr/6ph/3pg/fr L

OLD TAPPAN

Haring,Cosyn,House; see Herring,Dewerk Peter,House

Haring,David R. ,House
202 Old Tappan Rd.
HABS NJ-703
HABS NJ,2-TAPO,4-
13dr/3ph/6pg/fr L

Haring,Frederick,House
Old Tappan & DeWolfe Rds.
HABS NJ-487
HABS NJ,2-TAPO,3-
19dr/4ph/2pg/fr L

Haring,Gerrit J. ,House
W. Old Tappan Rd.
HABS NJ-459
HABS NJ,2-TAPO,2-
19dr/5ph/3pg/fr L

Herring,Dewerk Peter,House
(Haring,Cosyn,House)
166 Pearl River Rd.
HABS NJ-154
HABS NJ,2-TAPO,1-
9dr/6ph/4pg/fr L

OLD TAPPAN VIC.

Holdrom,William,House (Vanderbilt House)
Prospect & Rivervale Ave.
HABS NJ-686
HABS NJ,2-TAPO.V,1-
15dr/4ph/3pg/fr L

Vanderbilt House; see Holdrom,William,House

PARAMUS

Banta House & Barn
Howland Ave.
HABS NJ-163
HABS NJ,2-PARA,3-
7dr/2ph/2pg/fr L

Van Saun House
Howland Ave.
HABS NJ-343
HABS NJ,2-PARA,5-
11dr/3ph/2pg/fr L

Zabriskie,Albert J. ,House
Glen Ave.
HABS NJ-271
HABS NJ,2-PARA,4-
12dr/6ph/3pg/fr L

Zabriskie,Jacob,Farm Group
S. Paramus Rd.
HABS NJ-157
HABS NJ,2-PARA,2-
13dr/6ph/3pg/fr L

PARK RIDGE

Ackerson & Demarest Trading Post
Main St. & Mill Rd.
HABS NJ-176
HABS NJ,2-PARK,1-
12dr/5ph/3pg/fr L

PARK RIDGE VIC.

Nortendyke Barn (Wortendyke Barn)
HABS NJ-735
HABS NJ,2-PARK.V,1-
1ph L

Wortendyke Barn; see Nortendyke Barn

RIDGEFIELD

De Groot,John,House
1008 De Groot Ave.
HABS NJ-170
HABS NJ,2-RIDG,2-
12dr/4ph/3pg/fr L

Reformed Church of English Neighborhood
Edgewater Ave.
HABS NJ-552
HABS NJ,2-RIDG,1-
26dr/3ph/4pg/fr L

RIDGEFIELD PARK

Brinkerhoff-Christie-Paulison Homestead
8 Homestead Place
HABS NJ-160
HABS NJ,2-RIDGP,1-
9dr/1ph/2pg/fr L

RIDGEWOOD

Ackerman-Naugle,David,House
415 E. Saddle River Rd.
HABS NJ-155
HABS NJ,2-RIDGWO,1-
5dr/3ph/9pg/fr L

RIVER EDGE

Wilson,Peter,House
1027 Main St.
HABS NJ-655
HABS NJ,2-RIVED,2-
14dr/4ph/5pg/fr L

Zabriskie-Steuben House
New Bridge Rd.
HABS NJ-47
HABS NJ,2-RIVED,1-
10dr/6ph/2pg/2ct/fr L

ROCHELLE PARK

Demarest,Samuel C. ,House
12 Rochelle Ave.
HABS NJ-90
HABS NJ,2-ROCH,1-
9dr/3ph/4pg/fr L

Lutkins House
Passaic St.
HABS NJ-159
HABS NJ,2-ROCH,2-
4dr/2ph/2pg/fr L

ROCKLEIGH

Haring,Nicholas,House
Piermont Rd.
HABS NJ-169
HABS NJ,2-NORVA,1-
11dr/12ph/2pg/fr L

RUTHERFORD

Berry,John W. ,House
(Jurianson,Juria,House)
Meadow Rd. & Crane Ave.
HABS NJ-468
HABS NJ,2-RUTH,1-
20dr/6ph/2pg/fr L

Jurianson,Juria,House; see Berry,John W. ,House

SADDLE RIVER

Ackerman-Washington Feed & Flour Mill; see Washington Feed & Flour Mill

Ackerman,Abram,House
199 E. Saddle River Rd.
HABS NJ-156
HABS NJ,2-SADR,1-
10dr/5ph/3pg/fr L

Bond Farm House; see Van Buskirk,Thomas,House

Van Buskirk-Arkerman House
E. Saddle River Rd.
HABS NJ-331
HABS NJ,2-SADR,4-
7dr/1ph/2pg/fr L

Van Buskirk,Thomas,House (Bond Farm House)
E. Saddle River Rd.
HABS NJ-300
HABS NJ,2-SADR,2-
11dr/3ph/4pg L

Washington Feed & Flour Mill
(Ackerman-Washington Feed & Flour Mill)
E. Saddle River Rd.
HABS NJ-486
HABS NJ,2-SADR,5-
5dr/1ph/2pg L

Zion Evangelical Lutheran Church
Allendale Ave.
HABS NJ-330
HABS NJ,2-SADR,3-
15dr/1ph/2pg/fr L

SADDLE RIVER TWP.

Demarest,Samuel C. ,House
511 Market St.
HABS NJ-542
HABS NJ,2- ,1-
18dr/6ph/4pg/fr L

TEANECK

Ackerman,John,House
1286 River Rd.
HABS NJ-298
HABS NJ,2-TEA,4-
12dr/4ph/2pg/fr L

Banta,Samuel,House
1485 Teaneck Rd.
HABS NJ-171
HABS NJ,2-TEA,3-
13dr/2ph/2pg L

Brinkerhoff-Demarest (Homestead,Old)
493 Teaneck Rd.
HABS NJ-110
HABS NJ,2-TEA,1-
8dr/3ph/3pg/fr L

Homestead,Old; see Brinkerhoff-Demarest

Westervelt House
190 Teaneck Rd.
HABS NJ-113
HABS NJ,2-TEA,2-
8dr/1ph/2pg/fr L

TENAFLY

Westervelt House
256 Tenafly Rd.
HABS NJ-9
HABS NJ,2-TENF,1-
14dr/15ph/3pg/fr L

TENALFY

Christie-Parsils House
195 Jefferson Ave.
HABS NJ-470
HABS NJ,2-TENF,2-
14dr/5ph/3pg L

UPPER SADDLE RIVER

Saddle River Reformed Church
E. Saddle River & Upper Saddle River Rds.
HABS NJ-255
HABS NJ,2-SADRU,1-
12dr/4ph/2pg/fr L

WYCKOFF

Branford,John,House (Van Blarcom-Van Horn House)
Lafayette & Wyckoff
HABS NJ-391
HABS NJ,2-WYCK,4-
13dr/7ph/3pg/fr L

Brown Stone Inn; see Quackenbush,Corines,House

Quackenbush,Corines,House (Brown Stone Inn)
Wyckoff & Franklin Aves.
HABS NJ-702
HABS NJ,2-WYCK,5-
24dr/7ph/8pg/fr L

Van Blarcom-Van Horn House; see Branford,John,House

Van Voorhis,Albert,House
Maple & Franklin Aves.
HABS NJ-161
HABS NJ,2-WYCK,1-
18dr/10ph/3pg/fr L

Willis,Samuel & Abram,House
Main St.
HABS NJ-378
HABS NJ,2-WYCK,3-
9dr/2ph/2pg/fr L

Wycoff Reformed Church
Main St.
HABS NJ-338
HABS NJ,2-WYCK,2-
14dr/1ph/3pg/fr L

WYCKOFF VIC.

Packer House
600 Ewing Ave.
HABS NJ-528
HABS NJ,2-WYCK.V,1-
19dr/4ph/2pg/fr L

Stagg,John C. ,House
Sicomac Rd. & Cedar Hill Ave.
HABS NJ-678
HABS NJ,2-WYCK.V,2-
16dr/3ph/5pg/fr L

BURLINGTON COUNTY

ARNEYTOWN

Arneytown Tavern; see Lawrie House

Emley-Wildes House (Myrtlebank)
HABS NJ-303
HABS NJ,3-ARNTO,2-
32dr/5ph/2pg/fr L

Lawrie House (Arneytown Tavern)
HABS NJ-134
HABS NJ,3-ARNTO,1-
24dr/6ph/3pg/fr L

Myrtlebank; see Emley-Wildes House

BATSTO

Atsion Stove & Pattern for stove casting
HABS NJ-40-A
HABS NJ,3-BATO,7-
2ph/fr L

Babington,Rosanna Ireland,Cast Iron Gravestone
Batsto Museum (moved from ME,Weymouth)
HABS NJ-882
HABS NJ,3-BATO,5-
1ph L

Batsto Village, Typical Workman's Cottage
HABS NJ-40-D
HABS NJ,3-BATO,2-
3dr/1ph/fr L

General Store & Post Office
HABS NJ-366
HABS NJ,3-BATO,8-
11dr/4ph/1pg/fr L

Ironmaster's Mansion; see Manor House

Manor House (Ironmaster's Mansion; Richards Mansion)
Batsto Village
HABS NJ-40-C
HABS NJ,3-BATO,3-
4ph/fr L

Richards Grist Mill
HABS NJ-367
HABS NJ,3-BATO,9-
9dr/2ph/1pg/fr L

Richards Mansion; see Manor House

Richards Store House
HABS NJ-443
HABS NJ,3-BATO,10-
9dr/2ph/1pg/fr L

Richards,Jess,Burial Plot
Pleasant Mill Cemetery
HABS NJ-881
HABS NJ,3-BATO,4-
1ph L

Slag Heap
Batsto Village
HABS NJ-879
HABS NJ,3-BATO,6-
1ph L

Village,Old-General View
Batsto Village
HABS NJ-880
HABS NJ,3-BATO,1-
1ph/4pg L

BORDENTOWN

Barton,Clara,School
142 Crosswicks & Burlington Sts.
HABS NJ-84
HABS NJ,3-BORD,2-
3dr/1ph/5pg/fr L

Friends Meetinghouse
HABS NJ-322
HABS NJ,3-BORD,5-
1ph/2pg L

Hopkinson,Francis,House
Park St. & Farnsworth Ave.
HABS NJ-64
HABS NJ,3-BORD,1-
15dr/3ph/3pg/fr L

Lovell-Maron,John,House
223 Farnsworth Ave.
HABS NJ-324
HABS NJ,3-BORD,7-
9dr/4ph/3pg/fr L

Sayre House
25 Farnsworth Ave.
HABS NJ-323
HABS NJ,3-BORD,6-
1ph/2pg L

Watson-Gilder,Richard,House (Watson,Richard,House)
HABS NJ-315
HABS NJ,3-BORD,4-
22dr/6ph/4pg L

Watson,Richard,House; see Watson-Gilder,Richard,House

Wright,Joseph & Patience,House
100 Farnsworth Ave.
HABS NJ-314
HABS NJ,3-BORD,3-
1ph/4pg L

BRIDGEBORO

Anderson,Ellis,House; see Bridgeboro Historic District

Bridgeboro Historic District (Anderson,Ellis,House)
22 Bridgeboro St.
HABS NJ-899-4
HABS NJ,3-BRIBO,1/4-
3ph/1pg/1pc L

Bridgeboro Historic District (Bright,Widow Fannie,House)
26 S. Bridgeboro St.
HABS NJ-899-6
HABS NJ,3-BRIBO,1/6-
3ph/1pg/1pc L

Bridgeboro Historic District (Gaskill,Charles,House)
14 S. Bridgeboro St.
HABS NJ-899-2
HABS NJ,3-BRIBO,1/2-
2ph/1pg/1pc L

Bridgeboro Historic District (Haines,Thomas,House)
12 S. Bridgeboro St.
HABS NJ-899-1
HABS NJ,3-BRIBO,1/1-
1ph/1pg/1pc L

Bridgeboro Historic District (Lippincott,Wallace,House)
18-20 S. Bridgeboro St.
HABS NJ-899-3
HABS NJ,3-BRICO,1/3-
2ph/1pg/1pc L

Bridgeboro Historic District (Lowden,J. S. ,House)
Rt. 130,Section 9F Parcel 160
HABS NJ-899-11
HABS NJ,3-BRIBO,1/11-
3ph/1pg/1pc L

Bridgeboro Historic District (Meyers,Aaron,House)
24 S. Bridgeboro St.
HABS NJ-899-5
HABS NJ,3-BRIBO,1/5-
3ph/1pg/1pc L

Bridgeboro Historic District (Ridgeway,Andrew,House)
30 S. Bridgeboro St.
HABS NJ-899-8
HABS NJ,3-BRIBO,1/8-
3ph/1pg/1pc L

Bridgeboro Historic District (32-34 South Bridgeboro Street (Apartment House))
HABS NJ-899-9
HABS NJ,3-BRIBO,1/9-
2ph/1pg/1pc L

Bridgeboro Historic District (28 South Bridgeboro Street (House))
HABS NJ-899-7
HABS NJ,3-BRIBO,1/7-
2ph/1pg/1pc L

Bright,Widow Fannie,House; see Bridgeboro Historic District

Fortnum Motor Company
Rt. 130 & S. Bridgeboro St.
HABS NJ-937
HABS NJ,3-BRIBO,2-
9ph/5pg/1pc L

Gaskill,Charles,House; see Bridgeboro Historic District

Haines,Thomas,House; see Bridgeboro Historic District

Lippincott,Wallace,House; see Bridgeboro Historic District

Lowden,J. S. ,House; see Bridgeboro Historic District

Meyers,Aaron,House; see Bridgeboro Historic District

Ridgeway,Andrew,House; see Bridgeboro Historic District

32-34 South Bridgeboro Street (Apartment House); see Bridgeboro Historic District

28 South Bridgeboro Street (House); see Bridgeboro Historic District

BURLINGTON

Bishop's House; see Riverside

Burlington Library
23 W. Union St.
HABS NJ-319
HABS NJ,3-BURL,17-
1ph/3pg L

Chapel of the Holy Innocents (St. Mary's Hall)
HABS NJ-317
HABS NJ,3-BURL,16-
1ph/2pg L

Cooper-Lawrence House
457-459 High St.
HABS NJ-73
HABS NJ,3-BURL,6-
12dr/4ph/4pg/1pc/fr L

Doane House; see Riverside

Documentation: **ct** color transparencies **dr** measured drawings **fr** field records
pc photograph captions **pg** pages of text **ph** photographs

Fleetwood,Joseph,Cottage (Toll House,Old)
Burlington Pike
HABS NJ-244
HABS NJ,3-BURL,7-
2dr/2ph/2pg/fr L

Grant,Gen. ,House
309 Wood St.
HABS NJ-320
HABS NJ,3-BURL,18-
1ph/4pg L

Hutchinson-Revell House
8 E. Pearl St.
HABS NJ-30
HABS NJ,3-BURL,5-
4dr/1ph/2pg/fr L

Neale-Collins, Isaac, House
Broad & York Sts.
HABS NJ-312
HABS NJ,3-BURL,8-
22dr/4ph/3pg/fr L

Pearson-How,Hartshorn,House
453 High St.
HABS NJ-251
HABS NJ,3-BURL,15-
11dr/1ph/3pg/fr L

Riverside (Bishop's House; Doane House)
W. Delaware St.
HABS NJ-318
HABS NJ,3-BURL,3-
44dr/11ph/2pg/fr L

St. Mary's Church,New
HABS NJ-393
HABS NJ,3-BURL,2-
7ph/2pg L

St. Mary's Church,Old
W. Broad & Wood Sts.
HABS NJ-72
HABS NJ,3-BURL,1-
21dr/9ph/3pg/fr L

St. Mary's Hall; see Chapel of the Holy Innocents

Toll House,Old; see Fleetwood,Joseph,Cottage

Wright-Carey House
406 High St.
HABS NJ-321
HABS NJ,3-BURL,19-
1ph/2pg L

CHARLESTON VIC.

Rodman-Creely House
HABS NJ-369
HABS NJ,3-CHAR.V,4-
7dr/4ph/2pg/fr L

COLUMBUS

Atkinson-Shinn,William R. ,House
Route 39
HABS NJ-313
HABS NJ,3-COLU,1-
17dr/6ph/2pg/fr L

COOKSTOWN

Cookstown Tavern
Main St. & Bunting Bridge Rd.
HABS NJ-508
HABS NJ,3-COOK,1-
28dr/6ph/2pg/fr L

COOKSTOWN VIC.

Hockamick Log Cabin
HABS NJ-532
HABS NJ,3-COOK.V,1-
1dr/fr L

CROSSWICKS

Chesterfield Friends Meetinghouse
Front & Church Sts.
HABS NJ-25
HABS NJ,3-CROWI,1-
11dr/8ph/3pg/fr L

Middletown-Braislin House
Main St.
HABS NJ-368
HABS NJ,3-CROWI,2-
16dr/8ph/2pg/fr L

EAYRESTOWN

Eayres-Githens Farm Buildings
HABS NJ-136
HABS NJ,3-EARTO,2-
3dr/2ph/2pg/fr L

EAYRESTOWN VIC.

Black,John Jr. ,Barn (Stone Barn)
Newbold's Corner
HABS NJ-254
HABS NJ,3-EARTO.V,1-
7dr/3ph/2pg/fr L

Stone Barn; see Black,John Jr. ,Barn

EVESBORO VIC.

Clinton,Gen. ,Headquarters
Evesboro Rd.
HABS NJ-504
HABS NJ,3-EVBO.V,1-
16dr/6ph/4pg/fr L

Hewlings House
Mt. Laurel Rd.
HABS NJ-537
HABS NJ,3-EVBO.V,2-
16dr/8ph/2pg/fr L

EWANSVILLE

Woolston,John,House
Rt. 39
HABS NJ-365
HABS NJ,3-EWAV.V,1-
14dr/5ph/4pg/fr L

FIELDSBORO

Field-Stevens House (White Hill)
Delaware River
HABS NJ-203
HABS NJ,3-FIELB,1-
25dr/7ph/2pg/fr L

White Hill; see Field-Stevens House

JOBSTOWN

Newbold-Hoffman House
Monmouth Rd.
HABS NJ-135
HABS NJ,3-JOBTO,1-
3dr/1ph/2pg/fr L

JOBSTOWN VIC.

Black,Thomas,Smokehouse (Ockanickon Farm)
Monmouth Rd.
HABS NJ-636
HABS NJ,3-JOBTO.V,4A-
2dr/1ph/4pg/fr L

Ockanickon Farm; see Black,Thomas,Smokehouse

Ridgway,Job,House
HABS NJ-600
HABS NJ,3-JOBTO.V,1-
8dr/2ph/4pg/fr L

JOBSTOWN VICINITY

Black,John,Smokehouse
Monmouth Rd.
HABS NJ-263
HABS NJ,3-JOBTO.V,3-A-
3dr/1ph/4pg/fr L

KINKORA

Biddle,William,House
HABS NJ-527
HABS NJ,3-KINK,1-
16dr/4ph/5pg/fr L

LUMBERTON VIC.

Haines-Budd House (Jones Farmhouse)
HABS NJ-438
HABS NJ,3-LUMTO.V,3-
12dr/5ph/2pg/fr L

Jones Farmhouse; see Haines-Budd House

Log Stables; see Moore-Stiles Farm

Moore-Stiles Farm (Log Stables)
Bulls Head Rd.
HABS NJ-453
HABS NJ,3-LUMTO.V,2A-
10dr/4ph/2pg L

MAPLE SHADE

Matlack,Reuben,Blacksmith & Wheelwright Shop
HABS NJ-264
HABS NJ,3-MAPSH,1A-
10dr/6ph/3pg/fr L

MARLTON VIC.

Evans,Jacob,House
Marlton-Medford Rd.
HABS NJ-540
HABS NJ,3-MART.V,5-
24dr/11ph/6pg/fr L

Lippincott,Daniel,House
HABS NJ-596
HABS NJ,3-MART.V,2-
2ph/3pg L

Wills,Jacob,House
HABS NJ-597
HABS NJ,3-MART.V,1-
20dr/6ph/3pg/fr L

MOORESTOWN

Tallman Smokehouse
Long Crossing Rd.
HABS NJ-137
HABS NJ,3-MORTO.V,4-A-
1dr/1ph/2pg/fr L

MOORESTOWN VIC.

Cowperthwaite House
King's Hwy.
HABS NJ-471
HABS NJ,3-MORTO.V,3-
20dr/7ph/2pg/fr L

MOUNT HOLLY

Ashhusrt Estate,Summer House
Garden St.
HABS NJ-448
HABS NJ,3-MOUHO,12A-
4dr/1ph/1pg/fr L

Bispham Farmhouse
Rt. 138 & Madison Ave.
HABS NJ-400
HABS NJ,3-MOUHO,11-
21dr/8ph/2pg/fr L

Brainard,John,School
35 Brainard St.
HABS NJ-100
HABS NJ,3-MOUHO,3-
2dr/1ph/3pg/fr L

Burlington County Courthouse
(Surrogate's Office)
High St.
HABS NJ-27
HABS NJ,3-MOUHO,1-
28dr/8ph/3pg/fr L

Burlington County Prison
128 High St.
HABS NJ-340
HABS NJ,3-MOUHO,8-
24dr/7ph/12pg/fr L

Curtis House; see Shinn-Curtis Log Cabin

Farmer's Trust Company Bank Building
21 Mill St.
HABS NJ-397
HABS NJ,3-MOUHO,10-
18dr/4ph/2pg/fr L

Fire Department Building,Old
S. Pine St.
HABS NJ-353
HABS NJ,3-MOUHO,9-
2dr/1ph/2pg/fr L

Girard,Stephen,House
HABS NJ-316
HABS NJ,3-MOUHO,7-
1ph/4pg L

Shinn-Curtis House; see Shinn-Curtis Log Cabin

Shinn-Curtis Log Cabin (Shinn-Curtis House; Curtis House)
23 Washington St. (moved from Rancocas Blvd.)
HABS NJ-890
HABS NJ,3-MOUHO,14-
8ph/1pg/2pc L

Surrogate's Office; see Burlington County Courthouse

Three Tun Tavern
HABS NJ-230
HABS NJ,3-MOUHO,6-
1ph/2pg L

Woolman,John,Memorial
99 Branch St.
HABS NJ-71
HABS NJ,3-MOUHO,2-
7dr/3ph/2pg/fr L

Woolman,John,Shop
47 Mill St.
HABS NJ-457
HABS NJ,3-MOUHO,13-
19dr/7ph/3pg/fr L

MOUNT LAUREL

Evesham Friends Meetinghouse
Mt. Laurel Rd.
HABS NJ-31
HABS NJ,3-MOULA,1-
14dr/3ph/2pg/fr L

MOUNT LAUREL VIC.

Haines-Darnell House
Mt. Laurel Rd.
HABS NJ-589
HABS NJ,3-MOULA.V,2-
8ph/4pg L

Hewlings,Joseph,House
HABS NJ-547
HABS NJ,3-MOULA.V,1-
32dr/10ph/4pg/fr L

NEW GRETNA

New Jersey Coastal Heritage Trail; see St. Paul's United Methodist Church

St. Paul's United Methodist Church
(New Jersey Coastal Heritage Trail)
U.S. Hwy. 9
HABS NJ-1132
1ph/1pc H

NEW LISBON

Burlington County Almshouse
HABS NJ-290
HABS NJ,3-NEWLI,1-
4ph/2pg L

RANCOCAS

Friends Meetinghouse & School
HABS NJ-130
HABS NJ,3-RANC,1-
6dr/1ph/2pg/fr L

Friends School
Main St.
HABS NJ-250
HABS NJ,3-RANC,3-
3dr/1ph/2pg/fr L

Haines,Ezre,House
Main St.
HABS NJ-246
HABS NJ,3-RANC,2-
10dr/1ph/2pg/fr L

RANCOCAS VIC.

Buzby,Thomas,House
Rancocas River
HABS NJ-439
HABS NJ,3-RANC.V,2-
19dr/10ph/2pg/fr L

Green-Grovatt House
HABS NJ-204
HABS NJ,3-RANC.V,1-
13dr/5ph/8pg/fr L

Rogers-Bitting House
HABS NJ-426
HABS NJ,3-RANC.V,7-
11dr/10ph/2pg/fr L

RANCOCAS VICINITY

Wills,Aaron,House
HABS NJ-541
HABS NJ,3-RANC.V,3-
21dr/9ph/9pg/fr L

RED LION VICINITY

Sooy Place
HABS NJ-59
HABS NJ,3-REDLI.V,1-
13dr/4ph/4pg/fr L

RIVERTON VIC.

Wright,Joseph,House
Taylor's Lane
HABS NJ-683
HABS NJ,3-RIVTO.V,1-
16dr/12ph/3pg/fr L

SANDTOWN

Prickett-Wilkins House
HABS NJ-456
HABS NJ,3-SAND,1-
14dr/4ph/2pg/fr L

SOUTH PEMBERTON

Burr,Hudson,Mansion
HABS NJ-238
HABS NJ,3-PEMBS,1-
29dr/8ph/3pg/fr L

Covered Bridge & Flood Gates,Old
HABS NJ-654
HABS NJ,3-PEMBS,2-
5dr/fr L

SPRINGFIELD TWP.

Merritt,Jacob,House
HABS NJ-631
HABS NJ,3-MOUHO.V,3-
17dr/7ph/4pg/fr L

SPRINGSIDE VIC.

Rogers,John,House
HABS NJ-241
HABS NJ,3-SPRI.V,1-
10dr/8ph/2pg/fr L

SYKESVILLE

Plattsburg Presbyterian Church
HABS NJ-382
HABS NJ,3-SYKVI,1-
10dr/1ph/2pg/fr L

UPPER MILL

Bard,Peter,Log Cabin
Lebanon State Forest
HABS NJ-101
HABS NJ,3-UPMI,1-
2dr/1ph/2pg/fr L

VINCETOWN

Woolston,John,House
51-53 Mill St.
HABS NJ-494
HABS NJ,3-VINTO,1-
28dr/4ph/2pg/fr L

VINCETOWN VICINITY

Hollingshead-Peacock House
Pemberton-Vincetown Rd.
HABS NJ-239
HABS NJ,3-VINTO.V,1-
11dr/2ph/2pg/fr L

WASHINGTON TWP.

Quigley,John,House; see Wading River Tavern

Wading River Tavern
(Quigley,John,House)
HABS NJ-444
HABS NJ,3-WADRI,1-
19dr/9ph/2pg/fr L

WASHINGTON TWSP. VIC

Lower Bank Road Bridge
See Atlantic Co.,Egg Harbor City Vic. for document
HAER NJ-73
HAER DLC/PP-1993:NJ-3
33ph/16pg/3pc L

CAMDEN COUNTY

ANCORA

Spring Garden Inn
HABS NJ-534
HABS NJ,4-ANCO,1-
16dr/7ph/3pg/fr L

BELLMAWR

Hugg-Lippincott House; see Lippincott,Samuel B. ,House

Hugg,Samuel,House
Big Timber Creek
HABS NJ-284
HABS NJ,4-BELM,3-
23dr/3ph/4pg/fr L

Kay House
HABS NJ-282
HABS NJ,4-BELM,1-
9dr/4ph/4pg/fr L

Lippincott,Samuel B. ,House
(Hugg-Lippincott House)
Creek Rd.
HABS NJ-283
HABS NJ,4-BELM,2-
1ph/3pg L

BELLMAWR VIC.

Dobbs House
(Hugg-Brasilia-Crispin-Dobbs House)
HABS NJ-292
HABS NJ,4-BELM.V,1-
17dr/2ph/3pg/fr L

Glover House
Bellmawr Ave.
HABS NJ-380
HABS NJ,4-BELM.V,2-
13dr/3ph/3pg/fr L

Hugg-Brasilia-Crispin-Dobbs House; see Dobbs House

BLUE ANCHOR

Blue Anchor Tavern
Folsom Rd.
HABS NJ-131
HABS NJ,4-BLUA,1-
13dr/1ph/3pg/fr L

CAMDEN

Broadway Subway Station
30-32 & 33-37 S. Broadway
HABS NJ-928
HABS NJ,4-CAM,10-
28ph/2pg/2pc L

Camden Historical Society; see Pomona Hall

Cooper,Benjamin,House
Point & Erie Sts.
HABS NJ-304
HABS NJ,4-CAM,7-
9dr/2ph/3pg/fr L

Cooper,Joseph,House
Pyne Point Park
HABS NJ-70
HABS NJ,4-CAM,2-
4dr/2ph/4pg/fr L

Cooper,Samuel,House
1104 N. Twenty-second St.
HABS NJ-209
HABS NJ,4-CAM,5-
18dr/5ph/4pg/fr L

Grieveson House
1218 N. Thirty-second St.
HABS NJ-212
HABS NJ,4-CAM,6-
4dr/1ph/2pg/fr L

Harned,John,House
728 Cooper St.
HABS NJ-931
HABS NJ,4-CAM,11-
2ph/2pg/1pc L

New Jersey Transit Bus Operations, Inc.; see Public Service Railway Co:Newton Avenue Car Shops

Newton Avenue Bus Garage; see Public Service Railway Co:Newton Avenue Car Shops

Newton Friend's Meeting House
Cooper St.
HABS NJ-843
HABS NJ,4-CAM,12-
5dr/8ph/1pc/fr L

Newton Friend's Meeting,Guildhouse; see Newton Friend's Meeting,Schoolhouse

Newton Friend's Meeting,Schoolhouse
(Newton Friend's Meeting,Guildhouse)
Cooper St.
HABS NJ-843-A
HABS NJ,4-CAM,12-A-
1dr/fr L

Nicholson House
Admiral Wilson Blvd.
HABS NJ-102
HABS NJ,4-CAM,3-
5dr/3ph/3pg/fr L

Plummer,Frederick,House
1242 S. Front St.
HABS NJ-446
HABS NJ,4-CAM,8-
8dr/4ph/2pg/fr L

Pomona Hall (Camden Historical Society)
Park Blvd. & Euclid Ave.
HABS NJ-206
HABS NJ,4-CAM,4-
10dr/16ph/6pg/fr L

Public Service Railway Co:Newton Avenue Car Shops (New Jersey Transit Bus Operations, Inc.; Newton Avenue Bus Garage)
Bounded by 10th,Mt. Ephraim,Border & Newton Ave.
HAER NJ-65
HAER NJ,4-CAM,9-
26ph/15pg/2pc L

Rex,Frederick A. ,House
726 Cooper St.
HABS NJ-930
HABS NJ,4-CAM,13-
2ph/2pg/1pc L

Taylor,Dr. H. Genet,House & Offices
305 Cooper St.
HABS NJ-844
HABS NJ,4-CAM,14-
20ph/2pg/2pc L

Whitman,Walt,House
328 Mickle St.
HABS NJ-69
HABS NJ,4-CAM,1-
3dr/1ph/4pg/fr L

CHEWS LANDING VIC.

Hampton Hospital House (Hillman House)
HABS NJ-285
HABS NJ,4-CHEWL.V,1-
13dr/3ph/3pg/fr L

Hillman House; see Hampton Hospital House

COLLINGSWOOD

Hopkins-Burr House (Hopkins,Ebenezer,House)
King's Hwy.
HABS NJ-395
HABS NJ,4-COLWO,1-
8dr/1ph/3pg/fr L

Hopkins,Ebenezer,House; see Hopkins-Burr House

DELAWARE TWP.

Burrough-Wick Farm,Outbuildings
Church Rd.
HABS NJ-223
HABS NJ,4-MERCH.V,1-
1dr/2ph/3pg/fr L

FELLOWSHIP-DEL. TWP.

Childs-French Farm
Springdale Rd.
HABS NJ-211
HABS NJ,4- ,1-
11dr/3ph/3pg L

GLENDALE

Kay-Cooper Tenant House
HABS NJ-210
HABS NJ,4-GLEND,1-
2dr/1ph/2pg/fr L

HADDONFIELD

Boxwoods,The; see Gill,John,House

Dobbins-Eggman House
24 Potter St.
HABS NJ-103
HABS NJ,4-HADFI,3-
4dr/1ph/2pg/fr L

Gill,John,House (Boxwoods,The)
343 Kings Highway East
HABS NJ-403
HABS NJ,4-HADFI,9-
23dr/5ph/2pg/fr L

Haddon,Elizabeth,House; see Wood-Haddon House

Hip-Roof House; see Mickle House

Hopkins House
Birdwood-Hopkins Rd.
HABS NJ-133
HABS NJ,4-HADFI,5-
8dr/1ph/3pg/fr L

Hopkins-Elkinton House
Haddon Ave. & Lake St.
HABS NJ-205
HABS NJ,4-HADFI,6-
12dr/1ph/2pg/fr L

Indian King Tavern
233 King Highway E.
HABS NJ-99
HABS NJ,4-HADFI,2-
8dr/1ph/6pg/fr L

Mickle House (Hip-Roof House)
23 Ellis St.
HABS NJ-132
HABS NJ,4-HADFI,4-
2dr/1ph/6pg/fr L

Roberts,John,House
344 E. Kings Hwy.
HABS NJ-401
HABS NJ,4-HADFI,7-
27dr/9ph/2pg/fr L

Wood-Haddon House (Haddon,Elizabeth,House)
201 Wood Lane & Hawthorne Ave.
HABS NJ-402
HABS NJ,4-HADFI,8-
27dr/7ph/3pg/fr L

PENNSAUKEN TWP.

Burrough-Dover Farmhouse
HABS NJ-252
HABS NJ,4-MERCH.V,2-
5dr/5ph/2pg/fr L

Wood-Phillips House
HABS NJ-208
HABS NJ,4-DELA.V,1-
9dr/5ph/2pg/fr L

PENNSAUKEN VIC.

Burrough-Steelman House
Irving & Colonial Aves.
HABS NJ-301
HABS NJ,4-PENSA.V,1-
8dr/5ph/2pg/fr L

SOMERDALE VIC.

Warrick House
Warrick Rd.
HABS NJ-345
HABS NJ,4-SOM.V,1-
10dr/4ph/2pg/fr L

TAVISTOCK

Gill Homestead at Tavistock
HABS NJ-207
HABS NJ,4-TAV,1-
9dr/2ph/2pg/fr L

CAPE MAY COUNTY

AVALON

Avalon Life Saving Station (New Jersey Coastal Heritage Trail)
76 W. Fifteenth St.
HABS NJ-1109
1ph/1pc H

New Jersey Coastal Heritage Trail; see Avalon Life Saving Station

BEESLEYS POINT

Beesley House,Old
U. S. Hwy. 9
HABS NJ-482
HABS NJ,5-BEEPO,1-
16dr/5ph/3pg/fr L

Burnell House,Old
HABS NJ-495
HABS NJ,5-BEEPO,2-
13dr/6ph/2pg/fr L

CAPE MAY

Allen,George,House (Victorian House)
720 Washington St.
HABS NJ-845
HABS NJ,5-CAPMA,66-
4dr/1ph/1pc/1ct L

Atlantic Terrace House
20 Jackson St.
HABS NJ-846
HABS NJ,5-CAPMA,44-
4dr/1pg L

Bailey,Julius A. ,House
907 Stockton St.
HABS NJ-598
HABS NJ,5-CAPMA,62-
1ph/1pc L

Baronet,The; see Lewis,Joseph,House

Documentation: **ct** color transparencies **dr** measured drawings **fr** field records
pc photograph captions **pg** pages of text **ph** photographs

1001 Beach Avenue (House)
HABS NJ-462
HABS NJ,5-CAPMA,11-
1ph/1pc L

937 Beach Avenue (House)
HABS NJ-417
HABS NJ,5-CAPMA,10-
1ph/1pc L

901-931 Beach Avenue (Houses)
HABS NJ-412
HABS NJ,5-CAPMA,9-
2ph/1pc L

Boyd,George W. ,House
1501 Beach Ave.
HABS NJ-847
HABS NJ,5-CAPMA,14-
2dr/1ph/1pg/1pc L

Breezeway Hotel; see
Ware,Lambert,Drug Store

10 Broadway (House)
HABS NJ-574
HABS NJ,5-CAPMA,17-
1ph/1pc L

12 Broadway (House)
HABS NJ-575
HABS NJ,5-CAPMA,18-
1ph/1pc L

Cape Island Baptist Church
Columbia Ave. & Gurney St.
HABS NJ-593
HABS NJ,5-CAPMA,19-
1ph/1pc L

Cape Island Baptist Church (Franklin Street United Methodist Church)
727 Franklin St.
HABS NJ-848
HABS NJ,5-CAPMA,31-
3dr/1pg L

Cape Island Marina
Schellinger's Creek,N. side
HABS NJ-570
HABS NJ,5-CAPMA,61-
1ph/1pc L

Cape Island Presbyterian Church (Community Center)
417 Lafayette St.
HABS NJ-742
HABS NJ,5-CAPMA,50-
1dr/3ph/1pg/1pc/2ct L

Cape May Buildings
HABS NJ-919
HABS NJ,5-CAPMA,1-
6dr L

Carroll Villa
19 Jackson St.
HABS NJ-849
HABS NJ,5-CAPMA,43-
2dr/2ph/1pg/1pc/2ct L

Chalfonte Hotel
Howard & Sewell Sts.
HABS NJ-743
HABS NJ,5-CAPMA,36-
5dr/9ph/1pg/1pc/12ct L

Chalfonte Hotel,Cottages
Howard & Sewell Sts.
HABS NJ-743-A
HABS NJ,5-CAPMA,36A-
1dr L

Christian Science Society; see
McCreary,John B. ,House

Church of Our Lady Star of the Sea;
see St. Mary's Roman Catholic Church

Church of the Advent; see St. John's Church

Colonial Hotel
Beach & Ocean Aves.
HABS NJ-850
HABS NJ,5-CAPMA,5-
2dr/3ph/1pg/3ct L

Community Center; see Cape Island Presbyterian Church

Congress Hall
Beach & Congress Sts.
HABS NJ-744
HABS NJ,5-CAPMA,2-
2dr/4ph/1pg/1pc/2ct L

208 Congress Street (House)
HABS NJ-581
HABS NJ,5-CAPMA,25-
1ph/1pc L

210 Congress Street (House)
HABS NJ-586
HABS NJ,,5-CAPMA,27-
1ph/1pc L

Cook's Villa; see Fryer's Cottage

132 Decatur Street (House)
HABS NJ-590
HABS NJ,5-CAPMA,30-
1ph/1pc L

Delsea
621 Columbia Ave.
HABS NJ-906
HABS NJ,5-CAPMA,20-
3ph/1pc/8ct L

Denizot House
Decatur St. & Beach Ave.
HABS NJ-577
HABS NJ,5-CAPMA,29-
2ph/1pc L

Evans,Joseph R. ,Cottage
207 Congress Place
HABS NJ-893
HABS NJ,5-CAPMA,24-
1dr L

Evening Star Villa
1312 New Jersey Ave.
HABS NJ-578
HABS NJ,5-CAPMA,54-
1ph/1pc L

Ferguson,Charles,House
101 S. Lafayette St.
HABS NJ-587
HABS NJ,5-CAPMA,49-
1ph/1pc L

Franklin Street United Methodist Church; see Cape Island Baptist Church

Fryer's Cottage (Cook's Villa)
9 Perry St.
HABS NJ-860
HABS NJ,5-CAPMA,60-
1dr/2ph/1pg/1pc/2ct L

Gallagher,Christopher,House
45 Jackson St.
HABS NJ-905
HABS NJ,5-CAPMA,45-
1ph/1pc L

Hall,Joseph,Cottage
645 Hughes St.
HABS NJ-894
HABS NJ,5-CAPMA,39-
1dr/2ph/1pc/3ct L

Herzberg Family Cottage
8 Broadway
HABS NJ-895
HABS NJ,5-CAPMA,16-;(DLC/PP-1992:NJ-5)
2dr/1ph/1pc/1ct L

Hildreth,George,House (Lyhano)
17 Jackson St.
HABS NJ-851
HABS NJ,5-CAPMA,42-
1dr/1pg/1pc/2ct L

511 Hughes Street (House)
HABS NJ-594
HABS NJ,5-CAPMA,37-
1ph/1pc L

605 Hughes Street (Store & Residence)
HABS NJ-550
HABS NJ,5-CAPMA,38-
1ph/1pc L

Hunt,Dr. Henry F. ,House
209 Congress Place
HABS NJ-898
HABS NJ,5-CAPMA,26-
1dr/2ph/1pc/1ct L

Huntington House
107 Grant St.
HABS NJ-573
HABS NJ,5-CAPMA,32-
2ph/1pc/2ct L

Jackson's Clubhouse (Victorian Mansion)
635 Columbia Ave.
HABS NJ-748
HABS NJ,5-CAPMA,21-
3dr/6ph/1pg/1pc/1ct L

Johnson,Eldridge,House (Pink House)
33 Perry St. (moved from 225 Congress St.)
HABS NJ-853
HABS NJ,5-CAPMA,28-
2dr/2ph/1pg/1pc/6ct L

815 Kearny Avenue (House)
HABS NJ-407
HABS NJ,5-CAPMA,46-
1ph/1pc L

817 Kearny Avenue (House)
HABS NJ-394
HABS NJ,5-CAPMA,47-
1ph/1pc L

Knight,Edward C. ,Cottage
203 Congress Place
HABS NJ-892
HABS NJ,5-CAPMA,23-
1dr/1ph/1pc L

Lafayette Hotel
Beach Ave. & Decatur St.
HABS NJ-745
HABS NJ,5-CAPMA,3-
3ph/1pg/1pc L

Lewis,Joseph,House (Baronet,The)
819 Beach St.
HABS NJ-854
HABS NJ,5-CAPMA,8-
4dr/1ph/1pg/1pc L

Ludlam,S. R. ,House
839 Kearny St.
HABS NJ-386
HABS NJ,5-CAPMA,48-
1ph/1pc L

Lyhano; see Hildreth,George,House

Macomber Hotel
Beach & Howard Sts.
HABS NJ-852
HABS NJ,5-CAPMA,4-
2dr L

200 Madison Street (House)
HABS NJ-909
HABS NJ,5-CAPMA,52-
1ph/1pc L

McConnell,John,House
15 Jackson St.
HABS NJ-857
HABS NJ,5-CAPMA,41-
1dr/2ph/1pc L

McCreary,John B. ,House (Christian Science Society)
34 Gurney St.
HABS NJ-855
HABS NJ,5-CAPMA,35-
5dr/1ph/1pg/1pc/1ct L

McCreary,Kate,House
1005 Beach Ave.
HABS NJ-510
HABS NJ,5-CAPMA,12-
1ph/1pc L

Morning Star Villa
Beach Ave. ,1300 Block
HABS NJ-538
HABS NJ,5-CAPMA,13-
2ph/1pc L

Neafie-Levy House
28-30 Congress St.
HABS NJ-896
HABS NJ,5-CAPMA,22-
1dr L

1120 New Jersey Avenue (House)
HABS NJ-908
HABS NJ,5-CAPMA,53-
1ph/1pc L

New Jersey Trust & Safe Deposit Company
526 Washington St.
HABS NJ-856
HABS NJ,5-CAPMA,65-
3dr/1ph/1pg/1pc L

102 Ocean Street (House)
HABS NJ-588
HABS NJ,5-CAPMA,58-
1ph/1pc L

107 Ocean Street (House)
HABS NJ-567
HABS NJ,5-CAPMA,59-
4ph/1pc/1ct L

Physick,Emlen,House
1048 Washington St.
HABS NJ-746
HABS NJ,5-CAPMA,68-
9dr/9ph/1pg/1pc L

Pink House; see Johnson,Eldridge,House

Pumping Station
Washington St. ,900 Block
HABS NJ-910
HABS NJ,5-CAPMA,67-
1ph/1pc L

Schellinger,Jeremiah,House
1286 Lafayette St.
HABS NJ-747
HABS NJ,5-CAPMA,51-
3ph/1pg/1pc/1ct L

Seaside House
201-209 Grant St.
HABS NJ-572
HABS NJ,5-CAPMA,33-
1ph/1pc L

Seaview House
19 Ocean St.
HABS NJ-907
HABS NJ,5-CAPMA,56-
1ph/1pc/1ct L

Sewell House
1507 Beach Ave.
HABS NJ-932
HABS NJ,5-CAPMA,15-
2ph/1pc/2ct L

St. John's Church (Church of the Advent)
Washington & Franklin Sts.
HABS NJ-858
HABS NJ,5-CAPMA,64-
4dr/1ph/1pc/1ct L

St. Mary's Roman Catholic Church (Church of Our Lady Star of the Sea)
Ocean & Washington Sts.
HABS NJ-933
HABS NJ,5-CAPMA,55-
1ph/1pc L

Stockton Cottage
26 Gurney St.
HABS NJ-859
HABS NJ,,5-CAPMA,34-
4dr/2ph/1pg/1pc/2ct L

Stockton Manor
805 Beach Ave.
HABS NJ-599
HABS NJ,5-CAPMA,7-
1ph/1pc L

Victorian House; see Allen,George,House

Victorian Mansion; see Jackson's Clubhouse

Wales,Thomas Roger,House
1033 Lafayette St.
HABS NJ-926
HABS NJ,5-CAPMA,69-
1ph/1pg/1pc L

Ware,J. Stratton,House
655 Hughes St.
HABS NJ-897
HABS NJ,5-CAPMA,40
1dr/1ph/1pc/3ct L

Ware,Lambert,Drug Store (Breezeway Hotel)
101-103 Ocean St.
HABS NJ-566
HABS NJ,5-CAPMA,57-
1ph/1pc L

Weightman,William,Jr. ,House
Trenton Ave. ,btwn. Beach & New Jersey Aves.
HABS NJ-549
HABS NJ,5-CAPMA,63-
1dr/2ph/1pc/1ct L

Windsor Hotel
Beach Ave. ,btwn. Windsor & Congress Sts.
HABS NJ-749
HABS NJ,5-CAPMA,6-
7ph/1pg/1pc/1ct L

CAPE MAY COURT HOUSE

Cape May County Historical Museum; see Holmes,John,House

Courthouse Building,Old (New Jersey Coastal Heritage Trail)
N. Main St. (U.S. Hwy. 9)
HABS NJ-1112
2ph/1pc H

First United Methodist Church (New Jersey Coastal Heritage Trail)
1 Church St.
HABS NJ-1110
2ph/1pc H

Holmes,John,House (Cape May County Historical Museum; New Jersey Coastal Heritage Trail)
504 U.S. Hwy. 9
HABS NJ-1113
2ph/1pc H

New Ashbury Methodist Meeting House (New Jersey Coastal Heritage Trail)
Shore Rd.
HABS NJ-1111
2ph/1pc H

New Jersey Coastal Heritage Trail; see Courthouse Building,Old

New Jersey Coastal Heritage Trail; see First United Methodist Church

New Jersey Coastal Heritage Trail; see Holmes,John,House

New Jersey Coastal Heritage Trail; see New Ashbury Methodist Meeting House

CAPE MAY COURTHOUSE

Holmes House; see Way,Judge,House

Stites,Benjamin,House
400 Shore Rd. (U. S. Rt. 9)
HABS NJ-750
HABS NJ,5-CAPMAC,1-
7ph/1pg/1pc L

Way,Judge,House (Holmes House)
U. S. Hwy. 9
HABS NJ-465
HABS NJ,5-CAPMA.V,15-
16dr/11ph/2pg/fr L

CAPE MAY POINT

Beadle Memorial Presbyterian Church
HABS NJ-911
HABS NJ,5-CAPMAP,3-
1ph/1pc L

Cape May Point Lighthouses
HABS NJ-912
HABS NJ,5-CAPMAP,2-
1ph/1pc L

Coast Guard Station
Delaware Bay
HABS NJ-450
HABS NJ,5-CAPMAP,1-
9dr/1ph/2pg/fr L

New Jersey Coastal Heritage Trail; see Shoreham Hotel

New Jersey Coastal Heritage Trail; see St. Peter's by the Sea Episcopal Church

Shoreham Hotel (St. Mary's by the Sea; New Jersey Coastal Heritage Trail)
Lincoln & Lehigh Aves.
HABS NJ-1115
3ph/12pg/1pc H

St. Mary's by the Sea; see Shoreham Hotel

St. Peter's by the Sea Episcopal Church (New Jersey Coastal Heritage Trail)
Ocean Ave. at Lake Ave.
HABS NJ-1114
4ph/1pc H

COLD SPRING

Cold Spring Presbyterian Church (New Jersey Coastal Heritage Trail)
W. side Seashore Rd.
HABS NJ-270
HABS NJ,5-COLSP,1-
11ph/3pg/1pc/fr L H

New Jersey Coastal Heritage Trail; see Cold Spring Presbyterian Church

DENNISVILLE

Belle-Carroll House
Main St.
HABS NJ-751
HABS NJ,5-DEN,1-
4ph/1pg/1pc L

Holmes,Nathaniel,House (Holmestead)
36 Main St.
HABS NJ-752
HABS NJ,5-DEN,2-
7ph/1pg/1pc L

Holmes,Nathaniel,House,Privy (Holmestead,Privy)
36 Main St.
HABS NJ-752-A
HABS NJ,5-DEN,2-A-
1ph/1pc L

Holmestead; see Holmes,Nathaniel,House

Holmestead,Privy; see Holmes,Nathaniel,House,Privy

Townsend,William S. ,House,Outbuilding
96 Delsea Drive (State Rt. 47)
HABS NJ-753-A
HABS NJ,5-DEN,3-A-
1ph/1pc L

Townsend,William S.,House
96 Delsea Dr. (State Rt. 47)
HABS NJ-753
HABS NJ,5-DEN,3-
11ph/1pg/1pc L

GOSHEN

Goshen Public School (New Jersey Coastal Heritage Trail)
Delsea Dr. (St. Rt. 47)
HABS NJ-1191
1ph/1pg/1pc H

Ludlam,James,House
Delsea Dr. (State Rt. 47)
HABS NJ-754
HABS NJ,5-GOSH,1-
6ph/1pg/1pc L

New Jersey Coastal Heritage Trail; see Goshen Public School

OCEAN CITY

Flanders Hotel (New Jersey Coastal Heritage Trail)
Boardwalk at Eleventh St.
HABS NJ-1116
1ph/1pc H

New Jersey Coastal Heritage Trail; see Flanders Hotel

OCEAN VIEW

Rising Sun Tavern
158 Shore Rd. (U. S. Rt. 9)
HABS NJ-755
HABS NJ,5-OCEV,1-
7ph/1pg/1pc L

SEAVILLE VIC.

Friends' Meetinghouse
Shore Rd. ,W. side (State Rt. 9)
HABS NJ-74
HABS NJ,5-SEAV.V,1-
9dr/7ph/3pg/1pc/fr L

SOUTH DENNIS

Falkenburg,Joseph,House
922 Delsea Dr. (State Rt. 47)
HABS NJ-756
HABS NJ,5-DENS,1-
8ph/1pg/1pc L

Farmhouse (New Jersey Coastal Heritage Trail)
Mile 16.5 on State Rt. 47
HABS NJ-1182
1ph/1pc H

New Jersey Coastal Heritage Trail; see Farmhouse

New Jersey Coastal Heritage Trail; see Trinity Union School Church

Trinity Union School Church (New Jersey Coastal Heritage Trail)
Mile 17 on State Rt. 47
HABS NJ-1181
4ph/1pc H

SOUTH DENNIS VIC.

Ludlam, Christopher House (New Jersey Coastal Heritage Trail)
Delsea Dr.,S. of County Rd. 657
HABS NJ-1206
1ph/2pg/1pc H

Ludlam, Thomas House (New Jersey Coastal Heritage Trail)
Delsea Dr.,S. of County Rd. 657
HABS NJ-1205
1ph/2pg/1pc H

New Jersey Coastal Heritage Trail; see Ludlam, Christopher House

New Jersey Coastal Heritage Trail; see Ludlam, Thomas House

SOUTH SEAVILLE

New Jersey Coastal Heritage Trail; see South Seaville Methodist Camp Meeting,Auditorium

New Jersey Coastal Heritage Trail; see South Seaville Methodist Camp Meeting,Cottage

New Jersey Coastal Heritage Trail; see South Seaville Methodist Camp Meeting,Cottage 87

New Jersey Coastal Heritage Trail; see South Seaville Methodist Meeting Camp

South Seaville Methodist Camp Meeting,Auditorium (New Jersey Coastal Heritage Trail)
Intersection of County Rds. 628 & 608
HABS NJ-1049-A
H

South Seaville Methodist Camp Meeting,Cottage (New Jersey Coastal Heritage Trail)
2 Morris Ave.
HABS NJ-1049-B
H

South Seaville Methodist Camp Meeting,Cottage 87 (New Jersey Coastal Heritage Trail)
4 S.S. Wesley Park
HABS NJ-1049-C
2ph/1pc H

South Seaville Methodist Meeting Camp (New Jersey Coastal Heritage Trail)
Intersection of County Rds. 628 & 608
HABS NJ-1049
1ph/3pg/1pc H

TUCKAHOE VIC.

New Jersey Coastal Heritage Trail; see Tuckahoe River Bridge

Tuckahoe River Bridge (New Jersey Coastal Heritage Trail)
Spanning Tuckahoe River at St. Rt. 50
HAER NJ-89
1ph/1pc H

WILDWOOD

Coast Guard Station (New Jersey Coastal Heritage Trail)
Central Ave.
HABS NJ-1183
1ph/1pc H

Ebb Tide Motel (New Jersey Coastal Heritage Trail)
5711 Atlantic Ave.
HABS NJ-1185
1ph/1pc H

El Ray Motel (New Jersey Coastal Heritage Trail)
4711 Atlantic Ave.
HABS NJ-1189
1ph/1pc H

Knoll's Resort Motel (New Jersey Coastal Heritage Trail)
4111 Atlantic Ave.
HABS NJ-1184
1ph/1pc H

New Jersey Coastal Heritage Trail; see Coast Guard Station

New Jersey Coastal Heritage Trail; see Ebb Tide Motel

New Jersey Coastal Heritage Trail; see El Ray Motel

New Jersey Coastal Heritage Trail; see Knoll's Resort Motel

WILDWOOD CREST

Caribbean Motel (New Jersey Coastal Heritage Trail)
5600 Ocean Ave.
HABS NJ-1186
1ph/10pg/1pc H

New Jersey Coastal Heritage Trail; see Caribbean Motel

WOODBINE

Woodbine Brotherhood Synagogue
612 Washington Ave.
HABS NJ-866
HABS NJ,5-WOBI,1-
4dr/13ph/7pg/2pc/fr L

CUMBERLAND COUNTY

BACON'S NECK

Bacon House
HABS NJ-354
HABS NJ,6-BACO,2-
10dr/8ph/2pg/fr L

Davis,Gabriel S. ,House
HABS NJ-267
HABS NJ,6-BAC0,1-
7dr/1ph/2pg L

BACON'S NECK VIC.

Maskell,Thomas,House (Vauxhall Gardens)
Bacon's Neck Rd.
HABS NJ-582
HABS NJ,6-BACO.V,1-
9dr/3ph/3pg/fr L

Vauxhall Gardens; see Maskell,Thomas,House

BAYSIDE VIC.

Dennis,Philip,House
HABS NJ-583
HABS NJ,6-BAYSI.V,1-
9dr/8ph/3pg/fr L

BOWENTON VIC.

Hope Grange No. 43 (New Jersey Coastal Heritage Trail)
Hope Grange Rd.
HABS NJ-998
1ph/1pg/1pc H

New Jersey Coastal Heritage Trail; see Hope Grange No. 43

BRIDGETON

Buck-Elmer House (Buck,Jeremiah,House)
297 E. Commerce St.
HABS NJ-530
HABS NJ,6-BRIG,5-
35dr/9ph/3pg/fr L

Buck,Jeremiah,House; see Buck-Elmer House

Cumberland National Bank (New Jersey Coastal Heritage Trail)
59-61 E. Commerce St.
HABS NJ-1193
1ph/2pg/1pc H

Elmer,Robert,House
230 E. Commerce St.
HABS NJ-404
HABS NJ,6-BRIG,3-
26dr/7ph/2pg/fr L

Ferracute Machine-Works (New Jersey Coastal Heritage Trail)
E. Commerce St.
HABS NJ-1192
4ph/2pg/1pc H

First Presbyterian Church
W. Broad St.
HABS NJ-272
HABS NJ,6-BRIG,2-
18dr/4ph/6pg/2ct/fr L

Giles,James,House
143 W. Broad St.
HABS NJ-221
HABS NJ,6-BRIG,1-
7dr/5ph/2pg/fr L

Lee,James House; see Woodruff-Lee House

New Jersey Coastal Heritage Trail; see Cumberland National Bank

New Jersey Coastal Heritage Trail; see Ferracute Machine-Works

Seeley House
274 E. Commerce St.
HABS NJ-497
HABS NJ,6-BRIG,4-
7dr/2ph/2pg/fr L

163-165 West Broad Street (House)
HABS NJ-934
HABS NJ,6-BRIG,7-
8pg/fr L

Woodruff-Lee House (Lee,James House)
330 Fayette St.
HABS NJ-670
HABS NJ,6-BRIG,6-
9dr/2ph/2pg/fr L

BRIDGETON VIC.

Cumberland County Hospital (New Jersey Coastal Heritage Trail)
Cumberland Dr. (County Rd. 613)
HABS NJ-1151
2pg/1pc H

New Jersey Coastal Heritage Trail; see Cumberland County Hospital

CEDARVILLE

Bateman Estate; see Ogden House

Cedarville Methodist Church (NJCH Trail)
Main St.
HABS NJ-1162
1ph/2pg/1pc H

New Jersey Coastal Heritage Trail; see Ogden House

NJCH Trail; see Cedarville Methodist Church

Ogden House (Bateman Estate; Padgett Funeral Home; New Jersey Coastal Heritage Trail)
100 N. Main St.
HABS NJ-1207
1ph/1pg/1pc H

Padgett Funeral Home; see Ogden House

DEERFIELD VIC.

Sneathen House
Deerfield St.
HABS NJ-344
HABS NJ,6-DERF.V,1-
5dr/1ph/2pg/fr L

DORCHESTER VIC.

Mauricetown Freight Station (NJ Coastal Heritage Trail-Cumberland & Maurice RR)
S. Delsea Dr. (St. Rt. 47)
HABS NJ-1159
3pg/1pc H

NJ Coastal Heritage Trail-Cumberland & Maurice RR; see Mauricetown Freight Station

Reeve-Marshall Log House
HABS NJ-215
HABS NJ,6-DORCH.V,1-
5dr/3ph/2pg/fr L

DUTCH NECK

Brick,John III,House
County Rd. 50
HABS NJ-585
HABS NJ,6-GREWI.V,5-
13dr/3ph/4pg/fr L

Wheaton,William,House
County Rd. 50
HABS NJ-584
HABS NJ,6-GREWI.V,4-
17dr/8ph/4pg/fr L

FAIRTON

Fairfield Presbyterian Church
HABS NJ-273
HABS NJ,6-FAIRT,1-
10dr/2ph/4pg/fr L

GREENWICH

Ewing Homestead
Main St.
HABS NJ-138
HABS NJ,6-GREWI,4-
6dr/3ph/2pg/fr L

Ferry Tavern & Jail
HABS NJ-268
HABS NJ,6-GREWI,6-
8dr/5ph/2pg/fr L

Friends Meetinghouse,Old
Main St.
HABS NJ-105
HABS NJ,6-GREWI,2-
6dr/1ph/3pg/fr L

Gibbon,Leonard,Homestead
Main St.
HABS NJ-129
HABS NJ,6-GREWI,3-
9dr/1ph/2pg/fr L

School House,Old Stone
Greenwich St.
HABS NJ-222
HABS NJ,6-GREWI,5-
3dr/1ph/2pg/fr L

Sheppard,John,House
Main St.
HABS NJ-641
HABS NJ,6-GREWI,9-
18dr/6ph/3pg/fr L

Tavern,Old Stone
Main St.
HABS NJ-104
HABS NJ,6-GREWI,1-
8dr/1ph/3pg/fr L

Wood,Richard,House
Main St. & Bacon's Neck Rd.
HABS NJ-269
HABS NJ,6-GREWI,7-
11dr/4ph/3pg/fr L

Wood,Richard,Store
Main & Willow Sts.
HABS NJ-269-A
HABS NJ,6-GREWI,8-
3dr/2ph/3pg L

GREENWICH VIC.

Ewing,Samuel,House
Main St.
HABS NJ-635
HABS NJ,6-GREWI.V,6-
11dr/2ph/4pg/fr L

Maskell,Thomas,Store
Main & Pine Sts.
HABS NJ-660
HABS NJ,6-GREWI.V,7-
7dr/7ph/5pg/fr L

Old Davis Mill; see Seeley-Davis Mill

Seeley-Davis Homestead
Davis Mill Rd.
HABS NJ-220-B
HABS NJ,6-GREWI.V,2-
11dr/5ph/2pg/fr L

Seeley-Davis Mill (Old Davis Mill)
Davis Mill Rd.
HABS NJ-220-A
HABS NJ,6-GREWI.V,1-
4dr/1ph/2pg/fr L

HEISLERVILLE

House (New Jersey Coastal Heritage Trail)
Main St. & Glade Rd.
HABS NJ-1194
1ph/2pg/1pc H

New Jersey Coastal Heritage Trail; see House

MAURICETOWN

Compton-Bowen House (New Jersey Coastal Heritage Trail)
Front St.
HABS NJ-1195
2ph/2pg/1pc H

Maurice River Pratt Through-Truss Swing Bridge
Spanning Maurice River
HAER NJ-20
HAER NJ,6-MAUR,1-
20ph/1pg/2pc L

Mauricetown Academy (New Jersey Coastal Heritage Trail)
118 High St.
HABS NJ-1152
1ph/1pg/1pc H

New Jersey Coasta Heritage Trail; see Peterson,Capt. Isaac,House

New Jersey Coastal Heritage Trail; see Compton-Bowen House

New Jersey Coastal Heritage Trail; see Mauricetown Academy

Peterson,Capt. Isaac,House (New Jersey Coasta Heritage Trail)
Front St.
HABS NJ-1196
1ph/2pg/1pc H

MILLVILLE

Millville Manufacturing Company (Wheaton Industries; New Jersey Coastal Heritage Trail)
Btwn. Columbia Ave. & Maurice Riv.,SE. of Union Lk
HABS NJ-1198
4ph/2pg/1pc H

New Jersey Coastal Heritage Trail; see Millville Manufacturing Company

New Jersey Coastal Heritage Trail; see Wood,David,Mansion

NJCH Trail; see Town of Millville

Town of Millville (NJCH Trail)
South of union Lake
HABS NJ-1165
4ph/5pg/1pc H

WaWa Farm Markets Office; see Wood,David,Mansion

Wheaton Industries; see Millville Manufacturing Company

Locations: **H** HABS/HAER, National Park Service **L** Library of Congress

Wood,David,Mansion (WaWa Farm Markets Office; New Jersey Coastal Heritage Trail)
821 Columbia Ave.
HABS NJ-1197
2ph/3pg/1pc H

MILLVILLE VIC.

Migrant Worker Housing (Multi-Residence) (New Jersey Coastal Heritage Trail)
Cedarville Rd. (Rt. 410)
HABS NJ-996
1ph/2pg/1pc H

New Jersey Coastal Heritage Trail; see Migrant Worker Housing (Multi-Residence)

PORT ELIZABETH

Camp's Big Oaks Farm Market
South Delsea Dr.
HABS NJ-997
2ph/3pg/1pc H

PORT NORRIS

NJCH Trail; see Town of Port Norris

Town of Port Norris (NJCH Trail)
HABS NJ-1163
2ph/1pc H

ROADSTOWN

Cohansey Baptist Church
HABS NJ-463
HABS NJ,6-ROATO,2-
19dr/5ph/2pg/fr L

Gilman House; see Wood Tavern

Howell Homestead
Roadstown Rd.
HABS NJ-76
HABS NJ,6-ROATO.V,1-
6dr/1ph/3pg/fr L

NJCH Trail; see Town of Roadstown

Town of Roadstown (NJCH Trail)
HABS NJ-1164
2ph/1pg/1pc H

Wood Tavern (Gilman House)
HABS NJ-44
HABS NJ,6-ROATO,1-
5dr/2ph/3pg/fr L

SEA BREEZE

Sheppard,David,House
HABS NJ-554
HABS NJ,6-GREWI.V,3-
16dr/5ph/2pg/1pc/fr L

SEELEY

Seeley,Josiah,Homestead
Finley Station Rd.
HABS NJ-75
HABS NJ,6-SEEL,1-
9dr/2ph/2pg/fr L

SEELEY VIC.

Loper,Uriah,House
Beebe Run Rd.
HABS NJ-514
HABS NJ,6-SEEL.V,1-
6dr/4ph/2pg/fr L

SHILOH

New Jersey Coastal Heritage Trail; see Noyes Service Center

Noyes Service Center (New Jersey Coastal Heritage Trail)
Main St. (St. Rt. 49) & South Ave.
HABS NJ-1153
1ph/1pg/1pc H

VINELAND

New Jersey Memorial Home
524 Northwest Blvd.
HABS NJ-979
HABS DLC/PP-1993:NJ-1
9pg L

New Jersey Memorial Home,Main Building
524 Northwest Blvd.
HABS NJ-979-A
HABS DLC/PP-1993:NJ-1
28ph/6pg/2pc L

ESSEX COUNTY

BELLEVILLE

Brandt House
205 Main St.
HABS NJ-387
HABS NJ,7-BELVI,2-
22dr/4ph/2pg/fr L

Christ Episcopal Church
HABS NJ-565
HABS NJ,7-BELVI,7-
11dr L

Coeyman House
502 Belleville Ave.
HABS NJ-449
HABS NJ,7-BELVI,6-
14dr/6ph/2pg/fr L

Lloyd House; see Rose Cottage

Macomb,Gen. Alexander,House
125 Main St.
HABS NJ-390
HABS NJ,7-BELVI,5-
10dr/2ph/6pg/fr L

Rose Cottage (Lloyd House)
221 Main St.
HABS NJ-153
HABS NJ,7-BELVI,1-
16dr/6ph/3pg/fr L

Speer House
319 Main St.
HABS NJ-389
HABS NJ,7-BELVI,4-
17dr/1ph/2pg/fr L

Ward,Dr. Samuel L. ,House
191 Main St.
HABS NJ-388
HABS NJ,7-BELVI,3-
14dr/2ph/2pg/fr L

BLOOMFIELD

Davis House; see First Presbyterian Church on-the-Green,The Manse

Dodd,Daniel,House
339 Franklin St.
HABS NJ-688
HABS NJ,7-BLOFI,4-
6ph/4pg L

First Presbyt. Church on-the-Green,Parish House
HABS NJ-371
HABS NJ,7-BLOFI,3-
6dr/1ph/2pg/fr L

First Presbyterian Church on-the-Green
HABS NJ-60
HABS NJ,7-BLOFI,1-
8dr/5ph/3pg/fr L

First Presbyterian Church on-the-Green,The Manse (Davis House)
HABS NJ-370
HABS NJ,7-BLOFI,2-
17dr/4ph/2pg/fr L

CALDWELL

Cleveland,Grover,Birthplace
207 Bloomfield Ave.
HABS NJ-179
HABS NJ,7-CALD,2-
12dr/2ph/2pg/fr L

Cory,John,House (House,Little)
485 Bloomfield Ave.
HABS NJ-143
HABS NJ,7-CALD,1-
6dr/2ph/2pg/fr L

House,Little; see Cory,John,House

CEDAR GROVE

Jacobus House
178 Grove Ave.
HABS NJ-475
HABS NJ,7-CEGRO,1-
15dr/3ph/2pg/fr L

Personett House
727 Pompton Ave.
HABS NJ-496
HABS NJ,7-CEGRO,2-
12dr/2ph/3pg/fr L

FAIRFIELD VIC.

Speer,Peter,House
Fairfield Rd.
HABS NJ-669
HABS NJ,7-FAIRF.V,2-
11dr/3ph/5pg/fr L

Van Ness,Peter,Farmhouse
Fairfield Rd.
HABS NJ-625
HABS NJ,7-FAIRF.V,1-
11dr/9ph/5pg/fr L

IRVINGTON

Osborn,Henry,House
506 Stuyvesant Ave.
HABS NJ-618
HABS NJ,7-IRV,1-
14dr/3ph/6pg/fr L

LIVINGSTON

Force,William,House
343 S. Livingston Ave.
HABS NJ-556
HABS NJ,7-LIV,1-
17dr/8ph/4pg/fr L

Wade,Henry W. ,House
554 S. Livingston Ave.
HABS NJ-619
HABS NJ,7-LIV,2-
13dr/3ph/8pg/fr L

MAPLEWOOD

Ball,Timothy,House (Washington Inn)
425 Ridgewood Rd.
HABS NJ-50
HABS NJ,7-MAPWO,1-
9dr/2ph/2pg/fr L

Henderson,Robert,House; see Ogden,Montgomery,House

Ogden,Montgomery,House
(Henderson,Robert,House)
22 Jefferson Ave.
HABS NJ-337
HABS NJ,7-MAPWO,2-
13dr/6ph/2pg/fr L

Washington Inn; see Ball,Timothy,House

MILLBURN

Parsil,William Jr. ,House
Parsonage Hill & White Oak Ridge Rds.
HABS NJ-627
HABS NJ,7-MILB,2-
13dr/5ph/4pg/fr L

Smith-Henderson Homestead
155 Millburn Ave.
HABS NJ-107
HABS NJ,7-MILB,1-
13dr/3ph/3pg/fr L

MONTCLAIR

Crane,King,House
159 Glenridge Ave.
HABS NJ-152
HABS NJ,7-MONC,1-
15dr/4ph/2pg/fr L

Grove Street Bridge
Grove St. ,spanning RR tracks
HAER NJ-52
HAER NJ,7-MONC,3-
11ph/2pg/1pc L

Munn Tavern (Swedish Church Parish House)
19 Valley Rd.
HABS NJ-372
HABS NJ,7-MONC,2-
11dr/2ph/2pg/fr L

Swedish Church Parish House; see Munn Tavern

NEWARK

Alling House
1012 Broad St.
HABS NJ-187
HABS NJ,7-NEARK,8-
8dr/2ph/2pg/fr L

American Red Cross Chapterhouse; see Feigenspan House

Ballantine,John Holme,House (Newark Museum Offices)
43 Washington St.
HABS NJ-757
HABS NJ,7-NEARK,30-
5ph/1pc L

Ballantine,John Holme,House,Stables
(Newark Museum Offices)
43 Washington St.
HABS NJ-757-A
HABS NJ,7-NEARK,30-A-
1ph/1pc L

Bascule Trunnion Lift Bridge; see Erie Railway:New York Division,Bridge 8.04 (c.1900

Beam,Anthony,House
(Crane,Stephen,Birthplace)
14 Mulberry Place
HABS NJ-310
HABS NJ,7-NEARK,12-
16dr/1ph/4pg/fr L

103 Bleeker Street (House)
HABS NJ-936
HABS NJ,7-NEARK,21-
3ph/2pg/1pc L

79 Bleeker Street (House)
HABS NJ-921
HABS NJ,7-NEARK,28-
5ph/2pg/1pc L

83 Bleeker Street (House)
HABS NJ-939
HABS NJ,7-NEARK,29-
2ph/2pg/1pc L

Broad Street,900 Block (House)
HABS NJ-708
HABS NJ,7-NEARK,14-
2ph L

Carter,Anthony,House
3 Clay St.
HABS NJ-253
HABS NJ,7-NEARK,10-
3dr/1ph/2pg/fr L

102 Central Avenue (House)
HABS NJ-917
HABS NJ,7-NEARK,20-
4ph/2pg/1pc L

106 Central Avenue (House)
HABS NJ-940
HABS NJ,7-NEARK,22-
4ph/2pg/1pc L

132 Central Avenue (House)
HABS NJ-920
HABS NJ,7-NEARK,23-
9ph/2pg/1pc L

Central RR of NJ:Newark Bay Lift Bridge
Spanning Newark Bay
HAER NJ-37
HAER NJ,7-NEARK,16-
71ph/1pg/4pc L

Chancellor Avenue School; see Lyons Farm Schoolhouse

Crane,Stephen,Birthplace; see Beam,Anthony,House

Davis-Agnew-Lloyd Houses
86-88 Plane St.
HABS NJ-180
HABS NJ,7-NEARK,6-
25dr/5ph/2pg/fr L

Erie Railway:New York Division,Bridge 8.04 (c.1875
Spanning Passaic River
HAER NJ-25-A
HAER NJ,7-NEARK,17-A-
1ph/1pc L

Erie Railway:New York Division,Bridge 8.04 (c.1900 (Bascule Trunnion Lift Bridge)
Spanning Passaic River
HAER NJ-25-B
HAER NJ,7-NEARK,17-B-
1ph/1pc L

Essex County Jail
Newark,New & Wilsey Sts.
HABS NJ-758
HABS NJ,7-NEARK,31-
5ph/1pc L

Feigenspan House (American Red Cross Chapterhouse)
710 High St.
HABS NJ-759
HABS NJ,7-NEARK,32-
5ph/1pc L

First Baptist Peddie Memorial Church
Broad & Fulton Sts.
HABS NJ-760
HABS NJ,7-NEARK,33-
5ph/1pg/1pc L

First Presbyterian Church
820 Broad St.
HABS NJ-33
HABS NJ,7-NEARK,3-
16dr/5ph/3pg/fr L

Gaddis,Elisha B. ,House
1016 Broad St.
HABS NJ-696
HABS NJ,7-NEARK,13-
2ph/1pg/fr L

Hobart,George S. ,House
599 Mount Prospect Ave.
HABS NJ-867
HABS NJ,7-NEARK,34-
21ph/5pg/2pc L

House of Prayer,Rectory
(Plume,Isaac,House)
407 Broad St.
HABS NJ-14
HABS NJ,7-NEARK,2-
12dr/4ph/4pg/fr L

Jackson Street Bridge
Spanning Passaic River
HAER NJ-54
HAER NJ,7-NEARK,18-
55ph/14pg/6pc L

James Street Commons Historic District
Halsey,Warren,Boyden,Bleeker,Orange & Broad Sts.
HABS NJ-335
HABS NJ,7-NEARK,35-
2ph/1pc L

Kiersted,Aaron,House; see Pierson,Abraham,House

Kiersted,John,House; see Nichols,David,House

La Grange Apartment Building (Park Lane Hotel)
81 Lincoln Park
HABS NJ-902
HABS NJ,7-NEARK,36-
4ph/2pg/1pc L

Lyons Farm Schoolhouse (Chancellor Avenue School)
Chancellor & Elizabeth Aves.
HABS NJ-3
HABS NJ,7-NEARK,1-
1dr/2ph/2pg/fr L

320 Martin Luther King Boulevard (House)
HABS NJ-913
HABS NJ,7-NEARK,24-
1ph/2pg/1pc L

322 Martin Luther King Boulevard (House)
HABS NJ-914
HABS NJ,7-NEARK,25-
3ph/2pg/1pc L

324 Martin Luther King Boulevard (House)
HABS NJ-935
HABS NJ,7-NEARK,26-
3ph/2pg/1pc L

326 Martin Luther King Boulevard (House)
HABS NJ-916
HABS NJ,7-NEARK,27-
4ph/2pg/1pc L

Mount Pleasant Cemetery,Cook Tomb
375 Broadway St.
HABS NJ-761-B
HABS NJ,7-NEARK,37-B-
1ph/1pc L

Mount Pleasant Cemetery,Gateway
375 Broadway St.
HABS NJ-761-A
HABS NJ,7-NEARK,37-A-
3ph/1pc L

Mount Pleasant Cemetery,Opdyke,George,Tomb
375 Broadway St.
HABS NJ-761-C
HABS NJ,7-NEARK,37-C-
1ph/1pc L

Newark City Hall
920 Broad St.
HABS NJ-229
HABS NJ,7-NEARK,15-
7ph/4pg/1pc/fr L

Newark Museum Offices; see Ballantine,John Holme,House

Newark Museum Offices; see Ballantine,John Holme,House,Stables

Nichols,David,House
(Kiersted,John,House)
229 Mulberry
HABS NJ-242
HABS NJ,7-NEARK,9-
5dr/4ph/3pg/fr L

Northeast Corridor; see Northeast Railroad Corridor

Northeast Railroad Corridor
(Northeast Corridor)
Amtrak Rt. btwn. PA/NJ & NJ/NY State Lines
HAER NJ-40
HAER NJ,7-NEARK,19-
37ph/4pc/fr L

Park Lane Hotel; see La Grange Apartment Building

Pierson,Abraham,House
(Kiersted,Aaron,House)
231 Mulberry St.
HABS NJ-302
HABS NJ,7-NEARK,11-
10dr/1ph/2pg/fr L

Plume,Isaac,House; see House of Prayer,Rectory

South Park Presbyterian Church
Broad St. & Clinton Ave.
HABS NJ-182
HABS NJ,7-NEARK,7-
21dr/5ph/3pg/fr L

Sydenham,John,House
Old Road to Bloomfield
HABS NJ-148
HABS NJ,7-NEARK,5-
11dr/20ph/6pg/1pc/fr L

82 1/2 to 84 University Avenue (Rowhouse)
HABS NJ-981
HABS DLC/PP-1993:NJ-1
7ph/8pg/1pc L

Trinity Cathedral Church
Rector & Broad Sts.
HABS NJ-34
HABS NJ,7-NEARK,4-
10dr/3ph/3pg/fr L

NORTH CALDWELL

Francisco,Henry,House
Allen Rd.
HABS NJ-653
HABS NJ,7-CALDN,1-
12dr/5ph/6pg/fr L

NUTLEY

Feland House
63 Enclosure
HABS NJ-373
HABS NJ,7-NUT,4-
27dr/4ph/2pg/fr L

Hay,James R. ,House
385 Passaic Ave.
HABS NJ-186
HABS NJ,7-NUT,3-
16dr/5ph/2pg/fr L

Kingsland House
3 Kingsland Rd.
HABS NJ-150
HABS NJ,7-NUT,2-
18dr/8ph/5pg/fr L

Rutandt House
123 Prospect Ave.
HABS NJ-876
HABS NJ,7-NUT,5-
6dr L

Vreeland Homestead
226 Chestnut St.
HABS NJ-6
HABS NJ,7-NUT,1-
6dr/4ph/12pg/fr L

ORANGE

Hillyer,Rev. Asa,Parsonage
59 Main St.
HABS NJ-656
HABS NJ,7-ORA,2-
22dr/8ph/4pg/fr L

Lighthipe House
548 Main St.
HABS NJ-245
HABS NJ,7-ORA,1-
22dr/2ph/2pg/fr L

ROSELAND

Williams-Harrison House
126 Eagle Rock Rd.
HABS NJ-109
HABS NJ,7-ROSLA,1-
13dr/6ph/2pg/fr L

Documentation: **ct** color transparencies **dr** measured drawings **fr** field records
pc photograph captions **pg** pages of text **ph** photographs

UPPER MONTCLAIR

Sigler-DeForest House
471 Valley Rd.
HABS NJ-308
HABS NJ,7-MONCU,1-
9dr/2ph/2pg/fr L

WEST CALDWELL

Bond House
Runnymeade Rd.
HABS NJ-184
HABS NJ,7-CALDW,4-
9dr/2ph/2pg L

Cadmus House
159 Fairfield Ave.
HABS NJ-918
HABS NJ,7-CALDW,5-
39ph/41pg/3pc L

Cory,Joseph,House; see Lane-Cory House

Crane,Nathaniel S. ,House
29 Clinton Rd.
HABS NJ-151
HABS NJ,7-CALDW,2-
15dr/4ph/2pg/fr L

Harrison House
Orton Rd.
HABS NJ-183
HABS NJ,7-CALDW,3-
10dr/2ph/2pg/fr L

Lane-Cory House (Cory,Joseph,House)
633 Bloomfield Ave.
HABS NJ-108
HABS NJ,7-CALDW,1-
10dr/6ph/3pg/fr L

WEST ORANGE

Edison National Historic Site; see Edison,Thomas A. ,Laboratories

Edison National Historic Site; see Edison,Thomas A.,Lab.,Machine Shop & Library

Edison National Historic Site; see Edison,Thomas A.,Laboratories,Gatehouse (Bldg. 9)

Edison National Historic Site; see Glenmont

Edison National Historic Site; see Glenmont,Barn

Edison National Historic Site; see Glenmont,Concrete Garage

Edison National Historic Site; see Glenmont,Gardener's Cottage & Greenhouse

Edison National Historic Site; see Glenmont,Hose House

Edison National Historic Site; see Glenmont,Pump House

Edison,Thomas A. ,House; see Glenmont

Edison,Thomas A. ,Laboratories (Edison National Historic Site)
Main St. & Lakeside Ave.
HABS NJ-808
HABS NJ,7-ORAW,5-
1ph/1pc L

Edison,Thomas A.,Lab.,Machine Shop & Library (Edison National Historic Site)
Main St. & Lakeside Ave.
HABS NJ-808-B
HABS NJ,7-ORAW,5-B-ıDLC/PP-1992:NJ-5°
6ph/2pc L

Edison,Thomas A.,Lab,Chem Lab; see Edison,Thomas A.,Lab,Chemistry Lab (Bldg. 2)

Edison,Thomas A.,Lab,Chemistry Lab (Bldg. 2) (Edison,Thomas A.,Lab,Chem Lab)
HAER NJ-70-A
HAER NJ,7-ORAW,4-A-
17ph/2pc L

Edison,Thomas A.,Laboratories
Main St. & Lakeside Ave.
HAER NJ-70
HAER NJ,7-ORAW,4-
16ph/3pg/2pc L

Edison,Thomas A.,Laboratories,Gatehouse (Bldg. 9) (Edison National Historic Site)
HABS NJ-808-A
HABS NJ,7-ORAW,5-A-
5ph/1pg/1pc L

Edison,Thomas A.,Labs,Bldg. No. 3 (Edison,Thomas A.,Labs,Woodworking Pattern Shop)
HAER NJ-70-B
HAER NJ,7-ORAW,4-B-
6ph/1pc L

Edison,Thomas A.,Labs,Bldg. No. 5 (Edison,Thomas A.,Labs,Main Bldg.)
HAER NJ-70-C
HAER NJ,7-ORAW,4-C-
93ph/2pg/6pc L

Edison,Thomas A.,Labs,Main Bldg.; see Edison,Thomas A.,Labs,Bldg. No. 5

Edison,Thomas A.,Labs,Woodworking Pattern Shop; see Edison,Thomas A.,Labs,Bldg. No. 3

Freeman House
61 S. Valley Rd.
HABS NJ-651
HABS NJ,7-ORAW,3-
22dr/8ph/5pg/fr L

Glenmont (Edison,Thomas A. ,House; Edison National Historic Site)
Llewellyn Park
HABS NJ-729
HABS NJ,7-ORAW,6-
13dr/31ph/11pg/3pc/fr L

Glenmont,Barn (Edison National Historic Site)
Llewellyn Park
HABS NJ-729-B
HABS NJ,7-ORAW,6-B-
3ph/1pc L

Glenmont,Concrete Garage (Edison National Historic Site)
Llewellyn Park
HABS NJ-729-C
HABS NJ,7-ORAW,6-C-
5ph/1pg/1pc/fr L

Glenmont,Gardener's Cottage & Greenhouse (Edison National Historic Site)
Llewellyn Park
HABS NJ-729-A
HABS NJ,7-ORAW,6-A-
3ph/1pc L

Glenmont,Hose House (Edison National Historic Site)
Llewellyn Park
HABS NJ-729-E
HABS 1984(HABS):280
fr L

Glenmont,Pump House (Edison National Historic Site)
Llewellyn Park
HABS NJ-729-D
HABS NJ,7-ORAW,6-D-
3ph/1pc L

Harrison,Caleb,House (Mountain Foot)
93 Northfield Ave.
HABS NJ-643
HABS NJ,7-ORAW,2-
23dr/12ph/7pg/fr L

Mountain Foot; see Harrison,Caleb,House

Williams House
30 Ashwood Terrace
HABS NJ-624
HABS NJ,7-ORAW,1-
13dr/3ph/5pg/fr L

GLOUCESTER COUNTY

GLASSBORO

St. Thomas' Episcopal Church
Main & Focer Sts.
HABS NJ-376
HABS NJ,8-GLASB,1-
ıDLC/PP-1993:NJ-1°
20dr/7ph/3pg/2pc L

MALAGA VIC.

Zion Methodist Church
HABS NJ-665
HABS NJ,8-MAL.V,1-
13dr/2ph/3pg/fr L

MANTUA

Carpenter,Thomas,House
(Eastlake-Carpenter House)
Main & Martel Sts.
HABS NJ-68
HABS NJ,8-MANT,1-
23dr/5ph/4pg/fr L

Eastlake-Carpenter House; see Carpenter,Thomas,House

MANTUA VIC.

Moffett,Archibald,House
HABS NJ-311
HABS NJ,8-MANT.V,1-
17dr/7ph/2pg/fr L

MICKLETON

Mickleton Friends School
Democrat Rd.
HABS NJ-256
HABS NJ,8-MICK,2-
5dr/1ph/2pg/fr L

Otto-Tonkin House
Kings Highway
HABS NJ-46
HABS NJ,8-MICK,1-
7dr/2ph/4pg/fr L

MOUNT ROYAL

Death-of-the-Fox Inn
HABS NJ-231
HABS NJ,8-MOURO,1-
1ph/2pg L

MULLICA HILL

Mullica Hill Town Hall
S. Main St. (Bridgeton Pike) & Woodstown Rd.
HABS NJ-839
HABS NJ,8-MUL,1-
3dr/8ph/9pg L

St. Stephen's Episcopal Church
51 N. Main St.
HABS NJ-889
HABS NJ,8-MUL,2-
9ph/1pg/1pc L

NATIONAL PARK

Whitall House
Delaware River & Hessian Ave.
HABS NJ-79
HABS NJ,8-NAPA,1-
18dr/7ph/5pg/fr L

Whitall,James Jr. ,House
HABS NJ-576
HABS NJ,8-NAPA,2-
2ph/3pg L

PAULSBORO

Paul House
HABS NJ-405
HABS NJ,8-PABO,1-
11dr/4ph/2pg/fr L

PAULSBORO VIC.

Francis,Tench,House & Barn
Manuta Creek
HABS NJ-410
HABS NJ,8-PABO.V,2-
14dr/8ph/3pg/fr L

Hopkins House (Paradise Farm)
HABS NJ-473
HABS NJ,8-PABO.V,3-
11dr/5ph/2pg/fr L

Paradise Farm; see Hopkins House

Rambo,John,House
Mantua Grove Rd.
HABS NJ-485
HABS NJ,8-PABO.V,4-
13dr/4ph/2pg/fr L

Swedesboro-Paulsboro Road (Log House)
HABS NJ-10
HABS NJ,8-PABO.V,1-
1dr/2ph/1pg L

PITMAN

Pitman Grave Camp Meeting
North,South,East, & West Aves.
HABS NJ-730
HABS NJ,8-PIT,1-
21ph/4pg L

SWEDESBORO

Trinity Church
Church & Main Sts.
HABS NJ-85
HABS NJ,8-SWEBO,1-
24dr/5ph/5pg/fr L

SWEDESBORO VIC.

Adams Methodist Episcopal Church
Road to Hendrickson's Mill
HABS NJ-83
HABS NJ,8-SWEBO.V,5-
3dr/1ph/2pg/fr L

Moravian Church
Sharptown Rd.
HABS NJ-81-A
HABS NJ,8-SWEBO.V,1-
12dr/1ph/3pg/fr L

Moravian Church,Rectory
HABS NJ-81-B
HABS NJ,8-SEWBO.V,2-
4dr/1ph/3pg/fr L

Stille,Peter,House
HABS NJ-82-B
HABS NJ,8-SWEBO.V,4-
2dr/1ph/2pg/fr L

West-Newbold House
HABS NJ-307
HABS NJ,8-SWEBO.V,7-
1ph/2pg L

SWEDESBORO VICINITY

Stratton Mansion
HABS NJ-82-A
HABS NJ,8-SWEBO.V,3-
9dr/2ph/6pg/fr L

Vanleer Cedar Log Cabin
HABS NJ-92
HABS NJ,8-SWEBO.V,6-
4dr/2ph/3pg/fr L

WOODBURY

Friends Meetinghouse
120 N. Broad St.
HABS NJ-80
HABS NJ,8-WOBU,1-
19dr/2ph/3pg/fr L

HUDSON COUNTY

BAYONNE

Bayonne Bridge
Spanning Kill Van Kull between Bayonne & Staten I.
HAER NJ-66
HAER NJ,9-BAYO,1-
10ph/1pg/1pc/fr L

BAYONNE VIC.

Shooters Island:Ships Graveyard
Newark Bay
HAER NY-162
HAER NY,43-SHOOTI,1-
1dr/6ph/49pg/1pc L

HOBOKEN

Castle Point; see Stevens,Col. John,House

Erie-Lackawana Railroad Ferry Terminal & Warehouse
Hudson Place
HABS NJ-763
HABS NJ,9-HOBO,4-
7ph/1pg/1pc L

Erie/Lackawanna RR/Ferry Terminal:Slips & Bridges
Bounded by Observer,Newark & River Sts,Hudson Riv.
HAER NJ-59
HAER NJ,9-HOBO,2-
20ph/26pg/2pc L

Hoboken City Hall
86-98 Washington St.
HABS NJ-51
HABS NJ,9-HOBO,1-
10ph/6pg/1pc/fr L

Hoboken Fire Engine Company Number Two
1313 Washington St.
HABS NJ-764
HABS NJ,9-HOBO,5-
2ph/1pc L

Hoboken Piers Headhouse
River St. at Hudson River
HAER NJ-63
HAER NJ,9-HOBO,3-
72ph/37pg/6pc L

Stevens Gatehouse
Castle Point
HABS NJ-809
HABS NJ,9-HOBO,7-
3ph/1pc L

Stevens,Col. John,House (Castle Point)
HABS NJ-765
HABS NJ,9-HOBO,6-
5ph/1pc L

JERSEY CITY

(Documentation filed under New York City,New York); see Holland Tunnel

Apple Tree House; see Van Wagenen House

Bergen Church,Old
Bergen & Highland Aves.
HABS NJ-466
HABS NJ,9-JERCI,1-
20dr/3ph/4pg/fr L

Central Railroad of New Jersey,Engine Terminal
HAER NJ-27-A
HAER NJ,9-JERCI,4-A-
46ph/73pg/4pc L

Central Railroad of New Jersey,Pier 19
Hudson River waterfront
HAER NJ-27-B
HAER NJ,9-JERCI,4-B-
24ph/21pg/2pc L

Central RR of N. J. ,Jersey City Ferry Terminal
Johnson Ave. at Hudson River
HAER NJ-27
HAER NJ,9-JERCI,4-
37ph/51pg/3pc L

Delaware,Lackawanna & Western RR:Pier 6:Grain Tres (Pier No. 6 Grain Trestle; Grain Trestle)
Erie Lackawanna Railroad Yard
HAER NJ-50
HAER NJ,9-JERCI,5-
3dr/27ph/10pg/2pc L

Erie Railway:Bergen Hill Open Cut
Palisade Ave. to Tonnele Ave.
HAER NJ-22
HAER NJ,9-JERCI,6-
19ph/2pc L

Erie Railway:Ferryboat Susquehanna
HAER NJ-23
HAER NJ,9-JERCI,7-
3ph/1pc L

Erie Railway:Pier 5 Immigrant's Waiting Room
HAER NJ-24
HAER NJ,9-JERCI,8-
2ph/1pc L

Grace Episcopal Church (Van Vorst Episcopal Church)
Second & Erie Sts.
HABS NJ-766
HABS NJ,9-JERCI,12-
4ph/1pg/1pc L

Grain Trestle; see Delaware,Lackawanna & Western RR:Pier 6:Grain Tres

Greenville Yard
Upper New York Bay
HAER NJ-49
HAER NJ,9-JERCI,9-
19ph/102pg/1pc L

Gregory House
31 Erie St.
HABS NJ-503
HABS NJ,9-JERCI,3-
11dr/3ph/2pg/fr L

Holland Tunnel ((Documentation filed under New York City,New York)
Beneath Hudson River btwn Jersey City & New York
HAER NY-161
HAER NY,31-NEYO,166-
43ph/3pg/3pc L

Hudson County Courthouse
583 Newark Ave.
HABS NJ-841
HABS NJ,9-JERCI,13-
42ph/4pg/3pc L

Jersey City Hospital, Nurses Homes (Jersey City Medical Ctr., Nurses Homes Nos. 1 & 2)
112-114 Clifton Place
HABS NJ-891-A
HABS NJ,9-JERCI,14-A-
5ph/16pg/1pc L

Jersey City Hospital,Powerhouse & Laundry (Jersey City Medical Ctr., Powerhouse & Laundry)
112-114 Clifton Place
HABS NJ-891-B
HABS NJ,9-JERCI,14-B-
5ph/4pg/1pc L

Jersey City Medical Ctr., Nurses Homes Nos. 1 & 2; see Jersey City Hospital, Nurses Homes

Jersey City Medical Ctr., Powerhouse & Laundry; see Jersey City Hospital,Powerhouse & Laundry

Lehigh Valley Railroad,Pier G
HAER NJ-27-C
HAER NJ,9-JERCI,4-C-
26ph/23pg/2pc L

Montgomery Gateway East,One & Two
Montgomery & Monmouth St.
HABS NJ-868
HABS NJ,9-JERCI,15-
50ph/1pg/3pc L

Pier No. 6 Grain Trestle; see Delaware,Lackawanna & Western RR:Pier 6:Grain Tres

Pulaski Skyway
Spanning Passaic & Hackensack Rivers
HAER NJ-34
HAER NJ,9-JERCI,10-
7ph/1pg/1pc L

Roosevelt Stadium
State Rt. 440 & Danforth Ave.
HABS NJ-819
HABS NJ,9-JERCI,16-
1dr/88ph/20pg/3pc L

273-273 1/2 Tenth Street (Houses)
HABS NJ-900
HABS NJ,9-JERCI,11-
4ph/1pg/1pc L

Van Vorst Episcopal Church; see Grace Episcopal Church

Van Vorst House
531 Palisade Ave.
HABS NJ-501
HABS NJ,9-JERCI,2-
11dr/6ph/2pg/fr L

Van Wagenen House (Apple Tree House)
298 Academy St.
HABS NJ-767
HABS NJ,9-JERCI,17-
5ph/1pc L

KEARNY

Conrail Bridge (Penn Central Bridge)
Spanning Hackensack River
HAER NJ-43
HAER NJ,9-KEAR,1-
1ph/1pg/1pc L

Delaware,Lackawanna & Western Railroad Bridge; see Erie & Lackawanna Railroad Bridge

Erie & Lackawanna Railroad Bridge (Delaware,Lackawanna & Western Railroad Bridge)
Spanning Hackensack River
HAER NJ-42
HAER NJ,9-KEAR,2-
10ph/1pg/1pc L

Path Transit System Bridge (Port Authority Bridge)
Spanning Hackensack River
HAER NJ-44
HAER NJ,9-KEAR,3-
6ph/1pg/1pc L

Penn Central Bridge; see Conrail Bridge

Port Authority Bridge; see Path Transit System Bridge

UNION CITY

Alcorn,William,House
91 Palisade Ave.
HABS NJ-502
HABS NJ,9-UNCI,1-
13dr/4ph/2pg/fr L

Browning,Cyrus S. ,House
161 Palisade Ave.
HABS NJ-506
HABS NJ,9-UNCI,2-
14dr/3ph/2pg/fr L

WEST NEW YORK

West Shore Railroad,Pier 7 Grain Elevator
Hudson River & Pershing Rd. vic.
HAER NJ-47
HAER NJ,9-NEYOW,1-
19ph/25pg/2pc L

HUNTERDON COUNTY

CALIFON VIC.

Trimmer,William,House
HABS NJ-650
HABS NJ,10-CALIF.V,1-
11dr/4ph/4pg/fr L

CLINTON

(3 drawings in HABS/HAER); see Lowthorp Truss Bridge

Lowthorp Truss Bridge ((3 drawings in HABS/HAER))
Spanning Raritan River at W. Main St.
HAER NJ-19
HAER NJ,10-CLIN,1-
3dr/17ph/5pg/2pc/fr L H

CLINTON VIC.

Hamden Bridge; see Raritan River Fink Through-Truss Bridge

Raritan River Fink Through-Truss Bridge (Hamden Bridge)
Spanning S. Branch Raritan River
HAER NJ-18
HAER NJ,10-CLIN.V,1-
13ph/3pg/1pc/fr L

FLEMINGTON

Emery,William E. ,House (Roselawn)
3 E. Main St.
HABS NJ-768
HABS NJ,10-FLEM,5-
7ph/1pg/1pc L

Fisher,Mahlon,House
116 Main St.
HABS NJ-769
HABS NJ,10-FLEM,6-
2ph/1pg/1pc L

Fleming Castle
5 Bonnel St.
HABS NJ-406
HABS NJ,10-FLEM,2-
12dr/4ph/3pg/fr L

Hopewell,John C. ,House
55 E. Main St.
HABS NJ-770
HABS NJ,10-FLEM,7-
3ph/1pg/1pc L

Hunterdon County Courthouse
Main & Court Sts.
HABS NJ-771
HABS NJ,10-FLEM,8-
3ph/1pg/1pc L

Reading-Large House
119 Main St.
HABS NJ-396
HABS NJ,10-FLEM,1-
22dr/11ph/5pg/fr L

Reading,Gov. John,Dependency
River Rd.
HABS NJ-773-A
HABS NJ,10-FLEM,9-A-
1ph/1pc L

Reading,Gov. John,House
River Rd.
HABS NJ-773
HABS NJ,10-FLEM,9-
5ph/1pc L

Reading,John G. ,House
151-153 Main St.
HABS NJ-731
HABS NJ,10-FLEM,3-
5ph/6pg L

Roselawn; see Emery,William E. ,House

Union Hotel
76 Main St.
HABS NJ-732
HABS NJ,10-FLEM,4-
3ph/5pg L

Wurts,Alexander,Law Office
59 Main St.
HABS NJ-772
HABS NJ,10-FLEM,10-
2ph/1pg/1pc L

GLEN GARDNER

Glen Gardner Bridge (Mill Street Bridge; Pennsylvania Railroad)
Spanning Spruce Run
HAER NJ-92
H

Mill Street Bridge; see Glen Gardner Bridge

Pennsylvania Railroad; see Glen Gardner Bridge

LAMBERTVILLE

Holcombe House
HABS NJ-56
HABS NJ,10-LAMB,1-
2ph/3pg L

MOUNTAINVILLE

Main Street (Commercial Building)
HABS NJ-887
HABS NJ,10-MTVI,1-
2ph/1pc L

Oldstone Barn (Philhower,C. ,Barn)
HABS NJ-888
HABS NJ,10-MITVI,2-
2ph/1pc L

Philhower,C. ,Barn; see Oldstone Barn

NEW HAMPTON

Musconetcong River Bridge; see New Hampton Bridge

New Hampton Bridge (Shoddy Mill Road Bridge; Musconetcong River Bridge; Pennsylvania Railroad)
Spanning the Musconetcong River
HAER NJ-91
13ph/1pg/1pc H

Pennsylvania Railroad; see New Hampton Bridge

Shoddy Mill Road Bridge; see New Hampton Bridge

OLDWICK

Alpaugh House (Illif House)
HABS NJ-886
HABS NJ,10-OLWI,1-
4ph/1pc L

Barnet House; see Barnet,Dr. Oliver,House

Barnet,Dr. Oliver,House (Barnet House; Dillon House)
Vliettown Rd.
HABS NJ-774
HABS NJ,10-OLWI,2-
6ph/1pc L

Barnett Hall Academy (Oldwick Commumity Center)
High St.
HABS NJ-775
HABS NJ,10-OLWI,3-
2ph/1pg/1pc L

Beavers House
Main St. (County Rt. 517)
HABS NJ-776
HABS NJ,10-OLWI,4-
3ph/1pc L

Clark House; see Dickerson,Charles E. ,House

Coughlin House; see Honeyman,Robert M. ,House

Crater-Slack House
High St.
HABS NJ-784
HABS NJ,10-OLWI,5-
4ph/1pc L

Dickerson,Charles E. ,House (Clark House)
Main St.
HABS NJ-777
HABS NJ,10-OLWI,6-
2ph/1pc L

Dillon House; see Barnet,Dr. Oliver,House

Durand,Garet,House; see Johnson House

Fisher,Jacob R. ,House
High St.
HABS NJ-779
HABS NJ,10-OLWI,7-
6ph/1pc L

Honeyman,Robert M. ,House (Coughlin House)
Joliet St.
HABS NJ-781
HABS NJ,10-OLWI,8-
5ph/1pc L

Illif House; see Alpaugh House

Johnson House (Durand,Garet,House)
Homestead Rd.
HABS NJ-778
HABS NJ,10-OLWI,9-
4ph/1pg/1pc L

Miller,Henry,House
Main St.
HABS NJ-782
HABS NJ,10-OLWI,10-
27ph/2pc L

Oldwick Commumity Center; see Barnett Hall Academy

Oldwick Methodist Church
Main St.
HABS NJ-783
HABS NJ,10-OLWI,11-
7ph/1pc L

Stryker House
High St.
HABS NJ-885
HABS NJ,10-OLWI,12-
7ph/1pc L

Van Doren House
Main St.
HABS NJ-785
HABS NJ,10-OLWI,13-
3ph/1pc L

Zion Lutheran Church
Main & Church Sts.
HABS NJ-786
HABS NJ,10-OLWI,14-
6ph/1pg/1pc L

Zion Lutheran Church, Dependency
HABS NJ-786-A
HABS NJ,10-OLWI,14-A-
1ph/1pc L

PATTENBURG VIC.

Clifford-Williamson House
HABS NJ-698
HABS NJ,10-PAT.V,1-
13dr/7ph/7pg/fr L

RAVEN ROCK VIC.

Saxton,Quimby,House; see Saxtonville Tavern

Saxtonville Tavern (Saxton,Quimby,House)
HABS NJ-616
HABS NJ,10-RAVRO.V,1-
14dr/8ph/6pg/fr L

RINGOES

Amwell Academy
HABS NJ-513
HABS NJ,10-RING,2-
11dr/6ph/4pg/fr L

Frame Grist Mill
Rt. 30
HABS NJ-451
HABS NJ,10-RING,1-
13dr/5ph/2pg/fr L

RINGOES VIC.

Williamson House
HABS NJ-235
HABS NJ,10-RING.V,1-
13dr/4ph/2pg/fr L

SERGEANTSVILLE

Miller's House (Opdyke,John,Farm)
Rosemont Rd.
HABS NJ-455
HABS NJ,10-SERG,1-
11dr/5ph/2pg/fr L

Opdyke,John,Farm; see Miller's House

SERGEANTSVILLE VIC.

Covered Bridge
Wickecheoke Creek
HABS NJ-442
HABS NJ,10-SERG.V,1-
5dr/2ph/2pg/fr L

MERCER COUNTY

HOPEWELL

Brown's College
19 Broad St.
HABS NJ-232
HABS NJ,11-HOP,2-
1ph/2pg L

School Baptist Church,Old
Main St.
HABS NJ-199
HABS NJ,11-HOP,1-
8dr/2ph/2pg/fr L

HOPEWELL VIC.

Weart-Hunt House
Stoutsburg-Amwell Rd.
HABS NJ-289
HABS NJ,11-HOP.V,1-
18dr/7ph/2pg/fr L

HUTCHINSON'S MILL

Hutchinson House
HABS NJ-483
HABS NJ,11-HUTMI,1-
16dr/4ph/3pg/fr L

LAWRENCEVILLE

Brearly House
HABS NJ-342
HABS NJ,11-LAWR,3-
1ph/3pg L

Glencairn (Opdyke-Hunt House)
Lawrence Rd.
HABS NJ-296
HABS NJ,11-LAWR.V,1-
15dr/6ph/2pg/fr L

Green House; see Harmony Hall

Harmony Hall (Green House)
Main St.
HABS NJ-52
HABS NJ,11-LAWR,1-
12dr/3ph/2pg/fr L

Opdyke-Hunt House; see Glencairn

Presbyterian Church
Main St.
HABS NJ-53
HABS NJ,11-LAWR,2-
5dr/1ph/2pg/fr L

LAWRENCEVILLE VIC.

Brearley,John,House; see Spring Grove

Spring Grove (Brearley,John,House)
Lewisville Rd. & Princeton Pike
HABS NJ-810
HABS NJ,11-LAWR.V,2-
8dr/12ph/1pc L

PENNINGTON

Hart,John D. ,House
Curlis Ave.
HABS NJ-454
HABS NJ,11-PENT,2-
14dr/4ph/2pg/fr L

Welling,John,House
Curlis Ave.
HABS NJ-409
HABS NJ,11-PENT,1-
13dr/3ph/2pg/fr L

PENNINGTON VIC.

Woolsey,Jeremiah M. ,House
HABS NJ-201
HABS NJ,11-PENT.V,1-
11dr/2ph/2pg L

PRINCETON

Alexander Hall; see Princeton Theological Seminary

20 Alexander St. (House)
HABS NJ-795
HABS NJ,11-PRINT,15-
2ph/1pc L

29 Alexander St. (House)
HABS NJ-796
HABS NJ,11-PRINT,24-
6ph/1pc L

Bainbridge House
158 Nassau St.
HABS NJ-336
HABS NJ,11-PRINT,6-
14dr/5ph/2pg/fr L

Beatty,Col. Jacob,House; see Hyer,Col. Jacob,House

Belgarde; see Princeton University,Borough Hall

Breckenridge,Professor John,House (Ridge,The)
72 Library Place
HABS NJ-790
HABS NJ,11-PRINT,23-
6ph/1pc L

Chancellor Green Library; see Princeton University,Library

Chancellor Green Student Center; see Princeton University,Library

Clarke,Thomas,House; see Mercer,Gen.,House

Dean's House (President's House,Old; Princeton University)
73 Nassau St.
HABS NJ-88
HABS NJ,11-PRINT,4A-
9dr/3ph/2pg/fr L

Drumthwacket,Italianate Garden
344 Stockton St. (U. S. Rt. 206)
HABS NJ-903
HABS NJ,11-PRINT,26-
12dr/24ph/14pg/2pc/fr L

Field,Richard Stockton,House; see Princeton University,Guernsey Hall

Fieldwood; see Princeton University,Guernsey Hall

First Presbyterian Church
61 Nassau St.
HABS NJ-793
HABS NJ,11-PRINT,25-
6ph/1pc L

Gulick-Hudge-Scott House
Herrontown Rd.
HABS NJ-794
HABS NJ,11-PRINT,27-
7ph/1pg/1pc L

Hyer,Col. Jacob,House (Beatty,Col. Jacob,House)
19 Vandeventer St.
HABS NJ-789
HABS NJ,11-PRINT,10-
6ph/1pc L

Leonard,Judge Thomas,House; see Nassau Inn

Mercer,Gen.,House
(Clarke,Thomas,House)
Mercer Rd.
HABS NJ-548
HABS NJ,11-PRINT,9-
15dr/8ph/3pg/fr L

Morven (Stockton,Richard,House; Signer,The)
55 Stockton St. (U.S. Hwy. 206)
HABS NJ-408
HABS NJ,11-PRINT,7- ι1991(HABS):22
10dr/17ph/2pg/1pc/fr L

Morven,Icehouse
(Stockton,Richard,Icehouse)
55 Stockton St. (U.S. Hwy. 206)
HABS NJ-408-A
HABS 1991(HABS):22
2dr/fr L

Nassau Hall (Old North; Princeton University)
Nassau St.
HABS NJ-249
HABS NJ,11-PRINT,4B-
25dr/2ph/5pg L

Nassau Inn (Leonard,Judge Thomas,House)
HABS NJ-434
HABS NJ,11-PRINT,8-
1ph/2pg L

Old North; see Nassau Hall

Olden,Thomas,House
344 Stockton Rd.
HABS NJ-797
HABS NJ,11-PRINT,16-
3ph/1pc L

Potter,Thomas F. ,House
Princeton University Campus
HABS NJ-865
HABS NJ,11-PRINT,21-
1ph/1pc L

President's House,Old; see Dean's House

Princeton Bank & Trust
12-14 Nassau St.
HABS NJ-798
HABS NJ,11-PRINT,13-
4ph/1pc L

Princeton Theological Seminary
(Alexander Hall; Seminary,Old)
Mercer St.
HABS NJ-787
HABS NJ,11-PRINT,18A-
7ph/1pc L

Princeton University; see Dean's House

Princeton University; see Nassau Hall

Princeton University,Alexander Hall
Nassau St. & Palmer Sq.
HABS NJ-788
HABS NJ,11-PRINT,4C-
8ph/1pc L

Princeton University,Borough Hall
(Thomas,Senator John R. ,House; Belgarde)
50 Stockton St.
HABS NJ-799
HABS NJ,11-PRINT,12-
12ph/2pg/1pc L

Princeton University,Guernsey Hall
(Field,Richard Stockton,House; Fieldwood)
63 Lovers Lane
HABS NJ-792
HABS NJ,11-PRINT,20-
11ph/4pg/1pc L

Princeton University,Library
(Chancellor Green Library; Chancellor Green Student Center)
Nassau St. btw. Witherspoon & Tulane Sts.
HABS NJ-791
HABS NJ,11-PRINT,4D-
6ph/1pc L

Ridge,The; see Breckenridge,Professor John,House

Seminary,Old; see Princeton Theological Seminary

Signer,The; see Morven

Stockton,Richard,House; see Morven

Stockton,Richard,Icehouse; see Morven,Icehouse

Stony Brook Bridge
Rt. 27
HABS NJ-29
HABS NJ,11-PRINT,3-
1dr/1ph/2pg/fr L

Stony Brook Quaker Meetinghouse
Quaker Rd.
HABS NJ-140
HABS NJ,11-PRINT,5-
4dr/2ph/2pg/fr L

Thomas,Senator John R. ,House; see Princeton University,Borough Hall

Tusculum; see Witherspoon,John,House

Tusculum Barn; see Witherspoon,John,Barn

Tusculum Springhouse; see Witherspoon,John,Springhouse

Witherspoon,John,Barn (Tusculum Barn)
166 Cherry Hill Rd.
HABS NJ-801
HABS NJ,11-PRINT,22-
3ph/1pc L

Witherspoon,John,House (Tusculum)
166 Cherry Hill Rd.
HABS NJ-800
HABS NJ,11-PRINT,17-
9ph/1pc L

Witherspoon,John,Springhouse
(Tusculum Springhouse)
166 Cherry Hill Rd.
HABS NJ-802
HABS NJ,11-PRINT,14-
1ph/1pc L

PRINCETON VIC.

Golden,John,House
Pretty Brook Rd.
HABS NJ-358
HABS NJ,11-PRINT.V,1-
11dr/4ph/2pg/fr L

TRENTON

Anchor (Stangl) Pottery Company
940 New York Ave.
HAER NJ-26
HAER NJ,11-TRET,11-
19ph/1pg/1pc L

Barracks,Old
S. Willow St.
HABS NJ-39
HABS NJ,11-TRET,4-
9dr/4ph/3pg/5ct/fr L

Bloomsbury Court; see Trent House

Bow Hill; see De Klyn House

Bright-Douglass House
Mahlon Stacy Park
HABS NJ-237
HABS NJ,11-TRET,8-
5dr/1ph/3pg/fr L

Caulkins,Victor,House; see 403-521 Market Street (Houses & Commercial Bldgs.)

De Klyn House (Bow Hill)
Deutzville
HABS NJ-224
HABS NJ,11-TRET,7-
2ph/3pg L

Dunham's Department Store; see 22-26 East State Street (Commercial Building)

25-27 East Hanover Street (Commercial Building)
25-27 E. Hanover St.
HABS NJ-971
HABS 1991(HABS):22
5ph/13pg/1pc L

27 East Hanover Street (Commercial Building)
HABS NJ-972
HABS 1991(HABS):22
1ph/3pg/1pc L

29 East Hanover Street (Commercial Building)
29 E. Hanover St.
HABS NJ-973
HABS 1991(HABS):22
1ph/3pg/1pc L

33 East Hanover Street (Commercial Building) (Trenton Odd Fellows Hall Lodge No. 3)
33 E. Hanover St.
HABS NJ-970
HABS 1991(HABS):22
2ph/3pg/1pc L

12-14 East State Street (Commercial Building)
12-14 E. State St.
HABS NJ-963
HABS 1991(HABS):22
2ph/3pg/1pc L

16 East State Street (Commercial Building)
16 E. State St.
HABS NJ-964
HABS 1991(HABS):22
1ph/3pg/1pc L

18 East State Street (Commercial Building)
18 E. State St.
HABS NJ-965
HABS 1991(HABS):22
1ph/3pg/1pc L

2-6 East State Street (Commercial Building)
2-6 E. State St.
HABS NJ-961
HABS 1991(HABS):22
10ph/15pg/1pc L

20 East State Street (Commercial Building)
20 E. State St.
HABS NJ-966
HABS 1991 (HABS):22
1ph/2pg/1pc L

22-26 East State Street (Commercial Building) (Dunham's Department Store)
HABS NJ-967
HABS 1991(HABS):22
1ph/3pg/1pc L

8-10 East State Street (Commercial Building)
8-10 E. State St.
HABS NJ-962
HABS 1991(HABS):22
6ph/17pg/1pc L

88 East State Street (Commercial Building); see Wallach Building

Ellarslie (Mansion House; McCall House)
Cadwalader Park
HABS NJ-980
fr H

Kingsbury Hall; see Trent House

Mansion House; see Ellarslie

407 Maret Street (House); see 403-521 Market Street (Houses & Commercial Bldgs.)

Margerum,John,House; see 403-521 Market Street (Houses & Commercial Bldgs.)

501 Market Street (Commercial Building); see 403-521 Market Street (Houses & Commercial Bldgs.)

413 Market Street (House); see 403-521 Market Street (Houses & Commercial Bldgs.)

415 Market Street (House); see 403-521 Market Street (Houses & Commercial Bldgs.)

417 Market Street (House); see 403-521 Market Street (Houses & Commercial Bldgs.)

503 Market Street (House); see 403-521 Market Street (Houses & Commercial Bldgs.)

505 Market Street (House); see 403-521 Market Street (Houses & Commercial Bldgs.)

507 Market Street (House); see 403-521 Market Street (Houses & Commercial Bldgs.)

509 Market Street (House); see 403-521 Market Street (Houses & Commercial Bldgs.)

511 Market Street (House); see 403-521 Market Street (Houses & Commercial Bldgs.)

513 Market Street (House); see 403-521 Market Street (Houses & Commercial Bldgs.)

515 Market Street (House); see 403-521 Market Street (Houses & Commercial Bldgs.)

517 Market Street (House); see 403-521 Market Street (Houses & Commercial Bldgs.)

519 Market Street (House); see 403-521 Market Street (Houses & Commercial Bldgs.)

521 Market Street (House); see 403-521 Market Street (Houses & Commercial Bldgs.)

403-521 Market Street (Houses & Commercial Bldgs.)
(Caulkins,Victor,House; Mill Hill Historic District)
403 Market St.
HABS NJ-901-A
HABS NJ,11-TRET,12-A-
2ph/1pg/1pc L

403-521 Market Street (Houses & Commercial Bldgs.) (407 Maret Street (House); Mill Hill Historic District)
HABS NJ-901-C
HABS NJ,11-TRET,12-C-
1ph/1pg/1pc L

403-521 Market Street (Houses & Commercial Bldgs.)
(Margerum,John,House; Mill Hill Historic District)
405 Market St.
HABS NJ-901-B
HABS NJ,11-TRET,12-B-
2ph/1pg/1pc L

403-521 Market Street (Houses & Commercial Bldgs.) (501 Market Street (Commercial Building); Mill Hill Historic District)
HABS NJ-901-I
HABS NJ,11-TRET,12-I-
2ph/1pg/1pc L

403-521 Market Street (Houses & Commercial Bldgs.) (413 Market Street (House); Mill Hill Historic District)
HABS NJ-901-E
HABS NJ,11-TRET,12-E-
1ph/1pg/1pc L

403-521 Market Street (Houses & Commercial Bldgs.) (415 Market Street (House); Mill Hill Historic District)
HABS NJ-901-F
HABS NJ,11-TRET,12-F-
1pg L

403-521 Market Street (Houses & Commercial Bldgs.) (417 Market Street (House); Mill Hill Historic District)
HABS NJ-901-G
HABS NJ,11-TRET,12-G-
1ph/1pg/1pc L

403-521 Market Street (Houses & Commercial Bldgs.) (503 Market Street (House); Mill Hill Historic District)
HABS NJ-901-J
HABS NJ,11-TRET,12-J-
2ph/1pg/1pc L

403-521 Market Street (Houses & Commercial Bldgs.) (505 Market Street (House); Mill Hill Historic District)
HABS NJ-901-K
HABS NJ,11-TRET,12-K-
2ph/1pg/1pc L

403-521 Market Street (Houses & Commercial Bldgs.) (507 Market Street (House); Mill Hill Historic District)
HABS NJ-901-L
HABS NJ,11-TRET,12-L-
1ph/1pg/1pc L

403-521 Market Street (Houses & Commercial Bldgs.) (509 Market Street (House); Mill Hill Historic District)
HABS NJ-901-M
HABS NJ,11-TRET,12-M-
1ph/1pg/1pc L

403-521 Market Street (Houses & Commercial Bldgs.) (511 Market Street (House); Mill Hill Historic District)
HABS NJ-901-N
HABS NJ,11-TRET,12-N-
1ph/1pg/1pc L

403-521 Market Street (Houses & Commercial Bldgs.) (513 Market Street (House); Mill Hill Historic District)
HABS NJ-901-O
HABS NJ,11-TRET,12-O-
1ph/1pg/1pc L

403-521 Market Street (Houses & Commercial Bldgs.) (515 Market Street (House); Mill Hill Historic District)
HABS NJ-901-P
HABS NJ,11-TRET,12-P-
2ph/1pg/1pc L

403-521 Market Street (Houses & Commercial Bldgs.) (517 Market Street (House); Mill Hill Historic District)
HABS NJ-901-Q
HABS NJ,11-TRET,12-Q-
2ph/1pg/1pc L

403-52i Market Street (Houses & Commercial Bldgs.) (519 Market Street (House); Mill Hill Historic District)
HABS NJ-901-R
HABS NJ,11-TRET,12-R-
1ph/1pg/1pc L

403-521 Market Street (Houses & Commercial Bldgs.) (521 Market Street (House); Mill Hill Historic District)
HABS NJ-901-S
HABS NJ,11-TRET,12-S-
2ph/1pg/1pc L

403-521 Market Street (Houses & Commercial Bldgs.) (Nutt,John,Jr. ,House; Mill Hill Historic District)
HABS NJ-901-D
HABS NJ,11-TRET,12-D-
1ph/1pg/1pc L

403-521 Market Street (Houses & Commercial Bldgs.) (Pratt,Charles W. ,Grocery; Mill Hill Historic District)
419 Market St.
HABS NJ-901-H
HABS NJ,11-TRET,12-H-
2ph/1pg/1pc L

Masonic Temple,Old
S. Willow & W. Lafaytette Sts.
HABS NJ-141
HABS NJ,11-TRET,5-
8dr/2ph/3pg/fr L

McCall House; see Ellarslie

McPherson Building; see 8 North Warren Sreet (Commercial Building)

Mill Hill Historic District; see 403-521 Market Street (Houses & Commercial Bldgs.)

12 N. Warren Street (Commercial Building)
HABS NJ-957
HABS 1991(HABS):22
2ph/13pg/1pc H

New Jersey State Prison
Second & Federal Sts.
HABS NJ-874
HABS NJ,11-TRET,13-
19ph/104pg/3pc/fr L

11-15 North Broad Street (Commercial Building)
11-15 N. Broad St.
HABS NJ-969
HABS 1991(HABS):22
5ph/15pg/1pc L

8 North Warren Sreet (Commercial Building) (McPherson Building)
8 N. Warren St.
HABS NJ-955
HABS 1991(HABS):22
1ph/3pg/1pc L

10 North Warren Street (Commercial Building)
10 North Warren Street
HABS NJ-956
HABS 1991(HABS):22
7ph/12pg/1pc L

16 North Warren Street (Commercial Building)
HABS NJ-959
HABS 1991(HABS):22
4ph/13pg/1pc L

Nutt,John,Jr. ,House; see 403-521 Market Street (Houses & Commercial Bldgs.)

Pratt,Charles W. ,Grocery; see 403-521 Market Street (Houses & Commercial Bldgs.)

Roeblin's,J.A.,Sons Co.,and Am. Steel and Wire Co.
HAER NJ-46
1dr/1ct H

Russell-Stokes House
HABS NJ-425
HABS NJ,11-TRET,9-
6ph/3pg L

Trent House (Kingsbury Hall; Bloomsbury Court; Woodlawn)
539 S. Warren St.
HABS NJ-200
HABS NJ,11-TRET,6-
19dr/11ph/4pg/3ct/fr L

Trenton City Hall & City Hall Annex; see Trenton Municipal Building

Trenton House Hotel
20-24 N. Warren St. and 1-19 E. Hanover St.
HABS NJ-960
HABS 1991(HABS):22
19ph/24pg/2pc L

Trenton Municipal Building (Trenton City Hall & City Hall Annex)
319 E. State St.
HABS NJ-279
HABS NJ,11-TRET,10-
9ph/7pg/1pc L

Trenton Odd Fellows Hall Lodge No. 3; see 33 East Hanover Street (Commercial Building)

True American Building
14 N. Warren St.
HABS NJ-958
HABS 1991(HABS):22
8ph/14pg/1pc L

Wallach Building (88 East State Street (Commercial Building))
88 E. State St.
HABS NJ-968
HABS 1991(HABS):22
12ph/12pg/1pc L

Woodlawn; see Trent House

WASHINGTON CROSSING

Johnson-McKonkey Ferry House
HABS NJ-19
HABS NJ,11-WASHC,1-
7dr/3ph/6pg/fr L

MIDDLESEX COUNTY

BONHAMTOWN

Ford,Charles,House
Old Post Rd.
HABS NJ-467
HABS NJ,12-BONTO,1-
12dr/3ph/3pg/fr L

BOUND BROOK VIC.

Perry,Kenneth,Cottage
River Rd.
HABS NJ-710
HABS NJ,12-BOUB.V,2-
1ph/1pg L

Perry,Kenneth,House
River Rd.
HABS NJ-709
HABS NJ,12-BOUB.V,1-
5ph/3pg L

CARTERET

Williams,Ichabod T., & Sons:Sawmill & Veneer Plant
Roosevelt Ave. at Carteret Ave.
HAER NJ-28
HAER NJ,12-CART,1-
26ph/2pg/2pc/fr L

FRANKLIN PARK VIC.

Williamson House
Cozzens Lane
HABS NJ-89
HABS NJ,12-FRAPA.V,1-
11dr/3ph/2pg/fr L

HIGHLAND PARK VIC.

Antill,Dr. ,House (Ross Hall)
River Rd.
HABS NJ-362
HABS NJ,12-HILPA.V,1-
17dr/3ph/2pg/fr L

Ross Hall; see Antill,Dr. ,House

KINGSTON

Delaware & Raritan:Drawbridge,Lock & Tollhouse (Drawbridge,Lock & Tollhouse)
Delaware & Raritan Canal
HABS NJ-359
HABS NJ,12-PLABO.V,3-
14dr/5ph/3pg/fr L

Drawbridge,Lock & Tollhouse; see Delaware & Raritan:Drawbridge,Lock & Tollhouse

METUCHEN

Borough Improvement League House (Franklin School)
491 Middlesex Ave.
HABS NJ-226
HABS NJ,12-METU,2-
7dr/1ph/3pg/fr L

Fairweather,Thomas,House
191 Middlesex Ave.
HABS NJ-216
HABS NJ,12-METU,1-
6dr/1ph/2pg/fr L

Franklin School; see Borough Improvement League House

St. Luke's Episcopal Church
Middlesex & Oaks Aves.
HABS NJ-711
HABS NJ,12-METU,3-
6ph/3pg L

METUCHEN VIC.

Shotwell-Runyon House
Happy Valley Lane
HABS NJ-55
HABS NJ,12-METU.V,1-
9dr/2ph/2pg/fr L

NEW BRUNSWICK

Bishop,James,House
College Ave. & Bartlett St.
HABS NJ-712
HABS NJ,12-NEBRU,6-
9ph/4pg L

Christ Episcopal Church
HABS NJ-38
HABS NJ,12-NEBRU,1-
4ph/2pg L

Deep Lock; see Delaware & Raritan Canal:Lock

Delaware & Raritan Canal:Lock (Deep Lock)
Raritan River btw. George & Hamilton Sts.
HABS NJ-713
HAER NJ-60-A
HABS/HAER NJ,12-NEBRU,13-
1dr/26ph/9pg/2pc L

Delaware & Raritan Canal:Locktender's House
N. of Hamilton, E. of George & E. of Pumping Stat.
HAER NJ-60-B
HAER NJ,12-NEBRU,13-B-
9dr/13ph/2pg/1pc L

Delaware & Raritan Canal:Outlet Locks
Between State Rt. 18 & Raritan River
HAER NJ-61
HAER NJ,12-NEBRU,18-
12ph/1pc L

Doolittle-Demarest House; see Rutgers University

Farley Blacksmith Shop
82 Memorial Pky.(moved to Johnson Park,Piscataway)
HABS NJ-715
HABS NJ,12-NEBRU,10-
7ph/3pg L

First Reformed Church of New Brunswick
Neilson St.
HABS NJ-716
HABS NJ,12-NEBRU,2-
10ph/4pg L

Guest,Henry,House
HABS NJ-499
HABS NJ,12-NEBRU,5-
14dr/5ph/6pg L

Hertzog,Peter,Theological Hall; see New Brunswick Theological Seminary

Indian Queen Tavern
Albany Ave. & Rt. 27
HABS NJ-875
HABS NJ,12-NEBRU,20-
6ph/1pc L

Jarrad,Levi D. ,House; see Rutgers University

177-179 Neilson Street (Commercial Building) (Thrift Shop)
HABS NJ-904
HABS NJ,12-NEBRU,19-
2ph/7pg/1pc L

New Brunswick Theological Seminary (Hertzog,Peter,Theological Hall)
17 Seminary Place
HABS NJ-717
HABS NJ,12-NEBRU,7-
4ph/4pg L

New Brunswick Theological Seminary,Library (Sage,Gardener A. ,Library)
21 Seminary Place
HABS NJ-722
HABS NJ,12-NEBRU,8-
7ph/5pg L

New Jersey Rubber Shoe Company Building No. 1
Albany St.
HABS NJ-719
HABS NJ,12-NEBRU,11A-
2ph/2pg L

New Jersey Rubber Shoe Company Building No. 9
Burnet St.
HABS NJ-720
HABS NJ,12-NEBRU,11B-
2ph/2pg L

Norfolk & New Brunswick Hosiery Company
George & Hamilton Sts.
HABS NJ-721
HABS NJ,12-NEBRU,12-
3ph/3pg L

Queen's Building
Somerset St.
HABS NJ-119
HABS NJ,12-NEBRU,4-
11dr/2ph/3pg/fr L

Raritan Railroad Station
Sanford St.
HABS NJ-974
HABS 1990 (HABS):6
9ph/7pg/1pc L

Rutgers University (Doolittle-Demarest House)
George St. & Seminary Pl.
HABS NJ-714
HABS NJ,12-NEBRU,15-
6ph/3pg L

Rutgers University (Jarrad,Levi D. ,House)
George St.
HABS NJ-718
HABS NJ,12-NEBRU,9-
6ph/5pg L

Rutgers University,Observatory (Schanck,Daniel S. ,Observatory)
George St.
HABS NJ-723
HABS NJ,12-NEBRU,14-
6ph/2pg L

Sage,Gardener A. ,Library; see New Brunswick Theological Seminary,Library

Schanck,Daniel S. ,Observatory; see Rutgers University,Observatory

Smith Stable & Carriage House
29 Remson Ave.
HABS NJ-725
HABS NJ,12-NEBRU,16A-
1ph/1pg L

Smith,Emily,House
29 Remson Ave.
HABS NJ-724
HABS NJ,12-NEBRU,16-
8ph/3pg L

Strong,Judge Woodbridge,House (Stronghold)
272 Hamilton St.
HABS NJ-726
HABS NJ,12-NEBRU,17-
10ph/2pg L

Stronghold; see Strong,Judge Woodbridge,House

Thrift Shop; see 177-179 Neilson Street (Commercial Building)

White-Buccleuch Mansion
River Rd.
HABS NJ-22
HABS NJ,12-NEBRU,3-
26dr/3ph/3pg/fr L

NEW BRUNSWICK VIC.

Nevius House; see Smock,Matthias,House

Smock,Matthias,House (Nevius House)
River Rd.
HABS NJ-478
HABS NJ-12 NEBRU.V.4-
10dr/2ph/3pg/fr L

NEW MARKET

Our Lady of Fatima R. C. Church,Rectory; see Vail,William,House

Vail,William,House (Valmere; Our Lady of Fatima R. C. Church,Rectory)
501 New Market St.
HABS NJ-727
HABS NJ,12-NEWM,1-
3ph/4pg L

Valmere; see Vail,William,House

NEWTOWN

Dunn,Walter G. ,Farmhouse
Hoe's Lane
HABS NJ-287
HABS NJ,12-NEBRU.V,2-
14dr/1ph/3pg/fr L

Fitz-Randolph,Ephraim,House
S. Randolphville Rd.
HABS NJ-277
HABS NJ,12-NEBRU.V,1-
13dr/3ph/2pg/fr L

NORTH STELTON VIC.

Dunn,Jeremiah,House
Stelton Rd.
HABS NJ-458
HABS NJ,12-STELN,1-
9dr/4ph/2pg/fr L

PERTH AMBOY

Anaconda Copper Works,Old (Records Storage Building)
Elm & Market Sts.
HAER NJ-32
HAER NJ,12-PERAM,4-
17ph/6pg/1pc L

Governor's House
149 Kearny Ave.
HABS NJ-341
HABS NJ,12-PERAM,2-
70dr/11ph/7pg/fr L

Kearny Cottage
Catalpa Ave.
HABS NJ-637
HABS NJ,12-PERAM,3-
10dr/4ph/6pg/fr L

Parker Castle
Front & Water Sts.
HABS NJ-118
HABS NJ,12-PERAM,1-
8dr/4ph/3pg/fr L

Records Storage Building; see Anaconda Copper Works,Old

PISCATAWAY

St. James Episcopal Church
HABS NJ-197
HABS NJ,12-PISC,1-
10dr/2ph/3pg/fr L

PISCATAWAY TWP.

Ivy Hall (Low,Cornelius,House)
1225 River Rd.
HABS NJ-360
HABS NJ,12-NEBRU.V,3-
22dr/4ph/5pg/fr L

Low,Cornelius,House; see Ivy Hall

PLAINSBORO VIC.

Britton,Col. Dean,House
Dey Rd.
HABS NJ-225
HABS NJ,12-PLABO.V,2-
12dr/6ph/4pg/fr L

SCHALK STATION

Groendyke House
HABS NJ-95
HABS NJ,12-PLABO.V,1-
13dr/4ph/2pg/fr L

SOUTH AMBOY

New Jersey Coastal Heritage Trail; see New Jersey Transit Railroad Station

New Jersey Transit Railroad Station (New Jersey Coastal Heritage Trail)
N.E. side of railroad tracks
HABS NJ-1187
3ph/1pc H

WOODBRIDGE

Barron Library
Rahway Ave. & Port Reading Ave.
HABS NJ-861
HABS NJ,12-WOBRI,1-
7ph/1pc L

MONMOUTH COUNTY

ALLAIRE

Camp Burton; see Deserted Village,The

Deserted Village,The (Howell Iron Works; Camp Burton)
HABS NJ-28
HABS NJ,13-ALAR,1-
29dr/10ph/6pg L

Deserted Village,The,Bakery
HABS NJ-28-A
HABS NJ,13-ALAR,1E-
L

Deserted village,The,Blacksmith Shop
HABS NJ-28-B
HABS NJ,13-ALAR,1J-
L

Deserted Village,The,Blast Furnace
HABS NJ-28-C
HABS NJ,13-ALAR,1A-
L

Documentation: **ct** color transparencies **dr** measured drawings **fr** field records
pc photograph captions **pg** pages of text **ph** photographs

Deserted Village,The,Carpenter Shop
HABS NJ-28-D
HABS NJ,13-ALAR,1H-
L

Deserted Village,The,Church
HABS NJ-28-E
HABS NJ,13-ALAR,1B-
L

Deserted Village,The,Double House
HABS NJ-28-F
HABS NJ,13-ALAR,1C-
L

Deserted Village,The,Enameling House
HABS NJ-28-G
HABS NJ,13-ALAR,1F-
L

Deserted Village,The,Foreman's Cottage
HABS NJ-28-J
HABS NJ,13-ALAR,1D-
L

Deserted Village,The,Fuel Depot
HABS NJ-28-H
HABS NJ,13-ALAR,1K-
L

Deserted Village,The,Store
HABS NJ-28-I
HABS NJ,13-ALAR,1G-
L

Howell Iron Works; see Deserted Village,The

ALLENTOWN

Imlay,John,Mansion
28 S. Main St.
HABS NJ-24
HABS NJ,13-ALTO,1-
29dr/5ph/4pg/fr L

ARNEYTOWN VIC.

Mackenzie,Duncan,Place
(Woodward,Thomas,Homestead)
Province Line Rd.
HABS NJ-202
HABS NJ,13- ,1-
23dr/5ph/6pg L

Woodward,Thomas,Homestead; see Mackenzie,Duncan,Place

ASBURY PARK

ASBURY PARK CASINO (New Jersey Coastal Heritage Trail)
Ocean Ave. & Asbury Ave.
HABS NJ-1176
6ph/1pc H

Asbury Park Casino, Carousel (New Jersey Coastal Heritage Trail)
Ocean Ave. & Asbury Ave.
HABS NJ-1176-A
3ph/1pc H

Asbury Park Convention Hall (New Jersey Coastal Heritage Trail)
Ocean Ave. & Fifth Ave.
HABS NJ-1175
3ph/1pc H

Berkeley-Carteret Hotel (New Jersey Coastal Heritage Trail)
1401 Ocean Ave.
HABS NJ-1174
1ph/1pc H

Fort Monmouth (Fort Monmouth,Evans Area; Fort Monmouth,Charles Wood Area)
HAER NJ-41
HAER NJ,13-ASPA,1-
108pg/fr L

Fort Monmouth,Charles Wood Area; see Fort Monmouth

Fort Monmouth,Evans Area; see Fort Monmouth

705 Grand Avenue (Commercial) (New Jersey Coastal Heritage Trail)
HABS NJ-1077
HABS NJ,13-HOLM.V,1-
1ph/1pc H

New Jersey Coastal Heritage Trail; see ASBURY PARK CASINO

New Jersey Coastal Heritage Trail; see Asbury Park Casino, Carousel

New Jersey Coastal Heritage Trail; see Asbury Park Convention Hall

New Jersey Coastal Heritage Trail; see Berkeley-Carteret Hotel

New Jersey Coastal Heritage Trail; see 705 Grand Avenue (Commercial)

New Jersey Coastal Heritage Trail; see Palace Amusements

New Jersey Coastal Heritage Trail; see Steinbeck Department Store

Palace Amusements (New Jersey Coastal Heritage Trail)
Kingsley St. between Lake & Cookman Aves.
HABS NJ-1075
HABS NJ,13-HOLM.V,1-
H

Steinbeck Department Store (New Jersey Coastal Heritage Trail)
Cookman & Summerfield Aves.
HABS NJ-1076
HABS NJ,13-HOLM.V,1-
1ph/1pc H

ATLANTIC HIGHLANDS

(No Assgd 3-31-93 C. Madrid); see 198 Ocean Boulevard (House)

New Jersey Coastal Heritage Trail; see 198 Ocean Boulevard (House)

New Jersey Coastal Heritage Trail; see White Crystal Diner

198 Ocean Boulevard (House) ((No Assgd 3-31-93 C. Madrid); New Jersey Coastal Heritage Trail)
HABS NJ-1173
3ph/1pc H

White Crystal Diner (New Jersey Coastal Heritage Trail)
20 Center Ave.
HABS NJ-1078
HABS NJ,13-HOLM.V,1-
2ph/1pc H

AVON-BY-THE-SEA

(N0. assigned WASO 3-3-93 Chris M.); see Avon-by-the-Sea,Town of

Avon-by-the-Sea,Town of ((N0. assigned WASO 3-3-93 Chris M.); New Jersey Coastal Heritage Trail)
HABS NJ-1069
3ph/1pc H

New Jersey Coastal Heritage Trail; see Avon-by-the-Sea,Town of

BELMAR

Belmar Boardwalk,Ladies' Bathroom (New Jersey Coastal Heritage Trail)
On the Boardwalk
HABS NJ-1080-B
1ph/1pc H

Belmar Boardwalk,Men's Bathroom (New Jersey Coastal Heritage Trail)
On the Boardwalk
HABS NJ-1080-A
HABS NJ,13-HOLM.V,1-
1ph/1pc H

Belmar Fishing Club (New Jersey Coastal Heritage Trail)
Ocean Ave. & First St.,on the boardwalk
HABS NJ-1079
HABS NJ,13-HOLM.V,1-
1ph/11pg/1pc H

New Jersey Coastal Heritage Trail; see Belmar Boardwalk,Ladies' Bathroom

New Jersey Coastal Heritage Trail; see Belmar Boardwalk,Men's Bathroom

New Jersey Coastal Heritage Trail; see Belmar Fishing Club

BRADLEY BEACH

New Jersey Coastal Heritage Trail; see 709 Ocean Avenue (House)

709 Ocean Avenue (House) (New Jersey Coastal Heritage Trail)
HABS NJ-1081
HABS 1991(HABS):22
1ph/1pc H

CHAPEL HILL

Conover Farm
Mountain Hill Rd.
HABS NJ-276
HABS NJ,13-CHAP,1-
15dr/1ph/3pg L

CREAMRIDGE VIC.

Meirs,William,House
HABS NJ-509
HABS NJ,13-CREM.V,1-
33dr/8ph/4pg/fr L

DEAL

New Jersey Coastal Heritage Trail; see 248 Ocean Boulevard (House)

248 Ocean Boulevard (House) (New Jersey Coastal Heritage Trail)
HABS NJ-1082
HABS 1991(HABS):22
2ph/1pc H

ENGLISHTOWN

Newell,Robert,House; see Village Inn

Village Inn (Newell,Robert,House)
Main & Water Sts.
HABS NJ-65
HABS NJ,13-ENGTO,1-
12dr/18ph/48pg/1pc/fr L

EVERETT VIC.

Hendrickson,Denise,House
Everett Rd.
HABS NJ-679
HABS NJ,13-EV.V,2-
17dr/6ph/4pg/fr L

Hendrickson,Hendrick,House
HABS NJ-544
HABS NJ,13-EV.V,1-
15dr/9ph/5pg/fr L

FREEHOLD VIC.

Craig,John,House
HABS NJ-543
HABS NJ,13-FREHO.V,1-
17dr/2ph/8pg/fr L

HIGHLANDS

Life Saving Station,Original
Spermacetti Cove (moved from Sandy Hook)
HABS NJ-42
HABS NJ.13-SANHO,1-
3dr/2ph/2pg/fr L

HOLLAND

Luyster,Johannes,House
Laurel Ave. & Middleton Rd.
HABS NJ-668
HABS NJ,13-HOL,2-
15dr/10ph/5pg/fr L

HOLMDEL

Cooke,Dr. Robert W. ,Office
HABS NJ-666
HABS NJ,13-HOLM,2-
7dr/3ph/5pg/fr L

Duncan,William J. ,House; see Longstreet House

Longstreet House (Duncan,William J. ,House)
HABS NJ-411
HABS NJ,13-HOLM,1-
20dr/7ph/3pg/fr L

HOLMDEL VIC.

Couwenhoven,Corneles,House
HABS NJ-646
HABS NJ,13-HOLM.V,1-
15dr/3ph/6pg/fr L

KEANSBURG

Keansburg Amusement Park (New Jersey Coastal Heritage Trail)
Beachway Rd.
HABS NJ-1177
2ph/1pc H

New Jersey Coastal Heritage Trail; see Keansburg Amusement Park

LONG BRANCH

Church of the Presidents (Long Branch Historical Museum; New Jersey Coastal Heritage Trail)
1260 Ocean Ave.
HABS NJ-1083
HABS 1991(HABS):22
3ph/1pc H

Congregation Brothers of Israel Synagogue
85 Second Ave.
HABS NJ-924
HABS NJ,13-LOBRA,1-
7ph/3pg/1pc L

Grant,Ulysses S.,Cottage (Potter,Howard,House)
995 Ocean Ave.
HABS NJ-884
HABS NJ,13-LOBRA,2-
21ph/4pg/1pc L

Long Branch Historical Museum; see Church of the Presidents

Monmouth College, Library; see Murray Guggenheim House

Monmouth College,Administration Building; see Shadow Lawn

Murray Guggenheim House (Monmouth College, Library; New Jersey Coastal Heritage Trail)
Cedar & Norwood Aves.
HABS NJ-1178
2ph/1pc H

New Jersey Coastal Heritage Trail; see Church of the Presidents

New Jersey Coastal Heritage Trail; see Murray Guggenheim House

New Jersey Coastal Heritage Trail; see Shadow Lawn

Potter,Howard,House; see Grant,Ulysses S.,Cottage

Reservation,The,(Site Map)
New Ocean & Joline Aves.
HABS NJ-883
HABS NJ,13-LOBRA,3-
1dr L

Reservation,The,Building No. 2
New Ocean & Joline Aves.
HABS NJ-883-A
HABS NJ,13-LOBRA,3-A-
2dr/4ph/1pc/fr L

Reservation,The,Building No. 5
New Ocean & Joline Aves.
HABS NJ-883-B
HABS NJ,13-LOBRA,3-B-
2dr/4ph/1pc/fr L

Shadow Lawn (Monmouth College,Administration Building; New Jersey Coastal Heritage Trail)
Cedar & Norwood Aves.
HABS NJ-1188
1ph/1pc H

MATAWAN

Burrowes Mansion (New Jersey Coastal Heritage Trail)
94 Main St.
HABS NJ-198
HABS NJ,13-MAT,1-
22dr/8ph/10pg/1pc/fr L H

First Presbyterian Church (New Jersey Coastal Heritage Trail)
33 State Rt. 34
HABS NJ-1179
1ph H

226 Main Street (House) (New Jersey Coastal Heritage Trail)
HABS NJ-1084
HABS 1991(HABS):22
1ph/1pc H

Matawan Passenger Railroad Station (New Jersey Coastal Heritage Trail)
1 RR Plaza bwt. Main St. & Atlantic Ave.
HABS NJ-873
HABS NJ,13-MAT,2-
12ph/3pg/2pc L H

New Jersey Coastal Heritage Trail; see Burrowes Mansion

New Jersey Coastal Heritage Trail; see First Presbyterian Church

New Jersey Coastal Heritage Trail; see 226 Main Street (House)

New Jersey Coastal Heritage Trail; see Matawan Passenger Railroad Station

MIDDLETON

Christ Episcopal Church
Church St. & King's Highway
HABS NJ-325
HABS NJ,13-MIDTO,2-
13dr/3ph/4pg/fr L

Franklin Academy
King's Highway
HABS NJ-424
HABS NJ,13-MIDTO,3-
9dr/1ph/2pg/fr L

Marlpit Hall; see Taylor,Edward I. ,House

Taylor,Edward I. ,House (Marlpit Hall)
King's Highway
HABS NJ-275
HABS NJ,13-MIDTO,1-
16dr/6ph/4pg/fr L

MIDDLETOWN

Hendrickson,Daniel,House
Holland Rd.
HABS NJ-498
HABS NJ,13-HOL,1-
16dr/5ph/8pg/fr L

MONMOUTH BEACH

13 Beach Road (House) (New Jersey Coastal Heritage Trail)
HABS NJ-1087
2ph/1pc H

Ice House (New Jersey Coastal Heritage Trail)
Park Dr. & Ice House Rd.
HABS NJ-1086
1ph/1pc H

Monmouth Beach Bathing Pavilion (Monmouth Beach Bathing, Bath and Tennis Club; New Jersey Coastal Heritage Trail)
Ocean Ave.
HABS NJ-1180
1ph/1pc H

Monmouth Beach Bathing, Bath and Tennis Club; see Monmouth Beach Bathing Pavilion

Monmouth Beach,Town of (New Jersey Coastal Heritage Trail)
HABS NJ-1070
4ph/1pc H

New Jersey Coastal Heritage Trail; see 13 Beach Road (House)

New Jersey Coastal Heritage Trail; see Ice House

New Jersey Coastal Heritage Trail; see Monmouth Beach Bathing Pavilion

New Jersey Coastal Heritage Trail; see Monmouth Beach,Town of

New Jersey Coastal Heritage Trail; see Normandy Inn

Normandy Inn (New Jersey Coastal Heritage Trail)
21 Tuttle Ave.
HABS NJ-1085
1ph/1pc H

OCEAN GROVE

6 Atlantic Avenue (Hotel) (New Jersey Coastal Heritage Trail)
HABS NJ-1088
1ph/1pc H

New Jersey Coastal Heritage Trail; see 6 Atlantic Avenue (Hotel)

New Jersey Coastal Heritage Trail; see Ocean Grove,Town of,Centennial Cottage

New Jersey Coastal Heritage Trail; see Ocean Grove,Town of,Great Auditorium

Ocean Grove,Town of,Centennial Cottage (New Jersey Coastal Heritage Trail)
44 Ocean Pathway
HABS NJ-1007-B
1ph/1pc H

Ocean Grove,Town of,Great Auditorium (New Jersey Coastal Heritage Trail)
Auditorium Sq.
HABS NJ-1007-A
1ph/1pc H

PHALANX

North American Phalanx
Country Route 537
HABS NJ-842
HABS NJ,13-PHAL,1-
19ph/1pg L

PHALANX VIC.

Polhemus,Daniel,Farmhouse
HABS NJ-693
HABS NJ,13-PHAL.V,1-
16dr/6ph/6pg/fr L

PROSPERTOWN VIC.

Coward,John,House
HABS NJ-555
HABS NJ,13-REDVA.V,1-
16dr/8ph/5pg/fr L

RED BANK

Bergen House; see Fortune,T. Thomas,House

Fortune,T. Thomas,House (Bergen House; Maple Hall)
94 W. Bergen Pl.
HABS NJ-877
HABS NJ,13-REBA,1-
1ph/7pg/1pc L

Maple Hall; see Fortune,T. Thomas,House

Molly Pitcher Inn (New Jersey Coastal Heritage Trail)
88 Riverside Ave.
HABS NJ-1091
1ph/1pc H

New Jersey Coastal Heritage Trail; see Molly Pitcher Inn

SANDY HOOK

Life Saving Station,Original
Spermacetti Cove (moved to Highlands)
HABS NJ-42
HABS NJ,13-SANHO,1-
3dr/2ph/2pg/fr L

Sandy Hook Lighthouse
HABS NJ-326
HABS NJ,13-SANHO,2-
5dr/2ph/6pg/fr L

SHREWSBURY

Allen Homestead
Broad St. & Sycamore Ave.
HABS NJ-228
HABS NJ,13-SHREW,3-
18dr/11ph/3pg/fr L

Christ Episcopal Church
Broad St. & Sycamore Ave.
HABS NJ-37
HABS NJ,13-SHREW,1-
19dr/5ph/5pg/fr L

Friends Meetinghouse
Sycamore Ave.
HABS NJ-568
HABS NJ,13-SHREW,2-
16dr/fr L

SPRING LAKE

Essex & Sussex Hotel Condominiums (New Jersey Coastal Heritage Trail)
HABS NJ-1199
3ph/1pc H

New Jersey Coastal Heritage Trail; see Essex & Sussex Hotel Condominiums

New Jersey Coastal Heritage Trail; see Spring Lake Bathing Pavilion,North

New Jersey Coastal Heritage Trail; see Spring Lake Bathing Pavilion,South

Spring Lake Bathing Pavilion,North (New Jersey Coastal Heritage Trail)
Between Tuttle & Ludlow Aves. on the boardwalk
HABS NJ-1092
1ph/7pg/1pc H

Spring Lake Bathing Pavilion,South (New Jersey Coastal Heritage Trail)
At Atlantic Ave. on the boardwalk
HABS NJ-1093
1ph/6pg/1pc H

TENNENT

First Presbyterian Church (Tennent Church,Old)
HABS NJ-26
HABS NJ,13-TENT,1-
11dr/4ph/3pg/fr L

Tennent Church,Old; see First Presbyterian Church

WALNFORD VIC.

Tilton House
HABS NJ-484
HABS NJ,13-WALF.V,1-
33dr/10ph/3pg/fr L

WEST FREEHOLD

Clinton Gen. ,Headquarters (Conover-Hankinson House)
W. Main St.
HABS NJ-227
HABS NJ,13-FREHOW,1-
19dr/6ph/3pg/fr L

Conover-Hankinson House; see Clinton Gen. ,Headquarters

WRIGHTSVILLE

Merino Hill; see Wright House

Wright House (Merino Hill)
Old Shrewsbury Rd.
HABS NJ-526
HABS NJ,13-WRIT,1-
71dr/15ph/6pg/fr L

MORRIS COUNTY

BOONTON VIC.

Kingsland Homestead
Vreeland Ave.
HABS NJ-96
HABS NJ,14-BOONT.V,1-
18dr/6ph/2pg/fr L

CHATHAM

Crane House (Pitt,William,Tavern)
HABS NJ-94
HABS NJ,14-CHAT,1-
2ph/2pg L

Day-Hamblen House
142 Main St.
HABS NJ-356
HABS NJ,14-CHAT,3-
9dr/3ph/3pg/fr L

Day-Munn House
25 Main St.
HABS NJ-490
HABS NJ,14-CHAT,4-
12dr/4ph/2pg/fr L

Day,Stephen,House
62 Elmwood Rd.
HABS NJ-125
HABS NJ,14-CHAT,2-
7dr/4ph/3pg/fr L

Pitt,William,Tavern; see Crane House

CHESTER

Chester House Hotel
HABS NJ-61
HABS NJ,14-CHEST,1-
20dr/6ph/2pg/fr L

Corwin,Issac,House
HABS NJ-628
HABS NJ,14-CHEST,2-
18dr/4ph/5pg/fr L

Drake,John,House
Main St.
HABS NJ-647
HABS NJ,14-CHEST,3-
20dr/4ph/3pg/fr L

DENVILLE VIC.

Cook,Peter,House
Morris Rd.
HABS NJ-642
HABS NJ,14-DENV.V,1-
19dr/5ph/5pg/fr L

DOVER VIC.

Friends Meetinghouse of Randolph
HABS NJ-145
HABS NJ,14-DOV,1-
4dr/2ph/3pg L

Picatinny Arsenal
State Rt. 15 near I-80
HAER NJ-36
HAER NJ,14-DOV.V,2-
1dr/74ph/142pg/7pc/fr L

Picatinny Arsenal,Complete Rounds/Melt Loading Dis; see Picatinny Arsenal:800 Area,Complete Rnds/Melt Load

Picatinny Arsenal,Gun Bag Loading District; see Picatinny Arsenal:400 Area,Gun Bag Loading Distrct

Picatinny Arsenal,Powder Factory & Power Hse Distr; see Picatinny Arsenal:500 Area,Powder Fac & Power Hse

Picatinny Arsenal,Shell Component Loading District; see Picatinny Arsenal:200 Area,Shell Component Loading

Picatinny Arsenal,Test Areas District; see Picatinny Arsenal:600 Area,Test Areas District

Picatinny Arsenal:200 Area,Shell Component Loading (Picatinny Arsenal,Shell Component Loading District
State Rt. 15 near I-80
HAER NJ-36-A
HAER NJ,14-DOV.V,2-A-
2dr/37ph/1pg/4pc L

Picatinny Arsenal:400 Area,Gun Bag Loading Distrct (Picatinny Arsenal,Gun Bag Loading District)
State Rt. 15 near I-80
HAER NJ-36-B
HAER NJ,14-DOV.V,2-B-
2dr/46ph/1pg/6pc L

Picatinny Arsenal:500 Area,Powder Fac & Power Hse (Picatinny Arsenal,Powder Factory & Power Hse Distr
State Rt. 15 near I-80
HAER NJ-36-C
HAER NJ,14-DOV.V,2-C-
4dr/103ph/1pg/11pc L

Picatinny Arsenal:600 Area,Test Areas District (Picatinny Arsenal,Test Areas District)
State Rt. 15 near I-80
HAER NJ-36-D
HAER NJ,14-DOV.V,2-D-
1dr/15ph/1pg/2pc L

Picatinny Arsenal:800 Area,Complete Rnds/Melt Load (Picatinny Arsenal,Complete Rounds/Melt Loading Dis
State Rt. 15 near I-80
HAER NJ-36-E
HAER NJ,14-DOV.V,2-E-
1dr/13ph/1pg/2pc L

Washington Arms Tavern
HABS NJ-196
HABS NJ,14-DOV.V,1-
12dr/4ph/2pg/fr L

FLORHAM PARK

Campfield,James A. ,House (Cory-Campfield House)
HABS NJ-522
HABS NJ,14-FLORP,1-
17dr/4ph/5pg/fr L

Cory-Campfield House; see Campfield,James A. ,House

Hopping,John,House
Ridgedale Ave. & Park Ave.
HABS NJ-692
HABS NJ,14-FLORP,3-
14dr/4ph/5pg/fr L

Hopping,Silas,House
Park St.
HABS NJ-687
HABS NJ,14-FLORP,2-
12dr/8ph/5pg/fr L

HANOVER

Ball,Aaron,House
Mt. Pleasant Tpk.
HABS NJ-561
HABS NJ,14-HANO,3-
15dr/3ph/3pg/fr L

Green,Calvin,House
HABS NJ-517
HABS NJ,14-HANO,2-
13dr/3ph/5pg/fr L

Halfway House (Merry-Hopping House)
HABS NJ-676
HABS NJ,14-HANO,4-
15dr/9ph/6pg/fr L

Hopping,Daniel,House
Hanover Rd.
HABS NJ-195
HABS NJ,14-HANO,1-
11dr/6ph/4pg/fr L

Merry-Hopping House; see Halfway House

Woodruff,John,House
28 Hanover Rd.
HABS NJ-681
HABS NJ,14-HANO,5-
17dr/5ph/4pg/fr L

HANOVER NECK

Tuttle,John O. ,House
Eagle Rock Ave.
HABS NJ-511
HABS NJ,14-HANO.V,1-
7dr/2ph/2pg/fr L

HANOVER TWP.

Pierson,Lewis,House
Horsehill Rd.
HABS NJ-689
HABS NJ,14-MORTO.V,2-
13dr/7ph/4pg/fr L

LINCOLN PARK

Dey,Thomas,House
Lincoln Park Blvd.
HABS NJ-536
HABS NJ,14-LINPA,3-
12dr/4ph/4pg/fr L

Dods,John,House
Highland St.
HABS NJ-93
HABS NJ,14-LINPA,2-
16dr/5ph/2pg/fr L

Mead,Peter,House
Pine Brook Rd.
HABS NJ-87
HABS NJ,14-LINPA,1-
1ph/7pg L

MADISON

Bottle Hill Tavern
127 Main St. & Alexander Ave.
HABS NJ-58
HABS NJ,14-MAD,1-
7dr/2ph/2pg/fr L

Bruen,Jonathan B. ,House
250 Main St.
HABS NJ-529
HABS NJ,14-MAD,4-
23dr/3ph/4pg/fr L

Miller,Andrew,House
105 Ridgedale Ave.
HABS NJ-124
HABS NJ,14-MAD,2-
12dr/4ph/3pg/fr L

Sayre,Daniel,House
(Sayre,Ephrim,House)
31 Ridgedale Ave.
HABS NJ-146
HABS NJ,14-MAD,3-
10dr/2ph/2pg/fr L

Sayre,Ephrim,House; see Sayre,Daniel,House

MENDHAM

Hill Top Church
HABS NJ-63
HABS NJ,14-MEND,2-
15dr/1ph/2pg/fr L

Howell,Abraham,House; see Wolfe,Peter,House

Hudson,Aaron,House
Hilltop Rd.
HABS NJ-564
HABS NJ,14-MEND,4-
16dr/5ph/3pg/fr L

Ladies Seminary (Phoenix House)
HABS NJ-62
HABS NJ,14-MEND,1-
13dr/3ph/2pg/fr L

Phoenix House; see Ladies Seminary

Thompson House
HABS NJ-194
HABS NJ,14-MEND,3-
10dr/6ph/2pg/fr L

Wolfe,Peter,House
(Howell,Abraham,House)
Hill Top Rd.
HABS NJ-623
HABS NJ,14-MEND,5-
20dr/6ph/2pg/fr L

MIDDLE VALLEY

Miller,David,House
HABS NJ-519
HABS NJ,14-MIDVA,1-
21dr/4ph/4pg/fr L

MONTVILLE

Van Duyne,Abraham,House
State Rt. 32
HABS NJ-489
HABS NJ,14-MONV,1-
14dr/2ph/2pg/fr L

MONTVILLE VIC.

Demarest Farmhouse
Changebridge Rd.
HABS NJ-309
HABS NJ,14-MONVI.V,2-
7dr/2ph/2pg/fr L

Parlaman,Johannes,House
River Rd.
HABS NJ-49
HABS NJ,14-MONVI.V,1-
17dr/1ph/3pg/fr L

MORRISTOWN

Abbett Avenue Bridge
Spanning Whippany River at Abbett Ave.
HAER NJ-35
HAER NJ,14-MORTO,12-
14ph/4pg/1pc L

Campfield,Dr. Jabez,House; see Schuyler-Hamilton House

Este,Capt. Moses,House
62 Water St. (moved to Speedwell Village)
HABS NJ-677
HABS NJ,14-MORTO,9-
26dr/13ph/5pg/fr L

Ford,Col. Jacob Jr. ,House
(Washington's Headquarters)
230 Morris St.
HABS NJ-32
HABS NJ,14-MORTO,2-
26dr/18ph/4pg/1pc/2ct/fr L

Guerin House
Jockey Hollow Rd.
HABS NJ-144
HABS NJ,14-MORTO,5-
9dr/17ph/2pg/fr L

Hatfield,Moses,House
21 DeHart St.
HABS NJ-695
HABS NJ,14-MORTO,11-
16dr/6ph/5pg/fr L

Kemble House
Mt. Kemble Ave.
HABS NJ-48
HABS NJ,14-MORTO,4-
10dr/4ph/3pg/fr L

Liddell Mill
Jockey Hollow
HABS NJ-682
HABS NJ,14-MORTO,10-
3ph L

Macculloch,George P. ,Mansion
45 Macculloch Ave.
HABS NJ-658
HABS NJ,14-MORTO,7-
14ph/4pg L

Mills,Timothy,House
27 Mills St.
HABS NJ-632
HABS NJ,14-MORTO,6-
11dr/2ph/4pg/fr L

Russell,Sylvester D. ,House
89 Western Ave.
HABS NJ-659
HABS NJ,14-MORTO,8-
16dr/2ph/4pg/fr L

Schuyler-Hamilton House
(Campfield,Dr. Jabez,House)
5 Oliphant Pl.
HABS NJ-35
HABS NJ,14-MORTO,3-
8dr/1ph/3pg/fr L

Washington's Headquarters; see Ford,Col. Jacob Jr. ,House

Wick,Tempe,House
Mendham Rd. ,Jockey Hollow
HABS NJ-15
HABS NJ,14-MORTO,1-
13dr/36ph/14pg/fr L

MOUNT FREEDOM VIC.

Pool,Henry,House
County Rd. No. 20
HABS NJ-671
HABS NJ,14-MOUFR.V,1-
16dr/6ph/5pg/fr L

MOUNT TABOR VIC.

Dickerson,Thomas,House
HABS NJ-644
HABS NJ,14-MOUTA.V,1-
14dr/5ph/5pg/fr L

NEWFOUNDLAND

DeMouth-Snyder House
Green Pond Rd.
HABS NJ-217
HABS NJ,14-NEWFO,1-
14dr/4ph/3pg/fr L

NEWFOUNDLAND VIC.

Weaver-Hough House
HABS NJ-427
HABS NJ,14-NEWFO.V,1-
14dr/2ph/3pg/fr L

PARSIPPANY VIC.

Bowers-Benedict House; see
Osborn,Thomas,House

Osborn,Thomas,House (Bowers-Benedict House)
Parsippany Rd.
HABS NJ-630
HABS NJ,14-PAR.V,1-
16dr/6ph/4pg/fr L

PINE BROOK

Van Duyne,Simon,House
Maple Lane & Hook Mt. Rd.
HABS NJ-147
HABS NJ,14-PIBR,1-
11dr/4ph/2pg/fr L

POMPTON PLAINS

Berry,Martin,House
Jackson Ave. & Rt. 23
HABS NJ-546
HABS NJ,14-POMPL,2-
22dr/5ph/3pg/fr L

Van Ness House
Jackson Ave. & Pompton Pine
HABS NJ-545
HABS NJ,14-POMPL,1-
19dr/3ph/3pg/fr L

POWERVILLE

Miller,Adam,House at Powerville
HABS NJ-193
HABS NJ,14-POWVI,1-
7dr/2ph/2pg/fr L

Scott,William,Mansion House
Powerville Rd.
HABS NJ-558
HABS NJ,14-POWVI,2-
29dr/4ph/5pg/fr L

RALSTON

Post Office (Ralston Manor House)
HABS NJ-357
HABS NJ,14-RAL,2,2B-
22dr/6ph/4pg/fr L

Ralston Manor House; see Post Office

Ralston,John,Mill
HABS NJ-339
HABS NJ,14-RAL,1-
8dr/8ph/2pg/fr L

ROCKAWAY

Jackson House
82 E. Main St.
HABS NJ-507
HABS NJ,14-ROCK,1-
20dr/4ph/2pg/fr L

SPEEDWELL VILLAGE

Este,Capt. Moses,House
(moved from Morristown,62 Water St.)
HABS NJ-677
HABS NJ,14-MORTO,9-
26dr/13ph/5pg/fr L

SPLIT ROCK

Split Rock Furnance
HABS NJ-553
HABS NJ,14- 1-
3dr/7ph/7pg/fr L

SPRINGTOWN VIC.

Dernberger,Philip,House
HABS NJ-633
HABS NJ,14-MIDVA.V,2-
8dr/4ph/5pg/fr L

Sager,Adam,House
HABS NJ-626
HABS NJ,14-MIDVA.V,1-
11dr/3ph/4pg/fr L

TOWACO

Bott,Elmer E. ,House
State Highway No. 32
HABS NJ-452
HABS NJ,14-TOWA,1-
10dr/1ph/2pg/fr L

Jacobus,Abram,Out Kitchen
U. S. 202
HABS NJ-492
HABS NJ,14-TOWA,2A-
2dr/1ph/2pg/fr L

Jacobus,John T. ,House
(Mandeville-Jacobus House)
HABS NJ-474
HABS NJ,14-TOWA.V,1-
7dr/1ph/2pg/fr L

Mandeville-Jacobus House; see
Jacobus,John T. ,House

Vreeland,John H. ,Out Kitchen
HABS NJ-493
HABS NJ,14-TOWA,3A-
3dr/1ph/2pg/fr L

TOWACO VIC.

Doremus,Henry,House
State Route 32
HABS NJ-488
HABS NJ,14-TOWA.V,2-
6dr/1ph/3pg/fr L

TROY HILLS

Parritt,Dr. Joseph,House
S. Beverwyck Rd.
HABS NJ-562
HABS NJ,14-TROHI,1-
15dr/6ph/5pg/fr L

WASHINGTON VALLEY

Smith,John,House
HABS NJ-398
HABS NJ,14-MORTO.V,1-
20dr/4ph/2pg/fr L

WHIPPANY

Methodist Episcopal Church
Route 10,Troy Hills Rd.
HABS NJ-518
HABS NJ,14-WHIP,2-
15dr/2ph/2pg/fr L

Tuttle,Joseph,House
Mount Pleasant Ave.
HABS NJ-469
HABS NJ,14-WHIP,1-
18dr/3ph/2pg/fr L

WHIPPANY VIC.

Green-Cook House
Rt. 10
HABS NJ-639
HABS NJ,14-WHIP.V,1-
13dr/4ph/5pg/fr L

OCEAN COUNTY

BARNEGAT

Barnegat Historical Society Museum;
see Lippencott-Falkinburg House

Barnegat Lifesaving Station (New Jersey Coastal Heritage Trail)
Decateur & Ocean Blvds.
HABS NJ-1094
2ph/1pc H

Barnegat Lighthouse
HABS NJ-43
HABS NJ,15-BAR,1-
2ph/2pg L

593 East Bay Avenue (House) (New Jersey Coastal Heritage Trail)
HABS NJ-1097
1ph/1pc H

First National Antiques; see First National Bank of Barnegat

First National Bank of Barnegat (First National Antiques; New Jersey Coastal Heritage Trail)
708 West Bay Ave.
HABS NJ-1095
1ph/1pc H

Lippencott-Falkinburg House (Barnegat Historical Society Museum; New Jersey Coastal Heritage Trail)
East Bay St.
HABS NJ-1096
1ph/1pc H

New Jersey Coastal Heritage Trail; see Barnegat Lifesaving Station

New Jersey Coastal Heritage Trail; see 593 East Bay Avenue (House)

New Jersey Coastal Heritage Trail; see First National Bank of Barnegat

New Jersey Coastal Heritage Trail; see Lippencott-Falkinburg House

New Jersey Coastal Heritage Trail; see Quaker Meeting House

Quaker Meeting House (New Jersey Coastal Heritage Trail)
East Bay Ave.
HABS NJ-1098
1ph/1pc H

BAYHEAD

Elmer Cottage (New Jersey Coastal Heritage Trail)
32 North St.
HABS NJ-1099
1ph/1pc H

New Jersey Coastal Heritage Trail; see Elmer Cottage

BAYVILLE

Bayview Convalescent Center; see Royal Pines Hotel

Bayville Town Hall (Berkeley Township Historical Society Museum; New Jersey Coastal Heritage Trail)
U.S. Highway 9
HABS NJ-1100
1ph/1pc H

Berkeley Township Historical Society Museum; see Bayville Town Hall

New Jersey Coastal Heritage Trail; see Bayville Town Hall

New Jersey Coastal Heritage Trail; see Royal Pines Hotel

Royal Pines Hotel (Bayview Convalescent Center; New Jersey Coastal Heritage Trail)
395 Lakeside Ave.
HABS NJ-1101
1ph/1pc H

BEACH HAVEN

Holy Innocents Episcopal Church (Long Beach Historical Society and Museum; New Jersey Coastal Heritage Trail)
Beach Ave. at Engleside St.
HABS NJ-1102
1ph/1pc H

Liberty Hall; see Sherborne Farm

Little Egg Harbor Yacht Club (New Jersey Coastal Heritage Trail)
Ocean St. between Berkeley & Ocean Aves.
HABS NJ-1105
1ph/16pg/1pc H

Long Beach Historical Society and Museum; see Holy Innocents Episcopal Church

New Jersey Coastal Heritage Trail; see Holy Innocents Episcopal Church

New Jersey Coastal Heritage Trail; see Little Egg Harbor Yacht Club

New Jersey Coastal Heritage Trail; see Pharo House

New Jersey Coastal Heritage Trail; see Sherborne Farm

New Jersey Coastal Heritage Trail; see The Log

Pharo House (New Jersey Coastal Heritage Trail)
125 Second St.
HABS NJ-1103
2ph/1pc H

Sherborne Farm (The Farm; Liberty Hall; The White House of New Jersey; New Jersey Coastal Heritage Trail)
319 Liberty Ave.
HABS NJ-1106
1ph/13pg/1pc H

The Farm; see Sherborne Farm

The Log (New Jersey Coastal Heritage Trail)
Coral St. at S. Bay Ave.
HABS NJ-1104
4pg/1pc H

The White House of New Jersey; see Sherborne Farm

BRICK VIC.

Brick Plaza (New Jersey Coastal Heritage Trail)
Chambers Bridge Rd. at St. Rt. 70
HABS NJ-1107
1ph/1pc H

New Jersey Coastal Heritage Trail; see Brick Plaza

CEDAR BRIDGE

Cedar Bridge Tavern
HABS NJ-41
HABS NJ,15- ,1-
18dr/4ph/5pg/fr L

FORKED RIVER

Forked River Game Farm (Woodmansee Estate; New Jersey Coastal Heritage Trail)
Main St. (U.S. Hwy. 9) N. of Lacey Rd.
HABS NJ-1200
3ph/1pc H

Forked River Game Farm,Gatehouse (New Jersey Coastal Heritage Trail)
U.S. Hwy. 9
HABS NJ-1200-A
1ph/1pc H

Forked River House (New Jersey Coastal Heritage Trail)
U.S. Hwy. 9
HABS NJ-1108
1ph/1pc H

New Jersey Coastal Heritage Trail; see Forked River Game Farm

New Jersey Coastal Heritage Trail; see Forked River Game Farm,Gatehouse

New Jersey Coastal Heritage Trail; see Forked River House

Woodmansee Estate; see Forked River Game Farm

HARVEY CEDARS

Harvey Cedars Bible Conference Center; see Harvey Cedars Hotel

Harvey Cedars Hotel (Harvey Cedars Bible Conference Center; New Jersey Coastal Heritage Trail)
Cedars Ave.
HABS NJ-1143
1ph/8pg/1pc H

Maris-Stella Sisters of Charity Convent Station (New Jersey Coastal Heritage Trail)
Convent St. & Long Beach Blvd.
HABS NJ-1142
1ph/1pc H

New Jersey Coastal Heritage Trail; see Harvey Cedars Hotel

New Jersey Coastal Heritage Trail; see Maris-Stella Sisters of Charity Convent Station

HERBERTSVILLE

Herbertsville,Town of (New Jersey Coastal Heritage Trail)
HABS NJ-1074
2ph/1pc H

New Jersey Coastal Heritage Trail; see Herbertsville,Town of

New Jersey Coastal Heritage Trail; see Osborn Farmhouse

Osborn Farmhouse (New Jersey Coastal Heritage Trail)
610 Herbertsville Rd.
HABS NJ-1167
2ph/1pc H

ISLAND HEIGHTS

Arbutus Lodge (House) (New Jersey Coastal Heritage Trail)
60 River Ave.
HABS NJ-1201
1ph/1pc H

English,John,House (New Jersey Coastal Heritage Trail)
236 Ocean Ave.
HABS NJ-1146
1ph/1pc H

Island Queen House (New Jesrey Coastal Heritage Trail)
70 River Ave.
HABS NJ-1145
1ph/1pc H

New Jersey Coastal Heritage Trail; see Arbutus Lodge (House)

New Jersey Coastal Heritage Trail; see English,John,House

New Jersey Coastal Heritage Trail; see Wanamaker Hall

New Jesrey Coastal Heritage Trail; see Island Queen House

Wanamaker Hall (New Jersey Coastal Heritage Trail)
E. End & Van Sant Aves.
HABS NJ-1144
1ph/17pg/1pc H

LAKEHURST VIC.

Charcoal Pits
HABS NJ-291
HABS NJ,15-LAK.V,1-
1dr/8ph/2pg/fr L

LANOKA HARBOR

Potter,Thomas,House
Murray Grove Rd.
HABS NJ-840
HABS NJ,15-LAHA,1-
18ph/1pg/2pc L

LAVALLETTE

New Jersey Coastal Heritage Trail; see Union Church of Lavalette (Interdenominational)

Union Church of Lavalette (Interdenominational) (New Jersey Coastal Heritage Trail)
25 Philadelphia Ave.
HABS NJ-1147
1ph/1pc H

MANAHAWKIN

Baptist Church (Stafford Township Historical Society; New Jersey Coastal Heritage Trail)
N. Main St. (Rt. 9) & N. Lakeshore Dr.
HABS NJ-1148
1ph/1pc H

Manahawkin Station (New Jersey Coastal Heritage Trail)
Paul King Park,W. Bay Ave & St. Rt. 72
HABS NJ-1150
1ph/1pc H

New Jersey Coastal Heritage Trail; see Baptist Church

New Jersey Coastal Heritage Trail; see Manahawkin Station

New Jersey Coastal Heritage Trail; see Stafford Avenue Bridge

New Jersey Coastal Heritage Trail; see Stone Store,Old

Stafford Avenue Bridge (New Jersey Coastal Heritage Trail)
E. end of Stafford Ave.
HAER NJ-87
2ph/1pc H

Stafford Township Historical Society; see Baptist Church

Stone Store,Old (New Jersey Coastal Heritage Trail)
Paul King Park,W. Bay Ave. & St. Rt. 72
HABS NJ-1149
1ph/1pc H

MURRAY GROVE

New Jersey Coastal Heritage Trail; see Unitarian Church

Unitarian Church (New Jersey Coastal Heritage Trail)
Church Ln. off U.S. Hwy. 9
HABS NJ-1133
1ph/1pc H

OCEAN GATE

American Telephone & Telegraph Building (New Jersey Coastal Heritage Trail)
Bayview Ave. (Rt. 617)
HABS NJ-1134
1ph/1pc H

New Jersey Coastal Heritage Trail; see American Telephone & Telegraph Building

New Jersey Coastal Heritage Trail; see Ocean Gate,Town of

Ocean Gate,Town of (New Jersey Coastal Heritage Trail)
HABS NJ-1073
1dr/1ph/1pc H

PARKERTOWN

New Jersey Coastal Heritage Trail; see Schoolhouse

Schoolhouse (New Jersey Coastal Heritage Trail)
Bay Ave.
HABS NJ-1135
2ph/1pc H

PINE BEACH

Farragut,Admiral,Academy (New Jersey Coastal Heritage Trail)
601 Riverside Dr.
HABS NJ-1160
1ph/1pc H

New Jersey Coastal Heritage Trail; see Farragut,Admiral,Academy

New Jersey Coastal Heritage Trail; see Pine Beach Chapel

New Jersey Coastal Heritage Trail; see Pine Beach,Town of

Pine Beach Chapel (New Jersey Coastal Heritage Trail)
Hillside & Huntingdon Drs.
HABS NJ-1136
1ph/1pc H

Pine Beach,Town of (New Jersey Coastal Heritage Trail)
HABS NJ-1072
2ph/1pc H

POINT PLEASANT

112 New Jersey Avenue (House) (New Jersey Coastal Heritage Trail)
HABS NJ-1137
2ph/1pc H

New Jersey Coastal Heritage Trail; see 112 New Jersey Avenue (House)

New Jersey Coastal Heritage Trail; see Point Pleasant Hardware Company

Point Pleasant Hardware Company (New Jersey Coastal Heritage Trail)
528 Arnold Ave.
HABS NJ-1138
2ph/1pc H

SEASIDE HEIGHTS

Moreland Dentzel,Floyd L.-Loof Carousel (New Jersey Coastal Heritage Trail)
Casino Pier (The Boardwalk) btw. Grant & Sherman
HABS NJ-1141
1ph/5pg H

New Jersey Coastal Heritage Trail; see Moreland Dentzel,Floyd L.-Loof Carousel

SEASIDE PARK

Jennings,Isaac,House (New Jersey Coastal Heritage Trail)
13-17 W. Central Ave.
HABS NJ-1139
1ph/1pc H

New Jersey Coastal Heritage Trail; see Jennings,Isaac,House

SEASIDE PARK VIC.

Island Beach State Park (New Jersey Coastal Heritage Trail)
Island Beach,E. of Barnegat Bay
HABS NJ-1071
2ph/1pc H

New Jersey Coastal Heritage Trail; see Island Beach State Park

SOUTH TOMS RIVER

Birdville (New Jersey Coastal Heritage Trail)
Flint Rd. at Mill St.
HABS NJ-1140
3ph/1pc H

New Jersey Coastal Heritage Trail; see Birdville

TOMS RIVER

New Jersey Coastal Heritage Trail; see Ocean County Courthouse

Ocean County Courthouse (New Jersey Coastal Heritage Trail)
118 Washington St.
HABS NJ-1117
1ph/1pc H

TUCKERTON

New Jersey Coastal Heritage Trail; see Quaker Meeting House

New Jersey Coastal Heritage Trail; see Tuckerton Emporium

New Jersey Coastal Heritage Trail; see Tuckerton Library

Quaker Meeting House (New Jersey Coastal Heritage Trail)
W. Main & N. Green Sts.
HABS NJ-1118
3ph/1pc H

Tuckerton Emporium (New Jersey Coastal Heritage Trail)
W. Main & Water Sts.
HABS NJ-1120
2ph/1pc H

Tuckerton Library (New Jersey Coastal Heritage Trail)
380 Bay Ave.
HABS NJ-1119
2ph/1pc H

WARETOWN

Cranberry Sorting House (New Jersey Coastal Heritage Trail)
29 Old Main
HABS NJ-1121
1ph/1pc H

Dugan House (New Jersey Coastal Heritage Trail)
Birdsall St. & Old Main Shore Rd.
HABS NJ-1122
1ph/1pc H

New Jersey Coastal Heritage Trail; see Cranberry Sorting House

New Jersey Coastal Heritage Trail; see Dugan House

WEST CREEK

Municipal Building; see Schoolhouse

New Jersey Coastal Heritage Trail; see Schoolhouse

New Jersey Coastal Heritage Trail; see West Creek United Methodist Church

Schoolhouse (Municipal Building; New Jersey Coastal Heritage Trail)
Division St.
HABS NJ-1123
1ph/1pc H

West Creek United Methodist Church (New Jersey Coastal Heritage Trail)
Church St.
HABS NJ-1190
1ph/1pc H

PASSAIC COUNTY

CLIFTON

Dundee Canal: Headgates,Guardlock & Upper Sections
250 Ft. NE of Randolph Ave. opposite E. Clifton
HAER NJ-45
HAER NJ,16-CLIF,5-
18ph/37pg/2pc L

Erie Railway:Clifton Station
HAER NJ-21
HAER NJ,16-CLIF,6-
4ph/1pc L

Jacobus,Peter,House
Allwood Rd.
HABS NJ-559
HABS NJ,16-CLIF,3-
9dr/3ph/3pg/fr L

Minett Varnish Kiln
Delawanna Ave.
HABS NJ-560
HABS NJ,16-CLIF,4-
6dr/4ph/5pg/fr L

Speer,John Jacobus,House (Vreeland-Speer House)
Bloomfield Ave.
HABS NJ-149
HABS NJ,16-CLIF,1-
8dr/2ph/3pg/fr L

Vanderhoof House
Weasel Brook Park
HABS NJ-328
HABS NJ,16-CLIF,2-
9dr/2ph/2pg/fr L

Vreeland-Speer House; see Speer,John Jacobus,House

HASKELL

Van Wagoner House
891 Ringwood Ave.
HABS NJ-520
HABS NJ,16-HASK,1-
12dr/2ph/3pg/fr L

HAWTHORNE

Doremus House; see Rea,John W. ,House

Knapik Inn; see Rea,John W. ,House

Lafayette Headquarters (Ryerson,Johannes,House)
Goffle Brook Park
HABS NJ-165
HABS NJ,16-HAWTH,1-
10dr/2ph/4pg/fr L

Marcellus-Vreeland House
Goffle Rd.
HABS NJ-258
HABS NJ,16-HAWTH,3-
10dr/3ph/2pg/fr L

Rea,John W. ,House (Doremus House; Knapik Inn)
675 Goffle Rd.
HABS NJ-178
HABS NJ,16-HAWTH,2-
17dr/1ph/4pg/fr L

Ryerson,Johannes,House; see Lafayette Headquarters

Van Winkle,Judge John S. ,House
868 Goffle Rd.
HABS NJ-531
HABS NJ,16-HAWTH,4-
15dr/4ph/6pg/fr L

LITTLE FALLS

Brower House
50 Paterson Ave.
HABS NJ-521
HABS NJ,16-LITFA,2-
24dr/2ph/5pg/fr L

Matches-Beattie House
53-55 Main St.
HABS NJ-164
HABS NJ,16-LITFA,1-
11dr/1ph/2pg/fr L

Matches,Robert,House
Browertown Rd.
HABS NJ-595
HABS NJ,16-LITFA,3-
12dr/3ph/3pg/fr L

LOWER PREAKNESS

Bloomsbury Manor; see Dey Mansion

Dey Mansion (Bloomsbury Manor)
199 Totowa Rd.
HABS NJ-17
HABS NJ,16-PREK,1-
26dr/14ph/5pg/1pc/fr L

MOUNTAIN VIEW

Van Duyne House
636 Fairfield Rd.
HABS NJ-464
HABS NJ,16-MOUV,1-
11dr/5ph/2pg/fr L

PASSAIC

Anderson House; see Passaic Home & Orphan Asylum

Aycrigg Mansion (Masonic Temple)
Main Ave.
HABS NJ-413
HABS NJ,16-PASA,3-
19dr/7ph/2pg/fr L

Botany Worsted Mills
Bounded by President St.,Parker & Sherman Aves.
HABS NJ-982
HABS DLC/PP-1993:NJ-5
7pg L

Botany Worsted Mills,Bag Factory
176 Parker Ave.
HABS NJ-982-B
HABS DLC/PP-1993:NJ-5
5ph/4pg/1pc L

Botany Worsted Mills,Locomotive House
30a Sherman St.
HABS NJ-982-E
HABS DLC/PP-1993:NJ-5
6ph/4pg/1pc L

Botany Worsted Mills,Waste Picker House
176 Parker Ave.
HABS NJ-982-A
HABS DLC/PP-1993:NJ-5
12ph/4pg/1pc L

Botany Worsted Mills,Wool & Waste Storage
176 Parker Ave.
HABS NJ-982-C
HABS DLC/PP-1993:NJ-5
2ph/4pg/1pc L

Botany Worsted Mills,Wool Storage Building
99 President St.
HABS NJ-982-D
HABS DLC/PP-1993:NJ-5
6ph/4pg/1pc L

95-97 Dayton Ave. (House)
95-97 Dayton Ave.
HABS NJ-977
HABS 1991(HABS):22
5ph/4pg/1pc L

77 Dayton Avenue (Apartment Building)
77 Dayton Ave.
HABS NJ-978
HABS 1991(HABS):22
6ph/4pg/1pc L

Dutch Reformed Parsonage,Old; see Van Schott House

Masonic Temple; see Aycrigg Mansion

Passaic Home & Orphan Asylum (Anderson House)
River Rd. & Lafayette Ave.
HABS NJ-811
HABS NJ,16-PASA,4-
11dr L

Van Schott House (Dutch Reformed Parsonage,Old)
125 Lexington Ave.
HABS NJ-121
HABS NJ,16-PASA,2-
6dr/3ph/3pg/fr L

PATERSON

Allied Textile Printers (Gun Mill,The)
Van Houten & Mill Sts.
HAER NJ-17
HAER NJ,16-PAT,6-
7ph/7pg/1pc L

Barbour Flax Spinning Company
Spruce & Barbour Sts.
HAER NJ-11
HAER NJ,16-PAT,7-
1ph/7pg/1pc L

Barbour Flax Spinning Company,Granite Mill
Spruce & Barbour Sts.
HAER NJ-11-A
HAER NJ,16-PAT,7-A-
3ph/1pc L

Barbour Flax Spinning Company,Machine Shop
Spruce & Barbour Sts.
HAER NJ-11-C
HAER NJ,16-PAT,7-C-
2ph/1pc L

Barbour Flax Spinning Company,Spruce Street Mill
Spruce & Barbour Sts.
HAER NJ-11-B
HAER NJ,16-PAT,7-B-
2ph/1pc L

Barkalow House
22 Van Houten St.
HABS NJ-327
HABS NJ,16-PAT,2-
10dr/2ph/2pg/fr L

City of Paterson Board of Health; see Public School No. 2

Cooke Locomotive & Machine Works; see Danforth Locomotive & Machine Co. ,Blacksmith Shop

Cooke Locomotive & Machine Works; see Danforth Locomotive & Machine Co. ,Erecting Shop

Cooke Locomotive & Machine Works; see Danforth Locomotive & Machine Company

Danforth Locomotive & Machine Co. ,Blacksmith Shop (Danforth,Cooke, & Co.; Cooke Locomotive & Machine Works)
Market St.
HAER NJ-8-B
HAER NJ,16-PAT,8-B-
8ph/2pc L

Danforth Locomotive & Machine Co. ,Erecting Shop (Danforth,Cooke, & Co.; Cooke Locomotive & Machine Works)
Market St.
HAER NJ-8-A
HAER NJ,16-PAT,8-A-
1ph/1pc L

Danforth Locomotive & Machine Company (Danforth,Cooke, & Company; Cooke Locomotive & Machine Works)
Market St.
HAER NJ-8
HAER NJ,16-PAT,8-
5ph/11pg/1pc L

Danforth,Cooke, & Co.; see Danforth Locomotive & Machine Co. ,Blacksmith Shop

Danforth,Cooke, & Co.; see Danforth Locomotive & Machine Co. ,Erecting Shop

Danforth,Cooke, & Company; see Danforth Locomotive & Machine Company

Dolphin Jute Mill; see Dolphin Manufacturing Company

Dolphin Manufacturing Company (Dolphin Jute Mill)
Spruce & Barbour Sts.
HAER NJ-12
HAER NJ,16-PAT,9-
3ph/5pg/1pc L

Erie Railway:Paterson Station
HAER NJ-38
HAER NJ,16-PAT,10-
1ph/1pc L

Essex Mill
Mill & Van Houten Sts.
HAER NJ-6
HAER NJ,16-PAT,11-
3dr/3ph/7pg/1pc/fr L

Franklin Manufacturing Company,Waverley Mill
Van Houten & Mill Sts.
HABS 3
HAER NJ-7
HABS/HAER J,16-PAT,12-
3ph/4pg/1pc/fr L

Godwin Mill,Boiler & Engine House (Hamil Mill)
Mill & Market Sts.
HAER NJ-14
HAER NJ,16-PAT,13-
1ph/4pg/1pc/fr L

Grant Locomotive Works
Market & Spruce Sts.
HAER NJ-9
HAER NJ,16-PAT,14-
7ph/5pg/2pc L

Great Falls/S. U. M. Historic District (Society for the Estab. of Useful Manufactures)
Oliver St.
HAER NJ-1
HAER NJ,16-PAT,15-
5dr/34ph/1pg/3pc L

Great Falls/S. U. M. Power Canal System
HAER NJ-2
HAER NJ,16-PAT,16-
37ph/51pg/3pc/fr L

Gun Mill,The; see Allied Textile Printers

Hamil Mill; see Godwin Mill,Boiler & Engine House

Hartley,Bernard,House
158-160 W. Broadway
HABS NJ-505
HABS NJ,16-PAT,4-
13dr/4ph/2pg/fr L

Industry Mill
Van Houten & Prospect St.
HAER NJ-15
HAER NJ,16-PAT,17-
6ph/5pg/1pc L

Ivanhoe Mill,Wheelhouse
Spruce & Market Sts.
HAER NJ-10
HAER NJ,16-PAT,18-
6ph/6pg/1pc L

Morrisse Building
55 Ward St. & 312 Main St.
HABS NJ-945
HABS 1991(HABS):22
9ph/12pg/1pc L

179-181 Oliver Street (Commercial Building)
179-181 Oliver St.
HABS NJ-953
HABS 1991(HABS):22
1ph/3pg/1pc L

144 Oliver Street (House)
144 Oliver St.
HABS NJ-946
HABS 1991(HABS):22
1ph/3pg/1pc L

146 Oliver Street (House)
146 Oliver St.
HABS NJ-947
HABS 1991(HABS):22
1ph/3pg/1pc L

150-152 Oliver Street (House)
150-152 Oliver St.
HABS NJ-948
HABS 1991(HABS):22
1ph/3pg/1pc L

169 Oliver Street (House)
169 Oliver St.
HABS NJ-949
HABS 1991(HABS):22
1ph/3pg/1pc L

171 Oliver Street (House)
171 Oliver St.
HABS NJ-950
HABS 1991(HABS):22
1ph/3pg/1pc L

173 Oliver Street (House)
173 Oliver St.
HABS NJ-951
HABS 1991(HABS):22
1ph/3pg/1pc L

177 Oliver Street, Rear (House)
177 Oliver St.
HABS NJ-952-A
HABS 1991(HABS):22
1ph/3pg/1pc L

177 Oliver Street,Front (House)
177 Oliver St.
HABS NJ-952
HABS 1991(HABS):22
1ph/3pg/1pc L

Passaic County Jail & Sheriff's House
Main St.
HABS NJ-381
HABS NJ,16-PAT,3-
19dr/5ph/2pg/fr L

Phoenix Mill
Van Houten & Cianci Sts.
HAER NJ-4
HAER NJ,16-PAT,19-
2dr/7ph/6pg/2pc/fr L

Public School No. 2 (City of Paterson Board of Health)
Mill & Passaic Sts.
HABS NJ-927
HABS NJ,16-PAT,24-
5ph/2pg/1pc L

Rogers Locomotive & Machine Works
Spruce & Market Sts.
HAER NJ-3
HAER NJ,16-PAT,20-
1dr/9ph/2pg/1pc L

Rogers Locomotive & Machine Works,Admin. Building
Spruce & Market Sts.
HAER NJ-3-D
HAER NJ,16-PAT,10-D-
1dr/3ph/1pg/2pc/fr L

Rogers Locomotive & Machine Works,Erecting Shop
Spruce & Market Sts.
HAER NJ-3-A
HAER NJ,16-PAT,20-A-
3dr/7ph/1pg/1pc/fr L

Rogers Locomotive & Machine Works,Fitting Shop
Spruce & Market Sts.
HAER NJ-3-B
HAER NJ,16-PAT,20-B-
2dr/4ph/1pg/1pc/fr L

Rogers Locomotive & Machine Works,Millwright Shop
Spruce & Market Sts.
HAER NJ-3-C
HAER NJ,16-PAT,20-C-
2dr/1ph/1pg/1pc/fr L

Rosen Mill; see Union Works

S. U. M. Hydroelectric Plant
McBride Ave.
HAER NJ-16
HAER NJ,16-PAT,21-
6ph/4pg/1pc L

Society for the Estab. of Useful Manufactures; see Great Falls/S. U. M. Historic District

St. Michael's Sisters' Home; see 45-47 Ward Street (House)

Thompson,Daniel,House
11 Mill St.
HABS NJ-652
HABS NJ,16-PAT,5-
15dr/4ph/2pg/fr L

Todd & Rafferty Machine Company (Todd Mill)
Van Houten St. & McGee Alley
HAER NJ-5
HAER NJ,16-PAT,22-
3dr/7ph/11pg/2pc/fr L

Todd Mill; see Todd & Rafferty Machine Company

Union Works (Rosen Mill)
Spruce & Market Sts.
HAER NJ-13
HAER NJ,16-PAT,23-
2ph/5pg/1pc L

Van Houten House
Totowa Ave.
HABS NJ-120
HABS NJ,16-PAT,1-
9dr/6ph/3pg/fr L

30 Ward Street (House)
30 Ward St.
HABS NJ-942
HABS 1991(HABS):22
1ph/3pg/1pc L

45-47 Ward Street (House) (St. Michael's Sisters' Home)
45-47 Ward St.
HABS NJ-943
HABS 1991(HABS):22
7ph/12pg/1pc L

49-53 Ward Street (House)
49-53 Ward St.
HABS NJ-944
HABS 1991(HABS):22
2ph/4pg/1pc L

PATERSON VIC.

Van Riper House
HABS NJ-218
HABS NJ,16-PAT.V,1-
10dr/1ph/2pg/fr L

POMPTON FALLS VIC.

Colfax-Dawes House
Paterson-Hamburg Turnpike
HABS NJ-123
HABS NJ,16-POMLA.V,2-
13dr/1ph/2pg/fr L

Schuyler-Colfax House
Paterson-Hamburg Turnpike
HABS NJ-122
HABS NJ,16-POMLA.V,1-
16dr/6ph/4pg/fr L

PREAKNESS

Laruwe House; see Van Saun House

Van Saun House (Laruwe House)
Preakness Ave. & Singac Brook
HABS NJ-166
HABS NJ,16-PREK,2-
8dr/1ph/3pg/fr L

RINGWOOD

Ringwood Manor (Ryerson House)
HABS NJ-12-A
HABS NJ,16-RING,1-
11ph/2pg/1ct L

Ringwood Manor,Smithy
HABS NJ-12
HABS NJ,16-RING,1A-
1dr/2ph/fr L

Ryerson House; see Ringwood Manor

TOTOWA

Van Allen-Garretson House
Totowa Rd.
HABS NJ-480
HABS NJ,16-TOTO,1-
12dr/6ph/3pg/fr L

UPPER PREAKNESS

Merselis-Van Houten House
Paterson-Hamburg Pike
HABS NJ-257
HABS NJ,16-POMLA.V,3-
20dr/3ph/2pg/fr L

WANAQUE

Lines,Conrad House
Ringwood & Highland Aves.
HABS NJ-512
HABS NJ,16-WANA,1-
12dr/4ph/4pg/fr L

WAYNE

Fosberg-Sisco House
3 Edgemont Rd.
HABS NJ-870
HABS NJ,16-WAYN,1-
10ph/2pg/1pc L

Jacobus,Cornelius R. ,Blacksmith Shop
110 Boonton Rd.
HABS NJ-871
HABS NJ,16-WAYN,2-
4ph/2pg/1pc L

Sears House
958 Rt. 23
HABS NJ-872
HABS NJ,16-WAYN,3-
10ph/2pg/1pc L

WEST MILFORD

Long Pond Ironworks Historic District; see Ward-Ryerson-Patterson House

Rydner House; see Whritenour House

Ward-Ryerson-Patterson House (Long Pond Ironworks Historic District)
1266 Greenwood Lake Turnpike
HABS NJ-923
HABS NJ,16-MILFW,1-
12ph/22pg/1pc/fr L

Whritenour House (Rydner House)
1293 Greenwood Lake Turnpike
HABS NJ-922
HABS NJ,16-MILFW,2-
17ph/19pg/2pc L

SALEM COUNTY

ALDINE VIC.

Gamble Farmhouse; see Sinnickson,Thomas,House

Newkirk-Ballingers Mill & Houses
Tonard Rd.
HABS NJ-139
HABS NJ,17-ALD.V,1-
12dr/7ph/4pg/fr L

Sinnickson,Thomas,House (Gamble Farmhouse)
HABS NJ-638
HABS NJ,17-ALD.V,2-
10dr/4ph/5pg/fr L

ALLOWAY

Alloway Tavern
Main & Greenwich Sts.
HABS NJ-306
HABS NJ,17-ALLO,3-
16dr/3ph/2pg/fr L

Evans House; see Holme-Reeves House

Fogg-Hopkins House
HABS NJ-262-D
HABS NJ,17-ALLO,2-
1dr/1ph/2pg/fr L

Holme-Reeves House (Evans House; Oak Log Cabin)
HABS NJ-262-A
HABS NJ,17-ALLO,1-
3dr/1ph/2pg/fr L

Oak Log Cabin; see Holme-Reeves House

ALLOWAY VIC.

Dickinson House (Oakland Station)
HABS NJ-243
HABS NJ,17-OAKL,1-
10dr/4ph/2pg/fr L

Emmell Log Cabin
Elmer Rd.
HABS NJ-262-B
HABS NJ,17-ALLO.V,2-
3dr/2ph/2pg/fr L

Oakford,William,House
Telegraph & Greenwich Rds.
HABS NJ-127
HABS NJ,17-ALLO.V,1-
8dr/5ph/2pg/1pc/fr L

Oakland Station; see Dickinson House

AUBURN

Scull House
Auburn Rd.
HABS NJ-214
HABS NJ,17-AUB,1-
29dr/2ph/2pg/fr L

DARETOWN

Pittsgrove Presbyterian Church,Old
Aldine Rd.
HABS NJ-213
HABS NJ,17-DARTO,1-
6dr/1ph/3pg/fr L

ELSINBORO

Nicholson,Abel,House
HABS NJ-305
HABS NJ,17-HANBR.V,3-
22dr/11ph/2pg/fr L

ELSINBORO TWP.

Morris-Goodwin House
Fort Elfsboro Rd.
HABS NJ-690
HABS NJ,17-SAL.V,6-
23dr/10ph/5pg/fr L

FRIESBURG

Mench-Reall Log Cabin
HABS NJ-262-C
HABS NJ,17-FRIBU.V,1-
1dr/2ph/2pg/fr L

HANCOCK'S BRIDGE VIC

New Bridge Road Alloways Creek Bridge (NJHC Trail)
Spanning Alloways Creek on New Bridge Road
HAER NJ-88
3ph/2pg/1pc H

NJHC Trail; see New Bridge Road Alloways Creek Bridge

HANCOCKS BRIDGE

Cedar Plank House
(Tyler,William,House)
Locust Island Rd. & Main St.
HABS NJ-106
HABS NJ,17-HANBR,2-
2dr/2ph/2pg/fr L

Hancock House
Loucst Island Rd. & Main St.
HABS NJ-54
HABS NJ,17-HANBR,1-
19dr/7ph/5pg/2ct/fr L

Tyler,William,House; see Cedar Plank House

HANCOCKS BRIDGE VIC.

Chambless,Nathaniel,House (New Jersey Coastal Heritage Trail)
HABS NJ-1202
2ph/3pg/1pc H

New Jersey Coastal Heritage Trail; see Chambless,Nathaniel,House

LOWER ALLOWAYS CREEK

Denn,John Maddox,House
HABS NJ-260
HABS NJ,17-HANBR.V,2-
7dr/5ph/3pg/fr L

Oakford,John & Hannah,House
HABS NJ-349
HABS NJ,17-HANBR.V,4-
6dr/5ph/2pg/fr L

Stretch-Padgett House
HABS NJ-234
HABS NJ,17-HANBR.V,1-
7dr/2ph/2pg/fr L

LOWER PENNS NECK

Goslin,Leon,House; see Johnson-Goslin House

Johnson-Goslin House
(Goslin,Leon,House)
HABS NJ-347
HABS NJ,17-HARVI.V,1-
14dr/5ph/3pg/fr L

MANNINGTON VIC.

Fox,Jacob,House
HABS NJ-248
HABS NJ,17-MANT.V,1-
9dr/5ph/3pg/fr L

PITTSGROVE VIC.

Richman,Michael,House
HABS NJ-350
HABS NJ,17-PIT.V,1-
2ph/4pg L

QUINTON VIC.

Tyler,William,House
HABS NJ-128
HABS NJ,17-QUINT.V,1-
14dr/12ph/2pg/fr L

SALEM

Bradway House (Governor's House; Lighthouse)
32 W. Broadway
HABS NJ-379
HABS NJ,17-SAL,10-
1ph/7pg L

City of Salem (NJCH Trail)
Adjacent to Salem River
HABS NJ-1166
2ph/4pg/1pc H

City of Salem Municipal Building; see Salem National Banking Company

Clement-Redstrake House
West Broadway
HABS NJ-377
HABS NJ,17-SAL,9-
11dr/4ph/2pg/fr L

First Prebyterian Church (New Jersey Coastal Heritage Trail)
88 Market St.
HABS NJ-1154
2ph/1pg/1pc H

Friends Meetinghouse
E. Broadway & Walnut St.
HABS NJ-77
HABS NJ,17-SAL,1-
10dr/5ph/2pg/fr L

Governor's House; see Bradway House

Grant,Alexander,House
81-83 Market St.
HABS NJ-78
HABS NJ,17-SAL,6-
30dr/7ph/2pg/fr L

Hampton,John T.,House (New Jersey Coastal Heritage Trail)
67 Market St.
HABS NJ-1204
3ph/2pg/1pc H

Hancock,Morris,House
314 E. Broadway
HABS NJ-591
HABS NJ,17-SAL,12-
1ph/2pg L

Johnson House
90 Market St.
HABS NJ-219
HABS NJ,17-SAL,7-
68dr/6ph/3pg/fr L

Jones,John,Law Office
W. Broadway & New Market St.
HABS NJ-261
HABS NJ,17-SAL,8-
2dr/5ph/2pg/fr L

Keasby
HABS NJ-804
HABS NJ,17-SAL,2-
1ph/1pg L

Lighthouse; see Bradway House

Mount Pisgah A.M.E. Church (New Jersey Coastal Heritage Trail)
15 Yorke St. (County Rd. 658)
HABS NJ-1156
1ph/1pg/1pc H

New Jersey Coastal Heritage Trail; see First Prebyterian Church

New Jersey Coastal Heritage Trail; see Hampton,John T.,House

New Jersey Coastal Heritage Trail; see Mount Pisgah A.M.E. Church

New Jersey Coastal Heritage Trail; see Salem Free Public Library

New Jersey Coastal Heritage Trail; see Salem National Banking Company

New Jersey Coastal Heritage Trail; see Salem Oak Diner

New Jersey Coastal Heritage Trail; see Sharp,William S.,House

NJCH Trail; see City of Salem

Salem Free Public Library
(Tyler,John,Building; New Jersey Coastal Heritage Trail)
112 W. Broadway (St. Rt. 49)
HABS NJ-1155
1ph/1pg/1pc H

Salem National Banking Company
(City of Salem Municipal Building; New Jersey Coastal Heritage Trail)
Moved to New Market St.
HABS NJ-1158
1ph/2pg/1pc H

Salem Oak Diner (New Jersey Coastal Heritage Trail)
113 W. Broadway (St. Rt. 49)
HABS NJ-1157
1ph/1pg/1pc H

Sharp,William S.,House (New Jersey Coastal Heritage Trail)
31 Market St.
HABS NJ-1203
1ph/2pg/1pc H

Sinnickson House
HABS NJ-806
HABS NJ,17-SAL,13-
1ph/1pg L

Thompson,Hedge,House
HABS NJ-805
HABS NJ,17-SAL,3-
1ph/1pg L

Tyler,John,Building; see Salem Free Public Library

Victorian Cottage
HABS NJ-803
HABS NJ,17-SAL,4-
1ph/1pg L

Worledge,John,House
323 E. Broadway
HABS NJ-383
HABS NJ,17-SAL,11-
13dr/4ph/2pg/fr L

SALEM VIC.

Holmeland; see Holmes,Benjamin,House

Holmes,Benjamin,House (Holmeland)
HABS NJ-481
HABS NJ,17-SAL.V,5-
20dr/10ph/2pg/fr L

Lambson Tavern
HABS NJ-384
HABS NJ,17-SAL.V,4-
2ph/2pg L

Mecum,William,House
HABS NJ-233
HABS NJ,17-SAL.V,1-
1ph/2pg L

Nicholson,Samuel,House
Oakwood Beach Rd.
HABS NJ-259
HABS NJ,17-SAL.V,2-
8dr/3ph/2pg L

Pledger House
HABS NJ-385
HABS NJ,17-MANT.V,2-
13dr/9ph/3pg/fr L

Smith,Richard,House
HABS NJ-348
HABS NJ,17-SAL.V,3-
1ph/2pg L

SHARPTOWN VIC.

Robinson-Kiger House
HABS NJ-445
HABS NJ,17-SHARP.V,1-
10dr/8ph/4pg/fr L

WOODSTOWN

Clawson House (Shinn House)
68 N. Main St.
HABS NJ-461
HABS NJ,17-WOOTO,1-
18dr/fr L

Shinn House; see Clawson House

WOODSTOWN VIC.

Brick,Richard,House; see Dolbow House

Dolbow House (Brick,Richard,House)
Compromise Rd.
HABS NJ-615
HABS NJ,17-WOOTO.V,4-
19dr/9ph/5pg/fr L

Pissant House
HABS NJ-346
HABS NJ,17-WOOTO.V,2-
6ph/2pg L

Seven Star Tavern
HABS NJ-126
HABS NJ,17-WOOTO.V,1-
19dr/16ph/3pg/fr L

WOODSTOWN VICINITY

Bassett,Samuel & Anne,House
HABS NJ-355
HABS NJ,17-WOOTO.V,3-
21dr/2ph/2pg/fr L

SOMERSET COUNTY

BASKING RIDGE

Presbyterian Church
Finley Ave.
HABS NJ-97
HABS NJ,18-BASK,1-
17dr/5ph/4pg/fr L

Washington Tavern
HABS NJ-707
HABS NJ,18-BASK,2-
2ph L

BERNARDS TWP.

McMurtry's Saw Mill
Hardscrabble Rd.
HABS NJ-533
HABS NJ,18- ,2-
10dr/4ph/4pg/fr L

BERNARDSVILLE

Van Doren's Mill
HABS NJ-67
HABS NJ,18-BERVI,1-
5dr/5ph/2pg/fr L

BOUND BROOK VIC.

Island Farm; see Smock-Hodge House

Kells Hall; see Smock-Hodge House

Schenck-Polhemus House
Easton Tpk. Rd.
HABS NJ-524
HABS NJ,18-BOUB.V,3-
17dr/4ph/5pg/fr L

Smock-Hodge House (Kells Hall; Island Farm)
HABS NJ-525
HABS NJ,18-BOUB.V,4-
17dr/4ph/14pg/fr L

BOUND BROOK VICINITY

Van Horn,Philip,House
Somerset Ave.
HABS NJ-523
HABS NJ,18-BOUB.V,2-
14dr/4ph/16pg/fr L

BRIDGEWATER TWP.

Finderne Avenue Bridge
County Rt. 533,spanning RR tracks
HAER NJ-57
HAER NJ,18-BRIWA,1-
6ph/1pg/1pc L

EAST MILLSTONE

Franklin House (Hotel); see Van Liew House

Van Liew House (Franklin House (Hotel))
Amwell Rd.
HABS NJ-648
HABS NJ,18-MILE,1-
16dr/4ph/6pg/fr L

EAST MILLSTONE VIC.

Delaware & Raritan Canal: Six Mile Run Culvert
.2 mi. S of Blackwells Mills Rd.
HAER NJ-67
HAER NJ,18-MILE.V,1-
4ph/8pg/2pc L

Delaware & Raritan Canal: Ten Mile Run Culvert
1.5 mi. S of Blackwells Rd.
HAER NJ-68
HAER NJ,18-MILE.V,2-
8ph/8pg/2pc L

FINDERNE VIC.

Van Veghten House
HABS NJ-661
HABS NJ,18-FIND.V,1-
12dr/4ph/13pg/fr L

FRANKFORT

Du Bois,Abraham,House
HABS NJ-334
HABS NJ,18-FRAFO,1-
10dr/2ph/8pg/fr L

FRANKLIN PARK

Voorhees House; see Wyckoff,Jacobus,House

Wyckoff,Jacobus,House (Voorhees House)
Lincoln Hwy. (Countyline Rd.)
HABS NJ-447
HABS NJ,18-----,1-
13dr/5ph/2pg/fr L

LIBERTY CORNER

Compton House; see De Mott,William F. ,House

Compton House (House,Old Stone)
Valley Rd.
HABS NJ-247
HABS NJ,18-LIBCO,2-
11dr/7ph/5pg/fr L

Documentation: **ct** color transparencies **dr** measured drawings **fr** field records
pc photograph captions **pg** pages of text **ph** photographs

De Mott,William F. ,House (Compton House)
Valley Rd.
HABS NJ-185
HABS NJ,18-LIBCO,1-
12dr/4ph/4pg/fr L

House,Old Stone; see Compton House

LIBERTY CORNER VIC.

Annin-Smalley House
Valley Rd.
HABS NJ-240
HABS NJ,18-LIBCO.V,1-
13dr/3ph/4pg/fr L

MIDDLEBUSH VIC.

Hageman,Aaron,House
Cortelyou Lane
HABS NJ-620
HABS NJ,18-MID.V,1-
14dr/6ph/6pg/fr L

MILLSTONE

Dutch Reformed Church
Amwell Rd. & Main St.
HABS NJ-295
HABS NJ,18-MIL,2-
13dr/3ph/4pg/fr L

Van Doren,John,House (Washington's Headquarters)
HABS NJ-293
HABS NJ,18-MIL,1-
8ph/3pg L

Washington's Headquarters; see Van Doren,John,House

NESHANIC STATION

Bridge C 0601; see Neshanic Station Lenticular Truss Bridge

Neshanic Station Bridge; see Neshanic Station Lenticular Truss Bridge

Neshanic Station Lenticular Truss Bridge (Neshanic Station Bridge; Bridge C 0601)
State Rt. 567,spanning S. Branch of Raritan River
HAER NJ-31
HAER NJ,18-NESTA,1-
18ph/2pg/2pc/9ct/fr L

NEW BRUNSWICK VIC.

Suydam House; see Van Wickle,Symen,House

Van Wickle,Symen,House (Suydam House)
Easton Tpk.
HABS NJ-479
HABS NJ,18-BOUB.V,1-
12dr/4ph/4pg/fr L

PLUCKEMIN

Fenner,John,House
HABS NJ-188
HABS NJ,18-PLUK,1-
10dr/3ph/4pg/fr L

RARITAN

Cornell Homestead (Northwood)
Somerset St.
HABS NJ-333
HABS NJ,18-RAR,2-
27dr/3ph/2pg/fr L

Frelinghuysen,Gen. John,House
54 E. Somerset St.
HABS NJ-332
HABS NJ,18-RAR,1-
19dr/5ph/2pg/1pc/fr L

Northwood; see Cornell Homestead

ROCKY HILL

Berrien,Judge John,House (Rockingham; Washington's Headquarters)
Rocky Hill Rd.
HABS NJ-18
HABS NJ,18-ROHI,1-
29dr/7ph/5pg/fr L

Berrien,Peter,House
Old Rocky Hill Rd.
HABS NJ-91
HABS NJ,18-ROHI,2-
16dr/4ph/3pg/fr L

Rockingham; see Berrien,Judge John,House

Washington's Headquarters; see Berrien,Judge John,House

S. MIDDLEBUSH

Nevius,David,House (Voorhees,Jacques,House)
HABS NJ-673
HABS NJ,18-MID.V,2-
17dr/8ph/6pg/fr L

Stoothoff,Cornelius,House (Suydam House)
County Rd. 31
HABS NJ-674
HABS NJ,18-MID.V,3-
10dr/4ph/6pg/fr L

Suydam House; see Stoothoff,Cornelius,House

Voorhees,Jacques,House; see Nevius,David,House

SOMERVILLE

Dutch Parsonage,Old; see Frelinghuysen Parsonage

Frelinghuysen Parsonage (Dutch Parsonage,Old)
Washington Place
HABS NJ-294
HABS NJ,18-SOMVI,2-
14dr/3ph/3pg/fr L

Lindsley,John,House
10 W. End Ave.
HABS NJ-374
HABS NJ,18-SOMVI,3-
28dr/3ph/2pg/fr L

Wallace House (Washington Headquarters)
Washington Place
HABS NJ-20
HABS NJ,18-SOMVI,1-
13dr/5ph/3pg/fr L

Washington Headquarters; see Wallace House

SOUTH BOUND BROOK

Staats-Latourette; see Staats,Abraham,House

Staats,Abraham,House (Staats-Latourette; Von Steuben,Baron,Headquarters)
Canal Rd. (165 Main St.)
HABS NJ-57
HABS NJ,18-BOUBS,1-
17dr/3ph/4pg/fr L

Von Steuben,Baron,Headquarters; see Staats,Abraham,House

SUSSEX COUNTY

FLATBROOKVILLE VIC.

Smith-Rosenkrans House
Old Mine Rd.
HABS NJ-812
HABS NJ,19-FLABRO.V,1-
11dr/11ph/8pg/1pc/fr L

HAINESVILLE VIC.

Nyce-Depue Farm
Old Mine Rd.
HABS NJ-737
HABS NJ,19-HAIN.V,1-
9dr/9ph/8pg/1pc/fr L

HAMBURG

Haines,Gov. ,Mansion (Sharp House; Wheatsworth Inn)
HABS NJ-278
HABS NJ,19-HAMB,1-
19dr/4ph/2pg/fr L

Sharp House; see Haines,Gov. ,Mansion

Wheatsworth Inn; see Haines,Gov. ,Mansion

HOPATCONG VIC.

Ennes,William,House
Old Mine Rd.
HABS NJ-431
HABS NJ,19-HOPAT.V,1-
4dr/3ph/10pg/1pc/fr L

Morris Canal,Scotch Turbine
HAER NJ-29-L
HAER NJ,21-PHIL,1-L-
3ph/1pg/1pc L

Westbrook-Bell House
Old Mine Rd.
HABS NJ-435
HABS NJ,19-HOPAT.V,2-
6dr/6ph/9pg/1pc/fr L

MILLVILLE VIC.

Shimer,Jacob,House
Old Mine Rd.
HABS NJ-818
HABS NJ,19-MOGU.V,5-
4dr/5ph/6pg/1pc/fr L

MONTAGUE

Clark-Herman House (House,Brick; Hotel,Brick)
HABS NJ-437
HABS NJ,19-MONT,1-
1ph/2pg L

Hotel,Brick; see Clark-Herman House

House,Brick; see Clark-Herman House

MONTAGUE VIC.

Everitt House
Old Mine Rd.
HABS NJ-823
HABS NJ,19-MOGU.V,1-
2ph/3pg/1pc L

Fort Namanock; see Westbrook,Cornelius,House

Foster-Armstrong Farm
Old Mine Rd.
HABS NJ-817
HABS NJ,19-MOGU.V,2-
10dr/15ph/8pg/2pc/fr L

Foster-Armstrong Farm,Barn
Old Mine Rd.
HABS NJ-817-A
HABS NJ,19-MOGU.V,2-A-
2ph/1pc L

Montague Ferry Keeper's House
Old Bridge Rd.
HABS NJ-821
HABS NJ,19-MOGU.V,3-
3ph/3pg/1pc L

Westbrook,Cornelius,House (Fort Namanock)
Old Mine Rd.
HABS NJ-741
HABS NJ,19-MOGU.V,4-
1ph/1pg/1pc L

SMITH FERRY VIC.

Knight Farm
Old Mine Rd.
HABS NJ-814
HABS NJ,19-SMIF.V,1-
6pg L

Knight Farm,Corn Crib
HABS NJ-814-A
HABS NJ,19-SMIF.V,1-A-
2dr/3ph/1pc/fr L

WALLPACK CENTER

Wallpack Center
HABS NJ-827
HABS NJ,19-WALPAC,1-
1ph/1pc L

WALLPACK CENTER VIC.

Hull,David R. ,Farm; see Shoemaker,Daniel,Farm

Shoemaker,Daniel,Farm (Hull,David R. ,Farm)
Mountain Rd.
HABS NJ-820
HABS NJ,19-WALPAC.V,1-
1ph/5pg/1pc/fr L

Shoemaker,Daniel,Farm,House
HABS NJ-820-A
HABS NJ,19-WALPAC.V,1-A-
11dr/5ph/1pc/fr L

Shoemaker,Daniel,Farm,Springhouse
HABS NJ-820-B
HABS NJ,19-WALPAC.V,1-B-
3dr/2ph/1pc/fr L

Snable-Rundle House
Old Mine Rd.
HABS NJ-828
HABS NJ,19-WALPAC.V,2-
2ph/3pg/1pc L

Van Campen Inn; see Van Campen,Isaac,House

Van Campen-Dewitt Barn (Van Campen,Isaac,Barn)
HABS NJ-736
HABS NJ,19-WALPAC.V,3-
6dr/6ph/8pg/1pc/fr L

Van Campen,Isaac,Barn; see Van Campen-Dewitt Barn

Van Campen,Isaac,House (Van Campen Inn)
Old Mine Rd.
HABS NJ-436
HABS NJ,19-SHAP.V,1-
14dr/15ph/15pg/2pc/fr L

WANTAGE

Titsworth House
State Hwy. 32
HABS NJ-433
HABS NJ,19-SUSX.V,1-
10dr/2ph/2pg/fr L

WATERLOO VIC.

Morris Canal
HAER NJ-29-J
HAER NJ,21-PHIL,1-J-
6ph/1pg/1pc L

Morris Canal,Cassedy's Store
HAER NJ-29-K
HAER NJ,21-PHIL,1-K-
3ph/1pg/1pc L

UNION COUNTY

CRANFORD

Crane House
124 Union Ave,N.
HABS NJ-189
HABS NJ,20-CRANF,1-
4dr/2ph/2pg/fr L

ELIZABETH

Belcher,Gov. ,Mansion
1046 E. Jersey St.
HABS NJ-13
HABS NJ,20-ELI,6-
13dr/7ph/5pg/fr L

Boudinot Mansion (Boxwood Hall)
1073 E. Jersey Ave.
HABS NJ-476
HABS NJ,20-ELI,11-
35dr/11ph/25pg/2ct/fr L

Boxwood Hall; see Boudinot Mansion

Carteret Arms (Thomas,Robinson House)
16 S. Broad St.
HABS NJ-66
HABS NJ,20-ELI,7-
10dr/2ph/11pg/fr L

Chateau,Old; see Jouet,Cavalier,Mansion

Crane,Nathaniel,House
HABS NJ-418
HABS NJ,20-ELI,10-
2pg L

First Presbyterian Church
Broad St.
HABS NJ-21
HABS NJ,20-ELI,1-
8dr/3ph/3pg/fr L

Hampton House; see St. John's Church,Parsonage

Jouet,Cavalier,Mansion (Chateau,Old)
HABS NJ-2
HABS NJ,20-ELI,5-
7dr/4ph/8pg/fr L

Magie House
330 Elmora Ave.
HABS NJ-351
HABS NJ,20-ELI,9-
14dr/4ph/2pg/fr L

Singer Manufacturing Company (Singer Sewing Machine Manufacturing Company)
321 First St.
HAER NJ-51
HAER NJ,20-ELI,13-
15ph/20pg/1pc L

Singer Sewing Machine Manufacturing Company; see Singer Manufacturing Company

South Broad Street Bridge
Spanning Elizabeth River
HAER NJ-39
HAER NJ,20-ELI,14-
12ph/52pg/1pc L

St. John's Church,Parsonage (Hampton House)
633 Pearl St.
HABS NJ-672
HABS NJ,20-ELI,12-
39dr/10ph/4pg/fr L

Thomas,Robinson House; see Carteret Arms

Wilcox House
1000 Magie Ave.
HABS NJ-286
HABS NJ,20-ELI,8-
14dr/3ph/3pg/fr L

FANWOOD

Fanwood Station,New Jersey Transit Shelter; see Fanwood Station,South Side Waiting Room

Fanwood Station,South Side Waiting Room (Fanwood Station,New Jersey Transit Shelter)
238 North Ave., Raritan Valley Line
HABS NJ-941
HABS NJ,20-FANWO,1-
18ph/9pg/2pc L

MOUNTAINSIDE

Williams,Smith,House
Springfield Rd.
HABS NJ-86
HABS NJ,20-MOUSI,1-
16dr/3ph/3pg/fr L

NEW PROVIDENCE

Presbyterian Church
Springfield Ave. & Passaic St.
HABS NJ-297
HABS NJ,20-NEWP,1-
14dr/4ph/2pg/fr L

PLAINFIELD

Plainfield Friend's Meetinghouse
Watchung Ave. & East Third St.
HABS NJ-142
HABS NJ,20-PLAFI,1-
18dr/2ph/6pg/fr L

RAHWAY

Lufberry Homestead
30 E. Grand Ave.
HABS NJ-329
HABS NJ,20-RAH,2-
21dr/4ph/2pg/fr L

Merchant and Drovers Tavern (Von Tuyl Tavern)
Saint George's & Westfield Aves.
HABS NJ-36
HABS NJ,20-RAH,1-
11dr/6ph/2pg/fr L

Von Tuyl Tavern; see Merchant and Drovers Tavern

RAHWAY VIC.

Rahway River Park,Swimming Pool
Rahway River Park
HAER NJ-55
HAER NJ,20-RAH.V,1-
2ph/2pg/1pc L

SCOTCH PLAINS

Baker House
2511 Mountain Ave. & Jerusalem Rd.
HABS NJ-491
HABS NJ,20-SCOPL,4-
15dr/4ph/2pg/fr L

Baptist Parsonage
347 Park Ave.
HABS NJ-419
HABS NJ,20-SCOPL,3-
1ph/2pg L

Frazee House
Front St.
HABS NJ-415
HABS NJ,20-SCOPL,2-
1ph/2pg L

Historic Inn,Old; see Stanberry,Recompense,Inn

Stanberry,Recompense,Inn (Historic Inn,Old)
E. Front St. & Park Ave.
HABS NJ-414
HABS NJ,20-SCOPL,1-
9dr/4ph/2pg/fr L

SPRINGFIELD

Bonnel House (Hemlocks,The)
504 Morris Ave.
HABS NJ-181
HABS NJ,20-SPRIF,2-
23dr/6ph/3pg/fr L

Cannon Ball House; see Hutchings House

First Presbyterian Church
Main St. & Springfield Ave.
HABS NJ-1
HABS NJ,20-SPRIF,1-
5dr/1ph/3pg/fr L

First Presbyterian Church,Parsonage
41 Main St.
HABS NJ-416
HABS NJ,20-SPRIF,5-
15dr/3ph/3pg/fr L

Hemlocks,The; see Bonnel House

Hutchings House (Cannon Ball House)
126 Morris Ave.
HABS NJ-190
HABS NJ,20-SPRIF,3-
12dr/5ph/3pg/fr L

Swaim Homestead
S. Springfield Ave.
HABS NJ-191
HABS NJ,20-SPRIF,4-
12dr/9ph/2pg/fr L

UNION

Brandt-Headley Farm House
1827 Vauxhall Rd.
HABS NJ-266
HABS NJ,20-UNI,2-
16dr/4ph/2pg/fr L

Connecticut Farms Presbyterian Church
Stuyvesant Ave.
HABS NJ-539
HABS NJ,20-UNI,5-
21dr/3ph/3pg/fr L

Liberty Hall
Morris Ave.
HABS NJ-515
HABS NJ,20-UNI,3-
13dr/9ph/4pg/fr L

Townley House
Morris & Potter Aves.
HABS NJ-192
HABS NJ,20-UNI,1-
14dr/9ph/2pg/fr L

Townley,James,House
Morris Ave. & Green Lane
HABS NJ-535
HABS NJ,20-UNI,4-
15dr/3ph/4pg/fr L

Townley,Richard,House
1407 Morris Ave.
HABS NJ-557
HABS NJ,20-UNI,6-
42dr/7ph/5pg/fr L

WESTFIELD

Varleth-Sip Manor
5 Cherry Lane
HABS NJ-265
HABS NJ,20-WESF,1-
9dr/3ph/3pg/fr L

WARREN COUNTY

ASBURY

Castner,Rev. Jacob R. ,Parsonage
Main St.
HABS NJ-699
HABS NJ,21-ASBU,1-
25dr/10ph/5pg/fr L

DELAWARE

Albertson House
HABS NJ-460
HABS NJ,21-DEL,1-
10dr/fr L

HOPE

American House Hotel
Union St. & Moravian Alley
HABS NJ-704
HABS NJ,21-HOP,4-
19dr/12ph/9pg/fr L

Blacksmith's Shop & Wheelwright's Shop; see Moravian Grist Mill Complex

Moravian Grist Mill; see Moravian Grist Mill Complex

Moravian Grist Mill Complex (Blacksmith's Shop & Wheelwright's Shop)
High St. & Hackettstown Rd.
HABS NJ-569-A
HABS NJ,21-HOP,2-A-
2ph/1pc L

Moravian Grist Mill Complex (Moravian Grist Mill)
High St. & Hackettstown Rd.
HABS NJ-569
HABS NJ,21-HOP,2-
13ph/18pg/1pc L

Moravian Grist Mill Complex (Toll House and Bridge)
HABS NJ-569-B
HABS NJ,21-HOP,2-B-
3ph/1pc L

Schenk,John,House (Swayze House)
Union St. & Moravian Alley
HABS NJ-580
HABS NJ,21-HOP,3-
1ph/6pg L

St. Luke's Episcopal Church
High St. & Hickory St.
HABS NJ-432
HABS NJ,21-HOP,1-
22dr/7ph/3pg/fr L

Swayze House; see Schenk,John,House

Toll House and Bridge; see Moravian Grist Mill Complex

HOPE VIC.

Eight-Square Stone School,Old
HABS NJ-429
HABS NJ,21-HOP.V,1-
3dr/2ph/2pg/fr L

Moravian Farm House (Newton-Davis Farm)
HABS NJ-705
HABS NJ,21-HOP.V,2-
14dr/10ph/11pg/fr L

Newton-Davis Farm; see Moravian Farm House

Swayze,Israel,House & Kitchen
HABS NJ-706
HABS NJ,21-HOP.V,3-
8dr/12ph/9pg/fr L

JOHNSONBURG

Dennis Stone Barn (Storehouse)
Greendell Rd.
HABS NJ-441
HABS NJ,21-JONBU,2-
5dr/1ph/3pg/fr L

Gibbs House (Octagon House)
Greendell Rd.
HABS NJ-440
HABS NJ,21-JONBU,1-
9dr/1ph/2pg/fr L

Octagon House; see Gibbs House

MILLBROOK

Millbrook Methodist Episcopal Church
HABS NJ-738
HABS NJ,21-MILBRO,2-
1ph/1pg/1pc L

Millbrook Village
HABS NJ-813
HABS NJ,21-MILBRO,1-
1ph/1pc L

MILLBROOK VIC.

Copper Mine Inn; see Union Hotel

Ferry,Dimmick,Farm; see Shoemaker,Moses,Farm

Millbrook Schoolhouse
HABS NJ-739
HABS NJ,21-MILBRO.V,1-
1ph/1pg/1pc L

Miller,E. ,Farm; see Van Campen,James,Farm

Shoemaker,Moses,Farm (Ferry,Dimmick,Farm)
Old Mine Rd.
HABS NJ-824
HABS NJ,21-MILBRO.V,2-
3ph/9pg/1pc L

Shoemaker,Moses,Farm,Barn
Old Mine Rd.
HABS NJ-824-B
HABS NJ,21-MILBRO.V,2-B-
1ph/1pc L

Shoemaker,Moses,Farm,Small House
HABS NJ-824-A
HABS NJ,21-MILBRO.V,2-A-
2dr/4ph/1pc/fr L

Union Hotel (Copper Mine Inn)
Old Mine Rd.
HABS NJ-740
HABS NJ,21-MILBRO.V,3-
2ph/8pg/1pc L

Van Campen,Abraham,House
Old Mine Rd.
HABS NJ-822
HABS NJ,21-MILBRO.V,4-
13dr/7ph/10pg/1pc/fr L

Van Campen,Col. Abraham,House
Old Mine Rd.
HABS NJ-430
HABS NJ,21-CAL,1-
10dr/8ph/8pg/1pc/fr L

Van Campen,James,Farm (Miller,E. ,Farm)
Old Mine Rd.
HABS NJ-825
HABS NJ,21-MILBRO.V,5-
5ph/11pg/1pc L

Van Campen,James,Farm,Wagon Shed-Corn Crib
HABS NJ-825-A
HABS NJ,21-MILBRO.V,5-A-
1ph/1pc L

Van Campen,Moses,House
Old Mine Rd.
HABS NJ-826
HABS NJ,21-MILBRO.V,6-
4ph/7pg/1pc L

OXFORD

Oxford Furnace
HABS NJ-236
HABS NJ,21-OXFO,1-
8dr/10ph/4pg/fr L

PHILLIPSBURG

Morris Canal
HAER NJ-29
HAER NJ,21-PHIL,1-
173ph/9pg/17pc L

PHILLIPSBURG VIC.

Morris Canal,Delaware River Portal
HAER NJ-29-A
HAER NJ,21-PHIL,1-A-
7ph/1pg/2pc L

Morris Canal,Hotel
HAER NJ-29-B
HAER NJ,21-PHIL,1-B-
1ph/1pg/1pc L

Morris Canal,Inclined Plane 10 West
HAER NJ-30
HAER NJ,21-PHIL.V,1-
9ph/8pg/2pc L

Morris Canal,Spillway
HAER NJ-29-C
HAER NJ,21-PHIL,1-C-
1ph/1pg/1pc L

PORT WARREN VIC.

Morris Canal,Inclined Plane 9 West
HAER NJ-29-D
HAER NJ,21-PHIL,1-D-
2ph/1pg/1pc L

ROCKPORT VIC.

Morris Canal
HAER NJ-29-H
HAER NJ,21-PHIL,1-H-
2ph/1pg/1pc L

SAXTON FALLS

Morris Canal,Guard Lock 5 West
HAER NJ-29-I
HAER NJ,21-PHIL,1-I-
3ph/1pg/1pc L

STEWARTSVILLE

Morris Canal
HAER NJ-29-E
HAER NJ,21-PHIL,1-E-
2ph/1pg/1pc L

STEWARTSVILLE VIC.

Morris Canal,Greene's Mill Vicinity
HAER NJ-29-F
HAER NJ,21-PHIL,1-F-
4ph/1pg/1pc L

WASHINGTON VIC.

Morris Canal
HAER NJ-29-G
HAER NJ,21-PHIL,1-G-
1ph/1pg/1pc L

Musconetcong River Bridge; see New Hampton Bridge

New Hampton Bridge (Shoddy Mill Road Bridge; Musconetcong River Bridge; Pennsylvania Railroad)
Spanning the Musconetcong River
HAER NJ-91
H

Pennsylvania Railroad; see New Hampton Bridge

Shoddy Mill Road Bridge; see New Hampton Bridge

San Jose de Gracia Church, Trampas, Taos County, New Mexico. Detail of main door. Photograph by Jack E. Boucher, October 1961 (HABS NM,28-TRAMP,1-4).

New Mexico

BERNALILLO COUNTY

ALBUQUERQUE

Alvarado Hotel
First St.
HABS NM-123
HABS NM,1-ALBU,5-
33ph/2pc L

Building
HABS NM-32
HABS NM1-ALBU,1-
3ph L

Charles Ilfeld Company Warehouse
200 First St. NW
HABS NM-105
HABS NM,1-ALBU,3-
25ph/5pg/2pc L

1-25 Hazeldine Plaza (Building)
1-25 Hazeldine Plaza,First & Second Sts. NW
HABS NM-22
HABS NM,1-ALBU,4-
1ph/1pc L

House
HABS NM-33
HABS NM1-ALB,2-
1ph L

Kimo Theater
421 Central NW
HABS NM-20
HABS NM,1-ALBU,6-
1ph/1pc/2ct L

Rosenwald Brothers Building
320 Central SW
HABS NM-26
HABS NM,1-ALBU,7-
1ph/1pc L

San Felipe de Neri Church
Old Town Plaza,NW
HABS NM-176
7dr/fr H

St. Anthony's Orphanage
1500 Indian School Rd.,N.W.
HABS NM-149
HABS 1989(HABS):15
7ph/22pg/1pc L

St. Anthony's Orphanage,Auditorium
1500 Indian School Rd. NW
HABS NM-149-B
HABS 1989(HABS):15
7ph/1pc L

St. Anthony's Orphanage,Chapel
1500 Indian School Rd. NW
HABS NM-149-C
HABS 1989(HABS):15
11ph/1pc L

St. Anthony's Orphanage,Classroom & Dormitory
1500 Indian School Rd. NW
HABS NM-149-A
HABS 1989(HABS):15
11ph/1pc L

U. S. Veteran's Administration Medical Center
2100 Ridgecrest SE
HABS NM-133
HABS NM,1-ALBU,8-
28ph/1pg/2pc/fr L

Wool Warehouse
516-522 First St. NW
HABS NM-21
HABS NM,1-ALBU,9-
1ph/1pc L

ISLETA PUEBLO

House,Adobe (Walled Forecourt)
HABS NM-121
HABS NM,1-ISLEP,3-
1ph L

House,Adobe & Sod
HABS NM-79
HABS NM,1-ISLEP,1-
1pg L

Houses,Row of,& Sod Wall
HABS NM-120
HABS NM,1-ISLEP,4-
1ph L

ISLETO PUEBLO

House,Adobe (Recessed Portal)
HABS NM-122
HABS NM,1-ISLEP,2-
1ph L

COLFAX COUNTY

CIMARRON

Aztec Mill,Old
HABS NM-119
HABS NM,4-CIM,1-
2ph L

Blacksmith Shop
HABS NM-38
HABS NM,4-CIM,2-
1ph L

Cimarron Church
HABS NM-114
HABS NM,4-CIM,3-
3ph L

County Courthouse,Old
HABS NM-118
HABS NM,4-CIM,4-
2ph L

Diego,Don,Hotel; see St. James Hotel

Government Trading Store
HABS NM-116
HABS NM,4-CIM,6-
2ph L

Jail,Old Stone
HABS NM-117
HABS NM,4-CIM,5-
3ph L

St. James Hotel (Diego,Don,Hotel)
HABS NM-115
HABS NM,4-CIM,7-
4ph L

DONA ANA COUNTY

LAS CRUCES

Ascarate,Frank,House
HABS NM-80
HABS NM,7-LACRU,1-
5ph L

House #127 (House Opposite Amador Hotel)
HABS NM-81
HABS NM,7-LACRU,2-
1ph L

House Opposite Amador Hotel; see House #127

RODEY

St. Francis de Sales Church
HABS NM-43
HABS NM,7-ROD,1-
1ph L

WHITE SANDS MSL RANG

Utah Launch Complex; see White Sands Missile Range

V-2 Rocket Facilities; see White Sands Missile Range,V-2 Rocket Facilities

White Sands Missile Range (Utah Launch Complex)
HAER NM-1
HAER NM,7-ALMOG.V,1-
128pg/fr L

White Sands Missile Range,V-2 Rocket Facilities (V-2 Rocket Facilities)
Near Headquarters Area
HAER NM-1-B
6dr/72ph/117pg/5pc/fr L

GRANT COUNTY

GILA

L. C. Ranch Headquarters
HABS NM-144
HABS NM,9-GILA,1A-
1ph/2pg/1pc/fr L

SILVER CITY

Commercial Building (Peddler's Square)
HABS NM-151
HABS NM,9-SILCI,3-
1ph/1pg/1pc/fr L

Commercial Building (Western Stationers; Southern Union Gas Company)
HABS NM-150
HABS NM,9-SILCI,2-
1ph/1pg/1pc/fr L

Peddler's Square; see Commercial Building

Silver City Museum
312 W. Broadway
HABS NM-143
HABS NM,9-SILCI,1-
2ph/2pg/1pc/fr L

Southern Union Gas Company; see Commercial Building

Western Stationers; see Commercial Building

GUADALUPE COUNTY

PUERTO DE LUNA

House
State Hwy. 91, 10 mi. S of Santa Rosa
HABS NM-138
HABS NM,10-PUEDEL,1-
6dr L

HIDALGO COUNTY

LORDSBURG VIC.

Shakespeare,Town of
HABS NM-23
HABS NM,12-LORBU.V,1-
1ph/2pg/1pc/fr L

LOS ALAMOS COUNTY

LOS ALAMOS

Fuller Lodge
Central & Twentieth Sts.
HABS NM-25
HABS NM,32-LOSAL,1-
1ph/1pc L

LOS ALAMOS VIC.

Romero Cabin
Pajarito Rd.
HABS NM-148
HABS NM,32-LOSAL.V,1-
3dr L

MCKINLEY COUNTY

GALLUP

Fort Wingate Depot Activity
HAER NM-3
HAER NM,16-GALUP,1-
36pg/fr L

ZUNI PUEBLO

Pueblo of Zuni,Central & Original Portion
Vic. of State Rds. 32 & 53
HABS NM-78
HABS NM,16-ZUNIP,1-
6dr/1ph/8pg/1pc/fr L

ZUNI VIC.

Mission Nuestra Senora de Guadalupe de Zuni (Zuni-Cibola National Historical Park)
Zuni Pueblo
HABS NM-124
HABS NM,16-ZUNIP,2-;(DLC/PP-1992:NM-5)
12dr/3ph/1pc L

Zuni-Cibola National Historical Park; see Mission Nuestra Senora de Guadalupe de Zuni

MORA COUNTY

TIPTONVILLE

Tipton House & Barn
HABS NM-19
HABS NM,17-TIP,1-
4dr/22ph/4pg/fr L

VALMORA VIC.

Fort Union
NM 161
HABS NM-164
H

Fort Union,Fort
NM 161
HABS NM-164-A
HABS DLC/PP-1992:NM-4
1ph/1pc L

Fort Union,Post Officers' Houses (Officers' Row)
NM 161
HABS NM-164-B
HABS DLC/PP-1992:NM-4
1ph/1pc L

Officers' Row; see Fort Union,Post Officers' Houses

WATROUS VIC.

Watrous House
HABS NM-18
HABS NM,17-WATRO.V,1-
25dr/29ph/9pg/fr L

OTERO COUNTY

ALAMOGORDO VIC.

La Luz,Town of
La Luz
HABS NM-141
HABS NM,18-LALUZ,1-
3ph/3pg/1pc/fr L

CIENEGA

House,Double
HABS NM-82
HABS NM,18-CINEG,1-
2pg L

QUAY COUNTY

TUCUMCARI

Baca-Goodman House
Third & Aber Sts.
HABS NM-108
HABS NM,19-TUCUM,1-
4dr/13ph/5pg/2pc/fr L

RIO ARRIBA COUNTY

ALCALDE

Alcalde Village
Site of San Gabriel
HABS NM-83
HABS NM,20-ALCA,1-
2ph L

Church
HABS NM-84
HABS NM,20-ALCA,2-
1pg L

Los Luceros Chapel
Between U. S. Rt. 64; Rio Grande R. ; Los Luceros
HABS NM-54
HABS NM,20-LOLUC,2-
5dr L

Los Luceros House
Between U. S. Rt. 64; Rio Grande R. ; Los Luceros
HABS NM-53
HABS NM,20-LOLUC,1-
9dr L

Merrill House (Door)
HABS NM-34
HABS NM,20-ALCA,3-
2pg L

CHAMITA

House next to Church
HABS NM-37
HABS NM,20-CHAM,1-
1ph L

CHIMAYO

Plaza de San Buenaventura; see Plaza del Cerro

Plaza del Cerro (Plaza de San Buenaventura)
State Rts. 76 & 4 vic.
HABS NM-128
HABS NM,20-CHIM,1-
2dr/3pg/fr L

SAN JUAN PUEBLO

Pueblo of San Juan
Espanola Vic.
HABS NM-101
HABS NM,20-SAJUP,1
1ph/4pg/1pc/fr L

SANTA CLARA PUEBLO

Pueblo of Santa Clara,Central Portion
State Rd. 30 Vic. ,Espanola Vic.
HABS NM-98
HABS NM,20-SACLAP,1-
4dr/1ph/6pg/1pc/fr L

SAN JUAN COUNTY

AZTEC VIC.

Aztec Ruins
NM 44
HABS NM-165
H

Aztec Ruins,Great Kiva
NM 44
HABS NM-165-B
HABS DLC/PP-1992:NM-4
2ph/1pc L

Aztec Ruins,West Ruin
NM 44
HABS NM-165-A
HABS DLC/PP-1992:NM-4
6ph/1pc L

CHACO CANYON

Bonito,Pueblo (Chaco Canyon National Monument; Chaco Culture National Historical Park)
S. terminus of NM56 & N. terminus of NM164
HABS NM-30
HABS NM,23- ,1-
9dr L

Chaco Canyon National Monument; see Bonito,Pueblo

Chaco Culture National Historical Park; see Bonito,Pueblo

Chacu Culture National Historical Park; see Pueblo Del Arroyo

Pueblo Del Arroyo (Chacu Culture National Historical Park)
HABS NM-163
HABS DLC/PP-1992:NM-5
3dr/3ph/1pc/fr L

CHACO CANYON VIC.

Chaco Canyon National Monument; see Kin Klizhin

Kin Klizhin (Chaco Canyon National Monument)
HABS NM-31
HABS NM,23- ,2-
5dr L

SAN MIGUEL COUNTY

EL CERRITO

El Cerrito,Village of (Spanish-American Villages of the Pecos River Val.)
Pecos River Valley
HABS NM-127
HABS NM,24-ELCERT,1-
5dr/1ph/3pg/1pc/fr L

Spanish-American Villages of the Pecos River Val.; see El Cerrito,Village of

LAS VEGAS

Castaneda Hotel
HABS NM-29
HABS NM,24-LAVEG,2-
5ph/3pg/1pc/fr L

City Hall,Old; see Las Vegas City Hall

Las Vegas City Hall (Las Vegas City Police & Fire Department; City Hall,Old)
626 Sixth St.
HABS NM-99
HABS NM,24-LAVEG,1-
4ph/7pg/1pc/fr L

Las Vegas City Police & Fire Department; see Las Vegas City Hall

LAS VEGAS VIC.

Baca,Don Jose Albino,House
Old Santa Fe Trail
HABS NM-12
HABS NM,24-LAVEG.V,1-
19dr/15ph/4pg/fr L

Montezuma Hotel
HABS NM-28
HABS NM,24-LAVEG.V,2-
10ph/4pg/1pc/fr L

PECOS

Pecos Church (Ruins) (Pecos National Monument; Pecos Mission Church)
HABS NM-85
HABS NM,24-PECO,1-
14dr/7ph/fr L

Pecos Mission Church; see Pecos Church (Ruins)

Pecos National Monument; see Pecos Church (Ruins)

ROMEROVILLE

Houses on Plaza
HABS NM-87
HABS NM,24-ROMVI,3-
1ph L

Romero Barn
HABS NM-44
HABS NM,24-ROMVI,1-
2ph L

Romeroville Church
HABS NM-86
HABS NM,24-ROMVI,2-
1ph L

SAN JOSE

San Jose Dal Vado,Village of (Spanish-American Villages of the Pecos River Val.)
Upper Pecos River Valley
HABS NM-126
HABS NM,24-SAJOS,1-
3dr/1ph/2pg/1pc/fr L

Spanish-American Villages of the Pecos River Val.; see San Jose Dal Vado,Village of

SAN MIGUEL

San Miguel Del Vado,General View (Spanish-American Villages of the Pecos River Val.)
Upper Pecos River Valley
HABS NM-139
HABS NM,24-SAMIG,1-
4dr/1ph/2pg/1pc/fr L

Spanish-American Villages of the Pecos River Val.; see San Miguel Del Vado,General View

Spanish-American Villages of the Pecos River Val.; see Territorial House, San Miguel del Vado

Spanish-American Villages of the Pecos River Val.; see Warehouse & Stable

Territorial House, San Miguel del Vado (Spanish-American Villages of the Pecos River Val.)
Upper Pecos River Valleyy
HABS NM-139-B
HABS NM,24-SAMIG,3-
2dr/fr L

Warehouse & Stable (Spanish-American Villages of the Pecos River Val.)
Upper Pecos River Valley
HABS NM-139-A
HABS NM,24-SAMIG,2-
1dr L

VILLANUEVA

Spanish-American Villages of the Pecos River Val.; see Villanueva,Village of

Villanueva,Village of (Spanish-American Villages of the Pecos River Val.)
Upper Pecos River Valley
HABS NM-135
HABS NM,24-VILLA,1-
1ph/4pg/1pc/fr L

VILLANUEVA VIC.

General View; see Spanish American Villages of the Pecos River Val.

Spanish American Villages of the Pecos River Val. (General View)
Upper Pecos River Valley
HABS NM-131
HABS NM,24-VILLA.V,1-
1dr/57pg L

SANDOVAL COUNTY

BLAND VIC.

Bandelier National Monument; see Ceremonial Cave

Bandelier National Monument; see Kiva,Large

Ceremonial Cave (Bandelier National Monument)
HABS NM-17
HABS NM,22-BLAND.V,2-
2dr/8ph/1pg L

Kiva,Large (Bandelier National Monument)
HABS NM-16
HABS NM,22-BLAND.V,1-
2dr/4ph/1pg L

JEMEZ PUEBLO

Jemez,Pueblo of
HABS NM-145
HABS NM,22-JEMEP,1-
5ph/4pg/1pc/fr L

SANTA ANA PUEBLO

Santa Ana Mission Church,Pueblo of
Jemez River vic.
HABS NM-125
HABS NM,22-SANAP,2-
4dr L

Santa Ana,Pueblo of
Jemez River Vic.
HABS NM-106
HABS NM,22-SANAP,1-
1dr L

ZIA PUEBLO

Zia,Pueblo of
San Ysidro Vic.
HABS NM-104
HABS NM,22-ZIAP,1-
1ph/2pg/1pc/fr L

SANTA FE COUNTY

CANONCITA

Church
HABS NM-36
HABS NM,25-CANCI,1-
1ph L

CHIMAYO

El Santuario del Senor Esquipula
HABS NM-9
HABS NM,25-CHIM,1-
32dr/21ph/2pg/1pc/2ct/fr L

GALISTEO

House
HABS NM-39
HABS NM,25-GAL,1-
1ph L

Lucero House
HABS NM-129
HABS NM,25-GAL,2-
6dr L

NAMBE PUEBLO

Kiva
HABS NM-8
HABS NM,25-NAMP,1-
6dr/4ph/1pg/fr L

Nambe,Pueblo of
State Rd. 4 Vic.
HABS NM-107
HABS NM,25-NAMP,2-
2dr/1ph/2pg/1pc/fr L

POJOAQUE VIC.

Bouquet Ranch House
HABS NM-88
HABS NM,25-POJU.V,1-
3ph L

SAN ILDEFONSO PUEBLO

Kiva
HABS NM-90
HABS NM,25-SAILFOP,2-
1ph L

San Ildefonso,Pueblo of
State Rd. 4 Vic.
HABS NM-89
HABS NM,25-SAILFOP,1-
2dr/3ph/4pg/1pc/fr L

SANTA CRUZ

Santa Cruz Mission
HABS NM-45
HABS NM,25-SANCRU,1-
2ph L

SANTA FE

Applegate,Frank,House
Camino del Monte Sal
HABS NM-113
HABS NM,25-SANFE,6-
4ph L

Borrego House (McCormick Prize House)
724 Canyon Rd.
HABS NM-14
HABS NM,25-SANFE,4-
5dr/8ph/3pg L

Christo Rey Church; see Reredos of Our Lady of Light (church)

El Palacio Real de Santa Fe (Palace of the Governors)
Palace Ave.
HABS NM-2
HABS NM,25-SANFE,2-
26dr/12ph/8pg/fr L

Garcia House
202 Closson St.
HABS NM-13
HABS NM,25-SANFE,3-
5dr/3ph/2pg L

Grade School at Loretto Academy
Don Gaspar Ave. & E. Water St.
HABS NM-134
HABS NM,25-SANFE,9-
7dr L

McCormick Prize House; see Borrego House

Mignardot House
HABS NM-91
HABS NM,25-SANFE,7-
1ph L

Nuestra Senora de Guadalupe
HABS NM-112
HABS NM,25-SANFE,8-
1ph L

Palace of the Governors; see El Palacio Real de Santa Fe

Rael House
663,667,669 Canyon Rd.
HABS NM-15
HABS NM,25-SANFE,5-
4dr/7ph/2pg L

Reredos of Our Lady of Light (church) (Christo Rey Church)
Canyon Rd. & Christo Rey St.
HABS NM-140
HABS NM,25-SANFE,10-
1ph/1pc L

SANTA FE VIC.

San Miguel Church
HABS NM-1
HABS NM,25-SANFE,1-
18dr/11ph/3pg/fr L

TESUQUE

Tesuque Central Portion,Pueblo of
Tesuque River Vic.
HABS NM-103
HABS NM,25-TESUP,1-ι1991(HABS):20°
9dr/5ph/2pg/2pc/fr L H

SIERRA COUNTY

HILLSBORO

Hillsboro,Town of
HABS NM-142
HABS NM,26-HILLSB,1-
5ph/3pg/1pc/fr L

SOCORRO COUNTY

GRAN QUIVIRA

Church of San Buenaventura; see Missions of San Buenaventura & San Isidro

Church of San Isidro; see Missions of San Buenaventura & San Isidro

Missions of San Buenaventura & San Isidro (Church of San Isidro; Church of San Buenaventura; Pueblo de las Humanas)
NM Hwy. 14, Salinas National Monument
HABS NM-147
HABS NM,27-GRAQI,1-
11dr/fr L

Pueblo de las Humanas; see Missions of San Buenaventura & San Isidro

SOCORRO

Baca Store
HABS NM-46
HABS NM,27-SOCO,1-
2ph L

Opera House
HABS NM-47
HABS NM,27-SOCO,2-
1ph L

Park Hotel
HABS NM-48
HABS NM,27-SOCO,3-
1ph L

San Miguel Mission
HABS NM-49
HABS NM,27-SOCO,4-
2ph L

WHITE SANDS MSL RANG

Trinity Site; see White Sands Missile Range,Trinity Site

White Sands Missile Range,Trinity Site (Trinity Site)
Vic. of Rts. 13 & 20
HAER NM-1-A
HAER NM,27-ALMOG.V,1A-
11dr/106ph/115pg/8pc/fr L H

TAOS COUNTY

ARROYO HONDO

Penitente Morada; see Upper Penitente Morada Chapel

Upper Penitente Morada Chapel (Penitente Morada)
HABS NM-60
HABS NM,28-ARROY,1-
6dr/5ph/4pg L

LLANO QUEMADO

Fernandez,Sofio,House
HABS NM-67
HABS NM,28-LLANO,1-
4dr L

PENASCO

Romero House
Embado Watershed Vic.
HABS NM-73
HABS NM,28-PENA,1-
6dr L

PICURIS

Picuris,Pueblo of (San Lorenzo Pueblo)
Vadito Vic.
HABS NM-100
HABS NM,28-PICUP,1-
1ph/2pg/1pc/fr L

San Lorenzo Pueblo; see Picuris,Pueblo of

PLACITA DE TAOS

Chapel at Placita de Taos; see La Capilla de Nuestra Senora de Dolores

La Capilla de Nuestra Senora de Dolores (Chapel at Placita de Taos)
HABS NM-93
HABS NM,28-TAO.V,1-
2ph L

RANCHITO

Maritnez,Pascual,House
HABS NM-70
HABS NM,28-RANCHI,2-
8dr L

Martinez,Jose Maria,House
HABS NM-71
HABS NM,28-RANCHI,3-
8dr L

Martinez,Leandro,House
HABS NM-64
HABS NM,28-RANCHI,1-
7dr L

RANCHOS DE TAOS

Caretaker's House
HABS NM-94
HABS NM,28-RANTA,2-
2ph L

House (Recessed Portal)
HABS NM-95
HABS NM,28-RANTA,3-
1ph L

House,Adobe (Typical Roof Construction)
HABS NM-42
HABS NM,28-RANTA,5-
1ph L

House,Territorial Period
HABS NM-96
HABS NM,28-RANTA,4-
1ph L

Long,Horace G. ,House
HABS NM-62
HABS NM,28-RANTA,6-
9dr L

Mission Church of Ranchos de Taos
HABS NM-7
HABS NM,28-RANTA,1-
32dr/13ph/3pg/1pc/fr L

TALPA

La Capilla de Nuestra Senora de Talpa
HABS NM-10
HABS NM,28-TALP,1-
12dr/6ph/2pg/fr L

La Morada de Talpa
State Rd. 3 Vic.
HABS NM-130
HABS NM,28-TALP,3-
3dr L

Trujillo House
HABS NM-74
HABS NM,28-TALP,2-
5dr L

TAOS

Adair House
Pueblo St.
HABS NM-50
HABS NM,28-TAO,1-
1ph L

Carson,Kit,House
Kit Carson Ave.
HABS NM-111
HABS NM,28-TAO,2-
1ph L

Chapel of Padre Antonio Jose Martinez
Garden of Irving Couse
HABS NM-110
HABS NM,28-TAO,3-
2ph L

Meyers,Ralph,House (Corbels)
HABS NM-51
HABS NM,28-TAO,4-
1pg L

Romero,Santiago,House
HABS NM-136
HABS NM,28-TAO,5-
3dr L

Valdez,Don Antonio Jose,House
Santa Fe & Pueblo Rds. Vic.
HABS NM-137
HABS NM,28-TAO,6-
4dr L

TAOS PUEBLO

San Geronimo Mission
HABS NM-109
HABS NM,28-TAOP,1-
1ph L

Taos Central Portion,Pueblo of
HABS NM-102
HABS NM,28-TAOP,2-
8dr/1ph/4pg/1pc/fr L

TRAMPAS

Atencio House
HABS NM-76
HABS NM,28-TRAMP,3-
7dr L

de Cruz,Jose,House
HABS NM-75
HABS NM,28-TRAMP,2-
6dr L

San Jose de Gracia Church
HABS NM-61
HABS NM,28-TRAMP,1-
5dr/13ph/5pg L

VADITO

Casita Martinez
State Rt. 75
HABS NM-72
HABS NM,28-VADI,1-
3dr L

TORRANCE COUNTY

ABO

Mision San Gregorio de Abo
State Hwy. 513,Mountainair vic.
HABS NM-146
HABS NM,29-ABOP,1-
14dr/fr L

MANZANO

Torreon,The
HABS NM-11
HABS NM,29-MANZ,1-
3dr/4ph/4pg/fr L

VALENCIA COUNTY

ACOMA PUEBLO

Acoma,Pueblo of (Sky City)
Casa Blanca vic.
HABS NM-6
HABS NM,31-ACOMP,1-
86dr/87ph/6pg/1pc/fr L

San Esteban del Rey Mission
HABS NM-5
HABS NM,31-ACOMP,2-
32dr/34ph/5pg/fr L

Sky City; see Acoma,Pueblo of

BELEN

Chavez House
Chihuahua,Santa Fe Trail
HABS NM-35
HABS NM,31-BEL,1-
2ph L

LAGUNA PUEBLO

Houses (near Mission)
HABS NM-97
HABS NM,31-LAGUP,3-
1ph L

Laguna,Pueblo of
HABS NM-27
HABS NM,31-LAGUP,4-
1ph/5pg/1pc/fr L

Meetinghouse
HABS NM-4
HABS NM,31-LAGUP,2-
4dr/2ph/2pg/fr L

San Jose de Laguna Mission Church & Convento
HABS NM-3
HABS NM,31-LAGUP,1-
22dr/21ph/3pg/fr L

PERALTA

Alverete House (Door & Zaguan)
HABS NM-41
HABS NM,31-PERAL,2-
1ph L

Church at Peralta; see Our Lady of Guadalupe

Our Lady of Guadalupe (Church at Peralta)
State Hwy. 47
HABS NM-40
HABS NM,31-PERAL,1-
11dr/1ph L

VALENCIA VIC.

Aragon,Don Simon,House
HABS NM-52
HABS NM,31-VAL.V,1-
1ph L

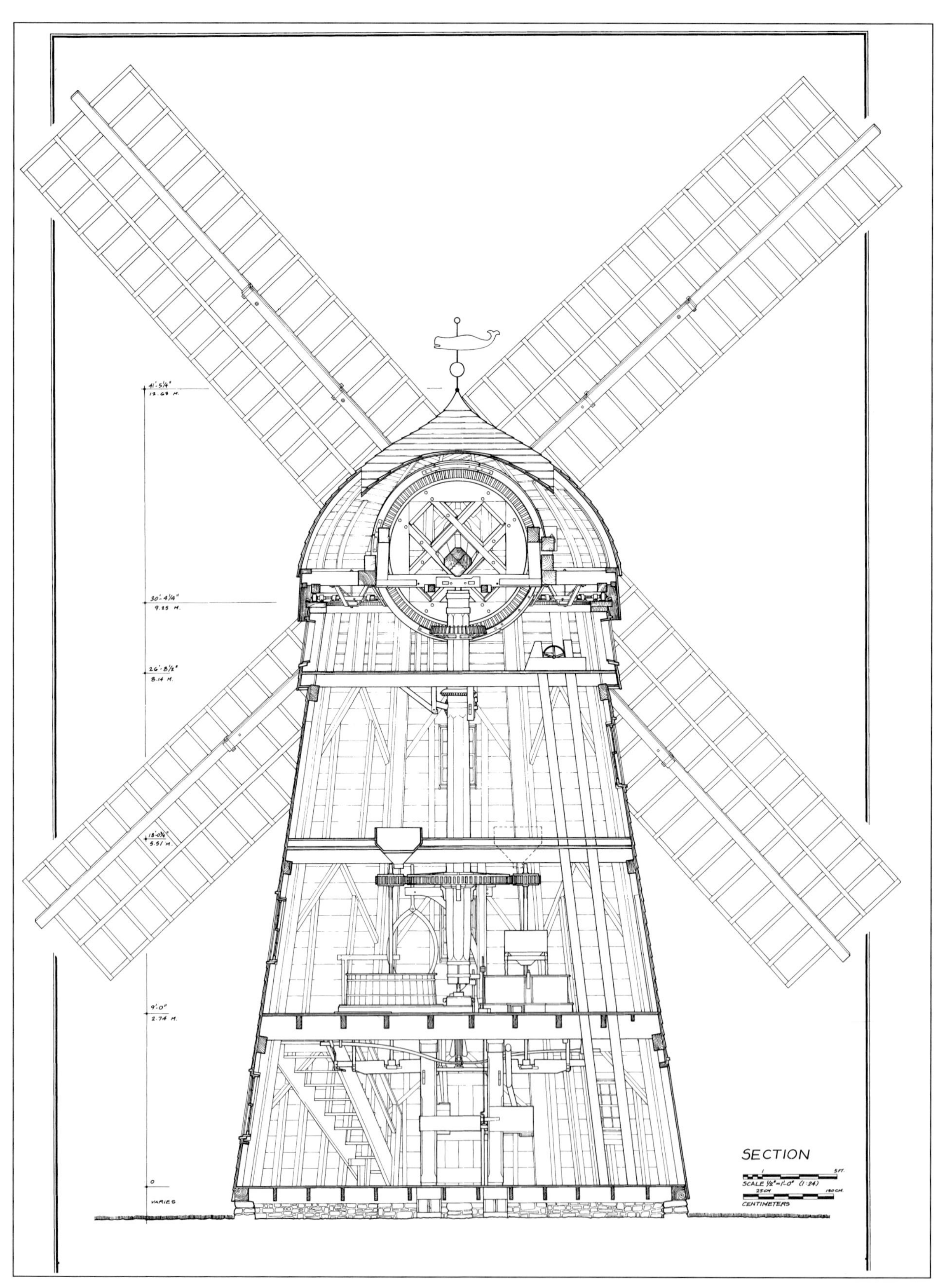

Beebe Windmill, Bridgehampton, Suffolk County, Long Island, New York. Section. Measured drawing delineated by Chalmers G. Long, Jr., 1976 (HAER NY-67, sheet 4 of 6; negative number LC-USZA2-13).

New York

PATTERSON

Hayt Farmstead,Cool Storage Shed
Rt. 311
HABS NY-6300-C
HABS DLC/PP-1993:NY-5
2ph/2pg/1pc L

ALBANY COUNTY

ALBANY

Albany Card & Paper Company Building Addition; see Hudson Theater Building

Bernstein Building (Entrance)
669 Broadway
HABS NY-3201
HABS NY,1-ALB,12-
1ph L

922 Broadway (House)
HABS NY-378
HABS NY,1-ALB,7-
3dr/2ph/fr L

Buel,Jesse,House
637 Western Ave.
HABS NY-5-A-6
HABS NY,1-ALB,4-
12dr/1ph/2pg/fr L

Church,Old Dutch
State,Market & Court Sts.
HABS NY-3129
HABS NY,1-ALB,10-
1ph L

Church,Old Dutch (Pulpit)(Now in First Church)
Broadway & State Sts.
HABS NY-3129-A
HABS NY,1-ALB,11A-
4dr L

City Hall
Eagle St.
HABS NY-342
HABS NY,1-ALB,22-
11ph/3pg/1pc/fr L

Court of Appeals (Interiors)
(moved from State Capitol Building)
HABS NY-6001
HABS NY,1-ALB,13-
3ph L

Doyle Building
Clinton Ave. & Broadway
HABS NY-3202
HABS NY,1-ALB,14-
1ph L

Exchange,The; see Lansing-Pemberton House

First Church in Albany; see First Reformed Church

First Reformed Church (First Church in Albany; North Dutch Church; Reformed Protestant Dutch Church)
N. Pearl & Orange Sts.
HABS NY-3128
HABS NY,1-ALB,11-
8dr/3ph/1pg/fr L

Gable,Dutch
HABS NY-3111
HABS NY,1-ALB,9-
1ph L

Hawk Street Bridge; see Hawk Street Viaduct

Hawk Street Viaduct (Hawk Street Bridge)
HAER NY-10
HAER NY,1-ALB,20-
10ph/5pg L

Homeopathic Hospital,Old (Interiors)
123 N. Pearl St.
HABS NY-6002
HABS NY,1-ALB,15-
4ph/1pg L

House,Dutch Gable
674 Broadway
HABS NY-376
HABS NY,1-ALB,6-
1dr/2ph/fr L

Hudson River Day Line Building
Broadway St.
HABS NY-5710
HABS NY,1-ALB,24-
10dr L

Hudson Theater Building (Albany Card & Paper Company Building Addition)
270-276 Hudson Ave.
HABS NY-6265
HABS NY,1-ALB,25A-
5ph/2pg L

Hun House
149 Washington Ave.
HABS NY-5-A-12
HABS NY,1-ALB,5-
10dr/7ph/2pg/fr L

Lansing-Pemberton House
(Exchange,The)
N. Pearl & Columbia Sts.
HABS NY-3203
HABS NY,1-ALB,16-
2ph/1pg L

New York State Capitol
Capitol Park
HABS NY-404
HABS NY,1-ALB,26-
2ph L

Nipper; see RCA Building

North Dutch Church; see First Reformed Church

Pastures,The; see Schuyler Mansion (Ironwork)

Public School Number 15 (School Number 15)
75 Herkimer St.
HABS NY-5707
HABS NY,1-ALB,21-
8pg/fr L

RCA Building (Nipper)
Broadway & Loudonville Rd.
HABS NY-5711
HABS NY,1-ALB,27-
2ph L

Reformed Protestant Dutch Church; see First Reformed Church

School Number 15; see Public School Number 15

Schuyler Mansion (Ironwork)
(Pastures,The)
HABS NY-6256
HABS NY,1-ALB,2-
1ph L

65 South Ferry Street (House)
HABS NY-6004
HABS NY,1-ALB,18-
1ph L

Sturtevant,Widow,House
Pearl St.
HABS NY-6003
HABS NY,1-ALB,17-
1ph L

Visscher,William,Building
100-102 N. Pearl St.
HABS NY-389
HABS NY,1-ALB,8-
6dr/1ph L

116 Washington Avenue (House & Office)
HABS NY-6041
HABS NY,1-ALB,23-
16dr/5ph/fr L

Whipple Cast & Wrought Iron Bowstring Truss Br.
Normans Kill Vic.
HAER NY-4
HAER NY,1-ALB,19-
5dr/13ph/14pg/fr L

ALTAMONT

Severson House
HABS NY-3205
HABS NY,1-ALTA,1-
4ph L

Severson,George,Inn
HABS NY-3205
HABS NY,1-ALTA,2-
1ph L

ALTAMONT VIC.

Crounse Homestead
HABS NY-6005
HABS NY,1-ALTA.V,1-
4ph L

BERNE VIC.

Building,Old Stone
Old Indian Ladder Rd.
HABS NY-3164
HABS NY,1- ,3-
1ph L

Livingston,Peter,House
Old Indian Ladder Rd.
HABS NY-5713
HABS NY,1- ,1-
1ph L

BETHLEHEM

Bethlehem (Nicoll,Rensselaer,House)
HABS NY-5-A-4
HABS NY,1-BETH,1-
11dr/2ph/2pg/fr L

Nicoll,Rensselaer,House; see Bethlehem

Sunnybrook
HABS NY-5-A-13
HABS NY,1-BETH,2-
11dr/3ph/2pg/fr L

Van Wie,Hendrick,House
HABS NY-4204
HABS NY,1-ALB.V,1-
2ph L

CLARKSVILLE

Chapman,W.,House
HABS NY-6006
HABS NY,1-CLARK,1-
1ph L

Zeh House
HABS NY-6007
HABS NY,1-CLARK,2-
1ph L

COEYMANS

Coeymans,Ariaantje,House
Coeymans Creek
HABS NY-333
HABS NY,1-COEY,1-
3dr/5ph/fr L

Coyemans-Bronck House (Niles House)
State Rt. 144
HABS NY-390
HABS NY,1-COEY.V,1-
8dr/2ph L

Niles House; see Coyemans-Bronck House

COHOES

Cohoes Co. Power Canal System: Head Gate House; see Cohoes Company,Gate House No. 1

Cohoes Company Power Canal System,Level 2
N. Mohawk St.
HAER NY-9
HAER NY,1-COHO,3-
5ph/15pg L

Cohoes Company Stable
Champlain & Oneida Sts.
HABS NY-6123
HABS NY,1-COHO,8A-
1ph/4pg L

Cohoes Company,Gate House No. 1
(Cohoes Co. Power Canal System: Head Gate House)
On Mohawk R. ,N. end of Canal abutting E. bank
HAER NY-8
HAER NY,1-COHO,3B-
24ph/4pg/1pc L

Eagle's Nest Creek Culvert
Erie Canal to Whitehall St. near Lock No. 2
HAER NY-157
HAER NY,1-COHO,5B-
2ph/4pg/1pc L

Erie Canal (Enlarged),Double Lock; see Erie Canal (Enlarged),Lock Number 18

Erie Canal (Enlarged),Lock Number 18 (Erie Canal (Enlarged),Double Lock)
252 N. Mohawk St.
HAER NY-11
HAER NY,1-COHO,5-
11ph/15pg L

Harmony Manufacturing Co.,Mastodon Mill; see Harmony Manufacturing Co.,Mill Number 3

Harmony Manufacturing Co.,Mill Number 3 (Harmony Manufacturing Co.,Mastodon Mill)
100 N. Mohawk St.
HAER NY-5
HAER NY,1-COHO,2-
26ph/13pg/1pc/fr L

198-200 Saratoga Street (House & Commercial Bldg.)
HABS NY-6027
HABS NY,1-COHO,6-
7ph/4pg L

Van Schaick,Wessel,House
Van Schaick Ave. & Delaware & Hudson R.R. Tracks
HABS NY-3121
HABS NY,1-COHO,1-
17dr/4ph/1pg/fr L

COLONIE

Cohoes Company,Gate House No. 1
Mohawk River,near river's mouth
HAER NY-151
HAER NY,1-COL,40A-
20ph/8pg/1pc L

Erie Canal (Enlarged),Oothout Culvert & Waste Weir
Lock No. 4 vic. ,near Maplewood village
HAER NY-152
HAER NY,1-MAPL,1A-
8ph/28pg/1pc L

COLONIE TWP.

Flatts,The; see Schuyler,Gen. Philip,House

Flatts,The,Kitchen; see Schuyler,Gen. Philip,Kitchen

Schuyler,Gen. Philip,House (Flatts,The)
Troy Rd. Vic.
HABS NY-3102
HABS NY,1-COL,39-
4ph L

Schuyler,Gen. Philip,Kitchen
(Flatts,The,Kitchen)
Troy Rd. Vic.
HABS NY-3102-A
HABS NY,1-COL,39A-
4dr L

DUNNSVILLE

Wemple Farm
HABS NY-3156
HABS NY,1-DUNV,1-
4ph L

FEURA BUSH

Bleeker House & Outbuildings
(Vadney,John,House)
HABS NY-3163
HABS NY,1-FEURB,1-
6ph L

Vadney House
HABS NY-3213
HABS NY,1-FEURB,2-
2ph/1pg L

Vadney,John,House; see Bleeker House & Outbuildings

GREEN ISLAND

Rensselaer & Saratoga R.R.,Green Island Shops
Tibbitts Ave. & Delaware & Hudson R.R. Tracks
HAER NY-15
HAER NY,1-GRENI,1-
15ph/7pg L

GUILDERLAND CENTER

Freeman House
HABS NY-6009
HABS NY,1-GUILC,1-
5ph/1pg L

GUILDERLAND VIC.

Case Homestead
HABS NY-6008
HABS NY,1-GUIL.V,2-
3ph/1pg L

Fort,Old Indian
HABS NY-3141
HABS NY,1-GUIL.V,1-
3ph L

HOUCKS CORNERS

Houck Hall; see Tavern,Old

Tavern,Old (Houck Hall)
Feura Bush Vic.
HABS NY-6000
HABS NY,1- ,4-
1ph/1pg L

JOHNSON CITY

C. F. J. Pool; see Johnson,Charles F. ,Pool

Johnson City Pool; see Johnson,Charles F. ,Pool

Johnson,Charles F. ,Pool (C. F. J. Pool; Johnson City Pool)
Charles F. Johnson Park
HAER NY-57
HAER NY,4-JOCI,1A-
20ph/18pg/2pc L

NEW SCOTLAND TWP.

Bradt House
HABS NY-3225
HABS NY,1-NESCO,2-
2ph L

Slingerland,Teunis Cornelius,House
HABS NY-3162
HABS NY,1-NESCO,1-
4ph L

Van Rensselaer,Steven,House
HABS NY-3150
HABS NY,1- ,2-
2ph L

NEW SCOTLAND VIC.

Slingerlands Hill Farm
HABS NY-3232
HABS NY,1-NESCO.V,1-
2ph L

NEWTONVILLE

Newton House
HABS NY-3234
HABS NY,1-NEWT,1-
1ph L

ONESQUETHAW

Austin Homestead
HABS NY-3154
HABS NY,1-ONES,4-
1ph L

Mead,Judge Henry,House
HABS NY-3153
HABS NY,1-ONES,3-
1ph L

Onesquethaw Church
HABS NY-3152
HABS NY,1-ONES,2-
1ph L

Scott,John,House
HABS NY-3236
HABS NY,1-ONES,5-
1ph L

Van Dyke Homestead
HABS NY-3151
HABS NY,1-ONES,1-
1ph L

RENSSELAERVILLE

Conklin,Gurdon,House (Quaint Acres)
HABS NY-3224
HABS NY,1-RENLA,3-
1ph L

Episcopal Church
HABS NY-3155
HABS NY,1-RENLA,2-
1ph L

House,Old Stone
HABS NY-3143
HABS NY,1-RENLA,1-
2ph L

Hutchinson,Eli,House (Rider,James,House)
HABS NY-6010
HABS NY,1-RENLA,4-
2ph L

Quaint Acres; see Conklin,Gurdon,House

Rider,James,House; see Hutchinson,Eli,House

UNIONVILLE

McCullock House
Clipp Rd.
HABS NY-3149
HABS NY,1-UNVI,1-
2ph L

WATERVIELT

Shaker West Family Barn
Watervliet Shaker Rd.,Colonie Township
HABS NY-3292
HABS NY,1-COL,6-
1ph L

WATERVLIET

Shaker Chruch Family Office; see Shaker Church Family Trustee's Office

Shaker Church Family (General Views)
Watervliet Shaker Rd.,Colonie Township
HABS NY-3306
HABS NY,1-COL,25-
8ph L

Shaker Church Family Brethren's Workshop
Watervliet Shaker Rd.,Colonie Township
HABS NY-3307
HABS NY,1-COL,29-
5ph L

Shaker Church Family Dwelling House (second)
Watervliet Shaker Rd.,Colonie Township
HABS NY-3308
HABS NY,1-COL,30-
1ph L

Shaker Church Family Herb House
Watervliet Shaker Rd.,Colonie Twp.
HABS NY-3309
HABS NY,1-COL,31-
5ph L

Shaker Church Family Laundry & Canning Factory; see Shaker Church Family Washhouse & Canning Factory

Shaker Church Family Main Dwelling House (first)
Watervliet Shaker Rd.,Colonie Township
HABS NY-3310
HABS NY,1-COL,32-
1ph L

Shaker Church Family Mill
Watervliet Shaker Rd.,Colonie Township
HABS NY-3311
HABS NY,1-COL,33-
1ph L

Shaker Church Family New Meetinghouse; see Shaker Meetinghouse (second)

Shaker Church Family Old Meetinghouse; see Shaker Meetinghouse (first)

Shaker Church Family School; see Shaker Schoolhouse

Shaker Church Family Seed House
Watervliet Shaker Rd.,Colonie Township
HABS NY-3316
HABS NY,1-COL,38-
2ph L

Shaker Church Family Sisters' Workshop
Watervliet Shaker Rd.,Colonie Township
HABS NY-3277
HABS NY,1-COL,28-
4ph/fr L

Shaker Church Family Trustee's Office (Shaker Chruch Family Office)
Watervliet Shaker Rd.,Colonie Township
HABS NY-3313
HABS NY,1-COL,35-
3ph L

Shaker Church Family Washhouse & Canning Factory (Shaker Church Family Laundry & Canning Factory)
Watervliet Shaker Rd.,Colonie Township
HABS NY-3275
HABS NY,1-COL,26-
6ph L

Shaker Church Ministry's House; see Shaker Ministry's House

Shaker Meetinghouse (first) (Shaker Church Family Old Meetinghouse)
Watervliet Shaker Rd.,Colonie Township
HABS NY-3314
HABS NY,1-COL,36-
1ph L

Shaker Meetinghouse (second) (Shaker Church Family New Meetinghouse)
Watervliet Shaker Rd.,Colonie Township
HABS NY-3276
HABS NY,1-COL,27
7ph L

Shaker Ministry's House (Shaker Church Ministry's House)
Watervliet Shaker Rd.,Colonie Township
HABS NY-3312
HABS NY,1-COL,34-
2ph L

Shaker North Family (General Views)
Albany Shaker Rd.,Colonie Township
HABS NY-3294
HABS NY,1-COL,7-
2ph L

Shaker North Family Dwelling House
Albany Shaker Rd.,Colonie Township
HABS NY-3295
HABS NY,1-COL,8-
1ph L

Shaker North Family Old Second House
Albany Shaker Rd.,Colonie Township
HABS NY-3296
HABS NY,1-COL,9-
1ph L

Shaker North Farm Barn
Albany Shaker Rd.,Colonie Township
HABS NY-3318
HABS NY,1-COL,10-
1ph L

Shaker Schoolhouse (Shaker Church Family School)
Watervliet Shaker Rd.,Colonie Township
HABS NY-3315
HABS NY,1-COL,37-
10ph L

Shaker South Family (General Views)
Watervliet Shaker Rd.,Colonie Township
HABS NY-3272
HABS NY,1-COL,11-
1dr/6ph/6pg L

Shaker South Family Ash House
Watervliet Shaker Rd.,Colonie Township
HABS NY-3289
HABS NY,1-COL,24-
1ph L

Shaker South Family Brothers' Dormitory (Shaker South Family Building Number 2)
Watervliet Shaker Rd.,Colonie Township
HABS NY-3260
HABS NY,1-COL,13-
8dr/2ph/3pg L

Shaker South Family Brothers' Workshop; see Shaker South Family Trustees' Office

Shaker South Family Building Number 1; see Shaker South Family Cottage

Shaker South Family Building Number 10; see Shaker South Family Horse & Wagon Barn

Shaker South Family Building Number 11; see Shaker South Family Icehouse

Shaker South Family Building Number 12; see Shaker South Family Cow & Hay Barn

Shaker South Family Building Number 15; see Shaker South Family Woodshed

Shaker South Family Building Number 2; see Shaker South Family Brothers' Dormitory

Shaker South Family Building Number 3; see Shaker South Family Dwelling House

Shaker South Family Building Number 4; see Shaker South Family Trustees' Office

Shaker South Family Building Number 5; see Shaker South Family Cottage

Shaker South Family Building Number 6; see Shaker South Family Sisters' Workshop

Shaker South Family Building Number 7; see Shaker South Family Washhouse

Shaker South Family Building Number 8; see Shaker South Family Cannery

Shaker South Family Cannery (Shaker South Family Building Number 8)
Watervliet Shaker Rd.,Colonie Township
HABS NY-3262
HABS NY,1-COL,19-
2dr/1ph L

Shaker South Family Cottage (Shaker South Family Building Number 1)
Watervliet Shaker Rd.,Colonie Township
HABS NY-3258
HABS NY,1-COL,12-
2dr/2ph/2pg L

Shaker South Family Cottage (Shaker South Family Building Number 5)
Watervielt Shaker Rd.,Colonie Township
HABS NY-3242
HABS NY,1-COL,16-
5dr/2pg L

Shaker South Family Cow & Hay Barn (Shaker South Family Building Number 12)
Watervliet Shaker Rd.,Colonie Township
HABS NY-3245
HABS NY,1-COL,21-
8dr/6ph/3pg L

Shaker South Family Dwelling House (Shaker South Family Residence; Shaker South Family Building Number 3)
Watervliet Shaker Rd.,Colonie Township
HABS NY-3261
HABS NY,1-COL,14-
13dr/7ph/5pg L

Shaker South Family Horse & Wagon Barn (Shaker South Family Wagon Shed; Shaker South Family Building Number 10)
Watervliet Shaker Rd.,Colonie Township
HABS NY-3244
HABS NY,1-COL,20-
4dr L

Shaker South Family Icehouse (Shaker South Family Building Number 11)
Watervliet Shaker Rd.,Colonie Township
HABS NY-3246
HABS NY,1-COL,22-
1dr L

Shaker South Family Residence; see Shaker South Family Dwelling House

Shaker South Family Sisters' Workshop (Shaker South Family Building Number 6)
Watervliet Shaker Rd.,Colonie Township
HABS NY-3290
HABS NY,1-COL,17-
5ph L

Shaker South Family Trustees' Office (Shaker South Family Brothers' Workshop; Shaker South Family Building Number 4)
Watervliet Shaker Rd.,Colonie Township
HABS NY-3241
HABS NY,1-COL,15-
13dr/3ph/4pg L

Shaker South Family Wagon Shed; see Shaker South Family Horse & Wagon Barn

Shaker South Family Washhouse (Shaker South Family Building Number 7)
Watervliet Shaker Rd.,Colonie Township
HABS NY-3243
HABS NY,1-COL,18-
3dr/2ph/2pg L

Shaker South Family Woodshed (Shaker South Family Building Number 15)
Watervliet Shaker Rd.,Colonie Township
HABS NY-3247
HABS NY,1-COL,23-
1dr/2ph L

Shaker West Family (General Views)
Watervliet Shaker Rd.,Colonie Township
HABS NY-3274
HABS NY,1-COL,1-
4ph L

Shaker West Family Broom Shop (Shaker West Family Workshop; Shaker West Family Building Number 3)
Watervliet Shaker Rd.,Colonie Township
HABS NY-3263
HABS NY,1-COL,3-
13dr/2ph L

Shaker West Family Building Number 1; see Shaker West Family Main Dwelling House

Shaker West Family Building Number 3; see Shaker West Family Broom Shop

Shaker West Family Building Number 7; see Shaker West Family Smokehouse

Shaker West Family Building Number 8; see Shaker West Family Privy

Shaker West Family Main Dwelling House (Shaker West Family Building Number 1)
Watervliet Shaker Rd.,Colonie Township
HABS NY-3257
HABS NY,1-COL,2-
10dr/6ph L

Shaker West Family Privy (Shaker West Family Building Number 8)
Watervliet Shaker Rd.,Colonie Township
HABS NY-3265
HABS NY,1-COL,5-
1dr L

Shaker West Family Smokehouse (Shaker West Family Building Number 7)
Watervliet Shaker Rd.,Colonie Township
HABS NY-3264
HABS NY,1-COL,4-
1dr L

Shaker West Family Workshop; see Shaker West Family Broom Shop

Watervliet Arsenal
S. Broadway
HAER NY-1-A
HAER NY,1-WAVL,1-
7dr/83ph/27pg/6pc/fr L

Watervliet Arsenal, Building 101 (Watervliet Arsenal, Oil Storage Building)
S. Broadway, on the Hudson River
HAER NY-226
HAER NY,1-WAVL,1/101-
2ph/1pc/fr L

Watervliet Arsenal, Building 103 (Watervliet Arsenal, Latrine Building)
S. Broadway, on the Hudson River
HAER NY-227
HAER NY,1-WAVL,1/103-
2ph/1pc/fr L

Watervliet Arsenal, Building 104 (Watervliet Arsenal, Steel Stock Storage Building)
S. Broadway,on the Hudson River
HAER NY-228
HAER NY,1-WAVL,1/104-
3ph/1pc/fr L

Watervliet Arsenal, Building 105 (Watervliet Arsenal, Facilities Engineering Bldg.)
S. Broadway, on the Hudson River
HAER NY-229
HAER NY,1-WAVL,1/105-
18ph/1pg/2pc/fr L

Watervliet Arsenal, Building 106 (Watervliet Arsenal, Storage Shed (open))
S. Broadway,on the Hudson River
HAER NY-230
HAER NY,1-WAVL,1/106-
2ph/1pc/fr L

Watervliet Arsenal, Building 108 (Watervliet Arsenal, Operations Maintenance Office)
S. Broadway,on the Hudson River
HAER NY-231
HAER NY,1-WAVL,1/108-
3ph/1pc/fr L

Watervliet Arsenal, Building 112 (Watervliet Arsenal, Proof Range)
S. Broadway,on the Hudson River
HAER NY-232
HAER NY,1-WAVL,1/112-
2ph/1pc/fr L

Watervliet Arsenal, Building 116 (Watervliet Arsenal, Oil Storage Building)
S. Broadway,on the Hudson River
HAER NY-233
HAER NY,1-WAVL,1/116-
4ph/1pc/fr L

Watervliet Arsenal, Building 14 (Watervliet Arsenal, Machine Rebuild Shop)
S. Broadway, on the Hudson River
HAER NY-218
HAER NY,1-WAVL,1/14-
10ph/2pg/1pc/fr L

Watervliet Arsenal, Building 26 (Watervliet Arsenal, Storage Shed (Bldg. Materials)
S. Broadway, on the Hudson River
HAER NY-219
HAER NY,1-WAVL,1/26-
2ph/1pc/fr L

Watervliet Arsenal, Building 27 (Watervliet Arsenal, Storage Shed (Lumber))
S. Broadway, on the Hudson River
HAER NY-220
HAER NY,1-WAVL,1/27-
2ph/1pc/fr L

Watervliet Arsenal, Building 28 (Watervliet Arsenal, Storage Shed (Bldg. Materials)
S. Broadway, on the Hudson River
HAER NY-221
HAER NY,1-WAVL,1/28-
3ph/1pc/fr L

Watervliet Arsenal, Building 30 (Watervliet Arsenal, Carpenter Shop)
S. Broadway, on the Hudson River
HAER NY-222
HAER NY,1-WAVL,1/30-
4ph/1pc/fr L

Watervliet Arsenal, Building 31 (Watervliet Arsenal, Condensate Return Pump House)
S. Broadway, on the Hudson River
HAER NY-223
HAER NY,1-WAVL,1/31-
1ph/1pc/fr L

Watervliet Arsenal, Building 32 (Watervliet Arsenal, Gate House)
S. Broadway,on the Hudson River
HAER NY-234
HAER NY,1-WAVL,1/32-
2ph/1pc/fr L

Watervliet Arsenal, Building 33 (Watervliet Arsenal, Storage Shed (Bldg. Materials)
S. Broadway, on the Hudson River
HAER NY-224
HAER NY,1-WAVL,1/33-
2ph/1pc/fr L

Watervliet Arsenal, Building 34 (Watervliet Arsenal, Storage Bldg. (Paint))
S. Broadway, on the Hudson River
HAER NY-225
HAER NY,1-WAVL,1/34-
1ph/1pc/fr L

Watervliet Arsenal, Carpenter Shop; see Watervliet Arsenal, Building 30

Watervliet Arsenal, Condensate Return Pump House; see Watervliet Arsenal, Building 31

Watervliet Arsenal, Facilities Engineering Bldg.; see Watervliet Arsenal, Building 105

Watervliet Arsenal, Gate House; see Watervliet Arsenal, Building 32

Watervliet Arsenal, Latrine Building; see Watervliet Arsenal, Building 103

Watervliet Arsenal, Machine Rebuild Shop; see Watervliet Arsenal, Building 14

Watervliet Arsenal, Oil Storage Building; see Watervliet Arsenal, Building 101

Watervliet Arsenal, Oil Storage Building; see Watervliet Arsenal, Building 116

Watervliet Arsenal, Operations Maintenance Office; see Watervliet Arsenal, Building 108

Watervliet Arsenal, Proof Range; see Watervliet Arsenal, Building 112

Watervliet Arsenal, Steel Stock Storage Building; see Watervliet Arsenal, Building 104

Watervliet Arsenal, Storage Bldg. (Paint); see Watervliet Arsenal, Building 34

Watervliet Arsenal, Storage Shed (Bldg. Materials); see Watervliet Arsenal, Building 26

Watervliet Arsenal, Storage Shed (Bldg. Materials); see Watervliet Arsenal, Building 28

Watervliet Arsenal, Storage Shed (Bldg. Materials); see Watervliet Arsenal, Building 33

Watervliet Arsenal, Storage Shed (Lumber); see Watervliet Arsenal, Building 27

Watervliet Arsenal, Storage Shed (open); see Watervliet Arsenal, Building 106

Watervliet Arsenal,Assistant Officer's Quarters; see Watervliet Arsenal,Building No. 6

Watervliet Arsenal,Barracks; see Watervliet Arsenal,Building No. 24

Watervliet Arsenal,Big Gun Shop; see Watervliet Arsenal,Building No. 110

Watervliet Arsenal,Broadway Shops; see Watervliet Arsenal,Building No. 40

Watervliet Arsenal,Building No. 1
(Watervliet Arsenal,South Stone Quarters; Watervliet Arsenal,Commandant's Quarters)
Mettler Rd. between Dalliba Ave. & Bricker Lane
HABS NY-5521-B
HABS NY,1-WAVL,1/1-
15ph/14pg/2pc L

Watervliet Arsenal,Building No. 10
(Watervliet Arsenal,Campbell Hall; Watervliet Arsenal,Headquarters)
Buffington St. W. of Dalliba Ave.
HABS NY-5521-A
HABS NY,1-WAVL,1/10-
11ph/14pg/2pc L

Watervliet Arsenal,Building No. 110
(Watervliet Arsenal,Seacoast Gun Shop; Watervliet Arsenal,Big Gun Shop)
Hagner Rd. between Schull & Whittemore Rds.
HAER NY-1-B
HAER NY,1-WAVL,1/110- & 1/110A-
63ph/24pg/7pc/fr L

Watervliet Arsenal,Building No. 119
(Watervliet Arsenal,East Magazine)
Munroe St. between Hagner & Worth Rds.
HAER NY-1-D
HAER NY,1-WAVL,1/119-
3ph/8pg/1pc/fr L

Watervliet Arsenal,Building No. 12
(Watervliet Arsenal,Greenhouse; Watervliet Arsenal,Community Facility)
Farley Drive, SE of Bricker Lane
HABS NY-5521-H
HABS NY,1-WAVL,1/12-
7ph/7pg/1pc L

Watervliet Arsenal,Building No. 129
(Watervliet Arsenal,West Magazine)
Worth Rd. near Baker Rd.
HAER NY-1-E
HAER NY,1-WAVL,1/129-
6ph/7pg/1pc/fr L

Watervliet Arsenal,Building No. 135
(Watervliet,Large Caliber Gun Tube Manufactng Bldg)
Gillespie Rd. ,S. of Parker Rd.
HAER NY-1-J
HAER NY,1-WAVL,1/135-
20ph/9pg/2pc/fr L

Watervliet Arsenal,Building No. 15
(Watervliet Arsenal,North Carriage House; Watervliet Arsenal,Motor Pool Garage)
Buffington St. btwn Symington St. & Dalliba Ave.
HAER NY-1-I
HAER NY,1-WAVL,1/15-
5ph/8pg/1pc/fr L

Watervliet Arsenal,Building No. 17
(Watervliet Arsenal,Roads & Grounds Shop; Watervliet Arsenal,Nitre Storehouse)
Arnold Lane, S. of Dalliba Ave.
HAER NY-1-F
HAER NY,1-WAVL,1/17-
5ph/8pg/1pc/fr L

Watervliet Arsenal,Building No. 2
(Watervliet Arsenal,Officer's Quarters)
Bricker Lane,S. of Stewart Rd.
HABS NY-5521-E
HABS NY,1-WAVL,1/2-
12ph/13pg/2pc L

Watervliet Arsenal,Building No. 22
(Watervliet Arsenal,Fire Station; Watervliet Arsenal,South Carriage Storehouse)
Westervelt Ave. & Buffington St.
HAER NY-1-H
HAER NY,1-WAVL,1/22-
8ph/8pg/1pc/fr L

Watervliet Arsenal,Building No. 24
(Watervliet Arsenal,Barracks; Watervliet Arsenal,Operations Directorate Office)
Arnold Lane, S. of Westervelt Ave.
HABS NY-5521-G
HABS NY,1-WAVL,1/24-
8ph/10pg/1pc L

Watervliet Arsenal,Building No. 3
(Watervliet Arsenal,Officer's Quarters)
Mordecai Drive S. of Stewart Rd.
HABS NY-5521-F
HABS NY,1-WAVL,1/3-
8ph/12pg/1pc L

Watervliet Arsenal,Building No. 4
(Watervliet Arsenal,Officer's Quarters)
Mordecai Drive,W. of Mettler Rd.
HABS NY-5521-D
HABS NY,1-WAVL,1/4-
14ph/13pg/2pc L

Watervliet Arsenal,Building No. 40
(Watervliet Arsenal,Broadway Shops; Watervliet,Benet Research & Engineering Labs)
Broadway between Dalliba & Watervliet Aves.
HAER NY-1-C
HAER NY,1-WAVL,1/40-
20ph/20pg/3pc/fr L

Watervliet Arsenal,Building No. 41
(Watervliet Arsenal,Officer's Club; Watervliet Arsenal,Power Laboratory)
Gibson St. & Dalliba St.
HAER NY-1-G
HAER NY,1-WAVL,1/41-
4ph/8pg/1pc/fr L

Watervliet Arsenal,Building No. 6
(Watervliet Arsenal,North Stone Quarters; Watervliet Arsenal,Assistant Officer's Quarters)
Mettler Rd. ,N. of Mordecai Drive
HABS NY-5521-C
HABS NY,1-WAVL,1/6-
12ph/12pg/2pc L

Watervliet Arsenal,Campbell Hall; see Watervliet Arsenal,Building No. 10

Watervliet Arsenal,Cast-Iron Storehouse
Westervelt Ave. & Gibson St.
HAER NY-1
HAER NY,1-WAVL,1/38-
8dr/24ph/20pg/fr L

Watervliet Arsenal,Commandant's Quarters; see Watervliet Arsenal,Building No. 1

Watervliet Arsenal,Community Facility; see Watervliet Arsenal,Building No. 12

Watervliet Arsenal,East Magazine; see Watervliet Arsenal,Building No. 119

Watervliet Arsenal,Fire Station; see Watervliet Arsenal,Building No. 22

Watervliet Arsenal,Greenhouse; see Watervliet Arsenal,Building No. 12

Watervliet Arsenal,Headquarters; see Watervliet Arsenal,Building No. 10

Watervliet Arsenal,Motor Pool Garage; see Watervliet Arsenal,Building No. 15

Watervliet Arsenal,Nitre Storehouse; see Watervliet Arsenal,Building No. 17

Watervliet Arsenal,North Carriage House; see Watervliet Arsenal,Building No. 15

Watervliet Arsenal,North Stone Quarters; see Watervliet Arsenal,Building No. 6

Watervliet Arsenal,Officer's Club; see Watervliet Arsenal,Building No. 41

Watervliet Arsenal,Officer's Quarters; see Watervliet Arsenal,Building No. 2

Watervliet Arsenal,Officer's Quarters; see Watervliet Arsenal,Building No. 3

Watervliet Arsenal,Officer's Quarters; see Watervliet Arsenal,Building No. 4

Watervliet Arsenal,Operations Directorate Office; see Watervliet Arsenal,Building No. 24

Watervliet Arsenal,Power Laboratory; see Watervliet Arsenal,Building No. 41

Watervliet Arsenal,Roads & Grounds Shop; see Watervliet Arsenal,Building No. 17

Watervliet Arsenal,Seacoast Gun Shop; see Watervliet Arsenal,Building No. 110

Watervliet Arsenal,South Carriage Storehouse; see Watervliet Arsenal,Building No. 22

Watervliet Arsenal,South Stone Quarters; see Watervliet Arsenal,Building No. 1

Watervliet Arsenal,West Magazine; see Watervliet Arsenal,Building No. 129

Watervliet,Benet Research & Engineering Labs; see Watervliet Arsenal,Building No. 40

Watervliet,Large Caliber Gun Tube Manufactng Bldg; see Watervliet Arsenal,Building No. 135

ALLEGANY COUNTY

BELFAST VIC.

Erie Railway:Allegany Division,Bridge 375.41 (Genesee River Viaduct)
Genesee River,State Rt. 19
HAER NY-43
HAER NY,2-BELF.V,1-
5ph/1pc L

Genesee River Viaduct; see Erie Railway:Allegany Division,Bridge 375.41

BELVIDERE VIC.

Belvidere
S. of intersection Camp Rd. & Gibson Hill Rd.
HABS NY-6011
HABS NY,2-BELVI,1-
15ph/9pg/fr L

Belvidere,Barn
S. of intersection Camp Rd. & Gibson Hill Rd.
HABS NY-6011-A
HABS NY,2-BELVI,1A-
1ph/fr L

Belvidere,Gazebo
S. of intersection Camp Rd. & Gibson Hill Rd.
HABS NY-6011-B
HABS NY,2-BELVI,1B-
1ph/fr L

FILLMORE VIC.

Erie Railway:Allegany Division,Bridge 367.33 (Rush Creek Viaduct)
Rush Creek,Botsford Hollow Rd.
HAER NY-42
HAER NY,2-FILM.V,2-
2ph/1pc L

Fillmore Bridge
Spanning Genesee River at County Rd. 4
HAER NY-140
HAER NY,2-FILM.V,1-
10ph/5pg/1pc L

Rush Creek Viaduct; see Erie Railway:Allegany Division,Bridge 367.33

WELLSVILLE

Erie Railway:Wellsville Station
Pearl & Depot Sts.
HAER NY-103
HAER NY,2-WELV,1-
7ph/1pc L

BRONX COUNTY

BRONX

Bartow Mansion
Pelham Bay Park
HABS NY-456
HABS NY,3-BRONX,6-
10dr/18ph/fr L H

Bartow-Pell Carriage House
Shore Rd.
HABS NY-456-A
1dr H

Ferris Mansion
Ferris Ave.
HABS NY-432
HABS NY,3-BRONX,4-
9dr/4ph/3pg/fr L

Fordham Manor Reformed Church
71 Kingsbridge Rd. & Reservoir Ave.
HABS NY-4-22
HABS NY,3-BRONX,1-
6dr/3ph/4pg/fr L

Fort Schuyler
Throgg's Neck
HABS NY-4-30
HABS NY,3-BRONX,3-
12dr/14ph/8pg/fr L

Francis Mansion
Girard Ave. & E. 146th St.
HABS NY-457
HABS NY,3-BRONX,7-
9ph L

Hawkswood; see Marshall House

High Bridge; see Old Croton Aqueduct,Harlem River Crossing

Hunter Island Mansion
Hunter Island
HABS NY-460
HABS NY,3-BRONX,8-
3ph L

Lorillard Snuff Mill
Botanical Gardens,Bronx Park
HABS NY-462
HABS NY,3-BRONX,9-
3dr/2ph L

Macombs Dam Bridge
(See NEW YORK CO.,NEW YORK CITY for documentatn.)
HAER NY-269
L

Marshall House (Hawkswood)
Rodman's Neck
HABS NY-467
HABS NY,3-BRONX,10-
1ph L

Messiah Home for Children (Salvation Army School for Officers' Training)
1771 Andrews Ave.
HABS NY-5699
HABS NY,3-BRONX,11-
7ph/6pg/1pc L

Old Croton Aqueduct,Harlem River Crossing (High Bridge)
Spanning Harlem River
HAER NY-119
HAER NY,3-BRONX,12A-
13ph/1pg/2pc/fr L

Salvation Army School for Officers' Training; see Messiah Home for Children

Van Cortlandt,Frederick,Mansion
Broadway & Two-hundred-forty-second St.
HABS NY-455
HABS NY,3-BRONX,5-
8ph/fr L

Varian,Isaac,House
277 Van Cortlandt Ave.
HABS NY-4-23
HABS NY,3-BRONX,2-
7dr/2ph/5pg/fr L

NEW YORK CITY

Interborough Rapid Transit Co:3rd Ave. Elevated Ln
Borough of the Bronx
HAER NY-68
HAER NY,3-BRONX,13-
85ph/1pg/5pc/3ct L

Interborough Rapid Transit,149th St. Subway Kiosk
Melrose Ave. & 149th St.
HAER NY-87
HAER NY,3-BRONX,13A-
fr L

BROOME COUNTY

BINGHAMTON

Andrews,Dr.,House (Dobson Club)
272 Washington St.
HABS NY-5589
HABS NY,4-BING,1-
4ph/2pg L

Binghamton City Hall
Collier St.
HABS NY-5568
HABS NY,4-BING,3-
13ph/8pg L

Broome County Courthouse
Court St.
HABS NY-5617
HABS NY,4-BING,19-
5pg L

Christ Church
Washington & Henry Sts.
HABS NY-5566
HABS NY,4-BING,10-
8ph/3pg L

Church of the First Presbyterian Society
Chenango St.
HABS NY-5564
HABS NY,4-BING,18-
11ph/3pg L

City National Bank
49 Court St.
HABS NY-5636
HABS NY,4-BING,8-
9ph L

Delaware,Lackawana,& Western Railroad Station
Lewis & Chenango Sts.
HABS NY-5567
HABS NY,4-BING,26-
7ph/fr L

1 Dickinson Street (House)
HABS NY-5502
HABS NY,4-BING,12-
3ph/12pg/1pc/fr L

3 Dickinson Street (House)
HABS NY-5503
HABS NY,4-BING,13-
1ph/12pg/1pc/fr L

4 Dickinson Street (House)
N side of Dickinson St.
HABS NY-5504
HABS NY,4-BING,14-
2ph/12pg/1pc/fr L

8 Dickinson Street (House)
HABS NY-5505
HABS NY,4-BING,15-
2ph/12pg/1pc/fr L

Dobson Club; see Andrews,Dr.,House

Dunk,Alfred,House
4 Pine St.
HABS NY-5565
HABS NY,4-BING,9-
5ph/3pg L

Dwightsville, History of
HABS NY-6317
4pg L

Ely-Hawley House; see Jones,Joseph R. ,House

Erie Railway:Binghamton Freight Station
Lewis & Chenango Sts.
HAER NY-31
HAER NY,4-BING,25B-
3ph/1pc L

Erie Railway:Binghamton Station
Lewis & Chenango Sts.
HAER NY-30
HAER NY,4-BING,25A-
3ph/1pc L

Hills,McLean & Haskins Department Store; see Perry Block

Jones,Joseph R. ,House (Ely-Hawley House)
8 Riverside Dr.
HABS NY-5562
HABS NY,4-BING,4-
8ph/4pg L

Mason-Randall House (Two River Gallery of Roberson Memorial)
22 Front St.
HABS NY-434
HABS NY,4-BING,24-
1ph L

Monday Afternoon Club Clubhouse,The; see Phelps,Sherman,House

New York State Inebriate Asylum
425 Robinson St.
HABS NY-5588
HABS NY,4-BING,5-
1ph/4pg L

Perry Block (Hills,McLean & Haskins Department Store)
89 Court St.
HABS NY-5443
HABS NY,4-BING,2-
7ph/3pg L

Phelps,Sherman,House (Monday Afternoon Club Clubhouse,The)
191 Court St.
HABS NY-5544
HABS NY,4-BING,7-
5ph/4pg L

Roberson Memorial; see Roberson,Alonzo,House

Roberson,Alonzo,House (Roberson Memorial)
30 Front St.
HABS NY-5545
HABS NY,4-BING,23-
4ph/4pg/fr L

Two River Gallery of Roberson Memorial; see Mason-Randall House

U. S. Courthouse & Post Office
HABS NY-5587
HABS NY,4-BING,20-
3ph L

Wells,J. Stuart,House
71 Main St.
HABS NY-5546
HABS NY,4-BING,6-
8ph/2pg L

Whitney,Franklin,House
63 Front St.
HABS NY-5563
HABS NY,4-BING,22-
6ph/3pg L

1 Winding Way (House)
HABS NY-5506
HABS NY,4-BING,16-
2ph/12pg/1pc/fr L

3 Winding Way (House)
HABS NY-5507
HABS NY,4-BING,17-
3ph/12pg/1pc/fr L

DEPOSIT

Delaware Division,Bridge 176.88; see Erie Railway:Oquaga Creek Bridge

Deposit Lumber Company Mill
Borden St.
HAER NY-75
HAER NY,4-DEPO,6-
2ph/1pc L

Erie Railroad Company; see Erie Railway

Erie Railway (New York & Lake Erie Railroad; New York,Lake Erie & Western Railroad Company; Erie Railroad Company; Erie-Lackawanna Railroad)
New Jersey,New York,Pennsylvania
HAER NY-124
HAER NY,4-DEPO,2-
3dr/9ph/471pg/14pc L

Erie Railway:Delaware Division,Bridge 175.53
Delaware River & Front St.
HAER NY-28
HAER NY,4-DEPO,4-
3ph/1pc L

Erie Railway:Deposit Station
Front St.
HAER NY-26
HAER NY,4-DEPO,3-
9ph/1pc L

Erie Railway:Oquaga Creek Bridge (Delaware Division,Bridge 176.88)
Spanning Oquaga Creek at State Rt. 17
HAER NY-27
HAER NY,4-DEPO,5-
3ph/1pc L

Erie-Lackawanna Railroad; see Erie Railway

Hyde,Sheldon,House (Hyde's Castle; Pemberton,Doctor,House)
97 Second St.
HABS NY-5542
HABS NY,4-DEPO,1-
6ph/4pg L

Hyde's Castle; see Hyde,Sheldon,House

New York & Lake Erie Railroad; see Erie Railway

New York,Lake Erie & Western Railroad Company; see Erie Railway

Documentation: **ct** color transparencies **dr** measured drawings **fr** field records
pc photograph captions **pg** pages of text **ph** photographs

Pemberton,Doctor,House; see Hyde,Sheldon,House

ENDWELL

Patterson,Amos,House (Washingtonian Hall)
3725 River Rd.
HABS NY-5541
HABS NY,4-END,1-
13ph/8pg L

Washingtonian Hall; see Patterson,Amos,House

MAINE VIC.

Gates,Cyrus,House
Old Nanticoke Rd.
HABS NY-5540
HABS NY,4-MAIN.V,1-
4ph/3pg L

OUAQUAGA

Ouaquaga Bridge
Dutchtown Road, spanning the Susquehanna River
HAER NY-166
HAER 1991(HAER):5
4dr/19ph/6pg/2pc/fr L

VESTAL

D. L. & W. RR,Vestal Passenger & Freight Station
N. Main St.
HAER NY-50
HAER NY,4-VES,1-
6ph/1pg/1pc L

WHITNEY POINT

Daniels,G. H.,Clock Shop
Main St.
HABS NY-5539
HABS NY,4-WHIT,1-
1ph/2pg L

CATTARAUGUS COUNTY

COLLINS

Erie Railway:Collins Station
HAER NY-135
HAER NY,5-COL,1A-
1ph/1pc L

DAYTON

Erie Railway:Dayton Tunnel
Allen St. Vic.
HAER NY-46
HAER NY,5-DAYT,1-
2ph/1pc L

LIMESTONE VIC.

Baltimore & Ohio RR:Parallel Pratt Thru-Truss Brdg
HAER NY-44
HAER NY,5-LIM.V,1-
2ph/1pc L

Baltimore & Ohio RR:Riverside Jctn Interlckng Towe
Allegheny River Vic.
HAER NY-45
HAER NY,5-LIM.V,2-
2ph/1pc L

NAPOLI

Gladden Wind Turbine
Pigeon Valley Rd.
HAER NY-82
HAER NY,5-NAP,1-
3dr/7pg/fr L

SALAMANCA

B & O RR,East Salamanca Passenger Station
Columbia Ave.
HAER NY-98
HAER NY,5-SAL,3A-
3ph/1pc L

B & O RR,Salamanca Repair Shops
Columbia Ave.
HAER NY-100
HAER NY,5-SAL,3-
4ph/1pc L

Baltimore & Ohio RR:Downtown Salamanca Psngr. Stn. (Salamanca Station)
HAER NY-99
HAER NY,5-SAL,2A-
1ph/1pc L

Erie Railway:Salamanca Station
Atlantic St.
HAER NY-37
HAER NY,5-SAL,1A-
1ph/1pc L

Erie Railway:Salamanca Turntable
Atlantic St.
HAER NY-38
HAER NY,5-SAL,1B-
2ph/1pc L

Salamanca Station; see Baltimore & Ohio RR:Downtown Salamanca Psngr. Stn.

SALAMANCA VIC.

Baltimore & Ohio RR:Balt. Skewed Thru-Truss Bridge
HAER NY-101
HAER NY,5-SAL.V,1-
2ph/1pc L

CAYUGA COUNTY

AUBURN

Flat Iron Building
1-3 Genesee St.
HABS NY-5702
HABS NY,6-AUB,8-
7dr/4ph/5pg L

Marshall,Capt. Alexander,House
Auburn-Aureling Rd.
HABS NY-219
HABS NY,6-AUB.V,2-
10dr/6ph/1pg/fr L

AURORA

Scipio Lodge Number 110 (F. & A. M.)
Main St.
HABS NY-229
HABS NY,6-AURO,4-
13dr/14ph/2pg/fr L

CHAUTAUQUA COUNTY

ASHVILLE

Atherly House
406 W. Main St.
HABS NY-5607
HABS NY,7-ASHV,1-
7ph/5pg L

Bly,Smith,House
4 N. Maple St.
HABS NY-5462
HABS NY,7-ASHV,2-
6ph/5pg L

CHATAUQUA

Chautauqua Institute; see Miller,Lewis,Cottage

Miller,Lewis,Cottage (Chautauqua Institute)
HABS NY-6015
HABS NY,7-CHAUT,1A-
3ph L

DUNKIRK

Abel House
429 Central Ave.
HABS NY-6016
HABS NY,7-DUNK,1-
9dr L

American Locomotive Company,Foundry
320 S. Roberts St.
HAER NY-40
HAER NY,7-DUNK,2A-
1ph/1pg/1pc L

Combined Railroad Right-of-Way
Middle & Brigham Rds.
HAER NY-77
4ph H

Erie Railway:Central Avenue Pier
Central Ave.
HAER NY-78
HAER NY,7-DUNK,3-
2ph/1pc L

JAMESTOWN

Boatlanding Bridge (Fairmount Avenue Bridge; Sixth Avenue Bridge)
Sixth Ave.,spanning Chadakoin Rv. at L. Chautauqua
HAER NY-167
HAER 1991(HAER):5
2ph/6pg/1pc/fr L

Erie Railway:Jamestown Station
E. Second & Lafayette Sts.
HAER NY-59
HAER NY,7-JAMTO,1A-
2ph/1pc L

Fairmount Avenue Bridge; see Boatlanding Bridge

Sixth Avenue Bridge; see Boatlanding Bridge

SINCLAIRVILLE

Copp,Timothy,House
Church,Joy,East & Okerlund Sts.
HABS NY-6017
HABS NY,7-SINC,1-
8ph/1pg L

Copp,Timothy,Rose Trellis & Barn
HABS NY-6017-A
HABS NY,7-SINC,1A-
1ph L

WESTFIELD

Peck House
180 E. Main St.
HABS NY-6018
HABS NY,7-WESF,2-
1ph/1pg L

Rynd House
34 Pearl St. (corner of Pearl & Washington)
HABS NY-6258
HABS NY,7-WESF,2-
5ph/1pg L

CHEMUNG COUNTY

ELMIRA

Elmira College,Cowles Hall; see Elmira Female College,Cowles Hall

Elmira Female College,Cowles Hall (Elmira College,Cowles Hall)
Park Pl. & W. Washington Ave.
HABS NY-6019
HABS NY,7-ELM,1A-
2ph/3pg L

Elmira Rolling Mill
Hatch & State Sts.
HAER NY-25
2ph H

Erie Railway:Elmira Station
Railroad Ave.
HAER NY-36
HAER NY,8-ELM,2A-
1ph/1pc L

HORSEHEADS

Erie R.R. & Penn. R.R.,Horseheads Tower
State Rt. 328
HAER NY-32
3ph L

Erie Railway:Horseheads Interlocking Tower
HAER NY-32
HAER NY,8-HORSE,1A-
3ph/1pc L

HORSEHEADS VIC.

Horseheads High School Annex
Grand Central Ave.
HABS NY-6301
HABS 1989(HABS):17
25ph/6pc L

CLINTON COUNTY

KEESEVILLE

Upper Bridge
River Street, spanning the AuSable River
HAER NY-169
HAER 1991(HAER):5
3dr/18ph/19pg/2pc/fr L

COLUMBIA COUNTY

BLUE STORES VIC.

Hermitage,The (Livingston,Peter,House)
Linlithgo Hamlet Vic.
HABS NY-362
HABS NY,11-BLUSTO.V,1-
9dr/5ph/1pg/fr L

Livingston,Peter,House; see Hermitage,The

CHATHAM CENTER

Van Walkenburg,John,House
State Rt. 66
HABS NY-5-A-20
HABS NY,11-CHATC,1-
11dr/7ph/2pg/fr L

CLAVERACK

Miller,Clifford,House (Van Rensselaer,Jacob,House)
State Rt. 23
HABS NY-5-A-22
HABS NY,11-CLAV,2-
14dr/10ph/2pg/fr L

Van Rensselaer,Jacob,House; see Miller,Clifford,House

CLERMONT TWP.

Clermont (Livingston Manor; Clermont Livingston Manor)
Clermont State Historic Site
HABS NY-403
HABS NY,11-CLER,1-
20dr/11ph/1pc/fr L

Clermont Livingston Manor; see Clermont

Clermont,Livingston Farm House (Livingston Farm House; Sylvan Cottage)
Clermont State Historic Site
HABS NY-403-A
HABS NY,11-CLER,2-
1dr/2ph/fr L

Livingston Farm House; see Clermont,Livingston Farm House

Livingston Manor; see Clermont

Sylvan Cottage; see Clermont,Livingston Farm House

COPAKE

Miller's Tavern
HABS NY-354
HABS NY,11-COPA,1-
2ph/1pg L

COPAKE VIC.

House
HABS NY-3240
HABS NY,11-COPA.V,1-
1ph L

CORTLAND

Randall,W. R.,Garden House
7 Reynolds Ave. (moved from 76 Main St.)
HABS NY-5596
HABS NY,12-CORT,4A-
4ph/4pg L

GERMANTOWN VIC.

Lasher House
State Rt. 9G Vic.
HABS NY-4358
HABS NY,11-GERM.V,1-
7dr/9ph/fr L

GREENPORT

Centre,Job,House; see Turtle House,Old

Turtle House,Old (Centre,Job,House)
Post Rd.
HABS NY-5-A-21
HABS NY,11-GREPO,1-
9dr/3ph/2pg/fr L

HUDSON

Church,Frederic Edwin,Barn; see Olana,Barn

Church,Frederic Edwin,Coach House; see Olana,Coach House

Church,Frederic Edwin,Horse Barn; see Olana,Horse Barn

Church,Frederic Edwin,House; see Olana

Church,Frederic Edwin,Pump House; see Olana,Pump House

Church,Frederic Edwin,Shed; see Olana,Shed

Church,Frederick,Farmhouse; see Olana,Farmhouse

Olana (Church,Frederic Edwin,House)
State Rt. 9G
HABS NY-5501
HABS NY,11-HUD,1-
15dr/33ph/4pg/3pc/fr L

Olana,Barn (Church,Frederic Edwin,Barn)
State Rt. 9G
HABS NY-5501-B
HABS NY,11-HUD,1B-
4dr/fr L

Olana,Coach House (Church,Frederic Edwin,Coach House)
State Rt. 9G
HABS NY-5501-A
HABS NY,11-HUD,1A-
4dr/fr L

Olana,Farmhouse (Church,Frederick,Farmhouse)
State Rt. 9G
HABS NY-5501-F
HABS NY,11-HUD,1F-
5dr/fr L

Olana,Horse Barn (Church,Frederic Edwin,Horse Barn)
State Rt. 9G
HABS NY-5501-C
HABS NY,11-HUD,1C-
4dr/fr L

Olana,Pump House (Church,Frederic Edwin,Pump House)
State Rt. 9G
HABS NY-5501-E
HABS NY,11-HUD,1E-
3dr/fr L

Olana,Shed (Church,Frederic Edwin,Shed)
State Rt. 9G
HABS NY-5501-D
HABS NY,11-HUD,1D-
2dr/fr L

10 Power Avenue (House); see Simpsonville

11 Power Avenue (House); see Simpsonville

12 Power Avenue (House); see Simpsonville

13 Power Avenue (House); see Simpsonville

16 Power Avenue (House); see Simpsonville

20 Power Avenue (House); see Simpsonville

6 Power Avenue (House); see Simpsonville

7 Power Avenue (House); see Simpsonville

8 Power Avenue (House); see Simpsonville

Simpsonville
Power Ave. btwn. S. Third St. & E. Court St.
HABS NY-6284
HABS NY,11-HUD,3-
5pg L

Simpsonville (10 Power Avenue (House))
HABS NY-6284-D
HABS NY,11-HUD,7-
4ph/1pg L

Simpsonville (11 Power Avenue (House))
HABS NY-6284-E
HABS NY,11-HUD,8-
3ph/1pg L

Simpsonville (12 Power Avenue (House))
HABS NY-6284-F
HABS NY,11-HUD,9-
5ph/1pg L

Simpsonville (13 Power Avenue (House))
HABS NY-6284-G
HABS NY,11-HUD,10-
6ph/1pg L

Simpsonville (16 Power Avenue (House))
HABS NY-6284-H
HABS NY,11-HUD,11-
6ph/1pg L

Simpsonville (20 Power Avenue (House))
HABS NY-6284-I
HABS NY,11-HUD,12-
4ph/1pg L

Simpsonville (6 Power Avenue (House))
HABS NY-6284-A
HABS NY,11-HUD,4-
3ph/1pg L

Simpsonville (7 Power Avenue (House))
HABS NY-6284-B
HABS NY,11-HUD,5-
6ph/1pg L

Simpsonville (8 Power Avenue (House))
HABS NY-6284-C
HABS NY,11-HUD,6-
7ph/1pg L

Worth,General,Hotel
213-215 Main St.
HABS NY-6023
HABS NY,11-HUD,2-
17ph/fr L

HUDSON VIC.

Livingston House (Proper House)
State Rt. 9E,Livingston Township
HABS NY-3158
HABS NY,11-HUD.V,1-
1ph/1pg L

Proper House; see Livingston House

KINDERHOOK

Spencer-Hinds House
HABS NY-3132
HABS NY,11-KINHO,2-
3ph L

Van Alen,Adam,House (Van Tassell,Katrina,House)
Kinderhook Creek Vic.
HABS NY-5-A-11
HABS NY,11-KINHO,1-
9dr/4ph/2pg/fr L

Van Tassell,Katrina,House; see Van Alen,Adam,House

KINDERHOOK VIC.

Lindenwald (Van Buren,Martin,House)
Old Post Rd.
HABS NY-6021
HABS NY,11-KINMO,1-
6ph/3pg L

Van Buren,Martin,House; see Lindenwald

LIVINGSTON VIC.

Callander House; see Ten Broeck House

Livingston,Mary,House
HABS NY-6022
HABS NY,11-LIV.V,2-
3ph L

Ten Broeck House (Callander House)
County Hwy. 82
HABS NY-357
HABS NY,11-LIV.V,1-
13dr/7ph/1pg L

MALDEN BRIDGE

Lippitt House
State Rts. 204 & 66
HABS NY-5-A-23
HABS NY,11-MALB,1-
10dr/3ph/2pg L

MOUNT LEBANON

Shaker Centre Family (General View)
Shaker Rd.
HABS NY-3337
HABS NY,11-NELEB.V,35-
1ph L

Shaker Centre Family Ann Lee Cottage; see Shaker Centre Family Dwelling House (second)

Shaker Centre Family Building Number 13; see Shaker Centre Family Southwest Work Cottage

Shaker Centre Family Building Number 15; see Shaker Centre Family Smithy

Shaker Centre Family Dwelling House (second) (Shaker Centre Family Ann Lee Cottage)
Shaker Rd.
HABS NY-3339
HABS NY,11-NELEB.V,39-
3ph L

Shaker Centre Family Medicine Factory
Shaker Rd.
HABS NY-3341
HABS NY,11-NELEB.V,40-
3ph L

Shaker Centre Family Smithy (Shaker Centre Family Building Number 15)
Shaker Rd.
HABS NY-3256
HABS NY,11-NELEB.V,37-
3dr/3ph L

Shaker Centre Family Southwest Work Cottage (Shaker Centre Family Building Number 13)
Shaker Rd.
HABS NY-3266
HABS NY,11-NELEB.V,36-
1dr/1ph L

Shaker Centre Family Washhouse (Shaker Medicine Shop)
Shaker Rd.
HABS NY-3338
HABS NY,11-NELEB.V,38-
3ph L

Shaker Church Family (General Views)
Shaker Rd.
HABS NY-3291
HABS NY,11-NELEB.V,1-
1dr/2ph/9pg/fr L

Shaker Church Family Apple Drying Kiln
Shaker Rd.
HABS NY-3304
HABS NY,11-NELEB.V,14-
1ph L

Shaker Church Family Brethren's Workshop (Shaker Church Family Building Number 3)
Shaker Rd.
HABS NY-3293
HABS NY,11-NELEB.V,4-
7ph L

Shaker Church Family Building Number 1; see Shaker Church Family Dwelling House

Shaker Church Family Building Number 12; see Shaker Church Family Trustees' Office

Shaker Church Family Building Number 13; see Shaker Church Family Nurse Shop

Shaker Church Family Building Number 18; see Shaker Church Family Sisters' Workshop

Shaker Church Family Building Number 2; see Shaker Meetinghouse (second)

Shaker Church Family Building Number 20; see Shaker Church Family Waterpower Building

Shaker Church Family Building Number 3; see Shaker Church Family Brethren's Workshop

Shaker Church Family Building Number 4; see Shaker Church Family Seed House

Shaker Church Family Building Number 5; see Shaker Ministry's Shop

Shaker Church Family Building Number 9; see Shaker Church Family Tannery

Shaker Church Family Building SS; see Shaker Schoolhouse

Shaker Church Family Dwelling House (Shaker Church Family Main Dwelling; Shaker Wickersham House; Shaker Church Family Building Number 1)
Shaker Rd.
HABS NY-3298
HABS NY,11-NELEB.V,2-
6ph L

Shaker Church Family Herb House
Shaker Rd.
HABS NY-3305
HABS NY,11-NELEB.V,15-
1ph L

Shaker Church Family Infirmary; see Shaker Church Family Nurse Shop

Shaker Church Family Main Dwelling; see Shaker Church Family Dwelling House

Shaker Church Family Ministry's Residence; see Shaker Ministry's Shop

Shaker Church Family Nurse Shop (Shaker Church Family Infirmary; Shaker Hinckley House; Shaker Church Family Building Number 13)
Shaker Rd.
HABS NY-3297
HABS NY,11-NELEB.V,9-
4ph L

Shaker Church Family Office; see Shaker Church Family Trustees' Office

Shaker Church Family Reservoir
Shaker Rd.
HABS NY-3300
HABS NY,11-NELEB.V,13-
1ph L

Shaker Church Family School; see Shaker Schoolhouse

Shaker Church Family Seed House (Shaker Whittaker House; Shaker Church Family Building Number 4)
Shaker Rd.
HABS NY-3301
HABS NY,11-NELEB.V,5-
3ph L

Shaker Church Family Sisters' Workshop (Shaker Church Family Washhouse; Shaker Church Family Building Number 18)
Shaker Rd.
HABS NY-3302
HABS NY,11-NELEB.V,11-
10ph L

Shaker Church Family Tannery (Shaker Church Family Building Number 9)
Shaker Rd.
HABS NY-3303
HABS NY,11-NELEB.V,7-
2ph L

Shaker Church Family Trustees' Office (Shaker Church Family Office; Shaker Church Family Building Number 12)
Shaker Rd.
HABS NY-3299
HABS NY,11-NELEB.V,8-
3ph L

Shaker Church Family Washhouse; see Shaker Church Family Sisters' Workshop

Shaker Church Family Waterpower Building (Shaker Church Family Building Number 20)
Shaker Rd.
HABS NY-3267
HABS NY,11-NELEB.V,12-
1dr L

Shaker Hinckley House; see Shaker Church Family Nurse Shop

Shaker Medicine Shop; see Shaker Centre Family Washhouse

Shaker Meetinghouse (second) (Shaker Church Family Building Number 2)
Shaker Rd.
HABS NY-3254
HABS NY,11-NELEB.V,3-
13dr/17ph/6pg L

Shaker Ministry's Shop (Shaker Church Family Ministry's Residence; Shaker Church Family Building Number 5)
Shaker Rd.
HABS NY-3255
HABS NY,11-NELEB.V,6-
4dr/6ph L

Shaker North Familly Building Number 6; see Shaker North Family Washhouse (second)

Shaker North Family (General Views)
Shaker Rd.
HABS NY-3319
HABS NY,11-NELEB.V,23-
7ph L

Shaker North Family Barn (Shaker North Family Stone Barn; Shaker North Family Building Number 14)
State Rt. 22 & U.S. Rt. 20
HABS NY-3251
HABS NY,11-NELEB.V,30-
5dr/5ph L

Shaker North Family Brethren's Dwelling House; see Shaker North Family Dwelling House (second)

Shaker North Family Brethren's Shop; see Shaker North Family Washhouse (first)

Shaker North Family Building Number 1; see Shaker North Family Dwelling House (first)

Shaker North Family Building Number 14; see Shaker North Family Barn

Shaker North Family Building Number 18; see Shaker North Family Washhouse (first)

Shaker North Family Building Number 19; see Shaker North Family Smithy

Shaker North Family Building Number 2; see Shaker North Family Office & Store

Shaker North Family Building Number 20; see Shaker North Family Lumber & Grist Mill

Shaker North Family Building Number 3; see Shaker North Family Icehouse

Shaker North Family Building Number 7; see Shaker North Family Dwelling House (second)

Shaker North Family Building Number 8; see Shaker North Family Farm,Deacon's Shop

Shaker North Family Dwelling House (first) (Shaker North Family Residence; Shaker North Family Building Number 1)
Shaker Rd.
HABS NY-3249
HABS NY,11-NELEB.V,24-
11dr/19ph L

Shaker North Family Dwelling House (second) (Shaker North Family Second House; Shaker North Family Brethren's Dwelling House; Shaker North Family Building Number 7)
State Rt. 22 & U.S. Rt. 20
HABS NY-3321
HABS NY,11-NELEB.V,28-
16ph L

Shaker North Family Farm,Deacon's Shop (Shaker North Family Men's Quarters & Shop; Shaker North Family Building Number 8)
Shaker Rd.
HABS NY-3325
HABS NY,11-NELEB.V,29-
1ph L

Shaker North Family Granary
Shaker Rd.
HABS NY-3320
HABS NY,11-NELEB.V,34-
2ph L

Shaker North Family Icehouse (Shaker North Family Building Number 3)
Shaker Rd.
HABS NY-3322
HABS NY,11-NELEB.V,26-
2ph L

Shaker North Family Laundry & Water Power Bldg.; see Shaker North Family Washhouse (first)

Shaker North Family Laundry & Woodstore Building; see Shaker North Family Washhouse (second)

Shaker North Family Lumber & Grist Mill (Shaker North Family Building Number 20)
Shaker Rd.
HABS NY-3253
HABS NY,11-NELEB.V,33-
4dr/8ph L

Shaker North Family Men's Quarters & Shop; see Shaker North Family Farm,Deacon's Shop

Shaker North Family Office & Store (Shaker North Family Building Number 2)
Shaker Rd.
HABS NY-3323
HABS NY,11-NELEB.V,25-
3ph L

Shaker North Family Residence; see Shaker North Family Dwelling House (first)

Shaker North Family Second House; see Shaker North Family Dwelling House (second)

Shaker North Family Smithy (Shaker North Family Building Number 19)
Shaker Rd.
HABS NY-3268
HABS NY,11-NELEB.V,32-
4dr/5ph L

Shaker North Family Stone Barn; see Shaker North Family Barn

Shaker North Family Washhouse (first) (Shaker North Family Laundry & Water Power Bldg.; Shaker North Family Brethren's Shop; Shaker North Family Building Number 18)
Shaker Rd.
HABS NY-3252
HABS NY,11-NELEB.V,31-
4dr/8ph L

Shaker North Family Washhouse (second) (Shaker North Family Laundry & Woodstore Building; Shaker North Familly Building Number 6)
Shaker Rd.
HABS NY-3250
HABS NY,11-NELEB.V,27-
5dr/16ph L

Shaker Schoolhouse (Shaker Church Family School; Shaker Church Family Building SS)
Shaker Rd.
HABS NY-3259
HABS NY,11-NELEB.V,10-
4dr/5ph L

Shaker Second Family (General Views)
Shaker Rd.
HABS NY-3326
HABS NY,11-NELEB.V,41-
2ph L

Shaker Second Family Brethren's Workshop (Shaker Second Family Building Number 2)
Shaker Rd.
HABS NY-3330
HABS NY,11-NELEB.V,42-
2ph L

Shaker Second Family Building Number 2; see Shaker Second Family Brethren's Workshop

Shaker Second Family Chair Factory
Shaker Rd.
HABS NY-3328
HABS NY,11-NELEB,44-
4ph L

Shaker Second Family Dwelling House
Shaker Rd.
HABS NY-3327
HABS NY,11-NELEB.V,43-
4ph L

Shaker Second Family Herb House
Shaker Rd.
HABS NY-3329
HABS NY,11-NELEB.V,45-
1ph L

Shaker Second Family Sisters' Workshop & Barn
Shaker Rd.
HABS NY-3331
HABS NY,11-NELEB.V,46-
10ph L

Shaker South Family (General Views)
Shaker Rd.
HABS NY-3332
HABS NY,11-NELEB.V,16-
6ph L

Shaker South Family Barn
Shaker Rd.
HABS NY-3342
HABS NY,11-NELEB.V,48-
1ph L

Shaker South Family Building Number 1; see Shaker South Family Dwelling House (second)

Shaker South Family Building Number 2; see Shaker South Family Dwelling House (first)

Shaker South Family Building Number 6; see Shaker South Family Washhouse

Shaker South Family Building Number 7; see Shaker South Family Chair Factory

Shaker South Family Chair Factory (Shaker South Family Chair Shop; Shaker South Family Building Number 7)
Shaker Rd.
HABS NY-3335
HABS NY,11-NELEB.V,21-
3ph L

Shaker South Family Chair Shop; see Shaker South Family Chair Factory

Shaker South Family Dwelling House (first) (Shaker South Family Office; Shaker South Family Building Number 2)
Shaker Rd.
HABS NY-3334
HABS NY,11-NELEB.V,18-
3ph L

Shaker South Family Dwelling House (second) (Shaker South Family Building Number 1)
Shaker Rd.
HABS NY-3333
HABS NY,11-NELEB.V,17-
3dr/14ph L

Shaker South Family Infirmary; see Shaker South Family Nurse Shop

Shaker South Family Laundry & Chairmaking Shop; see Shaker South Family Washhouse

Shaker South Family Nurse Shop (Shaker South Family Infirmary)
Shaker Rd.
HABS NY-3336
HABS NY,11-NELEB.V,22-
3ph L

Shaker South Family Office; see Shaker South Family Dwelling House (first)

Shaker South Family Privy
Shaker Rd.
HABS NY-3248
HABS NY,11-NELEB.V,19-
3dr L

Shaker South Family Washhouse (Shaker South Family Laundry & Chairmaking Shop; Shaker South Family Building Number 6)
Shaker Rd.
HABS NY-3269
HABS NY,11-NELEB.V,20-
11dr/20ph L

Shaker Upper Canaan Family
Shaker Rd.
HABS NY-3340
HABS NY,11-NELEB.V,47-
1ph L

Shaker Village (Sketch Map)
HABS NY-6261
HABS NY,11-NELEB.V,49-
1dr/fr L

Shaker Whittaker House; see Shaker Church Family Seed House

Shaker Wickersham House; see Shaker Church Family Dwelling House

NEW CONCORD

House,Gingerbread
HABS NY-3231
HABS NY,11-NECON,4-
1ph L

Pratt,Anson,House
HABS NY-355
HABS NY,11-NECON,1-
13dr/5ph/1pg L

Reformed Church
HABS NY-3218
HABS NY,11-NECON,3-
1ph L

Tompkins,Thomas L.,House
HABS NY-3147
HABS NY,11-NECON,2-
2ph L

NORTH GERMANTOWN

Hake's House
HABS NY-6020
HABS NY,11-GERMN,1-
1ph/1pg L

OLD CHATHAM

Antinore Farm; see Van Walkenburg House

Parsonage,Old
HABS NY-5493
HABS NY,11-CHATO,3-
1ph L

Root-Harper House
HABS NY-5494
HABS NY,11-CHATO,2-
2ph L

Run House (Porch)
HABS NY-5496
HABS NY,11-CHATO,4-
1ph L

Van Walkenburg House (Antinore Farm)
HABS NY-5495
HABS NY,11-CHATO,5-
5ph L

Wilbor,Samuel,House
HABS NY-5-A-24
HABS NY,11-CHATO,1-
9dr/6ph/2pg L

STOCKPORT

Lathrope House
HABS NY-6024
HABS NY,11-STOCPO,1-
1ph/1pg L

Macy Woolen Mill,Old; see Print Works

Mill,Stone
HABS NY-6026
HABS NY,11-STOCPO,3-
2ph L

Print Works (Macy Woolen Mill,Old)
HABS NY-6025
HABS NY,11-STOCPO,2-
1ph L

CORTLAND COUNTY

CINCINNATUS

Kingman,Col. John,House
Main St.
HABS NY-5600
HABS NY,11-CINC,1-
4ph/7pg L

CORTLAND

Church,Cobblestone; see Unitarian-Universalist Church

Delaware,Lackawana & Western RR,Crossing Guard Hse (Delaware,Lackawana & Western RR,Elevated Watch Twr
Central Ave. at Pendleton St.
HABS NY-5595
HABS NY,12-CORT,7A-
3ph/8pg/fr L

Delaware,Lackawana & Western RR,Elevated Watch Twr; see Delaware,Lackawana & Western RR,Crossing Guard Hse

Dibble,Horace A.,House
90 N. Main St.
HABS NY-5591
HABS NY,12-CORT,1-
8ph/6pg L

Hathaway Hall; see Hathaway,Samuel Gilbert,House

Hathaway,Samuel Gilbert,House (Hathaway Hall)
Solon Rd. (State Rt. 41)
HABS NY-5592
HABS NY,12-SOL,1-
12ph/5pg L

Lehigh Valley Railroad Station
7 South Ave.
HABS NY-5594
HABS NY,12-CORT,6A-
10ph/7pg/fr L

Randall,Henry Stephens,House
18 Tompkins St.
HABS NY-5593
HABS NY,12-CORT,2-
2ph/2pg L

Unitarian-Universalist Church (Church,Cobblestone)
3 Church St.
HABS NY-5590
HABS NY,12-CORT,5-
5ph L

HOMER

Barber,Jedediah,House
18 N. Main St.
HABS NY-5597
HABS NY,12-HOM,4-
9ph/6pg/fr L

Calvary Episcopal Church
Park St.
HABS NY-5435
HABS NY,12-HOM,1-
4dr/5ph/7pg/fr L

Donnelly,Augustus,House
(Harum,David,House)
80 S. Main St.
HABS NY-5598
HABS NY,11-HOM,3-
6ph/6pg L

Harum,David,House; see
Donnelly,Augustus,House

Satterly,George,House; see
Sautelle,Sig,Circus Training House

Sautelle,Sig,Circus Training House
(Satterly,George,House)
S. Main St. (State Rt. 11)
HABS NY-5599
HABS NY,12-HOM,2-
9ph/5pg L

MCGRAW

Lamont Library; see
McGraw,Marcus,House

McGraw,Marcus,House (Lamont
Library)
Main St.
HABS NY-5601
HABS NY,12-MCGRA,1-
8ph/7pg L

DELAWARE COUNTY

DEPOSIT

Edick,Conrad,House
1 River St.
HABS NY-5543
HABS NY,13-DEPO,1-
8ph/3pg L

HANCOCK

Erie Railway:Hancock Freight Station
Front & Leonard Sts.
HAER NY-48
HAER NY,13-HANK,1A-
3ph/1pc L

Erie Railway:Hancock Station
Front St.
HAER NY-47
HAER NY,13-HANK,1-
4ph/1pc L

New York,Ontario & Western RR,Delaware River Bridg
HAER NY-66
HAER NY,13-HANK,2-
2ph/1pc L

HANCOCK VIC.

Lordville Suspension Bridge
Spanning Delaware River on Warren Rd.
HAER NY-79
HAER NY,13-HANK.V,1-
1ph/1pc L

DUTCHESS COUNTY

BARRYTOWN VIC.

Edgewater
Station Rd.
HABS NY-5621
HABS NY,14-BARTO.V,1-
5dr/23ph/7pg/2pc/fr L

Edgewater,North Gatehouse
Station Rd.
HABS NY-5621-B
HABS NY,14-BARTO.V,1B-
1dr/1ph/1pg/fr L

Edgewater,South Gatehouse
Station Rd.
HABS NY-5621-A
HABS NY,14-BARTO.V,1A-
1dr/1ph/1pg/1pc/fr L

La Bergerie (Rokeby)
River Rd.
HABS NY-5623
HABS NY,14-BARTO.V,2-
11dr/70ph/21pg/1pc/fr L

Montgomery Place
Annandale Rd.
HABS NY-5625
HABS NY,14-BARTO.V,3-
1dr/13ph/10pg/1pc/fr L

Montgomery Place,Farmhouse
Annandale Rd.
HABS NY-5625-A
HABS NY,14-BARTO.V,3A-
1dr/3ph/1pg/1pc/fr L

Montgomery Place,Swiss Cottage
Annandale Rd.
HABS NY-5625-B
HABS NY,14-BARTO.V,3B-
1dr/2ph/7pg/1pc/fr L

Rokeby; see La Bergerie

BEACON

Brett House; see Teller House

Locust Grove; see Teller House

Mount Gulian; see Verplank House

Teller House (Brett House; Locust Grove)
De Windt St.
HABS NY-360
HABS NY,14-BEAC,1-
10dr/fr L

Tioronda Bridge
South Ave. spanning Fishkill Creek
HAER NY-168
HAER 1991(HAER):5
4dr/19ph/8pg/2pc/fr L

Verplank House (Mount Gulian)
HABS NY-4380
HABS NY,14-BEAC,2-
1ph L

BEACON VIC.

Bannerman's Castle (Bannerman's
Island Arsenal)
Pollepel Island (Bannerman's Island)
,Hudson River
HABS NY-246
HABS NY,14-POLI,1-
17ph L

Bannerman's Island Arsenal; see
Bannerman's Castle

BRINCKERHOFF

Brinckerhoff,Col. John,House
State Rt. 82
HABS NY-4130
HABS NY,14-BRINC,1-
18dr/4ph/3pg/fr L

DOVER PLAINS

Taber-Wing House
State Rt. 22
HABS NY-4117
HABS NY,14-DOVP,1-
18dr/9ph/4pg/fr L

FISHKILL

Classic House
Brinkerhoff Rd.
HABS NY-3101
HABS NY,14-FISH,3-
1ph L

First Dutch Reformed Church
Main St.
HABS NY-4-202
HABS NY,14-FISH,2-
11dr/5ph/8pg/fr L

Trinity Church
E. Main St.
HABS NY-4-201
HABS NY,14-FISH,1-
10dr/3ph/7pg/fr L

Van Wyck House; see Wharton House

Wharton House (Van Wyck House)
U.S. Rt. 9
HABS NY-6028
HABS NY,14-FISH,4-
3pg/fr L

HYDE PARK

Bellefield Barn
Old Post Rd.
HABS NY-5665
HABS NY,14-HYP,7-
5dr/fr L

Crumwold (Fencepost & Gate)
(Rogers,Col. Archibald,House)
Fuller Ln.
HABS NY-4354
HABS NY,14-HYP,4-
1dr L

Eleanor Roosevelt National Historic Site; see Val-Kill

Eleanor Roosevelt National Historic Site; see Val-Kill,Factory

Eleanor Roosevelt National Historic Site; see Val-Kill,Stone Cottage

Home of Franklin D. Roosevelt Nat'l. Historic Site; see Springwood

Hyde Park; see Springwood

Milestone
Old Albany Post Rd.
HABS NY-4353
HABS NY,14-HYP,3-
1dr/fr L

Rogers,Col. Archibald,House; see Crumwold (Fencepost & Gate)

Roosevelt,Franklin D. ,House; see Springwood

Springwood (Roosevelt,Franklin D. ,House; Hyde Park; Home of Franklin D. Roosevelt Nat'l. Historic Site
HABS NY-4355
HABS NY,14-HYP,5-
35dr/78ph/fr L

Springwood,Ice House
HABS NY-4355-B
HABS NY,14-HYP,5B-
4ph L

Springwood,Superintendent's Cottage
HABS NY-4355-A
HABS NY,14-HYP,5A-
5ph L

Stoutenburch,John,House (Porch)
HABS NY-4351
HABS NY,14-HYP,2-
1dr L

Tombstone of Bard Family
St. James' Churchyard,Albany Post Rd.
HABS NY-4352
HABS NY,14-HYP,6-
5dr L

Val-Kill (Eleanor Roosevelt National Historic Site)
State Rt. 9G
HABS NY-5666
HABS NY,14-HYP,8-
2dr/fr L

Val-Kill,Factory (Eleanor Roosevelt National Historic Site)
State Rt. 9G
HABS NY-5666-B
HABS NY,14-HYP,8B-
5dr/fr L

Val-Kill,Stone Cottage (Eleanor Roosevelt National Historic Site)
State Rt. 9G
HABS NY-5666-A
HABS NY,14-HYP,8A-
3dr L

Vanderbilt Boathouse (Vanderbilt Mansion National Historic Site)
HABS NY-3200
HABS NY,14-HYP,1-
2dr L

Vanderbilt Mansion National Historic Site; see Vanderbilt Boathouse

MILAN

Rowe Estate,1766 House
HABS NY-6280
HABS NY,14-MILAN,1-
2ph L

Rowe Estate,1818 House
HABS NY-6280-A
HABS NY,14-MILAN,1A-
6ph L

MILLBROOK

Nine Partners Meetinghouse
State Rt. 82 Vic.
HABS NY-4129
HABS NY,14-MILB,1-
8dr/4ph/1pg/fr L

PLEASANT VALLEY

Dye House; see Mill & Office,Old Stone

Mill & Office,Old Stone (Dye House)
HABS NY-3238
HABS NY,14-PLEAV,2-
1ph L

Store Building,Old Stone
State Rt. 44
HABS NY-356
HABS NY,14-PLEAV,1-
6dr/2ph/1pg/fr L

POUGHKEEPSIE

Clinton,Gov. George,House; see Van Kleeck-Hay House

Flicker House; see Glebe House

Glebe House (Flicker House)
635 Main St.
HABS NY-5-A-203
HABS NY,14-POKEP,1-
11dr/5ph/7pg/fr L

Harmon Printing Building
207-209 Main St.
HABS NY-6029
HABS NY,14-POKEP,4-
4ph/1pg/fr L

Mid Hudson Suspension Bridge
Spanning Hudson River
HAER NY-160
HAER NY,14-POKEP,7-
4ph/1pg/1pc L

Poughkeepsie Bridge
Spanning Hudson River
HAER NY-131
HAER NY,14-POKEP,8-
27ph/1pg/2pc L

Springside (Vassar,Mathew,Estate)
Academy St.
HABS NY-5489
HABS NY,14-POKEP,6-
16ph/1pg L

Springside,Barn & Stable (Vassar,Mathew,Estate,Barn & Stables)
Academy St.
HABS NY-5489-A
HABS NY,14-POKEP,6A-
5ph L

Springside,Carriage House (Vassar,Mathew,Estate,Carriage House)
Academy St.
HABS NY-5489-B
HABS NY,14-POKEP,6B-
2ph L

Springside,Gatehouse (Vassar,Mathew,Estate,Gatehouse)
Market St.
HABS NY-5489-C
HABS NY,14-POKEP,6C-
1ph L

150 Union Street (Commercial Building)
HABS NY-6030
HABS NY,14-POKEP,5-
5ph L

Van Kleeck-Hay House (Clinton,Gov. George,House)
549 Main St.
HABS NY-373
HABS NY,14-POKEP,2-
20dr/fr L

Vassar,Mathew,Estate; see Springside

Vassar,Mathew,Estate,Barn & Stables; see Springside,Barn & Stable

Vassar,Mathew,Estate,Carriage House; see Springside,Carriage House

Vassar,Mathew,Estate,Gatehouse; see Springside,Gatehouse

Winslow,James,Gatehouse
U. S. Rt. 9
HABS NY-4389
HABS NY,14-POKEP,3-
7ph/4pg L

QUAKER HILL

Hicksite Meetinghouse
Pawling vic.
HABS NY-6282
HABS NY,14-QUAHI,1-
8ph L

RED HOOK

House,Dutch (Interior)
HABS NY-3108
HABS NY,14-RED,2-
1ph L

Mansion
HABS NY-3112
HABS NY,14-RED,3-
1ph L

Martin Homestead
U. S. Rt. 9
HABS NY-341
HABS NY,14-RED,1-
9dr/6ph/1pg L

RHINEBECK

Delamater,Henry,House
44 Montgomery St.
HABS NY-5638
HABS NY,14-RHINB,5-
13ph/1pc/fr L

Edgewater; see Rhinebeck Area Historic Survey

Rhinebeck Area Historic Survey (Edgewater)
Hudson River
HABS NY-5624
HABS NY,14-RHINB.V,1-
1dr/1pc L

RHINEBECK VIC.

Leacote; see Meadows,The

Leacote,Stable Cottage; see Meadows,The,Stable Cottage

Leacote,Stables & Carriage House; see Meadows,The,Stables & Carriage House

Linden Grove; see Wyndcliffe

Meadows,The (Leacote)
River Rd.
HABS NY-5622
HABS NY,14-RHINB.V,5-
4dr/17ph/7pg/1pc/fr L

Meadows,The,Stable Cottage (Leacote,Stable Cottage)
River Rd.
HABS NY-5622-B
HABS NY,14-RHINB.V,5B-
1dr/1ph/2pg/1pc/fr L

Meadows,The,Stables & Carriage House (Leacote,Stables & Carriage House)
River Rd.
HABS NY-5622-A
HABS NY,14-RHINB.V,5A-
2dr/3ph/2pg/1pc/fr L

Wildercliff
Morton Rd.
HABS NY-5628
HABS NY,14-RHINB.V,3-
5dr/11ph/10pg/1pc/fr L

Wilderstein
Morton Rd.
HABS NY-5629
HABS NY,14-RHINB.V,4-
8dr/54ph/72pg/3pc/fr L

Wyndcliffe (Linden Grove)
Mill Rd.
HABS NY-5627
HABS NY,14-RHINB.V,2-
3dr/43ph/9pg/3pc/5ct/fr L

TIORONDA

De Peyster,Abraham,House (Newlin House)
Town of Fishkill
HABS NY-4-205
HABS NY,14-TIOR,1-
16dr/fr L

Newlin House; see De Peyster,Abraham,House

TIVOLI VIC.

Rose Hill
Woods Rd.
HABS NY-5626
HABS NY,14-TIV.V,1-
5dr/16ph/7pg/1pc/fr L

UPPER RED HOOK

Lyle House
HABS NY-6031
HABS NY,14-REDU,1-
7ph L

WAPPINGERS FALLS

Mesier House
Mesier Park,Mesier Ave.
HABS NY-372
HABS NY,14-WAP,1-
11dr/fr L

WINGDALE

Morehouse Tavern
HABS NY-6281
HABS NY,14-WING,1-
1ph L

ERIE COUNTY

BUFFALO

Blessed Trinity Roman Catholic Church
317 Leroy Ave.
HABS NY-5709
HABS NY,15-BUF,15-
5ph/2pg L

Buffalo City Hall (City Hall)
65 Niagara Square
HABS NY-6033
HABS NY,15-BUF,13-
27ph/14pg/2pc/fr L

Buffalo Gas Light Company
249 W. Genesee St.
HAER NY-64
HAER NY,15-BUF,23-
2ph/1pg/1pc L

Buffalo Lighthouse
Buffalo Harbor,Buffalo River & Lake Erie
HABS NY-60
HABS NY,15-BUF,17-
7dr/2ph/4pg L

Buffalo State Hospital; see State Lunatic Asylum

Cary House
184 Delaware Ave.
HABS NY-5613
HABS NY,15-BUF,1-
5ph/2pg L

City Hall; see Buffalo City Hall

Cyclorama Building
369 Franklin St.
HABS NY-6297
HABS 1991(HABS):21
44ph/8pg/4pc L

D. L. & W. Railroad,Lackawanna Terminal
Main St. & Buffalo River
HAER NY-63
HAER NY,15-BUF,22-
4dr/16ph/4pg/4pc/fr L

Dorsheimer,William,House
438 Delaware Ave.
HABS NY-5608
HABS NY,15-BUF,2-
5ph/5pg L

Erie County Hall
HABS NY-6034
HABS NY,15-BUF,16-
1ph L

Erie County Savings Bank
16 Niagara St.
HABS NY-5615
HABS NY,15-BUF,3-
12ph/5pg L

Erie Railway:East Buffalo Station
HAER NY-71
HAER NY,15-BUF,21-
1ph/1pc L

Erie Railway:Kensington Avenue Station
Kensington Ave.
HAER NY-72
HAER NY,15-BUF,18-
1ph/1pc L

Erie Railway:Main Street Station
Main St.
HAER NY-73
HAER NY,15-BUF,19-
1ph/1pc L

Erie Railway:Walden Avenue Station
Walden Ave.
HAER NY-74
HAER NY,15-BUF,20-
1ph/1pc L

Guaranty Building; see Prudential Building

Heath,W. R.,House
76 Soldiers Place
HABS NY-6035
HABS NY,15-BUF,14-
3ph L

Kremlin Building
Pearl & Eagle Sts.
HABS NY-5614
HABS NY,15-BUF,4-
2ph/2pg L

Martin,Darwin,House
125 Jewett Parkway
HABS NY-5611
HABS NY,15-BUF,5-
27dr/15ph/13pg/fr L

Prudential Building (Guaranty Building)
28 Church St.
HABS NY-5487
HABS NY,15-BUF,6-
16ph/9pg L

St. Louis Roman Catholic Church
Main & Edward Sts.
HABS NY-5488
HABS NY,15-BUF,7-
12ph/6pg L

St. Paul's Episcopal Cathedral
Shelton Square
HABS NY-5612
HABS NY,15-BUF,8-
12ph/8pg L

State Lunatic Asylum (Buffalo State Hospital)
400 Forest Ave.
HABS NY-5606
HABS NY,15-BUF,9-
8ph/7pg L

Theodore Roosevelt Inaugural Nat'l Hist. Site; see Wilcox,Ansley,House

U. S. Custom House
Washington & Seneca Sts.
HABS NY-5609
HABS NY,15-BUF,10-
9ph/8pg L

U. S. Post Office
121 Ellicott St.
HABS NY-5605
HABS NY,15-BUF,11-
18ph/7pg L

Wilcox,Ansley,House (Theodore Roosevelt Inaugural Nat'l Hist. Site)
641 Delaware Ave.
HABS NY-5610
HABS NY,15-BUF,12-
7ph/12pg L

BUFFALO VIC.

Bethlehem Steel Corporation,Lackawanna Plant (Lackawanna Steel Company)
Rt. 5 on Lake Erie
HAER NY-198
HAER NY,15-LACK,1-
8dr/fr L

Lackawanna Steel Company; see Bethlehem Steel Corporation,Lackawanna Plant

IRVING

Thomas Asylum for Orph. & Dest. Indians,Admin.Bldg (Thomas Indian School,Administration Building)
Rt. 438,Cattaraugas Reservation
HABS NY-6012-A
HABS NY,15-CATRES,1A-
21ph/1pg L

Thomas Asylum for Orph. & Dest. Indians,Dining Hal (Thomas Indian School,Dining Hall)
Rt. 438,Cattaraugas Reservation
HABS NY-6012-B
HABS NY,15-CATRES,1B-
8ph/1pg L

Thomas Asylum for Orph. & Dest. Indians,Dormitory (Thomas Indian School,Dormitory)
Rt. 438,Cattaraugas Reservation
HABS NY-6012-C
HABS NY,15-CATRES,1C-
6ph/7pg L

Thomas Asylum for Orphan & Destitute Indians (Thomas Indian School)
Rt. 438,Cattaraugas Reservation
HABS NY-6012
HABS NY,15-CATRES,1-
7pg L

Thomas Indian School; see Thomas Asylum for Orphan & Destitute Indians

Thomas Indian School,Administration Building; see Thomas Asylum for Orph. & Dest. Indians,Admin.Bldg

Thomas Indian School,Dining Hall; see Thomas Asylum for Orph. & Dest. Indians,Dining Hal

Thomas Indian School,Dormitory; see Thomas Asylum for Orph. & Dest. Indians,Dormitory

LAWTONS VIC.

Buffalo & South Western Division,Bridge 20.18; see Erie Railway:Clear Creek Viaduct

Erie Railway:Clear Creek Viaduct (Buffalo & South Western Division,Bridge 20.18)
Spanning Clear Creek at U.S. Rt. 62
HAER NY-29
HAER NY,15-LAWT.V,1-
3ph/1pc L

SUSPENSION BRIDGE

Erie Railway:Suspension Bridge Station
HAER NY-139
HAER NY,15-SUSBR,1-
1ph/1pc L

ESSEX COUNTY

AU SABLE FORKS

Grove Road Bridge; see Rolling Hill Mill Road Bridge

Rolling Hill Mill Road Bridge (Grove Road Bridge)
Grove Rd.,spanning the east branch of AuSable Rv.
HAER NY-171
HAER 1991(HAER):5
5ph/4pg/1pc L

FORT TICONDEROGA

Fort Ticonderoga
HABS NY-3212
HABS NY,16-FOTI,1-
5ph L

JAY

Jay Covered Bridge
Count Route 22, spans the E. Branch of AuSable Riv
HAER NY-170
HAER 1991(HAER):5
2dr/7ph/5pg/1pc/fr L

LAKE PLACID VIC.

Brown,John,Farm State Historic Site,Farmhouse
State Rt. 73 (North Elba Twp.)
HABS NY-245
HABS NY,16-LAPLA.V,1A-
6dr L

NORTH ELBA

Lake Placid Club,Forest Wing
E. side of Mirror Lake Dr.,N. of St. Rt. 86 & Main
HABS NY-6306
HABS DLC/PP-1993:NY-5
78ph/59pg/9pc L

TAHAWUS

Adirondack Iron & Steel Company,New Furnace
Hudson River
HAER NY-123
HAER NY,16-TAHA,1-
13dr/32ph/202pg/3pc/fr L

FULTON COUNTY

BROADALBIN

Hemlock Church
HABS NY-3210
HABS NY,18-BROD,1-
1ph L

GLOVERSVILLE

Burr,Nathaniel,House
153 Kingsboro Ave.
HABS NY-6036
HABS NY,18-GLOV,2-
2ph/1pg L

Kingsboro Presbyterian Church
N. Kingsboro Ave.
HABS NY-381
HABS NY,18-GLOV,1-
3ph/1pg L

JOHNSTOWN

Black Horse Tavern
HABS NY-3126
HABS NY,18-JONTO,4-
3ph L

Courthouse,Old
N. William St.
HABS NY-3139
HABS NY,18-JONTO,2-
3ph/1pg L

Drumm Homestead
W. State & Green Sts.
HABS NY-3233
HABS NY,18-JONTO,5-
1ph L

Fort Johnstown,Old (Fulton County Jail)
Montgomery & S. Perry Sts.
HABS NY-394
HABS NY,18-JONTO,3-
3ph L

Fulton County Jail; see Fort Johnstown,Old

Johnson Hall
HABS NY-3107
HABS NY,18-JONTO,1-
17ph/1pg/fr L

Johnson Hall,Blockhouse
HABS NY-392
HABS NY,18-JONTO,1A-
3dr/2ph L

Union Hall
E. Main St.
HABS NY-6259
HABS NY,18-JONTO,6-
1ph/1pg L

MAYFIELD

Rice Homestead
Rt. 30
HABS NY-365
HABS NY,18-MAYF,1-
17dr/4ph/2pg/fr L

PERTH

McIntyre,Duncan,House
HABS NY-3237
HABS NY,18-PERTH,2-
1ph L

United Presbyterian Church
State Hwy. 30 Vic.
HABS NY-363
HABS NY,18-PERTH,1-
15dr/4ph/1pg/fr L

United Presbyterian Church,Parsonage
State Rt. 30 Vic.
HABS NY-363-A
HABS NY,18-PERTH,1A-
1ph/1pg L

GENESEE COUNTY

BATAVIA

Batavia Gas Light Company,Gasholder Houses
Evans & Ellicott Sts.
HAER NY-41
HAER NY,19-BAT,4A-
3ph/1pg/1pc L

Holland Land Office
W. Main St.
HABS NY-6038
HABS NY,19-BAT,3-
5ph L

BATAVIA VIC.

Lehigh Valley R.R.,Baltimore Through-Truss Bridge
State Rt. 5 Vic.
HAER NY-51
HAER 1984(HAER):33
2ph/1pc L

GREENE COUNTY

ATHENS

Hudson-Athens Lighthouse
Hudson River
HABS NY-6286
HABS NY,20-ATH,2-
9dr/fr L

CAIRO

First Presbyterian Church
Main St.
HABS NY-4-25
HABS NY,20-CARO,1-
10dr/4ph/4pg/fr L

CATSKILL

Uncle Sam Bridge
County Rt. 385,spanning the Catskill Creek
HAER NY-172
HAER 1991(HAER):5
3ph/4pg/1pc L

CATSKILL MTS.

Van Winkle,Rip,House
HABS NY-383
HABS NY,20- ,
1ph L

LEEDS

Church,Stone
HABS NY-387
HABS NY,20-LEED,2-
1ph/1pg L

Leeds Bridge
State Hwy. 23
HABS NY-4-8
HABS NY,20-LEED,1-
2dr/5ph/2pg/fr L

WEST COXSACKIE

Bronck,Peter,House
HABS NY-3114
HABS NY,20-COXW,1-
8ph/1pg/fr L

HERKIMER COUNTY

DANUBE

Indian Castle Church
State Rt. 55
HABS NY-243
HABS NY,22-INCA.V,1-
4ph/1pg L

FORT HERKIMER

Schoolhouse,Old
HABS NY-3217
HABS NY,22-HERK,4-
1ph/1pg L

FRANKFORT

Erie Canal,North Lock
Moyer Creek Crossing
HABS NY-231-C
HABS NY,22-FRAFO,1-
2ph L

Erie Canal,South Towpath Crossing
Moyer Creek Crossing
HABS NY-231-B
HABS NY,22-FRAFO,1-
2ph L

Erie Canal,Viaduct
Moyer Creek Crossing
HABS NY-231-A
HABS NY,22-FRAFO,1-
5ph L

HERKIMER

Fort Herkimer Church
HABS NY-242
HABS NY,22-HERK,1-
9ph/1pg L

Herkimer Jail
HABS NY-249
HABS NY,22-HERK,3-
2ph L

Reformed Church
HABS NY-6039
HABS NY,22-HERK,2-
1ph L

ILION

Erie Canal Locks
HABS NY-6040
HABS NY,22-ILIO,1-
3ph L

INDIAN CASTLE VIC.

Van Wie House
HABS NY-3204
HABS NY,22-INCA.V,2-
1ph L

LITTLE FALLS

Fink,Major,House
HABS NY-248
HABS NY,22-LITFA,1-
1ph L

RUSSIA

Butler House
State Rd.
HABS NY-5-U-2
HABS NY,22-RUS,1-
3dr/3ph/2pg/fr L

JEFFERSON COUNTY

WATERTOWN

Court Street Bridge
Court St.,Rt.11,spanning the Black River
HAER NY-173
HAER 1991(HAER):5
10ph/11pg/1pc/fr L

Jefferson County Courthouse,Old
Arsenal & Sherman Sts.
HABS NY-5438
HABS NY,23-WATO,2-
5ph L

New York State Armory (second)
Arsenal & Jackman Sts.
HABS NY-5437
HABS NY,23-WATO,1-
2ph L

125 Washington Street (Commercial Building)
HABS NY-5439
HABS NY,23-WATO,3-
1ph L

Watertown National Bank Building
Washington & Stone Sts.
HABS NY-5440
HABS NY,23-WATO,4-
1ph L

KINGS COUNTY

BROOKLYN

Bennett House; see Wyckoff-Bennett House

Bergen House
HABS NY-6042
HABS NY,24-BROK,13-
1ph L

Bethany Deaconess Hospital
237 Saint Nicholas Ave.
HABS NY-5731
HABS NY,24-BROK,47-
15ph/10pg L

Brooklyn Army Supply Base (Brooklyn Military Ocean Terminal; Brooklyn Army Terminal)
Upper NY Bay, Fifty-eighth thru Sixty-fourth Sts.
HAER NY-202
HAER 1991(HAER):5
1ph/20pg/2pc L

Brooklyn Army Supply Base: Pier 1 (Brooklyn Military Ocean Terminal: Pier 1; Brooklyn Army Terminal: Pier 1)
Upper NY Bay, opp. the end of Sixty-third St.
HAER NY-202-A
HAER 1991(HAER):5
4ph/8pg/2pc H

Brooklyn Army Terminal; see Brooklyn Army Supply Base

Brooklyn Army Terminal: Pier 1; see Brooklyn Army Supply Base: Pier 1

Brooklyn Borough Hall; see Brooklyn City Hall

Brooklyn City Hall (Brooklyn Borough Hall)
209 Joralemon St.
HABS NY-6260
HABS NY,24-BROK,42-
11dr/6ph/17pg L

Brooklyn Military Ocean Terminal; see Brooklyn Army Supply Base

Brooklyn Military Ocean Terminal: Pier 1; see Brooklyn Army Supply Base: Pier 1

Bush Terminal; see Bush Terminal Company

Bush Terminal Company (Bush Terminal)
Btwn. Second & Third Aves. from 39th to 50th Sts.
HAER NY-201
HAER 1991(HAER):5
3ph/22pg/2pc L

Bush Terminal Company: Pier 5 (Bush Terminal: Pier 5)
Opposite end of Forty-first St. on upper NY Bay
HAER NY-201-B
HAER 1991(HAER):5
12ph/10pg/2pc L

Bush Terminal Company: Pier 7 (Bush Terminal: Pier 7)
End of Forty-first St. on Upper NY Bay
HAER NY-201-A
HAER 1991(HAER):5
9ph/13pg/2pc/fr L

Bush Terminal: Pier 5; see Bush Terminal Company: Pier 5

Bush Terminal: Pier 7; see Bush Terminal Company: Pier 7

Columbia Street Pier; see New York Barge Canal:Gowanus Bay Terminal Pier

Cutting House; see Tillary,Dr. James,House

Ditmas House; see Van Nuyse,Johannes,House

Erasmus Hall (Academy)
Flatbush Ave.
HABS NY-519
HABS NY,24-BROK,4-
18dr/4ph/fr L

Flatbush Town Hall
35 Snyder Ave.
HABS NY-332
HABS NY,24-BROK,43-
3ph/3pg/fr L

Flushing Avenue (House)
Junk yard
HABS NY-6266
HABS NY,24-BROK,45-
2ph L

Fox Theatre
20 Flatbush Ave. & 1 Nevins St.
HABS NY-5554
HABS NY,24-BROK,41-
23ph/51pg/2pc L

Gowanus; see Vechte-Cortelyou House

Gowanus Bay Terminal Pier; see New York Barge Canal:Gowanus Bay Terminal Pier

Isbrantsen Pier; see South Brooklyn Freight Terminal:29th Street Pier

Jefferson Mansion (Unity Democratic League)
HABS NY-6267
HABS NY,24-BROK,49-
1ph L

Lefferts House
Prospect Park (moved from 563 Flatbush Ave.)
HABS NY-511
HABS NY,24-BROK,2-
14dr/15ph/7pg/fr L

Long Island Historical Society Building
128 Pierrepont St.
HABS NY-6100
HABS NY,24-BROK,46-
8pg/fr L

N. Y. State Barge Canal,Grain Elevator Terminal
Henry St. Basin
HAER NY-69
HAER NY,24-BROK,51B-
1ph/1pg/1pc L

Documentation: **ct** color transparencies **dr** measured drawings **fr** field records
pc photograph captions **pg** pages of text **ph** photographs

New Utrecht Reformed Church
HABS NY-6268
HABS NY,24-BROK,50-
1ph L

New York Barge Canal:Gowanus Bay Terminal Pier (Gowanus Bay Terminal Pier; Columbia Street Pier)
E. of bulkhead supporting Columbia St.
HAER NY-154
HAER NY,24-BROK,51A-
29ph/38pg/3pc L

Plymouth Church
Orange & Hicks Sts.
HABS NY-4-11
HABS NY,24-BROK,31-
12dr/4ph/5pg L

Pratt Institute,Power Generating Plant
Willoughby Ave. between Classen & Hall Sts.
HAER NY-70
HAER NY,24-BROK,52A-
2ph/1pg/1pc L

Rheingold Brewery Office Building
74 Stanwix St.
HABS NY-6120
HABS NY,24-BROK,48A-
6ph/2pg L

Robb House
Bedford Ave. & Clarkson
HABS NY-6043
HABS NY,24-BROK,44-
11dr L

Schenck House
Canarsie Park (fragments in Brooklyn Museum)
HABS NY-513
HABS NY,24-BROK,18-
8dr/12ph/3pg/fr L

Schenck-Crooke House
21-23 E. Sixty-third St.
HABS NY-4-12
HABS NY,24-BROK,9-
10dr/4ph/5pg/fr L

Schenck,Judge Teunis,House
Highland Park,Jamaica Ave.
HABS NY-517
HABS NY,24-BROK,38-
15dr/15ph L

South Brooklyn Freight Terminal:29th Street Pier (Twenty-Ninth Street Pier; Isbrantsen Pier)
Opposite end of Twenty-ninth St. on upper NY Bay
HAER NY-203
HAER 1991(HAER):5
16ph/18pg/3pc L

Szold,Harold J.,House
57 Willow St.
HABS NY-4-34
HABS NY,24-BROK,33-
8dr/4ph/fr L

Tillary,Dr. James,House (Cutting House)
15 Tillary St.
HABS NY-512
HABS NY,24-BROK,35-
11dr/17ph/3pg L

Twenty-Ninth Street Pier; see South Brooklyn Freight Terminal:29th Street Pier

Unity Democratic League; see Jefferson Mansion

Van Nuyse-Magaw House
1041 E. Twenty-second St.
HABS NY-514
HABS NY,24-BROK,36-
15dr/13ph/fr L

Van Nuyse,Johannes,House (Ditmas House)
150 Amersfort Place
HABS NY-4-15
HABS NY,24-BROK,3-
8dr/8ph/9pg/fr L

Van Pelt Manor House
Eighty-first St. & Eighteenth Ave.
HABS NY-516
HABS NY,24-BROK,37-
10ph L

Vechte-Cortelyou House (Gowanus)
HABS NY-5112
HABS NY,24-BROK,40-
2ph L

Wyckoff Homestead
1325 Flushing Ave.
HABS NY-518
HABS NY,24-BROK,12-
9ph L

Wyckoff-Bennett House (Bennett House)
Kings Hwy. & 1669 E. Twenty-second St.
HABS NY-5110
HABS NY,24-BROK.39-
15dr/22ph/fr L

Wyckoff,Peter,House
5902 Canarsie Ln.
HABS NY-4-28
HABS NY,24-BROK,32-
9dr/4ph/4pg/fr L

LIVINGSTON COUNTY

AVON

Erie Railway:Avon Freight Station
Rochester St.
HAER NY-53
HAER NY,26-AVO,1A-
1ph/1pc L

Erie Railway:Avon Station
Railroad Ave.
HAER NY-52
HAER NY,26-AVO,1-
5ph/1pc L

CALEDONIA

Clark,James R.,House
Main St.
HABS NY-213
HABS NY,26-CAL,1-
9dr/4ph/8pg/fr L

EAST AVON

Pearson,Joseph,House (Taintor House)
HABS NY-216
HABS NY,26-AVNE,1-
8dr/5ph/6pg/fr L

Taintor House; see Pearson,Joseph,House

MADISON COUNTY

CANASTOTA

Buda House; see Sowter,Lewis,House

Sowter,Lewis,House (Buda House)
142 Canal St.
HABS NY-6262
HABS NY,27-CANA,1-
9ph/2pg L

CANASTOTA VIC.

Roberts,Judge Nathan,House
State Hwy. 5
HABS NY-5-S-4
HABS NY,27-CANA.V,1-
13dr/4ph/2pg L

CAZENOVIA

Lincklaen,Col. John,House; see Lorenzo Mansion

Lorenzo Mansion (Lincklaen,Col. John,House)
HABS NY-5454
HABS NY,27-CAZNO,1-
8ph L

CHITTENANGO

St. Paul's Episcopal Church
HABS NY-5453
HABS NY,27-CHIT,1-
4ph L

EATON VILLAGE

House,Stone; see Morse,Joseph,House

Morse,Joseph,House (House,Stone)
State Rt. 26 & Mill St.
HABS NY-5603
HABS NY,27-EATO,1-
12ph/12pg L

GEORGETOWN

Brown,Timothy,House (Brown's Temple; Spirit House)
S. Main St. & State Rt. 26
HABS NY-5602
HABS NY,27-GEO,1-
13ph/6pg L

Brown's Temple; see Brown,Timothy,House

Spirit House; see Brown,Timothy,House

ONEIDA VIC.

Oneida Community Mansion; see Perfectionist Community Building

Perfectionist Community Building (Oneida Community Mansion)
Kenwood Ave. ,Kenwood
HABS NY-5616
HABS NY,27-KEN,1A-
3pg L

MONROE COUNTY

BRIGHTON

Orringh Stone Tavern
2370 East Ave.
HABS NY-5-R-8
HABS NY,28-BRIT,1-
10dr/2ph/3pg/fr L

CLARKSON

Jewett,Simeon B.,House
Lake & Ridge Rds.
HABS NY-218
HABS NY,28-CLAR,1-
9dr/6ph/3pg/fr L

HENRIETTA

Kirby,Elihu,House
E. Henrietta & Lehigh Station Rds.
HABS NY-215
HABS NY,28-HEN,1-
9dr/5ph/2pg/fr L

ROCHESTER

Allison House
12 Vick Park-A
HABS NY-6044
HABS NY,28-ROCH,39-
1pg/fr L

Anthony,Susan B.,House
17 Madison St.
HABS NY-6045
HABS NY,28-ROCH,37-
7ph/fr L

Anthony,Susan B.,School (School No. 27)
First St. & Central Park
HABS NY-5722
HABS NY,28-ROCH,41-
45ph/11pg/5pc L

Barry,Patrick,House
692 Mount Hope Ave.
HABS NY-5651
HABS NY,28-ROCH,25-
8ph/8pg L

Bates-Ryder House
1399 East Ave.
HABS NY-5639
HABS NY,28-ROCH,13-
6ph/8pg L

Bissell,Charles,House
666 East Ave.
HABS NY-5640
HABS NY,28-ROCH,14-
4ph/8pg L

Board of Education Building; see Rochester Free Academy

Boynton,E. E.,House
16 East Blvd.
HABS NY-5655
HABS NY,28-ROCH,29-
7ph/10pg L

Brewster,Henry A.,House
Spring & Washington Sts.,NW
HABS NY-220
HABS NY,28-ROCH,9-
10dr/5ph/2pg/fr L

Bronson,Amon,House
263 S. Plymouth Ave.
HABS NY-5662
HABS NY,28-ROCH,35-
4ph/6pg L

Campbell,Benjamin,House (Whittelsey House)
Troup & S. Fitzhugh Sts.
HABS NY-5-R-6
HABS NY,28-ROCH,5-
12dr/6ph/2pg/fr L

Charlotte Lighthouse,Old; see Genessee Lighthouse

Child,Jonathan,House
37 S. Washington St.
HABS NY-5-R-1
HABS NY,28-ROCH,3-
14dr/4ph/2pg/fr L

City Hall; see U. S. Post Office & Courthouse

Convention Hall; see New York State Arsenal

Crombie-Mathews House
135 Spring St.
HABS NY-5653
HABS NY,28-ROCH,27-
4ph/6pg L

Culver,Oliver,House
70 East Blvd.
HABS NY-5-R-5
HABS NY,28-ROCH,4-
9dr/4ph/2pg/fr L

D. A. R.,Irondequoit Chapter House; see Ely,Hervey,House

Danforth,George,House
200 West Ave.
HABS NY-5642
HABS NY,28-ROCH,16-
2ph/5pg L

Dann,Dr. Archibald,House
12 Vick Park
HABS NY-5657
HABS NY,28-ROCH,30-
5ph/6pg L

Driving Park Avenue Bridge (Seneca Park Bridge)
Spanning Genesee River Gorge
HAER NY-150
HAER NY,28-ROCH,42-
12ph/16pg/1pc L

Ellwanger & Barry Nursery Office
668 Mt. Hope Ave.
HABS NY-5650
HABS NY,28-ROCH,24-
3ph/7pg L

Ely,Hervey,House (D. A. R.,Irondequoit Chapter House)
138 Troup St.
HABS NY-5661
HABS NY,28-ROCH,2-
6ph/9pg L

Federal Building
NE corner of N. Fitzhugh & Church Sts.
HABS NY-6046
HABS 1991(HABS):21
9ph/13pg/1pc L

Female Academy of the Sacred Heart
8 Prince St.
HABS NY-5644
HABS NY,28-ROCH,18-
6ph/9pg L

First Presbyterian Church
101 Plymouth Ave South
HABS NY-5652
HABS NY,28-ROCH,26-
5ph/6pg L

First Universalist Church
S. Clinton Ave. & Court St.
HABS NY-5433
HABS NY,28-ROCH,12-
7ph/17pg L

Genessee Lighthouse (Charlotte Lighthouse,Old)
Lake Ave.
HABS NY-228
HABS NY,28-ROCH,10-
4dr/4ph/3pg/fr L

Harris-Hollister-Spencer House
1005 East Ave.
HABS NY-5646
HABS NY,28-ROCH,20-
6ph/6pg L

Hills,Isaac,House
135 Plymouth Ave. South
HABS NY-5-R-10
HABS NY,28-ROCH,8-
13dr/2ph/2pg/fr L

Livingston Park Seminary
1 Livingston Park
HABS NY-5-R-9
HABS NY,28-ROCH,7-
11dr/5ph/3pg/fr L

Main Street Bridge
Main St. E,spanning the Genesee River
HAER NY-175
HAER 1991(HAER):5
18ph/4pg/2pc/fr L

Miner,Edward,House
2 Argyle St.
HABS NY-6048
HABS NY,28-ROCH,38-
2pg/fr L

Monroe County Courthouse (Monroe County Office Building)
39 W. Main St.
HABS NY-5641
HABS NY,28-ROCH,15-
6ph/7pg L

Monroe County Office Building; see Monroe County Courthouse

Monroe County Penitentiary; see Workhouse

Moore,Lindley M.,House
22 Lake View Park
HABS NY-5432
HABS NY,28-ROCH,11-
8dr/4ph/9pg/fr L

Naval Armory Building; see New York State Arsenal

New York State Arsenal (Convention Hall; Naval Armory Building)
75 Woodbury Blvd.
HABS NY-6189
HABS NY,28-ROCH,40-
25ph/8pg L

Powers Building
16 Main St. West
HABS NY-5649
HABS NY,28-ROCH,23-
7ph/8pg L

Rochester Free Academy (Board of Education Building)
13 Fitzhugh St.
HABS NY-5656
HABS NY,28-ROCH,36-
3ph/7pg L

School No. 27; see Anthony,Susan B.,School

Seneca Park Bridge; see Driving Park Avenue Bridge

Sibley,Hiram W.,House
400 East Ave.
HABS NY-5648
HABS NY,28-ROCH,22-
5ph/6pg L

Smith,Silas O.,House (Willard,Ernest R.,House)
485 East Ave.
HABS NY-5-R-7
HABS NY,28-ROCH,6-
11dr/2ph/2pg/fr L

St. Luke's Church (Episcopal)
17 S. Fitzhugh St.
HABS NY-5654
HABS NY,28-ROCH,28-
5ph/7pg L

Thompson,George,House
546 East Ave.
HABS NY-5645
HABS NY,28-ROCH,19-
5ph/7pg L

Treat-Witherspoon House
25 Clarissa St.
HABS NY-5659
HABS NY,28-ROCH,32-
2ph/5pg L

U. S. Post Office & Courthouse (City Hall)
30 Church St.
HABS NY-5647
HABS NY,28-ROCH,21-
18ph/15pg/1pc L

Warehouse,Stone
1 Mt. Hope St.
HABS NY-5658
HABS NY,28-ROCH,31-
3ph/6pg L

Watts,Ebenezer,House
47 S. Fitzhugh St.
HABS NY-5660
HABS NY,28-ROCH,33-
4ph/6pg L

Whittelsey House; see Campbell,Benjamin,House

Willard,Ernest R.,House; see Smith,Silas O.,House

Workhouse (Monroe County Penitentiary)
1360 S. Ave.
HABS NY-5643
HABS NY,28-ROCH,17-
3ph/6pg L

MONTGOMERY COUNTY

AMSTERDAM

Allen,James,House
HABS NY-3206
HABS NY,29-AMST,3-
1ph L

Guy Park Manor
W. Main St.
HABS NY-369
HABS NY,29-AMST,1-
8ph/2pg L

Inman Manufacturing Company
53 Guy Park Ave.
HAER NY-158
HAER NY,29-AMST,4-
8ph/36pg/1pc L

Prospect Street Bridge
Prospect St.,spanning the Chuctanunda Creek
HAER NY-176
HAER 1991(HAER):5
2ph/3pg/1pc L

CANAJOHARIE

Fort Rensselaer (Van Alstyne House)
HABS NY-3116
HABS NY,29-CANA,1-
14dr/8ph/1pg/fr L

Van Alstyne House; see Fort Rensselaer

CHARLESTON

Baptist Church
State Rt. 148
HABS NY-385
HABS NY,29-CHARF,1-
1ph/1pg/fr L

FONDA

House,Greek Revival
HABS NY-3115
HABS NY,29-FOND,1-
1ph L

FORT HUNTER

Barn,Old Dutch
Wemple Farm
HABS NY-386
HABS NY,29-FORHU,1-
1ph/1pg/fr L

Erie Canal,Empire Lock Number 29
HAER NY-17
HAER NY,29-FORHU,2C-
4ph/1pg L

Erie Canal,Schoharie Creek Aqueduct
Spanning Schoharie Creek
HAER NY-6
HAER NY,29-FORHU,2A-
3dr/30ph/9pg/fr L

Erie Canal,Yankee Hill Lock Number 28
Schoharie Creek Aqueduct Vic.
HAER NY-16
HAER NY,29-FORHU,2B-
4ph/1pg L

FORT JOHNSON

Fort Johnson; see Johnson,Sir William,House

Johnson,Sir William,House (Fort Johnson)
State Rts. 5 & 67
HABS NY-391
HABS NY,29-FORJO,1-
27dr/23ph/6pg/fr L

FORT PLAIN

Bleeker House; see Parris,Isaac,House & Trading Post

Bridge,Stone
HABS NY-3106
HABS NY,29-FORPL,1-
1ph L

Parris,Isaac,House & Trading Post (Bleeker House)
HABS NY-3118
HABS NY,29-FORPL,2-
4ph/1pg L

FULTONVILLE

Van Epps House
Franklin St.
HABS NY-377
HABS NY,29-FULT,1-
14dr/5ph/2pg/fr L

GLEN

Edwards House
HABS NY-3216
HABS NY,29-GLEN,1-
1ph L

MINDEN

Widanka,Peter,House
HABS NY-6049
HABS NY,29-MIND,1-
2ph L

NELLISTON VIC.

Cochrane,General,House
State Rt. 5
HABS NY-384
HABS NY,29-NEL.V,2-
8ph/1pg L

Palatine Church
State Rt. 5
HABS NY-364
HABS NY,29-NEL.V,1-
12dr/17ph/5pg/fr L

PALATINE BRIDGE

Fort Henrick Frey
State Rt. 5 Vic. (Grand St.)
HABS NY-396
HABS NY,29-PALBR,2-
9dr/14ph/1pg/fr L

Frey House
State Rt. 5 (Grand St.)
HABS NY-367
HABS NY,29-PALBR,1-
2ph/1pg L

Lime Kiln
Fort Frey Vic.
HABS NY-6047
HABS NY,29-PALBR,3-
1ph L

PALATINE BRIDGE VIC.

"Fort Ehle"; see Ehle House

Ehle House ("Fort Ehle")
Old Kings Hwy. Vic.
HABS NY-3104
HABS NY,29-NEL,1-
6ph/3pg L

Fort Wagner
HABS NY-368
HABS NY,29-PALBR.V,1-
4ph/2pg L

PATTERSONVILLE

Staley House
HABS NY-3148
HABS NY,29- ,1-
2ph L

ST. JOHNSVILLE VIC

Fort Klock
U.S. Rt. 5
HABS NY-370
HABS NY,29-SAIJO.V,2-
17ph/1pg L

STONE ARABIA

Dutch Reformed Church
State Rt. 10
HABS NY-361
HABS NY,29-STONAR,1-
15dr/8ph/1pg/fr L

Trinity Lutheran Church
State Rt. 10
HABS NY-3161
HABS NY,29-STONAR,2-
3ph/1pg L

NASSAU COUNTY

EAST ROCKAWAY

Hewlett,Oliver,House
86 Main St.
HABS NY-536
HABS NY,30-ROCKE,1-
10dr/7ph/3pg L

EAST WILLISTON

Willis-Post House
Willis Ave.
HABS NY-533
HABS NY,30-WILTE,1-
12dr/9ph/5pg L

FARMINGDALE

Old Maids' Home; see Powell House

Powell House (Old Maids' Home)
HABS NY-5311
HABS NY,30-FARM,1-
1ph L

GLEN COVE

Pratt,Harold I.,House
Crescent Beach Rd.
HABS NY-6242
HABS NY,30-GLENC,1-
5ph/2pg/fr L

GREAT NECK

Eldridge Mill
HABS NY-539
HABS NY,30-GRE,1-
6ph L

HEMPSTEAD

Carman-Irish House
160 Marvin Ave.
HABS NY-4-408
HABS NY,30-HEMP,5-
8dr/2ph/1pg L

Catholic Rectory
104 Greenwich St.
HABS NY-535
HABS NY,30-HEMP,7-
1dr/1ph/2pg L

Harper House,Old
68 Washington St.
HABS NY-4-406
HABS NY,30-HEMP,3-
3dr L

Jones Beach Causeway Bridge No. 1 (Wantagh Parkway Bridge)
Rt. 908 T,spanning Seamans Island Creek
HAER NY-163
HAER 1991(HAER):5
3pg/fr L

Jones Beach St. Prkwy. Channel Bascue Br. LP-2 (Loop State Parkway Bridge)
Rt. 908 C,spanning Long Creek SE of Middle Bay
HAER NY-177
HAER 1991(HAER):5
3ph/3pg/1pc L

Jones Beach St. Prkwy. Channel Bascule Br. MP-3 (Meadowbrook State Parkway Bridge MP-3)
Rt. 908 E,spanning Sloop Channel SE of East Bay
HAER NY-178
HAER 1991(HAER):5
4ph/4pg/1pc L

Loop State Parkway Bridge; see Jones Beach St. Prkwy. Channel Bascue Br. LP-2

Meadowbrook State Parkway Bridge MP-3; see Jones Beach St. Prkwy. Channel Bascule Br. MP-3

Snedecker,Isaac,House
359 Front St.
HABS NY-4-407
HABS NY,30-HEMP,4-
13dr/1pg L

St. George's Church
Front St.
HABS NY-4-403
HABS NY,30-HEMP,1-
10dr/1ph L

St. George's Rectory
Prospect & Greenwich Sts.
HABS NY-4-401
HABS NY,30-HEMP,2-
10dr/5ph/3pg L

Wantagh Parkway Bridge; see Jones Beach Causeway Bridge No. 1

Wright,Constance,House
90 Greenwich St.
HABS NY-532
HABS NY,30-HEMP,6-
7dr/4ph/3pg L

LAWRENCE

Rock Hall
Broadway
HABS NY-534
HABS NY,30-LAWR,1-
19dr/13ph/6pg L

MANHASSET

Onderdonk,Judge Horatio Gates,House
Strathmore Rd. & Rolling Hill Rd.
HABS NY-537
HABS NY,30-MANHA,1-
8dr/12ph/5pg/fr L

MASSAPEQUA

Fort Neck (House) (Tryon Hall)
HABS NY-4-402
HABS NY,30-MASAP,1-
18dr/9ph/5pg L

Tryon Hall; see Fort Neck (House)

MATINECOCK

Matinecock Quaker Meetinghouse
HABS NY-6050
HABS NY,30, ,1-
1ph L

NEW HYDE PARK

Kelsey House
Lakeville Rd.
HABS NY-531
HABS NY,30-NEHYP,1-
8dr/4ph/7pg L

NORTH HEMPSTEAD

Great Neck & Port Wash. RR,Cow's Neck Bridge; see Long Island Railroad,Manhasset Bridge

Long Island Railroad,Manhasset Bridge (Great Neck & Port Wash. RR,Cow's Neck Bridge)
Manhasset Shore Rd. Vic.
HAER NY-81
HAER NY,30-HEMPN,1-
1ph/1pg/1pc L

Sands Point Lighthouse
Middle Neck Rd.
HAER NY-93
HAER NY,30-HEMPN,2-
1ph/1pg/1pc L

OLD WESTBURY

Turnpike House,Old
HABS NY-5310
HABS NY,30-WESBO,1-
2ph L

OYSTER BAY

Laurelton Hall (Tiffany Mansion)
Laurel Hollow & Ridge Rds.
HABS NY-5663
HABS NY,30-OYSTB,1-
20ph L

Roosevelt,Theodore,House; see Sagamore Hill

Roosevelt,Theodore,House,Grey Cottage; see Sagamore Hill,Grey Cottage

Sagamore Hill
(Roosevelt,Theodore,House; Sagamore Hill National Historic Site)
HABS NY-6051
HABS NY,30-OYSTB,2-
13dr/35ph/4pg/3pc/fr L

Sagamore Hill National Historic Site; see Sagamore Hill

Sagamore Hill National Historic Site; see Sagamore Hill,Grey Cottage

Sagamore Hill,Grey Cottage
(Roosevelt,Theodore,House,Grey Cottage; Sagamore Hill National Historic Site)
HABS NY-6051-A
HABS NY,30-OYSTB,2A-
1ph L

Tiffany Mansion; see Laurelton Hall

ROSLYN

Godwin,F. B. ,House; see Montrose

Montrose (Godwin,F. B. ,House)
HABS NY-6052
HABS NY,30-ROS,4-
10ph L

Robeson-Williams Grist Mill
HABS NY-6053
HABS NY,30-ROS,3-
1dr/17ph L

Roslyn Presbyterian Church
33 E. Broadway
HABS NY-6054
HABS NY,30-ROS,5-
7dr/5ph/2pg L

Smith,James & William,Barn
106 Main St.
HABS NY-6055-A
HABS NY,30-ROS,6A-
1dr/1ph L

Smith,James & William,House
106 Main St.
HABS NY-6055
HABS NY,30-ROS,6-
10dr/4ph/2pg L

Wilkey,Warren,House
190 Main St.
HABS NY-6056
HABS NY,30-ROS,7-
5ph/2pg L

SEAFORD

Verity,Stephen,Homestead
Montauk Hwy. & Washington Ave.
HABS NY-538
HABS NY,30-SEAF,1-
12dr/21ph/fr L

WANTAGH

Friends' Meetinghouse of Jerusalem
Wantagh Ave.
HABS NY-4-405
HABS NY,30-WANT,2-
4dr/3pg L

Jones,Jackson,Homestead
Merrick Rd.
HABS NY-4-404
HABS NY,30-WANT,1-
14dr L

NEW YORK COUNTY

NEW YORK CITY

Albano Building
305-311 E. Forty-sixth St.
HABS NY-6057
HABS NY,31-NEYO,107-
3ph L

All Saint's Church
286-290 Henry St.
HABS NY-4-10
HABS NY,31-NEYO,14-
10dr/3ph/6pg/fr L

Allied Arts Building
304-320 E. Forty-fifth St.
HABS NY-6058
HABS NY,31-NEYO,105-
1ph/1pg L

Apothecary Shop (Interiors)
10 Greenwich St.
HABS NY-475-A
HABS NY,31-NEYO,54DI-
3dr/3ph/fr L

Auchmuty,Ellen S. ,Building; see South Street Seaport Museum

Battery Maritime Building; see Whitehall Street Ferry Terminal

Bayard-Condict Building
65-69 Bleecker St.
HABS NY-5485
HABS NY,31-NEYO,82-
5ph/6pg L

Beaux Arts Apartments
307-317 & 308-320 E. Forty-fourth St.
HABS NY-6059
HABS NY,31-NEYO,101-
4ph/1pg L

127-137 Beekman Street; see South Street Seaport Museum

142-144 Beekman Street/211 Front Street; see South Street Seaport Museum

Beekman Tower; see Panhellenic Tower

Beekman,John,House
29-29 1/2 Cherry St.
HABS NY-452
HABS NY,31-NEYO,42-
8dr/19ph/6pg/fr L

Block Houses (Numbers 1 & 2)
Central (110th St.) & Morningside Pks. (123rd St.)
HABS NY-443
HABS NY,31-NEYO,33-
2dr/4ph/1pg/fr L

Block 96W; see South Street Seaport Museum

165 Broadway (Building); see City Investing Building

Brooklyn Bridge (East River Bridge)
Spanning East River btwn Brooklyn & Manhattan
HAER NY-18
HAER NY,31-NEYO,90-
1dr/73ph/3pg/6pc/26ct L

Building No. 104; see Governors Island,New York Arsenal,Storehouse No. 1

Building No. 105; see Governors Island,New York Arsenal,Office

Building No. 107; see Governors Island,New York Arsenal,Storehouse

Building No. 110; see Governors Island,New York Arsenal,Storehouse

Building No. 125; see Governors Island,Second Corps Area Headquarters

Building No. 135; see Governors Is.,New York Arsenal,Storehse & C.O. Qtr

Building No. 140; see Governors Island,New York Arsenal,Storehouse

Building No. 298; see Governors Island,Half Moon Battery

Building No. 3; see Governors Island,Commissary Storehouse

Building No. 400; see Governors Island,Infantry Regimental Barracks

Building No. 501; see Governors Island,Castle Williams

Building No. 550; see Governors Island,Barracks

Building No. 9; see Governors Island,Post Hospital

Buildings No. 403-409; see Governors Island,Brick Row

Carle Building
151-153 Water St.,134-136 Maiden Ln.
HABS NY-4390
HABS NY,31-NEYO,63-
2ph/4pg L

Carnegie Hall; see Music Hall

Castle Clinton
Battery Park
HABS NY-6336
HABS DLC/PP-1992:NY-5
5ph/1pg/1pc L

Central Park Bridges,Bow Bridges
(Central Park Bridges,Bridge No. 5)
Spanning the Lake,Central Park
HAER NY-195
HAER NY,31-NEYO,153A-
6ph/1pg/1pc L

Central Park Bridges,Bridge No. 15; see Central Park Bridges,Pinebank Arch,Bridge No. 15

Central Park Bridges,Bridge No. 24
Central Park,SW of Reservoir
HAER NY-192
HAER NY,31-NEYO,153E-
3ph/1pc L

Central Park Bridges,Bridge No. 27
Central Park, SW of Reservoir
HAER NY-193
HAER NY,31-NEYO,153D-
4ph/1pc L

Central Park Bridges,Bridge No. 28; see Central Park Bridges,Gothic Arch

Central Park Bridges,Bridge No. 5; see Central Park Bridges,Bow Bridges

Central Park Bridges,Gothic Arch
(Central Park Bridges,Bridge No. 28)
Central Park,NW of Reservoir
HAER NY-194
HAER NY,31-NEYO,153C-
6ph/1pc/2ct L

Central Park Bridges,Pinebank Arch,Bridge No. 15 (Central Park Bridges,Bridge No. 15)
Near Columdus Circle entrance,Central Park
HAER NY-196
HAER NY,31-NEYO,153B-
3ph/2pg/1pc L

Central Park,Ladies' Pavilion
Central Park,W side of Lake
HAER NY-197
HAER NY,31-NEYO,153F-
1ph/1pg/1pc L

Chamber of Commerce Building
65 Liberty St.
HABS NY-397
HABS NY,31-NEYO,156-
1ph L

Charles & Company Building
335-341 E. Forty-fourth St.
HABS NY-6060
HABS 1984(HABS):50
2ph/1pg L

Church of St. John the Evangelist
Eleventh St. & Wavery Place
HABS NY-437
HABS NY,31-NEYO,27-
5dr/4ph/3pg/fr L

Church of St. Paul the Apostle
Fifty-ninth St. & Ninth Ave.
HABS NY-269
HABS NY,31-NEYO,154-
6ph L

Church of the Ascension
Fifth Ave. & Tenth St.
HABS NY-6061
HABS NY,31-NEYO,95-
12dr L

Church of the Covenant
310 E. Forty-second St.
HABS NY-6062
HABS NY,31-NEYO,97-
1ph L

Church of the Epiphany
Lexington Ave. & Thirty-fifth St.
HABS NY-454
HABS NY,31-NEYO,43-
9ph L

Church of the Nativity
46-48 Second Ave.
HABS NY-5461
HABS NY,31-NEYO,93-
6ph/9pg L

Church,Brick (Interiors)
Fifth Ave. & Thirty-seventh St.
HABS NY-468
HABS NY,31-NEYO,50-
7ph L

City Hospital; see Island Hospital

City Investing Building (165 Broadway (Building))
HABS NY-5498
HABS NY,31-NEYO,80-
3ph L

City Pier A
Battery Place at Hudson River
HAER NY-84
HAER NY,31-NEYO,148-
10ph/3pg/1pc L

Colonnade Row; see La Grange Terrace

Cook,Will Marion,House (Strivers Row)
221 W. One-hundred-thirty-eighth St.
HABS NY-5721
HABS NY,31-NEYO,111A-
2ph/5pg/1pc L

Cooper Union for the Advancement of Science & Art
Third & Fourth Aves.,Astor Pl.,Seventh St.
HAER NY-20
HAER NY,31-NEYO,81-
20dr/32ph/67pg L

Corbin Hall; see Governors Island,Half Moon Battery

Crocheron,Jacob,House
47 Whitehall St.
HABS NY-5456
HABS NY,31-NEYO,125-
4dr/2ph/1pc L

Documentation: **ct** color transparencies **dr** measured drawings **fr** field records
pc photograph captions **pg** pages of text **ph** photographs

Daily News Building
220-226 E. Forty-second St.
HABS NY-6063
HABS NY,31-NEYO,99-
2ph L

Dakota,The (Apartments)
1 W. Seventy-second St.,Central Park West
HABS NY-5467
HABS NY,31-NEYO,74-
7ph/11pg L

Dunbar Apartments; see Henson,Matthew,Apartment

Dyckman House
Broadway & Two-hundred-fourth St.
HABS NY-4-4
HABS NY,31-NEYO,11-
11dr/4ph/7pg/fr L

East River Bridge; see Brooklyn Bridge

555 Edgecomb Ave. (APARTMENT BUILDING) (Robeson,Paul,Residence)
HABS NY-5692
HABS NY,31-NEYO,117-
4ph L

Eitel,John,Building; see South Street Seaport Museum

Ellington,Edward Kennedy-Residence; see 935 St. Nicholas Ave. ,Apt. 4-A

Ellis Island (U.S. Immigration Station)
New York Harbor
HABS NY-6086
HABS NY,31-ELLIS,1-
13ph/1pc L

Ellis Island,Baggage & Dormitory Building
New York Harbor,Statue of Liberty Nat'l Monument
HABS NY-6086-E
HABS NY,31-ELLIS,1E-
2ph/1pc L

Ellis Island,Ferry Building
New York Harbor,Statue of Liberty Nat'l Monument
HABS NY-6086-D
HABS NY,31-ELLIS,1D-
5ph/1pc/1ct L

Ellis Island,Greenhouse (U. S. Immigration Station,Greenhouse; Statue of Liberty National Monument)
New York Harbor
HABS NY-6086-A
HABS NY,31-ELLIS,1A-
3ph/9pg/fr L

Ellis Island,Hospital
New York Harbor,Statue of Liberty Nat'l Monument
HABS NY-6086-G
HABS NY,31-ELLIS,1G-
1ph/1pc L

Ellis Island,Incinerator (U. S. Immigration Station,Incinerator; Statue of Liberty National Monument)
New York Harbor
HABS NY-6086-B
HABS NY,31-ELLIS,1B-
6ph/6pg/fr L

Ellis Island,Kitchen,Restaurant & Bath House
HABS NY-6086-F
HABS NY,31-ELLIS,1F-
5ph/1pc L

Ellis Island,Main Building
New York Harbor,Statue of Liberty Nat'l Monument
HABS NY-6086-C
HABS NY,31-ELLIS,1C-
33ph/1pg/2pc L

Ellis Island,Water Towers
New York Harbor,Statue of Liberty Nat'l Monument
HABS NY-6086-H
HABS NY,31-ELLIS,1H-
2ph/1pc L

Erie Railway:Chambers Street Ferry Terminal
Chambers St.
HAER NY-85
HAER NY,31-NEYO,150-
5ph/1pc L

Erie Railway:Twenty-third Street Ferry Terminal
Twenty-third St.
HAER NY-86
HAER NY,31-NEYO,149-
6ph/1pc L

Faile,Edward G. ,Building; see South Street Seaport Museum

Federal Hall National Memorial; see U. S. Custom House

Field's Building
168-170 John St. (formerly 32-38 Burling Slip)
HABS NY-4391
HABS NY,31-NEYO,64-
1ph/3pg L

Fish,Hamilton,House
21 Stuyvesant St.
HABS NY-398
HABS NY,31-NEYO,155-
1ph L

Folies Bergere Theatre (Fulton Theatre; Hayes,Helen,Theatre)
210 W. Forty-sixth St.
HABS NY-5673
HABS NY,31-NEYO,84-
7dr/8ph/2pg/fr L

Fordham,George,House
329 Cherry St.
HABS NY-445
HABS NY,31-NEYO,35-
10dr/10ph/3pg/fr L

Forrest,Edwin,House
436 W. Twenty-second St.
HABS NY-4-14
HABS NY,31-NEYO,16-
8dr/9ph/2pg/fr L

Fort Jay; see Governors Island,Fort Columbus

Fort Jay,Building No. 202; see Governors Island,Fort Columbus

Fort Jay,Building No. 206; see Governors Island,Fort Columbus

Fort Jay,Building No. 210; see Governors Island,Fort Columbus

Fort Jay,Building No. 214; see Governors Island,Fort Columbus

Fraunces Tavern Block
Bounded by Pearl St,Coeties Slip,Water St,Broad St
HABS NY-267
HABS NY,31-NEYO,128-
4ph L

Fraunces Tavern Museum Complex
54-58 Pearl St.,101-103 Broad St. & 24-26 Water
HABS NY-6321
15dr H

Front & Whitehall Streets Study
Bounded by Front & Whitehall Sts.
HABS NY-6064
HABS NY,31-NEYO,123-
3ph/1pc L

207 Front Street (Commercial Building); see South Street Seaport Museum

Front Street (Warehouse)
HABS NY-4378
HABS NY,31-NEYO,60-
4dr L

203-204 Front Street; see South Street Seaport Museum

205 Front Street; see South Street Seaport Museum

206 Front Street; see South Street Seaport Museum

232-234 Front Street; see South Street Seaport Museum

236 Front Street; see South Street Seaport Museum

21-25 Fulton Street; see South Street Seaport Museum

Fulton Theatre; see Folies Bergere Theatre

George Washington Bridge
Spanning Hudson River btwn Manhattan & Fort Lee
HAER NY-129
HAER NY,31-NEYO,161-
63ph/1pg/4pc/8ct L

Govenors Island,Quarters No. 8
New York Harbor,Nolan Park
HABS NY-5715-14
HABS NY,31-GOVI,14-
4ph/6pg/1pc/fr L

Governor's Island Ferry Terminal; see Whitehall Street Ferry Terminal

Governors Is.,New York Arsenal,Storehse & C.O. Qtr (Building No. 135)
New York Harbor near Andes Rd.
HABS NY-5715-6A
HABS NY,31-GOVI,6A-
12ph/15pg/1pc/fr L

Governors Island,Barracks (Building No. 550)
New York Harbor,Short & Wheeler Aves.
HABS NY-5715-9
HABS NY,31-GOVI,9-
5dr/6ph/7pg/1pc/fr L

Governors Island,Brick Row (Officer's Quarters; Buildings No. 403-409)
New York Harbor,Clayton & Hay Rds.
HABS NY-5715-12
HABS NY,31-GOVI,12-
10ph/3pg/1pc/fr L

Governors Island,Building No. 2
New York Harbor,Nolan Park near Barry & Andes Rds.
HABS NY-5715-4
HABS NY,31-GOVI,4-
10ph/17pg/2pc/fr L

Governors Island,Building No. 25
New York Harbor,Nolan Park near Andes Rd.
HABS NY-5715-7
HABS NY,31-GOVI,7-
3ph/16pg/1pc/fr L

Governors Island,Castle Williams (Building No. 501)
New York Harbor near Hay & Andes Rds.
HABS NY-5715-2
HABS SY,31-GOVI,19-
28ph/22pg/2pc/fr L

Governors Island,Commanding Officer's House (Quarters No. 1)
New York Harbor,Nolan Park near Barry Rd.
HABS NY-5715-3
HABS NY,31-GOVI,3-
35ph/23pg/3pc/fr L

Governors Island,Commissary Storehouse (Officers' Quarters; Building No. 3)
New York Harbor,Nolan Park
HABS NY-5715-13
HABS NY,31-GOVI,13-
1ph/4pg/1pc L

Governors Island,Fort Columbus (Fort Jay)
New York Harbor
HABS NY-4-6
HABS NY,31-GOVI,1-
10dr/34ph/44pg/2pc/fr L

Governors Island,Fort Columbus (Fort Jay,Building No. 202)
New York Harbor
HABS NY-5715-1A
HABS NY,31-GOVI,1A-
8ph/17pg/1pc/fr L

Governors Island,Fort Columbus (Fort Jay,Building No. 206)
New York Harbor
HABS NY-5715-1B
HABS NY,31-GOVI,1B-
9ph/21pg/1pc/fr L

Governors Island,Fort Columbus (Fort Jay,Building No. 210)
New York Harbor
HABS NY-5715-1C
HABS NY,31-GOVI,1C-
7ph/18pg/1pc/fr L

Governors Island,Fort Columbus (Fort Jay,Building No. 214)
New York Harbor
HABS NY-5715-1D
HABS NY,31-GOVI,1D-
9ph/17pg/1pc/fr L

Governors Island,Half Moon Battery (South Battery; Corbin Hall; Officers' Club; Building No. 298)
New York Harbor near Comfort & Barry Rds.
HABS NY-5715-11
HABS NY,31-GOVI,11-
8ph/11pg/1pc/fr L

Governors Island,Infantry Regimental Barracks (Liggett Hall; Building No. 400)
New York Harbor,Clayton Rd. betwn Wheeler & King
HABS NY-5715-8
HABS NY,31-GOVI,8-
14ph/45pg/1pc/fr L

Governors Island,New York Arsenal,Building No. 109
HABS NY-5715-6F
HABS NY,31-GOVI,6F-
2ph/7pg/1pc/fr L

Governors Island,New York Arsenal,Office (Building No. 105)
New York Harbor near Andes Rd.
HABS NY-5715-6G
HABS NY,31-GOVI,6G-
5ph/1pg/1pc/fr L

Governors Island,New York Arsenal,Storehouse (Building No. 107)
New York Harbor near Andes Rd.
HABS NY-5715-6C
HABS NY,31-GOVI,6C-
5ph/8pg/1pc/fr L

Governors Island,New York Arsenal,Storehouse (Building No. 110)
New York Harbor near Andes Rd.
HABS NY-5715-6D
HABS NY,31-GOVI,6D-
4ph/15pg/1pc/fr L

Governors Island,New York Arsenal,Storehouse (Building No. 140)
New York Harbor near Carder Rd.
HABS NY-5715-6E
HABS NY,31-GOVI,6E-
3dr/5ph/12pg/1pc/fr L

Governors Island,New York Arsenal,Storehouse No. 1 (Building No. 104)
New York Harbor near Andes Rd.
HABS NY-5715-6B
HABS NY,31-GOVI,6B-
1dr/9ph/14pg/1pc/fr L

Governors Island,Overview
New York Harbor
HABS NY-5715
HABS NY,31-GOVI,2-
1dr/15ph/49pg/1pc/3ct/fr L

Governors Island,Post Hospital (Building No. 9)
New York Harbor,Nolan Park near Barry Rd.
HABS NY-5715-5
HABS NY,31-GOVI,5-
8ph/34pg/2pc/fr L

Governors Island,Quarters No. 10
New York Harbor,Nolan Park
HABS NY-5715-15
HABS NY,31-GOVI,15-
5ph/1pg/1pc/fr L

Governors Island,Quarters No. 16
New York Harbor,Nolan Park
HABS NY-5715-16
HABS NY,31-GOVI,16-
1ph/1pg/1pc/fr L

Governors Island,Quarters No. 19
New York Harbor,Nolan Park
HABS NY-5715-17
HABS NY,31-GOVI,17-
1ph/7pg/1pc/fr L

Governors Island,Quarters No. 20
New York Harbor,Nolan Park
HABS NY-5715-18
HABS NY,31-GOVI,18-
9ph/2pg/1pc/fr L

Governors Island,Second Corps Area Headquarters (U. S. Army Headquarters,First; Pershing Hall; Building No. 125)
New York Harbor near Andes Rd.
HABS NY-5715-10
HABS NY,31-GOVI,10-
2dr/6ph/8pg/1pc/fr L

Grace Church
Broadway,Tenth St. , & Fourth Ave.
HABS NY-399
HABS NY,31-NEYO,67-
18ph/6pg/3pc/fr L

Grace Church Houses
Fourth Ave. & Eleventh St.
HABS NY-268
HABS NY,31-NEYO,68A-
2ph L

Documentation: **ct** color transparencies **dr** measured drawings **fr** field records **pc** photograph captions **pg** pages of text **ph** photographs

Gracie Mansion
Carl Schurz Park,E. 68th St.
HABS NY-461
HABS NY,31-NEYO,46-
57ph/3pc L

Grand Central Post Office Annex
Forty-fifth St. & Lexington Ave.,SW corner
HABS NY-6302
HABS 1991(HABS):21
41ph/29pg/3pc L

Grant,General,National Memorial; see Grant's Monument

Grant's Monument (Grant's Tomb; Grant,General,National Memorial)
Riverside Drive & W. 122nd St.
HABS NY-5429
HABS NY,31-NEYO,69-
13dr/29ph/9pg/2pc/fr L

Grant's Tomb; see Grant's Monument

10 Greenwich Street (House)
HABS NY-475
HABS NY,31-NEYO,54D-
9dr/13ph/fr L

14 Greenwich Street (House)
HABS NY-476
HABS NY,31-NEYO,54E-
1dr/2ph/fr L

16 Greenwich Street (House)
HABS NY-477
HABS NY,31-NEYO,54F
3dr/5ph/fr L

18 Greenwich Street (House)
HABS NY-478
HABS NY,31-NEYO,54G-
13dr/7ph/fr L

20 Greenwich Street (House)
HABS NY-479
HABS NY,31-NEYO,54H-
2dr/7ph/fr L

4 Greenwich Street (House)
HABS NY-472
HABS NY,31-NEYO,54A-
3dr/fr L

6 Greenwich Street (House)
HABS NY-473
HABS NY,31-NEYO,54B-
7dr/11ph/fr L

8 Greenwich Street (House)
HABS NY-474
HABS NY,31-NEYO,54C-
8dr/7ph/fr L

Greenwich Street Study (Plot plan)
HABS NY-472-A
HABS NY,31-NEYO,54-
1dr/11ph L

Gridley,John V.,House
37 Charlton St.
HABS NY-441
HABS NY,31-NEYO,31-
6dr/8ph/3pg/fr L

4-10 Grove Street (Row Houses)
HABS NY-449
HABS NY,31-NEYO,39-
7dr/6ph/fr L

Hall of Records; see Surrogates Court

Hamilton Grange
(Moved Frm)237 W.141 St. to 141st St. & Amsterdam
HABS NY-6335
HABS DLC/PP-1992:NY-4
25ph/3pc L

Harlem Fire Watchtower
Marcus Garvey Park
HAER NY-104
HAER NY,31-NEYO,163A-
13ph/3pg/1pc L

Harper,James,House
4 Gramercy Park
HABS NY-4-7
HABS NY,31-NEYO,12-
8dr/6ph/3pg/fr L

Hart-Carpenter-Havens Building; see South Street Seaport Museum

Hart-Havens-Lauderback Building; see South Street Seaport Museum

Haughwout,E. V. & Company,Building
488-492 Broadway
HABS NY-5459
HABS NY,31-NEYO,70-
5dr/10ph/6pg L

Hayes,Helen,Theatre; see Folies Bergere Theatre

Hazlet,John,House
204-206 W. Thirteenth St.
HABS NY-444
HABS NY,31-NEYO,34-
3dr/6ph/4pg/fr L

48 Henry Street (Row House)
HABS NY-6065
HABS NY,31-NEYO,55-
10ph/6pg/fr L

Henson,Matthew,Apartment (Dunbar Apartments)
246 W. One-hundred-fiftieth St.
HABS NY-5697
HABS NY,31-NEYO,118A-
10ph/3pg/2pc L

Holland Tunnel
Beneath Hudson River btwn New York & Jersey City
HAER NY-161
HAER NY,31-NEYO,166-
43ph/3pg/3pc L

Hotel Astor
1511-1515 Broadway
HABS NY-5464
HABS NY,31-NEYO,72-
3ph/9pg L

Houseman,Jacob,House
49 Whitehall St.
HABS NY-5457
HABS NY,31-NEYO,126-
3dr/3ph/1pc L

Houseman,Jacob,House & Office
2 Front St.
HABS NY-5458
HABS NY,31-NEYO,127-
5dr/11ph/1pc L

Howell,Matthew,Building; see South Street Seaport Museum

India House
1 Hanover Square
HABS NY-4-2
HABS NY,31-NEYO,9-
8dr/2ph/4pg L

Interborough Rapid Transit Subway (Original Line)
HAER NY-122
HAER NY,31-NEYO,86-
72ph/614pg/4pc L

Island Hospital (City Hospital)
Roosevelt Island
HABS NY-6285
HABS DLC/PP-1993:NY-5
27ph/21pg/3pc L

Jefferson Market Courthouse; see Third Judicial District Courthouse

Jerome,Leonard W.,Mansion
32 E. Twenty-sixth St.
HABS NY-5470
HABS NY,31-NEYO,77-
7ph/14pg L

John Street Methodist Episcopal Church,Old
44-46 John St.
HABS NY-4-27
HABS NY,31-NEYO,23-
9dr/3ph/2pg/fr L

Johnson,James Weldon-Residence; see 187 W. 135th St. (APARTMENT BUILDING)

48 & 50 King Street (Houses)
HABS NY-4-20
HABS NY,31-NEYO,21-
8dr/5ph/3pg/fr L

Kingsbridge Bus Depot (Kingsbridge Car House)
4069-79 Tenth Ave. between 216th & 218th Sts.
HABS NY-6324
HABS DLC/PP-1993:NY-3
11ph/28pg/2pc L

Kingsbridge Car House; see Kingsbridge Bus Depot

La Grange Terrace (Colonnade Row)
428-434 Lafayette Place
HABS NY-5604
HABS NY,31-NEYO,83-
5dr L

Laing,Edgar,Stores
Washington & Murray Sts.
HABS NY-5469
HABS NY,31-NEYO,76-
17dr/47ph/14pg/fr L

Lamppost
Second Ave. & E. Forty-ninth St.
HABS NY-6073
HABS NY,31-NEYO,92-
1ph L

Lawrence Building; see South Street Seaport Museum

Leake & Watts Orphanage,Old
Amsterdam Ave. & One-hundred-tenth St.
HABS NY-426
HABS NY,31-NEYO,22-
8dr/4ph/5pg L

9 Lexington Avenue (House)
HABS NY-465
HABS NY,31-NEYO,48-
2ph L

Liggett Hall; see Governors Island,Infantry Regimental Barracks

Livingston Building; see South Street Seaport Museum

Loew's Victoria Theater
235-237 W. One-hundred-and-twenty-fifth St.
HABS NY-6283
HABS NY,31-NEYO,109-
22ph/8pg L

Manhattan Bridge
Span. East Riv.at Flatbush Ave.bet.NYC & Brooklyn
HAER NY-127
HAER NY,31-NEYO,164-
7ph/1pg/1pc/5ct L

Mariners' Temple
Oliver & Henry Sts.
HABS NY-436
HABS NY,31-NEYO,26-
8dr/4ph/2pg/fr L

Matheson,William J. ,Building
145-155 John St.
HABS NY-6013
HABS NY,31-NEYO,56-
14ph/16pg/1pc L

McKay,Claude-Residence; see YMCA

Metal Exchange Building
234 Pearl St.
HABS NY-431
HABS NY,31-NEYO,24-
7dr/2ph/5pg/fr L

Metropolitan Opera House
1423 Broadway
HABS NY-5486
HABS NY,31-NEYO,79-
23ph/7pg L

Meyer's Hotel; see South Street Seaport Museum

Mills,Florence,House
220 W. One hundred thirty-fifth St.
HABS NY-5696
HABS NY,31-NEYO,114A-
5ph L

Minnie Building
303 E. Forty-sixth St.
HABS NY-6066
HABS NY,31-NEYO,106-
1ph L

Modernace Building
319 E. Forty-fourth St.
HABS NY-6067
HABS NY,31-NEYO,102-
1ph L

Morosco Theater
217-225 W. Forty-fifth St.
HABS NY-5718
HABS NY,31-NEYO,104-
36ph/47pg L

Morris-Jumel Mansion
Edgecomb Ave. & 160th-162nd Sts.
HABS NY-469
HABS NY,31-NEYO,51-
8ph L

Mott,Jordan L.,House
2122 Fifth Ave.
HABS NY-450
HABS NY,31-NEYO,40-
3dr/15ph/3pg/fr L

Mount Vernon Coach House & Stable (Smith,Abigail Adams,Museum; Teller,Jane,Mansiona)
421 E. Sixty-first St.
HABS NY-5631
HABS NY,31-NEYO,45-
10dr/2ph/fr L

Municipal Ferry Pier; see Whitehall Street Ferry Terminal

Music Hall (Carnegie Hall)
154 W. Fifty-seventh St.
HABS NY-5717
HABS NY,31-NEYO,18-
8ph/7pg L

National City Bank
55 Wall St.
HABS NY-400
HABS NY,31-NEYO,158-
1ph L

New York Amsterdam News Building
2293 Seventh Ave.
HABS NY-5693
HABS NY,3NEYO,98-
7ph/4pg/1pc L

New York City Hall
City Hall Park
HABS NY-234
HABS NY,31-NEYO,91-
9ph/5pg/1pc/fr L

New York Connecting RR,Hell Gate Bridge
Spanning East River,Wards Island & Astoria
HAER NY-88
2ph H

New York County Courthouse (Tweed Courthouse)
52 Chambers St.
HABS NY-5688
HABS NY,31-NEYO,116-
34ph L

New York Edison Company,Powerhouse
686-700 First Ave.
HABS NY-6068
HABS NY,31-NEYO,159A-
4ph L

New York Public Library,Jefferson Market Branch; see Third Judicial District Courthouse

New York Society Library
109 University Place
HABS NY-4-13
HABS NY,31-NEYO,15-
12dr/3ph/7pg/fr L

Northeast Corridor; see Northeast Railroad Corridor

Northeast Railroad Corridor (Northeast Corridor)
Amtrak Rt. btwn. NJ/NY & NY/CT State Lines
HAER NY-121
HAER NY,31-NEYO,167-
51ph/4pc/fr L

Northern Dispensary
165 Waverly Place
HABS NY-4-9
HABS NY,31-NEYO,13-
9dr/2ph/4pg/fr L

Officer's Quarters; see Governors Island,Brick Row

Officers' Club; see Governors Island,Half Moon Battery

Officers' Quarters; see Governors Island,Commissary Storehouse

Old Croton Aqueduct
HAER NY-120
HAER NY,31-NEYO,87-
1dr/53ph/184pg/7pc/fr L

Olliffe Pharmacy
6 Bowery
HABS NY-4-17
HABS NY,31-NEYO,20-
3dr/2ph/7pg/fr L

Onderdonk,Harriet,Building; see South Street Seaport Museum

Panhellenic Tower (Beekman Tower)
3-7 Mitchell Place
HABS NY-6069
HABS NY,31-NEYO,157-
3ph/1pg L

45 Peck Slip/151 South Street; see South Street Seaport Museum

Penn Station; see Pennsylvania Station

Documentation: **ct** color transparencies **dr** measured drawings **fr** field records **pc** photograph captions **pg** pages of text **ph** photographs

Pennsylvania Station (Penn Station)
370 Seventh Ave., W. 31st,31st-33rd Sts.
HABS NY-5471
HABS NY,31-NEYO,78-
22ph/6pg L

Pershing Hall; see Governors Island,Second Corps Area Headquarters

Phoenix-Shaw Warehouse
68-70 Front St.
HABS NY-4394
HABS NY,31-NEYO,66-
4ph/5pg L

Piers 95 & 96,North River; see West 55th Street & West 56th Street Piers

Quarters No. 1; see Governors Island,Commanding Officer's House

Queensboro Bridge
Spanning East river & Blackwell's Island
HAER NY-19
HAER NY,31-NEYO,160-
9ph/1pg/1pc L

Queensboro Bridge Trolley Station
Spanning East River & Blackwell's Island
HABS NY-6070
HABS NY,31-NEYO,160A-
3dr/7ph/fr L

Racquet & Tennis Club
370 Park Ave.,E. 52nd-53rd Sts.
HABS NY-5466
HABS NY,31-NEYO,73-
1ph/7pg L

Reeves Sound Studio
304 E. Forty-fourth St.
HABS NY-6071
HABS NY,31-NEYO,100-
3ph L

Rhinelander Row
Seventh Ave.,Twelfth-Thirteenth Sts.
HABS NY-463
HABS NY,31-NEYO,47-
2ph L

Robeson,Paul,Residence; see 555 Edgecomb Ave. (APARTMENT BUILDING)

Rogers,George P. ,Building; see South Street Seaport Museum

Rogers,Moses,House; see Watson,James,House

Roosevelt Island,Castle-Hospital; see Welfare Island,Castle-Hospital

Roosevelt Island,Church; see Welfare Island,Church

Roosevelt Island,Farmhouse; see Welfare Island,Farmhouse

Roosevelt Island,Insane Asylum; see Welfare Island,Insane Asylum

Roosevelt Island,Lighthouse; see Welfare Island,Lighthouse

Roosevelt Island,South Building; see Welfare Island,South Building

Roosevelt Island,Strecker Memorial Laboratory; see Welfare Island,Strecker Memorial Laboratory

Rose House; see South Street Seaport Museum

Schermerhorn Row; see South Street Seaport Museum

Sea & Land Church
Henry & Market Sts.
HABS NY-446
HABS NY,31-NEYO,36-
10dr/8ph/3pg/fr L

Seventh Regiment Armory
643 Park Ave.
HABS NY-6295
HABS NY,31-NEYO,121-
102ph/1pg/6pc L

Sinclair,Harry F. ,House
2 E. Seventy-ninth St.
HABS NY-395
HABS NY,31-NEYO,110-
1ph L

Singer Tower
149 Broadway
HABS NY-5463
HABS NY,31-NEYO,71-
20ph/10pg L

Smith,Abigail Adams,Museum; see Mount Vernon Coach House & Stable

Smith,Gershom,Building; see South Street Seaport Museum

Society of Friends Meetinghouse
15 Rutherford Place
HABS NY-4-1
HABS NY,31-NEYO,8-
6dr/3ph/3pg/fr L

South Battery; see Governors Island,Half Moon Battery

South Street Seaport Museum
HABS NY-5632
HABS NY,31-NEYO,129-
2dr L

South Street Seaport Museum (127-137 Beekman Street; Livingston Building)
HABS NY-5634
HABS NY,31-NEYO,136-
3dr/1ph/6pg/fr L

South Street Seaport Museum (142-144 Beekman Street/211 Front Street; Auchmuty,Ellen S. ,Building)
HABS NY-5674
HABS NY,31-NEYO,131-
1ph/5pg L

South Street Seaport Museum (Block 96W)
HABS NY-5687
HABS NY,31-NEYO,129B-
1dr/fr L

South Street Seaport Museum (207 Front Street (Commercial Building))
HABS NY-5678
HABS NY,31-NEYO,135-
5dr/9pg/fr L

South Street Seaport Museum (203-204 Front Street; Hart-Carpenter-Havens Building)
HABS NY-5675
HABS NY,31-NEYO,132-
5dr/4ph/9pg/fr L

South Street Seaport Museum (205 Front Street; Lawrence Building)
HABS NY-5676
HABS NY,31-NEYO,134-
3dr/8pg/fr L

South Street Seaport Museum (206 Front Street; Howell,Matthew,Building)
HABS NY-5677
HABS NY,31-NEYO,133-
3dr/9pg/fr L

South Street Seaport Museum (232-234 Front Street; Smith,Gershom,Building)
HABS NY-5679
HABS NY,31-NEYO,137-
1ph/6pg L

South Street Seaport Museum (236 Front Street; Faile,Edward G. ,Building)
236 Front St.
HABS NY-5680
HABS NY,31-NEYO,138-
1ph/6pg L

South Street Seaport Museum (21-25 Fulton Street; Rogers,George P. ,Building)
21-25 Fulton St.
HABS NY-5633
HABS NY,31-NEYO,130-
5dr/9pg/fr L

South Street Seaport Museum (Onderdonk,Harriet,Building; Meyer's Hotel)
116-119 South St.
HABS NY-5681
HABS NY,31-NEYO,139-
3ph/5pg L

South Street Seaport Museum (45 Peck Slip/151 South Street; Ward,Joseph,Building)
HABS NY-5682
HABS NY,31-NEYO,140-
2ph/9pg L

South Street Seaport Museum (Schermerhorn Row)
John,South,Fulton, & Front Sts. ,bounded by
HABS NY-6072
HABS NY,31-NEYO,129A-
1dr/3ph/fr L

South Street Seaport Museum (207-211 Water Street; Hart-Havens-Lauderback Building)
HABS NY-5683
HABS NY,31-NEYO,141-
3dr/1ph/10pg/fr L

South Street Seaport Museum (213-215 Water Street; Thompson,A. A. ,& Company)
HABS NY-5684
HABS NY,31-NEYO,142-
4dr/2ph/7pg/fr L

South Street Seaport Museum (251 Water Street; Eitel,John,Building)
HABS NY-5685
HABS NY,31-NEYO,143-
2ph/4pg L

South Street Seaport Museum (273 Water Street; Rose House)
HABS NY-5686
HABS NY,31-NEYO,144-
1ph/8pg L

South Street Seaport,Piers 17 & 18
South St. into East River at Fulton St.
HAER NY-156
HAER NY,31-NEYO,145A-
11ph/8pg/1pc L

St. Ann's Church
295 Saint Ann's Ave. & E. 140th St.
HABS NY-433
HABS NY,31-NEYO,4-
7dr/4ph/3pg L

St. George's Episcopal Church
Third Ave. & E. Sixteenth St., Stuyvesant Square
HABS NY-5720
HABS NY,31-NEYO,94-
2ph/4pg/1pc/4ct L

St. James Roman Catholic Church
St. James Place
HABS NY-458
HABS NY,31-NEYO,44-
2ph L

St. Luke's Chapel
447 Hudson St.
HABS NY-439
HABS NY,31-NEYO,29-
4dr/2ph/3pg/fr L

St. Mark's-in-the-Bouwerie
234 E. Eleventh St.
HABS NY-464
HABS NY,31-NEYO,3-
2ph L

935 St. Nicholas Ave. (APARTMENT BUILDING)
935 Saint Nicholas Ave. ,Apt. 4-A
HABS NY-5690
HABS NY,31-NEYO,119A-
9ph L

935 St. Nicholas Ave. ,Apt. 4-A (Ellington,Edward Kennedy-Residence)
935 St. Nicholas Ave. ,Apt. 4-A
HABS NY-5690-A
4ph/1pc L

St. Paul's Chapel
Broadway & Fulton Sts.
HABS NY-453
HABS NY,31-NEYO,2-
43ph/3pg/1pc/fr L

St. Peter's Episcopal Church
436 W. Twentieth St.
HABS NY-438
HABS NY,31-NEYO,28-
4ph/1pg/fr L

St. Peter's Roman Catholic Church
31 Barclay St.
HABS NY-4-3
HABS NY,31-NEYO,10-
12dr/3ph/5pg/fr L

St. Therese's Church
Henry & Rutgers Sts.
HABS NY-466
HABS NY,31-NEYO,49-
3ph L

St. Vincent's Hospital Complex
153 W. Eleventh St.
HABS NY-5698
HABS NY,31-NEYO,85-
4ph/1pg/1pc L

St. Vincent's Hospital,Elizabeth Seton Building
151-167 W. Eleventh St.
HABS NY-5698-A
HABS NY,31-NEYO,85A-
15ph/2pg/1pc L

St. Vincent's Hospital,Leon Lowenstein Clinic
7-15 Seventh Ave.
HABS NY-5698-B
HABS NY,31-NEYO,85B-
6ph/2pg/1pc L

Statue of Liberty (Statue of Liberty National Monument)
Liberty Island,Manhattan
HAER NY-138
HAER NY,31-NEYO,89- ι1991(HAER):5°
4dr/230ph/2pg/17pc/125ct L H

Statue of Liberty National Monument; see Ellis Island,Greenhouse

Statue of Liberty National Monument; see Ellis Island,Incinerator

Statue of Liberty National Monument; see Statue of Liberty

Strivers Row; see Cook,Will Marion,House

Stuyvesant Apartments
142 E. Eighteenth St.
HABS NY-435
HABS NY,31-NEYO,25-
6dr/7ph/4pg/fr L

Surrogates Court (Hall of Records)
31 Chambers St.
HABS NY-402
HABS NY,31-NEYO,115-
1ph L

Teller,Jane,Mansiona; see Mount Vernon Coach House & Stable

Third Judicial District Courthouse (Jefferson Market Courthouse; New York Public Library,Jefferson Market Branch)
425 Ave. of the Americas
HABS NY-4392
HABS NY,31-NEYO,65-
8ph/10pg L

Thompson,A. A. ,& Company; see South Street Seaport Museum

Tiffany & Company Building
401 Fifth Ave.
HABS NY-401
HABS NY,31-NEYO,96-
1ph L

Tredwell,Seabury,House
29 E. Fourth St.
HABS NY-440
HABS NY,31-NEYO,30-
9dr/21ph/3pg/fr L

Tribune Building
154 Printing House Sq.,Nassau & Spruce Sts.
HABS NY-5468
HABS NY,31-NEYO,75-
9ph/13pg L

Trinity Church
Broadway & Wall St.
HABS NY-6074
8pg H

Tudor City Complex
E. Fortieth to E. Fourty-third,btwn First & Second
HABS NY-6075
HABS NY,31-NEYO,122-
3ph/1pg L

Tudor City Complex,Cloister,The
321 E. Forty-third St.
HABS NY-6075-H
HABS NY,31-NEYO,122H-
5ph L

Tudor City Complex,Essex House
325 E. Forty-first St.
HABS NY-6075-E
HABS NY,31-NEYO,122E-
2ph L

Tudor City Complex,Haddon Hall
318-324 E. Forty-first St.
HABS NY-6075-D
HABS NY,31-NEYO,122D-
2ph L

Tudor City Complex,Hermitage,The
E. Forty-third St.
HABS NY-6075-J
HABS NY,31-NEYO,122J-
1ph L

Tudor City Complex,Hotel Tudor
304 E. Forty-second St.
HABS NY-6075-F
HABS NY,31-NEYO,122F-
3ph L

Tudor City Complex,Manor,The
333 E. Forty-third St.
HABS NY-6075-I
HABS NY,31-NEYO,122I-
2ph L

Tudor City Complex,Prospect Tower
45 Tudor City Place
HABS NY-6075-C
HABS NY,31-NEYO,122C-
3ph L

Tudor City Complex,Stewart Hall
310 Mitchell Place
HABS NY-6075-K
HABS NY,31-NEYO,122K-
1ph L

Tudor City Complex,Tudor Tower
25 Tudor City Place
HABS NY-6075-B
HABS NY,31-NEYO,122B-
2ph L

Tudor City Complex,Windsor Tower
5 Tudor City Place
HABS NY-6075-A
HABS NY,31-NEYO,122A-
2ph L

Tudor City Complex,Woodstock Tower
320 E. Forty-second St.
HABS NY-6075-G
HABS NY,31-NEYO,122G-
5ph L

Tweed Courthouse; see New York County Courthouse

U. S. Army Headquarters,First; see Governors Island,Second Corps Area Headquarters

U. S. Custom House (U. S. Sub-Treasury Building; Federal Hall National Memorial)
28 Wall St.
HABS NY-470
HABS NY,31-NEYO,53-
15dr/39ph/10pg/1ct/fr L

U. S. Immigration Station,Greenhouse; see Ellis Island,Greenhouse

U. S. Immigration Station,Incinerator; see Ellis Island,Incinerator

U. S. Sub-Treasury Building; see U. S. Custom House

U.S. Immigration Station; see Ellis Island

United Nations Headquarters
United Nations Plaza
HABS NY-6076
HABS NY,31-NEYO,151-
5ph/6pg L

United Nations Vicinity Area Study
Second Ave.,E.41,E.43,E.44,E.46,E.48, & E.49 Sts.
HABS NY-6254
HABS NY,31-NEYO,152-
32ph L

Villard Houses
451-457 Madison Ave. & 24 E. Fifty-first St.
HABS NY-5635
HABS NY,31-NEYO,120-
35dr/153ph/6pg/10pc/fr L

187 W. 135th St. (APARTMENT BUILDING) (Johnson,James Weldon-Residence)
187 W. One-hundred-thirty-fifth St.
HABS NY-5694
HABS NY,31-NEYO,113-
7ph L

Walker,David,House & Office
45 Whitehall St.
HABS NY-5455
HABS NY,31-NEYO,123-
5dr/2ph/1pc L

Ward,Joseph,Building; see South Street Seaport Museum

Washington Bridge
Spanning Harlem River at One-hundred-eighty-first
HAER NY-130
HAER NY,31-NEYO,162-
5ph/1pg L

Washington Square North (House)
Washington Sq. North & Fifth Ave.
HABS NY-4-16-A
HABS NY,31-NEYO,17-
1ph L

7 Washington Square North (House)
HABS NY-4-16-B
HABS NY,31-NEYO,19-
4ph/5pg L

8 Washington Square North (House)
HABS NY-4-16-C
HABS NY,31-NEYO,18-
10dr/5ph/8pg/fr L

61 Washington Square South (House)
HABS NY-447
HABS NY,31-NEYO,37-
9dr/7ph/2pg/fr L

71-77 Washington Street (House)
HABS NY-482
HABS NY,31-NEYO,54L-
1dr/7ph/fr L

15 Washington Street (Stairs)
HABS NY-482-A
HABS NY,31-NEYO,54K-
1ph L

13 Washington Street (Store Front)
HABS NY-481
HABS NY,31-NEYO,54I-
1dr/1ph L

29 Washington Street (Store Front)
HABS NY-481-A
HABS NY,31-NEYO,54J-
1ph L

739 Washington Street (Town House)
HABS NY-4379
HABS NY,31-NEYO,61-
3dr L

207-211 Water Street; see South Street Seaport Museum

213-215 Water Street; see South Street Seaport Museum

251 Water Street; see South Street Seaport Museum

273 Water Street; see South Street Seaport Museum

Watson,James,House
(Rogers,Moses,House)
7 State St.
HABS NY-442
HABS NY,31-NEYO,32-
5dr/16ph/3pg/1pc/fr L

Welfare Island,Castle-Hospital
(Roosevelt Island,Castle-Hospital)
HABS NY-6077
HABS NY,31-WELFI,4-
6ph L

Welfare Island,Church (Roosevelt Island,Church)
HABS NY-6078
HABS NY,31-WELFI,2-
6ph L

Welfare Island,Farmhouse (Roosevelt Island,Farmhouse)
HABS NY-6079
HABS NY,31-WELFI,1-
6ph L

Welfare Island,Insane Asylum
(Roosevelt Island,Insane Asylum)
HABS NY-6080
HABS NY,31-WELFI,6-
6ph L

Welfare Island,Lighthouse (Roosevelt Island,Lighthouse)
HABS NY-6081
HABS NY,31-WELFI,3-
4ph L

Welfare Island,South Building
(Roosevelt Island,South Building)
HABS NY-6082
HABS NY,31-WELFI,7-
7ph L

Welfare Island,Strecker Memorial Laboratory (Roosevelt Island,Strecker Memorial Laboratory)
HABS NY-6083
HABS NY,31-WELFI,5-
5ph L

116 West Eleventh Street (Building)
HABS NY-451
HABS NY,31-NEYO,41-
10dr/12ph/3pg L

132 West Fourth Street (Building)
HABS NY-448
HABS NY,31-NEYO,38-
10dr/6ph/4pg L

West Side Highway
HAER NY-133
HAER NY,31-NEYO,88-
23ph L

West 55th Street & West 56th Street Piers (Piers 95 & 96,North River)
Hudson River at W. 55th & W. 56th Sts. ,Manhattan
HAER NY-147
HAER NY,31-NEYO,147-
38ph/38pg/3pc L

Whitehall Street Ferry Terminal
(Governor's Island Ferry Terminal; Municipal Ferry Pier; Battery Maritime Building)
11 South St.
HAER NY-90
HAER NY,31-NEYO,146-
10ph/2pg/1pc L

Williamsburg Bridge
Span. East Riv.at S.Sixth St. bet.NYC & Brooklyn
HAER NY-128
HAER NY,31-NEYO,165-
4ph/1pg/1pc L

YMCA (McKay,Claude-Residence)
180 W. One-hundred-thirty-fifth St.
HABS NY-5695
HABS NY,31-NEYO,112-
7ph/1pc L

NIAGARA COUNTY

LEWISTON

Barton Hill
Center & River Sts.
HABS NY-6084
HABS NY,32-LEW,2-
6ph/1pg L

Cook,Bates Law Office
755 Center St.
HABS NY-6085
HABS NY,32-LEW,6-
2ph/1pg L

First Presbyterian Church
505 Cayuga St. at Fifth St.
HABS NY-6320
HABS NY,32-LEW,1-
2ph/1pg L

Frontier House
450 Center St.
HABS NY-6087
HABS NY,32-LEW,4- S
5ph L

Hennepin Hall
Center & Seventh Sts.
HABS NY-6088
HABS NY,32-LEW,3-
3ph L

Kelsey Tavern
625 Center St.
HABS NY-6089
HABS NY,32-LEW,7-
2ph L

LOCKPORT

Bissell-Spalding House
471 Market St.
HABS NY-6148
HABS NY,32-LOCK,5-
1ph/1pg L

Bond House
143 Ontario St.
HABS NY-6090
HABS NY,32-LOCK,8-
1ph/1pg L

Bouck,David,House
(Merritt,Ericsson,House)
532 Pine St.
HABS NY-6091
HABS NY,32-LOCK,9-
7ph/1pg L

Bouck,David,Well House & Garage
(Merritt,Ericsson,Well House & Garage)
532 Pine St.
HABS NY-6091-A
HABS NY,32-LOCK,9A-
1ph L

Christ Episcopal Church
425 Market St.
HABS NY-6092
HABS NY,32-LOCK,4-
2ph L

Dayton,Nathan,House
499 Market St.
HABS NY-6093
HABS NY,32-LOCK,7-
2ph L

Erie Canal,Combined Locks 67-71; see New York State Barge Canal,Lockport Locks

Hitchings,Francis,House
Summit St.
HABS NY-6095
HABS NY,31-NEYO,10-
2ph/1pg L

Hunt,Washington,House
363 Market St.
HABS NY-6096
HABS NY,32-LOCK,3-
2ph/1pg L

Jackson Block
Buffalo & Cottage Sts.
HABS NY-6097
HABS NY,32-LOCK,1-
1ph L

Lockport Bank Building
317-319 Market St.
HABS NY-6098
HABS NY,32-LOCK,2-
2ph/1pg L

Merritt,Ericsson,House; see Bouck,David,House

Merritt,Ericsson,Well House & Garage; see Bouck,David,Well House & Garage

New York Central R.R.:Lockport Passenger Station (New York Central R.R.:Union Station)
Washburn & Union Sts.
HAER NY-60
HAER NY,32-LOCK,13-
2ph/1pg/1pc L

New York Central R.R.:Union Station; see New York Central R.R.:Lockport Passenger Station

New York State Barge Canal,Lockport Locks (Erie Canal,Combined Locks 67-71)
Richmond Ave.
HAER NY-61
HAER NY,32-LOCK,14A-
6ph/2pg/1pc L

Second Presbyterian Church
71 Van Buren St.
HABS NY-6099
HABS NY,31-NEYO,11-
1ph/1pg L

Skinner,Josiah K. ,House
485 Market St.
HABS NY-6147
HABS NY,32-LOCK,6-
2ph L

Vine Street School
Vine & Garden Sts.
HABS NY-6149
HABS NY,32-LOCK,12-
2ph/1pg L

MARTINSVILLE

Erie Railway:Sawyer Creek Bridge
Spanning Sawyer Creek on U.S. Rt. 62
HAER NY-95
HAER NY,32-MARV,1-
1ph/1pc L

NIAGARA FALLS

Adams,Edward D. ,Station Power Plant
Niagara River & Buffalo Ave.
HABS NY-6150
HABS NY,32-NIAF,3-
15ph/fr L

Erie Railway:La Salle Station
HAER NY-92
HAER NY,32-LAS,1-
1ph/1pc L

Erie Railway:Niagara Falls Station
HAER NY-91
HAER NY,32-NIAF,4-
1ph/1pc L

U. S. Custom House
Whirlpool St. at Lower Arch Bridge
HABS NY-6152
HABS NY,31-NIAF,2-
14ph/4pg/fr L

University Club; see Whitney House

Whitney House (University Club)
355 Buffalo Ave.
HABS NY-6153
HABS NY,31-NIAF,1-
6ph/1pg L

NORTH TONAWANDA

Erie Railway:North Tonawanda Station
HAER NY-94
HAER NY,32-TONAN,1-
1ph/1pc L

SOMERSET

Thirty-mile Point Lighthouse
Golden Hill Park,Lake Ontario
HABS NY-6154
HABS NY,32-SOM,2-
3ph L

Van Wagoner,Morgan,Barn
Hosmer Rd.
HABS NY-5529-B
HABS NY,32-SOM,1B-
3dr/4ph/fr L

Van Wagoner,Morgan,House
Hosmer Rd.
HABS NY-5529-A
HABS NY,32-SOM,1A-
6dr/11ph/fr L

Van Wagoner,Morgan,House & Barn
Hosmer Rd.
HABS NY-5529
HABS NY,32-SOM,1-
1dr/19pg/fr L

YOUNGSTOWN

Fort Niagara
Fort Niagara State Park
HABS NY-6155
HABS NY,32-YOUNG,1-
7ph L

Fort Niagara,Administration Building
Fort Niagara State Park
HABS NY-6155-D
HABS NY,32-YOUNG,1D-
1ph L

Fort Niagara,East Gun Tower
Fort Niagara State Park
HABS NY-6155-B
HABS NY,32-YOUNG,1B-
1ph L

Fort Niagara,Entrance Gun Tower
Fort Niagara State Park
HABS NY-6155-C
HABS NY,32-YOUNG,1C-
1ph L

Fort Niagara,French Castle
Fort Niagara State Park
HABS NY-6155-A
HABS NY,32-YOUNG,1A-
17ph L

Fort Niagara,Hot Shot Battery Oven
Fort Niagara State Park
HABS NY-6155-E
HABS NY,32-YOUNG,1E-
1ph L

St. John's Episcopal Church
Main & Chestnut Sts.
HABS NY-6156
HABS NY,32-YOUNG,2-
3ph L

ONEIDA COUNTY

BOONVILLE VIC.

Black River Canal,Locks 39-43
State Rt. 46
HAER NY-83
HAER NY,33-BOONV.V,1A-
7ph/6pg/1pc L

ROME

Barnes-Mudge House (Rome Club)
115 E. Dominick St.
HABS NY-5509
HABS NY,33-ROM,2-
16ph/15pg L

Cole-Kingsley House (Women's Community Center)
110 E. Liberty St.
HABS NY-5512
HABS NY,33-ROM,5-
15ph/15pg L

Draper,Virgil,House
121 E. Dominick St.
HABS NY-5510
HABS NY,33-ROM,3-
2ph/5pg L

Empire House
111-113 E. Dominick St.
HABS NY-5508
HABS NY,33-ROM,1-
11ph/19pg L

Floyd,Gen. William,House
Westernville
HABS NY-5513
HABS NY,33-WESV,1-
5ph L

Golf Course Road Bridge; see Rome Westernville Road Bridge

Liberty Hall (Stryker,John,House)
112 E. Liberty St.
HABS NY-5511
HABS NY,33-ROM,4-
1dr/20ph/14pg L

Oneida County Courthouse
HABS NY-6111
HABS NY,33-ROM,6-
4ph L

Rome Club; see Barnes-Mudge House

Rome Westernville Road Bridge (Golf Course Road Bridge)
Spanning Mohawk River
HAER NY-179
HAER 1991(HAER):5
4ph/5pg/1pc L

Stryker,John,House; see Liberty Hall

Women's Community Center; see Cole-Kingsley House

UTICA

City Hall
Genesee & Pearl Sts.
HABS NY-5444
HABS NY,33-UTI,1-
4ph L

VERNON CENTER

Tuttle,Hiram,House
HABS NY-5-S-9
HABS NY,33-VERC,1-
4ph/2pg L

WHITESBORO

Town Hall
Park Ave.
HABS NY-5-U-1
HABS NY,33-WHIT,1-
2dr/2ph/3pg/fr L

ONONDAGA COUNTY

CAMILLUS

Camillus Baptist Church
Genesee St.
HABS NY-6159
HABS NY,34-CAM,1-
1ph/1pg L

DELPHI FALLS

Delphi Baptist Church; see Meetinghouse of the First Baptist Society

Meetinghouse of the First Baptist Society (Delphi Baptist Church)
Pompey
HABS NY-5431
HABS NY,34-DELF,1-
8dr/6ph/fr L

ELBRIDGE VIC

Munro,John,House
State Rt. 5
HABS NY-6160
HABS NY,34-ELBRI.V,1-
2ph/1pg L

FABIUS

Benson House
Ridge Rd.
HABS NY-6161
HABS NY,34-FAB,1-
1ph/1pg L

FAYETTEVILLE

Collin,Charles,House
7860 E. Genesee St.
HABS NY-6163
HABS NY,34-FAYV,2-
1ph/1pg L

McViciar,John,House
315 Genesee St.
HABS NY-6164
HABS NY,34-FAYV,1-
1ph L

JAMESVILLE

St. Mark's Episcopal Church
HABS NY-6165
HABS NY,34-JAMS,1-
1ph/1pg L

JAMESVILLE VIC.

Ives,Dr. ,House
E. Seneca Turnpike
HABS NY-6118
HABS NY,34-JAMS.V,1-
1ph/1pg L

JORDAN

Junod House
150 N. Main St.
HABS NY-6166
HABS NY,34-JORD,4-
1ph/1pg L

15 Main Street (Commercial Building)
HABS NY-6167
HABS NY,34-JORD,3-
1ph/1pg L

Rogers,W. C.,Block
Main & Mechanics Sts.
HABS NY-6168
HABS NY,34-JORD,2-
1ph/1pg L

Tanner,Dr. ,House
HABS NY-6169
HABS NY,34-JORD,1-
1ph/1pg L

LIVERPOOL

Gleason,Lucius,House
Sycamore & Second Sts.
HABS NY-6171
HABS NY,34-LIV,2-
1ph L

Hicks,J. P. ,Building; see
Hotel,Cobblestone

Hicks,Jonathan,House
609 Vine St.
HABS NY-6172
HABS NY,34-LIV,3-
1ph/1pg L

Hotel,Cobblestone (Hicks,J. P. ,Building)
HABS NY-6170
HABS NY,34-LIV,1-
1ph/1pg L

MANLIUS

Smith Hall
Seneca Turnpike
HABS NY-6173
HABS NY,34-MANLI,2-
1ph/1pg L

MARCELLUS

Bradley,Dan,House
HABS NY-6174
HABS NY,34-MARC,2-
1ph/1pg L

Marcellus Presbyterian Church
Seneca Turnpike & North St.
HABS NY-6175
HABS NY,34-MARC,1-
1ph/1pg L

MARCELLUS VIC.

District School Number 9
HABS NY-227
HABS NY,34-MARC.V,1-
4dr/4ph/2pg/fr L

MARTISCO

Martisco Station
Marcellus & Otisco Sts.
HABS NY-6176
HABS NY,34-MART,1-
2ph L

ONONDAGA HILL

Easton Storehouse
Seneca Turnpike
HABS NY-223
HABS NY,34-ONDA,1-
4dr/4ph/2pg L

Hutchinson,Gen. George,House
4311 W. Seneca Turnpike
HABS NY-6177
HABS NY,34-ONDA,2-
3ph/1pg L

Onondaga County Poorhouse
Onondaga Rd.
HABS NY-6162
HABS NY,34-ONDA,3-
1ph L

ORAN

Travelers' & Drovers' Tavern
Cherry Valley Turnpike
HABS NY-5-S-6
HABS NY,34-ORA,1-
7dr/3ph/2pg/fr L

PLAINVILLE VIC.

Voorhees,Colonel,House; see Whig Hall

Whig Hall (Voorhees,Colonel,House)
State Rt. 370 & Gates Rd.
HABS NY-6178
HABS NY,34-PLANK.V,1-
4ph/1pg L

POMPEY

Beard-Conan Store
HABS NY-225
HABS NY,34-POMP,3-
6dr/5ph/2pg/fr L

Marsh,Moses Seymour,Store
HABS NY-224
HABS NY,34-POMP,2-
6dr/4ph/2pg/fr L

Pompey Presbyterian Church
Fabius Pompey Rd.
HABS NY-5-S-5
HABS NY,34-POMP,1-
7dr/3ph/1pg/fr L

SKANEATELES

Benedict,Dr. ,House
43 State St.
HABS NY-6179
HABS NY,34-SKA,16-
1ph L

Community Place
HABS NY-6180
HABS NY,34-SKA,6-
2ph L

Dezeng,Richard,House (Roosevelt Hall)
W. Lake Rd.
HABS NY-6181
HABS NY,34-SKA,12-
2ph L

Jewett House,Small
81 Genesee St.
HABS NY-6182
HABS NY,34-SKA,10-
1ph L

Jewett,Freeborn,Mansion
11 Genesee St.
HABS NY-6183
HABS NY,34-SKA,9-
1ph L

Lamb,Alfred,House
Franklin St.
HABS NY-6184
HABS NY,34-SKA,7-
2ph L

Lee,Benoit,Law Office (Sphinx,The)
Skaneateles Public Library
HABS NY-6185
HABS NY,34-SKA,14A-
1ph L

Legg Hall
Genesee St.
HABS NY-6186
HABS NY,34-SKA,8-
1ph L

Loveless House
77 Jordan St.
HABS NY-6187
HABS NY,34-SKA,11-
2ph L

Meetinghouse of the Skaneateles Baptist Society
State St.
HABS NY-6188
HABS NY,34-SKA,15-
1ph L

Merriam House
W. Genesee St.
HABS NY-5-S-3
HABS NY,34-SKA,5-
7dr/3ph/1pg L

Roosevelt Hall; see
Dezeng,Richard,House

Smith,Reuel,House
W. Lake Rd.
HABS NY-5452
HABS NY,34-SKA,13-
18ph/1pg L

Documentation: **ct** color transparencies **dr** measured drawings **fr** field records
pc photograph captions **pg** pages of text **ph** photographs

Sphinx,The; see Lee,Benoit,Law Office

SKANEATELES VIC.

District School Number 17
W. Lake Rd.
HABS NY-226
HABS NY,34-SKA.V,3-
4dr/2ph/3pg L

SYRACUSE

Andrew Block
W. Fayette & Clinton Sts.
HABS NY-6190
HABS NY,34-SYRA,9-
1ph L

Botanic Infirmary,Old (Thompson,Dr. Cyrus,Block)
W. Genesee St.
HABS NY-5447
HABS NY,34-SYRA,11-
5ph/1pg L

Brown-Lipe-Chapin Division; see General Motors Factory

Brown,Alexander,House
726 W. Onondaga St.
HABS NY-6191
HABS NY,34-SYRA,32-
1ph/1pg L

Church of St. John the Baptist
Park & Court Sts.
HABS NY-6193
HABS NY,34-SYRA,34-
1ph/1pg L

Church of St. John the Evangelist
214 N. State St.
HABS NY-6194
HABS NY,34-SYRA,17-
1ph L

City Bank Building; see Kirk Fireproof Building

Crouse,John R. ,College
Syracuse University
HABS NY-6195
HABS NY,34-SYRA,25A-
1ph L

Dutch Reformed Church
HABS NY-6196
HABS NY,34-SYRA,24-
1ph L

Forman,Samuel,House
409 W. Seneca St.
HABS NY-5-S-2
HABS NY,34-SYRA,3-
13dr/2ph/2pg L

General Motors Factory
(Brown-Lipe-Chapin Division)
Marcellus St.
HABS NY-6192
HABS NY,34-SYRA,33-
1ph/1pg L

Gere,Robert,Bank Building
1212 E. Water St.
HABS NY-6197
HABS NY,34-SYRA,22-
1ph/1pg L

Grace Episcopal Church
819 Madison St.
HABS NY-6198
HABS NY,34-SYRA,30-
1ph L

Greenway Place
Hawley Ave. & McBridge St.
HABS NY-6199
HABS NY,34-SYRA,26-
1ph L

Gridley,John,House
205 E. Seneca Tpk.
HABS NY-222
HABS NY,34-SYRA,4-
12dr/11ph/2pg/1pc/fr L

Kellogg House
Lancaster & Euclid Ave.
HABS NY-6200
HABS NY,34-SYRA,29-
1ph L

Kirk Fireproof Building (City Bank Building)
HABS NY-6202
HABS NY,34-SYRA,23-
1ph L

Leavenworth,General,House
607 James St.
HABS NY-5-S-1
HABS NY,34-SYRA,2-
9dr/3ph/1pg L

McCarthy Warehouse,Edwards Annex
HABS NY-6203
HABS NY,34-SYRA,21-
1ph L

Onondaga County Courthouse,Old
(Third Onondaga County Courthouse)
Clinton Sq.
HABS NY-5430
HABS NY,34-SYRA,13-
6dr/5ph/fr L

Onondaga County Savings Bank,Old
Erie Blvd. & Salina St.
HABS NY-5450
HABS NY,34-SYRA,7-
6ph/1pg L

Park Avenue Methodist Church (St. Paul's Armenian Apostolic Church)
312 Geddes St.
HABS NY-6204
HABS NY,34-SYRA,10-
1ph L

Searle,Nathaniel,House
5323 S. Salina St.
HABS NY-6207
HABS NY,34-SYRA,15-
1ph L

Sedgewick House
742 James St.
HABS NY-5445
HABS NY,34-SYRA,27-
9ph/1pg L

Sedgewick House,Carriage House
742 James St.
HABS NY-5445-A
HABS NY,34-SYRA,27A-
1ph L

1622 South Salina Street (House)
HABS NY-6206
HABS NY,34-SYRA,14-
1ph L

St. Paul's Armenian Apostolic Church; see Park Avenue Methodist Church

St. Paul's Episcopal Church
Fayette & Montgomery Sts.
HABS NY-6205
HABS NY,34-SYRA,12-
2ph L

State Idiot Asylum; see Syracuse State School

Syracuse City Hall
Washington St.
HABS NY-379
HABS NY,34-SYRA,5-
9ph/10pg/fr L

Syracuse Savings Bank
102 N. Salina St.
HABS NY-5449
HABS NY,34-SYRA,35-
6ph L

Syracuse State School (State Idiot Asylum)
Burnet Park
HABS NY-6208
HABS NY,34-SYRA,36A-
1ph L

Syracuse University,Hall of Languages
Syrcause University Campus
HABS NY-5446
HABS NY,34-SYRA,25B-
15ph/1pg L

Teall,Oliver,House
105 S. Beech St.
HABS NY-6209
HABS NY,34-SYRA,6-
1ph L

Third Onondaga County Courthouse; see Onondaga County Courthouse,Old

Thompson,Dr. Cyrus,Block; see Botanic Infirmary,Old

Tolman,Harvey,House
5516 S. Salina St.
HABS NY-6210
HABS NY,34-SYRA,16-
1ph L

Weighlock Building
Erie Blvd. East & Montgomery St.
HABS NY-5451
HABS NY,34-SYRA,8A-
19ph/1pg L

Wesleyan Methodist Church
304 E. Onondaga St.
HABS NY-6211
HABS NY,34-SYRA,31-
1ph L

111 West Kennedy St. (House)
HABS NY-6201
HABS NY,34-SYRA,28-
2ph L

White Memorial Building
E. Washington & S. Salina Sts.
HABS NY-5448
HABS NY,34-SYRA,20-
6ph/1pg L

White,Hamilton,House
S. Townsend & E. Genesee St.
HABS NY-6212
HABS NY,34-SYRA,18-
1ph L

Wilkinson,Horace,House
703 Walnut Ave.
HABS NY-6213
HABS NY,34-SYRA,19-
1ph L

ONTARIO COUNTY

BRISTOL CENTER

Presbyterian Church
HABS NY-235
HABS NY,35-BRISC,1-
3ph L

CANANDAIGUA

Carr-Hayes House
Gibson & Hubbell Sts.
HABS NY-214
HABS NY,35-CANDA,3-
14dr/6ph/2pg/fr L

First Congregational Church
N. Main St.
HABS NY-5-R-11
HABS NY,35-CANDA,5-
15dr/10ph/2pg/fr L

Granger,Gideon,House
295 N. Main St.
HABS NY-5-R-2
HABS NY,35-CANDA,2-
16dr/8ph/2pg/fr L

Lansing,Henry,House
72 E. Gibson St.
HABS NY-212
HABS NY,35-CANDA,6-
8dr/6ph/2pg/fr L

GENEVA

Burns,Andrew,House
859 S. Main St.
HABS NY-230
HABS NY,35-GEN,3-
12dr/6ph/fr L

Chapman,Jebidiah,House
562 S. Main St.
HABS NY-232
HABS NY,35-GEN,4-
12dr/9ph/fr L

Chew House (Entrance)
600 S. Main St.
HABS NY-239
HABS NY,35-GEN,7-
1ph L

Hotel Geneva; see Nester Hotel

Jacobs Building
523 Exchange St.
HABS NY-5705
HABS NY,35-GEN,11-
2ph/4pg/1pc L

Nester Hotel (Hotel Geneva)
529-533 Exchange St.
HABS NY-5706
HABS NY,35-GEN,12-
30ph/12pg/2pc L

Truslow House
606 S. Main St.
HABS NY-238
HABS NY,35-GEN,6-
2ph L

Wheat House,The
584 S. Main St.
HABS NY-237
HABS NY,35-GEN,5-
3ph L

Williamson,Col. Charles,House
839 S. Main St.
HABS NY-233
HABS NY,35-GEN,2-
13dr/7ph/fr L

NAPLES

Cleveland,Ephraim,House
HABS NY-236
HABS NY,35-NAP,1-
2ph L

ORANGE COUNTY

GOSHEN

Erie Railway:Goshen Station
Grand & Erie Sts.
HAER NY-55
HAER NY,36-GOSH,1-
5ph/1pc/fr L

HARRIMAN

Erie Railway:Harriman Station
HAER NY-136
HAER NY,36-HAR,1-
1ph/1pc L

MIDDLETOWN

Erie Railway:Middletown Station
James St.
HAER NY-56
HAER NY,36-MID,1-
7ph/1pc/1ct L

NEW WINDSOR

Haskell,John,House
Windsor Hwy. (Rt. 32)
HABS NY-5664
HABS NY,36-NEWI,1-
15dr/16ph/13pg/fr L

NEWBURGH

71 Ann Street (House)
HABS NY-6214
HABS NY,36-NEWB,4-
1ph L

Anthony House
201 Montgomery St.
HABS NY-6215
HABS NY,36-NEWB,23A-
1ph L

55 Broad Street (House)
HABS NY-6216
HABS NY,36-NEWB,5-
2ph L

City Club; see Culbert,Dr. William A. M.,House

City Library
Grand St.
HABS NY-6217
HABS NY,36-NEWB,9-
5ph L

Clinton,George,Statue
Water St. at First St. (Clinton Sq.)
HABS NY-6231
HABS NY,36-NEWB,26-
1ph L

Colden Street Houses
HABS NY-6218
HABS NY,36-NEWB,6-
2ph L

Crawford,David,House
189 Montgomery St.
HABS NY-6219
HABS NY,36-NEWB,19-
10ph/1pg L

Culbert,Dr. William A. M.,House (City Club)
120 Grand St.
HABS NY-6220
HABS NY,36-NEWB,11-
9ph/1pg/fr L

Dutch Reformed Church
132 Grand St.
HABS NY-6221
HABS NY,36-NEWB,12-
16ph/9pg/fr L

Fowler,James,Walker,House
(Marvel,Capt. Thomas S. ,House; Walker-Marvel House)
53 Ann St.
HABS NY-6234
HABS NY,36-NEWB,3-
3ph/6pg L

288 Grand Street (House)
HABS NY-6224
HABS NY,36-NEWB,17-
2ph L

78-86 Grand Street (Houses)
HABS NY-6223
HABS NY,36-NEWB,10-
1ph L

Hasbrouck House (Washington's Headquarters)
Washington,Liberty,Lafayette,Colden Sts.
HABS NY-4131
HABS NY,36-NEWB,1-
13dr/26ph L

Hasbrouck,William C.,House (Tuscan Villa,The)
99 Montgomery St.
HABS NY-6255
HABS NY,36-NEWB,15-
15ph/6pg/fr L

Hodges Funeral Home; see Warren,W. E.,House

Leonard,C. M.,Company Firehouse
HABS NY-6225
HABS NY,36-NEWB,8-
4ph L

Mackies,Miss,School for Girls; see Roe,William,House

Marvel,Capt. Thomas S. ,House; see Fowler,James,Walker,House

Newburgh Savings Bank (Soul-Saving Church of God)
Smith & Second Sts.
HABS NY-6226
HABS NY,36-NEWB,24-
1ph L

Orange County Courthouse
Second & Grand Sts.
HABS NY-6227
HABS NY,36-NEWB,25-
10ph L

Reeve House
129-131 Montgomery St.
HABS NY-6228
HABS NY,36-NEWB,18-
10dr/7ph L

Ringgold Fire Company Firehouse
63 Colden St.
HABS NY-6229
HABS NY,36-NEWB,7-
4ph L

Roe,William,House (Mackies,Miss,School for Girls)
160 Grand St.
HABS NY-6230
HABS NY,36-NEWB,13-
15ph/4pg/fr L

Soul-Saving Church of God; see Newburgh Savings Bank

Stevens,Halsey,Carriage House
HABS NY-6232-A
HABS NY,36-NEWB,14A-
1ph L

Stevens,Halsey,Firehouse
HABS NY-6232-B
HABS NY,36-NEWB,14B-
3ph L

Stevens,Halsey,House
182 Grand St.
HABS NY-6232
HABS NY,36-NEWB,14-
9ph/3pg/fr L

Sunflower House
195 Montgomery St.
HABS NY-6233
HABS NY,36-NEWB,20-
2ph L

Tomb,Egyptian-Style
Calvary Cemetery
HABS NY-6222
HABS NY,36-NEWB,23-A-
3ph L

Tuscan Villa,The; see Hasbrouck,William C.,House

Walker-Marvel House; see Fowler,James,Walker,House

Warren,W. E.,House (Hodges Funeral Home)
196 Grand St.
HABS NY-6235
HABS NY,36-NEWB,16-
8ph L

Washington's Headquarters; see Hasbrouck House

Wright,William,House
Interstate Hwy. 84
HABS NY-5689
HABS NY,36-NEWB,2-
13ph/1pc L

OTISVILLE

Erie Railway:Otisville Tunnel
Sanitarium Rd. to Otisville Rd.
HAER NY-21
HAER NY,36-OTVI,1-
5ph/1pc L

PORT JERVIS

Erie Railway:Port Jervis Roundhouse
Pike St.
HAER NY-23
HAER NY,36-POJE,2A-
5ph/1pc L

Erie Railway:Port Jervis Station
Jersey Ave.
HAER NY-22
HAER NY,36-POJE,1-
9ph/1pc/2ct L

PORT JERVIS VIC.

Erie Railway:Port Jervis Rock Cut
Neversink & Shinhollow Rds. Vic.
HAER NY-24
HAER NY,36-POJE.V,1-
1ph/1pc L

SALISBURY MILLS VIC.

Erie Railway:Moodna Creek Viaduct
(Graham Line,Bridge 55.03)
Moodna Creek,Orrs Mill Rd.
HAER NY-62
HAER NY,36-SALMI.V,1-
4ph/1pc L

Graham Line,Bridge 55.03; see Erie Railway:Moodna Creek Viaduct

WEST POINT

Hotel Thayer; see U. S. Military Academy,Building 674

Queensboro Furnace; see U. S. Military Academy,Queensboro Furnace

U. S. M. A. ,Bartlett Hall; see U. S. Military Academy,East Academic Building

U. S. M. A. ,Benet Hall; see U. S. Military Academy,Ordnance Compound Office

U. S. M. A. ,Benton Hall; see U. S. Military Academy,Ordnance Comp. Blacksmth Sh

U. S. M. A. ,Benton Hall; see U. S. Military Academy,Ordnance Compound Barracks

U. S. M. A. ,Boodlers; see U. S. Military Academy,Confectionery

U. S. M. A. ,Building No. 100; see U. S. Military Academy,Officer's Quarters

U. S. M. A. ,Building No. 101; see U. S. Military Academy,Officer's Quarters

U. S. M. A. ,Building No. 102; see U. S. Military Academy,Officer's Quarters

U. S. M. A. ,Building No. 103; see U. S. Military Academy,Officer's Quarters

U. S. M. A. ,Building No. 105; see U. S. Military Academy,Officer's Quarters

U. S. M. A. ,Building No. 107; see U. S. Military Academy,Officer's Quarters

U. S. M. A. ,Building No. 109; see U. S. Military Academy,Officer's Quarters

U. S. M. A. ,Building No. 11; see U. S. Military Academy,Officer' Quarters

U. S. M. A. ,Building No. 116; see U. S. Military Academy,Officer's Quarters

U. S. M. A. ,Building No. 118; see U. S. Military Academy,Officer's Quarters

U. S. M. A. ,Building No. 1183; see U. S. Military Academy,Warner House

U. S. M. A. ,Building No. 120; see U. S. Military Academy,Officer's Quarters

U. S. M. A. ,Building No. 122; see U. S. Military Academy,Officer's Quarters

U. S. M. A. ,Building No. 126; see U. S. Military Academy,Soldiers' Hospital

U. S. M. A. ,Building No. 146; see U. S. Military Academy,Non-Commiss'd Off. Quarters

U. S. M. A. ,Building No. 147; see U. S. Military Academy,Confectionery

U. S. M. A. ,Building No. 21; see U. S. Military Academy,Officer's Quarters

U. S. M. A. ,Building No. 25; see U. S. Military Academy,Officer's Quarters

U. S. M. A. ,Building No. 32; see U. S. Military Academy,Officer's Quarters

U. S. M. A. ,Building No. 34; see U. S. Military Academy,Officer's Quarters

U. S. M. A. ,Building No. 344; see U. S. Military Academy,Married Enlisted Men's Qtrs

U. S. M. A. ,Building No. 352; see U. S. Military Academy,Married Enlisted Men's Qtrs

U. S. M. A. ,Building No. 374; see U. S. Military Academy,Hospital Steward's Quarters

U. S. M. A. ,Building No. 42; see U. S. Military Academy,Officer's Quarters

U. S. M. A. ,Building No. 45; see U. S. Military Academy,Officer's Quarters

U. S. M. A. ,Building No. 48; see U. S. Military Academy,Officer's Quarters

U. S. M. A. ,Building No. 60; see U. S. Military Academy,Chaplain's Quarters

U. S. M. A. ,Building No. 600; see U. S. Military Academy,Administration Building

U. S. M. A. ,Building No. 601; see U. S. Military Academy,Riding Hall

U. S. M. A. ,Building No. 602; see U. S. Military Academy,Grant Hall & South Barracks

U. S. M. A. ,Building No. 604; see U. S. Military Academy,Power Plant

U. S. M. A. ,Building No. 605; see U. S. Military Academy,Cullum Memorial Hall

U. S. M. A. ,Building No. 618; see U. S. Military Academy,Gun Shed

U. S. M. A. ,Building No. 620; see U. S. Military Academy,Artillery Barracks

U. S. M. A. ,Building No. 622; see U. S. Military Academy,Artillery Stables

U. S. M. A. ,Building No. 624; see U. S. Military Academy,Cavalry Barracks

U. S. M. A. ,Building No. 626; see U. S. Military Academy,Cavalry Stables

U. S. M. A. ,Building No. 635; see U. S. Military Academy,Ordnance Comp. Blacksmth Sh

U. S. M. A. ,Building No. 637; see U. S. Military Academy,Ordnance Compound Barracks

U. S. M. A. ,Building No. 671; see U. S. Military Academy,Ordnan. Compound Wkshp/Wrhs

U. S. M. A. ,Building No. 671-A; see U. S. Military Academy,Ordnance Compound Office

U. S. M. A. ,Building No. 689; see U. S. Military Academy,Cadet Chapel

U. S. M. A. ,Building No. 692; see U. S. Military Academy,Bachelor Enlistd Men's Qtrs

U. S. M. A. ,Building No. 696; see U. S. Military Academy,West Shore RR Passenger Sta

U. S. M. A. ,Building No. 7; see U. S. Military Academy,Officer's Quarters

U. S. M. A. ,Building No. 722; see U. S. Military Academy,Cadet Chapel

U. S. M. A. ,Building No. 727; see U. S. Military Academy,Gymnasium

U. S. M. A. ,Building No. 735; see U. S. Military Academy,North Barracks

U. S. M. A. ,Building No. 747; see U. S. Military Academy,Central Barracks

U. S. M. A. ,Building No. 751; see U. S. Military Academy,West Academic Building

U. S. M. A. ,Building No. 753; see U. S. Military Academy,East Academic Building

U. S. M. A. ,Building No. 8; see U. S. Military Academy,Officer's Quarters

U. S. M. A. ,Building Nos. 635-A & 635-B; see U. S. Military Academy,Ordnance Compound Privies

U. S. M. A. ,Cadet Activities Club; see U. S. Military Academy,Ordnance Comp. Blacksmth Sh

U. S. M. A. ,Cadet Activity Club; see U. S. Military Academy,Ordnan. Compound Wkshp/Wrhs

U. S. M. A. ,Cadet Activity Club; see U. S. Military Academy,Ordnance Compound Barracks

U. S. M. A. ,Cadet Activity Club; see U. S. Military Academy,West Shore RR Passenger Sta

U. S. M. A. ,Cadet Chapel,Old; see U. S. Military Academy,Cadet Chapel

U. S. M. A. ,Commandant's Quarters; see U. S. Military Academy,Officer's Quarters

U. S. M. A. ,Company Headquarters & Barracks; see U. S. Military Academy,Artillery Barracks

U. S. M. A. ,Crozier Hall; see U. S. Military Academy,Ordnan. Compound Wkshp/Wrhs

U. S. M. A. ,Dean's Quarters; see U. S. Military Academy,Officer's Quarters

U. S. M. A. ,East Cadet Barracks; see U. S. Military Academy,West Academic Building

U. S. M. A. ,Eisenhower Hall; see U. S. Military Academy,Cadet Mess & Drwg. Academy

U. S. M. A. ,Elisted Men's Serv. Club & Post Libra; see U. S. Military Academy,Artillery Stables

U. S. M. A. ,Enlisted Men's Quarters; see U. S. Military Academy,Bachelor Enlistd Men's Qtrs

U. S. M. A. ,Family Housing; see U. S. Military Academy,Officer' Quarters

U. S. M. A. ,Family Housing; see U. S. Military Academy,Officer's Quarters

U. S. M. A. ,Family Housing; see U. S. Military Academy,Soldiers' Hospital

U. S. M. A. ,Heating Plant; see U. S. Military Academy,Power Plant

U. S. M. A. ,MacArthur Barracks; see U. S. Military Academy,Cadet Mess & Drwg. Academy

U. S. M. A. ,Madison Hall; see U. S. Military Academy,West Academic Building

U. S. M. A. ,Memorial Hall; see U. S. Military Academy,Cullum Memorial Hall

U. S. M. A. ,Mess Hall; see U. S. Military Academy,Cadet Mess & Drwg. Academy

U. S. M. A. ,NCO Quarters; see U. S. Military Academy,Ordnance Compound Office

U. S. M. A. ,New York City Railroad Station; see U. S. Military Academy,West Shore RR Passenger Sta

U. S. M. A. ,Ordnance Compound Towers; see U. S. Military Academy,Ordnance Compound Privies

U. S. M. A. ,Pershing Barracks; see U. S. Military Academy,West Academic Building

U. S. M. A. ,Post Headquarters; see U. S. Military Academy,Administration Building

U. S. M. A. ,Professors Row; see U. S. Military Academy,Officer's Quarters

U. S. M. A. ,Quarters No. 146; see U. S. Military Academy,Non-Commiss'd Off. Quarters

U. S. M. A. ,Scott Barracks; see U. S. Military Academy,North Barracks

U. S. M. A. ,South Barracks; see U. S. Military Academy,Grant Hall & South Barracks

U. S. M. A. ,Superintendent's Quarters; see U. S. Military Academy,Officer's Quarters

U. S. M. A. ,Thayer Hall; see U. S. Military Academy,Riding Hall

U. S. M. A. ,Washington Hall; see U. S. Military Academy,Cadet Mess & Drwg. Academy

U. S. Military Academy (West Point)
HABS NY-5708
HABS NY,36-WEPO,1-
39ph/259pg/2pc/3ct/fr L

U. S. Military Academy - Cemetery
HABS NY-5708-55
HABS NY,36-WEPO,1/55-
7ph/1pc/2ct L

U. S. Military Academy,Administration Building (U. S. M. A. ,Post Headquarters; U. S. M. A. ,Building No. 600)
HABS NY-5708-22
HABS NY,36-WEPO,1/22-
32ph/27pg/6ct/fr L

U. S. Military Academy,Artillery Barracks (U. S. M. A. ,Company Headquarters & Barracks; U. S. M. A. ,Building No. 620)
HABS NY-5708-27
HABS NY,36-WEPO,1/27-
3ph/7pg/fr L

U. S. Military Academy,Artillery Stables (U. S. M. A. ,Elisted Men's Serv. Club & Post Libra U. S. M. A. ,Building No. 622)
HABS NY-5708-46
HABS NY,36-WEPO,1/46-
7ph/7pg/fr L

U. S. Military Academy,Bachelor Enlistd Men's Qtrs (U. S. M. A. ,Building No. 692; U. S. M. A. ,Enlisted Men's Quarters)
HABS NY-5708-54
HABS NY,36-WEPO,1/54-
3ph/6pg/fr L

U. S. Military Academy,Building 674 (Hotel Thayer)
HABS NY-5708-60
HABS DLC/PP-1993:NY-5
48ph/37pg/7pc L

U. S. Military Academy,Cadet Chapel (U. S. M. A. ,Building No. 722)
HABS NY-5708-20
HABS NY,36-WEPO,1/20-
22ph/55pg/fr L

U. S. Military Academy,Cadet Chapel (U. S. M. A. ,Cadet Chapel,Old; U. S. M. A. ,Building No. 689)
HABS NY-5708-7
HABS NY,36-WEPO,1/55B-
8ph/12pg/fr L

U. S. Military Academy,Cadet Mess & Drwg. Academy (U. S. M. A. ,Mess Hall; U. S. M. A. ,Washington Hall; U. S. M. A. ,Eisenhower Hall; U. S. M. A. ,MacArthur Barracks)
HABS NY-5708-44
HABS NY,36-WEPO,1/44-
28ph/18pg/10ct/fr L

U. S. Military Academy,Cavalry Barracks (U. S. M. A. ,Building No. 624)
HABS NY-5708-28
HABS NY,36-WEPO,1/28-
3ph/6pg/fr L

U. S. Military Academy,Cavalry Stables (U. S. M. A. ,Building No. 626)
HABS NY-5708-47
HABS NY,36-WEPO,1/47-
4ph/7pg/fr L

U. S. Military Academy,Cemetery Gates
HABS NY-5708-55-A
HABS NY,36-WEPO,1/55A-
3ph/2pg/fr L

U. S. Military Academy,Central Barracks (U. S. M. A. ,Building No. 747)
HABS NY-5708-8
HABS NY,36-WEPO,1/8-
12ph/19pg/fr L

U. S. Military Academy,Chaplain's Quarters (U. S. M. A. ,Building No. 60)
HABS NY-5708-21
HABS NY,36-WEPO,1/21-
7ph/7pg/fr L

U. S. Military Academy,Confectionery (U. S. M. A. ,Boodlers; U. S. M. A. ,Building No. 147)
HABS NY-5708-19
HABS NY,36-WEPO,1/19-
2ph/6pg/fr L

U. S. Military Academy,Cullum Memorial Hall (U. S. M. A. ,Memorial Hall; U. S. M. A. ,Building No. 605)
HABS NY-5708-42
HABS NY,36-WEPO,1/42-
14ph/13pg/fr L

U. S. Military Academy,East Academic Building (U. S. M. A. ,Bartlett Hall; U. S. M. A. ,Building No. 753)
HABS NY-5708-25
HABS NY,36-WEPO,1/25-
16ph/12pg/fr L

U. S. Military Academy,Grant Hall & South Barracks (U. S. M. A. ,South Barracks; U. S. M. A. ,Building No. 602)
HABS NY-5708-26
HABS NY,36-WEPO,1/26-
12ph/22pg/fr L

U. S. Military Academy,Gun Shed (U. S. M. A. ,Building No. 618)
HABS NY-5708-56
HABS NY,36-WEPO,1/56-
3ph/6pg/fr L

U. S. Military Academy,Gymnasium (U. S. M. A. ,Building No. 727)
HABS NY-5708-43
HABS NY,36-WEPO,1/43-
22ph/13pg/fr L

U. S. Military Academy,Hospital Steward's Quarters (U. S. M. A. ,Building No. 374)
HABS NY-5708-18
HABS NY,36-WEPO,1/18-
3ph/6pg/fr L

U. S. Military Academy,Married Enlisted Men's Qtrs (U. S. M. A. ,Building No. 344)
HABS NY-5708-53
HABS NY,36-WEPO,1/53-
3ph/4pg/fr L

U. S. Military Academy,Married Enlisted Men's Qtrs (U. S. M. A. ,Building No. 352)
HABS NY-5708-52
HABS NY,36-WEPO,1/52-
3ph/4pg/fr L

U. S. Military Academy,Non-Commiss'd Off. Quarters (U. S. M. A. ,Quarters No. 146; U. S. M. A. ,Building No. 146)
HABS NY-5708-16
HABS NY,36-WEPO,1/16-
4ph/7pg/fr L

U. S. Military Academy,North Barracks (U. S. M. A. ,Scott Barracks; U. S. M. A. ,Building No. 735)
HABS NY-5708-45
HABS NY,36-WEPO,1/45-
19pg/fr L

U. S. Military Academy,Officer' Quarters (U. S. M. A. ,Family Housing; U. S. M. A. ,Building No. 11)
HABS NY-5708-51
HABS NY,36-WEPO,1/51-
2ph/5pg/fr L

U. S. Military Academy,Officer's Quarters (U. S. M. A. ,Commandant's Quarters; U. S. M. A. ,Building No. 101)
HABS NY-5708-2
HABS NY,36-WEPO,1/2-
12ph/11pg/fr L

U. S. Military Academy,Officer's Quarters (U. S. M. A. ,Dean's Quarters; U. S. M. A. ,Building No. 102)
HABS NY-5708-3
HABS NY,36-WEPO,1/3-
9ph/7pg/2ct/fr L

U. S. Military Academy,Officer's Quarters (U. S. M. A. ,Family Housing; U. S. M. A. ,Building No. 21)
HABS NY-5708-30
HABS NY,36-WEPO,1/30-
3ph/6pg/fr L

U. S. Military Academy,Officer's Quarters (U. S. M. A. ,Family Housing; U. S. M. A. ,Building No. 25)
HABS NY-5708-31
HABS NY,36-WEPO,1/31-
4ph/6pg/fr L

U. S. Military Academy,Officer's Quarters (U. S. M. A. ,Family Housing; U. S. M. A. ,Building No. 32)
HABS NY-5708-32
HABS NY,36-WEPO,1/32-
4ph/7pg/fr L

U. S. Military Academy,Officer's Quarters (U. S. M. A. ,Family Housing; U. S. M. A. ,Building No. 34)
HABS NY-5708-33
HABS NY,36-WEPO,1/33-
3ph/6pg/fr L

U. S. Military Academy,Officer's Quarters (U. S. M. A. ,Family Housing; U. S. M. A. ,Building No. 42)
HABS NY-5708-34
HABS NY,36-WEPO,1/34-
4ph/6pg/fr L

U. S. Military Academy,Officer's Quarters (U. S. M. A. ,Family Housing; U. S. M. A. ,Building No. 45)
HABS NY-5708-35
HABS NY,36-WEPO,1/35-
4ph/7pg/fr L

U. S. Military Academy,Officer's Quarters (U. S. M. A. ,Family Housing; U. S. M. A. ,Building No. 48)
HABS NY-5708-36
HABS NY,36-WEPO,1/50-
4ph/7pg/fr L

U. S. Military Academy,Officer's Quarters (U. S. M. A. ,Family Housing; U. S. M. A. ,Building No. 116)
HABS NY-5708-37
HABS NY,36-WEPO,1/37-
5ph/7pg/fr L

U. S. Military Academy,Officer's Quarters (U. S. M. A. ,Family Housing; U. S. M. A. ,Building No. 118)
HABS NY-5708-38
HABS NY,36-WEPO,1/38-
3ph/6pg/fr L

U. S. Military Academy,Officer's Quarters (U. S. M. A. ,Family Housing; U. S. M. A. ,Building No. 120)
HABS NY-5708-39
HABS NY,36-WEPO,1/39-
2ph/6pg/fr L

U. S. Military Academy,Officer's Quarters (U. S. M. A. ,Family Housing; U. S. M. A. ,Building No. 122)
HABS NY-5708-40
HABS NY,36-WEPO,1/40-
2ph/6pg/fr L

U. S. Military Academy,Officer's Quarters (U. S. M. A. ,Family Housing; U. S. M. A. ,Building No. 109)
HABS NY-5708-41
HABS NY,36-WEPO,1/41-
3ph/5pg/fr L

U. S. Military Academy,Officer's Quarters (U. S. M. A. ,Family Housing; U. S. M. A. ,Building No. 7)
HABS NY-5708-49
HABS NY,36-WEPO,1/49-
2ph/4pg/fr L

U. S. Military Academy,Officer's Quarters (U. S. M. A. ,Family Housing; U. S. M. A. ,Building No. 8)
HABS NY-5708-50
HABS NY,36-WEPO,1/50-
1ph/4pg/fr L

U. S. Military Academy,Officer's Quarters (U. S. M. A. ,Professors Row; U. S. M. A. ,Building No. 103)
HABS NY-5708-4
HABS NY,36-WEPO,1/4-
3ph/8pg/fr L

U. S. Military Academy,Officer's Quarters (U. S. M. A. ,Professors Row; U. S. M. A. ,Building No. 105)
HABS NY-5708-5
HABS NY,36-WEPO,1/5-
4ph/8pg/fr L

U. S. Military Academy,Officer's Quarters (U. S. M. A. ,Professors Row; U. S. M. A. ,Building No. 107)
HABS NY-5708-6
HABS NY,36-WEPO,1/6-
4ph/8pg/fr L

U. S. Military Academy,Officer's Quarters (U. S. M. A. ,Superintendent's Quarters; U. S. M. A. ,Building No. 100)
HABS NY-5708-1
HABS NY,36-WEPO,1/1-
18ph/15pg/8ct/fr L

U. S. Military Academy,Ordnan. Compound Wkshp/Wrhs (U. S. M. A. ,Crozier Hall; U. S. M. A. ,Cadet Activity Club; U. S. M. A. ,Building No. 671)
HABS NY-5708-10
HABS NY,36-WEPO,1/10-
2ph/10pg/fr L

U. S. Military Academy,Ordnance Comp. Blacksmth Sh (U. S. M. A. ,Cadet Activities Club; U. S. M. A. ,Benton Hall; U. S. M. A. ,Building No. 635)
HABS NY-5708-14
HABS NY,36-WEPO,1/14-
10pg/fr L

U. S. Military Academy,Ordnance Compound Barracks (U. S. M. A. ,Cadet Activity Club; U. S. M. A. ,Benton Hall; U. S. M. A. ,Building No. 637)
HABS NY-5708-9
HABS NY,36-WEPO,1/9-
1ph/21pg/fr L

U. S. Military Academy,Ordnance Compound Office (U. S. M. A. ,NCO Quarters; U. S. M. A. ,Benet Hall; U. S. M. A. ,Building No. 671-A)
HABS NY-5708-11
HABS NY,36-WEPO,1/11-
2ph/10pg/fr L

U. S. Military Academy,Ordnance Compound Privies (U. S. M. A. ,Ordnance Compound Towers; U. S. M. A. ,Building Nos. 635-A & 635-B)
HABS NY-5708-12
HABS NY,36-WEPO,1/12-
8pg/fr L

U. S. Military Academy,Power Plant (U. S. M. A. ,Heating Plant; U. S. M. A. ,Building No. 604)
HABS NY-5708-24
HABS NY,36-WEPO,1/24-
9ph/9pg/fr L

U. S. Military Academy,Queensboro Furnace (Queensboro Furnace)
HABS NY-5708-57
HABS NY,36-WEPO,1/57-
3ph/21pg/fr L

U. S. Military Academy,Riding Hall (U. S. M. A. ,Thayer Hall; U. S. M. A. ,Building No. 601)
HABS NY-5708-23
HABS NY,36-WEPO,1/23-
11ph/10pg/fr L

U. S. Military Academy,Soldiers' Hospital (U. S. M. A. ,Family Housing; U. S. M. A. ,Building No. 126)
HABS NY-5708-17
HABS NY,31-WEPO,1/17-
4ph/10pg/fr L

U. S. Military Academy,Warner House (U. S. M. A. ,Building No. 1183)
Constitution Island
HABS NY-5708-48
HABS NY,36-WEPO,1/48-
14ph/10pg/1ct/fr L

U. S. Military Academy,West Academic Building (U. S. M. A. ,Pershing Barracks; U. S. M. A. ,Madison Hall; U. S. M. A. ,East Cadet Barracks; U. S. M. A. ,Building No. 751)
HABS NY-5708-15
HABS NY,36-WEPO,1/15-
12ph/19pg/fr L

U. S. Military Academy,West Shore RR Passenger Sta (U. S. M. A. ,New York City Railroad Station; U. S. M. A. ,Cadet Activity Club; U. S. M. A. ,Building No. 696)
HABS NY-5708-29
HABS NY,36-WEPO,1/29-
5ph/10pg/fr L

U.S. Military Academy, Ice House (U.S.M.A. Bldg. No. 644)
Mills Road at Howze Place
HABS NY-5708-58
HABS NY,36-WEPO,1/58-
28ph/12pg/3pc/fr L

U.S. Military Academy,Bachelor Officers' Quarters (U.S. Military Academy,Building 149)
HABS NY-5708-59
HABS DLC/PP-1993:NY-5
12pg L

U.S. Military Academy,Building 149; see U.S. Military Academy,Bachelor Officers' Quarters

U.S.M.A. Bldg. No. 644; see U.S. Military Academy, Ice House

West Point; see U. S. Military Academy

ORLEANS COUNTY

ALBION

Blott-Bartlett House
135 W. Bank St.
HABS NY-6236
HABS NY,37-ALBI,5-
3ph/1pg L

D. A. R. House
N. Main St.
HABS NY-6237
HABS NY,37-ALBI,3-
7ph/2pg L

First Presbyterian Church
E. State St.
HABS NY-6238
HABS NY,37-ALBI,2-
3ph/1pg L

Lanson House
HABS NY-2
HABS NY,37-ALBI,1-
5ph L

Pratt Opera House
114-120 N. Main St.
HABS NY-6239
HABS NY,37-ALBI,4-
2ph L

CHILDS

First Universalist Church
Ridge Rd. (U.S. Rt. 104)
HABS NY-6240
HABS NY,37-CHILD,1-
9ph/1pg L

Schoolhouse,Cobblestone
(Schoolhouse,District Five)
Ridge Rd. (U.S. Rt. 104)
HABS NY-6241
HABS NY,37-CHILD,2-
7ph/1pg L

Schoolhouse,District Five; see Schoolhouse,Cobblestone

GAINES

Whipple House
Ridge Rd.
HABS NY-1
HABS NY,37-GAIN,1-
3ph L

LYNDONVILLE VIC.

Blood Road Bridge
Blood Rd.,spanning Johnson Creek,east of Lyndonvil
HAER NY-180
HAER 1991(HAER):5
3ph/5pg/1pc L

MURRAY

Hunn,John,House
Ridge & E. Holley Rds.
HABS NY-217
HABS NY,37-MUR,1-
5dr/2ph/2pg/fr L

ORANGEBURG VIC.

Saunders,I. V.,House
Ridge Rd.
HABS NY-3
HABS NY,37- ,1-
1ph L

OSWEGO COUNTY

OSWEGO

O'Brien Block
109-123 W. First St.
HABS NY-244
HABS NY,38-OSWE,2-
7dr/fr L

O'Brien Block (109-115 West First Street)
HABS NY-244-A
HABS NY,38-OSWE,2A-
7pg/fr L

O'Brien Block (117 West First Street)
HABS NY-244-B
HABS NY,38-OSWE,2B-
4pg/fr L

O'Brien Block (119 West First Street)
HABS NY-244-C
HABS NY,38-OSWE,2C-
3pg/fr L

O'Brien Block (121 West First Street)
HABS NY-244-D
HABS NY,38-OSWE,2D-
3pg/fr L

O'Brien Block (123 West First Street)
HABS NY-244-E
HABS NY,38-OSWE,2E-
3pg/fr L

Oswego City Library
E. Second & E. Oneida Sts.
HABS NY-5434
HABS NY,38-OSWE,3-
5dr/6ph/fr L

Public Market Building,Old
Bridge St. Vic.
HABS NY-5436
HABS NY,38-OSWE,1-
5ph L

109-115 West First Street; see O'Brien Block

117 West First Street; see O'Brien Block

119 West First Street; see O'Brien Block

121 West First Street; see O'Brien Block

123 West First Street; see O'Brien Block

PORT ONTARIO VIC.

Salmon River Lighthouse
Lake Ontario
HABS NY-6112
HABS NY,38-PORTO.V,1-
2ph L

OTSEGO COUNTY

CHERRY VALLEY

House
State Rt. 20
HABS NY-241
HABS NY,39-CHERVA,1-
3ph L

COOPERSTOWN

Building,Iron-clad
92 Main St.,Otsego Township
HABS NY-253
HABS NY,39-COOP,5-
4ph/2pg L

Byberry Cottage
River St.,Otsego Township
HABS NY-250
HABS NY,39-COOP,2-
3ph/2pg L

Clark Real Estate Office; see Otsego County Bank

Cory,Ellery,House
24 Pioneer St.,Otsego Township
HABS NY-252
HABS NY,39-COOP,4-
5ph/2pg L

Edgewater
Lake St.,Otsego Township
HABS NY-251
HABS NY,39-COOP,3-
6ph/2pg L

Lakelands
Main St.,Middlefield Township
HABS NY-254
HABS NY,39-COOP,6-
7ph/2pg L

Main Street (House)
HABS NY-247
HABS NY,39-COOP,1-
1ph L

Otsego County Bank (Clark Real Estate Office)
19 Main St.,Otsego Township
HABS NY-255
HABS NY,39-COOP,7-
4ph/2pg L

Pomeroy House
Main & River Sts.,Otsego Township
HABS NY-256
HABS NY,39-COOP,8-
4ph/3pg L

Presbyterian Church
Pioneer & Elm Sts.,Otsego Township
HABS NY-257
HABS NY,39-COOP,9-
5ph/2pg L

Smithy,The
55 Pioneer St.,Otsego Township
HABS NY-258
HABS NY,39-COOP,10-
3ph/2pg L

Woodside Hall
Main St.,Middlefield Township
HABS NY-259
HABS NY,39-COOP,11-
5ph/2pg L

Woodside Hall, Gate Tower
Main St.,Middlefield Township
HABS NY-262
HABS NY,39-COOP,11A-
2ph/1pg L

EAST SPRINGFIELD

Hyde Hall
E. Lake Rd. Vic.
HABS NY-260
HABS NY,39-SPRIFE,1-
10ph/3pg L

Hyde Hall,Covered Bridge
E. Lake Rd. Vic.
HABS NY-263
HABS NY,39-SPRIFE,1B-
2ph/1pg L

Hyde Hall,Gatehouse
E. Lake Rd.
HABS NY-264
HABS NY,39-SPRIFE,1A-
1ph/1pg L

MIDDLEFIELD CEN. VIC

Hop Barn & Kiln
HABS NY-265
HABS NY,39-MIDFI.V,1-
3ph/2pg L

OAKSVILLE

Williams-Childs House
State Rt. 28,Otsego Township
HABS NY-266
HABS NY,39-OAK,1-
3ph/3pg L

WESTVILLE VIC.

Cottage,Gothic
State Rt. 166 Vic.,Middlefield Township
HABS NY-261
HABS NY,39-WESVI.V,1-
4ph/2pg L

PUTNAM COUNTY

GARRISON

Boscobel
State Rt. 9D
HABS NY-5667
HABS NY,40-GARDI,3-
28dr L

Galloway Farmhouse
Manitou Rd.
HABS NY-4-107
HABS NY,40-GARI,1-
6dr/2ph/2pg/fr L

Grist Mill
Manitou Rd.
HABS NY-4-108
HABS NY,40-GARI,2-
7dr/4ph/3pg/fr L

PATTERSON

Hayt Farmstead
Rt. 311
HABS NY-6300
HABS DLC/PP-1993:NY-5
2ph/11pg/1pc L

Hayt Farmstead,Agricultural Building
Rt. 311
HABS NY-6300-H
HABS DLC/PP-1993:NY-5
1ph/2pg/1pc L

Hayt Farmstead,Barn
Rt. 311
HABS NY-6300-G
HABS DLC/PP-1993:NY-5
8ph/3pg/1pc L

Hayt Farmstead,Bowling Alley
Rt. 311
HABS NY-6300-D
HABS DLC/PP-1993:NY-5
7ph/2pg/1pc L

Hayt Farmstead,Corn Crib
Rt. 311
HABS NY-6300-M
HABS DLC/PP-1993:NY-5
3ph/2pg/1pc L

Hayt Farmstead,Farm Storage Shed
Rt. 311
HABS NY-6300-E
HABS DLC/PP-1993:NY-5
2ph/2pg/1pc L

Hayt Farmstead,Garage
Rt. 311
HABS NY-6300-K
HABS DLC/PP-1993:NY-5
2ph/2pg/1pc L

Hayt Farmstead,Mansion
Rt. 311
HABS NY-6300-A
HABS DLC/PP-1993:NY-5
22ph/12pg/2pc L

Hayt Farmstead,Poultry House I
Rt. 311
HABS NY-6300-I
HABS DLC/PP-1993:NY-5
2ph/2pg/1pc L

Hayt Farmstead,Poultry House II
Rt. 311
HABS NY-6300-J
HABS DLC/PP-1993:NY-5
2ph/2pg/1pc L

Hayt Farmstead,Poultry House III
Rt. 311
HABS NY-6300-L
HABS DLC/PP-1993:NY-5
2ph/2pg/1pc L

Hayt Farmstead,Recreation Building
Rt. 311
HABS NY-6300-F
HABS DLC/PP-1993:NY-5
3ph/2pg/1pc L

Hayt Farmstead,Storage Shed
Rt. 311
HABS NY-6300-B
HABS DLC/PP-1993:NY-5
2ph/2pg/1pc L

Seymour House (1830)
HABS NY-6269
HABS NY,40-PAT,1-
1ph L

QUEENS COUNTY

BOWERY BAY

Riker Homestead
Eightieth St.
HABS NY-4-29
HABS NY,41-BOWB,1-
10dr/3ph/1pg L

FLUSHING

Bowne House
37-01 Bowne St.
HABS NY-523
HABS NY,41-FLUSH,5-
17dr/33ph/fr L

Kingsland (Queens Historical Society Headquarters)
Weeping Beach Park,143-35 Thirty Seventh Ave.
HABS NY-6296
HABS NY,41-FLUSH,6A-
5dr L

Prince House
Northern Blvd. & Lawrence St.
HABS NY-4-19
HABS NY,41-FLUSH,4-
10dr/3ph/6pg L

Queens Historical Society Headquarters; see Kingsland

Documentation: **ct** color transparencies **dr** measured drawings **fr** field records
pc photograph captions **pg** pages of text **ph** photographs

Society of Friends Meetinghouse
Northern Blvd.
HABS NY-521
HABS NY,41-FLUSH,1-
15dr/14ph L

JACKSON HEIGHTS

LaGuardia Airport,Marine Air Terminal; see New York Municipal Airport,Marine Air Terminal

New York Municipal Airport,Marine Air Terminal (LaGuardia Airport,Marine Air Terminal)
Grand Central Pkwy. at Ninety-fourth St.
HAER NY-89
HAER NY,41-JAHT,1-
1ph/3pg/1pc L

KEW GARDENS

Bunche,Ralph,House
115-125 Grosvenor Rd.
HABS NY-5691
HABS NY,41-KEWG,1-
15ph/2pg L

LONG ISLAND CITY

American Chicle Company Factory
Thomson Ave.
HAER NY-80
1ph H

Bodine Castle
43-16 Vernon Blvd.
HABS NY-5465
HABS NY,41-LONGI,1-
9ph/5pg L

MASPETH

Hubb Estate
52-15 Flushing Ave.
HABS NY-522
HABS NY,41-MASP,2-
7dr/11ph/fr L

Woodward House
1891 Flushing Ave.
HABS NY-527
HABS NY,41-MASP,3-
9ph L

QUEENS

Astoria Studios,Barracks Buildings
Thirty-fourth Ave btwn Thirty-fifth & Thirty-sixth
HABS NY-5716
HABS NY,41-LONGI,2A-
2pg/fr L

Mel's Diner
3046 College Point Blvd.
HABS NY-6113
HABS NY,41-QUE,1-
2dr L

RIDGEWOOD

Covert House
1410 Flushing Ave.
HABS NY-525
HABS NY,41-RIDG,2-
14ph L

Van Anda House (Vander Ende-Onderdonk House)
1416 Flushing Ave.
HABS NY-524
HABS NY,41-RIDG,1-
9dr/16ph L

Vander Ende-Onderdonk House; see Van Anda House

Wyckoff Farmhand House
1306 Flushing Ave.
HABS NY-526
HABS NY,41-RIDG,3-
5ph L

RENSSELAER COUNTY

EAST GREENBUSH

Breese,Jan,House (De Bries,Hendrick,House)
Castleton Rd.
HABS NY-5-A-2
HABS NY,42-GREBUE,1-
4dr/6ph/1pg/fr L

De Bries,Hendrick,House; see Breese,Jan,House

MELROSE VIC.

Greens,Richard,House
HABS NY-3142
HABS NY,42-MELRO.V,1-
4ph L

PETERSBURG

Baptist Church
State Rt. 22
HABS NY-6114
HABS NY,42-PETBU,2-
1ph L

Gardner House
State Rt. 22
HABS NY-3136
HABS NY,42-PETBU,1-
2ph/1pg L

PETERSBURG VIC.

Reynolds,Elijah,House
State Rt. 22
HABS NY-6243
HABS NY,42-PETBU.V,1-
1ph/1pg L

RENSSELAER

Beverwyck (Van Rensselaer,William Patterson,House)
Washinghton Ave. ext.
HABS NY-5-A-10
HABS NY,42-RENLA,1-
14dr/6ph/1pg/fr L

Crailo,The (Fort Crailo; Van Rensselaer House)
10 Riverside Dr.
HABS NY-3105
HABS NY,42-RENLA,2-
4ph/1pg L

Fort Crailo; see Crailo,The

Genet,Citizen,House (Prospect Hill)
HABS NY-3160
HABS NY,42-RENLA,3-
3ph L

Prospect Hill; see Genet,Citizen,House

Van Rensselaer House; see Crailo,The

Van Rensselaer,William Patterson,House; see Beverwyck

SCHAGHTICOKE VIC.

Banker House
HABS NY-3130
HABS NY,42-SCHAG.V,1-
1ph L

TROY

Burden Iron Company; see Burden Iron Works

Burden Iron Company,Lower (Steam) Works; see Burden Iron Works,Lower (Steam) Works

Burden Iron Company,Office Building; see Burden Iron Works,Office Building

Burden Iron Company,Upper (Water) Works; see Burden Iron Works,Upper (Water) Works

Burden Iron Company,Water Wheel; see Burden Iron Works,Water Wheel

Burden Iron Works (Burden Iron Company)
Wynants Kill & Burden St.
HAER NY-7
HAER NY,42-TROY,7-
5ph/24pg L

Burden Iron Works,Lower (Steam) Works (Burden Iron Company,Lower (Steam) Works)
Hudson River,Wynants Kill Vic.
HAER NY-7-C
HAER NY,42-TROY,7C-
3ph L

Burden Iron Works,Office Building (Burden Iron Company,Office Building)
Polk St.
HAER NY-7-D
HAER NY,42-TROY,7D-
6ph/4pg L

Burden Iron Works,Upper (Water) Works (Burden Iron Company,Upper (Water) Works)
Burden St. & Wynants Kill
HAER NY-7-A
HAER NY,42-TROY,7A-
4ph L

Burden Iron Works,Water Wheel (Burden Iron Company,Water Wheel)
U.S. Rt. 4
HAER NY-7-B
HAER NY,42-TROY,7B-
4ph L

Church of the Holy Cross
Eighth & Grand Sts.
HABS NY-6257
HABS NY,42-TROY,10-
2dr/11ph/7pg/fr L

Cluett,Albert,House (Howard House; Hart House)
59 Second St.
HABS NY-5-A-3
HABS NY,42-TROY,1-
7dr/2ph/1pg/fr L

District School Number 1
N. Greenbush Rd.
HABS NY-329
HABS NY,42-TROY,3-
1dr/3ph/1pg L

Gurley,W. & L. E.,Building
514 Fulton St.
HAER NY-13
HAER NY,42-TROY,8-
6ph/10pg L

Hart House; see Cluett,Albert,House

House,Gothic Revival
HABS NY-3239
HABS NY,42-TROY,9-
1ph L

Howard House; see Cluett,Albert,House

Ludlow Valve Company; see Rensselaer Iron Works,Rail Mill

Rensselaer Iron Works,Rail Mill (Ludlow Valve Company)
Adams St. & Hudson River
HAER NY-3
HAER NY,42-TROY,6-
4dr/18ph/20pg/fr L

St. John's Rectory (Balcony)
First & Liberty Sts.
HABS NY-358
HABS NY,42-TROY,4-
1dr/1ph/1pg/fr L

Troy Gas Light Company,Gasholder House
Jefferson St. & Fifth Ave.
HAER NY-2
HAER NY,42-TROY,5-
4dr/15ph/11pg/fr L

Vail,Thomas Samuel,House
46 First St.
HABS NY-5-A-7
HABS NY,42-TROY,2-
11dr/4ph/1pg/fr L

Warren Family Chapel and Monuments
Oakwood Cemetery
HABS NY-6253
HABS NY,42-TROY,11A-
3dr/2pg/fr L

RICHMOND COUNTY

NEW BRIGHTON

Sailors' Snug Harbor
Richmond Terrace,Staten Island
HABS NY-5473
HABS NY,43-NEWBR,1-
2dr/16ph/10pg/2pc/fr L

Sailors' Snug Harbor,Bandstand
Richmond Terrace
HABS NY-6316
HABS NY,43-NEWBR,1C-
1ph L

Sailors' Snug Harbor,Building A; see Sailors' Snug Harbor,Dormitory A

Sailors' Snug Harbor,Building B; see Sailors' Snug Harbor,Dormitory B

Sailors' Snug Harbor,Building C; see Sailors' Snug Harbor,Dormitory C & Admin. Building

Sailors' Snug Harbor,Building D; see Sailors' Snug Harbor,Dormitory D

Sailors' Snug Harbor,Building E; see Sailors' Snug Harbor,Dormitory E

Sailors' Snug Harbor,Captain's Cottage No. 2
Richmond Terrace
HABS NY-6244
HABS NY,43-NEWBR,1L2-
6dr L

Sailors' Snug Harbor,Chapel
Richmond Terrace
HABS NY-5480
HABS NY,43-NEWBR,1K-
6dr/2ph/4pg L

Sailors' Snug Harbor,Dining Hall (Sailors' Snug Harbor,Infirmary)
Richmond Terrace
HABS NY-5479
HABS NY,43-NEWBR,1J-
1ph/4pg L

Sailors' Snug Harbor,Dormitory A (Sailors' Snug Harbor,Building A)
Richmond Terrace
HABS NY-5474
HABS NY,43-NEWBR,1D-
4pg L

Sailors' Snug Harbor,Dormitory B (Sailors' Snug Harbor,Building B)
Richmond Terrace
HABS NY-5475
HABS NY,43-NEWBR,1E-
4pg L

Sailors' Snug Harbor,Dormitory C & Admin. Building (Sailors' Snug Harbor,Building C)
Richmond Terrace
HABS NY-5476
HABS NY,43-NEWBR,1F-
7dr/7ph/7pg L

Sailors' Snug Harbor,Dormitory D (Sailors' Snug Harbor,Building D)
Richmond Terrace
HABS NY-5477
HABS NY,43-NEWBR,1G-
7dr/2ph/4pg L

Sailors' Snug Harbor,Dormitory E (Sailors' Snug Harbor,Building E)
Richmond Terrace
HABS NY-5478
HABS NY,43-NEWBR,1H-
6dr/4pg L

Sailors' Snug Harbor,East Gatehouse
Richmond Terrace
HABS NY-5484
HABS NY,43-NEWBR,1P-
1ph/2pg L

Sailors' Snug Harbor,Governor's House
Richmond Terrace
HABS NY-6115
HABS NY,43-NEWBR,1Q-
6dr L

Sailors' Snug Harbor,Infirmary; see Sailors' Snug Harbor,Dining Hall

Sailors' Snug Harbor,Music Hall
Richmond Terrace
HABS NY-6116
HABS NY,43-NEWBR,1A-
5dr/1ph L

Sailors' Snug Harbor,North Gatehouse
Richmond Terrace
HABS NY-5482
HABS NY,43-NEWBR,1M-
1dr/1ph/3pg L

Sailors' Snug Harbor,Recreation Building
Richmond Terrace
HABS NY-6245
HABS NY,43-NEWB,1B-
5dr/2ph L

Sailors' Snug Harbor,Residences
Richmond Terrace
HABS NY-5481
HABS NY,43-NEWBR,1L-
2ph/3pg L

Sailors' Snug Harbor,West Gatehouse
Richmond Terrace
HABS NY-5483
HABS NY,43-NEWBR,1N-
1dr/1ph/3pg L

Tysen,Jacob,House
355 Fillmore St.,Staten Island
HABS NY-6117
HABS NY,43-NEWBR,2-
18dr L

NEW DORP

Britton-Cubberly House
New Dorp Ln.
HABS NY-4-5
HABS NY,43-NEDO,1-
11dr/6ph/4pg L

Building No. 33; see Miller Field,North Hangar

Building No. 38; see Miller Field,Seaplane Hangar

Clausen House
291 New Dorp Ln.
HABS NY-4374
HABS NY,43-NEDO,3-
1ph L

Lake-Tysen House
Cobbs Ave.
HABS NY-4373
HABS NY,43-NEDO,2-
3ph L

Miller Field,North Hangar (Building No. 33)
New Dorp Lane,Staten Island
HABS NY-5669
HABS NY,43-NEDO,4A-
23ph L

Miller Field,Seaplane Hangar (Building No. 38)
New Dorp Lane,Staten Island
HABS NY-5671
HABS NY,43-NEDO,4B-
11dr/1ph L

RICHMOND

Cortelyou House
HABS NY-4372
HABS NY,43-RICH,2-
3ph L

RICHMONDTOWN

Courthouse
Staten Island
HABS NY-6322
10dr H

ROSEBANK

Austen,Elizabeth Alice,House
2 Hyland Blvd.
HABS NY-5472
HABS NY,43-ROSE,1-
10ph/7pg L

STATEN ISLAND

Bayonne Bridge
Spanning Kill Van Kull btwn Staen Island & Bayonne
HAER NJ-66
HAER 1988(HAER):64
10ph/1pg/1pc/fr L

Fort Wadsworth,Battery Duane
HAER NY-165
14ph/23pg/2pc H

Jane Moseley; see Shooters Island:Ships Graveyard,Vessel No. 53

Minerva; see Shooters Island:Ships Graveyard,Vessel No. 53

Shooters Island:Ships Graveyard
Newark Bay
HAER NY-162
HAER NY,43-SHOOTI,1-
1dr/6ph/49pg/1pc L

Shooters Island:Ships Graveyard,Vessel No. 37
Newark Bay
HAER NY-162-A
HAER NY,43-SHOOTI,2-
2dr/8ph/2pg/1pc L

Shooters Island:Ships Graveyard,Vessel No. 53 (Minerva; Jane Moseley)
Newark Bay
HAER NY-162-B
HAER NY,43-SHOOTI,3-
1dr/6ph/7pg/1pc L

Shooters Island:Ships Graveyard,Vessel No. 54
Newark Bay
HAER NY-162-C
HAER NY,43-SHOOTI,4-
1dr/5ph/2pg/1pc L

Shooters Island:Ships Graveyard,Vessel No. 84
Newark Bay
HAER NY-162-D
HAER NY,43-SHOOTI,5-
1dr/2ph/2pg/1pc L

TOTTENVILLE

Billop House (Conference House)
Hylan Blvd.
HABS NY-4370
HABS NY,43-TOTVI,1-
3ph L

Conference House; see Billop House

000

Dongan Hills; see Perine House

Perine House (Dongan Hills)
1476 Richmond Rd.
HABS NY-4371
HABS NY,43- ,1-
2ph L

ROCKLAND COUNTY

GERMONDS

Barn,The Old
HABS NY-4121
HABS NY,44-GERM,1-
3dr/2ph/fr L

NYACK

Erie Railway:Nyack Station
Railroad Ave.
HAER NY-96
HAER NY,44-NYACK,1-
2ph/1pc L

ORANGEBURG VIC.

Van Houten House
HABS NY-4120
HABS NY,44-ORABU.V,1-
11dr/7ph/fr L

PALISADES

House,the Big
State Rt. 9W Vic.
HABS NY-4122
HABS NY,44-PAL,1-
12dr/5ph/5pg/fr L

PEARL RIVER VIC.

Sickles House
HABS NY-4119
HABS NY,44-PERL.V,1-
10dr/5ph/fr L

SPARKILL

Erie Railway:Sparkill Station
HAER NY-137
HAER NY,44-SPARK,1-
1ph/1pc L

TAPPAN

'Seventy-six House; see Andre,Major,House (Prison)

Andre,Major,House (Prison) ('Seventy-six House)
Main St.
HABS NY-4-18
HABS NY,44-TAP,1-
7dr/7ph/8pg/fr L

Bake House,Old
HABS NY-4362
HABS NY,44-TAP,4-
1ph L

De Windt House
Livingston Ave. & Oak Tree Rd.
HABS NY-4123
HABS NY,44-TAP,2-
7dr/15ph/fr L

Dutch Reformed Church
Main St.
HABS NY-4357
HABS NY,44-TAP,3-
1ph L

TOMPKINS COVE

Boulderburg
HABS NY-6119
HABS NY,44-TOMC,1-
5dr/fr L

SARATOGA COUNTY

BALLSTON LAKE

Hawkwood Mansion
HABS NY-6246
HABS NY,46-BALA,1-
9ph L

BALLSTON LAKE VIC.

Buell House; see Palmer House

Palmer House (Buell House)
HABS NY-6247
HABS NY,46-BALA.V,1-
4ph L

BALLSTON SPA

First Presbyterian Church
High & Bath Sts.
HABS NY-3207
HABS NY,46-BALSP,1-
1ph L

BURNT HILLS

Kingsley,William,Tavern
Saratoga & Charlton Rds.
HABS NY-3209
HABS NY,46-BURHI,1-
1ph L

CHARLTON

Methodist Episcopal & Freehold Presbyt. Church
Charleston Rd.
HABS NY-3211
HABS NY,46-CHAR,1-
1ph/1pg L

GROOMS CORNERS

Best,Robert,House
HABS NY-3215
HABS NY,46-GROOM,1-
1ph L

HIGH BRIDGE VIC.

Pashley House
HABS NY-3137
HABS NY,46- ,1-
2ph L

REXFORD

Erie Canal (Enlarged),Rexford Aqueduct; see Erie Canal (Enlarged),Upper Mohawk River Aqueduct

Erie Canal (Enlarged),Upper Mohawk River Aqueduct (Erie Canal (Enlarged),Rexford Aqueduct)
Mohawk River,State Rt. 146
HAER NY-12
HAER NY,46-REX,1-
6ph/3pg L

SARATOGA

Bryan Inn
High Rock Spring
HABS NY-3131
HABS NY,46-SAR,1-
2ph L

Champlain & Hudson Canal
HABS NY-6121
HABS NY,46-SAR,2-
4ph L

Saratoga National Historic Park; see Schuyler House

Schuyler House (Saratoga National Historic Park)
HABS NY-6122
HABS NY,46-SAR,3-;(DLC/PP-1992:NY-5)
21ph/2pc L

SARATOGA VIC.

Bridge,Old
HABS NY-3157-C
HABS NY,46-SAR.V,1C-
1ph L

Main Mill Building
HABS NY-3157-A
HABS NY,46-SAR.V,1A-
2ph L

Mill Group,Old
HABS NY-3157
HABS NY,46-SAR.V,1-
1ph L

Mill Owner's House
HABS NY-3157-B
HABS NY,46-SAR.V,1B-
3ph L

Original Church (Ruins)
HABS NY-3157-D
HABS NY,46-SAR.V,2-
1ph L

STILLWATER

Neilson,John,House (Saratoga National Historical Park)
Bemis Heights
HABS NY-3317
HABS NY,46-BEMHI,1A-;(DLC/PP-1992:NY-5)
3dr/10ph/3pg/1pc/fr L

Saratoga National Historical Park; see Neilson,John,House

VISCHERS FERRY

Amity
HABS NY-3146
HABS NY,46-VICFE,1-
3ph L

WATERFORD

Champlain Canal,Waterford Locks
U.S. Rt. 4
HAER NY-14
HAER NY,46-WAFO,1-
9ph/5pg L

SCHENECTADY COUNTY

ALPLAUS

Alplaus School,Old
Maple Ave.
HABS NY-380
HABS NY,47-ALP,2-
1ph/1pg L

Governor's Inn; see Yates,Governor,Summer Home

Stevens House
Alplaus Rd.
HABS NY-366
HABS NY,47-ALP,1-
5dr/3ph/1pg/fr L

Stevens,Alex,Barn
HABS NY-3145
HABS NY,47-ALP,4-
2ph L

Yates,Governor,Summer Home (Governor's Inn)
Maple Ave.
HABS NY-3138
HABS NY,47-ALP,3-
2ph/fr L

DUANESBURG

Christ Episcopal Church
State Rt. 20 & Church Rd.
HABS NY-331
HABS NY,47-DUBU,2-
17ph/1pg/fr L

Duane House; see Featherstonhaugh Mansion

Featherstonhaugh Mansion (Duane House)
State Rt. 20
HABS NY-330
HABS NY,47-DUBU,1-
5ph/1pg/fr L

North,Gen. William,House
N. Mansion Rd.
HABS NY-346
HABS NY,47-DUBU,3-
3ph/1pg/fr L

GIFFORDS

Cheeseman's Tavern
Western Turnpike
HABS NY-339
HABS NY,47- ,1-
4ph/fr L

GLENVILLE

Glenville Centre Reformed Church
Bolt Rd.
HABS NY-3219
HABS NY,47-GLEN,1-
1ph L

Sanders,Joseph,House
HABS NY-6124
HABS NY,47-GLEN,2-
4ph L

Van Epps Hotel
HABS NY-3214
HABS NY,47-GLEN,3-
1ph L

GLENVILLE CENTER

Syman House
HABS NY-3140
HABS NY,46- ,2-
3ph L

NISKAYUNA

Erie Canal (Enlarged),Rexford Aqueduct; see Erie Canal (Enlarged),Upper Mohawk River Aqueduct

Erie Canal (Enlarged),Upper Mohawk River Aqueduct (Erie Canal (Enlarged),Rexford Aqueduct) (see NY,Rexford)
HAER NY-12
HAER NY,46-REX,1-
6ph/3pg L

Niskayuna Reformed Church
State Rt. 7 (Troy Rd.)
HABS NY-351
HABS NY,47-NISK,1-
4ph/1pg/fr L

Tymeson House
HABS NY-6125
HABS NY,47-NISK,2-
6ph L

PRINCETOWN

Liddle House
State Rt. 7 Vic.
HABS NY-352
HABS NY,47-PRINC,1-
3ph/1pg L

QUAKER STREET VIL.

Society of Friends Meetinghouse
State Rt. 7
HABS NY-347
HABS NY,47-QUAK,1-
10dr/3ph/4pg/fr L

ROTTERDAM

Bradt House
Schermerhorn Rd. (State Rt. 5S)
HABS NY-353
HABS NY,47-ROT,1-
3ph/1pg/fr L

Schermerhorn House
Schermerhorn Rd. & State Rt. 5S
HABS NY-371
HABS NY,47-ROT,2-
4ph/1pg L

ROTTERDAM JCT.

Mabie,John,House
River Rd. (State Rt. 55)
HABS NY-337
HABS NY,47-ROTJ,1-
16dr/13ph/4pg/fr L

Van Slyck House
State Rt. 5S
HABS NY-5712
HABS NY,47-ROT,3-
3ph L

ROTTERDAM TWP.

Veeder Farm
Wescott Rd.
HABS NY-3123
HABS NY,47-ROT,4-
3ph L

SCHENECTADY

Brandt,Capt. Arent,House
HABS NY-3223
HABS NY,47-SCHE,13-
1ph/1pg L

Brouwer-Rosa House (Rosa House)
14 N. Church St.
HABS NY-345
HABS NY,47-SCHE,8-
13dr/5ph/1pg/fr L

Courthouse,Old; see Schenectady County Courthouse

DeGraaf,Jeremiah,House
25-27 Front St.
HABS NY-3271
HABS NY,47-SCHE,17-
7ph/3pg L

First Presbyterian Church
215 Union St.
HABS NY-3288
HABS NY,47-SCHE,31-
3ph/2pg L

Forrest,David P.,House
39 Front St.
HABS NY-3278
HABS NY,47-SCHE,24-
6ph/3pg L

121 Front Street (House)
HABS NY-6126
HABS NY,47-SCHE,20-
1ph L

29 Front Street (House)
HABS NY-3221
HABS NY,47-SCHE,18-
1ph L

31 Front Street (House)
HABS NY-3222
HABS NY,47-SCHE,19-
1ph L

Glen,John,House
58 Washington Ave.
HABS NY-340
HABS NY,47-SCHE,7-
3ph/1pg/fr L

Kendall,Widow,House
10 N. Ferry St.
HABS NY-3282
HABS NY,47-SCHE,26-
5ph/3pg L

Miller Farm,Old
Consaul Rd.
HABS NY-3124
HABS NY,47-SCHE,12-
2ph L

Mohawk Bank,Old
1 N. Church St.
HABS NY-349
HABS NY,47-SCHE,10-
1ph/fr L

10-12 North Street (House)
HABS NY-6249
HABS NY,47-SCHE,21-
1ph L

13 North Street (House)
HABS NY-6248
HABS NY,47-SCHE,22-
1ph L

Peck,Jan,House
27 N. Ferry St.
HABS NY-3285
HABS NY,47-SCHE,29-
2ph/3pg L

Rosa House; see Brouwer-Rosa House

Sanders,Robert,House
43-45 Washington Ave.
HABS NY-335
HABS NY,47-SCHE,5-
5dr/13ph/1pg/fr L

Schenectady City Hall
100 Jay St.
HABS NY-393
HABS NY,47-SCHE,32-
9ph/1pg/1pc L

Schenectady County Clerk's Office
13 Union St.
HABS NY-6127
HABS NY,47-SCHE,34-
8dr L

Schenectady County Courthouse (Courthouse,Old)
108 Union St.
HABS NY-334
HABS NY,47-SCHE,4-
3dr/4ph/4pg L

9 South Church Street (Mantels)
HABS NY-3226
HABS NY,47-SCHE,16-
2ph L

St. George's Church
20-30 N. Ferry St.
HABS NY-344
HABS NY,47-SCHE,3-
5dr/8ph/5pg/fr L

State Theatre
238-244 Liberty St.
HABS NY-6264
HABS NY,47-SCHE,33-
18ph/18pg L

Tenant Houses
Cottage Row
HABS NY-3283
HABS NY,47-SCHE,27-
3ph/3pg L

Union College,North & South College,Old
Union St.
HABS NY-348
HABS NY,47-SCHE,9-
6ph/fr L

Union College,Nott Memorial Library
HABS NY-3270
HABS NY,47-SCHE,9C-
7ph/8pg L

201 Union Street (House)
HABS NY-3284
HABS NY,47-SCHE,28-
6ph/3pg L

Van Guysling House
HABS NY-374
HABS NY,47-SCHE,11-
5ph/1pg/fr L

Van Slyck,Adrian,House
114 Front St.
HABS NY-3273
HABS NY,47-SCHE,23-
5ph/3pg L

Veeder Farmhouse
2201 Rosendale Rd.
HABS NY-3279
HABS NY,47,SCHE.V,1-
6ph/3pg L

Veeder,Nicholas,House
104-106 Front St.
HABS NY-3281
HABS NY,47-SCHE,25-
5ph/3pg L

Veeder,Nicholas,Slave House
205 Green St.
HABS NY-3280
HABS NY,47-SCHE,25A-
5ph/3pg L

Vrooman,Adam,House
119 Front St.
HABS NY-3286
HABS NY,47-SCHE,30-
4ph/3pg L

Vrooman,Adam,Kitchen
119 Front St.
HABS NY-3287
HABS NY,47-SCHE,30A-
1ph/2pg L

Yates,Abraham,House
109 Union St.
HABS NY-336
HABS NY,47-SCHE,6-
8dr/8ph/4pg/fr L

Yates,Governor,House
17 Front St.
HABS NY-6250
HABS NY,47-SCHE,14-
4ph L

Yates,Joseph,House
26 Front St.
HABS NY-6128
HABS NY,47-SCHE,15-
1ph L

SCOTIA

Glen-Sanders House
2 Sanders Ave.
HABS NY-5-A-1
HABS NY,47-SCOT,1-
9dr/7ph/3pg/fr L

Glen,Abraham,House
Mohawk Ave.
HABS NY-338
HABS NY,47-SCOT,2-
4ph/2pg/fr L

SCHOHARIE COUNTY

BERNE VIC.

House,Stone
Old Schoharie Turnpike
HABS NY-6101
HABS NY,48- ,1-
1ph L

BREADABEEN

Chichester,L. H.,House
HABS NY-3208
HABS NY,48-BREAK,1-
1ph L

ESPERANCE

Presbyterian Church
HABS NY-3135
HABS NY,48-ESP,1-
1ph L

MIDDLEBURG

Reformed Church
HABS NY-3133
HABS NY,48-MIDBU,1-
1ph L

NORTH BLENHEIM

Blenheim Covered Bridge
Spanning Schoharie River
HABS NY-359
HABS NY,48-BLEN,1-
3dr/2ph/5pg L

Dutch Reformed Church
HABS NY-3235
HABS NY,48-BLEN,2-
1ph L

SCHOHARIE

Fort,Old Stone; see Reformed Dutch Church

Lutheran Church,Old
HABS NY-3144
HABS NY,48-SCHO,6-
3ph L

Lutheran Parsonage
HABS NY-5490
HABS NY,48-SCHO,2-
4ph L

Reform Church
HABS NY-375
HABS NY,48-SCHO,7-
1ph L

Reformed Dutch Church (Fort,Old Stone)
HABS NY-3134
HABS NY,48-SCHO,1-
4ph/fr L

Swart's Tavern
HABS NY-5492
HABS NY,48-SCHO,3-
2ph L

U.S. Frigate "Constitution",Cannon
(moved from MA,Charlestown)
HABS NY-5497
HABS NY,48-SCHO,5-
2ph L

Van Vrooman,Col. Peter,House
HABS NY-3125
HABS NY,48-SCHO,8-
3ph L

SCHOHARIE VIC.

Log Cabin
HABS NY-388
HABS NY,48-SCHO.V,1-
2ph/1pg L

SCHUYLER COUNTY

MECKLENBURG

Methodist Church
HABS NY-240
HABS NY,49-MECK,1-
1ph L

SENECA COUNTY

GENEVA VIC.

Rose Hill
HABS NY-6102
HABS NY,50-GEN.V,1-
3ph L

SENECA FALLS

Sackett,Garry V.,House
W. Bayard & Sackett Sts.
HABS NY-221
HABS NY,50-SENFA,1-
11dr/9ph/2pg L

Stanton,Elizabeth Cady,House (Women's Rights National Historical Park)
32 Washington St.
HABS NY-6103
HABS NY,50-SENFA,2-
7dr/3ph/fr L

Village Hall (Women's Rights National Historic Park)
136 Fall St. (State Rt. 5 & 20)
HABS NY-6305
HABS 1991(HABS):21
11dr/fr L

Wesleyan Chapel (Women's Rights National Historic Park)
126 Fall St. (State Rt. 5 & 20)
HABS NY-6304
HABS 1991S):21 21
10dr/fr L

Women's Rights National Historic Park; see Village Hall

Women's Rights National Historic Park; see Wesleyan Chapel

Women's Rights National Historical Park; see Stanton,Elizabeth Cady,House

TYRE

Lay,Hiram,Carriage House
Mays Point Road
HABS NY-6130-A
HABS NY,50-TYRE,1A-
26ph/25pg/2pc/fr L

WATERLOO

Locust Street Bridge
Locust St.,spanning the old channel of Seneca Rv.
HAER NY-181
HAER 1991(HAER):5
2ph/4pg/1pc L

M'Clintock House (Women's Rights National Historic Park)
14 East William St.
HABS NY-6303
HABS 1991(HABS):21
2dr/fr L

Women's Rights National Historic Park; see M'Clintock House

ST. LAWRENCE COUNTY

OGDENSBURG

Lafayette-Spring Street Bridge (Oswegatchie River Bridge)
Lafayette & Spring St.,spanning Oswegatchie River
HAER NY-174
HAER 1991(HAER):5
4ph/5pg/1pc L

Oswegatchie River Bridge; see Lafayette-Spring Street Bridge

STEUBEN COUNTY

ATLANTA

D. L. & W. RR, Atlanta Passenger & Freight Station
Main & Beecher Sts.
HAER NY-58
HAER NY,51-ATLA,1-
2ph/1pg/1pc L

CORNING

Erie Railway:Corning Station
Erie Ave. & Pine St.
HAER NY-76
HAER NY,51-CORN,1-
4ph/1pc L

CORNING VIC.

Erie Railway:Corning Side Hill Cut
Chemung River
HAER NY-35
HAER NY,51-CORN.V,1-
2ph/1pc L

HORNELL

Erie Railway:Hornell Erecting Shop
Canisteo River,Cedar St.
HAER NY-34
HAER NY,51-HORN,3-
1dr/3ph L

Erie Railway:Hornell Station
Loder St.
HAER NY-33
HAER NY,51-HORN,2-
2ph/1pc L

Merrill Silk Mill
233 Canisteo St.
HAER NY-126
HAER NY,51-HORN,1-
11ph/19pg/2pc L

PAINTED POST

Erie RR:Painted Post Passenger & Freight Station
Water St.
HAER NY-97
HAER NY,51-PAIPO,1-
3ph/1pc L

SUFFOLK COUNTY

AMAGANSETT

Cartwright House; see Conklin,Ananias,House

Conklin,Ananias,House (Cartwright House)
Main St.
HABS NY-5416
HABS NY,52-AMGA,1-
7dr/1ph/1pc L

AQUEBOQUE

Corwin House
HABS NY-5422
HABS NY,52-AQUBO,1-
1ph L

BABYLON

Conklin,Nat,House
280 Deer Park Ave.
HABS NY-542
HABS NY,52-BAB,1-
12dr/19ph/6pg/fr L

Merrick Road (House)
HABS NY-6104
HABS NY,52-BAB,2-
6dr L

BRIDGEHAMPTON

Bull's Head Tavern; see Wick's Tavern

Hampton House
HABS NY-6105
HABS NY,52-BRIG,2-
1ph L

Sayrelands
Montauk Hwy.
HABS NY-5619
HABS NY,52-BRIG,3-
11dr/fr L

Wick's Tavern (Bull's Head Tavern)
Montauk Hwy.
HABS NY-5419
HABS NY,52-BRIG,1-
10dr/fr L

BROOKHAVEN

Town Clerk's Office
HABS NY-5423
HABS NY,52-BROOK,1-
1ph L

CENTEREACH

First Congregational Church
HABS NY-5425
HABS NY,52-CEN,1-
2ph L

CENTERPORT

Suydam House
HABS NY-5420
HABS NY,52-CENPO,1-
4ph L

COMMACK

Smith,Caleb,House & Slave House
HABS NY-5411
HABS NY,52-COM,1-
8ph L

CUTCHOGUE

Fleet-Goldsmith-Kendrick House
New Suffolk Ln.
HABS NY-548
HABS NY,52-CUTCH,2-
26ph/1pc L

Horton-Wickham-Landon Barn
Kings Hwy.
HABS NY-5417
HABS NY,52-CUTCH,1A-
1dr/fr L

Horton-Wickham-Landon House
Kings Hwy. (moved from NY,Southhold)
HABS NY-546
HABS NY,52-CUTCH,1-
18dr/44ph/fr L

EAST HAMPTON

Clinton Academy
Main St.
HABS NY-4-24
HABS NY,52-HAMTE,1-
6dr/2ph/7pg/fr L

Dominy House
N. Main St.
HABS NY-5418
HABS NY,52-HAMTE,8-
14dr/10ph/1pc/fr L

Gardiner Windmill
36 James Ln.
HABS NY-4-21
HAER NY-141
HABS/HAER NY,52-HAMTE,4-
6dr/10ph/22pg/1pc/fr L

Hayground Windmill
Windmill Ln.
HAER NY-142
HAER NY,52-HAMTE,10-
8ph/7pg/1pc L

Home Sweet Home; see Payne,John Howard,Memorial

Hook Windmill
N. Main St. at Pantigo Rd.
HAER NY-105
HAER NY,52-HAMTE,2-
6dr/35ph/13pg/3pc/fr L

House
HABS NY-6106
HABS NY,52-HAMTE,9-
1ph L

Mulford Farm House; see Mulford House

Mulford House (Mulford Farm House)
James Lane
HABS NY-5412
HABS NY,52-HAMTE,7-
28dr/4ph/fr L

Pantigo Windmill
James Ln.
HAER NY-143
HAER NY,52-HAMTE,6-
15ph/4pg/2pc L

Payne,John Howard,Memorial (Home Sweet Home)
James Ln.
HABS NY-547
HABS NY,52-HAMTE,5-
21dr/30ph/fr L

Payne,John Howard,Memorial,Windmill
James Ln. (moved from Mill Hill & NY,Pantigo)
HABS NY-547-A
HABS NY,52-HAMTE,6-
1ph L

Wainscott Windmill
Village of Wainscott
HAER NY-144
HAER NY,52-WAISCO,3-
4ph/4pg/1pc L

EAST SETAUKET

Bruster,John,House (1670)
HABS NY-6277
HABS NY,52-SETEA,1-
1ph L

GARDINER'S ISLAND

Gardiner's Island Windmill
HAER NY-125
HAER NY,52-GARDI,1-
5dr/16ph/30pg/1pc/fr L

GREENLAWN

Cedarcroft; see Laurel Lodge

Cedarcroft,Apartments; see Laurel Lodge,Apartments

Cedarcroft,Log Cabin; see Laurel Lodge,Log Cabin

Cedarcroft,Studio; see Laurel Lodge,Studio

Laurel Lodge (Cedarcroft)
Arbutus Rd.
HABS NY-5703
HABS NY,52-GRENL,1-
12ph/3pg/1pc/4ct L

Laurel Lodge,Apartments (Cedarcroft,Apartments)
Arbutus Rd.
HABS NY-5703-A
HABS NY,52-GRENL,1A-
2ph/1pg/1pc L

Laurel Lodge,Log Cabin (Cedarcroft,Log Cabin)
Arbutus Rd.
HABS NY-5703-C
HABS NY,52-GRENL,1C-
10ph/1pg/1pc L

Laurel Lodge,Studio (Cedarcroft,Studio)
Arbutus Rd.
HABS NY-5703-B
HABS NY,52-GRENL,1B-
3ph/1pg/1pc L

HAUPPAUGE

Smith,Joshua Brewster,House
HABS NY-5414
HABS NY,52-HAUP,1-
3ph L

HUNTINGTON

First Presbyterian Church
125 E. Main St.
HABS NY-5410
HABS NY,52-HUNTO,1-
7dr/16ph/fr L

Lefferts Tide Mill (Van Wyck Mill)
Huntington Harbor,Southdown Rd.
HAER NY-106
HAER NY,52-LOHA,2-
8dr/19ph/24pg/2pc/fr L

Sammis,Silas,House
W. Neck Ave. & Sammis Rd.
HABS NY-544
HABS NY,52-HUNTO.V,1-
8dr/14ph/fr L

Van Wyck Mill; see Lefferts Tide Mill

HUNTINGTON VIC.

House
HABS NY-6272
HABS NY,52-HUNTO.V,3-
1ph L

House
HABS NY-6273
HABS NY,52-HUNTO.V,3-
1ph L

HUNTINGTON,SOUTH

Barker Estate; see Carll Homestead

Carll Homestead (Barker Estate)
Melville Blvd.
HABS NY-543
HABS NY,52-HUNTS,1-
15dr/29ph/fr L

LLOYD HARBOR

Lloyd,Joseph,Manor House
Lloyd Harbor Rd. & Lloyd Ln.
HABS NY-5670
HABS NY,52-LOHA,1-
8dr/24ph/2pc/fr L

LLOYD HARBOR VIC.

Caumsett Manor (Field,Marshall,Estate)
Lloyd Neck
HABS NY-6107
HABS NY,52-COSPHA,1-
18ph/2pg/2ct/fr L

Caumsett Manor,Guernsey Farm (Field,Marshall,Estate,Guernsey Farm)
Lloyd Neck
HABS NY-6107-C
HABS NY,52-COSPHA,1C-
2ph L

Caumsett Manor,Polo Stables (Field,Marshall,Estate,Polo Stables)
Lloyd Neck
HABS NY-6107-B
HABS NY,52-COSPHA,1B-
4ph L

Caumsett Manor,Winter Cottage (Field,Marshall,Estate,Winter Cottage)
Lloyd Neck
HABS NY-6107-A
HABS NY,52-COSPHA,1A-
1ph L

Field,Marshall,Estate; see Caumsett Manor

Field,Marshall,Estate,Guernsey Farm; see Caumsett Manor,Guernsey Farm

Field,Marshall,Estate,Polo Stables; see Caumsett Manor,Polo Stables

Field,Marshall,Estate,Winter Cottage; see Caumsett Manor,Winter Cottage

Fort Hill
Lloyd Neck
HABS NY-6108
HABS NY,52-LOHA.V,2-
20ph/2pg/fr L

LLOYD NECK VIC.

Caumsett Manor,Garage (Field,Marshall,Estate,Garage)
Lloyd Neck
HABS NY-6107-D
HABS NY,52-COSPHA,1D-
1ph L

Field,Marshall,Estate,Garage; see Caumsett Manor,Garage

MASTIC BEACH

Fire Island National Seashore; see Floyd,Gen. William,House

Floyd,Gen. William,House (Fire Island National Seashore; Floyd,Nicholl,House)
Washington Ave. & Wavecrest Dr.
HABS NY-5427
HABS NY,52-MAST,1-
11dr/15ph/13pg/fr L

Floyd,Nicholl,House; see Floyd,Gen. William,House

MELVILLE

Smith,Isaac,Farmhouse
Upper Hollow & Pine Lawn Rds.
HABS NY-545
HABS NY,52-MELV,1-
3dr/8ph/fr L

OAKDALE

Pepperidge Hall (fireplaces)
HABS NY-6279
HABS NY,52-OAK,1-
2ph L

SAG HARBOR

First Presbyterian Church (Whalers' Church)
HABS NY-6318
HABS NY,52-SAGHA,4-
6ph L

House
HABS NY-5426
HABS NY,52-SAGHA,2-
1ph L

Whalers' Church; see First Presbyterian Church

SELDEN VIC.

Lake Grove (House)
HABS NY-5424
HABS NY,52-SELD.V,1-
2ph L

SETAUKET

Castelma House
HABS NY-5413
HABS NY,52-SETA,4-
3ph L

Setauket Presbyterian Church
HABS NY-6276
HABS NY,52-SETA,1-
1ph L

Thompson,Benjamin,House
HABS NY-549
HABS NY,52-SETA,3-
6ph L

SHELTER ISLAND

Shelter Island Windmill
Manwaring Rd.
HAER NY-145
HAER NY,52-SHELI,2-
14ph/13pg/1pc L

SMITHTOWN

Hallock,Thomas,Tavern
HABS NY-6274
HABS NY,52-SMITO,3-
1ph L

Mills,Moses,House
HABS NY-5421
HABS NY,52-SMITO,2-
2ph L

New Mills House
HABS NY-6270
HABS NY,52-SMITO,6-
2ph L

Presbyterian Church
HABS NY-6109
HABS NY,52-SMITO,1-
8ph L

Smith,Obadiah,House
853 Saint Johnland Rd., San Remo
HABS NY-6110
HABS NY,52-SMITO,4-
9dr/19ph/3pg L

Stetson House
HABS NY-6275
HABS NY,52-SMITO,5-
2ph L

SOUTHAMPTON

Beebe Windmill
Ocean & Hildreath Sts.
HAER NY-67
HAER NY,52-BRIG,4-
6dr/11ph/18pg/1pc/fr L

Windmill at Water Mill
Montauk Hwy. & Halsey Ln.
HAER NY-134
HAER NY,52-WATMI,1-
6dr/11ph/59pg/1pc/fr L

SPEONK

Brick Mill; see Tuttle-Fordham Mill

Tuttle-Fordham Mill (Brick Mill)
Mill Rd. & Montauk Hwy.
HAER NY-102
HAER NY,52-SPEO,1-
1ph/2pg/1pc L

ST. JAMES VIC.

Mills Pond House
660 N. Country Rd. (State Rt. 25A)
HABS NY-5668
HABS NY,52-STJAM.V,1-
11dr/21ph/12pg/2pc/fr L

WAINSCOTT

Osborne,Thomas,House
Wainscott Rd.
HABS NY-5415
HABS NY,52-WAISCO,1-
8dr/fr L

Strong,Sylvester,House
HABS NY-6278
HABS NY,52-WAISCO,2-
1ph L

WEST HILLS

Whitman,Walt,Birthplace
Amityville Rd. (State Rt. 110)
HABS NY-541
HABS NY,52-WEHI,1-
11dr/20ph/5pg/fr L

WESTHAMPTON BEACH

Beach Lane Bridge; see Quantuck Canal Bridge

Quantuck Canal Bridge (Beach Lane Bridge)
Beach Lane,spanning Quantuck Canal,west of bay
HAER NY-182
HAER 1991(HAER):5
3ph/4pg/1pc L

SULLIVAN COUNTY

CALLICOON

Erie Railway:Callicoon Passenger & Freight Station
Main St.
HAER NY-65
HAER NY,53-CAL,1-
1ph/1pc L

MINISINK FORD

Delaware & Hudson Canal:Delaware Aqueduct Toll Hse
HAER NY-205
HAER 1991(HAER):5
10ph/1pc L

Delaware and Hudson Canal: Survey Locks 70-72
Downstream from Del. Aqdt. btwn Del. Riv. & Rt. 97
HAER NY-262
1dr H

PHILIPPSPORT

Store,Old
HABS NY-6129
HABS NY,53-PHILP,1-
2ph L

TIOGA COUNTY

OWEGO

Lovejoy,Dr. Ezekiel,House
100 Front St.
HABS NY-5428
HABS NY,54-OWEG,1-
1dr/9ph/6pg L

Pumpelly-Parker House; see Pumpelly,Harmon,House

Pumpelly,Harmon,House (Pumpelly-Parker House)
113 Front St.
HABS NY-5460
HABS NY,54-OWEG,2-
11ph/12pg L

TOMPKINS COUNTY

DANBY

Danby Federated Church
1859 Danby Rd.
HABS NY-5729
HABS NY,55-DANB,1-
8ph/1ct L

DRYDEN

West Dryden Community Center
HABS NY-6327
8dr/fr L

ITHACA

"The Station"; see Lehigh Valley Railroad Station

Clinton House
120 N. Cayuga St.
HABS NY-5723
HABS NY,55-ITH,9-
20ph L

Congregational Church
N. Geneva & W. Seneca Sts.
HABS NY-5441
HABS NY,55-ITH,5-
4ph L

Cornell University,Llenroc (Cornell,Ezra,House; Llenroc)
100 Cornell Ave.
HABS NY-5727
HABS NY,55-ITH,11A-
20ph L

Cornell,Ezra,House; see Cornell University,Llenroc

Lehigh Valley Railroad Station ("The Station")
W. Buffalo St. & Taughannock Blvd.
HABS NY-5630
HABS NY,55-ITH,6-
6ph L

Llenroc; see Cornell University,Llenroc

Sage Chapel,Cornell University
Central Ave.
HABS NY-5726
HABS NY,55-ITH,11B- ı1991(HABS):21°
24ph/66pg/2pc L

Second Tompkins County Courthouse
121 E. Court St.
HABS NY-5442
HABS NY,55-ITH,7-
15ph/4pg L

St. John's Episcopal Church & Parish House
210 N. Cayuga St.
HABS NY-5725
HABS NY,55-ITH,10-
14ph L

Williams,C. R. ,House
306 N. Cayuga St.
HABS NY-5724
HABS NY,55-ITH,8-
21ph L

ITHACA VIC.

Stainton House
1735 Ellis Hollow Rd.
HABS NY-5728
HABS NY,55-ITH.V,1-
10ph L

TRUMANSBURG

First Presbyterian Church of Ulysses
E. Main St.
HABS NY-5730
HABS NY,55-TRUM,1-
12ph/1pc L

First Presbyterian Church of Ulysses,Meeting Hall
E. Main St.
HABS NY-5730-A
HABS NY,55-TRUM,1A-
3ph/1pc L

ULSTER COUNTY

ELLENVILLE

Reformed Church
HABS NY-4381
HABS NY,56-ELVI,1-
1ph L

GARDINER

Deyo-Bevier House
Ireland's Corners
HABS NY-4365
HABS NY,56-GARD,1-
1ph L

Le Fevre,Matthew,House
HABS NY-4366
HABS NY,56-GARD,2-
1ph L

HIGH FALLS

Canal Locks & Dupuy House
HABS NY-4375
HABS NY,56-HIFA,1-
1ph L

De Motte House
Delaware & Hudson Canal
HABS NY-4383
HABS NY,56-HIFA,2-
1ph L

HURLEY

DuMond House (Spy House; Guard House,Old)
Main St. (State Hwy. 6)
HABS NY-4-302
HABS NY,56-HUR,5-
10dr/5ph/8pg L

Guard House,Old; see DuMond House

Hasbrouck House
HABS NY-4382
HABS NY,56-HUR,7-
1ph L

Hurley Street (House)
HABS NY-4376
HABS NY,56-HUR,6-
2ph L

Spy House; see DuMond House

Van Deusen,Capt. Jan,House
Hurley St.
HABS NY-4369
HABS NY,56-HUR,2-
2ph L

HURLEY VIC.

Well Head Cover
HABS NY-4377
HABS NY,56-HUR.V,1-
1ph/fr L

KERHONKSON

Hardenbergh,Johannes,House
HABS NY-4125
HABS NY,56-KER,1-
9dr/9ph/fr L

KINGSTON

Clinton Avenue Historic District
HABS NY-5561
HABS NY,56-KING,21-
2dr/12ph/44pg/fr L

Clinton Avenue Historic District (Newcomb House)
304 Clinton Ave.
HABS NY-5561-E
HABS NY,56-KING,21E-
2ph/6pg/1pc/fr L

Clinton Avenue Historic District (Nichols,Albert G.,House)
296-300 Clinton Ave.
HABS NY-5561-D
HABS NY,56-KING,21D-
1ph/5pg/1pc L

Clinton Avenue Historic District (Peters House)
306 Clinton Ave.
HABS NY-5561-F
HABS NY,56-KING,21F-
1ph/6pg/1pc L

Clinton Avenue Historic District (Smith House,North)
294 Clinton Ave.
HABS NY-5561-C
HABS NY,56-KING,21C-
1ph/8pg/1pc L

Clinton Avenue Historic District (Smith House,South)
290 Clinton Ave.
HABS NY-5561-B
HABS NY,56-KING,21B-
1ph/7pg/1pc L

Clinton Avenue Historic District (Van Gaasbeek,Thomas,House)
308 Clinton Ave.
HABS NY-5561-G
HABS NY,56-KING,21G-
2ph/7pg/1pc L

Clinton Avenue Historic Distrtict (Westbrook,Frederick L.,House)
286 Clinton Ave.
HABS NY-5561-A
HABS NY,56-KING,21A-
4ph/5pg/1pc L

Dutch Church,Old; see Reformed Protestant Dutch Church

Fair Street Reformed Dutch Church; see Second Reformed Dutch Church

Fireman's Hall
267 Fair St.
HABS NY-5672
HABS NY,56-KING,23-
1ph/1pc L

First Post Office; see Vandenburgh-Hasbrouck House

Jansen House
HABS NY-3230
HABS NY,56-KING,10-
1ph L

Kiersted,Dr. Luke,House
93 John St.
HABS NY-5559
HABS NY,56-KING,14-
5dr/7ph/9pg/1pc/fr L

Kingston Bank (Kingston Trust Company)
27 Main St.
HABS NY-5571
HABS NY,56-KING,17-
7ph/9pg/1pc/fr L

Kingston City Hall
408 Broadway
HABS NY-5570
HABS NY,56-KING,16-
15ph/12pg/2pc/1ct/fr L

Kingston Trust Company; see Kingston Bank

Loughran,Dr. Robert,House
296 Fair St.
HABS NY-5560
HABS NY,56-KING,15-
6dr/6ph/8pg/1pc/fr L

Newcomb House; see Clinton Avenue Historic District

Nichols,Albert G.,House; see Clinton Avenue Historic District

Pearl & Wall Streets (House)
HABS NY-3229
HABS NY,56-KING,9-
1ph L

Peters House; see Clinton Avenue Historic District

Philips,Christian F.,House
120 Saint James St.
HABS NY-5572
HABS NY,56-KING,18-
9dr/5ph/9pg/1pc/1ct/fr L

Reformed Protestant Dutch Church (Dutch Church,Old)
Main St.
HABS NY-5573
HABS NY,56-KING,25-
8ph/10pg/1pc/2ct/fr L

Second Reformed Dutch Church (Fair Street Reformed Dutch Church)
209 Fair St.
HABS NY-5569
HABS NY,56-KING,24-
10ph/9pg/1pc/1ct/fr L

Senate House (Ten Broeck House)
HABS NY-4360
HABS NY,56-KING,7-
3ph L

Slight,Henry,House
Green & Crown Sts.
HABS NY-3228
HABS NY,56-KING,2-
1ph L

Smith House,North; see Clinton Avenue Historic District

Smith House,South; see Clinton Avenue Historic District

Sudam,John,House
Wall & Main Sts.
HABS NY-4-301
HABS NY,56-KING,4-
10dr/5ph/5pg/fr L

Ten Broeck House; see Senate House

Tompkins,Edward,Well House
Grove St.
HABS NY-5574
HABS NY,56-KING,19-
2dr/fr L

Tremper,John,House
3 N. Front St.
HABS NY-5557
HABS NY,56-KING,12-
13dr/11ph/10pg/1pc/fr L

Van Gaasbeek,Thomas,House; see Clinton Avenue Historic District

Van Weye-Van Keuren House
138 Green St.
HABS NY-5575
HABS NY,56-KING,20-
13ph/12pg/1pc/2ct/fr L

Vandenburgh-Hasbrouck House (First Post Office; Weels,Jacobus,Cabinet Shop)
10 Crown St.
HABS NY-3227
HABS NY,56-KING,8-
13dr/5ph/12pg/1pc/fr L

Weeks,James B.,House
26 Pearl St.
HABS NY-3103
HABS NY,56-KING,26-
9dr/10ph/9pg/1pc/fr L

Weels,Jacobus,Cabinet Shop; see Vandenburgh-Hasbrouck House

Wells,George & Solomen,House
106 Saint James St.
HABS NY-5576
HABS NY,56-KING,22-
3ph/7pg/1pc/fr L

Westbrook,Frederick L.,House; see Clinton Avenue Historic Distrtict

Whittaker-Hoffman House
N. Front & Green Sts.
HABS NY-5556
HABS NY,56-KING,11-
11dr/10ph/12pg/1pc/fr L

KINGSTON VIC.

Fitch,S. & W. B.,Depot & Office Building
Abeel St.
HABS NY-5558
HABS NY,56-KING.V,9-
3dr/7ph/7pg/1pc/2ct/fr L

Ten Broeck,Benjamin,House
Flatbush
HABS NY-6131
HABS NY,56-KING.V,6-
3ph L

MARBLETOWN

Bevier,Louis,House
State Rt. 213 Vic.
HABS NY-4361
HABS NY,56-MARB,1-
10dr/3ph/fr L

NAPANOCH

Bevier,Cornelius,House
HABS NY-4132
HABS NY,56-NAP,2-
1ph L

Conrad-Bevier House (Ruins)
HABS NY-4126
HABS NY,56-NAP,1-
2ph L

NEW PALTZ

Bevier-Elting House
Hugenot St. & Broadhead Ave.
HABS NY-4-304
HABS NY,56-NEWP,2-
11dr/3ph/10pg/fr L

Fort Dubois
81 Huguenot St.
HABS NY-6132
HABS NY,56-NEWP,6-
7dr/11pg/fr L

Freer,Hughes,House
32 Hugenot St.
HABS NY-4-303
HABS NY,56-NEWP,5-
8dr/4ph/4pg/1pc/fr L

Hasbrouck,Abraham,House
Hugenot St.
HABS NY-4363
HABS NY,56-NEWP,4-
2ph/fr L

Hasbrouck,Jean,House
Hugenot St.
HABS NY-471
HABS NY,56-NEWP,3-
15dr/20ph/1pg/2pc/fr L

Hasbrouck,Oscar,House
Rt. 299 vic.
HABS NY-4364
HABS NY,56-NEWP,1-
3ph L

NEW PALTZ VIC.

Hasbrouck,Col. Josiah,House; see Locust Lawn

Hasbrouck,Col. Josiah,Well House; see Locust Lawn,Well House

House
HABS NY-4368
HABS NY,56-NEWP.V,2-
1ph L

LeFevre House,Old
Wallkill River
HABS NY-4386
HABS NY,56-NEWP.V,3-
1ph L

Locust Lawn (Hasbrouck,Col. Josiah,House)
State Rt. 32
HABS NY-4388
HABS NY,56-NEWP.V,1-
6dr/10ph/4pg/fr L

Locust Lawn,Well House
(Hasbrouck,Col. Josiah,Well House)
State Rt. 32
HABS NY-4367
HABS NY,56-NEWP.V,1A-
1ph/1pg L

Mohonk Mountain House
Mountain Rest Rd.
HABS NY-5700
HABS NY,56-NEWP.V,4-
89ph/5pc/20ct L

PHOENICIA VIC.

Snyder Hollow Bridge (Woodland Valley Road Bridge)
Woodland Valley Rd.,spanning Esopus Creek
HAER NY-183
HAER (HAER):5
4ph/5pg/1pc L

Woodland Valley Road Bridge; see Snyder Hollow Bridge

RIFTON

Perrine's Bridge
Spanning Wallkill River
HABS NY-4-204
HABS NY,56-RIF.V,1-
1dr/3ph/1pg/fr L

SHAWANGUNK

Decker,Johannes,Barn
HABS NY-6133
HABS NY,56-SHWA,3A-
6dr/2ph/fr L

Decker,Johannes,Coach House
HABS NY-6134
HABS NY,56-SHWA,3B-
1dr/1ph/fr L

Decker,Johannes,House
Red Mill Rd. & Shawangunk Kill vic.
HABS NY-6135
HABS NY,56-SHWA,3-
8dr/2pg/fr L

Decker,Johannes,Ice House
HABS NY-6136
HABS NY,56-SHWA,3C-
1dr/1ph/fr L

STONE RIDGE

Lounsberry House; see Wynkoop-Lounsberry House

Sally Tock Tavern; see Sally Tock's Inn

Sally Tock's Inn (Sally Tock Tavern)
HABS NY-4384
HABS NY,56-STORI,3-
1ph L

Wynkoop-Lounsberry House
(Lounsberry House)
HABS NY-4387
HABS NY,56-STORI,1-
1ph L

WAWARSING

Bruin House
HABS NY-4128
HABS NY,56-WAWAR,2-
6ph/fr L

DePuy House
HABS NY-4127
HABS NY,56-WAWAR,1-
6ph/fr L

WARREN COUNTY

WARRENSBURG

Emerson Sawmill (Warrensburg Mills)
Scroon River,River St.
HAER NY-146
HAER NY,57-WARBU,1-
17ph/3pg/1pc L

Warrensburg Mills; see Emerson Sawmill

WASHINGTON COUNTY

EASTON

Hegeman-Hill Street Bridge
Spanning Batten Kill,.65 mi W of Greenwich
HAER NY-153
HAER NY,58-EAS,1-
30ph/15pg/3pc L

FORT ANN

House,Old Stone (Library)
HABS NY-6139
HABS NY,58-FORA,3-
1ph L

House,Oldest
HABS NY-6137
HABS NY,58-FORA,1-
3ph L

House,Stone
HABS NY-6138
HABS NY,58-FORA,2-
2ph L

GRANVILLE

Odd Fellows Temple
98 Main St.
HABS NY-5719
HABS NY,58-GRANV,1-
2pg/fr L

HUDSON FALLS

Fenimore Bridge; see Sandy Hill Bridge

Sandy Hill Bridge (Fenimore Bridge)
Bridge St.,spanning Hudson River
HAER NY-185
HAER 1991(HAER):5
7ph/10pg/1pc L

KINGSBURY

Schoolhouse,Stone
HABS NY-6140
HABS NY,58-KING,1-
1ph L

SALEM

Cemetery Road Bridge
Cemetery Rd.,spans Black Crk, 2 mph SW of Salem
HAER NY-186
HAER 1991(HAER):5
3dr/7ph/4pg/1pc/fr L

WHITEHALL

Saunders Street Bridge
Saunders St.,spanning the Champlain Canal
HAER NY-184
HAER 1991(HAER):5
5ph/3pg/1pc L

WAYNE COUNTY

LYONS

Creager's Bridge
County Rt. 344,Cole Road,spanning Erie Canal
HAER NY-187
HAER 1991(HAER):5
2ph/4pg/1pc/fr L

Crisci-Hotchkiss Building; see Hotchkiss Building

Hotchkiss Building (Crisci-Hotchkiss Building)
1 Broad St.
HABS NY-6151
HABS NY,59-LYO,1-
1pg L

WESTCHESTER COUNTY

BEDFORD

Baylis House
Bedford Green
HABS NY-4112
HABS NY,60-BED,3-
12dr/5ph/4pg/fr L

Schoolhouse & Post Office
Bedford Green
HABS NY-4111-A
HABS NY,60-BED,1-
4dr/2ph/4pg/fr L

BRIARCLIFF MANOR

Old Croton Aqueduct,Ventilator No. 10
N. of Scarborough Rd.
HAER NY-207
1ph/1pc L

CHAPPAQUA

Greely,Horace,House; see Rehoboth

Rehoboth (Greely,Horace,House)
HABS NY-4124
HABS NY,60-CHAP,1-
5ph L

CHAPPAQUA VIC.

Society of Friends Meetinghouse
Pine's Bridge Rd.
HABS NY-4-102
HABS NY,60-CHAP.V,1-
8dr/5ph/4pg/fr L

CROTON-ON-HUDSON VIC

New Croton Dam & Reservoir
Croton River
HAER NY-132
HAER NY,60-CROTOH.V,1-
22ph/1pg/14ct L

DOBBS FERRY

Kendall,Messmore,House (Livingston House)
Albany Post Rd.
HABS NY-4-105
HABS NY,60-DOBF,1-
10dr/3ph/9pg/fr L

Livingston House; see Kendall,Messmore,House

Old Croton Aqueduct,Maintenance Building
Walnut St.
HAER NY-116
HAER NY,60-DOBF,2B-
1dr/fr L

Old Croton Aqueduct,Overseer's House
Walnut St.
HAER NY-115
HAER NY,60-DOBF,2A-
2dr/fr L

GOLDENS BRIDGE

Bridge L-158; see New York & Mahopac Railroad:Bridge L-158

New York & Mahopac Railroad:Bridge L-158 (Bridge L-158)
Schoolhouse Rd.
HAER NY-148
HAER NY,60-GOLBR,1-
2ph/2pg/1pc L

HARTSDALE

Hartsdale Railroad Station
E. Hartsdale Ave.
HABS NY-6293
HABS DLC/PP-1993:NY-5
16ph/12pg/2pc L

HASTINGS-ON-HUDSON

Cropsey House and Studio (Saunders,William,House)
49 Washington Ave.
HABS NY-6146
HABS NY,60-HAST,2-
11dr/fr L

Old Croton Aqueduct,Quarry Railroad Bridge
Aqueduct Lane at Williams St.
HAER NY-117
HAER NY,60-HAST,1A-
2dr/3ph/1pg/fr L

Saunders,William,House; see Cropsey House and Studio

IRVINGTON

Armour-Stiner House
45 W. Clinton Ave.
HABS NY-5620
HABS NY,60-IRV,3-
4dr/35ph/12pg/5ct/fr L

Armour-Stiner House,Gazebo
HABS NY-5620-A
HABS NY,60-IRV,3A-
1ph L

Odell Inn
S. Broadway
HABS NY-4109
HABS NY,60-IRV,1-
10dr/3ph/5pg/fr L

Old Croton Aqueduct,Jewels Brook Culvert
Spanning Station Rd.
HAER NY-114
HAER NY,60-IRV,4A-
4dr/8ph/1pg/fr L

Old Croton Aqueduct,Ventilator No. 18
S. of Main St.
HAER NY-208
1ph/1pc L

Poth,Anne E.,House; see Villa Lewaro

Villa Lewaro (Poth,Anne E.,House)
N. Broadway
HABS NY-5618
HABS NY,60-IRV,5-
2ph/5pg/1pc L

KATONAH

Jay,John,House
State Rt. 22
HABS NY-4393
HABS NY,60-KAT,1-
16ph/2ct L

MAMARONECK

Town Hall,Old
Prospect Ave.
HABS NY-4114
HABS NY,60-MAMA,1-
5dr/1ph/7pg/fr L

MOUNT PLEASANT

Philipse Manor Station: Pedestrian Bridge
Spanning Conrail,W. of Riverside Dr.,at Station
HAER NY-204
HAER 1991(HAER):5
12ph/2pg/1pc L

MOUNT VERNON

St. Paul's Church (St. Paul's Church National Historic Site)
897 S. Columbus Ave.
HABS NY-4121
HABS NY,60-MOUV,1-
9dr/5pg L

St. Paul's Church National Historic Site; see St. Paul's Church

NEW ROCHELLE

Paine,Thomas,House
Paine & North Aves.
HABS NY-6319
HABS NY,60-NEWRO,2-
1ph L

Parcot-Drake House (Door)
75 Eastchester Rd.
HABS NY-6142
HABS NY,60-NEWRO,1-
1ph L

NORTH SALEM

June House & Outhouse
HABS NY-4116
HABS NY,60-SALN,1- & 1A-
2dr/3ph/2pg/fr L

NORTH TARRYTOWN

First Dutch Reformed Church; see Old Dutch Reformed Church

Old Croton Aqueduct,Mill River Culvert
U. S. Rt. 9 at Sleepy Hollow Cemetery
HAER NY-112
HAER NY,60-TARYN,3A-
3dr/7ph/1pg/1pc/2ct/fr L

Old Croton Aqueduct,Mill River Waste Weir
U. S. Rt. 9 at Sleepy Hollow Cemetery
HAER NY-113
HAER NY,60-TARYN,3B-
3dr/5ph/1pg/1pc/fr L

Old Dutch Reformed Church (Sleepy Hollow Church; First Dutch Reformed Church)
Albany Post Rd. (U. S. Rt. 9)
HABS NY-6143
HABS NY,60-TARYN,1-
4dr/10ph L

Sleepy Hollow Church; see Old Dutch Reformed Church

OSSINING

Main Street Crescent
209-217 Main St.
HABS NY-5704
HABS NY,60-OSS,1-
32ph/8pg/2pc L

Old Croton Aqueduct,Northern Waste Weir
Snowden Ave. & Van Wick St.
HAER NY-109
HAER NY,60-OSS,2B-
2dr/4ph/1pg/fr L

Old Croton Aqueduct,Sing Sing Kill Bridge
Spanning Aqueduct St. & Broadway
HAER NY-110
HAER NY,60-OSS,2A-
4dr/18ph/1pg/fr L

Old Croton Aqueduct,Ventilator Number 9
Spring & Everett Sts.
HAER NY-111
HAER NY,60-OSS,2C-
1dr/1ph/1pg/1pc/2ct/fr L

OSSINING VIC.,CROTO.

Old Croton Aqueduct,Indian Creek Culvert
Reservoir & Quaker Bridge Rds.,Crotonville
HAER NY-108
HAER NY,60-CROTV,1A-
3dr/5ph/1pg/1pc/fr L

PLEASANTVILLE

Earle House; see St. John's Church,Rectory

St. John's Church,Rectory (Earle House)
Bedford Rd.
HABS NY-4110
HABS NY,60-PLEAV,3-
12dr/3ph/fr L

RYE

Kirby Mill; see Tide Mill Yacht Basin

Parsons-Lounsbury House
Boston Post Rd.
HABS NY-4115
HABS NY,60-RY,1-
14dr/5ph/3pg/fr L

Tide Mill Yacht Basin (Kirby Mill)
Kirby Ln.
HABS NY-6145
HABS NY,60-RY,2-
10dr/3ph/2pg L

SALEM CENTER

Town Hall
HABS NY-4118
HABS NY,60-SAL,1-
7dr/3ph/5pg/fr L

SCARSDALE

Drovers' Tavern,Old; see Wayside Inn

Popham House
1015 Post Rd.
HABS NY-4-103
HABS NY,60-SCARD,1-
9dr/4ph/5pg/fr L

Scarsdale Library; see Wayside Inn

Scarsdale Railroad Station
E. Parkway
HABS NY-6292
HABS DLC/PP-1993:NY-5
16ph/12pg/2pc L

Wayside Inn (Drovers' Tavern,Old; Scarsdale Library)
Post Rd. & Wayside Ln.
HABS NY-4-104
HABS NY,60-SCARD,2-
6dr/4ph/6pg/fr L

SOMERS

Elephant Hotel
State Rt. 116 Vic.
HABS NY-4-101
HABS NY,60-SOM,1-
11dr/5ph/6pg/fr L

TARRYTOWN

Gardener's Lodge,Bowling Alley,; see Lyndhurst,Outbuildings

Gatehouse/Entrance,Frame House,; see Lyndhurst,Outbuildings

Laundry/Guest Cottage; see Lyndhurst,Outbuildings

Lyndhurst,Boat Landing
635 S. Broadway
HABS NY-5538-F
HABS NY,60-TARY,1F-
3ph L

Lyndhurst,Greenhouse
635 S. Broadway
HABS NY-5538-B
HABS NY,60-TARY,1B-
38ph/2pg/4pc/fr L

Lyndhurst,Main House
635 S. Broadway
HABS NY-5538-A
HABS NY,60-TARY,1A-
16dr/98ph/2pg/8pc/fr L

Lyndhurst,Outbuildings
(Gatehouse/Entrance,Frame House,; Gardener's Lodge,Bowling Alley,; Northwest Cottage,Kennel &; Laundry/Guest Cottage)
635 S. Broadway
HABS NY-5538-C
HABS NY,60-TARY,1C-
8ph/1ct L

Lyndhurst,Stables
635 S. Broadway
HABS NY-5538-D
HABS NY,60-TARY,1D-
5ph L

Lyndhurst,Swimming Pool
635 S. Broadway
HABS NY-5538-E
HABS NY,60-TARY,1E-
4ph L

Northwest Cottage,Kennel &; see Lyndhurst,Outbuildings

Requa House
575 S. Broadway
HABS NY-5552
HABS NY,60-TARY,2-
8dr L

TARRYTOWN VIC.

Irving,Washington,House; see Sunnyside

Sunnyside (Irving,Washington,House)
U.S. Rt. 9
HABS NY-5637
HABS NY,60-TARY.V,1-
9dr/11ph/fr L

TUCKAHOE

Tuckahoe Railroad Station
Columbus Ave. & Main St.
HABS NY-6291
HABS DLC/PP-1993:NY-5
16ph/10pg/2pc L

VALHALLA VIC.

Miller,Elijah,House
W. Lake Dr.
HABS NY-4113
HABS NY,60-VAL.V,1-
13dr/5ph/4pg/fr L

VANCORTLANDVILLE

St. Peter's Church
Hillside Cemetery
HABS NY-4-106
HABS NY,60-VANCOV,1-
4dr/3ph/7pg/fr L

WHITE PLAINS

Westchester County Courthouse
166 Main St.
HABS NY-5701
HABS NY,60-WHIPL,1-
32dr/36ph/fr L

YONKERS

Moquette Row Housing
Moquette Row North & Moquette Row South
HABS NY-6263
HABS NY,60-YONK,6-
19ph/12pg L

Old Croton Aqueduct,Saw Mill River Culvert
Spanning Nepperhan Ave.
HAER NY-118
HAER NY,60-YONK,1A-
3dr/19ph/4pg/1pc/fr L

Public School No. 3
Hamilton Ave. btwn. Ludlow & Morris Sts.
HABS NY-6037
HABS NY,60-YONK,3-
20ph/24pg L

Public School No. 4
Trenchard St.
HABS NY-6298
HABS NY,60-YONK,4-
23ph/17pg/5pc L

Yonkers City Hall
Washington Park
HABS NY-382
HABS NY,60-YONK,2-
11ph/9pg/1pc L

Yonkers Public Library
Nepperhan Ave. & S. Broadway
HABS NY-6144
HABS NY,60-YONK,5-
21ph/11pg L

YORKTOWN HEIGHTS VIC

Old Croton Aqueduct,Entrance Entablature
New Croton Reservoir
HAER NY-107
HAER NY,60-CROTOH.V,2-
1dr/1ph/1pg/1pc/fr L

WYOMING COUNTY

PORTAGEVILLE VIC.

Erie Railway:Buffalo Division,Bridge 361.66 (Erie Railway:Portage Viaduct)
Genesee River,State Rt.436
HAER NY-54
HAER NY,61-PORT,1-
7ph/1pc L

Erie Railway:Portage Viaduct; see Erie Railway:Buffalo Division,Bridge 361.66

WARSAW

Erie Railway:Warsaw Passenger & Freight Station
U.S. Rt. 20
HAER NY-49
HAER NY,61-WARS,1-
3ph/1pc L

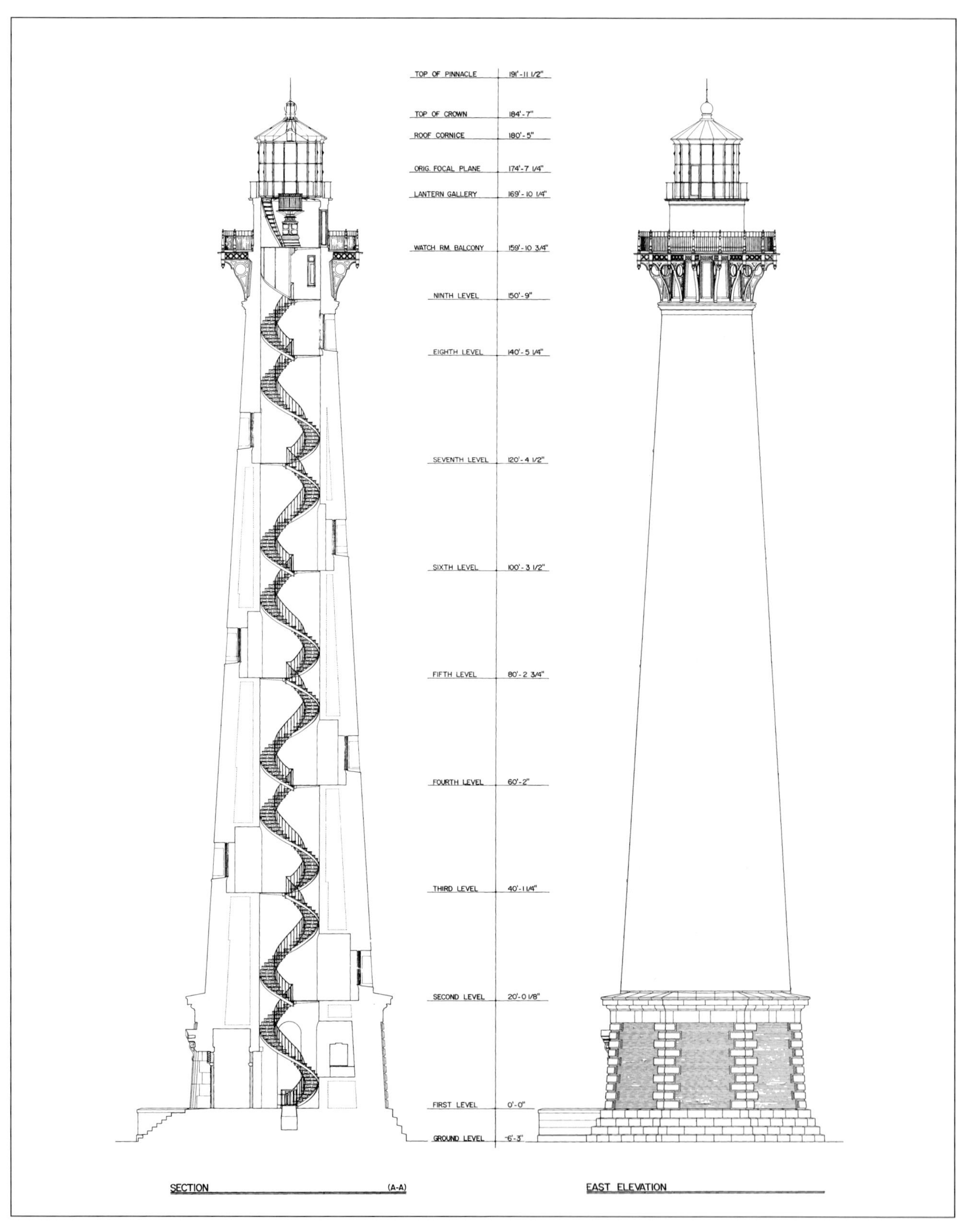

Cape Hatteras Lighthouse, Buxton, Dare County, North Carolina. East elevation; section. Measured drawing delineated by Judith E. Collins, 1989 (HABS NC-357, sheet 2 of 13).

North Carolina

ALAMANCE COUNTY

BURLINGTON

Tarheel Army Missle Plant
HAER NC-15
HAER NC,1-BURL,1-
35pg/fr L

GLENCOE

Glencoe Cotton Mills
State Rts. 1598 & 1600
HAER NC-6
HAER NC,1-GLEN,1-
3dr/17ph/22pg/2pc/fr L

SPARTA VIC.

Brinegar Cabin
Blue Ridge Pkwy.
HABS NC-188
HABS NC,97-SPART.V,1-
3dr/8ph/2pg L

ANSON COUNTY

MORVEN VIC.

Flowers Farm Cotton Press
State Rt. 1826
HAER NC-1
HAER NC,4-MORV.V,1-
3dr/3ph/1pc/fr L

BEAUFORT COUNTY

BATH

Bonner,Capt. Joseph,House
Front & Main Sts.
HABS NC-206
HABS NC,7-BATH,4-
8dr/8ph/1pg/1pc L

Glebe House; see Williams House

Lucas-Tompkins House; see Williams House

Marsh House; see Palmer-Marsh House

Marsh House, Smokehouse; see Palmer-Marsh Smokehouse

Palmer-Marsh House (Marsh House)
Main St.
HABS NC-310
HABS NC,7-BATH,1-
11ph/1pg/1pc L

Palmer-Marsh Smokehouse (Marsh House, Smokehouse)
Main St.
HABS NC-311
HABS NC,7-BATH,1A-
2ph/1pg/1pc L

St. Thomas' Episcopal Church
Craven St.
HABS NC-274
HABS NC,7-BATH,2-
5ph L

Williams House (Lucas-Tompkins House; Glebe House)
Main & Craven Sts.
HABS NC-275
HABS NC,7-BATH,3-
2ph L

WASHINGTON

Fowle Warehouse
Repass & Main Sts.
HABS NC-210
HABS NC,7-WASH,2-
4dr/2ph L

Haven Warehouse
Van Norden & Main Sts.
HABS NC-209
HABS NC,7-WASH,3-
10dr/3ph/1pg/1pc L

Leggett,Zophus,Store; see Washington Historic District

Washington Dry Goods Store; see Washington Historic District

Washington Historic District (Leggett,Zophus,Store; Washington Dry Goods Store)
302 Pierce St.
HABS NC-326-A
HABS NC,7-WASH,1-
4ph/3pg/1pc L

BLADEN COUNTY

ELIZABETHTOWN

Greek Revival House (McDowell House)
State Rt. 1198 & NC Rt. 87
HABS NC-173
HABS NC,9-ELITO,1-
1ph L

McDowell House; see Greek Revival House

ELIZABETHTOWN VIC.

Bridge No. 701-42-20N; see McGirt's Bridge

McGirt's Bridge (U. S. Route 701 Bridge; Bridge No. 701-42-20N)
Spanning Cape Fear River
HAER NC-29
HAER NC,9-ELITO.V,1-
16ph/1pg/1pc L

Neal-Brissom House; see Oakland

Oakland (Neal-Brissom House)
Cape Fear River & Rt. 21
HABS NC-135
HABS NC,9- ,1-
5ph/1pg L

U. S. Route 701 Bridge; see McGirt's Bridge

BRUNSWICK COUNTY

BRUNSWICK TOWN

St. Philip's Church (Ruins)
State Rt. 1533
HABS NC-109
HABS NC,10-BRU,1-
2pg L

SOUTHPORT

Bellamy House (Williamson House)
HABS NC-316
HABS NC,10-SOUPO,1-
1pc L

Fort Johnson
HABS NC-317
HABS NC,10-SOUPO,2-
1pc L

Williamson House; see Bellamy House

BUNCOMBE COUNTY

ASHEVILLE

Bunn,Robert D. ,Building (Commercial Building)
16 Biltmore Ave.
HABS NC-333
HABS NC,11-ASHV,5-
10ph/1pg/1pc L

Chateau Nollman; see Raven Cross Inn

12-16 Eagle Street (Commercial Building)
HABS NC-330
HABS NC,11-ASHV,3-
3ph/1pg/1pc L

Gibbs Building
18 Biltmore Ave.
HABS NC-334
HABS NC,11-ASHV,6-
2pg L

Henrietta House (White House Inn)
78 Biltmore St.
HABS NC-276
HABS NC,11-ASHV,1-
2ph L

Hutchinson Building
18 Eagle St.
HABS NC-331
HABS NC,11-ASHV,4-
4ph/1pg/1pc L

Raven Cross Inn (Ravenscroft Inn; Chateau Nollman)
29 Ravenscroft Dr.
HABS NC-277
HABS NC,11-ASHV,2-
1ph L

Ravenscroft Inn; see Raven Cross Inn

White House Inn; see Henrietta House

ASHEVILLE VIC.

Bridge No. 213; see North Carolina Route 2408 Bridge

North Carolina Route 2408 Bridge (Bridge No. 213)
Spanning Bull Creek
HAER NC-30
HAER NC,11-ASHV.V,1-
7ph/1pg/1pc L

FAIRVIEW VIC.

Sherrill's Inn
Lake Lure,U. S. Rt. 74
HABS NC-226
HABS NC,11-HICK,1-
20dr L

OLD TRAP VIC.

Cartwright House (Williams House)
NC Rt. 343
HABS NC-51
HABS NC,15-SHILO.V,1-
1ph/1pg L

Williams House; see Cartwright House

RIDGECREST VIC.

Swannanoa Tunnel
U. S. Rt. 70
HAER NC-12
HAER NC,11-RIDG.V,1-
10pg L

BURKE COUNTY

MARION VIC.

Bridge No. 126-85-10; see North Carolina Route 126 Bridge

North Carolina Route 126 Bridge (Bridge No. 126-85-10)
Spanning Lake James Canal
HAER NC-32
HAER NC,12-MAR.V,1-
8ph/1pg/1pc L

MORGANTOWN VIC.

Bridge No. 2; see Huffman Bridge

Huffman Bridge (North Carolina Route 1501 Bridge; Bridge No. 2)
Spanning Catawba River
HAER NC-31
HAER NC,12-MORG.V,1-
7ph/1pg/1pc L

North Carolina Route 1501 Bridge; see Huffman Bridge

CALDWELL COUNTY

LENOIR VIC.

Fort Defiance (Lenoir,Gen. William,House)
State Rt. 268,Yadkin Valley
HABS NC-106
HABS NC,14-YADVA,1-
2ph L

Lenoir,Gen. William,House; see Fort Defiance

PATTERSON

Clover Hill (Jones,Col. Edmond,House)
State Rt. 1514
HABS NC-142
HABS NC,14-LENO.V,1-
3ph L

Jones,Col. Edmond,House; see Clover Hill

PATTERSON VIC.

Davenport,Col. ,House; see Walnut Fountain

Walnut Fountain (Davenport,Col. ,House)
NC Rt. 268
HABS NC-143
HABS NC,14- ,1-
2ph L

CAMDEN COUNTY

CAMDEN

Camden County Courthouse
NC Rt. 343
HABS NC-69
HABS NC,15-CAMD,1-
1ph/1pg L

CAMDEN VIC.

Fairfield Hall; see Gregory,Gen. Isaac,House

Gregory,Gen. Isaac,House (Fairfield Hall)
State Rt. 1121
HABS NC-48
HABS NC,15-CAMD.V,2-
2ph/1pg L

Grice House (Grist House; Milford; Relfe-Grice-Sawyer House)
Ship Yard Ferry Rd.
HABS NC-16
HABS NC,15-CAMD.V,1-
3ph/1pg L

Grist House; see Grice House

Milford; see Grice House

Relfe-Grice-Sawyer House; see Grice House

SOUTH MILLS VIC.

Abbott House; see Gordon House

Gordon House (Hinton House; Abbott House; Mullen-Abbott House)
State Rt. 1224
HABS NC-56
HABS NC,15-SOUMI.V,2-
1ph/1pg L

Hinton House; see Gordon House

Morgan House
U. S. Rt. 17
HABS NC-27
HABS NC,15-SOUMI.V,1-
1ph/1pg L

Mullen-Abbott House; see Gordon House

CARTERET COUNTY

BEAUFORT

Beaufort High School
Broad St. (moved from Courthouse Sq.)
HABS NC-225
HABS NC,16-BEAUF,9-
13dr L

Beaufort Jail,Old
Courthouse Sq. on Cedar St.
HABS NC-228
HABS NC,16-BEAUF,8-
12dr L

Davis House (Inn,Old; Davis House Hotel)
121-123-125 Front St.
HABS NC-20
HABS NC,16-BEAUF,1-
1ph/1pg L

Davis House Hotel; see Davis House

Duncan House
107 Front St.
HABS NC-28
HABS NC,16-BEAUF,2-
1ph/1pg L

Easton House; see Thomas House

Henry,Jacob,House; see Thomas House

Hill,Micheal,House; see Thompson,Col. ,House

House,Joe,House (Nelson House)
205 Front St.
HABS NC-90
HABS NC,16-BEAUF,6-
1ph/1pg L

Inn,Old; see Davis House

Langdon House
135 Craven St. (House)
HABS NC-42
HABS NC,16-BEAUF,3-
1ph/1pg L

Mace House
619 Ann St.
HABS NC-84
HABS NC,16-BEAUF,4-
1ph/1pg L

Nelson House; see House,Joe,House

St. Paul's Episcopal Church
209 Ann St.
HABS NC-204
HABS NC,16-BEAUF,7-
8dr/1pg L

Stubbs,Vera,House; see Thompson,Col. ,House

Thomas House (Henry,Jacob,House; Easton House)
229 Front St.
HABS NC-87
HABS NC,16-BEAUF,5-
1ph/1pg L

Thompson,Col. ,House
(Hill,Micheal,House; Stubbs,Vera,House)
603 Front St.
HABS NC-8
HABS NC,16-BEAUF,10-
5ph/1pg/1pc L

BEAUFORT VIC.

Fort Macon
Bogue Point on Fort Macon Rd.
HABS NC-79
HABS NC,16-BEAUF.V,1-
11dr/2ph/28pg L

CASWELL COUNTY

HAMER VIC.

Melrose; see Williams House

Williams House (Melrose)
NC Rt. 62 & State Rt. 1596
HABS NC-119
HABS NC,17-YANV.V,1-
1ph L

LOCUST HILL VIC.

Moore House; see Stamp's Quarter

Stamp's Quarter (Moore House)
U. S. Rt. 158 Vic.
HABS NC-118
HABS NC,17- ,1-
1ph L

MILTON

Baptist Meetinghouse; see Milton Church

Clay House; see Irwin House

Irvine House; see Irwin House

Irwin House (Irvine House; Clay House)
Read & Broad Sts.
HABS NC-114
HABS NC,17-MILT,5-
1ph L

Milton Church (Baptist Meetinghouse)
Warehouse St.
HABS NC-113
HABS NC,17-MILT,4-
1ph L

Row Houses; see Union Tavern

Shops,Old
Broad St.
HABS NC-111
HABS NC,17-MILT,2-
1ph L

Stores,Old
Broad St.
HABS NC-112
HABS NC,17-MILT,3-
1ph L

Union Tavern (Row Houses; Yellow Tavern)
Main St. btwn. Lee St. & Farmer's Alley
HABS NC-110
HABS NC,17-MILT,1-
15ph/1pg/3pc L

Yellow Tavern; see Union Tavern

YANCEYVILLE

Caswell County Courthouse
Main St.
HABS NC-192
HABS NC,17-YANV,4-
8dr/4ph/1pg/3pc L

Caswell News Building (Store,Brick)
W. Main St.
HABS NC-117
HABS NC,17-YANV,3-
1ph L

Dongola; see Graves,Jeremiah,House

Forest House; see Poteat Inn

Graves,Jeremiah,House (Dongola)
Main St.
HABS NC-115
HABS NC,17-YANV,1-
6ph L

Poteat Inn (Forest House)
N. Main & N. First Sts.
HABS NC-116
HABS NC,17-YANV,2-
3ph L

Store,Brick; see Caswell News Building

Womack's Mill
HAER NC-14
HAER NC,17-YANV.V,3-
1dr/32ph/30pg/3pc/fr L

YANCEYVILLE VIC.

Graves House; see Pediment House

Pediment House (Graves House)
U. S. Rt. 158 & NC Rt. 86
HABS NC-120
HABS NC,17-YANV.V,2-
1ph L

CATAWBA COUNTY

HICKORY

Wilson,Joe,House
Old Robinson Cemetery (moved from Startown Rd.)
HABS NC-216
HABS NC,18-HICK,1-
8dr L

LONGVIEW VIC.

Bridge No. 58; see North Carolina Route 1116 Bridge

North Carolina Route 1116 Bridge
(Bridge No. 58)
Spanning Jacob Fork River
HAER NC-34
HAER NC,18-LONV.V,1-
5ph/1pg/1pc L

STONEY POINT VIC.

Bridge No. 1; see North Carolina Route 1006 Bridge

North Carolina Route 1006 Bridge
(Bridge No. 1)
Spanning Catawba River
HAER NC-33
HAER NC,18-STOPT.V,1-
5ph/1pg/1pc L

CHATHAM COUNTY

DURHAM VIC.

Mason,John,House
Rt. 751 vic.
HABS NC-91
HABS NC,19-DUR.,1-
1pg/fr L

MONCURE

Lockville Dam,Canal, & Powerhouse; see Lockville Hydroelectric Plant

Lockville Hydroelectric Plant
(Lockville Dam,Canal, & Powerhouse)
Deep River 3.5 mi. upstream from Haw River
HAER NC-35
HAER NC,19-MONC,1-
16ph/14pg/1pc L

CHOWAN COUNTY

EDENTON

Bandon
HABS NC-319
HABS NC,21-EDET,13-
2ph L

Beverley Hall (State Bank,Old)
114 W. King St.
HABS NC-190
HABS NC,21-EDET,14-
2ph L

Bockover House; see Everett House

Bond House; see Courthouse Green (House)

Booth House (William House; Burton House)
133 E. Church St. (moved to N. Granville St.)
HABS NC-77
HABS NC,21-EDET,5-
6ph/1pg L

Burton House; see Booth House

Charlton House; see Sawyer House

Chowan County Courthouse
E. King St.
HABS NC-12-G-3
HABS NC,21-EDET,2-
4dr/4ph/1pg/fr L

Courthouse Green (House) (Bond House)
405 Court St.
HABS NC-146
HABS NC,21-EDET,7-
1ph L

Cupola House (Eden,Gov. ,House)
408 S. Broad St.
HABS NC-2
HABS NC,21-EDET,3-
14dr/13ph/4pg/fr L

Custom House,East; see Custom House,Old

Custom House,Old (Custom House,East)
403 Court St.
HABS NC-151
HABS NC,21-EDET,11-
1ph L

Eden,Gov. ,House; see Cupola House

Everett House (Wool House; Bockover House; Leigh House)
120 W. Queen St.
HABS NC-152
HABS NC,21-EDET,12-
3ph L

Hewes House; see Jones House

Iredell,James,House
107 E. Church St.
HABS NC-150
HABS NC,21-EDET.10-
4ph/fr L

Jones House (Hewes House)
105 King St.
HABS NC-145
HABS NC,21-EDET,6-
1ph L

Leigh House; see Everett House

Page House (Pembroke Hall)
W. King St.
HABS NC-47
HABS NC,21-EDET,4-
1ph/1pg/fr L

Pembroke Hall; see Page House

Sawyer House (Charlton House)
206 W. Eden St.
HABS NC-147
HABS NC,21-EDET,8-
1ph L

St. Paul's Episcopal Church
W. Church & N. Broad Sts.
HABS NC-12-G-1
HABS NC,21-EDET,1-
5dr/14ph/1pg/fr L

St. Paul's Episcopal Church,Wall & Fence
W. Church & N. Broad Sts.
HABS NC-12-G-2
HABS NC,21-EDET,1-
1dr L

State Bank,Old; see Beverley Hall

Warren,Dr. ,House; see Wessington

Wessington (Warren,Dr. ,House)
120 W. King St.
HABS NC-171
HABS NC,21-EDET,16-
14ph/2pg L

William House; see Booth House

Wool House; see Everett House

EDENTON VIC.

Athol (Benbury Hall; Skinner,Joshua,House)
State Rt. 1114
HABS NC-45
HABS NC,21-EDET.V,2-
5ph/1pg L

Benbury Hall; see Athol

Blount House; see Mulberry Hill

Coffield House
209 E. King St.
HABS NC-64
HABS NC,21-EDET.V,5-
1ph/1pg L

Coke Farm; see Hoskins Place

Dillard's Mill
HABS NC-318
HABS NC,21-EDET.V,7-
1ph L

Hayes Manor (Hayes Plantation)
E. Water St. Vic.
HABS NC-3
HABS NC,21-EDET.V,1-
16dr/14ph/2pg/fr L

Hayes Plantation; see Hayes Manor

Hoskins Place (Coke Farm)
U. S. Rt. 17 (moved to NC,Somerset Vic.)
HABS NC-62
HABS NC,21-EDET.V,4-
1ph/1pg L

Mulberry Hill (Blount House)
Sound Shore Rd.
HABS NC-81
HABS NC,21-EDET.V,6-
5ph/1pg L

Sandy Point Plantation
Sound Shore Rd.
HABS NC-54
HABS NC,21-EDET.V,3-
1ph/1pg L

Skinner,Joshua,House; see Athol

SOMERSET VIC.

Coke Farm; see Hoskins Place

Hoskins Place (Coke Farm)
Locust Grove Rd. Vic. (moved from NC,Edenton Vic.)
HABS NC-62
HABS NC,21-EDET.V,8-
1ph/1pg L

CRAVEN COUNTY

NEW BERN

Academy,First (Central Elementary School)
New St. at Hancock
HABS NC-280
HABS NC,25-NEBER,15-
2ph L

108 Broad Street (House) (Hollister House; Swert-Shields House)
614 Broad St.
HABS NC-290
HABS NC,25-NEBER,26-
2ph L

109 Broad Street (House) (Hollister House)
613 Broad St.
HABS NC-70
HABS NC,25-NEBER,12-
3ph/1pg L

Bryan,James Washington,House; see Bryan,Washington,House & Office

Bryan,Washington,House & Office (Bryan,James Washington,House)
603 & 605 Pollack St.
HABS NC-12-F-2
HABS NC,25-NEBER,6-
8dr/6ph/1pg/fr L

45 Burn Street (House)
(Gill,James,House; Burns House)
823 Pollock St.
HABS NC-279
HABS NC,25-NEBER,7-
1ph L

Burns House; see 45 Burn Street (House)

Burnside's Headquarters; see Slover House

Central Elementary School; see Academy,First

Clark House; see Davis House

Clark-Gillespie House; see Davis House

Coor-Gaston House; see Gaston,Judge William,House

Coor,James,House; see Gaston,Judge William,House

130 Craven Street (House)
(Jerkins-Dufy House)
301 Johnson St.
HABS NC-291
HABS NC,25-NEBER,28-
1ph L

120 Craven Street (Office); see Smallwood,Dr. ,Office

Craven-Nixon House; see Taylor-Ward House

Daves,Maj. James,House; see Hanff House

Davis House (Clark House; Clark-Gillespie House)
419 Metcalf St.
HABS NC-281
HABS NC,25-NEBER,16-
1ph L

Donald,Judge,Law Office & House
(Donnell,Judge,Law Office & House)
163 Craven St.
HABS NC-12-F-3
HABS NC,25-NEBER,8A-
2dr/2ph/1pg/fr L

Donnell,Judge,Law Office & House; see Donald,Judge,Law Office & House

First Presbyterian Church
New & Middle Sts.
HABS NC-12-F-1
HABS NC,25-NEBER,1-
5dr/7ph/2pg/fr L

Gaston,Judge William,House
(Coor,James,House; Coor-Gaston House)
421 Craven St.
HABS NC-125
HABS NC,25-NEBER,13-
2ph L

Gill,James,House; see 45 Burn Street (House)

Hancock House; see Lee House

Hanff House (Daves,Maj. James,House; Hanff-Metz House; Metz House)
313 George St.
HABS NC-278
HABS NC,25-NEBER,3-
1ph L

Hanff-Metz House; see Hanff House

Harvey House (Harvey Mansion)
219 Tryon Palace Dr.
HABS NC-282
HABS NC,25-NEBER,18-
1ph L

Harvey Mansion; see Harvey House

Hollister House; see 108 Broad Street (House)

Hollister House; see 109 Broad Street (House)

Ives,Allen,House (Mitchell-Bryan House; Mitchell-Stevenson House)
211 Johnson St.
HABS NC-283
HABS NC,25-NEBER,19-
1ph L

Jarvis-Hand House; see Jarvis-Slover House

Jarvis-Slover House (Jones House; Jarvis-Hand House; Jones-Jarvis House)
528 E. Front St.
HABS NC-284
HABS NC,25-NEBER,20-
2ph L

Jerkins-Dufy House; see 130 Craven Street (House)

Jones House; see Jarvis-Slover House

Jones-Jarvis House; see Jarvis-Slover House

Lee House (Hancock House; McLin House)
507 Middle St.
HABS NC-52
HABS NC,25-NEBER,10-
3ph/1pg L

Leech,Col. ,House; see Louisiana House

Louisiana House (Moulton-Clark House; Vail-Moulton House; Leech,Col. ,House)
515 E. Front St.
HABS NC-285
HABS NC,25-NEBER,21-
1ph L

Masonic Opera House; see Masonic Temple

Masonic Temple (St. John's Lodge Number 3,A. F. & A. M.; Masonic Opera House)
Hancock & Johnson Sts.
HABS NC-286
HABS NC,25-NEBER,22-
1ph L

McLin House; see Lee House

Metz House; see Hanff House

Mitchell-Bryan House; see Ives,Allen,House

Mitchell-Stevenson House; see Ives,Allen,House

Moulton-Clark House; see Louisiana House

New Bern City Schools Administration Building; see Roberts House

Nixon-Ward House; see Taylor-Ward House

O'Hara,R. ,House (Oliver House)
185 Pollack St. (moved to 512 E. Front St.)
HABS NC-166
HABS NC,25-NEBER,14-
1ph/1pg L

Oaksmith House; see Simpson-Duffy House

Oliver House; see O'Hara,R. ,House

Roberts House (Tisdale-Jones House; New Bern City Schools Administration Building)
New & Metcalf Sts.
HABS NC-287
HABS NC,25-NEBER,23-
1ph L

Simpson-Duffy House (Oaksmith House; Simpson-Oaksmith-Patterson House)
E. Front & Pollack Sts.
HABS NC-288
HABS NC,25-NEBER,24-
1ph L

Simpson-Oaksmith-Patterson House; see Simpson-Duffy House

Slover House (Burnside's Headquarters; Slover-Bradham House; Slover-Guinon House)
E. Front & Johnson Sts.
HABS NC-289
HABS NC,25-NEBER,25-
1ph L

Slover-Bradham House; see Slover House

Slover-Guinon House; see Slover House

Smallwood-Jones House (Ward House; Smallwood,Eli,House)
524 E. Front St.
HABS NC-12-F-4
HABS NC,25-NEBER,9-
8dr/7ph/1pg/1pc/fr L

Smallwood,Dr. ,Office (120 Craven Street (Office))
505 Craven St.
HABS NC-247
HABS NC,25-NEBER,27-
1ph L

Smallwood,Eli,House; see Smallwood-Jones House

St. John's Lodge Number 3,A. F. & A. M.; see Masonic Temple

St. Paul's Roman Catholic Church
510 Middle St.
HABS NC-53
HABS NC,25-NEBER,11-
1ph/1pg L

Stanly,John Wright,House
New St. (moved to 307 George St.)
HABS NC-67
HABS NC,25-NEBER,4-
5ph/1pg L

Swert-Shields House; see 108 Broad Street (House)

Taylor-Ward House (Craven-Nixon House; Taylor,Isaac,House; Nixon-Ward House)
228 Craven St.
HABS NC-172
HABS NC,25-NEBER,17-
12ph/2pg L

Taylor,Isaac,House; see Taylor-Ward House

Tisdale-Jones House; see Roberts House

Vail-Moulton House; see Louisiana House

Ward House; see Smallwood-Jones House

CUMBERLAND COUNTY

FAYETTEVILLE

Cool Spring Inn (Davis Inn,Old; MacKethan House)
Cool Spring St.
HABS NC-292
HABS NC,26-FAYVI,4-
2ph L

Davis Inn,Old; see Cool Spring Inn

309 Dick Street (House) (Nimocks House)
225 Dick St.
HABS NC-298
HABS NC,26-FAYVI,8-
2ph L

First Presbyterian Church
Bow & Ann Sts.
HABS NC-294
HABS NC,26-FAYVI,6-
1ph L

Hotel,Old (Ironwork)
HABS NC-296
HABS NC,26-FAYVI,2-
1ph L

Liberty Point Store (Liberty Row)
Bow St. & Cool Spring Ln.
HABS NC-295
HABS NC,26-FAYVI,3-
1ph L

Liberty Row; see Liberty Point Store

MacKethan House; see Cool Spring Inn

Market House,Old
Hay,Green,Person & Gillespie Sts.
HABS NC-194
HABS NC,26-FAYVI,1-
10dr/2ph L

McLaughlin House; see 456 Person Street (House)

445 Moore Street (House)
HABS NC-299
HABS NC,26-FAYVI,9-
1ph L

Nimocks House; see 309 Dick Street (House)

456 Person Street (House) (McLaughlin House)
HABS NC-293
HABS NC,26-FAYVI,5-
1ph L

Thorton House
219 Maiden Ln.
HABS NC-297
HABS NC,26-FAYVI,7-
2ph L

CURRITUCK COUNTY

SHAWBORO VIC.

Culong; see Forbes House

Ferebee House; see Forbes House

Forbes House (Culong; Ferebee House)
State Rt. 1147
HABS NC-82
HABS NC,27-SHAWB.V,1-
3ph/1pg L

DARE COUNTY

BUXTON

Cape Hatteras Lighthouse
HABS NC-357
HABS DLC/PP-1993:NC-3
13dr/29ph/22pg/2pc/fr L

Cape Hatteras Lighthouse,Double Keeper's Dwelling (Cape Hatteras National Seashore)
Point of Cape Hatteras,Access Rd. from Rt. 12
HABS NC-357-A
HABS DLC/PP-1993:NC-3
8ph/6pg/1pc L

Cape Hatteras Lighthouse,Principal Keeper's Dwell. (Cape Hatteras National Seashore)
Point of Cape Hatteras,Access Rd. from Rt. 12
HABS NC-357-B
HABS DLC/PP-1993:NC-3
9ph/6pg/1pc L

Cape Hatteras National Seashore; see Cape Hatteras Lighthouse,Double Keeper's Dwelling

Cape Hatteras National Seashore; see Cape Hatteras Lighthouse,Principal Keeper's Dwell.

DUCK VIC.

Caffey's Inlet,Life-Saving Station
State Rt. 1200
HABS NC-207
HABS NC,27-DUCK.V,1-
9dr L

MANTEO VIC.

Fort Raleigh
U.S. 64-264
HABS NC-389
H

Fort Raleigh,Entrance Gate
U.S. 64-264
HABS NC-389-A
HABS DLC/PP-1992:NC-4
1ph/1pc L

Fort Raleigh,Fort
U.S. 64-264
HABS NC-389-D
HABS DLC/PP-1992:NC-4
2ph/1pc L

Fort Raleigh,Visitor Center (Lost Colony Activities Building)
U.S. 64-264
HABS NC-389-B
HABS DLC/PP-1992:NC-4
1ph/1pc L

Fort Raleigh,Waterside Theater (Lost Colony Production Amphitheater)
U.S. 64-264
HABS NC-389-C
HABS DLC/PP-1992:NC-4
1ph/1pc L

Lost Colony Activities Building; see Fort Raleigh,Visitor Center

Lost Colony Production Amphitheater; see Fort Raleigh,Waterside Theater

DAVIDSON COUNTY

LEXINGTON

Davidson County Courthouse,Old
Main & Center Sts.
HABS NC-300
HABS NC,29-LEX,1-
1ph L

LEXINGTON VIC.

Caldcleuch House
HABS NC-123
HABS NC,29-LEX.V,1-
2ph/1pg L

SOUTHMONT VIC.

Bridge No. 249
State Rt. 2294 spannning Abbotts Creek
HAER NC-21
HAER NC,29-SOUM.V,1-
4ph/1pg/1pc L

DAVIE COUNTY

MOCKSVILLE VIC.

Cooleemee Plantation (Hairston House)
U. S. Rt. 64
HABS NC-212
HABS NC,30-MOCK.V,1-
14dr/2pg L

Hairston House; see Cooleemee Plantation

DUPLIN COUNTY

FAISON VIC.

Hill,Buckner,House; see Taylor-Hill House

Taylor-Hill House (Hill,Buckner,House)
State Rt. 1354
HABS NC-174
HABS NC,31-FAISO.V,1-
1ph L

DURHAM COUNTY

DURHAM

American Tobacco Company
HAER NC-10
HAER NC,32-DURM,2-
7ph/10pg L

Liggett & Myers Tobacco Co.,Watts Tobacco Warehous (Watts,George W. ,Tobacco Warehouse)
Gregson & W. Peabody Sts.
HAER NC-5
HAER NC,32-DURM,3-
2dr/fr L

Orange Factory Village
Old Orange Factory Rd. (State Rt. 1628)
HABS NC-9
HABS NC,32-ORFA,1-
1dr/1ph/49pg/1pc L

Orange Factory Village,Dawson House (Supervisor's House)
Old Orange Factory Rd. (State Rt. 1628)
HABS NC-9-A
HABS NC,32-ORFA,2-
7ph/1pg/1pc L

Orange Factory Village,House No. 10
Old Orange Factory Rd. (State Rt. 1628)
HABS NC-9-E
HABS NC,32-ORFA,6-
2dr/3ph/7pg/1pc L

Orange Factory Village,House No. 12
Old Factory Rd. (State Rt. 1628)
HABS NC-9-F
HABS NC,32-ORFA,7-
2dr/3ph/7pg/1pc L

Orange Factory Village,House No. 13
Old Orange Factory Rd. (State Rt. 1628)
HABS NC-9-G
HABS NC,32-ORFA,8-
2dr/3ph/7pg/1pc L

Orange Factory Village,House No. 14
Old Orange Factory Rd. (State Rt. 1628)
HABS NC-9-H
HABS NC,32-ORFA,9-
2dr/3ph/7pg/1pc L

Orange Factory Village,House No. 16
Old Orange Factory Rd. (State Rt. 1628)
HABS NC-9-I
HABS NC,32-ORFA,10-
2dr/3ph/7pg/1pc L

Orange Factory Village,House No. 5
Old Orange Factory Rd. (State Rt. 1628)
HABS NC-9-B
HABS NC,32-ORFA,3-
2dr/3ph/7pg/1pc L

Orange Factory Village,House No. 8
Old Orange Factory Rd. (State Rt. 1628)
HABS NC-9-C
HABS NC,32-ORFA,4-
2dr/3ph/6pg/1pc L

Orange Factory Village,House No. 9
Old Orange Factory Rd. (State Rt. 1628)
HABS NC-9-D
HABS NC,32-ORFA,5-
2dr/3ph/7pg/1pc L

Supervisor's House; see Orange Factory Village,Dawson House

Watts,George W. ,Tobacco Warehouse; see Liggett & Myers Tobacco Co.,Watts Tobacco Warehous

DURHAM VIC.

Bridge No. 28
State Rt. 1004 spanning Flatt River
HAER NC-22
HAER NC,32-DURM.V,1-
6ph/1pg/1pc L

EDGECOMBE COUNTY

TARBORO

Cotton Press; see Norfleet Plantation,Cotton Press

Lanier House (Pender-Lanier House)
1002 Main St.
HABS NC-26
HABS NC,33-TARB,1-
1ph/1pg L

Norfleet Plantation,Cotton Press (Cotton Press)
Albermarle St. (moved from Norfleet Plantation)
HABS NC-60
HABS NC,33-TARB,2-
3dr/4ph/2pg/1pc L

Pender-Lanier House; see Lanier House

Taylor,Brinson,& Aycock Law Offices; see Williams,Dr. Don,House

Williams,Dr. Don,House (Taylor,Brinson,& Aycock Law Offices)
Saint James St.
HABS NC-100
HABS NC,33-TARB,3-
1ph L

TARBORO VIC.

Coolmore (Powell House)
U. S. Rt. 64
HABS NC-59
HABS NC,33-TARB.V,1-
1ph/1pg L

Powell House; see Coolmore

FORSYTH COUNTY

BETHABARA

Bethabara Parsonage (Brewers House; Mucke House; Mickey House)
U. S. Rt. 421
HABS NC-193
HABS NC,34-OLTO,2-
4dr/7ph/5pg L

Brewers House; see Bethabara Parsonage

Mickey House; see Bethabara Parsonage

Mucke House; see Bethabara Parsonage

BETHANIA

Jones Livestock Barn (Jones Plantation Barn; Salem Tavern Barn)
Tobaccoville Rd. (moved to NC,Winston-Salem)
HABS NC-240
HABS NC,34-BETH,1A-
14dr L

Jones Plantation Barn; see Jones Livestock Barn

Salem Tavern Barn; see Jones Livestock Barn

CLEMMONS

Fries Manufacturing & Power Company,Idols Station
Yadkin River
HAER NC-9
HAER NC,34-CLEM.V,1-
7ph/18pg/1pc L

KERNERSVILLE

Korner's Folly
271 S. Main St.
HABS NC-208
HABS NC,34-KERN,1-
10dr/10ph/1pg/1pc L

Korner's Folly,Brick Privy
271 S. Main St.
HABS NC-208-A
HABS NC,34-KERN,1A-
2ph/1pc L

OLD TOWN

Bethabara Moravian Church (Gemeinhaus)
2147 Bethabara Rd. (State Rt. 1681)
HABS NC-12-C-4
HABS NC,34-OLTO,1-
6dr/8ph/3pg/fr L

Gemeinhaus; see Bethabara Moravian Church

WINSTON-SALEM

Anstalt; see Salem Boys School

Arista Mill,Rehabilitation Center
HAER NC-17
5dr L

Belk Building; see Huntley-Hall-Stockton Building

Belo House
455 S. Main St.
HABS NC-103
HABS NC,34-WINSA,9-
4ph/1pg L

Bishop's House; see 519 Church Street (House)

Boner,John Henry,House; see Lick-Boner House

Cape Fear Bank; see Loesch,Israel,Bank & House

Chimney House
113 W. Walnut (moved to E. Tennessee)
HABS NC-242
HABS NC,34-WINSA,13-
2ph L

519 Church Street (House) (Bishop's House; Minister's House)
HABS NC-301
HABS NC,34-WINSA,18-
1ph L

Ebert-Reich House; see Reich,Christian,House

Girls Boarding School Annex; see Salem College,Old Chapel Annex

Gothic Revival House (Steiner House; Home Church Parsonage)
513 S. Church St.
HABS NC-246
HABS NC,34-WINSA,17-
1ph L

Hill,James S. ,House
914 Stadium Dr.
HABS NC-327
HABS NC,34-WINSA,20-
4ph/1pg/1pc L

Home Church Parsonage; see Gothic Revival House

Home Moravian Church
529 S. Church St.
HABS NC-134
HABS NC,34-WINSA,1-
3ph L

House of the Community Physician (Vierling House)
463 S. Church St.
HABS NC-162
HABS NC,34-WINSA,5-
3ph L

Huntley-Hall-Stockton Building (Belk Building)
450 N. Trade St.
HABS NC-324
HABS NC,34-WINSA,21-
7ph/3pg/1pc L

Jones Livestock Barn (Jones Plantation Barn; Salem Tavern Barn)
Old Salem,S. Main St. (moved from NC,Bethania)
HABS NC-240
HABS NC,34-BETH,1A-
14dr L

Jones Plantation Barn; see Jones Livestock Barn

Land Office Building,Old (Vorsteher House; Warden House; Moravian Archives & Music Foundation)
501 S. Main St.
HABS NC-104
HABS NC,34-WINSA,10-
1ph L

Leinbach,Henry,House
508 S. Main St.
HABS NC-12-C-2
HABS NC,34-WINSA,7-
6dr/4ph/1pg L

Lick-Boner House (Boner,John Henry,House)
512 Salt St.
HABS NC-241
HABS NC,34-WINSA,12-
2ph L

Loesch,Israel,Bank & House (Cape Fear Bank)
500 S. Main St.
HABS NC-243
HABS NC,34-WINSA,14-
4ph L

Minister's House; see 519 Church Street (House)

Moravian Archives & Music Foundation; see Land Office Building,Old

Reich,Christian,House (Ebert-Reich House)
731 S. Main St.
HABS NC-244
HABS NC,34-WINSA,15-
2ph L

Salem Boys School (Wachovia Historical Society Museum; Anstalt)
Main & Academy Sts.
HABS NC-12-C-1
HABS NC,34-WINSA,6-
6dr/10ph/3pg/fr L

Salem College,Administration Building; see Salem College,Office Building

Salem College,Alumnae House; see Salem College,Old Chapel Annex

Salem College,Brothers House (Single Brothers House; Single Brethren's House)
600 S. Main St.
HABS NC-102
HABS NC,34-WINSA,8C-
5ph/1pg L

Salem College,General View
Salem Square
HABS NC-141
HABS NC,34-WINSA,8-
1ph L

Salem College,Office Building (Salem College,Administration Building)
9-11 Academy St.
HABS NC-158
HABS NC,34-WINSA,2-
5ph L

Salem College,Old Chapel Annex (Girls Boarding School Annex; Salem College,Alumnae House)
601 S. Church St.
HABS NC-95
HABS NC,34-WINSA,8A-
1ph L

Salem College,Sisters House (Single Sisters House)
619-621 S. Church St.
HABS NC-101
HABS NC,34-WINSA,8B-
6ph/1pg L

Salem Manufacturing Company,Arista Cotton Mill
Brookstown & Marshall Sts.
HAER NC-3
HAER NC,34-WINSA,19-
6dr/13ph/8pg/1pc/fr L

Salem Tavern; see Tavern,The

Salem Tavern Barn; see Jones Livestock Barn

Schulz House & Shoe Shop; see Turner House

Single Brethren's House; see Salem College,Brothers House

Single Brothers House; see Salem College,Brothers House

Single Sisters House; see Salem College,Sisters House

Steiner House; see Gothic Revival House

Tavern,The (Salem Tavern)
800 S. Main St.
HABS NC-12-C-3
HABS NC,34-WINSA,4-
12dr/8ph/7pg/fr L

Turner House (Schulz House & Shoe Shop)
712-714 S. Main St.
HABS NC-245
HABS NC,34-WINSA,16-
1ph L

Vierling House; see House of the Community Physician

Vogler,Christoph,House
700 S. Main St.
HABS NC-105
HABS NC,34-WINSA,11-
2ph L

Vorsteher House; see Land Office Building,Old

Wachovia Historical Society Museum; see Salem Boys School

Warden House; see Land Office Building,Old

WINSTON-SALEM VIC.

Rock,Adam Spach,House; see Spach,Adam,House

Spach,Adam,House (Rock,Adam Spach,House)
HABS NC-94
HABS NC,34- ,1-
8ph L

FRANKLIN COUNTY

LOUISBURG

Person,Prudence,House
603 N. Main St.
HABS NC-180
HABS NC,35-LOUBU,1-
1ph L

Shaw House
114 Main St.
HABS NC-181
HABS NC,35-LOUBU,2-
1ph L

LOUISBURG VIC.

Bunn Road; see Green Hill Place

Cascine (Perry House)
State Rt. 1702
HABS NC-6
HABS NC,35-LOUBU.V,1-
12dr/9ph/2pg/fr L

Cascine Mill; see Perry Mill

Collins Place,Old
State Rt. 561 (moved to NC,Jacksonville)
HABS NC-224
HABS NC,35-LOUBU.V,5-
14dr L

Green Hill Place (Bunn Road)
State Rts. 1760 & 1761
HABS NC-183
HABS NC,35-LOUBU.V,3-
3ph L

House,Early
HABS NC-182
HABS NC,35-LOUBU.V,2-
1ph L

Perry House; see Cascine

Perry Mill (Cascine Mill)
U. S. Rt. 401
HABS NC-184
HABS NC,35-LOUBU.V,4-
1ph L

PEARCES

Las Perry Apple Mill & Press
HAER NC-13
HAER NC,35-PEARC.V,1-
5pg L

GASTON COUNTY

MC ADENVILLE

McAden Mill,Number 2
Main St.
HABS NC-199
HABS NC,36-McAD,1B-
7dr L

GATES COUNTY

BUCKLAND

Buckland; see Smith House

Smith House (Buckland)
NC Rt. 37
HABS NC-73
HABS NC,37-BUCLA,1-
2ph/1pg L

GATES VIC.

Riddick House
U. S. Rt. 13
HABS NC-71
HABS NC,37-GAT.V,1-
3ph/1pg L

Riddick House,Little (Riddick House,Old)
U. S. Rt. 13
HABS NC-80
HABS NC,37-GAT.V,2-
2ph/1pg L

Riddick House,Old; see Riddick House,Little

GATESVILLE VIC.

Carter Farmhouse
State Rt. 1100
HABS NC-32
HABS NC,37-GATV.V,1-
1ph/1pg L

Carter Farms,Barns
State Rt. 1100
HABS NC-33
HABS NC,37-GATV.V,1A-
1ph/1pg L

Hinton House
Main St.
HABS NC-50
HABS NC,37-GATV.V,3-
1ph/1pg L

Roberts,John,House
(moved to Carter Farm,State Rt. 1100)
HABS NC-34
HABS NC,37-GATV.V,2-
1ph/1pg L

HOBBSVILLE VIC.

Sumner-Winslow House; see Winslow House

Winslow House (Sumner-Winslow House)
NC Rt. 32
HABS NC-36
HABS NC,37-HOBV.V,1-
1ph/1pg L

MINTONSVILLE VIC.

Walton House
State Rt. 1101
HABS NC-140
HABS NC,37-HOBV.V,2-
2ph L

SANDY CROSS

Huffheimer House
HABS NC-88
HABS NC,37-SANC,1-
1ph/1pg L

TROTVILLE VIC.

Stallings,Whitmer,House (Whitstallings House)
State Rt. 1415
HABS NC-248
HABS NC,37-TROTV.V,1-
2ph L

Whitstallings House; see Stallings,Whitmer,House

GUILFORD COUNTY

GREENSBORO

Buick Motor Co. & Greensboro Motor Co. Dealerships
309 & 315 N. Elm St.
HABS NC-232
HABS NC,41-GREBO,2-
11ph/6pg L

Dick,Judge,House; see Dunleith

Dunleith (Dick,Judge,House)
677 Chestnut St.
HABS NC-231
HABS NC,41-GREBO,1-
29dr L

Henry,O. ,Hotel
N. Elm & Bellemeade Sts.
HABS NC-233
HABS NC,41-GREBO,3-
17ph/6pg L

Pomona Terra Cotta Manufacturing Company
W. Market St.
HAER NC-2
HAER NC,41-GREBO,4-
3dr/fr L

JAMESTOWN

Friends School & Meetinghouse (Jamestown Friends Meetinghouse; Quaker Meetinghouse)
High Point City Park
HABS NC-92
HABS NC,41-JAMTO,2-
1ph L

Jamestown Friends Meetinghouse; see Friends School & Meetinghouse

McCulloch Gold Mill
Copper Branch,N. of State Rt. 1153
HAER NC-7
HAER NC,41-JAMTO.V,1-
6dr/7ph/8pg/fr L

Mendenhall House
(Mendenhall,Richard,Plantation House)
U. S. Rt. 29-70A
HABS NC-37
HABS NC,41-JAMTO,1-
1ph/1pg L

Mendenhall,Richard,Plantation House; see Mendenhall House

Quaker Meetinghouse; see Friends School & Meetinghouse

JAMESTOWN VIC.

Bridge No. 53; see North Carolina Route 1334 Bridge

Mendenhall Counting House
HABS NC-97
HABS NC,41-JAMTO,3-
3ph L

North Carolina Route 1334 Bridge
(Bridge No. 53)
Spanning Deep River
HAER NC-24
HAER NC,41-JAMTO.V,2-
5ph/1pg/1pc L

OAK RIDGE

Benbow House
HABS NC-96
HABS NC,4-OAKRI.V,1-
1ph L

HALIFAX COUNTY

AIRLIE VIC.

Prospect Hill
HABS NC-157
HABS NC,42-AIRLI.V,1-
5ph/2pg L

ENFIELD VIC.

Cedar Grove (Whitaker,Jack,House; Strawberry Hill)
Scotland Neck Rd.
HABS NC-227
HABS NC,42-ENFI.V,
20dr L

Strawberry Hill; see Cedar Grove

Whitaker,Jack,House; see Cedar Grove

HALIFAX

Clerk's Office,Old; see Halifax County Clerk's Office

Constitution House
(Constitution-Burgess House)
E. of Market Sq.
HABS NC-29
HABS NC,42-HAL,3-
3ph/1pg L

Constitution-Burgess House; see Constitution House

Ferrell,Michael,Counting House
(McMahon,Michael,Store)
Main St.
HABS NC-13
HABS NC,42-HAL,1-
1ph/1pg L

Gaol,Old; see Halifax County Jail

Grove,The
HABS NC-177
HABS NC,42-HAL,5-
4pg L

Halifax County Clerk's Office (Clerk's Office,Old)
King & Market Sts.
HABS NC-15
HABS NC,42-HAL,2-
5dr/2ph/1pg L

Halifax County Jail (Gaol,Old)
King St.
HABS NC-200
HABS NC,42-HAL,6-
6dr L

House,Dutch Roof (Owens House)
Saint David St.
HABS NC-176
HABS NC,42-HAL,4-
1ph L

McMahon,Michael,Store; see Ferrell,Michael,Counting House

Owens House; see House,Dutch Roof

Pope House (Sally-Billy House)
Saint Andrew's St. (moved from NC,Scotland Neck)
HABS NC-76
HABS NC,42-SCON.V,2-
2ph/2pg L

Sally-Billy House; see Pope House

SCOTLAND NECK VIC.

Durham Farm; see Smith House

Kelvin Grove; see Smith House

Pope House (Sally-Billy House)
State Rt. 1117 (moved to NC,Halifax)
HABS NC-76
HABS NC,42-SCON.V,2-
2ph/2pg L

Sally-Billy House; see Pope House

Smith House (Durham Farm; Kelvin Grove)
State Rt. 1118
HABS NC-66
HABS NC,42-SCON.V,1-
3ph/1pg L

TILLERY VIC.

Glen Burne; see Tillery,Junius,House

Hermitage,The; see Tillery,Junius,House

Tillery,Junius,House (Hermitage,The; Glen Burne)
NC Rt. 481
HABS NC-17
HABS NC,42-TIL.V,1-
13ph/1pg L

HAYWOOD COUNTY

CATALOOCHEE

Conrad,Jim,Smokehouse; see Pioneer Farmstead,Meat House

Great Smoky Mountains National Park; see Pioneer Farmstead,Meat House

Great Smoky Mountains National Park; see Tyne,Woody,Cabin

Pioneer Farmstead,Meat House
(Conrad,Jim,Smokehouse; Great Smoky Mountains National Park)
(moved to NC,Cherokee Vic.)
HABS NC-202
HABS NC,87-NEWGA.V,1C-
1dr/5ph/1pc L

Tyne,Woody,Cabin (Great Smoky Mountains National Park)
HABS NC-5
HABS NC,44-CAT,1-
3dr/8ph/3pg L

HENDERSON COUNTY

FLAT ROCK

Buck House; see Memminger House

Church of St. John-in-the-Wilderness
U. S. Rt. 25
HABS NC-12-A-1
HABS NC,45-FLARO,1-
7dr/8ph/2pg L

Memminger House (Sandburg Estate; Buck House; Sandburg,Carl,National Historic Site)
State Rt. 1123
HABS NC-305
HABS NC,45-FLARO,2-
4dr L

Sandburg Estate; see Memminger House

Sandburg,Carl,National Historic Site; see Memminger House

FLETCHER

Calvery Episcopal Church
U. S. Rt. 25
HABS NC-12-A-3
HABS NC,45-FLECH,1-
4ph L

HENDERSONVILLE

Dixon's Sanitorium; see Judson College

Fletcher House
NC Rt. 69
HABS NC-264
HABS NC,91-HEND.V,2-
1ph L

Judson College (Western North Carolina Female College; Dixon's Sanitorium)
Third Ave. & W. Flemming St.
HABS NC-12-A-2
HABS NC,45-HENVI,1-
11dr/5ph/1pg L

St. James Episcopal Church
766 N. Main St.
HABS NC-249
HABS NC,45-HENVI,2-
1ph L

Western North Carolina Female College; see Judson College

MURFREESBORO

Melrose; see Murfree House

Murfree House (Melrose)
100 E. Broad St.
HABS NC-14
HABS NC,46-MURF,3-
2ph/1pg L

TUXEDO VIC.

Bridge No. 63; see North Carolina Route 1852 Bridge

North Carolina Route 1852 Bridge (Bridge No. 63)
Spanning Lake Summit
HAER NC-36
HAER NC,45-TUX.V,1-
10ph/1pg/1pc L

HERTFORD COUNTY

MURFREESBORO

Britton House
Main St.
HABS NC-12
HABS NC,46-MURF,2-
1ph/1pg L

Chowan College (Columns,The; McDowell Columns Building)
Jones Dr.
HABS NC-30
HABS NC,46-MURF,6-
2ph/1pg L

Columns,The; see Chowan College

Freeman House (Hertford Academy Building)
200 E. Broad St.
HABS NC-19
HABS NC,46-MURF,4-
2ph/1pg L

Harrell House (Pipkin,Dr. Isaac,House)
207 Wynne St.
HABS NC-11
HABS NC,46-MURF,1-
1ph/1pg L

Hertford Academy Building; see Freeman House

Hotel,Old (Lassiter Hotel)
417 W. Main St.
HABS NC-31
HABS NC,46-MURF,7-
2ph/1pg L

Lassiter Hotel; see Hotel,Old

McDowell Columns Building; see Chowan College

Methodist Church
HABS NC-98
HABS NC,46-MURF,11-
1ph L

Murfree Law Office; see Post Office,Old

Pipkin,Dr. Isaac,House; see Harrell House

Post Office,Old (Murfree Law Office)
318 Williams St.
HABS NC-129
HABS NC,46-MURF,12-
1ph L

Rea,William,Store; see White & Britton Store

Smith House
Williams & Fourth Sts.
HABS NC-74
HABS NC,46-MURF,9-
2ph/1pg L

Trader House (Wheeler,John,House)
403 E. Broad St.
HABS NC-57
HABS NC,46-MURF,8-
2ph/1pg L

Vaughn,Uriah,House (Yeates-Myrick-Vaughn House)
415 W. Main St.
HABS NC-21
HABS NC,46-MURF,5-
1ph/1pg L

Wheeler,John,House; see Trader House

White & Britton Store (Rea,William,Store)
Williams & Fifth Sts.
HABS NC-89
HABS NC,46-MURF,10-
1ph/1pg L

Williams House(Doorway)
320 Williams St.
HABS NC-130
HABS NC,46-MURF,13-
1ph L

Yeates-Myrick-Vaughn House; see Vaughn,Uriah,House

IREDELL COUNTY

MOUNT MOURNE

Houston Farmhouse
State Rt. 1102
HABS NC-155
HABS NC,49-MOUMO,1-
1ph L

Morrison House; see Mount Mourne

Mount Mourne (Morrison House)
State Rts. 1170 & 1189
HABS NC-154
HABS NC,49-MOUMO,2-
1ph L

STATESVILLE

Madison Building; see Statesville Commercial Historic District

Statesville Commercial Historic District (Madison Building)
Btwn. 125 & 145 E. Broad St.
HABS NC-322-B
HABS NC,49-STATV,2-
6ph/1pg/1pc L

Statesville Commercial Historic District (Sterns Building)
145-153 E. Broad St.
HABS NC-322-A
HABS NC,49-STATV,1-
15ph/4pg/1pc L

Sterns Building; see Statesville Commercial Historic District

JACKSON COUNTY

DILLSBORO VIC.

Bridge No. 63; see North Carolina Route 1392 Bridge

North Carolina Route 1392 Bridge (Bridge No. 63)
Spanning Tuckaseegee River
HAER NC-25
HAER NC,50-DILL.V,1-
7ph/1pg/1pc L

JOHNSTON COUNTY

SMITHFIELD

Hastings House
Johnston St. (moved to First St.)
HABS NC-303
HABS NC,51-SMIT,1-
4dr L

LINCOLN COUNTY

IRON STATION VIC.

Forney,David,Mansion; see Ingleside

Ingleside (Forney,David,Mansion)
State Rt. 1383
HABS NC-250
HABS NC,55-LINC.V,1-
2ph L

LABORATORY VIC.

Bridge No. 22; see North Carolina Route 1412 Bridge

North Carolina Route 1412 Bridge (Bridge No. 22)
Spanning Leepers Creek
HAER NC-26
HAER NC,55-LAB.V,1-
11ph/1pg/1pc L

LINCOLNTON VIC.

Brevard House (Mount Tisgah; Mount Tirzah)
State Rt. 1360 Vic.
HABS NC-251
HABS NC,55-LINC.V,2-
2ph L

Mount Tirzah; see Brevard House

Mount Tisgah; see Brevard House

MAIDEN VIC.

St. Matthew's Arbor (St. Matthew's Reformed Church Meeting Shed; St. Matthew's Reformed Church)
State Rt. 321
HABS NC-217
HABS NC,55-MAID.V,
7dr L

St. Matthew's Reformed Church; see St. Matthew's Arbor

St. Matthew's Reformed Church Meeting Shed; see St. Matthew's Arbor

MADISON COUNTY

MARSHALL

Marshall Mill.Co.Cmplx,Capitola Dam
French Broad River
HAER NC-19-B
HAER NC,58-MARSH,1B-
2ph/3pg/1pc L

Marshall Mill.Co.Cmplx,Capitola Mfg.Co.Cotton Mill
French Broad River,south side
HAER NC-19-C
HAER NC,58-MARSH,1C-
6pg L

Marshall Mill.Co.Cmplx,Grist Mill
French Broad River,south side
HAER NC-19-A
HAER NC,58-MARSH,1A-
12ph/8pg/1pc L

Marshall Milling Company Complex
French Broad River,south side
HAER NC-19
HAER NC,58-MARSH,1-
4ph/1pc L

MCDOWELL COUNTY

MARION VIC.

Carson House (Tavern,Old)
U. S. Rt. 70
HABS NC-144
HABS NC,56-MARI.V,1-
3ph L

Tavern,Old; see Carson House

NEBO VIC.

Lake James Spillway Bridge
Spanning Lake James Spillway
HAER NC-37
HAER NC,56-NEBO.V,1-
8ph/1pg/1pc L

MECKLENBURG COUNTY

CALDWELL VIC.

Hickory Grove; see Wilson House

Wilson House (Hickory Grove)
NC Rt. 115
HABS NC-12-B-3
HABS NC,60- ,2-
2dr/2ph/fr L

CHARLOTTE

Duke,James Buchanan,House (Lynnewood; White Oaks)
400 Hermitage
HABS NC-321
HABS NC,60-CHAR,1-
34ph/2pc/4ct L

Lynnewood; see Duke,James Buchanan,House

Sugaw Creek Presbyterian Church
101 Sugaw Creek Rd.
HABS NC-12-B-5
HABS NC,60-CHAR.V,3-
2dr/1ph/1pg L

White Oaks; see Duke,James Buchanan,House

CHARLOTTE VIC.

McIntyre Cabin; see McIntyre Log House

McIntyre Log House (McIntyre Cabin)
NC Rt. 271
HABS NC-12-B-4
HABS NC,60- ,3-
1dr/1ph/1pg/fr L

Wallis,Ezekial,Rock House
NC Rt. 27
HABS NC-12-B-1
HABS NC,60- ,1-
1dr/1ph/2pg/fr L

Whitley's Mill
State Rt. 2074
HABS NC-12-B-2
HABS NC,60-CHAR.V,2-
2dr/1ph/1pg/fr L

DAVIDSON

Davidson College,Chambers,Maxwell,Building
HABS NC-61
HABS NC,60-DAVSO,1C-
1ph/1pg L

Davidson College,Eumanean Hall
HABS NC-12-B-7
HABS NC,60-DAVSO,1A-
2dr/3ph/1pg/fr L

Davidson College,Philanthropic Hall
HABS NC-12-B-8
HABS NC,60-DAVSO,1B-
2dr/3ph/1pg/fr L

MITCHELL COUNTY

BURNSVILLE VIC.

Bridge No. 229; see North Carolina Route 1336 Bridge

North Carolina Route 1336 Bridge (Bridge No. 229)
Spanning North Toe River
HAER NC-27
HAER NC,61-BURV.V,1-
8ph/1pg/1pc L

MONTGOMERY COUNTY

ALBEMARLE

Coggins Gold Mine,Rich-Cog Mining Company
HAER NC-4
HAER NC,62-ALBE,1-
8dr/15ph/15pg/2pc/fr L

NASH COUNTY

DORTCHES

Dortch House
State Rt. 1527
HABS NC-68
HABS NC,64-BATBO.V,1-
4ph/1pg L

ROCKY MOUNT

Battle House
NC Rt. 43-48 (Falls Rd.)
HABS NC-201
HABS NC,64-ROCMO,1-
8dr L

ROCKY MOUNT MILLS

Bunn House; see Lewis House

House,The Brick; see Lewis House

Lewis House (Stonewall; Bunn House; House,The Brick)
HABS NC-58
HABS NC,64-ROCMO.V,1-
1ph/1pg L

Stonewall; see Lewis House

NEW HANOVER COUNTY

WILMINGTON

Bellamy Mansion
503 Market St.
HABS NC-198
HABS NC,65-WILM,3-
11dr/4pg L

Cassidey-Harper House; see Harper House

Dudley Mansion House (Dudley,Gov. ,House)
S. Front & Nun Sts.
HABS NC-307
HABS NC,65-WILM,1-
2ph L

Dudley,Gov. ,House; see Dudley Mansion House

Harper House (Cassidey-Harper House)
1-5 Church St.
HABS NC-252
HABS NC,65-WILM,2-
1ph L

Jowaha Building; see Wilmington Historic District

Wilmington City Hall-Thalian Hall
102 N. Third St.
HABS NC-7
HABS NC,65-WILM,4-
7ph/6pg/1pc L

Wilmington Historic District (Jowaha Building)
2 S. Water St.
HABS NC-325-A
HABS NC,65-WILM,5-
3ph/1pg/1pc L

NORTHAMPTON COUNTY

JACKSON VIC

Ransom,Matt Whittaker,House; see Verona

Verona (Ransom,Matt Whittaker,House)
U. S. Rt. 158
HABS NC-214
HABS NC,66-JACK.V,1-
10dr L

ONSLOW COUNTY

JACKSONVILLE

Collins Place,Old
Warrenton Way (moved from NC,Louisburg Vic.)
HABS NC-224
HABS NC,35-LOUBU.V,1-
14dr L

RICHLANDS VIC.

Ashley House
NC 258-24 South of SR 1229
HABS NC-374
HABS DLC/PP-1993:NC-5
6ph/3pg/1pc L

Brinson,Clarence,House
NC 258-24 South of SR 1229
HABS NC-375
HABS DLC/PP-1993:NC-5
6ph/3pg/1pc L

Richard House
NC 258-24 South of SR 1229
HABS NC-371
HABS DLC/PP-1993:NC-5
6ph/3pg/1pc L

ORANGE COUNTY

CHAPEL HILL

Chapel of the Cross
304 E. Franklin St.
HABS NC-195
HABS NC,68-CHAP,1-
7dr/6ph/4pg L

HILLSBOROUGH

Berry Brick House
208 W. Queen St.
HABS NC-315
HABS NC,68-HILBO,7-
2ph/4pg/1pc L

Burke-Heartt House; see Heartsease

Cottage,Frame,opposite Burke-Heartt House (Webb House)
E. Queen St.
HABS NC-267
HABS NC,68-HILBO,5-
1ph L

Eagle Lodge (Masonic Lodge; Masonic Hall; King Street Opera House)
142 W. King St.
HABS NC-268
HABS NC,68-HILBO,6-
3ph/3pg/1pc L

Forrest,R. O. ,House; see Twin Chimneys

Hasell-Nash House (Nash House)
116 W. Queen St.
HABS NC-160
HABS NC,68-HILBO,2-
7ph/3pg/1pc L

Heartsease (Burke-Heartt House)
113 E. Queen St.
HABS NC-159
HABS NC,68-HILBO,1-
8ph/3pg/1pc L

Hillsborough Presbyterian Church
Churton & W. Tryon Sts.
HABS NC-238
HABS NC,68-HILBO,8-
3ph/3pg/1pc L

King Street Opera House; see Eagle Lodge

Little Hawfields
HABS NC-164
HABS NC,68-HILBO,3-
1ph L

Lloyd House; see Nash Law Office

Masonic Hall; see Eagle Lodge

Masonic Lodge; see Eagle Lodge

Moorefields
State Rt. 1135
HABS NC-271
HABS NC,68-HILBO,9-
5ph/4pg/1pc L

Murphy,Dr. Robert,House; see Seven Hearths

Nash House; see Hasell-Nash House

Nash Law Office (Lloyd House)
143 W. Margaret Ln.
HABS NC-314
HABS NC,68-HILBO,11A-
4ph/4pg/1pc L

Nash-Hooper House
118 W. Tryon St.
HABS NC-272
HABS NC,68-HILBO,10-
3ph/4pg/1pc L

Nash-Hooper House,Outbuilding
118 W. Tryon St.
HABS NC-272-A
HABS NC,68-HILBO,10A-
1ph/1pc L

Orange County Courthouse
King & Churton Sts.
HABS NC-191
HABS NC,68-HILBO,4-
20dr/8ph/1pg/1pc L

Palmer House (Patterson-Palmer House)
173 W. Margaret Lane
HABS NC-222
HABS NC,68-HILBO,12-
11dr/4ph/10pg/1pc L

Patterson-Palmer House; see Palmer House

Ruffin House (Ruffin-Roulhac House)
Churton & Orange Sts.
HABS NC-312
HABS NC,68-HILBO.V,2-
1ph/1pc L

Ruffin-Roulhac House; see Ruffin House

Ruffin,Chief Justice Thomas,Law Office
Burnside,Cameron Park
HABS NC-270
HABS NC,68-HILBO,17A-
1ph/3pg/1pc L

Sans Souci
E. Corbin St. (formerly North St.)
HABS NC-221
HABS NC,68-HILBO,13-
4ph/3pg/1pc L

Sans Souci,Cain,William,Office
E. Corbin St. (formerly North St.)
HABS NC-221-B
HABS NC,68-HILBO,13B-
1ph L

Sans Souci,Kitchen
E. Corbin St. (formerly North St.)
HABS NC-221-A
HABS NC,68-HILBO,13A-
1ph L

Seven Hearths (Murphy,Dr. Robert,House)
157 E. King St.
HABS NC-223
HABS NC,68-HILBO,14-
14dr/5ph/5pg/1pc L

St. Matthew's Episcopal Church
St. Mary's Rd.
HABS NC-273
HABS NC,68-HILBO,16-
5ph/2pg/1pc L

Twin Chimneys (Forrest,R. O. ,House)
168 W. King St.
HABS NC-313
HABS NC,68-HILBO,15-
5ph/5pg/1pc L

Webb House; see Cottage,Frame,opposite Burke-Heartt House

HILLSBOROUGH VIC.

Ayr Mount (Kirkland Place)
Saint Mary's Rd.
HABS NC-220
HABS NC,68-HILBO,18-
20dr/9ph/5pg/1pc L

Barracks,The (Hillsborough Military Academy)
Barracks Rd.
HABS NC-269
HABS NC,68-HILBO.V,1-
2ph L

Hillsborough Military Academy; see Barracks,The

Kirkland Place; see Ayr Mount

PASQUOTANK COUNTY

ELIZABETH CITY

Charles House
710 W. Colonial Ave.
HABS NC-170
HABS NC,70-ELICI,4-
5ph/2pg L

Christ Church
Church & McMorine Sts.
HABS NC-46
HABS NC,70-ELICI,1-
1ph/1pg L

Fearing House; see Grice-Fearing House

Grice-Fearing House (Fearing House)
200 S. Road St.
HABS NC-169
HABS NC,70-ELICI,3-
4ph/2pg L

Smithson House (Whitehurst-Temple House)
Newland Hwy.
HABS NC-168
HABS NC,70-ELICI,2-
4ph/3pg L

Whitehurst-Temple House; see Smithson House

ELIZABETH CITY VIC.

Blackbeard House; see House,Brick

House,Brick (House,Old Brick; Teach,Edward,House; Blackbeard House; Jackson House)
182 Brick House Ln.
HABS NC-65
HABS NC,70-ELICI.V,1-
1ph/1pg L

House,Old Brick; see House,Brick

Jackson House; see House,Brick

Teach,Edward,House; see House,Brick

NIXONTON

Customs House; see Lane House

Lane House (Customs House)
State Rt. 1137
HABS NC-44
HABS NC,70-NIXTO,1-
3ph/1pg L

PENDER COUNTY

TOPSAIL SOUND

Ashe's Neck; see Sloop Point Plantation

MacMillan House; see Sloop Point Plantation

Sloop Point Plantation (MacMillan House; Ashe's Neck)
U. S. Rt. 17,Holly Ridge Vic.
HABS NC-219
HABS NC,71-HOL.V,1-
12dr L

PERQUIMANS COUNTY

BETHEL VIC.

Ashland (Skinner,John,House)
Harvey Point
HABS NC-25
HABS NC,72-BETH.V,2-
2ph/1pg L

Bateman House (Gilbert-Bateman House)
HABS NC-43
HABS NC,72-BETH.V,3-
1ph/1pg L

Cedar Vale (Gatling,John,House)
State Rt. 1339
HABS NC-49
HABS NC,72-BETH.V,4-
1ph/1pg L

Felton,Elisha,House; see Pender House

Gatling,John,House; see Cedar Vale

Gilbert-Bateman House; see Bateman House

Harrell,James,House
State Rt. 1347
HABS NC-253
HABS NC,72-BETH.V,8-
1ph L

Myers House (Myers-White House)
State Rt. 1347
HABS NC-22
HABS NC,72-BETH.V,1-
1ph/1pg L

Myers-White House; see Myers House

Documentation: **ct** color transparencies **dr** measured drawings **fr** field records
pc photograph captions **pg** pages of text **ph** photographs

Pender House (Felton,Elisha,House)
State Rt. 1339
HABS NC-99
HABS NC,72-BETH.V,6-
2ph L

Road Landing
State Rts. 1340 & 1339
HABS NC-86
HABS NC,72-BETH.V,5-
1ph/1pg L

Skinner,John,House; see Ashland

White,Isaac,House; see White,Thomas,House

White,Thomas,House (White,Isaac,House)
State Rt. 1339
HABS NC-127
HABS NC,72-BETH.V,7-
2ph L

HERTFORD VIC.

Cove Grove
State Rt. 1301
HABS NC-40
HABS NC,72-HERF.V,2-
2ph/1pg L

Davenport House (Sanders House)
State Rt. 1336
HABS NC-78
HABS NC,72-HERF.V,6-
2ph/1pg L

Fletcher-Skinner House; see Skinner House

Jones,William,House; see Riverside

Newbold-White House; see White-Newbold House

Newby,David,House
State Rt. 1336 (moved from State Rt. 1300)
HABS NC-41
HABS NC,72-NEHO.V,2-
1ph/1pg L

Nixon House (Nixon-Fleetwood House; Wilson,Thomas,House)
State Rt. 1341
HABS NC-126
HABS NC,72-HERF.V,8-
1ph L

Nixon-Fleetwood House; see Nixon House

Riverside (Jones,William,House; Winslow House)
State Rt. 1301
HABS NC-308
HABS NC,72-HERF.V,9-
1ph L

Sanders House; see Davenport House

Skinner House (Fletcher-Skinner House)
State Rt. 1301
HABS NC-55
HABS NC,72-HERF.V,3-
1ph/1pg L

Sumner House (Sumnerville)
State Rt. 1300
HABS NC-63
HABS NC,72-HERF.V,4-
1ph/1pg L

Sumnerville; see Sumner House

White House
State Rt. 1336
HABS NC-75-A
HABS NC,72-HERF.V,10-
2ph L

White-Newbold House (Newbold-White House)
State Rt. 1336
HABS NC-75
HABS NC,72-HERF.V,5-
4ph/1pg L

White,Theophilous,House
State Rt. 1336
HABS NC-254
HABS NC,72-HERF.V,10-
2ph L

Wilson,Thomas,House; see Nixon House

Winslow House; see Riverside

NEW HOPE VIC.

Clayton,Elizabeth Pointer,House; see Perry House

Davis House (Sutton-Newby House)
State Rt. 1300
HABS NC-85
HABS NC,72-NEHOP.V,3-
1ph/1pg L

Land's End; see Leigh House

Leigh House (Land's End)
State Rt. 1300
HABS NC-18
HABS NC,72-HERF.V,1-
1ph/1pg L

Perry House (Clayton,Elizabeth Pointer,House)
State Rt. 1300
HABS NC-133
HABS NC,72-NEHOP.V,4-
1ph/1pg L

Stockton
State Rt. 1329
HABS NC-83
HABS NC,72-HERF.V,7-
1ph/1pg L

Sutton-Newby House; see Davis House

Whedbee House
State Rt. 1316
HABS NC-39
HABS NC,72-NEHOP.V,1-
1ph/1pg L

WINFALL VIC.

Belvidere; see Newby,Exum,House

Newby,Exum,House (Belvidere)
NC Rt. 37
HABS NC-38
HABS NC,72-WINF.V,1-
1ph/1pg L

PERSON COUNTY

HURDLE MILLS VIC.

Person County Bridge No. 35
State Rt. 1120 spanning South Flat River
HAER NC-23
HAER NC,79-HUDMI.V,1-
8ph/1pg/1pc L

WOODSDALE

Woodsdale Station
State Rt. 1322
HABS NC-304
HABS NC,73-WOOD,1-
4dr L

POLK COUNTY

COLUMBUS

Baptist Church (Columbus Baptist Church)
Main St. & Huston Rd.
HABS NC-255
HABS NC,75-COLUM,1-
1ph L

Columbus Baptist Church; see Baptist Church

Polk County Courthouse
Courthouse St.
HABS NC-256
HABS NC,75-COLUM,2-
2ph L

Polk County Jail,Old
Walker St.
HABS NC-257
HABS NC,75-COLUM,3-
1ph L

RICHMOND COUNTY

ROCKINGHAM

Great Falls Mill (Richmond Manufacturing Company)
W. Washington & Broad Ave.
HABS NC-205
HABS NC,77-ROCHM,1-
8dr L

Richmond Manufacturing Company; see Great Falls Mill

ROBESON COUNTY

LUMBER BRIDGE

Presbyterian Church
HABS NC-165
HABS NC,78-LUMB,1-
1ph L

ROCKINGHAM COUNTY

EDEN VIC.

Berry Hill Bridge (State Line Bridge; Rockingham County Bridge No. 98)
Spanning Dan River at NC Rt. 1761 (VA Rt. 880)
HAER NC-38
HAER NC,79-EDEN.V,1-
27ph/18pg/2pc H

Rockingham County Bridge No. 98; see Berry Hill Bridge

State Line Bridge; see Berry Hill Bridge

WENTWORTH

Wright Tavern
NC Rt. 65
HABS NC-161
HABS NC,79-WENT,1-
2ph L

ROWAN COUNTY

GRANITE QUARRY VIC.

Braun,Michael,House (House,Old Stone)
State Rt. 2308
HABS NC-149
HABS NC,80-SALB.V,1-
5ph L

House,Old Stone; see Braun,Michael,House

MILL BRIDGE VIC.

Kerr Mill
Sloan Rd. (State Rt. 1768)
HABS NC-148
HABS NC,80-MILB.V,1A-
10dr/fr L

ROCKWELL VIC.

Grace Evangelical & Reformed Church; see Grace Lower Stone Church

Grace Lower Stone Church (Grace Evangelical & Reformed Church)
State Rts. 1221 & 2335
HABS NC-258
HABS NC,80-FAITH.V,1-
4ph L

Organ Evangelical Lutheran Church (Zion Evangelical Lutheran Church)
State Rt. 1006
HABS NC-259
HABS NC,80-FAITH.V,2-
3ph L

Zion Evangelical Lutheran Church; see Organ Evangelical Lutheran Church

SALISBURY

Beacham's Seafoods Complex; see Yadkin Railway Headquarters Building

Davis House
303 S. Main St.
HABS NC-260
HABS NC,80-SALB,2-
1ph L

Eames,Richard,Building (Salisbury Supply & Commission Company Building)
220-222 N. Depot St.
HABS NC-234
HABS NC,80-SALB,6-
6ph/4pg/1pc L

First Presbyterian Church
W. Innis & Jackson Sts.
HABS NC-218
HABS NC,80-SALB,5-
29dr L

Rowan County Courthouse
200 N. Main St.
HABS NC-12-B-6
HABS NC,80-SALB,1-
3dr/3ph/1pg L

Salisbury Supply & Commission Company Building; see Eames,Richard,Building

Swaringen Wholesale Grocery
210-216 N. Lee St.
HABS NC-235
HABS NC,80-SALB,7-
9ph/6pg/1pc L

Toll House
Cardwell St.
HABS NC-261
HABS NC,80-SALB,3-
1ph L

Whitehead,Marcellus,House
223 N. Fulton St.
HABS NC-262
HABS NC,80-SALB,4-
2ph L

Yadkin Railway Headquarters Building (Beacham's Seafoods Complex)
120-132 E. Council St.
HABS NC-236
HABS NC,80-SALB,8-
12ph/3pg/1pc L

SPENCER

Southern Railway Company:Spencer Shops
HAER NC-8
HAER NC,80-SPEN,1-
4dr/10ph/19pg/1pc/fr L

RUTHERFORD COUNTY

SPINDALE

Cox House; see Spindale Recreation House

Spindale Recreation House (Tavern,Old; Cox House)
101 Main St.
HABS NC-263
HABS NC,81-SPIND,1-
1ph L

Tavern,Old; see Spindale Recreation House

SAMPSON COUNTY

HARRELLS VIC.

Log Cabin
HABS NC-178
HABS NC,82-KER.V,1-
2ph L

Seavy House
HABS NC-179
HABS NC,82-KER.V,2-
1ph L

STANLY COUNTY

ALBEMARLE

Freeman-Marks House
112 N. Third St.
HABS NC-237
HABS NC,84-ALB,1-
4dr/30ph L

STOKES COUNTY

DANBURY VIC.

Bridge No. 75; see North Carolina Route 1417 Bridge

North Carolina Route 1417 Bridge (Bridge No. 75)
Spanning Dan River
HAER NC-39
HAER NC,85-DANB.V,1-
6ph/1pg/1pc L

SURRY COUNTY

MOUNT AIRY

Mount Airy Furniture Company
HAER NC-11
HAER NC,86-MTAIR,1-
14pg L

SWAIN COUNTY

CHEROKEE

Great Smoky Mountains National Park; see Oconaluftee Bridge

Oconaluftee Bridge (Great Smoky Mountains National Park)
Spanning Oconaluftee Bridge
HAER NC-40
HAER NC,87-CHER,1-
5ph/10pg/1pc/fr L

CHEROKEE VIC.

Conrad,Jim,Smokehouse; see Pioneer Farmstead,Meat House

Great Smoky Mountains National Park; see Pioneer Farmstead,Meat House

Pioneer Farmstead,Meat House (Conrad,Jim,Smokehouse; Great Smoky Mountains National Park)
U. S. Rt. 441 (moved from NC,Cataloochee)
HABS NC-202
HABS NC,87-NEWGA.V,1C-
1dr/5ph/1pc L

NEWFOUND GAP VIC.

Great Smoky Mountains National Park; see Pioneer Farmstead,Corn Crib

Pioneer Farmstead,Corn Crib (Queen,Joe,Place,Corn Crib; Great Smoky Mountains National Park)
U. S. 441 (moved from Deep Creek)
HABS NC-302
HABS NC,87-NEWGA.V,1B-
2dr L

Pounding Mill
Pioneer Museum,Rt. 441 (moved from Deep Creek)
HABS NC-4
HABS NC,87- ,1-
2dr/8ph/3pg L

Queen,Joe,Place,Corn Crib; see Pioneer Farmstead,Corn Crib

WAYNESVILLE

Great Smoky Mountains National Park; see Oconaluftee Ranger Station,Barn

Great Smoky Mountains National Park; see Oconaluftee Ranger Station,House

Oconaluftee Ranger Station,Barn (Great Smoky Mountains National Park)
U.S. Hwy. 441
HABS NC-390-B
HABS DLC/PP-1992:NC-5
4ph/1pc L

Oconaluftee Ranger Station,House (Great Smoky Mountains National Park)
U.S. Hwy. 441
HABS NC-390-A
HABS DLC/PP-1992:NC-5
3ph/1pc L

WAYNESVILLE VIC.

Great Smoky Mountains National Park; see Ocanaluftee Ranger Station,Chicken House

Great Smoky Mountains National Park; see Oconaluftee Ranger Station,Blacksmith Shop

Great Smoky Mountains National Park; see Oconaluftee Ranger Station,Corn Crib

Great Smoky Mountains National Park; see Oconaluftee Ranger Station,Ice House

Ocanaluftee Ranger Station,Chicken House (Great Smoky Mountains National Park)
U.S. Hwy. 441
HABS NC-390-D
HABS DLC/PP-1992:NC-5
1ph/1pc L

Oconaluftee Ranger Station
U.S. Hwy. 441
HABS NC-390
H

Oconaluftee Ranger Station,Blacksmith Shop (Great Smoky Mountains National Park)
U.S. Hwy. 441
HABS NC-390-E
HABS DLC/PP-1992:NC-5
1ph/1pc L

Oconaluftee Ranger Station,Corn Crib (Great Smoky Mountains National Park)
U.S. Hwy. 441
HABS NC-390-C
HABS DLC/PP-1992:NC-5
1ph/1pc L

Oconaluftee Ranger Station,Ice House (Great Smoky Mountains National Park)
U.S. Hwy. 441
HABS NC-390-F
HABS DLC/PP-1992:NC-5
1ph/1pc L

TYRRELL COUNTY

CRESWELL VIC.

Magnolia
State Rt. 1118
HABS NC-72
HABS NC,94-CRES.V,3-
2ph/1pg L

VANCE COUNTY

HENDERSON VIC.

Ashland Plantation House
Satterwhite Rd.
HABS NC-213
HABS NC,91-HEND.V,1-
8dr L

WILLIAMSBORO

Burnside Plantation (Hunt-Hamilton House)
State Rt. 1335
HABS NC-167
HABS NC,91-WILBO.V,1-
3ph L

House
HABS NC-187
HABS NC,91-WILBO,2-
1ph L

Hunt-Hamilton House; see Burnside Plantation

St. John's Episcopal Church
State Rt. 1329
HABS NC-136
HABS NC,91-WILBO,1-
2ph/2pg L

WAKE COUNTY

CARY

Bradford's Ordinary; see Page,A. T. House

Hines,Ambassador Walter,Birthplace; see Page,A. T. House

Page,A. T. House (Hines,Ambassador Walter,Birthplace; Bradford's Ordinary)
Wilkenson St.
HABS NC-306
HABS NC,92-CARY,1-
23dr L

FALLS

Falls of the Neuse Manufacturing Plant
W. bank of Neuse R. at SR 2000
HAER NC-18
HAER NC,92-FALLS,1-
8ph/13pg/1pc L

RALEIGH

Bank of the State of North Carolina; see Christ Church Rectory

Barber-Towler Building (Raleigh Office Supply)
123 E. Martin St.
HABS NC-10
HABS NC,92-RAL,10-
8ph/3pg L

Boylan Avenue Bridge
Boylan Ave. btwn. W. Martin & W. Hargett Sts.
HAER NC-20
HAER NC,92-RAL,13-
9ph/2pg/1pc L

Christ Church Rectory (Bank of the State of North Carolina)
Wilmington St. & New Bern Ave.
HABS NC-196
HABS NC,92-RAL,6-
11dr/6ph/1pg/1pc L

Christ Episcopal Church
120 E. Edenton St.
HABS NC-12-D-4
HABS NC,92-RAL,4-
26dr/1ph/1pg L

Craig's Building (Craig's Restaurant)
221 S. Wilmington St.
HABS NC-323
HABS NC,92-RAL,12-
7ph/3pg/1pc L

Craig's Restaurant; see Craig's Building

Haywood Hall
211 New Bern Ave.
HABS NC-229
HABS NC,92-RAL,8-
20dr L

Heck-Lee House; see Lee,Capt. ,House

Johnson,Andrew,Birthplace
Mordecai Place (moved from 123 Fayetteville St.)
HABS NC-12-D-1
HABS NC,92-RAL,1-
2dr/fr L

Lane,Joel,House (Wakefield Plantation)
728 Hargatt St.
HABS NC-12-D-2
HABS NC,92-RAL,2-
6dr/1pg L

Lee,Capt. ,House (Heck-Lee House)
503 E. Jones St.
HABS NC-230
HABS NC,92-RAL,9-
20dr L

Merriman-Wynne House; see Wynne House

Raleigh Office Supply; see Barber-Towler Building

State Capitol
Capitol Sq.
HABS NC-265
HABS NC,92-RAL,5-
3ph L

Vass,William,House
501 N. Halifax St.
HABS NC-12-D-3
HABS NC,92-RAWL,3-
11dr L

Wakefield Plantation; see Lane,Joel,House

White-Holman House
209 E. Morgan St.
HABS NC-329
HABS NC,92-RAL,11-
6ph/5pg/1pc L

Wynne House (Merriman-Wynne House)
209 Ashe Ave.
HABS NC-197
HABS NC,61-BURV.V,1-
8dr/5ph/1pg/1pc L

RALEIGH VIC.

Midway Plantation
U. S. Rt. 64
HABS NC-211
HABS NC,92-RAL.V,1-
11dr L

WARREN COUNTY

HENDERSON VIC.

Montmorenci
HABS NC-93
HABS NC,93-WARTO.V,1-
2ph L

LITTLETON

Little Manor; see Mosby Hall

Mosby Hall (Little Manor)
Mosby Ave.
HABS NC-156
HABS NC,42-LIT.V,1-
4ph L

WARRENTON

Davis,Peter,Store
Front St.
HABS NC-1
HABS NC,93-WARTO,1-
4dr/7ph/1pg/fr L

Fitts-Palmer House; see Palmer House

Green Tavern; see Green,Otis,House

Green,Otis,House (Green Tavern)
HABS NC-266
HABS NC,93-WARTO,3-
3ph L

House
HABS NC-186
HABS NC,93-WARTO,5-
1ph L

Mordecai House; see Palmer House

Palmer House (Fitts-Palmer House; Mordecai House)
210 Plummer St.
HABS NC-185
HABS NC,93-WARTO,4-
1ph L

WARRENTON VIC.

Buck Spring Plantation; see Macon,Nathaniel,House

Elgin
State Rt. 1509
HABS NC-121
HABS NC,93-WARTO.V,2-
8ph L

Hudgins House (Johnston-Plummer House)
Rt. 401
HABS NC-108
HABS NC,93-WARTO,2-
2ph L

Johnston-Plummer House; see Hudgins House

Macon,Nathaniel,House (Buck Spring Plantation; Williams-Reid-Macon House)
HABS NC-107
HABS NC,93-VAU,1-
2ph L

Williams-Reid-Macon House; see Macon,Nathaniel,House

WASHINGTON COUNTY

CRESWELL VIC.

Belgrade; see Pettigrew House

Collins,Josiah,House; see Somerset Place

Pettigrew House (Belgrade)
State Rt. 1158
HABS NC-35
HABS NC,94-CRES.V,2-
1ph/1pg L

Somerset Place (Collins,Josiah,House)
Lake Phelps,Pettigrew State Park
HABS NC-23
HABS NC,94-CRES.V,1-
2ph/3pg L

Somerset Place,Granary
Lake Phelps,Pettigrew State Park
HABS NC-24
HABS NC,94-CRES.V,1A-
1ph/1pg L

WAYNE COUNTY

FREMONT VIC.

Exum House
HABS NC-175
HABS NC,96-FREMO.V,1-
1ph L

YANCEY COUNTY

RELIEF VIC.

Bridge No. 194; see North Carolina Route 1314 Bridge

North Carolina Route 1314 Bridge
(Bridge No. 194)
Spanning Toe River
HAER NC-41
HAER NC,100-REL.V,1-
7ph/1pg/1pc L

Mott Rainbow Arch Bridge, Mott, Hettinger County, North Dakota. Center pier, arches, and stringers looking southwest. Photograph by Garry Redmann, April 1980 (HAER ND,21-MOTT,1-14).

Indian Dance Lodge, Elbowoods vicinity, McLean County, North Dakota. West elevation. Photograph by John A. Bryan, August 6, 1952 (HABS ND,28-ELBO,2-1).

North Dakota

BENSON COUNTY

DEVILS LAKE VIC.

Fort Totten (Fort Totten,State Historic Site)
HABS ND-17
HABS ND,3-FOTO,1-
1dr/14ph/17pg/2pc L

Fort Totten,Adjutant's Office
HABS ND-5
HABS ND,3-FOTO,1P-
2dr/4ph/2pg/1pc/fr L

Fort Totten,Bake House; see Fort Totten,Bakery Shop

Fort Totten,Bakery Shop (Fort Totten,Bake House)
HABS ND-14
HABS ND,3-FOTO,1N-
1dr/3ph/2pg/1pc/fr L

Fort Totten,Capt. & First Lt. Qtrs.,Bldg. 4
HABS ND-7
HABS ND,3-FOTO,1D-
5dr/7ph/1pg/1pc/fr L

Fort Totten,Capt. & First Lt. Qtrs.,Building 2
HABS ND-23
HABS ND,3-FOTO,1B-
8ph/1pc L

Fort Totten,Commanding Officers' Quarters
HABS ND-6
HABS ND,3-FOTO,1C-
5dr/10ph/1pg/1pc L

Fort Totten,Commissary (Fort Totten,Commissary Storehouse)
HABS ND-16
HABS ND,3-FOTO,1M-
1ph/1pg/1pc L

Fort Totten,Commissary Storehouse; see Fort Totten,Commissary

Fort Totten,Company Barracks,Building 11 (Fort Totten,Company Quarters)
HABS ND-13
HABS ND,3-FOTO,1J-
6dr/9ph/1pg/1pc/fr L

Fort Totten,Company Barracks,Building 12 (Fort Totten,Company Quarters)
HABS ND-24
HABS ND,3-FOTO,1K-
10ph/1pc L

Fort Totten,Company Barracks,Building 14 (Fort Totten,Company Quarters)
HABS ND-25
HABS ND,3-FOTO,1L-
11ph/1pc L

Fort Totten,Company Quarters; see Fort Totten,Company Barracks,Building 11

Fort Totten,Company Quarters; see Fort Totten,Company Barracks,Building 12

Fort Totten,Company Quarters; see Fort Totten,Company Barracks,Building 14

Fort Totten,Hospital
HABS ND-10
HABS ND,3-FOTO,1G-
7dr/7ph/2pg/1pc/fr L

Fort Totten,Magazine
HABS ND-11
HABS ND,3-FOTO,1H-
1dr/3ph/1pg/1pc/fr L

Fort Totten,Quartermaster's Storehouse (Fort Totten,Quartermasters's Warehouse)
HABS ND-12
HABS ND,3-FOTO,1I-
3dr/6ph/1pg/1pc/fr L

Fort Totten,Quartermasters's Warehouse; see Fort Totten,Quartermaster's Storehouse

Fort Totten,Second Lt. Qtrs.,Building 1
HABS ND-22
HABS ND,3-FOTO,1A-
7ph/1pc L

Fort Totten,Second Lt. Qtrs.,Building 5
HABS ND-9
HABS ND,3-FOTO,1E-
6dr/6ph/2pg/1pc/fr L

Fort Totten,State Historic Site; see Fort Totten

Fort Totten,Surgeon & Chaplains' Qtrs.
HABS ND-8
HABS ND,3-FOTO,1F-
4dr/7ph/2pg/1pc/1ct/fr L

BOTTINEAU COUNTY

KRAMER VIC.

Salyer,J. Clark,National Wildlife Refuge Dams
Along the Lower Souris River
HAER ND-4
HAER DLC/PP-1993:ND-1
6ph/15pg/1pc L

Salyer,J. Clark,National Wildlife Refuge,Dam 320
Along the Lower Souris River
HAER ND-4-A
HAER DLC/PP-1993:ND-1
13ph/3pg/2pc L

Salyer,J. Clark,National Wildlife Refuge,Dam 326
Along the Lower Souris River
HAER ND-4-B
HAER DLC/PP-1993:ND-1
13ph/3pg/2pc L

Salyer,J. Clark,National Wildlife Refuge,Dam 332
Along the Lower Souris River
HAER ND-4-C
HAER DLC/PP-1993:ND-1
11ph/3pg/1pc L

Salyer,J. Clark,National Wildlife Refuge,Dam 341
Along the Lower Souris River
HAER ND-4-D
HAER DLC/PP-1993:ND-1
14ph/3pg/2pc L

Salyer,J. Clark,National Wildlife Refuge,Dam 357
Along the Lower Souris River
HAER ND-4-E
HAER DLC/PP-1993:ND-1
25ph/3pg/2pc L

BURLEIGH COUNTY

BISMARCK

Liberty Memorial Bridge
Spanning Missouri River at I-94
HAER ND-7
HAER DLC/PP-1993:ND-2
56ph/27pg/4pc L

Roosevelt,Theodore,Cabin; see Roosevelt,Theodore,Maltese Cross-Ranch Cabin

Roosevelt,Theodore,Maltese Cross-Ranch Cabin (Roosevelt,Theodore,Cabin; Theodore Roosevelt National Park)
Roosevelt State Park (moved from ND,Medora Vic.)
HABS ND-1
HABS ND,8-BISMA,1-
1dr/3ph/1pg L

Theodore Roosevelt National Park; see Roosevelt,Theodore,Maltese Cross-Ranch Cabin

BISMARK

Bismarck Bridge
Spanning the Missouri River
HAER ND-2
HAER 1990 (HAER):10
8ph/1pc L

CAVALIER COUNTY

LANGDON VIC.

Mickelsen Safeguard Complex
(See PEMBINA COUNTY,MOUNTAIN VIC. for documntatn.)
HAER ND-9
L

NEKOMA VIC.

Mickelsen Safeguard Complex
(See PEMBINA COUNTY,MOUNTAIN VIC. for documntatn.)
HAER ND-9
L

GRAND FORKS COUNTY

GRAND FORKS

Grand Forks City Hall
404 Second Ave. N.
HABS ND-21
HABS ND,18-GRAFO,1-
1ph/3pg/1pc L

GRIGGS COUNTY

COOPERSTOWN VIC.

Griggs County Bridge
Spanning the Sheyenne River at Rt. 2
HAER ND-5
2dr/21ph/5pg/2pc L

HETTINGER COUNTY

MOTT

Mott Rainbow Arch Bridge
Spanning Cannonball River
HAER ND-1
HAER ND,21-MOTT,1-
27ph/96pg L

MCKENZIE COUNTY

GRASSY BUTTE

U. S. Post Office
Hwy. 85
HABS ND-19
HABS ND,27-GRABU,1-
4ph/1pg/1pc L

MCLEAN COUNTY

ELBOWOODS

Congregational Mission
Fort Berthold Indian Reservation
HABS ND-2
HABS ND,28-ELBO,1-
4dr/8ph/1pg L

ELBOWOODS VIC.

Indian Dance Lodge
Fort Berthold Indian Reservation
HABS ND-3
HABS ND,28-ELBO,2-
2dr/4ph/1pg L

MERCER COUNTY

STANTON VIC.

Knife River Indian Villages National Historic Site; see Olds,Milo,House

Olds,Milo,House (Knife River Indian Villages National Historic Site
HABS ND-20
HABS ND,29-STAN.V,1-
5dr L

MORTON COUNTY

MANDAN

Burlington Northern Overhead Railroad Bridge; see Northern Pacific Railroad Overhead Bridge

Liberty Memorial Bridge
See CCN ND0032,Burleigh Co.,Bismarck for document.
HAER ND-5
L

Northern Pacific Railroad Overhead Bridge (Burlington Northern Overhead Railroad Bridge)
Spanning Burlington Northern Railroad
HAER ND-6
20ph/16pg/2pc H

RAMSEY COUNTY

HAMPDEN VIC.

Mickelsen Safeguard Complex
(See PEMBINA COUNTY,MOUNTAIN VIC. for documntatn.)
HAER ND-9
L

RICHLAND COUNTY

WAHPETON

Bridge No. 90021; see Enloe Bridge

Enloe Bridge (Bridge No. 90021)
(See MN,WILKIN COUNTY,BRECKENRIDGE VIC. for doc.)
HAER MN-72
L

SHERIDAN COUNTY

GOODRICH VIC.

Winter,Daniel,House
HABS ND-18
HABS 1991(HABS):34
7dr/14ph/10pg/1pc/fr L

TRAILL COUNTY

MAYVILLE

Grinager,Inga,B. ,House; see Robinson,William,H. ,House

Robinson,William,H. ,House
(Grinager,Inga,B. ,House)
127 Fourth Ave. NE
HABS ND-15
HABS ND,49-MAYV,1-
9dr L

WALSH COUNTY

FAIRDALE VIC.

Mickelsen Safeguard Complex
(See PEMBINA COUNTY,MOUNTAIN VIC. for documntatn.)
HAER ND-9
L

WARD COUNTY

SOURIS RIVER BASIN

Upper Souris National Wildlife Refuge Dams
Souris River Basin
HAER ND-3
HAER DLC/PP-1992:ND-5
6ph/15pg/1pc L

Upper Souris National Wildlife Refuge,Dam 83
Souris River Basin
HAER ND-3-A
HAER DLC/PP-1992:ND-5
24ph/4pg/2pc L

Upper Souris National Wildlife Refuge,Dam 87
Souris River Basin
HAER ND-3-B
HAER DLC/PP-1992:ND-5
15ph/2pg/2pc L

Upper Souris National Wildlife Refuge,Dam 96
Souris River Basin
HAER ND-3-C
HAER DLC/PP-1992:ND-5
13ph/2pg/2pc L

WILLIAMS COUNTY

FORT BUFORD

Regimental Headquarters,Stable & Powder Magazine
HABS ND-4
HABS ND,53-FOBUF,1-
3dr/9ph/1pg L

Goodyear Airdock, Akron, Summit County, Ohio. Interior, looking north. Photograph by Jet Lowe, May 1985 (HAER OHIO,77-AKRO,6-18).

Ohio

ADAMS COUNTY

MANCHESTER

Massie,Gen. Nathaniel,House
Buckeye Station Bluff,Rt. 52
HABS OH-632
HABS OHIO,1-MANCH,1-
4dr/6ph/1pg/1pc/fr L

ALLEN COUNTY

LIMA

Dominion Building; see Holland Block Annex

Holland Block Annex (Dominion Building)
112-116 E. High St.
HABS OH-653
HABS OHIO,2-LIMA,1A-
15ph/13pg/1pc L

Lima Army Tank Plant
1155 Buckeye Rd.
HAER OH-31
HAER OHIO,2-LIMA,2-
38pg/fr L

ASHLAND COUNTY

ASHLAND VIC.

Freer House
Wooster Rd.
HABS OH-22-21
HABS OHIO,3-ASHLA.V,1-
2dr/2ph/1pg L

ASHTABULA COUNTY

ASHTABULA

Fourty-sixth Street Bridge (Spring Street Bridge)
Spanning Ashtabula River
HAER OH-24
HAER OHIO,4-ASH,1-
17ph/25pg/2pc L

Spring Street Bridge; see Fourty-sixth Street Bridge

COLEBROOK

Freewill Baptist Church
HABS OH-249
HABS OHIO,4-COLB,1-
2ph/2pg L

JEFFERSON

Giddings,Joshua R. ,Law Office
Chestnut & Walnut Sts.
HABS OH-268
HABS OHIO,4-JEF,2-
2dr/5ph/2pg L

Talcott House
Walnut St.
HABS OH-256
HABS OHIO,4-JEF,1-
1dr/2pg L

Wade,Benjamin,House
22 Jefferson St.
HABS OH-2237
HABS OHIO,4-JEF,3-
7ph/1pc L

UNIONVILLE VIC.

Harper,Col. Robert,House
HABS OH-22-26
HABS OHIO,4-UNVI.V,1-
1dr/4ph/1pg L

ATHENS COUNTY

ATHENS

Athens Foundry & Machine Company Building; see Athens Water Wheel

Athens Gas Light & Electric Company Building (Athens Lumber Company)
Factory St. ,Athens RR Station vic.
HABS OH-692-A
HABS OHIO,5-ATH,1-
1ph/1pg/1pc L

Athens Gas Light & Electric Company Office (Athens Lumber Company)
Factory St. ,Athens RR Station vic.
HABS OH-692-B
HABS OHIO,5-ATH,4B-
2ph/1pg/1pc L

Athens Ice & Storage Company House
17 Riverside Dr.
HABS OH-693
HABS OHIO,5-ATH,2-
1ph/1pg/1pc L

Athens Lumber Company; see Athens Gas Light & Electric Company Building

Athens Lumber Company; see Athens Gas Light & Electric Company Office

Athens Water Wheel (Athens Foundry & Machine Company Building)
Riverside Dr. ,across from 13-17
HABS OH-695
HABS OHIO,5-ATH,3-
4ph/1pg/1pc L

Hull Foster Homes
13 Riverside Dr.
HABS OH-694
HABS OHIO,5-ATH,1-
2ph/3pg/1pc L

BELMONT COUNTY

BELLAIRE

Anderson House (Dankworth House)
3678 Belmont St.
HABS OH-2324
HABS DLC/PP-1993:OH-5
15ph/17pg/2pc L

Dankworth House; see Anderson House

First Ward-South Ward Fire Station; see Independent Hose Company No. 3

4363 Guernsey Street (House)
HABS OH-2321
HABS DLC/PP-1993:OH-5
18ph/18pg/4pc L

4711 Guernsey Street (House)
4711 Guernsey St.
HABS OH-2358
HABS 1991(HABS):9
1ph/2pg/1pc L

4715 Guernsey Street (House)
4715 Guernsey Street
HABS OH-2359
HABS 1991(HABS):9
1ph/2pg/1pc L

Independent Hose Company No. 3 (First Ward-South Ward Fire Station)
Nineteenth & Belmont Sts.
HABS OH-2326
HABS DLC/PP-1993:OH-3
18ph/12pg/4pc L

Kelly,Willis,House
4735 Guernsey St.
HABS OH-2322
HABS 1991(HABS):9
17ph/16pg/1pc L

BLAINE

Bridge on Old National Road
HABS OH-2107
HABS OHIO,7-BLA.V,1-
2ph L

BLAINE VIC.

Bridge & Milestone
HABS OH-2108
HABS OHIO,7-BLA.V,3-
2ph L

Milestone on Old "S" Bridge
HABS OH-2109
HABS OHIO,7-BLA.V,2-
1ph L

ST. CLAIRSVILLE

Tavern
HABS OH-2111
HABS OHIO,7-SACLA,1-
1ph L

ST. CLAIRSVILLE VIC.

Arch Culvert (Old National Trail)
HABS OH-2110
HABS OHIO,7-SACLA.V,1-
1ph/1pg L

Old National Trail; see Arch Culvert

ZANESVILLE VIC.

Culvert
Between Cambridge & St. Clairsville
HABS OH-2106-B
HABS OHIO,- ,3-
2ph L

BROWN COUNTY

GEORGETOWN

Grant,Ulysses S. ,Boyhood House
219 Grant Ave.
HABS OH-2219
HABS OHIO,8-GEOTO,3-
2ph/1pc L

Schoolhouse
Water St.
HABS OH-629
HABS OHIO,8-GEOTO,1-
4dr/1ph/1pg L

Thompson,John,House
HABS OH-2218
HABS OHIO,8-GEOTO,2-
1ph L

GEORGETOWN VIC.

Thompson,Nettie,House
State Rd. 125, West
HABS OH-628
HABS OHIO,8-GEOTO.V,1-
7ph/1pg/1pc/fr L

RIPLEY

Rankin,Dr. John,House
Liberty Hill
HABS OH-630
HABS OHIO,8-RIP,1-
9dr/2ph/1pg L

BUTLER COUNTY

COLLINSVILLE VIC.

Covered Bridge
Spanning Seven Mile Creek
HABS OH-623
HABS OHIO,9-COL.V,1-
2dr L

DARRTOWN VIC.

Krebs,Charles,Place
S. of Morning Sun,State Rt. 224
HABS OH-2225
HABS OHIO,9-DART.V,1-
1ph L

HAMILTON VIC.

New London Pike Covered Bridge
Spanning Indian Creek
HABS OH-624
HABS OHIO,9-HAM.V,1-
3dr L

MONROE VIC.

Harkrader House
HABS OH-2234
HABS OHIO,9-MONRO.V,1-
2ph L

OXFORD

"Guest House" (Rodger's Place)
300 E. High St.
HABS OH-6-21
HABS OHIO,9-OXFO,1-
6dr/1ph/1pg L

Oxford Female College,Fisher Hall
Miami University Campus
HABS OH-2140
HABS OHIO,9-OXFO,3A-
4ph/5pg/1pc L

Presbyterian Parsonage
E. High St.
HABS OH-622
HABS OHIO,9-OXFO,2-
2ph/1pg L

Rodger's Place; see "Guest House"

WEST CHESTER

"Blue Shutters" Residence
Rt. 25
HABS OH-2235
HABS OHIO,9-CHESW,1-
2ph L

CLARK COUNTY

HARMONY

Tavern,Old; see Warren,Reuben,House

Warren,Reuben,House (Tavern,Old)
Rt. 40
HABS OH-635
HABS OHIO,12-HARM,1-
1ph L

SPRINGFIELD

Arcade Hotel
Fountain Ave.,bounded by High & Washington Sts.
HABS OH-2301
HABS DLC/PP-1993:OH-5
28ph/16pg/5pc L

Odd Fellow-Rebekah Home; see Odd Fellows' Home of Ohio

Odd Fellows' Home of Ohio (Odd Fellow-Rebekah Home)
404 E. McCreight Ave.
HABS OH-2284
HABS 1989(HABS):18
49ph/35pg/4pc L

Springfield City Hall (1979)
76 E. High St.
HABS OH-430
HABS OHIO,12-SPRIF,2-
9ph/6pg/1pc L

Springfield City Hall,1890
117 S. Fountain Ave.
HABS OH-417
HABS OHIO,12-SPRIF,1-
3ph/10pg/1pc L

CLERMONT COUNTY

BANTAM VIC.

Pinkham House & Farm
Ohio State Rt. 125,Amelia-Bantam Rd.
HABS OH-2204
HABS OHIO,13-BANT.V,1-
5dr/14ph/1pg/1pc L

MILFORD

Milford Bridge
Spans The Little Miami River on U.S. 50
HAER OH-77
14ph/9pg/3pc H

CLINTON COUNTY

CLARKSVILLE

Covered Bridge
Rt. 3
HABS OH-2224
HABS OHIO,14-CLARK,1-
2ph L

MIDLAND

Midland School Building
NW corner of Broadway & Cuba Ave.
HABS OH-2376
HABS DLC/PP-1993:OH-5
14ph/5pg/2pc L

NEW VIENNA VIC.

Harris,E. ,House (Snow Hill)
State Rt. No. 73
HABS OH-2250
HABS OHIO,14-NEVIE.V,1-
13dr/4ph/1pg/1pc/fr L

Snow Hill; see Harris,E. ,House

COSHOCTON COUNTY

ISLETA VIC.

Fort,Old Stone
N. of Isleta
HABS OH-410
HABS OHIO,16-ISLET.V,1-
2ph/1pg L

CRAWFORD COUNTY

CRESTLINE

Crestline City Hall
Bucyrus & Thoman Sts.
HABS 0H-2362
HABS DLC/PP-1993:OH-3
72ph/16pg/5pc L

LYKENS VIC.

Smith Road Bowstring Arch Bridge (Smith Road Bridge)
Spanning Sycamore Creek at Smith Rd.(TR 62)
HAER OH-46
HAER OHIO,17-LYK.V,1-
3dr/6ph/6pg/1pc/fr L

Smith Road Bridge; see Smith Road Bowstring Arch Bridge

CUYAHOGA COUNTY

BENTLEYVILLE

Bentley House
N. Miles Rd.
HABS OH-25
HABS OHIO,18-BENTV,1-
4dr/5ph/2pg L

BRECKSVILLE

Brecksville Inn
Brecksville Rd.
HABS OH-234
HABS OHIO,18-BRECK,2-
3dr/2ph/2pg L

Brecksville-Northfield High Level Bridge (Bridge No. 82; Bridge S.R. 114)
Spanning Cuyahoga River,Cuyahoga Valley NRA
HAER OH-66
HAER OHIO,18-BRECK,3-
8ph/1pg/1pc/2ct/fr L

Bridge No. 82; see Brecksville-Northfield High Level Bridge

Bridge S.R. 114; see Brecksville-Northfield High Level Bridge

Congregational Church
Highland Drive
HABS OH-22-30
HABS OHIO,18-BRECK,1-
3dr/4ph/1pg L

Station Road Bridge
Spanning Cuyahoga River,Cuyahoga Valley NRA
HAER OH-67
HAER OHIO,18-BRECK,4-
11ph/1pg/1pc L

CHAGRIN FALLS

Crawford,W. J. ,House
170 Cleveland St.
HABS OH-225
HABS OHIO,18-CHAFA,3-
3dr/4ph/2pg L

March,H. W. ,House
E. Washington St.
HABS OH-219
HABS OHIO,18-CHAFA,2-
2dr/1ph/2pg L

Warren-Hollis House
43 E. Orange St.
HABS OH-22-1
HABS OHIO,18-CHAFA,1-
2dr/1ph/1pg L

CHAGRIN FALLS VIC.

Sykes House
Rt. 232
HABS OH-253
HABS OHIO,18-CHAFA.V,2-
3dr/1ph/2pg L

CLEVELAND

Abbey Avenue Viaduct
Spanning Walworth Valley at Abbey Ave.
HAER OH-5
HAER OHIO,18-CLEV,20-
30ph/9pg/3pc L

Air Force Plant No. 47:Mesta 50,000-ton Forging Pr; see Alcoa Forging Div.:Mesta 50,000-ton Forging Press

Alcoa Forging Div.:Mesta 50,000-ton Forging Press (Air Force Plant No. 47:Mesta 50,000-ton Forging Pr
1600 Harvard Ave.
HAER OH-64
HAER OHIO,18-CLEV,41-
20ph/2pg/1pc L

B & O Railroad Bridge Number 464 (Scherzer Rolling Lift Bridge)
Spanning Old Ship Canal & Cuyahoga River
HAER OH-15
HAER OHIO,18-CLEV,27-
3ph/1pc L

Baker Motor Vehicle Company; see Rauch & Lang Carriage Company

Baker,R. & L. ,Company; see Rauch & Lang Carriage Company

Baldwin Filtration Plant & Reservoir; see Division Avenue Pumping Station & Filtration Plant

Beehive School
4345 Lee Rd.
HABS OH-689
HABS OHIO,18-CLEV,36-
12ph/12pg/1pc L

Brookside Park Bridge
Spanning Big Creek & Cleveland Metroparks
HAER OH-14
HAER OHIO,18-CLEV,26-
5ph/2pc L

Brotherhood of Locomotive Engineers Building (Engineers' Building)
1365 Ontario Street
HABS OH-2357
HABS DLC/PP-1993:OH-5
126ph/9pg/25pc L

Carling Brewing Company Building; see Peerless Motor Car Company

Carter Road Lift Bridge
Spanning Cuyahoga River at Carter Rd.
HAER OH-56
HAER OHIO,18-CLEV,37-
17ph/7pg/2pc L

Case,Leonard,Homestead
1295 E. Twentieth St.
HABS OH-22
HABS OHIO,18-CLEV,3-
4dr/1ph/2pg L

Cedar Avenue House; see Mould,H. ,House

Center Street Swing Bridge
SW of Public Square
HAER OH-10
HAER OHIO,18-CLEV,29-
22ph/9pg/2pc L

Central Furnaces
2650 Broadway,E. bank of Cuyahoga River
HAER OH-12
HAER OHIO,18-CLEV,32-
33ph/11pg/5pc L

Church,Old Stone; see First Presbyterian Church

Cleveland & Pittsburgh Ore Dock; see Pennsylvania Railway Ore Dock

Cleveland Arcade
401 Euclid Ave.
HABS OH-2119
HABS OHIO,18-CLEV,6-
22dr/5ph/11pg/1ct L

Cleveland Automobile Industry
HAER OH-11
HAER OHIO,18-CLEV,25-
34pg L

Cleveland Breakwater at Cleveland Harbor
HAER OH-1
HAER OHIO,18-CLEV,17-
18ph/37pg L

Cleveland City Hall
601 Lakeside Ave.
HABS OH-428
HABS OHIO,18-CLEV,35-
14ph/16pg/1pc L

Cleveland Municipal Airport
HAER OH-2
HAER OHIO,18-CLEV,19-
17ph/16pg L

Cleveland-Chandler Motors Corporation
300 E. One-hundred-and-thirty-first St.
HAER OH-11-G
HAER OHIO,18-CLEV,25G-
20ph/19pg/3pc L

Collinwood Railroad Yard Coal Tipple
Between E. 146th St. & E. 152nd St.
HAER OH-26
HAER OHIO,18-CLEV,40A-
4ph/1pg/1pc L

Columbus Road Lift Bridge
Spanning Cuyahoga River at Columbus Rd.
HAER OH-55
HAER OHIO,18-CLEV,38-
12ph/8pg/1pc L

Corrigan,McKinney,Steel Company (Republic Steel Company)
3100 W. Forty-fifth St. ,E. & W. banks of Cuyahoga
HAER OH-13
HAER OHIO,18-CLEV,34-
57ph/17pg/6pc L

Detroit Street Bridge,Old
HAER OH-8
HAER OHIO,18-CLEV,24-
5pg L

Detroit Superior High Level Bridge
HAER OH-6
HAER OHIO,18-CLEV,22-
25ph/24pg/4pc L

Diebolt Brewing Company Stable
2695 Pittsburgh Ave.
HAER OH-20
HAER OHIO,18-CLEV,31-
10ph/1pc L

Division Avenue Pumping Station & Filtration Plant (Baldwin Filtration Plant & Reservoir)
HAER OH-3
HAER OHIO,18-CLEV,18-
45ph/38pg L

Dunham,Rufus,Tavern
6709 Euclid Ave.
HABS OH-22-29
HABS OHIO,18-CLEV,1-
9dr/1ph/1pg/fr L

Engineers' Building; see Brotherhood of Locomotive Engineers Building

First Presbyterian Church (Church,Old Stone)
91 Public Square
HABS OH-2124
HABS OHIO,18-CLEV,10-
4ph/6pg L

Fisher Body Company,Ohio
E. One-hundred-and-fourtieth St. & Coit Rd.
HAER OH-11-H
HAER OHIO,18-CLEV,25H-
9ph/13pg/2pc L

Ford Motor Company Branch Assembly Plant; see Ford Motor Company,Cleveland Branch Assembly Plant

Ford Motor Company,Cleveland Branch Assembly Plant (Ford Motor Company Branch Assembly Plant)
Euclid Ave. & E. One-hundred-and-sixteenth St.
HAER OH-11-E
HAER OHIO,18-CLEV,25E-
6ph/10pg/2pc L

Garfield,Pres. James Abram,Monument
12316 Euclid Ave.
HABS OH-2122
HABS OHIO,18-CLEV,8-
4ph/5pg L

Hotel St. Regis
8205 Euclid Ave.
HABS OH-2336
HABS 1991(HABS):9
8ph/3pg/1pc L

Lorain-Carnegie Bridge
Lorain-Carnegie Ave. spanning Cuyahoga River
HAER OH-16
HAER OHIO,18-CLEV,39-
1ph/1pg/1pc L

May,T. P. ,Residence
1458 E. Twelfth St.
HABS OH-24
HABS OHIO,18-CLEV,5-
4dr/2pg L

Mould,H. ,House (Cedar Avenue House)
2637 Cedar Ave.
HABS OH-21
HABS OHIO,18-CLEV,2-
2dr/1ph L

Peerless Motor Car Company (Carling Brewing Company Building; Peerless Motor Company,Plant No. 1)
Quincy Ave. & E. Ninety-third St.
HABS OH-2123
HAER OH-11-D
HABS/HAER OHIO,18-CLEV,9-
13ph/21pg/2pc L

Peerless Motor Company,Plant No. 1; see Peerless Motor Car Company

Pennsylvania Railway Ore Dock (Cleveland & Pittsburgh Ore Dock)
Lake Erie at Whiskey Island
HAER OH-18
HAER OHIO,18-CLEV,33-
40ph/21pg/5pc L

Rauch & Lang Carriage Company (Baker Motor Vehicle Company; Baker,R. & L. ,Company)
W. Twenty-fifth St. & Monroe Ave.
HAER OH-11-B
HAER OHIO,18-CLEV,25B-
17ph/17pg/2pc L

Republic Steel Company; see Corrigan,McKinney,Steel Company

Rockefeller Building
614 Superior Ave.
HABS OH-2125
HABS OHIO,18-CLEV,11-
10ph/7pg L

Scherzer Rolling Lift Bridge; see B & O Railroad Bridge Number 464

Shaker Heights Rapid Transit Line
HAER OH-4
HAER OHIO,18-CLEV,28-
18ph/15pg/2pc L

Sidaway Avenue Footbridge (Suspension Bridge)
Jackowo & Garden Valley neighborhood Vic.
HAER OH-9
HAER OHIO,18-CLEV,23-
4ph/5pg L

Society National Bank Building
127-45 Public Square
HABS OH-2128
HABS OHIO,18-CLEV,14-
10ph/12pg L H

St. John's Episcopal Church
2600 Church Ave.
HABS OH-2126
HABS OHIO,18-CLEV,12-
4ph/5pg L

St. Michael the Archangel Roman Catholic Church
3114 Scranton Rd.
HABS OH-2127
HABS OHIO,18-CLEV,13-
5ph/4pg L

Stearns,F. B. ,Company
Euclid & Lakeview Aves.
HAER OH-11-F
HAER OHIO,18-CLEV,25F-
10ph/10pg/2pc L

Superior Avenue Viaduct
Cleveland E. & W. side,Cuyahoga Valley Vic.
HAER OH-7
HAER OHIO,18-CLEV,21-
16ph/12pg/3pc L

Suspension Bridge; see Sidaway Avenue Footbridge

Terminal Tower Bldg., Cleveland Union Terminal (Tower City Center)
50 Public Square
HABS OH-2280
HABS 1991(HABS):9
161ph/25pg/15pc L

Tower City Center; see Terminal Tower Bldg., Cleveland Union Terminal

Trinity Episcopal Church
Euclid Ave. & E. Twenty-Second St.
HABS OH-2129
HABS OHIO,18-CLEV,15-
8ph/6pg L

U. S. Post Office,Customs House & Courthouse
Public Square
HABS OH-2121
HABS OHIO,18-CLEV,7-
14ph/7pg L

Wade Park Avenue Bridge
Liberty Blvd. ,Rockefeller Park
HABS OH-2130
HABS OHIO,18-CLEV,16-
7ph/4pg L

Weddell,Peter,House
W. Sixth St. & Frankfort Ave.
HABS OH-23
HABS OHIO,18-CLEV,4-
10dr/1ph L

2332-2334 West 10th Street, House
HABS OH-2281
HABS OHIO,18-CLEV,42-
5ph/3pg/1pc L

White Company (White Motor Company)
E. Seventy-ninth St. & Saint Clair Ave.
HAER OH-11-C
HAER OHIO,18-CLEV,25C-
25ph/15pg/2pc L

White Motor Company; see White Company

Winton Motor Carriage Company
Berea Rd. & Madison Ave.
HAER OH-11-A
HAER OHIO,18-CLEV,25A-
11ph/15pg/2pc L

CLEVELAND HEIGHTS

Tremaine-Gallagher House
3001 Fairmount Blvd.
HABS OH-2131
HABS OHIO,18-CLEVHI,1-
10ph/7pg L

CLEVELAND VIC.

Fosdick House
Canal Rd.
HABS OH-228
HABS OHIO,18-CLEV.V,1-
3dr/1ph/2pg L

DOVER

Hurst,Thomas,Residence
31156 Detroit Rd.
HABS OH-231
HABS OHIO,18-DOV,1-
7dr/5ph/2pg L

GATES MILLS

Chagrin Valley Hunt Club (Doorway)
Mayfield & River Rds.
HABS OH-215
HABS OHIO,18-GATMI,2-
1dr/1ph/4pg L

St. Christopher's-By-The-River
Old Mill Rd.
HABS OH-212
HABS OHIO,18-GATMI,1-
14dr/3ph/7pg/fr L

LAKEWOOD

Hall House; see Honam,John,House

Honam,John,House (Hall House)
1396 St. Charles Ave. (moved to Lakewood Park)
HABS OH-27
HABS OHIO,18-LAKWO,1-
2dr/2ph/3pg L

Nicholson,Ezra,House
1335 Detroit Ave.
HABS OH-210
HABS OHIO,18-LAKWO,3-
6dr/4ph/5pg L

Warren House
Warren & Fisher Rds.
HABS OH-28
HABS OHIO,18-LAKWO,2-
3dr/2ph/5pg L

NORTH OLMSTED

Carpenter,F. D. ,House
Lorain Rd.
HABS OH-213
HABS OHIO,18-OLMN,1-
6dr/4ph/4pg L

Universalist Church
Lorain & Butternut Ridge Rds.
HABS OH-222
HABS OHIO,18-OLMN,2-
3dr/1ph/2pg L

PARMA

Gilchrist House
6515 York Rd.
HABS OH-214
HABS OHIO,18-PARM,2-
3dr/2ph/2pg L

PARMA HEIGHTS

Fay Homestead
Wooster Pike
HABS OH-22-23
HABS OHIO,18-PARMH,1-
4dr/1ph/1pg L

ROCKY RIVER

Detroit Avenue Crossing; see Rocky River Bridge

Rocky River Bridge (Detroit Avenue Crossing)
Spanning Beaver Dam River
HAER OH-21
HAER OHIO,18-RORI,1-
23ph/38pg/2pc L

SOLON VIC.

Blackman House
Pettibone Rd.
HABS OH-233
HABS OHIO,18-SOLO.V,1-
2dr/2ph/2pg L

STRONGSVILLE

Pomeroy,Alanson,House
Pearl & Westwood Rds.
HABS OH-2132
HABS OHIO,18-STROVI,1-
8ph/3pg/1pc L

VALLEY VIEW

Alexander's Grist Mill (Wilson's Mill)
Lock 37 on Ohio & Erie Canal,S. of Cleveland
HAER OH-58
HAER OHIO,18-VAVI,2-
13dr/25ph/13pg/4pc/fr L

Frazee,Stephen,House
7733 Canal Rd.,Cuyahoga Valley NRA
HABS OH-2307
HABS OHIO,18-VAVI,1-
3ph/1pg/1pc L

Ohio & Erie Canal,Lock No. 38
Canal & Hillside Rds.
HAER OH-59-C
HAER DLC/PP-1992:OH-2
1dr/4ph/1pc/fr L

Ohio & Erie Canal,Lock No. 39
West side of Canal Rd.,3400 ft. north of Stone Rd.
HAER OH-59-D
HAER DLC/PP-1992:OH-2
1dr/6ph/1pc/fr L

Ohio & Erie Canal,Tinker's Creek Aqueduct
Cnl Rd.,S. Tinkers Crk. Rd.,Cuy. Val Nat. Rec. Ar.
HAER OH-59-F
HAER DLC/PP-1992:OH-2
8ph/1pc L

Wilson's Mill; see Alexander's Grist Mill

VALLEY VIEW VIC.

Ohio & Erie Canal,Typical Lock Gates
Canal Rd. btwn. Rockside Rd. & Fitzwater Rd.
HAER OH-60
HAER DLC/PP-1992:OH-2
3dr/fr L

WHITESBURG

White House at Whitesburg
High St.
HABS OH-224
HABS OHIO,18-CHAFA.V,1-
4dr/2ph/2pg L

ERIE COUNTY

MILAN

Edison,Thomas A. ,Birthplace
Front St. & Choate Ave.
HABS OH-22-22
HABS OHIO,22-MILA,1-
2dr/3ph/1pg/1pc L

MILAN VIC.

Abbott-Page House
Mason Rd. ,State Rt. 13 vic.
HABS OH-2141
HABS OHIO,22-MILA.V,1A-
8ph/1pg/1pc/fr L

VERMILION VIC.

Rosedale; see Swift,Joseph,House

Swift Hollow; see Swift,Joseph,House

Swift,Joseph,House (Rosedale; Swift Hollow)
S. of Vermillion,on Vermillion River
HABS OH-26
HABS OHIO,22-VERM.V,1-
3dr/1ph/4pg L

FAIRFIELD COUNTY

CARROLL VIC.

Bright,John,No. 1 Iron Bridge
Spanning Poplar Creek at Havenport Rd.(TR 263)
HAER OH-44
HAER OHIO,23-CAR.V,1-
5dr/5ph/15pg/1pc/fr L

Bright,John,No. 2 Covered Bridge
Bish Rd.(Twp Rt. 263) over Poplar Creek
HAER OH-45
HAER OHIO,23-CAR.V,2-
5dr/6ph/5pg/1pc/fr L

LANCASTER

Devol-Dallow House
118 E. Wheeling St.
HABS OH-413
HABS OHIO,23-LANC,4-
3dr/13ph/4pg/2pc/fr L

Duplar,E. ,House
Rt. 22
HABS OH-2232
HABS OHIO,23-LANC.V,1-
1ph L

Effinger,Samuel,House (Reber Tavern)
HABS OH-41
HABS OHIO,23-LANC,1-
12ph/3pg L

Giani-Mumaugh Memorial
Main & High Sts.
HABS OH-419
HABS OHIO,23-LANC,2-
7dr/12ph/4pg/2pc/fr L

MacCracken-Hoffman House
105 E. Wheeling St.
HABS OH-414
HABS OHIO,23-LANC,3-
3dr L

Reber Tavern; see Effinger,Samuel,House

Stanbery-Rising House
High St. ,at corner of Wheeling St.
HABS OH-415
HABS OHIO,23-LANC,5-
3dr/18ph/5pg/2pc/fr L

135 West Wheeling Street (House)
135 W. Wheeling St.
HABS OH-2325
HABS 1991(HABS):9
7ph/3pg/1pc L

STOUTSVILLE VIC.

Fosnaugh Truss Leg Bedstead Bridge (Scippo Bridge)
Spanning Scippo Creek at Township Rt. 128
HAER OH-43
HAER OHIO,23-STOVI.V,1-
4dr/6ph/8pg/1pc/fr L

Scippo Bridge; see Fosnaugh Truss Leg Bedstead Bridge

FRANKLIN COUNTY

COLUMBUS

American Savings Bank; see Central National Bank Building

Baker Art Gallery
232 S. High St.
HABS OH-2213
HABS OHIO,25-COLB,33-
9ph/4pg/1pc L

Battelle Memorial Institute,First HIP Vessels
505 King Ave.,Ohio State University
HAER OH-65-B
HAER OHIO,25-COLB,38B-
8ph/1pg/1pc L

Battelle Memorial Institute,Xerography
505 King Ave.,Ohio State University
HAER OH-65-A
HAER OHIO,25-COLB,38A-
3ph/1pc L

Boylston,The
1228 E. Main St.
HABS OH-687
HABS OHIO,25-COLB,28-
2ph/1pg/1pc L

Central National Bank Building (American Savings Bank)
152-156 S. High St.
HABS OH-2214
HABS OHIO,25-COLB,32-
8ph/4pg/1pc L

Columbus Near East Side Historic District
Bounded by I-71,Norf. & Wester RR,E. Broad,E. Main
HABS OH-654
HABS OHIO,25-COLB,8-
6pg L

Columbus Near East Side Historic District; see 1600 East Rich Street (House)

Columbus Near East Side Historic District; see 1156-1158 East Rich Street (Houses)

Columbus Near East Side Historic District; see 1326-1328 Fair Avenue (Houses)

Columbus Near East Side Historic District; see 1092 Franklin Avenue (House)

Columbus Near East Side Historic District; see 1566-1568 Franklin Avenue (Houses)

Columbus Near East Side Historic District; see 250-252 Kelton Avenue (Houses)

Columbus Near East Side Historic District; see 168-170 Latta Avenue (Houses)

Columbus Near East Side Historic District; see 158 Linwood Avenue (House)

Columbus Near East Side Historic District; see 361 Loeffler Avenue (House)

Columbus Near East Side Historic District; see 347-349 Loeffler Avenue (Houses)

Columbus Near East Side Historic District; see 1037 Madison Avenue (House)

Columbus Near East Side Historic District; see 1102-1112 Oak Street (Commercial Buildings)

Columbus Near East Side Historic District; see 1022 Oak Street (House)

Columbus Near East Side Historic District; see 1310 Oak Street (House)

Columbus Near East Side Historic District; see 1372-1374 Oak Street (House)

Columbus Near East Side Historic District; see 1540-1542 Oak Street (Houses)

Columbus Near East Side Historic District; see 244-246 South Eighteenth Street (Houses)

Columbus Near East Side Historic District; see 29 South Monroe Avenue (House)

Columbus Near East Side Historic District; see 212 South Ohio Avenue (House)

Columbus Near East Side Historic District; see 274 South Ohio Avenue (House)

Commercial & Apartment Building,Brick
82-86 E. Town St.
HABS OH-2210
HABS OHIO,25-COLB,37-
5ph/4pg/1pc L

Corzelius House (German Village Historic District)
85 Deshler Ave.
HABS OH-416
HABS OHIO,25-COLB,7-
4dr/fr L

970-972 Delaware Avenue (Houses)
HABS OH-676
HABS OHIO,25-COLB,6-
2pg L

894-894.5 E. Engler St. (House)
HABS OH-2298
HABS OHIO,25-COLB,44-
1ph/4pg/1pc L

1847 E. Rich St.,(House)
HABS OH-2296
HABS OHIO,25-COLB,42-
2ph/4pg/1pc L

1105-1107 East Rich (House)
HABS OH-2292
HABS OHIO,25-COLB,40-
2ph/4pg/1pc L

1600 East Rich Street (House)
(Columbus Near East Side Historic District)
HABS OH-675
HABS OHIO,25-COLB,22-
2ph/1pg/1pc L

1156-1158 East Rich Street (Houses)
(Columbus Near East Side Historic District)
HABS OH-669
HABS OHIO,25-COLB,10-
2ph/1pg/1pc L

1041 East Whittier (House)
HABS OH-2291
HABS OHIO,25-COLB,39-
2ph/4pg/1pc L

Empress Theater; see Knickerbocker Theater

1326-1328 Fair Avenue (Houses)
(Columbus Near East Side Historic District)
HABS OH-670
HABS OHIO,25-COLB,11-
2ph/1pg L

1004-1006 Franklin (House)
1004-1006 Franklin Ave.
HABS OH-2339
HABS 1991(HABS):9
1ph/2pg/1pc L

1092 Franklin Avenue (House)
(Columbus Near East Side Historic District)
HABS OH-679
HABS OHIO,25-COLB,20-
2pg L

1566-1568 Franklin Avenue (Houses)
(Columbus Near East Side Historic District)
HABS OH-677
HABS OHIO,25-COLB,21-
2ph/1pg/1pc L

Gayety Theater; see Knickerbocker Theater

German Village Historic District; see Corzelius House

Greene,Thurman,Building (La Salle Wine Shop)
242-244 S. High St.
HABS OH-2211
HABS OHIO,25-COLB,34-
7ph/3pg/1pc L

Hartman Building & Theater
73-87 E. State St.
HABS OH-2215
HABS OHIO,25-COLB,5-
47ph/6pg/3pc L

Kelley,Alfred,House
282 E. Broad St.
HABS OH-47
HABS OHIO,25-COLB,2-
7dr/12ph/6pg/1pc/1ct/fr L

250-252 Kelton Avenue (Houses)
(Columbus Near East Side Historic District)
HABS OH-668
HABS OHIO,25-COLB,9-
2ph/1pg/1pc L

257-259 Kelton St.,(House)
HABS OH-2299
HABS OHIO,25-COLB,43-
2ph/4pg/1pc L

374 Kendall Place (House)
374 Kendall Pl.
HABS OH-2341
HABS 1991(HABS):9
2ph/2pg/1pc L

Knickerbocker Theater (Empress Theater; Gayety Theater)
246-254 S. High St.
HABS OH-2212
HABS OHIO,25-COLB,35-
5ph/4pg/1pc L

La Salle Wine Shop; see Greene,Thurman,Building

168-170 Latta Avenue (Houses)
(Columbus Near East Side Historic District)
HABS OH-672
HABS OHIO,25-COLB,13-
2ph/1pg/1pc L

158 Linwood Avenue (House)
(Columbus Near East Side Historic District)
HABS OH-680
HABS OHIO,25-COLB,23-
2pg L

373 Livingston Avenue (House)
HABS OH-678
HABS OHIO,25-COLB,31-
2pg L

361 Loeffler Avenue (House) (Columbus Near East Side Historic District)
HABS OH-682
HABS OHIO,25-COLB,25-
2pg L

347-349 Loeffler Avenue (Houses)
(Columbus Near East Side Historic District)
HABS OH-681
HABS OHIO,25-COLB,24-
2pg L

Loew's & United Artists Ohio Theatre
39 E. State St.
HABS OH-2148
HABS OHIO,25-COLB,4-
84ph/1pg L

1037 Madison Avenue (House)
(Columbus Near East Side Historic District)
HABS OH-686
HABS OHIO,25-COLB,29-
1ph/1pg/1pc L

461 North Monroe Street (House)
461 N. Monroe Ave.
HABS OH-2340
HABS 1991(HABS):9
2ph/2pg/1pc L

1102-1112 Oak Street (Commercial Buildings) (Columbus Near East Side Historic District)
HABS OH-667
HABS OHIO,25-COLB,17-
2ph/2pg/1pc L

1022 Oak Street (House) (Columbus Near East Side Historic District)
HABS OH-688
HABS OHIO,25-COLB,14-
1ph/1pg/1pc L

1310 Oak Street (House) (Columbus Near East Side Historic District)
HABS OH-673
HABS OHIO,25-COLB,15-
2ph/1pg/1pc L

1372-1374 Oak Street (House)
(Columbus Near East Side Historic District)
HABS OH-683
HABS OHIO,25-COLB,16-
2pg L

1635-1637 Oak Street (House)
1635-1637 Oak St.
HABS OH-2338
HABS 1991(HABS):9
2ph/2pg/1pc L

1540-1542 Oak Street (Houses)
(Columbus Near East Side Historic District)
HABS OH-684
HABS OHIO,25-COLB,18-
2pg L

Ohio Statehouse & Annex
High & Broad Sts.
HABS OH-2220
HABS OHIO,25-COLB,36-
1ph/1pc L

244-246 South Eighteenth Street (Houses) (Columbus Near East Side Historic District)
HABS OH-647
HABS OHIO,25-COLB,30-
1ph/1pg/1pc L

29 South Monroe Avenue (House)
(Columbus Near East Side Historic District)
HABS OH-671
HABS OHIO,25-COLB,12-
2ph/1pg/1pc L

212 South Ohio Avenue (House)
(Columbus Near East Side Historic District)
HABS OH-685
HABS OHIO,25-COLB,26-
2pg L

274 South Ohio Avenue (House)
(Columbus Near East Side Historic District)
HABS OH-646
HABS OHIO,25-COLB,27-
1ph/1pg/1pc L

270 South Twenty-first Street (House)
HABS OH-674
HABS OHIO,25-COLB,19-
2ph/1pg/1pc L

156 Wilson Avenue (House)
HABS OH-2290
HABS OHIO,25-COLB,41-
2ph/4pg/1pc L

Wyandotte Building
21 W. Broad St.
HABS OH-48
HABS OHIO,25-COLB,3-
8ph/6pg/1pc/fr L

WORTHINGTON

St. John's Episcopal Church
High St. & Granville Rd.
HABS OH-2238
HABS OHIOI,25-WORTH,1-
10dr L

Worthington Female Seminary
HABS OH-423
HABS OHIO,25-WORTH,2-
6ph/2pg/1pc/fr L

GALLIA COUNTY

GALLIPOLIS

"Our House" (432 First Avenue (House))
HABS OH-631
HABS OHIO,27-GAL,1-
13dr/6ph/2pg L

432 First Avenue (House); see "Our House"

Gallipolis Post Office
First Ave.
HABS OH-633
HABS OHIO,27-GAL,2-
4dr/1ph/1pg L

GALLIPOLIS VIC.

Byrd,Richard C.,Locks and Dam; see Gallipolis Locks and Dam

Gallipolis Locks and Dam
(Byrd,Richard C.,Locks and Dam)
(See WV,MASON CO.,POINT PLEASANT VIC. for docum.)
HAER WV-58
L

GEAUGA COUNTY

AURORA

Treat House
Rt. 43
HABS OH-230
HABS OHIO,28-AURO,1-
5dr/2ph/2pg L

BURTON

Cook,Meriman,House
Claridon & Burton Rds.
HABS OH-278
HABS OHIO,28-BURT,2-
3dr/1pg L

Lawyer,Lew,Residence
HABS OH-258
HABS OHIO,28-BURT,1-
2dr/1ph/1pg L

CLAIRDON VIC.

Moffett,Chester,House
HABS OH-279
HABS OHIO,28-CLAR.V,2-
9dr/2pg L

CLARIDON

Congregational Church
Rt. 85
HABS OH-237
HABS OHIO,28-CLAR,1-
4dr/3ph/2pg L

CLARIDON VIC.

Taylor,Corydon,House
Taylor Rd.
HABS OH-274
HABS OHIO,28-CLAR.V,1-
7dr/2ph/2pg L

GREENE COUNTY

WILBERFORCE

Young,Col. Charles,House
Columbia Pike btwn. Clifton & Stevenson Rds.
HABS OH-2249
HABS OHIO,29-WILB,1-
9ph/3pg/1pc L

YELLOW SPRINGS

Antioch College,Main Hall
Livermore St. & N. College Ave.
HABS OH-644
HABS OHIO,29-YEL,1A-
5dr/10ph/3pg/1pc/fr L

GUERNSEY COUNTY

CAMBRIDGE

Bridge on Old National Road
N. of U. S. Hwy. 40 at Saltfork
HABS OH-2113
HABS OHIO,30-CAMB.V,2-
1ph L

CAMBRIDGE VIC.

"S" Bridge
W. of Cambridge
HABS OH-2114
HABS OHIO,30-CAMB.V,3-
4ph L

Bridge on Old National Road
W. Cambridge on U. S. Hwy. 40
HABS OH-2112
HABS OHIO,30-CAMB.V,1-
4ph/5pg L

MIDDLEBOURNE VIC.

"S" Bridge
HABS OH-2116
HABS OHIO,30-MIDBO.V,2-
4ph L

Bridge
HABS OH-2115
HABS OHIO,30-MIDBO.V,1-
2ph L

HAMILTON COUNTY

CAMP DENNISON

Camp Dennison,Officers' Quarters & Guard House
(Waldschmidt,Christian,House)
7567 Glendale-Milford Rd.
HABS OH-6-18
HABS OHIO,31-CAMD,1-
15dr/6ph/1pg/1pc L

Waldschmidt,Christian,House; see Camp Dennison,Officers' Quarters & Guard House

CINCINNATI

Allen House
2711 Park Ave.
HABS OH-2343
HABS OHIO,31-CINT,67-
6ph/1pg/1pc L

American Oak Leather Company
1220-1236 Kenner St.
HABS OH-2263
HABS OHIO,31-CINT,38A-
13ph/12pg/1pc L

Anderson House
1111 Myrtle Ave.
HABS OH-2348
HABS OHIO,31-CINT,65-
3ph/1pg/1pc L

410-412 Armory Avenue (Commercial Building)
HABS OH-699
HABS OHIO,31-CINT,16-
2ph/1pg/1pc L

414 Armory Avenue (House)
HABS OH-700
HABS OHIO,31-CINT,17-
2ph/1pg/1pc L

428-430 Armory Avenue (Houses)
HABS OH-701
HABS OHIO,31-CINT,18-
2ph/1pg/1pc L

Augsburger Building
(Duennes,August,Building)
5811-13 Hamilton Ave.
HABS OH-2378
HABS DLC/PP-1993:OH-5
13ph/16pg/3pc L

Bender,Dr. Arthur C.,Office; see 817 Vine Street (Commercial Building)

Betts-Longworth (Houses & Commercial Buildings)
Ezzard Charles Dr,Central Ave,Old Court & Mound St
HABS OH-655
HABS OHIO,31-CINT,20-
8ph/4pg/1pc L

Bird Custom Hearing Aid; see 6-8 Garfield Place (Commercial Building)

Booktrader Books; see 4 Garfield Place (Commercial Building)

Brighton Car Barn & Employees Club & Office Bldg.
1143-1145 Harrison Ave.
HABS OH-661
HABS OHIO,31-CINT,36-
8ph/5pg/1pc L

Cathedral of St. Peter in Chains (St. Peter's Cathedral)
Eighth & Plum Sts.
HABS OH-638
HABS OHIO,31-CINT,8-
12ph/4pg/1pc L

1507-1509 Central Avenue (Commercial Building) (Fishman Building)
HABS OH-702
HABS OHIO,31-CINT,23-
1ph/1pg/1pc L

1521-1523 Central Avenue (Commercial Building)
HABS OH-703
HABS OHIO,31-CINT,24-
3ph/1pg/1pc L

707-709 Central Avenue (Commercial Building)
HABS OH-660
HABS OHIO,31-CINT,21-
1ph/1pg/1pc L

904-908 Central Avenue (Commercial Buildings)
HABS OH-2268
HABS OHIO,31-CINT,22-
3ph/1pg/1pc L

Chesapeake & Ohio Railroad Bridge
Spanning Ohio River
HAER OH-27
HAER OHIO,31-CINT,44-
2ph/1pg/1pc L

Christ Child Day Nursery Building; see 112 Findlay Street (House)

Cincinatti Union Depot,Mail Handling Building
Bounded by McLean,Sherman,Liberty Aves.& ConrailRR
HABS OH-705-A
HABS DLC/PP-1993:OH-3
16ph/12pg/2pc L

Cincinnati City Hall
801 Plum St.
HABS OH-418
HABS OHIO,31-CINT,15-
7ph/5pg/1pc/fr L

Cincinnati Suspension Bridge
Spanning Ohio River
HAER OH-28
HAER OHIO,31-CINT,45-
10ph/4pg/1pc/9ct L

Cincinnati Union Terminal
1301 Western Ave.
HABS OH-705
HABS OHIO,31-CINT,29-
56ph/10pg/4pc/fr L

Cooksey House
856 Lincoln Ave.
HABS OH-2206
HABS OHIO,31-CINT,39-
4ph/1pg/1pc L

46 Court (House)
Raleigh Alley Vic.
HABS OH-641
HABS OHIO,31-CINT,11-
1ph L

808 Dayton Street (House) (Dayton Street Historic District)
Note: See HABS No. OH-2200 for drawings.
HABS OH-2200-A
HABS OHIO,31-CINT,47-
4ph/4pg/1pc/fr L

816 Dayton Street (House) (Dayton Street Historic District)
Note: See HABS No. OH-2200 for drawings.
HABS OH-2200-C
HABS OHIO,31-CINT,49-
5ph/5pg/1pc/fr L

829 Dayton Street (House) (Dayton Street Historic District)
Note: See HABS No. OH-2200 for drawings.
HABS OH-2200-F
HABS OHIO,31-CINT,52-
3ph/4pg/1pc/fr L

837 Dayton Street (House) (Dayton Street Historic District)
Note: See HABS No. OH-2200 for drawings.
HABS OH-2200-H
HABS OHIO,31-CINT,54-
5ph/4pg/1pc/fr L

932 Dayton Street (House) (Dayton Street Historic District)
HABS OH-2200-M
HABS OHIO,31-CINT,59-
5ph/3pg/1pc L

936 Dayton Street (House) (Dayton Street Historic District)
HABS OH-2200-N
HABS OHIO,31-CINT,60-
3ph/3pg/1pc L

938 Dayton Street (House) (Dayton Street Historic District)
HABS OH-2200-O
HABS OHIO,31-CINT,61-
3ph/3pg/1pc L

808-938 Dayton Street & 923 Bank Street (Dayton Street Historic District)
808-938 Dayton St. & 923 Bank St.
HABS OH-2200
HABS OHIO,31-CINT,13-
14dr/5ph/1pc/5ct/fr L

Dayton Street Historic District; see 808 Dayton Street (House)

Dayton Street Historic District; see 816 Dayton Street (House)

Dayton Street Historic District; see 829 Dayton Street (House)

Dayton Street Historic District; see 837 Dayton Street (House)

Dayton Street Historic District; see 932 Dayton Street (House)

Dayton Street Historic District; see 936 Dayton Street (House)

Dayton Street Historic District; see 938 Dayton Street (House)

Dayton Street Historic District; see 808-938 Dayton Street & 923 Bank Street

Dayton Street Historic District; see Gazlay,Allan,House

Dayton Street Historic District; see Hatch,George,House

Dayton Street Historic District; see Hickenlooper,Andrew,House

Dayton Street Historic District; see Howell,Elizabeth,House

Dayton Street Historic District; see Hurtt,Francis,House

Dayton Street Historic District; see Laws,James,House

Dayton Street Historic District; see Murch,Chauncey,House

Dayton Street Historic District; see Skaats-Hauck House

Dayton Street Historic District; see St. Augustine School

Duennes,August,Building; see Augsburger Building

629-31 E. Third St. (House)
HABS OH-2199
HABS OHIO,31-CINT,10-
1ph L

Earnshaw,Joseph,House; see Murch,Chauncey,House

Eighth Street District (Queensgate II)
W. Eighth,John & W. Seventh Sts.
HABS OH-2208
HABS OHIO,31-CINT,25-
30ph/2pg L

425-435 Elm Street (Commercial Buildings)
HABS OH-691
HABS OHIO,31-CINT,32-
8ph/1pg/1pc L

Evanston School
1825 Dana Ave.
HABS OH-663
HABS OHIO,31-CINT,28-
11ph/1pg/1pc L

Farmers College
5553 Belmont Ave.
HABS OH-23-3
HABS OHIO,31-CINT,3-
6dr/3ph/1pg L

112 Findlay Street (House) (Christ Child Day Nursery Building)
HABS OH-2267
HABS OHIO,31-CINT,33-
9ph/1pg/1pc L

Fishman Building; see 1507-1509 Central Avenue (Commercial Building)

Fourth & Laurence Streets (House)
HABS OH-640
HABS OHIO,31-CINT,9-
1ph L

4 Garfield Place (Commercial Building) (Image Maker's Gallery; Booktrader Books; Stage Door Lounge; Hocking Barber Shop)
HABS OH-2349
HABS OHIO,31-CINT,70-
7ph/1pg/1pc L

6-8 Garfield Place (Commercial Building) (Paul's Flowers; Bird Custom Hearing Aid; Vivianne's Gift Shop)
HABS OH-2350
HABS OHIO,31-CINT,71-
2ph/1pg/1pc L

Gazlay,Allan,House (Dayton Street Historic District)
824 Dayton St. (See HABS No. OH-2200 for drwgs.)
HABS OH-2200-E
HABS OHIO,31-CINT,51-
5ph/4pg/1pc/fr L

2935 Gilbert Avenue (House)
HABS OH-2207
HABS OHIO,31-CINT,35-
6ph/1pg/1pc L

Glassmeyer Apartment Building
2712-2718 Park Ave.
HABS OH-2344
HABS OHIO,31-CINT,68-
11ph/1pg/1pc L

Hatch,George,House (Dayton Street Historic District)
830 Dayton St. (See HABS No. OH-2200 for drwgs.)
HABS OH-2200-G
HABS OHIO,31-CINT,53-
10ph/5pg/1pc/fr L

Hickenlooper,Andrew,House (Dayton Street Historic District)
838 Dayton St. (See HABS No. OH-2200 for drwgs.)
HABS OH-2200-I
HABS OHIO,31-CINT,55-
3ph/4pg/1pc/fr L

Hilberg,John,Sr.; see Murch,Chauncey,House

Hocking Barber Shop; see 4 Garfield Place (Commercial Building)

Howell,Elizabeth,House (Dayton Street Historic District)
842 Dayton St. (See HABS No. OH-2200 for drwgs.)
HABS OH-2200-J
HABS OHIO,31-CINT,56-
3ph/4pg/1pc/fr L

Hurtt,Francis,House (Dayton Street Historic District)
850 Dayton St. (See HABS No. OH-2200 for drwgs.)
HABS OH-2200-L
HABS OHIO,31-CINT,58-
2ph/3pg/1pc/fr L

Image Maker's Gallery; see 4 Garfield Place (Commercial Building)

Jordon House
857 Beecher St.
HABS OH-2205
HABS OHIO,31-CINT,19-
5ph/1pg/1pc L

Kemper,James,Log Cabin
Zoological Gardens
HABS OH-23-2
HABS OHIO,31-CINT,2-
4dr/3ph/1pg L

Lane Seminary Project Area
2711,2712-2718,2715,2723,2801 Park & 1111 Myrtle
HABS OH-2252
HABS OHIO,31-CINT,66-
3ph/2pg/1pc L

Laws,James,House (Dayton Street Historic District)
818 Dayton St. (See HABS No. OH-2200 for drwgs.)
HABS OH-2200-D
HABS OHIO,31-CINT,50-
4ph/5pg/1pc/fr L

Magrue,Joseph,House
1413 Western Ave.
HABS OH-2216
HABS OHIO,31-CINT,30-
15ph/10pg/1pc L

Marine Hospital
Third & Kilgour Sts.
HABS OH-23-10
HABS OHIO,31-CINT,6-
12dr/9ph/1pg/fr L

Methodist Episcopal Church (Wesley Chapel)
322 E. Fifth St.
HABS OH-23-1
HABS OHIO,31-CINT,1-
9dr/2ph/1pg/fr L

Metropolitan Gallery; see 821 Vine Street (Commercial Building)

Murch,Chauncey,House (Earnshaw,Joseph,House; Hilberg,John,Sr.; Dayton Street Historic District)
846 Dayton St. (See HABS No. OH-2200 for drwgs.)
HABS OH-2200-K
HABS OHIO,31-CINT,57-
7ph/4pg/1pc/fr L

National Theater
312 Sycamore St.
HABS OH-23-7
HABS OHIO,31-CINT,4-
5dr/3ph/1pg L

Nelson Building
2501-2507 Kemper La.
HABS OH-651
HABS OHIO,31-CINT,37-
6ph/3pg/1pc L

Ohio National Guard Armory
1417-1437 Western Ave.
HABS OH-2264
HABS OHIO,31-CINT,31-
17ph/10pg/1pc L

3022 Park Avenue (Commercial Building)
HABS OH-658
HABS OHIO,31-CINT,40-
3ph/1pg/1pc L

2801 Park Avenue (House)
HABS OH-2347
HABS OHIO,31-CINT,64-
7ph/1pg/1pc L

Paul's Flowers; see 6-8 Garfield Place (Commercial Building)

Pendleton Subdivision (Residen/Commercial Bldgs.)
Bounded by Liberty St. ,Reading Rd. & Sycamore St.
HABS OH-656
HABS OHIO,31-CINT,43-
8ph/4pg/1pc L

Plum Street Temple; see Wise,Isaac M. ,Temple

Queensgate II; see Eighth Street District

418-420 Reading Rd. (Commercial Bldg.)
HABS OH-2332
HABS 1989(HABS):18
8ph/7pg/1pc L

River Pumping Station:Cincinnati Water Works
5800 Kellogg Ave. ,California District
HAER OH-29
HAER OHIO,31-CINT,46A-
11ph/2pg/1pc L

Sinton,David,House (Taft,Charles P. ,Museum)
316 Pike St.
HABS OH-23-9
HABS OHIO,31-CINT,5-
18dr/7ph/2pg/1pc/fr L

Skaats-Hauck House (Dayton Street Historic District)
812 Dayton St. (See HABS No. OH-2200 for drwgs.)
HABS OH-2200-B
HABS OHIO,31-CINT,48-
14ph/5pg/1pc/fr L

Sleep Out Louis' Annex; see 823 Vine Street (Commercial Building)

St. Augustine School (Dayton Street Historic District)
923 Bank St.
HABS OH-2200-P
HABS OHIO,31-CINT,62-
6ph/4pg/1pc L

St. Heinrich's Roman Catholic Church
1057 Flint St.
HABS OH-2203
HABS OHIO,31-CINT,14-
11ph/1pg/1pc L

St. Peter's Cathedral; see Cathedral of St. Peter in Chains

Stage Door Lounge; see 4 Garfield Place (Commercial Building)

Strong House (Wilbur House)
2715 Park Ave.
HABS OH-2345
HABS OHIO,31-CINT,69-
12ph/1pg/1pc L

Taft,Charles P. ,Museum; see Sinton,David,House

Thomson,John,House; see Willowburn

813-815 Vine Street (Commercial Building) (Will's Pawn Shop)
HABS OH-2351
HABS OHIO,31-CINT,72-
3ph/2pg/1pc L

817 Vine Street (Commercial Building) (Bender,Dr. Arthur C.,Office)
HABS OH-2352
HABS OHIO,31-CINT,73-
5ph/1pg/1pc L

819 Vine Street (Commercial Building)
HABS OH-2353
HABS OHIO,31-CINT,74-
1ph/1pg/1pc L

821 Vine Street (Commercial Building) (Metropolitan Gallery)
HABS OH-2354
HABS OHIO,31-CINT,75-
3ph/1pg/1pc L

823 Vine Street (Commercial Building) (Sleep Out Louis' Annex)
HABS OH-2355
HABS OHIO,31-CINT,76-
8ph/1pg/1pc L

Vivianne's Gift Shop; see 6-8 Garfield Place (Commercial Building)

Walnut Hill Steam Laundry
1032 Foraker St.
HABS OH-659
HABS OHIO,31-CINT,34-
9ph/3pg/1pc L

Washington Elementary School
1326 Hopple St.
HABS OH-2377
HABS DLC/PP-1993:OH-5
22ph/18pg/5pc L

Wesley Chapel; see Methodist Episcopal Church

413 West Eighth Street (Commercial Building)
HABS OH-649
HABS OHIO,31-CINT,26-
1ph/1pg/1pc L

201-205 West Fifth Street (Commercial Building)
HABS OH-648
HABS OHIO,31-CINT,41-
5ph/1pg/1pc L

213-215 West Fifth Street (Commercial Buildings)
HABS OH-690
HABS OHIO,31-CINT,42-
2ph/1pg/1pc L

White House
2723 Park Ave.
HABS OH-2346
HABS OHIO,31-CINT,63-
8ph/1pg/1pc L

Wilbur House; see Strong House

Will's Pawn Shop; see 813-815 Vine Street (Commercial Building)

Willowburn (Thomson,John,House)
1562 Hobart Ave.
HABS OH-6-16
HABS OHIO,31-CINT,7-
7dr/2ph/1pg/fr L

Wise,Isaac M. ,Temple (Plum Street Temple)
Eighth & Plum Sts.
HABS OH-643
HABS OHIO,31-CINT,12-
2dr/13ph/6pg/2pc/fr L

Wolf Building
412-416 W. Seventh St.
HABS OH-657
HABS OHIO,31-CINT,27-
3ph/1pg/1pc L

CINCINNATI VIC.

Baxter,William,House
Ridge Ave.
HABS OH-23-12
HABS OHIO,31-CINT.V,1-
4dr/1pg/fr L

Covington & Cincinnati Suspension Bridge
Spanning Ohio River,Covington,KY-Cincinnati,OH
HAER KY-20
HAER 1988(HAER):10
4ph/1pg/1pc L

ELIZABETHTOWN

Presbyterian Church
HABS OH-23-11
HABS OHIO,31-ELITO,1-
2dr/3ph/1pg/fr L

GREENHILLS

Whallon,James,House
Winton Rd.
HABS OH-6-17
HABS OHIO,31-MOUH.V,1-
13dr/10ph/1pg/1pc/fr L

HARRISON

Looker,Othniel,House
New Haven Rd.
HABS OH-23-5
HABS OHIO,31-NARSO.V,2-
6dr/2ph/1pg L

HARRISON VIC.

Eighteen Mile House
E. on U. S. Rt. 52
HABS OH-23-4
HABS OHIO,31-HARSO.V,1-
8dr/1ph/1pg L

LOCKLAND

Benson Street Concrete Bowstring Bridge
Spanning Mill Creek at Benson St.
HAER OH-50
HAER OHIO,31-LOCK,1-
6ph/10pg/1pc/fr L

MARIEMONT

Ferris,Elithalet,House (Mariemont Historical Museum)
3905 Plainville Rd.
HABS OH-23-15
HABS OHIO,31-MARMO,1-
8dr/4ph/1pg/fr L

Mariemont Historical Museum; see Ferris,Elithalet,House

MARIEMONT VIC.

Ferris,Joseph,House
5801 Wooster Pike
HABS OH-23-8
HABS OHIO,31-MARMO.V,1-
10dr/4ph/1pg/fr L

MIAMITOWN

Harrison Road Camelback Through Truss Bridge
Spanning Great Miami River at Harrison Rd.(Rt.457)
HAER OH-49
HAER OHIO,31-MIAM,1-
9ph/8pg/1pc L

MILFORD

Milford Bridge
(See Clermont,Milford for Documentation
HAER OH-77
L

MONTGOMERY VIC.

Barn,Frame
U. S. Rt. 3
HABS OH-2221
HABS OHIO,31-MONT.V,1-
6ph L

MOUNT HEALTHY

Mount Healthy Mill
Covered Bridge Rd.
HAER OH-25
HAER OHIO,31-MOUH,1-
14dr/24ph/3pg/2pc L

MT. CARMEL VIC.

Campbell,John,Residence
Mt. Carmel Rd.
HABS OH-23-13
HABS OHIO,31- ,1-
7dr/3ph/1pg/fr L

NEWTOWN

Harrison House (Landers' House)
Newtown Rd.
HABS OH-620
HABS OHIO,31-NEWT,1-
2ph/1pg L

Landers' House; see Harrison House

NORTH BEND VIC.

Harrison,Scott,House
Brower Rd.
HABS OH-23-6
HABS OHIO,31-NORB.V,1-
7dr/2ph/1pg L

NORWOOD

(No assigned MARO 11-13-92 Tina L.); see LeBlond,R.K.,Machine Tool Co.,Shotblast Filter Str

LeBlond,R.K.,Machine Tol Co.,Service Garage
2980 Madison Rd.
HAER OH-71-F
2ph/4pg/2pc H

LeBlond,R.K.,Machine Tool Co.,Dairy Barn
2980 Madison Rd.
HAER OH-71-G
3ph/4pg/2pc H

LeBlond,R.K.,Machine Tool Co.,Executive Garage
2980 Madison Rd.
HAER OH-71-C
3ph/5pg/2pc H

LeBlond,R.K.,Machine Tool Co.,Front Office Block
2980 Madison Rd.
HAER OH-71-B
36ph/9pg/5pc H

LeBlond,R.K.,Machine Tool Co.,Madison & Edwards Rd
2980 Madison Rd.
HAER OH-71
65ph/18pg/3pc H

LeBlond,R.K.,Machine Tool Co.,Ornamtl.Lndscp.Pavln
2980 Madison Rd.
HAER OH-71-E
3ph/4pg/2pc H

LeBlond,R.K.,Machine Tool Co.,Power Hse.& Outbldgs
2980 Madison Rd.
HAER OH-71-D
17ph/5pg/4pc H

LeBlond,R.K.,Machine Tool Co.,Production Building
2980 Madison Rd.
HAER OH-71-A
20ph/10pg/4pc H

LeBlond,R.K.,Machine Tool Co.,Shotblast Filter Str ((No assigned MARO 11-13-92 Tina L.))
2980 Madison Rd.
HAER OH-71-H
1ph/4pg/2pc H

Norwood City Hall
Montgomery & Elm
HABS OH-2134
HABS OHIO,31-NOWD,1-
3ph/5pg/1pc L

ROSS VIC.

Old Colerain Pennsylvania Through Truss Bridge
Spanning Great Miami River at County Rte. 463
HAER OH-54
HAER OHIO,31-ROSS.V,1-
4ph/16pg/1pc L

WHITEWATER

Shaker Centre Family,Broom Shop
E. side of Oxford Rd.
HABS OH-2190
HABS OHIO,31-WHIT,1-
3ph L

Shaker Centre Family,Trustees' Office
Oxford Rd.
HABS OH-2191
HABS OHIO,31-WHIT,2-
3ph L

Shaker Centre Family,Washhouse
Oxford Rd.
HABS OH-2192
HABS OHIO,31-WHIT,3-
5ph L

Shaker Meetinghouse
Oxford Rd.
HABS OH-2189
HABS OHIO,31-WHIT,4-
3ph L

Shaker North Family,Dwelling House
Oxford Rd.
HABS OH-2196
HABS OHIO,31-WHIT,5-
1ph L

Shaker North Family,General View
Oxford Rd.
HABS OH-2197
HABS OHIO,31-WHIT,6-
1ph L

Shaker North Family,Milkhouse
Oxford Rd.
HABS OH-2194
HABS OH,31-WHIT,7-
1ph L

Shaker North Family,Seed House
Oxford Rd.
HABS OH-2195
HABS OHIO,31-WHIT,8-
1ph L

Shaker North Family,Smokehouse
Oxford Rd.
HABS OH-2198
HABS OHIO,31-WHIT,9-
1ph L

Shaker North Family,Woodshed
Oxford Rd.
HABS OH-2193
HABS OHIO,31-WHIT,10-
2ph L

WYOMING

Woodruff Building
500 Worthington Ave.
HABS OH-650
HABS OHIO,31-WYO,1-
3ph/1pg/1pc L

HANCOCK COUNTY

FINDLAY

Wolf,Jesse,House
210 E. Main Cross St.
HABS OH-2300
HABS 1989(HABS):18
8ph/2pg/1pc L

FINDLAY VIC.

Ewing,P. W. ,House
Rt. 68
HABS OH-22-11
HABS OHIO,32-FIND.V,1-
6dr/1ph/1pg L

HIGHLAND COUNTY

SINKING SPRING

Octagonal Schoolhouse
HABS OH-2233
HABS OHIO,36-SINSP,1-
1ph L

HOCKING COUNTY

ADELPHI VIC.

Spencer,Jesse,House
HABS OH-46
HABS OHIO,37-ADEL.V,1-
2ph L

HURON COUNTY

MONROEVILLE

Schug,Albert F. ,House
29 Brown St.
HABS OH-22-19
HABS OHIO,39-MONVI,1-
2dr/1ph/1pg L

NORWALK

Fulstow,Dr. P. H. ,House
99 W. Main St.
HABS OH-211
HABS OHIO,39-NOWA,2-
6dr/2ph/4pg L

Martin,E. G. ,House
54 W. Main St.
HABS OH-22-20
HABS OHIO,39-NOWA,1-
3dr/4ph/1pg L

KNOX COUNTY

BLADENSBURG VIC.

Bladensburg Concrete Bowstring Bridge
Spanning Wakatomika Creek at State Rte. 541
HAER OH-52
HAER OHIO,42-BLAD.V,1-
5ph/13pg/1pc L

GAMBIER

Kenyon College,Neff,Peter,Cottage
Wiggin St.
HABS OH-49
HABS OHIO,42-GAMB,1-
1dr/5ph/6pg/1pc/fr L

MT. VERNON

Curtis-Devin House
101 N. Main St.
HABS OH-22-18
HABS OHIO,42-MOVER,1-
5dr/1ph/1pg L

LAKE COUNTY

KIRTLAND VILLAGE

Kirtland Temple (Mormon)
9020 Chillicoth Rd.
HABS OH-22-25
HABS OHIO,43-KIRT,1-
6dr/18ph/5pg/1pc/fr L

MENTOR

Bolton,Thomas,House
Euclid Rd. & E. Seventy-first St.
HABS OH-22-28
HABS OHIO,43-MENT,1-
2dr/2ph/1pg L

Garfield,James A. ,National Historic Site; see Lawnfield,Granary

Garfield,James A.,Barn; see Lawnfield,Barn

Garfield,James A.,Campaign Office; see Lawnfield,Campaign Office

Garfield,James A.,Carriage House & Gasholder; see Lawnfield,Carriage House & Gasholder

Garfield,James A.,Chicken Coop; see Lawnfield,Chicken Coop

Garfield,James A.,Cottage; see Lawnfield,Cottage

Garfield,James A.,House; see Lawnfield

Garfield,James A.,Second Tenant House; see Lawnfield,Second Tenant House

Garfield,James A.,Tenant House; see Lawnfield,Tenant House

Garfield,James A.,Windmill; see Lawnfield,Windmill

Lawnfield (Garfield,James A.,House)
8095 Mentor Ave. (U. S. Rt. 20)
HABS OH-2254
HABS OHIO,43-MENT,2-
14dr/17ph/1pc/fr L

Lawnfield,Barn (Garfield,James A.,Barn)
8095 Mentor Ave. (U. S. Rte. 20)
HABS OH-2254-E
HABS OHIO,43-MENT,2E-
1dr/1ph/1pc/fr L

Lawnfield,Campaign Office (Garfield,James A.,Campaign Office)
8095 Mentor Ave. (U. S. Route 20)
HABS OH-2254-G
HABS OHIO,43-MENT,2G-
1dr/3ph/1pc/fr L

Lawnfield,Carriage House & Gasholder (Garfield,James A.,Carriage House & Gasholder)
8095 Mentor Ave. (U. S. Rt. 20)
HABS OH-2254-A
HABS OHIO,43-MENT,2A-
5dr/5ph/1pc/fr L

Lawnfield,Chicken Coop
(Garfield,James A.,Chicken Coop)
8095 Mentor Ave. (U. S. Rte. 20)
HABS OH-2254-F
HABS OHIO,43-MENT,2F-
1dr/1ph/1pc/fr L

Lawnfield,Cottage (Garfield,James A.,Cottage)
8095 Mentor Ave. (U. S. Rte. 20)
HABS OH-2254-I
HABS OHIO,43-MENT,2I-
2ph/1pc L

Lawnfield,Granary (White Barn; Garfield,James A. ,National Historic Site)
8095 Mentor Ave. (U. S. Rte. 20)
HABS OH-2254-C
HABS OHIO,43-MENT,2C-
1dr/fr L

Lawnfield,Second Tenant House
(Garfield,James A.,Second Tenant House)
8095 Mentor Ave. (U. S. Rte. 20)
HABS OH-2254-H
HABS OHIO,43-MENT,2H-
1ph/1pc L

Lawnfield,Tenant House
(Garfield,James A.,Tenant House)
8095 Mentor Ave. (U. S. Rte. 20)
HABS OH-2254-B
HABS OHIO,43-MENT,2B-
1dr/2ph/1pc/fr L

Lawnfield,Windmill (Garfield,James A.,Windmill)
8095 Mentor Ave. (U. S. Rte. 20)
HABS OH-2254-D
HABS OHIO,43-MENT,2D-
1dr/2ph/1pc/fr L

White Barn; see Lawnfield,Granary

White,Florence Graves,House
Mentor Ave. (U. S. Rte. 20)
HABS OH-2239
HABS OHIO,43-MENT,3-
9dr L

PAINESVILLE

City Hall; see Courthouse,Old

Courthouse,Old (City Hall)
Richmond & Mentor Aves.
HABS OH-235
HABS OHIO,43-PAINV,2-
3dr/2ph/2pg L

Lockwood House
S. Park Place
HABS OH-255
HABS OHIO,43-PAINV,5-
2dr/2pg L

Main Street Bridge
Spanning Grand River at Main St.
HAER OH-34
HAER OHIO,43-PAINV,7-
16ph/13pg/2pc L

Malin House
30 S. Park Place
HABS OH-240
HABS OHIO,43-PAINV,4-
2dr/1ph/2pg L

Marshall,Seth,Residence
375 Bank St.
HABS OH-236
HABS OHIO,43-PAINV,3-
4dr/5ph/2pg L

Mathews,Dr. John H. ,House
309 N. State St.
HABS OH-22-24
HABS OHIO,43-PAINV,1-
9dr/5ph/1pg/1pc L

Rider Tavern
HABS OH-269
HABS OHIO,43-PAINV,6-
2ph/1pg L

UNIONVILLE

Unionville Tavern
County Line Rd.
HABS OH-246
HABS OHIO,43-UNIV,1-
3dr/2ph/2pg L

WILLOUGHBY

Elwell House; see Robinson,William P. ,House

Robinson,William P. ,House (Elwell House)
3742 Erie St.
HABS OH-2120
HABS OHIO,43-WILL,1- 5
8ph/6pg/1pc L

LICKING COUNTY

GRANVILLE

St. Luke's Episcopal Church
200 E. Broadway
HABS OH-400
HABS OHIO,45-GRAN,1-
14ph/7pg/2pc/fr L

LOGAN COUNTY

N. LEWISBURG VIC.

Gray,Matt,House
HABS OH-22-14
HABS OHIO,46- ,1-
8dr/1ph L

LORAIN COUNTY

AVON TOWNSHIP

Baldauf,William,House
Avon Center Rd.
HABS OH-238
HABS OHIO,47-AVO,1-
2dr/3ph/2pg L

Hardwick House
Detroit Rd.
HABS OH-226
HABS OHIO,47- ,2-
4dr/1ph/2pg L

Hurst,W. & L. E. ,House
Detroit Rd.
HABS OH-221
HABS OHIO,47- ,1-
5dr/5ph/2pg L

AVON VIC.

Sweet House
Detroit Rd.
HABS OH-229
HABS OHIO,47-AVO.V,1-
4dr/2ph/1pg L

AVON VILLAGE

Lewis House
Avon Center Rd.
HABS OH-245
HABS OHIO,47-AVO,4-
3dr/1ph/2pg L

Robinson-Fitch House
Avon Center Rd.
HABS OH-241
HABS OHIO,47-AVO,3-
2dr/2ph/3pg L

Wilson-Riegelsberger House
Rieglsberger Rd.
HABS OH-239
HABS OHIO,47-AVO,2-
3dr/1ph/2pg L

HUNTINGTON VIC.

Barker,Orlando,House; see Dirlam-Allen House

Clark-Pratt-Kemery Residence
Rt. 58
HABS OH-277
HABS OHIO,47-HUNT.V,3-
3dr/2ph/2pg L

Dirlam-Allen House
(Barker,Orlando,House)
State Rt. 58
HABS OH-266
HABS OHIO,47-HUNT.V,1-
5dr/4ph/2pg/1pc L

Roice-Tipton House; see Tracey,Captain,House

Tracey,Captain,House (Roice-Tipton House)
Ashland-Overlin & Bursley Rds.
HABS OH-273
HABS OHIO,47-HUNT.V,2-
8dr/3ph/2pg/1pc L

OBERLIN

First Church in Oberlin (Congregational)
N. Main & W. Lorain Sts.
HABS OH-2117
HABS OHIO,47-OBER,1-
7dr/22ph/8pg/3pc/fr L

Langston,John Mercer,House
207 E. College St.
HABS OH-2226
HABS OHIO,47-OBER,2-
2ph/3pg/1pc L

WELLINGTON

Gillette,H. M. ,Residence
Rt. 18,Blue Goose Corners
HABS OH-276
HABS OHIO,47-WEL,1-
4dr/1ph/2pg L

Warner House
370 S. Main St.
HABS OH-2118
HABS OHIO,47-WEL,2-
2ph/1pg L

Wellington Town Hall
Main St.
HABS OH-2228
HABS OHIO,47-WEL,3-
2ph/1pc L

LUCAS COUNTY

MAUMEE

St. Paul's Episcopal Church
E. Wayne & Elizabeth Sts.
HABS OH-19
HABS OHIO,48-MAUM,1-
8dr L

TOLEDO

Brand Building (Western Shoe Company)
120-124 Saint Clair St.
HABS OH-2258
HABS OHIO,48-TOLED,7-
13ph/9pg/1pc L

First National Bank (Securities Bank)
312 Summit St.
HABS OH-2201
HABS OHIO,48-TOLED,1-
22ph/2pc/fr L

Lockwood/Coghlin Buildings
119 & 121-123 Saint Clair St.
HABS OH-2257
HABS OHIO,48-TOLED,6-
14ph/13pg/1pc L

Oliver House (Hotel)
27 Broadway & Ottawa Sts.
HABS OH-2242
HABS OHIO,48-TOLED,2-
10ph/1pc L

Securities Bank; see First National Bank

Swiss Hall
410-412 Monroe St.
HABS OH-2259
HABS OHIO,48-TOLED,4-
7ph/12pg/1pc L

Toledo Parking Garage
114-134 Superior St.
HABS OH-2256
HABS OHIO,48-TOLED,5-
11ph/12pg/1pc L

Western Shoe Company; see Brand Building

Wheeler Block
402 Monroe St. & 109-111 Saint Clair St.
HABS OH-2255
HABS OHIO,48-TOLED,3-
19ph/15pg/1pc L

WATERVILLE

Columbian House (Tavern)
River Rd.
HABS OH-22-17
HABS OHIO,48-WATVI,1-
8dr/3ph/1pg L

MADISON COUNTY

LAFAYTETTE

Tavern,Red Brick
U. S. Rt. 40
HABS OH-2246
HABS OHIO,49-LAFA,1-
1ph L

MAHONING COUNTY

POLAND

Main St. Parker Pony Truss Bridge
Main St. (Rt. 170) spanning Yellow Creek
HAER OH-40
HAER OHIO,50-POL,1-
4ph/5pg/1pc/fr L

White Bowstring Arch Truss Bridge
Spanning Yellow Creek at Cemetery Dr.(Riverside Dr
HAER OH-39
HAER OHIO,50-POL,2-
3dr/10ph/14pg/1pc/2ct/fr L

YOUNGSTOWN

Carnegie Steel-Ohio Works,Steam Engines (U. S. Steel-Ohio Works,Steam Engines)
912 Salt Springs Rd.
HAER OH-33
HAER OHIO,50-YOUNG,1A-
22ph/2pc/fr L

Eagle's Hall
270-278 West Rayen Ave.
HABS OH-2289
HABS OHIO,50-YOUNG,3-
20ph/1pc L

258 Federal Plaza West (Commercial Building)
HABS OH-2342
HABS DLC/PP-1993:OH-5
5ph/5pg/1pc L

Mahoning Ave. Pratt Double-Deck Bridge
Spanning Mill Creek at Mahoning Ave. (C.R. 319)
HAER OH-41
HAER OHIO,50-YOUNG,2-
23ph/10pg/2pc/2ct L

Pollock,Porter,Estate;Caretaker's House (Youngstown State University,Groundskeeper's House)
603 Wick Ave.
HABS OH-2329
HABS 1989(HABS):18
15ph/5pg/1pc L

Republic Steel Bessemer Plant
South Ave. at Mahoning River
HAER OH-63
HAER OHIO,50-YOUNG,4-
8ph/1pc/1ct L

U. S. Steel-Ohio Works,Steam Engines; see Carnegie Steel-Ohio Works,Steam Engines

Youngstown State University,Groundskeeper's House; see Pollock,Porter,Estate;Caretaker's House

MEDINA COUNTY

SELVILLE

Maukee Inn; see St. John House

St. John House (Wallick & Whiteside Residence; Maukee Inn)
HABS OH-217
HABS OHIO,52-SEVI,2-
2dr/1ph/3pg L

Wallick & Whiteside Residence; see St. John House

SEVILLE

Welday House
HABS OH-216
HABS OHIO,52-SEVI,1-
2dr/1ph/4pg L

WEYMOUTH

First Congregational Church
State Rt. 3
HABS OH-257
HABS OHIO,52-WEYM,1-
3dr/2pg L

MEIGS COUNTY

CHESTER

Meigs County Courthouse,Old
HABS OH-642
HABS OHIO,53-CHEST,1-
3ph/3pg L

POMEROY

Meigs County Children's Home
Mulberry Rd.
HABS OH-2261
HABS OHIO,53-POM,1-
7ph/8pg L

MERCER COUNTY

FORT RECOVERY VIC.

Burrville Road Bridge
Spanning Toti Creek at Burrville Rd. ,Recovery Twp
HAER OH-35
HAER OHIO,54-FORE.V,1-
8ph/8pg/1pc L

MIAMI COUNTY

COVINGTON

Steinhilber,Martin,House
402 S. High St.
HABS OH-2277
HABS OHIO,55-COV,1-
12ph/15pg/2pc L

PIQUA

Central Union Telephone Company Bldg. (Ohio Bell Telephone Company Bldg.)
311 N. Wayne St.
HABS OH-2274
HABS OHIO,55-PIQU,1-
14ph/6pg/1pc L

Ohio Bell Telephone Company Bldg.; see Central Union Telephone Company Bldg.

Shannon/Kiser Building
313-315 N. Wayne St.
HABS OH-2275
HABS OHIO,55-PIQU,2-
11ph/7pg/1pc L

PLEASANT HILL

Newton Township Building
S. Main St. near Hill St.
HABS OH-2276
HABS OHIO,55-PLEAH,1-
12ph/17pg/1pc L

MONTGOMERY COUNTY

DAYTON

Building No. 57; see Wright-Patterson A.F.B.,Air Corps Supply Warehouse

City of Dayton Municipal Building (Young Men's Christian Association (YMCA))
101 W. Third St.
HABS OH-427
HABS OHIO,57-DAYT,3-
8ph/12pg/1pc/fr L

Dayton Mental Health Center; see Southern Ohio Lunatic Asylum

Dunbar,Paul Laurence,Barn
219 N. Summit St.
HABS OH-218-A
HABS OHIO,57-DAYT,4A-
2dr/fr L

Dunbar,Paul Laurence,House
219 N. Summit St.
HABS OH-218
HABS OHIO,57-DAYT,4-
5dr/6pg/fr L

Log Cabin,Old; see Newcom Tavern

Montgomery County Courthouse,Old
Third & Main Sts.
HABS OH-51
HABS OHIO,57-DAYT,2-
8dr/35ph/7pg/3pc/fr L

Newcom Tavern (Log Cabin,Old)
Van Cleve Park,E. Monument Ave.
HABS OH-627
HABS OHIO,57-DAYT,1-
7dr/5ph/2pg/1pc/fr L

Southern Ohio Lunatic Asylum
(Dayton Mental Health Center)
2335 Wayne Ave.
HABS OH-2222
HABS OHIO,57-DAYT,5-
13ph/19pg/1pc L

Wright-Patterson A.F.B.,Air Corps Supply Warehouse (Building No. 57)
HAER OH-79-AF
H

Young Men's Christian Association (YMCA); see City of Dayton Municipal Building

KETTERING

Kettering Government Center
3600 Shroyer Rd.
HABS OH-429
HABS OHIO,57-KET,1-
8ph/12pg/fr L

MORGAN COUNTY

MCCONNELSVILLE VIC.

Morgan County Home
State Rt. 376
HABS OH-2135
HABS OHIO,58-MCCON.V,1-
5ph/2pg/1pc L

Morgan County Home for the Insane
State Rt. 376
HABS OH-2151
HABS OHIO,58-MCCON.V,2-
4ph/2pg/1pc L

STOCKPORT

McKibben's Grocery
Second St. & SR 266,Stockport Historic District
HABS OH-2149
HABS OHIO,58-STOCK,1-
4ph/5pg/1pc L

MORROW COUNTY

MOUNT GILEAD

Trimble,James,House
HABS OH-2335
11dr H

MUSKINGUM COUNTY

HOPEWELL VIC.

Bridge on Old National Road; see Covered Bridge,Old

Covered Bridge,Old (Bridge on Old National Road)
W. of Zanesville P. O. ,U. S. Hwy. 40
HABS OH-45
HABS OHIO,60-ZANV.V,1-
4ph L

ROSEVILLE

First Street Reinforced Concrete Bridge
Spanning Moxahala Creek at First St. (CR 7)
HAER OH-47
HAER OHIO,60-ROSE,1-
1dr/6ph/9pg/1pc/fr L

ZANESVILLE

Bridge
Between Cambridge,OH & Wheeling,W. VA
HABS OH-2106-F
HABS OHIO, - ,1-
1ph L

Bridge,Stone
Rt. 40
HABS OH-43
HABS OHIO,60-ZANV.V,4-
2ph L

Buckingham,Alvah,House
405 Moxahala Ave.
HABS OH-420
HABS OHIO,60-ZANV,2-
2dr L

Nye-Potts House
Adams St.
HABS OH-421
HABS OHIO,60-ZANV,1-
2dr L

Y-Bridge
Spanning confluence of Muskingham & Licking Rivers
HAER OH-22
HAER OHIO,60-ZANV,3-
15ph/13pg/2pc L

ZANESVILLE VIC.

"S" Bridge
Between St. Clairsville & Zanesville
HABS OH-2106-D
HABS OHIO, - ,5-
2ph L

Bridge
HABS OH-43-A
HABS OHIO,60-ZANV.V,5-
2ph L

Bridge
Between St. Clairsville & Zanesville
HABS OH-2106-E
HABS OHIO, - ,4-
1ph L

Bridge
Between Zanesville & Cambridge
HABS OH-2106-C
HABS OHIO, - ,6-
2ph L

Covered Bridge,Old
HABS OH-45
HABS OHIO,60-ZANV.V,2-
4ph L

Headley,Usual,Inn
Rt. 40
HABS OH-2217
HABS OHIO,60-ZANV.V,3-
2ph L

House,Stone
HABS OH-2106-A
HABS OHIO,- ,2-
1ph L

Structures on Old National Trail
Between Batlimore,MD & Zanesville,OH
HABS OH-2106
HABS OHIO, - , -
2pg L

OTTAWA COUNTY

LIMESTONE VIC.

Bridge
HABS OH-18
HABS OHIO,62-LIM.V,1-
2ph L

PUT-IN-BAY

Perry's Victory and International Peace Memorial
Green Island
HABS OH-2395
HABS DLC/PP-1992:OH-5
2ph/1pc L

PAULDING COUNTY

ANTWERP VIC.

"Forder" Pratt Through Truss Bridge
Spanning Maumee River at County Rte. 73
HAER OH-42
HAER OHIO,63-ANT.V,1-
7ph/14pg/1pc L

PERRY COUNTY

NEW LEXINGTON VIC.

Mount Aloysius; see St. Aloysius Academy

St. Aloysius Academy (Mount Aloysius)
Tile Plant Rd. at Thorn Rd.
HABS OH-2150
HABS OHIO,64-NELE.V,1-
33ph/14pg/1pc L

SOMERSET

Perry County Courthouse,Old
Town Square
HABS OH-412
HABS OHIO,64-SOM,1-
2dr/11ph/7pg/2pc/fr L

PICKAWAY COUNTY

KINDERHOOK VIC.

Milestone of Zane's Trace
Rt. 22
HABS OH-42
HABS OHIO,65-KINHO.V,1-
1ph L

PIKE COUNTY

JASPER

Jones House (Stone)
State Hwy. 24
HABS OH-634
HABS OHIO,66-JASP,1-
9dr/3ph/1pg L

PIKETON VIC.

Lucas,Gov. ,House
HABS OH-636
HABS OHIO,66-PIKT.V,1-
13dr L

PORTAGE COUNTY

ATWATER

Congregational Church
HABS OH-22-7
HABS OHIO,67-ATWA,1-
5dr/3ph/2pg L

AURORA

Egglestone,Chauncey,House; see Hopwood House

Hopwood House
(Egglestone,Chauncey,House)
Egglestone Rd.
HABS OH-243
HABS OHIO,67-AURO,3-
2dr/1ph/2pg L

Howard,C. R. ,House
Rt. 17
HABS OH-244
HABS OHIO,67-AURO,4-
2dr/1ph/2pg L

Root,Emery,House
Chillicothe Rd.
HABS OH-242
HABS OHIO,67-AURO,2-
3dr/4ph/2pg L

Willard,Archibald M. ,Residence
Rt. 82
HABS OH-232
HABS OHIO,67-AURO,1-
1dr/1ph/2pg L

DEERFIELD

Day,Judge Alva,House; see Shively,Lois,House (Entrance Doorway)

Shively,Lois,House (Entrance Doorway) (Day,Judge Alva,House)
HABS OH-22-10
HABS OHIO,67-DEER,1-
1dr/1ph/1pg L

FREEDOM

Freedom Congregational Church
HABS OH-2236
HABS OHIO,67-FREE,1-
8dr L

KENT

First Universalist Church
Gougler St.
HABS OH-2244
HABS OHIO,67-KENT,1-
7dr L

Franklin Town Hall; see Franklin Township Hall

Franklin Township Hall (Franklin Town Hall)
218 Gougler Ave.
HABS OH-2245
HABS OHIO,67-KENT,2-
11dr L

RAVENNA

Ravenna Army Ammunition Plant
HAER OH-30
HAER OHIO,67-RAV,1-
68pg/fr L

ROOTSTOWN

Rootstown Town Hall
State Rtes. 18 & 44
HABS OH-2243
HABS OHIO,67-ROOT,1-
6dr L

STREETSBORO

Baptist Church,Old (Methodist Church)
Rt. 43 & 14
HABS OH-251
HABS OHIO,67-STREBO,1-
2dr/1ph/2pg L

Methodist Church; see Baptist Church,Old

PREBLE COUNTY

EATON VIC.

Roberts Bridge
Old Camden Pike,Spanning Seven Mile Creek
HABS OH-2229
HABS OHIO,68-EATO.V,1-
4ph/1pc L

RICHLAND COUNTY

MANSFIELD

Gardner Apartments; see Sturges,Dimon,House

Sturges,Dimon,House (Windemere,The; Gardner Apartments)
114 Park Avenue W
HABS OH-2269
HABS OHIO,70-MAN,1-
15ph/14pg/1pc L

Windemere,The; see Sturges,Dimon,House

ROSS COUNTY

CHILLICOTHE

Barret,Vernon,House
(Greene,Judge,House)
HABS OH-2230
HABS OHIO,71-CHILC,1-
5ph L

Greene,Judge,House; see Barret,Vernon,House

CHILLICOTHE VIC.

Adena (Mount Prospect Hall; Worthington,Gov. Thomas,House)
St. Margaret's Cemetery Vic.
HABS OH-645
HABS OHIO,71-CHILC.V,1-
7dr/4ph/3pg L

Mount Prospect Hall; see Adena

Worthington,Gov. Thomas,House; see Adena

SANDUSKY COUNTY

FREMONT

Bidwell & Gallagher Factory (Fremont Glass Warehouse)
315 Bidwell Ave.
HAER OH-38
HAER OHIO,72-FREMO,3-
4ph/8pg/1pc L

Edgerton House
Buckland Ave.
HABS OH-22-16
HABS OHIO,72-FREMO,2-
4dr/3ph/1pg L

Fremont Glass Warehouse; see Bidwell & Gallagher Factory

Sandusky County Courthouse
S. Park St.
HABS OH-22-15
HABS OHIO,72-FREMO,1-
6dr/2ph/2pg L

SCIOTO COUNTY

PORTSMOUTH

All Saints Episcopal Church
610 Fourth St.
HABS OH-2312
HABS 1988(HABS):106
3ph/1pg/1pc L

Excelsior Shoe Factory
1015-1017 Gallia St.
HABS OH-2317
HABS OHIO,73-PORT,7-
2ph/1pg/1pc L

Fowler Building; see Reed,Joseph G. ,Company

Greyhound Bus Depot
1129-1135 Gallia St.
HABS OH-2320
HABS OHIO,73-PORT,8-
3ph/1pg/1pc L

Hall,William,House
429 Second St.
HABS OH-2309
HABS OHIO,73-PORT,10-
6ph/1pg/1pc L

Holly Store
Chillicothe & Fourth Sts.
HABS OH-2319
HABS OHIO,73-PORT,10-
5ph/1pg/1pc L

Hoobler,Emerson & Grace,House
935 Second St.
HABS OH-2313
HABS OHIO,73-PORT,11
4ph/1pg/1pc L

Independent Order of Odd Fellows
Court & Fifth Sts.
HABS OH-2316
HABS OHIO,73-PORT,12-
9ph/1pg/1pc L

Kehoe,Murtaugh,House
708 Second St.
HABS OH-666
HABS OHIO,73-PORT,3-
1pg L

Kinney,Peter,House
622 Front St.
HABS OH-2310
HABS OHIO,73-PORT,13-
5ph/1pg/1pc L

Kirby's Flower Shop
923 Gallia St.
HABS OH-2318
HABS OHIO,73-PORT,14-
3ph/1pg/1pc L

McDowell,John,House
701 Market St.
HABS OH-2308
HABS OHIO,73-PORT,15-
5ph/1pg/1pc L

Newman,William,House
716 Second St.
HABS OH-664
HABS OHIO,73-PORT,5-
15ph/8pg/2pc L

O'Neill,Andrew,House
712 Second St.
HABS OH-652
HABS OHIO,73-PORT,4-
9ph/7pg/1pc L

Portsmouth Foundry
401 Third St.
HABS OH-2315
HABS OHIO,73-PORT,16-
5ph/1pg/1pc L

Reed,Joseph G. ,Company (Fowler Building)
700 Second St.
HABS OH-665
HABS OHIO,73-PORT,2-
2ph/2pg/1pc L

Scioto Pennsylvania Through Truss Bridge
Spanning Scioto River at State Rte. 73
HAER OH-53
HAER OHIO,73-PORT,1-
13ph/9pg/1pc L

Tracey House
626 Fourth St.
HABS OH-2314
HABS OHIO,73-PORT,17-
5ph/1pg/1pc L

SENECA COUNTY

TIFFIN

Gordon Lumber Co.; see 15-17 S. Washington (Commercial Bldg)

Gordon Lumber Co.; see 19-21 S. Washington St. (Commercial Bldg.)

Kildow Bldg.; see 15-17 S. Washington (Commercial Bldg)

15-17 S. Washington (Commercial Bldg) (Tiffin Wood Mill; Kildow Bldg.; Gordon Lumber Co.)
HABS OH-2327
HABS OHIO,74-TIF,1-
4ph/5pg/1pc L

19-21 S. Washington St. (Commercial Bldg.) (Tiffin Wood Mill; Gordon Lumber Co.)
HABS OH-2328
HABS OHIO,74-TIF,2-
2ph/5pg/1pc L

Tiffin Wood Mill; see 15-17 S. Washington (Commercial Bldg)

Tiffin Wood Mill; see 19-21 S. Washington St. (Commercial Bldg.)

TIFFIN VIC.

Abbott's Parker Through Truss Bridge
Spanning Sandusky R. at Abbott Rd. (Pleasant Twp.)
HAER OH-48
HAER OHIO,74-TIF.V,1-
8ph/7pg/1pc L

SHELBY COUNTY

LOCKINGTON

Miami & Erie Canal Locks
Loramie Portage site Vic.
HABS OH-411
HABS OHIO,75-LOCK,1-
1ph/1pg L

STARK COUNTY

CANTON

Church of the Savior (United Methodist); see First Methodist Church

First Methodist Church (Church of the Savior (United Methodist))
Cleveland Ave. & W. Tuscarawas St.
HABS OH-2152
HABS OHIO,76-CANT,3-
1ph/1pc L

McKinley High School (Pottorf Education Center)
800 N. Market St.
HABS OH-2260
HABS OHIO,76-CANT,1-
19ph/3pg/1pc L

Pottorf Education Center; see McKinley High School

Renkert,Harry S. ,Carriage House
1414 N. Market Ave.
HABS OH-2265
HABS OHIO,76-CANT,2A-
6ph/3pg/1pc L

Third Street Southeast Bridge
Spanning Nimishillen Creek
HAER OH-23
HAER OHIO,76-CANT,4-
13ph/24pg/1pc L

LIMAVILLE

Baldwin,Alonzo,House (Entrance Doorway)
State Rt. 225
HABS OH-22-9
HABS OHIO,76-LIMAV,1-
1dr/1ph/1pg L

SUMMIT COUNTY

AKRON

Elizabeth Park Pavilion
Stuber & E. North St.
HABS OH-2253
HABS OHIO,77-AKRO,4A-
9dr/fr L

Goodyear Airdock
1210 Massillon Rd.
HAER OH-57
HAER OHIO,77-AKRO,6-
30ph/1pg/2pc/9ct/fr L

O'Neil,M. ,Company (O'Neil's Department Store)
226 S. Main St.
HABS OH-2262
HABS OHIO,77-AKRO,3-
8ph/13pg/1pc L

O'Neil's Department Store; see O'Neil,M. ,Company

Perkins Hill; see Perkins,Col. Simon,House

Perkins,Col. Simon,House (Perkins Hill)
Maple St.
HABS OH-22-8
HABS OHIO,77-AKRO,1-
3dr/2ph/1pg L

Quaker Oats Cereal Factory
SE corner of Broadway & Mill Streets
HAER OH-17
HAER OHIO,77-AKRO,7-
23ph/8pg/2pc L

Stan Hywet Hall
714 N. Portage Path
HABS OH-50
HABS OHIO,77-AKRO,5-
145ph/5pg/7pc/14ct/fr L

Stan Hywet Hall,Carriage House & Garage
714 N. Portage Path
HABS OH-50-A
HABS OHIO,77-AKRO,5A-
18ph/2pc/2ct/fr L

Stan Hywet Hall,Garden House & Garden
714 N. Portage Path
HABS OH-50-B
HABS OHIO,77-AKRO,5B-
6ph/1pc/fr L

Stan Hywet Hall,Gate House & Entrance Gates
714 N. Portage Path
HABS OH-50-C
HABS OHIO,77-AKRO,5C-
6ph/1pc/fr L

Stan Hywet Hall,Lookouts
714 N. Portage Path
HABS OH-50-E
HABS OHIO,77-AKRO,5E-
3ph/1pc L

Stan Hywet Hall,Service Bldg./Gardener's House
714 N. Portage Path
HABS OH-50-D
HABS OHIO,77-AKRO,5D-
5ph/1pc/fr L

Y. W. C. A.; see Young Women's Christian Association

Young Women's Christian Association (Y. W. C. A.)
146 S. High St.
HABS OH-2266
HABS OHIO,77-AKRO,2-
33ph/11pg/2pc L

BATH

Hopkins House (Entrance)
Rt.21
HABS OH-262
HABS OHIO,77-BATH,1-
1dr/1ph/2pg L

BOSTON TWP.

Kendall Lake Shelter
Truxell Rd.,Cuyahoga Valley Nat'l Recreation Area
HABS OH-2304
HABS OHIO,77-PEN.V,1-
10ph/1pg/1pc L

COPLEY

Arnold House
HABS OH-220
HABS OHIO,77-COP,1-
2dr/1ph/1pg L

EVERETT VIC.

Ohio & Erie Canal,Furnace Run Aqueduct
1100 ft. south of Everett Rd.
HAER OH-61
HAER DLC/PP-1992:OH-2
1dr/fr L

HUDSON

Baldwin-Buss House
(Baldwin,Augustus,House & Tavern)
Main St. & Streetsboro Rd.
HABS OH-22-4
HABS OHIO,77-HUD,1-
2dr/3ph/1pg/1pc L

Baldwin,Augustus,House & Tavern; see Baldwin-Buss House

Chapel; see Western Reserve Academy,Chapel

Dining Hall Dormitory; see Western Reserve Academy,Bliss-Slaughter House

First National Bank of Hudson
Aurora & Main Streets
HABS OH-2240
HABS OHIO,77-HUD,4-
7dr L

Hudson Library & Historical Society
49 E. Main St.
HABS OH-2241
HABS OHIO,77-HUD,5-
9dr L

Loomis Observatory; see Western Reserve Academy,Loomis Observatory

North Hall; see Western Reserve Academy,North Hall

Nutting House; see Western Reserve Academy,Bliss-Slaughter House

President's House; see Western Reserve Academy,President's House

Western Reserve Academy,Bliss-Slaughter House
(Nutting House; Dining Hall Dormitory)
79 Hudson St.
HABS OH-271
HABS OHIO,77-HUD,2D-
1dr/3ph/2pg/1pc L

Western Reserve Academy,Chapel
(Chapel)
Western Reserve University
HABS OH-22-2
HABS OHIO,77-HUD,2A-
3dr/4ph/2pg/1pc L

Western Reserve Academy,Loomis Observatory (Loomis Observatory)
Western Reserve University
HABS OH-22-5
HABS OHIO,77-HUD,2C-
7dr/4ph/1pg/1pc L

Western Reserve Academy,North Hall
(North Hall)
Western Reserve Academy
HABS OH-22-3
HABS OHIO,77-HUD,2B-
1dr/2ph/1pg L

Western Reserve Academy,President's House (President's House)
Hudson & College Sts.
HABS OH-275
HABS OHIO,77-HUD,2E-
8dr/4ph/2pg/1pc L

IRA (VILLAGE) VIC.

Hale,Jonathan,House
Oak Hill Rd.
HABS OH-250
HABS OHIO,77-IRA,1-
6dr/1ph/3pg L

NORTHFIELD CENTER VI

Wallace,James,Barn
8230 Brandywine Rd.,Cuyahoga Valley NRA
HABS OH-2306-A
HABS OHIO,77-NORCE.V,1A-
6ph/1pg/1pc L

Wallace,James,House
8230 Brandywine Rd.,Cuyahoga Valley NRA
HABS OH-2306
HABS OHIO,77-NORCE.V,1-
6ph/6pg/1pc L

Wallace,James,Outbuilding
8230 Brandywine Rd.,Cuyahoga Valley NRA
HABS OH-2306-B
HABS OHIO,77-NORCE.V,1B-
1ph/1pc L

NORTHFIELD VIC.

French House
Town Line Rd. ,Rt. 8 Vic.
HABS OH-252
HABS OHIO,77-NORF.V,1-
2dr/2pg L

PENINSULA

Bronson,H. V. ,House
Rt. 303
HABS OH-267
HABS OHIO,77-PEN,1-
5dr/2ph/2pg L

Ohio & Erie Canal,Lock No. 29
On Cuyahoga Riv.,600 ft. north of Main St.(Rt 303)
HAER OH-59-A
HAER DLC/PP-1992:OH-2
1dr/5ph/1pc/fr L

PENINSULA VIC.

Happy Days Shelter
434 W. Streetsboro Rd.(St. Rte. 303)
Cuyahoga NRA
HABS OH-2302
HABS OHIO,77-PEN.V,2-
5ph/1pg/1pc L

Ledges Shelter
Truxell Rd.,Cuyahoga Valley Nat'l Recreation Area
HABS OH-2303
HABS OHIO,77-PEN.V,3-
8ph/1pg/1pc L

Octagon Shelter
Truxell Rd.,Cuyahoga Vally Nat'l Recreation Area
HABS OH-2305
HABS OHIO,77-PEN.V,4-
5ph/1pg/1pc L

Ohio & Erie Canal
Links Lake Erie at Cleveland & Ohio Riv. at Ports.
HAER OH-59
HAER DLC/PP-1992:OH-2
1dr/2ph/10pg/1pc/fr L

Ohio & Erie Canal,Lock No. 28
E Junt. Mjr.&Rivrvw. Rds.,Cuy. Val. Nat. Rec. Area
HAER OH-59-E
HAER DLC/PP-1992:OH-2
3ph/1pc L

SAGAMORE HILLS

Baltimore & Ohio Railroad: Cuyahoga River Bridge; see Jaite Company Railroad Bridge

Cuyahoga Valley National Recreation Area; see Jaite Paper Mill

Jaite Company Railroad Bridge
(Baltimore & Ohio Railroad: Cuyahoga River Bridge)
1200 W. Highland Rd.
HAER OH-62
HAER 1991(HAER):27
5dr/fr L

Jaite Paper Mill (Cuyahoga Valley National Recreation Area)
1200 W. Highland Rd.
HAER OH-36
HAER OHIO,77-SAGHI,1-
13dr/26ph/2pc/fr L

TALLMADGE

Congregational Church
Village Green
HABS OH-22-6
HABS OHIO,77-TALM,1-
4dr/6ph/1pg/1pc L

TWINSBURG

Elliott Building
Rt. 14
HABS OH-227
HABS OHIO,77-TWINB,2-
2dr/2ph/2pg L

Twinsburg Congregational Church
Rt. 14
HABS OH-29
HABS OHIO,77-TWINB,1-
4dr/6ph/2pg L

TWINSBURG VIC.

Herrick House
Rt. 91
HABS OH-223
HABS OHIO,77-TWINB.V,1-
3dr/1ph/2pg L

VALLEY VIEW

Ohio & Erie Canal,Lock No. 37
At Canal and Fitzwater Rds.
HAER OH-59-B
HAER DLC/PP-1992:OH-2
1dr/2ph/1pc/fr L

TRUMBULL COUNTY

BRISTOLVILLE

Congregational Church
State Rt. 45 & 88
HABS OH-263
HABS OHIO,78-BRISVI,2-
3dr/1ph/2pg L

Methodist Church,Old
HABS OH-260
HABS OHIO,78-BRISVI,1-
1ph/2pg L

KINSMAN

Congregational-Presbyterian Church
State Rt. 5
HABS OH-247
HABS OHIO,78-KIN,1-
3dr/5ph/2pg/1pc L

KINSMAN VIC.

Allen,Peter,House
State Rt. 7
HABS OH-248
HABS OHIO,78-KIN.V,1-
13dr/2ph/2pg L

NEWTON FALLS

Covered Bridge
Spanning Mahoney River
HABS OH-270
HABS OHIO,78-NEWT,1-
3dr/3ph/2pg L

NORTH BLOOMFIELD

Brownwood Farm
HABS OH-261
HABS OHIO,78-BLOMN,1-
2ph/1pg L

NORTH BRISTOL

White House
State Rt. 45
HABS OH-259
HABS OHIO,78-BRISTN,1-
4dr/2ph/2pg L

WARREN

Basso Block (Commercial Building)
140 S. Park Ave.
HABS OH-2273
HABS OHIO,78-WAR,6-
2pg/fr L

Edwards-Webb House (Iddings House)
303 Monroe St.,NW,moved from 259 South St.,SE
HABS OH-272
HABS OHIO,78-WAR,2-;DLC/PP-1992:OH-3
7dr/1ph/3pg L

Guarnieri,Fred Building
140-146 E. MARKET ST.
HABS OH-2288
HABS OHIO,78-WAR,7-
3ph/5pg/1pc L

Iddings House; see Edwards-Webb House

Kinsman,F. ,Office
303 Mahoning Ave.
HABS OH-265
HABS OHIO,78-WAR,1A-
1dr/2pg L

Kinsman,Judge Frederick,House
303 Mahoning Ave.
HABS OH-264
HABS OHIO,78-WAR,1-
10dr/3ph/2pg L

126 South Park Avenue (Commercial Building)
HABS OH-2270
HABS OHIO,78-WAR,3-
2pg/fr L

136 South Park Avenue (Commercial Building)
HABS OH-2272
HABS OHIO,78-WAR,5-
2pg/fr L

Weil Building
130 S. Park Ave.
HABS OH-2271
HABS OHIO,78-WAR,4-
1ph/2pg/1pc L

TUSCARAWAS COUNTY

ZOAR

Beiter House Number 3
Fourth & Main Sts.
HABS OH-284
HABS OHIO,79-ZOAR,6-
3dr/1ph/1pg L

Blacksmith Shop
HABS OH-298
HABS OHIO,79-ZOAR,21-
2dr/3ph/1pg L

Brewery
Fifth & Park Sts.
HABS OH-291
HABS OHIO,79-ZOAR,13-
3dr/3ph/1pg L

Cider Mill,Planing Mill & Cabinet Shop
Second & Foltz Sts.
HABS OH-293
HABS OHIO,79-ZOAR,15-
5dr/3ph/1pg L

Cobbler Shop
Main St.
HABS OH-2103
HABS OHIO,79-ZOAR,26-
2dr/2ph/1pg L

Cow Barn
Second & Park Streets
HABS OH-283
HABS OHIO,79-ZOAR,5-
2dr/1ph/1pg L

Dormitory
Third St.
HABS OH-2101
HABS OHIO,79-ZOAR,24-
5dr/1ph/1pg L

Epsicopal Church
Main St.
HABS OH-281
HABS OHIO,79-ZOAR,3-
5dr/4ph/1pg/1pc L

First & Main Streets (House)
HABS OH-2105
HABS OHIO,79-ZOAR,28-
1ph/1pg L

First Meetinghouse
Fourth St.
HABS OH-286
HABS OHIO,79-ZOAR,8-
2dr/4ph/1pg/1pc L

Garden (Tree of Life)
HABS OH-286
HABS OHIO,79-ZOAR,4B-
1ph/1pc L

Gardener's Cottage
Fourth St.
HABS OH-282
HABS OHIO,79-ZOAR,4-
3dr/5ph/1pg L

General Store & Post Office
HABS OH-2100
HABS OHIO,79-ZOAR,23-
4dr/2ph/1pg L

Grist Mill
First St.
HABS OH-288
HABS OHIO,79-ZOAR,10-
4dr/1ph/1pg L

Gunn,Alexander,Cottage; see Hermitage (Log Cabin)

Hermitage (Log Cabin)
(Gunn,Alexander,Cottage)
Third St.
HABS OH-296
HABS OHIO,79-ZOAR,19-
1dr/2ph/1pg L

House on Hill
Planing Mill Vic.
HABS OH-294-A
HABS OHIO,79-ZOAR,17-
1ph/1pg L

Jebenhauschen (Log Cabin) (Schlather House)
Fourth & Pulta Streets.
HABS OH-287
HABS OHIO,79-ZOAR,9-
3dr/3ph/1pg L

Kappel House
Third & Main Sts.
HABS OH-289
HABS OHIO,79-ZOAR,11-
3dr/1ph/1pg L

Keucherer House
Third & Main Sts.
HABS OH-290
HABS OHIO,79-ZOAR,12-
3dr/2ph/1pg L

Number One (King's Palace)
Main & Third Sts.
HABS OH-297
HABS OHIO,79-ZOAR,20-
13dr/11ph/1pg/1pc L

Planing Mill,Old
HABS OH-294
HABS OHIO,79-ZOAR,16-
1ph/1pg L

Rieker Residence
Third St.
HABS OH-2104
HABS OHIO,79-ZOAR,27-
1ph/1pg L

Saddler Shop
Second St.
HABS OH-299
HABS OHIO,79-ZOAR,22-
1dr/1ph/1pg L

Schlather House; see Jebenhauschen (Log Cabin)

Sewing House
Second & Park Sts.
HABS OH-285
HABS OHIO,79-ZOAR,7-
6dr/2ph/1pg/1pc L

Woolen Water Mill
HABS OH-2102
HABS OHIO,79-ZOAR,25-
4dr/1pg L

Zeeb House (Log Cabin)
Fourth & Park Sts.
HABS OH-295
HABS OHIO,79-ZOAR,18-
1dr/2ph/1pg/1pc L

Zoar Hotel
Second & Main Sts.
HABS OH-280
HABS OHIO,79-ZOAR,2-
11dr/9ph/1pg/1pc L

Zoar Jail
Foltz St.
HABS OH-292
HABS OHIO,79-ZOAR,14-
1dr/1ph/1pg L

Zoar School
Fifth St.
HABS OH-2231
HABS OHIO,79-ZOAR,29-
1ph/1pc L

Zoar-Maps & General History
HABS OH-297
HABS OHIO,79-ZOAR,1-
2ph/3pg L

UNION COUNTY

NORTH LEWISBURG VIC.

Covered Bridge
Spanning Darby Creek
HABS OH-22-13
HABS OHIO,80- ,2-
3dr/1ph/1pg L

Covered Bridge
Spanning Spain's Creek
HABS OH-22-12
HABS OHIO,80- ,1-
3dr/1ph/1pg L

VAN WERT COUNTY

VAN WERT VIC.

Town Creek Truss-leg Bedstead Bridge
Spanning Town Creek at County Rte. 82
HAER OH-51
HAER OHIO,81-VAWT.V,1-
5ph/5pg/1pc L

WARREN COUNTY

CORWIN VIC.

McKay,Moses,House
New Burlington Rd.
HABS OH-2202
HABS OHIO,83-COR.V,1-
4dr/15ph/3pg L

FOSTER

Morrow,Gov. ,House
HABS OH-2248
HABS OHIO,83-FOS,1-
6dr/1ph/1pc/fr L

HARVEYSBURG VIC.

Lukins,Levi,House
Middletown Rd. ,R. R. # 3
HABS OH-2209
HABS OHIO,83-HARV.V,1-
3dr/9ph/1pg/1pc L

LEBANON

Golden Lamb Hotel
Main St.
HABS OH-625
HABS OHIO,83-LEBA,1-
7dr/1ph/1pg/fr L

LEBANON VIC.

Scott,Thomas P. ,House
HABS OH-637
HABS OHIO,83-LEVA.V,1-
8dr L

MORROW VIC.

Millgrove Road Bridge (Strout Road Bridge)
Spanning Little Miami Scenic River at County Rd 38
HAER OH-37
HAER OHIO,83-MOR.V,1-
4dr/18ph/10pg/1pc L

Strout Road Bridge; see Millgrove Road Bridge

UNION VILLAGE

Shaker South Family,Dwelling House
State Rts. 63 & 741 intersection
HABS OH-639
HABS OHIO,83-UNION,1-
7dr/2ph/fr L

WAYNESVILLE

Quaker Meetinghouse
HABS OH-426
HABS OHIO,83-WAYV,1-
6dr/2ph/1pc/fr L

WAYNE COUNTY

WOOSTER

Moore-Brewster House
202 Market St.
HABS OH-254
HABS OHIO,85-WOOST,1-
11dr/2ph/3pg L

WYANDOT COUNTY

MC CUTCHENVILLE

Greek Revival House (Shoemaker House)
HABS OH-22-27
HABS OHIO,88-MACUV,1-
1dr/1ph/1pg L

Shoemaker House; see Greek Revival House

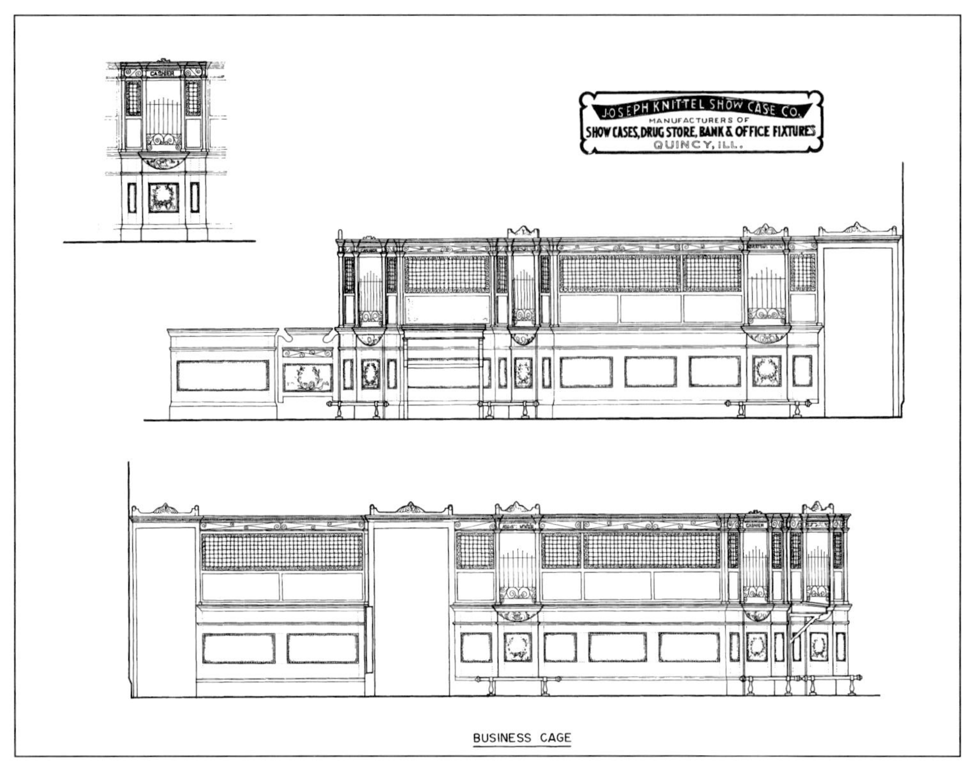

State Capitol Company Building, 301 W. Harrison, Guthrie, Logan County, Oklahoma. Business cage. Measured drawing delineated by Barry R. Gryb, 1973 (HABS OK-17, sheet 10 of 10).

Dr. Irvin D. Leoser's Log Cabin, Tahlequah, Cherokee County, Oklahoma. North (rear) and west elevations. Photograph by Walter Smalling, Jr., October 1979 (HABS OKLA,11-TAHL,5-3).

Oklahoma

ADAIR COUNTY

STILLWELL

Adair County Courthouse
Courthouse Square
HABS OK-32
HABS OKLA,1-STIL,1-
6ph/9pg/1pc L

CHEROKEE COUNTY

PARK HILL VIC.

"Hunter's Home"; see Murrell,George M.,House

First Cherokee Female Seminary
(Three Columns at Tsa-La-Gi)
Tsa-La-Gi,Cherokee Cultural Center
HABS OK-50
HABS OKLA,11-PARHI.V,1A-
2ph/2pg/1pc L

Murrell,George M.,House ("Hunter's Home")
Murrell Rd.
HABS OK-28
HABS OKLA,11-PARHI.V,2-
9dr/20ph/13pg/2pc/1ct/fr L

Three Columns at Tsa-La-Gi; see First Cherokee Female Seminary

TAHLEQUAH

"Leoser's Cabin"; see Leoser,Dr. Irvin D.,Log Cabin

Cherokee County Court Building; see Cherokee National Capitol Building

Cherokee County Jail; see Cherokee National Penitentiary

Cherokee Female Seminary
(Northeastern Oklahoma State Univ. ,Seminary Halll)
Northeastern Oklahoma State Univ. Campus
HABS OK-23
HABS OKLA,11-TAHL,1A-
10ph/13pg/1pc/1ct L

Cherokee National Capitol Building
(Cherokee County Court Building)
101-29 S. Muskogee Ave.
HABS OK-24
HABS OKLA,11-TAHL,2-
6dr/8ph/14pg/1pc/fr L

Cherokee National Penitentiary
(Cherokee County Jail)
124 E. Choctaw St.
HABS OK-25
HABS OKLA,11-TAHL,4-
2dr/3ph/7pg/1pc/fr L

Cherokee Supreme Court Building
130 E. Keetoowah St.
HABS OK-26
HABS OKLA,11-TAHL,3-
7dr/3ph/8pg/1pc/fr L

Leoser,Dr. Irvin D.,Log Cabin
("Leoser's Cabin")
119 W. Smith St.
HABS OK-27
HABS OKLA,11-TAHL,5-
4ph/6pg/1pc L

Northeastern Oklahoma State Univ. ,Seminary Halll; see Cherokee Female Seminary

COMANCHE COUNTY

FORT SILL

Fort Sill
HABS OK-43
HABS OKLA,16-FOSIL,1-
1ph/1pc L

Fort Sill,Commanding Officer's Quarters; see Fort Sill,Sherman House

Fort Sill,Old Post Headquarters
Quanah Rd.
HABS OK-35
HABS OKLA,16-FOSIL,1A-
1ph/1pg/1pc L

Fort Sill,Sherman House (Fort Sill,Commanding Officer's Quarters)
HABS OK-36
HABS OKLA,16-FOSIL,1B-
1pg L

DELAWARE COUNTY

FLINT VIC.

Beck's Mill; see Hildebrand's Mill

Hildebrand's Mill (Beck's Mill)
HABS OK-29
HABS OKLA,21-FLINT.V,1A-
7ph/9pg/1pc L

ROSE VIC.

Saline Courthouse
HABS OK-33
HABS OKLA,21-ROSE.V,1-
3ph/12pg/1pc L

LOGAN COUNTY

GUTHRIE

Carnegie Library
402 E. Oklahoma Ave.
HABS OK-14
HABS OK,42-GUTH,1D-
8dr/12ph/9pg/1pc/fr L

Cooperative Publishing Company Building; see State Capitol Company Building

Ferd-Heim Brewing Company (Heim Brewing Company)
424 W. Oklahoma Ave.
HABS OK-19
HABS OK,42-GUTH,1I-
1ph/1pc L

Gray Brothers Block
101 W. Oklahoma Ave.
HABS OK-12
HABS OK,42-GUTH,1B-
6dr/7ph/6pg/1pc/fr L

Guthrie Historic District; see Guthrie,Town of

Guthrie Waterworks
S. Division St.
HABS OK-20
HABS OK,42-GUTH,1J-
1ph/1pc L

Guthrie,Town of (Guthrie Historic District)
U.S. Rt. 77 & State Rd. 33
HABS OK-10
HABS OK,42-GUTH,1-
54ph/16pg/4pc/fr L

Heilman,P. J.,House
401 E. Cleveland Ave.
HABS OK-15
HABS OK,42-GUTH,1E-
9dr/15ph/7pg/1pc/fr L

Heim Brewing Company; see Ferd-Heim Brewing Company

Logan County Courthouse; see Oklahoma State Capitol

Oklahoma State Capitol (Logan County Courthouse)
301 E. Harrison Ave.
HABS OK-21
HABS OK,42-GUTH,1K-
1ph/1pc L

Stapleton Block
114 N. Division St.
HABS OK-16
HABS OK,42-GUTH,1F-
4dr/5pg/fr L

State Capitol Company Building (Cooperative Publishing Company Building)
301 W. Harrison Ave.
HABS OK-17
HABS OK,42-GUTH,1G-
10dr/10ph/15pg/1pc/fr L

Trinity Episcopal Church
310 E. Noble Ave.
HABS OK-11
HABS OK,42-GUTH,1A-
4dr/8ph/6pg/1pc/fr L

Union Station
W. Oklahoma & Railroad Aves.
HABS OK-18
HABS OK,42-GUTH,1H-
1ph/1pc L

Victor Block
202 W. Harrison Ave.
HABS OK-13
HABS OK,42-GUTH,1C-
4dr/12ph/6pg/1pc/fr L

MUSKOGEE COUNTY

FORT GIBSON

Dragoon Headquarters; see Fort Gibson,Howard House

Fort Gibson,Bake Oven
Garrison Ave.
HABS OK-34-7
HABS OKLA,51-FOGIB,1F-
1dr/2ph/1pg/fr L

Fort Gibson,Barracks Building
Garrison Ave.
HABS OK-34-1
HABS OKLA,51-FOGIB,1A-
14dr/3ph/3pg/fr L

Fort Gibson,Blacksmith Shop
Garrison Ave.
HABS OK-34-8
HABS OKLA,51-FOGIB,1G-
2dr/2ph/1pg/fr L

Fort Gibson,Commanding Officer's Quarters
Coppinger Ave.
HABS OK-34-2
HABS OKLA,51-FOGIB,1B-
16dr/7ph/2pg/fr L

Fort Gibson,Commissary Building
Garrison Ave.
HABS OK-34-5
HABS OKLA,51-FOGIB,1D-
10dr/3ph/2pg/fr L

Fort Gibson,Headquarters Building
Garrison Ave.
HABS OK-34-4
HABS OKLA,51-FOGIB,1C-
5dr/4ph/2pg/fr L

Fort Gibson,Howard House (Dragoon Headquarters)
Creek St.
HABS OK-34-3
HABS OKLA,51-FOGIB,2-
3dr/5ph/2pg/fr L

Fort Gibson,Powder House; see Fort Gibson,Powder Magazine

Fort Gibson,Powder Magazine (Fort Gibson,Powder House)
Garrison Ave.
HABS OK-34-6
HABS OKLA,51-FOGIB,1E-
2dr/2ph/1pg/fr L

Houston,Sam,Cabin
HABS OK-9
HABS OKLA,73- ,1-
7dr/3ph/5pg/fr L

MUSKOGEE

Central Baptist Church (Central Missionary Baptist Church)
515 N. Fourth St.
HABS OK-44
HABS OKLA,51-MUSK,1-
7ph/7pg/1pc L

Central Missionary Baptist Church; see Central Baptist Church

Honor Heights Park
Agency Hill
HABS OK-53
HABS DLC/PP-1993:OK-1
7dr/fr L

The Union Agency
Honor Heights Park
HABS OK-54
HABS DLC/PP-1993:OK-1
9dr/fr L

NOBLE COUNTY

PERRY

Atchison,Topeka,Santa Fe Railroad Station
HABS OK-37
HABS OKLA,52-PERRY,1-
7ph/1pc L

St. Louis,San Francisco Railroad Station
HABS OK-38
HABS OKLA,52-PERRY,2-
7ph/1pc L

OKFUSKEE COUNTY

OKEMAH VIC.

Guthrie,Woodie,Birthplace
HABS OK-22
HABS OKLA,54-OKE.V,1-
4ph/1pc L

OKLAHOMA COUNTY

OKLAHOMA CITY

Fulton House
14 Stiles Circle
HABS OK-48
HABS OKLA,55-OKLA,2-
4ph/4pg/1pc L

Maywood Presbyterian Church
400 N.E. Ninth St.
HABS OK-45
HABS OKLA,55-OKLA,4-
12ph/8pg/1pc L

Municipal Building
200 N. Walker
HABS OK-40
HABS OKLA,55-OKLA,1-
10ph/4pg/1pc L

Sealy House
15 Stiles Circle
HABS OK-49
HABS OKLA,55-OKLA,3-
5ph/4pg/1pc L

Wilson's Edible Fats Factory
2801 SW 15th St.
HAER OK-4-C
HAER OKLA,55-OKLA,5C-
5ph L

Wilson's Lard Refinery
2801 SW 15th St.
HAER OK-4-A
HAER OKLA,55-OKLA,5A-
3ph L

Wilson's Oil House
2801 SW 15th St.
HAER OK-4-B
HAER OKLA,55-OKLA,5B-
3ph L

Wilson's Oil House,Lard Refinery & Fats Factory
2801 SW 15th Street
HAER OK-4
HAER OKLA,55-OKLA,5-
8pg/1pc L

OSAGE COUNTY

AVANT

Bridge over Bird Creek
Spanning Bird Creek
HAER OK-2
HAER OKLA,57-AVA,1-
11ph/6pg/1pc L

NORTH OF HOMINY

Hominy Creek Bridge
Spanning Hominy Creek
HAER OK-5
16ph/23pg/1pc H

PAWNEE COUNTY

STILLWATER

Oklahoma State University Campus
HABS OK-52
10dr L

PAYNE COUNTY

STILLWATER

Berry,Thomas N.,Estate
U. S. Route 177
HABS OK-51
HABS 1991(HABS):35
7dr/4pg/fr L

PITTSBURG COUNTY

MCALESTER

McAlester Army Ammunition Plant
HAER OK-1
HAER OKLA,61-MCAL,1-
56pg/fr L

ROGER MILLS COUNTY

ROLL VIC.

Pack Saddle Bridge (U. S. 283 Pack Saddle Bridge)
Spanning South Canadian River,U. S. Rt. 283
HAER OK-3
HAER OKLA,65-ROLL.V,1-
9ph/4pg/1pc L

U. S. 283 Pack Saddle Bridge; see Pack Saddle Bridge

SEQUOYAH COUNTY

MARBLE CITY

Citizen's State Bank
Seminole & Main Sts.
HABS OK-30
HABS OKLA,68-MARCI,1-
3ph/5pg/1pc L

SALISAW

Dwight Mission,Administration Building
Rural Rt.
HABS OK-31
HABS OKLA,68-SALSA,1A-
5ph/9pg/1pc L

TULSA COUNTY

TULSA

Philbrook Museum of Art; see Villa Philbrook

Villa Philbrook (Philbrook Museum of Art)
2727 S. Rockford Rd.
HABS OK-55
13dr/fr H

Oregon Caves National Monument, Cave Junction, Josephine County, Oregon. Measured drawing delineated by Ranne Rhee, 1989 (HAER OR-145, sheet 1 of 3).

Coos Bay Bridge (Conde B. McCullough Memorial Bridge), North Bend, Coos County, Oregon. Perspective view from southwest. Photograph by Jet Lowe, Summer 1990 (accession number 1993(HAER):OR-2; photo number HAER-OR-46-10).

Oregon

BENTON COUNTY

CORVALLIS VIC.

Albany Bridge
See same name under Linn Co.,Albany
HAER OR-34
HAER DLC/PP-1993:OR-2
4ph/6pg/1pc/fr L

HOSKINS

Watson,James,House
HABS OR-30
HABS ORE,2-HOSK,1-
6dr/2ph/1pg L

CLACKAMAS COUNTY

CANBY

Canby Railroad Depot
HABS OR-131
HABS ORE,3-CAN,1-
11ph/2pg/1pc L

MILWAUKIE

Earl Bronaugh House
18121 River Rd.
HABS OR-150
12ph/19pg/2pc H

Earl Bronaugh House, Garage
18121 River Rd.
HABS OR-150-C
1ph H

Earl Bronaugh House, House
18121 River Rd.
HABS OR-150-A
2ph H

Earl Bronaugh House,Main Garage
18121 River Rd.
HABS OR-150-B
1ph H

Lewelling,Seth,House
Lot 5
HABS OR-1
HABS ORE,3-MILWA,1-
3ph/1pg L

MOLALLA VIC.

Copper Creek Bridge; see Four Mile Bridge

Dibble House
HABS OR-7
HABS ORE,3-MOLA.V,2-
8dr/2ph/1pg L

Four Mile Bridge (Copper Creek Bridge)
Copper Creek Rd.,Spans Table Rock Fork,Mollala Riv
HAER OR-13
HAER 2(HAER):OR-1
5ph/5pg/1pc/fr L

MOLLALA VIC.

Dickey,John K. ,House
HABS OR-6
HABS ORE,3-MOLA.V,1-
9dr/3ph/1pg L

MT. PLEASANT

Ainsworth,John C. ,House
HABS OR-4
HABS ORE,3-MOUPL,2-
2ph/1pg L

Holmes,William,House (Rose Farm)
HABS OR-3
HABS ORE,3-MOUPL,1-
14dr/3ph/1pg L

Locust Farm; see McCarver,Morton,House

McCarver,Morton,House (Locust Farm)
HABS OR-5
HABS ORE,3-MOUPL,3-
10dr/2ph/1pg L

Rose Farm; see Holmes,William,House

OREGON CITY

McLoughlin House National Historic Site; see McLoughlin,John,House

McLoughlin,John,House (McLoughlin House National Historic Site)
McLoughlin Park (moved from Second & Third Sts.)
HABS OR-2
HABS ORE,3-ORGCI,1-
2ph/2pg L

Williamette River Bridge
Spanning Williamette River at Oswego Hwy. 3
HAER OR-31
HAER DLC/PP-1993:OR-2
5ph/7pg/1pc/fr L

WEST LINN

Willamette Falls Lock ChambeR,No.1
Willamette River
HAER OR-1
HAER ORE,3-WELIN,1A-
14ph/4pg/2pc L

WILSONVILLE VIC.

Curry,George L. ,House
HABS OR-8
HABS ORE,3-WILSO.V,1-
14dr/2ph/1pg L

CLATSOP COUNTY

ASTORIA

Columbia River Bridge at Astoria
Spans Columbia River at Oregon Coast Hwy.
HAER OR-50
HAER DLC/PP-1993:OR-2
3ph/1pc L

COLUMBIA COUNTY

CHAPMAN VIC.

Nehalem Divide Railroad Tunnel; see Portland & Southwestern Railroad Tunnel

Portland & Southwestern Railroad Tunnel (Nehalem Divide Railroad Tunnel)
Willamette Meridian
HAER OR-3
HAER ORE,5-CHAP.V,1-
17ph/14pg/2pc L

COOS COUNTY

COQUILLE

Coquille River Bridge
Spanning Coquille River at St. Rt. 244
HAER 0R-32
HAER DLC/PP-1993:OR-2
4ph/6pg/1pc/fr L

NORTH BEND

Coos Bay Bridge (McCullough, Conde B. Memorial Bridge)
Spans Coos Bay at U.S. Hwy. 101
HAER OR-46
HAER DLC/PP-1993:OR-2
17ph/7pg/1pc/fr L

McCullough, Conde B. Memorial Bridge; see Coos Bay Bridge

CROOK COUNTY

PRINEVILLE VIC.

Building No. 2200,Ochoco National Forest; see Ochoco Ranger Station,Warehouse No. 2200

Ochoco Ranger Station,Warehouse No. 2200 (Building No. 2200,Ochoco National Forest)
U. S. Hwy. 42
HABS OR-126-A
HABS ORE,7-PRINV.V,1A-
6ph/3pg/1pc L

CURRY COUNTY

Agness Guard Station, Warehouse (Agness Guard Station,Building No. 2207)
Confluence of Rogue and Illinois Rivers
HABS OR-154-C
3ph/1pc H

Agness Guard Station,Building No. 1302; see Agness Guard Station,Crewhouse

Agness Guard Station,Building No. 2207; see Agness Guard Station, Warehouse

Agness Guard Station,Crewhouse (Agness Guard Station,Building No. 1302)
Confluence of Rogue and Illinois Rivers
HABS OR-154-D
4ph/1pc H

AGNESS

Agness Guard Station
Confluence of the Rogue and Illinois Rivers
HABS OR-154
2ph/4pg/1pc H

Agness Guard Station, Building No. 1009; see Agness Guard Station, Residence

Agness Guard Station, Residence (Agness Guard Station, Building No. 1009)
Confluence of Rogue and Illinois Rivers
HABS OR-154-B
8ph/3pg H

Agness Guard Station,Building No. 2004; see Agness Guard Station,Office

Agness Guard Station,Office (Agness Guard Station,Building No. 2004)
Confluence of Rogue and Illinois Rivers
HABS OR-154-A
4ph/3pg/1pc H

GOLD BEACH

Bridge at Mouth of Rogue River (Patterson,Isaac Lee Memorial Bridge)
Spans Rogue River at Oregon Coast Hwy.
HAER OR-38
HAER DLC/PP-1993:OR-2
4dr/15ph/11pg/1pc/fr L

Patterson,Isaac Lee Memorial Bridge; see Bridge at Mouth of Rogue River

DESCHUTES COUNTY

LA PINE VIC.

Paulina Lake IOOF Organization Camp
Deschutes National Forest
HABS OR-132
HABS ORE,7-PRINV.V,1A-
14ph/38pg/4pc L

Paulina Lake IOOF Organization Camp,Cabin No. 10
Deschutes National Forest
HABS OR-132-G
HABS ORE,9-LAPI.V,1G-
7ph L

Paulina Lake IOOF Organization Camp,Cabin No. 11
Deschutes National Forest
HABS OR-132-H
HABS ORE,9-LAPI.V,1H-
7ph L

Paulina Lake IOOF Organization Camp,Cabin No. 3
Deschutes National Forest
HABS OR-132-A
HABS OR,9-LAPI.V,1A-
6ph L

Paulina Lake IOOF Organization Camp,Cabin No. 5
Deschutes National Forest
HABS OR-132-B
HABS ORE,9-LAPI.V,1B-
5ph L

Paulina Lake IOOF Organization Camp,Cabin No. 6
Deschutes National Forest
HABS OR-132-C
HABS ORE,9-LAPI.V,1C-
8ph L

Paulina Lake IOOF Organization Camp,Cabin No. 7
Deschutes National Forest
HABS OR-132-D
HABS ORE,9-LAPI.V,1D-
6ph L

Paulina Lake IOOF Organization Camp,Cabin No. 8
Deschutes National Forest
HABS OR-132-E
HABS ORE,9-LAPI.V,1E-
5ph L

Paulina Lake IOOF Organization Camp,Cabin No. 9
Deschutes National Forest
HABS OR-132-F
HABS ORE,9-LAPI.V,1F-
5ph L

Paulina Lake IOOF Organization Camp,Lodge
Deschutes National Forest
HABS OR-132-I
HABS ORE,9-LAPI.V,1I-
7ph L

TERREBONNE

Oregon Trunk Railroad Bridge
Spans Crooked River at Oregon Trunk Railroad
HAER OR-51
HAER DLC/PP-1993:OR-2
1ph/1pc L

DOUGLAS COUNTY

OAKLAND

Powell,Louis,House
Second Ave. & Maple St.
HABS OR-36
HABS ORE,10-OAK,1-
7dr/2ph/1pg L

Young,Edward G. ,House
Second Ave. & Maple St.
HABS OR-37
HABS ORE,10-OAK,2-
8dr/3ph/1pg L

REEDSPORT

Umpqua River Bridge
Spans Umpqua River at Oregon Coast Hwy.
HAER OR-45
HAER DLC/PP-1993:OR-2
16ph/5pg/1pc/fr L

WINCHESTER

Booth, Robert A. Bridge; see Winchester Bridge

Winchester Bridge (Booth, Robert A. Bridge)
Spanning N. Umpqua River at Pacific Hwy.
HAER OR-33
HAER DLC/PP-1993:OR-2
4ph/4pg/1pc/fr L

YONCALLA VIC.

Ambrose,Alfred T. ,House
HABS OR-35
HABS ORE,10-YONC.V,2-
2ph/1pg L

Applegate,Charles,House
HABS OR-34
HABS ORE,10-YONC.V,1-
12dr/3ph/1pg L

GRANT COUNTY

DAYVILLE VIC.

Cant Ranch (John Day Fossil Beds National Monument)
E. side of St. Rt. 19,N. of U.S. 26
HABS OR-142
HABS 1989(HABS):19;DLC/PP-1993:OR-2
1dr/3ph/9pg/1pc/fr L

Documentation: **ct** color transparencies **dr** measured drawings **fr** field records
pc photograph captions **pg** pages of text **ph** photographs

Cant Ranch,Barn (John Day Fossil Beds National Monument)
E. side of St. Rt. 19,N. of U.S. 26
HABS OR-142-B
5dr/4ph/1pc L

Cant Ranch,Barn (John Day Fossil Beds National Monument)
E. side of St. Rt. 19,N. of U.S. 26
HABS 0R-142-B
HABS 1989(HABS):19;DLC/PP-1993:OR-2
5dr/4ph/1pc L

Cant Ranch,Hayfork (John Day Fossil Beds National Monument)
E. side of St. Rt. 19,N. of U.S. 26
HABS OR-142-C
HABS DLC/PP-1993:OR-2
1ph/1pc L

Cant Ranch,House (John Day Fossil Beds National Monument)
E. side of St. Rt. 19,N. of U.S. 26
HABS OR-142-A
HABS 1989(HABS):19;DLC/PP-1993:OR-2
6dr/9ph/1pc L

John Day Fossil Beds National Monument; see Cant Ranch

John Day Fossil Beds National Monument; see Cant Ranch,Barn

John Day Fossil Beds National Monument; see Cant Ranch,Hayfork

John Day Fossil Beds National Monument; see Cant Ranch,House

JACKSON COUNTY

ASHLAND VIC.

Tolman,James C. ,House
Pacific Hwy.
HABS OR-42
HABS ORE,15-ASH.V,1-
17dr/2ph/1pg L

CENTRAL POINT

McCredie,William,House
2606 Old Stage Rd.
HABS OR-128
HABS ORE,15-CENTPT,1-
18ph/4pg/fr L

GOLD HILL

Gold Hill Bridge
Spans Rogue Riv. at Oregon Rte. 234
HAER OR-37
HAER DLC/PP-1993:OR-2
3ph/4pg/1pc/fr L

Rock Point Arch Bridge (Rogue River Bridge at Rock Point)
Spanning Rogue River & Old Pacific Hwy.,Rt.271
HAER OR-29
HAER DLC/PP-1993:OR-2
2ph/4pg/1pc/fr L

Rogue River Bridge at Rock Point; see Rock Point Arch Bridge

GOLD HILL VIC.

Rock Point Tavern
HABS OR-40
HABS ORE,15-GOLHI.V,1-
3ph/2pg L

JACKSONVILLE

Anderson & Glenn Store
125 W. California St.
HABS OR-61
HABS ORE,15-JACVI,71-
1ph/4pg L

Applegate House
750 S. Third St.
HABS OR-56
HABS ORE,15-JACVI,36-
1ph/fr L

Applegate,Mark,House
655 S. Third St.
HABS OR-57
HABS ORE,15-JACVI,35-
1ph/fr L

Armstrong,Minerva,House; see Cool House

Barn,B. & B.
N. Third & D Sts.
HABS OR-58
HABS ORE,15-JACVI,70-
1ph L

Beekman Bank
110 W. California St.
HABS OR-59
HABS ORE,15-JACVI,38-
2ph/3pg L

Beekman House
E. California St.
HABS OR-60
HABS ORE,15-JACVI,49-
8ph/fr L

Bilger House
540 Blackstone Alley
HABS OR-62
HABS ORE,15-JACVI,34-
1ph/fr L

Briethbarth House
180 Oregon St.
HABS OR-63
HABS ORE,15-JACV,33-
1ph/fr L

Britt House
201 S. First St.
HABS OR-49
HABS ORE,15,JACVI,3-
5dr/11ph/4pg L

Brunner Brothers Store
170 S. Oregon St.
HABS OR-64
HABS ORE,15-JACVI,40-
1ph/4pg L

Building,Brick (Dowell's,B. F. ,Law Office)
125 S. Third St.
HABS OR-73
HABS ORE,15-JACVI,43-
1ph/5pg L

Colvig House
410 S. Oregon St.
HABS OR-67
HABS ORE,15-JACVI,32-
1ph/fr L

Cool House (Armstrong,Minerva,House)
E. California St. & Sixth St.
HABS OR-68
HABS ORE,15-JACVI,31-
1ph/fr L

Davidson House
503 N. Sixth St.
HABS OR-70
HABS ORE,15-JACVI,30-
1ph/fr L

Davis-Kubli House
HABS OR-101
HABS ORE,15-JACVI,12-
4ph/fr L

Deroboam House
390 E. California St.
HABS OR-71
HABS ORE,15-JACVI,29-
1ph/fr L

Dowell,B. F. ,House
470 N. Fifth St.
HABS OR-72
HABS ORE,15-JACVI,28-
7ph/1ct/fr L

Dowell's,B. F. ,Law Office; see Building,Brick

Drew,Ben,Commission House
160 E. California St.
HABS OR-74
HABS ORE,15-JACVI,44-
1ph/4pg L

Duncan,Judge,House
285 S. First St.
HABS OR-75
HABS ORE,15-JACVI,27-
1ph/fr L

Fisher Brothers Store & Bella Union Saloon
180 & 170 W. California St.
HABS OR-76
HABS ORE,15-JACVI,45-
1ph/7pg L

Greenman-Jackson House
E. California & Fifth Sts.
HABS OR-77
HABS ORE,15-JACVI,26-
1ph/fr L

Greer,Dr. G. W. ,House (Reed House)
250 N. Oregon St.
HABS OR-43
HABS ORE,15-JACVI,1-
6dr/3ph/2pg/1pc L

Gwinn House
415 E. C St. (moved from Courthouse Lot)
HABS OR-78
HABS ORE,15-JACVI,25-
1ph/fr L

Haines Brothers House,Brick
110 S. Oregon St.
HABS OR-79
HABS ORE,15-JACVI,46-
2ph/3pg/fr L

Harbaugh House
425 Huener Lane
HABS OR-81
HABS ORE,15-JACVI,23-
1ph/fr L

Harris-Chambers House
210 N. Third St.
HABS OR-82
HABS ORE,15-JACVI,22-
1ph/fr L

Helms House
320 S. Oregon St.
HABS OR-83
HABS ORE,15-JACVI,21-
1ph/fr L

I. O. O. F. Lodge; see McCully Building

Jackson County Courthouse
(Jacksonville Museum)
N. Fifth St.
HABS OR-69
HABS ORE,15-JACVI,42-
6ph/9pg/2ct L

Jacksonville City Hall
205 W. Main St.
HABS OR-66
HABS ORE,15-JACVI,41-
2ph/6pg L

Jacksonville Historic District
HABS OR-127
HABS ORE,15-JACVI,37-
14ph/24pg/fr L

Jacksonville Inn; see Ryan's,P. J. ,First Brick Store Building

Jacksonville Museum; see Jackson County Courthouse

Judge & Nunan's Saddlery
165 E. California St.
HABS OR-87
HABS ORE,15-JACVI,48-
1ph/4pg L

Kahler-Reuter House
410 E. E St.
HABS OR-91
HABS ORE,15-JACVI,17-
1ph/fr L

Kahler,C. W. ,Law Office
105 N. Third St.
HABS OR-90
HABS ORE,15-JACVI,50-
1ph/4pg L

Kahler,William,House
310 N. Sixth St.
HABS OR-89
HABS ORE,15-JACVI,18-
1ph/fr L

Kahler's Drugstore
120 W. California St.
HABS OR-88
HABS ORE,15-JACVI,39-
1ph/3pg L

Keegan,Chris,House
105 E. D St.
HABS OR-92
HABS ORE,15-JACVI,4-
2ph/fr L

Keegan,Owen,House
455 Huener Lane
HABS OR-93
HABS ORE,15-JACVI,16-
1ph/fr L

Klippel House
220 Eighth St.
HABS OR-94
HABS ORE,15-JACVI,15-
1ph/fr L

Langell House (Catholic Rectory)
210 N. Fourth St.
HABS OR-96
HABS ORE,15-JACVI,52-
1ph L

Love & Bilger Tin Shop
150 W. California St.
HABS OR-97
HABS ORE,15-JACVI,53-
1ph/4pg/fr L

Love House
175 N. Third St.
HABS OR-98
HABS ORE,15-JACVI,14-
1ph/7pg/fr L

Magruder House
455 E. California St.
HABS OR-99
HABS ORE,15-JACVI,13-
1ph/fr L

Masonic Building
California & Oregon Sts.
HABS OR-100
HABS ORE,15-JACVI,54-
4ph/7pg L

McCully Building (I. O. O. F. Lodge)
175 S. Oregon St.
HABS OR-102
HABS ORE,15-JACVI,55-
1ph/7pg L

McCully House
240 E. California St.
HABS OR-103
HABS ORE,15-JACVI,11-
1ph/fr L

Methodist Episcopal Church
Fifth & D Sts.
HABS OR-104
HABS ORE,15-JACVI,56-
5ph/4pg L

Moore House
635 S. Third St.
HABS OR-106
HABS ORE,15-JACVI,10-
1ph/fr L

Muller,Max,House
465 E. California St.
HABS OR-107
HABS ORE,15-JACVI,9-
1ph/fr L

Neuber's Jewelry Store
130 W. California St.
HABS OR-108
HABS ORE,15-JACVI,57-
1ph/3pg L

305 North Fourth Street (House)
HABS OR-110
HABS ORE,15-JACVI,8-
1ph/fr L

525 North Sixth Street (House)
HABS OR-84
HABS ORE,15-JACVI,19-
1ph/fr L

Nunan,Jeremiah,House
635 Oregon St.
HABS OR-109
HABS ORE,15-JACVI,58-
8ph/6pg/1ct L

Orth Building
140 S. Oregon St.
HABS OR-111
HABS ORE,15-JACVI,59-
1ph/5pg L

Orth House
Main & Third St.
HABS OR-112
HABS ORE,15-JACVI,7-
4ph/fr L

Orth House
425 S. Third St. (moved from 105 S. Third St.)
HABS OR-85
HABS ORE,15-JACVI,47-
1ph L

Presbyterian Church
California & Sixth Sts.
HABS OR-113
HABS ORE,15-JACVI,60-
8ph/7pg L

Reames,Thomas G. ,House
540 E. California St.
HABS OR-114
HABS ORE,15-JACVI,6-
3ph/fr L

Redmen's Lodge & Kubli Building
105 & 115 W. California St.
HABS OR-95
HABS ORE,15-JACVI,51-
3ph/8pg L

Reed House; see Greer,Dr. G. W. ,House

Rogue River Valley,Electric Power Substation
225 W. California St.
HABS OR-116
HABS ORE,15-JACVI,5-
1ph L

Rogue River Valley,Railroad Station
Oregon & W. C. Sts.
HABS OR-117
HABS ORE,15-JACVI,61-
1ph/2pg L

Ryan's,P. J. ,First Brick Store Building (Jacksonville Inn)
175 E. California St.
HABS OR-118
HABS ORE,15-JACVI,62-
2ph/4pg L

Ryan's,P. J. ,Store
135 W. California St.
HABS OR-119
HABS ORE,15-JACVI,63-
1ph/4pg L

Sachs Brothers Store
140 W. California St.
HABS OR-120
HABS ORE,15-JACVI,64-
1ph/4pg L

Schumpf & Miller Stores
155 & 157 W. California St.
HABS OR-122
HABS ORE,15-JACVI,66-
1ph/5pg L

Sifers-Savage House
160 W. C St.
HABS OR-44
HABS ORE,15-JACVI,2-
9dr/4ph/1pg/1pc L

325 Sixth Street (House)
HABS OR-86
HABS ORE,15-JACVI,20-
1ph L

St. Joseph's Roman Catholic Church
Fourth & D Sts.
HABS OR-121
HABS ORE,15-JACVI,65-
4ph/6pg/1ct L

Table Rock Billiard Saloon (Facade)
S. Oregon St.
HABS OR-123
HABS ORE,15-JACVI,67-
1ph/4pg L

U. S. Hotel
California & Third Sts.
HABS OR-124
HABS ORE,15-JACVI,68-
5ph/8pg/2ct L

JACKSONVILLE VIC.

Bybee,William,House
HABS OR-45
HABS ORE,15-JACVI.V,1-
13dr/3ph/1pg L

Hanley House
1053 Hanley Rd.
HABS OR-80
HABS ORE,15-JACVI.V,3-
5ph L

Miller,J. N. T. ,House
Old Stage Rd.
HABS OR-105
HABS ORE,15-JACV1.V,2-
1ph/fr L

Steamboat Stamp Mill
Brush Creek Canyon
HAER OR-57
4dr/10ph/3pg/1pc/fr H

PHOENIX

Colver,Hiram,House
Pacific Hwy.
HABS OR-41
HABS ORE,15-PHENIX,1-
6dr/2ph/1pg L

PROSPECT VIC.

Union Creek Water Tower
West Side of St. Hwy. 62
HABS OR-152
5ph/3pg/1pc H

ROGUE RIVER VIC.

Birdseye,David N. ,House
HABS OR-39
HABS ORE,15-ROGRI.V,1-
4ph/2pg/1pc L

JEFFERSON COUNTY

TERREBONNE VIC.

Crooked River High Bridge
Spans Crooked Riv. Gorge at the Dalles-CA Hwy.
HAER OR-35
HAER DLC/PP-1993:OR-2
5ph/4pg/1pc/fr L

JOSEPHINE COUNTY

CAVE JUNCTION

Oregon Caves Concession Cottages
Oregon Rt. 46,Oregon Caves National Monument
HABS OR-147
HABS 1989(HABS):19
1ph/7pg/1pc L

Oregon Caves National Monument
HABS OR-145
H

Oregon Caves National Monument,Chalet
HABS OR-145-B
H

Oregon Caves National Monument,Chateau
HABS OR-145-A
H

Oregon Caves National Monument,Ranger Residence
HABS OR-145-C
H

CAVE JUNCTION VIC.

Oregon Caves Concession Cottages,Cottage No. 11-12
Oregon Rt. 46,Oregon Caves National Monument
HABS OR-147-A
HABS 1989(HABS):19
4ph/1pc L

Oregon Caves Concession Cottages,Cottage No. 21-22
Oregon Rt. 46,Oregon Caves National Monument
HABS OR-147-B
HABS 1989(HABS):19
2ph/1pc L

Oregon Caves Concession Cottages,Cottage No. 31-32
Oregon Rt. 46,Oregon Caves National Monument
HABS OR-147-C
HABS 1989(HABS):19
1ph/1pc L

Oregon Caves Concession Cottages,Cottage No. 41-42
Oregon Rt. 46,Oregon Caves National Monument
HABS OR-147-D
HABS 1989(HABS):19
2ph/1pc L

Oregon Caves Concession Cottages,Cottage No. 61-62
Oregon Rt. 46,Oregon Caves National Monument
HABS OR-147-F
HABS 1989(HABS):19
1ph/1pc L

Oregon Caves Concession Cottages,Cottage No. 71-72
Oregon Rt. 46,Oregon Caves National Monument
HABS OR-147-G
HABS 1989(HABS):19
5ph/1pc L

CAVEJUNCTION VIC.

Oregon Caves Concession Cottages,Cottage No. 51-52
Oregon Rt. 46,Oregon Caves National Monument
HABS OR-147-E
HABS 1989(HABS):19
1ph/1pc L

GRANTS PASS

Caveman Bridge; see Rogue River Bridge

Rogue River Bridge (Caveman Bridge)
Spans Rogue River at Redwood Hwy. 25
HAER OR-52
HAER DLC/PP-1993:OR-2
4ph/1pc L

WOLF CREEK

Wolf Creek Tavern
Pacific Hwy.
HABS OR-38
HABS ORE,17-WOLF,1-
14dr/5ph/1pg L

KLAMATH COUNTY

CRATER LAKE

Crater Lake Admin Complex, Headquarters; see Crater Lake Administrative Complex, Admin Bldg.

Crater Lake Admin Complex, Merel S. Sager Bldg.; see Crater Lake Administrative Complex, Admin Bldg.

Crater Lake Administration Complex, Mess Hall (Crater Lake Administration Complex,Bunk House; Crater Lake Administration Complex,Canfield Bldg.)
Munson Valley,Off St. Hwy 62, Crater Lake Nat. Pk.
HABS OR-144-C
5ph/11pg/1pc H

Crater Lake Administration Complex, Ranger Dorm. (Crater Lake Administration Complex,Wm. Steel Ctr.; Crater Lake Administration Complex,Steel Ctr.)
Munson Valley,Off Hwy 62,Crater Lake Nat. Prk.
HABS OR-144-B
7ph/12pg/1pc H

Crater Lake Administration Complex,Bunk House; see Crater Lake Administration Complex, Mess Hall

Crater Lake Administration Complex,Canfield Bldg.; see Crater Lake Administration Complex, Mess Hall

Crater Lake Administration Complex,Steel Ctr.; see Crater Lake Administration Complex, Ranger Dorm.

Crater Lake Administration Complex,Wm. Steel Ctr.; see Crater Lake Administration Complex, Ranger Dorm.

Crater Lake Administrative Complex
Munson Valley,Off St. Hyw 62,Crater Lake Nat. Pk.
HABS OR-144
11pg H

Crater Lake Administrative Complex, Admin Bldg. (Crater Lake Admin Complex, Headquarters; Crater Lake Admin Complex, Merel S. Sager Bldg.)
Munson Valley,Off St. Hwy 62, Crater Lake Nat. Pk.
HABS OR-144-A
9ph/10pg/1pc H

Crater Lake Lodge (Crater Lake National Park)
Off Rt. 62
HABS OR-48
HABS ORE,18-CRALA,1-
25dr L

Crater Lake National Park; see Crater Lake Lodge

LANE COUNTY

EUGENE

Eugene Mill & Elevator
500 E. Fourth Ave.
HABS OR-140
HABS ORE,20-EUG,2-
10dr/fr L

University of Oregon,Deady Hall
University of Oregon Campus
HABS OR-53
HABS ORE,20-EUG,1B-
3ph/9pg L

University of Oregon,Villard Hall
Uiversity of Oregon Campus
HABS OR-50
HABS ORE,20-EUG,1A-
3ph/6pg L

FLORENCE

Cape Creek Bridge
Spans Cape Creek at Oregon Coast Hwy.
HAER OR-41
HAER DLC/PP-1993:OR-2
6ph/6pg/1pc/fr L

Siuslaw River Bridge
Spanning Siuslaw Riv. at Oregon Coast Hwy.
HAER OR-58
HAER DLC/PP-1993:OR-2
12ph/7pg/1pc/fr L

FLORENCE VIC.

Camp Cleawox Organizational Tract
Oregon Dunes Nat'l Rec. Area,Siuslaw Nat'l Forest
HABS OR-137
HABS ORE,20-FLO.V,1-
18pg/fr L

Camp Cleawox Organizational Tract,Lodge Bldg.
Oregon Dunes Nat'l Rec. Area,Siuslaw Nat'l Forest
HABS OR-137-A
HABS ORE,20-FLO.V,1A-
14ph/1pc/fr L

Camp Cleawox, Lafitte; see Camp Cleawox,Adirondack Sleeping Shelter

Camp Cleawox,Adirondack Sleeping Shelter (Camp Cleawox, Lafitte)
Oregon Dunes Nat'l Rec. Area,Siuslaw Nat'l Forest
HABS OR-137-B
HABS ORE,20-FLO.V,1B-
6ph/1pc/fr L

LORANE VIC.

Cartwright,Darius B. ,House
HABS OR-33
HABS ORE,20-LORA.V,1-
8dr/3ph/1pg L

MCKENZIE VIC.

Horse Creek Covered Bridge
Spanning Horse Creek Rd. at Milepost 1.28
HAER OR-15
10ph/1pg/1pc L

PLEASANT HILL VIC.

Mitchell House
HABS OR-156
HABS DLC/PP-1992:OR-2
6ph/3pg/1pc L

SPRINGFIELD

Dorris Ranch
201 Dorris St.
HABS OR-155
HABS DLC/PP-1992:OR-3
16dr L

Hayden Bridge
Spanning McKenzie River at Southern Pacific RR
HAER OR-19
HAER DLC/PP-1993:OR-2
4dr/15ph/4pg/1pc/fr L

WALTON VIC.

Prineville Bridge; see Siuslaw River Bridge

Richardson Bridge; see Siuslaw River Bridge

Siuslaw River Bridge (Richardson Bridge; Prineville Bridge)
Spanning Siuslaw River,Richardson Rd.,Co. Rd. 5018
HAER OR-10
HAER ORE,20-WALT.V,1-
12ph/8pg/1pc L

LINCOLN COUNTY

DEPOE BAY

Depoe Bay Bridge
Spans Depoe Bay at the Oregon Coast Hwy. (U.S.101)
HAER OR-36
HAER DLC/PP-1993:OR-2
6ph/5pg/1pc/fr L

NEWPORT

Yaquina Bay Bridge
Spans Yaquina Bay at Oregon Coast Hwy.
HAER OR-44
HAER DLC/PP-1993:OR-2
13ph/7pg/1pc/fr L

WALDPORT

Alsea Bay Bridge
Spanning Alsea Bay at Oregon Coast Hwy. 9
HAER OR-14
HAER DLC/PP-1993:OR-2
2dr/39ph/9pg/2pc/fr L

WALDPORT VIC.

Alsea Bay Bridge,New
Spanning Alsea Bay at Oregon Coast Highway
HAER OR-64
2ph/1pc H

Camp Angell Barracks (Camp Angell,Building No. 1381)
Angell Job Corps Center,Hwy 101
HABS OR-141
7ph/5pg/1pc H

Camp Angell,Building No. 1381; see Camp Angell Barracks

LINN COUNTY

ALBANY

Albany Bridge
Spanning Williamette River at U.S. Hwy. 20
HAER OR-34
HAER DLC/PP-1993:OR-2
4ph/6pg/1pc/fr L

JEFFERSON VIC.

Baber,Granville H. ,House
HABS OR-32
HABS ORE,22-JEF.V,1-
8dr/3ph/1pg L

SCIO VIC.

Jordan Covered Bridge
Spanning Thomas Creek,County Rd. 829
HAER OR-8
HAER ORE,22-SCIO.V,1-
18ph/12pg L

MALHEUR COUNTY

NYSSA VIC.

Owyhee Dam
Across the Owyhee River
HAER OR-17
193ph/123pg/20pc H

MARION COUNTY

AURORA

Keil,Elias,House
HABS OR-9
HABS ORE,24-AURO,1-
14dr/2ph/1pg L

GERVAIS VIC.

Brown,Samuel,House
HABS OR-10
HABS ORE,24-GERV,1-
14dr/4ph/1pg L

HOWELL PRAIRIE

McCorkle,George F. ,House
HABS OR-11
HABS ORE,24-HOPRA,1-
2ph/1pg L

JEFFERSON

Conser,Jacob Bridge; see Santiam River Bridge

Conser,Jacob,House
HABS OR-31
HABS ORE,24-JEFSO,1-
11dr/3ph/1pg L

Santiam River Bridge (Conser,Jacob Bridge)
Spans Santiam River at State Rte. 164
HAER OR-42
HAER DLC/PP-1993:OR-2
5ph/4pg/1pc/fr L

PARKERSVILLE

Parker,William,House
HABS OR-46
HABS ORE,24-GERV.V,1-
10dr/1ph/1pg L

SALEM

Chemawa Indian School
5495 Chugach Ave.
HABS OR-129
HABS ORE,24-SAL,1-
1ph/1pc L

Chemawa Indian School,Electrical Shop
5495 Chugach St. NE
HABS OR-129-M
HABS ORE,24-SAL,1M-
5ph/1pg/1pc L

Chemawa Indian School,Hawley Hall
5495 Chugach St. NE
HABS OR-129-L
HABS ORE,24-SAL,1L-
9ph/1pg/1pc L

Chemawa Indian School,House
2974 Misty St.
HABS OR-129-J
HABS ORE,24-SAL,1J-
4ph/1pc L

Chemawa Indian School,House
2984 Misty St.
HABS OR-129-I
HABS ORE,24-SAL,1I-
4ph/1pc L

Chemawa Indian School,House
2994 Misty St.
HABS OR-129-H
HABS ORE,24-SAL,1H-
4ph/1pc L

Chemawa Indian School,House
2995 Misty St.
HABS OR-129-G
HABS ORE,24-SAL,1G-
4ph/1pc L

Chemawa Indian School,House
3004 Misty St.
HABS OR-129-B
HABS ORE,24-SAL,1B-
5ph/1pg/1pc L

Chemawa Indian School,House
3005 Misty St.
HABS OR-129-A
HABS ORE,24-SAL,1A-
3ph/1pg/1pc L

Chemawa Indian School,House
3014 Misty St.
HABS OR-129-D
HABS ORE,24-SAL,1D-
4ph/1pg/1pc L

Chemawa Indian School,Industrial Shops
5495 Chugach St. NE
HABS OR-129-F
HABS ORE,24-SAL,1F-
5ph/1pg/1pc L

Chemawa Indian School,McBride Hall
5495 Chugach St. NE
HABS OR-129-C
HABS ORE,24-SAL,1C-
10ph/1pg/1pc L

Chemawa Indian School,McNary Hall
5495 Chugach St. NE
HABS OR-129-K
HABS ORE,24-SAL,1K-
7ph/1pg/1pc L

Chemawa Indian School,Winowa Hall
5495 Chugach St. NE
HABS OR-129-E
HABS ORE,24-SAL,1E-
7ph/1pg/1pc L

Kay,Thomas,Woolen Mill (Mission Mill Museum)
260 Twelfth St.
HABS OR-54
HABS ORE,24-SAL,2-
39dr/fr L

McCullough, Conde B., Bridges; see Oregon Historic Highway Bridges

Mission Mill Museum; see Kay,Thomas,Woolen Mill

Oregon Historic Highway Bridges (McCullough, Conde B., Bridges)
HAER OR-54
HAER DLC/PP-1993:OR-2
1dr/22pg L

SILVERTON

Brown,James,House
Fifth & Main Sts.
HABS OR-12
HABS ORE,24-SILV,1-
7dr/2ph/1pg L

MORROW COUNTY

HEPPNER VIC.

Ditch Creek Guard Station,Barn/Storage Shed (Ditch Creek Guard Station,Building No. 2404)
W. side of Forest Development Rd.
HABS OR-151-B
4ph/6pg/1pc H

Ditch Creek Guard Station,Building No. 1504; see Ditch Creek Guard Station,Garage

Ditch Creek Guard Station,Building No. 2404; see Ditch Creek Guard Station,Barn/Storage Shed

Ditch Creek Guard Station,Garage (Ditch Creek Guard Station,Building No. 1504)
W. side of Forest Development Rd. 21
HABS OR-151-A
3ph/6pg/1pc H

MULTNOMAH COUNTY

BONNEVILLE

Bonneville Power Admin. South Bank Substation
I-84,S. of Bonneville Dam Powerhouse
HAER OR-4
HAER ORE,26-BONV,1-
20ph/9pg/2pc L

Bonneville Project
Columbia River,1 mi. NE of Exit 40,off Intst. 84
HAER OR-11
HAER DLC/PP-1992:OR-2
42ph/75pg/4pc L

Bonneville Project,Administration Building
S. side of main entrance,Bonneville Project
HAER OR-11-B
HAER 1991(HAER):24
12ph/1pc L

Bonneville Project,Auditorium
Columbia River,1 mi. NE of Exit 40,Interstate 84
HAER OR-11-A
HAER 1991(HAER):24
22ph/2pc L

Bonneville Project,Bonneville Dam
Columbia River
HAER OR-11-F
HAER 1991(HAER):24
129ph/12pc L

Bonneville Project,Fish Hatchery
On Columbia R. bordered on S. by Union Pacific
HAER OR-11-C
HAER 1991(HAER):24
14ph/2pc L

Bonneville Project,Navigation Lock No. 1
Oregon shore of Columbia Rvr. near first Powerhse.
HAER OR-11-D
HAER 1991(HAER):24
32ph/3pc L

Bonneville Project,Powerhouse No.1
Spanning the Bradford Slough,from Bradford Island
HAER OR-11-E
HAER 1991(HAER):24
146ph/12pc L

LATOURELL

Latourell Creek Bridge
Spanning Latourell Creek at Columbia River Hwy.
HAER OR-24
HAER DLC/PP-1993:OR-2
6ph/6pg/1pc/fr L

LATOURELL VIC.

Shepperd's Dell Bridge (Young Creek Bridge)
Spanning Young Creek at Columbia River Hwy.
HAER OR-23
HAER DLC/PP-1993:OR-2
4ph/6pg/1pc/fr L

Young Creek Bridge; see Shepperd's Dell Bridge

PORTLAND

Broadway Bridge
Spanning Williamette Riv. at Broadway St.
HAER OR-22
HAER DLC/PP-1993:OR-2
16ph/7pg/1pc/fr L

Building A; see Portland General Electric Co.,Pepco Building

Building B; see Portland General Electric Co.,Storage Building

Building C; see Portland General Electric Co.,Storage/Office Bldg.

Building F; see Portland General Electric Co.,Welding Shop

Building G; see Portland General Electric Co.,Office Building

Building J; see Portland General Electric Company,Equipment Bldg.

Building K; see Portland General Electric Co.,Equipment Building

Building L1; see Portland General Electric Co.,Turbine Building

Building L10(P); see Portland General Electric Company,Shop Building

Building L2; see Portland General Electric Co.,L.P. Boiler Room

Building L3; see Portland General Electric Co.,Lincoln Substation

Building L4; see Portland General Electric Co.,H.P. Boiler Room

Building L5; see Portland General Electric Co.,Powerhouse Extension

Building L6; see Portland General Electric Co.,Stephens Substation

Building L7; see Portland General Electric Company,Machine Shop

Building 18; see Portland General Electric Company,Boiler No. 16

Buildings D and E; see Portland General Electric Co.,Office/Equip. Bldgs.

Burlington Northern Railroad Bridge (Willamette River Bridge No. 5.1)
Spanning Willamette River at River Mile 6.9
HAER OR-7
HAER ORE,26-PORT,8-
101ph/22pg/8pc/fr L

Columbia River Bridge; see Longview Bridge

Columbia River Highway Bridges
Spanning various creeks along Columbia River Hwy.
HAER OR-56
HAER DLC/PP-1993:OR-2
1dr/15pg L

Columbia River Interstate Bridge; see Vancouver-Portland Interstate Bridge

Hamilton Hotel; see Venable Hotel

Hawthorne Bridge
Spanning Williamette Bridge,at SE Hawthorne Blvd.
HAER OR-20
HAER DLC/PP-1993:OR-2
12ph/5pg/1pc/fr L

Hotel Lenox (Lenox Hotel,New)
1100-1116 SW Third St.
HABS OR-130
HABS ORE,26-PORT,5-
40ph/15pg/2pc L

Interstate Toll Bridge; see Longview Bridge

Lenox Hotel,New; see Hotel Lenox

Lewis & Clark Bridge; see Longview Bridge

Longview Bridge (Lewis & Clark Bridge; Columbia River Bridge; Interstate Toll Bridge)
(See WA,COWLITZ COUNTY,LONGVIEW for documentation)
HAER WA-89
L

Market Block,New & Theatre
1035 SW Second Ave.
HABS OR-51
HABS ORE,26-PORT,1-
2ph/7pg L

Odd Fellows Building
1019 SW Tenth St.
HABS OR-135
HABS ORE,26-PORT,6-
25ph/2pg/2pc L

Oriental Theatre
828 SE Grand Ave.
HABS OR-55
HABS ORE,26-PORT,3-
32ph/32pg L

Pioneer Post Office
Fifth St. between Yamhill & Morrison Sts.
HABS OR-52
HABS ORE,26-PORT,2-
4ph/9pg/1pc L

Portland City Hall
1220 SW Fifth Ave.
HABS OR-125
HABS ORE,26-PORT,4-
13ph/8pg/1pc L

Portland General Electric Co.,Equipment Building (Building K)
1841 SE Water St.
HAER OR-12-G
HAER 1991(HAER):24
1ph/1pc L

Portland General Electric Co.,H.P. Boiler Room (Building L4)
1841 SE Water St.
HAER OR-12-L
HAER 1991(HAER):24
24ph/2pc L

Portland General Electric Co.,L.P. Boiler Room (Building L2)
1841 SE Water St.
HAER OR-12-J
HAER 1991(HAER):24
17ph/1pc L

Portland General Electric Co.,Lincoln Substation (Building L3)
1841 SE Water St.
HAER OR-12-K
HAER 1991(HAER):24
7ph/1pc L

Portland General Electric Co.,Office Building (Building G)
1841 SE Water St.
HAER OR-12-F
HAER 1991(HAER):24
9ph/1pc L

Portland General Electric Co.,Office/Equip. Bldgs. (Buildings D and E)
1841 SE Water St.
HAER OR-12-D
HAER 1991(HAER):24
2ph/1pc L

Portland General Electric Co.,Pepco Building (Building A)
1841 SE Water St.
HAER OR-12-A
HAER 1991(HAER):24
13ph/1pc L

Portland General Electric Co.,Powerhouse Extension (Building L5)
1841 SE Water St.
HAER OR-12-M
HAER 1991(HAER):24
19ph/2pc L

Portland General Electric Co.,Station L
1841 SE Water St.
HAER OR-12
HAER 1991(HAER):24
57ph/24pg/7pc L

Portland General Electric Co.,Stephens Substation (Building L6)
1841 SE Water St.
HAER OR-12-N
HAER 1991(HAER):24
17ph/2pc L

Portland General Electric Co.,Storage Building (Building B)
1841 SE Water St.
HAER OR-12-B
HAER 1991(HAER):24
1ph/1pc L

Portland General Electric Co.,Storage/Office Bldg. (Building C)
1841 SE Water St.
HAER OR-12-C
HAER 1991(HAER):24
1ph/1pc L

Portland General Electric Co.,Turbine Building (Building L1)
1841 SE Water St.
HAER OR-12-H
HAER 1991(HAER):24
21ph/2pc L

Portland General Electric Co.,Water Intake System
1841 SE Water St.
HAER OR-12-I
HAER 1991(HAER):24
2ph/1pc L

Portland General Electric Co.,Welding Shop (Building F)
1841 SE Water St.
HAER OR-12-E
HAER 1991(HAER):24
2ph/1pc L

Portland General Electric Company,Boiler No. 16 (Building 18)
1841 SE Water St.
HAER OR-12-P
HAER 1991(HAER):24
3ph/1pc L

Portland General Electric Company,Equipment Bldg. (Building J)
1841 SE Water St.
HAER OR-12-R
HAER 1991(HAER):24
1ph/1pc L

Portland General Electric Company,Machine Shop (Building L7)
1841 SE Water St.
HAER OR-12-O
HAER 1991(HAER):24
1ph/1pc L

Portland General Electric Company,Shop Building (Building L10(P))
1841 SE Water St.
HAER OR-12-Q
HAER 1991(HAER):24
1ph/1pc L

Portland Reservoir No.2
6007 S.E. Division Street
HAER OR-48
1ph/14pg/2pc/fr H

St. John's Bridge
Spans Williamette River atU.S. Hwy. 30
HAER OR-40
HAER DLC/PP-1993:OR-2
13ph/6pg/1pc/fr L

Steel Bridge
Spanning Williamette River at St. Rt. 99
HAER OR-21
HAER DLC/PP-1993:OR-2
8ph/7pg/1pc/fr L

U. S. Courthouse
620 SW Main St.
HABS OR-134
HABS ORE,26-PORT,7-
36ph/32pg/2pc/fr L

Vancouver-Portland Interstate Bridge (Columbia River Interstate Bridge)
(See WA,CLARK COUNTY,VANCOUVER for documentation)
HAER WA-86
L

Venable Hotel (Hamilton Hotel)
1024 SW. Third Ave.
HABS OR-159
20ph/13pg/1pc/fr H

Willamette River Bridge No. 5.1; see Burlington Northern Railroad Bridge

Willamette River Bridges
Spanning Williamette River at various locations
HAER OR-55
HAER DLC/PP-1993:OR-2
1dr/6pg L

SAUVIE'S ISLAND

Bybee,James F. ,House
HABS OR-47
HABS ORE,26-SAUVI,1-
7dr/2ph/1pg L

WARRENDALE

Moffett Creek Bridge
Spans Moffett Creek at Old Columbia River Hwy.
HAER OR-49
HAER DLC/PP-1993:OR-2
2dr/fr L

POLK COUNTY

DALLAS

Lyle,John E. ,House
State Hwy. 22
HABS OR-27
HABS ORE,27-DAL,1-
2ph/1pg L

ELLENDALE

Boarding House
HABS OR-28
HABS ORE,27-DAL.V,1-
7dr/2ph/1pg L

PEDEE

Johnson,John,House
HABS OR-29
HABS ORE,27-PEDEE,1-
7dr/2ph/1pg L

PERRYDALE

Richmond,T. G. ,House
HABS OR-26
HABS ORE,27-PER.V,1-
7dr/2ph/1pg L

RICKREALL

Nesmith,James W. ,House
HABS OR-25
HABS ORE,34-RICK.V,1-
9dr/2ph/1pg L

TILLAMOOK COUNTY

HEBO VIC.

Dolph Toll Road
State Hwy. 22 Vic. ,Sinslaw National Forest
HAER OR-2
HAER ORE,29-HEBO.V,1-
20ph/12pg/2pc L

TILLAMOOK

Tillamook County Courthouse
201 Laurel Ave.
HABS OR-158
11ph/8pg/1pc H

Wilson River Bridge
Spans Wilson River at U.S. Hwy. 101
HAER OR-39
HAER DLC/PP-1993:OR-2
5ph/4pg/1pc/fr L

UMATILLA COUNTY

HERMISTON

U. S. Army Depot Activity,Umatilla (Umatilla Army Depot)
HAER OR-5
HAER ORE,30-HERM,1-
40pg/fr L

Umatilla Army Depot; see U. S. Army Depot Activity,Umatilla

UNION COUNTY

UNION

Union Ranger Distric Compd.,Rangers Residence (Union Ranger Station,Eagle Ranger District)
Fronting State Hwy. 203,at W. edge of Union
HABS OR-139-B
7ph H

Union Ranger District Compd.,Equipmt. Storage Shed (Union Ranger Station, Eagle Ranger District)
Fronting State Hwy. 203,at W. edge of Union
HABS OR-139-H
2ph H

Union Ranger District Compd.,Garage,Guard Res. (Union Ranger Station,Eagle Ranger District)
Fronting State Hwy. 203,at W. edge of Union
HABS OR-139-E
1ph H

Union Ranger District Compd.,Garage,Rangers Res. (Union Ranger Station,Eagle Ranger District)
Fronting State Hwy. 203,at W. edge of Union
HABS OR-139-C
3ph H

Union Ranger District Compd.,Guard Residence (Union Ranger Station,Eagle Ranger District)
Fronting State Hwy. 203,at W. edge of Union
HABS OR-139-D
11ph H

Union Ranger District Compd.,Office (Union Ranger Station,Eagle Ranger District)
Fronting State Hwy. 203,at W. edge of Union
HABS OR-139-A
11ph H

Union Ranger District Compd.,Oil and Gas House (Union Ranger Station,Eagle Ranger District)
Fronting State Hwy. 203,at W. edge of Union
HABS OR-139-F
4ph H

Union Ranger District Compd.,Warehouse (Union Ranger Station,Eagle Ranger District)
Fronting State Hwy. 203,at W. edge of Union
HABS OR-139-G
5ph H

Union Ranger District Compound (Union Ranger Station, Eagle Ranger District)
Fronting State Hwy. 203, at W. edge of Union
HABS OR-139
8ph/19pg/6pc H

Union Ranger Station, Eagle Ranger District; see Union Ranger District Compd.,Equipmt. Storage Shed

Union Ranger Station, Eagle Ranger District; see Union Ranger District Compound

Union Ranger Station,Eagle Ranger District; see Union Ranger Distric Compd.,Rangers Residence

Union Ranger Station,Eagle Ranger District; see Union Ranger District Compd.,Garage,Guard Res.

Union Ranger Station,Eagle Ranger District; see Union Ranger District Compd.,Garage,Rangers Res.

Union Ranger Station,Eagle Ranger District; see Union Ranger District Compd.,Guard Residence

Union Ranger Station,Eagle Ranger District; see Union Ranger District Compd.,Office

Union Ranger Station,Eagle Ranger District; see Union Ranger District Compd.,Oil and Gas House

Union Ranger Station,Eagle Ranger District; see Union Ranger District Compd.,Warehouse

WALLOWA COUNTY

WALLOWA

Wallowa Ranger Station
602 First St.
HABS OR-157
2ph/14pg/1pc H

Wallowa Ranger Station,Fire Equipment Building (Wallowa Ranger Station,Warehouse No. 2208)
602 First St.
HABS OR-157-C
8ph/2pg/1pc H

Wallowa Ranger Station,Garage
602 First St.
HABS OR-157-D
5ph/1pg/1pc H

Wallowa Ranger Station,Gas House
602 First St.
HABS OR-157-E
5ph/1pg/1pc H

Wallowa Ranger Station,Office (Wallowa Ranger Station,Office No. 2006)
602 First St.
HABS OR-157-A
7ph/2pg/1pc H

Wallowa Ranger Station,Office No. 2006; see Wallowa Ranger Station,Office

Wallowa Ranger Station,Residence (Wallowa Ranger Station,Residence No. 1010)
602 First St.
HABS OR-157-B
12ph/2pg/1pc H

Wallowa Ranger Station,Residence No. 1010; see Wallowa Ranger Station,Residence

Wallowa Ranger Station,Warehouse No. 2208; see Wallowa Ranger Station,Fire Equipment Building

WASCO COUNTY

ROWENA VIC.

Dry Canyon Creek Bridge
Spanning Dry Canyon Creek at Mosier-Dallas Hwy.
HAER OR-30
HAER DLC/PP-1993:OR-2
2ph/5pg/1pc/fr L

THE DALLES

Columbia River Highway Bridges
See same name under Multnomah Co. Portland
HAER OR-56
HAER DLC/PP-1993:OR-2
1dr/15pg L

Mill Creek Bridge
Spanning Mill Creek at W. Sixth St.
HAER OR-27
HAER DLC/PP-1993:OR-2
3ph/4pg/1pc/fr L

WASHINGTON COUNTY

FOREST GROVE

Pacific University,Old College Hall
HABS OR-15
HABS ORE,34-FOGRO,1-
4dr/2ph/1pg L

Smith,Alvin T. ,House
HABS OR-16
HABS ORE,34-FOGRO,2-
2ph/1pg L

REEDVILLE

Reed,Simeon G. ,House
HABS OR-13
HABS ORE,34-REEDV,1-
2ph/1pg L

WEST UNION

West Union Baptist Church
HABS OR-14
HABS ORE,34-UNIW,1-
6dr/3ph/1pg L

WHEELER COUNTY

DAYVILLE VIC.

Antone Mining District; see Rock Creek Mining Dist:Upper,Lower &Waterman Ditch

Rock Creek Mining Dist:Upper,Lower &Waterman Ditch (Antone Mining District)
Near inter. US Rt. 26 & Antone Rd.
HAER OR-9
HAER ORE,35-DAYV.V,1-
9ph/13pg/1pc/fr L

YAMHILL COUNTY

DAYTON

Fort Yamhill
U. S. Hwy. 99
HABS OR-21
HABS ORE,36-DAYT,1-
3dr/2ph/1pg L

DUNDEE

Hagey,Levi,House
HABS OR-20
HABS ORE,36-DUND,1-
8dr/2ph/1pg L

HOPEWELL VIC.

Gay,George K. ,House
HABS OR-24
HABS ORE,36-HOP.V,1-
7dr/2ph/1pg L

LAFAYETTE

Cook,Amos T. ,House
HABS OR-22
HABS ORE,36-LAFA.V,1-
9dr/2ph/1pg L

LAFAYETTE VIC.

Fletcher,Francis,House
HABS OR-23
HABS ORE,36-LAFA.V,2-
9dr/2ph/1pg L

YAMHILL

Bedwell,Elisha,House
HABS OR-18
HABS ORE,36-YAMHI.V,2-
10dr/2ph/1pg L

YAMHILL VIC.

Merchant,Robert,House
HABS OR-19
HABS ORE,36-YAMHI.V,3-
6dr/2ph/1pg L

Morris,Eliam Small,House
HABS OR-17
HABS ORE,36-YAMHI.V,1-
7dr/2ph/1pg L

Fallingwater (Edgar J. Kaufmann House), Ohiopyle vicinity, Fayette County, Pennsylvania. View from southwest of house as seen from downstream. Photograph by Jack E. Boucher, February or March 1985 (HABS PA,26-OHPY.V,1-3).

Pennsylvania

ALTOONA

St. Luke's Protestant Episcopal Mission
HABS PA-5856
H

BLAIR

St. Mary's Roman Catholic Church,Grounds
HABS PA-5847
H

JOHNSTOWN

Price,Charles S. & Sarah,Estate
(Westmont Neighborhood)
HABS PA-5734
H

St. Casimir's Roman Catholic Church,Grounds
HABS PA-5743
H

St. Columba's Roman Catholic Church, Grounds
HABS PA-5741
H

St. Mary's Greek Byzantine Catholic Church,Grounds
HABS PA-5742
H

Westmont Neighborhood; see Price,Charles S. & Sarah,Estate

MCALEVY'S FORT VIC.

Greenwood Furnace
E. of McAlevy's Fort on SR305y line
HAER PA-287
H

NAZARETH

Inspector's House; see Principal's House

Principal's House (Inspector's House)
Nazareth Hall Tract
HABS PA-1268
HABS 1991(HABS):1
7dr L

PHILADELPHIA

Frankford Arsenal,Building 34
SW corner Mordecai Rd. & Mellon St.
HAER PA-74-AL
1ph/3pg/1pc L

ADAMS COUNTY

BERMUDIAN VIC.

Christ Evangelical Lutheran Church
(Latimore Township)
HABS PA-348
HABS PA,1-YORSP.V,2-
1ph/1pg L

EAST BERLIN VIC.

Kuhn's Fording Bridge
Spanning Conewago Creek on Twp. Rd. 552
HAER PA-68
HAER PA,1-EBER.V,1-
12ph/14pg/1pc L

FAIRFIELD BOR.

Fairfield Inn; see Miller,William,House

Miller,William,House (Fairfield Inn)
HABS PA-350
HABS PA,1-FAIRF,1-
1ph/1pg L

FLORADALE VIC.

Peters,George,House
(Peters,John,House)
(Menallen Township)
HABS PA-362
HABS PA,1-FLORDA.V,1-
1ph/1pg L

Peters,John,House; see Peters,George,House

GETTYSBURG

Gettysburg College,Glatfelder Hall
Old Quadrangle,W. side
HABS PA-5442
HABS 1991(HABS):1
10ph/14pg/1pc L

GETTYSBURG BOR.

Adams County Courthouse
HABS PA-265
HABS PA,1-GET,9-
1ph/1pg/1pc L

Bushman House
HABS PA-365
HABS PA,1-GET,8-
2ph L

Gettysburg College,Old Dorm; see Pennsylvania College,Pennsylvania Hall

Gettysburg National Military Park; see McPherson Barn

Lutheran Theological Seminary,Main Building
HABS PA-359
HABS PA,1-GET,6-
3ph/1pg L

McPherson Barn (Gettysburg National Military Park)
HABS PA-5139
HABS PA,1-GET,10A-
4dr L

Pennsylvania College,Pennsylvania Hall (Gettysburg College,Old Dorm)
HABS PA-360
HABS PA,1-GET,7-
1ph/1pg L

GETTYSBURG VIC.

Bender,Theodore,House (James J. Wills Farm)
E. of Herr's Ridge Rd.,W. of Buford Ave.
HABS PA-1964
HABS PA,1-GET.V,9-
9dr L

Biggs Farm,House (Gettysburg National Military Park)
HABS PA-5940-A
HABS DLC/PP-1992:PA-5
2ph/1pc L

Black Horse Tavern
(Cumberland Township)
HABS PA-361
HABS PA,1-GET.V,5-
1ph/1pg L

Blocher House
Tablerock Road,off Rt. 34.
HABS PA-1963
HABS PA,1-GET.V,10-
3dr/fr L

Bricker Outdoor Bake Oven (Fox Outdoor Bake Oven)
Taneytown & Wheat Fields Rds.
HABS PA-355
HABS PA,1-GET.V,4-
4dr/4ph/1pg/fr L

Bryan House (Gettysburg National Military Park)
Hancock Ave.
HABS PA-342
HABS PA,1-GET.V,2-
8dr/4ph/1pg/fr L

Bushman Barn
Bus. U.S. 15,Emmitsburg Rd.,Gettysburg NMP
HABS PA-365-A
HABS PA,1-GET,8A-
12dr/fr L

Cobean Farm
State Rt. 34
HABS PA-1965
HABS PA,1-GET.V,11-
4dr/fr L

Conewago (Huntingtown) Presbyterian Church,doorway
HABS PA-345
HABS PA,1-HUNTO,1-
1ph L

Culp Farm & Smokehouse
W. of Rock Creek
HABS PA-5379
HABS PA,1-GET,12-
1dr/fr L

Culp Farm,Barn
W. of Rock Creek
HABS PA-5379-A
HABS PA,1-GET,12A-
6dr/fr L

Culp Farm,House (Gettysburg National Military Park)
HABS PA-354
HABS PA,1-GET,3-
6dr/2ph/1pg/fr L

Culp Farm,Springhouse
W. of Rock Creek
HABS PA-5379-B
HABS PA,1-GET,12B-
1dr/fr L

Culp Farm,Woodshed
W. of Rock Creek
HABS PA-5379-C
HABS PA,1-GET,12C-
1dr/fr L

Eisenhower Farm One
Eisenhower Nat'l Historic Site
HABS PA-5372
HABS PA,1-GET.V,12-
1dr/fr L

Eisenhower Farm One,Bank Barn
Emmitsburg Rd. (U.S. 15)
HABS PA-5372-A
HABS PA,1-GET.V,13A-
11dr/fr L

Eisenhower Farm Two
Emmitsburg Rd. (U.S. 15)
HABS PA-5373
HABS PA,1-GET.V,13-
1dr/fr L

Eisenhower Farm Two,Bank Barn
Emmitsburg Rd. (U.S. 15)
HABS PA-5373-A
HABS 1988(HABS):124
7dr/fr L

Eisenhower Farm Two,Breeding & Equipment Shed
Emmitsburg Rd. (U.S. 15)
HABS PA-5373-B
HABS PA,1-GET.V,13B-
2dr/fr L

Eisenhower Farm Two,Showbarn
Emmitsburg Rd. (U.S. 15)
HABS PA-5373-C
HABS PA,1-GET.V,13C-
6dr/1pg/fr L

Eisenhower Farms,Guard Huts
Back Lane & Nevins Lane off U.S. 15
HABS PA-5374
HABS PA,1-GET.V,14-
2dr/fr L

Fox Outdoor Bake Oven; see Bricker Outdoor Bake Oven

Gettysburg National Military Park; see Biggs Farm,House

Gettysburg National Military Park; see Bryan House

Gettysburg National Military Park; see Culp Farm,House

Gettysburg National Military Park; see Klingel Farm

Gettysburg National Military Park; see Klingel Farm,House

Gettysburg National Military Park; see Riggs Farm

Gettysburg National Military Park; see Rose Barn

Gettysburg National Military Park; see Slyder House

Gettysburg National Military Park; see Slyder House,Kitchen

Gettysburg National Military Park; see Spangler,Henry,Farm,House

Hummelbaugh Farm
Pleasonton Ave.,Gettysburg NMP
HABS PA-1961
HABS PA,1-GET.V,15-
1dr/fr L

Hummelbaugh Farm,House
Pleasonton Ave.,Gettysburg NMP
HABS PA-1961-A
HABS PA,1-GET.V,15A-
1dr/fr L

James J. Wills Farm; see Bender,Theodore,House

Klingel Farm (Gettysburg National Military Park)
HABS PA-5939
H

Klingel Farm,House (Gettysburg National Military Park)
HABS PA-5939-A
HABS DLC/PP-1992:PA-5
2ph/1pc L

Leister,Lydia,Barn
Taneytown Rd. (State Rt. 134) & Hunt Ave.
HABS PA-341-A
HABS PA,1-GET.V,1A-
8dr/fr L

Leister,Lydia,House
Taneytown Rd.
HABS PA-341
HABS PA,1-GET.V,1-
10dr/1ph L

McClean House
Mummasburg Rd. (Cumberland Twp.)
HABS PA-1187
HABS PA,1-GET.V,8-
7dr/fr L

Patterson,William,House
Taneytown Rd. (Rt. 134) ,Pleasonton Ave. vic.
HABS PA-580
HABS PA,1-GET.V,16-
5dr/fr L

Riggs Farm (Gettysburg National Military Park)
HABS PA-5940
H

Rose Barn (Gettysburg National Military Park)
HABS PA-5348
1dr/19ph H

Slyder Barn
Near Plum Run,W. of Big Round Top
HABS PA-356-B
HABS PA,1-GET,4B-
5dr/fr L

Slyder House (Gettysburg National Military Park)
Plum Run
HABS PA-356
HABS PA,1-GET,4-
8dr/3ph/1pg/fr L

Slyder House,Kitchen (Gettysburg National Military Park)
Plum Run
HABS PA-356-A
HABS PA,1-GET,4A-
3dr/fr L

Spangler Barn; see Spangler Farm,Carriage House

Spangler Farm
Emmitsburg Rd. (U. S. 15)
HABS PA-1960
HABS PA,1-GET,11-
1dr/fr L

Spangler Farm,Carriage House
(Spangler Barn)
Emmitsburg Rd. (U.S. Rt. 15)
HABS PA-357
HABS PA,1-GET,5-
2dr/1ph/1pg/fr L

Spangler Farm,Storage House & Woodshed
Emmitsburg Rd. (U. S. 15)
HABS PA-1960-C
HABS PA,1-GET,11C-
1dr/fr L

Spangler Farm,Summer Kitchen
Emmitsburg Rd. (U. S. 15)
HABS PA-1960-B
HABS PA,1-GET,11B-
2dr/fr L

Spangler,Henry,Farm,House
(Gettysburg National Military Park)
Emmitsburg Rd. (U. S. 15)
HABS PA-1960-A
HABS PA,1-GET,11A-;(DLC/PP-1992:PA-5)
2dr/2ph/1pc/fr L

Trostle Barn
Emmitsburg Rd. (U.S. 15),Gettysburg NMP
HABS PA-1962
HABS PA,1-GET.V,17A-
10dr/fr L

Weikert Barn
Emmitsburg Road,US 15 Gettysburg Nat'l Military Pk
HABS PA-358
HABS PA,1-GET.V,6B-
8dr/2ph/1pg/fr L

Weikert House
(Cumberland Township)
HABS PA-363
HABS PA,1-GET.V,6-
2ph/1pg L

Weikert Summer Kitchen
(Cumberland Township)
HABS PA-353
HABS PA,1-GET.V,6A-
3ph/1pg L

HEIDLERSBURG VIC.

Rock Chapel (Methodist)
(Huntington Township)
HABS PA-352
HABS PA,1-HEID.V,1-
1ph/1pg L

HUNTERSTOWN VIC.

Covered Bridge over Conewago Creek; see Snyder's Fording Covered Bridge

Snyder's Fording Covered Bridge
(Covered Bridge over Conewago Creek)
(Straban-Tyrone Township)
HABS PA-351
HABS PA,1-HUNTO.V,1-
1ph/1pg L

IRON SPRINGS VIC.

Stevens Furnace (Ruins)
(Hamiltonban Township)
HABS PA-346
HABS PA,1-IRONSP.V,2-
1ph/1pg L

Stevens Viaduct
Spanning Tom's Creek (Hamiltonban Township)
HABS PA-347
HABS PA,1-IRONSP.V,1-
1ph/1pg L

LITTLESTOWN VIC.

St. John's Lutheran Church
State Rt. 194 (Germany Township)
HABS PA-269
HABS PA,1-LIT.V,1-
1ph/1pc L

ZORA

Mason-Dixon Line Marker
HABS PA-349
HABS PA,1-ZORA.V,1-
1ph/1pg L

ALLEGHENY COUNTY

ASPINWALL VIC.

(Building No. 1); see VA Med. Center,Aspinwall Div.,Infirmary Bldg.

(Building No. 2); see VA Med. Center,Aspinwall Div.,Ambulatory Quarters

(Building No. 22); see VA Med. Center,Aspinwall Div.,Attnd.'s Qtrs. Annex

(Building No. 26); see VA Med. Center,Aspinwall Div.,Animal House

(Building No. 27); see VA Med. Center,Aspinwall Div.,Laundry Bldg.

(Building No. 3); see VA Med. Center,Aspinwall Div.,Station Garage

(Building No. 31); see VA Med. Center,Aspinwall Div.,Garage

(Building No. 32); see VA Med. Center,Aspinwall Div.,Administration Bldg.

(Building No. 4); see VA Med. Center,Aspinwall Div.,Boiler House

(Building No. 45); see VA Med. Center,Aspinwall Div.,Elevated Tank

(Building No. 5); see VA Med. Center,Aspinwall Div.,Storehouse

(Building No. 6); see VA Med. Center,Aspinwall Div.,Attendent's Quarters

VA Med. Center,Aspinwall Div.,Administration Bldg. ((Building No. 32))
5103 Delafield Ave.
HABS PA-5438-K
HABS DLC/PP-1993:PA-5
13ph/8pg/2pc L

VA Med. Center,Aspinwall Div.,Ambulatory Quarters ((Building No. 2))
5103 Delafield Ave.
HABS PA-5438-B
HABS DLC/PP-1993:PA-5
17ph/8pg/2pc L

VA Med. Center,Aspinwall Div.,Animal House ((Building No. 26))
5103 Delafield Ave.
HABS PA-5438-H
HABS DLC/PP-1993:PA-5
2ph/3pg/1pc L

VA Med. Center,Aspinwall Div.,Attendent's Quarters ((Building No. 6))
5103 Delafield Ave.
HABS PA-5438-F
HABS DLC/PP-1993:PA-5
10ph/8pg/1pc L

VA Med. Center,Aspinwall Div.,Attnd.'s Qtrs. Annex ((Building No. 22))
5103 Delafield Ave.
HABS PA-5438-G
HABS DLC/PP-1993:PA-5
10ph/8pg/1pc L

VA Med. Center,Aspinwall Div.,Boiler House ((Building No. 4))
5103 Delafield Ave.
HABS PA-5438-D
HABS DLC/PP-1993:PA-5
4ph/3pg/1pc L

VA Med. Center,Aspinwall Div.,Elevated Tank ((Building No. 45))
5103 Delafield Ave.
HABS PA-5438-M
HABS DLC/PP-1993:PA-5
3ph/3pg/1pc L

VA Med. Center,Aspinwall Div.,Garage ((Building No. 31))
5103 Delafield Ave.
HABS PA-5438-J
HABS DLC/PP-1993:PA-5
2ph/3pg/1pc L

VA Med. Center,Aspinwall Div.,Infirmary Bldg. ((Building No. 1))
5103 Delafield Ave.
HABS PA-5438-A
HABS DLC/PP-1993:PA-5
38ph/9pg/5pc L

VA Med. Center,Aspinwall Div.,Laundry Bldg. ((Building No. 27))
5103 Delafield Ave.
HABS PA-5438-I
HABS DLC/PP-1993:PA-5
8ph/8pg/1pc L

VA Med. Center,Aspinwall Div.,Station Garage ((Building No. 3))
5103 Delafield Ave.
HABS PA-5438-C
HABS DLC/PP-1993:PA-5
4ph/3pg/1pc L

VA Med. Center,Aspinwall Div.,Storehouse ((Building No. 5))
5103 Delafield Ave.
HABS PA-5438-E
HABS DLC/PP-1993:PA-5
4ph/3pg/1pc L

VA Medical Center,Aspinwall Division
5103 Delafield Ave.
HABS PA-5438
HABS DLC/P--1993:PA-5
10ph/15pg/2pc L

ASPIWALL VIC.

(Building No. 42); see VA Med. Center,Aspinwall Div.,Water Softener Bldg.

VA Med. Center,Aspinwall Div.,Water Softener Bldg. ((Building No. 42))
5103 Delafield Ave.
HABS PA-5438-L
HABS DLC/PP-1993:PA-5
3ph/3pg/1pc L

BEN AVON BOR.

Dalzell House
228 Dalzell Ave.
HABS PA-605
HABS PA,2-BENAV,1-
5dr L

CHURCHILL BOR.

Beulah Presbyterian Church
Beulah Rd. (State Rt. 130)
HABS PA-602
HABS PA,2-CHURCHL,1-
8dr L

CLAIRTON

U.S. Steel Corp:Clairton Works
Monongela River & State St. vic.
HAER PA-49
HAER PA,2-CLAIR,1-
2ph/1pc L

U.S. Steel Corp:Clairton Works,Blowing Engine Bldg
400 State St.
HAER PA-49-A
HAER PA,2-CLAIR,1A-
6ph/2pg/1pc L

U.S. Steel Corp:Clairton Works,14-Inch Mill Engs.
400 State St.
HAER PA-49-B
HAER PA,2-CLAIR,1B-
2ph/2pg/1pc L

U.S. Steel Corp:Clairton Works,22-Inch Mill Engine
400 State St.
HAER PA-49-C
HAER PA,2-CLAIR,1C-
1ph/1pg/1pc L

DRAVOSBURG VIC.

Rhodes,A. S. ,Springhouse
Bull Run Rd.
HABS PA-413
HABS PA,2-DRAVO.V,1-
3dr/4ph/1pg/fr L

DUQUESNE

Carnegie Steel Company; see USX Duquesne Works

USX Duquesne Works (Carnegie Steel Company)
Monongahela River bounded by West Mifflin
HAER PA-115
10dr/62ph/3pg/fr H

EVERGREEN HAMLET

Hampton-Kelly House; see Hampton,Wade,House

Hampton,Wade,House (Hampton-Kelly House; Kelly House)
Evergreen Hamlet Rd. (Ross Twp.)
HABS PA-606
HABS PA,2-EVGHM,1-
10dr L

Kelly House; see Hampton,Wade,House

HARRISON

16 Blue Ridge Avenue (Rowhouse)
HABS PA-5377
HABS DLC/PP-1993:PA-5
3ph/2pg/1pc L

36 Wood Street (Rowhouse)
HABS PA-5376
HABS DLC/PP-1993:PA-5
5ph/2pg/1pc L

MC KEESPORT

McConnell House; see Muse,John J. ,House

Muse,John J. ,House (McConnell House)
Muse's Lane
HABS PA-603
HABS PA,2-MCKSPT,1-
7dr L

MCKEES ROCKS

St. Mary's Roman Catholic School
NW corner of Church Ave. and Guthrie St.
HABS PA-5481
HABS DLC/PP-1993:PA-5
18ph/11pg/2pc L

PITTSBURGH

Allegheny County Courthouse & Jail
436 Grant St. (Courthouse) ,420 Ross St. (Jail)
HABS PA-610
HABS PA,2-PITBU,29-
35dr/13ph/1pg/1pc L

Allegheny Post Office,Old; see U. S. Allegheny Post Office

Arbuthnot Building; see Penn & Liberty Avenues (Commercial Buildings)

Beau Brummell Club
954 Liberty Ave.
HABS PA-625
HABS PA,2-PITBU,30-
10dr L

Bedford,Dr. Nathaniel,Monument
Trinity Cathedral Churchyard
HABS PA-44
HABS PA,20-PITBU,10-
1dr/2ph/3pg/fr L

Bouquet's Redoubt; see Fort Pitt Blockhouse

Bracken,John M.,Hotel
100-104 Anderson St.
HABS PA-5443
14ph/14pg/4pc H

Brady Street Bridge (South Twenty-Second Street Bridge)
Spanning Monongahela River
HABS PA-614
HAER PA-3
HABS/HAER PA,2-PITBU,31-
14dr/28ph/39pg/4pc/2ct/fr L

Brewer,Charles,House
1131 Western Ave.
HABS PA-41
HABS PA,2-PITBU,7-
11dr/3ph/3pg/fr L

Byers-Lyons House
901 Ridge St.
HABS PA-1158
HABS PA,2-PITBU,51-
8ph/1pc L

Carnegie Inst. of Technology,Administration Bldg. (Carnegie-Mellon University,Baker Hall)
Frew St.
HABS PA-1172
HABS PA,2-PITBU,24B-
14dr/4ph/1pc L

Carnegie Inst. of Technology,Machinery Hall Tower (Carnegie-Mellon University,Machinery Hall Tower)
Carnegie Mellon University Campus
HABS PA-1174
HABS PA,2-PITBU,24A-
6dr L

Carnegie-Mellon University,Baker Hall; see Carnegie Inst. of Technology,Administration Bldg.

Carnegie-Mellon University,Machinery Hall Tower; see Carnegie Inst. of Technology,Machinery Hall Tower

Chatham College,Berry Hall; see Wilson House

City-County Building
414 Grant St.
HABS PA-5193
HABS PA,2-PITBU,34-
6ph/3pg/1pc/fr L

Coltart,Joseph,House
3431 Forbes St.
HABS PA-47
HABS PA,2-PITBU,13-
4dr/1ph/2pg L

Documentation: **ct** color transparencies **dr** measured drawings **fr** field records
pc photograph captions **pg** pages of text **ph** photographs

Croghan House (Schenley House; Picnic Place)
Stanton Heights
HABS PA-8-8
HABS PA,2-PITBU,3-
14dr/10ph/4pg/fr L

Emmanuel Protestant Episcopal Church
North & Allegheny Sts.
HABS PA-426
HABS PA,2-PITBU,18-
6dr/7ph/4pg L

English-Oliver House (Oliver House)
845 Ridge Ave.
HABS PA-425
HABS PA,2-PITBU,17-
9dr/7ph/5pg L

Fahnestock,Benjamin A. ,House
408 Penn Ave.
HABS PA-45
HABS PA,2-PITBU,11-
3dr/1ph/2pg L

124 Fancourt St. (Brick Cornices); see 442 Third Avenue (Brick Cornices)

Forks of the Ohio; see Fort Pitt Blockhouse

Fort Pitt Blockhouse (Bouquet's Redoubt; Forks of the Ohio)
Point State Park
HABS PA-430
HABS PA,2-PITBU,20-
4dr/3ph/3pg L

Fulton Theater
101 Sixth St.
HABS PA-1180
HABS PA,2-PITBU,27-;1988(HABS):107
11dr L

Garden Theater,The
10-12-14 W. North Ave.
HABS PA-1278
HABS PA,2-PITBU,28-
1dr/6ph/14pg L

101 Grant Street (Brick Cornices); see 442 Third Avenue (Brick Cornices)

Harper Building; see Penn & Liberty Avenues (Commercial Buildings)

Harter,Eva,House
2557 Beechwood Blvd.
HABS PA-622
HABS PA,2-PITBU,32-
10dr L

Hays Army Ammunition Plant
300 Mifflin Rd.
HAER PA-77
HAER PA,2-PITBU,61-
46pg/fr L

Heathside Cottage
416 Catoma St.
HABS PA-623
HABS PA,2-PITBU,33-
6dr L

Heidelberg Apartments & Cottages
Braddock Ave. & Waverly St. Vic.
HABS PA-431
HABS PA,2-PITBU,21-
21dr/6ph/5pg L

Hogg-Brunot House
216 Stockton Ave.
HABS PA-428
HABS PA,2-PITBU,19-
3dr/4ph/4pg L

Jones & Laughlin Steel Corporation (Morgan Billet Mill Engine)
550' North of E. Carson St.,opposte S. 27th St.
HAER PA-48
HAER PA,2-PITBU,62A-
8ph/1pc L

Karns,John,House
900 N. Canal St.
HABS PA-424
HABS PA,2-PITBU,16-
4dr/2ph/3pg L

King Building; see Penn & Liberty Avenues (Commercial Buildings)

Kingsbacher's
637 Liberty Ave.
HABS PA-5151
HABS PA,2-PITBU,43-
2dr/3ph/22pg L

Klages,Allen M. ,House
5525 Beverly Pl.
HABS PA-621
HABS PA,2-PITBU,35-
11dr L

334 Liberty Avenue (Brick Cornices); see 442 Third Avenue (Brick Cornices)

Lipson Building; see Penn & Liberty Avenues (Commercial Buildings)

Loyal Order of Moose Building (Moose Hall)
628-634 Penn Ave.
HABS PA-5149
HABS PA,2-PITBU,49-
13dr/21ph/26pg/fr L

Manchester Bridge; see North Side Point Bridge

McCormick Building; see Penn & Liberty Avenues (Commercial Buildings)

7211-7225 Meade Street (Houses)
HABS PA-1096
HABS PA,2-PITBU,50-
4ph/5pg/1pc L

Miller,James,House
HABS PA-410
HABS PA,2-PITBU.V,1-
8dr/3ph/2pg/fr L

Mitchell,John M. ,House
524 Third Ave.
HABS PA-42
HABS PA,2-PITBU,8-
2dr/1ph/2pg L

Moose Hall; see Loyal Order of Moose Building

Morgan Billet Mill Engine; see Jones & Laughlin Steel Corporation

Morse School Annex
Sarah St. btwn. Twenty-fourth & Twenty-fifth Sts.
HABS PA-5199
HABS PA,2-PITBU,52A-
14ph/17pg/1pc L

Neal,Robert,Cabin
Schenley Park
HABS PA-46
HABS PA,2-PITBU,12-
2dr/3ph/2pg L

North Side Market
Federal & E. Ohio Sts.
HABS PA-601
HABS PA,2-PITBU,36-
10dr L

North Side Point Bridge (Manchester Bridge)
Spanning Allegheny River
HAER PA-4
HAER PA,2-PITBU,59-
24ph/1pg/3pc L

North Side Post Office; see U. S. Allegheny Post Office

Oliver House; see English-Oliver House

Penn & Liberty Avenues (Commercial Buildings) (Arbuthnot Building)
719-721 Liberty Ave.
HABS PA-5152-D
HABS PA,2-PITBU,46-
5ph/28pg/fr L

Penn & Liberty Avenues (Commercial Buildings) (Harper Building)
723-725 Liberty Ave.
HABS PA-5152-E
HABS PA,2-PITBU,47-
5ph/25pg/fr L

Penn & Liberty Avenues (Commercial Buildings) (King Building)
639 Liberty Ave.
HABS PA-5152-B
HABS PA,2-PITBU,44-
3ph/23pg/fr L

Penn & Liberty Avenues (Commercial Buildings) (Lipson Building)
636 Penn Ave.
HABS PA-5152-F
HABS PA,2-PITBU,48-
1ph/18pg/fr L

Penn & Liberty Avenues (Commercial Buildings) (McCormick Building)
635 Liberty Ave.
HABS PA-5152-A
HABS PA,2-PITBU,42-
2ph/23pg/fr L

Penn & Liberty Avenues (Commercial Buildings) (Whitten Building)
641 Liberty Ave.
HABS PA-5152-C
HABS PA,2-PITBU,45-
2ph/22pg/fr L

Penn RR Stn,Open Concourse & Concourse Roof Ext. (Union Stn.,Open Concourse & Concourse Roof Ext.)
1101 Liberty Ave.
HABS PA-1175-B
HABS PA,2-PITBU,37C-
4ph/6pg/1pc L

Penn. RR Stn.,South Baggage Passage & Canopy (Union Station,South Baggage Passage & Canopy)
1101 Liberty Ave.
HABS PA-1175-A
HABS PA,2-PITBU,37B-
4ph/8pg/1pc L

Pennsylvania & Liberty Avenues (Commercial Bldgs.)
600 & 700 blocks Liberty Ave. ,600 block Penn Ave.
HABS PA-5152
HABS PA,2-PITBU,40-
3dr/9ph/28pg/fr L

Pennsylvania Railroad Station Rotunda (Union Railroad Station Rotunda)
Liberty,Grant & Eleventh Sts.
HABS PA-1175
HABS PA,2-PITBU,37A-
6dr/7ph/1pg/1pc L

Picnic Place; see Croghan House

Pittsburgh & Lake Erie Station
Smithfield & Carson Sts.
HABS PA-1231
HABS PA,2-PITBU,55-
2ph/1pg/1pc L

Pittsburgh & Steubenville Extension RR Tunnel
Btwn. Fifth & Sixth Sts.
HAER PA-70
HAER PA,2-PITBU,60-
8ph/6pg/1pc L

Point Bridge
Spanning Monongahela River
HABS PA-604
HAER PA-5
HABS/HAER PA,2-PITBU,38-
6dr/6ph/1pc L

Post Office Museum,Old; see U. S. Allegheny Post Office

Schenley House; see Croghan House

132 Second Avenue (Brick Cornices); see 442 Third Avenue (Brick Cornices)

Shadyside Presbyterian Church
Amberson Ave. & Westminister Pl. Vic.
HABS PA-432
HABS PA,2-PITBU,22-
11ph/5pg L

Shoenberger,John H. ,House
425 Penn Ave.
HABS PA-43
HABS PA,2-PITBU,9-
6dr/1ph/2pg/fr L

Singer,John F. ,House
1318 Singer Pl.
HABS PA-433
HABS PA,2-PITBU,23-
6dr/11ph/5pg L

Smithfield Street Bridge
Spanning Monongahela River on Smithfield St.
HAER PA-2
HAER PA,2-PITBU,58-
28ph/42pg/3pc/4ct/fr L

Snider Buildings
2400,2402,2402 1/2 Sarah St.
HABS PA-5200
HABS PA,2-PITBU,54-
8ph/14pg/1pc L

South Twenty-Second Street Bridge; see Brady Street Bridge

St. Peter's Protestant Episcopal Church
Forbes St. & Craft Ave. (moved from Grant St.)
HABS PA-48
HABS PA,2-PITBU,14-
6dr/1ph/2pg L

442 Third Avenue (Brick Cornices) (132 Second Avenue (Brick Cornices); 124 Fancourt St. (Brick Cornices); 334 Liberty Avenue (Brick Cornices); 101 Grant Street (Brick Cornices))
HABS PA-49
HABS PA,2-PITBU,15-
2dr/1pg L

U. S. Allegheny Arsenal
Fortieth & Butler Sts.
HABS PA-8-1
HABS PA,2-PITBU,6-
2dr/2pg/fr L

U. S. Allegheny Arsenal,Armory
HABS PA-8-1-F
HABS PA,2-PITBU,6F-
3dr/2ph/fr L

U. S. Allegheny Arsenal,Barracks Building
Thirty-ninth St.
HABS PA-8-1-C
HABS PA,2-PITRBU,6C-
4dr/6ph/fr L

U. S. Allegheny Arsenal,Boiler House
HABS PA-8-1-G
HABS PA,2-PITBU,6G-
2dr/1ph/fr L

U. S. Allegheny Arsenal,Carriage House
HABS PA-8-1-L
HABS PA,2-PITBU,6L-
1ph/fr L

U. S. Allegheny Arsenal,Commandants' Quarters
Fortieth St.
HABS PA-8-1-A
HABS PA,2-PITBU,6A-
8dr/4ph/fr L

U. S. Allegheny Arsenal,Entrance Gates
Thirty-ninth St.
HABS PA-8-1-J
HABS PA,2-PITBU,6J
1dr/4ph/fr L

U. S. Allegheny Arsenal,Guardhouse
Butler St.
HABS PA-8-1-K
HABS PA,2-PITBU,6K-
2dr/2ph/fr L

U. S. Allegheny Arsenal,Machine Shop
HABS PA-8-1-H
HABS PA,2-PITBU,6H-
2dr/2ph/fr L

U. S. Allegheny Arsenal,N. C. O. Quarters
Thirty-ninth St.
HABS PA-8-1-D
HABS PA,2-PITBU,6D-
7dr/3ph/fr L

U. S. Allegheny Arsenal,Officers' Quarters
Thirty-ninth St.
HABS PA-8-1-B
HABS PA,2-PITBU,6B-
4dr/5ph/fr L

U. S. Allegheny Arsenal,Storehouse Number 2
HABS PA-8-1-E
HABS PA,2-PITBU,6E-
4dr/2ph/fr L

U. S. Allegheny Post Office (Allegheny Post Office,Old; North Side Post Office; Post Office Museum,Old)
Ohio St.
HABS PA-1178
HABS PA,2-PITBU,25-
13dr L

U. S. Bureau of Mines,Experimentation Station
Forbes Ave.
HABS PA-1166
HABS PA,2-PITBU,39-
1dr L

Union Railroad Station Rotunda; see Pennsylvania Railroad Station Rotunda

Union Station,South Baggage Passage & Canopy; see Penn. RR Stn.,South Baggage Passage & Canopy

Union Stn.,Open Concourse & Concourse Roof Ext.; see Penn RR Stn,Open Concourse & Concourse Roof Ext.

Wallace & McAlister Buildings
631-633 Liberty Ave.
HABS PA-5150
HABS PA,2-PITBU,41-
2dr/3ph/36pg/fr L

Washington Crossing Bridge
Fortieth St.
HABS PA-1179
HABS PA,2-PITBU,26-
14dr L

815-817 Western Avenue (House)
HABS PA-1247
HABS PA,2-PITBU,56-
2ph/1pg/1pc L

Whitten Building; see Penn & Liberty Avenues (Commercial Buildings)

Wilson House (Chatham College,Berry Hall)
Woodland Rd.
HABS PA-1250
HABS PA,2-PITBU,57-
1ph/1pg L

PITTSBURGH VIC.

Davis Island Dam & Lock No. 1 (Davis Island Lock & Dam No. 1)
Ohio River
HAER PA-65
HAER PA,2-PITBU.V,2-
4ph/35pg/1pc L

Davis Island Lock & Dam No. 1; see Davis Island Dam & Lock No. 1

West End Bridge; see West End-North Avenue Bridge

West End-North Avenue Bridge (West End Bridge)
Spanning Ohio River
HAER PA-96
HAER 1989(HAER):18
50ph/18pg/5pc L

SEWICKLEY

Sewickley Bridge
Spanning Ohio River
HAER PA-53
HAER PA,2-SEW,1-
32ph/88pg/2pc L

SEWICKLEY HTS. BOR.

Fairacres (Jones,B. F. ,House)
Blackburn Rd.
HABS PA-607
HABS PA,2-SEWICH,1-
9dr L

Jones,B. F. ,House; see Fairacres

SHARPSBURG VIC.

Ferry House
403 Dorseyville Rd. (O'Hara Twp.)
HABS PA-616
HABS PA,2-SHARP.V,1-
3dr L

SWISSVALE BOR.

Trevanion Avenue (House)
HABS PA-626
HABS PA,2-SWISV,1-
4dr L

BEAVER COUNTY

AMBRIDGE BOR.

Economy Feast Hall
Church St.
HABS PA-612
HABS PA,4-AMB,1A-
11dr L

Economy Meetinghouse (St. John's Lutheran Church)
Church St.
HABS PA-627
HABS PA,4-AMB,1B-
6dr L

Economy Tailor Shop & Wine Cellar
Church St.
HABS PA-613
HABS PA,4-AMB,1C-
9dr L

Economy Town Plan
HABS PA-1176
HABS PA,4-AMB,1-
5dr L

St. John's Lutheran Church; see Economy Meetinghouse

MONOCA

Washington,George,School
Eleventh & Pennsylvania Ave.
HABS PA-1356
HABS PA,4-MONO,1-
10ph/20pg/1pc L

SHIPPINGPORT

Shippingport Atomic Power Station
On Ohio River at Shippingport,25 mi. NW Pittsburgh
HAER PA-81
HAER PA,4-SHIP,1-
177ph/30pg/6pc L

BERKS COUNTY

BAUMSTOWN VIC.

Boone,Daniel,Birthplace
State Rt. 422 Vic. (Exeter Twp.)
HABS PA-149
HABS PA,6-BAUM.V,1-
6ph/3pg L

BERNVILLE

Heister Mill; see Pleasant Valley Roller Mill

Pleasant Valley Roller Mill (Heister Mill; Reber's Mill)
Gruber Rd.
HAER PA-59
HAER PA,6-BERN.V,4-
16ph/17pg/1pc L

Reber's Mill; see Pleasant Valley Roller Mill

BERNVILLE VIC.

Conrad's Warehouse
Btwn. Locks 38 & 39 on Union Canal
HAER PA-57
HAER PA,6-BERN.V,6-
3dr/6ph/5pg/1pc/fr L

Gruber Wagon Works
State Route 183 at Red Bridge Park
HAER PA-14
HAER PA,6-BERN.V,8-
11dr/215ph/29pg/17pc/fr L

Haag-Haak Log House
State RT. 183 (Penn Twp.)
HABS PA-254
HABS PA,6-BERN.V,2-
1ph/1pg/1pc L

House,Log
Host Rd. Vic. (N. Heidelberg Township)
HABS PA-255
HABS PA,6-BERN.V,3-
1ph/1pg/1pc L

Lamm's Mill
Sterner & Sleepy Hollow Rd. (N. Heidelburg Twp.)
HAER PA-58
HAER PA,6-BERN.V,10-
2ph/1pg/1pc L

South Bernville Hotel
Bernville-Robesonia & Host Rds. Vic.
HABS PA-257
HABS PA,6-0BERN.V,1-
9ph/10pg/1pc L

Speicher Bridge
Church Rd. over Tulpehocken Creek between Twps.
HAER PA-60
HAER PA,6-BERN.V,9-
3dr/14ph/10pg/1pc/fr L

Union Canal Locks
HAER PA-66
HAER PA,6-BERN.V,7-
32ph/10pg/2pc L

BIRDSBORO

Bird,William,Mansion
Mill & Main Sts.
HABS PA-1024
HABS PA,6-BIRD,1-
2ph/2pg L

Brooke Manor
Furnace St.
HABS PA-1075
HABS PA,6-BIRD,2-
3dr/2ph/4pg L

BROWNSVILLE VIC.

Dundore Farm (Hottenstein Farm) (moved from Mt. Pleasant Vic.)
HABS PA-261
HABS PA,6-MTPLES.V,7-
1dr/8ph/20pg/5pc L

Hottenstein Farm; see Dundore Farm

Lauer-Gerhard Farm (Reifsnyder Farm)
Farm Lane
HABS PA-1954
HABS PA,6-BROWV.V,1-
2dr/3ph/28pg/2pc/fr L

Lauer-Gerhard Farm,Barn (Reifsnyder Farm,Barn)
Farm Lane
HABS PA-1954-C
HABS PA,6-BROWV.V,1C-
8ph/fr L

Lauer-Gerhard Farm,Garage (Reifsnyder Farm,Garage)
Farm Lane
HABS PA-1954-E
HABS PA,6-BROWV.V,1E-
1ph/fr L

Lauer-Gerhard Farm,Main House (Reifsnyder Farm,Main House)
Farm Lane
HABS PA-1954-A
HABS PA,6-BROWV.V,1A-
6dr/8ph/fr L

Lauer-Gerhard Farm,Small House (Reifsnyder Farm,Small House)
Farm Lane
HABS PA-1954-B
HABS PA,26-BROWV.V,1B-
2dr/3ph/fr L

Lauer-Gerhard Farm,Wagon House (Reifsnyder Farm,Wagon House)
Farm Lane
HABS PA-1954-D
HABS PA,6-BROWV.V,1D-
1ph/fr L

Reifsnyder Farm; see Lauer-Gerhard Farm

Reifsnyder Farm,Barn; see Lauer-Gerhard Farm,Barn

Reifsnyder Farm,Garage; see Lauer-Gerhard Farm,Garage

Reifsnyder Farm,Main House; see Lauer-Gerhard Farm,Main House

Reifsnyder Farm,Small House; see Lauer-Gerhard Farm,Small House

Reifsnyder Farm,Wagon House; see Lauer-Gerhard Farm,Wagon House

CENTERPORT VIC.

Reber Barn (1770)
Centre Twp.
HABS PA-5275
HABS PA,6-CENPO.V,1A-
4ph/1pc L

DAUBERVILLE

Dauberville Bridge
Spanning Schuykill River at Belleman's Church Rd.
HAER PA-129
18ph/7pg/1pc H

DOUGLASVILLE

Building,Old; see St. Gabriel's Church

Jones,Mouns,House (Ruins)
U. S. Rt. 422 (Amity Township)
HABS PA-1032
HABS PA,6-DOUG,1-
1dr/2ph/4pg L

St. Gabriel's Church (Building,Old)
U. S. Rt. 422 (Amity Township)
HABS PA-1038
HABS PA,6-DOUG,2-
4ph/2pg L

EXETER TWP.

Barn
Oley Pike vic.
HABS PA-5262
HABS PA,6-EXTO,1-
1ph/1pc L

FRIEDENSBURG VIC.

Barn (1787)
State Rt. 73,Oley Twp.
HABS PA-5278
HABS PA,6-FRIEB.V,1A-
2ph L

Cricket Slope Farm,Barn
HABS PA-5276
HABS PA,6-FRIEB.V,2A-
1ph L

Farm Group
State Rt. 73
HABS PA-5265
HABS PA,6-FRIEB.V,3-
1ph/1pc L

Leinbach Barn (1851)
State Rt. 73 vic.
HABS PA-5267
HABS PA,6-FRIEB.V,4A-
2ph/1pc L

GABELSVILLE

Barn,Decorated
State Rt. 73 (Colebrookdale Twp.)
HABS PA-5264
HABS PA,6-GABEL,1-
1ph/1pc L

HAY CREEK

Hay Creek Forge
Birdsboro,Pa.
HAER PA-62
2ph/1pg H

HOPEWELL VILLAGE

Hopewell Village National Historic Site
State Rt. 345 vic.
HABS PA-5157
HABS PA,6-HOPVI,1-
1pg L

Hopewell Village National Historic Site; see Hopewell Village,Boarding House,Building No. 24

Hopewell Village National Historic Site; see Hopewell Village,Charcoal House,Building No. One

Hopewell Village National Historic Site; see Hopewell Village,Church,Alex,Stable

Hopewell Village National Historic Site; see Hopewell Village,Furnace & Bridge House

Hopewell Village National Historic Site; see Hopewell Village,Furnace Office-Store,Bldg Three

Hopewell Village National Historic Site; see Hopewell Village,Ironmaster's House

Hopewell Village National Historic Site; see Hopewell Village,Tenant House,Number One

Hopewell Village National Historic Site; see Hopewell Village,Tenant House,Number Three

Hopewell Village National Historic Site; see Hopewell Village,Tenant House,Number Two

Hopewell Village National Historic Site; see Hopewell Village,Village Barn

Hopewell Village,Boarding House,Building No. 24 (Hopewell Village National Historic Site)
State Rt. 345 vic.
HABS PA-5157-B
HABS PA,6-HOPVI,22-
6dr/1pg/fr L

Hopewell Village,Charcoal House,Building No. One (Hopewell Village National Historic Site)
State Rt. 345 vic.
HABS PA-5157-C
HABS PA,6-HOPVI,5-
3dr/1pg/fr L

Hopewell Village,Church,Alex,Stable (Hopewell Village National Historic Site)
Near State Rt. 345
HABS PA-5157-I
HABS PA,6-HOPVI,26A-
fr L

Hopewell Village,Furnace & Bridge House (Hopewell Village National Historic Site)
State Rt. 345 vic.
HABS PA-5157-A
HABS PA.6-HOPVI,3-
2ph L

Hopewell Village,Furnace Office-Store,Bldg Three (Hopewell Village National Historic Site)
Near State Rt. 345
HABS PA-5157-D
HABS PA,6-HOPVI,7-
6dr/1ph/1pg/fr L

Documentation: **ct** color transparencies **dr** measured drawings **fr** field records
pc photograph captions **pg** pages of text **ph** photographs

Hopewell Village,Ironmaster's House (Hopewell Village National Historic Site)
HABS PA-5162
HABS PA,6-HOPVI,8-
5dr/2ph L

Hopewell Village,Tenant House,Number One (Hopewell Village National Historic Site)
State Rt. 345 vic.
HABS PA-5157-F
HABS PA,6-HOPVI,19-
7dr/1pg/fr L

Hopewell Village,Tenant House,Number Three (Hopewell Village National Historic Site)
State Rt. 345 vic.
HABS PA-5157-H
HABS PA,6-HOPVI,21-
2dr/1pg/fr L

Hopewell Village,Tenant House,Number Two (Hopewell Village National Historic Site)
State Rt. 345 vic.
HABS PA-5157-G
HABS PA,6-HOPVI,20-
5dr/1pg L

Hopewell Village,Village Barn (Hopewell Village National Historic Site)
HABS PA-5166
HABS PA,6-HOPVI,16-
3dr/1ph L

JACKSONWALD

Hock,C. ,Farmhouse
HABS PA-150
HABS PA,6-JACSO,1-
3ph L

KUTZTOWN VIC.

Le Van Mill
Kutztown Rd. Vic.
HABS PA-1030
HABS PA,6-KUTZ.V,1-
3dr/6ph/3pg L

LENHARTSVILLE

Berger Farm; see Konig-Speicher Farm

Konig-Speicher Farm (Berger Farm) (moved from Mt. Pleasant Vic.)
HABS PA-258
HABS PA,6-MTPLES.V,13-
1dr/3ph/11pg/3pc L

LIMEKILN VIC.

Bertolet-Herbein Cabin (Snyder Farm)
Eastern Lime Co. Rd., Oley Twp.
HABS PA-1047
HABS PA,6-LIMKI.V,5-
2dr/7ph/5pg/fr L

Ha Penny Farm; see Knabb,Abraham,Barn

Ha Penny Farm; see Knabb,Abraham,House

Knabb-Bieber Mill
Monocacy Creek (Exeter Township)
HABS PA-1031
HABS PA,6-LIMKI.V,1-
5ph/2pg L

Knabb,Abraham,Barn (Ha Penny Farm)
Oley Line Rd. Vic. (Exeter Township)
HABS PA-1043
HABS PA,6-LIMKI.V,3A-
2ph/1pg L

Knabb,Abraham,House (Ha Penny Farm)
Oley Line Rd. Vic. (Exeter Township)
HABS PA-1045
HABS PA,6-LIMKI.V,3-
2ph/2pg L

Schneider,David,House
(Oley Township)
HABS PA-1044
HABS PA,6-LIMKI.V,2-
2ph/2pg L

Snyder Farm; see Bertolet-Herbein Cabin

LOBACHSVILLE VIC.

Keim Barn
Pike Twp.
HABS PA-1182
HABS PA,6-LOBA.V,2B-
2ph L

Keim House
Pike Twp.
HABS PA-1039
HABS PA,6-LOBA.V,2-
3ph/2pg L

Keim Stone Cabin
Pike Twp.
HABS PA-1041
HABS PA,6-LOBA.V,2A-
5ph/2pg L

Yoder Barn
(Pike Township)
HABS PA-1060
HABS PA,6-LOBA.V,1B-
2ph/1pg L

Yoder Stone Cabin
(Pike Township)
HABS PA-1040
HABS PA,6-LOBA.V,1A-
1ph/2pg L

Yoder,Jacob,House
(Pike Township)
HABS PA-1036
HABS PA,6-LOBA.V,1-
3ph/2pg L

MAIDEN CREEK VIC.

Barn,Decorated White
Maiden Creek Twp.
HABS PA-5273
HABS PA,6-MAICR.V,1A-
1ph/1pc L

MOSELEM SPRINGS VIC.

Barn A (1779)
HABS PA-5271-A
HABS PA,6-MOSP.V,2A-
4ph/1pc L

Barn B
HABS PA-5271-B
HABS PA,6-MOSP.V,2B-
1ph/1pc L

Barn,Decorated (1849)
State Rt. 122
HABS PA-5270
HABS PA.6-MOSP.V,1A-
1ph/1pc L

Barn,Decorated Red
State Rt. 135
HABS PA-5272
HABS PA,6-MOSP.V,3A-
1ph/1pc L

MT. PLEASANT VIC.

Berger Farm; see Konig-Speicher Farm

Conrad,John,House (Sheidy House)
Sheidy Rd. (Penn Township)
HABS PA-259
HABS PA,6-MTPLES.V,3-
6dr/24ph/20pg/3pc/fr L

Conrad,Joseph,Farm (Miller's Farm)
State Rt. 183 & Bright School Rd. (Penn Twp.)
HABS PA-260
HABS PA,6-MTPLES.V,6-
1dr/15pg/3pc L

Conrad,Joseph,Farm,Barn
St. Rt. 183 & Bright School Rd. (Penn Twp.)
HABS PA-260-B
HABS PA,6-MTPLES.V,6B-
5dr/6ph/fr L

Conrad,Joseph,Farm,House
State Rt. 83 & Bright School Rd. (Penn Twp.)
HABS PA-260-A
HABS PA,6-MTPLES.V,6A-
4dr/14ph/fr L

Conrad,Joseph,Farm,Pig House
St. Rt. 183 & Bright School Rd. (Penn Twp.)
HABS PA-260-C
HABS PA,6-MTPLES.V,6C-
2ph L

Conrad,Joseph,Farm,Springhouse
St. Rt. 183 & Bright School Rd. (Penn Twp.)
HABS PA-260-D
HABS PA,6-MTPLES.V,6D-
2ph L

Dundore Farm (Hottenstein Farm) (moved to Brownsville Vic.)
HABS PA-261
HABS PA,6-MTPLES.V,7-
1dr/8ph/20pg/5pc L

Dundore Farm,Barn
State Rt. 183 Vic. (Penn Township)
HABS PA-261-B
HABS PA,6-MTPLES.V,7B-
4dr/9ph L

Dundore Farm,Corn Crib & Wagon Shed
State Rt. 183 Vic. (Penn Township)
HABS PA-261-C
HABS PA,6-MTPLES.V,7C-
1dr/4ph L

Dundore Farm,Granary
State Rt. 183 Vic. (Penn Township)
HABS PA-261-D
HABS PA,6-MTPLES.V,7D-
1dr/6ph L

Dundore Farm,House
State Rt. 183 (Penn Township)
HABS PA-261-A
HABS PA,6-MTPLES.V,7A-
2dr/9ph L

Dundore Farm,Milk Shed
State Rt. 183 Vic. (Penn Township)
HABS PA-261-E
HABS PA,6-MTPLES.V,7E-
1dr/1ph L

Dundore Farm,Root Cellar
State Rt. 183 Vic. (Penn Township)
HABS PA-261-F
HABS PA,6-MTPLES.V,7F-
1dr/3ph L

Dundore Farm,Smokehouse
State Rt. 183 Vic. (Penn Township)
HABS PA-261-G
HABS PA,6-MTPLES.V,7G-
1dr/5ph L

Dundore Farm,Springhouse
State Rt. 183 (Penn Township)
HABS PA-261-H
HABS PA,6-MTPLES.V,7H-
1dr/5ph L

Dundore Farm,Wheat Barn
State Rt. 183 Vic. (Penn Township)
HABS PA-261-I
HABS PA,6-MTPLES.V,7I-
1ph L

Gruber House; see Penn,William,Tavern

Gruber,Jacob,House (Speicher House)
Mt. Pleasant Rd. (Penn Township)
HABS PA-262
HABS PA,6-MTPLES.V,8-
6ph/8pg/1pc L

Heck-Stamm-Unger Farm; see Stamm Farm

Hottenstein Farm; see Dundore Farm

Konig-Speicher Farm (Berger Farm)
(moved to Lenhartsville)
HABS PA-258
HABS PA,6-MTPLES.V,13,-
1dr/3ph/11pg/3pc L

Konig-Speicher Farm-Barn
Church Rd. (N. Heidelberg Township)
HABS PA-258-C
HABS PA,6-MTPLES.V,13C-
3ph L

Konig-Speicher Farm-House
Church Rd. (N. Heidelberg Township)
HABS PA-258-B
HABS PA,6-MTPLES.V,13B-
2ph L

Konig-Speicher Farm,Log House
Church Rd. ,(N. Heidelberg Township)
HABS PA-258-A
HABS PA,6-MTPLES.V,13A-
11ph L

Konig-Speicher Farm,Outdoor Bake Oven
Church Rd. (N. Heidelberg Township)
HABS PA-258-D
HABS PA,6-MTPLES.V,13D-
2ph L

Konig-Speicher Farm,Smokehouse
Church Rd. (N. Heidelberg Township)
HABS PA-258-E
HABS PA,6-MTPLES.V,13E-
1dr/1ph L

Miller's Farm; see Conrad,Joseph,Farm

Moorehead House; see Stamm,Eliza,House

Octagon House; see Stoudt,George,House

Penn,William,Tavern (Gruber House)
Gruber Rd. & State Rt. 183 (Penn Twp.)
HABS PA-263
HABS PA,6-MTPLES.V,9-
13ph/8pg/2pc L

Penn,William,Tavern,Privy
Gruber Rd. & State Rt. 183 (Penn Twp.)
HABS PA-263-A
HABS PA,6-MTPLES.V,9A-
1ph L

Penn,William,Tavern,Smokehouse
Gruber Rd. & State Rt. 183 (Penn Twp.)
HABS PA-263-B
HABS PA,6-MTPLES.V,9B-
1ph L

Penn,William,Tavern,Washhouse & Butcher Shop
Gruber Rd. & State Rt. 183 (Penn Twp.)
HABS PA-263-C
HABS PA,6-MTPLES.V,9C-
3ph L

Querean House; see Stamm,Isaac,House

Reber Farm
Gruber Rd. Vic. (Bern Township)
HABS PA-256
HABS PA,6-MTPLES.V,5-
11pg/2pc L

Reber Farm,Barn
Gruber Rd. Vic. (Bern Township)
HABS PA-256-B
HABS PA,6-MTPLES.V,5B-
4ph L

Reber Farm,Canal Store
Gruber Rd. Vic. (Bern Township)
HABS PA-256-C
HABS PA,6-MTPLES.V,5C-
6ph L

Reber Farm,House
Gruber Rd. Vic. (Bern Township)
HABS PA-256-A
HABS PA,6-MTPLES.V,5A-
7ph L

Reifsnyder Farm; see Riem-Schmidt-Deppen Farm

Riem-Schmidt-Deppen Farm
(Reifsnyder Farm)
State Rt. 183 & Church Rd. (Penn Twp.)
HABS PA-264
HABS PA,6-MTPLES.V,10-
11pg/1pc L

Riem-Schmidt-Deppen Farm,Barn
State Rt. 183 & Church Rd. (Penn Twp.)
HABS PA-264-A
HABS PA,6-MTPLES.V,10A-
2ph L

Sheidy House; see Conrad,John,House

Speicher House; see Gruber,Jacob,House

Stamm Farm (Heck-Stamm-Unger Farm)
Gruber Rd. Vic. (Penn Township)
HABS PA-266
HABS PA,6-MTPLES.V,11-
4ph/12pg/2pc L

Stamm Farm,Barn
Gruber Rd. (Penn Township)
HABS PA-266-B
HABS PA,6-MTPLES.V,11B-
7ph L

Stamm Farm,Butcher Shed,Wash House,Root Cellar
Gruber Rd. (Penn Township)
HABS PA-266-E
HABS PA,6-MTPLES.V,11E-
3ph L

Stamm Farm,Chicken & Brooder Houses
Gruber Rd. (Penn Township)
HABS PA-266-C
HABS PA,6-MTPLES.V,11C-
2ph L

Stamm Farm,Corn Crib & Wagon Shed
Gruber Rd. (Penn Township)
HABS PA-266-D
HABS PA,6-MTPLES.V,11D-
3ph L

Stamm Farm,House
Gruber Rd. Vic. (Penn Township)
HABS PA-266-A
HABS PA,6-MTPLES.V,11A-
6ph L

Stamm Farm,Summer Kitchen,Smokehouse
Gruber Rd. (Penn Township)
HABS PA-266-F
HABS PA,6-MTPLES.V,11F-
2ph L

Stamm,Eliza,House (Moorehead House)
Gruber Rd. (Penn Township)
HABS PA-113
HABS PA,6-MTPLES.V,2-
6dr/2ph/11pg/1pc L

Stamm,Isaac,House (Querean House)
Gruber Rd. (Penn Township)
HABS PA-112
HABS PA,6-MTPLES.V,1-
5dr/10ph/12pg/1pc L

Stoudt,George,House (Octagon House)
Eight Cornered House Rd. (Penn Twp.)
HABS PA-267
HABS PA,6-MTPLES.V,12-
4ph/12pg/1pc L

NEW BERLINVILLE

Barn
State Rt. 100 vic.
HABS PA-5259
HABS PA,6-NEBER,1A-
2ph/1pc L

OLEY

Barn
Oley Township
HABS PA-5261-A
HABS PA,6-OLEY,2A-
3ph/1pc L

DeTurck House
State Rt. 662 vic. ,Oley Twp.
HABS PA-1023
HABS PA,6-OLEY,1-
2dr/7ph/3pg/1pc/fr L

DeTurck House,Barn
State Rt. 662 vic. ,Oley Twp.
HABS PA-1023-A
HABS PA,6-OLEY,1A-
2ph/1pc L

Farmhouse,Stone
Oley Township
HABS PA-5261
HABS PA,6-OLEY,2-
1ph/1pc L

OLEY VIC.

Hoffman,Guy,Farm
HABS PA-5266
HABS PA,6-OLEY.V,2-
1ph/1pc L

Hoffman,Guy,Farm,Barn
HABS PA-5266-A
HABS PA,6-OLEY.V,2A-
2ph/1pc L

Hoffman,Guy,Farm,Original Farmhouse
HABS PA-5266-B
HABS PA,6-OLEY.V,2B-
1ph/1pc L

Hoffman,Guy,Farm,Shed
HABS PA-5266-C
HABS PA,6-OLEY.V,2C-
1ph/1pc L

Kaufman Barns
State Rt. 662 Vic. (Oley Township)
HABS PA-1059
HABS PA,6-OLEY.V,1B-
3ph/1pg L

Kaufman House
State Rt. 662 Vic. (Oley Township)
HABS PA-1042
HABS PA,6-OLEY.V,1-
6ph/3pg L

Kaufman House,Small
State Rt. 662 Vic. (Oley Township)
HABS PA-1046
HABS PA,6-OLEY.V,1A-
4ph/1pg L

PIKEVILLE

Barn,Decorated Red
(Pike Twp.)
HABS PA-5274
HABS PA,6-PIKVI,IA-
1ph/1pc L

PLEASANTVILLE VIC.

Barn
State Rt. 73, (Oley Twp.)
HABS PA-5281
HABS PA,6-PLEAS.V,1A-
3ph/1pc L

Barn,Decorated
State Rt. 73,(Oley Twp.)
HABS PA-5260
HABS PA,6-PLEAS.V,2A-
2ph/1pc L

Barn,Stone
HABS PA-5351
HABS PA,6-PLEAS.V,6A-
2ph L

Lee,A. & S. ,Barn (1797)
State Rt. 73 & Manutawny Creek
HABS PA-5277
HABS PA,6-PLEAS.V,3A-
2ph L

Maul Stone Barn (1791)
Oley Twp. ,Gen. Lesher's grave vic.
HABS PA-5280
HABS PA,6-PLEAS.V,4A-
2ph L

Stolzfus Stone Barn
State Rt. 73 vic. ,Oley Twp.
HABS PA-5279
HABS PA,6-PLEAS.V,5A-
1ph/1pc L

PRICETOWN

Barn,Decorated
(Ruscombmanor Twp.)
HABS PA-5269
HABS PA,6-PRICE,1A-
1ph/1pc L

READING

12 North Fifth Street (House)
HABS PA-5143
HABS PA,6-READ,8-
5ph/6pg/1pc L

16-20 North Fifth Street (House)
HABS PA-5144
HABS PA,6-READ,7-
5ph/7pg/1pc L

26 North Fifth Street (House)
HABS PA-5146
HABS PA,6-READ,5-
5ph/7pg/1pc L

Outer Station; see Philadelphia & Reading RR:Reading Depot

401 Penn Street (House)
HABS PA-5147
HABS PA,6-READ,4-
5ph/3pg/1pc L

Philadelphia & Reading RR:Pedestrian Suspension Br (Swinging Bridge)
Spanning Reading mainline at Reading Depot
HAER PA-120
3ph H

Philadelphia & Reading RR:Reading Depot (Reading Depot; Outer Station)
6th & Oley Sts.
HAER PA-121
5ph/1pg H

Philadelphia & Reading RR:Reading Depot Bridge (Reading Depot Bridge)
N. Sixth St. at Woodward St.
HAER PA-117
3ph H

Philadelphia & Reading RR:Skew Arch Bridge (Skew Arch Bridge)
N. Sixth St. at Woodward St.
HABS PA-1025
HAER PA-116
HABS/HAER PA,6-READ,1-
6ph/1pg L H

Philadelphia & Reading RR:Walnut Street Bridge (Walnut Street Bridge)
Spanning Reading mainline at Walnut St.
HAER PA-119
2ph H

Reading Depot; see Philadelphia & Reading RR:Reading Depot

Reading Depot Bridge; see Philadelphia & Reading RR:Reading Depot Bridge

Reading Friends Meeting
N. Sixth St.
HABS PA-1048
HABS PA,6-READ,2-
2ph/1pg L

Reading News Building (Sharp Building)
22-24 N. Fifth St.
HABS PA-5145
HABS PA,6-READ,6-
8ph/12pg/1pc L

Rennas Hotel,The (State Store Building)
403 Penn St.
HABS PA-5148
HABS PA,6-READ,3C-
4ph/3pg/1pc L

Sharp Building; see Reading News Building

Skew Arch Bridge; see Philadelphia & Reading RR:Skew Arch Bridge

State Store Building; see Rennas Hotel,The

Swinging Bridge; see Philadelphia & Reading RR:Pedestrian Suspension Br

Walnut Street Bridge; see Philadelphia & Reading RR:Walnut Street Bridge

READING VIC.

Barn
State Rt. 122 detour
HABS PA-5268
HABS PA,6-READ.V,1A-
1ph/1pc L

Peacock's Lock Viaduct; see Philadelphia & Reading RR:Peacock's Lock Viaduct

Philadelphia & Reading RR:Peacock's Lock Viaduct (Peacock's Lock Viaduct)
Reading RR spanning Schuylkill River
HAER PA-118
4ph H

ROBESONIA

Ege,George,Mansion
U. S. Rt. 422 Vic.
HABS PA-1026
HABS PA,6-ROBSO,1-
9ph/2pg L

SPANGSVILLE VIC.

Griesemer Mill
State Rt. 562 (Oley Township)
HABS PA-1019
HABS PA,6-YEL.V,1-
3ph/2pg L

Griesemer Mill Covered Bridge
State Rt. 662 Vic. (Oley Twp.)
HABS PA-1020
HABS PA,6-YEL.V,2-
2ph/1pg L

Hunter House
State Rt. 662 Vic. (Oley Twp.)
HABS PA-1034
HABS PA,6-YEL.V,6-
4ph/2pg L

Spang House
State Rt. 662 Vic. (Oley Twp.)
HABS PA-1033
HABS PA,6-YEL.V,5-
2ph/2pg L

STONERSVILLE

Blacksmith Shop,Log
HABS PA-148
HABS PA,6-STONV,1-
2ph L

STONERSVILLE VIC.

Exeter Friends Meetinghouse
State Rt. 662 (Exeter Twp.)
HABS PA-1021
HABS PA,6-STONV.V,1-
2dr/8ph/2pg L

Mill Tract Farm
Mill Rd. (Exeter Township)
HABS PA-1037
HABS PA,6-STONV.V,2-
9dr/14ph/2pg L

WOMELSDORF VIC.

Brown House
U. S. Rt. 422 Vic. (Marion Township)
HABS PA-1049
HABS PA,6-WOM.V,1-
4ph/2pg L

Charming Forge,Ironmaster's House
Tulpehocken Creek (Marion Township)
HABS PA-1022
HABS PA,6-WOM.V,1-
9ph/3pg L

Lime Kilns
State Rt. 419
HABS PA-142
HABS PA,6-WOM.V,2-
1ph L

YELLOW HOUSE

Yellow House Hotel
Rts. 662 & 562 (Amity Twp.)
HABS PA-1035
HABS PA,6-YEL,1-
2ph/2pg L

YELLOW HOUSE VIC.

Barn
State Rt. 100 vic.
HABS PA-5263
HABS PA,6-YEL.V,7A-
1ph/1pc L

De Benneville,Dr. George,House
State Rt. 662 Vic. (Oley Township)
HABS PA-1029
HABS PA,6-YEL.V,4-
2ph/2pg L

Fisher,Henry,House
State Rt. 622 (Oley Twp.)
HABS PA-1027
HABS PA,6-YEL.V,3-
17ph/2pg L

BLAIR COUNTY

ALTOONA

Agudah Achim Synagogue (Intown Neighborhood)
Seventeenth St. and Thirteenth St.
HABS PA-5938
HABS DLC/PP-1993:PA-3
4ph/1pc L

Alto Tower (Pennsylvania Railroad)
W. of 17th St. on N. side of the main line
HAER PA-229
HAER DLC/PP-1993:PA-2
8ph/2pg/1pc L

Altoona Area High School,Annex (Fourth Ward Neighborhood)
Sixth Ave. & Fourteenth St.
HABS PA-5851-A
HABS DLC/PP-1993:PA-3
1ph/2pg/1pc L

Altoona Car Shops (Pennsylvania Railroad,Altoona Works)
E. of Chestnut Ave.,S. of First St.
HAER PA-230
H

Altoona Car Shops,Cabinet,Tin & Machine Shop (Pennsylvania Railroad,Altoona Works)
201 Chestnut Ave.
HAER PA-230-C
HAER DLC/PP-1993:PA-2
1ph/2pg/1pc L

Altoona Car Shops,Fire Engine House No. 8 (Pennsylvania Railroad,Altoona Works)
201 Chestnut Ave.
HAER PA-230-A
HAER DLC/PP-1993:PA-2
1ph/2pg/1pc L

Altoona Car Shops,Foreman's Office & Stores (Pennsylvania Railroad,Altoona Works)
201 Chestnut Ave.
HAER PA-230-B
HAER DLC/PP-1993:PA-2
1ph/2pg/1pc L

Altoona City Hall (Intown Neighborhood)
Twelfth St. & Thirteenth Ave.
HABS PA-5520
HABS DLC/PP-1993:PA-3
3ph/6pg/1pc L

Altoona Gymnasium (Y.M.C.A.; First Ward Neighborhood)
Lexington Ave. & Ninth St.
HABS PA-5815
HABS DLC/PP-1993:PA-3
1ph/1pg/1pc L

Altoona Mirror Building (First Ward Neighborhood)
1000 Green Ave.
HABS PA-5814
HABS DLC/PP-1993:PA-3
1ph/1pg/1pc L

Altoona Trust Company Building (Intown Neighborhood)
1128-30 Twelfth Ave.
HABS PA-551
HABS DLC/PP-1993:PA-3
5ph/6pg/1pc L

Altoona,City of
HABS PA-5784
H

Baird,John M. & Minnie,House (Llyswen Neighborhood)
200 Coleridge Ave.
HABS PA-5876
HABS DLC/PP-1993:PA-2
2ph/1pg/1pc L

Baker Elementary School (Llyswen Neighborhood)
Ward Ave. at Coleridge Ave.
HABS PA-5908
HABS DLC/PP-1993:PA-3
1ph/1pg/1pc L

Ball,Frederick & Lisette,House (First Ward Neighborhood)
707 Lexington Ave.
HABS PA-5811
HABS DLC/PP-1993:PA-3
1ph/1pg/1pc L

Beahm's Garage; see Pielmeier,Peter,Blacksmith Shop

Beezer,Louis,House (Llyswen Neighborhood)
306 Logan Blvd.
HABS PA-5900
HABS DLC/PP-1993:PA-3
5ph/1pg/1pc L

Beezer,Michael J.,House (Llyswen Neighborhood)
308 Logan Blvd.
HABS PA-5901
HABS DLC/PP-1993:PA-3
2ph/3pg/1pc/fr L

Bell,Charles R. & Lettie L.,House (Fourth Ward Neighborhood)
200 Thirteenth St.
HABS PA-5862
HABS DLC/PP-1993:PA-2
1ph/2pg/1pc L

Belmar Hotel; see Green,Martin Asbury,House

Bentley,Alfred,House (Fourth Ward Neighborhood)
1509 Fourth Ave.
HABS PA-5845
HABS DLC/PP-1993:PA-2
2ph/2pg/1pc L

Black & Yon Building; see Silverman Building

Blumenthal,Solomon,House (First Ward Neighborhood)
1308 Ninth St.
HABS PA-5791
HABS DLC/PP-1993:PA-2
4ph/1pg/1pc L

Bott,Harry & Harriet,House (Llyswen Neighborhood)
100 Coleridge Ave.
HABS PA-5872
HABS DLC/PP-1993:PA-2
2ph/1pg/1pc L

Bowers,Edward H.,House (Llyswen Neighborhood)
302 Logan Blvd.
HABS PA-5899
HABS DLC/PP-1993:PA-2
1ph/1pg/1pc L

Brett Building (Intown Neighborhood)
1210-16 Eleventh Ave.
HABS PA-5507
HABS DLC/PP-1993:PA-3
3ph/8pg/1pc L

Brett,Jacob & Ida,House (Llyswen Neighborhood)
208 Logan Blvd.
HABS PA-5896
HABS DLC/PP-1993:PA-2
4ph/1pg/1pc L

109 Browning Avenue (House) (Llyswen Neighborhood)
HABS PA-5869
HABS DLC/PP-1993:PA-2
1ph/1pc L

Bush,John & Ellie,House (Fourth Ward Neighborhood)
1214 Third Ave.
HABS PA-5834
HABS DLC/PP-1993:PA-2
1ph/2pg/1pc L

Casanave Building (Intown Neighborhood)
1211-15 Eleventh St.
HABS PA-5519
HABS DLC/PP-1993:PA-3
2ph/6pg/1pc L

Cathedral of Christ the Good Shepherd; see Second Presbyterian Church

Cathedral of the Blessed Sacrament (Intown Neighborhood)
1301 Thirteenth Ave.
HABS PA-5516
HABS DLC/PP-1993:PA-5
10ph/5pg/1pc L

Caum,E. A.,Jr., & Marguerite,House (Llyswen Neighborhood)
104 Coleridge Ave.
HABS PA-5874
HABS DLC/PP-1993:PA-2
1ph/1pg/1pc L

Central Trust Company Building (Intown Neighborhood)
1218 Eleventh Ave.
HABS PA-5508
HABS DLC/PP-1993:PA-3
14ph/4pg/1pc L

Christ Reformed Church (First United Church of Christ; Intown Neighborhood)
1500-07 Twelfth Ave.
HABS PA-5514
HABS DLC/PP-1993:PA-3
3ph/5pg/1pc L

Corl's Store (Llyswen Neighborhood)
208 Coleridge Ave.
HABS PA-5880
HABS DLC/PP-1993:PA-2
1ph/1pg/1pc L

Davis,Isabel A.,House (First Ward Neighborhood)
704-06 Lexington Ave.
HABS PA-5798
HABS DLC/PP-1993:PA-2
1ph/2pg/1pc/fr L

Davis,Isabel A.,House II (First Ward Neighborhood)
700 Lexington Ave.
HABS PA-5806
HABS DLC/PP-1993:PA-3
1ph/1pg/1pc L

Dinkle,Charles F.,House (First Ward Neighborhood)
805 Lexington Ave.
HABS PA-5797
HABS DLC/PP-1993:PA-2
1ph/1pg/1pc L

Dudley,Charles B.,House (First Ward Neighborhood)
802 Lexington Ave.
HABS PA-5502
HABS DLC/PP-1993:PA-3
5dr/9ph/6pg/1pc/fr L

Eagles Building (Intown Neighborhood)
1106 Twelvth Ave.
HABS PA-5510
HABS DLC/PP-1993:PA-3
13pg L

East Altoona Freight Locomotive Terminal (Pennsylvania Railroad)
NE. of Furnace Rd. Bridge
HAER PA-228
H

East Altoona Freight Locomotive Termnl.,Roundhouse (Pennsylvania Railroad)
NE. of Furnace Rd. Bridge
HAER PA-228-A
HAER DCL/PP-1993:PA-2
4ph/2pg/1pc L

Eighth Avenue Methodist Episcopal Church (Faith United Methodist Church; Fourth Ward Neighborhood)
1227-31 Eighth Ave.
HABS PA-5855
HABS DLC/PP-1993:PA-2
2ph/1pg/1pc L

Eirhart,John & Ellen,House (Fourth Ward Neighborhood)
1220 Sixth Ave.
HABS PA-5849
HABS DLC/PP-1993:PA-2
1ph/1pg/1pc L

Engelman Outbuilding (LLyswen Neighborhood)
320 Morningside Dr.
HABS PA-5905
HABS DLC/PP-1993:PA-3
1ph/1pg/1pc L

Engelman,Emil A. & Geraldine,House (Llyswen Neighborhood)
318 Morningside Dr.
HABS PA-5904
HABS DLC/PP-1993:PA-3
2ph/1pg/1pc L

England,Sylvester & Margaret,House (Llyswen Neighborhood)
300 Coleridge Ave.
HABS PA-5884
HABS DLC/PP-1993:PA-2
4ph/1pg/1pc L

Faith United Methodist Church; see Eighth Avenue Methodist Episcopal Church

Fay,Robert H. & Patty,House (Llyswen Neighborhood)
109 Coleridge Ave.
HABS PA-5875
HABS DLC/PP-1993:PA-2
5ph/1pg/1pc L

Fearbeck,John & Annie,House (Fourth Ward Neighborhood)
1323 Eighth Ave.
HABS PA-5858
HABS DLC/PP-1993:PA-2
1ph/1pg/1pc L

Filer,John M. & Martha S.,House (Fourth Ward Neighborhood)
1508 First Ave.
HABS PA-5822
HABS DLC/PP-1993:PA-3
1ph/1pg/1pc L

Finney,Alfred F.,House (First Ward Neighborhood)
1011 Howard Ave.
HABS PA-5934
HABS DLC/PP-1993:PA-3
1ph/1pg/1pc L

First Evangelical Lutheran Chrurch (Intown Neighborhood)
1401-05 Twelfth Ave.
HABS PA-5513
HABS DLC/PP-1993:PA-3
9ph/5pg/1pc L

First Methodist Episcopal Church (Intown Neighborhood)
1208 Thirteenth St.
HABS PA-5521
HABS DLC/PP-1993:PA-3
11ph/4pg/1pc L

First National Bank (Mellon Bank Central; Intown Neighborhood)
1206 Eleventh Ave.
HABS PA-5506
HABS DLC/PP-1993:PA-3
12ph/6pg/1pc L

First United Church of Christ; see Christ Reformed Church

First Ward Neighborhood
HABS PA-5788
HABS DLC/PP-1993:PA-2
6ph/22pg/1pc L

First Ward Neighborhood; see Altoona Gymnasium

First Ward Neighborhood; see Altoona Mirror Building

First Ward Neighborhood; see Ball,Frederick & Lisette,House

First Ward Neighborhood; see Blumenthal,Solomon,House

First Ward Neighborhood; see Davis,Isabel A.,House

First Ward Neighborhood; see Davis,Isabel A.,House II

First Ward Neighborhood; see Dinkle,Charles F.,House

First Ward Neighborhood; see Dudley,Charles B.,House

First Ward Neighborhood; see Finney,Alfred F.,House

First Ward Neighborhood; see Hostler,W. S.,House

First Ward Neighborhood; see Kantner,William & Amanda,House

First Ward Neighborhood; see 1015 Lexington Ave. (House)

First Ward Neighborhood; see 1011-13 Lexington Avenue (House)

First Ward Neighborhood; see Little,David A.,House I

First Ward Neighborhood; see Little,David A.,House II

First Ward Neighborhood; see MacDonald,Albert P.,House

First Ward Neighborhood; see MacDonald,Alice,House

First Ward Neighborhood; see Matthews,Ann,House

First Ward Neighborhood; see Oburn,Harrison,House

First Ward Neighborhood; see Seeds,John S.,House I

First Ward Neighborhood; see Stouffer,Joseph,House I

First Ward Neighborhood; see Stouffer,Joseph,House II

First Ward Neighborhood; see Stouffer,Joseph,House III

First Ward Neighborhood; see Weston House

First Ward Neighborhood; see White,Joseph,House

First Ward Neighborhood; see Wilson,Mary,House

First Ward Neighborhood; see Wolf,Martha J.,House

Fleck,Howard & Effie,House (Llyswen Neighborhood)
312 Logan Blvd.
HABS PA-5902
HABS DLC/PP-1993:PA-3
1ph/1pg/1pc L

Fleig,Joseph & Barbara,House (Fourth Ward Neighborhood)
1329 Fourth Ave.
HABS PA-5842
HABS DLC/PP-1993:PA-2
2ph/1pg/1pc L

Fourth Ward; see St. Luke's Protestant Episcopal Mission,Rectory

Fourth Ward Neighborhood
HABS PA-5786
HABS DLC/PP-1993:PA-2
24ph/32pg/2pc L

Fourth Ward Neighborhood; see Altoona Area High School,Annex

Fourth Ward Neighborhood; see Bell,Charles R. & Lettie L.,House

Fourth Ward Neighborhood; see Bentley,Alfred,House

Fourth Ward Neighborhood; see Bush,John & Ellie,House

Fourth Ward Neighborhood; see Eighth Avenue Methodist Episcopal Church

Fourth Ward Neighborhood; see Eirhart,John & Ellen,House

Fourth Ward Neighborhood; see Fearbeck,John & Annie,House

Fourth Ward Neighborhood; see Filer,John M. & Martha S.,House

Fourth Ward Neighborhood; see Fleig,Joseph & Barbara,House

Fourth Ward Neighborhood; see Good,Jacob,House

Fourth Ward Neighborhood; see Goodwill Fire Engine & Hose Company Engine House

Fourth Ward Neighborhood; see Green,Martin Asbury,House

Fourth Ward Neighborhood; see Haller's Eagle Bakery

Fourth Ward Neighborhood; see Healy,Timothy & Mary C.,House

Fourth Ward Neighborhood; see Howarth,E.C.,House

Fourth Ward Neighborhood; see Huber,John,House

Fourth Ward Neighborhood; see Kerlin,Cloyd,House

Fourth Ward Neighborhood; see Kimmel,Lawrence,Jr.,& Caroline Long,House

Documentation: **ct** color transparencies **dr** measured drawings **fr** field records
pc photograph captions **pg** pages of text **ph** photographs

Fourth Ward Neighborhood; see Kimmel,Phillip,House

Fourth Ward Neighborhood; see Leix,Ludwig & Frances,House I

Fourth Ward Neighborhood; see Leix,Ludwig & Frances,House II

Fourth Ward Neighborhood; see Lyman,Thomas M. & Catherine,House

Fourth Ward Neighborhood; see Maennerchor Singing Society Hall

Fourth Ward Neighborhood; see Mason,Charles D.,House

Fourth Ward Neighborhood; see McCarthy,Samuel L. & Lettie,House

Fourth Ward Neighborhood; see Neher,Jacob & Pauline,House

Fourth Ward Neighborhood; see Nixon,Joseph & Sarah,House I

Fourth Ward Neighborhood; see Our Lady of Mount Carmel School

Fourth Ward Neighborhood; see Our Lady of Mt. Carmel Catholic Church

Fourth Ward Neighborhood; see Pielmeier,Peter,Blacksmith Shop

Fourth Ward Neighborhood; see Putz,Xavier (Frank X.),House

Fourth Ward Neighborhood; see Renner, Annie & George House

Fourth Ward Neighborhood; see Roosevelt,Theodore,Junior High School

Fourth Ward Neighborhood; see Scherdon,James & Mary,House

Fourth Ward Neighborhood; see Schmitt,Henry,Grocery Store

Fourth Ward Neighborhood; see Schraff,Theophilus,House

Fourth Ward Neighborhood; see Second Presbyterian Church

Fourth Ward Neighborhood; see St. James German Evangelical Lutheran Church

Fourth Ward Neighborhood; see St. Luke's Protestant Epis. Mission,Parish House

Fourth Ward Neighborhood; see St. Luke's Protestant Episcopal Mission,Church

Fourth Ward Neighborhood; see St. Mary's Roman Catholic Yard,Church

Fourth Ward Neighborhood; see St. Mary's Roman Catholic Yard,School

Fourth Ward Neighborhood; see 1105 Third Ave. (House)

Fourth Ward Neighborhood; see 1210 Third Ave. (House)

Fourth Ward Neighborhood; see 1224 Third Ave. (House)

Fourth Ward Neighborhood; see Union Brewery Stable

Fourth Ward Neighborhood; see Walton,Angus & Sarah L.,House

Fourth Ward Neighborhood; see Ward,Elizabeth & Blair,House

Fourth Ward Neighborhood; see Westley,John H.,House

Fourth Ward Neighborhood; see Wigton,Theodore & Mary,House

Fourth Ward Neighborhood; see Williams,Frank L. & Ella,House

Fourth Ward Neighborhood; see Wright,John & Emma,House

Fourth Ward Neighborhood; see Wright,John & Emma,House I

Fourth Ward Neighborhood; see Zierer,Bertha & Joseph,House

Gilden Barton Funeral Home; see McCarthy,Samuel L. & Lettie,House

Good,Jacob,House (Fourth Ward Neighborhood)
1225-1225 1/2-1227 Seventh Ave.
HABS PA-5853
HABS DLC/PP-1993:PA-2
1ph/2pg/1pc L

Goodwill Fire Engine & Hose Company Engine House (Fourth Ward Neighborhood)
1231 Sixth Ave.
HABS PA-5850
HABS DLC/PP-1993:PA-2
1ph/1pg/1pc L

Green,Martin Asbury,House (Belmar Hotel; Fourth Ward Neighborhood)
1501 Fourth Ave.
HABS PA-5844
HABS DLC/PP-1993:PA-2
2ph/2pg/1pc L

Haines,William & Della,House (Llyswen Neighborhood)
216 Coleridge Ave.
HABS PA-5885
HABS DLC/PP-1993:PA-2
1ph/1pg/1pc L

Haller's Eagle Bakery (Pacifico Bakery; Fourth Ward Neighborhood)
1206-10 Fifth Ave.
HABS PA-5846
HABS DLC/PP-1993:PA-2
1ph/3pg/1pc L

Healy,Timothy & Mary C.,House (Fourth Ward Neighborhood)
1415 Third Ave.
HABS PA-5839
HABS DLC/PP-1993:PA-2
2ph/1pg/1pc/fr L

Hebrew Reform Temple (Holy Trinity Greek Orthodox Church; Intown Neighborhood)
1433 Thirteenth Ave.
HABS PA-5517
4ph/5pg/1pc L

Henninger,W. Glenn & Doris,House (Llyswen Neighborhood)
317 Morningside Dr.
HABS PA-5903
HABS DLC/PP-1993:PA-3
2ph/1pg/1pc L

Hite,Christopher & Lana,House (Llyswen Neighborhood)
213-213A Coleridge Ave.
HABS PA-5882
HABS DLC/PP-1993:PA-2
1ph/1pg/1pc L

Holy Trinity Greek Orthodox Church; see Hebrew Reform Temple

Hoover,Joseph & Emma May,House (Llyswen Neighborhood)
203 1/2 W. Whittier Ave.
HABS PA-5910
HABS DLC/PP-1993:PA-3
1ph/1pg/1pc L

Hostler,W. S.,House (First Ward Neighborhood)
1303 Ninth St.
HABS PA-5807
HABS DLC/PP-1993:PA-3
1ph/1pg/1pc L

Howarth,E.C.,House (Fourth Ward Neighborhood)
1308 Third Ave.
HABS PA-5836
HABS DLC/PP-1993:PA-2
1ph/1pg/1pc L

Huber,John,House (Fourth Ward Neighborhood)
1424 Second Ave.
HABS PA-5828
HABS DLC/PP-1993:PA-2
3ph/1pg/1pc L

Intown Neighborhood
HABS PA-5789
HABS DLC/PP-1993:PA-2
2ph/9pg/1pc L

Intown Neighborhood; see Agudah Achim Synagogue

Intown Neighborhood; see Altoona City Hall

Intown Neighborhood; see Altoona Trust Company Building

Intown Neighborhood; see Brett Building

Intown Neighborhood; see Casanave Building

Intown Neighborhood; see Cathedral of the Blessed Sacrament

Intown Neighborhood; see Central Trust Company Building

Intown Neighborhood; see Christ Reformed Church

Intown Neighborhood; see Eagles Building

Intown Neighborhood; see First Evangelical Lutheran Chrurch

Intown Neighborhood; see First Methodist Episcopal Church

Intown Neighborhood; see First National Bank

Intown Neighborhood; see Hebrew Reform Temple

Intown Neighborhood; see Jaggard Building

Intown Neighborhood; see Lincoln Deposit & Trust Company

Intown Neighborhood; see Masonic Temple

Intown Neighborhood; see Mishler Theatre

Intown Neighborhood; see Penn Alto Hotel

Intown Neighborhood; see Rudisill,George,House

Intown Neighborhood; see Silverman Building

Intown Neighborhood; see U.S. Post Office

Jackson,John C. & Catherine,House (Llyswen Neighborhood)
215 Ruskin Dr.
HABS PA-5907
HABS DLC/PP-1993:PA-3
3ph/2pg/1pc/fr L

Jaggard Building (Klevan Building; Intown Neighborhood)
1300-02 Eleventh Ave.
HABS PA-5509
HABS DLC/PP-1993:PA-3
1ph/5pg/1pc L

Juniata Shops (Pennsylvania Railroad,Altoona Works)
E. side of Chestnut Ave.,S. of Sixth St.
HAER PA-232
HAER DLC/PP-1993:PA-2
5ph/1pg/1pc L

Juniata Shops,Blacksmith Shop No. 1 (Pennsylvania Railroad,Altoona Works)
E. of Fourth Ave. at Second St.
HAER PA-232-A
HAER DLC/PP-1993:PA-2
6ph/2pg/1pc L

Juniata Shops,Blacksmith Shop No. 2 (Pennsylvania Railroad,Altoona Works)
E. of Fourth Ave.,between First & Second Sts.
HAER PA-232-B
HAER DLC/PP-1993:PA-2
10ph/2pg/1pc L

Juniata Shops,Erecting Shop (Pennsylvania Railroad,Altoona Works)
E. of Fourth Ave. at Third St.
HAER PA-232-C
HAER DLC/PP-1993:PA-2
4ph/2pg/1pc L

Juniata Shops,Erecting Shop & Machine Shop (Pennsylvania Railroad,Altoona Works)
E. of Fourth Ave,between Fourth & Fifth Sts.
HAER PA-232-D
HAER DLC/PP-1993:PA-2
23ph/2pg/2pc L

Juniata Shops,Flue Shed (Pennsylvania Railroad,Altoona Works)
E. of Fourth Ave.,N. of First St.
HAER PA-232-E
HAER DLC/PP-1993:PA-2
1ph/2pg/1pc L

Juniata Shops,Machine Shop No. 1 (Pennsylvania Railroad,Altoona Works)
E. of Fourth Ave. at Thrid St.
HAER PA-232-F
HAER DLC/PP-1993:PA-2
9ph/2pg/1pc L

Juniata Shops,Machine Shop No. 2 (Pennsylvania Railroad,Altoona Works)
E. of Fourth Ave. at Third St.
HAER PA-232-G
HAER DLC/PP-1993:PA-2
1ph/2pg/1pc L

Juniata Shops,Paint Stores (Pennsylvania Railroad,Altoona Works)
E. of Fourth Ave.,S. of First St.
HAER PA-232-H
HAER DLC/PP-1993:PA-2
1ph/2pg/1pc L

Juniata Shops,Power Plant & Boiler House (Pennsylvania Railroad,Altoona Works)
E. of Fourth Ave. at Second St.
HAER PA-232-I
HAER DLC/PP-1993:PA-2
15ph/2pg/2pc L

Juniata Shops,Store House (Pennsylvania Railroad,Altoona Works)
E. of Fourth Ave. at Third St.
HAER PA-232-J
HAER DLC/PP-1993:PA-2
4ph/2pg/1pc L

Juniata Shops,Turntable (Pennsylvania Railroad,Altoona Works)
S. of Sixth St. at Third Ave.
HAER PA-232-K
HAER DLC/PP-1993:PA-2
10ph/1pg/2pc L

Kantner,William & Amanda,House (First Ward Neighborhood)
808 Lexington Ave.
HABS PA-5805
HABS DLC/PP-1993:PA-3
1ph/2pg/1pc/fr L

Kerlin,Cloyd,House (Fourth Ward Neighborhood)
1213 Fourth Ave.
HABS PA-5841
HABS DLC/PP-1993:PA-2
2ph/1pg/1pc L

Kimmel,Lawrence,Jr.,& Caroline Long,House (Fourth Ward Neighborhood)
1331 Second Ave.
HABS PA-5826
HABS DLC/PP-1993:PA-2
3ph/2pg/1pc L

Kimmel,Phillip,House (Fourth Ward Neighborhood)
104-6 Fourteenth St.
HABS PA-5863
HABS DLC/PP-1993:PA-2
1ph/2pg/1pc L

Kirk,Joseph L. & Catherine,House (Llyswen Neighborhood)
101 Halleck Pl.
HABS PA-5889
HABS DLC/PP-1993:PA-2
1ph/1pg/1pc L

Klevan Building; see Jaggard Building

Knickerbocker Rowhouse Complex
HABS PA-5785
HABS DLC/PP-1993:PA-2
11ph/1pc L

Krall,Franklin J. & Josephine,House (Llyswen Neighborhood)
201 Coleridge Ave.
HABS PA-5877
HABS DLC/PP-1993:PA-2
1ph/1pg/1pc L

Lamont,Joseph & Mary Ann,House (Llyswen Neighborhood)
208 Browning Ave.
HABS PA-5871
HABS DLC/PP-1993:PA-2
2ph/1pg/1pc L

Leix,Ludwig & Frances,House I (Fourth Ward Neighborhood)
1329 Third Ave.
HABS PA-5819
HABS DLC/PP-1993:PA-3
2ph/1pg/1pc L

Leix,Ludwig & Frances,House II (Fourth Ward Neighborhood)
210-12 Fourteenth St.
HABS PA-5865
HABS DLC/PP-1993:PA-5
1ph/1pg/1pc L

1015 Lexington Ave. (House) (First Ward Neighborhood)
HABS PA-5794
HABS DLC/PP-1993:PA-2
1ph/1pg/1pc L

1011-13 Lexington Avenue (House) (First Ward Neighborhood)
HABS PA-5792
HABS DLC/PP-1993:PA-3
1ph/1pc L

Lincoln Deposit & Trust Company (Intown Neighborhood)
1108-10 Twelfth Ave.
HABS PA-5937
HABS DLC/PP-1993:PA-3
3ph/1pc L

Little,David A.,House I (First Ward Neighborhood)
1301 Seventh St.
HABS PA-5809
HABS DLC/PP-1993:PA-5
1ph/1pg/1pc L

Little,David A.,House II (First Ward Neighborhood)
1303-05 Seventh St.
HABS PA-5813
HABS DLC/PP-1993:PA-3
1ph/1pg/1pc L

Llyswen Methodist Episcopal Church (Llyswen Neighborhood)
308 Coleridge Ave.
HABS PA-5887
1ph/1pg/1pc L

Llyswen Neighborhood
HABS PA-5787
HABS DLC/PP-1993:PA-3
29pg L

Llyswen Neighborhood; see Baird,John M. & Minnie,House

Llyswen Neighborhood; see Baker Elementary School

Llyswen Neighborhood; see Beezer,Louis,House

Llyswen Neighborhood; see Beezer,Michael J.,House

Llyswen Neighborhood; see Bott,Harry & Harriet,House

Llyswen Neighborhood; see Bowers,Edward H.,House

Llyswen Neighborhood; see Brett,Jacob & Ida,House

Llyswen Neighborhood; see 109 Browning Avenue (House)

Llyswen Neighborhood; see Caum,E. A.,Jr., & Marguerite,House

Llyswen Neighborhood; see Corl's Store

LLyswen Neighborhood; see Engelman Outbuilding

Llyswen Neighborhood; see Engelman,Emil A. & Geraldine,House

Llyswen Neighborhood; see England,Sylvester & Margaret,House

Llyswen Neighborhood; see Fay,Robert H. & Patty,House

Llyswen Neighborhood; see Fleck,Howard & Effie,House

Llyswen Neighborhood; see Haines,William & Della,House

Llyswen Neighborhood; see Henninger,W. Glenn & Doris,House

Llyswen Neighborhood; see Hite,Christopher & Lana,House

Llyswen Neighborhood; see Hoover,Joseph & Emma May,House

Llyswen Neighborhood; see Jackson,John C. & Catherine,House

Llyswen Neighborhood; see Kirk,Joseph L. & Catherine,House

Llyswen Neighborhood; see Krall,Franklin J. & Josephine,House

Llyswen Neighborhood; see Lamont,Joseph & Mary Ann,House

Llyswen Neighborhood; see Llyswen Methodist Episcopal Church

Llyswen Neighborhood; see Llyswen Station

Llyswen Neighborhood; see Long,Walter S. & Alice,House

Llyswen Neighborhood; see McLaughlin,Alexander & Mary,House

Llyswen Neighborhood; see Miller,Jacob & Mintie,House II

Llyswen Neighborhood; see Miller,Jacob E. & Mintie,House I

Llyswen Neighborhood; see Oaks,The

Llyswen Neighborhood; see Rudoplh,A.W. & Lavinia,House

Llyswen Neighborhood; see Seeds,John S.,House II

Llyswen Neighborhood; see Shank,Clair F. & Jean,House

Llyswen Neighborhood; see Skyles,James M. & Lizzie N,House

Llyswen Neighborhood; see Spence,James E. & Flora Neff,House

Llyswen Neighborhood; see Stewart,David G. & Margaret,House

Llyswen Neighborhood; see Stuckey,I. Bruce & Mary,House

Llyswen Neighborhood; see Talley,Maude Closson,House

Llyswen Neighborhood; see Ward Avenue Presbyterian Parsonage

Llyswen Neighborhood; see Ward Avenue United Presbyterian Church

Llyswen Neighborhood; see Warsing,Martin L.,House

Llyswen Neighborhood; see Weaver,Warren R.,House

Llyswen Neighborhood; see Weidner,Royal & Agnes Kane House

Llyswen Neighborhood; see Zimmerman,Frank L.,House

Llyswen Neighborhood; see Zimmerman's Store

Llyswen Station (Llyswen Neighborhood)
218 Logan Blvd.
HABS PA-5898
HABS DLC/PP-1993:PA-2
3ph/1pg/1pc L

Long,Walter S. & Alice,House (Llyswen Neighborhood)
308 Wordsworth Ave.
HABS PA-5913
HABS DLC/PP-1993:PA-3
1ph/1pg/1pc L

Lyman,Thomas M. & Catherine,House (Fourth Ward Neighborhood)
1300 Third Ave.
HABS PA-5835
HABS DLC/PP-1993:PA-2
1ph/2pg/1pc L

MacDonald,Albert P.,House (First Ward Neighborhood)
1307-09 Ninth St.
HABS PA-5802
HABS DLC/PP-1993:PA-3
2ph/1pg/1pc L

MacDonald,Alice,House (First Ward Neighborhood)
1305 Ninth St.
HABS PA-5810
HABS DLC/PP-1993:PA-3
1ph/1pg/1pc L

Maennerchor Singing Society Hall (Fourth Ward Neighborhood)
1313-15 Second Ave.
HABS PA-5825
HABS DLC/PP-1993:PA-2
1ph/2pg/1pc L

Mason,Charles D.,House (Fourth Ward Neighborhood)
1201 Fourth Ave.
HABS PA-5840
HABS DLC/PP-1993;PA-2
2ph/1pg/1pc L

Masonic Temple (Intown Neighborhood)
1111-19 Eleventh St.
HABS PA-5518
HABS DLC/PP-1993:PA-3
15dr/66ph/7pg/4pc/fr L

Matthews,Ann,House (First Ward Neighborhood)
1001-03 Lexington Ave.
HABS PA-5796
HABS DLC/PP-1993:PA-2
1ph/1pg/1pc L

McCarthy,Samuel L. & Lettie,House (Gilden Barton Funeral Home; Fourth Ward Neighborhood)
1329 Eighth Ave.
HABS PA-5859
HABS DLC/PP-1993:PA-2
2ph/2pg/1pc L

McLaughlin,Alexander & Mary,House (Llyswen Neighborhood)
210-12 Loga Blvd.
HABS PA-5897
HABS DLC/PP-1993:PA-2
1ph/1pg/1pc L

Mellon Bank Central; see First National Bank

Miller,Jacob & Mintie,House II
(Llyswen Neighborhood)
202 Coleridge Ave.
HABS PA-5878
HABS DLC/PP-1993:PA-2
2ph/1pg/1pc L

Miller,Jacob E. & Mintie,House I
(Llyswen Neighborhood)
107 Browning Ave.
HABS PA-5870
HABS DLC/PP-1993:PA-3
2ph/1pg/1pc L

Mishler Theatre (Intown Neighborhood)
1208 Twelfth Ave.
HABS PA-5512
HABS DLC/PP-1993:PA-3
2ph/6pg/1pc L

Neher,Jacob & Pauline,House (Fourth Ward Neighborhood)
1325 First Ave.
HABS PA-5821
HABS DLC/PP-1993:PA-3
1ph/1pg/1pc L

1117 Ninth Avenue (Commercial)
HABS PA-5960
HABS DLC/PP-1993:PA-3
1ph/1pg/1pc L

Nixon,Joseph & Sarah,House I (Fourth Ward Neighborhood)
1204 Sixth Ave.
HABS PA-5848
HABS DLC/PP-1993:PA-2
2ph/2pg/1pc L

Oaks,The (Llyswen Neighborhood)
112 Logan Blvd.
HABS PA-5894
HABS DLC/PP-1993:PA-2
6ph/1pg/1pc L

Oburn,Harrison,House (First Ward Neighborhood)
915-17 Lexington Ave.
HABS PA-5804
HABS DLC/PP-1993:PA-3
1ph/1pg/1pc L

Our Lady of Mount Carmel School
(Fourth Ward Neighborhood)
1012 8th Ave.
HABS PA-5936
HABS DLC/PP-1993:PA-3
1pg L

Our Lady of Mt. Carmel Catholic Church (Fourth Ward Neighborhood)
Eighth Ave. & Eleventh St.
HABS PA-5854
HABS DLC/PP-1993:PA-2
7ph/1pg/1pc L

Pacifico Bakery; see Haller's Eagle Bakery

Penn Alto Hotel (Intown Neighborhood)
1120-30 Thirteenth Ave.
HABS PA-5515
HABS DLC/PP-1993:PA-3
4ph/7pg/1pc L

Penn Central Building; see Silverman Building

Pennsylvania Railroad; see Alto Tower

Pennsylvania Railroad; see East Altoona Freight Locomotive Terminal

Pennsylvania Railroad; see East Altoona Freight Locomotive Termnl.,Roundhouse

Pennsylvania Railroad Company,House
1121-23 Eighth Ave.
HABS PA-5503
HABS DLC/PP-1993:PA-3
1ph/7pg/1pc/fr L

Pennsylvania Railroad,Altoona Works
Bounded by Sixth & 16th Sts.,Chestnut & Tenth Aves
HAER PA-108
HAER DLC/PP-1993:PA-2
11pg L

Pennsylvania Railroad,Altoona Works; see Altoona Car Shops

Pennsylvania Railroad,Altoona Works; see Altoona Car Shops,Cabinet,Tin & Machine Shop

Pennsylvania Railroad,Altoona Works; see Altoona Car Shops,Fire Engine House No. 8

Pennsylvania Railroad,Altoona Works; see Altoona Car Shops,Foreman's Office & Stores

Pennsylvania Railroad,Altoona Works; see Juniata Shops

Pennsylvania Railroad,Altoona Works; see Juniata Shops,Blacksmith Shop No. 1

Pennsylvania Railroad,Altoona Works; see Juniata Shops,Blacksmith Shop No. 2

Pennsylvania Railroad,Altoona Works; see Juniata Shops,Erecting Shop

Pennsylvania Railroad,Altoona Works; see Juniata Shops,Erecting Shop & Machine Shop

Pennsylvania Railroad,Altoona Works; see Juniata Shops,Flue Shed

Pennsylvania Railroad,Altoona Works; see Juniata Shops,Machine Shop No. 1

Pennsylvania Railroad,Altoona Works; see Juniata Shops,Machine Shop No. 2

Pennsylvania Railroad,Altoona Works; see Juniata Shops,Paint Stores

Pennsylvania Railroad,Altoona Works; see Juniata Shops,Power Plant & Boiler House

Pennsylvania Railroad,Altoona Works; see Juniata Shops,Store House

Pennsylvania Railroad,Altoona Works; see Juniata Shops,Turntable

Pennsylvania Railroad,Altoona Works; see Twelfth Street Car Shops

Pennsylvania Railroad,Altoona Works; see Twelfth Street Car Shops,Erecting Shop No. 3

Pennsylvania Railroad,Altoona Works; see Twelfth Street Car Shops,Fire Engine House No. 7

Pennsylvania Railroad,Altoona Works; see Twelfth Street Car Shops,Master Mechanic's Office

Pennsylvania RR:Pratt Arch Truss Bridge
1300 Ninth Ave. ,Railroaders' Memorial Museum
HAER PA-95
fr H

Pielmeier,Peter,Blacksmith Shop
(Beahm's Garage; Fourth Ward Neighborhood)
208 Sixteenth St.
HABS PA-5868
HABS DLC/PP-1993:PA-2
1ph/2pg/1pc L

Putz,Xavier (Frank X.),House (Fourth Ward Neighborhood)
208 Fourteenth St.
HABS PA-5864
HABS DLC/PP-1993:PA-2
1ph/1pg/1pc L

Renner, Annie & George House (Fourth Ward Neighborhood)
1222 Second Ave.
HABS PA-5823
HABS DLC/PP-1993:PA-2
1ph/2pg/1pc L

Roosevelt,Theodore,Junior High School (Fourth Ward Neighborhood)
Sixth Ave. & Fourteenth St.
HABS PA-5852
HABS DLC/PP-1993:PA-2
1ph/2pg/1pc L

Rudisill,George,House (Intown Neighborhood)
111 Twelfth Ave.
HABS PA-5790
HABS DLC/PP-1993:PA-2
1ph/1pc L

Rudoplh,A.W. & Lavinia,House
(Llyswen Neighborhood)
210 Holmes Ave.
HABS PA-5892
HABS DLC/PP-1993:PA-2
1ph/1pg/1pc L

Scherdon,James & Mary,House (Fourth Ward Neighborhood)
1426 Second Ave.
HABS PA-5829
HABS DLC/PP-1993:PA-2
1pg L

Schmitt,Henry,Grocery Store (Fourth Ward Neighborhood)
1224 Second Ave.
HABS PA-5824
HABS DLC/PP-1993:PA-2
1ph/2pg/1pc L

Schraff,Theophilus,House (Fourth Ward Neighborhood)
1327 Third Ave.
HABS PA-5837
HABS DLC/PP-1993:PA-2
1ph/1pg/1pc L

Second Presbyterian Church (Cathedral of Christ the Good Shepherd; Fourth Ward Neighborhood)
1315 Eighth Ave.
HABS PA-5857
HABS DLC/PP-1993:PA-2
9ph/2pg/1pc L

Seeds,John S.,House I (First Ward Neighborhood)
801 Lexington Ave.
HABS PA-5812
HABS DLC/PP-1993:PA-3
2ph/1pg/1pc L

Seeds,John S.,House II (Llyswen Neighborhood)
204 Coleridge Ave.
HABS PA-5879
HABS DLC/PP-1993:PA-2
2ph/1pg/1pc L

Shank,Clair F. & Jean,House (Llyswen Neighborhood)
300 Wordsworth Ave.
HABS PA-5912
HABS DLC/PP-1993:PA-3
1ph/1pg/1pc L

Silverman Building (Penn Central Building; Black & Yon Building; Intown Neighborhood)
1200-04 Eleventh Ave.
HABS PA-5504
HABS DLC/PP-1993:PA-3
3ph/5pg/1pc L

Skyles,James M. & Lizzie N,House (Llyswen Neighborhood)
108 Holmes Ave.
HABS PA-5891
HABS DLC/PP-1993:PA-2
2ph/1pg/1pc L

Spence,James E. & Flora Neff,House (Llyswen Neighborhood)
312 Coleridge Ave.
HABS PA-5888
HABS DLC/PP-1993:PA-2
1ph/1pg/1pc L

St. James German Evangelical Lutheran Church (Fourth Ward Neighborhood)
1401-05 Eighth Ave.
HABS PA-5860
HABS DLC/PP-1993:PA-2
4ph/2pg/1pc L

St. Luke's Protestant Epis. Mission,Parish House (Fourth Ward Neighborhood)
Eighth Ave. & Thirteenth St.
HABS PA-5856-B
HABS DLC/PP-1993:PA-3
1pg L

St. Luke's Protestant Episcopal Mission,Church (Fourth Ward Neighborhood)
Eighth Ave. & Thirteenth St.
HABS PA-5856-A
HABS DLC/PP-1993:PA-3
3ph/2pg/1pc L

St. Luke's Protestant Episcopal Mission,Rectory (Fourth Ward)
806 Thirteenth St.
HABS PA-5856-C
HABS DLC/PP-1993:PA-3
1pg L

St. Mary's Roman Catholic Yard,Church (Fourth Ward Neighborhood)
1401 Fifth Ave.
HABS PA-5847-A
HABS DLC/PP-1993:PA-3
4ph/2pg/1pc L

St. Mary's Roman Catholic Yard,School (Fourth Ward Neighborhood)
1400 Fourth Ave.
HABS PA-5847-B
HABS DLC/PP-1993:PA-2
1ph/1pc L

Stewart,David G. & Margaret,House (Llyswen Neighborhood)
209 Coleridge Ave.
HABS PA-5881
HABS DLC/PP-1993:PA-2
1ph/1pg/1pc L

Stouffer,Joseph,House I (First Ward Neighborhood)
803 Lexington Ave.
HABS PA-5795
HABS DLC/PP-1993:PA-2
1ph/1pg/1pc L

Stouffer,Joseph,House II (First Ward Neighborhood)
1301-03 Eighth St.
HABS PA-5800
HABS DLC/PP-1993:PA-3
1ph/1pg/1pc L

Stouffer,Joseph,House III (First Ward Neighborhood)
1305 Eighth St.
HABS PA-5803
HABS DLC/PP-1993:PA-3
1pg L

Stuckey,I. Bruce & Mary,House (Llyswen Neighborhood)
106 Hallech Pl.
HABS PA-5890
HABS DLC/PP-1993:PA-2
1ph/1pg/1pc L

Talley,Maude Closson,House (Llyswen Neighborhood)
206 Logan Blvd.
HABS PA-5895
HABS DLC/PP-1993:PA-2
1ph/1pg/1pc L

1105 Third Ave. (House) (Fourth Ward Neighborhood)
HABS PA-5816
HABS DLC/PP-1993:PA-3
1ph/1pc L

1210 Third Ave. (House) (Fourth Ward Neighborhood)
HABS PA-5818
HABS DLC/PP-1993:PA-3
1ph/1pc L

1224 Third Ave. (House) (Fourth Ward Neighborhood)
HABS PA-5817
HABS DLC/PP-1993:PA-3
1ph/1pc L

820 Twelfth Street (Commercial)
HABS PA-5959
HABS DLC/PP-1993:PA-3
2ph/1pg/1pc L

Twelfth Street Car Shops (Pennsylvania Railroad,Altoona Works)
S. of 11th St.,between 9th & 10th Aves.
HAER PA-231
H

Twelfth Street Car Shops,Erecting Shop No. 3 (Pennsylvania Railroad,Altoona Works)
Ninth Ave. at Twelfth St.
HAER PA-231-A
HAER DLC/PP-1993:PA-2
1ph/2pg/1pc L

Twelfth Street Car Shops,Fire Engine House No. 7 (Pennsylvania Railroad,Altoona Works)
1128 Ninth Ave.
HAER PA-231-B
HAER DLC/PP-1993:PA-2
2ph/2pg/1pc L

Twelfth Street Car Shops,Master Mechanic's Office (Pennsylvania Railroad,Altoona Works)
Ninth Ave. & Twelfth St.
HAER PA-231-C
HAER DLC/PP-1993:PA-2
5ph/2pg/1pc L

U.S. Post Office (Intown Neighborhood)
1201 Eleventh Ave.
HABS PA-5505
HABS DLC/PP-1993:PA-3
6ph/6pg/1pc L

Union Brewery Stable (Fourth Ward Neighborhood)
1425 1/2 Fourth Ave.
HABS PA-5843
HABS DLC/PP-1993:PA-2
1ph/2pg/1pc L

Walton,Angus & Sarah L.,House (Fourth Ward Neighborhood)
117 Fifteenth St.
HABS PA-5866
HABS DLC/PP-1993:PA-2
1ph/1pg/1pc L

Ward Avenue Presbyterian Parsonage (Llyswen Neighborhood)
101 Coleridge Ave.
HABS PA-5873
HABS DLC/PP-1993:PA-2
1ph/1pg/1pc L

Ward Avenue United Presbyterian Church (Llyswen Neighborhood)
NE Corner Ward & Coleridge Aves.
HABS PA-5909
HABS DLC/PP-1993:PA-3
1ph/1pg/1pc L

Ward,Elizabeth & Blair,House (Fourth Ward Neighborhood)
1537 Second Ave.
HABS PA-5832
HABS DLC/PP-1993:PA-2
1ph/2pg/1pc L

Warsing,Martin L.,House (Llyswen Neighborhood)
108 Wordsworth Ave.
HABS PA-5911
HABS DLC/PP-1993:PA-3
1ph/1pg/1pc L

Weaver,Warren R.,House (Llyswen Neighborhood)
106 Logan Blvd.
HABS PA-5893
HABS DLC/PP-1993:PA-2
2ph/1pg/1pc L

Weidner,Royal & Agnes Kane House (Llyswen Neighborhood)
211 Ruskin Dr.
HABS PA-5906
HABS DLC/PP-1993:PA-3
1ph/1pg/1pc L

Westley,John H.,House (Fourth Ward Neighborhood)
1200 Third Ave.
HABS PA-5833
HABS DLC/PP-1993:PA-2
2ph/2pg/1pc L

Weston House (First Ward Neighborhood)
1016-18 Howard Ave.
HABS PA-5793
HABS DLC/PP-1993:PA-3
2pg/fr L

White,Joseph,House (First Ward Neighborhood)
1401 Tenth St.
HABS PA-5801
HABS DLC/PP-1993:PA-3
2ph/1pg/1pc L

Wigton,Theodore & Mary,House (Fourth Ward Neighborhood)
211-13 Twelfth St.
HABS PA-5861
HABS DLC/PP-1993:PA-2
2ph/1pg/1pc L

Williams,Frank L. & Ella,House (Fourth Ward Neighborhood)
1515 Second Ave.
HABS PA-5831
HABS DLC/PP-1993:PA-2
1ph/2pg/1pc L

Wilson,Mary,House (First Ward Neighborhood)
708-10 Lexington Ave.
HABS PA-5799
HABS DLC/PP-1993:PA-2
1ph/1pg/1pc L

Wolf,Martha J.,House (First Ward Neighborhood)
1009 Chestnut St.
HABS PA-5808
HABS DLC/PP-1993:PA-3
2ph/1pg/1pc L

Wright,John & Emma,House (Fourth Ward Neighborhood)
1506 Second Ave.
HABS PA-5830
HABS DLC/PP-1993:PA-2
2ph/1pg/1pc L

Wright,John & Emma,House I (Fourth Ward Neighborhood)
205 Fifteenth St.
HABS PA-5867
HABS DLC/PP-1993:PA-2
1ph/2pg/1pc L

Y.M.C.A.; see Altoona Gymnasium

Zierer,Bertha & Joseph,House (Fourth Ward Neighborhood)
1404 Second Ave.
HABS PA-5827
HABS DLC/PP-1993:PA-2
1ph/1pg/1pc L

Zimmerman,Frank L.,House (Llyswen Neighborhood)
303 Coleridge Ave.
HABS PA-5885
HABS DLC/PP-1993:PA-2
1ph/1pg/1pc L

Zimmerman's Store (Llyswen Neighborhood)
305 Coleridge Ave.
HABS PA-5886
HABS DLC/PP-1993:PA-2
1ph/1pg/1pc L

CLAYSBURG

Claysburg High School
HABS PA-5980
1ph/1pc H

Claysburg,Town of (Refractories Company Towns)
HABS PA-5970
H

Fries,Jacob & Eliza,House (Standard Refractories Company Plant,Clubhouse)
HABS PA-5979
1ph/1pc H

Gazzara's Store
HABS PA-5981
1ph/1pc H

Refractories Company Towns; see Claysburg,Town of

Standard Refractories Company Plant,Clubhouse; see Fries,Jacob & Eliza,House

CRESSON VIC.

Allegheny Portage Railroad National Historic Site; see Skew Arch Bridge

Skew Arch Bridge (Allegheny Portage Railroad National Historic Site)
Crossing Incline No. 6 at old U.S. 22
HABS PA-1232
HAER PA-239
HABS/HAER PA,7-CRES.V,1-(DLC/PP-1992:PA-5);DLC/PP-1993:PA-2
5dr/6ph/2pg/2pc/fr L

SPROUL

General Refractories Company Plant; see Standard Refractories Company Plant

Refractories Company Towns; see Sproul,Town of

Sproul,Town of (Refractories Company Towns)
HABS PA-5971
H

Standard Refractories Co. Plant,House
14 Reed St.
HABS PA-5998
2ph/1pc H

Standard Refractories Co. Plant,Manager's House
4 Railroad St.
HABS PA-5982
1ph/1pc H

Standard Refractories Company Plant (General Refractories Company Plant)
HAER PA-282
3ph/1pc H

SPROUL VIC.

Sarah Furnace
Old U.S. 220
HAER PA-180
HAER DLC/PP-1993:PA-2
2pg L

Sarah Furnace,Grist Mill (Yingly Mill)
HAER PA-180-A
HAER DLC/PP-1993:PA-2
5ph/2pg/1pc L

Yingly Mill; see Sarah Furnace,Grist Mill

TYRONE VIC.

Birmingham Bridge
Spans L. Juniata Riv. at local rd. S. of PA 453
HAER PA-236
HAER DLC/PP-1993:PA-2
6ph/2pg/1pc L

WILLIAMSBURG

Isett,Jacob,House; see Mt. Etna Iron Works,Ironmaster's House

Mount Etna Iron Works,Church
E. of U.S. 20 on T.R. 463
HAER PA-224-K
HAER DLC/PP-1993:PA-5
1ph/1pg/1pc L

Mt. Etna Iron Works
East of U.S. 22 on T.R. 463
HAER PA-224
HAER DLC/PP-1993:PA-5
1dr/59ph/fr L

Mt. Etna Iron Works,Blacksmith Shop
East of U.S. 22 on T.R. 463
HAER PA-224-C
HAER DLC/PP-1993:PA-5
2ph/1pg/1pc L

Mt. Etna Iron Works,Boarding House
East of U.S. 22 on T.R. 463
HAER PA-224-I
HAER DLC/PP-1993:PA-5
1ph/1pg/1pc L

Mt. Etna Iron Works,Charcoal House
East of U.S. 22 on T.R. 463
HAER PA-224-B
HAER DLC/PP-1993:PA-5
3ph/1pg/1pc L

Mt. Etna Iron Works,Company Store-Residence
East of U.S. 22 on T.R. 463
HAER PA-224-E
HAER DLC/PP-1993:PA-5
2dr/1ph/1pg/1pc/fr L

Mt. Etna Iron Works,Etna Furnace
East of U.S. 22 on T.R. 463
HAER PA-224-A
HAER DLC/PP-1993:PA-5
5ph/1pg/1pc/fr L

Mt. Etna Iron Works,Forgeman's House No. 1
L.R. 07020 between junctions of T.R. 461 & 463
HAER PA-224-G
HAER DLC/PP-1993:PA-2;1993:PA-5
1dr/2ph/1pg/1pc/fr L

Mt. Etna Iron Works,Ironmaster's House (Isett,Jacob,House)
L.R. 07020 & T.R. 461
HAER PA-224-D
HAER DLC/PP-1993:PA-5
8dr/3ph/1pg/1pc/fr L

Mt. Etna Iron Works,Mule Barn
East of U.S. 22 on T.R. 463
HAER PA-224-J
HAER DLC/PP-1993:PA-5
8dr/3ph/1pg/1pc/fr L

Mt. Etna Iron Works,Residence
East of U.S. 22 on T.R. 463
HAER PA-224-F
HAER DLC/PP-1993:PA-5
1ph/1pg/1pc L

Mt. Etna Iron Works,Tenant House
East of U.S. 22 on T.R. 463
HAER PA-224-H
HAER DLC/PP-1993:PA-5
4dr/2ph/1pg/1pc/fr L

BRADFORD COUNTY

ATHENS TOWNSHIP

Franklin,Col. John,House
HABS PA-226
HABS PA,8- ,1-
5ph/9pg L

SAYRE

Lehigh Valley Railroad,Sayre Repair Shops
Lehigh Ave. (Northeast Side)
HAER PA-33
HAER PA,8-SAYRE,2-
9ph L

Lehigh Valley Railroad,Sayre Station
Lehigh Ave. (East Side)
HAER PA-32
HAER PA,8-SAYRE,1-
5ph/1pc L

TERRYTOWN

Log Cabin
HABS PA-227
HABS PA,8-TERTO,1-
15dr/7ph/5pg L

WYSOX

Presbyterian Church,Brick
State Rt. 187
HABS PA-222
HABS PA,8-WYSO,1-
17dr/8ph/5pg L

BUCKS COUNTY

ANDALUSIA

Andalusia (Biddle,Nicholas,Estate)
State Rd. Vic. ,(Bensalem Twp.)
HABS PA-1248
HABS PA,9-ANDA,1-
15dr/38ph/6pg/3pc/34ct/fr L

Andalusia,Billiard Room,The (house) (Biddle,Nicholas,Estate,Billiard Room,The (house))
State Rd. Vic. ,(Bensalem Twp.)
HABS PA-1248-C
HABS PA,9-ANDA,1C-
1dr/2ph/2pg/1pc/fr L

Andalusia,Cottage,The
(Biddle,Nicholas,Estate,Cottage,The)
State Rd. vic. ,(Bensalem Twp.)
HABS PA-1248-A
HABS PA,9-ANDA,1A-
2dr/4ph/2pg/1pc/fr L

Andalusia,Graperies,The
(Biddle,Nicholas,Estate,Graperies,The)
State Rd. vic. ,(Bensalem Twp.)
HABS PA-1248-D
HABS PA,9-ANDA,1D-
1dr/2pg/fr L

Andalusia,Grotto,The
State Rd. Vic. ,(Bensalem Twp.)
HABS PA-1248-B
HABS PA,9-ANDA,1B-
2dr/2ph/2pg/1pc/fr L

Biddle,Nicholas,Estate; see Andalusia

Biddle,Nicholas,Estate,Billiard Room,The (house); see Andalusia,Billiard Room,The (house)

Biddle,Nicholas,Estate,Cottage,The; see Andalusia,Cottage,The

Biddle,Nicholas,Estate,Graperies,The; see Andalusia,Graperies,The

AQUETONG VIC.

Barn,Stone
Aquetong Rd. ,(Solebury Twp.)
HABS PA-5298
HABS PA,9-AQUE.V,1A-
1ph/1pc L

BENSALEM

Bensalem African Methodist Episcopal Church (Little Jerusalem; Little Bethel)
1200 Bridgewater Rd.
HABS PA-1721
HABS PA,9-BRIDWA,2-
6ph/1pg/1pc/fr L

Little Bethel; see Bensalem African Methodist Episcopal Church

Little Jerusalem; see Bensalem African Methodist Episcopal Church

BRISTOL BOR.

Lenox-Keene House
710 Radcliffe St. ,(Bristol Twp.)
HABS PA-1234
HABS PA,9-BRIST,1-
10ph/1pg/1pc L

BUCKINGHAM

Farm Group
State Rt. 263,(Buckingham Twp.)
HABS PA-5295
HABS PA,9-BUCK,2-
1ph/1pc L

Fell Farm,House
Rt. 202 and Mechanicsville Rd.
HABS PA-5598
21ph/1pg/2pc H

CARVERSVILLE

Meadowrise Farm,House
5525 Carversville Rd.
HABS PA-5599
11ph/1pg/1pc H

CURLEY HILL VIC.

Barn
U. S. Rt. 611,(Plumstead Twp.)
HABS PA-5286
HABS PA,9-CURHI,1A-
1ph/1pc L

DOYLESTOWN

Bucks County Historical Society; see Mercer Museum

Harvey House
15 E. State St.
HABS PA-1006
HABS PA,9-DOYLT,2-
1ph/1pg L

Mercer Museum (Bucks County Historical Society)
Pine & Ashland Sts.
HABS PA-1007
HABS PA,9-DOYLT,3-
21ph/6pg L

DOYLESTOWN VIC.

Barn,Stone
State Rt. 113
HABS PA-5285
HABS PA,9-DOYLT.V,6A-
6ph L

Barn,Stone
Stone Rt. 212,(east of Doylestown)
HABS PA-5292
HABS PA,9-DOYLT.V,4A-
2ph/1pc L

Barn,Stone
U. S. Rt. 202
HABS PA-5284
HABS PA,9-DOYLT.V,1A-
2ph/1pc L

Barn,Stone
U. S. Rt. 202 vic.
HABS PA-5282
HABS PA,9-DOYLT.V,2A-
3ph/1pc L

Barn,Stone
U. S. Rt. 202,(west of Doylestown)
HABS PA-5191
HABS PA,9-DOYLT.V,3A-
2ph/1pc L

Fonthill (Mercer,Henry Chapman,House)
E. Court St. ,State Rt. 313 vic.
HABS PA-1140
HABS PA,9-DOYLT.V,7-
24ph/4pg/2pc/fr L

Fonthill,Farmhouse (Mercer,Henry Chapman,Farmhouse)
E. Court St. ,State Rt. 313 vic.
HABS PA-1140-B
HABS PA,9-DOYLT.V,7B-
1ph L

Fonthill,Garage (Mercer,Henry Chapman,Garage)
E. Court St. ,State Rt. 313 vic.
HABS PA-1140-A
HABS PA,9-DOYLT.V,7A-
2ph L

Mercer,Henry Chapman,Farmhouse; see Fonthill,Farmhouse

Mercer,Henry Chapman,Garage; see Fonthill,Garage

Mercer,Henry Chapman,House; see Fonthill

Mercer,Henry Chapman,Tile Works; see Moravian Pottery & Tile Works

Moore,William,Barn (1797)
Doylestown Twp. (2 mi. N. of Doylestown)
HABS PA-5297
HABS PA,9-DOYLT.V,5A-
3ph/1pc L

Moravian Pottery & Tile Works (Mercer,Henry Chapman,Tile Works)
State Rt. 313 (Swamp Rd.)
HABS PA-5381
HAER PA-107
HABS/HAER PA,9-DOYLT.V,8-
88ph/4pg/2pc L H

FALLSINGTON

Gambrel Roof House
3 S. Main St. ,(Falls Twp.)
HABS PA-5344
HABS PA,9-FALLSI,2-
4ph/1pc L

Gambrel Roof House, South Dependency
3 S. Main St., Falls Twp.
HABS PA-5344-A
HABS PA,9-FALLSI,2A-
2ph/1pc L

Gambrel Roof House, West Dependency
3 S. Main St., Falls Twp.
HABS PA-5344-B
HABS PA,9-FALLSI,2B-
1ph/1pc L

Moon-Williamson House
Yardley Rd. ,(Falls Twp.)
HABS PA-5343
HABS PA,9-FALLSI,1-
13ph/1pc/2ct L

HOLICONG

Bye Estate,Barn
HABS PA-5588-A
2ph/1pg H

Bye Estate,House (Byecroft; Old Congress)
Barcroft Ln.,south of Rt. 202
HABS PA-5588
16ph H

Byecroft; see Bye Estate,House

Old Congress; see Bye Estate,House

JOHNSVILLE

Craven Hall
SE corner of Street Rd. and Newtown Rd.
HABS PA-5600
14ph/1pc H

KINTNERSVILLE VIC.

Barn,Log
(Nockamixon Twp.)
HABS PA-5301
HABS PA,9-KINVI.V,2A-
3ph/1pc L

Hoffman Barn
State Rt. 611,(Nockamixon Twp.)
HABS PA-5300
HABS PA,9-KINVI.V,1A-
3ph/1pc L

MORRISVILLE

Barclay,Thomas,Barn; see Summerseat,Barn

Barclay,Thomas,House; see Summerseat

Barclay,Thomas,House,Outbuildings; see Summerseat, Outbuildings

Clymer,George,Barn; see Summerseat,Barn

Clymer,George,House; see Summerseat

Clymer,George,House,Outbuildings; see Summerseat, Outbuildings

Summerseat (Clymer,George,House; Barclay,Thomas,House)
Clymer St. & Morris Ave. ,Morrisville Bor.
HABS PA-5345
HABS PA,9-MORVI,1-
24ph/2pc/4ct L

Summerseat, Outbuildings (Clymer,George,House,Outbuildings; Barclay,Thomas,House,Outbuildings)
Clymer St. & Morris Ave., Morrisville Borough
HABS PA-5345-A
HABS PA,9-MORVI,1A-
3ph/1pc L

Summerseat,Barn (Clymer,George,Barn; Barclay,Thomas,Barn)
Clymer & Morris Ave. (Morrisville Borough)
HABS PA-5345-B
HABS PA,9-MORVI,1B-
1ph/1pc L

NESHAMINY VIC.

Barn A,Stone
State Rt. 132,(Warrington Twp.)
HABS PA-5294-A
HABS PA,9-NESH.V,1A-
2ph/1pc L

Barn B,Stone
State Rt. 132,(Warrington Twp.)
HABS PA-5294-B
HABS PA,9-NESH.V,1B-
2ph/1pc L

NEW BRITAIN VIC.

Barn,Stone
U. S. Rt. 202
HABS PA-5283
HABS PA,9-NEBRI.V,1A-
1ph/1pc L

NEWTON VIC.

Jenks' Hall
Ellis Rd. (Middletown Township)
HABS PA-1235
HABS PA,9-NETO.V,1-
1pg L

NEWTOWN

Temora Farm,House
372 Swamp Rd.
HABS PA-5601
13ph/1pg/1pc H

NEWTOWN VIC.

Barn,Stone (1810)
Newtown Twp.
HABS PA-5332
HABS PA,9-NETO.V,2A-
3ph/1pc L

OTTSVILLE VIC.

Barn,Stone (circa 1815)
State Rt. 611,(Tinicum Twp.)
HABS PA-5290
HABS PA,9-OTVI.V,1A-
2ph/1pc L

PERKASIE

High Farm,Barn
HABS PA-5591-C
8ph/1pc H

High Farm,Spring House (Underground)
HABS PA-5591-B
3ph/1pc H

Open Gate Farm,Barn
HABS PA-5589-A
7ph/1pc H

Open Gate Farm,House
Ridge Rd.,1 mi. east of Elephant Rd.
HABS PA-5589
19ph H

Standing Stone Farm,Barn
HABS PA-5590-A
4ph/1pc H

Standing Stone Farm,House
1950 Branch Rd.
HABS PA-5590
13ph H

PETER'S CORNER VIC.

Barn
Solebury Twp.
HABS PA-5291
HABS PA,9-PETCO.V,1-
1ph/1pc L

PIPERSVILLE

Cabin Run Covered Bridge
Schlentz Hill Rd. across Cabin Run
HAER PA-197
3ph/1pc H

High Farm,House
Creek Rd.,1 mi. W. of Easton Rd.
HABS PA-5591
31ph H

High Farm,Kitchen
HABS PA-5591-A
4ph/1pc H

Loux Covered Bridge
Carversville-Wismer Rd. across Cabin Run
HAER PA-198
3ph/1pc H

PIPERSVILLE VIC.

Krout,H.,Mill,House
Quarry Rd. at Creek Rd.
HABS PA-5597
14ph/1pg/1pc H

PLEASANT VALLEY VIC.

Finady,W. A. ,Barn (1829)
State Rt. 212
HABS PA-5287
HABS PA,9-PLEVA.V,1A-
2ph/1pc L

POINT PLEASANT

Dougal,Truss Bridge
Across Pennsylvania Canal,Cobbler's Way (LR 920)
HAER PA-196
10ph/1pc H

Swartz,Thomas,House
4902 River Rd.
HABS PA-5592
7ph/1pc H

POINT PLEASANT VIC.

Pennslyvania Canal:Delaware Division
Btwn Locks 13 & 14,S of Pt. Pleasant,Plumstead Twp
HAER PA-103
HAER PA,9-POPLE.V,1-
13pg L

QUAKERTOWN

Foulke,Burgess,House
26 N. Main St.
HABS PA-5594
16ph/1pc H

Liberty Hall
1235 W. Broad St.
HABS PA-5593
7ph/1pc H

RIEGELSVILLE

Delaware River Bridge
Spng Delaware River on Delaware Rd. betwn PA & NJ
HAER PA-31
HAER PA,9-RIEG,1-
5ph/1pc L

RUSHLAND

Foxheath,House
Swamp Rd.,2 mi. above Rushland
HABS PA-5595
14ph H

SOLEBURY VIC.

Paxson Barn
(Solebury Twp.)
HABS PA-5299
HABS PA,9-SOLBU.V,1A-
1ph/1pc L

SPRINGTOWN VIC.

Barn,Stone
State Rt. 212,(Springfield Twp.)
HABS PA-5289
HABS PA,9-SPRITO.V,1A-
2ph/1pc L

Barn,Stone (1790)
State Rt. 212,(Springfield Twp.)
HABS PA-5288
HABS PA,9-SPRITO.V,2A-
2ph/1pc L

STOOPVILLE VIC.

Barn,Stone
Stoopville Rd.
HABS PA-5334
HABS PA,9-STOVI.V,1A-
3ph L

UPPER MAKEFIELD

Minkel,Lester,Property; see VanHorn,William,House

VanHorn,William,House
(Minkel,Lester,Property)
Taylorsville Rd.
HABS PA-5596
17ph H

WASHINGTON CROS. VIC

Stone Barn; see
Thompson-Neeley-Pedcock Barn

Thompson-Neeley-Pedcock Barn (Stone Barn)
River Rd. (S.R. 32),Washington Crossing State Park
HABS PA-5293
HABS PA,9-WACRO.V,1A-
5ph/1pc L

WESTBORO VIC.

Barn (1813)
State Rt. 232
HABS PA-5296
HABS PA,9-WEBO.V,1A-
3ph L

WRIGHTSTOWN

Eight-Square School House; see Penns Park Octagonal School House

Penns Park Octagonal School House
(Wrightstown Octagonal School House; Eight-Square School House)
South corner St. Rd. 232 and Swamp Rd.
HABS PA-5603
4ph/1pg/1pc H

Smith,William,House
Corner Mud Rd. and Penn's Park Rd.
HABS PA-5602
7ph/1pg/1pc H

Wrightstown Octagonal School House; see Penns Park Octagonal School House

BUTLER COUNTY

HARMONY VIC.

Stauffer,David,Farm Buildings
HABS PA-414
HABS PA,10-HARM.V,1-
24dr/10ph/2pg L

CAMBRIA COUNTY

BEAVERDALE VIC.

Allendale Coal Proc. Plant.,Tipple,Separtr. & Col.
(Johnstown Coal & Coke Corporation)
S. of PA 869
HAER PA-181-A
HAER DLC/PP-1993:PA-2
2ph/1pg/1pc L

Allendale Coal Proc. Plant,Tipple & Conveyor (Johnstown Coal & Coke Corporation)
S. of PA 869
HAER PA-181-B
HAER DLC/PP-1993:PA-2
2ph/1pc L

Allendale Coal Processing Plant
(Johnstown Coal & Coke Corporation)
S. of PA 869
HAER PA-181
HAER DLC/PP-1993:PA-2
1ph/2pg/1pc L

Johnstown Coal & Coke Corporation; see Allendale Coal Proc. Plant.,Tipple,Separtr. & Col.

Johnstown Coal & Coke Corporation; see Allendale Coal Proc. Plant,Tipple & Conveyor

Johnstown Coal & Coke Corporation; see Allendale Coal Processing Plant

BLANDBURG

Bland,Fred,House
HABS PA-5984
2ph/1pc H

Blandburg,Town of (Refractories Company Towns)
HABS PA-5972
H

Harbison-Walker Refractories Co.,Community Bldg.
HABS PA-6003
1ph/1pc H

Harbison-Walker Refractories Co.,House
4 Boyd St.
HABS PA-6001
2ph/1pc H

Harbison-Walker Refractories Co.,House
5 Boyd St.
HABS PA-6002
1ph/1pc H

Harbison-Walker Refractories Co.,Office
Reade St.
HABS PA-5999
1ph/1pc H

Harbison-Walker Refractories Co.,Superint.'s House
HABS PA-6000
1ph/1pc H

Lloydsville Station Hotel
HABS PA-5986
1ph/1pc H

Reade Township School
HABS PA-5983
1ph/1pc H

Refractories Company Towns; see Blandburg,Town of

COLVER

Colver Mine; see Ebensburg Coal Co. Processing Plant & Powerhouse

Ebensburg Coal Co. Processing Plant & Powerhouse (Colver Mine)
Reese St. between Third & Fourth Sts.
HAER PA-237
HAER DCL/PP-1993:PA-2
1ph/2pg/1pc L

COLVER VIC.

Cambria & Indiana Railroad
HAER PA-238
HAER DCL/PP-1993:PA-2
2ph/2pg/1pc L

Cambria & Indiana Railroad,Blacksmith Shop
HAER PA-238-C
HAER DCL/PP-1993:PA-2
3ph/1pg/1pc

Cambria & Indiana Railroad,Car & Wheel Shops
HAER PA-238-D
HAER DCL/PP-1993:PA-2
3ph/1pg/1pc L

Cambria & Indiana Railroad,Engine House No. 1
HAER PA-238-A
HAER DCL/PP-1993:PA-2
2ph/2pg/1pc L

Cambria & Indiana Railroad,Engineer House No. 2
HAER PA-238-B
HAER DCL/PP-1993:PA-2
2ph/2pg/1pc L

CRESSON VIC.

Allegheny Portage RR National Historic Site; see Lemon,Samuel,House

Lemon,Samuel,House (Allegheny Portage RR National Historic Site)
Gallitzin Rd. (LR07068) ,U. S. Rt. 22 vic.
HABS PA-1236
HABS PA,11-CRES.V,1-;(DLC/PP-1992:PA-5)
12dr/1ph/1pc/fr L

GEISTOWN VIC.

Allegheny Portage Railroad National Historic Site; see Allegheny Portage Railroad,Staple Bend Tunnel

Allegheny Portage Railroad,Staple Bend Tunnel (Allegheny Portage Railroad National Historic Site)
Conemaugh Borough,E. of Cambria RR Bridge
HABS PA-1233
HAER PA-240
HABS/HAER PA,11-GETTO.V,1-;(DLC/PP-1992:PA-5); 1993:PA-2
2dr/4ph/4pg/2pc L

JOHNSTOWN

Allendorfer,John H.,House (Westmont Neighborhood)
834-36 Edgehill Dr.
HABS PA-5704
HABS DLC/PP-1993:PA-2
1pg L

Benshoff,Benjamin,House (Minersville Neighborhood)
144-46 Iron St.
HABS PA-5779
HABS DLC/PP-1993:PA-2
2pg L

Berkebile,Foster H. & Edna,House (Westmont Neighborhood)
534 Wayne St.
HABS PA-5728
HABS DLC/PP-1993:PA-2
1pg L

Blimmel,George,Building; see Fifth Avenue Hotel

100 Block Clinton Street (Downtown Neighborhood)
HABS PA-5673
HABS DLC/PP-1993:PA-2
1ph/1pg/1pc L

615 Brallier Alley (Cambria City Neighborhood)
HABS PA-5924
HABS DLC/PP-1993:PA-2
1ph/1pc L

Bratz,Paukratz,House (Cambria City Neighborhood)
207 Chestnut St.
HABS PA-5756
HABS DLC/PP-1993:PA-2
1pg L

Buchanan,Frank M. & Mary E.,House (Westmont Ave.)
434 Bucknell Ave.
HABS PA-5700
HABS DLC/PP-1993:PA-2
1pg L

Burkhard,William H. & Louise,House (Westmont Neighborhood)
603 Tioga St.
HABS PA-5696
HABS DLC/PP-1993:PA-2
1ph/2pg/1pc L

Burns,James P.,House (Minersville Neighborhood)
171-73 Iron St.
HABS PA-5932
HABS DLC/PP-1993:PA-2
2pg L

Butler,Elmer,House (Westmont Neighborhood)
152 Fayette St.
HABS PA-5708
HABS DLC/PP-1993:PA-2
1pg L

Cambria City & Minersville; see Fehse,William,House

Cambria City & Minersville Neighborhoods (Johnstown,City of)
HABS PA-5672
HABS DLC/PP-1993:PA-2
7ph/23pg/1pc L

Cambria City Neighborhood; see 615 Brallier Alley

Cambria City Neighborhood; see Bratz,Paukratz,House

Cambria City Neighborhood; see Cambria Fire Hook & Ladder Company Building

Cambria City Neighborhood; see Chestnut Street Public School

Cambria City Neighborhood; see Croatian Hall

Cambria City Neighborhood; see European Hotel

Cambria City Neighborhood; see Faith,Victor & Etella,House

Cambria City Neighborhood; see Faith,Victor,Building

Cambria City Neighborhood; see Fifth Avenue Hotel

Cambria City Neighborhood; see First Catholic Slovak Band Hall

Cambria City Neighborhood; see Germania Brewing Company Building

Cambria City Neighborhood; see Greiner,Albrecht & Josephine,House

Cambria City Neighborhood; see Holy Cross Evangelical Lutheran Church

Cambria City Neighborhood; see Hungarian Reformed Church

Cambria City Neighborhood; see Immaculate Conception Church of the Blessed Virgin

Cambria City Neighborhood; see Kelly,Joseph & Catherine,House

Cambria City Neighborhood; see Komara,Joseph,House I

Cambria City Neighborhood; see Komara,Joseph,House II

Cambria City Neighborhood; see Lorditch,George & Catherine,House

Cambria City Neighborhood; see Mannechor Singing Society Hall

Cambria City Neighborhood; see Pesch,Matilda,House

Cambria City Neighborhood; see Pollak,Samuel,Meat Market

Cambria City Neighborhood; see Roth,John Casper & Elizabeth,House

Cambria City Neighborhood; see St. Casimir's Roman Catholic Church,Church

Cambria City Neighborhood; see St. Casimir's Roman Catholic Church,Rectory I

Cambria City Neighborhood; see St. Casimir's Roman Catholic Church,Rectory II

Cambria City Neighborhood; see St. Casimir's School

Cambria City Neighborhood; see St. Casimir's Society Hall

Cambria City Neighborhood; see St. Columba's Roman Catholic Church,Church I

Cambria City Neighborhood; see St. Columba's Roman Catholic Church,Church II

Cambria City Neighborhood; see St. Columba's Roman Catholic Church,Convent

Cambria City Neighborhood; see St. Columba's Roman Catholic Church,Rectory

Cambria City Neighborhood; see St. Emerich's Roman Catholic Church

Cambria City Neighborhood; see St. Mary's Greek Byzantine Catholic Church,Church

Cambria City Neighborhood; see St. Mary's Greek Byzantine Catholic Church,Rectory

Cambria City Neighborhood; see St. Mary's Syrian Orthodox Church

Cambria City Neighborhood; see St. Rochus Croatian Catholic Church

Cambria City Neighborhood; see St. Stephen's Slovak Catholic Church

Cambria City Neighborhood; see Stenger,John & Anna Maria,House

Cambria City Neighborhood; see Third Avenue Hotel

Cambria City Neighborhood; see Wagner,George,House

Cambria City Neighborhood; see Wass,John & Eva,House

Cambria City United Church of Christ; see Hungarian Reformed Church

Cambria Fire Hook & Ladder Company Building (Cambria City Neighborhood)
624 Broad St.
HABS PA-5739
HABS DLC/PP-1993:PA-2
1ph/1pg/1pc L

Cambria Iron Co.,Blow. Eng. Hs. & Blst Furn. Comp.
E. Bank of Conemaugh River
HAER PA-109-F
7dr H

Cambria Iron Company
E. Bank of Conemaugh River
HAER PA-109
8dr H

Cambria Iron Company House; see 195-97 Iron St. (House)

Cambria Iron Company House; see 248-50 Iron Street (House)

Cambria Iron Company House I; see 203-05 Iron Street (House)

Cambria Iron Company House I; see 18 Wyoming Street (House)

Cambria Iron Company House II; see 114 Clarion Street (House)

Cambria Iron Company House II; see 227-9 Iron Street (House)

Cambria Iron Company House II; see 132 Wyoming Street (House)

Cambria Iron Company House III; see 272-74 Iron Street (House)

Cambria Iron Company House III; see 144 Wyoming Street (house)

Cambria Iron Company House III; see 216-18 Wyoming Street (House)

Cambria Iron Company House IV; see 42 Lehigh Street (House)

Cambria Iron Company House V; see 59 Lehigh Street (House)

Cambria Iron Company House VI; see 403 Luzerne Street (House)

Cambria Iron Company House VII; see 115 Montour Strret (House)

Cambria Iron Company House VIII; see 117-19 Wyoming Street (House)

Cambria Iron Company,Blacksmith Shop
E. BAnk of Conemaugh River
HAER PA-109-A
6dr H

Cambria Iron Company,Car Shop
E. Bank of Conemaugh River
HAER PA-109-D
3dr H

Cambria Iron Company,Foundry and Foundry Wing
E. Bank of Conemaugh River
HAER PA-109-E
10dr H

Cambria Iron Company,Pattern Shop
E. Bank of Conemaugh River
HAER PA-109-B
3dr H

Cambria Iron Company,Rolling Mill
E. Bank of Conemaugh River
HAER PA-109-C
2dr H

Cambria Steel Company House; see 800 Luzerne Street (House)

Cambria Steel Company House I; see 146 Colgate Avenue (House)

Cambria Steel Company House III; see 134 Tioga Street (House)

Cambria Steel Company House IV; see 238 Greene Street (House)

Cambria Steel Company House V; see 238 Tioga Street (House)

Cambria Steel Company House VII; see 140 Colgate Avenue (House)

Cambria Steel Company House VIII; see 244 Tioga Street (House)

Chestnut Street Public School (Cambria City Neighborhood)
500 Chestnut St.
HABS PA-5759
HABS DLC/PP-1993:PA-2
1pg L

114 Clarion Street (House) (Cambria Iron Company House II; Westmont Neighborhood)
HABS PA-5702
HABS DLC/PP-1993:PA-2
1pg L

Clinton Hotel
100 Clinton St.
HABS PA-5915
HABS DLC/PP-1993:PA-2
1pg L

102-04 Clinton Street (Saloon)
HABS PA-5916
HABS DLC/PP-1993:PA-2
1pg L

140 Colgate Avenue (House) (Cambria Steel Company House VII; Westmont Neighborhood)
HABS PA-5683
HABS DLC/PP-1993:PA-2
1ph/2pg/1pc L

146 Colgate Avenue (House) (Cambria Steel Company House I; Westmont Neighborhood)
HABS PA-5684
HABS DLC/PP-1993:PA-2
1ph/2pg/1pc L

Connelly,James,House (Minersville Neighborhood)
159 Iron St.
HABS PA-5775
HABS DLC/PP-1993:PA-2
1ph/1pg/1pc L

Cooper,Mary J.,House (Westmont Neighborhood)
204-06 Erie St.
HABS PA-5706
HABS DLC/PP-1993:PA-2
2pg L

Croatian Hall (Hrvatska Dvorana; Cambria City Neighborhood)
612 Broad St.
HABS PA-5753
HABS DLC/PP-1993:PA-2
1pg L

Dennison,Mary A.,House (Westmont Neighborhood)
245 Fayette St.
HABS PA-5694
HABS DLC/PP-1993:PA-2
1ph/1pg/1pc L

Dibert,David,Building (Downtown Neighborhood)
500 Main St.
HABS PA-5674
HABS DLC/PP-1993:PA-2
1ph/1pc L

Dom Polski; see St. Casimir's Society Hall

Downtown Neighborhood (Johnstown,City of)
HABS PA-5670
HABS DLC/PP-1993:PA-2
2ph/29pg/1pc L

Downtown Neighborhood; see 100 Block Clinton Street

Downtown Neighborhood; see Dibert,David,Building

Downtown Neighborhood; see Franklin Street Methodist Church

Downtown Neighborhood; see Glosser Brothers Department Store

Downtown Neighborhood; see Glosser Brothers Department Store,Annex

Downtown Neighborhood; see Harrigan-Sturver Building

Downtown Neighborhood; see Johnstown Tribune Building

Downtown Neighborhood; see St. John Gaulbert Roman Catholic Church

Endsley,Harry S.,House (Westmont Neighborhood)
144 Fayette St.
HABS PA-5732-A
HABS DLC/PP-1993:PA-2
1ph/1pg/1pc L

Endsley,Harry S.,Stable (Westmont Neighborhood)
144 Fayette St.
HABS PA-5732-B
HABS DLC/PP-1993:PA-2
1ph/1pc L

European Hotel (Cambria City Neighborhood)
313-15 Fourth Ave.
HABS PA-5767
HABS DLC/PP-1993:PA-2
1pg L

Faith,Victor & Etella,House (Cambria City Neighborhood)
122-24 Chestnut St.
HABS PA-5748
HABS DLC/PP-1993:PA-2
1ph/2pg/1pc L

Faith,Victor,Building (Cambria City Neighborhood)
322-24 Second Ave.
HABS PA-5749
HABS DLC/PP-1993:PA-2
1ph/1pg/1pc L

Fehse,William,House (Cambria City & Minersville)
521-23 Power St.
HABS PA-5768
HABS DLC/PP-1993:PA-2
2pg L

Fifth Avenue Hotel (Blimmel,George,Building; Cambria City Neighborhood)
502-04 Broad St.
HABS PA-5735
HABS DLC/PP-1993:PA-2
1ph/2pg/1pc L

First Catholic Slovak Band Hall (Cambria City Neighborhood)
716 Chestnut St.
HABS PA-5745
HABS DLC/PP-1993:PA-2
1ph/1pg/1pc L

Fisher,Rose,House (Westmont Neighborhood)
120 Erie St.
HABS PA-5705
HABS DLC/PP-1993:PA-2
1pg L

Franklin Street Methodist Church (Downtown Neighborhood)
131 Franklin St.
HABS PA-5677
HABS DLC/PP-1993:PA-2
1ph/1pc L

Fronheiser,Jacob & Marguerite Haymaker,House (Westmont Neighborhood)
201-05 Luzerne St.
HABS PA-5716
HABS DLC/PP-1993:PA-2
1pg L

Gardner,Jonathan,House (Westmont Neighborhood)
203-09 Greene St.
HABS PA-5689
HABS DLC/PP-1993:PA-2
1ph/1pg/1pc L

Germania Brewing Company Building (Cambria City Neighborhood)
200 Sixth Ave.
HABS PA-5770
HABS DLC/PP-1993:PA-2
1pg L

Glosser Brothers Department Store (Downtown Neighborhood)
435-49 Franklin St.
HABS PA-5783
HABS DLC/PP-1993:PA-2
1ph/1pc L

Glosser Brothers Department Store,Annex (Downtown Neighborhood)
435-49 Franklin St.
HABS PA-5783-A
HABS DLC/PP-1993:PA-2
1ph/1pc L

Grazier,Harvey F.,House (Westmont Neighborhood)
345 Luzerne St.
HABS PA-5718
HABS DLC/PP-1993:PA-2
1pg L

238 Greene Street (House) (Cambria Steel Company House IV; Westmont Neighborhood)
HABS PA-5685
HABS DLC/PP-1993:PA-2
2ph/1pg/1pc L

Greiner,Albrecht & Josephine,House (Cambria City Neighborhood)
902 Chestnut St.
HABS PA-5765
HABS DLC/PP-1993:PA-2
1pg L

Hamilton,James A.,House (Westmont Neighborhood)
200 Fayette St.,at Bucknell Ave.
HABS PA-5709
HABS DLC/PP-1993:PA-2
1pg L

Hamilton,Thomas E.,House (Westmont Neighborhood)
528 Edgehill Dr.
HABS PA-5703
HABS DLC/PP-1993:PA-2
1pg L

Hannan,Louise Fayon,House (Westmont Neighborhood)
300 Luzerne St.
HABS PA-5717
HABS DLC/PP-1993:PA-2
1pg L

Harrigan-Sturver Building (Downtown Neighborhood)
134 Iron St.
HABS PA-5782
HABS DLC/PP-1993:PA-2
1ph/2pg/1pc L

Hay,Harry M.,House (Westmont Neighborhood)
143 Greene St.
HABS PA-5686
HABS DLC/PP-1993:PA-2
2ph/1pg/1pc L

Holy Cross Evangelical Lutheran Church (Cambria City Neighborhood)
711 Chestnut St.
HABS PA-5761
HABS DLC/PP-1993:PA-2
2pg L

Hrvatska Dvorana; see Croatian Hall

Hungarian Reformed Church (Cambria City United Church of Christ; Cambria City Neighborhood)
822-24 Chestnut St.
HABS PA-5764
HABS DLC/PP-1993:PA-2
1pg L

Immaculate Conception Church of the Blessed Virgin (Cambria City Neighborhood)
308 Broad St.
HABS PA-5738
HABS DLC/PP-1993:PA-2
2ph/2pg/1pc L

195-97 Iron St. (House) (Cambria Iron Company House; Minersville Neighborhood)
HABS PA-5771
HABS DLC/PP-1993:PA-2
1ph/2pg/1pc L

203-05 Iron Street (House) (Cambria Iron Company House I; Minersville Neighborhood)
HABS PA-5772
HABS DLC/PP-1993:PA-2
1ph/2pg/1pc L

227-9 Iron Street (House) (Cambria Iron Company House II; Minersville Neighborhood)
HABS PA-5781
HABS DLC/PP-1993:PA-2
2pg L

248-50 Iron Street (House) (Cambria Iron Company House; Minersville Neighborhood)
HABS PA-5773
HABS DLC/PP-1993:PA-2
1ph/1pg/1pc L

272-74 Iron Street (House) (Cambria Iron Company House III; Minersville Neighborhood)
HABS PA-5774
HABS DLC/PP-1993:PA-2
1ph/1pg/1pc L

Johnson Company; see Johnson Steel Street Rail Company

Johnson Steel Street Rail Co.; see Johnstown and Stony Creek Railroad

Johnson Steel Street Rail Co.; see Johnstown and Stony Creek Railroad,Engine House

Johnson Steel Street Rail Co.,Drawg. Rm. & Laying (Johnson Steel Street Rail Co.,Engineering Bldg.)
525 Central Ave.
HAER PA-271-A
4ph/1pg/1pc H

Johnson Steel Street Rail Co.,Electl. Dept. & Boil
525 Central Ave.
HAER PA-271-B
3ph/1pg/1pc H

Johnson Steel Street Rail Co.,Engineering Bldg.; see Johnson Steel Street Rail Co.,Drawg. Rm. & Laying

Johnson Steel Street Rail Co.,General Office Bldg.
525 Central Ave.
HAER PA-271-C
2ph/1pg/1pc H

Johnson Steel Street Rail Co.,Iron Foundry
525 Central Ave.
HAER PA-271-D
H

Johnson Steel Street Rail Co.,Pattern Shop
525 Central Ave.
HAER PA-271-F
1ph/1pg/1pc H

Johnson Steel Street Rail Co.,Pattern Storage Bldg
525 Central Ave.
HAER PA-271-G
2ph/1pg/1pc H

Johnson Steel Street Rail Co.,Rolling Mill
525 Central Ave.,along Stony Creek River
HAER PA-271-I
2ph/1pc H

Johnson Steel Street Rail Co.,Steel Casting Molds
525 Central Ave.
HAER PA-271-E
3ph/1pg/1pc H

Johnson Steel Street Rail Co.,Switch Works; see Johnson Steel Street Rail Co.,Upper Shops

Johnson Steel Street Rail Co.,Upper Shops (Johnson Steel Street Rail Co.,Switch Works)
525 Central Ave.
HAER PA-271-H
1ph H

Johnson Steel Street Rail Company (U.S. Steel,Moxham Works; Johnstown Corporation; Johnson Company)
525 Central Ave.
HAER PA-271
1ph/1pc H

Johnstown and Stony Creek Railroad (Johnson Steel Street Rail Co.)
W. of Central Ave.,N. of Ohio St. along Stony Crk.
HAER PA-272
HAER DLC/PP-1993:PA-3
1pg L

Johnstown and Stony Creek Railroad,Conductor's Hse (Johnstown Steel St. Rail Co.)
W. of Central Ave.,N. of Ohio St. along Stony Crk.
HAER PA-272-B
HAER DLC/PP-1993:PA-3
1ph/1pc L

Johnstown and Stony Creek Railroad,Engine House (Johnson Steel Street Rail Co.)
W. of Central Ave.,N. of Ohio St. along Stony Crk.
HAER PA-272-A
HAER DLC/PP-1993:PA-3
1ph/1pc L

Johnstown City Hall
NE corner of Main & Market Sts.
HABS PA-5387
HABS DLC/PP-1993:PA-2
1ph/5pg/1pc L

Johnstown Corporation; see Johnson Steel Street Rail Company

Johnstown Inclined Plane
W. side of Stony Creek,S. of Little Conemaugh Riv.
HAER PA-234
HAER DLC/PP-1993:PA-2
2ph/2pg/1pc L

Johnstown Passenger Railway Co.,Baumer St. Powerho
Baumer St.,15 mile S. of PA 56.
HAER PA-258-C
HAER DLC/PP-1993:PA-3
1ph/2pg/1pc L

Johnstown Passenger Railway Co.,Car Barns
726 Central Ave.
HAER PA-258-A
HAER DLC/PP-1993:PA-3
3ph/2pg/1pc L

Johnstown Passenger Railway Co.,Conductor's Shed
Central Ave.
HAER PA-258-B
HAER DLC/PP-1993:PA-3
1ph/1pc L

Johnstown Passenger Railway Company
Central Ave.
HAER PA-258
HAER DLC/PP-1993:PA-3
1ph/1pc L

Johnstown Public Library
304 Washington St.
HABS PA-5386
HABS DLC/PP-1993:PA-2
2ph/8pg/1pc L

Johnstown Steel St. Rail Co.; see Johnstown and Stony Creek Railroad,Conductor's Hse

Johnstown Steel St. Rail Co.; see Moxham,Borough of

Johnstown Tribune Building (Downtown Neighborhood)
425 Locust St.
HABS PA-5675
HABS DLC/PP-1993:PA-2
1ph/1pc L

Johnstown,City of
HABS PA-5669
HABS DLC/PP-1993:PA-2
44pg L

Johnstown,City of; see Cambria City & Minersville Neighborhoods

Johnstown,City of; see Downtown Neighborhood

Johnstown,City of; see Westmont Neighborhood

Keedy,Thomas P.,House (Westmont Neighborhood)
202 Greene St.
HABS PA-5713
HABS DLC/PP-1993:PA-2
1pg L

Kelly,Joseph & Catherine,House (Cambria City Neighborhood)
816 1/2 Chestnut St.
HABS PA-5740
HABS DLC/PP-1993:PA-2
1ph/2pg/1pc L

Komara,Joseph,House I (Cambria City Neighborhood)
403-403 1/2 Chestnut St.
HABS PA-5750
HABS DLC/PP-1993:PA-2
1ph/2pg/1pc L

Komara,Joseph,House II (Cambria City Neighborhood)
403 Brallier Place (rear:403-403 1/2 Chestnut St.)
HABS PA-5754
HABS DLC/PP-1993:PA-2
1pg L

Krieger,William C.,House (Westmont Neighborhood)
444 Wayne St.
HABS PA-5727
1pg H

Krieger,William C.,House (Westmont Neighborhood)
444 Wayne St.
HABS PA-5922
HABS DLC/PP-1993:PA-2
1pg L

42 Lehigh Street (House) (Cambria Iron Company House IV; Westmont Neighborhood)
HABS PA-5679
HABS DLC/PP-1993:PA-2
1ph/2pg/1pc L

59 Lehigh Street (House) (Cambria Iron Company House V; Westmont Neighborhood)
HABS PA-5714
HABS DLC/PP-1993:PA-2
2pg L

Lenhart Building
106 Clinton St.
HABS PA-5917
HABS DLC/PP-1993:PA-2
1pg L

Lloyd,Evan A.,House I (Westmont Neighborhood)
926 Bucknell Ave.
HABS PA-5710
HABS DLC/PP-1993:PA-2
1pg L

Lloyd,Evan A.,House II (Westmont Neighborhood)
60 Clarion St.
HABS PA-5715
HABS DLC/PP-1993:PA-2
1pg L

Lorditch,George & Catherine,House (Cambria City Neighborhood)
202 Chestnut St.
HABS PA-5755
HABS DLC/PP-1993:PA-2
1pg L

Love,Russel C. & Lucy,House (Westmont Neighborhood)
535 Tioga St.
HABS PA-5733-A
HABS DLC/PP-1993:PA-2
1ph/4pg/1pc L

Love,Russel C. & Lucy,Stable (Westmont Neighborhood)
535 Tioga St.
HABS PA-5733-B
HABS DLC/PP-1993:PA-2
1ph/2pg/1pc L

403 Luzerne Street (House) (Cambria Iron Company House VI; Westmont Neighborhood)
HABS PA-5923
HABS DLC/PP-1993:PA-2
1pg L

800 Luzerne Street (House) (Cambria Steel Company House; Westmont Neighborhood)
HABS PA-5722
HABS DLC/PP-1993:PA-2
1pg L

Mannechor Singing Society Hall (Cambria City Neighborhood)
210 Chestnut St.
HABS PA-5757
HABS DLC/PP-1993:PA-2
1pg L

Mayer,L.H.,Building
414 Locust St.
HABS PA-5385
HABS DLC/PP-1993:PA-2
1ph/10pg/1pc L

McCreary House (Minersville Neighborhood)
169 Iron St.
HABS PA-5776
HABS DLC/PP-1993:PA-2
1ph/1pg/1pc L

Minersville Neighborhood; see Benshoff,Benjamin,House

Minersville Neighborhood; see Burns,James P.,House

Minersville Neighborhood; see Connelly,James,House

Minersville Neighborhood; see 195-97 Iron St. (House)

Minersville Neighborhood; see 203-05 Iron Street (House)

Minersville Neighborhood; see 227-9 Iron Street (House)

Minersville Neighborhood; see 248-50 Iron Street (House)

Minersville Neighborhood; see 272-74 Iron Street (House)

Minersville Neighborhood; see McCreary House

Minersville Neighborhood; see Polish National Alliance Building

Minersville Neighborhood; see Roach,Denis,House

115 Montour Strret (House) (Cambria Iron Company House VII; Westmont Neighborhood)
HABS PA-5724
HABS DLC/PP-1993:PA-2
1pg L

Morris,Fannie,House (Westmont Neighborhood)
105 Fayette St.
HABS PA-5707
HABS DLC/PP-1993:PA-2
1pg L

Morris,William H.,House (Westmont Neighborhood)
202 Mifflin St.
HABS PA-5723
HABS DLC/PP-1993:PA-2
1pg L

Moxham,Borough of (Johnstown Steel St. Rail Co.)
HAER PA-270
HAER DLC/PP-1993:PA-3
2ph/1pc L

Mulvehill,Peter,House (Westmont Neighborhood)
212 Mifflin St.
HABS PA-5688
HABS DLC/PP-1993:PA-2
1ph/1pg/1pc L

Oakley,William,House (Westmont Neighborhood)
27 Clarion St.
HABS PA-5691
HABS DLC/PP-1993:PA-2
1ph/1pg/1pc L

Our Mother of Sorrows Roman Catholic Church (Westmont Neighborhood)
424 Tioga St.
HABS PA-5727
HABS DLC/PP-1993:PA-2
2pg L

Owen,Moses & Mary,House (Westmont Neighborhood)
233 Greene St.
HABS PA-5690
HABS DLC/PP-1993:PA-2
1ph/1pg/1pc L

Palmer,George G. & Sarah,House (Westmont Neighborhood)
44-46 Bucknell Ave.
HABS PA-5699
HABS DLC/PP-1993:PA-2
1pg L

Penn Traffic Building
319 Washington St.
HABS PA-5388
HABS DLC/PP-1993:PA-2
2ph/9pg/1pc L

Pennsylvania Railroad Station
47 Walnut St.
HABS PA-5389
HABS DLC/PP-1993:PA-2
4ph/8pg/1pc L

Pesch,Matilda,House (Cambria City Neighborhood)
317 Second Ave.
HABS PA-5769
HABS DLC/PP-1993:PA-2
1pg L

Polish National Alliance Building (Minersville Neighborhood)
153 Benshoff St.
HABS PA-5777
HABS DLC/PP-1993:PA-2
1pg L

Pollak,Samuel,Meat Market (Cambria City Neighborhood)
314-16 Broad St.
HABS PA-5751
HABS DLC/PP-1993:PA-2
1pg L

Price,Charles S. & Sarah,House (Westmont Neighborhood)
510 Edgehill Dr.
HABS PA-5734-A
HABS DLC/PP-1993:PA-2
1ph/2pg/1pc L

Price,Charles S. & Sarah,Stable (Westmont Neighborhood)
510 Edgehill Dr.
HABS PA-5734-B
HABS DLC/PP-1993:PA-2
1ph/1pc L

Replogle,J. Leonard & Blanche McMillen,House (Westmont Neighborhood)
131 Fayette St.
HABS PA-5693
HABS DLC/PP-1993:PA-2
1ph/1pg/1pc L

Reynolds,Thomas E.,House (Westmont Neighborhood)
728 Bucknell Ave.
HABS PA-5701
HABS DLC/PP-1993:PA-2
1pg L

Roach,Denis,House (Minersville Neighborhood)
215-17 Honan Ave.
HABS PA-5778
HABS DLC/PP-1993:PA-2
1ph/1pg/1pc L

Rogers,Henry & Elfrieda,House (Westmont Neighborhood)
418 Luzerne St.
HABS PA-5719
HABS DLC/PP-1993:PA-2
1pg L

Roth,John Casper & Elizabeth,House (Cambria City Neighborhood)
601-601 1/2-603 Chestnut St.
HABS PA-5760
HABS DLC/PP-1993:PA-2
1ph/2pg/1pc L

Schondardt,John,House (Westmont Neighborhood)
600 Luzerne St.
HABS PA-5695
HABS DLC/PP-1993:PA-2
1ph/1pg/1pc L

St. Casimir's Roman Catholic Church,Church (Cambria City Neighborhood)
500 Power St.
HABS PA-5743-A
HABS DLC/PP-1993:PA-2
2ph/2pg/1pc L

St. Casimir's Roman Catholic Church,Rectory I (Cambria City Neighborhood)
511 Power St.
HABS PA-5743-B
HABS DLC/PP-1993:PA-2
1pg L

St. Casimir's Roman Catholic Church,Rectory II (Cambria City Neighborhood)
501 Power St.
HABS PA-5743-C
HABS DLC/PP-1993:PA-2
1pg L

St. Casimir's School (Cambria City Neighborhood)
400 Fifth Ave.
HABS PA-5766
HABS DLC/PP-1993:PA-2
1pg L

St. Casimir's Society Hall (Dom Polski; Cambria City Neighborhood)
306 Power St.
HABS PA-5737
HABS DLC/PP-1993:PA-2
1ph/1pg/1pc L

St. Columba's Roman Catholic Church,Church I (West End Catholic School; Cambria City Neighborhood)
917 Chestnut St.
HABS PA-5741-A
HABS DLC/PP-1993:PA-2
1pg L

St. Columba's Roman Catholic Church,Church II (Cambria City Neighborhood)
918 Broad St.
HABS PA-5741-B
HABS DLC/PP-1993:PA-2
1ph/2pg/1pc L

St. Columba's Roman Catholic Church,Convent (Cambria City Neighborhood)
915 Chestnut St.
HABS PA-5741-D
HABS DLC/PP-1993:PA-2
1pg L

St. Columba's Roman Catholic Church,Rectory (Cambria City Neighborhood)
916 Broad St.
HABS PA-5741-C
HABS DLC/PP-1993:PA-2
1pg L

St. Emerich's Roman Catholic Church (Cambria City Neighborhood)
600 Chestnut St.
HABS PA-5747
HABS DLC/PP-1993:PA-2
1ph/1pg/1pc L

St. George's Serbian Orthodox Church; see St. Mary's Syrian Orthodox Church

St. John Gaulbert Roman Catholic Church (Downtown Neighborhood)
117 Clinton St.
HABS PA-5676
HABS DLC/PP-1993:PA-2
1ph/1pc L

St. Mary's Greek Byzantine Catholic Church,Church (Cambria City Neighborhood)
401 Power St.
HABS PA-5742-A
HABS DLC/PP-1993:PA-2
8ph/2pg/1pc L

St. Mary's Greek Byzantine Catholic Church,Rectory (Cambria City Neighborhood)
413 Power St.
HABS PA-5742-B
HABS DLC/PP-1993:PA-2
1pg L

St. Mary's Syrian Orthodox Church (St. George's Serbian Orthodox Church; Cambria City Neighborhood)
300 Chestnut St.
HABS PA-5746
HABS DLC/PP-1993:PA-2
1ph/1pg/1pc L

St. Rochus Croatian Catholic Church (Cambria City Neighborhood)
800 Chestnut St.
HABS PA-5762
HABS DLC/PP-1993:PA-2
2pg L

St. Stephen's Slovak Catholic Church (Cambria City Neighborhood)
414 Fourth Ave.
HABS PA-5744
HABS DLC/PP-1993:PA-2
1ph/2pg/1pc L

Stenger,John & Anna Maria,House (Cambria City Neighborhood)
313-25 Chestnut St.
HABS PA-5758
HABS DLC/PP-1993:PA-2
1pg L

Stimmel,Elmer E.,House (Westmont Neighborhood)
434 Luzerne St.
HABS PA-5720
HABS DLC/PP-1993:PA-2
1pg L

Temple,Charles H. & Catherine,House (Westmont Neighborhood)
227 Fayette St.
HABS PA-5711
HABS DLC/PP-1993:PA-2
1pg L

Thackray,George E.,House (Westmont Neighborhood)
126 Fayette St.
HABS PA-5692
HABS DLC/PP-1993:PA-2
2ph/1pg/1pc L

Third Avenue Hotel (Weber,John,House; Cambria City Neighborhood)
222-24 Chestnut St.
HABS PA-5736
HABS DLC/PP-1993:PA-2
1ph/2pg/1pc L

134 Tioga Street (House) (Cambria Steel Company House III; Westmont Neighborhood)
HABS PA-5681
HABS DLC/PP-1993:PA-2
1ph/1pg/1pc L

238 Tioga Street (House) (Cambria Steel Company House V; Westmont Neighborhood)
HABS PA-5726
HABS DLC/PP-1993:PA-2
1pg L

244 Tioga Street (House) (Cambria Steel Company House VIII; Westmont Neighborhood)
HABS PA-5682
HABS DLC/PP-1993:PA-2
1ph/1pg/1pc L

Tioga Street Market (Westmont Neighborhood)
202 Tioga St.
HABS PA-5697
HABS DLC/PP-1993:PA-2
1ph/1pg/1pc L

Trent,Albert & Replogle,Jacob Z.,House (Westmont Neighborhood)
142-48 Tioga St.
HABS PA-5687
HABS DLC/PP-1993:PA-2
1ph/1pg/1pc L

U.S. Post Office
131 Market St.
HABS PA-5390
HABS DLC/PP-1993:PA-2
2ph/9pg/1pc L

U.S. Steel,Moxham Works; see Johnson Steel Street Rail Company

Varner,F. J.,House (Westmont Neighborhood)
120 Blair St.
HABS PA-5698
HABS DLC/PP-1993:PA-2
1pg L

Wagner,George,House (Cambria City Neighborhood)
418 Broad St.
HABS PA-5752
HABS DLC/PP-1993:PA-2
1pg L

Wass,John & Eva,House (Cambria City Neighborhood)
813 Chestnut St.
HABS PA-5763
HABS DLC/PP-1993:PA-2
1ph/2pg/1pc L

Wattingly,Minnie E.,House (Westmont Neighborhood)
233 Tioga St.
HABS PA-5725
HABS DLC/PP-1993:PA-2
1pg L

Weber,John,House; see Third Avenue Hotel

Wehn's Building
108 Clinton St.
HABS PA-5918
HABS DLC/PP-1993:PA-2
1pg L

West End Catholic School; see St. Columba's Roman Catholic Church,Church I

Westmont Ave.; see Buchanan,Frank M. & Mary E.,House

Westmont Neighborhood
(Johnstown,City of)
HABS PA-5671
HABS DLC/PP-1993:PA-2
1ph/33pg/1pc L

Westmont Neighborhood; see Allendorfer,John H.,House

Westmont Neighborhood; see Berkebile,Foster H. & Edna,House

Westmont Neighborhood; see Burkhard,William H. & Louise,House

Westmont Neighborhood; see Butler,Elmer,House

Westmont Neighborhood; see 114 Clarion Street (House)

Westmont Neighborhood; see 140 Colgate Avenue (House)

Westmont Neighborhood; see 146 Colgate Avenue (House)

Westmont Neighborhood; see Cooper,Mary J.,House

Westmont Neighborhood; see Dennison,Mary A.,House

Westmont Neighborhood; see Endsley,Harry S.,House

Westmont Neighborhood; see Endsley,Harry S.,Stable

Westmont Neighborhood; see Fisher,Rose,House

Westmont Neighborhood; see Fronheiser,Jacob & Marguerite Haymaker,House

Westmont Neighborhood; see Gardner,Jonathan,House

Westmont Neighborhood; see Grazier,Harvey F.,House

Westmont Neighborhood; see 238 Greene Street (House)

Westmont Neighborhood; see Hamilton,James A.,House

Westmont Neighborhood; see Hamilton,Thomas E.,House

Westmont Neighborhood; see Hannan,Louise Fayon,House

Westmont Neighborhood; see Hay,Harry M.,House

Westmont Neighborhood; see Keedy,Thomas P.,House

Westmont Neighborhood; see Krieger,William C.,House

Westmont Neighborhood; see 42 Lehigh Street (House)

Westmont Neighborhood; see 59 Lehigh Street (House)

Westmont Neighborhood; see Lloyd,Evan A.,House I

Westmont Neighborhood; see Lloyd,Evan A.,House II

Westmont Neighborhood; see Love,Russel C. & Lucy,House

Westmont Neighborhood; see Love,Russel C. & Lucy,Stable

Westmont Neighborhood; see 403 Luzerne Street (House)

Westmont Neighborhood; see 800 Luzerne Street (House)

Westmont Neighborhood; see 115 Montour Strret (House)

Westmont Neighborhood; see Morris,Fannie,House

Westmont Neighborhood; see Morris,William H.,House

Westmont Neighborhood; see Mulvehill,Peter,House

Westmont Neighborhood; see Oakley,William,House

Westmont Neighborhood; see Our Mother of Sorrows Roman Catholic Church

Westmont Neighborhood; see Owen,Moses & Mary,House

Westmont Neighborhood; see Palmer,George G. & Sarah,House

Westmont Neighborhood; see Price,Charles S. & Sarah,House

Westmont Neighborhood; see Price,Charles S. & Sarah,Stable

Westmont Neighborhood; see Replogle,J. Leonard & Blanche McMillen,House

Westmont Neighborhood; see Reynolds,Thomas E.,House

Westmont Neighborhood; see Rogers,Henry & Elfrieda,House

Westmont Neighborhood; see Schondardt,John,House

Westmont Neighborhood; see Stimmel,Elmer E.,House

Westmont Neighborhood; see Temple,Charles H. & Catherine,House

Westmont Neighborhood; see Thackray,George E.,House

Westmont Neighborhood; see 134 Tioga Street (House)

Westmont Neighborhood; see 238 Tioga Street (House)

Westmont Neighborhood; see 244 Tioga Street (House)

Westmont Neighborhood; see Tioga Street Market

Westmont Neighborhood; see Trent,Albert & Replogle,Jacob Z.,House

Westmont Neighborhood; see Varner,F. J.,House

Westmont Neighborhood; see Wattingly,Minnie E.,House

Westmont Neighborhood; see Westmont Presbyterian Church

Westmont Neighborhood; see 117-19 Wyoming Street (House)

Westmont Neighborhood; see 132 Wyoming Street (House)

Westmont Neighborhood; see 144 Wyoming Street (house)

Westmont Neighborhood; see 18 Wyoming Street (House)

Westmont Neighborhood; see 216-18 Wyoming Street (House)

Westmont Neighborhood; see Zimmerman,G. A. & Jennie A.,House

Westmont Presbyterian Church
(Westmont Neighborhood)
601 Luzerne St.
HABS PA-5721
HABS DLC/PP-1993:PA-2
2pg L

117-19 Wyoming Street (House)
(Cambria Iron Company House VIII; Westmont Neighborhood)
HABS PA-5729
HABS DLC/PP-1993:PA-2
1pg L

132 Wyoming Street (House) (Cambria Iron Company House II; Westmont Neighborhood)
HABS PA-5730
HABS DLC/PP-1993:PA-2
1pg L

144 Wyoming Street (house) (Cambria Iron Company House III; Westmont Neighborhood)
HABS PA-5731
HABS DLC/PP-1993:PA-2
2pg L

18 Wyoming Street (House) (Cambria Iron Company House I; Westmont Neighborhood)
HABS PA-5678
HABS DLC/PP-1993:PA-2
1ph/2pg/1pc L

216-18 Wyoming Street (House) (Cambria Iron Company House III; Westmont Neighborhood)
HABS PA-5680
HABS DLC/PP-1993:PA-2
1ph/1pg/1pc L

Zimmerman,G. A. & Jennie A.,House (Westmont Neighborhood)
131 Greene St.
HABS PA-5712
HABS DLC/PP-1993:PA-2
1pg L

JONHSTOWN

Cambria City Neighborhood; see Mayer,August G. & Louisa,Building

Mayer,August G. & Louisa,Building (Cambria City Neighborhood)
410 Eighth Ave.
HABS PA-5925
HABS DLC/PP-993:PA-2
1pg L

REVLOC VIC.

Revloc Mine
Between Cambria & Indiana spur and mainline
HAER PA-235
HAER DLC/PP-1993:PA-2
3ph/2pg/1pc L

Revloc Mine,Boiler & Hoist House
Between Cambria & Indiana spur and mainline
HAER PA-235-A
HAER DLC/PP-1993:PA-2
1ph/2pg/1pc L

Revloc Mine,Wash House
Between Cambria & Indiana Spur Mainline
HAER PA-235-B
HAER DLC/PP-1993:PA-2
1ph/1pg/1pc L

SCALP LEVEL

Berwind White Coal Mining Company; see Eureka No. 40,Wash House

Berwind-White Coal Mining Comapany; see Eureka No. 40,Fan House

Berwind-White Coal Mining Company; see Eureka No. 40

Berwind-White Coal Mining Company; see Eureka No. 40,Motor Barn

Berwind-White Coal Mining Company; see Eureka No. 40,Powerhouse

Berwind-White Coal Mining Company; see Eureka No. 40,Sand House & Tank

Berwind-White Coal Mining Company; see Eureka No. 40,Tipple & Cleaning Plant

Eureka No. 40 (Berwind-White Coal Mining Company)
East of PA 56,north of Little Paint Creek
HAER PA-184
HAER DCL/PP-1993:PA-2
3ph/98pg/1pc L

Eureka No. 40,Fan House (Berwind-White Coal Mining Comapany)
E. of PA 56,north of Little Paint Creek
HAER PA-184-A
HAER DCL/PP-1993:PA-2
3ph/2pg/1pc L

Eureka No. 40,Motor Barn (Berwind-White Coal Mining Company)
E. of PA 56,N. of Little Paint Creek
HAER PA-184-B
HAER DCL/PP-1993:PA-2
2ph/2pg/1pc L

Eureka No. 40,Powerhouse (Berwind-White Coal Mining Company)
W. side of PA 160
HAER PA-184-C
HAER DCL/PP-1993:PA-2
4ph/3pg/1pc L

Eureka No. 40,Sand House & Tank (Berwind-White Coal Mining Company)
E. of PA 56,N. of Little Paint Creek
HAER PA-184-D
HAER DLC/PP-1993:PA-2
2ph/1pc L

Eureka No. 40,Tipple & Cleaning Plant (Berwind-White Coal Mining Company)
E. of PA 56,north of Little Paint Creek
HAER PA-184-E
HAER DLC/PP-1993:PA-2
12ph/2pg/1pc L

Eureka No. 40,Wash House (Berwind White Coal Mining Company)
E. of PA 56,N. of Little Paint Creek
HAER PA-184-F
HAER DLC/PP-1993:PA-2
3ph/2pg/1pc L

SOUTH FORK

Fifficktown Bridge
Spanning Little Conemaugh River
HAER PA-233
HAER DLC/PP-1993:PA-2
8ph/2pg/1pc L

VINTONDALE VIC

Eliza Furnace
North side of PA 3045, .75 mile NW of PA 3047
HAER PA-257
HAER DLC/PP-1993:PA-3
6ph/3pg/1pc L

WILMORE VIC.

Berwind-White Coal Mining Company; see Maryland Shaft No. 2

Berwind-White Coal Mining Company; see Maryland Shaft No. 2,Blacksmith Shop

Berwind-White Coal Mining Company; see Maryland Shaft No. 2,Headframe

Maryland Shaft No. 2 (Berwind-White Coal Mining Company)
E. of PA 160
HAER PA-182
HAER DLC/PP-1993:PA-2
2pg L

Maryland Shaft No. 2,Blacksmith Shop (Berwind-White Coal Mining Company)
E. of PA 160
HAER PA-182-A
HAER DLC/PP-1993:PA-2
2ph/1pc L

Maryland Shaft No. 2,Headframe (Berwind-White Coal Mining Company)
E. of PA 160
HAER PA-182-B
HAER DLC/PP-1993:PA-2
6ph/1pc L

CARBON COUNTY

JIM THORPE

Central RR of New Jersey,Jim Thorpe Station (Jim Thorpe Station)
HAER PA-170
HAER PA,13-JIMTH,1-
1ph/1pc L

Courthouse Square
HABS PA-5473
HABS PA,13-JIMTH,2-
2ph/1pc L

Dimmick Memorial Library
HABS PA-5459
HABS PA,13-JIMTH,3-
1ph/1pc L

Jim Thorpe Station; see Central RR of New Jersey,Jim Thorpe Station

Lehigh Coal & Navigation Building
Susquehanna St. at Courthouse Square
HAER PA-169
HAER PA,13-JIMTH,4-
3ph/1pg/1pc L

Packer,Asa,Mansion
HABS PA-5330
HABS DLC/PP-1993:PA-3
15dr/fr L

St. Mark's Episcopal Church
Race St.
HABS PA-5457
HABS PA,13-JIMTH,6-
2ph/1pc L

Stone Row (Houses)
25-55 Race St.
HABS PA-5458
HABS PA,13-JIMTH,5-
2ph/1pg/1pc L

LEHIGHTON

Baer Silk Mill
Bridge & S. Seventh Sts.
HAER PA-167
HAER PA,13-LEHIT,1-
3ph/1pg/1pc L

LOWER TOWAMENSING

Lehigh Canal,Aquashicola Creek Aqueduct
Lehigh Canal at Aquashicola Creek
HAER PA-178
HAER PA,13-TOWLO,2-
1ph/1pg/1pc L

Lehigh Canal,Lock 20 (Lehigh Gap Lock)
S. of Aquashicola Creek
HAER PA-162
HAER PA,13-TOWLO,1A-
2ph/1pg/1pc L

Lehigh Gap Lock; see Lehigh Canal,Lock 20

PACKERTON

Lehigh Valley Railroad,Packerton Shops
Between Packerton Yards of LVRR & Lehigh River
HAER PA-168
HAER PA,13-PACKT,2-
1ph/1pg/1pc L

PALMERTON

Marshall Hill
HABS PA-5455
HABS PA,13-PALM,2-
3ph/1pg/1pc L

New Jersey Zinc Company,Palmerton Plant
Between Rt. 248 & Hazard Rd. at the Hazard Hamlet
HAER PA-163
HAER PA,13-PALM,1-
1ph/1pg/1pc L

PARRYVILLE

Carbon Iron Company Stables
Lehigh Gap Rd.
HABS PA-5456
HABS PA,13-PARVI,2-
1ph/1pg/1pc L

Parryville Mill (Souder's Supply Store)
Main & Maria Sts.
HAER PA-164
HAER PA,13-PARVI,1-
1ph/1pg/1pc L

Souder's Supply Store; see Parryville Mill

WEISSPORT

Rickert's Coal & Freight Company
Canal St. S. of Lock 8
HAER PA-166
HAER PA,13-WEISS,2-
1ph/1pg/1pc L

WEISSPORT VIC.

Lehigh Canal,Lock 10
S. of Weissport-Lehighton Bridge
HAER PA-165
HAER PA,13-WEISS.V,1A-
1ph/1pg/1pc L

Weider's Crossing,Stone House
HABS PA-5454
HABS PA,13-WEISS.V,2-
1ph/1pc L

CENTRE COUNTY

BELLEFONTE

Brockerhoff House
Bishop & Springs Sts.
HABS PA-333
HABS PA,14-BELF,3-
12dr/3ph/1pg/fr L

Harris,James,House (Willowbank)
S. Potter St.
HABS PA-331
HABS PA,14-BELF,2-
10dr/4ph/1pg/fr L

Linn,Henry S. ,House
N. Allegheny St.
HABS PA-8-5
HABS PA,14-BELF,1-
11dr/3ph/3pg/fr L

Willowbank; see Harris,James,House

BOALSBURG

Boalsburg Tavern
HABS PA-8-7
HABS PA,14-BOLBU,1-
8dr/7ph/2pg/fr L

CENTRE HALL VIC.

Fort Tavern
HABS PA-336
HABS PA,14-CENHA.V,1-
10dr/3ph/1pg L

CURTIN

Bathurst House (Ruins) (Curtin Village,Workers Houses)
Legislative Rt. 14010,(Boggs Twp.)
HABS PA-5356
HABS PA,14-CURT,1-
8ph/1pc/fr L

Curtin Village,Workers Houses; see Bathurst House (Ruins)

Curtin Village,Workers Houses; see Gingher House (Ruins)

Curtin Village,Workers Houses; see Schultz,Charles,House (Ruins)

Gingher House (Ruins) (Curtin Village,Workers Houses)
Legislative Rt. 14010
HABS PA-5355
HABS PA,14-CURT,2-
6ph/1pc/fr L

Schultz,Charles,House (Ruins) (Curtin Village,Workers Houses)
Legislative Rt. 14010
HABS PA-5357
HABS PA,14-CURT,3-
6ph/1pc/fr L

NITTANY

Schaeffer House
HABS PA-8-6
HABS PA,14-NIT,1-
6dr/5ph/2pg/fr L

PHILIPSBURG

Halehurst; see Philips,Hardman,House

Philips,Hardman,House (Halehurst)
E. Presqueisle St.
HABS PA-332
HABS PA,14-PHILBU,1-
10dr/2ph/1pg L

Union Church
E. Presqueisle St.
HABS PA-334
HABS PA,14-PHILBU,2-
7dr/3ph/1pg L

ROCK FORGE

Benner House
HABS PA-335
HABS PA,14-ROLFO,1-
9dr/3ph/fr L

CHESTER COUNTY

ANSELMA VIC.

Barn,Stone
State Rt. 41,(West Pikeland Twp.)
HABS PA-5244
HABS PA,15-ANS.V,1A-
2ph/1pc L

AVONDALE BOR.

Avondale; see Miller,William,House

Miller,William,Barn
Elliott Rd.
HABS PA-5137-A
HABS PA,15-AVON,1A-
1ph/1pc L

Miller,William,House (Avondale)
Elliott Rd.
HABS PA-5137
HABS PA,15-AVON,1-
16ph/9pg/1pc L

Miller,William,Tenant House
Elliot Rd.
HABS PA-5137-B
HABS PA,15-AVON,1B-
1ph/1pc L

BACTON

Hopper,Margaret,Log House; see Jacobs,John,House

House
(moved from Concordville)
HABS PA-174
HABS PA,23-CON,2-
14ph/2pc L

Jacobs,John,Barn
Conestoga Rd. (East Whiteland Township)
HABS PA-1209-A
HABS PA,15-BACT,1A-
1ph L

Jacobs,John,House
(Hopper,Margaret,Log House)
Conestoga Rd. (East Whiteland Township)
HABS PA-1209
HABS PA,15-BACT,1-
1ph/3pg/1pc L

BACTON VIC.

Barn
State Rt. 41
HABS PA-5243
HABS PA,15-BACT.V,2A-
1ph L

Gunkle,Michael,Spring,Mill
Moore Rd. (East Whiteland Township)
HABS PA-1113
HABS PA,15-BACT.V,1-
3ph/5pg/1pc/fr L

BERWYN VIC.

Bair,Mary A. ,House (Hunter-Bair House)
Conestoga Rd. & Cassatt Ave. (Tredyffrin Twp.)
HABS PA-117
HABS PA,15-BER.V,1-
20ph/1pg/2pc L

Hunter-Bair House; see Bair,Mary A. ,House

BIRMINGHAM

Birmingham Friends Meetinghouse
Birmingham & Meetinghouse Rds.
HABS PA-1193
HABS PA,15-BIRM,1-
5dr/5ph/6pg L

Birmingham Octagonal Schoolhouse
Birmingham & Meetinghouse Rds.
HABS PA-5138
HABS PA,15-BIRM,2-
1ph/1pc L

BIRMINGHAM VIC.

Darlington,Thomas,House (Spackman Corner Chimney House)
228 W. Street Rd. (Thornbury Township)
HABS PA-1110
HABS PA,15-BIRM.V,1-
1ph/4pg L

Sharpless House (Walker House)
Birmingham Rd. (Birmingham Township)
HABS PA-118
HABS PA,15-BIRM.V,2-
3ph/1pg/1pc L

Spackman Corner Chimney House; see Darlington,Thomas,House

Walker House; see Sharpless House

BULLTOWN

Bull,Thomas,House; see Mount Pleasant

Mount Pleasant (Bull,Thomas,House; Roberts' Plantation)
Bulltown Rd. (East Nantmeal Twp.)
HABS PA-248
HABS PA,15-BULT,1-
4ph/1pc L

Roberts' Plantation; see Mount Pleasant

CHADDS FORD VIC.

Barnes-Brinton House
U. S. Rt. 1 (Pennsbury Township)
HABS PA-173
HABS PA,15-CHAFO.V,1-
18ph/5pg/2pc L

Harvey,William,House
Brinton Bridge Rd. (Pennsbury Twp.)
HABS PA-1204
HABS PA,15-CHAFO.V,2-
4ph/6pg L

CHARLESTOWN

Charlestown Village Historic District; see Harvey,Job,House

Charlestown Village House; see Harvey,Job,House

Harvey,Job,House (Charlestown Village House; Charlestown Village Historic District)
Church Rd. (Charlestown Township)
HABS PA-1196
HABS PA,15-CHAST,1-
4ph/3pg/1pc L

CHARLESTOWN VIC.

Barn
State Rt. 29,(Charlestown Twp.)
HABS PA-5242
HABS PA,15-CHAST.V,1A-
5ph/1pc L

CHATHAM

Center Chimney House; see Half-Way House Tavern,New

Half-Way House Tavern,New (Center Chimney House)
State Rts. 41 & 841 (London Grove Twp.)
HABS PA-119
HABS PA,15-CHATH,1-
2ph/5pg/1pc L

CHATHAM VIC.

Morriseianna
State Rt. 41 (London Grove Twp.)
HABS PA-146
HABS PA,15-CHATM.V,1-
8ph/1pg/1pc L

Pusey House
Woodview Rd. (London Grove Twp.)
HABS PA-158
HABS PA,15-CHATM.V,2-
10ph/7pg/1pc/fr L

CHESTER SPRINGS

Chester Springs Hotel; see Yellow Springs Tavern

Good News Building; see Yellow Springs Tavern

Yellow Springs Bathhouse
Yellow Springs & Art School Rds.
HABS PA-1197
HABS PA,15-CHESP.1-
2ph/3pg/1pc L

Yellow Springs Summerhouse
Yellow Springs & Art School Rds.
HABS PA-1198
HABS PA,15-CHESP,2-
1ph/2pg/1pc L

Yellow Springs Tavern (Chester Springs Hotel; Good News Building)
Yellow Springs & Art School Rds.
HABS PA-1131
HABS PA,15-CHESP,3-
3ph/26pg/1pc L

CHESTER SPRINGS VIC.

Up-and-Down Sawmill
(moved to Smithsonian Inst. ,Wash. ,D. C.)
HABS PA-116
HABS PA,15-CHESP.V,1-
6ph/1pg/1pc L

CHROME

Chrome Hotel; see Cross Keys Tavern

Cross Keys Tavern (Chrome Hotel)
State Rts. 272 & 42 Vic. (East Nottingham Twp.)
HABS PA-1200
HABS PA,15-CHROM,1-
11ph/10pg/2pc L

CLONMELL VIC.

Pennock,Joseph House; see Primitive Hall

Primitive Hall (Pennock,Joseph House)
State Rt. 841 (W. Marlborough Twp.)
HABS PA-167
HABS PA,15-CLON.V,1-
13ph/1pg/2pc L

COATESVILLE

Thompson Building
163-167 E. Main St. (Lincoln Hwy.)
HABS PA-1955
HABS PA,15-COAT,1-
8ph/18pg/1pc L

COATESVILLE VIC.

Barn
State Rt. 82
HABS PA-5231
HABS PA,15-COAT.V,3A-
1ph/1pc L

Barn,Stone
U. S. Rt. 30
HABS PA-5230
HABS PA,15-COAT.V,2A-
3ph/1pc L

Stoltzfus House
U. S. Rt. 30 Vic. (Valley Township)
HABS PA-159
HABS PA,15-COAT.V,1-
5ph/1pg/1pc L

COPESVILLE

Brandywine Bridge; see Cope's Bridge

Cope's Bridge (Brandywine Bridge)
State Rt. 162 (East Bradford Twp.)
HABS PA-206
HABS PA,15-COPES,1-
3ph/5pg L

COPESVILLE VIC.

Taylor-Parke House
St. Rt. 162 (East Bradford Twp.)
HABS PA-205
HABS PA,15-COPES.V,1-
10ph L

Taylor,Abiah,House
Brandywine Creek Rd. (East Bradford Twp.)
HABS PA-204
HABS PA,15-COPES.V,2-
5ph/5pg L

COVENTRYVILLE

Coventry Forge Inn
(Nutt,Samuel,House)
Nantmeal Rd. (South Coventry Township)
HABS PA-1133
HABS PA,15-COV,1-
5ph/6pg L

Nutt,Samuel,House; see Coventry Forge Inn

DEVAULT VIC.

Bones,William & Rebecca,House
White Horse Rd. Vic. (Charlestown Township)
HABS PA-1189
HABS PA,15-DEV.V,2-
4ph/6pg L

Bones,William & Rebecca,Springhouse
White Horse Rd. Vic. (Charlestown Township)
HABS PA-1189-A
HABS PA,15-DEV.V,2A-
1ph L

Church of St. Peter-in-the-Great Valley (St. Peter's Protestant Episcopal Church)
Saint Peter's Rd. (East Whiteland Township)
HABS PA-1106
HABS PA,15-DEV.V,3-
4ph/6pg L

St. Peter's Protestant Episcopal Church; see Church of St. Peter-in-the-Great Valley

William Barn
Mine Rd. (Charlestown Township)
HABS PA-1216
HABS PA,15-DEV.V,1-
2ph/3pg L

DOWINGTOWN BOR.

Hunt-Pollock Mill
Race St.
HABS PA-170
HABS PA,15-DOWT,3-
2ph/5pg L

DOWNINGTOWN BOR.

Downingtown Public Library; see Todd,William A. ,House

Todd,William A. ,House (Downingtown Public Library)
330 E. Lancaster Ave.
HABS PA-169
HABS PA,15-DOWT.2-
6ph L

DOWNINGTOWN VIC.

Ashbridge House; see Baldwin-Sharpless House

Baldwin-Sharpless House (Ashbridge House)
U. S. Rt. 30 (East Caln Township)
HABS PA-1309
HABS PA,15-DOWT.V,8-
13ph/6pg L

Belle School
(East Caln Township)
HABS PA-168
HABS PA,15-DOWT.V,3-
1ph L

Downing House
Bell Tavern Rd. (East Caln Township)
HABS PA-171
HABS PA,15-DOWT.V,9-
7ph/1pg L

Hoopes Currying Shop
U. S. Rt. 322 (Caln Township)
HABS PA-1222
HABS PA,15-DOWT.V,4-
2ph/3pg L

Mendenhall-Valentine-Edge House
State Rt. 40 (Caln Twp.)
HABS PA-1201
HABS PA,15-DOWT.V,5-
2ph/5pg L

Parke House
Rock Raymond Rd. (Caln Twp.)
HABS PA-1211
HABS PA,15-DOWT.V,6-
1ph/3pg L

Valentine-Edge Mill
State Rt. 340
HABS PA-1202
HABS PA,15-DOWT.V,7-
1ph/4pg L

GLENLOCH

Loch Aerie (Lockwood,William E. ,House)
U. S. Rt. 30 (E. Whiteland Twp.)
HABS PA-181
HABS PA,15-GLENL,2-
7ph/7pg L

Lockwood,William E. ,House; see Loch Aerie

Zook Barn
King Rd. (East Whiteland Township)
HABS PA-1218
HABS PA,15-GLENL,1-
6ph/3pg L

GLENMOORE

Barn,Large
Old Creek Rd. ,(Wallace Twp.)
HABS PA-5232
HABS PA,15-GLENOR,1A-
1ph/1pc L

Barn,Small
Old Creek Rd. ,(Wallace Twp.)
HABS PA-5232-A
HABS PA,15-GLENOR,1B-
2ph/1pc L

GREEN LAWN VIC.

Marlboro Plank House; see Sharity Road (House)

Sharity Road (House) (Marlboro Plank House)
(West Marlborogh Township)
HABS PA-160
HABS PA,15-GRELA.V,1-
5ph/1pg L

GRUBBS MILL

Ivy House; see Wollerton,Charles,House

Log House; see Wollerton,Charles,House

Wollerton,Charles,House (Ivy House; Log House)
Valley Creek & Sunset Hollow Rds.
HABS PA-1208
HABS PA,15-GRUB,1-
3ph/6pg L

HAMORTON VIC.

Barn,Stone
State Rt. 52,(Pennsbury Twp.)
HABS PA-5240
HABS PA,15-HAMO.V,3A-
3ph/1pc L

HONEY BROOK VIC.

Barn
Legislative Rt. 15146,(Honeybrook Twp.)
HABS PA-5233
HABS PA,15-HOBRO.V,1A-
1ph/1pc L

HONEY BROOK VIC..

Barn
Legislative Rt. 15146,(Honeybrook Twp.)
HABS PA-5234
HABS PA,15-HOBRO.V,2A-
1ph/1pc L

HOPEWELL

Hopewell Academy
Hopewell Rd. (East Nottingham Twp.)
HABS PA-1311
HABS PA,15-HOPE,1-
4ph/11pg L

HOPEWELL VILLAGE

Big House (Iron Master's House; Hopewell Furnace National Historic Site)
East Head Race
HABS PA-5941
HABS DLC/PP-1992:PA-5
10ph/1pc L

Hopewell Furnace National Historic Site; see Big House

Hopewell Furnace National Historic Site; see Office Store

Hopewell Furnace National Historic Site; see Spring House

Hopewell Furnace National Historic Site; see Tenant House No. 1

Hopewell Furnace National Historic Site; see Village Barn

Hopewell Village National Historic Site; see Hopewell Village,Bethesda Baptist Church

Hopewell Village National Historic Site; see Hopewell Village,Employees Quarters,Number 71

Hopewell Village National Historic Site; see Hopewell Village,Harrison Lloyd House

Hopewell Village,Bethesda Baptist Church (Hopewell Village National Historic Site)
State Rt. 345 vic.
HABS PA-5157-J
HABS PA,15-HOPVI,3-
6dr/1pg/fr L

Hopewell Village,Employees Quarters,Number 71 (Lloyd House; Lucas House; Hopewell Village National Historic Site)
HABS PA-5160
HABS PA,15-HOPVI,2-
9dr/12ph/1pg L

Hopewell Village,Harrison Lloyd House (Hopewell Village National Historic Site)
HABS PA-5168
HABS PA,15-HOPVI,1-
6ph L

Iron Master's House; see Big House

Lloyd House; see Hopewell Village,Employees Quarters,Number 71

Lucas House; see Hopewell Village,Employees Quarters,Number 71

Office Store (Hopewell Furnace National Historic Site)
HABS PA-5943
HABS DLC/PP-1992:PA-5
11ph/2pc L

Spring House (Hopewell Furnace National Historic Site)
East Head Race
HABS PA-5942
HABS DLC/PP-1992:PA-5
10ph/1pc L

Tenant House No. 1 (Hopewell Furnace National Historic Site)
French Creek
HABS PA-5945
HABS DLC/PP-1992:PA-5
6ph/1pc L

Village Barn (Hopewell Furnace National Historic Site)
HABS PA-5944
HABS DLC/PP-1992:PA-5
3ph/1pc L

KAOLIN

Barn,Eighteenth Century
State Rt. 41,(New Garden Twp.)
HABS PA-5239
HABS PA,15-KAOL,1A-
2ph/1pc L

KAOLIN VIC.

Pyle,Walter C. ,Barn,1768
Legislative Rt. 15037
HABS PA-5238
HABS PA,15-KAOL.V,1A-
4ph/1pc L

KENNETT SQ. VIC.

Cedarcroft (Taylor,Bayard,House)
Bayard Dr. (East Marlborough Twp.)
HABS PA-172
HABS PA,15-KENSQ.V,3-
9ph L

Taylor,Bayard,House; see Cedarcroft

KENNETT SQUARE

121-127 South Union Street (Rowhouses)
121-127 S. Union St.,E. side of State Rte. 82
HABS PA-5444
HABS 1991(HABS):1
6ph/3pg/1pc L

KIMBERTON

Barn
Kimberton Rd. ,(East Pikeland Twp.)
HABS PA-5246
HABS PA,15-KIMB,1A-
1ph/1pc L

KNAUERTOWN

Halley House; see Rogers,Phillip,House

Penn Wick; see Rogers,Phillip,House

Documentation: **ct** color transparencies **dr** measured drawings **fr** field records
pc photograph captions **pg** pages of text **ph** photographs

Rogers,Philip,Barn
State Rt. 23 (Warwick Twp.)
HABS PA-114-A
HABS PA,15-KNATO,1A-
1ph L

Rogers,Phillip,House (Penn Wick; Halley House)
State Rt. 83 (Warwick Twp.)
HABS PA-114
HABS PA,15-KNATO,1
5ph L

KNAUERTOWN VIC.

Branson,William,House; see Warrenpoint

Templin House; see Warrenpoint

Warrenpoint (Branson,William,House; Templin House)
State Rt. 83 (Warwick Twp.)
HABS PA-115
HABS PA,15-KNATO.V,1-
18ph/4pg L

LANDENBERG VIC.

Miller-Pusey Mill
Broad Run Rd. (New Garden Township)
HABS PA-252
HABS PA,15-LAND.V,1-
8dr/fr L

LENAPE VIC.

Barn,Wood
State Rt. 52 Vic. ,at Denton's Bridge
HABS PA-5235
HABS PA,15-LENA.V,2A-
1ph/1pc L

Clark,Tom,Barn
State Rt. 52,(Pocopson Twp.)
HABS PA-5236
HABS PA,15-LENA.V,3A-
5ph/1pc L

LUDWIGS COR. VIC.

Buckwalter,John,House
State Rt. 401 (East Nantmeal Twp.)
HABS PA-1195
HABS PA,15-LUDCO.V,1-
5ph/3pg L

MARSH

Hause Smokehouse
State Rt. 401 (East Nantmeal Twp.)
HABS PA-1206
HABS PA,15-MAR,1-
1ph/3pg L

Hause Store
State Rt. 401 (East Nantmeal Twp.)
HABS PA-1205
HABS PA,15-MAR,2-
3ph/5pg L

MARSHALLTON

Bradford Friends Meetinghouse; see Marshallton Friends Meetinghouse

Cunningham Blacksmith Shop; see Marshallton Blacksmith Shop

Marshall,Humphry,House
State Rt. 162 (West Bradford Twp.)
HABS PA-203
HABS PA,15-MARSH,1-
9ph/6pg L

Marshallton Blacksmith Shop (Cunningham Blacksmith Shop)
State Rt. 162 (West Bradford Twp.)
HABS PA-1102
HABS PA,15-MARSH,2-
2ph/5pg L

Marshallton Friends Meetinghouse (Bradford Friends Meetinghouse)
Northbrook Rd. (West Bradford Twp.)
HABS PA-1105
HABS PA,15-MARSH,3-
11ph/5pg L

MARSHALLTON VIC.

Arnold-Temple House (Temple-Webster-Stoner House)
Broad Run Rd. (West Bradford Twp.)
HABS PA-1109
HABS PA,15-MARSH.V,1-
16ph/4pg L

Temple-Webster-Stoner House; see Arnold-Temple House

MARTINS'S CORNER

Martin's Corner House
Cedar Knoll Rd. (West Caln Township)
HABS PA-209
HABS PA,15-MARCO,1-
5ph/4pg L

MILLTOWN

Hickman House (Milltown Plank House)
St. Rt. 3 (East Goshen Township)
HABS PA-166
HABS PA,15-MILT,1-
5ph L

Milltown Plank House; see Hickman House

MOUNT ROCKY

Mount Rocky Methodist Church
Chrome & Chrome-New London Rds.
HABS PA-1210
HABS PA,15-MTROC,2-
2ph/3pg L

MT. ROCKY

Ankrim,Samuel,Shop (Brick Shop)
Chrome Rd. (Elk Township)
HABS PA-1194
HABS PA,15-MTROC,1-
1ph/3pg L

Brick Shop; see Ankrim,Samuel,Shop

NORTHBROOK VIC.

Allen House
Northbrook Rd. (Pocopson Township)
HABS PA-1190
HABS PA,15-NORB.V,1-
3ph/5pg L

PAOLI VIC.

Cedar Hollow Railroad Station
Cedar Hollow Rd. (Tredyffrin Twp.)
HABS PA-1199
HABS PA,15-PAOL.V,4-
3ph/3pg L

Diamond Rock Schoolhouse
Yellow Springs Rd. (Tredyffrin Twp.)
HABS PA-207
HABS PA,15-PAOL.V,2-
1ph/6pg L

Jerman-Walker Springhouse (Wilson Springhouse)
N. Valley Rd. (Tredyffrin Township)
HABS PA-1217
HABS PA,15-PAOL.V,3A-
2ph/3pg L

Waynesborough
2049 Waynesborough Rd. (Easttown Township)
HABS PA-208
HABS PA,15-PAOL.V,1-
5ph/6pg L

Wilson Springhouse; see Jerman-Walker Springhouse

PARKESBURG BOR.

Parke,David,House
40 E. Main St.
HABS PA-200
HABS PA,15-PARK,1-
7ph/1pg L

Parke,John,House
345 Main St.
HABS PA-1310
HABS PA,15-PARK,2-
12ph/5pg L

PARKESBURG VIC.

Upper Octoraro Presbyterian Church Session House
State Rt. 10 & Octoraro Rd.
HABS PA-201
HABS PA,15-PARK.V,1-
3ph/1pg L

PHOENIXVILLE VIC.

Moore Hall; see Moore,William,House

Moore,William,House (Moore Hall)
State Rt. 23 & Reading Railroad Tracks Vic.
HABS PA-1135
HABS PA,15-PHOEN.V,1-
7ph/14pg L

PUGHTOWN VIC.

Lundale Farm,House (Townsend,Samuel House)
State Rt. 100
HABS PA-1308
HABS PA,15-PUGH.V,1-
6dr/1ph/10pg/4ct/fr L

Lundale Farm,Springhouse (Pugh,James,Springhouse)
State Rt. 100
HABS PA-1308-A
HABS PA,15-PUGH.V,1A-
1dr/1pg/fr L

Pugh,James,Springhouse; see Lundale Farm,Springhouse

Townsend,Samuel House; see Lundale Farm,House

ROCKY HILL VIC.

Barn
State Rt. 352,(E. Goshen Twp.)
HABS PA-5241
HABS PA,15-ROHI.V,2A-
3ph/1pc L

Barn
State Rt. 352,(E. Goshen Twp.)
HABS PA-5333
HABS PA,15-ROHI.V,1A-
1ph/1pc L

ROMANSVILLE

Barn,1804; see Romans,John,Barn

Romans,John,Barn (Barn,1804)
Star Gazer Rd. (West Bradford Twp.)
HABS PA-165
HABS PA,15-ROMAV,2A-
3ph/3pg L

Romansville Friends Meetinghouse Sheds
Shadyside Rd.
HABS PA-1101
HABS PA,15-ROMAV,1-
2ph/3pg L

SCONNELLTOWN

Sconnelltown House
Birmingham Rd. (East Bradford Twp.)
HABS PA-202
HABS PA,15-SCON,1-
4ph/4pg L

SCONNELLTOWN VIC.

Strode's Grist Mill
Lenape & Birmingham Rds.
HABS PA-251
HABS PA,15-SCON.V,1-
2ph/4pg L

ST. MATTHEWS COR.

Barn
State Rt. 41,West Vincent Twp.
HABS PA-5245
HABS PA,15-SAMAC,1A-
4ph/1pc L

ST. PETERS VIC.

Mount Pleasant Grist Mill
Warwick Furnace & County Park Rds.
HAER PA-104
HAER 1989(HAER):18
25dr L

STRAFFORD

Eagle School
Old Eagle School Rd. (Tredyffrin Twp.)
HABS PA-1129
HABS PA,15-STRAFO,1-
4ph/7pg L

Strafford Railroad Station
Old Eagle School Rd. (Tredyffrin Twp.)
HABS PA-268
HABS PA,15-STRAFO,2-
2ph/3pg L

TANGUY VIC.

Hoopes,Daniel,House
State Rt. 926 (Westtown Twp.)
HABS PA-161
HABS PA,15-TANG.V,1-
10ph/7pg L

THORNDALE

Pim Hexagonal School (Six-Sided School)
Caln Twp. Municipal Park (moved from Bailey Rd.)
HABS PA-5136
HABS PA,15-THORN,1-
4ph/3pg L

Six-Sided School; see Pim Hexagonal School

TOWERVILLE

Fallowfield Octagonal House; see Pierce,Lukens,House

Pierce,Lukens,House (Fallowfield Octagonal House)
Wilmington Rd. (East Fallowfield Twp.)
HABS PA-1139
HABS PA,15-TOW,1-
2ph L

WAWASET

Stone Barn,circa 1795
Rt. 342,s. of Wawaset Bridge
HABS PA-5237
HABS PA,15-WAWA,1A-
7ph/1pc L

WEST CHESTER BOR.

Bank of Chester County (National Bank of Chester County; Southeast National Bank)
17 N. High St.
HABS PA-1126
HABS PA,15-WCHES,13-
9ph/8pg L

Baptist Church of West Chester
221 S. High St.
HABS PA-1191
HABS PA,15-WCHES,21-
2ph/10pg L

Brinton Serpentine House; see Brinton,Sibyla,House

Brinton,Sibyla,House (Brinton Serpentine House)
311 S. Church St.
HABS PA-249
HABS PA,15-WCHES,1-
1ph L

Chester County Courthouse
10 N. High St.
HABS PA-1119
HABS PA,15-WCHES,3-
7ph/22pg L

Chester County Historical Society; see Chester County Horticultural Hall

Chester County Horticultural Hall (Chester County Historical Society)
225 N. High St.
HABS PA-1121
HABS PA,15-WCHES,4-
8ph/12pg L

Chester County Hotel (Mansion House Hotel)
36 W. Market St.
HABS PA-1112
HABS PA,15-WCHES,17-
4ph/4pg L

Chester County Prison
235 W. Market St.
HABS PA-1134
HABS PA,15-WCHES,5-
19ph/18pg L

136 East Gay Street (Bakery) (Sorber Brick Store)
HABS PA-244
HABS PA,15-WCHES,2-
2ph L

Ebbs,William,House; see Mayfield

Everhart,William,Building (Highley Building)
28 W. Market St.
HABS PA-1207
HABS PA,15-WCHES,11-
3ph/3pg L

First Presbyterian Church
130 W. Miner St.
HABS PA-1115
HABS PA,15-WCHES,6-
3ph/13pg L

Hickman Fountain
225 N. Matlack St. (moved from Chester Courthouse)
HABS PA-247
HABS PA,15-WCHES,7-
3ph L

Highley Building; see Everhart,William,Building

Holy Trinity Protestant Episcopal Church
238 S. High St.
HABS PA-1223
HABS PA,15-WCHES,18-
3ph/10pg L

Mansion House Hotel; see Chester County Hotel

Matlack-Townsend House (Townsend,David,House)
225 N. Matlack St.
HABS PA-243
HABS PA,15-WCHES,10-
8ph/10pg L

Mayfield (Ebbs,William,House)
600 N. New St.
HABS PA-1104
HABS PA,15-WCHES,19-
2ph/5pg L

National Bank of Chester County; see Bank of Chester County

Pennsylvania Railroad Station
Market St.
HABS PA-246
HABS PA,15-WCHES,8-
6ph L

Sharples,Philip,House
400 S. Church St.
HABS PA-164
HABS PA,15-WCHES,20-
2ph/1pg L

Sorber Brick Store; see 136 East Gay Street (Bakery)

Southeast National Bank; see Bank of Chester County

Townsend,David,House; see Matlack-Townsend House

Villa Maria Convent; see West Chester Young Ladies Seminary (School)

West Chester State College; see West Chester State Normal School

West Chester State Normal School (West Chester State College)
S. High St.
HABS PA-250
HABS PA,15-WCHES,9-
3ph L

West Chester Young Ladies Seminary (School) (Villa Maria Convent)
300 Maple Ave.
HABS PA-1215
HABS PA,15-WCHES,12-
4ph/5pg L

WEST CHESTER VIC.

Barn,Stone
U. S. Rt. 322,Shady Side & Creek Rds.
HABS PA-5229
HABS PA,15-WCHES.V,5A-
4ph/1pc L

Collins,Joseph,House
633 Goshen Rd.
HABS PA-1114
HABS PA,15-WCHES.V,2-
8ph/5pg L

Matlack,George,House
409 Westtown Rd.
HABS PA-1221
HABS PA,15-WCHES.V,3-
3ph/3pg L

Rogers-Hoopes House (Rogers,William & Mary,House)
1121 Fernhill Rd.
HABS PA-1212
HABS PA,15-WCHES.V,4-
8ph/4pg L

Rogers,William & Mary,House; see Rogers-Hoopes House

Taylor,Lowndes,Barn
937 Pottstown Pike
HABS PA-1100
HABS PA,15-WCHES.V,1-
6ph/4pg L

Taylor,Lowndes,Carriage House
937 Pottstown Pike
HABS PA-1100-A
HABS PA,15-WCHES.V,1A-
1ph L

Taylor,Lowndes,Smokehouse
937 Pottstown Pike
HABS PA-1100-B
HABS PA,15-WCHES.V,1B-
1ph L

WEST GROVE VIC.

Jackson,Joseph,House
Old Baltimore Pike (London Grove Twp.)
HABS PA-1224
HABS PA,15-WGRO.V,1-
15ph/7pg L

WESTTOWN VIC.

Beehive,The; see Woodward,Richard,House

Woodward,Richard,House (Beehive,The)
Concord Rd. (Thornbury Township)
HABS PA-1192
HABS PA,15-WESTO.V,1-
4ph/4pg L

WHITEHORSE VIC.

Bartram's Covered Bridge
Spanning Crum Creek (Willistown-Newtown Townships)
HABS PA-1108
HABS PA,15-WHIHO.V,3-
4ph/5pg L

Plumsock; see Yarnall-Hibberd House

Thomas Mill
Crum Creek (Willistown Township)
HABS PA-1214
HABS PA,15-WHIHO.V,2-
11ph/3pg L

Vogdes,Jacob,House
Providence Rd. (Willistown Township)
HABS PA-1219
HABS PA,15-WHIHO.V,4-
3ph/4pg L

Yarnall-Hibberd House (Plumsock)
Plumsock Rd. (Willistown Township)
HABS PA-182
HABS PA,15-WHIHO.V,1-
3ph/3pg L

WILLISTOWN VIC.

Yarnall-Garrett House
West Chester Pike (Willistown Township)
HABS PA-1203
HABS PA,15-WILS.V,1-
5ph/4pg L

WILLOWDALE

Pyle House
State Rt. 926 (East Marlborough Twp.)
HABS PA-162
HABS PA,15-WIL,1-
5ph L

WYEBROOKE VIC.

Isabella Furnace
Bollinger Dr. (West Nantmeal Twp.)
HABS PA-163
HABS PA,15-WYBRO.V,1-
3ph/7pg L

CLINTON COUNTY

LOCK HAVEN

Aspley House; see Vosburg,Andrew,House

Frank-Harvey House
229 N. Jay St.
HABS PA-1304
HABS PA,18-LOKHA,4-
8dr/1ph/2pg/1pc/fr L

McCormick,John F. ,House
234 E. Church St.
HABS PA-1305
HABS PA,18-LOKHA,1-
11dr/1ph/3pg/1pc/fr L

Mussina,Lyons,House
123 N. Jay St.
HABS PA-1306
HABS PA,18-LOKHA,3-
11dr/1ph/2pg/1pc/fr L

Vosburg,Andrew,House (Aspley House)
302 E. Church St.
HABS PA-1303
HABS PA,18-LOKHA,2-
10dr/1ph/3pg/1pc/fr L

COLUMBIA COUNTY

BLOOMSBURG

East Bloomsburg Bridge
Spanning Susquehanna River at Rt. 487 (LR 283)
HAER PA-100
HAER PA,19-BLOOM,1-
41ph/13pg/3pc L

BRIAR CREEK

Methodist Episcopal Church
HABS PA-213
HABS PA,19-BER.V,1-
4dr/3ph/3pg L

CATAWISSA

Quaker Meetinghouse
Third & South Sts.
HABS PA-212
HABS PA,19-CAT,1-
4dr/2ph/3pg L

CATAWISSA VIC.

Catawissa Bridge (Pennsylvania Traffic Route 42 Bridge)
N Branch,Susquehanna River,3.5 mi. S of Bloomsburg
HAER PA-90
HAER PA,19-CAT,2-
58ph/5pg/2pc L

Pennsylvania Traffic Route 42 Bridge; see Catawissa Bridge

MILLVILLE

Friends Meetinghouse
HABS PA-218
HABS PA,19-MILV,1-
4dr/1ph/3pg L

CRAWFORD COUNTY

CAMBRIDGE SPR. VIC.

Erie Railway:Diverging French Creek Bridges (Meadville Division,Bridges 82.88 & 83.09)
Spanning French Creek
HAER PA-27
HAER PA,20-CAMSP.V,1-
5ph L

Erie Railway:Parallel French Creek Bridges (Meadville Division,Bridges 86.88 & 87.14)
Spanning French Creek
HAER PA-28
HAER PA,20-CAMSP.V,2-
4ph L

Meadville Division,Bridges 82.88 & 83.09; see Erie Railway:Diverging French Creek Bridges

Meadville Division,Bridges 86.88 & 87.14; see Erie Railway:Parallel French Creek Bridges

CAMBRIDGE SPRINGS

Erie Railway:Cambridge Springs Station
U. S. Rt. 6/19 & Railroad St.
HAER PA-26
HAER PA,20-CAMSP,1-
2ph L

COCHRANTON

Erie Railway:Cochranton Pasenger & Freight Station
State Rt. 173
HAER PA-29
HAER PA,20-COCH,1-
4ph/1pc L

CONNEAUTVILLE

Conneautville Baptist Church; see Trinity Protestant Episcopal Church

Trinity Protestant Episcopal Church (Conneautville Baptist Church)
1301 Water St.
HABS PA-609
HABS PA,20-CONT.V,1-
8dr L

EAST TITUSVILLE VIC.

Chase House
Old Enterprise-Titusville Rd.
HABS PA-1237
HABS PA,20-TITVE.V,1-
1ph/1pc L

HYDETOWN

Ridgeway House
HABS PA-543
HABS PA,20-HYD,1-
1ph L

Ridgeway,Charles,House
HABS PA-5130
HABS PA,20-HYD,2-
3ph L

MEADVILLE

Allegheny College,Bentley Hall
HABS PA-5955
HABS PA,20-MEDVI,2A-
1ph L

Atlantic & Great Western Railroad (Meadville Blacksmith Shop; Erie Railway)
U. S. Rt. 6/19
HAER PA-11-B
HAER PA,20-MEDVI,4B-
4dr/12ph/1pc/fr L

Atlantic & Great Western Railroad (Meadville Machine & Erecting Shop; Erie Railway)
U. S. Rt. 6/19
HAER PA-11-A
HAER PA,20-MEDVI,4A-
2dr/12ph/1pc/fr L

Atlantic & Great Western Railroad (Meadville Repair Shops; Erie Railway)
U. S. Rt. 6/19
HAER PA-11
HAER PA,20-MEDVI,4-
4ph/1pc L

Atlantic & Great Western Railroad (Meadville Storehouse; Erie Railway)
U. S. Rt. 6/19
HAER PA-11-C
HAER PA,20-MEDVI,4C-
4dr/6ph/1pc/fr L

Erie Railway; see Atlantic & Great Western Railroad

Erie Railway:Meadville Roundhouse
U. S. Rt. 6/19 & North St.
HAER PA-13
HAER PA,20-MEDVI,4D-
5ph/1pc L

Erie Railway:Meadville Station
McHenry & Chestnut Sts.
HAER PA-12
HAER PA,20-MEDVI,5-
2ph/1pc L

Independent Congregational Church
HABS PA-524
HABS PA,20-MEDVI,1-
1ph L

Mead Avenue Bridge
HAER PA-19
HAER PA,20-MEDVI,6-
9ph/1pc L

Meadville Blacksmith Shop; see Atlantic & Great Western Railroad

Meadville Machine & Erecting Shop; see Atlantic & Great Western Railroad

Meadville Repair Shops; see Atlantic & Great Western Railroad

Meadville Storehouse; see Atlantic & Great Western Railroad

Reynolds House
HABS PA-548
HABS PA,20-MEDVI,3-
1ph L

MEADVILLE VIC.

Erie Railway:Buchanan Junction Interlocking Tower
U. S. 322 Vic.
HAER PA-20
HAER PA,20-MEDVI.V,2A-
6ph/1pc L

Documentation: **ct** color transparencies **dr** measured drawings **fr** field records **pc** photograph captions **pg** pages of text **ph** photographs

Thomas,Albert,Summerhouse
Rt. 98
HABS PA-563
HABS PA,20-MEDVI.V,1-
1ph L

NEW RICHMOND VIC.

Flint House
HABS PA-576
HABS PA,20-NEWRI.V,1-
1ph L

RICEVILLE

Congregational Church
State Rt. 77
HABS PA-514
HABS PA,20-RICVI,1-
4dr/2ph/3pg/fr L

Grist Mill
Oil Creek
HABS PA-532
HABS PA,20-RICVI,4-
2ph/2pg L

Hendryx House
State Rt. 77
HABS PA-520
HABS PA,20-RICVI,3-
11dr/3ph/3pg/fr L

Westgate-Bruner House
State Rt. 77
HABS PA-519
HABS PA,20-RICVI,2-
3dr/3ph/3pg/fr L

SAEGERTOWN

Saeger,Edward,House
HABS PA-523
HABS PA,20-SAGTO,1-
1ph L

TITUSVILLE

Drake,Col. ,House
HABS PA-5108
HABS PA,20-TITVI,1-
1ph L

Kelly,William,Homestead
HABS PA-5115
HABS PA,20-TITVI,2-
1ph L

TOWNVILLE

Stevens House
HABS PA-5126
HABS PA,20-TOWNV,1-
2ph L

WOODCOCK

McPheeter House
HABS PA-546
HABS PA,20-WOOD,1-
1ph L

Methodist Church
HABS PA-5135
HABS PA,20-WOOD,2-
1ph L

CUMBERLAND COUNTY

NEWVILLE VIC.

Sterrett,David,House
State Game Lands Plot No. 169 (Upper Mifflin Twp.)
HABS PA-5354
HABS PA,21-NEWVI.V,1-
20ph/2pg/2pc/fr L

DAUPHIN COUNTY

FORT HUNTER

Fort Hunter Mansion
HABS PA-38
HABS PA,22-FOHUN,1-
9dr/8ph/2pg/fr L

HARRISBURG

2533 Agate Street (House); see North Sixth Street (Houses)

2535 Agate Street (House); see North Sixth Street (Houses)

2537 Agate Street (House); see North Sixth Street (Houses)

2539 Agate Street (House); see North Sixth Street (Houses)

Allison Hill (Houses)
State,Berryhill,Crescent,Royal Terrace & 17th Sts.
HABS PA-5203
HABS PA,22-HARBU,11-
6ph/7pg L

Allison Hill (Houses) (1618 Hunter Street (House))
HABS PA-5203-A
HABS PA,22-HARBU,12-
1ph/2pg L

Allison Hill (Houses) (1620 Hunter Street (House))
HABS PA-5203-B
HABS PA,22-HARBU,13-
4ph/2pg L

Allison Hill (Houses) (1152 Market Street (House))
HABS PA-5203-C
HABS PA,22-HARBU,14A-
3ph/2pg L

Allison Hill (Houses) (1152 1/2 Market Street (House))
HABS PA-5203-D
HABS PA,22-HARBU,14B-
3ph/2pg L

Allison Hill (Houses) (63 North Sixteenth Street (House))
HABS PA-5203-S
HABS PA,22-HARBU,22E-
2ph/2pg L

Allison Hill (Houses) (65 North Sixteenth Street (House))
HABS PA-5203-T
HABS PA,22-HARBU,22D-
1ph/2pg L

Allison Hill (Houses) (67 North Sixteenth Street (House))
HABS PA-5203-U
HABS PA,22-HARBU,22C-
3ph/2pg L

Allison Hill (Houses) (69 North Sixteenth Street (House))
HABS PA-5203-V
HABS PA,22-HARBU,22B-
1ph/2pg L

Allison Hill (Houses) (71 North Sixteenth Street (House))
HABS PA-5203-W
HABS PA,22-HARBU,22A-
4ph/2pg L

Allison Hill (Houses) (38 North Twelfth Street (House))
HABS PA-5203-Q
HABS PA,22-HARBU,21A-
2ph/2pg L

Allison Hill (Houses) (40 North Twelfth Street (House))
HABS PA-5203-R
HABS PA,22-HARBU,21B-
2ph/2pg L

Allison Hill (Houses) (1400 Regina Street (Commercial Building/House))
HABS PA-5203-E
HABS PA,22-HARBU,15A-
6ph/2pg L

Allison Hill (Houses) (1400 1/2 Regina Street (House))
HABS PA-5203-F
HABS PA,22-HARBU,15B-
1ph/2pg L

Allison Hill (Houses) (1402 Regina Street (House))
HABS PA-5203-G
HABS PA,22-HARBU,15C-
2pg L

Allison Hill (Houses) (1404 Regina Street (House))
HABS PA-5203-H
HABS PA,22-HARBU,16-
1ph/2pg L

Allison Hill (Houses) (1406 Regina Street (House))
HABS PA-5203-I
HABS PA,22-HARBU,17-
2ph/2pg L

Allison Hill (Houses) (1408 Regina Street (House))
HABS PA-5203-J
HABS PA,22-HARBU,18-
2ph/2pg L

Allison Hill (Houses) (1526 Regina Street (House))
HABS PA-5203-K
HABS PA,22-HARBU,19A-
2ph/2pg L

Allison Hill (Houses) (1528 Regina Street (House))
HABS PA-5203-L
HABS PA,22-HARBU,19B-
3ph/2pg L

Allison Hill (Houses) (1415 Shoop Street (House))
HABS PA-5203-M
HABS PA,22-HARBU,20D-
2ph/2pg L

Allison Hill (Houses) (1417 Shoop Street (House))
HABS PA-5203-N
HABS PA,22-HARBU,20C-
1ph/2pg L

Allison Hill (Houses) (1419 Shoop Street (House))
HABS PA-5203-O
HABS PA,22-HARBU,20B-
1ph/2pg L

Allison Hill (Houses) (1421 Shoop Street (House))
HABS PA-5203-P
HABS PA,22-HARBU,20A-
4ph/2pg L

Broad Street Market,Frame Wing
Verbeke & Capitol Sts.
HABS PA-1156
HABS PA,22-HARBU,4A-
3dr/4ph/1pg/1pc/fr L

First Capitol Buildings
HABS PA-37
HABS PA,22-HARBU,1-
3dr/4ph/2pg/fr L

Harrisburg Station & Trainshed; see Pennsylvania RR,Harrisburg Station & Trainshed

1618 Hunter Street (House); see Allison Hill (Houses)

1620 Hunter Street (House); see Allison Hill (Houses)

Maclay,William,Mansion
Front & South Sts.
HABS PA-310
HABS PA,2-HARBU,3-
5dr/1ph/2pg L

1152 Market Street (House); see Allison Hill (Houses)

1152 1/2 Market Street (House); see Allison Hill (Houses)

63 North Sixteenth Street (House); see Allison Hill (Houses)

65 North Sixteenth Street (House); see Allison Hill (Houses)

67 North Sixteenth Street (House); see Allison Hill (Houses)

69 North Sixteenth Street (House); see Allison Hill (Houses)

71 North Sixteenth Street (House); see Allison Hill (Houses)

North Sixth Street (Houses)
Maclay,Jefferson, & Radner Sts. & Bersinger Alley
HABS PA-5204
HABS PA,22-HARBU,6-
6pg L

North Sixth Street (Houses) (2533 Agate Street (House))
HABS PA-5204-A
HABS PA,22-HARBU,7-
6ph/2pg L

North Sixth Street (Houses) (2535 Agate Street (House))
HABS PA-5204-B
HABS PA,22-HARBU,8-
1ph/2pg L

North Sixth Street (Houses) (2537 Agate Street (House))
HABS PA-5204-C
HABS PA,22-HARBU,9-
1ph/2pg L

North Sixth Street (Houses) (2539 Agate Street (House))
HABS PA-5204-D
HABS PA,22-HARBU,10-
2ph/2pg L

38 North Twelfth Street (House); see Allison Hill (Houses)

40 North Twelfth Street (House); see Allison Hill (Houses)

Pennsylvania RR,Harrisburg Station & Trainshed (Harrisburg Station & Trainshed)
Market & S. Fourth Sts.
HAER PA-85
HAER PA,22-HARBU,23-
16dr/58ph/3pg/4pc/fr L

1400 Regina Street (Commercial Building/House); see Allison Hill (Houses)

1400 1/2 Regina Street (House); see Allison Hill (Houses)

1402 Regina Street (House); see Allison Hill (Houses)

1404 Regina Street (House); see Allison Hill (Houses)

1406 Regina Street (House); see Allison Hill (Houses)

1408 Regina Street (House); see Allison Hill (Houses)

1526 Regina Street (House); see Allison Hill (Houses)

1528 Regina Street (House); see Allison Hill (Houses)

1415 Shoop Street (House); see Allison Hill (Houses)

1417 Shoop Street (House); see Allison Hill (Houses)

1419 Shoop Street (House); see Allison Hill (Houses)

1421 Shoop Street (House); see Allison Hill (Houses)

St. Stephen's P. E. Church,Residence of Dean
215 N. Front St.
HABS PA-39
HABS PA,22-HARBU,2-
16dr/5ph/1pg/fr L

Telegram Building
227 Walnut St.
HABS PA-5370
HABS 1989(HABS):20
11ph/19pg/1pc L

U. S. Post Office & Courthouse
Third & Walnut Sts.
HABS PA-1255
HABS PA,22-HARBU,5-
6ph/1pg/1pc L

HIGHSPIRE VIC.

Burd,Col. James,House; see Tinian

Tinian (Burd,Col. James,House)
HABS PA-34
HABS PA,22-HISPI.V,1-
9dr/3ph/5pg L

LINGELESTOWN VIC.

Mackey,Capt. James,House
HABS PA-312
HABS PA,22-LING.V,1-
13dr L

MIDDLETOWN

St. Peter's Church,United Lutheran
N. Union St.
HABS PA-36
HABS PA,22-MIDTO,1-
5dr/4ph/1pg/fr L

PAXTANG

Elder,John,House & Barn
Twenty-fourth & Ellerslie Sts.
HABS PA-32
HABS PA,22-PAX,2-
7dr/2ph/2pg/fr L

Paxton Presbyterian Church
Sharon St.
HABS PA-31
HABS PA,22-PAX,1-
8dr/4ph/1pg/fr L

Rutherford Stone House (Springhouse)
HABS PA-33
HABS PA,22-PAX,3-
4dr/1ph/1pg/fr L

Springhouse; see Rutherford Stone House

PAXTANG VIC.

Willow Dale Farm,Brick House
HABS PA-35
HABS PA,22-PAX.V,1-
5dr/2ph/2pg/fr L

DELAWARE COUNTY

BROOMALL VIC.

Massey,Thomas,House
Lawrence & Springhouse Rds. (Marple Twp.)
HABS PA-1257
HABS PA,23-BROOM.V,1-
24ph/1pg/2pc L

CHADDS FORD

Chad,John,House
State Rt. 100,U. S. Rt. 1 vic.
HABS PA-1256
HABS PA,23-CHAF,2-
17ph/4pg/2pc L

Chad,John,Spring House
State Rt. 100,U. S. Rt. 1 vic.
HABS PA-1256-A
HABS PA,23-CHAF,2A-
1ph/1pc L

Gilpin,Joseph,Cart House
U. S. Rt. 1 (Birmingham Twp.)
HABS PA-1116-A
HABS PA,23-CHAF.V,1A-
1ph/1pc L

Gilpin,Joseph,House (Lafayette Quarters)
U. S. Rt. 1 (Birmingham Township)
HABS PA-1116
HABS PA,23-CHAF.V,1-
9ph/10pg L

Gilpin,Joseph,Root House
U. S. Rt. 1 (Birmingham Twp.)
HABS PA-1116-B
HABS PA,23-CHAF.V,1B-
1ph/1pc L

Gilpin,Joseph,Springhouse
U. S. Rt. 1 (Birmingham Twp.)
HABS PA-1116-C
HABS PA,23-CHAF.V,1C-
1ph/1pc L

Lafayette Quarters; see Gilpin,Joseph,House

CONCORDVILLE

House
U. S. Rt. 1 Vic. (moved to Bacton)
HABS PA-174
HABS PA,23-CON,2-
14ph/2pc L

DARBY

Bonsall House
1009 Main St.
HABS PA-127
HABS PA,23-DARB,1-
3ph L

DARBY VIC.

Blue Bell Tavern
7303 Woodland Ave.
HABS PA-131
HABS PA,23-DARB.V,1-
12ph/2pg L

Swedish Log Cabin,Lower
Darby Creek Vic.
HABS PA-135
HABS PA,23-DARB.V,2-
7dr/4ph/1pg/1pc/fr L

Swedish Log Cabin,Upper
Darby Creek Vic.
HABS PA-136
HABS PA,23-DARB.V,3-
4dr/4ph/1pg/1pc/fr L

DILWORTHTOWN VIC.

Brinton 1704 House
Oakland Rd. (Birmingham Twp.)
HABS PA-1258
HABS PA,23-DIL.V,1-
11ph/12pg/1pc L

Brinton 1704 House,Privy
Oakland Rd. (Birmingham Twp.)
HABS PA-1258-A
HABS PA,23-DIL.V,1A-
1ph/1pc L

ESSINGTON

Lazaretto,The
Delaware River Vic.
HABS PA-125
HABS PA,23-ESTO,1-
9ph/3pg/1pc L

HAVERTOWN VIC.

Flintlock (Reese,Joseph,House)
1543 Lawrence Rd. (Haverford Twp.)
HABS PA-1230
HABS PA,23-HAVTO.V,1-
5ph/1pg L

Lawrence Cabin
State Rt. 3
HABS PA-1238
HABS PA,23-HAVTO.V,2-
12ph/1pg L

Nitre Hall Powder Magazine
(Haverford Twp.)
HABS PA-1279
HABS PA,23-HAVTO.V,3A-
2dr L

Pont Reading House
2713 Haverford Rd. (Haverford Township)
HABS PA-1239
HABS PA,23-HAVTO.V,4-
3ph/1pg/1pc L

Reese,Joseph,House; see Flintlock

ITHAN

Academy of Notre Dame de Namur; see Godfrey,Lincoln,House

Godfrey,Lincoln,House (Academy of Notre Dame de Namur)
560 Sproul Rd.
HABS PA-1241
HABS PA,23-ITH,2-
1ph/1pg/1pc L

MEDIA VIC.

Quaker Meetinghouse
HABS PA-180
HABS PA,23-MED.V,1-
1ph L

NORWOOD

Mortensen,Morton,House
Winona Ave. & Amosland Rd.
HABS PA-1240
HABS PA,23-NOR,1-
7dr/1pc L

RADNOR

Bel Orme
County Line Rd. (Radnor Township)
HABS PA-1001
HABS PA,23- ,3-
3ph/4pg L

Bolingbroke
King of Prussia Rd. (Radnor Twp.)
HABS PA-1000
HABS PA,23-RAD,2-
6ph/5pg/1pc L

Gaybrook; see Hillside

Hillside (Gaybrook)
King of Prussia Rd. (Radnor Township)
HABS PA-1002
HABS PA,23- 4-
3ph/4pg L

Morgan Barn
Matsons Ford Rd. (Radnor Township)
HABS PA-1003
HABS PA,23- 5A-
1ph/2pg L

Morgan Farmhouse
Matsons Ford Rd. (Radnor Township)
HABS PA-1004
HABS PA,23- ,5-
9ph/7pg L

St. Martin's Church (Episcopal)
King of Prussia Rd. (Radnor Twp.)
HABS PA-1242
HABS PA,23-RAD,3-
2ph/1pg/1pc L

Vanor
Lancaster Ave. & Radnor Railroad Station Vic.
HABS PA-193
HABS PA,23- ,2-
7ph/5pg L

ST. DAVIDS

Nantmell Hall
Lancaster Ave. ,Radnor-Chester Rd. Vic.
HABS PA-192
HABS PA,23- ,1-
3ph/4pg L

Nantmell Hall,Tenant House
Lancaster Ave. & Radnor-Chester Rd.
HABS PA-1066
HABS PA,23- ,1A-
3ph/3pg L

SWARTHMORE

Pennock,William,House
Swarthmore Ave. (moved to PA,Upland)
HABS PA-1243
HABS PA,23-SWAM,1-
15ph/1pg L

UPLAND

Pennock,William,House
Race St. (moved from PA,Swarthmore)
HABS PA-1243
HABS PA,23-SWAM,1-
15ph/1pg L

Pusey,Caleb,House
Race St.
HABS PA-1079
HABS PA,23-UPLA,1-
4dr/20ph/1pg L

VILLANOVA

Ashwood
208 Ashwood Rd. (Radnor Township)
HABS PA-194
HABS PA,23-VILLA,1-
6ph/5pg L

Chuckswood (House, Brick)
Spring Mill Rd. (Radnor Township)
HABS PA-195
HABS PA,23-VILLA,2-
8ph/5pg L

House, Brick; see Chuckswood

Woodstock
South Spring Mill Rd. (Radnor Township)
HABS PA-196
HABS PA,23-VILLA,3-
13ph/9pg L

Woodstock,Barn
South Spring Mill Rd. (Radnor Township)
HABS PA-197
HABS PA,23-VILLA,3A-
7ph/4pg L

WALLINGFORD

Avondale; see Leiper,Thomas,House

Avondale,Vault; see Leiper,Thomas,House,Vault

Furness,Horace H. ,Estate,House; see Lindenshade,House

Furness,Horace H. ,Estate,Kitchen & Serv. Quarters; see Lindenshade,Kitchen & Servants' Quarters

Furness,Horace H. ,Estate,Library; see Lindenshade,Library

Horace,Jayne,House; see Subrosa

Leiper,Thomas,House (Avondale)
519 Avondale Rd. (Nether Providence Twp.)
HABS PA-1244
HABS PA,23-WALF,1-
9ph/1pg/1pc L

Leiper,Thomas,House,Vault
(Avondale,Vault)
519 Avondale Rd. (Nether Providence Twp.)
HABS PA-1244-A
HABS PA,23-WALF,1A-
2ph/1pc L

Lindenshade,House (Furness,Horace H. ,Estate,House)
Furness Lane
HABS PA-1245-A
HABS PA,23-WALF,2-
3ph/1pg/1pc L

Lindenshade,Kitchen & Servants' Quarters (Furness,Horace H. ,Estate,Kitchen & Serv. Quarters
Furness Lane
HABS PA-1245-C
HABS PA,23-WALF,2B-
1ph/1pc L

Lindenshade,Library (Furness,Horace H. ,Estate,Library)
Furness Lane
HABS PA-1245-B
HABS PA,23-WALF,2A-
5ph/1pc L

Subrosa (Horace,Jayne,House)
Turner Rd. (Nether Providence Twp.)
HABS PA-1213
HABS PA,23-WALF,3-
1ph/1pc L

WAYNE

Jones Farm,Springhouse
Lancaster Pike & Farm Rd. (Radnor Twp.)
HABS PA-199
HABS PA,23-WAYN,1A-
1ph/2pg L

Jones Farmhouse
Lancaster Pike (Radnor Township)
HABS PA-198
HABS PA,23-WAYN,1-
8ph/6pg L

St. David's Church (Episcopal)
Valley Forge Rd.
HABS PA-176
HABS PA,23-RAD,1-
10ph/6pg/1pc/fr L

St. David's Church,Grave of Gen. Anthony Wayne
Valley Forge Rd.
HABS PA-176-B
HABS PA,23-RAD,1B-
1ph/1pg/1pc L

St. David's Church,Horse Shed
Valley Forge Rd.
HABS PA-176-A
HABS PA,23-RAD,1A-
1ph/1pc L

ERIE COUNTY

CORRY

Hatch School
HABS PA-515
HABS PA,25-COR,1-
4ph/3pg L

CORRY VIC.

Penna. Railroad,Erie Railroad Bridge
State Rt. 89
HAER PA-34
HAER PA,25-COR.V,1-
3ph/1pc L

EDINBORO

First Constitutional Presbyterian Church
HABS PA-5114
HABS PA,25-EDBO,2-
1ph L

Hencke House
HABS PA-5113
HABS PA,25-EDBO,1-
2ph L

ERIE

Arbuckle House (Carey-Murphy House)
140 E. Fifth St.
HABS PA-311
HABS PA,25-ERI,10-
12ph/3pg L

Arbuckle House,Carriage House
(Carey-Murphy House,Carriage House)
140 E. Fifth St.
HABS PA-311-A
HABS PA,25-ERI,10A-
1ph L

Carey-Murphy House; see Arbuckle House

Carey-Murphy House,Carriage House; see Arbuckle House,Carriage House

Colt,George P.,House
628.5 E Sixth St.
HABS PA-5359
HABS PA,25-ERI,14-
10ph/7pg/1pc L

Crittenton,Florence,Home; see Sterrett,James M. ,House

Customs House,Old
415 State St.
HABS PA-53
HABS PA,25-ERI,2-
13dr/5ph/3pg/fr L

Dickson Tavern; see Perry Memorial Building

Empire Stores (Gage Hotel)
501-505 State St.
HABS PA-5142
HABS PA,25-ERI,9-
30ph/9pg/2pc L

Frank's Hotel; see Reed,C. M. ,Block

Gage Hotel; see Empire Stores

Hughes Log House
136 E. Third St.
HABS PA-5117
HABS PA,25-ERI,7-
1ph L

Land Lighthouse
Front St.
HABS PA-517
HABS PA,25-ERI,5-
2dr/3ph/4pg/fr L

Perry Memorial Building (Dickson Tavern; Tavern,Old)
Second & French Sts.
HABS PA-52
HABS PA,25-ERI,1-
13dr/11ph/7pg L

Presque Isle Lighthouse
Peninsula Dr. ,Presque Isle State Park
HABS PA-624
HABS PA,25-ERI,8-
6dr L

Reed Mansion
Sixth & Peach Sts.
HABS PA-57
HABS PA,25-ERI,4-
17ph/3pg L

Reed,C. M. ,Block (Frank's Hotel)
22-26 E. Fifth St.
HABS PA-1957
HABS PA,25-ERI,13-
4ph/3pg/1pc L

Sterrett,James M. ,House (Crittenton,Florence,Home)
501-503 Holland St.
HABS PA-178
HABS PA,25-ERI,11-
17ph/4pg/1pc L

Tavern,Old; see Perry Memorial Building

Tracy Building
532-527 French St.
HABS PA-5154
HABS PA,25-ERI,12-
20ph/5pg/2pc L

Whitman,Benjamin,House
Ninth & Peach Sts.
HABS PA-542
HABS PA,25-ERI,6-
1ph L

Woodruff House
417 State St.
HABS PA-56
HABS PA,25-ERI,3-
6dr/1ph/3pg/fr L

ERIE VIC.

Strong House
Perry Highway
HABS PA-559
HABS PA,25-ERI.V,1-
1ph L

GIRARD

Hutchinson House
155 E. Main St.
HABS PA-59
HABS PA,25-GIRA,1-
7dr/3ph/3pg/fr L

GIRARD VIC.

Blair Cabin
Blair Rd.
HABS PA-510
HABS PA,25-GIRA.V,2-
2dr/4ph/3pg/fr L

Thompson,Denman,House
Blair Rd.
HABS PA-58
HABS PA,25-GIRA.V,1-
1dr/2ph/3pg L

HARBORCREEK

Davidson House
HABS PA-5110
HABS PA,25-HARB,1-
1ph L

Dodge House
HABS PA-5121
HABS PA,25-HARB,2-
1ph L

MOORHEADVILLE

Backus House
HABS PA-5120
HABS PA,25-MOOR,2-
1ph L

Moorhead House
HABS PA-51
HABS PA,25-MOOR,1-
11dr/7ph/4pg L

NORTH EAST

First Baptist Church
Railroad St.
HABS PA-513
HABS PA,25-NORE,2-
3dr/4ph/3pg L

Octagon Barn
HABS PA-574
HABS PA,25-NORE,3-
1ph L

Silliman-Phillips House
HABS PA-512
HABS PA,25-NORE,1-
1ph/3pg L

NORTH SPRINGFIELD

Stevenson House
Lake Rd.
HABS PA-55
HABS PA,25-SPRIFN,1-
9dr/4ph/3pg L

STERRETTANIA

Sterrett Cabin (Interiors)
Conneaut Rd.
HABS PA-511
HABS PA,25-STER,1-
8dr/5ph/3pg L

SUMMIT

Summit Stone School
HABS PA-5122
HABS PA,25-SUM,1-
1ph L

UNION CITY

Bridge Street Bridge
Spanning Little French Creek at Bridge St.
HAER PA-91
HAER PA,25-UNCI,2-
24ph/26pg/2pc L

Erie Railway:Crossing Gate Tower
Lincoln St.
HAER PA-47
HAER PA,25-UNCI,5A-
1ph L

Erie Railway:Union City Freight Station
HAER PA-46
HAER PA,25-UNCI,4-
2ph L

Erie Railway:Union City Station
Lincoln St.
HAER PA-45
HAER PA,25-UNCI,3-
4ph L

Rockwell House
HABS PA-5124
HABS PA,25-UNCI,1-
1ph L

WATERFORD

Brotherton House
HABS PA-5102
HABS PA,25-WAFO,6-
1ph L

Doctor's Office
HABS PA-5134
HABS PA,25-WAFO,7-
1ph L

Eagle Hotel
HABS PA-521
HABS PA,25-WAFO,2-
1ph L

Judson,Amos,House
HABS PA-5954
HABS PA,25-WAFO,3-
1ph L

St. Peter's Episcopal Church
Cherry St.
HABS PA-544
HABS PA,25-WAFO,5-
1ph L

Waterford Academy
Fourth & Cherry Sts.
HABS PA-54
HABS PA,25-WAFO,1-
8dr/3ph/2pg L

Waterford Covered Bridge
Spanning Le Boeuf Creek
HABS PA-535
HABS PA,25-WAFO,4-
1dr/2ph/3pg L

WATTSBURG

Chaffe House
HABS PA-590
HABS PA,25-WATBU,1-
1ph L

Howard Double House
HABS PA-5116
HABS PA,25-WATBU,2-
1ph L

FAYETTE COUNTY

ALLISON

Allison No. 1 Mine and Coke Works,Coke Ovens (W.J. Rainey Coke Company)
S. of the mining complex, E. side of Redstone Ck.
HAER PA-261-A
HAER DLC/PP-1993:PA-3
1ph/3pg/1pc L

W.J. Rainey Coke Company; see Allison No. 1 Mine and Coke Works,Coke Ovens

BROWNSVILLE

Dunlap's Creek Bridge
Spanning Dunlap's Creek
HAER PA-72
HAER PA,26-BROVI,2-
6ph/2pg/1pc L

BROWNSVILLE BOR.

Bowman's Castle (Nemacolin Castle)
Front & Second Sts.
HABS PA-429
HABS PA,26-BROVI,1-
7dr/11ph/1pg L

Bowman's Castle,Barn (Nemacolin Castle,Barn)
Front & Second Sts.
HABS PA-429-A
HABS PA,26-BROVI,1A-
1ph L

Bowman's Castle,Outbuildings (Nemacolin Castle,Outbuildings)
Front & Second Sts.
HABS PA-429-B
HABS PA,26-BROVI,1B-
1ph/1pc L

Nemacolin Castle; see Bowman's Castle

Nemacolin Castle,Barn; see Bowman's Castle,Barn

Nemacolin Castle,Outbuildings; see Bowman's Castle,Outbuildings

CHALKHILL VIC.

Hagan,Isaac N.,House
Kentuck Knob,U.S. RT. 40 vic.,Stewart Twp.
HABS PA-5347
HABS PA,26-CHALK,1-
39ph/2pc/12ct L

CONNELLSVILLE

Carnegie Free Library
301 S. Pittsburgh St.
HABS PA-5476
HABS DLC/PP-1993:PA-1
10ph/28pg/1pc L

DUNBAR TOWNSHIP

Meason,Isaac,House (Mt. Braddock)
U.S. Rt. 119
HABS PA-5475
HABS DLC/PP-1993:PA-1
20ph/2pg/2pc L

Mt. Braddock; see Meason,Isaac,House

FAIRCHANCE

Nixon Tavern
Fairchance Rd.
HABS PA-8-3
HABS PA,26-FACHA,1-
7dr/7ph/3pg L

FAYETTE CITY VIC.

Cook,Col. Edward,House
HABS PA-412
HABS PA,26-FACI.V,1-
9dr/3ph/3pg/fr L

HOPWOOD

Hayden,Ben,House
HABS PA-8-4
HABS PA,26-HOP,1-
5dr/6ph/3pg/fr L

LEISENRING

H.C. Frick Coke Company; see Town of Leisenring

H.C. Frick Coke Company; see Town of Leisenring,Company Store

H.C. Frick Coke Company; see Town of Leisenring,Manager's House No. 1

H.C. Frick Coke Company; see Town of Leisenring,Manager's House No. 2

Town of Leisenring (H.C. Frick Coke Company)
HAER PA-298
1ph/3pg/1pc H

Town of Leisenring,Company Store (H.C. Frick Coke Company)
HAER PA-298-A
3ph/1pc H

Town of Leisenring,Manager's House No. 1 (H.C. Frick Coke Company)
HAER PA-298-B
2ph/1pc H

Town of Leisenring,Manager's House No. 2 (H.C. Frick Coke Company)
HAER PA-298-C
1ph/1pc H

MASONTOWN VIC.

Bessemer Coke Company; see Griffin No. 1 Coke Works

Griffin No. 1 Coke Works (Bessemer Coke Company)
Along Cats Run, SE of Mansontown Bourough
HAER PA-260
HAER DLC/PP-1993:PA-3
4ph/2pg/1pc L

NEW GENEVA VIC.

Friendship Hill National Historic Site; see Painter,Charles Albert,House

Painter,Charles Albert,House (Friendship Hill National Historic Site)
State Rt. 166
HABS PA-5201
HABS PA,26-NEGEN.V,1-
11dr L

OHIOPYLE VIC.

Fallingwater (Kaufmann,Edgar J. ,House)
State Rt. 381,Stewart Twp.
HABS PA-5346
HABS PA,26-OHPY.V,1-
84ph/6pc/27ct L

Fallingwater,Guest House (Kaufmann,Edgar J.,Guesthouse)
State Rte. 381,Stewart Township
HABS PA-5346-A
HABS PA,26-OHPY.V,1A-
22ph/2pc L

Kaufmann,Edgar J. ,House; see Fallingwater

Kaufmann,Edgar J.,Guesthouse; see Fallingwater,Guest House

PENN-CRAFT

Penn-Craft,Town of
HABS PA-5920
HABS DLC/PP-1993:PA3
18ph/23pg/1pc/fr L

Subsistence-Homestead Towns
HABS PA-5919
HABS DLC/PP-1993:PA-3
25pg L

SHOAF

H.C. Frick Coke Company; see Shoaf Mine & Coke Works

Shoaf Mine & Coke Works (H.C. Frick Coke Company)
Off T472, East of Shoaf
HAER PA-259
HAER DLC/PP-1993:PA-3
6ph/3pg/1pc L

SOUTH UNION TWP.

Fort Gaddis; see Gaddis,Thomas,House

Gaddis,Thomas,House (Fort Gaddis)
U.S. Rt. 119 near intersection of Rt. 859
HABS PA-5474
HABS DLC/PP-1993:PA-1
8ph/13pg/1pc L

UNIONTOWN VIC.

Fort Necessity Museum; see Mount Washington Tavern

Mount Washington Tavern (Fort Necessity Museum)
U.S. 40,Old National Trail
HABS PA-5587
HABS PA,26-UNITO.V,1-
ıDLC/PP-1992:PA-4°
3ph/1pc L

Springer,Levi,House
Fan Hollow Rd.
HABS PA-5482
HABS DLC/PP-1993:PA-1
9dr/25ph/22pg/2pc/fr L

Springer,Levi,Smoke Hse.,Spring Hse.,& Summer Kitc
Fan Hollow Rd.
HABS PA-5482-A
HABS DLC/PP-1993:PA-1
1dr/5ph/2pg/1pc/fr L

FRANKLIN COUNTY

CHAMBERSBURG

Letterkenny Army Depot
HAER PA-79
HAER PA,28-CHAMB,5-
55pg/fr L

CHAMBERSBURG BOR.

Brand Stable,The; see Fisher,Rev. Samuel R. ,Stable

Fisher,Rev. Samuel R. ,Stable (Brand Stable,The)
123-125 S. Main St.
HABS PA-5155
HABS PA,28-CHAMB,4A-
2ph/4pg/1pc L

59 West Queen Street (House)
HABS PA-5156
HABS PA,28-CHAMB,3-
10ph/8pg/1pc L

GREENE COUNTY

BROCK

Valley Methodist Manse (Wayne Township)
HABS PA-619
HABS PA,30-BROC,1-
4dr L

RUFF CREEK VIC.

Covered Bridge
Spanning Ruff Creek (Washington Twp.)
HABS PA-618
HABS PA,30-RUFCR.V,1-
5dr L

HUNTINGDON COUNTY

ALEXANDRIA

Alexandria High School (Canal Towns,Alexandria)
Main St. & Church St.
HABS PA-5411
HABS DLC/PP-1992:PA-3
2ph/6pg/1pc L

Alexandria Memorial Public Library (Memorial Free Library; Canal Towns,Alexandria)
Hartslog & Main Sts.
HABS PA-5414
HABS DLC/PP-1942:PA-3
8ph/6pg/1pc L

Alexandria Presbyterian Church (Canal Towns,Alexandria)
Hartslog St. & Shelton Ave.
HABS PA-5413
HABS DLC/PP-1992:PA-3
2ph/5pg/1pc L

Alexandria School
Second St.
HABS PA-5927
HABS DLC/PP-1993:PA-1
2ph/1pc L

Alexandria,Town of (Canal Towns)
HABS PA-5407
HABS DLC/PP-1992:PA-3
1ph/21pg/1pc L

Baker,Soloman,House (Canal Towns,Alexandria)
Shelton Ave.
HABS PA-5404
HABS DLC/PP-1992:PA-3
1ph/4pg/1pc L

Cameron,James,House (Canal Towns,Alexandria)
Main St. (at western borough boundary)
HABS PA-5394
HABS DLC/PP-1992:PA-3
3ph/5pg/1pc L

Canal Towns
See also:Canal Towns,Indiana Co.,Saltsburg
HABS PA-5666
HABS DLC/PP-1992:PA-3
22pg L

Canal Towns; see Alexandria,Town of

Canal Towns,Alexandria; see Alexandria High School

Canal Towns,Alexandria; see Alexandria Memorial Public Library

Canal Towns,Alexandria; see Alexandria Presbyterian Church

Canal Towns,Alexandria; see Baker,Soloman,House

Canal Towns,Alexandria; see Cameron,James,House

Canal Towns,Alexandria; see Charlton,Dr. James,House

Canal Towns,Alexandria; see Connor,Francis,House

Canal Towns,Alexandria; see Cresswell,John,House

Canal Towns,Alexandria; see Cross,Benjamin,House

Canal Towns,Alexandria; see German Reformed Church

Canal Towns,Alexandria; see Grafius,Israel,House

Canal Towns,Alexandria; see Houtz,Dr. Daniel,House

Canal Towns,Alexandria; see Houtz,Dr. Daniel,Office

Canal Towns,Alexandria; see McManus,Patrick,House

Canal Towns,Alexandria; see Neff,Benjamin,House

Canal Towns,Alexandria; see Pennsylvania Canal Lockkeeper's House

Canal Towns,Alexandria; see Pennsylvania Railroad Station

Canal Towns,Alexandria; see Porter,John,House

Canal Towns,Alexandria; see Stewart,Thomas,House

Canal Towns,Alexandria; see Stitt,Alexander,House

Canal Towns,Alexandria; see Thompson Carriage House

Canal Towns,Alexandria; see Walker,Evander P.,Store

Canal Towns,Alexandria; see Willibrand,Henry,Brewery

Charlton,Dr. James,House (Odd Fellows Hall; Canal Towns,Alexandria)
Main St. & Bridge St.
HABS PA-5398
HABS DLC/PP-1992:PA-3
5ph/5pg/1pc L

Christ Reformed Church; see German Reformed Church

Connor,Francis,House (Canal Towns,Alexandria)
Shelton Ave.
HABS PA-5403
HABS DLC/PP-1992:PA-3
4ph/5pg/1pc L

Cresswell,John,House (Canal Towns,Alexandria)
Main St.
HABS PA-5400
HABS DLC/PP-1992:PA-3
5ph/5pg/1pc L

Cross,Benjamin,House (Canal Towns,Alexandria)
Main St.
HABS PA-5395
HABS DLC/PP-1992:PA-3
3ph/5pg/1pc L

Dorfgrange Farm,Barn (Harstlog Farm,Barn)
HABS PA-5926-B
HABS DLC/PP-1993:PA-1
1ph/1pg/1pc L

Dorfgrange Farm,House (Hartslog Farm,House)
HABS PA-5926-A
HABS DLC/PP-1993:PA-1
1ph/1pg/1pc L

German Reformed Church (Christ Reformed Church; Canal Towns,Alexandria)
Main St. & Church St.
HABS PA-5412
HABS DLC/PP-1992:PA-3
6ph/5pg/1pc L

Grafius,Israel,House (Canal Towns,Alexandria)
215 Main St.
HABS PA-5399
HABS DLC/PP-1992:PA-3
3ph/6pg/1pc L

Harstlog Farm,Barn; see Dorfgrange Farm,Barn

Hartslog Farm,House; see Dorfgrange Farm,House

Houtz,Dr. Daniel,House (Canal Towns,Alexandria)
Main St.
HABS PA-5401
HABS DLC/PP-1992:PA-3
5ph/6pg/1pc L

Houtz,Dr. Daniel,Office (Canal Towns,Alexandria)
Main St.
HABS PA-5402
HABS DLC/PP-1992:PA-3
1ph/4pg/1pc L

Kilmarnock Hall Carriage House; see Thompson Carriage House

310 Main Street (House)
HABS PA-5951
HABS DLC/PP-1993:PA-1
1ph/1pc L

318 Main Street (House)
HABS PA-5952
HABS DLC/PP-1993:PA-1
1ph/1pc L

405 Main Street (House)
HABS PA-5953
HABS DLC/PP-1993:PA-1
2ph/1pc L

McManus,Patrick,House (Canal Towns,Alexandria)
710 Main St.
HABS PA-5393
HABS DLC/PP-1992:PA-3
2ph/5pg/1pc L

Memorial Free Library; see Alexandria Memorial Public Library

Neff,Benjamin,House (Canal Towns,Alexandria)
Second St.
HABS PA-5668
HABS DLC/PP-1992:PA-3
2ph/1pc L

Odd Fellows Hall; see Charlton,Dr. James,House

Pennsylvania Canal Lockkeeper's House (Canal Towns,Alexandria)
Hartslog St. & Shelton Ave.
HABS PA-5406
HABS DLC/PP-1992:PA-3
1ph/5pg/1pc L

Pennsylvania Railroad Station (Canal Towns,Alexandria)
Shelton Ave.
HABS PA-5415
HABS DLC/PP-1992:PA-3
1ph/1pg/1pc L

Porter,John,House (Canal Towns,Alexandria)
Brisge & Main Sts.
HABS PA-5397
HABS DLC/PP-1992:PA-3
2ph/5pg/1pc L

Shelter Inn-Canal Inn; see Stewart,Thomas,House

Stewart,Thomas,House (Shelter Inn-Canal Inn; Canal Towns,Alexandria)
Shelton Ave.
HABS PA-5408
HABS DLC/PP-1992:PA-3
2ph/6pg/1pc L

Stitt,Alexander,House (Canal Towns,Alexandria)
Main St.
HABS PA-5396
HABS DLC/PP-1992:PA-3
5pg L

Thompson Carriage House (Kilmarnock Hall Carriage House; Canal Towns,Alexandria)
Canal Rd.
HABS PA-5405
HABS DLC/PP-1992:PA-3
2ph/2pg/1pc L

Walker,Evander P.,Store (Canal Towns,Alexandria)
Main St.
HABS PA-5410
HABS DLC/PP-1992:PA-3
2ph/5pg/1pc L

Willibrand,Henry,Brewery (Canal Towns,Alexandria)
700 Block,Main St.
HABS PA-5409
HABS DLC/PP-1992:PA-3
1ph/6pg/1pc L

FRANKLINVILLE VIC.

Colerain Forge House
State Rt. 45 Vic. (Franklin Twp.)
HABS PA-615
HABS PA,31-FRNK.V,1-
7dr L

Huntingdon Furnace
NW. of Twnshp. Rd. 31106 & St. Rt. 45 intersection
HAER PA-243
HAER DLC/PP-1993:PA-2
2ph/3pg/1pc L

Huntingdon Furnace,Grist Mill
NW. of Twnshp. Rd. 31106 & St. Rt. 45 intersection
HAER PA-243-A
HAER DLC/PP-1993:PA-2
14ph/2pc L

Huntingdon Furnace,Ironmaster's Mansion
NW. of Twnshp. Rd. 31106 & St. Rt. 45 intersection
HAER PA-243-B
HAER DLC/PP-1993:PA-2
2ph/1pc L

Huntingdon Furnace,Office
NW. of Twnshp. Rd. 31106 & St. Rt. 45 intersection
HAER PA-243-C
HAER DLC/PP-1993:PA-2
1ph/1pc L

Huntingdon Furnace,Stack
NW. of Twnshp. Rd. 31106 & St. Rt. 45 intersection
HAER PA-243-E
HAER DLC/PP-1993:PA-2
4ph/1pc L

Huntingdon Furnace,Store
NW. of Twnshp. Rd. 31106 & St. Rt. 45 intersection
HAER PA-243-D
HAER DLC/PP-1993:PA-2
1ph/1pc L

HUNTINGDON

Blair,J.C.,Co. Complex
Bounded by Sixth,Penn,Seventh & Allegheny Sts.
HAER PA-241
HAER DLC/PP-1993:PA-2
3pg L

Blair,J.C.,Co. Complex,Building A
Sixth & Penn St.
HAER PA-241-A
HAER DLC/PP-1993:PA-2
3ph/1pg/1pc L

Blair,J.C.,Co. Complex,Building B
Sixth & Allegheny Sts.
HAER PA-241-B
HAER DCL/PP-1993:PA-2
1ph/1pg/1pc L

Blair,J.C.,Co. Complex,Building E
Penn & Seventh Sts.
HAER PA-241-C
HAER DCL/PP-1993:PA-2
1ph/1pg/1pc L

Hunt Tower (Pennsylvania Railroad)
Fifth and Alleghny Streets
HAER PA-245
HAER DLC/PP-1993:PA-2
1ph/2pg/1pc L

Huntingdon Station (Pennsylvania Railroad)
Fourth and Allegheny Streets
HAER PA-244
HAER DLC/PP-1993:PA-2
7ph/3pg/1pc L

Pennslvania Railroad; see Stone Creek Bridge II

Pennsylvania Railroad; see Hunt Tower

Pennsylvania Railroad; see Huntingdon Station

Pennsylvania Railroad; see Stone Creek Bridge I

Stone Creek Bridge I (Pennsylvania Railroad)
South of Penn St. between First and Second Sts.
HAER PA-246
HAER DLC/PP-1993:PA-2
1ph/2pg/1pc L

Stone Creek Bridge II (Pennslvania Railroad)
S. of Penn St. between First and Second Sts.
HAER PA-247
HAER DLC/PP-1993:PA-2
2ph/2pg/1pc L

HUNTINGDON VIC.

Corbin Bridge
SE on road to Raystown Dam
HAER PA-248
HAER DCL/PP-1993:PA-2
2ph/2pg/1pc L

MCALEVY'S FORT VIC.

Greenwood Furnace,Blacksmith Shop
W. of SR305,on McAlevy's Fort vic.
HAER PA-287-D
H

Greenwood Furnace,Bookkeeper's House
E. of McAlevy's Fort on SR305
HAER PA-287-F
H

Greenwood Furnace,Ironmaster's Mansion
E. of McAlevy's Fort on SR305
HAER PA-287-C
H

Greenwood Furnace,Stack No. 1
E. of McAlevy's Fort on SR305
HAER PA-287-A
H

Greenwood Furnace,Stack No. 2
E. of McAlevy's Fort on SR305
HAER PA-287-B
H

McAlevy's Fort
PA Rts. 26 & 305
HABS PA-5382
HABS 1991(HABS):1
1dr/fr L

McAlevy's Fort,General Store
PA Rts. 26 & 305
HABS PA-5382-A
HABS 1991(HABS):1
2dr/fr L

McBurney's Bakeoven
PA Rts. 26 & 305
HABS PA-5382-C
HABS 1991(HABS):1
1dr/fr L

McBurney's Manor House
PA Rts. 26 & 305
HABS PA-5382-B
HABS 1991(HABS):1
5dr/fr L

MCALEVYS FORT VIC.

Greenwood Furnace,Nursery Buildings
SR305
HAER PA-287-H
2ph/1pc H

MOUNT UNION

General Refarctories Co.,Superintendent's House
Market St.
HABS PA-6005
1ph/1pc H

General Refractories Co.,Office
Market St.
HABS PA-6006
1ph/1pc H

Giacobello,T.A.,Foreign Supplies Store
Shirley St.
HABS PA-5992
2ph/1pc H

Harbison Walker Refractory Co.,Rot. Dry. & Stor. S
W. end of Shirley St.
HAER PA-242-E
HAER DLC/PP-1993:PA-2
2ph/1pc L

Harbison-Walker Refrac. Co.,Molding Room
W. end of Shirley St.
HAER PA-242-C
HAER DLC/PP-1993:PA-2
1ph/1pc L

Harbison-Walker Refrac. Co.,Packing Shed
W. end of Shirley St.
HAER PA-242-D
HAER DLC/PP-1993:PA-2
1ph/1pc L

Harbison-Walker Refractories Co.,Manager's House
213 Shirley St.
HABS PA-6004
1ph/1pc H

Harbison-Walker Refractories Company
W. end of Shirley St.
HAER PA-242
HAER DLC/PP-1993:PA-2
5ph/4pg/1pc L

Harbison-Walker Refractory Co.,Kiln
W. end of Shirley St.
HAER PA-242-B
HAER DLC/PP-1993:PA-2
1ph/1pc L

Mount Union,Town of (Refractories Company Towns)
HABS PA-5974
H

Mt. Hope Baptist Church
Chestnut & Division Sts.
HABS PA-5988
1ph/1pc H

Refractories Company Towns
HABS PA-5973
H

Refractories Company Towns; see Mount Union,Town of

Sharrar,John,House
HABS PA-5993
1ph/1pc H

SS. Peter & Paul Orthodox Church
N. Jefferson & Sherman Sts.
HABS PA-5987
1ph/1pc H

U.S. Post Office
HABS PA-5989
3ph/1pc H

ORBISONIA VIC.

East Broadtop Railroad
HAER PA-127
150ph H

PENNA. FURNACE

Lyons,John,House (Mansion House)
Penna. Furnace Rd. (Franklin Twp.)
HABS PA-611
HABS PA,31-PENFN,1-
9dr L

Mansion House; see Lyons,John,House

Pennsylvania Furnace
W. of SR45,S. of County line
HAER PA-286
H

Pennsylvania Furnace,Ironmaster's Mansion
W. of SR45,S. of Centre County line
HAER PA-286-A
H

Pennsylvania Furnace,Ironmaster's Privy
W. of SR45,S. of Centre County line
HAER PA-286-B
H

Pennsylvania Furnace,Worker House
W. od SR45,S. of Centre County line
HAER PA-286-C
H

ROBERTSDALE

Carney,J.A.,House
13-15 S. Main St.
HABS PA-5552
HABS DLC/PP-1993:PA-2
1ph/1pc L

29-31 Cliff Street (House)
HABS PA-5548
HABS DLC/PP-1993:PA-2
1ph/1pc L

13-15 East Street (House)
HABS PA-5549
HABS DLC/PP-1993:PA-2
1ph/1pc L

Engineer's House
9-11 Lincoln St.
HABS PA-5560
HABS DLC/PP-1993:PA-2
2ph/1pc L

21-23 Lincoln Street (House)
HABS PA-5562
HABS DLC/PP-1993:PA-2
1ph/1pc L

McClain,Jesse O.,Store
Lincoln St.
HABS PA-5561
HABS DLC/PP-1993:PA-2
2ph/1pg/1pc L

Paymaster's House
9-11 S. Main St.
HABS PA-5551
HABS DLC/PP-1993:PA-2
1ph/1pc L

Reality Theater
S. Main St. opposite Rte. 913
HABS PA-5557
HABS DLC/PP-1993:PA-2
1ph/1pg/1pc L

Robertsdale East Broad Top Railroad Depot
Main St.
HABS PA-5556
HABS DLC/PP-1993:PA-2
1ph/1pg/1pc L

Robertsdale Hotel (Rockhill Iron & Coal Company Hotel)
14 S. Main St.
HABS PA-5563
HABS DLC/PP-1993:PA-2
1ph/1pg/1pc L

Robertsdale Methodist Church Parsonage
15 Lincoln St.
HABS PA-5559
HABS DLC/PP-1993:PA-2
1ph/1pg/1pc L

Robertsdale Post Office; see Rockhill Iron & Coal Company Office

Robertsdale,Town of (Rockhill Iron & Coal Comany Towns)
HABS PA-5484
HABS DLC/PP-1993:PA-2
9ph/1pc L

Rockhill Iron & Coal Comany Towns; see Robertsdale,Town of

Rockhill Iron & Coal Company Hotel; see Robertsdale Hotel

Rockhill Iron & Coal Company Office (Robertsdale Post Office)
Main St.
HABS PA-5555
HABS DLC/PP-1993:PA-2
2ph/1pg/1pc L

Rockhill Iron & Coal Company Store
68 N. Main St.
HABS PA-5554
HABS DLC/PP-1993:PA-2
2ph/1pg/1pc L

Rockhill Iron & Coal Company Towns (Towns of Roberstdale & Woodvale)
HABS PA-5553
HABS DLC/PP-1993:PA-2
45pg L

103-05 South Main Street (House)
HABS PA-5565
HABS DLC/PP-1993:PA-2
1ph/1pc L

107-09 South Main Street (House)
HABS PA-5566
HABS DLC/PP-1993:PA-2
1ph/1pc L

56-58 South Main Street (House)
HABS PA-5564
HABS DLC/PP-1993:PA-2
1ph/1pc L

22 Spring Street (House)
HABS PA-5558
HABS DLC/PP-1993:PA-2
1ph/1pc L

Superintendent's House
9 Church St.
HABS PA-5550
HABS DLC/PP-1993:PA-2
1ph/1pc L

Towns of Roberstdale & Woodvale; see Rockhill Iron & Coal Company Towns

WOODVALE

19-21 Broad Street (House)
HABS PA-5578
HABS DLC/PP-1993:PA-2
1ph/1pc L

58-60 Broad Street (House)
HABS PA-5581
HABS DLC/PP-1993:PA-2
2ph/1pc L

2-4 Elm Street (House)
HABS PA-5568
HABS DLC/PP-1993:PA-2
2ph/1pc L

13 Fulton Street (House)
HABS PA-5579
HABS DLC/PP-1993:PA-2
1ph/1pc L

17 Fulton Street (House)
HABS PA-5580
HABS DLC/PP-1993:PA-2
1ph/1pc L

21-23 Main Street (House)
HABS PA-5577
HABS DLC/PP-1993:PA-2
1ph/1pc L

2 North Street (House)
HABS PA-5574
HABS DLC/PP-1993:PA-2
2ph/1pc L

5 North Street (House)
HABS PA-5576
HABS DLC/PP-1993:PA-2
1ph/1pc L

11-12 Pine Street (House)
HABS PA-5572
HABS DLC/PP-1993:PA-2
2ph/1pc L

9-10 Pine Street (House)
HABS PA-5571
HABS DLC/PP-1993:PA-2
2ph/1pc L

Rockhill Iron & Coal Comp.,Substation & Generator
HABS PA-5567-C
HABS DLC/PP-1993:PA-2
1ph/1pc L

Rockhill Iron & Coal Company Town; see Woodvale,Town of

Rockhill Iron & Coal Company Towns (Towns of Robertsdale and Woodvale)
See documentation under Huntingdon Co.,Robertsdale
HABS PA-5553
HABS DLC/PP-1993:PA-2
45pg L

Rockhill Iron & Coal Company,Boiler House
HABS PA-5567-A
HABS DLC/PP-1993:PA-2
2ph/1pc L

Rockhill Iron & Coal Company,Machine Shop
HABS PA-5567-B
HABS DLC/PP-1993:PA-2
2ph/1pc L

Rockhill Iron & Coal Company,Mule Barn
HABS PA-5567-E
HABS DLC/PP-1993:PA-2
2ph/1pc L

Rockhill Iron & Coal Company,Storage Building
HABS PA-5567-D
HABS DLC/PP-1993:PA-2
1ph/1pc L

St. Michael's Greek Orthodox Church
High St.
HABS PA-5570
HABS DLC/PP-1993:PA-2
3ph/1pg/1pc L

St. Michael's Greek Orthodox Social Hall
High St.
HABS PA-5569
HABS DLC/PP-1993:PA-2
1ph/1pg/1pc L

Towns of Robertsdale and Woodvale; see Rockhill Iron & Coal Company Towns

Woodvale Methodist Church
Huntingdon Square
HABS PA-5573
HABS DLC/PP-1993:PA-2
1ph/1pg/1pc L

Woodvale Post Office
5-7 Main St.
HABS PA-5575
HABS DLC/PP-1993:PA-2
1ph/1pg/1pc L

Woodvale,Town of (Rockhill Iron & Coal Company Town)
HABS PA-5485
HABS DLC/PP-1993:PA-2
3ph/1pc L

INDIANA COUNTY

ARMAGH VIC.

Buena Vista Furnace
W. of St. Hwy. 56,north bank of Blacklick Creek
HAER PA-265
HAER DLC/PP-1993:PA-3
4ph/2pg/1pc L

BLAIRSVILLE VIC.

East Tunnel Viaduct (Pennsylvania Railroad)
Spanning Conemaugh River,S. of Conemaugh Dam
HAER PA-267
HAER DLC/PP-1993:PA-3
2ph/2pg/1pc L

Pennsylvania Railroad; see East Tunnel Viaduct

ERNEST

Buffalo,Rochester & Pittsburgh Railway; see Ernest Mines Railroad Bridge

Ernest Mines Railroad Bridge (Buffalo,Rochester & Pittsburgh Railway)
Spanning McKee Run, at Ernest Mines Site
HAER PA-262
2ph/2pg/1pc H

GOODVILLE VIC.

Buffalo,Rochester & Pittsburgh Railway; see Mahoning Creek Trestle

Mahoning Creek Trestle (Buffalo,Rochester & Pittsburgh Railway)
Spanning Mahoning Creek, 1 mile W. of Goodville
HAER PA-266
HAER DLC/PP-1993:PA-3
4ph/2pg/1pc L

INDIANA

Buffalo,Rochester & Pittsburgh Railroad,Depot
Philadelphia St.
HAER PA-274-A
HAER DLC/PP-1993:PA-3
2ph/1pc L

LUCERNE

34 Eighth Street (House)
34 Eighth Street
HABS PA-5962
HABS DLC/PP-1993:PA-3
1ph/1pc L

Lucerne,Town of (Lucernmines,Town of; Rochester,Pittsburgh Coal & Iron Co.)
E. of U.S. Rt. 119,adjacent to Yellow Creek
HAER PA-263
HAER DLC/PP-1993:PA-3
3ph/2pg/1pc L

Lucernmines,Town of; see Lucerne,Town of

172 Ninth Street (House)
172 Ninth Street
HABS PA-5961
HABS DLC/PP-1993:PA-3
1ph/1pc L

Rochester,Pittsburgh Coal & Iron Co.; see Lucerne,Town of

LUCERNE VIC.

Lucernemines Coke Works,Coal Tipple (Rochester & Pittsburgh Coal & Iron Company)
.5 miles E. of Lucerne
HAER PA-264-C
HAER DLC/PP-1993:PA-3
1ph/1pg/1pc L

Lucernemines Coke Works,Coke Ovens (Rochester & Pittsburgh Coal & Iron Company)
.5 ml. E. of Lucerne,adjacent
HAER PA-264-A
HAER DLC/PP-1993:PA-3
4ph/2pg/1pc L

Lucernemines Coke Works,Larry Car Tipple (Rochester & Pittsburgh Coal & Iron Company)
.5 miles E. of Lucerne
HAER PA-264-B
HAER DLC/PP-1993:PA-3
2ph/1pg/1pc L

Lucernmines Coke Works (Rochester & Pittsburgh Coal & Iron Company)
.2 miles East of Lucerne
HAER PA-264
HAER DLC/PP-1993:PA-3
2ph/2pg/1pc L

Rochester & Pittsburgh Coal & Iron Company; see Lucernemines Coke Works,Coal Tipple

Rochester & Pittsburgh Coal & Iron Company; see Lucernemines Coke Works,Coke Ovens

Rochester & Pittsburgh Coal & Iron Company; see Lucernemines Coke Works,Larry Car Tipple

Rochester & Pittsburgh Coal & Iron Company; see Lucernmines Coke Works

ROBINSON

Refractories Company Towns; see Robinson,Town of

Robinson,Town of (Refractories Company Towns)
HABS PA-5975
H

SALTSBURG

Andre,Andrew,House (Canal Towns,Saltsburg)
821 High St.
HABS PA-5423
3ph/6pg/1pc L

Canal Towns
See Also: Canal Towns,Huntingdon Co.,Alexandria
HABS PA-5666
HABS DLC/PP-1992:PA-3
22pg L

Canal Towns; see Saltsburg,Town of

Canal Towns,Saltsburg; see Andre,Andrew,House

Canal Towns,Saltsburg; see First National Bank of Saltsburg

Canal Towns,Saltsburg; see Martin,John,House

Canal Towns,Saltsburg; see McFarland,Dr. John,House

Canal Towns,Saltsburg; see McGlaughlin,James,House

Canal Towns,Saltsburg; see McIlwaine,William,House

Canal Towns,Saltsburg; see Moore,Samuel S.,House & Store

Canal Towns,Saltsburg; see Murray,Dr. Thomas,House

Canal Towns,Saltsburg; see Pennsylvania Railroad Station

Canal Towns,Saltsburg; see 105 Point Street (House)

Canal Towns,Saltsburg; see Robinson,James,House

Canal Towns,Saltsburg; see Robinson,Thomas & John,House

Canal Towns,Saltsburg; see Robinson,William C.,House

Canal Towns,Saltsburg; see Rombach,Mathias,House

Canal Towns,Saltsburg; see 706-08 Salt Street (House)

Canal Towns,Saltsburg; see Saltsburg Academy

Canal Towns,Saltsburg; see Shupe,P. D.,Hardware Store

Canal Towns,Saltsburg; see Sons of Zebedee Evangelical Lutheran Church

Canal Towns,Saltsburg; see St. Matthew's Catholic Church

Canal Towns,Saltsburg; see Stewart,William,House

Canal Towns,Saltsburg; see Taylor,Robert J.,House

Canal Towns,Saltsburg; see United Presbyterian Church

Canal Towns,Saltsburg; see Wray House

First National Bank of Saltsburg (Lions Activity Center; Canal Towns,Saltsburg)
214 Point St.
HABS PA-5431
HABS DLC/PP-1992:PA-3
3ph/6pg/1pc L

Lions Activity Center; see First National Bank of Saltsburg

Martin,John,House (Canal Towns,Saltsburg)
502 High St.
HABS PA-5422
HABS DLC/PP-1992:PA-3
7ph/6pg/1pc L

Masonic Hall-White Church; see United Presbyterian Church

McFarland,Dr. John,House (Canal Towns,Saltsburg)
216 Washington St.
HABS PA-5425
HABS DLC/PP-1992:PA-3
1ph/5pg/1pc L

McGlaughlin,James,House (Canal Towns,Saltsburg)
803 Water St.
HABS PA-5429
HABS DLC/PP-1992:PA-3
2ph/7pg/1pc L

McIlwaine,William,House (Canal Towns,Saltsburg)
241 Washington St.
HABS PA-5424
HABS DLC/PP-1992:PA-3
1ph/6pg/1pc L

Memorial Institute; see Saltsburg Academy

Moore,Samuel S.,House & Store (Canal Towns,Saltsburg)
222 Point St.
HABS PA-5421
HABS DLC/PP-1992:PA-3
2ph/6pg/1pc L

Murray,Dr. Thomas,House (Canal Towns,Saltsburg)
101 Point St.
HABS PA-5417
HABS DLC/PP-1922:PA-3
2ph/6pg/1pc L

Pennsylvania Railroad Station (Canal Towns,Saltsburg)
Point St.
HABS PA-5437
HABS DLC/PP-1992:PA-3
2ph/6pg/1pc L

105 Point Street (House) (Stone House Museum; Canal Towns,Saltsburg)
HABS PA-5419
HABS DLC/PP-1992:PA-3
3ph/6pg/1pc L

Robinson,James,House (Canal Towns,Saltsburg)
425 Salt St.
HABS PA-5427
HABS DLC/PP-1992:PA-3
2ph/6pg/1pc L

Robinson,Thomas & John,House (Canal Towns,Saltsburg)
711 Water St.
HABS PA-5428
HABS DLC/PP-1992:PA-3
3ph/6pg/1pc L

Robinson,William C.,House (Canal Towns,Saltsburg)
103 Point St.
HABS PA-5418
HABS DLC/PP-1992:PA-3
1ph/6pg/1pc L

Rombach,Mathias,House (Saltsburg General Hospital; Canal Towns,Saltsburg)
321 Basin St.
HABS PA-5430
HABS DLC/PP-1992:PA-3
3ph/6pg/1pc L

706-08 Salt Street (House) (Canal Towns,Saltsburg)
HABS PA-5665
HABS DLC/PP-1992:PA-3
3ph/1pc L

Saltsburg Academy (Memorial Institute; Canal Towns,Saltsburg)
High & Point Sts.
HABS PA-5433
3ph/6pg/1pc L

Saltsburg General Hospital; see Rombach,Mathias,House

Saltsburg,Town of (Canal Towns)
HABS PA-5438
HABS DLC/PP-1992:PA-3
8ph/30pg/1pc L

Shupe,P. D.,Hardware Store (Canal Towns,Saltsburg)
202 Point St.
HABS PA-5432
HABS DLC/PP-1992:PA-3
9ph/7pg/1pc L

Sons of Zebedee Evangelical Lutheran Church (Canal Towns,Saltsburg)
422 Salt St.
HABS PA-5435
HABS DLC/PP-1992:PA-3
6ph/6pg/1pc L

St. Matthew's Catholic Church (Canal Towns,Saltsburg)
Cathedral St.
HABS PA-5436
HABS DLC/PP-1992:PA-3
4ph/6pg/1pc L

Stewart,William,House (Canal Towns,Saltsburg)
232 Point St.
HABS PA-5416
18pg/fr L

Documentation: **ct** color transparencies **dr** measured drawings **fr** field records
pc photograph captions **pg** pages of text **ph** photographs

Stone House Museum; see 105 Point Street (House)

Taylor,Robert J.,House (Canal Towns,Saltsburg)
211 Point St.
HABS PA-5420
HABS DLC/PP-1992:PA-3
5ph/6pg/1pc L

United Presbyterian Church (Masonic Hall-White Church; Canal Towns,Saltsburg)
High St. & Ash Alley
HABS PA-5434
1ph/6pg/1pc L

Wray House (Canal Towns,Saltsburg)
500 Market St.
HABS PA-5426
HABS DLC/PP-1992:PA-3
4ph/6pg/1pc L

TUNNELTON VIC.

Pennsylvania Railroad; see West Tunnel Viaduct

West Tunnel Viaduct (Pennsylvania Railroad)
Spanning Conemaugh Riv.,25 ml. S. of Conemaugh Dam
HAER PA-268
HAER DLC/PP-1993:PA-3
3ph/2pg/1pc L

JEFFERSON COUNTY

BROCKWAY

Ross Leffler Training School Complex
Synder Twp.
HABS PA-5361
HABS PA,33-BROWA.V,1-
2ph/2pg/1pc L

BROCKWAY VIC.

Leffler,Ross,Training School Complex,Classroom Bld
Synder Twp.
HABS PA-5361-B
HABS PA,33-BROWA.V,1B-
7ph/8pg/1pc L

Leffler,Ross,Training School Complex,Main Bldg.
Synder Twp.
HABS PA-5361-A
HABS PA,33-BROWA.V,1A-
13ph/9pg/1pc L

LACKAWANNA COUNTY

CARBONDALE

Miners & Mechanics Bank Building
13 N. Main St.
HABS PA-5153
HABS PA,35-CARB,1-
4dr/11ph/4pg/1pc/fr L

CLARKS GREEN

Clark,William,House (Matthews House)
Abington Rd.
HABS PA-231
HABS PA,35-CLAR,1-
16dr/8ph/4pg L

Matthews House; see Clark,William,House

Stone,Lemuel,House
HABS PA-220
HABS PA,35-WAV,2-
8dr/3ph/3pg L

SCRANTON

D L & W RR,Scranton Yards,Bridge 60 (Delaware,Lackawanna & Western Railroad)
Spanning Lackawanna River,Seventh Ave. & Bridge St
HAER PA-132-A
HAER DLC/PP-1992:PA-2
3dr/9ph/10pg/1pc L

D L & W RR,Scranton Yards,Cedar Avenue Bridge (Delaware,Lackawanna & Western Railroad)
Spanning Cedar Ave. at Railroad Alley
HAER PA-132-J
HAER DLC/PP-1992:PA-2
1dr/8ph/11pg/1pc L

D L & W RR,Scranton Yards,Coal Trestle
685 ft. S. of Bridge St. & Lackawanna Ave.
HAER PA-132-D
HAER DLC/PP-1992:PA-2
1dr/6ph/12pg/1pc L

D L & W RR,Scranton Yards,Gas House (Delaware,Lackawanna & Western Railroad)
100 Blk. of S. Wash. Ave.,Westside
HAER PA-132-G
HAER DLC/PP-1992:PA-2
3dr/10ph/18pg/1pc/fr L

D L & W RR,Scranton Yards,Mattes St. Signal Tower (Delaware,Lackawanna & Western Railroad)
80 ft. SW of Railroad Alley & Cedar Ave.
HAER PA-132-I
HAER DLC/PP-1992:PA-2
2dr/7ph/18pg/1pc L

D L & W RR,Scranton Yards,Oil House
650 ft. SE of Cliff & Mechanic Sts.
HAER PA-132-E
HAER DLC/PP-1992:PA-2
2dr/7ph/9pg/1pc L

D L & W RR,Scranton Yards,Roundhouse (Delaware,Lackawanna & Western Railroad)
HAER PA-132-K
HAER DLC/PP-1992:PA-2
4ph/1pc L

D L & W RR,Scranton Yards,Scrap Platform (Delaware,Lackawanna & Western Railroad)
350 ft. S. of S. Washington Ave. & River St.
HAER PA-132-F
HAER DLC/PP-1992:PA-2
1dr/7ph/12pg/1pc/fr L

D L & W RR,Scranton Yards,Switch Shanty (Delaware,Lackawanna & Western Railroad)
350 ft. SE of Bridge No. 60
HAER PA-132-B
HAER DLC/PP-1992:PA-2
1dr/1ph/10pg/1pc L

D L & W RR,Scranton Yards,Track Scales (Delaware,Lackawanna & Western Railroad)
500 ft. SE of Bridge No. 60
HAER PA-132-C
HAER DLC/PP-1992:PA-2
1dr/5ph/15pg/1pc L

D L & W RR,Scranton Yards,Washington Avenue Bridge (Delaware,Lackawanna & Western Railroad)
Spanning Washington Ave. at Railroad Alley
HAER PA-132-H
HAER DLC/PP-1992:PA-2
1dr/6ph/11pg/1pc/fr L

Delaware,Lackawanna & Western Railroad; see D L & W RR,Scranton Yards,Bridge 60

Delaware,Lackawanna & Western Railroad; see D L & W RR,Scranton Yards,Cedar Avenue Bridge

Delaware,Lackawanna & Western Railroad; see D L & W RR,Scranton Yards,Gas House

Delaware,Lackawanna & Western Railroad; see D L & W RR,Scranton Yards,Mattes St. Signal Tower

Delaware,Lackawanna & Western Railroad; see D L & W RR,Scranton Yards,Roundhouse

Delaware,Lackawanna & Western Railroad; see D L & W RR,Scranton Yards,Scrap Platform

Delaware,Lackawanna & Western Railroad; see D L & W RR,Scranton Yards,Switch Shanty

Delaware,Lackawanna & Western Railroad; see D L & W RR,Scranton Yards,Track Scales

Delaware,Lackawanna & Western Railroad; see D L & W RR,Scranton Yards,Washington Avenue Bridge

Delaware,Lackawanna & Western RR:Scranton Yards
Lackawanna Ave.,Cedar Ave.,River St. & Seventh Ave
HAER PA-132
HAER DLC/PP-1992:PA-2
3dr/29ph/81pg/2pc L

Marvine Colliery
W. side Boulevard Ave.,b/w E. Parker St. & Rt. 380
HAER PA-183
10ph/23pg/3pc L

Marvine Colliery, Heavy Rail Scales Office
W. side Boulevard Ave.,b/w E. Parker St. & Rt. 380
HAER PA-183-B
5ph/4pg/2pc L

Marvine Colliery,Boiler House No. 2
W. side Boulevard Ave.,b/w E. Parker St. & Rt. 380
HAER PA-183-A
11ph/7pg/3pc L

Marvine Colliery,Breaker No. 2
W. side Boulevard Ave.,b/w E. Parker St. & Rt. 380
HAER PA-183-C
24ph/6pg/4pc L

Marvine Colliery,Dorr Thickener Plant No. 1
W. side Boulevard Ave.,b/w E. Parker St. & Rt. 380
HAER PA-183-D
5ph/4pg/2pc L

Marvine Colliery,Fan House No. 2
W. side Boulevard Ave.,b/w E. Parker St. & Rt. 380
HAER PA-183-G
2pg L

Marvine Colliery,Oil House
W. side Boulevard Ave.,b/w E. Parker St. & Rt. 380
HAER PA-183-E
6ph/4pg/2pc L

Marvine Colliery,Shed
W. side Boulevard Ave.,b/w E. Parker St. & Rt. 380
HAER PA-183-F
3ph/3pg/2pc L

Marvine Colliery,Washery Pump
W. side Boulevard Ave.,b/w E. Parker St. & Rt. 380
HAER PA-183-H
2pg L

Sanderson Avenue Bridge
Sanderson Ave. spanning Lackawanna River
HAER PA-173
HAER 1991(HAER):12
20ph/12pg/2pc L

Scranton Army Ammunition Plant
156 Cedar Ave.
HAER PA-76
HAER PA,35-SCRAN,3-
60pg/fr L

Silkman House
2006 N. Main Ave.
HABS PA-217
HABS PA,35-SCRAN,1-
12dr/3ph/3pg L

U. S. Post Office
N. Washington & Linden Sts.
HABS PA-1251
HABS PA,35-SCRAN,2-
1ph/1pc L

WAVERLY

Main Street School,One Room
HABS PA-214
HABS PA,35-WAV,1-
6dr/2ph/2pg L

LANCASTER COUNTY

???

Barns
HABS PA-5222
HABS PA,36- ,1-
1ph/1pc L

BIRD-IN-HAND VIC.

Barn
State Rt. 340
HABS PA-5212-B
HABS PA,36-BIRDI.V,1A-
3ph/1pc L

Grain Mill
State Rt. 340
HABS PA-5212-A
HABS PA,36-BIRDI.V,1B-
1ph/1pc L

BRICKERVILLE

Emanuel Evangelical Lutheran Church
HABS PA-364
HABS PA,36-BRICK,1-
1ph L

CHRISTIANA BOROUGH

Christiana Borough Bridge
Bridge St. at Pennsylvania RR
HAER PA-88
HAER PA,36-CHRIS,1-
1dr/47ph/22pg/2pc L

CHURCHTOWN VIC.

Barn
HABS PA-5221
HABS PA,36-CHUR.V,1A-
2ph/1pc L

COCALICO

Cook House,Outdoor Stone
HABS PA-155
HABS PA,36-COCAL,2-
1ph L

Cotton Mill,Old
HABS PA-156
HABS PA,36-COCAL,3-
2ph L

Farm Group & Mill Pond
HABS PA-154
HABS PA,36-COCAL,1-
2ph L

DRUMORE VIC.

Cider Press at Hesse's Mill
(Drumore Township)
HABS PA-367
HABS PA,36-DRUM.V,1A-
1dr L

EPHRATA

Buck,Adam R. ,Barn
Rt. 1
HABS PA-5210
HABS PA,36-EPH.V,2A-
4ph L

Cloisters,Bake House Oven
HABS PA-320-C
HABS PA,36-EPH,1D-
2dr/1ph L

Cloisters,Cabin Number 3
HABS PA-320-E
HABS PA,36-EPH,1G-
1dr L

Cloisters,Clockmaker's Cottage
HABS PA-320-F
HABS PA,36-EPH,1E-
5dr/2ph L

Cloisters,Graveyard
HABS PA-320-G
HABS PA,36-EPH,1M-
2ph L

Cloisters,House on Hill
HABS PA-320-H
HABS PA,36-EPH,1L-
2ph L

Cloisters,Mill
HABS PA-320-I
HABS PA,36-EPH,1K-
3ph L

Cloisters,The
HABS PA-320
HABS PA,36-EPH,1-
60dr/5pg/fr L

Cloisters,The Academy
HABS PA-320-A
HABS PA,36-EPH,1J-
2ph L

Cloisters,The Almonry
HABS PA-320-B
HABS PA,36-EPH,1C-
10dr/6ph L

Cloisters,The Bethania
HABS PA-320-D
HABS PA,36-EPH,1H-
7ph L

Cloisters,The Saal
HABS PA-320-J
HABS PA,36-EPH,1B-
37dr/50ph L

Documentation: **ct** color transparencies **dr** measured drawings **fr** field records
pc photograph captions **pg** pages of text **ph** photographs

Cloisters,The Saron
HABS PA-320-K
HABS PA,36-EPH,1A-
16dr/20ph L

Cloisters,Whitehaus & Summer Kitchen (Community Physicians House)
HABS PA-320-L
HABS PA,36-EPH,1F-
3dr/3ph L

Community Physicians House; see Cloisters,Whitehaus & Summer Kitchen

FARMERVILLE VIC.

Victorian Barn
Conestoga Creek at covered bridge
HABS PA-5209
HABS PA,36-FARM.V,1A-
2ph/1pc L

GAP VIC.

Barn
Rt. 572 vic.
HABS PA-5219
HABS PA,36-GAP.V,1A-
1ph/1pc L

HINKLETOWN

Red Barn,Old
HABS PA-157
HABS PA,36-HINK,1-
2ph L

HINKLETOWN VIC.

Barn
U. S. Rt. 322 on Conestoga Creek
HABS PA-5220
HABS PA,36-HINK.V,1A-
1ph L

IRONVILLE VIC.

Barn
County Rd.
HABS PA-5214-A
HABS PA,36-IRON.V,1A-
2ph L

Farmhouse
County Rd.
HABS PA-5214
HABS PA,36-IRON.V,1-
1ph L

LANCASTER

City Hall,Old (Heritage Center)
Penn Square
HABS PA-1343
HABS PA,36-LANC,2-
7ph/9pg L

Heritage Center; see City Hall,Old

125 Howard Avenue (House)
HABS PA-1355
HABS PA,36-LANC,4-
3ph/1pg/1pc L

Lancaster Municipal Building; see U. S. Post Office & Courthouse

Lutheran Church of the Holy Trinity
31 S. Duke St.
HABS PA-575
HABS PA,36-LANC,1-
17ph/1pg/1pc L

Montgomery,William,House
21 S. Queen St.
HABS PA-1061
HABS PA,36-LANC,5-
7ph/1pg/1pc L

Musser-Reigart House
323 W. King St.
HABS PA-373
HABS PA,36-LANC,6-
8ph/1pg/1pc L

Sehner-Ellicott House
123 N. Prince St.
HABS PA-372
HABS PA,36-LANC,7-
15dr/13ph/5pg/1pc L

Smith,Judge Charles,House
22 S. Queen St.
HABS PA-369
HABS PA,36-LANC.V,8-
5ph/1pg/1pc L

U. S. Post Office & Courthouse
(Lancaster Municipal Building)
120 N. Duke St.
HABS PA-370
HABS PA,36-LANC,3-
8ph/4pg L

LANCASTER VIC.

Barn
Rt. 280
HABS PA-5213
HABS PA,36-LANC.V,5A-
1ph/1pc L

Barn
U. S. Rt. 30 vic.
HABS PA-5227
HABS PA,36-LANC.V,4A-
1ph L

Landis,Christian & Fanny,Barn (1842)
U. S. Rt. 222
HABS PA-5223
HABS PA,36-LANC.V,3A-
2ph L

Landis,Henry,Barn
County Road
HABS PA-5224
HABS PA,36-LANC.V,2A-
3ph/1pc L

Long,Jacob E. ,Barn
County Road
HABS PA-5225
HABS PA,36-LANC.V,84-
3ph/1pc L

Miller,Jacob & Elizabeth,Barn (1804)
U. S. Rt. 30 vic.
HABS PA-5228
HABS PA,36-LANC.V,6A-
5ph L

Rock Ford
Rock Ford Rd. (West Lampeter Twp.)
HABS PA-368
HABS PA,36-LANC.V,1-
13dr/14ph/10pg/fr L

Rock Ford,Springhouse
Rock Ford Rd. (West Lampeter Twp.)
HABS PA-368-A
HABS PA,36-LANC.V,1A-
1dr/1pc L

Wheatland
1120 Marietta Ave.
HABS PA-1265
HABS PA,36-LANC.V,7-
19dr/1pc L

LANDISVILLE

Bachman-Landis-Kauffman House
Kauffman Rd. (East Hempfield Twp.)
HABS PA-1246
HABS PA,36-LAND,1-
5dr L

LITITZ

Schriner,John H. ,Barn (1827)
Rt. 3
HABS PA-5226
HABS PA,36-LIT,1A-
3ph/1pc L

LITITZ VIC.

Hollinger,C. H. ,Barn
County Rd.
HABS PA-5216
HABS PA,36-LIT.V,1A-
3ph/1pc L

MANHEIM VIC.

Barn,Pink
HABS PA-5215
HABS PA,36-MAN.V,1A-
1ph/1pc L

MAPLE GROVE VIC.

Stoneroads Mill Bridge
Spanning Little Conestoga Creek
HABS PA-321
HABS PA,36-MAP.V,1-
2dr L

MARIETTA VIC.

Johnson's Mill Bridge
(East Donegal-Rapho Township)
HABS PA-1173
HABS PA,36-CHICK,1-
7dr L

MECHANICSVILLE VIC.

Barn
State Rt. 23
HABS PA-5208
HABS PA,36-MECH.V,1A-
2ph/1pc L

PINETOWN

Leaman Rifle Works Bridge
Spanning Conestoga Creek
HABS PA-319
HABS PA,36-PINTO,1-
1dr L

SCOTTDALE

Scottdale Iron & Steel Works
Uptegraff Dr.
HAER PA-297
1ph/3pg/1pc H

STRASBURG VIC.

Barn
County Rd.
HABS PA-5218
HABS PA,36-STRAS.V,1A-
1ph/1pc L

Barn,1809
County Rd.
HABS PA-5217
HABS PA,36-STRAS.V,2A-
4ph/1pc L

SWARTZVILLE VIC.

Decorated Barn,circa 1910
U. S. Rt. 222
HABS PA-5211
HABS PA,36-SWAR.V,1A-
3ph/1pc L

WILLOW STREET VIC.

Herr,Hans,House
1851 Hans Herr Dr. ,West Lampeter Twp.
HABS PA-371
HABS PA,36-WILST.V,1-
3ph/1pg/1pc L

LEBANON COUNTY

KLEINFELTERSVILLE

Barn,Brick End
HABS PA-153
HABS PA,38-KLEIN,1-
1ph L

MILLBACH

Illig's Mill; see Miller House & Mill

Miller House & Mill (Mueller House; Illig's Mill)
Newmanstown-Klienfeltersville Rd.
HABS PA-151
HABS PA,38-MILB,1-
8ph/2pg L

Mueller House; see Miller House & Mill

NEWMANSTOWN VIC.

Fort Zeller; see Zeller,Heinrich,House

Zeller,Heinrich,House (Fort Zeller)
Mill Creek (Millcreek Twp.)
HABS PA-141
HABS PA,38-NEWM.V,1-
7dr/22ph/fr L

SCHAEFFERSTOWN

Stiegel House
E. side SR 419,N. of intersection of SR 419 &SR897
HABS PA-5341
HABS PA,38-SCHAF,1-
7dr/23ph/1pg/2pc/fr L

SHERIDAN

Brick Stone Barn
HABS PA-152
HABS PA,38-SHER,1-
1ph L

LEHIGH COUNTY

ALBURTIS VIC.

Barn,Decorated
HABS PA-5320
HABS PA,39-ALB.V,1A-
1ph/1pc L

Barn,Decorated Red
HABS PA-5319
HABS PA,39-ALB.V,2A-
1ph/1pc L

ALLENTOWN

Allentown Station; see Central Railroad of New Jersey,Allentown Station

520 Brush Street (House)
520 Brush St.
HABS PA-5439
HABS 1991(HABS):1
2pg/fr L

Central Railroad of New Jersey,Allentown Station (Allentown Station)
Race & Hamilton Sts.
HAER PA-150
HAER PA,39-ALLEN,4-
2ph/1pg/1pc L

Dam No. 7; see Hamilton Street Dam

Germania BreweryN (Neuweiler Brewery; Nuding-Neuweiler Brewing Company)
Front & Gordon Sts.
HAER PA-152
HAER PA,39-ALLEN,5-
6ph/1pg/1pc L

Hamilton Street Dam (Dam No. 7)
Lehigh River upstream of Hamilton St. Bridge
HAER PA-89
HAER PA,39-ALLEN,3A-
26ph/5pg/2pc L

Lehigh Canal,Lock 40
Lehigh Canal where River & Canal turn North
HAER PA-149
HAER PA,39-ALLEN,3B-
1ph/1pg/1pc L

Neuweiler Brewery; see Germania BreweryN

Newhorter,Thomas,House (Nunnemacher,Daniel,House)
Lehigh & Lawrence Sts.
HABS PA-1271
HABS PA,39-ALLEN,1-
2dr/1ph/4pg L

414 North Law Street (House)
414 N. Law St.
HABS PA-5440
HABS 1991(HABS):1
2pg/fr L

Nuding-Neuweiler Brewing Company; see Germania BreweryN

Nunnemacher,Daniel,House; see Newhorter,Thomas,House

Rialto Theater
943 Hamilton Mall
HABS PA-5340
HABS PA,39-ALLEN,2-
37ph/1pg/2pc/fr L

ALLENTOWN VIC.

Barn,Wood
HABS PA-5324
HABS PA,39-ALLEN.V,1A-
2ph/1pc L

Powder Valley Pottery; see Stahl Pottery

Stahl Pottery (Powder Valley Pottery)
Upper Milford Twp.
HAER PA-124
35pg H

BETHLEHEM

Ashbury Graphite Mill; see Pettinos Brothers Graphite Manufacturing Mill

Bethlehem Station; see Central Railroad of New Jersey,Bethlehem Station

Central Railroad of New Jersey,Bethlehem Station (Bethlehem Station)
Lehigh St.
HABS PA-1149
HAER PA-145
HABS/HAER PA,39-BETH,1-
6ph/1pg/2pc L

Hill-to-Hill Bridge
(See Northampton,Bethlehem
HAER PA-131
L

Documentation: **ct** color transparencies **dr** measured drawings **fr** field records
pc photograph captions **pg** pages of text **ph** photographs

Pettinos Brothers Graphite Manufacturing Mill (Ashbury Graphite Mill)
Sand Island,S. side of Lehigh Canala
HAER PA-147
HAER pa,39-BETH,2-
1ph/1pg/1pc L

Rossmaessler Mill; see Saquoit Silk Mill

Saquoit Silk Mill (Rossmaessler Mill)
Sand Island,S. bank of Lehigh Canal
HAER PA-148
HAER PA,39-BETH,3-
2ph/1pg/1pc L

CATASAUQUA

Combs House
N. Dauphin St. at Catasauqua Lake (Hanover Twp.)
HABS PA-5447
HABS PA,39-CATS,3-
2ph/1pg/1pc L

Lehigh Crane Iron Works (Thomas Iron Works)
Front St.
HAER PA-154
HAER PA,39-CATS,1-
3ph/1pg/1pc L

2 Race Street (House)
HABS PA-5448
HABS PA,39-CATS,2-
1ph/1pg/1pc L

Thomas Iron Works; see Lehigh Crane Iron Works

CENTER VALLEY

Barn,Decorated Red
State Rt. 309 vic.
HABS PA-5321
HABS PA,39-CENVA,1A-
2ph L

COPLAY

Coplay Cement Company
N. Main St.
HAER PA-156
HAER PA,39-COP,1-
1ph/1pg/1pc L

EAST TEXAS VIC.

Barn (1839)
HABS PA-5308
HABS PA,39-ETEX.V,1A-
2ph L

Barn (1853)
HABS PA-5307
HABS PA,39-ETEX.V,2A-
1ph L

Barn,Decorated (1857)
HABS PA-5309
HABS PA,39-ETEX.V,3A-
3ph L

EMMAUS

Tank Farm Road Bridge
Tank Farm Road Crossing Reading RR tracks
HAER PA-123
HAER 1991(HAER):12
7ph/1pg/1pc L

EMMAUS VIC.

Barn
HABS PA-5306
HABS PA,39-EMMA.V,1A-
1ph L

Barn,Decorated Red
State Rt. 29
HABS PA-5315
HABS PA,39-EMMA.V,2A-
1ph L

Dorfer,Abraham,Barn A
HABS PA-5316-A
HABS PA,39-EMMA.V,3A-
1ph L

Dorfer,Abraham,Barn B
HABS PA-5316-B
HABS PA,39-EMMA.V,3B-
1ph L

Wenner,Howard W. ,Barn A
State Rt. 29 vic.
HABS PA-5314-A
HABS PA,39-EMMA.V,4A-
2ph L

Wenner,Howard W. ,Barn B
State Rt. 29 vic.
HABS PA-5314-B
HABS PA,39-EMMA.V,4B-
1ph/1pc L

FOGELSVILLE VIC.

Barn
(Between Haase Mill & Steton School)
HABS PA-5323
HABS PA,39-FOGVI.V,1A-
3ph/1pc L

Barn,Decorated (circa 1845)
U.S. Rt. 22 (Interstate 78) vic.
HABS PA-5322
HABS PA,39-FOGVI.V,2A-
2ph/1pc L

LIMEPORT VIC.

Barn,Decorated Red
Btwn. Limeport & Steinberg
HABS PA-5317
HABS PA,39-LIM.V,1A-
1ph/1pc L

LYNNVILLE VIC.

Betz's Mill
Bausch Rd.
HAER PA-64
HAER PA,39-LYNVI.V,1-
9dr/fr L

LYON VALLEY

Barn,Red
(New Tripoli Vic.)
HABS PA-5325
HABS PA,39-LYVA,1A-
5ph/1pc L

MACUNGIE

Singmaster,John Adam,Barn
State Rt. 100
HABS PA-5303
HABS PA,39-MAC,1A-
4ph/1pc L

MACUNGIE VIC.

Barn
State Rt. 100 vic.
HABS PA-5305
HABS PA,39-MAC.V,1A-
2ph L

Barn A (1834)
HABS PA-5310-A
HABS PA,39-MAC.V,2A-
1ph L

Barn B
HABS PA-5310-B
HABS PA,39-MAC.V,2B-
3ph L

Barn,Decorated Red
State Rt. 100
HABS PA-5312
HABS PA,39-MAC.V,3A-
1ph L

Barn,Stone
State Rt. 100 vic.
HABS PA-5304
HABS PA,39-MAC.V,4-
2ph L

Farm Groups
HABS PA-5311
HABS PA,39-MAC.V,5-
1ph L

Roeder,S. & R. G. ,Barn
HABS PA-5313
HABS PA,39-MAC.V,6A-
2ph L

NEW SMITHFIELD

Barn,Decorated Red
U. S. Rt. 22 vic.
HABS PA-5302
HABS PA,39-NESMI,1A-
2ph L

SCHNECKSVILLE

House,Leader Head
HABS PA-5628
HABS 1991(HABS):1
1dr L

SHIMERVILLE VIC.

Barn,Decorated Red
HABS PA-5318
HABS PA,39-SHIM.V,1A-
1ph L

SLATINGTON

Barn
375 Main St. ,behind Kern's Mill
HAER PA-177
HAER PA,39-SLAT,1-
1ph/1pc L

Kern's Mill (Slatington Roller Mill)
375 Main St.
HAER PA-161
HAER PA,39-SLAT,2-
1ph/1pg/1pc L

Main Street (Houses)
HABS PA-5453
HABS PA,39-SLAT,3-
4ph/1pc L

Slatington Roller Mill; see Kern's Mill

WANAMAKERS

Ontelaunee Creek Bridge
Spanning Ontelaunee Creek
HAER PA-122
HAER 1991(HAER):12
6ph/2pg/1pc L

WHITEHALL

Whitehall Cement Company
Whitehall Twp.
HAER PA-157
HAER PA,39-WHITO,1-
1ph/1pc L

Whitehall Township,General Views (Houses)
HABS PA-5450
HABS PA,39-WHITO,2-
3ph/1pc L

LUZERNE COUNTY

ASHLEY

Huber Coal Breaker,Breaker
101 S. Main St.
HAER PA-204-A
H

Huber Coal Breaker,Foothouse
101 S. Main St.
HAER PA-204-C
H

Huber Coal Breaker,Power Plant
101 S. Main St.
HAER PA-204-B
H

EXETER

Coray,Elisha Atherton,House
HABS PA-27
HABS PA,40-EXT,1-
6dr/3ph/1pg L

Coray,Elisha Atherton,Mill
Sutton's Creek
HABS PA-216
HABS PA,40-EXT.V,1-
11dr/6ph/4pg L

FORTY FORT BOR.

Culver,William,House
278 River St.
HABS PA-240
HABS PA,40-FOFO,7-
8dr/3ph/3pg L

Denison House
Wyoming Ave.
HABS PA-25
HABS PA,40-FOFO,3-
6dr/5ph/2pg L

Elm Lawn; see Shoemaker House

Forty Fort Meetinghouse
River St.
HABS PA-21
HABS PA,40-FOFO,1-
8dr/4ph/2pg L

Perkins House
HABS PA-232
HABS PA,40-FOFO,8-
1ph L

Real,Benjamin,Homestead
318 River St.
HABS PA-233
HABS PA,40-FOFO,5-
5dr/2ph/3pg L

Shoemaker House (Elm Lawn)
1577 Wyoming Ave.
HABS PA-22
HABS PA,40-FOFO,2-
6dr/8ph/4pg L

Snowden,Father,House
991 Wyoming Ave.
HABS PA-223
HABS PA,40-FOFO,4-
15dr/7ph/4pg L

Tripp House,The
1086 Wyoming House
HABS PA-236
HABS PA,40-FOFO,6-
18dr/6ph/7pg L

HANOVER GREEN

Hanover Green Meetinghouse
Nanticoke Vic.
HABS PA-26
HABS PA,40-HANO,1-
8dr/5ph/2pg L

KINGSTON

Helme Tavern,The
238 Wyoming Ave.
HABS PA-235
HABS PA,40-KING,1-
16dr/8ph/5pg L

Meyers,Lawrence,House
98 Main St.
HABS PA-245
HABS PA,40-KING,2-
8dr/2ph/3pg L

NANTICOKE

Mill,Samantha,House
493 E. Main St.
HABS PA-24
HABS PA,40-NANT,1-
6dr/8ph/4pg L

NANTICOKE VIC.

Harvey House
72-74 McDonald St.
HABS PA-237
HABS PA,40-NANTW,1-
17dr/7ph/7pg L

PLYMOUTH

Gaylord,Henderson,House
135 W. Main St.
HABS PA-28
HABS PA,40-PLYM,1-
8dr/4ph/1pg L

Wright,Col. H. B. ,House
843-845 W. Main St.
HABS PA-224
HABS PA,40-PLYM,2-
9dr/6ph/4pg L

WAPWALLOPEN

Union Reformed & Lutheran Church
HABS PA-219
HABS PA,40-WAP,1-
8dr/7ph/4pg L

WILKES BARRE

Bowman,Capt. Samuel,House
220 N. Main St.
HABS PA-241
HABS PA,40-WILB,3-
15dr/4ph/2pg L

Butler,Col. Zebulon, Homestead
313 S. River St.
HABS PA-239
HABS PA,40-WILB,2-
11dr/4ph/5pg L

McLean,Alexander,House
156 Carey Ave.
HABS PA-242
HABS PA,40-WILB,4-
11dr/5ph/3pg L

Pickering,Timothy,House (Ross House)
130 S. Main St.
HABS PA-230
HABS PA,40-WILB,1-
7dr/9ph/5pg L

Ross House; see Pickering,Timothy,House

WILKES-BARRE

Dorrance Colliery Fan Complex
Susquehanna River at Rt. 115 & Richard St.
HAER PA-61
HAER PA,40-WILB,5-
7dr/24ph/fr L

South Street Bridge
Spans Penn. Ave.,Wilkes-Barre Blvd.,Pocono NE RR
HAER PA-105
HAER 1991(HAER):12
42ph/8pg/3pc L

WYOMING

Crawford House
482 Wyoming Ave.
HABS PA-234
HABS PA,40-WYOM,4-
17dr/8ph/4pg L

Swetland House
885 Wyoming Ave.
HABS PA-23
HABS PA,40-WYOM,1-
7dr/6ph/2pg L

Swetland Store
828 Wyoming Ave.
HABS PA-211
HABS PA,40-WYOM,3-
9dr/3ph/5pg L

Wyoming Institute
Institute St.
HABS PA-29
HABS PA,40-WYOM,2-
2dr/2ph/1pg L

LYCOMING COUNTY

MUNCY VIC.

Reading-Halls Station Bridge
U.S. Rt. 220,spanning RR near Halls Station
HAER PA-55
HAER PA,41-MUNC.V,1-
5dr/30ph/41pg/3pc/fr L

WILLIAMSPORT

Memorial Avenue Bridge
Spanning Lycoming Creek
HAER PA-102
HAER PA,41-WILPO,3-
42ph/21pg/3pc L

Parson,Judge A. V. ,Mansion
5 E. Fourth St.
HABS PA-326
HABS PA,41-WILPO,1-
19dr/16ph L

Updegraff,Thomas,House
Reach Rd.
HABS PA-327
HABS PA,41-WILPO,2-
8dr L

Updegraff,Thomas,Log Granary
Reach Rd.
HABS PA-327-A
HABS PA,41-WILPO,2A-
3dr L

MCKEAN COUNTY

BETULA

Shattuck,Richard,Lodge
HABS PA-5106
HABS PA,42-BETU,1-
5ph L

CROSBY VIC.

Marsh Stone House
State Rt. 46
HABS PA-5105
HABS PA,42-CROSB.V,1-
6dr/1ph/3pg L

ELDRED

Chrisman House
HABS PA-551
HABS PA,42-ELD,1-
1ph L

KING'S RUN ROAD

Chevalier House
HABS PA-5104
HABS PA,42-CER.V,1-
5dr/1ph/3pg/fr L

MT. JEWETT VIC.

Erie Railway:Bradford Division,Bridge 27.66 (Kinzua Viaduct)
Spanning Kinzua Creek
HAER PA-7
HAER PA,42-MOJEW.V,1-
27ph/3pc L

Erie Railway:Mount Jewett Station
U. S. Rt. 6 & Kushequa Rd.
HAER PA-21
HAER PA,42-MOJEW,1-
6ph/1pc L

Kinzua Viaduct; see Erie Railway:Bradford Division,Bridge 27.66

PORT ALLEGANY VIC.

Coleman House
HABS PA-557
HABS PA,42-PORAL.V,1-
5ph L

SMETHPORT

Backus House
HABS PA-533
HABS PA,42-SMETH,1-
6dr/7ph/1pg/1pc L

Medbury Place
604 Main St.
HABS PA-5103
HABS PA,42-SMETH,2-
7dr/3ph L

WEST ELDRED VIC.

Lamphier House
HABS PA-552
HABS PA,42-ELDW,1-
4ph/5pg L

MERCER COUNTY

GREENVILLE

College Avenue Bridge
Spanning Little Shenango River
HAER PA-83
HAER PA,43-GRENV,4-
21ph/31pg/2pc L

Goodwin House
36 S. Mercer St.
HABS PA-567
HABS PA,43-GRENV,1-
3ph L

Penn High School
Penn. Ave. at Main St.
HABS PA-547
HABS PA,43-GRENV,3-
33ph/4pg/2pc L

Stewart,Vance,House
HABS PA-568
HABS PA,43-GRENV,2-
4ph L

MERCER

Bell House
HABS PA-564
HABS PA,43-MERC,5-
2ph L

Garrett Cenotaph
HABS PA-534
HABS PA,43-MERC,1-
1ph/3pg L

Jail,Old Stone
HABS PA-560
HABS PA,43-MERC,2-
1ph L

Magoffin House
119 S. Pitt St.
HABS PA-565
HABS PA,43-MERC,6-
2ph L

Magoffin,Dr. Beriah,House
116 Venago St.
HABS PA-561
HABS PA,43-MERC,3-
3ph L

Robinson,W. J. ,House
HABS PA-562
HABS PA,43-MERC,4-
1ph L

MERCER VIC.

Johnson House
Springfield Falls
HABS PA-581
HABS PA,43-MERC.V,1-
1ph L

SHEAKLEYVILLE

Scrivens House
HABS PA-558
HABS PA,43-SHEAK,2-
4ph L

Scrivens Store
Main St.
HABS PA-537
HABS PA,43-SHEAK,1-
5dr/2ph/4pg/fr L

MIFFLIN COUNTY

KISTLER

Kistler,Town of (Refractories Company Towns)
HABS PA-5976
H

Refractories Company Towns; see Kistler,Town of

MONROE COUNTY

BUSHKILL VIC.

Clark-Heller Mill
U. S. Rt. 209 (Middle Smithfield Township)
HABS PA-1159
HABS PA,45-BUSH.V,1-
2ph/3pg/1pc L

DELAWARE WATER GAP

Delaware Water Gap Railroad Station (Delaware-Lackawanna-Western Railroad Station)
U. S. Rt. 611
HABS PA-1168
HABS PA,45-DELWA,1-
3ph/1pg/1pc L

Delaware-Lackawanna-Western Railroad Station; see Delaware Water Gap Railroad Station

SHAWNEE-ON-DEL. VIC.

Camp Ministerium; see Turn,John,Farm

Camp Ministerium,Barn; see Turn,John,Farm,Barn

Camp Ministerium,House; see Turn,John,Farm,House

Camp Ministerium,Lime Kiln; see Turn,John,Farm,Lime Kiln

Camp Ministerium,Smokehouse; see Turn,John,Farm,Smokehouse

Camp Ministerium,Weaver House; see Turn,John,Farm,Weave House

Coldspring Farm; see Dewitt Farm

Dewitt Farm (Coldspring Farm)
River Rd. ,South of U. S. Rt. 209
HABS PA-1165
HABS PA,45-SHAWD.V,1-
3dr/3ph/13pg/fr L

Dewitt Farm,Barn
(Middle Smithfield Township)
HABS PA-1165-A
HABS PA,45-SHAWD.V,1A-
7dr/4ph/fr L

Dewitt Farm,Springhouse
(Middle Smithfield Township)
HABS PA-1165-B
HABS PA,45-SHAWD.V,1B-
3dr/6ph/fr L

Dewitt Farm,Woodshed
(Middle Smithfield Township)
HABS PA-1165-C
HABS PA,45-SHAWD.V,1C-
2dr/1ph/fr L

Farrington House; see Michael,Samuel,House

Michael Barn
River Rd. (Middle Smithfield Twp.)
HABS PA-1259
HABS PA,45-SHAWD.V,2A-
15dr/3ph/8pg/fr L

Michael,George,House (Theune House)
River Rd. (Middle Smithfield Township)
HABS PA-1160
HABS PA,45-SHAWD.V,2-
1ph/7pg L

Michael,Samuel,Barn
HABS PA-1170-C
HABS PA,45-SHAWD.V,3C-
1ph L

Michael,Samuel,House (Farrington House)
River Rd. (Middle Smithfield Twp.)
HABS PA-1170
HABS PA,45-SHAWD.V,3-
6ph/8pg/2pc L

Michael,Samuel,Schoolhouse
HABS PA-1170-B
HABS PA,45-SHAWD.V,3B-
1ph L

Michael,Samuel,Smokehouse
HABS PA-1170-A
HABS PA,45-SHAWD.V,3A-
1ph L

River Schoolhouse (Stone Schoolhouse)
River Rd. (Smithfield Township)
HABS PA-1167
HABS PA,45-SHAWD.V,5-
4dr/2ph/7pg/fr L

Robacker House; see Weaver,Valentine,House

Rouch House; see Treible,Peter,House

Stone Schoolhouse; see River Schoolhouse

Theune House; see Michael,George,House

Treible,Peter,House (Rouch House)
River Rd. (Smithfield Twp.)
HABS PA-1161
HABS PA,45-SHAWD.V,6-
13dr/10ph/9pg/fr L

Turn,John,Farm (Camp Ministerium)
River Rd. (Middle Smithfield Twp.)
HABS PA-1274
HABS PA,45-SHAWD.V,7-
1ph/9pg/1pc/fr L

Turn,John,Farm,Barn (Camp Ministerium,Barn)
River Rd. (Middle Smithfield Twp.)
HABS PA-1274-B
HABS PA,45-SHAWD.V,7B-
2ph/1pc L

Turn,John,Farm,House (Camp Ministerium,House)
River Rd. (Middle Smithfield Twp.)
HABS PA-1274-A
HABS PA,45-SHAWD.V,7A-
2ph/1pc L

Turn,John,Farm,Lime Kiln (Camp Ministerium,Lime Kiln)
River Rd. (Middle Smithfield Twp.)
HABS PA-1274-C
HABS PA,45-SHAWD.V,7C-
3dr/2ph/1pc/fr L

Turn,John,Farm,Smokehouse (Camp Ministerium,Smokehouse)
River Rd. (Middle Smithfield Twp.)
HABS PA-1274-D
HABS PA,45-SHAWD.V,7D-
2dr/1ph/1pc/fr L

Turn,John,Farm,Weave House (Camp Ministerium,Weaver House)
River Rd. (Middle Smithfield,Twp.)
HABS PA-1274-E
HABS PA,45-SHAWD.V,7E-
3dr/3ph/fr L

Walter-Kautz Farm
River Rd. (Smithfield Twp.)
HABS PA-1169
HABS PA,45-SHAWD.V,8-
4ph/15pg/1pc L

Walter-Kautz Farm,Barn
River Rd. (Smithfield Twp.)
HABS PA-1169-B
HABS PA,45-SHAWD.V,8B-
13dr/15ph/2pc/fr L

Walter-Kautz Farm,Corn Crib-Wagon Shed
River Rd. (Smithfield Twp.)
HABS PA-1169-C
HABS PA,45-SHAWD.V,8C-
7dr/3ph/1pc/fr L

Walter-Kautz Farm,House
River Rd. (Smithfield Twp.)
HABS PA-1169-A
HABS PA,45-SHAWD.V,8A-
2ph/1pc L

Walter-Kautz Farm,Icehouse
River Rd. (Smithfield Twp.)
HABS PA-1169-D
HABS PA,45-SHAWD.V,8D-
3dr/1ph/1pc/fr L

Walter-Kautz Farm,Washhouse & Woodshed
River Rd.
HABS PA-1169-E
HABS PA,45-SHAWD.V,8E-
1ph L

Weaver,Valentine,House (Robacker House)
River Rd. (Smithfield Twp.)
HABS PA-1164
HABS PA,45-SHAWD.V,9-
12dr/5ph/10pg/fr L

Zion Evangelical Lutheran Church
River Rd.
HABS PA-1136
HABS PA,45-SHAWD.V,10-
7dr/4ph/5pg/fr L

TOBYHANNA

Tobyhanna Army Depot
West of Rt. 423
HAER PA-78
HAER PA,45-TOBY,1-
33pg/fr L

MONTGOMERY COUNTY

???

Barn,Decorated Red
HABS PA-5349
HABS PA,46- ,7-
2ph L

AMBLER VIC.

Barn,Stone
Mt. Pleasant Rd.
HABS PA-5256
HABS PA,46-AMB.V,9-
3ph L

Mathers Mill
Mathers Lane
HABS PA-126
HABS PA,46-AMB.V,6-
5ph/2pg L

BALA CYNWYD

Pencoyd Farm,Barn (Roberts Estate)
355 E. City Ave. (Lower Merion Twp.)
HABS PA-1090
HABS PA,46-BALA,1B-
1ph L

Pencoyd Farm,Smokehouse (Roberts Estate)
355 E. City Ave. (Lower Merion Twp.)
HABS PA-1089
HABS PA,46-BALA,1A-
1ph L

Roberts Estate; see Pencoyd Farm,Barn

Roberts Estate; see Pencoyd Farm,Smokehouse

BALA-CYNWYD

Pencoyd Farm (Roberts Estate)
355 E. City Ave. (Lower Merion Twp.)
HABS PA-1087
HABS PA,46-BALA,1-
16ph/21pg L

Roberts Estate; see Pencoyd Farm

BARREN HILL

Lukens Stone Barn
Park Ave. ,Whitemarsh Twp.
HABS PA-5255
HABS PA,46-BARRHI,1A-
2ph L

BLUE BELL VIC.

Barn,Stone
Walton Rd. ,Whitpain Twp.
HABS PA-5250
HABS PA,46-BLUEB.V,1A-
1ph L

BRYN MAWR

Bryn Mawr Hospital Thrift Shop; see Whitehall Railroad Station

First Bryn Mawr Railroad Station; see Whitehall Railroad Station

Pennsylvania Railroad Bryn Mawr Station
Bryn Mawr & Morris Aves.
HABS PA-1081
HABS PA,46-BRYN,1-
5ph/5pg L

Whitehall Railroad Station (Bryn Mawr Hospital Thrift Shop; First Bryn Mawr Railroad Station)
Glenbrook Ave. & Haverford Rd.
HABS PA-577
HABS PA,46-BRYN,2-
1ph/1pg L

CENTER SQUARE VIC.

Barn,Stone
State Rt. 23,Whitpain Twp.
HABS PA-5251
HABS PA,46-CENSQ.V,1A-
4ph L

CONSHOHOCKEN VIC.

Andorra Inn Barn
Ridge & Butler Pikes
HABS PA-5254
HABS PA,46-CONSH.V,1A-
5ph L

EAST GREENVILLE VIC.

Mack,Abraham,Barn (1858)
State Rt. 29
HABS PA-5257
HABS PA,46-GRENVE.V,1A-
3ph L

FRANCONIA

Allentown Road Bridge
Spanning the Skippack Creek on Allentown Rd.
HAER PA-112
HAER 1989(HAER):18
18ph/8pg/2pc L

HAVERFORD

Quaker Meetinghouse
HABS PA-179
HABS PA,46-HAV,1-
1ph L

HORSHAM VIC.

Graeme Park,Barn
Keith Valley Rd. (Horsham Twp.)
HABS PA-579-A
HABS PA,46-HORM,1A-
2ph L

Graeme Park,House
Keith Valley Rd. (Horsham Twp.)
HABS PA-579
HABS PA,46-HORM,1-
5ph L

JENKINTOWN

Alvethorpe
HABS PA-130
HABS PA,46-JENK,1-
7ph/3pg L

KING OF PRUSSIA

Commercial Building (King of Prussia Antique Shop)
U.S. Rt. 202, Upper Merion Township
HABS PA-5360
HABS PA,46-KING,2-
4dr/1pg L

King of Prussia Antique Shop; see Commercial Building

King of Prussia Inn
U. S. Rt. 202 (Upper Merion Twp.)
HABS PA-1009
HABS PA,46-KING,1-
5dr/15ph/9pg L

KING OF PRUSSIA VIC.

Barn
Beidler Rd. ,Upper Merion Twp.
HABS PA-5247
HABS PA,46-KING.V,1A-
1ph L

Barn
Beidler Rd. ,Upper Merion Twp.
HABS PA-5248
HABS PA,46-KING.V,2A-
1ph L

Barn,1790
State Rt. 23,Upper Merion Twp.
HABS PA-5249
HABS PA,46-KING.V,3A-
3ph L

LOWER PROVIDENCE TWP

Barn,Stone
Germantown Pike vic. ,Lower Providence Twp.
HABS PA-5258
HABS PA,46-PROVL,3A-
2ph L

Vaux-Wetherill Stone Barn
Pawling Rd.
HABS PA-5350
HABS PA,46-PROVL,1A-
4ph L

MERION

Wayne,Gen. Anthony,Inn
625 Montgomery Ave.
HABS PA-144
HABS PA,46-MER,1-
1ph L

NARBERTH VIC.

Lower Merion Friends Meetinghouse (Merion Friends Meetinghouse)
Montgomery Ave. & Meetinghouse Lane
HABS PA-145
HABS PA,46-NARB.V,1-
4ph/1pg L

Lower Merion Friends Meetinghouse,Carriage House (Merion Friends Meetinghouse,Carriage House)
Montgomery Ave. & Meetinghouse Lane
HABS PA-145-A
HABS PA,46-NARB.V,1A-
3ph L

Merion Friends Meetinghouse; see Lower Merion Friends Meetinghouse

Merion Friends Meetinghouse,Carriage House; see Lower Merion Friends Meetinghouse,Carriage House

NIANTIC VIC.

Barn
Hill Rd. ,Rural Rt. 46012
HABS PA-5329
HABS PA,46-NIANT.V,1A-
3ph L

NORRISTOWN

West Marshall Street Bridge
Marshall St. over Stony Creek
HAER PA-54
HAER PA,46-NOR,1-
10ph/8pg/2pc L

PORT KENNEDY

Kennedy Mansion (Valley Forge National Historical Park)
1050 Port Kennedy Rd.
HABS PA-1959
HABS PA,46-POKEN,1-
12dr/27ph/fr L

Valley Forge National Historical Park; see Kennedy Mansion

POTTSTOWN VIC.

Barn,Decorated Red (1852)
State Rt. 100 vic.
HABS PA-5253
HABS PA,46-POTTS.V,1A-
2ph L

Hoffman,H. & S. ,Barn (1853)
HABS PA-5252
HABS PA,46-POTTS.V,2A-
2ph L

TRAPPE

Augustus Lutheran Church; see Trappe Church,Old

Trappe Church,Old (Augustus Lutheran Church)
HABS PA-175
HABS PA,46-TRAP,1-
10ph L

VALLEY FORGE

Jones House
Trace Rd.,Valley Forge Nat'l Historic Park
HABS PA-5369
HABS PA,46-VALFO,3-
2pg L

Mount Joy Observation Tower; see Valley Forge Observation Tower

Valley Forge Observation Tower (Mount Joy Observation Tower)
Valley Forge National Historic Park
HAER PA-114
HAER 1989(HAER):18
10ph/6pg/1pc L

VALLEY FORGE VIC.

Potts,Isaac,House (Washington's Headquarters; Valley Forge National Historical Park)
HABS PA-1171
HABS PA,46-VALFO,1-
25ph L

Valley Forge National Historical Park; see Potts,Isaac,House

Washington's Headquarters; see Potts,Isaac,House

WHITEMARSH

Hope Lodge
Bethehem & Skippack Pikes
HABS PA-18
HABS PA,46-WHIM,2-
12dr/6ph/2pg L

MONTOUR COUNTY

WASHINGTONVILLE VIC.

Washingtonville Bridge
Spanning Chillisquaque Creek (Derry Twp.) Rt.47036
HAER PA-98
HAER PA,47-WASH.V,1-
12ph/5pg/1pc L

NORTHAMPTON COUNTY

BELFAST VIC.

Henry Gun Factory
HABS PA-122
HABS PA,48-BOLT,1-
11dr/12ph/7pg L

Henry Gun Factory,Workman's House
HABS PA-123
HABS PA,48-BOLT,2-
7dr/4ph/3pg L

BETHELEHEM

Widows' House
53 W. Church St.
HABS PA-1155
HABS PA,48-BETH,5-
1ph L

BETHLEHEM

Bell House (Moravian Seminary,Bell House)
56 W. Church St.
HABS PA-1152
HABS PA,48-BETH,3C-
4ph L

Bethlehem Steel Corp: Treatment Shop # 3 CA. 1915; see Bethlehem Steel Corporation: High House

Bethlehem Steel Corporation: Beth Forge Division
Along the Lehigh River,North of Fourth St.
HAER PA-186
2dr H

Bethlehem Steel Corporation: Forge Shop CA. 1900
Along the Lehigh River,North of Fourth St.
HAER PA-186-A
2dr H

Bethlehem Steel Corporation: High House (Bethlehem Steel Corp: Treatment Shop # 3 CA. 1915)
Along the Lehigh River,North of Fourth St.
HAER PA-186-C
3dr H

Bethlehem Steel Corporation: Treatment Shop No. 2
Along the Lehigh River, North of Fourth St.
HAER PA-186-B
3dr H

Bethlehem Union Station
Betwn Lehigh Valley RR & Reading RR Tracks
HAER PA-146
HAER PA,48-BETH,15-
1ph/1pg/1pc L

Central Moravian Church (Moravian Seminary,Church)
406 Main St.
HABS PA-1147
HABS PA,48-BETH,2-
9ph/1pg/1pc L

Eighteenth Century Moravian Industrial Area
Monocacy Creek Vic.
HABS PA-1151
HABS PA,48-BETH,7-
1ph/1pc L

Gemein Haus
62-66 W. Church St.
HABS PA-1142
HABS PA,48-BETH,34-
10dr/12ph/1pc L

Goundie House
501 Main St.
HABS PA-1145
HABS PA,48-BETH,12-
9dr/11ph/1pg/1pc L

Grist Miller's House
459 Old York Rd.
HABS PA-1144
HABS PA,48-BETH,7D-
5ph/1pc L

Hill to Hill Bridge
Spans Lehigh River at PA. Rt. 378
HAER PA-131
66ph/28pg/6pc H

Lehigh Canal,Monocacy Creek Aqueduct (Monocacy Creek Aqueduct)
Lehigh Canal across Monocacy Creek
HAER PA-144
HAER PA,48-BETH,17A-
1ph/1pg/1pc L

Lester House
HABS PA-1005
HABS PA,48-BETH,1-
1ph L

Luckenbach Flour Mill
Monocacy Creek Vic.
HAER PA-50
HAER PA,48-BETH,10-
5dr/24ph/24pg/fr L

Luckenbach Grist Mill
Ohio Rd. ,Monocacy Creek Vic.
HABS PA-1148
HABS PA,48-BETH,7C-
3ph/1pc L

Monocacy Creek Aqueduct; see Lehigh Canal,Monocacy Creek Aqueduct

Moravian Seminary,Bell House; see Bell House

Moravian Seminary,Church; see Central Moravian Church

Schnitz House
38 W. Church St.
HABS PA-1154
HABS PA,48-BETH,6-
1ph L

Single Brethren's House
89 W. Church St.
HABS PA-1141
HABS PA,48-BETH,4-
21dr/22ph/2pc L

Single Sisters' House
44 W. Church St.
HABS PA-1153
HABS PA,48-BETH,3B-
1ph L

Sun Inn
564 Main St.
HABS PA-1150
HABS PA,48-BETH,13-
5dr L

Tannery
Monocacy Creek Vic.
HABS PA-1143
HABS PA,48-BETH,7B-
16dr/25ph/2pg/2pc L

Waterworks
Monocacy Creek Vic.
HABS PA-1146
HABS PA,48-BETH,7A-
9ph/1pg/1pc L

EASTON

Cinruss Building; see 31 North Fourth Street (Commercial Building)

Easton Dam (Dam 9); see Lehigh Canal,Easton Dam

Engine House No. 1
219 Ferry St.
HABS PA-5547
HABS DLC/PP-1993:PA-3
6ph/5pg/1pc L

217 Ferry Street (Commercial Building)
HABS PA-5546
HABS DLC/PP-1993:PA-3
3ph/5pg/1pc L

Hellick,George,Coffee Company
215 Ferry St.
HABS PA-5545
HABS DLC/PP-1993:PA-3
5ph/4pg/1pc L

Hellick,George,Coffee Warehouse No. 3
38-40 Sitgreaves St.
HABS PA-5522
HABS DLC/PP-1993:PA-3
5ph/4pg/1pc L

Lehigh Canal,Easton Dam (Easton Dam (Dam 9))
Confluence of Lehigh & Delaware Rivers
HAER PA-133
HAER PA,48-EATO,6B-
3ph/1pg/1pc L

Lehigh Canal,Lock 48; see Lehigh Canal,Outlet Lock

Lehigh Canal,Outlet Lock (Lehigh Canal,Lock 48)
Canal St.
HAER PA-136
HAER PA,48-EATO,6A-
1ph/1pg/1pc L

Lehigh Valley RR,Easton Car Shops
Canal St.
HAER PA-137-B
HAER PA,48-EATO,5B-
3ph/1pg/1pc L

Lehigh Valley RR,Easton Station
Canal St. & Smith Ave. at Third St. Bridge
HAER PA-137-A
HAER PA,48-EATO,5A-
1ph/1pg/1pc L

Lehigh Valley RR,Easton Steam Laundry & Dining Car
Canal St. near Easton Station
HAER PA-137-C
HAER PA,48-EATO,5C-
2ph/1pg/1pc L

31 North Fourth Street (Commercial Building) (Cinruss Building)
HABS PA-5140
HABS PA,48-EATO,2-
5ph/19pg/1pc L

33-35 North Fourth Street (Commercial Building) (Patio Club Building)
HABS PA-5141
HABS PA,48-EATO,3-
4ph/17pg/1pc L

Parsons-Taylor House
S. Fourth & Ferry Sts.
HABS PA-1008
HABS PA,48-EATO,1-
1ph/1pg L

Patio Club Building; see 33-35 North Fourth Street (Commercial Building)

Phoenix Hose Driver's House
48 Sitgreaves St.
HABS PA-5582
HABS DLC/PP-1993:PA-3
6ph/4pg/1pc L

520 Pine Street (House)
HABS PA-5342
HABS PA,48-EATO,4-
1ph/1pg L

FREEMANSBURG

Canal Manager's House
HAER PA-142
HAER PA,48-FREEB,2-
2ph/1pc L

Freemansburg Lock; see Lehigh Canal,Lock 44

Freemansburg-Steel City Bridge
Span. Lehigh River betwn Freemansburg & Steel City
HAER PA-141
HAER PA,48-FREEB,3-
1ph/1pg/1pc L

Lehigh Canal,Freemansburg
HAER PA-176
HAER PA,48-FREEB,1-
4ph/1pc L

Lehigh Canal,Lock 44 (Freemansburg Lock)
N. end of Freemansburg Borough
HAER PA-140
HAER PA,48-FREEB,1A-
1ph/1pg/1pc L

GLENDON

Glendon Hotel
Main St.
HABS PA-5445
HABS PA,48-GLEN,1-
1ph/1pg/1pc L

Glendon Iron Company
Hugh Moore Park near Old Glendon Bridge
HAER PA-138
HAER PA,48-GLEN,3-
1ph/1pg/1pc L

Lehigh Canal,Guard Lock 8 & Lockhouse
Island Park Rd.
HAER PA-139
HAER PA,48-GLEN,2A-
2ph/1pg/1pc L

HELLERTOWN

Barn,Stone
Water St. ,Lower Saucon Twp.
HABS PA-5328
HABS PA,48-HELLT,1A-
3ph L

County Bridge No. 16; see Old Mill Road Bridge

Old Mill Road Bridge (County Bridge No. 16)
Spanning Saucon Creek,Old Mill Rd.
HAER PA-93
11ph/1pc/fr H

HELLERTOWN VIC.

Barn,Decorated
Lower Saucon Twp.
HABS PA-5327
HABS PA,48-HELLT.V,1A-
3ph L

LAURY'S STATION VIC.

Laury's Dam; see Lehigh Canal,Slate Dam

Lehigh Canal,Guard Lock 5
Upstream fm Cementon-Northampton Bridge(Allen Twp)
HAER PA-158
HAER PA,48-LAST.V,1A-
3ph/1pg/1pc L

Lehigh Canal,Slate Dam (Slate Dam (Dam 5); Laury's Dam)
Lehigh Canal opposite Laury's Station (Allen Twp.)
HAER PA-171
HAER PA,48-LAST.V,1B-
1ph/1pg/1pc L

Slate Dam (Dam 5); see Lehigh Canal,Slate Dam

LEITHSVILLE VIC.

Mountain View Dairy Farm,Barn
State Rt. 412,Lower Saucon Twp.
HABS PA-5326
HABS PA,48-LEITH.V,1A-
3ph L

NAZARETH

First Room; see Parsonage

Hall Square; see Nazareth Hall Tract

137 Main Street,Shop Window
HABS PA-1655
HABS PA,48-NAZ,1-
1dr L

1840 Moravian Church
Nazareth Hall Tract
HABS PA-1269
HABS 1991(HABS):1
3dr L

Nazareth Hall
Nazareth Hall Tract
HABS PA-1266
HABS 1991(HABS):1
8dr L

Nazareth Hall Tract (Hall Square)
HABS PA-5627
HABS 1991(HABS):1
1dr L

Parsonage (First Room)
Nazareth Hall Tract
HABS PA-1270
HABS 1991(HABS):1
1dr L H

Single Sister's House
Nazareth Hall Tract
HABS PA-1267
HABS 1991(HABS):1
4dr L

NORTH CATASAUQUA

Hokendauqua Dam (Dam 6); see Lehigh Canal,Hokendauqua Dam

Lehigh Canal,Hokendauqua Dam (Hokendauqua Dam (Dam 6); Swartz' Dam)
Lehigh Riv. N. of Hokendauqua-N. Catasauqua Bridge
HAER PA-153
HAER PA,48-CATSN,1A-
1ph/1pg/1pc L

Swartz' Dam; see Lehigh Canal,Hokendauqua Dam

NORTHAMPTON

Main Street (Houses)
HABS PA-5449
HABS PA,48-NORTH,2-
2ph/1pc L

Northampton Brewery
Newport Ave. N. of Laubach Ave.
HAER PA-155
HAER PA,48-NORTH,1-
1ph/1pg/1pc L

PORTLAND VIC.

Mount Minsi Farm; see Slateford House

Munsch House; see Slateford House

Slateford House (Munsch House; Mount Minsi Farm)
U. S. Rt. 611 & T709
HABS PA-1249
HABS PA,48-PORT.V,1-
14dr/16ph/5pg/fr L

Slateford House,Small Dwelling
U. S. Rt. 611 & T709 (Upper Mt. Bethel Township)
HABS PA-1249-A
HABS PA,48-PORT.V,1A-
3dr/5ph/fr L

Slateford House,Springhouse
(Upper Mt. Bethel Township)
HABS PA-1249-B
HABS PA,48-PORT.V,1B-
2dr/4ph/fr L

TREICHLERS

Mauser Mill Company (White Star Mills)
Breadfruit Drive at Lehigh Canal
HAER PA-159
HAER PA,48-TREIC,1-
2ph/1pg/1pc L

Treichlers Cafe
HABS PA-5451
HABS PA,48-TREIC,2-
1ph/1pc L

White Star Mills; see Mauser Mill Company

WALNUTPORT

Anchor Hotel
Main & Canal Sts.
HABS PA-5471
HABS PA,48-WALNPO,2-
1ph/1pg/1pc L

Houses (General Views)
Banks of Lehigh Canal
HABS PA-5452
HABS PA,48-WALNPO,3-
3ph/1pc L

Kelchner's Lock; see Lehigh Canal,Lock 23

Lehigh Canal,Lock 23 (Kelchner's Lock)
S. of Walnutport-Slatington Bridge
HAER PA-160
HAER PA,48-WALNPO,1A-
1ph/1pg/1pc L

WIND GAP VIC.

Ross-Common Manor
HABS PA-177
HABS PA,48-WIGAP.V,1-
1ph L

PHILADELPHIA COUNTY

FRANKFORD

Lardner House; see Lynfield House

Lynfield House (Lardner House)
HABS PA-132
HABS PA,51-PHILA,221-
3ph/1pg L

GERMANTOWN

Johnson House
6306 Germantown Ave.
HABS PA-7-7
HABS PA,51-GERM,55-
12dr/4ph/3pg/fr L

Keyser House
6205 Germantown Ave.
HABS PA-11
HABS PA,51-GERM,52-
7dr/2pg/fr L

PHILADELPHIA

(HABS Photos,HAER Stereoplates); see Strawberry Mansion Bridge

Abercrombie,Capt. James,House (Perelman Antique Toy Museum)
268-270 S. Second St.
HABS PA-1316
HABS PA,51-PHILA,621-
5dr/10ph/fr L

Academy of Music; see American Academy of Music

Academy of Notre Dame (Rittenhouse Square)
208 S. Nineteenth St. ,Rittenhouse Sq.
HABS PA-1492
HABS PA,51-PHILA,680-
3ph L

American Academy of Music (Academy of Music)
232-246 S. Broad St.
HABS PA-1491
HABS PA,51-PHILA,294-
15ph L

American Fire Insurance Company Building
308-310 Walnut St.
HABS PA-1386
HABS PA,51-PHILA,316-
1ph/1pc L

American Life Insurance Company Building (Manhattan Building)
330-336 Walnut St.
HABS PA-1064
HABS PA,51-PHILA,257-
9ph/10pg L

American Philosophical Society
104 S. Fifth St.
HABS PA-1464
HABS PA,51-PHILA,46-
5ph L

Annan,William,House
776 S. Front St.
HABS PA-1539
HABS PA,51-PHILA,444-
1ph L

Arbour,William,House
HABS PA-1051
HABS PA,51-PHILA,250-
1dr/3ph/4pg L

Arcade Building (Commercial Trust Building)
Fifteenth & Market Sts.
HABS PA-1493
HABS PA,51-PHILA,676-
11ph/9pg L

501 Arch Street (House)
HABS PA-1092
HABS PA,51-PHILA,465-
1ph L

620 Arch Street (House)
HABS PA-1423
HABS PA,51-PHILA,468-
1ph/2pg L

628-630 Arch Street (House)
HABS PA-1424
HABS PA,51-PHILA,469-
1ph/2pg L

503-527 Arch Street (Houses)
HABS PA-1387
HABS PA,51-PHILA,466-
2ph L

Arch Street Friends Meetinghouse
330 Arch St.
HABS PA-1388
HABS PA,51-PHILA,10-
4ph/1pc L

Arch Street Methodist Episcopal Church
Broad & Arch Sts.
HABS PA-1494
HABS PA,51-PHILA,312-
1ph/1pg L

Arch Street Opera House (Troc,The)
1003-1005 Arch St.
HABS PA-1495
HABS PA,51-PHILA,470-
2ph L

Arch Street Presbyterian Church; see West Arch Street Presbyterian Church

Armat,Thomas,House
5450 Germantown Ave.
HABS PA-1671
HABS PA,51-GERM,31-
2ph L

Ashmead,Albert,House
5430 Germantown Ave.
HABS PA-1672
HABS PA,51-GERM,27-
1ph L

Ashmead,William,House
5434 Germantown Ave.
HABS PA-1673
HABS PA,51-GERM,28-
1ph L

Askins-Jones House; see 720-724 South Front Street (House)

Ayer,N. W. & Company Building (N. W. Ayer and Son,Incorporated,Building)
204-212 S. Seventh St.
HABS PA-1390
HABS PA,51-PHILA,664-
2ph L

Baird,Donald L. ,Company Warehouse
327-329 S. Water St.
HABS PA-1378
HABS PA,51-PHILA,612-
3ph L

Bake House & Oven
423 S. Second St.
HABS PA-1317
HABS PA,51-PHILA,292-
2ph/1pg L

Baltimore & Ohio Railroad Station
Twenty-fourth & Chestnut Sts.
HABS PA-1220
HABS PA,51-PHILA,405-
3dr/18ph L

Bank of North America
305-307 Chestnut St.
HABS PA-1391
HABS PA,51-PHILA,383-
4ph/4pg L

Bank of Pennsylvania (Philadelphia Bank; Philadelphia National Bank)
421 Chestnut St.
HABS PA-1392
HABS PA,51-PHILA,376-
5ph/4pg/3pc/fr L

Bank Row
407-431 Chestnut St.
HABS PA-1667
HABS PA,51-PHILA,374-
2ph/2pg/1pc/fr L

Barron,Com. James,House
5106 Germantown Ave.
HABS PA-1674
HABS PA,51-GERM,13-
2ph L

Bartram,John,Hotel; see Hotel Walton

Bartram,John,House
Fifty-fourth St.
HABS PA-1132
HABS PA,51-PHILA,38-
8dr/11ph L

Baugh Warehouse; see Beck-Care Warehouse

Baynton House; see Germantown Historical Society Area Study

111-113 Beck Street (Houses)
HABS PA-1581
HABS PA,51-PHILA,337-
1ph L

Beck Street Area Study (Court of Homes)
Beck St. ,200 Block
HABS PA-1542
HABS PA,51-PHILA,338-
2ph L

Beck-Care Warehouse (Baugh Warehouse)
18-20 S. Delaware Ave.
HABS PA-1188
HABS PA,51-PHILA,392-
5dr/4ph/fr L

Beggarstown School
6669 Germantown Ave.
HABS PA-1675
HABS PA,51-GERM,72-
1ph/1pc L

Bel Air (Belleaire; Singley House; Lasse Cock's Manor House)
League Island Park (Passyunk Twp.)
HABS PA-1124
HABS PA,51-PHILA,228-
30dr/8ph L

Belfield; see Peale,Charles Willson,House

Belleaire; see Bel Air

Bellevue-Stratford Hotel
Broad & Walnut Sts.
HABS PA-1226
HABS PA,51-PHILA,344-
34ph/8ct L

Belmont Mansion
Belmont Mansion Dr.
HABS PA-1649
HABS PA,51-PHILA,304-
5ph L

Berry-Blair House
415 Locust St.
HABS PA-1063
HABS PA,51-PHILA,492-
2ph/1pg L

Berry-Coxe House
413 Locust St.
HABS PA-1062
HABS PA,51-PHILA,168-
10dr/15ph/7pg L

Bethel African Methodist Episcopal Church (Mother Bethel African Methodist Espiscopal Church)
419 S. Sixth St.
HABS PA-1318
HABS PA,51-PHILA,288-
2ph L

Bethel Christian Center; see Mariners' Bethel Church

Billmeyer,Michael,House; see 6505-6507 Germantown Avenue (House)

Binney,H. Esq. ,House
HABS PA-1903
HABS PA,51-PHILA,686-
2ph L

Bird,Joseph,Houses
813-815 S. Hancock St.
HABS PA-1543
HABS PA,51-PHILA,482-
1ph L

Bishop-Sparks House
948 S. Front St.
HABS PA-1544
HABS PA,51-PHILA,457-
1ph L

Blackwell,Reverend Robert,House (St. Peter's Church House (Episcopal))
313 Pine St.
HABS PA-1319
HABS PA,51-PHILA,322-
1ph/1pg L

Blair,Samuel Jr. ,House
6105 Germantown Ave.
HABS PA-7-5
HABS PA,51-GERM,49-
7dr/4ph/2pg L

Bleakley House; see Cannonball Farm

Blight Warehouse
101-103 S. Front St.
HABS PA-1393
HABS PA,51-PHILA,420-
1ph L

200 Block Spruce Street (House)
HABS PA-1713
HABS PA,51-PHILA,688-
3ph L

Boat House Row
E. River Drive
HABS PA-1650
HABS PA,51-PHILA,561-
1ph/2pg L

Bonsall,John,House
706 Locust St. (Washington Sq.)
HABS PA-1394
HABS PA,51-PHILA,320-
5ph L

Bourse Building; see Philadelphia Bourse

Bridges-LaTour House
509 S. Front St.
HABS PA-1321
HABS PA,51-PHILA,429-
10ph/1pg L

Bridges,Robert,House; see 507 South Front Street (House)

Bringhurst House
5448 Germantown Ave.
HABS PA-1679
HABS PA,51-GERM,181-
15ph L

British Building; see International Exhibition of 1876,St. George's Hse.

Brock,John, & Sons,Warehouse
242-244 N. Delaware Ave.
HABS PA-1395
HABS PA,51-PHILA,278-
9ph/1pg/fr L

Bromley,John & Sons,Building
201-263 Lehigh Ave.
HABS PA-1744
HABS PA,51-PHILA,305-
3ph L

Bulletin Building
1315-1325 Filbert St.
HABS PA-1496
HABS PA,51-PHILA,410-
2ph/1pg L

Burden,Joseph,House
132 S. Fourth St.
HABS PA-1949
HABS PA,51-PHILA,645-
3ph L

Burholme (Ryers Mansion)
Burholme Park,Cottman & Central Aves.
HABS PA-186
HABS PA,51-PHILA,273-
10dr/2ph/3ct L

Burholme,Stables (Ryerss Mansion,Stables)
Burholme Park,Coltman & Central Aves.
HABS PA-186-A
HABS PA,51-PHILA,273A-
1ph L

Burk,Alfred E. ,House
1500 N. Broad St.
HABS PA-1722
HABS PA,51-PHILA,313-
2ph/1pg L

Burnham,George,House
3401 Powelton Ave.
HABS PA-1627
HABS PA,51-PHILA,279-
2ph/1pg L

Burnside; see Hamilton-Hoffman House

Bussey-Poulson House
320 S. Front St.
HABS PA-1323
HABS PA,51-PHILA,144-
1dr/3ph L

Busti,Paul,House (Kirkbride Residence)
Forty-sixth St. & Haverford Ave.
HABS PA-1628
HABS PA,51-PHILA,483-
8ph/1pg/fr L

Byrne-Cavenaugh Houses
130-132 Queen St.
HABS PA-1545
HABS PA,51-PHILA,285-
2ph/1pg L

Callowhill Street Bridge (Spring Garden Street Bridge; Fairmount Bridge)
Schuylkill Riv. at Spring Garden & Callowhill Sts.
HAER PA-86
HAER PA,51-PHILA,702-
10ph/1pg/1pc L

Cannonball Farm (Bleakley House)
HABS PA-134
HABS PA,51-PHILA,222-
10dr/6ph/1pg L

Carpenters' Company Hall (Carpenters' Hall)
320 Chestnut St. & Carpenters' Ct.
HABS PA-1398
HABS PA,51-PHILA,229-
3dr/10ph/8pg/8ct L

Carpenters' Company,Front Store
322 Chestnut St. & Carpenters' Ct.
HABS PA-1398-A
HABS PA,51-PHILA,229A-
3dr/5ph/7pg/fr L

Carpenters' Company,New Hall
Carpenters' Ct. & 322 Chestnut St. (rear)
HABS PA-1398-B
HABS PA,51-PHILA,229B-
2ph/1pg L

Carpenters' Company,Pemberton House
322 Chestnut St. & Carpenters' Ct.
HABS PA-1398-C
HABS PA,51-PHILA,229C-
1ph L

Carpenters' Company,Rule Book (carpentry manual)
HABS PA-1398-D
HABS PA,51-PHILA,229D-
39ph L

Carpenters' Hall; see Carpenters' Company Hall

Carpenters' Mansion
615-619 Chestnut St.
HABS PA-1397
HABS PA,51-PHILA,230-
1ph/1pg L

Cast Iron Sidewalk
1907 N. Seventh St.
HABS PA-1723
HABS PA,51-PHILA,291-
5ph L

Cathedral of Saints Peter & Paul
Eighteenth & Race Sts.
HABS PA-1497
HABS PA,51-PHILA,552-
3ph L

29-31 Catherine Street (Alley)
HABS PA-5181
HABS PA,51-PHILA,360-
1ph L

Catherine Street (courtyard)
HABS PA-1128
HABS PA,51-PHILA,368-
1ph L

30 Catherine Street (House)
HABS PA-1573
HABS PA,51-PHILA,365-
2ph L

33 1/2 Catherine Street (House)
HABS PA-1069
HABS PA,51-PHILA,359-
2dr/5ph/1pg/fr L

19-35 Catherine Street (Houses)
HABS PA-5182
HABS PA,51-PHILA,357-
1ph L

27 Catherine Street (stoop)
HABS PA-1928
HABS PA,51-PHILA,361-
1ph L

Cedar Grove
Landsdowne Dr.
HABS PA-1651
HABS PA,51-PHILA,231
3ph/1pc L

Centennial Guard Box
Traffic Triangle,Benjamin Franklin Pky. Vic.
HABS PA-1652
HABS PA,51-PHILA,289-
1ph/1pg L

Centennial National Bank
Thirty-second & Market Sts.
HABS PA-1095
HABS PA,51-PHILA,525-
3dr/1ph/fr L

Chalkley Hall
Wheatsheaf La. & Sepviva St.
HABS PA-110
HABS PA,51-PHILA,62-
24dr/12ph/9pg L

Chamounix Mansion
Chamounix Dr.
HABS PA-1653
HABS PA,51-PHILA,281-
2ph/1pg L

Chestnut Hill Academy; see Wissahickon Inn

213-243 Chestnut Street (Commercial Buildings); see Chestnut Street Area Study

Chestnut Street Area Study (213-243 Chestnut Street (Commercial Buildings))
HABS PA-1402
HABS PA,51-PHILA,373-
3ph/2pg L

Chestnut Street Bridge
Schuykill River,Chestnut St. Vic.
HABS PA-1054
HABS PA,51-PHILA,253-
5ph/3pg L

Chew Mansion,The; see Cliveden

Chinatown YMCA (Chinese Cultural & Community Center)
125 N. Tenth St.
HABS PA-1498
HABS PA,51-PHILA,315-
5ph/1pg L

Chinese Cultural & Community Center; see Chinatown YMCA

Christ Church
22-26 N. Second St.
HABS PA-1071
HABS PA,51-PHILA,7-
19dr/36ph/2pc/1ct/fr L

Church of St. James the Less
3200 W. Clearfield St.
HABS PA-1725
HABS PA,51-PHILA,318-
3ph/1pg L

Church of St. Luke (Church of St. Luke & Epiphany)
330 S. Thirteenth St.
HABS PA-1499
HABS PA,51-PHILA,300-
3ph/1pg/2ct L

Church of St. Luke & Epiphany; see Church of St. Luke

Church of St. Philip de Neri
220-228 Queen St.
HABS PA-1547
HABS PA,51-PHILA,550-
3ph L

Church of St. Vincent de Paul
101-107 E. Price St.
HABS PA-1680
HABS PA,51-PHILA,309-
3ph L

Church of the Gesu
Eighteenth & Thompson Sts.
HABS PA-1724
HABS PA,51-PHILA,284-
2ph/1pg/1ct L

Church of the Holy Trinity (Protestant Episcopal)
200 S. Nineteenth St.
HABS PA-1085
HABS PA,51-PHILA,677-
6ph/5pg L

Church of the Immaculate Conception
1020 N. Front St.
HABS PA-1901
HABS PA,51-PHILA,419-
1ph L

Church of the Redeemer
101-107 Queen St.
HABS PA-1077
HABS PA,51-PHILA,263-
8ph/5pg L

Civil War Memorial; see Smith Memorial Arch

Clarkson-Watson House
5275-5277 Germantown Ave.
HABS PA-1681
HABS PA,51-GERM,25-
1ph L

Cliffs,The
Columbia Ave. ,Fairmount Park
HABS PA-185
HABS PA,51-PHILA,274-
14dr/4ph/1pg L

Cliveden (Chew Mansion,The)
6401 Germantown Ave.
HABS PA-1184
HABS PA,51-GERM,64-
17dr/87ph/9pg/26ct/fr L

Clunie; see Mount Pleasant

Clunie Kitchen; see Mount Pleasant Kitchen

Clunie Office; see Mount Pleasant Office

Clymers Alley (Clymers Court)
770 S. Front St.
HABS PA-1582
HABS PA,51-PHILA,441-
1ph L

Clymers Court; see Clymers Alley

Collins,Samuel,House; see 783 South Front Street (House)

Columbia Engine Company
3420 Market St.
HABS PA-1629
HABS PA,51-PHILA,522-
1ph L

Commandant's House; see Schuylkill Arsenal,Building No. 1A

Commercial Exchange
135 S. Second St.
HABS PA-1406
HABS PA,51-PHILA,314-
4ph/1pg L

Commercial Trust Building; see Arcade Building

Commercial Union Assurance Company Building
416-420 Walnut St.
HABS PA-1076
HABS PA,51-PHILA,262-
7ph/6pg L

Compton (Morris House)
Meadowbrook Ave.
HABS PA-1682
HABS PA,51-GERM,188-
12ph/4pg L

Concord School
6309 Germantown Ave.
HABS PA-12
HABS PA,51-GERM,59-
6dr/1ph/4pg/1pc L

Congress Hall (Philadelphia County Courthouse; Independence Hall Complex,Congress Hall; Independence National Historical Park)
Sixth & Chestnut Sts.
HABS PA-1431
HABS PA,51-PHILA,6A-
35dr/24ph/3pg/3pc/19ct/fr L

Conyngham-Hacker House; see Germantown Historical Society Area Study

Cooper,Jacob,House
118 Cuthbert St.
HABS PA-1407
HABS PA,51-PHILA,692-
3ph L

Cope,Caleb & Company Store
429 Market St.
HABS PA-1408
HABS PA,51-PHILA,516-
2ph L

Cope,Edward Drinker,Houses
2100-2102 Pine St.
HABS PA-1500
HABS PA,51-PHILA,539-
4ph/2pg L

Court of Homes; see Beck Street Area Study

Cove Cornice House; see Stafford's Tavern-Paschall House

Covered Bridge
Thomas Mill Rd. (Spanning Wissahickon Creek)
HABS PA-19
HABS PA,51-GERM,62-
1dr/2ph L

Currie,Dr. William,House
271 S. Fifth St.
HABS PA-191
HABS PA,51-PHILA,240-
2ph/2pg L

Curtis Publishing Company Building
Sixth & Walnut Sts.
HABS PA-1902
HABS PA,51-PHILA,585-
2ph L

Curtis,John,House
785 S. Front St.
HABS PA-1550
HABS PA,51-PHILA,446-
1ph L

Customs House; see Second Bank of the United States

Davis-Lenox House
217 Spruce St.
HABS PA-1324
HABS PA,51-PHILA,324-
2ph/1pg L

305 Delancey Street (House)
HABS PA-1399
HABS PA,51-PHILA,386-
2ph L

307 Delancey Street (House)
HABS PA-1927
HABS PA,51-PHILA,387-
1ph L

1800-1836 Delancey Street (Houses); see Delancey Street Area Study I

105 Delancey Street (Warehouse)
HABS PA-1377
HABS PA,51-PHILA,464-
1ph L

Delancey Street Area Study (II)
(2301-2319 Delancey Street)
HABS PA-1502
HABS PA,51-PHILA,390-
3ph L

Delancey Street Area Study I
(1800-1836 Delancey Street (Houses))
HABS PA-1501
HABS PA,51-PHILA,389-
8ph L

2301-2319 Delancey Street; see Delancey Street Area Study (II)

Deshler-Morris House
5442 Germantown Ave.
HABS PA-1683
HABS PA,51-GERM,30-
5ph L

Detweiler House
8226 Germantown Ave.
HABS PA-1684
HABS PA,51-GERM,187-
1ph L

1601-1635 Diamond Street (Houses); see Diamond Street Area Study

Diamond Street Area Study (1601-1635 Diamond Street (Houses))
HABS PA-1726
HABS PA,51-PHILA,393-
2ph/1pg L

Dilworth-Todd-Moylan House
(Independence National Historical Park)
343 Walnut St.
HABS PA-1409
HABS PA,51-PHILA,593-
14dr/1ph L

Dilworth-Todd-Moylan House,Rear Wing (Independence National Historical Park)
149 S. Fourth St.
HABS PA-1409-A
HABS PA,51-PHILA,593A-
11dr L

Dobson,J. & J., Carpet Mill (W. Parcel),Bldg. 10
4041-4055 Ridge Ave.
HABS PA-5383-J
7ph/5pg/1pc H

Dobson,J. & J.,Carpet Mill (W. Parcel),Bdlg. 16
4041-4055 Ridge Ave.
HABS PA-5385-O
4ph/6pg/1pc H

Dobson,J. & J.,Carpet Mill (W. Parcel),Bdlg. 33
4041-4055 Ridge Ave.
HABS PA-5383-W
3ph/1pg/1pc H

Documentation: **ct** color transparencies **dr** measured drawings **fr** field records
pc photograph captions **pg** pages of text **ph** photographs

Dobson,J. & J.,Carpet Mill (W. Parcel),Bldg. 1
4041-4055 Ridge Ave.
HABS PA-5383-A
5ph/1pg/1pc H

Dobson,J. & J.,Carpet Mill (W. Parcel),Bldg. 11
4041-4055 Ridge Ave.
HABS PA-5383-K
10ph/6pg/1pc H

Dobson,J. & J.,Carpet Mill (W. Parcel),Bldg. 12
4041-4055 Ridge Ave.
HABS PA-5383-L
8ph/5pg/1pc H

Dobson,J. & J.,Carpet Mill (W. Parcel),Bldg. 15
4041-4055 Ridge Ave.
HABS PA-5383-N
6ph/6pg/1pc H

Dobson,J. & J.,Carpet Mill (W. Parcel),Bldg. 17
4041-4055 Ridge Ave.
HABS PA-5383-P
4ph/6pg/1pc H

Dobson,J. & J.,Carpet Mill (W. Parcel),Bldg. 22
4041-4055 Ridge Ave.
HABS PA-5383-S
6ph/5pg/1pc H

Dobson,J. & J.,Carpet Mill (W. Parcel),Bldg. 24
4041-4055 Ridge Ave.
HABS PA-5383-U
4ph/5pg/1pc H

Dobson,J. & J.,Carpet Mill (W. Parcel),Bldg. 25
4041-4055 Ridge Ave.
HABS PA-5383-V
5ph/6pg/1pc H

Dobson,J. & J.,Carpet Mill (W. Parcel),Bldg. 4
4041-4055 Ridge Ave.
HABS PA-5383-D
5ph/6pg/1pc H

Dobson,J. & J.,Carpet Mill (W. Parcel),Bldg. 5
4041-4055 Ridge Ave.
HABS PA-5383-E
7ph/6pg/1pc H

Dobson,J. & J.,Carpet Mill (W. Parcel),Bldg. 7
4041-4055 Ridge Ave.
HABS PA-5383-F
9ph/6pg/1pc H

Dobson,J. & J.,Carpet Mill (W. Parcel),Bldg. 8
4041-4055 Ridge Ave.
HABS PA-5383-G
7ph/6pg/1pc H

Dobson,J. & J.,Carpet Mill (W. Parcel),Bldg. 9
4041-4055 Ridge Ave.
HABS PA-5383-H
7ph/6pg/1pc H

Dobson,J. & J.,Carpet Mill (W. Parcel),Bldg. 9A
4041-4055 Ridge Ave.
HABS PA-5383-I
2ph/1pg/1pc H

Dobson,J. & J.,Carpet Mill (W. Parcel),Bldg.18
4041-4055 Ridge Ave.
HABS PA-5383-Q
5ph/6pg/1pc H

Dobson,J. & J.,Carpet Mill (W. Parcel),Tower,The
4041-4055 Ridge Ave.
HABS PA-5383-B
5ph/6pg/1pc H

Dobson,J.& J.,Carpet Mill (W. Parcel),Bldg. 3
4041-4055 Ridge Ave.
HABS PA-5383-C
5ph/6pg/1pc H

Dobson,John & James,Carpet Mill (West Parcel)
4041-4055 Ridge Ave.
HABS PA-5383
19ph/9pg/3pc H

Dock Street Sewer
Dock & Third Sts. Vic.
HABS PA-1072
HABS PA,51-PHILA,407-
1dr L

Dorfenille House
5139 Germantown Ave.
HABS PA-1685
HABS PA,51-GERM,176-
1ph L

Dowers-Okill House
115 N. Water St.
HABS PA-1410
HABS PA,51-PHILA,609-
4ph/1pg L

Drexel & Company
135-143 S. Fifteenth St.
HABS PA-1503
HABS PA,51-PHILA,311-
1ph/1pg L

Drexel Institute (Drexel University)
Thirty-second & Chestnut Sts.
HABS PA-1630
HABS PA,51-PHILA,302-
3ph/1pg L

Drexel University; see Drexel Institute

Drinker,John,House
241 Pine St.
HABS PA-1325
HABS PA,51-PHILA,317-
3ph/1pg L

Drinker,John,House; see Krider Gun Shop

Drinker's Court
236-238 Delancey St.
HABS PA-1326
HABS PA,51-PHILA,303-
6ph/1pg L

Duche House
24 Catherine St.
HABS PA-1552
HABS PA,51-PHILA,362-
6ph L

Duche-Walker House
26 Catherine St.
HABS PA-1553
HABS PA,51-PHILA,363-
4ph/1pg L

Dunlap-Eyre House
1003 Spruce St.
HABS PA-1504
HABS PA,51-PHILA,295-
1ph/1pg L

Eagle Hotel
601-607 W. Girard Ave.
HABS PA-1727
HABS PA,51-PHILA,355-
4ph/1pg L

Eakins,Thomas,House
1729 Mt. Vernon St.
HABS PA-1728
HABS PA,51-PHILA,528-
1ph L

Eastburn Mariners' Bethel Church (Presbyterian)
Front & Delancey Sts.
HABS PA-1327
HABS PA,51-PHILA,463-
2ph/2pg L

Eastern State Penitentiary
Fairmount,Corinthian,Brown & Twenty-second Sts.
HABS PA-1729
HABS PA,51-PHILA,354-
9ph/1pg L

Eckert-Tarrant House
38 Catherine St.
HABS PA-1554
HABS PA,51-PHILA,366-
4ph L

Elfreth,Jeremiah,House
126 Elfreth's Alley
HABS PA-1413
HABS PA,51-PHILA,272A-
6ph L

Elfreth's Alley (Houses)
HABS PA-1103
HABS PA,51-PHILA,272-
19dr/10ph L

Elliot,John,House
37 Queen St.
HABS PA-1555
HABS PA,51-PHILA,548-
6ph L

Elliot,John,House; see Marshall's Court Area Study

Ellison,John B. & Sons,Building
22-26 S. Sixth St.
HABS PA-1414
HABS PA,51-PHILA,290-
2ph/1pg L

Locations: **H** HABS/HAER, National Park Service **L** Library of Congress

Elwell,Henry,House
812 S. Front St.
HABS PA-1556
HABS PA,51-PHILA,449-
1ph L

Enlisted Men's Barracks; see Schuylkill Arsenal,Building No. 1

Episcopal Hospital; see Hospital of Protestant Episcopal Church in Phila.

Estlack,Thomas,House
413 Lombard St.
HABS PA-1328
HABS PA,51-PHILA,506-
1ph L

Executive Officers' Quarters; see Schuylkill Arsenal,Building No. 1A

Fairmount Bridge; see Callowhill Street Bridge

Fairmount Waterworks
Aquarium Dr. ,Fairmount Park
HABS PA-1654
HAER PA-51
HABS/HAER PA,51-PHILA,328-
36dr/170ph/198pg/14pc/23ct/fr L

Falls Bridge
Span. Schuylkill Riv. connect. E.& W. River Drives
HAER PA-35
HAER PA, 51-PHILA, 701-
12ph/2pg/1pc/2ct/fr L

Falls Bridge; see Philadelphia & Reading RR,Schuylkill River Viaduct

Far East Chinese Restaurant; see 907-909 Race Street (Commercial Buildings)

Farmers' & Mechanics' Bank
427 Chestnut St.
HABS PA-1415
HABS PA,51-PHILA,377-
4ph/3pg L

Federal Reserve Bank (Federal Reserve Bank of Philadelphia)
921-939 Chestnut St.
HABS PA-1506
HABS PA,51-PHILA,301-
6ph/1pg L

Federal Reserve Bank of Philadelphia; see Federal Reserve Bank

Fell-Van Rensselaer House (Pennsylvania Athletic Club)
Eighteenth & Walnut Sts.
HABS PA-1507
HABS PA,51-PHILA,586-
10ph L

Fielding,Mantle,House
28 W. Walnut Lane
HABS PA-1687
HABS PA,51-PHILA,286-
1ph/1pg L

Finlow-Nichell House
770 S. Front St.
HABS PA-1558
HABS PA,51-PHILA,442-
3ph L

Fire Association Building (Irvin Building)
401-403 Walnut St.
HABS PA-1434
HABS PA,51-PHILA,594-
1ph L

Fireman's Hall; see Philadelphia Fire Department,Engine Co. Number 8

First Bank of the United States (Girard's,Stephen,Bank)
120 S. Third St.
HABS PA-1417
HABS PA,51-PHILA,235-
17dr/7ph/fr L

First Baptist Church of Germantown
36-42 E. Price St.
HABS PA-1688
HABS PA,51-PHILA,299-
2ph/1pg L

First German Reformed Church
322-330 Race St.
HABS PA-1910
HABS PA,51-PHILA,554-
1ph L

First German Reformed Church Area Study (129-151 North Fourth Street (Houses))
HABS PA-1418
HABS PA,51-PHILA,643-
5ph/1pg L

First National Bank (First Pennsylvania Banking & Trust Company)
315 Chestnut St.
HABS PA-1011
HABS PA,51-PHILA,241-
2ph/4pg/9ct L

First Pennsylvania Banking & Trust Company; see First National Bank

First Pennsylvania Banking & Trust Company; see Kensington National Bank

First Polish Baptist Church; see Mariners' Bethel Church

First Presbyterian Church
Seventh St. & Washington Sq. Vic.
HABS PA-1117
HABS PA,51-PHILA,124-
15dr L

First Unitarian Church
2121 Chestnut St.
HABS PA-1508
HABS PA,51-PHILA,296-
4ph/1pg L

Fitzgerald,Thomas,House
437 Lombard St.
HABS PA-1329
HABS PA,51-PHILA,508-
1ph L

11-23 Fitzwater Street (Houses); see Fitzwater Street Area Study I

24-32 Fitzwater Street (Houses); see Fitzwater Street Area Study II

Fitzwater Street Area Study I (11-23 Fitzwater Street (Houses))
HABS PA-1559
HABS PA,51-PHILA,411-
3ph L

Fitzwater Street Area Study II (24-32 Fitzwater Street (Houses))
HABS PA-1560
HABS PA,51-PHILA,412-
2ph L

Fleisher,Samuel S. ,Art Memorial
711-721 Catharine St.
HABS PA-1229
HABS PA,51-PHILA,369-
10dr L

Flickwir-Williamson Houses
809-811 S. Hancock St.
HABS PA-1561
HABS PA,51-PHILA,481-
1ph L

Folwell House
5281 Germantown Ave.
HABS PA-1689
HABS PA,51-GERM,179-
1ph L

Fort Mifflin
Mud Island,Marine & Penrose Ferry Rds.
HABS PA-1225
HABS PA,51-PHILA,111-
9dr/73ph/128pg/9ct/fr L

Fort Mifflin Arsenal; see Fort Mifflin,Guard House

Fort Mifflin Officers' Quarters
Mud Island,Marine & Penrose Ferry Rds.
HABS PA-1225-F
HABS PA,51-PHILA,111F-
6dr/17ph/7pg/fr L

Fort Mifflin,Artillery Shed
Mud Island,Marine & Penrose Ferry Rds.
HABS PA-1225-B
HABS PA,51-PHILA,111B-
5dr/7ph/5pg/fr L

Fort Mifflin,Commandant's House (Headquarters)
Mud Island,Marine & Penrose Ferry Rds.
HABS PA-1225-C
HABS PA,51-PHILA,111C-
8dr/33ph/11pg/fr L

Fort Mifflin,Commissary; see Fort Mifflin,Storehouse

Fort Mifflin,Frame Guard House
Mud Island,Marine & Penrose Ferry Rds.
HABS PA-1225-J
HABS PA,51-PHILA,111J-
1ph L

Documentation: **ct** color transparencies **dr** measured drawings **fr** field records
pc photograph captions **pg** pages of text **ph** photographs

Fort Mifflin,Guard House (Fort Mifflin Arsenal)
Mud Island,Marine & Penrose Ferry Rds.
HABS PA-1225-A
HABS PA,51-PHILA,111A-
2dr/6ph/5pg/fr L

Fort Mifflin,Hospital (Fort Mifflin,Mess House)
Mud Island,Marine & Penrose Ferry Rds.
HABS PA-1225-I
HABS PA,51-PHILA,111I-
6dr/4ph/6pg/fr L

Fort Mifflin,Mess House; see Fort Mifflin,Hospital

Fort Mifflin,Powder Magazine
Mud Island,Marine & Penrose Ferry Rds.
HABS PA-1225-G
HABS PA,51-PHILA,111G-
3dr/13ph/8pg/fr L

Fort Mifflin,Smith's Shop
Mud Island,Marine & Penrose Ferry Rds.
HABS PA-1225-H
HABS PA,51-PHILA,111H-
4dr/12ph/5pg/fr L

Fort Mifflin,Soldiers' Barracks
Mud Island,Marine & Penrose Ferry Rds.
HABS PA-1225-E
HABS PA,51-PHILA,111E-
5dr/16ph/7pg/fr L

Fort Mifflin,Storehouse (Fort Mifflin,Commissary)
Mud Island,Marine & Penrose Ferry Rds.
HABS PA-1225-D
HABS PA,51-PHILA,111D-
2dr/5ph/4pg/fr L

Fountain of the Sea Horses
Aquarium Lane
HABS PA-1656
HABS PA,51-PHILA,287-
2ph/1pg L

Frankford Arensal,Building 35
Bridge & Tacony Sts.
HAER PA-74-A
10ph/3pg/1pc L

Frankford Arsenal
Bridge & Tacony Sts.
HAER PA-74
HAER PA,51-PHILA,693-
6ph/24pg/1pc L

Frankford Arsenal,Building Substation
SE corner CraigRd. & Montgomery St.
HAER PA-74-BX
1ph/3pg/1pc L

Frankford Arsenal,Building 106
Bridge & Tacony Sts.
HAER PA-74-D
13ph/4pg/2pc L

Frankford Arsenal,Building 113
SW corner Craig Rd. & Baker St.
HAER PA-74-AQ
1ph/3pg/1pc L

Frankford Arsenal,Building 117
East side Montgomery St. btwn Worth & Crozier Rds.
HAER PA-74-AR
1ph/3pg/1pc L

Frankford Arsenal,Building 118
West side Mellon St. btwn Worth & Crozier Rds.
HAER PA-74-AS
1ph/3pg/1pc L

Frankford Arsenal,Building 129
NE corner of Craig Rd. & Thomas St.
HAER PA-74-AT
1ph/3pg/1pc L

Frankford Arsenal,Building 130
NE corner of Williams S. & Craig Rd.
HAER PA-74-U
8ph/3pg/1pc L

Frankford Arsenal,Building 131
NE corner of Craid Rd. & Clay St.
HAER PA-74-AU
1ph/3pg/1pc L

Frankford Arsenal,Building 133
North side Craid Rd.,west of Eakin St.
HAER PA-74-AV
1ph/3pg/1pc L

Frankford arsenal,Building 135
NE cornerof Mellon St. & Craig Rd.
HAER PA-74-AW
1ph/3pg/1pc L

Frankford Arsenal,Building 137
NW corner Craig Rd. & Walbach St.
HAER PA-74-AX
2ph/3pg/1pc L

Frankford Arsenal,Building 138
East side Eakin St.,north of Craig St.
HAER PA-74-AY
1ph/3pg/1pc L

Frankford Arsenal,Building 140
SE corner Eakin St. & Worth Rd.
HAER PA-74-AZ
1ph/3pg/1pc L

Frankford Arsenal,Building 141-143
South side Worth Rd. btwn Eakin St. & Walbach St.
HAER PA-74-V
3ph/3pg/1pc L

Frankford Arsenal,Building 148
Bridge & Tacony Sts.
HAER PA-74-H
6ph/3pg/1pc L

Frankford Arsenal,Building 148A
East side Eakin St. btwn Craid & Worth Rds.
HAER PA-74-BA
1ph/3pg/1pc L

Frankford Arsenal,Building 151
East side Dearborn St.,north of Craig Rd.
HAER PA-74-BB
3ph/3pg/1pc L

Frankford Arsenal,Building 20
North side of Mordecai Rd.,West of Mellon St.
HAER PA-74-AJ
1ph/3pg/1pc L

Frankford Arsenal,Building 202A
North side Hagner Rd. btwn Heath & Whittemore Sts.
HAER PA-74-BC
1ph/3pg/1pc L

Frankford Arsenal,Building 203
SE corner of Heath St. & Hagner Rd.
HAER PA-74-BD
1ph/3pg/1pc L

Frankford Arsenal,Building 204
NE corner of Craid Rd. & Heath St.
HAER PA-74-BE
1ph/3pg/1pc L

Frankford Arsenal,Building 206
Bridge & Tacony Sts.
HAER PA-74-I
9ph/3pg/1pc L

Frankford Arsenal,Building 207
NW corner Baker St. & Hagner Rd.
HAER PA-74-W
7ph/3pg/1pc L

Frankford Arsenal,Building 211
Bridge & Tacony Sts.
HAER PA-74-E
11ph/4pg/1pc L

Frankford Arsenal,Building 213-214
Bridge & Tacony Sts.
HAER PA-74-J
11ph/3pg/1pc L

Frankford Arsenal,Building 216
Bridge & Tacony Sts.
HAER PA-74-K
6ph/3pg/1pc L

Frankford Arsenal,Building 217
Bridge & Tacony Sts.
HAER PA-74-L
7ph/3pg/1pc L

Frankford Arsenal,Building 221
NE corner of Mellon St. & Farley Rd.
HAER PA-74-X
3ph/3pg/1pc L

Frankford Arsenal,Building 223
South side Hagner Rd. btwn. Mellow & Ripley Sts.
HAER PA-74-M
7ph/3pg/1pc L

Frankford Arsenal,Building 227
South side of Hagner Rd. btwn Ripley & Mellon Sts.
HAER PA-74-Y
15ph/3pg/2pc L

Frankford Arsenal,Building 232
East side Ripley St.,north of Hagner Rd.
HAER PA-74-BF
1ph/3pg/1pc L

Frankford Arsenal,Building 233
South side Craig Rd. btwn Bldgs. 201 & 202
HAER PA-74-BG
1ph/3pg/1pc L

Frankford Arsenal,Building 238
NE corner Clay St. & Hagner Rd.
HAER PA-74-Z
7ph/3pg/1pc L

Frankford Arsenal,Building 239-239A
SE corner of Clay St. & Cray Rd.
HAER PA-74-AA
16ph/3pg/2pc L

Frankford Arsenal,Building 240
NE corner Hagner Rd. & Clay St.
HAER PA-74-AB
9ph/3pg/1pc L

Frankford Arsenal,Building 242-246A
South side Craig Rd. btwn Eakin & Walbach Sts.
HAER PA-74-AC
20ph/4pg/2pc L

Frankford Arsenal,Building 249
NW corner of Hagner Rd. & Eakin St.
HAER PA-74-BJ
1ph/3pg/1pc L

Frankford Arsenal,Building 251
NE corner Hagner Rd. & Walbach St.
HAER PA-74-N
12ph/3pg/1pc L

Frankford Arsenal,Building 252
NW corner of Hagner Rd. & Dearborn St.
HAER PA-74-O
8ph/3pg/1pc L

Frankford Arsenal,Building 253
SW corner of Craig Rd. & Montgomery St.
HAER PA-74-BK
1ph/3pg/1pc L

Frankford Arsenal,Building 254-255
Montgomery St., btwn Hagner & Craid Rds.
HAER PA-74-BL
1ph/3pg/1pc L

Frankford Arsenal,Building 256
West side of Mellon St. btwn Farley & Craid Rds.
HAER PA-74-BM
1ph/3pg/1pc L

Frankford Arsenal,Building 261
East of Clay St. btwn Craid & Hagner Rds.
HAER PA-74-BN
1ph/3pg/1pc L

Frankford Arsenal,Building 264
SE coner Eakin St. & Craid Rd.
HAER PA-74-BO
1ph/3pg/1pc L

Frankford Arsenal,Building 265
NE corner of Farley Rd. & Mellon St.
HAER PA-74-BP
1ph/3pg/1pc L

Frankford Arsenal,Building 266
NE corner Farley Rd. & Mellon St.
HAER PA-74-BQ
1ph/3pg/1pc L

Frankford Arsenal,Building 267
SW corner of Craig Rd. & Eakin St.
HAER PA-74-BR
1ph/3pg/1pc L

Frankford Arsenal,Building 29
SE corner of Mellon St. & Mordecai Rd.
HAER PA-74-R
7ph/3pg/1pc L

Frankford Arsenal,Building 30/31
Bridge & Tacony Sts.
HAER PA-74-F
2ph/3pg/1pc L

Frankford Arsenal,Building 301
SE conrner of Hagner Rd. & Thomas St.
HAER PA-74-P
16ph/3pg/1pc L

Frankford Arsenal,Building 303
NW corner Bricker Rd. & Eakin St.
HAER PA-74-BS
1ph/3pg/1pc L

Frankford Arsenal,Building 305
Bridge & Tacony Sts.
HAER PA-74-AD
6ph/3pg/1pc L

Frankford Arsenal,Building 308
North side Laidley Rd. btwn Walbach & Eakin Sts.
HAER PA-74-AE
6ph/3pg/1pc L

Frankford Arsenal,Building 309
South of Hagner Rd. to west of Clay St.
HAER PA-74-AF
4ph/3pg/1pc L

Frankford Arsenal,Building 310
SW corner Eakin St. & Munroe Rd.
HAER PA-74-BT
1ph/3pg/1pc L

Frankford Arsenal,Building 311
SW corner of Hagner Rd. & Eakin St.
HAER PA-74-AG
4ph/3pg/1pc L

Frankford Arsenal,Building 312
NE Corner of Walbach S. & Monroe Rd.
HAER PA-74-AH
7ph/3pg/1pc L

Frankford Arsenal,Building 316
NW corner Eakin St. & Treadwell Rd.
HAER PA-74-Q
10ph/3pg/1pc L

Frankford Arsenal,Building 318
West Eakin St. btwn Hagner & Munroe Rds.
HAER PA-74-BU
1ph/3pg/1pc L

Frankford Arsenal,Building 319
SW corner of Eakin St. & Treadwell Rd.
HAER PA-74-AI
3ph/3pg/1pc L

Frankford Arsenal,Building 320
South side of Laidley Rd. btwn Eakin St. & Walbach
HAER PA-74-BV
2ph/3pg/1pc L

Frankford Arsenal,Building 322
South side of Bricker Rd. btwn Eakin & Walbach Sts
HAER PA-74-BW
1ph/3pg/1pc L

Frankford Arsenal,Building 38A
West side Rodman St. btwn Benet Rd. & Worth Rd.
HAER PA-74-AM
3ph/3pg/1pc L

Frankford Arsenal,Building 40
Bridge & Tacony Sts.
HAER PA-74-B
9ph/3pg/1pc L

Frankford Arsenal,Building 43
SE corner of Mordecai Rd. & Mellon St.
HAER PA-74-AN
1ph/3pg/1pc L

Frankford Arsenal,Building 46
Bridge & Tacony Sts.
HAER PA-74-G
9ph/3pg/1pc L

Frankford Arsenal,Building 59
SE corner Mordecai Rd. & Ripley Sts.
HAER PA-74-AO
1ph/3pg/1pc L

Frankford Arsenal,Building 65
Bridge & Tacony Sts.
HAER PA-74-C
9ph/3pg/1pc L

Frankford Arsenal,Building 66
North of Benet Rd. & east of Walbach St.
HAER PA-74-S
5ph/3pg/1pc L

Frankford Arsenal,Building 68
SE corner of Walbach St. & Benet Rd.
HAER PA-74-T
10ph/3pg/1pc L

Frankford Arsenal,Building 72
West side Walbach St. north of Benet Rd.
HAER PA-74-AP
1ph/3pg/1pc L

Frankford Arsenl,Building 24
North side of Mordecai Rd.,West of Mellon St.
HAER PA-74-AK
1ph/3pg/1pc L

Frankford Town Hall
4255 Frankford Ave.
HABS PA-1758
HABS PA,51-PHILA,293-
1ph/1pg L

Franklin Hose Company,No. 28
(Harmony Engine Company,No. 6)
730-732 S. Broad St.
HABS PA-1566
HABS PA,51-PHILA,349-
2ph L

Franklin Institute
(Kent,Atwater,Museum)
15 S. Seventh St.
HABS PA-121
HABS PA,51-PHILA,153-
7dr/1ph/3pg/1pc L

Franklin Row; see Sims,Joseph,House

Franklin Sugar Refinery (Merchants Warehouse Company)
701-715 S. Front St.
HABS PA-1562
HABS PA,51-PHILA,438-
1ph/1pg L

Free Quakers Meetinghouse
500 Arch St.
HABS PA-1120
HABS PA,51-PHILA,158-
22dr/11ph/1pg/fr L

Friends Select School,Log Cabin (Two Story Log House)
Sixteenth & Race Sts.
HABS PA-143
HABS PA,51-PHILA,227-
2ph L

Friendship Engine Company,Number Fifteen (Hook & Ladder Company C)
2200-2204 E. Norris St.
HABS PA-1759
HABS PA,51-PHILA,533-
1ph/2pg L

Fromberger,John,Houses (Germantown Insurance Company)
5501 Germantown Ave.
HABS PA-1690
HABS PA,51-PHILA,298-
1ph/1pg L

Fullerton,John,Houses; see 606-608 South Front Street (Houses)

Garden,C. H. ,& Company,Building
606 Market St.
HABS PA-1419
HABS PA,51-PHILA,517-
2ph/1pg L

Garrett-Buchanan Company,Paper Dealers; see Megargee Brothers Paper Warehouse

Gaul-Forrest House
1326 N. Broad St.
HABS PA-1730
HABS PA,51-PHILA,323-
1ph/1pg L

Gentilhommiere; see Girard,Stephen,Country House

George,Henry,Birthplace
413 S. Tenth St.
HABS PA-1509
HABS PA,51-PHILA,310-
9dr/1ph/1pg L

Germantown Academy (Germantown Union School)
110 Schoolhouse Lane
HABS PA-7-4
HABS PA,51-GERM,33-
17dr/8ph/2pg/fr L

6000-6002 Germantown Avenue (House)
HABS PA-1698
HABS PA,51-PHILA,185-
1ph L

6377 Germantown Avenue (House)
HABS PA-1699
HABS PA,51-GERM,186-
4ph/2pg L

6505-6507 Germantown Avenue (House) (Billmeyer,Michael,House)
HABS PA-1677
HABS PA,51-GERM,67-
1ph/1pg/1pc L

Germantown Cricket Club (Manheim Club)
5140 Morris St.
HABS PA-1693
HABS PA,51-PHILA,104-
2ph/1pc L

Germantown Historic District (Green Tree Tavern; Pastorius House)
6023 Germantown Ave.
HABS PA-1695
HABS PA,51-GERM,45-
1ph/1pc L

Germantown Historical Society Area Study
5208-5214-5218 Germantown Ave.
HABS PA-1694
HABS PA,51-GERM,177-
1ph L

Germantown Historical Society Area Study (Baynton House)
5208 Germantown Ave.
HABS PA-1694-A
HABS PA,51-GERM,178-
1ph L

Germantown Historical Society Area Study (Conyngham-Hacker House)
5214 Germantown Ave.
HABS PA-1694-B
HABS PA,51-GERM,20-
1ph L

Germantown Historical Society Area Study (Howell House)
5218 Germantown Ave.
HABS PA-1694-C
HABS PA,51-GERM,96-
2ph L

Germantown Insurance Company; see Fromberger,John,Houses

Germantown Union School; see Germantown Academy

Girard Avenue Bridge
Girard Ave. ,spanning Schuykill River
HABS PA-1657
HABS PA,51-PHILA,461-
16ph L

Girard Bank; see Girard Trust Corn Exchange Bank

Girard College,Founder's Hall
Girard & Corinthian Aves.
HABS PA-1731
HABS PA,51-PHILA,459A-
7ph/3ct L

Girard Row (Houses)
326-334 Spruce St.
HABS PA-1330
HABS PA,51-PHILA,687-
1dr/6ph/fr L

Girard Trust Corn Exchange Bank (Girard Bank)
34-36 S. Broad St.
HABS PA-1510
HABS PA,51-PHILA,319-
2ph/1pg L

Girard,Stephen,Country House (Gentilhommiere)
Shunk & Twenty-first Sts.
HABS PA-140
HABS PA,51-PHLA,226-
11dr/24ph/20pg L

Girard,Stephen,Country House (Utility Building)
Shunk & Twenty-first Sts.
HABS PA-1082
HABS PA,51-PHILA,226A-
3dr/5ph/4pg L

Girard's,Stephen,Bank; see First Bank of the United States

Gladstone Hotel (Greystone Apartments)
328-338 S. Front St.
HABS PA-1511
HABS PA,51-PHILA,425-
2ph/1pg L

Glebe House
HABS PA-139
HABS PA,51-PHILA,225-
14dr/2ph L

Glen Fern; see Livezey House

Gloria Dei (Church) (Swedes Church,Old)
929 S. Water St.
HABS PA-120
HABS PA,51-PHILA,174-
10dr/15ph/2pg/fr L

Gloria Dei,Rectory
929 S. Water St.
HABS PA-120-A
HABS PA,51-PHILA,174B-
2ph L

Godley,Jesse,Warehouse
19-27 Queen St.
HABS PA-1564
HABS PA,51-PHILA,544-
4ph L

Godley's Stores; see Granite Street Vaults

Gordon,George,Building
300 Arch St.
HABS PA-1065
HABS PA,51-PHILA,258-
4dr/5ph/5pg L

Granite Street Vaults (Godley's Stores)
100-112 & 101-127 Granite St.
HABS PA-1420
HABS PA,51-PHILA,543-
3ph/1pg/fr L

2201-2205 Green Street (House)
(Kemble-Bergdol House)
HABS PA-1732
HABS PA,51-PHILA,472-
3ph L

2219 Green Street (House)
HABS PA-1907
HABS PA,51-PHILA,474-
1ph L

2221 Green Street (House)
HABS PA-1908
HABS PA,51-PHILA,475-
2ph L

2223 Green Street (House)
HABS PA-1909
HABS PA,51-PHILA,476-
4ph L

2213-2215 Green Street (Houses)
HABS PA-1906
HABS PA,51-PHILA,473-
3ph L

2225-2227 Green Street (Houses)
HABS PA-1911
HABS PA,51-PHILA,477-
1ph L

2229-2231 Green Street (Houses)
HABS PA-1912
HABS PA,51-PHILA,478-
1ph L

Green Tree Tavern; see Germantown Historic District

Greystone Apartments; see Gladstone Hotel

Griffith-Peale House
8100 Frankford Ave.
HABS PA-1761
HABS PA,51-PHILA,413-
3ph/1pg L

Grumblethorpe (Wister's Big House)
5267 Germantown Ave.
HABS PA-7-1
HABS PA,51-GERM,23-
10dr/6ph/4pg L

Grumblethorpe Tenant House (Wister's Tenant House)
5269 Germantown Ave.
HABS PA-7-6
HABS PA,51-GERM,24-
9dr/4ph/1pg L

Haines House; see Wyck

Hall-Wister House
330 S. Third St.
HABS PA-1332
HABS PA,51-PHILA,640A-
3ph/1pg L

Hall,John,House
327 S. Third St.
HABS PA-1331
HABS PA,51-PHILA,638-
1dr/5ph L

Hamilton Village; see Woodlands

Hamilton-Hoffman House (Burnside)
Coggs Creek Parkway
HABS PA-1053
HABS PA,51-PHILA,252-
13ph/8pg L

Hamilton,Andrew,House; see Woodlands

Hansell,John,House
153 N. Sixth St.
HABS PA-1012
HABS PA,51-PHILA,242-
1ph/4pg L

Harmony Engine Company,No. 6; see Franklin Hose Company,No. 28

Harper,Thomas,House,Wall Stencil
421 S. Second St.
HABS PA-5197
HABS PA,51-PHILA,624-
1dr L

Harrison Building
4 S. Fifteenth St.
HABS PA-1088
HABS PA,51-PHILA,268-
15ph/7pg L

Harrison House
Point No Point (Richmond Ave.)
HABS PA-1458
HABS PA,51-PHILA,232-
2ph L

Harrison,Charles C. ,Building
1001-1005 Market St.
HABS PA-550
HABS PA,51-PHILA,520-
7ph/6pg/fr L

Harrison,Henry,Houses
112-116 Cuthbert St.
HABS PA-1421
HABS PA,51-PHILA,692-
1dr/4ph/3pg L

Hart-Patterson House; see 603 South Front Street (House)

Hart,John,House
601 S. Front St.
HABS PA-1568
HABS PA,51-PHILA,433-
1ph L

Hatfield House
Thirty-third St. & Girard Ave.
HABS PA-1658
HABS PA,51-PHILA,233-
14ph/2pg/1pc/fr L

Hellings,Benjamin,House
931 S. Front St.
HABS PA-1570
HABS PA,51-PHILA,455-
1ph L

Hensel,Colladay & Company Factory
45-51 N. Seventh St.
HABS PA-1422
HABS PA,51-PHILA,308-
2ph/3pg L

Hill-Physick House (Hill-Physick-Keith House)
321 S. Fourth St.
HABS PA-1334
HABS PA,51-PHILA,36-
5ph/2pg/fr L

Hill-Physick-Keith House; see Hill-Physick House

Hill,David,House
309 S. Third St.
HABS PA-1333
HABS PA,51-PHILA,283-
7ph/1pg/1ct L

Hilyard,Eber,House
427 Lombard St.
HABS PA-1335
HABS PA,51-PHILA,507-
1ph L

Historical Society of Pennsylvania (mantlepiece)
1300 Locust St.
HABS PA-1942
HABS PA,51-PHILA,496-
1ph L

Hockley,Thomas,House
235 S. Twenty-first St.
HABS PA-1512
HABS PA,51-PHILA,282-
1ph/1pg L

Holloway,Thomas,Houses
125-131 Ellen St.
HABS PA-1763
HABS PA,51-PHILA,408-
2ph L

Holy Redeemer Chinese Catholic Church & School
Vine St. & Ridge Ave.
HABS PA-1513
HABS PA,51-PHILA,557-
2ph L

Holy Trinity Roman Catholic Church (German)
601-609 Spruce St.
HABS PA-1336
HABS PA,51-PHILA,573-
4ph L

Hood Cemetery,Entrance
4901 Germantown Ave.
HABS PA-1697
HABS PA,51-PHILA,325-
2ph L

Hook & Ladder Company C; see Friendship Engine Company,Number Fifteen

Hope Engine Company,Number Seventeen
733 S. Sixth St.
HABS PA-1572
HABS PA,51-PHILA,659-
2ph/2pg L

Hope Hose Co. No. 6 & Fellowship Engine Co. No. 29 (New Market,Head House)
Second St. between Pine & Lombard
HABS PA-1351
HABS PA,51-PHILA,28-
2ph L

Hopkinson House; see Williams-Hopkinson House

Hospital of Protestant Episcopal Church in Phila. (Episcopal Hospital)
Front St. & Lehigh Ave.
HABS PA-1764
HABS PA,51-PHILA,416-
14ph L

Hotel Walton (Bartram,John,Hotel)
Broad & Locust Sts.
HABS PA-1091
HABS PA,51-PHILA,269-
6ph/11pg L

House on Old Turnpike
Frankford Ave.
HABS PA-1429
HABS PA,51-PHILA,236-
2ph L

Houston-Sauveur House
8205 Seminole Ave.
HABS PA-1700
HABS PA,51-PHILA,565-
2ph L

Howell & Brothers Building
12-14 S. Sixth St.
HABS PA-1428
HABS PA,51-PHILA,657-
1ph/1pg L

Howell House; see Germantown Historical Society Area Study

Independence Hall Complex,City Hall; see Philadelphia City Hall

Independence Hall Complex,Congress Hall; see Congress Hall

Independence Hall Complex,Independence Hall (State House of Pennsylvania; Independence National Historical Park)
Chestnut St.
HABS PA-1430
HABS PA,51-PHILA,6-
45dr/130ph/10pc/35ct/fr L

Independence National Historical Park
Walnut,Sixth,Chestnut, & Second Sts.
HABS PA-1951
HABS PA,51-PHILA,6D-
18ph L

Independence National Historical Park; see Congress Hall

Independence National Historical Park; see Dilworth-Todd-Moylan House

Independence National Historical Park; see Dilworth-Todd-Moylan House,Rear Wing

Independence National Historical Park; see Independence Hall Complex,Independence Hall

Independence National Historical Park; see Philadelphia City Hall

Independence National Historical Park; see Philadelphia Exchange Company

Independence National Historical Park; see Second Bank of the United States

Independence National Historical Park; see Stable & Carriage House

Independent Order of Odd Fellows
Third & Brown Sts.
HABS PA-1771
HABS PA,51-PHILA,353-
4ph/7pg L

Institute of the Penn. Hospital,Dept. for Males; see Pennsylvania Hosp. for the Insane,Dept. for Males

Insurance Patrol Building
509 Arch St.
HABS PA-1433
HABS PA,51-PHILA,329-
1ph/2pg/fr L

International Exhibition of 1876,Memorial Hall
Belmont Ave. ,Fairmount Park
HABS PA-1659
HABS PA,51-PHILA,265B-
4ph/3pg L

International Exhibition of 1876,Ohio Building (Ohio House)
Belmont Ave. ,Fairmount Park
HABS PA-1660
HABS PA,51-PHILA,265C-
5ph L

International Exhibition of 1876,St. George's Hse. (British Building)
State's Dr.
HABS PA-1080
HABS PA,51-PHILA,265A-
7ph/4pg L

Irish,Nathaniel,House
704 S. Front St.
HABS PA-1013
HABS PA,51-PHILA,243-
1dr/8ph/8pg L

Irvin Building; see Fire Association Building

Italian Villa; see Lea,Henry Charles,House

Iungerich Warehouse
147 S. Front St.
HABS PA-1403
HABS PA,51-PHILA,421-
1ph L

Ivy Lodge
29 E. Penn St.
HABS PA-1701
HABS PA,51-PHILA,535-
1ph L

Jacoby,Wigard,House
8327 Germantown Ave.
HABS PA-1702
HABS PA,51-GERM,153-
1ph/1pg L

Jayne Building (Jayne,Dr. ,Granite Building)
242-244 Chestnut St.
HABS PA-188
HABS PA,51-PHILA,237-
16dr/15ph/3pg/fr L

Jayne,Dr. ,Granite Building; see Jayne Building

Jefferson Fire Insurance Company
425 Walnut St.
HABS PA-1435
HABS PA,51-PHILA,597-
2ph L

Jefferson,Joseph,House
600 Spruce St.
HABS PA-1340
HABS PA,51-PHILA,572-
1ph L

Jordan-Stoddart House
404 S. Fifth St.
HABS PA-1341
HABS PA,51-PHILA,656-
1ph L

Justi,Henry D. ,House
Thirty-fourth & Baring Sts.
HABS PA-1632
HABS PA,51-PHILA,336-
2ph L

Keen,James,House
946 S. Front St.
HABS PA-1587
HABS PA,51-PHILA,456-
1ph/1pg L

Kemble-Bergdol House; see 2201-2205 Green Street (House)

121-123 Kenilworth Street (alley door)
HABS PA-1446
HABS PA,51-PHILA,488A-
1ph L

109 Kenilworth Street (House)
HABS PA-1588
HABS PA,51-PHILA,486-
2ph L

117 Kenilworth Street (House)
HABS PA-1437
HABS PA,51-PHILA,487-
1ph L

Kensington National Bank (First Pennsylvania Banking & Trust Company)
2-8 W. Girard Ave.
HABS PA-1773
HABS PA,51-PHILA,460-
2ph L

Kent,Atwater,Museum; see Franklin Institute

Keyser Brothers Iron Works
4041 Ridge Ave.
HAER PA-40
HAER PA,51-GERM,192-
16ph/2pc L

Kid-Chandler & Kid-Physick Houses
323-325 Walnut St.
HABS PA-1436
HABS PA,51-PHILA,591-
3ph/1pg/fr L

Kid-Chandler House
323 Walnut St.
HABS PA-1436-A
HABS PA,51-PHILA,591A-
49ph/fr L

Kid-Physick House
325 Walnut St.
HABS PA-1436-B
HABS PA,51-PHILA,591B-
20ph/fr L

Kirkbride Residence; see Busti,Paul,House

Kirkbride's Hospital; see Pennsylvania Hospital for Mental & Nervous Disease

Kosciuszko,Thaddeus,House
301 Pine St.
HABS PA-1342
HABS PA,51-PHILA,536-
2ph L

Krider Gun Shop (Drinker,John,House)
133-135 Walnut St.
HABS PA-1055
HABS PA,51-PHILA,186-183(HABS):118°
16dr/6ph/9pg/1pc/fr L

Lamb,Peter,House
28 Catherine St.
HABS PA-1590
HABS PA,51-PHILA,364-
1ph L

Land Title Bank & Trust Company (Land Title Building)
100-118 S. Broad St.
HABS PA-1514
HABS PA,51-PHILA,345-
2ph/1pg L

Land Title Building; see Land Title Bank & Trust Company

Lasse Cock's Manor House; see Bel Air

Latour Warehouse
508 S. Water St.
HABS PA-1056
HABS PA,51-PHILA,254-
8dr/9ph/5pg/fr L

Laurel Hill (Rawle,Randolph,House)
Farimount Park
HABS PA-13
HABS PA,51-PHILA,12-
10dr/1ph/2pg/fr L

Laurel Hill Cemetery
3822 Ridge Ave. ,Fairmount Park
HABS PA-1811
HABS PA,51-PHILA,100-
2ph/1ct L

Laurel Hill Cemetery Gatehouse
3822 Ridge Ave.
HABS PA-1811-A
HABS PA,51-PHILA,100A-
2ph L

Lea,Henry Charles,House (Italian Villa)
3903 Spruce St.
HABS PA-1633
HABS PA,51-PHILA,580-
18ph L

123-125 League Street (Houses)
HABS PA-1583
HABS PA,51-PHILA,490-
1ph L

Lee,Robert M. ,House & Law Office
109-111 N. Sixth St.
HABS PA-1052
HABS PA,51-PHILA,251-
3dr/8ph/11pg/fr L

Leidy,Joseph Jr. ,House (Poor Richard Club)
1319 Locust St.
HABS PA-1515
HABS PA,51-PHILA,498-
1ph L

Leland Building
37-39 S. Third St.
HABS PA-1086
HABS PA,51-PHILA,267-
7ph/7pg L

Lemon Hill
Lemon Hill Dr. ,Fairmount Park
HABS PA-1010
HABS PA,51-PHILA,234-
2dr/4ph/1pg/fr L

Letitia Street House
Lansdowne Dr. ,W. Fairmount Park
HABS PA-184
HABS PA,51-PHILA,45-
4dr/3ph L

Library Company of Philadelphia,Ridgway Branch
900 S. Broad St.
HABS PA-1616
HABS PA,51-PHILA,350-
24ph/1pg L

Lippincott,Joshua B. ,House
204 S. Nineteenth St.
HABS PA-1516
HABS PA,51-PHILA,679-
8ph/1pg L

Lit Brothers Store
701-739 Market St.
HABS PA-1438
HABS PA,51-PHILA,519-
3ph/2pg L

Livezey House (Glen Fern)
Livezey Lane & Wissahickon Creek
HABS PA-14
HABS PA,51-GERM,91-
12dr/1ph/4pg/1pc/fr L

1314-1320 Locust Street (Buildings)
HABS PA-1917
HABS PA,51-PHILA,497-
1ph L

404-406-408 Locust Street (Houses)
HABS PA-1915
HABS PA,51-PHILA,491-
1ph L

117 Lombard Street (House) (Palmer,John,House)
HABS PA-1353
HABS PA,51-PHILA,500-
1ph/1pg L

323 Lombard Street (House)
HABS PA-1678
HABS PA,51-PHILA,502-
2ph L

325 Lombard Street (House)
HABS PA-1913
HABS PA,51-PHILA,503-
1ph L

327-329 Lombard Street (Houses)
HABS PA-1914
HABS PA,51-PHILA,504-
1ph L

331-333 Lombard Street (Houses)
HABS PA-1916
HABS PA,51-PHILA,505-
1ph L

Loudoun
4650 Germantown Ave.
HABS PA-1705
HABS PA,51-GERM,3-
2ph L

Luding Hall; see Schuylkill Arsenal,Building No. 1

Lyle-Newman Houses
905-907 S. Front St.
HABS PA-1592
HABS PA,51-PHILA,454-
1ph/1pg L

Mack,Connie,Stadium; see Shibe Park (stadium)

Maloby,Thomas,House & Tavern
700 S. Front St.
HABS PA-1595
HABS PA,51-PHILA,437-
1ph L

Man Full of Trouble Tavern; see Stafford's Tavern-Paschall House

Manhattan Building; see American Life Insurance Company Building

Manheim Club; see Germantown Cricket Club

Mariners' Bethel Church (First Polish Baptist Church; Bethel Christian Center)
923 S. Front St.
HABS PA-1596
HABS PA,51-PHILA,306-
1ph/1pg L

Market Street Area Study (Commercial Buildings) (617-637 Market Street)
HABS PA-1441
HABS PA,51-PHILA,518-
5ph/2pg/fr L

Market Street National Bank Building (One East Penn Square Building)
1-21 Juniper St.
HABS PA-1517
HABS PA,51-PHILA,484-
4ph L

617-637 Market Street; see Market Street Area Study (Commercial Buildings)

Marks-Dunbar House
849 S. Front St.
HABS PA-1597
HABS PA,51-PHILA,451-
4ph L

Marshall-Morris House
774 S. Front St.
HABS PA-1599
HABS PA,51-PHILA,443-
1ph/1pg L

Marshall,Joseph,Houses
854 S. Front St.
HABS PA-1598
HABS PA,51-PHILA,453-
1ph/1pg L

Marshall's Court Area Study (Elliot,John,House)
407 Marshall's Court
HABS PA-1345-B
HABS PA,51-PHILA,523B-
6ph L

Marshall's Court Area Study (403-411 Marshall's Court)
HABS PA-1345
HABS PA,51-PHILA,523-
3ph L

Marshall's Court Area Study (Shinn,Samuel,House)
403 Marshall's Court
HABS PA-1345-A
HABS PA,51-PHILA,523A-
3ph L

Marshall's Court Area Study (Simpson,David,House)
411 Marshall's Court
HABS PA-1345-C
HABS PA,51-PHILA,523G-
5ph L

403-411 Marshall's Court; see Marshall's Court Area Study

Mason,James S. & Company,Store
138-140 N. Front St.
HABS PA-1442
HABS PA,51-PHILA,418-
7ph/1pg L

Massey & Janney Leather Warehouse
355 N. Third St.
HABS PA-1782
HABS PA,51-PHILA,628-
3ph/1pg L

Maxfield-Elliott House
35 Queen St.
HABS PA-1600
HABS PA,51-PHILA,547-
4ph L

Maxwell,Ebenezer,House
200 W. Tulpehocken St.
HABS PA-1098
HABS PA,51-GERM,190-
7dr/11ph/9pg/fr L

McClare-Hutchinson Building
20 S. Third St.
HABS PA-1439
HABS PA,51-PHILA,629-
2ph L

McCraig,George,House
810 S. Front St.
HABS PA-1593
HABS PA,51-PHILA,448-
1ph L

McCrea,James,Houses
108-110 Sansom St.
HABS PA-1440
HABS PA,51-PHILA,564-
11dr/36ph/11pg/fr L

McKean,Thomas Jr. ,House
269 S. Fifth St.
HABS PA-190
HABS PA,51-PHILA,239-
1dr/5ph/4pg/fr L

McMullin,Robert,House
411 Pine St.
HABS PA-1344
HABS PA,51-PHILA,537-
8ph L

Mears-Heaton House
240 Delancey St.
HABS PA-1070
HABS PA,51-PHILA,385-
4dr/fr L

Mechanics' Bank (Norwegian Seamen's Church)
22 S. Third St.
HABS PA-1443
HABS PA,51-PHILA,630-
2ph/1pg L

Megargee Brothers Paper Warehouse (Garrett-Buchanan Company,Paper Dealers)
18-20 S. Sixth St.
HABS PA-1444
HABS PA,51-PHILA,658-
1ph L

Mehl House
4821 Germantown Ave.
HABS PA-1706
HABS PA,51-GERM,6-
1ph/1pg L

Mellon,Thomas,House
716 Spruce St.
HABS PA-1346
HABS PA,51-PHILA,574-
1ph/fr L

Mellor & Meigs Architectural Office
205 S. Juniper St.
HABS PA-1519
HABS PA,51-PHILA,485-
1ph/2pg L

Mennonite Meeting House
6119 Germantown Ave.
HABS PA-15
HABS PA,51-GERM,51-
7dr/1ph/2pg L

Mercer,Thomas,Houses
2-12 Christian St.
HABS PA-1601
HABS PA,51-PHILA,381-
5ph L

Merchants Warehouse Company; see Franklin Sugar Refinery

Merchants' Exchange; see Philadelphia Exchange Company

Merchants' Hotel (Washington Hotel)
40-50 N. Fourth St.
HABS PA-1445
HABS PA,51-PHILA,642-
12ph/7pg L

Met,The; see Philadelphia Opera House

Mifflin Building; see Schuylkill Arsenal,Building No. 2

Mikveh Israel Cemetery Gatehouse
1114 Federal St.
HABS PA-1602
HABS PA,51-PHILA,409A-
2ph L

Mitchell,Thomas,House
276 S. Third St.
HABS PA-1348
HABS PA,51-PHILA,636-
7ph L

Moffett-Urquhart House; see Moffett,Robert,House

Moffett,Robert,House (Moffett-Urquhart House)
35 Catherine St.
HABS PA-1603
HABS PA,51-PHILA,358-
1ph L

Monastery
Kitchen's Lane
HABS PA-183
HABS PA,51-GERM,90-
23dr/2ph/fr L

Moore,Clarence B. ,House
1321 Locust St.
HABS PA-1521
HABS PA,51-PHILA,499-
1ph L

Moore,John,House
734 S. Front St.
HABS PA-1605
HABS PA,51-PHILA,440-
1ph/1pg L

Morris Brewery Vaults
210 Chancellor St.
HABS PA-5331
HABS PA,51-PHILA,331A-
1pg/fr L

Morris House; see Compton

Morris House; see Reynolds-Morris House

Mother Bethel African Methodist Espiscopal Church; see Bethel African Methodist Episcopal Church

Mount Moriah Cemetery Gatehouse
6299 Kingsessing Ave.
HABS PA-1634
HABS PA,51-PHILA,489A-
4ph L

Mount Pleasant (Clunie)
East Fairmount Park
HABS PA-1130
HABS PA,51-PHILA,15-
31dr/24ph/1pc/1ct L

Mount Pleasant Dependency; see Mount Pleasant Kitchen

Mount Pleasant Kitchen (Mount Pleasant Dependency; Clunie Kitchen)
Mount Pleasant Dr.,Fairmount Park
HABS PA-1130-A
HABS PA,51-PHILA,15A-
1ph L

Mount Pleasant Office (Clunie Office)
Mount Pleasant Dr.,Fairmont Park
HABS PA-1130-B
1ph/1pc L

Mount Sinai Cemetery,Chapel
Bridge & Cottage Sts.
HABS PA-1783
HABS PA,51-PHILA,339A-
4ph/2ct L

Moyamensing Prison; see Philadelphia County Prison

Moyamensing Prison,Debtors' Wing; see Philadelphia County Prison,Debtors' Wing

Murphy-Johnson House
42 Catherine St.
HABS PA-1606
HABS PA,51-PHILA,367-
2ph L

Museum of Science & Art; see University of Pennsylvania,University Museum

Musical Fund Hall (Musical Fund Society Hall)
808 Locust St.
HABS PA-1447
HABS PA,51-PHILA,494-
1ph/1pg L

Musical Fund Society Hall; see Musical Fund Hall

Mutual Fire Insurance Company Building
Germantown Ave. & School House Lane
HABS PA-1014
HABS PA,51-PHILA,244-
6ph/6pg L

N. W. Ayer and Son,Incorporated,Building; see Ayer,N. W. & Company Building

National Bank of Northern Liberties
Third & Vine Sts.
HABS PA-1784
HABS PA,51-PHILA,583-
3ph L

National Guard's Hall
518-20 Race St.
HABS PA-1015
HABS PA,51-PHILA,245-
8ph/6pg L

National Park Service,Mid-Atlantic Region Office; see Philadelphia Exchange Company

Navigator Statue; see Riggs & Brother,Navigator Statue

Neave,Samuel,House & Store
272-274 S. Second St.
HABS PA-1349
HABS PA,51-PHILA,622-
10dr/19ph/fr L

Nevel,Thomas,House
338 S. Fourth St.
HABS PA-1350
HABS PA,51-PHILA,649-
6ph L

New Century Club
124 S. Twelfth St.
HABS PA-1522
HABS PA,51-PHILA,675-
9ph/1pg L

New Market,Head House; see Hope Hose Co. No. 6 & Fellowship Engine Co. No. 29

New Public Buildings,The (Philadelphia City Hall)
Penn Square,Broad & Market Sts.
HABS PA-1530
HABS PA,51-PHIL,327-
58ph/22pg/3pc L

New York Mutual Life Insurance Company Building (Victory Building)
1001-1005 Chestnut St.
HABS PA-1523
HABS PA,51-PHILA,379-
3ph L

39-43 Norfolk Street (Houses)
HABS PA-1584
HABS PA,51-PHILA,532-
1ph L

Norris-Cadwalader House
240 S. Fourth St.
HABS PA-1352
HABS PA,51-PHILA,646-
18ph L

129-151 North Fourth Street (Houses); see First German Reformed Church Area Study

2-66 North Front Street (Commercial Buildings); see North Front Street Area Study

North Front Street Area Study (2-66 North Front Street (Commercial Buildings))
HABS PA-1448
HABS PA,51-PHILA,417-
9ph L

110 North Ninth Street (Restaurant & Apt. Bldg.)
HABS PA-1536
HABS P51-PHILA,670-
2ph/1pg L

9 North Seventh Street (Commercial Building)
HABS PA-1939
HABS PA,51-PHILA,661-
1ph L

North Seventh Street Area Study (Comm. Bldgs.)
21-33 N. Seventh St.
HABS PA-1449
HABS PA,51-PHILA,662-
1ph L

17-63 North Third Street (Commercial Buildings); see North Third Street Area Study

North Third Street Area Study (17-63 North Third Street (Commercial Buildings))
HABS PA-1450
HABS PA,51-PHILA,625-
6ph/fr L

113 North Water Street (House)
HABS PA-1425
HABS PA,51-PHILA,608-
2ph L

Northeast Corridor; see Northeast Railroad Corridor

Northeast Railroad Corridor (Northeast Corridor)
Amtrak Rt. btwn. DE/PA & PA/NJ State Lines
HAER PA-71
HAER PAS,51-PHILA,694-
32ph/fr L

Northern Liberty Hose Company Number Four (Snappers,The)
714 New Market St.
HABS PA-1785
HABS PA,51-PHILA,530-
1ph/1pg L

Northern Saving Fund,Safe Deposit & Trust Co.
600 Spring Garden St.
HABS PA-1733
HABS PA,51-PHILA,326-
5dr/13ph/1pg L

Norwegian Seamen's Church; see Mechanics' Bank

Ohio House; see International Exhibition of 1876,Ohio Building

Old Pine Street Church; see Third Presbyterian Church

Documentation: **ct** color transparencies **dr** measured drawings **fr** field records **pc** photograph captions **pg** pages of text **ph** photographs

One East Penn Square Building; see Market Street National Bank Building

Ormiston House
Reservoir Dr. ,Fairmount Park
HABS PA-187
HABS PA,51-PHILA,275-
9dr/1ph L

Overbrook School for the Blind; see Pennsylvania Institute for the Blind

Palmer,John,House; see 117 Lombard Street (House)

Pancake,Philip,House
333 S. Fifth St.
HABS PA-1354
HABS PA,51-PHILA,654-
1ph L

Pancoast-Lewis-Wharton House
336 Spruce St.
HABS PA-1083
HABS PA,51-PHILA,27-
10dr/7ph/10pg L

Parry House
1921 Arch St.
HABS PA-1524
HABS PA,51-PHILA,333-
27ph/2pg L

Parry House,Carriage House & Stable
1921 Arch St. (rear)
HABS PA-1524-A
HABS PA,51-PHILA,33A-
1ph L

Paschall House
Spruce & Mattis Sts.
HABS PA-128-B
HABS PA,51-PHILA,276B-
3dr/3ph/fr L

Paschall,Jonathan,House
36 Christian St.
HABS PA-1607
HABS PA,51-PHILA,384-
2ph L

Pastorius House; see Germantown Historic District

Peale,Charles Willson,House (Belfield)
5500 N. Twentieth St.
HABS PA-1676
HABS PA,51-GERM,191-
6ph L

Penn Mutual Building; see Penn Mutual Life Insurance Company Building

Penn Mutual Life Insurance Company Building (Penn Mutual Building)
Third & Dock Sts.
HABS PA-1451
HABS PA,51-PHILA,406-
1ph/1pg L

Penn. Co. for Insurances on Lives & Grant. Annuiti
431 Chestnut St.
HABS PA-1452
HABS PA,51-PHILA,378-
4ph/3pg/2pc/fr L

Pennsylvania Academy of the Fine Arts
Broad & Cherry Sts.
HABS PA-1525
HABS PA,51-PHILA,340-
14ph L

Pennsylvania Athletic Club; see Fell-Van Rensselaer House

Pennsylvania Company for Insurances on Lives
304 Walnut St.
HABS PA-1453
HABS PA,51-PHILA,588-
6ph/2pg L

Pennsylvania Fire Insurance Company
508-510 Walnut St.
HABS PA-1454
HABS PA,51-PHILA,600-
6ph/2pg L

Pennsylvania Hosp. for the Insane,Dept. for Males (Institute of the Penn. Hospital,Dept. for Males)
111 N. Forty-ninth St.
HABS PA-1635
HABS PA,51-PHILA,512-
1ph L

Pennsylvania Hospital
Eighth & Ninth,Pine & Spruce Sts.
HABS PA-1123
HABS PA,51-PHILA,39-
19dr/33ph/1pg/2ct/fr L

Pennsylvania Hospital for Mental & Nervous Disease (Kirkbride's Hospital)
Forty-fourth & Market Sts.
HABS PA-1636
HABS PA,51-PHILA,511-
10ph/2pg L

Pennsylvania Institute for the Blind (Overbrook School for the Blind)
Sixty-fourth St. & Malvern Ave.
HABS PA-1637
HABS PA,51-PHILA,510-
5ph L

Pennsylvania Institution for the Deaf & Dumb (Philadelphia College of Art)
320 S. Broad St.
HABS PA-1526
HABS PA,51-PHILA,348-
5ph L

Pennsylvania Railroad Station,Broad Street Station
Broad & Market Sts.
HABS PA-1527
HABS PA,51-PHILA,341-
7ph L

Pennsylvania Railroad,Brick Viaduct
Parallel to Schuylkill Riv. NW of Spring Garden St
HAER PA-38
HAER PA,51-PHILA,696-
2ph/2pg/1pc/fr L

Pennsylvania Railroad,Chestnut Hill Line
Chelton Ave.
HABS PA-1943
HABS PA,51-GERM,184-
1ph L

Pennsylvania Railroad,Germantown Junction
HABS PA-1941
HABS PA,51-GERM,183-
1ph L

Pennsylvania Railroad,Mantua Junction Viaduct
Spanning Schuylkill River,n. of Girard Ave. Bridge
HAER PA-37
HAER PA,51-PHILA,695-
7ph/3pg/1pc/fr L

Pennypack Creek Bridge
8300 Frankford Ave.
HABS PA-1786
HABS PA,51-PHILA,414-
2ph L

Perelman Antique Toy Museum; see Abercrombie,Capt. James,House

Perseverance Hose Company,Number Five
316 Race St.
HABS PA-1455
HABS PA,51-PHILA,553-
1ph L

Philadelphia & Reading Railroad,Terminal Station (Reading Terminal)
1115-1141 Market St.
HABS PA-1528
HABS PA,51-PHILA,521-
11ph/1ct L

Philadelphia & Reading RR,Schuylkill River Viaduct (Reading RR,Schuylkill River Viaduct; Falls Bridge)
Span. Schuylkill Riv. SE of Roosevelt Blvd. Bridge
HAER PA-39
HAER PA,51-PHILA,697-
7ph/3pg/1pc/fr L

Philadelphia & Reading RR,Wissahickon Creek Viaduc (Reading RR,Wissahickon Creek Viaduct)
Spanning Wissahickon Creek,n. of Ridge Ave. Bridge
HAER PA-36
HAER PA,51-PHILA,698-
8ph/3pg/1pc/fr L

Philadelphia Art Club
220 S. Broad St.
HABS PA-1529
HABS PA,51-PHILA,329-
4ph L

Philadelphia Athenaeum
219 S. Sixth St. (E. Washington Sq.)
HABS PA-1389
HABS PA,51-PHILA,116-
1dr/3ph L

Philadelphia Athenaeum,Brick Privy
219 S. Sixth St. (E. Washington Sq.)
HABS PA-1389-A
HABS PA,51-PHILA,116A-
1dr/2ph/fr L

Philadelphia Bank; see Bank of Pennsylvania

Philadelphia Bourse (Bourse Building)
11-21 S. Fifth St.
HABS PA-1456
HABS PA,51-PHILA,651-
7ph L

Philadelphia City Hall; see New Public Buildings,The

Philadelphia City Hall (U. S. Supreme Court Building; Independence Hall Complex,City Hall; Independence National Historical Park)
Fifth & Chestnut Sts.
HABS PA-1432
HABS PA,51-PHILA,6B-
2dr/6ph/2pg/1pc/fr L

Philadelphia College of Art; see Pennsylvania Institution for the Deaf & Dumb

Philadelphia Contributionship,House Fire Insurance
212 S. Fourth St.
HABS PA-1457
HABS PA,51-PHILA,141-
7ph/2pg L

Philadelphia County Courthouse; see Congress Hall

Philadelphia County Prison (Moyamensing Prison)
Tenth St.
HABS PA-1097
HABS PA,51-PHILA,672-
10ph/2pg L

Philadelphia County Prison,Debtors' Wing (Moyamensing Prison,Debtors' Wing)
Reed St. & Passyunk Ave.
HABS PA-1097-A
HABS PA,51-PHILA,672A-
7dr/5ph/2pg/fr L

Philadelphia Exchange Company (Merchants' Exchange; National Park Service,Mid-Atlantic Region Office; Independence National Historical Park)
143 S. Third St.
HABS PA-1028
HABS PA,51-PHILA,137-
16dr/21ph L

Philadelphia Fire Department,Engine Co. Number 21
826-828 New Market St.
HABS PA-1787
HABS PA,51-PHILA,531-
1ph L

Philadelphia Fire Department,Engine Co. Number 8 (Fireman's Hall)
826-828 New Market St.
HABS PA-1459
HABS PA,51-PHILA,619-
1dr/1ph L

Philadelphia Fire Department,No. 3 & Patrol House; see Weccacoe Engine Company,No. 9

Philadelphia Gas Works,Point Breeze Meter House
Passyunk Ave.
HAER PA-41
HAER PA,51-PHILA,699A-
6dr/17pg L

Philadelphia Hose Company Number One
Seventh & Filbert Sts.
HABS PA-1460
HABS PA,51-PHILA,660-
4ph/2pg L

Philadelphia Masonic Temple
HABS PA-1532
39ph/13pg H

Philadelphia Museum of Art
Benjamin Franklin Pkwy.
HABS PA-1661
HABS PA,51-PHILA,335-
6ph/13ct L

Philadelphia National Bank; see Bank of Pennsylvania

Philadelphia Opera House (Met,The)
1400-1418 Poplar St.
HABS PA-1734
HABS PA,51-PHILA,540-
4ph L

Philadelphia Saving Fund Society
306 Walnut St.
HABS PA-1461
HABS PA,51-PHILA,589-
3ph L

Philadelphia Saving Fund Society
700 Walnut St.
HABS PA-1462
HABS PA,51-PHILA,601-
2ph L

Philadelphia Saving Fund Society (PSFS)
12th & Market Sts.
HABS PA-1533
HABS PA,51-PHILA,584-
33ph/3pc/11ct L

Philadelphia Trust,Safe Deposit & Insurance Co.
415 Chestnut St.
HABS PA-1181
HABS PA,51-PHILA,375-
1dr/3ph L

Philadelphia Zoological Gardens,Bear Pits
Fairmount Park
HABS PA-1662
HABS PA,51-PHILA,394B-
4ph L

Philadelphia Zoological Gardens,Entrance Pavilions
Girard Ave. & 34th St. ,Fairmount Park
HABS PA-1663
HABS PA,51-PHILA,394A-
1ph L

Philadelphia,Germ. & Norris. RR,Germantown Depot
5731-5735 Germantown Ave.
HABS PA-1707
HABS PA,51-GERM,182-
1ph L

Philadelphia,Wilmington & Balt. RR,Freight Station (Semple Company Warehouse)
Fifteenth & Carpenter Sts.
HABS PA-1611
HABS PA,51-PHILA,356A-
10ph L

Picklands,Thomas,House
307 S. Third St.
HABS PA-1357
HABS PA,51-PHILA,637-
4ph L

Piles,John,House
328 S. Third St.
HABS PA-1358
HABS PA,51-PHILA,640B-
2ph L

524 Pine Street (House) ,Rainwater Conductor Head
HABS PA-5196
HABS PA,51-PHILA,538-
1dr L

Poe,Edgar Allan,House
530 N. Seventh St. (rear)
HABS PA-1735
HABS PA,51-PHILA,663A-
5ph L

Poor Richard Club; see Leidy,Joseph Jr. ,House

Port Royal (Stiles-Lukens House)
Tacony St.
HABS PA-111
HABS PA,51-PHILA,5-
7dr/5ph/5pg L

Portico Row; see Portico Square

Portico Square (Portico Row)
900-930 Spruce St.
HABS PA-1534
HABS PA,51-PHILA,576-
5ph L

Potts House
3905 Spruce St.
HABS PA-1638
HABS PA,51-PHILA,581-
10ph/1pg L

Potts House,Carriage House & Stable
3905 Spruce St.
HABS PA-1638-A
HABS PA,51-PHILA,581A-
1ph L

Documentation: **ct** color transparencies **dr** measured drawings **fr** field records
pc photograph captions **pg** pages of text **ph** photographs

Potts,Horace T. & Company,Warehouse
316-320 N. Third St.
HABS PA-1789
HABS PA,51-PHILA,627-
7dr/3ph/2pg/fr L

Powder Magazine
Magazine Lane
HABS PA-124
HABS PA,51-PHILA,220-
2dr/5ph/2pg L

Powder Magazine; see Schuylkill Arsenal,Building No. 8

Powel,Samuel,House
244 S. Third St.
HABS PA-1359
HABS PA,51-PHILA,25-
19ph/1pg L

Preston Retreat
Twentieth & Hamilton Sts.
HABS PA-1736
HABS PA,51-PHILA,480-
24ph/6pg L

Protestant Episcopal City Mission; see St. Paul's Protestant Episcopal Church

Provident Life & Trust Co. Bank,1888-1890 Addition
401-407 Chestnut St.
HABS PA-1058-A
HABS PA,51-PHILA,256A-
1ph L

Provident Life & Trust Company Bank
407-409 Chestnut St.
HABS PA-1058
HABS PA,51-PHILA,256-
2dr/19ph/14pg/1pc/fr L

PSFS; see Philadelphia Saving Fund Society

523-525 Quarry Street (Houses)
NE corner of Quarry & Fairhill Sts.
HABS PA-1426
HABS PA,51-PHILA,524-
1ph L

31-33 Queen Street (stoops)
HABS PA-5194
HABS PA,51-PHILA,546-
1ph L

Queen Street Area Study (Houses)
(26-28 Queen Street)
HABS PA-1613
HABS PA,51-PHILA,545-
2ph L

26-28 Queen Street; see Queen Street Area Study (Houses)

907-909 Race Street (Commercial Buildings) (Far East Chinese Restaurant)
HABS PA-1505
HABS PA,51-PHILA,297-
2ph L

Ralston School
625 S. American St.
HABS PA-1614
HABS PA,51-PHILA,334-
1ph/1pg L

Ralston,Robert,House
521 Arch St.
HABS PA-1016
HABS PA,51-PHILA,246-
8ph/3pg L

Rawle,Randolph,House; see Laurel Hill

Reading RR,Schuylkill River Viaduct; see Philadelphia & Reading RR,Schuylkill River Viaduct

Reading RR,Wissahickon Creek Viaduct; see Philadelphia & Reading RR,Wissahickon Creek Viaduc

Reading Terminal; see Philadelphia & Reading Railroad,Terminal Station

Reed,Samuel & Joseph,Houses
518-520 S. Front St.
HABS PA-1615
HABS PA,51-PHILA,431-
4ph L

Reliance Insurance Company of Philadelphia
429 Walnut St.
HABS PA-1465
HABS PA,51-PHILA,598-
5ph/1pg L

Reynolds-Morris House (Morris House)
225 S. Eighth St.
HABS PA-1107
HABS PA,51-PHILA,40-
9dr/5ph/2pg L

Rhoads-Barclay House
217 Delancey St.
HABS PA-1057
HABS PA,51-PHILA,255-
7dr/7ph/6pg L

Rich-Truman House
320 Delancey St.
HABS PA-1074
HABS PA,51-PHILA,261-
12dr/4ph/8pg L

Rich,Comly,House
4276 Orchard St.
HABS PA-1794
HABS PA,51-PHILA,534-4:63°
4dr/13ph/2ct L

Ridge Avenue Farmers' Market Company
1810 Ridge Ave.
HABS PA-1737
HABS PA,51-PHILA,558-
4ph L

Ridgeland
Chamounix Dr. ,Fairmount Park
HABS PA-1664
HABS PA,51-PHILA,395-
8ph L

Riggs & Brother,Navigator Statue (Navigator Statue)
310 Market St.
HABS PA-1466
HABS PA,51-PHILA,513A-
1ph/1pg L

Rittenhouse House
Lincoln Dr. & Rittenhouse St.
HABS PA-16
HABS PA,51-GERM,78-
7dr/3ph/1pg/fr L

Rittenhouse Square; see Academy of Notre Dame

Robeson House; see Shoomac Park

Robinson,William,House
23 Clymer St.
HABS PA-1361
HABS PA,51-PHILA,689-
1ph L

Rogers-Cassatt House
202 S. Nineteenth St.
HABS PA-1537
HABS PA,51-PHILA,678-
9ph/1pg L

Roney,John,House
117 N. Sixth St.
HABS PA-1017
HABS PA,51-PHILA,247-
1ph/3pg L

Rowley-Pullman House
238 S. Third St.
HABS PA-1467
HABS PA,51-PHILA,632-
7ph L

Royal House
5011 Germantown Ave.
HABS PA-1709
HABS PA,51-GERM,175-
1ph/1pg L

Royal Insurance Company Building
212 S. Third St.
HABS PA-1468
HABS PA,51-PHILA,631-
3ph L

Rumpp,C. F. & Sons,Inc. ,Factory
114-130 N. Fifth St. at Cherry St.
HABS PA-1469
HABS PA,51-PHILA,650-
2ph/1pg L

Rush,Benjamin,Birthplace
Red Lion Rd.
HABS PA-1796
HABS PA,51-PHILA,556-
4ph/4pg L

Rush,Benjamin,Birthplace,Spring House
Red Lion Rd.
HABS PA-1796-A
HABS PA,51-PHILA,556A-
1ph L

Ryers Mansion; see Burholme

Ryerss Mansion,Stables; see Burholme,Stables

Sansom,William,House
707 Walnut St.
HABS PA-1476
HABS PA,51-PHILA,602-
1ph L

Schaeffer,Harriet,House
433 W. Stafford St.
HABS PA-1712
HABS PA,51-PHILA,582-
1ph L

Schenck Building
535-537 Arch St.
HABS PA-1078
HABS PA,51-PHILA,264-
3ph/5pg L

Schively,Henry,House
329 S. Third St.
HABS PA-1364
HABS PA,51-PHILA,639-
2ph L

Schuylkill Arsenal
2620 Gray's Ferry Ave.
HABS PA-1540
HABS PA,51-PHILA,578-
2pg/fr L

Schuylkill Arsenal,Building No. 1 (U. S. Laboratory; Enlisted Men's Barracks; Luding Hall)
2620 Gray's Ferry Ave.
HABS PA-1540-A
HABS PA,51-PHILA,578A-
4ph/1pg/fr L

Schuylkill Arsenal,Building No. 1A (Commandant's House; Executive Officers' Quarters)
2620 Gray's Ferry Ave.
HABS PA-1540-B
HABS PA,51-PHILA,578B-
6ph/1pg/fr L

Schuylkill Arsenal,Building No. 2 (Mifflin Building)
2620 Gray's Ferry Ave.
HABS PA-1540-C
HABS PA,51-PHILA,578C-
2ph/1pg L

Schuylkill Arsenal,Building No. 2A (Surgeon's House)
2620 Gray's Ferry Ave.
HABS PA-1540-D
HABS PA,51-PHILA,578D-
2ph/1pg/fr L

Schuylkill Arsenal,Building No. 6
2620 Gray's Ferry Ave.
HABS PA-1540-E
HABS PA,51-PHILA,578E-
3ph/1pg/fr L

Schuylkill Arsenal,Building No. 8 (Powder Magazine)
2620 Gray's Ferry Ave.
HABS PA-1540-F
HABS PA,51-PHILA,578F-
2ph/1pg/fr L

Schuylkill Hose,Hook & Ladder Company,No. 24
1227 Locust St.
HABS PA-1577
HABS PA,51-PHILA,495-
1ph L

Scott-Wanamaker House
2032 Walnut St.
HABS PA-1578
HABS PA,51-PHILA,607-
11ph/1pg/1ct L

Second Bank of the United States (Customs House; Independence National Historical Park)
420 Chestnut St.
HABS PA-137
HABS PA,51-PHILA,223-
19dr/43ph/1ct/fr L

Sedgeley Guard House; see Sedgeley Porter's House

Sedgeley Porter's House (Sedgeley Guard House)
Fairmount Park
HABS PA-1665
HABS PA,51-PHILA,397A-
2ph L

Semple Company Warehouse; see Philadelphia,Wilmington & Balt. RR,Freight Station

Shibe Park (stadium) (Mack,Connie,Stadium)
2701 N. Twenty-first St.
HABS PA-1738
HABS PA,51-PHILA,683-
12ph/2pg/2ct L

Shinn,Samuel,House; see Marshall's Court Area Study

Shippen-Wistar House
238 S. Fourth St.
HABS PA-1365
HABS PA,51-PHILA,647-
3ph L

Shoomac Park (Robeson House)
Ridge Ave. & Wissahickon Dr.
HABS PA-1067
HABS PA,51-PHILA,259-
6dr/7ph/9pg/fr L

Shur's Lane Mill
428 Shur's Lane
HAER PA-73
HAER PA,51-PHILA,700-
1ph/1pg L

Siddons,William,House
851 S. Front St.
HABS PA-1618
HABS PA,51-PHILA,452-
1ph L

Simpson,David,House; see Marshall's Court Area Study

Sims,Joseph,House (Franklin Row)
228 S. Ninth St.
HABS PA-1186
HABS PA,51-PHILA,671-
5dr/9ph/5pg/fr L

Singer,John,Warehouse
319 1/2 Market St.
HABS PA-1478
HABS PA,51-PHILA,515-
1ph/1pg L

Singley House; see Bel Air

Sink-Burgin House; see 331 South Fifth Street (House)

Sisk Houses; see Stafford's Tavern-Paschall House

Smith Memorial Arch (Civil War Memorial)
Fairmount Park
HABS PA-1666
HABS PA,51-PHILA,398A-
1ph L

Smith,Daniel,Jr. ,House; see 505 South Front Street (House)

Snappers,The; see Northern Liberty Hose Company Number Four

Solitude
Fairmount Park,Zoo grounds
HABS PA-1127
HABS PA,51-PHILA,30-
9dr/22ph/fr L

Somerton; see Strawberry Mansion

Sons of Temperance Fountain
Independence Sq. (moved from Belmont & Fount.)
HABS PA-1480
HABS PA,51-PHILA,265E-
2ph/1pg L

Souder,Charles F. ,House
514 Race St.
HABS PA-1018
HABS PA,51-PHILA,248-
1ph/3pg L

246 South Eighth Street (House)
HABS PA-5206
HABS PA,51-PHILA,665-
3ph/5pg L

248 South Eighth Street (House)
HABS PA-5207
HABS PA,51-PHILA,666-
3ph/5pg L

331 South Fifth Street (House) (Sink-Burgin House)
HABS PA-1366
HABS PA,51-PHILA,653-
1ph L

315-317-319 South Fifth Street (Townhouses)
HABS PA-1322
HABS PA,51-PHILA,652-
1ph/1pg L

919 South Front Street (Doorway) (Wharton,John,House)
HABS PA-1624
HABS PA,51-PHILA,690-
1ph L

312 South Front Street (House)
HABS PA-1950
HABS PA,51-PHILA,422-
2ph L

319 South Front Street (House)
HABS PA-1337
HABS PA,51-PHILA,423-
1ph L

321 South Front Street (House)
HABS PA-1905
HABS PA,51-PHILA,424-
1ph L

505 South Front Street (House)
(Smith,Daniel,Jr. ,House)
HABS PA-1367
HABS PA,51-PHILA,427-
1ph L

507 South Front Street (House)
(Bridges,Robert,House)
HABS PA-1320
HABS PA,51-PHILA,428-
1ph L

510 South Front Street (House)
(Wharton,Isaac,House)
HABS PA-1381
HABS PA,51-PHILA,430-
1ph L

603 South Front Street (House)
(Hart-Patterson House)
HABS PA-1569
HABS PA,51-PHILA,434-
1ph L

626 South Front Street (House)
(Spafford,William,House)
HABS PA-1620
HABS PA,51-PHILA,436-
4ph L

720-724 South Front Street (House)
(Askins-Jones House)
HABS PA-1541
HABS PA,51-PHILA,439-
3ph L

783 South Front Street (House)
(Collins,Samuel,House)
HABS PA-1549
HABS PA,51-PHILA,445-
1ph L

836 South Front Street (House)
HABS PA-1952
HABS PA,51-PHILA,450-
1ph L

600-858 South Front Street (Houses)
W. side Front St. btw. South & Catherine Sts.
HABS PA-1812
HABS PA,51-PHILA,432-
4ph L

606-608 South Front Street (Houses)
(Fullerton,John,Houses)
HABS PA-1563
HABS PA,51-PHILA,435-
1ph L

806-808 South Front Street (Houses)
HABS PA-1594
HABS PA,51-PHILA,447-
2ph L

125-127 South Second Street (Commercial Bldgs.)
HABS PA-1405
HABS PA,51-PHILA,620-
1dr L

252 South Second Street (House)
HABS PA-1934
HABS PA,51-PHILA,188-
1ph L

252 South Third Street (House)
HABS PA-1945
HABS PA,51-PHILA,633-
1ph L

266-276 South Third Street (Houses)
HABS PA-1936
HABS PA,51-PHILA,635-
1ph L

532 South Water Street (House)
HABS PA-1809
HABS PA,51-PHILA,614-
1ph L

South Water Street (Houses)
S. Water & Fitzwater Sts.
HABS PA-1953
HABS PA,51-PHILA,610-
1ph L

512-526 South Water Street (Houses)
(South Water Street Area Survey)
HABS PA-1619
HABS PA,51-PHILA,613-
3ph L

100-150 South Water Street (Warehouses); see South Water Street Area Study

South Water Street Area Study
(100-150 South Water Street (Warehouses))
HABS PA-1810
HABS PA,51-PHILA,611-
1ph L

South Water Street Area Survey; see 512-526 South Water Street (Houses)

Southern Loan Company of Philadelphia (Tradesmen's National Bank of Philadelphia)
300 S. Second St.
HABS PA-1368
HABS PA,51-PHILA,623-
2ph L

Southwark Hose Company,No. 9
512 S. Third St.
HABS PA-1369
HABS PA,51-PHILA,641-
1ph L

Sower House (Trinity Lutheran Church House)
5300 Germantown Ave.
HABS PA-1717
HABS PA,51-GERM,26-
1ph/1pg L

Spafford,William,House; see 626 South Front Street (House)

Sparks Shot Tower
129-131 Carpenter St.
HABS PA-1621
HABS PA,51-PHILA,195-
2ph/1ct L

Spring Garden Institute
523-525 N. Broad St.
HABS PA-1739
HABS PA,51-PHILA,351-
2ph L

Spring Garden Insurance Company Building
431 Walnut St.
HABS PA-1481
HABS PA,51-PHILA,599-
2ph/1pg L

Spring Garden Street Bridge; see Callowhill Street Bridge

2009-2045 Spruce Street (Houses); see Spruce Street Area Study

700-714 Spruce Street (Houses)
HABS PA-253
HABS PA,51-PHILA,321-
4dr/28ph/32pg L

722-730 Spruce Street (Houses)
HABS PA-1339
HABS PA,51-PHILA,575-
5ph L

Spruce Street Area Study (2009-2045 Spruce Street (Houses))
HABS PA-1579
HABS PA,51-PHILA,579-
11ph L

St. Agatha's Roman Catholic Church
3801 Spring Garden St.
HABS PA-1639
HABS PA,51-PHILA,568-
3ph/1ct L

St. Andrew's Protestant Episcopal Church (St. George's Greek Orthodox Cathedral)
250-254 S. Eighth St.
HABS PA-1362
HABS PA,51-PHILA,667-
1ph/1pg L

St. Augustine's Roman Catholic Church
Fourth & New Sts.
HABS PA-1471
HABS PA,51-PHILA,529-
1ph/2pg L

St. Charles Borromeo Roman Catholic Church
900 S. Twentieth St.
HABS PA-1546
HABS PA,51-PHILA,682-
3ph L

St. Charles Hotel
60-66 N. Third St.
HABS PA-1472
HABS PA,51-PHILA,626-
3ph/2pg L

St. Clement's Protestant Episcopal Church
128 N. Twentieth St.
HABS PA-1538
HABS PA,51-PHILA,681-
7ph L

St. Elizabeth Roman Catholic Church
1845 N. Twenty-third St.
HABS PA-1940
HABS PA,51-PHILA,684-
1ph L

St. Francis DeSales Roman Catholic Church
4629-4635 Springfield Ave.
HABS PA-1640
HABS PA,51-PHILA,567-
4ph/5ct L

St. Francis Xavier's Church (Roman Catholic)
2321 Green St.
HABS PA-1933
HABS PA,51-PHILA,479-
1ph L

St. George's Greek Orthodox Cathedral; see St. Andrew's Protestant Episcopal Church

St. George's Methodist Episcopal Church
235 N. Fourth St.
HABS PA-1473
HABS PA,51-PHILA,644-
6ph L

St. James Roman Catholic Church
3278 Chestnut St.
HABS PA-1641
HABS PA,51-PHILA,380-
4ph L

202 St. James Street (House)
HABS PA-1474
HABS PA,51-PHILA,562-
2ph L

206 St. James Street (House)
HABS PA-5195
HABS PA,51-PHILA,563-
5ph L

St. John's Lutheran Church
511-523 Race St.
HABS PA-1935
HABS PA,51-PHILA,555-
4ph L

St. Mark's Church (Episcopal)
1625 Locust St.
HABS PA-1093
HABS PA,51-PHILA,270-
9ph/10pg L

St. Mary's Protestant Episcopal Church
3916 Locust Walk
HABS PA-1642
HABS PA,51-PHILA,509-
3ph L

St. Mary's Roman Catholic Church
244 S. Fourth St.
HABS PA-1363
HABS PA,51-PHILA,648-
2ph L

St. Mary's Roman Catholic Church, Grave
244 S. Fourth St.
HABS PA-1363-A
HABS PA,51-PHILA,648A-
1ph L

St. Paul's Protestant Episcopal Church (Protestant Episcopal City Mission)
225 S. Third St.
HABS PA-1475
HABS PA,51-PHILA,98-
1dr/1ph L

St. Peter's Church House (Episcopal); see Blackwell,Reverend Robert,House

St. Peter's Protestant Episcopal Church
Third & Pine Sts.
HABS PA-1118
HABS PA,51-PHILA,108-
17dr/13ph/1ct L

St. Stephen's Methodist Episcopal Church,Rectory
5213 Germantown Ave.
HABS PA-1708
HABS PA,51-GERM,19-
1ph/1pg L

St. Stephen's Protestant Episcopal Church
19 S. Tenth St.
HABS PA-1576
HABS PA,51-PHILA,673-
2ph/1pg L

St. Timothy's Protestant Episcopal Church
5720 Ridge Ave.
HABS PA-1710
HABS PA,51-PHILA,560-
3ph L

St. Timothy's Protestant Episcopal Church,Gateway
5720 Ridge Ave.
HABS PA-1710-A
HABS PA,51-PHILA,561-
2ph L

St. Timothy's Working Men's Club & Institute
5164 Ridge Ave.
HABS PA-1711
HABS PA,51-PHILA,559-
2ph L

Stable & Carriage House (Independence National Historical Park)
422 Walnut St. (rear)
HABS PA-1401
HABS PA,51-PHILA,595A-
2dr/11ph L

Stafford's Tavern
Spruce & Mattis Sts.
HABS PA-128-A
HABS PA,51-PHILA,276A-
5dr/7ph/fr L

Stafford's Tavern-Paschall House (Man Full of Trouble Tavern; Cove Cornice House; Sisk Houses)
Spruce & Mattis Sts.
HABS PA-128
HABS PA,51-PHILA,276-
4dr/6ph/fr L

Stanfield House; see Woods,Capt. John,House

State House of Pennsylvania; see Independence Hall Complex,Independence Hall

Stenton
Courtland & Eighteenth Sts.
HABS PA-1714
HABS PA,51-PHILA,8-
4ph L

Stetson Hat Factory; see Stetson,John B. ,Company

Stetson,John B. ,Company (Stetson Hat Factory)
Germantown & Columbia Aves.
HABS PA-1227
HABS PA,51-PHILA,458-
21ph/18pg/fr L

Stewart,Thomas,House
410 Locust St.
HABS PA-189
HABS PA,51-PHILA,238-
7dr/2ph/3pg/fr L

Stiles-Lukens House; see Port Royal

Stiles,William,House
310 Cypress St.
HABS PA-1371
HABS PA,51-PHILA,462-
8ph L

Stocker,John Clement,House
402 S. Front St.
HABS PA-1068
HABS PA,51-PHILA,22-
6dr/15ph/11pg/fr L

Stone-Penrose House
700 Locust St.
HABS PA-1483
HABS PA,51-PHILA,493-
3ph L

Strawberry Mansion (Summerville; Somerton)
Fairmount Park
HABS PA-1668
HABS PA,51-PHILA,219-
6ph L

Strawberry Mansion Bridge ((HABS Photos,HAER Stereoplates))
Ford Rd. & E. River Dr. ,Fairmount Park
HABS PA-1669
HAER PA-92
HABS/HAER PA,51-PHILA,404-
3ph/2ct L

Documentation: **ct** color transparencies **dr** measured drawings **fr** field records
pc photograph captions **pg** pages of text **ph** photographs

Stride-Madison House
429 Spruce St.
HABS PA-1073
HABS PA,51-PHILA,260-
6dr/10ph/8pg L

Sully,Thomas,House
530 Spruce St.
HABS PA-1372
HABS PA,51-PHILA,571-
6ph L

Summers-Worrell House
505 Delancey St.
HABS PA-1373
HABS PA,51-PHILA,388-
1ph L

Summerville; see Strawberry Mansion

Surgeon's House; see Schuylkill Arsenal,Building No. 2A

Swedes Church,Old; see Gloria Dei (Church)

Sweetbrier
Fairmount Park
HABS PA-1670
HABS PA,51-PHILA,395-
5ph L

Tabernacle Presbyterian Church
3700 Chestnut St.
HABS PA-1099
HABS PA,51-PHILA,271-
18ph/7pg L

Tanner,Henry O. ,House
2908 W. Diamond St.
HABS PA-1740
HABS PA,51-PHILA,391-
4ph/1pg L

Third Presbyterian Church (Old Pine Street Church)
422 Pine St.
HABS PA-1374
HABS PA,51-PHILA,203-
5ph L

Toby-Shaw House
12 Queen St.
HABS PA-1937
HABS PA,51-PHILA,542-
1ph L

Tradesmen's National Bank of Philadelphia; see Southern Loan Company of Philadelphia

Trinity Church,Oxford (Episcopal)
6900-6902 Oxford Ave.
HABS PA-17
HABS PA,51-PHILA,37-
6dr/5ph/4pg/2ct/fr L

Trinity Lutheran Church
19 N. Queen Lane
HABS PA-1716
HABS PA,51-GERM,189-
3ph L

Trinity Lutheran Church House; see Sower House

Troc,The; see Arch Street Opera House

Tuttleman Brothers & Faggen Building
56-60 N. Second St.
HABS PA-1485
HABS PA,51-PHILA,618-
1ph L

Twelfth Street Meeting House
20 S. Twelfth St.
HABS PA-1944
HABS PA,51-PHILA,674-
9dr/48ph/1pg/fr L

Two Story Log House; see Friends Select School,Log Cabin

U. S. Bonded Warehouse
415-419 S. Front St.
HABS PA-1375
HABS PA,51-PHILA,426-
3ph L

U. S. Hose Company,No. 14
423 Buttonwood St.
HABS PA-1804
HABS PA,51-PHILA,119-
1ph/1pg L

U. S. Laboratory; see Schuylkill Arsenal,Building No. 1

U. S. Mint
Sixteenth & Garden Sts.
HABS PA-1741
HABS PA,51-PHILA,372-
2ph L

U. S. Mint,Old
Chestnut & Juniper Sts.
HABS PA-1938
HABS PA,51-PHILA,371-
2ph L

U. S. Naval Asylum,Biddle Hall (U. S. Naval Home,Biddle Hall)
Gray's Ferry Ave.
HABS PA-1622-A
HABS PA,51-PHILA,577A-
23ph/9pg L

U. S. Naval Asylum,Governor's Residence (U. S. Naval Home,Governor's Residence)
Gray's Ferry Ave.
HABS PA-1622-B
HABS PA,51-PHILA,577B-
5ph/4pg L

U. S. Naval Asylum,Laning Hall (U. S. Naval Home,Laning Hall,Building No. 2)
Gray's Ferry Ave.
HABS PA-1622-D
HABS PA,51-PHILA,577D-
9ph/3pg L

U. S. Naval Asylum,Stable Building (U. S. Naval Home,Stable Building)
Gray's Ferry Ave.
HABS PA-1622-E
HABS PA,51-PHILA,577E-
1ph L

U. S. Naval Asylum,Surgeon's Residence (U. S. Naval Home,Surgeon's Residence)
Gray's Ferry Ave.
HABS PA-1622-C
HABS PA,51-PHILA,577C-
3ph/4pg L

U. S. Naval Home,Biddle Hall; see U. S. Naval Asylum,Biddle Hall

U. S. Naval Home,Governor's Residence; see U. S. Naval Asylum,Governor's Residence

U. S. Naval Home,Laning Hall,Building No. 2; see U. S. Naval Asylum,Laning Hall

U. S. Naval Home,Stable Building; see U. S. Naval Asylum,Stable Building

U. S. Naval Home,Surgeon's Residence; see U. S. Naval Asylum,Surgeon's Residence

U. S. Supreme Court Building; see Philadelphia City Hall

Union League of Philadelphia
140 S. Broad St.
HABS PA-1626
HABS PA,51-PHILA,346-
2ph/1pg/fr L

University of Pennsylvania,College Hall
Woodland Ave.
HABS PA-1643
HABS PA,51-PHILA,566C-
2ph/1pg L

University of Pennsylvania,Furness Building
HABS PA-1644
HABS PA,51-PHILA,566D-
10ph L

University of Pennsylvania,Mask & Wig Club; see Welsh Coach House and Stable

University of Pennsylvania,Men's Dormitories
Spruce St.
HABS PA-1645
HABS PA,51-PHILA,566B-
5ph/2ct L

University of Pennsylvania,University Museum (Museum of Science & Art)
3620 South St.
HABS PA-1646
HABS PA,51-PHILA,566A-
4ph L

Upper Ferry Bridge
Spring Garden St.
HABS PA-1946
HABS PA,51-PHILA,569-
1ph L

Upsula
6430 Germantown Ave.
HABS PA-1718
HABS PA,51-GERM,65-
3ph L

Valley Green Inn
Wissahickon Dr.
HABS PA-1719
HABS PA,51-PHLIA,83-
11dr/1ph L

Vaults
Front & Walnut Sts. (Beneath Sidewalk)
HABS PA-1486
HABS PA,51-PHILA,415-
1pg/fr L

Vernon
Germantown Ave. ,Vernon Park
HABS PA-7-2
HABS PA,51-GERM,38-
17dr/6ph/3pg/fr L

Victory Building; see New York Mutual Life Insurance Company Building

Waln,Isaac,House
259 S. Third St.
HABS PA-1376
HABS PA,51-PHILA,634-
6ph L

131 Walnut Street (Casement Window)
HABS PA-1948
HABS PA,51-PHILA,587-
2dr L

329 Walnut Street (mantlepiece)
HABS PA-1947
HABS PA,51-PHILA,592-
1ph L

423 Walnut Street (Railing)
HABS PA-1715
HABS PA,51-PHILA,596-
1ph L

Walnut Street Theater
829-833 Walnut St.
HABS PA-1487
HABS PA,51-PHILA,605-
16ph/fr L

Wanamaker,John,Store
Thirteenth & Chestnut Sts.
HABS PA-1692
HABS PA,51-PHILA,370-
2ph L

Washington Hose Company,No. 10
35 N. Ninth St.
HABS PA-1488
HABS PA,51-PHILA,669-
1ph L

Washington Hotel; see Merchants' Hotel

Washington Square Area Study
Sixth,Seventh,Walnut & Locust Sts.
HABS PA-1489
HABS PA,51-PHILA,603-
9ph L

Water Trough and Fountain
Ninth St.
HABS PA-1379
HABS PA,51-PHILA,668-
2ph L

Wayne,Gen. ,Hotel
5060 Germantown Ave.
HABS PA-1691
HABS PA,51-GERM,10-
1ph/1pg L

Weccacoe Engine Company,No. 9
(Philadelphia Fire Department,No. 3 & Patrol House)
117-121 Queen St.
HABS PA-1610
HABS PA,51-PHILA,549-
3ph L

Welsh Coach House and Stable
(University of Pennsylvania,Mask & Wig Club)
310 S. Quince St.
HABS PA-1518
HABS PA,51-PHILA,551A-
1ph/3pg L

West Arch Street Presbyterian Church
(Arch Street Presbyterian Church)
1726-32 Arch St.
HABS PA-1696
HABS PA,51-PHILA,280-
8ph L

Western Saving Fund Society of Philadelphia
1000-1008 Walnut St.
HABS PA-1703
HABS PA,51-PHILA,606-
5ph/1pg L

Wetherill,Joseph,House
233 Delancey St.
HABS PA-1380
HABS PA,51-PHILA,330-
4ph L

Wharton-Stewart House
27 Christian St.
HABS PA-1185
HABS PA,51-PHILA,382-
5dr/4ph/fr L

Wharton,Isaac,House; see 510 South Front Street (House)

Wharton,John,House; see 919 South Front Street (Doorway)

Wharton,Joseph,House
119 Lombard St.
HABS PA-1382
HABS PA,51-PHILA,501-
6ph/1pg L

White,Bishop William,House
309 Walnut St.
HABS PA-1490
HABS PA,51-PHILA,590-
1ph L

Widener,Peter A. B. ,House
1200 N. Broad St.
HABS PA-1742
HABS PA,51-PHILA,352-
2ph/1pg L

Williams-Hopkinson House (Hopkinson House)
338 Spruce St.
HABS PA-1084
HABS PA,51-PHILA,266-
13dr/10ph/11pg/fr L

Williams-Mathurin House
427 Spruce St.
HABS PA-1383
HABS PA,51-PHILA,570-
9ph/2pg L

Winder,William H. ,Houses
232-234 S. Third St.
HABS PA-1384
HABS PA,51-PHILA,9-
4ph L

Winemore,Phillip,House
220 Spruce St.
HABS PA-1050
HABS PA,51-PHILA,249-
1dr/3ph/5pg L

Wissahickon Inn (Chestnut Hill Academy)
500 W. Willow Grove Ave.
HABS PA-1720
HABS PA,51-PHILA,614-
2ph L

Wister's Big House; see Grumblethorpe

Wister's Tenant House; see Grumblethorpe Tenant House

Wood,George,Houses
335-337 S. Fifth St.
HABS PA-1385
HABS PA,51-PHILA,655-
1ph L

Woodford
Fairmount Pk.
HABS PA-1307
HABS PA,51-PHILA,13-
31ph L

5901 Woodland Avenue (Cottage)
HABS PA-138
HABS PA,51-PHILA,224-
4dr/1ph L

Woodland Avenue Car Barn
Woodland Ave. & Fourty-ninth St.
HABS PA-1956
HABS PA,51-PHILA,616-
7ph/1pg L

Woodland Terrace Area Study (Houses)
Woodland Terrace,East & West sides
HABS PA-1647
HABS PA,51-PHILA,617-
8ph L

Woodlands (Hamilton,Andrew,House; Hamilton Village)
Thirty-ninth St. & Woodland Ave.
HABS PA-1125
HABS PA,51-PHILA,29-
18dr/6ph L

Documentation: **ct** color transparencies **dr** measured drawings **fr** field records
pc photograph captions **pg** pages of text **ph** photographs

Woods,Capt. John,House (Stanfield House)
Front & Lombard Sts.
HABS PA-1111
HABS PA,51-PHILA,277-
9dr/3pg L

Woolfall-Huddell House
9 Queen St.
HABS PA-1625
HABS PA,51-PHILA,541-
2ph L

Workman Place
742-746 S. Front St.
HABS PA-133
HABS PA,51-PHILA,42-
7ph/3pg L

Wyck (Haines House)
6026 Germantown Ave.
HABS PA-7-3
HABS PA,51-GERM,46-
22dr/8ph/3pg L

Wynnestay
Fifty-second St. & Woodbine Ave.
HABS PA-1648
HABS PA,51-PHILA,26-
1ph L

PHILADEPHIA

Dobson,J. & J.,Carpet Mill (W. Parcel),Bldg. 13/14
4041-4055 Ridge Ave.
HABS PA-5383-M
10ph/6pg/1pc H

Dobson,J. & J.,Carpet Mill (W. Parcel),Bldg. 19
4041-4055 Ridge Ave.
HABS PA-5383-R
7ph/6pg/1pc H

Dobson,J. & J.,Carpet Mill (W. Parcel),Bldg. 22A
4041-4055 Ridge Ave.
HABS PA-5383-T
1ph/4pg/1pc H

PIKE COUNTY

BUSHKILL

Bushkill Mill; see Peters Mill

Peters House Hotel
U. S. Rt. 209 & T301
HABS PA-1138
HABS PA,52-BUSH,1-
1ph/5pg L

Peters Mill (Bushkill Mill)
U. S. Rt. 209 & T301
HABS PA-1137
HABS PA,52-BUSH,2-
9dr/14ph/8pg/fr L

DINGMAN'S FERRY

Delaware House Hotel
U. S. Rt. 209
HABS PA-1162
HABS PA,52-DING,2-
1ph/1pg L

Dutch Reformed Church
HABS PA-1273
HABS PA,52-DING,3-
2ph/5pg L

St. John the Evangelist Episcopal Church
HABS PA-1254
HABS PA,52-DING,4-
6dr/4ph/6pg/fr L

DINGMANS FERRY

Delaware River Bridge; see Dingmans Ferry Bridge

Dingmans Ferry Bridge (Delaware River Bridge)
U. S. Rt. 209 & State Rt. 739 Vic.
HAER PA-15
HAER PA,52-DING,1-
3dr/3ph/1pc/fr L

EGYPT MILLS VIC.

Eshback House; see Nyce,William,House

Eshback Tenant House; see Van Gorden,Jacobus,House

Nyce,William,House (Eshback House)
U. S. Rt. 209
HABS PA-1163
HABS PA,52-EGYMI.V,1-
2ph/1pg L

Van Gorden,Jacobus,House (Eshback Tenant House)
U. S. Rt. 209
HABS PA-5180
HABS PA,52-EGYMI.V,2-
3dr/5ph/7pg/fr L

LACKAWAXEN

Delaware & Hudson Canal,Delaware Aqueduct
Spanning Delaware River
HAER PA-1
HAER PA,52-LACK,1- ι1991(HAER):12°
8dr/56ph/12pg/2pc/1ct/fr L

Erie Railway:Delaware Division,Bridge 110.54
Spanning Lackawaxen River,State Rt. 590 Vic.
HAER PA-24
HAER PA,52-LACK,2-
19ph/2pc L

Grey,Zane,House
W. side of Scenic Dr.
HABS PA-5371
HABS 1991(HABS):1
9dr/18ph/29pg/1pc/fr L

MILFORD

Milford Jail
Broad & High Sts.
HABS PA-221
HABS PA,52-MILF,1-
7dr/4ph/3pg L

MILFORD VIC.

Callahan House; see Helm,Jacob,House

Delaware Water Gap National Recreation Area; see Peirce,Charles S. ,House

Erie Railway:Pond Eddy Side Hill Cut & Fill
Delaware River,South Bank
HAER PA-30
HAER PA,52-MILF.V,3-
3ph L

Grey Towers
Old Rt. 6
HABS PA-1400
HABS PA,52-MILF.V,4-
8dr L

Grey Towers,Bait Box
Old Rt. 6
HABS PA-1400-B
HABS PA,52-MILF.V,4B-
1dr L

Grey Towers,Gate House
Old Rt. 6
HABS PA-1400-A
HABS PA,52-MILF.V,4A-
2dr L

Grey Towers,Letter Box
Old Rt. 6
HABS PA-1400-C
HABS PA,52-MILF.V,4C-
1dr L

Helm,Jacob,House (Callahan House)
U. S. Rt. 209 (Dingman Township)
HABS PA-1275
HABS PA,52-MILF.V,1-
2ph/8pg L

Peirce,Charles S. ,House (Delaware Water Gap National Recreation Area)
U. S. Rt. 209
HABS PA-5198
HABS PA,52-MILF.V,2-
1dr L

MILLRIFT

Erie Railway:Delaware River Bridge
Spanning Delaware River,S. of Cherry Island
HAER PA-23
HAER PA,52-MILRI,2-
1ph/1pc L

SHOHOLA

Delaware Division,Bridge 105.90; see Erie Railway:Shohola Creek Bridge

Erie Railway:Shohola Creek Bridge
(Delaware Division,Bridge 105.90)
Spanning Shohola Creek at State Rt. 434
HAER PA-43
HAER PA,52-SHOH,1-
8ph/1pc/fr L

Erie Railway:Shohola Station
Rohman Ave. & Richardson St.
HAER PA-42
HAER PA,52-SHOH,2-
7ph/1pc L

SHOHOLA VIC.

Erie Railway:Shohola Side Hill Cut & Revetment
Delaware River
HAER PA-44
HAER PA,52-SHOH.V,1-
3ph/1pc L

POTTER COUNTY

COUDERSPORT

Barn,Log
Rt. 6 (Lyman Run Rd.)
HABS PA-5127
HABS PA,53- ,1-
2dr/2ph/3pg/fr L

Coudersport Jail
HABS PA-5132
HABS PA,53-COUD,4-
1ph L

Ives House
Third & East Sts.
HABS PA-528
HABS PA,53-COUD,1-
13dr/4ph/5pg/fr L

Lillibridge House
HABS PA-5107
HABS PA,53-COUD,3-
3ph L

Presbyterian Church
HABS PA-529
HABS PA,53-COUD,2-
1ph L

ROULETTE

Wiedrich House
HABS PA-5129
HABS PA,53-ROUL,1-
1ph L

SCHUYLKILL COUNTY

BUTLER

Lavelle School
Township Rd. 905,Main St.,Village of Lavelle
HABS PA-5441
HABS DLC/PP-1993:PA-1
17ph/11pg/2pc L

POTTSVILLE

Capitol Theatre
218-220 N. Centre St.
HABS PA-5202
HABS PA,54-POTTS,1-
6ph/3pg L

SKUYLKILL HAVEN BOR.

Schuylkill Canal,Bausman's Lock No. 12
Coal St. & Garfield Creek
HAER PA-69
HAER PA,54-SCHUYH,1A-
6ph/4pg/1pc L

SNYDER COUNTY

BEAVER SPRINGS VIC.

Beaver Springs Covered Bridge; see Gross Covered Bridge

Gross Covered Bridge (Klinepeter's Covered Bridge; Beaver Springs Covered Bridge)
Spanning Middle Creek,Rt. 574
HAER PA-67
HAER PA,55-BEAVS.V,1-
22ph/1pg/1pc L

Klinepeter's Covered Bridge; see Gross Covered Bridge

SELINSGROVE

Academy,Old
Market & W. Snyder Sts.
HABS PA-325
HABS PA,55-SELI,1-
19dr/7ph/3pg L

SOMERSET COUNTY

ADDISON

Toll House
U. S. Rt. 40 (Cumberland Rd.)
HABS PA-5177
2ph L

ROCKWOOD VIC.

Shaulis,W. L. ,House
HABS PA-416
HABS PA,56-ROCHO.V,1-
4ph L

SULLIVAN COUNTY

GANOGA LAKE

Ricketts,William R. ,House
North Mountain Colley
HABS PA-210
HABS PA,57-COL,1-
5dr/3ph/5pg L

SUSQUEHANNA COUNTY

LANESBORO

Erie Railway:Delaware Division Bridge,189.46 (Starrucca Viaduct)
Spanning Starrucca Creek Valley
HAER PA-6
HAER PA,58-LANBO,1-
3dr/16ph/2pc/3ct L

Erie Railway:Delaware Division,Bridge 190.13
Spanning Canawacta Creek at State Rt. 171
HAER PA-16
HAER PA,58-LANBO,2-
6ph L

Erie Railway:Delaware Division,Culvert 190.21
Spanning Canawacta Creek at State Rt. 171
HAER PA-17
HAER PA,58-LANBO,3-
1ph L

Starrucca Viaduct; see Erie Railway:Delaware Division Bridge,189.46

LANESBORO VIC.

Erie Railway:Cascade Bridge Site
Cascade Creek
HAER PA-18
HAER PA,58-LANBO.V,1-
2ph L

MONTROSE

Lyons,John,House; see Mulford,Sylvanus,House

Mulford,Sylvanus,House
(Lyons,John,House)
65 Church St.
HABS PA-215
HABS PA,58-MONT-1-
6dr/2ph/6pg L

SUSQUEHANNA

Erie Railway:Susquehanna Blacksmith Shop
Main & Drinker Sts.
HAER PA-10-C
HAER PA,58-SUSQ,1C-
3ph/1pc L

Erie Railway:Susquehanna Boiler Shop
Main & Drinker Sts.
HAER PA-10-D
HAER PA,58-SUSQ,1D-
3ph/1pc L

Erie Railway:Susquehanna Boiler Shop,1900
Main & Drinker Sts.
HAER PA-10-E
HAER PA,58-SUSQ,1E-
2ph/1pc L

Erie Railway:Susquehanna Carpenter Shop
Main & Drinker Sts.
HAER PA-10-B
HAER PA,58-SUSQ,1B-
3ph/1pc L

Erie Railway:Susquehanna Freight Station
Front St.
HAER PA-9
HAER PA,58-SUSQ,2-
1ph L

Erie Railway:Susquehanna Machine & Erecting Shop (Long Shop)
Main & Drinker Sts.
HAER PA-10-A
HAER PA,58-SUSQ,1A-
3dr/4ph/1pc L

Erie Railway:Susquehanna Repair Office Building
Main & Drinker Sts.
HAER PA-10-F
HAER PA,58-SUSQ,1F-
4ph/1pc L

Erie Railway:Susquehanna Repair Shops
Main & Drinker Sts.
HAER PA-10
HAER PA,58-SUSQ,1-
2dr/4ph/1pc/fr L

Erie Railway:Susquehanna Station & Hotel (Starracca House)
Front St.
HAER PA-8
HAER PA,58-SUSQ,3-
7dr/22ph/2pc/fr L

Erie Railway:Susquehanna Transfer Table
Main & Drinker Sts.
HAER PA-10-G
HAER PA,58-SUSQ,1G-
3ph L

Long Shop; see Erie Railway:Susquehanna Machine & Erecting Shop

Starracca House; see Erie Railway:Susquehanna Station & Hotel

UNION COUNTY

ALLENWOOD

Allenwood Bridge
Spanning Susquehanna River at St. Rt. 44
HAER PA-130
22ph/13pg/2pc H

LEWISBURG

St. Anthony Street Bridge
Spanning Buffalo Creek,Legislative Rt. 59024
HAER PA-99
HAER PA,60-LEWB,1-
24ph/18pg/2pc L

VENANGO COUNTY

CHERRY TREE

Cherry Tree Presbyterian Church
HABS PA-530
HABS PA,61-CHERT,1-
5dr/4ph/5pg/fr L

Public School
HABS PA-539
HABS PA,61-CHERT,2-
1ph L

EMLENTON

Emlenton Bridge
Spanning Allegheny River,Travel Rt. 38 (LR 75)
HAER PA-101
HAER PA,61-EML,1-
39ph/19pg/3pc L

FRANKLIN

Ridgeway Log House
HABS PA-578
HABS PA,61-FRANK,1-
1ph L

OIL CITY

Erie Railway:Meadville Division,Bridge 33.14
Spanning Oil Creek
HAER PA-63
HAER PA,61-OICI,1-
1ph L

Pennsylvania Railroad,Allegheny River Bridge
River St. Vic.
HAER PA-22
HAER PA,61-OICI,2-
5ph L

PLEASANTVILLE

Free Methodist Church
HABS PA-531
HABS PA,61-PLEAV,2-
4dr/2ph/4pg L

Quinn House
HABS PA-518
HABS PA,61-PLEAV,1-
2dr/5ph/4pg L

WARREN COUNTY

GARLAND

Mill,Old (Interior)
HABS PA-540
HABS PA,62-GARL,1-
1ph L

IRVINE

Irvine Estate,House by the Pines
HABS PA-522
HABS PA,62-IRV,2F-
1ph/1pg L

Irvine Estate,Irvine Farmhouse
HABS PA-525
HABS PA,62-IRV,2A-
14dr/1ph/6pg L

Irvine Estate,Miller's House
HABS PA-526
HABS PA,62-IRV,2B-
7dr/2ph/3pg L

Irvine Estate,Tenant House
HABS PA-527
HABS PA,62-IRV,2C-
9dr/1ph/4pg/fr L

Irvine Presbyterian Church
HABS PA-516
HABS PA,62-IRV,1-
7dr/5ph/4pg/fr L

PITTSFIELD

Acock House
HABS PA-554
HABS PA,62-PITFI,1-
1ph L

Hotel,Old
HABS PA-553
HABS PA,62-PITFI,3-
1ph L

Rhodes House
HABS PA-556
HABS PA,62-PITFI,4-
1ph L

Terry House
HABS PA-555
HABS PA,62-PITFI,5-
1ph L

TIDIOUTE

Hotel,Old (Ryan House)
HABS PA-585
HABS PA,62-TIDI,1-
1ph L

Ryan House; see Hotel,Old

WARREN

Henry-Windsor House
203 Market St.
HABS PA-5205
HABS PA,62-WAR,1-
13ph/2pg L

YMCA; see Young Men's Christian Association

Young Men's Christian Association (YMCA)
310 Liberty St.
HABS PA-5352
HABS PA,62-WAR,2-
12ph/12pg L

WASHINGTON COUNTY

BENTLEYVILLE

116 Main Street (Commercial) (Sokol Club)
HABS PA-5384
HABS DLC/PP-1993:PA-1
7ph/6pg/1pc L

Sokol Club; see 116 Main Street (Commercial)

BROWNSVILLE VIC.

Krepps,John Tavern (Malden Inn)
U.S. 40, Old National Trail, 2.5m W. of Brownsvill
HABS PA-417
HABS PA,63-BROVI.V,1-
7ph/4pg L

Malden Inn; see Krepps,John Tavern

CANONSBURG

Gowern Bldg
35-43 N. Jefferson Ave.
HABS PA-5368
HABS PA,63-CANON,2-
6ph/12pg/1pc L

Roberts,John,Stone House
225 N. Central Ave.
HABS PA-1177
HABS PA,63-CANON,1-
11dr L

CARROLL TOWNSHIP

Taylor Run-Yorty Run Schoolhouse
Legislative Rts. 62175 (PA Hwy. 481) & 62161
HABS PA-1157
HABS PA,63-CARTO,1-
2dr/14ph/16pg L

CHARLEROI

First Christian Church
553 Fallowfield Ave.
HABS PA-5358
HABS PA,63-CHAR,1-
18ph/8pg/1pc L

101-11 Tenth Street (Rowhouse)
HABS PA-5391
HABS DLC/PP-1993:PA-5
5ph/4pg/1pc L

FINLEYVILLE VIC.

Methodist Church,James Chapel
Gill Hall Rd. ,Union Twp.
HABS PA-600
HABS PA,63-FINV.V,1-
4dr L

MEADOW LANDS VIC.

Wylie-Miller Barn
U. S. Rt. 19 (North Strabane Twp.)
HABS PA-427
HABS PA,63-WASH.V,1-
6dr/6ph/3pg L

MONOGAHELA

109 Second Street (Commercial Building)
109 Second St.
HABS PA-5479
HABS 1991(HABS):1
2ph/5pg/1pc L

111 Second Street (Commercial Building)
HABS PA-5480
HABS DLC/PP-1993:PA-1
2ph/5pg/1pc L

WASHINGTON

Washington & Jefferson College,Admin. Building
HABS PA-8-2
HABS PA,63-WASH,3-
7dr/3ph/2pg/fr L

WEST BROWNSVILLE VIC

Dorsey House
113 Cherry Ave.
HABS PA-5176
HABS PA,63-BROVW.V,1-
3ph/1pg L

WAYNE COUNTY

BETHANY

Wilmot,David,House
Wayne St.
HABS PA-225
HABS PA,64-BETH,1-
9dr/5ph/5pg L

HAWLEY

Erie Railway:Hawley Coaling Station
HAER PA-25
HAER PA,64-HAW,1-
5ph/1pc L

HONESDALE

Honesdale Coal Pockets
Main & Commercial Sts. ,btwn. 700 & 800 Blocks
HAER PA-82
HAER PA,64-HOND,3-
11ph/8pg/1pc L

House,Italian Villa
HABS PA-5175
HABS PA,64-HOND,2-
1ph L

Thompson,Andrew,House
HABS PA-229
HABS PA,64-HOND,1-
50dr/18ph/7pg L

WHITES VALLEY

Octagon School House
HABS PA-228
HABS PA,64-WHIVA,1-
5dr/2ph/3pg L

WESTMORELAND COUNTY

ALVERTON

Alverton Coke Ovens (H.C. Frick Coke Company)
SE. section of town,adjacent to railroad tracks
HAER PA-288
H

H.C. Frick Coke Company; see Alverton Coke Ovens

BOLIVAR

Bolivar,Town of (Refractories Company Towns)
HABS PA-5977
H

Refractories Company Towns; see Bolivar,Town of

BRENIZER VIC.

East Tunnel Viaduct (Pennsylvania Railroad)
See INDIANA CO.,BLAIRSVILLE VIC. for documentation
HAER PA-267
HAER DLC/PP-1993:PA-3
2ph/2pg/1pc L

Pennsylvania Railroad; see East Tunnel Viaduct

FELLSBURG

Fellsburg Methodist Episcopal Church
Webster Rd. & State Rt. 201 (Rostraver Twp.)
HABS PA-608
HABS PA,65-FELB,1-
12dr L

GREENSBURG

General Greene Hotel; see Rappe Hotel

Greensburg Station (Pennsylvania Railroad)
HAER PA-249
H

Greensburger Hotel; see Rappe Hotel

Pennsylvania Railroad; see Greensburg Station

Rappe Hotel (General Greene Hotel; Greensburger Hotel)
40 E. Pennsylvania Ave.
HABS PA-5192
HABS PA,65-GREEB,1-
15ph/5pg L

IRWIN

Penn-Borough Freight Depot (Pennsylvania Railroad)
HAER PA-252
H

Pennsylvania Railroad; see Penn-Borough Freight Depot

JEANNETTE

American Window Glass Company
HAER PA-221
H

633-635 Division Street (House)
HABS PA-5948
H

Hotel Colombe
HABS PA5606
H

Jeannette Bottle Works; see Jeannette Glass Company

Jeannette Glass Company (Jeannette Bottle Works)
Chambers Ave. extension on Brush Creek
HAER PA-285
H

108 North Second Street (House)
HABS PA-5949
H

313 South Fifth Street (House)
HABS PA-5947
H

326 South Fifth Street (House)
HABS PA-5950
H

425 South Fifth Street (House)
HABS PA-5946
H

LATROBE

Pearce Manufacturing Company
Harrison Ave. W.
HAER PA-291
H

Pearce Manufacturing Company,Building H
Harrison Ave. W.
HAER PA-291-B
H

Pearce Manufacturing Company,Factory A
Harrison Ave. W.
HAER PA-291-A
H

Pearce Manufacturing Company,Long Garage
Harrison Ave. W.
HAER PA-291-D
H

Pearce Manufacturing Company,Small Garage
Harrison Ave. W.
HAER PA-291-E
H

Pearce Manufacturing Company,Wool Storage Building
Harrison Ave. W.
HAER PA-291-C
H

LATROBE VIC.

Connelsville Coal & Coke Region (See FAYETTE COUNTY,CONNELSVILLE for documtatn.)
HAER PA-283
L

LAUGHLINTOWN VIC.

Penguin Court; see Scaife,Alan M. ,House

Scaife,Alan M. ,House (Penguin Court)
U. S. Rt. 30 (Ligonier Twp.)
HABS PA-620
HABS PA,65-LAULT.V,1-
12dr L

LOWER BURRELL

Braeburn Alloy Steel
Braeburn Ed. at Allegheny River
HAER PA-254
3pg H

MAMMOTH

H.C. Frick Coke Company; see Mammoth,Town of

Mammoth,Town of (H.C. Frick Coke Company)
S.R. 982,N. of I-76
HAER PA-289
H

MONESSEN

Monessen Works (Pittsburgh Steel Company)
HAER PA-253
H

Pittsburgh Steel Company; see Monessen Works

NEW ALEXANDRIA

Alter's Halfway House
HABS PA-5477
HABS DLC/PP-1993:PA-1
4ph/10pg/1pc L

NEW ALEXANDRIA VIC.

Bow Ridge Tunnel (Pennsylvnia Railroad)
Through Box Ridge,.3 ml. S. of Conemaugh Dam
HAER PA-269
HAER DLC/PP-1993:PA-3
2ph/2pg/1pc L

Pennsylvania Railroad; see West Tunnel Viaduct

Pennsylvnia Railroad; see Bow Ridge Tunnel

West Tunnel Viaduct (Pennsylvania Railroad)
See INDIANA CO.,TUNELTON VIC. for documentation
HAER PA-268
HAER DLC/PP-1993:PA-3
3ph/2pg/1pc L

NEW FLORENCE

Laurel Hill Furnace
HAER PA-251
H

NEW KENSINGTON

Alcoa Research Laboratory (New Kensington Research Laboratory; Aluminum Company of America)
Freeport Road
HAER PA-295
8ph/3pg/1pc H

Aluminum Company of America; see Alcoa Research Laboratory

New Kensington Research Laboratory; see Alcoa Research Laboratory

NEW KENSINGTON VIC.

Milligan,Samuel,Mill (Water Power Grist Mill)
Little Pucketos Creek
HABS PA-411
HABS PA,65-MILTO,1-
9dr/2ph/2pg/fr L

Water Power Grist Mill; see Milligan,Samuel,Mill

NORVELT

Norvelt,Town of (Westmoreland Homesteads)
HABS PA-5921
HABS DLC/PP-1993:PA-3
22ph/18pg/2pc L

Subsistence-Homestead Towns
See FAYETTE COUNTY,PENN-CRAFT for documentation
HABS PA-5919
HABS DLC/PP-1993:PA-3
25pg L

Westmoreland Homesteads; see Norvelt,Town of

SAILNA

Bell Township Elementary School; see Salina High School

Salina High School (Bell Township Elementary School)
HABS PA-5997
1ph/1pc H

SALINA

Kier Fire Company Hotel (Salina Inn)
HABS PA-5996
1ph/1pc H

Refractories Company Towns; see Salina,Town of

Salina Inn; see Kier Fire Company Hotel

Salina State Bank (U.S. Post Office)
HABS PA-5995
1ph/1pc H

Salina,Town of (Refractories Company Towns)
HABS PA-5978
H

Superintendent's House; see Whiteseel,George,House

U.S. Post Office; see Salina State Bank

Whiteseel,George,House (Superintendent's House)
HABS PA-5994
2ph/1pc H

SCOTTDALE

Duraloy Foundry
HAER PA-255
H

SLICKVILLE

Slickville,Town of
HAER PA-256
HAER DLC/PP-1993:PA-2
2ph/4pg/1pc L

SMITHTON

Smithton Bridge
Spanning Youghiogheny River on State Rd. 981
HAER PA-97
HAER PA,65-SMIT,1-
24ph/5pg/2pc L

STANDARD

H.C. Frick Coke Company; see Standard,Town of

Standard,Town of (H.C. Frick Coke Company)
S.R. 819
HAER PA-290
H

STANDARD SHAFT

H.C. Frick Coke Company; see Standard Shaft,Town of

Standard Shaft,Town of (H.C. Frick Coke Company)
N. of SR819
HAER PA-292
H

TRAUGER

St. Mary's Byzantine Catholic Church
HABS PA-6007
H

TRAUGER VIC.

H.C. Frick Coke Company; see Hecla No. 2 Mine and Coke Works

Hecla No. 2 Mine and Coke Works (H.C. Frick Coke Company)
Between T571 and Rt. 981, west of Trauger
HAER PA-293
4ph/3pg/1pc H

VANDERGRIFT

(NO. assigned WASO 2-11-93 Chris M.); see Vandergrift Station

Allegheny Ludlum Steel Works; see Apollo Iron and Steel Works

Apollo Iron and Steel Works (Allegheny Ludlum Steel Works; U.S. Steel Corporation)
West of Washington and Lincoln Avenues
HAER PA-296
4ph/2pg/1pc H

Apollo Iron and Steel Works,Company Housing
West of Washington and Lincoln Avenues
HAER PA-296-A
3ph/2pg/1pc H

Pennsylvania Railroad; see Vandergrift Station

U.S. Steel Corporation; see Apollo Iron and Steel Works

Vandergrift Station ((NO. assigned WASO 2-11-93 Chris M.); Pennsylvania Railroad)
HAER PA-250
H

WEST NEWTON BOROUGH

Plumer,John C. ,House
131 S. Water St.
HABS PA-617
HABS PA,65-NEWTW,1-
6dr L

WEST NEWTON VIC.

Bells Mill Bridge
Sewickley Creek
HABS PA-415
HABS PA,65-NEWTW.1-
2dr/2ph/1pg/fr L

WEST OVERTON

(HABS No. cancelled per K. Hoagland 12-3-91); see Overton,Henry S.,House

(HAER No. cancelled per K. Hoagland 12-3-91); see Overholt,Christian S.,House

Overholt Co. Workers House C
HABS PA-5662
H

Overholt Co. Workers House D
HABS PA-5663
H

Overholt Co. Workers House F
HABS PA-5664
H

Overholt,A. & H. S.,Coke Oven (Replica)
HABS PA-5660
H

Overholt,A. & H. S.,Distillery
HABS PA-5659
H

Overholt,Abraham,Barn
HABS PA-5661-C
H

Overholt,Abraham,Farm Complex
HABS PA-5661
H

Overholt,Abraham,Farm House
HABS PA-5661-A
H

Overholt,Abraham,House
HABS PA-5658
H

Overholt,Abraham,Large Barn
HABS PA-5661-B
H

Overholt,Abraham,Smokehouse
HABS PA-5658-B
H

Overholt,Abraham,South Stables
HABS PA-5658-D
H

Overholt,Abraham,Springhouse
HABS PA-5658-A
H

Overholt,Abraham,Stables
HABS PA-5661-D
H

Overholt,Abraham,Summerhouse and Shed
HABS PA-5658-C
H

Overholt,Christian S.,House ((HAER No. cancelled per K. Hoagland 12-3-91))
HABS PA-5656
H

Overton,Henry S.,House ((HABS No. cancelled per K. Hoagland 12-3-91))
HABS PA-5655
H

Worker's House B
HABS PA-5657
H

WESTMORELAND

(HAER No. cancelled per K. Hoagland 12-3-91); see West Overton

West Overton ((HAER No. cancelled per K. Hoagland 12-3-91))
HABS PA-5654
H

YUKON

Magee Mine (Westmoreland Coal Company)
Northern border of Sewickley Creek and PA Railroad
HAER PA-294
3ph/3pg/1pc H

Magee Mine,Hoist House (Westmoreland Coal Company)
Northern border of Sewickley Creek and PA Railroad
HAER PA-294-A
4ph/1pc H

Magee Mine,Powerhouse (Westmoreland Coal Company)
Northern border of Sewickley Creek & PA Railroad
HAER PA-294-B
3ph/1pc H

Westmoreland Coal Company; see Magee Mine

Westmoreland Coal Company; see Magee Mine,Hoist House

Westmoreland Coal Company; see Magee Mine,Powerhouse

WYOMING COUNTY

NICHOLSON

Erie-Lackawanna RR:Tunkhannock Viaduct
HAER PA-87
HAER PA,66-NICH,1-
10ph/1pg L

NORTH MEHOOPANY

Kintner Mill
HABS PA-238
HABS PA,66-MEHOPN,1-
11dr/2ph/5pg L

YORK COUNTY

DAVIDSBURG VIC.

Kleiser House; see Wertz-Lashee House

Wertz-Lashee House (Kleiser House)
Julius Ln. ,near Davidsburg Rd.
HABS PA-5183
HABS PA,67-DAVBU.V,1-
5ph/1pg L

DETTERS MILL

Detters Mill Covered Bridge
Harmony Grove Rd. ,spanning Conewago Ck.
HABS PA-5184
HABS PA,67-DETMI,1-
2ph/1pg L

DOVER

Barn
Rural Delivery Rt. 1
HABS PA-129
HABS PA,67-DOV,1-
4ph/1pg L

HALLAM BOROUGH

Schultz,Martin,House
Emig St. ,near Hellam St.
HABS PA-5185
HABS PA,67-HAL,1-
7ph/1pg L

LAUREL VIC.

Guinston United Presbyterian Church
Old Forge Rd. ,Guinston-Laurel Rd. vic.
HABS PA-5187
HABS PA,67-LAUR.V,1-
7ph/1pg L

NEW CUMBERLAND

New Cumberland Army Depot
HAER PA-80
HAER PA,67-NECUB,1-
44pg/fr L

PITTSFIELD

Church
HABS PA-5133
HABS PA,62-PITFI,2-
1ph L

YORK

Acco Industries; see American Chain & Cable Company

American Chain & Cable Company (Acco Industries)
E. Princess St. (400 Block)
HAER PA-52
HAER PA,67-YORK,16-
18ph/10pg/2pc L

Billmeyer House (York House)
225 E. Market St.
HABS PA-5188
HABS PA,67-YORK,10-
4ph/1pg L

Chambers,Joseph,House (Gates,Horatio,House)
157 W. Market St.
HABS PA-5189
HABS PA,67-YORK,11-
1pg L

Christ Lutheran Church
S. George St.
HABS PA-366
HABS PA,67-YORK,1-
2ph L

Cookes House
438-440 Codorus St.
HABS PA-5190
HABS PA,67-YORK,13-
3ph/6pg L

Direct Hotel; see North George Street Historic District

339 East Prospect Street (House)
HABS PA-5101
HABS PA,67-YORK,4-
2ph/2pg L

Gates,Horatio,House; see Chambers,Joseph,House

Golden Plough Tavern
159 W. Market St.
HABS PA-5169
HABS PA,67-YORK,12-
9ph/1pg L

105 North George Street (Commercial Building); see North George Street Historic District

109-111 North George Street (Commercial Building); see North George Street Historic District

107 North George Street (Commerical Building); see North George Street Historic District

101-103 North George Street (Hotel); see North George Street Historic District

North George Street Historic District
HABS PA-573
HABS PA,67-YORK,3-
4ph/1pc/fr L

North George Street Historic District (105 North George Street (Commercial Building))
HABS PA-570
HABS PA,67-YORK,3B-
1ph/4pg/1pc/fr L

North George Street Historic District (109-111 North George Street (Commercial Building))
HABS PA-572
HABS PA,67-YORK,3D-
1ph/4pg/1pc/fr L

North George Street Historic District (107 North George Street (Commerical Building))
HABS PA-571
HABS PA,67-YORK,3C-
1ph/4pg/1pc/fr L

North George Street Historic District (101-103 North George Street (Hotel); Direct Hotel)
HABS PA-569
HABS PA,67-YORK,3A-
2ph/4pg/1pc/fr L

415-421 Short Way (Houses)
HABS PA-5337
HABS PA,67-YORK,5-
3ph/2pg L

443 South Court Street (House)
HABS PA-5339
HABS PA,67-YORK,9-
2ph/1pg L

439-441 South Court Street (Houses)
HABS PA-5338
HABS PA,67-YORK,8-
2ph/3pg L

428 South Duke Street (House)
HABS PA-5335
HABS PA,67-YORK,6-
2ph/3pg L

431 South Duke Street (House)
HABS PA-5336
HABS PA,67-YORK,7-
3ph/4pg L

21-23 West Market Street (Commercial Building)
HABS PA-1313
HABS PA,67-YORK,2-
6ph/6pg L

Willis House
190 Willis Rd.
HABS PA-5170
HABS PA,67-YORK,14-
4ph/5pg L

York County Courthouse,Doorway
250 E. Market St.
HABS PA-5171
HABS PA,67-YORK,15-
3ph/1pg L

York House; see Billmeyer House

YORK VIC.

Barn
Bull Rd. ,U. S. Rt. 30 vic.
HABS PA-5174
HABS PA,67-YORK.V,3-
3ph/1pg L

Beard Tavern (Olde York Inn; Valley Inn)
2805 E. Market St.
HABS PA-5172
HABS PA,67-YORK.V,1-
12ph/1pg L

Dietz House (Hermit's House)
Pleasant Valley Rd. ,near Alpine Rd.
HABS PA-5173
HABS PA,67-YORK.V,2-
3ph/1pg L

Hermit's House; see Dietz House

Olde York Inn; see Beard Tavern

Valley Inn; see Beard Tavern

Hacienda Azucarera La Esperanza (Sugar Plantation), Steam engine mill, Manati, Municipality of Manati, Puerto Rico. Detail viewing of steam engine showing flywheel spokes and hub sector. Photograph by Fred Gjessing, June 1976 (HAER PR,55-MANA,1A-7).

Puerto Rico

AGUADILLA

BORINQUEN

Faro de Punta Borinquen (Punta Borinquen Light)
Punta Borinquen
HAER PR-19
HAER PR,11-BORN,1-
20ph/3pg/2pc L

Punta Borinquen Light; see Faro de Punta Borinquen

VICTORIA

Hacienda Azucarera La Concepcion,Sugar Mill Ruins (La Concepcion Sugar Mill Ruins)
.3 Mi. W. of Junction of Rts. 418 & 111
HAER PR-2
HAER PR,11-VICT,1A-
5dr/23ph/2pc/fr L

La Concepcion Sugar Mill Ruins; see Hacienda Azucarera La Concepcion,Sugar Mill Ruins

ARECIBO

ARECIBO VIC.

Arecibo Light; see Faro de los Morillos de Arecibo

Faro de los Morillos de Arecibo (Arecibo Light)
Punta Morillos,end of Rt. 655
HAER PR-13
HAER PR,15-AREC,1-
16ph/3pg/1pc L

ARROYO

PALMAS

Faro de Punta de Las Figuras (Punta de Las Figuras Light)
Punta de las Figuras
HAER PR-10
HAER PR,16-PALM,1-
11ph/2pg/1pc L

Punta de Las Figuras Light; see Faro de Punta de Las Figuras

CABO ROJO

CABO ROJO VIC.

Cabo Rojo Light; see Faro de los Morillos de Cabo Rojo

Faro de los Morillos de Cabo Rojo (Cabo Rojo Light; Los Morillos de Cabo Rojo)
Los Morillos de Cabo Rojo
HAER PR-11
HAER PR,20-CARO.V,1-
15ph/3pg/1pc L

Los Morillos de Cabo Rojo; see Faro de los Morillos de Cabo Rojo

CULEBRA

FRAILE (BARRIO)

Faro Isla de Culebritas (Isla de Culebrita Light)
South side of Isla Culebrita
HAER PR-12
HAER PR,33-FRAI,1-
13ph/2pg/1pc L

Isla de Culebrita Light; see Faro Isla de Culebritas

FAJARDO

CABEZAS

Cabezas de San Juan Light; see Faro de las Cabezas de San Juan

Faro de las Cabezas de San Juan (Cabezas de San Juan Light)
Cabezas de San Juan
HAER PR-18
HAER PR,35-CABEZ,1-
16ph/5pg/1pc L

GUANICA

CARENERO

Faro del Puerto de Guanica (Guanica Light)
Punta Meseta
HAER PR-14
HAER PR,37-CARN,1-
19ph/3pg/1pc L

Guanica Light; see Faro del Puerto de Guanica

GUANICA VIC.

Hacienda Azucarera La Igualdad:Sugar Mill Ruins (La Igualdad Sugar Mill Ruins & Steam Engine; Sugar Mill Ruins & Steam Engine)
KM 28.3,PR Rt. 332
HAER PR-7
HAER PR,37-GUAN.V,1A-
6dr/24ph/2pc/fr L

La Igualdad Sugar Mill Ruins & Steam Engine; see Hacienda Azucarera La Igualdad:Sugar Mill Ruins

Sugar Mill Ruins & Steam Engine; see Hacienda Azucarera La Igualdad:Sugar Mill Ruins

GUAYAMA

MACHETE (BARRIO)

Hacienda Azucarera Vives (Vives Sugar Mill Ruins)
HAER PR-28
HAER PR,38-MACH,1-
25ph/2pc L

Vives Sugar Mill Ruins; see Hacienda Azucarera Vives

GUAYANILLA

BOCA

San Francisco Sugar Central
HAER PR-26
HAER PR,39-BOCA,1-
22ph/2pc L

ISABELA

COTO (BARRIO)

American Railroad,Guajataca Tunnel (Guajataca Tunnel)
PR Rt. 2,KM 104.2
HAER PR-32
HAER PR,45-COTO,1-
7ph/1pc L

Guajataca Tunnel; see American Railroad,Guajataca Tunnel

LAJAS

COSTA (BARRIO)

Salinas Fortuna Salt Works
PR Rts. 323 & 324
HAER PR-31
HAER PR,49-COSTA,1-
16ph/2pc L

MANATI

TIERRAS NUEVAS PONIE

Hacienda Azucarera La Esperanza (La Esperanza Sugar Plantation)
2.65 mi. N of Rte. 2 bridge over Manati River
HAER PR-1
HAER PR,55-TINUP,1-
2dr/fr L

Hacienda Azucarera La Esperanza:House (La Esperanza Sugar Plantation:House)
2.65 Mi. N of PR Rt. 2 Bridge Over Manati River
HAER PR-1-C
HAER PR,55-TINUP,1C-
5dr/9ph/1pc/fr L

Hacienda Azucarera La Esperanza:Lime Kiln (La Esperanza Sugar Plantation:Lime Kiln)
2.65 mi. N. of Rte 2 bridge over Manati River
HAER PR-1-D
HAER PR,2-MANA,1D-ι83(HAER):104°
1dr/fr L

Hacienda Azucarera La Esperanza:Mill (Ruins) (La Esperanza Sugar Plantation:Mill (Ruins))
2.65 Mi. N of PR Rt. 2 Bridge Over Manati River
HAER PR-1-B
HAER PR,55-TINUP,1B-
2dr/30ph/2pc/fr L

Hacienda Azucarera La Esperanza:Steam Engine &Mill (La Esperanza Sugar Plantation:Steam Engine & Mill)
2.65 Mi. N of PR Rt. 2 Bridge over Manati River
HAER PR-1-A
HAER PR,55-TINUP,1A-
4dr/18ph/2pc/fr L

La Esperanza Sugar Plantation; see Hacienda Azucarera La Esperanza

La Esperanza Sugar Plantation:House; see Hacienda Azucarera La Esperanza:House

La Esperanza Sugar Plantation:Lime Kiln; see Hacienda Azucarera La Esperanza:Lime Kiln

La Esperanza Sugar Plantation:Mill (Ruins); see Hacienda Azucarera La Esperanza:Mill (Ruins)

La Esperanza Sugar Plantation:Steam Engine & Mill; see Hacienda Azucarera La Esperanza:Steam Engine &Mill

MAUNABO

EMAJAGUA (BARRIO)

Faro de Punta Tuna (Punta Tuna Light)
Punta Tuna
HAER PR-9
HAER PR,57-EMAG,1-
27ph/3pg/2pc L

Punta Tuna Light; see Faro de Punta Tuna

MAYAGUEZ

ISLA DE MONA

Faro de La Isla de Mona (Mona Light)
Isla de Mona
HAER PR-24
HAER PR,58-IMON,1-
41ph/3pg/2pc L

Mona Light; see Faro de La Isla de Mona

PONCE

MAGUEYES

Buena Vista Plantation; see Hacienda Buena Vista

Hacienda Buena Vista (Hacienda Vives; Buena Vista Plantation)
KM 16.5,PR Rt. 10 (Ponce to Arecibo)
HAER PR-4
HAER PR,6-MAGU,1-,1-A- THROUGH 1-I-
15dr/72ph/28pg/5pc/fr L

Hacienda Vives; see Hacienda Buena Vista

PONCE

Armstrong,Carlos,Casa
9 Plaza Munoz Rivera
HABS PR-74
HABS PR,6-PONCE,2-
4dr/17ph/1pg/1pc/5ct/fr L

Bestard,Margarita,Casa
118 Calle Reina
HABS PR-69
HABS PR,6-PONCE,7-
4dr/10ph/5pg/1pc/1ct/fr L

Catedral de Nuestra Senora de Guadalupe
Plaza Munoz Rivera
HABS PR-78
HABS PR,6-PONCE,3-
5ph/1pc/2ct L

Faro de La Isla Caja de Muertos (Isla Caja de Muertos Light)
Isla Caja de Muertos,Puerto de Ponce
HAER PR-17
HAER PR,6-PONCE,11-
10ph/2pg/1pc L

Firehouse; see Parque de Bombas

Font,Fredrico,Casa
34 Calle Castillo
HABS PR-71
HABS PR,6-PONCE,6-
5dr/12ph/1pc/8ct/fr L

Godreau,Miguel C. ,Casa
Calle Reina 146
HABS PR-80
HABS PR,6-PONCE,12-
9dr/fr L

Irizarry,Ramon,Casa
121 Calle Reina
HABS PR-70
HABS PR,6-PONCE,8-
5dr/3ph/1pc L

Isla Caja de Muertos Light; see Faro de La Isla Caja de Muertos

Lara,Rita,Casa
Calle Virtud & Calle Estrella
HABS PR-73
HABS PR,6-PONCE,9-
3dr/3ph/1pc/fr L

Parque de Bombas (Firehouse)
Plaza Munoz Rivera
HABS PR-77
HABS PR,6-PONCE,4-
7ph/1pc/6ct L

Plaza de Ponce
Route 14
HABS PR-76
HABS PR,6-PONCE,10-
2ph/1pc/2ct L

Ponce Historic Zone (Partial Map)
HABS PR-75
HABS PR,6-PONCE,1-
1dr L

Toro,Fernando Luis,Casa
Casa Obispado 3
HABS PR-125
HABS PR,6-PONCE,13-
6dr/fr L

Vendrell,Fernando,Casa
3 Calle Amor
HABS PR-72
HABS PR,6-PONCE,5-
5dr/11ph/1pg/1pc/fr L

PONCE VIC.

Cayo Cardona Light; see Faro del Puerto de Ponce

Faro del Puerto de Ponce (Cayo Cardona Light; Puerto de Ponce Light)
Calo Cardona,Puerto de Ponce
HAER PR-16
HAER PR,6-PONCE.V,1-
13ph/2pg/1pc L

Puerto de Ponce Light; see Faro del Puerto de Ponce

SABANETAS (BARRIO)

Hacienda Mercedita Foundry (Mercedita Foundry; Mercedita Sugar Mill Foundry)
HAER PR-8
HAER PR,6-SABA,1A-
21ph/15pg/2pc L

Mercedita Foundry; see Hacienda Mercedita Foundry

Mercedita Sugar Mill Foundry; see Hacienda Mercedita Foundry

RINCON

PUNTAS (BARRIO)

Faro de Punta Higuero (Punta Higuero Light)
Punta Higuero
HAER PR-21
HAER PR,67-PUNTS,1-
10ph/2pg/1pc L

Punta Higuero Light; see Faro de Punta Higuero

SALINAS

LAPAS (BARRIO)

Canal de Riego (Riego Irrigation Canal)
HAER PR-5
HAER PR,70-LAPAS,1-
9ph/1pc L

Riego Irrigation Canal; see Canal de Riego

SAN GERMAN

SABANA GRANDE ABAJO

El Coto Sugar Mill Ruins; see Hacienda Azucarera El Coto:Sugar Mill Ruins

Hacienda Azucarera El Coto:Sugar Mill Ruins (El Coto Sugar Mill Ruins)
.5 Mi. SW of Rt. 347 Bridge Over Guanajibo River
HAER PR-3
HAER PR,5-SAGRO,1A-
3dr/11ph/1pc/fr L

SAN GERMAN

Acosta y Fores,Jaime,Casa
Calle Dr. Santiago Veve No. 70
HABS PR-122
HABS PR,5-SANG,3-
8dr/fr L

Museo de Arte Religioso; see Templo de Porta Coeli

Templo de Porta Coeli (Museo de Arte Religioso)
HABS PR-45
HABS PR,5-SANG,1-
9dr/26ph/1pg/1pc/fr L

SAN JUAN

SAN GERMAN

Ortiz Perichi,Juan,Casa
Calle Luna No. 94
HABS PR-123
HABS PR,5-SANG,4-
11dr/fr L

SAN JUAN

Arsenal,Chapel
Calle Puntilla & Arsenal
HABS PR-99-A
5dr H

Arsenal,Entrance Portico
Calle Puntilla & Arsenal
HABS PR-99-B
4dr H

Arsenal,Naval Storehouses (Spanish Naval Headquarters)
Calle Puntilla & Arsenal
HABS PR-99
10dr/27ph/4pg H

Block Study
Plaza de Armas & the Alcadia Vic.
HABS PR-120
9pg H

100 Calle De La Cruz (Commercial/Residential Bldg)
HABS PR-79
HABS PR,7-SAJU,20-
6ph/1pc L

102 Calle de la Cruz (House)
HABS PR-113
HABS PR,7-SAJU,19-
7ph/1pc L

104 Calle de la Cruz (House) (20 Calle de la Cruz (House))
HABS PR-64
HABS PR,7-SAJU,18-
3dr/7ph/1pg/1pc/fr L

106 Calle de la Cruz (House)
HABS PR-103
7ph/1pc H

108 Calle de la Cruz (House)
HABS PR-119
HABS PR,7-SAJU,16-
5ph/1pc L

20 Calle de la Cruz (House); see 104 Calle de la Cruz (House)

151 Calle de la Luna (House)
HABS PR-114
HABS PR,7-SAJU,31-
3ph/1pc L

153 Calle de la Luna (House)
HABS PR-118
HABS PR,7-SAJU,32-
1ph/1pc L

155 Calle de la Luna (House)
HABS PR-115
HABS PR,7-SAJU,33-
2ph/1pc L

150 Calle del Sol (House)
HABS PR-117
HABS PR,7-SAJU,24-
3ph/1pc L

152 Calle del Sol (House)
HABS PR-108
HABS PR,7-SAJU,23-
1ph/1pc L

154 Calle del Sol (House)
HABS PR-107
HABS PR,7-SAJU,22-
3ph/1pc L

156 Calle del Sol (House)
HABS PR-111
HABS PR,7-SAJU,21-
3ph/1pc L

101 Calle Fortaleza (House)
HABS PR-104
HABS PR,7-SAJU,15-
6dr L

103 Calle San Jose (Commercial/Residential Bldg.)
HABS PR-63
HABS PR,7-SAJU,26-
3dr/7ph/1pg/1pc/fr L

105 Calle San Jose (House)
HABS PR-68
HABS PR,7-SAJU,27-
5ph/1pc L

106 Calle San Jose (House)
106 Calle San Jose
HABS PR-124
HABS PR,7-SAJU,41-
5dr L

107 Calle San Jose (House)
HABS PR-116
HABS PR,7-SAJU,28-
3ph/1pc L

109 Calle San Jose (Casa de los Dos Zaguanes; House of Two Entrances)
109 Calle San Jose
HABS PR-67
HABS PR,7-SAJU,29-
5dr/12ph/1pc L

Capilla del Cristo
Cristo & Tetuan Sts.
HABS PR-42
HABS PR,7-SAJU,2-
8dr/5ph/1pg/fr L

Casa Blanca Complex; see Old San Juan Historic District

Casa Blanca Complex,Casa del Sargento,Guard Corps; see Old San Juan Historic District

Casa Blanca Complex,Casa Fuerte de Ponce de Leon; see Old San Juan Historic District

Casa Blanca Complex,Soldiers Barracks,El Teatrito; see Old San Juan Historic District

Casa Blanca Complex,Stables (La Cochera); see Old San Juan Historic District

Casa Blanca Complex,Storehouse & Cell (El Manuela); see Old San Juan Historic District

Casa de los Azulejos (Palacio Berrocal)
101 Calle San Jose
HABS PR-62
HABS PR,7-SAJU,25-
4dr/19ph/1pg/2pc L

Casa de los Dos Zaguanes; see 109 Calle San Jose

Casa de Ratones
251 Calle de Cristo
HABS PR-105
HABS PR,7-SAJU,14-
7dr L

Castillo de San Cristobal,Cistern Heads (San Juan National Historic Site)
HABS PR-102
2dr/3pg H

Castillo de San Cristobal,Entrance (San Juan National Historic Site)
Blvd. Norzagaray
HABS PR-56
5dr H

Castillo de San Cristobal,Fuerte El Albanico (San Juan National Historic Site)
Blvd. Norzagaray
HABS PR-94
18dr H

Castillo de San Cristobal,Fuerte La Princesa (San Juan National Historic Site)
Fuerta Le Princesa
HABS PR-95
12dr H

Castillo de San Cristobal,Guardhouse (San Juan National Historic Site)
Fuerte El Abanico
HABS PR-59
7dr H

Castillo de San Cristobal,La Trinidad Counterguard (San Juan National Historic Site)
Blvd. Norzagaray
HABS PR-121
17dr/5ph/fr H

Castillo de San Cristobal,Northeast Gate (San Juan National Historic Site)
Blvd. Norzagaray
HABS PR-58
12dr H

Castillo de San Cristobal,Officer's Quarters (San Juan National Historic Site)
Blvd. Norzagaray
HABS PR-98
4dr H

Castillo de San Cristobal,Quarters Number 210 (San Juan National Historic Site)
Blvd. Norezagaray
HABS PR-96
4dr/3pg H

Castillo de San Cristobal,Quarters Number 211 (San Juan National Historic Site)
Blvd. Norzagaray
HABS PR-97
5dr/2pg H

Castillo de San Cristobal,Quarters Number 9 (San Juan National Historic Site)
Blvd. Norzagaray
HABS PR-60
4dr H

Castillo de San Cristobal,San Carlos Ravelin (San Carlos Ravelin; San Juan National Historic Site)
HABS PR-93
14dr H

Castillo de San Cristobal,South Gate (San Juan National Historic Site)
Blvd. Norzagaray
HABS PR-57
8dr H

Castillo de San Felipe del Morro (El Morro; San Juan National Historic Site)
NW end of San Juan
HABS PR-48
HABS PR,7-SAJU,6-
15dr/74ph/1pg/4pc/fr L

Castillo de San Felipe del Morro,Sally Port,Chapel (El Morro,Sally Port & Chapel; San Juan National Historic Site)
NW end of San Juan Island
HABS PR-55
HABS PR,7-SAJU,13-
10dr/fr L

Castillo San Cristobal,Ravelin (Ravelin,Second Line of Defense; Fortifications of San Juan,Second Line of Defense)
Puerta de Tierra
HABS PR-51
HABS PR,7-SAJU,10-
3dr/4ph/3pg/fr L

Castillo San Juan (Fort San Cristobal)
HABS PR-47
HABS PR,7-SAJU,5-
1dr/14ph/4pg L

El Morro; see Castillo de San Felipe del Morro

El Morro,Sally Port & Chapel; see Castillo de San Felipe del Morro,Sally Port,Chapel

El Polvorin; see Fortin de San Jeronimo,Powder House

Escambron Bateria (Escambron Battery; Fortifications of San Juan,First Line of Defense)
Puerta de Tierra
HABS PR-50
HABS PR,7-SAJU,9-
3dr/5ph/8pg/1pc/fr L

Escambron Battery; see Escambron Bateria

Fort of El Canuelo; see Fuerte de El Canuelo

Fort of San Geronimo; see Fortin de San Jeronimo de Boqueron

Fort San Cristobal; see Castillo San Juan

Fortifications of San Juan,First Line of Defense; see Escambron Bateria

Fortifications of San Juan,First Line of Defense; see Fortin de San Jeronimo de Boqueron

Fortifications of San Juan,First Line of Defense; see Fortin de San Jeronimo,Powder House

Fortifications of San Juan,Outer Defenses (Outer Defenses)
Puerta de Tierra
HABS PR-53
HABS PR,7-SAJU,12-
1dr/8ph/6pg L

Fortifications of San Juan,Second Line of Defense; see Castillo San Cristobal,Ravelin

Fortin de San Jeronimo de Boqueron (Fort of San Geronimo; Fortifications of San Juan,First Line of Defense)
Puerta de Tierra
HABS PR-49
HABS PR,7-SAJU,8-
9dr/9ph/15pg/fr L

Fortin de San Jeronimo,Powder House (El Polvorin; Fortifications of San Juan,First Line of Defense)
HABS PR-46
HABS PR,7-SAJU,4-
5dr/9ph/1pg/fr L

Fuerte de El Canuelo (Fort of El Canuelo; San Juan National Historic Site)
Cabras Island
HABS PR-52
HABS PR,7-SAJU,11-
5dr/9ph/fr L

Giorgetti,Eduardo,House
Ponce de Leon Ave.,Santurce
HABS PR-65
HABS PR,7-SAJU,36-
3dr/18ph/1pg/1pc/fr L

Governor's Palace; see La Fortaleza

Historic Zone,Block Study
Calle de las Cruz,Sol,Luna & San Jose
HABS PR-61
HABS PR,7-SAJU,42-
12dr/3pg/fr L

House of Two Entrances; see 109 Calle San Jose

Iglesia San Jose (San Jose Church)
Calle San Sebatian
HABS PR-41
HABS PR,7-SAJU,1-
13dr/20ph/1pg/fr L

Documentation: **ct** color transparencies **dr** measured drawings **fr** field records
pc photograph captions **pg** pages of text **ph** photographs

Iglesia San Mateo de Cangrejos (San Mateo de Cangrejos Church)
NW of Calle San Jorge at Calle San Mateo,Santurce
HABS PR-66
HABS PR,7-SAJU,38-
6dr/10ph/1pg/1pc L

Jewish Synagogue; see Korber,William,House

Korber,William,House (Jewish Synagogue)
903 Ponce de Leon Ave.,Santurce
HABS PR-109
HABS PR,7-SAJU,37-
9ph/1pg L

La Fortaleza (Governor's Palace)
Calle Fortaleza
HABS PR-54
HABS PR,7-SAJU,7-
5ph L

Los Frailes Bridge; see Puente de los Frailes

Norzagaray Bridge; see Puente de los Frailes

Old San Juan Historic District (Casa Blanca Complex)
San Sebastian St. (West End)
HABS PR-106
2dr/5pg/fr H

Old San Juan Historic District (Casa Blanca Complex,Casa del Sargento,Guard Corps)
San Sebastian St. (West End)
HABS PR-106-E
2dr/fr H

Old San Juan Historic District (Casa Blanca Complex,Casa Fuerte de Ponce de Leon)
San Sabastian St. (West End)
HABS PR-106-A
7dr/fr H

Old San Juan Historic District (Casa Blanca Complex,Soldiers Barracks,El Teatrito)
San Sebastian St. (West End)
HABS PR-106-B
2dr/fr H

Old San Juan Historic District (Casa Blanca Complex,Stables (La Cochera))
San Sebastian St. (West End)
HABS PR-106-C
2dr/fr H

Old San Juan Historic District (Casa Blanca Complex,Storehouse & Cell (El Manuela)
San Sebastian St. (West End)
HABS PR-106-D
2dr/fr H

Outer Defenses; see Fortifications of San Juan,Outer Defenses

Palacio Berrocal; see Casa de los Azulejos

Porto Rico Hotel & Chalet
HABS PR-110
HABS PR,7-SAJU,35-
1ph/1pc L

Puente de los Frailes (Norzagaray Bridge; Los Frailes Bridge)
Spanning Frailes Creek,PR Rt. 873,KM 18.85
HAER PR-29
HAER PR,7-SAJU,40-
11ph/1pc L

Puerta de San Juan (San Juan Gate)
N. of La Fortaleza at Caleta San Juan
HABS PR-43
HABS PR,7-SAJU,3-
7dr/3ph/1pg/fr L

Ravelin,Second Line of Defense; see Castillo San Cristobal,Ravelin

San Carlos Ravelin; see Castillo de San Cristobal,San Carlos Ravelin

San Jose Church; see Iglesia San Jose

San Juan Gate; see Puerta de San Juan

San Juan National Historic Site; see Castillo de San Cristobal,Cistern Heads

San Juan National Historic Site; see Castillo de San Cristobal,Entrance

San Juan National Historic Site; see Castillo de San Cristobal,Fuerte El Albanico

San Juan National Historic Site; see Castillo de San Cristobal,Fuerte La Princesa

San Juan National Historic Site; see Castillo de San Cristobal,Guardhouse

San Juan National Historic Site; see Castillo de San Cristobal,La Trinidad Counterguard

San Juan National Historic Site; see Castillo de San Cristobal,Northeast Gate

San Juan National Historic Site; see Castillo de San Cristobal,Officer's Quarters

San Juan National Historic Site; see Castillo de San Cristobal,Quarters Number 210

San Juan National Historic Site; see Castillo de San Cristobal,Quarters Number 211

San Juan National Historic Site; see Castillo de San Cristobal,Quarters Number 9

San Juan National Historic Site; see Castillo de San Cristobal,San Carlos Ravelin

San Juan National Historic Site; see Castillo de San Cristobal,South Gate

San Juan National Historic Site; see Castillo de San Felipe del Morro

San Juan National Historic Site; see Castillo de San Felipe del Morro,Sally Port,Chapel

San Juan National Historic Site; see Fuerte de El Canuelo

San Juan Railroad Terminal
Calle Commercio & Calle Harding
HABS PR-112
HABS PR,7-SAJU,34-
9ph/1pg/1pc L

San Mateo de Cangrejos Church; see Iglesia San Mateo de Cangrejos

Spanish Naval Headquarters; see Arsenal,Naval Storehouses

Superintendent of Lighthouses Dwelling
Punta Puntilla
HAER PR-20
HAER PR,7-SAJU,39-
4ph/5pg/1pc L

SAN JUAN ANTIGUO

Castillo de San Felipe del Morro:Lighthouse (Puerto San Juan Light; Faro del Castillo de San Felipe del Morro)
Summit of Castillo de San Felipe del Morro
HAER PR-23
HAER PR,7-SAJU,6A-
1ph/3pg/1pc L

Faro del Castillo de San Felipe del Morro; see Castillo de San Felipe del Morro:Lighthouse

Puerto San Juan Light; see Castillo de San Felipe del Morro:Lighthouse

TOA BAJA

TOA BAJA

Hacienda Azucarera Santa Elena:Sugar Mill Ruins (Santa Elena Sugar Plantation:Sugar Mill Ruins)
1.44 Mi. N of PR Rt. 2 Bridge Over Rio De La Plata
HAER PR-6
HAER PR,75-TOBA,1A-
5dr/51ph/13pg/3pc/fr L

Santa Elena Sugar Plantation:Sugar Mill Ruins; see Hacienda Azucarera Santa Elena:Sugar Mill Ruins

VIEQUES

ISABEL II (VIEQUES)

Faro de Punta Mulas (Punta Mulas Light)
Punta Mulas
HAER PR-15
HAER PR,8-VIEQUI,2-
14ph/3pg/1pc L

Fort Vieques; see Fuerte de Vieques

Fuerte de Vieques (Fort Vieques)
Isla de Vieques
HABS PR-44
HABS PR,8-VIEQUI,1-
6dr/19ph/1pg L H

Punta Mulas Light; see Faro de Punta Mulas

PUERTO FERRO

Faro de Puerto Ferro (Puerto Ferro Light)
Isla de Vieques
HAER PR-22
HAER PR,8-PUFE,1-
14ph/2pg/1pc L

Puerto Ferro Light; see Faro de Puerto Ferro

YABUCOA

CAMINO NUEVO (BARIO)

Hacienda Azucarera La Lucia:Sugar Mill (Ruins) (La Lucia Sugar Mill (Ruins))
HAER PR-30
HAER PR,81-CANUE,1A-
20ph/2pc L

La Lucia Sugar Mill (Ruins); see Hacienda Azucarera La Lucia:Sugar Mill (Ruins)

YAUCO

RIO PRIETO (BARRIO)

Hacienda Cafetalera Santa Clara,House
Km 19,PR Rte. 372
HAER PR-27-B
HAER PR,82-RIPRI,1-B-
4ph/1pc L

Hacienda Cafetalera Santa Clara:Coffee Mill (Santa Clara Coffee Plantation Mill)
KM 19,PR Rt. 372
HAER PR-27-A
HAER PR,82-REPRI,1-A-
22ph/2pc L

Santa Clara Coffee Plantation Mill; see Hacienda Cafetalera Santa Clara:Coffee Mill

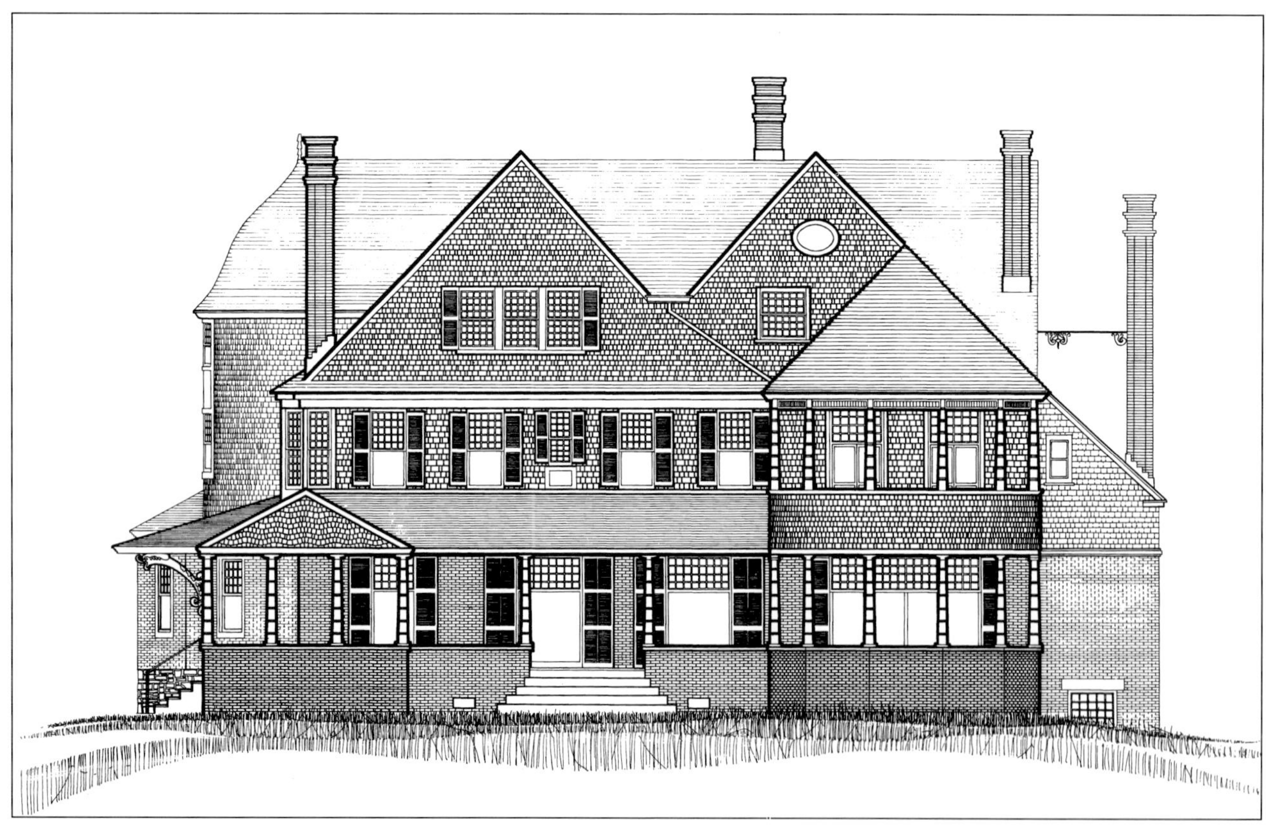

William G. Low House, Bristol, Bristol County, Rhode Island. Exterior from northwest. Photograph by Cervin Robinson, September 18, 1962 (HABS RI,1-BRIST,18-1).

Isaac Bell House, Newport, Newport County, Rhode Island. Front east elevation. Measured drawing by Thomas B. Schubert, 1969 (HABS RI-308, sheet 4 of 8; negative number LC-USZA1-390).

Rhode Island

BRISTOL COUNTY

BRISTOL

Borden,Capt. Parker,House
736 Hope St.
HABS RI-265
HABS RI,1-BRIST,17-
2ph L

Bosworth,Nathaniel,House
814 Hope St.
HABS RI-109
HABS RI,1-BRIST,8-
1ph L

Bourn,John,House
417 Hope St.
HABS RI-260
HABS RI,1-BRIST,12-
1ph L

Bradford,Deputy Gov. William,House; see Royall,Isaac,House

Bristol Congregational Church
HABS RI-375
HABS RI,1-BRIST,11-
1ph L

DeWolf-Middleton House (Hey Bonnie Hall)
Poppasquash Rd.
HABS RI-3-12
HABS RI,1-BRIST,6-
13dr/3ph/2pg L

DeWolf,Gen. George,House; see Linden Place

DeWolf,Mark Anthony,House
Poppasquash Neck
HABS RI-262
HABS RI,1-BRIST,14-
1ph L

Dimond,Francis M. ,Carriage House
HABS RI-128-A
HABS RI,1-BRIST,19A-
1dr/fr L

Dimond,Francis M. ,House
617 Hope St.
HABS RI-128
HABS RI,1-BRIST,19-
7dr/3ph/9pg/1pc/fr L

Gibson House; see Longfield

Herreshoff House
Pleasant Point
HABS RI-126
HABS RI,1-BRIST,10-
1ph L

Hey Bonnie Hall; see DeWolf-Middleton House

Howe,John,House
341 Hope St.
HABS RI-131
HABS RI,1-BRIST,7-
3ph L

Linden Place (DeWolf,Gen. George,House)
500 Hope St.
HABS RI-263
HABS RI,1-BRIST,15-
12dr/8ph/1pc/fr L

Longfield (Gibson House)
1200 Hope St.
HABS RI-129
HABS RI,1-BRIST,20-
10dr/4ph/6pg/1pc/fr L

Low,William G.,House
3 Low Ln.
HABS RI-346
HABS RI,1-BRIST,18-
8ph L

Morice-Babbitt House
328 Hope St.
HABS RI-264
HABS RI,1-BRIST,16-
1ph L

Reynolds,Joseph,House
956 Hope St.
HABS RI-70
HABS RI,1-BRIST,9-
5ph L

Royall,Isaac,House (Bradford,Deputy Gov. William,House)
Metacom Ave.
HABS RI-261
HABS RI,1-BRIST,13-
2ph L

Warren-Bache House (Warren,Russel,House)
86 State St.
HABS RI-259
HABS RI,1-BRIST,1-
7dr/3ph/12pg/1pc L

Warren,Russel,House; see Warren-Bache House

WARREN

Bliss-Ruisden House
606 Main St.
HABS RI-266
HABS RI,1-WAR,6-
3ph L

12 Croade Street (House)
HABS RI-389
HABS RI,1-WAR,10-
3ph/2pg/1pc L

18 Croade Street (House)
HABS RI-390
HABS RI,1-WAR,11-
3ph/2pg/1pc L

Warren Ladies Seminary
HABS RI-267
HABS RI,1-WAR,7-
1ph L

Waterman House
392 S. Water St.
HABS RI-268
HABS RI,1-WAR,8-
1ph L

KENT COUNTY

ANTHONY

Greene,Gen. Nathaniel,House
Greene St.
HABS RI-269
HABS RI,2-ANTH,1-
2ph L

APPONAUG

Northeast Railroad Corridor
HAER RI-19
L

BUTTONWOODS

Greene,James,House
698 Buttonwoods Ave.
HABS RI-270
HABS RI,2-BUTWO,1-
3ph L

EAST GREENWICH

Eldredge,James,House
40 Division St.
HABS RI-58
HABS RI,2-GREWIE,4-
5ph L

Gorton,Samuel Jr.,House
777 Love Ln.
HABS RI-271
HABS RI,2-GREWIE,6-
1ph L

Kent County Courthouse
Main St. (Post Rd.)
HABS RI-57
HABS RI,2-GREWIE,3-
12ph L

Northeast Railroad Corridor
HAER RI-19
L

Union Mill
Main St.
HABS RI-59
HABS RI,2-GREWIE,5-
2ph L

Varnum,Gen. James M.,House
57 Pierce St.
HABS RI-56
HABS RI,2-GREWIE,2-
1ph L

63 Water Street (House)
HABS RI-386
HABS RI,2-GREWIE,7-
4ph/3pg/1pc L

Weaver,Clement,House
125 Howland Rd.
HABS RI-46
HABS RI,2-GREWIE,1-
9dr/19ph L

SPRING GREEN

Greene,John,House
Spring Green Rd.
HABS RI-54
HABS RI,2-SPRI,1-
7ph/1pg L

WARWICK

Greene,Job,House
W. Shore Rd. (Hoxie)
HABS RI-20
HABS RI,2-WAR,1-
13dr/9ph/2pg L

WEST GREENWICH

Grist Mill
State Rt. 3
HABS RI-376
HABS RI,2-GREWIW,2-
5ph/1pc L

Hopkins Mill
State Rt. 3 & Nooseneck River
HABS RI-303
HABS RI,2-GREWIW,1-
11ph/5pg L

WEST WARWICK

Lippitt Mill
825 Main St.
HABS RI-338
HABS RI,2-WAR,1-
4dr/11ph/6pg/fr L

NEWPORT COUNTY

JAMESTOWN

Cajacet; see Paine,Capt. Thomas,House

Carr,Gov. Caleb,House
Conanicut Island
HABS RI-272
HABS RI,3-JAMTO,1-
1ph L

Paine,Capt. Thomas,House (Cajacet)
E. Shore Rd.
HABS RI-273
HABS RI,3-JAMTO,2-
1ph L

MIDDLETOWN

Bannister,John,House
Broadway (Parts in Winterthur Museum)
HABS RI-141
HABS RI,3-MIDTO,2-
9ph/1pg L

Berkeley,Bishop George,House; see Whitehall

Elam,Gervais,House; see Vaucluse

Lazy Lawn
528 Third Beach Rd.
HABS RI-392
HABS 1991(HABS):32
11dr L

Vaucluse (Elam,Gervais,House)
Wapping Rd. (Parts in Metropolitan Museum,NY)
HABS RI-16
HABS RI,3-MIDTO,3-
29dr/8ph/2pg L

Whitehall (Berkeley,Bishop George,House)
Berkeley Ave.
HABS RI-52
HABS RI,3-MIDTO,1-
2ph L

NEWPORT

Armed Services YMCA; see Armed Services Young Mens' Christian Association

Armed Services Young Mens' Christian Association (Armed Services YMCA)
50 Washington St.
HABS RI-391
HABS RI,3-NEWP,79-
28ph/12pg/2pc L

Art Association of Newport,The; see Griswold,John N. A. ,House

Audrain Building
220-230 Bellevue Ave.
HABS RI-333
HABS RI,3-NEWP,41-
3ph/5pg L

Ayrault,Daniel,House (Doorway)
Thames & Ann Sts. (moved to Newport Hist. Soc.)
HABS RI-275
HABS RI,3-NEWP,25-
1ph L

Baldwin,Charles H.,House (Gamir Doon)
Bellevue Ave.
HABS RI-334
HABS RI,3-NEWP,42-
7ph/10pg L

Banister,John,House (Sayer-Banister House)
56 Pelham St.
HABS RI-139
HABS RI,3-NEWP,23-
1ph L

Barney,Jonathan,House (Maxon-Jeffers House; Maxon House)
Spring & Barney Sts.
HABS RI-140
HABS RI,3-NEWP,24-
2dr L

Bedlow,Henry,House; see Malbone

Bell,Isaac,House (Edna Villa)
70 Perry St.
HABS RI-308
HABS RI,3-NEWP,44-
8dr/10ph/13pg L

Berwind,Edward J.,House; see Elms,The

Bliss,Elder John,House (House,Stone End)
2 Wilbur Ave.
HABS RI-104
HABS RI,3-NEWP,18-
1ph L

Bowen's Wharf Warehouse Number 1; see Stevens,Robert,Ship Chandlery

Bowen's Wharf Warehouse Number 2; see Stevens,Robert,Warehouse

Breakers,The
(Vanderbilt,Cornelius,House)
Ochre Point Ave.
HABS RI-339
HABS RI,3-NEWP,67-
41ph/10pg/2pc L

Brenton,Jahleel,House
Thames St. (Mantels at Mill St. & Prospect St.)
HABS RI-36
HABS RI,3-NEWP,14-
7ph L

Bull,Jireh,House; see Maudsley,Capt. John,House

Challoner,Ninyon,House
HABS RI-105
HABS RI,3-NEWP,19-
1ph L

Chateau-sur-Mer (Wetmore House)
Bellevue Ave.
HABS RI-313
HABS RI,3-NEWP,59-
12dr/34ph/16pg/2pc/fr L

Clagget,Caleb,House
22 Bridge St.
HABS RI-348
HABS RI,3-NEWP,55-
2ph L

Clarke,John,House; see Pitt's Head Tavern

Cliff Walk
Leroy & Narragansett Aves. (portion btwn.)
HAER RI-18
HAER RI,3-NEWP,80-
16pg L

Documentation: **ct** color transparencies **dr** measured drawings **fr** field records
pc photograph captions **pg** pages of text **ph** photographs

Coddington,Gov. Williams,House
Marlborough St. (Parts in R.I. Hist. Society)
HABS RI-101
HABS RI,3-NEWP,16-
3ph L

Colony House (State House,Old)
Washington Square
HABS RI-33
HABS RI,3-NEWP,9-
41ph/2pg/2pc/fr L

Covell,William King,House; see Sanford-Covell House

Dennis House; see Grafton,William,House

Edgar,Commodore William,House
29 Old Beach Rd.
HABS RI-318
HABS RI,3-NEWP,35-
7ph/8pg L

Edna Villa; see Bell,Isaac,House

Elms,The (Berwind,Edward J.,House)
Bellevue Ave.
HABS RI-344
HABS RI,3-NEWP,60-
29ph/16pg/1ct L

Fort Adams
Newport Neck
HABS RI-347
HABS RI,3-NEWP,54-
50dr/1ph/25pg/fr L H

Fort Adams,Battery Bankhead
Brenton Point
HABS RI-347-H
1dr/fr H

Fort Adams,Battery Belton
Brenton Point
HABS RI-347-E
1dr/fr H

Fort Adams,Battery Reilly
Brenton Point
HABS RI-347-F
2dr/fr H

Fort Adams,Battery Talbot
Brenton Point
HABS RI-347-G
1dr/fr H

Fort Adams,Redoubt
Brenton Point
HABS RI-347-D
9dr/14pg/fr H

Fort Adams,Stables
Brenton Point
HABS RI-347-J
1dr/fr H

Friends Meeting House
30 Farewell St.
HABS RI-310
HABS RI,3-NEWP,70-
12ph/12pg L

Gale,Levi,House (Jewish Community Center)
89 Touro St. (moved from Washington Square)
HABS RI-328
HABS RI,3-NEWP,52-
6ph/8pg L

Gamir Doon; see Baldwin,Charles H.,House

General Electric Wiring Device Department Plant 2; see Perry Mill

Gibbs-Gardner-Bowler House; see Vernon House

Grafton,William,House (Dennis House)
65 Poplar St.
HABS RI-349
HABS RI,3-NEWP,56-
3ph L

Greene,Amanda,House (Mantel)
Spring & Bridge Sts.
HABS RI-277
HABS RI,3-NEWP,28-
1ph L

Griswold,John N. A. ,House (Art Association of Newport,The)
76 Bellevue Ave.
HABS RI-322
HABS RI,3-NEWP,36-
4dr/7ph/7pg L

Hall-Bedlow House; see Malbone

Hall,J. Prescott,House; see Malbone

Hazard Block (Peckham Coal & Oil Company)
405-411 Thames St.
HABS RI-379
HABS RI,3-NEWP,74-
2ph/6pg/1pc L

House,Stone End; see Bliss,Elder John,House

Hunt,Richard Morris,House; see Hypotenuse

Hypotenuse (Hunt,Richard Morris,House)
33 Catherine St.
HABS RI-315
HABS RI,3-NEWP,33-
4ph/9pg L

Izard,Ralph S.,House
10 Pell St.
HABS RI-319
HABS RI,3-NEWP,69-
4ph/4pg/1pc L

Jewish Community Center; see Gale,Levi,House

Jones-King House; see Kingscote

Jones,George,House; see Kingscote

King Block
204-214 Bellevue Ave.
HABS RI-332
HABS RI,3-NEWP,40-
1ph/5pg L

King,David,House
20 Catherine St.
HABS RI-317
HABS RI,3-NEWP,34-
6ph/5pg L

King,William H. ,House; see Kingscote

Kingscote (Jones,George,House; King,William H. ,House; Jones-King House)
Bellevue Ave. & Bowery St.
HABS RI-307
HABS RI,3-NEWP,61-
6dr/20ph/10pg/fr L

Lillibridge House; see Pitt's Head Tavern

Linden Gate (Marquand,Henry G. ,House)
Old Beach Rd.
HABS RI-335
HABS RI,3-NEWP,64-
13ph/8pg/1pc/fr L

Lucas,Augustus,House
40 Division St.
HABS RI-336
HABS RI,3-NEWP,53-
10ph L

Malbone (Hall,J. Prescott,House; Bedlow,Henry,House; Hall-Bedlow House; Malbone Hall)
Malbone Rd.
HABS RI-340
HABS RI,3-NEWP,62-
14ph/9pg/1pc L

Malbone Hall; see Malbone

Market,Brick (Public Granary)
127 Thames St.
HABS RI-276
HABS RI,3-NEWP,26-
3ph L

Marquand,Henry G. ,House; see Linden Gate

23 Mary Street (Doorway)
HABS RI-137
HABS RI,3-NEWP,21-
1ph L

Mason,George Champlin,House
31 Old Beach Rd.
HABS RI-341
HABS RI,3-NEWP,39-
3ph/5pg L

Maudsley,Capt. John,House (Bull,Jireh,House)
228 Spring St.
HABS RI-35
HABS RI,3-NEWP,13-
9ph L

Maxon House; see Barney,Jonathan,House

Maxon-Jeffers House; see Barney,Jonathan,House

41 Mill Street (Doorway)
HABS RI-136
HABS RI,3-NEWP,20-
1ph L

Mill,Stone (Viking Tower)
Touro Park
HABS RI-103
HABS RI,3-NEWP,3-
3ph L

Mumford,Stephen,House; see
Wanton-Lyman-Hazard House

Newport Casino
186-202 Bellevue Ave.
HABS RI-331
HABS RI,3-NEWP,39-
21ph/20pg/1pc/fr L

Newport Steam Factory
449 Thames St.
HABS RI-324
HABS RI,3-NEWP,75-
4dr/8ph/10pg/1pc/fr L

Nichols-Wanton-Hunter House
(Wanton-Hunter House)
54 Washington St.
HABS RI-7
HABS RI,3-NEWP,11-
35dr/30ph/5pg/fr L

Olmsted,A. H. ,House; see Wildacre

Peckham Coal & Oil Company; see
Hazard Block

10 Pelham Street (House)
HABS RI-138
HABS RI,3-NEWP,22-
1ph L

Perry Mill (General Electric Wiring
Device Department Plant 2)
337 Thames St.
HABS RI-380
HABS RI,3-NEWP,73-
2ph/1pg/1pc L

Pitt's Head Tavern (Clarke,John,House;
Lillibridge House)
Bridge St. (moved from Clarke St. & 5
Charles St.)
HABS RI-279
HABS RI,3-NEWP,30-
1ph L

Porter,Mary T.,House
25 Greenough Pl.
HABS RI-314
HABS RI,3-NEWP,47-
8ph/5pg L

Powel,James C.,House
28 Greenough Pl.
HABS RI-320
HABS RI,3-NEWP,49-
4ph/5pg L

Public Granary; see Market,Brick

Redwood Library
50 Bellevue Ave.
HABS RI-100
HABS RI,3-NEWP,15-
5dr/18ph/18pg/fr L

Redwood,Abraham,Garden House
(Redwood,Abraham,Summerhouse)
50 Bellevue Rd. (moved from original
location)
HABS RI-274
HABS RI,3-NEWP,15A-
1ph L

Redwood,Abraham,Summerhouse; see
Redwood,Abraham,Garden House

Richardson-Blatchford House
37 Catherine St.
HABS RI-316
HABS RI,3-NEWP,48-
5ph/6pg L

Richardson,Thomas,House; see
Spencer,Micah,House

Robinson,Thomas,House
64 Washington St.
HABS RI-280
HABS RI,3-NEWP,31-
15ph/12pg L

Sabbatarian Meetinghouse
82 Touro St. (moved from Spring &
Barney Sts.)
HABS RI-113
HABS RI,3-NEWP,2-
14dr/2ph L

Sanford-Covell House (Sanford,Milton
H. ,House; Covell,William King,House;
Villa Marina)
72 Washington St.
HABS RI-345
HABS RI,3-NEWP,66-
9ph/10pg/1pc L

Sanford,Milton H. ,House; see
Sanford-Covell House

Sayer-Banister House; see
Banister,John,House

Second Congregational Church
13-17 Clarke St.
HABS RI-325
HABS RI,3-NEWP,71-
5ph/4pg L

Sherman,William Watts,House (Watts
Sherman House)
2 Shepard Ave.
HABS RI-342
HABS RI,3-NEWP,68-
10ph/14pg/2pc/fr L

Spencer,Micah,House
(Richardson,Thomas,House)
85-87 Thames St.
HABS RI-3
HABS RI,3-NEWP,10-
15dr/6ph/2pg/fr L

State House,Old; see Colony House

Stevens,Robert,House
261-265 Thames St.
HABS RI-306
HABS RI,3-NEWP,76-
5dr/3ph/fr L

Stevens,Robert,Ship Chandlery
(Bowen's Wharf Warehouse Number 1)
Bowen's Wharf
HABS RI-304
HABS RI,3-NEWP,78-
4dr/6ph/2pg/fr L

Stevens,Robert,Warehouse (Bowen's
Wharf Warehouse Number 2)
Bowen's Wharf
HABS RI-305
HABS RI,3-NEWP,77-
2dr/5ph/2pg/fr L

Swinburne,Daniel T.,House
6 Greenough Pl.
HABS RI-312
HABS RI,3-NEWP,46-
10ph/5pg L

Thames Street Area Survey (Thames
Street Business District)
Thames St. ,between Wash. Sq. &
Memorial Blvd.
HABS RI-337
HABS RI,3-NEWP,72-
13ph/7pg/1pc L

Thames Street Business District; see
Thames Street Area Survey

Tilton,Samuel,House
12 Sunnyside Pl.
HABS RI-309
HABS RI,3-NEWP,45-
4dr/14ph/8pg/fr L

Tompkins,Tillinghast,House
11 Redwood St.
HABS RI-311
HABS RI,3-NEWP,32-
2dr/7ph/5pg L

**Touro Synagogue,Congregation
Jeshuat Israel**
85 Touro St.
HABS RI-278
HABS RI,3-NEWP,29-
27dr/12ph/11pg L

Travers Block
166-184 Bellevue Ave.
HABS RI-330
HABS RI,3-NEWP,38-
3ph/6pg L

Trinity Church
141 Spring St.
HABS RI-102
HABS RI,3-NEWP,17-
19ph/8pg L

Tripp,John,House
88 Washington St. (moved from
RI,Manton)
HABS RI-23
HABS RI,4-MANT,2-
9dr/6ph/1pg L

United Congregational Church
Spring & Pelham Sts.
HABS RI-326
HABS RI,3-NEWP,37-
5ph/7pg L

Vanderbilt,Cornelius,House; see Breakers,The

Vernon House (Gibbs-Gardner-Bowler House)
46 Clarke St.
HABS RI-34
HABS RI,3-NEWP,1-
10dr/14ph/14pg/fr L

Viking Tower; see Mill,Stone

Villa Marina; see Sanford-Covell House

Wanton-Hunter House; see Nichols-Wanton-Hunter House

Wanton-Lyman-Hazard House (Mumford,Stephen,House)
17 Broadway
HABS RI-13
HABS RI,3-NEWP,12-
16dr/12ph L

Warren,Capt. John,House
62 Washington St.
HABS RI-350
HABS RI,3-NEWP,57-
5ph L

Watts Sherman House; see Sherman,William Watts,House

Wetmore House; see Chateau-sur-Mer

White,Isaac P.,House
66 Ayrault St.
HABS RI-321
HABS RI,3-NEWP,58-
8ph/5pg L

Whitehorne,Samuel,House
414 Thames St.
HABS RI-323
HABS RI,3-NEWP,50-
12dr/9ph/19pg/fr L

Wildacre (Olmsted,A. H. ,House)
Ocean Dr.
HABS RI-343
HABS RI,3-NEWP,63-
7ph/1pc L

Williams,John W. ,House
33 S. Baptist St.
HABS RI-327
HABS RI,3-NEWP,51-
2ph/4pg L

PROVIDENCE COUNTY

ALBION VIC.

Blackstone Canal
HAER RI-11
HAER RI,4-LINC,14-
3ph/2pg L

ASHTON VIC.

Blackstone Canal
Blackstone River & Washington Hwy. (Quinnville)
HAER RI-10
HAER RI,4-ASH.V,1-
5ph/2pg/1pc L

Blackstone Canal,Canal Tender's House
Blackstone River,Washington Hwy. Vic.
HAER RI-10-A
HAER RI,4-ASH.V,1-A-
1ph/2pg/1pc L

CENTERDALE

Allendale Mill
494 Woonasquatucket Ave.
HABS RI-302
HABS RI,4-CENT,2-
5dr/16ph/6pg L

Olney,Epenetus,House
370 Woonasquatucket Ave.
HABS RI-89
HABS RI,4-CENT,1-
1ph L

CENTRAL FALLS

Blackstone Canal
State Rt. 126
HAER RI-8
HAER RI,4-CENFA,1-
1ph/1pg/1pc L

Northeast Railroad Corridor
HAER RI-19
L

CHEPACHET

Plante Grist Mill
U.S. Rt. 44
HAER RI-5
HAER RI,4-CHEP,2A-
15ph/2pg/fr L

CUMBERLAND

Albion Bridge
School St., Spanning Blackstone River
HAER RI-21
HAER 1991(HAER):26
11ph/1pc L

Albion Trench Bridge
School St. spanning Albion Mill Race
HAER RI-22
HAER 1991(HAER):26
6ph/1pc L

Grant's Grist & Saw Mill
Wrentham Rd.
HAER RI-13
HAER RI,4-CUMB,3-
1ph/1pc/fr L

CUMBERLAND HILL

Ballou,Elder,Meetinghouse
Ballou Meetinghouse Rd. & W. Wrentham Rd.
HABS RI-14
HABS RI,4-CUMB,1-
8dr/2ph/3pg/fr L

Cooke,Cyrus,House
W. Wrentham Rd.
HABS RI-281
HABS RI,4-CUMB,2-
1ph L

GREENVILLE

Windsor,Daniel,House
Austin Ave.
HABS RI-282
HABS RI,4-GRENV,1-
1ph L

JOHNSTON

Clemence-Irons House; see Clemence,Thomas,House

Clemence,Thomas,House (Clemence-Irons House)
38 George Waterman Rd.
HABS RI-6
HABS RI,4-JONTO,1-
12dr/25ph/7pg/1pc L

Thornton Homestead
Atwood Ave. & Memorial Ave.
HABS RI-80
HABS RI,4-JONTO,2-
3ph L

LIMEROCK

Manton,T. H.,House
Wilbur Rd.
HABS RI-93
HABS RI,4-LIMRO,2-
1ph L

Masonic Temple
Great Rd. & Anna Sayles Rd.
HABS RI-94
HABS RI,4-LIMRO,3-
1ph L

Whitman,Valentine Jr.,House
Great Rd. & Meetinghouse Rd.
HABS RI-8
HABS RI,4-LIMRO,1-
12dr/7ph/3pg/fr L

LIMEROCK VIC.

Whipple,Eleazer,House
Great Rd.
HABS RI-95
HABS RI,4-LIMRO.V,1-
3ph L

LINCOLN

Angell,Widow Anthony,House
Louisquisset Pike (State Rt. 146)
HABS RI-96
HABS RI,4-LINC,12
5ph L

Arnold,Benjamin,House
Entrance "A" Rd. to Lincoln Woods Reservation
HABS RI-86
HABS RI,4-LINC,6-
1ph L

Arnold,Eleazer,House
Great Rd.
HABS RI-87
HABS RI,4-LINC,7-
8ph L

Arnold,Israel,House
Great Rd.
HABS RI-91
HABS RI,4-LINC,10-
10dr/5ph L

Butterfly Factory
Great Rd.
HABS RI-48
HABS RI,4-LINC,3-
1ph/1pg L

Croade Tavern
Great Rd. (moved from RI,Pawtucket)
HABS RI-88
HABS RI,4-LINC,8-
1ph L

Fireplace House
Entrance "A" Rd. to Lincoln Woods Reservation
HABS RI-85
HABS RI,4-LINC,5-
4ph L

Friends Meetinghouse
Great Rd.
HABS RI-17
HABS RI,4-LINC,1-
19dr/6ph/2pg/fr L

Hearthside (Smith,Stephen H.,House)
Great Rd.
HABS RI-47
HABS RI,4-LINC,2-
8ph L

Jenks,Capt. John,House
Great Rd.
HABS RI-92
HABS RI,4-LINC,11-
1ph L

Milk Can,The
Louisquisset Tpk. ,Rt. 146
HABS RI-384
HABS RI,4-LINC,13-
11ph/5pg/1pc L

Millstone
Barneys Pond Bridge Vic.
HABS RI-84
HABS RI,4-LINC,4-
1ph L

Moffatt Mill; see Olney,George,Machine Shop

Olney,George,Machine Shop (Moffatt Mill)
Great Rd.
HABS RI-90
HABS RI,4-LINC,9-
3ph L

Smith,Stephen H.,House; see Hearthside

LONSDALE VIC.

Blackstone Canal
Front St. & Lonsdale Ave. (Lonsdale)
HAER RI-9
HAER RI,4-LONS.V,1-
2ph/1pg/1pc L

MANTON

Tripp,John,House
953 1/2 Manton Ave.(moved to Newport,RI)
HABS RI-23
HABS RI,4-MANT,2-
9dr/6ph/1pg L

Tripp,John,House
981 Manton Ave.
HABS RI-79
HABS RI,4-MANT,3-
1ph L

NORTH PROVIDENCE

Olney,Capt. Stephen,House
138 Smithfield Rd.
HABS RI-77
HABS RI,4-PROVN,2-
4ph L

Smith,Joseph,House
109 Cushing St.
HABS RI-76
HABS RI,4-PROVN,1-
5ph L

NORTH SCITUATE

Lapham Institute (Smithfield Seminary)
Seminary Ln.
HABS RI-291
HABS RI,4-SCITN,1-
1ph L

Smithfield Seminary; see Lapham Institute

NORTH SMITHFIELD

Arnold,Capt. Daniel,House
71 Great Rd. (State Rt. 146)
HABS RI-294
HABS RI,4-SMIFN,1-
1ph L

OAKLAWN

Searle,Edward,House
107 Wilbur Ave.
HABS RI-11
HABS RI,4-OAK,1-
11dr/1ph/2pg/fr L

PAWTUCKET

Croade Tavern
13-15 Dexter St. (moved to RI,Lincoln)
HABS RI-88
HABS RI,4-LINC,8-
1ph L

Dagget,John,House
Slater Park
HABS RI-83
HABS RI,4-PAWT,4-
4ph L

Modern Diner
13 Dexter St.
HABS RI-385
HABS RI,4-PAWT,5-
11ph/2pg/1pc L

Northeast Railroad Corridor
HAER RI-19
L

Pidge Tavern
586 Pawtucket Ave.
HABS RI-29
HABS RI,4-PAWT,1-
14dr/2ph/fr L

Slater Mill,Old
Roosevelt Ave.
HABS RI-82
HAER RI-1
HABS/HAER RI,4-PAWT,3-
7ph/2pg/1pc L

Starkweather-Stearns House
60 Summit Ave. (moved from 57 Summit Ave.)
HABS RI-81
HABS RI,4-PAWT,2-
2ph L

Wilkinson Mill
Roosevelt Ave.
HAER RI-2
HAER RI,4-PAWT,6-
3ph/2pg/1pc L

PAWTUCKET VIC.

Blackstone Canal
HAER RI-16
HAER RI,4-PAWT,7-
6ph/1pg L

PROVIDENCE

Adams,Seth,House
26 Benevolent St.
HABS RI-168
HABS RI,4-PROV,68-
2ph/4pg L

Allen,Amos,House
62 Benefit St.
HABS RI-148
HABS RI,4-PROV,51-
2ph/4pg L

Allen,Candace,Coach House
12 Benevolent St.
HABS RI-170
HABS RI,4-PROV,69A-
1ph L

Allen,Candace,House
12 Benevolent St.
HABS RI-169
HABS RI,4-PROV,69-
13ph/5pg L

American Screw Company
Stevens St.
HAER RI-6
HAER RI,4-PROV,172-
2dr/42ph/3pg/2pc/fr L

Ammadon's,Alpheus,Inn; see Golden Ball Inn

Antram,William,House
953 1/2 Smith St.
HABS RI-381
HABS RI,4-PROV,16-
6dr L

Arcade,The
130 Westminster St.
HABS RI-206
HABS RI,4-PROV,106-
2ph/4pg L

Arnold,Christopher,House
7 Arnold St.
HABS RI-171
HABS RI,4-PROV,71-
1ph/4pg L

Ashton,William Jr.,House
368 Benefit St.
HABS RI-26
HABS RI,4-PROV,30-
27dr/3ph/2pg L

Baker,Josiah,House
23 Arnold St.
HABS RI-190
HABS RI,4-PROV,90-
1ph/4pg L

Barker,William C.,Building
266-268 S. Main St.
HABS RI-209
HABS RI,4-PROV,109-
1ph/5pg L

Barnes,Joanna,House
49 Benefit St.
HABS RI-144
HABS RI,4-PROV,47-
2ph/5pg L

Barney,Cromwell,House
91 Williams St.
HABS RI-252
HABS RI,4-PROV,149-
1ph/4pg L

Beckwith,Truman,House (Handicraft Club)
42 College St.
HABS RI-21
HABS RI,4-PROV,26-
56dr/5ph/7pg L

Beneficent Congregational Church (Round Top)
300 Weybosset St.
HABS RI-210
HABS RI,4-PROV,110-
4ph/19pg L

Benson,George,House
64 Angell St.
HABS RI-172
HABS RI,4-PROV,72-
12ph/5pg L

Binney,William,House
72 Prospect St.
HABS RI-224
HABS RI,4-PROV,124-
1ph/4pg L

Bishop's House; see Ives,Moses B.,House

Blackstone Canal (Northeast Corridor Project)
Charles & Randall Sts.,Canal & Haymarket Sts.
HAER RI-7
HAER RI,4-PROV,173-
11ph/7pg/1pc L

Blanding,Shubael,House
20 Cooke St.
HABS RI-211
HABS RI,4-PROV,111-
1ph/5pg L

Block,Granite (Hotel Bristol)
6-18 Market Sq.
HABS RI-30
HABS RI,4-PROV,33-
20dr/6ph/fr L

Bowen,Isaac Jr.,House
312 Benefit St.
HABS RI-161
HABS RI,4-PROV,62-
7ph/4pg L

Bowen,Jabez,House
39 Bowen St.
HABS RI-173
HABS RI,4-PROV,73-
3ph/5pg L

Bowen,Tully,House
389 Benefit St.
HABS RI-167
HABS RI,4-PROV,67-
1ph/4pg L

Brown University,Brown Library; see Brown University,Robinson Hall

Brown University,Manning Hall
Prospect St.
HABS RI-181
HABS RI,4-PROV,81B-
2ph/4pg L

Brown University,Robinson Hall (Brown University,Brown Library)
Waterman & Prospect Sts.
HABS RI-185
HABS RI,4-PROV,81C-
5ph/4pg L

Brown University,University Hall
Prospect St.
HABS RI-283
HABS RI,4-PROV,81A-
1ph L

Brown,Gov. Elisha,House
537 N. Main St.
HABS RI-9
HABS RI,4-PROV,20-
12dr/3ph/2pg/fr L

Brown,James,Warehouse
142-152 S. Water St.
HABS RI-246
HABS RI,4-PROV,143-
1ph/2pg L

Brown,John,House
52 Power St.
HABS RI-75
HABS RI,4-PROV,5-
16ph/1pg L

Brown,Joseph,House
50 S. Main St.
HABS RI-53
HABS RI,4-PROV,4-
6ph/5pg L

Brown,Moses,School; see Friends' School

Brown,Nicholas,House
29 S. Main St.
HABS RI-99
HABS RI,4-PROV,45-
2ph L

Brown,Richard,House
587 Rochambeau Ave.
HABS RI-31
HABS RI,4-PROV,34-
12dr/4ph/fr L

Brown,Riley,House
2 Thayer St.
HABS RI-174
HABS RI,4-PROV,74-
2ph/4pg L

Brown,William L.,House
23 John St.
HABS RI-225
HABS RI,4-PROV,125-
4ph/4pg L

Bucklin-Eddy Building
283-297 S. Main St.
HABS RI-254
HABS RI,4-PROV,151-
1ph/5pg L

Bucklin,George,House
10 Arnold St.
HABS RI-175
HABS RI,4-PROV,75-
2ph/4pg L

Bullock,Richmond,House
288-292 S. Main St.
HABS RI-248
HABS RI,4-PROV,145-
2pg L

Buonanno Garage,Old
Crockett St.
HABS RI-372
HABS RI,4-PROV,15-
9ph L

Burnside,Gen. Ambrose,House
314 Benefit St.
HABS RI-162
HABS RI,4-PROV,63-
2ph/4pg L

Burrough,James,House
160 Power St.
HABS RI-226
HABS RI,4-PROV,126-
5ph/5pg L

Burroughs,Robert S. ,House
6 Cooke St.
HABS RI-212
HABS RI,4-PROV,12-
1ph/5pg L

Burroughs,Robert S.,House; see Tobey,Dr. S. B.,House

Carlile,Samuel,House
87 Williams St.
HABS RI-251
HABS RI,4-PROV,148-
2ph/3pg L

Carpenter,Zachariah,House
20 Arnold St.
HABS RI-176
HABS RI,4-PROV,76-
7ph/4pg L

Carrington,Edward,House
66 Williams St.
HABS RI-19
HABS RI,4-PROV,25-
55dr/11ph/9pg/fr L

Carter,John,House (Shakespeare's Head)
21 Meeting St.
HABS RI-1
HABS RI,4-PROV,17-
15dr/11ph/6pg/fr L

Cathedral of St. John; see St. John's Church

Church,John,House (Pearce,Levi,House)
25-27 John St.
HABS RI-240
HABS RI,4-PROV,137-
1ph/5pg L

Church,William,House
22 Arnold St.
HABS RI-177
HABS RI,4-PROV,77-
1ph/4pg L

City Hall (Providence City Hall)
Exchange Place,Kennedy Plaza
HABS RI-192
HABS RI,4-PROV,92-
9ph/9pg/1pc/fr L

City Poor Farm; see Dexter Asylum

Clark & Nightingale Block
247-259 S. Main St.
HABS RI-253
HABS RI,4-PROV,150-
2ph/8pg L

Colony House; see State House,Old

Comstock Block
265-277 S. Main St.
HABS RI-228
HABS RI,4-PROV,128-
1ph/8pg L

Cooke,Benoni,House
110 S. Main St.
HABS RI-213
HABS RI,4-PROV,10-
4ph/4pg L

Corliss,George H.,House
45 Prospect St.
HABS RI-229
HABS RI,4-PROV,14-
2ph/5pg L

Cushing,Benjamin,House
38 1/2 N. Court St.
HABS RI-193
HABS RI,4-PROV,93-
6ph/4pg L

Daggett's Tavern; see Golden Ball Inn

Dexter Asylum (City Poor Farm)
Hope St. & Lloyd Ave.
HABS RI-231
HABS RI,4-PROV,131-
3ph/1pg L

Dexter,Ebenezer Knight,House
300 Angell St.
HABS RI-178
HABS RI,4-PROV,78-
1ph/5pg L

Dexter,Edward,House
72 Waterman St. (moved from George St.)
HABS RI-15
HABS RI,4-PROV,23-
53dr/7ph/3pg L

Dexter,Jeremiah,House
957 N. Main St.
HABS RI-5
HABS RI,4-PROV,19-
9dr/7ph/3pg/fr L

Dike,Henry A.,House
101 Prospect St.
HABS RI-250
HABS RI,4-PROV,147-
9ph/4pg L

Dodge,Seril,House
10 Thomas St.
HABS RI-3-7
HABS RI,4-PROV,13-
15dr/5ph/6pg L

Dorr,Sullivan,House
109 Benefit St.
HABS RI-284
HABS RI,4-PROV,158-
1ph L

East Side Railroad Tunnel
Benefit St. to Seekonk River
HAER RI-29
HAER RI,4-PROV,184-
7ph/2pg/1pc L

Ellis,Cyrus,House
31 John St.
HABS RI-232
HABS RI,4-PROV,132-
7ph/4pg L

Exchange Bridge
Spanning Providence River
HAER RI-17
HAER RI,4-PROV,181-
8ph/15pg/1pc L

Exchange Coffee House
1-5 Market Square
HABS RI-98
HABS RI,4-PROV,44-
1ph L

Fenner,Gov. James,House
41 Waterman St.
HABS RI-55
HABS RI,4-PROV,38-
6ph/1pg L

First Baptist Meetinghouse
75 N. Main St.
HABS RI-38
HABS RI,4-PROV,1-
37ph/4pg L

First Congregational Church (First Unitarian Church)
301 Benefit St.
HABS RI-159
HABS RI,4-PROV,43-
13ph/6pg L

First Unitarian Church; see First Congregational Church

Fleur De Lys Studio
7 Thomas St.
HABS RI-393
HABS 992(HABS):RI-1
5dr/fr L

Francis Street Bridge
Beneath Providence Union Station & Viaduct
HAER RI-33
HAER RI,4-PROV,185-
13ph/1pg/1pc L

Franklin House Hotel
32 Market Sq.
HABS RI-22
HABS RI,4-PROV,27-
7dr/1ph L

Franklin Institute Building; see Williams,Roger,Bank

Friends' School (Brown,Moses,School)
257 Hope St.
HABS RI-255
HABS RI,4-PROV,152-
1ph/2pg L

Gardiner House; see Hale,Joseph,House

Gaspee Street Bridge
Gaspee St. at Providence Union Station Viaduct
HAER RI-32
HAER RI,4-PROV,186-
3ph/1pg/1pc L

Glove Tavern; see Golden Ball Inn

Goddard,Francis W.,House
71 George St.
HABS RI-194
HABS RI,4-PROV,94-
4ph/4pg L

Goddard,William,House
38 Brown St.
HABS RI-195
HABS RI,4-PROV,95-
1ph/5pg L

Golden Ball Inn (Daggett's Tavern; Williams,Roger,Hotel; Ammadon's,Alpheus,Inn; Glove Tavern)
159 Benefit St.
HABS RI-73
HABS RI,4-PROV,41-
3ph/1pg L

Gorham,Jabez,House
56 Benefit St.
HABS RI-146
HABS RI,4-PROV,49-
2ph/5pg L

Greene,John Holden,House
150 Power St.
HABS RI-196
HABS RI,4-PROV,96-
1ph/4pg L

Greenman,William,House
24 Thayer St.
HABS RI-179
HABS RI,4-PROV,79-
1ph/4pg L

Guild,Samuel,House
(Pearce,Daniel,House; Lightning Splitter House)
53 Transit St.
HABS RI-258
HABS RI,4-PROV,155-
1ph/3pg L

Haile,Joseph,House; see
Hale,Joseph,House

Hale,Joseph,House (Haile,Joseph,House; Gardiner House)
106 George St.
HABS RI-197
HABS RI,4-PROV,97-
9ph/4pg L

Hall,Abner,House
116 Hope St.
HABS RI-198
HABS RI,4-PROV,98-
1ph/3pg L

Halsey,Thomas L.,House
140 Prospect St.
HABS RI-233
HABS RI,4-PROV,133-
1ph/3pg L

Hamilton Building
Westminster & Exchange Sts.
HABS RI-285
HABS RI,4-PROV,159-
1ph L

Handicraft Club; see
Beckwith,Truman,House

Harding,William,House
278-282 S. Main St.
HABS RI-234
HABS RI,4-PROV,134-
1ph/2pg L

Harris,Stephen,House
135 Benefit St.
HABS RI-151
HABS RI,4-PROV,54-
1ph/4pg L

Holden,Thomas R.,House
(Humphrey,Josiah,House)
118 Benefit St.
HABS RI-150
HABS RI,4-PROV,53-
4ph/5pg L

Holroyd,William,House
106 Angell St.
HABS RI-180
HABS RI,4-PROV,80-
11ph/4pg L

Hopkins,Stephen,House
12 Hopkins St.
HABS RI-28
HABS RI,4-PROV,32-
15dr/8ph/5pg/fr L

Hoppin,Benjamin,Homestead
Snow & Westminster Sts.
HABS RI-286
HABS RI,4-PROV,160-
1ph L

Hoppin,Thomas F.,House
383 Benefit St.
HABS RI-166
HABS RI,4-PROV,66-
2ph/7pg L

Hotel Bristol; see Block,Granite

Humphrey,Josiah,House; see
Holden,Thomas R.,House

Ives,Moses B.,House (Bishop's House)
10 Brown St.
HABS RI-199
HABS RI,4-PROV,99-
2ph/5pg L

Ives,Thomas P.,Block
270-276 Benefit St.
HABS RI-158
HABS RI,4-PROV,60-
1ph/5pg L

Ives,Thomas P.,House
66 Power St.
HABS RI-235
HABS RI,4-PROV,12-
7ph/7pg L

Ives,Thomas P.,Stable & Coach House
66 Power St.
HABS RI-236
HABS RI,4-PROV,12A-
3ph/2pg L

Jastram,Mawney,House
61 Benefit St.
HABS RI-147
HABS RI,4-PROV,50-
1ph/4pg L

Jenckes,John,House
(Jenckes,Joseph,House)
43 Benefit St.
HABS RI-12
HABS RI,4-PROV,22-
16dr/4ph/8pg/fr L

Jenckes,Joseph,House; see
Jenckes,John,House

Jenckes,Thomas A.,House
2 Angell St.
HABS RI-214
HABS RI,4-PROV,114-
7ph/5pg L

Kilton-Wilkinson House
201 S. Main St.
HABS RI-230
HABS RI,4-PROV,130-
1ph/5pg L

Kimball,James M.,House
108 Prospect St.
HABS RI-237
HABS RI,4-PROV,135-
1ph/4pg L

King,Dr. William J.,House
48 College St.
HABS RI-200
HABS RI,4-PROV,100-
1ph/4pg L

Larcher,John,House
282 Benefit St.
HABS RI-32
HABS RI,4-PROV,35-
23dr/7ph/4pg/fr L

Lightning Splitter House; see
Guild,Samuel,House

Lippitt-Green House
14 John St.
HABS RI-223
HABS RI,4-PROV,123-
3ph/5pg L

Lippitt,Gov. Henry,House
199 Hope St.
HABS RI-239
HABS RI,4-PROV,136-
34ph/5pg L

Market House
Market Sq.
HABS RI-74
HABS RI,4-PROV,42-
9ph/2pg L

Mason,John B.,House (Tockwotten Hall Hotel)
Tockwotten & East Sts.
HABS RI-288
HABS RI,4-PROV,162-
1ph L

Mason,John,House (Mantel)
Weybosset St. (moved to R.I. School of Design)
HABS RI-287
HABS RI,4-PROV,161-
1ph L

Mason,Nathan,House
33 Arnold St.
HABS RI-182
HABS RI,4-PROV,82-
3ph/4pg L

Mason,Nathan,House
(Sweet,Menzies,House)
34 Arnold St.
HABS RI-215
HABS RI,4-PROV,115-
3ph/4pg L

Merchants Cold Storage Warehouse
160 Kingsley Ave.
HAER RI-12
HAER RI,4-PROV,171-
16ph/4pg/2pc L

Metcalf,Stephen O.,House
132 Bowen St.
HABS RI-216
HABS RI,4-PROV,116-
1ph/5pg L

Mortgage Guarantee & Title Company Building; see Phenix National Bank

Nightingale,Col. Joseph,House
357 Benefit St.
HABS RI-164
HABS RI,4-PROV,7-
8ph/6pg L

Northeast Corridor; see Northeast Railroad Corridor

Northeast Corridor Project; see Blackstone Canal

Northeast Corridor Project; see Promenade Street Interlocking Tower

Northeast Corridor Project; see Providence Cove Lands

Northeast Corridor Project; see Providence Union Station

Northeast Corridor Project; see Union Station Viaduct

Northeast Railroad Corridor
(Northeast Corridor)
Amtrak Rt. btwn. CT/RI & RI/MA State Lines
HAER RI-19
HAER RI,4-PROV,174-
35ph/4pc/fr L

Owen,George & Smith,Building
9 Steeple St.
HABS RI-256
HABS RI 4-PROV,153-1
1ph/4pg L

Pearce,Daniel,House; see Guild,Samuel,House

Pearce,Earle D.,House
225-227 Benefit St.
HABS RI-154
HABS RI,4-PROV,57-
1ph/2pg L

Pearce,Edward,House
2 Benevolent St.
HABS RI-201
HABS RI,4-PROV,101-
1ph/3pg L

Pearce,Levi,House; see Church,John,House

Pearce,Nathaniel,House
305 Brook St. (moved from 41 George St.)
HABS RI-184
HABS RI,4-PROV,84-
4ph/6pg L

Pearson,Luther,House
6 Thayer St.
HABS RI-183
HABS RI,4-PROV,83-
1ph/4pg L

Phenix National Bank (Mortgage Guarantee & Title Company Building)
85-89 Westminster St.
HABS RI-329
HABS RI,4-PROV,167-
3ph/1pg L

Pine Street (House,Interior)
(Plantations Club)
(Fragments in Plantations Club,Weybosset St.)
HABS RI-289
HABS RI,4-PROV,163-
1ph L

Pioneer Fire Company Building
296-302 S. Main St.
HABS RI-247
HABS RI,4-PROV,144-
2pg L

Plantations Club; see Pine Street (House,Interior)

Pope,West,House
97 Williams St.
HABS RI-249
HABS RI,4-PROV,146
2ph/5pg L

Post Office Covered Walkway
HAER RI-31
HAER RI,4-PROV,187-
2ph/1pc L

Potter,Charles,House
154 Waterman St.
HABS RI-217
HABS RI,4-PROV,117-
1ph/3pg L

Potter,Russell,House
26 John St.
HABS RI-241
HABS RI,4-PROV,138-
8ph/3pg L

Promenade Street Bridge
Spanning Woonasquatucket & Moshassuck Rivers
HAER RI-30
HAER RI,4-PROV,188-
12ph/1pg/1pc L

Promenade Street Interlocking Tower
(Northeast Corridor Project)
Promenade St btwn Union Sta & E Side Tunnel Viaduc
HAER RI-23
HAER RI,4-PROV,178-
6ph/2pg/1pc L

Providence & Worcester RR,Freight House (Providence & Worcester RR,South Freight House; Providence & Worcester RR,Merchandise House)
Canal St.
HAER RI-3
HAER RI,4-PROV,176A-
5dr/22ph/2pg/1pc L

Providence & Worcester RR,Merchandise House; see Providence & Worcester RR,Freight House

Providence & Worcester RR,South Freight House; see Providence & Worcester RR,Freight House

Providence Athenaeum
251 Benefit St.
HABS RI-156
HABS RI,4-PROV,59-
1ph/4pg L

Providence Biltmore Hotel
11 Dorrance St.
HABS RI-49
HABS RI,4-PROV,183-
12ph/18pg/1pc L

Providence City Hall; see City Hall

Providence College,Bailey,William M. ,House (Providence College,Hillwood; Providence College,Dominic Hall)
Eaton St.
HABS RI-382
HABS RI,4-PROV,169-
1ph/1pg L

Providence College,Bradley,George M. ,House (Providence College,Martin Hall)
189 Eaton St.
HABS RI-383
HABS RI,4-PROV,170-
3ph/1pg L

Providence College,Dominic Hall; see Providence College,Bailey,William M. ,House

Providence College,Hillwood; see Providence College,Bailey,William M. ,House

Providence College,Martin Hall; see Providence College,Bradley,George M. ,House

Providence Cove Lands (Northeast Corridor Project)
Smith St,Moshassuck Riv,Exchange St & Prov/Worc RY
HAER RI-24
HAER RI,4-PROV,175-
23pg L

Providence Marine Corps Arsenal
176 Benefit St.
HABS RI-152
HABS RI,4-PROV,55-
2ph/4pg L

Providence Union Station (Northeast Corridor Project)
Exchange Terrace
HABS RI-388
HABS RI,4-PROV,177-
23ph/3pg/1pc L

Purkis,Robert,House
37 Charles Field St.
HABS RI-202
HABS RI,4-PROV,102-
1ph/4pg L

Reynolds,Benjamin & John,House
88 Benefit St.
HABS RI-149
HABS RI,4-PROV,52-
1ph/4pg L

Reynolds,John,House
81 Power St. (moved from 31 Benevolent St.)
HABS RI-71
HABS RI,4-PROV,40-
17dr/15ph L

Rhode Island State House
90 Smith St.
HABS RI-155
HABS RI,4-PROV,180-
7ph/7pg L

Rhodes,James T.,House
367 Benefit St.
HABS RI-165
HABS RI,4-PROV,65-
1ph/6pg L

Richmond,Samuel,House
36 Bowen St.
HABS RI-203
HABS RI,4-PROV,103-
5ph/4pg L

Roffee,Caleb,House
92 Williams St.
HABS RI-257
HABS RI,4-PROV,154-
2ph/3pg L

Round Top; see Beneficent Congregational Church

Russell,Joseph,House
118 N. Main St. (fragments in Brooklyn Museum)
HABS RI-242
HABS RI,4-PROV,139-
1ph/2pg L

Schoolhouse,Brick
24 Meeting St.
HABS RI-191
HABS RI,4-PROV,91-
1ph/4pg L

Seamans,Nathan,House
15 Arnold St.
HABS RI-186
HABS RI,4-PROV,86-
5ph/4pg L

Shakespeare's Head; see Carter,John,House

Sheldon House
336 Benefit St.
HABS RI-163
HABS RI,4-PROV,64-
2ph/4pg L

Sheldon,Christopher,Warehouse
369-371 S. Main St.
HABS RI-218
HABS RI,4-PROV,118-
2ph/4pg L

Sheldon,Remington,Business Building
379-381 S. Main St.
HABS RI-219
HABS RI,4-PROV,119-
1ph/5pg L

Smith,C. Morris,House
112 Benevolent St.
HABS RI-187
HABS RI,4-PROV,87-
1ph/5pg L

Smith,Franklin,House
9 Hidden St.
HABS RI-220
HABS RI,4-PROV,120-
1ph/4pg L

Smith,Martha,House; see Smith,Rev. Francis,House

Smith,Rev. Francis,House
(Smith,Martha,House)
35 Benefit St.
HABS RI-143
HABS RI,4-PROV,46-
1ph/4pg L

Snow,Peter W.,House
104 Benevolent St.
HABS RI-188
HABS RI,4-PROV,88-
1ph/6pg L

St. John's Church (Cathedral of St. John)
271 N. Main St.
HABS RI-204
HABS RI,4-PROV,104-
6ph/9pg L

St. Stephen's Church
114 George St.
HABS RI-189
HABS RI,4-PROV,89-
2ph/4pg L

Staples,Samuel,House
52 Benefit St.
HABS RI-145
HABS RI,4-PROV,48-
1ph/4pg L

State House,Old (Colony House)
155 N. Main St.
HABS RI-18
HABS RI,4-PROV,24-
20dr/15ph/10pg/fr L

Sweet,Menzies,House; see Mason,Nathan,House

Taft,Robert W.,House
154 Hope St.
HABS RI-205
HABS RI,4-PROV,105-
1ph/4pg L

Taylor,Deacon Edward,House
9 Thomas St.
HABS RI-243
HABS RI,4-PROV,8-
1ph/5pg L

Tillinghast,Capt. Joseph,House
403 S. Main St.
HABS RI-4
HABS RI,4-PROV,18-
16dr/7ph/4pg/fr L

Tobey,Dr. S. B.,House
(Burroughs,Robert S.,House)
110 Benevolent St.
HABS RI-227
HABS RI,4-PROV,127-
1ph/6pg L

Tockwotten Hall Hotel; see Mason,John B.,House

Townsend,Solomon,House
35 Charles Field St.
HABS RI-221
HABS RI,4-PROV,121-
2ph/5pg L

Underwood,Edward S.,House
28 John St.
HABS RI-244
HABS RI,4-PROV,141-
1ph/3pg L

Union Station Railroad Bridge; see Woonasquatucket Bridge

Union Station Viaduct (Northeast Corridor Project)
Spanning Gaspee,Francis,Promenade & Canal Sts.
HAER RI-14
HAER RI,4-PROV,179-
20ph/4pg/3pc L

Ward,Eliza,House
2 George St.
HABS RI-207
HABS RI,4-PROV,107-
21ph/6pg L

Warner,Samuel,House
362 S. Main St.
HABS RI-10
HABS RI,4-PROV,21-
12dr/2pg/fr L

Waterman,Richard,House
219 Benefit St.
HABS RI-153
HABS RI,4-PROV,9-
1ph/5pg L

Watson,William,House; see Wilkinson,William,House

Wells,Elisha,House
30 John St.
HABS RI-245
HABS RI,4-PROV,142-
4ph/3pg L

Westcott,Samuel,House
240 Benefit St.
HABS RI-25
HABS RI,4-PROV,29-
8dr L

Westminster Congregational Church
119 Mathewson St.
HABS RI-290
HABS RI,4-PROV,164-
1ph L

Wheaton & Anthony Building (First)
33-39 Kennedy Plaza
HABS RI-377
HABS RI,4-PROV,165-
3ph/1pg L

Wheaton & Anthony Building (Second)
75 Westminster St.
HABS RI-378
HABS RI,4-PROV,166-
10ph/6pg L

Whipple,John,House
54 College St.
HABS RI-208
HABS RI,4-PROV,108-
1ph/5pg L

Wilkinson,William,House (Watson,William,House)
69 College St.
HABS RI-24
HABS RI,4-PROV,28-
38dr/1ph/2pg L

Williams,Betsy,Cottage
Roger Williams Park
HABS RI-69
HABS RI,4-PROV,39-
2ph L

Williams,Roger,Bank (Franklin Institute Building)
27 Market Sq.
HABS RI-37
HABS RI,4-PROV,36-
5ph L

Williams,Roger,Hotel; see Golden Ball Inn

Woods,Marshall,House
62 Prospect St.
HABS RI-222
HABS RI,4-PROV,122-
1ph/10pg L

Woodward,William,House
22 James St.
HABS RI-27
HABS RI 4-PROV,31-
2ph/4pg L

Woonasquatucket Bridge (Union Station Railroad Bridge)
Spanning Woonasquatucket River
HAER RI-28
HAER RI,4-PROV,189-
5ph/1pg/1pc L

World War I Monument
Memorial Square
HABS RI-387
HABS RI,4-PROV,182-
18ph/9pg/3pc L

SLATERSVILLE

Mill House "K"; see Slater Mill,House "K"

Slater Mill,House "K" (Mill House "K")
20 School St.
HABS RI-293
HABS RI,4-SLATV,2-
1ph L

Slatersville Green
Green & School Sts.
HABS RI-292
HABS RI,4-SLATV,1-
1ph L

SMITHFIELD

St. Michael's Catholic Church
15 Homestead Ave.
HABS RI-110
HABS RI,4-SMIF,1-
6ph/1pg/1pc L

THORNTON

Fenner,Thomas,House
1538 Plainfield St.
HABS RI-72
HABS RI,4-THOR,1-
16ph L

WOONSOCKET

Clinton Mill
93 Clinton St.
HABS RI-299
HABS RI,4-WOON,1-
2dr/18ph/5pg L

Club Marquette; see St. Anne's Gymnasium

Holbrook,Capt.,House
383 S. Main St.
HABS RI-295
HABS RI,4-WOON,4-
1ph L

Providence & Worcester Railroad Station
1 Depot Square
HABS RI-373
HABS RI,4-WOON,6-
4ph/1pc L

St. Anne's Gymnasium (Club Marquette)
74 Cumberland St.
HABS RI-374
HABS RI,4-WOON,5-
16ph/3pg/fr L

Woonsocket Company,Number 1 Mill
100 Front St.
HABS RI-300
HABS RI,4-WOON,2-
4dr/9ph/8pg L

Woonsocket Company,Number 2 Mill
115 Front St.
HABS RI-301
HABS RI,4-WOON,3-
5dr/11ph/6pg L

WASHINGTON COUNTY

ALTON

Northeast Railroad Corridor
HAER RI-19
L

BELLEVILLE

Mobra Castle; see Phillips,Samuel,House

Phillips,Samuel,House (Mobra Castle)
Tower Hill Rd. (U. S. Rt. 1)
HABS RI-50
HABS RI,5-BELVI,1-
9dr/13ph/fr L

BURDICKVILLE

Northeast Railroad Corridor
HAER RI-19
L

KENYON

Clarke,Samuel,House
Lewiston Ave.
HABS RI-296
HABS RI,5-KEN.V,1-
2ph L

KINGSTON

Carpenter,Solomon,House (Indian Acres)
144 South Rd.
HABS RI-61
HABS RI,5-KING,4-
2ph L

Congregational Church (Kingston Congregational Church)
Kingstown Rd. (State Rt. 138)
HABS RI-64
HABS RI,5-KING,6-
2ph L

Douglas House
Kingstown Rd. (State Rt. 138)
HABS RI-60
HABS RI,5-KING,3-
1ph L

Fayerweather House
Mooresfield Rd. (State Rt. 138) & Kingston Rd.
HABS RI-62
HABS RI,5-KING,5-
4ph L

French,Gen. Cyrus,House
Kingstown Rd. (State Rt. 138) & College Rd.
HABS RI-51
HABS RI,5-KING,2-
11dr/12ph/1pg/fr L

Hagadorn House; see Taylor,Thomas Stafford,House

Indian Acres; see Carpenter,Solomon,House

Kingston Congregational Church; see Congregational Church

Taylor,Thomas Stafford,House (Hagadorn House)
1305 Kingstown Rd. (State Rt. 138)
HABS RI-297
HABS RI,5-KING,7-
1ph L

KINGSTON HILL

Kingston Inn (Kingstown Hill)
HABS RI-44
HABS RI,5-KING,1-
4ph L

Kingstown Hill; see Kingston Inn

NEW SHOREHAM

Block Island Southeast Light (Block Island Southeast Lighthouse)
Spring St. & Mohegan Trail at Mohegan Bluffs
HAER RI-27
HAER DLC/PP-1992:RI-2
12dr/53ph/54pg/4pc/fr L

Block Island Southeast Lighthouse; see Block Island Southeast Light

NORTH KINGSTON

Hammond,Benjamin,Grist Mill
Hammond Hill Rd.
HABS RI-2
HABS RI,5-KINGN,2-
7dr/4ph/4pg/fr L

Northrup,Palmer,House
7919 Post Rd. (U.S. Rt. Alt. 1)
HABS RI-40
HABS RI,5-KINGN,4-
12dr/10ph/fr L

Quonset Point Naval Air Station
Roger Williams Way
HAER RI-15
HAER 1991(HAER):26
274ph/113pg/19pc L

Reynolds-Lawrence House; see Reynolds,Joseph,House

Reynolds,Joseph,House
(Reynolds-Lawrence House)
Forge Rd.
HABS RI-3-8
HABS RI,5-KINGN,1-
9dr/2ph/3pg L

Smith,Richard Jr.,House
Post Rd. (U.S. Rt. Alt. 1)
HABS RI-39
HABS RI,5-KINGN,3-
10ph L

Stuart,Gilbert,Birthplace; see Stuart,Gilbert,House

Stuart,Gilbert,House
(Stuart,Gilbert,Birthplace)
Hammond Hill Rd.
HABS RI-120
HABS RI,5-KINGN,5-
3ph L

SAUNDERSTOWN

Casey,Edward P.,House
Boston Neck Rd. (State Rt. 138)
HABS RI-41
HABS RI,5-SAUTO,1-
6ph L

SOUTH KINGSTON

Glebe,The
Tower Hill Rd.
HABS RI-42
HABS RI,5-KINGS,1-
4ph L

WAKEFIELD

Dockray,John,House
Dockray St.
HABS RI-43
HABS RI,5-WAKF,1-
6ph L

WEST KINGSTON

Noetheast Railroad Corridor
HAER RI-19
L

WESTERLY

Babcock,Dr. Joshua,House
124 Granite St.
HABS RI-142
HABS RI,5-WEST,1-
3ph/1pg L

Northeast Railroad Corridor
HAER RI-19
L

WICKFORD

Bailey,George,House
(Wall,Daniel,House)
79 Main St.
HABS RI-68
HABS RI,5-WICK,10-
1ph L

Barney,Capt. Richard,House
115 Main St.
HABS RI-67
HABS RI,5-WICK,9-
1ph L

Case,Immanuel,House (Gardiner House)
41 Main St.
HABS RI-3-13
HABS RI,5-WICK,5-
14dr/2ph/2pg L

Cooper,Thomas,House (Doorway)
75 Main St.
HABS RI-66
HABS RI,5-WICK,8-
1ph L

Gardiner House; see Case,Immanuel,House

Narragansett Church,Old; see St. Paul's Episcopal Church

Northrup,Cyrus,House
90 Main St.
HABS RI-298
HABS RI,5-WICK,4-
2ph L

Reynolds,Jonathan,House
85 Main St.
HABS RI-65
HABS RI,5-WICK,7-
1ph L

Smith,John,House
4 Gold St.
HABS RI-63
HABS RI,5-WICK,6-
1ph L

St. Paul's Episcopal Church
(Narragansett Church,Old)
Church Lane (moved from Tower Hill)
HABS RI-45
HABS RI,5-WICK,1-
15ph L

Wall,Daniel,House; see Bailey,George,House

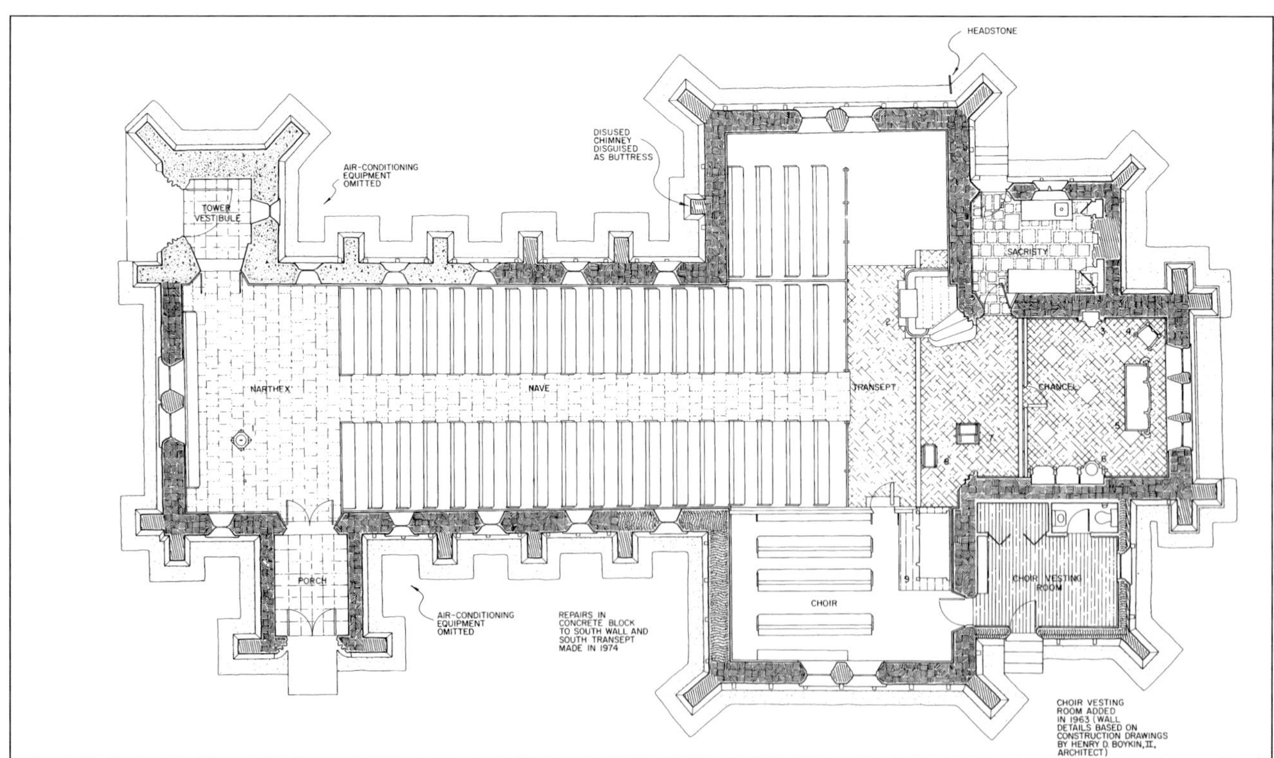

Drayton Hall, Charleston vicinity, Charleston County, South Carolina. Section B-B. Measured drawing delineated by Belmont Freeman, 1974 (HABS SC-377, sheet 11/14 of 15; negative number LC-USZA1-803).

Church of the Holy Cross, Stateburg, Sumter County, South Carolina. Plan. Measured drawing delineated by Michael L. Lafond, Timothy Buehner, Caroline Guay, summer 1984 (HABS SC-13-14, sheet 3 of 17).

South Carolina

ABBEVILLE COUNTY

ABBEVILLE

Trinity Episcopal Church
Church St.
HABS SC-38
HABS SC,1-ABVI,1-
1ph/1pg L

ABBEVILLE VIC.

Frazier-Pressley House
Intersection County Roads 33,112 & 47
HABS SC-589
HABS SC,1-ABVI.V,1-
13ph/1pg/1pc L

Frazier-Pressley House,Privy
intersection County Roads 33,112 & 47
HABS SC-589-A
HABS SC,ABVI.V,1A-
5ph/1pc L

LOWNDESVILLE VIC.

Caldwell-Hutchison Farm
County Rd. 93
HABS SC-382
HABS SC,1-LOWN.V,4-
6dr/31ph/13pg/2pc/6ct/fr L

Featherstone Tenant Farm
County Rd. 81
HABS SC-381
HABS SC,1-LOWN.V,3-
2dr/13ph/4pg/1pc/fr L

Harper-Featherstone Farm
County Rd. 81
HABS SC-379
HABS SC,1-LOWN.V,1-
1dr/29ph/19pg/2pc/fr L

Harper-Featherstone Farm,Well House
County Rd. 81
HABS SC-379-A
HABS SC,1-LOWN.V,1D-
1dr/9ph/fr L

Harper-Featherstone Tenant Farm
County Rd. 81
HABS SC-380
HABS SC,1-LOWN.V,2-
2dr/17ph/5pg/1pc/2ct/fr L

Long-Hutchison Farm
County Rd. 123
HABS SC-383
HABS SC,1-LOWN.V,5-
4pg/1pc L

Long-Hutchison Farm,House
County Rd. 123
HABS SC-383-A
HABS SC,1-LOWN.V,5A-
9ph L

Long-Hutchison Farm,Tenant Barn
County Rd. 123
HABS SC-383-B
HABS SC,1-LOWN.V,5B-
1dr/7ph/fr L

ROCKY RIVER

Abbeville Hydroelectric Power Plant
State Hwy. 284
HAER SC-5
HAER SC,1-ROCRO,1-
35ph/6pg/4ct L

SAVANNAH RIVER

Seaboard Coast Line Railroad Bridge
Calhoun Falls Vic. ,Spanning Savannah River
HAER SC-6
HAER SC,1-SAVRI,1-
4ph/4pg L

ANDERSON COUNTY

ANDERSON

Capers-Watson House; see Orange Grove

Carolina Lunch; see Johnson,H. G.,& Sons

Harrison,W. H.,Grocery; see Johnson,H. G.,& Sons

Ideal Pawn Shop; see Johnson,H. G.,& Sons

Ideal Pawn Shop; see Victor Theater

Johnson,H. G.,& Sons (Harrison,W. H.,Grocery; Carolina Lunch; Ideal Pawn Shop)
117 W. Church St.
HABS SC-628
HABS 1989(HABS):21
2ph/1pg/1pc L

Maxwell,Jeff,House
1109 W. Whitner St. & Maxwell Ave.
HABS SC-322
HABS SC,4-AND,3-
3ph/3pg L

Morris House
220 E. Morris Street at S. Manning Street
HABS SC-323
HABS SC,4-AND,4-
1ph/2pg L

Orange Grove (Capers-Watson House; Silcox House)
1092 N. Main St.
HABS SC-120
HABS SC,4-AND,1-
2dr/9ph/1pg/fr L

Poppe House
805 S. McDuffie St.
HABS SC-324
HABS SC,4-AND,5-
2ph/1pg L

Prevost,Nick,House
105 N. Prevost St.
HABS SC-325
HABS SC,4-AND,6-
4ph/3pg L

Reynolds,C. C.,Skating Rink; see 123 West Church Street (Commercial Building)

Sears Warehouse; see 123 West Church Street (Commercial Building)

Sheppard,Gordon,Motor Company; see 123 West Church Street (Commercial Building)

Silcox House; see Orange Grove

Sullivan House
E. Franklin St.
HABS SC-123
HABS SC,4-AND,2-
3ph L

U. S. Soil Conservation Svc. Warehouse & Garage; see 123 West Church Street (Commercial Building)

Victor Theater (Ideal Pawn Shop)
119 W. Church St.
HABS SC-629
HABS 1989(HABS):21
5ph/1pg/1pc L

123 West Church Street (Commercial Building) (U. S. Soil Conservation Svc. Warehouse & Garage; Reynolds,C. C.,Skating Rink; Sears Warehouse; Sheppard,Gordon,Motor Company)
HABS SC-630
HABS 1989(HABS):21
4ph/1pg/1pc L

ANDERSON VIC.

Varennes Tavern
HABS SC-5
HABS SC,4-AND.V,1-
11dr/10ph L

BELTON

Belton Depot; see Southern Railway Combined Depot

Southern Railway Combined Depot (Belton Depot)
W side of Belton Public Square
HABS SC-621
HABS SC,4-BELT,1A-
7ph/2pg/1pc/2ct L

LOWNDESVILLE VIC.

Gregg Shoals Dam & Power Plant
Spanning Savannah River
HAER SC-7
HAER SC, 4-SAVRI,2-
17ph/9pg/2pc/3ct L

PENDLETON

Farmers' Hall
Village Green
HABS SC-13-12
HABS SC,4-PEND,1-
7dr/4ph/3pg L

Maverick,Samuel,Plantation House; see Montpelier

Montpelier (Van Wyck-Maverick House; Maverick,Samuel,Plantation House)
Old Greenville Hwy.
HABS SC-329
HABS SC,4-PEND,4-
2dr/7ph/fr L

Pendleton Presbyterian Church
Broad & S. Mechanic Sts.
HABS SC-326
HABS SC,4-PEND,2-
6ph/1pg L

St. Paul's Episcopal Church
E. Queen St.
HABS SC-327
HABS SC,4-PEND,3-
4ph/1pg L

Van Wyck-Maverick House; see Montpelier

PENDLETON VIC.

Altamont (Pinckney,Col. Thomas,House)
HABS SC-282
HABS SC,4-PEND.V,3-
2dr L

Ashtabula (Gibbes,Lewis Ladson,House)
State Rt. 88
HABS SC-328
HABS SC,4-PEND.V,2-
3ph/4pg L

Burt,Frank,House; see Oaklawn

Gibbes,Lewis Ladson,House; see Ashtabula

Oaklawn (Burt,Frank,House)
HABS SC-279
HABS SC,4-PEND.V,1-
2dr L

Pickens,Col. T.S.,House; see Sycamore Avenue

Pinckney,Col. Thomas,House; see Altamont

Sycamore Avenue (Pickens,Col. T.S.,House)
HABS SC-283
HABS SC,4-PEND.V,4-
1dr L

Woodburn
Woodburn Rd. ,U. S. Rt. 76 vic.
HABS SC-285
HABS SC,4-PEND.V,5-
21ph/1pg L

SAVANNAH RIVER

Sanders Ferry Bridge
State Hwy. 184,Spanning Savannah River
HAER SC-2
HAER SC,4-SAVRI,1-
12ph/3pg L

BAMBERG COUNTY

BAMBERG

Bamberg Cotton Mill (Santee Cotton Mill)
Main St.
HAER SC-20
HAER 1989(HAER):19
30ph/2pg/2pc L

Santee Cotton Mill; see Bamberg Cotton Mill

BAMBERG VIC.

Coffee Pot Diner
SC Rt. 301 at Rt. 601
HABS SC-627
HABS 1989(HABS):21
1ph/1pc L

Simms,William Gilmore,House; see Woodlands (Ruins)

Woodlands (Ruins) (Simms,William Gilmore,House)
U. S. Rt. 78
HABS SC-219
HABS SC,5-BAMB.V,1-
3ph L

EHRHARDT VIC.

Confederate Memorial Pavilion
Rivers Bridge State Park
HABS SC-388
HABS SC,5-EHR.V,2-
5dr/2pg L

Murdock House
HABS SC-231
HABS SC,5-EHR.V,1-
1ph L

BEAUFORT COUNTY

BEAUFORT

Baptist Church; see Beaufort Baptist Church

Barnwell House; see Hepworth,Thomas,House

Beaufort Baptist Church (Baptist Church)
600 Charles St.
HABS SC-290
HABS SC,7-BEAUF,3-
17ph/4pg L

Beaufort County Arsenal; see Beaufort Volunteer Artillery

Beaufort Volunteer Artillery (Beaufort County Arsenal)
713 Craven St.
HABS SC-462
HABS SC,7-BEAUF,13-
5ph L

Cassena (House)
315 Federal St.
HABS SC-540
HABS SC,7-BEAUF,23-
11ph L

Cuthbert,John,House
1203 Bay St.
HABS SC-281
HABS SC,7-BEAUF,18-
15ph L

Cuthbert,Louis,House
915 Port Republic St.
HABS SC-457
HABS SC,7-BEAUF,31-
14ph L

Danner,Porter,House; see Johnson,Dr. Joseph,House

Farmer,Henry,House
412 East St.
HABS SC-490
HABS S,7-BEAUF,20-
12ph L

First African Baptist Church (circa 1865)
601 New St.
HABS SC-280
HABS SC,7-BEAUF,28-
8ph L

Fraser,Frederick,House
901 Prince St.
HABS SC-487
HABS SC,7-BEAUF,33-
12ph L

Fripp,Edgar,House; see Tidalholm

Fripp,William,House; see Tidewater

Fuller,Thomas,House (Tabby Manse)
1211 Bay & Harrington Sts.
HABS SC-287
HABS SC,7-BEAUF,2-
34ph/4pg L

Gough,Elizabeth Barnwell,House
705 Washington St.
HABS SC-542
HABS SC,7-BEAUF,34-
16ph L

Documentation: **ct** color transparencies **dr** measured drawings **fr** field records
pc photograph captions **pg** pages of text **ph** photographs

Habersham House
802-806 Bay St.
HABS SC-461
HABS SC,7-BEAUF,17-
6ph L

Hamilton,Paul,House; see Oaks,The

Hepworth,Thomas,House (Barnwell House)
214 New St.
HABS SC-16
HABS SC,7-BEAUF,4-
10dr/14ph/1pg/fr L

Hext House
207 Handcock St.
HABS SC-289
HABS SC,7-BEAUF,11-
10ph/3pg L

Jenkins,W. J. ,House
901 Craven St.
HABS SC-489
HABS SC,7-BEAUF,14-
9ph L

Jervey,James,Dependencies
55 Laurens St.
HABS SC-485-A
HABS SC,7-BEAUF,25A-
1ph L

Jervey,James,House
55 Laurens St.
HABS SC-485
HABS SC,7-BEAUF,25-
3ph L

Johnson,Dr. Joseph,House (Danner,Porter,House)
411 Craven St.
HABS SC-187
HABS SC,7-BEAUF,7-
17ph L

Lafayette House; see Verdier,John Mark,House

Ledbetter,Thomas E.,House
411 Bayard St.
HABS SC-221
HABS SC,7-BEAUF,9-
14ph/2pc L

Marshlands; see Verdier,James Robert,House

Maxcy-Rhett House
1111 Craven & Church Sts.
HABS SC-288
HABS SC,7-BEAUF,10-
4ph/4pg L

McKee-Smalls House (Smalls,Robert,House)
511 Prince St.
HABS SC-398
HABS SC,7-BEAUF,32-
11ph/1pg/1pc L

McKee,Henry,House
511 Prince St.
HABS SC-486
HABS SC,7-BEAUF,32-
9ph L

McLeod House; see Smith,John Joyner,House

Means,Col. Edward,House
604 Pinckney St.
HABS SC-220
HABS SC,7-BEAUF,8-
23ph L

Means,Robert,House
1207 Bay St.
HABS SC-459
HABS SC,7-BEAUF,19-
19ph L

Oaks,The (Hamilton,Paul,House)
100 Laurens St.
HABS SC-458
HABS SC,7-BEAUF,26-
21ph L

Rhett,James,House
303 Federal St.
HABS SC-538
HABS SC,7-BEAUF,22-
15ph L

Rhett,Thomas,House
1009 Craven St.
HABS SC-270
HABS SC,7-BEAUF,15-
16ph L

Sams,Berners B. ,Dependencies
201 Laurens St.
HABS SC-541-A
HABS SC,7-BEAUF,27A-
3ph L

Sams,Berners B. ,House
201 Laurens St.
HABS SC-541
HABS SC,7-BEAUF,27-
8ph L

Secession House
1113 Craven St.
HABS SC-190
HABS SC,7-BEAUF,16-
19ph L

Secession House,Dependency
1113 Craven St.
HABS SC-190-A
HABS SC,7-BEAUF,16A-
2ph L

Smith,John Joyner,House (McLeod House)
400 Wilmington St.
HABS SC-291
HABS SC,7-BEAUF,12-
26ph/4pg L

St. Helena's Episcopal Church
501 Church St.
HABS SC-460
HABS SC,7-BEAUF,1-
15ph L

Stoney,George Mosse,House
500 Port Republic St.
HABS SC-456
HABS SC,7-BEAUF,30-
10ph L

Tabby Manse; see Fuller,Thomas,House

Talbird House (Ruins); see Tolbert House (Ruins)

Tidalholm (Fripp,Edgar,House)
1 Laurens St.
HABS SC-539
HABS SC,7-BEAUF,24-
19ph L

Tidewater (Fripp,William,House)
302 Federal St.
HABS SC-488
HABS SC,7-BEAUF,21-
12ph L

Tolbert House (Ruins) (Talbird House (Ruins))
Hamilton & Hancock Sts.
HABS SC-138
HABS SC,7-BEAUF,5-
1ph L

Verdier,James Robert,House (Marshlands)
501 Pinckney St.
HABS SC-152
HABS SC,7-BEAUF,29-
13ph L

Verdier,John Mark,House (Lafayette House)
801 Bay & Scott Sts.
HABS SC-139
HABS SC,7-BEAUF,6-
40ph/6pg L

Whitehall (Ruins)
Whitehall Point,Ladies Island
HABS SC-222
HABS SC,7-BEAUF.V.1-
4ph L

BLUFFTON VIC.

Rose Hill Plantation House
2.5 mi. NW of intersection SC 278 & SC 46
HABS SC-592
HABS SC,7-BUFF.V,1-
16ph/1pg/1pc/3ct L

DATHA ISLAND

Sams Tabby Complex (Ruins)
Datha Island
HABS SC-622
HABS SC,7-DATIL,1-
20ph/1pg/1pc L

FROGMORE VIC.

Arnett House; see Penn School Historic District,Arnett House

Benezet House; see Penn School Historic District,Benezet House

Brick Church; see Penn School Historic District,Brick Church

Butler Bldg; see Penn School Historic District,Butler Bldg

Cafeteria; see Penn School Historic District,Cafeteria

Cedar Cottage; see Penn School Historic District,Cedar Cottage

Central Baptist Church; see Penn School Historic District,Brick Church

Cope Bldg; see Penn School Historic District,Cope Bldg

Darrah Bldg; see Penn School Historic District,Darrah Bldg

Frissell Community House; see Penn School Hist. Dist.,Frissell Community House

Gantt Cottage; see Penn School Historic District,Gantt Cottage

Hampton House; see Penn School Historic District,Hampton House

House,Small,next to Brick Church; see Penn School Historic District,House,Small

Implement Bldg; see Penn School Historic District,Implement Bldg

Jasmin Cottage; see Penn School Historic District,Jasmin Cottage

Johnson Fellowship Hall; see Penn School Hist. Dist.,Johnson Fellowship Hall

Lathers Dormitory; see Penn School Historic District,Lathers Dormitory

Liberty Bell; see Penn School Historic District,Liberty Bell

Old Laundry Bldg; see Penn School Historic District,Cafeteria

Old Milk Barn; see Penn School Historic District,Old Milk Barn

Paint Shop; see Penn School Historic District,Paint Shop

Penn Normal, Industrial & Agricultural School; see Penn School Historic District

Penn School Hist. Dist.,Frissell Community House (Frissell Community House)
SC Rt. 37,1 mile S. of Frogmore,St. Helena Island
HABS SC-588-J
HABS SC,7-FROG.V,11-
5ph/1pg/1pc L

Penn School Hist. Dist.,Johnson Fellowship Hall (Johnson Fellowship Hall)
SC Rt. 37,1 mile S. of Frogmore,St. Helena Island
HABS SC-588-G
HABS SC,7-FROG.V,8-
2ph/1pc L

Penn School Historic District (Penn Normal, Industrial & Agricultural School)
Rt. SC 37,1 mile S. of Frogmore,St. Helena Island
HABS SC-588
HABS SC,7-FROG.V,1-
8pg L

Penn School Historic District,Arnett House (Arnett House)
SC Rt. 37,1 mile S. of Frogmore,St. Helena Island
HABS SC-588-A
HABS SC,7-FROG.V,2-
3ph/1pg/1pc L

Penn School Historic District,Benezet House (Benezet House)
1 mile S. of Frogmore,Rt. 37,St Helena Island
HABS SC-588-B
HABS SC,7-FROG.V,3-
4ph/1pg/1pc L

Penn School Historic District,Brick Church (Brick Church; Central Baptist Church)
SC Rt. 37,1 mile S. of Frogmore,St. Helena Island
HABS SC-588-C
HABS SC,7-FROG.V,4-
14ph/2pg/2pc/2ct L

Penn School Historic District,Butler Bldg (Butler Bldg)
SC Rt. 37,1 mile S. of Frogmore,St. Helena Island
HABS SC-588-D
HABS SC,7-FROG.V,5-
4ph/1pg/1pc L

Penn School Historic District,Cafeteria (Old Laundry Bldg; Cafeteria)
SC Rt. 37,1 mile S. of Frogmore,St. Helena Island
HABS SC-588-E
HABS SC,7-FROG.V,6-
3ph/1pg/1pc L

Penn School Historic District,Cedar Cottage (Cedar Cottage)
SC Rt. 37,1 mile S. of Frogmore,St. Helena Island
HABS SC-588-F
HABS SC,7-FROG.V,7-
3ph/1pg/1pc L

Penn School Historic District,Cope Bldg (Cope Bldg)
SC Rt. 37,1 mile S. of Frogmore,St. Helena Island
HABS SC-588-H
HABS SC,7-FROG.V,9-
4ph/1pg/1pc L

Penn School Historic District,Darrah Bldg (Darrah Bldg)
SC Rt. 37,1 mile S. of Frogmore,St. Helena Island
HABS SC-588-I
HABS SC,7-FROG.V,10-
1ph/1pg/1pc L

Penn School Historic District,Gantt Cottage (Gantt Cottage)
SC Rt. 37,1 mile S. of Frogmore,St. Helena Island
HABS SC-588-K
HABS SC,7-FROG.V,12-
2ph/1pg/1pc L

Penn School Historic District,Hampton House (Hampton House)
SC Rt. 37,1 mile S. of Frogmore,St. Helena Island
HABS SC-588-L
HABS SC,7-FROG.V,13-
2ph/1pg/1pc L

Penn School Historic District,House,Small (House,Small,next to Brick Church)
Sc Rt. 37,next to Brick Church,St.Helena Island
HABS SC-588-U
HABS SC,7-FROG.V,22-
2ph/1pc L

Penn School Historic District,Implement Bldg (Implement Bldg)
SC Rt. 37,1 mile S. of Frogmore,St. Helena Island
HABS SC-588-M
HABS SC,7-FROG.V,14-
1ph/1pc L

Penn School Historic District,Jasmin Cottage (Jasmin Cottage)
SC Rt. 37,1 mile S. of Frogmore,St. Helena Island
HABS SC-588-N
HABS SC,7-FROG.V,15-
2ph/1pg/1pc L

Penn School Historic District,Lathers Dormitory (Lathers Dormitory)
SC Rt. 37,1 mile S. of Frogmore,St. Helena Island
HABS SC-588-O
HABS SC,7-FROG.V,16-
2ph/1pg/1pc L

Penn School Historic District,Liberty Bell (Liberty Bell)
SC Rt. 37,1 mile S. of Frogmore,St. Helena Island
HABS SC-588-P
HABS SC,7-FROG.V,17-
1ph/1pg/1pc L

Penn School Historic District,Old Milk Barn (Old Milk Barn)
SC Rt. 37,1 mile S. of Frogmore,St. Helena Island
HABS SC-588-Q
HABS SC,7-FROG.V,18-
2ph/1pc L

Penn School Historic District,Paint Shop (Paint Shop)
SC Rt. 37,1 mile S. of Frogmore,St. Helena Island
HABS SC-588-R
HABS SC,7-FROG.V,19-
2ph/1pc L

Penn School Historic District,Pine Cottage (Pine Cottage)
SC Rt. 37,1 mile S. of Frogmore,St. Helena Island
HABS SC-588-S
HABS SC,7-FROG.V,20-
2ph/1pg/1pc L

Penn School Historic District,Retreat House (Retreat House)
SC Rt. 37,1 mile S. of Frogmore,St. Helena Island
HABS SC-588-T
HABS SC,7-FROG.V,21-
2ph/1pg/1pc L

Pine Cottage; see Penn School Historic District,Pine Cottage

Retreat House; see Penn School Historic District,Retreat House

HUNTING ISLAND

Hunting Island Lighthouse Complex
Hunting Island State Park
HABS SC-385
HABS SC,7-HUNTIL,1-
1dr/4pg L

Hunting Island Lighthouse Complex,Lighthouse
Hunting Island State Park,US Rt 21,16 mi E Beaufor
HABS SC-385-A
HABS SC,7-HUNTIL,1A-
1dr/15ph/1pg/1pc/4ct L

Hunting Island Lighthouse Complex,Oil House
Hunting Island State Park,US Rt 21,16 mi E Beaufor
HABS SC-385-C
HABS SC,7-HUNTIL,1C-
2dr/1ph/1pc L

Hunting Island Lighthouse Complex,Storage Building
Hunting Island State Park
HABS SC-385-B
HABS SC,7-HUNTIL,1B-
3dr L

Hunting Island Lighthouse,Cottage HI-64
Hunting Island State Park,US Rt 21,16 mi E Beaufor
HABS SC-385-D
HABS SC,7-HUNTIL,1D-
4ph/1pc L

Hunting Island Lighthouse,Cottage HI-65
Hunting Island State Park,US Rt 21,16 mi E Beaufor
HABS SC-385-E
HABS SC,7-HUNTIL,1E-
3ph/1pc L

SHELDON VIC.

Prince William's Parish Church (Ruins)
HABS SC-137
HABS SC,7-SHELD,1-
3ph/1pg L

ST. HELENA ISLAND

Fripp,Edgar,Mausoleum; see St. Helena Island Parish,Edgar Fripp Mausoleum

St. Helena Island Chapel of Ease Ruins; see St. Helena Island Parish Church Ruins

St. Helena Island Parish Church Ruins (St. Helena Island Chapel of Ease Ruins)
Junction County Roads 45 & 37
HABS SC-590
HABS SC,7-SAHELI,1A-
14ph/1pg/1pc L

St. Helena Island Parish,Edgar Fripp Mausoleum (Fripp,Edgar,Mausoleum)
Junction County Roads 45 & 37
HABS SC-591
HABS SC,7-SAHELI,1B-
12ph/1pg/1pc L

YEMASSEE

Auldbrass (Old Brass)
River Rd.
HABS SC-354
HABS SC,7-YEMA,1-
6ph L

Auldbrass,Stable Complex (Old Brass,Stable Complex)
River Rd.
HABS SC-354-A
HABS SC,7-YEMA.1A-
8ph L

Old Brass; see Auldbrass

Old Brass,Stable Complex; see Auldbrass,Stable Complex

BERKELEY COUNTY

CORDSVILLE

Ball,Elias,Plantation House; see Comingtee

Comingtee (Ball,Elias,Plantation House)
Cooper River
HABS SC-132
HABS SC,8-CORD.V,4-
3ph/2pg L

CORDSVILLE VIC.

North Chachan Plantation,Stable
Cooper River,W. Branch
HABS SC-119
HABS SC,8-CORD.V,3-
1ph/1pg L

Pogson,Rev. Milward,Plantation House; see Wappaola

Strawberry Chapel
Cooper River,W. Branch
HABS SC-37
HABS SC,8-CORD.V,2-
8ph/2pg L

Wappahola; see Wappaola

Wappaola (Pogson,Rev. Milward,Plantation House; Wappahola; Wappoola)
Cooper River,W. Branch
HABS SC-82
HABS SC,8-MONCO.V,3-
2ph/2pg L

Wappoola; see Wappaola

CORDVILLE VIC.

Limerick (Mahon,Michael,Plantation)
Cooper River,E. Branch
HABS SC-8
HABS SC,8-CORD.V,1-
13dr/12ph/2pg L

Mahon,Michael,Plantation; see Limerick

CROSS

Cabin
HABS SC-35
HABS SC,8-CRO,1-
1ph/1pg L

CROSS VIC.

Cabin
HABS SC-230
HABS SC,8-CRO.V,1-
1ph L

EUTAW SPRINGS VIC.

Lawson Pond (Porcher,Charles Cordes,Plantation House)
HABS SC-57
HABS SC,8-EUTA.V,3-
24ph/1pg/3pc L

Porcher,Charles Cordes,Plantation House; see Lawson Pond

EUTAWVILLE VIC.

Loch Dhu
State Rd. 6 & County Rd. 59 vic.
HABS SC-56
HABS SC,8-EUTA.V,2-
14ph/1pg L

Loch Dhu,Barn
State Rt. 6 & County Rd. 59
HABS SC-56-B
HABS SC,8-EUTA.V,2B-
1ph L

Loch Dhu,Kitchen Building
State Rt. 6 & County Rd. 59 vic.
HABS SC-56-A
HABS SC,8-EUTA.V,2A-
1ph L

Loch Dhu,Smokehouse
State Rt. 6 & County Rd. 59 vic.
HABS SC-56-C
HABS SC,8-EUTA.V,2C-
1ph L

Palmer,Joseph,Plantation House; see Springfield

Palmer,Joseph,Plantation House,Kitchen Oven; see Springfield,Kitchen Oven

Springfield (Palmer,Joseph,Plantation House)
HABS SC-55
HABS SC,8-EUTA.V,1-
1ph/2pg L

Springfield,Kitchen Oven (Palmer,Joseph,Plantation House,Kitchen Oven)
HABS SC-55-A
HABS SC,8-EUTA.V,1A-
1ph L

GOOSE CREEK

St. James' Church; see St. James' Protestant Episcopal Church

St. James' Protestant Episcopal Church (St. James' Church)
HABS SC-79
HABS SC,8-GOOCR,1-
17ph/7pg L

GOOSE CREEK VIC.

Crowfield Ruins (Middleton,William,Plantation House)
HABS SC-6
HABS SC,8-GOOCR.V,1-
5dr/11ph/3pg/fr L

Middleton,William,Plantation House; see Crowfield Ruins

HOLLY HILL VIC.

Williams,Stephan,House
U. S. Rt. 176
HABS SC-483
HABS SC,8-HOHI.V,1-
8ph L

HUGER VIC.

Middleburg (Simons,Benjamin,Plantation House)
Cooper River,E. Branch
HABS SC-13
HABS SC,8-HUG.V,1-
3dr/7ph/2pg/fr L

Pompion Hill Chapel
Cooper River,S. Side
HABS SC-34
HABS SC,8-HUG.V,2-
30ph/5pg/3pc L

Simons,Benjamin,Plantation House; see Middleburg

LAKE MOULTRIE VIC.

Santee Canal Structures (Area Survey)
HABS SC-240
HABS SC,8- ,1-
4ph L

MONCKS CORNER VIC.

Berkeley Country Club; see Exeter

Biggin Church (Ruins)
Cooper River,W. Branch
HABS SC-30
HABS SC,8-MONCO.V,2-
3ph/2pg L

Broughton,Thomas,Plantation House; see Mulberry

Butler,Hugh,Plantation House; see Exeter

Exeter (Butler,Hugh,Plantation House; Berkeley Country Club)
Cooper River,W. Branch
HABS SC-12
HABS SC,8-MONCO.V,1-
9dr/17ph/1pg/fr L

Gippy (White,John Sims,Plantation House)
Cooper River,W. Branch
HABS SC-169
HABS SC,8-MONCO.V,4-
2ph/2pg L

Lewisfield
U. S. Rt. 52 vic.
HABS SC-484
HABS SC,8-MONCO.V,6-
18ph L

Mulberry (Broughton,Thomas,Plantation House)
Cooper River,W. Branch
HABS SC-393
HABS SC,8-MONCO.V,5-
34ph/4pc L

White,John Sims,Plantation House; see Gippy

PINE GROVE VIC.

Carson,William Augustus,Plantation House; see Dean Hall

Dean Hall (Carson,William Augustus,Plantation House)
Cooper River,W. Side
HABS SC-40
HABS SC,8-PIGRO.V,1-
5ph/2pg L

Medway Plantation
U. S. Rt. 52
HABS SC-140
HABS SC,8-PIGRO.V,2-
4ph/2pg L

PINEVILLE

Blueford Plantation (Oakland Club)
State Rt. 45
HABS SC-236
HABS SC,8-PIN.V,3-
2ph L

Oakland Club; see Blueford Plantation

PINEVILLE VIC.

Belle Isle Plantation,Washhouse
Upper Santee
HABS SC-241
HABS SC,8-PIN.V,2-
1ph L

House
State Rt. 45 & U. S. Rt. 52
HABS SC-237
HABS SC,8-PIN.V,1-
1ph L

PINOPOLIS VIC.

Black Oak Church
HABS SC-33
HABS SC,8-PINOP.V,11-
2ph L

Bunker Hill Plantation House
HABS SC-27
HABS SC,8-PINOP.V,9-
2ph/1pg/1pc L

Cedar Spring Plantation House
HABS SC-23
HABS SC,8-PINOP.V,5-
2ph/1pg/1pc L

de St. Julien,Paul,Plantation; see Hanover

de St. Julien,Paul,Plantation,Barn; see Hanover,Barn

Hanover (de St. Julien,Paul,Plantation) (moved to SC,Clemson,Clemson University Campus)
HABS SC-36
HABS SC,8-PINOP.V,12-
15dr/67ph/5pg/5pc/fr L

Hanover,Barn (de St. Julien,Paul,Plantation,Barn)
HABS SC-36-A
HABS SC,8-PINOP.V,12A-
4ph L

Indianfield Plantation House
HABS SC-26
HABS SC,8-PINOP.V,8-
2ph/1pg/1pc L

North Hampton Plantation House (Northampton Plantation House)
HABS SC-17
HABS SC,8-PINOP.V,1-
2ph/1pg/1pc L

North Hampton Plantation Outbuildings (Northampton Plantation Outbuildings)
HABS SC-18
HABS SC,8-PINOP.V,1-
2ph/1pg L

Northampton Plantation House; see North Hampton Plantation House

Northampton Plantation Outbuildings; see North Hampton Plantation Outbuildings

Documentation: **ct** color transparencies **dr** measured drawings **fr** field records **pc** photograph captions **pg** pages of text **ph** photographs

Ophir (Porcher,Col. Thomas,Plantation House)
HABS SC-19
HABS SC,8-PINOP.V,2-
6ph/3pg/1pc L

Pooshee Plantation House
HABS SC-22
HABS SC,8-PINOP.V,4-
2ph/1pg/1pc L

Porcher,Col. Thomas,Plantation House; see Ophir

Porcher,Thomas,Plantation House; see White Hall

Wampee Plantation House
HABS SC-24
HABS SC,8-PINOP.V,6-
2ph/1pg/1pc L

White Hall (Porcher,Thomas,Plantation House)
HABS SC-28
HABS SC,8-PINOP.V,10-
8ph/3pg/1pc L

Woodlawn Plantation House
Dover Plantation (moved from SC,Lake Moultrie)
HABS SC-25
HABS SC,8-PINOP.V,7-
4ph/1pg/1pc L

PINOPOLIS VIC.

Cain,William,Plantation House; see Somerset

Somerset (Cain,William,Plantation House)
HABS SC-20
HABS SC,8-PINOP.V,3-
5ph/2pg/1pc L

ST. STEPHENS

House
E. of Railroad Tracks
HABS SC-239
HABS SC,8-SAST,2-
1ph L

St. Stephen's Church (Episcopal)
HABS SC-74
HABS SC,8-SAST,1-
22ph/1pg L

WANDO RIVER

St. Thomas' & St. Dennis' Chapel of Ease; see St. Thomas' & St. Dennis' Church

St. Thomas' & St. Dennis' Church (St. Thomas' & St. Dennis' Chapel of Ease)
Clements Ferry Rd. Vic.
HABS SC-29
HABS SC,8-WAND.V,1-
8ph/1pg/2pc L

CALHOUN COUNTY

ST. MATTHEWS

Banks,Joseph,House
104 Dantzler St.
HABS SC-593
HABS SC,9-SMAT,1-
11ph/1pg/1pc/2ct L

CHARLESTON COUNTY

CHARLESTON

Aiken,Joseph,House
20 Charlotte St.
HABS SC-91
HABS SC,10-CHAR,116-
3ph/1pg L

Aiken,William,Carriage House; see South Carolina RR-Southern Rlwy Co. ,Carriage Hse.

Aiken,William,House; see South Carolina Railroad-Southern Railway Co.

Alston House
HABS SC-633
H

Alston House; see Edmonston,Charles,House

14 Amhearst St.
HABS SC-664
HABS 1992(HABS):SC-1
11ph/1pc L

Ashe,Col. John,Carriage House
32 S. Battery St.
HABS SC-321-A
HABS SC,10-CHAR,194A-
2ph L H

Ashe,Col. John,House
32 S. Battery
HABS SC-321
HABS SC,10-CHAR,194-
7ph L H

Ashe,Col. John,Kitchen Building
32 S. Battery St.
HABS SC-321-B
HABS SC,10-CHAR,194B-
1ph L H

192 Ashley Avenue (House)
(Beauregard's,Gen. G. T. ,Headquarters)
HABS SC-399
HABS SC,10-CHAR,199-
4ph L

1 Atlantic Street (House)
HABS SC-507
HABS SC,10-CHAR,200-
1ph L

3 Atlantic Street (House)
HABS SC-508
HABS SC,10-CHAR,201-
1ph L

Axson,Samuel Edward,House
4 Greenhill St.
HABS SC-197
HABS SC,10-CHAR,195-
9dr L

Bank of South Carolina; see Chamber of Commerce

Bank of U. S.; see Office of Discount & Deposit of U. S. Bank

56 Beaufain Street (House) (St. Michael's Church,Rectory)
HABS SC-134
HABS SC,10-CHAR,102-
3ph L

Beauregard's,Gen. G. T. ,Headquarters; see 192 Ashley Avenue (House)

Bee,Thomas,House
94 Church St.
HABS SC-455
HABS SC,10-CHAR,254-
2ph L

Belser,Christopher,House
2 Amherst St.
HABS SC-203
HABS SC,10-CHAR,155-
2dr/21ph/6pg/fr L

Bennett,Gov. Thomas,Dependency
1 Lucas St.
HABS SC-101-A
HABS SC,10-CHAR,124A-
3ph L

Bennett,Gov. Thomas,House
1 Lucas St.
HABS SC-101
HABS SC,10-CHAR,124-
39ph/1pg/1pc L

Bennett,Thomas,House
89 Smith St.
HABS SC-267
HABS SC,10-CHAR,175-
3ph/4pg L

Bennett's Rice Mill
Btwn. East Bay,Hasell,Concord & Laurens Sts.
HABS SC-13-7
HABS SC,10-CHAR,65-;1992(HABS):SC-1°
8dr/14ph/10pg/1pc L

Beth Elohim Synagogue; see Kahal Kadosh Beth Elohim Synagogue

Bethel Methodist Church
57 Pitt St.
HABS SC-153
HABS SC,10-CHAR,142-
3ph/1pg L

Bethel Methodist Church,Old
222 Calhoun St.
HABS SC-497
HABS SC,10-CHAR,4-
3ph L

Blacklock,William,Carriage House
18 Bull St.
HABS SC-272
HABS SC,10-CHAR,130B-
3ph/2pg L

Blacklock,William,Gazebo
18 Bull St.
HABS SC-273
HABS SC,10-CHAR,130C-
3ph/1pg L

Blacklock,William,House
18 Bull St.
HABS SC-109
HABS SC,10-CHAR,130-
45ph/6pg L

Blake Tenements
6-8 Courthouse Sq.
HABS SC-634
9dr/75ph/5pc/fr H

Blake,Daniel,Tenement
6-8 (2-4) Courthouse Sq.
HABS SC-128
HABS SC,10-CHAR,11-;DLC/PP-1993:SC-5
9dr/75ph/5pc/fr L

Bocquet,Maj. Peter,Jr. ,House
95 Broad St.
HABS SC-264
HABS SC,10-CHAR,172-
6ph/4pg/1pc L

Branford-Horry House
59 Meeting St.
HABS SC-513
HABS SC,10-CHAR,266-
3ph L

Brewton-Sawter House (Century House; Century Antiques House)
77 Church St.
HABS SC-191
HABS SC,10-CHAR,153-
2ph L

Brewton-Sawter Stable (Century House Stable)
75 Church St.
HABS SC-191-A
HABS SC,10-CHAR,153A-
1ph L

Brewton,Miles,House
27 King St.
HABS SC-78
HABS SC,10-CHAR,5-
11ph/1pg L

Brewton,Miles,House,Carriage House
27 King St.
HABS SC-78-A
HABS SC,10-CHAR,5A-
1ph L

Brewton,Miles,House,Kitchen
27 King St.
HABS SC-78-B
HABS SC,10-CHAR,5B-
3ph L

Brewton,Miles,House,Milk Room
27 King St.
HABS SC-78-D
HABS SC,10-CHAR,5D-
1ph L

Brewton,Miles,House,Slave Quarters
27 King St.
HABS SC-78-C
HABS SC,10-CHAR,5C-
3ph L

Brewton,Robert,House
71 Church St.
HABS SC-370
HABS SC,10-CHAR,247-
16ph/1pg L

13 Broad Street (Commercial Building)
HABS SC-410
HABS SC,10-CHAR,205-
1ph L

15 Broad Street (Commercial Building)
HABS SC-411
HABS SC,10-CHAR,206-
1ph L

17 Broad Street (Commercial Building)
HABS SC-412
HABS SC,10-CHAR,207-
1ph L

28 Broad Street (Commercial Building)
HABS SC-413
HABS SC,10-CHAR,232-
1ph L

29 Broad Street (Commercial Building)
HABS SC-414
HABS SC,10-CHAR,208-
1ph L

3 Broad Street (Commercial Building)
HABS SC-407
HABS SC,10-CHAR,203-
1ph L

30 Broad Street (Commercial Building)
HABS SC-415
HABS SC,10-CHAR,231-
1ph L

36 Broad Street (Commercial Building)
HABS SC-417
HABS SC,10-CHAR,230-
1ph L

37 Broad Street (Commercial Building)
HABS SC-418
HABS SC,10-CHAR,210-
1ph/1pc L

38 Broad Street (Commercial Building)
HABS SC-419
HABS SC,10-CHAR,229-
1ph L

40 Broad Street (Commercial Building)
HABS SC-420
HABS SC,10-CHAR,228-
1ph L

41 Broad Street (Commercial Building)
HABS SC-421
HABS SC,10-CHAR,211-
1ph L

42 Broad Street (Commercial Building)
HABS SC-422
HABS SC,10-CHAR,227-
1ph L

43-47 Broad Street (Commercial Building)
HABS SC-423
HABS SC,10-CHAR,212-
1ph L

63 Broad Street (Commercial Building)
HABS SC-425
HABS SC,10-CHAR,215-
1ph L

7-11 Broad Street (Commercial Buildings)
HABS SC-408
HABS SC,10-CHAR,204-
1ph L

85-87 Broad Street (Commercial-Residential Bldgs.)
HABS SC-519
HABS SC,10-CHAR,216-
4ph L

102 Broad Street (House)
HABS SC-503
HABS SC,10-CHAR,226-
2ph L

117 Broad Street (House)
HABS SC-427
HABS SC,10-CHAR,218-
4ph/1pc L

119 Broad Street (House)
HABS SC-527
HABS SC,10-CHAR,48-
2ph L

158 Broad Street (House)
HABS SC-428
HABS SC,10-CHAR,224-
1ph L

160 Broad Street (House)
HABS SC-429
HABS SC,10-CHAR,223-
1ph L

167 Broad Street (House)
HABS SC-430
HABS SC,10-CHAR,134-
1ph L

170 Broad Street (House)
HABS SC-431
HABS SC,10-CHAR,222-
1ph L

33 Broad Street (House)
HABS SC-416
HABS SC,10-CHAR,209-
2ph/2pc L

54 Broad Street (House)
HABS SC-424
HABS SC,10-CHAR,315-
2ph/2pc L

93 Broad Street (Residential Structure)
HABS SC-426
HABS SC,10-CHAR,217-
1ph L

101-107 Bull Street (Townhouses)
HABS SC-401
HABS SC,10-CHAR,236-
3ph L

Bull,Lt. Gov. William,House
43 Meeting St.
HABS SC-155
HABS SC,10-CHAR,143-
1ph L

Cabbage Row; see 89-91 Church Street (Houses)

276 Calhoun St. (House); see Cannon,Daniel,Kitchen Dependency

85 Calhoun Street (Building)
HABS SC-265
HABS SC,10-CHAR,173-
2ph/4pg L

Calhoun,Patrick,House,Stable (19 Church St. (House))
19 Church St.
HABS SC-506
HABS SC,10-CHAR,263A-
1ph L

Calhoun,Patrick,Mansion
16 Meeting St.
HABS SC-500
HABS SC,10-CHAR,263-
6ph L

Cannon,Daniel,House
274 Calhoun St.
HABS SC-375
HABS SC,10-CHAR,239-
12ph L

Cannon,Daniel,Kitchen Dependency
(276 Calhoun St. (House))
276 Calhoun St.
HABS SC-432
HABS SC,10-CHAR,239A-
1ph L

Capers,Richard,House
(Motte,Jacob,House)
69 Church St.
HABS SC-215
HABS SC,10-CHAR,163-
3ph L

Capers,Richard,Kitchen & Slave Building (Motte,Jacob,Kitchen & Slave Building)
69 Church St.
HABS SC-215-A
HABS SC,10-CHAR,163A-
1ph L

Capers,Richard,Laundry Building
(Motte,Jacob,Laundry Building)
69 Church St.
HABS SC-215-C
HABS SC,10-CHAR,163C-
2ph L

Capers,Richard,Stable
(Motte,Jacob,Stable)
69 Church St.
HABS SC-215-B
HABS SC,10-CHAR,163B-
1ph L

Carolina Hotel (Confederate Home)
60-64 Broad St.
HABS SC-510
HABS SC,10-CHAR,35-
13ph/2pc L

Castle Pickney
Charleston Harbor
HABS SC-195
HABS SC,10-CHAR.V,4-
2ph/3pg L

Catfish Row; see 89-91 Church Street (Houses)

Cathedral of St. John the Baptist (Roman Catholic)
122 Broad St.
HABS SC-504
HABS SC,10-CHAR,225-
3ph L

Centenary Methodist Church
60 Wentworth St.
HABS SC-550
HABS SC,10-CHAR,325-
4ph L

Century Antiques House; see Brewton-Sawter House

Century House; see Brewton-Sawter House

Century House Stable; see Brewton-Sawter Stable

17 Chalmers Street (House) (Pink House)
HABS SC-127
HABS SC,10-CHAR,134-
3ph/1pg L

36 Chalmers Street (House)
HABS SC-71
HABS SC,10-CHAR,86-
1ph L

Chamber of Commerce (Bank of South Carolina; Citizens & Southern Bank)
50 Broad St.
HABS SC-116
HABS SC,10-CHAR,132-
4ph/1pg L

Charleston Battery Project; see 19 East Battery (House)

Charleston Battery Project; see 27 East Battery (House)

Charleston Battery Project; see 28 South Battery Street (house)

Charleston Battery Project; see 30 South Battery Street (house)

Charleston Battery Project; see White Point Gardens

Charleston Battery Project; see White Point Gardens,Pavilion

Charleston Battery Project 1992; see East Battery

Charleston Battery Project 1992; see 13 East Battery (House)

Charleston Battery Project 1992; see 17 East Battery (House)

Charleston Battery Project 1992; see 29 East Battery (House)

Charleston Battery Project 1992; see 31 East Battery (House)

Charleston Battery Project 1992; see 39 East Battery (House)

Charleston Battery Project 1992; see 43 East Battery (House)

Charleston Battery Project 1992; see 5 East Battery (House)

Charleston Battery Project 1992; see South Battery

Charleston Battery Project 1992; see 2 South Battery Street (House)

1992 Charleston Battery Project; see 24 South Battery Street (House)

Charleston Battery Project 1992; see 2 Water Street (House)

Charleston City Hall; see Office of Discount & Deposit of U. S. Bank

Charleston County Courthouse
(County Court House)
82-86 Broad St.
HABS SC-131
HABS SC,10-CHAR,135-
5ph/1pg L

Charleston Gas & Light Company (141 Meeting St. (House))
141 Meeting St.
HABS SC-515
HABS SC,10-CHAR,269-
2ph L

Charleston Hotel
Meeting St.
HABS SC-77
HABS SC,10-CHAR,109-
4ph/3pg L

Charleston Insurance & Trust Company
12 Broad St.
HABS SC-409
HABS SC,10-CHAR,234-
1ph L

Charleston Orphan House,Chapel
13 Vanderhorst St.
HABS SC-146
HABS SC,10-CHAR,137-
1ph L

10 Charlotte Street (House)
HABS SC-85
HABS SC,10-CHAR,112-
3ph/1pg L

32 Charlotte Street (House)
HABS SC-96
HABS SC,10-CHAR,121-
1ph L

33 Charlotte Street (House)
HABS SC-159
HABS SC,10-CHAR,144-
1ph L

43 Charlotte Street (House)
HABS SC-93
HABS SC,10-CHAR,118-
1ph/1pg L

Chisholm Rice Mill
196 Tradd St.
HAER SC-10
HAER SC,10-CHAR,336-
2ph/1pc L

Chisholm-Alston House
172 Tradd St.
HABS SC-518
HABS SC,10-CHAR,323-
5ph L

Chisolm,Alexander Robert,House
6 Montague St.
HABS SC-260
HABS SC,10-CHAR,168-
5ph/7pg L

19 Church St. (House); see Calhoun,Patrick,House,Stable

131 Church Street (House)
HABS SC-448
HABS S,10-CHAR,256-
1ph L

143-145 Church Street (House) (Pirate House)
HABS SC-164
HABS SC,10-CHAR,89-
3ph L

20 Church Street (House)
HABS SC-433
HABS SC,10-CHAR,199-
2ph L

38 Church Street (House)
HABS SC-434
HABS SC,10-CHAR,245-
2ph L

76 Church Street (House)
HABS SC-452
HABS SC,10-CHAR,249-
1ph L

78 Church Street (House)
HABS SC-453
HABS SC,10-CHAR,248-
1ph L

92 Church Street (House) (St. Philip's Church,Rectory)
HABS SC-90
HABS SC,10-CHAR,115-
5ph/1pg L

89-91 Church Street (Houses) (Cabbage Row; Catfish Row)
HABS SC-447
HABS SC,10-CHAR,252-
1ph L

137-139 Church Street (Residential Buildings)
HABS SC-512
HABS SC,10-CHAR,259-
2ph L

133 Church Street
HABS SC-449
HABS SC,10-CHAR,257-
1ph L

Circular Congregational Church
138-150 Meeting St.
HABS SC-50-A
HABS SC,10-CHAR,90A-
4ph L

Circular Congregational Church,Parish House (Lance Hall)
138-150 Meeting St.
HABS SC-50
HABS SC,10-CHAR,90-
3ph L

Citadel Square Baptist Church
328 Meeting St.
HABS SC-498
HABS SC,10-CHAR,282-
5ph L

Citadel,Old; see South Carolina State Arsenal

Citizens & Southern Bank; see Chamber of Commerce

City Hall; see Office of Discount & Deposit of U. S. Bank

College of Charleston
66 George St.
HABS SC-175
HABS SC,10-CHAR,151-
1ph/1pg L

Commercial Building Front; see 227 Meeting Street (Commercial Building)

Commercial Building Front; see 229 Meeting Street (Commercial Building)

Confederate Home; see Carolina Hotel

County Court House; see Charleston County Courthouse

County Records Building (Mesne Conveyance Office; Fireproof Building)
100 Meeting St. (at Chalmers St.)
HABS SC-13-2
HABS SC,10-CHAR,64-
7dr/26ph/4pg/fr L

8 Courthouse Square (House)
HABS SC-446
HABS SC,10-CHAR,240-
2ph L

Crane,Dr. Samuel,House
4 Orange St.
HABS SC-537
HABS SC,10-CHAR,333-
10ph L

Crane,Dr. Samuel,Kitchen Building
4 Orange St.
HABS SC-537-A
HABS SC,10-CHAR,333A-
3ph L

de Saussure,Chancellor,House
18 Montague St.
HABS SC-94
HABS SC,10-CHAR,119-
1ph/1pg L

de Saussure,Louis,House
1 E. Battery
HABS SC-98
HABS SC,10-CHAR,82-
1ph/1pg L

Dictator; see Rutledge,John,House

Dock Street Theatre; see Planters Hotel

Doughty,Thomas,House
185 Rutledge Ave.
HABS SC-470
HABS SC,10-CHAR,311-
5ph L

Drayton,Charles H. ,House
25 E. Battery St.
HABS SC-472
HABS SC,10-CHAR,284-
4ph L H

Drayton,William,House (Parker-Drayton House)
6 Gibbes St.
HABS SC-70
HABS SC,10-CHAR,107-
7ph/1pg L

East Battery (Charleston Battery Project 1992)
HABS SC-675
H

13 East Battery (House) (Charleston Battery Project 1992)
HABS SC-677
H

17 East Battery (House) (Charleston Battery Project 1992)
HABS SC-678
H

19 East Battery (House) (Charleston Battery Project)
HABS SC-679
H

27 East Battery (House) (Charleston Battery Project)
HABS SC-680
H

29 East Battery (House) (Charleston Battery Project 1992)
HABS SC-681
H

Documentation: **ct** color transparencies **dr** measured drawings **fr** field records
pc photograph captions **pg** pages of text **ph** photographs

31 East Battery (House) (Charleston Battery Project 1992)
HABS SC-683
H

39 East Battery (House) (Charleston Battery Project 1992)
HABS SC-684
H

43 East Battery (House) (Charleston Battery Project 1992)
HABS SC-685
H

5 East Battery (House) (Charleston Battery Project 1992)
HABS SC-676
H

East Bay & Reid Streets (House)
HABS SC-205
HABS SC,10-CHAR,157-
2ph L

East Bay Street (Houses)
East Bay Street, near Tradd Street
HABS SC-226
HABS SC,10-CHAR,166-
1ph L

95-103 East Bay Street (Townhouses) (Rainbow Row)
HABS SC-405
HABS SC,10-CHAR,286-
2ph L

East Bay-Seaboard Airline,Railroad Freight Station
55 E. Bay St.
HABS SC-443
HABS SC,10-CHAR,331A-
6ph L

Edmonston,Charles,Dependency
21 E. Battery St.
HABS SC-54-A
HABS SC,10-CHAR,101A-
1ph L

Edmonston,Charles,House (Alston House; Middleton-Smith House)
21 E. Battery St.
HABS SC-54
HABS SC,10-CHAR,101-
26ph/4pg L H

Edwards-Smythe House; see Simmons,Francis,House

Edwards-Smythe Kitchen Building; see Simmons,Francis,Kitchen Building

Edwards-Smythe,Stable; see Simmons,Francis,Stable

Edwards,George,House; see Simmons,Francis,House

Edwards,George,Kitchen Building; see Simmons,Francis,Kitchen Building

Edwards,George,Stable; see Simmons,Francis,Stable

Edwards,John,House
15 Meeting St.
HABS SC-450
HABS SC,10-CHAR,262-
6ph L

Elfe,Thomas,Workshop; see 54 Queen Street (House)

Eliot,Charles,House; see 43 Legare Street (House)

Elliot House; see Middleton-Pinckney House

English,Col. James,House
49 S. Battery St.
HABS SC-546
HABS SC,10-CHAR,314-
2ph L

Eveleigh,George,House
39 Church St.
HABS SC-435
HABS SC,10-CHAR,244-
2ph/1pc L

Exchange Building & Custom House (Exchange,Old)
122-126 E. Bay St.
HABS SC-45
HABS SC,10-CHAR,72-
8ph/1pg L

Exchange,Old; see Exchange Building & Custom House

Faber House (Ward Mansion)
631 E. Bay St.
HABS SC-204
HABS SC,10-CHAR,156-
13ph L

Faber House,North Dependency (Ward Mansion,North Dependency)
631 E. Bay St.
HABS SC-204-A
HABS SC,10-CHAR,156A-
1ph L

Faber House,South Dependency (Ward Mansion,South Dependency)
631 East Bay Street
HABS SC-204-B
HABS SC,10-CHAR,156B-
1ph L

Farmers' & Exchange Bank
141 E. Bay St.
HABS SC-268
HABS SC,10-CHAR,176-
5ph/7pg L

Fayssoux,Dr. Peter,House
126 Tradd St.
HABS SC-468
HABS SC,10-CHAR,322-
2ph L

Fayssoux,Dr. Peter,Kitchen Building
126 Tradd St.
HABS SC-468-A
HABS SC,10-CHAR,322A-
4ph L

Federal Officer's Prison
180 Broad St.
HABS SC-561
HABS SC,10-CHAR,221-
2ph L

Ficken Servants' Quarters; see Mikell,I. Jenkins,Servants' Quarters

Fickin House; see Mikell,I. Jenkins,House

Fickin House,Kitchen Bldg; see Mikell,I. Jenkins,Kitchen Building

Fireproof Building; see County Records Building

First Baptist Church
61 Church St.
HABS SC-121
HABS SC,10-CHAR,70-
6ph/1pg L

First Scots Presbyterian Church (Presbyterian Church)
57 Meeting St.
HABS SC-80
HABS SC,10-CHAR,110-
5ph/1pg L

Fort Sumter (Fort Sumter National Monument)
HABS SC-194
HABS SC,10-CHAR.V,3-
23ph/5pg L

Fort Sumter National Monument; see Fort Sumter

Fraser,Charles,Carriage House & Slave Quarters
55 King St.
HABS SC-147-A
HABS SC,10-CHAR,138A-
2ph L

Fraser,Charles,House
55 King St.
HABS SC-147
HABS SC,10-CHAR,138-
1ph L

Fraser,Charles,Privy
55 King St.
HABS SC-147-B
HABS S,10-CHAR,138B-
2ph L

French Protestant Huguenot Church (Huguenot Church)
136 Church St.
HABS SC-105
HABS SC,10-CHAR,71-
10ph/2pg L

Fullerton,John,House
15 Legare St.
HABS SC-520
HABS SC,10-CHAR,305-
2ph L

Gaillard-Bennett Carriage House
60 Montague St.
HABS SC-516-B
HABS SC,10-CHAR,283B-
3ph L

Gaillard-Bennett House
60 Montague St.
HABS SC-516
HABS SC,10-CHAR,283-
9ph L

Gaillard-Bennett Kitchen Building
60 Montague St.
HABS SC-516-A
HABS SC,10-CHAR,283A-
2ph L

Gate
96 Ashley Ave.
HABS SC-108
HABS SC,10-CHAR,129-
1ph L

Gibbes House
64 S. Battery St.
HABS SC-445
HABS SC,10-CHAR,316-
28ph L

Gibbes House,Dependency
64 S. Battery St.
HABS SC-445-A
HABS SC,10-CHAR,316A-
5ph L

Gibbes House,Necessary
64 S. Battery St.
HABS SC-445-B
HABS SC,10-CHAR,316B-
1ph L

Gibbs House; see Lowndes Grove (House)

Glebe House (Smith,Bishop Robert,House)
6 Glebe St.
HABS SC-261
HABS SC,10-CHAR,169-
8dr/21ph/6pg/fr L

Glebe Street Presbyterian Church
(Mount Zion African Methodist Episcopal Church)
7 Glebe St.
HABS SC-266
HABS SC,10-CHAR,174-
6ph/5pg L

Glover House; see Smith,Josiah,House

Glover,Dr. Joseph,House
61 Rutledge Ave.
HABS SC-320
HABS SC,10-CHAR,193-
10ph/2pg L

Grace Episcopal Church
100 Wentworth St.
HABS SC-548
HABS SC,10-CHAR,326-
5ph L

14 Green Street (Entry Gates)
HABS SC-524
HABS SC,10-CHAR,290A-
1ph L

Harth,John,Dependency
68 S. Battery St.
HABS SC-474-A
HABS SC,10-CHAR,317A-
1ph/1pc L

Harth,John,House
68 S. Battery St.
HABS SC-474
HABS SC,10-CHAR,317-
10ph/1pc L

Hartley,James,House
43 E. Bay St.
HABS SC-471
HABS SC,10-CHAR,285-
1ph L

Harvey-Lining House & Pharmacy
Broad & Kings Sts.
HABS SC-106
HABS SC,10-CHAR,127-
8ph/10pg L

Harvey,William,Carriage House; see Izard,Ralph,Carriage House

Harvey,William,House; see Izard,Ralph,House

Harvey,William,Kitchen Bldg; see Izard,Ralph,Kitchen Building

Harvey,William,Privy; see Izard,Ralph,Privy

36 Hasell Street (door frontispiece)
HABS SC-406
HABS SC,10-CHAR,291-
1ph L

86 Hasell Street (House)
HABS SC-52
HABS SC,10-CHAR,99-
1ph L

64 Hasell Street (House,ca. 1840)
HABS SC-404
HABS SC,10-CHAR,294-
10ph L

60 Hasell Street (Mansion)
HABS SC-555
HABS SC,10-CHAR,293-
10ph L

33 Hayne Street (Commercial Building)
HABS SC-308
HABS SC,10-CHAR,192-
1ph/1pg L

Hendricks,William,House
83-85 Church St.
HABS SC-454
HABS SC,10-CHAR,250-
1ph L

Heyward-Washington House; see Heyward,Thomas Jr. ,House

Heyward,Hannah,House
31 Legare St.
HABS SC-571
HABS SC,10-CHAR,306-
2ph L

Heyward,Hannah,Kitchen Building
31 Legare St.
HABS SC-571-A
HABS SC,10-CHAR,306A-
3ph L

Heyward,Hannah,Stable & Carriage House
31 Legare St.
HABS SC-571-B
HABS SC,10-CHAR,306B-
2ph L

Heyward,Thomas Jr. ,House
(Heyward-Washington House)
87 Church St.
HABS SC-64
HABS SC,10-CHAR,103-
12ph/2pg L

Heyward,Thomas Jr. ,Kitchen Building
87 Church St.
HABS SC-64-A
HABS SC,10-CHAR,103A-
3ph L

Heyward,Thomas Jr. ,Privy
87 Church St.
HABS SC-64-C
HABS SC,10-CHAR,103C-
1ph L

Heyward,Thomas Jr. ,Stable Building
87 Church St.
HABS SC-64-B
HABS SC,10-CHAR,103B-
1ph L

Heyward,Thomas,Dependency
18 Meeting St.
HABS SC-160-A
HABS SC,10-CHAR,1A-
1ph L

Heyward,Thomas,House
(Manigault,Henry,House)
18 Meeting St.
HABS SC-160
HABS SC,10-CHAR,1-
7ph L

Hibernian Hall
105 Meeting St.
HABS SC-136
HABS SC,10-CHAR,88-
13ph/1pg L

Historic Charleston Foundation; see Russell,Nathaniel,House

House,Jerkinhead Roof; see 392-394 Meeting Street (House)

Huger,Daniel E. ,House
54 Meeting St.
HABS SC-525
HABS SC,10-CHAR,265-
13ph L

Huger,Daniel E. ,Kitchen Building
54 Meeting St.
HABS SC-525-A
HABS SC,10-CHAR,265A-
1ph L

Huger,Daniel E. ,Privy
54 Meeting St.
HABS SC-525-B
HABS SC,10-CHAR,265B-
1ph L

Huguenot Church; see French Protestant Huguenot Church

Documentation: **ct** color transparencies **dr** measured drawings **fr** field records
pc photograph captions **pg** pages of text **ph** photographs

Hunter,John,Building
(Sandburg,Annette,Antiques; Popular Loans & Finance)
244-246 King St.
HABS SC-585
HABS SC,10-CHAR,300-
3ph/1pg L

Independent Order of Odd Fellows Lodge
289 Meeting St.
HABS SC-499
HABS SC,10-CHAR,281-
2ph L

Islington Manor
135 Cannon St.
HABS SC-278
HABS SC,10-CHAR,179-
3ph/3pg L

Izard Carriage House; see Izard,Ralph,Carriage House

Izard House; see Izard,Ralph,House

Izard House,Kitchen Bldg; see Izard,Ralph,Kitchen Building

Izard Privy; see Izard,Ralph,Privy

Izard-Pinckney House
114 Broad St.
HABS SC-100
HABS SC,10-CHAR,122-
5ph/5pg L

Izard,Ralph,Carriage House (Izard Carriage House; Harvey,William,Carriage House)
110 Broad St.
HABS SC-65-B
HABS SC,10-CHAR,104B-
2ph L

Izard,Ralph,House (Izard House; Harvey,William,House)
110 Broad St.
HABS SC-65
HABS SC,10-CHAR,104-
13ph/1pg L

Izard,Ralph,Kitchen Building (Izard House,Kitchen Bldg; Harvey,William,Kitchen Bldg)
110 Broad St.
HABS SC-65-A
HABS SC,10-CHAR,104A-
9ph L

Izard,Ralph,Privy (Izard Privy; Harvey,William,Privy)
110 Broad St.
HABS SC-65-C
HABS SC,10-CHAR,104C-
1ph L

Jacobs,Rev. Ferdinand,Seminary for Girls
409 King St.
HABS SC-529
HABS SC,10-CHAR,303-
3ph L

Jewish Orphanage,Old
88 Broad St.
HABS SC-13-15
HABS SC,10-CHAR,68-
8dr/8ph/7pg L

8 Judith Street (Kitchen Dependency)
HABS SC-444
HABS SC,10-CHAR,295A-
3ph L

Kahal Kadosh Beth Elohim Synagogue
(Beth Elohim Synagogue)
90 Hasell St.
HABS SC-81
HABS SC,10-CHAR,41-
6dr/20ph/16pg/fr L

Kerrison,Charles,Gazebo
138 Wentworth St.
HABS SC-475-A
HABS SC,10-CHAR,328A-
4ph L

Kerrison,Charles,House
138 Wentworth St.
HABS SC-475
HABS SC,10-CHAR,328-
7ph L

183-185 King Street (Commercial Building)
HABS SC-301
HABS SC,10-CHAR,185-
1ph/1pg L

191 King Street (Commercial Building)
HABS SC-302
HABS SC,10-CHAR,186-
1ph/1pg L

211-213 King Street (Commercial Building)
HABS SC-303
HABS SC,10-CHAR,187-
1ph/1pg L

237 King Street (Commercial Building)
HABS SC-304
HABS SC,10-CHAR,188-
1ph/1pg L

238-242 King Street (Commercial Building)
HABS SC-586
HABS SC,10-CHAR,299-
7ph/1pg L

Ladson House
8 Meeting St.
HABS SC-95
HABS SC,10-CHAR,120-
1ph/1pg L

14 Lamboll Street (House)
HABS SC-570
HABS SC,10-CHAR,304-
4ph L

Lamboll,Thomas,House
19 King St.
HABS SC-569
HABS SC,10-CHAR,297-
2ph L

Lance Hall; see Circular Congregational Church,Parish House

8 Legare Street (Gates)
HABS SC-402
HABS SC,10-CHAR,335-
2ph L

10 Legare Street (House)
HABS SC-212
HABS SC,10-CHAR,161-
1ph L

43 Legare Street (House)
(Eliot,Charles,House)
HABS SC-162
HABS SC,10-CHAR,17-
1ph L

32 Legare Street (House,Drawing Room Wing); see Swordgate House

Legare,Thomas,House
90 Church St.
HABS SC-568
HABS SC,10-CHAR,253-
1ph L

Legare,Thomas,House
96 Church St.
HABS SC-509
HABS SC,10-CHAR,255-
1ph L

Legare,Thomas,Stable
90 Church St.
HABS SC-568-A
HABS SC,10-CHAR,253A-
1ph L

Levy,Moses C. ,House
301 E. Bay St.
HABS SC-99
HABS SC,10-CHAR,33-
8ph/9pg L

Lowndes Grove (House) (Gibbs House; Lowndes,William,House)
Saint Margaret St. & Sixth Ave.
HABS SC-178
HABS SC,10-CHAR,152-
5ph L

Lowndes,William,House; see Lowndes Grove (House)

Lucas,Jonathan,Dependency
286 Calhoun St.
HABS SC-41-A
HABS SC,10-CHAR,93A-
1ph L

Lucas,Jonathan,House
286 Calhoun St.
HABS SC-41
HABS SC,10-CHAR,93-
23ph/1pg L

4 Magazine Street (House)
HABS SC-103
HABS SC,10-CHAR,125-
1ph/1pg L

Manigault,Henry,House; see Heyward,Thomas,House

Manigault,Joseph,House
350 Meeting St. & Ashmead Place
HABS SC-67
HABS SC,10-CHAR,21-
11ph/1pg/1pc L

Manigault,Joseph,House,Gatehouse
350 Meeting St.
HABS SC-67-A
HABS SC,10-CHAR,21A-
2ph L

Marine Hospital,Old
20 Franklin St.
HABS SC-13-10
HABS SC,10-CHAR,66-
5dr/4ph/3pg L

Market Hall (Market,Old)
188 Meeting St.
HABS SC-135
HABS SC,10-CHAR,6-ı1992(HABS):SC-1°
14dr/75ph/1pg/5pc/1ct/fr L

Market Hall,Shed No. 1 (Old Market,Shed No. 1)
188 Meeting St.
HABS SC-135-A
HABS SC,10-CHAR,6A-
1ph L

Market Hall,Shed No. 2 (Old Market,Shed No. 2)
188 Meeting St.
HABS SC-135-B
HABS SC,10-CHAR,6B-
1ph L

Market Hall,Shed No. 3 (Old Market,Shed No. 3)
188 Meeting St.
HABS SC-135-C
HABS SC,10-CHAR,6C-
1ph L

Market Hall,Shed No. 4 (Old Market,Shed No. 4)
188 Meeting St.
HABS SC-135-D
HABS SC,10-CHAR,6D-
1ph L

Market Hall,Shed No. 5 (Old Market,Shed No. 5)
188 Meeting St.
HABS SC-135-E
HABS SC,10-CHAR,6E-
1ph L

Market,Old; see Market Hall

Martin,Robert,House
16 Charlotte St.
HABS SC-150
HABS SC,10-CHAR,141-
1ph L

Mathews,George,House
37 Church St.
HABS SC-451
HABS SC,10-CHAR,243-
1ph L

Mazyck,Isaac,House
86 Church St.
HABS SC-556
HABS SC,10-CHAR,251-
1ph L

Mazyck,Isaac,North Dependency
86 Church St.
HABS SC-556-B
HABS SC,10-CHAR,251B-
4ph L

Mazyck,Isaac,South Dependency
86 Church St.
HABS SC-556-A
HABS SC,10-CHAR,251A-
1ph L

McLeod Plantation
325 Country Club Dr.
HABS SC-665
HABS 1992(HABS):SC-1
7ph/1pc L

McLeod Plantation,Slave Quarters
325 Country Club Dr.
HABS SC-665-A
HABS 192(HABS):SC-1
3ph/1pc L

141 Meeting St. (House); see Charleston Gas & Light Company

207 Meeting Street (Commercial Building)
HABS SC-574
HABS SC,10-CHAR,270-
4ph/1pg L

211 Meeting Street (Commercial Building)
HABS SC-576
HABS SC,10-CHAR,272-
4ph/1pg L

213 Meeting Street (Commercial Building)
HABS SC-577
HABS SC,10-CHAR,273-
1ph/1pg L

215-215 1/2 Meeting Street (Commercial Building)
HABS SC-578
HABS SC,10-CHAR,274-
4ph/1pg L

217 Meeting Street (Commercial Building)
HABS SC-579
HABS SC,10-CHAR,275-
4ph/1pg L

219 Meeting Street (Commercial Building)
HABS SC-580
HABS SC,10-CHAR,276-
1ph/1pg L

221 Meeting Street (Commercial Building)
HABS SC-581
HABS SC,10-CHAR,277-
3ph/1pg L

223 Meeting Street (Commercial Building)
HABS SC-582
HABS SC,10-CHAR,278-
4ph/1pg L

225 Meeting Street (Commercial Building)
HABS SC-583
HABS SC,10-CHAR,279-
4ph/1pg L

226 Meeting Street (Commercial Building)
HABS SC-307
HABS SC,10-CHAR,191-
1ph/2pg L

227 Meeting Street (Commercial Building) (Commercial Building Front)
HABS SC-305
HABS SC,10-CHAR,189-
2ph/2pg L

229 Meeting Street (Commercial Building) (Commercial Building Front)
HABS SC-306
HABS SC,10-CHAR,190-
5ph/2pg L

231 Meeting Street (Commercial Building)
HABS SC-584
HABS SC,10-CHAR,280-
4ph/1pg L

27 Meeting Street (Entry Gate)
HABS SC-523
HABS SC,10-CHAR,24-
1ph L

135 Meeting Street (Fence and Gates)
HABS SC-563
HABS SC,10-CHAR,268A-
3ph L

1 Meeting Street (House)
HABS SC-521
HABS SC,10-CHAR,260-
3ph L H

2 Meeting Street (House)
HABS SC-522
HABS SC,10-CHAR,261-
1ph L H

392-394 Meeting Street (House) (House,Jerkinhead Roof)
HABS SC-42
HABS SC,10-CHAR,94-
2ph L

286 Meeting Street (House,ca. 1807)
HABS SC-403
HABS SC,10-CHAR,13-
8ph L

31 Meeting Street,Gate
Ladson Street
HABS SC-440-B
HABS SC,10-CHAR,264B-
1ph L

31 Meeting Street,Gazebo
HABS SC-440-A
HABS SC,10-CHAR,264A-
1ph L

Melcher-Enston House
105 Drake ST.
HABS SC-202
HABS SC,10-CHAR,154-
3ph L

Mesne Conveyance Office; see County Records Building

Middleton-Pinckney House (Elliot House)
14 George St.
HABS SC-51
HABS SC,10-CHAR,98-
25ph/1pg L

Middleton-Smith House; see Edmonston,Charles,House

Mikell,I. Jenkins,House (Fickin House)
Rutledge Ave. & Montague St.
HABS SC-43
HABS SC,10-CHAR,95-
11ph L

Mikell,I. Jenkins,Kitchen Building (Fickin House,Kitchen Bldg)
Rutledge Ave. & Montague St.
HABS SC-43-A
HABS SC,10-CHAR,95B-
1ph L

Mikell,I. Jenkins,Servants' Quarters (Ficken Servants' Quarters)
Rutledge Ave. & Montague St.
HABS SC-44
HABS SC,10-CHAR,95A-
1ph L

Mills,Clark,Studio
51 Broad St.
HABS SC-371
HABS SC,10-CHAR,214-
2ph/1pg L

Mixson Seed & Garden Supplies Building
217 E. Bay St.
HABS SC-372
HABS SC,10-CHAR,287-
1ph L

Moreland House
39 S. Battery St.
HABS SC-531
HABS SC,10-CHAR,47-
4ph L

Morris-Gadsden House
329 E. Bay St.
HABS SC-14
HABS SC,10-CHAR,49-
7dr/17ph/7pg/fr L

Motte,Col. Issac,House
30 Meeting St.
HABS SC-263
HABS SC,10-CHAR,171-
5ph/6pg L

Motte,Jacob,House; see Capers,Richard,House

Motte,Jacob,Kitchen & Slave Building; see Capers,Richard,Kitchen & Slave Building

Motte,Jacob,Laundry Building; see Capers,Richard,Laundry Building

Motte,Jacob,Stable; see Capers,Richard,Stable

Moultrie,Dr. James,House
20 Montague St.
HABS SC-209
HABS SC,10-CHAR,159-
9ph L

Moultrie,Dr. James,House,Dependency
20 Montague St.
HABS SC-209-A
HABS SC,10-CHAR,159A-
2ph/1pc L

Mount Zion African Methodist Episcopal Church; see Glebe Street Presbyterian Church

Northeastern Railroad:Charleston Freighthouses
2 & 4 Chapel St.
HAER SC-1
HAER SC,10-CHAR,337A-
1pg/fr L

O'Donnel Carriage House
21 King St.
HABS SC-437-A
HABS SC,10-CHAR,298A-
1ph L

O'Donnel House
21 King St.
HABS SC-437
HABS SC,10-CHAR,298-
8ph L

Office of Discount & Deposit of U. S. Bank (City Hall; Bank of U. S.; Charleston City Hall)
80 Broad St.
HABS SC-76
HABS SC,10-CHAR,108-
22ph/36pg/2pc/fr L

Old Market,Shed No. 1; see Market Hall,Shed No. 1

Old Market,Shed No. 2; see Market Hall,Shed No. 2

Old Market,Shed No. 3; see Market Hall,Shed No. 3

Old Market,Shed No. 4; see Market Hall,Shed No. 4

Old Market,Shed No. 5; see Market Hall,Shed No. 5

9-11 Orange Street (House)
HABS SC-501
HABS SC,10-CHAR,79-
2ph L

Osborne House
56 S. Battery St.
HABS SC-544
HABS SC,10-CHAR,28-
3ph L

Paine Studio; see 47 South Meeting Street (House)

Parker-Drayton House; see Drayton,William,House

Payne,Commodore,House
64 Vanderhorst St.
HABS SC-68
HABS SC,10-CHAR,106-
5ph/1pg L

Pelzer House
107 Ashley Ave.
HABS SC-104
HABS SC,10-CHAR,126-
4ph L

Penny,J. C. ,Building; see Seyle,Samuel,Building

Petigru,James Louis,Law Office
8 St. Michael's Place
HABS SC-148
HABS SC,10-CHAR,139-
1ph L

Pink House; see 17 Chalmers Street (House)

Pirate House; see 143-145 Church Street (House)

13 Pitt Street (Cornice)
HABS SC-573
HABS SC,10CHAR,334-
1ph/1pc L

Planters Hotel (Dock Street Theatre)
135 Church St.
HABS SC-467
HABS SC,10-CHAR,258-
1ph L

Popular Loans & Finance; see Hunter,John,Building

Porcher,Philip,House
19 Archdale St.
HABS SC-165
HABS SC,10-CHAR,147-
9ph L

Porter Academy; see U. S. Arsenal,Main Building

Porter Academy,Armory; see U. S. Arsenal,Powder Magazine

Porter Academy,Chapel; see U. S. Arsenal,Artillery Shed

Porter Academy,Colcock Hall; see U. S. Arsenal,Foundry Building

Porter Academy,Officers' Dwellings; see U. S. Arsenal,Building

Porter Academy,President's House; see U. S. Arsenal,Building

Powder Magazine,Old City
21 Cumberland St.
HABS SC-88
HABS SC,10-CHAR,114-
2ph/1pg L

Presbyterian Church; see First Scots Presbyterian Church

Primrose House
332 E. Bay & Vernon Sts.
HABS SC-107
HABS SC,10-CHAR,128-
3ph L

Pringle,Judge Robert,House
70 Tradd St.
HABS SC-166
HABS SC,10-CHAR,148-
6ph L

Pringle,Judge Robert,Kitchen Building
70 Tradd St.
HABS SC-166-A
HABS SC,10-CHAR,148A-
3ph L

5 Queen Street (Commercial Building)
HABS SC-566
HABS SC,10-CHAR,332-
4ph L

54 Queen Street (House)
(Elfe,Thomas,Workshop)
HABS SC-286
HABS SC,10-CHAR,180-
4dr/7ph/5pg/fr L

Radcliffe,Thomas,House; see
Ratcliffe,Thomas,House

Rainbow Row; see 95-103 East Bay Street (Townhouses)

Ramsey,Dr. David,House
92 Broad St.
HABS SC-13-1
HABS SC,10-CHAR,63-
6dr/10ph/5pg/fr L

Ratcliffe,Thomas,House
(Radcliffe,Thomas,House)
24 George St.
HABS SC-53
HABS SC,10-CHAR,100-
1ph/1pg L

Ravenel,Daniel,Dependency
68 Broad St.
HABS SC-133-A
HABS SC,10-CHAR,136A-
2ph L

Ravenel,Daniel,House
68 Broad St.
HABS SC-133
HABS SC,10-CHAR,136-
1ph/1pg L

Ravenel,William,House
13 E. Bay St.
HABS SC-161
HABS SC,10-CHAR,145-
1ph/1pg L

Rhett,Col. William,House
54 Hasell St.
HABS SC-171
HABS SC,10-CHAR,69-
7ph/1pg L

Rhett,Col. William,House,Dependency A
58 Hasell St.
HABS SC-171-A
HABS SC,10-CHAR,69A-
1ph L

Rhett,Col. William,House,Dependency B
62 Hasell St.
HABS SC-171-B
HABS SC,10-CHAR,69B-
2ph L

Rhett,Colonel William,House,Dependency C
56 Hassell St.
HABS SC-171-C
HABS SC,10-CHAR,69C-
1ph L

Robinson-Aiken Cow House
48 Elizabeth St.
HABS SC-274
HABS SC,10-CHAR,177A-
2dr/3ph/1pg L

Robinson-Aiken House
48 Elizabeth St.
HABS SC-269
HABS SC,10-CHAR,177-
10dr/54ph/9pg/3pc/fr L

Robinson-Aiken Necessary Building
48 Elizabeth St.
HABS SC-277
HABS SC,10-CHAR,177D-
2dr/3ph/2pg L

Robinson-Aiken Service Building & Stable
48 Elizabeth St.
HABS SC-275
HABS SC,10-CHAR,177B-
3dr/6ph/3pg L

Robinson-Aiken Slave Building & Kitchens
48 Elizabeth St.
HABS SC-276
HABS SC,10-CHAR,177C-
2dr/4ph/3pg L

Robinson,John,House
10 Judith St.
HABS SC-466
HABS SC,10-CHAR,296-
3ph L

Robinson,John,Kitchen Building
10 Judith St.
HABS SC-466-A
HABS SC,10-CHAR,296A-
7ph L

Rogers,Francis S. ,Carriage House
147-149 Wentworth St.
HABS SC-547-A
HABS SC,10-CHAR,329A-
1ph L

Rogers,Francis S. ,Mansion
147-149 Wentworth St.
HABS SC-547
HABS SC,10-CHAR,329-
8ph L

Rogers,Francis S. ,Stable
141 Wentworth St. (formerly 147-149 Wentworth St.)
HABS SC-547-B
HABS SC,10-CHAR,329B-
1ph L

Roper,Robert William,House; see
Roper,William,House

Roper,William,House (Roper,Robert William,House)
9 E. Battery
HABS SC-173
HABS SC,10-CHAR,149-
9ph L

Rose,Thomas,House
59 Church St.
HABS SC-436
HABS SC,10-CHAR,246-
3ph L

Russell,Nathaniel,Dependencies
51 Meeting St.
HABS SC-145-A
HABS SC,10-CHAR,2A-
2ph L

Russell,Nathaniel,House (Historic Charleston Foundation)
51 Meeting St.
HABS SC-145
HABS SC,10-CHAR,2-
11ph/2pg L

101 Rutledge Avenue (House)
HABS SC-465
HABS SC,10-CHAR,308-
1ph L

74 Rutledge Avenue (House)
HABS SC-210
HABS SC,10-CHAR,160-
2ph L

93 Rutledge Avenue (House)
HABS SC-572
HABS SC,10-CHAR,307-
9ph L

Rutledge,"Dictator",House; see
Rutledge,John,House

Rutledge,John,Carriage House
116 Broad St.
HABS SC-394-A
HABS SC,10-CHAR,123A-
3ph L

Rutledge,John,House (Dictator; Rutledge,"Dictator",House)
116 Broad St.
HABS SC-394
HABS SC,10-CHAR,123-
12ph/1pg L

Sandburg,Annette,Antiques; see
Hunter,John,Building

Savage,Thomas,House; see
Washington,William,House

Savage,Thomas,Stable; see
Washington,William,Stable

Seabrook,T. B. ,House
95 Rutledge Ave.
HABS SC-216
HABS SC,10-CHAR,164-
4ph L

Documentation: **ct** color transparencies **dr** measured drawings **fr** field records
pc photograph captions **pg** pages of text **ph** photographs

Second Bank of the United States (South Carolina National Bank)
16 Broad St.
HABS SC-562
HABS SC,10-CHAR,233-
5ph/2pc L

Second Presbyterian Church
342 Meeting St.
HABS SC-92
HABS SC,10-CHAR,117-
11ph/1pg L

Seyle,Samuel,Building (Penny,J. C. ,Building; Shroeder/Sussdorf Building)
209 Meeting St.
HABS SC-575
HABS SC,.10-CHAR,271-
4ph/2pg L

Shaffer,Frederick,House
214 Calhoun St.
HABS SC-560
HABS SC,10-CHAR,237-
2ph L

Shingler,William Pinckney,House
9 Limehouse St.
HABS SC-300
HABS SC,10-CHAR,184-
2ph/5pg L

Shirras,Alexander,House
271 Meeting St.
HABS SC-217
HABS SC,10-CHAR,12-
2ph L

Shrewsbury,Stephen,House
311 E. Bay
HABS SC-258
HABS SC,10-CHAR,167-
5ph/5pg L

Shroeder/Sussdorf Building; see Seyle,Samuel,Building

Siegling Music Shop
243 King St.
HABS SC-558
HABS SC,10-CHAR,301-
2ph L

Simmons,Francis,House (Edwards,George,House; Edwards-Smythe House; Smythe House)
14 Legare St.
HABS SC-47
HABS SC,10-CHAR,9-;
10ph/1pc L

Simmons,Francis,Kitchen Building (Edwards,George,Kitchen Building; Edwards-Smythe Kitchen Building)
14 Legare St.
HABS SC-47-A
HABS SC,10-CHAR,9A-
1ph L

Simmons,Francis,Stable (Edwards,George,Stable; Edwards-Smythe,Stable)
14 Legare St.
HABS SC-47-B
HABS SC,10-CHAR,9B-
1ph L

34 Smith Street (House)
HABS SC-553
HABS SC,10-CHAR,324-
2ph L

59 Smith Street (House)
HABS SC-84
HABS SC,10-CHAR,111-
3ph/1pg L

Smith,Benjamin,House
49 Broad St.
HABS SC-502
HABS SC,10-CHAR,213-
2ph L

Smith,Bishop Robert,House; see Glebe House

Smith,Josiah,House (Glover House)
7 Meeting St.
HABS SC-225
HABS SC,10-CHAR,165-
6ph L

Smith,William Mason,House
26 Meeting St.
HABS SC-149
HABS SC,10-CHAR,140-
3ph L

Smythe House; see Simmons,Francis,House

Sottile House
12 Green St.
HABS SC-517
HABS SC,10-CHAR,289-
4ph L

South Battery (Charleston Battery Project 1992)
HABS SC-668
H

4 South Battery (House) (Villa Margherita)
HABS SC-174
HABS SC,10-CHAR,150-
1ph L H

26 South Battery Street (Dependencies)
HABS SC-114-A
HABS SC,10-CHAR,313A-
2ph L

2 South Battery Street (House) (Charleston Battery Project 1992)
HABS SC-669
H

22 South Battery Street (House)
HABS SC-670
H

24 South Battery Street (House) (1992 Charleston Battery Project)
HABS SC-671
H

26 South Battery Street (House)
HABS SC-114
HABS SC,10-CHAR,313-
3ph L H

28 South Battery Street (house) (Charleston Battery Project)
HABS SC-672
H

30 South Battery Street (house) (Charleston Battery Project)
HABS SC-673
H

54 South Battery Street (Roof Decoration)
HABS SC-543
HABS SC,10-CHAR,315-
1ph L

South Carolina National Bank; see Second Bank of the United States

South Carolina Railroad-Southern Railway Co. (Aiken,William,House)
456 King St.
HABS SC-373-A
HABS SC,10-CHAR,54-
31ph/1pg L

South Carolina RR-Southern Railway Co. ,Warehouse
42 John St.
HABS SC-373-C
HABS SC,10-CHAR,330B-
1ph L

South Carolina RR-Southern Rlwy Co. ,Camden Depot
Anne St.
HABS SC-373-B
HABS SC,10-CHAR,330A-
4ph L

South Carolina RR-Southern Rlwy Co. ,Carriage Hse. (Aiken,William,Carriage House)
456 King Street
HABS SC-373-D
HABS SC,10-CHAR,54A-
2ph L

South Carolina Society Building
72 Meeting St.
HABS SC-514
HABS SC,10-CHAR,267-
3ph L

South Carolina State Arsenal (Citadel,Old)
Marion Square
HABS SC-184
HABS SC,10-CHAR,76-
11ph/6pg L

47 South Meeting Street (House) (Paine Studio)
HABS SC-46
HABS SC,10-CHAR,96-
5ph L

St. James United Methodist Church (ca. 1858)
68 Spring St.
HABS SC-374
HABS S,10-CHAR,36-
14ph L

St. Johannes Lutheran Church
48 Hasell St.
HABS SC-528
HABS S,10-CHAR,292-
3ph L

St. John's Lutheran Church
10 Archdale St.
HABS SC-168
HABS SC,10-CHAR,42-
15ph/1pg L

St. Luke's Episcopal Church
22 Elizabeth St.
HABS SC-535
HABS SC,10-CHAR,288-
4ph L

St. Mark's Episcopal Church
14 Thomas St.
HABS SC-552
HABS SC,10-CHAR,19-
2ph L

St. Mary's Roman Catholic Church
89 Hasell St.
HABS SC-48
HABS SC,10-CHAR,97-
4ph/1pg L

St. Matthew's Lutheran Church
405 King St.
HABS SC-557
HABS SC,10-CHAR,302-
4ph L

St. Matthew's Lutheran Church,Sunday School Bldg.
405 King St.
HABS SC-557-A
HABS SC,10-CHAR,302A-
2ph L

St. Michael's Church,Rectory; see 56 Beaufain Street (House)

St. Michael's Episcopal Church
80 Meeting St.
HABS SC-62
HABS SC,10-CHAR,8-
11dr/32ph/15pg/fr L

St. Philip's Church,Rectory; see 92 Church Street (House)

St. Philip's Protestant Episcopal Church
146 Church St.
HABS SC-75
HABS SC,10-CHAR,58-
34ph/2pg L

St. Philip's Protestant Episcopal Church,Parish Hs
146 Church St.
HABS SC-75-A
HABS SC,10-CHAR,58A-
1ph L

State Bank of South Carolina
1 Broad St.
HABS SC-559
HABS SC,10-CHAR,202-
7ph/2pc L

State Powder Magazines & Administration Bldgs.
Charleston Neck
HABS SC-13-13
HABS SC,10-CHAR,67-
2dr/7ph/4pg L

Steele,William,House
89 Beaufain St.
HABS SC-86
HABS SC,10-CHAR,52-
11ph/1pg L

Steinmeyer,John,Accessory Building
108 Beaufain St.
HABS SC-564-B
HABS SC,10-CHAR,196B-
2ph L

Steinmeyer,John,House
108 Beaufain St.
HABS SC-564
HABS SC,10-CHAR,196-
6ph L

Steinmeyer,John,Kitchen Building
108 Beaufain St.
HABS SC-564-A
HABS SC,10-CHAR,196A-
3ph L

Stevens-Lathers House
20 S. Battery St.
HABS SC-545
HABS SC,10-CHAR,312-
3ph L H

Stevens-Lathers Kitchen Dependency
20 S. Battery St.
HABS SC-545-A
HABS SC,10-CHAR,312A-
1ph L

Sts. Luke & Paul Cathedral
126 Coming St.
HABS SC-536
HABS SC,10-CHAR,45-
18ph L

Sts. Luke & Paul Cathedral,Johnston Mausoleum
126 Coming St.
HABS SC-536-A
HABS SC,10-CHAR,45A-
2ph L

Stuart,Col. John,Carriage House
106 Tradd St.
HABS SC-156-A
HABS SC,10-CHAR,81A-
2ph L

Stuart,Col. John,House
106 Tradd St.
HABS SC-156
HABS SC,10-CHAR,81-
10ph/1pg L

Swordgate House (32 Legare Street (House,Drawing Room Wing))
109 Tradd St. (moved from 32 Legare St.)
HABS SC-271
HABS SC.10-CHAR,178-
3ph/4pg L

Three Sisters (Building)
Calhoun & E. Bay Sts.
HABS SC-384
HABS SC,10-CHAR,238-
1ph L

123 Tradd Street (House)
HABS SC-532
HABS SC,10-CHAR,321-
2ph L

38 Tradd Street (House)
HABS SC-533
HABS SC,10-CHAR,318-
1ph L

46 Tradd Street (House)
HABS SC-66
HABS SC,10-CHAR,105-
3ph/2pg L

72 Tradd Street (House)
HABS SC-122
HABS SC,10-CHAR,133-
3ph/1pg L

41-43 Tradd Street (Houses)
HABS SC-534
HABS SC,10-CHAR,319-
1ph L

Trenholm,George A. ,Addition A
Ratcliff St.
HABS SC-565-C
HABS SC,10-CHAR,309C-
1ph L

Trenholm,George A. ,Addition B
172 Rutledge Ave.
HABS SC-565-D
HABS SC,10-CHAR,309D-
1ph L

Trenholm,George A. ,Carriage House
172 Rutledge Ave.
HABS SC-565-A
HABS SC,10-CHAR,309A-
2ph L

Trenholm,George A. ,Kitchen Building
172 Rutledge Ave.
HABS SC-565-B
HABS SC,10-CHAR,309B-
1ph L

Trenholm,George A. ,Mansion
172 Rutledge Ave.
HABS SC-565
HABS SC,10-CHAR,309-
54ph L

Trinity Methodist Church; see Westminster Presbyterian Church

U. S. Arsenal,Artillery Shed (Porter Academy,Chapel)
167 Ashley Ave.
HABS SC-296
HABS SC,10-CHAR,183C-
1ph/3pg L

U. S. Arsenal,Building (Porter Academy,Officers' Dwellings)
167 Ashley Ave.
HABS SC-295
HABS SC,10-CHAR,183B-
1ph/3pg L

Documentation: **ct** color transparencies **dr** measured drawings **fr** field records **pc** photograph captions **pg** pages of text **ph** photographs

U. S. Arsenal,Building (Porter Academy,President's House)
167 Ashley Ave.
HABS SC-299
HABS SC,10-CHAR,183F-
2ph/3pg L

U. S. Arsenal,Foundry Building (Porter Academy,Colcock Hall)
167 Ashley Ave.
HABS SC-297
HABS SC,10-CHAR,183D-
1ph/3pg L

U. S. Arsenal,Main Building (Porter Academy)
167 Ashley Ave.
HABS SC-294
HABS SC,10-CHAR,183A-
3ph/4pg L

U. S. Arsenal,Powder Magazine (Porter Academy,Armory)
167 Ashley Ave.
HABS SC-298
HABS SC,10-CHAR,183E-
2ph/3pg L

U. S. Customs House
200 E. Bay St.
HABS SC-39
HABS SC,10-CHAR,92-
27ph/2pg L

U. S. Post Office Building
Broad & Meeting Sts.
HABS SC-293
HABS SC,10-CHAR,182-
11ph/5pg L

Unitarian Church
6 Archdale St.
HABS SC-473
HABS SC,10-CHAR,197-
14ph L

Valk,Charles R. ,House
125 Broad St.
HABS SC-567
HABS SC,10-CHAR,219-
2ph L

VanderHorst Row
78 E. Bay St.
HABS SC-526
HABS SC,10-CHAR,10-
4ph L

14 Vanderhorst Street (House)
HABS SC-163
HABS SC,10-CHAR,146-
1ph L

67 Vanderhorst Street (House)
HABS SC-181
HABS SC,10-CHAR,113-
3ph L

Vanderhorst,William,House
54 Tradd St.
HABS SC-551
HABS SC,10-CHAR,320-
2ph L

Vanderhorst,William,Kitchen Building
54 Tradd St.
HABS SC-551-A
HABS SC,10-CHAR,320A-
1ph L

Villa Margherita; see 4 South Battery (House)

Wagener-Randolph Carriage & Stable House
179 Rutledge Ave.
HABS SC-469-A
HABS SC,10-CHAR,310A-
1ph L

Wagener-Randolph House
179 Rutledge Ave.
HABS SC-469
HABS SC,10-CHAR,310-
6ph L

Walker,John Falls,House
344 E. Bay St.
HABS SC-262
HABS SC,10-CHAR,170-
5ph/3pg L

Ward Mansion; see Faber House

Ward Mansion,North Dependency; see Faber House,North Dependency

Ward Mansion,South Dependency; see Faber House,South Dependency

Warren & Smith Streets (House)
HABS SC-208
HABS SC,10-CHAR,158-
3ph L

Washington Park (Gates)
90 Meeting St.
HABS SC-530
HABS SC,10-CHAR,44-
2ph L

Washington,William,Carriage House
8 S Battery St.
HABS SC-115-B
2ph/1pc H

Washington,William,House
(Savage,Thomas,House)
8 South Battery Street
HABS SC-115
HABS SC,10-CHAR,131-
8ph/1pg L H

Washington,William,Stable
(Savage,Thomas,Stable)
8 S. Battery St.
HABS SC-115-A
HABS SC,10-CHAR,131A-
1ph L

2 Water Street (House) (Charleston Battery Project 1992)
HABS SC-682
H

128 Wentworth Street (House)
HABS SC-554
HABS SC,10-CHAR,327-
2ph L

West Point Rice Mill
Ashley River,Near Calhoun St.
HABS SC-214
HABS SC,10-CHAR,162-ı1992(HABS):SC-1°
8ph/1pc L

Westminster Presbyterian Church
(Trinity Methodist Church)
273 Meeting St.
HABS SC-292
HABS SC,10-CHAR,181-
6dr/25ph/6pg/fr L

White Point Gardens (Charleston Battery Project)
HABS SC-687
H

White Point Gardens,Pavilion
(Charleston Battery Project)
HABS SC-687-A
3ph/1pc H

Willard-Tobias House
178 Ashley Ave.
HABS SC-439
HABS S,10-CHAR,198-
7ph L

Young,Thomas,House
35 Church St.
HABS SC-505
HABS SC,10-CHAR,242-
1ph L

CHARLESTON VIC.

Ball,John,House; see Marshlands

Drayton Hall
Ashley River Rd. (State Rt. 61)
HABS SC-377
HABS SC,10-CHAR.V,8-
14dr/12ph/17pg/fr L

Drayton Hall,Brick Office
State Rt. 61
HABS SC-377-A
HABS SC,10-CHAR.V,8A-
1dr L

Fort Johnson,Powder Magazine
James Island,Charleston Harbor
HABS SC-387
HABS 1983(HABS):172
3dr/3pg L

Marshlands (Ball,John,House)
College of Charleston (moved from Cooper River)
HABS SC-259
HABS SC,10-CHAR.V,6-
5ph/8pg L

St. Andrew's Episcopal Church
State Rt. 61
HABS SC-4
HABS SC,10-CHAR.V,1-
10dr/9ph/2pg L

EDISTO BEACH VIC.

Seaside (House)
State Hwy. 174 vic.
HABS SC-496
HABS SC,10-EDIB.V,1-
13ph L

EDISTO ISLAND

Brookland
HABS SC-141
HABS SC,10-EDIL,4-
3ph L

Cassina Point (House)
County Rd. 1989 vic.
HABS SC-493
HABS SC,10-EDIL,5-
9ph L

Edisto Island Presbyterian Church
(Presbyterian Church)
HABS SC-125
HABS SC,10-EDIL,3-
8ph L

Edisto Island Presbyterian Church,Session House
HABS SC-125-A
HABS SC,10-EDIL,3A-
1ph L

Hamilton,Paul,House (Ruins)
(House,Brick)
Russell Creek
HABS SC-1
HABS SC,10-EDIL,1-
8dr/10ph/5pg L

House,Brick; see Hamilton,Paul,House (Ruins)

Oak Island (House)
County Rd. 768 vic.
HABS SC-491
HABS SC,10-EDIL,6-
18ph L

Presbyterian Church; see Edisto Island Presbyterian Church

Prospect Hill (House)
State Rt. 174 vic.
HABS SC-492
HABS SC,10-EDIL,7-
9ph L

Seabrook,William,House
County Rd. 768
HABS SC-124
HABS SC,10-EDIL,2-
30ph/1pg L

Sunnyside Plantation
County Rd. 767
HABS SC-494
HABS SC,10-EDIL,8-
10ph L

Sunnyside Plantation,Barn
County Rd. 767
HABS SC-494-C
HABS SC,10-EDIL,8C-
1ph L

Sunnyside Plantation,Cotton Gin Building (Ruins)
County Rd. 767
HABS SC-494-D
HABS SC,10-EDIL,8D-
1ph L

Sunnyside Plantation,East Dependency
County Rd. 767
HABS SC-494-A
HABS SC,10-EDIL,8A-
1ph L

Sunnyside Plantation,West Dependency
County Rd. 767
HABS SC-494-B
HABS SC,10-EDIL,8B-
1ph L

GOOSE CREEK VIC.

Elms,The (Ruins)
(Izard,Henry,Plantation House)
University Blvd. (U. S. Rt. 78)
HABS SC-167
HABS SC,8-OTRAT,1-
3ph/1pg L

Izard,Henry,Plantation House; see Elms,The (Ruins)

MC CLELLANVILLE

Lucas,William,House (Wedge,The)
U. S. Rts. 17 & 701
HABS SC-144
HABS SC,10-MCCLEL.V,5-
2ph L

Wedge,The; see Lucas,William,House

MC CLELLANVILLE VIC.

Fairfield; see Lynch House

Hampton Plantation
Wambaw Creek,S. side
HABS SC-72
HABS SC,10-McCLEL.V,3-
14ph/1pg L

Harrietta Plantation
U. S. Rts. 17 & 701
HABS SC-143
HABS SC,10-MCCLEL.V,4-
2ph/1pg L

Lynch House (Fairfield)
U. S. Rts. 17 & 701
HABS SC-10
HABS SC,10-MCCLEL.V,2-
12dr/10ph/2pg/fr L

St. James' Episcopal Church
Wambaw Creek,S. side
HABS SC-69
HABS SC,10-MCCLEL.V,1-
5ph/1pg L

MEGGETT

Summit (House)
County Rd. 390
HABS SC-495
HABS SC,10-MEG,1-
10ph L

MOUNT PLEASANT VIC.

Boone Hall Quarters
HABS SC-102
HABS SC,10-MOUP.V,3-
1ph/1pg L

Oakland Plantation
HABS SC-9
HABS SC,10-MOUP.V,1-
11dr/6ph/1pg L

Snee Farm
1240 Long Point Rd.
HABS SC-87
HABS SC,10-MOUP.V,2-ı1992(HABS):SC-1°
21dr/48ph/32pg/3pc/fr L

SULLIVANS ISLAND

Fort Moultrie (Fort Sumter National Monument)
W. Fort St. & Central Ave.
HABS SC-196
HABS SC,10-CHAR.V,5-
50dr/17ph/6pg/fr L

Fort Moultrie,Cable Tank Storage Building (Fort Sumter National Monument)
Central Avenue, Fort Sumter National Monument
HABS SC-196-A
HABS SC,10-CHAR.V,5A-
6dr/fr L

Fort Sumter National Monument; see Fort Moultrie

Fort Sumter National Monument; see Fort Moultrie,Cable Tank Storage Building

CHESTER COUNTY

CHESTER VIC.

Sealy,Obadiah,House
State Rt. 9
HABS SC-130
HABS SC,12-CHEST.V,1-
2ph L

GREAT FALLS

Rock House (Ruins)
Catawba River
HABS SC-158
HABS SC,12-GREFA,1-
2ph L

GREAT FALLS VIC.

Rocky Mount Canal,Lock Keeper's House
HABS SC-386
HABS SC,12-GREFA.V,1A-
7dr/2pg L

CHESTERFIELD COUNTY

CHERAW

Cheraw Lyceum; see Equity Court,Old

Duvall House
226 Third St.
HABS SC-227
HABS SC,13-CHERA,6-
1ph L

Equity Court,Old (Cheraw Lyceum)
Market & Seaboard Sts.
HABS SC-179
HABS SC,13-CHERA,4-
1ph/1pg L

Lafayette House; see Pegues-McKay House

Lane House; see St. David's Episcopal Church,Rectory

Masonic Hall
Market & Second Sts.
HABS SC-180
HABS SC,13-CHERA,5-
1ph L

Pegues-McKay House (Lafayette House)
Kershaw & Third Sts.
HABS SC-172
HABS SC,13-CHERA,3-
3ph L

Police Station; see Town Hall

St. David's Episcopal Church
First & Church Sts.
HABS SC-112
HABS SC,13-CHERA,1-S
3ph/1pg L

St. David's Episcopal Church,Rectory (Lane House)
515 Market St.
HABS SC-378
HABS SC,13-CHERA,7-
9ph/1pg/fr L

Town Hall (Police Station)
Market & Second Sts.
HABS SC-151
HABS SC,13-CHERA,2-
1ph L

CHERAW VIC.

McLaurin,Tom,House
State Rt. 382
HABS SC-229
HABS SC,13-CHERA.V,1-
1ph L

Sessions,H. E. ,House
State Rt. 9
HABS SC-228
HABS SC,13-CHERA.V,1-
1ph L

CHESTERFIELD

Craig,John,House
Courthouse Vic.
HABS SC-188
HABS SC,13-CHESF,1-
1ph/1pg L

CLARENDON COUNTY

MANNING

Oakland (Wyndham,William,House)
HABS SC-235
HABS SC,14-MAN,1-
1ph L

Wyndham,William,House; see Oakland

COLLETON COUNTY

WALTERBORO

Library
Wichman St. & N. Miller (moved from Fishburne St.)
HABS SC-2
HABS SC,15-WALT,2-
1ph/1pg L

Mansion
HABS SC-192
HABS SC,15-WALT,3-
1ph L

WALTERBORO VIC.

Cabin
HABS SC-249
HABS SC,15-WALT.V,1-
1ph L

DARLINGTON COUNTY

MECHANICSVILLE VIC.

Flowers,B. C. ,House (Fountain,Wilson,House)
Cash's Ferry Rd.
HABS SC-111
HABS SC,16-DARL.V,1-
5ph/1pg L

Fountain,Wilson,House; see Flowers,B. C. ,House

SOCIETY HILL VIC.

Cedar Grove (Gandy,Lila,House)
Rt. 2
HABS SC-113
HABS SC,16-SOCHI.V,1-
3ph/1pg L

Gandy,Lila,House; see Cedar Grove

DILLON COUNTY

DILLON VIC.

Smith Tobacco Barn
1/4 mi s of Hwy 17-34 & 1/2 mi s of Hwy 17-155
HABS SC-594
HABS SC,17-DILL.V,1-
12ph/1pg/1pc/4ct L

LATTA VIC.

Cotton Press
Near RTes. 917 & 38,moved from Berry's Crossroads
HAER SC-11
HAER SC,17-LAT.V,1-
5ph/1pg/1pc L

Tobacco Barn
HABS SC-594-A
HABS 1989(HABS):21
4ph/1pc L

MULLINS

Warehouse,Old Brick
Main & Wine Sts. (corner)
HABS SC-620
HABS 1990 (HABS):7
4ph/1pg/1pc L

DORCHESTER COUNTY

ASHLEY RIVER

Middleton Place
Ashley River Rd.
HABS SC-218
HABS SC,18- ,3-
2pg L

ASHLEY RIVER,N. BANK

Dorchester Church Tower
Dorchester Creek Junction
HABS SC-189
HABS SC,18- ,1-
1ph L

Fort Dorchester
Dorchester Creek Junction
HABS SC-185
HABS SC,18- ,2-
3ph L

ST. GEORGE3VIC.

Indian Fields Methodist Campground
SC Rt 73, .7 mi. from SC Rt 15
HABS SC-595
HABS SC,18-SAGEO,1-SC,S8SAGEO,1A-0
35ph/2pg/2pc L

EDGEFIELD COUNTY

PLEASANT LANE VIC.

Edgefield County Bridge No. 3
Rd. S-63 spanning Log Creek
HAER SC-8
HAER SC,19-PLELA.V1-
6ph/1pg/1pc L

FAIRFIELD COUNTY

JENKINSVILLE VIC.

Church,Old Brick; see First Associate Reformed Presbyterian Church

Ebenezer Church; see First Associate Reformed Presbyterian Church

First Associate Reformed Presbyterian Church (Ebenezer Church; Church,Old Brick)
State Rt. 213
HABS SC-157
HABS SC,20-MONT.V,1-
17ph/1pg/1pc L

WINNSBORO

Fairfield County Courthouse
Congress & Washington Sts.
HABS SC-213
HABS SC,20-WINBO,2-
1ph/1pg L

Fire Station & Municipal Offices
Congress & Washington Sts.
HABS SC-182
HABS SC,20-WINBO,1-
1ph L

Gadsen,Christopher,Jr.,House; see Tocaland

Tocaland (Gadsen,Christopher,Jr.,House)
Secondary Rd. 344 near Hwy. 34
HABS SC-623
HABS SC,20-WINBO.V,1-
7ph/1pg/1pc/2ct L

Wolfe House
S. Congress St.
HABS SC-596
HABS 1989(HABS):21
12ph/1pg/1pc L

FLORENCE COUNTY

JOHNSONVILE VIC.

Browntown Cotton Gin
SC Rt. 341 between Johnsonville & Lake City
HAER SC-13
HAER SC,21-JOHVI.V,1-
16ph/2pg/1pc L

LAKE CITY

Tobacco Redrying Plant
Railroad Avenue
HAER SC-12
HAER SC,21-LACI,1-
12ph/1pg/1pc/2ct L

MARS BLUFF VIC.

Columns,The (Johnson,Dr. William R. ,Plantation House)
U. S. Rts. 76 & 301
HABS SC-117
HABS SC,21-MARB.V,1-
2ph/1pg L

Johnson,Dr. William R. ,Plantation House; see Columns,The

GEORGETOWN COUNTY

CAT ISLAND

Cat Island Plantation
By ferry via Etherville Minim Creek Canal
HABS SC-481
HABS SC,22-CATIL,1-
2ph L

GEORGETOWN

Allston House
405 Front St.
HABS SC-310
HABS SC,22-GEOTO,6-
5ph/3pg L

Church of Prince George Winyah
Broad & Highmarket Sts.
HABS SC-49
HABS SC,22-GEOTO,1-
4ph/1pg L

Crowley Store
936 Front St.
HABS SC-313
HABS SC,22-GEOTO,9-
1ph/2pg L

Georgetown County Courthouse
Screven & Prince Sts.
HABS SC-142
HABS SC,22-GEOTO,2-
4ph L

Henning-Ward House
614 Prince St.
HABS SC-309
HABS SC,22-GEOTO,5-
4ph/3pg L

Man,Mary,House
528 Front St.
HABS SC-317
HABS SC,22-GEOTO,13-
6ph/3pg L

Market Building (Police Department Building)
Front & Screven Sts.
HABS SC-198
HABS SC,22-GEOTO,3-
4ph L

Middleton House
15 Cannon St.
HABS SC-314
HABS SC,22-GEOTO,10-
3ph/1pg L

Pawley,George,House
1019 Front St.
HABS SC-312
HABS SC,22-GEOTO,8-
6ph/4pg L

Police Department Building; see Market Building

Pyatt,John S. ,House
630 Highmarket St.
HABS SC-311
HABS SC,22-GEOTO,7-
7ph/4pg L

Winyah Indigo Society Hall
Prince & Cannon Sts.
HABS SC-199
HABS SC,22-GEOTO,4-
3ph L

Withers House
316 Screven St.
HABS SC-318
HABS SC,22-GEOTO,14-
6ph/3pg L

Withers House
622 Highmarket St.
HABS SC-315
HABS SC,22-GEOTO,11-
6ph/3pg L

Withers,Frances,House
202 Cannon St.
HABS SC-316
HABS SC,22-GEOTO,12-
6ph/4pg L

GEORGETOWN VIC.

Allston Planatation,Kitchen Bldg; see Chicora Wood Plantation,Kitchen Building

Allston Plantation; see Chicora Wood Plantation

Allston Plantation Cabin; see Chicora Wood Plantation,Cabin

Allston Plantation Laundry Bldg; see Chicora Wood Plantation,Laundry Building

Allston Plantation Rice Shipping House; see Chicora Wood Plantation,Rice Shipping House

Allston Plantation Rice Threshing Mill; see Chicora Wood Plantation,Rice Threshing Mill

Allston Plantation,Smokehouse; see Chicora Wood Plantation,Smokehouse

Annandale Plantation,Dependency
State Rts. 30 & 18 vic.
HABS SC-232-A
HABS SC,22-GEOTO.V,4A-
1ph L

Arcadia Plantation (Prospect Hill Plantation)
U. S. Hwy. 17 vic.
HABS SC-463
HABS SC,22-GEOTO.V,5-
13ph L

Arundel Plantation,Slave Cabin
Intersection of Rts. 701 & 4
HABS SC-631-A
HABS SC,22-GEOTO.V,11A-
17ph/1pg/1pc/4ct L

Beneventum Plantation
Rd. S-22-431
HABS SC-480
HABS SC,22-GEOTO.V,6-
4ph L

Chicora Wood Plantation (Mantazas; Allston Plantation)
County Rd. 52
HABS SC-482
HABS SC,22-GEOTO.V,7-
13ph/2pc L

Chicora Wood Plantation,Cabin (Mantazas Cabin; Allston Plantation Cabin)
County Rd. 52
HABS SC-482-F
HABS SC,22-GEOTO.V,7F-
1ph L

Chicora Wood Plantation,Kitchen Building (Mantazas,Kitchen Bldg; Allston Planatation,Kitchen Bldg)
County Rd. 52
HABS SC-482-A
HABS SC,22-GEOTO.V,7A-
1ph L

Chicora Wood Plantation,Laundry Building (Mantazas Laundry Bldg; Allston Plantation Laundry Bldg)
County Rd. 52
HABS SC-482-C
HABS SC,22-GEOTO.V,7C-
1ph L

Chicora Wood Plantation,Rice Shipping House (Mantazas Rice Shipping House; Allston Plantation Rice Shipping House)
County Rd. 52
HABS SC-482-E
HABS SC,22-GEOTO.V,7E-
1ph L

Chicora Wood Plantation,Rice Threshing Mill (Mantazas Rice Threshing Mill; Allston Plantation Rice Threshing Mill)
County Rd. 52
HABS SC-482-D
HABS SC,22-GEOTO.V,7D-
3ph L

Chicora Wood Plantation,Smokehouse (Mantazas,Smokehouse; Allston Plantation,Smokehouse)
County Rd. 52
HABS SC-482-B
HABS SC,22-GEOTO.V,7B-
1ph L

Dirleton Plantation
Rd. S-22-52 vic.
HABS SC-477
HABS SC,22-GEOTO.V10-
2ph/1pc L

Hopsewee Plantation (Hopsewee-on-the-Santee)
U.S. Rts. 17&701,Santee River,North
HABS SC-200
HABS SC,22-GEOTO.V,3-
9ph L

Hopsewee Plantation,Slave Quarters (Hopsewee-on-the-Santee)
U.S. Rts. 17&701,Santee River,North
HABS SC-200-A
HABS SC,22-GEOTO.V,3A-
8ph L

Hopsewee-on-the-Santee; see Hopsewee Plantation

Hopsewee-on-the-Santee; see Hopsewee Plantation,Slave Quarters

House
Annandale Plantation Vic.
HABS SC-232
HABS SC,22-GEOTO.V,4-
4ph L

Mansfield Plantation
U. S. Rt. 701 vic.
HABS SC-476
HABS SC,22-GEOTO.V,8-
4ph L

Mansfield Plantation,Rice Threshing Mill
U. S. Rt. 701 vic.
HABS SC-476-B
HABS SC,22-GEOTO.V,8B-
6ph L

Mansfield Plantation,Schoolhouse
U. S. Rt. 701 vic.
HABS SC-476-C
HABS SC,22-GEOTO.V,8C-
1ph L

Mansfield Plantation,Slave Quarters
U. S. Rt. 701 vic.
HABS SC-476-D
HABS SC,22-GEOTO.V,8D-
3ph L

Mansfield Plantation,Winnowing House
U. S. Rt. 701 vic.
HABS SC-476-A
HABS SC,22-GEOTO.V,8A-
1ph L

Mantazas; see Chicora Wood Plantation

Mantazas Cabin; see Chicora Wood Plantation,Cabin

Mantazas Laundry Bldg; see Chicora Wood Plantation,Laundry Building

Mantazas Rice Shipping House; see Chicora Wood Plantation,Rice Shipping House

Mantazas Rice Threshing Mill; see Chicora Wood Plantation,Rice Threshing Mill

Mantazas,Kitchen Bldg; see Chicora Wood Plantation,Kitchen Building

Mantazas,Smokehouse; see Chicora Wood Plantation,Smokehouse

Prospect Hill Plantation; see Arcadia Plantation

Silver Hill Plantation
Friendfield Estate,Sampit River
HABS SC-89
HABS SC,22-GEOTO.V,1-
2ph L

Silver Hill Plantation,Negro Baptist Church
Friendfield Estate
HABS SC-89-A
HABS SC,22-GEOTO.V,2-
2ph/1pg L

Wicklow Hall Plantation
State Rt. 30
HABS SC-478
HABS SC,22-GEOTO.V,9-
3ph L

Wicklow Hall Plantation,Barn
State Rt. 30
HABS SC-478-C
HABS SC,22-GEOTO.V,9C-
1ph L

Wicklow Hall Plantation,Carriage House
State Route 30
HABS SC-478-B
HABS SC,22-GEOTO.V,9B-
1ph L

Wicklow Hall Plantation,Kitchen Building
State Rt. 30
HABS SC-478-A
HABS SC,22-GEOTO.V,9A-
1ph L

Wicklow Hall Plantation,Playhouse
State Rt. 30
HABS SC-478-D
HABS SC,22-GEOTO.V,9D-
1ph L

Wicklow Hall Plantation,Servants' Quarters
State Rt. 30
HABS SC-478-E
HABS SC,22-GEOTO.V,9E-
1ph L

PLANTERSVILLE VIC.

Prince Frederick's Chapel (Ruins)
U. S. Rt. 52
HABS SC-464
HABS SC,22-PLANT.V,1-
3ph L

GREENVILLE COUNTY

GREENVILLE

Broad Margin
9 W Avondale Drive
HABS SC-597
HABS SC,23-GRENV,2-
28ph/2pg/2pc/3ct L

Christ Episcopal Church
N. Church St.
HABS SC-13-6
HABS SC,23-GRENV,1-
14dr/5ph/4pg L

Lanneau-Norwood House
417 Belmont Ave.
HABS SC-599
HABS SC,23-GRENV,3-
17ph/2pg/1pc L

Lanneau-Norwood House,Carriage House & Garage
417 Belmont Ave.
HABS SC-599-A
HABS SC,23-GRENV,3A-
1ph/1pc L

GREENVILLE VIC.

Paris Mountain State Park,Bathhouse
Paris Mountain State Park,off SC Rt. 253
HABS SC-598
HABS 1989(HABS):21
9ph/2pg/1pc/1ct L

Poinsett,Joel,House
HABS SC-183
HABS SC,23-GRENV.V,1-
1ph L

TIGERVILLE VIC.

Poinsett Bridge
SC Rt 42 2 mi. NW of Rt 11,2.5 mi. E of SC Rt 25
HAER SC-14
HAER SC,23-TIGVI.V,1-
18ph/2pg/1pc/5ct L

GREENWOOD COUNTY

GREENWOOD (VIC.)

Stony Point
NE corner of SC 246 & SC 39
HABS SC-600
HABS SC,24-GRENW.V,1-
13ph/2pg/1pc/4ct L

HAMPTON COUNTY

CROCKETVILLE VIC.

Cohasset
US 601, 1 mi. N of Crocketville
HABS SC-601
HABS SC,25-CROV.V,1-
10ph/1pg/1pc L

Cohasset,Tenant House
U.S. 601,approx. 1 mi. N. of Crocketville
HABS SC-601-A
HABS SC,25-CROV.V,1A-
1ph/1pc L

Crocketville Country Store
US 601 & Rt. 14
HABS SC-602-B
4ph/1pc L

Crocketville Country Store
US 601 & Rt. 38
HABS SC-602-A
HABS 1989(HABS):21
4ph/1pg/1pc L

MCPHERSONVILLE

Stoney Creek Presbyterian Church
1 block N of SC Rt 17
HABS SC-603
HABS SC,25-MCPHE,1-
8ph/1pg/1pc L

KERSHAW COUNTY

CAMDEN

Alexander,Elizabeth G. ,House
612 Laurens St.
HABS SC-330
HABS SC,28-CAMD,4-
1ph/1pg L

Bethesda Presbyterian Church
Dekalb & Market Sts.
HABS SC-331
HABS SC,28-CAMD,3-
5ph/1pg L

Bloomsbury (Chesnut,James,House)
1707 Lyttleton St.
HABS SC-332
HABS SC,28-CAMD,5-
3ph/1pg L

Bloomsbury,Outbuilding
(Chesnut,James,House,Outbuilding)
1707 Lyttleton St.
HABS SC-332-A
HABS SC,28-CAMD,5A-
1ph L

Chesnut,Gen. James,House; see Kamchatka

Chesnut,James,House; see Bloomsbury

Chesnut,James,House,Outbuilding; see Bloomsbury,Outbuilding

Davis,Bishop,House
Broad & Walnut Sts.
HABS SC-333
HABS SC,28-CAMD,6-
2ph L

Dekalb,Baron,Monument
N. Dekalb & Market Sts.
HABS SC-13-8
HABS SC,28-CAMD,1-
4dr/1ph/2pg/fr L

Douglas,James K. ,House
York St.
HABS SC-334
HABS SC,28-CAMD,7-
3ph L

First National Bank of Camden,The
(South Carolina National Bank)
Broad St.
HABS SC-626
HABS 1989(HABS):21
1ph/1pg/1pc L

Flake,Samuel,House; see Greenleaf Villa

Greenleaf Villa (Flake,Samuel,House)
1307 Broad St.
HABS SC-335
HABS SC,28-CAMD,8-
2ph/1pg L

Holly Hedge (Johnson,William E. ,House)
302 Greene St.
HABS SC-336
HABS SC,28-CAMD,9-
2ph L

Horsebranch Hall (McRae House)
Kirkwood Ln.
HABS SC-337
HABS SC,28-CAMD,10-
1ph L

Johnson,William E. ,House; see Holly Hedge

Kamchatka (Chesnut,Gen. James,House)
Kirkwood Ln.
HABS SC-338
HABS SC,28-CAMD,11-
5ph/1pg L

Kershaw County Courthouse (Masonic Hall)
Broad & King Sts.
HABS SC-13-9
HABS SC,28-CAMP,2-
10dr/3ph/3pg L

Masonic Hall; see Kershaw County Courthouse

Mathis,Samuel,House
(Team,Alberta,House)
1409 Broad St.
HABS SC-339
HABS SC,28-CAMD,12-
1ph L

McRae House; see Horsebranch Hall

Price,Fanny,House & Store
Broad & York Sts.
HABS SC-340
HABS SC,28-CAMD,13-
2ph/1pg L

Shannon,Charles John,House
1502 Broad St.
HABS SC-341
HABS SC,28-CAMD,14-
2ph/1pg L

South Carolina National Bank; see First National Bank of Camden,The

Team,Alberta,House; see Mathis,Samuel,House

Documentation: **ct** color transparencies **dr** measured drawings **fr** field records
pc photograph captions **pg** pages of text **ph** photographs

CAMDEN VIC.

Boykin,John,Plantation House; see Coolspring

Chesnut,James,Plantation House; see Mulberry

Coolspring (Boykin,John,Plantation House)
U. S. Rts. 521 & 601
HABS SC-342
HABS SC,28-CAMD.V,1-
3ph/1pg L

Mulberry (Chesnut,James,Plantation House)
U. S. Rt. 521
HABS SC-343
HABS SC,28-CAMD.V,2-
9ph L

LANCASTER COUNTY

LANCASTER

Lancaster & Chester Railway Building
512 S. Main St.
HABS SC-625
HABS 1989(HABS):21
3ph/1pc/2ct L

Lancaster County Courthouse
104 N Main St. at Dunlap St.
HABS SC-604
HABS SC,29-LANC,1-
13ph/1pg/1pc/3ct L

Lancaster County Jail
208 W Gay St.
HABS SC-605
HABS SC,29-LANC,2-
11ph/1pg/1pc L

LAURENS COUNTY

LAURENS

Holmes,Zelotes,House (Octagon House)
619 E. Main St.
HABS SC-376
HABS SC,30-LAUR,1-
9dr/26ph/9pg/3pc/5ct L

Octagon House; see Holmes,Zelotes,House

Owings,John Calvin,House
787 W Main St.
HABS SC-606
HABS SC,30-LAUR,2-
21ph/1pg/2pc/11ct L

Owings,John Calvin,House,Outbuildings
787 W. Main St.
HABS SC-606-A
HABS SC,30-LAUR,2A-
2ph/1pc L

MARLBORO COUNTY

BENNETTSVILLE

Courthouse (Entrance)
HABS SC-223
HABS SC,35-BENVI,1-
1ph L

Ruins
Adjoining Golf Club
HABS SC-224
HABS SC,35-BENVI,2-
1ph L

MCCORMICK COUNTY

PARKSVILLE VIC.

Calliham's Mill (Stone's Mill; Park's Mill; Prices's Gristmill)
SC Rt 138 on Stevens Creek,2 mi. east of Parksvill
HAER SC-15
HAER SC,33-PARVI.V,1-
16ph/1pg/1pc/7ct L

Park's Mill; see Calliham's Mill

Prices's Gristmill; see Calliham's Mill

Stone's Mill; see Calliham's Mill

OCONEE COUNTY

CLEMSON

de St. Julien,Paul,Plantation; see Hanover

Hanover (de St. Julien,Paul,Plantation)
Clemson Univ. Campus (moved from SC,Pinopolis Vic)
HABS SC-36
HABS SC,8-PINOP.V,12-
15dr/67ph/5pg/5pc/fr L

CLEMSON VIC.

Church,Old Stone; see Hopewell Meetinghouse

Hopewell Meetinghouse (Church,Old Stone)
Anderson-Seneca Rd. ,U. S. Rt. 76 Vic.
HABS SC-347
HABS SC,37-CLEM.V,1-
6ph/1pg L

OCONEE STATION

Fort of Indian Trading Station,Old; see Oconee Station

Oconee Station (Fort of Indian Trading Station,Old)
HABS SC-348
HABS SC,37-OCOST,1-
3ph/1pg L

Richards,William,House
Walhalla Vic.
HABS SC-349
HABS SC,37-OCOST,2-
7ph/1pg L

TAMASSEE VIC.

Sharpe,Elam,Jr. ,Plantation House; see Tamassee

Tamassee (Tomassee; Sharpe,Elam,Jr. ,Plantation House)
HABS SC-284
HABS SC,37-TAM.V,1-
3dr/6ph/1pg L

Tomassee; see Tamassee

WEST UNION

Strother,J. R. ,House
State Rts. 28 & 11 (Old Georgian Rd.)
HABS SC-351
HABS SC,37-UNIW,1-
6ph/3pg L

WESTMINSTER

Robinson,Galbraith,House (Robinson,Horseshoe,House)
Horseshoe Bridge Rd.
HABS SC-350
HABS SC,37-WESM,1-
3ph/1pg L

Robinson,Horseshoe,House; see Robinson,Galbraith,House

ORANGEBURG COUNTY

EUTAW SPRINGS VIC.

Belvidere (Sinkler,James,Plantation House)
HABS SC-21
HABS SC,38-EUTA.V,1-
2ph/1pg L

Eutaw
HABS SC-61
HABS SC,38-EUTA.V,6-
3ph L

Gaillard,Capt. Peter,Plantation House; see Rocks,The

Numertia Plantation House
HABS SC-32
HABS SC,38-EUTA.V,3-
1ph L

Pond Bluff (Simons,Keating,Plantation House)
HABS SC-59
HABS SC,38-EUTA.V,5-
6ph/2pg L

Pond Bluff,Outbuildings
HABS SC-60
HABS SC,38-EUTA.V,5A-,B-
3ph/1pg L

Rocks,The (Gaillard,Capt. Peter,Plantation House)
HABS SC-58
HABS SC,38-EUTA.V,4-
19ph/2pg L

Rocks,The,Servant's Quarters
HABS SC-58-A
HABS SC,38-EUTA.V,4A-
1ph L

Rocks,The,Smokehouse
HABS SC-58-B
HABS SC,38-EUTA.V,4B-
1ph/1pc L

Simons,Keating,Plantation House; see Pond Bluff

Sinkler,James,Plantation House; see Belvidere

Walworth Plantation House
State Rt. 6
HABS SC-31
HABS SC,38-EUTA.V,2-
1ph L

EUTAWVILLE

Church of the Epiphany
Intersection S-38-1132 & S-38-1133
HABS SC-608
HABS SC,38-EUTV,1-
9ph/1pg/1pc L

HOLLY HILL VIC.

Target United Methodist Church
HABS SC-609
HABS 1989(HABS):21
3ph/1pc L

ORANGEBURG

Claflin College,Lee Library
College Ave.
HABS SC-607
HABS SC,38-ORAN,1A-
17ph/1pg/1pc/5ct L

PICKENS COUNTY

CLEMSON

Fort Hill (McElhenny-Calhoun-Clemson House)
Clemson University Campus
HABS SC-344
HABS SC,39-CLEM,1-
12ph/4pg L

Fort Hill,Kitchen (McElhenny-Calhoun-Clemson House,Kitchen)
Clemson University Campus
HABS SC-344-B
HABS SC,39-CLEM,1B-
2ph/1pg L

Fort Hill,Office (McElhenny-Calhoun-Clemson House,Office)
Clemson University Campus
HABS SC-344-A
HABS SC,39-CLEM,1A-
1ph/1pg L

McElhenny-Calhoun-Clemson House; see Fort Hill

McElhenny-Calhoun-Clemson House,Kitchen; see Fort Hill,Kitchen

McElhenny-Calhoun-Clemson House,Office; see Fort Hill,Office

CLEMSON VIC.

Old Stone Church & Cemetery
Off US Rt 76
HABS SC-610
HABS SC,39-CLEM.V,1-
13ph/1pg/1pc L

GOWENSVILLE VIC.

Chapman's Bridge
Hwy. 414,Keonee-Toxaway State Park
HABS SC-391
HABS SC,39-GOW.V,1-
1dr/1pg L

NORRIS VIC.

Lower Gassaway Bridge
State Rt. 137,spanning Twelve Mile Creek
HABS SC-396
HABS SC,39-NOR,1-
4dr L

RICHLAND COUNTY

COLUMBIA

Allen University,Chapelle Administration Building
1530 Harden St.
HABS SC-397
HABS SC,40-COLUM,10A-
1ph/2pg L

Central National Bank (Sylvan Building)
Hampton & Main Sts.
HABS SC-255
HABS SC,40-COLUM,8-
3ph/4pg L

Columbia Canal & Power Plant
Waterfront on the Broad River
HAER SC-17
HAER SC,40-COLUM,18-
68ph/1pg/4pc/5ct L

Consolidated Building
1328 N Main St.
HABS SC-614
HABS SC,40-COLUM,15-
3ph/1pg/1pc/2ct L

Crawford-Clarkson House
Bull & Blanding Sts.
HABS SC-250
HABS SC,40-COLUM,4-
15ph/5pg L

DeBruhl-Marshall House
1401 Laurel St.
HABS SC-13-3
HABS SC,40-COLUM,1-
13dr/8ph/5pg L

Ensor-Keenan Barn & Carriage House
801 Wildwood Ave.
HABS SC-395-A
HABS SC,40-COLUM,11A-
2dr/4ph/1pg L

First Baptist Church
Hampton St.
HABS SC-251
HABS SC,40-COLUM,5-
6ph/4pg L

First Presbyterian Church
Marion & Lady Sts.
HABS SC-352
HABS SC,40-COLUM,12-
7ph/1pg L

Fisher-Bachman House
1615 Hampton St.
HABS SC-353
HABS SC,40-COLUM,13-
5ph/1pg L

Gervais Street Bridge
Gervais St. spanning Congaree River
HAER SC-16
HAER SC,40-COLUM,19-
12ph/1pg/1pc/2ct L

Greyhound Bus Station
1200 Blanding St.
HABS SC-612
HABS SC,40-COLUM,16-
8ph/1pg/1pc/7ct L

Hall,Ainsley,Mansion
Blanding St.
HABS SC-13-16
HABS SC,40-COLUM,3-
10dr/25ph/18pg L

Lunatic Asylum (South Carolina State Hospital,Mills Building)
Bull St. & Elmwood Ave.
HABS SC-253
HABS SC,40-COLUM,7-
19ph/9pg/1pc L

O'Neal,Richard Jr. ,House
1028 Elmwood Ave.
HABS SC-252
HABS SC,40-COLUM,6-
5ph/3pg L

Palmetto Bldg.
1400 Main St. at Washington St.
HABS SC-611
HABS SC,40-COLUM,17-
9ph/1pg/1pc/4ct L

South Carolina State Hospital,Mills Building; see Lunatic Asylum

South Carolina State House
Capitol Sq.
HABS SC-319
HABS SC,40-COLUM,9-
9ph/15pg L

South Caroliniana Library; see University of South Carolina,Library

Sylvan Building; see Central National Bank

Trinity Episcopal Church
Sumter & Gervais Sts.
HABS SC-355
HABS SC,40-COLUM,14-
2ph/1pg L

University of South Carolina,Library
(South Caroliniana Library)
S. Sumter St.
HABS SC-13-11
HABS SC,40-COLUM,2A-
12dr/10ph/3pg/fr L

University of South Carolina,President's House
Sumter St.
HABS SC-110
HABS SC,40-COLUM,2B-
2ph L

COLUMBIA VIC.

Hampton,Wade,Mansion (Ruins); see Millwood (Ruins)

Millwood (Ruins)
(Hampton,Wade,Mansion (Ruins))
U. S. Rt. 76 (Garners Ferry Rd.)
HABS SC-256
HABS SC,40-COLUM.V,1-
2ph/2pg L

EASTOVER VIC.

Kensington Plantation,Lanham Residence
U. S. Rt. 601
HABS SC-129-E
HABS SC,40-EAST.V,1E-
1pg L

Kensington Plantation,Main House
U. S. Rt. 601
HABS SC-129
HABS S,40-EAST.V,1-
1dr/3ph/9pg/fr L

Kensington Plantation,Plantation Store
U. S. Rt. 601
HABS SC-129-B
HABS SC,40-EAST.V,1B-
2dr/3ph/2pg/fr L

Kensington Plantation,Singleton,Cleland,Residence
U. S. Rt. 601
HABS SC-129-D
HABS SC,40-EAST.V,1D-
1pg L

Kensington Plantation,Singleton,Matthew,Residence
U. S. Rt. 601
HABS SC-129-C
HABS SC,40-EAST.V,1C-
4ph/3pg L

Kensington Plantation,Summer Kitchen
U. S. Rt. 601
HABS SC-129-A
HABS SC,40-EAST.V,1A-
2dr/3ph/2pg/fr L

EAU CLAIRE

Eau Claire Survey Publishing Company Building
3904 Monticello Rd. (Rt. 215) at Main St.
HABS SC-617-B
HABS 1990 (HABS):7
1ph/1pc L

SALUDA COUNTY

CHAPPLES FERRY VIC.

Saluda 1 Bridge
Spanning Saluda River on SC Rt. 39
HAER SC-21
HAER 1990 (HAER):12
7ph/10pg/1pc L

JONES CROSSROADS VIC

Saluda County Bridge No. 4
Rd. S-26 spanning Clouds Creek
HAER SC-9
HAER SC,41-JOCRO.V,1-
5ph/1pg/1pc L

SPARTANBURG COUNTY

Williams Place,Frame Barn
SC secondary Rd 113,3/4 m N of SC secondary Rd 235
HABS SC-615-C
HABS SC,42-GLENS,1C-
7ph/1pc/2ct L

EAU CLAIRE

Eau Claire Town Hall
3904 Monticello Rd. (Rt. 215 at Main St.)
HABS SC-617-A
HABS 1990 (HABS):7
6ph/1pg/1pc L

GAFFNEY

Cowpens Iron Furnace
1000 ft E of County Road 34 & Cherokee Creek Bridg
HAER SC-18
HAER SC,11-GAFF,1-
11ph/2pg/1pc/3ct L

GLENN SPRINGS

Williams Place, Kitchen
SC secondary Rd 113,3/4 mi N of SC sec Rd 235
HABS SC-615-B
HABS SC,42-GLENS,1B-
7ph/1pc/1ct L

Williams Place,Commissary
SC secondary Rd 113,3/4 m N of SC secondary Rd 235
HABS SC-615-H
HABS SC,42-GLENS,1H-
7ph/1pc L

Williams Place,Crib
SC secondary Rd 113,3/4 m N of SC secondary Rd 235
HABS SC-615-G
HABS SC,42-GLENS,1G-
7ph/1pc/1ct L

Williams Place,Double Log Barn
SC secondary Rd 113,3/4 m N of SC secondary Rd 235
HABS SC-615-D
HABS SC,42-GLENS,1D-
5ph/1pc L

Williams Place,Main House
SC Secondary Road 113, .75 mi. N of SC 235
HABS SC-615
HABS SC,42-GLENS,1-
19ph/1pg/1pc/4ct L

Williams Place,Smithy
SC secondary Rd 113,3/4 m N of SC secondary Rd 235
HABS SC-615-I
HABS SC,42-GLENS,1I-
2ph/1pc L

Williams Place,Smokehouse
SC secondary Rd 113,3/4 m N of SC secondary Rd 235
HABS SC-615-E
HABS SC,42-GLENS,1E-
7ph/1pc/1ct L

Williams Place,Still House/Barn
SC secondary Rd 113,3/4 m N of SC secondary Rd 235
HABS SC-615-F
HABS SC,42-GLENS,1F-
9ph/1pc/2ct L

Williams Place,Tenant House
SC secondary Rd 113,3/4 m N of SC secondary Rd 235
HABS SC-615-A
HABS SC,42-GLENS,1A-
14ph/1pc/2ct L

MOORE

Walnut Grove,Wheat House Cabin
Rt. 1,1 mi. E. of intersection US 221 & I-26
HABS SC-616-B
HABS SC,42-ROE,1B-
2ph/1pc L

MOORE VIC.

Price House (Price's Post Office)
Intersection of SC Rts. 199,200 & 86
HABS SC-624
HABS 1989(HABS):21
13ph/1pg/1pc L

Price's Post Office; see Price House

ROEBUCK

Walnut Grove
Rt 1, 1 mi. E of intersection US 221 & I-26
HABS SC-616
HABS SC,42-ROE,1-
16ph/1pg/1pc/6ct L

Walnut Grove,Academy
Rt. 1,1 mi. E. of intersection US 221 & I-26
HABS SC-616-C
HABS SC,42-ROE,1C-
3ph/1pc L

Walnut Grove,Kitchen
Rt. 1,1 mi. E. of intersection US 221 & I-26
HABS SC-616-D
HABS SC,42-ROE,1D-
1ph/1pc L

Walnut Grove,Outbuildings
Rt. 1,1 mi. E. of intersection US 221 & I-26
HABS SC-616-A
HABS SC,42-ROE,1A-
2ph/1pc L

SUMTER COUNTY

PINEWOOD VIC.

Manning,Gov. John Lawrence,Plantation; see Milford

Milford (Manning,Gov. John Lawrence,Plantation)
Wedgefield-Rimini Rd.
HABS SC-257
HABS SC,43-PINWO.V,1-
4dr/20ph/5pg/2ct L

Milford Plantation,Accessory Building
Wedgefield-Rimini Rd.
HABS SC-356
HABS SC,43-PINWO.V,1A-
2ph/2pg L

Milford Plantation,Entrance Gateway
Wedgefield-Rimini Rd.
HABS SC-357
HABS SC,43-PINWO.V,1B-
1ph/2pg L

Milford Plantation,Porter's Lodge
Wedgefield-Rimini Rd.
HABS SC-358
HABS SC,43-PINO.V,1C-
2ph/2pg L

Milford Plantation,Spring House
Wedgefield-Rimini Rd.
HABS SC-359
HABS SC,43-PINWO.V,1D-
1ph/2pg L

Milford Plantation,Stables
Wedgefield-Rimini Rd.
HABS SC-360
HABS SC,43-PINWO.V,1E-
1ph/3pg L

Milford Plantation,Water Tower
Wedgefield-Rimini Rd.
HABS SC-361
HABS SC,43-PINWO.V,1F-
1ph/2pg L

POINSETT STATE PARK

Ramsey House
HABS SC-238
HABS SC,43- ,3-
1ph L

STATEBURG

(2 photos in HABS/HAER); see Borough House,Dr. Anderson's Office

(3 photos in HABS/HAER); see Borough House,Dry Well Shelter

(3 photos in HABS/HAER); see Borough House,Weaving House

(4 photos in HABS/HAER); see Borough House,Kitchen-Storehouse

(4 photos in HABS/HAER); see Borough House,School

(42 photos in HABS/HAER); see Borough House

Anderson,Gen. ,Plantation House; see Oaks,The

Borough House (Hill Crest; (42 photos in HABS/HAER))
State Rt. 261 & Garners Ferry Rd.
HABS SC-362
HABS SC,43-STATBU,1-
48ph/4pg/4ct L H

Borough House School Road (Cabin)
HABS SC-244
HABS SC,43-STABU,2-
1ph L

Borough House,Chicken Brooder
State Rt. 261 & Garners Ferry Rd.
HABS SC-511
2ph H

Borough House,Cook's House
State Rt. 261 & Garners Ferry Rd.
HABS SC-369
3ph H

Borough House,Dependency
State Rt. 261 & Garners Ferry Rd.
HABS SC-363
HABS SC,43-STATBU,1A-
1ph L

Borough House,Dr. Anderson's Office
((2 photos in HABS/HAER))
State Rt. 261 & Garners Ferry Rd.
HABS SC-242
HABS SC,43-STATBU,1B-
4ph L H

Borough House,Dry Well Shelter ((3 photos in HABS/HAER))
State Rt. 261 & Garners Ferry Rd.
HABS SC-364
HABS SC,43-STATBU,1C-
4ph L H

Borough House,Hay Barn
State Rt. 261 & Garners Ferry Rd.
HABS SC-346
2ph H

Borough House,Hooper Tombs
State Rt. 261 & Garners Ferry Rd.
HABS SC-365
HABS SC,43-STATBU,1D-
1ph L

Borough House,Kitchen-Storehouse ((4 photos in HABS/HAER))
State Rt. 261 & Garners Ferry Rd.
HABS SC-366
HABS SC,43-STATBU,1E-
8ph L H

Borough House,Playhouse
State Rt. 261 & Garners Ferry Rd.
HABS SC-345
2ph H

Borough House,School ((4 photos in HABS/HAER))
State Rt. 261 & Garners Ferry Rd.
HABS SC-367
HABS SC,43-STATBU,1F-
6ph/1ct L H

Borough House,Weaving House ((3 photos in HABS/HAER))
State Rt. 261 & Garners Ferry Rd.
HABS SC-368
HABS SC,43-STATBU,1G-
4ph L H

Brookland Plantation House
Old Charleston Rd. (State Rt. 261)
HABS SC-243
HABS SC,43-STATBU.V,2-
1ph L

Carson Plantation House; see Homefield

Church of the Holy Cross,The
State Rte. 261
HABS SC-13-14
HABS SC,43-STATBU.V,1-
17dr/91ph/23pg/6pc/11ct/fr L

DeLage Chapel; see Sumter,Gen. Thomas,Tomb

High Hills Baptist Church
Kings Hwy. (State Rt. 261)
HABS SC-13-5
HABS SC,43- ,2-
9dr/3ph/2pg/fr L

Hill Crest; see Borough House

Documentation: **ct** color transparencies **dr** measured drawings **fr** field records
pc photograph captions **pg** pages of text **ph** photographs

Homefield (Carson Plantation House)
HABS SC-245
HABS SC,43-STATBU.V,3-
1ph L

Marshton Plantation House
Camden Rd.
HABS SC-246
HABS SC,43-STATBU.V,4-
1ph L

Needwood Plantation House
HABS SC-247
HABS SC,43-STATBU.V,5-
1ph L

Oaks,The (Anderson,Gen. ,Plantation House)
Stateburg-Wedgefield Rd.
HABS SC-248
HABS SC,43-STATBU.V,6-
1ph L

Ruins,The
Barnwell Dr.
HABS SC-549
27ph/fr H

Sumter,Gen. Thomas,Tomb (DeLage Chapel)
HABS SC-13-4
HABS SC,43- ,1-
6dr/3ph/2pg/fr L

SUMTER VIC.

Cabin
HABS SC-63
HABS SC,43-SUMT.V,1-
1ph L

WEDGEFIELD VIC.

Melrose (Singleton,Capt. Matthew,Plantation)
Kings Hwy. (State Rt. 261)
HABS SC-7
HABS SC,43-WEDG.V,1-
5dr/8ph/1pg/fr L

Singleton,Capt. Matthew,Plantation; see Melrose

UNION COUNTY

BUFFALO

Buffalo Cotton Textile Mill,Mill Office
S.C. Rt. 215
HAER SC-19-B
HAER SC,44-BUF,1B-
8ph/1pc/4ct L

Buffalo Cotton Textile Mill,Mill,Bldg.
SC Rt 215
HAER SC-19
HAER SC,44-BUF,1-
6ph/1pg/1pc/2ct L

Buffalo Cotton Textile Mill,Power Plant
S.C. Rt. 215
HAER SC-19-A
HAER SC,44-BUF,1A-
1ph/1pc L

Buffalo Cotton Textile Mill,Worker's House
S.C. Rt. 215
HAER SC-19-C
HAER SC,44-BUF,1C-
4ph/1pc L

Buffalo Cotton Textile Mill,Worker's House
S.C. Rt. 215
HAER SC-19-D
HAER SC,44-BUF,1D-
1ph/1pc L

UNION

Carnegie Free Library
300 E South St.
HABS SC-618
HABS SC,44-UNI,1-
12ph/1pg/1pc/6ct L

UNION VIC.

Gist,William H. ,House
U. S. Rt. 176
HABS SC-390
HABS SC,44-UNI.V,1-
7dr/4pg L

WILLIAMSBURG COUNTY

KINGSTREE

Nelson House
HABS SC-233
HABS SC,45-KING,1-
1ph L

Williamsburg County Courthouse
Main St.
HABS SC-234
HABS SC,45-KING,2-
1ph L

NESMITH VIC.

Baptist Black Mingo Church,The; see Black Mingo Baptist Church

Belin Church; see Black Mingo Baptist Church

Black Mingo Baptist Church (Belin Church; Baptist Black Mingo Church,The)
S. C. Secondary Rd. 162
HABS SC-392
HABS SC,45-NESM.V,1-
8dr/12ph/9pg/fr L

YORK COUNTY

CLOVER VIC.

Hawthorne House
Catawba River
HABS SC-193
HABS SC,46- ,2-
8dr/9ph L

Houser,Henry, House (Kings Mountain National Military Park)
HABS SC-15
HABS SC,11- ,1-
7dr/3ph/fr L

Kings Mountain National Military Park; see Houser,Henry, House

ROCK HILL

Winthrop College, Withers Bldg.
Oakland Ave.
HABS SC-619-A
HABS SC,46-ROHI,1A-
15ph/1pg/1pc/1ct L

Winthrop College,Tillman Building (Winthrop Normal & Industrial College)
Winthrop College Campus
HABS SC-619-B
HABS SC,46-ROHI,1B-
15ph/1pg/1pc/3ct L

Winthrop Normal & Industrial College; see Winthrop College,Tillman Building

YORK VIC.

McElwee,William,House
Kings Mountain Recreational Area
HABS SC-11
HABS SC,46- ,1-
7dr/7ph/10pg/fr L

Oahe Congregational Mission, Rigg's Ranch, Pierre, Hughes County, South Dakota. East elevation. Photograph by John A. Bryan, July 9, 1952 (HABS SD,33-PIER.V,1-2).

Old Blacksmith Shop, Fort Bennett, Pierre vicinity, Hughes County, South Dakota. Northeast perspective. Photograph by John A. Bryan, July 8, 1952 (HABS SD,1-PIER.V, 1A-1).

South Dakota

BEADLE COUNTY

HURON

55 Fifth Street SW (House)
Block 15,Lots 15 & 16
HABS SD-19
HABS SD,3-HURO,1-
5ph/1pg/1pc L

73 Fifth Street SW (House)
Block 15,Lots 18 & 19
HABS SD-18
HABS SD,3-HURO,2-
4ph/1pg/1pc L

BON HOMME COUNTY

TABOR

Bon Homme Mill
Gavins Point Reservoir Vic.
HABS SD-6
HABS SD,5-TABOR,1-
4dr/9ph/1pg L

CLAY COUNTY

VERMILLION

(University of South Dakota,Alumni House); see Inman House

Austin-Whittemore House (Clay County Historic Society)
15 Austin St.
HABS SD-12
HABS SD,14-VERM,1-
8ph/2pg/1pc/2ct L

Clay County Historic Society; see Austin-Whittemore House

Inman House ((University of South Dakota,Alumni House))
415 E. Main St.
HABS SD-13
HABS SD,14-VERM,2-
2ph/2pg/1pc L

University of South Dakota,Old Main; see University of South Dakota,University Hall

University of South Dakota,University Hall (University of South Dakota,Old Main)
HABS SD-11
HABS SD,14-VERM,3-
11ph/2pg/1pc/4ct L

CUSTER COUNTY

CUSTER VIC.

Administration & Operator's Building; see Wind Cave National Park,Visitors Center

Wind Cave National Park,Visitors Center (Administration & Operator's Building)
U. S. Rt. 385 Vic.
HABS SD-9
HABS SD,17-CUST.V,1-
28ph/2pc L

DEWEY COUNTY

CHEYENNE RIVER AGCY.

St. John's Episcopal Mission,Chapel & Rectory
Fort Bennett Vic.
HABS SD-5
HABS SD,21- ,1-
9dr/11ph/1pg L

GREGORY COUNTY

PICKSTON VIC.

Fort Randall Church,Old
Right Bank,Missouri River
HABS SD-4
HABS SD,27- ,1-
11dr/33ph/14pg/fr L

HUGHES COUNTY

PIERRE VIC.

Fort Bennett,Blacksmith Shop & Barracks,Old
Fort Bennett
HABS SD-8
HABS SD,1-PIER.V,1-
1dr/6ph/1pg L

Oahe Congregational Mission
Oahe Reservior Vic.
HABS SD-7
HABS SD,33-PIER.V,1-
3dr/3ph/1pg L

MINNEHAHA COUNTY

SIOUX FALLS

Sioux Falls V.A. Medical & Regional Office Center
2501 West 22nd
HABS SD-20
HABS SD,50-SIOFA,1-
14ph/7pg/1pc L

PENNINGTON COUNTY

RAPID CITY

Main Street District
614-632 Main St.
HABS SD-10
HABS SD,52-RACI,1-
13ph/10pg/1pc L

WALL VIC.

Ellsworth A.F.B.,Delta Flight Launch Control Ctr. (Minuteman II ICBM)
See MEADE COUNTY,RAPID CITY VIC. for documentation
HAER SD-3
L

Ellsworth Air Force Base,Delta Flight Launch Fac. (Minuteman II ICBM)
See MEADE COUNTY,RAPID CITY VIC. for documentation
HAER SD-4
L

Minuteman II ICBM; see Ellsworth A.F.B.,Delta Flight Launch Control Ctr.

Minuteman II ICBM; see Ellsworth Air Force Base,Delta Flight Launch Fac.

ROBERTS COUNTY

(FORT) SISSETON

Fort Sisseton,Commandant's Quarters
HABS SD-1
HABS SD,55-SIST,1A-
1ph/1pg L

Fort Sisseton,North Barracks
HABS SD-2
HABS SD,55-SIST,1B-
1ph/1pg L

Fort Sisseton,Powder Magazine
HABS SD-3
HABS SD,55-SIST,1C-
1ph/1pg L

UNION COUNTY

ELK POINT

Union County Courthouse
Courthouse Square
HABS SD-17
HABS SD,64-ELPO,1-
32ph/2pc/9ct L

SIOUX CITY

Sioux City Bridge
Spanning Missouri River
HAER SD-1
HAER SD,64-SIOCI,1-
4ph/1pc L

YANKTON COUNTY

YANKTON

Gurney Seed Plant
Second & Capitol Sts.
HABS SD-15
HABS SD,68-YANK,1-
3ph/1pc L

Yankton College,Conservatory
HABS SD-14
HABS SD,68-YANK,2-
2ph/3pg/1pc/4ct L

First Presbyterian Church (Downtown Presbyterian Church), Nashville, Davidson County, Tennessee. Interior, detail of south wall. Photograph by Jack E. Boucher, August 1970 (HABS TENN,19-NASH,13-7)

Tennessee

ANDERSON COUNTY

LAKE CITY

Crosby,Caleb,Threshing Barn
Norris Dam State Park (moved from Morristown Vic.)
HABS TN-159-A
HABS TENN,32-NOET,1A-
15dr/36ph/3pc/fr L

NORRIS VIC.

Massengill Bridge
Coal Creek Rd. ,spanning Clinch River
HAER TN-2
HAER TENN,1-NOR.V,1-
17ph/9pg L

BEDFORD COUNTY

UNIONVILLE VIC.

Moore Road Bridge
Spannning North Fork Creek at Moore Rd.
HAER TN-3
HAER TENN,2-UNI.V,1-
10ph/8pg L

BLOUNT COUNTY

CADES COVE

Forge Creek Dam; see Forge Creek Dam-John Cable Mill

Forge Creek Dam-John Cable Mill (Forge Creek Dam; Great Smoky Mountains National Park)
HABS TN-118
HABS TENN,5-CADCO,1-
3dr/26ph/3pg/3pc/fr L

Garland,Townsend,Corn Crib (Great Smoky Mountains National Park)
Vicinity of Rich Mountain Rd.
HABS TN-119
HABS TENN,5-CADCO,2A-
2dr L

Great Smoky Mountains National Park; see Forge Creek Dam-John Cable Mill

Great Smoky Mountains National Park; see Garland,Townsend,Corn Crib

Great Smoky Mountains National Park; see Shields,Witt,Barn

Shields,Witt,Barn (Great Smoky Mountains National Park)
HABS TN-160
HABS TENN,5-CADCO,3A-
5dr/23ph/fr L

CADES COVE VIC.

Great Smoky Mountains National Park; see Whitehead,Henry,Place

Great Smoky Mountains National Park; see Whitehead,Henry,Place,Smokehouse

Whitehead,Henry,Place (Great Smoky Mountains National Park)
HABS TN-161
HABS TENN,5-CADCO.V,1-
11dr/11ph/4pg/fr L

Whitehead,Henry,Place,Smokehouse (Great Smoky Mountains National Park)
HABS TN-162
HABS TENN,5-CADCO.V,1A-
2dr/4ph/1pg/fr L

CADES GROVE

Cable,Becky,House (Great Smoky Mountains National Park)
HABS TN-247
HABS DLC/PP-1992:TN-5
2ph/1pc L

Great Smoky Mountains National Park; see Cable,Becky,House

Great Smoky Mountains National Park; see Oliver,John,Cabin

Oliver,John,Cabin (Great Smoky Mountains National Park)
HABS TN-248
HABS DLC/PP-1992:TN-5
3ph/1pc L

BRADLEY COUNTY

CLEVELAND

Hughes,W. J. ,Business House (Wilson,C. J. ,Clothing Store)
3202 Ocoee St.
HABS TN-204
HABS TENN,6-CLEVE,1-
2dr/5ph/7pg/fr L

Wilson,C. J. ,Clothing Store; see Hughes,W. J. ,Business House

EUREKA

McPherson Bridge
Spanning Candies Creek at County Rd. A165
HAER TN-4
HAER TENN,6-EURK.V,1-
11ph/4pg L

CARTER COUNTY

ELIZABETHTON

Carter,John & Landon,House
E. Broad St.
HABS TN-231
HABS TENN,10-ELIZ,1-
9dr L

Elizabethton Covered Bridge
Hattie Ave.
HABS TN-224
HABS TENN,10-ELIZ,2-
5ph L

ELIZABETHTON VIC.

Taylor,Gen. Nathaniel,House
State Hwy. 67
HABS TN-94
HABS TENN,10-ELIZ.V,1-
3ph/2pg L

CLAIBORNE COUNTY

HARROGATE

Huff,Daniel,Mill
Lincoln Memorial University
HABS TN-195
HABS TENN,13-HARRO,1-
1dr/5ph/fr L

COCKE COUNTY

COSBY VIC.

Great Smoky Mountains National Park; see Jenkins,Chandler,Cabin

Jenkins,Chandler,Cabin (Great Smoky Mountains National Park)
Indian Camp Rd.
HABS TN-120
HABS TENN,15-CROSBY.V,1-
2dr L

DAVIDSON COUNTY

ANTIOCH

Hays-Kiser House; see Hays,Charles,House

Hays,Charles,House (Hays-Kiser House)
834 Reeves Rd.
HABS TN-65
HABS TENN,19-ANT,1-
9ph/4pg L

DONELSON

McGavock House (Two Rivers Plantation)
3130 McGavock Pike
HABS TN-15
HABS TENN,19-DONEL,1-
10dr/10ph/8pg/fr L

Two Rivers Plantation; see McGavock House

DONELSON VIC.

Blue Brick,Old
Stewart's Ferry Pike
HABS TN-129
HABS TENN,19-DONEL.V,1-
3ph/1pg L

Ridley,James,House
Stewart Ferry Rd.
HABS TN-140
HABS TENN,19-DONEL.V,2-
5ph/1pg L

HERMITAGE

Hermitage,The (Jackson,Andrew,House)
U.S. Hwy. 70N
HABS TN-52
HABS TENN,19-NASH.V,1-
7dr/68ph/4pg/1ct L

Jackson,Andrew,House; see Hermitage,The

Tulip Grove
HABS TN-127
HABS TENN,19-NASH.V,3-
5ph/2pg L

HERMITAGE VIC.

Cleveland Hall
HABS TN-130
HABS TENN,19-NASH.V,5-
4ph/1pg L

Hermitage Church
HABS TN-136
HABS TENN,19-NASH.V,2-
3ph/1pg L

NASHVILLE

Acklen,Col. J. A. S. ,House; see Belmont

Belmont (Acklen,Col. J. A. S. ,House; Belmont College,Acklen Hall)
Belmont Blvd. & Wedgewood
HABS TN-56
HABS TENN,19-NASH,2-
24ph/15pg/1pc L

Belmont College,Acklen Hall; see Belmont

Belmont,Gazebos
Belmont Blvd. & Wedgewood
HABS TN-56-A
HABS TENN,19-NASH,2A-,C-,D-
4ph L

Belmont,Water Tower
Belmont Blvd. & Wedgewood
HABS TN-56-B
HABS TENN,19-NASH,2B-
1ph L

Children's Museum; see University of Nashville,Literary Department Bldg.

Davidson County Courthouse & Public Building
Public Square
HABS TN-168
HABS TENN,19-NASH,21-
35ph/5pg/1pc/fr L

Downtown Presbyterian Church; see First Presbyterian Church

Fine Arts Building; see Vanderbilt University,Gymnasium

First Baptist Church
Seventh & Broadway
HABS TN-42
HABS TENN,19-NASH,16-
1ph L

First Presbyterian Church (Downtown Presbyterian Church)
154 Fifth Ave.
HABS TN-17
HABS TENN,19-NASH,13-
2dr/8ph/11pg/1pc/fr L

Fisk University,Jubilee Hall
Seventeenth Ave. ,North
HABS TN-19
HABS TENN,19-NASH,7A-
20ph/10pg/2pc L

Grand Ole Opry House; see Union Gospel Tabernacle

Heiman,Adolphus,House
900 Jefferson St. ,NW
HABS TN-25
HABS TENN,19-NASH,4-
4ph/6pg L

Holy Trinity Episcopal Church
615 Sixth Ave. ,South
HABS TN-135
HABS TENN,19-NASH,3-
9dr/8ph/8pg/1pc/fr L

Morgan-Reeves Building (Morgan,S. S. , & Co. Building; Reeves Building)
208-210 Public Square
HABS TN-16
HABS TENN,19-NASH,9-
3dr/3ph/7pg/fr L

Morgan,S. S. , & Co. Building; see Morgan-Reeves Building

Overton,Judge John,House; see Traveller's Rest

Public Arcade
Fourth & Fifth Sts.
HABS TN-24
HABS TENN,19-NASH,17-
1ph/1pg L

Public Square Commercial Area
212,214,216 Public Sq.
HABS TN-57
HABS TENN,19-NASH,12-
7ph/1pg/1pc L

Reeves Building; see Morgan-Reeves Building

Riverwood
HABS TN-128
HABS TENN,19-NASH.V,4-
2ph/1pg L

Ryman Auditorium; see Union Gospel Tabernacle

Second Avenue North,Commercial District
Second Ave. North btw. Broadway & Church Sts.
HABS TN-20
HABS TENN,19-NASH,14-
26ph/7pg L

St. Mary's Cathedral (St. Mary's Church)
328 Fifth Ave. ,North
HABS TN-13
HABS TENN,19-NASH,8-
6dr/5ph/14pg/fr L

St. Mary's Church; see St. Mary's Cathedral

State Capitol
State Capitol Blvd. & Cedar St.
HABS TN-51
HABS TENN,19-NASH,1-
23dr/12ph/3pg/1pc/fr L

Tennessee Maufacturing Company Buildings (Werthan Bag Corporation)
HABS TN-22
HABS TENN,19-NASH,18-
3ph/1pg L

Tennessee State Penitentiary,Main Prison
West End,Centennial Ave.
HABS TN-33
HABS TENN,19-NASH,10-
8ph/10pg L

Traveller's Rest (Overton,Judge John,House)
Farrell Pky.
HABS TN-14
HABS TENN,19-NASH,11-
11ph/9pg/fr L

Union Gospel Tabernacle (Ryman Auditorium; Grand Ole Opry House)
116 Fifth Ave., North
HABS TN-23
HABS TENN,19-NASH,20-
33ph/10pg/4ct L

Union Station
1001 Broadway
HABS TN-21
HABS TENN,19-NASH,19-
18ph/18pg L

University of Nashville,Literary Department Bldg. (Children's Museum)
724 Second Ave. ,North
HABS TN-18
HABS TENN,19-NASH,15A-
6dr/4ph/11pg/fr L

Vanderbilt University,Gymnasium
(Fine Arts Building)
Twenty-third Ave. ,South & West End Blvd.
HABS TN-11
HABS TENN,19-NASH,5A-
9dr/6ph/12pg/fr L

Vanderbilt University,West Side Row
West End Ave. & Twenty-fourth Ave. ,South
HABS TN-34
HABS TENN,19-NASH,5-
7ph/5pg L

Werthan Bag Corporation; see
Tennessee Maufacturing Company Buildings

Windsor
HABS TN-133
HABS TENN,19-NASH.V,8-
3ph/1pg L

Worker's House
1724 N. Jefferson St.
HABS TN-26
HABS TENN,19-NASH,6-
2ph/3pg L

NASHVILLE VIC.

Belair
HABS TN-134
HABS TENN,19-NASH.V,9-
9ph/1pg L

Belle Meade
HABS TN-132
HABS TENN,19-NASH.V,6-
10ph/3pg L

Harding,John,Cabin-Belle Meade Estate
HABS TN-139
HABS TENN,19-NASH.V,7-
3ph L

Newsom's Mill Bridge
Spanning Harpeth River,Newsom's Station Rd.
HAER TN-15
HAER TENN,19-NASH.V,11-
13ph/8pg/1pc L

Spence House
Lebanon Pike
HABS TN-138
HABS TENN,19-NASH.V,10-
1ph/1pg L

DYER COUNTY

LENOX VIC.

Lenox Bridge
Spanning Obion River,Rural Rd. S8025
HAER TN-16
HAER TENN,23-LEN.V,1-
20ph/3pg/2pc L

FAYETTE COUNTY

LA GRANGE

Hancock Hall
Third St. (Hwy. 57)
HABS TN-174
HABS TENN,24-LAGRA,1-
8dr/9ph/8pg/fr L

Hancock Hall,Smokehouse
Third St. (Hwy. 57)
HABS TN-174-A
HABS TENN,24-LAGRA,1A-
2ph L

Hancock Hall,Storage Shed
Third St. (Hwy. 57)
HABS TN-174-B
HABS TENN,24-LAGRA,1B-
1ph L

Immanuel Episcopal Church
Second St.
HABS TN-173
HABS TENN,24-LAGRA,2-
7dr/12ph/8pg/fr L

FRANKLIN COUNTY

DECHARD

Boulevard Bridge
Spanning Wagner Creek at Old Dechard-Winchester Rd
HAER TN-17
HAER TENN,26-DECH,1-
12ph/8pg/1pc L

WINCHESTER

Hundred Oaks
Oak St. near U. S. Rt. 64
HABS TN-221
HABS TENN,26-WIN,1-
21ph/14pg L

GIBSON COUNTY

MILAN

Milan Army Ammunition Plant
HAER TN-9
HAER TENN,27-MILAN,1-
54pg/fr L

GREENE COUNTY

CHUCKEY VIC.

Earnest House
HABS TN-143
HABS TENN,30-CHUCK.V,1-
3ph/2pg L

Earnest Log House
HABS TN-144
HABS TENN,30-CHUCK.V,2-
1ph/2pg L

GREENEVILLE

Brown-Milligan House
Brown's Hill
HABS TN-145
HABS TENN,30-GRENV,2-
2ph/2pg L

Cumberland Presbyterian Church
N. Main & W. Church Sts.
HABS TN-146
HABS TENN,30-GRENV,3-
1ph/2pg L

Davis House
Maple Ave.
HABS TN-147
HABS TENN,30-GRENV,4-
2ph/2pg L

Dickson-Williams Mansion
N. Irish & W. Church Sts.
HABS TN-148
HABS TENN,30-GRENV,5-
4ph/2pg L

First Presbyterian Church
N. Main St.
HABS TN-149
HABS TENN,30-GRENV,6-
1ph/2pg L

Johnson,Andrew,First House; see
Kerbaugh

Johnson,Andrew,Homestead; see
Johnson,Andrew,House

Johnson,Andrew,House
(Johnson,Andrew,Homestead)
217 S. Main St.
HABS TN-142
HABS TENN,30-GRENV,1-
ιDLC/PP-1992:NM-4°
14dr/25ph/3pc/fr L

Kerbaugh (Johnson,Andrew,First House)
Depot & College Sts.
HABS TN-227
HABS TENN,30-GRENV,12-
ιDLC/PP-1992:TN-4°
6dr/18ph/1pc/fr L

Law Office
McKee & S. Irish Sts.
HABS TN-150
HABS TENN,30-GRENV,7-
1ph/2pg L

Locations: **H** HABS/HAER, National Park Service **L** Library of Congress

Rumbough-Doughty House
215 S. Irish St.
HABS TN-151
HABS TENN,30-GRENV,8-
1ph/2pg L

Sevier-Coles House
214 N. Main St.
HABS TN-153
HABS TENN,30-GRENV,10-
4ph/2pg L

Sevier-Coles House,Outbuildings
214 N. Main St.
HABS TN-153-A
HABS TENN,30-GRENV,10A-
1ph L

Sevier-Johnson-Susong-House
S. Main St.
HABS TN-154
HABS TENN,30-GRENV,11-
2ph/2pg L

St. James Episcopal Church
W. Church St.
HABS TN-152
HABS TENN,30-GRENV,9-
3ph/2pg L

GREENEVILLE VIC.

Reaves-Crislip House
HABS TN-155
HABS TENN,30-GRENV.V,1-
1ph/2pg L

TUSCULUM

Doak House
HABS TN-156
HABS TENN,30-TUSC,1-
3ph/2pg L

Doak House,Springhouse
State Rt. 107, Greeneville Vic.
HABS TN-156-A
HABS TENN,30-TUSC,1A-
1ph/1pc L

Old College; see Tusculum College

Tusculum College (Old College)
State Rt. 107,Greeneville Vic.
HABS TN-157
HABS TENN,30-TUSC,2A-
1ph/2pg L

Tusculum College,McCormick Hall
State Rt. 107,Greeneville Vic.
HABS TN-196
HABS TENN,30-TUSC,2B-
4dr/7ph/1pc/fr L

Tusculum College,Virginia Hall
State Rt. 107,Greenville Vic.
HABS TN-46
HABS TENN,30-TUSC,2C-
7ph/1pc L

GRUNDY COUNTY

BEERSHEBA SPRINGS

Armfield House; see Beersheba Inn,Old,Armfield House (Cottage)

Bass House; see Beersheba Inn,Old,Bass House (Cottage)

Beersheba Inn,Old (Beersheba Springs Hotel)
Armfield Ave.
HABS TN-54
HABS TENN,31-BERSP,1-
7dr/21ph/5pg/fr L

Beersheba Inn,Old,Armfield House (Cottage) (Beersheba Springs Hotel,Armfield House; Armfield House)
Armfield Ave.
HABS TN-54-K
HABS TENN,31-BERSP,9-
9ph/1pc L

Beersheba Inn,Old,Bass House (Cottage) (Beersheba Springs Hotel,Bass House; Bass House)
Armfield Ave.
HABS TN-54-J
HABS TENN,31-BERSP,8-
11ph/1pc L

Beersheba Inn,Old,Brick Row (Boarding Cabin) (Beersheba Springs Hotel,Brick Row)
Armfield Ave.
HABS TN-54-B
HABS TENN,31-BERSP,1B-
1ph L

Beersheba Inn,Old,Cross Row (Boarding Cabin) (Beersheba Springs Hotel,Cross Row)
Armsfield Ave.
HABS TN-54-C
HABS TENN,31-BERSP,1C-
4ph L

Beersheba Inn,Old,Dahlgren House (Cottage) (Beersheba Springs Hotel,Dahlgren House; Dahlgren House)
Armfield Ave.
HABS TN-54-F
HABS TENN,31-BERSP,4-
8ph/1pc L

Beersheba Inn,Old,Family Row (Boarding Cabin) (Beersheba Springs Hotel,Family Row)
Armfield Ave.
HABS TN-54-A
HABS TENN,31-BERSP,1A-
1ph L

Beersheba Inn,Old,Harding House (Cottage) (Beersheba Springs Hotel,Harding House; Harding House)
Armfield Ave.
HABS TN-54-I
HABS TENN,31-BERSP,7-
9ph/1pc L

Beersheba Inn,Old,Murfree House (Cottage) (Beersheba Springs Hotel,Murfree House; Murfree House)
Armfield Ave.
HABS TN-54-E
HABS TENN,31-BERSP,3-
9ph/1pc L

Beersheba Inn,Old,Northcut Store-Burch House (Beersheba Springs Hotel,Northcut Store-Burch House Northcut Store-Burch House)
Armfield Ave.
HABS TN-54-G
HABS TENN,31-BERSP,5-
4ph/1pc L

Beersheba Inn,Old,Otey House (Cottage) (Beersheba Springs Hotel,Otey House; Otey House)
Armfield Ave.
HABS TN-54-H
HABS TENN,31-BERSP,6-
4ph/1pc L

Beersheba Inn,Old,Polk House (Cottage) (Beersheba Springs Hotel,Polk House & Slave Quarter Polk House & Slave Quarters)
Armfield Ave.
HABS TN-54-D
HABS TENN,31-BERSP,2-
10ph/1pc L

Beersheba Springs Hotel; see Beersheba Inn,Old

Beersheba Springs Hotel,Armfield House; see Beersheba Inn,Old,Armfield House (Cottage)

Beersheba Springs Hotel,Bass House; see Beersheba Inn,Old,Bass House (Cottage)

Beersheba Springs Hotel,Brick Row; see Beersheba Inn,Old,Brick Row (Boarding Cabin)

Beersheba Springs Hotel,Cross Row; see Beersheba Inn,Old,Cross Row (Boarding Cabin)

Beersheba Springs Hotel,Dahlgren House; see Beersheba Inn,Old,Dahlgren House (Cottage)

Beersheba Springs Hotel,Family Row; see Beersheba Inn,Old,Family Row (Boarding Cabin)

Beersheba Springs Hotel,Harding House; see Beersheba Inn,Old,Harding House (Cottage)

Beersheba Springs Hotel,Murfree House; see Beersheba Inn,Old,Murfree House (Cottage)

Beersheba Springs Hotel,Northcut Store-Burch House; see Beersheba Inn,Old,Northcut Store-Burch House

Beersheba Springs Hotel,Otey House; see Beersheba Inn,Old,Otey House (Cottage)

Beersheba Springs Hotel,Polk House & Slave Quarter; see Beersheba Inn,Old,Polk House (Cottage)

Dahlgren House; see Beersheba Inn,Old,Dahlgren House (Cottage)

Harding House; see Beersheba Inn,Old,Harding House (Cottage)

Murfree House; see Beersheba Inn,Old,Murfree House (Cottage)

Northcut Store-Burch House; see Beersheba Inn,Old,Northcut Store-Burch House

Otey House; see Beersheba Inn,Old,Otey House (Cottage)

Polk House & Slave Quarters; see Beersheba Inn,Old,Polk House (Cottage)

HAMBLEN COUNTY

MORRISTOWN

Deadrick-Taylor House (Taylor,Frank W. ,House)
U. S. Hwy. 11-E
HABS TN-97
HABS TENN,32-MORTO.V,1-
5ph/4pg L

Taylor,Frank W. ,House; see Deadrick-Taylor House

MORRISTOWN VIC.

Crosby,Caleb,Farm Complex
Noeton
HABS TN-159
HABS TENN,32-NOET,1-
1dr L

Crosby,Caleb,Threshing Barn
Noeton (moved to Norris Dam State Park,Lake City)
HABS TN-159-A
HABS TENN,32-NOET,1A-
15dr/36ph/3pc/fr L

Rural Mount
State Rt. 160 vic.
HABS TN-203
HABS TENN,32-MORTO.V,2-
6dr/12ph/12pg/fr L

HAMILTON COUNTY

CHATTANOOGA

Brown Furniture Co. Warehouse; see Trigg,Dobbs & Co. Warehouse

Customs House & Post Office
Eleventh St.
HABS TN-30
HABS TENN,31-CHAT,1-
9ph L

Dome Building; see Times Building,The

Etheridge,D. S. ,Automobile Showroom & Tire Store
329 Market St.
HABS TN-206
HABS TENN,33-CHAT,2-
7ph/4pg L

First Presbyterian Church
McCallis Ave. & Douglas St.
HABS TN-28
HABS TENN,33-CHAT,4-
15ph L

Fort Wood Historic District (Knox House; White House)
841 Clark St.
HABS TN-238-A
HABS TENN,33-CHAT,9A-
1ph/2pg L

Fort Wood Historic District (Schroyer House; Secor House)
843 Clark St.
HABS TN-238-B
HABS TENN,33-CHAT,9B-
1ph/2pg L

Hixon,William House
Burnt Mill Rd. ,Rt. 8
HABS TN-245
HABS TENN,33-CHAT,13-
6ph/2pg/1pc L

Knox House; see Fort Wood Historic District

Orange Grove Housing for Industrial Workers
1031,1201-1209 E. Thirteenth St.
HABS TN-205
HABS TENN,33-CHAT,10-
2dr/6pg/fr L

Schroyer House; see Fort Wood Historic District

Secor House; see Fort Wood Historic District

Times Building,The (Dome Building)
Georgia Ave. & E. Eighth St.
HABS TN-199
HABS TENN,33-CHAT,5-
4dr/5ph/fr L

Tivoli Theater
709-713 Broad St.
HABS TN-207
HABS TENN,33-CHAT,8-
10ph/11pg/fr L

Trigg,Dobbs & Co. Warehouse (Brown Furniture Co. Warehouse)
1152 Market St.
HABS TN-229
HABS TENN,33-CHAT,3-
8ph/8pg/fr L

U. S. Post Office & Courthouse
Georgia Ave.
HABS TN-29
HABS TENN,33-CHAT,6-
18ph L

Union Depot
W. Ninth St. ,btwn. Chestnut & Broad Sts.
HABS TN-233
HABS TENN,33-CHAT,7-
3pg L

Volunteer Army Ammunition Plant
HAER TN-8
HAER TENN,33-CHAT,12-
53pg/fr L

Walnut Street Bridge
Spanning Tennessee River at Market St.
HAER TN-11
HAER TENN,33-CHAT,14-
38pg/fr L

Warner,Joseph H. ,Home
800 Vine St.
HABS TN-208
HABS TENN,33-CHAT,11-
11ph/8pg L

White House; see Fort Wood Historic District

HARDEMAN COUNTY

BOLIVAR

McNeal,Col. ,House
Union & Bills Sts.
HABS TN-10
HABS TENN,35-BOL,1-
16dr/19ph/11pg/fr L

HARDIN COUNTY

HOHENWALD VIC.

Log Cabin,Early (Meriwether Lewis National Monument Hwy. 48)
HABS TN-158
HABS TENN,36- ,1-
4ph L

Meriwether Lewis National Monument Hwy. 48; see Log Cabin,Early

SAVANNAH

Cherry Mansion
101 Main St.
HABS TN-141
HABS TENN,36-PITLA.V,1-
8dr/9ph/12pg/fr L

Cherry Mansion,Overlook
101 Main St.
HABS TN-141-A
HABS TENN,36-PITLA.V,1A-
1ph L

HAWKINS COUNTY

KINGSPORT VIC.

Holston Army Ammunition Plant,RDX-Composition-B (Holston Ordnance Works,Plant B)
HAER TN-10-B
HAER TENN,82-KINPO,2-B-
5dr/54ph/55pg/6pc L

Holston Ordnance Works,Plant B; see Holston Army Ammunition Plant,RDX-Composition-B

ROGERSVILLE

Clay,Nannie Bynum,Residence
265 E. Main St.
HABS TN-220
HABS TENN,37-ROGVI,1-
12ph/6pg L

HENRY COUNTY

PARIS

Atkins-Jackson House
Dresden Hwy. (State Hwy. 54)
HABS TN-180
HABS TENN,40-PARIS,2-
3ph/6pg L

Crawford-Gov. Porter House
407 Dunlap St.
HABS TN-176
HABS TENN,40-PARIS,2-
8dr/7ph/10pg/fr L

Crawford-Gov. Porter House,Service Building
407 Dunlap St.
HABS TN-176-A
HABS TENN,40-PARIS,2A-
1dr/1ph/1pg L

JEFFERSON COUNTY

JEFFERSON CITY

Glenmore
U. S. Rt. 11 E vic.
HABS TN-48
HABS TENN,45-JEFCI,1-
14ph L

WHITE PINE

Fairfax; see Franklin,Isaac,House

Fairfax,Smokehouse; see Franklin,Isaac,Smokehouse

Franklin,Isaac,House (Fairfax)
U. S. Rt. 25 E.
HABS TN-197
HABS TENN,45-WHIP,1-
6dr/11ph/fr L

Franklin,Isaac,Smokehouse (Fairfax,Smokehouse)
U. S. Rt. 25 E
HABS TN-197-A
HABS TENN,45-WHIP,1A-
1ph L

KNOX COUNTY

KNOXVILLE

Belcaro
2000 Belcaro Dr.
HABS TN-112
HABS TENN,47-KNOVI,6-
24ph/1ct L

Blount,William,Mansion
State St. & Hill Ave.
HABS TN-101
HABS TENN,47-KNOVI,1-
7dr/2ph/3pg/fr L

Campbell House
Cumberland Ave. & Central St.
HABS TN-103
HABS TENN,47-KNOVI,3-
5dr/2ph/2pg/fr L

Chisholm Tavern
Front & Gay Sts.
HABS TN-111
HABS TENN,47-KNOVI,4-
7dr/2ph/2pg/fr L

Commerce Avenue Fire Hall
201-205 Commerce Ave.
HABS TN-211
HABS TENN,47-KNOVI,7-
8ph/6pg/1ct L

Jackson Avenue Warehouse District
101-131 & 120-122 Jackson Ave.
HABS TN-212
HABS TENN,47-KNOVI,8-
20ph/5pg/6ct L

Jackson,Dr. George,House
State St. & Hill Ave.
HABS TN-102
HABS TENN,47-KNOVI,2-
5dr/2ph/2pg/fr L

Knoxville City Hall; see Tennessee School for the Deaf

McGhee,Lawson,Library
217 Market St.
HABS TN-213
HABS TENN,47-KNOVI,9-
5pg/fr L

Old Knoxville City Hall; see Tennessee School for the Deaf

Park Place
5201 N. Broadway
HABS TN-240
HABS TENN,47-KNOVI,10-
7dr L

St. John's Episcopal Church
413 W. Cumberland Ave. SW corner Walnut & Cumberla
HABS TN-243
HABS TENN,47-KNOVI,11-
12ph/1pc L

Tennessee School for the Deaf (Knoxville City Hall; Old Knoxville City Hall)
Summit Hill Dr. & Broadway
HABS TN-5
HABS TENN,47-KNOVI,5-
7ph/10pg L

Zeigler,Isaac B.,House
712 N. Fourth Ave.
HABS TN-216
HABS TENN,47-KNOVI,12-
4ph/3pg/1pc L

KNOXVILLE VIC.

Ramsey House (Swan Pond; Ramsey,J. G. M. ,House)
Thorngrove Pike
HABS TN-104
HABS TENN,47-KNOVI.V,1-
18dr/2ph/2pg/fr L

Ramsey,J. G. M. ,House; see Ramsey House

Swan Pond; see Ramsey House

LINCOLN COUNTY

COLDWATER VIC.

Hobbs Bridge
Spanning Elk River on Curtis Rd. (A494)
HAER TN-23
HAER 1989(HAER):20
20ph/12pg/2pc L

FAYETTEVILLE VIC.

Coldwater Bridge
Spanning Coldwater Creek on Old Railroad Bed Rd.
HAER TN-20
HAER TENN,52-FAY.V,1-
10ph/10pg/1pc L

LOUDON COUNTY

LENOIR CITY

Lenoir Cotton Mill
Near U. S. Rt. 11
HABS TN-198
HABS TENN,53-LENCI,1-
4dr/9ph/fr L

LOUDON

Arp,Charles W. ,Grocery; see Blair's Ferry Storehouse

Blair's Ferry Storehouse (Arp,Charles W. ,Grocery)
800 Main St.
HABS TN-41
HABS TENN,53-LOUD,1-
3ph/12pg/1pc L

MADISON COUNTY

JACKSON

Southern Engine & Boiler Works
342 N. Royal St.
HAER TN-12
HAER 1992(HAER):TN-1
1ph/7pg/1pc L

Union Station
N. Royal St.
HABS TN-184
HABS TENN,57-JACSO,1-
6ph/6pg L

Wisdom,John L. ,House
535 E. Main St.
HABS TN-177
HABS TENN,57-JACSO,2-
9dr/17ph/7pg/2ct/fr L

MARION COUNTY

SOUTH PITTSBURG

Christ Episcopal Church & Parish House
302 W. Third St.
HABS TN-45
HABS TENN,58-SPITBU,1-
10ph/8pg/1pc L

VICTORIA VIC.

Ketner Mill
Sequatchie River,E bank of
HABS TN-47
HABS TENN,58-VICT.V,1-
28ph L

MAURY COUNTY

COLUMBIA

Mercer Hall (Otey,Bishop James Hervey,Hall)
HABS TN-61
HABS TENN,60-COLUM,1-
2ph/2pg L

Otey,Bishop James Hervey,Hall; see Mercer Hall

COLUMBIA VIC.

Clifton Place (Pillow,Gen. Gideon J. ,House)
State Hwy. 6
HABS TN-62
HABS TENN,60-COLUM.V,1-
7ph/4pg L

Pillow,Gen. Gideon J. ,House; see Clifton Place

Polk-Granberry House; see Rattle & Snap

Rattle & Snap (Polk-Granberry House)
U. S. Rt. 43
HABS TN-63
HABS TENN,60-COLUM.V,2-
31ph/11pg/4ct L

Zion Church (Presbyterian)
State Rt. 1
HABS TN-64
HABS TENN,60-COLUM.V,3-
4dr/8ph/21pg/fr L

MCMINN COUNTY

ATHENS VIC.

Cleage,Samuel,House
Lee Hwy.
HABS TN-201
HABS TENN,54-ATH.V,1-
8dr/9ph/6pg/fr L

MONTGOMERY COUNTY

CLARKSVILLE

Clarksville Dept. of Electricity; see U. S. Post Office

Cunningham,John T. ,Memorial Bridge
Spanning Cumberland River,on Old State Rt. 13
HAER TN-21
HAER TENN,63-CLKSV,5-
15ph/13pg/1pc L

Federal Building; see U. S. Post Office

Grange Warehouse
Riverside St.
HABS TN-39
HABS TENN,63-CLKSV,1-
8ph/7pg L

Poston Block
126-130 Public Square
HABS TN-35
HABS TENN,63-CLKSV,2-
7dr/9ph/4pg/fr L

Southern Hotel; see Washington Hotel

U. S. Post Office (Clarksville Dept. of Electricity; Federal Building)
Commerce & S. Second Sts.
HABS TN-38
HABS TENN,63-CLKSV,3-
11ph/6pg L

Washington Hotel (Southern Hotel)
Corner Main & Telegraph Streets
HABS TN-6
HABS TENN,63-CLKSV,4-
5pg L

MORGAN COUNTY

RUGBY

Christ Episcopal Church
Central Ave. (State Rt. 52)
HABS TN-44
HABS TENN,65-RUGBY,1-
12ph/2ct L

Hughes,Thomas,Public Library
Central Ave. (State Rt. 52)
HABS TN-200
HABS TENN,65-RUGBY,2-
4dr/9ph/fr L

OVERTON COUNTY

LIVINGSTON

Roberts,Gov. Albert H. ,Law Office
114 E. Main St.
HABS TN-218
HABS TENN,67-LIV,1-
6ph/6pg L

POLK COUNTY

BENTON VIC.

Dentville Road Bridge
Spanning Hiawassee River on Dentville Rd.
HAER TN-5
HAER TENN,70-BEN.V,1-
18ph/10pg L

ROANE COUNTY

KINGSTON

Roane County Courthouse
Public Square (119 Court St.)
HABS TN-202
HABS TENN,73-KINGS,1-
7dr/9ph/13pg/fr L

KINGSTON VIC.

Weaver Road Bridge
Spanning Paint Rock Ck. on Weaver Rd (Cty Rd A323)
HAER TN-6
HAER TENN,75-KINGS.V,1-
12ph/5pg L

ROBERTSON COUNTY

CEDAR HILL VIC.

Glen Raven
Washington Rd.
HABS TN-59
HABS TENN,74-CEDHI.V,2-
6ph L

Washington,Joseph,Gazebo; see Wessyngton,Gazebo

Washington,Joseph,House; see Wessyngton

Washington,Joseph,Kitchen & Laundry; see Wessyngton,Kitchen & Laundry

Washington,Joseph,Tobacco Barn & Fields; see Wessyngton,Tobacco Barn & Fields

Washington,Joseph,Water Tower; see Wessyngton,Water Tower

Wessyngton (Washington,Joseph,House)
HABS TN-32
HABS TENN,74-CEDHI.V,1-
8ph/8pg L

Wessyngton,Gazebo (Washington,Joseph,Gazebo)
HABS TN-32-B
HABS TENN,74-CEDHI.V,1B-
1ph L

Wessyngton,Kitchen & Laundry (Washington,Joseph,Kitchen & Laundry)
HABS TN-32-A
HABS TENN,74-CEDHI.V,1A-
4ph L

Wessyngton,Tobacco Barn & Fields (Washington,Joseph,Tobacco Barn & Fields)
HABS TN-32-D
HABS TENN,74-CEDHI.V,1D-
3ph/1pc L

Wessyngton,Water Tower (Washington,Joseph,Water Tower)
HABS TN-32-C
HABS TENN,74-CEDHI.V,1C-
1ph L

RUTHERFORD COUNTY

MURFREESBORO

Oaklands
N. Maney Ave.
HABS TN-31
HABS TENN,75-MURFS,1-
14ph/7pg L

SEVIER COUNTY

GATLINBURG

Great Smoky Mountains National Park; see Walker Family Farm (General views)

Great Smoky Mountains National Park; see Walker Family Farm,Big House

Great Smoky Mountains National Park; see Walker Family Farm,Corn Crib

Great Smoky Mountains National Park; see Walker Family Farm,Log Barn

Great Smoky Mountains National Park; see Walker Family Farm,Log Blacksmith Shop

Great Smoky Mountains National Park; see Walker Family Farm,Log Pig Pen

Great Smoky Mountains National Park; see Walker Family Farm,Log Structure

Great Smoky Mountains National Park; see Walker Family Farm,Springhouse

Mingus Flour Mill
Great Smokey Mountains Nat'l Park
HAER TN-13
HAER TENN,78-GAT,2-
12ph/1pc L

Walker Family Farm (General views) (Great Smoky Mountains National Park)
HABS TN-121
HABS TENN,78-GAT,1-
10ph L

Walker Family Farm,Big House (Great Smoky Mountains National Park)
HABS TN-121-A
HABS TENN,78-GAT,1A-
5ph L

Walker Family Farm,Corn Crib (Great Smoky Mountains National Park)
HABS TN-121-C
HABS TENN,78-GAT,1C-
4ph L

Walker Family Farm,Log Barn (Great Smoky Mountains National Park)
HABS TN-121-E
HABS TENN,78-GAT,1E-
1ph L

Walker Family Farm,Log Blacksmith Shop (Great Smoky Mountains National Park)
HABS TN-121-F
HABS TENN,78-GAT,1F-
1ph L

Walker Family Farm,Log Pig Pen (Great Smoky Mountains National Park)
HABS TN-121-G
HABS TENN,78-GAT,1G-
1ph L

Walker Family Farm,Log Structure (Great Smoky Mountains National Park)
HABS TN-121-B
HABS TENN,78-GAT,1B-
3ph L

Walker Family Farm,Springhouse (Great Smoky Mountains National Park)
HABS TN-121-D
HABS TENN,78-GAT,1D-
3ph L

GATLINBURG VIC.

Bales,Ephraim,Place (Great Smoky Mountains National Park)
Roaring Fork Trail
HABS TN-117
HABS TENN,78-GAT.V,1-
8dr/15ph/2pg/fr L

Great Smoky Mountains National Park; see Bales,Ephraim,Place

Great Smoky Mountains National Park; see Junglebrook Barn

Great Smoky Mountains National Park; see Junglebrook Cabin

Great Smoky Mountains National Park; see McCarter,Tyson,Place (Barn,Corn Crib,Smokehouse)

Great Smoky Mountains National Park; see Raegan,Alfred,House

Great Smoky Mountains National Park; see Raegan,Alfred,Tub Mill

Junglebrook Barn (Great Smoky Mountains National Park)
Airport Rd.
HABS TN-123
HABS TENN,78-GAT.V,2B-
2ph L

Junglebrook Cabin (Great Smoky Mountains National Park)
Airport Rd.
HABS TN-122
HABS TENN,78-GAT.V,2A-
3ph L

Junglebrook Tub Mill
Cherokee Orchard Rd. ,Great Smoky Mountains N. P.
HABS TN-163
HABS TENN,78-GAT.V,2-
6dr/fr L

McCarter,Tyson,Place (Barn,Corn Crib,Smokehouse) (Great Smoky Mountains National Park)
HABS TN-226
HABS TENN,78-GAT.V,5A-
5dr L

Raegan,Alfred,House (Great Smoky Mountains National Park)
Roaring Fork Trail
HABS TN-164
HABS TENN,78-GAT.V,3-
11dr/1pg/fr L

Raegan,Alfred,Tub Mill (Great Smoky Mountains National Park)
Roaring Fork Trail
HABS TN-165
HABS TENN,78-GAT.V,4-
4dr/7ph/fr L

KNOXVILLE VIC.

Buckingham House
Sevierville Pike
HABS TN-110
HABS TENN,78- ,1-
3dr/2ph/2pg/fr L

WEARS VALLEY VIC.

Great Smoky Mountains National Park; see Little Greenbrier School & Church House

Little Greenbrier School & Church House (Great Smoky Mountains National Park)
HABS TN-116
HABS TENN,78-ELK.V,1-
3dr/19ph/5pg/fr L

SHELBY COUNTY

MEMPHIS

Allenberg Cotton Company
104-106 S. Front St.
HABS TN-188
HABS TENN,79-MEMPH,8-
4ph/7pg L

Annesdale
1325 Lamar Ave.
HABS TN-178
HABS TENN,79-MEMPH,14-
9ph/11pg/fr L

Beale Street Historic District
HABS TN-60
HABS TENN,79-MEMPH,6-
9ph/1pg L

Brinkley Female College (Ghost House)
683 S. Fifth St.
HABS TN-189
HABS TENN,79-MEMPH,13-
6pg L

Calvary Episcopal Church
102 N. Second St.
HABS TN-182
HABS TENN,79-MEMPH,12-
5ph/6pg L

Claiborne Temple; see Second Presbyterian Church

Driver-Hunt-Phelan House (Hunt-Phelan Residence)
533 Beale Ave.
HABS TN-19-3
HABS TENN,79-MEMPH,3-
3dr/2ph/10pg/fr L

Dunscomb House
584 S. Front St.
HABS TN-19-1
HABS TENN,79-MEMPH,1-
2dr/2ph/2pg/fr L

First Baptist Church
379 E. Beale Street
HABS TN-181
HABS TENN,79-MEMPH,7-
7ph/7pg L

Ghost House; see Brinkley Female College

Goyer-Lee House
690 E. Adams St.
HABS TN-171
HABS TENN,79-MEMPH,15-
9dr/9ph/12pg/2ct/fr L

Goyer-Lee House,Carriage Entrance Gate
690 E. Adams Ave.
HABS TN-171-A
HABS TENN,79-MEMPH,15A-
2dr L

Handwerker Gingerbread Playhouse
865 N. Thomas St.
HABS TN-169
HABS TENN,79-MEMPH,17-
2dr/3ph/6pg/fr L

Hunt-Phelan Residence; see Driver-Hunt-Phelan House

Littleton-Pettit House
496 Beale Ave.
HABS TN-7
HABS TENN,79-MEMPH,5-
8ph/2pg L

Memphis Bridge
Spanning Mississippi River
HAER TN-14
HAER TENN,79-MEMPH,19-
61ph/4pc L

North Memphis Driving Park (Race Track)
1450 N. Thomas St.
HABS TN-170
HABS TENN,79-MEMPH,18-
3dr/5pg/fr L

Second Presbyterian Church (Claiborne Temple)
Pontatoc Ave. & Hernando St.
HABS TN-186
HABS TENN,79-MEMPH,11-
10ph/5pg L

Titus Block
Third & Market Sts.
HABS TN-19-4
HABS TENN,79-MEMPH,4-
6dr/2ph/3pg/fr L

Topp,Robertson,House
565 Beale Ave.
HABS TN-19-2
HABS TENN,79-MEMPH,2-
3dr/2ph/2pg/fr L

Turnage-Young House
196 E. Court St.
HABS TN-172
HABS TENN,79-MEMPH,16-
6dr/8pg/fr L

45-47 Union Avenue (Cotton Brokerage House)
HABS TN-187
HABS TENN,79-MEMPH,9-
4ph/7pg L

Watkins,J. R. ,Building
70 W. Crump Blvd.
HABS TN-179
HABS TENN,79-MEMPH,10-
2ph/6pg L

MEMPHIS VIC.

Davies Manor
9336 Davies Plantation Rd.
HABS TN-183
HABS TENN,79-MEMPH.V,1-
6ph/5pg L

SMITH COUNTY

CARTHAGE VIC.

Buena Vista Ford Bridge
Spanning Round Lick Creek on McClanahan Rd.
HAER TN-18
HAER TENN,80-CARTH.V,1-
9ph/6pg/1pc L

STEWART COUNTY

DOVER

Dover Hotel (Surrender House; Fort Donaldson National Monument)
Petty St.
HABS TN-232
HABS DLC/PP-1992:TN-5
8ph/1pc/fr L

Fort Donaldson National Monument; see Dover Hotel

Surrender House; see Dover Hotel

DOVER VIC.

Bear Spring Furance
HABS TN-36
HABS TENN,81-DOVR.V,1-
4ph/5pg L

SULLIVAN COUNTY

BLOUNTVILLE

Deery Inn,Old
Old Rt. 4 S. & Rt. 11 W.
HABS TN-167
HABS TENN,82-BLOUNT,1-
8dr/17ph L

Deery Inn,Old,Dependencies
Old Rt. 4 S. & Rt. 11 W.
HABS TN-167-B
HABS TENN,82-BLOUNT,1B-
1ph L

Deery Inn,Old,Slave Quarters
Old Rt. 4 S. & Rt. 11 W.
HABS TN-167-A
HABS TENN,82-BLOUNT,1A-
1ph L

BLOUNTVILLE VIC.

Fain,John,Barn
Lone Oaks Estates,near State Rt. 126
HABS TN-194
HABS TENN,82-BLOUNT.V,1A-
4dr/13ph/2ct/fr L

BLUFF CITY VIC.

Riverside Bridge
Weaver Rd. spanning South Fork Holston River
HAER TN-7
HAER TENN,82-BLUCI.V,1-
10ph/3pg L

KINGSPORT

Holston Army Ammunition Plant (Holston Ordnance Works)
Along the Holston River
HAER TN-10
HAER TENN,82-KINPO,2-
1dr/91pg/fr L

Holston Army Ammunition Plant,Producer Gas Plant (Holston Ordnance Works,Plant A)
HAER TN-10-A
HAER TENN,82-KINPO,2-A-
2dr/13ph/38pg/2pc L

Holston Ordnance Works; see Holston Army Ammunition Plant

Holston Ordnance Works,Plant A; see Holston Army Ammunition Plant,Producer Gas Plant

Netherland Inn
2144 Knoxville Hwy.
HABS TN-166
HABS TENN,82-KINPO,1-
10dr/7ph/2pg L

SUMNER COUNTY

CASTALIAN SPRINGS

Castalian Springs; see Wynnewood

Wynne House; see Wynnewood

Wynnewood (Wynne House; Castalian Springs)
HABS TN-81
HABS TENN,83-CASPR,1-
19ph/14pg L

GALLATIN

Blythe,Sam,House
Hartsman Pike
HABS TN-137
HABS TENN,83-GAL,1-
2ph/1pg L

GALLATIN VIC.

Bridge,Stone at Bowling Green
HABS TN-236
HABS TENN, - ,1-
1ph L

Cragfont (Winchester,Gen. James,House)
Hwy. 25
HABS TN-82
HABS TENN,83-GAL.V,2-
9dr/33ph/16pg/1ct/fr L

Cragfont Cemetery
HABS TN-82-A
HABS TENN,83-GAL.V,2A-
1ph L

Fairvue (Franklin,Isaac,Plantation)
U. S. Hwy. 31-E
HABS TN-80
HABS TENN,83-GAL.V,1-
22ph/21pg/1ct/fr L

Fairvue,Stallion Barns
U. S. Hwy. 31-E
HABS TN-80-B
HABS TENN,83-GAL.V,1B-
1ph L

Fairvue,Wellhouse
U. S. Hwy. 31-E
HABS TN-80-A
HABS TENN,83-GAL.V,1A-
2ph L

Franklin,Isaac,Plantation; see Fairvue

Winchester,Gen. James,House; see Cragfont

HENDERSONVILLE VIC.

Priestly-Bradford House
Gallatin Pike
HABS TN-126
HABS TENN,83-HEND.V,1-
1ph/1pg L

Rock Castle (Smith,Gen. Daniel,House)
Indian Lake Rd. (Berry Lane)
HABS TN-131
HABS TENN,83-HEND.V,2-
9dr/21ph/14pg/1pc L

Rock Castle,Smokehouse (Smith,Gen. Daniel,Smokehouse)
Indian Lake Rd.
HABS TN-131-B
HABS TENN,83-HEND.V,2B-
3ph/1pc L

Rock Castle,Springhouse (Smith,Gen. Daniel,Springhouse)
Indian Lake Rd.
HABS TN-131-A
HABS TENN,83-HEND.V,2A-
2ph L

Smith,Gen. Daniel,House; see Rock Castle

Smith,Gen. Daniel,Smokehouse; see Rock Castle,Smokehouse

Smith,Gen. Daniel,Springhouse; see Rock Castle,Springhouse

TROUSDALE COUNTY

DIXON SPRINGS

McGee,John,House
State Hwy. 25 vic.
HABS TN-230
HABS TENN,85-DISP,1-
4dr/8ph/fr L

WARREN COUNTY

MCMINNVILLE

Northcut Plantation (Wheeler Place)
Wheeler Lane
HABS TN-219
HABS TENN,89-MCMIN,1-
16ph/3pg/1pc L

Wheeler Place; see Northcut Plantation

MCMINNVILLE VIC.

Northcut Plantation,Slave Quarters
Wheeler La.
HABS TN-219-A
HABS TENN,89-McMIN,1A-
1ph L

WASHINGTON COUNTY

JOHNSON CITY VIC.

Cobb House
U. S. Hwy. 41
HABS TN-92
HABS TENN,90-JONCI.V,1-
3ph/4pg L

Hammer,Issac,House
HABS TN-40
HABS TENN,90-JONCI.V,3-
9ph/1pg L

Mountain Home V. A. Medical Center
HAER TN-1
HAER TENN,90-JONCI.V,4-
14ph/4pg/1pc L

Mountain Home V. A. Cntr,Boiler Plant & Smokestack
HAER TN-1-A
HAER TENN,90-JONCI.V,4A-
5ph/1pg/1pc L

Tipton-Hayes House
U. S. Hwy. 19
HABS TN-93
HABS TENN,90-JONCI.V,2-
3ph/3pg L

JONESBORO

Hacker-Kennedy House
400 W. Main St.
HABS TN-210
HABS TENN,90-JONSBO,1-
3dr/6pg L

JONESBORO VIC.

Sulphur Springs Methodist Campground
Sulphur Springs Rd. (Sulphur Springs)
HABS TN-209
HABS TENN,90-SULSP,1-
7ph/6pg L

LEESBURG

DeVault Tavern
North Tennessee Rt. 81
HABS TN-217
HABS TENN,90-LEES,1-
16ph/7pg L

DeVault Tavern,Springhouse
Rt. 81
HABS TN-217-A
HABS TENN,90-LEES,1A-
1ph L

LIMESTONE

Stone House,Old
HABS TN-96
HABS TENN,90-LIM,1-
3ph/3pg L

WATAUGA FLATS VIC.

Gibson Bridge
Spanning Watauga River on Herb Hodge Rd.
HAER TN-19
HAER TENN,90-WATFLA.V,1-
8ph/13pg/1pc L

WAYNE COUNTY

CLIFTON VIC.

Stencil House
HABS TN-190
HABS TENN,91-CLIF.V,1-
11ph/6pg/2ct L

Stencil House,Log Barn
HABS TN-190-A
HABS TENN,91-CLIF.V,1A-
2ph L

Stencil House,Log Corn Crib
HABS TN-190-B
HABS TENN,91-CLIF.V,1B-
1ph L

Stencil House,Saddlehouse
HABS TN-190-D
HABS TENN,91-CLIF.V,1D-
2ph L

Stencil House,Smokehouse
HABS TN-190-C
HABS TENN,91-CLIF.V,1C-
2ph L

WHITE COUNTY

SPARTA

Lincoln,Jesse,House
Rt. 5
HABS TN-193
HABS TENN,93-SPART,1-
6dr/1ph/1pg/1pc L

WILLIAMSON COUNTY

FRANKLIN

Carter House
1140 Columbia Ave.
HABS TN-37
HABS TENN,94-FRANK,1-
6dr/12ph/8pg/fr L

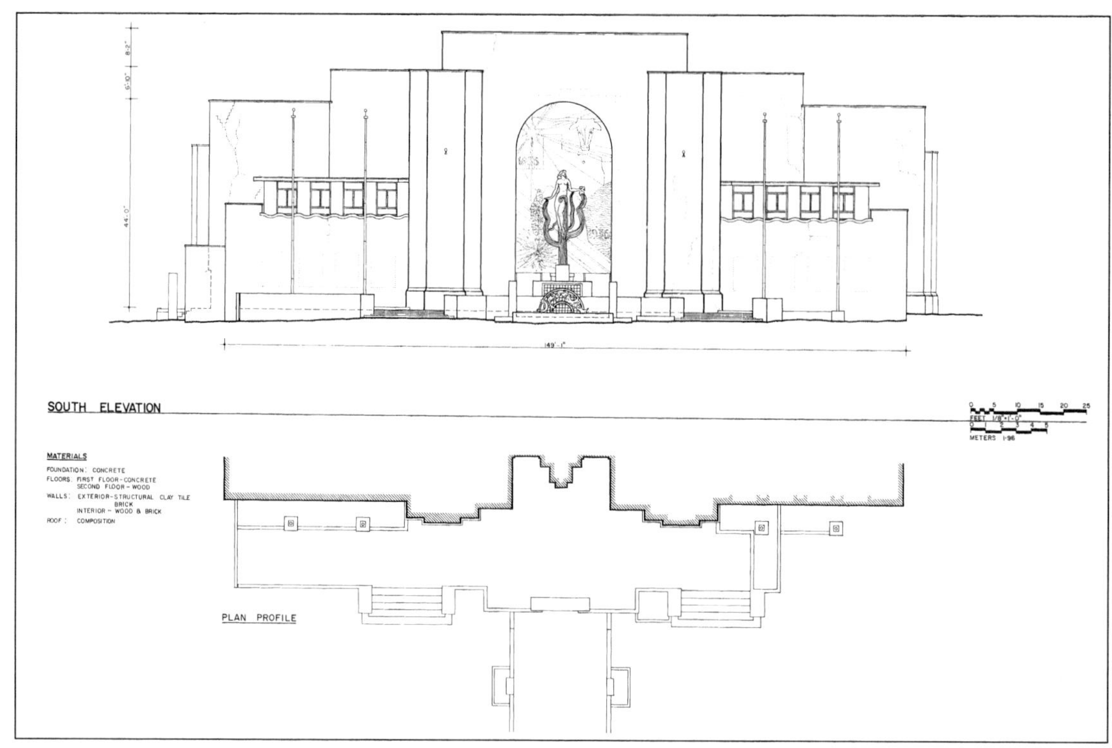

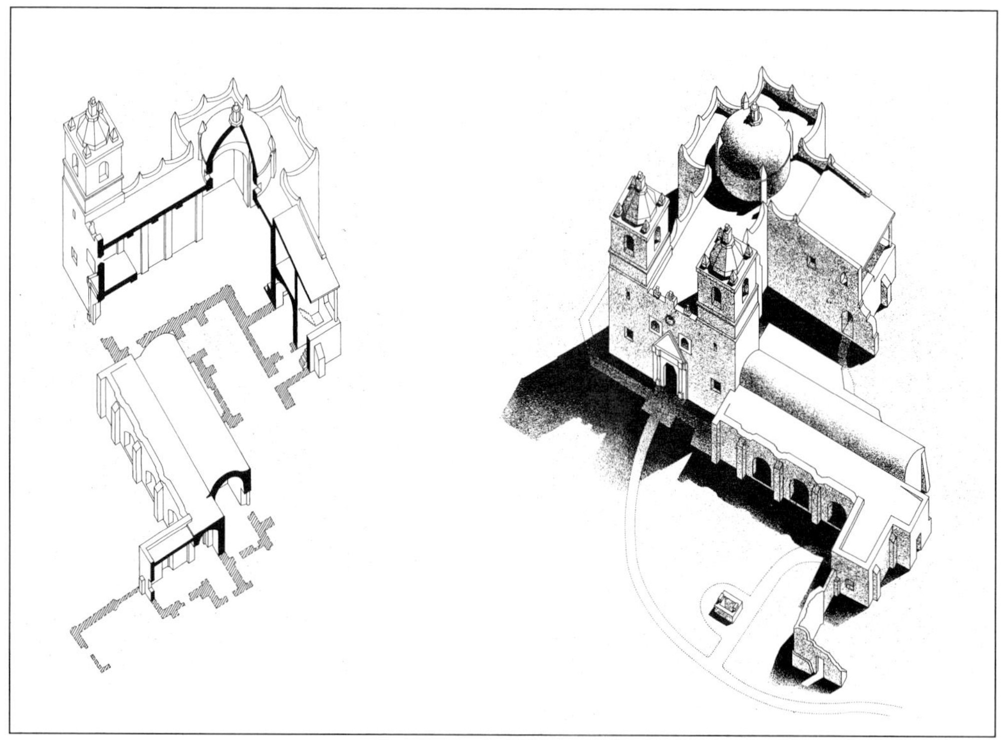

Fair Park — Coliseum, Dallas, Dallas County, Texas. South elevation and plan profile. Measured drawing delineated by Thomas Dreesen, 1986 (HABS TEX,57-DAL,3A, sheet 6 of 8).

Misión Nuestra Señora de la Purísima Concepción de Acuña, San Antonio, Bexar County, Texas. Sectional axonometric and axonometric view. Measured drawing delineated by Roland Rodriguez, 1983 (HABS TX-319, sheet 2 of 12).

Texas

ANDERSON COUNTY

PALESTINE

Dorsett House
HABS TX-127
HABS TEX,1-PAL,2-
2ph/1pg L

Egan House; see Schoolhouse,Red Brick

Gathright House; see Pessony,George,House

Mallard-Alexander-McNaughton House
407 E. Kolstad St.
HABS TX-128
HABS TEX,1-PAL,3-
3ph/1pg L

Pessony,George,House (Gathright House)
HABS TX-126
HABS TEX,1-PAL,1-
3ph/1pg L

Schoolhouse,Red Brick (Egan House)
HABS TX-129
HABS TEX,29-BOV1.V,1-
3ph/1pg L

Schwirter House
HABS TX-130
HABS TEX,1-PAL,5-
3ph/1pg L

ANGELINA COUNTY

LUFKIN VIC.

Gann,John,House
Rt. 94 Vic.
HABS TX-285
HABS TEX,3- ,1-
2ph/1pg L

ARANSAS COUNTY

FULTON

Fulton,George W. ,House
S. Beach St.
HABS TX-3116
HABS TEX,4-FULT,1-
2ph/2pg L

ROCKPORT

Mathis,T. H. ,House
612 S. Church St.
HABS TX-3115
HABS TEX,4-ROCPO,1-
7ph/1pg L

ARMSTRONG COUNTY

CLAUDE

"J. A. " Milk & Meat Cooler
TX Rt. 207 & Farm Rd. 2272 (moved from TX,Lubbock)
HABS TX-3236
HABS TEX,152-LUBBO,3-
3dr L

AUSTIN COUNTY

CAT SPRING

Cat Spring Agriculture Society Pavilion
HABS TX-386
HABS TEX,8-CASP,1-
5dr L

SHELBY

Ehrigson Cotton Gin
HABS TX-370
HABS TEX,8-SHEL,1-
6dr L

BASTROP COUNTY

BASTROP VIC.

Crocheron,Henry,House
1502 Wilson St.
HABS TX-335
HABS TEX, -BAST,3-
8dr/5ph/1pg L

Hill,A. Wiley,House
Rt. 304,Hill's Prairie Vic.
HABS TX-336
HABS TEX,11-HILPR,1-
7dr/11ph/1pg/fr L

Jung-Pearcy House
909 Pecan St.
HABS TX-3127
HABS TEX,11-BAST,4-
2ph/1pg L

Sayers,Gov. Joseph D. ,House
1903 Wilson St.
HABS TX-33-C-5
HABS TEX,11-BAST,1-
5dr/6ph/2pg L

Wilbarger House
1403 N. Main St.
HABS TX-33-C-6
HABS TEX,11-BAST,2-
5dr/6ph/1pg L

WEBBERVILLE VIC.

Burleson,Aaron,House
HABS TX-3126
HABS TEX,11- ,2-
5ph/2pg L

Dog-Run House; see Ireland,Tom,House

Ireland,Tom,House (Dog-Run House)
HABS TX-337
HABS TEX,11- ,1-
3ph/1pg L

BELL COUNTY

SALADO VIC.

"Shady Villa" (Stagecoach Inn)
E. access Rd. I-35
HABS TX-395
HABS TEX,14-SALA,2-
5ph/1pg L

Robertson,E. Sterling C. ,Plantation House
W. access Rd. I-35 Vic.
HABS TX-394
HABS TEX,14-SALA,1-
16dr/10ph/3pg L

Stagecoach Inn; see "Shady Villa"

BEXAR COUNTY

LEON SPRINGS

Aue Stagecoach Inn & Complex
Boerne Stage Rd.
HABS TX-3220
HABS TEX,15-LESP,1-
8dr/3pg/fr L

Aue Stagecoach Inn & Complex,Max Aue House
Boerne Stage Rd.
HABS TX-3220-A
HABS TEX,15-LESP,1A-
3ph/4pg L

Aue Stagecoach Inn & Complex,Max Aue Log House
Boerne Stage Rd.
HABS TX-3220-B
HABS TEX,15-LESP,1B-
2ph/4pg L

Aue Stagecoach Inn & Complex,1878 House
Boerne Stage Rd.
HABS TX-3220-C
HABS TEX,15-LESP,1C-
1ph/5pg L

SAN ANTONIO

Acequias of San Antonio
Hildebrand Ave. & Minita Creek
HAER TX-1
HAER TEX,15-SANT.V,4-
3dr/27pg/fr L

Alamo Madre Acequia
E. of Alamo St. ,N. of Durango Blvd.
HAER TX-1-C
HAER TEX,15-SANT.V,4C-
1dr/fr L

Alamo Roman & Portland Cement Company (San Antonio Portland Cement Company)
Brackenridge Park
HABS TX-3173
HABS TEX,15-SANT,35-
4dr/1ph/4pg/fr L

Alamo,The; see Mission San Antonio de Valero

Alamo,The,Church; see Mission San Antonio de Valero,Church

Alamo,The,Convent; see Mission San Antonio de Valero,Convent

Altgelt,Ernst H. ,House (Isbell,George P. ,House)
226 King William St.
HABS TX-3147
HABS TEX,15-SANT,22-
3ph/5pg L

Argyle House
924 Patterson & Argyle-Alamo Heights
HABS TX-36
HABS TEX,15-SANT,11-
7ph/1pg L

Ball,John,House
120 King William St.
HABS TX-3151
HABS TEX,15-SANT,27-
1ph/4pg L

Bexar County Courthouse
20 Dolorosa St.
HABS TX-3174
HABS TEX,15-SANT,36-
2dr/7ph/6pg/fr L

Boelhauwe,Joseph,House
321 N. Alamo
HABS TX-3153
HABS TEX,15-SANT,26-
2ph/4pg L

Building No. 102,Artillery Post; see Fort Sam Houston,Officer's Quarters

Building No. 109,Artillery Post; see Fort Sam Houston,Officer's Quarters

Building No. 11,Staff Post; see Fort Sam Houston,Officer's Quarters

Building No. 141,Cavalry Post; see Fort Sam Houston,Telephone Exchange

Building No. 143,Cavalry Post; see Fort Sam Houston,Barracks

Building No. 15,Staff Post; see Fort Sam Houston,Officer's Quarters

Building No. 151,Cavalry Post; see Fort Sam Houston,Latrine

Building No. 155,Cavalry Post; see Fort Sam Houston,Kitchen & Mess Hall

Building No. 179,Artillery Post; see Fort Sam Houston,Officer's Quarters

Building No. 2157; see Fort Sam Houston,Military Post of San Ant. Magazin

Building No. 2200; see Fort Sam Houston,Gift Chapel

Building No. 616,Infantry Post; see Fort Sam Houston,Military Post San Ant. Admin Bldg

Building No. 646,Infantry Post; see Fort Sam Houston,Band Quarters

Building Nos. 603-610,613,Infantry Post; see Fort Sam Houston,Military Post of San Antonio

Commanding Officer's Quarters; see Fort Sam Houston,Headqtrs. of the Dept. of Texas

Commanding Officer's Quarters; see Fort Sam Houston,Military Post of San Antonio

Company Barracks & Band Building; see Fort Sam Houston,Military Post of San Antonio

Concepcion Mission; see Mision Nuestra Senora de la Purisima Concepcion

Concepcion Mission,Church; see Mission Senora de la Purisima Concepcion,Church

Concepcion Mission,Convent; see Mission Senora de la Purisima Concepcion,Convent

Cos House
513 Paseo de la Villita
HABS TX-33-A-6
HABS TEX,15-SANT,4-
2dr/3ph/1pg/fr L

Dashiell,Col. Jeremiah Y. ,House
511 Villita St.
HABS TX-3169
HABS TEX,15-SANT,37-
7dr/5ph/7pg/fr L

Denman House; see Lewis,Nat. ,House

Des Mazieres,Francis Louis,Store Building & House
Martinez & S. Alamo Sts.
HABS TX-33-A-2
HABS TEX,15-SANT,2-
5dr/5ph/2pg/fr L

Devine,Judge Thomas J. ,House
HABS TX-332
HABS TEX,15-SANT,17-
7ph/1pg L

Espada Acequia:Diversion Dam
San Antonio River,Military Dr. vic.
HAER TX-1-B
HAER TEX,15-SANT.V,4B-
1dr/1ph L

Espada Acequia:Piedras Creek Aqueduct (Espada Aqueduct)
Espada Rd. & Piedra Creek
HABS TX-322
HAER TX-1-A
HABS/HAER TEX,15-SANT.V,4A-
1dr/13ph/4pg/1pc L

Espada Aqueduct; see Espada Acequia:Piedras Creek Aqueduct

Espada Mission; see Mission San Francisco de la Espada

Espada Mission,Church; see Mission San Francisco de la Espada,Church

Espada Mission,Rectory; see Mission San Francisco de la Espada,Rectory

Fairmount Hotel
857 E. Commerce St.
HABS TX-3310
HABS TEX,15-SANT,38-
31ph/8pg L

Fort Sam Houston (Fort Sam Houston National Historic Landmark)
HABS TX-3303
HABS TEX,15-SANT,39-
3dr/fr L

Fort Sam Houston National Historic Landmark; see Fort Sam Houston

Fort Sam Houston National Historic Landmark; see Fort Sam Houston,Band Quarters

Fort Sam Houston National Historic Landmark; see Fort Sam Houston,Barracks

Fort Sam Houston National Historic Landmark; see Fort Sam Houston,Gift Chapel

Fort Sam Houston National Historic Landmark; see Fort Sam Houston,Headqtrs. of the Dept. of Texas

Fort Sam Houston National Historic Landmark; see Fort Sam Houston,Kitchen & Mess Hall

Fort Sam Houston National Historic Landmark; see Fort Sam Houston,Latrine

Fort Sam Houston National Historic Landmark; see Fort Sam Houston,Military Post of San Ant. Magazin

Fort Sam Houston National Historic Landmark; see Fort Sam Houston,Military Post of San Antonio

Fort Sam Houston National Historic Landmark; see Fort Sam Houston,Military Post San Ant. Admin Bldg

Fort Sam Houston National Historic Landmark; see Fort Sam Houston,Officer's Quarters

Fort Sam Houston National Historic Landmark; see Fort Sam Houston,San Ant. Depot Water & Watch Towe

Fort Sam Houston National Historic Landmark; see Fort Sam Houston,San Antonio Quartermaster Depot

Fort Sam Houston National Historic Landmark; see Fort Sam Houston,Streetscape

Fort Sam Houston National Historic Landmark; see Fort Sam Houston,Telephone Exchange

Fort Sam Houston,Band Quarters (Building No. 646,Infantry Post; Fort Sam Houston National Historic Landmark)
Infantry Post Rd.
HABS TX-3303-10
HABS TEX,15-SANT,39J-
12ph/7pg L

Fort Sam Houston,Barracks (Building No. 143,Cavalry Post; Fort Sam Houston National Historic Landmark)
Stanley Rd. ,between Liscum & New Braunfels
HABS TX-3303-12
HABS TEX,15-SANT,39L
9ph/7pg L

Fort Sam Houston,Gift Chapel (Building No. 2200; Fort Sam Houston National Historic Landmark)
Wilson St. ,btwn. Hancock & Connell Rds.
HABS TX-3303-7
HABS TEX,15-SANT,39G-
11ph/10pg/4ct L

Fort Sam Houston,Headqtrs. of the Dept. of Texas (Commanding Officer's Quarters; Pershing House,Building No. 6,Staff Post; Fort Sam Houston National Historic Landmark)
6 Staff Post Rd.
HABS TX-3303-3
HABS TEX,15-SANT,39C-
15ph/12pg/2ct L

Fort Sam Houston,Kitchen & Mess Hall (Building No. 155,Cavalry Post; Fort Sam Houston National Historic Landmark)
Stanley Rd. ,behind Barracks Nos. 145 & 146
HABS TX-3303-14
HABS TEX,15-SANT,39N-
8ph/6pg L

Fort Sam Houston,Latrine (Building No. 151,Cavalry Post; Fort Sam Houston National Historic Landmark)
Stanley Rd. ,behind Barracks No. 143
HABS TX-3303-15
HABS TEX,15-SANT,39O-
3ph/4pg L

Fort Sam Houston,Military Post of San Ant. Magazin (Building No. 2157; Fort Sam Houston National Historic Landmark)
Cunningham Ave.
HABS TX-3303-6
HABS TEX,15-SANT,39F-
3ph/4pg/2ct L

Fort Sam Houston,Military Post of San Antonio (Commanding Officer's Quarters; Stilwell House,Building No. 626,Infantry Post; Fort Sam Houston National Historic Landmark)
626 Infantry Post Rd.
HABS TX-3303-9
HABS TEX,15-SANT,39I-
9ph/9pg/2ct L

Fort Sam Houston,Military Post of San Antonio (Company Barracks & Band Building; Building Nos. 603-610,613,Infantry Post; Fort Sam Houston National Historic Landmark)
603-610,613 Infantry Post Rd.
HABS TX-3303-11
HABS TEX,15-SANT,39K-
13ph/8pg/8ct L

Fort Sam Houston,Military Post San Ant. Admin Bldg (Building No. 616,Infantry Post; Fort Sam Houston National Historic Landmark)
616 Infantry Post Rd.
HABS TX-3303-8
HABS TEX,15-SANT,39H-
9ph/6pg/1ct L

Fort Sam Houston,Officer's Quarters (Building No. 102,Artillery Post; Fort Sam Houston National Historic Landmark)
102 Artillery Post Rd.
HABS TX-3303-18
HABS TEX,15-SANT,39R-
11ph/8pg/4ct L

Fort Sam Houston,Officer's Quarters (Building No. 109,Artillery Post; Fort Sam Houston National Historic Landmark)
109 Artillery Post Rd.
HABS TX-3303-17
HABS TEX,15-SANT,39Q-
8ph/8pg/2ct L

Fort Sam Houston,Officer's Quarters (Building No. 11,Staff Post; Fort Sam Houston National Historic Landmark)
11 Staff Post Rd.
HABS TX-3303-4
HABS TEX,15-SANT,39D-
9ph/10pg/2ct L

Fort Sam Houston,Officer's Quarters (Building No. 15,Staff Post; Fort Sam Houston National Historic Landmark)
15 Staff Post Rd.
HABS TX-3303-5
HABS TEX,15-SANT,39E-
9ph/9pg L

Fort Sam Houston,Officer's Quarters (Building No. 179,Artillery Post; Fort Sam Houston National Historic Landmark)
179 Artillery Post Rd.
HABS TX-3303-16
HABS TEX,15-SANT,39P-
4ph/9pg L

Fort Sam Houston,San Ant. Depot Water & Watch Towe (Quadrangle Building No. 40; Fort Sam Houston National Historic Landmark)
Grayson St. & New Braunfels Ave.
HABS TX-3303-2
HABS TEX,15-SANT,39B-
8ph/7pg/4ct L

Fort Sam Houston,San Antonio Quartermaster Depot (Quadrangle,Building No. 16; Fort Sam Houston National Historic Landmark)
New Braunfels Ave. & Grayson St.
HABS TX-3303-1
HABS TEX,15-SANT,39A-
21ph/9pg/4ct L

Fort Sam Houston,Streetscape (Fort Sam Houston National Historic Landmark)
HABS TX-3303-19
HABS TEX,15-SANT,39S-
19ph/11ct L

Fort Sam Houston,Telephone Exchange (Building No. 141,Cavalry Post; Fort Sam Houston National Historic Landmark)
Stanley Rd. ,behind Cavalry Post Barracks
HABS TX-3303-13
HABS TEX,15-SANT,39M-
2ph/5pg L

French Mansard House; see Kingsley,Dr. D. B. F. ,House

Henry,O. ,House (Porter,William Sydney,House)
Lone Star Brewery,600 Lane Star Blvd.
HABS TX-325
HABS TEX,15-SANT,16-
3ph/1pg L

Herrera Portones (Gates)
University of Texas,Institute of Texan Cultures
HABS TX-3343
HABS 1991(HABS):29
1dr/fr L

Isbell,George P. ,House; see Altgelt,Ernst H. ,House

Kampmann,John R. ,House
HABS TX-396
HABS TEX,15-SANT,19-
13ph/2pg L

317 King William Street (House)
HABS TX-302
HABS TEX,15-SANT,32-
1ph L

410-412 King William Street (Houses)
HABS TX-301
HABS TEX,15-SANT,34-
1ph/2ct L

King William Street,300 Block
HABS TX-303
HABS TEX,15-SANT,31-
1ph/3ct L

Kingsley,Dr. D. B. F. ,House (French Mansard House)
408 Elm St.
HABS TX-33-A-3
HABS TEX,15-SANT,3-
7dr/4ph/1pg/fr L

Lege,Charles L. ,House
533 W. Elmira St.
HABS TX-3172
HABS TEX,15-SANT,40-
4dr/1ph/8pg/fr L

Lewis,Nat. ,House (Denman House)
112 Lexington
HABS TX-393
HABS TEX,15-SANT,18-
8ph/1pg L

Menger Hotel
Alamo Plaza
HABS TX-35
HABS TEX,15-SANT,10-
17ph/2pg/1ct L

Mision Nuestra Senora de la Purisima Concepcion (Concepcion Mission)
807 Mission Rd.
HABS TX-319
HABS TEX,15-SANT.V1-
13dr/15ph/10pg/fr L

Mission San Antonio de Valero (Alamo,The; San Antonio Missions National Historical Park)
Alamo Plaza
HABS TX-318
HABS TEX,15-SANT,15-
17dr/26ph/14pg L

Mission San Antonio de Valero,Church (Alamo,The,Church; San Antonio Missions National Historical Park)
Alamo Plaza
HABS TX-318-A
HABS TEX,15-SANT,15A-
7pg L

Mission San Antonio de Valero,Convent (Alamo,The,Convent; San Antonio Missions National Historical Park)
Alamo Plaza
HABS TX-318-B
HABS TEX,15-SANT,15B-
3pg L

Mission San Francisco de la Espada (Espada Mission)
Berg's Mill Community
HABS TX-320
HABS TEX,15-SANT.V,2-
13dr/49ph/7pg/2pc/fr L

Mission San Francisco de la Espada,Church (Espada Mission,Church; San Antonio Missions National Historical Park)
Berg's Mill Community
HABS TX-320-A
HABS TEX,15-SANT.V,2-
10ph/3pg L

Mission San Francisco de la Espada,Rectory (Espada Mission,Rectory; San Antonio Missions National Historical Park)
Berg's Mill Community
HABS TX-320-B
HABS TEX,15-SANT.V,2B-
2ph L

Mission San Jose y San Miguel de Aguayo (San Jose Mission)
Mission Rd.
HABS TX-333
HABS TEX,15-SANT.V,5-
21dr/33ph/16pg/fr L

Mission San Jose y San Miguel de Aguayo,Chapel (San Jose Mission,Chapel; San Antonio Missions National Historical Park)
6539 San Jose
HABS TX-333-B
HABS TEX,15-SANT,5F-
5ph/3pg L

Mission San Jose y San Miguel de Aguayo,Church (San Jose Mission,Church; San Antonio Missions National Historical Park)
6539 San Jose
HABS TX-333-A
HABS TEX,15-SANT.V,5E-
19ph/4pg L

Mission San Jose y San Miguel de Aguayo,Convent (San Jose Mission,Convent; San Antonio Missions National Historical Park)
6539 San Jose Rd.
HABS TX-333-C
HABS TEX,15-SANT.V,5G-
3ph/3pg L

Mission San Jose y San Miguel de Aguayo,Granary (San Jose Mission,Granary; San Antonio Missions National Historical Park)
6539 San Jose
HABS TX-333-D
HABS TEX,15-SANT.V,5B-
3ph/2pg L

Mission San Jose y San Miguel de Aguayo,Ramparts (San Jose Mission,Ramparts; San Antonio Missions National Historical Park)
6539 San Jose Rd.
HABS TX-333-E
HABS TEX,15-SANT.V,5A-
3ph/5pg L

Mission San Juan de Capistrano (San Juan Mission)
Berg's Mill-Graf Rd.
HABS TX-321
HABS TEX,15-SANT.V,3-
19dr/25ph/6pg/1pc/fr L

Mission San Juan de Capistrano,Chapel (San Juan Misssion,Chapel; San Antonio Missions National Historical Park)
Berg's Mill-Graf Rd.
HABS TX-321-A
HABS TEX,15-SANT.V,3A-
10ph/5pg L

Mission San Juan de Capistrano,Convent (San Juan Mission,Convent; San Antonio Missions National Historical Park)
Berg's Mill-Graf Rd.
HABS TX-321-B
HABS TEX,15-SANT.V,3G-
2ph/3pg L

Mission San Juan de Capistrano,Habitation A (San Juan Mission,Habitation A; San Antonio Missions National Historical Park)
Berg's Mill-Graf Rd.
HABS TX-321-C
HABS TEX,15-SANT.V,3C-
3pg L

Mission San Juan de Capistrano,Habitation B (San Juan Mission,Habitation B; San Antonio Missions National Historical Park)
Berg's Mill-Graf Rd.
HABS TX-321-D
HABS TEX,15-SANT,3E-
1ph/3pg L

Mission San Juan de Capistrano,House (San Juan Mission,House; San Antonio Missions National Historical Park)
Berg's Mill-Graf Rd.
HABS TX-321-F
HABS TEX,15-SANT.V,3H-
2ph L

Mission San Juan de Capistrano,Old Church (San Juan Mission,Old Church; San Antonio Missions National Historical Park)
Berg's Mill-Graf Rd.
HABS TX-321-E
HABS TEX,15-SANT.V,3F-
2ph L

Mission San Juan de Capistrano,Outhouse (San Juan Mission,Outhouse; San Antonio Missions National Historical Park)
Berg's Mill-Graf Rd.
HABS TX-321-H
HABS TEX,15-SANT.V,3I-
2ph L

Mission San Juan de Capistrano,Tefu House (San Juan Mission,Tefu House)
Berg's Mill-Graf Rd.
HABS TX-321-G
HABS TEX,15-SANT.V,3B-
6ph/fr L

Mission Senora de la Purisima Concepcion,Church (Concepcion Mission,Church)
807 Mission Rd.
HABS TX-319-A
HABS TEX,15-SANT.V,1A-
17ph/6pg/1pc/fr L

Mission Senora de la Purisima Concepcion,Convent (Concepcion Mission,Convent)
807 Mission Rd.
HABS TX-319-B
HABS TEX,15-SANT.V,1B-
3ph/3pg/1pc/fr L

Mitchell,Newton A. ,Carriage House & Stable
257 Yellowstone St.
HABS TX-3171-A
HABS TEX,15-SANT,41A-
1dr L

Mitchell,Newton A. ,House
(Oge,Louis,House)
209 Washington St.
HABS TX-3171
HABS TEX,15-SANT,41-
8dr/3ph/9pg/fr L

Navarro,Jose Antonio,House
228 S. Laredo St.
HABS TX-3148
HABS TEX,15-SANT,23-
1ph/6pg L

Navarro,Jose Antonio,Store
232 S. Laredo St.
HABS TX-317
HABS TEX,15-SANT,14-
3dr/3ph/1pg L

Norton-Polk-Mathis House
401 King William St.
HABS TX-3225
HABS TEX,15-SANT,33-
12dr L

Oge,Louis,House; see Mitchell,Newton A. ,House

Pershing House,Building No. 6,Staff Post; see Fort Sam Houston,Headqtrs. of the Dept. of Texas

Porter,William Sydney,House; see Henry,O. ,House

Quadrangle Building No. 40; see Fort Sam Houston,San Ant. Depot Water & Watch Towe

Quadrangle,Building No. 16; see Fort Sam Houston,San Antonio Quartermaster Depot

Ruiz,Francisco,House
Witte Museum,3801 Broadway,Brackenridge Park
HABS TX-3117
HABS TEX,15-SANT,20-
2ph/1pg L

San Antonio City Hall
Military Plaza
HABS TX-222
HABS TEX,15-SANT,29-
6ph/3pg L

San Antonio Missions Nat'l Hist. Park (site plan) (San Antonio Missions National Historical Park)
HABS TX-334
HABS TEX,15-SANT.V,6-
1dr/fr L

San Antonio Missions National Historical Park; see Mission San Antonio de Valero

San Antonio Missions National Historical Park; see Mission San Antonio de Valero,Church

San Antonio Missions National Historical Park; see Mission San Antonio de Valero,Convent

San Antonio Missions National Historical Park; see Mission San Francisco de la Espada,Church

San Antonio Missions National Historical Park; see Mission San Francisco de la Espada,Rectory

San Antonio Missions National Historical Park; see Mission San Jose y San Miguel de Aguayo,Chapel

San Antonio Missions National Historical Park; see Mission San Jose y San Miguel de Aguayo,Church

San Antonio Missions National Historical Park; see Mission San Jose y San Miguel de Aguayo,Convent

San Antonio Missions National Historical Park; see Mission San Jose y San Miguel de Aguayo,Granary

San Antonio Missions National Historical Park; see Mission San Jose y San Miguel de Aguayo,Ramparts

San Antonio Missions National Historical Park; see Mission San Juan de Capistrano,Chapel

San Antonio Missions National Historical Park; see Mission San Juan de Capistrano,Convent

San Antonio Missions National Historical Park; see Mission San Juan de Capistrano,Habitation A

San Antonio Missions National Historical Park; see Mission San Juan de Capistrano,Habitation B

San Antonio Missions National Historical Park; see Mission San Juan de Capistrano,House

San Antonio Missions National Historical Park; see Mission San Juan de Capistrano,Old Church

San Antonio Missions National Historical Park; see Mission San Juan de Capistrano,Outhouse

San Antonio Missions National Historical Park; see San Antonio Missions Nat'l Hist. Park (site plan)

San Antonio Portland Cement Company; see Alamo Roman & Portland Cement Company

San Fernando Cathedral
115 Main Ave.
HABS TX-34
HABS TEX,15-SANT,9-
11ph/16pg L

San Jose Grist Mill
SW of San Jose Dr. ,E. of Espada Rd.
HAER TX-2
HAER TEX,15-SANT,30-
1dr/9ph/1pc L

San Jose Mission; see Mission San Jose y San Miguel de Aguayo

San Jose Mission,Chapel; see Mission San Jose y San Miguel de Aguayo,Chapel

San Jose Mission,Church; see Mission San Jose y San Miguel de Aguayo,Church

San Jose Mission,Convent; see Mission San Jose y San Miguel de Aguayo,Convent

San Jose Mission,Granary; see Mission San Jose y San Miguel de Aguayo,Granary

San Jose Mission,Ramparts; see Mission San Jose y San Miguel de Aguayo,Ramparts

San Juan Mission; see Mission San Juan de Capistrano

San Juan Mission,Convent; see Mission San Juan de Capistrano,Convent

San Juan Mission,Habitation A; see Mission San Juan de Capistrano,Habitation A

San Juan Mission,Habitation B; see Mission San Juan de Capistrano,Habitation B

San Juan Mission,House; see Mission San Juan de Capistrano,House

San Juan Mission,Old Church; see Mission San Juan de Capistrano,Old Church

San Juan Mission,Outhouse; see Mission San Juan de Capistrano,Outhouse

San Juan Mission,Tefu House; see Mission San Juan de Capistrano,Tefu House

San Juan Misssion,Chapel; see Mission San Juan de Capistrano,Chapel

Seng,Magnus,House
HABS TX-33-A-15
HABS TEX,15-SANT,5-
3dr/5ph/1pg/fr L

St. Mark's Episcopal Church
307 E. Pecan St.
HABS TX-33
HABS TEX,15-SANT,8-
4ph/3pg L

Steves Homestead; see Steves,Eduard,House

Steves,Eduard,House (Steves Homestead)
509 King William St.
HABS TX-3150
HABS TEX,15-SANT,25-
7ph/6pg L

Stilwell House,Building No. 626,Infantry Post; see Fort Sam Houston,Military Post of San Antonio

Twohig,John,House
Witte Museum,3801 Broadway,Brackenridge Park
HABS TX-31
HABS TEX,15-SANT,6-
4ph/1pg L

U. S. San Antonio Arsenal
San Antonio Arsenal
HABS TX-3175
HABS TEX,15-SANT,42-
9pg L

U. S. San Antonio Arsenal,Commanding Officers' Qtr
San Antonio Arsenal
HABS TX-3175-A
HABS TEX,15-SANT,42A-
9ph/4pg L

U. S. San Antonio Arsenal,Magazine
San Antonio Arsenal
HABS TX-3175-E
HABS TEX,15-SANT,42E-
3dr/5ph/4pg/fr L

U. S. San Antonio Arsenal,Office Building
San Antonio Arsenal
HABS TX-3175-B
HABS TEX,15-SANT,42B-
1ph/3pg L

U. S. San Antonio Arsenal,Servants' Quarters
San Antonio Arsenal
HABS TX-3175-C
HABS TEX,15-SANT,42D-
2ph/3pg L

U. S. San Antonio Arsenal,Stable
Arsenal Grounds
HABS TX-3175-D
HABS TEX,15-SANT,42D-
1ph/3pg L

U. S. San Antonio Arsenal,Storehouse
San Antonio Arsenal
HABS TX-3175-F
HABS TEX,15-SANT,42F-
4dr/5ph/5pg/fr L

Uhl Store
HABS TX-315
HABS TX,15-SANT,12-
7ph/1pg L

Uhl,Gustave,House
HABS TX-316
HABS TEX,15-SANT,13-
5ph/1pg L

Ursuline Academy
300 Augusta St.
HABS TX-32
HABS TEX,15-SANT,7-
21dr/14ph/13pg/fr L

Ursuline Academy,Academy Building
300 Augusta St.
HABS TX-32-A
HABS TEX,15-SANT,7A-
8ph/6pg/1pc L

Ursuline Academy,Academy Building Addition
300 Augusta St.
HABS TX-32-B
HABS TEX,15-SANT,7B-
3ph/7pg/1pc L

Ursuline Academy,Chapel
300 Augusta St.
HABS TX-32-C
HABS TEX,15-SANT,7C-
9ph/6pg/1pc L

Ursuline Academy,Dormitory Building
300 Augusta St.
HABS TX-32-D
HABS TEX,15-SANT,7D-
10ph/4pg/1pc L

Ursuline Academy,Laundry Building
300 Augusta St.
HABS TX-32-G
HABS TEX,15-SANT,7G-
4ph/6pg/1pc L

Ursuline Academy,Priest's House
300 Augusta St.
HABS TX-32-E
HABS TEX,15-SANT,7E-
5ph/5pg/1pc L

Ursuline Academy,1872 House
300 Augusta St.
HABS TX-32-F
HABS TEX,15-SANT,7F-
3ph/4pg L

Vance,James,House
HABS TX-33-A-1
HABS TEX,15-SANT,1-
9dr/6ph/2pg/fr L

Veramendi Palace (Veramendi,Don Fernando,Palace)
130 Soledad St.
HABS TX-3128
HABS TEX,15-SANT,21-
3ph/2pg L

Veramendi,Don Fernando,Palace; see Veramendi Palace

Vollrath House & Store
712 S. Alamo St.
HABS TX-3152
HABS TEX,15-SANT,28-
1ph/5pg L

Wohlfarth,Jacob,Store & Residence
823 W. Laurel
HABS TX-3374
5dr/fr H

Wulff,Anton,House
107 King William St.
HABS TX-3149
HABS TEX,15-SANT,24-
1ph/6pg L

SAN ANTONIO VIC.

"Old House"; see Casa Vieja

Casa Vieja ("Old House")
Blue Wing Rd.
HABS TX-323
HABS TEX,15- ,1-
5dr/5ph/2pg/fr L

Casa Vieja Lime Kiln & Arch
Blue Wing Rd.
HABS TX-324
HABS TEX,15- ,1A-
2ph/1pg L

SOMERSET VIC.

Cowan,I. M. ,House
HABS TX-382
HABS TEX,15-SOM,1-
3ph/1pg L

BLANCO COUNTY

HYE

Hye Post Office & General Store
Lyndon B. Johnson Nat'l Historical Park
HABS TX-3330
3dr L

BOSQUE COUNTY

KIMBALL

Kimball Academy
Rt. 174,Brazos River Vic.
HABS TX-139
HABS TEX,18-KIMB,1-
6ph/5pg L

BOWIE COUNTY

TEXARKANA

Lone Star Army Ammunition Plant
HAER TX-5
HAER TEX,19-TEX,3-
55pg/fr L

Municipal Building
Texas Blvd. at Third St.
HABS TX-230
HABS TEX,19-TEX,1-
6ph/8pg/1pc L

Red River Army Depot
HAER TX-4
HAER TEX,19-TEX,2-
52pg/fr L

BRAZORIA COUNTY

ANGLETON VIC.

Chenango Sugar Mill
Chenango Vic.
HABS TX-283
HABS TEX,20-CHEN,1-
3dr/1ph/1pg L

BRAZORIA

McCormick House (McCormick-Ashcomb House)
HABS TX-249
HABS TEX,20-BRAZ,1-
2ph/1pg L

McCormick-Ashcomb House; see McCormick House

WEST COLUMBIA VIC.

Varner-Hogg Plantation House
Varner Hogg State Park Museum
HABS TX-251
HABS TEX,20-COLW,1-
4ph/1pg L

BRAZOS COUNTY

BRYAN

Coulter Carriage House
500 Block East 26th St.
HABS TX-3389-A
HABS DLC/PP-1993:TX-1
8dr/fr L

Coulter House
HABS TX-3389
HABS DLC/PP-1993:TX-1
6dr/fr L

Temple Freda
205 Parker St.
HABS TX-288
HABS TEX,21-BRY,1-
9dr L

COLLEGE STATION VIC.

Bird Pond Road Bridge
Spanning Carter Creek on County Rd. 184
HAER TX-10
HAER TEX,21-COLST.V,1-
4ph/2pg/1pc L

MILLICAN

Harrington-Upham House
FM 2154
HABS TX-3342
HABS 1991(HABS):29
10dr L

Harrington-Upham House,Corn Crib
FM 2154
HABS TX-3342-A
HABS 1991(HABS):29
4dr/fr L

PEACH CREEK

Gay-MacGregor-Allen Cabin
Rock Prairie Rd.
HABS TX-3341
HABS 1991(HABS):29
10dr L

BREWSTER COUNTY

CASTOLON

Big Bend National Park; see Castolon,Alvino House

Big Bend National Park; see Castolon,Enlisted Men's Barracks/Store

Big Bend National Park; see Castolon,Noncommissioned Officers' Quarters

Big Bend National Park; see Castolon,Town of

Castolon,Alvino House (Big Bend National Park)
Rt. 5
HABS TX-3312-C
HABS TEX,22-CAST,2-
2dr/fr L

Castolon,Enlisted Men's Barracks/Store (Big Bend National Park)
Rt. 5
HABS TX-3312-B
HABS TEX,22-CAST,3B-
2dr/fr L

Castolon,Noncommissioned Officers' Quarters (Big Bend National Park)
Rt. 5
HABS TX-3312-A
HABS TEX,22-CAST,3A-S
1dr/fr L

Castolon,Town of (Big Bend National Park)
Rt. 5
HABS TX-3312
HABS TEX,22-CAST,1-
1dr/fr L

CASTOLON VIC.

Big Bend National Forest; see Chisos Basin Store

Chisos Basin Store (Big Bend National Forest)
HABS TX-3399
6dr/10ph/42pg/1pc H

TERLINGUA

Big Bend National Park; see Perry School

Big Bend National Park; see Perry,Howard E. ,House

Big Bend National Park; see St. Agnes' Church

Big Bend National Park; see Terlingua,Town of

Perry School (Big Bend National Park)
HABS TX-3334
HABS TEX,22-TERL,2-
3dr/fr L

Perry,Howard E. ,House (Big Bend National Park)
HABS TX-3333
HABS TEX,22-TERL,3-
5dr/fr L

St. Agnes' Church (Big Bend National Park)
HABS TX-3335
HABS TEX,22-TERL,4-
2dr/fr L

Terlingua,Town of (Big Bend National Park)
HABS TX-3332
HABS TEX,22-TERL,1-
1dr/fr L

CALDWELL COUNTY

LOCKHART VIC.

Blackwell,James,House
HABS TX-391
HABS TEX,28-LOCK.V,1-
5ph/1pg L

Lane,Dr. Pleasant,House
HABS TX-392
HABS TEX,28-LOCK,1-
5ph/1pg L

CAMERON COUNTY

BROWNSVILLE

Alonso Building
510-514 E. Saint Charles St.
HABS TX-3270
HABS TEX,31-BROWN,2-
12ph/9pg/fr L

Browne-Wagner House
245 E. Saint Charles St.
HABS TX-3271
HABS TEX,31-BROWN,3-
11ph/13pg L

Cameron County Courthouse
1150 E. Madison St.
HABS TX-3272
HABS TEX,31-BROWN,4-
23ph/9pg L

Cross Family House
911 E. Madison St.
HABS TX-3273
HABS TEX,31-BROWN,5-
9ph/6pg/fr L

Douglas Drug Store
1201 E. Elizabeth St.
HABS TX-3274
HABS TEX,31-BROWN,6-
5ph/9pg/fr L

El Globo Chiquito (Laiseca Store)
1054 E. Monroe St.
HABS TX-3275
HABS TEX,31-BROWN,7-
4dr/8ph/7pg/fr L

El Globo Nuevo
1502 E. Madison St.
HABS TX-3276
HABS TEX,31-BROWN,8-
3dr/14ph/9pg/fr L

Field-Pacheco Complex
1049 E. Monroe St.
HABS TX-3277
HABS TEX,31-BROWN,9-
7dr/15ph/18pg/fr L

Fort Brown Commissary & Guard House (Building 88) (Texas Southmost College)
May St. & Gorgas Dr. Vic.
HABS TX-3278
HABS TEX,31-BROWN,10A-
10ph/8pg/fr L

Fort Brown Medical Laboratory (Building 84) (Texas Southmost College)
May St. & Gorgas Dr. Vic.
HABS TX-3279
HABS TEX,31-BROWN,10B-
9ph/10pg/fr L

Garza House
1009 E. Thirteenth St.
HABS TX-3280
HABS TEX,31-BROWN,11-
6ph/7pg/fr L

La Madrilena (Ortiz,Adrian,House)
1002 E. Madison St.
HABS TX-3281
HABS TEX,31-BROWN,12-
4dr/9ph/6pg/fr L

Laiseca Store; see El Globo Chiquito

Neale House
230 Neale Rd. (moved from 625 E. Fourteenth St.)
HABS TX-3282
HABS TEX,31-BROWN,13-
15ph/8pg/fr L

Ortiz,Adrian,House; see La Madrilena

Sacred Heart Roman Catholic Church
E. Sixth & E. Elizabeth Sts.
HABS TX-3283
HABS TEX,31-BROWN,14-
9ph/10pg/fr L

Southern Pacific Railroad Passenger Station
601 E. Madison St.
HABS TX-3284
HABS TEX,31-BROWN,15-
16ph/5pg/fr L

Stillman House
1305 E. Washington St.
HABS TX-3285
HABS TEX,31-BROWN,16-
13ph/10pg L

Texas Southmost College; see Fort Brown Commissary & Guard House (Building 88)

Texas Southmost College; see Fort Brown Medical Laboratory (Building 84)

Tijerina,Tomas,House
333 E. Adams St.
HABS TX-3286
HABS TEX,31-BROWN,17-
3dr/10ph/9pg/fr L

Trevino House
1405 E. Jefferson St.
HABS TX-3287
HABS TEX,31-BROWN,18-
6dr/8ph/8pg/fr L

Valdez House
815 E. Fourteenth St.
HABS TX-3288
HABS TEX,31-BROWN,19-
7ph/6pg/fr L

BROWNSVILLE VIC.

Carmen Ranch House
(Cortina,Juan,Headquarters)
Rio Grande Vic.
HABS TX-33-AB-3
HABS TEX,31-BROWN.V,1-
4dr/7ph/1pg/fr L

Church of the Immaculate Conception
Twelfth & Jefferson Sts.
HABS TX-3139
HABS TEX,31-BROWN,1-
6ph/7pg L

Cortina,Juan,Headquarters; see Carmen Ranch House

PORT ISABEL

Point Isabel Lighthouse
NE of Brownsville
HABS TX-33-AB-1
HABS TEX,31-POISA,1-
4dr/5ph/1pg/fr L

CHAMBERS COUNTY

ANAHUAC

Chambers,Gen. Thomas Jefferson,House
Cummings St.
HABS TX-281
HABS TEX,36-ANA,1-
3dr/5ph/2pg/fr L

COLEMAN COUNTY

LEADAY

Leaday School
Farm Rds. 2134 & Leaday-Hill Rd.
HABS TX-3353
6ph/12pg/1pc/fr H

VOSS VIC.

Creswell-Rozzle Ranch
Approx. 2 mi. S. of Leaday
HABS TX-3352
3dr/10pg/1pc/fr H

Creswell-Rozzle Ranch,Cellar
HABS TX-3352-B
1ph H

Creswell-Rozzle Ranch,House
HABS TX-3352-A
9ph H

Creswell-Rozzle Ranch,Outbuildings
HABS TX-3352-D
3ph H

Creswell-Rozzle Ranch,Water Tower
HABS TX-3352-C
2ph H

Day Padgitt Ranch Tenant House
Approx. 1 mi. WSW of Leaday
HABS TX-3363
4ph/11pg/1pc/fr H

Elm Creek Silo
2.9 mi. SE of Leaday Townsite
HAER TX-15
HAER DLC/PP-1992:TX-3
4ph/7pg/1pc L

Leaday Townsite
Near Hwy. 2134 & Colorado River
HABS TX-3362
1dr/1ph/15pg/1pc/fr H

Leaday Townsite,Bungalow
HABS TX-3362-D
1ph H

Leaday Townsite,Livery Stable
HABS TX-3362-B
1ph H

Leaday Townsite,Post Office
HABS TX-3362-C
1ph H

Leaday Townsite,Store
HABS TX-3362-A
1ph H

Documentation: **ct** color transparencies **dr** measured drawings **fr** field records
pc photograph captions **pg** pages of text **ph** photographs

Mabel Doss Day Lea House
HABS TX-3351-J
1ph H

Mabel Doss Day Lea House,Chicken Coop
HABS TX-3351-E
1ph H

Mabel Doss Day Lea House,First Barn
HABS TX-3351-F
1ph H

Mabel Doss Day Lea House,First Cowshed
HABS TX-3351-H
1ph H

Mabel Doss Day Lea House,Main House
HABS TX-3351-A
7ph H

Mabel Doss Day Lea House,Office
HABS TX-3351-D
1ph H

Mabel Doss Day Lea House,Second Barn
HABS TX-3351-G
2ph H

Mabel Doss Day Lea House,Second Cowshed
HABS TX-3351-I
1ph H

Mabel Doss Day Lea House,Storm Cellar
HABS TX-3351-B
1ph H

Mabel Doss Day Lea House,Sugar Cane Press (ruins)
HABS TX-3351-K
1ph H

Mabel Doss Day Lea House,Water Tower
HABS TX-3351-C
1ph H

Red Wire Pasture,Lime Kiln
0.3 mi. E. of Colorado Riv.,1.3 mi. S. of Leaday
HAER TX-14
HAER DLC/PP-1992:TX-3
5ph/5pg/1pc L

Works Progress Administration,Bridge No. 232
(WPA,Bridge No. 232)
Elm Creek Rd. (Leaday-Hill Rd.)
HAER TX-16
1ph/4pg/1pc/fr L

Works Progress Administration,Bridge No. 234
(WPA,Bridge No. 234)
Spanning Elm Creek,on Elm Creek Rd.
HAER TX-18
HAER DLC/PP-1992:TX-3
1ph/4pg/1pc/fr L

WPA Dynamite Storage Facility
Approx. 1.2 mi. S. of Leaday
HABS TX-3360
2ph/7pg/1pc H

WPA,Bridge No. 232; see Works Progress Administration,Bridge No. 232

WPA,Bridge No. 234; see Works Progress Administration,Bridge No. 234

VOSS. VIC.

Mabel Doss Day Lea House
1.2 mi. S. of Leaday
HABS TX-3351
10dr/5ph/14pg/2pc/fr H

COLORADO COUNTY

COLUMBUS

Colorado County Courthouse
HABS TX-3400
23dr/fr H

COLUMBUS VIC.

Tait,Dr. Charles W. ,Plantation House
Rt. 71 Vic.
HABS TX-282
HABS TEX,45-COLUM.V,1-
3dr/3ph/1pg L

Tait,Dr. Charles W. ,Town House
526 Wallace St.
HABS TX-250
HABS TEX,45-COLUM,1-
3ph/1pg L

FRELSBURG

Zimmerscheidt-Leyendecker House
HABS TX-313
HABS TEX,45-FREBU,1-
10dr L

COMAL COUNTY

NEW BRAUNFELS

Evandberg Orphanage (Waisenhaus; West Texas Orphan Asylum)
Evandberg Ave. & Guadalupe River Vic.
HABS TX-3145
HABS TEX,46-NEBRA.V,1-
3ph/6pg L

First Protestant Church
HABS TX-3314
HABS TEX,46-NEBRA,8-
4ph L

Forke,J. L. ,House
593 Seguin St.
HABS TX-373
HABS TEX,46-NEBRA,4-
3ph/1pg L

Hinman,Heinrich,House
Castell Ave.
HABS TX-3253
HABS TEX,46-NEBRA,7-
7dr/6ph/6pg/fr L

Homann,Friederich,Saddlery & Residence (New Braunfels Coffee Company)
136 Seguin St.
HABS TX-33-A-11
HABS TEX,46-NEBRA,2-
3dr/13ph/2pg L

Klein-Naegelin House (Naegelin House)
511 S. Seguin Ave.
HABS TX-33-A-10
HABS TEX,46-NEBRA,1
3dr/8ph/5pg L

Landa Rock Mill
Landa St. ,Landa Park Vic.
HABS TX-3251
HABS TEX,46-NEBRA,6-
2ph/5pg L

Lindheimer,Ferdinand,House
491 S. Comal Ave.
HABS TX-374
HABS TEX,46-NEBRA,5-
5dr/10ph/7pg/fr L

Naegelin House; see Klein-Naegelin House

New Braunfels Coffee Company; see Homann,Friederich,Saddlery & Residence

Schmidt,Phillip,House
354 Bridge St.
HABS TX-372
HABS TEX,46-NEBRA,3-
2ph/1pg L

Waisenhaus; see Evandberg Orphanage

West Texas Orphan Asylum; see Evandberg Orphanage

CONCHO COUNTY

Colorado-Concho Rivers Confluence Area
HABS TX-3350
1dr/5ph/36pg/1pc H

VOSS VIC.

Creswell Half-Dugout
HABS TX-3356
2dr/7ph/8pg/1pc/fr H

Gann House
S. of Leaday
HABS TX-3358
2ph/9pg/1pc/fr H

Leaday Crossing
Spanning Colorado River on Farm-Ranch Rd. 2134
HAER TX-20
HAER DLC/PP-1992:TX-3
3ph/5pg/1pc/fr L

McLane-Hafner Ranch
Approx. 1.2 km W. of Elm Creek & Colorado River
HABS TX-3355
2dr/15pg/1pc/fr H

McLane-Hafner Ranch,Main House
HABS TX-3355-A
7ph H

McLane-Hafner Ranch,Stone Outbuilding
HABS TX-3355-B
2ph H

Rich Coffey Ranch
Approx. 3 mi. ENE of Leaday
HABS TX-3354
3dr/2ph/13pg/1pc/fr H

Rich Coffey Ranch,Barn
HABS TX-3354-C
1ph H

Rich Coffey Ranch,House
HABS TX-3354-A
10ph H

Rich Coffey Ranch,Stone Chicken Pen
HABS TX-3354-D
1ph H

Rich Coffey Ranch,Storm Cellar
HABS TX-3354-B
2ph H

Tickle House & Outbldgs.,Main House
HABS TX-3359-A
4ph H

Tickle House & Outbldgs.,Milk Pen,Gas Pump
HABS TX-3359-B
1ph H

Tickle House & Outbldgs.,Round Corral
HABS TX-3359-E
1ph H

Tickle House & Outbldgs.,Stone Barn
HABS TX-3359-C
2ph H

Tickle House & Outbldgs.,Tenant House
HABS TX-3359-D
1ph H

Tickle House & Outbuildings
Approx. 5.4 mi. SW of Leaday
HABS TX-3359
1ph/9pg/1pc/fr H

Tickle House and Outbldgs.,Lambing Shed
HABS TX-3359-F
1ph H

Tickle,E. T. Dam
NW of Concho River,SE of Concho Townsite
HAER TX-19
HAER DLC/PP-1992:TX-3
3ph/6pg/1pc L

Winkel-Blair House
S. of Leaday
HABS TX-3357
3dr/4ph/9pg/1pc/fr H

CROCKETT COUNTY

OZONA VIC.

Picket & Sotol House
Howard's Creek Vic. (moved to TX,Lubbock)
HABS TX-3316
HABS TEX,152-LUBBO,13-
4dr L

DALLAS COUNTY

DALLAS

A.,T. & SF Control Tower 19,Maintence Shed
Santa Fe Railway Milepost 51
HAER TX-22-A
4ph/2pg/1pc H

A.,T. & SF Control Tower 19,Tool Shed
Santa Fe Railway Milepost 51
HAER TX-22-B
4ph/2pg/1pc H

Atchison,Topeka & Santa Fe Control Tower 19
Santa Fe Railway Milepost 51
HAER TX-22
3dr/13ph/8pg/1pc/fr H

Brown,F. A.,Farmstead
4611 Kelton
HABS TX-3387
HABS DLC/PP-1993:TX-1
12dr/fr L

Dallas City Hall
City Hall Plaza
HABS TX-3325
HABS TEX,57-DAL,1-
12ph/3pg/1pc/fr L

Dreyfuss & Son Store
Main & Ervay Sts.
HABS TX-3125
HABS TEX,57-DAL,2-
12ph/16pg/fr L

Fair Park
Perry & Second Aves.
HABS TX-3336
HABS TEX,57-DAL,3A-
1dr L

Fair Park,Coliseum
Perry & Second Aves.
HABS TX-3336-A
HABS TEX,57-DAL,3A-
8dr/fr L

Fair Park,General Exhibits Bldg
NE of Parry & Second Aves.
HABS TX-3336-B
HABS TEX,57-DAL,3B-
12dr/fr L

Morehead-Gano Log House
Old City Park (moved from TX,Grapevine Vic.)
HABS TX-3269
HABS TEX,220,GRA.V,1-
5dr L

DE WITT COUNTY

THOMASTOWN VIC.

Murphree,Thomas,House
HABS TX-279
HABS TEX,62-THOM,1-
1ph/1pg L

DEAF SMITH COUNTY

BOVINA VIC.

Las Escarbadas Ranch House
Tierra Blanca Draw
HABS TX-3229
HABS TEX,59-BOVI.V,1-
5dr L

DICKENS COUNTY

DICKENS

Matador Half-Dugout
Dickens Vic. (moved to TX,Lubbock)
HABS TX-3232
HABS TEX,152-LUBBO,8-
2dr L

Spur-Swenson Granary
Dickens Vic. (moved to TX,Lubbock)
HABS TX-3230
HABS TEX,152-LUBBO,11-
6dr L

DONLEY COUNTY

CLARENDON

Bairfield School
Farm Rd. 262 (Moved to TX,Lubbock)
HABS TX-3243
HABS TEX,152-LUBBO,1-
4dr L

EL PASO COUNTY

EL PASO

Capri Theater; see South El Paso Street Historic District

County Jail,Old
San Elizario Plaza
HABS TX-3304
HABS TEX,71-ELPA,2-
4ph/1pc L

Ellanay Theater; see South El Paso Street Historic District

First National Bank Building (Star Jewelry)
100-102 E. San Antonio Ave.
HABS TX-3308
HABS TEX,71-ELPA,6-
4dr/4ph/13pg/1pc/fr L

Fort Bliss Building No.440; see Fort Bliss,7th Cavalry Mess Hall & Kitchen

Fort Bliss,Building No. 445; see Fort Bliss,7th Cavalry Mess Hall and Kitchen

Fort Bliss,Building No. 448; see Fort Bliss,7th Cavalry Barrack

Fort Bliss,Building No. 451; see Fort Bliss,7th Cavalry Barrack

Fort Bliss,Building No. 452; see Fort Bliss,7th Cavalry Barrack

Fort Bliss,Building No. 458; see Fort Bliss,7th Cavalry Post Exchange

Fort Bliss,7th Calvary Cantonment Barrack; see Fort Bliss,7th Cavalry Barrack

Fort Bliss,7th Cavalry Barrack (Fort Bliss,Building No. 448)
U. S. Army Air Defense Artillery Ctr & Fort Bliss
HABS TX-3339-C
HABS 1989(HABS):22
2ph/1pg/1pc L

Fort Bliss,7th Cavalry Barrack (Fort Bliss,Building No. 451; Fort Bliss,7th Calvary Cantonment Barrack)
U. S. Army Air Defense Artillery Ctr & Fort Bliss
HABS TX-3339-D
HABS 1989(HABS):22
3ph/1pg/1pc L

Fort Bliss,7th Cavalry Barrack (Fort Bliss,Building No. 452)
U. S. Army Air Defense Artillery Ctr. & Fort Bliss
HABS TX-3339-E
HABS 1989(HABS):22
2ph/1pg/1pc L

Fort Bliss,7th Cavalry Buildings
U. S. Army Air Defence Artillery Ctr & Fort Bliss
HABS TX-3339
HABS 1989(HABS):22
11ph/46pg/2pc L

Fort Bliss,7th Cavalry Mess Hall & Kitchen (Fort Bliss Building No.440)
U. S. Army Air Defence Artillery Ctr & Fort Bliss
HABS TX-3339-A
HABS 1989(HABS):22
3ph/1pg/1pc L

Fort Bliss,7th Cavalry Mess Hall and Kitchen (Fort Bliss,Building No. 445)
U. S. Army Air Defense Artillery Ctr & Fort Bliss
HABS TX-3339-B
HABS 1989(HABS):22
4ph/1pg/1pc L

Fort Bliss,7th Cavalry Post Exchange (Fort Bliss,Building No. 458)
U. S. Army Air Defense Artillery Ctr. & Fort Bliss
HABS TX-3339-F
HABS 1989(HABS):22
5ph/1pg/1pc L

Hart,Simeon,Grist Mill
HABS TX-3109
HABS TEX,71-ELPA,1-
1ph/1pg L

Hollywood Cafe; see Merrick Building

Merrick Building (St. Charles Hotel; Hollywood Cafe)
301-303 S. El Paso St.
HABS TX-3309
HABS TEX,71-ELPA,5-
4dr/5ph/12pg/1pc L

San Elizario Plaza Gazebo
San Elizario Plaza
HABS TX-3305
HABS TEX,71-ELPA,3-
3ph/1pc/1ct/fr L

South El Paso Street Historic District
S. El Paso,S. Oregon & S. Santa Fe Sts.
HABS TX-3307
HABS TEX,71-ELPA,4-
1dr/115ph/7pc/fr L

South El Paso Street Historic District (Ellanay Theater; Capri Theater)
107 S. El Paso Street
HABS TX-3307-A
HABS TEX,71-ELPA,4A-
14ph L

St. Charles Hotel; see Merrick Building

Star Jewelry; see First National Bank Building

SAN ELIZARIO

Casa Ronquillo; see Viceregal House

El Palacio; see Viceregal House

El Paso County Courthouse,First; see Los Portales

Garcia,Gregorio,House; see Los Portales

Iglesia de San Elceario (San Elizario Chapel)
San Elizario Plaza
HABS TX-3106
HABS TEX,71-SANEL,1-
7dr/13ph/14pg/2pc/5ct/fr L

Los Portales (El Paso County Courthouse,First; Garcia,Gregorio,House)
San Elizario Plaza
HABS TX-3107
HABS TEX,71-SANEL,2-
4dr/6ph/10pg/1pc/1ct/fr L

Lujan,Jesus,House
San Elizario Plaza
HABS TX-3108
HABS TEX,71-SANEL,3-
3ph/1pg L

San Elizario Chapel; see Iglesia de San Elceario

Viceregal House (El Palacio; Casa Ronquillo; Viceroy's Palace)
SE of San Elizario Plaza
HABS TX-3110
HABS TEX,71-SANEL,4-
3dr/18ph/14pg/2pc/3ct/fr L

Viceroy's Palace; see Viceregal House

SOCORRO

Mission Nuestra Senora del Socorro
Moon Rd. at Farm Rd. 258
HABS TX-3105
HABS TX,71-SOCO,1-
7dr/22ph/6pg/2pc/2ct/fr L

YSLETA

Mission de San Antonio de la Ysleta del Sur (Our Lady of Mount Carmel Church; Mission Nuestra Senora del Carmen)
Alameda Ave. & Zaragosa Drive
HABS TX-3104
HABS TEX,71-YSL,1-
7dr/17ph/21pg/2pc/3ct/fr L

Mission Nuestra Senora del Carmen; see Mission de San Antonio de la Ysleta del Sur

Our Lady of Mount Carmel Church; see Mission de San Antonio de la Ysleta del Sur

YSLETA-SAN ELIZARIO

El Camino de las Misiones
Ysleta,Socorro,San Elizario Vic.
HABS TX-3306
HABS TEX,71-YSL,2-
1dr/14pg/fr L

FAYETTE COUNTY

LA GRANGE

Etario Club; see Steihl,Judge J. C. ,House

Frede,Francis,House (Kaulbach House)
LaFayette St.
HABS TX-3120
HABS TEX,75-LAGR,1-
2ph/1pg L

Kaulbach House; see Frede,Francis,House

Kirsch,Anton,House
HABS TX-3122
HABS TEX,75-LAGR,3-
3ph/1pg L

Steihl,Judge J. C. ,House (Etario Club)
Fannin at Franklin Sts.
HABS TX-3121
HABS TEX,75-LAGR,2-
4ph/11pg L

ROUND TOP

Bethlehem Lutheran Church
White St.
HABS TX-3124
HABS TEX,75-ROUNT,2-
6dr/10ph/7pg/fr L

Henkel,Edward,House
Henkel Square,Live Oak & First Sts.
HABS TX-3196
HABS TEX,75-ROUNT,4-
5dr/6ph/5pg/fr L

Kneip,Ferdinand,House
HABS TX-3123
HABS TEX,75-ROUNT,1-
3ph/1pg L

Rummel,Carl Wilhelm,House
First St.
HABS TX-3200
HABS TEX,75-ROUNT,5-
5dr/6ph/5pg/fr L

Wantke-Pochmann House
White & Third Sts.
HABS TX-3188
HABS TEX,75-ROUNT,3-
3dr/4ph/4pg/fr L

Zapp-Von Rosenberg House
Henkel Square,Live Oak & First Sts.
HABS TX-3252
HABS TEX,75-ROUNT,6-
2ph/5pg L

FORT BEND COUNTY

RICHMOND

Moore House
HABS TX-3393
17dr/fr H

GALVESTON COUNTY

GALVESTON

Albert,J. T. ,House; see Turner Hall

Ashton Villa; see Brown,James Mareau,House

Austin,Edward T. ,House
1502 Market St. (Ave. D)
HABS TX-261
HABS TEX,84-GALV,14-
3ph/1pg L

B'nai Israel Synagogue
707 Twenty-second St.
HABS TX-3298
HABS TEX,84-GALV,16-
2ph/1pg L

Ball,George,House
1405 Twenty-fourth St.
HABS TX-27
HABS TEX,84-GALV,4-
7dr/5ph/5pg L

Ballinger Building
2201 Post Office St.
HABS TX-3297
HABS TEX,84-GALV,20-
1ph L

Berlocher,John,Building; see Strand Historic District

Bishop's Palace; see Gresham,Col. Walter,House

Blum,Leon & H. ,Building; see Strand Historic District

Bolton Estate Building; see Strand Historic District

Brown-Denison-Moore House
(Moore,Bartlett,House)
3112 Ave. O
HABS TX-257
HABS TEX,84-GALV,10-
2ph/1pg L

Brown,James Mareau,House (Ashton Villa; El Mina Shrine Temple)
2328 Broadway
HABS TX-33-B-3
HABS TEX,84-GALV,1-
8dr/18ph/8pg L

Cherry,Wilbur F. ,House
1602 Church St.
HABS TX-252
HABS TEX,84-GALV,7-
2ph/5pg L

Darragh,Mrs. John L. ,House
519 Fifteenth St.
HABS TX-2104
HABS TEX,84-GALV,21-
4ph/4pg L

Eaton Memorial Chapel of Trinity Episcopal Church
710 Twenty-second St.
HABS TX-295
HABS TEX,84-GALV,18-
2ph/5pg L

El Mina Shrine Temple; see Brown,James Mareau,House

Federal Building; see U. S. Custom House

First National Bank Building; see Strand Historic District

First Presbyterian Church
Church & Nineteenth Sts.
HABS TX-2106
HABS TEX,84-GALV,22-
5ph/8pg L

Galveston Baggage & Cordage Factory
Winnie St.
HABS TX-3319
HABS TEX,84-GALV,23-
5dr/2ph/6pg/fr L

Galveston News Building
2108 Mechanic St.
HABS TX-289
HABS TEX,84-GALV,24-
1ph/4pg L

Goldbeck College; see Marwitz,Herman,House

Grace Episcopal Church
1115 Thirty-sixth St.
HABS TX-3299
HABS TEX,84-GALV,25-
2ph L

Greenleve,Block & Company,Building; see Strand Historic District

Gresham,Col. Walter,House (Bishop's Palace)
1402 Broadway
HABS TX-2103
HABS TEX,84-GALV,26-
11dr/10ph/6pg/fr L

Grover,George Washington,House
1520 Market St.
HABS TX-296
HABS TEX,84-GALV,29-
3ph/4pg L

Heidenheimer Building; see Strand Historic District

Heidenheimer Castle; see Sydnor-Heidenheimer Building

Hendley Building
2000-2016 Strand
HABS TX-290
HABS TEX,84-GALV,37-
7dr/3ph/4pg/fr L

Hutchings,John Henry,House
2816 Ave. O
HABS TX-154
HABS TEX,84-GALV,30-
7ph/5pg L

Hutchings,Sealy & Company,Building; see Strand Historic District

Jefferson,Thomas League,Building; see Strand Historic District

Kaufman & Runge Building; see Strand Historic District

Landes,Henry A. ,House
1604 Post Office St.
HABS TX-2102
HABS TEX,84-GALV,31-
4ph/4pg L

Lasker,Morris,House
1718-1726 Broadway
HABS TX-2100
HABS TEX,84-GALV,27-
5ph/5pg L

Lewis,Allen,House
2328 Ave. G (moved from Ave. J & Twenty-fifth St.)
HABS TX-256
HABS TEX,84-GALV,9-
2ph/1pg L

Marwitz,Herman,House (Goldbeck College)
801 Twenty-second St.
HABS TX-2105
HABS TEX,84-GALV,19-
2ph/1pg L

2014 Mechanic Street (Commercial Building); see Strand Historic District

Menard,Michel B. ,House
1603 Thirty-third St.
HABS TX-26
HABS TEX,84-GALV,3-
5dr/6ph/6pg L

Merchants Mutual Insurance Company Building; see Strand Historic District

Moody Building; see Strand Historic District

Moody,M. L. ,House
Ave. M & Twenty-third St.
HABS TX-254
HABS TEX,84-GALV,8-
2ph/1pg L

Moore,Bartlett,House; see Brown-Denison-Moore House

Palmetto House Hotel; see Strand Historic District

Pix Building
2126 Post Office St.
HABS TX-3300
HABS TEX,84-GALV,32-
1ph L

Powhatan Hotel
3427 Ave. O
HABS TX-28
HABS TEX,84-GALV,5-
7dr/5ph/6pg L

Rice,Baulard & Company Building
Tremont St. (200 Block)
HABS TX-3301
HABS TEX,84-GALV,33-
1ph L

Rosenberg Building; see Strand Historic District

Rosenberg,Henry,House
1306 Market St.
HABS TX-260
HABS TEX,84-GALV,13-
5dr/8ph/6pg/fr L

Sealy,George,Carriage House
2424 Broadway
HABS TX-298-A
HABS TEX,84-GALV,28A-
1ph L

Sealy,George,House
2424 Broadway
HABS TX-298
HABS TEX,84-GALV,28-
7ph/6pg L

Smith,J. F. & Brothers,Building; see Strand Historic District

St. Mary's Cathedral
Twenty-first St. & Church Ave.
HABS TX-293
HABS TEX,84-GALV,34-
7dr/3ph/4pg/fr L

St. Patrick's Catholic Church
Thirty-fourth & K Sts.
HABS TX-3302
HABS TEX,84-GALV,38-
5ph L

Strand Historic District
Strand & Mechanic Sts.
HABS TX-3296
HABS TEX,84-GALV,38-
3pg/fr L

Strand Historic District
(Berlocher,John,Building)
2315 Mechanic St.
HABS TX-3296-C
HABS TEX,84-GALV,38C-
2ph/1pc L

Strand Historic District (Blum,Leon & H. ,Building)
2310-2328 Mechanic St.
HABS TX-3296-D
HABS TEX,84-GALV,38D-
2ph L

Strand Historic District (Bolton Estate Building; Smith,J. F. & Brothers,Building)
2321-2323 Strand
HABS TX-3296-N
HABS TEX,84-GALV,38N-
1ph/2pg/fr L

Strand Historic District (First National Bank Building)
2127 Strand
HABS TX-3296-E
HABS TEX,84-GALV,38E-
5ph/1pg L

Strand Historic District
(Greenleve,Block & Company,Building)
2310-2314 Strand
HABS TX-3296-G
HABS TEX,84-GALV,38G-
2ph/1pg L

Strand Historic District (Heidenheimer Building)
2127 Mechanic St.
HABS TX-3296-H
HABS TEX,84-GALV,38H-
1ph L

Strand Historic District
(Hutchings,Sealy & Company,Building)
2326-2328 Strand
HABS TX-3296-I
HABS TEX,84-GALV,38I-
1ph L

Strand Historic District
(Jefferson,Thomas League,Building)
2301-2307 Strand
HABS TX-3296-F
HABS TEX,84-GALV,38F-
1ph/3pg/fr L

Strand Historic District (Kaufman & Runge Building)
222 Twenty-second St.
HABS TX-3296-J
HABS TEX,84-GALV,38J-
2ph/2pg/fr L

Strand Historic District (2014 Mechanic Street (Commercial Building))
HABS TX-3296-A
HABS TEX,84-GALV,38A-
2ph L

Strand Historic District (Merchants Mutual Insurance Company Building)
2317-2319 Strand
HABS TX-3296-K
HABS TEX,84-GALV,38K-
1ph/2pg/fr L

Strand Historic District (Moody Building)
2202-2206 Strand
HABS TX-3296-Q
HABS TEX,84-GALV,38Q-
2ph L

Strand Historic District (Palmetto House Hotel)
2302 Mechanic St.
HABS TX-3296-L
HABS TEX,84-GALV,38L-
1ph L

Strand Historic District (Rosenberg Building)
2309-2311 Strand
HABS TX-3296-M
HABS TEX,-84-GALV,38M-
1ph L

Strand Historic District (Ufford Building)
303-309 Twenty-third St.
HABS TX-3296-O
HABS TEX,84-GALV,38O-
8ph/1pg/fr L

Strand Historic District (Washington Hotel)
Twenty-second St. & Ave. C
HABS TX-3296-P
HABS TEX,84-GALV,38P-
2ph/1pg L

Strand Historic District
(Wood-Rosenfield-House-Berlocher Buildings)
2213-2223 Strand
HABS TX-3296-B
HABS TEX,84-GALV,38B-
1ph/fr L

Sydnor-Heidenheimer Building
(Heidenheimer Castle)
1602 Sealy St.
HABS TX-2101
HABS TEX,84-GALV,39-
4ph/4pg L

Trinity Episcopal Church
708 Twenty-second St.
HABS TX-294
HABS TEX,84-GALV,17-
7dr/5ph/7pg/fr L

Trube,John C. ,House
1621-27 Sealy Ave.
HABS TX-299
HABS TEX,84-GALV,40-
3ph/4pg L

Trueheart-Adriance Building
(Trueheart,H. M. ,Building)
212 Twenty-second St.
HABS TX-291
HABS TEX,84-GALV,15-
5dr/4ph/5pg/fr L

Trueheart,H. M. ,Building; see Trueheart-Adriance Building

Turner Hall (Albert,J. T. ,House)
2015 Ave. I
HABS TX-21
HABS TEX,84-GALV,2-
4dr/11ph/1pg L

Twenty-seventh Avenue H (Part of Powhatan Hotel)
HABS TX-28-A
HABS TEX,84-GALV,6-
1ph/1pg L

U. S. Custom House (Federal Building)
Twentieth & Post Office Sts.
HABS TX-259
HABS TEX,84-GALV,12-
8dr/7ph/7pg/fr L

Ufford Building; see Strand Historic District

University of Texas Medical School Building
914-916 Strand
HABS TX-292
HABS TEX,84-GALV,36-
3ph/5pg L

Ursuline Convent
Ave. N & Twenty-fifth St.
HABS TX-3227
HABS TEX,84-GALV,41-
2ph/1pg L

Washington Hotel; see Strand Historic District

Williams-Tucker House
(Williams,Samuel May,House)
3601 Ave. P
HABS TX-297
HABS TEX,84-GALV,42-
6dr/5ph/8pg/fr L

Williams,Samuel May,House; see Williams-Tucker House

Wolston,John,House
1705 Thirty-fifth St.
HABS TX-258
HABS TEX,84-GALV,11-
1ph/1pg L

Wood-Rosenfield-House-Berlocher Buildings; see Strand Historic District

GARZA COUNTY

POST

"U Lazy S" Carriage,Saddle & Harness Shop
W. Farm Rd. 669,S. of Post (moved to TX,Lubbock)
HABS TX-3242
HABS TEX,152-LUBBO,12-
L

GILLESPIE COUNTY

CAVE CREEK

Althaus,Dr. Christian,House
HABS TX-3327
HABS TEX,86-CACRE,1-
5dr/fr L

CHERRY SPRING

Rode-Kothe House
E. of U. S. 87 at Cherry Spring
HABS TX-378
HABS TEX,86-CHESP,1-
8ph/1pg L

CHERRY SPRINGS

Rode-Kothe Sheep Barn
E. of U. S. 87 at Cherry Spring
HABS TX-33-A-14
HABS TEX,86-CHEP,1B-
5ph/1pg/fr L

FREDERICKSBURG

Dietz,Heinrich G. ,House
Creek & Bowie Sts.
HABS TX-380
HABS TEX,86-FREBU,7-
4ph/1pg L

First Courthouse (Post Office,Old)
Main & Crockett Sts.
HABS TX-33-A-7
HABS TEX,86-FREBU,1-
3dr/4ph/1pg/fr L

Kammlah,Heinrich,House
309 W. Main St.
HABS TX-379
HABS TEX,86-FREBU,6-
6ph/1pg L

Kiehne-Foerster House
405 E. Main St.
HABS TX-381
HABS TEX,86-FREBU,8-
3ph/1pg L

Pfeil House
125 W. San Antonio St.
HABS TX-33-A-13
HABS TEX,86-FREBU,4-
6dr/3ph/1pg/fr L

Post Office,Old; see First Courthouse

St. Mary's Catholic Church,Old
San Antonio St.
HABS TX-33-C-2
HABS TEX 86-FREBU.-5-
4dr/5ph/2pg L

Staudt,Sunday,House
512 W. Creek St.
HABS TX-33-A-8
HABS TEX,86-FREBU,2-
2dr/4ph/1pg/fr L

Tatsch,John Peter,House
210 N. Bowie St.
HABS TX-33-A-12
HABS TEX,86-FREBU,3-
2dr/6ph/1pg L

STONEWALL

Evangelical Lutheran Church,Congre. of the Trinity (Trinity Lutheran Church)
Ranch Rd. 1 at Lower Albert Rd.
HABS TX-3329
HABS TEX,86-STONE,2-
4dr L

Trinity Lutheran Church; see Evangelical Lutheran Church,Congre. of the Trinity

STONEWALL VIC.

Johnson,Lyndon B. ,National Historical Park; see Johnson,Lyndon B. ,Ranch

Johnson,Lyndon B. ,National Historical Park; see Johnson,Lyndon B. ,Ranch House

Johnson,Lyndon B. ,Ranch
(Johnson,Lyndon B. ,National Historical Park)
Park Rd. 49,LBJ National Historical Park
HABS TX-3328
1dr/fr H

Johnson,Lyndon B. ,Ranch House
(Johnson,Lyndon B. ,National Historical Park)
Park Rd. 49,LBJ National Historical Park
HABS TX-3328-A
3dr/fr H

Johnson,Lyndon B. ,Ranch,Junction School
Ranch Rd. 49 at Reagan Rd.
HABS TX-3328-B
2dr/fr H

GOLIAD COUNTY

GOLIAD

Davis House (McCampbell,John S. ,House)
HABS TX-385
HABS TEX,88-GOLI,3-
4ph/1pg L

McCampbell,John S. ,House; see Davis House

GOLIAD VIC.

Boyd,William H. ,House
HABS TX-383
HABS TEX,88-GOLI,1-
3ph/1pg L

La Bahia Presidio Chapel
S. on U. S. Rt. 183
HABS TX-387
HABS TEX,8-GOLI,4-
5ph/1pg L

Peck,Capt. Barton,House
S. of U. S. 59
HABS TX-384
HABS TEX,88-GOLI,2-
11ph/1pg L

GONZALES COUNTY

BELMONT VIC.

King,Tom,House
HABS TX-352
HABS TEX,89-BELM.V,1-
4ph/1pg L

GRIMES COUNTY

ANDERSON

Grimes County Courthouse
HABS TX-3344
HABS 1991(HABS):29
14dr/fr L

ANDERSON VIC.

Baptist Church
Main St.
HABS TX-276
HABS TEX,93-AND,10-
2ph/1pg L

Barnes,Gen. James W. ,Plantation House (Prairie Woods)
Farm Rd. 1774 Vic.
HABS TX-287
HABS TEX,93-AND.V,2-
8dr/4ph/5pg L

Black-Schroder Springhouse (Neblett Springhouse)
HABS TX-220
HABS TEX,93-AND,4-
1ph/1pg L

Bogess; see Boggess,H. H. ,House

Boggess,H. H. ,House (Bogess)
Fanthorp St. ,Farm Rd. 1774 Vic.
HABS TX-221
HABS TEX,93-AND,5-
1ph/1pg L

Bowman-Clarke-Kelley House; see Bowman,John,House

Bowman,John,House
(Bowman-Clarke-Kelley House; Clarke House,Old)
W. of Anderson
HABS TX-272
HABS TEX,93-AND,7-
1ph/1pg L

Buchanan,Dr. J. E. ,House
HABS TX-223
HABS TEX,93-AND,6-
1ph/1pg L

Cawthorn,E. W. ,House (Womack House)
Farm Rd. 149 Vic.
HABS TX-274
HABS TEX,93-AND,9-
2ph/1pg L

Clarke House,Old; see Bowman,John,House

Dickson,David C. ,House
Farm Rd. 1774
HABS TX-273
HABS TEX,93-AND,8-
2ph/1pg L

Fanthorp Tavern
S. Main St.
HABS TX-217
HABS TEX,93-AND,1-
2ph/1pg L

Fuqua,Ephraim,House
La Bahia Rd.
HABS TX-275
HABS TEX,93-AND.V,1-
1ph/1pg L

Green,Allen,House
HABS TX-218
HABS TEX,93-AND,2-
1ph/1pg L

Neblett Springhouse; see Black-Schroder Springhouse

Pahl,Henry,House
HABS TX-219
HABS TEX,93-AND,3-
1ph/1pg L

Prairie Woods; see Barnes,Gen. James W. ,Plantation House

Womack House; see Cawthorn,E. W. ,House

NAVASOTA

Railroad Avenue,100 Block (Buildings)
HABS TX-286
HABS TEX,93-NAVA,4-
18dr/fr L

NAVASOTA VIC.

Bechtol House (Navosota Beauty Shop)
HABS TX-216
HABS TEX,93-NAVA,2-
1ph/1pg L

Collins-Camp House (Foster House; Felder,Alfred,House)
HABS TX-215
HABS TEX,93-NAVA,1-
3ph/1pg L

Felder,Alfred,House; see Collins-Camp House

Foster House; see Collins-Camp House

Freeman,Ira M. ,House
HABS TX-271
HABS TEX,93-NAVA,3-
1ph/1pg L

Gibbs-Foster House
TX Rt. 90 Vic.
HABS TX-214
HABS TEX,93-NAVA.V,1-
2ph/1pg L

Navosota Beauty Shop; see Bechtol House

PLANTERSVILLE VIC.

Baker,Capt. Isaac,House; see Cedaar Hall

Cedaar Hall (Baker,Capt. Isaac,House)
HABS TX-225
HABS TEX,93-PLAN.V,1-
2ph/1pg L

College Dormitory,Old; see Markey's Seminary Dormitory

Easley,A. B. ,House
HABS TX-227
HABS TEX,93-PLANV,3-
2ph/1pg L

Markey's Seminary Dormitory (College Dormitory,Old)
W. edge of Plantersville
HABS TX-277
HABS TEX,93-PLANV,4-
2ph/1pg L

Walton,Maj. Peter,House
HABS TX-226
HABS TEX,93-PLAN.V,2-
1ph/1pg L

ROANS PRAIRIE VIC.

Kennard,Anthony D. ,House
HABS TX-229
HABS TEX,93-ROPR,2-
1ph/1pg L

Kennard,Mark,House
HABS TX-228
HABS TEX,93-ROPR,1-
1ph/1pg L

STONEHAM VIC.

Sanders-McIntyre House
HABS TX-224
HABS TEX,93-STO.V,1-
1ph/1pg L

GUADALUPE COUNTY

SEGUIN

Aunt Margaret's House
HABS TX-348
HABS TEX,94-SEGUI,12-
2ph/1pg L

Baxter-Fennell House (Fennell,Dr. J. D. ,House)
202 E. Walnut St.
HABS TX-347
HABS TEX,94-SEGUI,11-
4ph/2pg L

Campbell,Mosey,House
HABS TX-329
HABS TEX,94-SEGUI,4-
9ph/1pg L

Coopender,Luke,House
HABS TX-344
HABS TEX,94-SEGUI,8-
4ph/1pg L

Erskine House I; see Humphrey-Erskine House

Erskine House II
513 E. Nolte St.
HABS TX-343
HABS TEX,94-SEGUI,7-
6ph/1pg L

Fennell,Dr. J. D. ,House; see Baxter-Fennell House

Flores,Manuel,House
HABS TX-340
HABS TEX,94-SEGUI,5-
7ph/1pg L

Herron-Vaughn House (Vaughn,Tom,House)
S. Goodrich St.
HABS TX-346
HABS TEX,94-SEGUI,10-
5ph/1pg L

Herron,Parson Andrew,House
906 W. Court St.
HABS TX-345
HABS TEX,94-SEGUI,9-
5ph/1pg L

Hollomon House
315 Glen Cove Dr.
HABS TX-350
HABS TEX,94-SEGUI,14-
5ph/1pg L

Humphrey-Erskine House (Erskine House I)
902 N. Austin St.
HABS TX-328
HABS TEX,94-SEGUI,3-
4dr/10ph/1pg L

Isom's House
HABS TX-349
HABS TEX,94-SEGUI,13-
3ph/1pg L

Johnson-LeGette-Miller House (Miller,Thad B. ,House)
Johnson Ave.
HABS TX-341
HABS TEX,94-SEGUI,6-
9ph/2pg L

Magnolia Hotel
203 S. Crockett St.
HABS TX-327
HABS TEX,94-SEGUI,2-
4ph/1pg L

McCulloch,Ben,House
Kingsbury Vic.
HABS TX-353
HABS TEX,94-SEGUI,16-
2ph/1pg L

Miller,Thad B. ,House; see Johnson-LeGette-Miller House

Sebastopol; see Young,Col. Joshua,House

Vaughn,Tom,House; see Herron-Vaughn House

White,Judge John P. ,House
HABS TX-351
HABS TEX,94-SEGUI,15-
4ph/1pg L

Young,Col. Joshua,House (Sebastopol; Zorn,Joseph,House)
704 Mill Ave.
HABS TX-33-A-9
HABS TEX,94-SEGUI,1-
5dr/5ph/2pg/fr L

Zorn,Joseph,House; see Young,Col. Joshua,House

SEGUIN VIC.

Baume,Jose,de la,Cabin; see El Capote Cabin

El Capote Cabin (Baume,Jose,de la,Cabin)
Guadalupe River Vic. (moved to TX,Lubbock)
HABS TX-3317
HABS TEX,152-LUBBO,15-
3dr L

HALE COUNTY

ABERNATHY VIC.

Barton,Joseph J. ,House
Bartonsite (moved to TX,Lubbock)
HABS TX-3315
HABS TEX,152-LUBBO,14-
9dr L

HARRIS COUNTY

HOUSTON

Carrington,Dr. ,House
Crawford St. & Rusk Ave.
HABS TX-33-B-2
HABS TEX,101-HOUT,2-
4dr/9ph/1pg L

Houston City Hall
901 Bagby St.
HABS TX-3226
HABS TEX,101-HOUT,5-
16ph/16pg/1pc/fr L

Kellum-Noble House (Shelter House)
Sam Houston Park,212 Dallas Ave.
HABS TX-23
HABS TEX,101-HOUT,4-
4dr/2ph/1pg/fr L

Longcope,E. ,House
102 Chenevert St.
HABS TX-22
HABS TEX,101-HOUT,3-
3dr/7ph/1pg/fr L

Nichols-Rice-Cherry House
Sam Houston Park (moved from San Jacinto St.)
HABS TX-33-B-1
HABS TEX,101-HOUT,1-
4dr/10ph/1pg L

Shelter House; see Kellum-Noble House

HARRISON COUNTY

KARNACK VIC.

Andrews-Taylor House
State Rt. 43,Farm Rd. 2862 Vic.
HABS TX-147
HABS TEX,102-KARN.V,1-
11dr/8ph/6pg/fr L

MARSHALL VIC.

Alexander House
HABS TX-124
HABS TEX,102-MARSH,5-
3ph/1pg L

Carter House
HABS TX-121
HABS TEX,102-MARSH,2-
3ph/1pg L

First Methodist Church South
300 E. Houston St.
HABS TX-122
HABS TEX,102-MARSH,3-
2ph/1pg L

Henderson,J. B. ,House (Stage Coach Stop)
U. S. Rt. 59
HABS TX-120
HABS TEX,102-MARSH.V,1-
3ph/1pg L

Holcombe,Beverly Lafayette,House; see Wyalucing

Longhorn Army Ammunition Plant
HAER TX-8
HAER TEX,102-MARSH.V,2-
53pg/fr L

Munce House
HABS TX-123
HABS TEX,102-MARSH,4-
2ph/1pg L

Stage Coach Stop; see Henderson,J. B. ,House

Whetstone House
HABS TX-125
HABS TEX,102-MARSH,6-
3ph/1pg L

Wyalucing (Holcombe,Beverly Lafayette,House)
Bishop & W. Bush Sts.
HABS TX-33-D-4
HABS TEX,102-MARSH,1-
5dr/8ph/2pg/fr L

HAYS COUNTY

DRIFTWOOD VIC.

Camp Ben McCulloch; see Johnson's Institute

Friday Mountain Camp; see Johnson's Institute

Johnson's Institute (Camp Ben McCulloch; Friday Mountain Camp)
Farm Rd. 1826
HABS TX-398
HABS TEX,105-DRIF,1-
4ph/2pg L

HILL COUNTY

HILLSBORO

Hill County Courthouse
Public Squre,Waco,Elm,Covington & Franklin Sts.
HABS TX-138
HABS TEX,109-HILBO,1-
5ph/4pg L

ITASCA VIC.

Randle-Turner House
Farm Rd. 934
HABS TX-136
HABS TEX,109-ITASC,1-
5dr/8ph/4pg/fr L

HOCKLEY COUNTY

LEVELLAND

Slaughter Two-Story Dugout
Levelland Vic. (moved to TX,Lubbock)
HABS TX-3228
HABS TEX,152-LUBBO,9-
3dr L

HOUSTON COUNTY

CROCKETT VIC.

Collin,Tom,House; see Park Hill

Monroe-Coleman House
707 E. Houston St.
HABS TX-232
HABS TEX,113-CROC,1-
2ph/1pg L

Park Hill (Collin,Tom,House)
Between Farm Rds. 229 & 2076
HABS TX-233
HABS TEX,113-CROC.V,1-
3ph/2pg L

JEFF DAVIS COUNTY

FORT DAVIS

Fort Davis (Fort Davis National Historic Site)
TX Rt. 17
HABS TX-3102
HABS TEX,122-FODA,1-
5ph/2pg L

Fort Davis National Historic Site; see Fort Davis

Fort Davis National Historic Site; see Fort Davis,Officer's Row

Fort Davis,Hospital
TX Rt. 17
HABS TX-3158
HABS TEX,122-FODA,1B-
7dr L

Fort Davis,Magazine
TX Rt. 17
HABS TX-3159
HABS TEX,122-FODA,1C-
2dr L

Fort Davis,Officer's Row (Fort Davis National Historic Site)
State Route 17
HABS TX-3390
HABS DLC/PP-1992:TX-5
3ph/1pc L

Fort Davis,Quarters,HB-14
TX Rt. 17
HABS TX-3156
HABS TEX,122-FODA,1A-
7dr/fr L

Ft. Davis,Quarters,HB-12
HABS TX-3368
H

JEFFERSON COUNTY

BEAUMONT VIC.

Tryyell Farm,Farmstead House
6245 Fannet Rd. (Hwy 124)
HABS TX-3369-A
6ph/4pg/1pc H

Tyrrell Farm Complex
6245 Fannet Road (Hwy. 124)
HABS TX-3369
4dr/3ph/8pg/1pc/fr H

Tyrrell Farm,Barn
6245 Fannet Rd. (Hwy. 124)
HABS TX-3369-C
5ph/2pg/1pc H

Tyrrell Farm,Machine Shed
6245 Fannet Rd. (Hwy. 124)
HABS TX-3369-B
4ph/1pg/1pc H

JIM HOGG COUNTY

CUEVITAS

Roderiguez,Eugenio,House & Post Office
Farm Rd. 649
HABS TX-3138
HABS TEX,124-CUEV,1-
5ph/4pg L

KARNES COUNTY

CZESTOCHOWA

Nativity of the Blessed Virgin Mary Church
W. of Rt. 123
HABS TX-3261
HABS TEX,128-CESTA,1-
6dr L

PANNA MARIA VIC.

Moscygamba Houses
Off Farm Rd. 81,TX Rt. 123 Vic.
HABS TX-312
HABS TEX,128-PANA,2-
4ph/1pg L

Urbanczyk House
Farm Rd. 81 Vic.
HABS TX-311
HABS TEX,128-PANA,1-
3ph/1pg L

Whetstone Ranch House
Farm Rd. 81 Vic.
HABS TX-388
HABS TEX,128-PANA,3-
5ph/1pg L

PAWELEKVILLE

Pawelek,Machie,House
TX. 123 at Farm Rd. 887
HABS TX-314
HABS TEX,128-CRESTA.V,1-
3dr/7ph/1pg/fr L

KENDALL COUNTY

BOERNE VIC.

Becker House; see Schertz House

Schertz House (Becker House)
Farm Rd. 474 & Spring Creek Rd.
HABS TX-375
HABS TEX,130-BORN.V,1-
5ph/1pg L

COMFORT

Faltin House
Seventh St.
HABS TX-376
HABS TEX,130-COMF,1-
4dr/3ph/1pg/fr L

KERR COUNTY

CENTER POINT VIC.

Ganahl,Dr. Charles,House (Zanzenburg)
Historic marker at site on TX Rt. 27
HABS TX-377
HABS TEX,133-CENPO,1-
5dr/8ph/1pg/fr L

Zanzenburg; see Ganahl,Dr. Charles,House

KING COUNTY

TRUSCOTT

Masterson Rock Bunkhouse
Truscott Vic. (moved to TX,Lubbock)
HABS TX-3231
HABS TEX,152-LUBBO,6-
3dr L

LAVACA COUNTY

HACKBERRY

Neuhas Complex,Neuhaus Brothers General Store
Hwy. 532
HABS TX-3388-B
HABS DLC/PP-1993:TX-1
11dr/fr L

Neuhaus Complex
St. Hwy. 532 & Co. Rd. 219
HABS TX-3388
HABS DLC/PP-1993:TX-1
2dr/27pg/fr L

Neuhaus Complex,C. L. Neuhaus-King House
Hwy. 532
HABS TX-3388-C
HABS DLC/PP-1993:TX-1
8dr/fr L

Neuhaus Complex,Neuhaus,L. E. Homestead
Hwy. 532
HABS TX-3388-A
HABS DLC/PP-1993:TX-1
8dr/fr L

LUBBOCK COUNTY

LUBBOCK

"J. A. " Milk & Meat Cooler
The Ranch Headquarters (moved from TX,Claude)
HABS TX-3236
HABS TEX,152-LUBBO,3-
3dr L

"Long S" Box & Strip House
The Ranch Headquarters (moved from TX,Patricia)
HABS TX-3241
HABS TEX,152-LUBBO,5-
2dr L

"U Lazy S" Carriage,Saddle & Harness House
The Ranch Headquarters (moved from TX,Post)
HABS TX-3242
HABS TEX,152-LUBBO,12-
2dr L

Bairfield School
The Ranch Headquarters (moved from TX,Clarendon)
HABS TX-3243
HABS TEX,152-LUBBO,1-
4dr L

Barton,Joseph J. ,House
Ranching Heritage Center (moved from TX,Abernathy)
HABS TX-3315
HABS TEX,152-LUBBO,14-
9dr L

Baume,Jose,de la,Cabin; see El Capote Cabin

Chatman Hospital
2301 Cedar Ave.
HABS TX-3338
HABS TEX,152-LUBBO,18-
3dr L

El Capote Cabin (Baume,Jose,de la,Cabin)
Ranching Heritage Center (moved from TX,Seguin)
HABS TX-3317
HABS TEX,152-LUBBO,15-
3dr L

Hedwigs Hill Cabin
The Ranch Headquarters (moved from TX,Mason)
HABS TX-3233
HABS TEX,152-LUBBO,2-
6dr L

Jowell Ranch House
The Ranch Headquarters (moved from TX,Palo Pinto)
HABS TX-3237
HABS TEX,152-LUBBO,4-
3dr L

Masterson Rock Bunkhouse
The Ranch Headquarters (moved from TX,Truscott)
HABS TX-3231
HABS TEX,152-LUBBO,6-
3dr L

Matador Guest House & Office
The Ranch Headquarters (moved from TX,Matador)
HABS TX-3262
HABS TEX,152-LUBBO,7-
4dr L

Matador Half-Dugout
The Ranch Headquarters (moved from TX,Dickens)
HABS TX-3232
HABS TEX,152-LUBBO,8-
2dr L

Picket & Sotol House
Ranching Heritage Center (moved from TX,Ozona)
HABS TX-3316
HABS TEX,152-LUBBO,13-
4dr L

Renderbrook-Spade Blacksmith Shop
Ranching Heritage Center (moved from TX,Co. City)
HABS TX-3238
HABS TEX,152-LUBBO,16-
3dr L

Reynolds-Gentry Barn
Ranching Heritage Center (moved from TX,Albany)
HABS TX-3318
HABS TEX,152-LUBBO,17-
6dr L

Slaughter Two-Story Dugout
The Ranch Headquarters (moved from TX,Levelland)
HABS TX-3228
HABS TEX,152-LUBBO,9-
3dr L

Smith-Harrell House
The Ranch Headquarters (moved from TX,Snyder)
HABS TX-3235
HABS TEX,152-LUBBO,10-
5dr L

Spur-Swenson Granary
The Ranch Headquarters (moved from TX,Dickens)
HABS TX-3230
HABS TEX,152-LUBBO,11-
6dr L

MARION COUNTY

JEFFERSON

Alley,D.N.,-Woods House; see Wibler-Woods House

Christ Episcopal Church
Main & Taylor Sts.
HABS TX-143
HABS TEX,158-JEF,16-
5dr/2ph/4pg/fr L

Cockell House; see Cutrer-Key House

Cutrer-Key House (Cockell House)
State Rt. 59
HABS TX-116
HABS TEX,158-JEF.V,2-
10dr/6ph/7pg L

DeWare House
202 E. Dixon St.
HABS TX-149
HABS TEX,158-JEF,21-
4ph/4pg L

Epperson,Benjamin H. ,House; see House of the Seasons

House of the Seasons
(Epperson,Benjamin H. ,House)
409 S. Alley St.
HABS TX-142
HABS TEX,158-JEF,15-
14dr/12ph/6pg/1pc/fr L

Jefferson Historical Society Museum; see U. S. Courthouse & Post Office

Murphy-Dannelly House
410 Delte St.
HABS TX-148
HABS TEX,158-JEF,20-
8dr/2ph/5pg/fr L

Planters Bank Building & Warehouse
224 E. Austin St.
HABS TX-144
HABS TEX,158-JEF,17-
4dr/2ph/5pg/fr L

Presbyterian Church
600 E. Jefferson St.
HABS TX-150
HABS TEX,158-JEF,22-
5ph/5pg L

Sedberry House
211 N. Market St.
HABS TX-151
HABS TEX,158-JEF,23-
6ph/4pg L

St. Mary's Catholic School-Sinai Hebrew Synagogue
209 N. Henderson St.
HABS TX-141
HABS TEX,158-JEF,14-
10dr/6ph/5pg/fr L

U. S. Courthouse & Post Office
(Jefferson Historical Society Museum)
224 W. Austin St.
HABS TX-140
HABS TEX,158-JEF,13-
12dr/7ph/9pg/fr L

Wibler-Woods House (Alley,D.N.,-Woods House)
502 E. Walker St.
HABS TX-153
HABS TEX,158-JEF,25-
5ph/5pg L

Wright-Lester House
301 S. Friou St.
HABS TX-145
HABS TEX,158-JEF,18-
3dr/4ph/4pg L

JEFFERSON VIC.

Abernathy-Singleton House
204 N. Soda St.
HABS TX-146
HABS TEX,158-JEF,19-
8dr/5ph/4pg/fr L

Alley House; see Duke,W. S. ,House

Alley-Carlson House
501 E. Walker St.
HABS TX-152
HABS TEX,158-JEF,24-
4ph/4pg L

Alley,D. N. ,Sr. ,House (Ward House)
209 E. Broadway
HABS TX-117
HABS TEX,158-JEF,10-
4ph/1pg/fr L

Beard House; see Birge,Noble A. ,House

Birge,Noble A. ,House (Beard House)
212 N. Vale St.
HABS TX-113
HABS TEX,158-JEF,6-
3dr/3ph/1pg/fr L

Camp,J.,Building (Jefferson Journal Building)
112 N. Vale St.
HABS TX-111
HABS TEX,158-JEF,4-
3ph/1pg L

Culberson House
403 N. Walnut St.
HABS TX-114
HABS TEX,158-JEF,7-
3ph/1pg L

Duke,W. S. ,House (Keese House; Alley House)
112 S. Friou St.
HABS TX-119
HABS TEX,158-JEF,12-
2ph/1pg L

Excelsior Hotel (Irvine House)
Austin St.
HABS TX-112
HABS TEX,158-JEF,5-
7dr/10ph/8pg L

Freeman,Willamson M. ,House
Rt. 49
HABS TX-33-D-3
HABS TEX,158-JEF.V,1-
5dr/10ph/2pg/fr L

Immaculate Conception Roman Catholic Church
201 N. Vale St.
HABS TX-13
HABS TEX,158-JEF,1-
4dr/4ph/1pg/fr L

Irvine House; see Excelsior Hotel

Jefferson Courthouse,Old
304 W. Broadway
HABS TX-118
HABS TEX,158-JEF,11-
1ph/1pg L

Jefferson Journal Building; see Camp,J.,Building

Kahn Saloon Building
123 W. Austin St.
HABS TX-110
HABS TEX,158-JEF,3-
2ph/1pg L

Keese House; see Duke,W. S. ,House

Presbyterian Manse (Rogers,Gen. James Harrison,House)
221 Delta St.
HABS TX-14
HABS TEX,158-JEF,2-
6dr/6ph/1pg/fr L

Rogers,Gen. James Harrison,House; see Presbyterian Manse

Spellings,Solomon A. ,House
107 E. Clarkesville St.
HABS TX-115
HABS TEX,158-JEF,8-
3ph/1pg L

Ward House; see Alley,D. N. ,Sr. ,House

MARTIN COUNTY

PATRICIA

"Long S" Box & Strip House
Patricia Vic. (moved to TX,Lubbock)
HABS TX-3241
HABS TEX,152-LUBBO,5-
2dr L

MASON COUNTY

MASON

Hedgewigs Hill Cabin
U. S. 87 Vic. (moved to TX,Lubbock)
HABS TX-3233
HABS TEX,152-LUBBO,2-
L

MAVERICK COUNTY

EAGLE PASS

Fessman House
Washington St.
HABS TX-3257
HABS TEX,162-EAPA,1-
6dr L

Fort Duncan
HABS TX-3255
HABS TEX,162-EAPA,2-
1dr L

Fort Duncan,Adjutant's Office
HABS TX-3255-B
HABS TEX,162-EAPA,2B-
1dr L

Fort Duncan,Bakery Building
HABS TX-3255-A
HABS TEX,162-EAPA,2A-
1dr L

Fort Duncan,Blacksmith's Shop
HABS TX-3255-D
HABS TEX,162-EAPA,2D-
1dr L

Fort Duncan,Commisary Building
HABS TX-3255-E
HABS TEX,162-EAPA,2E-
1dr L

Fort Duncan,Lee Memorial Building
HABS TX-3255-G
HABS TEX,162-EAPA,2G-
1dr L

Fort Duncan,Post Commander's Office
HABS TX-3255-C
HABS TEX,162-EAPA,2C-
1dr L

Fort Duncan,Post Headquarters Building
HABS TX-3255-H
HABS TEX,162-EAPA,2H-
3dr L

Fort Duncan,Powder Magazine
HABS TX-3255-F
HABS TEX,162-EAPA,2F-
1dr L

Hartz,F. H. ,House
Commercial St.
HABS TX-3258
HABS TEX162-EAPA,3-
7dr L

Maverick County Courthouse
HABS TX-3256
HABS TEX,162-EAPA,4-
9dr L

Stone,Will,House
Ford & Adams Sts.
HABS TX-3254
HABS TEX,162-EAPA,5-
3dr L

MCLENNAN COUNTY

WACO

Waco Suspension Bridge
HAER TX-13
HAER 1991(HAER):10
8ph/1pc L

MEDINA COUNTY

CASTROVILLE

Landmark Inn; see Vance Hotel Complex

Simon Cabin; see Simon House

Simon House (Simon Cabin; Vance Hotel,Bathhouse)
Florence & Florella Sts.
HABS TX-354
HABS TEX,163-CAST,3-
2ph/1pg L

Vance Hotel Complex (Landmark Inn)
Florence & Fiorella Sts.
HABS TX-33-A-4
HABS TEX,163-CAST,1-
4dr/7ph/1pg/fr L

Vance Hotel,Bathhouse; see Simon House

CASTROVILLE VIC.

Bendele,Joe,House
Angelo St.
HABS TX-357
HABS TEX,163-CAST,6-
2ph/1pg L

Carle,Andrew,House
Main & Lafayette Sts.
HABS TX-33-A-5
HABS TEX,163-CAST,2-
3dr/1ph/1pg/fr L

Carle,Joseph,House & Store
Madird & Angelo Sts. (Houston Square)
HABS TX-390
HABS TEX,163-CAST,19-
5dr/4ph/1pg/fr L

Castro,Henry,Storehouse
HABS TX-356
HABS TEX,163-CAST,5-
2ph/2pg L

Courthouse,Old
On former site of present City Hall
HABS TX-364
HABS TEX,163-CAST,13-
2ph/1pg L

de Mentel,Charles,House
NW of Castroville
HABS TX-369
HABS TEX,163-CAST.V,1-
7ph/2pg L

First Catholic Church
Angelo St.
HABS TX-359
HABS TEX,163-CAST,8-
2ph/1pg L

First Lutheran Church
HABS TX-363
HABS TEX,163-CAST,12-
2ph/1pg L

Goldberg,C. F. ,House
HABS TX-358
HABS TEX,163-CAST,7-
3ph/1pg L

Haass,Louis,House
Florence St.
HABS TX-367
HABS TEX,163-CAST,16-
3ph/2pg L

Hoog,Peter,House; see Tondre,Nicholas,House

Ihnken,Gerhard,House & Store
HABS TX-365
HABS TEX,163-CAST,14-
4ph/1pg L

Merian,John,House
London & Angelo Sts.
HABS TX-368
HABS TEX,163-CAST,17-
3ph/1pg L

Pingenot,P. F. ,House
Petersburg St.
HABS TX-360
HABS TEX,163-CAST,9-
6ph/1pg L

Quintle & Haas Mill
Millrace,Medina River,S. of Florella St.
HABS TX-355
HABS TEX,163-CAST,4-
6ph/1pg L

Quintle,Laurent,House & Store
Medina River off Hwy. 90
HABS TX-362
HABS TEX,163-CAST,11-
5dr/3ph/1pg/fr L

Tarde Hotel
Florella & Madrid Sts.
HABS TX-389
HABS TEX,163-CAST,18-
6ph/2pg L

Tondre,Nicholas,House
(Hoog,Peter,House)
Florence & Amelia Sts.
HABS TX-366
HABS TEX,163-CAST,15-
3ph/1pg L

Vance,John,House
Florella St.
HABS TX-361
HABS TEX,163-CAST,10-
4ph/1pg L

D'HANIS

D'Hanis Brick Works
HAER TX-12
HAER 1991(HAER):10
36ph/2pc L

D'Hanis Brick Works, Workers Housing
HAER TX-12-B
HAER 1991(HAER):10
1ph/1pc L

D'Hanis Brick Works,Owner's House
HAER TX-12-A
HAER 1991(HAER):10
2ph/1pc L

Ney,Joseph,House
Parker's Creek,E. of Farm Rd. 2200
HABS TX-3100
HABS TEX,163-DHAN,1-
3ph/1pg L

QUIHI VIC.

Boehle,Louis,House
Quihi Rd.
HABS TX-33-A-18
HABS TEX,163-QUI,1-
2dr/6ph/1pg/fr L

Von Schorobiny,Rudolph,Houses I & II
S. of Quihi
HABS TX-371
HABS TEX,163-QUI.V,1-
5ph/2pg L

Documentation: **ct** color transparencies **dr** measured drawings **fr** field records
pc photograph captions **pg** pages of text **ph** photographs

MENARD COUNTY

FORT MC KAVET

Fort McKavett
W. of Menard on Farm Rd. 864
HABS TX-3111
HABS TEX,164-FOMAK,1-
16ph/5pg L

MITCHELL COUNTY

COLORADO CITY VIC.

Renderbrook-Spade Blacksmith Shop
SW of Colorado River (moved to TX,Lubbock)
HABS TX-3238
HABS DLC/ADE-1983(HABS):145
3dr L

MOTLEY COUNTY

MATADOR

Matador Guest House & Office
TX Rt. 70 Vic. (moved to TX,Lubbock)
HABS TX-3262
HABS TEX,152-LUBBO,7-
4dr L

NACOGDOCHES COUNTY

CHIRENO VIC.

Old Half-Way Inn
W. of Chireno on TX Rt. 21
HABS TX-33-D-5
HABS TEX,174-CHIR,1-
4dr/6ph/1pg L

NACOGDOCHES VIC.

Bean,Peter Ellis,House
Melrose Rd.
HABS TX-236
HABS TEX,174-NACO.V,1-
1ph/1pg L

Church of the Divine Infant (Sacred Heart Church)
Cotton Ford Rd.
HABS TX-266
HABS TEX,174-NACO,3-
1ph/1pg L

Hoya Library; see Sterne,Adolphus,House

Nacogdoches University
High School Grounds,Washington Square
HABS TX-235
HABS TEX,174-NACO,2-
1ph/1pg L

Sacred Heart Church; see Church of the Divine Infant

Sterne,Adolphus,House (Hoya Library)
211 LaNana St.
HABS TX-234
HABS TEX,174-NACO,1-
2ph/2pg L

Ybarbo Ranch House
Stephen F. Austin College Grounds
HABS TX-268
HABS TEX,174-NACO.V,2-
1ph/2pg L

NUECES COUNTY

CORPUS CHRISTI

Muely,Conrad,House & Store
210 Chaparral St.
HABS TX-3114
HABS TEX,178-CORP,1-
7dr/8ph/2pg/fr L

PALO PINTO COUNTY

PALO PINTO

Jowell Ranch House
Possum Kingdom Lake (moved to TX,Lubbock)
HABS TX-3237
HABS TEX,152-LUBBO,4-
3dr L

PANOLA COUNTY

CARTHAGE VIC.

Collins,Jasper,House
HABS TX-15
HABS TEX,183-CARTH,1-
4ph/1pg L

Morris,Dempsey,House
HABS TX-17
HABS TX,183-CARTH,3-
2ph/1pg L

Parker,J. B. ,House
201 W. Sabine
HABS TX-18
HABS TX,183-CARTH,4-
2ph/1pg L

Snow House
HABS TX-16
HABS TEX,183-CARTH,2-
2ph/1pg L

PECOS COUNTY

SHEFFIELD VIC.

Canon Ranch Eclipse Windmill
HAER TX-7
HAER TEX,186-SHEF.V,1-
9dr/6ph/44pg/fr L

PRESIDIO COUNTY

PRESIDIO VIC.

Fort Leaton
SE of Presidio between Farm Rd. 170 & Rio Grande
HABS TX-3103
HABS TEX,189-PRES.V,1-
6dr/16ph/2pg/fr L

SHAFTER VIC.

Fortin de Cibolo (Little Fort of Cibolo)
Cibolo Creek
HABS TX-3118
HABS TEX,189-SHAF.V,1-
8ph/2pg L

Fortin de Cienega
Cienega Creek
HABS TX-3119
HABS TEX,189-SHAF.V,2-
3dr/1ph/2pg L

Little Fort of Cibolo; see Fortin de Cibolo

REFUGIO COUNTY

REFUGIO

Rooke House,Cistern
US Hwy. 77 W,La Rosa Ranch
HABS TX-3371-A
HABS DLC/PP-1992:TX-3
1dr L

REFUGIO VIC.

Rooke House
La Rosa Ranch,U.S. Hwy. 77,W.
HABS TX-3371
HABS DLC/PP-1992:TX-3
14dr/5ph/1pc/fr L

ROBERTSON COUNTY

CALVERT

Gibson Gin Office & Weigh Station
HABS TX-253
HABS TEX,198-CALV,3-
6dr/fr L

Hammond House
604 Elm St.
HABS TX-3337
HABS TEX,198-CALV,4-
11dr/fr L

610 Main Street (Commercial Building)
HABS TX-244
HABS TEX,198-CALV,1-
4dr/fr L

Main Street,400-700 Blocks (Commercial Buildings)
HABS TX-243
HABS TEX,198-CALV,2-
25dr/fr L

HEARNE

Smith-Welch Memorial Library
HABS TX-255
HABS TEX,198-HEAR,1-
7dr/fr L

Southern Pacific Railroad Depot
HABS TX-269
HABS TEX,198-HEAR,2-
7dr L

WHEELOCK

Cavitt Cemetery
HABS TX-270-C
HABS TEX,198-WHEEL,1C-
1dr/fr L

Cavitt House
HABS TX-270-A
HABS TEX,198-WHEEL,1A-
10dr/fr L

Cavitt House & Log Cabin
HABS TX-270
HABS TEX,198-WHEEL,1-
2dr/fr L

Cavitt Log Cabin
HABS TX-270-B
HABS TEX,198-WHEEL,1B-
4dr/fr L

RUSK COUNTY

HENDERSON

Walling,Thomas Jefferson,Log Cabin
HABS TX-3321
HABS TEX,201-HEN,1-
5dr/8ph/4pg/fr L

SABINE COUNTY

MILAM VIC.

Gaines-McGowan House
Toledo Bend Reservoir site
HABS TX-267
HABS TEX,202- ,1-
1ph/1pg L

SAN AUGUSTINE COUNTY

SAN AUGUSTINE

Blount,Col. Stephen W. ,House
501 E. Columbia St.
HABS TX-33-D-1
HABS TEX,203-SAUG,1-
4dr/6ph/2pg L

Cartwright,Columbus,House
Sharp St.
HABS TX-239
HABS TEX,203-SAUG,4-
1ph/1pg L

Cartwright,Matthew,House
505 E. Main St.
HABS TX-238
HABS TEX,203-SAUG,2-
5dr/11ph/1pg/fr L

Cullen-Roberts House
Congress & Market Sts.
HABS TX-237
HABS TEX,203-SUAG,3-
2ph/1pg L

Johnson,C. C. ,House
Congress St.
HABS TX-242
HABS TEX,203-SAUG,6-
1ph/1pg L

SAN AUGUSTINE VIC.

Garrett,William,Plantation House
TX Rt. 21
HABS TX-33-D-2
HABS TEX,203-SAUG.V,1-
4dr/6ph/1pg L

Hale-Blount House
TX Rt. 21
HABS TX-240
HABS TEX,203-SAUG,5-
2ph/1pg L

Sublett,Col. Phillip A. ,House
TX Rt. 21
HABS TX-241
HABS TEX,203-SAUG.V,2-
2ph/1pg L

SCURRY COUNTY

SNYDER

Smith-Harrell House
N. of Snyder (moved to TX,Lubbock)
HABS TX-3235
HABS TEX,152-LUBBO,10-
5dr L

SHELBY COUNTY

CENTER VIC.

Jones,Louis,House
HABS TX-12
HABS TEX,210-CENT,2-
2ph/1pg L

Smith,Emzy C. ,House
N. of Farm Rd. 2026
HABS TX-11
HABS TEX,210-CENT,1-
2ph/1pg L

SMITH COUNTY

BULLARD VIC.

Dewberry,Col. John,Plantation House
Farm Rd. 346
HABS TX-133
HABS TEX,212- ,2-
3ph/1pg L

Douglas House
HABS TX-134
HABS TEX,212-BUL,1-
5ph/1pg L

Loftin,Pitt,House
Farm Rd. 344
HABS TX-132
HABS TEX,212- ,1-
4ph/1pg L

Loftkin,Alf,House
HABS TX-135
HABS TEX,212-BUL,2-
3ph/1pg L

STARR COUNTY

RIO GRANDE CITY

Courthouse,Old
Water St. at Texas Ave.
HABS TX-33-AB-2
HABS TEX,214-RIGCI,1-
4dr/2ph/1pg/fr L

Davis,Henry Clay,House
Britton Ave.
HABS TX-33-AB-4
HABS TEX,214-RIGCI,2-
6dr/8ph/1pg/fr L

Pena,Silverio De La,Drugstore & Post Office
Main & Lopez Sts.
HABS TX-3136
HABS TEX,214-RIGCI,4-
6ph/5pg L

Ramirez,Jose,House
Corpus & Third Sts.
HABS TX-3133
HABS TEX,214-RIGCI,3-
6ph/4pg L

ROMA

Church of our Lady of Refuge of Sinners
N. end of Main Plaza on Estrella St.
HABS TX-3135
HABS TEX,214-ROMA,4-
7ph/5pg L

Garcia,Leocadia Leandro,House
SW corner of Main Plaza
HABS TX-3131
HABS TEX,214-ROMA,2-
5ph/4pg L

Guerra,Manuel,Residence & Store
W. side of Main Plaza at Hidalgo St.
HABS TX-3146
HABS TEX,214-ROMA,5-
7ph/6pg L

Ramirez,Rafael Garcia,House
E. side of Main Plaza at Hidalgo St.
HABS TX-3134
HABS TEX,214-ROMA,3-
5ph/5pg L

Saens,Nextor,Store
Hidalgo St. & Juarez Alley
HABS TX-3129
HABS TEX,214-ROMA,1-
7dr/5ph/5pg/fr L

SWISHER COUNTY

TULIA

Jowell,W. E. ,House
SW Second St.
HABS TX-3331
HABS TEX,219-TUL,1-
3dr/fr L

Tulia Railroad Depot
State Hwy. 87
HABS TX-3323
HABS TEX,219-TUL,2-
2dr L

TARRANT COUNTY

FORT WORTH

Pollock-Capps Residence
1120 Penn St.
HABS TX-3240
HABS TEX,220-FOWOR,1-
13dr/14ph/2pg L

Wharton-Scott House
1509 Pennsylvania St.
HABS TX-3289
HABS TEX,220-FOWOR,2-
19dr/fr L

GRAPEVINE VIC.

Morehead-Gano Log House
Rt. 121,NW of Bethel Rd. (moved to TX,Dallas)
HABS TX-3269
HABS TEX,220-GRA.V,1-
5dr L

SAGINAW

Saginaw Army Aircraft Plant
HAER TX-3
HAER TEX,220-SAG,1-
32pg/fr L

THROCKMORTON COUNTY

ALBANY VIC.

Reynolds-Gentry Barn
Clearfork of Brazos River (moved to TX,Lubbock)
HABS TX-3318
HABS 1983(HABS):145
6dr L

TOM GREEN COUNTY

SAN ANGELO

Santa Fe Depot
Hardeman Pass,702 S. Chadbourne St.
HABS TX-3366
HABS 1991(HABS):29
5dr/fr L

TRAVIS COUNTY

AUSTIN

Bremond,Eugene,House
404 W. Seventh St.
HABS TX-3143
HABS TEX,227-AUST,11-
2ph/3pg L

Bremond,John,House
W. Seventh & Guadalupe Sts.
HABS TX-3140
HABS TEX,227-AUST,8-
10ph/5pg L

Carrington-Covert House
1511 Colorado St.
HABS TX-3311
HABS TEX,227-AUST,18-
11ph/1pg/1pc L

Enfield; see Pease,Gov. Elisha M. ,Mansion

French Legation to Republic of Texas
Seventh & San Marcos Sts.
HABS TX-33-C-1
HABS TEX,227-AUST,1-
4dr/14ph/4pg/1pc L

General Land Office; see Land Office

Gethsemane Lutheran Church
Sixteenth St. & Congress Ave.
HABS TX-3137
HABS TEX,227-AUST,7-
6dr/6ph/4pg/fr L

Goodman Building
202 W. Thirteenth St.
HABS TX-3263
HABS TEX,227-AUST,15-
7dr/5ph/7pg/1pc/fr L

Governor's Mansion
1010 Colorado St.
HABS TX-33-C-4
HABS TEX,226,-AUST,3-
11dr/21ph/2pg/1pc L

Houghton Carriage House
1111 Guadalupe St. ,rear of 307 W. Twelfth St.
HABS TX-3264-A
HABS TEX,227-AUST,16A-
3dr/5ph/5pg/1pc/fr L

Houghton,John H. ,House
307 W. Twelfth St.
HABS TX-3264
HABS TEX,227-AUST,16-
8dr/12ph/9pg/1pc/fr L

Land Office (General Land Office; Land Office,Old)
108 E. Eleventh St.
HABS TX-397
HABS TEX,227-AUST,6-
8dr/32ph/17pg/2pc/fr L

Land Office,Old; see Land Office

Lundberg Bakery
1006 Congress Ave.
HABS TX-3267
HABS TEX,227-AUST,19-
5dr/12ph/9pg/1pc/fr L

Millett,C. F. ,Mansion
Ninth & Brazos Sts.
HABS TX-3142
HABS TEX,227-AUST,10-
2ph/3pg L

Neill-Cochran,House
HABS TX-3391
H

Orsay Tenant House
310 E. Fourteenth St.
HABS TX-3265
HABS TEX,227-AUST,20-
4dr/3ph/7pg/1pc/fr L

Pease,Gov. Elisha M. ,Mansion
(Woodlawn; Enfield)
6 Niles Rd.
HABS TX-330
HABS TEX,227-AUST,4-
7ph/2pg/fr L

Raymond,Nathaniel,House
204 E. Twenty-fourth St.
HABS TX-331
HABS TEX,227-AUST,5-
6ph/2pg/fr L

Simms-Vance House
1802 San Gabriel St.
HABS TX-33-C-3
HABS TEX,227-AUST,2-
9dr/4ph/1pg L

Taylor-Hunnicutt House
405 W. Twelfth St. (moved from Guadalupe St.)
HABS TX-3268
HABS TEX,227-AUST,17-
4dr/8ph/7pg/1pc/fr L

Texas State Capitol
Eleventh St. at Congress Avenue
HABS TX-3326
HABS TEX,227-AUST,13-;1993:TX-3
79dr/21ph/1pg/2pc/fr L

Townsend,Angela,House
1802 West Ave.
HABS TX-3141
HABS TEX,227-AUST,9-
5ph/3pg L

504 W. Fourteenth Street (House)
HABS TX-3266
HABS TEX,227-AUST,14-
6dr/6ph/1pc L

502 West Thirteenth Street (House)
HABS TX-3295
HABS TEX,227-AUST,12-
7ph/1pg/1pc L

Woodlawn; see Pease,Gov. Elisha M. ,Mansion

AUSTIN VIC.

Sneed,Judge Sebron G. ,House
Rt. I-35 & Bluff Springs Rd.
HABS TX-399
HABS TEX,22-AUSTIN,.V,1-
8dr/4ph/2pg/fr L

VAL VERDE COUNTY

LANGTRY

Bean,Judge Roy,Saloon & Justice Court (Jersey Lilly Saloon)
HABS TX-3101
HABS TEX,223-LANG,1-
2ph/1pg L

Jersey Lilly Saloon; see Bean,Judge Roy,Saloon & Justice Court

VICTORIA COUNTY

MISSION VALLEY VIC.

Davidson,Quincy,House
HABS TX-248
HABS TEX,235-MIVA,2-
1ph/1pg L

De Leon,Patricio,Ranch House
HABS TX-278
HABS TEX,235-MIVA,3-
1ph/1pg L

Rives,James,House
HABS TX-246
HABS TEX,235-MIVA,1-
1ph/1pg L

VICTORIA

Callender,William L. ,House
404 W. Guadalupe St.
HABS TX-247
HABS TEX,235-VIC,2-
4dr/1ph/1pg/fr L

Goldman,A. ,House
HABS TX-245
HABS TEX,235-VIC,1-
1ph/1pg L

McNamara House
502 N. Liberty St.
HABS TX-3340
HABS TEX,235-VIC,4-
8dr/fr L

Rupley Building
HABS TX-280
HABS TEX,235-VIC,3-
1ph/1pg L

WALKER COUNTY

HUNTSVILLE VIC.

Yoakum,Henderson,House
HABS TX-231
HABS TEX,236-HUNVI.V,1-
1ph/1pg L

WALLER COUNTY

HEMPSTEAD VIC.

Groce,Leonard,Plantation House; see Liendo

Liendo (Groce,Leonard,Plantation House)
Farm Rd. 1488 & Wyatt Chapel Rd. Vic.
HABS TX-33-B-4
HABS TEX,239-HEMP.V,1-
5dr/8ph/3pg/fr L

WASHINGTON COUNTY

BRENHAM

Giddings-Wilkin House
805 Crockett St.
HABS TX-3364
HABS DLC/PP-1992:TX-3
16dr/fr L

Schmid Brothers Buildings
Commerce & Park Sts.
HABS TX-300
HABS TEX,239-BREN,1-
11dr/fr L

BURTON

Burton Farmer's Gin
Main St.
HABS TX-3365
HABS 1991(HABS):29
9dr/fr L

CHAPPELL HILL

Inge-Stoneham House
HABS TX-342
HABS TEX,239-CHAP.V,2-
10dr L

Stage Coach Tavern
Farm Rd. 1155 at Farm Rd. 2447
HABS TX-24
HABS TEX,239-CHAP,1-
6dr/3ph/1pg L

CHAPPELL HILL VIC.

Browning,Col. William W. ,House
Farm Rds. 1155 & 1371
HABS TX-265
HABS TEX,239-CHAP,2-
10dr/2ph/1pg L

Sledge,Col. William Madison,House (Smith,John,House)
W. of Chappell Hill
HABS TX-25
HABS TEX,239-CHAP.V,1-
5dr/2ph/1pg/fr L

Smith,John,House; see Sledge,Col. William Madison,House

INDEPENDENCE

Blue,J. M. ,House
HABS TX-210
HABS TEX,239-INDEP,4-
3ph/1pg L

INDEPENDENCE VIC.

Baptist Church
Farm Rds. 390 & 50
HABS TX-29
HABS TEX,239-INDEP,3-
2ph/1pg L

Clark House; see Holmes,Willett,House

Holmes,Willett,House (Clark House)
HABS TX-211
HABS TEX,239-INDEP,5-
2ph/1pg L

Houston,Sam,House
Farm Rd. 390
HABS TX-264
HABS TEX,239-INDEP,8-
1ph/1pg L

Mexican Jail (Toalson House)
Farm Rds. 390 & 50 Vic.
HABS TX-263
HABS TEX,239-INDEP,7-
2ph/1pg L

Robertson,Gen. Jerome B. ,House
Farm Rds. 50 & 390
HABS TX-33-B-9
HABS TEX,239-INDEP,2-
2dr/6ph/1pg L

Seward,John H. ,House
Farm Rd. 390
HABS TX-33-B-8
HABS TEX,239-INDEP,1-
4dr/7ph/1pg/fr L

Seward,Samuel,House
NE of Independence
HABS TX-262
HABS TEX,239-INDEP,6-
1ph/1pg L

Toalson House; see Mexican Jail

WASHINGTON VIC.

Barrington (House); see Jones,Anson,House

Brown,John M. ,House
Farm Rd. 912
HABS TX-213
HABS TEX,239-WASH.V,1-
5dr/3ph/1pg/fr L

Jones,Anson,House (Barrington (House))
Brazos State Park Vic.
HABS TX-212
HABS TEX,239-WASH,1-
3ph/1pg L

WEBB COUNTY

LAREDO

Bertani,Paul Prevost,House
604 Iturbide St.
HABS TX-3293
HABS TEX,240-LARD,2-
4dr/6ph/2pg/1pc L

de la Garza,Zoila,House
509 Iturbide St.
HABS TX-3291
HABS TEX,240-LARD,5-
2dr/6ph/1pg/1pc L

Leyendecker,Jo Emma,& Salinas,Dr. Guillermo,House
702 Iturbide St.
HABS TX-3290
HABS TEX,240-LARD,1-
3dr/5ph/2pg/1pc L

Montemayor,Jose A. ,House
(Vela,Carlos,House)
601 Zaragosa St.
HABS TX-3292
HABS TEX,240-LARD,3-
5dr/7ph/2pg/1pc L

Vela,Carlos,House; see Montemayor,Jose A. ,House

Viscaya de Leal,Rosario,House
620 Zaragosa St.
HABS TX-3294
HABS TEX,240-LARD,4-
3dr/4ph/2pg/1pc L

WILLIAMSON COUNTY

ROUND ROCK VIC.

Anderson,Washington,House (El Milagro)
TX Rt. 79 at NE edge of Round Rock
HABS TX-338
HABS TEX,246-ROURO,1-
6ph/1pg L

Cole,Dr. J. T. ,House (Stage Shop,Old)
W. of I-35 access Rd.
HABS TX-3144
HABS TEX,246-ROURO.V,2-
1ph/2pg L

El Milagro; see Anderson,Washington,House

Merrell,Capt. Nelson,House
E. of I-35 on TX Rt. 79
HABS TX-3132
HABS TEX,246-ROURO.V,1-
6ph/4pg L

Stage Shop,Old; see Cole,Dr. J. T. ,House

TAYLOR VIC.

McFadin,D. H. ,House
Farm Rd. 1331,E. of TX Rt. 95
HABS TX-339
HABS TEX,246-TAYL.V,1-
3ph/1pg L

WILSON COUNTY

FLORESVILLE VIC.

Seguin,Juan N. ,Ranch House
NW of Floresville
HABS TX-39
HABS TEX,247-FLOVI.V,1-
5dr/8ph/1pg/fr L

Yndo,Miguel,House
Farm Rd. 1303
HABS TX-37
HABS TEX,247- ,1-
4ph/1pg L

LABATT

Flores,Francisco,Ranch House
HABS TX-38
HABS TEX,247-LABAT,1-
4ph/1pg L

POTH VIC.

Beauregard Ranch Buildings
S. of Poth
HABS TX-310
HABS TEX,247-POTH.V,1-
7ph/1pg L

SUTHERLAND SPRINGS

Polley,Col. Joseph H. ,House; see Whitehall

Whitehall (Polley,Col. Joseph H. ,House)
Farm Rd. 539
HABS TX-326
HABS TEX,247-SUSPR.V,1-
7dr/9ph/2pg/fr L

YOUNG COUNTY

NEWCASTLE VIC.

Fort Belknap
S. on TX Rt. 251
HABS TX-33-D-7
HABS TEX,252-NEWC.V,1-
3dr/12ph/1pg/fr L

ZAPATA COUNTY

FALCON VIC.

Ramirez,Jose,House
Falcon Reservoir Site
HABS TX-3130
HABS TEX,253-RAMIR,1-
4dr L

SAN YGNACIO

San Ygnacio Ranch Buildings
(Trevino,Jesus,House)
Uribe & Trevino Sts.
HABS TX-3112
HABS TEX,253-SANYG,1-
5dr/17ph/2pg/fr L

Trevino,Jesus,House; see San Ygnacio Ranch Buildings

ZAPATA VIC.

San Bartolo Ranch Buildings
Falcon Reservoir Site
HABS TX-3113
HABS TEX,253-ZAP.V,1-
5ph/2pg L

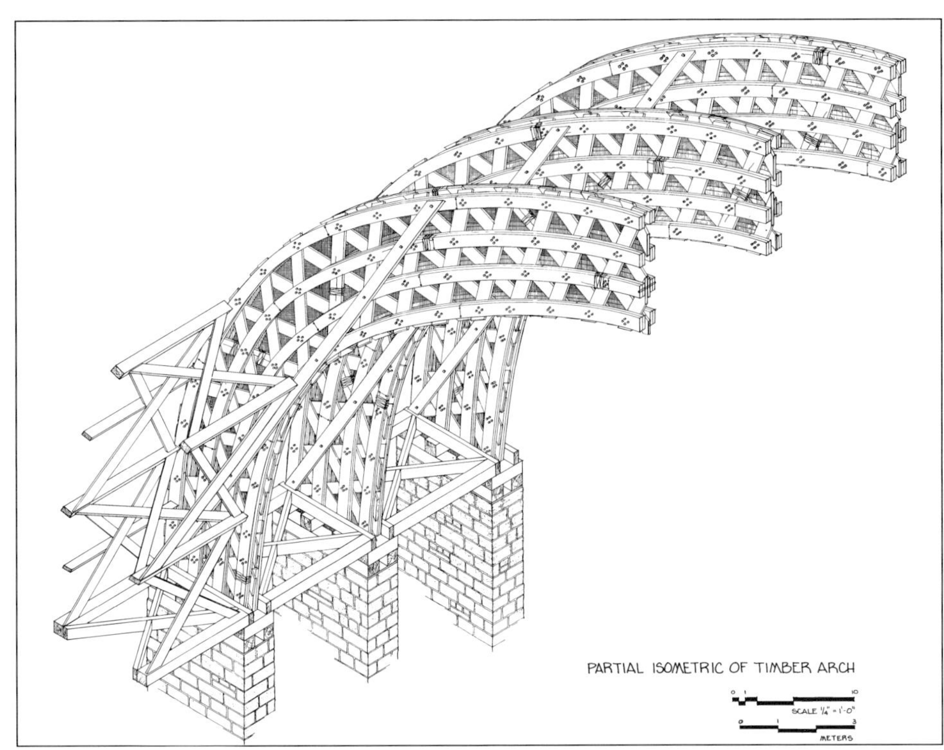

Church of Jesus Christ of the Latter-Day Saints, Salt Lake City Tabernacle, Salt Lake City, Salt Lake County, Utah. Partial isometric of timber arch. Measured drawing delineated by Toni Ristau, 1971 (HAER UT-1, sheet 5 of 5; negative number LC-USZA2-6).

District School, Fairfield, Utah County, Utah. West elevation. Photograph by Kent Fairbanks, July 11, 1967 (HABS UTAH,25-FAIRF,1-2).

Utah

BEAVER COUNTY

BEAVER

Beaver County Courthouse
Center & First East Sts.
HABS UT-61
HABS UTAH,1-BEAV,1-
8dr/4ph/6pg L

MILFORD VIC.

Frisco Charcoal Kilns
State Rt. 21 (Frisco)
HAER UT-25
HAER UTAH,1-FRIS,1-
4ph/15pg/1pc L

Frisco Charcoal Kilns,Kiln No. 2
State Rt. 21 (Frisco)
HAER UT-25-A
HAER UTAH,1-FRIS,1A-
5ph/1pc L

Frisco Charcoal Kilns,Kiln No. 3
State Rt. 21 (Frisco)
HAER UT-25-B
HAER UTAH,1-FRIS,1B-
5ph/1pc L

Frisco Charcoal Kilns,Kiln No. 4
State Rt. 21 (Frisco)
HAER UT-25-C
HAER UTAH,1-FRIS,1C-
2ph/1pc L

Frisco Charcoal Kilns,Smelter
State Rt. 21 (Frisco)
HAER UT-25-D
HAER UTAH,1-FRIS,1D-
1ph/1pc L

BOX ELDER COUNTY

BRIGHAM CITY

Fishburn Dry Goods Store; see Roxy Theatre

Mercantile & Manufacturing Association Tannery
First East St.
HABS UT-46
HABS UTAH,2-BRICI,1-
7ph/6pg L

Roxy Theatre (Fishburn Dry Goods Store)
106 S. Main St.
HABS UT-102
HABS UTAH,2-BRICI,4-
3ph/3pg L

Snow,Lorenzo,House
Forest St.
HABS UT-45
HABS UTAH,2-BRICI,2-
2ph/6pg L

BRIGHAM CITY VIC.

Southern Pacific RR,Ogden-Lucin Cutoff Trestle
Spanning Great Salt Lake
HAER UT-13
HAER UTAH,2-BRICI,3-
5dr/42ph/10pg/3pc/fr L

COLLINSTON VIC.

Bear River Hotel; see Hampton's Ford Stage Station

Hampton's Ford Stage Station (Bear River Hotel)
State Rt. 154
HABS UT-42
HABS UTAH,2-COL.V,1-
6dr/9ph/6pg/fr L

Hampton's Ford Stage Station,Barn
State Rt. 154
HABS UT-43
HABS UTAH,2-COL.V,1A-
6ph/3pg L

CORIINE VIC.

Promontory Route Railroad Trestles,Trestle 790B
11 miles W. of Corrine
HAER UT-64-E
5ph/3pg/1pc H

CORINNE

Methodist Episcopal Church
Colorado & S. Sixth Sts.
HABS UT-40
HABS UTAH,2-CORI,1-
6ph/5pg L

CORRINE

Hayden Bridge
Moved to Springfield,Lane County,Oregon
HAER OR-19
HAER DLC/PP-1993:OR-2
4dr/15ph/4pg/1pc/fr L

CORRINE VIC.

Promontory Route Railroad Trestle Complex
HAER UT-64
1dr/3ph/28pg/1pc H

Promontory Route Railroad Trestles,Tresle 789B
11 miles W. of Corrine
HAER UT-64-B
5ph/3pg/1pc H

Promontory Route Railroad Trestles,Trestle 788B
11 miles W. of Corrine
HAER UT-64-A
6ph/3pg/1pc H

Promontory Route Railroad Trestles,Trestle 789C
11 miles W. of Corrine
HAER UT-64-C
6ph/3pg/1pc H

Promontory Route Railroad Trestles,Trestle 790A
11 miles W. of Corrine
HAER UT-64-D
8ph/3pg/1pc H

Promontory Route Railroad Trestles,Trestle 790C
11 miles W. of Corrine
HAER UT-64-F
6ph/3pg/1pc H

Promontory Route Railroad Trestles,Trestle 791B
11 miles W. of Corrine
HAER UT-64-G
5ph/3pg/1pc H

FIELDING VIC.

Irrigation Diversion Canal
Bear River
HAER UT-9
HAER UTAH,2-FIELD,2-
1ph/1pc L

Utah Sugar Company,Wheelon Hydoelectric Plant
Bear River
HAER UT-8
HAER UTAH,2-FIELD,1-
8dr/2ph/1pc L

GARLAND VIC.

Utah Sugar Company,Garland Beet Sugar Refinery (Utah-Idaho Sugar Co. ,Garland Beet Sugar Refinery)
Factory St.
HAER UT-19
HAER UTAH,2-GARL.V,1-
8dr/8ph/1pc/fr L

Utah-Idaho Sugar Co. ,Garland Beet Sugar Refinery; see Utah Sugar Company,Garland Beet Sugar Refinery

MANTUA VIC.

Box Elder Creek Arch Bridge
Spans former channel of S. fork of Box Elder Creek
HAER UT-65
HAER DLC/PP-1993:UT-2
9ph/17pg/1pc L

Mantua Lime Kiln
HAER UT-66
HAER DLC/PP-1993:UT-2
6ph/24pg/1pc L

PROMONTORY VIC.

Golden Spike
State or county road 504
HABS UT-130
H

Golden Spike,Monument (Last Spike Monument)
State or Co. Rd. 504
HABS UT-130-B
HABS DLC/PP-1992:UT-4
2ph/1pc L

Golden Spike,Visitor Center
State or Co. Rd. 504
HABS UT-130-A
HABS DLC/PP-1992:UT-4
2ph/1pc L

Last Spike Monument; see Golden Spike,Monument

WILLARD

Baird,Robert Bell,House
195 W. Central St.
HABS UT-89
HABS UTAH,2-WILL,1-
3dr/3ph/6pg/fr L

Edwards,John L. ,Granary
55 S. Second West
HABS UT-90-A
HABS UTAH,2-WILL,2A-
1dr/2ph L

Edwards,John L. ,House
55 S. Second West
HABS UT-90
HABS UTAH,2-WILL,2-
3dr/4ph/6pg/1ct/fr L

Jones,Shadrach,House
101 W. Second South
HABS UT-86
HABS UTAH,2-WILL,3-
3dr/2ph/6pg/fr L

Mason,George,Barn
150 N. Second St.
HABS UT-92-B
HABS UTAH,2-WILL,4B-
2ph L

Mason,George,Granary
150 N. Second West St.
HABS UT-92-A
HABS UTAH,2-WILL,4A-
1dr/1ph L

Mason,George,House
150 N. Second West
HABS UT-92
HABS UTAH,2-WILL,4-
3dr/4ph/7pg/fr L

CACHE COUNTY

BENSON

Benson Bridge
Spanning Cutler Reservoir
HAER UT-48
HAER UTAH,3-BEN.V,1-
11ph/6pg/1pc L

CACHE JUNCTION

Cache Junction Beanery
Hwy. 23
HABS UT-113
HABS UTAH,3-CAJU,2-
5ph L

Oregon Short Line Railroad Depot (Union Pacific Railroad Depot)
Hwy. 23
HABS UT-114
HABS UTAH,3-CAJU,1-
3dr/2ph/4pg/fr L

Union Pacific Railroad Depot; see Oregon Short Line Railroad Depot

LOGAN

Logan Temple Barn
368 E. Second North
HABS UT-84
HABS UTAH,3-LOG,2A-
2dr/4ph/5pg/fr L

Oregon Short Line Railroad Station (Union Pacific Railroad Station)
Sixth West St.
HABS UT-44
HABS UTAH,3-LOG,1-
4dr/9ph/4pg/fr L

Union Pacific Railroad Station; see Oregon Short Line Railroad Station

CARBON COUNTY

GORDON CREEK

Sweet Mine
SW 1/4 section 17 Township 13 South,Range 8 East
HAER UT-56
HAER 1991(HAER):21
7ph/7pg/1pc L

HELPER

Bottino,James,Bldg; see Helper Commercial District

Carbon Hotel; see Helper Commercial District

Carbon Rubber & Repair Service Station; see Helper Commercial District

Day-Mutual Mine
Burnt Tree Fork,Spring Canyon
HAER UT-45
HAER 1989(HAER):21
4ph/10pg/1pc L

Floyd House; see Helper Commercial District

Helper Commercial District (Carbon Hotel)
258 S. Main St.
HABS UT-107-C
HABS UTAH,4-HELP,3-
1ph/1pg/fr L

Helper Commercial District (Carbon Rubber & Repair Service Station; Bottino,James,Bldg)
220 S. Main St.
HABS UT-107-E
HABS UTAH,4-HELP,5-
4ph/1pg/1pc L

Helper Commercial District (Floyd House)
276 S. Main St.
HABS UT-107-A
HABS UTAH,4-HELP,1-
1ph/1pg/fr L

Helper Commercial District (Floyd House)
290 S. Main St.
HABS UT-107-B
HABS UTAH,4-HELP,2-
1ph/1pg/fr L

Helper Commercial District (Rio Hotel)
210 S. Main St.
HABS UT-107-D
HABS UTAH,4-HELP,4-
3ph/1pg/fr L

Rio Hotel; see Helper Commercial District

HELPER VIC.

Rolapp Mine
Price Canyon,Mouth of Bear Canyon
HAER UT-53
HAER 1989(HAER):21
6pg L

Rolapp Mine,Lamphouse
Price Canyon (mouth of Bear Canyon)
HAER UT-53-A
HAER 1989(HAER):21
6ph/7pg/1pc L

Rolapp Mine,Tramway
Price Canyon (mouth of Bear Canyon)
HAER UT-53-B
HAER 1989(HAER):21
2ph/4pg/1pc L

KENILWORTH

Independent Coal & Coke Company (Kenilworth Mine Workings)
HAER UT-31
HAER UTAH,4-KENW,1-
32pg/fr L

Kenilworth Mine Workings; see
Independent Coal & Coke Company

SCOFIELD

Jones Mine
HAER UT-43
HAER 1989(HAER):21
17ph/8pg/1pc L

Winter Quarters Mine
HAER UT-44
HAER 1989(HAER):21
21ph/9pg/2pc L

STANDARDVILLE VIC.

Liberty Fuel Company,Mine Office
Old Latuda Townsite,Spring Canyon
HAER UT-52
HAER 1989(HAER):21
9ph/14pg/1pc/fr L

Rains Mine,Bathhouse
Old Rains Townsite,Spring Canyon
HAER UT-54
HAER 1989(HAER):21
13ph/10pg/1pc L

Standard Mine,Timber Trestle
Gilson Gulch
HAER UT-55
HAER 1989(HAER):21
4ph/12pg/1pc/fr L

DAVIS COUNTY

CENTERVILLE

Pettit, Arthur H.,Outbuilding
42 E. One-Hundred S.,Assessor's Plat A,Bl. 21,Lot3
HABS UT-122-A
HABS 1991(HABS):3
1ph/1pc L

Pettit,Arthur H.,House
42 E. One-Hundred S.
HABS UT-122
HABS 199(HABS):3
8ph/5pg/1pc L

FARMINGTON

Cotterell,Samuel & Eleanor,House
96 N. One Hundred East
HABS UT-124
HABS 1991(HABS):3
9ph/17pg/1pc L

DUCHESNE COUNTY

ALTAMONT

Irrig. Canals in Uintah Basin,U.S. Lake Fork Canal
HAER UT-30-D
6ph/2pg/1pc H

Irrig. Canals in Uintah Basin,Wissiup Homestead
HAER UT-30-E
8ph/1pc H

DUCHESNE

Irrig. Canals in Uintah Basin,Rocky Point Canal
HAER UT-30-K
13ph/3pg/1pc H

DUCHESNE VIC.

Irrig. Canals in Uintah Basin
HAER UT-30
4dr/19ph/115pg/2pc H

Irrig. Canals in Uintah Basin,Knight Ditch
HAER UT-30-I
13ph/3pg/1pc H

HANNA VIC.

High Mt. Dams in Upalco Unit,Brown Duck Lake Dam
Ashley Natl. Forest,4.4 mi. N of Miners Gulch Cmpg
HAER UT-42-B
HAER DLC/PP-1992:UT-3
6ph/3pg/1pc L

High Mt. Dams in Upalco Unit,Central Utah Project
See also:High Mt. Dams ...,at Mountain Home Vic.
HAER UT-42
HAER DLC/PP-1993:UT-1
1dr/7pg L

High Mt. Dams in Upalco Unit,Clements Lake Dam
Ashley Natl. Forest,6.5 mi. N of Miners Gulch Cmpg
HAER UT-42-C
HAER DLC/PP-1992:UT-3
5ph/3pg/1pc L

High Mt. Dams in Upalco Unit,Island Lake Dam
Ashley Natl. Forest,4.8 mi. N of Miners Gulch Cmpg
HAER UT-42-I
HAER DLC/PP-1992:UT-3
8ph/3pg/1pc L

High Mt. Dams in Upalco Unit,Kidney Lake Dam
Ashley Natl. Forest,4.7 mi. N of Miners Gulch Cmpg
HAER UT-42-J
HAER DLC/PP-1992:UT-3
9ph/3pg/1pc L

MOUNTAIN HOME VIC.

High Mt. Dams in Upaco Unit,Superior Lake Dam
Ashley Natl. Forest,12.4 mi. NW of Swift Creek Cmp
HAER UT-42-L
4ph/3pg/1pc L

High Mt. Dams in Upalco Unit,Bluebell Lake Dam
Ashley Natl. Forest,11.2 mi. NW of Swift Creek Cpg
HAER UT-42-A
HAER DLC/PP-1992:UT-3
8ph/3pg/1pc L

High Mt. Dams in Upalco Unit,Central Utah Project
See also:High Mt. Dams in Upalco Unit,at Hanna Vic
HAER UT-42
HAER DLC/PP-1992:UT-3
1dr/7pg L

High Mt. Dams in Upalco Unit,Deer Lake Dam
Ashley Natl. Forest,5.8 mi. N. of Swift Creek Cmpg
HAER UT-42-D
HAER DLC/PP-1992:UT-3
7ph/3pg/1pc L

High Mt. Dams in Upalco Unit,Drift Lake Dam
Ashley Natl. Forest,11.4 mi. NW of Swift Creek Cmp
HAER UT-42-E
HAER DLC/PP-1992:UT-3
6ph/3pg/1pc L

High Mt. Dams in Upalco Unit,East Timothy Lake Dam
Ashley Natl. Forest,8.4 mi. N of Swift Creek Cmpgd
HAER UT-42-F
9ph/3pg/1pc L

High Mt. Dams in Upalco Unit,Farmers Lake Tunnel
Ashley Natl. Forest,5.7 mi. N of Swift Creek Cmpgd
HAER UT-42-G
HAER DLC/PP-1992:UT-3
6ph/3pg/1pc L

High Mt. Dams in Upalco Unit,Five Point Lake Dam
Ashley Natl. Forest,12 mi. NW of Swift Creek Cmpgd
HAER UT-42-H
HAER DLC/PP-1992:UT-3
8ph/3pg/1pc L

High Mt. Dams in Upalco Unit,Milk Lake Dam
Ashley Natl. Forest,9.4 mi. NW of Swift Creek Cmpg
HAER UT-42-K
HAER DLC/PP-1992:UT-3
7ph/3pg/1pc L

High Mt. Dams in Upalco Unit,Twin Pots Dam
Ashley Natl. Forest,10.1 mi. N of Mountain Home
HAER UT-42-M
HAER DLC/PP-1992:UT-3
19ph/2pg/2pc L

High Mt. Dams in Upalco Unit,Water Lily Lake Dam
Ashley Natl. Forest,1.1 mi. NE of Swift Creek Cmpg
HAER UT-42-N
HAER DLC/PP-1992:UT-3
4ph/3pg/1pc L

High Mt. Dams in Upalco Unit,White Miller Lake Dam
Ashley Natl. Forest,6.9 mi. N of Swift Creek Cmpgd
HAER UT-42-O
HAER DLC/PP-1992:UT-3
5ph/3pg/1pc L

TABIONA

Irrig. Canals in Uintah Basin,Thomas,Jepp,Canal
HAER UT-30-G
2ph/2pg/1pc H

EMERY COUNTY

CASTLE DALE VIC.

San Rafael Bridge
Spanning San Rafael River near Buckhorn Wash
HAER UT-60
17ph/10pg/2pc L

EMERY

Emery Latter-Day Saints Church
Block 23
HABS UT-96
HABS UTAH,8-EMERY,1-
4dr/4ph/5pg/1ct/fr L

GARFIELD COUNTY

BOULDER VIC.

Capitol Reef Roads & Bridges
(See WAYNE COUNTY,TORREY VIC. for documentation)
HAER UT-77
L

BRYCE CANYON

Bryce Canyon Lodge
Bryce Canyon National Park
HABS UT-121
HABS 1991(HABS):3
37ph/2pc L

PANGUITCH

Bishop's Storehouse
Center St. & First St. E
HABS UT-95
HABS UTAH,9-PANGU,1-
5dr/4ph/5pg/fr L

GRAND COUNTY

GREEN RIVER

Irrigation Water Wheel
Hastings Ranch
HAER UT-18
HAER UTAH,10-GRENRI,1-
11ph/1pc L

IRON COUNTY

CEDAR CITY

Bladen,Mary,House
200 West St.
HABS UT-6
HABS UTAH,11-CEDCI,1-
3ph L

Haight,Isaac C.,House
200 North & 100 East Sts.
HABS UT-5
HABS UTAH,11-CEDCI,2-
1ph L

Hunter,Joseph S.,House
86 E. Center St.
HABS UT-7
HABS UTAH,11-CEDCI,3-
1ph L

Pioneer Cabin; see Wood,George Lamar,Cabin

Wood,George Lamar,Cabin (Pioneer Cabin)
City Park (moved from original location)
HABS UT-4
HABS UTAH,11-CEDCI,4-
2ph L

OLD IRONTOWN

Coke Oven
State Rt. 56 Vic.
HABS UT-59
HABS UTAH,11-OLDIR,1-
2dr/1ph/4pg L

JUAB COUNTY

EUREKA

Bullion Beck and Champion Mine,Headframe
Tintic Mining District
HAER UT-46
HAER 1991(HAER):21
9ph/10pg/1pc L

MILLARD COUNTY

COVE FORT

Cove Fort
State Rts. 4 & 161
HABS UT-57
HABS UTAH,14-COVFO,1-
5dr/7ph/5pg L

FILLMORE

Callister,Bishop Thomas,House
30 W. Center St.
HABS UT-75
HABS UTAH,14-FILL,3-
1ph L

Rock Schoolhouse
First West & First South Sts.
HABS UT-32
HABS UTAH,14-FILL,1-
4dr/6ph/4pg/fr L

Territorial Capital
Main,Center,First South & First West Sts.
HABS UT-33
HABS UTAH,14-FILL,4-
11ph/5pg L

PIUTE COUNTY

MARYSVALE

Marysvale Bridge
Spanning the Sevier River on Rio Grande St.
HAER UT-57
HAER DLC/PP-1992:UT-2
11ph/13pg/1pc L

SALT LAKE COUNTY

BINGHAM CANYON

Utah Copper Company,Bingham Canyon Mine
State Rt. 48
HAER UT-21
HAER UTAH,18-BINCA,1-
4dr/26ph/2pc L

HOLLADAY

Big Cottonwood Power Co. :Stairs Hydroelec. Statio; see Utah Power & Light Co. :Stairs Hydroelec. Station

Big Cottonwood Power Co. :Stairs Sta. Wooden Flume; see Utah Power & Light Co.:Stairs Station Wooden Flume

Big Cottonwood Power Co.,Hydroelectric Plant; see Utah Power Company,Granite Hydroelectric Plant

Stairs Hydroelectric Station; see Utah Power & Light Co. :Stairs Hydroelec. Station

Stairs Station Wooden Flume; see Utah Power & Light Co.:Stairs Station Wooden Flume

Utah Power & Light Co. :Stairs Hydroelec. Station (Big Cottonwood Power Co. :Stairs Hydroelec. Statio Stairs Hydroelectric Station)
HAER UT-3
HAER UTAH,18-HOLD,1-
7ph/1pc L

Utah Power & Light Co.:Stairs Station Wooden Flume (Big Cottonwood Power Co. :Stairs Sta. Wooden Flume Stairs Station Wooden Flume)
HAER UT-3-A
HAER UTAH,18-HOLD,1A-
4ph/1pc L

Utah Power Company,Granite Hydroelectric Plant (Big Cottonwood Power Co.,Hydroelectric Plant)
HAER UT-4
HAER UTAH,18-HOLD,2-
8ph/1pc L

MAGNA

Kennecott Copper Company,Magna Concentrator; see Utah Copper Company,Magna Concentrator

Utah Copper Company,Magna Concentrator (Kennecott Copper Company,Magna Concentrator)
HAER UT-24
HAER UTAH,18-MAGNA,1-
4dr/8ph/1pc L

RIVERTON

Jordan Narrows Hydroelectric Plant; see Salt Lake City Water & Electrical Power Co.

Salt Lake City Water & Electrical Power Co. (Jordan Narrows Hydroelectric Plant)
Jordan River
HAER UT-15
HAER UTAH,18-RIVER,1-
3ph/9pg/1pc L

SALT LAKE

Salt Lake City & County Building
451 Washington Square
HABS UT-104
HABS UTAH,18-SALCI,23-
3ph/14pg L

SALT LAKE CITY

Beehive House (Young,Brigham,House)
E. South Temple St.
HABS UT-36-U-1
HABS UTAH,18-SALCI,1-
13dr/8ph/2pg/fr L

Chase,Isaac Mill
Sixth East St.
HABS UT-49
HABS UTAH,18-SALCI,13-
6dr/4ph/6pg/fr L

Church of Jesus Christ of Latter-Day Saints; see Salt Lake Temple

Church of Jesus Christ of Latter-Day Saints; see Seventh Ward Chapel

Church of Jesus Christ of the Latter-Day Saints; see Salt Lake City Tabernacle

Conklin-Dern Mansion
711 E. South Temple St.
HABS UT-73
HABS UTAH,18-SALCI,18-
6ph/5pg L

Council Hall; see Salt Lake City Hall

Culmer,William H.,House
33 C St.
HABS UT-85
HABS UTAH,18-SALCI,28-
5dr/15ph/8pg/fr L

Deuel,Osmyn,Log Cabin
Temple Square (moved from original site)
HABS UT-36-U-3
HABS UTAH,18-SALCI,3-
1ph/1pg L

Devereaux; see Staines-Jennings Mansion

Dooly Building
109 W. Second South St.
HABS UT-91
HABS UTAH,18-SALCI,19-
1ph/3pg L

Eico Overhead Loader
HAER UT-33
HAER UTAH,18-SALCI,20-
2ph/1pc L

Fisher,Albert,Carriage House
1206 W. Second South St.
HABS UT-50
HABS UTAH,18-SALCI,14A-
9dr/4ph/4pg/fr L

Fort Douglas,Building Number 55; see Fort Douglas,Commander's Residence

Fort Douglas,Commander's Residence (Fort Douglas,Building Number 55)
HABS UT-68
HABS UTAH,18-SALCI,16B-
2ph L

Fort Douglas,Officers' Duplexes
Officers' Circle
HABS UT-67
HABS UTAH,18-SALCI,16A-
5dr/4ph/6pg/fr L

Fourteenth District School; see Fremont School

Fremont School (Fourteenth District School)
139 S. Second West St.
HABS UT-24
HABS UTAH,18-SALCI,7-
8dr/14ph/7pg L

Granite Paper Mill
6900 Big Cottonwood Canyon Rd.
HABS UT-39
HABS UTAH,18-SALCI,9-
8ph/5pg L

Great Salt Lake Base & Meridian
Temple Square
HAER UT-36
HAER UTAH,18-SALCI,32-
1ph/1pg/1pc L

Interstate Pressed Brick Company; see Salt Lake Pressed Brick Company

Keith-Brown Carriage House
529 E. South Temple
HABS UT-97-A
HABS UTAH,18-SALCI,26A-
1ph L

Keith-Brown House
529 E. South Temple
HABS UT-97
HABS UTAH,18-SALCI,26-
8dr/15ph/7pg/fr L

McCune,Alfred W. ,Carriage House
200 N. Main St.
HABS UT-87-A
HABS UTAH,18-SALCI,27A-
1ph/2ct L

McCune,Alfred W.,House
200 N. Main St.
HABS UT-87
HABS UTAH,18-SALCI,27-
8dr/21ph/7pg/fr L

Meyer,Frederick A. E. ,House
929 E. Second South St.
HABS UT-51
HABS UTAH,18-SALCI,15-
9dr/6ph/4pg/fr L

Mormon Tabernacle; see Salt Lake City Tabernacle

Mormon Temple; see Salt Lake Temple

Mountain Dell Dam
Interstate Hwy. 80
HAER UT-16
HAER UTAH,18-SALCI,22-
4dr/19ph/28pg/3pc/fr L

Perkins,Francis H.,House
77 S St.
HABS UT-98
HABS UTAH,18-SALCI,31-
4ph/1pg L

Salt Lake City Hall (Council Hall)
300 N. State St.
HABS UT-74
HABS UTAH,18-SALCI,24-
4ph/14pg/1pc/fr L

Salt Lake City Tabernacle (Church of Jesus Christ of the Latter-Day Saints; Mormon Tabernacle)
Temple Square
HABS UT-36-U-2
HAER UT-1
HABS/HAER UTAH,18-SALCI,2-
5dr/29ph/6pg/2pc/2ct/fr L

Salt Lake Pressed Brick Company (Interstate Pressed Brick Company)
1100 East St.
HAER UT-7
HAER UTAH,18-SALCI,21-
6ph/1pc L

Salt Lake Temple (Church of Jesus Christ of Latter-Day Saints; Mormon Temple)
Temple Square
HABS UT-2
HABS UTAH,18-SALCI,4-
4ph/2pg/1pc/fr L

Seventh Ward Chapel (Church of Jesus Christ of Latter-Day Saints)
116 W. Fifth South St.
HABS UT-22
HABS UTAH,18-SALCI,5-
7dr/5ph/5pg/fr L

Seventh Ward Recreation Hall; see Whittier School

St. Mark's Episcopal Cathedral
231 E. First South St.
HABS UT-41
HABS UTAH,18-SALCI,2-
9dr/16ph/30pg L

Staines-Jennings Mansion (Devereaux)
334 W. South Temple St.
HABS UT-37
HABS UTAH,18-SALCI,8-
19dr/28ph/12pg L

Union Pacific Depot; see Union Passenger Station

Union Passenger Station (Union Pacific Depot)
Third West & South Temple
HABS UT-88
HABS UTAH,18-SAlCI,25-
5dr/4ph/7pg/fr L

Utah Commercial & Savings Bank
22 E. First South St.
HABS UT-72
HABS UTAH,18-SALCI,17-
2dr/1ph/5pg/fr L

Varley,John,House
180 West 500 North
HABS UT-101
HABS UTAH,18-SALCI,30-
6ph/1pg/fr L

Whipple,Nelson Wheeler,House
564 W. 400 North
HABS UT-100
HABS UTAH,18-SALCI,29-
2dr/1pg/fr L

Whittier School (Seventh Ward Recreation Hall)
120 W. Fifth South St.
HABS UT-23
HABS UTAH,18-SALCI,6-
8ph/4pg L

Young,Brigham,House; see Beehive House

Z. C. M. I.; see Zion's Cooperative Mercantile Institution

Zion's Cooperative Mercantile Institution (Z. C. M. I.)
15 S. Main St.
HABS UT-47
HABS UTAH,18-SALCI,11-
3dr/12ph/20pg/fr L

Zion's First National Bank Clock
First South & Main sts.
HABS UT-48
HABS UTAH,18-SALCI,12A-
1ph/2pg L

SOUTH JORDAN

Fairbourn,Richard M.,Farm
170 West, 11,400 South
HABS UT-131
17ph/18pg/2pc H

Fairbourn,Richard M.,Farm,Barn
170 West, 11,400 South
HABS UT-131-C
1ph/1pc H

Fairbourn,Richard M.,Farm,Chicken Coop
170 West, 11,400 South
HABS UT-131-E
1ph/1pc H

Fairbourn,Richard M.,Farm,Equipment Shed
170 West, 11,400 South
HABS UT-131-F
1ph/1pc H

Fairbourn,Richard M.,Farm,Garage
170 West, 11,400 South
HABS UT-131-A
2ph/1pc H

Fairbourn,Richard M.,Farm,Horse Barn
170 West, 11,400 South
HABS UT-131-B
2ph/1pc H

Fairbourn,Richard,M.,Farm,Granary
170 West, 11,400 South
HABS UT-131-D
1ph/1pc H

UNION

Burgon,Horace W., House
7501 South 700 East
HABS UT-129
6ph/11pg/1pc H

SAN JUAN COUNTY

BLUFF VIC.

Hole-in-the-Rock Trail (Mormon Trail)
Running From Bluff Vic. to Escalante,Garfield Co.
HAER UT-29
HAER UTAH,19-BLUFF.V,1-
8ph/3pg L

Mormon Trail; see Hole-in-the-Rock Trail

SANPETE COUNTY

EPHRAIM

Ephraim Co-op Building; see Ephraim United Order Mercantile Institution

Ephraim United Order Mercantile Institution (Ephraim Co-op Building)
Main & First North Sts.
HABS UT-106
HABS UTAH,20-EPHRA,2-
6ph/10pg/fr L

Peterson,Canute,House
10 N. Main St.
HABS UT-64
HABS UTAH,20-EPHRA,1-
8dr/4ph/6pg/fr L

GUNNISON

Casino Theater (Star Theater)
Main St. (U. S. Rt. 89)
HABS UT-76
HABS UTAH,20-GUNNI,1-
1ph L

Star Theater; see Casino Theater

MANTI

Church of Jesus Christ of Latter-Day Saints; see Manti Temple

Manti Temple (Church of Jesus Christ of Latter-Day Saints)
Main St. (U. S. Rt. 89)
HABS UT-71
HABS UTAH,20-MANT,1-
8ph/6pg L

SPRING CITY

Bishop's Storehouse; see Spring City Area Study

Church of Jesus Christ of Latter-day Saints; see Spring City Area Study

City Hall; see Spring City Area Study

Hons,Peter,House; see Spring City Area Study

House,Adobe; see Spring City Area Study

House,Frame; see Spring City Area Study

House,Stone; see Spring City Area Study

Hyde,Orson,House; see Spring City Area Study

Log Cabin; see Spring City Area Study

Masonic Lodge; see Spring City Area Study

Public School; see Spring City Area Study

Spring City Area Study
HABS UT-70
HABS UTAH,20-SPRICI,1-
1dr/5ph/2pg L

Spring City Area Study (Bishop's Storehouse)
Fourth & E Sts.
HABS UT-70-B
HABS UTAH,20-SPRICI,3-
2ph L

Spring City Area Study (City Hall)
Main St.
HABS UT-70-C
HABS UTAH,20-SPRICI,4-
2ph L

Spring City Area Study (Hons,Peter,House)
Fourth & F Sts.
HABS UT-70-E
HABS UTAH,20-SPRICI,6-
1ph L

Spring City Area Study (House,Adobe)
First St.
HABS UT-70-A
HABS UTAH,20,SPRICI,2-
1ph L

Spring City Area Study (House,Frame)
Second & B Sts.
HABS UT-70-D
HABS UTAH,20-SPRICI,5-
2ph L

Spring City Area Study (House,Stone)
Main & F Sts.
HABS UT-70-K
HABS UTAH,20-SPRICI,12-
1ph L

Spring City Area Study (Hyde,Orson,House)
Main & C Sts.
HABS UT-70-F
HABS UTAH,20-SPRICI,7-
2ph L

Spring City Area Study (Log Cabin)
HABS UT-70-H
HABS UTAH,20-SPRICI,9-
2ph L

Spring City Area Study (Log Cabin)
First & B Sts.
HABS UT-70-G
HABS UTAH,20-SPRICI,8-
1ph L

Spring City Area Study (Masonic Lodge)
B St.
HABS UT-70-I
HABS UTAH,20-SPRICI,10-
2ph L

Spring City Area Study (Public School)
Fourth & E Sts.
HABS UT-70-J
HABS UTAH,20-SPRICI,11-
2ph L

Spring City Area Study (Tithing Barn)
Second St.
HABS UT-70-L
HABS UTAH,20-SPRICI,13-
1ph L

Spring City Area Study (Tithing Office)
Second St.
HABS UT-70-M
HABS UTAH,20-SPRICI,13-
2ph L

Spring City Area Study (Ward Chapel; Church of Jesus Christ of Latter-day Saints)
Main St.
HABS UT-70-N
HABS UTAH,20-SPRICI,14-
5ph L

Tithing Barn; see Spring City Area Study

Tithing Office; see Spring City Area Study

Ward Chapel; see Spring City Area Study

SUMMIT COUNTY

HENEFER

Henefer Bridge
Spanning Weber River at Center St.
HAER UT-49
HAER UTAH,22-HENF,1-
16ph/11pg/1pc L

HOYTSVILLE

Hoyt,Samuel Pierce,House
U. S. Rt. 189 Vic.
HABS UT-62
HABS UTAH,22-HOYT,1-
8dr/6ph/6pg/fr L

Hoyt,Samuel Pierce,Mill
U. S. Rt. 189 Vic.
HABS UT-63
HABS UTAH,22-HOYT,2-
2ph/3pg L

KAMAS VIC.

High Mt. Dams in Bonneville Unit,Big Elk Lake Dam
Wasatch National Forest
HAER UT-41-A
HAER DLC/PP-1992:UT-5
7ph/3pg/1pc L

High Mt. Dams in Bonneville Unit,Central Utah Proj (Wasatch National Forest)
HAER UT-41
HAER DLC/PP-1993:UT-1
2dr/3pg L

High Mt. Dams in Bonneville Unit,Crystal Lake Dam
Wasatch National Forest
HAER UT-41-B
HAER DLC/PP-1992:UT-5
5ph/3pg/1pc L

High Mt. Dams in Bonneville Unit,Duck Lake Dam (North Fork No. 6 Lake Dam)
Wasatch National Forest
HAER UT-41-C
HAER DLC/PP-1992:UT-5
6ph/3pg/1pc L

High Mt. Dams in Bonneville Unit,Fire Lake Dam (North Fork No. 5 Lake Dam)
Wasatch National Forest
HAER UT-41-D
HAER DLC/PP-1992:UT-5
8ph/3pg/1pc L

High Mt. Dams in Bonneville Unit,Island Lake Dam
Wasatch National Forest
HAER UT-41-E
HAER DLC/PP-1992:UT-5
7ph/3pg/1pc L

High Mt. Dams in Bonneville Unit,Long Lake Dam (North Fork No. 3 Lake Dam)
Wasatch National Forest
HAER UT-41-F
HAER DLC/PP-1992:UT-5
8ph/3pg/1pc L

High Mt. Dams in Bonneville Unit,Lost Lake Dam (Wasatch National Forest)
HAER UT-41-G
HAER DLC/PP-1993:UT-1
8ph/3pg/1pc L

High Mt. Dams in Bonneville Unit,Marjorie Lake Dam (North Fork No. 1 Lake Dam)
Wasatch National Forest
HAER UT-41-H
HAER DLC/PP-1992:UT-5
9ph/3pg/1pc L

High Mt. Dams in Bonneville Unit,Pot Lake Dam
Wasatch National Forest
HAER UT-41-I
HAER DLC/PP-1992:UT-5
6ph/3pg/1pc L

High Mt. Dams in Bonneville Unit,Star Lake Dam
Wasatch National Forest
HAER UT-41-J
HAER DLC/PP-1992:UT-5
6ph/3pg/1pc L

High Mt. Dams in Bonneville Unit,Teapot Lake Dam (Lost Lake No. 2 Dam; Wasatch National Park)
HAER UT-41-K
HAER DLC/PP-1993:UT-1
6ph/3pg/1pc L

High Mt. Dams in Bonneville Unit,Trial Lake Dam (Wasatch National Forest)
HAER UT-41-L
HAER DLC/PP-1993:UT-1
12ph/3pg/2pc L

High Mt. Dams in Bonneville Unit,Wall Lake Dam (Wasatch National Forest)
HAER UT-41-M
HAER DLC/PP-1993:UT-1
8ph/3pg/1pc L

High Mt. Dams in Bonneville Unit,Washington Lk Dam (Wasatch National Forest)
HAER UT-41-N
HAER DLC/PP-1993:UT-1
11ph/3pg/2pc L

High Mt. Dams in Bonneville Unit,Weir Lake Dam (North Fork No. 2 Lake Dam)
Wasatch National Forest
HAER UT-41-O
HAER DLC/PP-1992:UT-5
9ph/3pg/1pc L

Lost Lake No. 2 Dam; see High Mt. Dams in Bonneville Unit,Teapot Lake Dam

North Fork No. 1 Lake Dam; see High Mt. Dams in Bonneville Unit,Marjorie Lake Dam

North Fork No. 2 Lake Dam; see High Mt. Dams in Bonneville Unit,Weir Lake Dam

North Fork No. 3 Lake Dam; see High Mt. Dams in Bonneville Unit,Long Lake Dam

North Fork No. 5 Lake Dam; see High Mt. Dams in Bonneville Unit,Fire Lake Dam

North Fork No. 6 Lake Dam; see High Mt. Dams in Bonneville Unit,Duck Lake Dam

Wasatch National Forest; see High Mt. Dams in Bonneville Unit,Central Utah Proj

Wasatch National Forest; see High Mt. Dams in Bonneville Unit,Lost Lake Dam

Wasatch National Forest; see High Mt. Dams in Bonneville Unit,Trial Lake Dam

Wasatch National Forest; see High Mt. Dams in Bonneville Unit,Wall Lake Dam

Wasatch National Forest; see High Mt. Dams in Bonneville Unit,Washington Lk Dam

Wasatch National Park; see High Mt. Dams in Bonneville Unit,Teapot Lake Dam

PARK CITY

New Deal Market
204 Main St.
HABS UT-99
HABS UTAH,22-PARK,4-
2ph/1pg/fr L

Silver King Mining Company,Ore Loading Station
Park Ave.
HAER UT-11
HAER UTAH,22-PARK.V,4-
6dr/20ph/2pc/fr L

St. Mary of the Assumption Church
Park Ave.
HABS UT-35
HABS UTAH,22-PARK,2-
4ph/4pg L

St. Mary of the Assumption School
Park Ave.
HABS UT-34
HABS UTAH,22-PARK,1-
4dr/2ph/4pg/fr L

PARK CITY VIC.

California Comstock Mill
HAER UT-32
HAER UTAH,22-PARK.V,1-
10ph/1pc L

Keystone Mill
HAER UT-28
HAER UTAH,22-PARK.V,2-
8ph/1pc L

Silver King Mining Co.,Covered Tramway
Park City West
HAER UT-22-C
HAER UTAH,22-PARKW,3C-
10ph/6pg/1pc L

Silver King Mining Company,Mineshaft & Main Hoist
Woodside Gulch
HAER UT-22-A
HAER UTAH,22-PARK.V,3A-
3dr/6ph/10pg/1pc/fr L

Silver King Mining Company,Ore Mill
Park City West
HAER UT-22-B
HAER UTAH,22-PARK.V,3B-
12ph/6pg L

Silver King Mining Company,Warehouse
Park City West
HAER UT-22-D
HAER UTAH,22-PARK.V,3D-
2ph/1pc L

Silver King Mining Company,Water Tanks
Park City West
HAER UT-22-E
HAER UTAH,22-PARK.V,3E-
2ph/1pc L

SILVER CREEK JCT.

Kimball Hotel
U. S. Rt. 40
HABS UT-53
HABS UTAH,22-SILV.V,1-
5dr/6ph/6pg/fr L

TOOELE COUNTY

DUGWAY

Dugway Proving Ground
HAER UT-35
HAER UTAH,23-DUG,1-
43pg/fr L

KNOLLS/WENDOVER VIC.

Lincoln Highway,Wendover Cutoff
Great Salt Lake Desert
HAER UT-23
HAER UTAH,23-KNOL,1-
3dr/5ph/11pg L

OPHIR

DeLamar Mercur Mines Co.,Golden Gate Mill
HAER UT-10
HAER UTAH,23-OPHIR,2-
34ph/3pc L

Town Hall
43 Main St.
HABS UT-38
HABS UTAH,23-OPHIR,1-
3dr/7ph/4pg/fr L

TOOELE

Tooele Army Depot
HAER UT-34
HAER UTAH,23-TOO,3-
47pg/fr L

Tooele County Courthouse & City Hall
Vine St.
HABS UT-52
HABS UTAH,23-TOO,1-
5dr/3ph/5pg/fr L

TOOELE VIC.

International Smelting & Refining Company (Tooele Smelter)
State Rt. 178
HAER UT-20
HAER UTAH,23-TOO,2-
5dr/15ph/2pc L

International Smelting & Refining Company (Tooele Smelter,Blast Furnace Building)
State Rt. 178
HAER UT-20-K
HAER UTAH,23-TOO,2K-
6ph/1pc L

International Smelting & Refining Company (Tooele Smelter,Charge Bins)
State Rt. 178
HAER UT-20-J
HAER UTAH,23-TOO,2J-
3ph/1pc L

International Smelting & Refining Company (Tooele Smelter,Drossing Plant)
State Rt. 178
HAER UT-20-L
HAER UTAH,23-TOO,2L-
5ph/1pc L

International Smelting & Refining Company (Tooele Smelter,Miscellaneous Ore Bins)
State Rt. 178
HAER UT-20-H
HAER UTAH,23-TOO,2H-
1ph/1pc L

International Smelting & Refining Company (Tooele Smelter,Office Building)
State Rt. 178
HAER UT-20-B
HAER UTAH,23-TOO,2B-
1ph L

International Smelting & Refining Company (Tooele Smelter,Powerhouse)
State Rt. 178
HAER UT-20-A
HAER UTAH,23-TOO,2A-
3dr/7ph/1pc/fr L

International Smelting & Refining Company (Tooele Smelter,Receiving Bins)
78 te Rt. 1yon
HAER UT-20-C
HAER UTAH,23-TOO,2C-
3ph/1pc L

International Smelting & Refining Company (Tooele Smelter,Reverberatory,Converter & Casting B
State Rt. 178
HAER UT-20-G
HAER UTAH,23-TOO,2G-
8ph/1pc L

International Smelting & Refining Company (Tooele Smelter,Roaster Building)
State Rt. 178
HAER UT-20-F
HAER UTAH,23-TOO,2F-
5ph/1pc L

International Smelting & Refining Company (Tooele Smelter,Roaster Ore Bins)
State Route 178
HAER UT-20-E
HAER UTAH,23-TOO,2E-
2ph/1pc L

International Smelting & Refining Company (Tooele Smelter,Sample Mill)
State Rt. 178
HAER UT-20-D
HAER UTAH,23-TOO,2D-
1ph L

International Smelting & Refining Company (Tooele Smelter,Sinter Plant)
State Rt. 178
HAER UT-20-I
HAER 1986(HAER):71
1ph/1pc L

Tooele Smelter; see International Smelting & Refining Company

Tooele Smelter,Blast Furnace Building; see International Smelting & Refining Company

Tooele Smelter,Charge Bins; see International Smelting & Refining Company

Tooele Smelter,Drossing Plant; see International Smelting & Refining Company

Tooele Smelter,Miscellaneous Ore Bins; see International Smelting & Refining Company

Tooele Smelter,Office Building; see International Smelting & Refining Company

Tooele Smelter,Powerhouse; see International Smelting & Refining Company

Tooele Smelter,Receiving Bins; see International Smelting & Refining Company

Tooele Smelter,Reverberatory,Converter & Casting B; see International Smelting & Refining Company

Tooele Smelter,Roaster Building; see International Smelting & Refining Company

Tooele Smelter,Roaster Ore Bins; see International Smelting & Refining Company

Tooele Smelter,Sample Mill; see International Smelting & Refining Company

Tooele Smelter,Sinter Plant; see International Smelting & Refining Company

WENDOVER

Machine Shop; see Wendover Air Force Base,Building 104

Wendover Air Force Base,Building 104 (Machine Shop)
Wendover Air Force Base
HABS UT-105
HABS UTAH,23-WEND,1A-
10ph/1pg L

UINTAH COUNTY

GUSHER

Irrig. Canals in Uintah Basin,Ouray Park Canal
HAER UT-30-B
6ph/2pg/1pc H

JENSEN

Jensen Bridge
Spanning the Green River at the Town of Jensen
HAER UT-50
HAER DLC/PP-1992:UT-3
21ph/12pg/2pc L

LAPOINT

Irrig. Canals in Uintah Basin,Deep Creek Canal
HAER UT-30-C
7ph/2pg/1pc H

Irrig. Canals in Uintah Basin,Rhodes Canal
HAER UT-30-J
5ph/2pg/1pc H

LAPOINT VIC.

Irrigation Canals in Uintah Basin
HAER UT-30
L

VERNAL

Ashley Post Office
1335 W. 2000 North
HABS UT-94
HABS UTAH,24-VERN,1-
2dr/7ph/5pg/fr L

Irrig. Canals in Uintah Basin,Highline Canal
HAER UT-30-F
1ph/2pg/1pc H

WHITEROCKS

Irrig. Canals in Uintah Basin,U.S. Whiterocks Cana
HAER UT-30-A
12ph/2pg/1pc H

Irrig. Canals in Uintah Basin,Whiterocks & Ouray V
HAER UT-30-H
12ph/3pg/1pc H

UTAH COUNTY

AMERICAN FORK

Chipman Warehouse
Merchant St.,W. side, btwn. North St. & Main St.
HABS UT-120
HABS 1991(HABS):3
9ph/8pg/1pc L

FAIRFIELD

Carson,John,House (Stagecoach Inn)
Main St.
HABS UT-31
HABS UTAH,25-FAIRF,2-
4ph/6pg L

District School
N. Church St.
HABS UT-29
HABS UTAH,25-FAIRF,1-
6dr/5ph/7pg/fr L

District School Gymnasium
N. Church St.
HABS UT-30
HABS UTAH,25-FAIRF,1A-
2ph L

Stagecoach Inn; see Carson,John,House

GOSHEN VIC.

Tintic Standard Reduction Mill
Warm Springs Mtn.
HAER UT-12
HAER UTAH,25-GOSH,1-
4dr/13ph/5pg/1pc/fr L

OREM VIC.

Telluride Power Co. Olmsted Hydroelectric Plant
mouth of Provo River Canyon W. of U.S. Rt. 189
HAER UT-5
HAER UTAH,25-OREM,1B-
ιDLC/PP-1993:UT-1°
5dr/28ph/7pg/3pc/fr L

Telluride Power Co.,Nunn Hydroelectric Plant
SE side of Provo River,300 feet W. of US Route 189
HAER UT-2
HAER UTAH,25-OREM,1A-
ιDLC/PP-1993:UT-1°
11ph/20pg/2pc L

Telluride Power Company,Provo River Bridge
Spanning Provo River
HAER UT-2-A
HAER UTAH,25-OREM.V,1C-
5ph/1pc L

OREM VIC. (OLMSTEAD)

Denver & Rio Grande Western RR,Provo River Bridge
Spanning Provo River,Orem Vic.
HAER UT-14
HAER UTAH,25-OLMS,1-
4dr/4ph/4pg/1pc/fr L

PAYSON

Strawberry Valley Project
HAER UT-26
HAER UTAH,25-PAYS,1-
78ph/165pg/fr L

PLEASANT GROVE

Fugal Blacksmith Shop
650 N. Fourth East St.
HABS UT-56
HABS UTAH,25-PLEAS,1-
2dr/4ph/4pg/fr L

Halliday,John R.,House
90 E. Second North
HABS UT-93
HABS UTAH,25-PLEAS,2-
5dr/5ph/9pg/1ct/fr L

Nelson, Jeppa Residence and Log Granary
150 W. Eleven Hundred North St.
HABS UT-128
2ph/10pg/1pc H

Nelson,Jeppa Residence & Log Granary,Log Granary
150 West 1100 North Street
HABS UT-128-B
5ph/2pg/1pc H

Nelson,Jeppa Residence and Log Granary,Residence
150 West 1100 North St.
HABS UT-128-A
4ph/2pg/1pc H

PROVO

Columbia Lane Bridge; see Provo River Bridge

Provo Brickyard,Turbine House
1620 N. 200 West St.
HABS UT-36
HABS UTAH,25-PROVO,1-
5dr/3ph/4pg L

Provo River Bridge (Columbia Lane Bridge)
625 West Columbia Lane
HAER UT-61
12ph/12pg/1pc L

PROVO VIC.

Heber Creeper Railroad Line
Provo to Heber City
HAER UT-63
2ph/23pg/1pc H

Heber Creeper RR Line,Brid. Veil Fall to Vivian Pk
Provo to Heber City
HAER UT-63-A
19ph/3pg/2pc H

Heber Creeper RR Line,Vivian Park Bridge
Provo to Heber City
HAER UT-63-B
4ph/3pg/1pc H

Heeber Creeper RR Line,Olmstead Bridge
Provo to Heber City
HAER UT-63-C
7ph/3pg/1pc H

WASATCH COUNTY

HEBER CITY

Church of Jesus Christ of Latter-Day Saints; see Wasatch Stake Tabernacle

Hatch,Abram,House
81 E. Center St.
HABS UT-83
HABS UTAH,26-HEBER,5-
9dr/20ph/5pg/fr L

Heber Amusement Hall
100 North & 100 West Sts.
HABS UT-28
HABS UTAH,26-HEBER,4-
7dr/7ph/5pg/fr L

Wasatch County Courthouse
Main St.
HABS UT-25
HABS UTAH,26-HEBER,1-
6dr/7ph/5pg/fr L

Wasatch County Jail
Center St.
HABS UT-26
HABS UTAH,26-HEBER,2-
3dr/5ph/4pg/fr L

Wasatch Stake Tabernacle (Church of Jesus Christ of Latter-Day Saints)
Main St.
HABS UT-27
HABS UTAH,26-HEBER,3-
7dr/11ph/5pg/fr L

HEBER CITY VIC.

Heber Creeper Railroad Line
Heber City to Provo
HAER UT-63
L

Heber Light & Power Company:Hydroelectric Plant
U. S. Route 40/189
HAER UT-6
HAER UTAH,26-HEBER,7-
3dr/7ph/7pg/1pc/fr L

Jordanelle Valley
HABS UT-115
HABS 1989(HABS):23
1dr/24ph/2pc/fr L

Keetley Mine Complex; see Park Utah Mining Company:Keetley Mine Complex

Keetley Mine:Employee Garage; see Park Utah:Keetley Mine:Employee Garage

Keetley Mine:Employee Storage Sheds; see Park Utah:Keetley Mine:Employee Storage Sheds

Keetley Mine:Lime Storage Shed; see Park Utah:Keetley Mine:Lime Storage Shed

Keetley Mine:Machine/Welding Shop; see Park Utah:Keetley Mine:Machine/Welding Shop

Documentation: **ct** color transparencies **dr** measured drawings **fr** field records
pc photograph captions **pg** pages of text **ph** photographs

Keetley Mine:New Office & Storage; see Park Utah:Keetley Mine:New Office & Storage

Keetley Mine:Office Building; see Park Utah:Keetley Mine:Office Building

Keetley Mine:Powder Shed; see Park Utah:Keetley Mine:Powder Shed

Keetley Mine:Residential Area; see Park Utah:Keetley Mine:Residential Area

Keetley Mine:Sawmill/Carpenter Shop; see Park Utah:Keetley Mine:Sawmill/Carpenter Shop

Keetley Mine:Superintendent's House; see Park Utah:Keetley Mine:Superintendent's House

Keetley Mine:Tailing Car Snowshed; see Park Utah:Keetley Mine:Tailing Car Snowshed

Keetley Mine:Tipple/Ore Car Snowshed; see Park Utah:Keetley Mine:Tipple/Ore Car Snowshed

Park Utah Mining Company:Keetley Mine Complex (Keetley Mine Complex)
1 mi. E. of U. S. 40 at Keetley
HAER UT-47
HAER 1989(HAER):21
1dr/9ph/16pg/5pc/fr L

Park Utah:Keetley Mine:Employee Garage (Keetley Mine:Employee Garage)
1 mi. E. of U. S. 40 at Keetley
HAER UT-47-J
HAER 1989(HAER):21
3ph L

Park Utah:Keetley Mine:Employee Storage Sheds (Keetley Mine:Employee Storage Sheds)
1 mi. E. of U. S. 40 at Keetley
HAER UT-47-K
HAER 1989(HAER):21
2ph L

Park Utah:Keetley Mine:Lime Storage Shed (Keetley Mine:Lime Storage Shed)
1 mi. E. of U. S. 40 at Keetley
HAER UT-47-E
HAER 1989(HAER):21
1ph L

Park Utah:Keetley Mine:Machine/Welding Shop (Keetley Mine:Machine/Welding Shop)
1 mi. E. of U. S. 40 at Keetley
HAER UT-47-A
HAER 1989(HAER):21
5ph L

Park Utah:Keetley Mine:New Office & Storage (Keetley Mine:New Office & Storage)
1 mi. E. of U. S. 40 at Keetley
HAER UT-47-H
HAER 1989(HAER):21
1ph L

Park Utah:Keetley Mine:Office Building (Keetley Mine:Office Building)
1 mi. E. of U. S. 40 at Keetley
HAER UT-47-G
HAER 1989(HAER):21
2ph L

Park Utah:Keetley Mine:Powder Shed (Keetley Mine:Powder Shed)
1 mi. E. of U. S. 40 at Keetley
HAER UT-47-F
HAER 1989(HAER):21
1ph L

Park Utah:Keetley Mine:Residential Area (Keetley Mine:Residential Area)
1 mi. E. of U. S. 40 at Keetley
HAER UT-47-I
HAER 1989(HAER):21
4ph L

Park Utah:Keetley Mine:Sawmill/Carpenter Shop (Keetley Mine:Sawmill/Carpenter Shop)
1 mi. E. of U. S. 40 at Keetley
HAER UT-47-C
HAER 1989(HAER):21
2ph L

Park Utah:Keetley Mine:Superintendent's House (Keetley Mine:Superintendent's House)
1 mi. E. of U. S. 40 at Keetley
HAER UT-47-L
HAER 1989(HAER):21
3ph L

Park Utah:Keetley Mine:Tailing Car Snowshed (Keetley Mine:Tailing Car Snowshed)
1 mi. E. of U. S. 40 at Keetley
HAER UT-47-B
HAER 1989(HAER):21
3ph L

Park Utah:Keetley Mine:Tipple/Ore Car Snowshed (Keetley Mine:Tipple/Ore Car Snowshed)
1 mi. E. of U. S. 40 at Keetley
HAER UT-47-D
HAER 1989(HAER):21
10ph L

HERBER CITY VIC.

Cluff,Henry Ranch,Barn
(Fisher,George,Barn)
Keetley Mine Rd. & U.S. Rt. 40
HABS UT-115-C
3ph/1pc L

Cluff,Henry Ranch,Cabin
(Fisher,George,Ranch,Cabin)
Keetley Mine Rd. & U.S. Rt. 40
HABS UT-115-E
2ph/1pc L

Cluff,Henry,Ranch
(Fisher,George,Ranch)
Keetley Mine Road at U.S. Rt. 40
HABS UT-115-A
HABS 1989(HABS):23
13ph/1pg/2pc L

Cluff,Henry,Ranch,Ranch House
(Fisher,George,Ranch House)
Keetley Mine Rd. at U.S. Rt. 40
HABS UT-115-B
7ph/1pc L

Cluff,Henry,Ranch,Shed
(Fisher,George,Ranch,Shed)
Keetley Mine Rd. & U.S. Rt. 40
HABS UT-115-D
3ph/1pc L

Fisher,George,Barn; see Cluff,Henry Ranch,Barn

Fisher,George,Ranch; see Cluff,Henry,Ranch

Fisher,George,Ranch House; see Cluff,Henry,Ranch,Ranch House

Fisher,George,Ranch,Cabin; see Cluff,Henry Ranch,Cabin

Fisher,George,Ranch,Shed; see Cluff,Henry,Ranch,Shed

MIDWAY

Watkins-Coleman House
5 E. Main St.
HABS UT-54
HABS UTAH,26-MID,1-
10dr/6ph/8pg/fr L

WASHINGTON COUNTY

HURRICANE VIC.

Harrisburg Bridge; see Virgin River Bridge

Hurricane Irrigation Canal
State Rt. 15 Vic.
HAER UT-17
HAER UTAH,27-HURI,1-
3dr/19ph/10pg/2pc/fr L

Virgin River Bridge (Harrisburg Bridge)
Spanning Virgin River on State Hwy. 9
HAER UT-59
HAER DLC/PP-1992:UT-3
9ph/28pg/1pc L

LEEDS

Angell,George E. House; see Wilkinson,Charles,House

Stirling,William,House
HABS UT-77
HABS UTAH,27-LEED,1-
1ph L

Wilkinson,Charles,House (Angell,George E. House)
HABS UT-78
HABS UTAH,27-LEED,2-
1ph L

MIDDLETON

McDonald,Alexander F.,House
HABS UT-79
HABS UTAH,27-MID,1-
1ph L

PINE VALLEY

Church of Jesus Christ of Latter-Day Saints; see Pine Valley Ward Chapel

Pine Valley Tithing Office
Main St.
HABS UT-69
HABS UTAH,27-PINVA,2-
1ph/2pg L

Pine Valley Ward Chapel (Church of Jesus Christ of Latter-Day Saints)
Main & Grass Valley Sts.
HABS UT-60
HABS UTAH,27-PINVA,1-
5dr/5ph/5pg/fr L

ROCKVILLE

Deseret Telegraph & Post Office Building
State Rt. 15
HABS UT-36-U-4
HABS UTAH,27-ROCVI,1-
7dr/3ph/2pg/fr L

SILVER REEF

Wells,Fargo & Company Express Building
Main St.
HABS UT-58
HABS UTAH,27-SILV,1-
2dr/4ph/6pg/fr L

SPRINGDALE VIC.

Oak Creek Historic Complex
Zion National Park
HABS UT-110
HABS UTAH,27-SPDA.V,4-
3ph/1pc/fr L

Oak Creek Historic Complex,Carpenter Shop
Zion National Park
HABS UT-110-L
HABS UTAH, 27-SPDA.V,4L-
3ph/1pc/fr L

Oak Creek Historic Complex,Equipment Shop
Zion National Park
HABS UT-110-P
HABS UTAH,27-SPDA.V,4P-
1ph/1pc/fr L

Oak Creek Historic Complex,Firehouse
Zion National Park
HABS UT-110-M
HABS UTAH, 27-SPDA.V,4M-
2ph/1pc/fr L

Oak Creek Historic Complex,Machine Shop
Zion National Park
HABS UT-110-O
HABS UTAH,27-SPDA.V,40-
4ph/1pc/fr L

Oak Creek Historic Complex,Ranger's Dormitory
Zion National Park
HABS UT-110-A
HABS UTAH,27-SPDA.V,4A-
7ph/1pc/fr L

Oak Creek Historic Complex,Ranger's House
Zion National Park
HABS UT-110-B
HABS UTAH,27-SPDA.V,4B-
4ph/1pc/fr L

Oak Creek Historic Complex,Ranger's House
Zion National Park
HABS UT-110-C
HABS UTAH,27-SPDA.V,4C-
3ph/1pc/fr L

Oak Creek Historic Complex,Ranger's House
Zion National Park
HABS UT-110-D
HABS UTAH,27-SPDA.V,4D-
2ph/1pc/fr L

Oak Creek Historic Complex,Ranger's House
Zion National Park
HABS UT-110-E
HABS UTAH,27-SPDA.V,4E-
2ph/1pc L

Oak Creek Historic Complex,Ranger's House
Zion National Park
HABS UT-110-F
HABS UTAH,27-SPDA.V,4F-
3ph/1pc/fr L

Oak Creek Historic Complex,Ranger's House
Zion National Park
HABS UT-110-G
HABS UTAH,27-SPDA.V,4G-
2ph/1pc/fr L

Oak Creek Historic Complex,Ranger's House
Zion National Park
HABS UT-110-H
HABS UTAH,27-SPDA.V,4H-
2ph/1pc/fr L

Oak Creek Historic Complex,Three Stall Garage
Zion National Park
HABS UT-110-I
HABS UTAH,27-SPDA.V,4I-
1ph/1pc/fr L

Oak Creek Historic Complex,Two Stall Garage
Zion National Park
HABS UT-110-J
HABS UTAH,27-SPDA.V,4J-
1ph/1pc L

Oak Creek Historic Complex,Two Stall Garage
Zion National Park
HABS UT-110-K
HABS UTAH,27-SPDA.V,4K-
1ph/1pc/fr L

Oak Creek Historic Complex,Warehouse
Zion National Park
HABS UT-110-N
HABS UTAH,27-SPDA.V,4N-
3ph/1pc/fr L

Pine Creek Bridge; see Zion-Mount Carmel Highway,Pine Creek Bridge

Pine Creek Historic Complex,Asst. Supt's House
Zion National Park
HABS UT-109-B
HABS UTAH,27-SPDA.V,5B-
3ph/1pc/fr L

Pine Creek Historic Complex,Chief Ranger's House
Zion National Park
HABS UT-109-C
HABS UTAH,27-SPDA.V,5C-
3ph/1pc/fr L

Pine Creek Historic Complex,Superintendent's House
Zion National Park
HABS UT-109-A
HABS UTAH,27-SPDA.V,5A-
4ph/1pc/fr L

Pine Creek Historic Complex,Three Stall Garage
Zion National Park
HABS UT-109-E
HABS UTAH,27-SPDA.V,5E-
1ph/1pc/fr L

Pine Creek Historic Complex,Two Stall Garage
Zion National Park
HABS UT-109-D
HABS UTAH,27-SPDA.V,5D-
2ph/1pc/fr L

Virgin River Bridge; see Zion Mount Carmel Highway,N. Fork Virgin Riv. Brdg

Zion Lodge/Birch Creek Complex,Bake Shop
Zion National Park
HABS UT-112-E
HABS UTAH,27-SPDA.V,6D-
1ph/1pc/fr L

Zion Lodge/Birch Creek Complex,Barber Shop
Zion National Park
HABS UT-112-D
HABS UTAH,27-SPDA.V,6D-
1ph/1pc/fr L

Zion Lodge/Birch Creek Complex,Duplex Cabin
Zion National Park
HABS UT-112-B
HABS UTAH,27-SPDA.V,6B-
2ph/1pc/fr L

Documentation: **ct** color transparencies **dr** measured drawings **fr** field records
pc photograph captions **pg** pages of text **ph** photographs

Zion Lodge/Birch Creek Complex,Family Cabin
Zion National Park
HABS UT-112-C
HABS UTAH,27-SPDA.V,6C-
1ph/1pc/fr L

Zion Lodge/Birch Creek Complex,Five Stall Shed
Zion National Park
HABS UT-112-I
HABS UTAH,27-SPDA.V,6I-
1ph/1pc/fr L

Zion Lodge/Birch Creek Complex,Machine Shop
Zion National Park
HABS UT-112-J
HABS UTAH,27-SPDA.V,6J-
2ph/1pc/fr L

Zion Lodge/Birch Creek Complex,Mattress Stor. Cabn
Zion National Park
HABS UT-112-H
HABS UTAH,27-SPDA.V,6H-
1ph/1pc/fr L

Zion Lodge/Birch Creek Complex,Men's Dormitory
Zion National Park
HABS UT-112-F
HABS UTAH,27-SPA.V,6F-
3ph/1pc/fr L

Zion Lodge/Birch Creek Complex,Quadraplex Cabins
Cabins No. 523,528 & 529,Zion National Park
HABS UT-112-A
HABS UTAH,27-SPDA.V,6A-
3ph/1pc/fr L

Zion Lodge/Birch Creek Complex,Women's Dormitory
Zion National Park
HABS UT-112-G
HABS UTAH,27-SPDA.V,6G-
3ph/1pc/fr L

Zion Lodge/Birch Creek Historic Complex
Zion National Park
HABS UT-112
HABS UTAH,27-SPDA.V,6-
5ph/1pc/fr L

Zion Mount Carmel Highway,N. Fork Virgin Riv. Brdg (Virgin River Bridge; Zion National Park)
Spanning Virgin River
HAER UT-39-C
HAER UTAH,27-SPDA.V,3C-
3ph/3pg/1pc L

Zion Nat'l Park Hist Trails Sys.,Canyon Overlook
HAER UT-40-B
HAER UTAH,27-SPDA.V,1B-
2pg L

Zion Nat'l Park Hist Trails Sys.,East Rim Trail
Zion Nat'l Park
HAER UT-40-C
HAER UTAH,27-SPDA.V,1C-
2pg L

Zion Nat'l Park Hist Trails Sys.,Grotto Trail
Zion Nat'l Park
HAER UT-40-E
HAER UTAH,27-SPDA.V,1E
2pg L

Zion Nat'l Park Hist Trails Sys.,West Rim Trail
Zion Nat'l Park
HAER UT-40-G
HAER UT,27-SPDA.V,1G-
9ph/2pg/1pc L

Zion Nat'l Park Hist Trails Sys,Gateway to Narrows
Zion Nat'l Park
HAER UT-40-D
HAER UTAH,27-SPDA.V,1D-
2pg L

Zion Nat'l Park Hist Trails,Hidden Canyon Trail
Zion Nat'l Park
HAER UT-40-F
HAER UTAH,27-SPDA.V,1F-
3pg L

Zion Nat'l Park Hist. Trails Sys.,Angels Landing
Zion Nat'l Park
HAER UT-40-A
HAER UTAH,27-SPDA.V,1A-
2pg L

Zion Nat'l Park Irrig. Sys.,Crawford/Gifford Canal
Zion Nat'l Park
HAER UT-38-A
HAER UTAH,27-SPDA.V,2A-
4ph/2pg/1pc L

Zion Nat'l Park Irrigation Sys.,Oak Creek Canal
Zion Nat'l Park
HAER UT-38-B
HAER UTAH,27-SPDA.V,2B-
1ph/2pg/1pc L

Zion Nat'l Park Irrigation Sys.,Pine Creek Canal
Zion Nat'l Park
HAER UT-38-C
HAER UTAH,27-SPDA.V,2C-
3ph/1pc L

Zion Nat'l Park Irrigation Sys.,Springdale Canal
Zion Nat'l Park
HAER UT-38-D
HAER UTAH,27-SPDA.V,2D-
8ph/1pc L

Zion National Park
Zion National Park
HABS UT-108
HABS UTAH,27-SPDA.V,7-
24pg/fr L

Zion National Park; see Zion Mount Carmel Highway,N. Fork Virgin Riv. Brdg

Zion National Park,East Entrance Checking Station
Zion National Park
HABS UT-108-G
HABS UTAH,27-SPDA.V,7G-
2ph/1pc/fr L

Zion National Park,East Entrance Sign
Zion National Park
HABS UT-108-I
HABS UTAH,27-SPDA.V,7I-
1ph/1pc/fr L

Zion National Park,East Ranger's House
Zion National Park
HABS UT-108-H
HABS UTAH,27-SPDA.V,7H-
1ph/1pc/fr L

Zion National Park,Gateway to Narrows Int. Kiosk
Zion National Park
HABS UT-108-F
HABS UTAH,27-SPDA.V,7F-
1ph/1pc/fr L

Zion National Park,Grotto Comfort Station
Zion National Park
HABS UT-108-E
HABS UTAH,27-SPDA.V,7E-
1ph/1pc/fr L

Zion National Park,Grotto House; see Zion National Park,Zion Museum

Zion National Park,Pioneer Cabin (ZNP,Kolob Canyon Tack & Storage Shed)
Zion National Park
HABS UT-108-J
HABS UTAH,27-SPDA.V,7J-
2ph/1pc/fr L

Zion National Park,South Campground Amphitheatre
Zion National Park
HABS UT-108-B
HABS UTAH,27-SPDA.V,7B-
2ph/1pc/fr L

Zion National Park,South Campground Comfort Stn.
Zion National Park
HABS UT-108-C
HABS UTAH,27-SPDA.V,7C-
2ph/1pc/fr L

Zion National Park,Stone Quarry
Zion National Park
HABS UT-108-K
HABS UTAH,27-SPDA.V,7K-
2ph/1pc/fr L

Zion National Park,Zion Inn (Zion National Park,Zion Nature Center)
Zion National Park
HABS UT-108-A
HABS UTAH,27-SPDA.V,7A-
8ph/1pc/fr L

Zion National Park,Zion Museum (Zion National Park,Grotto House)
Zion National Park
HABS UT-108-D
HABS UTAH,27-SPDA.V,7D-
3ph/1pc/fr L

Zion National Park,Zion Nature Center; see Zion National Park,Zion Inn

Zion-Mount Carmel Highway
Zion Nat'l Park
HAER UT-39
HAER UTAH,27-SPDA.V,3-
10ph/3pg/1pc L

Zion-Mount Carmel Highway Tunnel
Zion Nat'l Park
HAER UT-39-A
HAER UTAH,27-SPDA.V,3A-
6ph/2pg/1pc L

Zion-Mount Carmel Highway,Pine Creek Bridge (Pine Creek Bridge)
Zion Nat'l Park
HAER UT-39-B
HAER UTAH,27-SPDA.V,3B-
4ph/2pg/1pc L

ZNP,Kolob Canyon Tack & Storage Shed; see Zion National Park,Pioneer Cabin

ST. GEORGE

Blake,B. F.,House
141 S. 100 East St.
HABS UT-80
HABS UTAH,27-SAGEO,14-
1ph L

Burgess,Melancthon W.,House
HABS UT-12
HABS UTAH,27-SAGEO,1-
1ph L

Cannon,David H.,House
49 E. 100 South St.
HABS UT-9
HABS UTAH,27-SAGEO,2-
2ph L

Chamber of Commerce; see Washington County Courthouse

Church of Jesus Christ of Latter-Day Saints; see St. George Tabernacle

Ivins,Anthony W.,House (Ivins,Israel,House)
157 N. 100 West St.
HABS UT-18
HABS UTAH,27-SAGEO,4-
1ph L

Ivins,Israel,House; see Ivins,Anthony W.,House

Lund,Robert,House
100 West & 200 North Sts.
HABS UT-15
HABS UTAH,27-SAGEO,5-
1ph L

McArthur,Daniel D.,House
159 W. Tabernacle St.
HABS UT-11
HABS UTAH,27-SAGEO,6-
1ph L

Saigmiller House
HABS UT-19
HABS UTAH,27,SAGEO,7-
1ph L

Snow,Erastus,House
150 N. Main St.
HABS UT-13
HABS UTAH,27-SAGEO,8-
1ph L

162 South 300 West Street (House)
HABS UT-81
HABS UTAH,27-SAGEO,15-
1ph L

St. George Tabernacle (Church of Jesus Christ of Latter-Day Saints)
Main St.
HABS UT-16
HABS UTAH,27-SAGEO,9-
9dr/11ph/6pg/fr L

St. George Tithing Office
Main & Tabernacle Sts.
HABS UT-8
HABS UTAH,27-SAGEO,10-
3ph L

Washington County Courthouse (Chamber of Commerce)
100 North St.
HABS UT-10
HABS UTAH,27-SAGEO,3-
1ph L

Woolley,Edwin G.,House
217 N. 100 West St.
HABS UT-14
HABS UTAH,27-SAGEO,11-
3ph L

Young,Brigham,Office
200 North St.
HABS UT-20
HABS UTAH,27-SAGEO,12-
3ph/3pg L

Young,Brigham,Winter House
200 North & 100 West Sts.
HABS UT-66
HABS UTAH,27-SAGEO,13-
6ph/4pg L

TOQUERVILLE

Naegle Winery
Spring St. (State Rt. 15)
HABS UT-65
HABS UTAH,27-TOQVI,1-
4ph/5pg L

Spilsbury,David,House
Spring St. (State Rt. 15)
HABS UT-82
HABS UTAH,27-TOQVI,2-
1ph L

WASHINGTON

Chapel of Jesus Christ of Latter-Day Saints; see Washington Ward Chapel

Covington,Bishop Robert D.,House
HABS UT-3
HABS UTAH,27-WASH,1-
1ph L

Pioneer Cotton Mill; see Washington Cotton Mill

Washington Cotton Mill (Pioneer Cotton Mill)
Mill Creek
HABS UT-1
HABS UTAH,27-WASH,3-
3dr/6ph/5pg/fr L

Washington Ward Chapel (Chapel of Jesus Christ of Latter-Day Saints)
HABS UT-17
HABS UTAH,27-WASH,2-
1ph L

WAYNE COUNTY

FRUITA

Capitol Reef National Monument; see Fruita School House

Capitol Reef National Park; see Fruita School House

Fruita School House (Capitol Reef National Monument; Capitol Reef National Park)
State Rt. 24
HABS UT-21
HABS UTAH,28-FRUITA,1-
3dr/5ph/4pg L

WEBER COUNTY

OGDEN

Goodyear,Miles,Cabin
Tabernacle Park
HABS UT-55
HABS UTAH,29-OGDEN,2-
3dr/6pg/fr L

Lewis Bldg
2463-65 Washington Blvd.
HABS UT-116
HABS UTAH,29-OGDEN,3-
8ph/2pg/1pc L

Odgen River Bridge,Odgen River Bridge Sign
Washington Blvd. near 17th Street
HAER UT-62-A
4ph/11pg/1pc L

Ogden River Bridge
Spanning Ogden River at Washington Blvd.
HAER UT-62
14ph/13pg/1pc L

Union Pacific Railroad,Gateway Bridge
Spanning Weber Canyon
HAER UT-27
HAER UTAH,29-OGDEN,1-
5dr/7ph/1pg/1pc L

OGDEN CANYON

Fairmont Bridge
Spanning Ogden River in Ogden Canyon
HAER UT-58
HAER 1991(HAER):21
10ph/9pg/1pc L

OGDEN VIC.

Ogden Canyon Conduit
HAER UT-51
29ph/31pg/2pc H

UINTAH

Uintah Bridge
Spanning Weber River at 6600 South St.
HAER UT-37
HAER UTAH,29-UINT,1-
6ph/3pg L

Job Lyman House, Woodstock, Windsor County, Vermont. Front (east) portico. Photograph by Jack E. Boucher, November 1959 (HABS VT,14-WOOD,1-4).

Vermont

ADDISON COUNTY

MIDDLEBURY

Congregational Church
Main & Seymour Sts.
HABS VT-11
HABS VT,1-MIDBU,1-
13ph/8pg L

Middlebury College,Administration Building; see Middlebury College,Old Chapel

Middlebury College,Old Chapel (Middlebury College,Administration Building)
Rt. 30
HABS VT-89
HABS VT,1-MIDBU,4A-
1ph L

Middlebury College,Painter Hall
Rt. 30
HABS VT-88
HABS VT,1-MIDBU,4B-
1ph L

Middlebury Community House; see Seymour,Horatio,House

Painter,Gamaliel,House
Court & S. Pleasant Sts.
HABS VT-84
HABS VT,1-MIDBU,2-
3ph L

Seymour,Horatio,House (Middlebury Community House)
Main & Seymour Sts.
HABS VT-85
HABS VT,1-MIDBU,3-
4ph L

ORWELL

Baptist Church (Community Hall)
Rt. 73
HABS VT-74
HABS VT,1-OR,1-
1ph L

Benson-Orwell Parish; see Congregational Church

Community Hall; see Baptist Church

Congregational Church (Benson-Orwell Parish; United Church of Christ)
Rt. 73
HABS VT-75
HABS VT,1-OR,2-
1ph L

United Church of Christ; see Congregational Church

ORWELL VIC.

Willcox-Cutts Mansion
Rt. 22A
HABS VT-72
HABS VT,1-OR.V,1-
2ph L

VERGENNES

Strong,Gen. Samuel,House
W. Main St.
HABS VT-12
HABS VT,1-VERG,1-
17dr/7ph/1pg L

BENNINGTON COUNTY

ARLINGTON

Canfield,Martha,Library; see Smith-Canfield House

Smith-Canfield House (Canfield,Martha,Library)
Rt. 7 Vic.
HABS VT-83
HABS VT,2-ARL,1-
2ph L

BENNINGTON

First Church,Old; see First Congregational Church

First Congregational Church (First Church,Old)
Monument Ave.
HABS VT-90
HABS VT,2-BEN,1-
8ph/3pg L

Robinson,Gen. David,House
HABS VT-21
HABS VT,2-BEN,2-
4ph/1pg L

NORTH BENNINGTON

Church,Old Stone; see Hindillville Methodist Episcopal Church

Hindillville Methodist Episcopal Church (Church,Old Stone)
Hillside St. & River Rd.
HABS VT-80
HABS VT,2-BENN,1-
1ph L

Orwell House
Bennington Rd.
HABS VT-81
HABS VT,2-BENN,2-
1ph L

SHAFTSBURY CENTER

Galusha,Gov. ,House
HABS VT-20
HABS VT,2-SHAFTCE,1-
11ph/2pg L

SOUTH SHAFTSBURY

Hawkins House (Monroe House)
HABS VT-19
HABS VT,2-SHAFTS,1-
11ph/5pg L

Monroe House; see Hawkins House

SOUTH SHAFTSBURY VIC

White Pillar
State Rt. 7
HABS VT-82
HABS VT,2-SHAFTS.V,1-
1ph L

CALEDONIA COUNTY

BARNET CENTER

Jack,Alexander,Dye & Print Works; see Thresher,Ben,Mill

Judkins Wagon & Woodworking Shop; see Thresher,Ben,Mill

Thresher,Ben,Mill (Jack,Alexander,Dye & Print Works; Judkins Wagon & Woodworking Shop)
HAER VT-10
HAER VT,3-BACEN,1-
11dr/25ph/36pg/3pc/fr L

ST. JOHNSBURY

Fairbanks-Morse Manufacturing Co.; see Fairbanks,E. & T. ,& Co. ,Two-Story Covered Bridge

Fairbanks-Morse Manufacturing Company; see Fairbanks,E. & T. ,& Company Factory

Fairbanks,E. & T. ,& Co. ,Two-Story Covered Bridge (Fairbanks-Morse Manufacturing Co.)
HAER VT-1-A
HAER VT,3-SAJON,1A-
2dr/15ph/2pg/1pc L

Fairbanks,E. & T. ,& Company Factory (Fairbanks-Morse Manufacturing Company)
HAER VT-1
HAER VT,3-SAJON,1-
4ph/1pg L

Mount Vernon Street Bridge (Sleepers River Lenticular Semi-deck Truss Bridge)
HAER VT-2
HAER VT,3-SAJON,2-
1ph/1pg/1pc L

Sleepers River Lenticular Semi-deck Truss Bridge; see Mount Vernon Street Bridge

CHITTENDEN COUNTY

BURLINGTON

First Church (First Congregational Church)
Winooski & Buell Sts.
HABS VT-73
HABS VT,4-BURL,3-
1ph L

First Congregational Church; see First Church

First Congregational Society Church (Unitarian Church)
Pearl St. & Elmwood Ave.
HABS VT-24
HABS VT,4-BURL,1-
6dr/8ph/5pg L

Isham,Deming,House
308 Pearl St.
HABS VT-71
HABS VT,4-BURL,2-
6ph L

Unitarian Church; see First Congregational Society Church

JERICHO

Ethan Allen Firing Range
Jericho,Underhill & Bolton Townships
HAER VT-4
HAER VT,4-JER,2-
35pg/fr L

JERICHO CENTER VIC.

Chittenden,Gov. Martin,House
Rt. 117
HABS VT-69
HABS VT,4-JER,1-
1ph L

RICHMOND

Round Church,Old; see Round Meetinghouse

Round Meetinghouse (Round Church,Old; Town Hall)
Town Common
HABS VT-70
HABS VT,4-RICH,1-
4ph L

Town Hall; see Round Meetinghouse

WINOOSKI

American Woolen Company (Champlain Mill)
E. Canal St.
HAER VT-11
HAER VT,4-WINO,2-
9ph/1pg/1pc/fr L

Champlain Mill; see American Woolen Company

Porter Screen Warehouse & Dist. Co. ,Warehouse 11
E. Spring St.
HABS VT-101-A
HABS VT,4-WINO,1A-
5ph/2pg L

Porter Screen Warehouse & Distributing Co. Complex
Spring St.
HABS VT-101
HABS VT,4-WINO,1-
8ph/1pc/fr L

FRANKLIN COUNTY

HIGHGATE FALLS

St. John's Church (Protestant Episcopal)
Highgate Falls Common
HABS VT-87
HABS VT,6-HIGH,2-
1ph L

Store
Highgate Falls Common
HABS VT-86
HABS VT,6-HIGH,1-
1ph L

ST. ALBANS

Central Vermont Railroad,Locomotive Shop
Bounded by Railroad Tracks,Lake & Pine Sts.
HAER VT-12
HAER VT,6-SALB,1A-
3pg/fr L

GRAND ISLE COUNTY

GRAND ISLE

Hyde-Jackson Log Cabin
Rt. 2 Vic.
HABS VT-66
HABS VT,7-GRAND,1-
3ph L

SOUTH HERO

Inn,Old Stone; see Island House

Island House (Inn,Old Stone)
Rt. 2
HABS VT-65
HABS VT,7-HEROS,1-
1ph L

ORANGE COUNTY

RANDOLPH

Chase-Redfield Barn
Main St.
HABS VT-54
HABS VT,9-RAND,3A-
1ph/2pg L

Chase-Redfield House
Main St.
HABS VT-39
HABS VT,9-RAND,2-
9ph/4pg L

RANDOLPH CENTER

Edgerton,Lebbeus,House
Main St.
HABS VT-38
HABS VT,9-RAND,1-
9ph/4pg L

STRAFFORD

Morrill,Sen. Justin Smith,House
HABS VT-55
HABS VT,9-STRAF,2-
4ph/4pg L

Strafford Meetinghouse
On the Green
HABS VT-36
HABS VT,9-STRAF,1-
7ph/4pg L

THETFORD VIC.

Latham House
HABS VT-56
HABS VT,9-THETN,1-
5ph/4pg L

ORLEANS COUNTY

BROWNINGTON

Brownington Congregational Church
Timothy Hinman Rd.
HABS VT-95
HABS VT,10-BROW,1-
5dr L

Eaton,Cyrus,House
Brownington Center Rd.
HABS VT-96
HABS VT,10-BROW,2-
6dr L

House,Old Stone
Brownington-Brownington Center Rd. at Derby Line
HABS VT-97
HABS VT,10-BROW,3-
15dr/11pg/fr L

TROY

River Road Bridge
Spanning Missisquoi River at River Rd.
HAER VT-15
16ph/12pg/2pc L

RUTLAND COUNTY

CASTLETON

Congregational Church of Christ in Castleton (Federated Church)
Main St.
HABS VT-17
HABS VT,11-CAST,4-
3dr/5ph/1pg L

Dake,Thomas Royal,House
South St.
HABS VT-77
HABS VT,11-CAST.V,1-
1ph L

Federated Church; see Congregational Church of Christ in Castleton

Gridley,Selah,House
Main St.
HABS VT-79
HABS VT,11-CAST,8-
1ph L

Harris,Josiah,House
Main & Mill Sts.
HABS VT-14
HABS VT,11-CAST,1-
9dr/7ph/2pg L

1810 House; see Meecham-Ainsworth House

Langdon,B. F. ,House
Main & North Sts.
HABS VT-76
HABS VT,11-CAST,6-
2ph L

Mallory,Rollin C. ,House
Main St.
HABS VT-78
HABS VT,11-CAST,7-
1ph L

Meecham-Ainsworth House (1810 House)
Main St.
HABS VT-15
HABS VT,11-CAST,2-
7ph/1pg L

Ransom House (Stairway)
South St.
HABS VT-18
HABS VT,11-CAST,5-
2ph/2pg L

Ransom,Justus,House
Main St.
HABS VT-91
HABS VT,11-CAST,9-
1ph L

Watters House
Main & South Sts.
HABS VT-16
HABS VT,11-CAST,3-
10dr/2ph/1pg L

RUTLAND

Googan House
HABS VT-13
HABS VT,11-RUT,2-
17dr/11ph/1pg L

WASHINGTON COUNTY

BARRE

Grearson & Lane Company,Granite Turning Shed
HAER VT-9
HAER VT,12-BARRE,1-
1pg/fr L

Smith,E. L. , & Co.,Sixteen-Sided Granite Shed
Burnham St.
HAER VT-8
HAER VT,12-BARRE,2-
3pg/fr L

Trow & Holden Company,Granite Tool Works
45-55 S. Main St.
HAER VT-7
HAER VT,12-BARRE,3-
2pg/fr L

MONTPELIER

Pavilion Hotel
State St.
HABS VT-93
HABS VT,12-MONT,3-
6dr/16ph/10pg/3pc/fr L

Reed,Hezekiah,House (Vermont Mutual Fire Insurance Company Building)
89 Brick St.
HABS VT-67
HABS VT,12-MONT,1-
1ph L

Vermont Mutual Fire Insurance Company Building; see Reed,Hezekiah,House

Vermont State House
State St. at Western Ave.
HABS VT-68
HABS VT,12-MONT,2-
1ph L

NORTHFIELD

Northfield Parker Truss Bridge
Over tracks of Central Vermont Railroad
HAER VT-13
HAER VT,12-NORF,1-
10ph/1pg/1pc L

WINDHAM COUNTY

GRAFTON

Congregational Church
HABS VT-23
HABS VT,13-GRAFT,1-
6dr/6ph/6pg L

ROCKINGHAM

Meetinghouse
HABS VT-22
HABS VT,13-ROCHA,1-
8ph/2pg L

Pulsifer,David,Inn
Rt. 103
HABS VT-41
HABS VT,13-ROCHA,2-
7ph/3pg L

WINDHAM

Olcott,Elias,House
Upper Meadows Settlement
HABS VT-42
HABS VT,13-ROCHA.V,1-
2ph/3pg L

WINDSOR COUNTY

BETHEL

Paige,Dr. Alfred,House
HABS VT-40
HABS VT,14-BETH,1-
9ph/4pg L

CAVENDISH

Dutton,Salmon,House
HABS VT-25
HABS VT,14-CAV,1-
10dr L

CHESTER

Congregational Church
Church & Main Sts.
HABS VT-49
HABS VT,14-CHEST,1A-
2ph/2pg L

CHESTER DEPOT

Edson,Dr. ,House (Stone Village Inn)
North St.
HABS VT-44
HABS VT,14-CHET,1-
4ph/3pg L

Spaulding,Granville,House
North St.
HABS VT-45
HABS VT,14-CHET,2-
3ph/3pg L

Stone Village Inn; see Edson,Dr. ,House

CHESTER VIC.

Earl House (Red House)
State Rt. 103
HABS VT-43
HABS VT,14-CHEST.V,1-
1ph/3pg L

Red House; see Earl House

NORWICH

Hatch-Peisch House
Main St.
HABS VT-52
HABS VT,14-NOR,1-
5ph/3pg L

Norwich Congregational Church (South Church)
Norwich Green
HABS VT-53
HABS VT,14-NOR,2-
9ph/7pg/1pc/fr L

South Church; see Norwich Congregational Church

NORWICH VIC.

Olcott-Johnson House
Old Norwich Center
HABS VT-51
HABS VT,14-NOR.V,1-
8dr/5ph/11pg L

PERKINSVILLE

Foster,Rev. Dan,House
Weathersfield Center
HABS VT-60
HABS VT,14-PERK.V,4-
2ph/3pg L

Weathersfield Congregational Church & Town Hall
Weathersfield Center
HABS VT-57
HABS VT,14-PERK.V,1-
5dr/4ph/4pg L

PERKINSVILLE VIC.

Stoughton Farmstead
Black River Vic. (moved to VT,Amsden Vic.)
HABS VT-59
HABS VT,14-PERK.V,3-
2dr/5ph/4pg L

Warren-Child House
Old Crown Point Rd.
HABS VT-58
HABS VT,14-PERK.V,2-
5dr/5ph/4pg L

ROYALTON VIC.

Fox Stand Inn
Rts. 14 & 107
HABS VT-37
HABS VT,14-ROY.V,1-
7ph/4pg L

SIMONSVILLE

Rowell's Inn
State Rt. 11
HABS VT-50
HABS VT,14-SIMO,1-
1ph/2pg L

SPRINGFIELD

Gould House
Parker Hill Rd.
HABS VT-46
HABS VT,14-SPRIF.V,1-
4ph/3pg L

WESTON

Farrar-Mansur House (Farrar,Capt. ,Inn)
Weston Green
HABS VT-48
HABS VT,14-WEST,1-
4ph/3pg L

Farrar,Capt. ,Inn; see Farrar-Mansur House

Vermont Country Store
Weston Common
HABS VT-47
HABS VT,14-WEST,1-
1ph/3pg L

WINDSOR

Conant-Hubbard House
52 Main St.
HABS VT-63
HABS VT,14-WIND,6-
3dr/2ph/3pg L

Constitution House,The Old
15 N. Main St.
HABS VT-35
HABS VT,14-WIND,3-
4ph/4pg L

Courthouse & Post Office
Main St.
HABS VT-62
HABS VT,14-WIND,5-
14ph/7pg L

South Congregational Church,Old
Main St.
HABS VT-64
HABS VT,14-WIND,7-
5dr/6ph/15pg/1pc/fr L

St. Paul's Episcopal Church
State & Court Sts.
HABS VT-61
HABS VT,14-WIND,4-
19ph/5pg L

Townsend House
5 Courthouse St.
HABS VT-34
HABS VT,14-WIND,2-
13ph/4pg L

Trask,Nahum,House
25 N. Main St.
HABS VT-33
HABS VT,14-WIND,1-
6ph/3pg L

WOODSTOCK

Aylwin House
48 Elm St.
HABS VT-32
HABS VT,14-WOOD,7-
5ph/3pg L

D. A. R. Historic Museum; see Parker,Tille,Tavern

Dana,Charles,House
26 Elm St.
HABS VT-31
HABS VT,14-WOOD,6-
11ph/4pg L

Elm Street Bridge
Spanning the Ottauquechee River
HAER VT-3
HAER VT,14-WOOD,8-
26ph/12pg/2pc/fr L

Lyman,Job,House
30 Elm St.
HABS VT-26
HABS VT,14-WOOD,1-
8ph/4pg L

Mower,Gen. Lyman,House
16 The Green
HABS VT-27
HABS VT,14-WOOD,2-
8ph/4pg L

Parker,Tille,Tavern (D. A. R. Historic Museum)
26 The Green
HABS VT-28
HABS VT,14-WOOD,3-
5ph/4pg L

Richardson,Capt. Israel,Tavern
9 The Green
HABS VT-29
HABS VT,14-WOOD,4-
8ph/4pg L

Swan,Benjamin,House
37 Elm St.
HABS VT-30
HABS VT,14-WOOD,5-
8ph/4pg L

Estate Reef Bay, Sugar Factory, Reef Bay Quarter, St. John Island, Virgin Islands. South elevation. Photograph by Jet Lowe, September 19, 1985 (HAER VI,2-REBA,1-C-16).

Caneel Bay Plantation, Sugar Factory, Caneel Bay, St. John Island, Virgin Islands. Interior of boiling house with boiling bench to the right, viewed from the north. Photograph by Jack E. Boucher, January 1960 (HABS VI,2-CANBA,1A-3).

Virgin Islands

ST. CROIX

CHRISTIANSTED

Anglican Church
27 King St.
HABS VI-21
HABS VI,1-CHRIS,40-
13ph/1pg/1pc L

Anglican Church,Grave Fence
27 King St.
HABS VI-21-A
HABS VI,1-CHRIS,40-A-
2ph/1pc L

Bjerget
56-58 Hill St.
HABS VI-36
HABS VI,1-CHRIS,11-
9ph/5pg/1pc L

Christiansted Lutheran Church (Dutch Reformed Church)
4 King St.
HABS VI-23
HABS VI,1-CHRIS,37-
7ph/6pg/1pc L

Christiansted National Historic Site; see Fort Christiansvaern

Christiansted,City of (General Views)
HABS VI-98
HABS VI,1-CHRIS,13-
10ph/2pc L

Customshouse,Old (Scalehouse)
Christiansted Warf Square Vic.
HABS VI-3
HABS VI,1-CHRIS,2-
11dr/11ph/8pg L

Drewes House
46B-47 King St.
HABS VI-22
HABS VI,1-CHRIS,43-
6ph/4pg/1pc L

Dronningens Tvaergade 42 (House)
42 Queens Cross St.
HABS VI-39
HABS VI,1-CHRIS,14-
1ph/1pc L

Dutch Reformed Church; see Christiansted Lutheran Church

67 East Street (House)
HABS VI-34
HABS VI,1-CHRIS,12-
8ph/1pg/1pc L

Fort Christiansvaern (Christiansted National Historic Site)
Company St. Vic.
HABS VI-5
HABS VI,1-CHRIS,4-
26dr/52ph/13pg/1pc L

Friedensthal; see Moravian Mission House

Government House
King St.
HABS VI-42
HABS VI,1-CHRIS,34-
28ph/3pc L

Hendricks' Butchery
Market St. (Company & Queen Sts. Vic.)
HABS VI-25
HABS VI,1-CHRIS,32-
2ph/2pg/1pc L

4-5 Hill Street (House)
HABS VI-35
HABS VI,1-CHRIS,10-
6ph/4pg/1pc L

Hospitalsgade 21-22 (House)
21-22 Hospital St.
HABS VI-93
HABS VI,1-CHRIS,15-
1ph/1pc L

Hospitalsgade 23 (House)
23 Hospital St.
HABS VI-94
HABS VI,1-CHRIS,16-
1ph/1pc L

Hospitalsgade 25 (House)
25 Hospital St.
HABS VI-104
HABS VI,1-CHRIS,17-
3ph/1pc L

Hospitalsgade 27 (House)
27 Hospital St.
HABS VI-105
HABS VI,1-CHRIS,18-
1ph/1pc L

Hospitalsgade 28 (House)
28 Hospital St.
HABS VI-106
HABS VI,1-CHRIS,19-
1ph/1pc L

King Street Area Study (Kongensgade 1,45-59 & Custom House,Old)
King St.
HABS VI-44
HABS VI,1-CHRIS,41-
9ph/2pc L

7 King's Cross Street (House)
HABS VI-40
HABS VI,1-CHRIS,54-
2ph/3pg/1pc L

Kirkegade 10 (House)
10 Church St.
HABS VI-109
HABS VI,1-CHRIS,21-
1ph/1pc L

Kirkegade 15 (House)
15 Church St.
HABS VI-110
HABS VI,1-CHRIS,22-
1ph/1pc L

Kirkegade 16A (House)
16A Church St.
HABS VI-121
HABS VI,1-CHRIS,24-
1ph/1pc L

Kirkegade 16B (House); see Markoe House

Kirkegade 17 (House)
17 Church St.
HABS VI-111
HABS VI,1-CHRIS,26-
3ph/1pc L

Kirkegade 18 (House)
18 Church St.
HABS VI-112
HABS VI,1-CHRIS,27-
1ph/1pc L

Kirkegade,General View
Church St.
HABS VI-108
HABS VI,1-CHRIS,20-
1ph/1pc L

Kompagnigade 1 (House)
1 Company St.
HABS VI-120
HABS VI,1-CHRIS,23-
1ph/1pc L

Kompagnigade 39 (House)
HABS VI-37
HABS VI,1-CHRIS,29-
4ph/1pc L

Kompagnigade 51 (House)
51 Company St.
HABS VI-38
HABS VI,1-CHRIS,30-
10ph/2pc L

Kompagnigade 51 (House),Kitchen
51 Company St.
HABS VI-38-A
HABS VI,1-CHRIS,30-A-
1ph/1pc L

Kongensgade 1,45-59 & Custom House,Old; see King Street Area Study

Kongensgade 21 (House)
HABS VI-113
HABS VI,1-CHRIS,39-
1ph/1pc L

Kongensgade 52 (House)
52 King St.
HABS VI-114
HABS VI,1-CHRIS,45-
10ph/1pc L

Kongensgade 53 (House)
53 King St.
HABS VI-115
HABS VI,1-CHRIS,46-
2ph/1pc L

Kongensgade 54 (House)
54 King St.
HABS VI-89
HABS VI,1-CHRIS,47-
1ph/1pc L

Kongensgade 55 (House)
55 King St.
HABS VI-116
HABS VI,1-CHRIS,48-
1ph/1pc L

Kongensgade 56-57 (House)
56-57 King St.
HABS VI-92
HABS VI,1-CHRIS,49-
2ph/1pc L

Kongensgade 58 (House)
58 King St.
HABS VI-117
HABS VI,1-CHRIS,50-
2ph/1pc L

Kongensgade 59 (House)
59 King St.
HABS VI-118
HABS VI,1-CHRIS,51-
2ph/1pc L

Kongensgade 7-8 (House)
7-8 King St.
HABS VI-164
HABS VI,1-CHRIS,38-
1ph/1pc L

La Princesse Public School
King St.
HABS VI-99
HABS VI,1-CHRIS,35-
6ph/1pc L

Lutheran Church of the Lord of Zebaoth (Steeple Building)
Company St.
HABS VI-1
HABS VI,1-CHRIS,1-
15dr/12ph/5pg/fr L

Lutheran Church of the Lord of Zebaoth,Weathervane (Steeple Building,Weathervane)
Company St.
HABS VI-1-A
HABS VI,1-CHRIS,1-A-
2dr L

Lutheran Parsonage
Kongensgade 51
HABS VI-26
HABS VI,1-CHRIS,44-
14ph/5pg/1pc L

Markoe House (Kirkegade 16B (House))
16B Church St.
HABS VI-27
HABS VI,1-CHRIS,25-
5ph/3pg/1pc L

Moravian Church
King St. Vic.
HABS VI-28
HABS VI,1-CHRIS,52-
9ph/3pg/1pc/fr L

Moravian Mission House (Moravian Parsonage; Friedensthal)
King St. Vic.
HABS VI-29
HABS VI,1-CHRIS,53-
21ph/3pg/2pc L

Moravian Parsonage; see Moravian Mission House

Newton House
56 Company St.
HABS VI-30
HABS VI,1-CHRIS,31-
4ph/7pg/1pc L

Pentheny Hotel
45A & 46B King St.
HABS VI-31
HABS VI,1-CHRIS,42-
8ph/6pg/1pc L

Post Office
Church & Company Sts.
HABS VI-43
HABS VI,1-CHRIS,28-
8ph/1pc L

Scalehouse; see Customshouse,Old

Steeple Building; see Lutheran Church of the Lord of Zebaoth

Steeple Building,Weathervane; see Lutheran Church of the Lord of Zebaoth,Weathervane

Strandgade (House)
Corner of Strand St. & Queen's Cross St.
HABS VI-102
HABS VI,1-CHRIS,8-
1ph/1pc L

33-35 Strandgade (House)
33-35 Strand St.
HABS VI-41
HABS VI,1-CHRIS,7-
5ph/4pg/1pc L

CHRISTIANSTED VIC.

Little La Grange Estate
HABS VI-100
HABS VI,1-CHRIS.V,1-
12ph/1pc L

COMPANY QUARTER

Little Princess
HABS VI-101
HABS VI,1-COMP,4-
6ph/1pc L

COMPANY'S QUARTER

Bulows Minde Estate House
Bulows Minde
HABS VI-7
HABS VI,1-COMP,3-
2dr/19ph/2pc L

Orange Grove
HABS VI-55
HABS VI,1-COMP,5-
3ph/1pc L

Richmond
HABS VI-119
HABS VI,1-COMP,1-
1ph/1pc L

Richmond Prison,Keeper's House
HABS VI-163-A
HABS VI,1-COMP,2-A-
1ph/1pc L

Richmond,Kitchen
HABS VI-119-A
HABS VI,1-COMP,1-A-
1ph/1pc L

FREDERIKSTED

Benjamin House; see Dronningensgade Area Study

Benjamin House (Peterson,Judge Reuban,House; Dronningensgade 48 (House))
48 Queen St.
HABS VI-45
HABS VI,1-FRED,12-
4ph/5pg/1pc L

Custom House
Custom House St.
HABS VI-46
HABS VI,1-FRED,2-
7ph/3pg/1pc L

Dronningensgade Area Study (Dronningensgade 46-48 (House); Benjamin House)
46-48 Queen St.
HABS VI-52-D
HABS VI,1-FRED,11-
1ph/1pc L

Dronningensgade 13 (House); see Queen Street Area Study

Dronningensgade 44 (House); see Queen Street Area Study

Dronningensgade 45 (House); see Queen Street Area Study

Dronningensgade 46-48 (House); see Dronningensgade Area Study

Dronningensgade 48 (House); see Benjamin House

Dronningensgade 64 (House); see Queen Street Area Study

Frederiksfort
King St. Vic.
HABS VI-47
HABS VI,1-FRED,3-
18ph/4pg/2pc L

King Street Area Study (Kongensgade 13 (House))
13 King St.
HABS VI-50-A
HABS VI,1-FRED,4-A-
2ph/1pc L

King Street Area Study (Kongensgade 18 (House))
18 King St.
HABS VI-50-B
HABS VI,1-FRED,4-B-
1ph/1pc L

King Street Area Study (Kongensgade 36 (House))
36 King St.
HABS VI-50-C
HABS VI,1-FRED,4-C-
1ph/1pc L

King Street Area Study (Kongensgade 37B (House))
37B King St.
HABS VI-50-D
HABS VI,1-FRED,4-D-
3ph/1pc L

King Street Area Study (Kongensgade 5-18,36,37B,51-58 (Houses))
5-18,36-37B,51-58 King St.
HABS 3I-50
HABS VI,1-FRED,4-
9ph/1pc L

Kongensgade 13 (House); see King Street Area Study

Kongensgade 18 (House); see King Street Area Study

Kongensgade 36 (House); see King Street Area Study

Kongensgade 37B (House); see King Street Area Study

Kongensgade 5-18,36,37B,51-58 (Houses); see King Street Area Study

Peterson,Judge Reuban,House; see Benjamin House

Queen Street Area Study (Dronningensgade 13 (House))
13 Queen St.
HABS VI-52-A
HABS VI,1-FRED,8-
4ph/1pc L

Queen Street Area Study (Dronningensgade 44 (House))
44 Queen St.
HABS VI-52-B
HABS VI,1-FRED,9-
1ph/1pc L

Queen Street Area Study (Dronningensgade 45 (House))
45 Queen St.
HABS VI-52-C
HABS VI,1-FRED,10-
1ph/1pc L

Queen Street Area Study (Dronningensgade 64 (House))
64 Queen St.
HABS VI-52-E
HABS VI,1-FRED,13-
3ph/1pc L

Strandgade 10-13 (Houses)
10-13 Strand St.
HABS VI-129
HABS VI,1-FRED,5-
1ph/1pc L

Strandgade 14-17 (House)
14-17 Strand St.
HABS VI-130
HABS VI,1-FRED,6-
1ph/1pc L

Torvegade 1A (House)
1A Market St.
HABS VI-54
HABS VI,1-FRED,7-
2ph/1pc L

FREDERIKSTED ET AL.

Sugar Cane Industry in the Virgin Islands
Islands of Saint Croix,Saint Thomas,& Saint John
HAER VI-7
HAER VI,1-FRED,1-
26pg L

FRIEDENSFELD

Moravian Church
HABS VI-57
HABS VI,1-FRIE,1-
7ph/7pg/1pc L

Moravian Parsonage
HABS VI-58
HABS VI,1-FRIE,2-
2ph/2pg/1pc L

KING'S QUARTER

Estate Clinton Hill,Sugar Factory & Rum Distillery
S. Central St.
HAER VI-4
HAER VI,1-KING,2-A-;DLC/PP-1993:VI-2
5dr/48ph/11pg/3pc/fr L

Slob Great House
Centerline Rd. Vic.
HABS VI-56
HABS VI,1-KING,1-
2ph/2pg/1pc L

NEVIS,BRIT.W.INDIES

Estate Clay Gut,Windmill
HABS VI-95
HABS VI,4-NEVIS,1A-
8dr L

NORTHSIDE A QUARTER

Estate Annaly:Sugar Mill
HAER VI-8
HAER VI,1-NORA,1-
11ph/1pc/9ct L

NORTHSIDE B QTR

Estate Belvedere:Jamaican Train
HAER VI-9
HAER VI,1-NORT,2-
3ph/1pc L

NORTHSIDE QUARTER

Estate Rust-Op-Twist:Steam Engine & Cane Mill
HAER VI-3
HAER VI,1-NORT,1-A-
4dr/10ph/9pg/1pc/fr L

PRINCE'S QUARTERS

Mount Pleasant
HABS VI-59
HABS VI,1-PRIN,1-
2ph/1pc L

PRINCESS' QUARTER

Diamond School
HABS VI-133
HABS VI,1-PRISS,2-
4ph/1pc L

QUEEN'S QUARTER

Castle Coakley,Bell Tower & Letterbox
HABS VI-96-D
HABS VI,1-QUEEN,5-D-
1ph/1pc L

Castle Coakley,Outbuilding
HABS VI-96-C
HABS VI,1-QUEEN,5-C-
1ph/1pc L

Castle Coakley,Slave Quarters
HABS VI-96-B
HABS VI,1-QUEEN,5-B-
2ph/1pc L

Castle Coakley,Sugar Mill
HABS VI-96-A
HABS VI,1-QUEEN,5-A-
4ph/1pc L

Gateway (Ruins)
Centerline Rd.
HABS VI-134
HABS VI,1-QUEEN,2-A-
1ph/1pc L

Peter's Rest Estate,Letterbox
HABS VI-132
HABS VI,1-QUEEN,7-B-
1ph/1pc L

Peter's Rest Estate,Nursery
Centerline Rd.
HABS VI-131
HABS VI,1-QUEEN,7-A-
1ph/1pc L

Plantation Hope
HABS VI-97
HABS VI,1-QUEEN,6-
1ph/1pc L

Sion Farm,Great House
Centerline Rd. Vic.
HABS VI-60
HABS VI,1-QUEEN,3-
8ph/1pg/1pc L

Sion Hill Estate
HABS VI-64
HABS VI,1-QUEEN,1-
5ph/1pc L

Sion Hill Estate,Cook House
Centerline Rd. Vic.
HABS VI-64-D
HABS VI,1-QUEEN,1-D-
1ph/1pg/1pc L

Sion Hill Estate,Factory (Ruin)
Centerline Rd. Vic.
HABS VI-64-B
HABS VI,1-QUEEN,1-B-
11ph/7pg/1pc L

Sion Hill Estate,Great House
Centerline Rd. Vic.
HABS VI-64-A
HABS VI,1-QUEEN,1-A-
15ph/1pg/1pc L

Sion Hill Estate,Mill
Centerline Rd. Vic.
HABS VI-64-C
HABS VI,1-QUEEN,1-C-
4ph/1pg/1pc L

Sion Hill Estate,Privy
Centerline Rd. Vic.
HABS VI-64-F
HABS VI,1-QUEEN,1-F-
1ph/1pc L

Sion Hill Estate,Stable
Centerline Rd. Vic.
HABS VI-64-E
HABS VI,1-QUEEN,1-E-
1ph/1pg/1pc L

St. John,Bell Tower
HABS VI-161
HABS VI,1-QUEEN,4-A-
1ph/1pc L

WESTEND QUARTER

Estate Whim,Great House
Centerline Rd.
HABS VI-49-A
HABS VI,1-WEST,1A-
3ph/1pg/1pc L

Estate Whim,Horizontal Steam Engine
Frederiksted Vic.
HAER VI-5-A
HAER 1991(HAER):23
4ph/1pc L

Estate Whim,Horse Mill
Frederiksted Vic.
HAER VI-5-C
HAER 1991(HAER):23
1ph/1pc L

Estate Whim,Overhead Crank Steam Engine & Cane Mil
Centerline Rd.,Frederiksted Vic.
HABS VI-49-C
HAER VI-5
HABS/HAER VI,1-WEST,1-C-;DLC/PP-1991:23
2dr/7ph/1pc/2ct L

Estate Whim,Rum Still
Frederiksted Vic.
HAER VI-5-B
HAER 1991(HAER):23
1ph/1pc L

Estate Whim,Wind Mill
Centerline Rd.,Frederiksted Vic.
HAER VI-5-D
HAER 1991(HAER):23
6ph/1pc L

Estate Whim,Windmill
Centerline Rd.
HABS VI-49-B
HABS VI,1-WEST,1-B-
5dr/2ph/1pc L

Prosperity
HABS VI-103
HABS VI,1-WEST,2-
4ph/1pc L

ST. JOHN

CORAL BAY

Frederiks Fort
Fortberg Hill
HABS VI-74
HABS VI,2-CORBA,1-
6ph/2pg/1pc L

CORAL BAY QUARTER

Estate Carolina,Windmill
North of King Hill Rd.
HABS VI-136
HABS VI,2-CORBA,2-A-
4dr L

CRUZ BAY QTR.

Estate Adrian
HAER VI-6
HAER VI,2-CRUZBA,3-
11ph/1pc/7ct L

CRUZ BAY QUARTER

Caneel Bay Plantation,General Views
HABS VI-69
HABS VI,2-CANBA,1-
1ph/1pc L

Caneel Bay Plantation,Mill Round
HABS VI-69-B
HABS VI,2-CANBA,1-B-
3ph/1pg/1pc L

Caneel Bay Plantation,Overseer's House
HABS VI-69-C
HABS VI,2-CANBA,1-C-
4ph/1pc L

Caneel Bay Plantation,Sugar Factory
HABS VI-69-A
HABS VI,2-CANBA,1-A-
8ph/1pc L

Christians Fort
Cruz Bay Vic.
HABS VI-70
HABS VI,2-CRUZBA,1-
1ph/1pc L

Estate Denis Bay,Windmill
HABS VI-160
HABS VI,2-DENBA,1-A-
5dr L

Estate Hammer Farms,Windmill Tower Ruins
HABS VI-75
HABS VI,2-CRUZBA,2-A-
7dr/2ph/1pc L

Estate Susannaberg,Windmill
HABS VI-78
HABS VI,3-CRUZBA,2A-
4dr/3ph/1pg L

MAHO BAY QTR

Estate Cinnamon Bay:Sugar Mill Ruins
Cinnamon Bay
HAER VI-10
HAER VI,2-MABA,3-
10ph/1pc L

MAHO BAY QUARTER

Estate Annaberg
HABS VI-18
HABS VI,2-MABA,1-
14ph/5pg/1pc/fr L

Estate Annaberg,Bake Oven
HABS VI-18-D
HABS VI,2-MABA,1-D-
2dr L

Estate Annaberg,Cookhouse
HABS VI-18-C
HABS VI,2-MABA,1-C-
2dr L

Estate Annaberg,Sugar Factory
HABS VI-18-A
HABS VI,2-MABA,1-A-
5dr/fr L

Estate Annaberg,Windmill
HABS VI-18-B
HABS VI,2-MABA,1-B-
5dr/fr L

Estate Mary Point,Great House
HABS VI-159
HABS VI,2-MAYPO,1-A-
6dr/2ph/1pc L

Indian Petroglyphs
HABS VI-76
HABS VI,2-REBA,2-
1ph/1pc L

REEF BAY QTR

Estate Reef Bay,Sugar Factory
HABS VI-2-C
HAER VI-2
HABS/HAER VI,2-REBA,1-C-
11dr/35ph/10pg/3pc/3ct/fr L

REEF BAY QUARTER

Estate Reef Bay,Great House
HABS VI-2-A
HABS VI,2-REBA,1-A-
17dr/6ph/1pc/fr L

Estate Reef Bay,Service Buildings
HABS VI-2-B
HABS VI,2-REBA,1-B-
4dr/3ph/1pc L

Estate Reef Bay,Wattle House
HABS VI-2-D
HABS VI,2-REBA,1-D-
5ph/1pc L

WHISTLING CAY

Custom House
HABS VI-87
HABS VI,2-WHICA,1-
3dr L

ST. THOMAS

CHARLOTTE AMALIE

Berg,Gov. Hans Hendrik,House; see Catharineberg

Bethania; see Frederick Lutheran Church,Parish Hall

Bluebeard's Castle (Bluebeard's Hill; Frederiksfort)
HABS VI-16
HABS VI,3-CHAM,7-
4ph/7pg/1pc L

Bluebeard's Hill; see Bluebeard's Castle

Catharineberg (Berg,Gov. Hans Hendrik,House; Denmark Hill; Estate Number 8,Store Nordside Quarter)
HABS VI-12
HABS VI,3-CHAM,5-
13ph/10pg L

Catharineberg Porter's House & Cookhouse (Estate Number 8,Store Nordside Quarter)
HABS VI-13
HABS VI,3-CHAM,5-A-
2ph L

Christiansfort
Waterfront
HABS VI-137
HABS VI,3-CHAM,30-
13ph/2pc L

Commercial Building; see Dronningensgade 22 (Commercial Building)

Commercial Building; see Kronprinsensgade Area Study

Commercial Hotel & Coffee House (Grand Hotel)
44-45 Northern St.
HABS VI-8
HABS VI,3-CHAM,1-
6ph/5pg L

Crystalgade 5 (House)
5 Crystal St.
HABS VI-88
HABS VI,3-CHAM,31-
1ph/1pc L

Denmark Hill; see Catharineberg

Dronningensgade Area Study (Ninty-nine Steps)
30-31 Queen St.
HABS VI-83-A
HABS VI,3-CHAM,19-
1ph/1pc L

Dronningensgade 10 (House)
HABS 3I-141
HABS VI,3-CHAM,15-B-
1ph/1pc L

Dronningensgade 14 (House)
14 Queen St.
HABS VI-152
HABS VI,3-CHAM,15-C-
1ph/1pc L

Dronningensgade 15 (House)
15 Queen St.
HABS VI-142
HABS VI,3-CHAM,15-D-
1ph/1pc L

Dronningensgade 2 (House)
2 Queen St.
HABS VI-138
HABS VI,3-CHAM,14-
1ph/1pc L

Dronningensgade 22 (Commercial Building) (Commercial Building)
22 Queen St.
HABS VI-144
HABS VI,3-CHAM,16-
3ph/1pc L

Dronningensgade 25B (House)
HABS VI-145
HABS VI,3-CHAM,17-
1ph/1pc L

Dronningensgade 30-31 (House)
30-31 Queen St.
HABS VI-146
HABS VI,3-CHAM,18-
3ph/1pc L

Dronningensgade 32 (House)
32 Queen St.
HABS VI-153
HABS VI,3-CHAM,20-
10ph/1pc L

Dronningensgade 8B (House)
8B Queen St.
HABS VI-139
HABS VI,3-CHAM,15-A-
6ph/2pc L

Dronningensgade 8B-18 (House)
8B-18 Queen St.
HABS VI-140
HABS VI,3-CHAM,15-
4ph/1pc L

Estate Number 8,Store Nordside Quarter; see Catharineberg

Estate Number 8,Store Nordside Quarter; see Catharineberg Porter's House & Cookhouse

Frederick Lutheran Church,Parish Hall (Lind,Jacob H. S. ,House; Bethania)
Norre Gade 6
HABS VI-15
HABS VI,3-CHAM,6-
9ph/7pg L

Frederiks Lutheran Church
Norregade
HABS VI-80
HABS VI,3-CHAM,11-
6ph/3pg/1pc L

Frederiksfort; see Bluebeard's Castle

Government House
Kongensgade 21-22
HABS VI-17
HABS VI,3-CHAM,8-
4ph/40pg L

Grand Hotel; see Commercial Hotel & Coffee House

Hotel 1829 (Lavalette,A. (House))
Kongensgade 30A
HABS VI-11
HABS VI,3-CHAM,4-
8ph/6pg/1pc L

Kongensgade 1B (House)
HABS VI-154
HABS VI,3-CHAM,23-
1ph/1pc L

Kronprinsensgade Area Study (Commercial Building)
Crown Prince St.
HABS VI-84-F
HABS VI,3-CHAM,29-
1ph/1pc L

Kronprinsensgade Area Study (Kronprinsensgade 11 (House))
11 Crown Prince St.
HABS VI-84-B
HABS VI,3-CHAM,25-
1ph/1pc L

Kronprinsensgade Area Study (Kronprinsensgade 22 (House))
22 Crown Prince St.
HABS VI-84-C
HABS VI,3-CHAM,26-
2ph/1pc L

Kronprinsensgade Area Study (Kronprinsensgade 5 (House))
5 Crown Prince St.
HABS VI-84-A
HABS VI,3-CHAM,24-
1ph/1pc L

Kronprinsensgade Area Study (Kronprinsensgade 76 (House))
76 Crown Prince St.
HABS VI-84-D
HABS VI,3-CHAM,27-
3ph/1pc L

Kronprinsensgade Area Study (Kronprinsensgade 78 (House))
HABS VI-157
HABS VI,3-CHAM,9-
1ph L

Kronprinsensgade Area Study (Kronprinsensgade 80 (House))
80 Crown Prince St.
HABS VI-84-E
HABS VI,3-CHAM,28-
1ph/1pc L

Kronprinsensgade 11 (House); see Kronprinsensgade Area Study

Kronprinsensgade 22 (House); see Kronprinsensgade Area Study

Kronprinsensgade 5 (House); see Kronprinsensgade Area Study

Kronprinsensgade 76 (House); see Kronprinsensgade Area Study

Kronprinsensgade 78 (House); see Kronprinsensgade Area Study

Kronprinsensgade 80 (House); see Kronprinsensgade Area Study

Lavalette,A. (House); see Hotel 1829

Lind,Jacob H. S. ,House; see Frederick Lutheran Church,Parish Hall

Lutheran Cemetery
Hospital Grounds
HABS VI-147
HABS VI,3-CHAM,10-
1ph/1pc L

Lutheran Parsonage
Kongensgade 23
HABS VI-81
HABS VI,3-CHAM,21-
5ph/4pg/1pc L

Ninty-nine Steps; see Dronningensgade Area Study

Norregade 29-40B (Houses)
HABS VI-148
HABS VI,3-CHAM,13-
6ph/1pc L

Norregade 6 (House)
HABS VI-77
HABS VI,3-CHAM,12-
1ph/1pc L

Quarters B
Kongensgade 32-33
HABS VI-82
HABS VI,3-CHAM,22-
5ph/3pg/1pc L

St. Thomas Reformed Church
Nye Gade 4B
HABS VI-9
HABS VI,3-CHAM,2-
6ph/14pg L

Synagogue of Beracha Veshalom Vegemiluth Hasidim (Synagogue of Blessing & Peace & Acts of Piety)
Krystalgade 16A & B
HABS VI-10
HABS VI,3-CHAM,3-
7ph/8pg/1pc L

Synagogue of Blessing & Peace & Acts of Piety; see Synagogue of Beracha Veshalom Vegemiluth Hasidim

Wimmelskaftsgade 6B (House)
6B Wimmelskafts St.
HABS VI-85
HABS VI,3-CHAM,32-
1ph/1pc L

CHRISTIANSTED

Christiansted Library; see Customhouse & Post Office

Customhouse & Post Office
(Christiansted Library)
Christiansted Warf Square Vic.
HABS VI-4
HABS VI,1-CHRIS,3-
9dr/18ph/10pg L

CRUZ BAY QUARTER

Estate Contant,Windmill
HABS VI-149
HABS VI,3-CRUZBA,1A-
3dr L

HASSEL ISLAND

Creque Marine Railway (St. Thomas Marine Repairslip)
HAER VI-1
HAER VI,3-HASI,1-
9dr/19ph/19pg/1pc/3ct/fr L

Fort Willoughby
HABS VI-90
HABS VI,3-HASI,2-
3ph/1pc/1ct L

St. Thomas Marine Repairslip; see Creque Marine Railway

KRONPRINDSENS QTR

Beth Ha-Chaim (House of Life; Jewish Cemetery Chapel)
Kronprindsensgade Vic.
HABS VI-14
HABS VI,3-CHAM.V,1-
3ph/3pg L

House of Life; see Beth Ha-Chaim

Jewish Cemetery Chapel; see Beth Ha-Chaim

LITTLE N. SIDE QTR

Estate Solberg,Windmill
HABS VI-150
HABS VI,3-NORTL,1A-
6dr L

NEW QUARTER

Windmill Tower
Raphune
HABS VI-151
HABS VI,3-NEW,1A-
5dr L

SOUTHSIDE QUARTER

Nisky Moravian Mission
Harwood Hwy. Vic.
HABS VI-86
HABS VI,3-SOUTH,1-
15ph/1pc L

Documentation: **ct** color transparencies **dr** measured drawings **fr** field records **pc** photograph captions **pg** pages of text **ph** photographs

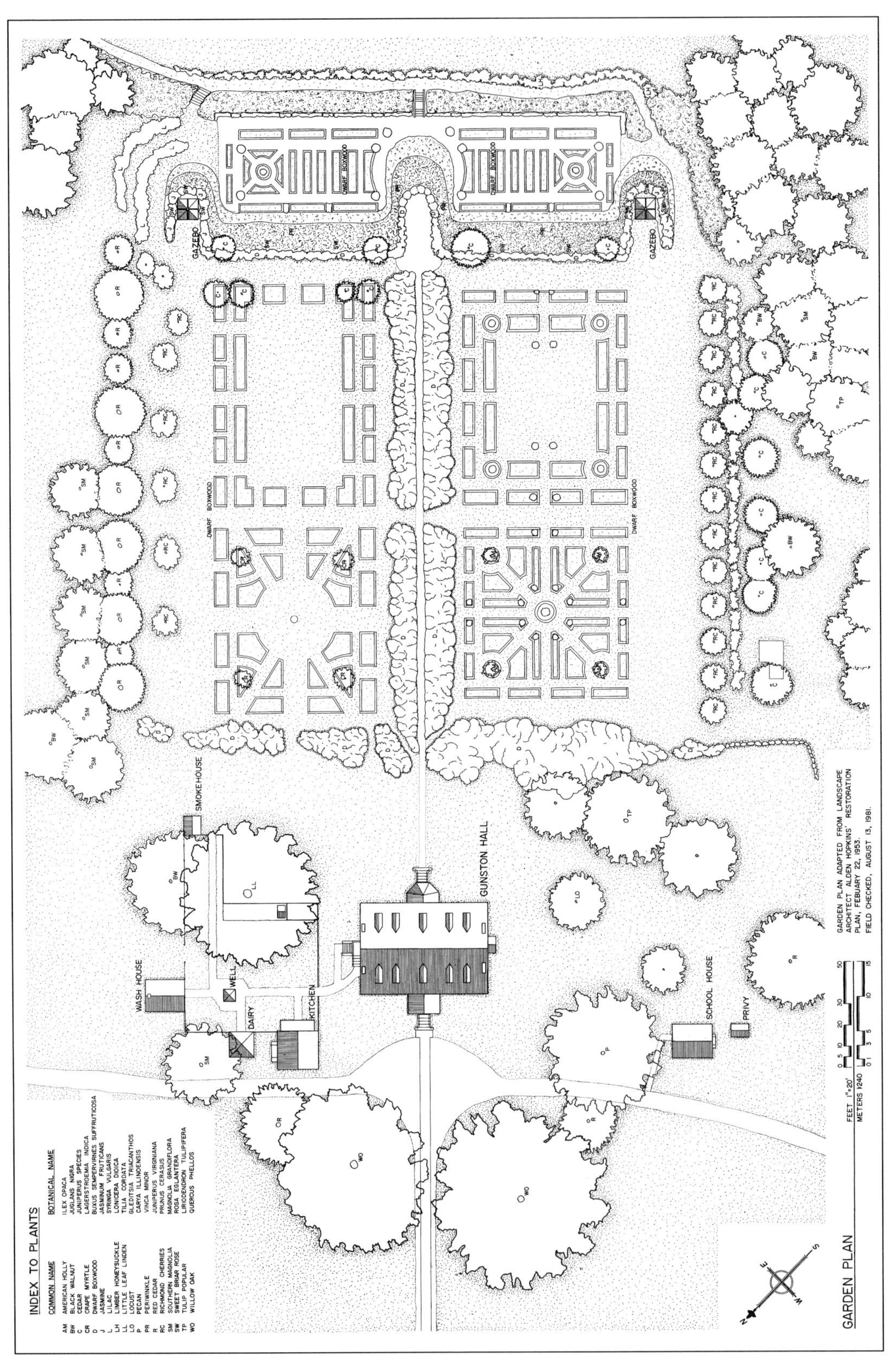

Gunston Hall, Lorton vicinity, Fairfax County, Virginia. Garden plan. Measured drawing delineated by Richard J. Cronenberger, 1981 (HABS VA-141, sheet 3 of 30; negative number LC-USZA1-1438).

Virginia

ACCOMACK COUNTY

ACCOMAC

Bayly,Richard D.,House (St. James Rectory; Episcopal Rectory)
Back St.
HABS VA-622
HABS VA,1-AC,6-
11ph/3pg L

Debtor's Prison (Jailor's House)
State Rt. 764
HABS VA-623
HABS VA,1-AC,4-
4ph/2pg L

Episcopal Rectory; see Bayly,Richard D.,House

Fisher-Seymour House
State Rt. 13
HABS VA-624
HABS VA,1-AC,9-
5ph/4pg L

Fisher-Seymour Icehouse
State Rt. 13
HABS VA-636
HABS VA,1-AC,9A-
1ph/1pg L

Jailor's House; see Debtor's Prison

St. James Rectory; see Bayly,Richard D.,House

ACCOMAC VIC

Folly Farm Dovecote; see Folly,The,Dovecote

Folly,The,Dovecote (Smith-Custis Dovecote; Folly Farm Dovecote; Nock Farm Dovecote)
Folly Creek
HABS VA-633
HABS VA,1-AC.V,2B-
1ph/1pg L

Nock Farm Dovecote; see Folly,The,Dovecote

Smith-Custis Dovecote; see Folly,The,Dovecote

ACCOMAC VIC.

Bowman's Folly (Cropper,Gen. John,House)
Folly Creek
HABS VA-625
HABS VA,1-AC.V,1-
8ph/4pg L

Bowman's Folly,Dovecote (Cropper,Gen. John,Dovecote)
Folly Creek
HABS VA-634
HABS VA,1-AC.V,1A-
1ph/1pg L

Bowman's Folly,Privy (Cropper,Gen. John,Privy)
Folly Creek
HABS VA-635
HABS VA,1-AC.V,1B-
2ph/1pg L

Cropper,Gen. John,Dovecote; see Bowman's Folly,Dovecote

Cropper,Gen. John,House; see Bowman's Folly

Cropper,Gen. John,Privy; see Bowman's Folly,Privy

Cropper,Thomas,House; see Runnymede

Folly Farm; see Folly,The

Folly Farm Icehouse; see Folly,The,Icehouse

Folly,The (Smith-Custis House; Folly Farm; Nock Farm)
Folly Creek
HABS VA-626
HABS VA,1-AC.V,2-
5ph/4pg L

Folly,The,Icehouse (Smith-Custis Icehouse; Folly Farm Icehouse; Nock Farm Icehouse)
Folly Creek
HABS VA-632
HABS VA,1-AC.V,2A-
1ph/1pg L

Mount Custis
State Rt. 662
HABS VA-627
HABS VA,1-AC.V,3-
8ph/2pg L

Nock Farm; see Folly,The

Nock Farm Icehouse; see Folly,The,Icehouse

Runnymede (Cropper,Thomas,House)
Walston Creek
HABS VA-628
HABS VA,1-AC.V,4-
4ph/3pg L

Smith-Custis House; see Folly,The

Smith-Custis Icehouse; see Folly,The,Icehouse

ATLANTIC VIC.

Mount Wharton
Wishart Point
HABS VA-551
HABS VA,1- ,3-
2ph L

CASHVILLE VIC.

Topping House
Dahl Swamp
HABS VA-482
HABS VA,1-CASH.V,1-
3ph/1pg L

CHESCONESSEX VIC.

Ohio; see Wise House

West,Revell,House
Deep Creek
HABS VA-931
HABS VA,1- ,7-
3ph/1pg L

Wise House (Ohio)
Deep Creek
HABS VA-486
HABS VA,1- ,4-
1ph L

CRADDOCKVILLE

Hermitage (Rogers House; Nealy Place)
Craddock Creek
HABS VA-483
HABS VA,1- ,5-
2ph/1pg L

Nealy Place; see Hermitage

Rogers House; see Hermitage

CRADDOCKVILLE VIC.

Hedra Cottage (Farm) (Hedrick Cottage (Farm))
Scarborough Cut
HABS VA-484
HABS VA,1-CRAD.V,1-
1ph L

Hedrick Cottage (Farm); see Hedra Cottage (Farm)

GREENBUSH VIC.

Bull House (Bull-Coard House; Slave Trader's House)
State Rt. 764
HABS VA-493
HABS VA,1-ONACO,2-
1ph L

Bull-Coard House; see Bull House

Slave Trader's House; see Bull House

GUILFORD

Clayton,George,House
State Rt. 73 Vic.
HABS VA-629
HABS VA,1-GUIL,1-
7ph/3pg L

GUILFORD VIC.

Hinman-Mason House (Mason House; Thoroughgood House)
HABS VA-630
HABS VA,1-GUIL.V,1-
5dr/23ph/3pg L

Mason House; see Hinman-Mason House

Thoroughgood House; see Hinman-Mason House

HALLWOOD

Wessel's Root Cellar
State Rts. 701 & 692 Vic.
HABS VA-953
HABS VA,1-HALL,1-
2dr L

HORNTOWN VIC.

Chincoteague Farm (Corbin Hall; Corbin)
Chincoteague Bay
HABS VA-489
HABS VA,1-HORT.V,1-
3ph L

Corbin; see Chincoteague Farm

Corbin Hall; see Chincoteague Farm

Douglas Hall; see Poplar Grove

Poplar Grove (Wallop House; Douglas Hall)
Mosquito Creek
HABS VA-932
HABS VA,1-HORT.V,2-
4ph/2pg L

Wallop House; see Poplar Grove

LEE MONT VIC.

Drummond House
Drummond Pond
HABS VA-487
HABS VA,1-AC,11-
2ph L

Drummond Store
Drummond Pond
HABS VA-488
HABS VA,1- ,2-
1ph L

LOCUSTVILLE VIC.

Mount Hope
HABS VA-1030
HABS VA,1-LOCT.V,1-
1ph/1pc L

MAPPSVILLE VIC.

Wharton Place
Assawaman Creek Vic.
HABS VA-490
HABS VA,1-MAP.V,1-
2ph/1pg L

MODEST TOWN

Salt Box House
State Rts. 679 & 772
HABS VA-491
HABS VA,1-MOD,1-
5ph L

NEW CHURCH VIC.

Pitts Neck Farm
State Rt. 709
HABS VA-492
HABS VA,1-NECH.V,2-
3ph L

ONANCOCK

Kerr Place
Crockett Ave & Market St.
HABS VA-494
HABS VA,1-ONACO,1-
2ph L

PAINTER VIC.

Thunder Castle (Thunder Cottage)
State Rt. 607 Vic.
HABS VA-496
HABS VA,1- ,6-
2ph L

Thunder Cottage; see Thunder Castle

PUNGOTEAGUE

Siamese Twin House
HABS VA-1031
HABS VA,1-PUNG,2-
2ph/1pc L

St. George's Church
State Rt. 178
HABS VA-497
HABS VA,1-PUNG,1-
1ph L

PUNGOTEAGUE VIC.

Ker,Edward,House; see Shepherd's Plain

Melrose; see Shepherd's Plain

Shepherd's Plain (Melrose; Ker,Edward,House)
State Rt. 178
HABS VA-631
HABS VA,1-PUNG.V,1-
8ph/2pg L

QUINBY VIC.

Warwick
Upshur Bay Vic.
HABS VA-495
HABS VA,1-PAINT.V,1-
3ph L

TASLEY VIC.

Custis House
Deep Creek Vic.
HABS VA-485
HABS VA,1- ,1-
3ph/1pg L

ALBEMARLE COUNTY

ALBERENE

Company House,The
State Rt. 719
HABS VA-1032
HABS VA,2-ALB,1-
8dr/9pg/fr L

BATESVILLE

Mount Ed Baptist Church
State Rt. 635
HABS VA-999
HABS VA,2-BATE,1-
7dr/8pg/fr L

Walters-Page House
State Rt. 692,opposite State Rt. 635
HABS VA-1033
HABS VA,2-BATE,2-
10dr/4pg/fr L

BATESVILLE VIC.

Sutherland Barn
State Rt. 692
HABS VA-1078
HABS VA,2-BATE.V,1-
7dr/3pg/fr L

CARTERS BRIDGE VIC.

Carter,Robert,House; see Redlands

Coles, Tucker, House; see Tallwood

Redlands (Carter,Robert,House)
State Route 708
HABS VA-1245
HABS VA,2-CARB.V,2-
6dr/11pg/fr L

Solitude
State Rt. 20
HABS VA-1074
HABS VA,2-CARB.V,1-
8dr/29pg/fr L

Tallwood (Coles, Tucker, House)
Green Mountain Road (State Road 627)
HABS VA-1244
HABS VA,2-CARB.V,3-
5dr/16pg/fr L

CHARLOTTESVILLE VIC.

Birdwood Ice House
U. S. Rt. 250 W
HABS VA-1077
HABS VA,2-CHAR.V,7A-
5dr/11pg/fr L

Documentation: **ct** color transparencies **dr** measured drawings **fr** field records
pc photograph captions **pg** pages of text **ph** photographs

Blenheim Library
State Rt. 727
HABS VA-1004
HABS VA,2-CHAR.V,5A-
8dr/6pg/fr L

Carrsbrook
South Fork River Vic.
HABS VA-150
HABS VA,2-CHAR.V,3-
5ph/1pg L

D. S. Tavern
U. S. Rt. 250 W
HABS VA-1019
HABS VA.2-CHAR.V,8-
5dr/14pg/fr L

Darby's Folly
Barracks Rd (State Rt. 658)
HABS VA-981
HABS VA,2-CHAR.V,6-
9dr/12pg/fr L

Farmington (Farmington Country Club)
U. S. Rt. 250 Vic.
HABS VA-253
HABS VA,2-CHAR.V,4-
1ph L

Farmington Country Club; see Farmington

Fry,Col. Joshua,House; see Viewmont

Malvern; see Mills House

Mills House (Oaklands; Malvern)
State Rt. 708
HABS VA-1086
HABS VA,2-CHAR.V,9-
6dr/16pg/fr L

Monticello
State Rt. 53 Vic.
HABS VA-241
HABS VA,2-CHAR.V,1-
1dr/38ph/1pg/11ct L H

Oaklands; see Mills House

Viewmont (Fry,Col. Joshua,House)
State Rts. 20 & 712 vic.
HABS VA-11-12
HABS VA,2-CHAR.V,2-
4dr/5ph/2pg/fr L

COVESVILLE

Cove Presbyterian Church
U. S. Rt. 29
HABS VA-982
HABS VA,2-LOVS,1-
8dr/7pg/fr L

CROZET VIC.

Brown-Parrott House
State Rt. 680
HABS VA-992
HABS VA,2-CROZ,1-
11dr/11pg/fr L

EARLYSVILLE

Buck Mountain Episcopal Church
State Rt. 743
HABS VA-971
HABS VA,2-EARL,1-
6dr/fr L

ESMONT VIC.

Coles,Walter,House (Woodville,Old)
State Route 627 at junction with Route 715
HABS VA-1246
HABS VA,2-ESM.V,2-
5dr/6pg/fr L

Harris,Benjamin,House (Mountain Grove)
State Rt. 717
HABS VA-1081
HABS VA,2-ESM.V,1-
9dr/10pg/fr L

Mountain Grove; see Harris,Benjamin,House

Woodville,Old; see Coles,Walter,House

GLENDOWER

Christ Church (Episcopal)
State Rts. 713 & 712
HABS VA-972
HABS VA,2-GLEN,1-
8dr/12pg/fr L

GREENWOOD VIC.

Blue Ridge Railroad,Greenwood Tunnel (Chesapeake & Ohio Railroad,Greenwood Tunnel)
Hwy. 690 Vic.
HAER VA-3
HAER VA,2-GREN.V,1-
2dr/5ph/4pg/1pc L

Chesapeake & Ohio Railroad,Greenwood Tunnel; see Blue Ridge Railroad,Greenwood Tunnel

HATTON

Hatton Grange Mill
State Rt. 625 vic.
HABS VA-990
HABS VA.2-HAT,1-
8dr/fr L

HOWARDSVILLE

George Lodge Number 32 (Masonic Lodge Number 32)
State Rt. 602
HABS VA-975
HABS ,2-HOWRD,1-
9dr/5pg/fr L

Masonic Lodge Number 32; see George Lodge Number 32

IVY

Spring Hill Claim House
State Rt. 637
HABS VA-980
HABS VA,2-IVY,1-
5dr/fr L

KEENE VIC.

Coles, Juliana, House; see Enniscorthy

Enniscorthy (Coles, Juliana, House)
State Route 627
HABS VA-1243
HABS VA,2-KEE.V,1-
5dr/fr L

KESWICK

Monroe Law Office,Limestone Plantation
VA Rte. 250
HABS VA-988
HABS VA,2-KESW,1A-
8dr/10pg/fr L

KESWICK VIC.

South Plains Presbyterian Church
State Rts. 22 & 648 vic.
HABS VA-942
HABS VA,2-KESW.V,1-
7dr/10pg/fr L

NORTH GARDEN

Crossroads Tavern
State Rt. 692
HABS VA-993
HABS VA,2-NOGAR,1-
10dr/fr L

NORTH GARDEN VIC.

Old Zion Baptist Church
U. S. Rt. 29
HABS VA-995
HABS VA,2-NOGAR.V,1-
5dr/6pg/fr L

Sunny Bank
State Rt. 712 vic.
HABS VA-996
HABS VA,2-NOGAR.V,2-
7dr/6pg/fr L

OWENSVILLE VIC.

Garth Chapel (St. James Church)
Garth Rd. (State Rt. 676)
HABS VA-1023
HABS VA,2-OWEN.V,1-
5dr/8pg/fr L

St. James Church; see Garth Chapel

SCOTTSVILLE

Barclay House
Main St.
HABS VA-1289
HABS DLC/PP-1993:VA-1
9dr/fr L

Blair House (Tipton House)
Harrison St.
HABS VA-1332
9dr H

Canal Warehouse
HABS VA-1331
9dr H

Chesapeake & Ohio Railway Station
Main St. btwn. Union & Ferry Sts.
HABS VA-977
HABS VA,2-SCOTS,30-
6dr/11pg/fr L

Disciples of Christ Church; see Scottsville Disciples of Christ Church

Jefferies-Bruce House (Scottsville Historic District)
Harrison St.
HABS VA-1292
HABS DLC/PP-1993:VA-1
8dr/fr L

Mason,James W. ,House (Old Hall)
Byrd & Harrison Sts.
HABS VA-1201
HABS VA,2-SCOTS,6-
6dr/12pg/fr L

Mount Walla; see Scott,John,House

Old Hall; see Mason,James W. ,House

Scott,John,House (Mount Walla)
Jackson St.
HABS VA-986
HABS VA,2-SCOTS,4-
8dr/fr L

Scottsville Disciples of Christ Church (Disciples of Christ Church; Scottsville Museum)
Main St. (State Rt. 6)
HABS VA-974
HABS VA,2-SCOTS,2-
9dr/fr L

Scottsville Historic District; see Jefferies-Bruce House

Scottsville Museum; see Scottsville Disciples of Christ Church

Sowell House
State Rt. 20
HABS VA-1016
HABS VA,2-SCOTS,5-
5dr/8pg/fr L

St. John's Church (Episcopal)
Harrison & Bird Sts.
HABS VA-973
HABS VA,2-SCOTS,1-
6dr/10pg/fr L

Tipton House; see Blair House

SCOTTSVILLE VIC.

Scott,Daniel,House (Valmont)
Warren Rd. ,Rt. 726
HABS VA-1001
HABS VA,2-SCOTS.V,1-
7dr/16pg/fr L

Valmont; see Scott,Daniel,House

SHADWELL

Chesapeake & Ohio Railway Station
U. S. Rt. 250 & Chesapeake & Ohio RR
HABS VA-1013
HABS VA,2-SHAD,1-
5dr/6pg/fr L

SIMEON

Ashlawn
College of William & Mary
HABS VA-1017
HABS VA,2-SIM,1-
9dr/11pg/fr L

Colle Mission Chapel; see St. Luke's Chapel

St. Luke's Chapel (Colle Mission Chapel)
State Rt. 53 & State Rt. 732
HABS VA-1025
HABS VA,2-SIM,2-
5dr/8pg/fr L

SIMEON VIC.

Springdale Farm
Buck Island Creek Vic.
HABS VA-1024
HABS VA,2-SIM.V,1-
7dr/23pg/fr L

ALEXANDRIA (CITY)

Adam Silver Shop
318 King St.
HABS VA-667
HABS VA,7-ALEX,136-
1ph/3pg L

Adam,Robert,House; see Fairfax-Adam-Hodgson House

Alexandria Alms House
HABS VA-134
HABS VA,7-ALEX.V,1-
8dr/fr L

Alexandria City Hall; see Alexandria Market House & City Hall (Masonic Hall)

Alexandria Market House & City Hall (Masonic Hall) (Alexandria City Hall)
301 King St.
HABS VA-33
HABS VA,7-ALEX,171-
24ph/52pg/fr L

Alfriend Building; see Gordon,John,House

Alley House; see Queen Street Area Survey

Appich Buildings
408-414 King St.
HABS VA-677
HABS VA,7-ALEX,141
6ph/3pg L

Arch Hall; see Lewis,Lawrence,House

Atheneum,The; see Old Dominion Bank

Ayres Gun Shop
324 King St.
HABS VA-456
HABS VA,7-ALEX,73-
2ph/1pg L

Bank of Alexandria
133 N. Fairfax St.
HABS VA-449
HABS VA,7-ALEX,11-
4ph/1pg/1pc L

Bank of Potomac (Capitol,Northern & West Virginia (Civil War))
415 Prince St.
HABS VA-458
HABS VA,7-ALEX,75-
1ph/1pg L

Barrett,Kate Waller,House; see Dick-Janney House

Bayne-Moore-House (Bayne-Moore-Mourot House)
811 Prince St.
HABS VA-453
HABS VA,7-ALEX,70-
1ph L

Bayne-Moore-Mourot House; see Bayne-Moore-House

Bird House; see Dalton House

Black,Justice Hugo L. ,House; see Vowell-Snowden-Black House

Black,Justice Hugo L.,Stable; see Vowell-Snowden-Black Stable

Blue Door,The,Antique Shop; see Lynch,Captain,House

Braddock's Headquarters; see Carlyle,John,House

Brown,Bedford,Building
113-115 S. Fairfax St.
HABS VA-669
HABS VA,7-ALEX,154-
1ph/3pg L

Brown,Dr. William,House
212 S. Fairfax St.
HABS VA-466
HABS VA,7-ALEX,82-
4ph/2pg L

Bunch of Grapes Tavern; see Dalton-Herbert Houses

Burson House; see Wilson-Hopkins House

Capitol,Northern & West Virginia (Civil War); see Bank of Potomac

Carlin House; see Washington Street Area Survey

Carlyle,John,House (Braddock's Headquarters)
123 N. Fairfax St.
HABS VA-101
HABS VA,7-ALEX,13-
8dr/13ph/2pg/fr L

Carne School; see St. John's Academy

Documentation: **ct** color transparencies **dr** measured drawings **fr** field records
pc photograph captions **pg** pages of text **ph** photographs

Caton,James R.,House
111 S. Fairfax St.
HABS VA-668
HABS VA,7-ALEX,153-
1ph/4pg L

Chatham,Henry,House
106-108 Pitt St.
HABS VA-680
HABS VA,7-ALEX,161-
1ph/4pg L

Chequire,Bernard,House
202 King St.
HABS VA-455
HABS VA,7-ALEX,72-
4ph/2pg L

Christ Church (Episcopal)
Columbus & Cameron Sts.
HABS VA-479
HABS VA,7-ALEX,2-
13dr/60ph/9pg/2pc/fr L

City Hotel; see Mason's Ordinary (Coffee House)

City Tavern; see Mason's Ordinary (Coffee House)

Coryton,Catharine,House
522-524 King St.
HABS VA-686
HABS VA,7-ALEX,150-
1ph/2pg L

Craddock House; see DeNeale-Craddock-Crocker House

Craik,Dr. James,House (Murry-Craik House)
210 Duke St.
HABS VA-583
HABS VA,7-ALEX,3-
1ph L

Crocker House; see DeNeale-Craddock-Crocker House

Dalton House (Bird House)
209 N. Fairfax St.
HABS VA-460
HABS VA,7-ALEX,76-
2ph/2pg L

Dalton-Herbert Houses
(Lee,Anne,Memorial Home for the Aged; Wise's Tavern; Bunch of Grapes Tavern)
201 N. Fairfax St.
HABS VA-934
HABS VA,7-ALEX,14-
1ph/1pg L

DeNeale-Craddock-Crocker House
(Craddock House; Crocker House)
323 S. Fairfax St.
HABS VA-229
HABS VA,7-ALEX,7-
3ph L

Devaughan,James H.,House (Shuman's)
516 King St.
HABS VA-679
HABS VA,7-ALEX,148-
5ph/4pg L

Dick-Janney House (Barrett,Kate Waller,House)
408 Duke St.
HABS VA-696
HABS VA,7-ALEX,160-
1ph/8pg L

Duffey House
203 S. Fairfax St.
HABS VA-454
HABS VA,7-ALEX,71-
1ph/2pg L

200 Duke Street (House); see Duke Street Area Survey

201 Duke Street (House); see McConnell,Alexander,House

700 Duke Street (House); see Duke Street Area Survey

Duke Street Area Survey (200 Duke Street (House))
HABS VA-1050
HABS VA,7-ALEX,176-
2ph/1pc L

Duke Street Area Survey (700 Duke Street (House))
HABS VA-1051
HABS VA,7-ALEX,177-
2ph/1pc L

Dulany,Benjamin,House
601 Duke St.
HABS VA-697
HABS VA,7-ALEX,65-
9ph/6pg L

Dulany,Benjamin,Stable
601 Duke St.
HABS VA-447
HABS VA,7-ALEX,65A-
1ph/1pg L

Eden,Charles Gregory,House; see 113 Prince Street (House)

Evans,John T.,Building
320 King St.
HABS VA-666
HABS VA,7-ALEX,137-
1ph/3pg L

Fairfax-Adam-Hodgson House
(Fairfax,George William,House; Adam,Robert,House)
207 Prince St.
HABS VA-230
HABS VA,7-ALEX,28-
3ph L

Fairfax,George William,House; see Fairfax-Adam-Hodgson House

Fairfax,Lord,House (Yeaton-Fairfax House; Yeaton-Crilly House)
607 Cameron St.
HABS VA-211
HABS VA,7-ALEX,10-
12ph/1pg L

Farmer's Bank of Alexandria; see 200 Prince & 201 South Lee Streets (House)

Fawcett House; see Murray-Dick-Fawcett House

Fendall House
611 Oronoco St.
HABS VA-1049
HABS VA,7-ALEX,178-
2ph/1pc L

First National Bank
503-507 King St.
HABS VA-672
HABS VA,7-ALEX,147-
5ph/5pg L

Fitzgerald,John,Warehouse; see Patterson-Fitzgerald Warehouse

Flounder House
317 S. Saint Asaph St.
HABS VA-462
HABS VA,7-ALEX,78-
1ph/1pg L

Flounder Tavern Building
Sharpskin & Market Square Alleys
HABS VA-621
HABS VA,7-ALEX,132 & 132A-
6dr/4ph/5pg L

Flounder Warehouse (Little Theater Workshop)
207 Ramsay's Alley
HABS VA-474
HABS VA,7-ALEX,87-
1ph/1pg L

Fortney,Jacob,House; see Royal Street Area Survey

Fowle-Taylor House; see Fowle,William,House

Fowle,William,House (Fowle-Taylor House)
711 Prince St.
HABS VA-574
HABS VA,7-ALEX,31-
4ph L

Free Methodist Church; see Old Dominion Bank

Friendship Fire Company (Friendship Veteran's Fire Engine Company)
107 S. Alfred St.
HABS VA-463
HABS VA,7-ALEX,79-
5dr/5ph/5pg/fr L

Friendship Veteran's Fire Engine Company; see Friendship Fire Company

Gadsby's Tavern; see Mason's Ordinary (Coffee House)

Gordon,John,House (Alfriend Building)
631 King St.
HABS VA-938
HABS VA,7-ALEX,12-
3ph/5pg L

Greene Funeral Home; see Jockey Club,The

Gregory,William,Building (first)
400-402 King St.
HABS VA-674
HABS VA,7-ALEX,139-
1ph/5pg L

Gregory,William,Building (second)
404-406 King St.
HABS VA-690
HABS VA,7-ALEX,140-
1ph/2pg L

Gregory,William,House (Leadbeater House,Old)
329 N. Washington St.
HABS VA-416
HABS VA,7-ALEX,62-
3ph/1pg L

Hallowell School; see Wilson-Hopkins House

Hallowell-Carlin House; see Washington Street Area Survey

Hallowell,James,School For Young Ladies; see 213-215 North Fairfax Street (Houses)

Hampson,Bryan,House (Wales House)
120 S. Fairfax St.
HABS VA-468
HABS VA,7-ALEX,85-
5ph/1pg L

Harper-Buckingham-Berry Building
312 King St.
HABS VA-664
HABS VA,7-ALEX,134-
2ph/4pg L

Harper-Vowell House
213 Prince St.
HABS VA-939
HABS VA,7-ALEX,29-
2ph L

Hill,George R. ,House; see Shadows,The

Hollinsbury,John,House; see Queen Street Area Survey

House
Princess St.
HABS VA-1212
HABS VA,7-ALEX,179-
1ph/1pc L

House of the Smiling Face; see Ladd House

House,Greek Revival
801 Duke St.
HABS VA-461
HABS VA,7-ALEX,77-
1ph L

House,Little; see Queen Street Area Survey

Howard House; see Washington Street Area Survey

Jacobs-Miner House
113 S. Royal St.
HABS VA-673
HABS VA,7-ALEX,167-
1ph/3pg L

Janney,Elisha,House
404 Duke St.
HABS VA-703
HABS VA,7-ALEX,159-
6ph/7pg L

215 Jefferson Street (House); see Jefferson Street Area Survey

222 Jefferson Street (House); see Jefferson Street Area Survey

Jefferson Street Area Survey (215 Jefferson Street (House))
HABS VA-1052
HABS VA,7-ALEX,174-
2ph/1pc L

Jefferson Street Area Survey (222 Jefferson Street (House))
HABS VA-1053
HABS VA,7-ALEX,175-
2ph/1pc L

Jockey Club,The (Greene Funeral Home)
814 Franklin St.
HABS VA-102
HABS VA,7-ALEX,45-
7dr/8ph/fr L

Johnston-Vowell House
224 S. Lee St.
HABS VA-451
HABS VA,7-ALEX,68-
1ph/2pg L

Johnston,George,Homesite; see Old Dominion Bank

Johnston,Reuben,House; see South Fairfax Street Area Survey

Kennedy Buildings
416-418 King St.
HABS VA-670
HABS VA,7-ALEX,142-
2ph/3pg L

300-320 King Street (Buildings) (King Street,300 Block (General Views))
HABS VA-920
HABS VA,7-ALEX,133-
2ph L

400-430 King Street (Buildings) (King Street,400 Block (General View))
HABS VA-921
HABS VA,7-ALEX,138-
1ph L

500-532 King Street (Buildings) (King Street,500 Block (General View))
HABS VA-922
HABS VA,7-ALEX,144-
1ph L

King Street,300 Block (General Views); see 300-320 King Street (Buildings)

King Street,400 Block (General View); see 400-430 King Street (Buildings)

King Street,500 Block (General View); see 500-532 King Street (Buildings)

Korn & Wisemiller Building
202 S. Saint Asaph & 502 Prince Sts.
HABS VA-704
HABS VA,7-ALEX,155-
4ph/10pg L

Ladd House (House of the Smiling Face)
320 N. Fairfax St.
HABS VA-212
HABS VA,7-ALEX,4-
1ph L

LaFayette-Lawrason-Cazenove House; see Lawrason,Thomas,House

Lannon's Opera House
500-508 King St.
HABS VA-675
HABS VA,7-ALEX,146-
2ph/5pg L

Lawrason,Thomas,House (LaFayette-Lawrason-Cazenove House)
301 S. Saint Asaph St.
HABS VA-467
HABS VA,7-ALEX,83-
7ph/2pg L

Leadbeater Drug Store; see Stabler-Leadbeater Drug Corporation

Leadbeater House
414 N. Washington St.
HABS VA-457
HABS VA,7-ALEX,74-
1ph/1pg L

Leadbeater House,Old; see Gregory,William,House

Leadbeater-Barrett House; see Leadbeater,James,House

Leadbeater-Stabler Apothecary Shop; see Stabler-Leadbeater Apothecary Shop

Leadbeater,James,House (Leadbeater-Barrett House)
213 S. Pitt St.
HABS VA-1067
HABS VA,7-ALEX,173-
4dr L

Lee Street Area Survey (403 South Lee Street (House))
HABS VA-620-A
HABS VA,7-ALEX,128-
2ph L

Lee Street Area Survey (601 South Lee Street (House))
HABS VA-620-B
HABS VA,7-ALEX,129-
1ph L

Lee Street Area Survey (605 South Lee Street (House))
HABS VA-620-C
HABS VA,7-ALEX,130-
1ph L

Lee Street Area Survey (615 South Lee Street (House))
HABS VA-620-D
HABS VA,7-ALEX,131-
1ph L

Lee,Anne,Memorial Home for the Aged; see Dalton-Herbert Houses

Lee,Charles,House; see Washington Street Area Survey

Lee,Edmund Jennings,House
428 N. Washington St.
HABS VA-452
HABS VA,7-ALEX,69-
2ph/1pg L

Lee,Robert E.,House; see Potts-Fitzhugh House

Lewis,Lawrence,House (Arch Hall)
815 Franklin St. (moved to VA,Lorton)
HABS VA-109
HABS VA,7-ALEX,52-
11dr/7ph/1pg L

Little Theater Workshop; see Flounder Warehouse

Lloyd House; see Wise-Hooe-Lloyd House

Lockwood-Cross Building
314 King St.
HABS VA-665
HABS VA,7-ALEX,135-
1ph/3pg L

Longden,John,House
111 S. Royal St.
HABS VA-689
HABS VA,7-ALEX,166-
1ph/3pg L

Longden,John,Houses
105-107 S. Royal St.
HABS VA-685
HABS VA,7-ALEX,164-
1ph/4pg L

Lyceum (McGuire House)
201 S. Washington St.
HABS VA-185
HABS VA,7-ALEX,56-
10dr/20ph/1pg/fr L

Lynch,Captain,House (Blue Door,The,Antique Shop)
708 Wolfe St.
HABS VA-476
HABS VA,7-ALEX,41-
3ph/1pg L

Lynn,Adam,House (first)
518-520 King St.
HABS VA-676
HABS VA,7-ALEX,149-
6ph/9pg L

Lynn,Adam,House (second)
532 King St.
HABS VA-687
HABS VA,7-ALEX,151-
1ph/2pg L

Lynn,Adam,House (third)
104 S. Saint Asaph St.
HABS VA-688
HABS VA,7-ALEX,169-
1ph/3pg L

Married Houses; see Thompson,Jonah,Houses

Mason's Ordinary (Coffee House) (Gadsby's Tavern; City Hotel; City Tavern)
128 N. Royal St.
HABS VA-100
HABS VA,7-ALEX,19-
7dr/14ph/4pg L

McConnell,Alexander,House (201 Duke Street (House))
HABS VA-459
HABS VA,7-ALEX,37-
1ph/1pg L

McConnell,Alexander,Tenement Houses
223-225 S. Lee St.
HABS VA-475-A
HABS VA,7-ALEX,88-
1ph/1pg L

McGuire House; see Lyceum

Miller,Mordecai,House; see South Fairfax Street Area Survey

Miller,Samuel,Building
420 King St.
HABS VA-671
HABS VA,7-ALEX,143-
1ph/3pg L

Murray-Dick-Fawcett House (Fawcett House)
517 Prince St.
HABS VA-104
HABS VA,7-ALEX,51-
6dr/3ph/fr L

Murry-Craik House; see Craik,Dr. James,House

New Virginia Market
1221-1223 King St.
HABS VA-1333
6dr H

213-215 North Fairfax Street (Houses) (Hallowell,James,School For Young Ladies; St. Mary's Academy)
HABS VA-448
HABS VA,7-ALEX,66-
2ph L

310 North Lee Street (Doorway)
HABS VA-940
HABS VA,7-ALEX,91-
1ph L

110-112 North Pitt Street (Houses)
HABS VA-683
HABS VA,7-ALEX,163-
1ph L

109 North Royal Street (Building); see Royal Street Area Survey

207 North Royal Street (House); see Royal Street Area Survey

217 North Royal Street (House); see Royal Street Area Survey

219 North Royal Street (House)
HABS VA-293
HABS VA,7-ALEX,18-
1ph L

221 North Royal Street (House); see Royal Street Area Survey

215 North Washington Street (House); see Washington Street Area Survey

407 North Washington Street (House); see Washington Street Area Survey

Old Dominion Bank (Free Methodist Church; Atheneum,The; Johnston,George,Homesite)
201 Prince St.
HABS VA-428
HABS VA,7-ALEX,63-
1ph L

Orange & Alexandria RR,Wilkes Street Tunnel (Southern Railway,Wilkes Street Tunnel)
Wilkes Street Vic.
HAER VA-18
HAER VA,7-ALEX,172-
3dr/fr L

Patterson-Fitzgerald Warehouse (Fitzgerald,John,Warehouse)
101-105 S. Union St.
HABS VA-132
HABS VA,7-ALEX,53-
7dr/7ph/1pg/fr L

Pharmaceutical Museum; see Stabler-Leadbeater Apothecary Shop

Plain,George,House; see South Fairfax Street Area Survey

Potts-Fitzhugh House (Lee,Robert E.,House)
607 Oronoco St.
HABS VA-707
HABS VA,7-ALEX,17-
12ph/10pg L

Presbyterian Church; see Presbyterian Meetinghouse

Presbyterian Meetinghouse (Presbyterian Church)
321 S. Fairfax St.
HABS VA-231
HABS VA,7-ALEX,17-
4ph L

200 Prince & 201 South Lee Streets (House) (Farmer's Bank of Alexandria)
HABS VA-937
HABS VA,7-ALEX,92-
1ph L

113 Prince Street (House) (Eden,Charles Gregory,House)
113 Prince St.
HABS VA-700
HABS VA,7-ALEX,24A-
7dr L

605 Prince Street (House)
HABS VA-964
HABS VA,7-ALEX,157-
1ph L

607 Prince Street (House)
HABS VA-965
HABS VA,7-ALEX,158-
3ph L

103-133 Prince Street (Row Houses,General View)
HABS VA-924
HABS VA,7-ALEX,24-
1ph L

Pythian Temple
319 Cameron St.
HABS VA-252
HABS VA,7-ALEX,58-
1ph L

214 Queen Street (House)
HABS VA-446
HABS VA,7-ALEX,64-
2ph/1pg L

308 Queen Street (House); see Queen Street Area Survey

312 Queen Street (House); see Queen Street Area Survey

317 Queen Street (House); see Queen Street Area Survey

510 Queen Street (House); see Queen Street Area Survey

511 Queen Street (House); see Queen Street Area Survey

517 Queen Street (House); see Queen Street Area Survey

519 Queen Street (House); see Queen Street Area Survey

523 Queen Street (House); see Queen Street Area Survey

525 Queen Street (House); see Queen Street Area Survey

513-515 Queen Street (Houses); see Queen Street Area Survey

301-303 Queen Street (Row Houses); see Queen Street Area Survey

305-307 Queen Street (Row Houses); see Queen Street Area Survey

319-325 Queen Street (Row Houses); see Queen Street Area Survey

Queen Street Area Survey (308 Queen Street (House))
HABS VA-600-C
HABS VA,7-ALEX,93-
3ph L

Queen Street Area Survey (312 Queen Street (House); Summers-Scott House)
HABS VA-600-D
HABS VA,7-ALEX,94-
3ph L

Queen Street Area Survey (317 Queen Street (House))
HABS VA-600-E
HABS VA,7-ALEX,96-
1ph L

Queen Street Area Survey (510 Queen Street (House))
HABS VA-600-G
HABS VA,7-ALEX,97-
3ph L

Queen Street Area Survey (511 Queen Street (House))
HABS VA-600-H
HABS VA,7-ALEX,98-
1ph L

Queen Street Area Survey (517 Queen Street (House))
HABS VA-600-J
HABS VA,7-ALEX,100-
1ph L

Queen Street Area Survey (519 Queen Street (House))
HABS VA-600-K
HABS VA,7-ALEX,101-
1ph L

Queen Street Area Survey (523 Queen Street (House); House,Little; Alley House)
HABS VA-600-L
HABS VA,7-ALEX,102-
1ph L

Queen Street Area Survey (525 Queen Street (House); Hollinsbury,John,House)
HABS VA-600-M
HABS VA,7-ALEX,103-
1ph L

Queen Street Area Survey (513-515 Queen Street (Houses))
HABS VA-600-I
HABS VA,7-ALEX,99-
1ph L

Queen Street Area Survey (301-303 Queen Street (Row Houses))
HABS VA-600-A
HABS VA,7-ALEX,32-
2ph L

Queen Street Area Survey (305-307 Queen Street (Row Houses))
HABS VA-600-B
HABS VA,7-ALEX,32-
1ph L

Queen Street Area Survey (319-325 Queen Street (Row Houses))
HABS VA-600-F
HABS VA,7-ALEX,95-
4ph L

Ramsay-Atkinson House
113 N. Fairfax St.
HABS VA-464
HABS VA,7-ALEX,80-
3ph/2pg L

Ramsay,Dennis,House
221 S. Lee St.
HABS VA-475-B
HABS VA,7-ALEX,89-
6ph L

Ramsay,William,House
221 King St.
HABS VA-103
HABS VA,7-ALEX,50-
4dr/2ph/fr L

Roberdeau,Gen. Daniel,House
418 S. Lee St.
HABS VA-469
HABS VA,7-ALEX,86-
3ph/1pg L

Roberts,Reuben,House; see Shadows,The

103-107 Royal Street (Commercial Building); see Royal Street Area Survey

Royal Street Area Survey (109 North Royal Street (Building))
HABS VA-619-B
HABS VA,7-ALEX,121-
1ph L

Royal Street Area Survey (207 North Royal Street (House); Fortney,Jacob,House)
HABS VA-619-F
HABS VA,7-ALEX,125-
1ph L

Royal Street Area Survey (217 North Royal Street (House))
HABS VA-619-G
HABS VA,7-ALEX,126-
1ph L

Royal Street Area Survey (221 North Royal Street (House))
HABS VA-619-H
HABS VA,7-ALEX,127-
1ph L

Royal Street Area Survey (103-107 Royal Street (Commercial Building))
HABS VA-619-A
HABS VA,7-ALEX,120-
1ph L

Royal Street Area Survey (112 South Royal Street (House))
HABS VA-619-C
HABS VA,7-ALEX,122-
1ph L

Royal Street Area Survey (120 South Royal Street (House))
HABS VA-619-D
HABS VA,7-ALEX,123-
1ph L

Royal Street Area Survey (122 South Royal Street (House))
HABS VA-619-E
HABS VA,7-ALEX,124-
1ph L

Second Presbyterian Church,Westminster Bldg.
521-523 Prince St.
HABS VA-682
HABS VA,7-ALEX,156-
1ph/5pg L

Shadows,The (Roberts,Reuben,House; Hill,George R. ,House)
617 S. Washington St.
HABS VA-906
HABS VA,7-ALEX,181-
1pg/fr L

Shuman's; see Devaughan,James H.,House

Simmonds,Samuel,House
109 S. Royal St.
HABS VA-684
HABS VA,7-ALEX,165-
1ph/4pg L

Snowden House; see Vowell-Snowden-Black House

Snowden Stable; see Vowell-Snowden-Black Stable

207-209 South Fairfax Street (Double House); see South Fairfax Street Area Survey

109 South Fairfax Street (House); see South Fairfax Street Area Survey

117 South Fairfax Street (House); see South Fairfax Street Area Survey

118 South Fairfax Street (House); see South Fairfax Street Area Survey

124 South Fairfax Street (House); see South Fairfax Street Area Survey

213 South Fairfax Street (House); see South Fairfax Street Area Survey

227 South Fairfax Street (House); see South Fairfax Street Area Survey

405 South Fairfax Street (House); see South Fairfax Street Area Survey

131-137 South Fairfax Street (Row Houses); see South Fairfax Street Area Survey

511-517 South Fairfax Street (Row Houses); see South Fairfax Street Area Survey

South Fairfax Street Area Survey (207-209 South Fairfax Street (Double House))
HABS VA-618-F
HABS VA,7-ALEX,114-
1ph L

South Fairfax Street Area Survey (109 South Fairfax Street (House); Miller,Mordecai,House)
HABS VA-618-A
HABS VA,7-ALEX,109-
2ph/4pg L

South Fairfax Street Area Survey (117 South Fairfax Street (House))
HABS VA-618-B
HABS VA,7-ALEX,110-
1ph L

South Fairfax Street Area Survey (118 South Fairfax Street (House))
HABS VA-618-C
HABS VA,7-ALEX,111-
1ph L

South Fairfax Street Area Survey (124 South Fairfax Street (House); Wilson,James,House)
HABS VA-618-D
HABS VA,7-ALEX,112-
1ph L

South Fairfax Street Area Survey (213 South Fairfax Street (House); Johnston,Reuben,House)
HABS VA-618-G
HABS VA,7-ALEX,115-
1ph L

South Fairfax Street Area Survey (227 South Fairfax Street (House); Plain,George,House)
HABS VA-618-H
HABS VA,7-ALEX,116-
1ph L

South Fairfax Street Area Survey (405 South Fairfax Street (House))
HABS VA-618-I
HABS VA,7-ALEX,117-
1ph L

South Fairfax Street Area Survey (131-137 South Fairfax Street (Row Houses))
HABS VA-618-E
HABS VA,7-ALEX,113-
2ph L

South Fairfax Street Area Survey (511-517 South Fairfax Street (Row Houses))
HABS VA-618-J
HABS VA,7-ALEX,118-
1ph L

South Fairfax Street,100 Block (General View)
HABS VA-919
HABS VA,7-ALEX,152-
1ph L

106 South Lee Street (House)
HABS VA-465
HABS VA,7-ALEX,81-
1ph L

310 South Lee Street (House)
HABS VA-584
HABS VA,7-ALEX,90-
1ph L

403 South Lee Street (House); see Lee Street Area Survey

601 South Lee Street (House); see Lee Street Area Survey

605 South Lee Street (House); see Lee Street Area Survey

615 South Lee Street (House); see Lee Street Area Survey

221-225 South Lee Street (Houses)
HABS VA-475
HABS VA,7-ALEX,88-
1ph/1pg L

110 South Pitt Street (House); see South Pitt Street Area Survey

South Pitt Street Area Survey (110 South Pitt Street (House))
HABS VA-1054
HABS VA,7-ALEX,180-
1ph/1pc L

112 South Royal Street (House); see Royal Street Area Survey

120 South Royal Street (House); see Royal Street Area Survey

122 South Royal Street (House); see Royal Street Area Survey

308 South Union Street (House)
HABS VA-267
HABS VA,7-ALEX,59-
1ph L

415-417 South Washington Street (Double House); see Washington Street Area Survey

207 South Washington Street (House); see Washington Street Area Survey

209 South Washington Street (House); see Washington Street Area Study

411 South Washington Street (Row House); see Washington Street Area Survey

Southern Railway,Wilkes Street Tunnel; see Orange & Alexandria RR,Wilkes Street Tunnel

St. John's Academy (Carne School)
Duke & S. Columbus Sts.
HABS VA-450
HABS VA,7-ALEX,67-
1ph/3pg L

St. Mary's Academy; see 213-215 North Fairfax Street (Houses)

St. Paul's Episcopal Church
216 S. Pitt St.
HABS VA-340
HABS HABS VA,7-ALEX,60-
3ph/2pg L

St. Paul's Episcopal Church,Rectory
417 Duke St.
HABS VA-708
HABS VA,7-ALEX,61-
1ph/2pg L

Stabler-Leadbeater Apothecary Shop (Leadbeater-Stabler Apothecary Shop; Pharmaceutical Museum)
107 S. Fairfax St.
HABS VA-175
HABS VA,7-ALEX,55-
2dr/13ph/2pg/fr L

Stabler-Leadbeater Drug Corporation (Leadbeater Drug Store)
King & S. Fairfax Sts.
HABS VA-948
HABS VA,7-ALEX,119-
1ph L

Stockton House; see Vowell-Snowden-Black House

Stockton Stable; see Vowell-Snowden-Black Stable

Summers-Scott House; see Queen Street Area Survey

Swope,Col. Michael,House
210 Prince St.
HABS VA-292
HABS VA,7-ALEX,44-
1ph L

Taylor-Fraser House
414 Franklin St. (moved from 109 S. Pitt St.)
HABS VA-678
HABS VA,7-ALEX,162-
4ph/4pg L

Thompson,Jonah,Houses (Twin Houses; Married Houses)
211 N. Fairfax St.
HABS VA-251
HABS VA,7-ALEX,57-
10ph/2pg L

Twin Houses; see Thompson,Jonah,Houses

Van Havre-Daingerfield House
608 Cameron St.
HABS VA-710
HABS VA,7-ALEX,168-
6ph/9pg L

Vowell-Snowden-Black House (Snowden House; Black,Justice Hugo L. ,House; Stockton House)
619 S. Lee St.
HABS VA-709
HABS VA,7-ALEX,170-
25ph/7pg L

Vowell-Snowden-Black Stable (Snowden Stable; Black,Justice Hugo L.,Stable; Stockton Stable)
Franklin St.
HABS VA-711
HABS VA,7-ALEX,170A-
3ph/4pg L

Wales House; see Hampson,Bryan,House

Warehouse Area Survey
Gazette & Market Square Alleys
HABS VA-1269
HABS VA,7-ALEX,132-
3ph L

Warehouse,Small; see Water Street (Warehouse)

Warfield Building
501 King St.
HABS VA-681
HABS VA,7-ALEX,145-
4ph/4pg L

Washington Street Area Study (209 South Washington Street (House))
HABS VA-617-B
HABS VA,7-ALEX,106-
1ph L

Washington Street Area Survey (215 North Washington Street (House); Hallowell-Carlin House; Carlin House)
HABS VA-617-C
HABS VA,7-ALEX,20-
1ph L

Washington Street Area Survey (407 North Washington Street (House); Lee,Charles,House)
HABS VA-617-D
HABS VA,7-ALEX,104-
2ph L

Washington Street Area Survey (415-417 South Washington Street (Double House))
HABS VA-617-F
HABS VA,7-ALEX,108-
1ph L

Washington Street Area Survey (207 South Washington Street (House); Howard House)
HABS VA-617-A
HABS VA,7-ALEX,105-
1ph L

Washington Street Area Survey (411 South Washington Street (Row House))
HABS VA-617-E
HABS VA,7-ALEX,107-
1ph L

Washington,George,Town House (reconstructed)
508 Cameron St.
HABS VA-597
HABS VA,7-ALEX,9-
1ph/14pg L

Water Street (Warehouse) (Warehouse,Small)
HABS VA-133
HABS VA,7-ALEX,54-
3dr/2ph L

Wilson-Hopkins House (Hallowell School; Burson House)
609 Oronoco St.
HABS VA-933
HABS VA,7-ALEX,42-
1ph L

Wilson,James,House; see South Fairfax Street Area Survey

Wise-Hooe-Lloyd House (Lloyd House)
220 N. Washington St.
HABS VA-582
HABS VA,7-ALEX,15-
16dr/33ph/6pg L

Wise's Tavern; see Dalton-Herbert Houses

Yeaton-Crilly House; see Fairfax,Lord,House

Yeaton-Fairfax House; see Fairfax,Lord,House

Jones Point Lighthouse
Jones Point,Potomac River
HABS VA-641
HABS VA,7-ALEX.V,2-
6dr/6ph/7pg L

ALLEGHANY COUNTY

COVINGTON VIC.

Humpback Covered Bridge
Spanning Dunlap Creek
HAER VA-1
HAER VA,3-COV.V,1-
4dr/19ph/4pg/1pc/fr L

SWEET CHALYBEATE

Red Springs,Bandstand; see Sweet Chalybeate Springs,Bandstand

Red Sweet Springs; see Sweet Chalybeate Springs

Red Sweet Springs, N. Guest Range and Cottages; see Sweet Chalybeate Springs,N. Guest Range & Cottages

Red Sweet Springs,Southern Guest Range; see Sweet Chalybeate Springs,Southern Guest Range

Red Sweet Springs,Spring House; see Sweet Chalybeate Springs,Spring House

Sweet Chalybeate Springs (Red Sweet Springs)
State Rt. 311
HABS VA-1035
HABS VA,3-SWECH,1-
1ph/1pg/1pc L

Sweet Chalybeate Springs,Bandstand (Red Springs,Bandstand)
State Rt. 311
HABS VA-1035-D
HABS VA,3-SWECH,1D-
1ph/1pc L

Sweet Chalybeate Springs,Main Building
State Rt. 311
HABS VA-1035-A
HABS VA,3-SWECH,1A-
3ph/1pc L

Sweet Chalybeate Springs,N. Guest Range & Cottages (Red Sweet Springs, N. Guest Range and Cottages)
State Rt. 311
HABS VA-1035-B
HABS VA,3-SWECH,1B-
1ph/1pc L

Sweet Chalybeate Springs,Southern Guest Range (Red Sweet Springs,Southern Guest Range)
HABS VA-1035-C
HABS VA,3-SWECH,1C-
1ph/1pc L

Sweet Chalybeate Springs,Spring House (Red Sweet Springs,Spring House)
State Rte. 311
HABS VA-1035-E
HABS VA,3-SWECH,1E-
1ph/1pc L

AMELIA COUNTY

AMELIA VIC.

Archer-Hindle House; see Woodlands

Hindle House; see Woodlands

Woodlands (Hindle House; Archer-Hindle House)
Amelia Courthouse Vic.
HABS VA-269
HABS VA,4-AMELCH.V,1-
2dr/1pg/fr L

MATTOAX VIC.

Oaks,The
(moved to VA,Richmond)
HABS VA-157
HABS VA,4-MATOX.V,1-
8ph/1pg L

AMHERST COUNTY

CLIFFORD

House,Brick
State Rt. 151
HABS VA-54
HABS VA,5-CLIF,1-
2ph/1pg L

DILLWYN VIC.

Bellmont
State Rt. 667 Vic.
HABS VA-11-14
HABS VA,15-DIL.V,1-
4dr/3ph/2pg/fr L

LYNCHBURG VIC.

Ninemile Bridge
(See CAMPBELL CO.,LYNCHBURG VIC. for documentatn.)
HAER VA-93
L

APPOMATTOX COUNTY

APPOMATTOX

Appomattox Court House National Historical Park; see Appomattox Courthouse

Appomattox Court House National Historical Park; see Store,Old

Appomattox Court House National Historical Park; see Wright,Mariah,House

Appomattox Court House NHP; see Bagby,Luke,House

Appomattox Court House NHP; see Sweeney Farm,House

Appomattox Court House NHP; see Sweeney Farm,Prizery

Appomattox Court House NHP; see Trent House

Appomattox Court House NHP; see Webb,Martin,House

Appomattox Court House NHP; see Woodson Law Office

Appomattox Courthouse (Appomattox Court House National Historical Park)
HABS VA-716
HABS VA,6-APPO,6-;(DLC/PP-1992:VA-5)
5ph/1pg/2pc L

Bagby,Luke,House (Appomattox Court House NHP)
HABS VA-1313
HABS DLC/PP-1992:VA-5
1ph/1pc L

Bocock-Isbell House
Bocock Ln.
HABS VA-1314
HABS DLC/PP-1992:VA-5
1ph/1pc L

Clover Hill Tavern; see Tavern

Jail,The
Appomattox Courthouse National Historical Park
HABS VA-436
HABS VA,6-APPO,4-;(DLC/PP-1992:VA-5)
2ph/1pc/fr L

Kelly House
Main St.
HABS VA-1315
HABS DLC/PP-1992:VA-5
12ph/2pc L

LeGrand House
State Rt. 631
HABS VA-715
HABS VA,6-APPO,10-
1ph/1pc L

McDearmon-Tibbs House
State Rt. 24 Vic.
HABS VA-714
HABS VA,6-APPO,8-
2ph/1pc L

McLean House (Raine-McLean House; Surrender House)
Appomattox Courthouse National Historical Park
HABS VA-240
HABS VA,6-APPO,1-;(DLC/PP-1992:VA-5)
8dr/4ph/26pg/1pc/fr L

Patterson House; see Tavern

Peers House
Old Richmond-Lynchburg Stage Rd.
HABS VA-1316
HABS DLC/PP-1992:VA-5
2ph/1pc L

Plunkett-Meeks Store & House
Appomattox Courthouse National Historical Park
HABS VA-432
HABS VA,6-APPO,2-;(DLC/PP-1992:VA-5)
17ph/2pc/fr L

Raine-McLean House; see McLean House

Sears,J. ,House
State Rt. 631
HABS VA-713
HABS VA,6-APPO,9-;(DLC/PP-1992:VA-5)
3ph/2pc L

Store,Old (Appomattox Court House National Historical Park)
HABS VA-435
HABS VA,6-APPO,3-
1ph L

Surrender House; see McLean House

Sweeney Farm,House (Appomattox Court House NHP)
HABS VA-1317-A
HABS DLC/PP-1992:VA-5
1ph/1pc L

Sweeney Farm,Prizery (Appomattox Court House NHP)
HABS VA-1317-B
HABS DLC/PP-1992:VA-5
5ph/1pc L

Tavern (Clover Hill Tavern; Patterson House)
Appomattox Courthouse National Historical Park
HABS VA-439
HABS VA,6-APPO,5-;(DLC/PP-1992:VA-5)
4ph/1pc/fr L

Tavern Kitchen-Gueshouse; see Tavern,Tavern Kitchen

Tavern,Tavern Guesthouse
Main St.
HABS VA-439-B
HABS DLC/PP-1992:VA-5
6ph/1pc L

Tavern,Tavern Kitchen (Tavern Kitchen-Gueshouse)
Main St.
HABS VA-439-A
HABS DLC/PP-1992:VA-5
5ph/1pc L

Trent House (Appomattox Court House NHP)
HABS VA-1318
HABS DLC/PP-1992:VA-5
2ph/1pc L

Webb,Martin,House (Appomattox Court House NHP)
HABS VA-1319
HABS DLC/PP-1992:VA-5
1ph/1pc L

Woodson Law Office (Appomattox Court House NHP)
HABS VA-1320
HABS DLC/PP-1992:VA-5
4ph/1pc L

Wright,Mariah,House (Appomattox Court House National Historical Park)
HABS VA-947
HABS VA,6-APPO,7-;(DLC/PP-1992:VA-5)
7dr/14ph/2pc/fr L

ARLINGTON COUNTY

ARLINGTON

Adams,Porter & Radigan Building; see Moncure Building

Arlington Hall Station
4000 Arlington Blvd.
HABS VA-1270
12ph/15pg/2pc H

Arlington Hall Station, Building No. 125
4000 Arlington Blvd.
HABS VA-1270-I
3ph/3pg/1pc H

Arlington Hall Station, Building No. 401
4000 Arlington Blvd.
HABS VA-1270-V
20ph/8pg/2pc H

Arlington Hall Station,Building No. 100
4000 Arlington Blvd.
HABS VA-1270-B
3ph/3pg/1pc H

Arlington Hall Station,Building No. 101
4000 Arlington Blvd.
HABS VA-1270-C
5ph/3pg/1pc H

Arlington Hall Station,Building No. 102
4000 Arlington Blvd.
HABS VA-1270-D
4ph/3pg/1pc H

Arlington Hall Station,Building No. 110
4000 Arlington Blvd.
HABS VA-1270-E
4ph/3pg/1pc H

Arlington Hall Station,Building No. 111
4000 Arlington Blvd.
HABS VA-1270-F
3ph/3pg/1pc H

Arlington Hall Station,Building No. 114
4000 Arlington Blvd.
HABS VA-1270-G
3ph/3pg/1pc H

Arlington Hall Station,Building No. 115
4000 Arlington Blvd.
HABS VA-1270-H
4ph/3pg/1pc H

Arlington Hall Station,Building No. 126
4000 Arlington Blvd.
HABS VA-1270-J
4ph/3pg/1pc H

Arlington Hall Station,Building No. 127
4000 Arlington Blvd.
HABS VA-1270-K
3ph/3pg/1pc H

Arlington Hall Station,Building No. 128
4000 Arlington Blvd.
HABS VA-1270-L
3ph/3pg/1pc H

Arlington Hall Station,Building No. 300
4000 Arlington Blvd.
HABS VA-1270-M
3ph/3pg/1pc H

Arlington Hall Station,Building No. 301
4000 Arlington Blvd.
HABS VA-1270-N
3ph/3pg/1pc H

Arlington Hall Station,Building No. 305
4000 Arlington Blvd.
HABS VA-1270-P
3ph/3pg/1pc H

Arlington Hall Station,Building No. 315
4000 Arlington Blvd.
HABS VA-1270-S
3ph/3pg/1pc H

Arlington Hall Station,Building No. 316
4000 Arlington Blvd.
HABS VA-1270-T
4ph/3pg/1pc H

Arlington Hall Station,Building No. 320
4000 Arlington Blvd.
HABS VA-1270-U
3ph/3pg/1pc H

Arlington Hall Station,Building No. 420
4000 Arlington Blvd.
HABS VA-1270-W
5ph/3pg/1pc H

Arlington Hall Station,Building No. 423
4000 Arlington Blvd.
HABS VA-1270-X
3ph/3pg/1pc H

Arlington Hall Station,Building No. 500
4000 Arlington Blvd.
HABS VA-1270-Y
3ph/3pg/1pc H

Arlington Hall Station,Building No. 501
4000 Arlington Blvd.
HABS VA-1270-Z
3ph/3pg/1pc H

Arlington Hall Station,Building No. 502
4000 Arlington Blvd.
HABS VA-1270-AA
3ph/3pg/1pc H

Arlington Hall Station,Building No. 503
4000 Arlington Blvd.
HABS VA-1270-AB
3ph/3pg/1pc H

Arlington Hall Station,Building No. 504
4000 Arlington Blvd.
HABS VA-1270-AC
3ph/3pg/1pc H

Arlington Hall Station,Building No. 505
4000 Arlington Blvd.
HABS VA-1270-AD
3ph/3pg/1pc H

Arlington Hall Station,Building No. 506
HABS VA-1270-AE
3ph/3pg/1pc H

Arlington Hall Station,Building No. 507
4000 Arlington Blvd.
HABS VA-1270-AF
3ph/3pg/1pc H

Arlington Hall Station,Building No. 508
4000 Arlington Blvd.
HABS VA-1270-AG
3ph/3pg/1pc H

Arlington Hall Station,Building No. 509
4000 Arlington Blvd.
HABS VA-1270-AH
3ph/3pg/1pc H

Arlington Hall Station,Building No. 510
4000 Arlington Blvd.
HABS VA-1270-AI
3ph/3pg/1pc H

Arlington Hall Station,Building No. 511
4000 Arlington Blvd.
HABS VA-1270-AJ
3ph/3pg/1pc H

Arlington Hall Station,Building No. 512
4000 Arlington Blvd.
HABS VA-1270-AK
3ph/3pg/1pc H

Arlington Hall Station,Building No. 513
4000 Arlington Blvd.
HABS VA-1270-AL
4ph/3pg/1pc H

Arlington Hall Station,Building No. 550
4000 Arlington Blvd.
HABS VA-1270-AM
3ph/3pg/1pc H

Arlington Hall Station,Building Nos. 302-304
4000 Arlington Blvd.
HABS VA-1270-O
10ph/3pg/1pc H

Arlington Hall Station,Building Nos. 306-307
4000 Arlington Blvd.
HABS VA-1270-Q
9ph/3pg/1pc H

Arlington Hall Station,Main Building,Bldg. No. 1
4000 Arlington Blvd.
HABS VA-1270-A
37ph/9pg/3pc H

Arlington Hill Station,Building No. 314
4000 Arlington Blvd.
HABS VA-1270-R
3ph/3pg/1pc H

Arlington House (Custis-Lee Mansion; Lee,Robert E.,House; Arlington House,Robert E. Lee Memorial; Arlington National Cemetery Grounds)
HABS VA-443
HABS VA,7-ARL,1- ı1991(HABS):7
18dr/4ct/fr L

Arlington House,Robert E. Lee Memorial; see Arlington House

Arlington Memorial Bridge (Memorial Bridge)
Spanning Potomac River btwn Lin. Mem. & Arl. Cemt.
HAER DC-7
HAER 1990 (HAER):5
19ph/8pg/2pc L

Arlington Memorial Bridge: Watergate & Bridge Plz. (Watergate & Bridge Plaza)
Adjacent to Arlington Mem. Bridge & Lincoln Mem.
HAER DC-7-A
HAER 1990 (HAER):5
3ph/5pg/1pc L

Arlington National Cemetery Grounds; see Arlington House

Ball Building
1437 N. Court House Rd.
HABS VA-1272
HABS DLC/PP-1993:VA-1
5ph/8pg/1pc L

Custis-Lee Mansion; see Arlington House

Fort Myer,Building No. 42; see Fort Myer,Commissary Sergeant's Quarters

Fort Myer,Building No. 43; see Fort Myer,First Sergeant's Quarters

Fort Myer,Building No. 45; see Fort Myer,Non-Commissioned Officers Quarters

Fort Myer,Building No. 46; see Fort Myer,Non-Commissioned Officers Quarters

Fort Myer,Commissary Sergeant's Quarters (Fort Myer,Building No. 42)
Washington Ave. btwn. Johnson Lane & Custer Rd.
HABS VA-1253-A
HABS 1991(HABS)
10ph/25pg/2pc L

Fort Myer,First Sergeant's Quarters (Fort Myer,Building No. 43)
Washington Ave. btwn. Johnson Lane & Custer
HABS VA-1253-B
HABS 1991(HABS):7
6ph/4pg/1pc L

Fort Myer,Non-Commissioned Officers Quarters (Fort Myer,Building No. 45)
Wahington Ave. btwn. Johnson Lane & Custer Rd.
HABS VA-1253-C
HABS 1991(HABS):7
12ph/5pg/2pc L

Fort Myer,Non-Commissioned Officers Quarters (Fort Myer,Building No. 46)
Washington Ave. btwn. Johnson Lane & Custer Rd.
HABS VA-1253-D
HABS 1991(HABS):7
9ph/6pg/1pc L

Jesse-Hosmer Building
1419 N. Court House Rd.
HABS VA-1276
HABS DLC/PP-1993:VA-1
2ph/5pg/1pc L

Jesse,Charles,Building
1423-27 N. Court House Rd.
HABS VA-1273
HABS DLC/PP-1993:VA-1
5ph/9pg/1pc L

Lawyers' Row Block
N. Court House Rd. between 14th & 15th Sts.
HABS VA-1277
HABS DLC/PP-1993:VA-1
2ph/14pg/1pc L

Lee,Robert E.,House; see Arlington House

Memorial Bridge; see Arlington Memorial Bridge

Moncure Building (Adams,Porter & Radigan Building)
1415 N. Court House Rd.
HABS VA-1275
HABS DLC/PP-1993:VA-1
9ph/10pg/1pc L

Rucker Building
1403 N. Court House Rd.
HABS VA-1274
HABS DLC/PP-1993:VA-1
9ph/5pg/1pc L

Simmonds Building
2041 N. Fifteenth St.
HABS VA-1280
HABS DLC/PP-1993:VA-1
2ph/8pg/1pc L

Watergate & Bridge Plaza; see Arlington Memorial Bridge: Watergate & Bridge Plz.

AUGUSTA COUNTY

CRIMORA VIC.

South River Bridge; see South River Pratt Through-Truss Bridge

South River Pratt Through-Truss Bridge (South River Bridge)
State Rt. 612,spanning South River
HAER VA-19
HAER VA,8-CRIM.V,1-
2ph/1pc L

FISHERSVILLE VIC.

Tinkling Spring Church
State Rt. 608
HABS VA-717
HABS VA,8-FISH.V,1-
5dr L

FORT DEFIANCE

Church,Old Stone
U. S. Rt. 11
HABS VA-11-10
HABS VA,8-FORDEF,1-
9dr/3ph/3pg/fr L

GROTTOES VIC.

Harnsberger Octagonal Barn (Mt. Meridian Octagonal Barn)
Va. Rt. 256, W. of Intersection with Va. Rt. 865
HABS VA-1211
HABS VA,8-GROTT.V,1-
2ph/1pc L

Mt. Meridian Octagonal Barn; see Harnsberger Octagonal Barn

STAUNTON VIC.

Folly Farm
Folly Mills Creek
HABS VA-11-8
HABS VA,8-STAU.V,1-
10dr/7ph/3pg/fr L

WAYNESBORO VIC.

Blue Ridge (C&O) Railroad,Culvert (Chesapeake & Ohio Railroad,Culvert)
S. of U. S. Rt. 250,2.2 miles SE of Waynesboro
HAER VA-12
HAER VA,8-WANBO.V,1-
1ph/1pg L

Chesapeake & Ohio Railroad,Culvert; see Blue Ridge (C&O) Railroad,Culvert

Rockfish Service Station
Virginia Rt. 865
HABS VA-962
HABS VA,8-WANBO.V,2-
6dr/6ph L

WEYERS CAVE VIC.

Middle River Bridge; see Middle River Pratt Through-Truss Bridge

Middle River Pratt Through-Truss Bridge (Middle River Bridge)
State Rt. 256,spanning Middle River
HAER VA-26
HAER VA,WEYCA.V,1-
1ph/1pc L

BATH COUNTY

BACOVA VIC.

"Buckhorn Manor",Kitchen (McClintic House,Kitchen)
State Rt. 603
HABS VA-966-A
HABS VA,9-BACO.V,1A-
1dr/4ph/fr L

Buckhorn Manor (McClintic House)
State Rt. 603
HABS VA-966
HABS VA,9-BACO.V,1-
10dr/20ph/8pg/fr L

Buckhorn Manor,Housekeeping Cabin; see Buckhorn Manor,Log Dwelling

Buckhorn Manor,Log Dwelling (Buckhorn Manor,Housekeeping Cabin; McClintic House,Log Dwelling; McClintic House,Housekeeping Cabin)
State Rt. 603
HABS VA-966-C
HABS VA,9-BACO.V,1C-
3ph L

Buckhorn Manor,Log Outbuilding (McClintic House,Log Outbuilding)
State Rt. 603
HABS VA-966-D
HABS VA,9-BACO.V,1D-
1ph L

Buckhorn Manor,Springhouse (McClintic House,Springhouse)
State Rt. 603
HABS VA-966-B
HABS VA,9-BACO.V,1B-
1dr/3ph/fr L

McClintic House; see Buckhorn Manor

McClintic House,Housekeeping Cabin; see Buckhorn Manor,Log Dwelling

McClintic House,Kitchen; see "Buckhorn Manor",Kitchen

McClintic House,Log Dwelling; see Buckhorn Manor,Log Dwelling

McClintic House,Log Outbuilding; see Buckhorn Manor,Log Outbuilding

McClintic House,Springhouse; see Buckhorn Manor,Springhouse

BEDFORD (CITY)

Roaring Run Bowstring Truss Bridge
Spanning Roaring Run, State Rt. 657
HAER VA-7
HAER VA,10-BED.V,2-
3dr/6ph/5pg/1pc/fr L

BEDFORD COUNTY

FOREST VIC.

Poplar Forest
State Rt. 661
HABS VA-303
HABS VA,10-BED.V,1-ı87(HABS):48°
22dr/74ph/4pg/4pc/15ct/fr L

Poplar Forest, Barns
State Rte. 661
HABS VA-303-D
HABS VA,10-BED.V,1D-
7ph/1pc L

Poplar Forest, Dairy
State Rte. 661
HABS VA-303-B
HABS VA,10-BED.V,1B-
5ph/1pc/4ct L

Poplar Forest, Privies
State Rte. 661
HABS VA-303-E
HABS VA,10-BED.V,1E-
16ph/1pc/3ct L

Poplar Forest, Slave Quarters (Poplar Forest, Tenant Houses)
State Rte. 661
HABS VA-303-C
HABS VA,10-BED.V,1C-
3dr/17ph/1pc/1ct/fr L

Poplar Forest, Summer Kitchen
State Rte. 661
HABS VA-303-A
HABS VA,10-BED.V,1A-
16ph/2pc L

Poplar Forest, Tenant Houses; see Poplar Forest, Slave Quarters

BOTETOURT COUNTY

BUCHANAN

James River Suspension Bridge
Spanning James River,Rt. 11
HAER VA-17
HAER VA,12-BUCH,1-
9ph L

CAMPBELL COUNTY

GLADYS VIC.

Marysville Covered Bridge
Seneca Creek,W. of SR 633,4.8 mi. SW of Gladys
HAER VA-20
HAER VA,16-GLAD.V,4-
1ph/1pg/1pc L

LONG ISLAND VIC.

Green Hill Plantation & Main House
State Rt. 728
HABS VA-419
HABS VA,16-LONI.V,1-
12ph/6pg L

Green Hill Plantation,Brick Dependency
State Rt. 728
HABS VA-604
HABS VA,16-LONI.V,I-
2ph/2pg L

Green Hill Plantation,Cobblestone Walks & Drives
State Rt. 728
HABS VA-615
HABS VA,16-LONI.V,1R-
1ph/1pg L

Green Hill Plantation,Duck House
State Rt. 728
HABS VA-608
HABS VA,16-LONI.V,1L-
1ph/2pg L

Green Hill Plantation,Frame Barn
State Rt. 728
HABS VA-610
HABS VA,16-LONI.V,1M-
1ph/2pg L

Green Hill Plantation,Frame Dependency
State Rt. 728
HABS VA-602
HABS VA,16-LONI.V,1G-
1ph/1pg L

Green Hill Plantation,Gateposts
State Rt. 728
HABS VA-616
HABS VA,16-LONI.V,1S-
1ph/1pg L

Green Hill Plantation,Granary
State Rt. 728
HABS VA-613
HABS VA,16-LONI.V,1F-
3ph/3pg L

Green Hill Plantation,Icehouse
State Rt. 728
HABS VA-603
HABS VA,16-LONI.V,1H-
2ph/1pg L

Green Hill Plantation,Kitchen
State Rt. 728
HABS VA-606
HABS VA,16-LONI.V,1B-
3ph/3pg L

Green Hill Plantation,Laundry
State Rt. 728
HABS VA-609
HABS VA,16-LONI.V,1C-
4ph/3pg L

Green Hill Plantation,Log Barn
State Rt. 728
HABS VA-611
HABS VA,16-LONI.V,1N-
1ph/2pg L

Green Hill Plantation,Log Quarters (Detail)
HABS VA-419-A
HABS VA,16-LONI.V,1T-
1ph L

Green Hill Plantation,Slave Auction Block
State Rt. 728
HABS VA-605
HABS VA,16-LONI.V,1J-
2ph/1pg L

Green Hill Plantation,Slave Quarters
State Rt. 728
HABS VA-607
HABS VA,16-LONI.V,1K-
1ph/2pg L

Green Hill Plantation,Stable (Ruins)
State Rt. 728
HABS VA-612
HABS VA,16-LONI.V,1P-
1ph/1pg L

Green Hill Plantation,Tobacco Barn
State Rt. 728
HABS VA-614
HABS VA,16-LONI.V,1D-
3ph/3pg L

LYNCHBURG VIC.

Johnson,Christopher,Cottage
State Rt. 126
HABS VA-11-11
HABS VA,16-LYNBU.V,1-
3dr/3ph/3pg/fr L

RUSTBURG VIC.

White Hall
State Rt. 637
HABS VA-66
HABS VA,16-RUST.V,1-
4ph/1pg L

CAROLINE COUNTY

BOWLING GREEN

Caroline County Courthouse
U. S. Rt. 301 & Courthouse Ln.
HABS VA-718
HABS VA,17-BOGR,2-
3ph L

Mansion,The Old
State Rt. 2 Vic.
HABS VA-128
HABS VA,17-BOGR,1-
16dr/8ph/7pg/fr L

BOWLING GREEN VIC.

Mulberry Place
Tanyard Swamp Vic.
HABS VA-719
HABS VA,17-BOGR.V,1-
2ph L

Oak Ridge
Elliot's Pond Vic.
HABS VA-720
HABS VA,17-BOGR.V,2-
5ph L

PORT ROYAL

Roy House
HABS VA-721
HABS VA,17-PORO,
4ph L

St. Peter's Episcopal Church & Bell Tower
Water St. (State Rt. 1006)
HABS VA-261
HABS VA,17-PORO,7-
2ph L

St. Peter's Episcopal Church,Rectory
Water St. (State Rt. 1006)
HABS VA-260
HABS VA,17-PORO,8-
1ph L

PORT ROYAL VIC.

Camden
Rappahannock River
HABS VA-184
HABS VA,17-PORO.V,2-
38ph/2pg/2pc L

Catlett House; see Gaymont

Gaymont (Rose Hill; Catlett House)
U. S. Rt. 17 Vic.
HABS VA-306
HABS VA,17-PORO.V,3-
20ph/1pg L

Rose Hill; see Gaymont

WOODFORD

Flippo House (Sycamore Tavern,Old)
HABS VA-344
HABS VA,17-WODF,1-
6ph/1pg L

Sycamore Tavern,Old; see Flippo House

CHARLES CITY COUNTY

CHARLES CITY

Charles City County Courthouse
State Rt. 5
HABS VA-60
HABS VA,19-CHARC,1-
2ph/1pg L

CHARLES CITY VIC.

Berkeley (Harrison Family Home)
State Rt. 5 Vic.
HABS VA-363
HABS VA,19-CHARC.V,4-
16dr/30ph/2pg/11ct/fr L

Farmington
Morris Creek Vic.
HABS VA-95
HABS VA,19-CHARC.V,2-
11dr/1pc/fr L

Glebe House
State Rt. 615 Vic.
HABS VA-723
HABS VA,19-CHARC,2-
3ph L

Greenway (Marlee; Tyler,President John,Birthplace)
State Rt. 5 Vic.
HABS VA-11-23
HABS VA,19-CHARC.V,1-
17dr/12ph/8pg/4ct/fr L

Harrison Family Home; see Berkeley

Indian Field
State Rt. 5
HABS VA-376
HABS VA,19- ,9-
1ph L

Lower Weyanoke; see Weyanoke

Marlee; see Greenway

Sherwood Forest (Tyler,John,House)
State Rt. 5 Vic.
HABS VA-722
HABS VA,19-CHARC.V,3-
30ph/1pg L

Sherwood Forest,Dairy
(Tyler,John,House,Dairy)
State Rt. 5 Vic.
HABS VA-722-A
HABS VA,19-CHARC.V,3A-
2ph L

Sherwood Forest,Necessary
(Tyler,John,House,Necessary)
State Rt. 5 Vic.
HABS VA-722-B
HABS VA,19-CHARC.V,3B-
L

Sherwood Forest,Smokehouse
(Tyler,John,House,Smokehouse)
State Rt. 5 Vic.
HABS VA-722-C
HABS VA,19-CHARC.V,3C-
2ph L

Sherwood Forest,Wine House
(Tyler,John,House,Wine House)
State Rt. 5 Vic.
HABS VA-722-D
HABS VA,19-CHARC.V,3D-
1ph L

Shirley
State Rt. 608 Vic.
HABS VA-388
HABS VA,19-SHIR,1-
21ph/3pg/2pc L

Shirley,Brick Outbuilding
State Rt. 608 Vic.
HABS VA-388-C
HABS VA,19-SHIR,1C-
1ph L

Shirley,Dependency
State Rt. 608 Vic.
HABS VA-388-A
HABS VA,19-SHIR,1-2 and 1-3
2ph L

Shirley,Log Barn
State Rt. 608 Vic.
HABS VA-388-E
HABS VA,19-SHIR,1E-
1ph L

Shirley,Log Shed
State Rt. 608 Vic.
HABS VA-388-B
HABS VA,19-SHIR,1B-
1ph L

Shirley,Pigeon House
State Rt. 608 Vic.
HABS VA-388-G
HABS VA,19-SHIR,1G-
1ph L

Shirley,Quarters
State Rt. 608 Vic.
HABS VA-388-I
HABS VA,19-SHIR,1A-
1ph L

Shirley,Smokehouse
State Rt. 608 Vic.
HABS VA-388-F
HABS VA,19-SHIR,1F-
1ph L

Shirley,Stable
State Rt. 608 Vic.
HABS VA-388-D
HABS VA,19-SHIR,1D-
1ph L

Shirley,Stable
State Rt. 608 Vic.
HABS VA-388-H
HABS VA,19-SHIR,1H-
2ph L

Tyler,John,House; see Sherwood Forest

Tyler,John,House,Dairy; see Sherwood Forest,Dairy

Tyler,John,House,Necessary; see Sherwood Forest,Necessary

Tyler,John,House,Smokehouse; see Sherwood Forest,Smokehouse

Tyler,John,House,Wine House; see Sherwood Forest,Wine House

Tyler,President John,Birthplace; see Greenway

Westover
State Rt. 633
HABS VA-402
HABS VA,19-WEST,1-
33dr/75ph/1pg/5pc/9ct/fr L

Westover,Kitchen Building
State Rt. 633
HABS VA-402-A
HABS VA,19-WEST,1B-
2ph/1pc L

Westover,Office Building
State Rt. 633
HABS VA-402-B
HABS VA,19-WEST,1C-
3ph/1pc L

Westover,Tool Shed
State Rt. 633
HABS VA-402-C
HABS VA,19-WEST,1D-
2ph/1pc L

Weyanoke (Lower Weyanoke)
Weyanoke Rd.
HABS VA-290
HABS VA,19-WEY,1-
2ph/2pg L

TETTINGTON VIC.

Rowe,The
James River Vic.
HABS VA-142
HABS VA,19-TET.V,1-
2ph/1pg L

CHARLOTTE COUNTY

BROOKNEAL VIC.

National Memorial to Patrick Henry; see Red Hill

Patrick Henry National Memorial; see Red Hill,Dwelling

Patrick Henry National Memorial; see Red Hill,Kitchen

Patrick Henry National Memorial; see Red Hill,Law Office

Patrick Henry National Memorial; see Red Hill,Privy

Patrick Henry National Memorial; see Red Hill,Smokehouse

Patrick Henry National Memorial; see Red Hill,Stables and Carriage House

Red Hill (National Memorial to Patrick Henry)
7 mi. SW of Brookneal,VA, south of State Rt. 619
HABS VA-1034
HABS 1991(HABS):7
66pg L

Red Hill,Dwelling (Patrick Henry National Memorial)
State Rt. 619
HABS VA-1034-B
HABS 1991(HABS):7
15pg L

Red Hill,Kitchen (Patrick Henry National Memorial)
State Rt. 619
HABS VA-1034-C
HABS 1991(HABS):7
4pg L

Red Hill,Law Office (Patrick Henry National Memorial)
State Rt. 619
HABS VA-1034-A
HABS VA,20-BROOK,1A- ι1991(HABS):7°
1ph/6pg/1pc L

Red Hill,Privy (Patrick Henry National Memorial)
State Rt. 619
HABS VA-1034-E
HABS 1991(HABS):7
3pg L

Red Hill,Slave Cabin
State Rt. 619,Brookneal Vic.
HABS VA-1034-G
HABS 1991(HABS):7
4pg L

Red Hill,Smokehouse (Patrick Henry National Memorial)
State Rt. 619
HABS VA-1034-D
HABS 1991(HABS):7
3pg L

Red Hill,Stables and Carriage House (Patrick Henry National Memorial)
State Rt. 619
HABS VA-1034-F
HABS 1991(HABS):7
4pg L

Staunton Hill
State Rt. 619
HABS VA-1020
HABS VA,20-BROOK.V,1-
12dr L

CHARLOTTESVILLE (CITY)

Albemarle County Courthouse
Court Square
HABS VA-976
HABS VA,2-CHAR,2-
6dr/14pg/fr L

Bailey-Parrot Cottage; see Fowler House

Belmont; see Winn,John, House

Buckingham Palace
Carr's Hill,University of Virginia Campus
HABS VA-979
HABS VA,2-CHAR,3A-
3dr/9pg/fr L

Calvary Baptist Church; see Woolen Mills Chapel

Carter-Gilmer House
E. Jefferson St. at N. Eighth St.
HABS VA-1079
HABS VA,2-CHAR,7-
9dr/4pg/fr L

1 Cottage Lane (House)
HABS VA-1005
HABS VA,2-CHAR,4A-
7dr/fr L

220 Court Square (House)
Sixth St. ,NE
HABS VA-1199
HABS VA,2-CHAR,5-
5dr/7pg/fr L

117 Cream Street (House)
HABS VA-1007
HABS VA,2-CHAR,16-
5dr/8pg/fr L

Davis,John A.G.,House (Farm,The)
1201 Jefferson St.
HABS VA-1335
9dr H

1901 East Market Street (House)
HABS VA-989
HABS VA,2-CHAR,13B-
6dr/fr L

Farm,The; see Davis,John A.G.,House

Fowler House (Bailey-Parrot Cottage)
204 Ridge St.
HABS VA-1072
HABS VA,2-CHAR,14-
7dr/8pg/1pc/fr L

Fry's Spring Filling Station
2115 Jefferson Park Ave.
HABS VA-1021
HABS VA,2-CHAR,17-
4dr/7pg/fr L

Hughes House
307 Market St.
HABS VA-1338
9dr H

Inge's Store (Pitt,Johnson W. ,House)
331-333 Main St.
HABS VA-1015
HABS VA,2-CHAR,15-
8dr/17pg/fr L

Locust Grove Kitchen
810 Locust Ave.
HABS VA-1022
HABS VA,2-CHAR,19A-
6dr/6pg/fr L

Massie-Wills House
Fourth St.,NE
HABS VA-1337
5dr H

Monroe Hill Law Office
McCormick Rd. ,University of Virginia
HABS VA-1027
HABS VA,2-CHAR,8A-
4dr/6pg/fr L

Norris-McCue Building
415 E. Jefferson St.
HABS VA-1003
HABS VA,2-CHAR,6-
9dr/8pg/fr L

Norris-Preston Cottage
611 Preston Pl.
HABS VA-1075
HABS VA,2-CHAR,18-
5dr/14pg/fr L

Pitt,Johnson W. ,House; see Inge's Store

Price-Poore House
427 Park St.
HABS VA-1334
7dr H

104 Twelfth Street (Outbuilding)
HABS VA-1006
HABS VA,2-CHAR,12A-
6dr/fr L

Union Chapel; see Woolen Mills Chapel

University of Virginia
University Ave. & Rugby Rd.
HABS VA-193
HABS VA,2-CHAR,1-
1ph L

University of Virginia, Hotel E
West Range
HABS VA-193-M
HABS VA,2-CHAR,1Q-
8dr/10pg/fr L

University of Virginia, Pavilion VIII
East Lawn
HABS VA-193-L
HABS VA,2-CHAR,1L-
9dr/13pg/fr L

University of Virginia,Hotel A
West Range
HABS VA-193-N
HABS 1991(HABS):7
10dr/fr L

University of Virginia,Hotel C
West Range,University of Virginia
HABS VA-193-J
HABS VA,2-CHAR,1P-
8dr/fr L

University of Virginia,Pavilion I
W. Lawn
HABS VA-193-P
HABS 1991(HABS):7
12dr/fr L

University of Virginia,Pavilion II
East Lawn,University of Virginia
HABS VA-193-H
HABS VA,2-CHAR,1B-
6dr/30pg/fr L

University of Virginia,Pavilion III
West Lawn, University of Virginia Campus
HABS VA-193-C
HABS VA,2-CHAR,1D-
10dr/44pg/fr L

University of Virginia,Pavilion IV
East Lawn,University of Virginia campus
HABS VA-193-K
HABS VA,2-CHAR,1J-
10dr/fr L

University of Virginia,Pavilion IX
West Lawn,University of Virginia
HABS VA-193-G
HABS VA,2-CHAR,1G-;1991(HABS):7
17dr/12pg/fr L

University of Virginia,Pavilion VI
E. Lawn
HABS VA-193-O
HABS 1991(HABS):7
12dr/fr L

University of Virginia,Pavilion VII
West Lawn,University of Virginia Campus
HABS VA-193-F
HABS VA,2-CHAR,1F-
5dr/5pg/fr L

University of Virginia,Pavilion X
East Lawn,University of Virginia
HABS VA-193-E
HABS VA,2-CHAR,1M-
8dr/15pg/fr L

University of Virginia,Pavilions and Hotels
University Ave. & Rugby Rd.
HABS VA-193-B
HABS VA,2-CHAR,1B-
1dr/4ph L H

University of Virginia,Rotunda
University Ave. & Rugby Rd.
HABS VA-193-A
HABS VA,2-CHAR,1A-
1dr/3ph L H

University of Virginia,Serpentine Wall
University Ave. & Rugby Rd.
HABS VA-193-D
HABS VA,2-CHAR,1H-
4ph L

University of Virginia,The Crackerbox
East Range Drive
HABS VA-193-I
HABS VA,2-CHAR,1U-
3dr/6pg/fr L

Vowles Townhouses
1111-1113 W. Main St.
HABS VA-1336
H

Watson,Judge,House
713 Park St.
HABS VA-1076
HABS VA,2-CHAR,9-
8dr/fr L

1213 West Main Street (House)
HABS VA-1205
HABS VA,2-CHAR,10-
5dr/fr L

Winn,John, House (Belmont)
759 Belmont Avenue
HABS VA-1247
HABS VA,2-CHAR,20-
12dr/13pg/fr L

Woolen Mills Chapel (Union Chapel; Calvary Baptist Church)
1819 E. Market St.
HABS VA-1068
HABS VA,2-CHAR,13A-
6dr/7pg/fr L

CHESAPEAKE (CITY)

Powers House
U. S. Rt. 17
HABS VA-228
HABS VA,65-HICK.V,2-
4ph L

House (Ruins)
HABS VA-249
HABS VA,65-SABRI.V,1-
1ph L

CHESTERFIELD COUNTY

RICHMOND VIC.

Ampthill
(moved to VA,Richmond)
HABS VA-159
HABS VA,21- ,1-
1dr/11ph/2pg L

Bellona Arsenal,Workshops
State Rt. 673 Vic.
HABS VA-139
HABS VA,21- ,3-
10ph/4pg L

SKINQUARTER

Skinquarter House
U. S. Rt. 360
HABS VA-724
HABS VA,21-SKI,1-
1ph L

SOUTH RICHMOND

Dunlop Mills
HABS VA-925
HABS VA,21-RICHS,1-
2ph L

CLARKE COUNTY

BERRYVILLE VIC.

Clifton
State Rt. 610 Vic.
HABS VA-725
HABS VA,22-GAYLO.V,1-
3ph L

BOYCE

Summerville
Page Run
HABS VA-180
HABS VA,22-BOYC.V,1-
3dr/1ph/1pg/fr L

BOYCE VIC.

Annefield
State Rt. 633 Vic.
HABS VA-256
HABS VA,22-BERVI.V,1-
4ph/1pg L

Lee Headquarters; see Saratoga,Main House & Outbuildings

Saratoga,Main House & Outbuildings
(Lee Headquarters)
Roseville Run
HABS VA-246
HABS VA,22-BOYC.V,2-
3ph/1pg L

MILLWOOD

Burwell Mill (Millwood Mill)
State Rt. 723
HABS VA-354
HABS VA,22-MILWO,1-
1ph L

Carter Hall
State Rt. 723 Vic.
HABS VA-358
HABS VA,22-MILWO,3-
2ph/1pg L

Millwood Mill; see Burwell Mill

MILLWOOD VIC.

Chapel,Old
HABS VA-352
HABS VA,22-MILWO.V,1-
1ph/1pg L

WHITE POST VIC.

Greenway Court
HABS VA-108
HABS VA,22-WHIPO.V,1-
4dr/17ph/2pg L

Greenway Court,Estate Office
State Rt. 658 Vic.
HABS VA-332
HABS VA,22-WHIPO.V,1-
7ph/1pg L

Greenway Court,Outbuilding
State Rt. 658 Vic.
HABS VA-108-A
HABS VA,22-WHIPO.V,1C-
4ph L

Greenway Court,Powder House
State Rt. 658 Vic.
HABS VA-108-B
HABS VA,22-WHIPO.V,1B-
4dr/6ph/1pg L

Tuleyries,The
State Rt. 628 Vic.
HABS VA-353
HABS VA,22-MILWO.V,2-
1ph/1pg L

COLONIAL HEIGHTS (CITY)

Archer's Hill; see Oak Hill

Dunn Hill; see Oak Hill

Hector's Hill; see Oak Hill

Oak Hill (Dunn Hill; Hector's Hill; Archer's Hill)
151 Carroll Ave.
HABS VA-135
HABS VA,21- ,2-
6ph/1pg L

Violet Bank
U. S. Rt. 1 Vic.
HABS VA-322
HABS VA,21- ,4-
8ph/1pg L

CULPEPER COUNTY

BRANDY STATION VIC.

Little Fork Church
State Rts. 624 & 627
HABS VA-147
HABS VA,24-BRAND.V,1-
3dr L

JEFFERSONTON VIC.

Greenfield
State Rt. 621 Vic.
HABS VA-433
HABS VA,24-CUL.V,1-
1ph L

CUMBERLAND COUNTY

CA IRA

Grace Episcopal Church
State Rt. 632
HABS VA-970
HABS VA,25-CAIR,1-
6dr/5pg/fr L

CARTERSVILLE VIC.

Cartersville Bridge
Rt. 25,spanning James River
HAER VA-11
HAER VA,25-CART.V,1-
7ph/5pg/2pc/1ct/fr L

CUMBERLAND

Cumberland County Courthouse
U. S. Rt. 60
HABS VA-192
HABS VA,25-CUMB,1-
3ph/1pg L

Cumberland County Courthouse,Clerk's Office
U. S. Rt. 60
HABS VA-192-A
HABS VA,25-CUMB,1A-
1ph L

CUMBERLAND VIC.

Covered Bridge (Trent's Bridge)
Spanning Willis River
HABS VA-11-13
HABS VA,25-CUMB.V,1-
2dr/2ph/1pg/fr L

Trent's Bridge; see Covered Bridge

DINWIDDIE COUNTY

DINWIDDIE VIC.

Burnt Quarter
State Rt. 613 Vic.
HABS VA-386
HABS VA,27- ,2-
1ph/1pg L

Kingston
State Rt. 619 Vic.
HABS VA-384
HABS VA,27- ,1-
2ph/1pg L

Plank House
State Rt. 647
HABS VA-314
HABS VA,27-DIN,1-
1ph/1pg L

FORD VIC.

Roseberry,House & Outbuildings
State Rt. 640 & U. S. Rt. 460 Vic.
HABS VA-727
HABS VA,27-FORD.V,1-
2ph L

HEBRON VIC.

Harris House
U. S. Rt. 460
HABS VA-726
HABS VA,27-HEB.V,1-
1ph L

PETERSBURG VIC.

Mayfield
U. S. Rt. 460 (moved from original location)
HABS VA-958
HABS VA,27-PET.V,2-
10dr L

Wales
U. S. Rt. 460 Vic.
HABS VA-152
HABS VA,27-PET.V,1-
17dr/26ph/2pg/fr L

ESSEX COUNTY

CARET VIC.

Blandfield
U. S. Rt. 17 & State Rt. 624
HABS VA-1198
HABS VA,29-CAR.V,1-
21dr/6pc/fr L

Blandfield,Smokehouse
HABS VA-1198-A
HABS VA,29-CAR.V,1A-
3ph/1pc/fr L

CENTER CROSS VIC.

Bowlers,Frame House & Kitchen
State Rt. 684
HABS VA-728
HABS VA,29-BOWL,1-
5ph L

Mount Verde (Omnium Hill)
State Rt. 660
HABS VA-729
HABS VA,29-DUNV.V,3-
2ph L

Omnium Hill; see Mount Verde

CHAMPLAIN VIC.

Cloverfield; see St. Anne's Parish Glebe House

Fonthill
State Rt. 631 Vic.
HABS VA-330
HABS VA,29-LLOYD.V,1-
1ph/1pg L

Glebe House; see St. Anne's Parish Glebe House

St. Anne's Parish Glebe House
(Cloverfield; Glebe House)
U.S. Rt. 17 near Rt. 632
HABS VA-232
HABS VA,29-CHAMP.V,1-
5dr/2ph/1pg L

DUNNSVILLE VIC.

Bathurst
Piscataway Creek
HABS VA-129
HABS VA,29-DUNV.V,1-
11dr/7ph/6pg/fr L

Ben Lomond
U. S. Rt. 17 Vic.
HABS VA-730
HABS VA,29-DUNV.V,2-
2ph L

LORETTO VIC.

Brooke's Bank
U. S. Rt. 17 Vic.
HABS VA-731
HABS VA,29-LOR.V,3-
15dr L

Elmwood
State Rt. 640 Vic.
HABS VA-323
HABS VA,29-LOR.V,2-
18ph/3pg L

Kinloch
State Rt. 41 Vic.
HABS VA-387
HABS VA,29-SUP.V,1-
2ph/1pg L

Vauter's Episcopal Church
U. S. Rt. 17
HABS VA-410
HABS VA,29-LOR.V,1-
1ph/1pg L

PAUL'S CROSSROADS

Woodlawn
U. S. Rt. 360
HABS VA-991
HABS VA,29-PAUL,1-
13dr/17pg/fr L

TAPPAHANNOCK

Customs House,Old
109 Prince St.
HABS VA-499
HABS VA,29-TAP,8-
1ph L

Debtor's Prison; see Lawyer's Office,Old

Emerson's Ordinary,House No. 1
314 Water Ln.
HABS VA-498
HABS VA,29-TAP,5-
1ph L

Emerson's Ordinary,House No. 2
(Henly House)
314 Water Ln.
HABS VA-573
HABS VA,29-TAP,6-
1ph L

Henly House; see Emerson's Ordinary,House No. 2

Lawyer's Office,Old (Debtor's Prison)
321 Prince St.
HABS VA-500
HABS VA,29-TAP,3-
1ph L

Ritchie House
227 Prince St.
HABS VA-501
HABS VA,29-TAP,7-
4dr/1ph L

FAIRFAX (CITY)

Earp's Ordinary
Main St.
HABS VA-963
HABS VA,30-FAIRF,2-
3dr/fr L

C & O Canal National Historical Park; see Potowmack Company:Great Falls Canal:Lock No. 1

C & O Canal National Historical Park; see Potowmack Company:Great Falls Canal:Lock No. 2

C & O Canal National Historical Park; see Potowmack Company:Great Falls Canal:Locks No.3,4,5

Potowmack Company:Great Falls Canal:Lock No. 1 (C & O Canal National Historical Park)
HAER VA-13-A
HAER VA,30-GREFA,1A-
1dr/14ph L

Potowmack Company:Great Falls Canal:Lock No. 2 (C & O Canal National Historical Park)
HAER VA-13-B
HAER VA,30-GREFA,1B-
1dr/11ph L

Potowmack Company:Great Falls Canal:Locks No.3,4,5 (C & O Canal National Historical Park)
HAER VA-13-C
HAER VA,30-GREFA,1C-
4ph L

FAIRFAX COUNTY

ACCOTINK VIC.

Belvoir (Fairfax House)
HABS VA-179
HABS VA,30-ACO.V,1-
1dr/1ph L

Fairfax House; see Belvoir

ALEXANDRIA VIC.

Alexandria Avenue Bridge; see Mount Vernon Memorial Hwy:Alexandria Ave. Bridge

Hunting Creek Bridge; see Mount Vernon Memorial Hwy:Hunting Creek Bridge

Mount Vernon Memorial Hwy:Alexandria Ave. Bridge (Alexandria Avenue Bridge; Wellington Underpass)
Mount Vernon Memorial Hwy:3.5 Miles South of I-95
HAER VA-42-B
HAER 1989(HAER):22
4ph/4pg/1pc L

Mount Vernon Memorial Hwy:Hunting Creek Bridge (Hunting Creek Bridge)
.3 Miles South of I-95
HAER VA-42-A
HAER 1989(HAER):22
3ph/5pg/1pc L

Wellington Underpass; see Mount Vernon Memorial Hwy:Alexandria Ave. Bridge

ANNANDALE

Ossian Hall
5001 Regina Dr.
HABS VA-598
HABS VA,30-ANDA,1-
11dr/11ph L

ANNANDALE VIC.

Green Spring Farm (Moss House)
4601 Green Spring Rd.
HABS VA-277
HABS VA,30-ANDA.V,1-
2ph L

Moss House; see Green Spring Farm

BUSH HILL

Bush Hill (Gunnell House)
HABS VA-507
HABS VA,30-BUSHI,1-
2ph L

Gunnell House; see Bush Hill

CENTREVILLE

Jameson,Malcom,House (Mount Gilead)
5634 Mt. Gilead Rd.
HABS VA-280
HABS VA,30-CENT,1-
1ph L

Mount Gilead; see Jameson,Malcom,House

Newgate Tavern (Spread Eagle Tavern)
HABS VA-1038
HABS VA,30-CENT,2-
1ph L

Plank Meat House
HABS VA-282
HABS VA,30-CENT.V,1-
1ph L

Spread Eagle Tavern; see Newgate Tavern

CHANTILLY VIC.

Leeton
4619 Centreville Rd.
HABS VA-599
HABS VA,30-CHANT.V,2-
2ph/2pg L

Sully (Sully Plantation)
3601 Sully Rd.
HABS VA-250
HABS VA,30-CHANT.V,1-
17dr/46ph/7pg/fr L

Sully Plantation; see Sully

COLCHESTER

Metzer House
HABS VA-580
HABS VA,30-COLCH,2-
2ph/1pg L

FAIRFAX VIC.

Hope Park
11807 Pope's Head Rd.
HABS VA-107
HABS VA,30-FAIRF.V,1-
6dr/9ph/fr L

Hope Park Mill; see Piney Branch Water Mill

House,Stone (Innisfail)
11800 Fairfax Station Rd.
HABS VA-279
HABS VA,30-FAIRF.V,2-
1ph L

Innisfail; see House,Stone

Piney Branch Water Mill (Robey's Mill; Hope Park Mill)
1212 Pope's Head Rd.
HABS VA-741
HABS VA,30-FAIR,1-
5dr/3ph L

Robey's Mill; see Piney Branch Water Mill

FALLS CHURCH VIC.

Collier,Mr. & Mrs. Charles,House (Reno,Mr. & Mrs. William Lawson,House)
6080 Leesburg Pike
HABS VA-1084
HABS VA,30-FALCH.V,3-
23ph/1pg/2pc/5ct L

Dulin House
Graham Rd.
HABS VA-278
HABS VA,30-FALCH.V,1-
6ph L

Reno,Mr. & Mrs. William Lawson,House; see Collier,Mr. & Mrs. Charles,House

GREAT FALLS

C & O Canal National Historical Park; see Potowmack Company:Great Falls Canal & Locks

Potomac Canal; see Potowmack Company:Great Falls Canal & Locks

Potowmack Canal; see Potowmack Company:Great Falls Canal & Locks

Potowmack Company:Great Falls Canal & Locks (Potomac Canal; Potowmack Canal; C & O Canal National Historical Park)
HAER VA-13
HAER VA,30-GREFA,1-
2dr/5ph/44pg/6pc/fr L

GREAT FALLS VIC.

Colvin Run Mill
10017 Colvin Run Rd.
HABS VA-502
HABS VA,30-COLV,1-
2ph L

HERNDON VIC.

Dranesville Tavern; see Tavern,Old

Tavern,Old (Dranesville Tavern)
11919 Leesburg Pike (moved from orig. location)
HABS VA-503
HABS VA,30-DRANV,1-ı83(HABS):125°
8dr/1ph L

LORTON

Arch Hall; see Lewis,Lawrence,House

Lewis,Lawrence,House (Arch Hall)
11701 River Dr. (moved from VA,Alexandria)
HABS VA-109
HABS VA,7-ALEX,52-
11dr/7ph/1pg L

LORTON VIC.

Belmont; see Washington,Edward,House

Cocke-Washington House; see Washington,Edward,House

Colchester Inn (Fairfax Arms Tavern)
10712 Old Colchester Rd.
HABS VA-413
HABS VA,30-COLCH,1-
7ph/1pg L

Fairfax Arms Tavern; see Colchester Inn

Gunston Hall
10709 Gunston Rd.
HABS VA-141
HABS VA,30-LORT,1-
30dr/71ph/52pg/3pc/9ct/fr L

Pohick Church
9301 Richmond Hwy.
HABS VA-190
HABS VA,30-POHI,1-
4ph/3pg L

Washington,Edward,House (Belmont; Cocke-Washington House)
10913 Belmont Blvd.
HABS VA-578
HABS VA,30-COLCH.V,1-
8ph/2pg L

MANASSAS VIC.

Groveton Monument (Manassas National Battlefield Park)
HABS VA-1039-B
HABS VA,30-MAN.V,1B-
1dr L

Hill,Henry,Monument (Manassas National Battlefield Park)
HABS VA-1039-A
HABS VA,30-MAN.V,1A-
1dr L

Manassas National Battlefield Park; see Groveton Monument

Manassas National Battlefield Park; see Hill,Henry,Monument

Manassas National Battlefield Park; see Monuments

Monuments (Manassas National Battlefield Park)
HABS VA-1039
HABS VA,30-MAN.V,1-
1dr/1pc L

MCLEAN VIC.

Maplewood (Villa Nuova)
7676 Old Springhouse Rd.
HABS VA-739
HABS VA,30-MCLA.V,1-
7ph/1pg L

Maplewood,Springhouse (Villa Nuova,Springhouse)
7676 Old Springhouse Rd.
HABS VA-739-A
HABS VA,30-MCLA.V,1A-
2ph L

Villa Nuova; see Maplewood

Villa Nuova,Springhouse; see Maplewood,Springhouse

MOUNT VERNON

George Washington Memorial Parkway; see Mount Vernon Memorial Highway

Mount Vernon
Mt. Vernon Memorial Hwy.
HABS VA-505
HABS VA,30- ,2-
8ph/2pg L

Mount Vernon Memorial Highway (George Washington Memorial Parkway)
Parallels Potomac River from Mount Vernon to D. C.
HAER VA-42
HAER VA,30- ,6-ı1989(HAER):22°
8pg L

Mount Vernon,Barn
Mount Vernon Memorial Hwy.
HABS VA-505-C
HABS VA,30- ,2C-
1ph L

Mount Vernon,Butler's House
Mount Vernon Memorial Hwy.
HABS VA-505-M
HABS VA,30- ,2M-
1ph L

Mount Vernon,Smoke House
Mount Vernon Memorial Hwy.
HABS VA-505-D
HABS VA,30- ,2D-
1ph L

Mount Vernon,Washington Tomb
Mount Vernon Memorial Hwy.
HABS VA-505-E
HABS VA,30- ,2E-
1ph L

MOUNT VERNON VIC.

Fort Hunt Overpass; see Mount Vernon Memorial Hwy:Fort Hunt Overpass

Grand View (Troth,Jacob M. & Ann Walton,House)
9000 Richmond Hwy. (U. S. Rt. 1)
HABS VA-1207
HABS VA,30- ,7-
4dr L

Little Hunting Creek Bridge; see Mount Vernon Mem. Hwy:Little Hunting Creek Bridge

Mount Vernon Mem. Hwy:Little Hunting Creek Bridge (Little Hunting Creek Bridge)
8.6 Miles South of I-95
HAER VA-42-D
HAER 1989(HAER):22
4ph/5pg/1pc L

Mount Vernon Memorial Hwy:Fort Hunt Overpass (Fort Hunt Overpass)
Mount Vernon Mem. Hwy,5.9 Miles South of I-95
HAER VA-42-C
HAER 1989(HAER):22
2ph/4pg/1pc L

Troth,Jacob M. & Ann Walton,House; see Grand View

Washington's Grist Mill
55414 Mt. Vernon Memorial Hwy.
HABS VA-506
HABS VA,30- ,4-
1ph L

MT. VERNON VIC.

Pope-Leighey House (Pope,Loren B.,House)
9000 Richmond Hwy. (moved from VA,Falls Church)
HABS VA-638
HABS VA,30-FALCH,2-
9dr/33ph/4pg/2pc/fr L

Pope,Loren B.,House; see Pope-Leighey House

Woodlawn
9000 Richmond Hwy.
HABS VA-337
HABS VA,30- ,3-
13dr/22ph/1pg/1pc/8ct/fr L

Woodlawn,Dairy
9000 Richmond Hwy.
HABS VA-337-B
HABS VA,55-TREV.V,6-
1ph/1pc L

Woodlawn,Smokehouse
9000 Richmond Hwy.
HABS VA-337-A
HABS VA,30- ,3A-
1ph L

RAVENSWORTH VIC.

Lee Estate,House & Stable; see Ravensworth,House & Stable

Ravensworth,House & Stable (Lee Estate,House & Stable)
5200 Port Royal Rd.
HABS VA-105
HABS VA,30-RAV.V,1-
4dr/16ph/fr L

VIENNA VIC.

Ash Grove
8900 Ash Grove Ln.
HABS VA-504
HABS VA,30-FALCH.V,2-
16dr/28ph/3pg/fr L

FALLS CHURCH (CITY)

Bartlett-Lawton House (Home Hill)
203 Lawton St.
HABS VA-732
HABS VA,30-FALCH,5-
8ph/1pg/1pc L

Biggs,W. W. ,House
Little Falls & Great Falls Sts.
HABS VA-735
HABS VA,30-FALCH,6-
1ph/1pg/1pc L

Cherry Hill (Harvey-Riley House)
312 Park Ave.
HABS VA-733
HABS VA,30-FALCH,7-
9ph/1pc L

Crossman,Charles,House
421 N. Washington St.
HABS VA-734
HABS VA,30-FALCH,8-
1ph/1pg/1pc L

170 East Broad Street (House)
HABS VA-736
HABS VA,30-FALCH,4-
9ph/1pg/1pc L

Falls Church (Episcopal)
115 E. Fairfax St.
HABS VA-288
HABS VA,30-FALCH,1-
6ph L

Harvey-Riley House; see Cherry Hill

Home Hill; see Bartlett-Lawton House

Pond-Copeland House
407 E. Columbia St.
HABS VA-737
HABS VA,30-FALCH,9-
1ph/1pg/1pc L

Pope-Leighey House (Pope,Loren B.,House)
1005 Locust St. (moved to VA,Mt. Vernon Vic.)
HABS VA-638
HABS VA,30-FALCH,2-
9dr/33ph/4pg/2pc/fr L

Pope,Loren B.,House; see Pope-Leighey House

Rollins,George F.,House
109 E. Columbia St.
HABS VA-738
HABS VA,30-FALCH,3-
4ph/1pg/1pc L

FAUQUIER COUNTY

DELAPLANE

Delaplane Post Office
State Rts. 623 & 712 Vic.
HABS VA-968
HABS VA,31-DELA,1-
2ph/1pc L

Delaplane Store
State Rts. 623 & 712 Vic.
HABS VA-969
HABS VA,31-DELA,2-
2ph/1pc L

Delaplane,John,House
State Rt. 623
HABS VA-967
HABS VA,31-DELA,3-
9dr/24ph/2pc L

Delaplane,John,Stonehouse
State Rt. 623
HABS VA-967-A
HABS VA,31-DELA,3A-
2dr/4ph L

MARSHALL VIC.

Marshall,John,House (Oak Hill)
U. S. Rt. 17 Vic.
HABS VA-11-5
HABS VA,31-MARSH.V,1-
34dr/7ph/3pg/fr L

Oak Hill; see Marshall,John,House

PARIS

Watts Ashby Tavern
State Rts. 759 & 701
HABS VA-743
HABS VA,31-PAR,1-
6ph L

THE PLAINS VIC.

Gordonsdale Cabin; see Log House

Log Cabin; see Log House

Log House (Gordonsdale Cabin; Log Cabin)
State Rt. 750 Vic.
HABS VA-11-6
HABS VA,31-THEPLA.V,1-
9dr/1ph/3pg/fr L

UPPERVILLE

House,Old
U.S. Rt. 50
HABS VA-478
HABS VA,31-UPVI,1-
5dr/fr L

FLOYD COUNTY

WILLIS VIC.

Mabry Mill
Blue Ridge Pkwy.
HABS VA-165
HABS VA,32- ,1-
7dr/6ph/1pg/fr L

FLUVANNA COUNTY

BREMO BLUFF VIC.

Bremo
State Rt. 656 Vic.
HABS VA-302
HABS VA,33-FORKU.V,1-
29ph/2pg L

COHASSET

Fork Union Depot
State Rt. 6
HABS VA-978
HABS VA,33-COHAS,1-
6dr/8pg/fr L

FREDERICK COUNTY

CLEARBROOK VIC.

Hopewell Friends Meeting House
Interstate 81
HABS VA-693
HABS VA,35-CLEAR.V,1-
8dr/1pg/fr L

MIDDLETOWN VIC.

Belle Grove
State Rt. 727
HABS VA-259
HABS VA,35-MIDTO.V,2-
15dr/19ph/3pg/fr L

Fort,Old Stone; see House,Stone

House,Stone (Fort,Old Stone)
Middle Marsh Brook
HABS VA-210
HABS VA,35-MIDTO.V,1-
5ph/1pg L

WINCHESTER VIC.

Red Lion Tavern; see Tavern Number One,Old

Tavern Number One,Old (Red Lion Tavern)
204-208 S. Loudoun St.
HABS VA-508
HABS VA,35-WIN.V,1-
1ph L

Tavern Number Two,Old
HABS VA-509
HABS VA,35-WIN.V,2-
1ph L

FREDERICKSBURG (CITY)

Braxton,W. W. ,House; see Dixon-Maury House

Brompton
Sunken Rd. & Hanover St.
HABS VA-569
HABS VA,89-FRED,8-183:125°
7dr/3ph L

Dixon-Maury House (Braxton,W. W. ,House)
214 Caroline St.
HABS VA-1213
HABS VA,89-FRED,29-
8ph/1pc L

Doggett House; see Stevenson House

Doggett House,Quarters; see Stevenson House,Quarters

Federal Hill,Summerhouse
510 Hanover St.
HABS VA-11-4
HABS VA,89-FRED,19A-
1dr/1ph/3pg/fr L

100 Hanover Street (House)
HABS VA-204
HABS VA,89-FRED,23-
1ph L

House (Long House,Old)
607 Sophia St.
HABS VA-263
HABS VA,89-FRED,28-
1ph L

Jail,Old; see Warehouse,Stone

Kenmore
1201 Washington Ave.
HABS VA-305
HABS VA,89-FRED,1-
19dr/63ph/2pg/fr L

Kenmore,Kitchen (Kenmore,North Dependency)
1201 Washington Ave.
HABS VA-305-B
HABS VA,89-FRED,1C-
1ph L

Kenmore,North Dependency; see Kenmore,Kitchen

Kenmore,Office (Kenmore,South Dependency)
1201 Washington Ave.
HABS VA-305-A
HABS VA,89-FRED,1B-
1ph L

Kenmore,South Dependency; see Kenmore,Office

Long House,Old; see House

Mercer,Gen. Hugh,Apothecary Shop
1020 Caroline St.
HABS VA-1080
HABS VA,89-FRED,30-
6ph/1pc L

National Bank Building
George St. & Princess Ann St.
HABS VA-389
HABS VA,89-FRED,6-
2ph L

Rising Sun Tavern
1306 Caroline St.
HABS VA-11-1
HABS VA,89-FRED,4-
6dr/14ph/6pg/fr L

Sentry Box House
133 Caroline St.
HABS VA-300
HABS VA,89-FRED,22-
3ph L

511-519 Sophia Street (Houses)
HABS VA-205
HABS VA,89-FRED,26-
1ph L

710-716 Sophia Street (Houses)
HABS VA-207
HABS VA,89-FRED,27-
1ph L

Stevenson House (Doggett House)
303 Amelia St.
HABS VA-601
HABS VA,89-FRED,10-
1ph/1pc L

Stevenson House,Quarters (Doggett House,Quarters)
303 1/2 Amelia St.
HABS VA-601-A
HABS VA,89-FRED,10A-
1ph/1pc L

Warehouse & Miscellaneous Buildings
307-313 Sophia St.
HABS VA-206
HABS VA,89-FRED,25-
2ph L

Warehouse,Stone (Jail,Old)
915 Sophia St.
HABS VA-262
HABS VA,89-FRED,24-
1ph L

Washington,Mary,House
1200 Charles St.
HABS VA-11-2
HABS VA,89-FRED,2-
12dr/11ph/4pg/fr L

GLOUCESTER COUNTY

BELLAMY VIC.

Baytop (Capahosic House; York River Lodge)
State Rt. 618
HABS VA-744
HABS VA,37-CAP,1-
2ph L

Capahosic House; see Baytop

York River Lodge; see Baytop

BENA VIC.

Little England (Sara's Creek House)
State Rt. 672 Vic.
HABS VA-515
HABS VA,37-GLOPO,1-
1ph L

Sara's Creek House; see Little England

GLOUCESTER

Botetourt Hotel; see Botetourt Inn & Barn (Ruins)

Botetourt Inn & Barn (Ruins) (Botetourt Hotel)
Main St.
HABS VA-513
HABS VA,37-GLO,1-
5ph L

Gloucester County Courthouse
U. S. Rt. 17
HABS VA-511
HABS VA,37-GLO,2-
1ph L

Gloucester Women's Club (Longbridge Ordinary)
U. S. Rt. 17 & State Rt. 14
HABS VA-512
HABS VA,37-GLO,3-
11dr/24ph/2pc/fr L

Hay's Store
HABS VA-1040
HABS VA,37-GLO,4-
1ph/1pc L

Longbridge Ordinary; see Gloucester Women's Club

GLOUCESTER VIC.

Abingdon Glebe House
U. S. Rt. 17 Vic.
HABS VA-746
HABS VA,37-WHIMA,1-
8ph L

Belroi; see Reed,Dr. Walter,House

Reed,Dr. Walter,House (Belroi)
State Rts. 614 & 616
HABS VA-57
HABS VA,37-BEL,1-
2ph/2pg L

Roaring Springs
State Rt. 616 Vic.
HABS VA-983
HABS VA,37-GLO.V,4-
9dr/22ph/2pc/1ct L

Ware Church
State Rt. 3
HABS VA-408
HABS VA,37-GLO.V,2-
6ph/1pg L

NAXERA VIC.

Land's End
Severn River
HABS VA-518
HABS VA,37-NAX.V,1-
5ph/1pg L

NUTTALL VIC.

Toddsbury
Vic. of State Rts. 622 & 3-14 Intersection
HABS VA-417
HABS VA,37-NUT.V,1-
9dr/37ph/2pg/2pc/8ct/fr L

Toddsbury,Outbuildings & Gardens
Vic. of State Rts. 622 & 3-14 Intersection
HABS VA-417-A
HABS VA,37-NUT.V,1A-,B-,D-
7ph/2pc L

ORDINARY

House,Old (Sewall's Ordinary)
U. S. Rt. 17 (moved from original location)
HABS VA-519
HABS VA,37-ORD,1-
1ph L

Sewall's Ordinary; see House,Old

ORDINARY VIC.

Belle Farm
State Rt. 656 (moved to VA.Williamsburg)
HABS VA-69
HABS VA,37-ORD.V,1-
1ph/2pg L

WARE NECK VIC.

Belleville
North River & Belleville Creek vic.
HABS VA-994
HABS VA,37-WARNE.V,1-
7dr/13pg/fr L

WHITE MARSH

White Marsh Store
U. S. Rt. 17
HABS VA-520
HABS VA,37-WHIMA,2-
3ph L

WHITE MARSH VIC.

Abingdon Church
U. S. Rt. 17
HABS VA-182
HABS VA,37-WHIMA.V,1-
4dr/10ph/2pg/fr L

Carter's Creek House; see Fairfield

Fairfield (Carter's Creek House)
HABS VA-272
HABS VA,37-WHIMA.V,3-
2ph/2pg L

Rosewell
Carter Creek
HABS VA-61
HABS VA,37-WHIMA.V,2-
12ph/1pg L

WOODS CROSSROADS VIC

Marlfield
State Rt. 612 Vic.
HABS VA-514
HABS VA,37- ,1-
3ph L

Mount Prodigal (Roane House)
U. S. Rt. 17 Vic.
HABS VA-510
HABS VA,37-GLO.V,3-
7ph L

Roane House; see Mount Prodigal

GOOCHLAND COUNTY

ASHLAND VIC.

Fork Church
State Rt. 738
HABS VA-409
HABS VA,43-ASH.V,2-
4ph/1pg L

GOOCHLAND

Goochland County Courthouse
E. Side of U. S. Rt. 522
HABS VA-224
HABS VA,38-GOOCH,1-
4ph/1ct L

Lawyer's Office
U. S. Rt. 522
HABS VA-225
HABS VA,38-GOOCH,2-
1ph L

GOOCHLAND VIC.

James R. & Kanawha Canal,Lickinghole Ck. Aqueduct
Spanning Lickinghole Creek
HAER VA-10
HAER VA,38-GOOCH.V,1-
3dr/fr L

MANAKIN

House,Old
State Rt. 21
HABS VA-315
HABS VA,38-MANA,5-
1ph L

Manakin Village
State Rts. 6 & 621
HABS VA-218
HABS VA,38-MANA,1-
1ph/4pg L

Manakin Village,Structure Number 1
State Rt. 621
HABS VA-219
HABS VA,38-MANA,2-
1ph L

Manakin Village,Structure Number 2
State Rt. 621
HABS VA-220
HABS VA,38-MANA,3-
1ph L

Manakin Village,Structure Number 3
State Rt. 621
HABS VA-221
HABS VA,38-MANA,4-
1ph L

MANAKIN VIC.

Powell's Tavern
State Rt. 650
HABS VA-748
HABS VA,38-MANA.V,
1ph L

Tuckahoe Plantation
River Rd. ,Richmond Vic.
HABS VA-712
HABS VA,38-MANA.V,1-
8dr L

SABOT

Saddlebag House
State Rt. 6
HABS VA-215
HABS VA,38-SABO,1-
1ph L

GREENE COUNTY

STANARDSVILLE VIC.

Locust Grove
State Rt. 641
HABS VA-1073
HABS VA,40-STANA.V,1-
8dr/17pg/fr L

HALIFAX COUNTY

SOUTH BOSTON VIC.

Berry Hill Plantation
State Rt. 659 Vic.
HABS VA-304
HABS VA,42-BOSTS.V,1-
17ph/1pg L

HAMPTON (CITY)

Campbellton Smokehouse
HABS VA-480
HABS VA,95- ,1-
1ph L

Eagle Point
HABS VA-481
HABS VA,28- ,1-
1ph L

Fort Monroe
HABS VA-595
7dr H

Fort Monroe,Building No. 209; see Fort Monroe,M.A.R.S. Station

Fort Monroe,Building No. 226
Fenwick Rd.
HABS VA-595-D
5ph/2pg/1pc H

Fort Monroe,Chapel of the Centurion
HABS VA-595-B
3dr H

Fort Monroe,M.A.R.S. Station (Fort Monroe,Building No. 209)
HABS VA-595-C
2dr H

Fort Monroe,Quarters No. 1
HABS VA-595-A
7dr/fr H

Fortress Monroe,Main Gate (Fortress Monroe,Main Sally Port)
U. S. Rts. 60 & 258
HABS VA-595-E
HABS VA,28-HAMP,
8dr L

Fortress Monroe,Main Sally Port; see Fortress Monroe,Main Gate

Veterans Admin. Medical Center,Building No. 21; see Veterans Administration Medical Center,Stable

Veterans Admin. Medical Center,Building No. 34; see Veterans Administration Medical Center,Greenhouse

Veterans Admin. Medical Center,Motor Transpo. Ctr.; see Veterans Administration Medical Center,Stable

Veterans Administration Medical Center,Greenhouse (Veterans Admin. Medical Center,Building No. 34)
HABS VA-1210-A
HABS VA,28-HAMP,3A-
5ph/2pg/1pc L

Veterans Administration Medical Center,Stable (Veterans Admin. Medical Center,Building No. 21; Veterans Admin. Medical Center,Motor Transpo. Ctr.
HABS VA-1210-B
HABS VA,28-HAMP,3B-
2ph/2pg/1pc L

HANOVER COUNTY

ASHLAND VIC.

Church Quarter
State Rt. 738
HABS VA-751
HABS VA,43-TAYL.V,1-
1ph L

Fairfield; see Rocky Mills Mansion

Rocky Mills Mansion (Fairfield) (moved to Va,Richmond Vic.)
HABS VA-146
HABS VA,43-ASH.V,1-
6dr/40ph/6pg/fr L

BEAVER DAM

Scotchtown
State Rt. 685 Vic.
HABS VA-117
HABS VA,43-BEVDA,1-
11dr/12ph/5pg/fr L

BEAVER DAM VIC.

Edgewood
Newfound River
HABS VA-749
HABS VA,43-BEVDA,2-
4ph L

Mount Olivet Church
State Rt. 671
HABS VA-750
HABS VA,43- ,3-
1ph L

COLD HARBOR

Richmond National Battlefield Park; see Watt,Hugh,House

Watt,Hugh,House (Richmond National Battlefield Park)
HABS VA-477
HABS VA,43-COLD,2-;(DLC/PP-1992:VA-5)
6dr/11ph/3pg/1pc/fr L

GUMTREE VIC.

Dewberry
Little River Vic.
HABS VA-752
HABS VA,43- ,2-
3ph L

HANOVER

Barksdale Theater; see Tavern at Hanover Courthouse

Hall of Justice; see Tavern at Hanover Courthouse

Hanover County Courthouse
U. S. Rt. 301
HABS VA-429
HABS VA,43-HANO,1-
3ph L

Hanover Tavern; see Tavern at Hanover Courthouse

Tavern at Hanover Courthouse (Hanover Tavern; Barksdale Theater; Hall of Justice)
State Rt. 1002
HABS VA-521
HABS VA,43-HANO,2-
1ph L

MECHANICSVILLE VIC.

Fairfield Farm; see Gaines,William,House (Quarters)

Gaines,Doctor,House; see Powhite

Gaines,William,House (Quarters) (Fairfield Farm)
State Rt. 615 Vic.
HABS VA-78
HABS VA,43-MECHA.V,1-
3dr/5ph/1pg/fr L

Pollard House (Williamsville)
Studley Rd.
HABS VA-343
HABS VA,43-MECHA.V,3-
2ph/1pg L

Powhite (Gaines,Doctor,House; Richmond National Battlefield Park)
HABS VA-335
HABS VA,43-MECHA.V,1-
2ph L

Richmond National Battlefield Park; see Powhite

Rural Plains
State Rt. 606
HABS VA-753
HABS VA,43-MECHA.V,4-
3ph L

Williamsville; see Pollard House

OLD COLD HARBOR VIC.

Gathwright House
Rt. 156
HABS VA-76
HABS VA,43-COLD,1-
13dr/2ph/1pg L

HARRISONBURG (CITY)

106 North Liberty Street (House)
HABS VA-907
HABS VA,83-HARBU,1-
2ph L

HENRICO COUNTY

GLEN ALLEN

Cardwell,Virginia,Cottage; see Randolph,Viginia E. ,Cottage

Home Economics Cottage; see Randolph,Viginia E. ,Cottage

Randolph,Viginia E. ,Cottage (Cardwell,Virginia,Cottage; Home Economics Cottage)
2200 Mountain Rd.
HABS VA-65
HABS VA,44-GLAL,1-
3ph/2pg/1pc L

GLEN ALLEN VIC.

Quarters Cabin
Gayton Rd. Vic.
HABS VA-222
HABS VA,44-GAYT,1-
3ph L

RICHMOND VIC.

Cox House (Richmond National Battlefield Park)
HABS VA-396
HABS VA,44-RICH.V,5-
5ph L

Fairfield; see Rocky Mills Mansion

Malvern Hill
State Rt. 156 Vic.
HABS VA-89
HABS VA,44-RICH.V,1-
6dr/4ph/2pg L

Richmond National Battlefield Park; see Cox House

Rocky Mills Mansion (Fairfield)
211 Ross Rd. (moved from Va,Ashland Vic.)
HABS VA-146
HABS VA,43-ASH.V,1-
6dr/40ph/6pg/fr L

Wilton
Wilton Rd. (moved to VA,Richmond)
HABS VA-158
HABS VA,44-RICH.V,3-
26ph/4pg L

TUCKAHOE VIC.

Double House
HABS VA-223
HABS VA,44- ,1-
1ph L

HOPEWELL (CITY)

Appomattox Manor
Cedar Lane
HABS VA-824
HABS VA,75-HOPE,1-
8ph/1pg/1pc L

Appomattox Manor,Dependencies
Cedar Lane
HABS VA-824-B
HABS VA,75-HOPE,1B-
1ph/1pc L

Appomattox Manor,Kitchen
Cedar Lane
HABS VA-824-A
HABS VA,75-HOPE,1A-
2ph/1pc L

ISLE OF WIGHT COUNTY

SMITHFIELD

Barrett House
S. Church St.
HABS VA-140
HABS VA,47-SMIF,3-
5ph/1pg L

Clerk's Office; see Office,Small Brick

Grove Hotel (Pierce,Thomas,House)
Mason St.
HABS VA-301
HABS VA,47-SMIF,5-
3ph L

Isle of Wight County Courthouse
Main & Mason Sts.
HABS VA-294
HABS VA,47-SMIF,4-
3ph L

Mason's Hall
Mason St.
HABS VA-424
HABS VA,47-SMIF,6-
1ph L

Office,Small Brick (Clerk's Office)
Mason & Main Sts.
HABS VA-754
HABS VA,47-SMIF,7-
1ph L

Pierce,Thomas,House; see Grove Hotel

SMITHFIELD VIC.

St. Luke's Church
State Rt. 10 Vic.
HABS VA-11-20
HABS VA,47-SMIF.V,1-
10dr/15ph/2pg/fr L

WINDSOR VIC.

Saunders,Capt. Henry,House:Virginia Room
US Rte. 460
HABS DC-525-A
HABS DC,WASH,515A-
4dr/fr H

JAMES CITY COUNTY

CROAKER VIC.

Richardson House
HABS VA-88
HABS VA,48-CROK.V,1-
7dr/4ph/1pg L

JAMESTOWN ISLAND

Architectural Remains (Project 103,Structure 123)
HABS VA-472
HABS VA,48-JAM,12-
1dr L

Architectural Remains (Project 103,Structure 125)
HABS VA-473
HABS VA,48-JAM,13-
1dr L

Architectural Remains (Project 194,Structure 115)
HABS VA-470
HABS VA,48-JAM,10-
3dr L

Architectural Remains (Project 194,Structure 117)
HABS VA-471
HABS VA,48-JAM,11-
1dr L

Architectural Remains (Unit A,Sub-unit 39)
HABS VA-26
HABS VA,48-JAM,1-
10dr/4ph/7pg L

Architectural Remains (Unit B,Structure 110)
HABS VA-444
HABS VA,48-JAM,8-
3dr/3ph L

Architectural Remains (Unit B,Structure 112)
HABS VA-445
HABS VA,48-JAM,9-
3dr/12ph/fr L

Architectural Remains (Unit B,Sub-unit 101)
HABS VA-31
HABS VA,48-JAM,7-
1dr L

Architectural Remains (Unit B,Sub-unit 62)
HABS VA-28
HABS VA,48-JAM,4-
4dr/4ph/5pg L

Architectural Remains (Unit B,Sub-unit 76)
HABS VA-30
HABS VA,48-JAM,6-
7dr L

Architectural Remains (Unit B,Sub-unit 86)
HABS VA-29
HABS VA,48-JAM,5-
4dr L

Architectural Remains (Unit B,Sub-units 59 & 73)
HABS VA-27
HABS VA,48-JAM,3-
3dr/4ph/6pg L

Architectural Remains (Unit B,Sub-units 89 & 97)
HABS VA-25
HABS VA,48-JAM,2-
14dr/7ph/7pg L

Project 103,Structure 123; see Architectural Remains

Project 103,Structure 125; see Architectural Remains

Project 194,Structure 115; see Architectural Remains

Project 194,Structure 117; see Architectural Remains

Unit A,Sub-unit 39; see Architectural Remains

Unit B,Structure 110; see Architectural Remains

Unit B,Structure 112; see Architectural Remains

Unit B,Sub-unit 101; see Architectural Remains

Unit B,Sub-unit 62; see Architectural Remains

Unit B,Sub-unit 76; see Architectural Remains

Unit B,Sub-unit 86; see Architectural Remains

Unit B,Sub-units 59 & 73; see Architectural Remains

Unit B,Sub-units 89 & 97; see Architectural Remains

LIGHTFOOT VIC.

Pinewoods; see Warburton House

Warburton House (Pinewoods)
Pinewoods Pond Vic.
HABS VA-532
HABS VA,48- ,1-
3ph L

TOANO

Marston House (Chimney)
HABS VA-319
HABS VA,48-TOA,2-
1ph/1pg L

TOANO VIC.

Hickory Neck Church
U. S. Rt. 60
HABS VA-214
HABS VA,48-TOA,1-
2ph L

Martin Farmhouse; see Martin's Farm

Martin's Farm (Martin Farmhouse)
U. S. Rt. 60
HABS VA-756
HABS VA,48-TOA.V,2-
1ph L

Windsor Castle
State Rt. 610
HABS VA-254
HABS VA,48-TOA.V,1-
3ph/1pg L

WILLIAMSBURG VIC.

Berkeley,Gov. William,House; see Greenspring

Carter's Grove
U. S. Rt. 60 Vic.
HABS VA-351
HABS VA,48-WIL.V,1-
27dr/84ph/3pg/5pc/1ct L

Greenspring (Berkeley,Gov. William,House)
State Rt. 614 Vic.
HABS VA-440
HABS VA,48-WIL.V,6-
1dr L

Keith's Creek House; see Skiff's Creek House

Kingsmill Plantation,Dependencies
Kingsmill Pond Vic.
HABS VA-208
HABS VA,48-WIL.V,4-
7dr/2ph/2pg/fr L

Maine Farm
State Rt. 614 Vic.
HABS VA-71
HABS VA,48-WIL.V,2-
6ph/1pg L

Poplar Hall
Skiff's Creek Vic.
HABS VA-755
HABS VA,48-WIL.V,7-
2ph L

Powhatan (Powhatan Farm)
Powhatan Creek
HABS VA-177
HABS VA,48-WIL.V,3-
1dr/1ph/1pg L

Powhatan Farm; see Powhatan

Skiff's Creek House (Keith's Creek House)
Skiff's Creek Vic.
HABS VA-407
HABS VA,48-WIL.V,5-
3ph/1pg L

KING AND QUEEN COUNTY

NEWTOWN VIC.

Ballentine House (Dewsville)
(moved to VA,Yorktown)
HABS VA-596
HABS VA,100-YORK,16-
3ph/3pg L

Dewsville; see Ballentine House

Drysdale Glebe House
HABS VA-398
HABS VA,49-NEWT.V,3-
3ph/2pg L

Jackson Farm (Buildings)
HABS VA-361
HABS VA,49-NEWT.V,2-
1ph L

Southworth House
HABS VA-313
HABS VA,49-NEWT.V,1-
2ph/1pg L

WALKERTON VIC.

Hillsborough
HABS VA-125
HABS VA,49-WALK.V,1-
12dr/13ph/5pg L

KING GEORGE COUNTY

COMORN VIC.

Lamb's Creek Church (Episcopal)
State Rt. 694
HABS VA-98
HABS VA,50-COMO.V,1-
3dr/3ph/fr L

Marmion
State Rt. 649 Vic.
HABS VA-145
HABS VA,50-COMO.V,2-
25dr/30ph/fr L

OWENS VIC.

St. Paul's Church (Episcopal)
State Rts. 206 & 218
HABS VA-266
HABS VA,50- ,2-
1pg L

PORT ROYAL VIC.

Belle Grove
Rappahannock River
HABS VA-274
HABS VA,50-POCON.V,2-
3ph/1pg L

Woodlawn
Rappahannock River
HABS VA-213
HABS VA,50-POCON.V,1-
1ph/1pg L

KING WILLIAM COUNTY

AYLETT VIC.

Cherry Grove,Servants' Quarters
State Rt. 30 Vic.
HABS VA-762
HABS VA,51-RUMF.V,4-
1ph L

Moeser House
State Rt. 30 Vic.
HABS VA-154
HABS VA,51-RUMF.V,1-
6dr/10ph/3pg/fr L

Rumford Academy
State Rt. 600 Vic.
HABS VA-258
HABS VA,51-RUMF,1-
2pg L

KING WILLIAM

King William County Courthouse & Stable
State Rt. 619
HABS VA-123
HABS VA,51-KIWI,1-
7dr/6ph/4pg/fr L

KING WILLIAM VIC.

Green Level
State Rt. 621 Vic.
HABS VA-759
HABS VA,51-KIWI.V,1-
3ph L

Winterham
State Rt. 629
HABS VA-761
HABS VA,51- ,1-
1ph L

LESTER MANOR VIC.

Elsing Green
State Rt. 632 Vic.
HABS VA-67
HABS VA,51-LESM.V,1-
8ph/2pg L

MANGOHICK

Cottage (House)
State Rt. 604
HABS VA-534
HABS VA,51-MANG,4-
1ph L

House; see Cottage

Mooklar House
State Rts. 604 & 30
HABS VA-764
HABS VA,51-MANG,2-
1ph L

MANGOHICK VIC.

Hornquarter Farm
State Rt. 614 Vic.
HABS VA-149
HABS VA,51-MANG.V,1-
4ph/1pg L

Mangohick Baptist Church
State Rt. 638
HABS VA-763
HABS VA,51-MANG,1-
1ph L

Palestine
State Rt. 604 Vic.
HABS VA-765
HABS VA,51-MANG,3-
2ph L

Retreat
State Rt. 604 Vic.
HABS VA-767
HABS VA,51-MANG.V,2-
3ph L

Roseville
State Rt. 604 Vic.
HABS VA-766
HABS VA,51-MANG.V,3-
3ph L

MANQUIN VIC.

Dabney House; see Seven Springs

Fontainebleu
State Rt. 618
HABS VA-379
HABS VA,51-RUMF.V,2-
1ph L

Seven Springs (Dabney House)
State Rt. 605 Vic.
HABS VA-244
HABS VA,51-ENF.V,1-
1ph/1pg L

RUMFORD VIC.

Acquinton Church (Upper Church of St. John's Parish)
State Rt. 629
HABS VA-760
HABS VA,51-RUMF.V,3-
1ph L

Upper Church of St. John's Parish; see Acquinton Church

SWEET HALL

Sweet Hall
Pamunkey River
HABS VA-385
HABS VA,51-SWEHA,1-
3ph/1pg L

SWEET HALL VIC.

House,Old (Seaton House)
State Rt. 634
HABS VA-533
HABS VA,51-KIWI.V,2-
1ph L

Seaton House; see House,Old

St. John's Church,Old
State Rt. 30 Vic.
HABS VA-758
HABS VA,51-WESPO.V,1-
3ph L

Waterville; see Windsor Shade

Windsor Shade (Waterville)
Pamunkey River
HABS VA-257
HABS VA,51-SWEHA.V,1-
1ph L

WEST POINT VIC.

Chelsea
Mattaponi River
HABS VA-399
HABS VA,51-WSPO.V,2-
2ph/1pg L

LANCASTER COUNTY

BERTRAND VIC.

Towles House
Rappahannock River
HABS VA-62
HABS VA,52-BERT.V,1-
12dr/17ph/2pg/fr L

FARNHAM

Edgehill
State Rt. 354 Vic.
HABS VA-431
HABS VA,52- ,6-
3ph L

KILMARNOCK VIC.

Christ Church
State Rt. 3
HABS VA-70
HABS VA,52-KILM.V,1-
13dr/16ph/1pg L

LANCASTER

Clerk's Office
State Rt. 3
HABS VA-360
HABS VA,52-LANC,1-
1ph/1pg L

Hughlett House
State Rt. 3
HABS VA-412
HABS VA,52-LANC,2-
6ph/1pg L

LIVELY VIC.

St. Mary's Whitechapel Church
State Rts. 354 & 201
HABS VA-59
HABS VA,52-LIV.V,1-
7ph/1pg/fr L

MERRY POINT

Verville
State Rt. 611
HABS VA-151
HABS VA,52-MERPO,1-
7ph/1pg L

MERRY POINT VIC.

Home of the Blind Preacher; see Waddel,James,House

Waddel,James,House (Home of the Blind Preacher)
State Rt. 604
HABS VA-297
HABS VA,52-MERPO.V,1-
2ph L

NUTTSVILLE VIC.

Oakley
State Rt. 622
HABS VA-535
HABS VA,52- ,5-
2ph L

OTTOMAN VIC.

Belmont
State Rt. 662
HABS VA-296
HABS VA,52-OTTO.V,1-
6ph L

Oak Hill
State Rt. 604 Vic.
HABS VA-298
HABS VA,52-OTTO.V,2-
2ph L

SOMERS VIC.

Belle Isle
State Rt. 683
HABS VA-64
HABS VA,52-SOM.V,1-
18dr/24ph/1pg L

WEEMS

Corotoman (Spinster's House)
Rappahannock River
HABS VA-153
HABS VA,52-WEEM,1-
1dr/1ph/5pg/fr L

Spinster's House; see Corotoman

LEXINGTON (CITY)

Alexander-Withrow House
2 N. Main St.
HABS VA-905
HABS VA,82-LEX,15-
6dr/11ph/6pg/2pc L

Baxter House; see Main Street Area Survey

Central Hotel; see Main Street Area Survey

Chesapeake & Ohio Railroad Station; see Valley Railroad Station

Jordan's Point; see Stono

Jordan's Point,Ice House; see Stono,Ice House

Jordan's Point,Office; see Stono,Office

Jordan's Point,Summer Kitchen; see Stono,Summer Kitchen

Main Street Area Survey
HABS VA-897
HABS VA,82-LEX.8-
3ph/1pg/1pc L

Main Street Area Survey (Baxter House)
18 N. Main St.
HABS VA-897-B
HABS VA,82-LEX,10-
1ph/1pg/1pc L

Main Street Area Survey (Central Hotel)
15 N. Main St.
HABS VA-897-A
HABS VA,82-LEX,8-
1ph/1pg/1pc L

Main Street Area Survey (Ruff,Jacob M. ,House)
21 N. Main St.
HABS VA-897-C
HABS VA,82-LEX,11-
1ph/1pg/1pc L

Main Street Area Survey (Sheridan Livery Stable)
29-33 N. Main St.
HABS VA-897-D
HABS VA,82-LEX,12-
1ph/1pg/1pc L

Main Street Area Survey (Troubadour Theatre)
N. Main St.
HABS VA-897-F
HABS VA,82-LEX,14-
1ph/1pg/1pc L

Main Street Area Survey (Willson-Walker House)
30 N. Main St.
HABS VA-897-E
HABS VA,82-LEX,13-
2ph/1pg/1pc L

Pendleton-Coles House
319 Letcher Ave.
HABS VA-898
HABS VA,82-LEX,4-
7ph/3pg/1pc L

Reid-White House
208 W. Nelson St.
HABS VA-955
HABS VA,82-LEX,5-
8dr/5ph/1pc L

Ruff,Jacob M. ,House; see Main Street Area Survey

Sheridan Livery Stable; see Main Street Area Survey

Stono (Jordan's Point)
Institute Hill
HABS VA-900
HABS VA,100-YORK,17-
8dr/13ph/6pg/1pc L

Stono,Ice House (Jordan's Point,Ice House)
Institute Hill
HABS VA-900-C
HABS VA,82-LEX,6C-
1ph L

Stono,Office (Jordan's Point,Office)
Institute Hill
HABS VA-900-B
HABS VA,82-LEX,6B-
2dr/1ph L

Stono,Summer Kitchen (Jordan's Point,Summer Kitchen)
Institute Hill
HABS VA-900-A
HABS VA,82-LEX,6A-
1ph L

Troubadour Theatre; see Main Street Area Survey

Valley Railroad Station (Chesapeake & Ohio Railroad Station)
McLaughlin & Glasgow Sts.
HABS VA-904
HABS VA,82-LEX,7-
5ph/4pg/1pc L

Virginia Military Inst.,Superintendent's Quarters
Virginia Military Institute Parade Grounds
HABS VA-901
HABS VA,82-LEX,3A-
8ph/4pg/1pc L

Virginia Military Institute,Barracks
Virginia Military Institute Parade Grounds
HABS VA-902
HABS VA,82-LEX,3B-
3ph/22pg/1pc L

Washington & Lee University
HABS VA-568
HABS VA,82-LEX,2-
1ph L

Washington & Lee University,Center Building; see Washington & Lee University,Washington Hall

Washington & Lee University,Lee Chapel
HABS VA-568-C
HABS VA,82-LEX,2-
10ph/9pg L

Washington & Lee University,Lee-Jackson House
4 University Place
HABS VA-568-B
HABS VA,82-LEX,2B-
1pg L

Washington & Lee University,Washington Hall (Washington & Lee University,Center Building)
Jefferson St.
HABS VA-568-A
HABS VA,82-LEX,2A-
4ph/7pg/1pc L

Willson-Walker House; see Main Street Area Survey

LOUDOUN COUNTY

LEESBURG

Bank,Old (Valley Bank)
1 N. Church St.
HABS VA-378
HABS VA,54-LEEB,3-
1ph L

House
HABS VA-1041
HABS VA,54-LEEB,16-
2ph/1pc L

Nichols Law Office (13 South King Street (Commercial Building))
13 S. King St.
HABS VA-438
HABS VA,54-LEEB,15-
2ph L

1-5 North King Street (Commercial Building); see 1-5 North King Street (Drug Store)

1-5 North King Street (Drug Store) (1-5 North King Street (Commercial Building))
HABS VA-375
HABS VA,54-LEEB,14-
1ph L

13 South King Street (Commercial Building); see Nichols Law Office

Valley Bank; see Bank,Old

LEESBURG VIC.

Cabin
Goose Creek Vic.
HABS VA-536
HABS VA,54- ,5-
1ph L

Carter's Mills; see Oatlands Historic District

Church of Our Savior; see Oatlands Historic District

Clapham's Double Lock; see Goose Creek & Little River Navigation:Double Lock

Goose Creek & Little River Navigation:Double Lock (Clapham's Double Lock)
Mouth of Goose Creek at Potomac River
HAER VA-39
HAER VA,54-LEEB.V,6-
3dr/2pg/fr L

Little Oatlands; see Oatlands Historic District

Mountain Gap School; see Oatlands Historic District

Oatlands Historic District
U. S. Rt. 15
HABS VA-949
HABS VA,54-LEEB.V,4-
2dr L

Oatlands Historic District (Carter's Mills)
U. S. Rt. 15
HABS VA-949-H
HABS VA,54-LEEB.V,4H-
2ph/2pg/1pc L

Oatlands Historic District (Church of Our Savior)
U. S. Rt. 15
HABS VA-949-L
HABS VA,54-LEEB.V,4L-
2ph/4pg/1pc L

Oatlands Historic District (Little Oatlands)
U. S. Rt. 15 Vic.
HABS VA-949-G
HABS VA,54-LEEB.V,4G-
2dr/4pg L

Oatlands Historic District (Mountain Gap School)
U. S. Rt. 15
HABS VA-949-K
HABS VA,54-LEEB.V,4K-
1dr/1ph/fr L

Oatlands Historic District (Oatlands,Bachelor Cottage)
U. S. Rt. 15
HABS VA-949-B
HABS VA,54-LEEB.V,4B-
1dr/4pg/fr L

Oatlands Historic District (Oatlands,Carter Barn)
U. S. Rt. 15
HABS VA-949-F
HABS VA,54-LEEB.V,4F-
2dr/1ph/4pg L

Oatlands Historic District (Oatlands,Greenhouse)
U. S. Rt. 15
HABS VA-949-C
HABS VA,54-LEEB.V,4C-
1dr/3pg/fr L

Oatlands Historic District (Oatlands,Main House)
U. S. Rt. 15
HABS VA-949-A
HABS VA,54-LEEB.V,4A-
13dr/9ph/5pg/fr L

Oatlands Historic District (Oatlands,Servants' Quarters)
U. S. Rt. 15
HABS VA-949-E
HABS VA,54-LEEB.V,4E-
4pg/fr L

Oatlands Historic District (Oatlands,Studio,The)
U. S. Rt. 15 Vic.
HABS VA-949-D
HABS VA,54-LEEB.V,4D-
1dr/1ph/3pg/fr L

Oatlands,Bachelor Cottage; see Oatlands Historic District

Oatlands,Carter Barn; see Oatlands Historic District

Oatlands,Greenhouse; see Oatlands Historic District

Oatlands,Main House; see Oatlands Historic District

Oatlands,Servants' Quarters; see Oatlands Historic District

Oatlands,Studio,The; see Oatlands Historic District

LENAH POST OFFICE

Cottage,The
HABS VA-537
HABS VA,54-LENA.V,1-
1ph L

WATERFORD

Apothecary Shop (Haines-Shuey House)
Main & Water Sts.
HABS VA-777
HABS VA,54-WATFO,37-
1ph L

Arch House; see Gover,Miriam,House

Atley-Huff House (Hough-Haines House)
Main St. Hill
HABS VA-779
HABS VA,54-WATFO,38-
1ph L

Bank Building,Old (Bank House)
Main St.
HABS VA-378-A
HABS VA,54-WATFO,18-
1ph L

Bank House; see Bank Building,Old

Baptist Church
High & Church Sts.
HABS VA-796
HABS VA,54-WATFO,8-
1ph L

Braden-Binker House; see Morland,Charles,House

Catoctin Creek
Second St.
HABS VA-941
HABS VA,54-WATFO,39-
3pg L

Clockmaker's House & Shop; see Nettle,William & Sarah,House

Cottage,Brick (Gover-Phillips Cottage)
Main St.
HABS VA-776
HABS VA,54-WATFO,9-
1ph L

Curtis,Lloyd,House (Myers,Mahlon,House)
Main St. Hill
HABS VA-785
HABS VA,54-WATFO,11-
1ph L

Divine,Charles W.,House; see Loudoun Hotel

Dormers,The; see Schooley,John,House

Dorsey,Edward,House; see Middle Huff House

Dutton,John B.,House; see Steer House

Documentation: **ct** color transparencies **dr** measured drawings **fr** field records
pc photograph captions **pg** pages of text **ph** photographs

Edwards Barn (Hough,William,Barn)
John Brown's Rdwy.
HABS VA-782
HABS VA,54-WATFO,12-
1ph L

Edwards House (Hough,William,House)
John Brown's Rdwy.
HABS VA-781
HABS VA,54-WATFO,12-
3ph L

Edwards-Hough House; see Edwards,Doctor,House

Edwards,Doctor,House (Edwards-Hough House)
Main St. Hill & Butcher's Row
HABS VA-772
HABS VA,54-WATFO,13-
1ph L

Fairfax Meetinghouse
State Rts. 665 & 698
HABS VA-773
HABS VA,54-WATFO,21-
1ph L

French-Atlee House; see Sidewell House

Gover-James House (Gover,Samuel A.,House)
Main St.
HABS VA-382
HABS VA,54-WATFO,36-
1ph L

Gover-Matthews Log House
Main St.
HABS VA-775
HABS VA,54-WATFO,7-
1ph L

Gover-Phillips Cottage; see Cottage,Brick

Gover,Miriam,House (Arch House)
Main St.
HABS VA-380
HABS VA,54-WATFO,2-
1ph L

Gover,Samuel A.,House; see Gover-James House

Haines-Shuey House; see Apothecary Shop

Hampier-Robinson House
(Robinson,Nancy,Log House)
Water St.
HABS VA-778
HABS VA,54-WATFO,26-
1ph L

Hough-Haines House; see Atley-Huff House

Hough,Hector,House
(Moore,James,House)
Main St. Hill
HABS VA-784
HABS VA,54-WATFO,14-
1ph L

Hough,John & Samuel,House; see Huff,Robert,House

Hough,William,Barn; see Edwards Barn

Hough,William,House; see Edwards House

House,Stuccoed Brick
(Schooley,Ephraim,House)
Second St.
HABS VA-790
HABS VA,54-WATFO,31-
2ph L

House,Yellow Brick
(Nettle,William,House)
Second St.
HABS VA-786
HABS VA,54-WATFO,34-
1ph L

Huff,Robert,House (Hough,John & Samuel,House)
Main St. Hill
HABS VA-780
HABS VA,54-WATFO,16-
1ph L

Loudoun Hotel (Divine,Charles W.,House)
Main St.
HABS VA-769
HABS VA,54-WATFO,19-
2ph L

Main Street (Log Cabin)
(moved from original location)
HABS VA-783
HABS VA,54-WATFO,17-
1ph L

Main Street (Shop) (Mount-Silcott House)
Main St.
HABS VA-381
HABS VA,54-WATFO,6-
1ph L

Mansfield,Virginia,House
(Walker-Phillips House)
Second St.
HABS VA-795
HABS VA,54-WATFO,20-
1ph L

Middle Huff House
(Dorsey,Edward,House)
Main St. Hill
HABS VA-770
HABS VA,54-WATFO,15-
1ph L

Mock House; see Shawen-Schooley House

Moore,James,House; see Hough,Hector,House

Morland,Charles,House (Braden-Binker House)
Main St. Hill
HABS VA-768
HABS VA,54-WATFO,24-
1ph L

Mount-Silcott House; see Main Street (Shop)

Myers,Mahlon,House; see Curtis,Lloyd,House

Nettle,William & Sarah,House
(Clockmaker's House & Shop)
Second St. ,btwn. Patrick & Church Sts.
HABS VA-787
HABS VA,54-WATFO,10-
1ph/3pg L

Nettle,William,House; see House,Yellow Brick

Noland Ferry House
Big Spring Rd.
HABS VA-538
HABS VA,54-WATFO,35-
1ph/1pg L

Old Mill; see Waterford Mill

Patton House; see Steer,James M.,House

Robinson,Nancy,Log House; see Hampier-Robinson House

Schooley,Elizabeth Hough,House
(Walker,Nathan,House)
Main St. & John Brown's Rdwy.
HABS VA-789
HABS VA,54-WATFO,32-
1ph L

Schooley,Ephraim,House; see House,Stuccoed Brick

Schooley,John,House (Dormers,The)
Second St.
HABS VA-791
HABS VA,54-WATFO,28-
1ph/2pg L

Schoolhouse; see Williams Warehouse

Shawen-Schooley House (Mock House)
Main St. Hill
HABS VA-793
HABS VA,54-WATFO,23-
2ph L

Sidewell House (French-Atlee House)
Second & Church Sts.
HABS VA-774
HABS VA,54-WATFO,29-
1ph L

Steer House (Dutton,John B.,House)
Second & Mahlon Sts.
HABS VA-771
HABS VA,54-WATFO,30-
1ph L

Steer,James M.,House (Patton House)
Second & Factory Sts.
HABS VA-794
HABS VA,54-WATFO,25-
2ph L

Walker-Phillips House; see Mansfield,Virginia,House

Walker,Nathan,House; see Schooley,Elizabeth Hough,House

Waterford Methodist Church
Main & High Sts.
HABS VA-935
HABS VA,54-WATFO,40-
3pg L

Waterford Mill (Old Mill)
Catoctin Creek at end of Main St.
HABS VA-788
HABS VA,54-WATFO,22-
1ph/3pg L

Waterford School
Second & Janney Sts.
HABS VA-1014
HABS VA,54-WATFO,41-
4dr/6pg/fr L

Waterford,Town of (General Views)
HABS VA-1042
HABS VA,54-WATFO,1-
5ph L

Williams Warehouse (Schoolhouse)
Second & Janney Sts.
HABS VA-798
HABS VA,54-WATFO,27-
1ph L

Williams,John B.,House
(Williams,William,House)
Second & Janney Sts.
HABS VA-797
HABS VA,54-WATFO,33-
1ph L

Williams,William,House; see
Williams,John B.,House

LOUISA COUNTY

BOSWELL'S TAVERN VIC

St. John's Church,Waldrop
State Rt. 22, .5 mi W of U. S. Rt. 15
HABS VA-1202
HABS VA,55-BOSWE.V,1-
5dr/14pg/fr L

BOSWELLS TAVERN VIC.

Barton House
Near Rt. 15, Green Springs Historic District
HABS VA-1235
HABS VA,55-BOSWE.V,2-
6ph/1pg L

Barton House,Shed No. 1
Rt. 15 vic., Green Springs Historic District
HABS VA-1235-A
HABS VA,55-BOSWE.V,2A-
2ph L

Barton House,Shed No. 2
Rt. 15 vic., Green Springs Historic District
HABS VA-1235-B
HABS VA,55-BOSWE.V,2B-
1ph L

St. John's Chapel
Intersection Rts. 617 & 638, Green Springs Hist. D
HABS VA-1238
HABS VA,55-BOSWE,V,3-
7dr/3ph/5pg/1pc/fr L

GORDONSVILLE

Ashleigh,Barn
Rt. 22 vic., Green Springs Historic District
HABS VA-1218-B
HABS VA,55-GORD.V,1B-
2ph/1pc L

GORDONSVILLE VIC.

Ashleigh,Clapboard Storage Building
Rt. 22 vic., Green Springs Historic District
HABS VA-1218-A
HABS VA,55-GORD.V,1A-
2ph/1pc L

Ashleigh,Main House
Rt. 22 vic., Green Springs Historic District
HABS VA-1218
HABS VA,55-GORD.V,1-
4ph/1pg/1pc L

Ashleigh,Small Barn
Rt. 22 vic., Green Springs Historic District
HABS VA-1218-C
HABS VA,55-GORD.V,1C-
2ph/1pc L

Ashleigh,Small Storage Building
Rt. 22 vic., Green Springs Historic District
HABS VA-1218-D
HABS VA,55-GORD.V,1D-
2ph/1pc L

Beau Allyn (Browns House,The)
Rt. 22 vic., Green Springs Historic District
HABS VA-1219
HABS VA,55-GORD.V,2-
6ph/1pg/1pc L

Belle Monte,Barn & Sheds
Rt. 22 vic., Green Springs Historic District
HABS VA-1216-C
HABS VA,55-GORD,3C-
1ph/1pc L

Belle Monte,Cottage
Rt. 22 vic., Green Springs Historic District
HABS VA-1216-A
HABS VA,55-GORD.V,3A-
3ph/1pc L

Belle Monte,Main House
Rt. 22 vic., Green Springs Historic District
HABS VA-1216
HABS VA,55-GORD.V,3-
3ph/1pg/1pc L

Belle Monte,Smokehouse & Corn Crib
Rt. 22 vic., Green Springs Historic District
HABS VA-1216-B
HABS VA,55-GORD.V,3B-
2ph/1pc L

Boswell's Tavern
Rt. 22 vic., Green Springs Historic District
HABS VA-1217
HABS VA,55-GORD.V,4-
12ph/2pg/4ct L

Boswells Tavern,Smokehouse
Rt. 22 vic., Green Springs Historic District
HABS VA-1217-A
HABS VA,55-GORD.V,4A-
3ph/1pc L

Browns House,The; see Beau Allyn

Burnley Farm
Rt. 15 vic., Green Springs Historic District
HABS VA-1220
HABS VA,55-GORD.V,5-
7ph/2pg L

Buttonwood (Main House)
Rt. 22 vic., Green Springs Historic District
HABS VA-1221
HABS VA,55-GORD.V,6-
5ph/1pg L

Buttonwood,Green House
Rt. 22, Green Springs Historic District
HABS VA-1221-B
HABS VA,55-GORD.V,6B-
1ph L

Buttonwood,Storage Sheds
Rt. 22 vic., Green Springs Historic District
HABS VA-1221-A
HABS VA,55-GORD.V,6A-
1ph L

Elms,The; see Galway

Galway (Elms,The)
Near Rts. 22 & 636, Green Springs Historic Dist.
HABS VA-1224
HABS VA,55-GORD.V,7-
4ph/2pg L

Galway,Barn (The Elms, Barn)
Rts. 22 & 636 vic., Green Springs Historic Dist.
HABS VA-1224-C
HABS VA,55-GORD.V,7C-
2ph L

Galway,Guest Cottage (The Elms Guest Cottage)
Rts. 22 & 636 vic., Green Springs Historic Dist.
HABS VA-1224-A
HABS VA,55-GORD.V,7A-
3ph L

Galway,Service Building (The Elms, Service Building)
Rts. 22 & 636 vic., Green Springs Historic Dist.
HABS VA-1224-B
HABS VA,55-GORD.V,7B-
2ph L

Green "K" Acres (Oakleigh)
Rt. 617, Green Springs Historic District
HABS VA-1226
HABS VA,55-GORD.V,8-
4ph/1pg L

Green "K" Acres,Abandoned Barn,Old
Rt. 617, Green Springs Historic District
HABS VA-1226-A
HABS VA,55-GORD.V,8A-
1ph L

Green "K" Acres,Barn
Rt. 617, Green Springs Historic District
HABS VA-1226-B
HABS VA,55-GORD.V,8B-
1ph L

Hawkwood
Rt. 15, Green Springs Historic District
HABS VA-36
HABS VA,55-GORD.V,9-
19ph/2pg/2pc/2ct L

Hawkwood,Dependency No. 1
Rt. 15, Green Springs Historic District
HABS VA-36-C
HABS VA,55-GORD.V,9C-
2ph/1pc L

Hawkwood,Dependency No. 2
Rt. 15, Green Springs Historic District
HABS VA-36-D
HABS VA,55-GORD.V,9D-
2ph/1pc L

Hawkwood,Dependency No. 3
Rt. 15, Green Springs Historic District
HABS VA-36-E
HABS VA,55-GORD.V,9E-
3ph/1pc L

Hawkwood,Dependency No. 4
Rt. 15, Green Springs Historic District
HABS VA-36-F
HABS VA,55-GORD.V,9F-
1ph/1pc L

Hawkwood,Log Cabin
Rt. 15, Green Springs Historic District
HABS VA-36-A
HABS VA,55-GORD.V,9A-
3ph/1pc L

Hawkwood,Manager's House
Rt. 15, Green Springs Historic District
HABS VA-36-B
HABS VA,55-GORD.V,9B-
3ph/1pc L

Oakleigh; see Green "K" Acres

The Elms Guest Cottage; see Galway,Guest Cottage

The Elms, Barn; see Galway,Barn

The Elms, Service Building; see Galway,Service Building

TREVILIANS

Bracketts Farm,Barn
Rts. 638 & 640, Green Springs Historic Dist.
HABS VA-1215-E
HABS VA,55-TREV.V,1E-
2ph/1pc L

TREVILIANS VIC.

Bracketts Farm,Cemetery
Rts. 638 & 640 vic., Green Springs Hist. Dist.
HABS VA-1215-I
HABS VA,55-TREV.V,1I-
4ph/1pc L

Bracketts Farm,Corn Crib
Rts. 638 & 640 vic., Green Springs Hist. Dist.
HABS VA-1215-F
HABS VA,55-TREV.V,1F-
2ph/1pc L

Bracketts Farm,Depot House
Rts. 638 & 640 vic., Green Springs Hist. Dist.
HABS VA-1215-B
HABS VA,55-TREV.V,1B-
5ph/1pc L

Bracketts Farm,Guest House
Rts. 638 & 640 vic., Green Springs Hist. Dist.
HABS VA-1215-C
HABS VA,55-TREV.V,1C-
2ph/1pc L

Bracketts Farm,Horse Barn
Rts. 638 & 640 vic., Green Springs Hist. Dist.
HABS VA-1215-H
HABS VA,55-TREV.V,1H-
8ph/1pc L

Bracketts Farm,Main House
Rts. 638 & 640 vic., Green Springs Hist. Dist.
HABS VA-1215
HABS VA,55-TREV.V,1-
14ph/2pg/1pc L

Bracketts Farm,Slave Quarters
Rts. 638 & 640 vic., Green Springs Hist. Dist.
HABS VA-1215-A
HABS VA,55-TREV.V,1A-
8ph/1pc L

Bracketts Farm,Smokehouse
Rts. 638 & 640 vic., Green Springs Hist. Dist.
HABS VA-1215-D
HABS VA,55-TREV.V,1D-
2ph/1pc L

Bracketts Farm,Storage Shed
Rts. 638 & 640 vic., Green Springs Hist. Dist.
HABS VA-1215-G
HABS VA,55-TREV.V,1G-
2ph/1pc L

Clover Plains; see Ionia (Main House)

East View (Eastern View)
Near Rt. 613, Green Springs Historic District
HABS VA-1222
HABS VA,55-TREV.V,2-
4ph/1pg/1pc L

East View,Barn (Eastern View)
Rt. 613 vic., Green Springs Historic District
HABS VA-1222-B
HABS VA,55-TREV.V,2B-
2ph/1pc L

East View,Shed (Eastern View)
Rt. 613 vic., Green Springs Historic District
HABS VA-1222-A
HABS VA,55-TREV.V,2A-
1ph/1pc L

Eastern View; see East View

Eastern View; see East View,Barn

Eastern View; see East View,Shed

Ferncliff Farm
Rt. 613 & S. Anna Bridge Vic., Green Springs H. D.
HABS VA-1225
HABS VA,55-TREV.V,3-
3ph/1pg/1pc L

Ferncliff Farm,Tenant House
Rt. 613 & South Anna Bridge vic., Green Springs HD
HABS VA-1225-A
HABS VA,55-TREV.V,3A-
2ph/1pc L

Glen Burnie (Main House)
Rt. 613, Green Springs Historic District
HABS VA-1236
HABS VA,55-TREV.V,4-
7ph/2pg/1pc L

Glen Burnie,Barn
Rt. 613, Green Springs Historic District
HABS VA-1236-A
HABS VA,55-TREV.V,4A-
1ph/1pc L

Green Springs (Main House)
Near Rts. 617 & 15, Green Springs Historic Dist.
HABS VA-1227
HABS VA,55-TREV.V,5-
8ph/2pg/1pc L

Green Springs,Barn No. 1
Rts. 617 & 15 vic., Green Springs Historic Dist.
HABS VA-1227-F
HABS VA,55-TREV.V,5F-
3ph/1pc L

Green Springs,Barn No. 2
Rts. 617 & 15 vic., Green Springs Historic Dist.
HABS VA-1227-G
HABS VA,55-TREV.V,5G-
2ph/1pc L

Green Springs,Corn Crib
Rts. 617 & 15 vic., Green Springs Historic Dist.
HABS VA-1227-D
HABS VA,55-TREV.V,5D-
3ph/1pc L

Green Springs,Guest Cottage No. 1
Rts. 617 & 15 vic., Green Springs Historic Dist.
HABS VA-1227-A
HABS VA,55-TREV.V,5A-
3ph/1pc L

Green Springs,Guest Cottage No. 2
Rts. 617 & 15 vic., Green Springs Historic Dist.
HABS VA-1227-B
HABS VA,55-TREV.V,5B-
3ph/1pc L

Green Springs,Guest Cottage No. 3
Rts. 617 & 15 vic., Green Springs Historic Dist.
HABS VA-1227-C
HABS VA,55-TREV.V,5C-
2ph/1pc L

Green Springs,Tenant Houses
Rts. 617 & 15 vic., Green Springs Historic Dist.
HABS VA-1227-E
HABS VA,55-TREV.V,5E-
1ph/1pc L

Hard Bargain (Main House)
Near Rts. 695,636 & 613 vic. Green Springs Hist.D.
HABS VA-1231
7ph/2pg/1pc/1ct L

Hard Bargain,Barn
Rts. 695,636 & 613 vic., Green Springs Hist. Dist.
HABS VA-1231-B
HABS VA,55-TREV.V,6B-
2ph/1pc L

Hard Bargain,Cottage
Rts. 695,636 & 613 vic., Green Springs Hist. Dist.
HABS VA-1231-A
HABS VA,55-TREV.V,6A-
2ph/1pc L

Ionia (Main House) (Clover Plains)
Near Rt. 640, Green Springs Historic District
HABS VA-1232
HABS VA,55-TREV.V,7-
6ph/1pg/1pc L

Ionia,Barn
Rt. 640 vic., Green Springs Historic District
HABS VA-1000
HABS VA,55-TREV.V,7D-
6dr/5pg/fr L

Ionia,Milk House
Rt. 640 vic., Green Springs Historic District
HABS VA-1232-A
HABS VA,55-TREV.V,7A-
1ph/1pc L

Ionia,Outbuilding
Rt. 640 vic., Green Springs Historic District
HABS VA-1232-C
HABS VA,55-TREV.V,7C-
1ph/1pc L

Ionia,Smokehouse
Rt. 640 vic., Green Springs Historic District
HABS VA-1232-B
HABS VA,55-TREV.V,7B-
2ph/1pc L

Kenmuir (Main House)
Rt. 613, Green Springs Historic District
HABS VA-1229
HABS VA,55-TREV.V,8-
9ph/1pg/1pc L

Kenmuir,Barn
Rt. 613, Green Springs Historic District
HABS VA-1229-B
HABS VA,55-TREV.V,8B-
14ph/1pc L

Kenmuir,Carriage House
Rt. 613, Green Springs Historic District
HABS VA-1229-C
HABS VA,55-TREV.V,8C-
2ph/1pc L

Kenmuir,Corn Crib
Rt. 613, Green Springs Historic District
HABS VA-1229-E
HABS VA,55-TREV.V,8E-
2ph/1pc L

Kenmuir,Ragland House
Rt. 613, Green Springs Historic District
HABS VA-1229-A
HABS VA,55-TREV.V,8A-
8ph/1pc L

Kenmuir,Small Barn
Rt. 613, Green Springs Historic District
HABS VA-1229-D
HABS VA,55-TREV.V,8D-
1ph/1pc L

Kenmuir,Smokehouse
Rt. 613, Green Springs Historic District
HABS VA-1229-F
HABS VA,55-TREV.V,8F-
2ph/1pc L

Mill View (Main House) (Millview)
Near Rt. 613, Green Springs Historic District
HABS VA-1223
HABS VA,55-TREV.V,9-
4ph/1pg/1pc/1ct L

Mill View,Barns
Rt. 613 vic., Green Springs Historic District
HABS VA-1223-B
HABS VA,55-TREV.V,9B-
1ph/1pc L

Mill View,Ice House
Rt. 613 vic., Green Springs Historic District
HABS VA-1223-A
HABS VA,55-TREV.V,9A-
2ph/1pc L

Millview; see Mill View (Main House)

Misty Meadows
Near Rts. 613 & 607 Intersection, Green Springs HD
HABS VA-1230
HABS VA,55-TREV.V,10-
3ph/1pg/1pc L

Prospect Hill (Main House)
Near Rts. 613 & 607 Intersection, Green Springs HD
HABS VA-1234
HABS VA,55-TREV.V,11-
7ph/1pg/1pc/1ct L

Prospect Hill,Barn No. 1
Near Rts. 613 & 607 intersection, Green Springs HD
HABS VA-1234-B
HABS VA,55-TREV.V,11B-
1ph/1pc L

Prospect Hill,Barn No. 2
Near Rts. 613 & 607 intersection, Green Springs HD
HABS VA-1234-C
HABS VA,55-TREV.V,11C-
1ph/1pc L

Prospect Hill,Barn No. 3
Near Rts. 613 & 607 intersection, Green Springs HD
HABS VA-1234-D
HABS VA,55-TREV.V,11D-
2ph/1pc L

Prospect Hill,Barn No. 4
Near Rts. 613 & 607 intersection, Green Springs HD
HABS VA-1234-E
HABS VA,55-TREV.V,11E-
2ph/1pc L

Prospect Hill,Carriage House
Near Rts. 613 & 607 intersection, Green Springs HD
HABS VA-1234-A
HABS VA,55-TREV.V,11A-
5ph/1pc L

Prospect Hill,Guest House No. 1; see Prospect Hill,Slave Quarters No. 1

Prospect Hill,Guest House No. 2; see Prospect Hill,Slave Quarters No. 2

Prospect Hill,Guest House No. 3; see Prospect Hill,Slave Quarters No. 3

Prospect Hill,Shed
Near Rts. 613 & 607 intersection, Green Springs HD
HABS VA-1234-G
HABS VA,55-TREV.V,11G-
2ph/1pc L

Prospect Hill,Slave Quarters No. 1
(Prospect Hill,Guest House No. 1)
Near Rts. 613 & 607 intersection, Green Springs HD
HABS VA-1234-H
HABS VA,55-TREV.V,11H-
2ph/1pc L

Documentation: **ct** color transparencies **dr** measured drawings **fr** field records
pc photograph captions **pg** pages of text **ph** photographs

Prospect Hill,Slave Quarters No. 2
(Prospect Hill,Guest House No. 2)
Near Rts. 613 & 607 intersection, Green Springs HD
HABS VA-1234-I
HABS VA,55-TREV.V,11I-
3ph/1pc L

Prospect Hill,Slave Quarters No. 3
(Prospect Hill,Guest House No. 3)
Near Rts. 613 & 607 intersection, Green Springs HD
HABS VA-1234-J
HABS VA,55-TREV.V,11J-
4ph/1pc L

Prospect Hill,Slave Quarters No. 4
Near Rts. 613 & 607 intersection, Green Springs HD
HABS VA-1234-L
HABS VA,55-TREV.V,11L-
2ph/1pc L

Prospect Hill,Slave Quarters No. 5
Near Rts. 613 & 607 intersection, Green Springs HD
HABS VA-1234-M
HABS VA,55-TREV.V,11M-
2ph/1pc L

Prospect Hill,Tack Room
Near Rts. 613 & 607 intersection, Green Springs HD
HABS VA-1234-F
HABS VA,55-TREV.V,11F-
1ph/1pc L

Quaker Hill (Main House)
Rt. 613, Green Springs Historic District
HABS VA-1237
HABS VA,55-TREV.V,12-
6ph/1pg/1pc L

Quaker Hill,Barn & Shed
Rt. 613, Green Springs Historic District
HABS VA-1237-C
HABS VA,55-TRV.V,12C-
4ph/1pc L

Quaker Hill,Outbuildings
Rt. 613, Green Springs Historic District
HABS VA-1237-B
HABS VA,55-TREV.V,12B-
1ph/1pc L

Quaker Hill,Shed
Rt. 613, Green Springs Historic District
HABS VA-1237-A
HABS VA,55-TREV.V,12A-
1ph/1pc L

Sunny Banks (Main House)
Near Rt. 640, Green Springs Historic District
HABS VA-1228
HABS VA,55-TREV.V,13-
4ph/2pg/1pc/2ct L

Sunny Banks,Barn No. 1
Near Rt. 640, Green Springs Historic District
HABS VA-1228-A
HABS VA,55-TREV.V,13A-
2ph/1pc L

Sunny Banks,Barn No. 2
Near Rt. 640, Green Springs Historic District
HABS VA-1228-B
HABS VA,55-TREV.V,13B-
2ph/1pc L

Westend (Main House)
Rt. 638 vic., Green Springs Historic District
HABS VA-1233
HABS VA,55-TREV.V,14-
3ph/2pg/1pc/2ct L

Westend,Outbuilding No. 1
Rt. 638 vic., Green Springs Historic District
HABS VA-1233-A
HABS VA,55-TREV.V,14A-
2ph/1pc L

Westend,Outbuilding No. 2
Rt. 638 vic., Green Springs Historic District
HABS VA-1233-B
HABS VA,55-TREV.V,14B-
1ph/1pc L

Westend,Slave Quarters No. 1
Rt. 638 vic., Green Springs Historic District
HABS VA-1233-C
HABS VA,55-TREV.V,14C-
3ph/1pc L

Westend,Slave Quarters No. 2
Rt. 638 vic., Green Springs Historic District
HABS VA-1233-D
HABS VA,55-TREV.V,14D-
4ph/1pc L

LYNCHBURG (CITY)

Abbot,S. L. ,House,Mantel
104 Oakwood Place
HABS VA-1097
HABS VA,16-LYNBU,78-
1ph/1pc L

Academy of Music
Main & Sixth Sts.
HABS VA-1161
HABS VA,16-LYNBU,76-
1ph/1pc L

Adams,W. D. ,House
210 Cabell St.
HABS VA-1131
HABS VA,16-LYNBU,13-
1ph/1pc L

Allied Arts Building
Eighth & Church Sts.
HABS VA-1182
HABS VA,16-LYNBU,17-
2ph/1pc L

Atlantic,Miss. & Ohio RR,Jefferson Street Tunnel (Norfolk & Western RR,Jefferson Street Tunnel)
Norfolk & Western RY main line
HAER VA-9
HAER VA,16-LYNBU,10-
3ph/1pc L

Barksdale,A. D. ,House
2001 Link Rd.
HABS VA-1194
HABS VA,16-LYNBU,61-
1ph/1pc L

Blackford,Charles Minor,House
618 Pearl St.
HABS VA-1115
HABS VA,16-LYNBU,84-
1ph/1pc L

1500 Block Rivermont Avenue (Houses) (Rivermont Avenue,1500 Block (Houses))
HABS VA-1169
HABS VA,16-LYNBU,88-
1ph/1pc L

Bowman & Moore Leaf Tobacco Factory
Main & Thirteenth Sts.
HABS VA-1132
HABS VA,16-LYNBU,120-
1ph L

Bradley Cottage
1501 Church St.
HABS VA-1196
HABS VA,16-LYNBU,21-
1ph/1pc L

Brown,Edward S. ,House
818 Court St.
HABS VA-1138
HABS VA,16-LYNBU,34-
1ph/1pc L

1879 Building
Jefferson St. between Eighth & Ninth Sts.
HABS VA-1122
HABS VA,16-LYNBU,45-
1ph/1pc L

Burkholder,Robert Calhoun,House
Cabell & B Sts.
HABS VA-1126
HABS VA,16-LYNBU,12-
1ph/1pc L

Burroughs,Ambrose H. ,House
220 Madison St.
HABS VA-1153
HABS VA,16-LYNBU,66-
1ph/1pc L

Carrington,Richard A. ,House
508 Washington St.
HABS VA-1167
HABS VA,16-LYNBU,115-
3ph/1pc L

Carroll,John W. ,House
Harrison & Eleventh Sts.
HABS VA-1127
HABS VA,16-LYNBU,50-
1ph/1pc L

Carroll,William,House
Harrison & Eleventh Sts.
HABS VA-1128
HABS VA,16-LYNBU,49-
1ph/1pc L

Centenary Methodist Church
Rivermont Ave. & Marshall St.
HABS VA-1183
HABS VA,16-LYNBU,96-
1ph/1pc L

Chapel of the Good Shepherd (Episcopal)
Fourteenth & Wise Sts.
HABS VA-1165
HABS VA,16-LYNBU,118-
1ph/1pc L

Christian,Frank P. ,House
412 Madison St.
HABS VA-1150
HABS VA,16-LYNBU,70-
2ph/1pc L

City Court House (Court House; Court House,Old)
Court St. & Monument Terr.
HABS VA-1114
HABS VA,16-LYNBU,2-
4ph/1pc L

510-512 Clay Street (Double House)
HABS VA-1197
HABS VA,16-LYNBU,22-
2ph/1pc L

Court House; see City Court House

Court House,Old; see City Court House

Court Street Baptist Church
Court & Sixth Sts.
HABS VA-1125
HABS VA,16-LYNBU,29-
1ph/1pc L

Court Street Methodist Church
Court & Seventh Sts.
HABS VA-1147
HABS VA,16-LYNBU,30-
2ph/1pc L

Craddock-Terry Shoe Company
Ninth & Jefferson Sts.
HABS VA-1142
HABS VA,16-LYNBU,57-
1ph/1pc L

Craddock,C. G. ,House
222 Woodland Ave.
HABS VA-1186
HABS VA,16-LYNBU,119-
2ph/1pc L

Craddock,John W. ,House
208 Madison St.
HABS VA-1149
HABS VA,16-LYNBU,64-
1ph/1pc L

Crowe House
Eleventh & Jackson Sts.
HABS VA-1093
HABS VA,16-LYNBU,54-
1ph/1pc L

Dabney-Scott-Adams House (Dabney's Folly)
405 Cabell St.
HABS VA-1095
HABS VA,16-LYNBU,14-
3ph/1pc L

Dabney's Folly; see Dabney-Scott-Adams House

Daniel,John Warwick,Statue
Park Ave. between Floyd & Ninth Sts.
HABS VA-1174
HABS VA,16-LYNBU,81-
1ph/1pc L

Diamond Hill Fire Station; see Grace Street Fire Station

Dunnington-Garland-Noell House
(Garland,Samuel,Jr. ,House)
Third & Madison Sts.
HABS VA-1106
HABS VA,16-LYNBU,67-
1ph/1pc L

Early,Bishop John,House
HABS VA-1096
HABS VA,16-LYNBU,82-
3ph/1pc L

Edankrall; see Spencer,Anne,House,Study

Eighth Street Baptist Church
Eighth & Federal Sts.
HABS VA-1144
HABS VA,16-LYNBU,40-
1ph/1pc L

Elliott,Peter,House
Harrison & Seventh Sts.
HABS VA-1100
HABS VA,16-LYNBU,48-
1ph/1pc L

914 Federal Street (House)
HABS VA-1099
HABS VA,16-LYNBU,43-
3ph/1pc L

First Baptist Church
Court & Eleventh Sts.
HABS VA-1134
HABS VA,16-LYNBU,38-
3ph/1pc L

First Christian Church
Main & Fifth Sts.
HABS VA-1164
HABS VA,16-LYNBU,73-
1ph/1pc L

First Methodist Church; see First Presbyterian Church

First Presbyterian Church (First Methodist Church)
Ninth & Court Sts.
HABS VA-1145
HABS VA,16-LYNBU,35-
1ph/1pc L

First Unitarian Church
Monument Terr.
HABS VA-1181
HABS VA,16-LYNBU,39-
1ph/1pc L

Folly,The
Church St. between Thirteenth & Washington Sts.
HABS VA-1121
HABS VA,16-LYNBU,20-
1ph/1pc L

2560 Fort Avenue (House)
HABS VA-1103
HABS VA,16-LYNBU,45-
1ph/1pc L

Frye,Edward G. ,House
1 Easton Ave.
HABS VA-1159
HABS VA,16-LYNBU,42-
1ph/1pc L

Gannaway,John E. ,House
Washington & Clay Sts.
HABS VA-1157
HABS VA,16-LYNBU,112-
2ph/1pc L

Garland,Samuel,Jr. ,House; see Dunnington-Garland-Noell House

Garland,Samuel,Sr. ,House
215 Madison St.
HABS VA-1111
HABS VA,16-LYNBU,65-
1ph/1pc L

Gilliam,James R. ,Sr. ,House
Madison & Fourth Sts.
HABS VA-1179
HABS VA,16-LYNBU,68-
1ph/1pc L

Glass,Carter,House; see Wills-Davis-Glass House

Gleaves,R. Taylor,House
1700 Rivermont Ave.
HABS VA-1168
HABS VA,16-LYNBU,89-
1ph/1pc L

Grace Memorial Episcopal Church
1021 New Hampshire Ave.
HABS VA-1184
HABS VA,16-LYNBU,77-
1ph/1pc L

Grace Street Fire Station (Diamond Hill Fire Station)
Grace & Pearl Sts.
HABS VA-1129
HABS VA,16-LYNBU,47-
1ph/1pc L

Graves House; see Rosedale

Graves,William E. ,House
2102 Rivermont Ave.
HABS VA-1170
HABS VA,16-LYNBU,93-
2ph/1pc L

Hill City Masonic Lodge (Ward Building)
Church & Eleventh Sts.
HABS VA-1143
HABS VA,16-LYNBU,18-
2ph/1pc L

Holy Cross Catholic Church
Seventh & Clay Sts.
HABS VA-1124
HABS VA,16-LYNBU,27-
1ph/1pc L

Holy Cross Catholic Church,Campanile
Seventh & Clay Sts.
HABS VA-1124-A
HABS VA,16-LYNBU,27A-
1ph/1pc L

Horton,Lawrence W. ,House
1901 Link Rd.
HABS VA-1193
HABS VA,16-LYNBU,60-
1ph/1pc L

Ivey,William Christopher,House
2024 Rivermont Ave.
HABS VA-1171
HABS VA,16-LYNBU,92-
1ph/1pc L

Jackson & Seventh Streets (House)
HABS VA-1108
HABS VA,16-LYNBU,53-
1ph/1pc L

James River & Kanawha Canal Bridge (Ninth Street Bridge)
Ninth St. between Jefferson St. & James River
HABS VA-1109
HABS VA,16-LYNBU,53A-
2ph/1pc L

Jones Memorial Library
434 Rivermont Ave.
HABS VA-1160
HABS VA,16-LYNBU,90-
1ph/1pc L

Jordan,Ezekiah,House
Polk & Eighth Sts.
HABS VA-1102
HABS VA,16-LYNBU,41-
1ph/1pc L

Kean,Robert Garlick Hill,House
Pearl & Harrison Sts.
HABS VA-1119
HABS VA,16-LYNBU,51-
1ph/1pc L

Kentucky Hotel
Fifth & Jackson Sts.
HABS VA-1089
HABS VA,16-LYNBU,52-
1ph/1pc L

Kerr,George A. ,House (Seven Hills School)
2001 Rivermont Ave.
HABS VA-1172
HABS VA,16-LYNBU,91-
1dr/1ph/1pc L

Kinnier,John,House
Washington & Madison Sts.
HABS VA-1158
HABS VA,16-LYNBU,114-
1ph/1pc L

LaTour,Louis,House
Court & Eleventh Sts.
HABS VA-1154
HABS VA,16-LYNBU,37-
1ph/1pc L

Lewis,Henry Harrison,House
Church & Sixth Sts.
HABS VA-1117
HABS VA,16-LYNBU,16-
2ph/1pc L

Lewis,J. M. B. ,House
1314 Clay St.
HABS VA-1166
HABS VA,16-LYNBU,28-
1ph/1pc L

Loyd,Sidney B. ,House
1303 Langhorne Rd.
HABS VA-1188
HABS VA,16-LYNBU,59-
1ph/1pc L

Lynchburg City Armory
Church St. between Twelfth & Thirteenth Sts.
HABS VA-1190
HABS VA,16-LYNBU,19-
1ph/1pc L

Lynchburg City Hall; see U. S. Post Office & Court House

Lynchburg City Hall Annex; see U. S. Post Office & Court House

Lynchburg Furniture Company
1023 Main St.
HABS VA-1133
HABS VA,16-LYNBU,75-
1ph/1pc L

Lynchburg National Bank
Ninth & Main Sts.
HABS VA-1176
HABS VA,16-LYNBU,74-
1ph/1pc L

Lynchburg News & Daily Advance Building
Church St. at Monument Terr.
HABS VA-1191
HABS VA,16-LYNBU,15-
1ph/1pc L

1510 Madison Street (House)
HABS VA-1107
HABS VA,16-LYNBU,72-
1ph/1pc L

Main & Thirteenth Streets (Commercial Building)
HABS VA-1162
HABS VA,16-LYNBU,98-
1ph/1pc L

Manning,Thomas A. ,House
509 Cabell St.
HABS VA-1155
HABS VA,16-LYNBU,99-
1ph/1pc L

Marsan
1111 V. E. S. Rd.
HABS VA-1189
HABS VA,16-LYNBU,100-
1ph L

Massie,Robert Withers,House
Federal & Tenth Sts.
HABS VA-1156
HABS VA,16-LYNBU,101-
1ph/1pc L

McWane,Henry E. ,House
214 Cabell St.
HABS VA-1148
HABS VA,16-LYNBU,102-
1ph/1pc L

Miller-Claytor House
Miller-Claytor Lane & Treasure Island Rd.
HABS VA-1085
HABS VA,16-LYNBU,104-
3ph/1pc L

Miller,E. P. ,House
118 Oakwood Place
HABS VA-1185
HABS VA,16-LYNBU,103-
3ph/1pc L

Monument Terrace
Ninth St. between Church & Court Sts.
HABS VA-1180
HABS VA,16-LYNBU,105-
2ph/1pc L

Murrell,Edward,House
Madison & Second Sts.
HABS VA-1116
HABS VA,16-LYNBU,106-
1ph/1pc L

N & W Depot; see Norfolk & Western Freight Depot

Nichols,Joseph,Tavern; see Western Hotel

Ninth Street Bridge; see James River & Kanawha Canal Bridge

Norfolk & Western Freight Depot (N & W Depot)
Ninth & Eleventh Sts. at bank of James River
HABS VA-1130
HABS VA,16-LYNBU,107-
1ph/1pc L

Norfolk & Western RR,Jefferson Street Tunnel; see Atlantic,Miss. & Ohio RR,Jefferson Street Tunnel

Norvell,William Wiatt,House
822 Federal St.
HABS VA-1091
HABS VA,16-LYNBU,108-
1ph/1pc L

Oakwood Country Club
Rivermont Ave. opposite V. E. S. Rd.
HABS VA-1175
HABS VA,16-LYNBU,87-
1ph/1pc L

Oglesby-DeWitt Building
Tenth & Commerce Sts.
HABS VA-1163
HABS VA,16-LYNBU,109-
1ph/1pc L

Otey,John Matthews,House
1002 Federal St.
HABS VA-1090
HABS VA,16-LYNBU,110-
1ph/1pc L

Park View Methodist Church
Memorial Ave. & Wadsworth St.
HABS VA-1195
HABS VA,16-LYNBU,111-
1ph/1pc L

Paxton,James Dunlop,House
117 Oakwood Place
HABS VA-1187
HABS VA,16-LYNBU,79-
1ph/1pc L

Pettyjohn,C. R. ,House
3115 Rivermont Ave.
HABS VA-1192
HABS VA,16-LYNBU,95-
1ph/1pc L

Phaup,William,House
Sixth St. between Jackson & Polk Sts.
HABS VA-1101
HABS VA,16-LYNBU,97-
1ph/1pc L

Piedmont Mills
Jefferson St. & Horseford Rd.
HABS VA-1123
HABS VA,16-LYNBU,55-
1ph/1pc L

Point of Honor
Cabell St. between A & B Sts.
HABS VA-311
HABS VA,16-LYNBU,7-
1dr/5ph/1pg L

Powell House
307 Washington St.
HABS VA-1140
HABS VA,16-LYNBU,116-
1ph/1pc L

Price-Turner House
Sixth & Clay Sts.
HABS VA-1094
HABS VA,16-LYNBU,23-
2ph/1pc L

Price-Turner House,Dependency
Sixth St.
HABS VA-1094-A
HABS VA,16-LYNBU,23A-
1ph/1pc L

Quaker Meeting House; see South River Quaker Meeting House

9 Quinlan Street (House)
HABS VA-1098
HABS VA,16-LYNBU,86-
1ph/1pc L

Rivermont Avenue,1500 Block (Houses); see 1500 Block Rivermont Avenue (Houses)

Roane-Rodes House (Rodes House)
1008 Harrison St.
HABS VA-1092
HABS VA,16-LYNBU,4-
2ph L

Rodes House; see Roane-Rodes House

Rosedale (Graves House)
Old Graves Mill Rd.
HABS VA-1110
HABS VA,16-LYNBU,80-
3ph/1pc L

Schaefer,Edmund,House
714 Court St.
HABS VA-1137
HABS VA,16-LYNBU,31-
1ph/1pc L

Seven Hills School; see Kerr,George A. ,House

Sixth Street Bridge
Sixth St. ,Spanning Black Water Creek
HAER VA-6
HAER VA,16-LYNBU,11-
7ph/2pg/1pc L

South River Quaker Meeting House
(Quaker Meeting House)
5810 Fort Ave.
HABS VA-1087
HABS VA,16-LYNBU,46-
2ph/1pc L

Spencer,Anne,House
1313 Pierce St.
HABS VA-1173
HABS VA,16-LYNBU,85-
5ph/1pc L

Spencer,Anne,House,Study (Edankrall)
1313 Pierce St.
HABS VA-1173-A
HABS VA,16-LYNBU,85A-
3ph/1pc L

St. James C. M. E. Church
Forest Rd. & Old Forest Rd.
HABS VA-1146
HABS VA,16-LYNBU,44-
1ph/1pc L

St. Paul's Episcopal Church
Clay & Seventh Sts.
HABS VA-1135
HABS VA,16-LYNBU,25-
3ph/1pc L

Stabler,Robinson,House
Washington & Madison Sts.
HABS VA-1118
HABS VA,16-LYNBU,113-
4ph/1pc L

Tabb-Slaughter-Diggs House
117 Madison St.
HABS VA-1112
HABS VA,16-LYNBU,63-
2ph/1pc L

Tunstall House
801 Court St.
HABS VA-1139
HABS VA,16-LYNBU,33-
1ph/1pc L

Tyree-Slaughter House
Pearl & Harrison Sts.
HABS VA-1120
HABS VA,16-LYNBU,83-
1ph/1pc L

U. S. Post Office & Court House
(Lynchburg City Hall)
900 Church St.
HABS VA-38
HABS VA,16-LYNBU,9-
3ph/4pg/2pc L

U. S. Post Office & Court House
(Lynchburg City Hall Annex)
901 Church St.
HABS VA-1206
HABS VA,16-LYNBU,8-
6ph/4pg/1pc/fr L

Ward Building; see Hill City Masonic Lodge

Warwick,John Marshall,House
Eighth & Court Sts.
HABS VA-1104
HABS VA,16-LYNBU,32-
1ph/1pc L

Watkins,George P. ,House
400 Madison St.
HABS VA-1151
HABS VA,16-LYNBU,69-
2ph/1pc L

Watts,James W. ,House
1007 Court St.
HABS VA-1136
HABS VA,16-LYNBU,36-
1ph/1pc L

Western Hotel (Nichols,Joseph,Tavern)
Fifth & Madison Sts.
HABS VA-1088
HABS VA,16-LYNBU,71-
1ph/1pc L

Williams,Ernest,House
517 Washington St.
HABS VA-1178
HABS VA,16-LYNBU,117-
1ph/1pc L

Wills-Davis-Glass House
(Glass,Carter,House)
Clay & Sixth Sts.
HABS VA-1105
HABS VA,16-LYNBU,24-
2ph/1pc L

Wilson,William V. ,House
106 Madison St.
HABS VA-1152
HABS VA,16-LYNBU,62-
1ph/1pc L

Woodstock Apartments
2934 Rivermont Ave.
HABS VA-1177
HABS VA,16-LYNBU,94-
1ph L

Yancey,Elizabeth,House
707 Clay St.
HABS VA-1113
HABS VA,16-LYNBU,26-
1ph/1pc L

MADISON COUNTY

MADISON

Madison County Courthouse
U. S. Rt. 29
HABS VA-325
HABS VA,57-MAD,1-
1ph/33pg L

MADISON VIC.

Hebron Lutheran Church
State Rts. 638 & 653
HABS VA-411
HABS VA,57-MAD.V,1-
4dr/1ph/15pg/1pc/fr L

MECKLENBURG COUNTY

BUFFALO SPRINGS

Hotel Cottages
State Rt. 767 Vic.
HABS VA-186
HABS VA,59-BUF,1-
1ph L

CLARKSVILLE VIC.

Prestwould Plantation
U. S. Rt. 15 Vic.
HABS VA-320
HABS VA,59-CLARK.V,1-
23dr/4ph/1pg/fr L

SOUTH HILL

624 Mecklenburg Avenue (Tavern,Old)
HABS VA-312
HABS VA,59-SOUHI,1-
1ph L

MIDDLESEX COUNTY

CHRIST CHURCH VIC.

Christ Church
State Rt. 638
HABS VA-539
HABS VA,60- ,1-
1ph L

CHURCHVIEW VIC.

House
La Grange Creek Vic.
HABS VA-517
HABS VA,37- ,3-
1ph L

House,Old; see La Grange

La Grange (House,Old)
La Grange Creek Vic.
HABS VA-516
HABS VA,37- ,2-
1ph L

URBANNA

Customs House; see House,Old

House,Old (Customs House)
State Rt. 1002
HABS VA-799
HABS VA,60-URB,1-
1ph L

Mills,James & Co.,Storehouse; see Tobacco Warehouse

Tobacco Warehouse (Mills,James & Co.,Storehouse)
State Rt. 1002
HABS VA-589
HABS VA,60-URB,2-
27ph/6pg/fr L

URBANNA VIC.

Hewick House
State Rts. 615 & 602 Vic.
HABS VA-540
HABS VA,60-URB.V,1-
2ph L

MONTGOMERY COUNTY

ELLISTON VIC.

Fotheringay
U. S. Rt. 11 Vic.
HABS VA-348
HABS VA,61- ,1-
3ph/1pg L

RADFORD VIC.

New River Ordnance Plant; see Radford Army Ammunition Plant

New River Ordnance Works; see Radford Army Ammunition Plant

Radford Army Ammunition Plant (New River Ordnance Plant; Radford Ordnance Works; Radford Ordnance Plant; New River Ordnance Works)
HAER VA-37
HAER VA,61-RAD.V,1-
53pg/fr L

Radford Ordnance Plant; see Radford Army Ammunition Plant

Radford Ordnance Works; see Radford Army Ammunition Plant

NELSON COUNTY

AFTON VIC.

Blue Ridge Railroad,Blue Ridge Tunnel (Crozet Tunnel)
U. S. Rt. 250 at Rockfish Gap
HAER VA-2
HAER VA,63-AFT.V,1-
2dr/7ph/4pg/1pc/fr L

Chesapeake & Ohio Railroad,Blue Ridge Tunnel
Hwy. 250 at Rockfish Gap
HAER VA-5
HAER VA,63-AFT.V,2-
1ph/1pg/1pc L

Crozet Tunnel; see Blue Ridge Railroad,Blue Ridge Tunnel

GREENFIELD VIC.

Coles,Edward, House
State Route 635
HABS VA-1248
HABS VA,63-GREFI.V,1-
6dr/fr L

LOVINGSTON

Nelson County Courthouse
U. S. Rt.29
HABS VA-336
HABS VA,63-LOV,1-
2ph/1pg L

NEW KENT COUNTY

BARHAMSVILLE

Union Level
State Rt. 633 Vic.
HABS VA-442
HABS VA,64-BAR.V,1-
2ph/1pg L

BARHAMSVILLE VIC.

Smokehouse
State Rt. 30 Vic.
HABS VA-541
HABS VA,64-BAR,1-
1ph L

NEW KENT VIC.

Criss-Cross (Poindexter House)
State Rt. 617 Vic.
HABS VA-126
HABS VA,64-NEWK.V,1-
13dr/11ph/4pg/fr L

Poindexter House; see Criss-Cross

Woodland
HABS VA-803
HABS VA,64-NEWK.V,2-
1ph L

PROVIDENCE

Potts,Doctor,House; see Providence Forge House

Providence Forge House (Providence Hall; Potts,Doctor,House)
U.S. Rt. 60 (moved to VA,Williamsburg)
HABS VA-912
HABS VA,64-PROFO,2-
9ph L

Providence Hall; see Providence Forge House

PROVIDENCE FORGE VIC

Cedar Grove
State Rt. 609
HABS VA-802
HABS VA,64-PROFO.V,1-
4ph L

Grist Mill; see Providence Forge

Providence Forge (Grist Mill)
Old Forge Pond
HABS VA-110
HABS VA,64-PROFO,1-
9dr/17ph/2pg/fr L

QUINTON VIC.

Lucas,Doctor,House
State Rt. 33
HABS VA-121
HABS VA,64- ,3-
8dr/fr L

TUNSTALL VIC.

Castle,The
State Rt. 608 Vic.
HABS VA-124
HABS VA,64-TUN.V,2-
13dr/6ph/4pg/fr L

Ferry,The; see Poplar Grove

Poplar Grove (Ferry,The)
Pamunkey River
HABS VA-801
HABS VA,64-TUN.V,3-
4ph L

Road View Farm,Kitchen
State Rt. 609 Vic.
HABS VA-97
HABS VA,64-TUN.V,1-
5dr/5ph/3pg L

St. Peter's Church
State Rt. 642
HABS VA-127
HABS VA,64-TUN.V,4-
9dr/6ph/10pg/fr L

NEWPORT NEWS (CITY)

Davis & Kimpton Brickyard
W. Bank of Warwick River,Mulberry Island
HAER VA-43
5dr/12ph/9pg/2pc L

Denbigh Plantation,Milk House
Lukas Creek Rd.
HABS VA-1046-A
HABS VA,95-NEWNE,1A-
1ph/1pc L

Denbigh Plantation,Spring House
Lukas Creek Rd.
HABS VA-1046-B
HABS VA,95-NEWNE,1B-
1ph/1pc L

Jones,Matthew,House
HABS VA-163
HABS VA,95-LEHA,1-
7dr/10ph/1pg L

NORFOLK (CITY)

Academy,Old
State Rts. 625 & 170
HABS VA-227
HABS VA,65-HICK.V,1-
7ph L

MacArthur,General Douglas,Memorial; see Norfolk City Hall & Courthouse

Norfolk City Hall; see U. S. Post Office & Federal Courts Building

Norfolk City Hall & Courthouse (MacArthur,General Douglas,Memorial)
421 E. City Hall Ave.
HABS VA-32
HABS VA,65-NORF,10-
1ph/24pg L

Purdy-Whittle House; see Whittle House

U. S. Post Office & Federal Courts Building (Norfolk City Hall)
235 E. Plume St.
HABS VA-37
HABS VA,65-NORF,11-
3ph/16pg L

Whittle House (Purdy-Whittle House)
225 W. Freemason St.
HABS VA-11-15
HABS VA,65-NORF,6-
5dr/1ph/2pg/fr L

NORTHAMPTON COUNTY

BRIDGETOWN VIC.

Belote; see West House

Hungar's Church
State Rt. 619
HABS VA-542
HABS VA,66- ,1-
2ph L

Vaucluse
State Rt. 619
HABS VA-437
HABS VA,66- ,3-
2ph L

West House (Belote; Wester House)
Westerhouse Creek
HABS VA-544
HABS VA,66-BRIG.V,1-
3dr/1ph L

Wester House; see West House

Winona
Hungar Creek
HABS VA-543
HABS VA,66-BRIG.V,2-
8dr/2ph L

CAPEVILLE VIC.

Arlington,Custis Tombs
Old Plantation Creek & State Rt. 644
HABS VA-811
HABS VA,66-CAPE.V,1A-
3ph/1pg/1pc L

CHERITON VIC.

Eyre Hall
U. S. Rt. 13 & State Rt. 636 Vic.
HABS VA-809
HABS VA,66-CHER.V,1-
6ph/1pg/1pc L

Eyre Hall,Dairy
U. S. Rt. 13 & State Rt. 636 Vic.
HABS VA-809-A
HABS VA,66-CHER.V,1A-
1ph/1pc L

Eyre Hall,Graveyard
U. S. Rt. 13 & State Rt. 636 Vic.
HABS VA-809-D
HABS VA,66-CHER.V,1D-
2ph/1pc L

Eyre Hall,Orangery (Ruins)
U. S. Rt. 13 & State Rt. 636 Vic.
HABS VA-809-E
HABS VA,66-CHER.V,1E-
4ph/1pc L

Eyre Hall,Overseer's House
U. S. Rt. 13 & State Rt. 636
HABS VA-809-C
HABS VA,66-CHER.V,1C-
2ph/1pc L

Eyre Hall,Smokehouse
U. S. Rt. 13 & State Rt. 636 Vic.
HABS VA-809-B
HABS VA,66-CHER.V,1B-
1ph/1pc L

Stratton Manor
State Rt. 642 Vic.
HABS VA-545
HABS VA,66-CAPCHA,1-
2ph L

EASTVILLE

Cessford
U. S. Rt. 13
HABS VA-808
HABS VA,66-EAST.V,3-
11ph/1pg/1pc L

Courthouse Group Area Survey
U. S. Rt. 13
HABS VA-594
HABS VA,66-EAST,1-
8ph/6pg L

EASTVILLE VIC.

Caserta
Mattawoman Creek Vic.
HABS VA-591
HABS VA,66-EAST.V,1-
5ph/3pg L

Documentation: **ct** color transparencies **dr** measured drawings **fr** field records
pc photograph captions **pg** pages of text **ph** photographs

Cherry Grove
State Rt. 634 Vic.
HABS VA-592
HABS VA,66-EAST.V,4-
4ph/3pg/1pc L

Holly Brook
U. S. Rt. 13 Vic.
HABS VA-593
HABS VA,66-EAST.V,5-
11ph/3pg L

Kendall Grove
State Rt. 674
HABS VA-807
HABS VA,66-EAST.V,6-
12ph/1pg L

Kendall Grove,Connecting Passageway & Kitchen
State Rt. 674
HABS VA-807-A
HABS VA,66-EAST.V,6A-
8ph/1pg/3pc L

Kendall Grove,Dairy,Outhouse & Smokehouse
State Rt. 674
HABS VA-807-B
HABS VA,66-EAST.V,6B-
1ph L

Westover
State Rt. 630/U.S. Rt. 1 Vic. (Old Town Neck)
HABS VA-957
HABS VA,66-EAST.V,7-
7dr L

HADLOCK P.O. VIC.

Tankard's Rest
State Rts. 618 & 604 Vic.
HABS VA-806
HABS VA,66-HAD.V,1-
5ph L

JAMESVILLE VIC.

Mattissippi; see Sturgis House

Somers House
State Rt. 183 Vic.
HABS VA-546
HABS VA,66-JAM.V,1-
13dr/2ph L

Sturgis House (Mattissippi)
Occohannock Creek
HABS VA-547
HABS VA,66-JAM.V,2-
8dr/2ph L

NASSAWADOX

Brownsville,"Old Hall" (Ruins)
State Rts. 608 & 600 Vic.
HABS VA-810-B
HABS VA,66-NASA.V,6B-
1ph L

NASSAWADOX VIC.

Brownsville
State Rts. 608 & 600 Vic.
HABS VA-810
HABS VA,66-NASA.V,6-
13ph/1pg/1pc L

Brownsville,Outbuildings
State Rts. 608 & 600 Vic.
HABS VA-810-A
HABS VA,66-NASA.V,6B-
1ph L

Happy Union
Holly Grove Cove
HABS VA-805
HABS VA,66-NASA.V,2-
4ph/1pg/1pc L

Holly Grove
Holly Grove Cove
HABS VA-804
HABS VA,66-NASA.V,3-
6ph/1pg L

Woodlands
State Rt. 600 Vic.
HABS VA-590
HABS VA,66-NASA.V,1-
9ph/3pg L

SHADYSIDE VIC.

Pear Valley
State Rt. 628 Vic.
HABS VA-960
HABS VA,66-SHAD.V,1-
5dr L

TOWNSEND VIC.

Fitchett House (Point Pleasant)
State Rt. 600
HABS VA-548
HABS VA,66-KIPTO.V,1-
2ph L

Point Pleasant; see Fitchett House

WARDTOWN VIC.

Christian House; see Locust Grove

Fisher House
Holly Grove Cove
HABS VA-549
HABS VA,66-WARD.V,1-
2ph L

Locust Grove (Christian House)
Nassawadox Creek
HABS VA-550
HABS VA,66-WARD.V,2-
2ph L

NORTHUMBERLAND COUNTY

DITCHLEY

Ditchley
State Rt. 607
HABS VA-308
HABS VA,67-DITCH,1-
19ph/2pg L

NOTTOWAY COUNTY

BLACKSTONE

Anderson House; see Schwartz Tavern

Schwartz Tavern (Anderson House)
111 Tavern St.
HABS VA-813
HABS VA,68-BLACK,1-
1ph L

NOTTOWAY

Nottoway County Courthouse
State Rt. 625
HABS VA-812
HABS VA,68-NOT,1-
1ph L

ORANGE COUNTY

GORDONSVILLE VIC.

Montebello (Taylor,Zachary,Birthplace)
HABS VA-1044
HABS VA,69-GORD.V,1-
1ph/1pc L

Taylor,Zachary,Birthplace; see Montebello

MONTPELIER STA. VIC.

Montpelier
Near SR 693
HABS VA-1214
HABS VA,69-MONTS.V,2-
10dr L

Piedmont Log House
Near Junction of State Rts. 20 & 639
HABS VA-987
HABS VA,69-MONTS.V,1-
3dr/fr L

MONTPELIER STATION

Montpelier Depot
State Rt. 20 at Orange County Rd. 639
HABS VA-997
HABS VA,69-MONTS,1-
7dr/6pg/fr L

ORANGE VIC.

Howard Place (Mayhurst)
U. S. Rt. 15
HABS VA-1082
HABS VA,69-ORA.V,1-
4dr/8pg/fr L

Mayhurst; see Howard Place

PAGE COUNTY

LURAY VIC.

Fort Egypt
State Rt. 615
HABS VA-200
HABS VA,70-LURA.V,2-
11dr/14ph/3pg/fr L

Fort Massanutten
State Rt. 615 Vic.
HABS VA-341
HABS VA,70-LURA.V,3-
5ph/1pg L

Fort Stover
State Rt. 660 Vic.
HABS VA-194
HABS VA,70-LURA.V,1-
12dr/5ph/3pg/fr L

PETERSBURG (CITY)

Appomattox Iron Works
20-28 Old St.
HAER VA-25
HAER VA,27-PET,32-
6dr/58ph/13pg/3pc/fr L

Battersea
793 Appomattox St.
HABS VA-136
HABS VA,27-PET,3-
19dr/32ph/8pg/fr L

Bolling House; see Bollingbrook

Bolling,Robert,House; see Lawn,The

Bollingbrook (East Hill; Bolling House)
Franklin,Madison & Jefferson Sts. Vic.
HABS VA-79
HABS VA,27-PET,8-
5dr/23pg L

208-208A Bollingbrook Street (Double House) (Dunlop House)
HABS VA-816
HABS VA,27-PET,16-
1ph L

Bowers,William H.,House (Southworth's Drug Store)
254 N. Sycamore St.
HABS VA-68
HABS VA,27-PET,7-
5dr/9ph/9pg/fr L

Center Hill
Franklin St.
HABS VA-815
HABS VA,27-PET,15-
2ph L

City Hall; see U. S. Customs House & Post Office,Old

Clerk's House; see House,Stone

Cuthbert Law Office
220 N. Sycamore
HABS VA-1330
1dr H

Dunlop House; see 208-208A Bollingbrook Street (Double House)

Dunlop,David,Tobacco Factory
45-127 Old St.
HABS VA-663
HAER VA-29
HABS/HAER VA,27-PET,35-
2ph/6pg L

Dunn House & Outbuildings
105 S. Sycamore St.
HABS VA-130
HABS VA,27-PET,10-
16dr/13ph/2pg L

East Hill; see Bollingbrook

Elliot House
269 High St.
HABS VA-662
HABS VA,27-PET,34-
6ph/5pg L

Exchange,The
15-19 W. Bank St.
HABS VA-647
HABS VA,27-PET,6-
8dr/9ph/7pg/fr L

Farmers' Market,Old
W. Old & Rock Sts.
HABS VA-649
HABS VA,27-PET,26-
4dr/4ph/9pg/fr L

Friend,Nathaniel Jr.,House
27-29 Bollingbrook St.
HABS VA-651
HABS VA,27-PET,28-
4ph/6pg L

Gill,Erasmus,House
53 S. Market St.
HABS VA-650
HABS VA,27-PET,27-
8ph/6pg L

Gilliam Rowhouses; see Read's,John B.,Row

Golden Ball Tavern
Grove Ave. & N. Market St.
HABS VA-818
HABS VA,27-PET,18-
2ph L

706 Grove Avenue (House & Store); see Pig Alley Block Study

Harrison House; see Strachan,Dr. Alexander Glass,House

Hinton House
416 High St.
HABS VA-426
HABS VA,27-PET,12-
6ph L

House,Brick
Wills St.,Blandford
HABS VA-819
HABS VA,27-PET,14-
1ph L

House,Stone (Lloyd House; Clerk's House)
Crater Rd. & E. Washington St. (Blandford)
HABS VA-96
HABS VA,27-PET,9-
9dr/8ph/4pg L

406-408 Hurt Street (Double House); see Pig Alley Block Study

411-413 Hurt Street (Double House); see Pig Alley Block Study

412 Hurt Street (Store); see Pig Alley Block Study

Hustings Courthouse
Courthouse Ave. & N. Sycamore St.
HABS VA-657
HABS VA,27-PET,29-
6ph/12pg L

Jackson,John,House
410 High St.
HABS VA-661
HABS VA,27-PET,33-
6ph/8pg L

Lawn,The (Bolling,Robert,House)
224 S. Sycamore St.
HABS VA-814
HABS VA,27-PET,13-
2ph L

Lloyd House; see House,Stone

May's,David,Row
217-223 High St.
HABS VA-660
HABS VA,27-PET,32-
4ph/8pg L

Norfolk & Western RR,Petersburg Freight Station; see Southside Virginia RR,Petersburg Freight Station

O'Hara,Charles,House (Rat Castle; Trapezium House)
244 N. Market St.
HABS VA-820
HABS VA,27-PET,19-
1ph L

Petersburg Gas Light Company,Gasholder
Bank & Madison Sts. Vic.
HAER VA-14
HAER VA,27-PET,33A-
4dr/11ph/3pg/1pc/fr L

Pig Alley Block Study
Hurt St.,Plum St. & Grove Ave.
HABS VA-930
HABS VA,27-PET,23-
2ph L

Pig Alley Block Study (706 Grove Avenue (House & Store))
HABS VA-653
HABS VA,27-PET,23C-
5ph/5pg L

Pig Alley Block Study (406-408 Hurt Street (Double House))
HABS VA-654
HABS VA,27-PET,23D-
1ph/5pg L

Pig Alley Block Study (411-413 Hurt Street (Double House))
HABS VA-645
HABS VA,27-PET,23B-
7dr/2ph/5pg L

Pig Alley Block Study (412 Hurt Street (Store))
HABS VA-644
HABS VA,27-PET,23A-
8dr/3ph/5pg/fr L

Pig Alley Block Study (702-704 Plum Street (Double House))
HABS VA-656
HABS VA,27-PET,23F-
2ph/5pg L

Pig Alley Block Study (703-713 Plum Street (Row Houses))
HABS VA-655
HABS VA,27-PET,23E-
2ph/7pg L

702-704 Plum Street (Double House); see Pig Alley Block Study

703-713 Plum Street (Row Houses); see Pig Alley Block Study

Pride's Tavern
N. West & McKenzie Sts.
HABS VA-821
HABS VA,27-PET,20-
2ph L

Rat Castle; see O'Hara,Charles,House

Read's,John B.,Row (Gilliam Rowhouses)
102-104 W. Old St.
HABS VA-643
HABS VA,27-PET,5-
9dr/9ph/8pg/fr L

Romaine House; see Scott,Albert L.,House

Scott,Albert L.,House (Romaine House)
29 S. Market St.
HABS VA-648
HABS VA,27-PET,25-
8dr/7ph/6pg L

Smith's,John H.,Row
209-215 High St.
HABS VA-646
HABS VA,27-PET,24-
9dr/8ph/8pg/fr L

Southside Virginia RR,Petersburg Freight Station (Norfolk & Western RR,Petersburg Freight Station)
River St.
HAER VA-28
HAER VA,44-PET,34-
1ph/1pc L

Southworth's Drug Store; see Bowers,William H.,House

Spottswood House; see Stirling Castle

Stirling Castle (Spottswood House)
320 W. High St. (moved from original site)
HABS VA-822
HABS VA,27-PET,21-
1ph L

Strachan-Harrison House; see Strachan,Dr. Alexander Glass,House

Strachan,Dr. Alexander Glass,House (Harrison House; Strachan-Harrison House)
302 Cross St.
HABS VA-642
HABS VA,27-PET,4-
7dr/11ph/6pg L

Tabb Street Presbyterian Church
21 W. Tabb St.
HABS VA-658
HABS VA,27-PET,30-
7ph/9pg L

Trapezium House; see O'Hara,Charles,House

U. S. Customs House & Post Office,Old (City Hall)
129-141 N. Union St.
HABS VA-659
HABS VA,27-PET,31-
14ph/17pg/fr L

Warehouse,Stone
Market St.
HABS VA-823
HABS VA,27-PET,22-
1ph L

Washington Street Methodist Church
Washington & Adams St.
HABS VA-299
HABS VA,27-PET,11-
2ph L

PITTSYLVANIA COUNTY

CASCADE VIC.

Berry Hill Bridge (State Line Bridge; Pittsylvania County Bridge No. 6906) (See NC,ROCKINGHAM CO.,EDEN VIC. for documentatn.)
HAER NC-38
HAER NC,79-EDEN.V,1-
27ph/18pg/2pc L

Pittsylvania County Bridge No. 6906; see Berry Hill Bridge

State Line Bridge; see Berry Hill Bridge

CHATHAM

Pittsylvania County Courthouse
State Rt. 57 & U. S. Rt. 29
HABS VA-271
HABS VA,72-CHAT,1-
2ph/1pg L

DANVILLE

623 Monument Street (House)
HABS VA-1036
HABS VA,72-DANV,2-
3ph/2pg/1pc L

433 Shelton Street (House)
HABS VA-1037
HABS VA,72-DANV,3-
3ph/2pg/1pc L

Tobacco District Rehabilitation Project
HAER VA-31
HAER VA,72-DANV,1-
35ph/3pg/3pc/fr L

DANVILLE VIC.

Dan's Hill
State Rt. 1011 Vic.
HABS VA-11-24
HABS VA,72-DANV.V,1-
3dr/12ph/2pg/fr L

GRETNA

Yancy Cabin (Yates Tavern)
U. S. Rt. 29 Vic.
HABS VA-270
HABS VA,72-GRET,1-
3ph/1pg L

Yates Tavern; see Yancy Cabin

POWHATAN COUNTY

HUGUENOT VIC.

Keswick,Brick House (first)
State Rt. 711 Vic.
HABS VA-85-A
HABS VA,73-HUG.V,1A-
7dr/1ph/1pg/fr L

Keswick,Guest House
State Rt. 711 Vic.
HABS VA-85-C
HABS VA,73-HUG.V,1-
1ph L

Keswick,House & Quarters
State Rt. 711 Vic.
HABS VA-85
HABS VA,73-HUG.V,1-
11dr/16ph/3pg L

Keswick,Kitchen
State Rt. 711 Vic.
HABS VA-85-D
HABS VA,73-HUG.V,1-
2ph L

Keswick,Main House (second)
State Rt. 711 Vic.
HABS VA-164
HABS VA,73-HUG.V,2-
5ph/fr L

Keswick,Smokehouse
State Rt. 711 Vic.
HABS VA-85-E
HABS VA,73-HUG.V,1-
1ph L

Keswick,The Quarters
State Rt. 711 Vic.
HABS VA-85-B
HABS VA,73-HUG.V,1B-
4dr/7ph/2pg L

Malvern
State Rt. 711 Vic.
HABS VA-338
HABS VA,73-HUG.V,3-
11ph/1pg L

POWHATAN

Tavern,Old
State Rt. 30
HABS VA-441
HABS VA,73-POW,1-
1ph L

POWHATAN VIC.

Belnemus
U. S. Rt. 60 Vic.
HABS VA-86
HABS VA,73-POW.V,1-
3ph/3pg L

Woodberry Mill (Numbers One & Two)
State Rt. 614 Vic.
HABS VA-201
HABS VA,73-POW.V,2- & 2B-
5ph L

WYNDHAM VIC.

Norwood
State Rt. 711 Vic.
HABS VA-148
HABS VA,73-WYND.V,1-
4ph/1pg L

PRINCE EDWARD COUNTY

WORSHAM

Jail
U.S. Rt. 15
HABS VA-552
HABS VA,74- ,1-
1ph L

PRINCE GEORGE COUNTY

HOPEWELL VIC.

Flowerdew Hundred
State Rt. 639
HABS VA-295
HABS VA,75- ,2-
2ph L

PRINCE GEORGE VIC.

Brandon
State Rt. 611
HABS VA-143
HABS VA,75-BRAND.V,1-
1ph/2pg L

Merchants Hope Church
State Rt. 641
HABS VA-405
HABS VA,75-PRING.V,1-
6ph/1pg L

PRINCE WILLIAM COUNTY

ADEN

House,Green
State Rt. 646
HABS VA-825
HABS VA,76-AD,1-
1ph L

Pilgrim's Rest
State Rt. 607 Vic.
HABS VA-837
HABS VA,76-AD,2-
3ph L

ADEN VIC.

Effingham
State Rt. 646 Vic.
HABS VA-575
HABS VA,76-AD.V,1-
17ph/2pg L

BRENTSVILLE VIC.

Fleetwood (Gibson House)
State Rt. 611
HABS VA-275
HABS VA,76-BRENT.V,1-
4ph L

Gibson House; see Fleetwood

House,Old; see Moor Green

Lee House; see Park Gate

Moor Green (House,Old)
State Rt. 692
HABS VA-554
HABS VA,76-BRENT.V,3-
2ph L

Park Gate (Lee House)
State Rt. 653
HABS VA-555
HABS VA,76-BRENT.V,2-
1ph L

BULL RUN

Sudley
Sudley Rd.
HABS VA-427
HABS VA,76- ,1-
2ph L

BULL RUN VIC.

Carter House; see Mountain View

Mountain View (Carter House)
6421 Bull Run Post Office Rd.
HABS VA-291
HABS VA,76- ,2-
3ph L

CATHARDIN VIC.

Log Cabin
State Rt. 701
HABS VA-287
HABS VA,76-CATH,1-
3ph L

St. John's Church (Ruins)
HABS VA-286
HABS VA,76-CATH.V,1-
1ph L

DUMFRIES

Dumfries House; see Williams' Ordinary

Hotel,Old; see Williams' Ordinary

Love's Tavern; see Williams' Ordinary

Main Street (Frame House)
HABS VA-827
HABS VA,76-DUMF,4-
1ph L

Merchent House
Main St.
HABS VA-91
HABS VA,76-DUMF,1-
14dr/13ph/4pg L

Tebbs House; see Tebbs-Mundy House

Tebbs-Mundy House (Tebbs House)
Main St.
HABS VA-178
HABS VA,76-DUMF,2-
2dr/2ph/2pg L

Williams' Ordinary (Hotel,Old; Dumfries House; Love's Tavern)
Main St.
HABS VA-826
HABS VA,76-DUMF,3-
2ph L

DUMFRIES VIC.

Leesylvania (Ruins)
State Rt. 610
HABS VA-281
HABS VA,76- ,4-
2ph L

North Branch Quantico Creek Bridge
(Pyrite Mine Road Bridge)
Prince William Forest Park
HAER VA-50
HAER 1989(HAER):22
6ph/4pg/1pc L

Pyrite Mine Road Bridge; see North Branch Quantico Creek Bridge

South Branch Quantico Creek Bridge
Prince William Forest Park
HAER VA-49
HAER 1989(HAER):22
5ph/5pg/1pc L

GAINESVILLE VIC.

Dogan House
U. S. Rt. 29 & State Rt. 622
HABS VA-581
HABS VA,76-GROV,3-
3dr/39ph/3pg/fr L

GROVETON

Chinn House (Remains) (Manassas National Battlefield Park)
HABS VA-138
HABS VA,76-GROV,1-
3dr/14ph/2pg/fr L

Manassas National Battlefield Park; see Chinn House (Remains)

HAYMARKET

McCormack Cabin; see McCormack House

McCormack House (McCormack Cabin)
Fayette St.
HABS VA-283
HABS VA,76-HAYMA,1-
1ph L

HAYMARKET VIC.

Hagley (Tyler House)
State Rt. 601
HABS VA-276
HABS VA,76-WATFA.V,1-
5ph L

Harrison House; see La Grange

Hutchison House; see Prospect Hill

La Grange (Harrison House)
State Rt. 681
HABS VA-289
HABS VA,76-HAYMA.V,3-
5ph L

Poplar Hill (Tyler House)
State Rt. 601 Vic.
HABS VA-830
HABS VA,76-WATFA,3-
2ph L

Prospect Hill (Hutchison House)
State Rt. 624
HABS VA-832
HABS VA,76-HICK,1-
5ph L

Retreat,The (Woolsey; Shelter,The)
State Rts. 601 & 234 Vic.
HABS VA-285
HABS VA,76-HAYMA.V,2-
6ph L

Shelter,The; see Retreat,The

Tyler House; see Hagley

Tyler House; see Poplar Hill

Waverly Mills
State Rt. 679
HABS VA-284
HABS VA,76-HAYMA.V,1-
1ph L

Woolsey; see Retreat,The

MANASSAS

Beauregard,General,Headquarters; see Liberia

Liberia (Weir House; Beauregard,General,Headquarters)
627 Centreville Rd.
HABS VA-834
HABS VA,76-MAN,1-
4ph L

Tudor Hall
Tudor Lane
HABS VA-835
HABS VA,76-MAN,2-
1ph L

Weir House; see Liberia

MANASSAS VIC.

Ben Lomond (House,Stone)
State Rt. 234
HABS VA-836
HABS VA,76-STOHO,1-
2ph L

Brent House; see White House,The

House,Stone; see Ben Lomond

House,Stone (Mathews House)
Manassas National Battlefield Park
HABS VA-144
HABS VA,76-GROV,2-
9dr/29ph/2pg/fr L

Mathews House; see House,Stone

Stone Bridge
Spanning Bull Run
HAER VA-66
HAER DLC/PP-1992:VA-5
3ph/1pc L

White House,The (Brent House)
State Rt. 619
HABS VA-553
HABS VA,76-BRENT,1-
1ph L

MINNIEVILLE

Bel Air (Belle Air; Ewell House)
State Rt. 640 Vic.
HABS VA-99
HABS VA,76-MINVI,1-
7dr/8ph/fr L

Belle Air; see Bel Air

Ewell House; see Bel Air

OCCOQUAN

Den,The; see Rockledge

Merchant's Grist Mill & Mill House (Ruins)
Mill St.
HABS VA-576
HABS VA,76-OCCO,2-
1ph/1pg L

Rockledge (Den,The)
Mill St.
HABS VA-577
HABS VA,76-OCCO,1-
11dr/33ph/5pg/fr L

THOROUGHFARE

Beverley's Mill
State Rt. 55
HABS VA-828
HABS VA,76-THRORO,1-
1ph L

House (Ruins) (Meadowland (Ruins))
Beverley's Mill Vic. (State Rt. 55)
HABS VA-829
HABS VA,76-THORO,1-
1ph L

Meadowland (Ruins); see House (Ruins)

WATERFALL

Evergreen
State Rt. 630 Vic.
HABS VA-833
HABS VA,76-WATFA,1-
1ph L

Mount Atlas
State Rt. 731 Vic.
HABS VA-831
HABS VA,76-WATFA,2-
2ph L

WOODBRIDGE VIC.

Blackburn House; see Rippon Lodge

King's Highway (Remains)
Parallel to U. S. Rt. 1
HABS VA-579
HABS VA,76-WOOD.V,3-
2ph/2pg L

Rippon Lodge (Blackburn House)
State Rt. 638
HABS VA-106
HABS VA,76-WOOD.V,1-
9dr/9ph/fr L

Scarlit,Martin,Gravestone
Belmont Bay
HABS VA-838
HABS VA,76-WOOD.V,2-
1ph L

RAPPAHANNOCK COUNTY

SPERRYVILLE VIC.

Estes Mill
U. S. Rt. 211 & State Rt. 667
HABS VA-374
HABS VA,79-SPER.V,1-
4ph/1pg L

Sawmill
U.S. Rt. 11
HABS VA-839
HABS VA,79-SPER.V,2-
3ph L

WASHINGTON

Court Green Area Survey (Street Scene) (Courthouse & Lawyer's Office)
HABS VA-561
HABS VA,79-WASH,1-
1ph L

Courthouse & Lawyer's Office; see Court Green Area Survey (Street Scene)

RICHMOND (CITY)

(House)
HABS VA-1267
1dr H

Adams,Dr. John,Double House
2501-2503 E. Grace St.
HABS VA-865
HABS VA,44-RICH,56-
1ph L

Allen-Ellet House; see Ellet,Andrew,House

Allen,William C.,Double House
4-6 E. Main St.
HABS VA-869
HABS VA,44-RICH,64-
1ph L

Allison-Moore-Crump Building
1309 E. Main St.
HABS VA-846
HABS VA,44-RICH,95-
3ph/4pg L

Aluminum Building
215 Governor St.
HABS VA-652
HABS VA,44-RICH,109-
3ph/1pc L

Ampthill
211 Ampthill Rd. (moved from Va,Richmond Vic.)
HABS VA-159
HABS VA,21- ,1-
1dr/11ph/2pg L

2800 and 2900 Blocks Monument Avenue
HABS VA-1307
HABS DLC/PP-1993:VA-3
4ph/5pg/1pc L

Ballard Street & Tobacco Alley (House)
HABS VA-879
HABS VA,44-RICH,83-
1ph L

Barret,William,House
Fifth & Cary Sts.
HABS VA-425
HABS VA,44-RICH,43-
2ph L

Belgian Building
Lombardy St. & Brook Rd.
HABS VA-187
HABS VA,44-RICH,110-
7ph/1pc L

Bell Tower,The
Capitol Square
HABS VA-116
HABS VA,44-RICH,18-
1dr/2ph/5pg L

Belvin House (William,William C.,House)
412 N. Eighth St.
HABS VA-111
HABS VA,44-RICH,13-
5dr/8ph/3pg/fr L

1600 Block Monument Avenue
HABS VA-1299
HABS DLC/PP-1993:PA-3
15ph/9pg/2pc L

1800 Block Monument Avenue
HABS VA-1300
HABS DLC/PP-1993:VA-3
1dr/11ph/7pg/1pc L

2000 Block Monument Avenue
HABS VA-1301
HABS DLC/PP-1993:VA-3
7ph/8pg/1pc L

2200 Block Monument Avenue
HABS VA-1302
HABS DLC/PP-1993:VA-3
6ph/6pg/1pc L

2300 Block Monument Avenue
HABS VA-1303
HABS DLC/PP-1993:VA-3
11ph/4pg/1pc L

2500 Block Monument Avenue
HABS VA-1304
HABS DLC/PP-1993:VA-3
6ph/4pg/1pc L

2600 Block Monument Avenue
HABS VA-1305
HABS DLC/PP-1993:VA-3
1dr/4ph/5pg/1pc L

2700 Block Monument Avenue
HABS VA-1306
HABS DLC/PP-1993:VA-3
5ph/3pg/1pc L

2900 Block Monument Avenue
HABS VA-1308
H

3000 Block Monument Avenue
HABS VA-1309
HABS DLC/PP-1993:VA-3
9ph/6pg/1pc L

3100 Block Monument Avenue
HABS VA-1310
HABS DLC/PP-1993:VA-3
6ph/5pg/1pc L

3200 Block Monument Avenue
HABS VA-1311
HABS DLC/PP-1993:VA-3
1dr/4ph/5pg/1pc L

3300 Block Monument Avenue
HABS VA-1312
HABS DLC/PP-1993:VA-3
2ph/4pg/1pc L

1200 Block W. Franklin Street
HABS VA-1298
HABS DLC/PP-1993:VA-3
12ph/7pg/1pc L

Bott,Miles,House
216 Cowardin Ave.
HABS VA-119
HABS VA,44-RICH,20-
12dr/4ph/3pg/fr L

Bowser,Rosa D.,Branch Library; see Dill,Adolph,House

Branch-Glasgow House
(Glasgow,Ellen,House)
1 W. Main St.
HABS VA-857
HABS VA,44-RICH,29-
1ph L

Bransford House (Bransford,Frederick Cecil,House; Bransford-Cecil House; Cecil Memorial)
1005 Clay St. (moved from 13 N. Fifth St.)
HABS VA-161
HABS VA,44-RICH,73-
9ph L

Bransford-Cecil House; see Bransford House

Bransford,Frederick Cecil,House; see Bransford House

Bridge to Brown Island; see Seventh Street Bridge

Brockenbrough,Dr. John,House (White House of the Confederacy)
1201 E. Clay St.
HABS VA-861
HABS VA,44-RICH,7-
15dr/3ph L

Call,Daniel,House
217 W. Grace St.
HABS VA-866
HABS VA,44-RICH,79-
1ph L

Cameron,Alexander,House
519 E. Franklin St.
HABS VA-876
HABS VA,44-RICH,22-
1ph L

Carter-Crozet House; see Carter,Curtis,House

Carter,Curtis,House (Carter-Crozet House; Crozet House)
100 E. Main St.
HABS VA-1070
HABS VA,44-RICH,65-
5ph L

Caskie,Mrs. James,House
(Hancock-Palmer-Caskie House; Hancock,Michael,House; Hancock-Wirt-Caskie House)
2 N. Fifth St.
HABS VA-113
HABS VA,44-RICH,2-
12dr/5ph/2pg/fr L

Cecil Memorial; see Bransford House

Chamberlayne Avenue & Saint Peter Street (House) (Mann,William,House)
HABS VA-856
HABS VA,44-RICH,84-
1ph L

City Hall,Old; see Richmond City Hall

311-313 College Street (Double House)
HABS VA-875
HABS VA,44-RICH,47-
2ph L

Columbian Block
1301-1307 E. Cary St.
HABS VA-842
HABS VA,44-RICH,91-
7ph/6pg L

Courts Building; see Richmond City Hall

Crozet House; see Carter,Curtis,House

Davis Monument
Monument Ave. & Davis Ave.
HABS VA-1297
HABS DLC/PP-1993:VA-3
1ph/1pg/1pc L

De Saussure House
(Freeman,Samuel,House)
316 E. Main St.
HABS VA-114
HABS VA,44-RICH,16-
11dr/3ph/2pg/fr L

Dill,Adolph,House (Bowser,Rosa D.,Branch Library)
00 Clay St.
HABS VA-862
HABS VA,44-RICH,28-
1ph L

Donnan-Asher Iron Front Building
1207-1211 E. Main St.
HABS VA-853
HABS VA,44-RICH,66-
6ph/7pg L

107 East Cary Street (House)
HABS VA-859
HABS VA,44-RICH,41-
1ph L

402 East Cary Street (House)
HABS VA-891
HABS VA,44-RICH,42-
1ph L

1008 East Clay Street (House)
HABS VA-1061
HABS VA,44-RICH,46-
1ph L

804 East Clay Street (House) (Wiseham House)
HABS VA-889
HABS VA,44-RICH,27-
4ph L

206 East Leigh Street (House)
HABS VA-890
HABS VA,44-RICH,60-
1ph L

1109-1113 East Main Street (Commercial Buildings)
HABS VA-1058
HABS VA,44-RICH,112-
7ph/1pg L

2216-2218 East Main Street (Double House)
HABS VA-118
HABS VA,44-RICH,19-
12dr/2ph/2pg/fr L

2416 East Main Street (House)
HABS VA-864
HABS VA,44-RICH,86-
1ph L

1909 East Main Street (Store)
HABS VA-1064
HABS VA,44-RICH,67-
1ph L

1010 East Marshall Street (House)
HABS VA-1066
HABS VA,44-RICH,69-
1ph L

2600 East Marshall Street (House)
HABS VA-854
HABS VA,44-RICH,87-
1ph L

Eighteenth & Main Streets (House)
(Hampton-McCurdy House)
HABS VA-851
HABS VA,44-RICH,85-
1ph L

Ellet-Todd-Lawrence Building
1019-1021 E. Cary St.
HABS VA-844
HABS VA,44-RICH,93-
3ph/4pg L

Ellet,Andrew,House (Allen-Ellet House)
2702 E. Grace St.
HABS VA-850
HABS VA,44-RICH,57-
1ph L

Fifth & Leigh Streets (House)
HABS VA-888
HABS VA,44-RICH,63-
3ph L

Freeman,Samuel,House; see De Saussure House

Gentry-Stokes-Crew House; see Twenty-eighth & E. Franklin Streets (House)

George,William O.,House; see 116 South Third Street (House)

Gill House; see Grey House

Glasgow,Ellen,House; see Branch-Glasgow House

Gosden House (Tucker House)
Third & Leigh Sts.
HABS VA-852
HABS VA,44-RICH,61-
2ph L

Governor's Mansion
Capitol Square
HABS VA-1242
HABS VA.44-RICH,8-
16dr/fr L

Governor's Mansion,Summer Kitchen
Capitol Square
HABS VA-1242-A
HABS VA,44-RICH,8A-
1dr L

6 Granby Street (Cottage)
HABS VA-881
HABS VA,44-RICH,59-
1ph L

Greenhow House
403 E. Grace St.
HABS VA-112
HABS VA,44-RICH,14-
5dr/9ph/2pg/fr L

Grey House (Gill House)
1007 McDonough St.
HABS VA-131
HABS VA,44-RICH,21-
1dr/2ph/3pg/fr L

24 Hampton Hills Lane (House)
HABS VA-1263
HABS DLC/PP-1993:VA-3
1dr L

Hampton-McCurdy House; see Eighteenth & Main Streets (House)

Hancock-Palmer-Caskie House; see Caskie,Mrs. James,House

Hancock-Wirt-Caskie House; see Caskie,Mrs. James,House

Hancock,Michael,House; see Caskie,Mrs. James,House

Hawes House (Mann-Hawes House)
506 E. Leigh St.
HABS VA-115
HABS VA,44-RICH,17-
14dr/7ph/2pg/fr L

Haxall,Bolling W.,House (Women's Club)
211 E. Franklin St.
HABS VA-1057
HABS VA,44-RICH,30-
1ph L

Hickock House; see Ritter-Hickock House

Hobson-Nolting House (Nolting House)
409 E. Main St.
HABS VA-160
HABS VA,44-RICH,25-
8dr/21ph/2pg/fr L

Howard-Palmer House; see Palmer House

Jackson Ward Historic District
Bounded by Marshall,Fifth, & Gilmer Sts.
HABS VA-364
HABS VA,44-RICH,111-
2ph/1pc L

James River & Kanawha Canal,Locks 1-5 (Tidewater Connection Locks)
Tenth to Thirteenth Sts. ,north of Canal St.
HAER VA-23
HAER VA,44-RICH,100B-
8dr/21ph/5pg/2pc/fr L

James River & Kanawha Canal,Three Mile Locks (Kanawha Canal,First Grand Division,Locks 1 & 2)
Pumphouse Dr.
HAER VA-24
HAER VA,44-RICH,100C-
3dr/3ph/1pg/1pc/fr L

James River & Kanawha Canal:Pumphouse
HAER VA-34
HAER VA,44-RICH,100A-
11ph/1pg/1pc L

Jefferson Hotel
Main,Jefferson,Franklin & Adams Sts.
HABS VA-840
HABS VA,44-RICH,90-
24ph/10pg L

Kanawha Canal,First Grand Division,Locks 1 & 2; see James River & Kanawha Canal,Three Mile Locks

Kent-Valentine House; see Kent,Horace,House

Kent,Horace,House (Kent-Valentine House)
First & Franklin Sts.
HABS VA-858
HABS VA,44-RICH,49-
1ph L

Lee Monument
Monument Ave. & Allen Ave.
HABS VA-1295
HABS DLC/PP-1993:VA-3
2ph/1pg/1pc L

Lee,General,House; see Stewart,Norman,House

531 Leigh Street (House)
HABS VA-885
HABS VA,44-RICH,62-
1ph L

Linden Row
100-118 E. Franklin St.
HABS VA-247
HABS VA,44-RICH,50-
6ph L

315 Lock Lane (House)
HABS VA-1326
HABS DLC/PP-1993:VA-3
1dr L H

Main Street Station; see Union Station

Main Street Station Trainshed; see Union Station Trainshed

Malone,James,Row; see Twenty-third & Franklin Streets (Houses)

Manchester Cotton & Woolen Manufacturing Co. (Standard Paper Manufacturing Co.; Manchester Mill)
Southern Bank of James River at Mayo Bridge
HAER VA-44
HAER VA,44-RICH,114-
8dr/33ph/33pg/2pc/fr L

Manchester Mill; see Manchester Cotton & Woolen Manufacturing Co.

Mann-Hawes House; see Hawes House

Mann,William,House; see Chamberlayne Avenue & Saint Peter Street (House)

Marshall Street Viaduct
Marshall St. from College through Twenty-first Sts
HAER VA-27
HAER VA,44-RICH,102-
7ph/3pg/1pc L

Marshall,John,House
402 N. Ninth St.
HABS VA-309
HABS VA,44-RICH,4-
22ph/1pg L

Mason's Hall (Masonic Hall)
1805 E. Franklin St.
HABS VA-11-21
HABS VA,44-RICH,12-
12dr/2ph/3pg/fr L

Masonic Hall; see Mason's Hall

Monroe,James,Tomb
Hollywood Cemetery
HABS VA-843
HABS VA,44-RICH,92-
4ph/4pg L

Monument Avenue
HABS VA-1322
HABS DLC/PP-1993:VA-3
7dr L

1800 Monument Avenue (House)
HABS VA-1259
HABS DLC/PP-1993:VA-3
1dr L

1832 Monument Avenue (House)
HABS VA-1323
HABS DLC/PP-1993:VA-3
1dr L

2301 Monument Avenue (House)
HABS VA-1260
HABS DLC/PP-1993:VA-3
1dr L

2304 Monument Avenue (House)
HABS VA-1324
HABS DLC/PP-1993:VA-3
2dr L

2309 Monument Avenue (House)
HABS VA-1266
HABS DLC/PP-1993:VA-3
1dr L

2315 Monument Avenue (House)
HABS VA-1255
HABS DLC/PP-1993:VA-3
1dr L

2320 Monument Avenue (House)
HABS VA-1256
HABS DLC/PP-1993:VA-3
1dr L

2601 Monument Avenue (House)
HABS VA-1257
HABS DLC/PP-1993:VA-3
1dr L

2714 Monument Avenue (House)
HABS VA-1258
HABS DLC/PP-1993:VA-3
1dr L

3215 Monument Avenue (House)
HABS VA-1325
HABS DLC/PP-1993:VA-3
1dr L

Monumental Church
1224 E. Broad St.
HABS VA-1241
HABS VA,44-RICH,24-;DLC/PP-1993:VA-2
21dr/57ph/13pg/3pc/fr L

Morris,John,Cottage
2500 E. Grace St.
HABS VA-860
HABS VA,44-RICH,55-
1ph L

1200-1202 N. Seventeenth Street (Double House)
HABS VA-886
HABS VA,44-RICH,82-
1ph L

Nolting House; see Hobson-Nolting House

706 North Eighteenth Street (House)
HABS VA-887
HABS VA,44-RICH,39-
1ph L

778 North Ninth Street (Cottage)
HABS VA-877
HABS VA,44-RICH,37-
1ph L

616 North Ninth Street (House)
HABS VA-1065
HABS VA,44-RICH,36-
1ph L

516 North Third Street (House)
HABS VA-894
HABS VA,44-RICH,34-
2ph L

9 North Twenty-Third Street (House)
HABS VA-884
HABS VA,44-RICH,40-
1ph L

Oaks,The
307 Stockton Ln. (moved from VA,Mattoax Vic.)
HABS VA-157
HABS VA,4-MATOX.V,1-
8ph/1pg L

Old Stone House (Poe Museum; Poe Shrine)
1916 E. Main St.
HABS VA-120
HABS VA,44-RICH,10-
7dr/8ph/4pg L

Palmer House (Howard-Palmer House)
211 W. Franklin St.
HABS VA-867
HABS VA,44-RICH,80-
1ph L

Parsons,Samuel,House (Virginia Division of Youth Services)
601 Spring St.
HABS VA-434
HABS VA,44-RICH,78-
1ph L

Phillip Morris Leaf Storage Warehouse
1717-1721 E. Cary St.
HABS VA-849
HABS VA,44-RICH,98-
4ph/4pg L

Poe Museum; see Old Stone House

Poe Shrine; see Old Stone House

Pohlig Paper Box Factory (Yarbrough-Turpin Tobacco Factory)
Twenty-fifth & Franklin Sts.
HABS VA-863
HABS VA,44-RICH,53-
1ph L

Pratt's Castle
324 S. Fourth St.
HABS VA-162
HABS VA,44-RICH,74-
2ph/1pg L

Quarles,John D.,House
1 E. Main St.
HABS VA-871
HABS VA,44-RICH,68-
1ph L

Richmond City Hall (Courts Building; City Hall,Old)
1001 E. Broad St.
HABS VA-34
HABS VA,44-RICH,99-
12ph/14pg/1pc L

Ritter-Hickock House (Hickock House)
821 W. Franklin St.
HABS VA-855
HABS VA,44-RICH,81-
1ph L

6705 River Road (House)
HABS VA-1261
HABS DLC/PP-1993:VA-3
1dr L

8603 River Road (House)
HABS VA-1262
HABS DLC/PP-1993:VA-3
1dr L

Rutherfoord-Hobson House
2 W. Franklin St.
HABS VA-423
HABS VA,44-RICH,48-
3ph L

Scott-Clarke House
9 S. Fifth St.
HABS VA-421
HABS VA,44-RICH,76-
2ph L

Seventeenth & Venable Streets (House)
HABS VA-883
HABS VA,44-RICH,71-
1ph L

Seventh Street Bridge (Bridge to Brown Island)
HAER VA-41
HAER VA,44-RICH,103-
4ph/1pc L

Sixth & Franklin Streets (House)
HABS VA-1060
HABS VA,44-RICH,51-
1ph L

Smith,John D.,House
2617 E. Franklin St.
HABS VA-872
HABS VA,44-RICH,54-
1ph L

212-214 South First Street (Double House)
HABS VA-892
HABS VA,44-RICH,31-
1ph L

South Fourth & Byrd Streets (House)
HABS VA-1063
HABS VA,44-RICH,35-
1ph L

102 South Third Street (House)
HABS VA-893
HABS VA,44-RICH,32-
1ph L

116 South Third Street (House) (George,William O.,House)
HABS VA-868
HABS VA,44-RICH,33-
1ph L

St. John's Church (Episcopal)
E. Grace & Broad Sts.
HABS VA-11-22
HABS VA,44-RICH,1-
11dr/7ph/4pg/fr L

Standard Paper Manufacturing Co.; see Manchester Cotton & Woolen Manufacturing Co.

Stearns Iron Front Building
1007-1013 E. Main St.
HABS VA-847
HABS VA,44-RICH,96-
2ph/14pg L

Stewart-Lee House; see Stewart,Norman,House

Stewart,Norman,House (Stewart-Lee House; Lee,General,House)
707 E. Franklin St.
HABS VA-895
HABS VA,44-RICH,23-
1ph L

309 Stockton Lane (House)
HABS VA-1265
HABS DLC/PP-1993:VA-3
1dr L

Stuart Monument
Monument Ave. & N. Lombardy St.
HABS VA-1296
HABS DLC/PP-1993:VA-3
1ph/1pg/1pc L

4205 Sulgrave Road (House)
HABS VA-1264
HABS DLC/PP-1993:VA-3
1dr L

4207 Sulgrave Road (House)
HABS VA-1327
HABS DLC/PP-1993:VA-3
1dr L

Tenth & Clay Streets (House)
HABS VA-1062
HABS VA,44-RICH,45-
1ph L

Third & East Main Streets (House)
HABS VA-420
HABS VA,44-RICH,75-
1ph L

Third & Leigh Streets (House)
HABS VA-1059
HABS VA,44-RICH,61-
1ph L

Tidewater Connection Locks; see James River & Kanawha Canal,Locks 1-5

Tomlinson,A. M.,House; see Twenty-fifth & Venable Streets (House)

Tredegar Iron Works
U. S. Rt. 1,along James River
HAER VA-32
HAER VA,44-RICH,104-
5ph/6pg/1pc L

Triple Railroad Crossing
E. Byrd St. at Sixteenth St.
HAER VA-40
HAER VA,44-RICH,105-
2ph/1pc L

Tucker Cottage
612 N. Third St.
HABS VA-959
HABS VA,44-RICH,113-
1dr L

Tucker House; see Gosden House

Twenty-eighth & E. Franklin Streets (House) (Gentry-Stokes-Crew House)
HABS VA-873
HABS VA,44-RICH,58-
1ph L

Twenty-fifth & Venable Streets (House) (Tomlinson,A. M.,House)
HABS VA-926
HABS VA,44-RICH,89-
1ph L

Twenty-first & Venable Streets (House)
HABS VA-880
HABS VA,44-RICH,88-
1ph L

Twenty-third & Franklin Streets (Houses) (Malone,James,Row)
HABS VA-870
HABS VA,44-RICH,52-
1ph L

Union Station (Main Street Station)
1520 E. Main St.
HABS VA-848
HABS VA,44-RICH,97-
14ph/6pg L

Union Station Trainshed (Main Street Station Trainshed)
Main St.
HAER VA-4
HAER VA,44-RICH,97A-
3dr/11ph/1pg/1pc L

Valentine Museum; see Wickham-Valentine House

Venable & Tulip Streets (House)
HABS VA-878
HABS VA,44-RICH,70-
1ph L

Virginia Division of Youth Services; see Parsons,Samuel,House

Virginia Fire & Marine Insurance Building
1015 E. Main St.
HABS VA-845
HABS VA,44-RICH,94-
4dr/4ph/6pg/fr L

Virginia State Capitol
HABS VA-1254
HABS 1991(HABS):7;DLC/PP-1993:VA-2
48dr/74ph/84pg/5pc/fr L

Washington Monument,The
Capitol Square
HABS VA-1271
HABS 1991(HABS):7
4ph/1pc L

1322-1324 West Broad Street (Commercial Building)
HABS VA-326
HABS VA,44-RICH,107-
1ph/1pc L

504-510 West Broad Street (Commercial Buildings)
HABS VA-362
HABS VA,44-RICH,106-
1ph/1pc L

2028 West Cary Street (Commercial Building)
HABS VA-198
HABS VA,44-RICH,108-
1ph/1pc L

21 West Clay Street (House)
HABS VA-882
HABS VA,44-RICH,44-
1ph L

400 West Franklin Street (House)
HABS VA-422
HABS VA,44-RICH,77-
1ph L

White House of the Confederacy; see Brockenbrough,Dr. John,House

Whitlock Double House
628-630 N. Seventeenth St.
HABS VA-874
HABS VA,44-RICH,38-
1ph L

Wickham House; see Wickham-Valentine House

Wickham-Valentine House (Valentine Museum; Wickham House)
1015 E. Clay St.
HABS VA-310
HABS VA,44-RICH,5-
18dr/11ph/2pg/fr L

William,William C.,House; see Belvin House

Wilton
Wilton Rd. (moved from Va,Richmond Vic.)
HABS VA-158
HABS VA,44-RICH.V,3-
26ph/4pg L

Wiseham House; see 804 East Clay Street (House)

Women's Club; see Haxall,Bolling W.,House

Yarbrough-Turpin Tobacco Factory; see Pohlig Paper Box Factory

RICHMOND COUNTY

FARNHAM

Farnham Church (Episcopal)
State Rts. 602 & 607
HABS VA-562
HABS VA,80- ,1-
1ph L

SIMONSON VIC.

Morattico
Rappahannock River
HABS VA-73
HABS VA,52-MORAT,1-
1dr/1ph/1pg L

TIDEWATER VIC.

Indian Banks
State Rt. 606
HABS VA-74
HABS VA,80-SIMO,1-
7ph/1pg L

WARSAW

Clerk's Office
U.S. Rt. 360
HABS VA-331
HABS VA,80-WAR,1-
2ph/1pg L

Lawyer's Office
U.S. Rt. 360 & State Rt. 3
HABS VA-563
HABS VA,80-WAR,4-
1ph L

Richmond County Courthouse
U. S. Rt. 360
HABS VA-896
HABS VA,80-WAR,3-
2ph L

St. John's Episcopal Church
U. S. Rt. 360
HABS VA-564
HABS VA,80-WAR,2-
2ph L

WARSAW VIC.

Elmore House
State Rt. 3
HABS VA-63
HABS VA,80-WAR.V,5-
1dr/6ph L

Farmhouse
HABS VA-565
HABS VA,80-WAR.V,7-
1ph L

Linden Farm
Lancaster Rd.
HABS VA-566
HABS VA,80-WAR.V,8-
1ph L

Menokin
Menokin Bay
HABS VA-156
HABS VA,80-WAR.V,6-
20dr/16ph/2pg/fr L

Mount Airy (Tayloe,John,Plantation)
State Rt. 646 Vic.
HABS VA-72
HABS VA,80-WAR.V,4-
42ph/4pg/2pc/3ct L

Mount Airy,Barn (Tayloe,John,Plantation,Barn)
State Rt. 646 Vic.
HABS VA-72-A
HABS VA,80-WAR.V,4A-
1ph L

Mount Airy,Counting House (Tayloe,John,Plantation,Counting House)
State Rt. 646 Vic.
HABS VA-72-C
HABS VA,80/WAR.V,4C-
1ph/1pc L

Mount Airy,Dairy (Tayloe,John,Plantation,Dairy)
State Rt. 646 Vic.
HABS VA-72-B
HABS VA,80-WAR.V,4B-
1ph/1pc L

Mount Airy,Orangery (Ruins)
(Tayloe,John,Plantation,Orangery (Ruins))
State Rt. 646 Vic.
HABS VA-72-E
HABS VA,80-WAR.V,4E-
2ph/1pc L

Mount Airy,Smoke House
(Tayloe,John,Plantation,Smoke House)
State Rt. 646 Vic.
HABS VA-72-D
HABS VA,80-WAR.V,4D-
2ph/1pc L

Sabine Hall
State Rt. 624 Vic.
HABS VA-155
HABS VA,80-WAR.V,2-
24dr/40ph/5pg/fr L

Tayloe,John,Plantation; see Mount Airy

Tayloe,John,Plantation,Barn; see Mount Airy,Barn

Tayloe,John,Plantation,Counting House; see Mount Airy,Counting House

Tayloe,John,Plantation,Dairy; see Mount Airy,Dairy

Tayloe,John,Plantation,Orangery (Ruins); see Mount Airy,Orangery (Ruins)

Tayloe,John,Plantation,Smoke House; see Mount Airy,Smoke House

ROANOKE (CITY)

Courthouse & Municipal Building; see Roanoke Municipal Building & Annex

Roanoke Municipal Building & Annex
(Courthouse & Municipal Building)
216 Campbell Ave. SW & 215 Church Ave. SW
HABS VA-35
HABS VA,81-ROAN,1-,1A-,1B-
8ph/9pg L

Gartch Log House; see Showalter Log House

Showalter Log House (Gartch Log House)
HABS VA-359
HABS VA,81-SAL.V,1-
6ph/1pg L

ROANOKE COUNTY

SALEM

Moravian House (Williams-Brown House & Store)
423 E. Main St.
HABS VA-347
HABS VA,81-SAL,1-
1ph L

Williams-Brown House & Store; see Moravian House

ROCKBRIDGE COUNTY

EAST LEXINGTON VIC.

Mann,J. H. C. ,Bridge
Spanning Maury River on State Rt. 631
HAER VA-36
HAER VA,82-ELEX.V,1-
3ph/1pg/1pc L

LEXINGTON VIC

Winterview Farm Log Cabin
Interstate Hwy. 81
HABS VA-956
HABS VA,82-LEX.V,2-
5dr/3ph/1pc L

LEXINGTON VIC.

Covered Bridge
Spanning Maury River
HABS VA-567
HABS VA,82-LEX,1-
1ph L

James River & Kanawha Canal,Ben Salem Lock
Maury River
HAER VA-21
HAER VA,82-LEX.V,1A-
3ph/1pg/1pc L

James River & Kanawha Canal,South River Dam & Lock
Maury River
HAER VA-22
HAER VA,82-LEX.V,1B-
13ph/1pg/1pc L

Miller's Mill
Rt. 60,12 miles W. of Lexington
HABS VA-1208
HABS VA,82-LEX.V,3-
3ph/1pc L

Stone House
State Rt. 687
HABS VA-899
HABS VA,82-LEX.V,4-
6ph/5pg/1pc L

Thorn Hill
SW of Lexington, off VA Rt. 251
HABS VA-1209
HABS VA,82-LEX.V,5-
13ph/1pc L

Thorn Hill,Dependency
SW of Lexington, off VA Rt. 251
HABS VA-1209-B
HABS VA,82-LEX.V,5B-
1ph L

Thorn Hill,Detached Kitchen
SW of Lexington, off VA Rt. 251
HABS VA-1209-A
HABS VA,82-LEX.V,5A-
1ph L

Thorn Hill,Smokehouse
SW of Lexington, off VA Rt. 251
HABS VA-1209-C
HABS VA,82-LEX.V,5C-
1ph L

ROCKINGHAM COUNTY

BROADWAY

Daphna Creek Pratt Truss Bridge
State Rt. 1414,Holly Hill St.,Spanning Dahna Creek
HAER VA-33
HAER VA,83-BROAD,1-
6ph/2pg/1pc L

Thacher Truss Bridge
Spanning Linville Creek
HAER VA-35
HAER VA,83-BROAD,2-
10ph/3pg/1pc L

PLEASANT VALLEY

Pleasant Valley Depot
State Route 679
HABS VA-1249
HABS VA,83-PLEVA,1-
5dr/7pg/fr L

SCOTT COUNTY

CLINCHPORT

Clinchport Masonic Lodge No. 267
Second Ave.
HABS VA-984
HABS VA,85-CLIN,1-
5dr/1ph/4pg/1pc L

Flanary,Kathleen S.,House
Second Ave.
HABS VA-985
6dr/1ph/4pg/1pc/fr L

SHENANDOAH COUNTY

BIRDHAVEN

Barb Mill
Elks Run
HABS VA-137
HABS VA,86-BIRHA,1-
1ph/3pg L

QUICKSBURG VIC.

Shenandoah River Bridge
Spanning N. fork of Shenandoah River
HAER VA-52
19ph/17pg/2pc L

STRASBURG

Fort Bowman (Harmony Hall)
Frontage Rd.
HABS VA-909
HABS VA,86-STRASB.V,1-
7dr/16ph L

Frontier Fort (Hupp House)
HABS VA-908
HABS VA,86-STRASB,1-
1ph L

Harmony Hall; see Fort Bowman

Hupp House; see Frontier Fort

SMYTH COUNTY

MARION VIC.

Thomas,Abijah,House
Thomas Bridge Rd.
HABS VA-639
HABS VA,87-MAR.V,1-
13dr L

SOUTHAMPTON COUNTY

IVOR VIC.

Bailey House
Blackwater St.
HABS VA-349
HABS HABS,VA,88-IVOR.V,2-
6ph L

Binford House
HABS VA-235
HABS VA,88-IVOR.V,1-
10ph L

SPOTSYLVANIA COUNTY

CHANCELLORSVILLE

Chancellorsville (Ruins)
State Rts. 3 & 610
HABS VA-77
HABS VA,89-CHANVI,1-
11dr/5ph/3pg L

FREDERICKSBURG VIC.

Fredericksburg Country Club; see Smithfield Hall

Haley Farmhouse; see Todd House

Haney Farmhouse; see Todd House

Mannsfield
Rappahannock River
HABS VA-122
HABS VA,89-FRED.V,1-
27dr/44ph/12pg L

Salem Church
State Rt. 3
HABS VA-640
HABS 89/FRED.V,5-
10dr/fr L

Smithfield Hall (Fredericksburg Country Club)
Rappahannock River
HABS VA-570
HABS VA,89-FRED.V,4-
2ph L

Todd House (Haley Farmhouse; Haney Farmhouse)
HABS VA-367
HABS VA,89-FRED.V,2-
5ph L

GUINEA VIC.

Fredericksburg & Spotsylvania National Mltry. Park; see Jackson Shrine

Jackson Shrine (Thornton,John,House; Fredericksburg & Spotsylvania National Mltry. Park
State Rt. 606
HABS VA-637
HABS VA,89-GUIN.V,1-;(DLC/PP-1992:VA-5)
9dr/9ph/1pc L

Thornton,John,House; see Jackson Shrine

SALEM CHURCH

Steiger House
State Rt. 3
HABS VA-369
HABS VA,89- ,2-
3ph L

SPOTSYLVANIA

Harrison House (Ruins)
State Rt. 208
HABS VA-392
HABS VA,89-SPOT,1-
2ph L

Spotsylvania County Jail (Spotsylvania County Offices)
HABS VA-265
HABS VA,89-SPOT,2-
1ph L

Spotsylvania County Offices; see Spotsylvania County Jail

SPOTSYLVANIA VIC.

Danby Farm,Outbuildings
State Rt. 208
HABS VA-391
HABS VA,89-SPOT.V,2-
1ph L

Herndon House
State Rt. 612
HABS VA-372
HABS VA,89-SHAGR.V,1-
8ph L

Whig Hill (Wigg Hill)
State Rt. 208
HABS VA-373
HABS VA,89-SPOT.V,1-
5ph L

Wigg Hill; see Whig Hill

STAFFORD COUNTY

FALMOUTH

Barrett,Kate Waller,Birthplace; see 121 Prince Street (House)

Clifton; see 121 Prince Street (House)

Falmouth Baptist Church (Facade); see Union Church (Facade)

121 Prince Street (House) (Clifton; Barrett,Kate Waller,Birthplace)
HABS VA-264
HABS VA,90-FAL,11-
1ph L

Union Church (Facade) (Falmouth Baptist Church (Facade))
Carter St.
HABS VA-203
HABS VA,90-FAL,10-
2ph L

FALMOUTH VIC.

Chatham (Fitzhugh House)
State Rts. 3 & 607 Vic.
HABS VA-339
HABS VA,90-FAL.V,2-
58ph/1pg/3pc/24ct L

Chatham,Dairy Barn
.2 mi. NE of intersection State Rtes. 218 & 3
HABS VA-339-G
HABS VA,90-FAL.V,2G-
1ph/1pc L

Chatham,Farm Office
.2 mi. NE of intersection State Rtes. 218 & 3
HABS VA-339-D
HABS VA,90/FAL.V,2D-
2ph/1pc L

Chatham,Gardens,Garden Statuary & Grounds
.2 mi. NE of intersection of State Rtes. 218 & 3
HABS VA-339-A
HABS VA,90-FAL.V,2A-
20ph/2pc L

Chatham,Gazebo with Pan statue
.2 mi. NE of intersection State Rtes. 218 & 3
HABS VA-339-B
HABS VA,90-FAL.V,2B-
1ph/1pc L

Chatham,Greenhouses
.2 mi. NE of intersection State Rtes. 218 & 3
HABS VA-339-F
HABS VA,90-FAL.V,2F-
3ph/1pc L

Chatham,Kitchen
.2 mi. NE of intersection State Rtes. 218 & 3
HABS VA-339-C
HABS VA,90-FAL.V,2C-
3ph/1pc L

Chatham,Laundry
.2 mi. NE of intersection State Rtes. 218 & 3
HABS VA-339-H
HABS VA,90-FAL.V,2H-
3ph/1pc L

Chatham,Stable & Garage
.2 mi. NE of intersection State Rtes. 218 & 3
HABS VA-339-E
HABS VA,90-FAL.F,2E-
2ph/1pc L

Chatham,Summer House
.2 mi. NE of intersection State Rtes. 218 & 3
HABS VA-339-I
HABS VA,90-FAL.V,2I-
2ph/1pc L

Ferry Farm Surveying Office; see Washington,George,Surveying Office

Fitzhugh House; see Chatham

Washington,George,Surveying Office (Ferry Farm Surveying Office)
712 King's Hwy.
HABS VA-90
HABS VA,90-FAL.V,1-
7dr/2ph/3pg L

FREDERICKSBURG VIC.

Lansdown,Smokehouse (Reynolds House,Smokehouse)
571 Lansdown Rd.
HABS VA-368
HABS VA,89-FRED.V,3-
3ph L

Reynolds House,Smokehouse; see Lansdown,Smokehouse

STAFFORD

Stafford Co. Courthouse Complex,Clerk's Office
U. S. Rt. 1 & State Rt. 630
HABS VA-56-B
HABS VA,90-STAF,1A-
2ph L

Stafford County Courthouse Complex
U. S. Rt. 1 & State Rt. 630
HABS VA-56
HABS VA,90-STAF,1-
4ph/3pg L

Stafford County Courthouse Complex,Courthouse
U. S. Rt. 1 & State Rt. 630
HABS VA-56-A
HABS VA,90-STAF,1-
1ph/3pg L

Stafford County Courthouse Complex,Jail
U. S. Rt. 1 & State Rt. 630
HABS VA-56-C
HABS VA,90-STAF,1B-
1ph L

STAFFORD VIC.

Aquia Church
U. S. Rt. 1 & State Rt. 676
HABS VA-415
HABS VA,90-STAF.V,1-
15ph/5pg L

STAUNTON (CITY)

Cox,Lucretia,House
328 Green St.
HABS VA-1200
HABS VA,8-STAU,4-
4dr/8pg/fr L

Manse,The (Wilson,Woodrow,Birthplace)
Frederick & Coalter Sts.
HABS VA-11-9
HABS VA,8-STAU,2-
8dr/5ph/2pg/fr L

Putnam Organ Works Store (Valz,A. M. ,Building)
103 W. Beverley St.
HABS VA-1204
HABS VA,8-STAU,5-
5dr/18pg/fr L

Stuart-Robertson House (Entrance Gates)
120 Church St.
HABS VA-11-7
HABS VA,8-STAU,1-
1dr/2ph/2pg L

Valz,A. M. ,Building; see Putnam Organ Works Store

Wilson,Woodrow,Birthplace; see Manse,The

Baltimore & Ohio RR,Folly Mills Creek Viaduct; see Valley Railroad,Folly Mills Creek Viaduct

Valley Railroad,Folly Mills Creek Viaduct (Baltimore & Ohio RR,Folly Mills Creek Viaduct)
Interstate 81
HAER VA-8
HAER VA,8-STAU.V,2-
1dr/7ph/3pg/fr L

SUFFOLK (CITY)

Gateposts,Wood
State Rt. 125
HABS VA-800
HABS VA,62-CHUCK,3-
3ph L

Quarters,The
State Rt. 125
HABS VA-199
HABS VA,62-CHUCK,2-
1ph L

Pembroke
State Rt. 603
HABS VA-181
HABS VA,62-REIDF,1-
5dr/5ph/1pg/fr L

Dairy,Old
HABS VA-1043
HABS VA,62-SUF,2A-
1ph/1pc L

Joiner Farmhouse
HABS VA-324
HABS VA,62-SUF.V,1-
4ph/1pg L

SURRY COUNTY

BACON'S CASTLE VIC.

Allen's Brick House; see Bacon's Castle

Bacon's Castle (Allen's Brick House)
State Rt. 617
HABS VA-75
HABS VA,91- ,1-
22dr/46ph/5pg/5ct L

Crump House
State Rt. 617 Vic.
HABS VA-233
HABS VA,91-CABPO,2-
1ph L

CABIN POINT

House (Dutch Brickwork Detail)
State Rt. 10
HABS VA-390
HABS VA,91-CABPO,2-
1ph L

Ordinary,The
State Rts. 10 & 613
HABS VA-236
HABS VA,91-CABPO,1-
1ph L

CLAREMONT

Claremont,Manor Office
State Rt. 609 Vic.
HABS VA-430
HABS VA,91-CLAR,1A-
1ph L

OTTERDAM VIC.

Booth,Col. Samuel,House; see Snow Hill

Snow Hill (Booth,Col. Samuel,House)
State Rt. 40
HABS VA-1045
HABS VA,91-OTT.V,1-
10dr/6pg/fr L

SURRY VIC.

Clerestory House
State Rt. 31
HABS VA-248
HABS VA,91-SUR.V,4-
1ph L

Four-Mile Tree Plantation,Servants' Quarters
James River Vic.
HABS VA-55
HABS VA,91-SPRI.V,1-
7ph/1pg L

Point Pleasant
Surry County Courthouse Vic.
HABS VA-94
HABS VA,91-SUR.V,3-
1dr/2ph L

Rolfe House
Surry County Courthouse Vic.
HABS VA-397
HABS VA,91-SUR.V,2-
7ph/1pg L

SUSSEX COUNTY

SUSSEX

Windsor Farm (Winsor)
State Rt. 602
HABS VA-255
HABS VA,92-SUSX.V,1-
3ph L

Winsor; see Windsor Farm

VIRGINIA BEACH (CITY)

Ackiss,Francis,House
Pungo Ridge Rd.
HABS VA-226
HABS VA,77- ,7-
2ph L

Lovett,Reuben,House
State Rt. 627 Vic.
HABS VA-560
HABS VA,77-KEMP,3-
1ph L

Pleasant Hall; see Singleton House

Princess Anne County Courthouse
State Rt. 165
HABS VA-556
HABS VA,77-KEMP,2-
1ph L

Singleton House (Pleasant Hall)
State Rt. 165
HABS VA-238
HABS VA,77-KEMP,1-
1ph/1pg L

Cornick,Henry T.,House
Potters & Colonial Rds. Vic.
HABS VA-558
HABS VA,77-KEMP.V,1-
1ph L

Fairfield Plantation,Dependency (White House,The; Walke House)
State Rt. 190 Vic.
HABS VA-557
HABS VA,77-KEMP.V,2A-
1ph L

Walke House; see Fairfield Plantation,Dependency

White House,The; see Fairfield Plantation,Dependency

Eastwood
Great Neck Lake
HABS VA-242
HABS VA,77-LONBR.V,2-
5ph/1pg L

Hudgins House (Huggins House)
U. S. Rt. 58
HABS VA-243
HABS VA,77-LONBRI.V,3-
3ph/1pg L

Huggins House; see Hudgins House

Keeling,Adam,House
Keeling Rd.
HABS VA-11-17
HABS VA,77-LONBRI.V,1-
6dr/6ph/2pg/1pc/fr L

Boush House; see Wishart,James,House

Wishart,James,House (Boush House)
State Rt. 649 Vic.
HABS VA-11-16
HABS VA,77-LYNHA.V,2-
3dr/3ph/2pg/fr L

Brock Farm Quarters (Brook Farm Quarters)
State Rt. 615 Vic.
HABS VA-400
HABS VA,77-NIM.V,2-
6ph/2pg L

Brook Farm Quarters; see Brock Farm Quarters

Woodhouse,Jonathan,House
State Rt. 632 Vic.
HABS VA-239
HABS VA,77-NIM.V,1-
5ph/1pg L

Salisbury Plains
State Rt. 1002
HABS VA-559
HABS VA,77-OCEA.V,1-
1ph L

Thoroughgood,Adam,House
1636 Parish Road (Thoroughgood Road)
HABS VA-209
HABS VA,77-LYNHA.V,1-
9dr/3ph/2pg/1pc/fr L

WARREN COUNTY

FRONT ROYAL VIC.

Mount Zion
State Rt. 624
HABS VA-357
HABS VA,94-MILDA,1-
2ph/1pg L

WESTMORELAND COUNTY

HAGUE

Wilton
HABS VA-1047
HABS VA,97-HAG,1-
1ph L

MOUNT HOLLY VIC.

Spring Grove
State Rt. 202
HABS VA-1203
HABS VA,97-MOHO,1-
9dr/4pg/fr L

OAK GROVE

Blenheim
State Rt. 204 Vic.
HABS VA-571
HABS VA,97-OKGRO,1-
4dr/4ph L

STRATFORD

Stratford (Stratford Hall)
State Rt. 214
HABS VA-307
HABS VA,97- ,4-
34dr/14pg/fr L

Stratford Hall; see Stratford

TUCKER HILL VIC.

Yeocomico Church
State Rt. 606
HABS VA-268
HABS VA,97- ,1-
4ph/1pg L

WAKEFIELD CORNER VIC

George Washington Birthplace National Monument; see Wakefield

George Washington Birthplace National Monument; see Wakefield,Gardens & Grounds

George Washington Birthplace National Monument; see Wakefield,Kitchen

Wakefield (George Washington Birthplace National Monument)
State Rt. 204
HABS VA-393
HABS VA,97- ,3-
15ph/1pg L

Wakefield,Gardens & Grounds (George Washington Birthplace National Monument)
State Rt. 204
HABS VA-393-A
HABS VA,97- ,3-
2ph L

Wakefield,Kitchen (George Washington Birthplace National Monument)
State Rt. 204
HABS VA-393-B
HABS VA,-97- ,3B-
7ph L

WESTMORELAND

Nomoni Hall
HABS VA-1048
HABS VA,97- ,2-
2ph L

WILLIAMSBURG (CITY)

Audrey House; see Page,Gov. John,House

Barlow House; see De Neufville House

Barraud,Dr. Philip,House (Mercer House)
Francis & Botetourt Sts.
HABS VA-234
HABS VA,48-WIL,32-
1ph L

Belle Farm
(moved from VA,Ordinary Vic.)
HABS VA-69
HABS VA,37-ORD.V,1-
1ph/2pg L

Blair,Archibald,House
Nicholson St.
HABS VA-196
HABS VA,48-WIL,46-
1ph/1pg L

Blair,Archiblad,Dairy,Smokehouse & Privy
100 Nicholson St.
HABS VA-196
HABS VA,48-WIL,46A-,B-,C-
4dr/fr L

Blair,John,House
Duke of Gloucester St.
HABS VA-910
HABS VA,48-WIL,7-
2ph/1pg L

Bland-Wetherburn House; see Bland,Richard,House

Bland,Richard,House
(Bland-Wetherburn House; Wetherburn's Tavern)
Duke of Gloucester St.
HABS VA-403
HABS VA,48-WIL,18-
4ph/1pg L

Bowden-Armistead House
207 Duke of Gloucester St.
HABS VA-1026
HABS VA,48-WIL,64-
6dr/fr L

Bracken House; see Braken House

Braken House (Bracken House)
HABS VA-523
HABS VA,48-WIl,17-
1ph L

Bruton Parish Church
201 Duke of Gloucester St.
HABS VA-191
HABS VA,48-WIL,2-
4dr/2ph L

C & O RR Underpass; see Colonial National Monument Pkwy,C & O RR Underpass

Camm-Blair Apothecary Shop; see Prentis Store

Capitol Landing Underpass; see Colonial Natl Mon. Pkwy,Capitol Landing Underpass

Capitol,The (reconstructed)
Duke of Gloucester St.
HABS VA-365
HABS VA,48-WIL,51-
1ph/3pg L

Chiswell,Col. Charles,House (Interiors)
Francis St.
HABS VA-404
HABS VA,48-WIL,51-
2ph/2pg L

Coke-Garrett House
Nicholson St.
HABS VA-527
HABS VA,48-WIL,23-
1ph L

Colonial Hotel; see Spencer's Hotel

Colonial Nat. Monument Pkwy,Williamsburg Tunnel
(Williamsburg Tunnel; Colonial Pkwy,Williamsburg Tunnel)
.3 Miles South of C & O RR Underpass
HAER VA-48-D
HAER 1989(HAER):22
2ph/11pg/1pc L

Colonial National Monument Pkwy,C & O RR Underpass (C & O RR Underpass; Lafayette St. Bridge; Colonial Pkwy,C & O RR Underpass)
Milepost 12.54 of the Colonial Pkwy
HAER VA-48-C
HAER 1989(HAER):22
6ph/9pg/1pc L

Colonial Natl Mon. Pkwy,Capitol Landing Underpass (Capitol Landing Underpass; Colonial Pkwy,Capitol Landing Underpass)
Milepost 11.96 of Colonial Pkwy
HAER VA-48-B
HAER 1989(HAER):22
5ph/10pg/1pc L

Colonial Pkwy,C & O RR Underpass; see Colonial National Monument Pkwy,C & O RR Underpass

Colonial Pkwy,Capitol Landing Underpass; see Colonial Natl Mon. Pkwy,Capitol Landing Underpass

Colonial Pkwy,Williamsburg Tunnel; see Colonial Nat. Monument Pkwy,Williamsburg Tunnel

Courthouse,Old
Courthouse Green
HABS VA-528
HABS VA,48-WIL,53-
11dr/1ph/fr L

Custis-Maupin Necessary House
200 Duke of Gloucester St.
HABS VA-1071
HABS VA,48-WIL,63-
2dr/fr L

De Neufville House (Orr,Capt. Hugh,House; Barlow House)
Duke of Gloucester & Colonial Sts.
HABS VA-245
HABS VA,48-WIL,8-
1ph/1pg L

Foundation of Early Church
Bruton Parish Churchyard
HABS VA-176
HABS VA,48-WIL,2A-
1dr L

Galt,Anne,House; see Nelson-Galt House

Gaol,Old (Public Gaol)
Nicholson St.
HABS VA-530
HABS VA,48-WIL,52-
1ph L

Golden Ball Shop; see Hunter,Margaret,Shop

Governor's Palace (reconstructed)
Palace Green
HABS VA-327
HABS VA,48-WIL,41-
4ph/4pg L

Greenhow-Repiton Office; see Prison,Old

Griffin House
410 W. Francis St.
HABS VA-1008
HABS VA,48-WIL,62-
10dr/fr L

Hunter,Margaret,Shop (Golden Ball Shop)
Duke of Gloucester St.
HABS VA-526
HABS VA,48-WIL,55-
1ph L

Jackson,George,House & Store
(Lamb,Lucy,House)
York St.
HABS VA-524
HABS VA,48-WIL,57-
1ph L

Kerr House; see Palmer House

Lafayette St. Bridge; see Colonial National Monument Pkwy,C & O RR Underpass

Lamb,Lucy,House; see Jackson,George,House & Store

Little Christian House; see Timson,William,House

Ludwell-Paradise House (Paradise House)
Duke of Gloucester St.
HABS VA-189
HABS VA,48-WIL,45-
3ph/1pg L

Magazine,The (Powder Horn)
103 Duke of Gloucester St.
HABS VA-529
HABS VA,48-WIL,58-
7dr/1ph L

McClandish House (Orrell,John,House)
Francis St.
HABS VA-328
HABS VA,48-WIL,49-
1ph/1pg L

Mercer House; see Barraud,Dr. Philip,House

Moody House (Roper House)
Francis St.
HABS VA-237
HABS VA,48-WIL,36-
3ph/2pg L

Nelson-Galt House (Galt,Anne,House)
Francis St.
HABS VA-522
HABS VA,48-WIL,54-
1ph L

Nicholson,Robert,House
York St.
HABS VA-188
HABS VA,48-WIL,42-
1ph L

Orr,Capt. Hugh,House; see De Neufville House

Orrell,John,House; see McClandish House

Page,Gov. John,House (Audrey House)
Palace Green Vic.
HABS VA-273
HABS VA,48-WIL,10-
7ph/2pg L

Palmer House (Kerr House)
Duke of Gloucester St.
HABS VA-525
HABS VA,48-WIL,56-
1ph L

Paradise House; see Ludwell-Paradise House

Peachy House; see Randolph,Peyton,House

Peachy-Randolph House; see Randolph,Peyton,House

Powder Horn; see Magazine,The

Prentis Store (Camm-Blair Apothecary Shop)
214 Duke of Gloucester St.
HABS VA-316
HABS VA,48-WIL,48-
6dr/1ph/1pg L

Prison,Old (Greenhow-Repiton Office)
Duke of Gloucester St.
HABS VA-406
HABS VA,48-WIL,5-
1ph/1pg L

Public Gaol; see Gaol,Old

Public Records Office (Treasurer's House)
428 Duke of Gloucester St.
HABS VA-195
HABS VA,48-WIL,12-
5dr/1ph L

Randolph-Semple House; see Semple House

Randolph,Peyton,House
(Peachy-Randolph House; Peachy House)
Nicholson & N. England Sts.
HABS VA-197
HABS VA,48-WIL,47-
6ph/2pg L

Redwood Ordinary
449 Nicholson St.
HABS VA-1083
HABS VA,48-WIL,65-
13dr L

Reid,George,Wellhead
209 E. Duke of Gloucester St.
HABS VA-1011
HABS VA,48-WIL,61-
3dr L

Roper House; see Moody House

Semple House (Randolph-Semple House)
Francis St.
HABS VA-911
HABS VA,48-WIL,6-
1ph L

Spencer's Hotel (Colonial Hotel)
Duke of Gloucester & Queen Sts.
HABS VA-356
HABS VA,48-WIL,50-
1ph/1pg L

Taliaferro-Cole Shop
Duke of Gloucester St.
HABS VA-531
HABS VA,48-WIL,59-
1ph L

Tayloe Office
112 E. Nicholson St.
HABS VA-1010
HABS VA,48-WIL,60-
3dr L

Timson,William,House (Little Christian House)
Prince George & Nassau Sts.
HABS VA-383
HABS VA,48-WIL,14-
1ph/1pg L

Treasurer's House; see Public Records Office

Tucker,St. George,House
106 W. Nicholson St.
HABS VA-1012
HABS VA,48-WIL,33-
7dr L

Wetherburn's Tavern; see Bland,Richard,House

William & Mary College,Brafferton Hall (William & Mary College,First Indian School)
College Yard
HABS VA-346
HABS VA,48-WIL,4D-
7dr/4ph/3pg L

William & Mary College,First Indian School; see William & Mary College,Brafferton Hall

William & Mary College,Main Building (William & Mary College,Wren Building)
College Yard
HABS VA-401
HABS VA,48-WIL,4A-
14dr/4ph/1pg L

William & Mary College,President's House
College Yard
HABS VA-913
HABS VA,48-WIL,4B-
1ph L

William & Mary College,Wren Building; see William & Mary College,Main Building

Williamsburg Tunnel; see Colonial Nat. Monument Pkwy,Williamsburg Tunnel

Wythe,George,House
101 Palace Green St.
HABS VA-1009
HABS VA,48-WIL,16-
10dr/fr L

WINCHESTER (CITY)

Abram's Delight (Hollingsworth House)
Rouss Spring Ave.
HABS VA-692
HABS VA,35-WIN,14-
7dr/1pg/fr L

Amherst Street
HABS VA-694
HABS VA,35-WIN,6-
6dr/fr L

Amherst Street (Hottle,William F. ,House)
132 Amherst St.
HABS VA-694-C
HABS VA,35-WIN,9-
2pg L

Amherst Street (Long,Robert,House)
101 N. Washington St.
HABS VA-694-A
HABS VA,35-WIN,7-
6pg L

Amherst Street (McGuire,Dr. William P. ,House & Office)
120 & 124 Amherst St.
HABS VA-694-D
HABS VA,35-WIN,10-
7pg L

Amherst Street (McGuire,Edward,House)
103 N. Braddock St.
HABS VA-694-E
HABS VA,35-WIN,11-
5pg L

Amherst Street
(Tidball,Alexander,House)
138 Amherst St.
HABS VA-694-B
HABS VA,35-WIN,8-
5pg L

Glen Burnie
801 Amherst St.
HABS VA-698
HABS VA,35-WIN,8-
18pg L

Holliday Office Building; see Lawyer's Row

Hollingsworth House; see Abram's Delight

Hottle,William F. ,House; see Amherst Street

Kurtz,Adam,House (Washington's Headquarters)
S. Braddock & W. Cork Sts.
HABS VA-699
HABS VA,35-WIN,5-
11pg L

Lawyer's Row (Holliday Office Building)
30,32,34 & 36 Rouss Ave.
HABS VA-691
HABS VA,35-WIN,13-
5dr/1pg/fr L

Long,Robert,House; see Amherst Street

McGuire,Dr. William P. ,House & Office; see Amherst Street

McGuire,Edward,House; see Amherst Street

Tidball,Alexander,House; see Amherst Street

Washington's Headquarters; see Kurtz,Adam,House

YORK COUNTY

GRAFTON VIC.

Dairy House
York County Poor Farm (U.S. Rt. 17)
HABS VA-84
HABS VA,100-GRAF.V,1-
1dr/5ph L

YORKTOWN

Archer House (Colonial National Historical Park)
Lot #123,Water Street
HABS VA-914
HABS VA,100-YORK,17-;(DLC/PP-1992:VA-5)
3dr/11ph/1pc L

Archer House,Bake Oven (Architectural Remains) (Colonial National Historical Park)
Lot #117,Water Street
HABS VA-915
HABS VA,100-YORK,17A-
1dr L

Architectural Remains (Foundations)
Lot #30,Main & Church Sts.
HABS VA-92
HABS VA,100-YORK,11-
1dr L

Architectural Remains (Foundations)
Lot #30,Main & Church Sts.
HABS VA-93
HABS VA,100-YORK,12-
1dr L

Ballentine House (Dewsville)
Main St. (moved from VA,Newtown Vic.)
HABS VA-596
HABS VA,100-YORK,16-
3ph/3pg L

Blow,Capt. George P. ,House; see York Hall

Colonial Nat'l Historical Park,Lot 77 (Site Plan)
Main St.
HABS VA-917
HABS VA,100-YORK,9A-
1dr L

Colonial National Historical Park; see Archer House

Colonial National Historical Park; see Archer House,Bake Oven (Architectural Remains)

Colonial National Historical Park,Lot 77 (Digges,Dudley,(formerly West) House,Stone Steps)
Main St.
HABS VA-917-B
HABS VA,100-YORK,9B-
1dr L

Colonial National Historical Park,Lot 77 (Structures L & M)
Main St.
HABS VA-917-A
HABS VA,100-YORK,9A1-
1dr L

Colonial National Monument Parkway (Colonial Parkway)
Jamestown Is. to Yorktown,via Williamsburg
HAER VA-48
HAER 1989(HAER):22
15pg L

Colonial Natl Mon. Pkwy,Navy Mine Overpass (Mine Depot Overpass; Colonial Parkway,Mine Depot overpass)
Milepost 286 of the Colonial Parkway
HAER VA-48-A
HAER 1989(HAER):22
3ph/8pg/1pc L

Colonial Parkway; see Colonial National Monument Parkway

Colonial Parkway,Mine Depot overpass; see Colonial Natl Mon. Pkwy,Navy Mine Overpass

Customs House
Main & Read Sts.
HABS VA-202
HABS VA,100-YORK,4-
3ph L

Dewsville; see Ballentine House

Digges,Dudley,(formerly West) House,Stone Steps; see Colonial National Historical Park,Lot 77

Digges,Dudley,House; see West House

Lightfoot House (Somerwell House; Yorktown Hotel)
Church & Main Sts.
HABS VA-87
HABS VA,100-YORK,8-
3dr/6ph/1pg/fr L

Main Street (Medical Shop) (Main Street (Post Office))
HABS VA-395
HABS VA,100-YORK,15-
1ph L

Main Street (Post Office); see Main Street (Medical Shop)

Mine Depot Overpass; see Colonial Natl Mon. Pkwy,Navy Mine Overpass

Moore House (Temple Farm)
State Rt. 676
HABS VA-80
HABS VA,100-YORK.V,1-
16dr/10ph/4pg L

Nelson House; see York Hall

Nelson House,Dependency (Guest House); see York Hall,Dependency (Guest House)

Nelson House,Kitchen (Ruins); see York Hall,Kitchen (Ruins)

Powder Horn,Engraved
HABS VA-394
HABS VA,100-YORK,14-
1ph L

Sessions-Sheild House; see Sheild House

Sheild House (Sessions-Sheild House)
Pearl & Main Sts.
HABS VA-81
HABS VA,100-YORK,7-
11dr/4ph/1pg/fr L

Somerwell House; see Lightfoot House

Structures L & M; see Colonial National Historical Park,Lot 77

Swan Tavern
Main St.
HABS VA-83
HABS VA,100-YORK,10-
10dr/3ph/2pg/1pc L

Temple Farm; see Moore House

West House (Digges,Dudley,House)
HABS VA-82
HABS VA,100-YORK,9-
18dr/5ph/2pg L

Wharf Buildings
State Rt. 238
HABS VA-371
HABS VA,100-YORK,13-
2ph L

York Hall (Nelson House; Blow,Capt. George P. ,House)
State Rt. 1005 & Main St.
HABS VA-58
HABS VA,100-YORK,1-
41ph/4pg/2pc L

York Hall,Dependency (Guest House) (Nelson House,Dependency (Guest House))
State Rt. 1005 & Main St.
HABS VA-58-A
HABS VA,100-YORK,1B-
2ph/1pc L

York Hall,Kitchen (Ruins) (Nelson House,Kitchen (Ruins))
State Rt. 1005 & Main St.
HABS VA-58-B
HABS VA,100-YORK,1C-
2ph/1pc L

Yorktown Hotel; see Lightfoot House

YORKTOWN VIC.

Bellfield Cemetery (Digges Family Cemetery)
Digges Rd. Vic.
HABS VA-918
HABS VA,100-YORK.V,4-
1ph L

Digges Family Cemetery; see Bellfield Cemetery

End View
HABS VA-572
HABS VA,100- ,1-
1ph L

Kiskiack (Naval Mine Depot)
State Rt. 238 Vic.
HABS VA-183
HABS VA,100-YORK.V,2-
4dr L

Ringfield
King Creek
HABS VA-318
HABS VA,100-YORK.V,3-
1ph/3pg L

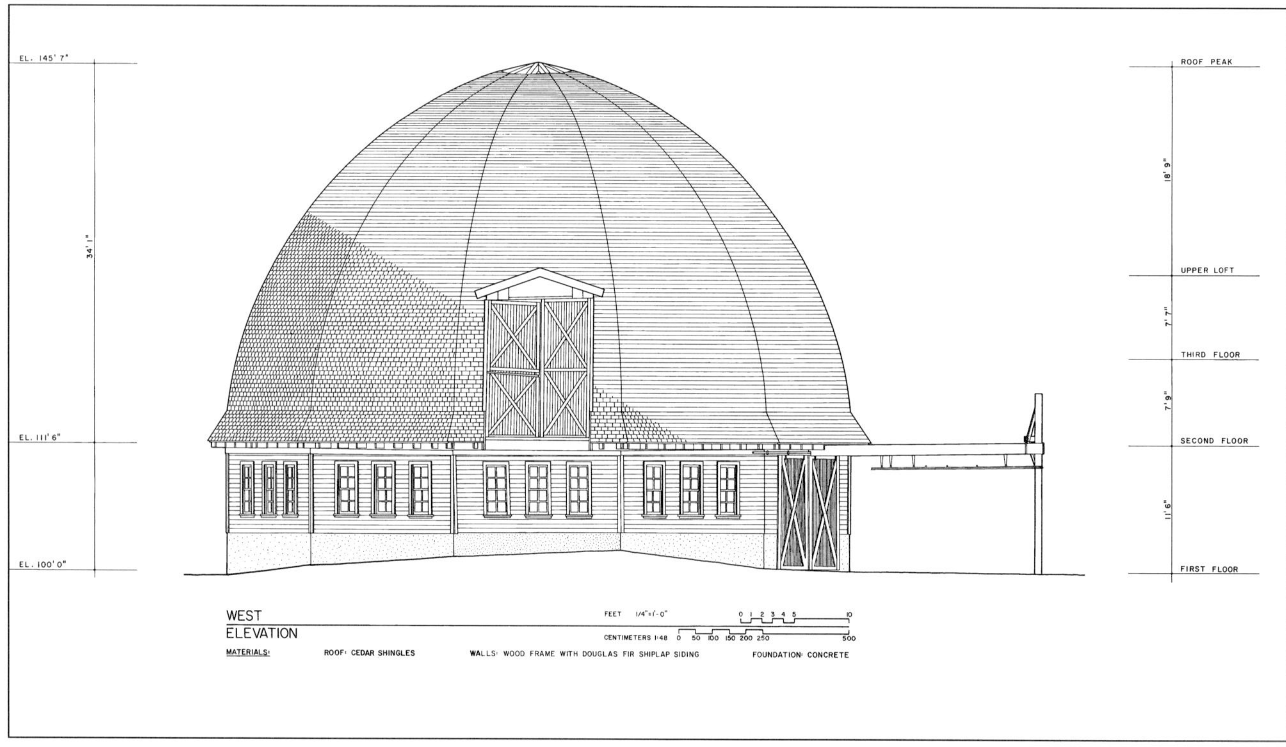

T. A. Leonard Barn, Pullman vicinity, Whitman County, Washington. Southwest elevation. Photograph by George Bedirian, August 31, 1985 (HABS WASH,38-PULL.V,1-4).

T.A. Leonard Barn, Pullman vicinity, Whitman County, Washington. West elevation. Measured drawing delineated by Steve E. Nys, 1985. Winner of the 1986 Charles E. Peterson Prize (HABS WA-168, sheet 8 of 10).

Washington

ASOTIN COUNTY

MISSION ORCHARD

Silcott House
HABS WA-114
HABS WASH,2-MISO,1-
2ph/1pg L

BENTON COUNTY

PROSSER

Grant Avenue Bridge (Prosser Steel Bridge)
Spanning Yakima River at Grant Ave.
HAER WA-4
HAER WASH,3-PROS,1-
13ph/2pg/fr L

Prosser Steel Bridge; see Grant Avenue Bridge

CHELAN COUNTY

CHELAN

U. S. Forest Service Chelan Ranger Sta.,Warehouse
428 W. Woodin Ave.
HABS WA-188-B
13ph H

U.S. Forest Service Chelan Ranger Sta.,Main Office
428 W. Woodin Ave.
HABS WA-188-A
15ph H

U.S. Forest Service Chelan Ranger Station
428 W. Woodin Ave.
HABS WA-188
5ph/20pg/3pc H

U.S. Forest Service Chelan Ranger Station,Annex
428 W. Woodin Ave.
HABS WA-188-C
4ph H

LEAVENWORTH

Leavenworth Ranger Station, Office No. 2084
Lvnwrth Rngr Dist, Wenatchee Natl Frst, U.S. Hwy 2
HABS WA-193-A
25ph/8pg/2pc H

STEHEKIN VIC.

Company Creek Bridge No. 2
(Harlequin Bridge; North Cascades National Park)
Spanning Stehekin River
HAER WA-115
5dr H

Harlequin Bridge; see Company Creek Bridge No. 2

North Cascades National Park; see Company Creek Bridge No. 2

CLALLAM COUNTY

DUNGENESS VIC.

Clallam County Courthouse (Weekly Farm)
HABS WA-70
HABS WASH,5-DUNG.V,1-
2ph/1pg L

Jail,First (Pettit Place)
Pettit Farm
HABS WA-71
HABS WASH,5-DUNG.V,2-
2ph/1pg L

Pettit Place; see Jail,First

Weekly Farm; see Clallam County Courthouse

LAKE CRESCENT VIC.

Olympic National Park; see Storm King Inn

Olympic National Park; see Storm King Ranger Station

Olympic National Park (Site Map)
HABS WA-164
HABS WASH,5-LACRE.V,1-
1dr L

Storm King Inn (Olympic National Park)
U. S. Hwy. 101 vic. ,near Barnes Point
HABS WA-156
HABS WASH,5-LACRE.V,3-
4dr/16ph/13pg/1pc/fr L

Storm King Ranger Station (Olympic National Park)
U. S. Hwy. 101 vic. ,near Barnes Point
HABS WA-155
HABS WASH,5-LACRE.V,2-
4dr/17ph/12pg/1pc L

PORT ANGELES (VIC.)

Rosemary Inn
Olympic Natl. For., Barnes Point, Lake Crescent
HABS WA-185
2ph/20pg/1pc H

Rosemary Inn, Alabam Cabin
(Rosemary Inn, Building No. 376)
OLYM Nat. For., Barnes Point, Lake Crescent
HABS WA-185-E
1ph/2pg/1pc H

Rosemary Inn, Barn; see Rosemary Inn, Tumble Inn

Rosemary Inn, Boathouse (Rosemary Inn, Building No. 399)
OLYM Natl. For., Barnes Point, Lake Crescent
HABS WA-185-P
1ph/2pg/1pc H

Rosemary Inn, Building No. 372; see Rosemary Inn, Lodge

Rosemary Inn, Building No. 373; see Rosemary Inn, Tumble Inn

Rosemary Inn, Building No. 374; see Rosemary Inn, Dreamerie Cabin

Rosemary Inn, Building No. 375; see Rosemary Inn, Indiana Cabin

Rosemary Inn, Building No. 376; see Rosemary Inn, Alabam Cabin

Rosemary Inn, Building No. 377; see Rosemary Inn, Honeysuckle Cabin

Rosemary Inn, Building No. 378; see Rosemary Inn, Wren Cabin

Rosemary Inn, Building No. 380; see Rosemary Inn, Red Wing Cabin

Rosemary Inn, Building No. 381; see Rosemary Inn, Silver Moon Cabin

Rosemary Inn, Building No. 382; see Rosemary Inn, Cara Mia Cabin

Rosemary Inn, Building No. 383; see Rosemary Inn, Dixie Cabin

Rosemary Inn, Building No. 384; see Rosemary Inn, Summerie Cabin

Rosemary Inn, Building No. 386; see Rosemary Inn, Rock-A-Bye Cabin

Rosemary Inn, Building No. 388; see Rosemary Inn, Dardenella Cabin

Rosemary Inn, Building No. 398; see Rosemary Inn, Inglenook

Rosemary Inn, Building No. 399; see Rosemary Inn, Boathouse

Rosemary Inn, Cara Mia Cabin
(Rosemary Inn, Building No. 382)
OLYM Natl. For., Barnes Point, Lake Crescent
HABS WA-185-J
1ph/2pg/1pc H

Rosemary Inn, Dardenella Cabin (Rosemary Inn, Building No. 388)
OLYM Natl. For., Barnes Point, Lake Crescent
HABS WA-185-N
1ph/2pg/1pc H

Rosemary Inn, Dixie Cabin (Rosemary Inn, Building No. 383)
OLYM Natl. For., Barnes Point, Lake Crescent
HABS WA-185-K
1ph/2pg/1pc H

Rosemary Inn, Dreamerie Cabin (Rosemary Inn, Building No. 374)
OLYM Natl. For., Barnes Point, Lake Crescent
HABS WA-185-C
1ph/2pg/1pc H

Rosemary Inn, Fireplace Shelter; see Rosemary Inn, Inglenook

Rosemary Inn, Honeysuckle Cabin (Rosemary Inn, Building No. 377)
OLYM Natl. For., Barnes Point, Lake Crescent
HABS WA-185-F
1ph/2pg/1pc H

Rosemary Inn, Indiana Cabin (Rosemary Inn, Building No. 375)
OLYM Natl. For., Barnes Point, Lake Crescent
HABS WA-185-D
1ph/2pg/1pc H

Rosemary Inn, Inglenook (Rosemary Inn, Fireplace Shelter; Rosemary Inn, Building No. 398)
OLYM Natl. For., Barnes Point, Lake Crescent
HABS WA-185-O
1ph/2pg/1pc H

Rosemary Inn, Lodge (Rosemary Inn, Building No. 372)
Olympic Natl. For., Barnes Point, Lake Crescent
HABS WA-185-A
4ph/3pg/1pc H

Rosemary Inn, Manager's Residence; see Rosemary Inn, Tumble Inn

Rosemary Inn, Men's Dormitory; see Rosemary Inn, Tumble Inn

Rosemary Inn, Red Wing Cabin (Rosemary Inn, Building No. 380)
OLYM Natl. For., Barnes Point, Lake Crescent
HABS WA-185-H
1ph/2pg/1pc H

Rosemary Inn, Rock-A-Bye Cabin (Rosemary Inn, Building No. 386)
OLYM Natl. For., Barnes Point, Lake Crescent
HABS WA-185-M
1ph/2pg/1pc H

Rosemary Inn, Silver Moon Cabin (Rosemary Inn, Building No. 381)
OLYM Natl. For., Barnes Point, Lake Crescent
HABS WA-185-I
1ph/2pg/1pc H

Rosemary Inn, Summerie Cabin (Rosemary Inn, Building No. 384)
OLYM Natl. For., Barnes Point, Lake Crescent
HABS WA-185-L
1ph/2pg/1pc H

Rosemary Inn, Tumble Inn (Rosemary Inn, Manager's Residence; Rosemary Inn, Men's Dormitory; Rosemary Inn, Barn; Rosemary Inn, Building No. 373)
OLYM Natl. For., Barnes Point Lake Crescent
HABS WA-185-B
1ph/2pg/1pc H

Rosemary Inn, Wren Cabin (Rosemary Inn, Building No. 378)
OLYM Nat. For., Barnes Point, Lake Crescent
HABS WA-185-G
1ph/2pg/1pc H

PORT ANGELES VIC.

Lake Crescent Lodge; see Singer's Lake Crescent Tavern

Lake Crescent Lodge,Building No. 1268; see Singer's Lake Crescent Tavern,Storage Bldg./Garage

Lake Crescent Lodge,Building No. 654; see Singer's Lake Crescent Tavern,Lodge Building

Lake Crescent Lodge,Building No. 656; see Singer's Lake Crescent Tavern,Outdoor Rec. Bldg.

Lake Crescent Lodge,Building No. 657; see Singer's Lake Crescent Tavern,Employees/Boys Dorm

Lake Crescent Lodge,Building No. 661; see Singer's Lake Crescent Tavern,Duplex 37/38

Lake Crescent Lodge,Building No. 662; see Singer's Lake Crescent Tavern,Cabin 36

Lake Crescent Lodge,Building No. 663; see Singer's Lake Crescent Tavern,Cabin 34

Lake Crescent Lodge,Building No. 664; see Singer's Lake Crescent Tavern,Cabin 35

Lake Crescent Lodge,Building No. 666; see Singer's Lake Crescent Tavern,Sleeping Quarters

Lake Crescent Lodge,Building No. 681; see Singer's Lake Crescent Tavern,Cabin 43

Lake Crescent Lodge,Building No. 682; see Singer's Lake Crescent Tavern,Storage Building

Lake Crescent Lodge,Building Nos. 668-674; see Singer's Lake Crescent Tavern,Cabins 3-21

Lake Crescent Lodge,Building Nos. 675-680; see Singer's Lake Crescent Tavern,Cabins 22-31

Singer's Lake Crescent Tavern (Lake Crescent Lodge)
Barnes Point,Lake Crescent,Olympic National Park
HABS WA-186
HABS 1991(HABS):10
24pg L

Singer's Lake Crescent Tavern,Cabin 34 (Lake Crescent Lodge,Building No. 663)
Barnes Point,Lake Crescent,Olympic National Park
HABS WA-186-H
HABS 1991(HABS):10
1ph/1pc L

Singer's Lake Crescent Tavern,Cabin 35 (Lake Crescent Lodge,Building No. 664)
Barnes Point,Lake Crescent,Olympic National Park
HABS WA-186-D
HABS 1991(HABS):10
1ph/1pc L

Singer's Lake Crescent Tavern,Cabin 36 (Lake Crescent Lodge,Building No. 662)
Barnes Point,Lake Crescent,Olympic National Park
HABS WA-186-C
HABS 1991(HABS):10
1ph/1pc L

Singer's Lake Crescent Tavern,Cabin 43 (Lake Crescent Lodge,Building No. 681)
Barnes Point,Lake Crescent,Olympic National Park
HABS WA-186-I
HABS 1991(HABS):10
1ph/2pg/1pc L

Singer's Lake Crescent Tavern,Cabins 22-31 (Lake Crescent Lodge,Building Nos. 675-680)
Barnes Point,Lake Crescent,Olympic National Park
HABS WA-186-J
HABS 1991(HABS):10
8ph/12pg/1pc L

Singer's Lake Crescent Tavern,Cabins 3-21 (Lake Crescent Lodge,Building Nos. 668-674)
Barnes Point,Lake Crescent,Olympic National Park
HABS WA-186-E
HABS 1991(HABS):10
9ph/14pg/1pc L

Singer's Lake Crescent Tavern,Duplex 37/38 (Lake Crescent Lodge,Building No. 661)
Barnes Point,Lake Crescent,Olympic National Park
HABS WA-186-B
HABS 1991(HABS):10
1ph/1pc L

Singer's Lake Crescent Tavern,Employees/Boys Dorm (Lake Crescent Lodge,Building No. 657)
Barnes Point,Lake Crescent,Olympic National Park
HABS WA-186-G
HABS 1991(HABS):10
1ph/2pg/1pc L

Singer's Lake Crescent Tavern,Lodge Building (Lake Crescent Lodge,Building No. 654)
Barnes Point,Lake Crescent,Olympic National Park
HABS WA-186-A
HABS 1991(HABS):10
8ph/9pg/1pc L

Singer's Lake Crescent Tavern,Outdoor Rec. Bldg. (Lake Crescent Lodge,Building No. 656)
Barnes Point,Lake Crescent,Olympic National Park
HABS WA-186-F
HABS 1991(HABS):10
1ph/2pg/1pc L

Singer's Lake Crescent Tavern,Sleeping Quarters (Lake Crescent Lodge,Building No. 666)
Banes Point,Lake Crescent,Olympic National Park
HABS WA-186-K
HABS 1991(HABS):10
1ph/2pg/1pc H

Singer's Lake Crescent Tavern,Storage Bldg./Garage (Lake Crescent Lodge,Building No. 1268)
Barnes Point,Lake Crescent,Olympic National Park
HABS WA-186-M
HABS 1991(HABS):10
1ph/2pg/1pc L

Singer's Lake Crescent Tavern,Storage Building (Lake Crescent Lodge,Building No. 682)
Barnes Point,Lake Crescent,Olympic National Park
HABS WA-186-L
HABS 1991(HABS):10
1ph/2pg/1pc L

CLARK COUNTY

VANCOUVER

Fort Vancouver
HABS WA-41
HABS WASH,6-VANCO,1-
1pg L

Fort Vancouver,Artillery Stables (Mule Barn,Old)
HABS WA-41-C
HABS WASH,6-VANCO,1H-
32ph/15pg/2pc L

Fort Vancouver,Barracks
HABS WA-41-A
HABS WASH,6-VANCO,1C-
2ph L

Fort Vancouver,Building No. 110 (Gun Shed)
HABS WA-41-E
HABS WASH,6-VANCO,1E-
3ph/2pg/1pc L

Fort Vancouver,Building No. 113 (Gun Shed)
HABS WA-41-F
HABS WASH,6-VANCO,1F-
3ph/2pg/1pc L

Fort Vancouver,Building No. 134 (Infantry Stables)
HABS WA-41-G
HABS WASH,6-VANCO,1G-
6ph/2pg/1pc L

Fort Vancouver,Gen. Grant's Headquarters
HABS WA-41-B
HABS WASH,6-VANCO,1-B-
4dr/3ph/fr L

Fort Vancouver,Officers' Club
HABS WA-39-W-14
HABS WASH,6-VANCO,1A-
1ph L

Fort Vancouver,Post Library
HABS WA-41-D
HABS WASH,6-VANCO,1-D-
10dr/4ph/fr L

Mule Barn,Old; see Fort Vancouver,Artillery Stables

Providence Academy
Tenth St.
HABS WA-99
HABS WASH,6-VANCO,3-
2ph/1pg L

Slocum House
Fifth & Daniel Sts.
HABS WA-81
HABS WASH,6-VANCO,2-
1ph/1pg/1pc L

VANCOUVER VIC.

Covington,Richard,Cabin
Loverich Park
HABS WA-38
HABS WASH,6-VANCO.V,1-
3dr/3ph/1pg/fr L

FERRY COUNTY

ORIENT

Orient Bridge
Spanning Kettle River at Richardson Rd.
HAER WA-32
HAER DLC/PP-1993:WA-2
15ph/11pg/2pc L

FRANKLIN COUNTY

KAHLOTUS VIC.

Lyons' Ferry Bridge; see Snake River Bridge at Lyons' Ferry

Snake River Bridge at Lyons' Ferry
(Lyons' Ferry Bridge)
(See COLUMBIA COUNTY,STARBUCK VIC. for documtatn.)
HAER WA-88
L

PASCO

Columbia River Crossing Towers; see Pasco-Kennewick Transmission Line,

Pasco-Kennewick Bridge
Spanning Columbia River
HAER WA-8
HAER WASH,11-PASC,1-
18ph/7pg L

Pasco-Kennewick Transmission Line,
(Columbia River Crossing Towers)
(See BENTON COUNTY,KENNEWICK for documentation)
HAER WA-118
L

WHITE BLUFFS VIC.

Hudson Bay Post
Columbia River Vic.
HABS WA-110
HABS WASH,11-WHIBL,1-
4ph/1pg L

GARFIELD COUNTY

STEMBER CREEK

Lee,Andrew E.,Barn
Alpowa Ridge Vic.
HABS WA-115
HABS WASH,12-SILC.V,1-
1ph/1pg L

GRANT COUNTY

ELECTRIC CITY VIC.

Columbia River Bridge at Grand Coulee Dam
(See OKANOGAN COUNTY,COULEE DAM for documentation)
HAER WA-102
L

GRAYS HARBOR COUNTY

ABERDEEN VIC.

West Wishkah Bridge
W. Wishkah Rd. Spanning Wishkah River Middle Fork
HAER WA-22
HAER 1992(HAER):WA-1
19ph/6pg/2pc L

MONTESANO

Byles,C. M.,House
Main & Spruce Sts.
HABS WA-101
HABS WASH,14-MONT,1-
2ph/1pg L

Methodist Episcopal Church
Church & Spruce Sts.
HABS WA-108
HABS WASH,14-MONT,2-
1ph/1pg L

QUINAULT

Building No. 1017,Olympic National Forest; see Quinault Ranger's Residence

Lake Quinault Lodge
Olympic National Forest
HABS WA-176
HABS WASH,14-QUIN,2-
11ph/4pg/1pc L

Quinault Ranger's Residence (Building No. 1017,Olympic National Forest)
Quinault Recreation Area
HABS WA-171
HABS WASH,14-QUIN,1-
31ph/14pg/3pc L

SOUTH MONTESANO

Scammon,Isaiah,House
Chehalis River Vic.
HABS WA-20
HABS WASH,14-MONTS,1-
6dr/3ph/1pg/fr L

STIMSON VIC.

Hicklin House
State Hwy. 110
HABS WA-105
HABS WASH,34- ,1-
2ph/1pg L

TOHOLAH VIC.

Chow Chow Suspension Bridge
(Quinault River Bridge)
Spanning Quinault River
HAER WA-5
HAER WASH,14-TOH.V,1-
11ph/1pg L

Quinault River Bridge; see Chow Chow Suspension Bridge

ISLAND COUNTY

COUPEVILLE

Alexander Blockhouse
Island Hwy. ,Main St. ,Whidby Island
HABS WA-39-W-8
HABS WASH,15-COUP,1-
4dr/2ph L

Cook Blockhouse; see Davis Blockhouse

Coupe,Capt. Thomas,House
Whidby Island
HABS WA-140
HABS WASH,15-COUP,8-
3ph/1pg L

Davis Blockhouse (Cook Blockhouse)
Cemetery Grounds Vic. ,Whidby Island
HABS WA-39-W-11
HABS WASH,15-COUP,2-
4dr/2ph L

Dow,Thomas J.,House
Front St.
HABS WA-39-W-12
HABS WASH,15-COUP,3-
5dr/2ph L

Ebey,Jacob,Homestead (original)
Whidby Island
HABS WA-104
HABS WASH,15-COUP,4-
2ph/1pg L

Haller,Maj. Granville O.,House (second)
Whidby Island
HABS WA-121
HABS WASH,15-COUP,6-
4ph/1pg L

Masonic Hall
Whidby Island
HABS WA-143
HABS WASH,15-COUP,9-
1ph/1pg L

Robertson,Capt. John,House
(Rosenfield House)
Front St.,Whidby Island
HABS WA-135
HABS WASH,15-COUP,7-
2ph/1pg L

Rosenfield House; see Robertson,Capt. John,House

Swift,Capt. James Henry,House
Front & Colbert Sts.
HABS WA-120
HABS WASH,15-COUP,5-
3ph/1pg L

COUPEVILLE VIC.

Doyle,R. L.,House
Whidby Island
HABS WA-141
HABS WASH,15-COUP.V,7-
2ph/1pg L

Ebey House (Ebey's Landing National Historical Reserve)
Ebey's Landing,Whidby Island
HABS WA-39-W-13
HABS WASH,15-COUP.V,2-
6dr/2ph L

Ebey,Jacob,Blockhouse
Sunnyside Cemetery Vic. ,Whidby Island
HABS WA-39-W-16
HABS WASH,15-COUP.V,4-
4dr/2ph L

Ebey's Landing National Historical Reserve; see Ebey House

Engle,William B.,House
Ebey's Prairie,Whidby Island
HABS WA-39-W-15
HABS WASH,15-COUP.V,3-
5dr/1ph L

Island Courthouse (first)
Whidby Island
HABS WA-39-W-7
HABS WASH,15-COUP.V,1-
7dr/2ph L

Kineth,John,House
Snakelumt Point,Whidby Island
HABS WA-39-W-19
HABS WASH,15-COUP.V,5-
7dr/2ph L

Terry,Charles T.,House
Ebey's Landing,Whidby Island
HABS WA-102
HABS WASH,15-COUP.V,6-
2ph/1pg L

FORT CASEY VIC.

Robertson,Capt. John,House (Sergeant House)
Whidby Island
HABS WA-119
HABS WASH,15-FOCA.V,1-
2ph/1pg L

Sergeant House; see Robertson,Capt. John,House

OAK HARBOR VIC.

Busby House
Whidby Island
HABS WA-118
HABS 15-OAKHA.V,2-
1ph/1pg L

Deception Pass Bridge
(See SKAGIT COUNTY,ANACORTES VIC. for documtatn.)
HAER WA-103
L

Gould House
Whidby Island
HABS WA-142
HABS WASH,15-OAKHA.V,4-
2ph/1pg L

Documentation: **ct** color transparencies **dr** measured drawings **fr** field records **pc** photograph captions **pg** pages of text **ph** photographs

Haller,Maj. Granville O.,House (first)
Whidby Island
HABS WA-130
HABS WASH,15-OAKHA.V,3-
2ph/1pg L

Izett,Capt. John M.,House
Whidby Island
HABS WA-39-W-23
HABS WASH,15-OAKHA.V,1-
5dr/2ph L

SAN DE FUCA

Crockett,Walter,Blockhouse
Whidby Island
HABS WA-97
HABS WASH,15-SANF,2-
3ph/1pg L

Power,I. B.,House
Whidby Island
HABS WA-76
HABS WASH,15-SANF,1-
3ph/1pg L

SAN DE FUCA VIC.

Hathaway,Capt. Eli,House
Penn Cove,Whidby Island
HABS WA-124
HABS WASH,15-SANF.V,1-
2ph/1pg L

JEFFERSON COUNTY

CHIMACUM

Bishop,Steven,House (son)
HABS WA-73
HABS WASH,16-CHIM,2-
1ph/1pg L

Nisbet Barn
Valley Rd.
HABS WA-72
HABS WASH,16-CHIM,1-
2ph/1pg L

Westergard House
West Valley Rd.
HABS WA-131
HABS WASH,16-CHIM,4-
2ph/1pg L

CHIMACUM VIC.

Glendale House
HABS WA-74
HABS WASH,16-CHIM,3-
1ph/1pg L

Peterson Place
HABS WA-75
HABS WASH,16-CHIM,5-
2ph/1pg L

PORT TOWNSEND

Buckley Jewelry Shop
Water & Quincy Sts.
HABS WA-125
HABS WASH,16-PORTO,3-
3ph/1pg L

Building 427,Combined Primary Station (Fort Worden State Park)
Fort Worden State Park
HABS WA-153
HABS WASH,16-PORTO,11-
10ph/5pg/1pc L

Clinger,J. G.,House
Water & Monroe Sts.
HABS WA-137
HABS WASH,16-PORTO,9-
2ph/1pg L

Eisenbeis House
Franklin & Clay Sts.
HABS WA-138
HABS WASH,16-PORTO,10-
2ph/1pg L

Fort Worden Balloon Hangar
Fort Worden State Park
HAER WA-23
2dr/18ph/7pg/1pc H

Fort Worden State Park; see Building 427,Combined Primary Station

Fowler House,Big (Fowler,E. S.,House)
Water & Quincy Sts.
HABS WA-136
HABS WASH,16-PORTO,8-
2ph/1pg L

Fowler House,Little (Fowler,E. S.,House)
Jefferson & Polks Sts.
HABS WA-123
HABS WASH,16-PORTO,2-
2ph/1pg L

Fowler,E. S.,House; see Fowler House,Big

Fowler,E. S.,House; see Fowler House,Little

Jefferson County Courthouse; see Leader Building

Leader Building (Jefferson County Courthouse)
HABS WA-128
HABS WASH,16-PORTO,6-
1ph/1pg L

Rothschild House
Jefferson & Taylor Sts.
HABS WA-127
HABS WASH,16-PORTO,5-
2ph/1pg L

St. Paul's Episcopal Church
Jefferson & Tyler Sts.
HABS WA-69
HABS WASH,16-PORTO,1-
2ph/1pg L

Starrett Building
Adams & Washington Sts.
HABS WA-126
HABS WASH,16-PORTO,4-
3ph/1pg L

Tucker,A. H.,House
Quincy & Franklin Sts.
HABS WA-129
HABS WASH,16-PORTO,7-
2ph/1pg L

PORT TOWNSEND VIC.

Irondale Iron & Steel Plant
HAER WA-7
HAER WASH,16-PORTO.V,1-
14dr/42ph/68pg/4pc L

KING COUNTY

CEDAR FALLS

Cedar Falls Hydroelectric Works
Cedar Falls Rd.,3.5 mi. S of Interstate 90
HAER WA-15
HAER WASH,17-CEDFA,1-
36ph/21pg/3pc/fr L

ENUMCLAW

Enumclaw High School (Enumclaw Junior High School,Old)
2222 Porter St.
HABS WA-175
HABS WASH,17-ENUM,1-
19ph/6pg/1pc L

Enumclaw Junior High School,Old; see Enumclaw High School

LESTER

Building No. 1036,Mt. Baker-Snoqualmie Nat. Forest; see Lester Guard Station,Ranger Station House

Building No. 1331,Mt. Baker-Snoqualmie Nat. Forest; see Lester Guard Station,Barclay Building

Building No. 2232,Mt. Baker-Snoqualmie Nat. Forest; see Lester Guard Station,Fire Warehouse

Building No. 2532,Mt. Baker-Snoqualmie Nat. Forest; see Lester Guard Station,Warehouse/Storehouse

Gas & Oil House; see Lester Guard Station,Warehouse/Storehouse

Guard Station Residence & Office; see Lester Guard Station,Barclay Building

Guard Station Residence & Office; see Lester Guard Station,Ranger Station House

Lester Guard Station
Forest Svc. Rd. No. 45,Mt. Baker-Snoqualmie N.F.
HABS WA-172
HABS WASH,17-LEST,1-
2ph/13pg/1pc L

Lester Guard Station,Barclay Building (Guard Station Residence & Office; Building No. 1331,Mt. Baker-Snoqualmie Nat. Forest
Forest Svc. Rd. No. 45
HABS WA-172-B
HABS WASH,17-LEST,1-B-
4ph/3pg/1pc L

Lester Guard Station,Fire Warehouse (Warehouse; Building No. 2232,Mt. Baker-Snoqualmie Nat. Forest
Forest Svc. Rd. No. 45
HABS WA-172-C
HABS WASH,17-LEST,1-C-
7ph/3pg/1pc L

Lester Guard Station,Ranger Station House (Guard Station Residence & Office; Building No. 1036,Mt. Baker-Snoqualmie Nat. Forest
Forest Svc. Rd. No. 45
HABS WA-172-A
HABS WASH,17-LEST,1-A-
6ph/3pg/1pc L

Lester Guard Station,Warehouse/Storehouse (Gas & Oil House; Building No. 2532,Mt. Baker-Snoqualmie Nat. Forest
Forest Svc. Rd. No. 45
HABS WA-172-D
HABS WASH,17-LEST,1-D-
3ph/3pg/1pc L

Warehouse; see Lester Guard Station,Fire Warehouse

RENTON

Longacres (Longacres Park)
1621 SW 16th St.
HABS WA-201
26ph/63pg/3pc/fr H

Longacres Park; see Longacres

Longacres Park,Barn 1; see Longacres,Testing Barn

Longacres Park,Barn 2; see Longacres,Receiving Barn

Longacres,Association Barn
1621 Sw 16th St.
HABS WA-201-34
2ph/1pc H

Longacres,Backstretch Cafe
1621 SW 16th St.
HABS WA-201-36
3ph/1pc H

Longacres,Barn E
1621 SW 16th St.
HABS WA-201-16
1ph/1pc H

Longacres,Barn F
1621 SW 16th St.
HABS WA-201-15
1ph/1pc H

Longacres,Barn K
1621 SW 16th St.
HABS WA-201-12
1ph/1pc H

Longacres,Barn L
1621 SW 16th St.
HABS WA-201-11
4ph/1pc H

Longacres,Barn 10A
1621 SW 16th St.
HABS WA-201-49
1ph/1pc H

Longacres,Barn 12
1621 SW 16th St.
HABS WA-201-28
1ph/1pc H

Longacres,Barn 16
1621 SW 16th St.
HABS WA-201-27
2ph/1pc H

Longacres,Barn 17
1621 SW 16th St.
HABS WA-201-26
1ph/1pc H

Longacres,Barn 2B
1621 SW 16th St.
HABS WA0201-39
1ph/1pc H

Longacres,Barn 20
1621 SW 16th St.
HABS WA-201-25
1ph/1pc H

Longacres,Barn 24
1621 SW 16th St.
HABS WA-201-24
1ph/1pc H

Longacres,Barn 25
1621 SW 16th St.
HABS WA-201-23
1ph/1pc H

Longacres,Barn 3
1621 SW 16th St.
HABS WA-201-31
2ph/1pc H

Longacres,Barn 31
1621 SW 16th St.
HABS WA-201-20
3ph/1pc H

Longacres,Barn 33
1621 SW 16th St.
HABS WA-201-19
1ph/1pc H

Longacres,Barn 34
1621 SW 16th St.
HABS WA-201-21
1ph/1pc H

Longacres,Barn 35
1621 SW 16th St.
HABS WA-201-22
2ph/1pc H

Longacres,Barn 36
1621 SW 16th St.
HABS WA-201-18
1ph/1pc H

Longacres,Barn 37
1621 SW 16th St.
HABS WA-201-27
1ph/1pc H

Longacres,Barn 4A
1621 Sw 16th St.
HABS WA-201-40
1ph/1pc H

Longacres,Barn 40
1621 SW 16th St.
HABS WA-201-14
2ph/1pc H

Longacres,Barn 41
1621 SW 16th St.
HABS WA-201-13
2ph/1pc H

Longacres,Barn 5A
1621 SW 16th St.
HABS WA-201-41
2ph/1pc H

Longacres,Barn 5B
1621 SW 16th St.
HABS WA-201-42
1ph/1pc H

Longacres,Barn 6
1621 SW 16th St.
HABS WA-201-30
1ph/1pc H

Longacres,Barn 6A
1621 Sw 16th St.
HABS WA-201-43
1ph/1pc H

Longacres,Barn 7
1621 SW 16th St.
HABS WA-201-29
1ph/1pc H

Longacres,Barn 7A
1621 Sw 16th St.
HABS WA-201-44
4ph/1pc H

Longacres,Barn 7B
1621 SW 16th St.
HABS WA-201-45
1ph/1pc H

Longacres,Barn 8A
1621 SW 16th St.
HABS WA-201-46
3ph/1pc H

Longacres,Barn 9A
u1621 SW 16th St.
HABS WA-201-47
2ph/1pc H

Longacres,Barn 9B
1621 SW 16th St.
HABS WA-201-48
1ph/1pc H

Longacres,Blacksmith Shop
1621 Sw 16th St.
HABS WA-201-38
1ph/1pc H

Longacres,Carpenter's Shop
1621 SW 16th St.
HABS WA-201-7
1ph/1pc H

Longacres,Clubhouse and Additions
1621 SW 16th St.
HABS WA-201-2
21ph/2pc H

Longacres,Gottstein Cottage
1621 SW 16th St.
HABS WA-201-10
3ph/1pc H

Longacres,Identifier's Stand
1621 SW 16th St.
HABS WA-201-37
1ph/1pc H

Longacres,Jockey Building
1621 SW 16th St.
HABS WA-201-3
6ph/1pc H

Longacres,Mechanic's Shop
1621 SW 16th St.
HABS WA-201-8
3ph/1pc H

Longacres,North Grandstand
1621 SW 16th St.
HABS WA-201-6
8ph/1pc H

Longacres,Original Grandstand
1621 SW 16th St.
HABS WA-201-1
22ph/2pc H

Longacres,Paddock Club
1621 SW 16th St.
HABS WA-201-4
8ph/1pc H

Longacres,Racing Secretary's Office
1621 SW 16th St.
HABS WA-201-35
3ph/1pc H

Longacres,Receiving Barn (Longacres Park,Barn 2)
1621 SW 16th St.
HABS WA-201-32
1ph/1pc H

Longacres,Second Grandstand
1621 SW 16th St.
HABS WA-201-5
9ph/1pc H

Longacres,Starting Gate Shed
1621 SW 16th St.
HABS WA-201-9
1ph/1pc H

Longacres,Testing Barn (Longacres Park,Barn 1)
1621 SW 16th St.
HABS WA-201-33
2ph/1pc H

Longacres,Vetinary Clinic
1621 SW 16th St.
HABS WA-201-50
1ph/1pc H

Longacres,WTBA Barn D
1621 SW 16th St.
HABS WA-201-52
2ph/1pc H

Longacres,WTBA C
1621 Sw 16th St.
HABS WA-201-51
2ph/1pc H

Longacres,WTBA Offices/Sales Pavilion
1621 SW 16th St.
HABS WA-201-53
2ph/1pc H

SEATTLE

Alaska-Yukon-Pacific Exposition Grounds,Building; see Hoo Hoo House

Boeing Airplane Company; see Pacific Aero Products Company

Buffalo Building; see Penney,J. C. ,Department Store

Fort Lawton
Discovery Park
HABS WA-150
HABS WASH,17-SEAT,7-
2dr/7ph/33pg/1pc/fr L

Fort Lawton,Administrative Building (Fort Lawton,Building No. 417)
Discovery Park
HABS WA-150-A
HABS WASH,17-SEAT,7-A-
3ph/2pg/1pc L

Fort Lawton,Bake House (Fort Lawton,Bldg. No. 735)
Discovery Park
HABS WA-150-B
HABS WASH,17-SEAT,7-B-
2ph/2pg/1pc L

Fort Lawton,Band Barracks (Fort Lawton,Bldg. No. 734)
Discovery Park
HABS WA-150-C
HABS WASH,17-SEAT,7-C-
3ph/2pg/1pc L

Fort Lawton,Bldg. No. 640; see Fort Lawton,Double Officers Qtrs.

Fort Lawton,Bldg. No. 642; see Fort Lawton,Double Officers Qtrs.

Fort Lawton,Bldg. No. 644; see Fort Lawton,Double Officers Qtrs.

Fort Lawton,Bldg. No. 670; see Fort Lawton,Single Officers Qtrs.

Fort Lawton,Bldg. No. 672; see Fort Lawton,Double Officers Qtrs.

Fort Lawton,Bldg. No. 676; see Fort Lawton,Double Officers Qtrs.

Fort Lawton,Bldg. No. 678; see Fort Lawton,Double Officers Qtrs.

Fort Lawton,Bldg. No. 730; see Fort Lawton,Double Barracks

Fort Lawton,Bldg. No. 731; see Fort Lawton,Double Barracks

Fort Lawton,Bldg. No. 733; see Fort Lawton,Post Exchange & Gymnasium

Fort Lawton,Bldg. No. 734; see Fort Lawton,Band Barracks

Fort Lawton,Bldg. No. 735; see Fort Lawton,Bake House

Fort Lawton,Bldg. No. 754; see Fort Lawton,Quartermaster Work Shops

Fort Lawton,Bldg. No. 755; see Fort Lawton,Civilian Employee Quarters

Fort Lawton,Bldg. No. 757; see Fort Lawton,Quartermaster Storehouse & Offices

Fort Lawton,Bldg. No. 759; see Fort Lawton,Guard House

Fort Lawton,Bldg. No. 903; see Fort Lawton,Double Non-Commissioned Officers Qtrs.

Fort Lawton,Bldg. No. 905; see Fort Lawton,Double Non-Commissioned Officers Qtrs.

Fort Lawton,Bldg. No. 906; see Fort Lawton,Hospital Stewards Qtrs.

Fort Lawton,Bldg. No. 907; see Fort Lawton,Double Non-Commissioned Officers Qtrs.

Fort Lawton,Bldg. No. 909; see Fort Lawton,Double Non-Commissioned Officers Qtrs.

Fort Lawton,Bldg. No. 915; see Fort Lawton,Quartermaster Storehouse

Fort Lawton,Bldg. No. 916; see Fort Lawton,Quartermaster Stables

Fort Lawton,Bldg. No. 917; see Fort Lawton,Quartermaster Stables

Fort Lawton,Building No. 417; see Fort Lawton,Administrative Building

Fort Lawton,Civilian Employee Quarters (Fort Lawton,Bldg. No. 755)
Discovery Park
HABS WA-150-D
HABS WASH,17-SEAT,7-D-
4ph/2pg/1pc L

Fort Lawton,Double Barracks (Fort Lawton,Bldg. No. 730)
Discovery Park
HABS WA-150-E
HABS WASH,17-SEAT,7-E-
6ph/2pg/1pc L

Fort Lawton,Double Barracks (Fort Lawton,Bldg. No. 731)
Discovery Park
HABS WA-150-F
HABS WASH,17-SEAT,1-F-
4dr/6ph/2pg/1pc/fr L

Fort Lawton,Double Non-Commissioned Officers Qtrs. (Fort Lawton,Bldg. No. 903)
Discovery Park
HABS WA-150-G
HABS WASH,17-SEAT,7-G-
3ph/2pg/1pc L

Fort Lawton,Double Non-Commissioned Officers Qtrs. (Fort Lawton,Bldg. No. 905)
Discovery Park
HABS WA-150-H
HABS WASH,17-SEAT,7-H-
2ph/2pg/1pc L

Fort Lawton,Double Non-Commissioned Officers Qtrs. (Fort Lawton,Bldg. No. 907)
Discovery Park
HABS WA-150-I
HABS WASH,17-SEAT,7-I-
3ph/2pg/1pc L

Fort Lawton,Double Non-Commissioned Officers Qtrs. (Fort Lawton,Bldg. No. 909)
Discovery Park
HABS WA-150-J
HABS WASH,17-SEAT,7-J-
2ph/2pg/1pc L

Fort Lawton,Double Officers Qtrs. (Fort Lawton,Bldg. No. 640)
Discovery Park
HABS WA-150-K
HABS WASH,17-SEAT,7-K-
2ph/2pg/1pc L

Fort Lawton,Double Officers Qtrs. (Fort Lawton,Bldg. No. 642)
Discovery Park
HABS WA-150-L
HABS WASH,17-SEAT,7-L-
2ph/2pg/1pc L

Fort Lawton,Double Officers Qtrs. (Fort Lawton,Bldg. No. 644)
Discovery Park
HABS WA-150-M
HABS WASH,17-SEAT,7-M-
4ph/2pg/1pc L

Fort Lawton,Double Officers Qtrs. (Fort Lawton,Bldg. No. 672)
Discovery Park
HABS WA-150-N
HABS WASH,17-SEAT,7-N-
6ph/2pg/1pc L

Fort Lawton,Double Officers Qtrs. (Fort Lawton,Bldg. No. 676)
Discovery Park
HABS WA-150-O
HABS WASH,17-SEAT,7-O-
3ph/2pg/1pc L

Fort Lawton,Double Officers Qtrs. (Fort Lawton,Bldg. No. 678)
Discovery Park
HABS WA-150-P
HABS WASH,17-SEAT,7-P-
3ph/2pg/1pc L

Fort Lawton,Guard House (Fort Lawton,Bldg. No. 759)
Discovery Park
HABS WA-150-Q
HABS WASH,17-SEAT,7-Q-
5dr/4ph/2pg/1pc/fr L

Fort Lawton,Hospital Stewards Qtrs. (Fort Lawton,Bldg. No. 906)
Discovery Park
HABS WA-150-R
HABS WASH,17-SEAT,7-R-
3ph/2pg/1pc L

Fort Lawton,Post Exchange & Gymnasium (Fort Lawton,Bldg. No. 733)
Discovery Park
HABS WA-150-S
HABS WASH,17-SEAT,7-S-
4dr/3ph/2pg/1pc/fr L

Fort Lawton,Quartermaster Stables (Fort Lawton,Bldg. No. 916)
Discovery Park
HABS WA-150-U
HABS WASH,17-SEAT,7-U-
3ph/2pg/1pc L

Fort Lawton,Quartermaster Stables (Fort Lawton,Bldg. No. 917)
Discovery Park
HABS WA-150-V
HABS WASH,17-SEAT,7-V-
3dr/3ph/2pg/1pc/fr L

Fort Lawton,Quartermaster Storehouse (Fort Lawton,Bldg. No. 915)
Discovery Park
HABS WA-150-W
HABS WASH,17-SEAT,7-W-
5ph/2pg/1pc L

Fort Lawton,Quartermaster Storehouse & Offices (Fort Lawton,Bldg. No. 757)
Discovery Park
HABS WA-150-Y
HABS WASH,17-SEAT,7-Y-
2ph/2pg/1pc L

Fort Lawton,Quartermaster Work Shops (Fort Lawton,Bldg. No. 754)
Discovery Park
HABS WA-150-T
HABS WASH,17-SEAT,7-T-
2ph/2pg/1pc L

Fort Lawton,Single Officers Qtrs. (Fort Lawton,Bldg. No. 670)
Discovery Park
HABS WA-150-X
HABS WASH,17-SEAT,7-X-
4ph/2pg/1pc L

Fox Theatre (Music Hall Theatre)
Seventh Ave. and Olive Way
HABS WA-197
62ph/50pg/5pc H

Georgetown Steam Plant
King County Airport
HAER WA-1
HAER WASH,17-SEAT,2-
8dr/37ph/49pg L

Hoo Hoo House (University of Washington,Faculty Club; Alaska-Yukon-Pacific Exposition Grounds,Building)
University of Washington Campus
HABS WA-148
HABS WASH,17-SEAT,1-
3ph/6pg L

Music Hall Theatre; see Fox Theatre

Mutual Life Building
601-607 First Ave.
HABS WA-42
HABS WASH,17-SEAT,3-
26ph/36pg/fr L

Olive Tower
1624 Boren Ave.
HABS WA-167
HABS WASH,17-SEAT,4-
10ph/1pg L

Pacific Aero Products Company (Boeing Airplane Company)
9404 E. Marginal Way S.
HABS WA-154
HABS WASH,17-SEAT,8-
17dr L

Penney,J. C. ,Department Store (Buffalo Building; Portland Building)
5403-5407 1/2 Ballard Ave.
HABS WA-169
HABS WASH,17-SEAT,5-
12ph/7pg L

Portland Building; see Penney,J. C. ,Department Store

San Mateo Ferry
South End of Lake Junction
HAER WA-17
HAER WASH,17-SEAT,9-
49ph/14pg/5pc L H

Schooner "Wawona" (Wawona)
1018 Valley St.
HAER WA-14
HAER WASH,17-SEAT,10-
7dr/62ph/4pg/4pc/7ct/fr L

U. S. Courthouse
1010 Fifth Ave.
HABS WA-152
HABS WASH,17-SEAT,6-
39ph/42pg/1pc L H

University of Washington,Faculty Club; see Hoo Hoo House

Wawona; see Schooner "Wawona"

KITSAP COUNTY

BREMERTON

Bldg. No. 106; see Central Power Station

Central Power Plant; see Central Power Station

Central Power Station (Central Power Plant; Bldg. No. 106)
Puget Sound Naval Shipyard
HABS WA-178
HABS WASH,18-BREM,1-
24ph/18pg/2pc L

KITTITAS COUNTY

LIBERTY

Alley Ranch; see Liberty Historic District

Anderson,Billy,Cabin; see Liberty Historic District

Assay Office; see Liberty Historic District

Barn; see Liberty Historic District

Bowman,Bob,Cabin; see Liberty Historic District

Brighton,Larry,Cabin; see Liberty Historic District

Caldwell Store & Post Office; see Liberty Historic District

Elliot,William,Cabin; see Liberty Historic District

Gold Placer's Incorporated Claim; see Liberty Historic District

Guse,Ed,Cabin; see Liberty Historic District

Jordin,Amos,Cabin; see Liberty Historic District

Killson,Ben,Cabin; see Liberty Historic District

Kirsh,Jack,Cabin No. 1; see Liberty Historic District

Kirsh,Jack,Cabin No. 2; see Liberty Historic District

Kirsh,Jack,Cabin No. 3; see Liberty Historic District

Liberty Historic District
Rt. 2,Cle Elum
HABS WA-163
HABS WASH,19-LIB,1-
3dr/1ph/15pg/fr L

Liberty Historic District (Alley Ranch)
Rt. 2,Cle Elum
HABS WA-163-A
HABS WASH,19-LIB,1A-
1ph/fr L

Liberty Historic District (Anderson,Billy,Cabin)
Rt. 2,Cle Elum
HABS WA-163-B
HABS WASH,19-LIB,1B-
1ph/fr L

Liberty Historic District (Assay Office)
Rt. 2,Cle Elum
HABS WA-163-C
HABS WASH,19-LIB,1C-
1ph/fr L

Liberty Historic District (Barn)
Rt. 2,Cle Elum
HABS WA-163-D
HABS WASH,19-LIB,1D-
1ph/fr L

Liberty Historic District (Bowman,Bob,Cabin)
Rt. 2,Cle Elum
HABS WA-163-E
HABS WASH,19-LIB,1E-
2ph/fr L

Liberty Historic District (Brighton,Larry,Cabin)
Rt. 2,Cle Elum
HABS WA-163-F
HABS WASH,19-LIB,1F-
1ph/fr L

Liberty Historic District (Caldwell Store & Post Office)
Rt. 2,Cle Elum
HABS WA-163-G
HABS WASH,19-LIB,1G-
2ph/fr L

Liberty Historic District (Elliot,William,Cabin)
Rt. 2,Cle Elum
HABS WA-163-H
HABS WASH,19-LIB,1H-
2ph/fr L

Liberty Historic District (Gold Placer's Incorporated Claim)
Rt. 2,Cle Elum
HABS WA-163-I
HABS WASH,19-LIB,1I-
1ph/fr L

Liberty Historic District (Guse,Ed,Cabin)
Rt. 2,Cle Elum
HABS WA-163-J
HABS WASH,19-LIB,1J-
1ph/fr L

Liberty Historic District (Jordin,Amos,Cabin)
Rt. 2,Cle Elum
HABS WA-163-K
HABS WASH,19-LIB,1K-
1ph/fr L

Liberty Historic District (Killson,Ben,Cabin)
Rt. 2,Cle Elum
HABS WA-163-L
HABS WASH,19-LIB,1L-
1ph/fr L

Liberty Historic District (Kirsh,Jack,Cabin No. 1)
Rt. 2,Cle Elum
HABS WA-163-M
HABS WASH,19-LIB,1M-
1ph/fr L

Liberty Historic District (Kirsh,Jack,Cabin No. 2)
Rt. 2,Cle Elum
HABS WA-163-N
HABS WASH,19-LIB,1N-
1ph/fr L

Liberty Historic District (Kirsh,Jack,Cabin No. 3)
Rt. 2,Cle Elum
HABS WA-163-O
HABS WASH,19-LIB,1O-
1ph/fr L

Liberty Historic District (Livery Stable & Barker Cabin)
Rt. 2,Cle Elum
HABS WA-163-P
HABS WASH,19-LIB,1P-
1ph/fr L

Liberty Historic District (Meagher Hotel & Boarding House)
Rt. 2,Cle Elum
HABS WA-163-R
HABS WASH,19-LIB,1R-
1ph/fr L

Liberty Historic District (Meagher,Thomas,Cabin)
Rt. 2,Cle Elum
HABS WA-163-Q
HABS WASH,19-LIB,1Q-
1ph/fr L

Liberty Historic District (Neal,Joe,Cabin)
Rt. 2,Cle Elum
HABS WA-163-S
HABS WASH,19-LIB,1S-
1ph/fr L

Liberty Historic District (Siegel,Gus,Cabin)
Rt. 2,Cle Elum
HABS WA-163-T
HABS WASH,19-LIB,1T-
1ph/fr L

Liberty Historic District (Stine,Eloise,Cabin)
Rt. 2,Cle Elum
HABS WA-163-U
HABS WASH,19-LIB,1U-
1ph/fr L

Liberty Historic District (Taxidermy Shop)
Rt. 2,Cle Elum
HABS WA-163-V
HABS WASH,19-LIB,1V-
1ph/fr L

Liberty Historic District (Water Powered Ore Mill)
Rt. 2,Cle Elum
HABS WA-163-W
HABS WASH,19-LIB,1W-
2ph/fr L

Liberty Historic District (York,A. F. ,Cabin)
Rt. 2,Cle Elum
HABS WA-163-X
HABS WASH,19-LIB,1X-
1ph/fr L

Livery Stable & Barker Cabin; see Liberty Historic District

Meagher Hotel & Boarding House; see Liberty Historic District

Meagher,Thomas,Cabin; see Liberty Historic District

Neal,Joe,Cabin; see Liberty Historic District

Siegel,Gus,Cabin; see Liberty Historic District

Stine,Eloise,Cabin; see Liberty Historic District

Taxidermy Shop; see Liberty Historic District

Water Powered Ore Mill; see Liberty Historic District

York,A. F. ,Cabin; see Liberty Historic District

KLICKITAT COUNTY

GLENWOOD VIC.

Whitcomb Cabin
BZ Corners,Glenwood Co. Rd. (Conboy Lake NWR)
HABS WA-179
HABS 1990 (HABS):8
18ph/14pg/1pc L

GOLDENDALE

Goldendale Blockhouse
Courthouse Park (moved from original location)
HABS WA-89
HABS WASH,20-GOLD,1-
3ph/1pg L

GOLDENDALE VIC.

Alexander House
HABS WA-86
HABS WASH,20-GOLD.V,1-
2ph/1pg L

Hopkins House & Barn
HABS WA-95
HABS WASH,20-GOLD.V,3-
3ph/1pg L

Potter,Myron,Cabin
HABS WA-88
HABS WASH,20-GOLD.V,2-
1ph/1pg L

LEWIS COUNTY

CENTRALIA

Borst Blockhouse
Borst Park
HABS WA-39-W-9
HABS WASH,21-CENT,1-
4dr/3ph/fr L

CHEHALIS

McFadden,O. B.,House
1639 Chehalis Ave.
HABS WA-83
HABS WASH,21-CHEHA,1-
2ph/1pg L

CHEHALIS VIC.

Jackson Prairie Courthouse
U. S. Hwy. 99
HABS WA-39-W-10
HABS WASH,21-CHEHAV,1-
4dr/1ph L

CLAQUATO

Claquato Church,Old (Protestant Episcopal Church)
HABS WA-39-W-6
HABS WASH,21-CLAQ,1-
5dr/2ph/fr L

Protestant Episcopal Church; see Claquato Church,Old

MOSSY ROCK VIC.

Riley,James,House
HABS WA-132
HABS WASH,21-MOSRO.V,1-
2ph/1pg L

MOUNT RAINIER

Box Canyon Tunnel (Mount Rainier National Park)
Stevens Canyon Hwy.
HAER WA-70
H

Mount Rainier National Park; see Box Canyon Tunnel

Mount Rainier National Park; see Stevens Canyon Viaduct

Stevens Canyon Viaduct (Mount Rainier National Park)
Stevens Canyon Hwy.
HAER WA-71
H

NAPAVINE VIC.

Bonneville Power Adm. Chehalis Subst.,Untank. Towr
St. Rt. 603,W. of Interstate 5
HAER WA-69-A
14ph/18pg/2pc H

RANDLE

Cispus Valley Bridge (Forest Service Bridge No. 2306-3.6)
Spanning Cispus River at Forest Service Rd. 2306
HAER WA-65
6ph/1pg/1pc H

Forest Service Bridge No. 2306-3.6; see Cispus Valley Bridge

Randle Ranger Residence,Building No. 1135
Silverbrook Rd.
HABS WA-187
HABS 1991(HABS):10
5ph/18pg/1pc/fr L

LINCOLN COUNTY

LINCOLN VIC.

Fort Spokane,Hospital
HABS WA-111-B
HABS WASH,22-LINC.V,1A-
3ph L

Fort Spokane,Indian School & Officers' Quarters
HABS WA-111-C
HABS WASH,22-LINC.V,1H-
2ph L

Fort Spokane,Jail
HABS WA-111-D
HABS WASH,22-LINC.V,1E-
3ph L

Fort Spokane,New Guardhouse
Miles
HABS WA-144
HABS WASH,22-LINC.V,1I-
4dr/fr L

Fort Spokane,Officers' Quarters
HABS WA-111-E
HABS WASH,22-LINC.V,1B- & 1C-
4ph L

Fort Spokane,Old Guardhouse
HABS WA-111-A
HABS WASH,22-LINC.V,1F-
2ph L

Fort Spokane,Powder Magazine
Miles
HABS WA-147
HABS WASH,22-LINC.V,1D-
2dr/2ph/fr L

Fort Spokane,Quartermaster Building
Miles
HABS WA-146
HABS WASH,22-LINC.V,1J-
2dr/fr L

Fort Spokane,Stable Barn
Miles
HABS WA-145
HABS WASH,22-LINC.V,1G-
5dr/2ph/fr L

REARDAN VIC.

Long Lake Hydroelectric Plant
See Stevens Co.,Reardan Vic. for documentation
HAER WA-33
HAER DLC/PP-1993:WA-2
4ph/8pg/1pc L

Long Lake Hydroelectric Plant,Spillway Dam
See Stevens Co.,Ford Vic. for documentation
HAER WA-33-A
HAER DLC/PP-1993:WA-2
16ph/6pg/2pc L

MASON COUNTY

HOODSPORT VIC.

Cushman No. 1 Hydroelectric Power Plant,Spillway
N. Fork of Skokomish River,5 mi. W. of Hood Canal
HAER WA-26-A
HAER 1991(HAER):11
29ph/14pg/3pc L

OKANOGAN COUNTY

MONSE VIC.

Columbia River Bridge at Bridgeport
(See DOUGLAS COUNTY,BRIDGEPORT VIC. for documtn.)
HAER WA-90
L

OMAK VIC.

St. Mary's Mission (Wayfarer's Cabin)
Colville Indian Reservation
HABS WA-35
HABS WASH,24-OMAK.V,1-
2dr/3ph/1pg/fr L

Wayfarer's Cabin; see St. Mary's Mission

OROVILLE VIC.

Enloe Dam
On the Similkameen River
HAER WA-6
HAER DLC/PP-1992:WA-2
30ph/10pg/3pc L

OROVILLE VICINITY

Enloe Dam,Power House
On the Similkameen River
HAER WA-6-A
HAER DLC/PP-1992:WA-2
19ph/2pc L

PACIFIC COUNTY

OYSTERVILLE

County Jail
HABS WA-109
HABS WASH,25-OYST,6-
1ph/1pg L

Crellen,John,House (Heckes Hotel)
HABS WA-103
HABS WASH,25-OYST,3-
2ph/1pg L

Crellen,Tom,House
HABS WA-106
HABS WASH,25-OYST,4-
2ph/1pg L

Espey Estate House
HABS WA-100
HABS WASH,25-OYST,2-
2ph/1pg L

Heckes Hotel; see Crellen,John,House

Nelson,Tom,House
HABS WA-107
HABS WASH,25-OYST,5-
3ph/1pg L

Wirt House
HABS WA-98
HABS WASH,25-OYST,1-
2ph/1pg L

PEND OREILLE COUNTY

NEWPORT

Newport Office; see Newport Ranger Station Office No. 2005

Newport Ranger Station Office No. 2005 (Newport Office)
315 N. Warren St.
HABS WA-174
HABS WASH,26-NEWP,1-
11ph/5pg/1pc L

USK

Kalispel Indian Log Cabin
HABS WA-77
HABS WASH,26-USK,1-
3ph/1pg L

USK VIC.

Calispell Diversion Canal
1.2 mi. SE of inter. State Rt. 20 & Flowery Trail
HAER WA-16
HAER WASH,26-USK.V,1-
15ph/15pg/2pc/fr L

PIERCE COUNTY

CARBONADO VIC.

Fairfax Bridge (O'Farrell,James R. Bridge)
Spanning the Carbon River at State Rt. 165
HAER WA-72
5ph H

O'Farrell,James R. Bridge; see Fairfax Bridge

DIERINGER

Puget Sound Power & Light Company
(White River Hydroelectric Project)
HAER WA-64
H

White River Hydroelectric Project
HAER WA-78
25dr/176ph/15pg/8pc H

White River Hydroelectric Project; see Puget Sound Power & Light Company

ELECTRON

Electron Hydroelectric Project
(Puyallup Project)
Along Puyallup River
HAER WA-12
HAER WASH,27-ELEC,1-
6dr/89ph/26pg/6pc/fr L

Puyallup Project; see Electron Hydroelectric Project

FORT LEWIS

Building No. 1-B-99; see Fort Lewis,Locomotive Shelter

Fort Lewis,Locomotive Shelter
(Building No. 1-B-99)
HABS WA-199-A
37ph/13pg/3pc/fr H

FORT STEILACOOM

Fort Stellacoom; see Officers' Houses

Officers' Houses (Fort Stellacoom)
HABS WA-39-W-18
HABS WASH,27-FOSTEI,1-
7dr/7ph L

GREENWATER VIC.

Suntop Lookout
Forest Rd. 510,Mt. Baker,Snoqualmie National Fores
HABS WA-190
HABS 1991(HABS):10
35ph/16pg/4pc L

LONGMIRE

Building L-209; see Longmire Garage

Longmire Garage (Building L-209; Mount Rainier National Park)
Tahoma Woods Star Rt., Mt. Ranier National Park
HABS WA-157
HABS WASH,27-LONG,1-
9pg/fr L

Longmire Springs Hotel; see National Park Inn

Mount Rainier National Park; see Longmire Garage

National Park Inn (Longmire Springs Hotel)
Mt. Rainier Nat'l. Pk. South side Nisqually Prd.Rd
HABS WA-184
HABS DLC/PP-1993:WA-1
6ph/23pg/1pc L

MCMILLIN

McMillin Bridge
Spanning Puyallup River at St. Rt. 162
HAER WA-73
6ph H

MOUNT RAINIER

East Side Tunnel (Mount Rainier Roads & Bridges)
HAER WA-75
1ph H

Mount Rainier Roads & Bridges; see East Side Tunnel

Mount Rainier Roads & Bridges; see Mowich Lake Road (No. 165)

Mount Rainier Roads & Bridges; see North Puyallup River Bridge

Mount Rainier Roads & Bridges; see Stevens Canyon Tunnel

Mount Rainier Roads & Bridges; see Sunbeam Creek Culvert

Mowich Lake Road (No. 165) (Mount Rainier Roads & Bridges)
HAER WA-35-C
H

North Puyallup River Bridge (Mount Rainier Roads & Bridges)
HAER WA-77
5ph H

Stevens Canyon Tunnel (Mount Rainier Roads & Bridges)
HAER WA-74
2ph H

Sunbeam Creek Culvert (Mount Rainier Roads & Bridges)
HAER WA-76
1ph H

PUYALLUP

Meeker,Ezra,House
Third & E. Meeker Sts.
HABS WA-96
HABS WASH,27-PUYAL,1-
3ph/1pg L

STEILACOOM

Black,Capt.,House
Seventh & Stevens Sts.
HABS WA-117
HABS WASH,27-STEIL,4-
3ph/1pg L

Catholic Church
Nisqually & Main Sts.
HABS WA-39-W-2
HABS WASH,27-STEIL,2-
8dr/2ph L

Gales House
Seventh & Stevens Sts.
HABS WA-134
HABS WASH,27-STEIL,6-
2ph/1pg L

Jail,Old Brick
HABS WA-39-W-1
HABS WASH,27-STEIL,1-
3ph/fr L

Judson,Stephen,House
Main St.
HABS WA-122
HABS WASH,27-STEIL,5-
2ph/1pg L

Keach,Philip,House
HABS WA-39-W-5
HABS WASH,27-STEIL,3-
5dr/3ph L

Wallus,Fred,House
Seventh St.
HABS WA-139
HABS WASH,27-STEIL,7-
2ph/1pg L

TACOMA

Buckley Gulch Brdige; see North Twenty-First Street Bridge

Fort Nisqually
Point Defiance Park
HABS WA-37
HABS WASH,27-TACO,1-
1dr/3pg/fr L

Fort Nisqually,Corner Bastion
Point Defiance Park
HABS WA-37-A
HABS WASH,27-TACO,1A-
1dr/1ph/fr L

Fort Nisqually,Factor's House
Point Defiance Park
HABS WA-37-B
HABS WASH,27-TACO,1B-
6dr/3ph/fr L

Fort Nisqually,Granary
Point Defiance Park
HABS WA-37-C
HABS WASH,27-TACO,1C-
2dr/2ph/fr L

Goodrich Silvertown Building
1955 Pacific Ave.
HABS WA-158
HABS WASH,27-TACO,4-
13ph/9pg/1pc L

North Twenty-First Street Bridge (Buckley Gulch Brdige; North Twenty-First Street Viaduct)
North 21st Street spanning Buckley Gulch
HAER WA-83
20ph/9pg/2pc H

North Twenty-First Street Viaduct; see North Twenty-First Street Bridge

Pantages Theatre & Jones Building
901-909 Broadway
HABS WA-151
HABS WASH,27-TACO,5-
21ph/6pg/2pc L

Post Office,First
Point Defiance Park
HABS WA-116
HABS WASH,27-TACO,2-
2ph/1pg L

Puget Sound Flouring Mill (Sperry Flour Company; Sperry Ocean Dock)
611 Schuster Pkwy.
HAER WA-27
24ph/12pg/3pc L

Rhodes Medical Arts Building; see Tacoma Rhodes Tower

Rhodes Medical Arts Tower; see Tacoma Rhodes Tower

Sperry Flour Company; see Puget Sound Flouring Mill

Sperry Ocean Dock; see Puget Sound Flouring Mill

Tacoma Municipal Administration Building; see Tacoma Rhodes Tower

Tacoma Rhodes Tower (Tacoma Municipal Administration Building; Rhodes Medical Arts Tower; Rhodes Medical Arts Building)
740 Saint Helens Ave.
HABS WA-173
HABS WASH,27-TACO,3-
15ph/9pg/1pc/fr L

Union Depot Area Study
HABS WA-165
HABS WASH,27-TACO,6-
51ph/1pg/5pc/fr L

Union Depot Area Study,Harmon,F. S.,Mattress Fact.
1953 S. C St.
HABS WA-165-A
HABS WASH,27-TACO,6A-
5ph/1pg/1pc L

Union Depot Area Study,Pacific Brewing & Malting
2500 Holgate St.
HABS WA-165-B
HABS WASH,27-TACO,6B-
5ph/1pg L

Union Passenger Station Concourse
1713 Pacific Ave.
HABS WA-159
HABS WASH,27-TACO,6C-
39ph/8pg L

SAN JUAN COUNTY

FRIDAY HARBOR

English Camp (Remains)
Garrison Bay,San Juan Island
HABS WA-39-W-17
HABS WASH,28-FRIHA,1-
9dr/10ph L

SKAGIT COUNTY

ANACORTES

Curtis Wharf
"O" and Second Sts.
HABS WA-198
HABS DLC/PP-1993:WA-1
22ph/79pg/4pc L

Curtis Wharf,Bottling Works
"O" & Second Sts.
HABS WA-198-J
HABS DLC/PP-1993:WA-1
4ph/1pc L

Curtis Wharf,Cement & Plaster Warehouse
"O" & Second Sts.
HABS WA-198-D
HABS DLC/PP-1993:WA-1
6ph/1pc L

Curtis Wharf,Cold Storage Warehouse
"O" & Second Sts.
HABS WA-198-G
HABS DLC/PP-1993:WA-1
3ph/1pc L

Curtis Wharf,Creamery
"O" & Second Sts.
HABS WA-198-I
HABS DLC/PP-1993:WA-1
6ph/1pc L

Curtis Wharf,Feed Mill
"O" & Second Sts.
HABS WA-198-H
HABS DLC/PP-1993:WA-1
4ph/1pc L

Curtis Wharf,Ferry Slip & Sand & Gravel Wharf
"O" & Second Sts.
HABS WA-198-K
HABS DLC/PP-1993:WA-1
1ph/1pc L

Curtis Wharf,Freight Warehouse
"O" & Second Sts.
HABS WA-198-B
HABS DLC/PP-1993:WA-1
8ph/1pc L

Curtis Wharf,Hay & Grain Warehouse
"O" & Second Sts.
HABS WA-198-F
HABS DLC/PP-1993:WA-1
4ph/1pc L

Curtis Wharf,Ice Plant
"O" & Second Sts.
HABS WA-198-E
HABS DLC/PP-1993:WA-1
3ph/1pc L

Curtis Wharf,Main Dock
"O" & Second Sts.
HABS WA-198-A
HABS DLC/PP-1993:WA-1
2ph/1pc L

Curtis Wharf,Ticket Office
"O" & Second Sts.
HABS WA-198-C
HABS DLC/PP-1993:WA-1
8ph/1pc L

SKAMANIA COUNTY

FORT RAINS

Fort Rains,Blockhouse
N. Bonnerville Vic.
HABS WA-90
HABS WASH,30-FORA.V,1-
2ph/1pg L

SNOHOMISH COUNTY

DARRINGTON

Building 2215; see Darrington Ranger Station,Road & Trail Warehouse

Building 2275; see Darrington Ranger Station,Fire & Truck Stor. Bldg.

Darrington Ranger Station (Mt. Baker-Snoqualmie National Forest)
1405 Emmens
HABS WA-191
HABS DLC/PP-1993:WA-1
1ph/3pc L

Darrington Ranger Station,Building 1229 (Mt. Baker-Snoqualmie National Forest)
1405 Emmens St.
HABS WA-191-G
HABS DLC/PP-1993:WA-1
1ph/1pc L

Darrington Ranger Station,Building 1230 (Mt. Baker-Snoqualmie National Forest)
1405 Emmens St.
HABS WA-191-E
HABS DLC/PP-1993:WA-1
1ph/1pc L

Darrington Ranger Station,Building 1232 (Mt. Baker-Snoqualmie National Forest)
1405 Emmens St.
HABS WA-191-H
HABS DLC/PP-1993:WA-1
1ph/1pc L

Darrington Ranger Station,Building 1575 (Mt. Baker-Snoqualmie National Forest)
1405 Emmens St.
HABS WA-191-F
HABS DLC/PP-1993:WA-1
1ph/1pc L

Darrington Ranger Station,Building 2013 (Mt. Baker-Snoqualmie National Forest)
1405 Emmens St.
HABS WA-191-D
HABS DLC/PP-1993:WA-1
1ph/1pc L

Darrington Ranger Station,Building 2315 (Mt. Baker-Snoqualmie National Forest)
1405 Emmens St.
HABS WA-191-A
HABS DLC/PP-1993:WA-1
7ph/10pg/1pc L

Darrington Ranger Station,Building 2415 (Mt. Baker-Snoqualmie National Forest)
1405 Emmens St.
HABS WA-191-I
HABS DLC/PP-1993:WA-1
1ph/1pc L

Darrington Ranger Station,Building 2515 (Mt. Baker-Snoqualmie National Forest)
1405 Emmens St.
HABS WA-191-J
HABS DLC/PP-1993:WA-1
1ph/1pc L

Darrington Ranger Station,Fire & Truck Stor. Bldg. (Building 2275; Mt. Baker-Snoqualmie National Forest)
1405 Emmens St.
HABS WA-191-C
HABS DLC/PP-1993:WA-1
6ph/10pg/1pc L

Darrington Ranger Station,Road & Trail Warehouse (Building 2215; Mt. Baker-Snoqualmie National Forest)
1405 Emmens St.
HABS WA-191-B
HABS DLC/PP-1993:WA-1
4ph/9pg/1pc L

Mt. Baker-Snoqualmie National Forest; see Darrington Ranger Station

Mt. Baker-Snoqualmie National Forest; see Darrington Ranger Station,Building 1229

Mt. Baker-Snoqualmie National Forest; see Darrington Ranger Station,Building 1230

Mt. Baker-Snoqualmie National Forest; see Darrington Ranger Station,Building 1232

Mt. Baker-Snoqualmie National Forest; see Darrington Ranger Station,Building 1575

Mt. Baker-Snoqualmie National Forest; see Darrington Ranger Station,Building 2013

Mt. Baker-Snoqualmie National Forest; see Darrington Ranger Station,Building 2315

Mt. Baker-Snoqualmie National Forest; see Darrington Ranger Station,Building 2415

Mt. Baker-Snoqualmie National Forest; see Darrington Ranger Station,Building 2515

Mt. Baker-Snoqualmie National Forest; see Darrington Ranger Station,Fire & Truck Stor. Bldg.

Mt. Baker-Snoqualmie National Forest; see Darrington Ranger Station,Road & Trail Warehouse

SPOKANE COUNTY

DEER PARK VIC.

Hazard Post Office
Wild Rose Prairie
HABS WA-28
HABS WASH,32-DERP.V,1-
3dr/2ph/1pg/fr L

HILLYARD

St. Michael's Mission Church
Mount St. Michaels
HABS WA-113
HABS WASH,32-HILYA,1-
2ph/1pg L

NINE MILE FALLS

Nine Mile Hydroelectric Development
St. Hwy. 291 along the Spokane River
HAER WA-84
6ph/41pg/1pc H

NINE MILE FALLS VIC.

Nine Mile Hydroelectric Development,Cottage No. 1
State Highway 291 along the Spokane River
HAER WA-84-C
9ph/2pc H

Nine Mile Hydroelectric Development,Cottage No. 10
State Highway 291 along the Spokane River
HAER WA-84-L
2ph/1pc H

Nine Mile Hydroelectric Development,Cottage No. 2
State Highway 291 along the Spokane River
HAER WA-84-D
8ph/1pc H

Nine Mile Hydroelectric Development,Cottage No. 3
State Highway 291 along the Spokane River
HAER WA-84-E
9ph/2pc H

Nine Mile Hydroelectric Development,Cottage No. 4
State Highway 291 along the Spokane River
HAER WA-84-F
4ph/1pc H

Nine Mile Hydroelectric Development,Cottage No. 5
State Highway 291 along the Spokane River
HAER WA-84-G
4ph/1pc H

Nine Mile Hydroelectric Development,Cottage No. 6
State Highway 291 along the Spokane River
HAER WA-84-H
2ph/1pc H

Nine Mile Hydroelectric Development,Cottage No. 7
State Highway 291 along the Spokane River
HAER WA-84-I
2ph/1pc H

Nine Mile Hydroelectric Development,Cottage No. 8
State Highway 291 along the Spokane River
HAER WA-84-J
4ph/1pc H

Nine Mile Hydroelectric Development,Cottage No. 9
State Highway 291 along the Spokane River
HAER WA-84-K
2ph/1pc H

Nine Mile Hydroelectric Development,Dam
State Highway 291 along the Spokane River
HAER WA-84-A
3ph/1pc H

Nine Mile Hydroelectric Development,Powerhouse
State Highway 291 along the Spokane River
HAER WA-84-B
19ph/2pc H

SPOKANE

Comstock Library; see Sears,Roebuck Department Store

Sears,Roebuck Department Store (Comstock Library)
W. 906 Main Ave.
HABS WA-194
25ph/33pg/2pc H

Washington Street Bridge
Spanning Spokane River at Washington St.
HAER WA-3
HAER WASH,32-SPOK,2-
17ph/3pg/2pc L

Washington Water Power Co. Monroe St. Plant,4 & 5
South Bank Spokane River,below Monroe St. Bridge
HAER WA-29
HAER DLC/PP-1992:WA-2
28ph/16pg/4pc L

West 1624 Pacific Avenue (House)
HABS WA-149
HABS WASH,32-SPOK,1-
4dr L

STEVENS COUNTY

ARDEN VIC.

Ayers Barn
HABS WA-94
HABS WASH,33-ARD.V,1-
1ph/1pg L

CHEWELAH

Douglas Cabin
HABS WA-26
HABS WASH,33-CHEW,1-
2dr/2ph/1pg/fr L

Indian Agency Building; see McPherson,Dr. F. P.,Cabin

McCrea,George,Cabin
HABS WA-80
HABS WASH,33-CHEW,3-
2ph/1pg L

McPherson,Dr. F. P.,Cabin (Indian Agency Building)
Third St. East
HABS WA-27
HABS WASH,33-CHEW,2-
5dr/1ph/1pg/fr L

CHEWELAH VIC.

King,Peter,Cabin
HABS WA-78
HABS WASH,33-CHEW.V,2-
2ph/1pg L

Regenary Cabin
HABS WA-30
HABS WASH,33-CHEW.V,1-
5dr/1ph/1pg/fr L

Waitt,George,Cabin
HABS WA-79
HABS WASH,33-CHEW.V,3-
2ph/1pg L

COLVILLE VIC.

Clugston,John,Barn
Clugston Rd.
HABS WA-34
HABS WASH,33-COLV.V,3-
4dr/3ph/1pg/fr L

Harbaugh,Dan,Homestead
HABS WA-36
HABS WASH,33-COLV.V,4-
3dr/1ph/1pg/fr L

Holst,John,Homestead (Stevens County Courthouse)
HABS WA-32
HABS WASH,33-COLV.V,1-
3dr/2ph/1pg/fr L

Stagecoach Station,Barn
HABS WA-33
HABS WASH,33-COLV.V,2-
2dr/3ph/1pg/fr L

Stevens County Courthouse; see Holst,John,Homestead

EVANS VIC.

Orient Bridge
See Orient,Ferry Co. for documentation
HAER WA-32
HAER DLC/PP-1993:WA-2
15ph/11pg/2pc L

FORD VIC.

Haines,Guy,Cottage
HABS WA-92
HABS WASH,33-FORD.V,2-
2ph/1pg L

Haines,Guy,House
HABS WA-93
HABS WASH,33-FORD.V,3-
2ph/1pg L

Long Lake Hydroelectric Plant
Across the Spokane River
HAER WA-33
HAER DLC/PP-1993:WA-2
4ph/8pg/1pc L

Long Lake Hydroelectric Plant,Spillway Dam
Across the Spokane River
HAER WA-33-A
HAER DLC/PP-1993:WA-2
16ph/6pg/2pc L

Tshimakain Mission
HABS WA-91
HABS WASH,33-FORD.V,1-
4ph/1pg L

KETTLE FALLS VIC.

St. Paul's Mission
HABS WA-31
HABS WASH,33-KETFA.V,1-
4dr/8ph/2pg/fr L

THURSTON COUNTY

CHAMBERS PRAIRIE

Chambers,David,House
HABS WA-21
HABS WASH,34-CHAMP,1-
5dr/3ph/1pg/fr L

OLYMPIA

Bigelow,Daniel T. ,House
918 E. Glass Ave.
HABS WA-161
HABS WASH,34-OLYM,2-
7dr/15ph/6pg/1pc L

Evans,Elwood,House (McMicken House)
Douglas St.
HABS WA-39-W-22
HABS WASH,34-OLYM,1-
8dr L

McMicken House; see Evans,Elwood,House

TUMWATER

Crosby,Nathaniel III,House
703 Deschutes Way
HABS WA-162
HABS WASH,34-TUM,1-
7dr/14ph/5pg/1pc L

WAHKIAKUM COUNTY

GRAYS RIVER VIC.

Grays River Covered Bridge
Worrel Rd. spanning Grays River
HAER WA-28
HAER DLC/PP-1992:WA-2
19ph/8pg/2pc L

WALLA WALLA COUNTY

WALLA WALLA VIC.

Clark,Ransom,Cabin
HABS WA-39
HABS WASH,36-WAL.V,1-
3dr/4ph/1pg/fr L

WHATCOM COUNTY

BELLINGHAM

Bellingham City Hall; see Whatcom City Hall,New

Courthouse,Old
1106 E St.
HABS WA-39-W-3
HABS WASH,37-BEL,1-
6dr/2ph L

Pickett,Capt. George E.,House
910 Bancroft St.
HABS WA-39-W-4
HABS WASH,37-BEL,2-
4dr/2ph L

Whatcom City Hall,New (Bellingham City Hall; Whatcom Museum of History & Art)
121 Prospect St.
HABS WA-22
HABS WASH,37-BEL,3-
11ph/8pg/1pc L

Whatcom Museum of History & Art; see Whatcom City Hall,New

BLAINE VIC.

Semiahmoo Cannery
On Boundary Bay near the Canadian Border
HAER WA-11
HAER WASH,37-BLAIN.V,1-
10ph/1pg/1pc L

GLACIER

Glacier Ranger Station
Mt. Baker-Snoqualmie Nat. Forest, WA State Rt.542
HABS WA-192
21ph/13pg/3pc H

Glacier Ranger Station,Protection Assistant's Res.
Mt. Baker-Snoqualmie Nat. For., WA State Rt. 542
HABS WA-192-A
4ph/1pc H

GLACIER VIC.

Austin Pass Warming Hut
HABS WA-195
HABS 1988(HAER):28
18ph/13pg/2pc H

Nooksack Falls Hydroelectric Plant
(Puget Sound Power and Light Company)
Rt. 542
HAER WA-18
6dr/42ph/32pg/5pc/fr L

Puget Sound Power and Light Company; see Nooksack Falls Hydroelectric Plant

NEWHALEM

Skagit Power Dev.,Skagit & Newhalem Hydro. Proj.
North Cascades National Park, on the Skagit River
HAER WA-24
HAER DLC/PP-1992:WA-2
3dr/31ph/99pg/3pc/fr L

Skagit Power Development,Gorge Powerhouse
On Skagit River,0.4 mi. upstream from Newhalem
HAER WA-24-B
HAER DLC/PP-1992:WA-2
3dr/29ph/3pc/fr L

Skagit Power Development,Newhalem Powerhouse & Dam
On Skagit River,0.3 mi. downstream from Newhalem
HAER WA-24-A
HAER DLC/PP-1992:WA-2
1dr/7ph/1pc/fr L

NEWHALEM VIC.

Goat Trail Mining Road
Hwy. 20, 1.5 mi. N of Newhalem
HAER WA-19
HAER 1992(HAER):WA-1;DLC/PP-1993:WA-2
4dr/16ph/7pg/2pc/fr L

Skagit Power Development,Diablo Dam
On Skagit River,6.9 mi. upstream from Newhalem
HAER WA-24-F
HAER DLC/PP-1992:WA-2
1dr/12ph/2pc/fr L

Skagit Power Development,Diablo Powerhouse
On Skagit River,6.1 mi. upstream from Newhalem
HAER WA-24-D
HAER DLC/PP-1992:WA-2
6dr/43ph/4pc/fr L

Skagit Power Development,Gorge High Dam
On Skagit River,2.9 mi. upstream from Newhalem
HAER WA-24-C
HAER DLC/PP-1992:WA-2
1dr/10ph/1pc/fr L

Skagit Power Development,Incline Railway
On Skagit River,6.1 mi. upstream from Newhalem
HAER WA-24-E
HAER DLC/PP-1992:WA-2
4ph/1pc L

Skagit Power Development,Ross Dam
11.0 mi. upstream from Newhalem on Skagit River
HAER WA-24-H
HAER DLC/PP-1992:WA-2
5ph/1pc L

Skagit Power Development,Ross Powerhouse
On Skagit River,10.7 mi. upstream from Newhalem
HAER WA-24-G
HAER DLC/PP-1992:WA-2
22ph/2pc L

SUMAS

U. S. Border Inspection Station
103 Cherry St.
HABS WA-182
HABS 1989(HABS):24
41ph/17pg/3pc L

WHITMAN COUNTY

CASHUP

Stagecoach Station
HABS WA-29
HABS WASH,38-CASH,1-
4dr/5ph/1pg/fr L

PALOUSE

"F" Street Bridge (Palouse Flour Mill Bridge)
Spanning Palouse River
HAER WA-31
HAER 1991(HAER):11
10ph/13pg/1pc L

Palouse Flour Mill Bridge; see "F" Street Bridge

PALOUSE VIC.

McClure Bridge
Spd.ning N. Fork of Palouse River on Altergott RD.
HAER WA-25
HAER 1991(HAER):11
13ph/10pg/1pc L

PULLMAN JUNCTION VIC

Collins,O. M.,House
HABS WA-112
HABS WASH,38-PULJ.V,1-
2ph/1pg L

PULLMAN VIC.

Leonard,T. A. ,Barn
Old Moscow Hwy.
HABS WA-168
HABS WASH,38-PULL.V,1-
10dr/12ph/14pg/1pc/fr L

YAKIMA COUNTY

COWICHE VIC.

Splawn,A. J.,House
HABS WA-84
HABS WASH,39-COWI.V,1-
2ph/1pg L

NACHES VIC.

Burge,Andy,Cabin
Reservoir Vic.
HABS WA-82
HABS WASH,39-NACH.V,1-
2ph/1pg L

Chinook Pass Work Center; see Naches Ranger Station Complex

Chinook Pass Work Center; see Naches Ranger Station,Building No. 1120

Chinook Pass Work Center; see Naches Ranger Station,Building No. 1320

Chinook Pass Work Center (Garage); see Naches Ranger Station,Building No. 1526

Chinook Pass Work Center (Garage); see Naches Ranger Station,Building No. 1527

Chinook Pass Work Center (House); see Naches Ranger Station,Building No. 1028

Chinook Pass Work Center (House); see Naches Ranger Station,Building No. 1029

Kiwanis Lodge (Wenatchee National Forest)
3200 Old River Rd.,Camp Roganunda
HABS WA-196
11ph/8pg/1pc H

Naches Ranger Station Complex (Chinook Pass Work Center)
State Hwy. 410,S. side,Wenatchee National Forest
HABS WA-181
HABS 1991(HABS):10
6ph/29pg/1pc L

Naches Ranger Station,Building No. 1028 (Chinook Pass Work Center (House))
State Hwy. 410,S. side,Wenatchee National Forest
HABS WA-181-A
HABS 1991(HABS):10
5ph/1pc L

Naches Ranger Station,Building No. 1029 (Chinook Pass Work Center (House))
State Hwy. 410,S. side,Wenatchee National Forest
HABS WA-181-B
HABS 1991(HABS):10
7ph/1pc L

Naches Ranger Station,Building No. 1120 (Chinook Pass Work Center)
State Hwy. 410,Wenatchee National Forest
HABS WA-181-C
HABS 1991(HABS):10
10ph/1pc L

Naches Ranger Station,Building No. 1320 (Chinook Pass Work Center)
State Hwy. 410,S. side,Wenatchee National Forest
HABS WA-181-D
HABS 1991(HABS):10
9ph/1pc L

Naches Ranger Station,Building No. 1526 (Chinook Pass Work Center (Garage))
State Hwy. 410,S. side,Wenatchee National Forest
HABS WA-181-E
HABS 1991(HABS):10
8ph/1pc L

Naches Ranger Station,Building No. 1527 (Chinook Pass Work Center (Garage))
State Hwy. 410,S. side,Wenatchee National Forest
HABS WA-181-F
HABS 1991(HABS):10
8ph/1pc L

Tieton Dam
S. and E. of State Hwy. 12
HAER WA-20
HAER 1992(HAER):WA-1
20ph/10pg/2pc L

Tieton Ranger Station (White Pass Work Center)
N. side State Hwy. 12,West of State Hwy. 410
HABS WA-180
HABS 1991(HABS):10
5ph/26pg/1pc L

Tieton Ranger Station,Building No. 1051 (White Pass Work Center (House))
North side of St. Hwy. 12,West of State Hwy. 410
HABS WA-180-A
HABS 1991(HABS):10
16ph/1pc L

Tieton Ranger Station,Building No. 1052 (White Pass Work Center (House))
North side of State Hwy. 12,West of State Hwy. 410
HABS WA-180-B
HABS 1991(HABS):10
11ph/1pc L

Tieton Ranger Station,Building No. 1053 (White Pass Work Center (House))
North side of State Hwy. 12,West of State Hwy. 410
HABS WA-180-C
HABS 1991(HABS):10
14ph/1pc L

Tieton Ranger Station,Building No. 1553 (White Pass Work Center (Garage))
North side of State Hwy. 12,West of State Hwy. 410
HABS WA-180-D
HABS 1991(HABS):10
6ph/1pc L

Wenatchee National Forest; see Kiwanis Lodge

White Pass Work Center; see Tieton Ranger Station

White Pass Work Center (Garage); see Tieton Ranger Station,Building No. 1553

White Pass Work Center (House); see Tieton Ranger Station,Building No. 1051

White Pass Work Center (House); see Tieton Ranger Station,Building No. 1052

White Pass Work Center (House); see Tieton Ranger Station,Building No. 1053

OUTLOOK

Outlook Irrigation Dist:Pump.Plant & Woodstave Pip (Pumping Plant & Woodstave Pipe)
Hudson Rd. & Snipes Lateral Rd. vic.
HAER WA-10
HAER WASH,39-OUT,1-
12ph/7pg/fr L

Pumping Plant & Woodstave Pipe; see Outlook Irrigation Dist:Pump.Plant & Woodstave Pip

SAWYER VIC.

Sawyer,W. P.,Cabin
HABS WA-24
HABS WASH,39-SAW.V,1-
2dr/4ph/1pg/fr L

TAMPICO VIC.

St. Joseph's Mission
Ahtanum Valley
HABS WA-40
HABS WASH,39-TAMP.V,1-
3dr/2ph/2pg L

UNION GAP

Garvis,P. T.,Store
HABS WA-85
HABS WASH,39-UNGA,1-
1ph/1pg L

WENAS

Longmire,David,House
HABS WA-87
HABS WASH,39-WENA,1-
2ph/1pg L

WHITE SWAN

Indian Methodist Episcopal Church (Indian Mission)
HABS WA-133
HABS WASH,39-WHIT,1-
1ph/1pg L

Indian Mission; see Indian Methodist Episcopal Church

WHITE SWAN VIC.

Fort Simcoe,Commandant's House & Blockhhouse
HABS WA-25
HABS WASH,39-WHIT.V,1-
13dr/4ph/2pg/fr L

YAKIMA

Douglas,Justice William O. ,Federal Building; see U. S. Post Office & Courthouse

U. S. Post Office & Courthouse (Douglas,Justice William O. ,Federal Building)
25 S. Third St.
HABS WA-170
HABS WASH,39-YAK,1-
26ph/1pg/2pc/fr L

YAKIMA VIC.

Naches River Bridge; see Yakima Valley Trans. Co.,Naches River Bridge

Yakima Valley Trans. Co. Interurban Railroad
Connects towns of Yakima,Selah & Wiley City
HAER WA-13
HAER WASH,39-YAK.V,1-
45ph/20pg/3pc L

Yakima Valley Trans. Co. RR,Electric Locomot. #297
HAER WA-13-H
HAER WASH,39-YAK.V,1-H-
4ph/1pc L

Yakima Valley Trans. Co. RR,Electric Locomot. #298
HAER WA-13-I
HAER WASH,39-YAK.V,1-I-
3ph/1pc L

Yakima Valley Trans. Co. RR,Main Power Substation
HAER WA-13-B
HAER WASH,39-YAK.V,1-B-
11ph/1pc L

Yakima Valley Trans. Co. RR,Wide Hollow Jct Substa
HAER WA-13-E
HAER WASH,39-YAK.V,1-E-
8ph/1pc L

Yakima Valley Trans. Co.,Naches River Bridge (Naches River Bridge)
HAER WA-13-F
HAER WASH,39-YAK.V,1-F-
7ph/1pc L

Yakima Valley Transportation Co. RR,Carbarn
Third Ave. & Pine St.
HAER WA-13-A
HAER WASH,39-YAK.V,1-A-
20ph/2pc L

Yakima Valley Transportation Co. RR,Flatcars
HAER WA-13-K
HAER WASH,39-YAK.V,1-K-
2ph/1pc L

Yakima Valley Transportation Co. RR,Line Car A
HAER WA-13-J
HAER WASH,39-YAK.V,1-J-
3ph/1pc L

Yakima Valley Transportation Co. RR,Storage Shed
HAER WA-13-C
HAER WASH,39-YAK.V,1-C-
5ph/1pc L

Yakima Valley Transportation Co. RR,Trackage
HAER WA-13-G
HAER WASH,39-YAK.V,1-G-
8ph/1pc L

Yakima Valley Transportation Co. RR,Warehouse
HAER WA-13-D
HAER WASH,39-YAK.V,1-D-
6ph/1pc L

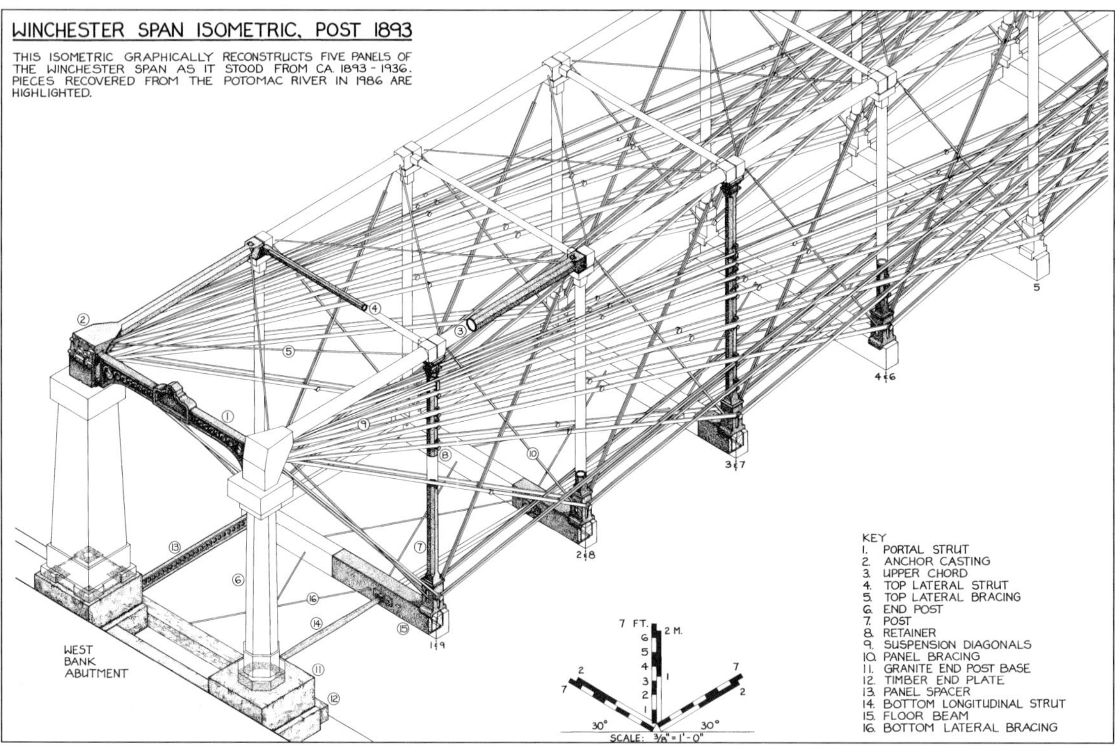

Wheeling Suspension Bridge, Wheeling, West Virginia. View through arch of east tower. Photograph by Jack E. Boucher, March 1977 (HAER WVA,35-WHEEL,35-44).

Baltimore and Ohio Railroad: Bollmann Bridge, Harper's Ferry, Jefferson County, West Virginia. Winchester span isometric, post 1893. Measured drawing delineated by Joanna Downs, Samuel Gaine, B rian D. Bartholomew, 1987 (HAER WV-36, sheet 5 of 6).

West Virginia

MARIETTA

Williamstown-Marietta Bridge
Span. Ohio River btwn Marietta & Williamstown,WV
HAER WV-40
HAER 1990(HAER):14
73ph/11pg/8pc L

BARBOUR COUNTY

PHILIPPI

Alderson-Broaddus College,Whitescarver Hall
W. side of U.S. 119/250,N. of covered bridge
HABS WV-246-A
HABS DLC/PP-1993:WV-5
13ph/21pg/1pc L

BERKELEY COUNTY

BUNKER HILL VIC.

Bunker Hill Mill (Cline & Chapman Roller Mill)
County Rt. 26
HAER WV-29
HAER WVA,2-BUNK.V,1-
38ph/20pg/3pc/1ct/fr L

Cline & Chapman Roller Mill; see Bunker Hill Mill

GERRARDSTOWN

Hollis,Trammell,House (Prospect Hill Farm)
HABS WV-153
HABS WVA,2-GERTO,1-
5ph L

Prospect Hill Farm; see Hollis,Trammell,House

HEDGESVILLE VIC.

Dam No. 5 Hydroelectric Plant
On Potomac River
HAER WV-28
HAER WVA,2-HEDVI.V,1-
63ph/1pg/6pc/fr L

MARTINSBURG

Baltimore & Ohio RR,Martinsburg East Roundhouse (Martinsburg East Roundhouse)
E. End of Race & Martin Sts.
HAER WV-1-B
HAER WVA,2-MART,1B-
3dr/4ph/1pg/1pc/fr L

Baltimore & Ohio RR,Martinsburg Machine Shop (Martinsburg Machine Shop)
W. Side of Tuscarora Creek Opp. E. End of Race St.
HAER WV-1-C
HAER WVA,2-MART,1C-
3ph/1pc L

Baltimore & Ohio RR,Martinsburg Repair Shops (Martinsburg Repair Shops)
W. Side of Tuscarora Creek Opp. E. End of Race St.
HAER WV-1
HAER WVA,2-MART,1-
11ph/3pg L

Baltimore & Ohio RR,Martinsburg West Roundhouse (Martinsburg West Roundhouse; Cast Iron Roundhouse)
E. End of Race & Martin Sts.
HAER WV-1-A
HAER WVA,2-MART,1A-
5dr/11ph/1pg/1pc/fr L

Cast Iron Roundhouse; see Baltimore & Ohio RR,Martinsburg West Roundhouse

Federal Aviation Administration Records Center (U. S. Courthouse,Old)
300 W. King St.
HABS WV-154
HABS WVA,2-MART,3-
1ph/1pc L

Martinsburg East Roundhouse; see Baltimore & Ohio RR,Martinsburg East Roundhouse

Martinsburg Machine Shop; see Baltimore & Ohio RR,Martinsburg Machine Shop

Martinsburg Repair Shops; see Baltimore & Ohio RR,Martinsburg Repair Shops

Martinsburg Station & Hotel
Martin St.
HAER WV-17
HAER WVA,2-MART,2-
1ph/1pc L

Martinsburg West Roundhouse; see Baltimore & Ohio RR,Martinsburg West Roundhouse

216 South Water Street (House)
HABS WV-249
H

U. S. Courthouse,Old; see Federal Aviation Administration Records Center

MARTINSBURG VIC.

Dam No. 4 Hydroelectric Plant
Potomac River
HAER WV-27
HAER WVA,2-SHEP.V,
6dr/167pg/fr L

BRAXTON COUNTY

BURNSVILLE

Burnsville Natural Gas Pumping Station
Saratoga Ave. btwn. Little Kanawha R. & C&O RR lin
HAER WV-33
HAER WVA,4-BURN,1-
45ph/4pg/3pc L

GASSAWAY VIC.

Baltimore & Ohio Railroad:Stone Bridges 1 & 2
Between Gassaway & Sutton
HAER WV-34
HAER WVA,4-GAS,1-
6ph/4pg/1pc L

BROOKE COUNTY

BETHANY

Bethany Church of Christ (Bethany Church,Old)
Main & Church Sts.
HABS WV-213
HABS WVA,5-BETH,2-
2ph/1pg/1pc L

Bethany Church,Old; see Bethany Church of Christ

Bethany College,"Old Main" Building
Rt. 67
HABS WV-118
HABS WVA,5-BETH,3-
30dr/22ph/24pg/2pc/14ct/fr L

Campbell,Alexander,Mansion
Rt. 67
HABS WV-212
HABS WVA,5-BETH,1A-
6dr/7ph/1pc/fr L

Campbell,Alexander,Study
Rt. 67
HABS WV-119
HABS WVA,5-BETH,1B-
1dr/5ph/1pc/fr L

CABELL COUNTY

HUNTINGTON

1302 Third Avenue (House)
1302 Third Avenue
HABS WV-233
HABS 1989(HABS):26
14ph/1pc L

MILTON

Milton Covered Bridge (Sink's Mill Covered Bridge; Mud River Covered Bridge)
County Rt. 25, U. S. Rt. 60 vic.
HAER WV-32
HAER WVA,6-MILT,1-
4ph/2pg/1pc L

Mud River Covered Bridge; see Milton Covered Bridge

Sink's Mill Covered Bridge; see Milton Covered Bridge

FAYETTE COUNTY

FAYETTEVILLE VIC.

Kay Moor Coal Mine
HAER WV-38
16dr/95ph/6ct/fr H

New River Gorge Bridge
Spanning New River near Fayetteville
HAER WV-41
HAER 1991(HAER):17
12ph/1pg/1pc/1ct L

GAULEY BRIDGE

Miller Tavern,Old
HABS WV-21-11
HABS WVA,10-GAUBR,1-
2pg/fr L

THURMOND

Chesapeake & Ohio Railroad: Coaling Station (Thurmond Coaling Station; Thurmond Coaling Tower)
Astride the tracks west end Thurmond Yards
HAER WV-42-C
HAER 1990 (HAER):14
2dr/3ph/1pc/fr L

Chesapeake & Ohio Railroad: Engine House (Thurmond Engine House)
Along south end Thurmond, west of New River Brdg.
HAER WV-42-B
HAER 1990 (HAER):14
2dr/10ph/1pc/fr L

Chesapeake & Ohio Railroad: Thurmond Depot (Thurmond Depot; Thurmond Passenger Station)
NE end of the New River Bridge
HAER WV-42-A
HAER 1990 (HAER):14
1dr/6ph/1pc/fr L

Chesapeake & Ohio Railroad: Thurmond Yards (Thurmond Yards)
East side New River,mouths of Arbuckle & Dunlop Cr
HAER WV-42
HAER 1990 (HAER):14
4dr/30ph/77pg/2pc/fr L

Thurmond Coaling Station; see Chesapeake & Ohio Railroad: Coaling Station

Thurmond Coaling Tower; see Chesapeake & Ohio Railroad: Coaling Station

Thurmond Depot; see Chesapeake & Ohio Railroad: Thurmond Depot

Thurmond Engine House; see Chesapeake & Ohio Railroad: Engine House

Thurmond Passenger Station; see Chesapeake & Ohio Railroad: Thurmond Depot

Thurmond Yards; see Chesapeake & Ohio Railroad: Thurmond Yards

GREENBRIER COUNTY

ALDERSON

107 Railroad Avenue (Commercial Building)
107 Railroad Ave.
HABS WV-241
HABS 1991(HABS):4
4ph/5pg/1pc L

LEWISBURG

Church,Old Stone (Presbyterian)
Church St.
HABS WV-21-1
HABS WVA,13-LEWBU,1-
13dr/4ph/3pg/1pc/fr L

Greenbrier County Courthouse
Randolph & Market Sts.
HABS WV-115
HABS WVA,13-LEWBU,2-
2ph L

RAINELLE

Meadow River Lumber Company
Hwy. 60
HAER WV-24
HAER WVA,13-RAIN,1-
2dr/56ph/27pg/5pc L

Meadow River Lumber Company,Powerhouse
State Rt. 20
HAER WV-24-B
HAER WVA,13-RAIN,1B-
1dr/fr L

Meadow River Lumber Company,Sawmill
State Rt. 20
HAER WV-24-A
HAER WVA,13-RAIN,1A-
2dr/fr L

Meadow River Lumber Company,Shops
State Rt. 20
HAER WV-24-C
HAER WVA,13-RAIN,1C-
2dr/fr L

RENICK

Renick House
U. S. Rt. 219
HABS WV-116
HABS WVA,13-RENI,1-
13ph/2pg L

RONCEVERTE

Church of the Incarnation (Episcopal)
Rt. 219
HABS WV-110
HABS WVA,13-RONC,1-
6ph L

Edgar House
Rt. 63 Vic.
HABS WV-111
HABS WVA,13-RONC,2-
2ph L

WHITE SULPHUR SPRING

Greenbrier,The; see White Sulphur Springs

Greenbrier,The,Alabama Row; see White Sulphur Springs,Alabama Row

Greenbrier,The,Bachelor's Row; see White Sulphur Springs,Paradise Row

Greenbrier,The,Baltimore Row; see White Sulphur Springs,Baltimore Row

Greenbrier,The,Colonnade Cottage; see White Sulphur Springs,Colonnade Cottage

Greenbrier,The,Georgia Row; see White Sulphur Springs,Georgia Row

Greenbrier,The,Louisiana Row; see White Sulphur Springs,Louisiana Row

Greenbrier,The,Paradise Row; see White Sulphur Springs,Paradise Row

Greenbrier,The,President's Cottage; see White Sulphur Springs,President's Cottage

Greenbrier,The,South Carolina Row; see White Sulphur Springs,South Carolina Row

Greenbrier,The,Spring House; see White Sulphur Springs,Spring House

Greenbrier,The,Tansas Row; see White Sulphur Springs,Tansas Row

Virginia Spings; see White Sulphur Springs

White Sulphur Springs (Greenbrier,The; Virginia Spings)
U. S. Rt. 60
HABS WV-131
HABS WVA,-13-WHISP,1-
1ph/2pg/1pc L

White Sulphur Springs,Alabama Row (Greenbrier,The,Alabama Row)
U. S. Rt. 60
HABS WV-131-C
HABS WVA,13-WHISP,1C-
2ph/1pg/1pc L

White Sulphur Springs,Bachelor's Row; see White Sulphur Springs,Paradise Row

White Sulphur Springs,Baltimore Row (Greenbrier,The,Baltimore Row)
U. S. Rt. 60
HABS WV-131-E
HABS WVA,13-WHISP,1E-
1ph/1pg/1pc L

White Sulphur Springs,Colonnade Cottage (Greenbrier,The,Colonnade Cottage)
U. S. Rt. 60
HABS WV-131-J
HABS WVA,13-WHISP,1J-
1ph/1pc L

White Sulphur Springs,Georgia Row (Greenbrier,The,Georgia Row)
U. S. Rt. 60
HABS WV-131-I
HABS WVA,13-WHISP,1I-
1ph L

White Sulphur Springs,Louisiana Row (Greenbrier,The,Louisiana Row)
U. S. Rt. 60
HABS WV-131-H
HABS WVA,13-WHISP,1H-
2ph/1pc L

White Sulphur Springs,Paradise Row (White Sulphur Springs,Bachelor's Row; Greenbrier,The,Paradise Row; Greenbrier,The,Bachelor's Row)
U. S. Rt. 60
HABS WV-131-B
HABS WVA,13-WHISP,1B-
2ph/1pg/1pc L

White Sulphur Springs,President's Cottage (Greenbrier,The,President's Cottage)
U. S. Rt. 60
HABS WV-131-D
HABS WVA,13-WHISP,1D-
2ph/1pg/1pc L

White Sulphur Springs,South Carolina Row (Greenbrier,The,South Carolina Row)
U. S. Rt. 60
HABS WV-131-F
HABS WASH,13-WHISP,1F-
1ph/1pc L

White Sulphur Springs,Spring House (Greenbrier,The,Spring House)
U. S. Rt. 60
HABS WV-131-A
HABS WVA,13-WHISP,1A-
2ph/1pg L

White Sulphur Springs,Tansas Row (Greenbrier,The,Tansas Row)
U. S. Rt. 60
HABS WV-131-G
HABS WVA,13-WHISP,1G-
1ph/1pc L

HAMPSHIRE COUNTY

ROMNEY

Valley Bank Building
HABS WV-44
HABS WVA,14-ROM,1-
3ph L

HARDY COUNTY

MOOREFIELD

Willow Wall
U. S. Rt. 220
HABS WV-220
HABS WVA,16-MORF,1-
4dr L

HARRISON COUNTY

BRIDGEPORT

Bridgeport Lamp Chimney Co.,Simpson Creek Bridge
Spanning Simpson Creek,State Rt. 58 vic.
HAER WV-23
HAER WVA,17-BRIPO,1-
2dr/6ph/3pg/1pc/fr L

JACKSON COUNTY

RIPLEY VIC.

Staats Mill Covered Bridge
Spanning Tug Fork River,Rts. 40W & 34
HAER WV-31
HAER WVA,18-RIP.V,1-
4ph/4pg/1pc/fr L

JEFFERSON COUNTY

CHARLES TOWN

Courthouse
George & Washington Sts.
HABS WV-21-4
HABS WVA,19-CHART,3-
12ph/1pg/fr L

Happy Retreat (Mordington)
HABS WV-10
HABS WVA,19-CHART,5-
8ph L

Log Cabin
212 Lawrence St.
HABS WV-16
HABS WVA,19-CHART,4-
2ph L

Mordington; see Happy Retreat

236 Washington Street (House,Doorway)
HABS WV-147
HABS WVA,19-CHART,6-
1ph L

CHARLES TOWN VIC.

"Level Green"
HABS WV-22
HABS WVA,19-CHART.V,9-
4ph L

Baptist Church,Old (Jones,C. W. ,House)
Shepherdstown Rd.
HABS WV-35
HABS WVA,19-SHENJ.V,4-
1ph L

Brick Mansion-Locust Hill
HABS WV-145
HABS WVA,19-CHART.V,12-
1ph L

Cassilis; see Manning,Vinton,House

Cedar Lawn (Poplar Hill)
Summit Point Rd.
HABS WV-15
HABS WVA,19-CHART.V,5-
2ph L

Claymont Court
Summit Point Rd.
HABS WV-13
HABS WVA,19-CHART.V,3-
4ph L

Flowing Spring
Shepherdstown Rd.
HABS WV-149
HABS WVA,19-CHART.V,7-
1ph L

Gap View Farm
HABS WV-11
HABS WVA,19-CHART.V,4-
2ph L

Harewood
HABS WV-2
HABS WVA,19-CHART.V,1-
20dr/14ph/2pg/fr L

Henderson,Henry,House
HABS WV-143
HABS WVA,19-CHART.V,8-
1ph L

Jones,C. W. ,House; see Baptist Church,Old

Kennedy,Andrew,House; see Manning,Vinton,House

Manning,Vinton,House (Cassilis; Kennedy,Andrew,House)
Berryville Rd.
HABS WV-144
HABS WVA,19-CHART.V,6-
1ph L

Piedmont (Quarry Banks)
HABS WV-50
HABS WVA,19-CHART.V,10-
13dr/1ph/fr L

Poplar Hill; see Cedar Lawn

Quarry Banks; see Piedmont

St. George's Chapel (Ruins)
HABS WV-3
HABS WVA,19-CHART.V,2-
3dr/7ph/1pg/fr L

Vestal House (Outbuildings)
HABS WV-17
HABS WVA,19-CHART.V,11A-
1ph L

DARKE

Darke,Gen. ,House
HABS WV-5
HABS WVA,19-DARK,1-
2ph L

DARKE VIC.

Hilliard Farm-Framing from Shepherdstown House
HABS WV-38-A
HABS WVA,19-DARK.V,2B-
3ph L

Hilliard's Farm Barn
HABS WV-38
HABS WVA,19-DARK.V,2A-
8ph L

Lucas,Robert,House
HABS WV-24
HABS WVA,19-DARK.V,1-
2ph L

HALLTOWN

Walnut Hill
HABS WV-29
HABS WVA,19-HALTO.V,1-
2ph L

HARPERS FERRY

Anderson,William,Building (Harpers Ferry National Historical Park)
Shenandoah St.
HABS WV-173
HABS WVA,19-HARF,21-
7dr/4pg/fr L

Anderson,William,House,Kitchen (Building 11-A; Harpers Ferry National Historical Park)
Shenandoah St.
HABS WV-173-A
HABS WVA,19-HARF,21A-
3dr/fr L

Annin,Samuel,House (Master Armorer's House,Building Numbers 34-35; Harpers Ferry National Historical Park)
Shenandoah St.
HABS WV-19
HABS WVA,19-HARF,4-
11dr/2ph/fr L

Armorer's Dwelling House (Harpers Ferry National Historical Park)
Shenandoah St.
HABS WV-230
HABS WVA,19-HARF,5-
5ph/1pg L

Armory Fire Engine House; see Brown,John,Fort

Armory Yard Gateway
Murphy Farm,.5 mile S of Hwy 340,Harpers Ferry NHP
HABS WV-162
HABS WVA,19-HARF.V,2-
1pg/fr L

Baltimore & Ohio Railroad: Bollman Bridge (Baltimore & Ohio Railroad: Potomac Crossing)
Spanning the Potomac River at Harpers Ferry
HAER WV-36
HAER WVA,19-HARF,28-;1991(HAER):17
6dr/fr L

Baltimore & Ohio Railroad: Potomac Crossing; see Baltimore & Ohio Railroad: Bollman Bridge

Bank of Harpers Ferry & Bank Annex (Stephenson,Ann G. ,House,Building Number 12; Harpers Ferry National Historical Park)
Shenandoah and High St.
HABS WV-152
HABS WVA,19-HARF,6-;(DLC/PP-1992:WV-5)
17dr/7ph/1pc/fr L

Bldg. 1-A; see Harper House

Bracket House; see Storer College,Brackett Hall

Brown,John,Fort (Armory Fire Engine House; Harpers Ferry National Historical Park)
Shenandoah St.
HABS WV-21-5
HABS WVA,19-HARF,2-(DLC/PP-1992:WV-5)
8dr/14ph/6pg/1pc/fr L

Building No. 20; see House

Building No. 6; see House

Building 11-A; see Anderson,William,House,Kitchen

Building 20; see House

Building 43; see McCabe-Marmion Building

Building 6; see House

Curtis Freewill Baptist Church (Harpers Ferry National Historical Park)
HABS WV-278
HABS DLC/PP-1992:WV-5
3ph/1pc L

Daingerfield,John E. P. ,House; see Master Armorer's New House

Downey,Susan,House,Building Number 15 (Harpers Ferry National Historical Park)
High St.
HABS WV-23
HABS WVA,19-HARF,9-
12dr/3ph/6pg/fr L

Harper House (Wager Mansion; Bldg. 1-A; Harpers Ferry National Historical Park)
HABS WV-168
HABS WVA,19-HARF,10-;(DLC/PP-1992;WV-5)
8dr/19ph/2pc/fr L

Harpers Ferry National Historical Park; see Anderson,William,Building

Harpers Ferry National Historical Park; see Anderson,William,House,Kitchen

Harpers Ferry National Historical Park; see Annin,Samuel,House

Harpers Ferry National Historical Park; see Armorer's Dwelling House

Harpers Ferry National Historical Park; see Bank of Harpers Ferry & Bank Annex

Harpers Ferry National Historical Park; see Brown,John,Fort

Harpers Ferry National Historical Park; see Curtis Freewill Baptist Church

Harpers Ferry National Historical Park; see Downey,Susan,House,Building Number 15

Harpers Ferry National Historical Park; see Harper House

Harpers Ferry National Historical Park; see Jewelry Store,Building Number 14

Harpers Ferry National Historical Park; see Masonic Hall

Harpers Ferry National Historical Park; see Master Armorer's New House

Harpers Ferry National Historical Park; see Morrell House

Harpers Ferry National Historical Park; see Paymaster's Quarters

Harpers Ferry National Historical Park; see Richards,William,Building

Harpers Ferry National Historical Park; see Roeder House

Harpers Ferry National Historical Park; see Roeder Store

Harpers Ferry National Historical Park; see Scottish Castle

Harpers Ferry National Historical Park; see St. John's Episcopal Church (Ruins)

Harpers Ferry National Historical Park; see Stagecoach Inn

Harpers Ferry National Historical Park; see Storer College

Harpers Ferry National Historical Park; see Storer College,Anthony Hall

Harpers Ferry National Historical Park; see Storer College,Anthony,Lewis,Library

Harpers Ferry National Historical Park; see Storer College,Brackett Hall

Harpers Ferry National Historical Park; see Storer College,Cook Hall

Harpers Ferry National Historical Park; see Storer College,Mosher Hall

Harpers Ferry National Historical Park; see Tearney Building

Harpers Ferry National Historical Park; see Unseld,John C. ,Building

Harpers Ferry National Historical Park; see Wager,Gerard B. ,Building

Harpers Ferry National Historical Park; see White Hall

Harpers Ferry National Historical Park,General
HABS WV-224
HABS WVA,19-HARF,3-
1pg/fr L

House (Building No. 20)
S. end of Arsenal Square
HABS WV-164
HABS WVA,19-HARF,26-
1pg/fr L

House (Building No. 6)
Potomac St. (Wager Lot #15-4)
HABS WV-163
HABS WVA,19-HARF,25-
1pg/fr L

House (Building 20)
S. of Shenandoah St. ,Block A,Lots 5 & 6
HABS WV-164
HABS WVA,19-HARF,26-
1pg/fr L

House (Building 6)
Potomac St. ,Wager Lot #15-4
HABS WV-163
HABS WVA,19-HARF,25-
1pg/fr L

Jewelry Store,Building Number 14
(Harpers Ferry National Historical Park)
HABS WV-226
HABS WVA,19-HARF,11-
2dr/fr L

Lockwood House; see Paymaster's Quarters

Masonic Hall (Richards Building; Harpers Ferry National Historical Park)
Shenandoah St.
HABS WV-279
HABS DLC/PP-1992:WV-5
3ph/1pc L

Master Armorer's House,Building Numbers 34-35; see Annin,Samuel,House

Master Armorer's New House (Daingerfield,John E. P. ,House; Harpers Ferry National Historical Park)
Shenandoah St.
HABS WV-232
HABS WVA,19-HARF,12-
4ph/1pg/fr L

McCabe-Marmion Building (Building 43)
Shenandoah St. ,Wager Lot 47,Harpers Ferry NH Park
HABS WV-165
HABS WVA,19-HARF,27-
3pg/fr L

Morrell House (Harpers Ferry National Historical Park; Paymaster Clerk's Quarters)
Columbia & Fillmore Sts.
HABS WV-171
HABS WVA,19-HARF,13-
14dr/6ph/5pg/fr L

Paymaster Clerk's Quarters; see Morrell House

Paymaster's Quarters (Lockwood House; Harpers Ferry National Historical Park)
E. End of Fillmore St.
HABS WV-179
HABS WVA,19-HARF,14-
17dr/8ph/4pg/fr L

Richards Building; see Masonic Hall

Richards,William,Building (Harpers Ferry National Historical Park)
Shenandoah St.
HABS WV-32
HABS WVA,19-HARF,15-
13dr L

Roeder House (Harpers Ferry National Historical Park)
High St. & Hog Alley
HABS WV-174
HABS WVA,19-HARF,16-
4dr/2ph/fr L

Roeder Store (Harpers Ferry National Historical Park)
Potomac St.
HABS WV-223
HABS WVA,19-HARF,17-
4dr/3ph/fr L

Scottish Castle (Harpers Ferry National Historical Park)
Bolivar Heights
HABS WV-228
HABS WVA,19-HARF.V,1-
8ph/1pg L

St. John's Episcopal Church (Ruins) (Harpers Ferry National Historical Park)
Church & Cliff Sts.
HABS WV-231
HABS WVA,19-HARF,19-
7ph/1pg L

Stagecoach Inn (Wilson,John G. ,Building; Harpers Ferry National Historical Park)
Shenandoah St.
HABS WV-229
HABS WVA,19-HARF,20-;(DLC/PP-1992:WV-5)
13ph/1pg/1pc/fr L

Stephenson,Ann G. ,House,Building Number 12; see Bank of Harpers Ferry & Bank Annex

Storer College (Harpers Ferry National Historical Park)
HABS WV-277
H

Storer College,Anthony Hall (Harpers Ferry National Historical Park)
HABS WV-277-A
HABS DLC/PP-1992:WV-5
4ph/1pc L

Storer College,Anthony,Lewis,Library (Harpers Ferry National Historical Park)
HABS WV-277-C
HABS DLC/PP-1992:WV-5
2ph/1pc L

Storer College,Brackett Hall (Bracket House; Harpers Ferry National Historical Park)
HABS WV-277-D
HABS DLC/PP-1992:WV-5
3ph/1pc L

Storer College,Cook Hall (Harpers Ferry National Historical Park)
HABS WV-277-E
HABS DLC/PP-1992:WV-5
2ph/1pc L

Storer College,Mosher Hall (Harpers Ferry National Historical Park)
HABS WV-277-B
HABS DLC/PP-1992:WV-5
2ph/1pc L

Tearney Building (Harpers Ferry National Historical Park)
Shenandoah St.
HABS WV-172
HABS WVA,19-HARF,8-;(DLC/PP-1992:WV-5)
12dr/2ph/1pc L

Unseld,John C. ,Building (Harpers Ferry National Historical Park)
Shenandoah St.
HABS WV-170
HABS WVA,19-HARF,22-
5dr/4ph/6pg/fr L

Virginius Island Hydraulic Works; see Waterpower on Virginius Island

Wager Mansion; see Harper House

Wager,Gerard B. ,Building (Harpers Ferry National Historical Park)
Shenandoah & Potomac Sts.
HABS WV-155
HABS WVA,19-HARF,23-
13dr/8ph/5pg/fr L

Waterpower on Virginius Island (Virginius Island Hydraulic Works)
On Shenandoah River near Potomac River
HAER WV-35
HAER WVA,19-HARF,29-
4dr/37pg/fr L

White Hall (Harpers Ferry National Historical Park)
Potomac St.
HABS WV-156
HABS WVA,19-HARF,18-
8dr/4pg/fr L

Wilson,John G. ,Building; see Stagecoach Inn

KEARNEYVILLE

McIntyre,Effie,House
HABS WV-27
HABS WVA,19-KEARN,1-
1ph L

Southwood
HABS WV-28
HABS WVA,19-KERN.V,1-
1ph L

LEETOWN

Hut; see Lee Barn & Outbuildings

Lee Barn & Outbuildings (Hut)
HABS WV-4
HABS WVA,19-LETO,1AB-
9dr/7ph/1pg/fr L

Woodberry
HABS WV-158
HABS WVA,19-LETO.V,3-
1ph L

LEETOWN VIC.

Royer House (Mantel)
HABS WV-21
HABS WVA,19-LETO.V,2-
1ph L

Traveler's Rest
HABS WV-1
HABS WVA,19-LETO.V,1-
8dr/10ph/1pg/fr L

MIDDLEWAY

Grantham House
HABS WV-51
HABS WVA,19-MIDWA,3-
1ph L

Stone,Gilbert,House
HABS WV-160
HABS WVA,19-MIDWA,2-
1ph L

MYERSTOWN VIC.

Lewis,Anne,House; see Rocks,The

Rocks,The (Lewis,Anne,House)
Shenandoah River
HABS WV-159
HABS WVA,19-MYRTO.V,1-
6ph L

RANSON

Ranson House
HABS WV-48
HABS WVA,19-RANSO,1-
3ph L

RIPPON VIC.

Beverly (Burns,Marshall,House)
Berryville Rd.
HABS WV-36
HABS WVA,19-RIP.V,1-
4ph L

Briscoe House (Bullskin Farm)
Berryville Rd.
HABS WV-39
HABS WVA,19-RIP.V,2-
1ph L

Bullskin Farm; see Briscoe House

Burns,Marshall,House; see Beverly

Mason House; see Rock Hall

Rock Hall (Mason House)
HABS WV-40
HABS WVA,19-RIP.V,3-
2ph L

Wheatland
Berryville Pike
HABS WV-49
HABS WVA,19-WHEAT,2-
4ph L

SHENANDOAH JUNC. VIC

Hazelfield
Warm Springs Rd. vic.
HABS WV-41
HABS WVA,19-SHENJ.V,7-
3dr/fr L

SHENANDOAH JUNCTION

Burr-McGarry House; see Burr,Peter,House

Burr-McGarry House,Springhouse; see Burr,Peter,House,Springhouse

Burr,Peter,House (Burr-McGarry House)
Vic. of State Rt. 9 & Ridge Rd.
HABS WV-42
HABS WVA,19-SHENJ.V,5-
27ph/1pg/2pc L

Burr,Peter,House,Springhouse (Burr-McGarry House,Springhouse)
Vic. of State Rt. 9 & Ridge Rd.
HABS WV-42-A
HABS WVA,19-SHENJ.V,5A-
7ph L

Clearland
Shepherdstown Rd.
HABS WV-31
HABS WVA,19-SHENJ.V,3-
2ph L

Elmwood (Lucas,Rion,House)
HABS WV-25
HABS WVA,19-SHENJ.V,1-
7ph L

Lucas,Rion,House; see Elmwood

Osborne House
Sandy Ridge Rd.
HABS WV-26
HABS WVA,19-SHENJ.C,2-
3ph L

Vickers,Newton,House
Shepherdstown Rd.
HABS WV-37
HABS WVA,19-SHENJ.V,6-
1ph L

SHEPHERDSTOWN

Hilliard Farmhouse
HABS WV-221
HABS WVA,19-SHEP,2-
1ph L

Market House,Old (Shepherdstown Public Library)
HABS WV-161
HABS WVA,19-SHEP,4-
6dr L

Morgan,Richard,House
High St.
HABS WV-166
HABS WVA,19-SHEP,1-
1ph L

Shepherd's Mill; see Shepherd's,Thomas,Grist Mill

Shepherd's,Thomas,Grist Mill (Shepherd's Mill)
High St. Vic.
HAER WV-5
HAER WVA,19-SHEP,3-
4dr/16ph/12pg/2pc/fr L

Shepherdstown Public Library; see Market House,Old

SHEPHERDSTOWN VIC.

Dandridge House; see Grove,The

Falling Spring; see Morgan,Jacob,House

Grove,The (Rose Break; Dandridge House)
HABS WV-34
HABS WVA,19-SHEP.V,3-
1ph L

Morgan,Jacob,House (Falling Spring; Steptoe House)
HABS WV-33
HABS WVA,19-SHEP.V,2-
2ph L

Rose Break; see Grove,The

Springdale
HABS WV-30
HABS WVA,19-SHEP.V,1-
1ph L

Steptoe House; see Morgan,Jacob,House

SUMMIT POINT

Thompson,Dr. ,House
HABS WV-18
HABS WVA,19-SUMPO,1-
3ph L

White House
HABS WV-12
HABS WVA,19-SUMPO,2-
2ph L

WHEATLAND

Locust Hill
HABS WV-9
HABS WVA,19-WHEAT,1-
1ph L

KANAWHA COUNTY

CEDAR GROVE

Church,Old Brick
HABS WV-21-12
HABS WVA,20-CEGRO,1-
2pg/fr L

CHARLES TOWN

Littlepage; see Mansion,Old Stone

Mansion,Old Stone (Littlepage)
HABS WV-21-10
HABS WVA,20-CHAR,1-
2pg/fr L

CHARLESTON

Craik-Patton House (Elm Grove)
Daniel Boone Park,U. S. Rt. 60
HABS WV-214
HABS WVA,20-CHAR,2-
2ph/1pg/1pc/1ct L

Elm Grove; see Craik-Patton House

Gates Building
108 Capitol St.
HABS WV-218
HABS WVA,20-CHAR,3-
1ph/1pg/1pc L

Glenwood (Laidley-Summers-Quarrier House)
800 Orchard St.
HABS WV-211
HABS WVA,20-CHAR,4-
2dr/16ph/16pg/fr L

Laidley-Summers-Quarrier House; see Glenwood

MacCorkle Mansion; see Sunrise

Ruffner Cabin
Daniel Boone Park,U. S. Rt. 60
HABS WV-219
HABS WVA,20-CHAR,5-
2ph/1pg/1ct L

St. John's Episcopal Church
1105 Quarrier St.
HABS WV-215
HABS WVA,20-CHAR,6-
1ph/1pg L

Sunrise (MacCorkle Mansion)
746 Myrtle Rd.
HABS WV-216
HABS WVA,20-CHAR,7-
1ph/1pg/1ct L

West Virginia Capitol
1800 Washington St. E.
HABS WV-217
HABS WVA,20-CHAR,8-
2ph/1pg/3ct L

MALDEN

African Zion Baptist Church; see Malden Historic District

Dickinson,J. Q. & Company,Office Building; see Malden Historic District

4212 Fallam Drive (House); see Malden Historic District

Kanawha Salines; see Malden Historic District

Kanawha Salines Presbyterian Church; see Malden Historic District

4300 Malden Drive (Commercial & Residential Bldg.); see Malden Historic District

4008 Malden Drive (Commercial Building); see Malden Historic District

4105 Malden Drive (House and Shop); see Malden Historic District

4001 Malden Drive (House); see Malden Historic District

4003 Malden Drive (House); see Malden Historic District

4004 Malden Drive (House); see Malden Historic District

4006 Malden Drive (House); see Malden Historic District

4007 Malden Drive (House); see Malden Historic District

4011 Malden Drive (House); see Malden Historic District

4012 Malden Drive (House); see Malden Historic District

4102 Malden Drive (House); see Malden Historic District

4103 Malden Drive (House); see Malden Historic District

4205 Malden Drive (House); see Malden Historic District

4207 Malden Drive (House); see Malden Historic District

4208 Malden Drive (House); see Malden Historic District

4301 Malden Drive (House); see Malden Historic District

4304 Malden Drive (House); see Malden Historic District

4306 Malden Drive (House); see Malden Historic District

4309 Malden Drive (House); see Malden Historic District

4312 Malden Drive (House); see Malden Historic District

4401 Malden Drive (House); see Malden Historic District

4402 Malden Drive (House); see Malden Historic District

4412 Malden Drive (House); see Malden Historic District

4414 Malden Drive (House); see Malden Historic District

4416 Malden Drive (House); see Malden Historic District

4502 Malden Drive (House); see Malden Historic District

4305 Malden Drive (Masonic Lodge); see Malden Historic District

4202 Malden Drive (Shop & House); see Malden Historic District

4203 Malden Drive (Shop); see Malden Historic District

4200 Malden Drive (Store & House); see Malden Historic District

4112 Malden Drive (Store); see Malden Historic District

Malden Historic District (African Zion Baptist Church)
4104 Malden Drive
HABS WV-210-6
HABS WVA,20-MALD,7-
2dr/3ph/6pg/fr L

Malden Historic District (Dickinson,J. Q. & Company,Office Building)
Malden Dr.
HABS WV-210-40
HABS WVA,20-MALD,41-
1dr/4ph/fr L

Malden Historic District (4212 Fallam Drive (House))
HABS WV-210-39
HABS WVA,20-MALD,40-
1dr/4ph/4pg/fr L

Malden Historic District (Kanawha Salines)
Georges,Malden,Planters Drs. & U. S. Rt. 60
HABS WV-210
HABS WVA,20-MALD,1-
9dr/9ph/5pg/fr L

Malden Historic District (Kanawha Salines Presbyterian Church)
4305 Salines Dr.
HABS WV-210-35
HABS WVA,20-MALD,36-
3dr/11ph/7pg L

Malden Historic District (4300 Malden Drive (Commercial & Residential Bldg.)
HABS WV-210-11
HABS WVA,20-MALD,12-
1ph/2pg L

Malden Historic District (4008 Malden Drive (Commercial Building))
HABS WV-210-3
HABS WVA,20-MALD,4-
1ph/2pg L

Malden Historic District (4105 Malden Drive (House and Shop))
HABS WV-210-29
HABS WVA,20-MALD,30-
1dr/1ph/4pg L

Malden Historic District (4001 Malden Drive (House))
HABS WV-210-34
HABS WVA,209-MALD,35-
1ph/4pg L

Malden Historic District (4003 Malden Drive (House))
HABS WV-210-33
HABS WVA,20-MALD,34-
2ph/4pg L

Malden Historic District (4004 Malden Drive (House))
HABS WV-210-1
HABS WVA,20-MALD,2-
1ph/3pg L

Malden Historic District (4006 Malden Drive (House))
HABS WV-210-2
HABS WVA,20-MALD,3-
1ph/2pg L

Malden Historic District (4007 Malden Drive (House))
HABS WV-210-32
HABS WVA,20-MALD,33-
1ph/2pg L

Malden Historic District (4011 Malden Drive (House))
HABS WV-210-31
HABS WVA,20-MALD,32-
1ph/2pg L

Malden Historic District (4012 Malden Drive (House))
HABS WV-210-4
HABS WVA,20-MALD,5-
1ph/2pg L

Malden Historic District (4102 Malden Drive (House))
HABS WV-210-5
HABS WVA,20-MALD,6-
1ph/2pg L

Malden Historic District (4103 Malden Drive (House))
HABS WV-210-30
HABS WVA,20-MALD,31-
1ph/3pg L

Malden Historic District (4205 Malden Drive (House))
HABS WV-210-27
HABS WVA,20-MALD,28-
1ph/4pg L

Malden Historic District (4207 Malden Drive (House))
HABS WV-210-26
HABS WVA,20-MALD,27-
1ph/2pg L

Malden Historic District (4208 Malden Drive (House))
HABS WV-210-10
HABS WVA,20-MALD,11-
2ph/4pg L

Malden Historic District (4301 Malden Drive (House))
HABS WV-210-25
HABS WVA,20-MALD,26-
2pg L

Malden Historic District (4304 Malden Drive (House))
HABS WV-210-12
HABS WVA,20-MALD,13-
2ph/2pg L

Malden Historic District (4306 Malden Drive (House))
HABS WV-210-13
HABS WVA,20-MALD,14-
1ph/2pg L

Malden Historic District (4309 Malden Drive (House))
HABS WV-210-23
HABS WVA,20-MALD,24-
1ph/2pg L

Malden Historic District (4312 Malden Drive (House))
HABS WV-210-15
HABS WVA,20-MALD,16-
4pg L

Malden Historic District (4401 Malden Drive (House))
HABS WV-210-22
HABS WVA,20-MALD,23-
1dr/10ph/4pg L

Malden Historic District (4402 Malden Drive (House))
HABS WV-210-16
HABS WVA,20-MALD,17-
1ph/4pg L

Malden Historic District (4412 Malden Drive (House))
HABS WV-210-18
HABS WVA,20-MALD,19-
1ph/2pg L

Malden Historic District (4414 Malden Drive (House))
HABS WV-210-19
HABS WVA,20-MALD,20-
1ph/2pg L

Malden Historic District (4416 Malden Drive (House))
HABS WV-210-20
HABS WVA,20-MALD,21-
1ph/2pg L

Malden Historic District (4502 Malden Drive (House))
HABS WV-210-21
HABS WVA,20-MALD,22-
4ph/2pg L

Malden Historic District (4305 Malden Drive (Masonic Lodge))
HABS WV-210-24
HABS WVA,20-MALD,25-
1ph/2pg L

Malden Historic District (4202 Malden Drive (Shop & House))
HABS WV-210-9
HABS WVA,20-MALD,10-
2pg L

Malden Historic District (4203 Malden Drive (Shop))
HABS WV-210-28
HABS WVA,20-MALD,29-
1ph/2pg L

Malden Historic District (4200 Malden Drive (Store & House))
HABS WV-210-8
HABS WVA,20-MALD,9-
1ph/2pg L

Malden Historic District (4112 Malden Drive (Store))
HABS WV-210-7
HABS WVA,20-MALD,8-
1ph/2pg L

Malden Historic District (Malden Methodist Church)
4308 Malden Dr.
HABS WV-210-14
HABS WVA,20-MALD,15-
3ph/3pg L

Malden Historic District (Malden Missionary Baptist Church)
202 Wise Dr.
HABS WV-210-38
HABS WVA,20-MALD,39-
1dr/4ph/2pg/fr L

Malden Historic District (Putney,Richard E. ,House)
4406 Malden Dr.
HABS WV-210-17
HABS WVA,20-MALD,18-
3dr/14ph/8pg/fr L

Malden Historic District (4101 Salines Drive (Commercial Building & House))
HABS WV-210-37
HABS WVA,20-MALD,38-
1dr/6ph/5pg/fr L

Malden Historic District (4103 Salines Drive (House))
HABS WV-210-36
HABS WVA,20-MALD,37-
1dr/3ph/3pg/fr L

Malden Methodist Church; see Malden Historic District

Malden Missionary Baptist Church; see Malden Historic District

Putney,Richard E. ,House; see Malden Historic District

4101 Salines Drive (Commercial Building & House); see Malden Historic District

4103 Salines Drive (House); see Malden Historic District

LEWIS COUNTY

ROANOKE

Bee's Shoe Shop & People's Telephone Exchange; see Roanoke,Town of

Bond Barn; see Roanoke,Town of

Bosley Store; see Roanoke,Town of

Conrad,John,House; see Roanoke,Town of

Craig Store; see Roanoke,Town of

Cutright Log House; see Roanoke,Town of

Cutright,James Lewis,House; see Roanoke,Town of

Feeney,Thomas,House; see Roanoke,Town of

Gillooly Hotel; see Roanoke,Town of

Hawkins Store; see Roanoke,Town of

Odd Fellows Lodge; see Roanoke,Town of

Post Store; see Roanoke,Town of

Rhodes Tenant House; see Roanoke,Town of

Rhodes,Erasmus,Barn; see Roanoke,Town of

Rhodes,Erasmus,House; see Roanoke,Town of

Rinehardt Store; see Roanoke,Town of

Roanoke Methodist Protestant Church; see Roanoke,Town of

Roanoke Methodist Protestant Church,Parsonage; see Roanoke,Town of

Roanoke,Town of
HABS WV-209
HABS WVA,21-ROAN,1-
59pg L

Roanoke,Town of (Bee's Shoe Shop & People's Telephone Exchange)
HABS WV-209-J
HABS WVA,21-ROAN,11-
21pg L

Roanoke,Town of (Bosley Store; Hawkins Store)
HABS WV-209-G
HABS WVA,21-ROAN,8-
12pg L

Roanoke,Town of (Conrad,John,House)
HABS WV-209-H
HABS WVA,21-ROAN,9-
27pg L

Roanoke,Town of (Craig Store; Post Store)
HABS WV-209-K
HABS WVA,21-ROAN,12-
19pg L

Roanoke,Town of (Cutright Log House)
Hwy. 38 (Brownsville Rd.)
HABS WV-209-O
HABS WVA,21-ROAN,16-
24pg L

Roanoke,Town of (Cutright,James Lewis,House)
Hwy. 38 (Brownsville Rd.)
HABS WV-209-N
HABS WVA,21-ROAN,15-
43pg L

Roanoke,Town of (Feeney,Thomas,House)
HABS WV-209-I
HABS WVA,21-ROAN,10-
38pg L

Roanoke,Town of (Odd Fellows Lodge; Whitesel Store)
HABS WV-209-L
HABS WVA,21-ROAN,13-
33pg L

Roanoke,Town of (Rhodes Tenant House; Bond Barn)
U. S. Hwy. 19
HABS WV-209-R
HABS WVA,21-ROAN,18-
29pg L

Roanoke,Town of (Rhodes,Erasmus,Barn)
County Rt. 19/7
HABS WV-209-Q
HABS WVA,21-ROAN,17A-
18pg L

Roanoke,Town of (Rhodes,Erasmus,House)
County Rt. 19/7
HABS WV-209-P
HABS WVA,21-ROAN,17-
42pg L

Roanoke,Town of (Rinehardt Store)
HABS WV-209-M
HABS WVA,21-ROAN,14-
32pg L

Roanoke,Town of (Roanoke Methodist Protestant Church)
HABS WV-209-A
HABS WVA,21-ROAN,2-
30pg L

Roanoke,Town of (Roanoke Methodist Protestant Church,Parsonage)
HABS WV-209-B
HABS WVA,21-ROAN,3-
26pg L

Roanoke,Town of (Smith House)
HABS WV-209-C
HABS WVA,21-ROAN,4-
37pg L

Roanoke,Town of (Smith Log House)
County Rt. 23/5
HABS WV-209-S
HABS WVA,21-ROAN,19-
21pg L

Roanoke,Town of (Whelan,M. E. ,House)
HABS WV-209-D
HABS WVA,21-ROAN,5-
47pg L

Roanoke,Town of (Whelan,M. E. ,Office)
HABS WV-209-E
HABS WVA,21-ROAN,6-
16pg L

Roanoke,Town of (White Hotel; Gillooly Hotel)
HABS WV-209-F
HABS WVA,21-ROAN,7-
49pg L

Smith House; see Roanoke,Town of

Smith Log House; see Roanoke,Town of

Whelan,M. E. ,House; see Roanoke,Town of

Whelan,M. E. ,Office; see Roanoke,Town of

White Hotel; see Roanoke,Town of

Whitesel Store; see Roanoke,Town of

MARION COUNTY

BARRACKSVILLE

Barracksville Covered Bridge
Spanning Buffalo Creek on Pike St.
HAER WV-8
HAER WVA,25-BARAC,1-
3dr/10ph/15pg/1pc/fr L

FAIRMONT

Club Deluxe; see 214 Madison Street (House)

High Gate Carriage House
801 Fairmont Ave. (faces Walnut St.)
HABS WV-256
HABS DLC/PP-1993:WV-3
5dr/34ph/17pg/2pc/fr L

Kenyon Hotel; see 312 Madison Street (Commercial Building)

Madison Hotel; see 312 Madison Street (Commercial Building)

312 Madison Street (Commercial Building) (Madison Hotel; Kenyon Hotel)
HABS WV-132
HABS WVA,25-FAIR,2-
2ph/8pg L

214 Madison Street (House) (Club Deluxe)
HABS WV-134
HABS WVA,25-FAIR,1-
7ph/9pg L

Yeager Building
329-331 Adams St.
HABS WV-133
HABS WVA,25-FAIR,3-
4ph/10pg L

FAIRMONT VIC.

Baltimore & Ohio Railroad,Fairmont Bridge
Spanning Monongahela River
HAER WV-14
HAER WVA,25-FAIR.V,1-
8ph/7pg/1pc L

MARSHALL COUNTY

BENWOOD

Baltimore & Ohio Railroad:Benwood Bridge
HAER WV-15
HAER WVA,26-BEN,1-
7ph/1pc L

LITTLETON VIC.

Board Tree Tunnel
HAER WV-37
HAER WVA,26-LIT.V,1-
11ph/1pg/1pc L

MASON COUNTY

POINT PLEASANT

Mansion House,Old
First & Main Sts.
HABS WV-21-2
HABS WVA,27-POPL,1-
20dr/fr L

MINERAL COUNTY

KEYSER VIC.

Baltimore & Ohio Railroad,Keyser Machine Shop
State Rt. 46 NW of Spring St.
HAER WV-22
HAER WVA,29-KEYS.V,1-
11ph/3pg/2pc L

NEW CREEK VIC.

House,Stone; see Tavern,Old Stone

Tavern,Old Stone (House,Stone)
Rt. 50
HABS WV-45
HABS WVA,29-NEWC.V,1-
2ph L

ROCKET CENTER

Washington Bottom Farmhouse
Allegany Ballistics Laboratory
HABS WV-244
HABS DLC/PP-1993:WV-3
18ph/15pg/1pc L

MONONGALIA COUNTY

DELLSLOW VIC.

Elkins Coal & Coke Company,Richard Ovens
Deckers Creek,State Rt. 7-92
HAER WV-21
HAER WVA,31-DELS.V,1-
2dr/9ph/12pg/1pc/fr L

MORGANTOWN

Seneca Glass Company Factory
Beechurst Ave. btwn. Sixth & Eighth Sts.
HAER WV-6
HAER WVA,31-MORG,1-
4dr/42ph/16pg/3pc/fr L

MORGANTOWN VIC.

Arnett,Carl,House
HABS WV-47
HABS WVA,31-MORG.V,1-
2ph L

Easton Roller Mill
West Run Rd.
HAER WV-4
HAER WVA,31-MORG,2-
4dr/24ph/9pg/fr L

Lake Lynn Hydroelectric Power House & Dam
Cheat River
HAER WV-30
HAER WVA,31-MORG.V,2-
58ph/6pg/3pc L

MONROE COUNTY

ALDERSON

102 North Monroe Street (Commercial Building)
102 N. Monroe St.
HABS WV-242
HABS 1991(HABS):4
4ph/5pg/1pc L

102 Railroad Avenue (House)
102 Railroad Ave.
HABS WV-239
HABS 1991(HABS):4
2ph/5pg/1pc L

104 Railroad Avenue (House)
104 Railroad Ave.
HABS WV-240
HABS 1991(HABS):4
3ph/5pg/1pc L

RED SULPHUR SPRINGS

Red Sulphur Springs
Rt. 12
HABS WV-120
HABS WVA,32-RESU,1-
2ph/2pg/1pc L

Red Sulphur Springs,Cottage
Rt. 12
HABS WV-120-A
HABS WVA,32-RESU,1A-
1ph L

SALT SULPHER SPRINGS

Salt Sulpher Springs
U.S. Rt. 219
HABS WV-117
HABS WVA,32-SALSU,1-
3ph/1pg/1pc L

SALT SULPHUR SP. VIC

House
U. S. Rt. 219
HABS WV-178
HABS WVA,32-SALSU.V,1-
2ph L

Documentation: **ct** color transparencies **dr** measured drawings **fr** field records
pc photograph captions **pg** pages of text **ph** photographs

SALT SULPHUR SPRINGS

Salt Sulphur Springs,Bath House
U. S. Rt. 219
HABS WV-117-F
HABS WVA,32-SALSU,1F-
1ph/1pg/1pc L

Salt Sulphur Springs,Chapel
U. S. Rt. 219
HABS WV-117-B
HABS WVA,32-SALSU,1B-
2ph/1pg/1pc L

Salt Sulphur Springs,Cottages
U. S. Rt. 219
HABS WV-117-D
HABS WVA,32-SALSU,1D-
1ph/1pg/1pc L

Salt Sulphur Springs,Erskine House (Ruins)
U. S. Rt. 219
HABS WV-117-E
HABS WVA,32-SALSU,1E-
1ph/1pg/1pc L

Salt Sulphur Springs,Main Building
U. S. Rt. 219
HABS WV-117-A
HABS WVA,32-SALSU,1A-
3ph/1pg/1pc L

Salt Sulphur Springs,Spring House
U. S. Rt. 219
HABS WV-117-G
HABS WVA,32-SALSU,1G-
1ph/1pc L

Salt Sulphur Springs,Store Building
U. S. Rt. 219
HABS WV-117-C
HABS WVA,32-SALSU,1C-
1ph/1pg/1pc L

SWEET SPRINGS

Lewis House; see Lynnside

Lynnside (Lewis House)
State Rts. 3 & 311
HABS WV-59
HABS WVA,32-SWESP,5-
2ph L

Rowan,Andrew S. ,Memorial Home; see Sweet Springs,General View

St. John the Evangelist Church (Roman Catholic)
State Rts. 3 & 311
HABS WV-60
HABS WVA,32-SWESP,6-
2ph L

Sweet Springs Bath House
State Rt. 311
HABS WV-56
HABS WVA,32-SWESP,2-
4ph L

Sweet Springs Cottages
State Rt. 311
HABS WV-57
HABS WVA,32-SWESP,3-
1ph L

Sweet Springs Hotel
State Rt. 311
HABS WV-58
HABS WVA,32-SWESP,4-
5ph/1pg L

Sweet Springs,General View
(Rowan,Andrew S. ,Memorial Home)
State Rt. 311
HABS WV-55
HABS WVA,32-SWESP,1-
1ph L

UNION

Church
HABS WV-121
HABS WVA,32-UNI,2-
1ph/1pc L

House
HABS WV-122
HABS WVA,32-UNI,3-
1ph/1pc L

Rehoboth Church
State Rt. 3
HABS WV-112
HABS WVA,32-UNI,1-
1ph L

MORGAN COUNTY

BERKELEY SPRINGS

Strother,David Hunter,House
HABS WV-43
HABS WVA,33-BERK,1-
2ph L

GREAT CACAPON

Baltimore & Ohio Railroad:Cacapon River Viaduct
HAER WV-20
HAER WVA,33-GRECA,1-
3ph/1pc L

OHIO COUNTY

ELM GROVE

Monument Place (Shepherd Hall)
HABS WV-21-8
HABS WVA,35-ELGRO,1-
14ph/3pg/fr L

Shepherd Hall; see Monument Place

WHEELING

Ackermann,Gregor,House
2319 Chapline St.
HABS WV-189
HABS WVA,35-WHEEL,16-
1dr/6ph/6pg/1pc/fr L

Baltimore & Ohio Railroad,Wheeling Freight Station
Fourteenth & South Sts.
HAER WV-3
HAER WVA,35-WHEEL,4-
5dr/15ph/2pc/fr L

Bank of Wheeling
1229 Main St.
HABS WV-182
HABS WVA,35-WHEEL,8-
1dr/2ph/7pg/1pc/fr L

Bridge on Old National Trail
HABS WV-14
HABS WVA,35-WHEEL,1-
4ph L

Bridgeport Bridge (Wheeling & Belmont Bridge)
Spanning W. Channel of Ohio River, U. S. Rt. 40
HAER WV-25
HAER WVA,35-WHEEL,5-ı1989(HAER):24°
3dr/28ph/1pg/6pc/fr L

Brues,Henry,House; see Irwin-Brues House

Centre Market (Centre Market Square Historic District)
Market St. btwn. Twenty-second & Twenty-third Sts.
HAER WV-26
HAER WVA,35-WHEEL,3-
2dr/15ph/2pg/2pc/fr L

Centre Market Square Historic District
Market St.
HABS WV-184
HABS WVA,35-WHEEL,25-
1dr L

Centre Market Square Historic District; see Centre Market

Centre Market Square Historic District; see Reed Building

Centre Market Square Historic District; see Thoner,John,House

Centre Market Square Historic District; see Zink,William T. ,Double House

Chapline Street Row Historic District
2301-2319 Chapline St.
HABS WV-188
HABS WVA,35-WHEEL,9-
3dr/3ph/1pc/fr L

Chapline Street Row Historic District; see Holliday-Schaefer House

Chapline Street Row Historic District; see Klieves,Bernard,House

Chapline Street Row Historic District; see Klieves,Theodore,House

Chapline Street Row Historic District; see Moore,Nancy,House

Chapline Street Row Historic District; see Schmulbach,Henry,House

Chapline Street Row Historic District; see Wells,Edgar,House

Eckhart,George W.,House
810 Main St.
HABS WV-253
HABS DLC/PP-1993:WV-3
5dr/20ph/20pg/2pc/fr L

First Presbyterian Church
1301 Chapline St.
HABS WV-202
HABS WVA,35-WHEEL,31-
8ph/8pg/1pc/1ct/fr L

Frissell,Dr. John,House
54 Fourteenth St.
HABS WV-197
HABS WVA,35-WHEEL,32-
1dr/4ph/8pg/1pc/fr L

Goering,William,House
701 Main St.
HABS WV-206
HABS WVA,35-WHEEL,33-
4ph/5pg/1pc/fr L

Hazlett,Edward,House
823 Main St.
HABS WV-252
HABS DLC/PP-1993:WV-3
6dr/25ph/26pg/2pc/fr L

Hess,Christian,House
811 Main St.
HABS WV-207
HABS WVA,35-WHEEL,34-
2dr/17ph/7pg/1pc/9ct/fr L

Holliday-Schaefer House (Holliday,John A. ,House; Chapline Street Row Historic District)
2307 Chapline St.
HABS WV-190
HABS WVA,35-WHEEL,12-
6ph/6pg/1pc/1ct/fr L

Holliday,John A. ,House; see Holliday-Schaefer House

Independence Hall; see U. S. Custom House

Irwin-Brues House (Brues,Henry,House; Irwin,Isaac,House)
201 N. Front St.
HABS WV-183
HABS WVA,35-WHEEL,17-
7ph/7pg/1pc/fr L

Irwin,Isaac,House; see Irwin-Brues House

Klieves,Bernard,House (Chapline Street Row Historic District)
2315 Chapline St.
HABS WV-192
HABS WVA,35-WHEEL,15-
1dr/2ph/5pg/1pc/fr L

Klieves,Theodore,House (Chapline Street Row Historic District)
2313 Chapline St.
HABS WV-193
HABS WVA,35-WHEEL,14-
6ph/5pg/1pc/fr L

LaBelle Iron Works
Thirtieth and Wood Sts.
HAER WV-47
HAER DLC/PP-1992:WV-4
5dr/62ph/52pg/5pc/fr L

List,Henry K. ,House
827 Main St.
HABS WV-208
HABS WVA,35-WHEEL,18-
3ph/4pg/1pc L

Main Street
Main St. (W. Side) betw. Fourteenth & Sixteenth
HABS WV-205
HABS WVA,35-WHEEL,19-
1ph/1pc L

Maroon's Department Store; see Reed Building

McColloch Street Cottages
McColloch St. (1300 Block)
HABS WV-203
HABS WVA,35-WHEEL,20-
3ph/10pg/1pc/fr L

Medical Tower Building
Twelfth & Main Sts.
HABS WV-227
HABS WVA,35-WHEEL,21-
3ph/1pc L

Monroe Street East Historic District; see Paxton-Reed House

Moore,Nancy,House (Chapline Street Row Historic District)
2305 Chapline St.
HABS WV-191
HABS WVA,35-WHEEL,11-
1dr/3ph/6pg/1pc/fr L

Paull,George,House
57 Fourteenth St.
HABS WV-198
HABS WVA,35-WHEEL,22-
1dr/4ph/6pg/1pc/fr L

Paull,Thomas,House
1314 Chapline St.
HABS WV-199
HABS WVA,35-WHEEL,23-
2dr/4ph/6pg/1pc/fr L

Paxton-Reed House (Monroe Street East Historic District)
100 Twelfth St.
HABS WV-200
HABS WVA,35-WHEEL,24-
7ph/5pg/1pc/fr L

Reed Building (Maroon's Department Store; Centre Market Square Historic District)
2125 Market St.
HABS WV-185
HABS WVA,35-WHEEL,26-
1dr/5ph/6pg/1pc/fr L

Ridgeley,Absalom,House
58 Fourteenth St.
HABS WV-201
HABS WVA,35-WHEEL,30-
1dr/3ph/5pg/1pc/fr L

Schmulbach,Henry,House (Chapline Street Row Historic District)
2311 Chapline St.
HABS WV-194
HABS WVA,35-WHEEL,13-
1dr/2ph/6pg/1pc/fr L

Speidel,Joseph & Company,Building
1417 Main St.
HABS WV-204
HABS WVA,35-WHEEL,7-
1dr/6ph/5pg/1pc/fr L

Thoner,John,House (Centre Market Square Historic District)
2238 Market St.
HABS WV-186
HABS WVA,35-WHEEL,28-
2dr/3ph/6pg/1pc/fr L

U. S. Custom House (Independence Hall)
Market & Sixteenth Sts.
HABS WV-53
HABS WVA,35-WHEEL,2-
15ph/2pg L

Vigilant Engine House
648-650 Main St.
HABS WV-196
HABS WVA,35-WHEEL,29-
3dr/5ph/7pg/1pc/2ct/fr L

Warwood Tool Company
Foot of Nineteenth St.
HAER WV-48
HAER DLC/PP-1992:WV-4
4dr/38ph/31pg/3pc/fr L

Warwood Tool Company,Worker's House
142 Eighteenth St.
HAER WV-48-A
HAER DLC/PP-1992:WV-4
1ph/1pc L

Wells,Edgar,House (Chapline Street Row Historic District)
2301-2303 Chapline St.
HABS WV-195
HABS WVA,35-WHEEL,10-
1dr/4ph/6pg/fr L

Wheeling & Belmont Bridge; see Bridgeport Bridge

Wheeling Project,1976
HABS WV-181
HABS WVA,35-WHEEL,6-
1dr L

Wheeling Suspension Bridge
U.S. Route 40,Spanning the Ohio River
HAER WV-2
HAER WVA,35-WHEEL,35-
4dr/56ph/30pg/3pc/15ct/fr L

Zink,William T. ,Double House (Centre Market Square Historic District)
2206-2208 Market St.
HABS WV-187
HABS WVA,35-WHEEL,27-
1dr/5ph/6pg/1pc/1ct/fr L

PENDLETON COUNTY

MOUTH OF SENECA

Sites Homestead
Monongahela National Forest (Tract 390) E of Rt.28
HABS WV-61
HABS WVA,36-MOSE,1-
2dr/10ph/8pg/1pc L

PARKERSBURG VIC.

Hammer Mill
Monogahela National Forest
HABS WV-8
HABS WVA,36- ,1-
1ph/1pg L

POCAHONTAS COUNTY

DUNMORE

Dunmore Methodist Church
State Rt. 28
HABS WV-54
HABS WVA,38-DUNM,1-
8ph L

HILLSBORO VIC.

Buck,Pearl S. ,Birthplace; see Stulting Place

Stulting Place (Buck,Pearl S. ,Birthplace)
U. S. Rt. 219
HABS WV-20
HABS WVA,38-HILBO.V,1-
11dr L

MARLINTON

McElwee Building
208 8th St. (Main St.)
HABS WV-234
HABS 1989(HABS):26
2ph/6pg/1pc L

People's Store
Intersection of Rt's 39 & 219
HABS WV-235
HABS 1989(HABS):26
3ph/7pg/1pc L

PRESTON COUNTY

BRETZ VIC.

Elkins Coal & Coke Company,Bretz Ovens
HAER WV-7
HAER WVA,39-BRETZ.V,1-
12ph/1pg/1pc L

ROWELSBURG VIC.

Baltimore & Ohio Railroad,Rowelsburg Bridge
Spanning Cheat River
HAER WV-13
HAER WVA,39-ROWBU.V,1-
4ph/1pg/1pc L

Baltimore & Ohio Railroad:Tray Run Viaduct
Spanning Tray Run
HAER WV-18
HAER WVA,39-ROWBU.V,2-
11ph/13pg/1pc L

TUNNELTON VIC.

Baltimore & Ohio Railroad,Kingwood Tunnel
HAER WV-16
HAER WVA,39-TUN.V,1-
4ph/6pg/1pc L

RITCHIE COUNTY

PENNSBORO

McGinnis Hotel
204 Collins Ave.
HABS WV-236
HABS WVA,43-PENBO,1-
5ph/2pg/1pc L

PETROLEUM VIC.

West Oil Company:Endless Wire Pumping Station
U. S. Rt. 50 (Volcano Vic.)
HAER WV-9
HAER WVA,43-PETRO.V,1-
5dr/48ph/16pg/fr L

SUMMERS COUNTY

ALDERSON VIC.

Federal Reformatory for Women
State Rt. 3,S. of Greenbriar River
HABS WV-113
HABS WVA,45-ALD;1-
2ph/2pg/1pc L

Federal Reformatory for Women,Adminstration Bldg.
State Rte. 3,South of Greenbrier River
HABS WV-113-A
HABS WVA,45-ALD.V,1-
1ph/1pc L

Federal Reformatory For Women,Cottages
State Rt. 3,South of Greenbrier River
HABS WV-113-C
HABS WVA,45-ALD.V,1-
1ph/1pc L

Federal Reformatory for Women,School & Chapel
State Rte. 3,South of Greenbrier River
HABS WV-113-B
HABS WVA,45-ALD.V,1-
1ph/1pc L

Federal Reformatory for Women,Warden's House
State Rt. 3,S. of Greenbrier River
HABS WV-113-D
HABS WVA,45-ALD.V,1D-
1ph L

HINTON

Chesapeake & Ohio Railraod: Hinton Yards (Hinton Yards)
HAER WV-43
HAER 1990 (HAER):14
1dr/fr L

Chesapeake & Ohio Railroad: Hinton Depot (Hinto Depot; Hinton Passenger Station)
Along New River near Greenbriar River
HAER WV-43-A
HAER 1990 (HAER):14
2dr/fr L

Hinto Depot; see Chesapeake & Ohio Railroad: Hinton Depot

Hinton Passenger Station; see Chesapeake & Ohio Railroad: Hinton Depot

Hinton Yards; see Chesapeake & Ohio Railraod: Hinton Yards

TALCOTT VIC.

Graham House
State Rt. 3
HABS WV-114
HABS WVA,45-TALC.V,1-
3ph/1pg/1pc L

TAYLOR COUNTY

GRAFTON

B & O RR, Grafton Bridge; see Northwestern RR,Grafton Bridge

Northwestern RR,Grafton Bridge (B & O RR, Grafton Bridge)
Spanning Tygart Valley River
HAER WV-11
HAER WVA,46-GRAFT,2-
7ph/5pg L

Northwsrn Va (B&O) RR,Grafton Mach. Shop & Foundry
U. S. 119 E of Tygart Valley River
HAER WV-10
HAER WVA,46-GRAFT,1-
5dr/25ph/20pg/2pc/fr L

TUCKER COUNTY

PARSONS VIC.

Parsons Nursery
S. side of U.S. Rt. 219
HABS WV-237
39ph/17pg/5pc H

Parsons Nursery,Cheat District Ranger Office
S. side of U.S. Rt. 219
HABS WV-237-G
HABS 1992(HAER):CA-1
4ph/9pg/1pc H

Parsons Nursery,Cheat District Ranger Residence
S. side of U.S. Rt. 219
HABS WV-237-P
6ph/12pg/1pc H

Parsons Nursery,Civ. Con. Corps. Blacksmith Shop
S. side of U.S. Rt. 219
HABS WV-237-R
1ph/8pg/1pc H

Parsons Nursery,Civ. Con. Corps. Garage
S. side of U.S. Rt. 219
HABS WV-237-Q
3ph/8pg/1pc H

Parsons Nursery,Cone Drying Shed
S. side of U.S. Rt. 219
HABS WV-237-J
7ph/8pg/1pc H

Parsons Nursery,Fernow Exper. Forest Bunkhouse
S. side of U.S. Rt. 219
HABS WV-237-N
5ph/8pg/1pc H

Parsons Nursery,Fernow Exper. Forest Residence
S. side of U.S. Rt. 219
HABS WV-237-M
6ph/11pg/1pc H

Parsons Nursery,Fernow Exper. Forest Well House
S. side of U.S. Rt. 219
HABS WV-237-O
2ph/7pg/1pc H

Parsons Nursery,Implement Building
S. side of U.S. Rt. 219
HABS WV-237-L
5ph/8pg/1pc H

Parsons Nursery,Manager's Residence
S. side of U.S. Rt. 219
HABS WV-237-E
9ph/10pg/1pc H

Parsons Nursery,Nursery Office
S. side of U.S. Rt. 219
HABS WV-237-D
6ph/8pg/1pc H

Parsons Nursery,Oil House
S. side of U.S. Rt. 219
HABS WV-237-H
HABS 1992(HAER):CA-1
2ph/8pg/1pc H

Parsons Nursery,Packing Building
S. side of U.S. Rt. 219
HABS WV-237-A
8ph/9pg/1pc H

Parsons Nursery,Pump House
S. side of U.S. Rt. 219
HABS WV-237-I
3ph/8pg/1pc H

Parsons Nursery,Seed Extractor Building
S. side of U.S. Rt. 219
HABS WV-237-K
6ph/9pg/1pc H

Parsons Nursery,Wash House
S. side of U.S. Rt. 219
HABS WV-237-F
HABS 1992(HAER):CA-1
12ph/10pg/2pc H

Parsons Nursery,Wash House,Original
S. side of U.S. Rt. 219
HABS WV-237-B
3ph/8pg/1pc H

Parsons Nursery,Workshop-Warehouse
S. side of U.S. Rt. 219
HABS WV-237-C
5ph/9pg/1pc H

WOOD COUNTY

PARKERSBURG

Baltimore & Ohio Railroad:Parkersburg Bridge
Ohio River
HAER WV-12
HAER WVA,54-PARK,2-
12ph/9pg/2pc L

Stephenson House
1131 Seventh St.
HABS WV-46
HABS WVA,54-PARK,1-
2ph L

Wood County Courthouse,Old
HABS WV-52
HABS WVA,54-PARK,4-
7ph/3pg/1pc/fr L

Wood County Jail
Market St.
HABS WV-225
HABS WVA,54-PARK,3-
4dr/4ph/2pg/1pc/fr L

WILLIAMSTOWN

Williamstown-Marietta Bridge
Spanning Ohio River btw. Williamstown & Marietta
HAER WV-40
HAER 1990 (HAER):14
73ph/11pg/8pc L

Johnson Wax Corporation Building, Racine, Racine County, Wisconsin. Exterior, close-up of tower from south. Photograph by Jack E. Boucher, August 1969 (HABS WIS,51-RAC,5-6).

Wisconsin

ASHLAND COUNTY

LAPOINTE

Apostle Island National Lakeshore; see LaPointe Light Station,Tower

LaPointe Light Station,Tower (Apostle Island National Lakeshore)
HABS WI-325-A
5dr H

LAPOINTE VIC.

Apostle Island National Lakeshore; see Devil's Island Light Station,Asst. Keeper's Qtrs.

Apostle Island National Lakeshore; see Devil's Island Light Station,Boat House

Apostle Island National Lakeshore; see Devil's Island Light Station,Keeper's Quarters

Apostle Island National Lakeshore; see Devil's Island Light Station,Tower

Apostle Island National Lakeshore; see Michigan Is. Light Sta.,Keeper's House

Apostle Island National Lakeshore; see Michigan Is. Light Sta.,Keeper's Qtrs. & Lighthous

Apostle Island National Lakeshore; see Michigan Is. Light Sta.,New Light Base (1880)

Apostle Island National Lakeshore; see Michigan Is. Light Sta.,Power House

Apostle Island National Lakeshore; see Outer Is. Light Sta.,Fog Signal Building

Apostle Island National Lakeshore; see Outer Is. Light Sta.,Lighthouse & Keeper's Qtrs.

Devil's Island Light Station,Asst. Keeper's Qtrs. (Apostle Island National Lakeshore)
HABS WI-324-C
3dr H

Devil's Island Light Station,Boat House (Apostle Island National Lakeshore)
HABS WI-324-D
1dr H

Devil's Island Light Station,Keeper's Quarters (Apostle Island National Lakeshore)
HABS WI-324-B
3dr H

Devil's Island Light Station,Tower (Apostle Island National Lakeshore)
HABS WI-324-A
6dr H

Michigan Is. Light Sta.,Keeper's House (Apostle Island National Lakeshore)
HABS WI-317-B
2dr H

Michigan Is. Light Sta.,Keeper's Qtrs. & Lighthous (Apostle Island National Lakeshore)
HABS WI-317-A
5dr H

Michigan Is. Light Sta.,New Light Base (1880) (Apostle Island National Lakeshore)
HABS WI-317-D
1dr H

Michigan Is. Light Sta.,Power House (Apostle Island National Lakeshore)
HABS WI-317-C
1dr H

Outer Is. Light Sta.,Fog Signal Building (Apostle Island National Lakeshore)
HABS WI-318-B
1dr H

Outer Is. Light Sta.,Lighthouse & Keeper's Qtrs. (Apostle Island National Lakeshore)
HABS WI-318-A
10dr H

BAYFIELD COUNTY

BAYFIELD

Apostle Islands National Lakeshore; see Light Stations of the Apostle Islands

Light Stations of the Apostle Islands (Apostle Islands National Lakeshore)
HABS WI-332
1dr H

BAYFIELD VIC.

Apostle Island National Lakeshore; see Raspberry Is. Light Sta.,Fog Signal Building

Apostle Island National Lakeshore; see Raspberry Is. Light Sta.,Lighthouse & Keeper's Qtr

Apostle Island National Lakeshore; see Sand Island Light Sta.,Lighthouse & Keeper's Qtrs.

Apostle Islands National Lakeshore; see Raspberry Island Light Station

Raspberry Is. Light Sta.,Fog Signal Building (Apostle Island National Lakeshore)
HABS WI-312-B
1dr H

Raspberry Is. Light Sta.,Lighthouse & Keeper's Qtr (Apostle Island National Lakeshore)
HABS WI-312-A
6dr H

Raspberry Island Light Station (Apostle Islands National Lakeshore)
HABS WI-312
8dr/fr H

Sand Island Light Sta.,Lighthouse & Keeper's Qtrs. (Apostle Island National Lakeshore)
HABS WI-313-A
4dr H

BROWN COUNTY

DE PERE

Wilcox,Randall,House
N. Broadway
HABS WI-28-20
HABS WIS,5-DEPER,1-
2pg L

GREEN BAY

Fairmont Dairy Complex
154-216 N. Broadway St.
HABS WI-310
HABS 1991(HABS):11
14ph/20pg/2pc L

Fort Howard Hospital
Chestnut Ave. & Kellogg St.
HABS WI-28-6
HABS WIS,5-GREBA,2-
6dr/2ph/2pg L

Moravian Church
Moravian St.
HABS WI-28-3
HABS WIS,5-GREBA,1-
7dr/1ph/3pg L

Tank Cottage
S. Tenth Ave.
HABS WI-165
HABS WIS,5-GREBA,3-
4dr/3ph/1pg L

WRIGHTSTOWN

Mallard Road Bridge; see Wrightstown Bridge

Wrightstown Bridge (Mallard Road Bridge)
Spanning East River,on Mallard Rd.
HAER WI-43
HAER 1990 (HAER):13
3ph/2pg/1pc L

BUFFALO COUNTY

ALMA

Upper Miss. River 9-Foot Channel,Lock & Dam No. 4
HAER WI-47
HAER WIS,6-ALMA,1-
118ph/12pg/7pc L

CHIPPEWA COUNTY

ARTHUR

Cobban Bridge; see Yellow River Bridge

Yellow River Bridge (Cobban Bridge)
Spanning Chippewa River on Co. Trunk T
HAER WI-28
HAER 1990 (HAER):13
4ph/9pg/1pc/fr L

CHIPPEWA FALLS

Bridge of Pines (Rumbly Bridge)
Ermatinger Dr. in Irvine Park
HAER WI-36
HAER 1990 (HAER):13
4ph/6pg/1pc/fr L

Marsh Rainbow Arch Bridge; see Spring Street Bridge

Rumbly Bridge; see Bridge of Pines

Spring Street Bridge (Marsh Rainbow Arch Bridge)
Spanning Duncan Creek
HAER WI-37
HAER 1990 (HAER):13
6ph/14pg/1pc L

CLARK COUNTY

LEVIS

Lynch Bridge
Spanning Black River at River Rd.
HAER WI-63
HAER DLC/PP-1993:WI-2
10ph/12pg/1pc L

WARNER TWP.

Hemlock Bridge
Spanning Black River on Warner Dr.
HAER WI-5
HAER WIS,10-WARNT,1-
19ph/29pg/2pc L

COLUMBIA COUNTY

PORTAGE

Indian Agency House
HABS WI-16
HABS WIS,11-PORT,1-
8dr/1ph/2pg L

CRAWFORD COUNTY

LYNXVILLE VIC.

Upper Miss. River 9-Foot Channel,Lock & Dam No. 9
HAER WI-50
HAER WIS,12-LYNX.V,1-
83ph/12pg/6pc L

PRAIRIE DU CHIEN

Benedict,Alonzo,House
HABS WI-244
HABS WIS,12-PRACH,3-
1ph/1pg L

Brisbois Warehouse
HABS WI-245
HABS WIS,12-PRACH,2-
1ph/1pg L

Brisbois,Michael,House
HABS WI-28-18
HABS WIS,12-PRACH,1-
6dr/1ph/3pg L

Dousman Hotel
Water St. at Fisher St. ,Saint Feriole Island
HABS WI-291
HABS WIS,12-PRACH,4-
3dr/28ph/30pg/2pc/fr L

Prairie du Chien,City of
HABS WI-302
HABS WIS,12-PRACH,5-
36pg/fr L

DANE COUNTY

DALEYVILLE VIC.

Hauge Norwegian Evangelical Lutheran Church
State Rt. 78
HABS WI-240
HABS WIS,13-DALY.V,1-
3dr/5ph/3pg L

MADISON

Austin,Albert & Lavinia,House
308 N. Pinckney St.
HABS WI-299
HABS WIS,13-MAD,2-
7ph/5pg/1pc L

Dudley House
508 N. Francis St.
HABS WI-234
HABS WIS,13-MAD,1-
6dr/5pg L

Kleinfelter,Henry G. & Frances,House
312 N. Pinckney St.
HABS WI-298
HABS WIS,13-MAD,3-
4ph/5pg/1pc L

Manchester's Department Store Building
2 E. Mifflin St.
HABS WI-292
HABS WIS,13-MAD,4-
12ph/14pg/1pc L

Schlimgen,Michael J. ,House
24 E. Johnson St.
HABS WI-297
HABS WIS,13-MAD,5-
5ph/2pg/1pc L

DODGE COUNTY

CHESTER TOWNSHIP

Chester Bridge
Spanning Rock River on Old Marsh Rd.
HAER WI-59
HAER 1989(HAER):23
7ph/4pg/1pc L

IRON RIDGE VIC.

Mueller House
County Trunk AP
HABS WI-150
HABS WIS,14-IRON.V,1-
4dr/4ph/4pg L

LEBANON TOWNSHIP

Christian Barn
State Rt. 109
HABS WI-148
HABS WIS,14-WATO.V,1-
3dr/3ph/3pg L

LOWELL

Sock Road Bridge (Westphal Bridge)
Spanning Beaver Dam River
HAER WI-2
HAER WIS,14-LOW,1-
16ph/4pg/1pc L

Westphal Bridge; see Sock Road Bridge

WATERTOWN VIC.

Kuenzi Barn
County Trunk EM
HABS WI-151
HABS WIS,14-WATO.V,3-
4dr/4ph/3pg L

Langholff House & Barn
State Rt. 109
HABS WI-149
HABS WIS,14-WATO.V,2-
6dr/4ph/4pg L

DOUGLAS COUNTY

SUPERIOR

Massachusetts Block
1525 Tower Avenue
HABS WI-314
22ph/14pg/2pc H

EAU CLAIRE COUNTY

EAU CLAIRE

Phoenix Manufacturing Company
Forest & Wisconsin Sts.
HAER WI-10
HAER WIS,18-ECLA,1-
10ph/12pg/1pc L

FOND DU LAC COUNTY

FOND DU LAC

Bragg,Edward S. ,School
149 E. First St.
HABS WI-288
HABS WIS,20-FONDU,1-
18ph/11pg/1pc L

Fountain Island Bridge
Lakeside Park bwtn. Promen Dr. & Fountain Island
HAER WI-23
HAER 1990 (HAER):13
5ph/4pg/1pc L

RIPON

Republican Schoolhouse
Second & Elm Sts.
HABS WI-15
HABS WIS,20-RIPO,1-
2dr/1ph/2pg L

ST. CLOUD

Palm Tree Road Bridge
Spanning Sheboygan River on Palm Tree Rd.
HAER WI-34
HAER 1990 (HAER):13
4ph/4pg/1pc L

FOREST COUNTY

LAONA VIC.

Forest Service Site 09-06-05-206; see Laona Ranger Dwelling & Garage

Laona Ranger Dwelling & Garage
(Forest Service Site 09-06-05-206)
Hwy. 8,Nicolet National Forest
HABS WI-309
8ph/10pg/1pc L

GRANT COUNTY

PATCH GROVE VIC.

Bridgeport Bridge
(See CRAWFORD COUNTY,BRIDGEPORT for documentation)
HAER WI-54
L

PATCH GROVE VILLAGE

Grant-Crawford Co-op Oil Company Building; see Paul,Alexander,Store

Paul,Alexander,Store (Grant-Crawford Co-op Oil Company Building)
Main & North Sts.
HABS WI-289
HABS WIS,22-PAGROVI,1-
6ph/2pg/1pc L

PLATTEVILLE

Mitchell-Roundtree House
HABS WI-28-4
HABS WIS,22-PLAVI,1-
5dr/2ph/3pg L

IOWA COUNTY

DODGERVILLE

Iowa County Courthouse
Main St.
HABS WI-28-15
HABS WIS,25-DODGV,1-
6dr/2ph/3pg L

MINERAL POINT

Cornish Miner's House,No. 1
114 Shakerag Alley
HABS WI-28-17
HABS WIS,25-MINPO,1-
1dr/1ph/4pg L

Cornish Miner's House,No. 2
HABS WI-28-14
HABS WIS,25-MINPO,2-
1dr/1ph/1pg L

Harris Cottage
425 Church St.
HABS WI-239
HABS WIS,25-MINPO,4-
3dr/3ph/2pg L

Odd Fellows Hall
Front & Vine Sts.
HABS WI-237
HABS WIS,25-MINPO,3-
4dr/1ph/1pg L

JEFFERSON COUNTY

PALMYRA

Enterprise Building,The
Main St.
HABS WI-17
HABS WIS,28-PALM,1-
2dr/1ph/1pg L

WATERTOWN

German Methodist Episcopal Church; see Wesley Methodist Church

Milford Bridge; see Tivoli Island Bridge

Milwaukee Street Bridge
Spanning Rock River
HAER WI-33
HAER 1990 (HAER):13
3ph/7pg/1pc L

Octagon House
HABS WI-135
HABS WIS,28-WATO,1-
5dr/1ph/4pg L

Tivoli Island Bridge (Milford Bridge)
Span. Rock Rvr. Chan. to Tivoli Is.(mov. fr. Mil.)
HAER WI-21
HAER 1990 (HAER):13
2dr/6ph/14pg/1pc/fr L

Wesley Methodist Church (German Methodist Episcopal Church)
201 N. Fifth St.
HABS WI-278
HABS WIS,28-WATO,2-
9ph/1pg/1pc L

Wesley Methodist Church,Parsonage
207 N. Fifth St.
HABS WI-279
HABS WIS,28-WATO,3-
9ph/1pg/1pc L

JUNEAU COUNTY

ARMENIA & NECEDAH

Ninth Street Bridge; see Sprague Bridge

Sprague Bridge (Ninth Street Bridge)
Over the Yellow River btwn. Armenia & Necedah
HAER WI-57
HAER 1991(HAER):15
7ph/24pg/1pc L

KENOSHA COUNTY

BRISTOL

Jackson,A.B. House
State Trunk Hwy. 50
HABS WI-301
HABS WIS,30-BRIS,1-
14ph/6pg/1pc L

LA CROSSE COUNTY

LA CROSSE

U. S. Courthouse & Post Office
Fourth & State Sts.
HABS WI-277
HABS WIS,47-LACR,1-
12dr/20ph/13pg/2pc L

LA CROSSE VIC.

McGilvray Road Bridge No. 1
Van Loon Wildlife Area
HAER WI-22
HAER 1990 (HAER):13
3dr/4ph/21pg/1pc/fr L

McGilvray Road Bridge No. 2
Van Loon Wildlife Area
HAER WI-22-A
HAER 1990 (HAER):13
4ph/1pc/fr L

McGilvray Road Bridge No. 3
Van Loon Wildlife Area
HAER WI-22-B
HAER 1990 (HAER):13
7ph/1pc/fr L

McGilvray Road Bridge No. 4
Van Loon Wildlife Area
HAER WI-22-C
HAER 1990 (HAER):13
7ph/1pc/fr L

McGilvray Road Bridge No. 6
Van Loon Wildlife Area
HAER WI-22-D
HAER 1990 (HAER):13
4ph/1pc/fr L

LAFAYETTE COUNTY

BENTON

Coltman Bridge
Spanning Fever River,on Horseshoe Bend Rd.
HAER WI-45
HAER 1990 (HAER):13
2ph/2pg/1pc L

NEW DIGGINGS

St. Augustine's Church
HABS WI-236
HABS WIS,33-NEDIG,1-
4dr/3pg L

LANGLADE COUNTY

ACKLEY

Hall Farm Bridge; see Range Line Road Bridge

Range Line Road Bridge (Hall Farm Bridge)
Spanning W. Branch of Eau Claire Rvr.,on Rang.Line
HAER WI-17
HAER 1990 (HAER):13
2dr/5ph/4pg/1pc/fr L

MANITOWOC COUNTY

FRANKLIN

Branch River Bridge
Spanning Branch River,on Hillcrest Rd.
HAER WI-44
HAER 1990 (HAER):13
2ph/2pg/1pc L

MARATHON COUNTY

MARATHON

Big Rib River Bridge; see Marathon City Bridge

Marathon City Bridge (Big Rib River Bridge)
Spanning Big Rib River,on state Trunk Hwy. 107
HAER WI-38
HAER 1990 (HAER):13
23ph/5pg/2pc L

PLOVER

Eau Claire Dells Bridge
Spanning Eau Claire River (Eau Claire Co. Prk.)
HAER WI-30
HAER 1990 (HAER):13
4ph/6pg/1pc L

SCHOFIELD

Eau Claire River Bridge (Schofield Bridge)
Spanning Eau Claire River,on U.S. Hwy. 51B
HAER WI-46
HAER 1990 (HAER):13
3ph/2pg/1pc L

Schofield Bridge; see Eau Claire River Bridge

WAUSAU

Baumann Building; see Third Street Historic District

Bing & Slimmer General Store; see Third Street Historic District

Fair Store; see Third Street Historic District

Frost Block; see Third Street Historic District

Gensmann Barber Shop; see Third Street Historic District

Gensmann Building; see Third Street Historic District

Halder Plumbing; see Third Street Historic District

Kickbusch Building; see Third Street Historic District

Lindsey Harness Shop; see Third Street Historic District

Miller Hotel; see Third Street Historic District

Northern Hotel
428 Jackson St.
HABS WI-282
HABS WIS,37-WASA,1-
5ph/8pg/1pc L

Paff Building; see Third Street Historic District

Pilot Building; see Third Street Historic District

Ringle Building; see Third Street Historic District

Third Street Historic District
Third & Washington Sts.
HABS WI-117
HABS WIS,37-WASA,2-
5ph/3pg/1pc L

Third Street Historic District (Baumann Building)
216-220 Third St.
HABS WI-117-E
HABS WIS,37-WASA,2E-
2ph/3pg/1pc L

Third Street Historic District (Bing & Slimmer General Store)
212-214 Third St.
HABS WI-117-F
HABS WIS,37-WASA,2F-
1ph/2pg/1pc L

Third Street Historic District (Fair Store)
222 Third St.
HABS WI-117-D
HABS WIS,37-WASA,2D-
1ph/4pg/1pc L

Third Street Historic District (Frost Block)
230 Third St.
HABS WI-117-C
HABS WIS,37-WASA,2C-
2ph/4pg/1pc L

Third Street Historic District (Gensmann Barber Shop)
311 Washington St.
HABS WI-117-M
HABS WIS,37-WASA,2M-
1ph/1pg/1pc L

Third Street Historic District (Gensmann Building)
225-227 Third St.
HABS WI-117-J
HABS WIS,37-WASA,2J-
4ph/5pg/1pc L

Third Street Historic District (Halder Plumbing)
303 Washington St.
HABS WI-117-L
HABS WIS,37-WASA,27-
2ph/1pg/1pc L

Third Street Historic District (Kickbusch Building)
215 Third St.
HABS WI-117-H
HABS WIS,37-WASA,2H-
1ph/5pg/1pc L

Third Street Historic District (Lindsey Harness Shop)
213 Washington St.
HABS WI-117-B
HABS WIS,37-WASA,2B-
1ph/3pg/1pc L

Third Street Historic District (Miller Hotel)
217-221 Third St.
HABS WI-117-I
HABS WIS,37-WASA,2I-
5ph/2pg/1pc L

Third Street Historic District (Paff Building)
200 Third St.
HABS WI-117-G
HABS WIS,37-WASA,2G-
3ph/2pg/1pc L

Third Street Historic District (Pilot Building)
229 Third St.
HABS WI-117-K
HABS WIS,37-WASA,2K-
2ph/3pg/1pc L

Third Street Historic District (Ringle Building)
313-315 Washington St.
HABS WI-117-N
HABS WIS,37-WASA,2N-
1ph/2pg/1pc L

Third Street Historic District (Woessner Tailor Shop)
211 Washington St.
HABS WI-117-A
HABS WIS,37-WASA,2A-
1ph/1pg/1pc L

Washington House
329 Washington St.
HABS WI-281
HABS WIS,37-WASA,3-
7ph/7pg/1pc L

Woessner Tailor Shop; see Third Street Historic District

MARINETTE COUNTY

WAGNER

Koss Bridge; see Wisconsin-Michigan Railroad Bridge

Wisconsin-Michigan Railroad Bridge (Koss Bridge)
Spanning Menominee River,on County Trunk Hwy. "JJ"
HAER WI-60
24ph/34pg/2pc L

WAUSAUKEE VIC.

Ferndale Road Bridge (Lake Road Bridge)
Spanning the Peshtigo River bwtn. Lake & Grover
HAER WI-58
HAER 1991(HAER):15
10ph/8pg/1pc L

Lake Road Bridge; see Ferndale Road Bridge

MILWAUKEE COUNTY

HALES CORNERS

Curtin,Jeremiah,House
Grange Rd.
HABS WI-120
HABS WIS,40-HALCO,1-
2dr/3ph/2pg L

MILWAUKEE

All Saints' Episcopal Cathedral
828 E. Juneau Ave.
HABS WI-265
HABS WIS,40-MILWA,23-
4ph/11pg L

American System-Built Homes
2720 W. Burnham St.
HABS WI-326
HABS DLC/PP-1992:WI-2
4dr/fr L

Basilica of St. Josaphat
601 W. Lincoln Ave.
HABS WI-258
HABS WIS,40-MILWA,28-
13ph/10pg L

Bogk,F. C. ,House
2420 N. Terrace Ave.
HABS WI-252
HABS WIS,40-MILWA,15-
11dr/12ph/8pg/fr L

Brandt House
1205 N. Eighth St.
HABS WI-129
HABS WIS,40-MILWA,4-
4dr/1ph/3pg L

Calvary Presbyterian Church
935 W. Wisconsin Ave.
HABS WI-264
HABS WIS,40-MILWA,22-
2ph/8pg L

Chamber of Commerce (Mackie Building)
611 N. Broadway
HABS WI-158
HABS WIS,40-MILWA,7-
1ph/2pg L

Church,Benjamin,House
1533 N. Fourth St.
HABS WI-13
HABS WIS,40-MILWA,3-
4dr/1ph/1pg L

City Hall
200 E. Wells St.
HABS WI-254
HABS WIS,40-MILWA,17-
21ph/24pg L

Diederichs,Edward,House
1241 N. Franklin Place
HABS WI-262
HABS WIS,40-MILWA,21-
4ph/9pg L

Downer,Jason,House
1201 N. Prospect Ave.
HABS WI-260
HABS WIS,40-MILWA,20-
9ph/9pg L

Evangelische Lutheran St. Johanneskirche (St. John's Evangelical Church)
804 W. Vliet St.
HABS WI-320
HABS 1991(HABS):11
4dr/fr L

First Unitarian Church
1009 E. Ogden Ave.
HABS WI-267
HABS WIS,40-MILWA,31-
11ph/16pg L

Fitzgerald,Robert P. ,House
1119 N. Marshall St.
HABS WI-266
HABS WIS,40-MILWA,30-
5ph/13pg L

Gipfel Brewery
423-427 W. Juneau Ave.
HABS WI-248
HABS WIS,40-MILWA,11-
8dr/7ph/7pg/fr L

Grand Avenue Viaduct (Wisconsin Avenue Viaduct)
West Wisconsin Ave.
HAER WI-27
HAER 1990 (HEAR):13
6ph/12pg/1pc L

Highland Boulevard Viaduct
Spanning Railroad Trcks on W. Highland Blvd.
HAER WI-26
HAER 1990 (HAER):13
4ph/7pg/1pc L

Holy Trinity Church
S. Fourth & W. Bruce Sts.
HABS WI-161
HABS WIS,40-MILWA,10-
7ph/3pg L

Immanuel Presbyterian Church
1100 N. Astor St.
HABS WI-263
HABS WIS,40-MILWA,25-
6ph/9pg L

Insurance Exchange Building (State Bank of Wisconsin)
210 E. Michigan Ave.
HABS WI-157
HABS WIS,40-MILWA,6-
1ph/1pg L

Iron Block
205 E. Wisconsin Ave.
HABS WI-251
HABS WIS,40-MILWA,14-
6dr/14ph/12pg/fr L

Jones Island Wastewater Treatment Plant; see Milwaukee Metropolitan Sewage Treatment Plant

Lake Park Brick Arch Bridge
Lake Park Drive (N. entrance to Lake Park)
HAER WI-20
HAER 1990 (HAER):13
2dr/5ph/9pg/1pc/fr L

Lake Park Lions Bridge
At the Lighthouse in Lake Park
HAER WI-19
HAER 1990 (HAER):13
4dr/6ph/8pg/1pc/fr L

Machek,Robert,House
1305 N. Nineteenth St.
HABS WI-250
HABS WIS,40-MILWA,13-
12dr/18ph/10pg/fr L

Mackie Building; see Chamber of Commerce

Miller,George P. ,House
1060 E. Juneau Ave.
HABS WI-276
HABS WIS,40-MILWA,38-
1ph/1pg/1pc L

Milwaukee County Historical Center; see Second Ward Savings Bank

Milwaukee Fire Department,Engine House Number 27
2647 N. Bartlett Ave.
HABS WI-328
HABS DLC/PP-1993:WI-1
4dr/fr L

Milwaukee Metropolitan Sewage Treatment Plant (Jones Island Wastewater Treatment Plant)
700 E. Jones St.
HAER WI-3
HAER WIS,40-MILWA,37-
95ph/57pg L

Milwaukee V. A. Medical Center,Building No. 38 (Milwaukee V. A. Medical Center,Duplex Qtrs)
5000 W. National Ave.
HABS WI-303-A
HABS WIS,40-MILWA,42-A-
19ph/5pg/1pc L

Milwaukee V. A. Medical Center,Building No. 47 (Milwaukee V. A. Medical Ctr,Single Family Dwelling
5000 W. National Ave.
HABS WI-303-B
HABS WIS,40-MILWA,42-B-
6ph/5pg/1pc L

Milwaukee V. A. Medical Center,Duplex Qtrs; see Milwaukee V. A. Medical Center,Building No. 38

Milwaukee V. A. Medical Ctr,Single Family Dwelling; see Milwaukee V. A. Medical Center,Building No. 47

Milwaukee V.A. Medical Center,Building No.40 (Milwaukee V.A. Medical Center,Greenhouse)
5000 West National Ave.
HABS WI-303-C
9ph/14pg/1pc H

Milwaukee V.A. Medical Center,Greenhouse; see Milwaukee V.A. Medical Center,Building No.40

Mitchell Building
N. Water & E. Michigan Sts.
HABS WI-156
HABS WIS,40-MILWA,5-
5ph/1pg L

North Avenue Viaduct
Spanning Milwk. Rvr. & Chic.,Milwk. & St. Paul RR
HAER WI-25
HAER 1990 (HAER):13
4ph/7pg/1pc/fr L

North Point Water Tower
E. North Ave.
HABS WI-249
HABS WIS,40-MILWA,12-
5dr/9ph/10pg/fr L

Northwestern Mutual Life Insurance Co. Home Office
605-623 N. Broadway
HABS WI-268
HABS WIS,40-MILWA,32-
10ph/24pg L

Pabst Theater
144 E. Wells St.
HABS WI-269
HABS WIS,40-MILWA,33-
12ph/22pg L

Plankinton,Elizabeth,House
1492 W. Wisconsin Ave.
HABS WI-280
HABS WIS,40-MILWA,40-
12dr/41ph/12pg/3pc/fr L

Public Library & Museum
814 W. Wisconsin Ave.
HABS WI-270
HABS WIS,40-MILWA,34-
7ph/23pg L

Public Service Building
231 W. Michigan St.
HABS WI-275
HABS WIS,40-MILWA,39-
4ph/1pg/1pc L

Second Ward Savings Bank (Milwaukee County Historical Center)
HABS WI-256
HABS WIS,40-MILWA,18-
10ph/10pg L

Small Block
704 N. Milwaukee St.
HABS WI-259
HABS WIS,40-MILWA,29-
4ph/9pg L

Smith,Lloyd R. ,House
2220 N. Terrace Ave.
HABS WI-272
HABS WIS,40-MILWA,36-
10ph/11pg L

St. James Episcopal Church
833 W. Wiconsin Ave.
HABS WI-255
HABS WIS,40-MILWA,27-
8ph/12pg L

St. John's Cathedral
812 N. Jackson St.
HABS WI-321
HABS 1991(HABS):11
4dr/fr L

St. John's Evangelical Church; see Evangelische Lutheran St. Johanneskirche

St. Mary's Church
836 N. Broadway
HABS WI-160
HABS WIS,40-MILWA,9-
5ph/4pg L

St. Paul's Episcopal Church & Parish House
904 E. Knapp St.
HABS WI-271
HABS WIS,40-MILWA,35-
10ph/17pg L

St. Peter's Church
2469 N. Murray Ave.
HABS WI-28-10
HABS WIS,40-MILWA,2-
4dr/1ph/4pg L

St. Stanislaus Church
524 W. Mitchell St.
HABS WI-159
HABS WIS,40-MILWA,8-
4ph/4pg L

State Bank of Wisconsin; see Insurance Exchange Building

Stevens Block
724-728 N. Milwaukee
HABS WI-257
HABS WIS,40-MILWA,19-
7ph/8pg L

Stewart,Alexander,House
2030 S. Kinnickinnic St.
HABS WI-28-9
HABS WIS,40-MILWA,1-
5dr/1ph/3pg L

Trinity Evangelical Lutheran Church
1046 N. Ninth St.
HABS WI-273
HABS WIS,40-MILWA,24-
5ph/6pg L

Uihlein,Alfred,House
1639 N. Fifth St.
HABS WI-253
HABS WIS,40-MILWA,16-
11dr/14ph/8pg/fr L

Wisconsin Avenue Viaduct; see Grand Avenue Viaduct

Wisconsin Club Gazebo
900 W. Wisconsin Ave.
HABS WI-274
HABS WIS,40-MILWA,41-
1ph/1pc L

PAYNESVILLE

Paynesville Cemetery Chapel
Rock Creek Vic.
HABS WI-114
HABS WIS,40-PAYNV,1-
2dr/3ph/2pg L

WAUWATOSA

Damon,Lowell,House
2107 Wauwatosa Ave. & Rogers St.
HABS WI-121
HABS WIS,40-WAWTO,1-
7dr/2ph/2pg L

WEST ALLIS

5th District School
8405 W. National Ave.
HABS WI-322
HABS 1992(HABS):WI-1
6dr/fr L

Milwaukee Light,Heat & Traction Company (West Allis Station)
8336 W. Lapham St.
HAER WI-9
HAER WIS,40-WESAL,1-
59ph/12pg/4pc L

West Allis Station; see Milwaukee Light,Heat & Traction Company

MONROE COUNTY

SPARTA

Barracks; see Fort McCoy,Building T-1129

Chapel; see Fort McCoy,Building T-1146

Fort McCoy,Building No. 1463 (Maintenance Shop)
HABS WI-308-E
HABS DLC/PP-1992:WI-4
21ph/10pg/2pc L

Fort McCoy,Building T-100 (Post Administration)
HABS WI-308-K
HABS DLC/PP-1992:WI-4
10ph/10pg/1pc L

Fort McCoy,Building T-1046 (Standard Ward)
HABS WI-308-I
HABS DLC/PP-1992:WI-4
20ph/10pg/2pc L

Fort McCoy,Building T-1129 (Barracks)
HABS WI-308-A
HABS DLC/PP-1992:WI-4
39ph/17pg/4pc L

Fort McCoy,Building T-1146 (Chapel)
HABS WI-308-H
HABS DLC/PP-1992:WI-4
11ph/11pg/1pc L

Fort McCoy,Building T-1551 (Theatre)
HABS WI-308-D
HABS DLC/PP-1992:WI-4
24ph/11pg/2pc L

Fort McCoy,Building T-1863 (Officer Quarters)
HABS WI-308-G
HABS DLC/PP-1992:WI-4
16ph/9pg/2pc L

Fort McCoy,Building T-2000 (Service Club)
HABS WI-308-J
HABS DLC/PP-1992:WI-4
30ph/10pg/2pc L

Fort McCoy,Building T-2002 (Guest House)
HABS WI-308-F
HABS DLC/PP-1992:WI-4
13ph/9pg/1pc L

Fort McCoy,Building T-635 (Mess Hall)
HABS WI-308-C
HABS DLC/PP-1992:WI-4
14ph/20pg/1pc L

Fort McCoy,Building T-801 (Storehouse,Administration & Recreation Building)
HABS WI-308-B
HABS DLC/PP-1992:WI-4
16ph/19pg/2pc L

Guest House; see Fort McCoy,Building T-2002

Maintenance Shop; see Fort McCoy,Building No. 1463

Mess Hall; see Fort McCoy,Building T-635

Officer Quarters; see Fort McCoy,Building T-1863

Post Administration; see Fort McCoy,Building T-100

Service Club; see Fort McCoy,Building T-2000

Standard Ward; see Fort McCoy,Building T-1046

Storehouse,Administration & Recreation Building; see Fort McCoy,Building T-801

Theatre; see Fort McCoy,Building T-1551

SPARTA VIC.

Camp McCoy; see Fort McCoy

Fort McCoy (Camp McCoy)
HABS WI-308
HABS DLC/PP-1992:WI-4
84ph/13pg/6pc/fr L

OCONTO COUNTY

LENA

Rosera,Paul,Barn; see Wood Block Masonry Barn,No. 1

Wood Block Masonry Barn,No. 1 (Rosera,Paul,Barn)
HABS WI-286
HABS WIS,42-LENA,1-
4ph/1pg/1pc L

Wood Block Masonry Barn,No. 2
HABS WI-285
HABS WIS,42-LENA,2-
1ph/1pc L

OUTAGAMIE COUNTY

APPLETON

Western Elevator Company
507 N. Appleton St.
HAER WI-62
6dr/25ph/10pg/2pc/fr L

KAUKAUNA

Grignon House
Augustin Rd.
HABS WI-28-13
HABS WIS,44-KAUK,1-
8dr/2ph/4pg L

NEW LONDON VIC.

New London Bridge (State Trunk Highway 54 Bridge)
Spanning Embarrass River on State Trunk Hwy. 54
HAER WI-29
HAER 1990 (HAER):13
4ph/3pg/1pc L

State Trunk Highway 54 Bridge; see New London Bridge

OZAUKEE COUNTY

CEDARBURG

Cedarburg Mill
215 E. Columbia Ave.
HABS WI-154
HABS WIS,45-CEDBU,1-
5dr/10ph/4pg L

CEDARBURG VIC.

Covered Bridge
Spanning Cedar Creek Vic.
HABS WI-28-12
HABS WIS,45-CEDBU.V,1-
2dr/1ph/1pg L

FREISTADT

Hilgendorf House
State Rt. 167
HABS WI-146
HABS WIS,45-FREI,1-
4dr/4ph/4pg L

HAMILTON

Concordia Mills
HABS WI-28-23
HABS WIS,45-HAM,1-
5dr/1ph/2pg L

MEQUON

Clark, Jonathan, Barn
Cedarburg Rd. & Bonniwell Rd.
HABS WI-311-A
HABS DLC/PP-1993:WI-1
6ph/6pg/1pc L

PORT WASHINGTON

Blake House
511 Grand Ave.
HABS WI-125
HABS WIS,45-POWASH,1-
5dr/2ph/2pg L

Sauk Creek Bridge
Spanning Sauk Creek in Port Washington Harbor
HAER WI-40
HAER 1990 (HAER):13
3ph/2pg/1pc L

THIENSVILLE

Green Bay Road Bridge (Pigeon Creek Bridge)
Spanning Pigeon Creek,on Green Bay Rd.
HAER WI-53
7ph/11pg/1pc H

Old Village Hall; see Thiensville Village Hall

Pigeon Creek Bridge; see Green Bay Road Bridge

Thiensville Village Hall (Old Village Hall)
101 Green Bay Road
HABS WI-307
9ph/9pg/1pc H

THIENSVILLE VIC.

Bonniwell,William T. ,House
Wauwatosa Ave.
HABS WI-28-7
HABS WIS,45-THIVI.V,1-
6dr/1ph/4pg L

Peuschel,Max E. ,House
County Trunk M
HABS WI-155
HABS WIS,45-THIVI.V,2-
7dr/3ph/4pg L

Peushel,Max E. ,Barn & Shed
State Rt. 167
HABS WI-164
HABS WIS,45-THIVI.V,2A-
2ph/2pg L

PEPIN COUNTY

PEPIN VIC.

Chippewa River Bridge
(See BUFFALO COUNTY,NELSON VIC. for documentatn.)
HAER WI-69
L

PIERCE COUNTY

PRESCOTT VIC.

Prescott Bridge
Spanning the St. Croix River on U. S. Hwy. 10
HAER WI-61
HAER DLC/PP-1992:WI-2
25ph/42pg/1pc L

RIVER FALLS

Cedar Street Bridge
Spanning Kinnickinnic River,on Cedar St.
HAER WI-52
HAER 1990 (HAER):13
12ph/3pg/1pc/fr L

SPRING VALLEY

Wagon Trail Road Bridge
Spanning Eau Galle River on Wagon Trail Rd.
HAER WI-31
HAER 1990 (HAER):13
4ph/4pg/1pc L

PORTAGE COUNTY

STEVENS POINT

Andrae,G. F. ,Opera House (Fox Theatre)
1124 Main St., Stevens Pt. Commercial Hist. Dist.
HABS WI-152
HABS WIS,49-STEPO,1-
15ph/10pg L

Andy's Coins; see Gignon,Louis,Upholstery Shop

Fox Theatre; see Andrae,G. F. ,Opera House

Gignon,Louis,Upholstery Shop (Andy's Coins)
1231-1233 Third St., Stevens Pt. Comm. Hist. Dist.
HABS WI-293
HABS WIS,49-STEPO,3-
4ph/2pg L

Iverson's Jewelers (Unique Bar & Liquor)
1217-1225 Third St., Stevens Pt. Comm. Hist. Dist.
HABS WI-296
HABS WIS,49-STEPO,4-
3ph/2pg/1pc L

1201-1211 Third Street (Commercial Building)
Stevens Point Commercial Historic District
HABS WI-294
HABS WIS,49-STEPO,2-
5ph/2pg L

Town Clown/Square Bar; see Zinda Saloon

Unique Bar & Liquor; see Iverson's Jewelers

Zinda Saloon (Town Clown/Square Bar)
844 Main St., Stevens Pt. Commercial Hist. Dist.
HABS WI-295
HABS WIS,49-STEPO,5-
3ph/2pg L

WHITING

Whiting-Plover Paper Mill
3243 Whiting Rd.
HAER WI-56
11ph/20pg/1pc/fr H

Whiting-Plover Paper Mill,Building No. 1
3243 Whiting Rd.
HAER WI-56-A
1ph/1pc H

Whiting-Plover Paper Mill,Building No. 17
3243 Whiting Rd.
HAER WI-56-G
1ph/1pc H

Whiting-Plover Paper Mill,Building No. 2
3243 Whiting Rd.
HAER WI-56-B
2ph/1pc H

Whiting-Plover Paper Mill,Building No. 3
3243 Whiting Rd.
HAER WI-56-C
2ph/1pc H

Whiting-Plover Paper Mill,Building No. 4
3243 Whiting Rd.
HAER WI-56-D
2ph/1pc H

Whiting-Plover Paper Mill,Building No. 5
3243 Whiting Rd.
HAER WI-56-E
3ph/1pc H

Whiting-Plover Paper Mill,Building No. 6
3243 Whiting Rd.
HAER WI-56-F
1ph/1pc H

PRICE COUNTY

KENNAN

Kennan-Jump River Bridge
Span. S. fork of Jump Rvr. on Co. Hwy. "N"
HAER WI-55
HAER 1990 (HAER):13
14ph/1pc L

PARK FALLS VIC.

Round Lake Logging Dam
Flambeau River,South Fork
HAER WI-7
HAER WIS,50-PATA.V,1-
4dr/13ph/63pg/1pc L

RACINE COUNTY

BURLINGTON

Bienemann Bridge; see White River Bridge

Immaculate Conception Church
HABS WI-126
HABS WIS,51-BURL,1-
2dr/2ph/2pg L

Luther Hall
Jefferson & Dyer Sts.
HABS WI-127
HABS WIS,51-BURL,2-
6dr/1ph/3pg L

Meinhardt Bank
Chestnut & Pine Sts.
HABS WI-131
HABS WIS,51-BURL,3-
2dr/1ph/3pg L

White River Bridge (Bienemann Bridge)
Spanning Honey Creek on Bieneman Rd.
HAER WI-16
HAER 1990 (HAER):13
3dr/7ph/7pg/1pc/fr L

BURLINGTON VIC.

Mormon House
Hwy. 20
HABS WI-130
HABS WIS,51-BURL.V,1-
2dr/1ph/4pg L

HONEY CREEK VIC.

Fraser,James,House
HABS WI-140
HABS WIS,51- ,1-
7dr/3ph/3pg L

RACINE

First Presbyterian Church
Seventh St. & College Ave.
HABS WI-28-8
HABS WIS,51-RACI,2-
8dr/2ph/3pg L

Fratt House,The
HABS WI-124
HABS WIS,51-RACI,3-
7dr/2ph/2pg L

Horlick Drive Bridge (Island Park/Horlick Park Bridge)
Carries Horlick Dr. over Root Creek
HAER WI-32
HAER 1990 (HAER):13
3ph/2pg/1pc L

Hunt House
1247 Main St.
HABS WI-28-1
HABS WIS,51-RACI,1-
5dr/1ph/3pg L

Island Park/Horlick Park Bridge; see Horlick Drive Bridge

Johnson Wax Corporation Building
1525 Howe St.
HABS WI-284
HABS WIS,51-RACI,5-
30ph/1pg/2pc L

Kinzie Avenue Bridge; see West Sixth Street Bridge

Kuehneman,William F. ,House
1135 S. Main St.
HABS WI-153
HABS WIS,51-RACI,4-
11dr/6ph/5pg L

Louis Morgensen-William Rowan Building
224-226 State St.
HABS WI-315
HABS 1991(HABS):11
6ph/15pg/1pc L

NW Trunk & Traveling Bag Mfg. Co.; see Secor,M.M.,Trunk Company

NW Trunk & Traveling Bag Mfg. Co.,Central Office; see Secor,M.M.,Trunk Company,Central Office

NW Trunk & Traveling Bag Mfg. Co.,Industrial Bldg.; see Secor,M.M.,Trunk Company,Industrial Bldg.

Secor,M.M.,Trunk Company (NW Trunk & Traveling Bag Mfg. Co.)
401,415,& 427 Lake Ave.
HABS WI-304
HABS WIS,51-RACI,6-
3ph/1pc L

Secor,M.M.,Trunk Company,Central Office (NW Trunk & Traveling Bag Mfg. Co.,Central Office)
401 Lake Ave.
HABS WI-304-A
HABS WIS,51-RACI,6-A-
5ph/7pg/1pc L

Secor,M.M.,Trunk Company,Industrial Bldg. (NW Trunk & Traveling Bag Mfg. Co.,Industrial Bldg.
415 Lake Ave.
HABS WI-304-B
HABS WIS,RACI,6-B-
5ph/6pg/1pc L

Secor,M.M.,Trunk Company,Industrial Bldg. (NW Trunk & Traveling Bag Mfg. Co.,Industrial Bldg.
427 Lake Ave.
HABS WI-304-C
HABS WIS,51-RACI,6-C-
5ph/6pg/1pc L

West Sixth Street Bridge (Kinzie Avenue Bridge)
Spanning Root River at W. Sixth St. & Kinzie Ave.
HAER WI-18
HAER 1990 (HAER):13
3dr/8ph/9pg/1pc/fr L

ROCHESTER VIC.

Russell,Henry,House
Old Hoyt Rd.
HABS WI-138
HABS WIS,51-ROCH.V,1-
3dr/1ph/2pg L

RICHLAND COUNTY

BUENA VISTA

Bear Creek Bridge
Spanning Bear Creek on St. Killian Rd.
HAER WI-42
HAER 1990 (HAER):13
4ph/2pg/1pc L

ROCKBRIDGE

Cunningham Lane Bridge
Spanning Pine River on Cunningham Lane near Hwy.80
HAER WI-51
HAER 1990 (HAER):13
7ph/9pg/1pc L

ROCK COUNTY

BELOIT VIC.

Lathers Road Bridge; see Turtleville Iron Bridge

Turtleville Iron Bridge (Lathers Road Bridge)
Spanning Turtle Creek,on Lathers Rd.
HAER WI-4
HAER 1990 (HAER):13
8ph/4pg/2pc L

MILTON

Inn,Old; see Milton House

Milton House (Inn,Old)
Fort Atkinson St.
HABS WI-119
HABS WIS,53-MILT,2-
6dr/1ph/2pg/fr L

Pioneer Log Cabin
Public Square Vic.
HABS WI-18
HABS WIS,53-MILT,1-
1dr/1ph/2pg L

TIFFANY

Chicago & North Western Railway Bridge No. 128 (Tiffany Stone Bridge)
Spanning Turtle Creek
HAER WI-24
HAER 1990 (HAER):13
8ph/5pg/1pc L

Tiffany Stone Bridge; see Chicago & North Western Railway Bridge No. 128

SAUK COUNTY

BARABOO

Badger Army Ammunition Plant
HAER WI-8
HAER WIS,56-BARAB,2-
50pg/fr L

Manchester Street Bridge
Spanning Baraboo River on Manchester St.
HAER WI-14
HAER WIS,56-BARAB,3-
10ph/8pg/1pc L

Ringling,AL. Theatre
136 Fourth St.
HABS WI-261
HABS WIS,56-BARAB,1-
7ph/20pg L

MERRIMACK VIC.

Chicago & North Western Railway Bridge No. 344 (Goette Road Bridge)
Spanning Goette Rd.
HAER WI-39
HAER 1990 (HAER):13
4ph/3pg/1pc L

Goette Road Bridge; see Chicago & North Western Railway Bridge No. 344

SHEBOYGAN COUNTY

GREENBUSH

Wade House
HABS WI-122
HABS WIS,59-GREBU,1-
7dr/3ph/4pg L

TAYLOR COUNTY

MEDFORD

Medford Soo Line Depot
109 West State Street
HABS WI-327
12ph/20pg/1pc H

TREMPEALEAU COUNTY

TREMPEALEAU VIC.

Upper Miss. River 9-Foot Channel,Lock & Dam No. 6
HAER WI-48
HAER WIS,61-TREM.V,1-
79ph/9pg/5pc L

VERNON COUNTY

GENOA VIC.

Upper Miss. River 9-Foot Channel,Lock & Dam No. 8
On Mississippi Riv. near Housto Co.,MN (see notes)
HAER WI-49
HAER 1992(HAER):WI-1
120ph/10pg/9pc L

LA FARGE

Bridge No. 18 (Old Hudson Toll Bridge)
Spanning Kickapoo River
HAER WI-65
HAER DLC/PP-1992:WI-4
17ph/5pg/2pc L

Old Hudson Toll Bridge; see Bridge No. 18

LA FARGE VIC.

Old Riverside Park Bridge; see State Highway Bridge No. 16

State Highway Bridge No. 16 (Old Riverside Park Bridge)
Spanning the Kickapoo River
HAER WI-64
HAER DLC/PP-1992:WI-4
17ph/5pg/1pc L

WESTBY

Thorson Block
200 Main St.
HABS WI-316
HABS DLC/PP-1993:WI-1
9ph/10pg/1pc L

WALWORTH COUNTY

EAST TROY VIC.

School,Stone
HABS WI-19
HABS WIS,64-TROYE.V,1-
2dr/1pg L

ELKHORN

Octagonal House
E. South St.
HABS WI-14
HABS WIS,64-ELK,1-
6dr/1ph/1pg L

LAKE GENEVA

Geneva Hotel
HABS WI-283
HABS WIS,64-LAGE,1-
6ph/1pc L

WASHINGTON COUNTY

ACKERVILLE VIC.

Lehner,Phillip,House
U. S. 41 Vic.
HABS WI-144
HABS WIS,66-ACKVI.V,1-
3dr L

ADDISON

Beaver Dam Road Bridge
Spanning Rock River,on Beaver Dam Rd.
HAER WI-41
HAER 1990 (HAER):13
2ph/2pg/1pc L

JACKSON

Koepsel House
HABS WI-147
HABS WIS,66-JACSO,1-
5dr L

JACKSON VIC.

Krueger House
State Rt. 60
HABS WI-142
HABS WIS,66-JACSO.V,1-
4dr L

Rusch Cottage
W. of Kirchhayn
HABS WI-143
HABS WIS,66-KIRHA.V,2-
3dr L

KIRCHHAYN VIC.

Turck,Christian,House
HABS WI-28-5
HABS WIS,66-KIRHA.V,1-
5dr/2ph/3pg L

KRICHHAYN

Krause House
Spring Valley & Maple Rds.
HABS WI-145
HABS WIS,66-KIRHA,1-
3dr L

RICHFIELD

Lehmann House
HABS WI-141
HABS WIS,66-RICH,1-
3dr L

Documentation: **ct** color transparencies **dr** measured drawings **fr** field records **pc** photograph captions **pg** pages of text **ph** photographs

WEST BEND VIC.

Maxon Farmhouse
HABS WI-112
HABS WIS,66-BENN.V,1-
6dr/2ph/1pg L

WAUKESHA COUNTY

BIG BEND VIC.

Smith,Jesse,Cobblestone Inn
HABS WI-28-16
HABS WIS,67-BIGB.V,1-
7dr/3ph/3pg L

CHAMBERLAIN

Martin Inn
HABS WI-113
HABS WIS,67-CHAM,1-
9dr/2pg L

DELAFIELD

Hawk's Inn
Main & Genesee Sts.
HABS WI-110
HABS WIS,67-DELA,1-
6dr/2ph/1pg L

St. John Chrysostom Church
Church St.
HABS WI-162
HABS WIS,67-DELA,2-
5ph/3pg L

MEONOMINEE FALLS VIC

Miller,Charles,House
County Line Rd.
HABS WI-28-11
HABS WIS,67-MENFA.V,1-
6dr/2ph/3pg L

MERTON

First Baptist Church; see Merton Baptist Church

Merton Baptist Church (First Baptist Church)
HABS WI-28-19
HABS WIS,67-MERT,1-
5dr/1ph/3pg L

MILWAUKEE VIC.

Dunkel,Robert,Inn
Bluemound Rd.
HABS WI-28-2
HABS WIS,67- ,1-
6dr/1ph/4pg L

NASHOTAH VIC.

Chapel of St. Mary the Virgin
Upper Nashotah Lake
HABS WI-163
HABS WIS,67-NASH.V,1-
2dr/6ph/4pg/1pc L

OKAUCHEE

Okauchee House (Okauchee Inn)
U. S. Hwys. 16 & 19
HABS WI-11
HABS WIS,67-OKAU,1-
8dr/2ph/2pg L

Okauchee Inn; see Okauchee House

PROSPECT

Baptist Church
State Hwy. 15
HABS WI-12
HABS WIS,67-PROSP,1-
5dr/3ph/2pg L

Smith,William,Farmhouse
HABS WI-116
HABS WIS,67-PROSP,3-
3dr/1ph/1pg L

Vanderpool Farmhouse
HABS WI-115
HABS WIS,67-PROSP,2-
5dr/2ph/1pg L

SAYLESVILLE

Booth House
HABS WI-132
HABS WIS,67-SAYVI.V,1-
6dr/1ph/3pg L

WAUKESHA

Lain-Estberg House
299 Wisconsin Ave.
HABS WI-133
HABS WIS,67-WAUK,2-
11dr/1ph/4pg L

Town Hall
Wisconsin Ave.
HABS WI-111
HABS WIS,67-WAUK,1-
4dr/1ph/2pg L

WAUPACA COUNTY

KING

onsin Home for Vets.,217 Bragg Ave. (House)
HABS WI-323-H
HABS MO,96-SALU,77-
2ph/1pg/1pc H

Wisconsin Home for Vet.,414 North Dr. (Cottage)
HABS WI-323-O
HABS MO,96-SALU,77-
2ph/1pg/1pc H

Wisconsin Home for Veterans
HABS WI-323
1dr/8ph/18pg/1pc H

Wisconsin Home for Vets.,113 Wright Ave. (House)
HABS WI-323-A
HABS MO,96-SALU,77-
2ph/1pg/1pc H

Wisconsin Home for Vets.,114 Wright Ave. (House)
HABS WI-323-B
HABS MO,96-SALU,77-
2ph/1pg/1pc H

Wisconsin Home for Vets.,115 Wright Ave. (House)
HABS WI-323-C
HABS MO,96-SALU,77-
2ph/1pg/1pc H

Wisconsin Home for Vets.,116 Bragg Ave. (House)
HABS WI-323-F
HABS MO,96-SALU,77-
4ph/1pg/1pc H

Wisconsin Home for Vets.,117 Bragg Ave. (House)
HABS WI-323-E
HABS MO,96-SALU,77-
4ph/1pg/1pc H

Wisconsin Home for Vets.,118 Bragg Ave. (House)
HABS WI-323-D
HABS MO,96-SALU,77-
2ph/1pg/1pc H

Wisconsin Home for Vets.,216 Bragg Ave. (House)
HABS WI-323-G
HABS MO,96-SALU,77-
4ph/2pg/1pc H

Wisconsin Home for Vets.,218 Bragg Ave. (House)
HABS WI-323-I
HABS MO,96-SALU,77-
2ph/1pg/1pc H

Wisconsin Home for Vets.,219 Bragg Ave. (House)
HABS WI-323-J
HABS MO,96-SALU,77-
2ph/1pg/1pc H

Wisconsin Home for Vets.,308N (House)
308N (Street Unnamed)
HABS WI-323-K
HABS MO,96-SALU,77-
2ph/1pg/1pc H

Wisconsin Home for Vets.,308S (Garage)
308S (Street Unnamed)
HABS WI-323-M
HABS MO,96-SALU,77-
2ph/1pg/1pc H

Wisconsin Home for Vets.,412 North Dr. (Cottage)
HABS WI-323-N
HABS MO,96-SALU,77-
4ph/1pg/1pc H

Wisconsin Home for Vets.,415 North Dr. (Cottage)
HABS WI-323-P
HABS MO,96-SALU,77-
4ph/1pg/1pc H

Wisconsin Home for Vets.,416 (Cottage)
416 (Street Unnamed)
HABS WI-323-L
HABS MO,96-SALU,77-
2ph/1pg/1pc H

SCANDINAVIA

Mill Bridge (Mill Street Bridge)
Spanning Little Wolf Rvr. on Mill St.
HAER WI-35
HAER 1990 (HAER):13
3ph/3pg/1pc L

Mill Street Bridge; see Mill Bridge

WAUPACA

Fisher-Fallgatter Mill
HAER WI-1
HAER HABS WIS,68-WAUP,1-
39ph/106pg/3pc L

WINNEBAGO COUNTY

MENASHA

Menasha City Hall & Fire Station
124 Main St.
HABS WI-306
HABS 1991(HABS):11
6ph/13pg/1pc L

MENASHAM

Marx,John House
108 Main St.
HABS WI-305
HABS WIS,70-MENA,1-
9ph/8pg/1pc L

NEENAH

Doty Loggery; see Grand Loggery

Grand Loggery (Doty Loggery)
E. Lincoln Ave.
HABS WI-118
HABS WIS,70-NENA,1-
5dr/2ph/2pg L

OSHKOSH

Borman,Henry,Saloon; see 15-27 North Main Street (Commercial Buildings)

Deltox Complex; see Oshkosh Grass Matting Company

Fox Valley Technical Institute Building
228 Algoma Blvd.
HABS WI-290
HABS WIS,70-OSH,2-
11ph/9pg L

Glatz,William J. ,Building; see 15-27 North Main Street (Commercial Buildings)

Good Knight's Bar; see 15-27 North Main Street (Commercial Buildings)

15-27 North Main Street (Commercial Buildings)
HABS WI-287
HABS WIS,70-OSH,1-
3ph/1pc/fr L

15-27 North Main Street (Commercial Buildings) (Borman,Henry,Saloon; Wharf Bar)
27 N. Main St.
HABS WI-287-E
HABS WIS,70-OSH,3E-
5pg L

15-27 North Main Street (Commercial Buildings) (Glatz,William J. ,Building; Seifeldt Carpet Store)
15 N. Main St.
HABS WI-287-A
HABS WIS,70-OSH,3A-
5pg L

15-27 North Main Street (Commercial Buildings) (Rahr Saloon; Good Knight's Bar)
25 N. Main St.
HABS WI-287-D
HABS WIS,70-OSH,3D-
5pg L

15-27 North Main Street (Commercial Buildings) (Seefluth Building; Seefluth Paint Store)
19-21 N. Main St.
HABS WI-287-B
HABS WIS,70-OSH,3B-
1ph/11pg/1pc L

15-27 North Main Street (Commercial Buildings) (Weisbrod's Hall)
23 N. Main St.
HABS WI-287-C
HABS WIS,70-OSH,3C-
2ph/4pg/1pc L

Oshkosh Grass Matting Company (Deltox Complex)
35 Wisconsin St.
HAER WI-11
HAER WIS,70-OSH,1-
35ph/28pg/3pc L

Rahr Saloon; see 15-27 North Main Street (Commercial Buildings)

Seefluth Building; see 15-27 North Main Street (Commercial Buildings)

Seefluth Paint Store; see 15-27 North Main Street (Commercial Buildings)

Seifeldt Carpet Store; see 15-27 North Main Street (Commercial Buildings)

Weisbrod's Hall; see 15-27 North Main Street (Commercial Buildings)

Wharf Bar; see 15-27 North Main Street (Commercial Buildings)

The Carrissa Mine, South Pass City vicinity, Fremont County, Wyoming. General view of smelter from west. Photograph by Jack E. Boucher, October 1974 (HABS WYO,7-SOPAC,3-12).

North Platte River Bowstring Truss Bridge, Fort Laramie vicinity, Goshen County, Wyoming. Bridge from northeast. Photograph by Jack E. Boucher, 1974 (HAER WYO,8-FOLA.V,1-1).

Wyoming

ALBANY COUNTY

BOSLER VIC.

Laramie River Bridge
County Rd. 740
HAER WY-17-J
HAER 1989(HAER):25
3ph/2pg/1pc L

CENTENNIAL

Knight,S. H. Science Camp
State Rt. 130
HABS WY-75
HABS WYO,1-CENT.V,1-
17ph/2ct L

CENTENNIAL VIC.

Cliff Mine
Centennial Ridge,Medicine Bow Nat'l Forest
HAER WY-18
HAER WYO,1-CENT.V,2-
9pg L

Cliff Mine,Bunkhouses
Centennial Ridge,Medicine Bow National Forest
HAER WY-18-A
HAER WYO,1-CENT.V,2-A-
5ph/1pg/1pc L

Cliff Mine,Log Mill
Centennial Ridge,Medicine Bow Nat'l Foraest
HAER WY-18-B
HAER WYO,1-CENT.V,2-B-
5ph/1pg/1pc L

Cliff Mine,Mine Tailings Pile
Centennial Ridge,Medicine Bow Nat'l Forest
HAER WY-18-C
HAER WYO,1-CENT.V,2-C-
1ph/1pg/1pc L

Queen Mine
Centennial Ridge,Medicine Bow Nat'l Forest
HAER WY-19
HAER WYO,1-CENT.V,3-
8pg L

Queen Mine,Log Structures
Centennial Ridge,Medicine Bow Nat'l Forest
HAER WY-19-C
HAER WYO,1-CENT.V,3-C-
1ph/1pg/1pc L

Queen Mine,Outhouse
Centennial Ridge,Medicine Bow Nat'l Forest
HAER WY-19-B
HAER WYO,1-CENT.V,3-B-
1ph/1pg/1pc L

Queen Mine,Shafthouse
Centennial Ridge,Medicine Bow Nat'l Forest
HAER WY-19-A
HAER WYO,1-CENT.V,3-A-
7ph/1pg/1pc L

KEYSTONE VIC.

Joker Mine
Medicine Bow National Forest,3.2 mi. NW of Keyston
HAER WY-45
HAER DLC/PP-1992:WY-2
1ph/22pg/1pc L

Joker Mine,Log Cabin
Medicine Bow National Forest,NW of Keystone
HAER WY-45-B
HAER DLC/PP-1992:WY-2
2ph/1pc L

Joker Mine,Shafthouse
Medicine Bow National Forest,NW of Keystone
HAER WY-45-A
HAER DLC/PP-1992:WY-2
12ph/1pc L

LARAMIE

Ames Monument
Interstate 80
HABS WY-72
HABS WYO,1-LARAM,1-
6ph/8pg/2ct L

Ivinson Mansion (Laramie Plains Museum)
603 Ivinson Ave.
HABS WY-74
HABS WYO,1-LARAM,2-
23ph/3ct L

Laramie Plains Museum; see Ivinson Mansion

ROCK RIVER

Rock Creek Station
Junction of Rock Creek & Union Pacific Railroad
HABS WY-55
HABS WYO,1-ROCRI.V,1-
30ph/11ct L

ROCK RIVER VIC.

Rock Creek Water Tower
Junction of Rock Creek & Union Pacific Railroad
HABS WY-55-A
HABS WYO,1-ROCRI.V,1A-
2dr/7ph/6pg/fr L

Rock River Union Pacific Snowshed Plant
.6 Mile N. of Rock River
HAER WY-6
HAER 1989(HAER):25
1dr/12ph/15pg/1pc L

W. LARAMIE

Wyoming Territorial Penitentiary
N. side of State Rt. 130
HABS WY-76
HABS WYO,1-WLARM,1-
16ph/3ct L

WHEATLAND VIC.

Padgett,William H. ,House
Flying X Ranch
HABS WY-84
HABS WYO,1-WHELA.V,1-
2dr L

WOODS LANDING VIC.

Boswell,N. K. Ranch
State Hwy. 10
HABS WY-85
HABS WYO,1-WOLAN.V,1-
1dr L

BIG HORN COUNTY

LOVELL VIC.

Shoshone River Bridge
County Rd. 111
HAER WY-17-V
HAER 1989(HAER):25
6ph/2pg/1pc L

SHELL VIC.

Shell Creek Bridge
County Rd. 57
HAER WY-17-U
HAER 1989(HAER):25
2ph/2pg/1pc L

CAMPBELL COUNTY

GILLETTE VIC.

Dunlap Ranch
Belle Ayr Coal Mine Permit Area
HABS WY-112
4ph/14pg/1pc H

Dunlap Ranch,Barn
Belle Ayr Coal Mine Permit Area
HABS WY-112-E
2ph/1pg/1pc H

Dunlap Ranch,Bunkhouse
Belle Ayr Coal Mine Permit Area
HABS WY-112-C
2ph/1pg/1pc H

Dunlap Ranch,Chicken House/Storage
Belle Ayr Coal Mine Permit Area
HABS WY-112-H
2ph/1pg/1pc H

Dunlap Ranch,Garage
Belle Ayr Coal Mine Permit Area
HABS WY-112-G
2ph/1pg/1pc H

Dunlap Ranch,Homestead Cabin
Belle Ayr Coal Mining Permit Area
HABS WY-112-J
2ph/1pg/1pc H

Dunlap Ranch,Homestead House
Belle Ayr Coal Mine Permit Area
HABS WY-112-F
2ph/2pg/1pc H

Dunlap Ranch,Privy
Belle Ayr Coal Mine Permit Area
HABS WY-112-D
1ph/1pg/1pc H

Dunlap Ranch,Pumphouse
Belle Ayr Coal Mine Permit Area
HABS WY-112-I
2ph/1pg/1pc H

Dunlap Ranch,Ranch House
Belle Ayr Coal Mine Permit Area
HABS WY-112-A
2ph/1pg/1pc H

Dunlap Ranch,Windmill
Belle Ayr Coal Mine Permit Area
HABS WY-112-B
1ph/1pg/1pc H

Dunlp Ranch,Chicken Coop
Belle Ayr Coal Minig Permit Area
HABS WY-112-K
1ph/1pg/1pc H

WRIGHT IC.

Rock Well Homestead,Rock Lined Well
(Thornburg Homestead,Rock Lined Well)
North Rochelle Coal Mine Permit Area
HABS WY-109-B
2ph H

Thornburg Homestead,Rock Lined Well; see Rock Well Homestead,Rock Lined Well

WRIGHT VIC.

(Thornburg Homestead); see RockWell Homestead

Rock Well Homestead,Dugout
(Thornburg Homestead,Dugout)
North Pacific Coal Mine Permit Area
HABS WY-109-A
7ph H

RockWell Homestead ((Thornburg Homestead))
North Rochelle Coal Mine Permit Area
HABS WY-109
2ph/33pg/1pc H

Thornburg Homestead,Dugout; see Rock Well Homestead,Dugout

CARBON COUNTY

ELK MOUNTAIN VIC.

Medicine Bow Bridge
Spanning Medicine Bow River on Co. Rd. No. 120-1
HAER WY-17-G
HAER 1989(HAER):25
3ph/2pg/1pc L

ENCAMPMENT VIC.

Butler Bridge
Spanning N. Platte River on County Rd. No. 203
HAER WY-17-I
HAER 1989(HAER):25
3ph/2pg/1pc L

FORT FRED STEELE

Fort Fred Steele
HABS WY-86
HABS WYO,4-FOFEST,1-
2dr L

Fort Fred Steele,Bridge Tenders House
HABS WY-86-D
HABS WYO,4-FOFEST,1D-
3dr L

Fort Fred Steele,Company Barracks
HABS WY-86-A
HABS WYO,4-FOFEST,1A-
3dr L

Fort Fred Steele,Officer's Quarters
HABS WY-86-B
HABS WYO,4-FOFEST,1B-
1dr L

Fort Fred Steele,Ordnance Magazine
HABS WY-86-C
HABS WYO,4-FOFEST,1C-
3dr L

SARATOGA VIC.

Pick Bridge
Spanning N. Platte River on County Rd. 508
HAER WY-22
HAER WYO,4-SARAT.V,1-
4ph/2pg/1pc L

CROOK COUNTY

HULETT VIC.

Missouri River Bridge
Spanning Missouri River on County Rd. 200
HAER WY-21
HAER WYO,6-HUL.V,1-
2ph/2pg/1pc L

FREMONT COUNTY

ATLANTIC CITY

Atlantic City
Southpass Rd.
HABS WY-60
HABS WYO,7-ATCI,1-
3pg L

Carpenter's Hall
HABS WY-61
HABS WYO,7-ATCI,2-
3ph/1ct L

Hyde's Hall
HABS WY-62
HABS WYO,7-ATCI,3-
2ph L

Mercantile Bar
HABS WY-63
HABS WYO,7-ATCI,4-
1ph L

St. Andrew's Episcopal Church
HABS WY-64
HABS WYO,7-ATCI,5-
4ph/1ct L

DUBOIS VIC.

Big Wind River Bridge
Spanning Big Wind River on County Rd. No. 21
HAER WY-17-W
HAER 1989(HAER):25
2ph/2pg/1pc L

ETHETE VIC.

Wind River Bridge
WY Hwy. 132
HAER WY-17-C
HAER 1989(HAER):25
2ph/2pg/1pc L

FORT WASHAKIE

Boarding School & Roberts Residence; see Shoshone Episcopal Mission

Church of the Redeemer; see Shoshone Episcopal Mission

Civ. Conservation Corps,Indian Div. Bldg. No. 1; see Fort Washakie,Building No. 67

Civ. Conservation Corps,Indian Div. Bldg. No. 2; see Fort Washakie,Building No. 68

Civ. Conservation Corps,Indian Div. Bldg. No. 3; see Fort Washakie,Building No. 69

Civ. Conservation Corps,Indian Div. Bldg. No. 4; see Fort Washakie,Building No. 70

Civ. Conservation Corps,Indian Div. Bldg. No. 5; see Fort Washakie,Building No. 71

Civ. Conservation Corps,Indian Div. Bldg. No. 6; see Fort Washakie,Building No. 72

Civ. Conservation Corps,Indian Div. Bldg. No. 7; see Fort Washakie,Building No. 73

Civ. Conservation Corps,Indian Div. Bldg. No. 8; see Fort Washakie,Building No. 74

Fort Washakie,Building No. 1
Washakie St.
HABS WY-107-I
HABS WYO,7-FOWA,1-I-
11ph/9pg/1pc L

Fort Washakie,Building No. 67 (Civ. Conservation Corps,Indian Div. Bldg. No. 1)
Sacajawea Cir.
HABS WY-107-A
2ph/8pg/1pc H

Fort Washakie,Building No. 68 (Civ. Conservation Corps,Indian Div. Bldg. No. 2)
Sacajawea Cir.
HABS WY-107-B
4ph/8pg/1pc H

Fort Washakie,Building No. 69 (Civ. Conservation Corps,Indian Div. Bldg. No. 3)
Sacajawea Cir.
HABS WY-107-C
3ph/8pg/1pc H

Fort Washakie,Building No. 70 (Civ. Conservation Corps,Indian Div. Bldg. No. 4)
Sacajawea Cir.
HABS WY-107-D
3ph/8pg/1pc H

Fort Washakie,Building No. 71 (Civ. Conservation Corps,Indian Div. Bldg. No. 5)
Sacajawea Cir.
HABS WY-107-E
3ph/8pg/1pc H

Fort Washakie,Building No. 72 (Civ. Conservation Corps,Indian Div. Bldg. No. 6)
Sacajawea Cir.
HABS WY-107-F
3ph/8pg/1pc H

Fort Washakie,Building No. 73 (Civ. Conservation Corps,Indian Div. Bldg. No. 7)
Sacajawea Cir.
HABS WY-107-G
3ph/8pg/1pc H

Fort Washakie,Building No. 74 (Civ. Conservation Corps,Indian Div. Bldg. No. 8)
Sacajawea Cir.
HABS WY-107-H
4ph/8pg/1pc H

Holy Saints John Chapel; see Shoshone Episcopal Mission

Mission House; see Shoshone Episcopal Mission

Roberts' Mission; see Shoshone Episcopal Mission

Shoshone Episcopal Mission (Boarding School & Roberts Residence; Mission House)
Wind River Indian Reservation
HABS WY-54-A
HABS WYO,7-FOWA.V,2A-
4dr/8ph/6pg L

Shoshone Episcopal Mission (Church of the Redeemer)
Wind River Indian Reservation
HABS WY-54-C
HABS WYO,7-FOWA.V,2C-
1ph/3pg L

Shoshone Episcopal Mission (Holy Saints John Chapel)
Wind River Indian Reservation
HABS WY-54-B
HABS WYO,7-FOWA.V,2B-
2dr/5ph/4pg/1ct L

Shoshone Episcopal Mission (Roberts' Mission; Shoshone School for Indian Girls)
Wind River Indian Reservation
HABS WY-54
HABS WYO,7-FOWA.V,2-
1dr/1ph/5pg/1ct/fr L

Shoshone Episcopal Mission (St. David's Church)
Wind River Indian Reservation
HABS WY-54-D
HABS WYO,7-FOWA.V,2D-
2ph/3pg L

Shoshone Indian Cemetary
Wind River Indian Reservation
HABS WY-52
HABS WYO,7-FOWA.V,1-
3ph/3pg L

Shoshone School for Indian Girls; see Shoshone Episcopal Mission

St. David's Church; see Shoshone Episcopal Mission

MINER'S DELIGHT

Hamilton City; see Miner's Delight

Miner's Delight (Hamilton City)
Atlantic City Vic.
HABS WY-59
HABS WYO,7-MINDE,1-
19ph/3pg/5ct L

MONETA

Sheep Shearing Shed
Moneta Access Rd.
HABS WY-53
HABS WYO,7-MONA,1-
4dr/8ph/5pg/1ct/fr L

MORTON VIC.

Wind River Diverson Dam Bridge
Spanning Wind River on County Rd. No. 24
HAER WY-17-X
HAER 1989(HAER):25
5ph/2pg/1pc L

SOUTH PASS CITY

B & H Mine,The
South Pass City Vic.
HABS WY-56
HABS WYO,7-SOPAC.V,1-
8ph/3ct L

Barney Tibbals Cabin
Price St. & South Pass Ave.
HABS WY-34
HABS WYO,7-SOPAC,7-
1dr/2ph/5pg/fr L

Black Horse Livery Stable
Grant St.
HABS WY-29
HABS WYO,7-SOPAC,2-
2dr/7ph/5pg/1ct L

Carissa Mine,The
South Pass City Vic.
HABS WY-30
HABS WYO,7-SOPAC,3-
27ph/8pg L

Carissa Saloon
South Pass Ave.
HABS WY-31
HABS WYO,7-SOPAC,4-
2dr/3ph/4pg/fr L

Cave,The (Fort Bourbon)
South Pass Ave.
HABS WY-32
HABS WYO,7-SOPAC,5-
2dr/3ph/4pg/fr L

Chipp,Jean,Cabin; see Dakota Street (Cabin)

Dakota Street (Cabin)
(Chipp,Jean,Cabin)
HABS WY-33
HABS WYO,7-SOPAC,6-
1dr/4ph/5pg/fr L

Dance Hall
South Pass Ave. & Dakota St.
HABS WY-35
HABS WYO,7-SOPAC,8-
1dr/6ph/4pg L

Duncan Mine
South Pass City Vic.
HABS WY-57
HABS WYO,7-SOPAC.V,2-
9ph/1ct L

Exchange Bank & Recorder's Office
South Pass Ave. & Price St.
HABS WY-36
HABS WYO,7-SOPAC,9-
1dr/1ph/4pg/1ct L

Fort Bourbon; see Cave,The

Grant & Price Streets (Commercial Building) (Morris,Esther,Hat Shop)
Grant & Price Sts.
HABS WY-41
HABS WYO,7-SOPAC,14-
3dr/9ph/5pg/fr L

Grecian Bend Saloon
South Pass Ave.
HABS WY-37
HABS WYO,7-SOPAC,10-
3dr/6ph/6pg/fr L

Houghton-Colter General Store
South Pass Ave.
HABS WY-38
HABS WYO,7-SOPAC,11-
2dr/4ph/6pg/fr L

Idaho House (South Pass Hotel; Sherlock Hotel)
South Pass Ave.
HABS WY-48
HABS WYO,7-SOPAC,21-
2dr/9ph/6pg/fr L

Libby Cabin (Pest House)
State Route 28,(moved from South Pass City Vic.)
HABS WY-39
HABS WYO,7-SOPAC,12-
1dr/3ph/5pg/fr L

Masonic Lodge
South Pass Ave.
HABS WY-40
HABS WYO,7-SOPAC,13-
3ph/3pg L

Morris,Esther,Hat Shop; see Grant & Price Streets (Commercial Building)

Palmetto Gulch Stamp Mill
Willow Creek,Palmetto Gulch Vic.
HABS WY-42
HABS WYO,7-SOPAC,15-
5ph/3pg/1ct L

Pest House; see Libby Cabin

Privy I & II
South Pass Ave.
HABS WY-44
HABS WYO,7-SOPAC,17-
2dr/4ph/4pg/fr L

Roberts-Payne House
Dakota St.
HABS WY-43
HABS WYO,7-SOPAC,16-
3dr/6ph/4pg/fr L

Schoolhouse
South Pass Ave.
HABS WY-46
HABS WYO,7-SOPAC,19-
3dr/8ph/5pg/1ct/fr L

Sherlock Hotel; see Idaho House

Sherlock House
South Pass Ave.
HABS WY-47
HABS WYO,7-SOPAC,20-
3dr/2ph/5pg/fr L

Shields,Carrie,Mine
South Pass City Vic.
HABS WY-58
HABS WYO,7-SOPAC.V,3-
5ph L

Smith-Sherlock Store
South Pass Ave.
HABS WY-49
HABS WYO,7-SOPAC,22-
4dr/9ph/5pg/2ct L

South Pass City,General View
HABS WY-27
HABS WYO,7-SOPAC,1-
3dr/12ph/10pg/5ct/fr L

South Pass Hotel; see Idaho House

Sweetwater County Jail
Grant St.
HABS WY-50
HABS WYO,7-SOPAC,23-
2dr/6ph/5pg/1ct/fr L

Tibbals-Sager Cabin
South Pass Ave.
HABS WY-45
HABS WYO,7-SOPAC,18-
2dr/3ph/4pg/fr L

GOSHEN COUNTY

CHEYENNE

Union Pacific Passenger Station
121 W. Fifteenth St.
HABS WY-80
HABS WYO,11-CHEY,5-
19ph L

FORT LARAMIE

Fort Laramie National Historic Site; see Fort Laramie,Administration Building

Fort Laramie National Historic Site; see Fort Laramie,N.C.O. Quarters

Fort Laramie National Historic Site; see Fort Laramie,New Bakery

Fort Laramie National Historic Site; see Fort Laramie,Officers' Quarters F

Fort Laramie National Historic Site; see Fort Laramie,Old Bedlam

Fort Laramie,Administration Building
(Fort Laramie National Historic Site)
HABS WY-14
HABS WYO,8-FOLA,3L-
3dr L

Fort Laramie,Calvary Barracks
HABS WY-5
HABS WYO,8-FOLA,3C-
8dr/5ph/2pg L

Fort Laramie,Commissary Storehouse
HABS WY-9
HABS WYO,8-FOLA,3G-
4dr/5ph/2pg L

Fort Laramie,Hospital (Ruins)
HABS WY-13
HABS WYO,8-FOLA,3K-
3dr/5ph/2pg L

Fort Laramie,Magazine
HABS WY-11
HABS WYO,8-FOLA,3I-
2dr/2ph/2pg L

Fort Laramie,N.C.O. Quarters (Fort Laramie National Historic Site)
HABS WY-16
HABS WYO,8-FOLA,3N-
1dr L

Fort Laramie,New Bakery (Fort Laramie National Historic Site)
HABS WY-15
HABS WYO,8-FOLA,3M-
1dr L

Fort Laramie,Officer's Quarters A
HABS WY-7
HABS WYO,8-FOLA,3E-
14dr/9ph/3pg L

Fort Laramie,Officers' Quarters F
(Fort Laramie National Historic Site)
HABS WY-4
HABS WYO,8-FOLA,3B-
12dr/2ph/3pg/1pc L

Fort Laramie,Old Bakery
HABS WY-10
HABS WYO,8-FOLA,3H-
3dr/2ph/2pg L

Fort Laramie,Old Bedlam (Fort Laramie National Historic Site)
HABS WY-1
HABS WYO,8-FOLA,1-
18dr/34ph/8pg/1pc L

Fort Laramie,Old Guard House
HABS WY-8
HABS WYO,8-FOLA,3F-
4dr/9ph/2pg L

Fort Laramie,Pit Toilet
HABS WY-3
HABS WYO,8-FOLA,3A-
2dr/2ph/2pg L

Fort Laramie,Stable
HABS WY-12
HABS WYO,8-FOLA,3J-
1dr/2ph/1pg L

Documentation: **ct** color transparencies **dr** measured drawings **fr** field records
pc photograph captions **pg** pages of text **ph** photographs

Fort Larmie,Officer's Ouarters E
HABS WY-6
HABS WYO,8-FOLA,3D-
10dr/5ph/3pg L

FORT LARAMIE VIC.

Fort Laramie National Historic Site; see Fort Laramie,Sutler's Store

Fort Laramie,Sutler's Store (Fort Laramie National Historic Site)
HABS WY-2
HABS WYO,8-FOLA,2-
7dr/17ph/2pg/1pc L

North Platte River Bowstring Truss Bridge
Spanning North Platte River
HAER WY-1
HAER WYO,8-FOLA.V,1-
29ph/8pg/3pc/fr L

HOT SPRINGS COUNTY

THERMOPLOIS VIC.

Owl Creek Bridge
County Rd. 287
HAER WY-17-T
HAER 1989(HAER):25
4ph/2pg/1pc L

THERMOPOLIS VIC.

Four Mile Bridge
Spanning Big Horn River on County Rd. No. 173
HAER WY-17-E
HAER 1989(HAER):25
11ph/2pg/1pc L

JOHNSON COUNTY

BUFFALO VIC.

Peloux Bridge
Spanning Clear Creek on County Rd. No. 40
HAER WY-20
HAER WYO,10-BUF.V,1-
2ph/2pg/1pc L

KAYCEE VIC.

South Fork Powder River Bridge
On West Service Rd. of I-25
HAER WY-17-B
HAER 1989(HAER):25
14ph/2pg/1pc L

SUSSEX VIC.

Irigary Bridge
Spanning Powder River on County Rd. No. 254
HAER WY-17-S
HAER 1989(HAER):25
3ph/2pg/1pc L

LARAMIE COUNTY

CHEYENNE

Atlas Theatre
213 W. Sixteenth St.
HABS WY-77
HABS WYO,11-CHEY,2-
7ph/3ct L

City & County Building
Nineteenth & Carey Ave.
HABS WY-73
HABS WYO,11-CHEY,6-
8ph/7pg/1pc/fr L

Fort David A. Russell Veterinary Hospital (Warren,Francis E. ,Air Force Base,Building 29)
Third St. & Second Ave.
HABS WY-66
HABS WYO,11-CHEY,1A-
6dr/11ph/16pg/1ct L

Fort David A. Russell,N. C. O. Quarters (Warren,Francis E. ,Air Force Base Building 74)
First Ave. & Eight St.
HABS WY-65
HABS WYO,11-CHEY,1B-
2dr/6ph/15pg L

St. Mark's Episcopal Church
1908 Central Ave.
HABS WY-78
HABS WYO,11-CHEY,3-
11ph/1ct L

State Capitol Building
Twenty-fourth St. & Capitol Ave.
HABS WY-79
HABS WYO,11-CHEY,4-
19ph/3ct L

W.A.N.G. Compound Cheyenne Airport; see Wyoming Air National Guard Base

Warren,Francis E. ,Air Force Base Building 74; see Fort David A. Russell,N. C. O. Quarters

Warren,Francis E. ,Air Force Base,Building 29; see Fort David A. Russell Veterinary Hospital

Wyoming Air National Guard Base (W.A.N.G. Compound Cheyenne Airport)
Cheyenne Airport
HAER WY-16
44ph/37pg/3pc/fr H

NATRONA COUNTY

CASPER VIC.

Bessemer Bend Bridge
Spanning N. Platte River on County Rd. 58
HAER WY-17-L
HAER 1989(HAER):25
3ph/2pg/1pc L

NIOBRARA COUNTY

RIVERVIEW VIC.

Cheyenne River Bridge
County Rd. 46
HAER WY-17-K
HAER 1989(HAER):25
3ph/2pg/1pc L

PARK COUNTY

CODY

Cody,Isaac,House
720 Sheridan Ave. (moved from Le Claire,IA)
HABS IA-56
HABS IOWA,82-LECLA,1-
1ph/1pg/1pc L

CODY VIC.

Buffalo Bill Dam (Shoshone River Dam)
HAER WY-2
HAER WYO,15-CODY,1-
12ph/3pg/1pc/1ct L

Hayden Arch Bridge
Spanning Shoshone River on Old U. S. 14/16
HAER WY-17-DD
HAER 1989(HAER):25
8ph/2pg/1pc L

Shoshone River Dam; see Buffalo Bill Dam

NORRIS JUNCTION

Norris Soldiers Station
Norris Campgrounds & Gibbon River Vic.
HABS WY-21
HABS WYO,24-NORJ,1-
6dr/7ph/5pg L

PLATTE COUNTY

CHUGWATER

Swan Land & Cattle Company (Two Bar Ranch)
State Rt. 313
HABS WY-71
HABS WYO,16-CHU6W,1-
1dr/3ph/2ct L

Swan Land & Cattle Company,Barn
State Rt. 313
HABS WY-71-A
HABS WYO,16-CHUGW,1A-
12ph/1ct L

Swan Land & Cattle Company,Main Office
State Rt. 313
HABS WY-71-B
HABS WYO,16-CHUGW,1B-
8ph L

Swan Land & Cattle Company,Manager's House
State Rt. 313
HABS WY-71-C
HABS WYO,16-CHUGW,1C-
4dr/8ph/17pg/fr L

Swan Land & Cattle Company,Mercantile Store
State Rt. 313
HABS WY-71-D
HABS WYO,16-CHUGW,1D-
3dr/13ph/7pg/fr L

Two Bar Ranch; see Swan Land & Cattle Company

GUERNSEY

Guernsey State Park Museum
Highway 317
HABS WY-81
HABS WYO,16-GUERN.V,1-
11ph/2ct L

PEPPERVILLE

Watertower
N. side of U. S. Rt. 26
HABS WY-82
HABS WYO,16-PEPV,1-
2ph L

WHEATLAND VIC.

East Channel of Laramie River Bridge; see Laramie River Bridge

Laramie River Bridge (East Channel of Laramie River Bridge)
County Rd. 204
HAER WY-17-CC
HAER 1989(HAER):25
4ph/2pg/1pc L

SHERIDAN COUNTY

ARVADA VIC.

Arvada Bridge
Spanning Power River on County Rd. No. 38
HAER WY-17-N
HAER 1989(HAER):25
3ph/2pg/1pc L

Powder River Bridge
US Hwy. 14/16
HAER WY-17-D
HAER 1989(HAER):25
16ph/2pg/1pc L

LEITER VIC.

Powder River Bridge
County Rd. 269
HAER WY-17-P
HAER 1989(HAER):25
4ph/2pg/1pc L

MONARCH VIC.

Kooi Bridge; see Tongue River Bridge

Tongue River Bridge (Kooi Bridge)
Spanning Tongue River on County Rd. No. 97
HAER WY-17-Q
HAER 1989(HAER):25
3ph/2pg/1pc L

SHERIDAN

Sheridan Inn
HABS WY-28
HABS HABS WYO,17-SHER,1-
14dr/25ph/5pg/fr L

SHERIDAN VIC.

Big Goose Creek Bridge
County Rd. 5
HAER WY-17-R
HAER 1989(HAER):25
3ph/2pg/1pc L

Twin Lakes Reservior No. 1
Big Goose Creek
HAER WY-52
6ph/10pg/1pc L

Twin Lakes Reservoir No. 1,Dam Structure
Head of Big Goose Creek
HAER WY-52-A
4ph/1pg/1pc L

Twin Lakes Reservoir No. 1,Valve Control House
Head of Big Goose Creek
HAER WY-52-B
3ph/1pg/1pc L

Twin Lakes Reservoir No.1,Intake & Outlet Struct.
Head of Big Goose Creek
HAER WY-52-C
5ph/2pg/1pc L

SUBLETTE COUNTY

BOULDER VIC.

New Fork River Bridge
County Rd. 136
HAER WY-17-F
HAER 1989(HAER):25
4ph/2pg/1pc L

DANIEL VIC.

Green River Bridge
Spanning Green River on County Rd. No. 145
HAER WY-17-Y
HAER 1989(HAER):25
3ph/2pg/1pc L

SWEETWATER COUNTY

FONTENELLE VIC.

Green River Bridge
Spanning Green River on County Road No. 8
HAER WY-17-AA
HAER 1989(HAER):25
2ph/2pg/1pc L

GRANGER

Granger Stage Station
Old Rt. 30 N.
HABS WY-67
HABS WYO,19-GRANG,1-
4dr/7ph/14pg/fr L

GREEN RIVER VIC.

Big Island Bridge
Spanning Green River on County Road No. 4
HAER WY-17-BB
HAER 1989(HAER):25
4ph/2pg/1pc L

POINT OF ROCKS

Point of Rocks Stage Station
Rock Springs Vic.
HABS WY-69
HABS WYO,19-PTROC.V,1-
4dr/5ph/8pg/fr L

Point of Rocks Stage Station,Stable
Rock Springs Vic.
HABS WY-69-A
HABS WYO,19-PTROC.V,1A-
2dr/4ph/6pg L

SUPERIOR

Superior Union Hall
State Hwy. 371,Block 9,part of lots 9 & 10
HABS WY-110
8dr/21ph/8pg/2pc H

TETON COUNTY

KELL VIC.

Chambers',Andy,Ranch House
Mormon Row Rd.
HABS WY-83
HABS WYO,20-KEL.V,1-
5dr/1ph/6pg/fr L

KELLY VIC.

Grand Teton National Park; see Moulton,T. A. ,Ranch

Moulton,T. A. ,Ranch (Grand Teton National Park)
Mormon Row Rd.
HABS WY-26
HABS WYO,20-KEL.V,2-
13dr/20ph/15pg/fr L

MOOSE

Menor's Ferry (Museum)
Snake River
HABS WY-24
HABS WYO,20-MOOS,2-
12dr/11ph/4pg L

Noble,Maud,Cabin
Menor's Ferry,Snake River,moved from Cottonwood Cr
HABS WY-23
HABS WYO,20-MOOS,1-
7dr/5ph/5pg L

MOOSE VIC.

Bar B C Ranch (Grand Teton National Park)
HABS WY-92
HABS WYO,20-MOOS.V,3-
1dr L

Crandall,Harrison,Studio (Jenny Lake Store; Grand Teton National Park)
HABS WY-90
HABS WYO,20-MOOS.V,4-
3dr L

Cunningham Cabin
Btw. Snake River & US Route 89
HABS WY-25
HABS WYO,20-MOOS.V,2-
5dr/3ph/4pg L

Grand Teton National Park; see Bar B C Ranch

Grand Teton National Park; see Crandall,Harrison,Studio

Grand Teton National Park; see Mangus,James H. ,Cabin

Grand Teton National Park; see Mangus,Lee,Cabin

Grand Teton National Park; see Pfeiffer,Joe,Homestead

Jenny Lake Store; see Crandall,Harrison,Studio

Lake,Jenny,Ranger Station; see Mangus,Lee,Cabin

Manges,James,Cabin; see Mangus,James H. ,Cabin

Mangus,James H. ,Cabin (Manges,James,Cabin; Grand Teton National Park)
HABS WY-22
HABS WYO,20-MOOS.V,1-
6dr/2ph/4pg L

Mangus,Lee,Cabin (Lake,Jenny,Ranger Station; Grand Teton National Park)
HABS WY-108
HABS WYO,20-MOOS.V,6-
4dr L

Pfeiffer,Joe,Homestead (Grand Teton National Park)
HABS WY-91
HABS WYO,20-MOOS.V,5-
1dr L

YELLOWSTONE NAT'L PK

Golden Gate Viaduct (Yellowstone National Park)
HAER WY-3
HAER WYO,20-YELNAP,2-
13ph/4pg/1pc L

Old Faithful Inn (Old Faithful Lodge; Old Faithful Tavern)
HABS WY-87
HABS WYO,20-YELNAP,1-
ıDLC/PP-1992:WY-4°
41ph/8pg/4pc L

Old Faithful Lodge; see Old Faithful Inn

Old Faithful Tavern; see Old Faithful Inn

Yellowstone National Park; see Golden Gate Viaduct

UINTA COUNTY

FORT BADGER VIC.

Black's Fork Bridge
Spanning Black's Fork River on County Rd. No. 217
HAER WY-17-Z
HAER 1989(HAER):25
1ph/2pg/1pc L

PIEDMONT

Piedmont Charcoal Kilns
Fort Bridger Vic.
HABS WY-68
HABS WYO,21-PIED,1-
3dr/12ph/5pg/2ct/fr L

WESTON COUNTY

OSAGE VIC.

Clay Spur Bentonite Plant & Camp
Clay Spur Siding on the Burlington Northern RR
HAER WY-23
HAER 1991(HAER):16
3ph/17pg/1pc L

Clay Spur Bentonite Plant & Camp, Stable
Clay Spur Siding on the Burlington Northern RR
HAER WY-23-A
HAER 1991(HAER):16
2ph/1pg/1pc L

Clay Spur Bentonite Plant & Camp,Bath House
Clay Spur Siding on the Burlington Northen RR
HAER WY-23-D
HAER 1991(HAER):16
2ph/2pg/1pc L H

Clay Spur Bentonite Plant & Camp,Bunhouses
Clay Spur Siding on the Burlington Northern RR
HAER WY-23-E
HAER 1991(HAER):16
2ph/2pg/1pc H

Clay Spur Bentonite Plant & Camp,Butler Storage
Clay Spur Siding on the Burlington Northern RR
HAER WY-23-H
HAER 1991(HAER):16
1ph/1pg/1pc H

Clay Spur Bentonite Plant & Camp,Cooler
Clay Spur Siding on the Burlington Northern RR
HAER WY-23-K
HAER 1991(HAER):16
2ph/1pg/1pc L

Clay Spur Bentonite Plant & Camp,Dwelling
Clay Spur Siding on the Burlington Northern RR
HAER WY-23-I
HAER 1991(HAER):16
4ph/2pg/1pc H

Clay Spur Bentonite Plant & Camp,Dwelling (1 Unit)
Clay Spur Siding on the Burlington Northern RR
HAER WY-23-R
HAER 1991(HAER):16
2ph/2pg/1pc L

Clay Spur Bentonite Plant & Camp,Garage
Clay Spur Siding on the Burlington Northern RR
HAER WY-23-B
HAER 1991(HAER):16
2ph/1pg/1pc L

Clay Spur Bentonite Plant & Camp,Garage/Mach. Shop
Clay Spur Siding o he Burlington Northern RR
HAER WY-23-L
HAER 1991(HAER):16
2ph/1pg/1pc L

Clay Spur Bentonite Plant & Camp,Laboratory
Clay Spur Siding on the Burlington Northern RR
HAER WY-23-F
HAER 1991(HAER):16
2ph/2pg/1pc H

Clay Spur Bentonite Plant & Camp,Office
Clay Spur Siding on the Burlington Northern RR
HAER WY-23-J
HAER 1991(HAER):16
3ph/2pg/1pc L

Clay Spur Bentonite Plant & Camp,Oil House
Clay Spur Siding on the Burlington Northern RR
HAER WY-23-N
HAER 1991(HAER):16
2ph/1pg/1pc L

Clay Spur Bentonite Plant & Camp,Outbuilding
Clay Spur Siding on the Burlington Northern RR
HAER WY-23-S
HAER 1991(HAER):16
1ph/1pg/1pc L

Clay Spur Bentonite Plant & Camp,Refining Mill
Clay Spur Siding on the Burlington Northern RR
HAER WY-23-O
HAER 1991(HAER):16
22ph/3pg/2pc L

Clay Spur Bentonite Plant & Camp,Scale House
Clay Spur Siding on the Burlington Northern RR
HAER WY-23-P
HAER 1991(HAER):16
4ph/1pg/1pc L

Clay Spur Bentonite Plant & Camp,Water Tower
Clay Spur Siding on the Burlington Northern RR
HAER WY-23-C
HAER 1991(HAER0:16
2ph/2pg/1pc L

Clay Spur Bentonite Plnt. & Camp,Dwelling(2 Unit)
Clay Spur Siding on the Burlington Northern RR
HAER WY-23-Q
HAER 1991(HAER):16
2ph/2pg/1pc L

Clay Spur Bentonite Plnt.&Camp,Power Plnt./Mach S.
Cly Spur Siding on the Burlington Northern RR
HAER WY-23-M
HAER 1991(HAER):16
4ph/2pg/1pc L

Clay Spur Bentonite,Garage/Storage
Clay Spur Siding on the Burlington Northern RR
HAER WY-23-G
HAER 1991(HAER):16
1ph/1pg/1pc H

Index to County by City

The arrangement of cities and towns within the preceding checklist is alphabetical **by county** within each state. To determine in which county a city or town is located, consult the following *Index to County by City*. This index lists all cities and towns in the checklist by state and indicates the county in which they are located.

Independent cities—those cities that are legally separate from any county—are identified by the word "(City)" following the city name without reference to a county name. In the preceding checklist, they are interfiled in the same alphabet as the counties.

Alabama

Abbeville, HENRY COUNTY
Akron vic., HALE COUNTY
Alexandria, CALHOUN COUNTY
Aliceville, PICKENS COUNTY
Aliceville vic., PICKENS COUNTY
Allenton, WILCOX COUNTY
Allsboro vic., COLBERT COUNTY
Alpine, TALLADEGA COUNTY
Alpine vic., TALLADEGA COUNTY
Andalusia vic., COVINGTON COUNTY
Anniston vic., CALHOUN COUNTY
Athens, LIMESTONE COUNTY
Athens vic., LIMESTONE COUNTY
Auburn, LEE COUNTY
Auburn vic., LEE COUNTY

Belle Mina, LIMESTONE COUNTY
Benton, LOWNDES COUNTY
Bessemer, JEFFERSON COUNTY
Bexar, MARION COUNTY
Birmingham, JEFFERSON COUNTY
Birmingham vic., JEFFERSON COUNTY
Blakely, BALDWIN COUNTY
Boligee, GREENE COUNTY
Boligee vic., GREENE COUNTY
Brewersville, SUMTER COUNTY
Brick vic., COLBERT COUNTY
Bridgeport vic., JACKSON COUNTY
Brierfield, BIBB COUNTY
Brookside, JEFFERSON COUNTY
Bucksville, TUSCALOOSA COUNTY
Burkville vic., LOWNDES COUNTY
Burnt Corn vic., MONROE COUNTY

Cahaba, DALLAS COUNTY
Calera, SHELBY COUNTY
Camden, WILCOX COUNTY
Camden vic., WILCOX COUNTY
Canton Bend, WILCOX COUNTY
Canton Bend vic., WILCOX COUNTY
Capell, WILCOX COUNTY
Carrollton, PICKENS COUNTY
Center Star vic., LAUDERDALE COUNTY
Chastang, MOBILE COUNTY
Cherokee vic., COLBERT COUNTY
Chewacla, LEE COUNTY
Citronelle, MOBILE COUNTY
Claiborne, MONROE COUNTY
Clifton Ferry, WILCOX COUNTY
Clinton, GREENE COUNTY
Coatopa, SUMTER COUNTY
Coatopa vic., SUMTER COUNTY
Columbia, HENRY COUNTY
Columbia, HOUSTON COUNTY
Columbia, SHELBY COUNTY
Cordova, WALKER COUNTY
Cordova vic., WALKER COUNTY
Cottonton, RUSSELL COUNTY
Courtland, LAWRENCE COUNTY
Courtland vic., LAWRENCE COUNTY
Coy vic., WILCOX COUNTY
Crawford, RUSSELL COUNTY
Crews Depot, LAMAR COUNTY

Dadeville, TALLAPOOSA COUNTY
Dadeville vic., TALLAPOOSA COUNTY
Dauphin Island, MOBILE COUNTY
Dawes, MOBILE COUNTY
Dayton, MARENGO COUNTY
Decatur, MORGAN COUNTY
Demopolis, MARENGO COUNTY
Dixon Mills vic., MARENGO COUNTY
Dora, WALKER COUNTY
Dudleyville vic., TALLAPOOSA COUNTY

Eastaboga vic., TALLADEGA COUNTY
Edwardsville, CLEBURNE COUNTY
Elmore vic., ELMORE COUNTY
Erie, GREENE COUNTY
Eufaula, BARBOUR COUNTY
Eutaw, GREENE COUNTY
Eutaw vic., GREENE COUNTY

Fairfield, JEFFERSON COUNTY
Fairfield vic., JEFFERSON COUNTY
Faunsdale vic., MARENGO COUNTY
Fayette vic., FAYETTE COUNTY
Florence, LAUDERDALE COUNTY
Florence vic., LAUDERDALE COUNTY
Forkland, GREENE COUNTY
Forkland vic., GREENE COUNTY
Forkland vic., HOUSTON COUNTY
Fort Mitchell, RUSSELL COUNTY
Franklin vic., MONROE COUNTY

Gallion, HALE COUNTY
Glenville, RUSSELL COUNTY
Gold Hill, LEE COUNTY
Gordon, HOUSTON COUNTY
Gordon vic., HOUSTON COUNTY
Greensboro, HALE COUNTY

Greensboro vic., HALE COUNTY
Greenville, BUTLER COUNTY
Greenville vic., BUTLER COUNTY
Grove Hill vic., CLARKE COUNTY
Gulf Shores vic., BALDWIN COUNTY

Haleburg vic., HENRY COUNTY
Harpersville vic., SHELBY COUNTY
Hayneville, LOWNDES COUNTY
Helena, SHELBY COUNTY
Helena vic., SHELBY COUNTY
Herrick, FAYETTE COUNTY
High Ridge vic., BULLOCK COUNTY
Holt, TUSCALOOSA COUNTY
Huntsville, MADISON COUNTY
Huntsville vic., MADISON COUNTY

Irondale, JEFFERSON COUNTY
Ishkouda, JEFFERSON COUNTY

Jacksonville, CALHOUN COUNTY
Jacksonville vic., CALHOUN COUNTY
Jasper, WALKER COUNTY
Jefferson, MARENGO COUNTY
Jefferson vic., MARENGO COUNTY

Lafayette, CHAMBERS COUNTY
Leighton, COLBERT COUNTY
Leighton vic., COLBERT COUNTY
Linden, MARENGO COUNTY
Livingston, SUMTER COUNTY
Livingston vic., SUMTER COUNTY
Loachapoka, LEE COUNTY
Loachapoka vic., LEE COUNTY
Lowndesboro, LOWNDES COUNTY
Lowndesboro vic., LOWNDES COUNTY
Luverne vic., CRENSHAW COUNTY

Manningham vic., BUTLER COUNTY
Marion, PERRY COUNTY
Marion vic., PERRY COUNTY
Martin's Station, DALLAS COUNTY
Mcintosh, WASHINGTON COUNTY
Memphis, PICKENS COUNTY
Millers Ferry, WILCOX COUNTY
Millers Ferry vic., WILCOX COUNTY
Mobile, MOBILE COUNTY
Mon Louis Island, MOBILE COUNTY
Monroeville vic., MONROE COUNTY
Montevallo, SHELBY COUNTY
Montgomery, MONTGOMERY COUNTY
Mooresville, LIMESTONE COUNTY
Moulton, LAWRENCE COUNTY
Moundville vic., HALE COUNTY
Mount Ida vic., CRENSHAW COUNTY
Mount Jefferson, LEE COUNTY
Mount Pleasant, MONROE COUNTY
Mount Vernon, MOBILE COUNTY
Mulberry vic., AUTAUGA COUNTY
Munford, TALLADEGA COUNTY

New Market, MADISON COUNTY
Newbern, HALE COUNTY
Northport, TUSCALOOSA COUNTY
Notasulga vic., LEE COUNTY

Oak Bowery, CHAMBERS COUNTY
Oak Hill, WILCOX COUNTY
Oakman, WALKER COUNTY
Opelika, LEE COUNTY
Opelika vic., LEE COUNTY
Orion, PIKE COUNTY
Orion vic., PIKE COUNTY
Orrville, DALLAS COUNTY
Orrville vic., DALLAS COUNTY
Oxford, CALHOUN COUNTY
Oxford vic., CALHOUN COUNTY

Peachburg, BULLOCK COUNTY
Peachburg vic., BULLOCK COUNTY
Perdue Hill, MONROE COUNTY
Pickensville, PICKENS COUNTY
Pine Apple, WILCOX COUNTY
Pittsview vic., RUSSELL COUNTY
Point Clear, BALDWIN COUNTY
Prairieville, HALE COUNTY
Prattville, AUTAUGA COUNTY
Prattville vic., AUTAUGA COUNTY

Ridgeville, BUTLER COUNTY
Robinson Springs, ELMORE COUNTY
Rogersville vic., LAUDERDALE COUNTY
Rogersville vic., LAUDERDALE COUNTY

Sawyerville vic., HALE COUNTY
Seale, RUSSELL COUNTY
Seale vic., RUSSELL COUNTY
Selma, DALLAS COUNTY
Selma vic., DALLAS COUNTY
Sheffield, COLBERT COUNTY
Sheffield vic., COLBERT COUNTY
Shelby, SHELBY COUNTY
Shorterville, HENRY COUNTY
Shorterville vic., HENRY COUNTY
Somerville, MORGAN COUNTY
Spring Hill, MOBILE COUNTY
Spring Valley vic., COLBERT COUNTY
St. Stephens, WASHINGTON COUNTY
Stockton, BALDWIN COUNTY
Suggsville, CLARKE COUNTY
Sulligent, LAMAR COUNTY
Summerfield, DALLAS COUNTY
Sylacauga, TALLADEGA COUNTY
Sylacauga vic., TALLADEGA COUNTY

Talladega, TALLADEGA COUNTY
Talladega vic., TALLADEGA COUNTY
Tallassee, ELMORE COUNTY
Tarrant, JEFFERSON COUNTY
Tensaw, BALDWIN COUNTY
Thomas, JEFFERSON COUNTY
Tombigbee Valley Vic, PICKENS COUNTY
Toulminville, MOBILE COUNTY
Town Creek vic., LAWRENCE COUNTY
Townley, WALKER COUNTY
Townley vic., WALKER COUNTY
Tuscaloosa, TUSCALOOSA COUNTY
Tuscaloosa vic., TUSCALOOSA COUNTY
Tuscumbia, COLBERT COUNTY
Tuscumbia vic., COLBERT COUNTY
Tuskegee, MACON COUNTY
Tuskegee vic., MACON COUNTY

Union Springs, BULLOCK COUNTY
Union Springs vic., BULLOCK COUNTY
Uniontown, PERRY COUNTY

Vilula, RUSSELL COUNTY

Watsonia, GREENE COUNTY
Weaver, CALHOUN COUNTY
Weaver vic., CALHOUN COUNTY
West Blocton, BIBB COUNTY
Wetumpka, ELMORE COUNTY
Wetumpka vic., ELMORE COUNTY
Wheeler Station, LAWRENCE COUNTY
White Plains, CALHOUN COUNTY
Winterboro, TALLADEGA COUNTY
Woodward, JEFFERSON COUNTY

Alaska

Afognak, KODIAK ISLAND COUNTY
Akhiok, KODIAK ISLAND COUNTY
Akutan, ALEUTIAN ISLANDS COUNTY
Anchorage, ANCHORAGE COUNTY
Angoon, SKAGWAY-YAKUTAT-ANGOON COUNTY

Barrow, NORTH SLOPE COUNTY
Barrow vic., NORTH SLOPE COUNTY
Bettles vic., YUKON-KOYUKUK COUNTY

Cape Nome, NOME COUNTY
Chatanika vic., FAIRBANKS NORTH STAR COUNTY
Chicken vic., MATANUSKA-SUSITNA COUNTY
Chignik Lake, DILLINGHAM COUNTY
Chisana, VALDEZ-CORDOVA COUNTY
Chisana vic., VALDEZ-CORDOVA COUNTY
Chitina, VALDEZ-CORDOVA COUNTY
Chitina vic., VALDEZ-CORDOVA COUNTY
Chuathbaluk, BETHEL COUNTY
Circle vic., YUKON-KOYUKUK COUNTY
Cold Bay, ALEUTIAN ISLANDS COUNTY
Coldfoot, YUKON-KOYUKUK COUNTY
Cordova, VALDEZ-CORDOVA COUNTY
Cordova vic., VALDEZ-CORDOVA COUNTY
Cordova-Mccarthy, VALDEZ-CORDOVA COUNTY

Delta Junction vic., SOUTHEAST FAIRBANKS COUNTY

Eagle, YUKON-KOYUKUK COUNTY
Eagle vic., YUKON-KOYUKUK COUNTY
Eklutna, ANCHORAGE COUNTY
Ekuk, DILLINGHAM COUNTY
English Bay, KENAI PENINSULA COUNTY
Ester, FAIRBANKS NORTH STAR COUNTY

Fairbanks, FAIRBANKS NORTH STAR COUNTY
Fort Greely, SOUTHEAST FAIRBANKS COUNTY
Fox, FAIRBANKS NORTH STAR COUNTY

Gakona, VALDEZ-CORDOVA COUNTY
Gakona vic., VALDEZ-CORDOVA COUNTY
Golovin, NOME COUNTY

Haines vic., HAINES COUNTY
Hoonah, SKAGWAY-YAKUTAT-ANGOON COUNTY
Hope, KENAI PENINSULA COUNTY

Igiugig, DILLINGHAM COUNTY

Juneau, JUNEAU COUNTY

Kenai, KENAI PENINSULA COUNTY
Ketchikan, KETCHIKAN GATEWAY COUNTY
Ketchikan vic., KETCHIKAN GATEWAY COUNTY
King Salmon, BRISTOL BAY COUNTY
King Salmon vic., BRISTOL BAY COUNTY
King Solmon vic., BRISTOL BAY COUNTY
Knik, MATANUSKA-SUSITNA COUNTY
Kodiak, KODIAK ISLAND COUNTY

Lime Village, BETHEL COUNTY
Lower Kalskag, BETHEL COUNTY
Lower Kalskag, YUKON-KOYUKUK COUNTY

Mccarthy, VALDEZ-CORDOVA COUNTY
Mccarthy vic., VALDEZ-CORDOVA COUNTY
Mckinley Station, YUKON-KOYUKUK COUNTY
Monk's Lagoon, KODIAK ISLAND COUNTY
Moses Point, NOME COUNTY

Naknek, BRISTOL BAY COUNTY
Napaskiak, BETHEL COUNTY
Nikolai, YUKON-KOYUKUK COUNTY
Nikolai vic., YUKON-KOYUKUK COUNTY
Nikolski, ALEUTIAN ISLANDS COUNTY
Ninilchik, KENAI PENINSULA COUNTY
Noatak vicinity, KOBUK
Nome, NOME COUNTY
Nome vic., NOME COUNTY
Nondalton, DILLINGHAM COUNTY

Old Harbor, KODIAK ISLAND COUNTY
Ouzinkie, KODIAK ISLAND COUNTY

Palmer, MATANUSKA-SUSITNA COUNTY
Palmer vic., MATANUSKA-SUSITNA COUNTY
Pedro Bay, DILLINGHAM COUNTY
Petersburg, FAIRBANKS NORTH STAR COUNTY
Petersburg, WRANGELL-PETERSBURG COUNTY
Point Hope, NORTH SLOPE COUNTY
Port Safety, NOME COUNTY
Portage, ANCHORAGE COUNTY
Pribilof Islands, ALEUTIAN ISLANDS COUNTY
Prudhoe Bay, NORTH SLOPE COUNTY
Prudhoe Bay vic., NORTH SLOPE COUNTY

Saxman, KETCHIKAN GATEWAY COUNTY
Seward, KENAI PENINSULA COUNTY
Seward To Nome, KENAI PENINSULA COUNTY
Sitka, SITKA COUNTY
Skagway, SKAGWAY-YAKUTAT-ANGOON COUNTY
Skagway vic., SKAGWAY-YAKUTAT-ANGOON COUNTY
Skwentna, MATANUSKA-SUSITNA COUNTY
Solomon, NOME COUNTY
South Naknek, BRISTOL BAY COUNTY
St. George, ALEUTIAN ISLANDS COUNTY
St. Paul, ALEUTIAN ISLANDS COUNTY
St. Paul, ANCHORAGE COUNTY
Summit, MATANUSKA-SUSITNA COUNTY
Sutton, MATANUSKA-SUSITNA COUNTY

Unalaska, ALEUTIAN ISLANDS COUNTY
Unalaska Island, ALEUTIAN ISLANDS COUNTY

Wiseman, YUKON-KOYUKUK COUNTY
Wrangell, WRANGELL-PETERSBURG COUNTY

Arizona

Ajo vic., PIMA COUNTY
Arivaca, PIMA COUNTY

Bowie vic., COCHISE COUNTY

Camp Verde, YAVAPAI COUNTY
Camp Verde vic., YAVAPAI COUNTY
Cave Creek vic., YAVAPAI COUNTY
Cavecreek, MARICOPA COUNTY
Chinle vic., APACHE COUNTY
Coconino vic., COCONINO COUNTY
Coolidge vic., PINAL COUNTY
Crown King vic., YAVAPAI COUNTY

Fairbank, COCHISE COUNTY
Fairbank vic., COCHISE COUNTY
Flagstaff vic., COCONINO COUNTY
Flasgstaff vic., COCONINO COUNTY
Florence, PINAL COUNTY

Ganado, APACHE COUNTY
Grand Canyon N. P., COCONINO COUNTY

Holbrook, NAVAJO COUNTY
Holbrook vic., APACHE COUNTY

Kayenta vic., NAVAJO COUNTY

Lukeville vic., PIMA COUNTY

Moccasin vic., MOHAVE COUNTY

Navajo vic., APACHE COUNTY
Nogales vic., SANTA CRUZ COUNTY

Page vic., COCONINO COUNTY
Patagonia, SANTA CRUZ COUNTY
Patagonia vic., SANTA CRUZ COUNTY
Peridot vic., PINAL COUNTY
Phoenix, MARICOPA COUNTY
Phoenix vic., MARICOPA COUNTY
Poston vic., PINAL COUNTY
Prescott, YAVAPAI COUNTY
Prescott vic., YAVAPAI COUNTY

Roosevelt vic., GILA COUNTY

Sacaton, PINAL COUNTY
Sacaton vic., PINAL COUNTY
Safford vic., GRAHAM COUNTY
Scottsdale, MARICOPA COUNTY
Showlow vic., NAVAJO COUNTY

Teec Nos Pos vic., APACHE COUNTY
Tempe, MARICOPA COUNTY
Tempe & Phoenix, MARICOPA COUNTY
Tohono O'odham Resv., PIMA COUNTY
Tombstone, COCHISE COUNTY
Tubac, SANTA CRUZ COUNTY
Tubac vic., SANTA CRUZ COUNTY
Tucson, PIMA COUNTY
Tucson vic., PIMA COUNTY

Walpi, COCONINO COUNTY
Wickenburg, MARICOPA COUNTY
Willcox, COCHISE COUNTY

Yuma, YUMA COUNTY

Arkansas

Augusta, WOODRUFF COUNTY

Beaver, CARROLL COUNTY
Belleville vic., YELL COUNTY
Benton, SALINE COUNTY
Blevins, HEMPSTEAD COUNTY

Calion, CALHOUN COUNTY
Calion vic., CALHOUN COUNTY
Camp Pioneer vic., POLK COUNTY
Center Point, HOWARD COUNTY
Clarendon, MONROE COUNTY
Clarksville vic., JOHNSON COUNTY
Cotter, BAXTER COUNTY
Cove City, CRAWFORD COUNTY

De Valls Bluff, PRAIRIE COUNTY

Eureka Springs, CARROLL COUNTY
Eureka Springs vic., CARROLL COUNTY

Fayetteville, WASHINGTON COUNTY
Fayettville vic., WASHINGTON COUNTY
Forrest City, ST. FRANCIS COUNTY
Fort Smith, SEBASTIAN COUNTY
Fountain Lake vic., GARLAND COUNTY
Ft. Douglas, JOHNSON COUNTY

Garland City, MILLER COUNTY
Gravette vic., BENTON COUNTY

Harrison vic., NEWTON COUNTY
Healing Springs vic., BENTON COUNTY
Heber Springs, CLEBURNE COUNTY
Hot Springs, GARLAND COUNTY
Hot Springs vic., GARLAND COUNTY

Imboden, LAWRENCE COUNTY

Jenny Lind vic., SEBASTIAN COUNTY
Johnson, WASHINGTON COUNTY
Judsonia, WHITE COUNTY

Lake City, CRAIGHEAD COUNTY
Lake Village, CHICOT COUNTY
Little Rock, PULASKI COUNTY
Lockesburg vic., SEVIER COUNTY

Malvern, HOT SPRING COUNTY
Milltown, SEBASTIAN COUNTY

Natural Dam, CRAWFORD COUNTY
Newport, JACKSON COUNTY
Norfolk, BAXTER COUNTY
North Little Rock, PULASKI COUNTY

Ola vic., YELL COUNTY
Old Rome vic., CLARK COUNTY
Osage vic., CARROLL COUNTY

Paragould, GREENE COUNTY
Pea Ridge vic., BENTON COUNTY
Perry vic., PERRY COUNTY
Petit Jean State Prk, CONWAY COUNTY
Pine Bluff, JEFFERSON COUNTY
Pocahontas, RANDOLPH COUNTY
Ponca, NEWTON COUNTY
Pruitt, NEWTON COUNTY

Rosston, NEVADA COUNTY

Siloan Springs, BENTON COUNTY
Springfield, CONWAY COUNTY

Van Buren, CRAWFORD COUNTY

Walnut Ridge, LAWRENCE COUNTY
War Eagle, BENTON COUNTY
Washington, HEMPSTEAD COUNTY
Washington vic., HEMPSTEAD COUNTY
Wilson, MISSISSIPPI COUNTY

California

Agua Fria, MARIPOSA COUNTY
Alameda, ALAMEDA COUNTY
Alameda, SANTA CLARA COUNTY
Alamo, CONTRA COSTA COUNTY
Alba, SAN JOAQUIN COUNTY
Albany Flat, CALAVERAS COUNTY
Albion, MENDOCINO COUNTY
Alhambra, LOS ANGELES COUNTY
Altaville, CALAVERAS COUNTY
Alton vic., HUMBOLDT COUNTY
Amador City, AMADOR COUNTY
Anaheim, ORANGE COUNTY
Angel Island, MARIN COUNTY
Angels Camp, CALAVERAS COUNTY
Angels Camp vic., CALAVERAS COUNTY
Arcata, HUMBOLDT COUNTY
Atherton, SAN MATEO COUNTY
Auburn, PLACER COUNTY

Bagby, MARIPOSA COUNTY
Baldwin Park, LOS ANGELES COUNTY
Bear River, YUBA COUNTY
Bear Valley, MARIPOSA COUNTY
Bell, LOS ANGELES COUNTY
Belmont, SAN MATEO COUNTY
Benicia, SOLANO COUNTY
Berkeley, ALAMEDA COUNTY
Beverly Hills, LOS ANGELES COUNTY
Bidwell Bar, BUTTE COUNTY
Big Oak Flat, TUOLUMNE COUNTY
Big Pine, FRESNO COUNTY
Bodie, MONO COUNTY
Bolinas, MARIN COUNTY
Brentwood vic., CONTRA COSTA COUNTY
Bridgeport, NEVADA COUNTY
Bridgeville, HUMBOLDT COUNTY
Brown's Valley vic., YUBA COUNTY
Buellton, SANTA BARBARA COUNTY
Buellton vic., SANTA BARBARA COUNTY
Buena Vista, AMADOR COUNTY
Burlingame, SAN MATEO COUNTY
Butte City, AMADOR COUNTY

Calabasas, LOS ANGELES COUNTY
Calabasas vic., LOS ANGELES COUNTY
Calistoga vic., NAPA COUNTY
Callahan, SISKIYOU COUNTY
Campbell, SANTA CLARA COUNTY
Campo Seco, CALAVERAS COUNTY
Carlotta vic., HUMBOLDT COUNTY
Carlsbad vic., SAN DIEGO COUNTY
Carmel, MONTEREY COUNTY
Carrville, TRINITY COUNTY
Carson Hill, CALAVERAS COUNTY
Castro Valley, ALAMEDA COUNTY
Centerville, BUTTE COUNTY
Cherokee, BUTTE COUNTY
Chico, BUTTE COUNTY
Chinese Camp, TUOLUMNE COUNTY
Chino vic., SAN BERNARDINO COUNTY
Chualar vic., MONTEREY COUNTY
Claremont, LOS ANGELES COUNTY
Clear Lake, LAKE COUNTY
Clear View, CALAVERAS COUNTY
Clipper Gap, PLACER COUNTY
Coloma, EL DORADO COUNTY
Coloma vic., EL DORADO COUNTY
Columbia, TUOLUMNE COUNTY
Colusa, COLUSA COUNTY
Concord, CONTRA COSTA COUNTY
Copperopolis, CALAVERAS COUNTY
Copperopolis Vic, CALAVERAS COUNTY
Copperopolis vic., CALAVERAS COUNTY
Coronado, SAN DIEGO COUNTY
Corral Hollow, SAN JOAQUIN COUNTY
Coulterville, MARIPOSA COUNTY
Coyote, SANTA CLARA COUNTY
Coyote vic., SANTA CLARA COUNTY
Crescent City vic., DEL NORTE COUNTY
Cupertino, SANTA CLARA COUNTY
Curry Village, MARIPOSA COUNTY

Danville vic., CONTRA COSTA COUNTY
Dardanelle vic., TUOLUMNE COUNTY
Death Valley, INYO COUNTY
Dobbins, YUBA COUNTY
Dobbins vic., YUBA COUNTY
Downieville, SIERRA COUNTY
Downieville vic., SIERRA COUNTY
Dragon Gulch, TUOLUMNE COUNTY
Drytown, AMADOR COUNTY

El Dorado, EL DORADO COUNTY
Eldoradotown, CALAVERAS COUNTY
Elizabeth Lake vic., LOS ANGELES COUNTY
Elk, MENDOCINO COUNTY
Escalon, SAN JOAQUIN COUNTY
Escondido, SAN DIEGO COUNTY
Eureka, HUMBOLDT COUNTY

Fairfield, SOLANO COUNTY
Felix, CALAVERAS COUNTY
Felix vic., CALAVERAS COUNTY
Ferndale vic., HUMBOLDT COUNTY
Fiddletown, AMADOR COUNTY
Folsom, SACRAMENTO COUNTY
Foresta vic., MARIPOSA COUNTY
Fort Bragg vic., MENDOCINO COUNTY
Fort Ross, SONOMA COUNTY
Fourth Crossing, CALAVERAS COUNTY
Fremont, ALAMEDA COUNTY
Fremont (Niles), ALAMEDA COUNTY
Fremont(Warm Spring), ALAMEDA COUNTY
French Camp, SAN JOAQUIN COUNTY

Garberville vic., HUMBOLDT COUNTY
Giant Forest Village, TULARE COUNTY
Gilroy, SANTA CLARA COUNTY
Gilroy vic., SANTA CLARA COUNTY
Glen Canyon, SANTA CRUZ COUNTY
Glencoe, CALAVERAS COUNTY
Glendale, LOS ANGELES COUNTY
Goodyear's Bar, SIERRA COUNTY
Grass Valley, NEVADA COUNTY
Groveland vic., TUOLUMNE COUNTY
Guadalupe, SANTA BARBARA COUNTY
Guadlupe, SANTA BARBARA COUNTY

Half Moon Bay, SAN MATEO COUNTY
Hamilton City vic., GLENN COUNTY
Happy Valley, CALAVERAS COUNTY
Hayward, ALAMEDA COUNTY
Herlong, LASSEN COUNTY
Hillsborough, SAN MATEO COUNTY
Honeydew, HUMBOLDT COUNTY
Hornitos, MARIPOSA COUNTY
Hume, FRESNO COUNTY
Huntington Beach, ORANGE COUNTY

Indian Gulch, MARIPOSA COUNTY
Indio vic., RIVERSIDE COUNTY
Inglewood, LOS ANGELES COUNTY
Irvine, ORANGE COUNTY
Isleton, SACRAMENTO COUNTY

Jackass Hill, TUOLUMNE COUNTY
Jackson, AMADOR COUNTY
Jackson Gate, AMADOR COUNTY
Jesus Maria, CALAVERAS COUNTY
Jolon vic., MONTEREY COUNTY
Julian, SAN DIEGO COUNTY

Keeler, INYO COUNTY
Kelsey, EL DORADO COUNTY
Knights Ferry, STANISLAUS COUNTY
Kyburz, EL DORADO COUNTY

La Jolla, SAN DIEGO COUNTY
Laguna Beach vic., ORANGE COUNTY
Lagunitas vic., MARIN COUNTY
Lassen Peak, SHASTA COUNTY
Lathrop, SAN JOAQUIN COUNTY
Lebec vic., KERN COUNTY
Littlerock vic., LOS ANGELES COUNTY
Livermore vic., ALAMEDA COUNTY
Locke, SACRAMENTO COUNTY
Lockeford, SAN JOAQUIN COUNTY
Lodi, SAN JOAQUIN COUNTY
Lompoc, SANTA BARBARA COUNTY
Lompoc vic., SANTA BARBARA COUNTY
Long Beach, LOS ANGELES COUNTY
Los Altos, SANTA CLARA COUNTY
Los Altos Hills, SANTA CLARA COUNTY
Los Angeles, LOS ANGELES COUNTY
Los Banos vic., MERCED COUNTY
Los Gatos, SANTA CLARA COUNTY
Lynwood, LOS ANGELES COUNTY

Mad River, HUMBOLDT COUNTY
Mare Island, SOLANO COUNTY
Mariposa, MARIPOSA COUNTY
Martinez, CONTRA COSTA COUNTY
Marysville, YUBA COUNTY
Melones vic., CALAVERAS COUNTY
Mendocino, MENDOCINO COUNTY
Menlo Park, SAN MATEO COUNTY
Michigan Bar, AMADOR COUNTY
Millbrae, SAN MATEO COUNTY
Millerton, EL DORADO COUNTY
Millerton, FRESNO COUNTY
Millerton vic., FRESNO COUNTY
Milpitas vic., SANTA CLARA COUNTY
Mokelumne Hill, CALAVERAS COUNTY
Monta Vista vic., SANTA CLARA COUNTY
Montecito, SANTA BARBARA COUNTY
Monterey, MONTEREY COUNTY
Monterey vic., MONTEREY COUNTY
Montezuma, TUOLUMNE COUNTY
Moraga Valley, CONTRA COSTA COUNTY
Morgan Hill, SANTA CLARA COUNTY
Morgan Hill vic., SANTA CLARA COUNTY
Morman Bar, MARIPOSA COUNTY
Mount Bullion, MARIPOSA COUNTY
Mount Ophir, MARIPOSA COUNTY
Murphy's, CALAVERAS COUNTY

Napa, NAPA COUNTY
Nashville, EL DORADO COUNTY
National City, SAN DIEGO COUNTY
Navaro River, MENDOCINO COUNTY
Nevada City, NEVADA COUNTY
Nevada City vic., NEVADA COUNTY
New Almaden, SANTA CLARA COUNTY
Newell, MODOC COUNTY
Newport Beach, ORANGE COUNTY
Nipomo vic., SAN LUIS OBISPO COUNTY
North Bloomfield, NEVADA COUNTY
North San Juan vic., NEVADA COUNTY

Oak Grove, SAN DIEGO COUNTY
Oakland, ALAMEDA COUNTY
Oceanside, SAN DIEGO COUNTY
Olema vic., MARIN COUNTY
Oleta, AMADOR COUNTY
Ontario, SAN BERNARDINO COUNTY
Oroville vic., BUTTE COUNTY

Pacific Palisades, LOS ANGELES COUNTY
Pala, SAN DIEGO COUNTY
Palo Alto, SANTA CLARA COUNTY
Palto Alto, SANTA CLARA COUNTY
Pasadena, LOS ANGELES COUNTY
Pescadero, SAN MATEO COUNTY
Pescadero vic., SAN MATEO COUNTY
Petaluma, SONOMA COUNTY
Petaluma vic., SONOMA COUNTY
Pilot Hill, CALAVERAS COUNTY
Pilot Hill, EL DORADO COUNTY
Pine Grove, AMADOR COUNTY
Piru vic., VENTURA COUNTY
Placerville, EL DORADO COUNTY
Placerville vic., EL DORADO COUNTY
Pleasanton, ALAMEDA COUNTY
Plumas, PLUMAS COUNTY
Plymouth, AMADOR COUNTY
Point Loma, SAN DIEGO COUNTY

Point Reyes, MARIN COUNTY
Pomona, LOS ANGELES COUNTY
Portola Valley, SAN MATEO COUNTY
Poverty Flat, CALAVERAS COUNTY
Prado vic., RIVERSIDE COUNTY
Priests, TUOLUMNE COUNTY

Quartz Mountain, TUOLUMNE COUNTY

Rancho Penasquitos, SAN DIEGO COUNTY
Rancho Santa Fe, SAN DIEGO COUNTY
Red Bluff vic., TEHAMA COUNTY
Red Dog, NEVADA COUNTY
Redding, SHASTA COUNTY
Redlands vic., SAN BERNARDINO COUNTY
Redwood City, SAN MATEO COUNTY
Richmond, CONTRA COSTA COUNTY
Riverbank, STANISLAUS COUNTY
Riverside, RIVERSIDE COUNTY
Roaring Camp, CALAVERAS COUNTY
Rough And Ready, NEVADA COUNTY
Round Top, AMADOR COUNTY

Sabastopol, SONOMA COUNTY
Sacramento, SACRAMENTO COUNTY
Salinas, MONTEREY COUNTY
Salinas vic., MONTEREY COUNTY
Salyer vic., TRINITY COUNTY
San Andreas, CALAVERAS COUNTY
San Bernardino, SAN BERNARDINO COUNTY
San Carlos, SAN MATEO COUNTY
San Diego, SAN DIEGO COUNTY
San Diego (Old Town), SAN DIEGO COUNTY
San Dimas vic., LOS ANGELES COUNTY
San Felipe vic., SANTA CLARA COUNTY
San Fernando, LOS ANGELES COUNTY
San Francisco, SAN FRANCISCO COUNTY
San Francisc0, SAN FRANCISCO COUNTY
San Gabriel, LOS ANGELES COUNTY
San Gregorio, SAN MATEO COUNTY
San Jose, SANTA CLARA COUNTY
San Juan, NEVADA COUNTY
San Juan Bautista, SAN BENITO COUNTY
San Juan Capistrano
San Juan Capistrano, ORANGE COUNTY
San Leandro, ALAMEDA COUNTY
San Luis Obispo, SAN LUIS OBISPO COUNTY
San Luis Rey (Vista), SAN DIEGO COUNTY
San Marino, LOS ANGELES COUNTY
San Martin, SANTA CLARA COUNTY
San Mateo, SAN MATEO COUNTY
San Miguel vic., SAN LUIS OBISPO COUNTY
San Pablo, CONTRA COSTA COUNTY
San Pedro, LOS ANGELES COUNTY
San Pedro Valley, SAN MATEO COUNTY
San Rafael, MARIN COUNTY
Santa Ana, ORANGE COUNTY
Santa Barbara, SANTA BARBARA COUNTY
Santa Catalina Isl., LOS ANGELES COUNTY
Santa Clara, SANTA CLARA COUNTY
Santa Clara vic., SANTA CLARA COUNTY
Santa Cruz, SANTA CRUZ COUNTY
Santa Margarita vic., SAN LUIS OBISPO COUNTY
Santa Monica, LOS ANGELES COUNTY
Santa Rosa, SONOMA COUNTY
Santa Rosa vic., SONOMA COUNTY
Saratoga, SANTA CLARA COUNTY
Saratoga vic., SANTA CLARA COUNTY
Sausalito, MARIN COUNTY
Sausalito vicinity, MARIN COUNTY
Sausalito Vicintiy, MARIN COUNTY
Sawyer's Bar, SISKIYOU COUNTY
Sawyers Bar, SISKIYOU COUNTY
Shasta, SHASTA COUNTY
Shaw's Flat, TUOLUMNE COUNTY
Shingle Springs, EL DORADO COUNTY
Shingletown vic., SHASTA COUNTY
Sierra City, SIERRA COUNTY
Sierra Madre vic., LOS ANGELES COUNTY
Sierraville, SIERRA COUNTY
Smartsville, YUBA COUNTY
Smith River, DEL NORTE COUNTY
Soledad, MONTEREY COUNTY
Solvang, SANTA BARBARA COUNTY
Sonoma, SONOMA COUNTY
Sonora, TUOLUMNE COUNTY
Sonora vic., TUOLUMNE COUNTY
Soquel, SANTA CRUZ COUNTY
South Pasadena, LOS ANGELES COUNTY
Spring Valley, SAN DIEGO COUNTY
Springfield, TUOLUMNE COUNTY
Springville vic., TULARE COUNTY
Stanford, SANTA CLARA COUNTY
Stent, TUOLUMNE COUNTY
Stockton, SAN JOAQUIN COUNTY
Stockton vic., SAN JOAQUIN COUNTY
Strawberry, EL DORADO COUNTY
Susanville vic., LASSEN COUNTY
Sweetland, NEVADA COUNTY
Sylmar vic., LOS ANGELES COUNTY

Terminal Island, LOS ANGELES COUNTY
Three Rivers vic., TULARE COUNTY
Timbuctoo, YUBA COUNTY
Tracy vic., ALAMEDA COUNTY
Tragedy Springs, EL DORADO COUNTY
Tulare, TULARE COUNTY
Tuolumne Meadows, TUOLUMNE COUNTY
Tuttletown, TUOLUMNE COUNTY
Tuttletown vic., TUOLUMNE COUNTY
Twenty-Nine Palms V., SAN BERNARDINO COUNTY

Ukiah vic., MENDOCINO COUNTY
Union City, ALAMEDA COUNTY

Vacaville, SOLANO COUNTY
Vallejo, SOLANO COUNTY
Ventura, VENTURA COUNTY
Ventura vic., VENTURA COUNTY
Volcano, AMADOR COUNTY

Warner Springs, SAN DIEGO COUNTY
Warner Springs vic., SAN DIEGO COUNTY
Wawona, MARIPOSA COUNTY
Weaverville, TRINITY COUNTY
West Sacramento, SACRAMENTO COUNTY
Westport, MENDOCINO COUNTY
Whittier, LOS ANGELES COUNTY
Willows, GLENN COUNTY
Winterhaven, IMPERIAL COUNTY
Woodbridge, SAN JOAQUIN COUNTY
Woodland, YOLO COUNTY
Woods Crossing, TUOLUMNE COUNTY
Woodside, SAN MATEO COUNTY

Yosemite Nat'l Park, MARIPOSA COUNTY
Yosemite Natl. Park, MARIPOSA COUNTY
Yosemite Village, MARIPOSA COUNTY

Canal Zone

Colon vic., CANAL ZONE

Colorado

Ames vic., SAN MIGUEL COUNTY
Arvada, JEFFERSON COUNTY
Aspen, PITKIN COUNTY
Aurora, ADAMS COUNTY

Battlement Mesa, GARFIELD COUNTY
Black Hawk, GILPIN COUNTY
Bondad vic., LA PLATA COUNTY
Boone vic., PUEBLO COUNTY
Boulder, BOULDER COUNTY
Brighton vic., ADAMS COUNTY
Buena Vista vic., CHAFFEE COUNTY

Central City, GILPIN COUNTY
Commerce City, ADAMS COUNTY
Cortez vic., MONTEZUMA COUNTY

Del Norte vic., RIO GRANDE COUNTY
Delta, DELTA COUNTY
Delta vic., DELTA COUNTY
Denver, DENVER COUNTY
Denver vic., ADAMS COUNTY
Denver vic., DENVER COUNTY
Dolores vic., MONTEZUMA COUNTY
Durango, LA PLATA COUNTY

Estes Park vic., LARIMER COUNTY

Fort Collins, LARIMER COUNTY

Georgetown, CLEAR CREEK COUNTY
Glenwood Springs, GARFIELD COUNTY
Grand Junction, MESA COUNTY
Grand Lake vic., GRAND COUNTY
Greeley, WELD COUNTY
Gunnison vic., GUNNISON COUNTY

Hotchkiss vic., DELTA COUNTY

Idaho Springs vic., CLEAR CREEK COUNTY
Iron City, CHAFFEE COUNTY

Kokomo, SUMMIT COUNTY

La Junta, BENT COUNTY
La Junta, OTERO COUNTY
Lakewood, JEFFERSON COUNTY
Littleton, ARAPAHOE COUNTY

Manzanola vic., CROWLEY COUNTY
Mcphee, MONTEZUMA COUNTY
Mesa Verde N. P., MONTEZUMA COUNTY
Morrison vic., JEFFERSON COUNTY
Mount Vernon, JEFFERSON COUNTY

Nathrop vic., CHAFFEE COUNTY

Parshall vic., GRAND COUNTY
Pueblo vic., PUEBLO COUNTY

Rangely vic., RIO BLANCO COUNTY
Rifle vic., GARFIELD COUNTY
Romley, CHAFFEE COUNTY

Sedalia vic. (Chr), DOUGLAS COUNTY
Segundo, LAS ANIMAS COUNTY
Silver Plume, CLEAR CREEK COUNTY
Silverton, SAN JUAN COUNTY
St. Elmo, CHAFFEE COUNTY
Steamboat Springs Vi, ROUTT COUNTY
Swink vic., OTERO COUNTY

Tacoma vic., LA PLATA COUNTY
Tijeras, LAS ANIMAS COUNTY
Trinidad, LAS ANIMAS COUNTY

Waterton vic., JEFFERSON COUNTY
Waterton vic., LAKE COUNTY
Watkins vic., ADAMS COUNTY
Weston vic., LAS ANIMAS COUNTY
Wolcott, EAGLE COUNTY

Connecticut

Barkhamsted, LITCHFIELD COUNTY
Bethany, NEW HAVEN COUNTY
Bolton (Center), TOLLAND COUNTY
Branford, NEW HAVEN COUNTY
Bridgeport, FAIRFIELD COUNTY
Bristol, HARTFORD COUNTY
Brooklyn, WINDHAM COUNTY

Canterbury, WINDHAM COUNTY
Cheshire, NEW HAVEN COUNTY
Chester, MIDDLESEX COUNTY
Clinton, MIDDLESEX COUNTY
Colchester, NEW LONDON COUNTY
Colebrook, LITCHFIELD COUNTY
Cornwall, LITCHFIELD COUNTY
Cos Cob, FAIRFIELD COUNTY

Danbury, FAIRFIELD COUNTY
Darien, FAIRFIELD COUNTY
Derby, NEW HAVEN COUNTY
Durham, MIDDLESEX COUNTY

East Canaan, LITCHFIELD COUNTY
East Granby, HARTFORD COUNTY
East Haddam, MIDDLESEX COUNTY
East Hampton, MIDDLESEX COUNTY
East Hartford, HARTFORD COUNTY
East Hartland, HARTFORD COUNTY
East Haven, NEW HAVEN COUNTY
East Lyme, NEW LONDON COUNTY
East Windsor Hill, HARTFORD COUNTY
Easton, FAIRFIELD COUNTY
Essex, MIDDLESEX COUNTY

Fairfield, FAIRFIELD COUNTY
Falls Village, LITCHFIELD COUNTY
Farmington, HARTFORD COUNTY
Fitchville, NEW LONDON COUNTY

Gaylordsville, LITCHFIELD COUNTY
Glastonbury, HARTFORD COUNTY
Goshen, LITCHFIELD COUNTY
Greenwich, FAIRFIELD COUNTY
Groton, NEW LONDON COUNTY
Guilford, NEW HAVEN COUNTY

Hadlyme, NEW LONDON COUNTY
Hamburg Cove, NEW LONDON COUNTY
Hamden, NEW HAVEN COUNTY
Hampton, WINDHAM COUNTY
Hartford, HARTFORD COUNTY
Harwinton, LITCHFIELD COUNTY

Kent, LITCHFIELD COUNTY
Killingworth, MIDDLESEX COUNTY

Lakeville, LITCHFIELD COUNTY
Lebanon, NEW LONDON COUNTY
Litchfield, LITCHFIELD COUNTY
Lyme, NEW LONDON COUNTY

Madison, NEW HAVEN COUNTY
Meriden, NEW HAVEN COUNTY
Middlefield, MIDDLESEX COUNTY
Middletown, MIDDLESEX COUNTY
Milford, NEW HAVEN COUNTY
Montowese, NEW HAVEN COUNTY
Moodus, MIDDLESEX COUNTY

Naugatuck, NEW HAVEN COUNTY
New Britain, HARTFORD COUNTY
New Canaan, FAIRFIELD COUNTY
New Canaan vic., FAIRFIELD COUNTY
New Haven, NEW HAVEN COUNTY
New London, NEW LONDON COUNTY
New Milford, LITCHFIELD COUNTY
New Preston, LITCHFIELD COUNTY
Norfolk, LITCHFIELD COUNTY
North Branford, NEW HAVEN COUNTY
North Branford vic., NEW HAVEN COUNTY
North Canaan, LITCHFIELD COUNTY
North Cornwall, LITCHFIELD COUNTY
North Greenwich, FAIRFIELD COUNTY
North Guilford, NEW HAVEN COUNTY
North Plain, MIDDLESEX COUNTY
North Stonington, NEW LONDON COUNTY
North Woodbury, LITCHFIELD COUNTY
Northford Center, NEW HAVEN COUNTY
Norwalk, FAIRFIELD COUNTY
Norwich, NEW LONDON COUNTY
Norwich vic., NEW LONDON COUNTY
Norwichtown, NEW LONDON COUNTY

Old Lyme, NEW LONDON COUNTY
Old Saybrook, MIDDLESEX COUNTY

Pawcatuck, NEW LONDON COUNTY
Phoenixville, WINDHAM COUNTY
Plainfield, WINDHAM COUNTY
Plainville, HARTFORD COUNTY
Portland, MIDDLESEX COUNTY
Preston City, NEW LONDON COUNTY
Putnam, WINDHAM COUNTY

Redding, FAIRFIELD COUNTY
Ridgefield, FAIRFIELD COUNTY
Rocky Hill, HARTFORD COUNTY

Scantic, HARTFORD COUNTY
Sharon, LITCHFIELD COUNTY
Silvermine, FAIRFIELD COUNTY
South Canaan, LITCHFIELD COUNTY
South Canterbury, WINDHAM COUNTY
South Glastonbury, HARTFORD COUNTY
South Norwalk, FAIRFIELD COUNTY
Southbury, NEW HAVEN COUNTY
Southport, FAIRFIELD COUNTY
Stamford, FAIRFIELD COUNTY
Stanwich vic., FAIRFIELD COUNTY
Sterling Hill, WINDHAM COUNTY
Stonington, NEW LONDON COUNTY
Straitsville, NEW HAVEN COUNTY
Stratford, FAIRFIELD COUNTY
Suffield, HARTFORD COUNTY
Suffield Center, HARTFORD COUNTY

Taftville, NEW LONDON COUNTY
Thomaston, LITCHFIELD COUNTY
Torrington, LITCHFIELD COUNTY
Trumbull, FAIRFIELD COUNTY

W. Stafford Springs, TOLLAND COUNTY
Wallingford, NEW HAVEN COUNTY
Waterbury, NEW HAVEN COUNTY
Watertown, LITCHFIELD COUNTY
West Goshen, LITCHFIELD COUNTY
West Hartford, HARTFORD COUNTY
West Haven, NEW HAVEN COUNTY
West Suffield, HARTFORD COUNTY
Westport, FAIRFIELD COUNTY
Wethersfield, HARTFORD COUNTY
Whitneyville, NEW HAVEN COUNTY
Willimantic, WINDHAM COUNTY
Wilton, FAIRFIELD COUNTY
Winchester Center, LITCHFIELD COUNTY
Windsor, HARTFORD COUNTY
Windsor Hill, HARTFORD COUNTY
Windsor Locks, HARTFORD COUNTY
Winsted, LITCHFIELD COUNTY
Woodbridge, NEW HAVEN COUNTY
Woodbury, LITCHFIELD COUNTY
Woodbury vic., LITCHFIELD COUNTY
Woodstock, WINDHAM COUNTY

Delaware

Armstrong Corner Vic, NEW CASTLE COUNTY
Ashland, NEW CASTLE COUNTY

Bethel, SUSSEX COUNTY
Biddles Corner, NEW CASTLE COUNTY
Biddles Corner vic., NEW CASTLE COUNTY
Blackiston vic., KENT COUNTY
Bridgeville, SUSSEX COUNTY

Camden, KENT COUNTY
Camden vic., KENT COUNTY
Centerville vic., NEW CASTLE COUNTY
Christiana, NEW CASTLE COUNTY
Christiana vic., NEW CASTLE COUNTY
Clarksville vic., SUSSEX COUNTY
Claymont vic., NEW CASTLE COUNTY
Clayton vic., KENT COUNTY
Collins Beach vic., NEW CASTLE COUNTY
Cool Spring vic., SUSSEX COUNTY
Corner Ketch, NEW CASTLE COUNTY
Corner Ketch vic., NEW CASTLE COUNTY
Cristiana vic., NEW CASTLE COUNTY

Dagsboro, SUSSEX COUNTY
Dover, KENT COUNTY
Dover vic., KENT COUNTY

Frederica, KENT COUNTY
Frederica vic., KENT COUNTY

Georgetown, SUSSEX COUNTY
Glasgow, NEW CASTLE COUNTY
Glasgow vic., NEW CASTLE COUNTY
Granogue vic., NEW CASTLE COUNTY
Greenville vic., NEW CASTLE COUNTY
Greenwood vic., SUSSEX COUNTY

Harrington vic., KENT COUNTY
Hockessin vic., NEW CASTLE COUNTY

Kenton vic., KENT COUNTY
Kirkwood vic., NEW CASTLE COUNTY

Laurel, SUSSEX COUNTY
Laurel vic., SUSSEX COUNTY
Leipsic, KENT COUNTY
Leipsic vic., KENT COUNTY
Lewes, SUSSEX COUNTY
Little Creek, KENT COUNTY
Little Creek vic., KENT COUNTY

Magnolia, KENT COUNTY
Marshallton, NEW CASTLE COUNTY
Marshallton vic., NEW CASTLE COUNTY

Mcconough vic., NEW CASTLE COUNTY
Mcdonough vic., NEW CASTLE COUNTY
Middletown vic., NEW CASTLE COUNTY
Milford, KENT COUNTY
Milford, SUSSEX COUNTY
Milford vic., KENT COUNTY
Milford vic., SUSSEX COUNTY
Millsboro, SUSSEX COUNTY
Milltown vic., NEW CASTLE COUNTY
Minquadale, NEW CASTLE COUNTY
Mt. Cuba vic., NEW CASTLE COUNTY
Mt. Pleasant vic., NEW CASTLE COUNTY

Naaman, NEW CASTLE COUNTY
New Castle, NEW CASTLE COUNTY
New Castle vic., NEW CASTLE COUNTY
Newark, NEW CASTLE COUNTY
Newark vic., NEW CASTLE COUNTY
Newport, NEW CASTLE COUNTY

Oak Orchard vic., SUSSEX COUNTY
Odessa, NEW CASTLE COUNTY
Odessa vic., NEW CASTLE COUNTY
Ogletown vic., NEW CASTLE COUNTY

Pea Patch Island, NEW CASTLE COUNTY
Port Penn vic., NEW CASTLE COUNTY
Price's Corner vic., NEW CASTLE COUNTY
Prices Corner vic., NEW CASTLE COUNTY

Rehobeth Beach, SUSSEX COUNTY
Rehobeth Beach vic., SUSSEX COUNTY
Rockland, NEW CASTLE COUNTY
Rockland vic., NEW CASTLE COUNTY

Seaford vic., SUSSEX COUNTY
Smyrna, KENT COUNTY
Smyrna vic., KENT COUNTY
Smyrna vic., NEW CASTLE COUNTY
Stanton, NEW CASTLE COUNTY
Summit Bridge vic., NEW CASTLE COUNTY

Taylor's Bridge, NEW CASTLE COUNTY
Taylor's Bridge vic., NEW CASTLE COUNTY
Thomas Landing vic., NEW CASTLE COUNTY
Townsend, NEW CASTLE COUNTY
Tybouts Corner vic., NEW CASTLE COUNTY

Wilmington, NEW CASTLE COUNTY
Wilmington vic., NEW CASTLE COUNTY
Woodland, SUSSEX COUNTY
Woodland vic., SUSSEX COUNTY

Yorklyn, NEW CASTLE COUNTY

District Of Columbia

Arlington

Washington, DISTRICT OF COLUMBIA

Florida

Altamonte Springs, SEMINOLE COUNTY
Apalachicola, FRANKLIN COUNTY
Auburdale, POLK COUNTY

Capps, JEFFERSON COUNTY
Coral Gables, DADE COUNTY
Cross Creek, ALACHUA COUNTY

Dry Tortugas Islands, MONROE COUNTY

Ellenton, MANATEE COUNTY

Fernandina Beach, NASSAU COUNTY
Fort George Island, DUVAL COUNTY
Fort Lauderdale, BROWARD COUNTY

Gainesville, ALACHUA COUNTY

Hampton Springs vic., TAYLOR COUNTY

Island Grove, ALACHUA COUNTY

Jacksonville, DUVAL COUNTY

Key Biscayne, DADE COUNTY
Key West, MONROE COUNTY
Knight Key, MONROE COUNTY

Lakeland, POLK COUNTY

Madison, MADISON COUNTY
Maitland, ORANGE COUNTY
Manalapan, PALM BEACH COUNTY
Marianna, JACKSON COUNTY
Miami, DADE COUNTY
Monticello, JEFFERSON COUNTY

New Smyrna, VOLUSIA COUNTY

Orlando, ORANGE COUNTY

Palm Beach, PALM BEACH COUNTY
Pensacola
Pensacola, ESCAMBIA COUNTY

Quincy, GADSDEN COUNTY

Rattlesnake Island, ST. JOHNS COUNTY

St. Augustine, ST. JOHNS COUNTY
St. Augustine vic., FLAGLER COUNTY
St. Johns Bluff, DUVAL COUNTY
St. Petersburg Beach, PINELLAS COUNTY
Starke, BRADFORD COUNTY

Tallahassee, LEON COUNTY
Tallahassee vic., LEON COUNTY
Tampa, HILLSBOROUGH COUNTY
Tampa,ybor City, HILLSBOROUGH COUNTY
Titusville vic., BREVARD COUNTY

White Springs, HAMILTON COUNTY

Georgia

Adairsville vic., BARTOW COUNTY
Arnoldsville vic., OGLETHORPE COUNTY
Athens, CLARKE COUNTY
Athens vic., CLARKE COUNTY
Atlanta, FULTON COUNTY
Atlanta, HARRIS COUNTY
Atlanta vic., COBB COUNTY
Augusta, RICHMOND COUNTY
Augusta vic., RICHMOND COUNTY

Barnesville vic., PIKE COUNTY
Between, WALTON COUNTY
Bibb City, MUSCOGEE COUNTY
Blairsville vic., UNION COUNTY
Broadfield vic., GLYNN COUNTY

Carlton vic., MADISON COUNTY
Cartersville vic., BARTOW COUNTY
Cash vic., GORDON COUNTY
Clarksville, HABERSHAM COUNTY
Cleveland, WHITE COUNTY
Clinton, JONES COUNTY
Cobbham, MCDUFFIE COUNTY
College Park, FULTON COUNTY
Colquitt vic., MILLER COUNTY
Columbus, MUSCOGEE COUNTY
Columbus vic., MUSCOGEE COUNTY
Covington, NEWTON COUNTY
Covington vic., NEWTON COUNTY
Crawfordville, TALIAFERRO COUNTY
Cumberland Island, CAMDEN COUNTY

Dahlenega, LUMPKIN COUNTY
Darien, MCINTOSH COUNTY
Darien vic., MCINTOSH COUNTY
Davidsboro vic., WASHINGTON COUNTY
Dial, FANNIN COUNTY

Eatonton, PUTNAM COUNTY
Eatonton vic., PUTNAM COUNTY
Elberton vic., ELBERT COUNTY
Ellerslie vic., HARRIS COUNTY

Fairburn, FULTON COUNTY
Fairburn vic., FULTON COUNTY
Fairmount vic., GORDON COUNTY
Fitzgerald, BEN HILL COUNTY
Fort Valley, PEACH COUNTY

Gainesville, HALL COUNTY
Glenwood vic., WHEELER COUNTY
Griffen, SPALDING COUNTY
Griffin, SPALDING COUNTY

Haddock vic., JONES COUNTY
Hartwell vic., HART COUNTY
Heardmont vic., ELBERT COUNTY
Hiawassee vic., TOWNS COUNTY
High Shoals, WALTON COUNTY
Homer vic., BANKS COUNTY
Hoschton vic., BARROW COUNTY

Irwinville vic., IRWIN COUNTY

Jacksonville vic., COFFEE COUNTY
Jefferson, JACKSON COUNTY
Jekyll Island, GLYNN COUNTY

Kennesaw, COBB COUNTY
Knoxville, CRAWFORD COUNTY

La Fayette, WALKER COUNTY
La Grange, TROUP COUNTY
La Grange vic., TROUP COUNTY
Lagrange, TROUP COUNTY
Lexington, OGLETHORPE COUNTY
Louisville, JEFFERSON COUNTY

Macon, BIBB COUNTY
Madison, MORGAN COUNTY
Marietta, COBB COUNTY
Marshallville, MACON COUNTY
Marshallville vic., MACON COUNTY
Mc Donough, HENRY COUNTY
Middleton, ELBERT COUNTY
Midway, LIBERTY COUNTY
Milledgeville, BALDWIN COUNTY
Milledgeville vic., BALDWIN COUNTY
Millegeville, BALDWIN COUNTY
Mineral Bluff, FANNIN COUNTY
Monroe, WALTON COUNTY
Montrose vic., LAURENS COUNTY

Mount Berry, FLOYD COUNTY

Nacoochee Valley, WHITE COUNTY
New Town vic., GORDON COUNTY
Newnan vic., COWETA COUNTY

Oxford, NEWTON COUNTY

Panola vic., DE KALB COUNTY
Pearl vic., ELBERT COUNTY
Plains, SUMTER COUNTY
Plains & Plains vic., SUMTER COUNTY
Plains vic., SUMTER COUNTY

Ranger vic., GORDON COUNTY
Rincon, EFFINGHAM COUNTY
Rising Fawn vic., DADE COUNTY
Rock Spring., WALKER COUNTY
Rome, FLOYD COUNTY
Roswell, FULTON COUNTY
Ruckersville, ELBERT COUNTY
Ruckersville vic., ELBERT COUNTY
Ruckerville vic., ELBERT COUNTY

Sapelo Island, MCINTOSH COUNTY
Savannah, CHATHAM COUNTY
Savannah, ELBERT COUNTY
Savannah vic., CHATHAM COUNTY
Savannah vic., ELBERT COUNTY
Scottdale, DE KALB COUNTY
Shoals vic., HANCOCK COUNTY
Snellsville vic., GWINNETT COUNTY
Snellville vic., GWINNETT COUNTY
Sparta, HANCOCK COUNTY
Spring Place, MURRAY COUNTY
St. Mary's, CAMDEN COUNTY
St. Mary's vic., CAMDEN COUNTY
St. Simons Island, GLYNN COUNTY

Talbotton, TALBOT COUNTY
Tallapoosa vic., HARALSON COUNTY
Thomasville, THOMAS COUNTY
Thomson vic., MCDUFFIE COUNTY
Tifton, TIFT COUNTY
Toccoa vic., STEPHENS COUNTY
Toomsboro vic., WILKINSON COUNTY

Warm Springs, MERIWETHER COUNTY
Warthen vic., WASHINGTON COUNTY
Washington, WILKES COUNTY
Washington vic., WILKES COUNTY
Watkinsville, OCONEE COUNTY
Waynesboro, BURKE COUNTY
West Point, TROUP COUNTY
Whitesville vic., HARRIS COUNTY
Woodbine vic., CAMDEN COUNTY

Guam

Orote Point, GUAM COUNTY

Hawaii

Hanalei, KAUAI COUNTY
Hanamaulu, KAUAI COUNTY
Hilo, HAWAII COUNTY
Honolulu, HONOLULU COUNTY

Kailua-Kona, HAWAII COUNTY
Kalaupapa, KALAWAO
Kalaupapa vic., KALAWAO
Kalawao, KALAWAO
Kaunakakai (Molokai), MAUI COUNTY
Kohala, HAWAII COUNTY
Kualapuu (Molokai Is, MAUI COUNTY

Lahaina, MAUI COUNTY
Lihue, KAUAI COUNTY

Olowalu, MAUI COUNTY

Paia, MAUI COUNTY
Pearl Harbor, HONOLULU COUNTY
Puako, HAWAII COUNTY
Pukoo vic. (Molokai), MAUI COUNTY

Spreckelsville, MAUI COUNTY

Ulupalakua, MAUI COUNTY

Wahiawa, HONOLULU COUNTY
Waiakoa, MAUI COUNTY
Waianae, HONOLULU COUNTY
Wailuku, MAUI COUNTY

Idaho

American Falls, POWER COUNTY
Ashton, FREMONT COUNTY
Atlanta, ELMORE COUNTY
Atlanta vic., ELMORE COUNTY
Avery, SHOSHONE COUNTY

Boise, ADA COUNTY
Boise vic., ADA COUNTY
Bonner's Ferry, BOUNDARY COUNTY
Bruneau Valley vic., OWYHEE COUNTY
Burley, CASSIA COUNTY

Cambridge vic., WASHINGTON COUNTY
Cascade vic., VALLEY COUNTY
Cataldo vic., KOOTENAI COUNTY
Coeur D'alene, KOOTENAI COUNTY

Eastport, BOUNDARY COUNTY
Elk City vic., IDAHO COUNTY

Garden Valley, BOISE COUNTY

Heise vic., JEFFERSON COUNTY

Idaho City, BOISE COUNTY
Idaho City vic., BOISE COUNTY
Island Park, FREMONT COUNTY
Island Park vic., FREMONT COUNTY

Kamiah vic., IDAHO COUNTY
Kuna, ADA COUNTY
Kuna vic., ADA COUNTY
Kuna vic., OWYHEE COUNTY

Leadore vic., LEMHI COUNTY
Lowman vic., BOISE COUNTY

Mccammon, BANNOCK COUNTY
Midvale, WASHINGTON COUNTY
Montour, GEM COUNTY
Montour vic., GEM COUNTY
Montpelier vic., BEAR LAKE COUNTY
Murtaugh vic., JEROME COUNTY

Nampa vic., CANYON COUNTY

Ola vic., GEM COUNTY
Oldtown, BONNER COUNTY

Paul, MINIDOKA COUNTY
Pocatello, BANNOCK COUNTY

Salmon, LEMHI COUNTY
Salmon vic., LEMHI COUNTY
Shelley vic., BINGHAM COUNTY
Smiths Ferry vic., VALLEY COUNTY
Spalding, NEZ PERCE COUNTY
Stanley vic., BLAINE COUNTY

Thatcher vic., FRANKLIN COUNTY
Twin Falls, TWIN FALLS COUNTY
Twin Falls vic., JEROME COUNTY

Wallace, SHOSHONE COUNTY
Warm Lake vic., VALLEY COUNTY
Woodville vic., BINGHAM COUNTY

Illinois

Addison, DU PAGE COUNTY
Albion, EDWARDS COUNTY
Alton, MADISON COUNTY
Alton vic., MADISON COUNTY
Anna, UNION COUNTY
Aurora, KANE COUNTY

Barry, PIKE COUNTY
Batavia, KANE COUNTY
Beardstown, CASS COUNTY
Belleville, ST. CLAIR COUNTY
Belvidere, BOONE COUNTY
Belvidere vic., BOONE COUNTY
Bement, PIATT COUNTY
Bement vic., PIATT COUNTY
Biggsville vic., HENDERSON COUNTY
Bishop Hill, HENRY COUNTY
Bishop Hill vic., HENRY COUNTY
Bloomingdale vic., DU PAGE COUNTY
Bloomington, MCLEAN COUNTY
Blue Island vic., COOK COUNTY
Brookfield, COOK COUNTY

Cahokia, ST. CLAIR COUNTY
Cairo, ALEXANDER COUNTY
Cairo, PULASKI COUNTY
Carbondale vic., JACKSON COUNTY
Carlinville, MACOUPIN COUNTY
Carlyle, CLINTON COUNTY
Channahon, WILL COUNTY
Channahon vic., WILL COUNTY
Cherry Valley, BOONE COUNTY
Chicago
Chicago, COOK COUNTY
Columbia, MONROE COUNTY

Decatur, MACON COUNTY
Delray, IROQUOIS COUNTY
Depue, BUREAU COUNTY

East Hannibal, PIKE COUNTY
East St. Louis, ST. CLAIR COUNTY
Eden vic., RANDOLPH COUNTY
Edwardsville, MADISON COUNTY
Edwardsville vic., MADISON COUNTY
Elgin, BROWN COUNTY
Elmhurst, DU PAGE COUNTY
Elmurst, DU PAGE COUNTY
Evanston, COOK COUNTY

Fall Creek vic., ADAMS COUNTY

Fayville, KANE COUNTY
Fort Gage, RANDOLPH COUNTY
Fort Sheridan, LAKE COUNTY
Frankfort vic., WILL COUNTY
Freeport vic., STEPHENSON COUNTY
Fullerburg vic., DU PAGE COUNTY
Fullersburg, DU PAGE COUNTY
Fulton vic., WHITESIDE COUNTY

Galena, JO DAVIESS COUNTY
Galena vic., JO DAVIESS COUNTY
Galesburg, KNOX COUNTY
Geneva, KANE COUNTY
Geneva vic., KANE COUNTY
Genoa vic., DOUGLAS COUNTY
Gladstone, HENDERSON COUNTY
Glencoe, COOK COUNTY
Godfrey, MADISON COUNTY
Grand Detour, OGLE COUNTY
Granite City, MADISON COUNTY

Halfday, LAKE COUNTY
Highland Park, LAKE COUNTY
Homer vic., CHAMPAIGN COUNTY

Jacksonville, MORGAN COUNTY
Joliet, WILL COUNTY
Jonesboro, UNION COUNTY
Jubilee, PEORIA COUNTY

Kaskaskia, RANDOLPH COUNTY
Keithsburg, MERCER COUNTY
Kenilworth, COOK COUNTY
Knoxville, KNOX COUNTY

La Salle, LA SALLE COUNTY
Lamoille vic., BUREAU COUNTY
Lasalle, LA SALLE COUNTY
Lebanon, ST. CLAIR COUNTY
Lee Center, LEE COUNTY
Lemont, COOK COUNTY
Lena vic., STEPHENSON COUNTY
Lewiston, FULTON COUNTY
Lisbon, KENDALL COUNTY
Little York vic., WARREN COUNTY
Lockport, WILL COUNTY
London Mills, KNOX COUNTY
London Mills vic., FULTON COUNTY

Mackinaw, TAZEWELL COUNTY
Marengo, MCHENRY COUNTY
Marion, WILLIAMSON COUNTY
Marseilles, LA SALLE COUNTY
Marseilles, WILL COUNTY
Mendota, LA SALLE COUNTY
Minnoka, GRUNDY COUNTY
Minooka vic., GRUNDY COUNTY
Monmouth, WARREN COUNTY
Monticello, PIATT COUNTY
Morris, GRUNDY COUNTY
Morris vic., GRUNDY COUNTY
Mossville, PEORIA COUNTY
Mount Vernon, JEFFERSON COUNTY
Mt. Carroll, CARROLL COUNTY
Mundelein, LAKE COUNTY

Naderville, DU PAGE COUNTY
Naperville, DU PAGE COUNTY
Naperville vic., DU PAGE COUNTY
Nauvoo, HANCOCK COUNTY
New Baden vic., ST. CLAIR COUNTY
New Boston, MERCER COUNTY
New Haven, GALLATIN COUNTY
Normal, MCLEAN COUNTY

Oak Park, COOK COUNTY
Oakland, COLES COUNTY
Onarga vic., IROQUOIS COUNTY
Oquawka, HENDERSON COUNTY
Oquawka vic., HENDERSON COUNTY
Ottawa, LA SALLE COUNTY
Ottawa vic., LA SALLE COUNTY

Paris, EDGAR COUNTY
Paxton, FORD COUNTY
Payson, ADAMS COUNTY
Penfield, CHAMPAIGN COUNTY
Peoria, PEORIA COUNTY
Peru, LA SALLE COUNTY
Petersburg, MENARD COUNTY
Pittsfield, PIKE COUNTY
Plainsfield, WILL COUNTY
Plano vic., KENDALL COUNTY
Pleasant Plains, SANGAMON COUNTY
Prairie Du Rocher, RANDOLPH COUNTY

Quincy, ADAMS COUNTY

Rantoul vic., CHAMPAIGN COUNTY
Redbud, RANDOLPH COUNTY
River Forest, COOK COUNTY
Riverside, COOK COUNTY
Rock Island, ROCK ISLAND COUNTY
Rockdale, WILL COUNTY
Rockdale Viv., WILL COUNTY
Rockford, WINNEBAGO COUNTY
Rockford vic., WINNEBAGO COUNTY
Rockton, WINNEBAGO COUNTY
Romeoville, WILL COUNTY

Saunemin vic., LIVINGSTON COUNTY
Savanna, CARROLL COUNTY
Seneca, LA SALLE COUNTY
Shawneetown, GALLATIN COUNTY
Sparta vic., RANDOLPH COUNTY
Springfield, SANGAMON COUNTY
St. Charles, KANE COUNTY
Sublette, LEE COUNTY
Summit, COOK COUNTY

Thebes, ALEXANDER COUNTY
Tilden vic., RANDOLPH COUNTY
Toulon, STARK COUNTY
Tremont, TAZEWELL COUNTY

Urbana vic., CHAMPAIGN COUNTY
Utica, LA SALLE COUNTY
Utica vic., LA SALLE COUNTY

Virginia vic., CASS COUNTY

Warrenville, DU PAGE COUNTY
Warsaw, HANCOCK COUNTY
Waterloo, MONROE COUNTY
Waterloo vic., MONROE COUNTY
Waukegan, LAKE COUNTY
Waukegan vic., LAKE COUNTY
White Heath vic., PIATT COUNTY
Wilmette, COOK COUNTY
Winchester, SCOTT COUNTY
Woodstock vic., MCHENRY COUNTY

Indiana

Alamo vic., MONTGOMERY COUNTY
Alton vic., CRAWFORD COUNTY
Anderson, MADISON COUNTY
Angola vic., STEUBEN COUNTY
Aurora, DEARBORN COUNTY
Aurora vic., OHIO COUNTY

Bloomingdale, PARKE COUNTY
Bloomington, MONROE COUNTY
Brownsville, UNION COUNTY
Butler, DE KALB COUNTY

Cambridge City, WAYNE COUNTY
Cannelton, PERRY COUNTY
Centerville, WAYNE COUNTY
Charlestown, CLARK COUNTY
Chesterton vic., PORTER COUNTY
Clarks Hill vic., TIPPECANOE COUNTY
Clay City vic., CLAY COUNTY
Columbus, BARTHOLOMEW COUNTY
Connersville, FAYETTE COUNTY
Connersville vic., FAYETTE COUNTY
Corydon, HARRISON COUNTY
Crawfordsville, MONTGOMERY COUNTY
Cutler, CARROLL COUNTY

Decatur, ADAMS COUNTY
Dunlapsville, UNION COUNTY

Elkhart, ELKHART COUNTY
Evansville, VANDERBURGH COUNTY

Fairfield, FRANKLIN COUNTY
Fort Wayne, ALLEN COUNTY
Fountain City, WAYNE COUNTY
Franklin, JOHNSON COUNTY

Gary, LAKE COUNTY
Geneva, ADAMS COUNTY
Gosport, OWEN COUNTY
Greensburg vic., DECATUR COUNTY

Harrison Twp., DELAWARE COUNTY
Hartford City, BLACKFORD COUNTY
Huntington, HUNTINGTON COUNTY
Hutsonville, CRAWFORD COUNTY

Independence vic., WARREN COUNTY
Indianapolis, MARION COUNTY
Indianapolis, MARSHALL COUNTY

Jeffersonville, CLARK COUNTY

Knightstown, HENRY COUNTY
Kokomo, HOWARD COUNTY

Lafayette, TIPPECANOE COUNTY
Logansport, CASS COUNTY

Madison, JEFFERSON COUNTY
Madison vic., JEFFERSON COUNTY
Mansfield, PARKE COUNTY
Marion, GRANT COUNTY
Matthews, GRANT COUNTY
Mccordsville vic., HANCOCK COUNTY
Medora, JACKSON COUNTY
Medora vic., JACKSON COUNTY
Metamora, FRANKLIN COUNTY
Michigan City, LA PORTE COUNTY
Milton, WAYNE COUNTY
Milton vic., WAYNE COUNTY
Mishawaka, ST. JOSEPH COUNTY
Mitchell, LAWRENCE COUNTY
Mongo, LAGRANGE COUNTY
Montezuma, PARKE COUNTY
Mooreland vic., HENRY COUNTY
Morris, RIPLEY COUNTY
Mount Auburn, WAYNE COUNTY
Muncie, DELAWARE COUNTY
Muncie vic., DELAWARE COUNTY

New Albany, FLOYD COUNTY
New Carlisle, LA PORTE COUNTY
New Harmony, POSEY COUNTY

Newburgh, WARRICK COUNTY
Newport, VERMILLION COUNTY
Noblesville, HAMILTON COUNTY
Noblesville vic., HAMILTON COUNTY
North Manchester, WABASH COUNTY

Paoli, ORANGE COUNTY
Patriot vic., SWITZERLAND COUNTY
Pendleton vic., MADISON COUNTY
Pennville, WAYNE COUNTY
Pinola, LA PORTE COUNTY
Pleasant Township, ALLEN COUNTY

Richmond, WAYNE COUNTY
Ridgeville, RANDOLPH COUNTY
Riverside vic., FOUNTAIN COUNTY
Rochester vic., FULTON COUNTY
Rushville, RUSH COUNTY
Rushville vic., RUSH COUNTY

Salem, WASHINGTON COUNTY
Seymour, JACKSON COUNTY
Shelbyville, SHELBY COUNTY
South Bend, ST. JOSEPH COUNTY
St. John, LAKE COUNTY

Terre Haute, VIGO COUNTY
Turkey Run St. Park, PARKE COUNTY

Union City, RANDOLPH COUNTY

Vera Cruz vic., WELLS COUNTY
Vernon, JENNINGS COUNTY
Versailles, RIPLEY COUNTY
Vevay, SWITZERLAND COUNTY
Vincennes, KNOX COUNTY

Washington, DAVIESS COUNTY
Waterloo vic., FAYETTE COUNTY
West Baden, ORANGE COUNTY
Wilkinson, HANCOCK COUNTY

Yorktown, DELAWARE COUNTY
Yorktown vic., DELAWARE COUNTY
Young America vic., CASS COUNTY

Iowa

Agency City, WAPELLO COUNTY
Amana, IOWA COUNTY
Amana vic., IOWA COUNTY
Ames, STORY COUNTY
Audubon, AUDUBON COUNTY

Bangor vic., MARSHALL COUNTY
Bellevue, JACKSON COUNTY
Bentonsport, VAN BUREN COUNTY
Bevington, MADISON COUNTY
Bloomfield vic., DAVIS COUNTY
Boone, BOONE COUNTY
Burlington, DES MOINES COUNTY
Burlington vic., DES MOINES COUNTY

Carlisle vic., WARREN COUNTY
Cedar Rapids, LINN COUNTY
Cherokee, CHEROKEE COUNTY
Clarinda, PAGE COUNTY
Clay Township, JONES COUNTY
Clermont vic., FAYETTE COUNTY
Clinton, CLINTON COUNTY
Council Bluffs, POTTAWATTAMIE COUNTY

Creston, UNION COUNTY

Davenport, SCOTT COUNTY
Decorah, WINNESHIEK COUNTY
Decorah vic., WINNESHIEK COUNTY
Des Moines, POLK COUNTY
Dow City, CRAWFORD COUNTY
Dubuque, DUBUQUE COUNTY
Dubuque vic., DUBUQUE COUNTY

Elkader, CLAYTON COUNTY

Fairfield, JEFFERSON COUNTY
Festina vic., WINNESHIEK COUNTY
Flores vic., WAPELLO COUNTY
Fort Dodge, WEBSTER COUNTY
Fort Madison, LEE COUNTY
Frankville vic., WINNESHIEK COUNTY

Gilbert vic., STORY COUNTY
Greene, BUTLER COUNTY
Grinell, POWESHIEK COUNTY
Guttenburg, CLAYTON COUNTY

Hampton, FRANKLIN COUNTY
Holy Cross vic., DUBUQUE COUNTY
Humboldt, HUMBOLDT COUNTY

Independence, BUCHANAN COUNTY
Iowa City, JOHNSON COUNTY

Jackson Twp., HENRY COUNTY

Kendallville vic., WINNESHIEK COUNTY
Keokuk, LEE COUNTY
Keosauqua, VAN BUREN COUNTY
Knoxville vic., MARION COUNTY

Le Claire, SCOTT COUNTY
Le Claire vic., SCOTT COUNTY
Lime Springs vic., HOWARD COUNTY

Maquoketa vic., JACKSON COUNTY
Marietta, MARSHALL COUNTY
Marshalltown, MARSHALL COUNTY
Marshalltown vic., MARSHALL COUNTY
Mason City, CERRO GORDO COUNTY
Middletown, DES MOINES COUNTY
Missouri Valley vic., HARRISON COUNTY
Monmouth Township, JACKSON COUNTY
Monroe, JASPER COUNTY
Mount Pleasant, HENRY COUNTY
Muscatine, MUSCATINE COUNTY
Muscatine vic., MUSCATINE COUNTY

Nashua vic., CHICKASAW COUNTY
Newton, JASPER COUNTY

Okoboji vic., DICKINSON COUNTY
Oskaloosa, MAHASKA COUNTY
Oskaloosa vic., MAHASKA COUNTY
Ottumwa, WAPELLO COUNTY

Pella, MARION COUNTY
Protivin, HOWARD COUNTY

Quasqueton, BUCHANAN COUNTY

Red Oak, MONTGOMERY COUNTY
Riverton vic., FREMONT COUNTY
Rock Rapids vic., LYON COUNTY

Sheldahl, STORY COUNTY
Sioux City, WOODBURY COUNTY
Solon vic., JOHNSON COUNTY
Spirit Lake, DICKINSON COUNTY
Springdale vic., CEDAR COUNTY

St. Donatus, JACKSON COUNTY

Valley Junction vic., POLK COUNTY
Vandalia, JASPER COUNTY
Vinton, BENTON COUNTY

Waterloo, BLACK HAWK COUNTY
Waukon, ALLAMAKEE COUNTY
Waverly vic., BREMER COUNTY
Webster City, HAMILTON COUNTY
West Branch, CEDAR COUNTY
Winterset, MADISON COUNTY

Kansas

Abilene, DICKINSON COUNTY
Albany, NEMAHA COUNTY

Baldwin, DOUGLAS COUNTY
Bloomington, OSBORNE COUNTY

Catherine, ELLIS COUNTY
Clinton vic., DOUGLAS COUNTY
Coffeyville, MONTGOMERY COUNTY
Council Grove, MORRIS COUNTY

De Soto, JOHNSON COUNTY

Enterprise, DICKINSON COUNTY

Fort Leavenworth, LEAVENWORTH COUNTY
Fort Riley, RILEY COUNTY

Hanover, WASHINGTON COUNTY
Hays, ELLIS COUNTY
Highland, DONIPHAN COUNTY
Hope vic., DICKINSON COUNTY

Inman vic., MCPHERSON COUNTY

Kansas City vic., JOHNSON COUNTY

Larned, PAWNEE COUNTY
Lawrence, DOUGLAS COUNTY
Leavenworth, LEAVENWORTH COUNTY
Lecompton, DOUGLAS COUNTY
Liebenthal, RUSH COUNTY

Manhattan, RILEY COUNTY
Meriden vic., JEFFERSON COUNTY
Miller vic., LYON COUNTY
Muncie, WYANDOTTE COUNTY
Munjor, ELLIS COUNTY

Nicodemus, GRAHAM COUNTY

Osawatomie, MIAMI COUNTY
Oskaloosa, JEFFERSON COUNTY
Overland Park, JOHNSON COUNTY

Paola, MIAMI COUNTY
Parsons, LABETTE COUNTY

Schoenchen, ELLIS COUNTY
Silver Lake vic., SHAWNEE COUNTY
Springdale vic., LEAVENWORTH COUNTY
Studley, SHERIDAN COUNTY
Studley vic., SHERIDAN COUNTY
Stull vic., DOUGLAS COUNTY

Valley Falls vic., JEFFERSON COUNTY
Vinland, DOUGLAS COUNTY

Wabaunsee, WABAUNSEE COUNTY

Kentucky

Bardstown, NELSON COUNTY
Bardstown vic., NELSON COUNTY
Beattyville, LEE COUNTY
Berea, MADISON COUNTY
Bowling Green, WARREN COUNTY
Bradfordsville, MARION COUNTY
Brandenburg, MEADE COUNTY
Buechel vic., JEFFERSON COUNTY
Burlington vic., BOONE COUNTY
Butler, PENDLETON COUNTY

Chaplin vic., NELSON COUNTY
Covington, KENTON COUNTY
Covington vic., KENTON COUNTY
Cynthiana, HARRISON COUNTY

Danville, BOYLE COUNTY
Danville vic., BOYLE COUNTY
Dixon vic., WEBSTER COUNTY

Fishtrap vic., JOHNSON COUNTY
Frankfort, FRANKLIN COUNTY
Frankfort vic., FRANKLIN COUNTY

Geneva vic., HENDERSON COUNTY
Georgetown, SCOTT COUNTY
Grahamton, MEADE COUNTY
Greensburg, GREEN COUNTY

Harrodsburg, MERCER COUNTY
Harrodsburg vic., MERCER COUNTY
Henderson, HENDERSON COUNTY
Hodgenville, LARUE COUNTY
Holbrook vic., GRANT COUNTY
Hopkinsville vic., CHRISTIAN COUNTY

Lexington, FAYETTE COUNTY
Lexington (vic.), FAYETTE COUNTY
Lexington vic., FAYETTE COUNTY
Loretto vic., MARION COUNTY
Louisville, JEFFERSON COUNTY
Louisville vic., JEFFERSON COUNTY
Loyall, HARLAN COUNTY
Ludlow, KENTON COUNTY

Mammoth Cave, EDMONSON COUNTY
Maysville, MASON COUNTY
Milford vic., BRACKEN COUNTY
Munfordville vic., HART COUNTY

Owensboro vic., DAVIESS COUNTY

Paducah, MCCRACKEN COUNTY
Paris, BOURBON COUNTY
Pikeville, PIKE COUNTY
Pikeville vic., PIKE COUNTY
Pineville, BELL COUNTY
Pisgah, WOODFORD COUNTY
Pleasant Hill, MERCER COUNTY
Pleasant Village, MERCER COUNTY

Richmond, MADISON COUNTY

Sampsonville, SHELBY COUNTY
Shelbyville, SHELBY COUNTY
Shelbyville vic., SHELBY COUNTY
South Union, LOGAN COUNTY
Springfield, WASHINGTON COUNTY
St. Matthews, JEFFERSON COUNTY
Stanford, LINCOLN COUNTY
Stanton, POWELL COUNTY

Talmage, MERCER COUNTY
Taylorsville vic., SPENCER COUNTY
Troy vic., WOODFORD COUNTY

Vanceburg vic., LEWIS COUNTY

Washington, MASON COUNTY
White Hall, MADISON COUNTY
Whitehall, MADISON COUNTY
Williamsburg, WHITLEY COUNTY
Williamsburg vic., WHITLEY COUNTY
Wolf Creek, MEADE COUNTY

Louisiana

Alexandria, RAPIDES PARISH
Alexandria vic., RAPIDES PARISH
Avery Island, IBERIA PARISH

Bains, WEST FELICIANA PARISH
Batchelor, POINTE COUPEE PARISH
Baton Rouge, EAST BATON ROUGE PARISH
Bermuda, NATCHITOCHES PARISH
Burnside, ASCENSION PARISH

Chambers vic., RAPIDES PARISH
Clinton, EAST FELICIANA PARISH
Convent vic., ST. JAMES PARISH

Destrehan, ST. CHARLES PARISH
Doyline, WEBSTER PARISH
Dubach vic., LINCOLN PARISH

Edgard, ST. JOHN THE BAPTIST PARISH

Franklin, RAPIDES PARISH

Geismar vic., ASCENSION PARISH
Grand Coteau, ST. LANDRY PARISH

Hahnville, ST. CHARLES PARISH
Hanhville, ST. CHARLES PARISH

Iberville vic., IBERVILLE PARISH

Krotz Springs, ST. LANDRY PARISH

La Place, ST. JOHN THE BAPTIST PARISH
Lafayette, LAFAYETTE PARISH
Lakeland, POINTE COUPEE PARISH
Larose vic., LAFOURCHE PARISH
Lecompte vic., RAPIDES PARISH
Longleaf, RAPIDES PARISH
Lucy, ST. JOHN THE BAPTIST PARISH

Melrose, NATCHITOCHES PARISH
Metairie, JEFFERSON PARISH
Mississippi River, ST. BERNARD PARISH
Monroe, OUACHITA PARISH

Napoleonville vic., ASSUMPTION PARISH
Natchitoches, NATCHITOCHES PARISH
Natchitoches vic., NATCHITOCHES PARISH
New Iberia, IBERIA PARISH
New Orleans, JEFFERSON PARISH
New Orleans, ORLEANS PARISH
New Orleans vic., ORLEANS PARISH
New Roads, POINTE COUPEE PARISH
New Roads vic., POINTE COUPEE PARISH

Opelousas, ST. LANDRY PARISH
Opelousas vic., ST. LANDRY PARISH
Oscar vic., POINTE COUPEE PARISH

Plaquemine, IBERVILLE PARISH

Reserve vic., ST. JOHN THE BAPTIST PARISH
Ruth, ST. MARTIN PARISH

Saint Francisville, WEST FELICIANA PARISH
Saint Rose, ST. CHARLES PARISH
Saint Rose vic., ST. CHARLES PARISH
Shreveport, CADDO PARISH
St. Gabriel, IBERVILLE PARISH
St. James, ST. JAMES PARISH
St. Martinville, ST. MARTIN PARISH
St. Martinville vic., ST. MARTIN PARISH
Sunset vic., ST. LANDRY PARISH
Sunshine vic., IBERVILLE PARISH

Thibodaux, LAFOURCHE PARISH

Union vic., ST. JAMES PARISH

Vacherie, ST. JAMES PARISH

Wallace, ST. JOHN THE BAPTIST PARISH
Washington, ST. LANDRY PARISH
Weyanoke, WEST FELICIANA PARISH
Weyanoke vic., WEST FELICIANA PARISH
White Castle vic., IBERVILLE PARISH

Maine

Alfred, YORK COUNTY
Alna, LINCOLN COUNTY
Andover, OXFORD COUNTY
Augusta, KENNEBEC COUNTY

Bailey Island, CUMBERLAND COUNTY
Baker Island, HANCOCK COUNTY
Bar Harbor vic., HANCOCK COUNTY
Bath, SAGADAHOC COUNTY
Belfast, WALDO COUNTY
Belfast vic., WALDO COUNTY
Biddeford, YORK COUNTY
Boon Island, YORK COUNTY
Bristol vic., LINCOLN COUNTY
Brunswick, CUMBERLAND COUNTY

Camden, KNOX COUNTY
Cape Elizabeth, CUMBERLAND COUNTY
Castine, HANCOCK COUNTY
Cedar Grove, LINCOLN COUNTY
Columbia Falls, WASHINGTON COUNTY

Damariscotta, LINCOLN COUNTY
Damariscotta Mills, LINCOLN COUNTY
Darmariscotta Mills, LINCOLN COUNTY

Edgecomb, LINCOLN COUNTY
Ellsworth, HANCOCK COUNTY

Falmouth vic., CUMBERLAND COUNTY

Gardiner, KENNEBEC COUNTY

Hallowell, KENNEBEC COUNTY
Harpswell, CUMBERLAND COUNTY
Head Tide, LINCOLN COUNTY

Jefferson vic., LINCOLN COUNTY

Kennebunk, YORK COUNTY
Kennebunkport, YORK COUNTY
Kittery Point, YORK COUNTY

Lewiston, ANDROSCOGGIN COUNTY
Lincolnville, WALDO COUNTY

Little Cranberry Is., HANCOCK COUNTY

Machias, WASHINGTON COUNTY
Monmouth, KENNEBEC COUNTY

New Portland, SOMERSET COUNTY
Newcastle, LINCOLN COUNTY
Newcastle vic., LINCOLN COUNTY
North Edgecomb, LINCOLN COUNTY

Ogunquit, YORK COUNTY

Paris, OXFORD COUNTY
Phippsburg, SAGADAHOC COUNTY
Phippsburg vic., SAGADAHOC COUNTY
Porter, OXFORD COUNTY
Portland, CUMBERLAND COUNTY

Richmond, SAGADAHOC COUNTY
Robinhood, SAGADAHOC COUNTY
Rockland, KNOX COUNTY
Rockland vic., KNOX COUNTY
Rockport, KNOX COUNTY
Rockport vic., KNOX COUNTY

Sabbathday Lake, CUMBERLAND COUNTY
Saco, YORK COUNTY
Scotland, YORK COUNTY
Searsport, WALDO COUNTY
South Portland, CUMBERLAND COUNTY
South Windham vic., CUMBERLAND COUNTY
Southwest Harbor Vic, HANCOCK COUNTY
St. Croix Island, WASHINGTON COUNTY
Stroudwater, CUMBERLAND COUNTY

Thomaston, KNOX COUNTY
Topsham, SAGADAHOC COUNTY
Topsham vic., SAGADAHOC COUNTY

Waldoboro vic., LINCOLN COUNTY
Walpole vic., LINCOLN COUNTY
Warren, KNOX COUNTY
Wells, YORK COUNTY
Westport Island, LINCOLN COUNTY
Windham Center vic., CUMBERLAND COUNTY
Winslow, KENNEBEC COUNTY
Wiscasset, LINCOLN COUNTY

York, YORK COUNTY

Maryland

Aberdeen, HARFORD COUNTY
Accokeek vic., PRINCE GEORGE'S COUNTY
Adelina, CALVERT COUNTY
Adelphi, PRINCE GEORGE'S COUNTY
Allen vic., WICOMICO COUNTY
Annapolis, ANNE ARUNDEL COUNTY
Annapolis vic., ANNE ARUNDEL COUNTY
Antietam vic., WASHINGTON COUNTY
Aquasco, PRINCE GEORGE'S COUNTY
Aquasco vic., PRINCE GEORGE'S COUNTY
Ashton, MONTGOMERY COUNTY

Baden, PRINCE GEORGE'S COUNTY
Baden vic., PRINCE GEORGE'S COUNTY
Baltimore (City)
Baltimore vic., BALTIMORE COUNTY
Baltimore vic., HOWARD COUNTY
Barstow vic., CALVERT COUNTY
Beallsville, MONTGOMERY COUNTY
Beallsville vic., MONTGOMERY COUNTY
Beaverdam vic., WORCESTER COUNTY
Bel Air, HARFORD COUNTY
Bel Air vic., HARFORD COUNTY
Belcamp, HARFORD COUNTY
Beltsville, PRINCE GEORGE'S COUNTY
Berlin, WORCESTER COUNTY
Berlin vic., WORCESTER COUNTY
Bethesda, MONTGOMERY COUNTY
Bethlehem, CAROLINE COUNTY
Big Spring vic., WASHINGTON COUNTY
Bladensburg, PRINCE GEORGE'S COUNTY
Blandensburg, PRINCE GEORGE'S COUNTY
Blossom Point, CHARLES COUNTY
Blue Ball, CECIL COUNTY
Bohemia River, CECIL COUNTY
Bowie, PRINCE GEORGE'S COUNTY
Bowie vic., PRINCE GEORGE'S COUNTY
Boyds, MONTGOMERY COUNTY
Brighton, MONTGOMERY COUNTY
Brookeville, MONTGOMERY COUNTY
Brookeville vic., MONTGOMERY COUNTY
Brookmont vic., MONTGOMERY COUNTY
Brunswick, FREDERICK COUNTY
Bryans Road vic., CHARLES COUNTY
Buena Vista, PRINCE GEORGE'S COUNTY
Buena Vista vic., PRINCE GEORGE'S COUNTY
Burtonsville, MONTGOMERY COUNTY
Bushwood, ST. MARY'S COUNTY
Butler vic., ANNE ARUNDEL COUNTY

Cabin John, MONTGOMERY COUNTY
Cabin John vic., MONTGOMERY COUNTY
Calvert vic., CECIL COUNTY
Cambridge vic., DORCHESTER COUNTY
Catoctin vic., FREDERICK COUNTY
Catoctin Village, FREDERICK COUNTY
Cecilton, CECIL COUNTY
Cecilton vic., CECIL COUNTY
Centreville vic., QUEEN ANNE'S COUNTY
Chaneyville vic., CALVERT COUNTY
Chaptico vic., ST. MARY'S COUNTY
Charlestown, CECIL COUNTY
Charlotte Hall, ST. MARY'S COUNTY
Chase vic., BALTIMORE COUNTY
Cheltenham, PRINCE GEORGE'S COUNTY
Cheltenham vic., PRINCE GEORGE'S COUNTY
Chesapeake City, CECIL COUNTY
Chestertown, KENT COUNTY
Chestertown vic., KENT COUNTY
Chesterville, KENT COUNTY
Cheverly, PRINCE GEORGE'S COUNTY
Chevy Chase vic., MONTGOMERY COUNTY
Church Creek, DORCHESTER COUNTY
Church Hill vic., QUEEN ANNE'S COUNTY
Churchville vic., HARFORD COUNTY
Clarksburg, MONTGOMERY COUNTY
Clearspring vic., WASHINGTON COUNTY
Clinton vic., PRINCE GEORGE'S COUNTY
Cockeysville, BALTIMORE COUNTY
Cockeysville vic., BALTIMORE COUNTY
Colesville, MONTGOMERY COUNTY
College Park, PRINCE GEORGE'S COUNTY
Collington vic., PRINCE GEORGE'S COUNTY
Collinsville vic., ANNE ARUNDEL COUNTY
Compton vic., ST. MARY'S COUNTY
Cononingo vic., CECIL COUNTY
Contee, PRINCE GEORGE'S COUNTY
Creswell vic., HARFORD COUNTY
Crisfield, SOMERSET COUNTY
Croom, PRINCE GEORGE'S COUNTY
Croom vic., PRINCE GEORGE'S COUNTY
Crownsville vic., ANNE ARUNDEL COUNTY
Cumberland, ALLEGANY COUNTY
Cumberland vic., ALLEGANY COUNTY
Cumberstone, ANNE ARUNDEL COUNTY
Cumberstone vic., ANNE ARUNDEL COUNTY
Dare's Wharf vic., CALVERT COUNTY
Darlington, HARFORD COUNTY
Darlington vic., HARFORD COUNTY
Darnestown vic., MONTGOMERY COUNTY
Davidsonville vic., ANNE ARUNDEL COUNTY
Dawsonville, MONTGOMERY COUNTY
Dawsonville vic., MONTGOMERY COUNTY
Denton, CAROLINE COUNTY
Dickerson, MONTGOMERY COUNTY
Dickerson vic., FREDERICK COUNTY
Dickerson vic., MONTGOMERY COUNTY
Drayden vic., ST. MARY'S COUNTY

Earleville vic., CECIL COUNTY
Easton, TALBOT COUNTY
Easton vic., TALBOT COUNTY
Ednor, MONTGOMERY COUNTY
Eldorado vic., DORCHESTER COUNTY
Elk Mills, CECIL COUNTY
Elk Mills vic., CECIL COUNTY
Elkridge, HOWARD COUNTY
Elkton, CECIL COUNTY
Elkton vic., CECIL COUNTY
Ellicott City, HOWARD COUNTY
Ellicott City vic., HOWARD COUNTY
Etchison, MONTGOMERY COUNTY

Fairhaven vic., ANNE ARUNDEL COUNTY
Fairlee Creek, KENT COUNTY
Fallston, HARFORD COUNTY
Fallston vic., HARFORD COUNTY
Federalsburg, CAROLINE COUNTY
Forestville vic., PRINCE GEORGE'S COUNTY
Forestville., PRINCE GEORGE'S COUNTY
Fork vic., BALTIMORE COUNTY
Fort Frederick vic., WASHINGTON COUNTY
Fort Washington vic., PRINCE GEORGE'S COUNTY
Franklinville vic., BALTIMORE COUNTY
Frederick, FREDERICK COUNTY
Frederick vic., FREDERICK COUNTY
Friendly vic., PRINCE GEORGE'S COUNTY
Friendship vic., ANNE ARUNDEL COUNTY
Frostburg, ALLEGANY COUNTY
Ft. Wash.forest vic., PRINCE GEORGE'S COUNTY
Ft.wash. Forest vic., PRINCE GEORGE'S COUNTY

Gaithersburg, MONTGOMERY COUNTY
Gaithersburg vic., MONTGOMERY COUNTY
Galena, KENT COUNTY
Galesville vic., ANNE ARUNDEL COUNTY
Gambrills vic., ANNE ARUNDEL COUNTY
Georgetown, KENT COUNTY
Girdletree, WORCESTER COUNTY
Girdletree vic., WORCESTER COUNTY
Glen Echo, MONTGOMERY COUNTY
Glen Echo vic., MONTGOMERY COUNTY
Glenville, HARFORD COUNTY
Granstville Vic, GARRETT COUNTY
Great Falls, MONTGOMERY COUNTY
Great Falls vic., MONTGOMERY COUNTY
Great Mills, ST. MARY'S COUNTY

Hagerstown, WASHINGTON COUNTY
Hagerstown vic.
Hagerstown vic., WASHINGTON COUNTY
Hancock vic., ALLEGANY COUNTY
Hancock vic., WASHINGTON COUNTY
Harpers Ferry vic., WASHINGTON COUNTY
Harwood vic., ANNE ARUNDEL COUNTY
Havre De Grace, HARFORD COUNTY
Havre De Grace vic., HARFORD COUNTY
Hebron vic., WICOMICO COUNTY
Hereford vic., BALTIMORE COUNTY

Hickory, HARFORD COUNTY
Hillsboro vic., QUEEN ANNE'S COUNTY
Hollywood vic., ST. MARY'S COUNTY
Huntingtown vic., CALVERT COUNTY
Hyattsville (Waso), PRINCE GEORGE'S COUNTY

Ilchester, BALTIMORE COUNTY
Ilchester vic., BALTIMORE COUNTY
Ilchester vic., HOWARD COUNTY

Jefferson, FREDERICK COUNTY
Jerusalem, HARFORD COUNTY
Jerusalem vic., HARFORD COUNTY
Joppatowne, HARFORD COUNTY

Keedysville vic., WASHINGTON COUNTY
Kent Island, QUEEN ANNE'S COUNTY
Keymar vic., CARROLL COUNTY
Kingston vic., SOMERSET COUNTY
Kingsville, BALTIMORE COUNTY
Kingsville vic., BALTIMORE COUNTY

La Plata vic., CHARLES COUNTY
Lander's Landing, FREDERICK COUNTY
Landover vic., PRINCE GEORGE'S COUNTY
Langford vic., CECIL COUNTY
Langley Park, PRINCE GEORGE'S COUNTY
Lapidum, HARFORD COUNTY
Lapidum vic., HARFORD COUNTY
Largo vic., PRINCE GEORGE'S COUNTY
Laurel Grove vic., ST. MARY'S COUNTY
Laurel vic., PRINCE GEORGE'S COUNTY
Laytonsville, MONTGOMERY COUNTY
Laytonsville vic., MONTGOMERY COUNTY
Leeland, PRINCE GEORGE'S COUNTY
Leeland vic., PRINCE GEORGE'S COUNTY
Leonardtown, ST. MARY'S COUNTY
Leonardtown vic., ST. MARY'S COUNTY
Level vic., HARFORD COUNTY
Lexington Park, ST. MARY'S COUNTY
Lexington Park vic., ST. MARY'S COUNTY
Liberty Town, FREDERICK COUNTY
Little Cove Point, CALVERT COUNTY
Locust Grove vic., KENT COUNTY
Long Green, BALTIMORE COUNTY
Lothian, ANNE ARUNDEL COUNTY
Lower Marlboro, CALVERT COUNTY
Lower Marlboro vic., CALVERT COUNTY
Lusby vic., CALVERT COUNTY

Mackall, CALVERT COUNTY
Maddox vic., ST. MARY'S COUNTY
Manokin, SOMERSET COUNTY
Manokin vic., SOMERSET COUNTY
Marbury vic., CHARLES COUNTY
Martinsburg vic., MONTGOMERY COUNTY
Matthews vic., TALBOT COUNTY
Mc Daniel vic., TALBOT COUNTY
Middletown, FREDERICK COUNTY
Middletown vic., FREDERICK COUNTY
Midland, ALLEGANY COUNTY
Millstone Landing, ST. MARY'S COUNTY
Millstone Landing Vi, ST. MARY'S COUNTY
Mitchellville, PRINCE GEORGE'S COUNTY
Monkton vic., BALTIMORE COUNTY
Morgantown, CHARLES COUNTY
Morganza, ST. MARY'S COUNTY
Mullikin, PRINCE GEORGE'S COUNTY
Mullikin vic., PRINCE GEORGE'S COUNTY

New Market, DORCHESTER COUNTY
New Market vic., ST. MARY'S COUNTY
Newport vic., CHARLES COUNTY
North East, CECIL COUNTY
Norwood, MONTGOMERY COUNTY
Norwood vic., MONTGOMERY COUNTY
Nottingham, PRINCE GEORGE'S COUNTY

Oakville vic., ST. MARY'S COUNTY
Oella, BALTIMORE COUNTY
Old Town vic., ALLEGANY COUNTY
Oldtown, ALLEGANY COUNTY
Oldtown vic., ALLEGANY COUNTY
Olney, MONTGOMERY COUNTY
Olney vic., MONTGOMERY COUNTY
Owings Mill, BALTIMORE COUNTY
Owings Mills vic., BALTIMORE COUNTY
Owings vic., CALVERT COUNTY
Oxford vic., TALBOT COUNTY
Oxon Hill, PRINCE GEORGE'S COUNTY
Oxon Hill vic., PRINCE GEORGE'S COUNTY

Papw Paw vic., ALLEGANY COUNTY
Parkton vic., BALTIMORE COUNTY
Paw Paw vic., ALLEGANY COUNTY
Paw Paw vic. (Wv), ALLEGANY COUNTY
Perryman, HARFORD COUNTY
Perryville vic., CECIL COUNTY
Phoenix vic., BALTIMORE COUNTY
Pikesville, BALTIMORE COUNTY
Pindell, ANNE ARUNDEL COUNTY
Piscataway, PRINCE GEORGE'S COUNTY
Piscataway vic., PRINCE GEORGE'S COUNTY
Pocomoke City vic., WORCESTER COUNTY
Point Of Rocks, FREDERICK COUNTY
Point Of Rocks vic., FREDERICK COUNTY
Pokomoke City, WORCESTER COUNTY
Poolesville, MONTGOMERY COUNTY
Poolesville vic., MONTGOMERY COUNTY
Port Deposit, CECIL COUNTY
Port Tobacco, CHARLES COUNTY
Port Tobacco vic., CHARLES COUNTY
Potomac vic., MONTGOMERY COUNTY
Prince Frederick Vic, CALVERT COUNTY
Princess Anne, SOMERSET COUNTY

Queen Anne, TALBOT COUNTY
Queenstown, QUEEN ANNE'S COUNTY

Randallstown vic., BALTIMORE COUNTY
Redland, MONTGOMERY COUNTY
Redland vic., MONTGOMERY COUNTY
Reisterstown vic., BALTIMORE COUNTY
Ridge, ST. MARY'S COUNTY
Ridge vic., ST. MARY'S COUNTY
Ridgely, CAROLINE COUNTY
Ritchie, PRINCE GEORGE'S COUNTY
Riverdale, PRINCE GEORGE'S COUNTY
Riverside, MONTGOMERY COUNTY
Riversie, MONTGOMERY COUNTY
Riviera Beach vic., ANNE ARUNDEL COUNTY
Robinson vic., ANNE ARUNDEL COUNTY
Rockville, MONTGOMERY COUNTY
Rocky Ridge vic., FREDERICK COUNTY
Romankoke, QUEEN ANNE'S COUNTY
Rosaryville, PRINCE GEORGE'S COUNTY
Round Bay vic., ANNE ARUNDEL COUNTY
Ruthsburg vic., QUEEN ANNE'S COUNTY

Salisbury, WICOMICO COUNTY
Samples Manor vic., WASHINGTON COUNTY
Sandy Bottom, KENT COUNTY
Sandy Spring, MONTGOMERY COUNTY
Savage, HOWARD COUNTY
Seat Pleasant, PRINCE GEORGE'S COUNTY
Seat Pleasant vic., PRINCE GEORGE'S COUNTY
Secretary, DORCHESTER COUNTY
Secretary vic., DORCHESTER COUNTY
Seneca vic., MONTGOMERY COUNTY
Sharpsburg, WASHINGTON COUNTY
Sharpsburg vic., WASHINGTON COUNTY
Sharptown vic., DORCHESTER COUNTY
Silver Spring, MONTGOMERY COUNTY
Snow Hill Landing, WORCESTER COUNTY
Snow Hill vic., WORCESTER COUNTY
Sollers vic., CALVERT COUNTY
Solomons, CALVERT COUNTY
Solomons Island vic., CALVERT COUNTY
Somerset vic., MONTGOMERY COUNTY
South River vic., ANNE ARUNDEL COUNTY
St. Augustine, CECIL COUNTY
St. Inigoes vic., ST. MARY'S COUNTY
St. Mary's City, ST. MARY'S COUNTY
St. Mary's City vic., ST. MARY'S COUNTY
St. Mary's vic., ST. MARY'S COUNTY
St. Michaels, TALBOT COUNTY
St. Michaels vic., TALBOT COUNTY
Stevensville, QUEEN ANNE'S COUNTY
Stevensville vic., QUEEN ANNE'S COUNTY
Still Pond, KENT COUNTY
Stoakley, CALVERT COUNTY
Stockton vic., HARFORD COUNTY
Sunderland vic., CALVERT COUNTY
Sunnybrook, BALTIMORE COUNTY
Sweet Air, BALTIMORE COUNTY
Sykesville, CARROLL COUNTY

Thomas Brook vic., PRINCE GEORGE'S COUNTY
Townsend vic., PRINCE GEORGE'S COUNTY
Towson, BALTIMORE COUNTY
Tracy's Landing vic., ANNE ARUNDEL COUNTY
Trappe, TALBOT COUNTY
Tunis Mills vic., TALBOT COUNTY
Tunis Mills vic.., TALBOT COUNTY

Union Bridge vic., FREDERICK COUNTY
Unity, MONTGOMERY COUNTY
Unity vic., MONTGOMERY COUNTY
Upper Marlboro, PRINCE GEORGE'S COUNTY
Upper Marlboro vic., PRINCE GEORGE'S COUNTY
Urbana, FREDERICK COUNTY

Valley Lee, ST. MARY'S COUNTY
Valley Lee vic., ST. MARY'S COUNTY
Vienna, DORCHESTER COUNTY

Waldore, CHARLES COUNTY
Warwick, CECIL COUNTY
Watervale, HARFORD COUNTY
Watervale vic., HARFORD COUNTY
Westernport, ALLEGANY COUNTY
Westminster, CARROLL COUNTY
Weverton vic., WASHINGTON COUNTY
Williampsort vic., WASHINGTON COUNTY
Williamsport, WASHINGTON COUNTY
Williamsport vic., WASHINGTON COUNTY
Williston Landing, CAROLINE COUNTY
Wilna vic., HARFORD COUNTY
Woodlawn, BALTIMORE COUNTY
Woodmore, PRINCE GEORGE'S COUNTY
Wye Mills, QUEEN ANNE'S COUNTY
Wye Mills, TALBOT COUNTY

Massachusetts

Acoaxet, BRISTOL COUNTY
Acton, MIDDLESEX COUNTY
Adams, BERKSHIRE COUNTY
Agawam, HAMPDEN COUNTY
Amesbury, ESSEX COUNTY
Amherst, HAMPSHIRE COUNTY
Andover, ESSEX COUNTY
Annisquam, ESSEX COUNTY

Arlington, MIDDLESEX COUNTY
Arlington Heights, MIDDLESEX COUNTY
Ashby, MIDDLESEX COUNTY
Ashfield, FRANKLIN COUNTY
Ashland, MIDDLESEX COUNTY
Athol, WORCESTER COUNTY
Attleboro, BRISTOL COUNTY
Attleboro vic., BRISTOL COUNTY
Attleboro-Plainville, BRISTOL COUNTY
Auburn, WORCESTER COUNTY
Auburndale, MIDDLESEX COUNTY

Barnstable, BARNSTABLE COUNTY
Bedford, MIDDLESEX COUNTY
Bedford vic., MIDDLESEX COUNTY
Belmont, MIDDLESEX COUNTY
Bernardston, FRANKLIN COUNTY
Beverly, ESSEX COUNTY
Billerica, MIDDLESEX COUNTY
Blackstone, WORCESTER COUNTY
Blandford, HAMPDEN COUNTY
Bolton, WORCESTER COUNTY
Boston, SUFFOLK COUNTY
Boston Harbor
Boston vic., SUFFOLK COUNTY
Bourne, BARNSTABLE COUNTY
Boxford, ESSEX COUNTY
Braintree, NORFOLK COUNTY
Brewster, BARNSTABLE COUNTY
Bridgewater, PLYMOUTH COUNTY
Brighton, SUFFOLK COUNTY
Brimfield, HAMPDEN COUNTY
Brockton, PLYMOUTH COUNTY
Brookfield, WORCESTER COUNTY
Brookline, NORFOLK COUNTY
Buckland, FRANKLIN COUNTY
Burlington, MIDDLESEX COUNTY
Buzzards Bay, BARNSTABLE COUNTY

Cambridge, MIDDLESEX COUNTY
Canton, NORFOLK COUNTY
Carlisle, MIDDLESEX COUNTY
Charlestown, SUFFOLK COUNTY
Charlton, WORCESTER COUNTY
Chatham, BARNSTABLE COUNTY
Chatham vic., BARNSTABLE COUNTY
Chathamport, BARNSTABLE COUNTY
Chelmsford, MIDDLESEX COUNTY
Chelsea, SUFFOLK COUNTY
Chester, FRANKLIN COUNTY
Chester, HAMPDEN COUNTY
Chicopee, HAMPDEN COUNTY
Clarksburg, BERKSHIRE COUNTY
Cohasset, NORFOLK COUNTY
Concord, MIDDLESEX COUNTY
Conway, FRANKLIN COUNTY
Cummington, HAMPSHIRE COUNTY

Dalton, BERKSHIRE COUNTY
Danvers, ESSEX COUNTY
Dartmouth, BRISTOL COUNTY
Dedham, NORFOLK COUNTY
Deerfield, FRANKLIN COUNTY
Deerfield vic., FRANKLIN COUNTY
Deerfield Village, FRANKLIN COUNTY
Dennis, BARNSTABLE COUNTY
Dighton, BRISTOL COUNTY
Dorchester, SUFFOLK COUNTY
Dover, NORFOLK COUNTY
Duxbury, PLYMOUTH COUNTY

East Brookfield, WORCESTER COUNTY
East Lexington, MIDDLESEX COUNTY
East Northfield, FRANKLIN COUNTY
East Sandwich, BARNSTABLE COUNTY
East Taunton, BRISTOL COUNTY
Eastham, BARNSTABLE COUNTY
Easthampton, HAMPSHIRE COUNTY
Easton, BRISTOL COUNTY
Egremont, BERKSHIRE COUNTY
Erving, FRANKLIN COUNTY
Essex, ESSEX COUNTY

Fairhaven, BRISTOL COUNTY
Fall River, BRISTOL COUNTY
Falmouth, BARNSTABLE COUNTY
Fitchburg, WORCESTER COUNTY
Framingham, MIDDLESEX COUNTY
Franklin, NORFOLK COUNTY
Freetown, BRISTOL COUNTY

Georgetown, ESSEX COUNTY
Gloucester, ESSEX COUNTY
Grafton, WORCESTER COUNTY
Granby, HAMPSHIRE COUNTY
Granville, HAMPDEN COUNTY
Great Barrington, BERKSHIRE COUNTY
Greenbush, PLYMOUTH COUNTY
Greenfield, FRANKLIN COUNTY
Greenfield vic., FRANKLIN COUNTY
Groton, MIDDLESEX COUNTY

Hadley, HAMPSHIRE COUNTY
Halifax, PLYMOUTH COUNTY
Hamilton-Ipswich, ESSEX COUNTY
Hancock, BERKSHIRE COUNTY
Hanover Center, PLYMOUTH COUNTY
Harvard, WORCESTER COUNTY
Hatfield, HAMPSHIRE COUNTY
Haverhill, ESSEX COUNTY
Hingham, PLYMOUTH COUNTY
Hinsdale, BERKSHIRE COUNTY
Holden, WORCESTER COUNTY
Holliston, MIDDLESEX COUNTY
Holyoke, HAMPDEN COUNTY
Hopkinton, MIDDLESEX COUNTY

Ipswich, ESSEX COUNTY

Jamaica Plain, SUFFOLK COUNTY

Kingston, PLYMOUTH COUNTY

Lakeville, PLYMOUTH COUNTY
Lancaster, WORCESTER COUNTY
Lancaster vic., WORCESTER COUNTY
Lanesborough, BERKSHIRE COUNTY
Lawrence, ESSEX COUNTY
Lawrence, MIDDLESEX COUNTY
Lee, BERKSHIRE COUNTY
Leicester, WORCESTER COUNTY
Lenox, BERKSHIRE COUNTY
Lexington, MIDDLESEX COUNTY
Lincoln, MIDDLESEX COUNTY
Longmeadow, HAMPDEN COUNTY
Lowell, MIDDLESEX COUNTY
Lowell-Somerville, MIDDLESEX COUNTY
Ludlow-Wilbraham, HAMPDEN COUNTY
Lynn, ESSEX COUNTY

Malden, MIDDLESEX COUNTY
Manchester, ESSEX COUNTY
Marblehead, ESSEX COUNTY
Marion, PLYMOUTH COUNTY
Marshfield, PLYMOUTH COUNTY
Marshfield Hills, PLYMOUTH COUNTY
Mashpee, BARNSTABLE COUNTY
Medfield, NORFOLK COUNTY
Medford, MIDDLESEX COUNTY
Melrose, MIDDLESEX COUNTY
Mendon, WORCESTER COUNTY
Middleboro, PLYMOUTH COUNTY
Middleborough, PLYMOUTH COUNTY
Middleton, ESSEX COUNTY
Milford, WORCESTER COUNTY
Millville, FRANKLIN COUNTY
Millville, WORCESTER COUNTY
Millville vic., WORCESTER COUNTY
Milton, NORFOLK COUNTY
Montague, FRANKLIN COUNTY
Montague City, FRANKLIN COUNTY

Nantucket, NANTUCKET COUNTY
Natick, MIDDLESEX COUNTY
Natick, NORFOLK COUNTY
New Bedford, BRISTOL COUNTY
New Marlborough, BERKSHIRE COUNTY
New Salem, FRANKLIN COUNTY
Newbury, ESSEX COUNTY
Newbury Old Town, ESSEX COUNTY
Newburyport, ESSEX COUNTY
Newton, MIDDLESEX COUNTY
Newton Centre, MIDDLESEX COUNTY
North Adams, BERKSHIRE COUNTY
North Andover, ESSEX COUNTY
North Attleboro, BRISTOL COUNTY
North Attleboro vic., BRISTOL COUNTY
North Billerica, MIDDLESEX COUNTY
North Brookfield, HAMPDEN COUNTY
North Carver, PLYMOUTH COUNTY
North Chatham, BARNSTABLE COUNTY
North Dighton, BRISTOL COUNTY
North Easton, BRISTOL COUNTY
North Hingham, PLYMOUTH COUNTY
North Pembroke, PLYMOUTH COUNTY
North Pepperell, MIDDLESEX COUNTY
North Reading, MIDDLESEX COUNTY
North Uxbridge, WORCESTER COUNTY
North Woburn, MIDDLESEX COUNTY
Northampton, HAMPSHIRE COUNTY
Northbridge, WORCESTER COUNTY
Northfield, FRANKLIN COUNTY
Northfield vic., FRANKLIN COUNTY
Norton, BRISTOL COUNTY
Norton vic., BRISTOL COUNTY
Norwell, PLYMOUTH COUNTY

Oakham, WORCESTER COUNTY
Orleans, BARNSTABLE COUNTY
Oxford, WORCESTER COUNTY

Palmer, HAMPDEN COUNTY
Peabody, ESSEX COUNTY
Pelham, HAMPSHIRE COUNTY
Pepperell, MIDDLESEX COUNTY
Pittsfield, BERKSHIRE COUNTY
Plainville, NORFOLK COUNTY
Plymouth, PLYMOUTH COUNTY
Prescott, HAMPSHIRE COUNTY
Provincetown, BARNSTABLE COUNTY

Quincy, NORFOLK COUNTY

Randolph, NORFOLK COUNTY
Reading, MIDDLESEX COUNTY
Rehoboth, BRISTOL COUNTY
Revere vic., SUFFOLK COUNTY
Richmond, BERKSHIRE COUNTY
Riverside, FRANKLIN COUNTY
Rockport, ESSEX COUNTY
Rowley, ESSEX COUNTY
Roxbury, SUFFOLK COUNTY
Russell, HAMPDEN COUNTY
Rutland, WORCESTER COUNTY

Salem, ESSEX COUNTY
Sandwich, BARNSTABLE COUNTY
Saugus, ESSEX COUNTY
Scituate, PLYMOUTH COUNTY

Scituate vic., PLYMOUTH COUNTY
Seekonk, BRISTOL COUNTY
Sharon, NORFOLK COUNTY
Sheffield, BERKSHIRE COUNTY
Shelburne, FRANKLIN COUNTY
Sherborn, MIDDLESEX COUNTY
Shirley, MIDDLESEX COUNTY
Siasconset, NANTUCKET COUNTY
Somerset, BRISTOL COUNTY
Somerville, MIDDLESEX COUNTY
South Boston, SUFFOLK COUNTY
South Deerfield, FRANKLIN COUNTY
South Hadley, HAMPSHIRE COUNTY
South Lee, BERKSHIRE COUNTY
South Orleans, BARNSTABLE COUNTY
South Pepperell vic., MIDDLESEX COUNTY
South Somerset, BRISTOL COUNTY
South Sudbury, MIDDLESEX COUNTY
South Westport, BRISTOL COUNTY
South Williamstown, BERKSHIRE COUNTY
Spencer, WORCESTER COUNTY
Springfield, HAMPDEN COUNTY
Sterling, WORCESTER COUNTY
Stockbridge, BERKSHIRE COUNTY
Stoneham, MIDDLESEX COUNTY
Stoughton, NORFOLK COUNTY
Sturbridge, WORCESTER COUNTY
Swampscott, ESSEX COUNTY
Swansea, BRISTOL COUNTY

Taunton, BRISTOL COUNTY
Templeton, WORCESTER COUNTY
Tisbury, DUKES COUNTY
Topsfield, ESSEX COUNTY
Townsend, MIDDLESEX COUNTY
Truro, BARNSTABLE COUNTY
Tyngsborough, MIDDLESEX COUNTY
Tyringham, BERKSHIRE COUNTY

Uxbridge, WORCESTER COUNTY

Vineyard Haven, DUKES COUNTY

Wakefield, MIDDLESEX COUNTY
Walpole, NORFOLK COUNTY
Waltham, MIDDLESEX COUNTY
Wareham, PLYMOUTH COUNTY
Watertown, MIDDLESEX COUNTY
Wayland, MIDDLESEX COUNTY
Webster, WORCESTER COUNTY
Wellesley, NORFOLK COUNTY
Wellfleet, BARNSTABLE COUNTY
Wenham, ESSEX COUNTY
West Brookfield, HAMPDEN COUNTY
West Brookfield, WORCESTER COUNTY
West Chatham, BARNSTABLE COUNTY
West Medford, MIDDLESEX COUNTY
West Northfield, FRANKLIN COUNTY
West Springfield, HAMPDEN COUNTY
West Stockbridge, BERKSHIRE COUNTY
Westboro, WORCESTER COUNTY
Westfield, HAMPDEN COUNTY
Westhampton, HAMPSHIRE COUNTY
Weston, MIDDLESEX COUNTY
Westwood, NORFOLK COUNTY
Weymouth, NORFOLK COUNTY
Wilkinsonville, WORCESTER COUNTY
Williamsburg, HAMPSHIRE COUNTY
Williamstown, BERKSHIRE COUNTY
Wilmington, MIDDLESEX COUNTY
Wilmington-Billerica, MIDDLESEX COUNTY
Windsor, BERKSHIRE COUNTY
Winthrop, SUFFOLK COUNTY
Woburn, MIDDLESEX COUNTY
Worcester, WORCESTER COUNTY
Worthington, HAMPSHIRE COUNTY
Wrentham, NORFOLK COUNTY

Yarmouth, BARNSTABLE COUNTY

Michigan

Adrian, LENAWEE COUNTY
Ann Arbor, WASHTENAW COUNTY

Bancroft vic., SHIAWASSEE COUNTY
Battle Creek, CALHOUN COUNTY
Battlecreek vic., CALHOUN COUNTY
Bay City, BAY COUNTY
Beacon Hill, HOUGHTON COUNTY
Benton vic., BERRIEN COUNTY
Brighton, LIVINGSTON COUNTY

Camden, HILLSDALE COUNTY
Canton Township, WAYNE COUNTY
Champion vic., MARQUETTE COUNTY
Charlotte, EATON COUNTY

Dearborn, WAYNE COUNTY
Detroit, WAYNE COUNTY
Detroit & Dearborn, WAYNE COUNTY
Dexter, WASHTENAW COUNTY
Dexter vic., WASHTENAW COUNTY
Dixboro, WASHTENAW COUNTY

East Grand Rapids, KENT COUNTY
East Munising, ALGER COUNTY
Eaton Rapids, EATON COUNTY
Eaton Township, EATON COUNTY
Empire vic., LEELANAU COUNTY

Frankenmuth vic., SAGINAW COUNTY

Glen Arbor, LEELANAU COUNTY
Glen Arbor vic., LEELANAU COUNTY
Grand Island, ALGER COUNTY
Grand Marais Vic, ALGER COUNTY
Grand Marais vic., ALGER COUNTY
Grand Rapids, KENT COUNTY
Grass Lake, JACKSON COUNTY
Grass Lake vic., JACKSON COUNTY

Hamilton vic., ALLEGAN COUNTY
Hamtramck, WAYNE COUNTY
Hancock, HOUGHTON COUNTY
Hastings vic., BARRY COUNTY
Houghton vic., KEWEENAW COUNTY

Ionia, IONIA COUNTY
Ishpeming, MARQUETTE COUNTY
Isle Royale, KEWEENAW COUNTY

Kalamazoo, KALAMAZOO COUNTY

Lansing, INGHAM COUNTY
Leland
Leland, LEELANAU COUNTY
Leland vic., LEELANAU COUNTY
Litchfield vic., HILLSDALE COUNTY

Mackinac Island, MACKINAC COUNTY
Marshall, CALHOUN COUNTY
Mason vic., INGHAM COUNTY
Menagerie Island, KEWEENAW COUNTY
Monroe, MONROE COUNTY
Muskegon, MUSKEGON COUNTY

Niles, BERRIEN COUNTY
Norton Shores, MUSKEGON COUNTY

Oshtemo vic., KALAMAZOO COUNTY
Ovid, CLINTON COUNTY

Passage Island, KEWEENAW COUNTY
Port Huron, ST. CLAIR COUNTY
Port Oneida, LEELANAU COUNTY
Presque Isle, PRESQUE ISLE COUNTY

Rock Of Ages, KEWEENAW COUNTY
Rushton, LIVINGSTON COUNTY

Sault Ste. Marie, CHIPPEWA COUNTY
Sharonville vic., WASHTENAW COUNTY
Springlake, OTTAWA COUNTY
St. Louis vic., GRATIOT COUNTY
Sumner vic., GRATIOT COUNTY

Tecumseh, LENAWEE COUNTY

Vermontville, EATON COUNTY

Warren, MACOMB COUNTY
Williamston Twp., INGHAM COUNTY

Ypsilanti, WASHTENAW COUNTY

Minnesota

Afton, WASHINGTON COUNTY
Anoka, ANOKA COUNTY
Artichoke, BIG STONE COUNTY

Babbit, ST. LOUIS COUNTY
Babitt, ST. LOUIS COUNTY
Bloomington, HENNEPIN COUNTY
Brown's Valley, TRAVERSE COUNTY

Center City, CHISAGO COUNTY
Chokio, STEARNS COUNTY
Cloquet, CARLTON COUNTY
Cloquet vic., CARLTON COUNTY
Cokato, WRIGHT COUNTY
Collegeville, STEARNS COUNTY

Detroit Lakes, BECKER COUNTY
Dresbach vic., WINONA COUNTY
Duluth, ST. LOUIS COUNTY
Duluth vic., ST. LOUIS COUNTY

Eden Prarie, HENNEPIN COUNTY
Elk River, SHERBURNE COUNTY
Elk River vic., SHERBURNE COUNTY
Ely vic., ST. LOUIS COUNTY
Elysian, LE SUEUR COUNTY
Excelsior, HENNEPIN COUNTY

Fort Ridgeley, NICOLLET COUNTY
Frontenac, GOODHUE COUNTY

Grand Marais, COOK COUNTY
Granite Falls, YELLOW MEDICINE COUNTY

Hennepin, HENNEPIN COUNTY
Herman, GRANT COUNTY
Hibbing vic., ST. LOUIS COUNTY
Houston vic., HOUSTON COUNTY

Jeffers vic., COTTONWOOD COUNTY

Kent vic., WILKIN COUNTY

La Cresent vic., HOUSTON COUNTY
Lake City, WABASHA COUNTY
Lake Itasca vic., CLEARWATER COUNTY
Lamberton, REDWOOD COUNTY

Le Sueur, LE SUEUR COUNTY
Little Falls, MORRISON COUNTY
Little Falls vic., MORRISON COUNTY

Madison, LAC QUI PARLE COUNTY
Mahnomen, MAHNOMEN COUNTY
Marine, WASHINGTON COUNTY
Mendota, DAKOTA COUNTY
Minneapolis, HENNEPIN COUNTY
Minneapolis vic., HENNEPIN COUNTY
Minnieska vic., WINONA COUNTY
Montevideo, CHIPPEWA COUNTY
Moorhead, CLAY COUNTY
Mountain Iron vic., ST. LOUIS COUNTY

Nerstand vic., RICE COUNTY
Nerstrand vic., RICE COUNTY
New Brighton, RAMSEY COUNTY
New Ulm, BROWN COUNTY
North Branch vic., ISANTI COUNTY
Northfield, RICE COUNTY

Owatonna, STEELE COUNTY

Pipestone, PIPESTONE COUNTY
Pipestone vic., PIPESTONE COUNTY

Red Wing vic., GOODHUE COUNTY
Rochester, OLMSTED COUNTY
Rockville, STEARNS COUNTY
Rushford, FILLMORE COUNTY

Sandy Lake, AITKIN COUNTY
Santiago, SHERBURNE COUNTY
Sauk Centre, STEARNS COUNTY
Saum vic., BELTRAMI COUNTY
Sawyer, CARLTON COUNTY
Seaforth vic., REDWOOD COUNTY
Silver Brook Twp., CARLTON COUNTY
Skyline vic., BLUE EARTH COUNTY
St. Clair, BLUE EARTH COUNTY
St. Louis Park, HENNEPIN COUNTY
St. Paul, RAMSEY COUNTY
Stillwater vic., WASHINGTON COUNTY

Taylors Falls, CHISAGO COUNTY
Tower vic., ST. LOUIS COUNTY
Troy vic., WINONA COUNTY
Two Harbor's vic., LAKE COUNTY
Two Harbors, LAKE COUNTY
Two Harbors vic., LAKE COUNTY

Underwood vic., OTTER TAIL COUNTY

Vineland, MILLE LACS COUNTY

Wabasha, WABASHA COUNTY
Watertown, CARVER COUNTY
Watson, CHIPPEWA COUNTY
Watson vic., CHIPPEWA COUNTY
Winona, WINONA COUNTY
Winona vic., WINONA COUNTY

Mississippi

Aberdeen, MONROE COUNTY
Alcorn vic., CLAIBORNE COUNTY

Bay St. Louis, HANCOCK COUNTY
Benoit, BOLIVAR COUNTY
Biloxi, HARRISON COUNTY
Biloxi vic., HARRISON COUNTY
Blakely, WARREN COUNTY
Bovina vicinity, WARREN COUNTY

Cannonsburg vic., JEFFERSON COUNTY
Carmen Church vic., LOWNDES COUNTY
Carrollton vic., CARROLL COUNTY
Chatham vic., WASHINGTON COUNTY
Church Hill, JEFFERSON COUNTY
Clinton, HINDS COUNTY
Coffeeville, YALOBUSHA COUNTY
Columbia (South), MARION COUNTY
Columbus, LOWNDES COUNTY
Columbus vic., LOWNDES COUNTY
Corinth, ALCORN COUNTY

Dennis vic., TISHOMINGO COUNTY

Edwards vic., HINDS COUNTY
Edwards vic., WARREN COUNTY

Foote vic., WASHINGTON COUNTY
Fort Adams, WILKINSON COUNTY
Fort Adams vic., WILKINSON COUNTY

Gloster vic., AMITE COUNTY
Gloster vicinity, AMITE COUNTY
Greenville vic., WASHINGTON COUNTY
Greenville vicinity, WASHINGTON COUNTY
Gulfport, HARRISON COUNTY

Holly Springs, MARSHALL COUNTY

Jackson, HINDS COUNTY

Kingston, ADAMS COUNTY

Lexington, HOLMES COUNTY
Lexington vic., HOLMES COUNTY
Liberty vic., AMITE COUNTY
Longwood, WASHINGTON COUNTY

Macon, NOXUBEE COUNTY
Macon vic., NOXUBEE COUNTY
Mannsdale, MADISON COUNTY
Mound Bayou, BOLIVAR COUNTY

Natchez, ADAMS COUNTY
Natchez vic., ADAMS COUNTY
New Site vicinity, PRENTISS COUNTY

Ocean Springs, JACKSON COUNTY
Oxford, LAFAYETTE COUNTY

Pascagoula, JACKSON COUNTY
Port Gibson, CLAIBORNE COUNTY
Port Gibson vic., CLAIBORNE COUNTY

Raymond, HINDS COUNTY
Raymond vic., HINDS COUNTY
Rienzi, ALCORN COUNTY
Rodney, JEFFERSON COUNTY
Rodney vic., JEFFERSON COUNTY

Steens vic., LOWNDES COUNTY

Tishomingo vicinity, TISHOMINGO COUNTY
Tombigbee Valley Vic, LOWNDES COUNTY

Vaiden vic., CARROLL COUNTY
Vicksburg, WARREN COUNTY
Vicksburg vic., WARREN COUNTY

Washington, ADAMS COUNTY
Washington vic., ADAMS COUNTY
Wayside, WASHINGTON COUNTY
West Point, CLAY COUNTY
West Point vic., CLAY COUNTY
Winona, MONTGOMERY COUNTY
Woodville, WILKINSON COUNTY
Woodville vic., WILKINSON COUNTY

Yazoo City vic., YAZOO COUNTY

Missouri

Affton, ST. LOUIS COUNTY
Affton vic., ST. LOUIS COUNTY
Afton vic., ST. LOUIS COUNTY
Allenville, CAPE GIRARDEAU COUNTY
Altenburg, PERRY COUNTY
Altenburg vic., PERRY COUNTY
Armstrong vic., HOWARD COUNTY
Arrow Rock, SALINE COUNTY
Arrow Rock vic., SALINE COUNTY
Ash Grove vic., GREENE COUNTY
Augusta, ST. CHARLES COUNTY
Auxvasse, CALLAWAY COUNTY
Auxvasse vic., CALLAWAY COUNTY

Bacon vic., MONITEAU COUNTY
Barnhart, JEFFERSON COUNTY
Barnhart vic., JEFFERSON COUNTY
Bay, GASCONADE COUNTY
Bay vic., GASCONADE COUNTY
Beaufort vic., FRANKLIN COUNTY
Beaufort vic., GASCONADE COUNTY
Beck, JEFFERSON COUNTY
Bellefontaine Neigh., ST. LOUIS COUNTY
Bellefontaine vic., ST. LOUIS COUNTY
Bethel, SHELBY COUNTY
Bethel vic., SHELBY COUNTY
Blackwater vic., COOPER COUNTY
Bloomdale, STE. GENEVIEVE COUNTY
Bloomsdale, STE. GENEVIEVE COUNTY
Bolivar vic., POLK COUNTY
Bonfils, ST. LOUIS COUNTY
Bonne Terre vic., ST. FRANCOIS COUNTY
Boonville, COOPER COUNTY
Boonville vic., COOPER COUNTY
Boonville vicinity, COOPER COUNTY
Brashear vic., ADAIR COUNTY
Brunswick, CHARITON COUNTY
Bufordville, CAPE GIRARDEAU COUNTY
Bunceton vic., COOPER COUNTY

Caledonia, WASHINGTON COUNTY
Caledonia vic., WASHINGTON COUNTY
Cannon Creek, WASHINGTON COUNTY
Canton, LEWIS COUNTY
Cap-Au-Gris, LINCOLN COUNTY
Cape Girardeau, CAPE GIRARDEAU COUNTY
Carondelet, ST. LOUIS COUNTY
Carthage vic., JASPER COUNTY
Center vic., RALLS COUNTY
Chesterfield, ST. LOUIS COUNTY
Clarksville, PIKE COUNTY
Clayton, ST. LOUIS COUNTY
Clinton, HENRY COUNTY
Clinton vic., HENRY COUNTY
Columbia, BOONE COUNTY
Columbia vic., BOONE COUNTY
Connelsville vic., ADAIR COUNTY
Cottleville, ST. CHARLES COUNTY
Cottleville vic., ST. CHARLES COUNTY
Cotton, COOPER COUNTY
Crestwood, ST. LOUIS COUNTY
Crosstown vic., PERRY COUNTY
Crystal City vic., JEFFERSON COUNTY

Danby, JEFFERSON COUNTY
Danville, MONTGOMERY COUNTY
Danville vic., MONTGOMERY COUNTY
Dardenne, ST. CHARLES COUNTY

Deepwater, HENRY COUNTY
Deepwater vic., HENRY COUNTY
Defiance, ST. CHARLES COUNTY
Defiance vic., ST. CHARLES COUNTY
Desloge vicinity, ST. FRANCOIS COUNTY
Detmold vic., FRANKLIN COUNTY
Dexter vic., STODDARD COUNTY
Diamond vic., NEWTON COUNTY
Dixon vic., PULASKI COUNTY
Doniphan vic., RIPLEY COUNTY
Dover, LAFAYETTE COUNTY
Drake vic., GASCONADE COUNTY
Dutzow vic., WARREN COUNTY
Duzow vic., WARREN COUNTY

Ellisville, ST. LOUIS COUNTY
Enon vic., MONITEAU COUNTY
Estill vic., HOWARD COUNTY
Etlah, FRANKLIN COUNTY
Excelsior Springs Vi, CLAY COUNTY
Excelsior Srings Vic, CLAY COUNTY

Fairfax vic., ATCHISON COUNTY
Fairfield vic., BENTON COUNTY
Farmington, ST. FRANCOIS COUNTY
Fayette, HOWARD COUNTY
Fayette vic., HOWARD COUNTY
Femme Osage, ST. CHARLES COUNTY
Femme Osage vic., ST. CHARLES COUNTY
Flat River vic., ST. FRANCOIS COUNTY
Flinthill vic., ST. CHARLES COUNTY
Florence, MORGAN COUNTY
Florida, MONROE COUNTY
Florissant, ST. LOUIS COUNTY
Florissant vic., ST. LOUIS COUNTY
Fredericksburg vic., GASCONADE COUNTY
Fredericktown vic., MADISON COUNTY
French Village, ST. FRANCOIS COUNTY
Fulton, CALLAWAY COUNTY

Gaines vic., HENRY COUNTY
Gasconade vic., GASCONADE COUNTY
Gentryville, GENTRY COUNTY
Gerald vic., FRANKLIN COUNTY
Glasgow, HOWARD COUNTY
Glasgow vic., HOWARD COUNTY
Glendale, ST. LOUIS COUNTY
Goldman vic., JEFFERSON COUNTY
Goss, MONROE COUNTY
Gravois Mills, MORGAN COUNTY
Green Bottom, ST. CHARLES COUNTY
Gumbo vic., ST. LOUIS COUNTY

Hannibal, MARION COUNTY
Hannibal vic., MARION COUNTY
Hannibal vic., RALLS COUNTY
Harvester, ST. CHARLES COUNTY
Herculaneum, JEFFERSON COUNTY
Hermann, GASCONADE COUNTY
Hermann vic., GASCONADE COUNTY
Hermitage, HICKORY COUNTY
Hermitage vic., HICKORY COUNTY
Hoover vic., PLATTE COUNTY
Hopkins vic., NODAWAY COUNTY

Independence, JACKSON COUNTY

Jackson, CAPE GIRARDEAU COUNTY
Jackson vic., CAPE GIRARDEAU COUNTY
Jameson vic., DAVIESS COUNTY
Jamesville vic., STONE COUNTY
Jefferson, COLE COUNTY
Jefferson City, COLE COUNTY
Jefferson City vic., CALLAWAY COUNTY
Jefferson City vic., COLE COUNTY
Joanna, RALLS COUNTY

Joplin, JASPER COUNTY

Kansas City, JACKSON COUNTY
Kimmswick, JEFFERSON COUNTY
Kingston vic., CALDWELL COUNTY
Kirkwood, ST. LOUIS COUNTY
Krakow, FRANKLIN COUNTY
Krakow vic., FRANKLIN COUNTY

Laclede, LINN COUNTY
Lamine vic., COOPER COUNTY
Lawson vic., CLAY COUNTY
Lees Summit, JACKSON COUNTY
Leopold, BOLLINGER COUNTY
Lexington, LAFAYETTE COUNTY
Lexington vic., LAFAYETTE COUNTY
Liberal, BARTON COUNTY
Lock Springs vic., DAVIESS COUNTY
Longwood vic., PETTIS COUNTY
Loose Creek, OSAGE COUNTY
Lowry City vic., ST. CLAIR COUNTY

Maplewood, ST. LOUIS COUNTY
Marthasville, WARREN COUNTY
Marthasville vic., WARREN COUNTY
Matson, ST. CHARLES COUNTY
Matson vic., ST. CHARLES COUNTY
Miami, SALINE COUNTY
Millersville, CAPE GIRARDEAU COUNTY
Mine La Motte, MADISON COUNTY
Mokane, CALLAWAY COUNTY
Morse Mill vic., JEFFERSON COUNTY
Moscow Mills, LINCOLN COUNTY

Nelson vic., SALINE COUNTY
Neosho vic., NEWTON COUNTY
New Franklin, HOWARD COUNTY
New Franklin vic., HOWARD COUNTY
New Hamburg, SCOTT COUNTY
New Haven vic., FRANKLIN COUNTY
New Lebanon, COOPER COUNTY
New London, RALLS COUNTY
New Madrid, NEW MADRID COUNTY
Nixa vic., CHRISTIAN COUNTY
North Fork vic., MONROE COUNTY
Northwoods, ST. LOUIS COUNTY

O'fallon, ST. CHARLES COUNTY
Old Appleton, CAPE GIRARDEAU COUNTY
Old Mines, WASHINGTON COUNTY
Old Mines vic., WASHINGTON COUNTY
Osceola, ST. CLAIR COUNTY
Osceola vic., ST. CLAIR COUNTY
Overland, ST. LOUIS COUNTY
Overton vic., COOPER COUNTY
Owensville vic., GASCONADE COUNTY

Palmyra, MARION COUNTY
Paradise vic., CLAY COUNTY
Paris vic., MONROE COUNTY
Pattonville, ST. LOUIS COUNTY
Perryville, PERRY COUNTY
Perryville vic., PERRY COUNTY
Petersburg vic., HOWARD COUNTY
Pevely, JEFFERSON COUNTY
Pevely vic., JEFFERSON COUNTY
Philadelphia vic., MARION COUNTY
Piedmont vic., WASHINGTON COUNTY
Pisgah, COOPER COUNTY
Pisgah vic., COOPER COUNTY
Platte City, PLATTE COUNTY
Pleasant Green vic., COOPER COUNTY
Poplar Bluff vic., BUTLER COUNTY
Portage Des Sioux, ST. CHARLES COUNTY
Potosi, WASHINGTON COUNTY

Racola, WASHINGTON COUNTY
Rayville vic., RAY COUNTY
Richfountain, OSAGE COUNTY
Ritchey vic., NEWTON COUNTY
Rocheport, BOONE COUNTY
Roscoe, ST. CLAIR COUNTY
Roscoe vic., ST. CLAIR COUNTY

Santa Fe vic., MONROE COUNTY
Saverton, RALLS COUNTY
Sedalia, PETTIS COUNTY
Sikeston, SCOTT COUNTY
Sikeston vic., SCOTT COUNTY
Smithville vic., CLAY COUNTY
Speed vic., COOPER COUNTY
Springfield, GREENE COUNTY
Springfield vic., GREENE COUNTY
St. Charles, ST. CHARLES COUNTY
St. Charles vic., ST. CHARLES COUNTY
St. Joseph, BUCHANAN COUNTY
St. Joseph vic., BUCHANAN COUNTY
St. Louis (City)
St. Louis vic., ST. LOUIS COUNTY
St. Peter's vic., ST. CHARLES COUNTY
St.louis (City)
Starkenburg, MONTGOMERY COUNTY
Ste. Genevieve
Ste. Genevieve, STE. GENEVIEVE COUNTY
Ste. Genevieve vic., STE. GENEVIEVE COUNTY
Stoutsville, MONROE COUNTY
Stoutsville vic., MONROE COUNTY
Sullivan, FRANKLIN COUNTY

Taos, COLE COUNTY
Tipton, MONITEAU COUNTY
Trimble vic., CLINTON COUNTY
Troy, LINCOLN COUNTY

University City, MERCER COUNTY

Vanzant vic., DOUGLAS COUNTY
Versailles, MORGAN COUNTY
Victor, MONROE COUNTY
Victor vic., MONROE COUNTY
Vineland vic., JEFFERSON COUNTY

Warrenton, WARREN COUNTY
Warrenton vic., WARREN COUNTY
Warsaw, BENTON COUNTY
Warsaw vic., BENTON COUNTY
Washington, FRANKLIN COUNTY
Washington vic., FRANKLIN COUNTY
Waverly, LAFAYETTE COUNTY
Webster Groves, ST. LOUIS COUNTY
Weingarten
Weldon Springs, ST. CHARLES COUNTY
Weldon Springs vic., ST. CHARLES COUNTY
Wellston, ST. LOUIS COUNTY
Westphalia, OSAGE COUNTY
Westphalia vic., OSAGE COUNTY

Zell

Montana

Alberton vic., MINERAL COUNTY
Alberton vic., MISSOULA COUNTY
Anaconda, DEER LODGE COUNTY
Anaconda vic., DEER LODGE COUNTY
Augusta vic., LEWIS AND CLARK COUNTY
Avon vic., POWELL COUNTY

Babb vic., GLACIER COUNTY

Bannack, BEAVERHEAD COUNTY
Barber, GOLDEN VALLEY COUNTY
Billings, YELLOWSTONE COUNTY
Billings vic., YELLOWSTONE COUNTY
Bozeman, GALLATIN COUNTY
Bozeman vic., GALLATIN COUNTY
Butte, SILVER BOW COUNTY
Butte vic., SILVER BOW COUNTY

Coburg, BLAINE COUNTY
Colstrip vic., ROSEBUD COUNTY
Coram vic., FLATHEAD COUNTY
Corvallis, RAVALLI COUNTY
Craig vic., LEWIS AND CLARK COUNTY
Custer Battlefield, BIG HORN COUNTY

Danvers vic., FERGUS COUNTY
Deer Lodge, POWELL COUNTY
Deer Lodge vic., POWELL COUNTY
Divide vic., SILVER BOW COUNTY

East Glacier Park V., GLACIER COUNTY
East Glacier vic., GLACIER COUNTY
Elkhorn, JEFFERSON COUNTY

Fort Belknap, BLAINE COUNTY
Fort Benton, CHOUTEAU COUNTY
Fort Benton vic., CHOUTEAU COUNTY
Fort Missoula, MISSOULA COUNTY
Fort Smith vic., CARBON COUNTY
Fortine vic., LINCOLN COUNTY
Fortine vicinity, LINCOLN COUNTY
Fromberg vic., CARBON COUNTY

Glasgow vic., VALLEY COUNTY
Goldcreek vic., GRANITE COUNTY
Goldcreek vic., POWELL COUNTY
Granite, GRANITE COUNTY
Great Falls, CASCADE COUNTY
Greycliff vic., SWEET GRASS COUNTY

Hall vic., GRANITE COUNTY
Hardin, BIG HORN COUNTY
Helena, LEWIS AND CLARK COUNTY
Helena vic., LEWIS AND CLARK COUNTY

Joliet, CARBON COUNTY

Kalispell, FLATHEAD COUNTY
Kalispell vic., FLATHEAD COUNTY

Lame Deer, ROSEBUD COUNTY
Livingston vic., PARK COUNTY
Lolo vic., MISSOULA COUNTY
Lombard vic., BROADWATER COUNTY

Maxville vic., GRANITE COUNTY
Miles City, CUSTER COUNTY
Miles City vic., CUSTER COUNTY
Milltown, MISSOULA COUNTY
Moore vic., FERGUS COUNTY

Ne Ennis, MADISON COUNTY
Nohly vic., RICHLAND COUNTY

Radersburg vic., BROADWATER COUNTY
Radersburg vic., JEFFERSON COUNTY
Red Lodge vic., CARBON COUNTY
Rocky Boy's Agency, HILL COUNTY
Roundup vic., MUSSELSHELL COUNTY

Springdale, PARK COUNTY
St. Mary, GLACIER COUNTY
St. Regis vic., MINERAL COUNTY
Stevensville, RAVALLI COUNTY
Stockett vic., CASCADE COUNTY

Terry vic., PRAIRIE COUNTY

Thompson Falls, SANDERS COUNTY
Toston vic., BROADWATER COUNTY
Triple Arch vic., FLATHEAD COUNTY
Troy, LINCOLN COUNTY
Twin Bridges, MADISON COUNTY

Victor vic., RAVALLI COUNTY
Virginia City, MADISON COUNTY

West Glacier, FLATHEAD COUNTY
White Sulphur Spring, MEAGHER COUNTY
Wibaux, WIBAUX COUNTY

Nebraska

Beatrice, GAGE COUNTY
Bellevue, SARPY COUNTY
Bellwood, BUTLER COUNTY
Blair vic., WASHINGTON COUNTY
Brownsville, NEMAHA COUNTY
Brownville, NEMAHA COUNTY

Crofton, KNOX COUNTY

Dakota City, DAKOTA COUNTY

Florence, DOUGLAS COUNTY

Grand Island, HALL COUNTY

Humboldt, RICHARDSON COUNTY

Lincoln, LANCASTER COUNTY

Millard, DOUGLAS COUNTY

Nebraka City, OTOE COUNTY
Nebraska City, OTOE COUNTY
Nebraska City vic., OTOE COUNTY
Niobrara, KNOX COUNTY

Omaha, DOUGLAS COUNTY

Plattsmouth vic., CASS COUNTY

Rulo, RICHARDSON COUNTY

Santee, KNOX COUNTY
Santee Reservation, KNOX COUNTY
Santee vic., KNOX COUNTY

Nevada

Aurora, MINERAL COUNTY

Baker vic., WHITE PINE COUNTY

Carson City (City)

Dayton, LYON COUNTY
Dayton vic., LYON COUNTY

Eureka, EUREKA COUNTY

Fallon, CHURCHILL COUNTY
Fallon vic., CHURCHILL COUNTY

Genoa, DOUGLAS COUNTY
Glendale Junction, CLARK COUNTY
Gold Hill, STOREY COUNTY

Hawthorne, MINERAL COUNTY
Hawthrone, MINERAL COUNTY
Humboldt City, PERSHING COUNTY

North Las Vegas, CLARK COUNTY

Pioche, LINCOLN COUNTY

Reno, WASHOE COUNTY
Rhyolite vic., NYE COUNTY

Silver City, LYON COUNTY

Tonopah, NYE COUNTY

Verdi, WASHOE COUNTY
Virginia, STOREY COUNTY
Virginia City, STOREY COUNTY

Weeks vic., LYON COUNTY

New Hampshire

Acworth, SULLIVAN COUNTY
Antrim, HILLSBOROUGH COUNTY

Bath, GRAFTON COUNTY
Boscawen, MERRIMACK COUNTY
Bow Mills vic., MERRIMACK COUNTY

Campton, GRAFTON COUNTY
Campton vic., GRAFTON COUNTY
Canterbury, MERRIMACK COUNTY
Canturbury, MERRIMACK COUNTY
Charleston, SULLIVAN COUNTY
Chesterfield, CHESHIRE COUNTY
Chichester, MERRIMACK COUNTY
Claremont, SULLIVAN COUNTY
Concord, MERRIMACK COUNTY
Cornish, SULLIVAN COUNTY

Derryville, ROCKINGHAM COUNTY
Durham, STRAFFORD COUNTY
Durham vic., STRAFFORD COUNTY

Easton, GRAFTON COUNTY
Enfield vic., GRAFTON COUNTY
Exeter, ROCKINGHAM COUNTY

Goshen, SULLIVAN COUNTY
Greenland, ROCKINGHAM COUNTY

Hampton, ROCKINGHAM COUNTY
Hampton Falls, ROCKINGHAM COUNTY
Hanover, GRAFTON COUNTY
Harrisville, CHESHIRE COUNTY
Henniker, MERRIMACK COUNTY
Hillsboro, HILLSBOROUGH COUNTY
Hillsborough, HILLSBOROUGH COUNTY
Hillsborough vic., HILLSBOROUGH COUNTY
Hinsdale, CHESHIRE COUNTY
Hopkinton, MERRIMACK COUNTY
Hopkinton vic., MERRIMACK COUNTY
Hopkinton Village, MERRIMACK COUNTY

Kensington, ROCKINGHAM COUNTY

Lancaster, COOS COUNTY
Lyme, GRAFTON COUNTY
Lyme vic., GRAFTON COUNTY

Manchester, HILLSBOROUGH COUNTY
Marlborough, HILLSBOROUGH COUNTY

Newington, ROCKINGHAM COUNTY
Newmarket, ROCKINGHAM COUNTY

Newport, SULLIVAN COUNTY
Northwood Narrows, ROCKINGHAM COUNTY

Orford, GRAFTON COUNTY

Portsmouth, ROCKINGHAM COUNTY

Raymond, ROCKINGHAM COUNTY
Rockingham, ROCKINGHAM COUNTY
Rye, ROCKINGHAM COUNTY

Salisbury, MERRIMACK COUNTY
Salisbury Heights, MERRIMACK COUNTY
Salmon Falls, STRAFFORD COUNTY
Sandown, ROCKINGHAM COUNTY
Somersworth, STRAFFORD COUNTY
Somersworth vic., STRAFFORD COUNTY
Stoddard vic., CHESHIRE COUNTY
Stratham, ROCKINGHAM COUNTY

Walpole, CHESHIRE COUNTY
Webster, MERRIMACK COUNTY
West Henniker, MERRIMACK COUNTY
West Henniker Villag, MERRIMACK COUNTY
Westminster
Westmoreland, CHESHIRE COUNTY

New Jersey

Absecon, ATLANTIC COUNTY
Aldine vic., SALEM COUNTY
Allaire, MONMOUTH COUNTY
Allentown, MONMOUTH COUNTY
Alloway, SALEM COUNTY
Alloway vic., SALEM COUNTY
Alpine, BERGEN COUNTY
Ancora, CAMDEN COUNTY
Arneytown, BURLINGTON COUNTY
Arneytown vic., MONMOUTH COUNTY
Asbury, WARREN COUNTY
Asbury Park, MONMOUTH COUNTY
Atlantic City, ATLANTIC COUNTY
Atlantic Highlands, MONMOUTH COUNTY
Auburn, SALEM COUNTY
Avalon, CAPE MAY COUNTY
Avon-By-The-Sea, MONMOUTH COUNTY

Bacon's Neck, CUMBERLAND COUNTY
Bacon's Neck vic., CUMBERLAND COUNTY
Barnegat, OCEAN COUNTY
Basking Ridge, SOMERSET COUNTY
Batsto, BURLINGTON COUNTY
Bayhead, OCEAN COUNTY
Bayonne, HUDSON COUNTY
Bayonne vic., HUDSON COUNTY
Bayside vic., CUMBERLAND COUNTY
Bayville, OCEAN COUNTY
Beach Haven, OCEAN COUNTY
Beesleys Point, CAPE MAY COUNTY
Belleville, ESSEX COUNTY
Bellmawr, CAMDEN COUNTY
Bellmawr vic., CAMDEN COUNTY
Belmar, MONMOUTH COUNTY
Bergenfield, BERGEN COUNTY
Bernards Twp., SOMERSET COUNTY
Bernardsville, SOMERSET COUNTY
Bloomfield, ESSEX COUNTY
Blue Anchor, CAMDEN COUNTY
Bonhamtown, MIDDLESEX COUNTY
Boonton vic., MORRIS COUNTY
Bordentown, BURLINGTON COUNTY
Bound Brook vic., MIDDLESEX COUNTY
Bound Brook vic., SOMERSET COUNTY
Bound Brook vicinity, SOMERSET COUNTY
Bowenton vic., CUMBERLAND COUNTY
Bradley Beach, MONMOUTH COUNTY
Brick vic., OCEAN COUNTY
Bridgeboro, BURLINGTON COUNTY
Bridgeton, CUMBERLAND COUNTY
Bridgeton vic., CUMBERLAND COUNTY
Bridgewater Twp., SOMERSET COUNTY
Brigantine, ATLANTIC COUNTY
Burlington, BURLINGTON COUNTY

Caldwell, ESSEX COUNTY
Califon vic., HUNTERDON COUNTY
Camden, CAMDEN COUNTY
Cape May, CAPE MAY COUNTY
Cape May Court House, CAPE MAY COUNTY
Cape May Courthouse, CAPE MAY COUNTY
Cape May Point, CAPE MAY COUNTY
Carteret, MIDDLESEX COUNTY
Cedar Bridge, OCEAN COUNTY
Cedar Grove, ESSEX COUNTY
Cedarville, CUMBERLAND COUNTY
Chapel Hill, MONMOUTH COUNTY
Charleston vic., BURLINGTON COUNTY
Chatham, MORRIS COUNTY
Chester, MORRIS COUNTY
Chews Landing vic., CAMDEN COUNTY
Clifton, PASSAIC COUNTY
Clinton, HUNTERDON COUNTY
Clinton vic., HUNTERDON COUNTY
Closter, BERGEN COUNTY
Cold Spring, CAPE MAY COUNTY
Collingswood, CAMDEN COUNTY
Columbus, BURLINGTON COUNTY
Cookstown, BURLINGTON COUNTY
Cookstown vic., BURLINGTON COUNTY
Cranford, UNION COUNTY
Creamridge vic., MONMOUTH COUNTY
Cresskill, BERGEN COUNTY
Crosswicks, BURLINGTON COUNTY

Daretown, SALEM COUNTY
Deal, MONMOUTH COUNTY
Deerfield vic., CUMBERLAND COUNTY
Delaware, WARREN COUNTY
Delaware Twp., CAMDEN COUNTY
Demarest, BERGEN COUNTY
Dennisville, CAPE MAY COUNTY
Denville vic., MORRIS COUNTY
Dorchester vic., CUMBERLAND COUNTY
Dover vic., MORRIS COUNTY
Dumont, BERGEN COUNTY
Dutch Neck, CUMBERLAND COUNTY

E. Rutherford, BERGEN COUNTY
East Millstone, SOMERSET COUNTY
East Millstone vic., SOMERSET COUNTY
Eayrestown, BURLINGTON COUNTY
Eayrestown vic., BURLINGTON COUNTY
Edgewater, BERGEN COUNTY
Egg Harbor City vic., ATLANTIC COUNTY
Elizabeth, UNION COUNTY
Elsinboro, SALEM COUNTY
Elsinboro Twp., SALEM COUNTY
Emerson, BERGEN COUNTY
Englewood, BERGEN COUNTY
Englishtown, MONMOUTH COUNTY
Everett vic., MONMOUTH COUNTY
Evesboro vic., BURLINGTON COUNTY
Ewansville, BURLINGTON COUNTY

Fair Lawn, BERGEN COUNTY
Fairfield vic., ESSEX COUNTY
Fairton, CUMBERLAND COUNTY
Fanwood, UNION COUNTY
Fellowship-Del. Twp., CAMDEN COUNTY
Fieldsboro, BURLINGTON COUNTY
Finderne vic., SOMERSET COUNTY
Flatbrookville vic., SUSSEX COUNTY
Flemington, HUNTERDON COUNTY
Florham Park, MORRIS COUNTY
Forked River, OCEAN COUNTY
Fort Lee, BERGEN COUNTY
Frankfort, SOMERSET COUNTY
Franklin Park, SOMERSET COUNTY
Franklin Park vic., MIDDLESEX COUNTY
Freehold vic., MONMOUTH COUNTY
Friesburg, SALEM COUNTY

Glassboro, GLOUCESTER COUNTY
Glen Gardner, HUNTERDON COUNTY
Glen Rock, BERGEN COUNTY
Glendale, CAMDEN COUNTY
Goshen, CAPE MAY COUNTY
Greenwich, CUMBERLAND COUNTY
Greenwich vic., CUMBERLAND COUNTY

Hackensack, BERGEN COUNTY
Haddonfield, CAMDEN COUNTY
Hainesville vic., SUSSEX COUNTY
Hamburg, SUSSEX COUNTY
Hancock's Bridge Vic, SALEM COUNTY
Hancocks Bridge, SALEM COUNTY
Hancocks Bridge vic., SALEM COUNTY
Hanover, MORRIS COUNTY
Hanover Neck, MORRIS COUNTY
Hanover Twp., MORRIS COUNTY
Harvey Cedars, OCEAN COUNTY
Haskell, PASSAIC COUNTY
Hawthorne, PASSAIC COUNTY
Head-Of-The-River, ATLANTIC COUNTY
Heislerville, CUMBERLAND COUNTY
Herbertsville, OCEAN COUNTY
Highland Park vic., MIDDLESEX COUNTY
Highlands, MONMOUTH COUNTY
Hillsdale, BERGEN COUNTY
Hoboken, HUDSON COUNTY
Hohokus, BERGEN COUNTY
Hohokus Twp., BERGEN COUNTY
Holland, MONMOUTH COUNTY
Holmdel, MONMOUTH COUNTY
Holmdel vic., MONMOUTH COUNTY
Hopatcong vic., SUSSEX COUNTY
Hope, WARREN COUNTY
Hope vic., WARREN COUNTY
Hopewell, MERCER COUNTY
Hopewell vic., MERCER COUNTY
Hutchinson's Mill, MERCER COUNTY

Irvington, ESSEX COUNTY
Island Heights, OCEAN COUNTY

Jersey City, HUDSON COUNTY
Jobstown, BURLINGTON COUNTY
Jobstown vic., BURLINGTON COUNTY
Jobstown vicinity, BURLINGTON COUNTY
Johnsonburg, WARREN COUNTY

Keansburg, MONMOUTH COUNTY
Kearny, HUDSON COUNTY
Kingston, MIDDLESEX COUNTY
Kinkora, BURLINGTON COUNTY

Lakehurst vic., OCEAN COUNTY
Lambertville, HUNTERDON COUNTY
Lanoka Harbor, OCEAN COUNTY
Lavallette, OCEAN COUNTY
Lawrenceville, MERCER COUNTY
Lawrenceville vic., MERCER COUNTY
Leeds Point, ATLANTIC COUNTY
Leonia, BERGEN COUNTY

Liberty Corner, SOMERSET COUNTY
Liberty Corner vic., SOMERSET COUNTY
Lincoln Park, MORRIS COUNTY
Little Falls, PASSAIC COUNTY
Livingston, ESSEX COUNTY
Long Branch, MONMOUTH COUNTY
Lower Alloways Creek, SALEM COUNTY
Lower Penns Neck, SALEM COUNTY
Lower Preakness, PASSAIC COUNTY
Lumberton vic., BURLINGTON COUNTY
Lyndhurst, BERGEN COUNTY

Madison, MORRIS COUNTY
Malaga vic., GLOUCESTER COUNTY
Manahawkin, OCEAN COUNTY
Mannington vic., SALEM COUNTY
Mantua, GLOUCESTER COUNTY
Mantua vic., GLOUCESTER COUNTY
Maple Shade, BURLINGTON COUNTY
Maplewood, ESSEX COUNTY
Margate City, ATLANTIC COUNTY
Marlton vic., BURLINGTON COUNTY
Matawan, MONMOUTH COUNTY
Mauricetown, CUMBERLAND COUNTY
Mays Landing, ATLANTIC COUNTY
Maywood, BERGEN COUNTY
Mendham, MORRIS COUNTY
Metuchen, MIDDLESEX COUNTY
Metuchen vic., MIDDLESEX COUNTY
Mickleton, GLOUCESTER COUNTY
Middle Valley, MORRIS COUNTY
Middlebush vic., SOMERSET COUNTY
Middleton, MONMOUTH COUNTY
Middletown, MONMOUTH COUNTY
Midland Park, BERGEN COUNTY
Millbrook, WARREN COUNTY
Millbrook vic., WARREN COUNTY
Millburn, ESSEX COUNTY
Millstone, SOMERSET COUNTY
Millville, CUMBERLAND COUNTY
Millville vic., CUMBERLAND COUNTY
Millville vic., SUSSEX COUNTY
Monmouth Beach, MONMOUTH COUNTY
Montague, SUSSEX COUNTY
Montague vic., SUSSEX COUNTY
Montclair, ESSEX COUNTY
Montvale Boro, BERGEN COUNTY
Montville, MORRIS COUNTY
Montville vic., MORRIS COUNTY
Moorestown, BURLINGTON COUNTY
Moorestown vic., BURLINGTON COUNTY
Morristown, MORRIS COUNTY
Mount Freedom vic., MORRIS COUNTY
Mount Holly, BURLINGTON COUNTY
Mount Laurel, BURLINGTON COUNTY
Mount Laurel vic., BURLINGTON COUNTY
Mount Royal, GLOUCESTER COUNTY
Mount Tabor vic., MORRIS COUNTY
Mountain View, PASSAIC COUNTY
Mountainside, UNION COUNTY
Mountainville, HUNTERDON COUNTY
Mullica Hill, GLOUCESTER COUNTY
Murray Grove, OCEAN COUNTY

National Park, GLOUCESTER COUNTY
Neshanic Station, SOMERSET COUNTY
New Brunswick, MIDDLESEX COUNTY
New Brunswick vic., MIDDLESEX COUNTY
New Brunswick vic., SOMERSET COUNTY
New Gretna, BURLINGTON COUNTY
New Hampton, HUNTERDON COUNTY
New Lisbon, BURLINGTON COUNTY
New Market, MIDDLESEX COUNTY
New Milford, BERGEN COUNTY
New Providence, UNION COUNTY
Newark, ESSEX COUNTY
Newfoundland, MORRIS COUNTY
Newfoundland vic., MORRIS COUNTY
Newtown, MIDDLESEX COUNTY
North Caldwell, ESSEX COUNTY
North Stelton vic., MIDDLESEX COUNTY
Nutley, ESSEX COUNTY

Oakland, BERGEN COUNTY
Ocean City, CAPE MAY COUNTY
Ocean Gate, OCEAN COUNTY
Ocean Grove, MONMOUTH COUNTY
Ocean View, CAPE MAY COUNTY
Old Tappan, BERGEN COUNTY
Old Tappan vic., BERGEN COUNTY
Oldwick, HUNTERDON COUNTY
Orange, ESSEX COUNTY
Oxford, WARREN COUNTY

Paramus, BERGEN COUNTY
Park Ridge, BERGEN COUNTY
Park Ridge vic., BERGEN COUNTY
Parkertown, OCEAN COUNTY
Parsippany vic., MORRIS COUNTY
Passaic, PASSAIC COUNTY
Paterson, PASSAIC COUNTY
Paterson vic., PASSAIC COUNTY
Pattenburg vic., HUNTERDON COUNTY
Paulsboro, GLOUCESTER COUNTY
Paulsboro vic., GLOUCESTER COUNTY
Pennington, MERCER COUNTY
Pennington vic., MERCER COUNTY
Pennsauken Twp., CAMDEN COUNTY
Pennsauken vic., CAMDEN COUNTY
Perth Amboy, MIDDLESEX COUNTY
Phalanx, MONMOUTH COUNTY
Phalanx vic., MONMOUTH COUNTY
Phillipsburg, WARREN COUNTY
Phillipsburg vic., WARREN COUNTY
Pine Beach, OCEAN COUNTY
Pine Brook, MORRIS COUNTY
Piscataway, MIDDLESEX COUNTY
Piscataway Twp., MIDDLESEX COUNTY
Pitman, GLOUCESTER COUNTY
Pittsgrove vic., SALEM COUNTY
Plainfield, UNION COUNTY
Plainsboro vic., MIDDLESEX COUNTY
Pleasantville, ATLANTIC COUNTY
Pluckemin, SOMERSET COUNTY
Point Pleasant, OCEAN COUNTY
Pompton Falls vic., PASSAIC COUNTY
Pompton Plains, MORRIS COUNTY
Port Elizabeth, CUMBERLAND COUNTY
Port Norris, CUMBERLAND COUNTY
Port Republic, ATLANTIC COUNTY
Port Warren vic., WARREN COUNTY
Powerville, MORRIS COUNTY
Preakness, PASSAIC COUNTY
Princeton, MERCER COUNTY
Princeton vic., MERCER COUNTY
Prospertown vic., MONMOUTH COUNTY

Quinton vic., SALEM COUNTY

Rahway, UNION COUNTY
Rahway vic., UNION COUNTY
Ralston, MORRIS COUNTY
Rancocas, BURLINGTON COUNTY
Rancocas vic., BURLINGTON COUNTY
Rancocas vicinity, BURLINGTON COUNTY
Raritan, SOMERSET COUNTY
Raven Rock vic., HUNTERDON COUNTY
Red Bank, MONMOUTH COUNTY
Red Lion vicinity, BURLINGTON COUNTY
Ridgefield, BERGEN COUNTY
Ridgefield Park, BERGEN COUNTY
Ridgewood, BERGEN COUNTY
Ringoes, HUNTERDON COUNTY
Ringoes vic., HUNTERDON COUNTY
Ringwood, PASSAIC COUNTY
River Edge, BERGEN COUNTY
Riverton vic., BURLINGTON COUNTY
Roadstown, CUMBERLAND COUNTY
Rochelle Park, BERGEN COUNTY
Rockaway, MORRIS COUNTY
Rockleigh, BERGEN COUNTY
Rockport vic., WARREN COUNTY
Rocky Hill, SOMERSET COUNTY
Roseland, ESSEX COUNTY
Rutherford, BERGEN COUNTY

S. Middlebush, SOMERSET COUNTY
Saddle River, BERGEN COUNTY
Saddle River Twp., BERGEN COUNTY
Salem, SALEM COUNTY
Salem vic., SALEM COUNTY
Sandtown, BURLINGTON COUNTY
Sandy Hook, MONMOUTH COUNTY
Saxton Falls, WARREN COUNTY
Schalk Station, MIDDLESEX COUNTY
Scotch Plains, UNION COUNTY
Sea Breeze, CUMBERLAND COUNTY
Seaside Heights, OCEAN COUNTY
Seaside Park, OCEAN COUNTY
Seaside Park vic., OCEAN COUNTY
Seaville vic., CAPE MAY COUNTY
Seeley, CUMBERLAND COUNTY
Seeley vic., CUMBERLAND COUNTY
Sergeantsville, HUNTERDON COUNTY
Sergeantsville vic., HUNTERDON COUNTY
Sharptown vic., SALEM COUNTY
Shiloh, CUMBERLAND COUNTY
Shrewsbury, MONMOUTH COUNTY
Smith Ferry vic., SUSSEX COUNTY
Smithville, ATLANTIC COUNTY
Somerdale vic., CAMDEN COUNTY
Somers Point, ATLANTIC COUNTY
Somerville, SOMERSET COUNTY
South Amboy, MIDDLESEX COUNTY
South Bound Brook, SOMERSET COUNTY
South Dennis, CAPE MAY COUNTY
South Dennis vic., CAPE MAY COUNTY
South Pemberton, BURLINGTON COUNTY
South Seaville, CAPE MAY COUNTY
South Toms River, OCEAN COUNTY
Speedwell Village, MORRIS COUNTY
Split Rock, MORRIS COUNTY
Spring Lake, MONMOUTH COUNTY
Springfield, UNION COUNTY
Springfield Twp., BURLINGTON COUNTY
Springside vic., BURLINGTON COUNTY
Springtown vic., MORRIS COUNTY
Stewartsville, WARREN COUNTY
Stewartsville vic., WARREN COUNTY
Swedesboro, GLOUCESTER COUNTY
Swedesboro vic., GLOUCESTER COUNTY
Swedesboro vicinity, GLOUCESTER COUNTY
Sykesville, BURLINGTON COUNTY

Tavistock, CAMDEN COUNTY
Teaneck, BERGEN COUNTY
Tenafly, BERGEN COUNTY
Tenalfy, BERGEN COUNTY
Tennent, MONMOUTH COUNTY
Toms River, OCEAN COUNTY
Totowa, PASSAIC COUNTY
Towaco, MORRIS COUNTY
Towaco vic., MORRIS COUNTY
Trenton, MERCER COUNTY
Troy Hills, MORRIS COUNTY
Tuckahoe vic., CAPE MAY COUNTY

Tuckerton, OCEAN COUNTY

Union, UNION COUNTY
Union City, HUDSON COUNTY
Upper Mill, BURLINGTON COUNTY
Upper Montclair, ESSEX COUNTY
Upper Preakness, PASSAIC COUNTY
Upper Saddle River, BERGEN COUNTY

Ventnor, ATLANTIC COUNTY
Vincetown, BURLINGTON COUNTY
Vincetown vicinity, BURLINGTON COUNTY
Vineland, CUMBERLAND COUNTY

Wallpack Center, SUSSEX COUNTY
Wallpack Center vic., SUSSEX COUNTY
Walnford vic., MONMOUTH COUNTY
Wanaque, PASSAIC COUNTY
Wantage, SUSSEX COUNTY
Waretown, OCEAN COUNTY
Washington Crossing, MERCER COUNTY
Washington Twp., BURLINGTON COUNTY
Washington Twsp. Vic, BURLINGTON COUNTY
Washington Valley, MORRIS COUNTY
Washington vic., WARREN COUNTY
Waterloo vic., SUSSEX COUNTY
Wayne, PASSAIC COUNTY
West Caldwell, ESSEX COUNTY
West Creek, OCEAN COUNTY
West Freehold, MONMOUTH COUNTY
West Milford, PASSAIC COUNTY
West New York, HUDSON COUNTY
West Orange, ESSEX COUNTY
Westfield, UNION COUNTY
Whippany, MORRIS COUNTY
Whippany vic., MORRIS COUNTY
Wildwood, CAPE MAY COUNTY
Wildwood Crest, CAPE MAY COUNTY
Woodbine, CAPE MAY COUNTY
Woodbridge, MIDDLESEX COUNTY
Woodbury, GLOUCESTER COUNTY
Woodstown, SALEM COUNTY
Woodstown vic., SALEM COUNTY
Woodstown vicinity, SALEM COUNTY
Wrightsville, MONMOUTH COUNTY
Wyckoff, BERGEN COUNTY
Wyckoff vic., BERGEN COUNTY

New Mexico

Abo, TORRANCE COUNTY
Acoma Pueblo, VALENCIA COUNTY
Alamogordo vic., OTERO COUNTY
Albuquerque, BERNALILLO COUNTY
Alcalde, RIO ARRIBA COUNTY
Arroyo Hondo, TAOS COUNTY
Aztec vic., SAN JUAN COUNTY

Belen, VALENCIA COUNTY
Bland vic., SANDOVAL COUNTY

Canoncita, SANTA FE COUNTY
Chaco Canyon, SAN JUAN COUNTY
Chaco Canyon vic., SAN JUAN COUNTY
Chamita, RIO ARRIBA COUNTY
Chimayo, RIO ARRIBA COUNTY
Chimayo, SANTA FE COUNTY
Cienega, OTERO COUNTY
Cimarron, COLFAX COUNTY

El Cerrito, SAN MIGUEL COUNTY

Galisteo, SANTA FE COUNTY
Gallup, MCKINLEY COUNTY
Gila, GRANT COUNTY
Gran Quivira, SOCORRO COUNTY

Hillsboro, SIERRA COUNTY

Isleta Pueblo, BERNALILLO COUNTY
Isleto Pueblo, BERNALILLO COUNTY

Jemez Pueblo, SANDOVAL COUNTY

Laguna Pueblo, VALENCIA COUNTY
Las Cruces, DONA ANA COUNTY
Las Vegas, SAN MIGUEL COUNTY
Las Vegas vic., SAN MIGUEL COUNTY
Llano Quemado, TAOS COUNTY
Lordsburg vic., HIDALGO COUNTY
Los Alamos, LOS ALAMOS COUNTY
Los Alamos vic., LOS ALAMOS COUNTY

Manzano, TORRANCE COUNTY

Nambe Pueblo, SANTA FE COUNTY

Pecos, SAN MIGUEL COUNTY
Penasco, TAOS COUNTY
Peralta, VALENCIA COUNTY
Picuris, TAOS COUNTY
Placita De Taos, TAOS COUNTY
Pojoaque vic., SANTA FE COUNTY
Puerto De Luna, GUADALUPE COUNTY

Ranchito, TAOS COUNTY
Ranchos De Taos, TAOS COUNTY
Rodey, DONA ANA COUNTY
Romeroville, SAN MIGUEL COUNTY

San Ildefonso Pueblo, SANTA FE COUNTY
San Jose, SAN MIGUEL COUNTY
San Juan Pueblo, RIO ARRIBA COUNTY
San Miguel, SAN MIGUEL COUNTY
Santa Ana Pueblo, SANDOVAL COUNTY
Santa Clara Pueblo, RIO ARRIBA COUNTY
Santa Cruz, SANTA FE COUNTY
Santa Fe, SANTA FE COUNTY
Santa Fe vic., SANTA FE COUNTY
Silver City, GRANT COUNTY
Socorro, SOCORRO COUNTY

Talpa, TAOS COUNTY
Taos, TAOS COUNTY
Taos Pueblo, TAOS COUNTY
Tesuque, SANTA FE COUNTY
Tiptonville, MORA COUNTY
Trampas, TAOS COUNTY
Tucumcari, QUAY COUNTY

Vadito, TAOS COUNTY
Valencia vic., VALENCIA COUNTY
Valmora vic., MORA COUNTY
Villanueva, SAN MIGUEL COUNTY
Villanueva vic., SAN MIGUEL COUNTY

Watrous vic., MORA COUNTY
White Sands Msl Rang, DONA ANA COUNTY
White Sands Msl Rang, SOCORRO COUNTY

Zia Pueblo, SANDOVAL COUNTY
Zuni Pueblo, MCKINLEY COUNTY
Zuni vic., MCKINLEY COUNTY

New York

Albany, ALBANY COUNTY
Albion, ORLEANS COUNTY
Alplaus, SCHENECTADY COUNTY
Altamont, ALBANY COUNTY
Altamont vic., ALBANY COUNTY
Amagansett, SUFFOLK COUNTY
Amsterdam, MONTGOMERY COUNTY
Aqueboque, SUFFOLK COUNTY
Ashville, CHAUTAUQUA COUNTY
Athens, GREENE COUNTY
Atlanta, STEUBEN COUNTY
Au Sable Forks, ESSEX COUNTY
Auburn, CAYUGA COUNTY
Aurora, CAYUGA COUNTY
Avon, LIVINGSTON COUNTY

Babylon, SUFFOLK COUNTY
Ballston Lake, SARATOGA COUNTY
Ballston Lake vic., SARATOGA COUNTY
Ballston Spa, SARATOGA COUNTY
Barrytown vic., DUTCHESS COUNTY
Batavia, GENESEE COUNTY
Batavia vic., GENESEE COUNTY
Beacon, DUTCHESS COUNTY
Beacon vic., DUTCHESS COUNTY
Bedford, WESTCHESTER COUNTY
Belfast vic., ALLEGANY COUNTY
Belvidere vic., ALLEGANY COUNTY
Berne vic., ALBANY COUNTY
Berne vic., SCHOHARIE COUNTY
Bethlehem, ALBANY COUNTY
Binghamton, BROOME COUNTY
Blue Stores vic., COLUMBIA COUNTY
Boonville vic., ONEIDA COUNTY
Bowery Bay, QUEENS COUNTY
Breadabeen, SCHOHARIE COUNTY
Briarcliff Manor, WESTCHESTER COUNTY
Bridgehampton, SUFFOLK COUNTY
Brighton, MONROE COUNTY
Brinckerhoff, DUTCHESS COUNTY
Bristol Center, ONTARIO COUNTY
Broadalbin, FULTON COUNTY
Bronx, BRONX COUNTY
Brookhaven, SUFFOLK COUNTY
Brooklyn, KINGS COUNTY
Buffalo, ERIE COUNTY
Buffalo vic., ERIE COUNTY
Burnt Hills, SARATOGA COUNTY

Cairo, GREENE COUNTY
Caledonia, LIVINGSTON COUNTY
Callicoon, SULLIVAN COUNTY
Camillus, ONONDAGA COUNTY
Canajoharie, MONTGOMERY COUNTY
Canandaigua, ONTARIO COUNTY
Canastota, MADISON COUNTY
Canastota vic., MADISON COUNTY
Catskill, GREENE COUNTY
Catskill Mts., GREENE COUNTY
Cazenovia, MADISON COUNTY
Centereach, SUFFOLK COUNTY
Centerport, SUFFOLK COUNTY
Chappaqua, WESTCHESTER COUNTY
Chappaqua vic., WESTCHESTER COUNTY
Charleston, MONTGOMERY COUNTY
Charlton, SARATOGA COUNTY
Chatauqua, CHAUTAUQUA COUNTY
Chatham Center, COLUMBIA COUNTY

Cherry Valley, OTSEGO COUNTY
Childs, ORLEANS COUNTY
Chittenango, MADISON COUNTY
Cincinnatus, CORTLAND COUNTY
Clarkson, MONROE COUNTY
Clarksville, ALBANY COUNTY
Claverack, COLUMBIA COUNTY
Clermont Twp., COLUMBIA COUNTY
Coeymans, ALBANY COUNTY
Cohoes, ALBANY COUNTY
Collins, CATTARAUGUS COUNTY
Colonie, ALBANY COUNTY
Colonie Twp., ALBANY COUNTY
Commack, SUFFOLK COUNTY
Cooperstown, OTSEGO COUNTY
Copake, COLUMBIA COUNTY
Copake vic., COLUMBIA COUNTY
Corning, STEUBEN COUNTY
Corning vic., STEUBEN COUNTY
Cortland, COLUMBIA COUNTY
Cortland, CORTLAND COUNTY
Croton-On-Hudson Vic, WESTCHESTER COUNTY
Cutchogue, SUFFOLK COUNTY

Danby, TOMPKINS COUNTY
Danube, HERKIMER COUNTY
Dayton, CATTARAUGUS COUNTY
Delphi Falls, ONONDAGA COUNTY
Deposit, BROOME COUNTY
Deposit, DELAWARE COUNTY
Dobbs Ferry, WESTCHESTER COUNTY
Dover Plains, DUTCHESS COUNTY
Dryden, TOMPKINS COUNTY
Duanesburg, SCHENECTADY COUNTY
Dunkirk, CHAUTAUQUA COUNTY
Dunnsville, ALBANY COUNTY

East Avon, LIVINGSTON COUNTY
East Greenbush, RENSSELAER COUNTY
East Hampton, SUFFOLK COUNTY
East Rockaway, NASSAU COUNTY
East Setauket, SUFFOLK COUNTY
East Springfield, OTSEGO COUNTY
East Williston, NASSAU COUNTY
Easton, WASHINGTON COUNTY
Eaton Village, MADISON COUNTY
Elbridge Vic, ONONDAGA COUNTY
Ellenville, ULSTER COUNTY
Elmira, CHEMUNG COUNTY
Endwell, BROOME COUNTY
Esperance, SCHOHARIE COUNTY

Fabius, ONONDAGA COUNTY
Farmingdale, NASSAU COUNTY
Fayetteville, ONONDAGA COUNTY
Feura Bush, ALBANY COUNTY
Fillmore vic., ALLEGANY COUNTY
Fishkill, DUTCHESS COUNTY
Flushing, QUEENS COUNTY
Fonda, MONTGOMERY COUNTY
Fort Ann, WASHINGTON COUNTY
Fort Herkimer, HERKIMER COUNTY
Fort Hunter, MONTGOMERY COUNTY
Fort Johnson, MONTGOMERY COUNTY
Fort Plain, MONTGOMERY COUNTY
Fort Ticonderoga, ESSEX COUNTY
Frankfort, HERKIMER COUNTY
Fultonville, MONTGOMERY COUNTY

Gaines, ORLEANS COUNTY
Gardiner, ULSTER COUNTY
Gardiner's Island, SUFFOLK COUNTY
Garrison, PUTNAM COUNTY
Geneva, ONTARIO COUNTY
Geneva vic., SENECA COUNTY
Georgetown, MADISON COUNTY
Germantown vic., COLUMBIA COUNTY
Germonds, ROCKLAND COUNTY
Giffords, SCHENECTADY COUNTY
Glen, MONTGOMERY COUNTY
Glen Cove, NASSAU COUNTY
Glenville, SCHENECTADY COUNTY
Glenville Center, SCHENECTADY COUNTY
Gloversville, FULTON COUNTY
Goldens Bridge, WESTCHESTER COUNTY
Goshen, ORANGE COUNTY
Granville, WASHINGTON COUNTY
Great Neck, NASSAU COUNTY
Green Island, ALBANY COUNTY
Greenlawn, SUFFOLK COUNTY
Greenport, COLUMBIA COUNTY
Grooms Corners, SARATOGA COUNTY
Guilderland Center, ALBANY COUNTY
Guilderland vic., ALBANY COUNTY

Hancock, DELAWARE COUNTY
Hancock vic., DELAWARE COUNTY
Harriman, ORANGE COUNTY
Hartsdale, WESTCHESTER COUNTY
Hastings-On-Hudson, WESTCHESTER COUNTY
Hauppauge, SUFFOLK COUNTY
Hempstead, NASSAU COUNTY
Henrietta, MONROE COUNTY
Herkimer, HERKIMER COUNTY
High Bridge vic., SARATOGA COUNTY
High Falls, ULSTER COUNTY
Homer, CORTLAND COUNTY
Hornell, STEUBEN COUNTY
Horseheads, CHEMUNG COUNTY
Horseheads vic., CHEMUNG COUNTY
Houcks Corners, ALBANY COUNTY
Hudson, COLUMBIA COUNTY
Hudson Falls, WASHINGTON COUNTY
Hudson vic., COLUMBIA COUNTY
Huntington, SUFFOLK COUNTY
Huntington vic., SUFFOLK COUNTY
Huntington,south, SUFFOLK COUNTY
Hurley, ULSTER COUNTY
Hurley vic., ULSTER COUNTY
Hyde Park, DUTCHESS COUNTY

Ilion, HERKIMER COUNTY
Indian Castle vic., HERKIMER COUNTY
Irving, ERIE COUNTY
Irvington, WESTCHESTER COUNTY
Ithaca, TOMPKINS COUNTY
Ithaca vic., TOMPKINS COUNTY

Jackson Heights, QUEENS COUNTY
Jamestown, CHAUTAUQUA COUNTY
Jamesville, ONONDAGA COUNTY
Jamesville vic., ONONDAGA COUNTY
Jay, ESSEX COUNTY
Johnson City, ALBANY COUNTY
Johnstown, FULTON COUNTY
Jordan, ONONDAGA COUNTY

Katonah, WESTCHESTER COUNTY
Keeseville, CLINTON COUNTY
Kerhonkson, ULSTER COUNTY
Kew Gardens, QUEENS COUNTY
Kinderhook, COLUMBIA COUNTY
Kinderhook vic., COLUMBIA COUNTY
Kingsbury, WASHINGTON COUNTY
Kingston, ULSTER COUNTY
Kingston vic., ULSTER COUNTY

Lake Placid vic., ESSEX COUNTY
Lawrence, NASSAU COUNTY
Lawtons vic., ERIE COUNTY
Leeds, GREENE COUNTY
Lewiston, NIAGARA COUNTY
Limestone vic., CATTARAUGUS COUNTY
Little Falls, HERKIMER COUNTY
Liverpool, ONONDAGA COUNTY
Livingston vic., COLUMBIA COUNTY
Lloyd Harbor, SUFFOLK COUNTY
Lloyd Harbor vic., SUFFOLK COUNTY
Lloyd Neck vic., SUFFOLK COUNTY
Lockport, NIAGARA COUNTY
Long Island City, QUEENS COUNTY
Lyndonville vic., ORLEANS COUNTY
Lyons, WAYNE COUNTY

Maine vic., BROOME COUNTY
Malden Bridge, COLUMBIA COUNTY
Mamaroneck, WESTCHESTER COUNTY
Manhasset, NASSAU COUNTY
Manlius, ONONDAGA COUNTY
Marbletown, ULSTER COUNTY
Marcellus, ONONDAGA COUNTY
Marcellus vic., ONONDAGA COUNTY
Martinsville, NIAGARA COUNTY
Martisco, ONONDAGA COUNTY
Maspeth, QUEENS COUNTY
Massapequa, NASSAU COUNTY
Mastic Beach, SUFFOLK COUNTY
Matinecock, NASSAU COUNTY
Mayfield, FULTON COUNTY
Mcgraw, CORTLAND COUNTY
Mecklenburg, SCHUYLER COUNTY
Melrose vic., RENSSELAER COUNTY
Melville, SUFFOLK COUNTY
Middleburg, SCHOHARIE COUNTY
Middlefield Cen. Vic, OTSEGO COUNTY
Middletown, ORANGE COUNTY
Milan, DUTCHESS COUNTY
Millbrook, DUTCHESS COUNTY
Minden, MONTGOMERY COUNTY
Minisink Ford, SULLIVAN COUNTY
Mount Lebanon, COLUMBIA COUNTY
Mount Pleasant, WESTCHESTER COUNTY
Mount Vernon, WESTCHESTER COUNTY
Murray, ORLEANS COUNTY

Napanoch, ULSTER COUNTY
Naples, ONTARIO COUNTY
Napoli, CATTARAUGUS COUNTY
Nelliston vic., MONTGOMERY COUNTY
New Brighton, RICHMOND COUNTY
New Concord, COLUMBIA COUNTY
New Dorp, RICHMOND COUNTY
New Hyde Park, NASSAU COUNTY
New Paltz, ULSTER COUNTY
New Paltz vic., ULSTER COUNTY
New Rochelle, WESTCHESTER COUNTY
New Scotland Twp., ALBANY COUNTY
New Scotland vic., ALBANY COUNTY
New Windsor, ORANGE COUNTY
New York City, BRONX COUNTY
New York City, NEW YORK COUNTY
Newburgh, ORANGE COUNTY
Newtonville, ALBANY COUNTY
Niagara Falls, NIAGARA COUNTY
Niskayuna, SCHENECTADY COUNTY
North Blenheim, SCHOHARIE COUNTY
North Elba, ESSEX COUNTY
North Germantown, COLUMBIA COUNTY
North Hempstead, NASSAU COUNTY
North Salem, WESTCHESTER COUNTY
North Tarrytown, WESTCHESTER COUNTY
North Tonawanda, NIAGARA COUNTY
Nyack, ROCKLAND COUNTY

Oakdale, SUFFOLK COUNTY
Oaksville, OTSEGO COUNTY

Ogdensburg, ST. LAWRENCE COUNTY
Old Chatham, COLUMBIA COUNTY
Old Westbury, NASSAU COUNTY
Oneida vic., MADISON COUNTY
Onesquethaw, ALBANY COUNTY
Onondaga Hill, ONONDAGA COUNTY
Oran, ONONDAGA COUNTY
Orangeburg vic., ORLEANS COUNTY
Orangeburg vic., ROCKLAND COUNTY
Ossining, WESTCHESTER COUNTY
Ossining vic.,croto., WESTCHESTER COUNTY
Oswego, OSWEGO COUNTY
Otisville, ORANGE COUNTY
Ouaquaga, BROOME COUNTY
Owego, TIOGA COUNTY
Oyster Bay, NASSAU COUNTY

Painted Post, STEUBEN COUNTY
Palatine Bridge, MONTGOMERY COUNTY
Palatine Bridge vic., MONTGOMERY COUNTY
Palisades, ROCKLAND COUNTY
Patterson
Patterson, PUTNAM COUNTY
Pattersonville, MONTGOMERY COUNTY
Pearl River vic., ROCKLAND COUNTY
Perth, FULTON COUNTY
Petersburg, RENSSELAER COUNTY
Petersburg vic., RENSSELAER COUNTY
Philippsport, SULLIVAN COUNTY
Phoenicia vic., ULSTER COUNTY
Plainville vic., ONONDAGA COUNTY
Pleasant Valley, DUTCHESS COUNTY
Pleasantville, WESTCHESTER COUNTY
Pompey, ONONDAGA COUNTY
Port Jervis, ORANGE COUNTY
Port Jervis vic., ORANGE COUNTY
Port Ontario vic., OSWEGO COUNTY
Portageville vic., WYOMING COUNTY
Poughkeepsie, DUTCHESS COUNTY
Princetown, SCHENECTADY COUNTY

Quaker Hill, DUTCHESS COUNTY
Quaker Street Vil., SCHENECTADY COUNTY
Queens, QUEENS COUNTY

Red Hook, DUTCHESS COUNTY
Rensselaer, RENSSELAER COUNTY
Rensselaerville, ALBANY COUNTY
Rexford, SARATOGA COUNTY
Rhinebeck, DUTCHESS COUNTY
Rhinebeck vic., DUTCHESS COUNTY
Richmond, RICHMOND COUNTY
Richmondtown, RICHMOND COUNTY
Ridgewood, QUEENS COUNTY
Rifton, ULSTER COUNTY
Rochester, MONROE COUNTY
Rome, ONEIDA COUNTY
Rosebank, RICHMOND COUNTY
Roslyn, NASSAU COUNTY
Rotterdam, SCHENECTADY COUNTY
Rotterdam Jct., SCHENECTADY COUNTY
Rotterdam Twp., SCHENECTADY COUNTY
Russia, HERKIMER COUNTY
Rye, WESTCHESTER COUNTY

Sag Harbor, SUFFOLK COUNTY
Salamanca, CATTARAUGUS COUNTY
Salamanca vic., CATTARAUGUS COUNTY
Salem, WASHINGTON COUNTY
Salem Center, WESTCHESTER COUNTY
Salisbury Mills vic., ORANGE COUNTY
Saratoga, SARATOGA COUNTY
Saratoga vic., SARATOGA COUNTY
Scarsdale, WESTCHESTER COUNTY
Schaghticoke vic., RENSSELAER COUNTY
Schenectady, SCHENECTADY COUNTY
Schoharie, SCHOHARIE COUNTY
Schoharie vic., SCHOHARIE COUNTY
Scotia, SCHENECTADY COUNTY
Seaford, NASSAU COUNTY
Selden vic., SUFFOLK COUNTY
Seneca Falls, SENECA COUNTY
Setauket, SUFFOLK COUNTY
Shawangunk, ULSTER COUNTY
Shelter Island, SUFFOLK COUNTY
Sinclairville, CHAUTAUQUA COUNTY
Skaneateles, ONONDAGA COUNTY
Skaneateles vic., ONONDAGA COUNTY
Smithtown, SUFFOLK COUNTY
Somers, WESTCHESTER COUNTY
Somerset, NIAGARA COUNTY
Southampton, SUFFOLK COUNTY
Sparkill, ROCKLAND COUNTY
Speonk, SUFFOLK COUNTY
St. James vic., SUFFOLK COUNTY
St. Johnsville Vic, MONTGOMERY COUNTY
Staten Island, RICHMOND COUNTY
Stillwater, SARATOGA COUNTY
Stockport, COLUMBIA COUNTY
Stone Arabia, MONTGOMERY COUNTY
Stone Ridge, ULSTER COUNTY
Suspension Bridge, ERIE COUNTY
Syracuse, ONONDAGA COUNTY

Tahawus, ESSEX COUNTY
Tappan, ROCKLAND COUNTY
Tarrytown, WESTCHESTER COUNTY
Tarrytown vic., WESTCHESTER COUNTY
Tioronda, DUTCHESS COUNTY
Tivoli vic., DUTCHESS COUNTY
Tompkins Cove, ROCKLAND COUNTY
Tottenville, RICHMOND COUNTY
Troy, RENSSELAER COUNTY
Trumansburg, TOMPKINS COUNTY
Tuckahoe, WESTCHESTER COUNTY
Tyre, SENECA COUNTY

Unionville, ALBANY COUNTY
Upper Red Hook, DUTCHESS COUNTY
Utica, ONEIDA COUNTY

Valhalla vic., WESTCHESTER COUNTY
Vancortlandville, WESTCHESTER COUNTY
Vernon Center, ONEIDA COUNTY
Vestal, BROOME COUNTY
Vischers Ferry, SARATOGA COUNTY

Wainscott, SUFFOLK COUNTY
Wantagh, NASSAU COUNTY
Wappingers Falls, DUTCHESS COUNTY
Warrensburg, WARREN COUNTY
Warsaw, WYOMING COUNTY
Waterford, SARATOGA COUNTY
Waterloo, SENECA COUNTY
Watertown, JEFFERSON COUNTY
Watervielt, ALBANY COUNTY
Watervliet, ALBANY COUNTY
Wawarsing, ULSTER COUNTY
Wellsville, ALLEGANY COUNTY
West Coxsackie, GREENE COUNTY
West Hills, SUFFOLK COUNTY
West Point, ORANGE COUNTY
Westfield, CHAUTAUQUA COUNTY
Westhampton Beach, SUFFOLK COUNTY
Westville vic., OTSEGO COUNTY
White Plains, WESTCHESTER COUNTY
Whitehall, WASHINGTON COUNTY
Whitesboro, ONEIDA COUNTY
Whitney Point, BROOME COUNTY
Wingdale, DUTCHESS COUNTY

Yonkers, WESTCHESTER COUNTY
Yorktown Heights Vic, WESTCHESTER COUNTY
Youngstown, NIAGARA COUNTY

North Carolina

Airlie vic., HALIFAX COUNTY
Albemarle, MONTGOMERY COUNTY
Albemarle, STANLY COUNTY
Asheville, BUNCOMBE COUNTY
Asheville vic., BUNCOMBE COUNTY

Bath, BEAUFORT COUNTY
Beaufort, CARTERET COUNTY
Beaufort vic., CARTERET COUNTY
Bethabara, FORSYTH COUNTY
Bethania, FORSYTH COUNTY
Bethel vic., PERQUIMANS COUNTY
Brunswick Town, BRUNSWICK COUNTY
Buckland, GATES COUNTY
Burlington, ALAMANCE COUNTY
Burnsville vic., MITCHELL COUNTY
Buxton, DARE COUNTY

Caldwell vic., MECKLENBURG COUNTY
Camden, CAMDEN COUNTY
Camden vic., CAMDEN COUNTY
Cary, WAKE COUNTY
Cataloochee, HAYWOOD COUNTY
Chapel Hill, ORANGE COUNTY
Charlotte, MECKLENBURG COUNTY
Charlotte vic., MECKLENBURG COUNTY
Cherokee, SWAIN COUNTY
Cherokee vic., SWAIN COUNTY
Clemmons, FORSYTH COUNTY
Columbus, POLK COUNTY
Creswell vic., TYRRELL COUNTY
Creswell vic., WASHINGTON COUNTY

Danbury vic., STOKES COUNTY
Davidson, MECKLENBURG COUNTY
Dillsboro vic., JACKSON COUNTY
Dortches, NASH COUNTY
Duck vic., DARE COUNTY
Durham, DURHAM COUNTY
Durham vic., CHATHAM COUNTY
Durham vic., DURHAM COUNTY

Eden vic., ROCKINGHAM COUNTY
Edenton, CHOWAN COUNTY
Edenton vic., CHOWAN COUNTY
Elizabeth City, PASQUOTANK COUNTY
Elizabeth City vic., PASQUOTANK COUNTY
Elizabethtown, BLADEN COUNTY
Elizabethtown vic., BLADEN COUNTY
Enfield vic., HALIFAX COUNTY

Fairview vic., BUNCOMBE COUNTY
Faison vic., DUPLIN COUNTY
Falls, WAKE COUNTY
Fayetteville, CUMBERLAND COUNTY
Flat Rock, HENDERSON COUNTY
Fletcher, HENDERSON COUNTY
Fremont vic., WAYNE COUNTY

Gates vic., GATES COUNTY
Gatesville vic., GATES COUNTY
Glencoe, ALAMANCE COUNTY
Granite Quarry vic., ROWAN COUNTY
Greensboro, GUILFORD COUNTY

Halifax, HALIFAX COUNTY
Hamer vic., CASWELL COUNTY

Harrells vic., SAMPSON COUNTY
Henderson vic., VANCE COUNTY
Henderson vic., WARREN COUNTY
Hendersonville, HENDERSON COUNTY
Hertford vic., PERQUIMANS COUNTY
Hickory, CATAWBA COUNTY
Hillsborough, ORANGE COUNTY
Hillsborough vic., ORANGE COUNTY
Hobbsville vic., GATES COUNTY
Hurdle Mills vic., PERSON COUNTY

Iron Station vic., LINCOLN COUNTY

Jackson Vic, NORTHAMPTON COUNTY
Jacksonville, ONSLOW COUNTY
Jamestown, GUILFORD COUNTY
Jamestown vic., GUILFORD COUNTY

Kernersville, FORSYTH COUNTY

Laboratory vic., LINCOLN COUNTY
Lenoir vic., CALDWELL COUNTY
Lexington, DAVIDSON COUNTY
Lexington vic., DAVIDSON COUNTY
Lincolnton vic., LINCOLN COUNTY
Littleton, WARREN COUNTY
Locust Hill vic., CASWELL COUNTY
Longview vic., CATAWBA COUNTY
Louisburg, FRANKLIN COUNTY
Louisburg vic., FRANKLIN COUNTY
Lumber Bridge, ROBESON COUNTY

Maiden vic., LINCOLN COUNTY
Manteo vic., DARE COUNTY
Marion vic., BURKE COUNTY
Marion vic., MCDOWELL COUNTY
Marshall, MADISON COUNTY
Mc Adenville, GASTON COUNTY
Mill Bridge vic., ROWAN COUNTY
Milton, CASWELL COUNTY
Mintonsville vic., GATES COUNTY
Mocksville vic., DAVIE COUNTY
Moncure, CHATHAM COUNTY
Morgantown vic., BURKE COUNTY
Morven vic., ANSON COUNTY
Mount Airy, SURRY COUNTY
Mount Mourne, IREDELL COUNTY
Murfreesboro, HENDERSON COUNTY
Murfreesboro, HERTFORD COUNTY

Nebo vic., MCDOWELL COUNTY
New Bern, CRAVEN COUNTY
New Hope vic., PERQUIMANS COUNTY
Newfound Gap vic., SWAIN COUNTY
Nixonton, PASQUOTANK COUNTY

Oak Ridge, GUILFORD COUNTY
Old Town, FORSYTH COUNTY
Old Trap vic., BUNCOMBE COUNTY

Patterson, CALDWELL COUNTY
Patterson vic., CALDWELL COUNTY
Pearces, FRANKLIN COUNTY

Raleigh, WAKE COUNTY
Raleigh vic., WAKE COUNTY
Relief vic., YANCEY COUNTY
Richlands vic., ONSLOW COUNTY
Ridgecrest vic., BUNCOMBE COUNTY
Rockingham, RICHMOND COUNTY
Rockwell vic., ROWAN COUNTY
Rocky Mount, NASH COUNTY
Rocky Mount Mills, NASH COUNTY

Salisbury, ROWAN COUNTY
Sandy Cross, GATES COUNTY
Scotland Neck vic., HALIFAX COUNTY
Shawboro vic., CURRITUCK COUNTY
Smithfield, JOHNSTON COUNTY
Somerset vic., CHOWAN COUNTY
South Mills vic., CAMDEN COUNTY
Southmont vic., DAVIDSON COUNTY
Southport, BRUNSWICK COUNTY
Sparta vic., ALAMANCE COUNTY
Spencer, ROWAN COUNTY
Spindale, RUTHERFORD COUNTY
Statesville, IREDELL COUNTY
Stoney Point vic., CATAWBA COUNTY

Tarboro, EDGECOMBE COUNTY
Tarboro vic., EDGECOMBE COUNTY
Tillery vic., HALIFAX COUNTY
Topsail Sound, PENDER COUNTY
Trotville vic., GATES COUNTY
Tuxedo vic., HENDERSON COUNTY

Warrenton, WARREN COUNTY
Warrenton vic., WARREN COUNTY
Washington, BEAUFORT COUNTY
Waynesville, SWAIN COUNTY
Waynesville vic., SWAIN COUNTY
Wentworth, ROCKINGHAM COUNTY
Williamsboro, VANCE COUNTY
Wilmington, NEW HANOVER COUNTY
Winfall vic., PERQUIMANS COUNTY
Winston-Salem, FORSYTH COUNTY
Winston-Salem vic., FORSYTH COUNTY
Woodsdale, PERSON COUNTY

Yanceyville, CASWELL COUNTY
Yanceyville vic., CASWELL COUNTY

North Dakota

Bismarck, BURLEIGH COUNTY
Bismark, BURLEIGH COUNTY

Cooperstown vic., GRIGGS COUNTY

Devils Lake vic., BENSON COUNTY

Elbowoods, MCLEAN COUNTY
Elbowoods vic., MCLEAN COUNTY

Fairdale vic., WALSH COUNTY
Fort Buford, WILLIAMS COUNTY

Goodrich vic., SHERIDAN COUNTY
Grand Forks, GRAND FORKS COUNTY
Grassy Butte, MCKENZIE COUNTY

Hampden vic., RAMSEY COUNTY

Kramer vic., BOTTINEAU COUNTY

Langdon vic., CAVALIER COUNTY

Mandan, MORTON COUNTY
Mayville, TRAILL COUNTY
Mott, HETTINGER COUNTY

Nekoma vic., CAVALIER COUNTY

Souris River Basin, WARD COUNTY
Stanton vic., MERCER COUNTY

Wahpeton, RICHLAND COUNTY

Ohio

Adelphi vic., HOCKING COUNTY
Akron, SUMMIT COUNTY
Antwerp vic., PAULDING COUNTY
Ashland vic., ASHLAND COUNTY
Ashtabula, ASHTABULA COUNTY
Athens, ATHENS COUNTY
Atwater, PORTAGE COUNTY
Aurora, GEAUGA COUNTY
Aurora, PORTAGE COUNTY
Avon Township, LORAIN COUNTY
Avon vic., LORAIN COUNTY
Avon Village, LORAIN COUNTY

Bantam vic., CLERMONT COUNTY
Bath, SUMMIT COUNTY
Bellaire, BELMONT COUNTY
Bentleyville, CUYAHOGA COUNTY
Bladensburg vic., KNOX COUNTY
Blaine, BELMONT COUNTY
Blaine vic., BELMONT COUNTY
Boston Twp., SUMMIT COUNTY
Brecksville, CUYAHOGA COUNTY
Bristolville, TRUMBULL COUNTY
Burton, GEAUGA COUNTY

Cambridge, GUERNSEY COUNTY
Cambridge vic., GUERNSEY COUNTY
Camp Dennison, HAMILTON COUNTY
Canton, STARK COUNTY
Carroll vic., FAIRFIELD COUNTY
Chagrin Falls, CUYAHOGA COUNTY
Chagrin Falls vic., CUYAHOGA COUNTY
Chester, MEIGS COUNTY
Chillicothe, ROSS COUNTY
Chillicothe vic., ROSS COUNTY
Cincinnati, HAMILTON COUNTY
Cincinnati vic., HAMILTON COUNTY
Clairdon vic., GEAUGA COUNTY
Claridon, GEAUGA COUNTY
Claridon vic., GEAUGA COUNTY
Clarksville, CLINTON COUNTY
Cleveland, CUYAHOGA COUNTY
Cleveland Heights, CUYAHOGA COUNTY
Cleveland vic., CUYAHOGA COUNTY
Colebrook, ASHTABULA COUNTY
Collinsville vic., BUTLER COUNTY
Columbus, FRANKLIN COUNTY
Copley, SUMMIT COUNTY
Corwin vic., WARREN COUNTY
Covington, MIAMI COUNTY
Crestline, CRAWFORD COUNTY

Darrtown vic., BUTLER COUNTY
Dayton, MONTGOMERY COUNTY
Deerfield, PORTAGE COUNTY
Dover, CUYAHOGA COUNTY

Eaton vic., PREBLE COUNTY
Elizabethtown, HAMILTON COUNTY
Everett vic., SUMMIT COUNTY

Findlay, HANCOCK COUNTY
Findlay vic., HANCOCK COUNTY
Fort Recovery vic., MERCER COUNTY
Foster, WARREN COUNTY
Freedom, PORTAGE COUNTY
Fremont, SANDUSKY COUNTY

Gallipolis, GALLIA COUNTY

Gallipolis vic., GALLIA COUNTY
Gambier, KNOX COUNTY
Gates Mills, CUYAHOGA COUNTY
Georgetown, BROWN COUNTY
Georgetown vic., BROWN COUNTY
Granville, LICKING COUNTY
Greenhills, HAMILTON COUNTY

Hamilton vic., BUTLER COUNTY
Harmony, CLARK COUNTY
Harrison, HAMILTON COUNTY
Harrison vic., HAMILTON COUNTY
Harveysburg vic., WARREN COUNTY
Hopewell vic., MUSKINGUM COUNTY
Hudson, SUMMIT COUNTY
Huntington vic., LORAIN COUNTY

Ira (Village) vic., SUMMIT COUNTY
Isleta vic., COSHOCTON COUNTY

Jasper, PIKE COUNTY
Jefferson, ASHTABULA COUNTY

Kent, PORTAGE COUNTY
Kettering, MONTGOMERY COUNTY
Kinderhook vic., PICKAWAY COUNTY
Kinsman, TRUMBULL COUNTY
Kinsman vic., TRUMBULL COUNTY
Kirtland Village, LAKE COUNTY

Lafaytette, MADISON COUNTY
Lakewood, CUYAHOGA COUNTY
Lancaster, FAIRFIELD COUNTY
Lebanon, WARREN COUNTY
Lebanon vic., WARREN COUNTY
Lima, ALLEN COUNTY
Limaville, STARK COUNTY
Limestone vic., OTTAWA COUNTY
Lockington, SHELBY COUNTY
Lockland, HAMILTON COUNTY
Lykens vic., CRAWFORD COUNTY

Manchester, ADAMS COUNTY
Mansfield, RICHLAND COUNTY
Mariemont, HAMILTON COUNTY
Mariemont vic., HAMILTON COUNTY
Maumee, LUCAS COUNTY
Mc Cutchenville, WYANDOT COUNTY
Mcconnelsville vic., MORGAN COUNTY
Mentor, LAKE COUNTY
Miamitown, HAMILTON COUNTY
Middlebourne vic., GUERNSEY COUNTY
Midland, CLINTON COUNTY
Milan, ERIE COUNTY
Milan vic., ERIE COUNTY
Milford, CLERMONT COUNTY
Milford, HAMILTON COUNTY
Monroe vic., BUTLER COUNTY
Monroeville, HURON COUNTY
Montgomery vic., HAMILTON COUNTY
Morrow vic., WARREN COUNTY
Mount Gilead, MORROW COUNTY
Mount Healthy, HAMILTON COUNTY
Mt. Carmel vic., HAMILTON COUNTY
Mt. Vernon, KNOX COUNTY

N. Lewisburg vic., LOGAN COUNTY
New Lexington vic., PERRY COUNTY
New Vienna vic., CLINTON COUNTY
Newton Falls, TRUMBULL COUNTY
Newtown, HAMILTON COUNTY
North Bend vic., HAMILTON COUNTY
North Bloomfield, TRUMBULL COUNTY
North Bristol, TRUMBULL COUNTY
North Lewisburg vic., UNION COUNTY
North Olmsted, CUYAHOGA COUNTY

Northfield Center Vi, SUMMIT COUNTY
Northfield vic., SUMMIT COUNTY
Norwalk, HURON COUNTY
Norwood, HAMILTON COUNTY

Oberlin, LORAIN COUNTY
Oxford, BUTLER COUNTY

Painesville, LAKE COUNTY
Parma, CUYAHOGA COUNTY
Parma Heights, CUYAHOGA COUNTY
Peninsula, SUMMIT COUNTY
Peninsula vic., SUMMIT COUNTY
Piketon vic., PIKE COUNTY
Piqua, MIAMI COUNTY
Pleasant Hill, MIAMI COUNTY
Poland, MAHONING COUNTY
Pomeroy, MEIGS COUNTY
Portsmouth, SCIOTO COUNTY
Put-In-Bay, OTTAWA COUNTY

Ravenna, PORTAGE COUNTY
Ripley, BROWN COUNTY
Rocky River, CUYAHOGA COUNTY
Rootstown, PORTAGE COUNTY
Roseville, MUSKINGUM COUNTY
Ross vic., HAMILTON COUNTY

Sagamore Hills, SUMMIT COUNTY
Selville, MEDINA COUNTY
Seville, MEDINA COUNTY
Sinking Spring, HIGHLAND COUNTY
Solon vic., CUYAHOGA COUNTY
Somerset, PERRY COUNTY
Springfield, CLARK COUNTY
St. Clairsville, BELMONT COUNTY
St. Clairsville vic., BELMONT COUNTY
Stockport, MORGAN COUNTY
Stoutsville vic., FAIRFIELD COUNTY
Streetsboro, PORTAGE COUNTY
Strongsville, CUYAHOGA COUNTY

Tallmadge, SUMMIT COUNTY
Tiffin, SENECA COUNTY
Tiffin vic., SENECA COUNTY
Toledo, LUCAS COUNTY
Twinsburg, SUMMIT COUNTY
Twinsburg vic., SUMMIT COUNTY

Union Village, WARREN COUNTY
Unionville, LAKE COUNTY
Unionville vic., ASHTABULA COUNTY

Valley View, CUYAHOGA COUNTY
Valley View, SUMMIT COUNTY
Valley View vic., CUYAHOGA COUNTY
Van Wert vic., VAN WERT COUNTY
Vermilion vic., ERIE COUNTY

Warren, TRUMBULL COUNTY
Waterville, LUCAS COUNTY
Waynesville, WARREN COUNTY
Wellington, LORAIN COUNTY
West Chester, BUTLER COUNTY
Weymouth, MEDINA COUNTY
Whitesburg, CUYAHOGA COUNTY
Whitewater, HAMILTON COUNTY
Wilberforce, GREENE COUNTY
Willoughby, LAKE COUNTY
Wooster, WAYNE COUNTY
Worthington, FRANKLIN COUNTY
Wyoming, HAMILTON COUNTY

Yellow Springs, GREENE COUNTY
Youngstown, MAHONING COUNTY

Zanesville, MUSKINGUM COUNTY
Zanesville vic., BELMONT COUNTY
Zanesville vic., MUSKINGUM COUNTY
Zoar, TUSCARAWAS COUNTY

Oklahoma

Avant, OSAGE COUNTY

Flint vic., DELAWARE COUNTY
Fort Gibson, MUSKOGEE COUNTY
Fort Sill, COMANCHE COUNTY

Guthrie, LOGAN COUNTY

Marble City, SEQUOYAH COUNTY
Mcalester, PITTSBURG COUNTY
Muskogee, MUSKOGEE COUNTY

North Of Hominy, OSAGE COUNTY

Okemah vic., OKFUSKEE COUNTY
Oklahoma City, OKLAHOMA COUNTY

Park Hill vic., CHEROKEE COUNTY
Perry, NOBLE COUNTY

Roll vic., ROGER MILLS COUNTY
Rose vic., DELAWARE COUNTY

Salisaw, SEQUOYAH COUNTY
Stillwater, PAWNEE COUNTY
Stillwater, PAYNE COUNTY
Stillwell, ADAIR COUNTY

Tahlequah, CHEROKEE COUNTY
Tulsa, TULSA COUNTY

Oregon

Agness, CURRY COUNTY
Albany, LINN COUNTY
Ashland vic., JACKSON COUNTY
Astoria, CLATSOP COUNTY
Aurora, MARION COUNTY

Bonneville, MULTNOMAH COUNTY

Canby, CLACKAMAS COUNTY
Cave Junction, JOSEPHINE COUNTY
Cave Junction vic., JOSEPHINE COUNTY
Cavejunction vic., JOSEPHINE COUNTY
Central Point, JACKSON COUNTY
Chapman vic., COLUMBIA COUNTY
Coquille, COOS COUNTY
Corvallis vic., BENTON COUNTY
Crater Lake, KLAMATH COUNTY

Dallas, POLK COUNTY
Dayton, YAMHILL COUNTY
Dayville vic., GRANT COUNTY
Dayville vic., WHEELER COUNTY
Depoe Bay, LINCOLN COUNTY
Dundee, YAMHILL COUNTY

Ellendale, POLK COUNTY
Eugene, LANE COUNTY

Florence, LANE COUNTY
Florence vic., LANE COUNTY
Forest Grove, WASHINGTON COUNTY

Gervais vic., MARION COUNTY
Gold Beach, CURRY COUNTY
Gold Hill, JACKSON COUNTY
Gold Hill vic., JACKSON COUNTY
Grants Pass, JOSEPHINE COUNTY

Hebo vic., TILLAMOOK COUNTY
Heppner vic., MORROW COUNTY
Hermiston, UMATILLA COUNTY
Hopewell vic., YAMHILL COUNTY
Hoskins, BENTON COUNTY
Howell Prairie, MARION COUNTY

Jacksonville, JACKSON COUNTY
Jacksonville vic., JACKSON COUNTY
Jefferson, MARION COUNTY
Jefferson vic., LINN COUNTY

La Pine vic., DESCHUTES COUNTY
Lafayette, YAMHILL COUNTY
Lafayette vic., YAMHILL COUNTY
Latourell, MULTNOMAH COUNTY
Latourell vic., MULTNOMAH COUNTY
Lorane vic., LANE COUNTY

Mckenzie vic., LANE COUNTY
Milwaukie, CLACKAMAS COUNTY
Molalla vic., CLACKAMAS COUNTY
Mollala vic., CLACKAMAS COUNTY
Mt. Pleasant, CLACKAMAS COUNTY

Newport, LINCOLN COUNTY
North Bend, COOS COUNTY
Nyssa vic., MALHEUR COUNTY

Oakland, DOUGLAS COUNTY
Oregon City, CLACKAMAS COUNTY

Parkersville, MARION COUNTY
Pedee, POLK COUNTY
Perrydale, POLK COUNTY
Phoenix, JACKSON COUNTY
Pleasant Hill vic., LANE COUNTY
Portland, MULTNOMAH COUNTY
Prineville vic., CROOK COUNTY
Prospect vic., JACKSON COUNTY

Reedsport, DOUGLAS COUNTY
Reedville, WASHINGTON COUNTY
Rickreall, POLK COUNTY
Rogue River vic., JACKSON COUNTY
Rowena vic., WASCO COUNTY

Salem, MARION COUNTY
Sauvie's Island, MULTNOMAH COUNTY
Scio vic., LINN COUNTY
Silverton, MARION COUNTY
Springfield, LANE COUNTY

Terrebonne, DESCHUTES COUNTY
Terrebonne vic., JEFFERSON COUNTY
The Dalles, WASCO COUNTY
Tillamook, TILLAMOOK COUNTY

Union, UNION COUNTY

Waldport, LINCOLN COUNTY
Waldport vic., LINCOLN COUNTY
Wallowa, WALLOWA COUNTY
Walton vic., LANE COUNTY
Warrendale, MULTNOMAH COUNTY
West Linn, CLACKAMAS COUNTY
West Union, WASHINGTON COUNTY
Wilsonville vic., CLACKAMAS COUNTY
Winchester, DOUGLAS COUNTY
Wolf Creek, JOSEPHINE COUNTY

Yamhill, YAMHILL COUNTY
Yamhill vic., YAMHILL COUNTY
Yoncalla vic., DOUGLAS COUNTY

Pennsylvania

Addison, SOMERSET COUNTY
Alburtis vic., LEHIGH COUNTY
Alexandria, HUNTINGDON COUNTY
Allentown, LEHIGH COUNTY
Allentown vic., LEHIGH COUNTY
Allenwood, UNION COUNTY
Allison, FAYETTE COUNTY
Altoona
Altoona, BLAIR COUNTY
Alverton, WESTMORELAND COUNTY
Ambler vic., MONTGOMERY COUNTY
Ambridge Bor., BEAVER COUNTY
Andalusia, BUCKS COUNTY
Anselma vic., CHESTER COUNTY
Aquetong vic., BUCKS COUNTY
Armagh vic., INDIANA COUNTY
Ashley, LUZERNE COUNTY
Aspinwall vic., ALLEGHENY COUNTY
Aspiwall vic., ALLEGHENY COUNTY
Athens Township, BRADFORD COUNTY
Avondale Bor., CHESTER COUNTY

Bacton, CHESTER COUNTY
Bacton vic., CHESTER COUNTY
Bala Cynwyd, MONTGOMERY COUNTY
Bala-Cynwyd, MONTGOMERY COUNTY
Barren Hill, MONTGOMERY COUNTY
Baumstown vic., BERKS COUNTY
Beaver Springs vic., SNYDER COUNTY
Beaverdale vic., CAMBRIA COUNTY
Belfast vic., NORTHAMPTON COUNTY
Bellefonte, CENTRE COUNTY
Ben Avon Bor., ALLEGHENY COUNTY
Bensalem, BUCKS COUNTY
Bentleyville, WASHINGTON COUNTY
Bermudian vic., ADAMS COUNTY
Bernville, BERKS COUNTY
Bernville vic., BERKS COUNTY
Berwyn vic., CHESTER COUNTY
Bethany, WAYNE COUNTY
Bethelehem, NORTHAMPTON COUNTY
Bethlehem, LEHIGH COUNTY
Bethlehem, NORTHAMPTON COUNTY
Betula, MCKEAN COUNTY
Bird-In-Hand vic., LANCASTER COUNTY
Birdsboro, BERKS COUNTY
Birmingham, CHESTER COUNTY
Birmingham vic., CHESTER COUNTY
Blair
Blairsville vic., INDIANA COUNTY
Blandburg, CAMBRIA COUNTY
Bloomsburg, COLUMBIA COUNTY
Blue Bell vic., MONTGOMERY COUNTY
Boalsburg, CENTRE COUNTY
Bolivar, WESTMORELAND COUNTY
Brenizer vic., WESTMORELAND COUNTY
Briar Creek, COLUMBIA COUNTY
Brickerville, LANCASTER COUNTY
Bristol Bor., BUCKS COUNTY
Brock, GREENE COUNTY
Brockway, JEFFERSON COUNTY
Brockway vic., JEFFERSON COUNTY
Broomall vic., DELAWARE COUNTY
Brownsville, FAYETTE COUNTY
Brownsville Bor., FAYETTE COUNTY
Brownsville vic., BERKS COUNTY
Brownsville vic., WASHINGTON COUNTY
Bryn Mawr, MONTGOMERY COUNTY
Buckingham, BUCKS COUNTY
Bulltown, CHESTER COUNTY
Bushkill, PIKE COUNTY
Bushkill vic., MONROE COUNTY
Butler, SCHUYLKILL COUNTY

Cambridge Spr. vic., CRAWFORD COUNTY
Cambridge Springs, CRAWFORD COUNTY
Canonsburg, WASHINGTON COUNTY
Carbondale, LACKAWANNA COUNTY
Carroll Township, WASHINGTON COUNTY
Carversville, BUCKS COUNTY
Catasauqua, LEHIGH COUNTY
Catawissa, COLUMBIA COUNTY
Catawissa vic., COLUMBIA COUNTY
Center Square vic., MONTGOMERY COUNTY
Center Valley, LEHIGH COUNTY
Centerport vic., BERKS COUNTY
Centre Hall vic., CENTRE COUNTY
Chadds Ford, DELAWARE COUNTY
Chadds Ford vic., CHESTER COUNTY
Chalkhill vic., FAYETTE COUNTY
Chambersburg, FRANKLIN COUNTY
Chambersburg Bor., FRANKLIN COUNTY
Charleroi, WASHINGTON COUNTY
Charlestown, CHESTER COUNTY
Charlestown vic., CHESTER COUNTY
Chatham, CHESTER COUNTY
Chatham vic., CHESTER COUNTY
Cherry Tree, VENANGO COUNTY
Chester Springs, CHESTER COUNTY
Chester Springs vic., CHESTER COUNTY
Christiana Borough, LANCASTER COUNTY
Chrome, CHESTER COUNTY
Churchill Bor., ALLEGHENY COUNTY
Churchtown vic., LANCASTER COUNTY
Clairton, ALLEGHENY COUNTY
Clarks Green, LACKAWANNA COUNTY
Claysburg, BLAIR COUNTY
Clonmell vic., CHESTER COUNTY
Coatesville, CHESTER COUNTY
Coatesville vic., CHESTER COUNTY
Cocalico, LANCASTER COUNTY
Cochranton, CRAWFORD COUNTY
Colver, CAMBRIA COUNTY
Colver vic., CAMBRIA COUNTY
Concordville, DELAWARE COUNTY
Conneautville, CRAWFORD COUNTY
Connellsville, FAYETTE COUNTY
Conshohocken vic., MONTGOMERY COUNTY
Copesville, CHESTER COUNTY
Copesville vic., CHESTER COUNTY
Coplay, LEHIGH COUNTY
Corry, ERIE COUNTY
Corry vic., ERIE COUNTY
Coudersport, POTTER COUNTY
Coventryville, CHESTER COUNTY
Cresson vic., BLAIR COUNTY
Cresson vic., CAMBRIA COUNTY
Crosby vic., MCKEAN COUNTY
Curley Hill vic., BUCKS COUNTY
Curtin, CENTRE COUNTY

Darby, DELAWARE COUNTY
Darby vic., DELAWARE COUNTY
Dauberville, BERKS COUNTY
Davidsburg vic., YORK COUNTY
Delaware Water Gap, MONROE COUNTY
Detters Mill, YORK COUNTY
Devault vic., CHESTER COUNTY
Dilworthtown vic., DELAWARE COUNTY
Dingman's Ferry, PIKE COUNTY
Dingmans Ferry, PIKE COUNTY

Douglasville, BERKS COUNTY
Dover, YORK COUNTY
Dowingtown Bor., CHESTER COUNTY
Downingtown Bor., CHESTER COUNTY
Downingtown vic., CHESTER COUNTY
Doylestown, BUCKS COUNTY
Doylestown vic., BUCKS COUNTY
Dravosburg vic., ALLEGHENY COUNTY
Drumore vic., LANCASTER COUNTY
Dunbar Township, FAYETTE COUNTY
Duquesne, ALLEGHENY COUNTY

East Berlin vic., ADAMS COUNTY
East Greenville vic., MONTGOMERY COUNTY
East Texas vic., LEHIGH COUNTY
East Titusville vic., CRAWFORD COUNTY
Easton, NORTHAMPTON COUNTY
Edinboro, ERIE COUNTY
Egypt Mills vic., PIKE COUNTY
Eldred, MCKEAN COUNTY
Emlenton, VENANGO COUNTY
Emmaus, LEHIGH COUNTY
Emmaus vic., LEHIGH COUNTY
Ephrata, LANCASTER COUNTY
Erie, ERIE COUNTY
Erie vic., ERIE COUNTY
Ernest, INDIANA COUNTY
Essington, DELAWARE COUNTY
Evergreen Hamlet, ALLEGHENY COUNTY
Exeter, LUZERNE COUNTY
Exeter Twp., BERKS COUNTY

Fairchance, FAYETTE COUNTY
Fairfield Bor., ADAMS COUNTY
Fallsington, BUCKS COUNTY
Farmerville vic., LANCASTER COUNTY
Fayette City vic., FAYETTE COUNTY
Fellsburg, WESTMORELAND COUNTY
Finleyville vic., WASHINGTON COUNTY
Floradale vic., ADAMS COUNTY
Fogelsville vic., LEHIGH COUNTY
Fort Hunter, DAUPHIN COUNTY
Forty Fort Bor., LUZERNE COUNTY
Franconia, MONTGOMERY COUNTY
Frankford, PHILADELPHIA COUNTY
Franklin, VENANGO COUNTY
Franklinville vic., HUNTINGDON COUNTY
Freemansburg, NORTHAMPTON COUNTY
Friedensburg vic., BERKS COUNTY

Gabelsville, BERKS COUNTY
Ganoga Lake, SULLIVAN COUNTY
Gap vic., LANCASTER COUNTY
Garland, WARREN COUNTY
Geistown vic., CAMBRIA COUNTY
Germantown, PHILADELPHIA COUNTY
Gettysburg, ADAMS COUNTY
Gettysburg Bor., ADAMS COUNTY
Gettysburg vic., ADAMS COUNTY
Girard, ERIE COUNTY
Girard vic., ERIE COUNTY
Glendon, NORTHAMPTON COUNTY
Glenloch, CHESTER COUNTY
Glenmoore, CHESTER COUNTY
Goodville vic., INDIANA COUNTY
Green Lawn vic., CHESTER COUNTY
Greensburg, WESTMORELAND COUNTY
Greenville, MERCER COUNTY
Grubbs Mill, CHESTER COUNTY

Hallam Borough, YORK COUNTY
Hamorton vic., CHESTER COUNTY
Hanover Green, LUZERNE COUNTY
Harborcreek, ERIE COUNTY
Harmony vic., BUTLER COUNTY
Harrisburg, DAUPHIN COUNTY
Harrison, ALLEGHENY COUNTY
Haverford, MONTGOMERY COUNTY
Havertown vic., DELAWARE COUNTY
Hawley, WAYNE COUNTY
Hay Creek, BERKS COUNTY
Heidlersburg vic., ADAMS COUNTY
Hellertown, NORTHAMPTON COUNTY
Hellertown vic., NORTHAMPTON COUNTY
Highspire vic., DAUPHIN COUNTY
Hinkletown, LANCASTER COUNTY
Hinkletown vic., LANCASTER COUNTY
Holicong, BUCKS COUNTY
Honesdale, WAYNE COUNTY
Honey Brook vic., CHESTER COUNTY
Honey Brook vic.., CHESTER COUNTY
Hopewell, CHESTER COUNTY
Hopewell Village, BERKS COUNTY
Hopewell Village, CHESTER COUNTY
Hopwood, FAYETTE COUNTY
Horsham vic., MONTGOMERY COUNTY
Hunterstown vic., ADAMS COUNTY
Huntingdon, HUNTINGDON COUNTY
Huntingdon vic., HUNTINGDON COUNTY
Hydetown, CRAWFORD COUNTY

Indiana, INDIANA COUNTY
Iron Springs vic., ADAMS COUNTY
Ironville vic., LANCASTER COUNTY
Irvine, WARREN COUNTY
Irwin, WESTMORELAND COUNTY
Ithan, DELAWARE COUNTY

Jacksonwald, BERKS COUNTY
Jeannette, WESTMORELAND COUNTY
Jenkintown, MONTGOMERY COUNTY
Jim Thorpe, CARBON COUNTY
Johnstown
Johnstown, CAMBRIA COUNTY
Johnsville, BUCKS COUNTY
Jonhstown, CAMBRIA COUNTY

Kaolin, CHESTER COUNTY
Kaolin vic., CHESTER COUNTY
Kennett Sq. vic., CHESTER COUNTY
Kennett Square, CHESTER COUNTY
Kimberton, CHESTER COUNTY
King Of Prussia, MONTGOMERY COUNTY
King Of Prussia vic., MONTGOMERY COUNTY
King's Run Road, MCKEAN COUNTY
Kingston, LUZERNE COUNTY
Kintnersville vic., BUCKS COUNTY
Kistler, MIFFLIN COUNTY
Kleinfeltersville, LEBANON COUNTY
Knauertown, CHESTER COUNTY
Knauertown vic., CHESTER COUNTY
Kutztown vic., BERKS COUNTY

Lackawaxen, PIKE COUNTY
Lancaster, LANCASTER COUNTY
Lancaster vic., LANCASTER COUNTY
Landenberg vic., CHESTER COUNTY
Landisville, LANCASTER COUNTY
Lanesboro, SUSQUEHANNA COUNTY
Lanesboro vic., SUSQUEHANNA COUNTY
Latrobe, WESTMORELAND COUNTY
Latrobe vic., WESTMORELAND COUNTY
Laughlintown vic., WESTMORELAND COUNTY
Laurel vic., YORK COUNTY
Laury's Station vic., NORTHAMPTON COUNTY
Lehighton, CARBON COUNTY
Leisenring, FAYETTE COUNTY
Leithsville vic., NORTHAMPTON COUNTY
Lenape vic., CHESTER COUNTY
Lenhartsville, BERKS COUNTY
Lewisburg, UNION COUNTY
Limekiln vic., BERKS COUNTY
Limeport vic., LEHIGH COUNTY
Lingelestown vic., DAUPHIN COUNTY
Lititz, LANCASTER COUNTY
Lititz vic., LANCASTER COUNTY
Littlestown vic., ADAMS COUNTY
Lobachsville vic., BERKS COUNTY
Lock Haven, CLINTON COUNTY
Lower Burrell, WESTMORELAND COUNTY
Lower Providence Twp, MONTGOMERY COUNTY
Lower Towamensing, CARBON COUNTY
Lucerne, INDIANA COUNTY
Lucerne vic., INDIANA COUNTY
Ludwigs Cor. vic., CHESTER COUNTY
Lynnville vic., LEHIGH COUNTY
Lyon Valley, LEHIGH COUNTY

Macungie, LEHIGH COUNTY
Macungie vic., LEHIGH COUNTY
Maiden Creek vic., BERKS COUNTY
Mammoth, WESTMORELAND COUNTY
Manheim vic., LANCASTER COUNTY
Maple Grove vic., LANCASTER COUNTY
Marietta vic., LANCASTER COUNTY
Marsh, CHESTER COUNTY
Marshallton, CHESTER COUNTY
Marshallton vic., CHESTER COUNTY
Martins's Corner, CHESTER COUNTY
Masontown vic., FAYETTE COUNTY
Mc Keesport, ALLEGHENY COUNTY
Mcalevy's Fort vic.
Mcalevy's Fort vic., HUNTINGDON COUNTY
Mcalevys Fort vic., HUNTINGDON COUNTY
Mckees Rocks, ALLEGHENY COUNTY
Meadow Lands vic., WASHINGTON COUNTY
Meadville, CRAWFORD COUNTY
Meadville vic., CRAWFORD COUNTY
Mechanicsville vic., LANCASTER COUNTY
Media vic., DELAWARE COUNTY
Mercer, MERCER COUNTY
Mercer vic., MERCER COUNTY
Merion, MONTGOMERY COUNTY
Middletown, DAUPHIN COUNTY
Milford, PIKE COUNTY
Milford vic., PIKE COUNTY
Millbach, LEBANON COUNTY
Millrift, PIKE COUNTY
Milltown, CHESTER COUNTY
Millville, COLUMBIA COUNTY
Monessen, WESTMORELAND COUNTY
Monoca, BEAVER COUNTY
Monogahela, WASHINGTON COUNTY
Montrose, SUSQUEHANNA COUNTY
Moorheadville, ERIE COUNTY
Morrisville, BUCKS COUNTY
Moselem Springs vic., BERKS COUNTY
Mount Rocky, CHESTER COUNTY
Mount Union, HUNTINGDON COUNTY
Mt. Jewett vic., MCKEAN COUNTY
Mt. Pleasant vic., BERKS COUNTY
Mt. Rocky, CHESTER COUNTY
Muncy vic., LYCOMING COUNTY

Nanticoke, LUZERNE COUNTY
Nanticoke vic., LUZERNE COUNTY
Narberth vic., MONTGOMERY COUNTY
Nazareth
Nazareth, NORTHAMPTON COUNTY
Neshaminy vic., BUCKS COUNTY
New Alexandria, WESTMORELAND COUNTY
New Alexandria vic., WESTMORELAND COUNTY
New Berlinville, BERKS COUNTY
New Britain vic., BUCKS COUNTY
New Cumberland, YORK COUNTY
New Florence, WESTMORELAND COUNTY

New Geneva vic., FAYETTE COUNTY
New Kensington, WESTMORELAND COUNTY
New Kensington vic., WESTMORELAND COUNTY
New Richmond vic., CRAWFORD COUNTY
New Smithfield, LEHIGH COUNTY
Newmanstown vic., LEBANON COUNTY
Newton vic., BUCKS COUNTY
Newtown, BUCKS COUNTY
Newtown vic., BUCKS COUNTY
Newville vic., CUMBERLAND COUNTY
Niantic vic., MONTGOMERY COUNTY
Nicholson, WYOMING COUNTY
Nittany, CENTRE COUNTY
Norristown, MONTGOMERY COUNTY
North Catasauqua, NORTHAMPTON COUNTY
North East, ERIE COUNTY
North Mehoopany, WYOMING COUNTY
North Springfield, ERIE COUNTY
Northampton, NORTHAMPTON COUNTY
Northbrook vic., CHESTER COUNTY
Norvelt, WESTMORELAND COUNTY
Norwood, DELAWARE COUNTY

Ohiopyle vic., FAYETTE COUNTY
Oil City, VENANGO COUNTY
Oley, BERKS COUNTY
Oley vic., BERKS COUNTY
Orbisonia vic., HUNTINGDON COUNTY
Ottsville vic., BUCKS COUNTY

Packerton, CARBON COUNTY
Palmerton, CARBON COUNTY
Paoli vic., CHESTER COUNTY
Parkesburg Bor., CHESTER COUNTY
Parkesburg vic., CHESTER COUNTY
Parryville, CARBON COUNTY
Paxtang, DAUPHIN COUNTY
Paxtang vic., DAUPHIN COUNTY
Penn-Craft, FAYETTE COUNTY
Penna. Furnace, HUNTINGDON COUNTY
Perkasie, BUCKS COUNTY
Peter's Corner vic., BUCKS COUNTY
Philadelphia
Philadelphia, PHILADELPHIA COUNTY
Philadephia, PHILADELPHIA COUNTY
Philipsburg, CENTRE COUNTY
Phoenixville vic., CHESTER COUNTY
Pikeville, BERKS COUNTY
Pinetown, LANCASTER COUNTY
Pipersville, BUCKS COUNTY
Pipersville vic., BUCKS COUNTY
Pittsburgh, ALLEGHENY COUNTY
Pittsburgh vic., ALLEGHENY COUNTY
Pittsfield, WARREN COUNTY
Pittsfield, YORK COUNTY
Pleasant Valley vic., BUCKS COUNTY
Pleasantville, VENANGO COUNTY
Pleasantville vic., BERKS COUNTY
Plymouth, LUZERNE COUNTY
Point Pleasant, BUCKS COUNTY
Point Pleasant vic., BUCKS COUNTY
Port Allegany vic., MCKEAN COUNTY
Port Kennedy, MONTGOMERY COUNTY
Portland vic., NORTHAMPTON COUNTY
Pottstown vic., MONTGOMERY COUNTY
Pottsville, SCHUYLKILL COUNTY
Pricetown, BERKS COUNTY
Pughtown vic., CHESTER COUNTY

Quakertown, BUCKS COUNTY

Radnor, DELAWARE COUNTY
Reading, BERKS COUNTY
Reading vic., BERKS COUNTY
Revloc vic., CAMBRIA COUNTY
Riceville, CRAWFORD COUNTY
Riegelsville, BUCKS COUNTY
Robertsdale, HUNTINGDON COUNTY
Robesonia, BERKS COUNTY
Robinson, INDIANA COUNTY
Rock Forge, CENTRE COUNTY
Rockwood vic., SOMERSET COUNTY
Rocky Hill vic., CHESTER COUNTY
Romansville, CHESTER COUNTY
Roulette, POTTER COUNTY
Ruff Creek vic., GREENE COUNTY
Rushland, BUCKS COUNTY

Saegertown, CRAWFORD COUNTY
Sailna, WESTMORELAND COUNTY
Salina, WESTMORELAND COUNTY
Saltsburg, INDIANA COUNTY
Sayre, BRADFORD COUNTY
Scalp Level, CAMBRIA COUNTY
Schaefferstown, LEBANON COUNTY
Schnecksville, LEHIGH COUNTY
Sconnelltown, CHESTER COUNTY
Sconnelltown vic., CHESTER COUNTY
Scottdale, LANCASTER COUNTY
Scottdale, WESTMORELAND COUNTY
Scranton, LACKAWANNA COUNTY
Selinsgrove, SNYDER COUNTY
Sewickley, ALLEGHENY COUNTY
Sewickley Hts. Bor., ALLEGHENY COUNTY
Sharpsburg vic., ALLEGHENY COUNTY
Shawnee-On-Del. vic., MONROE COUNTY
Sheakleyville, MERCER COUNTY
Sheridan, LEBANON COUNTY
Shimerville vic., LEHIGH COUNTY
Shippingport, BEAVER COUNTY
Shoaf, FAYETTE COUNTY
Shohola, PIKE COUNTY
Shohola vic., PIKE COUNTY
Skuylkill Haven Bor., SCHUYLKILL COUNTY
Slatington, LEHIGH COUNTY
Slickville, WESTMORELAND COUNTY
Smethport, MCKEAN COUNTY
Smithton, WESTMORELAND COUNTY
Solebury vic., BUCKS COUNTY
South Fork, CAMBRIA COUNTY
South Union Twp., FAYETTE COUNTY
Spangsville vic., BERKS COUNTY
Springtown vic., BUCKS COUNTY
Sproul, BLAIR COUNTY
Sproul vic., BLAIR COUNTY
St. Davids, DELAWARE COUNTY
St. Matthews Cor., CHESTER COUNTY
St. Peters vic., CHESTER COUNTY
Standard, WESTMORELAND COUNTY
Standard Shaft, WESTMORELAND COUNTY
Sterrettania, ERIE COUNTY
Stonersville, BERKS COUNTY
Stonersville vic., BERKS COUNTY
Stoopville vic., BUCKS COUNTY
Strafford, CHESTER COUNTY
Strasburg vic., LANCASTER COUNTY
Summit, ERIE COUNTY
Susquehanna, SUSQUEHANNA COUNTY
Swarthmore, DELAWARE COUNTY
Swartzville vic., LANCASTER COUNTY
Swissvale Bor., ALLEGHENY COUNTY

Tanguy vic., CHESTER COUNTY
Terrytown, BRADFORD COUNTY
Thorndale, CHESTER COUNTY
Tidioute, WARREN COUNTY
Titusville, CRAWFORD COUNTY
Tobyhanna, MONROE COUNTY
Towerville, CHESTER COUNTY
Townville, CRAWFORD COUNTY
Trappe, MONTGOMERY COUNTY
Trauger, WESTMORELAND COUNTY
Trauger vic., WESTMORELAND COUNTY
Treichlers, NORTHAMPTON COUNTY
Tunnelton vic., INDIANA COUNTY
Tyrone vic., BLAIR COUNTY

Union City, ERIE COUNTY
Uniontown vic., FAYETTE COUNTY
Upland, DELAWARE COUNTY
Upper Makefield, BUCKS COUNTY

Valley Forge, MONTGOMERY COUNTY
Valley Forge vic., MONTGOMERY COUNTY
Vandergrift, WESTMORELAND COUNTY
Villanova, DELAWARE COUNTY
Vintondale Vic, CAMBRIA COUNTY

Wallingford, DELAWARE COUNTY
Walnutport, NORTHAMPTON COUNTY
Wanamakers, LEHIGH COUNTY
Wapwallopen, LUZERNE COUNTY
Warren, WARREN COUNTY
Washington, WASHINGTON COUNTY
Washington Cros. Vic, BUCKS COUNTY
Washingtonville vic., MONTOUR COUNTY
Waterford, ERIE COUNTY
Wattsburg, ERIE COUNTY
Waverly, LACKAWANNA COUNTY
Wawaset, CHESTER COUNTY
Wayne, DELAWARE COUNTY
Weissport, CARBON COUNTY
Weissport vic., CARBON COUNTY
West Brownsville Vic, WASHINGTON COUNTY
West Chester Bor., CHESTER COUNTY
West Chester vic., CHESTER COUNTY
West Eldred vic., MCKEAN COUNTY
West Grove vic., CHESTER COUNTY
West Newton Borough, WESTMORELAND COUNTY
West Newton vic., WESTMORELAND COUNTY
West Overton, WESTMORELAND COUNTY
Westboro vic., BUCKS COUNTY
Westmoreland, WESTMORELAND COUNTY
Westtown vic., CHESTER COUNTY
Whitehall, LEHIGH COUNTY
Whitehorse vic., CHESTER COUNTY
Whitemarsh, MONTGOMERY COUNTY
Whites Valley, WAYNE COUNTY
Wilkes Barre, LUZERNE COUNTY
Wilkes-Barre, LUZERNE COUNTY
Williamsburg, BLAIR COUNTY
Williamsport, LYCOMING COUNTY
Willistown vic., CHESTER COUNTY
Willow Street vic., LANCASTER COUNTY
Willowdale, CHESTER COUNTY
Wilmore vic., CAMBRIA COUNTY
Wind Gap vic., NORTHAMPTON COUNTY
Womelsdorf vic., BERKS COUNTY
Woodcock, CRAWFORD COUNTY
Woodvale, HUNTINGDON COUNTY
Wrightstown, BUCKS COUNTY
Wyebrooke vic., CHESTER COUNTY
Wyoming, LUZERNE COUNTY
Wysox, BRADFORD COUNTY

Yellow House, BERKS COUNTY
Yellow House vic., BERKS COUNTY
York, YORK COUNTY
York vic., YORK COUNTY
Yukon, WESTMORELAND COUNTY

Zora, ADAMS COUNTY

Puerto Rico

Arecibo vic., ARECIBO

Boca, GUAYANILLA
Borinquen, AGUADILLA

Cabezas, FAJARDO
Cabo Rojo vic., CABO ROJO
Camino Nuevo (Bario), YABUCOA
Carenero, GUANICA
Costa (Barrio), LAJAS
Coto (Barrio), ISABELA

Emajagua (barrio), MAUNABO

Fraile (Barrio), CULEBRA

Guanica vic., GUANICA

Isabel Ii (Vieques), VIEQUES
Isla De Mona, MAYAGUEZ

Lapas (Barrio), SALINAS

Machete (Barrio), GUAYAMA
Magueyes, PONCE

Palmas, ARROYO
Ponce, PONCE
Ponce vic., PONCE
Puerto Ferro, VIEQUES
Puntas (Barrio), RINCON

Rio Prieto (Barrio), YAUCO

Sabana Grande Abajo, SAN GERMAN
Sabanetas (Barrio), PONCE
San German, SAN GERMAN
San German, SAN JUAN
San Juan, SAN JUAN
San Juan Antiguo, SAN JUAN

Tierras Nuevas Ponie, MANATI
Toa Baja, TOA BAJA

Victoria, AGUADILLA

Rhode Island

Albion vic., PROVIDENCE COUNTY
Alton, WASHINGTON COUNTY
Anthony, KENT COUNTY
Apponaug, KENT COUNTY
Ashton vic., PROVIDENCE COUNTY

Belleville, WASHINGTON COUNTY
Bristol, BRISTOL COUNTY
Burdickville, WASHINGTON COUNTY
Buttonwoods, KENT COUNTY

Centerdale, PROVIDENCE COUNTY
Central Falls, PROVIDENCE COUNTY
Chepachet, PROVIDENCE COUNTY
Cumberland, PROVIDENCE COUNTY
Cumberland Hill, PROVIDENCE COUNTY

East Greenwich, KENT COUNTY

Greenville, PROVIDENCE COUNTY

Jamestown, NEWPORT COUNTY
Johnston, PROVIDENCE COUNTY

Kenyon, WASHINGTON COUNTY
Kingston, WASHINGTON COUNTY
Kingston Hill, WASHINGTON COUNTY

Limerock, PROVIDENCE COUNTY
Limerock vic., PROVIDENCE COUNTY
Lincoln, PROVIDENCE COUNTY
Lonsdale vic., PROVIDENCE COUNTY

Manton, PROVIDENCE COUNTY
Middletown, NEWPORT COUNTY

New Shoreham, WASHINGTON COUNTY
Newport, NEWPORT COUNTY
North Kingston, WASHINGTON COUNTY
North Providence, PROVIDENCE COUNTY
North Scituate, PROVIDENCE COUNTY
North Smithfield, PROVIDENCE COUNTY

Oaklawn, PROVIDENCE COUNTY

Pawtucket, PROVIDENCE COUNTY
Pawtucket vic., PROVIDENCE COUNTY
Providence, PROVIDENCE COUNTY

Saunderstown, WASHINGTON COUNTY
Slatersville, PROVIDENCE COUNTY
Smithfield, PROVIDENCE COUNTY
South Kingston, WASHINGTON COUNTY
Spring Green, KENT COUNTY

Thornton, PROVIDENCE COUNTY

Wakefield, WASHINGTON COUNTY
Warren, BRISTOL COUNTY
Warwick, KENT COUNTY
West Greenwich, KENT COUNTY
West Kingston, WASHINGTON COUNTY
West Warwick, KENT COUNTY
Westerly, WASHINGTON COUNTY
Wickford, WASHINGTON COUNTY
Woonsocket, PROVIDENCE COUNTY

South Carolina

Abbeville, ABBEVILLE COUNTY
Abbeville vic., ABBEVILLE COUNTY
Anderson, ANDERSON COUNTY
Anderson vic., ANDERSON COUNTY
Ashley River, DORCHESTER COUNTY
Ashley River,n. Bank, DORCHESTER COUNTY

Bamberg, BAMBERG COUNTY
Bamberg vic., BAMBERG COUNTY
Beaufort, BEAUFORT COUNTY
Belton, ANDERSON COUNTY
Bennettsville, MARLBORO COUNTY
Bluffton vic., BEAUFORT COUNTY
Buffalo, UNION COUNTY

Camden, KERSHAW COUNTY
Camden vic., KERSHAW COUNTY
Cat Island, GEORGETOWN COUNTY
Chapples Ferry vic., SALUDA COUNTY
Charleston, CHARLESTON COUNTY
Charleston vic., CHARLESTON COUNTY
Cheraw, CHESTERFIELD COUNTY
Cheraw vic., CHESTERFIELD COUNTY
Chester vic., CHESTER COUNTY
Chesterfield, CHESTERFIELD COUNTY
Clemson, OCONEE COUNTY
Clemson, PICKENS COUNTY
Clemson vic., OCONEE COUNTY
Clemson vic., PICKENS COUNTY
Clover vic., YORK COUNTY
Columbia, RICHLAND COUNTY
Columbia vic., RICHLAND COUNTY
Cordsville, BERKELEY COUNTY
Cordsville vic., BERKELEY COUNTY
Cordville vic., BERKELEY COUNTY
Crocketville vic., HAMPTON COUNTY
Cross, BERKELEY COUNTY
Cross vic., BERKELEY COUNTY

Datha Island, BEAUFORT COUNTY
Dillon vic., DILLON COUNTY

Eastover vic., RICHLAND COUNTY
Eau Claire, RICHLAND COUNTY
Eau Claire, SPARTANBURG COUNTY
Edisto Beach vic., CHARLESTON COUNTY
Edisto Island, CHARLESTON COUNTY
Ehrhardt vic., BAMBERG COUNTY
Eutaw Springs vic., BERKELEY COUNTY
Eutaw Springs vic., ORANGEBURG COUNTY
Eutawville, ORANGEBURG COUNTY
Eutawville vic., BERKELEY COUNTY

Frogmore vic., BEAUFORT COUNTY

Gaffney, SPARTANBURG COUNTY
Georgetown, GEORGETOWN COUNTY
Georgetown vic., GEORGETOWN COUNTY
Glenn Springs, SPARTANBURG COUNTY
Goose Creek, BERKELEY COUNTY
Goose Creek vic., BERKELEY COUNTY
Goose Creek vic., CHARLESTON COUNTY
Gowensville vic., PICKENS COUNTY
Great Falls, CHESTER COUNTY
Great Falls vic., CHESTER COUNTY
Greenville, GREENVILLE COUNTY
Greenville vic., GREENVILLE COUNTY
Greenwood (vic.), GREENWOOD COUNTY

Holly Hill vic., BERKELEY COUNTY
Holly Hill vic., ORANGEBURG COUNTY
Huger vic., BERKELEY COUNTY
Hunting Island, BEAUFORT COUNTY

Jenkinsville vic., FAIRFIELD COUNTY
Johnsonvile vic., FLORENCE COUNTY
Jones Crossroads Vic, SALUDA COUNTY

Kingstree, WILLIAMSBURG COUNTY

Lake City, FLORENCE COUNTY
Lake Moultrie vic., BERKELEY COUNTY
Lancaster, LANCASTER COUNTY
Latta vic., DILLON COUNTY
Laurens, LAURENS COUNTY
Lowndesville vic., ABBEVILLE COUNTY
Lowndesville vic., ANDERSON COUNTY

Manning, CLARENDON COUNTY
Mars Bluff vic., FLORENCE COUNTY
Mc Clellanville, CHARLESTON COUNTY
Mc Clellanville vic., CHARLESTON COUNTY
Mcphersonville, HAMPTON COUNTY
Mechanicsville vic., DARLINGTON COUNTY
Meggett, CHARLESTON COUNTY
Moncks Corner vic., BERKELEY COUNTY
Moore, SPARTANBURG COUNTY
Moore vic., SPARTANBURG COUNTY
Mount Pleasant vic., CHARLESTON COUNTY
Mullins, DILLON COUNTY

Nesmith vic., WILLIAMSBURG COUNTY

Norris vic., PICKENS COUNTY

Oconee Station, OCONEE COUNTY
Orangeburg, ORANGEBURG COUNTY

Parksville vic., MCCORMICK COUNTY
Pendleton, ANDERSON COUNTY
Pendleton vic., ANDERSON COUNTY
Pine Grove vic., BERKELEY COUNTY
Pineville, BERKELEY COUNTY
Pineville vic., BERKELEY COUNTY
Pinewood vic., SUMTER COUNTY
Pinopolis vic., BERKELEY COUNTY
Pinop0lis vic., BERKELEY COUNTY
Plantersville vic., GEORGETOWN COUNTY
Pleasant Lane vic., EDGEFIELD COUNTY
Poinsett State Park, SUMTER COUNTY

Rock Hill, YORK COUNTY
Rocky River, ABBEVILLE COUNTY
Roebuck, SPARTANBURG COUNTY

Savannah River, ABBEVILLE COUNTY
Savannah River, ANDERSON COUNTY
Sheldon vic., BEAUFORT COUNTY
Society Hill vic., DARLINGTON COUNTY
St. George3vic., DORCHESTER COUNTY
St. Helena Island, BEAUFORT COUNTY
St. Matthews, CALHOUN COUNTY
St. Stephens, BERKELEY COUNTY
Stateburg, SUMTER COUNTY
Sullivans Island, CHARLESTON COUNTY
Sumter vic., SUMTER COUNTY

Tamassee vic., OCONEE COUNTY
Tigerville vic., GREENVILLE COUNTY

Union, UNION COUNTY
Union vic., UNION COUNTY

Walterboro, COLLETON COUNTY
Walterboro vic., COLLETON COUNTY
Wando River, BERKELEY COUNTY
Wedgefield vic., SUMTER COUNTY
West Union, OCONEE COUNTY
Westminster, OCONEE COUNTY
Winnsboro, FAIRFIELD COUNTY

Yemassee, BEAUFORT COUNTY
York vic., YORK COUNTY

South Dakota

(Fort) Sisseton, ROBERTS COUNTY

Cheyenne River Agcy., DEWEY COUNTY
Custer vic., CUSTER COUNTY

Elk Point, UNION COUNTY

Huron, BEADLE COUNTY

Pickston vic., GREGORY COUNTY
Pierre vic., HUGHES COUNTY

Rapid City, PENNINGTON COUNTY

Sioux City, UNION COUNTY
Sioux Falls, MINNEHAHA COUNTY

Tabor, BON HOMME COUNTY

Vermillion, CLAY COUNTY

Wall vic., PENNINGTON COUNTY

Yankton, YANKTON COUNTY

Tennessee

Antioch, DAVIDSON COUNTY
Athens vic., MCMINN COUNTY

Beersheba Springs, GRUNDY COUNTY
Benton vic., POLK COUNTY
Blountville, SULLIVAN COUNTY
Blountville vic., SULLIVAN COUNTY
Bluff City vic., SULLIVAN COUNTY
Bolivar, HARDEMAN COUNTY

Cades Cove, BLOUNT COUNTY
Cades Cove vic., BLOUNT COUNTY
Cades Grove, BLOUNT COUNTY
Carthage vic., SMITH COUNTY
Castalian Springs, SUMNER COUNTY
Cedar Hill vic., ROBERTSON COUNTY
Chattanooga, HAMILTON COUNTY
Chuckey vic., GREENE COUNTY
Clarksville, MONTGOMERY COUNTY
Cleveland, BRADLEY COUNTY
Clifton vic., WAYNE COUNTY
Coldwater vic., LINCOLN COUNTY
Columbia, MAURY COUNTY
Columbia vic., MAURY COUNTY
Cosby vic., COCKE COUNTY

Dechard, FRANKLIN COUNTY
Dixon Springs, TROUSDALE COUNTY
Donelson, DAVIDSON COUNTY
Donelson vic., DAVIDSON COUNTY
Dover, STEWART COUNTY
Dover vic., STEWART COUNTY

Elizabethton, CARTER COUNTY
Elizabethton vic., CARTER COUNTY
Eureka, BRADLEY COUNTY

Fayetteville vic., LINCOLN COUNTY
Franklin, WILLIAMSON COUNTY

Gallatin, SUMNER COUNTY
Gallatin vic., SUMNER COUNTY
Gatlinburg, SEVIER COUNTY
Gatlinburg vic., SEVIER COUNTY
Greeneville, GREENE COUNTY
Greeneville vic., GREENE COUNTY

Harrogate, CLAIBORNE COUNTY
Hendersonville vic., SUMNER COUNTY
Hermitage, DAVIDSON COUNTY
Hermitage vic., DAVIDSON COUNTY
Hohenwald vic., HARDIN COUNTY

Jackson, MADISON COUNTY
Jefferson City, JEFFERSON COUNTY
Johnson City vic., WASHINGTON COUNTY
Jonesboro, WASHINGTON COUNTY
Jonesboro vic., WASHINGTON COUNTY

Kingsport, SULLIVAN COUNTY
Kingsport vic., HAWKINS COUNTY
Kingston, ROANE COUNTY
Kingston vic., ROANE COUNTY
Knoxville, KNOX COUNTY
Knoxville vic., KNOX COUNTY
Knoxville vic., SEVIER COUNTY

La Grange, FAYETTE COUNTY
Lake City, ANDERSON COUNTY
Leesburg, WASHINGTON COUNTY
Lenoir City, LOUDON COUNTY
Lenox vic., DYER COUNTY
Limestone, WASHINGTON COUNTY
Livingston, OVERTON COUNTY
Loudon, LOUDON COUNTY

Mcminnville, WARREN COUNTY
Mcminnville vic., WARREN COUNTY
Memphis, SHELBY COUNTY
Memphis vic., SHELBY COUNTY
Milan, GIBSON COUNTY
Morristown, HAMBLEN COUNTY
Morristown vic., HAMBLEN COUNTY
Murfreesboro, RUTHERFORD COUNTY

Nashville, DAVIDSON COUNTY
Nashville vic., DAVIDSON COUNTY
Norris vic., ANDERSON COUNTY

Paris, HENRY COUNTY

Rogersville, HAWKINS COUNTY
Rugby, MORGAN COUNTY

Savannah, HARDIN COUNTY
South Pittsburg, MARION COUNTY
Sparta, WHITE COUNTY

Tusculum, GREENE COUNTY

Unionville vic., BEDFORD COUNTY

Victoria vic., MARION COUNTY

Watauga Flats vic., WASHINGTON COUNTY
Wears Valley vic., SEVIER COUNTY
White Pine, JEFFERSON COUNTY
Winchester, FRANKLIN COUNTY

Texas

Abernathy vic., HALE COUNTY
Albany vic., THROCKMORTON COUNTY
Anahuac, CHAMBERS COUNTY
Anderson, GRIMES COUNTY
Anderson vic., GRIMES COUNTY
Angleton vic., BRAZORIA COUNTY
Austin, TRAVIS COUNTY
Austin vic., TRAVIS COUNTY

Bastrop vic., BASTROP COUNTY
Beaumont vic., JEFFERSON COUNTY
Belmont vic., GONZALES COUNTY
Boerne vic., KENDALL COUNTY
Bovina vic., DEAF SMITH COUNTY
Brazoria, BRAZORIA COUNTY
Brenham, WASHINGTON COUNTY
Brownsville, CAMERON COUNTY
Brownsville vic., CAMERON COUNTY
Bryan, BRAZOS COUNTY
Bullard vic., SMITH COUNTY
Burton, WASHINGTON COUNTY

Calvert, ROBERTSON COUNTY
Carthage vic., PANOLA COUNTY
Castolon, BREWSTER COUNTY
Castolon vic., BREWSTER COUNTY
Castroville, MEDINA COUNTY
Castroville vic., MEDINA COUNTY
Cat Spring, AUSTIN COUNTY
Cave Creek, GILLESPIE COUNTY
Center Point vic., KERR COUNTY
Center vic., SHELBY COUNTY

Chappell Hill, WASHINGTON COUNTY
Chappell Hill vic., WASHINGTON COUNTY
Cherry Spring, GILLESPIE COUNTY
Cherry Springs, GILLESPIE COUNTY
Chireno vic., NACOGDOCHES COUNTY
Clarendon, DONLEY COUNTY
Claude, ARMSTRONG COUNTY
College Station vic., BRAZOS COUNTY
Colorado City vic., MITCHELL COUNTY
Columbus, COLORADO COUNTY
Columbus vic., COLORADO COUNTY
Comfort, KENDALL COUNTY
Corpus Christi, NUECES COUNTY
Crockett vic., HOUSTON COUNTY
Cuevitas, JIM HOGG COUNTY
Czestochowa, KARNES COUNTY

D'hanis, MEDINA COUNTY
Dallas, DALLAS COUNTY
Dickens, DICKENS COUNTY
Driftwood vic., HAYS COUNTY

Eagle Pass, MAVERICK COUNTY
El Paso, EL PASO COUNTY

Falcon vic., ZAPATA COUNTY
Floresville vic., WILSON COUNTY
Fort Davis, JEFF DAVIS COUNTY
Fort Mc Kavet, MENARD COUNTY
Fort Worth, TARRANT COUNTY
Fredericksburg, GILLESPIE COUNTY
Frelsburg, COLORADO COUNTY
Fulton, ARANSAS COUNTY

Galveston, GALVESTON COUNTY
Goliad, GOLIAD COUNTY
Goliad vic., GOLIAD COUNTY
Grapevine vic., TARRANT COUNTY

Hackberry, LAVACA COUNTY
Hearne, ROBERTSON COUNTY
Hempstead vic., WALLER COUNTY
Henderson, RUSK COUNTY
Hillsboro, HILL COUNTY
Houston, HARRIS COUNTY
Huntsville vic., WALKER COUNTY
Hye, BLANCO COUNTY

Independence, WASHINGTON COUNTY
Independence vic., WASHINGTON COUNTY
Itasca vic., HILL COUNTY

Jefferson, MARION COUNTY
Jefferson vic., MARION COUNTY

Karnack vic., HARRISON COUNTY
Kimball, BOSQUE COUNTY

La Grange, FAYETTE COUNTY
Labatt, WILSON COUNTY
Langtry, VAL VERDE COUNTY
Laredo, WEBB COUNTY
Leaday, COLEMAN COUNTY
Leon Springs, BEXAR COUNTY
Levelland, HOCKLEY COUNTY
Lockhart vic., CALDWELL COUNTY
Lubbock, LUBBOCK COUNTY
Lufkin vic., ANGELINA COUNTY

Marshall vic., HARRISON COUNTY
Mason, MASON COUNTY
Matador, MOTLEY COUNTY
Milam vic., SABINE COUNTY
Millican, BRAZOS COUNTY
Mission Valley vic., VICTORIA COUNTY

Nacogdoches vic., NACOGDOCHES COUNTY
Navasota, GRIMES COUNTY
Navasota vic., GRIMES COUNTY
New Braunfels, COMAL COUNTY
Newcastle vic., YOUNG COUNTY

Ozona vic., CROCKETT COUNTY

Palestine, ANDERSON COUNTY
Palo Pinto, PALO PINTO COUNTY
Panna Maria vic., KARNES COUNTY
Patricia, MARTIN COUNTY
Pawelekville, KARNES COUNTY
Peach Creek, BRAZOS COUNTY
Plantersville vic., GRIMES COUNTY
Port Isabel, CAMERON COUNTY
Post, GARZA COUNTY
Poth vic., WILSON COUNTY
Presidio vic., PRESIDIO COUNTY

Quihi vic., MEDINA COUNTY

Refugio, REFUGIO COUNTY
Refugio vic., REFUGIO COUNTY
Richmond, FORT BEND COUNTY
Rio Grande City, STARR COUNTY
Roans Prairie vic., GRIMES COUNTY
Rockport, ARANSAS COUNTY
Roma, STARR COUNTY
Round Rock vic., WILLIAMSON COUNTY
Round Top, FAYETTE COUNTY

Saginaw, TARRANT COUNTY
Salado vic., BELL COUNTY
San Angelo, TOM GREEN COUNTY
San Antonio, BEXAR COUNTY
San Antonio vic., BEXAR COUNTY
San Augustine, SAN AUGUSTINE COUNTY
San Augustine vic., SAN AUGUSTINE COUNTY
San Elizario, EL PASO COUNTY
San Ygnacio, ZAPATA COUNTY
Seguin, GUADALUPE COUNTY
Seguin vic., GUADALUPE COUNTY
Shafter vic., PRESIDIO COUNTY
Sheffield vic., PECOS COUNTY
Shelby, AUSTIN COUNTY
Snyder, SCURRY COUNTY
Socorro, EL PASO COUNTY
Somerset vic., BEXAR COUNTY
Stoneham vic., GRIMES COUNTY
Stonewall, GILLESPIE COUNTY
Stonewall vic., GILLESPIE COUNTY
Sutherland Springs, WILSON COUNTY

Taylor vic., WILLIAMSON COUNTY
Terlingua, BREWSTER COUNTY
Texarkana, BOWIE COUNTY
Thomastown vic., DE WITT COUNTY
Truscott, KING COUNTY
Tulia, SWISHER COUNTY

Victoria, VICTORIA COUNTY
Voss vic., COLEMAN COUNTY
Voss vic., CONCHO COUNTY
Voss. vic., COLEMAN COUNTY

Waco, MCLENNAN COUNTY
Washington vic., WASHINGTON COUNTY
Webberville vic., BASTROP COUNTY
West Columbia vic., BRAZORIA COUNTY
Wheelock, ROBERTSON COUNTY

Ysleta, EL PASO COUNTY
Ysleta-San Elizario, EL PASO COUNTY

Zapata vic., ZAPATA COUNTY

Utah

Altamont, DUCHESNE COUNTY
American Fork, UTAH COUNTY

Beaver, BEAVER COUNTY
Benson, CACHE COUNTY
Bingham Canyon, SALT LAKE COUNTY
Bluff vic., SAN JUAN COUNTY
Boulder vic., GARFIELD COUNTY
Brigham City, BOX ELDER COUNTY
Brigham City vic., BOX ELDER COUNTY
Bryce Canyon, GARFIELD COUNTY

Cache Junction, CACHE COUNTY
Castle Dale vic., EMERY COUNTY
Cedar City, IRON COUNTY
Centerville, DAVIS COUNTY
Collinston vic., BOX ELDER COUNTY
Coriine vic., BOX ELDER COUNTY
Corinne, BOX ELDER COUNTY
Corrine, BOX ELDER COUNTY
Corrine vic., BOX ELDER COUNTY
Cove Fort, MILLARD COUNTY

Duchesne, DUCHESNE COUNTY
Duchesne vic., DUCHESNE COUNTY
Dugway, TOOELE COUNTY

Emery, EMERY COUNTY
Ephraim, SANPETE COUNTY
Eureka, JUAB COUNTY

Fairfield, UTAH COUNTY
Farmington, DAVIS COUNTY
Fielding vic., BOX ELDER COUNTY
Fillmore, MILLARD COUNTY
Fruita, WAYNE COUNTY

Garland vic., BOX ELDER COUNTY
Gordon Creek, CARBON COUNTY
Goshen vic., UTAH COUNTY
Green River, GRAND COUNTY
Gunnison, SANPETE COUNTY
Gusher, UINTAH COUNTY

Hanna vic., DUCHESNE COUNTY
Heber City, WASATCH COUNTY
Heber City vic., WASATCH COUNTY
Helper, CARBON COUNTY
Helper vic., CARBON COUNTY
Henefer, SUMMIT COUNTY
Herber City vic., WASATCH COUNTY
Holladay, SALT LAKE COUNTY
Hoytsville, SUMMIT COUNTY
Hurricane vic., WASHINGTON COUNTY

Jensen, UINTAH COUNTY

Kamas vic., SUMMIT COUNTY
Kenilworth, CARBON COUNTY
Knolls/wendover vic., TOOELE COUNTY

Lapoint, UINTAH COUNTY
Lapoint vic., UINTAH COUNTY
Leeds, WASHINGTON COUNTY
Logan, CACHE COUNTY

Magna, SALT LAKE COUNTY
Manti, SANPETE COUNTY
Mantua vic., BOX ELDER COUNTY
Marysvale, PIUTE COUNTY
Middleton, WASHINGTON COUNTY

Midway, WASATCH COUNTY
Milford vic., BEAVER COUNTY
Mountain Home vic., DUCHESNE COUNTY

Ogden, WEBER COUNTY
Ogden Canyon, WEBER COUNTY
Ogden vic., WEBER COUNTY
Old Irontown, IRON COUNTY
Ophir, TOOELE COUNTY
Orem vic., UTAH COUNTY
Orem vic. (Olmstead), UTAH COUNTY

Panguitch, GARFIELD COUNTY
Park City, SUMMIT COUNTY
Park City vic., SUMMIT COUNTY
Payson, UTAH COUNTY
Pine Valley, WASHINGTON COUNTY
Pleasant Grove, UTAH COUNTY
Promontory vic., BOX ELDER COUNTY
Provo, UTAH COUNTY
Provo vic., UTAH COUNTY

Riverton, SALT LAKE COUNTY
Rockville, WASHINGTON COUNTY

Salt Lake, SALT LAKE COUNTY
Salt Lake City, SALT LAKE COUNTY
Scofield, CARBON COUNTY
Silver Creek Jct., SUMMIT COUNTY
Silver Reef, WASHINGTON COUNTY
South Jordan, SALT LAKE COUNTY
Spring City, SANPETE COUNTY
Springdale vic., WASHINGTON COUNTY
St. George, WASHINGTON COUNTY
Standardville vic., CARBON COUNTY

Tabiona, DUCHESNE COUNTY
Tooele, TOOELE COUNTY
Tooele vic., TOOELE COUNTY
Toquerville, WASHINGTON COUNTY

Uintah, WEBER COUNTY
Union, SALT LAKE COUNTY

Vernal, UINTAH COUNTY

Washington, WASHINGTON COUNTY
Wendover, TOOELE COUNTY
Whiterocks, UINTAH COUNTY
Willard, BOX ELDER COUNTY

Vermont

Arlington, BENNINGTON COUNTY

Barnet Center, CALEDONIA COUNTY
Barre, WASHINGTON COUNTY
Bennington, BENNINGTON COUNTY
Bethel, WINDSOR COUNTY
Brownington, ORLEANS COUNTY
Burlington, CHITTENDEN COUNTY

Castleton, RUTLAND COUNTY
Cavendish, WINDSOR COUNTY
Chester, WINDSOR COUNTY
Chester Depot, WINDSOR COUNTY
Chester vic., WINDSOR COUNTY

Grafton, WINDHAM COUNTY
Grand Isle, GRAND ISLE COUNTY

Highgate Falls, FRANKLIN COUNTY

Jericho, CHITTENDEN COUNTY
Jericho Center vic., CHITTENDEN COUNTY

Middlebury, ADDISON COUNTY
Montpelier, WASHINGTON COUNTY

North Bennington, BENNINGTON COUNTY
Northfield, WASHINGTON COUNTY
Norwich, WINDSOR COUNTY
Norwich vic., WINDSOR COUNTY

Orwell, ADDISON COUNTY
Orwell vic., ADDISON COUNTY

Perkinsville, WINDSOR COUNTY
Perkinsville vic., WINDSOR COUNTY

Randolph, ORANGE COUNTY
Randolph Center, ORANGE COUNTY
Richmond, CHITTENDEN COUNTY
Rockingham, WINDHAM COUNTY
Royalton vic., WINDSOR COUNTY
Rutland, RUTLAND COUNTY

Shaftsbury Center, BENNINGTON COUNTY
Simonsville, WINDSOR COUNTY
South Hero, GRAND ISLE COUNTY
South Shaftsbury, BENNINGTON COUNTY
South Shaftsbury Vic, BENNINGTON COUNTY
Springfield, WINDSOR COUNTY
St. Albans, FRANKLIN COUNTY
St. Johnsbury, CALEDONIA COUNTY
Strafford, ORANGE COUNTY

Thetford vic., ORANGE COUNTY
Troy, ORLEANS COUNTY

Vergennes, ADDISON COUNTY

Weston, WINDSOR COUNTY
Windham, WINDHAM COUNTY
Windsor, WINDSOR COUNTY
Winooski, CHITTENDEN COUNTY
Woodstock, WINDSOR COUNTY

Virgin Islands

Charlotte Amalie, ST. THOMAS
Christiansted, ST. CROIX
Christiansted, ST. THOMAS
Christiansted vic., ST. CROIX
Company Quarter, ST. CROIX
Company's Quarter, ST. CROIX
Coral Bay, ST. JOHN
Coral Bay Quarter, ST. JOHN
Cruz Bay Qtr., ST. JOHN
Cruz Bay Quarter, ST. JOHN
Cruz Bay Quarter, ST. THOMAS

Frederiksted, ST. CROIX
Frederiksted Et Al., ST. CROIX
Friedensfeld, ST. CROIX

Hassel Island, ST. THOMAS

King's Quarter, ST. CROIX
Kronprindsens Qtr, ST. THOMAS

Little N. Side Qtr, ST. THOMAS

Maho Bay Qtr, ST. JOHN
Maho Bay Quarter, ST. JOHN

Nevis,brit.w.indies, ST. CROIX
New Quarter, ST. THOMAS
Northside A Quarter, ST. CROIX
Northside B Qtr, ST. CROIX
Northside Quarter, ST. CROIX

Prince's Quarters, ST. CROIX
Princess' Quarter, ST. CROIX

Queen's Quarter, ST. CROIX

Reef Bay Qtr, ST. JOHN
Reef Bay Quarter, ST. JOHN

Southside Quarter, ST. THOMAS

Westend Quarter, ST. CROIX
Whistling Cay, ST. JOHN

Virginia

Accomac, ACCOMACK COUNTY
Accomac Vic, ACCOMACK COUNTY
Accomac vic., ACCOMACK COUNTY
Accotink vic., FAIRFAX COUNTY
Aden, PRINCE WILLIAM COUNTY
Aden vic., PRINCE WILLIAM COUNTY
Afton vic., NELSON COUNTY
Alberene, ALBEMARLE COUNTY
Alexandria (City)
Alexandria vic., FAIRFAX COUNTY
Alexandria vic. (City)
Amelia vic., AMELIA COUNTY
Annandale, FAIRFAX COUNTY
Annandale vic., FAIRFAX COUNTY
Appomattox, APPOMATTOX COUNTY
Arlington, ARLINGTON COUNTY
Ashland vic., GOOCHLAND COUNTY
Ashland vic., HANOVER COUNTY
Atlantic vic., ACCOMACK COUNTY
Aylett vic., KING WILLIAM COUNTY

Bacon's Castle vic., SURRY COUNTY
Bacova vic., BATH COUNTY
Barhamsville, NEW KENT COUNTY
Barhamsville vic., NEW KENT COUNTY
Batesville, ALBEMARLE COUNTY
Batesville vic., ALBEMARLE COUNTY
Beaver Dam, HANOVER COUNTY
Beaver Dam vic., HANOVER COUNTY
Bedford vic. (City)
Bellamy vic., GLOUCESTER COUNTY
Bena vic., GLOUCESTER COUNTY
Berryville vic., CLARKE COUNTY
Bertrand vic., LANCASTER COUNTY
Birdhaven, SHENANDOAH COUNTY
Blackstone, NOTTOWAY COUNTY
Blossom Hill (City)
Boswell's Tavern Vic, LOUISA COUNTY
Boswells Tavern vic., LOUISA COUNTY
Bowling Green, CAROLINE COUNTY
Bowling Green vic., CAROLINE COUNTY
Boyce, CLARKE COUNTY
Boyce vic., CLARKE COUNTY
Brandy Station vic., CULPEPER COUNTY
Bremo Bluff vic., FLUVANNA COUNTY
Brentsville vic., PRINCE WILLIAM COUNTY
Bridgetown vic., NORTHAMPTON COUNTY
Broadway, ROCKINGHAM COUNTY
Brookneal vic., CHARLOTTE COUNTY
Buchanan, BOTETOURT COUNTY
Buffalo Springs, MECKLENBURG COUNTY
Bull Run, PRINCE WILLIAM COUNTY
Bull Run vic., PRINCE WILLIAM COUNTY
Bush Hill, FAIRFAX COUNTY

Ca Ira, CUMBERLAND COUNTY
Cabin Point, SURRY COUNTY
Capeville vic., NORTHAMPTON COUNTY
Caret vic., ESSEX COUNTY
Carters Bridge vic., ALBEMARLE COUNTY
Cartersville vic., CUMBERLAND COUNTY
Cascade vic., PITTSYLVANIA COUNTY
Cashville vic., ACCOMACK COUNTY
Cathardin vic., PRINCE WILLIAM COUNTY
Center Cross vic., ESSEX COUNTY
Centreville, FAIRFAX COUNTY
Champlain vic., ESSEX COUNTY
Chancellorsville, SPOTSYLVANIA COUNTY
Chantilly vic., FAIRFAX COUNTY
Charles City, CHARLES CITY COUNTY
Charles City vic., CHARLES CITY COUNTY
Charlottesville (City)
Charlottesville vic., ALBEMARLE COUNTY
Chatham, PITTSYLVANIA COUNTY
Cheriton vic., NORTHAMPTON COUNTY
Chesapeake vic. (City)
Chesconessex vic., ACCOMACK COUNTY
Christ Church vic., MIDDLESEX COUNTY
Chuckatuck (City)
Churchview vic., MIDDLESEX COUNTY
Claremont, SURRY COUNTY
Clarksville vic., MECKLENBURG COUNTY
Clearbrook vic., FREDERICK COUNTY
Clifford, AMHERST COUNTY
Clinchport, SCOTT COUNTY
Cohasset, FLUVANNA COUNTY
Colchester, FAIRFAX COUNTY
Cold Harbor, HANOVER COUNTY
Colonial Heights (City)
Comorn vic., KING GEORGE COUNTY
Covesville, ALBEMARLE COUNTY
Covington vic., ALLEGHANY COUNTY
Craddockville, ACCOMACK COUNTY
Craddockville vic., ACCOMACK COUNTY
Crimora vic., AUGUSTA COUNTY
Croaker vic., JAMES CITY COUNTY
Crozet vic., ALBEMARLE COUNTY
Cumberland, CUMBERLAND COUNTY
Cumberland vic., CUMBERLAND COUNTY

Danville, PITTSYLVANIA COUNTY
Danville vic., PITTSYLVANIA COUNTY
Delaplane, FAUQUIER COUNTY
Dillwyn vic., AMHERST COUNTY
Dinwiddie vic., DINWIDDIE COUNTY
Ditchley, NORTHUMBERLAND COUNTY
Dumfries, PRINCE WILLIAM COUNTY
Dumfries vic., PRINCE WILLIAM COUNTY
Dunnsville vic., ESSEX COUNTY

Earlysville, ALBEMARLE COUNTY
East Lexington vic., ROCKBRIDGE COUNTY
Eastville, NORTHAMPTON COUNTY
Eastville vic., NORTHAMPTON COUNTY
Elliston vic., MONTGOMERY COUNTY
Esmont vic., ALBEMARLE COUNTY

Fairfax (City)
Fairfax vic., FAIRFAX COUNTY
Falls Church (City)
Falls Church vic., FAIRFAX COUNTY
Falmouth, STAFFORD COUNTY
Falmouth vic., STAFFORD COUNTY
Farnham, LANCASTER COUNTY
Farnham, RICHMOND COUNTY
Fishersville vic., AUGUSTA COUNTY
Ford vic., DINWIDDIE COUNTY
Forest vic., BEDFORD COUNTY
Fort Defiance, AUGUSTA COUNTY
Fredericksburg (City)
Fredericksburg vic., SPOTSYLVANIA COUNTY
Fredericksburg vic., STAFFORD COUNTY
Front Royal vic., WARREN COUNTY

Gainesville vic., PRINCE WILLIAM COUNTY
Gladys vic., CAMPBELL COUNTY
Glen Allen, HENRICO COUNTY
Glen Allen vic., HENRICO COUNTY
Glendower, ALBEMARLE COUNTY
Gloucester, GLOUCESTER COUNTY
Gloucester vic., GLOUCESTER COUNTY
Goochland, GOOCHLAND COUNTY
Goochland vic., GOOCHLAND COUNTY
Gordonsville, LOUISA COUNTY
Gordonsville vic., LOUISA COUNTY
Gordonsville vic., ORANGE COUNTY
Grafton vic., YORK COUNTY
Great Falls, FAIRFAX COUNTY
Great Falls (City)
Great Falls vic., FAIRFAX COUNTY
Greenbush vic., ACCOMACK COUNTY
Greenfield vic., NELSON COUNTY
Greenwood vic., ALBEMARLE COUNTY
Gretna, PITTSYLVANIA COUNTY
Grottoes vic., AUGUSTA COUNTY
Groveton, PRINCE WILLIAM COUNTY
Guilford, ACCOMACK COUNTY
Guilford vic., ACCOMACK COUNTY
Guinea vic., SPOTSYLVANIA COUNTY
Gumtree vic., HANOVER COUNTY

Hadlock P.o. vic., NORTHAMPTON COUNTY
Hague, WESTMORELAND COUNTY
Hallwood, ACCOMACK COUNTY
Hampton (City)
Hanover, HANOVER COUNTY
Harrisonburg (City)
Hatton, ALBEMARLE COUNTY
Haymarket, PRINCE WILLIAM COUNTY
Haymarket vic., PRINCE WILLIAM COUNTY
Hebron vic., DINWIDDIE COUNTY
Herndon vic., FAIRFAX COUNTY
Hickory vic. (City)
Hopewell (City)
Hopewell vic., PRINCE GEORGE COUNTY
Horntown vic., ACCOMACK COUNTY
Howardsville, ALBEMARLE COUNTY
Huguenot vic., POWHATAN COUNTY

Ivor vic., SOUTHAMPTON COUNTY
Ivy, ALBEMARLE COUNTY

Jamestown Island, JAMES CITY COUNTY
Jamesville vic., NORTHAMPTON COUNTY
Jeffersonton vic., CULPEPER COUNTY

Keene vic., ALBEMARLE COUNTY
Kempsville (City)
Kempsville vic. (City)
Keswick, ALBEMARLE COUNTY
Keswick vic., ALBEMARLE COUNTY
Kilmarnock vic., LANCASTER COUNTY
King William, KING WILLIAM COUNTY
King William vic., KING WILLIAM COUNTY

Lancaster, LANCASTER COUNTY
Lee Mont vic., ACCOMACK COUNTY
Leesburg, LOUDOUN COUNTY
Leesburg vic., LOUDOUN COUNTY
Lenah Post Office, LOUDOUN COUNTY
Lester Manor vic., KING WILLIAM COUNTY
Lexington (City)
Lexington Vic, ROCKBRIDGE COUNTY
Lexington vic., ROCKBRIDGE COUNTY
Lightfoot vic., JAMES CITY COUNTY
Lively vic., LANCASTER COUNTY
Locustville vic., ACCOMACK COUNTY
London Bridge vic. (City)
Long Island vic., CAMPBELL COUNTY
Loretto vic., ESSEX COUNTY
Lorton, FAIRFAX COUNTY
Lorton vic., FAIRFAX COUNTY
Lovingston, NELSON COUNTY
Luray vic., PAGE COUNTY
Lynchburg (City)
Lynchburg vic., AMHERST COUNTY
Lynchburg vic., CAMPBELL COUNTY
Lynnhaven vic. (City)

Madison, MADISON COUNTY
Madison vic., MADISON COUNTY
Manakin, GOOCHLAND COUNTY
Manakin vic., GOOCHLAND COUNTY
Manassas, PRINCE WILLIAM COUNTY
Manassas vic., FAIRFAX COUNTY
Manassas vic., PRINCE WILLIAM COUNTY
Mangohick, KING WILLIAM COUNTY
Mangohick vic., KING WILLIAM COUNTY
Manquin vic., KING WILLIAM COUNTY
Mappsville vic., ACCOMACK COUNTY
Marion vic., SMYTH COUNTY
Marshall vic., FAUQUIER COUNTY
Mattoax vic., AMELIA COUNTY
Mclean vic., FAIRFAX COUNTY
Mechanicsville vic., HANOVER COUNTY
Merry Point, LANCASTER COUNTY
Merry Point vic., LANCASTER COUNTY
Middletown vic., FREDERICK COUNTY
Millwood, CLARKE COUNTY
Millwood vic., CLARKE COUNTY
Minnieville, PRINCE WILLIAM COUNTY
Modest Town, ACCOMACK COUNTY
Montpelier Sta. vic., ORANGE COUNTY
Montpelier Station, ORANGE COUNTY
Mount Holly vic., WESTMORELAND COUNTY
Mount Vernon, FAIRFAX COUNTY
Mount Vernon vic., FAIRFAX COUNTY
Mt. Vernon vic., FAIRFAX COUNTY

Nassawadox, NORTHAMPTON COUNTY
Nassawadox vic., NORTHAMPTON COUNTY
Naxera vic., GLOUCESTER COUNTY
New Church vic., ACCOMACK COUNTY
New Kent vic., NEW KENT COUNTY
Newport News (City)
Newtown vic., KING AND QUEEN COUNTY
Nimmo vic. (City)
Norfolk (City)
North Garden, ALBEMARLE COUNTY
North Garden vic., ALBEMARLE COUNTY
Nottoway, NOTTOWAY COUNTY
Nuttall vic., GLOUCESTER COUNTY
Nuttsville vic., LANCASTER COUNTY

Oak Grove, WESTMORELAND COUNTY
Occoquan, PRINCE WILLIAM COUNTY
Oceana vic. (City)
Old Cold Harbor vic., HANOVER COUNTY
Onancock, ACCOMACK COUNTY
Orange vic., ORANGE COUNTY
Ordinary, GLOUCESTER COUNTY
Ordinary vic., GLOUCESTER COUNTY
Otterdam vic., SURRY COUNTY
Ottoman vic., LANCASTER COUNTY
Owens vic., KING GEORGE COUNTY
Owensville vic., ALBEMARLE COUNTY

Painter vic., ACCOMACK COUNTY
Paris, FAUQUIER COUNTY
Paul's Crossroads, ESSEX COUNTY
Petersburg (City)

Petersburg vic., DINWIDDIE COUNTY
Pleasant Valley, ROCKINGHAM COUNTY
Port Royal, CAROLINE COUNTY
Port Royal vic., CAROLINE COUNTY
Port Royal vic., KING GEORGE COUNTY
Powhatan, POWHATAN COUNTY
Powhatan vic., POWHATAN COUNTY
Prince George vic., PRINCE GEORGE COUNTY
Providence, NEW KENT COUNTY
Providence Forge Vic, NEW KENT COUNTY
Pungoteague, ACCOMACK COUNTY
Pungoteague vic., ACCOMACK COUNTY

Quicksburg vic., SHENANDOAH COUNTY
Quinby vic., ACCOMACK COUNTY
Quinton vic., NEW KENT COUNTY

Radford vic., MONTGOMERY COUNTY
Ravensworth vic., FAIRFAX COUNTY
Reids Ferry vic. (City)
Richmond (City)
Richmond vic., CHESTERFIELD COUNTY
Richmond vic., HENRICO COUNTY
Roanoke (City)
Rumford vic., KING WILLIAM COUNTY
Rustburg vic., CAMPBELL COUNTY

Sabot, GOOCHLAND COUNTY
Saint Brides vic. (City)
Salem, ROANOKE COUNTY
Salem Church, SPOTSYLVANIA COUNTY
Salem vic. (City)
Scottsville, ALBEMARLE COUNTY
Scottsville vic., ALBEMARLE COUNTY
Shadwell, ALBEMARLE COUNTY
Shadyside vic., NORTHAMPTON COUNTY
Simeon, ALBEMARLE COUNTY
Simeon vic., ALBEMARLE COUNTY
Simonson vic., RICHMOND COUNTY
Skinquarter, CHESTERFIELD COUNTY
Smithfield, ISLE OF WIGHT COUNTY
Smithfield vic., ISLE OF WIGHT COUNTY
Somers vic., LANCASTER COUNTY
South Boston vic., HALIFAX COUNTY
South Hill, MECKLENBURG COUNTY
South Richmond, CHESTERFIELD COUNTY
Sperryville vic., RAPPAHANNOCK COUNTY
Spotsylvania, SPOTSYLVANIA COUNTY
Spotsylvania vic., SPOTSYLVANIA COUNTY
Stafford, STAFFORD COUNTY
Stafford vic., STAFFORD COUNTY
Stanardsville vic., GREENE COUNTY
Staunton (City)
Staunton vic., AUGUSTA COUNTY
Staunton vic. (City)
Strasburg, SHENANDOAH COUNTY
Stratford, WESTMORELAND COUNTY
Suffolk (City)
Suffolk vic. (City)
Surry vic., SURRY COUNTY
Sussex, SUSSEX COUNTY
Sweet Chalybeate, ALLEGHANY COUNTY
Sweet Hall, KING WILLIAM COUNTY
Sweet Hall vic., KING WILLIAM COUNTY

Tappahannock, ESSEX COUNTY
Tasley vic., ACCOMACK COUNTY
Tettington vic., CHARLES CITY COUNTY
The Plains vic., FAUQUIER COUNTY
Thoroughfare, PRINCE WILLIAM COUNTY
Tidewater vic., RICHMOND COUNTY
Toano, JAMES CITY COUNTY
Toano vic., JAMES CITY COUNTY
Townsend vic., NORTHAMPTON COUNTY
Trevilians, LOUISA COUNTY
Trevilians vic., LOUISA COUNTY
Tuckahoe vic., HENRICO COUNTY
Tucker Hill vic., WESTMORELAND COUNTY
Tunstall vic., NEW KENT COUNTY

Upperville, FAUQUIER COUNTY
Urbanna, MIDDLESEX COUNTY
Urbanna vic., MIDDLESEX COUNTY

Vienna vic., FAIRFAX COUNTY
Virginia Beach (City)

Wakefield Corner Vic, WESTMORELAND COUNTY
Walkerton vic., KING AND QUEEN COUNTY
Wardtown vic., NORTHAMPTON COUNTY
Ware Neck vic., GLOUCESTER COUNTY
Warsaw, RICHMOND COUNTY
Warsaw vic., RICHMOND COUNTY
Washington, RAPPAHANNOCK COUNTY
Waterfall, PRINCE WILLIAM COUNTY
Waterford, LOUDOUN COUNTY
Waynesboro vic., AUGUSTA COUNTY
Weems, LANCASTER COUNTY
West Point vic., KING WILLIAM COUNTY
Westmoreland, WESTMORELAND COUNTY
Weyers Cave vic., AUGUSTA COUNTY
White Marsh, GLOUCESTER COUNTY
White Marsh vic., GLOUCESTER COUNTY
White Post vic., CLARKE COUNTY
Williamsburg (City)
Williamsburg vic., JAMES CITY COUNTY
Willis vic., FLOYD COUNTY
Winchester (City)
Winchester vic., FREDERICK COUNTY
Windsor vic., ISLE OF WIGHT COUNTY
Woodbridge vic., PRINCE WILLIAM COUNTY
Woodford, CAROLINE COUNTY
Woods Crossroads Vic, GLOUCESTER COUNTY
Worsham, PRINCE EDWARD COUNTY
Wyndham vic., POWHATAN COUNTY

Yorktown, YORK COUNTY
Yorktown vic., YORK COUNTY

Washington

Aberdeen vic., GRAYS HARBOR COUNTY
Anacortes, SKAGIT COUNTY
Arden vic., STEVENS COUNTY

Bellingham, WHATCOM COUNTY
Blaine vic., WHATCOM COUNTY
Bremerton, KITSAP COUNTY

Carbonado vic., PIERCE COUNTY
Cashup, WHITMAN COUNTY
Cedar Falls, KING COUNTY
Centralia, LEWIS COUNTY
Chambers Prairie, THURSTON COUNTY
Chehalis, LEWIS COUNTY
Chehalis vic., LEWIS COUNTY
Chelan, CHELAN COUNTY
Chewelah, STEVENS COUNTY
Chewelah vic., STEVENS COUNTY
Chimacum, JEFFERSON COUNTY
Chimacum vic., JEFFERSON COUNTY
Claquato, LEWIS COUNTY
Colville vic., STEVENS COUNTY
Coupeville, ISLAND COUNTY
Coupeville vic., ISLAND COUNTY
Cowiche vic., YAKIMA COUNTY

Darrington, SNOHOMISH COUNTY
Deer Park vic., SPOKANE COUNTY
Dieringer, PIERCE COUNTY
Dungeness vic., CLALLAM COUNTY

Electric City vic., GRANT COUNTY
Electron, PIERCE COUNTY
Enumclaw, KING COUNTY
Evans vic., STEVENS COUNTY

Ford vic., STEVENS COUNTY
Fort Casey vic., ISLAND COUNTY
Fort Lewis, PIERCE COUNTY
Fort Rains, SKAMANIA COUNTY
Fort Steilacoom, PIERCE COUNTY
Friday Harbor, SAN JUAN COUNTY

Glacier, WHATCOM COUNTY
Glacier vic., WHATCOM COUNTY
Glenwood vic., KLICKITAT COUNTY
Goldendale, KLICKITAT COUNTY
Goldendale vic., KLICKITAT COUNTY
Grays River vic., WAHKIAKUM COUNTY
Greenwater vic., PIERCE COUNTY

Hillyard, SPOKANE COUNTY
Hoodsport vic., MASON COUNTY

Kahlotus vic., FRANKLIN COUNTY
Kettle Falls vic., STEVENS COUNTY

Lake Crescent vic., CLALLAM COUNTY
Leavenworth, CHELAN COUNTY
Lester, KING COUNTY
Liberty, KITTITAS COUNTY
Lincoln vic., LINCOLN COUNTY
Longmire, PIERCE COUNTY

Mcmillin, PIERCE COUNTY
Mission Orchard, ASOTIN COUNTY
Monse vic., OKANOGAN COUNTY
Montesano, GRAYS HARBOR COUNTY
Mossy Rock vic., LEWIS COUNTY
Mount Rainier, LEWIS COUNTY
Mount Rainier, PIERCE COUNTY

Naches vic., YAKIMA COUNTY
Napavine vic., LEWIS COUNTY
Newhalem, WHATCOM COUNTY
Newhalem vic., WHATCOM COUNTY
Newport, PEND OREILLE COUNTY
Nine Mile Falls, SPOKANE COUNTY
Nine Mile Falls vic., SPOKANE COUNTY

Oak Harbor vic., ISLAND COUNTY
Olympia, THURSTON COUNTY
Omak vic., OKANOGAN COUNTY
Orient, FERRY COUNTY
Oroville vic., OKANOGAN COUNTY
Oroville vicinity, OKANOGAN COUNTY
Outlook, YAKIMA COUNTY
Oysterville, PACIFIC COUNTY

Palouse, WHITMAN COUNTY
Palouse vic., WHITMAN COUNTY
Pasco, FRANKLIN COUNTY
Port Angeles (vic.), CLALLAM COUNTY
Port Angeles vic., CLALLAM COUNTY
Port Townsend, JEFFERSON COUNTY
Port Townsend vic., JEFFERSON COUNTY
Prosser, BENTON COUNTY
Pullman Junction Vic, WHITMAN COUNTY
Pullman vic., WHITMAN COUNTY
Puyallup, PIERCE COUNTY

Quinault, GRAYS HARBOR COUNTY

Randle, LEWIS COUNTY
Reardan vic., LINCOLN COUNTY

Renton, KING COUNTY

San De Fuca, ISLAND COUNTY
San De Fuca vic., ISLAND COUNTY
Sawyer vic., YAKIMA COUNTY
Seattle, KING COUNTY
South Montesano, GRAYS HARBOR COUNTY
Spokane, SPOKANE COUNTY
Stehekin vic., CHELAN COUNTY
Steilacoom, PIERCE COUNTY
Stember Creek, GARFIELD COUNTY
Stimson vic., GRAYS HARBOR COUNTY
Sumas, WHATCOM COUNTY

Tacoma, PIERCE COUNTY
Tampico vic., YAKIMA COUNTY
Toholah vic., GRAYS HARBOR COUNTY
Tumwater, THURSTON COUNTY

Union Gap, YAKIMA COUNTY
Usk, PEND OREILLE COUNTY
Usk vic., PEND OREILLE COUNTY

Vancouver, CLARK COUNTY
Vancouver vic., CLARK COUNTY

Walla Walla vic., WALLA WALLA COUNTY
Wenas, YAKIMA COUNTY
White Bluffs vic., FRANKLIN COUNTY
White Swan, YAKIMA COUNTY
White Swan vic., YAKIMA COUNTY

Yakima, YAKIMA COUNTY
Yakima vic., YAKIMA COUNTY

West Virginia

Alderson, GREENBRIER COUNTY
Alderson, MONROE COUNTY
Alderson vic., SUMMERS COUNTY

Barracksville, MARION COUNTY
Benwood, MARSHALL COUNTY
Berkeley Springs, MORGAN COUNTY
Bethany, BROOKE COUNTY
Bretz vic., PRESTON COUNTY
Bridgeport, HARRISON COUNTY
Bunker Hill vic., BERKELEY COUNTY
Burnsville, BRAXTON COUNTY

Cedar Grove, KANAWHA COUNTY
Charles Town, JEFFERSON COUNTY
Charles Town, KANAWHA COUNTY
Charles Town vic., JEFFERSON COUNTY
Charleston, KANAWHA COUNTY

Darke, JEFFERSON COUNTY
Darke vic., JEFFERSON COUNTY
Dellslow vic., MONONGALIA COUNTY
Dunmore, POCAHONTAS COUNTY

Elm Grove, OHIO COUNTY

Fairmont, MARION COUNTY
Fairmont vic., MARION COUNTY
Fayetteville vic., FAYETTE COUNTY

Gassaway vic., BRAXTON COUNTY
Gauley Bridge, FAYETTE COUNTY
Gerrardstown, BERKELEY COUNTY
Grafton, TAYLOR COUNTY
Great Cacapon, MORGAN COUNTY

Halltown, JEFFERSON COUNTY
Harpers Ferry, JEFFERSON COUNTY
Hedgesville vic., BERKELEY COUNTY
Hillsboro vic., POCAHONTAS COUNTY
Hinton, SUMMERS COUNTY
Huntington, CABELL COUNTY

Kearneyville, JEFFERSON COUNTY
Keyser vic., MINERAL COUNTY

Leetown, JEFFERSON COUNTY
Leetown vic., JEFFERSON COUNTY
Lewisburg, GREENBRIER COUNTY
Littleton vic., MARSHALL COUNTY

Malden, KANAWHA COUNTY
Marietta
Marlinton, POCAHONTAS COUNTY
Martinsburg, BERKELEY COUNTY
Martinsburg vic., BERKELEY COUNTY
Middleway, JEFFERSON COUNTY
Milton, CABELL COUNTY
Moorefield, HARDY COUNTY
Morgantown, MONONGALIA COUNTY
Morgantown vic., MONONGALIA COUNTY
Mouth Of Seneca, PENDLETON COUNTY
Myerstown vic., JEFFERSON COUNTY

New Creek vic., MINERAL COUNTY

Parkersburg, WOOD COUNTY
Parkersburg vic., PENDLETON COUNTY
Parsons vic., TUCKER COUNTY
Pennsboro, RITCHIE COUNTY
Petroleum vic., RITCHIE COUNTY
Philippi, BARBOUR COUNTY
Point Pleasant, MASON COUNTY

Rainelle, GREENBRIER COUNTY
Ranson, JEFFERSON COUNTY
Red Sulphur Springs, MONROE COUNTY
Renick, GREENBRIER COUNTY
Ripley vic., JACKSON COUNTY
Rippon vic., JEFFERSON COUNTY
Roanoke, LEWIS COUNTY
Rocket Center, MINERAL COUNTY
Romney, HAMPSHIRE COUNTY
Ronceverte, GREENBRIER COUNTY
Rowelsburg vic., PRESTON COUNTY

Salt Sulpher Springs, MONROE COUNTY
Salt Sulphur Sp. Vic, MONROE COUNTY
Salt Sulphur Springs, MONROE COUNTY
Shenandoah Junc. Vic, JEFFERSON COUNTY
Shenandoah Junction, JEFFERSON COUNTY
Shepherdstown, JEFFERSON COUNTY
Shepherdstown vic., JEFFERSON COUNTY
Summit Point, JEFFERSON COUNTY
Sweet Springs, MONROE COUNTY

Talcott vic., SUMMERS COUNTY
Thurmond, FAYETTE COUNTY
Tunnelton vic., PRESTON COUNTY

Union, MONROE COUNTY

Wheatland, JEFFERSON COUNTY
Wheeling, OHIO COUNTY
White Sulphur Spring, GREENBRIER COUNTY
Williamstown, WOOD COUNTY

Wisconsin

Ackerville vic., WASHINGTON COUNTY
Ackley, LANGLADE COUNTY
Addison, WASHINGTON COUNTY
Alma, BUFFALO COUNTY
Appleton, OUTAGAMIE COUNTY
Armenia & Necedah, JUNEAU COUNTY
Arthur, CHIPPEWA COUNTY

Baraboo, SAUK COUNTY
Bayfield, BAYFIELD COUNTY
Bayfield vic., BAYFIELD COUNTY
Beloit vic., ROCK COUNTY
Benton, LAFAYETTE COUNTY
Big Bend vic., WAUKESHA COUNTY
Bristol, KENOSHA COUNTY
Buena Vista, RICHLAND COUNTY
Burlington, RACINE COUNTY
Burlington vic., RACINE COUNTY

Cedarburg, OZAUKEE COUNTY
Cedarburg vic., OZAUKEE COUNTY
Chamberlain, WAUKESHA COUNTY
Chester Township, DODGE COUNTY
Chippewa Falls, CHIPPEWA COUNTY

Daleyville vic., DANE COUNTY
De Pere, BROWN COUNTY
Delafield, WAUKESHA COUNTY
Dodgerville, IOWA COUNTY

East Troy vic., WALWORTH COUNTY
Eau Claire, EAU CLAIRE COUNTY
Elkhorn, WALWORTH COUNTY

Fond Du Lac, FOND DU LAC COUNTY
Franklin, MANITOWOC COUNTY
Freistadt, OZAUKEE COUNTY

Genoa vic., VERNON COUNTY
Green Bay, BROWN COUNTY
Greenbush, SHEBOYGAN COUNTY

Hales Corners, MILWAUKEE COUNTY
Hamilton, OZAUKEE COUNTY
Honey Creek vic., RACINE COUNTY

Iron Ridge vic., DODGE COUNTY

Jackson, WASHINGTON COUNTY
Jackson vic., WASHINGTON COUNTY

Kaukauna, OUTAGAMIE COUNTY
Kennan, PRICE COUNTY
King, WAUPACA COUNTY
Kirchhayn vic., WASHINGTON COUNTY
Krichhayn, WASHINGTON COUNTY

La Crosse, LA CROSSE COUNTY
La Crosse vic., LA CROSSE COUNTY
La Farge, VERNON COUNTY
La Farge vic., VERNON COUNTY
Lake Geneva, WALWORTH COUNTY
Laona vic., FOREST COUNTY
Lapointe, ASHLAND COUNTY
Lapointe vic., ASHLAND COUNTY
Lebanon Township, DODGE COUNTY
Lena, OCONTO COUNTY
Levis, CLARK COUNTY
Lowell, DODGE COUNTY
Lynxville vic., CRAWFORD COUNTY

Madison, DANE COUNTY
Marathon, MARATHON COUNTY
Medford, TAYLOR COUNTY
Menasha, WINNEBAGO COUNTY
Menasham, WINNEBAGO COUNTY
Meonominee Falls Vic, WAUKESHA COUNTY
Mequon, OZAUKEE COUNTY
Merrimack vic., SAUK COUNTY
Merton, WAUKESHA COUNTY
Milton, ROCK COUNTY
Milwaukee, MILWAUKEE COUNTY
Milwaukee vic., WAUKESHA COUNTY
Mineral Point, IOWA COUNTY

Nashotah vic., WAUKESHA COUNTY
Neenah, WINNEBAGO COUNTY
New Diggings, LAFAYETTE COUNTY
New London vic., OUTAGAMIE COUNTY

Okauchee, WAUKESHA COUNTY
Oshkosh, WINNEBAGO COUNTY

Palmyra, JEFFERSON COUNTY
Park Falls vic., PRICE COUNTY
Patch Grove vic., GRANT COUNTY
Patch Grove Village, GRANT COUNTY
Paynesville, MILWAUKEE COUNTY
Pepin vic., PEPIN COUNTY
Platteville, GRANT COUNTY
Plover, MARATHON COUNTY
Port Washington, OZAUKEE COUNTY
Portage, COLUMBIA COUNTY
Prairie Du Chien, CRAWFORD COUNTY
Prescott vic., PIERCE COUNTY
Prospect, WAUKESHA COUNTY

Racine, RACINE COUNTY
Richfield, WASHINGTON COUNTY
Ripon, FOND DU LAC COUNTY
River Falls, PIERCE COUNTY
Rochester vic., RACINE COUNTY
Rockbridge, RICHLAND COUNTY

Saylesville, WAUKESHA COUNTY
Scandinavia, WAUPACA COUNTY
Schofield, MARATHON COUNTY
Sparta, MONROE COUNTY
Sparta vic., MONROE COUNTY
Spring Valley, PIERCE COUNTY
St. Cloud, FOND DU LAC COUNTY
Stevens Point, PORTAGE COUNTY
Superior, DOUGLAS COUNTY

Thiensville, OZAUKEE COUNTY
Thiensville vic., OZAUKEE COUNTY
Tiffany, ROCK COUNTY
Trempealeau vic., TREMPEALEAU COUNTY

Wagner, MARINETTE COUNTY
Warner Twp., CLARK COUNTY
Watertown, JEFFERSON COUNTY
Watertown vic., DODGE COUNTY
Waukesha, WAUKESHA COUNTY
Waupaca, WAUPACA COUNTY
Wausau, MARATHON COUNTY
Wausaukee vic., MARINETTE COUNTY
Wauwatosa, MILWAUKEE COUNTY
West Allis, MILWAUKEE COUNTY
West Bend vic., WASHINGTON COUNTY
Westby, VERNON COUNTY
Whiting, PORTAGE COUNTY
Wrightstown, BROWN COUNTY

Wyoming

Arvada vic., SHERIDAN COUNTY
Atlantic City, FREMONT COUNTY

Bosler vic., ALBANY COUNTY
Boulder vic., SUBLETTE COUNTY
Buffalo vic., JOHNSON COUNTY

Casper vic., NATRONA COUNTY
Centennial, ALBANY COUNTY
Centennial vic., ALBANY COUNTY
Cheyenne, GOSHEN COUNTY
Cheyenne, LARAMIE COUNTY
Chugwater, PLATTE COUNTY
Cody, PARK COUNTY
Cody vic., PARK COUNTY

Daniel vic., SUBLETTE COUNTY
Dubois vic., FREMONT COUNTY

Elk Mountain vic., CARBON COUNTY
Encampment vic., CARBON COUNTY
Ethete vic., FREMONT COUNTY

Fontenelle vic., SWEETWATER COUNTY
Fort Badger vic., UINTA COUNTY
Fort Fred Steele, CARBON COUNTY
Fort Laramie, GOSHEN COUNTY
Fort Laramie vic., GOSHEN COUNTY
Fort Washakie, FREMONT COUNTY

Gillette vic., CAMPBELL COUNTY
Granger, SWEETWATER COUNTY
Green River vic., SWEETWATER COUNTY
Guernsey, PLATTE COUNTY

Hulett vic., CROOK COUNTY

Kaycee vic., JOHNSON COUNTY
Kell vic., TETON COUNTY
Kelly vic., TETON COUNTY
Keystone vic., ALBANY COUNTY

Laramie, ALBANY COUNTY
Leiter vic., SHERIDAN COUNTY
Lovell vic., BIG HORN COUNTY

Miner's Delight, FREMONT COUNTY
Monarch vic., SHERIDAN COUNTY
Moneta, FREMONT COUNTY
Moose, TETON COUNTY
Moose vic., TETON COUNTY
Morton vic., FREMONT COUNTY

Norris Junction, PARK COUNTY

Osage vic., WESTON COUNTY

Pepperville, PLATTE COUNTY
Piedmont, UINTA COUNTY
Point Of Rocks, SWEETWATER COUNTY

Riverview vic., NIOBRARA COUNTY
Rock River, ALBANY COUNTY
Rock River vic., ALBANY COUNTY

Saratoga vic., CARBON COUNTY
Shell vic., BIG HORN COUNTY
Sheridan, SHERIDAN COUNTY
Sheridan vic., SHERIDAN COUNTY
South Pass City, FREMONT COUNTY
Superior, SWEETWATER COUNTY
Sussex vic., JOHNSON COUNTY

Thermoplois vic., HOT SPRINGS COUNTY
Thermopolis vic., HOT SPRINGS COUNTY

W. Laramie, ALBANY COUNTY
Wheatland vic., ALBANY COUNTY
Wheatland vic., PLATTE COUNTY
Woods Landing vic., ALBANY COUNTY
Wright Ic., CAMPBELL COUNTY
Wright vic., CAMPBELL COUNTY

Yellowstone Nat'l Pk, TETON COUNTY

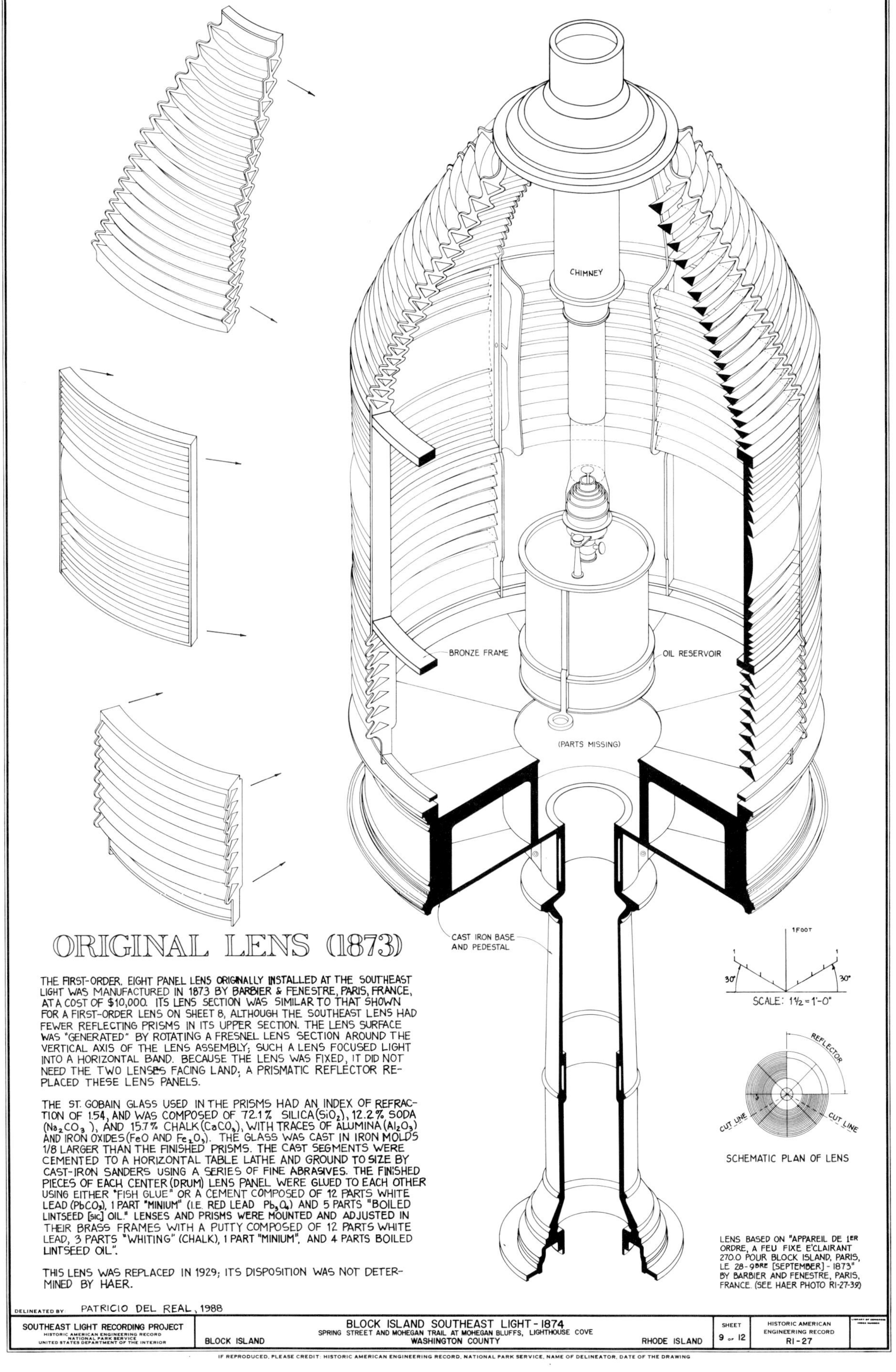
CHIMNEY
BRONZE FRAME
OIL RESERVOIR
(PARTS MISSING)
CAST IRON BASE
AND PEDESTAL
1 FOOT
30°
30°
SCALE: 1½ = 1'-0"
REFLECTOR
CUT LINE
CUT LINE
SCHEMATIC PLAN OF LENS
ORIGINAL LENS (1873)
THE FIRST-ORDER, EIGHT PANEL LENS ORIGINALLY INSTALLED AT THE SOUTHEAST LIGHT WAS MANUFACTURED IN 1873 BY BARBIER & FENESTRE, PARIS, FRANCE, AT A COST OF $10,000. ITS LENS SECTION WAS SIMILAR TO THAT SHOWN FOR A FIRST-ORDER LENS ON SHEET 8, ALTHOUGH THE SOUTHEAST LENS HAD FEWER REFLECTING PRISMS IN ITS UPPER SECTION. THE LENS SURFACE WAS "GENERATED" BY ROTATING A FRESNEL LENS SECTION AROUND THE VERTICAL AXIS OF THE LENS ASSEMBLY; SUCH A LENS FOCUSED LIGHT INTO A HORIZONTAL BAND. BECAUSE THE LENS WAS FIXED, IT DID NOT NEED THE TWO LENSES FACING LAND; A PRISMATIC REFLECTOR REPLACED THESE LENS PANELS.
THE ST. GOBAIN GLASS USED IN THE PRISMS HAD AN INDEX OF REFRACTION OF 1.54, AND WAS COMPOSED OF 72.1% SILICA (SiO_2), 12.2% SODA (Na_2CO_3), AND 15.7% CHALK ($CaCO_3$), WITH TRACES OF ALUMINA (Al_2O_3) AND IRON OXIDES (FeO AND Fe_2O_3). THE GLASS WAS CAST IN IRON MOLDS 1/8 LARGER THAN THE FINISHED PRISMS. THE CAST SEGMENTS WERE CEMENTED TO A HORIZONTAL TABLE LATHE AND GROUND TO SIZE BY CAST-IRON SANDERS USING A SERIES OF FINE ABRASIVES. THE FINISHED PIECES OF EACH CENTER (DRUM) LENS PANEL WERE GLUED TO EACH OTHER USING EITHER "FISH GLUE" OR A CEMENT COMPOSED OF 12 PARTS WHITE LEAD ($PbCO_3$), 1 PART "MINIUM" (I.E. RED LEAD Pb_3O_4) AND 5 PARTS "BOILED LINTSEED [SIC] OIL." LENSES AND PRISMS WERE MOUNTED AND ADJUSTED IN THEIR BRASS FRAMES WITH A PUTTY COMPOSED OF 12 PARTS WHITE LEAD, 3 PARTS "WHITING" (CHALK), 1 PART "MINIUM", AND 4 PARTS BOILED LINTSEED OIL".
THIS LENS WAS REPLACED IN 1929; ITS DISPOSITION WAS NOT DETERMINED BY HAER.
LENS BASED ON "APPAREIL DE 1ER ORDRE, A FEU FIXE E'CLAIRANT 270.0 POUR BLOCK ISLAND, PARIS, LE 28-9BRE [SEPTEMBER] - 1873" BY BARBIER AND FENESTRE, PARIS, FRANCE. (SEE HAER PHOTO RI-27-39)
DELINEATED BY: PATRICIO DEL REAL, 1988
SOUTHEAST LIGHT RECORDING PROJECT
HISTORIC AMERICAN ENGINEERING RECORD
NATIONAL PARK SERVICE
UNITED STATES DEPARTMENT OF THE INTERIOR
BLOCK ISLAND SOUTHEAST LIGHT - 1874
SPRING STREET AND MOHEGAN TRAIL AT MOHEGAN BLUFFS, LIGHTHOUSE COVE
BLOCK ISLAND
WASHINGTON COUNTY
RHODE ISLAND
SHEET
9 OF 12
HISTORIC AMERICAN
ENGINEERING RECORD
RI-27
IF REPRODUCED, PLEASE CREDIT: HISTORIC AMERICAN ENGINEERING RECORD, NATIONAL PARK SERVICE, NAME OF DELINEATOR, DATE OF THE DRAWING

◀ *The original lens (1873), Block Island Southeast Light, Block Island, Washington County, Rhode Island. Measured drawing delineated by Patricio Del Real, 1988 (HABS RI-27, sheet- 9 of 12)*

E 159 .A37 1995
America preserved
DATE DUE
GAYLORD No. 2333
PRINTED IN U.S.A.